WEBSTER'S Dictionary & Thesaurus for Students

WITH FULL~COLOR WORLD ATLAS

WEBSTER'S Dictionary & Thesaurus for Students

WITH FULL-COLOR WORLD ATLAS

THIRD EDITION

Created in Cooperation with the Editors of
MERRIAM-WEBSTER

FEDERAL STREET PRESS

A Division of Merriam-Webster, Incorporated
Springfield, Massachusetts

Federal Street Press books are available for bulk purchase for sales promotion and premium use. For details, write the manager of special sales, Federal Street Press, P.O. Box 281, Springfield, MA 01102.

This edition published by
Federal Street Press
A Division of Merriam-Webster, Incorporated
P.O. Box 281
Springfield, MA 01102

ISBN 978-1-59695-178-5

Printed in Canada

1st Printing Webcom, Toronto ON 7/2019 SRM

Contents

A FULL-COLOR ATLAS
OF THE WORLD FOLLOWS PAGE 500

Using the Dictionary

This newly updated volume defines more than 37,000 words and phrases that reflect the vocabulary level, curriculum requirements, and personal interests of students. One feature of this new edition that we are particularly proud of is the addition of special Canadian and British spellings, when they differ from the usual spelling in the U.S., which we believe will give the book wide appeal.

The features of this dictionary are similar to those of larger dictionaries. It is important to understand them to make best use of this valuable language tool.

The **bold** word that begins an entry is known as the main entry word. All of the material in the entry is related to the main entry word or to derived words or phrases that also appear in the entry.

> **co·la** *n, pl* **co·las :** a sweet brown carbonated soft drink that contains flavoring from the nut of a tropical tree
>
> **icon** *n* . . . **4 :** a small picture or symbol on a computer screen that represents a function that the computer can perform

Centered dots in the bold forms show where the words may be hyphenated at the end of a line on a page, and they may serve as an aid in sounding out the words.

Other bold forms may appear in this entry, such as **variant spellings** and **inflected forms** of the main entry word. Inflected forms are the plurals of nouns, the principal parts of verbs, or the comparative and superlative forms of adjectives.

> [1]**down·ward** *or* **down·wards** *adv* **:** from a higher place, amount, or level to a lower one
>
> [2]**witness** *vb* **wit·nessed; wit·ness·ing 1 :** to see or gain personal knowledge of something . . .

Other bold items in the entry may be defined **run-on phrases** that have the main entry word in the phrase, and **run-in entries** that are being explained in the definition itself.

> [1]**stand** *vb* **stood; stand·ing 1 :** to be in or take an upright position . . . — **stand by 1 :** to be or remain loyal or true to . . . — **stand for 1 :** to be a symbol for **:** REPRESENT . . .
>
> **ol·ive** *n* . . . **:** the oily fruit of an evergreen tree that is eaten both ripe and unripe and is the source of an edible oil (**olive oil**) . . .

One of the more common bold forms appearing at an entry is the **undefined run-on entry**. This is a word at the end of an entry that is derived from the main entry by the addition of a common word ending (suffix).

> **af·fa·ble** *adj* **:** friendly and easy to talk to — **af·fa·bly** *adv*

Since you know the meaning of the main entry word and the meaning of the suffix, the meaning of the run-on entry is self-explanatory.

The way a word is used in a sentence, its *function*, sometimes called its *part of speech*, is indicated by any of several *italic* abbreviations: *n* for *noun* (**cat, dog, mother**), *vb* for *verb* (**run, jump, cry**), *adj* for *adjective* (**blue, tall, happy**), *adv* for *adverb* (**easily, fast, nearby**), *pron* for *pronoun* (**who, them, none**), *conj* for *conjunction* (**and, but, if**), *prep* for *preposition* (**about, for, to**), and *interj* for *interjection* (**hello, ahoy**). Others include *helping verb* (**may, can**), *prefix* (**anti-, bio-**), and *suffix* (**-age, -er, -graph**).

When there are two or more words that have the same spelling but are different in their meanings or how they function in a sentence, these are distinguished by a small superscript numeral in front of the spelling. The numeral is not part of the spelling; it is there in this dictionary to distinguish these identically spelled words (called **homographs**).

> ^{1}**calf** *n, pl* **calves 1 :** a young cow . . .
>
> ^{2}**calf** *n, pl* **calves :** the muscular back part of the leg . . .
>
> ^{1}**dai·ly** *adj* **1 :** occurring, done, produced, appearing, or used every day . . .
>
> ^{2}**daily** *adv* **:** every day
>
> ^{3}**daily** *n, pl* **dai·lies :** a newspaper published every weekday

One very important way a dictionary saves space when two or more words have the same meaning is by putting the definition at the more common word and linking to that entry by means of a cross-reference in SMALL CAPITALS. This treatment tells you to look at the entry for the word in small capitals for the definition, and it tells you that the entry word and the word in small capitals are synonyms.

Sometimes the synonym cross-reference is used in place of a definition and sometimes following a definition.

> **lightning bug** *n* **:** FIREFLY
>
> **om·nip·o·tent** *adj* **:** having power or authority without limit **:** ALMIGHTY . . .

When the synonym cross-reference has a following sense number or has a superscript homograph number attached, it tells you which specific sense number and which homograph to look to for the shared meaning.

> **prince** *n* **1 :** MONARCH 1 . . .
>
> **con·fi·den·tial** *adj* **1 :** ^{1}SECRET 1 . . .

There is a special treatment for Canadian (*Can*) and British (*Brit*) spelling variants. These variants are usually listed along with the U.S. spelling.

> **cal·i·ber** *or Can and Brit* **cal·i·bre** *n* **1 :** level of excellence, skill, or importance . . .
>
> **the·ater** *or chiefly Can and Brit* **the·atre** *n* **1 :** a building in which plays, motion pictures, or shows are presented . . .

The *or Can and Brit* at **caliber** indicates that the following spelling is the typical spelling in Canada and Britain and is relatively uncommon in the U.S.; the *or chiefly Can and Brit* at **theater** indicates that the following spelling, while typical in Canada and Britain, has some currency in the U.S.

When the Canadian or British spelling would fall more than five entries away, it is also reentered with a cross-reference to the main entry.

> **cheque** *Can and Brit spelling of* CHECK n, sense 4
>
> **plough, ploughshare** *chiefly Brit spelling of* PLOW, PLOWSHARE

Your dictionary also guides you in the way a particular word is used. **Usage notes** may follow a definition or be used in place of a definition.

ath·let·ics *n pl* **:** games, sports, and exercises requiring strength, endurance, and skill — used as singular or plural

[3]**why** *interj* — used to express surprise, uncertainty, approval, disapproval, or impatience

Guidance on capitalization for entries where the main entry word is not shown capitalized is usually shown by an italic note at the beginning of the definition.

french fry *n, often cap 1st F* **:** a strip of potato fried in deep fat

cpu *n, often cap C&P&U* **:** the part of a computer that does most of the processing of data

DICTIONARY

A

¹a *n, pl* **a's** *or* **as** *often cap* **1 :** the first letter of the English alphabet **2 :** a grade that shows a student's work is excellent **3 :** a musical note referred to by the letter A
²a *indefinite article* **1 :** someone or something being mentioned for the first time **2 :** the same **3 :** ¹ANY 1 **4 :** for or from each **5 :** ²ONE 3 — used before words that do not begin with a vowel sound
a- *prefix* **1 :** on **:** in **:** at **2 :** in (such) a state, condition, or manner **3 :** in the act or process of
aard·vark *n* **:** an African animal with a long snout and a long sticky tongue that feeds mostly on ants and termites and is active at night
AB *abbr* Alberta
ab- *prefix* **:** from **:** differing from
aback *adv* **:** by surprise
aba·cus *n, pl* **aba·ci** *or* **aba·cus·es :** an instrument for doing arithmetic by sliding counters along rods or in grooves
ab·a·lo·ne *n* **:** a shellfish that is a mollusk which has a flattened shell with a pearly lining
¹aban·don *vb* **aban·doned; aban·don·ing 1 :** to leave and never return to **:** give up completely **2 :** to stop having or doing — **aban·don·ment** *n*
²abandon *n* **:** a feeling of complete freedom
aban·doned *adj* **:** given up **:** left empty or unused
abash *vb* **abashed; abash·ing :** EMBARRASS
abate *vb* **abat·ed; abat·ing :** to make or become less — **abate·ment** *n*
ab·bess *n* **:** the head of an abbey for women
ab·bey *n, pl* **abbeys 1 :** MONASTERY, CONVENT **2 :** a church that is connected to buildings where nuns or monks live
ab·bot *n* **:** the head of an abbey for men
abbr *abbr* abbreviation
ab·bre·vi·ate *vb* **ab·bre·vi·at·ed; ab·bre·vi·at·ing :** to make briefer **:** SHORTEN
ab·bre·vi·a·tion *n* **:** a shortened form of a word or phrase
ab·di·cate *vb* **ab·di·cat·ed; ab·di·cat·ing :** to give up a position of power or authority — **ab·di·ca·tion** *n*
ab·do·men *n* **1 :** the part of the body between the chest and the hips including the cavity containing the stomach and other digestive organs **2 :** the hind part of the body of an arthropod (as an insect)
ab·dom·i·nal *adj* **:** relating to or located in the abdomen
ab·duct *vb* **ab·duct·ed; ab·duct·ing :** to take a person away by force **:** KIDNAP — **ab·duc·tion** *n*
abed *adv or adj* **:** in bed
ab·er·ra·tion *n* **:** an instance of being different from what is normal or usual
ab·hor *vb* **ab·horred; ab·hor·ring :** to dislike very much **:** LOATHE
ab·hor·rent *adj* **:** causing or deserving strong dislike
abide *vb* **abode** *or* **abid·ed; abid·ing 1 :** to put up with patiently **:** TOLERATE **2 :** ¹LAST 1, ENDURE **3 :** to stay or live in a place — **abide by :** to accept the terms of **:** OBEY
abil·i·ty *n, pl* **abil·i·ties 1 :** power to do something **2 :** natural talent or acquired skill
-abil·i·ty *also* **-ibil·i·ty** *n suffix, pl* **-abil·i·ties** *also* **-ibil·i·ties :** ability, fitness, or tendency to act or be acted upon in (such) a way
ab·ject *adj* **1 :** very bad or severe **2 :** low in spirit, strength, or hope — **ab·ject·ly** *adv*
ablaze *adj* **1 :** on fire **2 :** glowing with light, color, or emotion
able *adj* **abler; ablest 1 :** having enough power, resources, or skill to do something **2 :** having the freedom or opportunity to do something **3 :** having or showing much skill
-able *also* **-ible** *adj suffix* **1 :** capable of, fit for, or worthy of being **2 :** tending or likely to — **-ably** *also* **-ibly** *adv suffix*
able–bod·ied *adj* **:** physically fit
ably *adv* **:** in a skillful way
ab·nor·mal *adj* **:** differing from the normal usually in a noticeable way — **ab·nor·mal·ly** *adv*
ab·nor·mal·i·ty *n, pl* **ab·nor·mal·i·ties :** something that is not usual, expected, or normal
¹aboard *adv* **:** on, onto, or within a ship, train, bus, or airplane
²aboard *prep* **:** on or into especially for passage
¹abode *past of* ABIDE
²abode *n* **:** the place where someone stays or lives
abol·ish *vb* **abol·ished; abol·ish·ing :** to do away with **:** put an end to
ab·o·li·tion *n* **:** a complete elimination of
ab·o·li·tion·ist *n* **:** a person favoring the abolition of slavery
A–bomb *n* **:** ATOMIC BOMB
abom·i·na·ble *adj* **1 :** deserving or causing disgust **2 :** very disagreeable or unpleasant — **abom·i·na·bly** *adv*
abominable snowman *n, often cap A&S* **:** a creature somewhat resembling a human being or ape that is reported to exist in the Himalaya mountains
abom·i·na·tion *n* **:** something that causes disgust

ab·orig·i·nal *adj* **1 :** being the first of its kind in a region **2 :** of or relating to the original people living in a region

ab·orig·i·ne *n, pl* **ab·orig·i·nes :** a member of the original people living in a region : NATIVE

abound *vb* **abound·ed; abound·ing 1 :** to be plentiful : TEEM **2 :** to be fully supplied

¹about *adv* **1 :** ALMOST, NEARLY **2 :** on all sides : AROUND **3 :** in the opposite direction **4 :** on the verge of

²about *prep* **1 :** having to do with **2 :** on every side of : AROUND **3 :** over or in different parts of **4 :** near or not far from in time

¹above *adv* **:** in or to a higher place

²above *prep* **1 :** higher than : OVER **2 :** too good for **3 :** more than **4 :** to a greater degree than **5 :** having more power or importance than

³above *adj* **:** said or written earlier

¹above·board *adv* **:** in an honest open way

²aboveboard *adj* **:** free from tricks and secrecy

ab·ra·ca·dab·ra *n* **:** a magical charm or word

abrade *vb* **abrad·ed; abrad·ing :** to wear away or irritate by rubbing

¹abra·sive *n* **:** a substance for grinding, smoothing, or polishing

²abrasive *adj* **1 :** causing damage or wear by rubbing **2 :** very unpleasant or irritating

abreast *adv or adj* **1 :** right beside one another **2 :** up to a certain level of knowledge

abridge *vb* **abridged; abridg·ing :** to shorten by leaving out some parts

abridg·ment *or* **abridge·ment** *n* **:** a shortened form of a written work

abroad *adv or adj* **1 :** over a wide area **2 :** in the open : OUTDOORS **3 :** in or to a foreign country **4 :** known to many people

abrupt *adj* **1 :** happening without warning : SUDDEN **2 :** ¹STEEP 1 **3 :** rudely brief — **abrupt·ly** *adv* — **abrupt·ness** *n*

ab·scess *n* **:** a collection of pus with swollen and red tissue around it — **ab·scessed** *adj*

ab·sence *n* **1 :** a failure to be present at a usual or expected place **2 :** ²LACK, WANT

ab·sent *adj* **1 :** not present **2 :** not existing **3 :** showing a lack of attention

ab·sen·tee *n* **:** a person who is not present

ab·sent·mind·ed *adj* **:** tending to forget or not pay attention — **ab·sent·mind·ed·ly** *adv* — **ab·sent·mind·ed·ness** *n*

ab·so·lute *adj* **1 :** ¹TOTAL 1, COMPLETE **2 :** not limited in any way **3 :** free from doubt : CERTAIN — **ab·so·lute·ly** *adv*

ab·solve *vb* **ab·solved; ab·solv·ing :** to make free from guilt or responsibility

ab·sorb *vb* **ab·sorbed; ab·sorb·ing 1 :** to take in or swallow up **2 :** to hold the complete attention of **3 :** to receive without giving back

ab·sor·ben·cy *n* **:** the quality or state of being able to draw in or soak up

ab·sor·bent *adj* **:** able to draw in or soak up

ab·sorp·tion *n* **1 :** the process of drawing in or soaking up : absorbing or being absorbed **2 :** complete attention

ab·stain *vb* **ab·stained; ab·stain·ing :** to choose not to do or have something — **ab·stain·er** *n*

ab·sti·nence *n* **:** an avoidance by choice especially of certain foods or of liquor

¹ab·stract *adj* **1 :** hard to understand **2 :** relating to general ideas or qualities rather than specific people, things, or actions — **ab·stract·ly** *adv*

²ab·stract *n* **:** ²SUMMARY

³ab·stract *vb* **ab·stract·ed; ab·stract·ing 1 :** to take away : SEPARATE **2 :** SUMMARIZE

ab·strac·tion *n* **1 :** the act of summarizing : the state of being summarized **2 :** a thought or thoughts about general qualities or ideas rather than people or things

ab·surd *adj* **:** very foolish, unreasonable, or untrue : RIDICULOUS — **ab·surd·ly** *adv*

ab·sur·di·ty *n, pl* **ab·sur·di·ties 1 :** the fact of being ridiculous **2 :** something that is ridiculous

abun·dance *n* **:** a large quantity : PLENTY

abun·dant *adj* **:** more than enough : PLENTIFUL — **abun·dant·ly** *adv*

¹abuse *n* **1 :** wrong or unfair treatment or use **2 :** the act or practice of improperly using or of using in harmful amounts **3 :** harmful treatment of a person or an animal **4 :** harsh insulting language **5 :** a dishonest practice

²abuse *vb* **abused; abus·ing 1 :** to treat in a cruel or harmful way **2 :** to use wrongly : MISUSE **3 :** to use improperly or in harmful amounts **4 :** to blame or scold rudely

abu·sive *adj* **1 :** using or involving harmful treatment **2 :** using harsh insulting language

abut *vb* **abut·ted; abut·ting :** to touch along an edge

abys·mal *adj* **:** extremely bad

abyss *n* **:** a gulf so deep or space so great that it cannot be measured

AC *abbr* **1** air-conditioning **2** alternating current **3** area code

ac·a·dem·ic *adj* **1 :** of or relating to schools and education **2 :** having no practical importance — **ac·a·dem·i·cal·ly** *adv*

acad·e·my *n, pl* **acad·e·mies 1 :** a private high school **2 :** a high school or college where special subjects are taught **3 :** an organization which supports art, science, or literature

ac·cede *vb* **ac·ced·ed; ac·ced·ing :** to agree to

ac·cel·er·ate *vb* **ac·cel·er·at·ed; ac·cel·er·at·ing 1 :** to move or cause to move faster **2 :** to cause to happen more quickly

ac·cel·er·a·tion *n* : the act or process of speeding up

ac·cel·er·a·tor *n* : a pedal in an automobile for controlling the speed of the motor

[1]**ac·cent** *vb* **ac·cent·ed; ac·cent·ing** **1** : to give a greater force or stress **2** : to mark with a written or printed accent

[2]**ac·cent** *n* **1** : a way of pronouncing words shared by the people of a particular country or region **2** : greater stress or force given to a syllable of a word in speaking or to a beat in music **3** : a mark (as ˈ or ˌ) used in writing or printing to show the place of greater stress on a syllable

ac·cen·tu·ate *vb* **ac·cen·tu·at·ed; ac·cen·tu·at·ing** : to make more noticeable

ac·cept *vb* **ac·cept·ed; ac·cept·ing** **1** : to receive or take willingly **2** : to agree to **3** : to stop resisting **4** : to admit deserving

ac·cept·able *adj* **1** : worthy of being accepted **2** : ADEQUATE 2 — **ac·cept·ably** *adv*

ac·cep·tance *n* **1** : the act of accepting **2** : the quality or state of being accepted or acceptable

[1]**ac·cess** *n* **1** : the right or ability to approach, enter, or use **2** : a way or means of approaching

[2]**access** *vb* **ac·cessed; ac·cess·ing** : to get at : get access to

ac·ces·si·ble *adj* **1** : able to be reached **2** : able to be used or obtained **3** : easily used or accessed by people with disabilities

ac·ces·sion *n* : the rise to a position of power

ac·ces·so·ry *n, pl* **ac·ces·so·ries** **1** : a person who helps another in doing wrong **2** : an object or device not necessary in itself but adding to the beauty or usefulness of something else

ac·ci·dent *n* **1** : something that happens by chance or from unknown causes and that often causes injury or damage : MISHAP **2** : [1]CHANCE 1

ac·ci·den·tal *adj* **1** : happening by chance or unexpectedly **2** : not happening or done on purpose — **ac·ci·den·tal·ly** *adv*

[1]**ac·claim** *vb* **ac·claimed; ac·claim·ing** : [1]PRAISE 1

[2]**acclaim** *n* : [2]PRAISE 1

ac·cli·mate *vb* **ac·cli·mat·ed; ac·cli·mat·ing** : to adjust or change to fit a new climate or new surroundings

ac·cli·ma·tize *vb* **ac·cli·ma·tized; ac·cli·ma·tiz·ing** : ACCLIMATE

ac·com·mo·date *vb* **ac·com·mo·dat·ed; ac·com·mo·dat·ing** **1** : to provide with a place to stay or sleep **2** : to provide with something needed : help out **3** : to have room for

ac·com·mo·dat·ing *adj* : ready to help

ac·com·mo·da·tion *n* **1 accommodations** *pl* : a place where travelers can sleep and find other services **2** : something supplied that is useful or handy

ac·com·pa·ni·ment *n* : music played in support of someone singing or playing an instrument

ac·com·pa·nist *n* : a musician who plays in support of someone else who is singing or playing an instrument

ac·com·pa·ny *vb* **ac·com·pa·nied; ac·com·pa·ny·ing** **1** : to go with as a companion **2** : to play a musical accompaniment for **3** : to go or occur with

ac·com·plice *n* : a partner in wrongdoing

ac·com·plish *vb* **ac·com·plished; ac·com·plish·ing** : to succeed in doing or reaching

ac·com·plished *adj* : skilled through practice or training : EXPERT

ac·com·plish·ment *n* **1** : the act of successfully doing or reaching **2** : something successfully done or reached especially through effort **3** : an ability or skill gained by practice or training

[1]**ac·cord** *vb* **ac·cord·ed; ac·cord·ing** **1** : [1]GIVE 3 **2** : to be in harmony : AGREE

[2]**accord** *n* **1** : AGREEMENT 1, HARMONY **2** : willingness to act or to do something

ac·cor·dance *n* : AGREEMENT 1

ac·cord·ing·ly *adv* **1** : in the necessary way : in the way called for **2** : as a result : CONSEQUENTLY, SO

ac·cord·ing to *prep* **1** : in agreement with **2** : as stated by

ac·cor·di·on *n* : a portable keyboard musical instrument played by forcing air from a bellows past metal reeds

ac·cost *vb* **ac·cost·ed; ac·cost·ing** : to approach and speak to in a demanding or aggressive way

[1]**ac·count** *n* **1** : a record of money received and money paid out **2** : an arrangement with a bank to hold money and keep records of transactions **3** : an arrangement for regular dealings with a business **4** : a statement of explanation or of reasons or causes **5** : a statement of facts or events : REPORT **6** : [2]WORTH 1, IMPORTANCE — **on account of** : for the sake of : because of — **on someone's account** : because of someone

[2]**account** *vb* **ac·count·ed; ac·count·ing** **1** : to think of as : CONSIDER **2** : to take into consideration **3** : to give an explanation **4** : to be the only or chief reason

ac·coun·tant *n* : someone whose job is keeping the financial records of a person or a business

ac·count·ing *n* : the work of keeping the financial records of a person or a business

ac·cu·mu·late *vb* **ac·cu·mu·lat·ed; ac·cu·mu·lat·ing** **1** : COLLECT 3, GATHER **2** : to increase in quantity or number

ac·cu·mu·la·tion *n* **1 :** an act of collecting or gathering **2 :** COLLECTION 2
ac·cu·ra·cy *n* **:** freedom from mistakes
ac·cu·rate *adj* **:** free from mistakes **:** RIGHT — **ac·cu·rate·ly** *adv*
ac·cursed *or* **ac·curst** *adj* **1 :** being under a curse **2 :** greatly or strongly disliked
ac·cu·sa·tion *n* **:** a claim that someone has done something bad or illegal
ac·cuse *vb* **ac·cused; ac·cus·ing :** to blame for something wrong or illegal — **ac·cus·er** *n*
ac·cus·tom *vb* **ac·cus·tomed; ac·cus·tom·ing :** to cause (someone) to get used to something
ac·cus·tomed *adj* **1 :** CUSTOMARY 2, USUAL **2 :** familiar with
[1]**ace** *n* **1 :** a playing card with one figure in its center **2 :** a person who is expert at something
[2]**ace** *adj* **:** of the very best kind
[1]**ache** *vb* **ached; ach·ing 1 :** to suffer a dull continuous pain **2 :** to desire very much **:** YEARN
[2]**ache** *n* **:** a dull continuous pain
achieve *vb* **achieved; achiev·ing 1 :** to get by means of hard work **2 :** to become successful
achieve·ment *n* **1 :** the state of having gotten through great effort **2 :** something gotten especially by great effort
[1]**ac·id** *adj* **1 :** having a taste that is sour, bitter, or stinging **2 :** harsh or critical in tone **3 :** of, relating to, or like an acid — **ac·id·ly** *adv*
[2]**acid** *n* **:** a chemical compound that tastes sour and forms a water solution which turns blue litmus paper red
acid·i·ty *n, pl* **acid·i·ties :** the quality, state, or degree of being acid
ac·knowl·edge *vb* **ac·knowl·edged; ac·knowl·edg·ing 1 :** to admit the truth or existence of **2 :** to make known that something has been received or noticed **3 :** to recognize the rights or authority of **4 :** to express thanks or appreciation for
ac·knowl·edged *adj* **:** generally accepted
ac·knowl·edg·ment *or* **ac·knowl·edge·ment** *n* **1 :** an act of admitting the truth or existence of **2 :** an act of praising or thanking for some deed or achievement **3 :** a usually written statement saying that a letter or message was received
ac·ne *n* **:** a skin condition in which pimples and blackheads are present
acorn *n* **:** the nut of the oak tree
acous·tic *or* **acous·ti·cal** *adj* **1 :** of or relating to hearing or sound **2 :** not having the sound changed by electrical devices
acous·tics *n pl* **:** the qualities in a room that affect how well a person in it can hear
ac·quaint *vb* **ac·quaint·ed; ac·quaint·ing 1 :** to cause to know personally **2 :** to make familiar
ac·quain·tance *n* **1 :** a person someone knows slightly **2 :** personal knowledge
ac·qui·esce *vb* **ac·qui·esced; ac·qui·esc·ing :** to accept, agree, or give consent by keeping silent or by not making objections
ac·qui·es·cence *n* **:** the act of agreeing, accepting, or giving consent
ac·quire *vb* **ac·quired; ac·quir·ing :** to get especially through effort **:** GAIN
ac·qui·si·tion *n* **1 :** the act of gaining especially through effort **2 :** something gained especially through effort
ac·quit *vb* **ac·quit·ted; ac·quit·ting 1 :** to declare innocent of a crime or of wrongdoing **2 :** to behave in a certain way
ac·quit·tal *n* **:** the act of declaring someone innocent of a crime or wrongdoing
acre *n* **:** a measure of land area equal to 43,560 square feet (about 4047 square meters)
acre·age *n* **:** area in acres
ac·rid *adj* **1 :** sharp or bitter in taste or odor **2 :** very harsh or unpleasant
ac·ro·bat *n* **:** a person skillful at performing stunts like jumping, balancing, tumbling, and swinging from a bar
ac·ro·bat·ic *adj* **:** relating to acrobats or acrobatics
ac·ro·bat·ics *n pl* **1 :** the art or performance of an acrobat **2 :** difficult or dangerous stunts — used either as a singular or a plural in writing
ac·ro·nym *n* **:** a word formed from the first letter or letters of the words of a compound term
[1]**across** *adv* **1 :** from one side to the other **2 :** a measurement from one side to another **3 :** on the opposite side
[2]**across** *prep* **1 :** to or on the opposite side of **2 :** so as to pass, go over, or intersect at an angle **3 :** in every part of
[1]**act** *n* **1 :** something that is done **:** DEED **2 :** a law made by a governing body **3 :** a main division of a play **4 :** one of the performances in a show **5 :** an insincere way of behaving
[2]**act** *vb* **act·ed; act·ing 1 :** to do something **:** MOVE **2 :** to behave oneself in a certain way **3 :** to perform as a character in a play **4 :** to perform a certain function **5 :** to have a result **:** make something happen **:** WORK — **act up :** to behave badly
act·ing *adj* **:** serving for a short time only or in place of another
ac·tion *n* **1 :** the process by which something produces a change in another thing **2 :** the doing of something **3 :** something done **4 :** the way something runs or works **5 :** combat in war

action figure *n* : a model often of a superhero used as a toy

ac·ti·vate *vb* **ac·ti·vat·ed; ac·ti·vat·ing** : to start working or cause to start working

ac·tive *adj* **1** : producing or involving action or movement **2** : showing that the subject of a sentence is the doer of the action represented by the verb **3** : quick in physical movement : LIVELY **4** : taking part in an action or activity — **ac·tive·ly** *adv*

ac·tiv·i·ty *n, pl* **ac·tiv·i·ties** **1** : energetic action **2** : something done especially for relaxation or fun

ac·tor *n* : a person who acts especially in a play or movie

ac·tress *n* : a woman or girl who acts especially in a play or movie

ac·tu·al *adj* : really existing or happening : not false

ac·tu·al·ly *adv* : in fact : REALLY

acute *adj* **acut·er; acut·est** **1** : measuring less than 90 degrees **2** : having or showing an ability to understand what is not obvious **3** : SEVERE 2, SHARP **4** : developing quickly and lasting only a short time **5** : CRITICAL 4, URGENT **6** : very strong and sensitive — **acute·ly** *adv* — **acute·ness** *n*

ad *n* : ADVERTISEMENT

A.D. *abbr* in the year of our Lord — abbreviation for Latin *anno Domini*, which means "in the year of our Lord"

ad·age *n* : an old familiar saying : PROVERB

ad·a·mant *adj* : not giving in

Ad·am's apple *n* : the lump formed in the front of a person's neck by cartilage in the throat

adapt *vb* **adapt·ed; adapt·ing** **1** : to change behavior so that it is easier to function in a particular place or situation **2** : to make or become suitable or able to function

adapt·able *adj* : capable of changing or being changed to better suit a situation

ad·ap·ta·tion *n* **1** : the act or process of changing to better suit a situation **2** : a body part or feature or a behavior that helps a living thing survive and function better in its environment

add *vb* **add·ed; add·ing** **1** : to combine numbers into a single sum **2** : to join or unite to something **3** : to cause to have **4** : to say something more — **add up** **1** : to be added together to equal the expected amount **2** : to make sense

ad·dend *n* : a number that is to be added to another number

ad·den·dum *n, pl* **ad·den·da** : something added (as to a book)

ad·der *n* **1** : a poisonous snake of Europe or Africa **2** : a harmless North American snake

ad·dict *n* **1** : a person who is not able to stop taking drugs **2** : a person who likes or enjoys something excessively

ad·dict·ed *adj* **1** : unable to stop using a drug **2** : having an unusually great need to do or have something — **ad·dic·tion** *n*

ad·di·tion *n* **1** : the act or process of adding numbers to obtain their sum **2** : something added — **in addition** : as something more — **in addition to** : along with or together with

ad·di·tion·al *adj* : [1]EXTRA — **ad·di·tion·al·ly** *adv*

ad·di·tive *n* : a substance added to another in small amounts

ad·dle *vb* **ad·dled; ad·dling** : to make or become confused

[1]**ad·dress** *vb* **ad·dressed; ad·dress·ing** **1** : to put directions for delivery on **2** : to speak or write to **3** : to use a specified name or title when speaking or writing to (someone) **4** : to deal with : give attention to

[2]**ad·dress** *n* **1** : the place where a person can usually be reached **2** : the directions for delivery placed on mail **3** : the symbols (as numerals or letters) that identify the location where particular information (as a home page) is stored on a computer especially on the Internet **4** : a formal speech **5** : the name of a computer account from which e-mail can be sent or received

ad·dress·ee *n* : the person to whom something is addressed

ad·e·noids *n pl* : fleshy growths near the opening of the nose into the throat

ad·ept *adj* : very good at something — **adept·ly** *adv* — **adept·ness** *n*

ad·e·quate *adj* **1** : [1]ENOUGH **2** : good enough — **ad·e·quate·ly** *adv*

ad·here *vb* **ad·hered; ad·her·ing** **1** : to stick tight : CLING **2** : to act in the way that is required by

ad·her·ence *n* : the act of doing what is required by

ad·her·ent *n* : a person who is loyal to a belief, an organization, or a leader

ad·he·sion *n* : the act or state of sticking

[1]**ad·he·sive** *adj* : tending to stick : STICKY

[2]**adhesive** *n* : a substance that is used to make things stick together

adj *abbr* adjective

ad·ja·cent *adj* : next to or near something

ad·jec·ti·val *adj* : of, relating to, or functioning as an adjective — **ad·jec·ti·val·ly** *adv*

ad·jec·tive *n* : a word that says something about a noun or pronoun

ad·join *vb* **ad·joined; ad·join·ing** : to be next to or in contact with

ad·journ *vb* **ad·journed; ad·journ·ing** : to bring or come to a close for a period of time — **ad·journ·ment** *n*

ad·just *vb* **ad·just·ed; ad·just·ing** **1 :** to change (something) in a minor way to make it work better **2 :** to change the position of (something) **3 :** to become used to
ad·just·able *adj* **:** possible to change to make work or be positioned better
ad·just·ment *n* **1 :** a small change that improves something or makes it work better **2 :** the act or process of changing or adjusting **3 :** the decision about and payment of a claim or debt
ad·ju·tant *n* **:** an officer who assists the officer in command
ad–lib *vb* **ad–libbed; ad–lib·bing :** to make up words or music during a performance **:** IMPROVISE
ad·min·is·ter *vb* **ad·min·is·tered; ad·min·is·ter·ing** **1 :** to be in charge of **:** MANAGE **2 :** to give out as deserved **3 :** to give officially **4 :** to give or supply as treatment
ad·min·is·tra·tion *n* **1 :** the act or process of administering **2 :** the work involved in managing something **3 :** the people who direct the business of something (as a city or school) **4 :** a government department
ad·min·is·tra·tive *adj* **:** of or assisting in administration
ad·min·is·tra·tor *n* **:** a person who administers business, school, or government affairs
ad·mi·ra·ble *adj* **:** deserving great respect and approval — **ad·mi·ra·bly** *adv*
ad·mi·ral *n* **:** a high-ranking commissioned officer in the navy or coast guard
ad·mi·ral·ty *adj* **:** of or relating to conduct on the sea
ad·mi·ra·tion *n* **:** a feeling of great respect and approval
ad·mire *vb* **ad·mired; ad·mir·ing :** to think very highly of **:** feel admiration for — **ad·mir·er** *n*
ad·mis·si·ble *adj* **:** able to be or deserving to be admitted or allowed **:** ALLOWABLE
ad·mis·sion *n* **1 :** acknowledgment by someone of something about him or her that has not been proved **2 :** the right or permission to enter **3 :** the price of entrance
ad·mit *vb* **ad·mit·ted; ad·mit·ting** **1 :** to make known usually with some unwillingness **2 :** to allow to enter **:** let in **3 :** [1]PERMIT 2, ALLOW
ad·mit·tance *n* **:** permission to enter
ad·mon·ish *vb* **ad·mon·ished; ad·mon·ish·ing** **1 :** to criticize or warn gently but seriously **2 :** to give friendly advice or encouragement
ad·mo·ni·tion *n* **:** a gentle or friendly criticism or warning
ado *n* **:** foolish or unnecessary trouble, activity, or excitement
ado·be *n* **1 :** brick made of earth or clay dried in the sun **2 :** a building made of adobe
ad·o·les·cence *n* **:** the period of life between childhood and adulthood
ad·o·les·cent *n* **:** a person who is no longer a child but not yet an adult
adopt *vb* **adopt·ed; adopt·ing** **1 :** to legally take a child of other parents to raise **2 :** to take up as someone's own **3 :** to accept and put into action
adop·tion *n* **:** the act of adopting **:** the state of being adopted
ador·able *adj* **:** CHARMING, LOVELY — **ador·ably** *adv*
ad·o·ra·tion *n* **:** deep love
adore *vb* **adored; ador·ing** **1 :** [2]WORSHIP 1 **2 :** to be very fond of
adorn *vb* **adorned; adorn·ing :** to make more attractive by adding something
adorn·ment *n* **:** something added to make a person or thing more attractive
adren·a·line *n* **1 :** EPINEPHRINE **2 :** excited energy
adrift *adv or adj* **:** in a drifting state
adroit *adj* **:** having or showing great skill or cleverness — **adroit·ly** *adv*
ad·u·la·tion *n* **:** very great admiration
[1]**adult** *adj* **:** fully developed and mature
[2]**adult** *n* **:** a fully grown person, animal, or plant
adul·ter·ate *vb* **adul·ter·at·ed; adul·ter·at·ing** **:** to make impure or weaker by adding something different or of poorer quality
adult·hood *n* **:** the period of being an adult
adv *abbr* adverb
[1]**ad·vance** *vb* **ad·vanced; ad·vanc·ing** **1 :** to move forward **2 :** to help the progress of **3 :** to raise to a higher rank **:** PROMOTE **4 :** to give ahead of time **5 :** PROPOSE 1
[2]**advance** *n* **1 :** a forward movement **2 :** progress in development **:** IMPROVEMENT **3 :** a rise in price, value, or amount **4 :** a first step or approach **5 :** money given ahead of the usual time — **in advance :** before an expected event
ad·vanced *adj* **1 :** being far along in years or progress **2 :** being beyond the elementary or introductory level
ad·vance·ment *n* **1 :** the action of moving forward in position or progress **:** the state of being moved forward in position or progress **2 :** the act of raising to a higher rank or position **:** the result of being raised to a higher rank or position
ad·van·tage *n* **1 :** something that benefits the one it belongs to **2 :** the fact of being in a better position or condition **3 :** personal benefit or gain
ad·van·ta·geous *adj* **:** giving a benefit especially that others do not have **:** giving an advantage — **ad·van·ta·geous·ly** *adv*
ad·vent *n* **:** the arrival or coming of something

ad·ven·ture *n* **1 :** an action that involves unknown dangers and risks **2 :** an unusual experience

ad·ven·tur·er *n* **:** a person who seeks dangerous or exciting experiences

ad·ven·ture·some *adj* **:** likely to take risks **:** DARING

ad·ven·tur·ous *adj* **1 :** ready to take risks or to deal with new or unexpected problems **2 :** DANGEROUS 1, RISKY

ad·verb *n* **:** a word used to modify a verb, an adjective, or another adverb and often used to show degree, manner, place, or time

ad·ver·bi·al *adj* **:** of, relating to, or used as an adverb — **ad·ver·bi·al·ly** *adv*

ad·ver·sary *n, pl* **ad·ver·sar·ies :** OPPONENT, ENEMY

ad·verse *adj* **1 :** acting against or in an opposite direction **2 :** not helping or favoring — **ad·verse·ly** *adv*

ad·ver·si·ty *n, pl* **ad·ver·si·ties :** hard times **:** MISFORTUNE

ad·ver·tise *vb* **ad·ver·tised; ad·ver·tis·ing 1 :** to call to public attention to persuade to buy **2 :** to announce publicly — **ad·ver·tis·er** *n*

ad·ver·tise·ment *n* **:** a notice or short film advertising something

ad·ver·tis·ing *n* **1 :** speech, writing, pictures, or films meant to persuade people to buy something **2 :** the business of preparing advertisements

ad·vice *n* **:** suggestions about a decision or action

ad·vis·able *adj* **:** reasonable or wise to do

ad·vise *vb* **ad·vised; ad·vis·ing 1 :** to give suggestions about a decision or action **:** give advice to **2 :** to give information about something — **ad·vis·er** *or* **ad·vi·sor** *n*

ad·vi·so·ry *adj* **:** having the power or right to advise

[1]**ad·vo·cate** *n* **1 :** a person who argues for or supports an idea or plan **2 :** a person who argues for another especially in court

[2]**ad·vo·cate** *vb* **ad·vo·cat·ed; ad·vo·cat·ing :** to speak in favor of **:** argue for

ad·ware *n* **:** computer software that is provided usually for free but contains advertisements

adze *also* **adz** *n, pl* **adz·es :** a cutting tool that has a thin curved blade at right angles to the handle and is used for shaping wood

ae·on *or* **eon** *n* **:** a very long period of time

aer- *or* **aero-** *prefix* **:** air **:** atmosphere **:** gas

aer·ate *vb* **aer·at·ed; aer·at·ing 1 :** to supply or cause to be filled with air **2 :** to supply (blood) with oxygen by breathing — **aer·a·tor** *n*

aer·a·tion *n* **:** the process of supplying or filling with air or gas

[1]**ae·ri·al** *adj* **1 :** performed or occurring in the air **2 :** of aircraft **3 :** taken from, used in, or performed using an airplane

[2]**aer·i·al** *n* **:** ANTENNA 2

aero·nau·ti·cal *adj* **:** of or relating to aeronautics

aero·nau·tics *n* **:** a science dealing with the building and flying of aircraft

aero·sol *n* **1 :** a substance (as an insect repellent or medicine) that is released from a container as a spray of tiny solid or liquid particles in gas **2 :** a container (as a can) that dispenses a substance as a spray

[1]**aero·space** *n* **1 :** the earth's atmosphere and the space beyond **2 :** a science dealing with aerospace

[2]**aerospace** *adj* **:** relating to aerospace, to the vehicles used in aerospace or their manufacture, or to travel in aerospace

aes·thet·ic *adj* **:** relating to beauty and what is beautiful — **aes·thet·i·cal·ly** *adv*

[1]**afar** *adv* **:** from, at, or to a great distance

[2]**afar** *n* **:** a long way off

af·fa·ble *adj* **:** friendly and easy to talk to — **af·fa·bly** *adv*

af·fair *n* **1 affairs** *pl* **:** work or activities done for a purpose **:** BUSINESS **2 :** something that relates to or involves someone **3 :** a social event or activity

[1]**af·fect** *vb* **af·fect·ed; af·fect·ing :** to pretend that a false behavior or feeling is natural or genuine

[2]**affect** *vb* **affected; affecting 1 :** to have an effect on **2 :** to cause strong emotions in **3 :** to cause illness in

af·fect·ed *adj* **:** not natural or genuine — **af·fect·ed·ly** *adv*

af·fec·tion *n* **:** a feeling of liking and caring for someone or something

af·fec·tion·ate *adj* **:** feeling or showing a great liking for a person or thing **:** LOVING — **af·fec·tion·ate·ly** *adv*

af·fi·da·vit *n* **:** a written statement signed by a person who swears that the information is true

af·fil·i·ate *vb* **af·fil·i·at·ed; af·fil·i·at·ing :** to associate as a member or partner

af·fin·i·ty *n, pl* **af·fin·i·ties :** a strong liking for or attraction to someone or something

af·firm *vb* **af·firmed; af·firm·ing :** to declare that something is true

af·fir·ma·tion *n* **:** an act of saying or showing that something is true

[1]**af·fir·ma·tive** *adj* **1 :** saying or showing that the answer is "yes" **2 :** being positive or helpful

[2]**affirmative** *n* **1 :** an expression (as the word *yes*) of agreement **2 :** the side that supports or votes for something

[1]**af·fix** *vb* **af·fixed; af·fix·ing 1 :** to attach firmly **2 :** to add to something else

DICTIONARY

[2]**af·fix** *n* : a letter or group of letters (as a prefix or suffix) that comes at the beginning or end of a word and has a meaning of its own
af·flict *vb* **af·flict·ed; af·flict·ing** : to cause pain or unhappiness to
af·flic·tion *n* **1** : the state of being affected by something that causes pain or unhappiness **2** : something that causes pain or unhappiness
af·flu·ence *n* : the state of having much money and expensive things : WEALTH
af·flu·ent *adj* : having plenty of money and expensive things : WEALTHY
af·ford *vb* **af·ford·ed; af·ford·ing** **1** : to be able to do or bear without serious harm **2** : to be able to pay for **3** : to supply or provide someone with
af·ford·able *adj* : within someone's ability to pay : reasonably priced
[1]**af·front** *vb* **af·front·ed; af·front·ing** : to insult openly : OFFEND
[2]**affront** *n* : an act or statement that insults or offends someone
Af·ghan *n* **1** : a person born or living in Afghanistan **2** *not cap* : a blanket or shawl made of wool or cotton knitted or crocheted into patterns
afield *adv* **1** : to, in, or into the countryside **2** : away from home **3** : out of a usual, planned, or proper course
afire *adj* **1** : being on fire **2** : in a state of great excitement or energy
afk *abbr* away from keyboard
aflame *adj* : burning with flames
afloat *adv or adj* : carried on or as if on water
aflut·ter *adj* **1** : flapping quickly **2** : very excited and nervous
afoot *adv or adj* **1** : on foot **2** : happening now : going on
afore·men·tioned *adj* : mentioned before
afore·said *adj* : named before
afraid *adj* **1** : filled with fear **2** : filled with concern or regret **3** : having a dislike for something
afresh *adv* : again from the beginning
[1]**Af·ri·can** *n* : a person born or living in Africa
[2]**African** *adj* : of or relating to Africa or African people
African–American *n* : an American having African and especially black African ancestors — **African–American** *adj*
African violet *n* : a tropical African plant often grown for its showy white, pink, or purple flowers and its velvety leaves
Af·ro–Amer·i·can *n* : AFRICAN-AMERICAN — **Afro–American** *adj*
aft *adv* : toward or at the back part of a ship or the tail of an aircraft
[1]**af·ter** *adv* : following in time or place : at a later time
[2]**after** *prep* **1** : behind in time or place **2** : for the reason of catching, seizing, or getting **3** : following in order or in a series **4** : following the actions or departure of **5** : with the name of
[3]**after** *conj* : following the time when
af·ter·ef·fect *n* : an effect that follows its cause after some time has passed
af·ter·glow *n* **1** : a glow remaining (as in the sky after sunset) where a light has disappeared **2** : a pleasant feeling that remains after some good experience
af·ter·life *n* : an existence after death
af·ter·math *n* **1** : a result or consequence **2** : the period of time following a bad and usually destructive event
af·ter·noon *n* : the part of the day between noon and evening
af·ter–par·ty *n* : a party for invited guests that follows a main party or event
af·ter·thought *n* : something done or said that was not thought of originally
af·ter·ward *or* **af·ter·wards** *adv* : at a later time
again *adv* **1** : for another time : once more **2** : on the other hand **3** : in addition
against *prep* **1** : opposed to **2** : not agreeing with or allowed by **3** : as protection from **4** : in or into contact with **5** : in a direction opposite to **6** : before the background of
agape *adj* : having the mouth open in wonder, surprise, or shock
ag·ate *n* : a mineral that is a form of quartz with colors arranged in stripes or patches and that is used especially in jewelry
aga·ve *n* : a plant that has sword-shaped leaves with spiny edges and is sometimes grown for its large stalks of flowers
[1]**age** *n* **1** : the amount of time during which someone or something has lived or existed **2** : the time of life when a person receives some right or capacity **3** : the later part of life **4** : the condition of being old **5** : a period of time associated with a person or thing **6** : a long period of time
[2]**age** *vb* **aged; ag·ing** *or* **age·ing** **1** : to become old or older **2** : to cause to become old or to appear to be old **3** : to remain or cause to remain undisturbed until fit for use : MATURE
-age *n suffix* **1** : total amount : collection **2** : action : process **3** : result of **4** : rate of **5** : house or place of **6** : state : condition **7** : fee : charge
aged *adj* **1** : very old **2** : having reached a specified age
age·less *adj* **1** : not growing old or showing the effects of age **2** : lasting forever : TIMELESS
agen·cy *n, pl* **agen·cies** **1** : a person or thing through which power is used or something is

achieved **2 :** a business that provides a particular service **3 :** a part of a government that is responsible for providing a particular service or performing a specific function

agen·da *n* **:** a list of things to be done or talked about

agent *n* **1 :** something that produces an effect **2 :** a person who acts or does business for another

ag·gra·vate *vb* **ag·gra·vat·ed; ag·gra·vat·ing** **1 :** to make worse or more serious **2 :** to make angry usually by bothering again and again

ag·gra·va·tion *n* **1 :** an act or the result of making worse or more serious **2 :** something that annoys or bothers someone

[1]ag·gre·gate *vb* **ag·gre·gat·ed; ag·gre·gat·ing :** to collect or gather into a mass or whole

[2]ag·gre·gate *n* **1 :** a mass or body of units or parts **2 :** the whole sum or amount

ag·gre·ga·tion *n* **1 :** the collecting of units or parts into a mass or whole **2 :** a group, body, or mass composed of many distinct parts

ag·gres·sion *n* **1 :** angry or violent behavior or feelings **2 :** hostile action made without reasonable cause

ag·gres·sive *adj* **1 :** showing a readiness to fight or argue **2 :** engaging in hostile action without reasonable cause **3 :** being forceful in getting things done — **ag·gres·sive·ly** *adv* — **ag·gres·sive·ness** *n*

ag·gres·sor *n* **:** a person or a country that engages in hostile action without reasonable cause

ag·grieved *adj* **1 :** having or showing a troubled or unhappy mind **2 :** having cause for complaint especially from unfair treatment

aghast *adj* **:** struck with terror, surprise, or horror

ag·ile *adj* **1 :** able to move quickly and easily **2 :** having a quick mind — **ag·ile·ly** *adv*

agil·i·ty *n* **:** the ability to move quickly and easily

aging *present participle of* AGE

ag·i·tate *vb* **ag·i·tat·ed; ag·i·tat·ing** **1 :** to move or stir up **2 :** to disturb, excite, or anger **3 :** to try to stir up public feeling — **ag·i·ta·tor** *n*

ag·i·ta·tion *n* **:** the act of agitating **:** the state of being agitated

aglow *adj* **1 :** glowing with light or color **2 :** feeling or showing excitement and happiness

ago *adv* **:** before this time

agog *adj* **:** full of excitement

ag·o·nize *vb* **ag·o·nized; ag·o·niz·ing :** to think or worry very much about something

ag·o·ny *n, pl* **ag·o·nies :** great physical pain or emotional distress

agree *vb* **agreed; agree·ing** **1 :** to give approval or permission **2 :** to have the same opinion **3 :** ADMIT 1 **4 :** to be alike **5 :** to come to an understanding **6 :** to be fitting or healthful

agree·able *adj* **1 :** pleasing to the mind or senses **2 :** willing to do, allow, or approve something **3 :** of a kind that can be accepted — **agree·ably** *adv*

agree·ment *n* **1 :** the act or fact of having the same opinion or an understanding **2 :** the act or fact of giving approval or permission **3 :** an arrangement by which people agree about what is to be done

ag·ri·cul·tur·al *adj* **:** relating to or used in farming or agriculture

ag·ri·cul·ture *n* **:** the cultivating of the soil, producing of crops, and raising of livestock

aground *adv or adj* **:** on or onto the shore or the bottom of a body of water

aha *interj* — used to express discovery or understanding

aha moment *n* **:** a moment of sudden realization, inspiration, or insight

ahead *adv or adj* **1 :** in or toward the front **2 :** into or for the future

ahead of *prep* **1 :** in front of **2 :** earlier than **3 :** having a lead over

ahoy *interj* — used in calling out to a passing ship or boat

[1]aid *vb* **aid·ed; aid·ing :** to provide what is useful or necessary **:** HELP

[2]aid *n* **1 :** the act of helping **2 :** help given **3 :** someone or something that is of help or assistance

aide *n* **:** a person who acts as an assistant

AIDS *n* **:** a serious disease of the human immune system in which large numbers of the cells that help the body fight infection are destroyed by the HIV virus carried in the blood and other fluids of the body

AIDS virus *n* **:** HIV

ail *vb* **ailed; ail·ing** **1 :** to be wrong with **2 :** to suffer especially with ill health

ail·ment *n* **:** a sickness or disease

[1]aim *vb* **aimed; aim·ing** **1 :** to point a weapon toward an object **2 :** INTEND **3 :** to direct toward an object or goal

[2]aim *n* **1 :** the ability to hit a target **2 :** the pointing of a weapon at a target **3 :** a goal or purpose

aim·less *adj* **:** lacking a goal or purpose — **aim·less·ly** *adv*

ain't **1 :** am not **:** are not **:** is not **2 :** have not **:** has not

[1]air *n* **1 :** the invisible mixture of odorless tasteless gases that surrounds the earth **2 :** the space or sky that is filled with air **3 :** air that is compressed **4 :** outward appearance **:** a quality that a person or thing has **5 :** AIR-

CRAFT **6 :** AVIATION 1 **7 :** a radio or television broadcast **8 airs** *pl* **:** an artificial way of acting

²air *vb* **aired; air·ing 1 :** to place in the air for cooling, freshening, or cleaning **2 :** to make known in public

air bag *n* **:** an automobile safety device consisting of a bag that inflates to cushion a rider in an accident

air base *n* **:** a base for military aircraft

air·borne *adj* **:** moving through the air

air–con·di·tion *vb* **air–con·di·tioned; air–con·di·tion·ing :** to equip with a device for cleaning air and controlling its humidity and temperature — **air con·di·tion·er** *n* — **air–con·di·tion·ing** *n*

air·craft *n, pl* **aircraft :** a vehicle (as an airplane or helicopter) that can travel through the air and that is supported either by its own lightness or by the action of the air against its surfaces

air·field *n* **:** a field or airport where airplanes take off and land

air force *n* **:** the military organization of a nation for air warfare

air·lift *vb* **air·lift·ed; air·lift·ing :** to move people or cargo by aircraft usually to or from an area that cannot be reached otherwise — **airlift** *n*

air·line *n* **:** a company that owns and operates many airplanes which are used for carrying passengers and cargo to different places

air·lin·er *n* **:** a large airplane used for carrying passengers

¹air·mail *n* **1 :** the system of carrying mail by airplanes **2 :** mail carried by airplanes

²airmail *vb* **air·mailed; air·mail·ing :** to send by airmail

air·man *n, pl* **air·men 1 :** an enlisted person in the air force in one of the ranks below sergeant **2 :** ¹PILOT 1, AVIATOR

airman basic *n* **:** an enlisted person of the lowest rank in the air force

airman first class *n* **:** an enlisted person in the air force ranking just below that of sergeant

air·plane *n* **:** an aircraft with wings which do not move, that is heavier than air, is driven by a propeller or jet engine, and is supported by the action of the air against its wings

aiplane mode *n* **:** a setting for an electronic device (as a cell phone or tablet) which prevents the device from connecting to wireless networks or accessing the Internet but allows other functions to remain usable

air·port *n* **:** a place where aircraft land and take off and where there are usually buildings for passengers to wait in and for aircraft and equipment to be kept

air sac *n* **:** one of the small pouches in the lungs where oxygen and carbon dioxide are exchanged

air·ship *n* **:** an aircraft lighter than air that is kept in the air by one or more compartments filled with gas and that has an engine and steering

air·strip *n* **:** a runway without places (as hangars) for the repair of aircraft or shelter of passengers or cargo

air·tight *adj* **:** so tightly sealed that no air can get in or out

air·wave *n* **:** the radio waves used to broadcast radio and television programs — usually used in pl.

air·way *n* **1 :** the passage through which air moves from the nose or mouth to the lungs in breathing **2 :** a route along which airplanes regularly fly **3 :** AIRLINE

airy *adj* **air·i·er; air·i·est 1 :** open to the air **:** BREEZY **2 :** high in the air **3 :** having a light or careless quality that shows a lack of concern **4 :** like air in lightness and delicacy — **air·i·ly** *adv*

aisle *n* **1 :** a passage between sections of seats (as in a church or theater) **2 :** a passage between shelves (as in a supermarket)

ajar *adv or adj* **:** slightly open

AK *abbr* Alaska

aka *abbr* also known as

akim·bo *adv or adj* **1 :** with the hands on the hips and the elbows turned outward **2 :** set in a bent position

akin *adj* **1 :** related by blood **2 :** SIMILAR

AL *abbr* Alabama

¹-al *adj suffix* **:** of, relating to, or showing

²-al *n suffix* **:** action **:** process

Ala. *abbr* Alabama

al·a·bas·ter *n* **:** a smooth usually white stone used for carving

à la carte *adv or adj* **:** with a separate price for each item on the menu

alac·ri·ty *n* **:** a cheerful readiness to do something

¹alarm *n* **1 :** a warning of danger **2 :** a device (as a bell) that warns or signals people **3 :** ALARM CLOCK **4 :** the feeling of fear caused by a sudden sense of danger

²alarm *vb* **alarmed; alarm·ing :** to cause to feel a sense of danger **:** worry or frighten

alarm clock *n* **:** a clock that can be set to sound an alarm at a desired time

alas *interj* — used to express unhappiness, pity, disappointment or worry

al·ba·tross *n* **:** a very large seabird with webbed feet

al·be·it *conj* **:** even though **:** ALTHOUGH

al·bi·no *n, pl* **al·bi·nos 1 :** a person or an animal that has little or no coloring matter in skin, hair, and eyes **2 :** a plant with little or no coloring matter

al·bum *n* **1 :** a book with blank pages in which to put a collection (as of photographs, stamps, or autographs) **2 :** one or more recordings (as on tape or disk) produced as a single collection

al·bu·men *n* **1 :** the white of an egg **2 :** ALBUMIN

al·bu·min *n* **:** any of various proteins that dissolve in water and occur in blood, the whites of eggs, and plant and animal tissues

al·che·my *n* **:** a science that was used in the Middle Ages with the goal of changing ordinary metals into gold

al·co·hol *n* **1 :** a colorless flammable liquid that in one form is the substance in liquors (as beer, wine, or whiskey) that can make a person drunk **2 :** a drink containing alcohol

¹al·co·hol·ic *adj* **1 :** of, relating to, or containing alcohol **2 :** affected with alcoholism

²alcoholic *n* **:** a person affected with alcoholism

al·co·hol·ism *n* **:** continued, uncontrolled, and greater than normal use of alcoholic drinks accompanied by physical and mental dependence on alcohol

al·cove *n* **:** a small part of a room set back from the rest of it

al·der *n* **:** a shrub or small tree that is related to the birch and usually grows in moist soil (as near a river or pond)

al·der·man *n* **:** a member of a lawmaking body in a city

ale *n* **:** an alcoholic drink made from malt and flavored with hops that is usually more bitter than beer

¹alert *adj* **1 :** watchful and ready especially to meet danger **2 :** quick to understand and act — **alert·ly** *adv* — **alert·ness** *n*

²alert *n* **1 :** an alarm or signal of danger **2 :** the period during which an alert is in effect — **on the alert :** watchful against danger

³alert *vb* **alert·ed; alert·ing :** to make aware of a need to get ready or take action **:** WARN

al·fal·fa *n* **:** a plant with purple flowers that is related to the clovers and is grown as a food for horses and cattle

al·ga *n, pl* **al·gae :** any of a large group of simple plants and plant-like organisms (as a seaweed) that usually grow in water and produce chlorophyll like plants but do not produce seeds

al·ge·bra *n* **:** a branch of mathematics in which symbols (as letters and numbers) are combined according to the rules of arithmetic

Al·gon·qui·an *or* **Al·gon·quin** *n* **1 :** a group of American Indian people of southeastern Ontario and southern Quebec or their language — usually *Algonquin* in this sense **2 :** a family of American Indian languages spoken by people from Newfoundland and Labrador to North Carolina and westward into the Great Plains **3 :** a member of the group of people speaking Algonquian languages

¹ali·as *adv* **:** otherwise known as

²alias *n* **:** a false name

al·i·bi *n, pl* **al·i·bis** **1 :** the explanation given by a person accused of a crime that he or she was somewhere else when the crime was committed **2 :** an excuse intended to avoid blame

¹alien *adj* **1 :** different from what is familiar **2 :** from another country and not a citizen of the country of residence **:** FOREIGN **3 :** from somewhere other than the planet earth

²alien *n* **1 :** a resident who was born elsewhere and is not a citizen of the country in which he or she now lives **2 :** a being that comes from somewhere other than the planet earth

alien·ate *vb* **alien·at·ed; alien·at·ing :** to cause (a person who used to be friendly or loyal) to become unfriendly or disloyal

¹alight *vb* **alight·ed; alight·ing** **1 :** to get down **:** DISMOUNT **2 :** to come down from the air and settle

²alight *adj* **:** full of light **:** lighted up

align *vb* **aligned; align·ing :** to arrange things so that they form a line or are in proper position

align·ment *n* **:** the state of being arranged in a line or in proper position

¹alike *adv* **:** in the same way

²alike *adj* **:** being like each other **:** similar in appearance, nature, or form

al·i·men·ta·ry canal *n* **:** DIGESTIVE TRACT

alimentary tract *n* **:** DIGESTIVE TRACT

al·i·mo·ny *n* **:** money for living expenses paid regularly by one spouse to another after their legal separation or divorce

alive *adj* **1 :** having life **:** not dead **2 :** still in force, existence, or operation **3 :** aware of the existence of **4 :** filled with life and activity

al·ka·li *n, pl* **al·ka·lies** *or* **al·ka·lis** **1 :** a substance that has a bitter taste and reacts with an acid to form a salt **:** BASE **2 :** a salt or a mixture of salts sometimes found in large amounts in the soil of dry regions

al·ka·line *adj* **1 :** having the properties of an alkali **2 :** containing an alkali

al·ka·lin·i·ty *n* **:** the quality, state, or degree of being alkaline

¹all *adj* **1 :** every one of **2 :** the whole of **3 :** the whole number of **4 :** any whatever **5 :** the greatest possible

²all *adv* **1 :** COMPLETELY **2 :** so much **3 :** ²VERY 1 **4 :** for each side

³all *pron* **1 :** the whole number or amount **2 :** EVERYTHING **3 :** the only thing

Al·lah *n* : God as named in Islam
all–around *also* **all–round** *adj* **1** : having many good aspects **2** : skillful or useful in many ways
al·lay *vb* **al·layed; al·lay·ing** **1** : to make less severe **2** : to put to rest
all but *adv* : very nearly : ALMOST
al·le·ga·tion *n* : a statement that is not supported by proof and that usually accuses someone of wrongdoing
al·lege *vb* **al·leged; al·leg·ing** : to state as fact but without proof
al·le·giance *n* : loyalty and service to a group, country, or idea
al·le·lu·ia *interj* : HALLELUJAH
al·ler·gen *n* : a substance that causes an allergic reaction
al·ler·gic *adj* : of, relating to, causing, or affected by allergy
al·ler·gist *n* : a medical doctor who specializes in treating allergies
al·ler·gy *n, pl* **al·ler·gies** : a condition in which a person is made sick by something that is harmless to most people
al·le·vi·ate *vb* **al·le·vi·at·ed; al·le·vi·at·ing** : to make less painful, difficult, or severe
al·ley *n, pl* **al·leys** **1** : a narrow passageway between buildings **2** : a special narrow wooden floor on which balls are rolled in bowling
all fours *n pl* : all four legs of a four-legged animal or both legs and both arms of a person
al·li·ance *n* **1** : a relationship in which people, groups, or countries agree to work together **2** : an association of people, groups, or nations working together for a specific purpose
al·lied *adj* **1** : being connected or related in some way **2** : joined in a relationship in which people, groups, or countries work together
al·li·ga·tor *n* : a large short-legged reptile that has a long body, thick skin, a long broad snout, and sharp teeth and is related to the crocodile and lizards
al·lo·cate *vb* **al·lo·cat·ed; al·lo·cat·ing** **1** : to divide and give out for a special reason or to particular people or things **2** : to set apart for a particular purpose
all·o·sau·rus *n* : a large meat-eating dinosaur related to the tyrannosaur
al·lot *vb* **al·lot·ted; al·lot·ting** : to give out as a share or portion
al·lot·ment *n* **1** : the act of giving out as a share or portion **2** : an amount of something that is given out as a share or portion
all–out *adj* : as great as possible
al·low *vb* **al·lowed; al·low·ing** **1** : to give permission to **2** : to fail to prevent **3** : to assign as a share or suitable amount (as of time or money) **4** : to accept as true : CONCEDE **5** : to consider when making a decision or a calculation **6** : to make it possible to have or do something
al·low·able *adj* : not forbidden
al·low·ance *n* **1** : an amount of money given regularly for a specific purpose **2** : a share given out **3** : the act of considering things that could affect a result
al·loy *n* : a substance made of two or more metals melted together
[1]**all right** *adv* **1** : fairly well : well enough **2** — used to show agreement, acceptance, annoyance, reluctance, pleasure, or excitement
[2]**all right** *adj* **1** : not ill, hurt, or unhappy : WELL **2** — used to tell someone not to be concerned **3** : within acceptable limits of behavior **4** : suitable or appropriate **5** : fairly good : SATISFACTORY
all–round *variant of* ALL-AROUND
All Saint's Day *n* : November 1 observed as a church holy day in honor of the Christian saints
all–star *adj* : made up mainly or entirely of outstanding participants
all–ter·rain vehicle *n* : a small open vehicle with three or four wheels for use on rough ground
al·lude *vb* **al·lud·ed; al·lud·ing** : to talk about or hint at without mentioning directly
[1]**al·lure** *vb* **al·lured; al·lur·ing** : to try to attract or influence by offering what seems to be a benefit or pleasure
[2]**allure** *n* : power to attract
al·lu·sion *n* : a statement that refers to something without mentioning it directly
[1]**al·ly** *n, pl* **allies** : a person, group, or nation associated or united with another in a common purpose
[2]**al·ly** *vb* **al·lied; al·ly·ing** : to form a connection between : join in an alliance
al·ma·nac *n* : a book containing a calendar of days, weeks, and months and usually facts about weather and astronomy and information of general interest
al·mighty *adj, often cap* : having absolute power over all
al·mond *n* : a nut that is the edible kernel of a small tree related to the peach tree
al·most *adv* : only a little less than : very nearly
alms *n, pl* **alms** : money given to help the poor : CHARITY
aloft *adv* **1** : at or to a great height **2** : in the air : in flight **3** : at, on, or to the top of the mast or the higher rigging of a ship
[1]**alone** *adj* **1** : separated from others **2** : not including anyone or anything else
[2]**alone** *adv* **1** : and nothing or no one else **2** : without company or help

[1]along *prep* **1 :** on or near in a lengthwise direction **2 :** at a point on

[2]along *adv* **1 :** farther forward or on **2 :** as a companion, associate, or useful item **3 :** at an advanced point — **all along :** all the time

[1]along·side *adv* **:** along or by the side

[2]alongside *prep* **:** parallel to

[1]aloof *adv* **:** at a distance

[2]aloof *adj* **:** not friendly or outgoing

aloud *adv* **:** in a voice that can be clearly heard

al·paca *n* **:** a South American animal related to the camel and llama that is raised for its long woolly hair which is woven into warm strong cloth

al·pha·bet *n* **:** the letters used in writing a language arranged in their regular order

al·pha·bet·i·cal *or* **al·pha·bet·ic** *adj* **:** arranged in the order of the letters of the alphabet — **al·pha·bet·i·cal·ly** *adv*

al·pha·bet·ize *vb* **al·pha·bet·ized; al·pha·bet·iz·ing :** to arrange in alphabetical order

al·ready *adv* **1 :** before a certain time **:** by this time **2 :** so soon

al·so *adv* **:** in addition **:** TOO

alt. *abbr* **1** alternate **2** altitude

Alta *abbr* Alberta

al·tar *n* **1 :** a platform or table used as a center of worship **2 :** a usually raised place on which sacrifices are offered

al·ter *vb* **al·tered; al·ter·ing :** to change partly but not completely

al·ter·ation *n* **1 :** the act or process of changing something **2 :** the result of changing **:** MODIFICATION

[1]al·ter·nate *adj* **1 :** occurring or following by turns **2 :** arranged one above, beside, or next to another **3 :** every other **:** every second — **al·ter·nate·ly** *adv*

[2]al·ter·nate *vb* **al·ter·nat·ed; al·ter·nat·ing :** to take place or cause to take place by turns

[3]al·ter·nate *n* **:** a person named to take the place of another whenever necessary

alternating current *n* **:** an electric current that reverses its direction of flow regularly many times per second

al·ter·na·tion *n* **:** the act, process, or result of taking place by turns

[1]al·ter·na·tive *adj* **:** offering or expressing a choice — **al·ter·na·tive·ly** *adv*

[2]alternative *n* **1 :** a chance to choose between two things **2 :** one of the things between which a choice is to be made

al·though *conj* **1 :** in spite of the fact that **2 :** [1]BUT 1

al·ti·tude *n* **1 :** height above a certain level and especially above sea level **2 :** the perpendicular distance from the base of a geometric figure to the vertex or to the side parallel to the base

al·to *n, pl* **altos 1 :** the lowest female singing voice **2 :** the second highest part in harmony that has four parts **3 :** a singer or an instrument having an alto range or part

al·to·geth·er *adv* **1 :** COMPLETELY **2 :** with everything taken into consideration **3 :** when everything is added together

al·um *n* **:** either of two aluminum compounds that are used especially in medicine (as to stop bleeding)

alu·mi·num *n* **:** a silver-white light metallic chemical element that is easily shaped, conducts electricity well, resists weathering, and is the most plentiful metal in the earth's crust

alum·na *n, pl* **alum·nae :** a girl or woman who has attended or has graduated from a school, college, or university

alum·nus *n, pl* **alum·ni :** a person who has attended or has graduated from a school, college, or university

al·ways *adv* **1 :** at all times **2 :** throughout all time **:** FOREVER **3 :** often, frequently, or repeatedly

am *present first person sing of* BE

Am. *abbr* **1** America **2** American

a.m., A.M. *abbr* before noon — abbreviation for Latin *ante meridiem,* which means "before noon."

amass *vb* **amassed; amass·ing :** to collect or gather together

[1]am·a·teur *n* **1 :** a person who takes part in sports or occupations for pleasure and not for pay **2 :** a person who takes part in something without having experience or skill in it — **am·a·teur·ish** *adj*

[2]amateur *adj* **:** not professional

amaze *vb* **amazed; amaz·ing :** to surprise or puzzle very much

amaze·ment *n* **:** great surprise

am·bas·sa·dor *n* **:** a person sent as the chief representative of his or her government in another country — **am·bas·sa·dor·ship** *n*

am·ber *n* **1 :** a hard yellowish to brownish clear substance that is a fossil resin from trees long dead and that can be polished and used in making ornamental objects (as beads) **2 :** a dark orange yellow **:** the color of honey

Amber Alert *n* **:** a widely publicized bulletin that alerts the public to a recently abducted or missing child

ambi- *prefix* **:** both

am·bi·dex·trous *adj* **:** using both hands with equal ease — **am·bi·dex·trous·ly** *adv*

am·bi·gu·i·ty *n, pl* **am·bi·gu·i·ties :** something that can be understood in more than one way

am·big·u·ous *adj* **:** able to be understood in more than one way — **am·big·u·ous·ly** *adv*

am·bi·tion *n* **1 :** a desire for success, honor, or power **2 :** something a person hopes to do or achieve **3 :** the drive to do things and be active
am·bi·tious *adj* **1 :** possessing a desire for success, honor, or power **2 :** not easily done or achieved — **am·bi·tious·ly** *adv*
am·ble *vb* **am·bled; am·bling :** to walk at a slow easy pace
am·bu·lance *n* **:** a vehicle used to carry a sick or injured person
¹am·bush *vb* **am·bushed; am·bush·ing :** to attack by surprise from a hidden place
²ambush *n* **1 :** a hidden place from which a surprise attack can be made **2 :** a surprise attack made from a hidden place
amen *interj* **1** — used at the end of a prayer **2** — used to express agreement
ame·na·ble *adj* **:** readily giving in or agreeing
amend *vb* **amend·ed; amend·ing 1 :** to change for the better **:** IMPROVE **2 :** to change the wording or meaning of **:** ALTER
amend·ment *n* **:** a change in wording or meaning especially in a law, bill, or motion
amends *n pl* **:** something done or given by a person to make up for a loss or injury he or she has caused — used as singular, but more common as plural
ame·ni·ty *n, pl* **ame·ni·ties 1 :** the quality or characteristic of being pleasant or agreeable **2** *amenities pl* **:** something that makes life easier or more pleasant
Amer. *abbr* **1** America **2** American
¹Amer·i·can *n* **1 :** a citizen of the United States **2 :** a person born or living in North or South America
²American *adj* **1 :** of or relating to the United States or its citizens **2 :** of or relating to North or South America or their residents
American Indian *n* **:** a member of any of the first groups of people to live in North and South America
AmerInd *abbr* American Indian
am·e·thyst *n* **:** a clear purple or bluish violet quartz used as a gem
ami·a·ble *adj* **:** having a friendly and pleasant manner — **ami·a·bly** *adv*
am·i·ca·ble *adj* **:** showing kindness or goodwill — **am·i·ca·bly** *adv*
amid *or* **amidst** *prep* **:** in or into the middle of
amid·ships *adv* **:** in or near the middle of a ship
ami·no acid *n* **:** any of various acids containing carbon and nitrogen that are building blocks of protein and are made by living plant or animal cells or are obtained from the diet
¹amiss *adv* **:** in the wrong way
²amiss *adj* **:** not right **:** WRONG
am·i·ty *n* **:** a feeling of friendship
am·me·ter *n* **:** an instrument for measuring electric current in amperes
am·mo·nia *n* **1 :** a colorless gas that is a compound of nitrogen and hydrogen, has a sharp smell and taste, can be easily made liquid by cold and pressure, and is used in cleaning products and in making fertilizers and explosives **2 :** a solution of ammonia and water
am·mu·ni·tion *n* **:** objects fired from weapons
am·ne·sia *n* **:** abnormal and usually complete loss of memory
amoe·ba *n, pl* **amoe·bas** *or* **amoe·bae :** a tiny water animal that is a single cell which flows about and takes in food
amok *or* **amuck** *adv* **:** in a wild or uncontrolled manner — usually used in the phrase "run amok" or "run amuck"
among *also* **amongst** *prep* **1 :** in or through the middle of **2 :** in the presence of **:** WITH **3 :** through all or most of **4 :** in shares to each of **5 :** in the number or group of being considered or compared
¹amount *vb* **amount·ed; amount·ing 1 :** to add up **2 :** to be the same in meaning or effect
²amount *n* **:** the total number or quantity
am·pere *n* **:** a unit for measuring the strength of an electric current
am·per·sand *n* **:** a character & standing for the word *and*
am·phet·amine *n* **:** a drug that makes the nervous system more active
am·phib·i·an *n* **1 :** any of a group of cold-blooded vertebrate animals (as frogs and toads) that have gills and live in water as larvae but breathe air as adults **2 :** an airplane designed to take off from and land on either land or water
am·phib·i·ous *adj* **1 :** able to live both on land and in water **2 :** meant to be used on both land and water **3 :** made by land, sea, and air forces acting together
am·phi·the·ater *n* **:** an arena with seats rising in curved rows around an open space
am·ple *adj* **am·pler; am·plest :** enough or more than enough of what is needed — **am·ply** *adv*
am·pli·fi·er *n* **:** a device that increases the strength of electric signals so that sounds played through an electronic system are louder
am·pli·fy *vb* **am·pli·fied; am·pli·fy·ing 1 :** to make louder or greater **2 :** to give more information about — **am·pli·fi·ca·tion** *n*
am·pu·tate *vb* **am·pu·tat·ed; am·pu·tat·ing :** to cut off
amt. *abbr* amount
amuck *variant of* AMOK
am·u·let *n* **:** a small object worn as a charm against evil
amuse *vb* **amused; amus·ing 1 :** to enter-

tain with something pleasant **2 :** to please the sense of humor of

amuse·ment *n* **1 :** something that amuses or entertains **2 :** the condition of being amused or entertained

amusement park *n* **:** a place for entertainment having games and rides

an *indefinite article* **:** ²A — used before words beginning with a vowel sound

¹**-an** *or* **-ian** *also* **-ean** *n suffix* **1 :** one that belongs to **2 :** one skilled in or specializing in

²**-an** *or* **-ian** *also* **-ean** *adj suffix* **1 :** of or relating to **2 :** like : resembling

an·a·bol·ic steroid *n* **:** a hormone that is used in medicine to help tissue grow and is sometimes abused by athletes to increase muscle size and strength even though it may have unwanted or harmful effects (as stunted growth in teenagers)

an·a·con·da *n* **:** a large South American snake that coils around and crushes its prey

anal·o·gy *n, pl* **anal·o·gies** **1 :** a comparison of things based on ways they are alike **2 :** the act of comparing things that are alike in some way

anal·y·sis *n, pl* **anal·y·ses** **1 :** an examination of something to find out how it is made or works or what it is **2 :** an explanation of the nature and meaning of something

an·a·lyst *n* **:** a person who studies or analyzes something

an·a·lyt·ic *or* **an·a·lyt·i·cal** *adj* **:** of, relating to, or skilled in the careful study of something — **an·a·lyt·i·cal·ly** *adv*

an·a·lyze *vb* **an·a·lyzed; an·a·lyz·ing** **1 :** to examine something to find out what it is or what makes it work **2 :** to study carefully to understand the nature or meaning of

an·a·tom·i·cal *or* **an·a·tom·ic** *adj* **:** of or relating to the structural makeup of living things

anat·o·my *n, pl* **anat·o·mies** **1 :** a science that has to do with the structure of living things **2 :** the structural makeup especially of a person or animal

-ance *n suffix* **1 :** action or process **2 :** quality or state **3 :** amount or degree

an·ces·tor *n* **1 :** a person from whom someone is descended **2 :** something from which something else develops

an·ces·tral *adj* **:** of, relating to, or coming from an ancestor

an·ces·try *n, pl* **an·ces·tries** **:** a person's ancestors

¹**an·chor** *n* **1 :** a heavy device attached to a ship by a cable or chain and used to hold the ship in place when thrown overboard **2 :** someone or something that provides strength and support

²**anchor** *vb* **an·chored; an·chor·ing** **1 :** to hold or become held in place with an anchor **2 :** to fasten tightly

an·chor·age *n* **:** a place where boats can be anchored

¹**an·cient** *adj* **1 :** very old **2 :** of or relating to a time long past or to those living in such a time

²**ancient** *n* **1 :** a very old person **2 ancients** *pl* **:** the civilized peoples of ancient times and especially of Greece and Rome

-an·cy *n suffix, pl* **-an·cies** **:** quality or state

and *conj* **1 :** added to **2 :** AS WELL AS **3** — used to describe an action that is repeated or that occurs for a long time **4** — used to indicate the purpose of an action — **and so forth :** and others or more of the same kind — **and so on :** and so forth

and·iron *n* **:** one of a pair of metal supports for firewood in a fireplace

an·ec·dote *n* **:** a short story about something interesting or funny in a person's life

ane·mia *n* **:** a sickness in which there is too little blood or too few red blood cells or too little hemoglobin in the blood

an·e·mom·e·ter *n* **:** an instrument for measuring the speed of the wind

anem·o·ne *n* **1 :** a plant that blooms in spring and is often grown for its large white or colored flowers **2 :** SEA ANEMONE

an·es·the·sia *n* **:** loss of feeling in all or part of the body with or without loss of consciousness

¹**an·es·thet·ic** *adj* **:** of, relating to, or capable of producing loss of feeling in all or part of the body

²**anesthetic** *n* **:** something that produces loss of feeling in all or part of the body

anew *adv* **1 :** over again **2 :** in a new or different form

an·gel *n* **1 :** a spiritual being serving God especially as a messenger **2 :** a person who is very good, kind, or beautiful

¹**an·ger** *vb* **an·gered; an·ger·ing** **:** to make strongly displeased : make angry

²**anger** *n* **:** a strong feeling of displeasure or annoyance and often of active opposition to an insult, injury, or injustice

¹**an·gle** *n* **1 :** the figure formed by two lines meeting at a point **2 :** POINT OF VIEW **3 :** a sharp corner **4 :** the slanting direction in which something is positioned

²**angle** *vb* **an·gled; an·gling** **:** to turn, move, or point in a direction that is not straight or flat

³**angle** *vb* **an·gled; an·gling** **1 :** to fish with hook and line **2 :** to try to get something in a sly way

an·gler *n* **:** a person who fishes with hook and line especially for pleasure

an·gling *n* **:** fishing with hook and line for pleasure

DICTIONARY

An·glo- *prefix* **1 :** English **2 :** English and

[1]**An·glo–Sax·on** *n* **1 :** a member of the German people who conquered England in the fifth century A.D. **2 :** a person whose ancestors were English

[2]**Anglo–Saxon** *adj* **:** relating to the Anglo-Saxons

an·go·ra *n* **:** cloth or yarn made from the long soft silky hair of a special usually white domestic rabbit (**Angora rabbit**) or from the long shiny wool of a goat (**Angora goat**)

an·gry *adj* **an·gri·er; an·gri·est :** feeling or showing great annoyance or displeasure **:** feeling or showing anger — **an·gri·ly** *adv*

an·guish *n* **:** great physical or emotional pain

an·guished *adj* **:** full of physical or emotional pain

an·gu·lar *adj* **1 :** having angles or sharp corners **2 :** lean and bony

an·i·mal *n* **1 :** any member of the kingdom of living things (as earthworms, crabs, birds, and people) that differ from plants typically in being able to move about, in not having cell walls made of cellulose, and in depending on plants and other animals as sources of food **2 :** any of the animals lower than humans in the natural order **3 :** MAMMAL

animal kingdom *n* **:** a basic group of natural objects that includes all living and extinct animals

[1]**an·i·mate** *adj* **:** having life

[2]**an·i·mate** *vb* **an·i·mat·ed; an·i·mat·ing 1 :** to give life or energy to **:** make alive or lively **2 :** to make appear to move

an·i·mat·ed *adj* **1 :** full of life and energy **:** LIVELY **2 :** appearing to be alive or moving

an·i·ma·tion *n* **1 :** a lively, enthusiastic, or eager state or quality **2 :** a way of making a movie that includes moving cartoons

an·i·me *n* **:** a style of animation that was created in Japan and that uses colorful images, strong characters, and action-filled plots

an·i·mos·i·ty *n, pl* **an·i·mos·i·ties :** [1]DISLIKE, HATRED

an·kle *n* **1 :** the joint between the foot and the leg **2 :** the area containing the ankle joint

an·klet *n* **1 :** something (as an ornament) worn around the ankle **2 :** a short sock reaching just above the ankle

an·ky·lo·saur *n* **:** a plant-eating dinosaur with bony plates covering the back

an·nals *n pl* **1 :** a record of events arranged in yearly sequence **2 :** historical records **:** HISTORY

an·neal *vb* **an·nealed; an·neal·ing :** to heat (as glass or steel) and then cool so as to toughen and make less brittle

[1]**an·nex** *vb* **an·nexed; an·nex·ing :** to add (something) to something else usually so as to become a part of it

[2]**an·nex** *n* **:** a building or part of a building attached to or near another building and considered part of it

an·nex·ation *n* **:** the act of adding new territory

an·ni·hi·late *vb* **an·ni·hi·lat·ed; an·ni·hi·lat·ing :** to destroy entirely **:** put completely out of existence — **an·ni·hi·la·tion** *n*

an·ni·ver·sa·ry *n, pl* **an·ni·ver·sa·ries :** a date remembered or celebrated every year because of something special that happened on it in an earlier year

an·nounce *vb* **an·nounced; an·nounc·ing 1 :** to make known publicly **2 :** to give notice of the arrival, presence, or readiness of

an·nounce·ment *n* **1 :** the act of making known publicly **2 :** a public notice making something known

an·nounc·er *n* **:** a person who gives information on television or radio

an·noy *vb* **an·noyed; an·noy·ing :** to cause to feel slightly angry or irritated

an·noy·ance *n* **1 :** slight anger or irritation **2 :** a source or cause of slight anger or irritation

an·noy·ing *adj* **:** causing slight anger or irritation — **an·noy·ing·ly** *adv*

[1]**an·nu·al** *adj* **1 :** coming, happening, done, made, or given once a year **2 :** completing the life cycle in one growing season — **an·nu·al·ly** *adv*

[2]**annual** *n* **:** an annual plant

annual ring *n* **:** the layer of wood produced by one year's growth of a woody plant (as in the trunk of a tree)

an·nu·ity *n, pl* **an·nu·ities :** a sum of money paid yearly or at other regular intervals

an·nul *vb* **an·nulled; an·nul·ling :** to cancel by law **:** take away the legal force of — **an·nul·ment** *n*

an·ode *n* **1 :** the positive electrode of an electrolytic cell **2 :** the negative end of a battery that is delivering electric current **3 :** the electron-collecting electrode of an electron tube

anoint *vb* **anoint·ed; anoint·ing 1 :** to rub or cover with oil or grease **2 :** to put oil on as part of a religious ceremony

anom·a·lous *adj* **:** not regular or usual

anom·a·ly *n, pl* **anom·a·lies :** something different, abnormal, strange, or not easily described

anon. *abbr* anonymous

anon·y·mous *adj* **1 :** not named or identified **2 :** made or done by someone unknown — **anon·y·mous·ly** *adv*

[1]**an·oth·er** *adj* **1 :** some other **2 :** one more

[2]**another** *pron* **1 :** one more **2 :** someone or something different

ans. *abbr* answer

[1]**an·swer** *n* **1 :** something said or written in reply (as to a question) **2 :** a solution of a problem

[2]**answer** *vb* **an·swered; an·swer·ing** **1 :** to speak or write in order to satisfy a question **2 :** to write a response to a letter or e-mail **3 :** to pick up (a ringing telephone) **4 :** to open (a door) when someone knocks on it **5 :** to react to something with an action **6 :** to take responsibility — **answer back :** to reply rudely

an·swer·able *adj* **1 :** RESPONSIBLE 1 **2 :** possible to answer

answering machine *n* **:** a machine that receives telephone calls and records messages from callers

ant *n* **:** a small insect related to the bees and wasps that lives in colonies and forms nests in the ground or in wood in which it stores food and raises its young

ant. *abbr* antonym

ant- *see* ANTI-

[1]**-ant** *n suffix* **1 :** one that does or causes a certain thing **2 :** thing that is acted upon in a certain way

[2]**-ant** *adj suffix* **1 :** doing a certain thing or being a certain way **2 :** causing a certain action

an·tag·o·nism *n* **:** a strong feeling of dislike or disagreement

an·tag·o·nist *n* **:** a person who is against something or someone else **:** OPPONENT

an·tag·o·nis·tic *adj* **:** showing dislike or opposition **:** HOSTILE, UNFRIENDLY

an·tag·o·nize *vb* **an·tag·o·nized; an·tag·o·niz·ing :** to stir up dislike or anger in

ant·arc·tic *adj, often cap* **:** of or relating to the south pole or to the region around it

ante- *prefix* **1 :** before in time **:** earlier **2 :** in front of

ant·eat·er *n* **:** an animal that has a long nose and long sticky tongue and feeds chiefly on ants and termites

an·te·lope *n* **:** an animal chiefly of Africa and southwest Asia that resembles a deer and has horns that extend upward and backward

an·ten·na *n* **1** *pl* **an·ten·nae :** one of two or four threadlike movable feelers on the head of insects and crustaceans (as lobsters) **2** *pl* **an·ten·nas :** a metallic device (as a rod or wire) for sending or receiving radio waves

an·te·room *n* **:** a room used as an entrance to another

an·them *n* **1 :** a patriotic song **2 :** a song that is important to a particular group

an·ther *n* **:** the enlargement at the tip of a flower's stamen that contains pollen

ant·hill *n* **:** a mound made by ants in digging their nest

an·thol·o·gy *n, pl* **an·thol·o·gies :** a collection of writings (as stories and poems)

an·thra·cite *n* **:** a hard glossy coal that burns without much smoke

an·thrax *n* **:** a serious bacterial disease of warm-blooded animals (as sheep) that can affect humans

an·thro·pol·o·gy *n* **:** a science that studies people and especially their history, development, distribution, and culture

anti- *or* **ant-** *prefix* **1 :** opposite in kind, position, or action **2 :** hostile toward

an·ti·bi·ot·ic *n* **:** a substance produced by living things and especially by bacteria and fungi that is used to kill or prevent the growth of harmful germs

an·ti·body *n, pl* **an·ti·bod·ies :** a substance produced by special cells of the body that counteracts the effects of a disease germ or its poisons

an·tic *n* **:** a wildly playful or funny act or action

an·tic·i·pate *vb* **an·tic·i·pat·ed; an·tic·i·pat·ing** **1 :** to foresee and deal with or provide for beforehand **2 :** to look forward to

an·tic·i·pa·tion *n* **1 :** excitement about something that's going to happen **2 :** the act of preparing for something

an·ti·cy·clone *n* **:** a system of winds that is like a cyclone but that rotates about a center of high atmospheric pressure instead of low

an·ti·dote *n* **:** something used to reverse or prevent the action of a poison

an·ti·freeze *n* **:** a substance added to the water in an automobile radiator to prevent its freezing

an·ti·mo·ny *n* **:** a silvery white metallic chemical element

an·tip·a·thy *n, pl* **an·tip·a·thies :** a strong feeling of dislike

an·ti·per·spi·rant *n* **:** a substance that is used to prevent sweating

an·ti·quat·ed *adj* **:** very old and no longer useful or popular **:** OLD-FASHIONED, OBSOLETE

[1]**an·tique** *n* **:** an object (as a piece of furniture) made at an earlier time

[2]**antique** *adj* **:** belonging to or like a former style or fashion

an·tiq·ui·ty *n* **1 :** ancient times **2 :** very great age

[1]**an·ti·sep·tic** *adj* **:** killing or preventing the growth or action of germs that cause decay or sickness

[2]**antiseptic** *n* **:** a substance that helps stop the growth or action of germs

an·ti·so·cial *adj* **1 :** violent or harmful to people **2 :** UNFRIENDLY 1

an·tith·e·sis *n, pl* **an·tith·e·ses :** the exact opposite

an·ti·tox·in *n* **:** a substance that is formed in the blood of one exposed to a disease and that prevents or acts against that disease

ant·ler *n* **:** a bony branching structure that grows from the head of a deer or related animal (as a moose) and that is cast off and grown anew each year — **ant·lered** *adj*

ant lion *n* **:** an insect having a larva form with long jaws that digs a cone-shaped hole in which it waits for prey (as ants)

an·to·nym *n* **:** a word of opposite meaning

ant·sy *adj* **ant·si·er; ant·si·est :** impatient and unable to keep still

an·vil *n* **:** an iron block on which pieces of metal are hammered into shape

anx·i·ety *n, pl* **anx·i·eties :** fear or nervousness about what might happen

anx·ious *adj* **1 :** afraid or nervous about what may happen **2 :** causing or showing fear or nervousness **3 :** wanting very much **:** EAGER — **anx·ious·ly** *adv*

[1]**any** *adj* **1 :** whichever one of **2 :** of whatever number or amount

[2]**any** *pron* **1 :** any one or ones of the people or things in a group **2 :** any amount

[3]**any** *adv* **:** to the least amount or degree

any·body *pron* **:** any person **:** ANYONE

any·how *adv* **1 :** in any way, manner, or order **2 :** ANYWAY 1

any·more *adv* **:** NOWADAYS

any·one *pron* **:** any person

any·place *adv* **:** ANYWHERE

any·thing *pron* **:** a thing of any kind

any·way *adv* **1 :** without regard to other considerations **2 :** as an additional consideration or thought

any·where *adv* **:** in, at, or to any place

aor·ta *n* **:** the main artery that carries blood from the heart for distribution to all parts of the body

Apache *n, pl* **Apache** *or* **Apach·es 1 :** a member of an American Indian people of the southwestern United States **2 :** any of the languages of the Apache people

apart *adv* **1 :** away from each other **2 :** separated by an amount of time **3 :** into parts **:** to pieces **4 :** one from another **5 :** as something separated **:** SEPARATELY

apart·ment *n* **:** a room or set of rooms rented as a home

apartment building *n* **:** a large building having several apartments

apartment house *n* **:** APARTMENT BUILDING

ap·a·thy *n* **:** lack of feeling or of interest **:** INDIFFERENCE

apato·sau·rus *n* **:** BRONTOSAURUS

[1]**ape** *n* **:** any of a group of animals (as gorillas or chimpanzees) that are primates most closely related to humans — **ape·like** *adj*

[2]**ape** *vb* **aped; ap·ing :** to imitate (someone) awkwardly

ap·er·ture *n* **:** an opening or open space **:** HOLE

apex *n, pl* **apex·es** *or* **api·ces 1 :** the highest point **:** PEAK **2 :** the most successful time

aphid *n* **:** a small insect that sucks the juices of plants

apiece *adv* **:** for each one

aplomb *n* **:** confidence and skill shown especially in a difficult situation

apol·o·get·ic *adj* **:** sorry for having done or said something wrong — **apol·o·get·i·cal·ly** *adv*

apol·o·gize *vb* **apol·o·gized; apol·o·giz·ing :** to express regret for having done or said something wrong

apol·o·gy *n, pl* **apol·o·gies :** an expression of regret for having done or said something wrong

apos·tle *n* **:** one of the twelve close followers of Jesus Christ

apos·tro·phe *n* **:** a mark ' used to show that letters or figures are missing (as in "can't" for "cannot" or "'76" for "1776") or to show the possessive case (as in "Mike's") or the plural of letters or figures (as in "cross your t's")

apoth·e·cary *n, pl* **apoth·e·car·ies :** PHARMACIST

app *n* **:** a program (as a word processor, spreadsheet, or game) that performs one of the major tasks for which a computer is used

ap·pall *vb* **ap·palled; ap·pall·ing :** to cause to feel shock, horror, or disgust

ap·pall·ing *adj* **:** being shocking and terrible

ap·pa·ra·tus *n, pl* **ap·pa·ra·tus·es** *or* **apparatus :** the equipment or material for a particular use or job

ap·par·el *n* **:** things that are worn **:** CLOTHING

ap·par·ent *adj* **1 :** clear to the understanding **:** EVIDENT **2 :** open to view **:** VISIBLE **3 :** appearing to be real or true — **ap·par·ent·ly** *adv*

ap·pa·ri·tion *n* **1 :** GHOST **2 :** an unusual or unexpected sight

[1]**ap·peal** *n* **1 :** the power to cause enjoyment **:** ATTRACTION **2 :** the act of asking for something badly needed or wanted **:** PLEA **3 :** a legal action by which a case is brought to a higher court for review

[2]**appeal** *vb* **ap·pealed; ap·peal·ing 1 :** to be pleasing or attractive **2 :** to ask for something badly needed or wanted **3 :** to take action to have a case or decision reviewed by a higher court

ap·pear *vb* **ap·peared; ap·pear·ing 1 :** to come into sight **2 :** to present oneself **3 :** SEEM 1 **4 :** to come before the public **5 :** to come into existence

ap·pear·ance *n* **1 :** the way something looks **2 :** the act or an instance of appearing

ap·pease *vb* **ap·peased; ap·peas·ing 1 :** to make calm or quiet **2 :** to make less severe

ap·pend *vb* **ap·pend·ed; ap·pend·ing :** to add as something extra

ap·pend·age *n* **:** something (as a leg) attached to a larger or more important thing

ap·pen·di·ci·tis *n* **:** a condition in which a person's appendix is painful and swollen

ap·pen·dix *n, pl* **ap·pen·dix·es** *or* **ap·pen·di·ces 1 :** a part of a book giving added and helpful information (as notes or tables) **2 :** a small tubelike part growing out from the large intestine

ap·pe·tite *n* **1 :** a natural desire especially for food **2 :** a desire or liking for something

ap·pe·tiz·er *n* **:** a food or drink served before a meal

ap·pe·tiz·ing *adj* **:** pleasing to the appetite

ap·plaud *vb* **ap·plaud·ed; ap·plaud·ing 1 :** to show approval especially by clapping the hands **2 :** [1]PRAISE 1

ap·plause *n* **:** approval shown especially by clapping the hands

ap·ple *n* **:** a round or oval fruit with red, yellow, or green skin and white flesh that grows on a spreading tree related to the rose

ap·ple·sauce *n* **:** a sweet sauce made from cooked apples

ap·pli·ance *n* **:** a piece of household equipment that performs a particular job

ap·pli·ca·ble *adj* **:** capable of being put to use or put into practice

ap·pli·cant *n* **:** a person who applies for something (as a job)

ap·pli·ca·tion *n* **1 :** the act or an instance of applying **2 :** something put or spread on a surface **3 :** [1]REQUEST 1 **4 :** a document used to make a request for something **5 :** ability to be put to practical use **6 :** a computer program (as a word processor or browser)

ap·pli·ca·tor *n* **:** a device for applying a substance (as medicine or polish)

ap·ply *vb* **ap·plied; ap·ply·ing 1 :** to request especially in writing **2 :** to lay or spread on **3 :** to place in contact **4 :** to have relation or a connection **5 :** to put to use **6 :** to give full attention

ap·point *vb* **ap·point·ed; ap·point·ing 1 :** to choose for some duty, job, or office **2 :** to decide on usually from a position of authority

ap·point·ment *n* **1 :** an agreement to meet at a fixed time **2 :** the act of choosing for a position or office or of being chosen for a position or office **3 :** a position or office to which a person is named **4 appointments** *pl* **:** FURNISHINGS

ap·po·si·tion *n* **:** a grammatical construction in which a noun is followed by another that explains it

ap·pos·i·tive *n* **:** the second of a pair of nouns in apposition

ap·prais·al *n* **:** an act or instance of setting a value on

ap·praise *vb* **ap·praised; ap·prais·ing :** to set a value on

ap·pre·cia·ble *adj* **:** large enough to be noticed or measured — **ap·pre·cia·bly** *adv*

ap·pre·ci·ate *vb* **ap·pre·ci·at·ed; ap·pre·ci·at·ing 1 :** to be grateful for **2 :** to admire greatly and with understanding **3 :** to be fully aware of **4 :** to increase in number or value

ap·pre·ci·a·tion *n* **1 :** a feeling of being grateful **2 :** awareness or understanding of worth or value **3 :** a rise in value

ap·pre·cia·tive *adj* **:** having or showing gratitude — **ap·pre·cia·tive·ly** *adv*

ap·pre·hend *vb* **ap·pre·hend·ed; ap·pre·hend·ing 1 :** [1]ARREST 1 **2 :** to look forward to with fear and uncertainty **3 :** UNDERSTAND 1

ap·pre·hen·sion *n* **1 :** [2]ARREST **2 :** fear of or uncertainty about what may be coming **3 :** an understanding of something

ap·pre·hen·sive *adj* **:** fearful of what may be coming — **ap·pre·hen·sive·ly** *adv*

[1]**ap·pren·tice** *n* **:** a person who is learning a trade or art by experience under a skilled worker

[2]**apprentice** *vb* **ap·pren·ticed; ap·pren·tic·ing :** to set at work as an apprentice

ap·pren·tice·ship *n* **1 :** service as an apprentice **2 :** the period during which a person serves as an apprentice

[1]**ap·proach** *vb* **ap·proached; ap·proach·ing 1 :** to come near or nearer **:** draw close **2 :** to begin to deal with **3 :** to start talking to for a specific purpose

[2]**approach** *n* **1 :** an act or instance of drawing near **2 :** a way of doing or thinking about something **:** a way of dealing with something **3 :** a path or road to get to a place

ap·proach·able *adj* **:** easy to meet or deal with

[1]**ap·pro·pri·ate** *adj* **:** especially fitting or suitable — **ap·pro·pri·ate·ly** *adv* — **ap·pro·pri·ate·ness** *n*

[2]**ap·pro·pri·ate** *vb* **ap·pro·pri·at·ed; ap·pro·pri·at·ing 1 :** to take possession of especially in an illegal or unfair way **2 :** to set apart for a certain purpose or use

ap·pro·pri·a·tion *n* **1 :** an act or instance of taking especially illegally or unfairly **2 :** the act or an instance of setting apart for a special purpose **3 :** a sum of money set apart for a special purpose

ap·prov·al *n* **1 :** the belief that something is good or acceptable **2 :** permission to do something

ap·prove *vb* **ap·proved; ap·prov·ing 1 :** to think of as good **2 :** to accept as satisfactory

[1]**ap·prox·i·mate** *adj* **:** nearly correct or exact — **ap·prox·i·mate·ly** *adv*

[2]**ap·prox·i·mate** *vb* **ap·prox·i·mat·ed; ap·prox·i·mat·ing :** to come near in position, value, or characteristics **:** APPROACH

ap·prox·i·ma·tion *n* **1 :** an estimate or figure that is not intended to be exact **2 :** an act or the result of coming near or close

appt. *abbr* appointment

Apr. *abbr* April

apri·cot *n* **:** a small oval orange-colored fruit that looks like the related peach and plum

DICTIONARY

April *n* : the fourth month of the year
apron *n* **1** : a piece of cloth worn on the front of the body to keep clothing from getting dirty **2** : a paved area for parking or handling airplanes
apt *adj* **1** : having a tendency : LIKELY **2** : just right : SUITABLE **3** : quick to learn — **apt·ly** *adv* — **apt·ness** *n*
ap·ti·tude *n* **1** : natural ability : TALENT **2** : capacity to learn
aqua *n* : a light greenish blue : the color of water in a swimming pool
aqua·ma·rine *n* : a transparent gem that is blue, blue-green, or green
aquar·i·um *n* **1** : a container (as a tank or bowl) in which fish and other water animals and plants can live **2** : a building in which water animals or water plants are exhibited
Aquar·i·us *n* **1** : a constellation between Capricorn and Pisces imagined as a man pouring water **2** : the eleventh sign of the zodiac or a person born under this sign
aquat·ic *adj* : growing, living, or done in water
aq·ue·duct *n* : an artificial channel used to carry water over a valley
aque·ous *adj* : made of, by, or with water
AR *abbr* Arkansas
-ar *adj suffix* : of or relating to
Ar·ab *n* : a person born or living in the Arabian Peninsula of southwestern Asia — **Arab** *adj*
[1]**Ara·bi·an** *n* : ARAB
[2]**Arabian** *adj* : of or relating to Arabs or to the Arabian Peninsula of southwestern Asia
[1]**Ar·a·bic** *n* : a language spoken in the Arabian Peninsula of southwestern Asia, Iraq, Jordan, Lebanon, Syria, Egypt, and parts of northern Africa
[2]**Arabic** *adj* : of or relating to the Arabian Peninsula of southwestern Asia, the Arabs, or Arabic
Arabic numeral *n* : one of the number symbols 1, 2, 3, 4, 5, 6, 7, 8, 9, and 0
ar·a·ble *adj* : fit for or cultivated by plowing : suitable for producing crops
Arap·a·ho *or* **Arap·a·hoe** *n, pl* **Arapaho** *or* **Arapahos** *or* **Arapahoe** *or* **Arapahoes** **1** : a member of an American Indian people of the plains region of the United States and Canada **2** : the language of the Arapaho people
ar·bi·trary *adj* **1** : made, chosen, or acting without thought of what is fair or right **2** : seeming to have been made or chosen by chance — **ar·bi·trari·ly** *adv* — **ar·bi·trar·i·ness** *n*
ar·bi·trate *vb* **ar·bi·trat·ed; ar·bi·trat·ing** **1** : to settle a disagreement after hearing the arguments of both sides **2** : to refer a dispute to others for settlement
ar·bi·tra·tion *n* : the settling of a disagreement in which both sides present their arguments to a third person or group for decision
ar·bi·tra·tor *n* : a person chosen to settle differences in a disagreement
ar·bor *n* : a shelter shaped like an arch over which vines grow
ar·bo·re·al *adj* **1** : living in or often found in trees **2** : of or relating to a tree
ar·bo·re·tum *n, pl* **ar·bo·re·tums** *or* **ar·bo·re·ta** : a place where trees and plants are grown to be studied
[1]**arc** *n* **1** : a glowing light across a gap in an electric circuit or between electrodes **2** : a part of a curved line between any two points on it
[2]**arc** *vb* **arced; arc·ing** **1** : to form an electric arc **2** : to follow a curved course
ar·cade *n* **1** : a row of arches supported by columns **2** : an arched or covered passageway between two rows of shops **3** : a place with electronic games that are operated by coins or tokens
[1]**arch** *n* **1** : a usually curved part of a structure that is over an opening and serves as a support (as for the wall above the opening) **2** : something that has a curved shape like an arch — **arched** *adj*
[2]**arch** *vb* **arched; arch·ing** **1** : to form or shape into an arch : CURVE **2** : to cover with an arch
[3]**arch** *adj* **1** : [2]CHIEF 2, PRINCIPAL **2** : being clever and mischievous — **arch·ly** *adv*
ar·chae·ol·o·gy *or* **ar·che·ol·o·gy** *n* : a science that deals with past human life and activities as shown by objects (as pottery, tools, and statues) left by ancient peoples
ar·cha·ic *adj* : of, relating to, or existing from an earlier time
arch·an·gel *n* : a chief angel
arch·bish·op *n* : the bishop of highest rank in a group of dioceses
ar·cher *n* : a person who shoots with a bow and arrow
ar·chery *n* : the sport or practice of shooting with bow and arrows
ar·chi·pel·a·go *n, pl* **ar·chi·pel·a·goes** *or* **ar·chi·pel·a·gos** : a group of islands
ar·chi·tect *n* : a person who designs buildings
ar·chi·tec·ture *n* **1** : the art of designing buildings **2** : a style of building — **ar·chi·tec·tur·al** *adj* — **ar·chi·tec·tur·al·ly** *adv*
ar·chive *n* : a place in which public records or historical papers are saved
arch·way *n* **1** : a passage under an arch **2** : an arch over a passage
-archy *n suffix, pl* **-archies** : rule : government
arc·tic *adj* **1** *often cap* : of or relating to the north pole or to the region around it **2** : very cold
ar·dent *adj* : showing or having warmth of feeling : PASSIONATE — **ar·dent·ly** *adv*

ar·dor *n* **1 :** warmth of feeling **2 :** great eagerness **:** ZEAL

ar·du·ous *adj* **:** DIFFICULT 1 — **ar·du·ous·ly** *adv*

are *present second person sing or present pl of* BE

ar·ea *n* **1 :** REGION 1 **2 :** the amount of surface included within limits **3 :** a part of the surface of something **4 :** a field of activity or study

area code *n* **:** a usually three-digit number that represents a telephone service area in a country

are·na *n* **1 :** an enclosed area used for public entertainment **2 :** a building containing an enclosed area used for public entertainment **3 :** a field of activity

aren't : are not

ar·gue *vb* **ar·gued; ar·gu·ing 1 :** to discuss some matter usually with different points of view **2 :** to give reasons for or against something **3 :** to persuade by giving reasons **4 :** to disagree or fight using angry words **:** QUARREL — **ar·gu·er** *n*

ar·gu·ment *n* **1 :** an angry disagreement **:** QUARREL **2 :** a reason for or against something **3 :** a discussion in which reasons for and against something are given

ar·id *adj* **:** not having enough rainfall to support agriculture

Ar·ies *n* **1 :** a constellation between Pisces and Taurus imagined as a ram **2 :** the first sign of the zodiac or a person born under this sign

aright *adv* **:** in a correct way

arise *vb* **arose; aris·en; aris·ing 1 :** to move upward **2 :** to get up from sleep or after lying down **3 :** to come into existence

ar·is·toc·ra·cy *n, pl* **ar·is·toc·ra·cies 1 :** a government that is run by a small class of people **2 :** an upper class that is usually based on birth and is richer and more powerful than the rest of a society **3 :** people thought of as being better than the rest of the community

aris·to·crat *n* **:** a member of an aristocracy

aris·to·crat·ic *adj* **:** of or relating to the aristocracy or aristocrats — **aris·to·crat·i·cal·ly** *adv*

arith·me·tic *n* **1 :** a science that deals with the addition, subtraction, multiplication, and division of numbers **2 :** an act or method of adding, subtracting, multiplying, or dividing — **arith·met·ic** *or* **ar·ith·met·i·cal** *adj*

ar·ith·met·ic mean *n* **:** a quantity formed by adding quantities together and dividing by their number

Ariz. *abbr* Arizona

ark *n, often cap* **1 :** the ship in which an ancient Hebrew of the Bible named Noah and his family were saved from a great flood that God sent down on the world because of its wickedness **2 :** a cabinet in a synagogue for the scrolls of the Torah

Ark. *abbr* Arkansas

¹arm *n* **1 :** a human upper limb especially between the shoulder and wrist **2 :** something like an arm in shape or position **3 :** SLEEVE 1 **4 :** ¹POWER 1 **5 :** a foreleg of a four-footed animal

²arm *vb* **armed; arm·ing 1 :** to provide with weapons **2 :** to provide with a way of fighting, competing, or succeeding

³arm *n* **1 :** WEAPON, FIREARM **2 :** a branch of an army or of the military forces **3 arms** *pl* **:** the designs on a shield or flag of a family or government **4 arms** *pl* **:** WAR

ar·ma·da *n* **:** a large fleet of warships

ar·ma·dil·lo *n, pl* **ar·ma·dil·los :** a small burrowing animal found from Texas to Argentina that has the head and body protected by small bony plates

ar·ma·ment *n* **1 :** the military strength and equipment of a nation **2 :** the supply of materials for war **3 :** the process of preparing for war

ar·ma·ture *n* **:** the part of an electric motor or generator that turns in a magnetic field

arm·chair *n* **:** a chair with armrests

¹armed *adj* **1 :** carrying weapons **2 :** involving the use of weapons

²armed *adj* **:** having arms of a specified kind or number

armed forces *n pl* **:** the military, naval, and air forces of a nation

arm·ful *n, pl* **arm·fuls** *or* **arms·ful :** as much as a person's arm can hold

ar·mi·stice *n* **:** a pause in fighting brought about by agreement between the two sides

ar·mor *or Can and Brit* **armour** *n* **1 :** a covering (as of metal) to protect the body in battle **2 :** a hard covering that provides protection **3 :** armored forces and vehicles (as tanks)

ar·mored *or Can and Brit* **armoured** *adj* **:** protected by or equipped with armor

ar·mory *or Can and Brit* **armoury** *n, pl* **ar·mor·ies** *or Can and Brit* **armouries 1 :** a supply of weapons **2 :** a place where weapons are kept and where soldiers are often trained **3 :** a place where weapons are made

arm·pit *n* **:** the hollow under a person's arm where the arm joins the shoulder

ar·my *n, pl* **ar·mies 1 :** a large body of soldiers trained for land warfare **2** *often cap* **:** the complete military organization of a nation for land warfare **3 :** a great number of people or things

aro·ma *n* **:** a noticeable and pleasant smell

ar·o·mat·ic *adj* **:** of, relating to, or having a noticeable and pleasant smell

arose *past of* ARISE

¹around *adv* **1 :** in circumference **2 :** in or

along a curving course **3 :** on all sides **4 :** NEARBY **5 :** in close so as to surround **6 :** in many different directions or places **7 :** to each in turn **8 :** in an opposite direction **9 :** almost but not exactly : APPROXIMATELY

²around *prep* **1 :** in a curving path along the outside boundary of **2 :** on every side of **3 :** on or to another side of **4 :** here and there in **5 :** near in number, time, or amount **6 :** in the area near to

arouse *vb* **aroused; arous·ing 1 :** to awaken from sleep **2 :** to cause to feel **3 :** to cause to become active or upset

ar·range *vb* **ar·ranged; ar·rang·ing 1 :** to put in order and especially a particular order **2 :** to make plans for **3 :** to come to an agreement about : SETTLE **4 :** to write or change (a piece of music) to suit particular voices or instruments — **ar·rang·er** *n*

ar·range·ment *n* **1 :** the act of putting things in order : the order in which things are put **2 :** something made by putting things together and organizing them **3 :** preparation or planning done in advance **4 :** a usually informal agreement **5 :** a piece of music written or changed to suit particular voices or instruments

ar·rant *adj* **:** of the worst kind

¹ar·ray *vb* **ar·rayed; ar·ray·ing 1 :** to place in order **2 :** to dress especially in fine or beautiful clothing

²array *n* **1 :** an impressive group **2 :** a group of persons (as soldiers) in a certain order **3 :** fine or beautiful clothing **4 :** regular order or arrangement **5 :** a group of mathematical elements (as numbers or letters) arranged in rows and columns

ar·rears *n pl* **1 :** the state of being behind in paying debts **2 :** unpaid and overdue debts

¹ar·rest *vb* **ar·rest·ed; ar·rest·ing 1 :** to take or keep control over (someone) by authority of law **2 :** to stop the progress or movement of : CHECK **3 :** to attract and hold the attention of

²arrest *n* **:** the act of taking or holding a person by authority of law

ar·riv·al *n* **1 :** the act of reaching a place **2 :** the time when something begins or happens **3 :** a person or thing that has come to a place

ar·rive *vb* **ar·rived; ar·riv·ing 1 :** to reach the place started out for **2 :** COME 4 **3 :** to be born — **arrive at :** to reach by effort or thought

ar·ro·gance *n* **:** a person's sense of his or her own importance that shows itself in a proud and insulting way

ar·ro·gant *adj* **:** showing the attitude of a person who is overly proud of himself or herself or of his or her own opinions — **ar·ro·gant·ly** *adv*

ar·row *n* **1 :** a weapon that is shot from a bow and is usually a stick with a point at one end and feathers at the other **2 :** a mark to show direction

ar·row·head *n* **:** the pointed end of an arrow

ar·row·root *n* **:** an edible starch obtained from the roots of a tropical plant

ar·se·nal *n* **:** a place where military equipment is made and stored

ar·se·nic *n* **:** a solid poisonous chemical element that is usually gray and snaps easily

ar·son *n* **:** the illegal burning of a building or other property

art *n* **1 :** works (as pictures, poems, or songs) made through use of the imagination and creative skills by artists **2 :** the methods and skills used for creative visual works (as painting, sculpting, and drawing) **3 :** an activity (as painting, music, or writing) whose purpose is making things that are beautiful to look at, listen to, or read **4 :** skill that comes through experience or study **5 :** an activity that requires skill

ar·tery *n, pl* **ar·ter·ies 1 :** one of the branching tubes that carry blood from the heart to all parts of the body **2 :** a main road or waterway

art·ful *adj* **1 :** done with or showing art or skill **2 :** clever at taking advantage — **art·ful·ly** *adv*

ar·thri·tis *n* **:** a condition in which the joints are painful and swollen

ar·thro·pod *n* **:** any of a large group of animals (as crabs, insects, and spiders) with jointed limbs and a body made up of segments

ar·ti·choke *n* **:** the immature flower head of a Mediterranean plant that is cooked and eaten as a vegetable

ar·ti·cle *n* **1 :** a piece of writing other than fiction or poetry that forms a separate part of a publication (as a magazine or newspaper) **2 :** one of a class of things **3 :** a word (as *a, an,* or *the*) used with a noun to limit it or make it clearer **4 :** a separate part of a document

¹ar·tic·u·late *adj* **1 :** clearly understandable **2 :** able to express oneself clearly and well — **ar·tic·u·late·ly** *adv*

²ar·tic·u·late *vb* **ar·tic·u·lat·ed; ar·tic·u·lat·ing :** to speak or pronounce clearly

ar·tic·u·la·tion *n* **:** the making of articulate sounds (as in speaking)

ar·ti·fact *n* **:** an object (as a tool or ornament) showing human work and remaining from the past

ar·ti·fice *n* **:** a clever trick or device

ar·ti·fi·cial *adj* **1 :** made by humans **2 :** not natural in quality **3 :** made to seem like something natural — **ar·ti·fi·cial·ly** *adv*

artificial respiration *n* **:** the forcing of air into and out of the lungs of a person whose breathing has stopped

ar·til·lery *n* **1 :** large firearms (as cannon or

rockets) **2 :** a branch of an army armed with artillery

ar·ti·san *n* **:** a person who makes things by using skill with the hands

art·ist *n* **1 :** a person skilled in one of the arts (as painting, music, or writing) **2 :** a person who is very good at something

ar·tis·tic *adj* **1 :** relating to art or artists **2 :** having or showing skill and imagination — **ar·tis·ti·cal·ly** *adv*

¹-ary *n suffix, pl* **-ar·ies :** thing or person belonging to or connected with

²-ary *adj suffix* **:** of, relating to, or connected with

¹as *adv* **1 :** to the same degree or amount **2 :** for example

²as *conj* **1 :** in equal amount or degree with **2 :** in the way that **3 :** at the same time that **4 :** for the reason that **:** BECAUSE

³as *pron* **1 :** ¹THAT 1, WHO, WHICH **2 :** a fact that

⁴as *prep* **1 :** ⁴LIKE 1 **2 :** in the position or role of

as·bes·tos *n* **:** a grayish mineral that separates easily into long flexible fibers and has been used especially in the past in making fireproof materials

as·cend *vb* **as·cend·ed; as·cend·ing 1 :** to go or move up **2 :** to rise to a higher or more powerful position

as·cen·sion *n* **:** the act or process of moving or rising up especially to a higher or more powerful position

as·cent *n* **1 :** the act of rising or climbing upward **2 :** the act of rising to a higher or more powerful position **3 :** an upward slope or path

as·cer·tain *vb* **as·cer·tained; as·cer·tain·ing :** to find out with certainty

as·cribe *vb* **as·cribed; as·crib·ing :** to think of as coming from a specified cause, source, or author

asex·u·al *adj* **:** formed by, characterized by, or being a process of reproduction (as the dividing of one cell into two cells) that does not involve the combining of male and female germ cells — **asex·u·al·ly** *adv*

¹ash *n* **:** a tree that has seeds with a winglike part, bark with grooves, and hard strong wood

²ash *n* **1 :** the solid matter left when something is completely burned **2 ashes** *pl* **:** the last remains of the dead human body

ashamed *adj* **1 :** feeling shame, guilt, or disgrace **2 :** kept from doing something by fear of shame or embarrassment

ash·en *adj* **1 :** of the color of ashes **2 :** very pale

ashore *adv* **:** on or to the shore

ashy *adj* **ash·i·er; ash·i·est 1 :** of or relating to ashes **2 :** very pale

¹Asian *adj* **:** of or relating to Asia or its people

²Asian *n* **:** a person born or living in Asia

Asian–Amer·i·can *n* **:** an American who has Asian ancestors

aside *adv* **1 :** to or toward the side **2 :** out of the way especially for future use **3 :** not included or considered

aside from *prep* **:** with the exception of

as if *conj* **1 :** the way it would be if **2 :** as someone would do if **3 :** ²THAT 1

ask *vb* **asked; ask·ing 1 :** to seek information by posing a question **2 :** to make a request **3 :** to set as a price **4 :** INVITE 1 **5 :** to behave as if seeking a result

askance *adv* **1 :** with a side glance **2 :** with distrust or disapproval

askew *adv or adj* **:** not straight **:** at an angle

aslant *adv or adj* **:** in a slanting direction

¹asleep *adj* **1 :** being in a state of sleep **2 :** having no feeling

²asleep *adv* **:** into a state of sleep

as of *prep* **:** ¹ON 8, AT

as·par·a·gus *n* **:** a vegetable that is the young shoots of a garden plant related to the lilies that lives for many years

as·pect *n* **1 :** the appearance of something **:** LOOK **2 :** a certain way in which something appears or may be thought of **3 :** a position facing a certain direction

as·pen *n* **:** a poplar tree whose leaves move easily in the breeze

as·phalt *n* **1 :** a dark-colored substance obtained from natural deposits in the earth or from petroleum **2 :** any of various materials made of asphalt that are used for pavements and as a waterproof cement

as·phyx·i·ate *vb* **as·phyx·i·at·ed; as·phyx·i·at·ing :** to cause (as a person) to become unconscious or die by cutting off the normal taking in of oxygen whether by blocking breathing or by replacing the oxygen of the air with another gas

as·pi·ra·tion *n* **1 :** a strong desire to achieve something **2 :** something that someone wants very much to achieve

as·pire *vb* **as·pired; as·pir·ing :** to very much want to have or achieve something

as·pi·rin *n* **:** a white drug used to relieve pain and fever

ass *n* **1 :** an animal that looks like but is smaller than the related horse and has shorter hair in the mane and tail and longer ears **:** DONKEY **2** *sometimes vulgar* **:** a stupid or stubborn person

as·sail *vb* **as·sailed; as·sail·ing 1 :** to attack violently or angrily with blows or words **2 :** to be troubled or bothered by

as·sail·ant *n* **:** a person who attacks someone violently

as·sas·sin *n* **:** someone who kills another

person usually for pay or from loyalty to a cause
as·sas·si·nate *vb* **as·sas·si·nat·ed; as·sas·si·nat·ing :** to murder a usually important person by a surprise or secret attack
as·sas·si·na·tion *n* **:** the act of murdering a usually important person by a surprise or secret attack
[1]**as·sault** *n* **1 :** a violent or sudden attack **2 :** an unlawful attempt or threat to harm someone
[2]**assault** *vb* **as·sault·ed; as·sault·ing :** to violently attack
as·sem·blage *n* **:** a collection of persons or things
as·sem·ble *vb* **as·sem·bled; as·sem·bling 1 :** to collect in one place or group **2 :** to fit together the parts of **3 :** to meet together in one place — **as·sem·bler** *n*
as·sem·bly *n, pl* **as·sem·blies 1 :** a group of people gathered together **2** *cap* **:** a group of people who make and change laws for a government or organization **3 :** the act of gathering together **4 :** the act of connecting together the parts of **5 :** a collection of parts that make up a complete unit
assembly line *n* **:** an arrangement for assembling a product mechanically in which work passes from one operation to the next in a direct line until the product is finished
[1]**as·sent** *vb* **as·sent·ed; as·sent·ing :** to agree to or approve of something
[2]**assent** *n* **:** an act of agreeing to or approving of something
as·sert *vb* **as·sert·ed; as·sert·ing 1 :** to state clearly and strongly **2 :** to make others aware of **3 :** to speak or act in a way that demands attention or recognition
as·ser·tion *n* **1 :** the act of stating clearly and strongly or making others aware **2 :** something stated as if certain
as·ser·tive *adj* **:** having a bold or confident manner
as·sess *vb* **as·sessed; as·sess·ing 1 :** to make a judgment about **2 :** to decide on the rate, value, or amount of (as for taxation) **3 :** to put a charge or tax on — **as·ses·sor** *n*
as·set *n* **1 :** someone or something that provides a benefit **2 assets** *pl* **:** all the property belonging to a person or an organization
as·sid·u·ous *adj* **:** showing great care, attention, and effort — **as·sid·u·ous·ly** *adv*
as·sign *vb* **as·signed; as·sign·ing 1 :** to give out as a job or responsibility **2 :** to give out to **:** PROVIDE **3 :** to give a particular quality, value, or identity to
as·sign·ment *n* **1 :** the act of giving out or assigning **2 :** something (as a job or task) that is given out
as·sim·i·late *vb* **as·sim·i·lat·ed; as·sim·i·lat·ing 1 :** to become or cause to become part of a different group or country **2 :** to take in and make part of a larger thing **3 :** to learn thoroughly
as·sim·i·la·tion *n* **:** the act or process of assimilating
[1]**as·sist** *vb* **as·sist·ed; as·sist·ing :** to give support or help
[2]**assist** *n* **:** an act of supporting or helping
as·sis·tance *n* **1 :** the act of helping **2 :** the help given
[1]**as·sis·tant** *adj* **:** acting as a helper to another
[2]**assistant** *n* **:** a person who assists another
assn. *abbr* association
[1]**as·so·ci·ate** *vb* **as·so·ci·at·ed; as·so·ci·at·ing 1 :** to join or come together as partners, friends, or companions **2 :** to connect in thought
[2]**as·so·ciate** *adj* **:** having a rank or position that is below the highest level
[3]**as·so·ciate** *n* **:** a person who you work with or spend time with
as·so·ci·a·tion *n* **1 :** a connection or relationship between things or people **2 :** an organization of persons having a common interest **3 :** a feeling, memory, or thought connected with a person, place, or thing
as·so·cia·tive *adj* **:** relating to or being a property of a mathematical operation (as addition or multiplication) in which the result does not depend on how the elements are grouped
as·sort *vb* **as·sort·ed; as·sort·ing :** to sort into groups of like kinds
as·sort·ed *adj* **1 :** made up of various kinds **2 :** suited to one another **:** matching or fitting together
as·sort·ment *n* **1 :** the act of sorting into groups **2 :** a group or collection of various or different things or persons
asst. *abbr* assistant
as·suage *vb* **as·suaged; as·suag·ing :** to make less severe or intense
as·sume *vb* **as·sumed; as·sum·ing 1 :** to begin to take on or perform **2 :** to take or begin to have **3 :** to pretend to have or be **4 :** to accept as true
as·sump·tion *n* **1 :** the act of taking on **2 :** something accepted as true
as·sur·ance *n* **1 :** the act of making sure or confident **2 :** the state of being sure or confident **3 :** SELF-CONFIDENCE
as·sure *vb* **as·sured; as·sur·ing 1 :** to give certainty, confidence, or comfort to **2 :** to inform positively **3 :** to provide a guarantee of
as·sured *adj* **1 :** made sure or certain **2 :** very confident — **as·sured·ly** *adv*
as·ter *n* **:** any of various herbs related to the daisies that have leafy stems and white, pink, purple, or yellow flower heads which bloom in the fall
as·ter·isk *n* **:** a symbol * used in printing or

in writing especially to refer a reader to a note usually at the bottom of a page

astern *adv* **1** : in, at, or toward the back of a boat or ship : in, at, or toward the stern **2** : in a reverse direction : BACKWARD

as·ter·oid *n* : one of thousands of rocky objects that move in orbits mostly between those of Mars and Jupiter and have diameters from a fraction of a mile to nearly 500 miles (800 kilometers)

asth·ma *n* : a lung disorder that causes periods of wheezing, coughing, and difficulty with breathing

as to *prep* **1** : with respect to : ABOUT **2** : ACCORDING TO 1

as·ton·ish *vb* **as·ton·ished; as·ton·ish·ing** : to strike with sudden wonder or surprise

as·ton·ish·ment *n* : great surprise or wonder : AMAZEMENT

as·tound *vb* **as·tound·ed; as·tound·ing** : to fill with puzzled wonder

astray *adv or adj* **1** : off the right path or route **2** : in or into error

astride *prep* : with one leg on each side of

as·trin·gent *n* : a substance that is able to shrink or tighten body tissues — **astringent** *adj*

astro- *prefix* : star : heavens : astronomical

as·trol·o·gy *n* : the study of the supposed influences of the stars and planets on people's lives and behavior

as·tro·naut *n* : a person who travels beyond the earth's atmosphere : a traveler in a spacecraft

as·tro·nau·tics *n* : the science of the construction and operation of spacecraft

as·tron·o·mer *n* : a person who is a specialist in astronomy

as·tro·nom·i·cal *or* **as·tro·nom·ic** *adj* **1** : of or relating to astronomy **2** : extremely or unbelievably large — **as·tro·nom·i·cal·ly** *adv*

as·tron·o·my *n* : a science concerned with objects and matter outside the earth's atmosphere and of their motions and makeup

as·tute *adj* : very alert and aware : CLEVER — **as·tute·ly** *adv*

asun·der *adv* : into parts

as well as *conj* : and in addition

asy·lum *n* **1** : a place of protection and shelter **2** : protection given especially to political refugees **3** : a place for the care of the poor or the physically or mentally ill

at *prep* **1** — used to indicate a particular place or time **2** — used to indicate the person or thing toward which an action, motion, or feeling is directed or aimed **3** — used to indicate position or condition **4** — used to tell how or why **5** — used to indicate time, age, or position on a scale

ate *past of* EAT

¹-ate *n suffix* : one acted upon in such a way

²-ate *n suffix* : office : rank : group of persons holding such an office or rank

³-ate *adj suffix* : marked by having

⁴-ate *vb suffix* **1** : cause to be changed or affected by **2** : cause to become **3** : furnish with

athe·ist *n* : a person who does not believe in the existence of a god or any gods — **athe·ism** *n*

ath·lete *n* : a person who is trained in or good at games and exercises that require physical skill, endurance, and strength

athlete's foot *n* : a fungus infection of the foot marked by blisters, itching, and cracks between and under the toes

ath·let·ic *adj* **1** : of, relating to, or characteristic of athletes or athletics **2** : used by athletes **3** : active in sports or exercises **4** : strong and muscular

ath·let·ics *n pl* : games, sports, and exercises requiring strength, endurance, and skill — used as singular or plural

-ation *n suffix* **1** : action or process **2** : something connected with an action or process

-ative *adj suffix* **1** : of, relating to, or connected with **2** : designed to do something **3** : tending to

at·las *n* : a book of maps

ATM *n* : a computerized machine that performs basic banking functions (as cash withdrawals)

at·mo·sphere *n* **1** : the whole mass of air that surrounds the earth **2** : the gas surrounding a celestial body (as a planet) **3** : the air in a particular place **4** : a surrounding influence or set of conditions

at·mo·spher·ic *adj* : of or relating to the atmosphere

atoll *n* : a ring-shaped coral island consisting of a coral reef surrounding a lagoon

at·om *n* **1** : the smallest particle of an element that can exist alone or in combination **2** : a tiny particle : BIT

atom·ic *adj* **1** : of or relating to atoms **2** : NUCLEAR 3

atomic bomb *n* : a bomb whose great power is due to the sudden release of the energy in the nuclei of atoms

at·om·iz·er *n* : a device for spraying a liquid (as a perfume or disinfectant)

atone *vb* **atoned; aton·ing** : to do something to make up for a wrong

atone·ment *n* : a making up for an offense or injury

atop *prep* : on top of

atri·um *n* : the part of the heart that receives blood from the veins

atro·cious *adj* **1** : extremely brutal, cruel, or wicked **2** : very bad — **atro·cious·ly** *adv*

atroc·i·ty *n, pl* **atroc·i·ties** : an extremely cruel or terrible act, object, or situation

DICTIONARY

at sign *n* **:** the symbol @ used especially as part of an e-mail address

at·tach *vb* **at·tached; at·tach·ing 1 :** to fasten or join one thing to another **2 :** to bind by feelings of affection **3 :** to think of as belonging to something

at·tach·ment *n* **1 :** connection by feelings of affection or regard **2 :** an extra part that can be attached to a machine or tool **3 :** a connection by which one thing is joined to another

¹at·tack *vb* **at·tacked; at·tack·ing 1 :** to take strong action against **:** try to hurt, injure, or destroy **2 :** to use harsh words against **:** criticize harshly **3 :** to begin to affect or to act upon harmfully **4 :** to start to work on in a determined and eager way — **at·tack·er** *n*

²attack *n* **1 :** a violent, harmful, or destructive act against someone or something **2 :** strong criticism **3 :** the setting to work on some undertaking **4 :** a sudden short period of suffering from an illness or of being affected by a strong emotion

at·tain *vb* **at·tained; at·tain·ing 1 :** to accomplish or achieve **2 :** to come into possession of **:** OBTAIN **3 :** to reach or come to gradually **:** arrive at — **at·tain·able** *adj*

at·tain·ment *n* **1 :** the act of obtaining or doing something difficult **:** the state of having obtained or done something difficult **2 :** ACHIEVEMENT 2

¹at·tempt *vb* **at·tempt·ed; at·tempt·ing :** to try to do, accomplish, or complete

²attempt *n* **:** the act or an instance of trying to do something

at·tend *vb* **at·tend·ed; at·tend·ing 1 :** to go to or be present at **2 :** to look after **:** take charge of **3 :** to direct attention **4 :** to pay attention to **5 :** to go with especially as a servant or companion **6 :** to care for

at·ten·dance *n* **1 :** presence at a place **2 :** a record of how often a person is present at a place **3 :** the number of people present

¹at·ten·dant *n* **1 :** a person who goes with or serves another **2 :** an employee who waits on or helps customers

²attendant *adj* **:** coming with or following closely as a result

at·ten·tion *n* **1 :** the act or the power of fixing the mind on something **:** careful listening or watching **2 :** notice, interest, or awareness **3 :** careful thinking about something so as to be able to take action on it **4 :** special care or treatment **5 :** an act of kindness or politeness **6 :** the way a soldier stands with the body stiff and straight, heels together, and arms at the sides

at·ten·tive *adj* **1 :** paying attention **2 :** very thoughtful about the needs of others — **at·ten·tive·ly** *adv* — **at·ten·tive·ness** *n*

at·test *vb* **at·test·ed; at·test·ing :** to show or give proof of **:** say to be true

at·tic *n* **:** a room or a space just under the roof of a building

¹at·tire *vb* **at·tired; at·tir·ing :** to put clothes and especially special or fine clothes on

²attire *n* **:** CLOTHING

at·ti·tude *n* **1 :** a feeling or way of thinking that affects a person's behavior **2 :** a way of positioning the body or its parts

at·tor·ney *n, pl* **at·tor·neys :** a person and usually a lawyer who acts for another in business or legal matters

at·tract *vb* **at·tract·ed; at·tract·ing 1 :** to draw by appealing to interest or feeling **2 :** to draw to or toward something else

at·trac·tion *n* **1 :** a feeling of interest in something or someone **2 :** the act or power of drawing toward something **3 :** something that interests or pleases

at·trac·tive *adj* **1 :** having the power or quality of drawing interest **2 :** having a pleasing appearance — **at·trac·tive·ly** *adv* — **at·trac·tive·ness** *n*

¹at·tri·bute *n* **:** a quality belonging to a particular person or thing

²at·trib·ute *vb* **at·trib·ut·ed; at·trib·ut·ing 1 :** to explain as the cause of **2 :** to think of as likely to be a quality of a person or thing

atty. *abbr* attorney

ATV *n* **:** ALL-TERRAIN VEHICLE

atyp·i·cal *adj* **:** not usual or normal **:** not typical — **atyp·i·cal·ly** *adv*

au·burn *adj* **:** of a reddish brown color

¹auc·tion *n* **:** a public sale at which things are sold to those who offer to pay the most

²auction *vb* **auc·tioned; auc·tion·ing :** to sell at an auction

auc·tion·eer *n* **:** a person who runs an auction

au·da·cious *adj* **1 :** very bold and daring **:** FEARLESS **2 :** disrespectful of authority **:** INSOLENT — **au·da·cious·ly** *adv*

au·dac·i·ty *n* **:** a bold and daring quality that is sometimes shocking or rude

au·di·ble *adj* **:** loud enough to be heard — **au·di·bly** *adv*

au·di·ence *n* **1 :** a group that listens or watches (as at a play or concert) **2 :** a chance to talk with a person of very high rank **3 :** those people who give attention to something said, done, or written

¹au·dio *adj* **1 :** of or relating to sound or its reproduction **2 :** relating to or used in the transmitting or receiving of sound (as in radio or television)

²audio *n* **1 :** the transmitting, receiving, or reproducing of sound **2 :** the section of television equipment that deals with sound

audio book *n* **:** a recording of a book being read

au·dio·tape *n* : a magnetic tape recording of sound
au·dio·vi·su·al *adj* : of, relating to, or using both sound and sight
[1]**au·dit** *n* : a thorough check of business accounts
[2]**audit** *vb* **au·dit·ed; au·dit·ing** : to thoroughly check the business records of
[1]**au·di·tion** *n* : a short performance to test the talents of someone (as a singer, dancer, or actor)
[2]**audition** *vb* **au·di·tioned; au·di·tion·ing** : to test or try out in a short performance
au·di·tor *n* : a person who checks the accuracy of business accounts
au·di·to·ri·um *n* **1** : the part of a building where an audience sits **2** : a large room where people gather as an audience
au·di·to·ry *adj* : of or relating to hearing
Aug. *abbr* August
au·ger *n* : a tool used for boring holes
aught *n* : ZERO 1
aug·ment *vb* **aug·ment·ed; aug·ment·ing** : to increase in size, amount, or degree
au·gust *adj* : being grand and noble : MAJESTIC
Au·gust *n* : the eighth month of the year
auk *n* : a black-and-white diving seabird of cold parts of the northern hemisphere
aunt *n* **1** : a sister of a person's parent **2** : the wife of a person's uncle or aunt
au·ra *n* : a feeling that seems to be given off by a person or thing
au·ral *adj* : of or relating to the ear or sense of hearing — **au·ral·ly** *adv*
au·ri·cle *n* : ATRIUM
au·ro·ra bo·re·al·is *n* : broad bands of light that have a magnetic and electrical source and that appear in the sky at night especially in the arctic regions
aus·pic·es *n pl* : support and guidance of a sponsor
aus·pi·cious *adj* : promising success — **aus·pi·cious·ly** *adv*
aus·tere *adj* **1** : seeming or acting serious and unfriendly **2** : [1]PLAIN 1 — **aus·tere·ly** *adv*
aus·ter·i·ty *n* : lack of all luxury
[1]**Aus·tra·lian** *adj* : of or relating to Australia or the Australians
[2]**Australian** *n* : a person born or living in Australia
aut- *or* **au·to-** *prefix* **1** : self : same one **2** : automatic
au·then·tic *adj* : being really what it seems to be : GENUINE — **au·then·ti·cal·ly** *adv*
au·then·ti·cate *vb* **au·then·ti·cat·ed; au·then·ti·cat·ing** : to prove or serve as proof that something is authentic
au·thor *n* : a person who writes something (as a novel)
au·thor·i·ta·tive *adj* : having or coming from authority — **au·thor·i·ta·tive·ly** *adv*
au·thor·i·ty *n, pl* **au·thor·i·ties** **1** : power to exercise control **2** : a person looked to as an expert **3** : people having powers to make decisions and enforce rules and laws **4** : a fact or statement used to support a position
au·tho·rize *vb* **au·tho·rized; au·tho·riz·ing** **1** : to give power to : give authority to **2** : to give legal or official approval to
au·thor·ship *n* : the profession of writing
au·to *n, pl* **au·tos** : [1]AUTOMOBILE
auto- — see AUT-
au·to·bi·og·ra·phy *n, pl* **au·to·bi·og·ra·phies** : the biography of a person written by that person
au·to·cor·rect *n* : a feature of an electronic device (as a computer or cell phone) that attempts to correct the spelling of a word as the user types it
[1]**au·to·graph** *n* : a person's signature written by hand
[2]**autograph** *vb* **au·to·graphed; au·to·graph·ing** : to write a person's own signature in or on
au·to·im·mune *adj* : of, relating to, or caused by antibodies or cells that attack molecules, cells, or tissues of the organism producing them — **au·to·im·mu·ni·ty** *n* — **au·to·im·mu·ni·za·tion** *n*
au·to·mate *vb* **au·to·mat·ed; au·to·mat·ing** : to run or operate something using machines instead of people
au·to·mat·ic *adj* **1** : INVOLUNTARY 1 **2** : being a machine or device that allows something to work without being directly controlled by a person — **au·to·mat·i·cal·ly** *adv*
au·to·ma·tion *n* **1** : the method of making a machine, a process, or a system work without being directly controlled by a person **2** : automatic working of a machine, process, or system by mechanical or electronic devices that take the place of humans
au·to·mo·bile *n* : a usually four-wheeled vehicle that runs on its own power and is designed to carry passengers
au·to·mo·tive *adj* : of or relating to automobiles
au·tumn *n* : the season between summer and winter
au·tum·nal *adj* : of or relating to autumn
[1]**aux·il·ia·ry** *adj* : available to provide something extra
[2]**auxiliary** *n, pl* **aux·il·ia·ries** **1** : a group that provides assistance **2** : HELPING VERB
[1]**avail** *vb* **availed; avail·ing** **1** : to be of use or help **2** : to make use of
[2]**avail** *n* : help in or toward reaching a goal : USE
avail·able *adj* **1** : SUITABLE, USABLE **2** : possible to get : OBTAINABLE — **avail·abil·i·ty** *n*
av·a·lanche *n* : a large mass of snow and ice or of earth or rock sliding down a mountainside or over a cliff

av·a·rice *n* : strong desire for riches : GREED
av·a·ri·cious *adj* : greedy for riches — **av·a·ri·cious·ly** *adv*
ave. *abbr* avenue
avenge *vb* **avenged; aveng·ing** : to take revenge for — **aveng·er** *n*
av·e·nue *n* **1** : a wide street **2** : a way of reaching a goal
[1]**av·er·age** *n* **1** : a number that is calculated by adding quantities together and dividing the total by the number of quantities : ARITHMETIC MEAN **2** : something usual in a group, class, or series
[2]**average** *adj* **1** : equaling or coming close to an average **2** : being ordinary or usual
[3]**average** *vb* **av·er·aged; av·er·ag·ing** **1** : to amount to usually **2** : to find the average of
averse *adj* : having a feeling of dislike
aver·sion *n* **1** : a strong dislike **2** : something strongly disliked
avert *vb* **avert·ed; avert·ing** **1** : to turn away **2** : to keep from happening
avi·ary *n, pl* **avi·ar·ies** : a place (as a large cage or a building) where birds are kept
avi·a·tion *n* **1** : the flying of aircraft **2** : the designing and making of aircraft
avi·a·tor *n* : the pilot of an aircraft
av·id *adj* : very eager — **av·id·ly** *adv*
av·o·ca·do *n, pl* **av·o·ca·dos** : a usually green fruit that is shaped like a pear or an egg, grows on a tropical American tree, and has a rich oily flesh
av·o·ca·tion *n* : an interest or activity that is not a regular job : HOBBY
avoid *vb* **avoid·ed; avoid·ing** **1** : to keep away from **2** : to keep from happening **3** : to keep from doing or being
avoid·ance *n* : the act of avoiding something
avow *vb* **avowed; avow·ing** : to declare openly and frankly
avow·al *n* : an open declaration
await *vb* **await·ed; await·ing** **1** : to wait for **2** : to be ready or waiting for
[1]**awake** *vb* **awoke; awo·ken** *or* **awaked; awak·ing** **1** : to stop sleeping : wake up **2** : to make or become conscious or aware of something
[2]**awake** *adj* : not asleep
awak·en *vb* **awak·ened; awak·en·ing** : [1]AWAKE
[1]**award** *vb* **award·ed; award·ing** **1** : to give as deserved or needed **2** : to give by official decision
[2]**award** *n* : something (as a prize) that is given in recognition of good work or a good act
aware *adj* : having or showing understanding or knowledge : CONSCIOUS — **aware·ness** *n*
awash *adj* : flooded or covered with water or other liquid
[1]**away** *adv* **1** : from this or that place **2** : in another place or direction **3** : out of existence **4** : from someone's possession **5** : without stopping or slowing down **6** : at or to a great distance in space or time : FAR
[2]**away** *adj* **1** : ABSENT 1 **2** : DISTANT 1
[1]**awe** *n* : a feeling of mixed fear, respect, and wonder
[2]**awe** *vb* **awed; aw·ing** : to fill with respect, fear, and wonder
awe·some *adj* **1** : causing a feeling of respect, fear, and wonder **2** : being extremely good
awe·struck *adj* : filled with awe
[1]**aw·ful** *adj* **1** : very disagreeable or unpleasant **2** : very much **3** : causing fear or terror
[2]**awful** *adv* : AWFULLY
aw·ful·ly *adv* **1** : to a very great degree : VERY **2** : in a disagreeable or unpleasant manner
awhile *adv* : for a while : for a short time
awk·ward *adj* **1** : not graceful : CLUMSY **2** : likely to embarrass **3** : difficult to use or handle — **awk·ward·ly** *adv* — **awk·ward·ness** *n*
awl *n* : a pointed tool for making small holes (as in leather or wood)
aw·ning *n* : a cover (as of canvas) that shades or shelters like a roof
awoke *past of* AWAKE
awoken *past participle of* AWAKE
awry *adv or adj* **1** : turned or twisted to one side : ASKEW **2** : out of the right course : AMISS
ax *or* **axe** *n* : a tool that has a heavy head with a sharp edge fixed to a handle and is used for chopping and splitting wood
ax·i·om *n* **1** : MAXIM **2** : a statement thought to be clearly true
ax·is *n, pl* **ax·es** : a straight line about which a body or a geometric figure rotates or may be thought of as rotating
ax·le *n* : a pin or shaft on or with which a wheel or pair of wheels turns
ax·on *n* : a long fiber that carries impulses away from a nerve cell
[1]**aye** *adv* : [1]YES 1
[2]**aye** *n* : a yes vote or voter
AZ *abbr* Arizona
aza·lea *n* : a usually small bush that has flowers of many colors which are shaped like funnels
azure *n* : the blue color of the clear daytime sky

B

b *n, pl* **b's** *or* **bs** *often cap* **1 :** the second letter of the English alphabet **2 :** a grade that shows a student's work is good **3 :** a musical note referred to by the letter B

¹baa *n* **:** the cry of a sheep

²baa *vb* **baaed; baa·ing :** to make the cry of a sheep

¹bab·ble *vb* **bab·bled; bab·bling 1 :** to make meaningless sounds **2 :** to talk foolishly **3 :** to make the sound of a brook

²babble *n* **1 :** talk that is not clear **2 :** the sound of a brook

babe *n* **:** ¹BABY 1

ba·boon *n* **:** a large monkey of Africa and Asia with a doglike face

¹ba·by *n, pl* **babies 1 :** a very young child **2 :** a very young animal **3 :** the youngest of a group **4 :** a childish person — **ba·by·ish** *adj*

²baby *adj* **1 :** ¹YOUNG 1 **2 :** very small

³baby *vb* **ba·bied; ba·by·ing :** to treat as a baby **:** to be overly kind to

ba·by·hood *n* **:** the time in a person's life when he or she is a baby

ba·by–sit *vb* **ba·by–sat; ba·by–sit·ting :** to care for a child while the child's parents are away

ba·by–sit·ter *n* **:** a person who cares for a child while the child's parents are away

baby tooth *n* **:** MILK TOOTH

bach·e·lor : a man who is not married — **bach·e·lor·hood** *n*

¹back *n* **1 :** the rear part of the human body from the neck to the end of the spine **:** the upper part of the body of an animal **2 :** the part of something that is opposite or away from the front part **3 :** a player in a team game who plays behind the forward line of players — **backed** *adj*

²back *adv* **1 :** to, toward, or at the rear **2 :** in or to a former time, state, or place **3 :** under control **4 :** in return or reply — **back and forth 1 :** toward the back and then toward the front **2 :** between two places or people

³back *adj* **1 :** located at the back **2 :** far from a central or main area **3 :** not yet paid **:** OVERDUE **4 :** no longer published

⁴back *vb* **backed; back·ing 1 :** to give support or help to **:** UPHOLD **2 :** to move back — **back·er** *n* — **back down :** to stop arguing or fighting for something — **back off :** to back down — **back out :** to decide not to do something after agreeing to do it

back·bone *n* **1 :** the column of bones in the back enclosing and protecting the spinal cord **:** SPINAL COLUMN **2 :** the strongest part of something **3 :** strength of character

¹back·fire *vb* **back·fired; back·fir·ing 1 :** to have a result opposite to what was planned **2 :** to make a loud engine noise caused by fuel igniting at the wrong time

²backfire *n* **1 :** a loud engine noise caused by fuel igniting at the wrong time **2 :** a fire that is set to stop the spread of a forest fire or a grass fire by burning off a strip of land ahead of it

back·ground *n* **1 :** the scenery or ground that is behind a main figure or object **2 :** a position that attracts little attention **3 :** the total of a person's experience, knowledge, and education

¹back·hand *n* **1 :** a stroke in sports played with a racket that is made with the back of the hand turned in the direction in which the hand is moving **2 :** a catch (as in baseball) made with the arm across the body and the palm turned away from the body

²backhand *adv or adj* **:** with a backhand

back·hand·ed *adj* **1 :** using or done with a backhand **2 :** not sincere

back·pack *n* **:** a bag worn on the back for carrying things

back·side *n* **1 :** RUMP 1 **2 :** the part of the body on which a person sits

back·stage *adv or adj* **:** in or to the area behind the stage

back·stop *n* **:** a fence behind the catcher to keep a baseball from rolling away

back·track *vb* **back·tracked; back·track·ing :** to go back over a course or a path

back·up *n* **:** a person who takes the place of or supports another

¹back·ward *or* **back·wards** *adv* **1 :** toward the back **2 :** with the back first **3 :** opposite to the usual way

²backward *adj* **1 :** turned toward the back **2 :** done backward **3 :** not as advanced in learning and development as others

back·woods *n pl* **1 :** wooded or partly cleared areas away from cities **2 :** a place that is backward in culture

back·yard *n* **:** an area in the back of a house

ba·con *n* **:** salted and smoked meat from the sides and the back of a pig

bac·te·ri·al *adj* **:** relating to or caused by bacteria

bac·te·ri·um *n, pl* **bac·te·ria :** any of a group of single-celled microscopic organisms that are important to humans because of their chemical activities and as causes of disease

bad *adj* **worse; worst 1 :** not good **:** POOR **2 :** not favorable **3 :** not fresh or sound **4 :** not good or right **:** EVIL **5 :** not behaving properly

6 : not enough **7 :** UNPLEASANT **8 :** HARMFUL **9 :** SERIOUS 5, SEVERE **10 :** not correct **11 :** not cheerful or calm **12 :** not healthy **13 :** SORRY 1 **14 :** not skillful — **bad·ness** *n*

bade *past of* BID

badge *n* **:** something worn to show that a person belongs to a certain group or rank

[1]bad·ger *n* **:** a furry burrowing animal with short thick legs and long claws on the front feet

[2]badger *vb* **bad·gered; bad·ger·ing :** to annoy again and again

bad·ly *adv* **worse; worst 1 :** in a bad manner **2 :** very much

bad·min·ton *n* **:** a game in which a shuttlecock is hit back and forth over a net by players using light rackets

baf·fle *vb* **baf·fled; baf·fling :** to completely confuse — **baffled** *adj*

[1]bag *n* **1 :** a container made of flexible material (as paper or plastic) **2 :** [1]PURSE 1, HANDBAG **3 :** SUITCASE

[2]bag *vb* **bagged; bag·ging 1 :** to swell out **2 :** to put into a bag **3 :** to kill or capture in hunting

ba·gel *n* **:** a bread roll shaped like a ring

bag·gage *n* **:** the bags, suitcases, and personal belongings of a traveler

bag·gy *adj* **bag·gi·er; bag·gi·est :** hanging loosely or puffed out like a bag

bag·pipe *n* **:** a musical instrument played especially in Scotland that consists of a tube, a bag for air, and pipes from which the sound comes

[1]bail *vb* **bailed; bail·ing :** to dip and throw out water (as from a boat) — **bail out :** to jump out of an airplane

[2]bail *n* **:** money given to free a prisoner until his or her trial

[3]bail *vb* **bailed; bailing :** to get the release of (a prisoner) by giving money as a guarantee of the prisoner's return for trial

[1]bait *n* **:** something that is used to attract fish or animals so they can be caught

[2]bait *vb* **bait·ed; bait·ing 1 :** to put something (as food) on or in to attract and catch fish or animals **2 :** to torment by mean or unjust attacks

bake *vb* **baked; bak·ing 1 :** to cook or become cooked in a dry heat especially in an oven **2 :** to dry or harden by heat

bak·er *n* **:** a person who bakes and sells bread, cakes, or pastry

baker's dozen *n* **:** THIRTEEN

bak·ery *n, pl* **bak·er·ies :** a place where bread, cakes, and pastry are made or sold

baking powder *n* **:** a powder used to make the dough rise in making baked goods

baking soda *n* **:** a white powder used in cooking and medicine

[1]bal·ance *n* **1 :** a steady position or condition **2 :** something left over **:** REMAINDER **3 :** an instrument for weighing **4 :** a state in which things occur in equal or proper amounts **5 :** the amount of money in a bank account **6 :** an amount of money still owed

[2]balance *vb* **bal·anced; bal·anc·ing 1 :** to make or keep steady **:** keep from falling **2 :** to make the two sides of (an account) add up to the same total **3 :** to be or make equal in weight, number, or amount

bal·co·ny *n, pl* **bal·co·nies 1 :** a platform enclosed by a low wall or a railing built out from the side of a building **2 :** a platform inside a theater extending out over part of the main floor

bald *adj* **bald·er; bald·est 1 :** lacking a natural covering (as of hair) **2 :** [1]PLAIN 3 — **bald·ness** *n*

bald eagle *n* **:** a North American eagle that when full-grown has white head and neck feathers

[1]bale *n* **:** a large bundle of goods tightly tied for storing or shipping

[2]bale *vb* **baled; bal·ing :** to press together and tightly tie or wrap into a large bundle — **bal·er** *n*

ba·leen *n* **:** a tough material that hangs down from the upper jaw of whales without teeth and is used by the whale to filter small ocean animals out of seawater

balk *vb* **balked; balk·ing 1 :** to stop short and refuse to go **2 :** to refuse to do something often suddenly

balky *adj* **balk·i·er; balk·i·est :** likely to stop or refuse to go

[1]ball *n* **1 :** something round or roundish **2 :** a round or roundish object used in a game or sport **3 :** a game or sport (as baseball) played with a ball **4 :** a solid usually round shot for a gun **5 :** the rounded bulge at the base of the thumb or big toe **6 :** a pitched baseball that is not hit and is not a strike

[2]ball *vb* **balled; ball·ing :** to make or come together into a ball

[3]ball *n* **1 :** a large formal party for dancing **2 :** a good time

bal·lad *n* **1 :** a short poem suitable for singing that tells a story in simple language **2 :** a simple song **3 :** a slow usually romantic song

ball–and–socket joint *n* **:** a joint (as in the shoulder) in which a rounded part can move in many directions in a socket

bal·last *n* **1 :** heavy material used to make a ship steady or to control the rising of a balloon **2 :** gravel or broken stone laid in a foundation for a railroad or used in making concrete

ball bearing *n* **1 :** a bearing in which the revolving part turns on metal balls that roll easily in a groove **2 :** one of the balls in a ball bearing

bal·le·ri·na *n* **:** a female ballet dancer

bal·let *n* **1 :** a stage dance that tells a story in movement and pantomime **2 :** a group that performs ballets

[1]**bal·loon** *n* **1 :** a bag that rises and floats above the ground when filled with heated air or with a gas that is lighter than air **2 :** a toy or decoration consisting of a rubber bag that can be blown up with air or gas **3 :** an outline containing words spoken or thought by a character (as in a cartoon)

[2]**balloon** *vb* **bal·looned; bal·loon·ing :** to swell or puff out

bal·lot *n* **1 :** a printed sheet of paper used in voting **2 :** the action or a system of voting **3 :** the right to vote **4 :** the number of votes cast

ball·park *n* **:** a park in which baseball games are played

ball·point *n* **:** a pen whose writing point is a small metal ball that rolls ink on a writing surface

ball·room *n* **:** a large room for dances

balm *n* **:** a greasy substance used for healing or protecting the skin

balmy *adj* **balm·i·er; balm·i·est :** warm, calm, and pleasant

bal·sa *n* **:** the very light but strong wood of a tropical American tree

bal·sam *n* **1 :** a material with a strong pleasant smell that oozes from some plants **2 :** a fir tree that yields balsam

bal·us·ter *n* **:** a short post that supports the upper part of a railing

bal·us·trade *n* **:** a row of balusters topped by a rail to serve as an open fence (as along the side of a bridge or a balcony)

bam·boo *n* **:** a tall treelike tropical grass with a hard hollow jointed stem that is used in making furniture and in building

[1]**ban** *vb* **banned; ban·ning :** to forbid especially by law or social pressure

[2]**ban** *n* **:** an official order forbidding something

ba·nana *n* **:** a fruit that is shaped somewhat like a finger, is usually yellow when ripe, and grows in bunches on a large treelike tropical plant with very large leaves

[1]**band** *n* **1 :** a strip of material that holds together or goes around something else **2 :** a strip of something that is different from what it goes around or across **3 :** a range of frequencies (as of radio waves)

[2]**band** *vb* **band·ed; band·ing 1 :** to put a strip of material on or around **:** tie together with a band **2 :** to unite in a group

[3]**band** *n* **1 :** a group of persons or animals **2 :** a group of musicians performing together

[1]**ban·dage** *n* **:** a strip of material used to cover and wrap up wounds

[2]**bandage** *vb* **ban·daged; ban·dag·ing :** to cover or wrap up (a wound) with a strip of material

ban·dan·na *or* **ban·dana** *n* **:** a large handkerchief usually with a colorful design printed on it

ban·dit *n* **:** a criminal who attacks and steals from travelers and is often a member of a group

band·stand *n* **:** an outdoor platform used for band concerts

band·wag·on *n* **1 :** a wagon carrying musicians in a parade **2 :** a candidate, side, or movement that attracts growing support

[1]**bang** *vb* **banged; bang·ing :** to beat, strike, or shut with a loud noise

[2]**bang** *n* **1 :** a sudden loud noise **2 :** a hard hit or blow **3 :** [2]THRILL 1

[3]**bang** *n* **:** hair cut short across the forehead — usually used in pl.

ban·ish *vb* **ban·ished; ban·ish·ing 1 :** to force to leave a country **2 :** to cause to go away

ban·ish·ment *n* **:** an act of forcing or of being forced to leave a country

ban·is·ter *n* **1 :** one of the slender posts used to support the handrail of a staircase **2 :** a handrail and its supporting posts **3 :** the handrail of a staircase

ban·jo *n, pl* **banjos :** a musical instrument with a round body, long neck, and four or five strings

[1]**bank** *n* **1 :** a mound or ridge especially of earth **2 :** the side of a hill **3 :** the higher ground at the edge of a river, lake, or sea **4 :** something shaped like a mound **5 :** an undersea elevation **:** SHOAL

[2]**bank** *vb* **banked; bank·ing 1 :** to build (a curve) in a road or track with a slope upward from the inside edge **2 :** to heap up in a mound or pile **3 :** to raise a pile or mound around **4 :** to tilt to one side when turning

[3]**bank** *n* **1 :** a business where people deposit and withdraw their money and borrow money **2 :** a small closed container in which money may be saved **3 :** a storage place for a reserve supply

[4]**bank** *vb* **banked; bank·ing 1 :** to have an account in a bank **2 :** to deposit in a bank

[5]**bank** *n* **:** a group or series of objects arranged together in a row

bank·er *n* **:** a person who is engaged in the business of a bank

bank·ing *n* **:** the business of a bank or banker

[1]**bank·rupt** *adj* **:** not having enough money to pay debts

[2]**bankrupt** *vb* **bank·rupt·ed; bank·rupt·ing :** to cause to not have enough money to pay debts

[3]**bankrupt** *n* **:** a person or business that does not have enough money to pay debts

bank·rupt·cy *n, pl* **bank·rupt·cies :** the state of not having enough money to pay debts

ban·ner *n* **1 :** [1]FLAG **2 :** a piece of cloth with a design, a picture, or some writing on it

ban·quet *n* **:** a formal dinner for many people usually to celebrate a special event

ban·tam *n* **:** a miniature breed of domestic chicken often raised for exhibiting in shows

[1]**ban·ter** *n* **:** good-natured teasing and joking

[2]**banter** *vb* **ban·tered; ban·ter·ing :** to tease or joke with in a friendly way

bap·tism *n* **:** the act or ceremony of baptizing

bap·tize *vb* **bap·tized; bap·tiz·ing 1 :** to dip in water or sprinkle water on as a part of the ceremony of receiving into the Christian church **2 :** to give a name to as in the ceremony of baptism **:** CHRISTEN

[1]**bar** *n* **1 :** a usually slender rigid piece (as of wood or metal) that has a specific use (as for a lever or barrier) **2 :** a rectangular solid piece or block of something **3 :** a counter on which alcoholic drinks are served **4 :** a place of business for the sale of alcoholic drinks **5 :** a part of a place of business where a particular food or drink is served **6 :** something that blocks the way **7 :** a submerged or partly submerged bank along a shore or in a river **8 :** a court of law **9 :** the profession of law **10 :** a straight stripe, band, or line longer than it is wide **11 :** a vertical line across a musical staff marking equal measures of time **12 :** [1]MEASURE 6

[2]**bar** *vb* **barred; bar·ring 1 :** to fasten with a bar **2 :** to block off **3 :** to shut out

[3]**bar** *prep* **:** with the exception of

barb *n* **:** a sharp point that sticks out and backward (as from the tip of an arrow or fishhook) — **barbed** *adj*

bar·bar·i·an *n* **:** an uncivilized person

bar·bar·ic *adj* **1 :** BARBAROUS **2 :** showing a lack of restraint

bar·ba·rous *adj* **1 :** not civilized **2 :** CRUEL 2, HARSH **3 :** very offensive

[1]**bar·be·cue** *vb* **bar·be·cued; bar·be·cu·ing :** to cook over hot coals or on an open fire often in a highly seasoned sauce

[2]**barbecue** *n* **1 :** an often portable grill **2 :** an outdoor meal or party at which food is cooked over hot coals or an open fire

barbed wire *n* **:** wire that has sharp points and is often used for fences

bar·ber *n* **:** a person whose business is cutting hair and shaving and trimming beards

bar code *n* **:** a group of thick and thin lines placed on a product that represents computerized information about the product (as price)

bard *n* **1 :** a person in ancient societies skilled at composing and singing songs about heroes **2 :** POET

[1]**bare** *adj* **bar·er; bar·est 1 :** having no covering **:** NAKED **2 :** [1]EMPTY 1 **3 :** having nothing left over or added **:** MERE **4 :** [1]PLAIN 3

[2]**bare** *vb* **bared; bar·ing :** UNCOVER

bare·back *adv or adj* **:** on the bare back of a horse **:** without a saddle

bare·foot *adv or adj* **:** with the feet bare

bare·ly *adv* **1 :** almost not **2 :** with nothing to spare **:** by a narrow margin

barf *vb* **barfed; barf·ing :** [2]VOMIT

[1]**bar·gain** *n* **1 :** an agreement settling what each person is to give and receive in a business deal **2 :** something bought or offered for sale at a good price

[2]**bargain** *vb* **bar·gained; bar·gain·ing :** to talk over the terms of a purchase or agreement

[1]**barge** *n* **:** a broad boat with a flat bottom used chiefly in harbors and on rivers and canals

[2]**barge** *vb* **barged; barg·ing :** to move or push in a fast and often rude way

bar graph *n* **:** a chart that uses parallel bars whose lengths are in proportion to the numbers represented

bari·tone *n* **1 :** a male singing voice between bass and tenor in range **2 :** a singer having a baritone voice

[1]**bark** *vb* **barked; bark·ing 1 :** to make the short loud cry of a dog or like a dog's **2 :** to shout or speak sharply

[2]**bark** *n* **:** the sound made by a barking dog or a similar sound

[3]**bark** *n* **:** the outside covering of the trunk, branches, and roots of a tree

[4]**bark** *or* **barque** *n* **1 :** a small sailing boat **2 :** a three-masted ship with foremast and mainmast square-rigged

[5]**bark** *vb* **barked; barking :** to rub or scrape the skin off

bark·er *n* **:** a person who stands at the entrance to a show and tries to attract customers

bar·ley *n* **:** a cereal grass grown for its grain which is used mostly to feed farm animals or make malt

bar mitz·vah *n, often cap B&M* **1 :** a Jewish boy who at 13 years of age takes on religious responsibilities **2 :** the ceremony recognizing a boy as a bar mitzvah

barn *n* **:** a building used for storing grain and hay and for housing farm animals

bar·na·cle *n* **:** a small saltwater animal that is a crustacean and becomes permanently attached (as to rocks or the bottoms of boats) as an adult

barn·yard *n* **:** a usually fenced area next to a barn

ba·rom·e·ter *n* **:** an instrument that measures air pressure and is used to forecast changes in the weather

bar·on *n* **:** a man who is a member of the lowest rank of British nobility

bar·on·ess *n* **1 :** the wife or widow of a baron **2 :** a woman who is a member of the lowest rank of British nobility

bar·on·et *n* **:** the holder of a rank of honor below a baron but above a knight

ba·ro·ni·al *adj* **:** of, relating to, or suitable for a baron

barque *variant of* [4]BARK

bar·rack *n* **:** a building or group of buildings in which soldiers live — usually used in pl.

bar·ra·cu·da *n* **:** any of several large fierce marine fishes of warm seas that have strong jaws and sharp teeth

bar·rage *n* **1 :** continuous artillery or machine-gun fire directed upon a narrow strip of ground **2 :** a great amount of something that comes quickly and continuously

[1]**bar·rel** *n* **1 :** a round container often with curved sides that is longer than it is wide and has flat ends **2 :** the amount contained in a full barrel **3 :** something shaped like a cylinder

[2]**barrel** *vb* **bar·reled** *or* **bar·relled; bar·rel·ing** *or* **bar·rel·ling :** to move at a high speed

bar·ren *adj* **1 :** unable to produce seed, fruit, or young **2 :** growing only poor or few plants

bar·rette *n* **:** a clasp or bar used to hold hair in place

[1]**bar·ri·cade** *vb* **bar·ri·cad·ed; bar·ri·cad·ing :** to block off with a temporary barrier

[2]**barricade** *n* **:** a temporary barrier for protection against attack or for blocking the way

bar·ri·er *n* **1 :** something (as a fence) that blocks the way **2 :** something that keeps apart or makes progress difficult

barrier reef *n* **:** a coral reef parallel to the shore and separated from it by a lagoon

bar·ring *prep* **:** aside from the possibility of

[1]**bar·row** *n* **1 :** WHEELBARROW **2 :** PUSHCART

[2]**barrow** *n* **:** a castrated male pig

[1]**bar·ter** *vb* **bar·tered; bar·ter·ing :** to trade by exchanging one thing for another without the use of money — **bar·ter·er** *n*

[2]**barter** *n* **:** the exchange of goods without the use of money

[1]**base** *n* **1 :** a thing or a part on which something rests **:** BOTTOM, FOUNDATION **2 :** a starting place or goal in various games **3 :** any of the four stations a runner in baseball must touch in order to score **4 :** the main place or starting place of an action or operation **5 :** a place where a military force keeps its supplies or from which it starts its operations **6 :** a line or surface of a geometric figure upon which an altitude is or is thought to be constructed **7 :** the main substance in a mixture **8 :** a number with reference to which a system of numbers is constructed **9 :** a chemical substance (as lime or ammonia) that reacts with an acid to form a salt and turns red litmus paper blue

[2]**base** *vb* **based; bas·ing 1 :** to make or develop from a starting point **2 :** to use as a main place of operation or action

[3]**base** *adj* **bas·er; bas·est 1 :** of low value and not very good in some ways **2 :** not honorable

base·ball *n* **1 :** a game played with a bat and ball by two teams of nine players on a field with four bases that mark the course a runner must take to score **2 :** the ball used in the game of baseball

base·board *n* **:** a line of boards or molding extending around the walls of a room and touching the floor

base·ment *n* **:** the part of a building that is partly or entirely below ground level

bash *vb* **bashed; bash·ing :** to hit very hard

bash·ful *adj* **1 :** uneasy in the presence of others **2 :** showing shyness

[1]**ba·sic** *adj* **1 :** relating to or forming the basis or most important part of something **2 :** relating to or characteristic of a chemical base — **ba·si·cal·ly** *adv*

[2]**basic** *n* **:** something that is one of the simplest and most important parts of something

ba·sil *n* **:** a fragrant mint used in cooking

ba·sin *n* **1 :** a wide shallow usually round dish or bowl for holding liquids **2 :** the amount that a basin holds **3 :** the land drained by a river and its branches **4 :** a partly enclosed area of water for anchoring ships

ba·sis *n, pl* **ba·ses :** something on which another thing is based or established **:** FOUNDATION

bask *vb* **basked; bask·ing 1 :** to lie or relax in pleasantly warm surroundings **2 :** to take pleasure or derive enjoyment

bas·ket *n* **1 :** a container usually made by weaving together materials (as reeds, straw, or strips of wood) **2 :** the contents of a basket **3 :** a net hanging from a metal ring through which a ball is shot in basketball **4 :** a shot that scores in basketball — **bas·ket·like** *adj*

bas·ket·ball *n* **1 :** a game in which two teams try to throw a ball through a hanging net **2 :** the ball used in basketball

bas·ket·ry *n* **1 :** the making of objects (as baskets) by weaving or braiding long slender pieces of material (as reed or wood) **2 :** objects made of interwoven material

bas mitzvah *variant of* BAT MITZVAH
[1]bass *n, pl* **bass** *or* **bass·es :** any of numerous freshwater or saltwater fishes that are caught for sport and food
[2]bass *n* **1 :** a tone of low pitch **2 :** the lowest part in harmony that has four parts **3 :** the lower half of the musical pitch range **4 :** the lowest male singing voice **5 :** a singer or an instrument having a bass range or part
[3]bass *adj* **:** having a very low sound or range
bas·soon *n* **:** a woodwind instrument with two bound reeds and with a usual range two octaves lower than an oboe
[1]baste *vb* **bast·ed; bast·ing :** to sew with long loose stitches so as to hold the cloth temporarily in place
[2]baste *vb* **bast·ed; bast·ing :** to moisten (as with melted fat or juices) while roasting
[1]bat *n* **1 :** a sharp blow or slap **2 :** an implement used for hitting the ball in various games **3 :** a turn at batting
[2]bat *vb* **bat·ted; bat·ting 1 :** to strike with or as if with a bat **2 :** to take a turn at bat
[3]bat *n* **:** any of a group of mammals that fly by means of long front limbs modified into wings
batch *n* **1 :** an amount used or made at one time **2 :** a group of persons or things
bate *vb* **bat·ed; bat·ing :** to reduce the force or intensity of
bath *n, pl* **baths 1 :** an act of washing the body usually in a bathtub **2 :** water for bathing **3 :** a place, room, or building where people may bathe **4 :** BATHROOM **5 :** BATHTUB
bathe *vb* **bathed; bath·ing 1 :** to take a bath **2 :** to give a bath to **3 :** to go swimming **4 :** to apply a liquid to for washing or rinsing **5 :** to cover with or as if with a liquid — **bath·er** *n*
bathing suit *n* **:** SWIMSUIT
bath·robe *n* **:** a robe that is worn especially before or after a bath
bath·room *n* **:** a room containing a sink and toilet and usually a bathtub or shower
bath·tub *n* **:** a tub in which to take a bath
bat mitz·vah *also* **bas mitz·vah** *n, often cap B&M* **1 :** a Jewish girl who at twelve or more years of age takes on religious responsibilities **2 :** the ceremony recognizing a girl as a bat mitzvah
ba·ton *n* **1 :** a thin stick with which a leader directs an orchestra or band **2 :** a rod with a ball at one or both ends that is carried by a person leading a marching band **3 :** a stick that is passed from one runner to the next in a relay race
bat·tal·ion *n* **:** a part of an army consisting of two or more companies
bat·ten *vb* **bat·tened; bat·ten·ing 1 :** to secure by or as if by fastening — often used with *down* **2 :** to prepare for possible trouble or difficulty — often used with *down*
[1]bat·ter *vb* **bat·tered; bat·ter·ing 1 :** to beat with repeated violent blows **2 :** to damage by blows or hard use
[2]batter *n* **:** a mixture made chiefly of flour and a liquid that is cooked and eaten
[3]batter *n* **:** the player whose turn it is to bat
bat·tered *adj* **:** worn down or injured by hard use
bat·ter·ing ram *n* **1 :** an ancient military machine that consisted of a heavy beam with an iron tip swung back and forth in order to batter down walls **2 :** a heavy metal bar with handles used (as by firefighters) to break down doors or walls
bat·tery *n, pl* **bat·ter·ies 1 :** two or more big military guns that are controlled as a unit **2 :** an electric cell or connected electric cells for providing electric current **3 :** a number of similar items or devices grouped together **4 :** an unlawful touching or use of force on a person against his or her will
bat·ting *n* **:** sheets of soft material (as cotton or wool) used mostly for stuffing quilts or packaging goods
[1]bat·tle *n* **1 :** a fight between armies, warships, or airplanes **2 :** a fight between two persons or animals **3 :** a long or hard struggle or contest **4 :** WARFARE 1, COMBAT
[2]battle *vb* **bat·tled; bat·tling 1 :** to engage in fighting **2 :** to try to stop or defeat
bat·tle–ax *or* **bat·tle–axe** *n* **:** an ax with a broad blade formerly used as a weapon
bat·tle·field *n* **:** a place where a military battle is fought or was once fought
bat·tle·ground *n* **:** BATTLEFIELD
bat·tle·ment *n* **:** a low wall (as at the top of a castle) with openings to shoot through
bat·tle·ship *n* **:** a large warship with heavy armor and large guns
bat·ty *adj* **bat·ti·er; bat·ti·est :** CRAZY 1
[1]bawl *vb* **bawled; bawl·ing 1 :** to shout or cry loudly **2 :** to weep noisily — **bawl out :** to scold severely
[2]bawl *n* **:** a loud cry
[1]bay *n* **1 :** a reddish-brown horse with black mane, tail, and lower legs **2 :** a reddish brown
[2]bay *vb* **bayed; bay·ing :** to bark or bark at with long deep tones
[3]bay *n* **1 :** a deep bark **2 :** the position of an animal or a person forced to face pursuers when it is impossible to escape **3 :** the position of someone or something held off or kept back
[4]bay *n* **:** a part of a large body of water extending into the land
[5]bay *n* **:** the laurel or a related tree or shrub

bay·ber·ry *n, pl* **bay·ber·ries** : a shrub with leathery leaves and clusters of small berries covered with grayish white wax

[1]**bay·o·net** *n* : a weapon like a dagger made to fit on the end of a rifle

[2]**bayonet** *vb* **bay·o·net·ted; bay·o·net·ting** : to stab with a bayonet

bay·ou *n* : a body of water (as a creek) that flows slowly through marshy land

bay window *n* : a large window or a set of windows that sticks out from the wall of a building

ba·zaar *n* **1** : a marketplace (as in southwestern Asia and northern Africa) that has rows of small shops **2** : a place where many kinds of goods are sold **3** : a fair for the sale of goods especially for charity

ba·zoo·ka *n* : a portable gun that rests on a person's shoulder and consists of a tube open at both ends that shoots an explosive rocket

BC *abbr* British Columbia

B.C. *abbr* before Christ

be *vb, past first person & third person sing* **was;** *second person sing* **were;** *pl* **were;** *past subjunctive* **were;** *past participle* **been;** *present participle* **be·ing;** *present first person sing* **am;** *second person sing* **are;** *third person sing* **is;** *pl* **are;** *present subjunctive* **be** **1** : to equal in meaning or identity **2** : to have a specified character, quality, or condition **3** : to belong to the group or class of **4** : to exist or live **5** : to occupy a place, situation, or position **6** : to take place **7** : [1]COST 1 **8** — used as a helping verb with other verbs

be- *prefix* **1** : on : around : over **2** : provide with or cover with : dress up with **3** : about : to : upon **4** : make : cause to be

[1]**beach** *n* : a sandy or gravelly part of the shore of an ocean or a lake

[2]**beach** *vb* **beached; beach·ing** : to run or drive ashore

bea·con *n* **1** : a guiding or warning light or fire on a high place **2** : a radio station that sends out signals to guide aircraft **3** : someone or something that guides or gives hope to others

[1]**bead** *n* **1** : a small piece of solid material with a hole through it by which it can be strung on a thread **2** : a small round drop of liquid

[2]**bead** *vb* **bead·ed; bead·ing** : to decorate or cover with beads

beady *adj* **bead·i·er; bead·i·est** : like a bead especially in being small, round, and shiny

bea·gle *n* : a small hound with short legs and a smooth coat

beak *n* **1** : the bill of a bird **2** : a part shaped like or resembling a bird's bill — **beaked** *adj*

bea·ker *n* : a cup or glass with a wide mouth and usually a lip for pouring that is used especially in science laboratories for holding and measuring liquids

[1]**beam** *n* **1** : a long heavy piece of timber or metal used as a main horizontal support of a building or a ship **2** : a ray of light **3** : a radio wave sent out from an airport to guide pilots

[2]**beam** *vb* **beamed; beam·ing** **1** : to send out beams of light **2** : to smile with joy **3** : to aim a radio broadcast by use of a special antenna

bean *n* **1** : the edible seed or pod of a bushy or climbing garden plant related to the peas and clovers **2** : a seed or fruit like a bean

[1]**bear** *n, pl* **bears** **1** *or pl* **bear** : a large heavy mammal with long shaggy hair and a very short tail **2** : a person resembling a bear in size or behavior

[2]**bear** *vb* **bore; borne; bear·ing** **1** : [1]SUPPORT 4 **2** : to move while holding up and supporting : CARRY **3** : to hold in the mind **4** : to put up with **5** : to assume or accept **6** : to have as a feature or characteristic **7** : to give birth to **8** : [1]PRODUCE 1 **9** : to push down on : [2]PRESS **10** : to move or lie in the indicated direction **11** : to have a relation to the matter at hand — **bear in mind** : to think of especially as a warning — **bear up** : to have strength or courage — **bear with** : to be patient with

bear·able *adj* : possible to put up with

beard *n* **1** : the hair that grows on a man's face often not including the mustache **2** : a hairy growth or tuft (as on the chin of a goat) — **beard·ed** *adj*

bear·er *n* **1** : someone or something that bears, supports, or carries **2** : a person who has a check or an order for payment

bear·ing *n* **1** : the manner in which a person carries or conducts himself or herself **2** : a part of a machine in which another part turns **3** : the position or direction of one point with respect to another or to the compass **4** : a determination of position **5** **bearings** *pl* : understanding of position or situation **6** : a relation or connection

beast *n* **1** : a mammal with four feet (as a bear or deer) especially as distinguished from human beings **2** : a wild animal that is large, dangerous, or unusual **3** : a farm animal especially when kept for work **4** : a horrid person

beast·ly *adj* : very unpleasant : HORRIBLE

[1]**beat** *vb* **beat; beat·en** *or* **beat; beat·ing** **1** : to hit or strike again and again **2** : to hit repeatedly in order to cause pain or injury — often used with *up* **3** : to mix by stirring rapidly **4** : to win against : DEFEAT **5**

: to come, arrive, or act before **6 :** [1]THROB 2, PULSATE **7 :** to flap against **8 :** to move with an up and down motion **:** FLAP **9 :** to do or be better than **10 :** to find hard to figure out **11 :** to make by walking or riding over — **beat·er** *n* — **beat it :** to go away quickly

[2]**beat** *n* **1 :** a blow or a stroke made again and again **2 :** a single pulse (as of the heart) **3 :** a sound produced by or as if by beating **4 :** a measurement of time in music **:** an accent or regular pattern of accents in music or poetry **5 :** an area or place regularly visited or traveled through as part of a job

[3]**beat** *adj* **:** very tired

beat·box *n* **:** an electronic device that adds a steady rhythm, alters sounds, and mimics musical instruments

beat·en *adj* **1 :** worn smooth by passing feet **2 :** having lost all hope or spirit

beat–up *adj* **:** badly worn or damaged by use or neglect

beau·te·ous *adj* **:** BEAUTIFUL

beau·ti·cian *n* **:** a person who gives beauty treatments (as to skin and hair)

beau·ti·ful *adj* **1 :** having qualities of beauty **:** giving pleasure to the mind or senses **2 :** very good **:** EXCELLENT — **beau·ti·ful·ly** *adv*

beau·ti·fy *vb* **beau·ti·fied; beau·ti·fy·ing :** to make beautiful

beau·ty *n, pl* **beauties 1 :** the qualities of a person or a thing that give pleasure to the senses or to the mind **2 :** a beautiful or excellent person or thing

beauty mark *n* **:** a small dark mark (as a mole) on the skin especially of the face

bea·ver *n* **:** an animal that has thick brown fur, webbed hind feet, and a broad flat tail, that cuts down trees with its teeth, and that builds dams and houses of sticks and mud in water

became *past of* BECOME

be·cause *conj* **:** for the reason that — **because of :** for the reason of

beck·on *vb* **beck·oned; beck·on·ing 1 :** to call or signal by a motion (as a wave or nod) **2 :** to appear inviting

be·come *vb* **be·came; become; be·com·ing 1 :** to come or grow to be **2 :** to be suitable to especially in a pleasing way — **become of :** to happen to

be·com·ing *adj* **:** having a flattering effect

[1]**bed** *n* **1 :** a piece of furniture on which a person sleeps or rests **2 :** a place for sleeping or resting **3 :** sleep or a time for sleeping **4 :** a piece of ground prepared for growing plants **5 :** the bottom of something **6 :** [1]LAYER 1

[2]**bed** *vb* **bed·ded; bed·ding :** to put or go to bed

bed·bug *n* **:** a small wingless insect that sucks blood and is sometimes found in houses and especially in beds

bed·clothes *n pl* **:** coverings (as sheets and blankets) for a bed

bed·ding *n* **1 :** BEDCLOTHES **2 :** material for a bed

be·deck *vb* **be·decked; be·deck·ing :** to dress up or decorate with showy things

be·dev·il *vb* **be·dev·iled; be·dev·ils :** to trouble or annoy again and again

bed·lam *n* **:** a place, scene, or state of uproar and confusion

be·drag·gled *adj* **:** limp, wet, or dirty from or as if from rain or mud

bed·rid·den *adj* **:** forced to stay in bed by sickness or weakness

bed·rock *n* **:** the solid rock found under surface materials (as soil)

bed·room *n* **:** a room used for sleeping

bed·side *n* **:** the place next to a bed

bed·spread *n* **:** a decorative top covering for a bed

bed·stead *n* **:** the framework of a bed

bed·time *n* **:** time to go to bed

bee *n* **1 :** an insect with four wings that is related to the wasps, gathers pollen and nectar from flowers from which it makes beebread and honey for food, and usually lives in large colonies **2 :** a gathering of people to do something together or engage in a competition

bee·bread *n* **:** a bitter yellowish brown food material prepared by bees from pollen and stored in their honeycomb

beech *n* **:** a tree with smooth gray bark, deep green leaves, and small edible nuts

[1]**beef** *n, pl* **beefs** *or* **beeves 1 :** the meat of a steer, cow, or bull **2 :** a steer, cow, or bull especially when fattened for food **3** *pl beefs* **:** COMPLAINT 2

[2]**beef** *vb* **beefed; beef·ing :** COMPLAIN — **beef up :** to add weight, strength, or power to

bee·hive *n* **:** HIVE

bee·line *n* **:** a straight direct course

been *past participle of* BE

[1]**beep** *n* **:** a sound that signals or warns

[2]**beep** *vb* **beeped; beep·ing :** to make or cause to make a sound that signals or warns

beer *n* **:** an alcoholic drink made from malt and flavored with hops

bees·wax *n* **:** wax made by bees and used by them in building honeycomb

beet *n* **1 :** a leafy plant with a thick juicy root that is used as a vegetable or as a source of sugar **2 :** the root of a beet plant

bee·tle *n* **1 :** any of a group of insects with four wings the outer pair of which are stiff cases that cover the others when folded **2 :** an insect that looks like a beetle

beeves *pl of* BEEF
be·fall *vb* **be·fell; be·fall·en; be·fall·ing :** to happen to
be·fit *vb* **be·fit·ted; be·fit·ting :** to be suitable to or proper for
[1]**be·fore** *adv* **1 :** at an earlier time **2 :** AHEAD
[2]**before** *prep* **1 :** in front of **2 :** earlier than **3 :** before in order **4 :** in the presence of
[3]**before** *conj* **1 :** ahead of the time when **2 :** sooner or quicker than **3 :** more willingly than **4 :** until the time that
be·fore·hand *adv* **:** at an earlier or previous time
be·friend *vb* **be·friend·ed; be·friend·ing :** to act as a friend to
be·fud·dle *vb* **be·fud·dled; be·fud·dling :** CONFUSE 1
beg *vb* **begged; beg·ging 1 :** to ask for money, food, or help as charity **2 :** to ask as a favor in an earnest or polite way **:** PLEAD
beg·gar *n* **:** a person who lives by begging
be·gin *vb* **be·gan; be·gun; be·gin·ning 1 :** to do the first part of an action **2 :** to come into existence **3 :** to start to have a feeling or thought **4 :** to have a starting point **5 :** to do or succeed in the least degree
be·gin·ner *n* **:** a person who is doing something for the first time
be·gin·ning *n* **1 :** the point at which something begins **2 :** the first part
be·gone *vb* **:** to go away — used as a command
be·go·nia *n* **:** a plant with a juicy stem, ornamental leaves, and bright waxy flowers
be·grudge *vb* **be·grudged; be·grudg·ing :** to give or allow reluctantly
be·guile *vb* **be·guiled; be·guil·ing 1 :** [2]TRICK, DECEIVE **2 :** to cause time to pass pleasantly **3 :** to attract or interest by or as if by charm
begun *past of* BEGIN
be·half *n* **:** a person's interest or support — **on behalf of** *or* **in behalf of 1 :** in the interest of **2 :** as a representative of
be·have *vb* **be·haved; be·hav·ing 1 :** to act in a particular manner **2 :** to act in a proper or acceptable way **3 :** to act or function in a particular way
be·hav·ior *or Can and Brit* **behaviour** *n* **1 :** the manner in which a person acts **2 :** the whole activity of something and especially a living being
be·head *vb* **be·head·ed; be·head·ing :** to cut off the head of
[1]**be·hind** *adv* **1 :** in a place that is being or has been left **2 :** in, to, or toward the back **3 :** not up to the general level **4 :** not keeping up to a schedule
[2]**behind** *prep* **1 :** at or to the back of **2 :** not up to the level of **3 :** out of the thoughts of **4 :** responsible for **5 :** in support of
be·hold *vb* **be·held; be·hold·ing :** to look upon **:** SEE — **be·hold·er** *n*
be·hold·en *adj* **:** owing the return of a gift or favor
be·hoove *vb* **be·hooved; be·hoov·ing :** to be necessary or proper for
beige *n* **:** a yellowish brown — **beige** *adj*
be·ing *n* **1 :** the state of having life or existence **2 :** a living thing **3 :** an entity believed to be divine
be·la·bor *vb* **be·la·bored; be·la·bor·ing :** to keep explaining or insisting on to excess
be·lat·ed *adj* **:** happening or coming very late or too late — **be·lat·ed·ly** *adv*
[1]**belch** *vb* **belched; belch·ing 1 :** to force out gas suddenly from the stomach through the mouth usually with a sound **2 :** to throw out or be thrown out with force
[2]**belch** *n* **:** a forcing out of gas from the stomach through the mouth
bel·fry *n, pl* **belfries :** a tower or room in a tower for a bell or set of bells
[1]**Bel·gian** *adj* **:** of or relating to Belgium or the Belgians
[2]**Belgian** *n* **:** a person born or living in Belgium
be·lie *vb* **be·lied; be·ly·ing 1 :** to give a false idea of **2 :** to show to be false
be·lief *n* **1 :** a feeling of being sure that a person or thing exists or is true or trustworthy **2 :** religious faith **3 :** something believed
be·liev·able *adj* **:** possible to believe
be·lieve *vb* **be·lieved; be·liev·ing 1 :** to have faith or confidence in the existence or worth of **2 :** to accept as true **3 :** to accept the word of **4 :** to hold an opinion **:** THINK
be·liev·er *n* **:** someone who has faith or confidence in the existence or worth of something
be·lit·tle *vb* **be·lit·tled; be·lit·tling :** to make (a person or a thing) seem small or unimportant
bell *n* **1 :** a hollow metallic device that is shaped somewhat like a cup and makes a ringing sound when struck **2 :** DOORBELL **3 :** the stroke or sound of a bell that tells the hour **4 :** the time indicated by the stroke of a bell **5 :** a half-hour period of watch on shipboard **6 :** something shaped like a bell
bell·boy *n* **:** BELLHOP
belle *n* **:** an attractive and popular girl or woman
bell·hop *n* **:** a hotel or club employee who takes guests to rooms, moves luggage, and runs errands
bel·lied *adj* **:** having a belly of a certain kind
[1]**bel·lig·er·ent** *adj* **1 :** carrying on war **2 :** feeling or showing readiness to fight

²belligerent *n* **1 :** a nation at war **2 :** a person taking part in a fight
bell jar *n* **:** a usually glass vessel shaped like a bell and used to cover objects, hold gases, or keep a vacuum
¹bel·low *vb* **bel·lowed; bel·low·ing 1 :** to shout in a deep voice **2 :** to make a deep and loud sound
²bellow *n* **:** a loud deep sound
bel·lows *n pl* **:** a device that produces a strong current of air when its sides are pressed together — used as singular or plural
bel·ly *n, pl* **bellies 1 :** the front part of the body between the chest and the hips **2 :** the under part of an animal's body **3 :** ¹STOMACH 1 **4 :** a space inside something
belly button *n* **:** NAVEL
be·long *vb* **be·longed; be·long·ing 1 :** to be in a proper place **2 :** to be the property of a person or group of persons **3 :** to be a part of **:** be connected with **:** go with
be·long·ings *n pl* **:** the things that belong to a person
be·lov·ed *adj* **:** greatly loved **:** very dear
¹be·low *adv* **1 :** in or to a lower place **2 :** below zero
²below *prep* **1 :** in or to a lower place than **:** BENEATH **2 :** at the bottom of **:** directly underneath **3 :** lower in number, size, or amount
¹belt *n* **1 :** a strip of flexible material (as leather or cloth) worn around a person's body for holding in or supporting something (as clothing or weapons) or for ornament **2 :** a flexible endless band running around wheels or pulleys and used for moving or carrying something **3 :** a region suited to or producing something or having some special feature — **belt·ed** *adj*
²belt *vb* **belt·ed; belt·ing 1 :** to put a belt on or around **2 :** to hit hard **3 :** to sing in a loud and forceful way
belying *present participle of* BELIE
be·moan *vb* **be·moaned; be·moan·ing :** to express sadness, distress, or displeasure over
be·muse *vb* **be·mused; be·mus·ing :** to cause to be confused and often also somewhat amused
bench *n* **1 :** a long seat for two or more persons **2 :** a long table for holding work and tools **3 :** the position or rank of a judge
¹bend *vb* **bent; bend·ing 1 :** to make, be, or become curved or angular rather than straight or flat **2 :** to move out of a straight line or position **3 :** to not follow or tell exactly
²bend *n* **:** something that is bent **:** a curved part of something
¹be·neath *adv* **1 :** in a lower place **2 :** directly under
²beneath *prep* **1 :** in or to a lower position than **:** BELOW **2 :** directly under (something or someone) **3 :** not worthy of
bene·dic·tion *n* **1 :** a short blessing said especially at the end of a religious service **2 :** an expression of good wishes
ben·e·fac·tor *n* **:** someone who helps another especially by giving money
ben·e·fi·cial *adj* **:** producing good results or effects **:** HELPFUL
ben·e·fi·cia·ry *n, pl* **ben·e·fi·cia·ries :** a person who benefits or will benefit from something
¹ben·e·fit *n* **1 :** a good or helpful result or effect **2 :** useful assistance **:** HELP **3 :** money paid in time of death, sickness, or unemployment or in old age (as by an insurance company)
²benefit *vb* **ben·e·fit·ed; ben·e·fit·ing 1 :** to be useful or profitable to **2 :** to be helped
be·nev·o·lence *n* **:** KINDNESS 1, GENEROSITY
be·nev·o·lent *adj* **1 :** having a desire to do good **:** KINDLY **2 :** marked by or suggestive of a kindly feeling — **be·nev·o·lent·ly** *adv*
be·nign *adj* **1 :** marked by gentleness and kindness **2 :** not causing death or serious harm — **be·nign·ly** *adv*
¹bent *adj* **1 :** changed by bending **:** CROOKED **2 :** strongly favorable to **:** quite determined
²bent *n* **:** a natural talent or interest
be·queath *vb* **be·queathed; be·queath·ing 1 :** to give or leave by means of a will **2 :** to hand down
be·quest *n* **1 :** the act of leaving property by means of a will **2 :** something given or left by a will
be·rate *vb* **be·rat·ed; be·rat·ing :** to scold in a loud and angry way
be·reaved *adj* **:** grieving over the death of a loved one
be·reft *adj* **1 :** not having something needed, wanted, or expected **2 :** BEREAVED
be·ret *n* **:** a soft round flat cap without a visor
berg *n* **:** ICEBERG
beri·beri *n* **:** a disease marked by weakness, wasting, and damage to nerves and caused by a lack of the vitamin thiamin in the diet
ber·ry *n, pl* **berries 1 :** a small juicy and usually edible fruit (as a strawberry) **2 :** a fruit (as a grape or tomato) in which the ripened ovary wall is fleshy **3 :** a dry seed (as of the coffee plant)
ber·serk *adj* **:** out of control especially due to extreme anger or excitement
berth *n* **1 :** a place in the water where a ship stops and stays when anchored or at a wharf **2 :** a bed on a ship or train **3 :** an amount of distance kept for the sake of safety
be·seech *vb* **be·sought** *or* **be·seeched; be·seech·ing :** to ask in a serious and emotional way
be·set *vb* **be·set; be·set·ting 1 :** to attack

violently **2 :** SURROUND **3 :** to cause problems or difficulties for

be·side *prep* **1 :** at or by the side of **2 :** compared with **3 :** [1]BESIDES **4 :** not relating to

[1]**be·sides** *prep* **1 :** in addition to **2 :** other than

[2]**besides** *adv* **:** in addition **:** ALSO

be·siege *vb* **be·sieged; be·sieg·ing 1 :** to surround with armed forces for the purpose of capturing **2 :** to crowd around **3 :** to overwhelm with questions or requests

[1]**best** *adj, superlative of* GOOD **1 :** better than all others **2 :** most appropriate, useful, or helpful — **best part :** [3]MOST

[2]**best** *adv, superlative of* WELL **1 :** in a way that is better than all the others **2 :** [2]MOST 1

[3]**best** *n* **1 :** a person or thing or part of a thing that is better than all the others **2 :** someone's greatest effort

[4]**best** *vb* **best·ed; best·ing :** to do better than **:** defeat or outdo

be·stir *vb* **be·stirred; be·stir·ring :** to stir up **:** rouse to action

be·stow *vb* **be·stowed; be·stow·ing :** to give as a gift or honor

[1]**bet** *n* **1 :** an agreement requiring the person who guesses wrong about the result of a contest or the outcome of an event to give something to the person who guesses right **2 :** the money or thing risked in a bet **3 :** a choice made by considering what might happen

[2]**bet** *vb* **bet** *or* **bet·ted; bet·ting 1 :** to risk in a bet **2 :** to make a bet with **3 :** to be sure enough to make a bet

bet. *abbr* between

be·tray *vb* **be·trayed; be·tray·ing 1 :** to give over to an enemy by treason or treachery **2 :** to be unfaithful to **3 :** to reveal or show without meaning to **4 :** to tell in violation of a trust

be·troth *vb* **be·trothed; be·troth·ing :** to promise to marry or give in marriage

be·troth·al *n* **:** an engagement to be married

[1]**bet·ter** *adj, comparative of* GOOD **1 :** more satisfactory or skillful than another **2 :** improved in health — **better part :** more than half

[2]**better** *vb* **bet·tered; bet·ter·ing :** to make or become more satisfactory

[3]**better** *adv, comparative of* WELL **1 :** in a superior or more excellent way **2 :** to a higher or greater degree

[4]**better** *n* **1 :** something that is more satisfactory **2 :** ADVANTAGE 2, VICTORY

bet·ter·ment *n* **:** the act or result of making something more satisfactory **:** IMPROVEMENT

bet·tor *or* **bet·ter** *n* **:** someone that bets

[1]**be·tween** *prep* **1 :** in the time or space that separates **2 :** functioning to separate or tell apart **3 :** by the efforts of each of **4 :** by comparing **5 :** shared by **6 :** in shares to each of **7 :** to and from

[2]**between** *adv* **:** in a position between others

be·twixt *prep* **:** BETWEEN 1

[1]**bev·el** *n* **:** a slant or slope of one surface or line against another

[2]**bevel** *vb* **bev·eled** *or* **bev·elled; bev·el·ing** *or* **bev·el·ling :** to cut or shape (an edge or surface) at an angle or slant

bev·er·age *n* **:** a liquid for drinking

be·ware *vb* **:** to be cautious or careful — used only in the forms *beware* or *to beware*

be·whis·kered *adj* **:** having whiskers

be·wil·der *vb* **be·wil·dered; be·wil·der·ing :** CONFUSE 1 — **be·wil·der·ment** *n*

be·witch *vb* **be·witched; be·witch·ing 1 :** to gain an influence over by means of magic or witchcraft **2 :** to attract or delight as if by magic

[1]**be·yond** *adv* **:** on or to the farther side

[2]**beyond** *prep* **1 :** on the other side of **2 :** out of the limits or range of

BFF *abbr* best friends forever

bi- *prefix* **1 :** two **2 :** coming or occurring every two **3 :** into two parts **4 :** twice **:** doubly **:** on both sides

[1]**bi·as** *n* **1 :** a seam, cut, or stitching running in a slant across cloth **2 :** a favoring of some ideas or people over others **:** PREJUDICE

[2]**bias** *vb* **bi·ased** *or* **bi·assed; bi·as·ing** *or* **bi·as·sing :** to give a prejudiced outlook to

bib *n* **1 :** a cloth or plastic shield tied under the chin (as of a young child) to protect the clothes **2 :** the upper part of an apron or of overalls

Bi·ble *n* **1 :** the book of sacred writings accepted by Christians as coming from God **2 :** a book containing the sacred writings of a religion

bib·li·cal *adj* **:** relating to, taken from, or found in the Bible

bib·li·og·ra·phy *n, pl* **bib·li·og·ra·phies 1 :** a list of materials (as books or magazine articles) used in the preparation of a written work or mentioned in a text **2 :** a list of writings about an author or a subject — **bib·lio·graph·ic** *also* **bib·lio·graph·i·cal** *adj*

bi·car·bon·ate of soda *n* **:** BAKING SODA

bi·ceps *n, pl* **biceps** *also* **bi·ceps·es :** a large muscle of the front of the upper arm

bick·er *vb* **bick·ered; bick·er·ing :** to quarrel in an irritating way especially over unimportant things

bi·cus·pid *n* **:** either of the two teeth with double points on each side of each jaw of a person

[1]**bi·cy·cle** *n* **:** a light vehicle having two

wheels one behind the other, handlebars, a seat, and pedals by which it is made to move
[2]**bicycle** *vb* **bi·cy·cled; bi·cy·cling** : to ride a bicycle
bi·cy·clist *n* : a person who rides a bicycle
[1]**bid** *vb* **bade** *or* **bid; bid·den** *or* **bid; bid·ding** **1** : [1]ORDER 2, COMMAND **2** : to express to **3** : to make an offer for something (as at an auction) — **bid·der** *n*
[2]**bid** *n* **1** : an offer to pay a certain sum for something or to do certain work at a stated fee **2** : an attempt to win, achieve, or attract
bide *vb* **bode** *or* **bid·ed; bid·ed; bid·ing** : to wait or wait for
[1]**bi·en·ni·al** *adj* **1** : occurring every two years **2** : growing stalks and leaves one year and flowers and fruit the next before dying — **bi·en·ni·al·ly** *adv*
[2]**biennial** *n* : a biennial plant
bier *n* : a stand on which a corpse or coffin is placed
big *adj* **big·ger; big·gest** **1** : large in size **2** : large in number or amount **3** : of great importance **4** : of great strength or force — **big·ness** *n*
Big Dipper *n* : a group of seven stars in the northern sky arranged in a form like a dipper with the two stars that form the side opposite the handle pointing to the North Star
big·horn *n* : a grayish brown wild sheep of mountainous western North America
big·ot *n* : a person who hates or refuses to accept the members of a particular group — **big·ot·ed** *adj*
big·ot·ry *n* : acts or beliefs characteristic of a bigot
big tree *n* : GIANT SEQUOIA
[1]**bike** *n* **1** : [1]BICYCLE **2** : MOTORCYCLE
[2]**bike** *vb* **biked; bik·ing** : [2]BICYCLE
bik·er *n* : a person who rides a bicycle or motorcycle
bile *n* : a thick bitter yellow or greenish fluid produced by the liver to aid in digestion of fats in the small intestine
bi·lin·gual *adj* **1** : using or expressed in two languages **2** : able to speak two languages
[1]**bill** *n* **1** : the jaws of a bird together with their horny covering **2** : a part of an animal (as a turtle) that resembles the bill of a bird — **billed** *adj*
[2]**bill** *n* **1** : a draft of a law presented to a legislature for consideration **2** : a record of goods sold, services performed, or work done with the cost involved **3** : a piece of paper money **4** : a sign or poster advertising something
[3]**bill** *vb* **billed; bill·ing** : to send a bill to
bill·board *n* : a flat surface on which outdoor advertisements are displayed
bill·fold *n* : WALLET
bil·liards *n* : a game played by driving solid balls with a cue into each other or into pockets on a large rectangular table
Bill of Rights *n* : the first ten amendments to the United States Constitution
bil·lion *n* **1** : a thousand millions **2** : a very large number
[1]**bil·lionth** *adj* : being last in a series of a billion
[2]**billionth** *n* : number 1,000,000,000 in a series
[1]**bil·low** *n* **1** : a large wave **2** : a moving cloud or mass (as of smoke or flame)
[2]**billow** *vb* **bil·lowed; bil·low·ing** **1** : to rise or roll in large waves **2** : to move as a large cloud or mass **3** : to bulge or swell out
bil·lowy *adj* **1** : full of large waves **2** : bulging or puffing out
bil·ly club *n* : NIGHTSTICK
billy goat *n* : a male goat
bin *n* : a box or enclosed place used for storage
bi·na·ry *adj* : of, relating to, or being a number system with a base of 2
[1]**bind** *vb* **bound; bind·ing** **1** : to tie or wrap securely (as with string or rope) **2** : to hold or restrict by force or obligation **3** : to wrap or cover with a bandage **4** : to cause to be joined together closely **5** : to fasten together and enclose in a cover
[2]**bind** *n* : a difficult situation
bind·er *n* **1** : a person who binds books **2** : a cover for holding together loose sheets of paper **3** : a machine that cuts grain and ties it into bundles
bind·ing *n* **1** : the cover and the fastenings of a book **2** : a narrow strip of fabric used along the edge of an article of clothing **3** : a device that attaches a boot to a ski
binge *vb* **binged; binge·ing** *or* **bing·ing** : to do a lot of something (as eating) in a short amount of time
bin·go *n* : a game of chance played by covering a numbered space on a card when the number is matched by one drawn at random and won by the first player to cover five spaces in a row
bin·oc·u·lar *adj* : of, using, or suited for the use of both eyes
bin·oc·u·lars *n pl* : a hand-held instrument for seeing at a distance that is made up of two telescopes usually having prisms and a focusing device
bio- *prefix* : life : living organisms
bio·de·grad·able *adj* : possible to break down into very small harmless parts by the action of living things (as bacteria)
bio·die·sel *n* : a fuel that is similar to diesel fuel and is usually derived from plants
bio·di·ver·si·ty *n* : the existence of many different kinds of plants and animals in an environment

bi·og·ra·pher *n* : someone who tells the account of a real person's life
bio·graph·i·cal *adj* : of or relating to an account of a real person's life
bi·og·ra·phy *n, pl* **bi·og·ra·phies** : a usually written account of a real person's life
bi·o·log·i·cal *adj* : of or relating to biology or to life and living things
bi·ol·o·gist *n* : a person specializing in biology
bi·ol·o·gy *n* : a science that deals with living things and their relationships, distribution, and behavior
bi·ome *n* : a major type of community of distinctive plants and animals living together in a particular climate and physical environment
bio·tech·nol·o·gy *n* : the use of techniques from genetics to combine inherited characteristics selected from different kinds of organisms into one organism in order to produce useful products (as drugs)
bi·ped *n* : an animal (as a person) that has only two feet
bi·plane *n* : an airplane with two wings on each side usually placed one above the other
birch *n* : a tree with hard wood and a smooth bark that can be peeled off in thin layers
bird *n* : an animal that lays eggs and has wings and a body covered with feathers
bird·bath *n* : a basin for birds to bathe in
bird·house *n* : an artificial nesting place (as a wooden box) for birds
bird of prey *n, pl* **birds of prey** : a bird (as an eagle or owl) that feeds almost entirely on meat taken by hunting
bird's–eye *adj* : seen from above as if by a flying bird
birth *n* **1** : the coming of a new individual from the body of its parent **2** : the act of bringing into life **3** : LINEAGE 1 **4** : ORIGIN 3
birth·day *n* **1** : the return each year of the date on which a person was born or something began **2** : the day on which a person is born **3** : a day of beginning
birth·mark *n* : an unusual mark or blemish on the skin at birth
birth·place *n* : the place where a person was born or where something began
birth·right *n* : a right belonging to a person because of his or her birth
birth·stone *n* : a gemstone associated with the month of a person's birth
bis·cuit *n* : a small light bread
bi·sect *vb* **bi·sect·ed; bi·sect·ing** **1** : to divide into two equal parts **2** : INTERSECT
bish·op *n* **1** : a member of the clergy of high rank **2** : a piece in the game of chess
bis·muth *n* : a heavy grayish white metallic chemical element that is used in alloys and in medicines
bi·son *n, pl* **bison** : a large animal with short horns and a shaggy mane that is related to the cows and oxen
[1]**bit** *n* **1** : a small piece or quantity **2** : a short time **3** : [1]SOMEWHAT — **bit by bit** : by small steps or amounts : GRADUALLY
[2]**bit** *n* **1** : a part of a bridle that is put in the horse's mouth **2** : the cutting or boring edge or part of a tool
[3]**bit** *n* : a unit of computer information that represents the selection of one of two possible choices (as *on* or *off*)
bitch *n* : a female dog
[1]**bite** *vb* **bit; bit·ten; bit·ing** **1** : to seize, grip, or cut into with or as if with teeth **2** : to wound or sting usually with a stinger or fang **3** : to take a bait
[2]**bite** *n* **1** : an act of seizing or cutting into with the teeth **2** : a wound made by biting : STING **3** : the amount of food taken at a bite **4** : a sharp or biting sensation
bit·ing *adj* : causing intense discomfort
bit·ter *adj* **bit·ter·er; bit·ter·est** **1** : sharp, biting, and unpleasant to the taste **2** : unhappy and angry because of unfair treatment **3** : hard to put up with **4** : caused by anger, distress, or sorrow **5** : very harsh or sharp : BITING — **bit·ter·ly** *adv* — **bit·ter·ness** *n*
bit·tern *n* : a brownish marsh bird which has a loud booming cry
[1]**bit·ter·sweet** *n* **1** : a poisonous vine originally of Europe and Asia with purple flowers and red berries **2** : a poisonous North American woody climbing plant with orange seedcases that open when ripe to reveal red seeds
[2]**bittersweet** *adj* : being partly bitter or sad and partly sweet or happy
bi·tu·mi·nous coal *n* : a soft coal that gives a lot of smoke when burned
bi·zarre *adj* : very strange or odd
blab *vb* **blabbed; blab·bing** **1** : to reveal a secret **2** : to talk too much
[1]**black** *adj* **black·er; black·est** **1** : of the color of coal : colored black **2** : very dark **3** *often cap* : of or relating to any peoples having dark skin and especially any of the original peoples of Africa south of the Sahara **4** : of or relating to Americans having ancestors from Africa south of the Sahara **5** : WICKED **6** : very sad or gloomy **7** : UNFRIENDLY — **black·ish** *adj* — **black·ness** *n*
[2]**black** *n* **1** : the color of coal : the opposite of white **2** : black clothing **3** : a person belonging to a race of people having dark skin **4** : an American having black African ancestors : AFRICAN-AMERICAN **5** : total or near total darkness **6** : the condition of making a profit
[3]**black** *vb* **blacked; black·ing** : BLACKEN 1

— **black out** : to lose consciousness or the ability to see for a short time

black–and–blue *adj* : darkly discolored (as from a bruise)

black·ber·ry *n, pl* **black·ber·ries** : the black or dark purple sweet juicy berry of a prickly plant related to the raspberry

black·bird *n* : any of several birds of which the males are mostly black

black·board *n* : a hard smooth dark surface used for writing or drawing on with chalk

black·en *vb* **black·ened; black·en·ing** **1** : to make or become dark or black **2** : [2]SPOIL 2

black–eyed Su·san *n* : a daisy with yellow or orange petals and a dark center

black·head *n* : a darkened bit of oily material that blocks the opening of a gland in the skin

black hole *n* : an object in outer space with such strong gravity that light cannot escape it and that is thought to be caused by the collapse of a massive star

[1]**black·mail** *n* **1** : the act of forcing someone to pay money by threatening to reveal a secret that might bring disgrace on him or her **2** : money paid under threat of revealing a secret

[2]**blackmail** *vb* **black·mailed; black·mail·ing** : to threaten with the revealing of a secret unless money is paid — **black·mail·er** *n*

black·out *n* **1** : a period of darkness enforced as a protection against enemy attack by airplanes during a war **2** : a period of darkness caused by power failure **3** : a temporary loss of vision or consciousness

black·smith *n* : a person who makes things out of iron by heating and hammering it

black·snake *n* : either of two harmless snakes of the United States with blackish skins

black·top *n* : a black material used especially to pave roads

black widow *n* : a poisonous spider the female of which is black with a red mark shaped like an hourglass on the underside of the abdomen

blad·der *n* **1** : an organ in the body resembling a pouch into which urine passes from the kidneys and is temporarily stored until discharged from the body **2** : a container that can be filled with air or gas

blade *n* **1** : a leaf of a plant and especially of a grass **2** : the broad flat part of a leaf **3** : something that widens out like the blade of a leaf **4** : the cutting part of a tool, machine, or weapon **5** : SWORD **6** : the runner of an ice skate — **blad·ed** *adj*

[1]**blame** *vb* **blamed; blam·ing** **1** : to find fault with **2** : to hold responsible **3** : to place responsibility for

[2]**blame** *n* **1** : responsibility for something that fails or is wrong **2** : expression of disapproval — **blame·less** *adj*

blame·wor·thy *adj* : deserving blame

blanch *vb* **blanched; blanch·ing** **1** : [1]BLEACH, WHITEN **2** : to scald so as to remove the skin from **3** : to turn pale

bland *adj* **bland·er; bland·est** **1** : not interesting or exciting **2** : not having much flavor **3** : not showing emotion

[1]**blank** *adj* **1** : not having any writing or marks **2** : having empty spaces to be filled in **3** : not showing emotion or understanding

[2]**blank** *n* **1** : an empty space in a line of writing or printing **2** : a paper with empty spaces to be filled in **3** : a cartridge loaded with powder but no bullet **4** : events or a time that cannot be remembered

[1]**blan·ket** *n* **1** : a heavy woven covering used especially for beds **2** : a covering layer

[2]**blanket** *vb* **blank·et·ed; blank·et·ing** : to cover with or as if with a blanket

[1]**blare** *vb* **blared; blar·ing** **1** : to sound loud and harsh **2** : to present in a harsh noisy manner

[2]**blare** *n* : a harsh loud noise

[1]**blast** *n* **1** : the sound made by a wind instrument **2** : EXPLOSION 1 **3** : a strong gust of wind **4** : a stream of air or gas forced through an opening **5** : a very enjoyable experience

[2]**blast** *vb* **blast·ed; blast·ing** **1** : to break to pieces by an explosion : SHATTER **2** : to hit with great force **3** : to make a loud unpleasant sound **4** : to strongly criticize **5** : [2]BLIGHT — **blast off** : to take off

blast–off *n* : an instance of taking off (as of a rocket)

bla·tant *adj* : completely obvious in a disagreeable way

[1]**blaze** *n* **1** : an intense and dangerous fire **2** : great brightness and heat **3** : a bright display **4** : OUTBURST 1

[2]**blaze** *vb* **blazed; blaz·ing** **1** : to burn brightly **2** : to shine as if on fire

[3]**blaze** *n* **1** : a white stripe down the center of an animal's face **2** : a mark made on a tree to show a trail

[4]**blaze** *vb* **blazed; blaz·ing** : to show a path by making marks on trees

bldg. *abbr* building

[1]**bleach** *vb* **bleached; bleach·ing** : to make white by removing the color or stains from

[2]**bleach** *n* : a chemical used for bleaching

bleach·er *n* : one of a set of open seats arranged like steps for people to sit on while watching a game or performance — usually used in pl.

bleak *adj* **bleak·er; bleak·est** **1** : open to wind or weather **2** : being cold and raw or uncheerful **3** : not hopeful or encouraging — **bleak·ly** *adv* — **bleak·ness** *n*

[1]bleat *vb* **bleat·ed; bleat·ing** : to make the cry of a sheep, goat, or calf
[2]bleat *n* : the sound made by a sheep, goat, or calf
bleed *vb* **bled; bleed·ing** **1** : to lose or shed blood **2** : to feel pain or pity **3** : to draw a liquid or gas from **4** : to spread into something else
[1]blem·ish *n* : a mark that makes something imperfect : an unwanted mark on a surface
[2]blemish *vb* **blem·ished; blem·ish·ing** : to spoil by or as if by an ugly mark
[1]blend *vb* **blend·ed; blend·ing** **1** : to mix so completely that the separate things mixed cannot be told apart **2** : to exist agreeably with each other — **blend in** : to look like part of something
[2]blend *n* **1** : a thorough mixture : a product made by blending **2** : a word formed by combining parts of two or more other words so that they overlap
blend·er *n* : an appliance used to chop, mix, blend, and liquefy
bless *vb* **blessed** *also* **blest; bless·ing** **1** : to make holy by a religious ceremony or words **2** : to ask the favor or protection of God for — used to wish good health especially to someone who has just sneezed **3** : to praise or honor as holy **4** : to give happiness or good fortune to
bless·ed *adj* **1** : HOLY 1 **2** : enjoying happiness — **bless·ed·ness** *n*
bless·ing *n* **1** : the act of one who blesses **2** : APPROVAL **3** : something that makes a person happy or content **4** : a short prayer
blew *past of* BLOW
[1]blight *n* : a disease that makes parts of plants dry up and die
[2]blight *vb* **blight·ed; blight·ing** : to injure or destroy by or as if by a blight
blimp *n* : an airship filled with gas like a balloon
[1]blind *adj* **blind·er; blind·est** **1** : unable or nearly unable to see **2** : lacking in judgment or understanding **3** : UNQUESTIONING **4** : closed at one end — **blind·ly** *adv* — **blind·ness** *n*
[2]blind *vb* **blind·ed; blind·ing** **1** : to cause the permanent loss of sight in **2** : to make it impossible to see well for a short time
[3]blind *n* **1** : a device to reduce sight or keep out light **2** : a place of hiding
[4]blind *adv* : with only instruments as guidance
[1]blind·fold *vb* **blind·fold·ed; blind·fold·ing** : to cover the eyes of with a piece of cloth
[2]blindfold *n* : a covering over the eyes
blind·man's buff *n* : a game in which a blindfolded player tries to catch and identify one of the other players
blink *vb* **blinked; blink·ing** **1** : to shut and open the eyes quickly **2** : to shine with a light that goes or seems to go on and off
blink·er *n* : a light that blinks to indicate that a vehicle will be turning
bliss *n* : great happiness : JOY — **bliss·ful** *adj* — **bliss·ful·ly** *adv*
[1]blis·ter *n* **1** : a small raised area of the skin filled with a watery liquid **2** : a swelling (as in paint) that looks like a blister of the skin
[2]blister *vb* **blis·tered; blis·ter·ing** **1** : to develop a blister or blisters **2** : to cause blisters on
blithe *adj* **blith·er; blith·est** : free from worry : MERRY, CHEERFUL — **blithe·ly** *adv*
bliz·zard *n* : a long heavy snowstorm
bloat *vb* **bloat·ed; bloat·ing** : to make swollen with or as if with fluid
blob *n* : a small lump or drop of something thick
[1]block *n* **1** : a solid piece of some material usually with one or more flat sides **2** : an area of land surrounded by four streets in a city **3** : the length of one side of a city block **4** : a number of things thought of as forming a group or unit **5** : a large building divided into separate houses or shops **6** : an action that stops or slows down an opponent (as in football) **7** : something that prevents a person from thinking about certain things **8** : something that stops or makes passage or progress difficult : OBSTRUCTION **9** : a case enclosing one or more pulleys
[2]block *vb* **blocked; block·ing** **1** : to stop or make passage through or through to difficult : OBSTRUCT **2** : to stop or make the passage of difficult **3** : to make an opponent's movement (as in football) difficult
[1]block·ade *vb* **block·ad·ed; block·ad·ing** : to close off a place to prevent the coming in or going out of people or supplies
[2]blockade *n* : the closing off of a place (as by warships) to prevent the coming in or going out of people or supplies
block and tackle *n* : an arrangement of pulleys in blocks with rope or cable for lifting or hauling
block·house *n* : a building (as of heavy timbers or of concrete) built with holes in its sides through which people inside may fire out at an enemy
block letter *n* : a capital letter often printed by hand that has all lines of equal thickness
blog *n* : a website that contains an online personal journal with reflections, comments, and often links provided by the writer — **blog·ger** *n*
[1]blond *or* **blonde** *adj* **blond·er; blond·est** **1** : of a golden or pale yellowish brown color **2** : having hair of a light color

[2]blond *or* **blonde** *n* **:** someone with golden or pale yellowish brown hair

blood *n* **1 :** the red fluid that circulates in the heart, arteries, capillaries, and veins of persons and animals and that brings nourishment and oxygen to and carries away waste products from all parts of the body **2 :** relationship through a common ancestor **:** KINSHIP — **blood·ed** *adj*

blood·cur·dling *adj* **:** causing great horror or fear

blood·hound *n* **:** a large hound with long drooping ears, a wrinkled face, and a very good sense of smell

blood pressure *n* **:** pressure of the blood on the walls of blood vessels and especially arteries

blood·shed *n* **:** serious injury or death caused by violence

blood·shot *adj* **:** red and sore

blood·stream *n* **:** the circulating blood in the living body

blood·suck·er *n* **:** an animal (as a leech) that sucks blood — **blood·suck·ing** *adj*

blood·thirsty *adj* **:** eager to kill or hurt

blood vessel *n* **:** an artery, vein, or capillary of the body

bloody *adj* **blood·i·er; blood·i·est 1 :** bleeding or covered with blood **2 :** causing or accompanied by bloodshed

[1]bloom *n* **1 :** [1]FLOWER 1 **2 :** the period or state of producing flowers **3 :** a condition or time of beauty, freshness, and strength **4 :** the rosy color of the cheek

[2]bloom *vb* **bloomed; bloom·ing 1 :** to produce flowers **2 :** to change, grow, or develop fully

[1]blos·som *n* **1 :** [1]FLOWER 1 **2 :** [1]BLOOM 2

[2]blossom *vb* **blos·somed; blos·som·ing 1 :** [2]BLOOM 1 **2 :** to appear, change, grow, or develop

[1]blot *n* **1 :** a spot or stain of dirt or ink **2 :** a mark of shame or dishonor

[2]blot *vb* **blot·ted; blot·ting 1 :** [2]SPOT 1 **2 :** to dry by pressing with paper or cloth — **blot out 1 :** to make (something) difficult to see **2 :** to destroy completely

blotch *n* **1 :** a blemish on the skin **2 :** a large irregular spot of color or ink — **blotched** *adj*

blotchy *adj* **blotch·i·er; blotch·i·est :** marked with irregular spots

blot·ter *n* **:** a piece of blotting paper

blot·ting paper *n* **:** a soft spongy paper used to absorb wet ink

blouse *n* **1 :** a loose garment for women covering the body from the neck to the waist **2 :** the jacket of a uniform

[1]blow *vb* **blew; blown; blow·ing 1 :** to move or be moved usually with speed and force **2 :** to move in or with the wind **3 :** to send forth a strong stream of air from the mouth or from a bellows **4 :** to make a sound or cause to sound by blowing **5 :** to clear by forcing air through **6 :** to shape by forcing air into **7 :** to enter or leave very quickly **8 :** to fail in performing or keeping — **blow·er** *n* — **blow over :** to pass without effect — **blow up 1 :** EXPLODE 1 **2 :** to fill with a gas

[2]blow *n* **:** a blowing of wind **:** GALE

[3]blow *n* **1 :** a hard hit with a part of the body or an object **2 :** a sudden happening that causes suffering or loss

blow·gun *n* **:** a tube from which a dart may be shot by the force of the breath

blow·torch *n* **:** a small portable burner in which the flame is made hotter by a blast of air or oxygen

[1]blub·ber *vb* **blub·bered; blub·ber·ing 1 :** to weep noisily **2 :** to utter while weeping

[2]blubber *n* **:** the fat of various sea mammals (as whales and seals) from which oil can be obtained

[1]blue *n* **1 :** the color of the clear daytime sky **2 :** blue clothing or cloth **3 :** SKY **4 :** SEA — **blu·ish** *adj* — **out of the blue :** suddenly and unexpectedly

[2]blue *adj* **blu·er; blu·est 1 :** of the color of the sky **:** of the color blue **2 :** SAD 1

blue·bell *n* **:** a plant with blue flowers shaped like bells

blue·ber·ry *n, pl* **blue·ber·ries :** a sweet blue or blackish berry that grows on a bush and has many small soft seeds

blue·bird *n* **:** a small North American songbird that is blue above and reddish brown or pale blue below

blue·bot·tle *n* **:** a large blue hairy fly

blue cheese *n* **:** cheese ripened by and full of greenish blue mold

blue·fish *n* **:** a saltwater fish that is bluish above with silvery sides and is often used for food

blue·grass *n* **1 :** a grass with bluish green stems **2 :** a type of traditional American music that is played on stringed instruments

blue jay *n* **:** a crested and mostly blue North American bird related to the crows

blue jeans *n pl* **:** pants made of blue denim

blue·print *n* **1 :** a photographic print made with white lines on a blue background and showing how something will be made **2 :** a detailed plan of something to be done

blue ribbon *n* **:** a decorative ribbon colored blue that is given to the winner in a competition

blues *n pl* **1 :** low spirits **2 :** a style of music that was created by African-Americans and that expresses feelings of sadness

blue whale *n* **:** a very large whale that is

generally considered the largest living animal
[1]bluff *adj* **1 :** rising steeply with a broad front **2 :** frank and outspoken in a rough but good-natured way
[2]bluff *n* **:** a high steep bank **:** CLIFF
[3]bluff *vb* **bluffed; bluff·ing :** to deceive or frighten by pretending to have more strength or confidence than is really true
[4]bluff *n* **:** an act or instance of pretending to have more strength, confidence, or ability than is really true
[1]blun·der *vb* **blun·dered; blun·der·ing 1 :** to move in a clumsy way **2 :** to make a mistake
[2]blunder *n* **:** a bad or stupid mistake
blun·der·buss *n* **:** a short gun that has a barrel which is larger at the end and that was used long ago for shooting at close range without taking exact aim
[1]blunt *adj* **blunt·er; blunt·est 1 :** having a thick edge or point **:** DULL **2 :** speaking or spoken in plain language without thought for other people's feelings — **blunt·ly** *adv*
[2]blunt *vb* **blunt·ed; blunt·ing :** to make or become less sharp
[1]blur *n* **1 :** something that cannot be seen clearly **2 :** something that is difficult to remember
[2]blur *vb* **blurred; blur·ring 1 :** to make unclear or hard to see or remember **2 :** to make or become unclear or confused
blur·ry *adj* **blur·ri·er; blur·ri·est :** not in sharp focus
blurt *vb* **blurt·ed; blurt·ing :** to say or tell suddenly and without thinking
[1]blush *vb* **blushed; blush·ing 1 :** to become red in the face from shame, confusion, or embarrassment **2 :** to feel ashamed or embarrassed
[2]blush *n, pl* **blush·es 1 :** a reddening of the face from shame, confusion, or embarrassment **2 :** a rosy color
[1]blus·ter *vb* **blus·tered; blus·ter·ing 1 :** to talk or act in a noisy boastful way **2 :** to blow hard and noisily
[2]bluster *n* **:** noisy violent action or speech
blvd. *abbr* boulevard
boa *n* **:** a large snake (as a python) that coils around and crushes its prey
boar *n* **1 :** a male pig **2 :** WILD BOAR
[1]board *n* **1 :** a sawed piece of lumber that is much broader and longer than it is thick **2 :** a usually rectangular piece of rigid material used for some special purpose **3 :** BLACKBOARD **4 :** a number of persons having authority to manage or direct something **5 :** meals given at set times for a price **6 boards** *pl* **:** the low wooden wall enclosing a hockey rink **7 :** a sheet of insulating material carrying electronic parts (as for a computer) — **on board :** [1]ABOARD
[2]board *vb* **board·ed; board·ing 1 :** to go aboard **2 :** to cover with boards **3 :** to give or get meals and a place to live for a price
board·er *n* **:** a person who pays for meals and a place to live at another's house
board·ing·house *n* **:** a house at which people are given meals and often a place to live
boarding school *n* **:** a school at which most of the students live during the school year
board·walk *n* **:** a walk made of planks especially along a beach
[1]boast *vb* **boast·ed; boast·ing 1 :** to express too much pride in a person's own qualities, possessions, or achievements **2 :** to have and be proud of having
[2]boast *n* **1 :** an act of expressing too much pride in a person's own qualities, possessions, or achievements **2 :** a cause for pride — **boast·ful** *adj* — **boast·ful·ly** *adv*
[1]boat *n* **1 :** a small vessel driven on the water by oars, paddles, sails, or a motor **2 :** [1]SHIP 1
[2]boat *vb* **boat·ed; boat·ing :** to use a boat — **boat·er** *n*
boat·house *n* **:** a house or shelter for boats
boat·man *n, pl* **boat·men :** a person who works on, handles, or operates boats
boat·swain *n* **:** a warrant officer on a warship or a petty officer on a commercial ship who has charge of the hull, anchors, boats, and rigging
[1]bob *vb* **bobbed; bob·bing 1 :** to move or cause to move with a short jerky up-and-down motion **2 :** to try to seize something with the teeth
[2]bob *n* **:** a short jerky up-and-down motion
[3]bob *n* **1 :** a float used to buoy up the baited end of a fishing line **2 :** a woman's or child's short haircut
[4]bob *vb* **bobbed; bob·bing 1 :** to cut (hair) in the style of a bob **2 :** to cut shorter
bob·by pin *n* **:** a flat metal hairpin with the two ends pressed close together
bob·cat *n* **:** a North American wildcat that is a small rusty brown type of lynx
bob·o·link *n* **:** a North American songbird related to the blackbirds
bob·sled *n* **:** a racing sled made with two sets of runners, a hand brake, and often a steering wheel
bob·tail *n* **1 :** a short tail **:** a tail cut short **2 :** an animal (as a dog) with a short tail
bob·white *n* **:** a North American quail with gray, white, and reddish brown coloring
[1]bode *vb* **bod·ed; bod·ing :** to be a sign of (a future event)
[2]bode *past of* BIDE
bod·ice *n* **:** the upper part of a dress

[1]**bodi·ly** *adj* : of or relating to the body
[2]**bodily** *adv* **1 :** by the body **2 :** as a whole
body *n, pl* **bod·ies** **1 :** the physical whole of a live or dead person or animal **2 :** the main part of a person, animal, or plant **3 :** a human being **4 :** the main or central part **5 :** the main part of a motor vehicle **6 :** a group of persons or things united for some purpose **7 :** a mass or portion of something distinct from other masses — **bod·ied** *adj*
body·guard *n* **:** a person or a group of persons whose duty it is to protect someone
body mass index *n* **:** a measure of body fat that is related to the body's weight and height
body·wash *n* **:** a liquid product for cleansing the body
[1]**bog** *n* **:** wet spongy ground that is usually acid and found next to a body of water (as a pond)
[2]**bog** *vb* **bogged; bog·ging :** to sink or stick fast in or as if in a bog
bo·gey *also* **bo·gie** *or* **bo·gy** *n, pl* **bogeys** *or* **bogies** **1 :** GHOST, GOBLIN **2 :** something a person is afraid of without reason
bo·gus *adj* **:** not genuine
[1]**boil** *n* **:** a red painful lump in the skin that contains pus and is caused by infection
[2]**boil** *vb* **boiled; boil·ing** **1 :** to heat or become heated to the temperature (**boiling point**) at which bubbles rise and break at the surface **2 :** to cook or become cooked in boiling water **3 :** to feel angry or upset
[3]**boil** *n* **:** the state of something that is boiling
boil·er *n* **1 :** a container in which something is boiled **2 :** a tank heating and holding water **3 :** a strong metal container used in making steam (as to heat buildings)
bois·ter·ous *adj* **:** being rough and noisy — **bois·ter·ous·ly** *adv*
bold *adj* **bold·er; bold·est** **1 :** willing to meet danger or take risks **:** DARING **2 :** not polite and modest **:** FRESH **3 :** showing or calling for courage or daring **4 :** standing out prominently — **bold·ly** *adv* — **bold·ness** *n*
bold·face *n* **:** a heavy black type — **bold–faced** *adj*
boll *n* **:** the seedpod of a plant (as cotton)
boll weevil *n* **:** a grayish or brown insect that lays its eggs in cotton bolls
bo·lo·gna *n* **:** a large smoked sausage usually made of beef, veal, and pork
[1]**bol·ster** *n* **:** a long pillow or cushion sometimes used to support bed pillows
[2]**bolster** *vb* **bol·stered; bol·ster·ing :** to support with or as if with a bolster
[1]**bolt** *n* **1 :** a stroke of lightning **:** THUNDERBOLT **2 :** a sliding bar used to fasten a door **3 :** the part of a lock worked by a key **4 :** a metal pin or rod with a head at one end and a screw thread at the other that is used to hold something in place **5 :** a roll of cloth or wallpaper
[2]**bolt** *vb* **bolt·ed; bolt·ing** **1 :** to move suddenly and rapidly **2 :** to run away **3 :** to fasten with a bolt **4 :** to swallow hastily or without chewing
[1]**bomb** *n* **1 :** a hollow case or shell filled with explosive material **2 :** a container in which something (as an insecticide) is stored under pressure and from which it is released in a fine spray **3 :** something that is a complete failure
[2]**bomb** *vb* **bombed; bomb·ing** **1 :** to attack with bombs **2 :** to fail completely
bom·bard *vb* **bom·bard·ed; bom·bard·ing** **1 :** to attack with heavy fire from big guns **:** SHELL **2 :** to attack again and again
bomb·er *n* **:** an airplane specially made for dropping bombs
bo·na fide *adj* **:** GENUINE 1
bon·bon *n* **:** a candy with a soft coating and a creamy center
[1]**bond** *n* **1 :** something that binds **2 :** the condition of being held together **3 :** a force or influence that brings or holds together **4 :** a chain or rope used to prevent someone from moving or acting freely **5 :** a promise to do something **6 :** a legal agreement in which a person agrees to pay a sum of money if he or she fails to do a certain thing **7 :** a government or business certificate promising to pay a certain sum by a certain day
[2]**bond** *vb* **bond·ed; bond·ing** **1 :** to stick or cause to stick together **2 :** to form a close relationship
bond·age *n* **:** SLAVERY
[1]**bone** *n* **1 :** any of the hard pieces that form the skeleton of most animals **2 :** the hard material of which the skeleton of most animals is formed — **bone·less** *adj*
[2]**bone** *vb* **boned; bon·ing :** to remove the bones from
bone marrow *n* **:** a soft tissue rich in blood vessels that fills the spaces of most bones and includes one type that is red and produces red blood cells and white blood cells and another type that is yellow and contains fat
bon·fire *n* **:** a large fire built outdoors
bong *n* **:** a deep sound like that of a large bell
bon·go *n, pl* **bongos** *also* **bongoes :** either of a pair of small drums of different sizes fitted together and played with the fingers
bon·net *n* **:** a child's or woman's hat usually tied under the chin by ribbons or strings
bon·ny *also* **bon·nie** *adj* **bon·ni·er; bon·ni·est** *chiefly British* **:** HANDSOME 1, BEAUTIFUL
bo·nus *n* **:** something given to somebody

(as a worker) in addition to what is usual or owed
bony *adj* **bon·i·er; bon·i·est** **1 :** of or relating to bone **2 :** like bone especially in hardness **3 :** having bones and especially large or noticeable bones **4 :** very thin
¹boo *interj* — used to express disapproval or to startle or frighten
²boo *n, pl* **boos :** a cry expressing disapproval
³boo *vb* **booed; boo·ing :** to express disapproval of with boos
boo·by trap *n* **1 :** a hidden bomb that explodes when the object connected to it is touched **2 :** a trap set for an unsuspecting person
boo·by–trap *vb* **boo·by–trapped; boo·by–trap·ping :** to set up as a booby trap
¹book *n* **1 :** a set of sheets of paper bound together **2 :** a long written work **3 :** a large division of a written work **4 :** a pack of small items bound together **5 :** the records of a business's accounts — often used in pl.
²book *vb* **booked; book·ing :** to reserve for future use
book·case *n* **:** a set of shelves to hold books
book·end *n* **:** a support at the end of a row of books to keep them standing up
book·keep·er *n* **:** a person who keeps financial records for a business
book·keep·ing *n* **:** the work of keeping business records
book·let *n* **:** a little book usually having paper covers and few pages
book·mark *n* **1 :** something placed in a book to show the page the reader wants to return to **2 :** something on a computer screen that serves as a shortcut (as to a website)
book·mo·bile *n* **:** a truck with shelves of books that is a traveling library
book·worm *n* **:** a person who reads a lot
¹boom *vb* **boomed; boom·ing** **1 :** to make a deep, hollow and loud sound **2 :** to increase or develop rapidly
²boom *n* **1 :** a deep, hollow, and loud sound **2 :** a rapid increase in activity or popularity
³boom *n* **1 :** a long pole attached to the bottom of a sail **2 :** a long beam sticking out from the mast of a derrick to support or guide something that is being lifted **3 :** a long pole for holding a microphone
boom box *n* **:** a large portable radio and CD or tape player
boo·mer·ang *n* **:** a curved club that can be thrown so as to return to the thrower
boom·ing *adj* **1 :** making a deep sound **2 :** forcefully or powerfully done
boon *n* **1 :** something asked or granted as a favor **2 :** something pleasant or helpful that comes at just the right time
¹boost *vb* **boost·ed; boost·ing** **1 :** to raise or push up from below **2 :** to make bigger or greater — **boost·er** *n*
²boost *n* **:** a push up **:** an act of boosting
¹boot *n* **:** a covering usually of leather or rubber for the foot and part of the leg
²boot *vb* **boot·ed; boot·ing :** ¹KICK 1
boo·tee *or* **boo·tie** *n* **:** an infant's knitted sock
booth *n, pl* **booths** **1 :** partly enclosed area or small building used for a particular purpose **2 :** table in a restaurant between two benches with high backs
boo·ty *n* **1 :** goods seized from an enemy in war or by robbery **:** PLUNDER **2 :** a valuable gain or prize
¹bop *vb* **bopped; bop·ping :** ¹HIT 1
²bop *n* **:** ²HIT 1
¹bor·der *n* **1 :** a boundary especially of a country or state **2 :** the outer edge of something **3 :** a decorative strip on or near the edge of something
²border *vb* **bor·dered; bor·der·ing** **1 :** to put a border on **2 :** to be close or next to
bor·der·line *adj* **:** not quite average, standard, or normal
¹bore *vb* **bored; bor·ing** **1 :** to make a hole in especially with a drill **2 :** to make by piercing or drilling — **bor·er** *n*
²bore *n* **1 :** a hole made by boring **2 :** a space (as in a gun barrel) shaped like a cylinder **3 :** the diameter of a hole or cylinder
³bore *past of* BEAR
⁴bore *n* **:** an uninteresting person or thing
⁵bore *vb* **bored; bor·ing :** to make tired and restless by being uninteresting
bore·dom *n* **:** the state of being bored
bo·ric acid *n* **:** a weak acid containing boron used to kill germs
bor·ing *adj* **:** dull and uninteresting
born *adj* **1 :** brought into life by birth **2 :** brought into existence **3 :** having a certain characteristic from or as if from birth
borne *past participle of* BEAR
bo·ron *n* **:** a powdery or hard solid chemical element that is used especially in making glass and detergents
bor·ough *n* **1 :** a town, village, or part of a large city that has its own government **2 :** one of the five political divisions of New York City
bor·row *vb* **bor·rowed; bor·row·ing** **1 :** to take and use something with the promise of returning it **2 :** to use something begun or thought up by another **:** ADOPT **3 :** to adopt into one language from another — **bor·row·er** *n*
¹bos·om *n* **1 :** the front of the human chest **2 :** the breasts of a woman

[2]**bosom** *adj* : very close
[1]**boss** *n* **1** : the person at a job who tells workers what to do **2** : the head of a group (as a political organization)
[2]**boss** *vb* **bossed; boss·ing** : to give orders to
bossy *adj* **boss·i·er; boss·i·est** : liking to order people around
bot *n* : a computer program that performs automatic, repetitive, and sometimes harmful tasks
bo·tan·i·cal *adj* : of or relating to the study of plants
bot·a·nist *n* : a person specializing in botany
bot·a·ny *n* : a branch of biology dealing with plants
[1]**botch** *vb* **botched; botch·ing** : to do clumsily and unskillfully : BUNGLE
[2]**botch** *n* : a badly done job
[1]**both** *pron* : each one of two things or people : the two
[2]**both** *conj* — used before two words or phrases connected with *and* to stress that each is included
[3]**both** *adj* : the two
[1]**both·er** *vb* **both·ered; both·er·ing** **1** : to trouble (someone) in body or mind : ANNOY **2** : to cause to worry **3** : to take the time or trouble **4** : to intrude upon : INTERRUPT
[2]**bother** *n* **1** : someone or something that is annoying **2** : COMMOTION **3** : a state of worry or annoyance
both·er·some *adj* : ANNOYING
[1]**bot·tle** *n* **1** : a container (as of glass or plastic) usually having a narrow neck and mouth and no handle **2** : the quantity held by a bottle
[2]**bottle** *vb* **bot·tled; bot·tling** **1** : to put into a bottle **2** : to shut up as if in a bottle
bot·tle·neck *n* : a place or condition where improvement or movement is held up
bot·tom *n* **1** : the lowest part of something **2** : the under surface of something **3** : a supporting surface or part : BASE **4** : the lowest or worst level or position **5** : clothing that covers the lower part of the body **6** : the bed of a body of water **7** : low land along a river **8** : the most basic part **9** : the second half of an inning of baseball
bot·tom·less *adj* **1** : having no bottom **2** : very deep
bough *n* : a usually large or main branch of a tree
bought *past and past participle of* BUY
bouil·lon *n* : a clear soup or stock made from meat or vegetables
boul·der *n* : a very large rounded piece of rock
bou·le·vard *n* : a wide usually major street often having strips with trees, grass, or flowers planted along its center or sides
[1]**bounce** *vb* **bounced; bounc·ing** **1** : to spring back or up after hitting a surface **2** : to cause to spring back **3** : to jump or move up and down **4** : to leap suddenly
[2]**bounce** *n* **1** : the action of springing back after hitting something **2** : a sudden leap — **bouncy** *adj*
[1]**bound** *adj* : going or intending to go
[2]**bound** *n* **1** : a boundary line **2** : a point or line beyond which a person or thing cannot go
[3]**bound** *past and past participle of* BIND
[4]**bound** *vb* **bound·ed; bound·ing** : to form the boundary of
[5]**bound** *adj* **1** : tied or fastened with or as if with bands **2** : required by law or duty **3** : under the control of something **4** : covered with binding **5** : firmly determined **6** : very likely : CERTAIN
[6]**bound** *n* : a leap or long jump
[7]**bound** *vb* **bounded; bounding** : to make a long leap or move in leaps
bound·ary *n, pl* **bound·aries** : something that points out or shows a limit or end : a dividing line
bound·less *adj* : having no limits
boun·te·ous *adj* **1** : GENEROUS 1 **2** : given in plenty : ABUNDANT
boun·ti·ful *adj* **1** : giving freely or generously **2** : PLENTIFUL 1
boun·ty *n, pl* **boun·ties** **1** : GENEROSITY 1 **2** : things given in generous amounts **3** : money given as a reward
bou·quet *n* : a bunch of flowers
bout *n* **1** : a contest of skill or strength **2** : [2]ATTACK 4, OUTBREAK
bou·tique *n* : a small fashionable shop
[1]**bow** *vb* **bowed; bow·ing** **1** : to bend the head or body as an act of politeness or respect **2** : to stop resisting : YIELD
[2]**bow** *n* : the act of bending the head or body to express politeness or respect
[3]**bow** *n* **1** : a weapon used for shooting arrows and usually made of a strip of wood bent by a cord connecting the two ends **2** : something shaped in a curve **3** : a knot made with one or more loops **4** : a rod with horsehairs stretched from end to end used for playing a stringed instrument (as a violin)
[4]**bow** *vb* **bowed; bow·ing** : to bend or cause to bend into a curve
[5]**bow** *n* : the forward part of a ship
bow·el *n* **1** : INTESTINE — usually used in pl. **2** : a part of the intestine
bow·er *n* : a shelter in a garden made of boughs of trees or vines
[1]**bowl** *n* **1** : a round hollow dish without handles **2** : the contents of a bowl **3** : something in the shape of a bowl (as part of a spoon or pipe)
[2]**bowl** *vb* **bowled; bowl·ing** **1** : to play a

game of bowling **2 :** to move rapidly and smoothly — **bowl over 1 :** to hit and push down while moving quickly **2 :** to surprise or impress very much

bow·legged *adj* **:** having the legs bowed outward

bow·line *n* **:** a knot used for making a loop that will not slip

bowl·ing *n* **:** a game in which large heavy balls are rolled so as to knock down pins

bow·sprit *n* **:** a large spar sticking out forward from the bow of a ship

bow·string *n* **:** the cord connecting the two ends of a bow

[1]**box** *n* **:** an evergreen shrub or small tree used for hedges

[2]**box** *n* **1 :** a container usually having four sides, a bottom, and a cover **2 :** the contents of a box **3 :** a four-sided shape on a piece of paper or computer screen **4 :** an enclosed place for one or more persons

[3]**box** *vb* **boxed; box·ing :** to enclose in or as if in a box

[4]**box** *vb* **boxed; boxing :** to fight with the fists

box·car *n* **:** a roofed freight car usually having sliding doors in the sides

box elder *n* **:** a North American maple with leaves divided into several leaflets

[1]**boxer** *n* **:** a person who engages in the sport of boxing

[2]**boxer** *n* **:** a compact dog of German origin that is of medium size with a square build and has a short and often tan coat

box·ing *n* **:** the sport of fighting with the fists

box office *n* **:** a place where tickets to public entertainments (as sports or theatrical events) are sold

boy *n* **1 :** a male child from birth to young manhood **2 :** SON **3** *often offensive* **:** a male servant

boy band *n* **:** a small group of teenage boys or young men who play pop songs geared especially to a young female audience

[1]**boy·cott** *vb* **boy·cot·ted; boy·cot·ting :** to join with others in refusing to deal with someone (as a person, organization, or country) as a way of protesting or forcing changes

[2]**boycott** *n* **:** the process or an instance of joining with others in refusing to deal with someone (as a person, organization, or country) as a way of protesting or forcing changes

boy·friend *n* **:** a man or boy involved in a romantic relationship

boy·hood *n* **:** the time or condition of being a boy

boy·ish *adj* **:** relating to or having qualities often felt to be typical of boys

Boy Scout *n* **:** a member of a scouting program (as the Boy Scouts of America)

bp *abbr* birthplace

Br. *abbr* **1** Britain **2** British

bra *n* **:** a woman's undergarment for breast support

[1]**brace** *vb* **braced; brac·ing 1 :** to make strong, firm, or steady **2 :** to get ready

[2]**brace** *n* **1 :** something that adds strength or support **2 brac·es** *pl* **:** a usually wire device worn to correct the position of teeth **3 :** one of a pair of marks { } used to connect words or items to be considered together **4 :** two of a kind **5 :** a tool with a U-shaped bend that is used to turn wood-boring bits

brace·let *n* **:** a decorative band or chain usually worn on the wrist or arm

brack·en *n* **:** a large branching fern

[1]**brack·et** *n* **1 :** a support for a weight (as a shelf) that is usually attached to a wall **2 :** one of a pair of marks [ ] (**square brackets**) used to enclose letters or numbers or in mathematics to enclose items to be treated together **3 :** one of a pair of marks ⟨ ⟩ (**angle brackets**) used to enclose letters or numbers **4 :** [1]GROUP 1, CATEGORY

[2]**bracket** *vb* **brack·et·ed; brack·et·ing 1 :** to place within brackets **2 :** to put into the same class **:** GROUP

brack·ish *adj* **:** somewhat salty

brad *n* **:** a thin nail with a small usually indented head

brag *vb* **bragged; brag·ging :** to speak in a way that shows too much pride **:** BOAST — **brag·ger** *n*

brag·gart *n* **:** a person who boasts a lot

[1]**braid** *vb* **braid·ed; braid·ing :** to weave three strands together

[2]**braid** *n* **:** a length of cord, ribbon, or hair formed of three or more strands woven together

braille *n, often cap* **:** a system of printing for the blind in which the letters are represented by raised dots

[1]**brain** *n* **1 :** the part of the nervous system that is inside the skull, consists of grayish nerve cells and whitish nerve fibers, and is the organ of thought and the central control point for the nervous system **2 :** the ability to think **:** INTELLIGENCE **3 :** someone who is very smart

[2]**brain** *vb* **brained; brain·ing :** to hit on the head very hard

brain·storm *n* **:** a sudden inspiration or idea

brainy *adj* **brain·i·er; brain·i·est :** very smart

[1]**brake** *n* **:** a device for slowing or stopping motion (as of a wheel) usually by friction

[2]**brake** *vb* **braked; brak·ing :** to slow or stop by using a brake

brake·man *n, pl* **brake·men :** a crew member on a train who inspects the train and helps the conductor

bram·ble *n* : a rough prickly bush or vine — usually used in pl.
bran *n* : the broken coat of the seed of cereal grain separated (as by sifting) from the flour or meal
[1]**branch** *n* **1** : a part of a tree that grows out from the trunk or from a main division of the trunk **2** : something extending from a main line or body like a branch **3** : a division or subordinate part of something — **branched** *adj*
[2]**branch** *vb* **branched; branch·ing** : to spread or divide into smaller or attached parts : send out a branch
[1]**brand** *n* **1** : a mark made by burning (as on cattle) or by stamping or printing (as on manufactured goods) to show ownership, maker, or quality **2** : a category of goods identified by a name as being made by a certain company **3** : TRADEMARK **4** : a particular type **5** : a mark of disgrace
[2]**brand** *vb* **brand·ed; brand·ing** **1** : put a mark on to show ownership **2** : to show or claim (something) to be bad or wrong
bran·dish *vb* **bran·dished; bran·dish·ing** : to wave or shake in a threatening manner
brand–new *adj* : completely new
bran·dy *n, pl* **brandies** : an alcoholic liquor made from wine or fruit juice
brass *n* **1** : an alloy made by combining copper and zinc **2** : the musical instruments of an orchestra or band that are usually made of brass and include the cornets, trumpets, trombones, French horns, and tubas
brat *n* : a naughty annoying child
[1]**brave** *adj* **brav·er; brav·est** : feeling or showing no fear — **brave·ly** *adv*
[2]**brave** *vb* **braved; brav·ing** : to face or handle without fear
[3]**brave** *n* : an American Indian warrior
brav·ery *n* : COURAGE
[1]**brawl** *vb* **brawled; brawl·ing** : to quarrel or fight noisily
[2]**brawl** *n* : a noisy quarrel or fight
brawn *n* : muscular strength
brawny *adj* **brawn·i·er; brawn·i·est** : having large strong muscles
[1]**bray** *vb* **brayed; bray·ing** : to make the loud harsh cry of a donkey
[2]**bray** *n* : the loud harsh cry of a donkey
bra·zen *adj* **1** : made of brass **2** : sounding loud and usually harsh **3** : done or acting in a very bold and shocking way without shame
Bra·zil nut *n* : a dark three-sided nut with a white kernel
[1]**breach** *n* **1** : a failure to act in a promised or required way **2** : an opening made by breaking
[2]**breach** *vb* **breached; breach·ing** **1** : to fail to do as promised or required by **2** : to make a break in
[1]**bread** *n* **1** : a baked food made from flour or meal **2** : FOOD 1
[2]**bread** *vb* **bread·ed; bread·ing** : to cover with bread crumbs
breadth *n* **1** : distance measured from side to side **2** : SCOPE 2
[1]**break** *vb* **broke; bro·ken; break·ing** **1** : to separate into parts especially suddenly or forcibly **2** : to cause (a bone) to separate into two or more pieces **3** : to stop working or cause to stop working because of damage or wear **4** : to fail to keep **5** : to force a way **6** : to cut into and turn over **7** : to go through : PENETRATE **8** : [2]TAME 1 **9** : to do better than **10** : to interrupt or put an end to : STOP **11** : to reduce the force of **12** : to develop or burst out suddenly **13** : to make known **14** : SOLVE **15** : [1]CHANGE 4 **16** : to run or flee suddenly — **break down** **1** : to stop working properly **2** : to separate or become separated into simpler substances : DECOMPOSE **3** : to be overcome by emotion **4** : to knock down — **break out** **1** : to develop a skin rash **2** : to start up suddenly — **break up** **1** : to separate into parts **2** : to bring or come to an end **3** : to end a romantic relationship
[2]**break** *n* **1** : an act of breaking **2** : something produced by breaking **3** : a period of time when an activity stops **4** : an accidental event
break·down *n* **1** : a failure to function properly **2** : a sudden failure of mental or physical health
brea·ker *n* **1** : a person or thing that breaks something **2** : a wave that breaks on shore
[1]**break·fast** *n* : the first meal of the day
[2]**breakfast** *vb* **break·fast·ed; break·fast·ing** : to eat breakfast
break·neck *adj* : very fast or dangerous
break·through *n* : a sudden advance or successful development
break·wa·ter *n* : an offshore wall to protect a beach or a harbor from the sea
breast *n* **1** : either of the two enlarged soft parts on a woman's chest that contain a gland that produces milk when she has a baby **2** : the front part of the body between the neck and the stomach **3** : the front part of a bird's body below the neck — **breast·ed** *adj*
breast·bone *n* : a flat narrow bone in the middle of the chest to which the ribs are connected
breast–feed *vb* **breast–fed; breast–feed·ing** : to feed (a baby) from a mother's breast
breast·plate *n* : a piece of armor for covering the breast

breast·work *n* : a wall thrown together to serve as a defense in battle

breath *n* **1 :** ability to breathe : ease of breathing **2 :** air taken in or sent out by the lungs **3 :** a slight breeze — **out of breath :** breathing very rapidly as a result of hard exercise — **under someone's breath :** very quietly

breathe *vb* **breathed; breath·ing 1 :** to draw air into and expel it from the lungs **2 :** to take in by inhaling **3 :** [1]LIVE 1 **4 :** [1]SAY 1, UTTER

breath·er *n* : a pause for rest

breath·less *adj* **1 :** panting from exertion **2 :** filled with excitement or tension — **breath·less·ly** *adv*

breath·tak·ing *adj* : very exciting or beautiful

breech·es *n pl* **1 :** short pants fastening below the knee **2 :** PANTS

[1]**breed** *vb* **bred; breed·ing 1 :** to produce or increase (animals or plants) by sexual reproduction **2 :** to produce offspring by sexual reproduction **3 :** to bring up : TRAIN **4 :** to bring about : CAUSE — **breed·er** *n*

[2]**breed** *n* **1 :** a kind of animal or plant that is found only under human care and is different from related kinds **2 :** [1]CLASS 6, KIND

breed·ing *n* : training especially in manners

breeze *n* **1 :** a gentle wind **2 :** something that is easy to do

breezy *adj* **breez·i·er; breez·i·est 1 :** somewhat windy **2 :** lively and somewhat carefree — **breez·i·ly** *adv*

breth·ren *pl of* BROTHER — used chiefly in formal situations

breve *n* : a mark ˘ placed over a vowel to show that the vowel is short

brev·i·ty *n* : the condition of being short or brief

[1]**brew** *vb* **brewed; brew·ing 1 :** to make (beer) from water, malt, and hops **2 :** to prepare by soaking in hot water **3 :** [2]PLAN 2 **4 :** to start to form — **brew·er** *n*

[2]**brew** *n* : something made by brewing

brew·ery *n, pl* **brew·er·ies :** a place where malt liquors are brewed

bri·ar *also* **bri·er** *n* : a plant (as the rose or blackberry) with a thorny or prickly stem

[1]**bribe** *n* : something given or promised to a person in order to influence dishonestly a decision or action

[2]**bribe** *vb* **bribed; brib·ing :** to influence or try to influence dishonestly by giving or promising something

brib·ery *n, pl* **brib·er·ies :** the act of giving or taking a bribe

[1]**brick** *n* **1 :** a building or paving material made from clay molded into blocks and baked **2 :** a block made of brick

[2]**brick** *vb* **bricked; brick·ing :** to close, face, or pave with bricks

brick·lay·er *n* : a person who builds or paves with bricks

brid·al *adj* : of or relating to a bride or a wedding

bride *n* : a woman just married or about to be married

bride·groom *n* : a man just married or about to be married

brides·maid *n* : a woman who attends a bride at her wedding

[1]**bridge** *n* **1 :** a structure built over something (as water, a low place, or a railroad) so people can cross **2 :** the place on a ship where the ship is steered **3 :** something that joins or connects : something like a bridge

[2]**bridge** *vb* **bridged; bridg·ing :** to make a bridge over or across

[3]**bridge** *n* : a card game for four players in two teams

[1]**bri·dle** *n* : a device for controlling a horse made up of a set of straps enclosing the head, a bit, and a pair of reins

[2]**bridle** *vb* **bri·dled; bri·dling 1 :** to put a bridle on **2 :** RESTRAIN 2 **3 :** to hold the head high and draw in the chin as an expression of resentment

[1]**brief** *adj* **brief·er; brief·est :** not very long : SHORT — **brief·ly** *adv*

[2]**brief** *vb* **briefed; brief·ing :** to give information or instructions to

brief·case *n* : a flat case for carrying papers or books

briefs *n pl* : short snug underpants

brier *variant of* BRIAR

brig *n* : a square-rigged sailing ship with two masts

bri·gade *n* **1 :** a body of soldiers consisting of two or more regiments **2 :** a group of persons organized for acting together

brig·a·dier general *n* : a commissioned officer in the army, air force, or marine corps ranking above a colonel

bright *adj* **1 :** giving off or filled with much light **2 :** very clear or vivid in color **3 :** INTELLIGENT 1, CLEVER **4 :** CHEERFUL 1 **5 :** likely to be good — **bright·ly** *adv* — **bright·ness** *n*

bright·en *vb* **bright·ened; bright·en·ing 1 :** to add more light to **2 :** to make or become cheerful

bril·liance *n* : great brightness

bril·liant *adj* **1 :** flashing with light : very bright **2 :** very impressive **3 :** very smart or clever — **bril·liant·ly** *adv*

[1]**brim** *n* **1 :** the edge or rim of something hollow **2 :** the part of a hat that sticks out around the lower edge

[2]**brim** *vb* **brimmed; brim·ming :** to be or become full to overflowing

brin·dled *adj* : having dark streaks or spots on a gray or brownish background
brine *n* **1 :** a mixture of salty water used especially to preserve or season food **2 :** the salty water of the ocean
bring *vb* **brought; bring·ing 1 :** to cause to come by carrying or leading : take along **2 :** to cause to reach a certain state or take a certain action **3 :** to cause to arrive or exist **4 :** to sell for — **bring·er** *n* — **bring about** : to cause to happen — **bring back :** to cause to return to a person's memory — **bring forth :** to cause to happen or exist : PRODUCE — **bring on :** to cause to happen to — **bring out 1 :** to produce and make available **2 :** to cause to appear — **bring to :** to bring back from unconsciousness : REVIVE — **bring up 1 :** to bring to maturity through care and education **2 :** to mention when talking
brink *n* **1 :** the edge at the top of a steep place **2 :** a point of beginning
briny *adj* **brin·i·er; brin·i·est :** SALTY
brisk *adj* **1 :** done or spoken with quickness and energy **2 :** quick and efficient **3 :** very refreshing — **brisk·ly** *adv*
[1]**bris·tle** *n* **1 :** a short stiff hair **2 :** a stiff hair or something like a hair fastened in a brush
[2]**bristle** *vb* **bris·tled; bris·tling 1 :** to rise up and stiffen like bristles **2 :** to show signs of anger **3 :** to be covered with
bris·tly *adj* **bris·tli·er; bris·tli·est :** of, like, or having many bristles
Brit. *abbr* **1** Britain **2** British
britch·es *n pl* **1 :** BREECHES 1 **2 :** PANTS
[1]**Brit·ish** *adj* : of or relating to Great Britain (England, Scotland, and Wales) or the British
[2]**British** *n pl* : the people of Great Britain
brit·tle *adj* **brit·tler; brit·tlest :** hard but easily broken — **brit·tle·ness** *n*
bro *abbr* brother
broach *vb* **broached; broach·ing :** to bring up as a subject for discussion
broad *adj* **broad·er; broad·est 1 :** not narrow : WIDE **2 :** extending far and wide : SPACIOUS **3 :** [1]COMPLETE 1, FULL **4 :** not limited **5 :** covering only the main points : GENERAL — **broad·ly** *adv*
broad·band *n* : a high-speed electronic network that carries more than one type of communication (as Internet and cable television signals)
[1]**broad·cast** *vb* **broadcast; broad·cast·ing 1 :** to send out by radio or television from a transmitting station **2 :** to make widely known **3 :** to scatter far and wide — **broad·cast·er** *n*
[2]**broadcast** *n* **1 :** an act of broadcasting **2 :** a radio or television program
broad·cloth *n* : a fine cloth with a firm smooth surface
broad·en *vb* **broad·ened; broad·en·ing :** to make or become wide or wider
broad–mind·ed *adj* : willing to consider unusual or different opinions, beliefs, and practices
[1]**broad·side** *n* **1 :** the part of a ship's side above the waterline **2 :** a firing of all of the guns that are on the same side of a ship
[2]**broadside** *adv* **1 :** with one side forward **2 :** from the side
broad·sword *n* : a sword having a broad blade
bro·cade *n* : a cloth with a raised design woven into it — **bro·cad·ed** *adj*
broc·co·li *n* : a vegetable that has green stalks and green or purplish clustered flower buds
brogue *n* : an Irish or Scottish accent
broil *vb* **broiled; broil·ing 1 :** to cook or be cooked directly over or under a heat source **2 :** to make or feel extremely hot
broil·er *n* : a young chicken suitable for broiling
[1]**broke** *past of* BREAK
[2]**broke** *adj* : having no money
[1]**broken** *past participle of* BREAK
[2]**bro·ken** *adj* **1 :** separated into parts or pieces **2 :** not working properly **3 :** having gaps or breaks **4 :** not kept or followed **5 :** imperfectly spoken
bro·ken·heart·ed *adj* : very sad
bro·ker *n* : a person who acts as an agent for others in the buying or selling of property
bro·mine *n* : a chemical element that is a deep red liquid giving off an irritating smelly vapor
bron·chi·al *adj* : of or relating to either of the two branches (**bronchial tubes**) of the trachea that carry air into the lungs
bron·chi·tis *n* : a sore raw state of the bronchial tubes
bron·co *n, pl* **bron·cos :** MUSTANG
bron·to·sau·rus *n* : a huge plant-eating dinosaur with a long neck and tail and four thick legs
[1]**bronze** *n* **1 :** an alloy of copper and tin and sometimes other elements **2 :** a yellowish brown color **3 :** a medal made of bronze given to the third place winner in a competition
[2]**bronze** *adj* **1 :** made of bronze **2 :** having a yellowish brown color
brooch *n* : a piece of jewelry fastened to clothing with a pin
[1]**brood** *vb* **brood·ed; brood·ing 1 :** to sit on eggs to hatch them **2 :** to cover (young) with the wings for warmth and protection **3 :** to think long and anxiously about something
[2]**brood** *n* **1 :** the young of birds hatched at

the same time **2 :** a group of young children or animals having the same mother

brood·er *n* **:** a building or a compartment that can be heated and is used for raising young fowl

brook *n* **:** a small stream

broom *n* **1 :** a brush with a long handle used for sweeping **2 :** a plant with long slender branches along which grow many yellow flowers

broom·stick *n* **:** the handle of a broom

bros *abbr* brothers

broth *n* **:** the liquid in which a meat, fish, or vegetable has been cooked

broth·er *n, pl* **brothers** *also* **breth·ren 1 :** a male person or animal related to another person or animal by having one or both parents in common **2 :** a fellow member of an organization

broth·er·hood *n* **1 :** the state of being a brother **2 :** a group of people who are engaged in the same business or have a similar interest **3 :** feelings of friendship, support, and understanding between people

broth·er–in–law *n, pl* **broth·ers–in–law 1 :** the brother of a person's husband or wife **2 :** the husband of a person's sister or brother

broth·er·ly *adj* **1 :** of or relating to brothers **2 :** [1]KINDLY 1, AFFECTIONATE

brought *past and past participle of* BRING

brow *n* **1 :** EYEBROW **2 :** FOREHEAD **3 :** the upper edge of a steep slope

[1]**brown** *adj* **1 :** of the color of coffee **:** colored brown **2 :** having a dark or tanned complexion

[2]**brown** *n* **:** a color like that of coffee or chocolate — **brown·ish** *adj*

[3]**brown** *vb* **browned; brown·ing :** to make or become brown

brown·ie *n* **1 :** a small square piece of chewy chocolate cake **2** *cap* **:** a member of a program of the Girl Scouts for girls in the first through third grades in school **3 :** a cheerful elf believed to perform helpful services at night

brown sugar *n* **:** sugar that contains molasses

browse *vb* **browsed; brows·ing 1 :** to read or look in a casual way **2 :** to nibble young shoots and foliage

brows·er *n* **1 :** a person or animal that browses **2 :** a computer program providing access to sites on the World Wide Web

bru·in *n* **:** [1]BEAR 1

[1]**bruise** *vb* **bruised; bruis·ing :** to injure the flesh (as by a blow) without breaking the skin

[2]**bruise** *n* **:** a black-and-blue spot on the body or a dark spot on fruit caused by an injury or damage

brunch *n* **:** a meal that combines breakfast and lunch and is usually eaten in late morning

bru·net *or* **bru·nette** *adj* **:** having dark brown or black hair and dark eyes — spelled *brunet* when used of a boy or man and usually *brunette* when used of a girl or woman — **brunet** *or* **brunette** *n*

brunt *n* **:** the main force or stress (as of an attack)

[1]**brush** *n* **1 :** a tool made of bristles set in a handle and used for cleaning, smoothing, or painting **2 :** an act of smoothing or scrubbing with a brush **3 :** a light stroke **4 :** a bushy tail

[2]**brush** *vb* **brushed; brush·ing 1 :** to scrub or smooth with a brush **2 :** to remove with or as if with a brush **3 :** to pass lightly across

[3]**brush** *n* **1 :** branches and twigs cut from trees **2 :** a heavy growth of small trees and bushes

[4]**brush** *n* **:** a brief fight or quarrel

brush·wood *n* **:** [3]BRUSH

brusque *adj* **:** so abrupt and frank in manner or speech as to be impolite — **brusque·ly** *adj* — **brusque·ness** *n*

brus·sels sprouts *n pl, often cap B* **:** small leafy heads resembling tiny cabbages and eaten as a vegetable

bru·tal *adj* **:** cruel and harsh — **bru·tal·ly** *adv*

bru·tal·i·ty *n, pl* **bru·tal·i·ties 1 :** the quality of being cruel and harsh **2 :** a cruel and harsh act or course of action

[1]**brute** *adj* **:** typical of beasts **:** like that of a beast

[2]**brute** *n* **1 :** a four-footed animal especially when wild **2 :** a cruel or rough person

brut·ish *adj* **:** being unfeeling and stupid

BSA *abbr* Boy Scouts of America

BTW *abbr* by the way

bu. *abbr* bushel

[1]**bub·ble** *n* **1 :** a tiny round body of air or gas in a liquid **2 :** a round body of air within a solid **3 :** a thin film of liquid filled with air or gas — **bub·bly** *adj*

[2]**bubble** *vb* **bub·bled; bub·bling 1 :** to form or produce bubbles **2 :** to flow with a gurgle

bu·bon·ic plague *n* **:** a dangerous disease which is spread by rats and in which fever, weakness, and swollen lymph nodes are present

buc·ca·neer *n* **:** PIRATE

[1]**buck** *n* **1 :** the male of an animal (as a deer or rabbit) the female of which is called *doe* **2 :** DOLLAR **3 :** [1]MAN 1, FELLOW

[2]**buck** *vb* **bucked; buck·ing 1 :** to spring or jump upward with head down and back arched **2 :** to charge or push against **3 :** to go against **:** OPPOSE — **buck up :** to become more confident

buck·board *n* **:** a lightweight carriage with four wheels that has a seat supported by a springy platform

buck·et *n* **1 :** a usually round container with a handle for holding or carrying liquids or solids **2 :** a large container that is part of a machine and is used for collecting, scooping, or carrying **3 :** BUCKETFUL

buck·et·ful *n, pl* **buck·et·fuls** *or* **buck·ets·ful** **1 :** as much as a bucket will hold **2 :** a large quantity

buck·eye *n* **:** a tree with showy clusters of flowers and large brown inedible nutlike seeds

[1]**buck·le** *n* **:** a fastening device which is attached to one end of a belt or strap and through which the other end is passed and held

[2]**buckle** *vb* **buck·led; buck·ling** **1 :** to fasten with a buckle **2 :** to start to work hard — usually used with *down* **3 :** to bend, crumple, or give way

buck·skin *n* **:** a soft flexible leather usually having a suede finish

buck·wheat *n* **:** a plant with pinkish white flowers that is grown for its dark triangular seeds which are used as a cereal grain

[1]**bud** *n* **1 :** a small growth at the tip or on the side of a stem that later develops into a flower, leaf, or branch **2 :** a flower that has not fully opened **3 :** an early stage of development

[2]**bud** *vb* **bud·ded; bud·ding** **1 :** to form or put forth a small growth that develops into a flower, leaf, or branch **2 :** to reproduce by asexual means by forming a small growth that pinches off and develops into a new organism

Bud·dha *n* **1 :** the founder of Buddhism originally known as Siddhartha Gautama **2 :** a statue that represents Buddha

Bud·dhism *n* **:** a religion of eastern and central Asia based on the teachings of Gautama Buddha — **Bud·dhist** *n*

bud·dy *n, pl* **buddies :** a close friend

budge *vb* **budged; budg·ing** **1 :** to move or cause to move especially slightly **2 :** to give in

[1]**bud·get** *n* **1 :** a statement of estimated income and expenses for a period of time **2 :** a plan for using money

[2]**budget** *vb* **bud·get·ed; bud·get·ing** **1 :** to include in a plan for using money **2 :** to plan for efficient use

[1]**buff** *n* **1 :** a pale orange yellow **2 :** a stick or wheel with a soft surface for applying polish **3 :** [3]FAN

[2]**buff** *vb* **buffed; buff·ing :** to polish with or as if with a buff

buf·fa·lo *n, pl* **buffalo** *or* **buf·fa·loes :** any of several wild oxen and especially the American bison

buffalo wing *n* **:** a deep-fried chicken wing coated with a spicy sauce and usually served with blue cheese dressing

[1]**buf·fet** *vb* **buf·fet·ed; buf·fet·ing :** to pound repeatedly **:** BATTER

[2]**buf·fet** *n* **1 :** a cabinet or set of shelves for the display of dishes and silver **:** SIDEBOARD **2 :** a meal set out on a buffet or table from which people may serve themselves

buf·foon *n* **:** a foolish or stupid person

[1]**bug** *n* **1 :** any of a large group of insects that have four wings, suck liquid food (as plant juices or blood), and have young which resemble the adults but lack wings **2 :** an insect or other small creeping or crawling animal **3 :** FLAW

[2]**bug** *vb* **bugged; bug·ging** **1 :** [1]BOTHER 1, ANNOY **2 :** to stick out — often used with *out*

bug·gy *n, pl* **buggies :** a light carriage with a single seat that is usually drawn by one horse

bu·gle *n* **:** an instrument like a simple trumpet used chiefly for giving military signals

[1]**build** *vb* **built; build·ing** **1 :** to make by putting together parts or materials **2 :** to produce or create gradually by effort **3 :** to grow or increase to a high point or level

[2]**build** *n* **:** the shape and size of a person's or animal's body

build·er *n* **:** a person whose business is the construction of buildings

build·ing *n* **1 :** a permanent structure built as a dwelling, shelter, or place for human activities or for storage **2 :** the art, work, or business of assembling materials into a structure

built–in *adj* **:** forming a permanent part of a structure

bulb *n* **1 :** LIGHT BULB **2 :** a resting stage of a plant that is formed underground and consists of a very short stem with one or more flower buds surrounded by special thick leaves **3 :** a plant structure (as a tuber) that is somewhat like a bulb **4 :** a rounded object or part

bul·bous *adj* **:** round or swollen

[1]**bulge** *vb* **bulged; bulg·ing :** to swell or curve outward

[2]**bulge** *n* **:** a swelling part **:** a part that sticks out

bulk *n* **1 :** greatness of size or volume **2 :** the largest or chief part — **in bulk :** in large amounts

bulk·head *n* **:** a wall separating sections in a ship

bulky *adj* **bulk·i·er; bulk·i·est** **1 :** great in size or volume **2 :** being large and awkward to handle

bull *n* **:** an adult male ox or an adult male of certain other large animals (as the elephant and the whale)

bull·dog *n* **:** a dog of English origin with short hair and a stocky powerful build

bull·doz·er *n* **:** a motor vehicle with tracks instead of tires and a large wide blade for pushing (as in clearing land of trees)

bul·let *n* : a small piece of metal made to be shot from a firearm

bul·le·tin *n* : a short public notice usually coming from an informed or official source

bulletin board *n* : a board for posting bulletins and announcements

bul·let·proof *adj* : made to stop bullets from going through

bull·fight *n* : a public entertainment popular especially in Spain in which a person (**bull·fight·er**) displays skill in escaping the charges of a bull and usually finally kills it with a sword

bull·finch *n* : a European songbird that has a thick bill and a red breast

bull·frog *n* : a large heavy frog that makes a booming or bellowing sound

bull·head *n* : any of various fishes with large heads

bul·lion *n* : gold or silver metal in bars or blocks

bull·ock *n* **1** : a young bull **2** : [1]STEER

bull's–eye *n* **1** : the center of a target **2** : a shot that hits the center of a target

[1]**bul·ly** *n, pl* **bul·lies** : a person who teases, hurts, or threatens smaller or weaker persons

[2]**bully** *vb* **bul·lied; bul·ly·ing** : to tease, hurt, or threaten a smaller or weaker person : to act like a bully toward

bul·rush *n* : any of several large rushes or sedges that grow in wet places

bul·wark *n* **1** : a solid structure like a wall built for defense against an enemy **2** : something that defends or protects

[1]**bum** *n* **1** : a person who avoids work **2** : [2]TRAMP 1, HOBO

[2]**bum** *vb* **bummed; bum·ming** : to obtain by asking or begging

bum·ble *vb* **bum·bled; bum·bling** : to act, move, or speak in a clumsy way

bum·ble·bee *n* : a large hairy bee that makes a loud humming sound

[1]**bump** *n* **1** : a rounded swelling of flesh as from an injury **2** : a small raised area on a surface **3** : a sudden heavy impact or jolt

[2]**bump** *vb* **bumped; bump·ing** **1** : to strike or knock against something **2** : to move along unevenly : JOLT

[1]**bump·er** *n* : a bar across the front or back of a motor vehicle intended to lessen shock or damage from collision

[2]**bum·per** *adj* : larger or finer than usual

bumpy *adj* **bump·i·er; bump·i·est** **1** : having or covered with bumps **2** : having sudden up-and-down movements

bun *n* : a sweet or plain round roll

[1]**bunch** *n* **1** : a number of things of the same kind growing together **2** : [1]GROUP 1

[2]**bunch** *vb* **bunched; bunch·ing** : to gather in a bunch

[1]**bun·dle** *n* : a number of things fastened or wrapped together : PACKAGE

[2]**bundle** *vb* **bun·dled; bun·dling** **1** to fasten, tie, or wrap a group of things together **2** : to move or push into or out of a place quickly — **bundle up** : to dress warmly

bung *n* : a stopper that closes or covers a hole in a barrel

bun·ga·low *n* : a house with a main level and a smaller second level above

bun·gle *vb* **bun·gled; bun·gling** : to act, do, make, or work badly — **bun·gler** *n*

bun·ion *n* : a sore reddened swelling of the first joint of a big toe

[1]**bunk** *n* **1** : BUNK BED **2** : a built-in bed (as on a ship or train) **3** : a sleeping place

[2]**bunk** *vb* **bunked; bunk·ing** : to stay overnight

bunk bed *n* : one of two single beds usually placed one above the other

bun·ny *n, pl* **bunnies** : RABBIT

bunt *vb* **bunt·ed; bunt·ing** : to hit a baseball lightly so that the ball rolls for a short distance — **bunt** *n*

[1]**bun·ting** *n* : a bird similar to a sparrow in size and habits but having a stout bill

[2]**bunting** *n* : flags or decorations made of a thin cloth

[1]**buoy** *n* **1** : a floating object anchored in a body of water to mark a channel or to warn of danger **2** : LIFE BUOY

[2]**buoy** *vb* **buoyed; buoy·ing** **1** : to keep from sinking : keep afloat **2** : to brighten the mood of

buoy·an·cy *n* **1** : the power of rising and floating (as on water or in air) **2** : the power of a liquid to hold up a floating body

buoy·ant *adj* **1** : able to rise and float in the air or on the top of a liquid **2** : able to keep a body afloat **3** : LIGHTHEARTED, CHEERFUL

bur *or* **burr** *n* : a rough or prickly covering or shell of a seed or fruit

[1]**bur·den** *n* **1** : something carried : LOAD **2** : something that is hard to take **3** : the capacity of a ship for carrying cargo

[2]**burden** *vb* **bur·dened; bur·den·ing** **1** : to have a heavy load or put a heavy load on **2** : to cause to have to deal with

bur·den·some *adj* : so heavy or hard to take as to be a burden

bur·dock *n* : a tall weed related to the thistles that has prickly purplish heads of flowers

bu·reau *n* **1** : a low chest of drawers for use in a bedroom **2** : a division of a government department **3** : a business office that provides services

bur·ger *n* **1** : HAMBURGER 1 **2** : a sandwich like a hamburger

bur·glar *n* **:** a person who commits burglary
bur·glary *n, pl* **bur·glar·ies :** the act of breaking into a building especially at night with the intent to commit a crime (as theft)
buri·al *n* **:** the act of placing a dead body in a grave or tomb
bur·lap *n* **:** a rough cloth made usually from jute or hemp and used mostly for bags
bur·ly *adj* **bur·li·er; bur·li·est :** strongly and heavily built
¹burn *vb* **burned** *or* **burnt; burn·ing 1 :** to be on fire or to set on fire **2 :** to destroy or be destroyed by fire or heat **3 :** to make or produce by fire or heat **4 :** to give light **5 :** to injure or affect by or as if by fire or heat **6 :** to ruin by cooking too long or with too much heat **7 :** to feel or cause to feel as if on fire **8 :** to feel a strong emotion **9 :** to record music or data on a computer disk **10 :** to get a sunburn
²burn *n* **:** an injury produced by burning or by something rubbing away the skin
burn·er *n* **:** the part of a stove or furnace where the flame or heat is produced
bur·nish *vb* **bur·nished; bur·nish·ing :** to make shiny
¹burp *vb* **burped; burp·ing 1 :** ¹BELCH 1 **2 :** to help (a baby) let out gas from the stomach especially by patting or rubbing the baby's back
²burp *n* **:** ²BELCH
burr *variant of* BUR
bur·ro *n, pl* **burros :** a small donkey often used to carry loads
¹bur·row *n* **:** a hole in the ground made by an animal (as a rabbit or fox) for shelter or protection
²burrow *vb* **bur·rowed; bur·row·ing 1 :** to hide in or as if in a burrow **2 :** to make a burrow **3 :** to proceed by or as if by digging
¹burst *vb* **burst; burst·ing 1 :** to break open or in pieces (as by an explosion from within) **2 :** to suddenly show one's feelings **3 :** to come or go suddenly **4 :** to be filled to the maximum
²burst *n* **:** a sudden release or effort
bury *vb* **bur·ied; bury·ing 1 :** to place in the ground and cover over for concealment **2 :** to put (a dead body) in a grave or tomb **3 :** to cover with something **4 :** to cover up **:** HIDE
bus *n, pl* **bus·es** *or* **bus·ses :** a large motor vehicle for carrying passengers
bus·boy *n* **:** a person hired by a restaurant to clear and set tables
bush *n* **1 :** a usually low shrub with many branches **2 :** a stretch of uncleared or lightly settled country
bush·el *n* **:** a unit of measure (as of grain, produce, or seafood) equal to four pecks or 32 quarts (about 35 liters)
bushy *adj* **bush·i·er; bush·i·est 1 :** being thick and spreading **2 :** overgrown with bushes
busi·ness *n* **1 :** the activity of making, buying, and selling goods or services **2 :** a commercial enterprise **3 :** the normal activity of a person or group **4 :** personal concerns **5 :** ¹MATTER 1
busi·ness·man *n, pl* **busi·ness·men :** a man in business especially as an owner or a manager
busi·ness·wom·an *n, pl* **busi·ness·wom·en :** a woman in business especially as an owner or a manager
¹bust *n* **1 :** a piece of sculpture representing the upper part of the human figure including the head and neck **2 :** a woman's bosom
²bust *vb* **bust·ed; bust·ing 1 :** to hit with the fist **2 :** ¹BREAK 1
¹bus·tle *vb* **bus·tled; bus·tling :** to move about in a busy or noisy way
²bustle *n* **:** busy or noisy activity
¹busy *adj* **busi·er; busi·est 1 :** actively at work **2 :** being used **3 :** full of activity — **busi·ly** *adv*
²busy *vb* **bus·ied; busy·ing :** to make busy
busy·body *n, pl* **busy·bod·ies :** a person who is too interested in the affairs of other people
¹but *conj* **1 :** yet nevertheless **2 :** while just the opposite **3 :** except that **:** UNLESS
²but *prep* **:** other than **:** EXCEPT
³but *adv* **:** ²ONLY 1
¹butch·er *n* **1 :** a person whose business is killing animals for sale as food **2 :** a dealer in meat **3 :** a person who kills in large numbers or in a brutal manner
²butcher *vb* **butch·ered; butch·er·ing 1 :** to kill and prepare (an animal) for food **2 :** ²MASSACRE **3 :** to make a mess of **:** BOTCH
but·ler *n* **:** the chief male servant of a household
¹butt *n* **:** a target of ridicule or hurtful humor
²butt *n* **1 :** the part of the body on which a person sits **2 :** the thicker or bottom end of something **3 :** an unused remainder
³butt *vb* **butt·ed; butt·ing :** to strike or thrust with the head or horns — **butt in :** to intrude on someone else's activity or conversation
⁴butt *n* **:** a blow or thrust with the head or horns
butte *n* **:** an isolated hill with steep sides
¹but·ter *n* **1 :** a solid yellowish fatty food obtained from cream or milk by churning **2 :** a spreadable food made of cooked and crushed nuts or fruit
²butter *vb* **but·tered; but·ter·ing :** to spread with or as if with butter
but·ter·cup *n* **:** a common wildflower with bright yellow blossoms

but·ter·fat *n* **:** the natural fat of milk that is the chief ingredient of butter
but·ter·fly *n, pl* **but·ter·flies :** an insect that has a slender body and large colored wings covered with tiny overlapping scales and that flies mostly in the daytime
but·ter·milk *n* **:** the liquid left after churning butter from milk or cream
but·ter·nut *n* **:** an eastern North American tree that has sweet egg-shaped nuts and is related to the walnuts
but·ter·scotch *n* **:** a candy made from sugar, corn syrup, and water
but·tock *n* **1 :** the back of the hip which forms one of the rounded parts on which a person sits **2 buttocks** *pl* **:** RUMP 1
[1]**but·ton** *n* **1 :** a small ball or disk used for holding parts of a garment together or as an ornament **2 :** a small often round part of a machine that makes the machine do something when pushed
[2]**button** *vb* **but·toned; but·ton·ing :** to close or fasten with buttons
but·ton·hole *n* **:** a slit or loop for fastening a button
but·ton·wood *n* **:** SYCAMORE 2
[1]**but·tress** *n* **1 :** a structure built against a wall or building to give support and strength **2 :** something that supports, props, or strengthens
[2]**buttress** *vb* **but·tressed; but·tress·ing :** to support or strengthen **:** to support with or as if with a buttress
bux·om *adj* **:** having a healthy plump form
[1]**buy** *vb* **bought; buy·ing :** to get by paying for **:** PURCHASE — **buy·er** *n*
[2]**buy** *n* **:** [1]BARGAIN 2
[1]**buzz** *vb* **buzzed; buzz·ing 1 :** to make a low humming sound like that of bees **2 :** to be filled with a low hum or murmur **3 :** to fly an airplane low over
[2]**buzz** *n* **:** a low humming sound
buz·zard *n* **:** a usually large bird of prey that flies slowly
buzz·er *n* **:** an electric signaling device that makes a buzzing sound
[1]**by** *prep* **1 :** close to **:** NEAR **2 :** so as to go on **3 :** so as to go through **4 :** so as to pass **5 :** AT 1, DURING **6 :** no later than **7 :** with the use or help of **8 :** through the action of **9 :** ACCORDING TO 1 **10 :** with respect to **11 :** to the amount of **12** — used to join two or more measurements or to join the numbers in a statement of multiplication or division
[2]**by** *adv* **1 :** near at hand **2 :** [4]PAST — **by and by :** after a while
[1]**by·gone** *adj* **:** gone by **:** PAST
[2]**by·gone** *n* **:** an event that is over and done with
[1]**by·pass** *n* **:** a road serving as a substitute route around a blocked or crowded area
[2]**bypass** *vb* **by·passed; by·pass·ing 1 :** to make a detour around **2 :** AVOID 1, FORGO
by–prod·uct *n* **:** something produced (as in manufacturing) in addition to the main product
by·stand·er *n* **:** a person present or standing near but taking no part in what is going on
byte *n* **:** a group of eight bits that a computer handles as a unit
by·way *n* **:** a road that is not used very much

C

c *n, pl* **c's** *or* **cs** *often cap* **1 :** the third letter of the English alphabet **2 :** the number 100 in Roman numerals **3 :** a musical note referred to by the letter C **4 :** a grade that shows a student's work is fair or average
c. *abbr* **1** carat **2** cent **3** centimeter **4** century **5** chapter **6** cup
C *abbr* **1** Celsius **2** centigrade
CA *abbr* California
cab *n* **1 :** a light closed carriage pulled by a horse **2 :** TAXICAB **3 :** the covered compartment for the engineer and the controls of a locomotive or for the operator of a truck, tractor, or crane
ca·bana *n* **:** a shelter usually with an open side used by people at a beach or swimming pool
cab·bage *n* **:** a garden plant related to the turnips that has a round firm head of leaves used as a vegetable
cab·in *n* **1 :** a small simple dwelling usually having only one story **2 :** a private room on a ship **3 :** a place below deck on a small boat for passengers or crew **4 :** a part of an airplane for cargo, crew, or passengers
cab·i·net *n* **1 :** a case or cupboard with shelves or drawers for storing or displaying things **2 :** a group of people who act as advisers (as to the head of a country)
[1]**ca·ble** *n* **1 :** a very strong rope, wire, or

chain **2 :** a bundle of wires to carry electric current **3 :** TELEGRAM **4 :** CABLE TELEVISION

[2]**cable** *vb* **ca·bled; ca·bling :** to send a message by telegraph

cable television *n* **:** a television system in which paying customers receive the television signals over electrical wires

ca·boose *n* **:** a car usually at the rear of a freight train for the use of the train crew

ca·cao *n, pl* **cacaos :** a South American tree with fleshy yellow pods that contain fatty seeds from which chocolate is made

[1]**cache** *n* **1 :** a place for hiding, storing, or preserving treasure or supplies **2 :** something hidden or stored in a cache

[2]**cache** *vb* **cached; cach·ing :** to put or store so as to be safe or hidden **:** place in a cache

[1]**cack·le** *vb* **cack·led; cack·ling 1 :** to make the noise or cry a hen makes especially after laying an egg **2 :** to laugh or chatter noisily

[2]**cackle** *n* **:** a sound made by a hen or like that made by a hen

cac·tus *n, pl* **cac·ti** *or* **cac·tus·es :** any of a large group of flowering plants of dry regions that have thick juicy stems and branches with scales or spines

ca·dav·er *n* **:** CORPSE

[1]**cad·die** *or* **cad·dy** *n, pl* **cad·dies :** a person who carries a golfer's clubs

[2]**caddie** *or* **caddy** *vb* **cad·died; cad·dy·ing :** to carry a golfer's clubs

cad·dis fly *n* **:** an insect that has four wings and a larva which lives in water in a silk case covered especially with bits of wood, gravel, sand, or plant matter

ca·dence *n* **:** a regular beat or rhythm

ca·det *n* **:** a student in a military school or college

ca·fé *also* **ca·fe** *n* **:** a small restaurant serving usually simple meals

caf·e·te·ria *n* **:** a place where people get food at a counter and carry it to a table for eating

caf·feine *n* **:** a substance found especially in coffee and tea that makes a person feel more awake

[1]**cage** *n* **1 :** a box or enclosure that has large openings covered usually with wire net or bars and is used for keeping birds or animals **2 :** an enclosure like a cage in shape or purpose

[2]**cage** *vb* **caged; cag·ing :** to put or keep in or as if in a cage

ca·gey *adj* **ca·gi·er; ca·gi·est 1 :** unwilling to act or speak in a direct or open way **2 :** clever in a tricky way

ca·hoot *n* **:** a secret partnership — usually used in pl.

ca·jole *vb* **ca·joled; ca·jol·ing :** to coax or persuade especially by flattery or false promises

[1]**cake** *n* **1 :** a baked food made from a sweet batter or dough **2 :** a usually flat round piece of food that is baked or fried **3 :** a substance hardened or molded into a solid piece

[2]**cake** *vb* **caked; cak·ing 1 :** ENCRUST **2 :** to become dry and hard

Cal. *abbr* California

cal·a·mine *n* **:** a skin lotion used especially to reduce itching (as from an insect bite or poison ivy)

ca·lam·i·ty *n, pl* **ca·lam·i·ties 1 :** great distress or misfortune **2 :** an event that causes great harm and suffering **:** DISASTER — **ca·lam·i·tous** *adj*

cal·ci·um *n* **:** a silvery soft metallic chemical element that is essential for strong healthy bones

calcium carbonate *n* **:** a solid substance that is found as limestone and marble and in plant ashes, bones, and shells

cal·cu·late *vb* **cal·cu·lat·ed; cal·cu·lat·ing 1 :** to find by adding, subtracting, multiplying, or dividing **:** COMPUTE **2 :** [1]ESTIMATE **3 :** to plan by careful thought **:** INTEND

cal·cu·lat·ing *adj* **:** carefully thinking about and planning actions for selfish or improper reasons

cal·cu·la·tion *n* **:** the process or result of adding, subtracting, multiplying, or dividing

cal·cu·la·tor *n* **1 :** a person who calculates **2 :** a usually small electronic device for solving mathematical problems

cal·cu·lus *n* **:** an advanced branch of mathematics that deals mostly with rates of change and with finding lengths, areas, and volumes

caldron *variant of* CAULDRON

cal·en·dar *n* **1 :** a chart showing the days, weeks, and months of the year **2 :** a schedule of planned events or activities

[1]**calf** *n, pl* **calves 1 :** a young cow **2 :** the young of various large animals (as the elephant, moose, or whale)

[2]**calf** *n, pl* **calves :** the muscular back part of the leg below the knee

calf·skin *n* **:** leather made from the skin of a calf

cal·i·ber *or Can and Brit* **cal·i·bre** *n* **1 :** level of excellence, skill, or importance **2 :** the diameter of a bullet or of the hole in the barrel of a gun

[1]**cal·i·co** *n, pl* **cal·i·coes** *or* **cal·i·cos :** cotton cloth especially with a colored pattern printed on one side

[2]**calico** *adj* **:** marked with blotches of color

Calif. *abbr* California

cal·i·per *n* **:** an instrument with two adjustable legs used to measure the thickness of objects or the distance between surfaces — usually used in pl.

ca·liph *or* **ca·lif** *n* **:** an important Muslim political and religious leader

cal·is·then·ics *n pl* : exercises (as push-ups and jumping jacks) to develop strength and flexibility that are done without special equipment — used as singular or plural

[1]**call** *vb* **called; call·ing** **1** : to speak in a loud clear voice so as to be heard at a distance : SHOUT **2** : to say loudly or with authority **3** : to tell, order, or ask to come **4** : to give the order for **5** : to utter a cry **6** : to make a request or demand **7** : to get in touch with by telephone **8** : to make a short visit **9** : [2]NAME 1 **10** : to address someone or something as **11** : to regard as being of a certain kind **12** : to say or guess what the result will be **13** : to estimate as being **14** : SUSPEND 3, END — **call for** : to require as necessary or suitable — **call off** **1** : CANCEL 2 **2** : to cause or tell to stop attacking or chasing — **call on** : to choose to answer

[2]**call** *n* **1** : a loud shout or cry **2** : a cry of an animal **3** : a loud sound or signal **4** : a public request or command **5** : [1]REQUEST 1 **6** : a short visit **7** : something called or announced **8** : the act of calling on the telephone **9** : DECISION 1 **10** : the attraction or appeal of a particular place or condition

call·er *n* : someone who calls

cal·li·gra·phy *n* **1** : beautiful artistic handwriting **2** : the art of producing beautiful handwriting

call·ing *n* : a profession especially that a person feels strongly about

cal·lous *adj* : feeling or showing no sympathy for others

cal·lus *n, pl* **cal·lus·es** : a hard thickened area on the skin and especially on the hands and feet

[1]**calm** *n* **1** : a period or condition of freedom from storm, wind, or rough water **2** : a quiet and peaceful state

[2]**calm** *vb* **calmed; calm·ing** : to make or become less active or disturbed — often used with *down*

[3]**calm** *adj* **calm·er; calm·est** **1** : not stormy or windy **2** : not excited or upset — **calm·ly** *adv* — **calm·ness** *n*

cal·o·rie *n* **1** : a unit for measuring heat equal to the amount of heat required to raise the temperature of one gram of water one degree Celsius **2** : a unit of heat used to indicate the amount of energy foods produce in the human body that is equal to 1000 calories

calve *vb* **calved; calv·ing** : to give birth to a calf

calves *pl of* CALF

ca·lyp·so *n, pl* **calypsos** : a lively folk song or style of singing of the West Indies

ca·lyx *n, pl* **ca·lyx·es** *or* **ca·ly·ces** : the usually green outer part of a flower consisting of sepals

cam·bi·um *n, pl* **cam·bi·ums** *or* **cam·bia** : soft tissue in woody plants from which new wood and bark grow

cam·cord·er *n* : a small video camera

came *past of* COME

cam·el *n* : a large hoofed animal that has one or two large humps on its back and is used in the deserts of Asia and Africa for carrying passengers and loads

cam·era *n* : a device that is used to record visual images (as photographs or movies)

[1]**cam·ou·flage** *n* **1** : the hiding or disguising of something by covering it up or changing the way it looks **2** : something (as color or shape) that protects an animal from attack by making it difficult to see in the area around it

[2]**camouflage** *vb* **cam·ou·flaged; cam·ou·flag·ing** : to hide or disguise by covering or making harder to see

[1]**camp** *n* **1** : a place where temporary shelters are erected **2** : a place or program for recreation or instruction usually during the summer

[2]**camp** *vb* **camped; camp·ing** **1** : to make or occupy a camp **2** : to sleep outdoors usually in a tent

[1]**cam·paign** *n* **1** : a series of activities meant to produce a particular result **2** : a series of military operations in a certain area or for a certain purpose

[2]**campaign** *vb* **cam·paigned; cam·paign·ing** : to take part in activities meant to produce a particular result — **campaign·er** *n*

camp·er *n* **1** : a person who sleeps outdoors (as in a tent) **2** : a type of vehicle or special trailer that people can live and sleep in when they are traveling or camping **3** : a young person who goes to a camp during the summer

Camp Fire Girl *n* : a member of a national organization for girls from ages 5 to 18

camp·ground *n* : an area used for a camp or for camping

cam·phor *n* : a white fragrant solid that comes from the wood and bark of a tall Asian tree (**camphor tree**) and is used mostly in medicine, in making plastics, and to repel moths

camp·site *n* : a place used for camping

cam·pus *n* : the grounds and buildings of a college or school

[1]**can** *helping verb, past* **could;** *present sing & pl* **can** **1** : know how to **2** : be able to **3** : be permitted by conscience or feeling to **4** : have permission to **5** : to be possible

[2]**can** *n* **1** : a metal container usually shaped like a cylinder **2** : the contents of a can

[3]**can** *vb* **canned; can·ning** : to prepare for later use by sealing in an airtight can or jar

Can., Canad. *abbr* **1** Canada **2** Canadian

Canada Day *n* : July 1 observed in Canada as a legal holiday commemorating the anniversary of the proclamation of dominion status in 1867

Can·a·da goose *n, pl* **Canada geese** : a goose of North America that is mostly gray and brown with a black head and neck

[1]**Ca·na·di·an** *adj* : of or relating to Canada or its people

[2]**Canadian** *n* : a person born or living in Canada

ca·nal *n* **1** : an artificial waterway for boats or for irrigation of land **2** : a tubelike passage in the body

ca·nary *n, pl* **ca·nar·ies** : a small usually yellow songbird often kept in a cage

can·cel *vb* **can·celed** *or Can and Brit* **can·celled; can·cel·ing** *or Can and Brit* **can·cel·ling** **1** : to take back : stop from being in effect **2** : to cause to not happen **3** : to be equal in force or importance but have opposite effect **4** : to remove (a common divisor) from numerator and denominator : remove (equivalents) on opposite sides of an equation **5** : to cross out or strike out with a line **6** : to mark (as a postage stamp) so as to make impossible to use again

can·cel·la·tion *n* **1** : an act of causing something to end or to no longer be in effect **2** : a mark that makes something impossible to use again

can·cer *n* : a serious sometimes deadly disease characterized by the growth of abnormal cells that form tumors which may damage or destroy normal body tissue

can·de·la·bra *n* : a candlestick or lamp that has several branches for lights

can·de·la·brum *n, pl* **can·de·la·bra** *also* **can·de·la·brums** : CANDELABRA

can·did *adj* **1** : marked by or showing honesty : FRANK **2** : relating to photography of people acting naturally without being posed — **can·did·ly** *adv*

can·di·da·cy *n, pl* **can·di·da·cies** : the position of a person who is trying to be elected : the state of being a candidate

can·di·date *n* **1** : a person who is trying to be elected **2** : a person who is being considered for a position or honor

can·died *adj* : cooked in or coated with sugar

[1]**can·dle** *n* : a stick of tallow or wax containing a wick and burned to give light

[2]**candle** *vb* **can·dled; can·dling** : to examine (an egg) by holding between the eye and a light — **can·dler** *n*

can·dle·light *n* : the light of a candle — **can·dle·lit** *adj*

can·dle·stick *n* : a holder for a candle

can·dor *or Can and Brit* **candour** *n* : sincere and honest expression

[1]**can·dy** *n, pl* **can·dies** : a sweet made of sugar often with flavoring and filling

[2]**candy** *vb* **can·died; can·dy·ing** : to coat or become coated with sugar often by cooking

cane *n* **1** : an often hollow, slender, and somewhat flexible plant stem **2** : a tall woody grass or reed (as sugarcane) **3** : a rod made especially of wood or metal that often has a curved handle and is used to help someone walk **4** : a rod for beating

[1]**ca·nine** *n* **1** : a pointed tooth next to the incisors **2** : a domestic dog or a related animal (as a wolf or fox)

[2]**canine** *adj* **1** : of or relating to the domestic dog or a related animal **2** : like or typical of a dog

can·is·ter *n* : a small box or can for holding a dry product

can·ker sore *n* : a small painful sore of the mouth

can·nery *n, pl* **can·ner·ies** : a factory where foods are canned

can·ni·bal *n* **1** : a human being who eats human flesh **2** : an animal that eats other animals of its own kind

can·non *n, pl* **cannons** *or* **cannon** : a large heavy weapon consisting mostly of a metal tube that is mounted on wheels and is used for firing cannonballs

can·non·ball *n* **1** : a usually round solid missile (as of stone or metal) for firing from a cannon **2** : a jump into water made with the arms holding the knees tight against the chest

can·not : can not

can·ny *adj* **can·ni·er; can·ni·est** : clever especially in taking advantage of opportunities : SHREWD — **can·ni·ly** *adv*

[1]**ca·noe** *n* : a long light narrow boat with pointed ends and curved sides that is usually moved by a paddle

[2]**canoe** *vb* **ca·noed; ca·noe·ing** : to travel or carry in a canoe — **ca·noe·ist** *n*

can·on *n* **1** : a rule or law of a church **2** : an accepted rule

can·o·py *n, pl* **can·o·pies** **1** : a covering fixed over a bed or throne or carried on poles (as over a person of high rank) **2** : something that hangs over and shades or shelters something else **3** : the uppermost spreading layer of a forest

can't : can not

can·ta·loupe *n* : a melon usually with a hard rough skin and reddish orange flesh

can·tan·ker·ous *adj* : CRABBY, QUARRELSOME

can·ta·ta *n* : a piece of music that features solos, duets, and choruses with instrumental accompaniment and is sometimes based on a poem, play, or story

can·teen *n* **1** : a store (as in a camp or factory) in which food, drinks, and small supplies are sold **2 :** a place of recreation and entertainment for people in military service **3 :** a small container for carrying water or another liquid

¹can·ter *n* **:** a horse's gait resembling but slower than a gallop

²canter *vb* **can·tered; can·ter·ing :** to run with a movement that resembles but is slower than a gallop

can·ti·le·ver *n* **1 :** a beam or similar support fastened (as by being built into a wall) only at one end **2 :** either of two structures that stick out from piers toward each other and when joined form a span in a bridge (**canti-lever bridge**)

can·to *n, pl* **can·tos :** one of the major divisions of a long poem

can·ton *n* **:** a division of a country (as Switzerland)

can·tor *n* **1 :** a synagogue official who sings religious music and leads the congregation in prayer **2 :** a leader of a choir in a church

can·vas *n* **1 :** a strong cloth of hemp, flax, or cotton **2 :** a specially prepared piece of cloth used as a surface for painting

can·vas·back *n* **:** a North American wild duck with reddish brown head and grayish back

can·vass *vb* **can·vassed; can·vass·ing :** to go to (people) to ask for votes, contributions, or orders for goods or to determine public opinion — **can·vass·er** *n*

can·yon *n* **:** a deep valley with steep sides and often a stream flowing through it

cap. *abbr* **1** capital **2** capitalize **3** capitalized

¹cap *n* **1 :** a head covering and especially one having a visor and no brim **2 :** something that serves as a cover or protection for something **3 :** a part that forms the top of something **4 :** an upper limit **5 :** a paper or metal container holding a small explosive charge

²cap *vb* **capped; cap·ping 1 :** to cover or provide with a top or cover **2 :** to bring to a high point or end **3 :** to match or follow with something equal or better **4 :** to put an upper limit on

ca·pa·bil·i·ty *n, pl* **ca·pa·bil·i·ties :** ABILITY 1

ca·pa·ble *adj* **1 :** having the qualities or abilities that are needed to do or accomplish something **2 :** able to do something well — **ca·pa·bly** *adv*

ca·pa·cious *adj* **:** able to hold a great deal

ca·pac·i·ty *n, pl* **ca·pac·i·ties 1 :** ability to contain or deal with something **2 :** mental or physical power **3 :** VOLUME 3 **4 :** ROLE 1, STATUS

¹cape *n* **:** a point of land that juts out into the sea or into a lake

²cape *n* **:** a sleeveless garment worn so as to hang over the shoulders, arms, and back

¹ca·per *vb* **ca·pered; ca·per·ing :** to leap about in a lively way

²caper *n* **1 :** a playful or mischievous trick **2 :** a lively leap or spring **3 :** an illegal or questionable act

¹cap·il·lary *adj* **1 :** having a long slender form and a small inner diameter **2 :** of or relating to capillary action or a capillary

²capillary *n, pl* **cap·il·lar·ies :** one of the slender hairlike tubes that are the smallest blood vessels and connect arteries with veins

capillary action *n* **:** the action by which the surface of a liquid where it is in contact with a solid (as in a capillary tube) is raised or lowered

¹cap·i·tal *adj* **1 :** being like the letters A, B, C, etc. rather than a, b, c, etc. **2 :** being the location of a government **3 :** punishable by or resulting in death **4 :** of or relating to accumulated wealth **5 :** EXCELLENT

²capital *n* **: 1 :** a capital letter **2 :** a capital city **3 :** the money and property that a person owns **4 :** profitable use

³capital *n* **:** the top part of an architectural column

cap·i·tal·ism *n* **:** a system under which the ownership of land and wealth is for the most part in the hands of private individuals

cap·i·tal·ist *n* **1 :** a person who has usually a lot of money which is used to make more money **2 :** a person who supports capitalism

cap·i·tal·ize *vb* **cap·i·tal·ized; cap·i·tal·iz·ing 1 :** to write with a beginning capital letter or in all capital letters **2 :** to provide money needed to start or develop (a business) **3 :** to gain by turning something to advantage — **cap·i·tal·i·za·tion** *n*

cap·i·tol *n* **1 :** the building in which a state legislature meets **2** *cap* **:** the building in Washington, D.C., in which the United States Congress meets

ca·pon *n* **:** a castrated male chicken

ca·price *n* **:** a sudden change in feeling, opinion, or action **:** WHIM

ca·pri·cious *adj* **1 :** moved or controlled by a sudden desire **2 :** likely to change suddenly — **ca·pri·cious·ly** *adv*

cap·size *vb* **cap·sized; cap·siz·ing :** to turn over **:** UPSET

cap·stan *n* **:** a device that consists of a drum to which a rope is fastened and that is used especially on ships for raising the anchor

cap·sule *n* **1 :** a case enclosing the seeds or spores of a plant **2 :** a small case of material that contains medicine to be swallowed **3 :** a closed compartment for travel in space

Capt. *abbr* captain

¹cap·tain *n* **1 :** the commanding officer of

a ship **2 :** a leader of a group **:** one in command **3 :** an officer of high rank in a police or fire department **4 :** a commissioned officer in the navy or coast guard ranking above a commander **5 :** a commissioned officer in the army, air force, or marine corps ranking below a major

[2]**captain** *vb* **cap·tained; cap·tain·ing :** to be captain of

cap·tion *n* **:** a comment or title that goes with a picture

cap·ti·vate *vb* **cap·ti·vat·ed; cap·ti·vat·ing :** to fascinate by some special charm

[1]**cap·tive** *adj* **1 :** taken and held prisoner **2 :** kept within bounds or under control **3 :** as a prisoner **4 :** unable to avoid watching or listening to something

[2]**captive** *n* **:** someone who is held prisoner

cap·tiv·i·ty *n* **:** the state of being held prisoner **:** the state of being captive

cap·tor *n* **:** someone who has captured a person or thing

[1]**cap·ture** *vb* **cap·tured; cap·tur·ing 1 :** to take and hold especially by force **2 :** to get and hold **3 :** to put into a lasting form

[2]**capture** *n* **:** the act of taking and holding especially by force

car *n* **1 :** a vehicle that moves on wheels **2 :** a separate section of a train **3 :** the part of an elevator that holds passengers

ca·rafe *n* **:** a bottle that has a wide mouth and is used to hold water or beverages

car·a·mel *n* **1 :** a firm chewy candy **2 :** burnt sugar used for coloring and flavoring

car·at *n* **:** a unit of weight for gemstones (as diamonds) equal to 200 milligrams

car·a·van *n* **1 :** a group (of people or animals) traveling together on a long journey **2 :** a group of vehicles traveling together one behind the other

car·a·vel *n* **:** a small sailing ship of the 15th and 16th centuries with a broad bow and high stern and three or four masts

car·a·way *n* **:** the dried seeds of a white-flowered plant that are used especially in seasoning foods

car·bine *n* **:** a short light rifle

car·bo·hy·drate *n* **:** a substance (as a starch or sugar) that is rich in energy and is made up of carbon, hydrogen, and oxygen

car·bon *n* **:** a chemical element occurring as diamond and graphite, in coal and petroleum, and in plant and animal bodies

car·bon·ate *vb* **car·bon·at·ed; car·bon·at·ing :** to fill with carbon dioxide which escapes in the form of bubbles

carbon di·ox·ide *n* **:** a heavy colorless gas that is formed by burning fuels, by the breakdown or burning of animal and plant matter, and by the act of breathing and that is absorbed from the air by plants in photosynthesis

carbon footprint *n* **:** the amount of carbon dioxide produced by something (as a person's activities or a product's manufacture and transport) during a given period

carbon mon·ox·ide *n* **:** a colorless odorless very poisonous gas formed by incomplete burning of carbon

car·bu·re·tor *n* **:** the part of an engine in which liquid fuel (as gasoline) is mixed with air to make it burn easily

car·cass *n* **:** the body of an animal prepared for use as meat

card *n* **1 :** a decorated piece of thick paper that contains a greeting or is used to write a message **2 :** a thick stiff piece of paper or plastic that contains information about a person or business **3 :** PLAYING CARD **4 cards** *pl* **:** a game played with playing cards **5 :** a thick stiff piece of paper that has a picture on one side and is traded or collected **6 :** CREDIT CARD

card·board *n* **:** a stiff material made of wood pulp that has been pressed and dried

car·di·ac *adj* **:** of, relating to, or affecting the heart

[1]**car·di·nal** *n* **1 :** a high official of the Roman Catholic Church ranking next below the pope **2 :** a bright red songbird with a crest and a whistling call

[2]**cardinal** *adj* **:** of first importance **:** MAIN, PRINCIPAL

cardinal number *n* **:** a number (as 1, 5, 22) that is used in simple counting and answers the question "how many?"

cardinal point *n* **:** one of the four chief points of the compass which are north, south, east, west

car·dio·pul·mo·nary re·sus·ci·ta·tion *n* **:** a method used in an emergency to save the life of a person whose heart has stopped beating that involves breathing into the victim's mouth to force air into the lungs and pressing on the victim's chest to cause blood to flow through the body

[1]**care** *n* **1 :** serious attention **2 :** PROTECTION 1, SUPERVISION **3 :** proper maintenance of property or equipment **4 :** a feeling of concern or worry

[2]**care** *vb* **cared; car·ing 1 :** to feel interest or concern **2 :** to provide help, protection, or supervision to **:** look after **3 :** to have a liking or desire

ca·reen *vb* **ca·reened; ca·reen·ing :** to go at high speed without control

ca·reer *n* **1 :** a period of time spent in a job or profession **2 :** a job followed as a life's work

care·free *adj* **:** free from care or worry

care·ful *adj* **1 :** using care **2 :** made, done, or said with care — **care·ful·ly** *adv*

care·less *adj* **1 :** not taking proper care **2 :** done, made, or said without being careful **3 :** CAREFREE — **care·less·ly** *adv* — **care·less·ness** *n*

¹ca·ress *n* **:** a tender or loving touch or hug

²caress *vb* **ca·ressed; ca·ress·ing :** to touch in a tender or loving way

care·tak·er *n* **:** a person who takes care of property for someone else

car·go *n, pl* **cargoes** *or* **cargos :** the goods carried by a ship, airplane, or vehicle

car·i·bou *n* **:** a large deer of northern and arctic regions that has antlers in both the male and female — used especially for one in the New World

car·ies *n, pl* **caries :** a decayed condition of a tooth or teeth

car·il·lon *n* **:** a set of bells sounded by hammers controlled by a keyboard

car·nage *n* **:** ¹SLAUGHTER 3

car·na·tion *n* **:** a fragrant usually white, pink, or red garden or greenhouse flower

car·ne·lian *n* **:** a hard reddish quartz used as a gem

car·ni·val *n* **1 :** a form of entertainment that travels from town to town and includes rides and games **2 :** an organized program of entertainment or exhibition **:** FESTIVAL

car·ni·vore *n* **:** an animal that feeds on meat

car·niv·o·rous *adj* **:** feeding on animal flesh or tissue

¹car·ol *n* **:** a usually religious song of joy

²carol *vb* **car·oled** *or* **car·olled; car·ol·ing** *or* **car·ol·ling 1 :** to sing in a joyful manner **2 :** to sing carols and especially Christmas carols — **car·ol·er** *or* **car·ol·ler** *n*

¹car·om *n* **:** the act of bouncing back at an angle

²carom *vb* **car·omed; car·om·ing :** to hit and bounce back at an angle

car·ou·sel : MERRY-GO-ROUND

¹carp *vb* **carped; carp·ing :** to complain in an annoying way

²carp *n* **:** a freshwater fish that lives a long time and is often used for food

car·pel *n* **:** the female reproductive structure of a flower that encloses the ovules

car·pen·ter *n* **:** a worker who builds or repairs wooden things

car·pen·try *n* **:** the skill or work of building or repairing wooden things

¹car·pet *n* **1 :** a heavy woven fabric used especially as a floor covering **2 :** a covering like a carpet

²carpet *vb* **car·pet·ed; car·pet·ing :** to cover with or as if with a carpet

car pool *n* **:** an arrangement by a group of automobile owners in which each takes turns driving his or her own car and giving the others a ride

car·riage *n* **1 :** a vehicle with wheels used for carrying people **2 :** a support with wheels used for carrying a load **3 :** a movable part of a machine that carries or supports some other moving part **4 :** the manner of holding the body **:** POSTURE

car·ri·er *n* **1 :** a person or thing that carries **2 :** a person or business that transports passengers or goods or provides a certain service **3 :** a person, animal, or plant that carries disease germs without showing symptoms and passes them on to others

car·ri·on *n* **:** dead and decaying flesh

car·rot *n* **:** a long orange root of a garden plant that is eaten as a vegetable

car·ry *vb* **car·ried; car·ry·ing 1 :** to take or transfer from one place to another **2 :** to contain and direct the course of **3 :** to wear or have on or within the body **4 :** to have as an element, quality, or part **5 :** to have for sale **6 :** to go over or travel a distance **7 :** ¹SUPPORT 4, BEAR **8 :** WIN 4 **9 :** to hold or bear the body or some part of it **10 :** to sing in correct pitch **11 :** to present to the public — **carry away :** to cause strong feeling in — **carry on 1 :** to behave in an improper or excited manner **2 :** MANAGE 1 **3 :** to continue in spite of difficulties — **carry out :** to put into action or effect

car seat *n* **:** a seat for a small child that attaches to an automobile seat and holds the child safely

¹cart *n* **1 :** a heavy vehicle with two wheels usually drawn by horses and used for hauling **2 :** a light vehicle pushed or pulled by hand

²cart *vb* **cart·ed; cart·ing 1 :** to carry in a cart **2 :** CARRY 1 — **cart·er** *n*

car·ti·lage *n* **:** tough flexible tissue that makes up most of the skeleton of vertebrates during early development and except for in a few places in the body (as the nose or outer ear) is replaced by bone

car·ti·lag·i·nous *adj* **:** relating to or made of cartilage

car·ton *n* **:** a cardboard container

car·toon *n* **1 :** a movie or television program made by photographing a series of drawings **2 :** a drawing (as in a newspaper) making people or objects look funny or foolish **3 :** COMIC STRIP

car·toon·ist *n* **:** a person who draws cartoons

car·tridge *n* **1 :** a case or shell containing gunpowder and shot or a bullet for use in a firearm **2 :** a container that is inserted into a machine to make it work

cart·wheel *n* **:** a handspring made to the side with arms and legs sticking out

carve *vb* **carved; carv·ing 1 :** to cut with

care **2 :** to make or get by cutting **3 :** to slice and serve (meat) — **carv·er** *n*

carv·ing *n* **1 :** the art or act of a person who carves **2 :** an object or design that has been carved

¹cas·cade *n* **:** a steep usually small waterfall

²cascade *vb* **cas·cad·ed; cas·cad·ing :** to flow or fall rapidly and in large quantity

¹case *n* **1 :** a particular instance, situation, or example **2 :** a situation or an object that calls for investigation or action (as by the police) **3 :** a question to be settled in a court of law **4 :** a form of a noun, pronoun, or adjective showing its grammatical relation to other words **5 :** the actual situation **6 :** a convincing argument **7 :** an instance of disease, injury, or discomfort — **in any case :** no matter what has happened or been said — **in case :** for the purpose of being ready for something that might happen

²case *n* **1 :** a container (as a box) for holding something **2 :** a box and its contents **3 :** an outer covering

ca·sein *n* **:** a whitish to yellowish protein that is found in milk and cheese and is used in making paints, plastics, and adhesives

case·ment *n* **1 :** a window sash opening on hinges **2 :** a window with a casement

¹cash *n* **1 :** money in the form of coins or bills **2 :** money or its equivalent (as a check) paid for goods at the time of purchase or delivery

²cash *vb* **cashed; cash·ing :** to give or get cash for

cash·ew *n* **:** a curved edible nut that comes from a tropical American tree

cash·ier *n* **:** a person who is responsible for giving out or taking in money (as in a bank or store)

cash·mere *n* **:** a soft yarn or fabric once made from the fine wool of an Indian goat but now often from sheep's wool

cash register *n* **:** a machine used in a business to calculate the amount of cash due for a sale and having a drawer to hold money

cas·ing *n* **:** something that covers or encloses

cask *n* **1 :** a container that is shaped like a barrel and is usually used for liquids **2 :** the amount contained in a cask

cas·ket *n* **1 :** COFFIN **2 :** a small box for storage or safekeeping (as for jewels)

cas·se·role *n* **1 :** a mix of food baked and served in a deep dish **2 :** a deep dish in which food can be baked and served

cas·sette *n* **1 :** a container that holds audiotape or videotape and in which the tape passes from one reel to another when being played **2 :** a container holding photographic film or plates that can be easily loaded into a camera

¹cast *vb* **cast; cast·ing 1 :** ¹THROW 1 **2 :** to direct to or toward something or someone **3 :** to send out or forward **4 :** to put under the influence of **5 :** to throw out, off, or away **:** SHED **6 :** to make (a vote) formally **7 :** to assign a part or role to **8 :** to give shape to liquid material by pouring it into a mold and letting it harden

²cast *n* **1 :** an act of throwing **2 :** the characters or the people acting in a play or story **3 :** a stiff dressing (as of plaster) hardened around a part of the body to allow a broken bone to heal **4 :** a hint of color **5 :** the container used to give a shape to the thing made in it **6 :** something formed by casting in a mold or form **7 :** the distance to which a thing can be thrown **8 :** ²SHAPE 1 **9 :** something (as the skin of an insect or the waste of an earthworm) that is shed or thrown out or off

cas·ta·net *n* **:** a rhythm instrument that consists of two small flat round parts fastened to the thumb and clicked by the fingers — usually used in pl.

¹cast·away *adj* **1 :** thrown away **2 :** cast adrift or ashore

²castaway *n* **:** a person who is stranded in a place where there are no other people (as because of a shipwreck)

caste *n* **1 :** one of the classes into which the Hindu people of India were formerly divided **2 :** a division or class of society based on wealth, rank, or occupation **3 :** social rank **:** PRESTIGE

cast·er *n* **:** one of a set of small wheels on a piece of furniture that makes it easier to move

cas·ti·gate *vb* **cas·ti·gat·ed; cas·ti·gat·ing :** to punish or criticize harshly

cast·ing *n* **1 :** the act or action of one that casts **2 :** something that is cast in a mold **3 :** ²CAST 9

cast iron *n* **:** a hard and brittle alloy of iron, carbon, and silicon shaped by being poured into a mold while melted

cas·tle *n* **1 :** a large building or group of buildings usually having high walls with towers that was built in the past to protect against attack **2 :** a large or impressive house

cast·off *n* **:** a person or thing that has been thrown aside or rejected

cast–off *adj* **:** thrown away or aside

cas·tor oil *n* **:** a thick yellowish liquid that comes from the seeds (**castor beans**) of a tropical herb and is used as a lubricant and as a strong laxative

cas·trate *vb* **cas·trat·ed; cas·trat·ing :** to remove the sex glands of

ca·su·al *adj* **1 :** happening unexpectedly or by chance **:** not planned or foreseen **2 :** occurring without regularity **:** OCCASIONAL **3**

: showing or feeling little concern : NONCHALANT **4** : meant for informal use — **ca·su·al·ly** *adv*

ca·su·al·ty *n, pl* **ca·su·al·ties** **1** : a person who is hurt or killed in a war, disaster, or accident **2** : a person or thing injured, lost, or destroyed

cat *n* **1** : a common furry meat-eating animal kept as a pet or for catching mice and rats **2** : any of a family of mammals (as the lion, tiger, and leopard) to which the domestic cat belongs

[1]**cat·a·log** *or* **cat·a·logue** *n* **1** : a book containing brief descriptions of things that can be purchased or signed up for **2** : a list of names, titles, or articles arranged by some system

[2]**catalog** *or* **catalogue** *vb* **cat·a·loged** *or* **cat·a·logued; cat·a·log·ing** *or* **cat·a·logu·ing** **1** : to make a catalog of **2** : to enter in a catalog — **cat·a·log·er** *or* **cat·a·logu·er** *n*

ca·tal·pa *n* : a tree of North America and Asia with broad leaves, showy flowers, and long pods

[1]**cat·a·pult** *n* **1** : an ancient military machine for hurling stones and arrows **2** : a device for launching an airplane from the deck of a ship

[2]**catapult** *vb* **cat·a·pult·ed; cat·a·pult·ing** **1** : to throw by or as if by a catapult **2** : to quickly advance

cat·a·ract *n* **1** : a clouding of the lens of the eye or of the cover around the lens that blocks the passage of light **2** : a large waterfall **3** : a sudden rush or flow like a waterfall

ca·tas·tro·phe *n* **1** : a sudden disaster **2** : complete failure : FIASCO

cat·bird *n* : a dark gray songbird that has a call like a cat's meow

cat·boat *n* : a sailboat with a single mast set far forward and a single large sail with a long boom

cat·call *n* : a sound like the cry of a cat or a noise expressing disapproval (as at a sports event)

[1]**catch** *vb* **caught; catch·ing** **1** : to capture and hold **2** : to discover unexpectedly **3** : to stop suddenly before doing something **4** : to take hold of **5** : to become affected by **6** : to take or get briefly or quickly **7** : to be in time for **8** : to grasp by the senses or the mind **9** : to play catcher on a baseball team **10** : to get tangled **11** : to hold firmly : FASTEN **12** to recover by resting — **catch on** **1** : to realize something **2** : to become popular — **catch up** : to move or progress fast enough to join another

[2]**catch** *n* **1** : something caught : the amount caught at one time **2** : the act of catching **3** : a pastime in which a ball is thrown and caught **4** : something that checks, fastens, or holds immovable **5** : a hidden difficulty

catch·er *n* **1** : someone or something that catches **2** : a baseball player who plays behind home plate

catch·ing *adj* **1** : INFECTIOUS 1, CONTAGIOUS **2** : likely to spread as if infectious

catchy *adj* **catch·i·er; catch·i·est** : likely to attract and be remembered

cat·e·chism *n* **1** : a series of questions and answers used in giving religious instruction **2** : a set of formal questions

cat·e·go·ry *n, pl* **cat·e·go·ries** : a basic division or grouping of things

ca·ter *vb* **ca·tered; ca·ter·ing** **1** : to provide a supply of food **2** : to supply what is needed or wanted — **ca·ter·er** *n*

cat·er·pil·lar *n* : a wormlike often hairy larva of an insect and usually a butterfly or moth

cat·fish *n* : a fish with a large head and feelers about the mouth

cat·gut *n* : a tough cord made from intestines of animals (as sheep) and used for strings of musical instruments and rackets and for sewing in surgery

ca·the·dral *n* : the principal church of a district headed by a bishop

cath·o·lic *adj* **1** : including many different things or types **2** *cap* : of or relating to the Roman Catholic church

Catholic *n* : a member of the Roman Catholic church

cat·kin *n* : a flower cluster (as of the willow and birch) in which the flowers grow in close circular rows along a slender stalk

cat·nap *n* : a very short light nap

cat·nip *n* : a plant that is a mint with a smell especially attractive to cats

catsup *variant of* KETCHUP

cat·tail *n* : a tall plant with long flat leaves and tall furry stalks that grows in marshy areas

cat·tle *n, pl* **cattle** : domestic animals with four feet and especially cows, bulls, and calves

cat·walk *n* : a narrow walk or way (as along a bridge)

caught *past and past participle of* CATCH

caul·dron *also* **cal·dron** *n* : a large kettle

cau·li·flow·er *n* : a vegetable that is a white head of undeveloped flowers and is related to the cabbage

[1]**caulk** *vb* **caulked; caulk·ing** : to fill up a crack, seam, or joint so as to make it watertight

[2]**caulk** *also* **caulk·ing** *n* : material used to fill up a crack, seam, or joint so as to make it watertight

[1]**cause** *n* **1** : a person or thing that brings about a result **2** : a good or good enough reason for something **3** : something supported or deserving support

[2]cause *vb* **caused; caus·ing :** to make happen or exist

[3]cause *conj* **:** BECAUSE

cause·way *n* **:** a raised road or way across wet ground or water

caus·tic *adj* **1 :** capable of eating away by chemical action **:** CORROSIVE **2 :** very harsh and critical

[1]cau·tion *n* **1 :** care taken to avoid trouble or danger **:** PRECAUTION **2 :** WARNING

[2]caution *vb* **cau·tioned; cau·tion·ing :** to warn about danger

cau·tious *adj* **:** showing or using care to avoid trouble or danger — **cau·tious·ly** *adv*

cav·al·cade *n* **1 :** a procession especially of riders or carriages **2 :** a dramatic series (as of related events)

[1]cav·a·lier *n* **1 :** a mounted soldier **2 :** a brave and courteous gentleman

[2]cavalier *adj* **1 :** easy and lighthearted in manner **2 :** having or showing no concern for a serious or important matter

cav·al·ry *n, pl* **cav·al·ries :** a unit of troops mounted on horseback or moving in motor vehicles

[1]cave *n* **:** a hollow underground place with an opening on the surface

[2]cave *vb* **caved; cav·ing :** to fall or cause to fall in or down **:** COLLAPSE

cave·man *n, pl* **cave·men :** a person living in a cave especially during the Stone Age

cav·ern *n* **:** a cave often of large or unknown size

cav·ern·ous *adj* **1 :** having caverns or hollow places **2 :** like a cavern in being large and hollow

cav·i·ty *n, pl* **cav·i·ties 1 :** a small hole formed in a tooth by decay **2 :** a hollow place

ca·vort *vb* **ca·vort·ed; ca·vort·ing :** to move or hop about in a lively way

[1]caw *n* **:** the cry of a crow or a raven

[2]caw *vb* **cawed; caw·ing :** to make the sound of a crow or raven

cay *n* **:** [4]KEY

cay·enne pepper *n* **:** dried ripe hot peppers ground and used to add flavor to food

CD *n* **:** a small plastic disk on which information (as music or computer data) is recorded

CD–ROM *n* **:** a CD that contains computer data that cannot be changed

cease *vb* **ceased; ceas·ing :** to come or bring to an end **:** STOP

cease·less *adj* **:** occurring without stop or over and over again

ce·cro·pia moth *n* **:** a colorful moth that is the largest moth of North America

ce·dar *n* **:** a tree having cones and a strong wood with a pleasant smell

cede *vb* **ced·ed; ced·ing :** to give up especially by treaty

ceil·ing *n* **1 :** the overhead inside surface of a room **2 :** the greatest height at which an airplane can fly properly **3 :** the height above the ground of the bottom of the lowest layer of clouds **4 :** an upper limit

cel·e·brate *vb* **cel·e·brat·ed; cel·e·brat·ing 1 :** to observe (a holiday or important occasion) in some special way **2 :** to perform (a religious ceremony) **3 :** [1]PRAISE 1

cel·e·brat·ed *adj* **:** widely known and praised

cel·e·bra·tion *n* **1 :** the act of doing something to observe a special occasion **2 :** the activities or ceremonies for observing a special occasion

ce·leb·ri·ty *n, pl* **ce·leb·ri·ties 1 :** FAME **2 :** a famous person

cel·ery *n* **:** a vegetable that has crisp light green leafstalks that are eaten raw or cooked

ce·les·tial *adj* **1 :** of, relating to, or suggesting heaven **2 :** of or relating to the sky or outer space

cell *n* **1 :** a very small room (as in a prison or a monastery) **2 :** the basic structural unit of living things that is made up of cytoplasm enclosed by a membrane and that typically includes a nucleus and other smaller parts (as mitochondria or chloroplasts) which perform specific functions necessary for life **3 :** a small enclosed part or division (as in a honeycomb) **4 :** a container with substances which can produce an electric current by chemical action **5 :** a device that converts light (as sunlight) that falls on it into electrical energy that is used as a power source **6 :** CELL PHONE — **celled** *adj*

cel·lar *n* **:** a room or set of rooms below the surface of the ground **:** BASEMENT

cell membrane *n* **:** the thin outside layer that surrounds the cytoplasm of a cell and controls the movement of materials into and out of the cell

cel·lo *n, pl* **cel·los :** a large stringed instrument of the violin family that plays the bass part

cel·lo·phane *n* **:** a thin clear material made from cellulose and used as a wrapping

cell phone *n* **:** a portable telephone that connects to other telephones by radio through a system of transmitters each of which covers a limited geographical area

cel·lu·lar *adj* **1 :** of, relating to, or made up of cells **2 :** of, relating to, or being a cell phone

cel·lu·lose *n* **:** a substance that is the chief part of the cell walls of plants and is used in making various products (as paper and rayon)

cell wall *n* **:** the firm outer nonliving layer that surrounds the cell membrane and encloses and supports the cells of most plants, bacteria, and fungi

Cel·si·us *adj* : relating to or having a thermometer scale on which the interval between the freezing point and the boiling point of water is divided into 100 degrees with 0 representing the freezing point and 100 the boiling point

[1]ce·ment *n* **1 :** a powder that is made mainly from compounds of aluminum, calcium, silicon, and iron heated together and then ground and mixed with water to make mortar and concrete **2 :** [2]CONCRETE, MORTAR **3 :** a substance used to make things stick together firmly

[2]cement *vb* **ce·ment·ed; ce·ment·ing 1 :** to join together with or as if with cement **2 :** to make stronger

ce·men·tum *n* : a thin bony layer covering the part of a tooth inside the gum

cem·e·tery *n, pl* **cem·e·ter·ies :** a place where dead people are buried : GRAVEYARD

Ce·no·zo·ic *n* : an era of geological history lasting from 70 million years ago to the present time in which there has been a rapid evolution of mammals and birds and of flowering plants

[1]cen·sor *n* : an official who checks writings or movies to take out things considered offensive or immoral

[2]censor *vb* **cen·sored; cen·sor·ing :** to examine (as a book) to take out things considered offensive or immoral

cen·sor·ship *n* : the system or practice of examining writings or movies and taking out things considered offensive or immoral

[1]cen·sure *n* **1 :** the act of finding fault with or blaming **2 :** an official criticism

[2]censure *vb* **cen·sured; cen·sur·ing :** to find fault with especially publicly

cen·sus *n* : a count of the number of people in a country, city, or town

cent *n* **1 :** a hundredth part of the unit of the money system in a number of different countries **2 :** a coin, token, or note representing one cent

cent. *abbr* **1** centigrade **2** century

cen·taur *n* : a creature in Greek mythology that is part man and part horse

cen·ten·ni·al *n* : a 100th anniversary or a celebration of it — **centennial** *adj*

[1]cen·ter *or Can and Brit* **centre** *n* **1 :** the middle part of something **2 :** a person or thing characterized by a particular concentration or activity **3 :** a place used for a particular purpose **4 :** the middle point of a circle or a sphere equally distant from every point on the circumference or surface **5 :** a player occupying a middle position on a basketball, football, hockey, lacrosse, or soccer team

[2]center *or Can and Brit* **centre** *vb* **cen·tered/centred; cen·ter·ing/centring 1 :** to place or fix at or around a center or central area **2 :** to collect or concentrate at or around one point, group, or person

center of gravity *or Can and Brit* **centre of gravity** *n, pl* **centers of gravity/centres of gravity :** the point at which the entire weight of a body may be thought of as centered so that if supported at this point the body would balance perfectly

cen·ter·piece *or Can and Brit* **centrepiece** *n* : a piece put in the center of something and especially a decoration (as flowers) for a table

centi- *prefix* : hundredth part — used in terms of the metric system

cen·ti·grade *adj* : CELSIUS

cen·ti·gram *n* : a unit of weight equal to $^1/_{100}$ gram

cen·ti·li·ter *or Can and Brit* **centilitre** *n* : a unit of liquid capacity equal to $^1/_{100}$ liter

cen·ti·me·ter *or Can and Brit* **centimetre** *n* : a unit of length equal to $^1/_{100}$ meter

cen·ti·pede *n* : an animal that is an arthropod with a long somewhat flattened body with one pair of legs on most of its many body sections

cen·tral *adj* : **1 :** located or placed at, in, or near the center **2 :** most important : CHIEF — **cen·tral·ly** *adv*

[1]Central American *adj* : of or relating to Central America or the Central Americans

[2]Central American *n* : a person born or living in Central America

central angle *n* : an angle with its vertex at the center of a circle and with sides that are radii of the circle

cen·tral·ize *vb* **cen·tral·ized; cen·tral·iz·ing :** to bring to a central point or under a single control

central processing unit *n* : PROCESSOR 3

cen·tre *Can and Brit spelling of* CENTER

cen·trif·u·gal force *n* : the force that tends to cause a thing or parts of a thing to go outward from a center of rotation

cen·tu·ry *n, pl* **cen·tu·ries :** a period of 100 years

ce·ram·ic *n* **1 ceramics** *pl* : the art of making things (as pottery or tiles) of baked clay **2 :** a product made by baking clay

cereal *n* **1 :** a plant (as a grass) that produces grain for food **2 :** a food prepared from grain

cer·e·bel·lum *n, pl* **cer·e·bel·lums** *or* **cer·e·bel·la :** the lower back part of the brain whose chief functions are controlling the coordination of muscles and keeping the body in proper balance

ce·re·bral *adj* **1 :** of or relating to the brain or mind **2 :** of, relating to, or affecting the cerebrum

ce·re·brum *n, pl* **ce·re·brums** *or* **ce·re·bra** : the enlarged front and upper part of the brain that is the center of thinking

¹cer·e·mo·ni·al *adj* : of, used in, or being a ceremony — **cer·e·mo·ni·al·ly** *adv*

²ceremonial *n* : a special ceremony

cer·e·mo·ni·ous *adj* **1** : ¹CEREMONIAL **2** : ¹FORMAL 1 — **cer·e·mo·ni·ous·ly** *adv*

cer·e·mo·ny *n, pl* **cer·e·mo·nies** **1** : an act or series of acts performed in some regular way according to fixed rules especially as part of a social or religious event **2** : very polite behavior : FORMALITY

¹cer·tain *adj* **1** : without any doubt : SURE **2** : known to be true **3** : known but not named **4** : being fixed or settled **5** : bound by the way things are **6** : sure to have an effect

²certain *pron* : known ones that are not named

cer·tain·ly *adv* **1** : without fail **2** : without doubt

cer·tain·ty *n, pl* **cer·tain·ties** **1** : something that is sure **2** : the quality or state of being sure

cer·tif·i·cate *n* **1** : a written or printed statement that is proof of some fact **2** : a paper showing that a person has met certain requirements **3** : a paper showing ownership

cer·ti·fi·ca·tion mark *n* : a mark used to identify a product or service that has been certified to conform to a certain set of standards

cer·ti·fy *vb* **cer·ti·fied; cer·ti·fy·ing** **1** : to show to be true or as claimed by a formal or official statement **2** : to guarantee the quality, fitness, or value of officially **3** : to show to have met certain requirements

ces·sa·tion *n* : a coming to a stop

ch. *abbr* **1** chapter **2** church

chafe *vb* **chafed; chaf·ing** **1** : to become irritated or impatient **2** : to rub so as to wear away or make sore

¹chaff *n* **1** : the husks of grains and grasses separated from the seed in threshing **2** : something worthless

²chaff *vb* **chaffed; chaff·ing** : to tease in a friendly way

cha·grin *n* : a feeling of being annoyed by failure or disappointment

¹chain *n* **1** : a series of connected links or rings usually of metal **2** : a series of things joined together as if by links **3** : a group of businesses that have the same name and sell the same products or services

²chain *vb* **chained; chain·ing** : to fasten, bind, or connect with or as if with a chain

chain reaction *n* : a series of events in which each event causes the next one

chain saw *n* : a portable saw that cuts using teeth that are linked together to form a continuous chain

chair *n* **1** : a seat for one person usually having a back and four legs **2** : a person who leads a meeting, group, or event

chair·man *n, pl* **chair·men** **1** : CHAIR 2 **2** : a person who is in charge of a company — **chair·man·ship** *n*

chair·per·son *n* : CHAIR 2

chair·wom·an *n, pl* **chair·wom·en** **1** : a woman who leads a meeting, group, or event : CHAIR **2** : a woman who is in charge of a company

cha·let *n* **1** : a Swiss dwelling with a steep roof that sticks far out past the walls **2** : a cottage or house built to look like a Swiss chalet

chal·ice *n* : GOBLET

¹chalk *n* **1** : a soft white, gray, or buff limestone made up mainly of the shells of tiny saltwater animals **2** : a material like chalk especially when used for writing or drawing

²chalk *vb* **chalked; chalk·ing** : to rub, mark, write, or draw with chalk — **chalk up** **1** : to attribute to a supposed cause or source **2** : to earn or achieve

chalk·board *n* : BLACKBOARD

chalky *adj* **chalk·i·er; chalk·i·est** **1** : made of or like chalk **2** : very pale

¹chal·lenge *vb* **chal·lenged; chal·leng·ing** **1** : to object to as bad or incorrect : DISPUTE **2** : to confront or defy boldly **3** : to invite or dare to take part in a contest **4** : to be difficult enough to be interesting to : test the skill or ability of **5** : to halt and demand identification from — **chal·leng·er** *n*

²challenge *n* **1** : an objection to something as not being true, genuine, correct, or proper or to a person (as a juror) as not being correct, qualified, or approved **2** : a call or dare for someone to compete in a contest or sport **3** : a difficult task or problem **4** : an order to stop and provide identification

challenged *adj* : having a disability or deficiency

cham·ber *n* **1** : an enclosed space, cavity, or compartment **2** : a room in a house and especially a bedroom **3** : a room used for a special purpose **4** : a meeting hall of a government body **5** : a room where a judge conducts business outside of the courtroom **6** : a group of people organized into a lawmaking body **7** : a board or council of volunteers (as businessmen) — **cham·bered** *adj*

cham·ber·lain *n* **1** : a chief officer in the household of a ruler or noble **2** : TREASURER

cham·ber·maid *n* : a maid who takes care of bedrooms (as in a hotel)

chamber music *n* : instrumental music to be performed in a room or small hall

cha·me·leon *n* : a lizard that has the ability to change the color of its skin

cham·ois *n, pl* **cham·ois** **1** : a goatlike animal of the mountains of Europe and Asia **2 :** a soft yellowish leather made from the skin of the chamois or from sheepskin

[1]**champ** *vb* **champed; champ·ing :** to bite and chew noisily — **champing at the bit :** waiting in an impatient way

[2]**champ** *n* **1 :** [1]CHAMPION 2 **2 :** [1]CHAMPION 3

[1]**cham·pi·on** *n* **1 :** a person who fights or speaks for another person or in favor of a cause **2 :** a person accepted as better than all others in a sport or in a game of skill **3 :** the winner of first place in a competition

[2]**champion** *vb* **cham·pi·oned; cham·pi·on·ing :** to fight or speak publicly in support of

cham·pi·on·ship *n* **:** the position or title of best or winning player or team in a sport or game of skill **2 :** a contest held to determine the best or winning player or team in a sport or game

[1]**chance** *n* **1 :** the unplanned or uncontrolled happening of events **2 :** OPPORTUNITY 1 **3 :** [1]RISK 1, GAMBLE **4 :** the possibility that something will happen **5 :** a ticket in a raffle

[2]**chance** *vb* **chanced; chanc·ing 1 :** to take place without planning **:** to happen by luck **2 :** to find or meet unexpectedly **3 :** to accept the danger of **:** RISK

[3]**chance** *adj* **:** happening without being planned

chan·cel·lor *n* **1 :** a high government official (as in Germany) **2 :** the head of a university

chan·de·lier *n* **:** a lighting fixture with several branches that usually hangs from the ceiling

[1]**change** *vb* **changed; chang·ing 1 :** to make or become different **2 :** to give a different position, course, or direction to **3 :** to put one thing in the place of another **:** SWITCH **4 :** to give or receive an equal amount of money in usually smaller units of value or in the money of another country **5 :** to put fresh clothes or covering on **6 :** to put on different clothes — **change hands :** to pass from one person's possession or ownership to another's

[2]**change** *n* **1 :** the act, process, or result of making or becoming different **2 :** something that is different from what is usual or expected **3 :** a fresh set of clothes **4 :** money in small units of value received in exchange for an equal amount in larger units **5 :** money returned when a payment is more than the amount due **6 :** money in coins

change·able *adj* **:** able or likely to become different

[1]**chan·nel** *n* **1 :** the bed of a stream **2 :** the deeper part of a waterway (as a river or harbor) **3 :** a strait or a narrow sea **4 :** a passage (as a tube) through which something flows **5 :** a long groove **6 :** a means by which something is passed or carried from one place or person to another **7 :** a band of frequencies used by a single radio or television station in broadcasting

[2]**channel** *vb* **chan·neled** *or* **chan·nelled; chan·nel·ing** *or* **chan·nel·ling :** to direct into or through a passage or channel

[1]**chant** *vb* **chant·ed; chant·ing 1 :** to sing using a small number of musical tones **2 :** to recite or speak in a rhythmic usually loud way

[2]**chant** *n* **1 :** a melody in which several words or syllables are sung on one tone **2 :** something spoken in a rhythmic usually loud way

Chanukah *variant of* HANUKKAH

cha·os *n* **:** complete confusion and disorder

cha·ot·ic *adj* **:** in a state of or characterized by complete confusion and disorder

[1]**chap** *vb* **chapped; chap·ping :** to open in slits **:** CRACK

[2]**chap** *n* **:** [1]FELLOW 1

chap·el *n* **1 :** a building or a room or place for prayer or special religious services **2 :** a religious service or assembly held in a school or college

[1]**chap·er·one** *or* **chap·er·on** *n* **:** a person who goes with and is responsible for a group of young people

[2]**chaperone** *or* **chaperon** *vb* **chap·er·oned; chap·er·on·ing :** to go with and supervise a group of young people **:** act as a chaperone

chap·lain *n* **:** a member of the clergy who performs religious services for a special group (as the army)

chaps *n pl* **:** leather coverings for the legs worn over pants

chap·ter *n* **1 :** a main division of a book or story **2 :** a local branch of a club or organization

char *vb* **charred; char·ring :** to burn slightly

char·ac·ter *n* **1 :** a mark, sign, or symbol (as a letter or figure) used in writing or printing **2 :** the group of qualities that make a person, group, or thing different from others **3 :** a distinguishing feature **:** CHARACTERISTIC **4 :** a person who says or does funny or unusual things **5 :** a person in a story or play **6 :** the usually good opinions that most people have about a particular person **:** REPUTATION **7 :** moral excellence

[1]**char·ac·ter·is·tic** *n* **:** a special quality or appearance that makes an individual or a group different from others

[2]**characteristic** *adj* **:** serving to distinguish an individual or a group **:** typical of a person, thing, or group — **char·ac·ter·is·ti·cal·ly** *adv*

char·ac·ter·ize *vb* **char·ac·ter·ized; char·ac·ter·iz·ing** **1 :** to describe the special qualities of **2 :** to be a typical or distinguishing quality of

char·coal *n* **:** a black or dark absorbent fuel made by heating wood in the absence of air

[1]**charge** *n* **1 :** the responsibility of managing, controlling, or caring for **2 :** a task or duty given to a person **:** OBLIGATION **3 :** a person or thing given to someone to look after **4 :** the price asked especially for a service **5 :** an amount listed as a debt on an account **6 :** ACCUSATION **7 :** an instruction or command based on authority **8 :** the amount of an explosive material (as dynamite) used in a single blast **9 :** an amount of electricity **10 :** a rushing attack **11 :** the signal for attack

[2]**charge** *vb* **charged; charg·ing** **1 :** to give an electric charge to **2 :** to refill (as an exhausted battery) with available energy **3 :** to give a task, duty, or responsibility to **4 :** to instruct or command with authority **5 :** to accuse especially formally **6 :** to rush toward or against **7 :** to ask for payment from **8 :** to ask or set as a price or fee **9 :** to enter as a debt or responsibility on a record

charg·er *n* **1 :** a device that restores energy to an exhausted battery **2 :** a cavalry horse

char·i·ot *n* **:** a vehicle of ancient times that had two wheels, was pulled by horses, and was used in battle and in races and parades

char·i·ta·ble *adj* **1 :** freely giving money or help to needy persons **:** GENEROUS **2 :** given for the needy **:** of service to the needy **3 :** kindly especially in judging other people

char·i·ty *n, pl* **char·i·ties** **1 :** love for others **2 :** kindliness especially in judging others **3 :** the giving of aid to the needy **4 :** aid (as food or money) given to those in need **5 :** an organization or fund for helping the needy

char·la·tan *n* **:** a person who falsely pretends to know or be something

char·ley horse *n* **:** a painful cramp in a muscle (as of the leg)

[1]**charm** *n* **1 :** an action, word, or phrase believed to have magic powers **2 :** something believed to keep away evil and bring good luck **3 :** a small decorative object worn on a chain or bracelet **4 :** a quality that attracts and pleases

[2]**charm** *vb* **charmed; charm·ing** **1 :** to affect or influence by or as if by a magic spell **2 :** FASCINATE 2, DELIGHT **3 :** to attract by being graceful, beautiful, or welcoming **4 :** to protect by or as if by a charm

charm·ing *adj* **:** very pleasing

[1]**chart** *n* **1 :** a sheet giving information in a table or lists or by means of diagrams **2 :** a map showing features (as coasts, currents, and depths of water) of importance to sailors **3 :** a diagram of an area showing information other than natural features

[2]**chart** *vb* **chart·ed; chart·ing** **1 :** to make a map or chart of **2 :** to make a plan for

[1]**char·ter** *n* **1 :** an official document setting out the rights and duties of a group **2 :** a document which declares that a city, town, school, or corporation has been established **3 :** a document that describes the basic laws or principles of a group

[2]**charter** *vb* **char·tered; char·ter·ing** **1 :** to grant a charter to **2 :** to hire (as a bus or an aircraft) for temporary use

charter school *n* **:** a public school that is established by a charter describing its programs and goals and is supported by taxes but does not have to be run according to many of the rules of a city or state

[1]**chase** *n* **:** the act of following quickly in order to capture or catch up with **:** PURSUIT

[2]**chase** *vb* **chased; chas·ing** **1 :** to follow quickly in order to catch up with or capture **2 :** to drive away or out

chasm *n* **:** a deep split or gap in the earth

chas·sis *n, pl* **chas·sis** **:** the supporting frame of a structure (as an automobile or television)

chaste *adj* **chast·er; chast·est** **1 :** pure in thought and act **:** MODEST **2 :** simple or plain in design

chas·ten *vb* **chas·tened; chas·ten·ing** **:** to correct by punishment **:** DISCIPLINE

chas·tise *vb* **chas·tised; chas·tis·ing** **1 :** to punish severely (as by whipping) **2 :** to criticize harshly — **chas·tise·ment** *n*

chas·ti·ty *n* **:** the quality or state of being pure in thought and act

[1]**chat** *vb* **chat·ted; chat·ting** **:** to talk in a friendly way about things that are not serious

[2]**chat** *n* **:** a light friendly conversation

châ·teau *n, pl* **châ·teaus** *or* **châ·teaux** **:** a castle or a large house especially in France

chat room *n* **:** a website or computer program that allows people to send messages to each other instantly over the Internet

[1]**chat·ter** *vb* **chat·tered; chat·ter·ing** **1 :** to talk fast without thinking or without stopping **2 :** to make quick sounds that suggest speech but lack meaning **3 :** to make clicking sounds by hitting together again and again

[2]**chatter** *n* **1 :** the act or sound of chattering **2 :** quick or unimportant talk

chat·ter·box *n* **:** a person who talks a lot

chat·ty *adj* **chat·ti·er; chat·ti·est** **1 :** tending to talk a lot **:** TALKATIVE **2 :** having the style and manner of friendly conversation

chauf·feur *n* : a person hired to drive people around in a car

[1]**cheap** *adj* **cheap·er; cheap·est** **1** : not costing much **2** : charging low prices **3** : worth little : of low quality **4** : gained without much effort **5** : having little self-respect **6** : not willing to share or spend money : STINGY — **cheap·ly** *adv*

[2]**cheap** *adv* : at low cost

cheap·en *vb* **cheap·ened; cheap·en·ing** : to cause to be of lower quality, value, or importance

cheap·skate *n* : a stingy person

[1]**cheat** *vb* **cheat·ed; cheat·ing** **1** : to use unfair or dishonest methods to gain an advantage **2** : to take something away from or keep from having something by dishonest tricks — **cheat·er** *n*

[2]**cheat** *n* : a dishonest person

[1]**check** *n* **1** : a sudden stopping of progress : PAUSE **2** : something that delays, stops, or holds back **3** : EXAMINATION 1, INVESTIGATION **4** *US* **check** *or Can and Brit* **cheque** : a written order telling a bank to pay out money from a person's account to the one named on the order **5** : a ticket or token showing a person's ownership, identity, or claim to something **6** : a slip of paper showing the amount due **7** : a pattern in squares **8** : a mark ✓ typically placed beside a written or printed item to show that something has been specially noted **9** : an act of hitting or stopping a player in hockey **10** : a situation in chess in which a player's king can be captured on the opponent's next turn — **in check** : under control

[2]**check** *vb* **checked; check·ing** **1** : to slow or bring to a stop **2** : to hold back or under control **3** : to make sure that something is correct or satisfactory **4** : to get information by examining **5** : to mark with a check **6** : to leave or accept for safekeeping or for shipment **7** : to stop or hit (a player) in hockey — **check out** **1** : to look at **2** : to borrow from a library **3** : to pay for purchases

checked *adj* : CHECKERED

check·er·board *n* : a board marked with 64 squares in two colors and used for games (as checkers)

check·ered *adj* : having a pattern made up of squares of different colors

check·ers *n* : a game played on a checkerboard by two players each having twelve pieces

checking account *or Can* **chequing account** *n* : an account in a bank from which the depositor can draw money by writing checks

check·mate *n* : a situation in chess in which a player loses because the player's king is in a position from which it cannot escape capture

check·up *n* **1** : INSPECTION, EXAMINATION **2** : a general physical examination made by a doctor or veterinarian

cheek *n* **1** : the side of the face below the eye and above and to the side of the mouth **2** : disrespectful speech or behavior

cheeky *adj* **cheek·i·er; cheek·i·est** : showing disrespect : RUDE

[1]**cheep** *vb* : [3]PEEP, CHIRP

[2]**cheep** *n* : [1]CHIRP

[1]**cheer** *n* **1** : a happy feeling : good spirits **2** : something that gladdens **3** : a shout of praise or encouragement

[2]**cheer** *vb* **cheered; cheer·ing** **1** : to give hope to or make happier : COMFORT **2** : to grow or be cheerful — usually used with *up* **3** : to urge on especially with shouts or cheers **4** : to shout with joy, approval, or enthusiasm

cheer·ful *adj* **1** : feeling or showing happiness **2** : causing good feelings or happiness **3** : pleasantly bright — **cheer·ful·ly** *adv* — **cheer·ful·ness** *n*

cheer·less *adj* : offering no happiness or cheer : GLOOMY

cheery *adj* **cheer·i·er; cheer·i·est** : merry and bright in manner or effect : CHEERFUL — **cheer·i·ly** *adv* — **cheer·i·ness** *n*

cheese *n* : the curd of milk pressed for use as food

cheese·cloth *n* : a thin loosely woven cotton cloth

cheesy *adj* **chees·i·er; chees·i·est** **1** : resembling cheese especially in appearance or smell **2** : containing cheese **3** : of poor quality : lacking style or good taste

chee·tah *n* : a long-legged spotted African and formerly Asian animal of the cat family that is the fastest animal on land

chef *n* **1** : a professional cook who is usually in charge of a kitchen in a restaurant **2** : [1]COOK

[1]**chem·i·cal** *adj* : of or relating to chemistry or chemicals — **chem·i·cal·ly** *adv*

[2]**chemical** *n* : any substance (as an acid) that is formed when two or more other substances act upon one another or that is used to produce a change in another substance

chem·ist *n* : a person trained or engaged in chemistry

chem·is·try *n* **1** : a science that deals with the composition and properties of substances and of the changes they undergo **2** : chemical composition and properties

cheque *Can and Brit spelling of* CHECK n, sense 4

chequing account *Can spelling of* CHECKING ACCOUNT

cher·ish *vb* **cher·ished; cher·ish·ing 1 :** to hold dear : feel or show affection for **2 :** remember or hold in a deeply felt way

Cher·o·kee *n, pl* **Cherokee** *or* **Cherokees 1 :** a member of an American Indian people originally of Tennessee and North Carolina **2 :** the language of the Cherokee people

cher·ry *n, pl* **cherries 1 :** the small round yellow to deep red smooth-skinned fruit of a tree that is related to the plum tree **2 :** a medium red

cher·ub *n* **1 :** a beautiful child usually with wings in paintings and drawings **2 :** a cute chubby child

chess *n* **:** a game for two players in which each player moves 16 pieces according to fixed rules across a checkerboard and tries to place the opponent's king in a position from which it cannot escape

chest *n* **1 :** a container (as a box or case) for storing, safekeeping, or shipping **2 :** the front part of the body enclosed by the ribs and breastbone **3 :** a fund of public money — **chest·ed** *adj*

chest·nut *n* **1 :** a sweet edible nut that grows in burs on a tree related to the beech **2 :** a reddish brown

chev·ron *n* **:** a sleeve badge of one or more bars or stripes usually in the shape of an upside-down V indicating the wearer's rank (as in the armed forces)

[1]**chew** *vb* **chewed; chew·ing :** to crush or grind with the teeth

[2]**chew** *n* **1 :** the act of crushing or grinding with the teeth **2 :** something that a person or animal chews

chew·ing gum *n* **:** a sweetened and flavored soft material (as of chicle) that is chewed but not swallowed

chewy *adj* **chew·i·er; chew·i·est :** requiring a lot of chewing

Chey·enne *n, pl* **Cheyenne** *or* **Chey·ennes :** a member of an American Indian people of the western plains ranging between the Arkansas and Missouri rivers **2 :** the language of the Cheyenne people

[1]**chic** *n* **:** fashionable style

[2]**chic** *adj* **chic·er; chic·est :** STYLISH, FASHIONABLE

Chi·ca·na *n* **:** an American woman or girl of Mexican ancestry

[1]**Chi·ca·no** *n, pl* **Chicanos :** an American of Mexican ancestry

[2]**Chicano** *adj* **:** of or relating to Chicanos

chick *n* **:** a baby bird and especially a baby chicken

chick·a·dee *n* **:** a small mostly grayish bird with the top of the head black

[1]**chick·en** *n* **1 :** a bird that is commonly raised by people for its eggs and meat **:** a hen or rooster **2 :** the meat of a chicken used as food **3 :** COWARD

[2]**chicken** *adj* **:** COWARDLY 1

chicken out *vb* **chickened out; chicken·ing out :** to become too scared to do something

chicken pox *n* **:** a contagious illness especially of children in which there is fever and the skin breaks out in watery blisters

chick·pea *n* **:** an edible roundish pale yellow seed from the pod of an Asian plant that is cooked and eaten as a vegetable

chi·cle *n* **:** a gum obtained from the sap of a tropical American tree and used in making chewing gum

chide *vb* **chid·ed; chid·ing :** to scold gently

[1]**chief** *n* **:** the head of a group **:** LEADER — **in chief :** in the highest ranking position or place

[2]**chief** *adj* **1 :** highest in rank or authority **2 :** most important **:** MAIN

chief·ly *adv* **1 :** above all **:** most importantly **2 :** for the most part

chief master sergeant *n* **:** a noncommissioned officer in the air force ranking above a senior master sergeant

chief petty officer *n* **:** a petty officer in the navy or coast guard ranking above a petty officer first class

chief·tain *n* **:** a chief especially of a band, tribe, or clan

chief warrant officer *n* **:** a warrant officer in any of the three top grades

chig·ger *n* **:** the six-legged larva of a mite that clings to the skin and causes itching

chil·blain *n* **:** a red swollen itchy condition caused by cold that occurs especially on the hands or feet

child *n, pl* **chil·dren 1 :** an unborn or recently born person **2 :** a young person of either sex between infancy and youth **3 :** a son or daughter of any age

child·birth *n* **:** the act or process of giving birth to a child

child·hood *n* **:** the period of life between infancy and youth

child·ish *adj* **1 :** of, like, or thought to be suitable to children **2 :** showing the less pleasing qualities (as silliness) often thought to be those of children

child·like *adj* **1 :** like that of a child **2 :** showing the more pleasing qualities (as innocence and trustfulness) often thought to be those of children

child·proof *adj* **1 :** made to prevent opening by children **2 :** made safe for children

chili *also* **chile** *or* **chil·li** *n, pl* **chil·ies** *also* **chil·es** *or* **chil·is** *or* **chil·lies 1 :** a small pepper with a very hot flavor **2 :** a spicy stew of ground beef and chilies usually with beans

[1]**chill** *n* **1 :** coldness that is unpleasant but not

extreme **2 :** a feeling of coldness accompanied by shivering **3 :** a feeling of coldness caused by fear

[2]**chill** *adj* **1 :** unpleasantly cold **:** RAW **2 :** not friendly

[3]**chill** *vb* **chilled; chill·ing 1 :** to make or become cold or chilly **2 :** to make cool especially without freezing **3 :** to cause to feel cold from fear

chill·ing *adj* **:** very upsetting or frightening

chilly *adj* **chill·i·er; chill·i·est :** noticeably cold

[1]**chime** *vb* **chimed; chim·ing 1 :** to make sounds like a bell **2 :** to call or indicate by chiming — **chime in :** to interrupt or join in a conversation

[2]**chime** *n* **1 :** a set of bells tuned to play music **2 :** the sound from a set of bells — usually used in pl.

chim·ney *n, pl* **chimneys :** a structure that allows smoke to escape (as from a fireplace) and that is often made of brick

chimney sweep *n* **:** a person who cleans soot from chimneys

chimney swift *n* **:** a small dark gray bird with long narrow wings that often builds its nest inside chimneys

chimp *n* **:** CHIMPANZEE

chim·pan·zee *n* **:** an African ape that lives mostly in trees and is smaller than the related gorilla

chin *n* **:** the part of the face below the mouth and including the point of the lower jaw

chi·na *n* **1 :** PORCELAIN **2 :** dishes of pottery or porcelain for use as tableware

chin·chil·la *n* **:** a South American animal that is somewhat like a squirrel and is often raised for its soft silvery gray fur

[1]**Chi·nese** *adj* **:** of or relating to China, the Chinese people, or the languages of China

[2]**Chinese** *n, pl* **Chinese 1 :** a person born or living in China **2 :** a group of related languages used in China

chink *n* **:** a narrow slit or crack (as in a wall)

[1]**chip** *n* **1 :** a small piece cut or broken off **2 :** a thin crisp piece of food and especially potato **3 :** a small bit of candy used in baking **4 :** a flaw left after a small piece has been broken off **5 :** INTEGRATED CIRCUIT **6 :** a small slice of silicon containing a number of electronic circuits (as for a computer)

[2]**chip** *vb* **chipped; chip·ping 1 :** to cut or break a small piece from **2 :** to break off in small pieces

chip·munk *n* **:** a small striped animal related to the squirrels

[1]**chirp** *n* **:** the short high-pitched sound made by crickets and some small birds

[2]**chirp** *vb* **chirped; chirp·ing :** to make a short high-pitched sound

[1]**chis·el** *n* **:** a metal tool with a sharp edge at the end of a usually flat piece used to chip away stone, wood, or metal

[2]**chisel** *vb* **chis·eled** *or* **chis·elled; chis·el·ing** *or* **chis·el·ling :** to cut, shape, or carve with a chisel

chit·chat *n* **:** friendly conversation

chiv·al·rous *adj* **1 :** of or relating to a knight or knighthood **2 :** having or showing honor, generosity, and courtesy **3 :** showing special courtesy and regard to women

chiv·al·ry *n* **1 :** the system, spirit, ways, or customs of knighthood **2 :** very honorable and courteous behavior

chlo·rine *n* **:** a chemical element that is a greenish yellow irritating gas of strong odor used as a bleach and as a disinfectant to purify water

chlo·ro·form *n* **:** a colorless heavy liquid used especially to dissolve fatty substances

chlo·ro·phyll *n* **:** the green coloring matter found mainly in the chloroplasts of plants that absorbs energy from sunlight to produce carbohydrates from carbon dioxide and water during photosynthesis

chlo·ro·plast *n* **:** one of the tiny parts in a plant cell that contains chlorophyll and is the place where photosynthesis occurs

chock–full *adj* **:** very full

choc·o·late *n* **1 :** a food prepared from ground roasted cacao beans **2 :** a candy made or coated with chocolate **3 :** a beverage of chocolate in water or milk — **chocolate** *adj*

Choc·taw *n, pl* **Choctaw** *or* **Choc·taws 1 :** a member of an American Indian people of Mississippi, Alabama, and Louisiana **2 :** the language of the Choctaw people

[1]**choice** *n* **1 :** the act of picking between two or more possibilities **2 :** the power of choosing **:** OPTION **3 :** a person or thing chosen **4 :** a range of possibilities to choose from

[2]**choice** *adj* **choic·er; choic·est :** of very good quality

choir *n* **1 :** an organized group of singers especially in a church **2 :** the part of a church set aside for the singers

choke *vb* **choked; chok·ing 1 :** to keep from breathing in a normal way by cutting off the supply of air **2 :** to have the trachea blocked entirely or partly **3 :** to slow or prevent the growth or action of **4 :** to block by clogging — **choke down :** to eat with difficulty — **choke up :** to become too emotional to speak

choke·cher·ry *n, pl* **choke·cher·ries :** a wild cherry tree with clusters of bitter reddish black fruits

chol·era *n* **:** a serious disease that causes severe vomiting and diarrhea

choose *vb* **chose; cho·sen; choos·ing** **1** : to select freely and after careful thought **2** : to decide what to do **3** : to see fit
choosy *adj* **choos·i·er; choos·i·est** : careful in making choices
[1]**chop** *vb* **chopped; chop·ping** **1** : to cut by striking especially over and over with something sharp **2** : to cut into small pieces : MINCE
[2]**chop** *n* **1** : a sharp downward blow or stroke (as with an ax) **2** : a small cut of meat often including a part of a rib
chop·per *n* **1** : someone or something that chops **2** : HELICOPTER
choppy *adj* **chop·pi·er; chop·pi·est** **1** : rough with small waves **2** : marked by sudden stops and starts : not smooth
chops *n pl* : the fleshy covering of the jaws
chop·stick *n* : one of two thin sticks used chiefly in Asian countries to pick up and eat food
cho·ral *adj* : of or relating to a choir or chorus
cho·rale *n* **1** : a hymn sung by the choir or congregation at a church service **2** : CHORUS 1
[1]**chord** *n* : a group of tones sounded together to form harmony
[2]**chord** *n* : a straight line joining two points on a curve
chore *n* **1** : a small job that is done regularly **2** : a dull, unpleasant, or difficult task
cho·re·og·ra·phy *n* **1** : the art of arranging the movements of dancers for a performance and especially a ballet **2** : the arrangement of a dance — **cho·re·og·ra·pher** *n*
chor·tle *vb* **chor·tled; chor·tling** : to chuckle in amusement or joy
[1]**cho·rus** *n* **1** : a group of singers : CHOIR **2** : a group of dancers and singers (as in a musical comedy) **3** : a part of a song or hymn that is repeated every so often : REFRAIN **4** : a song meant to be sung by a group : group singing **5** : sounds uttered by a group of persons or animals together
[2]**chorus** *vb* **cho·rused; cho·rus·ing** : to speak, sing, or sound at the same time or together
chose *past of* CHOOSE
[1]**chosen** *past participle of* CHOOSE
[2]**cho·sen** *adj* **1** : carefully selected **2** : picked to be shown favor or given special privilege
chow·der *n* : a soup or stew made of fish, clams, or a vegetable usually simmered in milk
Christ *n* : JESUS CHRIST
chris·ten *vb* **chris·tened; chris·ten·ing** **1** : BAPTIZE 1 **2** : to name at baptism **3** : [2]NAME 1 **4** : to name or dedicate (as a ship) in a ceremony
chris·ten·ing *n* : BAPTISM
[1]**Chris·tian** *n* **1** : a person who believes in Jesus Christ and follows his teachings **2** : a member of a Christian church
[2]**Christian** *adj* **1** : of or relating to Jesus Christ or the religion based on his teachings **2** : of or relating to people who follow the teachings of Jesus Christ **3** : being what a person who practices Christianity should be or do
Chris·tian·i·ty *n* : the religion based on the teachings of Jesus Christ
Christian name *n* : the personal name given to a person at birth or christening
Christ·mas *n* : December 25 celebrated in honor of the birth of Jesus Christ
Christ·mas·tide *n* : the season of Christmas
Christmas tree *n* : a usually evergreen tree decorated at Christmas
chro·mat·ic scale *n* : a musical scale that has all half steps
chrome *n* **1** : CHROMIUM **2** : something plated with an alloy of chromium
chro·mi·um *n* : a bluish white metallic chemical element used especially in alloys
chro·mo·some *n* : one of the rod-shaped or threadlike structures of a cell nucleus that contain genes and divide when the cell divides
chron·ic *adj* **1** : continuing for a long time or returning often **2** : happening or done frequently or by habit — **chron·i·cal·ly** *adv*
[1]**chron·i·cle** *n* : an account of events in the order that they happened : HISTORY
[2]**chronicle** *vb* **chron·i·cled; chron·i·cling** : to record in the order of occurrence
chron·o·log·i·cal *adj* : arranged in or according to the order of time — **chron·o·log·i·cal·ly** *adv*
chrys·a·lis *n* **1** : a moth or butterfly pupa that is enclosed in a hardened protective case **2** : the hardened protective case made by and enclosing a moth or butterfly pupa
chry·san·the·mum *n* : a plant related to the daisies that has brightly colored flower heads
chub·by *adj* **chub·bi·er; chub·bi·est** : somewhat fat
chuck *vb* **chucked; chuck·ing** **1** : to give a pat or tap to **2** : [1]TOSS 2
[1]**chuck·le** *vb* **chuck·led; chuck·ling** : to laugh in a quiet way
[2]**chuckle** *n* : a low quiet laugh
chuck wagon *n* : a wagon carrying a stove and food for cooking
chug *vb* **chugged; chug·ging** : to move with repeated low sounds like that of a steam engine
[1]**chum** *n* : a close friend : PAL
[2]**chum** *vb* **chummed; chum·ming** : to spend time with as a friend

chum·my *adj* **chum·mi·er; chum·mi·est** : very friendly

chunk *n* : a short thick piece

chunky *adj* **chunk·i·er; chunk·i·est** **1** : heavy, thick, and solid **2** : having a short and thick body **3** : containing many solid pieces

church *n* **1** : a building for public worship and especially Christian worship **2** *often cap* : an organized body of religious believers **3** : public worship

church·yard *n* : an area of land that belongs to and usually surrounds a church and that is often used as a burial ground

[1]**churn** *n* : a container in which milk or cream is stirred or shaken in making butter

[2]**churn** *vb* **churned; churn·ing** **1** : to stir or shake in a churn (as in making butter) **2** : to stir or shake forcefully **3** : to feel the effects of an emotion (as fear) **4** : to move by or as if by forceful stirring action

chute *n* **1** : a tube or passage down or through which people slide or things are slid or dropped **2** : [1]PARACHUTE

ci·ca·da *n* : an insect that has transparent wings and a stout body and the males of which make a loud buzzing noise

-cide *n suffix* **1** : killer **2** : killing

ci·der *n* : the juice pressed out of fruit (as apples) and used especially as a drink and in making vinegar

ci·gar *n* : a small roll of tobacco leaf for smoking

cig·a·rette *n* : a small roll of cut tobacco wrapped in paper for smoking

cil·i·um *n, pl* **cil·ia** : a tiny hairlike structure on the surface of some cells

[1]**cinch** *n* **1** : a sure or an easy thing **2** : GIRTH 2

[2]**cinch** *vb* **cinched; cinch·ing** : to fasten (as a belt or strap) tightly

cin·cho·na *n* : a South American tree whose bark yields quinine

cin·der *n* **1** : a piece of partly burned coal or wood that is not burning **2** : EMBER **3 cinders** *pl* : [2]ASH 1

cin·e·ma *n* **1** : a movie theater **2** : the movie industry

cin·na·mon *n* : a spice that is made from the fragrant bark of a tropical Asian tree and is used especially in cooking and baking

[1]**ci·pher** *n* **1** : ZERO 1 **2** : a method of secret writing or the alphabet or letters and symbols used in such writing **3** : a message in code

[2]**cipher** *vb* **ci·phered; ci·pher·ing** : to use figures in doing a problem in arithmetic : CALCULATE

[1]**cir·cle** *n* **1** : a line that is curved so that its ends meet and every point on the line is the same distance from the center **2** : something in the form of a circle or part of a circle **3** : [1]CYCLE 2, ROUND **4** : a group of people sharing a common interest

[2]**circle** *vb* **cir·cled; cir·cling** **1** : to form or draw a circle around **2** : to move or revolve around **3** : to move in or as if in a circle

cir·cuit *n* **1** : a boundary line around an area **2** : an enclosed space **3** : movement around something **4** : a regular tour of service (as by a judge) around an assigned territory : a course so traveled **5** : a series of performances, competitions, or appearances held at many different places **6** : the complete path of an electric current **7** : a group of electronic parts

circuit breaker *n* : a switch that automatically stops the flow of electric current if a circuit becomes overloaded

[1]**cir·cu·lar** *adj* **1** : shaped like a circle or part of a circle : ROUND **2** : passing or going around in a circle **3** : not said in simple or sincere language

[2]**circular** *n* : a printed notice or advertisement given or sent to many people

cir·cu·late *vb* **cir·cu·lat·ed; cir·cu·lat·ing** **1** : to move around in a course **2** : to pass or be passed from place to place or from person to person

cir·cu·la·tion *n* **1** : movement through something **2** : passage from place to place or person to person **3** : the average number of copies (as of a newspaper) sold in a given period

cir·cu·la·to·ry *adj* : of or relating to circulation and especially the circulation of blood in the body

circulatory system *n* : the system of the body that circulates blood and lymph and includes the heart and blood vessels

circum- *prefix* : around : about

cir·cum·fer·ence *n* **1** : the line that goes around a circle **2** : a boundary line enclosing an area **3** : the distance around something

cir·cum·nav·i·gate *vb* **cir·cum·nav·i·gat·ed; cir·cum·nav·i·gat·ing** : to go completely around (as the earth) especially by water

cir·cum·po·lar *adj* **1** : continually visible above the horizon **2** : surrounding or found near a pole of the earth

cir·cum·stance *n* **1** : a fact or event that affects a situation **2 circumstances** *pl* : conditions at a certain time or place **3 circumstances** *pl* : the way something happens **4 circumstances** *pl* : the conditions in which someone lives **5** : an uncontrollable event or situation

cir·cum·vent *vb* **cir·cum·vent·ed; cir·cum·vent·ing** : to avoid the force or effect of by cleverness

cir·cus *n* **:** a traveling show that often takes place under a tent and that usually includes acts performed by acrobats, clowns, and trained animals

cir·rus *n, pl* **cir·ri :** a thin white cloud of tiny ice crystals that forms at a very high altitude

cis·tern *n* **:** an artificial reservoir or tank for storing water usually underground

cit·a·del *n* **:** a fortress that sits high above a city

ci·ta·tion *n* **1 :** an official order to appear in court **2 :** an act or instance of quoting **3 :** QUOTATION **4 :** a formal public statement praising a person for doing something good

cite *vb* **cit·ed; cit·ing 1 :** to order to appear in court **2 :** to quote as an example, authority, or proof **3 :** to refer to especially in praise

cit·i·zen *n* **1 :** a person who lives in a particular place **2 :** a person who legally belongs to, gives allegiance to, and has the rights and protections of a country

cit·i·zen·ry *n* **:** all the citizens of a place

cit·i·zen·ship *n* **1 :** the state of being a citizen **2 :** the behavior expected of a person as a member of a community

cit·ron *n* **1 :** a citrus fruit like the smaller lemon and having a thick rind that is preserved for use in cakes and puddings **2 :** a small hard watermelon used especially in pickles and preserves

cit·rus *n, pl* **citrus** *or* **cit·rus·es :** a juicy fruit (as a lemon, orange, or grapefruit) with a thick rind that comes from a tree or shrub that grows in warm regions

city *n, pl* **cit·ies 1 :** a place in which people live and work that is larger than a town **2 :** the people of a city

city hall *n* **:** the main administrative building of a city

civ·ic *adj* **:** of or relating to a citizen, a city, or citizenship

civ·ics *n* **:** the study of the rights and duties of citizens and of how government works

civ·il *adj* **1 :** of or relating to citizens **2 :** of or relating to matters within a country **3 :** of or relating to the regular business of citizens or government that is not connected to the military or a religion **4 :** polite without being friendly **5 :** relating to laws about private rights rather than criminal laws — **civ·il·ly** *adv*

¹ci·vil·ian *n* **:** a person who is not a member of a military, police, or firefighting force

²civilian *adj* **:** of or relating to people who are not members of a military, police, or firefighting force

ci·vil·i·ty *n, pl* **ci·vil·i·ties 1 :** polite behavior **2 :** a polite act or thing to say

civ·i·li·za·tion *n* **1 :** an advanced stage (as in art, science, and government) in the development of society **2 :** the way of life of a people **3 :** all the societies of the world

civ·i·lize *vb* **civ·i·lized; civ·i·liz·ing :** to cause to have a more advanced or modern way of living

civil rights *n* **:** the nonpolitical rights of a citizen guaranteed by the Constitution and acts of Congress

civil service *n* **:** the branch of a government that takes care of the business of running the government and its programs but that does not include the legislature, the military, or the courts

civil war *n* **:** a war between opposing groups of citizens of the same country

¹clack *vb* **clacked; clack·ing 1 :** to talk rapidly and without stopping **2 :** to make or cause to make a short sharp sound

²clack *n* **1 :** rapid continuous talk **2 :** a sound of clacking

¹clad *past and past participle of* CLOTHE

²clad *adj* **1 :** being covered **2 :** being dressed

¹claim *vb* **claimed; claim·ing 1 :** to ask for as something that is a right or is deserved **2 :** to take as the rightful owner **3 :** to state as a fact **:** insist to be true **4 :** to cause the end or death of

²claim *n* **1 :** a demand for something owed or believed to be owed **2 :** a right to something **3 :** something (as an area of land) claimed as one's own **4 :** a statement that others may dispute

clam *n* **:** a shellfish that lives in sand or mud and has a soft body surrounded by a hinged shell with two parts and that is often eaten as food

clam·bake *n* **:** an outdoor party where clams and other foods are cooked usually on heated rocks covered by seaweed

clam·ber *vb* **clam·bered; clam·ber·ing :** to climb in an awkward way

clam·my *adj* **clam·mi·er; clam·mi·est :** unpleasantly damp, sticky, and cool

¹clam·or *or Can and Brit* **clamour** *n* **1 :** a noisy shouting **2 :** a loud continuous noise **3 :** strong and loud demand

²clamor *or Can and Brit* **clamour** *vb* **clamored/clamoured; clam·or·ing/clamouring :** to make a loud noise or demand

¹clamp *n* **:** a device that holds or presses parts together firmly

²clamp *vb* **clamped; clamp·ing :** to fasten or to hold tightly with or as if with a clamp

clan *n* **1 :** a group (as in the Scottish Highlands) made up of households whose heads claim to have a common ancestor **2 :** a large family

¹clang *vb* **clanged; clang·ing :** to make or

cause to make the loud ringing sound of metal hitting something

[2]**clang** *n* **:** a loud ringing sound like that made by pieces of metal striking together

[1]**clank** *vb* **clanked; clank·ing** **1 :** to make or cause to make a clank or series of clanks **2 :** to move with a clank

[2]**clank** *n* **:** a sharp short ringing sound

[1]**clap** *vb* **clapped; clap·ping** **1 :** to hit (the palms of the hands) together usually more than once **2 :** to hit or touch with the open hand **3 :** to hit together noisily **4 :** to put or place quickly or with force

[2]**clap** *n* **1 :** a loud sharp sound **2 :** a hard or a friendly slap

clap·board *n* **:** a narrow board thicker at one edge than at the other used as siding for a building

clap·per *n* **:** the part hanging inside a bell that hits the sides to make the bell ring

clar·i·fy *vb* **clar·i·fied; clar·i·fy·ing** **1 :** to make or to become pure or clear **2 :** to make or become more easily understood

clar·i·net *n* **:** a woodwind instrument with a single reed, a straight body formed like a tube, and keys

clar·i·ty *n* **:** clear quality or state

[1]**clash** *vb* **clashed; clash·ing** **1 :** to make or cause to make the loud sound of metal objects hitting **2 :** to come into conflict **3 :** to not go together well

[2]**clash** *n* **1 :** a loud sharp sound usually of metal striking metal **2 :** a struggle or strong disagreement

[1]**clasp** *n* **1 :** a device for holding together objects or parts of something **2 :** a firm hold with the hands or arms

[2]**clasp** *vb* **clasped; clasp·ing** **1 :** to fasten with or as if with a clasp **2 :** to hold firmly with the hands or arms

[1]**class** *n* **1 :** a group of students who are taught together regularly **2 :** one of the meetings of students being taught **3 :** a course of instruction **4 :** a group of students who graduate together **5 :** a group of people in a society who are at the same level of wealth or social status **6 :** a group of related living things (as plants or animals) that ranks above the order and below the phylum or division in scientific classification **7 :** a category (as of goods or services) based on quality

[2]**class** *vb* **classed; class·ing :** CLASSIFY

[1]**clas·sic** *adj* **1 :** serving as a model of the best of its kind **2 :** fashionable year after year **3 :** of or relating to the ancient Greeks and Romans or their culture **4 :** being typical of its kind

[2]**classic** *n* **1 :** a written work or author of ancient Greece or Rome **2 :** a great work of art **3 :** something long regarded as outstanding of its kind

clas·si·cal *adj* **1 :** of a kind that has long been considered great **2 :** of or relating to the ancient Greek and Roman world and especially to its language and arts **3 :** relating to music in a European tradition that includes opera and symphony and that is generally considered more serious than other kinds of music **4 :** concerned with a general study of the arts and sciences

clas·si·fi·ca·tion *n* **1 :** the act of arranging into groups of similar things **2 :** an arrangement into groups of similar things

clas·si·fied *adj* **1 :** arranged in groups with other similar things **2 :** kept secret from all but a few people in government

clas·si·fy *vb* **clas·si·fied; clas·si·fy·ing :** to arrange in groups based on similarities

class·mate *n* **:** a member of the same class in a school or college

class·room *n* **:** a room where classes are held in a school

[1]**clat·ter** *vb* **clat·tered; clat·ter·ing** **1 :** to make or cause to make a rattling sound **2 :** to move or go with a rattling sound

[2]**clatter** *n* **1 :** a rattling sound (as of hard objects striking together) **2 :** COMMOTION

clause *n* **1 :** a separate part of a document (as a will) **2 :** a group of words having its own subject and predicate

clav·i·cle *n* **:** COLLARBONE

[1]**claw** *n* **1 :** a sharp usually thin and curved nail on the finger or toe of an animal (as a cat or bird) **2 :** the end of a limb of some animals (as an insect, scorpion, or lobster) that is pointed or used for grasping

[2]**claw** *vb* **clawed; claw·ing :** to scratch, seize, or dig with claws or fingers

clay *n* **1 :** an earthy material that is sticky and easily molded when wet and hard when baked **2 :** a substance like clay that is used for modeling

[1]**clean** *adj* **clean·er; clean·est** **1 :** free of dirt or pollution **2 :** not yet used **3 :** not involving or showing involvement with anything wrong or illegal **4 :** not offensive **5 :** THOROUGH 1 **6 :** having a simple graceful form **:** TRIM **7 :** [1]SMOOTH 1 — **clean·ly** *adv*

[2]**clean** *adv* **:** all the way **:** COMPLETELY

[3]**clean** *vb* **cleaned; clean·ing :** to make or become free of dirt or disorder — **clean·er** *n*

clean·li·ness *n* **:** the condition of being clean **:** the habit of keeping clean

cleanse *vb* **cleansed; cleans·ing :** to make clean

cleans·er *n* **:** a substance (as a scouring powder) used for cleaning

[1]**clear** *adj* **clear·er; clear·est** **1 :** easily heard,

seen, noticed, or understood **2 :** free of clouds, haze, or mist **3 :** free from feelings of guilt **4 :** easily seen through **5 :** free from doubt or confusion **:** SURE **6 :** free of blemishes **7 :** not blocked **8 :** BRIGHT 1, LUMINOUS — **clear·ly** *adv* — **clear·ness** *n*

[2]**clear** *vb* **cleared; clear·ing 1 :** to free of things blocking **2 :** to make or become free of clouds, haze, or mist **3 :** to get rid of **:** REMOVE **4 :** to go over or by without touching **5 :** to go away **:** DISPERSE **6 :** EXPLAIN 1 **7 :** to free from blame **8 :** to approve or be approved by **9 :** to make as profit

[3]**clear** *adv* **1 :** in a way that is easy to hear **2 :** all the way

clear·ance *n* **1 :** the act or process of removing something **2 :** the distance by which one object avoids hitting or touching another **3 :** official permission

clear·ing *n* **:** an open area of land in which there are no trees

cleat *n* **1 :** a wooden or metal device used to fasten a line or a rope **2 :** a strip or projection fastened to the bottom of a shoe to prevent slipping **3** *pl* **:** shoes equipped with cleats

cleav·age *n* **1 :** the tendency of a rock or mineral to split readily in one or more directions **2 :** the action of splitting **3 :** the state of being split

[1]**cleave** *vb* **cleaved** *or* **clove; cleav·ing :** to cling to a person or thing closely

[2]**cleave** *vb* **cleaved** *also* **cleft** *or* **clove; cleaved** *also* **cleft** *or* **clo·ven; cleav·ing :** to divide by or as if by a cutting blow **:** SPLIT

cleav·er *n* **:** a heavy knife used for cutting up meat

clef *n* **:** a sign placed on the staff in writing music to show what pitch is represented by each line and space

[1]**cleft** *n* **1 :** a space or opening made by splitting or cracking **:** CREVICE **2 :** [1]NOTCH 1

[2]**cleft** *adj* **:** partly split or divided

clem·en·cy *n, pl* **clemencies 1 :** MERCY 1 **2 :** an act of mercy

clench *vb* **clenched; clench·ing 1 :** to hold tightly **:** CLUTCH **2 :** to set or close tightly

cler·gy *n, pl* **clergies :** the group of religious officials (as priests, ministers, and rabbis) specially prepared and authorized to lead religious services

cler·gy·man *n, pl* **cler·gy·men :** a member of the clergy

cler·i·cal *adj* **1 :** relating to the clergy **2 :** relating to a clerk or office worker

[1]**clerk** *n* **1 :** a person whose job is to keep records or accounts **2 :** a salesperson in a store

[2]**clerk** *vb* **clerked; clerk·ing :** to act or work as a clerk

clev·er *adj* **clev·er·er; clev·er·est 1 :** having a quick inventive mind **2 :** showing intelligence, wit, or imagination **3 :** showing skill in using the hands — **clev·er·ly** *adv* — **clev·er·ness** *n*

[1]**click** *vb* **clicked; click·ing 1 :** to make or cause to make a slight sharp noise **2 :** to fit in or work together smoothly **3 :** to select or make a selection especially on a computer by pressing a button on a control device (as a mouse)

[2]**click** *n* **:** a slight sharp noise

click·er *n* **:** REMOTE CONTROL 1

cli·ent *n* **:** a person who uses the professional advice or services of another

cli·en·tele *n* **:** a group of clients

cliff *n* **:** a high steep surface of rock

cli·mate *n* **:** the average weather conditions of a place over a period of years

cli·max *n* **:** the most interesting, exciting, or important time or part of something

[1]**climb** *vb* **climbed; climb·ing 1 :** to move in a way that involves going up or down **2 :** to go up or down on often with the help of the hands **3 :** to rise little by little to a higher point **4 :** to go upward in growing (as by winding around something) **5 :** to increase in amount, value, or level — **climb·er** *n*

[2]**climb** *n* **1 :** a place where climbing is necessary **2 :** the act of climbing

clime *n* **:** CLIMATE

clinch *vb* **clinched; clinch·ing :** to show to be certain or true

cling *vb* **clung; cling·ing 1 :** to hold fast by grasping or winding around **2 :** to remain close **3 :** to hold fast or stick closely to a surface **4 :** to continue to believe in

clin·ic *n* **1 :** a place where people can receive medical treatment usually for minor ailments **2 :** a group meeting for teaching a certain skill and working on individual problems

[1]**clink** *vb* **clinked; clink·ing :** to make or cause to make a slight short sound like that of metal being struck

[2]**clink** *n* **:** a slight sharp ringing sound

[1]**clip** *n* **:** a device that holds or hooks

[2]**clip** *vb* **clipped; clip·ping :** to fasten with a clip

[3]**clip** *vb* **clipped; clip·ping 1 :** to shorten or remove by cutting **2 :** to cut off or trim the hair or wool of **3 :** to cut out or off

[4]**clip** *n* **1 :** a sharp blow **2 :** a rapid pace **3 :** a short section of a recording

clip·board *n* **1 :** a small board with a clip at the top for holding papers **2 :** a part of computer memory that is used to store data (as items to be copied to another file) temporarily

clip·per *n* **1 clippers** *pl* **:** a device used for clipping **2 :** a fast sailing ship with three tall masts and large square sails **3 :** a person who clips

clip·ping *n* **:** something cut out or off

clique *n* **:** a small group of friends who are not friendly to others

¹cloak *n* **1 :** a long loose outer garment **2 :** something that hides or covers

²cloak *vb* **cloaked; cloak·ing :** to cover or hide completely

cloak·room *n* **:** a room (as in a school) in which coats and hats may be kept

clob·ber *vb* **clob·bered; clob·ber·ing 1 :** to hit with force **2 :** to defeat very easily

¹clock *n* **:** a device for measuring or telling the time and especially one not meant to be worn or carried by a person — **around the clock :** at every hour of the day

²clock *vb* **clocked; clock·ing 1 :** to measure the amount of time it takes to do something **2 :** to show (as time or speed) on a recording device

clock·wise *adv or adj* **:** in the direction in which the hands of a clock turn

clock·work *n* **:** machinery that makes the parts of a device move — **like clockwork :** in a very regular or exact way

clod *n* **1 :** a lump or mass especially of earth or clay **2 :** a clumsy or stupid person

¹clog *vb* **clogged; clog·ging :** to make passage through difficult or impossible **:** PLUG

²clog *n* **1 :** something that hinders or holds back **2 :** a shoe having a thick usually wooden sole

clois·ter *n* **1 :** MONASTERY, CONVENT **2 :** a covered passage with arches along or around the walls of a courtyard

clomp *vb* **clomped; clomp·ing :** to walk with loud heavy steps

clop *n* **:** a sound like that of a hoof against pavement

¹close *vb* **closed; clos·ing 1 :** to cover the opening of **2 :** to change the position of so as to prevent passage through an opening **:** SHUT **3 :** to bring or come to an end **4 :** to end the operation of for a period of time or permanently **5 :** to bring the parts or edges of together **6 :** ¹APPROACH 1 **7 :** ¹DECREASE — **close in :** to come or move nearer or closer

²close *n* **:** the point at which something ends

³close *adj* **clos·er; clos·est 1 :** not far apart in space, time, degree, or effect **2 :** very similar **3 :** almost reaching a particular condition **4 :** having a strong liking each one for the other **5 :** strict and careful in attention to details **6 :** decided by a narrow margin **7 :** ¹SHORT 1 **8 :** having little extra space **9 :** kept secret or tending to keep secrets **10 :** lacking fresh or moving air — **close·ly** *adv* — **close·ness** *n*

⁴close *adv* **clos·er; clos·est :** a short distance or time away

close call *n* **:** a barely successful escape from a difficult or dangerous situation

closed *adj* **:** not open

clos·et *n* **:** a small room for clothing or for supplies for the house

close–up *n* **:** a photograph taken at close range

clo·sure *n* **1 :** an act of closing **2 :** the condition of being closed

¹clot *n* **:** a lump made by some substance getting thicker and sticking together

²clot *vb* **clot·ted; clot·ting :** to become thick and partly solid

cloth *n, pl* **cloths 1 :** a woven or knitted material (as of cotton or nylon) **2 :** a piece of cloth for a certain use **3 :** TABLECLOTH

clothe *vb* **clothed** *or* **clad; cloth·ing 1 :** to cover with or as if with clothing **:** DRESS **2 :** to provide with clothes

clothes *n pl* **:** CLOTHING

clothes·pin *n* **:** a small object used for holding clothes in place on a line

cloth·ing *n* **:** the things people wear to cover their bodies

¹cloud *n* **1 :** a visible mass of tiny bits of water or ice hanging in the air usually high above the earth **2 :** a visible mass of small particles in the air **3 :** a large number of things that move together in a group **4 :** an overwhelming feeling **5 :** the computers and connections that support cloud computing — **cloud·less** *adj*

²cloud *vb* **cloud·ed; cloud·ing 1 :** to make or become cloudy **2 :** to have a bad effect on **3 :** to make confused

cloud·burst *n* **:** a sudden heavy rainfall

cloud computing *n* **:** the practice of storing regularly used computer data on multiple computers that can be accessed through the Internet

cloudy *adj* **cloud·i·er; cloud·i·est 1 :** overspread with clouds **2 :** not clear — **cloud·i·ness** *n*

¹clout *n* **1 :** a blow especially with the hand **2 :** the power to influence or control situations

²clout *vb* **clout·ed; clout·ing :** to hit hard

¹clove *n* **:** the dried flower bud of a tropical tree used in cooking as a spice

²clove *past of* CLEAVE

cloven *past participle of* ²CLEAVE

cloven hoof *n* **:** a hoof (as of a sheep or cow) with the front part divided into two sections

clo·ver *n* **:** a small plant that has leaves with three leaflets and usually roundish red, white, yellow, or purple flower heads and is sometimes grown for hay or pasture

¹clown *n* **1 :** a performer (as in a circus)

who entertains by playing tricks and who usually wears comical clothes and makeup **2 :** someone who does things to make people laugh

[2]**clown** *vb* **clowned; clown·ing :** to act in a funny or silly way : act like a clown

[1]**club** *n* **1 :** a heavy usually wooden stick used as a weapon **2 :** a stick or bat used to hit a ball in various games **3 :** a group of people associated because of a shared interest **4 :** the meeting place of a club

[2]**club** *vb* **clubbed; club·bing :** to beat or strike with or as if with a club

club·house *n* **1 :** a building used by a club **2 :** locker rooms used by an athletic team

[1]**cluck** *vb* **clucked; cluck·ing :** to make the low sound of or like a hen

[2]**cluck** *n* **:** the sound made by a hen

clue *n* **:** something that helps a person to find something or to solve a mystery

[1]**clump** *n* **1 :** a group of things clustered together **2 :** a cluster or lump of something **3 :** a heavy tramping sound

[2]**clump** *vb* **clumped; clump·ing 1 :** to form or cause to form a clump or clumps **2 :** to walk with loud heavy steps : CLOMP

clum·sy *adj* **clum·si·er; clum·si·est 1 :** lacking skill or grace in movement **2 :** awkwardly or carelessly made or done **3 :** awkward to handle — **clum·si·ly** *adv* — **clum·si·ness** *n*

clung *past and past participle of* CLING

clunk *n* **:** a loud dull sound

[1]**clus·ter** *n* **:** a number of similar things growing or grouped closely together : BUNCH

[2]**cluster** *vb* **clus·tered; clus·ter·ing :** to grow, collect, or assemble in a bunch

[1]**clutch** *vb* **clutched; clutch·ing 1 :** to grasp or hold tightly with or as if with the hands or claws **2 :** to make a grab

[2]**clutch** *n* **1 :** control or power someone has over someone else — usually used in pl. **2 :** a coupling for connecting and disconnecting a driving and a driven part in machinery **3 :** a lever or pedal operating a clutch

[3]**clutch** *n* **1 :** a group of eggs that is laid by a bird at one time **2 :** a small group of things or people

[1]**clut·ter** *vb* **clut·tered; clut·ter·ing :** to fill or cover with scattered things

[2]**clutter** *n* **:** a collection of scattered things

cm *abbr* centimeter

co. *abbr* **1** company **2** county

CO *abbr* Colorado

co- *prefix* **1 :** with : together : joint : jointly **2 :** in or to the same degree **3 :** fellow : partner

[1]**coach** *n* **1 :** a large carriage that has four wheels and a raised seat outside in front for the driver and is drawn by horses **2 :** a person who instructs or trains a performer or team **3 :** a person who teaches students individually **4 :** a railroad passenger car without berths **5 :** the least expensive seats on an airplane or a train

[2]**coach** *vb* **coached; coach·ing :** to teach and train

coach·man *n, pl* **coach·men :** a person who drives a coach or carriage

co·ag·u·late *vb* **co·ag·u·lat·ed; co·ag·u·lat·ing :** to become a thick compact mass : CLOT

coal *n* **1 :** a piece of glowing or charred wood : EMBER **2 :** a black solid mineral substance that is formed by the partial decay of plant matter under the influence of moisture and often increased pressure and temperature within the earth and is mined for use as a fuel

coarse *adj* **coars·er; coars·est 1 :** having a harsh or rough quality **2 :** made up of large particles **3 :** crude in taste, manners, or language **4 :** of poor or ordinary quality — **coarse·ly** *adv* — **coarse·ness** *n*

coars·en *vb* **coars·ened; coars·en·ing :** to make or become rough or rougher

[1]**coast** *n* **:** the land near a shore

[2]**coast** *vb* **coast·ed; coast·ing 1 :** to move downhill by the force of gravity **2 :** to sail close to shore along a coast

coast·al *adj* **:** of, relating to, or located on, near, or along a coast

coast·er *n* **1 :** a ship that sails or trades along a coast **2 :** a small mat on which a glass is placed to protect the surface of a table

coast guard *n* **:** a military force that guards a coast and helps people on boats and ships that are in trouble

[1]**coat** *n* **1 :** an outer garment worn especially for warmth **2 :** the outer covering (as fur or feathers) of an animal **3 :** a layer of material covering a surface — **coat·ed** *adj*

[2]**coat** *vb* **coat·ed; coat·ing :** to cover with a coat or covering

coat·ing *n* **:** [1]COAT 3, COVERING

coat of arms *n, pl* **coats of arms :** a special group of pictures or symbols belonging to a person, family, or group and shown on a shield

coat of mail *n, pl* **coats of mail :** a garment of metal scales or rings worn long ago as armor

co·au·thor *n* **:** an author who works with another author

coax *vb* **coaxed; coax·ing 1 :** to influence by gentle urging, special attention, or flattering **2 :** to get or win by means of gentle urging or flattery

cob *n* **1 :** a male swan **2 :** CORNCOB

co·balt *n* **:** a tough shiny silvery white metallic chemical element found with iron and nickel

cob·bled *adj* : paved or covered with cobblestones

cob·bler *n* **1** : a person who mends or makes shoes **2** : a fruit pie with a thick upper crust and no bottom crust that is baked in a deep dish

cob·ble·stone *n* : a rounded stone used especially in the past to pave streets

co·bra *n* : a very poisonous snake of Asia and Africa that puffs out the skin around its neck into a hood when threatened

cob·web *n* **1** : SPIDERWEB **2** : tangles of threads of old spiderwebs usually covered with dirt and dust

co·caine *n* : a habit-forming drug obtained from the leaves of a South American shrub and sometimes used as a medicine to deaden pain

coc·cus *n, pl* **coc·ci** : a bacterium shaped like a ball

co·chlea *n, pl* **co·chle·as** *or* **co·chle·ae** : a coiled tube in the inner part of the ear that contains the endings of the nerve which carries information about sound to the brain

[1]**cock** *n* **1** : a male bird : ROOSTER **2** : a faucet or valve for controlling the flow of a liquid or a gas

[2]**cock** *vb* **cocked; cock·ing** **1** : to turn or tip upward or to one side **2** : to set or draw back in readiness for some action **3** : to draw back the hammer of (a gun) in readiness for firing

[3]**cock** *n* : the act of tipping or turning at an angle : TILT

cock·a·too *n, pl* **cock·a·toos** : a large, noisy, and usually brightly colored crested parrot mostly of Australia

cock·eyed *adj* **1** : tilted to one side **2** : FOOLISH

cock·le *n* : an edible shellfish with a shell that has two parts and is shaped like a heart

cock·le·bur *n* : a plant with prickly fruit that is related to the thistles

cock·le·shell *n* : a shell of a cockle

cock·pit *n* **1** : an open space in the deck from which a small boat (as a yacht) is steered **2** : a space in an airplane for the pilot

cock·roach *n* : a black or brown insect that is active chiefly at night and can be a troublesome pest in homes

cocky *adj* **cock·i·er; cock·i·est** : very sure of oneself : boldly self-confident

co·coa *n* **1** : a brown powder that is made from the roasted seeds (**cocoa beans**) of the cacao tree after some of its fat is removed and that is used to make chocolate **2** : a hot drink made from cocoa powder mixed with water or milk

co·co·nut *n* : a large nutlike fruit that has a thick husk with white flesh and a watery liquid inside it and that grows on a tall tropical palm (**coconut palm**)

co·coon *n* : the silky covering which moth caterpillars make around themselves and in which they are protected while changing into a moth

cod *n, pl* **cod** : a large fish found in the deep colder parts of the northern Atlantic Ocean and often used for food

COD *abbr* **1** cash on delivery **2** collect on delivery

cod·dle *vb* **cod·dled; cod·dling** : to treat with too much care : PAMPER

[1]**code** *n* **1** : a system of rules or principles **2** : a system of signals or letters and symbols with special meanings used for sending messages **3** : a collection of laws **4** : GENETIC CODE **5** : a set of instructions for a computer

[2]**code** *vb* **cod·ed; cod·ing** : to put in the form of a code

cod·fish *n, pl* **codfish** *or* **cod·fish·es** : COD

cod·ger *n* : an odd or cranky man

co·erce *vb* **co·erced; co·erc·ing** : [2]FORCE 1, COMPEL

cof·fee *n* **1** : a drink made from the roasted and ground seeds (**coffee beans**) of a tropical plant **2** : the roasted seeds of the coffee plant when whole or ground

coffee table *n* : a low table usually placed in front of a sofa

cof·fer *n* : a box used especially for holding money and valuables

cof·fin *n* : a box or case to hold a dead body for burial

cog *n* : a tooth on the rim of a wheel or gear

cog·i·tate *vb* **cog·i·tat·ed; cog·i·tat·ing** : to think over : PONDER

cog·i·ta·tion *n* : careful consideration

cog·wheel *n* : a wheel with cogs on the rim

co·her·ent *adj* **1** : logical and well-organized **2** : able to speak well

co·he·sion *n* **1** : the action of sticking together **2** : the force of attraction between the molecules in a mass

[1]**coil** *n* **1** : a circle, a series of circles, or a spiral made by coiling **2** : a long thin piece of material that is wound into circles

[2]**coil** *vb* **coiled; coil·ing** **1** : to wind into rings or a spiral **2** : to form or lie in a coil

[1]**coin** *n* **1** : a piece of metal put out by government authority as money **2** : metal money

[2]**coin** *vb* **coined; coin·ing** **1** : to make coins especially by stamping pieces of metal : MINT **2** : to make metal (as gold or silver) into coins **3** : to make up (a new word or phrase)

coin·age *n* **1** : the act or process of making coins **2** : money in the form of coins **3** : a word or phrase that has recently been invented

co·in·cide *vb* **co·in·cid·ed; co·in·cid·ing** **1**

: to happen at the same time **2** : to agree exactly **3** : to occupy the same space

co·in·ci·dence *n* **1** : a situation in which things happen at the same time without planning **2** : a condition of coming together in space or time

coke *n* : gray lumps of fuel made by heating soft coal in a closed chamber until some of its gases have passed off

col. *abbr* column

Col. *abbr* **1** colonel **2** Colorado

col- — see COM-

co·la *n, pl* **co·las** : a sweet brown carbonated soft drink that contains flavoring from the nut of a tropical tree

col·an·der *n* : a bowl-shaped utensil with small holes for draining foods

[1]**cold** *adj* **cold·er; cold·est** **1** : having a low temperature or one much below normal **2** : suffering from lack of warmth **3** : cooled after being cooked **4** : served at a low temperature or with ice **5** : lacking warmth of feeling : UNFRIENDLY — **cold·ly** *adv* — **cold·ness** *n* — **in cold blood** : with planning beforehand

[2]**cold** *n* **1** : a condition of low temperature : cold weather **2** : the bodily feeling produced by lack of warmth : CHILL **3** : COMMON COLD

cold–blood·ed *adj* **1** : having a body temperature that varies with the temperature of the environment **2** : lacking or showing a lack of normal human feelings

cold cuts *n pl* : slices of cold cooked meats

cole·slaw *n* : a salad made with chopped raw cabbage

co·le·us *n* : a plant grown as a houseplant or a garden plant for its many-colored leaves

col·ic *n* **1** : sharp pain in the intestines **2** : a condition in which a healthy baby is uncomfortable and cries for long periods of time — **col·icky** *adj*

col·i·se·um *n* : a large structure (as a stadium) for athletic contests or public entertainment

col·lab·o·rate *vb* **col·lab·o·rat·ed; col·lab·o·rat·ing** **1** : to work with others (as in writing a book) **2** : to cooperate with an enemy force that has taken over a person's country

col·lage *n* : a work of art made by gluing pieces of different materials to a flat surface

[1]**col·lapse** *vb* **col·lapsed; col·laps·ing** **1** : to break down completely : fall in **2** : to completely relax **3** : to suffer a physical or mental breakdown **4** : to fail or stop working suddenly **5** : to fold together

[2]**collapse** *n* : the act or an instance of breaking down

col·laps·ible *adj* : capable of collapsing or possible to collapse

[1]**col·lar** *n* **1** : the part of a piece of clothing that fits around a person's neck **2** : a band of material worn around an animal's neck **3** : a ring used to hold something (as a pipe) in place — **col·lar·less** *adj*

[2]**collar** *vb* **col·lared; col·lar·ing** : to seize by or as if by the collar : CAPTURE, GRAB

col·lar·bone *n* : a bone of the shoulder joined to the breastbone and the shoulder blade

col·league *n* : an associate in a profession : a fellow worker

col·lect *vb* **col·lect·ed; col·lect·ing** **1** : to gather from a number of sources **2** : to receive payment for **3** : to bring or come together into one body or place **4** : to gain or regain control of **5** : to increase in amount **6** : to get and bring

col·lect·ed *adj* : [3]CALM 2

col·lect·ible *adj* : considered valuable by collectors — **collectible** *n*

col·lec·tion *n* **1** : the act or process of gathering together **2** : a group of things that have been gathered **3** : a group of objects gathered for study or exhibition or as a hobby **4** : the act of gathering money (as for charitable purposes) **5** : money gathered for a charitable purpose

col·lec·tive *adj* **1** : having to do with a number of persons or things thought of as a whole **2** : done or shared by a number of persons as a group — **col·lec·tive·ly** *adv*

col·lec·tor *n* **1** : a person or thing that collects **2** : a person whose business it is to collect money

col·lege *n* : a school that offers more advanced classes than a high school

col·le·giate *adj* **1** : having to do with a college **2** : of, relating to, or characteristic of college students

col·lide *vb* **col·lid·ed; col·lid·ing** **1** : to strike against each other with strong force **2** : [1]CLASH 2

col·lie *n* : a large usually long-haired dog of Scottish origin that has been used to herd sheep

col·li·sion *n* : an act or instance of colliding

col·lo·qui·al *adj* : used in or suited to familiar and informal conversation

col·lo·qui·al·ism *n* : a word or expression used in or suited to familiar and informal conversation

co·logne *n* : a perfumed liquid made up of alcohol and fragrant oils

[1]**co·lon** *n* : the main part of the large intestine

[2]**colon** *n* : a punctuation mark : used mostly to call attention to what follows (as a list, explanation, or quotation)

col·o·nel *n* : a commissioned officer in the army, air force, or marine corps ranking above a major and below a general

[1]**co·lo·nial** *adj* **1** : of, relating to, or charac-

teristic of a colony **2** *often cap* **:** of or relating to the original 13 colonies that formed the United States
[2]**colonial** *n* **:** a member of or a person living in a colony
col·o·nist *n* **1 :** a person living in a colony **2 :** a person who helps to found a colony
col·o·nize *vb* **col·o·nized; col·o·niz·ing 1 :** to establish a colony in or on **2 :** to settle in a colony
col·on·nade *n* **:** a row of columns usually supporting a roof
col·o·ny *n, pl* **col·o·nies 1 :** a distant territory belonging to or under the control of a nation **2 :** a group of people sent out by a government to a new territory **3 :** a group of living things of one kind living together **4 :** a group of people with common qualities or interests located in close association
[1]**col·or** *or Can and Brit* **colour** *n* **1 :** the appearance of a thing apart from size and shape when light strikes it **2 :** skin tone as a mark of race **3 :** the rosy tint of a light-skinned person's face **4 :** [2]BLUSH 1 **5** **colors** *or Can and Brit* **colours** *pl* **:** an identifying flag **6 :** [1]INTEREST 2
[2]**color** *or Can and Brit* **colour** *vb* **col·ored/coloured; col·or·ing/colouring 1 :** to give color to **2 :** to change the color of **3 :** to fill in the outlines of a shape or picture with color **4 :** to take on or change color **:** BLUSH **5 :** [2]INFLUENCE
col·or·ation *n* **:** use or arrangement of colors or shades **:** COLORING
col·or–blind *or Can and Brit* **colour–blind** *adj* **:** unable to see the difference between certain colors
col·ored *or Can and Brit* **coloured** *adj* **:** having color
col·or·ful *or Can and Brit* **colourful** *adj* **1 :** having bright colors **2 :** full of variety or interest
col·or·ing *or Can and Brit* **colouring** *n* **1 :** the act of applying colors **2 :** something that produces color **3 :** the effect produced by the use of color **4 :** natural color **5 :** COMPLEXION
coloring book *or Can and Brit* **colouring book** *n* **:** a book of drawings made in solid lines for coloring
col·or·less *or Can and Brit* **colourless** *adj* **1 :** having no color **2 :** WAN, PALE **3 :** [1]DULL 3
co·los·sal *adj* **:** very large **:** HUGE
col·our *Can and Brit spelling of* COLOR
colt *n* **:** a young male horse
col·um·bine *n* **:** a plant that has leaves with three parts and showy flowers usually with five petals that are thin and pointed
col·umn *n* **1 :** one of two or more vertical sections of a printed page **2 :** a group of items shown one under the other down a page **3 :** a regular feature in a newspaper or magazine **4 :** a pillar used to support a building **5 :** something that is tall or thin in shape or arrangement **6 :** a long straight row
col·um·nist *n* **:** a writer of a column in a newspaper or magazine
com *abbr* commercial organization
com- *or* **col-** *or* **con-** *prefix* **:** with **:** together **:** jointly — usually *com-* before *b, p,* or *m, col-* before *l* and *con-* before other sounds
co·ma *n* **:** a deep sleeplike state caused by sickness or injury
Co·man·che *n, pl* **Comanche** *or* **Co·man·ches 1 :** a member of an American Indian people ranging from Wyoming and Nebraska into New Mexico and northwestern Texas **2 :** the language of the Comanche people
[1]**comb** *n* **1 :** a toothed implement used to smooth and arrange the hair or worn in the hair to hold it in place **2 :** a soft fleshy part on top of the head of a chicken or some related birds **3 :** HONEYCOMB
[2]**comb** *vb* **combed; comb·ing 1 :** to smooth, arrange, or untangle with a comb **2 :** to search over or through carefully
[1]**com·bat** *n* **1 :** a fight or contest between individuals or groups **2 :** active military fighting
[2]**com·bat** *vb* **com·bat·ed** *or* **com·bat·ted; com·bat·ing** *or* **com·bat·ting :** to fight with **:** fight against **:** OPPOSE
com·bat·ant *n* **:** a person who takes part in a combat
com·bi·na·tion *n* **1 :** a result or product of combining or being combined **2 :** a series of numbers or letters that is used to open a lock
combination lock *n* **:** a lock with one or more dials or rings marked usually with numbers which are used to open the lock by moving them in a certain order to certain positions
[1]**com·bine** *vb* **com·bined; com·bin·ing 1 :** to mix together so as to make or to seem one thing **2 :** to be or cause to be together for a purpose
[2]**com·bine** *n* **1 :** a union of persons or groups that work together to achieve a common goal **2 :** a machine that harvests and threshes grain
com·bus·ti·ble *adj* **:** catching fire or burning easily
com·bus·tion *n* **:** the process of burning
come *vb* **came; come; com·ing 1 :** to move toward **:** APPROACH **2 :** to go or travel to a place **3 :** ORIGINATE 2, ARISE **4 :** to reach the point of being or becoming **5 :** to add

up : AMOUNT **6 :** to happen or occur **7 :** to be available **8 :** [1]REACH 3 — **come about** : HAPPEN 1 — **come across :** to meet or find by chance — **come along 1 :** to go somewhere with someone **2 :** to make progress **3 :** to appear or occur as a possibility — **come by 1 :** to make a visit to **2 :** ACQUIRE — **come down :** to fall sick — **come over :** to affect suddenly and strangely — **come to :** to become conscious again — **come upon :** to meet or find by chance

co·me·di·an *n* **1 :** a performer who makes people laugh **2 :** an amusing person

com·e·dy *n, pl* **com·e·dies 1 :** an amusing play that has a happy ending **2 :** an amusing and often ridiculous event

come·ly *adj* **come·li·er; come·li·est :** physically attractive

com·et *n* **:** a small bright celestial body that develops a cloudy tail as it moves in an orbit around the sun

[1]**com·fort** *vb* **com·fort·ed; com·fort·ing :** to ease the grief or trouble of

[2]**comfort** *n* **1 :** acts or words that bring relief from grief or trouble **2 :** the feeling of being cheered **3 :** something that makes a person comfortable

com·fort·able *adj* **1 :** giving physical ease **2 :** more than what is needed **3 :** physically at ease — **com·fort·ably** *adj*

com·fort·er *n* **1 :** a person or thing that gives relief to someone suffering grief or trouble **2 :** [1]QUILT

com·ic *adj* **1 :** of, relating to, or characteristic of comedy **2 :** [1]FUNNY 1

com·i·cal *adj* **:** [1]FUNNY 1, RIDICULOUS — **com·i·cal·ly** *adv*

comic book *n* **:** a magazine made up of a series of comic strips

comic strip *n* **:** a series of cartoons that tell a story or part of a story

com·ma *n* **:** a punctuation mark , used chiefly to show separation of words or word groups within a sentence

[1]**com·mand** *vb* **com·mand·ed; com·mand·ing 1 :** to order with authority **2 :** to have power or control over : be commander of **3 :** to demand as right or due : EXACT **4 :** to survey from a good position

[2]**command** *n* **1 :** an order given **2 :** the authority, right, or power to command : CONTROL **3 :** the ability to control and use : MASTERY **4 :** the people, area, or unit (as of soldiers and weapons) under a commander **5 :** a position from which military operations are directed

com·man·dant *n* **:** an officer who is in charge of a group of soldiers

com·mand·er *n* **:** a commissioned officer in the navy or coast guard ranking above a lieutenant and below a captain

commander in chief *n, pl* **commanders in chief :** a person who holds supreme command of the armed forces of a nation

com·mand·ment *n* **1 :** something given as a command **2 :** one of ten rules given by God that are mentioned in the Bible

com·man·do *n, pl* **com·man·dos** *or* **com·man·does 1 :** a unit of troops trained for making surprise raids into enemy territory **2 :** a member of a commando

command sergeant major *n* **:** a noncommissioned officer in the army ranking above a first sergeant

com·mem·o·rate *vb* **com·mem·o·rat·ed; com·mem·o·rat·ing 1 :** to observe with a ceremony **2 :** to serve as a memorial of

com·mem·o·ra·tion *n* **1 :** the act of commemorating **2 :** something (as a ceremony) that commemorates

com·mence *vb* **com·menced; com·menc·ing :** BEGIN 1, START

com·mence·ment *n* **1 :** graduation exercises **2 :** the act or the time of beginning

com·mend *vb* **com·mend·ed; com·mend·ing 1 :** to give into another's care : ENTRUST **2 :** to speak or write of with approval : PRAISE

com·mend·able *adj* **:** deserving praise or approval

com·men·da·tion *n* **1 :** [2]PRAISE 1, APPROVAL **2 :** an expression of approval

[1]**com·ment** *n* **1 :** an expression of opinion either in speech or writing **2 :** mention of something that deserves notice

[2]**comment** *vb* **com·ment·ed; com·ment·ing :** to make a statement about someone or something : make a comment

com·men·ta·tor *n* **:** a person who describes or analyzes a news, sports, or entertainment event (as over radio or on television)

com·merce *n* **:** the buying and selling of goods especially on a large scale and between different places : TRADE

[1]**com·mer·cial** *n* **:** an advertisement broadcast on radio or television

[2]**commercial** *adj* **1 :** having to do with the buying and selling of goods and services **2 :** used to earn a profit — **com·mer·cial·ly** *adv*

com·mer·cial·ize *vb* **com·mer·cial·ized; com·mer·cial·iz·ing :** to handle with the idea of making a profit

[1]**com·mis·sion** *n* **1 :** an order granting the power to perform various acts or duties : the right or duty to be performed **2 :** a certificate that gives military or naval rank and authority : the rank and authority given **3 :** authority to act as agent for another : a

task or piece of business entrusted to an agent **4 :** a group of persons given orders and authority to perform specified duties **5 :** an act of doing something wrong **6 :** a fee paid to an agent for taking care of a piece of business

[2]**commission** *vb* **com·mis·sioned; com·mis·sion·ing 1 :** to give a commission to **2 :** to put (a ship) into service

commissioned officer *n* **:** an officer in the armed forces who ranks above the enlisted persons or warrant officers and who is appointed by the President

com·mis·sion·er *n* **1 :** a member of a commission **2 :** an official who is the head of a government department

com·mit *vb* **com·mit·ted; com·mit·ting 1 :** to bring about **:** PERFORM **2 :** to make secure or put in safekeeping **:** ENTRUST **3 :** to place in or send to a prison or mental hospital **4 :** to pledge to do some particular thing — **com·mit·ment** *n*

com·mit·tee *n* **:** a group of persons appointed or elected to study a problem, plan an event, or perform a specific duty

com·mod·i·ty *n, pl* **com·mod·i·ties :** something produced by agriculture, mining, or manufacture

com·mo·dore *n* **:** an officer of high rank in the navy

[1]**com·mon** *adj* **1 :** affecting, belonging to, needed by, or used by everybody **2 :** shared by two or more individuals or by the members of a family or group **3 :** [1]GENERAL 1 **4 :** occurring, appearing, or used frequently **5 :** not above the average in rank or status **6 :** not privileged or elite **7 :** expected from polite and decent people — **in common :** shared together

[2]**common** *n* **:** land (as a park) owned and used by a community

common cold *n* **:** a contagious illness which causes the lining of the nose and throat to be sore, swollen, and red and in which there is usually much mucus and coughing and sneezing

common denominator *n* **:** a common multiple of the denominators of a number of fractions

com·mon·er *n* **:** a person who is not privileged or high in social status

common multiple *n* **:** a multiple of each of two or more numbers

common noun *n* **:** a noun that names a class of persons or things or any individual of a class and that may occur with a limiting modifier (as *a*, *the*, *some*, or *every*)

[1]**com·mon·place** *adj* **:** often seen or met with **:** ORDINARY

[2]**commonplace** *n* **:** something that is often seen or met with

common sense *n* **:** ordinary good sense and judgment — **com·mon·sense** *adj*

com·mon·wealth *n* **1 :** a political unit (as a nation or state) **2 :** one of four states of the United States — Kentucky, Massachusetts, Pennsylvania, or Virginia

com·mo·tion *n* **:** noisy excitement and confusion **:** TURMOIL

com·mune *vb* **com·muned; com·mun·ing :** to be in close accord or communication with someone or something

com·mu·ni·ca·ble *adj* **:** able to be passed to another person

com·mu·ni·cate *vb* **com·mu·ni·cat·ed; com·mu·ni·cat·ing 1 :** to get in touch **2 :** to make known **3 :** to pass (as a disease) from one to another **:** SPREAD

com·mu·ni·ca·tion *n* **1 :** the exchange (as by speech or letter) of information between persons **2 :** information exchanged **3 communications** *pl* **:** a system of sending information **4 communications** *pl* **:** a system of routes for transportation

com·mu·nion *n* **1 :** a close relationship **2** *cap* **:** a Christian ceremony commemorating with bread and wine the last supper of Jesus Christ **3 :** a body of Christians having similar beliefs

com·mu·nism *n* **:** a social system or theory in which property and goods are held in common

com·mu·nist *n* **:** a person who supports communism

com·mu·ni·ty *n, pl* **com·mu·ni·ties 1 :** the people living in a certain place (as a village or city) **:** the area itself **2 :** a natural group (as of kinds of plants and animals) living together and depending on one another for various necessities of life (as food or shelter) **3 :** a group of people with common interests **4 :** a feeling of caring about others in a group

com·mu·ta·tive *adj* **:** being a property of a mathematical operation (as addition or multiplication) in which the result does not depend on the order of the elements

com·mute *vb* **com·mut·ed; com·mut·ing 1 :** to travel back and forth regularly **2 :** to change (as a penalty) to something less severe — **com·mut·er** *n*

[1]**com·pact** *adj* **1 :** closely united or packed **2 :** arranged so as to save space — **com·pact·ly** *adv* — **com·pact·ness** *n*

[2]**compact** *vb* **com·pact·ed; com·pact·ing 1 :** to draw together **:** COMBINE **2 :** to press together tightly

[3]**com·pact** *n* **1 :** a small case for cosmetics **2 :** a somewhat small automobile

[4]**com·pact** *n* **:** AGREEMENT 3

compact disc *n* **:** CD

com·pan·ion *n* **1 :** a person or thing that accompanies another **2 :** one of a pair of things that go together **3 :** a person employed to live with and assist another

com·pan·ion·ship *n* **:** FELLOWSHIP 1, COMPANY

com·pa·ny *n, pl* **com·pa·nies 1 :** an association of persons operating a business **2 :** the presence of someone who brings comfort **3 :** a person or thing someone enjoys being with **4 :** a person's companions or associates **5 :** guests or visitors especially at a person's home **6 :** a group of persons or things **7 :** a body of soldiers **8 :** a band of musical or dramatic performers

com·pa·ra·ble *adj* **:** being similar or about the same

[1]**com·par·a·tive** *adj* **1 :** not entirely but more so than others **:** RELATIVE **2 :** of or relating to the form of an adjective or adverb that shows an increase in the quality that the adjective or adverb expresses — **com·par·a·tive·ly** *adv*

[2]**comparative** *n* **:** the degree or form in a language that indicates an increase in the quality expressed by an adjective or adverb

com·pare *vb* **com·pared; com·par·ing 1 :** to point out as similar **:** LIKEN **2 :** to examine for similarity or differences **3 :** to appear in relation to others **4 :** to state the positive, comparative, and superlative forms of an adjective or adverb

com·par·i·son *n* **1 :** the act of examining things to see if they are similar or different **:** the condition of being examined to find similarity or difference **2 :** SIMILARITY **3 :** change in the form and meaning of an adjective or an adverb (as by adding *-er* or *-est* to the word or by adding *more* or *most* before the word) to show different levels of quality, quantity, or relation

com·part·ment *n* **1 :** a small chamber, receptacle, or container **2 :** one of the separate areas of a train, airplane, or automobile

com·pass *n* **1 :** a device having a magnetic needle that indicates direction on the earth's surface by pointing toward the north **2 :** an instrument for drawing circles or marking measurements consisting of two pointed legs joined at the top by a pivot — usually used in pl. **3 :** [1]RANGE 2, SCOPE

com·pas·sion *n* **:** pity for and a desire to help someone

com·pas·sion·ate *adj* **:** having or showing pity for and desire to help someone

com·pat·i·ble *adj* **:** capable of existing together in harmony

com·pa·tri·ot *n* **:** a person from the same country as someone else

com·pel *vb* **com·pelled; com·pel·ling 1 :** to make (as a person) do something by the use of physical, moral, or mental pressure **:** FORCE **2 :** to make happen by force

com·pen·sate *vb* **com·pen·sat·ed; com·pen·sat·ing 1 :** to make up for **2 :** to give money to make up for something

com·pen·sa·tion *n* **1 :** something that makes up for or is given to make up for something else **2 :** money paid regularly

com·pete *vb* **com·pet·ed; com·pet·ing :** to strive for something (as a prize or a reward) for which another is also striving

com·pe·tence *n* **:** the quality or state of being capable

com·pe·tent *adj* **:** CAPABLE 2, EFFICIENT — **com·pe·tent·ly** *adv*

com·pe·ti·tion *n* **1 :** the act or process of trying to get or win something others are also trying to get or win **2 :** a contest in which all who take part strive for the same thing **3 :** all of a person's competitors

com·pet·i·tive *adj* **:** characterized by or based on a situation in which more than one person is striving for the same thing

com·pet·i·tor *n* **:** someone or something that is trying to beat or do better than others in a contest or in the selling of goods or services **:** RIVAL

com·pile *vb* **com·piled; com·pil·ing 1 :** to create by gathering things together **2 :** to put things together in a publication or collection

com·pla·cen·cy *n* **:** a feeling of being satisfied with the way things are and not wanting to make them better

com·pla·cent *adj* **:** feeling or showing satisfaction and lack of worry or caution

com·plain *vb* **com·plained; com·plain·ing :** to express grief, pain, or discontent **:** find fault — **com·plain·er** *n*

com·plaint *n* **1 :** expression of grief, pain, or discontent **2 :** a cause or reason for expressing grief, pain, or discontent **3 :** a sickness or disease of the body **4 :** a charge of wrongdoing against a person

[1]**com·ple·ment** *n* **1 :** something that makes whole or better **2 :** the number or quantity of something that is needed or used

[2]**com·ple·ment** *vb* **com·ple·ment·ed; com·ple·ment·ing :** to serve as something necessary to make whole or better

com·ple·men·ta·ry *adj* **:** serving to make whole or improve something

[1]**com·plete** *adj* **1 :** having all necessary parts **:** not lacking anything **2 :** entirely done **3 :** THOROUGH 1 — **com·plete·ness** *n*

[2]**complete** *vb* **com·plet·ed; com·plet·ing 1 :** to bring to an end **:** FINISH **2 :** to make whole or perfect

com·plete·ly *adv* **:** as much as possible **:** in every way or detail

com·ple·tion *n* **:** the act or process of making whole or finishing **:** the condition of being whole or finished

com·plex *adj* **1 :** not easy to understand or explain **:** not simple **2 :** having parts that go together in complicated ways

complex fraction *n* **:** a fraction with a fraction or mixed number in the numerator or denominator or both

com·plex·ion *n* **:** the color or appearance of the skin and especially of the face

com·plex·i·ty *n, pl* **com·plex·i·ties 1 :** the quality or condition of being difficult to understand or of lacking simplicity **2 :** something difficult to understand or lacking simplicity

com·pli·cate *vb* **com·pli·cat·ed; com·pli·cat·ing :** to make or become difficult or lacking in simplicity

com·pli·cat·ed *adj* **:** difficult to understand or explain

com·pli·ca·tion *n* **:** something that makes a situation more difficult

¹com·pli·ment *n* **1 :** an act or expression of praise, approval, respect, or admiration **2 compliments** *pl* **:** best wishes

²com·pli·ment *vb* **com·pli·ment·ed; com·pli·ment·ing :** to express praise, approval, respect, or admiration to

com·pli·men·ta·ry *adj* **1 :** expressing or containing praise, approval, respect, or admiration **2 :** given free as a courtesy or favor

com·ply *vb* **com·plied; com·ply·ing :** to act in agreement with another's wishes or in obedience to a rule

com·po·nent *n* **:** one of the parts or units of a combination, mixture, or system

com·pose *vb* **com·posed; com·pos·ing 1 :** to form by putting together **2 :** to be the parts or materials of **3 :** to create and write **4 :** to make calm **:** get under control

com·posed *adj* **:** being calm and in control emotionally

com·pos·er *n* **:** a writer of music

com·pos·ite *adj* **:** made up of different parts or elements

composite number *n* **:** an integer that is a product of two or more whole numbers each greater than 1

com·po·si·tion *n* **1 :** a short piece of writing done as a school exercise **2 :** the act of writing words or music **3 :** the manner in which the parts of a thing are put together **:** MAKEUP, CONSTITUTION **4 :** a literary, musical, or artistic production

com·post *n* **:** decayed organic material (as of leaves and grass) used to improve soil especially for growing crops

com·po·sure *n* **:** calmness especially of mind, manner, or appearance

¹com·pound *vb* **com·pound·ed; com·pound·ing 1 :** to form by combining separate things **2 :** to make worse **3 :** to pay (interest) on both an original amount of money and on the interest it has already earned

²com·pound *adj* **:** made of or by the union of two or more parts

³com·pound *n* **1 :** a word made up of parts that are themselves words **2 :** something (as a chemical) that is formed by combining two or more parts or elements

⁴com·pound *n* **:** an enclosed area containing a group of buildings

com·pre·hend *vb* **com·pre·hend·ed; com·pre·hend·ing 1 :** to understand fully **2 :** to take in **:** INCLUDE

com·pre·hen·sion *n* **:** ability to understand

com·pre·hen·sive *adj* **:** including much **:** INCLUSIVE

¹com·press *vb* **com·pressed; com·press·ing 1 :** to press or squeeze together **2 :** to reduce in size, quantity, or volume by or as if by pressure

²com·press *n* **:** a pad (as of folded cloth) applied firmly to a part of the body (as to stop bleeding)

com·pres·sion *n* **:** the act, process, or result of pressing something together

com·pres·sor *n* **:** a machine for reducing the volume of something (as air) by pressure

com·prise *vb* **com·prised; com·pris·ing 1 :** to be made up of **:** consist of **2 :** ²FORM 3

¹com·pro·mise *n* **1 :** an agreement over a dispute reached by each side changing or giving up some demands **2 :** something agreed upon as a result of each side changing or giving up some demands

²compromise *vb* **com·pro·mised; com·pro·mis·ing 1 :** to settle by agreeing that each side will change or give up some demands **2 :** to expose to risk, suspicion, or disgrace

com·pul·sion *n* **1 :** a very strong urge to do something **2 :** a force that makes someone do something **3 :** an act or the state of forcing an action

com·pul·so·ry *adj* **1 :** required by or as if by law **2 :** having the power of forcing someone to do something

com·pu·ta·tion *n* **1 :** the act or action of determining by use of mathematics **2 :** a result obtained by using mathematics

com·pute *vb* **com·put·ed; com·put·ing :** to find out by using mathematics

com·put·er *n* **:** an automatic electronic machine that can store and process data

com·put·er·ize *vb* **com·put·er·ized; com·put·er·iz·ing 1 :** to carry out, control, or produce on a computer **2 :** to equip with computers **3 :** to put in a form that a computer can use

com·rade *n* : COMPANION 1

¹con *adv* : on the negative side

²con *n* : an opposing argument, person, or position

con- — see COM-

con·cave *adj* : hollow or rounded inward like the inside of a bowl

con·ceal *vb* **con·cealed; con·ceal·ing** **1** : to hide from sight **2** : to keep secret

con·ceal·ment *n* **1** : the act of hiding : the state of being hidden **2** : a hiding place

con·cede *vb* **con·ced·ed; con·ced·ing** **1** : to admit to be true **2** : to grant or yield usually unwillingly

con·ceit *n* : too much pride in a person's own abilities or qualities : excessive self-esteem

con·ceit·ed *adj* : VAIN 2

con·ceiv·able *adj* : possible to imagine or understand

con·ceive *vb* **con·ceived; con·ceiv·ing** **1** : to form an idea of : IMAGINE **2** : THINK 2

con·cen·trate *vb* **con·cen·trat·ed; con·cen·trat·ing** **1** : to focus thought or attention on something **2** : to bring or come to or direct toward a common center **3** : to make stronger or thicker by removing something (as water)

con·cen·tra·tion *n* **1** : close attention to or thought about a subject **2** : the ability to pay close attention **3** : a large amount of something or a large number of people in one place

con·cept *n* : something thought of : a general idea

¹con·cern *vb* **con·cerned; con·cern·ing** **1** : to relate to : be about **2** : to be of interest or importance to : AFFECT **3** : to make worried **4** : ENGAGE 2, OCCUPY

²concern *n* **1** : a feeling of worry or care about a person or thing **2** : something that causes worry or is regarded as important **3** : something that relates to or involves a person : AFFAIR **4** : a business organization

con·cerned *adj* : feeling interest and worry

con·cern·ing *prep* : relating to : ABOUT

con·cert *n* : a musical performance by several voices or instruments or by both — **in concert** : TOGETHER 5

con·cer·ti·na *n* : a small musical instrument like an accordion

con·cer·to *n, pl* **con·cer·tos** : a musical composition usually in three parts for orchestra with one or more principal instruments

con·ces·sion *n* **1** : the act or an instance of giving up or admitting something **2** : something given up **3** : a right to engage in business given by an authority **4** : a small business where things are sold (as at a sports facility or public place)

conch *n, pl* **conchs** *or* **conch·es** : a very large sea snail with a tall thick spiral shell

con·cil·i·ate *vb* **con·cil·i·at·ed; con·cil·i·at·ing** **1** : to bring into agreement : RECONCILE **2** : to gain or regain the goodwill or favor of — **con·cil·ia·to·ry** *adj*

con·cise *adj* : expressing much in few words

con·clude *vb* **con·clud·ed; con·clud·ing** **1** : to bring or come to an end : FINISH **2** : to decide after a period of thought or research **3** : to bring about as a result

con·clu·sion *n* **1** : final decision reached by reasoning **2** : the last part of something **3** : a final settlement

con·clu·sive *adj* : DECISIVE 1 — **con·clu·sive·ly** *adv*

con·coct *vb* **con·coct·ed; con·coct·ing** **1** : to prepare (as food) by putting several different things together **2** : to make up : DEVISE

con·cord *n* : a state of agreement

con·course *n* **1** : a flocking, moving, or flowing together (as of persons or streams) : GATHERING **2** : an open space or hall (as in a mall or airport)

¹con·crete *adj* **1** : made of or relating to concrete **2** : being specific and useful **3** : being real and useful

²con·crete *n* : a hardened mixture of cement, sand, and water with gravel or broken stone used in construction

con·cur *vb* **con·curred; con·cur·ring** **1** : to act or happen together **2** : to be in agreement (as in action or opinion) : ACCORD

con·cus·sion *n* : injury to the brain caused by a hard hit on the head

con·demn *vb* **con·demned; con·demn·ing** **1** : to cause to suffer or live in difficult or unpleasant conditions **2** : to sentence to a usually severe punishment **3** : to declare to be wrong **4** : to declare to be unfit for use

con·dem·na·tion *n* **1** : CRITICISM 1, DISAPPROVAL **2** : the act of condemning or state of being condemned

con·den·sa·tion *n* **1** : the act or process of making more compact or concise **2** : something that has been made more compact or concise **3** : the conversion of a vapor to a liquid (as by cooling)

con·dense *vb* **con·densed; con·dens·ing** **1** : to make or become more compact or concise **2** : to change or cause to change from a vapor to a liquid (as by cooling)

con·de·scend *vb* **con·de·scend·ed; con·de·scend·ing** **1** : to stoop to the level of someone considered less important **2** : to grant favors with a show of being better than others

con·di·ment *n* : something added to food to make it taste better

¹con·di·tion *n* **1** : state of physical fitness

or readiness for use **2 :** something agreed upon or necessary if some other thing is to take place **3 conditions** *pl* **:** the way things are at a certain time or in a certain place **4 :** state of being **5 :** situation in life

[2]**condition** *vb* **con·di·tioned; con·di·tion·ing 1 :** to put into the proper or desired state **2 :** to change the habits of usually by training

con·di·tion·al *adj* **:** of or relating to something that will happen only if something else happens

con·do *n, pl* **con·dos :** CONDOMINIUM

con·do·min·i·um *n* **:** an individually owned unit in a building with many units

con·dor *n* **:** a very large American vulture having a bare head and neck and a frill of feathers on the neck

[1]**con·duct** *vb* **con·duct·ed; con·duct·ing 1 :** to plan and put into operation from a position of command **:** LEAD **2 :** [2]GUIDE 1 **3 :** BEHAVE 1 **4 :** to direct the performance of (musicians or singers) **5 :** to have the quality of transmitting light, heat, sound, or electricity

[2]**con·duct** *n* **1 :** personal behavior **2 :** the act or way of managing something

con·duc·tion *n* **1 :** the act of transporting something **2 :** transmission through a conductor

con·duc·tor *n* **1 :** a person in charge of a public means of transportation (as a train) **2 :** a person or thing that directs or leads **3 :** a substance or body capable of transmitting light, electricity, heat, or sound

cone *n* **1 :** a thin crisp cookie shaped to hold ice cream **2 :** a scaly structure of certain trees (as the pine or fir) that produces pollen or egg cells and seeds **3 :** a shape with a circular base and sides that taper evenly to a point **4 :** a cell of the retina of the eye that is sensitive to colored light

con·fec·tion *n* **:** a very fancy and usually sweet food

con·fec·tion·er *n* **:** a maker of or dealer in sweet foods (as candies)

con·fed·er·a·cy *n, pl* **con·fed·er·a·cies 1 :** a league of persons, parties, or states **2** *cap* **:** the eleven southern states that seceded from the United States in 1860 and 1861 to form their own government

[1]**con·fed·er·ate** *adj* **1 :** united in a league **2** *cap* **:** of or relating to the southern Confederacy

[2]**confederate** *n* **1 :** a member of a league of persons, parties, or states **2 :** ACCOMPLICE **3** *cap* **:** a soldier of or a person who sided with the southern Confederacy

con·fer *vb* **con·ferred; con·fer·ring 1 :** BESTOW, PRESENT **2 :** to compare views especially in studying a problem

con·fer·ence *n* **:** a meeting for discussion or exchange of opinions

con·fess *vb* **con·fessed; con·fess·ing 1 :** to tell of doing something wrong or illegal or of something embarrassing **:** ADMIT **2 :** to admit committing sins to God or to a priest

con·fes·sion *n* **1 :** an act of telling of sins or wrong, illegal, or embarrassing acts **2 :** a written or spoken admission of guilt of a crime

con·fet·ti *n* **:** small bits of brightly colored paper made for throwing at celebrations

con·fide *vb* **con·fid·ed; con·fid·ing 1 :** to have or show faith **2 :** to display trust by telling secrets **3 :** to tell without anyone else knowing **4 :** ENTRUST 2

con·fi·dence *n* **1 :** a feeling of trust or belief **2 :** SELF-CONFIDENCE **3 :** reliance on another's secrecy or loyalty **4 :** [2]SECRET

con·fi·dent *adj* **:** having or showing sureness and optimism — **con·fi·dent·ly** *adv*

con·fi·den·tial *adj* **1 :** [1]SECRET 1 **2 :** indicating a need for secrecy **3 :** trusted with secret matters — **con·fi·den·tial·ly** *adv*

con·fine *vb* **con·fined; con·fin·ing 1 :** to keep within limits **2 :** to shut up **:** IMPRISON **3 :** to keep indoors — **con·fine·ment** *n*

con·fines *n pl* **:** the boundary or limits of something

con·firm *vb* **con·firmed; con·firm·ing 1 :** to make sure of the truth of **2 :** to make firm or firmer (as in a habit, in faith, or in intention) **:** STRENGTHEN **3 :** APPROVE 2, ACCEPT **4 :** to perform a ceremony admitting a person into a church or synagogue

con·fir·ma·tion *n* **1 :** an act of ensuring the truth of, strengthening, or approving **2 :** a religious ceremony admitting a person to full privileges in a church or synagogue **3 :** something that ensures the truth of, strengthens, or approves

con·firmed *adj* **:** unlikely to change

con·fis·cate *vb* **con·fis·cat·ed; con·fis·cat·ing :** to seize by or as if by public authority — **con·fis·ca·tion** *n*

con·fla·gra·tion *n* **:** a large destructive fire

[1]**con·flict** *n* **1 :** an extended struggle **:** BATTLE **2 :** a clashing disagreement (as between ideas or interests)

[2]**con·flict** *vb* **con·flict·ed; con·flict·ing :** to be in opposition

con·form *vb* **con·formed; con·form·ing 1 :** to make or be like **:** AGREE, ACCORD **2 :** COMPLY

con·for·mi·ty *n, pl* **con·for·mi·ties 1 :** agreement in form, manner, or character **2 :** action in accordance with some standard or authority

con·found *vb* **con·found·ed; con·found·ing :** CONFUSE 1

con·front *vb* **con·front·ed; con·front·ing 1** : to face especially in challenge : OPPOSE **2** : to cause to face or meet — **con·fron·ta·tion** *n*

con·fuse *vb* **con·fused; con·fus·ing 1** : to make uncertain or unable to understand : PERPLEX **2** : to fail to tell apart

con·fu·sion *n* **1** : difficulty in understanding or in being able to tell one thing from a similar thing **2** : a feeling or state of uncertainty

con·geal *vb* **con·gealed; con·geal·ing 1** : to change from a fluid to a solid state by or as if by cold : FREEZE **2** : to make or become hard, stiff, or thick

con·ge·nial *adj* **1** : alike or sympathetic in nature, disposition, or tastes **2** : existing together in harmony **3** : tending to please or satisfy **4** : FRIENDLY 1

con·gest *vb* **con·gest·ed; con·gest·ing** : to make too crowded or full : CLOG

con·gest·ed *adj* : blocked or clogged with fluid and especially mucus

con·glom·er·ate *n* **1** : a mass (as a rock) formed of fragments from various sources **2** : a corporation engaging in many different kinds of business

con·grat·u·late *vb* **con·grat·u·lat·ed; con·grat·u·lat·ing** : to express pleasure on account of success or good fortune — **con·grat·u·la·to·ry** *adj*

con·grat·u·la·tion *n* **1** : the act of expressing pleasure at another person's success or good fortune **2** : an expression of pleasure at another person's success or good fortune — usually used in pl.

con·gre·gate *vb* **con·gre·gat·ed; con·gre·gat·ing** : to collect or gather into a crowd or group : ASSEMBLE

con·gre·ga·tion *n* **1** : an assembly of persons gathered for religious worship **2** : a gathering or collection of people or things **3** : the membership of a church or synagogue

con·gress *n* **1** : the chief lawmaking body of a republic that in the United States is made up of the Senate and the House of Representatives **2** : a formal meeting of delegates for discussion and action : CONFERENCE — **con·gres·sio·nal** *adj*

con·gress·man *n, pl* **con·gress·men** : a member of a congress and especially of the United States House of Representatives

con·gress·wom·an *n, pl* **con·gress·wom·en** : a woman member of a congress and especially of the United States House of Representatives

con·gru·ent *adj* : having the same size and shape

con·i·cal *adj* : shaped like a cone

co·ni·fer *n* : any of a group of mostly evergreen trees and shrubs (as pines) that typically produce cones and have leaves resembling needles or scales in shape — **co·nif·er·ous** *adj*

conj *abbr* conjunction

[1]**con·jec·ture** *n* : [2]GUESS

[2]**conjecture** *vb* **con·jec·tured; con·jec·tur·ing** : [1]GUESS 1, SURMISE

con·ju·gate *vb* **con·ju·gat·ed; con·ju·gat·ing** : to give the various forms of a verb in order — **con·ju·ga·tion** *n*

con·junc·tion *n* **1** : a joining together : UNION **2** : a word or expression that joins together sentences, clauses, phrases, or words

con·jure *vb* **con·jured; con·jur·ing 1** : to practice magical arts **2** : IMAGINE 1 **3** : to produce by or as if by magic

Conn. *abbr* Connecticut

con·nect *vb* **con·nect·ed; con·nect·ing 1** : to join or link together **2** : to have something to do with **3** : to bring together in thought — **con·nec·tor** *n*

con·nec·tion *n* **1** : the act of linking together **2** : the fact or condition of having a link : RELATIONSHIP **3** : a thing that links **4** : a person having a relationship with another by kinship, friendship, or common interest **5** : a social, professional, or commercial relationship **6** : the act or the means of continuing a journey by transferring (as to another train)

con·nois·seur *n* : a person qualified to act as a judge in matters involving taste and appreciation

con·quer *vb* **con·quered; con·quer·ing 1** : to get or gain by force : win by fighting **2** : OVERCOME 1

con·quer·or *n* : a person who gains something by force

con·quest *n* **1** : the act or process of getting or gaining especially by force **2** : something that is gotten or gained especially by force

con·quis·ta·dor *n, pl* **con·quis·ta·do·res** *or* **con·quis·ta·dors** : a leader in the Spanish conquest especially of Mexico and Peru in the 16th century

con·science *n* : a sense of right and wrong and a feeling that what is right should be done

con·sci·en·tious *adj* **1** : guided by or agreeing with a sense of doing what is right **2** : using or done with care

con·scious *adj* **1** : aware of facts, feelings, or some particular condition or situation **2** : known or felt by a person's inner self **3** : mentally awake or active **4** : INTENTIONAL — **con·scious·ly** *adv*

con·scious·ness *n* **1** : the condition of being mentally awake and active **2** : the part of the mind involving thought and awareness **3 :** knowledge of something specified

con·se·crate *vb* **con·se·crat·ed; con·se·crat·ing :** to declare to be sacred or holy **:** set apart for a sacred purpose

con·sec·u·tive *adj* **:** following one another in order without gaps

¹con·sent *vb* **con·sent·ed; con·sent·ing :** to express willingness or approval **:** AGREE

²consent *n* **:** approval of or agreement with what is done or suggested by another person

con·se·quence *n* **1 :** something produced by a cause or following from a condition **2 :** real importance

con·se·quent *adj* **:** following as a result or effect

con·se·quent·ly *adv* **:** as a result

con·ser·va·tion *n* **:** planned management of something (as natural resources or historic places) to prevent waste, destruction, damage, or neglect

¹con·ser·va·tive *adj* **1 :** favoring a policy of keeping things as they are **:** opposed to change **2 :** favoring established styles and standards **3 :** likely to be lower than what the real amount or number is — **con·ser·va·tive·ly** *adv*

²conservative *n* **:** a person who is opposed to change **:** a cautious person

con·ser·va·to·ry *n, pl* **con·ser·va·to·ries 1 :** a place of instruction in some special study (as music) **2 :** GREENHOUSE

¹con·serve *vb* **con·served; con·serv·ing 1 :** to prevent the waste of **2 :** to keep in a safe condition **:** SAVE

²con·serve *n* **:** a rich fruit preserve

con·sid·er *vb* **con·sid·ered; con·sid·er·ing 1 :** to think over carefully **:** PONDER, REFLECT **2 :** to treat in a kind or thoughtful way **3 :** to think of in a certain way **:** BELIEVE

con·sid·er·able *adj* **:** rather large in extent, amount, or size — **con·sid·er·ably** *adv*

con·sid·er·ate *adj* **:** thoughtful of the rights and feelings of others

con·sid·er·ation *n* **1 :** careful thought **:** DELIBERATION **2 :** thoughtfulness for other people **3 :** something that needs to be thought over carefully before deciding or acting **4 :** a payment made in return for something

con·sid·er·ing *prep* **:** taking into account

con·sign *vb* **con·signed; con·sign·ing 1 :** to send (as goods) to an agent to be sold or cared for **2 :** to put (something) in a place to store it or get rid of it — **con·sign·ment** *n*

con·sist *vb* **con·sist·ed; con·sist·ing :** to be made up or composed

con·sis·ten·cy *n, pl* **con·sis·ten·cies 1 :** degree of compactness, firmness, or stickiness **2 :** agreement or harmony between parts or elements **3 :** a pattern of sticking with one way of thinking or acting

con·sis·tent *adj* **1 :** always the same **2 :** being in harmony — **con·sis·tent·ly** *adv*

con·so·la·tion *n* **1 :** something that lessens disappointment, misery, or grief **2 :** the act of comforting or the state of being comforted

¹con·sole *vb* **con·soled; con·sol·ing :** to comfort in a time of grief or distress

²con·sole *n* **1 :** a panel on which are dials and switches for controlling an electronic or mechanical device **2 :** a cabinet (as for a television) that stands on the floor **3 :** the part of an organ at which the organist sits and which contains the keyboard and controls

con·sol·i·date *vb* **con·sol·i·dat·ed; con·sol·i·dat·ing 1 :** to join together into one whole **:** UNITE **2 :** STRENGTHEN

con·so·nant *n* **1 :** a letter in the English alphabet other than *a, e, i, o,* or *u* **2 :** a speech sound (as \p\, \n\, or \s\) produced by partly or completely stopping the flow of air breathed out of the mouth

¹con·sort *n* **:** a wife or husband especially of a king or queen

²con·sort *vb* **con·sort·ed; con·sort·ing :** to spend time with as a companion **:** ASSOCIATE

con·spic·u·ous *adj* **1 :** easily seen **2 :** attracting attention **:** PROMINENT — **con·spic·u·ous·ly** *adv*

con·spir·a·cy *n, pl* **con·spir·a·cies 1 :** a secret agreement to do something harmful or unlawful **2 :** the act of plotting with others to do something harmful or unlawful **3 :** a group of people plotting to do something unlawful

con·spir·a·tor *n* **:** a person who plots with others to do something harmful or unlawful

con·spire *vb* **con·spired; con·spir·ing 1 :** to make an agreement with others especially in secret to do an unlawful act **2 :** to act together

con·sta·ble *n* **:** a police officer usually of a village or small town

con·stan·cy *n* **:** firmness and loyalty in beliefs or personal relationships

con·stant *adj* **1 :** remaining steady and unchanged **2 :** occurring continuously or following one after another **3 :** always faithful and true — **con·stant·ly** *adv*

con·stel·la·tion *n* **:** any of 88 named groups of stars forming patterns

con·ster·na·tion *n* **:** amazement, alarm, or disappointment that results in a feeling of helplessness or confusion

con·sti·pa·tion *n* **:** difficult or infrequent passage of dry hard material from the bowels

[1]con·stit·u·ent *n* **1 :** one of the parts or materials of which something is made **:** ELEMENT, INGREDIENT **2 :** any of the voters who elect a person to represent them

[2]constituent *adj* **:** forming part of a whole

con·sti·tute *vb* **con·sti·tut·ed; con·sti·tut·ing** **1 :** to form the whole of **2 :** to establish or create

con·sti·tu·tion *n* **1 :** the physical makeup of an individual **2 :** the basic structure of something **3 :** the basic beliefs and laws of a nation, state, or social group by which the powers and duties of the government are established and certain rights are guaranteed to the people or a document that sets forth these beliefs and laws

[1]con·sti·tu·tion·al *adj* **1 :** having to do with a person's physical or mental makeup **2 :** relating to or in agreement with a constitution (as of a nation)

[2]constitutional *n* **:** a walk taken to maintain health

con·strain *vb* **con·strained; con·strain·ing** **1 :** COMPEL 1, FORCE **2 :** to restrict or limit

con·straint *n* **1 :** control that limits or restricts **2 :** something that limits or restricts

con·strict *vb* **con·strict·ed; con·strict·ing** **:** to make narrower, smaller, or tighter by drawing together **:** SQUEEZE

con·stric·tion *n* **:** an act or instance of drawing together

con·stric·tor *n* **:** a snake (as a boa) that kills its prey by coiling around and crushing it

con·struct *vb* **con·struct·ed; con·struct·ing** **:** to make or form by combining parts

con·struc·tion *n* **1 :** the process, art, or manner of building something **2 :** something built or put together **:** STRUCTURE **3 :** the arrangement of words and the relationship between words in a sentence

construction paper *n* **:** a thick paper available in many colors for school art work

con·struc·tive *adj* **:** helping to develop or improve something — **con·struc·tive·ly** *adv*

con·strue *vb* **con·strued; con·stru·ing** **:** to understand or explain the sense or intention of

con·sul *n* **:** an official appointed by a government to live in a foreign country in order to look after the commercial interests of citizens of the appointing country

con·sult *vb* **con·sult·ed; con·sult·ing** **1 :** to seek the opinion or advice of **2 :** to seek information from **3 :** to talk something over

con·sul·tant *n* **:** a person who gives professional advice or services

con·sul·ta·tion *n* **1 :** a meeting held to talk things over **2 :** the act of talking things over

con·sume *vb* **con·sumed; con·sum·ing** **1 :** to destroy by or as if by fire **2 :** to eat or drink up **3 :** to use up **4 :** to take up the interest or attention of

con·sum·er *n* **:** a person who buys and uses up goods

con·sump·tion *n* **1 :** the act or process of using up something (as food or coal) **2 :** a wasting away of the body especially from tuberculosis of the lungs

cont. *abbr* continued

[1]con·tact *n* **1 :** a meeting or touching of persons or things **2 :** communication with other people **3 :** a person someone knows who serves as a connection especially in the business or political world **4 :** CONTACT LENS

[2]contact *vb* **con·tact·ed; con·tact·ing** **1 :** to touch or make touch physically **2 :** to get in touch or communication with

[3]contact *adj* **:** involving or activated by physical interaction

contact lens *n* **:** a thin lens used to correct bad eyesight and worn over the cornea of the eye

con·ta·gion *n* **1 :** the passing of a disease from one individual to another as a result of some contact between them **2 :** a contagious disease

con·ta·gious *adj* **1 :** able to be passed from one individual to another through contact **2 :** having a sickness that can be passed to someone else **3 :** causing other people to feel or act a similar way

con·tain *vb* **con·tained; con·tain·ing** **1 :** to have within **:** HOLD **2 :** to consist of or include **3 :** to keep within limits **:** RESTRAIN

con·tain·er *n* **:** something into which other things can be put (as for storage)

con·tam·i·nate *vb* **con·tam·i·nat·ed; con·tam·i·nat·ing** **1 :** to soil, stain, or infect by contact or association **2 :** to make unfit for use by adding something harmful or unpleasant

con·tem·plate *vb* **con·tem·plat·ed; con·tem·plat·ing** **1 :** to look at with careful and thoughtful attention **2 :** to think about deeply and carefully **3 :** to have in mind **:** plan on

con·tem·pla·tion *n* **1 :** the act of thinking about spiritual things **:** MEDITATION **2 :** the act of looking at or thinking about something for some time

[1]con·tem·po·rary *adj* **1 :** living or occurring at the same period of time **2 :** MODERN 1

[2]contemporary *n, pl* **con·tem·po·rar·ies** **:** a person who lives at the same time or is about the same age as another

con·tempt *n* **1 :** a feeling of disrespect or disapproval of something or someone **2 :** the state of being despised **3 :** lack of proper respect for a judge or court

con·tempt·ible *adj* **:** deserving or causing a person to be despised

con·temp·tu·ous *adj* **:** SCORNFUL

con·tend *vb* **con·tend·ed; con·tend·ing** **1** : COMPETE **2** : to try hard to deal with **3** : to argue or state earnestly

con·tend·er *n* : a person who is in competition with others

[1]con·tent *n* **1** : the things that are within — usually used in pl. **2** : the subject or topic treated (as in a book) — usually used in pl. **3** : the important part or meaning (as of a book) **4** : a certain amount

[2]con·tent *adj* : pleased and satisfied

[3]content *vb* **con·tent·ed; con·tent·ing** : to make pleased : SATISFY

[4]content *n* : freedom from care or discomfort

con·tent·ed *adj* : satisfied or showing satisfaction — **con·tent·ed·ly** *adv*

con·ten·tion *n* **1** : something that is argued **2** : anger and disagreement **3** : a state or situation of having a chance to win

con·tent·ment *n* : freedom from worry or restlessness : peaceful satisfaction

[1]con·test *n* : a struggle for victory : COMPETITION

[2]con·test *vb* **con·test·ed; con·test·ing** : to make (something) a cause of dispute or fighting

con·tes·tant *n* : a person who takes part in a competition

con·text *n* **1** : the words that are used with a certain word in writing or speaking **2** : the situation in which something happens

con·ti·nent *n* : one of the great divisions of land on the globe — Africa, Antarctica, Asia, Australia, Europe, North America, or South America

con·ti·nen·tal *adj* **1** : being the mainland part and not including islands **2** *often cap* : of the colonies later forming the United States

con·tin·gent *adj* : depending on something else that may or may not exist or occur

con·tin·u·al *adj* **1** : going on or lasting without stop **2** : occurring again and again within short periods of time — **con·tin·u·al·ly** *adv*

con·tin·u·ance *n* : the act of going on or lasting for a long time

con·tin·u·a·tion *n* **1** : something that begins where something else ends and follows a similar pattern **2** : the act of beginning again after an interruption

con·tin·ue *vb* **con·tin·ued; con·tinu·ing** **1** : to do or cause to do the same thing without changing or stopping **2** : to begin again after stopping

con·ti·nu·i·ty *n, pl* **con·ti·nu·i·ties** : the quality or state of going on without stop

con·tin·u·ous *adj* : going on without stop — **con·tin·u·ous·ly** *adv*

con·tort *vb* **con·tort·ed; con·tort·ing** : to give an unusual appearance or unnatural shape to by twisting

con·tor·tion *n* : the act or result of twisting out of shape

con·tour *n* : the outline of a figure, body, or surface

contra- *prefix* **1** : against : contrary : contrasting **2** : pitched below normal bass

con·tra·band *n* : goods forbidden by law to be owned or to be brought into or out of a country

[1]con·tract *n* **1** : a legal agreement **2** : a written document that shows the terms and conditions of a legal agreement

[2]con·tract *vb* **con·tract·ed; con·tract·ing** **1** : to agree by contract **2** : to become sick with : CATCH **3** : to draw together and make shorter and broader **4** : to make or become smaller : SHRINK **5** : to make (as a word) shorter by dropping sounds or letters

con·trac·tion *n* **1** : the act, process, or result of making or becoming smaller or shorter and broader **2** : a short form of a word or word group (as *don't* or *they've*) produced by leaving out a letter or letters

con·tra·dict *vb* **con·tra·dict·ed; con·tra·dict·ing** **1** : to deny the truth of a statement : say the opposite of what someone else has said **2** : to be opposed to

con·tra·dic·tion *n* : something (as a statement) that is the opposite of or is much different from something else

con·tra·dic·to·ry *adj* : involving, causing, or being the opposite of or much different from something else

con·tral·to *n, pl* **con·tral·tos** **1** : the lowest female singing voice : ALTO **2** : a singer with a low female singing voice

con·trap·tion *n* : GADGET

[1]con·trary *n, pl* **con·trar·ies** : something opposite — **on the contrary** : just the opposite : NO

[2]con·trary *adj* **1** : exactly opposite **2** : being against what is usual or expected **3** : not favorable **4** : unwilling to accept control or advice

[1]con·trast *vb* **con·trast·ed; con·trast·ing** **1** : to show noticeable differences **2** : to compare two persons or things so as to show the differences between them

[2]con·trast *n* **1** : something that is different from another **2** : difference or the amount of difference (as in color or brightness) between parts **3** : difference or amount of difference between related or similar things

con·trib·ute *vb* **con·trib·ut·ed; con·trib·ut·ing** **1** : to give along with others **2** : to have a share in something **3** : to supply (as an article) for publication especially in a magazine — **con·trib·u·tor** *n*

con·tri·bu·tion *n* : the act of giving something or something given : DONATION
con·trite *adj* : feeling or showing sorrow for some wrong that one has done : REPENTANT
con·triv·ance *n* : something (as a scheme or a mechanical device) produced with skill and cleverness
con·trive *vb* **con·trived; con·triv·ing** **1** : [2]PLAN 1, PLOT **2** : to form or make in some skillful or clever way **3** : to manage to bring about or do
[1]**con·trol** *vb* **con·trolled; con·trol·ling** **1** : to have power over **2** : to direct the actions or behavior of **3** : to keep within bounds : RESTRAIN **4** : to direct the function of
[2]**control** *n* **1** : the power or authority to manage **2** : ability to keep within bounds or direct the operation of **3** : SELF-RESTRAINT **4** : REGULATION 1 **5** : a device used to start, stop, or change the operation of a machine or system **6** : something that is not treated or exposed to testing in an experiment in order to serve as a comparison to others that have undergone treatment or exposure
con·tro·ver·sial *adj* : relating to or causing disagreement or argument
con·tro·ver·sy *n, pl* **con·tro·ver·sies** **1** : an often long or heated discussion of something about which there is great difference of opinion **2** : [1]QUARREL 1
co·nun·drum *n* : [1]RIDDLE 1
con·va·lesce *vb* **con·va·lesced; con·va·lesc·ing** : to regain health and strength gradually after sickness or injury
con·va·les·cence *n* : the period or process of becoming well again after a sickness or injury
[1]**con·va·les·cent** *adj* : going through or used for the process of becoming well again after a sickness or injury
[2]**convalescent** *n* : a person who is in the process of becoming well again after a sickness or injury
con·vec·tion *n* : motion in a gas (as air) or a liquid in which the warmer portions rise and the colder portions sink
con·vene *vb* **con·vened; con·ven·ing** : to come or bring together as an assembly
con·ve·nience *n* **1** : the quality or state of being available, easy to use, useful, or helpful **2** : personal comfort **3** : OPPORTUNITY 1 **4** : something that gives comfort or advantage
con·ve·nient *adj* **1** : suited to a person's comfort or ease **2** : suited to a certain use **3** : easy to get to — **con·ve·nient·ly** *adv*
con·vent *n* **1** : a group of nuns living together **2** : a house or a set of buildings occupied by a community of nuns
con·ven·tion *n* **1** : a meeting of people for a common purpose **2** : a custom or a way of acting and doing things that is widely accepted and followed **3** : AGREEMENT 3
con·ven·tion·al *adj* **1** : following the usual or widely accepted way of doing things **2** : used or accepted through general agreement
con·ver·sa·tion *n* : a talk between two or more people : the act of talking — **con·ver·sa·tion·al** *adj*
con·verse *vb* **con·versed; con·vers·ing** : to talk to another person or to other people
con·ver·sion *n* **1** : the act of changing : the process of being changed **2** : a change of religion
[1]**con·vert** *vb* **con·vert·ed; con·vert·ing** **1** : to change from one form to another **2** : to change from one belief, religion, view, or party to another **3** : to exchange for an equivalent
[2]**con·vert** *n* : a person who has been convinced to change to a different belief, religion, view, or party
[1]**con·vert·ible** *adj* : possible to change in form or use
[2]**convertible** *n* **1** : an automobile with a top that can be raised, lowered, or removed **2** : something that can be changed into a different form
con·vex *adj* : rounded like the outside of a ball or circle
con·vey *vb* **con·veyed; con·vey·ing** **1** : to carry from one place to another : TRANSPORT **2** : to make known : COMMUNICATE
con·vey·ance *n* **1** : the act of carrying from one place to another **2** : something used to carry goods or passengers
[1]**con·vict** *vb* **con·vict·ed; con·vict·ing** : to prove or find guilty
[2]**con·vict** *n* : a person serving a prison sentence
con·vic·tion *n* **1** : a strong belief or opinion **2** : the state of mind of a person who is sure that what he or she believes or says is true **3** : the act of proving or finding guilty : the state of being proven guilty
con·vince *vb* **con·vinced; con·vinc·ing** : to argue so as to make a person agree or believe
con·vinc·ing *adj* : causing someone to believe or agree : PERSUASIVE — **con·vinc·ing·ly** *adv*
[1]**con·voy** *n, pl* **con·voys** : a group traveling together for protection
[2]**con·voy** *vb* **con·voyed; con·voy·ing** : to travel with and protect
con·vulse *vb* **con·vulsed; con·vuls·ing** : to shake violently or with jerky motions
con·vul·sion *n* : an attack of powerful involuntary muscular contractions

con·vul·sive *adj* : causing or marked by violent, frantic, or jerky movement — **con·vul·sive·ly** *adv*

[1]**coo** *vb* **cooed; coo·ing** **1 :** to make the soft sound made by doves and pigeons or a similar sound **2 :** to talk or say fondly or lovingly

[2]**coo** *n, pl* **coos :** a sound of or similar to that made by doves and pigeons

[1]**cook** *n* : a person who prepares food for eating

[2]**cook** *vb* **cooked; cook·ing** **1 :** to prepare food for eating by the use of heat **2 :** to go through the process of being heated in preparation for being eaten **3 :** to create through thought and imagination — usually used with *up*

cook·book *n* : a book of recipes and directions for the preparation of food

cook·ie *n, pl* **cook·ies :** a small sweet cake

cook·out *n* : an outing at which a meal is cooked and served outdoors

[1]**cool** *adj* **cool·er; cool·est** **1 :** somewhat cold : not warm **2 :** not letting or keeping in heat **3 :** [3]CALM 2 **4 :** not friendly or interested : INDIFFERENT **5 :** fashionable, stylish, or attractive in a way that is widely approved of — **cool·ly** *adv* — **cool·ness** *n*

[2]**cool** *vb* **cooled; cool·ing :** to make or become less warm

[3]**cool** *n* **1 :** a time or place that is not warm **2 :** a calm state of mind

cool·er *n* : a container for keeping food or drink somewhat cold

coon *n* : RACCOON

[1]**coop** *n* : a cage or small building for keeping poultry

[2]**coop** *vb* **cooped; coop·ing :** to restrict to a small space

coo·per *n* : a worker who makes or repairs wooden casks, tubs, or barrels

co·op·er·ate *vb* **co·op·er·at·ed; co·op·er·at·ing** : to act or work together so as to get something done

co·op·er·a·tion *n* : the act or process of working together to get something done

[1]**co·op·er·a·tive** *adj* **1 :** willing to work with others **2 :** relating to an organization owned by and operated for the benefit of the people who use its services

[2]**cooperative** *n* : an organization owned by and operated for the benefit of the people who use its services

[1]**co·or·di·nate** *n* : any of a set of numbers used to locate a point on a line or surface or in space

[2]**co·or·di·nate** *vb* **co·or·di·nat·ed; co·or·di·nat·ing :** to work or cause to work together smoothly

co·or·di·na·tion *n* : smooth working together (as of parts)

cop *n* : POLICE OFFICER

cope *vb* **coped; cop·ing :** to struggle or try to manage especially with some success

copi·er *n* : a machine for making duplicates

co·pi·lot *n* : a person who assists in flying an airplane

co·pi·ous *adj* : very plentiful : ABUNDANT — **co·pi·ous·ly** *adv*

cop·per *n* **1 :** a tough reddish metallic chemical element that is one of the best conductors of heat and electricity **2 :** a coin having little value

cop·per·head *n* : a poisonous snake of the eastern and central United States with a reddish brown head

cop·pice *n* : a thicket, grove, or growth of small trees

copse *n* : COPPICE

[1]**copy** *n, pl* **cop·ies** **1 :** something that is made to look exactly like something else : DUPLICATE **2 :** one of the total number of books, magazines, or papers printed at one time **3 :** written material to be published

[2]**copy** *vb* **cop·ied; copy·ing** **1 :** to make a duplicate of **2 :** IMITATE 1

copy·cat *n* : a person who imitates another person

[1]**copy·right** *n* : the legal right to be the only one to reproduce, publish, and sell the contents and form of a literary or artistic work — **copyright** *vb*

[2]**copyright** *vb* **copy·right·ed; copy·right·ing** : to get a copyright on

[1]**cor·al** *n* **1 :** a stony material consisting of the skeletons of tiny sea animals that live in colonies and that are related to the jellyfish **2 :** one or a colony of the animals that form coral **3 :** a dark pink

[2]**coral** *adj* **1 :** made of coral **2 :** of a dark pink color

coral reef *n* : a long line of coral that lies in warm, shallow water

coral snake *n* : a small poisonous tropical American snake brightly ringed with red, black, and yellow or white

cord *n* **1 :** a covered electrical wire used to connect an electrical appliance with an outlet **2 :** material like a small thin rope that is used mostly for tying things **3 :** an amount of firewood equal to a pile of wood eight feet long, four feet high, and four feet wide or 128 cubic feet (about 3.6 cubic meters) **4 :** a rib or ridge woven into cloth **5** : a ribbed fabric

cor·dial *adj* : warm and friendly — **cor·dial·ly** *adv*

cor·du·roy *n* **1 :** a heavy ribbed usually cotton cloth **2 corduroys** *pl* **:** trousers made of a heavy ribbed cloth

[1]**core** *n* **1 :** the usually inedible central part

of some fruits (as a pineapple or pear) **2** **:** the central part of a celesital body (as the earth or sun) **3 :** the central or most important part of something

[2]**core** *vb* **cored; cor·ing :** to remove the core from

[1]**cork** *n* **1 :** the light but tough material that is the outer layer of bark of a tree (**cork oak**) and is used especially for stoppers and insulation **2 :** a stopper for a bottle or jug

[2]**cork** *vb* **corked; cork·ing :** to stop with a stopper

[1]**cork·screw** *n* **:** a pointed spiral piece of metal with a handle that is screwed into corks to pull them from bottles

[2]**corkscrew** *adj* **:** having a spiral shape

cor·mo·rant *n* **:** a black seabird with webbed feet, a long neck, and a slender hooked beak

[1]**corn** *n* **1 :** a tall American cereal grass plant widely grown for its large ears of starchy grain which come in many varieties **2 :** the seeds of a corn plant that are used especially as food for humans and animals and are typically yellow or whitish **3 :** an ear of corn with or without its leafy outer covering

[2]**corn** *n* **:** a hardening and thickening of the skin (as on a person's toe)

corn bread *n* **:** bread made with cornmeal

corn·cob *n* **:** the woody core on which grains of corn grow

cor·nea *n* **:** the transparent outer layer of the front of the eye covering the pupil and iris

corned beef *n* **:** beef that has been preserved in salt water

[1]**cor·ner** *n* **1 :** the point or place where edges or sides meet **2 :** the place where two streets or passageways meet **3 :** a position from which escape or retreat is difficult or impossible **4 :** a place away from ordinary life or business — **cor·nered** *adj*

[2]**corner** *adj* **1 :** located at a corner **2 :** used or usable in or on a corner

[3]**corner** *vb* **cor·nered; cor·ner·ing :** to force into a place from which escape is difficult or into a difficult position

cor·net *n* **:** a brass musical instrument similar to but shorter than a trumpet

corn·flow·er *n* **:** a European plant related to the daisies that is often grown for its bright heads of blue, pink, or white flowers

cor·nice *n* **1 :** an ornamental piece that forms the top edge of the front of a building or pillar **2 :** an ornamental molding placed where the walls meet the ceiling of a room

corn·meal *n* **:** coarse flour made from ground corn

corn·stalk *n* **:** a stalk of corn

corn·starch *n* **:** a fine powder made from corn and used to thicken foods when cooking

corn syrup *n* **:** a syrup made from cornstarch

cor·nu·co·pia *n* **:** a container in the shape of a horn overflowing with fruits and flowers used as a symbol of plenty

corny *adj* **corn·i·er; corn·i·est :** so simple, sentimental, or old-fashioned as to be annoying

co·rol·la *n* **:** the part of a flower that is formed by the petals

cor·o·nary *adj* **:** of or relating to the heart or its blood vessels

cor·o·na·tion *n* **:** the act or ceremony of crowning a king or queen

cor·o·ner *n* **:** a public official responsible for determining the causes of deaths which are not due to natural causes

cor·o·net *n* **1 :** a small crown worn by a person of noble but less than royal rank **2 :** an ornamental wreath or band worn around the head

[1]**cor·po·ral** *adj* **:** of or relating to the body

[2]**corporal** *n* **:** a noncommissioned officer ranking above a private in the army or above a lance corporal in the marine corps

cor·po·ra·tion *n* **:** a business or organization authorized by law to carry on an activity with the rights and duties of a single person

cor·po·re·al *adj* **:** having, consisting of, or relating to a physical body

corps *n, pl* **corps 1 :** an organized branch of a country's military forces **2 :** a group of persons acting under one authority

corpse *n* **:** a dead body

cor·pu·lent *adj* **:** very fat

cor·pus·cle *n* **:** a very small cell (as a red blood cell) that floats freely in the blood

[1]**cor·ral** *n* **:** an enclosure for keeping or capturing animals

[2]**corral** *vb* **cor·ralled; cor·ral·ling 1 :** to confine in or as if in an enclosure **2 :** to gather or get control over

[1]**cor·rect** *vb* **cor·rect·ed; cor·rect·ing 1 :** to make or set right **2 :** to change or adjust so as to bring to some standard or to a required condition **3 :** to punish in order to improve **4 :** to show how a thing can be improved or made right

[2]**correct** *adj* **1 :** free from mistakes **:** ACCURATE **2 :** meeting or agreeing with some standard **:** APPROPRIATE — **cor·rect·ly** *adv* — **cor·rect·ness** *n*

cor·rec·tion *n* **1 :** the act of making something agree with what is right or standard **2 :** a change that makes something right **3** **:** PUNISHMENT 1 — **cor·rec·tion·al** *adj*

cor·re·spond *vb* **cor·re·spond·ed; cor·re·spond·ing 1 :** to be alike **:** AGREE **2 :** to compare closely **3 :** to communicate with a person by exchanging letters

cor·re·spon·dence *n* **1 :** communication by means of letters or e-mail **:** the letters or

e-mail exchanged **2 :** agreement between certain things
cor·re·spon·dent *n* **1 :** a person with whom another person communicates by letter or e-mail **2 :** a person who sends news stories or comments to a newspaper, magazine, or broadcasting company especially from a distant place
cor·ri·dor *n* **:** a passage into which rooms open
cor·rob·o·rate *vb* **cor·rob·o·rat·ed; cor·rob·o·rat·ing :** to support with evidence or authority
cor·rode *vb* **cor·rod·ed; cor·rod·ing 1 :** to wear away little by little (as by rust or acid) **2 :** to gradually destroy or weaken
cor·ro·sion *n* **:** the process or effect of destroying, weakening, or wearing away little by little
cor·ro·sive *adj* **:** tending or able to destroy, weaken, or wear away little by little
cor·ru·gat·ed *adj* **:** having a wavy surface
[1]**cor·rupt** *vb* **cor·rupt·ed; cor·rupt·ing 1 :** to change (as in morals, manners, or actions) from good to bad **2 :** to influence a public official in an improper way (as by a bribe)
[2]**corrupt** *adj* **1 :** behaving in a bad or improper way **2 :** morally bad **:** EVIL
cor·rup·tion *n* **1 :** dishonest or illegal behavior **2 :** the process of causing someone else to do something wrong **3 :** the act of changing or damaging something
cor·sage *n* **:** a small bouquet of flowers usually worn on the shoulder
corse·let *or* **cors·let** *n* **:** the body armor worn by a knight especially on the upper part of the body
cor·set *n* **:** a tight undergarment worn to support or give shape to waist and hips
cos·met·ic *n* **:** a material (as a cream, lotion, or powder) used to improve a person's appearance
cos·mic *adj* **:** of or relating to the whole universe
cosmic ray *n* **:** a stream of very penetrating particles that enter the earth's atmosphere from outer space at high speed
cos·mo·naut *n* **:** a Russian or Soviet astronaut
cos·mos *n* **1 :** the universe especially as thought of as an orderly system **2 :** a tall garden plant related to the daisies that has showy white, pink, or rose-colored flower heads
[1]**cost** *vb* **cost; cost·ing 1 :** to have a price of **2 :** to cause the payment, spending, or loss of
[2]**cost** *n* **1 :** the amount paid or charged for something **:** PRICE **2 :** loss or penalty involved in gaining something
cost·ly *adj* **cost·li·er; cost·li·est 1 :** having a high price or value **:** EXPENSIVE **2 :** causing loss or suffering
[1]**cos·tume** *n* **1 :** special or fancy dress (as for wear on the stage or at a masquerade) **2 :** style of clothing, ornaments, and hair used during a certain period, in a certain region, or by a certain class or group
[2]**costume** *vb* **cos·tumed; cos·tum·ing :** to provide with a special or fancy outfit
cot *n* **:** a narrow bed often made to fold up
cot·tage *n* **:** a small house usually in the country or for vacation use
cottage cheese *n* **:** a very soft white cheese made from soured skim milk
cot·ton *n* **1 :** a soft fluffy usually white material made up of twisted hairs that surrounds the seeds of a tall plant of warm regions and is spun into thread or yarn **2 :** thread, yarn, or cloth made from cotton — **cotton** *adj*
cotton gin *n* **:** a machine for removing seeds from cotton
cot·ton·mouth *n* **:** WATER MOCCASIN
cot·ton·seed *n* **:** the seed of the cotton plant from which comes an oil used especially in cooking and a protein-rich meal used in livestock feed
cot·ton·tail *n* **:** a small rabbit with a white tail
cot·ton·wood *n* **:** a poplar tree that has seeds with bunches of hairs resembling cotton
couch *n* **:** a long piece of furniture that a person can sit or lie on
couch potato *n* **:** a person who spends a lot of time watching television
cou·gar *n* **:** a large yellowish brown wild animal of North and South America related to the domestic cat
[1]**cough** *vb* **coughed; cough·ing 1 :** to force air from the lungs suddenly with a sharp short noise or series of noises **2 :** to get rid of by coughing
[2]**cough** *n* **1 :** a condition in which there is severe or frequent coughing **2 :** an act or sound of coughing
could *past of* CAN **1** — used as a helping verb in the past **2** — used as a polite form instead of *can* **3** — used to say something is possible
couldn't : could not
coun·cil *n* **:** a group of people appointed or elected to make laws or give advice
coun·cil·lor *or* **coun·cil·or** *n* **:** a member of a group of people appointed or elected to make laws or give advice **:** a member of a council
[1]**coun·sel** *n* **1 :** advice given **2** *pl* **counsel :** a lawyer representing someone in court
[2]**counsel** *vb* **coun·seled** *or chiefly Can and Brit* **coun·selled; coun·sel·ing** *or chiefly Can and Brit* **coun·sel·ling 1 :** to give advice to **:** ADVISE **2 :** to suggest or recommend
coun·sel·or *or chiefly Can and Brit* **coun·sel·lor** *n* **1 :** a person who gives advice **2**

DICTIONARY

: a supervisor of campers or activities at a summer camp **3 :** LAWYER

[1]**count** *vb* **count·ed; count·ing** **1 :** to add one by one in order to find the total number **2 :** to name the numbers one by one, by groups, or in order up to a particular point **3 :** to include in thinking about **4 :** to rely or depend on **5 :** [2]PLAN 1 **6 :** to have value, force, or importance **7 :** to consider or judge to be

[2]**count** *n* **1 :** the act or process of naming numbers or adding one by one **2 :** a total arrived at by adding **3 :** any one crime that a person is charged with

[3]**count** *n* **:** a European nobleman whose rank is like that of a British earl

count·down *n* **:** the process of subtracting the time remaining before an event (as the launching of a rocket)

[1]**coun·te·nance** *n* **:** the human face or its expression

[2]**countenance** *vb* **coun·te·nanced; coun·te·nanc·ing :** to give approval or tolerance to

[1]**count·er** *n* **1 :** a level surface usually higher than a table that is used especially for selling, serving food, displaying things, or working on **2 :** a piece used in games or to find a total in adding

[2]**count·er** *n* **1 :** a person whose job is to determine a total **2 :** a device for showing a number or amount

[3]**coun·ter** *vb* **coun·tered; coun·ter·ing** **1 :** to say in response to something said **2 :** to act in opposition to **:** OPPOSE

[4]**coun·ter** *adv* **:** in another or opposite direction

[5]**coun·ter** *n* **:** an answering or opposing force or blow

coun·ter- *prefix* **1 :** opposite **2 :** opposing **3 :** like **:** matching **4 :** duplicate **:** substitute

coun·ter·act *vb* **coun·ter·act·ed; coun·ter·act·ing :** to make (something) have less of an effect or no effect at all

coun·ter·clock·wise *adv or adj* **:** in a direction opposite to that in which the hands of a clock move

[1]**coun·ter·feit** *adj* **1 :** made in exact imitation of something genuine and meant to be taken as genuine **2 :** not sincere

[2]**counterfeit** *vb* **coun·ter·feit·ed; coun·ter·feit·ing** **1 :** to imitate or copy especially in order to deceive **2 :** [1]PRETEND 2 — **coun·ter·feit·er** *n*

[3]**counterfeit** *n* **:** something made to imitate another thing with the desire to deceive

coun·ter·part *n* **:** a person or thing that is very like or equivalent to another person or thing

coun·ter·sign *n* **:** a secret signal that must be given by a person wishing to pass a guard **:** PASSWORD

count·ess *n* **1 :** the wife or widow of a count or an earl **2 :** a woman who holds the rank of a count or an earl in her own right

counting number *n* **:** NATURAL NUMBER

count·less *adj* **:** too many to be counted

coun·try *n, pl* **coun·tries** **1 :** a land lived in by a people with a common government **2 :** REGION 1, DISTRICT **3 :** open rural land away from big towns and cities **4 :** the people of a nation

country and western *n* **:** COUNTRY MUSIC

coun·try·man *n, pl* **coun·try·men** **1 :** a person born in the same country as another **:** a fellow citizen **2 :** a person living or raised in a place away from big towns and cities

country music *n* **:** a style of music that developed in the southern and western United States, that is similar to folk music, and that often has lyrics about people who live in the country

coun·try·side *n* **:** a rural area or its people

coun·ty *n, pl* **coun·ties :** a division of a state or country for local government

cou·pé *or* **coupe** *n* **1 :** a carriage with four wheels and an enclosed body seating two persons and with an outside seat for the driver in front **2 :** an enclosed two-door automobile for two persons

[1]**cou·ple** *n* **1 :** two people who are married or in a romantic relationship **2 :** two people or things paired together **3 :** two things that are of the same kind or that are thought of together

[2]**couple** *vb* **cou·pled; cou·pling** **1 :** to join or link together **:** CONNECT **2 :** to join in pairs

cou·plet *n* **:** two rhyming lines of verse one after another

cou·pling *n* **1 :** the act of bringing or coming together **2 :** something that connects two parts or things

cou·pon *n* **1 :** a ticket or form that allows the holder to receive some service, payment, or discount **2 :** a part of an advertisement meant to be cut out for use as an order blank

cour·age *n* **:** the ability to meet danger and difficulties with firmness

cou·ra·geous *adj* **:** having or showing the ability to meet danger and difficulties with firmness — **cou·ra·geous·ly** *adv*

cou·ri·er *n* **:** MESSENGER

[1]**course** *n* **1 :** motion from one point to another **:** progress in space or time **2 :** the path over which something moves **3 :** a natural channel for water **4 :** a way of doing something **5 :** the ordinary way something happens over time **6 :** a series of acts or proceedings arranged in regular order **7 :** a series of classes in a subject **8 :** a part of a meal served separately — **of course :** as might be expected

²course *vb* **coursed; cours·ing** **1 :** to run through or over **2 :** to move rapidly **:** RACE

¹court *n* **1 :** a space arranged for playing a certain game **2 :** an official meeting led by a judge for settling legal questions or the place where it is held **3 :** a judge or the judges presiding in a courtroom **4 :** the home of a ruler (as a king) **5 :** a ruler's assembly of advisers and officers as a governing power **6 :** the family and people who follow a ruler **7 :** an open space completely or partly surrounded by buildings **8 :** a short street **9 :** respect meant to win favor

²court *vb* **court·ed; court·ing** **1 :** to seek the love or companionship of **2 :** to try to gain or get the support of **:** SEEK **3 :** to seem to be asking for **:** TEMPT

cour·te·ous *adj* **:** showing respect and consideration for others **:** POLITE — **cour·te·ous·ly** *adv*

cour·te·sy *n, pl* **cour·te·sies** **1 :** the quality or state of being respectful and considerate of others **2 :** a polite or generous act or expression **3 :** something that is a favor and not a right

court·house *n* **1 :** a building in which courts of law are held **2 :** a building in which county offices are housed

court·i·er *n* **:** a member of a royal court

court·ly *adj* **court·li·er; court·li·est** **:** polite and graceful in a formal way

court·room *n* **:** a room in which formal legal meetings and trials take place

court·ship *n* **:** the act of seeking the love or companionship of someone

court·yard *n* **:** ¹COURT 7

cous·in *n* **:** a child of a person's uncle or aunt

cove *n* **:** a small sheltered inlet or bay

cov·e·nant *n* **:** a formal or serious agreement or promise

¹cov·er *vb* **cov·ered; cov·er·ing** **1 :** to place or spread something over **2 :** to be spread with or extend over much or all of the surface of **3 :** to form a covering over **4 :** to pass over or through **5 :** to provide protection to or against **6 :** to maintain a check on by patrolling **7 :** to hide from sight or knowledge **8 :** to deal with as a subject **9 :** to have as a field of activity or interest **10 :** to provide insurance for

²cover *n* **1 :** something that protects, shelters, or hides **2 :** a covering (as a blanket) used on a bed **3 :** a binding or a protecting case **4 :** something that is placed over or about another thing **:** LID, TOP

cov·er·age *n* **1 :** insurance against something **2 :** the value or amount of insurance **3 :** treatment of an event or subject

cov·er·all *n* **:** an outer garment that combines shirt and pants and is worn to protect a person's regular clothes — usually used in pl.

covered wagon *n* **:** a large long wagon with a curving canvas top

cov·er·ing *n* **:** something that shelters, protects, or conceals

cov·er·let *n* **:** BEDSPREAD

¹co·vert *adj* **:** made or done secretly — **co·vert·ly** *adv*

²covert *n* **1 :** a hiding place (as a thicket that gives shelter to game animals) **2 :** one of the small feathers around the bottom of the quills on the wings and tail of a bird

cov·et *vb* **cov·et·ed; cov·et·ing** **:** to wish for greatly or with envy

cov·et·ous *adj* **:** having or showing too much desire for wealth or possessions or for something belonging to another person

cov·ey *n, pl* **coveys** **1 :** a small flock of birds **2 :** ¹GROUP 1

¹cow *n* **:** the adult female of cattle or of any of various other large animals (as moose or seals)

²cow *vb* **cowed; cow·ing** **:** to make afraid

cow·ard *n* **:** a person who shows shameful fear

cow·ard·ice *n* **:** shameful fear

cow·ard·ly *adj* **1 :** shamefully fearful **2 :** showing shameful fear — **cow·ard·li·ness** *n*

cow·bell *n* **:** a bell hung around the neck of a cow to tell where it is

cow·bird *n* **:** a small North American blackbird that lays its eggs in the nests of other birds

cow·boy *n* **:** a man or boy who works on a ranch or performs at a rodeo

cow·catch·er *n* **:** a strong frame on the front of a railroad engine for moving things blocking the track

cow·er *vb* **cow·ered; cow·er·ing** **:** to shrink away or crouch down shivering (as from fear)

cow·girl *n* **:** a girl or woman who works on a ranch or performs at a rodeo

cow·hand *n* **:** a person who works on a cattle ranch

cow·herd *n* **:** a person who tends cows

cow·hide *n* **1 :** the hide of cattle or leather made from it **2 :** a whip of rawhide or braided leather

cowl *n* **:** a hood or long hooded cloak especially of a monk

cow·lick *n* **:** a small bunch of hair that sticks out and will not lie flat

cox·swain *n* **:** the person who steers or directs the rowers of a boat

coy *adj* **:** falsely shy or modest

coy·ote *n* **:** a yellowish to reddish gray doglike animal chiefly of western North America that is closely related to but smaller than the wolf

^{1}**co·zy** *adj* **co·zi·er; co·zi·est :** enjoying or providing warmth and comfort — **co·zi·ly** *adv* — **co·zi·ness** *n*

^{2}**cozy** *n, pl* **co·zies :** a padded covering for a container (as a teapot) to keep the contents hot

CPR *abbr* cardiopulmonary resuscitation

cpu *n, often cap C&P&U* **:** the part of a computer that does most of the processing of data

^{1}**crab** *n* **:** a sea animal that is a crustacean related to the lobsters and has a short broad flat shell and a front pair of legs with small claws

^{2}**crab** *n* **:** a person who is usually grouchy

^{3}**crab** *vb* **crabbed; crab·bing :** COMPLAIN

crab apple *n* **1 :** an apple tree grown for its white, pink, or red flowers or its small usually brightly colored sour fruit **2 :** the small sour fruit of a crab apple tree

crab·bed *adj* **:** CRABBY

crab·by *adj* **crab·bi·er; crab·bi·est :** GROUCHY

crab·grass *n* **:** a weedy grass with coarse stems that root at the joints

^{1}**crack** *vb* **cracked; crack·ing 1 :** to break or cause to break with a sudden sharp sound **2 :** to break often without completely separating into parts **3 :** to make or cause to make a sound as if breaking **4 :** to open a small amount **5 :** to tell (a joke) especially in a clever way **6 :** to lose self-control **7 :** to change in tone quality **8 :** to strike or receive a sharp blow **9 :** SOLVE — **crack up 1 :** to have a reputation as a result of praise **2 :** to damage or destroy (a vehicle) by crashing **3 :** to laugh or cause to laugh

^{2}**crack** *n* **1 :** a narrow break or opening **2 :** a sudden sharp noise **3 :** a sharp clever remark **4 :** a broken tone of the voice **5 :** the beginning moment **6 :** a sharp blow **7 :** ^{2}ATTEMPT

^{3}**crack** *adj* **:** of high quality or ability

crack·er *n* **:** a dry thin baked food made of flour and water

^{1}**crack·le** *vb* **crack·led; crack·ling 1 :** to make many small sharp noises **2 :** to form little cracks in a surface

^{2}**crackle** *n* **:** the noise of repeated small cracks (as of burning wood)

crack–up *n* **1 :** BREAKDOWN 2 **2 :** ^{2}CRASH 3, WRECK

^{1}**cra·dle** *n* **1 :** a baby's bed usually on rockers **2 :** place of beginning **3 :** the earliest period of life **4 :** a framework or support resembling a baby's bed in appearance or use

^{2}**cradle** *vb* **cra·dled; cra·dling :** to hold or support in or as if in a cradle

^{1}**craft** *n* **1 :** skill in making things especially with the hands **2 :** an occupation or trade requiring skill with the hands or as an artist **3** *pl usually* **craft :** a boat especially when of small size **4** *pl usually* **craft :** AIRCRAFT **5 :** skill and cleverness often used to trick people

^{2}**craft** *vb* **craft·ed; craft·ing :** to make or produce with care or skill

crafts·man *n, pl* **crafts·men 1 :** a person who works at a trade or handicraft **2 :** a highly skilled worker

crafty *adj* **craft·i·er; craft·i·est :** skillful at tricking others **:** CUNNING — **craft·i·ly** *adv* — **craft·i·ness** *n*

crag *n* **:** a steep rock or cliff

crag·gy *adj* **crag·gi·er; crag·gi·est :** having many steep rocks or cliffs

cram *vb* **crammed; cram·ming 1 :** to stuff or pack tightly **2 :** to fill full **3 :** to study hard just before a test

^{1}**cramp** *n* **1 :** a sudden painful tightening of a muscle **2 :** sharp pain in the abdomen — usually used in pl.

^{2}**cramp** *vb* **cramped; cramp·ing 1 :** to cause or experience a sudden painful muscular tightening in **2 :** to hold back from free action or expression **:** HAMPER

cramped *adj* **1 :** having too little space **2 :** unable to move freely because of lack of space

cran·ber·ry *n, pl* **cran·ber·ries :** a sour bright red berry that is eaten in sauces and jelly and is the fruit of an evergreen swamp plant related to the blueberries

^{1}**crane** *n* **1 :** a large tall wading bird with a long neck, bill, and legs **2 :** a machine with a swinging arm for lifting and carrying heavy weights

^{2}**crane** *vb* **craned; cran·ing :** to stretch the neck to see better

cra·ni·al *adj* **:** of or relating to the skull and especially the part enclosing the brain

cra·ni·um *n, pl* **cra·ni·ums** *or* **cra·nia 1 :** SKULL **2 :** the part of the skull enclosing the brain

^{1}**crank** *n* **1 :** a bent part with a handle that is turned to start or run machinery **2 :** a person with strange ideas **3 :** a cross or irritable person

^{2}**crank** *vb* **cranked; crank·ing 1 :** to start or run by or as if by turning a part with a handle **2 :** to make or become greater in speed or intensity — **crank out :** to produce quickly and often carelessly

cranky *adj* **crank·i·er; crank·i·est :** easily angered or irritated — **crank·i·ness** *n*

cran·ny *n, pl* **cran·nies 1 :** a small break or slit (as in a cliff) **2 :** a place that is not generally known or noticed

crap·pie *n* **:** either of two silvery sunfish that are caught for sport or for food

^{1}**crash** *vb* **crashed; crash·ing 1 :** to break or go to pieces with or as if with violence and noise : SMASH **2 :** to fall or strike something with noise and damage **3 :** to hit or cause to hit something with force and noise **4 :** to make or cause to make a loud noise **5 :** to move roughly and noisily **6 :** to stay for a short time where someone else lives

²crash *n* **1 :** a loud sound (as of things smashing) **2 :** an instance of hitting something with force **3 :** a collision involving a vehicle **4 :** a sudden weakening or failure (as of a business or prices)

¹crate *n* **:** a box or frame of wooden slats or boards for holding and protecting something in shipment

²crate *vb* **crat·ed; crat·ing :** to pack in a wooden box or frame

cra·ter *n* **1 :** the area around the opening of a volcano or geyser that is shaped like a bowl **2 :** a hole (as in the surface of the earth or moon) formed by an impact (as of a meteorite)

cra·vat *n* **:** NECKTIE

crave *vb* **craved; crav·ing 1 :** to want greatly : long for **2 :** to ask for earnestly

cra·ven *adj* **:** COWARDLY

crav·ing *n* **:** a great desire or longing

craw *n* **1 :** ¹CROP 3 **2 :** the stomach of an animal

craw·fish *n, pl* **crawfish 1 :** CRAYFISH **2 :** SPINY LOBSTER

¹crawl *vb* **crawled; crawl·ing 1 :** to move slowly with the body close to the ground : move on hands and knees **2 :** to go very slowly or carefully **3 :** to be covered with or have the feeling of being covered with creeping things

²crawl *n* **1 :** the act or motion of going very slowly **2 :** a swimming stroke performed by moving first one arm over the head and then the other while kicking the legs

cray·fish *n, pl* **crayfish 1 :** a freshwater shellfish that looks like the related lobster but is much smaller **2 :** SPINY LOBSTER

¹cray·on *n* **:** a stick of colored wax or sometimes chalk used for writing or drawing

²crayon *vb* **cray·oned; cray·on·ing :** to draw or color with a crayon

craze *n* **:** something that is very popular for a short while

cra·zy *adj* **cra·zi·er; cra·zi·est 1** *usually offensive* **:** having a severe mental illness : INSANE **2 :** not sensible or logical **3 :** very excited or pleased **4 :** very annoyed — **cra·zi·ly** *adv* — **cra·zi·ness** *n*

¹creak *vb* **creaked; creak·ing :** to make a long scraping or squeaking sound

²creak *n* **:** a long squeaking or scraping noise

creaky *adj* **creak·i·er; creak·i·est :** making or likely to make a long squeaking or scraping sound

¹cream *n* **1 :** the thick yellowish part of milk that contains butterfat **2 :** a food prepared with cream **3 :** a very thick liquid used to soften, protect, or heal the skin **4 :** the best part **5 :** a pale yellow

²cream *vb* **creamed; cream·ing 1 :** to stir (as butter) until smooth and soft **2 :** to defeat easily and completely

cream cheese *n* **:** a soft white cheese made from whole milk enriched with cream

cream·ery *n, pl* **cream·er·ies :** a place where milk is made into other products (as cream and cheese)

creamy *adj* **cream·i·er; cream·i·est 1 :** full of or containing cream **2 :** smooth and soft — **cream·i·ness** *n*

¹crease *n* **:** a line or mark made by folding, pressing, or wrinkling

²crease *vb* **creased; creas·ing :** to make a line or lines in or on

cre·ate *vb* **cre·at·ed; cre·at·ing :** to cause to exist : bring into existence : PRODUCE

cre·a·tion *n* **1 :** the act of bringing the world into existence out of nothing **2 :** the act of making, inventing, or producing something **3 :** something produced by human intelligence or imagination **4 :** a wide range of places **5 :** a living thing or living things

cre·a·tive *adj* **:** able to invent or produce new and original things — **cre·a·tive·ly** *adv* — **cre·a·tive·ness** *n*

cre·a·tor *n* **1 :** someone that invents or produces **2** *cap* **:** GOD 1

crea·ture *n* **1 :** a lower animal **2 :** PERSON 1 **3 :** an imaginary or strange being

cred·i·ble *adj* **:** possible to believe : deserving belief — **cred·i·bly** *adv*

¹cred·it *n* **1 :** recognition or honor received for some quality or work **2 :** the balance in an account in a person's favor **3 :** money or goods or services allowed to a person by a bank or business with the expectation of payment later **4 :** good reputation especially for honesty : high standing **5 :** a source of honor or pride **6 :** a unit of schoolwork **7 :** belief or trust in the truth of something

²credit *vb* **cred·it·ed; cred·it·ing 1 :** to give recognition or honor to for something **2 :** to place something in a person's favor on (a business account) **3 :** BELIEVE 2

cred·it·able *adj* **:** good enough to deserve praise

credit card *n* **:** a card with which a person can buy things and pay for them later

cred·i·tor *n* **:** a person to whom a debt is owed

creed *n* **1 :** a statement of the basic beliefs of a religious faith **2 :** a set of guiding rules or beliefs

creek *n* **:** a stream of water usually larger than a brook and smaller than a river

Creek *n* **1 :** a confederacy of American Indian people once occupying most of Alabama and Georgia **2 :** the language of the Creek people

creel *n* **:** a basket for holding caught fish

[1]**creep** *vb* **crept; creep·ing 1 :** to move along with the body close to the ground or floor **:** move slowly on hands and knees **:** CRAWL **2 :** to move or advance slowly, timidly, or quietly **3 :** to grow or spread along the ground or along a surface

[2]**creep** *n* **1 :** a strange or unlikable person **2 :** a slow, timid, or quiet movement **3 :** a feeling of nervousness or fear — usually used in pl.

creep·er *n* **1 :** a person or animal that moves slowly, timidly, or quietly **2 :** a small bird that creeps about trees and bushes in search of insects **3 :** a plant (as ivy) that grows by spreading over a surface

creepy *adj* **creep·i·er; creep·i·est 1 :** EERIE **2 :** annoyingly unpleasant — **creep·i·ness** *n*

cre·mate *vb* **cre·mat·ed; cre·mat·ing :** to burn (as a dead body) to ashes — **cre·ma·tion** *n*

crepe *n* **1 :** a thin crinkled fabric (as of silk or wool) **2 :** a very thin pancake

crepe paper *n* **:** paper with a crinkled or puckered look and feel

crept *past and past participle of* CREEP

cre·scen·do *n, pl* **cre·scen·dos :** a gradual increase in the loudness of music

[1]**cres·cent** *n* **1 :** the shape of the visible part of the moon when it is less than half full **2 :** something shaped like a crescent moon

[2]**crescent** *adj* **:** shaped like the crescent moon

cress *n* **:** a small plant having leaves with a sharp taste that are eaten in salads

crest *n* **1 :** a showy growth (as of flesh or feathers) on the head of an animal **2 :** the highest part or point of something **3 :** an emblem or design used to represent a family, group, or organization — **crest·ed** *adj*

crest·fall·en *adj* **:** feeling disappointment and loss of pride

crev·ice *n* **:** a narrow opening (as in the earth) caused by cracking or splitting **:** FISSURE

crew *n* **1 :** the group of people who operate a ship, train, or airplane **2 :** a group of people working together **3 :** a gathering of people

crib *n* **1 :** a small bed frame with high sides for a child **2 :** a building or bin for storage **3 :** a long open box for feeding animals

[1]**crick·et** *n* **:** a small leaping insect noted for the chirping sound made by the males rubbing part of the wings together

[2]**cricket** *n* **:** a game played on a large field with bats, ball, and wickets by two teams of eleven players

cri·er *n* **:** a person whose job is to call out orders or announcements

crime *n* **1 :** the act of doing something forbidden by law or the failure to do an act required by law **2 :** an act that is foolish or wrong

[1]**crim·i·nal** *adj* **1 :** being or guilty of an act that is unlawful, foolish, or wrong **2 :** relating to unlawful acts or their punishment — **crim·i·nal·ly** *adv*

[2]**criminal** *n* **:** a person who has committed an unlawful act

crimp *vb* **crimped; crimp·ing :** to make wavy or bent

crim·son *n* **:** a deep purplish red

cringe *vb* **cringed; cring·ing 1 :** to shrink in fear **:** COWER **2 :** to show disgust or embarrassment at something

crin·kle *vb* **crin·kled; crin·kling 1 :** to form or cause little waves or wrinkles on the surface **:** WRINKLE **2 :** [1]RUSTLE 1

crin·kly *adj* **crin·kli·er; crin·kli·est :** full of small wrinkles

[1]**crip·ple** *n, sometimes offensive* **:** a disabled person who is unable to fully use one or both of his or her arms or legs

[2]**cripple** *vb* **crip·pled; crip·pling 1 :** to cause to lose the use of one or more arms or legs **2 :** to make useless or powerless

cri·sis *n, pl* **cri·ses :** a difficult or dangerous situation that needs serious attention

[1]**crisp** *adj* **crisp·er; crisp·est 1 :** being thin, hard, and easily crumbled **2 :** pleasantly firm and fresh **3 :** being clear and brief **4 :** pleasantly cool and invigorating **:** BRISK **5 :** having clear details — **crisp·ly** *adv* — **crisp·ness** *n*

[2]**crisp** *vb* **crisped; crisp·ing :** to make or keep something crispy or fresh

crispy *adj* **:** pleasantly thin, dry, and crunchy

criss·cross *vb* **criss·crossed; criss·cross·ing 1 :** to go, pass, or extend back and forth or cover with something that extends back and forth **2 :** to mark with or make lines that go across one another

crit·ic *n* **1 :** a person who makes or gives a judgment of the value, worth, beauty, or quality of something **2 :** a person who finds fault or complains

crit·i·cal *adj* **1 :** likely or eager to find fault **2 :** consisting of or involving judgment of value, worth, beauty, or quality **3 :** using or involving careful judgment **4 :** extremely important — **crit·i·cal·ly** *adv*

crit·i·cism *n* **1 :** the act of finding fault **2 :** a remark that expresses disapproval **3 :** a careful judgment or review especially by a person whose job is to judge the value, worth, beauty, or quality of something

crit·i·cize *vb* **crit·i·cized; crit·i·ciz·ing 1 :** to examine and judge **2 :** to find fault with

crit·ter *n* : a small animal

[1]**croak** *vb* **croaked; croak·ing** **1** : to utter with a rough low voice **2** : to make a deep harsh sound

[2]**croak** *n* : a hoarse harsh sound or cry

[1]**cro·chet** *vb* **cro·cheted; cro·chet·ing** : to make (something) or create a fabric with a hooked needle by forming and weaving loops in a thread

[2]**crochet** *n* : work done or a fabric formed by weaving loops in a thread using a hooked needle

crock *n* : a thick pot or jar of baked clay

crock·ery *n* : EARTHENWARE

croc·o·dile *n* : a reptile that resembles the related alligator but that has a long narrow snout

cro·cus *n* : a small plant having grasslike leaves and colorful flowers that bloom in the spring

cro·ny *n, pl* **cro·nies** : a close companion : CHUM

[1]**crook** *vb* **crooked; crook·ing** : [1]BEND 1, CURVE

[2]**crook** *n* **1** : a dishonest person (as a thief) **2** : a shepherd's staff with one end curved into a hook **3** : a curved or hooked part of a thing : BEND

crook·ed *adj* **1** : having bends and curves **2** : not set or placed straight **3** : DISHONEST — **crook·ed·ly** *adv* — **crook·ed·ness** *n*

croon *vb* **crooned; croon·ing** : to hum or sing in a low soft voice

[1]**crop** *n* **1** : the amount gathered or harvested : HARVEST **2** : a short riding whip **3** : an enlargement just above the stomach of a bird or insect in which food is temporarily stored **4** : BATCH 2, LOT **5** : a close cut of the hair

[2]**crop** *vb* **cropped; crop·ping** **1** : to remove (as by cutting or biting) the upper or outer parts of : TRIM **2** : to grow or yield a crop (as of grain) : cause (land) to bear a crop **3** : to come or appear when not expected

cro·quet *n* : a game in which players hit wooden balls with mallets through a series of wickets set out on a lawn

cro·quette *n* : a roll or ball of hashed meat, fish, or vegetables fried in deep fat

[1]**cross** *n* **1** : a structure, object, or mark consisting of one line or bar extending across another at right angles **2** *often cap* : the structure on which Jesus Christ was crucified used as a symbol of Christianity **3** : sorrow or suffering as a test of patience or virtue **4** : mixture of two different things, types, or qualities

[2]**cross** *vb* **crossed; cross·ing** **1** : to move, pass, or extend across or past **2** : to place one over the other **3** : to lie or be situated across **4** : to go across : INTERSECT **5** : to turn (the eyes) toward the nose **6** : to occur to **7** : to make a gesture by touching the hand to the forehead, breast, and shoulders (as in prayer) **8** : to draw a line across **9** : to cancel by drawing a line through **10** : to act against : OPPOSE **11** : to cause (an animal or plant) to breed with one of another kind : produce hybrids **12** : to pass going in opposite directions

[3]**cross** *adj* **cross·er; cross·est** **1** : hard to get along with : IRRITABLE **2** : lying, falling, or passing across — **cross·ly** *adv*

cross·bar *n* : a piece or stripe placed crosswise or across something

cross·bones *n pl* : two leg or arm bones placed or pictured as lying across each other

cross·bow *n* : a short strip mounted crosswise near the end of a wooden stock that shoots short arrows

cross–ex·am·ine *vb* **cross–ex·am·ined; cross–ex·am·in·ing** : to question (a witness) in an effort to show that statements or answers given earlier in the legal hearing were false

cross–eyed *adj* : having one or both eyes turned toward the nose

cross·ing *n* **1** : a point where a line, track, or street intersects another line, track, or street **2** : a place provided for going across a street, railroad tracks, or a stream **3** : a voyage across a body of water

cross·piece *n* : something placed so as to lie across something else

cross–ref·er·ence *n* : a note (as in a dictionary) that directs a user to information at another place

cross·road *n* : a place where roads run across each other — usually used in pl.

cross section *n* **1** : a cutting made across something (as a log or an apple) **2** : a view showing what the inside of something looks like after a cut has been made through it **3** : a small group that includes examples of the different types of people or things in a larger group

cross·walk *n* : a specially marked path for people to walk across a street

cross·wise *adv* : so as to cross something

cross·word puzzle *n* : a puzzle in which words are filled into a pattern of numbered squares in answer to clues so that they read across and down

crotch *n* **1** : the part of the body where the legs join together **2** : an angle formed by the spreading apart of two legs or branches or of a limb from its trunk

crotch·ety *adj* : very grumpy or unpleasant

[1]**crouch** *vb* **crouched; crouch·ing** : to stoop

or bend low with the arms and legs close to the body
[2]crouch *n* **:** the position of stooping with the arms and legs close to the body
croup *n* **:** an illness that usually affects young children and causes a hoarse cough and difficult breathing
[1]crow *n* **1 :** a glossy black bird that has a harsh cry **2** *cap* **:** a member of an American Indian people of Montana **3 :** the language of the Crow people
[2]crow *vb* **crowed; crow·ing 1 :** to make the loud cry of a rooster **2 :** to make sounds of delight **3 :** [1]BOAST 1 **4 :** to say with delight
[3]crow *n* **1 :** the cry of a rooster **2 :** a cry of triumph
crow·bar *n* **:** a metal bar used as a lever (as for prying things apart)
[1]crowd *vb* **crowded; crowd·ing 1 :** to push into a small space **2 :** to form a tight group **3 :** to collect in numbers **4 :** to fill or pack by pressing together
[2]crowd *n* **1 :** a large number of people in one place **2 :** the population as a whole **:** ordinary people **3 :** a group of people who spend time together or have a common interest
[1]crown *n* **1 :** a royal headdress **2 :** a wreath or band worn especially as a symbol of victory or honor **3 :** the top of the head **4 :** the highest part (as of a tree or mountain) **5** *often cap* **:** royal power or authority, a person having such power, or the government of a country ruled by a king or queen **6 :** any of various coins (as a British coin worth five shillings) **7 :** the top part of a hat **8 :** the part of a tooth outside of the gum or an artificial substitute for it — **crowned** *adj*
[2]crown *vb* **crowned; crown·ing 1 :** to place a royal headdress on **:** give the title of king or queen to **2 :** to declare officially to be **3 :** to cover or be situated on the top of **4 :** to bring to a conclusion **5 :** to put an artificial crown on a damaged tooth **6 :** to hit on the head
crow's nest *n* **:** a partly enclosed place to stand high on the mast of a ship for use as a lookout
cru·cial *adj* **1 :** being a final or very important test or decision **:** DECISIVE **2 :** very important **:** SIGNIFICANT
cru·ci·ble *n* **:** a pot in which metals or other substances are heated to a very high temperature or melted
cru·ci·fix *n* **:** a cross with a figure representing Jesus crucified on it
cru·ci·fix·ion *n* **1 :** the act of killing someone by nailing his or her feet and hands to a cross **2** *cap* **:** the crucifying of Jesus on a cross
cru·ci·fy *vb* **cru·ci·fied; cru·ci·fy·ing 1 :** to put to death by nailing or binding the hands and feet to a cross **2 :** to treat cruelly or harshly
crude *adj* **crud·er; crud·est 1 :** in a natural state and not changed by special treatment **:** RAW **2 :** planned or done in a rough or unskilled way **3 :** not having or showing good manners **:** VULGAR — **crude·ly** *adv* — **crude·ness** *n*
cru·el *adj* **cru·el·er** *or* **cru·el·ler; cru·el·est** *or* **cru·el·lest 1 :** wanting to cause others to suffer **2 :** causing or helping to cause suffering — **cru·el·ly** *adv*
cru·el·ty *n, pl* **cru·el·ties 1 :** the quality or state of causing or wanting to cause suffering **2 :** treatment that causes suffering
[1]cruise *vb* **cruised; cruis·ing 1 :** to travel by ship often stopping at a series of ports **2 :** to travel at a steady pace
[2]cruise *n* **:** a trip on a ship
cruis·er *n* **1 :** a police car used for patrolling streets and equipped with radio for communicating with headquarters **2 :** a warship that is smaller than a battleship **3 :** a motorboat equipped for living aboard
crumb *n* **1 :** a very small piece of food **2 :** a little bit
crum·ble *vb* **crum·bled; crum·bling 1 :** to break into small pieces **2 :** to fall to pieces **:** fall into ruin
crum·bly *adj* **crum·bli·er; crum·bli·est :** easily broken into small pieces
crum·my *adj* **crum·mi·er; crum·mi·est :** very poor
crum·ple *vb* **crum·pled; crum·pling 1 :** to press or crush out of shape **2 :** to become full of wrinkles **3 :** [1]COLLAPSE 1
[1]crunch *vb* **crunched; crunch·ing 1 :** to chew or grind with a crushing noise **2 :** to make the sound of being crushed or squeezed
[2]crunch *n* **:** an act or sound of crushing
crunchy *adj* **crunch·i·er; crunch·i·est :** being firm and making a sharp sound when chewed or crushed
[1]cru·sade *n* **1** *cap* **:** one of the military expeditions made by Christian countries in the eleventh, twelfth, and thirteenth centuries to win the Holy Land from the Muslims **2 :** a campaign to get things changed for the better
[2]crusade *vb* **cru·sad·ed; cru·sad·ing 1 :** to take part in a medieval military expedition to win the Holy Land **2 :** to take part in a campaign to make things better — **cru·sad·er** *n*
[1]crush *vb* **crushed; crush·ing 1 :** to squeeze together so as to change or destroy the natural shape or condition **2 :** to break into fine pieces by pressure **3 :** OVERWHELM 1 **4 :** to defeat in spirit
[2]crush *n* **1 :** a tightly packed crowd **2 :** a foolish or very strong liking **:** INFATUATION

crust *n* **1 :** the hardened outside surface of bread **2 :** a hard dry piece of bread **3 :** the pastry cover of a pie **4 :** a hard outer covering or surface layer **5 :** the outer part of the earth

crus·ta·cean *n* **:** any of a large group of mostly water animals (as crabs, lobsters, and shrimps) with a body made of segments, a tough outer shell, two pairs of antennae, and limbs that are jointed

crusty *adj* **crust·i·er; crust·i·est** **1 :** having a thick or crispy crust **2 :** [3]CROSS 1

crutch *n* **1 :** a long stick usually made with a piece at the top to fit under the armpit that is used as an aid in walking **2 :** something that a person depends on to help deal with problems

[1]cry *vb* **cried; cry·ing** **1 :** to shed tears **:** WEEP **2 :** to make a loud call **:** SHOUT, EXCLAIM **3 :** to utter a special sound or call

[2]cry *n, pl* **cries** **1 :** a loud call or shout (as of pain, fear, or joy) **2 :** [1]APPEAL 2 **3 :** an act or period of weeping **4 :** the special sound made by an animal

cry·ba·by *n, pl* **cry·ba·bies** **:** a person who cries easily or who complains often

cryp·tic *adj* **:** difficult to understand or make sense of

[1]crys·tal *n* **1 :** quartz that is colorless and clear or nearly so **2 :** a body formed by a substance hardening so that it has flat surfaces in an even arrangement **3 :** a clear colorless glass of very good quality **4 :** something clear like colorless quartz **5 :** the clear cover over a clock or watch dial

[2]crystal *adj* **1 :** made of or being like a clear colorless glass of very good quality **2 :** [1]CLEAR 4

crys·tal·line *adj* **1 :** made of crystal or composed of crystals **2 :** [1]CLEAR 4

crys·tal·lize *vb* **crys·tal·lized; crys·tal·liz·ing** **1 :** to form or cause to form crystals or grains **2 :** to take or cause to take definite form

ct. *abbr* **1** cent **2** court

CT *abbr* Connecticut

cu. *abbr* cubic

cub *n* **1 :** the young of various animals (as the bear, fox, or lion) **2 :** CUB SCOUT

cub·by·hole *n* **:** a snug place (as for storing things)

[1]cube *n* **1 :** a solid body having six equal square sides **2 :** the product obtained by multiplying the square of a number by the number itself

[2]cube *vb* **cubed; cub·ing** **1 :** to take (a number) as a factor three times **2 :** to cut food into solid squares

cu·bic *adj* **1 :** having the shape of a cube **2 :** being the volume of a cube whose edge has a specified length

cu·bit *n* **:** a unit of length usually equal to about 18 inches (46 centimeters)

Cub Scout *n* **:** a member of a program of the Boy Scouts for boys in the first through fifth grades in school

cuck·oo *n, pl* **cuckoos** **1 :** a grayish brown European bird that lays eggs in the nests of other birds which hatch and raise them **2 :** the call of the cuckoo

cu·cum·ber *n* **:** a long usually green-skinned vegetable that is used in salads and for making pickles and is the fruit of a vine related to the melons and gourds

cud *n* **:** a portion of food brought up from the first stomach compartment of some animals (as the cow and sheep) to be chewed again

cud·dle *vb* **cud·dled; cud·dling** **1 :** to hold close for warmth or comfort or in affection **2 :** to lie close **:** NESTLE, SNUGGLE

[1]cud·gel *n* **:** a short heavy club

[2]cudgel *vb* **cud·geled** *or* **cud·gelled; cud·gel·ing** *or* **cud·gel·ling** **:** to beat with or as if with a short heavy club

[1]cue *n* **1 :** something serving as a signal or suggestion **:** HINT **2 :** a word, phrase, or action in a play serving as a signal for the next actor to speak or to do something

[2]cue *n* **:** a straight tapering stick used in playing billiards and pool

[1]cuff *n* **1 :** a band or turned-over piece at the end of a sleeve **2 :** the turned-back hem of a pant leg

[2]cuff *vb* **cuffed; cuff·ing** **:** to strike especially with or as if with the palm of the hand **:** SLAP

[3]cuff *n* **:** [2]SLAP 1

cu·li·nary *adj* **:** of or relating to the kitchen or cooking

[1]cull *vb* **culled; cull·ing** **1 :** to select from a group **2 :** to identify and remove less desirable members from

[2]cull *n* **:** something rejected from a group because it is not as good as the rest

cul·mi·nate *vb* **cul·mi·nat·ed; cul·mi·nat·ing** **:** to reach the end or the final result of

cul·prit *n* **:** a person accused of, charged with, or guilty of a crime or fault

cul·ti·vate *vb* **cul·ti·vat·ed; cul·ti·vat·ing** **1 :** to prepare land for the raising of crops **2 :** to raise or assist the growth of crops by tilling or by labor and care **3 :** to improve or develop by careful attention, training, or study **:** devote time and thought to **4 :** to seek the company and friendship of

cul·ti·vat·ed *adj* **1 :** raised or grown on a farm or under other controlled conditions **2 :** having or showing good education and proper manners

cul·ti·va·tion *n* **1 :** the act or process of preparing the soil for the raising of crops **2** : REFINEMENT 2

cul·ti·va·tor *n* : a tool or machine for loosening the soil between rows of a crop

cul·tur·al *adj* **1** : relating to the habits, beliefs, and traditions of a certain people **2** : relating to the arts (as music, dance, or painting) — **cul·tur·al·ly** *adv*

cul·ture *n* **1** : CULTIVATION 1 **2** : the raising or development (as of a crop or product) by careful attention **3** : the appreciation and knowledge of the arts (as music, dance, and painting) **4** : the habits, beliefs, and traditions of a particular people, place, or time

cul·tured *adj* **1** : having or showing refinement in taste, speech, or manners **2** : produced under artificial conditions

cul·vert *n* : a drain or waterway crossing under a road or railroad

cum·ber·some *adj* : hard to handle or manage because of size or weight

cu·mu·la·tive *adj* : increasing (as in force, strength, amount, or importance) over time

cu·mu·lus *n, pl* **cu·mu·li** : a massive cloud form having a flat base and rounded outlines often piled up like a mountain

cu·ne·i·form *adj* : made up of or written with marks or letters shaped like wedges — **cuneiform** *n*

[1]**cun·ning** *adj* **1** : skillful and clever at using special knowledge or at getting something done **2** : showing craftiness and trickery

[2]**cunning** *n* **1** : SKILL 1, DEXTERITY **2** : cleverness in getting what one wants often by tricks or deception

[1]**cup** *n* **1** : a container to drink out of in the shape of a small bowl usually with a handle **2** : the contents of a small drinking container : CUPFUL **3** : a unit of measure that equals half a pint or eight fluid ounces **4** : a trophy in the shape of a cup with two handles **5** : something like a small bowl in shape or use

[2]**cup** *vb* **cupped; cup·ping** **1** : to curve the hand or hands into the shape of a small bowl **2** : to put the hands in a curved shape around

cup·board *n* : a closet usually with shelves for dishes or food

cup·cake *n* : a small cake baked in a mold shaped like a cup

cup·ful *n, pl* **cup·fuls** *also* **cups·ful** **1** : the amount held by a cup **2** : a half pint : eight ounces (about 236 milliliters)

cu·pid *n* **1** *cap* : the god of love in ancient Roman mythology **2** : a picture or statue of a naked child with wings holding a bow and arrow and symbolizing love

cu·po·la *n* **1** : a small structure built on top of a roof **2** : a rounded roof or ceiling : DOME

cur *n* : a worthless or mongrel dog

cur·able *adj* : possible to bring about recovery from : possible to cure

cu·rate *n* : a member of the clergy who is in charge of a parish or who assists the rector or vicar of a church

cu·ra·tor *n* : a person in charge of a museum or zoo

[1]**curb** *n* **1** : an enclosing border (as of stone or concrete) often along the edge of a street **2** : [1]CHECK 2

[2]**curb** *vb* **curbed; curb·ing** : to control or limit

curb·ing *n* **1** : material for making an enclosing border along the edge of a street **2** : [1]CURB 1

curd *n* : the thickened or solid part of milk that separates from the whey after milk sours and is used to make cheese

cur·dle *vb* **cur·dled; cur·dling** : to thicken or cause to become thickened with or as if with curds

[1]**cure** *n* **1** : something (as a drug or medical treatment) that brings about recovery from a disease or illness : REMEDY **2** : recovery or relief from a disease **3** : something that solves a problem or improves a bad situation

[2]**cure** *vb* **cured; cur·ing** **1** : to make or become healthy or sound again **2** : to bring about recovery from **3** : to prepare by or undergo a chemical or physical process for use or storage **4** : to provide a solution for

cur·few *n* : a rule requiring certain or all people to be off the streets or at home at a stated time

cu·rio *n, pl* **cu·ri·os** : a rare or unusual article : CURIOSITY

cu·ri·os·i·ty *n, pl* **cu·ri·os·i·ties** **1** : an eager desire to learn and often to learn things that are another's concern **2** : something strange or unusual **3** : an object or article valued because it is strange or rare

cu·ri·ous *adj* **1** : eager to learn : INQUISITIVE **2** : showing an eagerness to learn **3** : attracting attention by being strange or unusual : ODD — **cu·ri·ous·ly** *adv*

[1]**curl** *vb* **curled; curl·ing** **1** : to twist or form into ringlets **2** : to take or move in a curved form — **curl up** : to arrange the body into a ball

[2]**curl** *n* **1** : a lock of hair that coils : RINGLET **2** : something having a spiral or winding form : COIL

cur·li·cue *n* : a fancy shape having curves in it

curly *adj* **curl·i·er; curl·i·est** **1** : having coils **2** : having a curved shape

cur·rant *n* **1 :** a small seedless raisin used in baking and cooking **2 :** a sour red, white, or black edible berry that is often used in making jams and jellies

cur·ren·cy *n, pl* **cur·ren·cies** **1 :** common use or acceptance **2 :** money in circulation

[1]**cur·rent** *adj* **1 :** now passing **2 :** occurring in or belonging to the present time **3 :** generally and widely accepted, used, or practiced

[2]**current** *n* **1 :** a body of fluid (as air or water) moving in a specified direction **2 :** the swiftest part of a stream **3 :** the general course **:** TREND **4 :** a flow of electricity

cur·ric·u·lum *n, pl* **cur·ric·u·la** *also* **cur·ric·u·lums :** all the courses of study offered by a school

cur·ry favor *vb* **cur·ried favor; cur·ry·ing favor :** to try to win approval by saying or doing nice things

[1]**curse** *n* **1 :** a series of words calling for harm to come to someone **2 :** a word or an expression used in swearing or in calling for harm to come to someone **3 :** evil or misfortune that comes as if in answer to someone's request **4 :** a cause of great harm or evil

[2]**curse** *vb* **cursed; curs·ing** **1 :** to call upon divine power to send harm or evil upon **2 :** SWEAR 5 **3 :** to bring unhappiness or evil upon **:** AFFLICT **4 :** to say or think bad things about (someone or something)

cur·sive *n* **:** a type of handwriting in which all the letters of a word are connected to each other — **cursive** *adj*

cur·sor *n* **:** a symbol (as an arrow or blinking line) on a computer screen that shows where the user is working

cur·so·ry *adj* **:** done or made quickly

curt *adj* **curt·er; curt·est :** rudely brief in language — **curt·ly** *adv*

cur·tail *vb* **cur·tailed; cur·tail·ing :** to shorten or reduce by cutting off the end or a part of

[1]**cur·tain** *n* **1 :** a piece of material (as cloth) hung up to darken, hide, divide, or decorate **2 :** something that covers, hides, or separates like a curtain

[2]**curtain** *vb* **cur·tained; cur·tain·ing** **1 :** to furnish with cloth that darkens, hides, divides, or decorates **2 :** to hide or shut off

[1]**curt·sy** *also* **curt·sey** *vb* **curt·sied** *also* **curt·seyed; curt·sy·ing** *also* **curt·sey·ing :** to lower the body slightly by bending the knees as an act of politeness or respect

[2]**curtsy** *also* **curtsey** *n, pl* **curtsies** *also* **curtseys :** an act of politeness or respect made by women and consisting of a slight lowering of the body by bending the knees

cur·va·ture *n* **:** a part having a somewhat round shape

[1]**curve** *vb* **curved; curv·ing :** to turn or cause to turn from a straight line or course

[2]**curve** *n* **1 :** a smooth rounded line or surface **2 :** something having a somewhat round shape **3 :** a ball thrown so that it moves away from a straight course

[1]**cush·ion** *n* **1 :** a soft pillow or pad to rest on or against **2 :** something soft like a pad **3 :** something that serves to soften or lessen the effects of something bad or unpleasant

[2]**cushion** *vb* **cush·ioned; cush·ion·ing** **1 :** to place on or as if on a soft pillow or pad **2 :** to furnish with a soft pillow or pad **3 :** to soften or lessen the force or shock of

cusp *n* **:** a point or pointed end

cus·pid *n* **:** [1]CANINE 1

cuss *vb* **cussed; cuss·ing :** SWEAR 5

cus·tard *n* **:** a sweetened mixture of milk and eggs baked, boiled, or frozen

cus·to·di·an *n* **:** a person who guards and protects or takes care of

cus·to·dy *n* **1 :** direct responsibility for care and control **2 :** the state of being arrested or held by police

[1]**cus·tom** *n* **1 :** the usual way of doing things **:** the usual practice **2 customs** *pl* **:** duties or taxes paid on imports or exports **3 :** support given to a business by its customers

[2]**custom** *adj* **1 :** made or done to personal order **2 :** specializing in work done to personal order

cus·tom·ary *adj* **1 :** usual in a particular situation or at a particular place or time **2 :** typical of a particular person

cus·tom·er *n* **:** a person who buys from or uses the services of a company especially regularly

[1]**cut** *vb* **cut; cut·ting** **1 :** to penetrate or divide with or as if with an edged tool **:** CLEAVE **2 :** to undergo shaping or penetrating with an edged tool **3 :** to divide into two or more parts **4 :** to shorten or remove with scissors, a knife, or clippers **5 :** to go by a short or direct path or course **6 :** to destroy the connection of **7 :** to intentionally not attend **8 :** to move quickly or suddenly **9 :** to make less **10 :** to experience the growth of through the gum **11 :** to stop or cause to stop **12 :** to cause painful feelings **13 :** to shape by carving or grinding — **cut down** **1 :** to knock down and wound or kill **2 :** to reduce the size or amount of — **cut off** **1 :** ISOLATE **2 :** DISCONTINUE **3 :** to stop or interrupt while speaking — **cut out** **1 :** to form by removing with scissors, a knife, or a saw **2 :** to assign through necessity **3 :** to put an end to

[2]**cut** *n* **1 :** something (as a gash or wound) produced by a sharp object **2 :** REDUCTION 1 **3 :** something resulting from shortening,

division, or removal **4 :** [1]SHARE 1 **5 :** a sharp stroke or blow **6 :** the way in which a thing is styled, formed, or made **7 :** something done or said that hurts someone's feelings

cute *adj* **cut·er; cut·est** **1 :** attractive in looks or actions **2 :** CLEVER 2 **3 :** clever in a way that annoys

cu·ti·cle *n* **1 :** an outer layer (as of skin or a leaf) often produced by the cells beneath **2 :** a dead or hard layer of skin especially around a fingernail

cut·lass *n* **:** a short heavy curved sword

cut·lery *n* **1 :** cutting tools (as knives and scissors) **2 :** utensils used in cutting, serving, and eating food

cut·let *n* **1 :** a small thin slice of meat **2 :** meat, fish, or vegetables pressed into a flat piece, covered with bread crumbs, and fried

cut·out *n* **:** a shape or picture that has been formed or removed with scissors, a knife, or a saw

cut·ter *n* **1 :** someone or something that cuts **2 :** a boat used by warships for carrying passengers and stores to and from the shore **3 :** a small sailing boat with one mast **4 :** a small military ship

cut·ting *n* **:** a part (as a shoot) of a plant able to grow into a whole new plant

cutting edge *n* **1 :** the foremost part or place **2 :** the forefront of an action or movement — **cutting–edge** *adj*

cut·tle·fish *n* **:** a sea animal with ten arms that is related to the squid and octopus

cut·up *n* **:** a person who behaves in a silly way and tries to make other people laugh

cut·worm *n* **:** a moth caterpillar that has a smooth body and feeds on the stems of plants at night

-cy *n suffix, pl* **-cies** **1 :** action **:** practice **2 :** rank **:** office **3 :** body **:** class **4 :** state **:** quality

cy·a·nide *n* **:** any of several compounds containing carbon and nitrogen and including two very poisonous substances

cyber- *prefix* **:** relating to computers or computer networks

cy·ber·bul·ly·ing *n* **:** the act of bullying someone through electronic means (as by posting mean or threatening messages about the person online)

cy·ber·space *n* **:** the online world of computer networks and especially the Internet

cy·cad *n* **:** a tropical plant like a palm but related to the conifers

[1]**cy·cle** *n* **1 :** a period of time taken up by a series of events or actions that repeat themselves again and again in the same order **2 :** a complete round or series **3 :** [1]BICYCLE **4 :** MOTORCYCLE

[2]**cycle** *vb* **cy·cled; cy·cling :** to ride a bicycle or motorcycle

cy·clist *n* **:** a person who rides a bicycle

cy·clone *n* **1 :** a storm or system of winds that rotates about a center of low atmospheric pressure and that moves forward at a speed of 20 to 30 miles (30 to 50 kilometers) an hour and often brings heavy rain **2 :** TORNADO

cyl·in·der *n* **:** a long round body whether hollow or solid

cy·lin·dri·cal *adj* **:** having a long round shape

cym·bal *n* **:** a musical instrument in the form of a brass plate that is struck with a drumstick or is used in pairs struck together

cyn·i·cal *adj* **:** believing that people are selfish and dishonest

cy·press *n* **:** an evergreen tree or shrub with small overlapping leaves resembling scales

cyst *n* **1 :** an abnormal lump or sac that forms in or on the body **2 :** a saclike structure with a protective covering or a body (as a spore) with such a covering

cy·to·plasm *n* **:** the jellylike material that fills most of the space in a cell and surrounds the nucleus

CZ *abbr* Canal Zone

czar *n* **:** the ruler of Russia before 1917

cza·ri·na *n* **:** the wife of a czar

D

d *n, pl* **d's** *or* **ds** *often cap* **1 :** the fourth letter of the English alphabet **2 :** 500 in Roman numerals **3 :** a grade that shows a student's work is poor **4 :** a musical note referred to by the letter D

d. *abbr* **1** day **2** dead **3** deceased **4** penny

¹dab *n* **1 :** a small amount **2 :** a light quick touch

²dab *vb* **dabbed; dab·bing 1 :** to strike or touch lightly **2 :** to apply with light or uneven strokes

dab·ble *vb* **dab·bled; dab·bling 1 :** to wet by splashing **:** SPATTER **2 :** to paddle or play in or as if in water **3 :** to work without any deep involvement — **dab·bler** *n*

dace *n, pl* **dace :** a small freshwater fish related to the carp

dachs·hund *n* **:** a small dog of German origin with a long body, short legs, and long drooping ears

dad *n* **:** ¹FATHER 1

dad·dy *n, pl* **daddies :** ¹FATHER 1

dad·dy long·legs *n, pl* **daddy longlegs 1 :** a small animal like the related spider but with longer more slender legs **2 :** a two-winged fly with long legs that resembles a large mosquito but does not bite

daf·fo·dil *n* **:** a plant that grows from a bulb and has long slender leaves and usually yellow or white flowers with petals whose inner parts are arranged to form a trumpet-shaped tube

daf·fy *adj* **daf·fi·er; daf·fi·est :** silly or oddly funny

daft *adj* **daft·er; daft·est :** FOOLISH, CRAZY

dag·ger *n* **:** a short knife used for stabbing

dahl·ia *n* **:** a plant related to the daisies and grown for its brightly colored flowers

¹dai·ly *adj* **1 :** occurring, done, produced, appearing, or used every day or every weekday **2 :** figured by the day

²daily *adv* **:** every day

³daily *n, pl* **dai·lies :** a newspaper published every weekday

¹dain·ty *n, pl* **dain·ties :** a delicious food **:** DELICACY

²dainty *adj* **dain·ti·er; dain·ti·est 1 :** tasting good **2 :** pretty in a delicate way **3 :** having or showing delicate or finicky taste — **dain·ti·ly** *adv*

dairy *n, pl* **dair·ies 1 :** a place where milk is stored or is made into butter and cheese **2 :** a farm that produces milk **3 :** a company or a store that sells milk products

da·is *n* **:** a raised platform (as in a hall or large room)

dai·sy *n, pl* **daisies :** a plant with flower heads consisting of one or more rows of white or colored flowers like petals around a central disk of tiny often yellow flowers closely packed together

Da·ko·ta *n, pl* **Da·ko·tas** *also* **Dakota 1 :** a member of an American Indian people of the area that is now Minnesota, North Dakota, and South Dakota **2 :** the language of the Dakota people

dale *n* **:** VALLEY

dal·ly *vb* **dal·lied; dal·ly·ing 1 :** to act playfully **2 :** to waste time **3 :** LINGER 1, DAWDLE

dal·ma·tian *n, often cap* **:** a large dog having a short white coat with black or brown spots

¹dam *n* **:** the female parent of a domestic animal (as a dog or horse)

²dam *n* **:** a barrier (as across a stream) to hold back a flow of water

³dam *vb* **dammed; dam·ming :** to hold back or block with or as if with a dam

¹dam·age *n* **1 :** loss or harm caused by injury to a person's body or property **2 damages** *pl* **:** money demanded or paid according to law for injury or damage

²damage *vb* **dam·aged; dam·ag·ing :** to cause harm or loss to

dame *n* **:** a woman of high rank or social position

¹damn *vb* **damned; damn·ing 1 :** to condemn to everlasting punishment especially in hell **2 :** to declare to be bad or a failure **3 :** to swear at **:** CURSE

²damn *or* **damned** *adj* **1 :** very bad **2 —** used to make a statement more forceful

¹damp *n* **1 :** MOISTURE **2 :** a harmful gas found especially in coal mines

²damp *vb* **damped; damp·ing :** DAMPEN

³damp *adj* **damp·er; damp·est :** slightly wet **:** MOIST — **damp·ness** *n*

damp·en *vb* **damp·ened; damp·en·ing 1 :** to make or become slighty wet **2 :** to make dull or less active

damp·er *n* **1 :** something that discourages or deadens **2 :** a valve or movable plate for controlling a flow of air

dam·sel *n* **:** GIRL 1, MAIDEN

¹dance *vb* **danced; danc·ing 1 :** to step or move through a series of movements usually in time to music **2 :** to move about or up and down quickly and lightly — **danc·er** *n*

²dance *n* **1 :** an act of stepping or moving through a series of movements usually in time to music **2 :** a social gathering for

dancing **3 :** a set of movements or steps for dancing usually in time to special music **4 :** the art of dancing
dan·de·li·on *n* **:** a weedy plant that has bright yellow flowers with hollow stems and long deeply toothed leaves that are often eaten
dan·der *n* **1 :** tiny scales from hair, feathers, or skin that may cause allergic reactions **2 :** ²ANGER
dan·druff *n* **:** thin dry whitish flakes of dead skin that form on the scalp and come off freely
¹**dan·dy** *n, pl* **dandies 1 :** a man who is extremely interested in his clothes and appearance **2 :** something excellent or unusual
²**dandy** *adj* **dan·di·er; dan·di·est :** very good
Dane *n* **:** a person born or living in Denmark
dan·ger *n* **1 :** the state of not being protected from harm or evil **:** PERIL **2 :** something that may cause injury or harm
dan·ger·ous *adj* **1 :** involving possible harm or death **:** full of danger **2 :** able or likely to injure — **dan·ger·ous·ly** *adv*
dan·gle *vb* **dan·gled; dan·gling 1 :** to hang loosely especially with a swinging motion **2 :** to cause to hang loosely
¹**Dan·ish** *adj* **:** belonging to or relating to Denmark, the Danes, or the Danish language
²**Danish** *n* **1 :** the language of the Danes **2 :** a piece of Danish pastry
Danish pastry *n* **:** a pastry made of rich raised dough
dank *adj* **dank·er; dank·est :** unpleasantly wet or moist
dap·per *adj* **:** neat and trim in dress or appearance
dap·ple *vb* **dap·pled; dap·pling :** to mark or become marked with rounded spots of color
¹**dare** *vb* **dared; dar·ing 1 :** to have courage enough for some purpose **:** be bold enough — sometimes used as a helping verb **2 :** to challenge to do something especially as a proof of courage **3 :** to face with courage
²**dare** *n* **:** a challenge to do something as proof of courage
dare·dev·il *n* **:** a person who does dangerous things especially for attention
¹**dar·ing** *adj* **:** ready to take risks **:** BOLD, VENTURESOME
²**daring** *n* **:** bold fearlessness **:** readiness to take chances
¹**dark** *adj* **dark·er; dark·est 1 :** without light or without much light **2 :** not light in color **3 :** not bright and cheerful **:** GLOOMY **4 :** arising from or characterized by evil
²**dark** *n* **1 :** absence of light **:** DARKNESS **2 :** a place or time of little or no light
Dark Ages *n pl* **:** the period of history from about A.D. 476 to about 1000
dark·en *vb* **dark·ened; dark·en·ing 1 :** to make or grow dark or darker **2 :** to make or become gloomy
dark·ly *adv* **1 :** with a dark or blackish color **2 :** with a gloomy or threatening manner or quality
dark·ness *n* **1 :** absence of light **2 :** NIGHT 1 **3 :** ²EVIL 1, WICKEDNESS
dark·room *n* **:** a usually small dark room used in developing photographic plates and film
¹**dar·ling** *n* **1 :** a dearly loved person **2 :** ¹FAVORITE
²**darling** *adj* **1 :** dearly loved **2 :** very pleasing **:** CHARMING
¹**darn** *vb* **darned; darn·ing :** to mend by sewing
²**darn** *interj* — used to express anger or annoyance
³**darn** *or* **darned** *adj* **1 :** very bad **2** — used to make a statement more forceful
darning needle *n* **:** DRAGONFLY
¹**dart** *n* **1 :** a small pointed object that is meant to be thrown **2 darts** *pl* **:** a game in which darts are thrown at a target **3 :** a quick sudden movement **4 :** a fold sewed into a piece of clothing
²**dart** *vb* **dart·ed; dart·ing :** to move or shoot out suddenly and quickly
¹**dash** *vb* **dashed; dash·ing 1 :** to knock, hurl, or shove violently **2 :** ²SMASH 1 **3 :** ¹SPLASH 2 **4 :** ¹RUIN 2 **5 :** to complete or do hastily **6 :** to move with sudden speed
²**dash** *n* **1 :** a sudden burst or splash **2 :** a punctuation mark — that is used most often to show a break in the thought or structure of a sentence **3 :** a small amount **:** TOUCH **4 :** liveliness in style and action **5 :** a sudden rush or attempt **6 :** a short fast race **7 :** a long click or buzz forming a letter or part of a letter (as in Morse code) **8 :** DASHBOARD
dash·board *n* **:** a panel across an automobile or aircraft below the windshield usually containing dials and controls
dash·ing *adj* **:** very attractive
das·tard·ly *adj* **:** very mean and tricky
da·ta *n pl* **1 :** facts about something that can be used in calculating, reasoning, or planning **2 :** information expressed as numbers for use especially in a computer — used as singular or plural
da·ta·base *n* **:** a collection of data that is organized especially to be used by a computer
¹**date** *n* **:** the sweet brownish fruit of an Old World palm (**date palm**)
²**date** *n* **1 :** the day, month, or year on which an event happens or happened **2 :** a statement of time on something (as a coin, letter, book, or building) **3 :** APPOINTMENT 1 **4 :** an arrangement to meet between two people usually with romantic feelings for each

other **5 :** either of two people who meet for a usually romantic social engagement

³date *vb* **dat·ed; dat·ing 1 :** to write the date on **2 :** to find or show the date or age of **3 :** to belong to or have survived from a time **4 :** to make or have a date with **5 :** to go together regularly on romantic social engagements

da·tum *n, pl* **da·ta** *or* **da·tums :** a single piece of information **:** FACT

¹daub *vb* **daubed; daub·ing :** to cover with something soft and sticky

²daub *n* **:** a small amount of something

daugh·ter *n* **1 :** a female child or offspring **2 :** a woman or girl associated with or thought of as a child of something (as a country, race, or religion)

daugh·ter–in–law *n, pl* **daugh·ters–in–law :** the wife of a person's son or daughter

daunt *vb* **daunt·ed; daunt·ing :** DISCOURAGE 1, FRIGHTEN

daunt·ing *adj* **:** likely to discourage or frighten

daunt·less *adj* **:** bravely determined

daw·dle *vb* **daw·dled; daw·dling 1 :** to spend time wastefully **:** DALLY **2 :** to move slowly and without purpose

¹dawn *vb* **dawned; dawn·ing 1 :** to begin to grow light as the sun rises **2 :** to start becoming plain or clear

²dawn *n* **1 :** the time when the sun comes up in the morning **2 :** a first appearance **:** BEGINNING

day *n* **1 :** the time between sunrise and sunset **:** DAYLIGHT **2 :** the time a planet or moon takes to make one turn on its axis **3 :** a period of 24 hours beginning at midnight **4 :** a specified day or date **5 :** a particular time **:** AGE **6 :** the time set apart by custom or law for work

day·break *n* **:** ²DAWN 1

day care *n* **:** a program in which or a place where care is provided during the day for young children

¹day·dream *n* **:** a person's pleasant and usually wishful thoughts about life

²daydream *vb* **day·dreamed; day·dream·ing :** to think pleasant and usually wishful thoughts while awake

day·light *n* **1 :** the light of day **2 :** DAYTIME **3 :** ²DAWN 1

daylight saving time *n* **:** time usually one hour ahead of standard time

day·time *n* **:** the period of daylight

¹daze *vb* **dazed; daz·ing 1 :** to stun by or as if by a blow **2 :** to dazzle with light

²daze *n* **:** a state of not being able to think or act as quickly as normal

daz·zle *vb* **daz·zled; daz·zling 1 :** to overpower with too much light **2 :** to confuse, surprise, or delight by being or doing something special and unusual — **daz·zling·ly** *adv*

DC *abbr* **2** District of Columbia **1** direct current

DDS *abbr* doctor of dental surgery

DDT *n* **:** a chemical that was used as an insecticide until it was found to damage the environment

DE *abbr* Delaware

de- *prefix* **1 :** do the opposite of **2 :** reverse of **3 :** remove or remove from something **4 :** reduce **5 :** get off of

dea·con *n* **1 :** an official in some Christian churches ranking just below a priest **2 :** a church member in some Christian churches who has special duties

¹dead *adj* **1 :** no longer living **2 :** having the look of death **3 :** ¹NUMB 1 **4 :** very tired **5 :** lacking motion, activity, energy, or power to function **6 :** no longer in use **7 :** no longer active **8 :** lacking warmth or vigor **9 :** not lively **10 :** ACCURATE, PRECISE **11 :** being sudden and complete **12 :** ¹COMPLETE 1, TOTAL **13 :** facing certain punishment

²dead *n, pl* **dead 1 :** a person who is no longer alive — usually used for all people who are no longer alive **2 :** the time of greatest quiet or least activity

³dead *adv* **1 :** in a whole or complete manner **2 :** suddenly and completely **3 :** ²STRAIGHT

dead·en *vb* **dead·ened; dead·en·ing :** to take away some of the force of **:** make less

dead end *n* **:** an end (as of a street) with no way out

dead·line *n* **:** a date or time by which something must be done

¹dead·lock *n* **:** a situation in which a disagreement cannot be ended because neither side will give in

²deadlock *vb* **dead·locked; dead·lock·ing :** to be unable to end a disagreement because neither side will give in

¹dead·ly *adj* **dead·li·er; dead·li·est 1 :** causing or capable of causing death **2 :** meaning or hoping to kill or destroy **3 :** very accurate **4 :** ¹EXTREME 1

²deadly *adv* **1 :** in a way suggestive of death **2 :** to an extreme degree

deaf *adj* **1 :** wholly or partly unable to hear **2 :** unwilling to hear or listen — **deaf·ness** *n*

deaf·en *vb* **deaf·ened; deaf·en·ing :** to make unable to hear

¹deal *n* **1 :** an indefinite amount **2 :** a person's turn to pass out the cards in a card game

²deal *vb* **dealt; deal·ing 1 :** to give out as a person's share **2 :** ¹GIVE 8, ADMINISTER **3**

: to have to do **4 :** to take action **5 :** to buy and sell regularly : TRADE — **deal·er** *n*

³deal *n* **1 :** an agreement to do business **2 :** treatment received **3 :** an arrangement that is good for everyone involved

deal·ing *n* **1 deal·ings** *pl* **:** friendly or business relations **2 :** a way of acting or doing business

dean *n* **1 :** a church official in charge of a cathedral **2 :** the head of a section (as a college) of a university **3 :** an official in charge of students or studies in a school or college

¹dear *adj* **1 :** greatly loved or cared about **2** — used as a form of address especially in letters **3 :** having a high price **4 :** deeply felt : EARNEST — **dear·ly** *adv*

²dear *adv* **:** with love

³dear *n* **:** a loved one : DARLING

dearth *n* **:** SCARCITY, LACK

death *n* **1 :** the end or ending of life **2 :** the cause of loss of life **3 :** the state of being dead **4 :** ²RUIN 1, EXTINCTION — **death·like** *adj* — **to death :** VERY, EXTREMELY

death·bed *n* **:** the bed a person dies in — **on someone's deathbed :** very close to death

¹death·ly *adj* **:** relating to or suggesting death

²deathly *adv* **:** in a way suggesting death

de·bat·able *adj* **:** possible to question or argue about

¹de·bate *n* **1 :** a discussion or argument carried on between two teams or sides **2 :** a discussion of issues

²debate *vb* **de·bat·ed; de·bat·ing 1 :** to discuss a question by giving arguments on both sides : take part in a debate **2 :** to consider reasons for and against : give serious and careful thought to — **de·bat·er** *n*

de·bil·i·tate *vb* **de·bil·i·tat·ed; de·bil·i·tat·ing :** to make feeble : WEAKEN

de·bil·i·ty *n, pl* **de·bil·i·ties :** a weakened state especially of health

¹deb·it *vb* **deb·it·ed; deb·it·ing :** to record as money paid out or as a debt

²debit *n* **:** an entry in a business record showing money paid out or owed

deb·o·nair *adj* **:** gracefully charming

de·bris *n, pl* **de·bris :** the junk or pieces left from something broken down or destroyed

debt *n* **1 :** ¹SIN 1 **2 :** something owed to another **3 :** the condition of owing something

debt·or *n* **:** a person who owes a debt

¹de·but *n* **1 :** a first public appearance **2 :** the formal entrance of a young woman into society

²debut *vb* **de·but·ed; de·but·ing 1 :** to make a first public appearance **2 :** to present to the public for the first time

deb·u·tante *n* **:** a young woman making her debut

Dec. *abbr* December

deca- *or* **dec-** *or* **deka-** *or* **dek-** *prefix* **:** ten

de·cade *n* **:** a period of ten years

deca·gon *n* **:** a closed figure having ten angles and ten sides

de·cal *n* **:** a design made to be transferred (as to glass) from specially prepared paper

de·camp *vb* **de·camped; de·camp·ing 1 :** to pack up gear and leave a camp **2 :** to go away suddenly

de·cant·er *n* **:** an ornamental glass bottle used especially for serving wine

de·cap·i·tate *vb* **de·cap·i·tat·ed; de·cap·i·tat·ing :** to cut off the head of : BEHEAD

¹de·cay *vb* **de·cayed; de·cay·ing 1 :** to break down or cause to break down slowly by natural processes **2 :** to slowly worsen in condition

²decay *n* **1 :** the process or result of slowly breaking down by natural processes **2 :** a gradual worsening in condition **3 :** a natural change of a radioactive element into another form of the same element or into a different element

de·ceased *n, pl* **deceased :** a dead person

de·ce·dent *n* **:** a dead person

de·ceit *n* **1 :** the act or practice of making someone believe something that is not true : DECEPTION **2 :** a statement or act that misleads a person or causes him or her to believe something that is not true : TRICK **3 :** the quality of being dishonest

de·ceit·ful *adj* **:** not honest : full of deceit

de·ceive *vb* **de·ceived; de·ceiv·ing 1 :** to cause to believe what is not true : MISLEAD **2 :** to be dishonest and misleading

de·cel·er·ate *vb* **de·cel·er·at·ed; de·cel·er·at·ing :** to slow down

De·cem·ber *n* **:** the twelfth month of the year

de·cen·cy *n, pl* **de·cen·cies :** a way or habit of behaving with good manners or good morals

de·cent *adj* **1 :** meeting an accepted standard of good taste (as in speech, dress, or behavior) **2 :** being moral and good **3 :** not offensive **4 :** fairly good — **de·cent·ly** *adv*

de·cep·tion *n* **1 :** the act of making someone believe something that is not true **2 :** ¹TRICK 1

de·cep·tive *adj* **:** tending or able to deceive — **de·cep·tive·ly** *adv*

deci- *prefix* **:** tenth part

deci·bel *n* **:** a unit for measuring the loudness of sounds

de·cide *vb* **de·cid·ed; de·cid·ing 1 :** to make a judgment on **2 :** to bring to an end in a particular way **3 :** to make a choice especially after careful thought

de·cid·ed *adj* **1 :** UNMISTAKABLE **2 :** free from doubt — **de·cid·ed·ly** *adv*

de·cid·u·ous *adj* **:** made up of or having a

part that falls off at the end of a period of growth and use

[1]**dec·i·mal** *adj* **1 :** based on the number 10 **:** numbered or counting by tens **2 :** expressed in or including a decimal

[2]**decimal** *n* **:** a proper fraction in which the denominator is 10 or 10 multiplied one or more times by itself and is indicated by a point placed at the left of the numerator

decimal point *n* **:** the dot at the left of a decimal (as .05) or between the decimal and whole parts of a mixed number (as 3.125)

dec·i·mate *vb* **dec·i·mat·ed; dec·i·mat·ing 1 :** to destroy a large number of **2 :** to severely damage or destroy a large part of

deci·me·ter *n* **:** a unit of length equal to one tenth of a meter

de·ci·pher *vb* **de·ci·phered; de·ci·pher·ing 1 :** to translate from secret or mysterious writing **:** DECODE **2 :** to make out the meaning of something not clear

de·ci·sion *n* **1 :** the act or result of making a choice especially after careful thought **2 :** the ability to make choices quickly and confidently

de·ci·sive *adj* **1 :** causing something to end in a certain way **2 :** UNMISTAKABLE, UNQUESTIONABLE **3 :** firmly determined — **de·ci·sive·ly** *adv*

[1]**deck** *n* **1 :** a floor that goes from one side of a ship to the other **2 :** something like the deck of a ship **3 :** a pack of playing cards

[2]**deck** *vb* **decked; deck·ing :** to dress or decorate especially in a fancy way

dec·la·ra·tion *n* **1 :** an act of formally or confidently stating something **2 :** something formally or confidently stated or a document containing such a statement

de·clar·a·tive *adj* **:** making a statement

de·clare *vb* **de·clared; de·clar·ing 1 :** to make known in a clear or formal way **2 :** to state as if certain

[1]**de·cline** *vb* **de·clined; de·clin·ing 1 :** to bend or slope downward **2 :** to pass toward a lower, worse, or weaker level **3 :** to refuse to accept, do, or agree

[2]**decline** *n* **1 :** a process of becoming worse or weaker in condition **2 :** a change to a lower state or level **3 :** the time when something is nearing its end

de·code *vb* **de·cod·ed; de·cod·ing :** to change a message in code into ordinary language

de·com·pose *vb* **de·com·posed; de·com·pos·ing 1 :** to break down or be broken down into simpler parts or substances especially by the action of living things (as bacteria and fungi) **2 :** to separate a substance into simpler compounds

de·com·pos·er *n* **:** a living thing (as a bacterium, fungus, or insect) that feeds on and breaks down plant and animal matter into simpler parts or substances

de·com·po·si·tion *n* **:** the process of breaking down or being broken down into simpler parts or substances especially by the action of living things

dec·o·rate *vb* **dec·o·rat·ed; dec·o·rat·ing 1 :** to make more attractive by adding beautiful or festive things **2 :** to award a badge of honor to

dec·o·ra·tion *n* **1 :** the act of adding things to improve the appearance of something **2 :** something that adds beauty **3 :** a badge of honor

dec·o·ra·tive *adj* **:** serving to improve appearance **:** ORNAMENTAL

dec·o·ra·tor *n* **:** a person who decorates especially the rooms of houses

de·co·rum *n* **:** proper behavior

[1]**de·coy** *n* **:** a person or thing (as an artificial bird) used to lead or lure into a trap or snare

[2]**decoy** *vb* **de·coy·ed; de·coy·ing :** to lure by or as if by a decoy

[1]**de·crease** *vb* **de·creased; de·creas·ing :** to grow less or cause to grow less

[2]**de·crease** *n* **1 :** the process of growing less **2 :** the amount by which something grows less

[1]**de·cree** *n* **:** an order or decision given by a person or group in authority

[2]**decree** *vb* **de·creed; de·cree·ing :** to give an order as an authority

de·crep·it *adj* **:** broken down with age **:** WORN-OUT

de·cre·scen·do *n* **:** a gradual decrease in the loudness of music

ded·i·cate *vb* **ded·i·cat·ed; ded·i·cat·ing 1 :** to set apart for some purpose **:** DEVOTE **2 :** to commit to a goal or way of life **3 :** to say or write that something (as a book or song) is written or performed as a compliment to someone

ded·i·ca·tion *n* **1 :** an act of setting apart for a special purpose **2 :** a message at the beginning of a work of art (as a book or a song) saying that it is written or performed to honor someone **3 :** extreme devotion

de·duce *vb* **de·duced; de·duc·ing :** to figure out by using reason or logic

de·duct *vb* **de·duct·ed; de·duct·ing :** to take away an amount of something **:** SUBTRACT

de·duc·tion *n* **1 :** SUBTRACTION **2 :** an amount deducted **3 :** a conclusion reached by reasoning

[1]**deed** *n* **1 :** something that is done **:** ACT **2 :** a legal document by which a person transfers land or buildings to another

[2]**deed** *vb* **deed·ed; deed·ing :** to transfer by a deed

deem *vb* **deemed; deem·ing :** to have as an opinion

[1]**deep** *adj* **deep·er; deep·est 1 :** reaching far down below the surface **2 :** reaching far inward or back from the front or outer part **3 :** located well below the surface or well within the boundaries of **4 :** coming from well within **5 :** completely absorbed **6 :** hard to understand **7 :** MYSTERIOUS **8 :** extreme in degree **:** HEAVY **9 :** dark and rich in color **10 :** low in tone — **deep·ly** *adv*

[2]**deep** *adv* **deep·er; deep·est 1 :** to a great depth **:** DEEPLY **2 :** [2]LATE 1

[3]**deep** *n* **1 :** a very deep place or part **2 :** OCEAN 1 **3 :** the middle or most intense part

deep·en *vb* **deep·ened; deep·en·ing :** to make or become deep or deeper

deep fat *n* **:** hot fat or oil deep enough in a cooking utensil to cover the food to be fried

deep–fry *vb* **deep–fried; deep–fry·ing :** to cook in deep fat

deep·ly *adv* **1 :** at or to a great depth **:** far below the surface **2 :** in a high degree **:** THOROUGHLY **3 :** with intensity of color

deer *n, pl* **deer :** a mammal that has cloven hoofs and in the male antlers which are often branched

deer·skin *n* **:** leather made from the skin of a deer or a garment made of such leather

de·face *vb* **de·faced; de·fac·ing :** to damage the face or surface of

[1]**de·fault** *n* **:** failure to do something especially that is required by law or duty

[2]**default** *vb* **de·fault·ed; de·fault·ing :** to fail to do something required

[1]**de·feat** *vb* **de·feat·ed; de·feat·ing 1 :** to win victory over **2 :** to cause to fail or be destroyed

[2]**defeat** *n* **:** loss of a contest or battle

de·fect *n* **1 :** something that makes a thing imperfect **:** FLAW **2 :** a lack of something needed for perfection

de·fec·tive *adj* **:** FAULTY

de·fence *Can and Brit spelling of* DEFENSE

de·fend *vb* **de·fend·ed; de·fend·ing 1 :** to protect from danger or attack **2 :** to act or speak in favor of when others are opposed

de·fend·er *n* **1 :** a person or thing that protects from danger or attack **2 :** a player in a sport who tries to keep the other team from scoring

de·fense *or Can and Brit* **defence** *n* **1 :** the act of protecting or defending **2 :** something that defends or protects **3 :** the players on a team who try to stop the other team from scoring — **de·fense·less** *or Can and Brit* **defenceless** *adj*

[1]**de·fen·sive** *adj* **1 :** serving or meant to defend or protect **2 :** relating to the attempt to keep an opponent from scoring **3 :** showing a dislike for criticism — **de·fen·sive·ly** *adv*

[2]**defensive** *n* **:** a position or attitude that is meant to defend

[1]**de·fer** *vb* **de·ferred; de·fer·ring :** to put off to a future time **:** POSTPONE

[2]**defer** *vb* **de·ferred; de·fer·ring :** to give in or yield to the opinion or wishes of another

def·er·ence *n* **:** respect and consideration for the wishes of another

de·fer·ment *n* **:** the act of postponing

de·fi·ance *n* **1 :** a refusal to obey **2 :** a willingness to resist

de·fi·ant *adj* **:** showing a willingness to resist — **de·fi·ant·ly** *adv*

de·fi·cien·cy *n, pl* **de·fi·cien·cies :** the condition of being without something necessary and especially something required for health

de·fi·cient *adj* **:** lacking something necessary for completeness or health

def·i·cit *n* **:** a shortage especially in money

de·fine *vb* **de·fined; de·fin·ing 1 :** to explain the meaning of **2 :** to make clear especially in outline

def·i·nite *adj* **1 :** having certain or distinct limits **2 :** clear in meaning **3 :** UNQUESTIONABLE — **def·i·nite·ly** *adv*

definite article *n* **:** the article *the* used to show that the following noun refers to one or more specific persons or things

def·i·ni·tion *n* **1 :** a statement of the meaning of a word or a word group **2 :** clearness of outline or detail

de·flate *vb* **de·flat·ed; de·flat·ing 1 :** to let the air or gas out of something that has been blown up **2 :** to reduce in size or importance

de·flect *vb* **de·flect·ed; de·flect·ing :** to change or cause to change direction

de·for·est *vb* **de·for·est·ed; de·for·est·ing :** to clear of forests — **de·for·es·ta·tion** *n*

de·form *vb* **de·formed; de·form·ing :** to spoil the form or the natural appearance of

de·for·mi·ty *n, pl* **de·for·mi·ties 1 :** the condition of having a physical flaw **2 :** a flaw in something and especially in the body of a person or animal

de·fraud *vb* **de·fraud·ed; de·fraud·ing :** to get something from by trickery: CHEAT

de·frost *vb* **de·frost·ed; de·frost·ing 1 :** to thaw out **2 :** to remove ice from — **de·frost·er** *n*

deft *adj* **deft·er; deft·est :** quick and skillful in action — **deft·ly** *adv*

de·fy *vb* **de·fied; de·fy·ing 1 :** to refuse boldly to obey or yield to **2 :** to challenge to do something thought to be impossible **:** DARE **3 :** to resist attempts at **:** WITHSTAND

de·grade *vb* **de·grad·ed; de·grad·ing 1 :** to lower in character or dignity **2 :** to break

down or separate into simpler parts or substances **3** : to reduce from a higher to a lower rank or degree
de·gree *n* **1** : a step in a series **2** : amount of something as measured by a series of steps **3** : one of the three forms an adjective or adverb may have when it is compared **4** : a title given (as to students) by a college or university **5** : one of the divisions marked on a measuring instrument **6** : a 360th part of the circumference of a circle **7** : a line or space of the staff in music or the difference in pitch between two notes
de·hu·mid·i·fy *vb* **de·hu·mid·i·fied; de·hu·mid·i·fy·ing** : to take moisture from (as the air) — **de·hu·mid·i·fi·er** *n*
de·hy·drate *vb* **de·hy·drat·ed; de·hy·drat·ing** **1** : to take water from (as foods) **2** : to lose water or body fluids — **de·hy·dra·tion** *n*
deign *vb* **deigned; deign·ing** : to do something a person considers below his or her dignity
de·i·ty *n, pl* **de·i·ties** **1** *cap* : GOD 1 **2** : GOD 2, GODDESS
de·ject·ed *adj* : SAD 1 — **de·ject·ed·ly** *adv*
de·jec·tion *n* : a feeling of sadness
deka- *or* **dek-** — see DECA-
Del. *abbr* Delaware
Del·a·ware *n, pl* **Delaware** *or* **Del·a·wares** **1** : a member of an American Indian people originally of the region from southeastern New York to northern Delaware **2** : the language of the Delaware people
[1]**de·lay** *n* **1** : a putting off of something **2** : the time during which something is delayed
[2]**delay** *vb* **de·layed; de·lay·ing** **1** : to put off **2** : to stop or prevent for a time **3** : to move or act slowly
de·lec·ta·ble *adj* **1** : very pleasing : DELIGHTFUL **2** : DELICIOUS
[1]**del·e·gate** *n* : a person sent with power to act for another or others
[2]**del·e·gate** *vb* **del·e·gat·ed; del·e·gat·ing** **1** : to entrust to another **2** : to make responsible for getting something done
del·e·ga·tion *n* **1** : the act of giving someone authority or responsibility for **2** : one or more persons chosen to represent others
de·lete *vb* **de·let·ed; de·let·ing** : to take out especially by erasing, crossing out, or cutting
de·le·tion *n* **1** : an act of taking out **2** : something taken out
deli *n, pl* **del·is** : DELICATESSEN
[1]**de·lib·er·ate** *vb* **de·lib·er·at·ed; de·lib·er·at·ing** : to think about carefully
[2]**de·lib·er·ate** *adj* **1** : showing careful thought **2** : done or said on purpose **3** : slow in action : not hurried — **de·lib·er·ate·ly** *adv*
de·lib·er·a·tion *n* **1** : careful thought : CONSIDERATION **2** : the quality of being deliberate
del·i·ca·cy *n, pl* **del·i·ca·cies** **1** : something pleasing to eat that is rare or a luxury **2** : fineness of structure **3** : weakness of body : FRAILTY **4** : a need for careful treatment **5** : consideration for the feelings of others
del·i·cate *adj* **1** : pleasing because of fineness or mildness **2** : able to sense very small differences **3** : calling for skill and careful treatment **4** : easily damaged **5** : SICKLY 1 **6** : requiring tact — **del·i·cate·ly** *adv*
del·i·ca·tes·sen *n* : a store where prepared foods (as salads and meats) are sold
de·li·cious *adj* : giving great pleasure especially to the taste or smell — **de·li·cious·ly** *adv*
[1]**de·light** *n* **1** : great pleasure or satisfaction : JOY **2** : something that gives great pleasure
[2]**delight** *vb* **de·light·ed; de·light·ing** **1** : to take great pleasure **2** : to give joy or satisfaction to
de·light·ed *adj* : very pleased
de·light·ful *adj* : giving delight : very pleasing — **de·light·ful·ly** *adv*
de·lin·quent *n* : a usually young person who is guilty of improper or illegal behavior
de·lir·i·ous *adj* **1** : not able to think or speak clearly usually because of a high fever or other illness **2** : wildly excited — **de·lir·i·ous·ly** *adv*
de·lir·i·um *n* **1** : a condition of mind in which thought and speech are confused usually because of a high fever or other illness **2** : wild excitement
de·liv·er *vb* **de·liv·ered; de·liv·er·ing** **1** : to take and give to or leave for another **2** : to set free : RESCUE **3** : to give birth to or help in giving birth to **4** : [1]SAY 1 **5** : to send to an intended target **6** : to do what is expected — **de·liv·er·er** *n*
de·liv·er·ance *n* : a setting free
de·liv·ery *n, pl* **de·liv·er·ies** **1** : the transfer of something from one place or person to another **2** : a setting free from something that restricts or burdens **3** : the act of giving birth **4** : speaking or manner of speaking (as of a formal speech) **5** : the act or way of throwing
dell *n* : a small valley with trees and grass
del·ta *n* : a piece of land in the shape of a triangle or fan made by deposits of mud and sand at the mouth of a river
de·lude *vb* **de·lud·ed; de·lud·ing** : DECEIVE 1, MISLEAD
[1]**del·uge** *n* **1** : a flooding of land by water : FLOOD **2** : a drenching rain **3** : a sudden huge stream of something
[2]**deluge** *vb* **del·uged; del·ug·ing** **1** : [2]FLOOD 1 **2** : to overwhelm as if with a flood

de·lu·sion *n* : a false belief that continues in spite of the facts
de·luxe *adj* : very fine or luxurious
delve *vb* **delved; delv·ing** **1** : to dig or work hard with or as if with a shovel **2** : to work hard looking for information
[1]**de·mand** *n* **1** : a forceful expression of what is desired **2** : something claimed as owed **3** : an expressed desire to own or use something **4** : a seeking or being sought after
[2]**demand** *vb* **de·mand·ed; de·mand·ing** **1** : to claim as a right **2** : to ask earnestly or in the manner of a command **3** : to call for : REQUIRE — **on demand** : when requested or needed
de·mand·ing *adj* : requiring or expecting much effort
[1]**de·mean** *vb* **de·meaned; de·mean·ing** : BEHAVE 2
[2]**demean** *vb* **de·meaned; de·mean·ing** : to lower in character or dignity
de·mean·or *or Can and Brit* **demeanour** *n* : outward manner or behavior
de·ment·ed *adj* : INSANE 1, MAD
de·mer·it *n* : a mark placed against a person's record for doing something wrong
demi- *prefix* : half or partly
de·mise *n* **1** : DEATH 1 **2** : an ending of existence or activity
de·mo·bi·lize *vb* **de·mo·bi·lized; de·mo·bi·liz·ing** **1** : to let go from military service **2** : to change from a state of war to a state of peace
de·moc·ra·cy *n, pl* **de·moc·ra·cies** **1** : government by the people : majority rule **2** : government in which the highest power is held by the people and is usually used through representatives **3** : a political unit (as a nation) governed by the people **4** : belief in or practice of the idea that all people are socially equal
dem·o·crat *n* **1** : a person who believes in or practices democracy **2** *cap* : a member of the Democratic party of the United States
dem·o·crat·ic *adj* **1** : relating to or favoring political democracy **2** : relating to a major political party in the United States that is associated with helping common people **3** : believing in or practicing the idea that all people are equal — **dem·o·crat·i·cal·ly** *adv*
de·mol·ish *vb* **de·mol·ished; de·mol·ish·ing** **1** : to destroy by breaking apart **2** : to ruin completely : SHATTER
de·mo·li·tion *n* : the act of destroying by breaking apart especially using explosives
de·mon *n* **1** : an evil spirit : DEVIL **2** : a person of great energy or enthusiasm
dem·on·strate *vb* **dem·on·strat·ed; dem·on·strat·ing** **1** : to show clearly **2** : to prove or make clear by reasoning **3** : to explain (as in teaching) by use of examples or experiments **4** : to show to people the good qualities of an article or a product **5** : to make a public display (as of feelings or military force)
dem·on·stra·tion *n* **1** : an outward expression (as a show of feelings) **2** : an act or a means of showing **3** : a showing or using of an article for sale to display its good points **4** : a parade or a gathering to show public feeling
de·mon·stra·tive *adj* **1** : pointing out the one referred to and showing that it differs from others **2** : showing feeling freely
dem·on·stra·tor *n* **1** : a person who makes or takes part in a demonstration **2** : a manufactured article (as an automobile) used for demonstration
de·mor·al·ize *vb* **de·mor·al·ized; de·mor·al·iz·ing** : to weaken the spirit or confidence of
de·mote *vb* **de·mot·ed; de·mot·ing** : to reduce to a lower grade or rank
de·mure *adj* **1** : proper and reserved in behavior and speech **2** : pretending to be proper and reserved : COY — **de·mure·ly** *adv*
den *n* **1** : the shelter or resting place of a wild animal **2** : a quiet or private room in a home **3** : a hiding place (as for thieves)
den·drite *n* : any of the usually branched fibers that carry nerve impulses toward a nerve cell body
de·ni·al *n* **1** : a refusal to give or agree to something asked for **2** : a refusal to admit the truth of a statement **3** : a refusal to accept or believe in someone or something **4** : a cutting down or limiting
den·im *n* **1** : a firm often coarse cotton cloth **2** **denims** *pl* : overalls or pants of usually blue denim
de·nom·i·na·tion *n* **1** : a value in a series of values (as of money) **2** : a name especially for a class of things **3** : a religious body made up of a number of congregations having the same beliefs
de·nom·i·na·tor *n* : the part of a fraction that is below the line
de·note *vb* **de·not·ed; de·not·ing** **1** : to serve as a mark or indication of **2** : to have the meaning of : MEAN
de·nounce *vb* **de·nounced; de·nounc·ing** **1** : to point out as wrong or evil : CONDEMN **2** : to inform against : ACCUSE
dense *adj* **dens·er; dens·est** **1** : having its parts crowded together : THICK **2** : STUPID 1 — **dense·ly** *adv*
den·si·ty *n, pl* **den·si·ties** **1** : the condition of having parts that are close together **2** : the amount of something in a specified volume or area
[1]**dent** *vb* **dent·ed; dent·ing** **1** : to make a

hollow mark in or on **2 :** to become damaged by a hollow mark

[2]**dent** *n* **:** a notch or hollow mark made in a surface by a blow or by pressure

den·tal *adj* **:** relating to the teeth or dentistry

dental floss *n* **:** a special thread used for cleaning between teeth

den·tin *or* **den·tine** *n* **:** a calcium-containing material that is similar to bone but harder and that makes up the main part of a tooth

den·tist *n* **:** a person whose profession is the care, treatment, and repair of the teeth

den·tist·ry *n* **:** the profession or practice of a dentist

de·nude *vb* **de·nud·ed; de·nud·ing :** to make bare

de·ny *vb* **de·nied; de·ny·ing 1 :** to declare not to be true **2 :** to refuse to grant **3 :** to refuse to admit

de·odor·ant *n* **:** something used to remove or hide unpleasant odors

de·odor·ize *vb* **de·odor·ized; de·odor·iz·ing :** to remove odor and especially a bad smell from

de·part *vb* **de·part·ed; de·part·ing 1 :** to go away or go away from **:** LEAVE **2 :** [1]DIE 1 **3 :** to turn away from

de·part·ment *n* **:** a special part or division of an organization (as a government or college)

department store *n* **:** a store having individual departments for different kinds of goods

de·par·ture *n* **1 :** an act of leaving or setting out **2 :** an act of turning away or aside (as from a way of doing things)

de·pend *vb* **de·pend·ed; de·pend·ing 1 :** to rely for support **2 :** to be determined by or based on a person, action, or condition **3 :** [2]TRUST 1, RELY

de·pend·able *adj* **:** TRUSTWORTHY, RELIABLE

de·pen·dence *n* **1 :** a condition of being influenced and caused by something else **2 :** a state of having to rely on someone or something **3 :** [1]TRUST 1, RELIANCE **4 :** the reliance on or addiction to a drug or alcohol

[1]**de·pen·dent** *adj* **1 :** determined by something or someone else **2 :** relying on someone else for support **3 :** requiring or addicted to a drug or alcohol

[2]**dependent** *n* **:** a person who depends upon another for support

de·pict *vb* **de·pict·ed; de·pict·ing 1 :** to represent by a picture **2 :** to describe in words

de·pic·tion *n* **1 :** a representation of something using a picture **2 :** DESCRIPTION 1

de·plete *vb* **de·plet·ed; de·plet·ing :** to reduce in amount by using up

de·plor·able *adj* **1 :** deserving to be deplored **:** REGRETTABLE **2 :** very bad **:** WRETCHED

de·plore *vb* **de·plored; de·plor·ing 1 :** to regret strongly **2 :** to disapprove of

de·port *vb* **de·port·ed; de·port·ing 1 :** BEHAVE 1, CONDUCT **2 :** to force (a person who is not a citizen) to leave a country

de·por·ta·tion *n* **:** the removal from a country of a person who is not a citizen

de·pose *vb* **de·posed; de·pos·ing :** to remove from a high office

[1]**de·pos·it** *vb* **de·pos·it·ed; de·pos·it·ing 1 :** to place for or as if for safekeeping **2 :** to give as a pledge that a purchase will be made or a service used **3 :** to lay down **:** PUT **4 :** to let fall or sink

[2]**deposit** *n* **1 :** the state of being deposited **2 :** money that is deposited **3 :** something given as a pledge or as part payment **4 :** something laid or thrown down **5 :** mineral matter built up in nature

de·pos·i·tor *n* **:** a person who makes a deposit especially of money in a bank

de·pot *n* **1 :** a place where military supplies are kept **2 :** STOREHOUSE 1 **3 :** a railroad or bus station

de·pre·ci·ate *vb* **de·pre·ci·at·ed; de·pre·ci·at·ing 1 :** BELITTLE **2 :** to lower the price or value of **3 :** to lose value

de·press *vb* **de·pressed; de·press·ing 1 :** to press down **2 :** to make sad or discouraged **3 :** to lessen the activity or strength of

de·pres·sant *n* **:** a drug that slows the activity of the nervous system

de·pressed *adj* **1 :** SAD 1 **2 :** suffering from bad economic times

de·pres·sion *n* **1 :** an act of pressing down **2 :** a hollow place or part **3 :** a feeling of sadness **4 :** a period of low activity in business with much unemployment

de·pri·va·tion *n* **1 :** a taking or keeping away **2 :** the state of having something taken away

de·prive *vb* **de·prived; de·priv·ing :** to take something away from or keep from having something

de·prived *adj* **:** not having the things that are needed for a good or healthful life

dept. *abbr* department

depth *n* **1 :** measurement from top to bottom or from front to back **2 :** a place far below a surface or far inside something (as a sea or a forest) **3 :** the middle of time **4 :** INTENSITY 2 **5 :** ABUNDANCE, COMPLETENESS

dep·u·tize *vb* **dep·u·tized; dep·u·tiz·ing :** to appoint as deputy

dep·u·ty *n, pl* **dep·u·ties :** a person who officially acts for or in place of another

de·rail *vb* **de·railed; de·rail·ing 1 :** to leave or cause to leave the rails **2 :** to make progress or success difficult for

der·by *n, pl* **der·bies** **1 :** a race for three-year-old horses usually held every year **2 :** a race or contest open to anyone **3 :** a stiff felt hat with a narrow brim and a rounded top

[1]**der·e·lict** *adj* **1 :** abandoned by the owner or occupant **2 :** in poor condition **:** RUN-DOWN **3 :** failing to do what should be done

[2]**derelict** *n* **1 :** something abandoned (as a boat) **2 :** [1]BUM 1, VAGRANT

de·ride *vb* **de·rid·ed; de·rid·ing :** to laugh at in scorn **:** make fun of **:** RIDICULE

de·ri·sion *n* **:** a feeling of dislike or disrespect often shown by the use of insults

der·i·va·tion *n* **1 :** the formation of a word from an earlier word or root **2 :** ETYMOLOGY **3 :** ORIGIN 1, SOURCE **4 :** an act or process by which one thing is formed from another

[1]**de·riv·a·tive** *n* **1 :** a word formed from an earlier word or root **2 :** something that is formed from something else

[2]**derivative** *adj* **:** formed from something else — **de·riv·a·tive·ly** *adv*

de·rive *vb* **de·rived; de·riv·ing** **1 :** to take or get from a source **2 :** to come from a certain source **3 :** to trace the origin or source of

der·mal *adj* **:** of or relating to skin

der·mis *n* **:** the inner sensitive layer of the skin

de·rog·a·to·ry *adj* **:** expressing a low opinion of a person or thing

der·rick *n* **1 :** a machine for moving or lifting heavy weights by means of a long arm fitted with ropes and pulleys **2 :** a framework or tower over an oil well used to support machinery

de·scend *vb* **de·scend·ed; de·scend·ing** **1 :** to come or go down from a higher place or level to a lower one **2 :** to move down or down along **3 :** to slope or lead downward **4 :** to come down from an earlier time **5 :** to come down from a source or ancestor **:** DERIVE **6 :** to be handed down to an heir **7 :** to arrive from or as if from the sky **8 :** to sink in dignity or respectability **:** STOOP **9 :** to sink to a worse condition

de·scen·dant *n* **1 :** someone related to a person or group of people who lived at an earlier time **2 :** a thing that comes from something that existed at an earlier time

de·scent *n* **1 :** an act of coming or going down in location or condition **2 :** a downward slope **3 :** a person's ancestors

de·scribe *vb* **de·scribed; de·scrib·ing** **1 :** to write or tell about **2 :** to draw the outline of

de·scrip·tion *n* **1 :** a written or spoken statement about something that enables a reader or listener to picture it **2 :** [1]SORT 1, KIND

de·scrip·tive *adj* **:** giving information about what something is like

des·e·crate *vb* **des·e·crat·ed; des·e·crat·ing** **:** to treat a sacred place or sacred object shamefully or with great disrespect

de·seg·re·gate *vb* **de·seg·re·gat·ed; de·seg·re·gat·ing :** to end by law the separation of members of different races

de·seg·re·ga·tion *n* **:** the act or process or an instance of ending a law or practice that separates people of different races

de·se·lect *vb* **:** to cause (something previously selected) to no longer be selected in a software program

[1]**des·ert** *n* **:** a dry land with few plants and little rainfall

[2]**de·sert** *n* **:** a reward or punishment that a person deserves

[3]**de·sert** *vb* **de·sert·ed; de·sert·ing** **1 :** to leave usually without intending to return **2 :** to leave a person or a thing that one should stay with **3 :** to fail in time of need — **de·sert·er** *n*

de·serve *vb* **de·served; de·serv·ing :** to have earned because of some act or quality

de·served·ly *adv* **:** as earned by acts or qualities

de·serv·ing *adj* **:** WORTHY

[1]**de·sign** *vb* **de·signed; de·sign·ing** **1 :** to think up and plan out in the mind **2 :** to set apart for or have as a special purpose **:** INTEND **3 :** to make a pattern or sketch of

[2]**design** *n* **1 :** an arrangement of parts in a structure or a work of art **2 :** the art or process of planning and creating something **3 :** a sketch, model, or plan of something made or to be made **4 :** a decorative pattern **5 :** [1]PLAN 1, SCHEME **6 :** a planned intention **7 :** a secret purpose **:** PLOT

des·ig·nate *vb* **des·ig·nat·ed; des·ig·nat·ing** **1 :** to appoint or choose for a special purpose **2 :** to call by a name or title **3 :** to mark or point out **:** INDICATE

des·ig·na·tion *n* **1 :** an act of choosing to be or do something **2 :** a name, sign, or title that identifies something

de·sign·er *n* **:** a person who plans how to make or change something

de·sir·able *adj* **1 :** having pleasing qualities **:** ATTRACTIVE **2 :** worth having or seeking

[1]**de·sire** *vb* **de·sired; de·sir·ing** **1 :** to long for **:** wish for in earnest **2 :** to express a wish for **:** REQUEST

[2]**desire** *n* **1 :** a strong wish **:** LONGING **2 :** something longed for

de·sist *vb* **de·sist·ed; de·sist·ing :** to stop doing something

desk *n* **1 :** a piece of furniture with a flat or sloping surface for use in writing or reading

2 : a counter at which a person works especially to help customers

desk·top *n* **1** : the top of a desk **2** : a computer that is used on a desk or table and is too big to be moved easily **3** : an area on a computer screen in which items are arranged as if they were objects on top of a desk

[1]**des·o·late** *adj* **1** : having no comfort or companionship : LONELY **2** : left neglected or in ruins **3** : without signs of life : BARREN **4** : CHEERLESS, GLOOMY — **des·o·late·ly** *adv*

[2]**des·o·late** *vb* **des·o·lat·ed; des·o·lat·ing** : to ruin or leave without comfort or companionship

des·o·la·tion *n* **1** : the state of being deserted or ruined **2** : sadness resulting from grief or loneliness

[1]**de·spair** *vb* **de·spaired; de·spair·ing** : to give up or lose all hope or confidence

[2]**despair** *n* **1** : loss of hope : a feeling of complete hopelessness **2** : a cause of hopelessness

de·spair·ing *adj* : having or showing no hope — **de·spair·ing·ly** *adv*

des·per·ate *adj* **1** : very sad and worried and with little or no hope **2** : showing great worry and loss of hope **3** : giving little reason to hope : causing despair **4** : reckless because of despair : RASH **5** : very severe

des·per·ate·ly *adv* **1** : in a way showing great worry and weakening hope **2** : in such a way as to leave little hope **3** : with great intensity

des·per·a·tion *n* : a condition of hopelessness often leading to recklessness

de·spi·ca·ble *adj* : very bad : deserving to be despised

de·spise *vb* **de·spised; de·spis·ing** : to feel scorn and dislike for

de·spite *prep* : in spite of

de·spon·den·cy *n* : DEJECTION, SADNESS

de·spon·dent *adj* : very sad — **de·spon·dent·ly** *adv*

des·pot *n* : a ruler having absolute power and authority and especially one who rules cruelly

des·sert *n* : a sweet food eaten at the end of a meal

des·ti·na·tion *n* : a place that a person starts out for or that something is sent to

des·tine *vb* **des·tined; des·tin·ing** **1** : to decide in advance on the future condition, use, or action of **2** : to be bound or directed

des·ti·ny *n, pl* **des·ti·nies** **1** : what happens to someone or something in the future **2** : the course of events believed to be controlled by a superhuman power **3** : a power that is believed to control the future

des·ti·tute *adj* **1** : lacking something needed or desirable **2** : very poor

des·ti·tu·tion *n* : the condition of being very poor

de·stroy *vb* **de·stroyed; de·stroy·ing** **1** : to put an end to : do away with **2** : [1]KILL 1

de·stroy·er *n* **1** : someone or something that ruins or ends something **2** : a small fast warship armed with guns, torpedoes, and sometimes missiles

de·struc·tion *n* **1** : the act or process of killing, ruining, or putting an end to something **2** : the state or fact of being killed, ruined, or brought to an end

de·struc·tive *adj* **1** : causing great damage or ruin **2** : not positive or helpful

de·tach *vb* **de·tached; de·tach·ing** : to separate from something else or from others especially for a certain purpose — **de·tach·able** *adj*

de·tached *adj* **1** : not joined or connected : SEPARATE **2** : not taking sides or being influenced by others

de·tach·ment *n* **1** : SEPARATION 1 **2** : the sending out of a body of troops or ships on a special duty **3** : a small unit of troops or ships sent out for a special duty **4** : lack of interest in worldly concerns **5** : freedom from the favoring of one side over another

[1]**de·tail** *n* **1** : a dealing with something with attention to each item **2** : a small part of something larger : ITEM **3** : a soldier or group of soldiers picked for special duty

[2]**detail** *vb* **de·tailed; de·tail·ing** **1** : to report with attention to each item **2** : to select for some special duty

de·tailed *adj* : including many small items or parts

de·tain *vb* **de·tained; de·tain·ing** **1** : to hold or keep in or as if in prison **2** : to stop especially from going on : DELAY

de·tect *vb* **de·tect·ed; de·tect·ing** : to learn that something or someone is or was there — **de·tec·tor** *n*

de·tec·tion *n* : the act of learning that something or someone is or was there : DISCOVERY

de·tec·tive *n* : a person (as a police officer) whose business is solving crimes and catching criminals or gathering information that is not easy to get

de·ten·tion *n* **1** : the act of holding back or delaying : the condition of being held or delayed **2** : the punishment of being kept after school

de·ter *vb* **de·terred; de·ter·ring** : to discourage or prevent from doing something

de·ter·gent *n* : a substance that cleans

de·te·ri·o·rate *vb* **de·te·ri·o·rat·ed; de·te·ri·o·rat·ing** : to make or become worse or of less value

de·ter·mi·na·tion *n* **1** : firm or fixed intention **2 :** an act of deciding or the decision reached **3 :** an act of making sure of the position, size, or nature of something

de·ter·mine *vb* **de·ter·mined; de·ter·min·ing** **1 :** to come to a decision **2 :** to learn or find out exactly **3 :** to be the cause of or reason for **4 :** to fix exactly and with certainty

de·ter·mined *adj* **1 :** free from doubt about doing something **2 :** not weak or uncertain **:** FIRM

de·ter·min·er *n* **:** a word belonging to a group of noun modifiers that can occur before descriptive adjectives modifying the same noun

de·test *vb* **de·test·ed; de·test·ing :** to dislike very much

de·throne *vb* **de·throned; de·thron·ing :** to drive from a throne **:** DEPOSE

¹de·tour *n* **:** a roundabout way that temporarily replaces part of a regular route

²detour *vb* **de·toured; de·tour·ing :** to go or make go on a different route than usual

de·tract *vb* **de·tract·ed; de·tract·ing :** to take away (as from value or importance)

det·ri·ment *n* **:** injury or damage or its cause **:** HARM

dev·as·tate *vb* **dev·as·tat·ed; dev·as·tat·ing** **1 :** to destroy entirely or nearly entirely **2 :** to cause to suffer emotionally

dev·as·ta·tion *n* **:** the action of destroying or damaging greatly **:** the state of being greatly damaged or destroyed

de·vel·op *vb* **de·vel·oped; de·vel·op·ing** **1 :** to make or become plain little by little **:** UNFOLD **2 :** to apply chemicals to exposed photographic material (as a film) in order to bring out the picture **3 :** to bring out the possibilities of **:** IMPROVE **4 :** to make more available or usable **5 :** to begin to have gradually **6 :** to begin to exist or be present gradually **7 :** to create over time **8 :** to grow or cause to grow bigger or more advanced — **de·vel·op·er** *n*

de·vel·oped *adj* **1 :** having many large industries and a complex economic system **2 :** bigger or more advanced

de·vel·op·ment *n* **1 :** the act, process, or result of developing **2 :** the state of being developed

de·vi·ate *vb* **de·vi·at·ed; de·vi·at·ing :** to follow a course, principle, standard, or topic that is different from usual

de·vice *n* **1 :** a piece of equipment made for a special purpose **2 :** choice of what to do **3 :** a thing or act used to deceive **:** TRICK

dev·il *n* **1** *often cap* **:** the most powerful spirit of evil **2 :** an evil spirit **:** DEMON, FIEND **3 :** a wicked or cruel person **4 :** an attractive, mischievous, or unfortunate person

dev·iled *adj* **:** spicy or highly seasoned

dev·il·ish *adj* **1 :** evil and cruel **2 :** MISCHIEVOUS 2

dev·il·ment *n* **:** MISCHIEF 2

de·vi·ous *adj* **1 :** SNEAKY, DISHONEST **2 :** not straight **:** having many twists and turns

de·vise *vb* **de·vised; de·vis·ing :** to think up **:** PLAN, INVENT

de·void *adj* **:** completely without

de·vote *vb* **de·vot·ed; de·vot·ing** **1 :** to set apart for a special purpose **2 :** to give up to entirely or in part

de·vot·ed *adj* **1 :** completely loyal **2 :** AFFECTIONATE, LOVING — **de·vot·ed·ly** *adv*

de·vo·tion *n* **1 :** deep love or loyalty **2 :** an act of giving (as effort or time) to something **3 :** a religious exercise or practice (as prayers) especially that is private

de·vour *vb* **de·voured; de·vour·ing** **1 :** to eat up hungrily **2 :** to take in eagerly by the senses or mind **3 :** to destroy as if by eating

de·vout *adj* **1 :** deeply religious **2 :** strongly loyal or devoted **3 :** warmly sincere and earnest — **de·vout·ly** *adv*

dew *n* **:** moisture that collects on cool surfaces at night

dew·lap *n* **:** loose skin hanging under the neck of some animals (as cows)

dew point *n* **:** the temperature at which the moisture in the air begins to turn to dew

dewy *adj* **dew·i·er; dew·i·est :** moist with or as if with dew

dex·ter·i·ty *n, pl* **dex·ter·i·ties** **1 :** skill and ease in the use of the hands or body **2 :** the ability to think and act quickly and cleverly

dex·ter·ous *adj* **1 :** skillful with the hands **2 :** CLEVER 2 **3 :** done with skill — **dex·ter·ous·ly** *adv*

di·a·be·tes *n* **:** a disease in which too little or no insulin is produced or insulin is produced but cannot be used normally resulting in high levels of sugar in the blood

di·a·bet·ic *n* **:** a person with diabetes

di·a·crit·i·cal mark *n* **:** a mark that is placed over, under, or through a letter in some languages to show that the letter should be pronounced in a particular way

di·ag·nose *vb* **di·ag·nosed; di·ag·nos·ing :** to recognize (as a disease) by signs and symptoms

di·ag·no·sis *n, pl* **di·ag·no·ses** **1 :** the act of recognizing a disease from its signs and symptoms **2 :** the conclusion that is reached following examination and testing

¹di·ag·o·nal *adj* **1 :** running from one corner to the opposite corner of a four-sided shape (as a square) **2 :** running in a slanting direction — **di·ag·o·nal·ly** *adv*

²diagonal *n* **:** a line, direction, or pattern that runs in a slanting direction

¹di·a·gram *n* **:** a drawing, plan, or chart that makes something clearer or easier to understand

²diagram *vb* **di·a·grammed** *or* **di·a·gramed; di·a·gram·ming** *or* **di·a·gram·ing** : to put in the form of a drawing, plan, or chart

¹di·al *n* **1** : the face of a watch or clock **2** : SUNDIAL **3** : a usually flat round part of a piece of equipment with numbers or marks to show some measurement usually by means of a pointer **4** : a part of a machine or device (as a radio) that may be turned to operate or adjust it

²dial *vb* **di·aled** *or* **di·alled; di·al·ing** *or* **di·al·ling** : to use a knob, button, or other control to operate or select

di·a·lect *n* : a form of a language that is spoken in a certain region or by a certain group

di·a·logue *also* **di·a·log** *n* **1** : conversation given in a written story or a play **2** : a conversation between two or more people or groups

di·am·e·ter *n* **1** : a straight line that runs from one side of a figure and passes through the center **2** : the distance through the center of an object from one side to the other : THICKNESS

di·a·mond *n* **1** : a very hard mineral that is a form of carbon, is usually nearly colorless, and is used especially in jewelry **2** : a flat figure ◇ like one of the surfaces of certain cut diamonds **3** : INFIELD 1

di·a·per *n* : a piece of absorbent material for a baby worn pulled up between the legs and fastened around the waist

di·a·phragm *n* **1** : a muscular wall that separates the lungs from the stomach area and assists in breathing in **2** : a thin disk (as in a microphone) that vibrates when sound strikes it

di·ar·rhea *n* : abnormally frequent and watery bowel movements

di·a·ry *n, pl* **di·a·ries** **1** : a daily written record especially of personal experiences and thoughts **2** : a book for keeping a record of experiences and thoughts

¹dice *n, pl* **dice** : ²DIE 1

²dice *vb* **diced; dic·ing** : to cut into small cubes

¹dic·tate *vb* **dic·tat·ed; dic·tat·ing** **1** : to speak or read for someone else to write down or for a machine to record **2** : to say or state with authority : ORDER **3** : to make necessary

²dictate *n* **1** : a statement made or direction given with authority : COMMAND **2** : a guiding rule or principle

dic·ta·tion *n* : the act of speaking words for someone else to write down or for a machine to record the words spoken

dic·ta·tor *n* : a person who rules with total power and often in a cruel manner — **dic·ta·tor·ship** *n*

dic·tion *n* **1** : choice of words especially with regard to correctness, clearness, and effectiveness **2** : the ability to say words

dic·tio·nary *n, pl* **dic·tio·nar·ies** **1** : a book giving the meaning and usually the pronunciation of words listed in alphabetical order **2** : a reference book explaining words of a particular subject listed in alphabetical order **3** : a book listing words of one language in alphabetical order with definitions in another language

did *past of* DO

didn't : did not

¹die *vb* **died; dy·ing** **1** : to stop living **2** : to come to an end **3** : to disappear little by little **4** : to want badly **5** : to stop working or running — **die out** : to disappear gradually

²die *n* **1** *pl* **dice** : a small cube marked on each side with one to six spots and used in games **2** *pl* **dies** : a device for forming or cutting material by pressure

die·sel *n* **1** : DIESEL ENGINE **2** : a vehicle that has a diesel engine **3** : DIESEL FUEL

diesel engine *n* : an engine in which the mixture of air and fuel is compressed until enough heat is created to ignite the mixture that uses diesel fuel instead of gasoline

diesel fuel *n* : a heavy oil used as fuel in diesel engines

¹di·et *n* **1** : the food and drink that a person or animal usually takes **2** : the kind and amount of food selected or allowed in certain circumstances (as poor health)

²diet *vb* **di·et·ed; di·et·ing** : to eat less or according to certain rules in order to lose weight — **di·et·er** *n*

³diet *adj* : reduced in calories

di·e·tary *adj* : relating to a diet

di·e·ti·tian *or* **di·e·ti·cian** *n* : a person trained to give advice about diet and nutrition

dif·fer *vb* **dif·fered; dif·fer·ing** **1** : to be unlike : be different **2** : DISAGREE 1

dif·fer·ence *n* **1** : what makes two or more persons or things not the same **2** : a disagreement about something **3** : the number that is left after subtracting one number from another **4** : an important change

dif·fer·ent *adj* **1** : not of the same kind **2** : not the same **3** : not ordinary — **dif·fer·ent·ly** *adv*

dif·fer·en·ti·ate *vb* **dif·fer·en·ti·at·ed; dif·fer·en·ti·at·ing** **1** : to make or become different **2** : to recognize or state the difference between

dif·fer·en·ti·a·tion *n* : the process of change by which immature living structures develop to maturity

dif·fi·cult *adj* **1** : not easy : hard to do or make **2** : hard to deal with **3** : hard to understand

dif·fi·cul·ty *n, pl* **dif·fi·cul·ties** **1 :** the state of being hard to do **2 :** great effort **3 :** something that makes something hard to do : OBSTACLE **4 :** a troublesome situation
dif·fi·dent *adj* **1 :** lacking confidence **2 :** cautious about acting or speaking
dif·fuse *vb* **dif·fused; dif·fus·ing :** to spread or allow to spread freely
dif·fu·sion *n* **1 :** the act of spreading or allowing to spread freely **2 :** the mixing of particles of liquids or gases so that they move from a region of high concentration to one of lower concentration
[1]**dig** *vb* **dug; dig·ging** **1 :** to turn up, loosen, or remove the soil **2 :** to turn up or remove with a shovel or by similar means **3 :** to form by removing earth **4 :** to uncover or search by or as if by turning up earth **5 :** [1]PROD 1, POKE — **dig in :** to begin eating — **dig into** **1 :** to begin eating **2 :** to try to discover information — **dig up** **1 :** to uncover or remove (as from soil) **2 :** DISCOVER
[2]**dig** *n* **1 :** [2]POKE **2 :** a place where buried objects are being uncovered **3 :** a project to uncover buried objects **4 :** a nasty remark
[1]**di·gest** *n* **:** information in shortened form
[2]**di·gest** *vb* **di·gest·ed; di·gest·ing** **1 :** to change or become changed into simpler forms that can be used by the body **2 :** to think over and try to understand
di·gest·ible *adj* **:** possible to digest
di·ges·tion *n* **:** the body's process or power of changing food into simpler forms that can be taken up and used
di·ges·tive *adj* **:** relating to or functioning in the body's process of changing food into simpler forms that can be taken up and used
digestive system *n* **:** the system of the body that takes in, breaks down, and absorbs food and discharges solid waste and consists of the digestive tract and related glands (as the salivary glands and pancreas)
digestive tract *n* **:** the tube-shaped passage including the mouth, pharynx, esophagus, stomach, and intestines that is concerned with taking in, breaking down, and absorbing food and discharging solid waste
dig·it *n* **1 :** any of the numerals 1 to 9 and the symbol 0 **2 :** a finger or toe
dig·i·tal *adj* **1 :** relating to or using calculation directly with digits rather than through measurable physical quantities **2 :** of or relating to data in the form of numerical digits **3 :** providing displayed or recorded information in numerical digits from an automatic device — **dig·i·tal·ly** *adv*
digital camera *n* **:** a camera that takes pictures without using film by recording the images as electronic data
dig·ni·fied *adj* **:** having or showing dignity
dig·ni·fy *vb* **dig·ni·fied; dig·ni·fy·ing** **1 :** to give dignity or importance to **2 :** to treat with respect or seriousness that is not deserved
dig·ni·tary *n, pl* **dig·ni·tar·ies** **:** a person of high position or honor
dig·ni·ty *n, pl* **dig·ni·ties** **1 :** the quality or state of being worthy of honor and respect **2 :** a serious and admirable look or way of behaving
dike *n* **1 :** a long trench dug in the earth to carry water **2 :** a mound of earth built to control water
di·lap·i·dat·ed *adj* **:** falling apart or ruined from age or from lack of care
di·late *vb* **di·lat·ed; di·lat·ing** **:** to make or grow larger or wider
di·lem·ma *n* **:** a situation in which a person has to choose between things that are all bad or unsatisfactory
dil·i·gence *n* **:** careful and continued hard work
dil·i·gent *adj* **:** showing steady and earnest care and hard work — **dil·i·gent·ly** *adv*
dill *n* **:** an herb that is related to the carrot plant and has fragrant leaves and seeds used in flavoring foods and especially pickles
dil·ly·dal·ly *vb* **dil·ly·dal·lied; dil·ly·dal·ly·ing** **:** to waste time : DAWDLE
di·lute *vb* **di·lut·ed; di·lut·ing :** to make thinner or more liquid by adding something
di·lu·tion *n* **1 :** the act of making thinner or more liquid : the state of being made thinner or more liquid **2 :** something (as a solution) that has had something added to it to make it thinner or more liquid
[1]**dim** *adj* **dim·mer; dim·mest** **1 :** not bright or distinct : FAINT **2 :** not seeing or understanding clearly — **dim·ly** *adv* — **dim·ness** *n*
[2]**dim** *vb* **dimmed; dim·ming :** to make or become less bright or clear
dime *n* **:** a United States coin worth ten cents
di·men·sion *n* **:** the length, width, or height of something
di·men·sion·al *adj* **:** relating to the length, width, or height of something
di·min·ish *vb* **di·min·ished; di·min·ish·ing** **1 :** to make less or cause to seem less **2 :** BELITTLE **3 :** to become gradually less or smaller : DWINDLE — **di·min·ish·ment** *n*
di·min·u·en·do *n, pl* **di·min·u·en·dos** *or* **di·min·u·en·does :** DECRESCENDO
di·min·u·tive *adj* **:** very small : TINY
dim·ple *n* **:** a slight hollow spot especially in the cheek or chin
din *n* **:** loud confused noise
dine *vb* **dined; din·ing :** to eat dinner — **dine out :** to eat at a restaurant
din·er *n* **1 :** a person eating dinner **2 :** a railroad dining car or a restaurant that looks like one

di·nette *n* : a small room or separate area near a kitchen that is used for dining

ding·dong *n* : the sound of a bell ringing

din·ghy *n, pl* **dinghies** **1** : a small light rowboat **2** : a rubber life raft

din·gy *adj* **din·gi·er; din·gi·est** : rather dark and dirty

din·ky *adj* **din·ki·er; din·ki·est** : very small and not impressive

din·ner *n* **1** : the main meal of the day **2** : a usually large formal event at which a meal is served

di·no·saur *n* : any of a group of extinct often very large mostly land-dwelling reptiles that lived millions of years ago

dint *n* : the force or power of something — used in the phrase *by dint of.*

di·o·cese *n* : the area that is under the authority of a bishop

[1]**dip** *vb* **dipped; dip·ping** **1** : to lower or push briefly into a liquid to wet or coat **2** : to take out or serve with or as if with a ladle **3** : to lower and quickly raise again : drop or sink and quickly rise again **4** : to sink out of sight **5** : to slope downward

[2]**dip** *n* **1** : a short swim **2** : something obtained by or as if by a ladle **3** : a sauce into which solid food may be dipped **4** : a downward slope

diph·the·ria *n* : a contagious disease that often makes breathing and swallowing difficult

diph·thong *n* : two vowel sounds joined in one syllable to form one speech sound

di·plo·ma *n* : a certificate that shows a person has finished a course or graduated from a school

di·plo·ma·cy *n* **1** : the work of keeping good relations between the governments of different countries **2** : skill in dealing with people

dip·lo·mat *n* **1** : a person whose work is keeping good relations between the governments of different countries **2** : a person who is good at dealing with people in a way that avoids bad feelings

dip·lo·mat·ic *adj* **1** : of or relating to keeping good relations between the governments of different countries **2** : not causing bad feelings — **dip·lo·mat·i·cal·ly** *adv*

dip·per *n* : [1]LADLE

dire *adj* **1** : causing horror or worry : DREADFUL **2** : very great

[1]**di·rect** *vb* **di·rect·ed; di·rect·ing** **1** : to cause to point or move in a particular direction **2** : to cause to focus on **3** : to show or tell the way **4** : to put an address on **5** : [1]ORDER 2, COMMAND **6** : to manage or control the making or activities of

[2]**direct** *adj* **1** : going from one point to another without turning or stopping : STRAIGHT **2** : coming straight from a cause or source **3** : going straight to the point **4** : being in an unbroken family line — **di·rect·ness** *n*

[3]**direct** *adv* : DIRECTLY 1

direct current *n* : an electric current flowing in one direction only

di·rec·tion *n* **1** : the path along which something moves, lies, or points **2** : an order or instruction to be followed **3** : instructions on how to get somewhere **4** : SUPERVISION, MANAGEMENT

di·rect·ly *adv* **1** : in a straight course or line **2** : straight to or from a source : without interference **3** : IMMEDIATELY 2

direct object *n* : a word that represents the main goal or the result of the action of a verb

di·rec·tor *n* **1** : a person who manages something **2** : a person in charge of making a movie or play

di·rec·to·ry *n, pl* **di·rec·to·ries** : a book containing an alphabetical list of names, addresses, and telephone numbers

di·ri·gi·ble *n* : AIRSHIP

dirk *n* : a long dagger with a straight blade

dirt *n* **1** : [2]SOIL 1 **2** : a substance (as mud or dust) that makes things unclean

[1]**dirty** *adj* **dirt·i·er; dirt·i·est** **1** : not clean **2** : UNFAIR, MEAN **3** : not pleasant but usually necessary **4** : being vulgar : not decent **5** : showing dislike or anger — **dirt·i·ness** *n*

[2]**dirty** *adv* : in an unfair or dishonest way

[3]**dirty** *vb* **dirt·ied; dirty·ing** : to make or become unclean

dis- *prefix* **1** : do the opposite of **2** : deprive of **3** : opposite or absence of **4** : not

dis·abil·i·ty *n, pl* **dis·abil·i·ties** : a condition (as one present at birth or caused by injury) that damages or limits a person's abilities : the state of being disabled

dis·able *vb* **dis·abled; dis·abling** : to make unable or incapable

dis·abled *adj* : not having the ability to do certain mental or physical tasks (as because of illness, injury, or a condition present at birth) that a person is typically capable of doing

dis·ad·van·tage *n* : a state or condition that favors someone else

dis·ad·van·ta·geous *adj* : making it harder for a person or thing to succeed or do something

dis·agree *vb* **dis·agreed; dis·agree·ing** **1** : to have different ideas or opinions **2** : to be unlike each other : be different **3** : to make ill

dis·agree·able *adj* **1** : UNPLEASANT **2** : difficult to get along with

dis·agree·ment *n* **1** : failure to agree **2** : ARGUMENT 1

dis·ap·pear *vb* **dis·ap·peared; dis·ap·pear-**

ing **1 :** to stop being visible **:** pass out of sight **2 :** to stop existing
dis·ap·pear·ance *n* **:** the act of passing out of sight or existence
dis·ap·point *vb* **dis·ap·point·ed; dis·ap·point·ing :** to fail to satisfy the hope or expectation of
dis·ap·point·ment *n* **1 :** unhappiness from the failure of something hoped for or expected to happen **2 :** someone or something that fails to satisfy hopes or expectations
dis·ap·prov·al *n* **:** the feeling of not liking or agreeing with something or someone
dis·ap·prove *vb* **dis·ap·proved; dis·ap·prov·ing :** to dislike or be against someone or something
dis·arm *vb* **dis·armed; dis·arm·ing** **1 :** to take weapons from **2 :** to reduce the size and strength of the armed forces of a country **3 :** to make harmless **4 :** to end dislike or mistrust **:** win over — **dis·ar·ma·ment** *n*
dis·ar·ray *n* **:** a confused or messy condition
dis·as·sem·ble *vb* **dis·as·sem·bled; dis·as·sem·bling :** to take apart
di·sas·ter *n* **:** something (as a flood or a tornado) that happens suddenly and causes much suffering or loss
di·sas·trous *adj* **1 :** causing great suffering or loss **2 :** very bad
dis·band *vb* **dis·band·ed; dis·band·ing :** to break up and stop being a group
dis·be·lief *n* **:** refusal or inability to believe
dis·be·lieve *vb* **dis·be·lieved; dis·be·liev·ing :** to think not to be true or real
dis·burse *vb* **dis·bursed; dis·burs·ing :** to pay out — **dis·burse·ment** *n*
disc *variant of* DISK
[1]**dis·card** *vb* **dis·card·ed; dis·card·ing** **1 :** to get rid of as useless or unwanted **2 :** to throw down an unwanted card from a hand of cards
[2]**dis·card** *n* **:** something thrown away or rejected
dis·cern *vb* **dis·cerned; dis·cern·ing :** to see, recognize, or understand something
[1]**dis·charge** *vb* **dis·charged; dis·charg·ing** **1 :** to allow to leave or get off **2 :** to dismiss from service **3 :** to free of a load or burden **:** UNLOAD **4 :** [1]SHOOT 2 **5 :** to cause to shoot out of **6 :** to pour forth fluid or other contents **7 :** to get rid of by paying or doing
[2]**dis·charge** *n* **1 :** the release of someone from a place **2 :** the release from a duty or debt **3 :** a certificate of release or payment **4 :** the act of firing a person from a job **5 :** an end of a person's military service **6 :** an act of firing off **7 :** something that flows out
dis·ci·ple *n* **1 :** a person who accepts and helps to spread the teachings of another **2 :** APOSTLE
dis·ci·plin·ary *adj* **:** relating to the correction or punishment of bad behavior
[1]**dis·ci·pline** *n* **1 :** PUNISHMENT 1 **2 :** strict training that corrects or strengthens **3 :** habits and ways of acting that are gotten through practice **4 :** control that is gained by insisting that rules be followed
[2]**discipline** *vb* **dis·ci·plined; dis·ci·plin·ing** **1 :** to punish as a way to bring about good behavior **2 :** to train in self-control or obedience **3 :** to bring under control
disc jockey *n* **:** someone who plays recorded music on the radio or at a party
dis·claim *vb* **dis·claimed; dis·claim·ing :** to deny being part of or responsible for
dis·close *vb* **dis·closed; dis·clos·ing :** to make known **:** REVEAL
dis·clo·sure *n* **1 :** an act of making known **2 :** something made known
dis·col·or *vb* **dis·col·ored; dis·col·or·ing :** to change in color especially for the worse
dis·col·or·a·tion *n* **1 :** change of color **2 :** a spot that is changed in color
dis·com·fort *n* **:** the condition of being uncomfortable
dis·con·cert *vb* **dis·con·cert·ed; dis·con·cert·ing :** to make confused and a little upset
dis·con·nect *vb* **dis·con·nect·ed; dis·con·nect·ing :** to undo or break the connection of
dis·con·so·late *adj* **:** too sad to be cheered up — **dis·con·so·late·ly** *adv*
[1]**dis·con·tent** *n* **:** the condition of being dissatisfied
[2]**discontent** *adj* **:** not satisfied
dis·con·tent·ed *adj* **:** not satisfied
dis·con·tin·ue *vb* **dis·con·tin·ued; dis·con·tinu·ing :** to bring to an end **:** STOP
dis·cord *n* **:** lack of agreement or harmony **:** CONFLICT
dis·cor·dant *adj* **:** being in disagreement
[1]**dis·count** *n* **:** an amount taken off a regular price
[2]**dis·count** *vb* **dis·count·ed; dis·count·ing** **1 :** to lower the amount of a bill, debt, or price **2 :** to think of as not important or serious
dis·cour·age *vb* **dis·cour·aged; dis·cour·ag·ing** **1 :** to make less determined, hopeful, or confident **2 :** to make less likely to happen **3 :** to try to persuade not to do something — **dis·cour·age·ment** *n*
[1]**dis·course** *n* **1 :** CONVERSATION **2 :** a long talk or essay about a subject
[2]**dis·course** *vb* **dis·coursed; dis·cours·ing :** to talk especially for a long time
dis·cour·te·ous *adj* **:** not polite **:** RUDE
dis·cour·te·sy *n, pl* **dis·cour·te·sies** **1 :** rude behavior **2 :** a rude act
dis·cov·er *vb* **dis·cov·ered; dis·cov·er·ing**

: to find out, see, or learn of especially for the first time : FIND — **dis·cov·er·er** *n*

dis·cov·ery *n, pl* **dis·cov·er·ies** **1 :** an act of finding out or learning of for the first time **2 :** something found or learned of for the first time

[1]**dis·cred·it** *vb* **dis·cred·it·ed; dis·cred·it·ing** **1 :** to cause to seem dishonest or untrue **2 :** to harm the reputation of

[2]**discredit** *n* **:** loss of good name or respect

dis·creet *adj* **:** careful not to attract attention or let out private information — **dis·creet·ly** *adv*

dis·crep·an·cy *n* **:** a difference between things that are expected to be the same

dis·crete *adj* **:** [2]SEPARATE 3, DISTINCT

dis·cre·tion *n* **1 :** care in not attracting attention or letting out private information **2 :** the power to decide what to do

dis·crim·i·nate *vb* **dis·crim·i·nat·ed; dis·crim·i·nat·ing** **1 :** to unfairly treat a person or group differently from other people or groups **2 :** to be able to tell the difference between things

dis·crim·i·na·tion *n* **1 :** the practice of unfairly treating a person or group differently from other people or groups of people **2 :** the ability to see differences

dis·crim·i·na·to·ry *adj* **:** showing discrimination : being unfair

dis·cus *n, pl* **dis·cus·es** **:** an object that is shaped like a disk and hurled for distance in a track-and-field event

dis·cuss *vb* **dis·cussed; dis·cuss·ing** **1 :** to talk about **2 :** to argue or consider fully and openly

dis·cus·sion *n* **:** conversation for the purpose of understanding or debating a question or subject

[1]**dis·dain** *n* **:** a feeling of dislike for someone or something considered not good enough — **dis·dain·ful** *adj* — **dis·dain·ful·ly** *adv*

[2]**disdain** *vb* **dis·dained; dis·dain·ing** **1 :** to feel dislike for something or someone usually for not being good enough **2 :** to refuse because of feelings of dislike

dis·ease *n* **:** a change in a living body (as of a person or plant) that prevents it from functioning normally : SICKNESS

dis·eased *adj* **:** having a sickness

dis·em·bark *vb* **dis·em·barked; dis·em·bark·ing** **:** to leave or remove from a ship or airplane

dis·en·fran·chise *vb* **dis·en·fran·chised; dis·en·fran·chis·ing** **:** to deprive of the right to vote

dis·en·tan·gle *vb* **dis·en·tan·gled; dis·en·tan·gling** **:** UNTANGLE

dis·fa·vor *n* **1 :** DISAPPROVAL **2 :** the condition of being disliked

dis·fig·ure *vb* **dis·fig·ured; dis·fig·ur·ing** **:** to spoil the looks of

dis·fig·ure·ment *n* **:** something that spoils the appearance of a person or thing

dis·fran·chise *vb* **dis·fran·chised; dis·fran·chis·ing** **:** DISENFRANCHISE — **dis·fran·chise·ment** *n*

[1]**dis·grace** *vb* **dis·graced; dis·grac·ing** **:** to bring shame to

[2]**disgrace** *n* **1 :** the condition of being looked down on : loss of respect **2 :** a cause of shame

dis·grace·ful *adj* **:** bringing or deserving shame — **dis·grace·ful·ly** *adv*

dis·grun·tled *adj* **:** GROUCHY

[1]**dis·guise** *vb* **dis·guised; dis·guis·ing** **1 :** to change the looks or sound of to avoid being recognized **2 :** to keep from revealing

[2]**disguise** *n* **1 :** clothing worn to avoid being recognized **2 :** an outward appearance that hides what something really is

[1]**dis·gust** *n* **:** a strong feeling of dislike or annoyance for something considered sickening or bad

[2]**disgust** *vb* **dis·gust·ed; dis·gust·ing** **:** to cause to feel strong dislike or annoyance by being sickening or bad — **dis·gust·ed·ly** *adv*

dis·gust·ing *adj* **:** very sickening or bad

dish *n* **1 :** a usually round shallow container used for cooking or serving food **2 dish·es** *pl* **:** all items (as plates and silverware) used for cooking and eating food **3 :** the food in a container for serving or eating **4 :** food that is prepared in a particular way **5 :** a round shallow object

dis·heart·en *vb* **dis·heart·ened; dis·heart·en·ing** **:** DISCOURAGE 1

di·shev·eled *or* **di·shev·elled** *adj* **:** MESSY 1

dis·hon·est *adj* **:** not honest or trustworthy — **dis·hon·est·ly** *adv*

dis·hon·es·ty *n* **:** the quality of being untruthful : lack of honesty

[1]**dis·hon·or** *n* **1 :** loss of honor or good name **2 :** a cause of disgrace

[2]**dishonor** *vb* **dis·hon·ored; dis·hon·or·ing** **:** to bring shame on : DISGRACE

dis·hon·or·able *adj* **:** SHAMEFUL — **dis·hon·or·ably** *adv*

dis·il·lu·sion *vb* **dis·il·lu·sioned; dis·il·lu·sion·ing** **:** to cause to stop having a mistaken belief that something is good, valuable, or true — **dis·il·lu·sion·ment** *n*

dis·in·fect *vb* **dis·in·fect·ed; dis·in·fect·ing** **:** to cleanse of germs that might cause disease

dis·in·fec·tant *n* **:** something that kills germs

dis·in·her·it *vb* **dis·in·her·it·ed; dis·in·her·it·ing** **:** to take away the legal right to receive money or property from at death

dis·in·te·grate *vb* **dis·in·te·grat·ed; dis·in·te·grat·ing** **:** to separate or break up into small parts or pieces

dis·in·te·gra·tion *n* : the act or process of breaking into small pieces : the condition of being broken into small pieces
dis·in·ter·est·ed *adj* **1** : not interested **2** : not influenced by personal feelings or concerns
dis·joint·ed *adj* : not clear and orderly — **dis·joint·ed·ly** *adv*
disk *or* **disc** *n* **1** : something that is or appears to be flat and round **2** usually disc : CD **3** : a round, thin, flat plate coated with a magnetic substance on which data for a computer is stored **4** usually disc : a phonograph record — **disk·like** *adj*
disk drive *n* : the part of a computer that moves data to and from a disk
disk·ette *n* : FLOPPY DISK
[1]**dis·like** *n* : a strong feeling of not liking or approving
[2]**dislike** *vb* **dis·liked; dis·lik·ing** : to not like or approve of
dis·lo·cate *vb* **dis·lo·cat·ed; dis·lo·cat·ing** : to displace a bone from its normal connections with another bone
dis·lo·ca·tion *n* : the condition of being moved out of a normal location
dis·lodge *vb* **dis·lodged; dis·lodg·ing** : to force out of a place of resting, hiding, or defense
dis·loy·al *adj* : failing to support or be true
dis·loy·al·ty *n, pl* **dis·loy·al·ties** **1** : lack of faithfulness or support **2** : an act that shows a lack of faithfulness or support
dis·mal *adj* : very gloomy
dis·man·tle *vb* **dis·man·tled; dis·man·tling** **1** : to take completely apart (as for storing or repair) **2** : to strip of furniture or equipment
[1]**dis·may** *vb* **dis·mayed; dis·may·ing** : to feel worry, disappointment, fear, or shock
[2]**dismay** *n* : a feeling of fear, disappointment, shock, or worry
dis·miss *vb* **dis·missed; dis·miss·ing** **1** : to allow or cause to leave **2** : to remove from a job or position **3** : to decide not to think about
dis·miss·al *n* : the act of dismissing : the state or fact of being dismissed
dis·mount *vb* **dis·mount·ed; dis·mount·ing** : to get down from something (as a horse or bicycle)
dis·obe·di·ence *n* : an act of failing or refusing to behave as told or taught
dis·obe·di·ent *adj* : not behaving as told or taught — **dis·obe·di·ent·ly** *adv*
dis·obey *vb* **dis·obeyed; dis·obey·ing** : to refuse or fail to behave as told or taught
[1]**dis·or·der** *vb* **dis·or·dered; dis·or·der·ing** : to disturb the regular or normal arrangement or functioning of
[2]**disorder** *n* **1** : a confused or messy state **2** : unruly behavior **3** : a physical or mental condition that is not normal or healthy
dis·or·der·ly *adj* **1** : not behaving quietly or well : UNRULY **2** : not neat or orderly
dis·or·ga·ni·za·tion *n* : lack of order
dis·or·ga·nized *adj* **1** : not having order **2** : not able to manage or plan things well
dis·own *vb* **dis·owned; dis·own·ing** : to refuse to accept any longer a relationship with or connection to
dis·par·age *vb* **dis·par·aged; dis·par·ag·ing** : to speak of as unimportant or bad : BELITTLE — **dis·par·age·ment** *n*
dis·pas·sion·ate *adj* : not influenced by strong feeling or personal involvement : CALM, IMPARTIAL — **dis·pas·sion·ate·ly** *adv*
[1]**dis·patch** *vb* **dis·patched; dis·patch·ing** **1** : to send away quickly to a certain place or for a certain reason **2** : to get done quickly **3** : [1]KILL 1 — **dis·patch·er** *n*
[2]**dispatch** *n* **1** : MESSAGE 1 **2** : a news story sent in to a newspaper **3** : [1]SPEED 1
dis·pel *vb* **dis·pelled; dis·pel·ling** : to make go away
dis·pense *vb* **dis·pensed; dis·pens·ing** **1** : to give out in small amounts **2** : to give out as deserved **3** : to put up or prepare medicine in a form ready for use — **dispense with** : to do or get along without
dis·pens·er *n* : a container that gives out something in small amounts
dis·perse *vb* **dis·persed; dis·pers·ing** : to break up and scatter
dis·pir·it·ed *adj* : not cheerful or enthusiastic — **dis·pir·it·ed·ly** *adv*
dis·place *vb* **dis·placed; dis·plac·ing** **1** : to remove from the usual or proper place **2** : to take the place of : REPLACE **3** : to move out of position — **dis·place·ment** *n*
[1]**dis·play** *vb* **dis·played; dis·play·ing** **1** : to put (something) in plain sight **2** : to make clear the existence or presence of : show plainly
[2]**display** *n* **1** : a presentation of something **2** : an arrangement of something where it can be easily seen **3** : an electronic device (as a computer monitor) that shows information
dis·please *vb* **dis·pleased; dis·pleas·ing** : to cause to feel unhappy or unsatisfied
dis·plea·sure *n* : a feeling of dislike and irritation : DISSATISFACTION
dis·pos·able *adj* : made to be thrown away after use
dis·pos·al *n* **1** : the act of getting rid of **2** : right or power to use : CONTROL
dis·pose *vb* **dis·posed; dis·pos·ing** : to put in place : ARRANGE — **dispose of** **1** : to finish with **2** : to get rid of
dis·posed *adj* **1** : having the desire or ten-

dency to **2 :** feeling or thinking in a particular way about

dis·po·si·tion *n* **1 :** a person's usual attitude or mood **2 :** TENDENCY 2, LIKING **3 :** ARRANGEMENT 1

dis·pro·por·tion *n* **:** a marked difference in the size, number, or amount of something as compared to another thing

dis·prove *vb* **dis·proved; dis·prov·ing :** to show to be false or wrong

[1]**dis·pute** *vb* **dis·put·ed; dis·put·ing 1 :** to question or deny the truth or rightness of **2 :** ARGUE 1 **3 :** to fight over

[2]**dispute** *n* **1 :** [1]DEBATE 3 **2 :** [1]QUARREL 1

dis·qual·i·fy *vb* **dis·qual·i·fied; dis·qual·i·fy·ing :** to make or declare not fit to have, do, or take part in

[1]**dis·qui·et** *vb* **dis·qui·et·ed; dis·qui·et·ing :** to make uneasy or worried

[2]**disquiet** *n* **:** an uneasy feeling

[1]**dis·re·gard** *vb* **dis·re·gard·ed; dis·re·gard·ing :** to pay no attention to

[2]**disregard** *n* **:** the act of paying no attention to

dis·re·pair *n* **:** the condition of needing to be fixed

dis·rep·u·ta·ble *adj* **:** not respectable or honest

dis·re·spect *n* **:** lack of respect **:** DISCOURTESY — **dis·re·spect·ful** *adj* — **dis·re·spect·ful·ly** *adv*

dis·rupt *vb* **dis·rupt·ed; dis·rupt·ing 1 :** to cause disorder in **2 :** to interrupt the normal course of — **dis·rup·tion** *n* — **dis·rup·tive** *adj*

dis·sat·is·fac·tion *n* **:** a feeling of unhappiness or disapproval

dis·sat·is·fy *vb* **dis·sat·is·fied; dis·sat·is·fy·ing :** to fail to give what is desired or expected **:** DISPLEASE

dis·sect *vb* **dis·sect·ed; dis·sect·ing :** to cut or take apart especially for examination

dis·sec·tion *n* **:** the act of cutting something or taking something apart for examination

dis·sen·sion *n* **:** difference in opinion

[1]**dis·sent** *vb* **dis·sent·ed; dis·sent·ing :** DISAGREE 1 — **dis·sent·er** *n*

[2]**dissent** *n* **:** difference of opinion

dis·ser·vice *n* **:** a harmful, unfair, or unjust act

dis·sim·i·lar *adj* **:** DIFFERENT 1

dis·si·pate *vb* **dis·si·pat·ed; dis·si·pat·ing 1 :** to cause to break up and disappear: DISPERSE **2 :** to scatter or waste foolishly **:** SQUANDER

dis·si·pat·ed *adj* **:** indulging in bad, foolish, or harmful activities

dis·si·pa·tion *n* **1 :** the act of causing to break up and disappear **2 :** indulgence in too much pleasure

dis·solve *vb* **dis·solved; dis·solv·ing 1 :** to become part of a liquid **2 :** to bring to an end **:** TERMINATE **3 :** to fade away as if by melting or breaking up **4 :** to be overcome by a strong feeling

dis·so·nance *n* **:** an unpleasant combination of musical sounds

dis·suade *vb* **dis·suad·ed; dis·suad·ing :** to persuade or advise not to do something

dis·tance *n* **1 :** how far from each other two points or places are **2 :** a point or place that is far away **3 :** the quality or state of not being friendly **:** RESERVE

dis·tant *adj* **1 :** existing or happening at a place far away **2 :** far away in time **3 :** not closely related **4 :** [1]COLD 5, UNFRIENDLY — **dis·tant·ly** *adv*

dis·taste *n* **:** [1]DISLIKE

dis·taste·ful *adj* **:** UNPLEASANT

dis·tend *vb* **dis·tend·ed; dis·tend·ing :** EXPAND 2, SWELL

dis·till *also* **dis·til** *vb* **dis·tilled; dis·till·ing :** to make (a liquid) pure by heating it until it becomes a gas and then cooling it until it becomes a liquid — **dis·till·er** *n*

dis·til·la·tion *n* **:** the process of heating a liquid until it gives off a gas and then cooling the gas until it becomes liquid

dis·tinct *adj* **1 :** different from each other **2 :** easy to notice or understand — **dis·tinct·ly** *adv*

dis·tinc·tion *n* **1 :** DIFFERENCE 1 **2 :** the act of seeing or pointing out a difference **3 :** great worth **:** EXCELLENCE **4 :** something that makes a person or thing special or different

dis·tinc·tive *adj* **1 :** clearly marking a person or a thing as different from others **2 :** having or giving a special look or way — **dis·tinc·tive·ly** *adv*

dis·tin·guish *vb* **dis·tin·guished; dis·tin·guish·ing 1 :** to recognize one thing from others by some mark or quality **2 :** to hear or see clearly **3 :** to know the difference **4 :** to set apart as different or special

dis·tin·guish·able *adj* **:** possible to recognize or tell apart from others

dis·tin·guished *adj* **:** widely known and admired

dis·tort *vb* **dis·tort·ed; dis·tort·ing 1 :** to twist out of shape **2 :** to change so as to make untrue or inaccurate

dis·tor·tion *n* **:** the act of twisting out of shape or making inaccurate **:** the state or fact of being twisted out of shape or made inaccurate

dis·tract *vb* **dis·tract·ed; dis·tract·ing :** to draw a person's thoughts or attention to something else

dis·trac·tion *n* **1 :** something that makes it hard to pay attention **2 :** the act of having thoughts or attention drawn away **:** the state of drawing thoughts or attention away **3** : confusion of thoughts or feelings

dis·traught *adj* : very upset

¹dis·tress *n* **1** : physical or mental pain or suffering **2** : a state of danger or desperate need

²distress *vb* **dis·tressed; dis·tress·ing** : to cause to suffer — **distressing** *adj*

dis·trib·ute *vb* **dis·trib·ut·ed; dis·trib·ut·ing** **1** : to give out to or deliver to **2** : to divide among many or several **3** : to spread out so as to cover something

dis·tri·bu·tion *n* **1** : the act of giving out or delivering to or dividing among **2** : the way things are given out or delivered to or divided among **3** : something given out or delivered to or divided among

dis·trib·u·tive *adj* **1** : of or relating to the act of giving or spreading out **2** : producing the same answer when operating on the sum of several numbers as when operating on each and collecting the results

dis·trib·u·tor *n* : a person or company that supplies stores or businesses with goods

dis·trict *n* **1** : an area or section (as of a city or nation) set apart for some purpose **2** : an area or region with some special feature

¹dis·trust *n* : a lack of belief or confidence in : SUSPICION — **dis·trust·ful** *adj*

²distrust *vb* **dis·trust·ed; dis·trust·ing** : to have no belief or confidence in

dis·turb *vb* **dis·turbed; dis·turb·ing** **1** : to interfere with : INTERRUPT **2** : to change the position or arrangement of **3** : UPSET, WORRY **4** : to make confused or disordered

dis·tur·bance *n* **1** : the act of interrupting, changing the arrangement of, or upsetting : the state of being interrupted, changed in arrangement, or upset **2** : ²DISORDER 2, COMMOTION

dis·turbed *adj* : showing signs of mental or emotional illness

dis·use *n* : lack of use

dis·used *adj* : not used any more

¹ditch *n* : a long narrow channel or trench dug in the earth

²ditch *vb* **ditched; ditch·ing** **1** : to get rid of : DISCARD **2** : to end a relationship with

dith·er *n* : a very nervous or excited state

dit·ty *n, pl* **ditties** : a short simple song

¹dive *vb* **dived** *or* **dove; div·ing** **1** : to plunge into water headfirst **2** : to swim underwater especially while using special equipment **3** : SUBMERGE 1 **4** : to fall fast **5** : to descend in an airplane at a steep angle **6** : to move forward suddenly into or at something — **div·er** *n*

²dive *n* **1** : an act of plunging headfirst into water **2** : an act of swimming underwater especially while using special equipment **3** : an act of submerging a submarine **4** : a quick drop (as of prices) **5** : a sudden movement forward into or at something

di·verse *adj* **1** : different from each other : UNLIKE **2** : made up of people or things that are different from each other

di·ver·si·fy *vb* **di·ver·si·fied; di·ver·si·fy·ing** : to change to include many different things

di·ver·sion *n* **1** : an act or instance of changing the direction or use of **2** : something that relaxes, distracts, or entertains

di·ver·si·ty *n, pl* **di·ver·si·ties** : the condition or fact of being different

di·vert *vb* **di·vert·ed; di·vert·ing** **1** : to turn from one path or use to another **2** : to turn the attention away : DISTRACT **3** : to give pleasure to : AMUSE

di·vide *vb* **di·vid·ed; di·vid·ing** **1** : to separate into two or more parts or pieces **2** : to give out in shares **3** : to be or make different in opinion or interest **4** : to subject to or perform mathematical division **5** : to branch off : FORK — **di·vid·er** *n*

div·i·dend *n* **1** : a number to be divided by another number **2** : an amount of a company's profits that is paid to the owners of its stock

div·i·na·tion *n* : the art or practice of using signs and omens or magic powers to foretell the future

¹di·vine *adj* **1** : of or relating to God or a god **2** : being in praise of God : RELIGIOUS, HOLY **3** : like a god **4** : very good — **di·vine·ly** *adv*

²divine *vb* **di·vined; di·vin·ing** **1** : to discover or understand something by using intuition **2** : to foretell the future by using signs and omens or magic powers

di·vin·i·ty *n, pl* **di·vin·i·ties** **1** : the quality or state of being God or a god **2** : a god or goddess **3** : the study of religion

di·vis·i·ble *adj* : possible to divide or separate

di·vi·sion *n* **1** : the act or process of dividing or separating : the state of being divided or separated **2** : the mathematical process of finding out how many times one number is contained in another **3** : something that divides, separates, or marks off **4** : one of the parts or groups that make up a whole **5** : a large military unit **6** : a level of competitors **7** : a group of plants that ranks above the class and below the kingdom and in scientific classification is typically equal to a phylum

di·vi·sor *n* : the number by which a dividend is divided

¹di·vorce *n* : a legal ending of a marriage

²divorce *vb* **di·vorced; di·vorc·ing** : to end a marriage legally : get a divorce

di·vulge *vb* **di·vulged; di·vulg·ing** : to make known to others : REVEAL, DISCLOSE

DIY *n* : DO-IT-YOURSELF
diz·zy *adj* **diz·zi·er; diz·zi·est** **1** : having the feeling of spinning **2** : causing a feeling of spinning **3** : overwhelmed with emotion — **diz·zi·ness** *n*
DMD *abbr* doctor of dental medicine
DNA *n* : a complicated organic acid that carries genetic information in the chromosomes
[1]**do** *vb* **did; done; do·ing; does** **1** : to cause (as an act or action) to happen : PERFORM **2** : [2]ACT 2, BEHAVE **3** : to make progress : SUCCEED **4** : to finish working on — used in the past participle **5** : to put forth : EXERT **6** : to work on, prepare, produce, or put in order **7** : to work at as a paying job **8** : to serve the purpose : SUIT **9** : to have an effect **10** : to travel at a speed of **11** — used as a helping verb (1) before the subject in a question, (2) in a negative statement, (3) for emphasis, and (4) as a substitute for a predicate that has already been stated — **do away with** **1** : to get rid of **2** : [1]KILL 1
[2]**do** *n* : the first note of the musical scale
DOB *abbr* date of birth
doc·ile *adj* : easily taught, led, or managed — **doc·ile·ly** *adv*
[1]**dock** *vb* **docked; dock·ing** **1** : to cut off the end of **2** : to take away a part of
[2]**dock** *n* **1** : an artificial basin for ships that has gates to keep the water in or out **2** : a waterway usually between two piers to receive ships **3** : a wharf or platform for loading or unloading materials
[3]**dock** *vb* **docked; dock·ing** **1** : to haul or guide into a dock **2** : to come or go into a dock **3** : to join (as two spacecraft) mechanically while in space
[1]**doc·tor** *n* : a person (as a physician or veterinarian) skilled and specializing in the art of healing
[2]**doctor** *vb* **doc·tored; doc·tor·ing** **1** : to use remedies on or for **2** : to practice medicine
doc·trine *n* : something (as a rule or principle) that is taught, believed in, or considered to be true
[1]**doc·u·ment** *n* **1** : a written or printed paper that gives information about or proof of something **2** : a computer file containing data entered by a user
[2]**document** *vb* **doc·u·ment·ed; doc·u·ment·ing** **1** : to record (as on paper or in film) the details about **2** : to prove through usually written records
doc·u·men·ta·ry *n* : a film that tells the facts about something
[1]**dodge** *n* **1** : a sudden movement to one side **2** : a trick done to avoid something
[2]**dodge** *vb* **dodged; dodg·ing** **1** : to move suddenly aside or to and fro **2** : to avoid especially by moving quickly **3** : EVADE — **dodg·er** *n*
dodge ball *n* : a game in which players try to knock other players out of the game by hitting them with a ball
do·do *n, pl* **do·does** *or* **do·dos** : a large heavy bird unable to fly that once lived on some of the islands of the Indian Ocean
doe *n* : the female of an animal (as a deer or kangaroo) the male of which is called *buck*
do·er *n* : a person who tends to act rather than talk or think about things
does *present third person sing of* DO
doesn't : does not
doff *vb* **doffed; dof·fing** : to take off
[1]**dog** *n* **1** : a domestic animal that eats meat and is closely related to the wolves **2** : any of the group of mammals (as wolves, foxes, and jackals) to which the domestic dog belongs **3** : PERSON 1 — **dog·like** *adj*
[2]**dog** *vb* **dogged; dog·ging** **1** : to hunt, track, or follow like a hound **2** : PESTER **3** : cause problems for
dog·catch·er *n* : an official paid to catch and get rid of stray dogs
dog days *n pl* : the hot period between early July and early September
dog–eared *adj* : having a lot of pages with corners turned over
dog·fish *n* : a small shark often seen near shore
dog·ged *adj* : stubbornly determined — **dog·ged·ly** *adv*
dog·gy *or* **dog·gie** *n, pl* **doggies** : a usually small or young dog
dog·house *n* : a shelter for a dog — **in the doghouse** : in trouble over some wrongdoing
dog·ma *n* **1** : something firmly believed **2** : a belief or set of beliefs taught by a church
dog·sled *n* : a sled pulled by dogs
dog·wood *n* : a shrub or small tree with clusters of small flowers often surrounded by four showy leaves that look like petals
doi·ly *n, pl* **doilies** : a small often lacy cloth or paper used to protect the surface of furniture
do·ing *n* **1** : the act of performing : ACTION **2 doings** *pl* : things that are done or that go on
do–it–your·self *n* : the activity of doing something oneself without professional training or assistance — **do–it–your·self·er** *n*
dol·drums *n pl* **1** : a spell of sadness **2** : a period of no activity or improvement **3** : a part of the ocean near the equator known for its calms
[1]**dole** *n* **1** : an act of giving out food, clothing, or money to the needy **2** : something given out to the needy especially at regular times

²dole *vb* **doled; dol·ing :** to give out
dole·ful *adj* **:** very sad — **dole·ful·ly** *adv*
doll *n* **1 :** a child's toy in the form of a baby or small person **2 :** a kind or loveable person
dol·lar *n* **:** any of various coins or pieces of paper money (as of the United States or Canada) equal to 100 cents
dolly *n, pl* **dollies 1 :** DOLL 1 **2 :** a platform on a roller or on wheels for moving heavy things
dol·phin *n* **1 :** a small whale with teeth and a long nose **2 :** either of two large fish usually of warm seas that are often used for food
-dom *n suffix* **1 :** the area ruled by **2 :** state or fact of being **3 :** the group having a certain office, occupation, interest, or character
do·main *n* **1 :** land under the control of a ruler or a government **2 :** a field of knowledge or activity **3 :** DOMAIN NAME
domain name *n, pl* **domain names :** the characters (as Merriam-Webster.com) that form the main part of an Internet address
dome *n* **1 :** a rounded top or roof that looks like half of a ball **2 :** a rounded structure
domed *adj* **:** having a rounded shape like a dome
do·mes·tic *adj* **1 :** relating to a household or a family **2 :** relating to, made in, or done in a person's own country **3 :** living with or under the care of human beings **:** TAME — **do·mes·ti·cal·ly** *adv*
do·mes·ti·cate *vb* **do·mes·ti·cat·ed; do·mes·ti·cat·ing :** to bring under the control of and make usable by humans
do·mi·cile *n* **:** a place where someone lives
dom·i·nance *n* **:** the state or fact of being in control of or having more power than another
dom·i·nant *adj* **1 :** controlling or being more powerful or important than all others **2 :** being or produced by a form of a gene that prevents or hides the effect of another form
dom·i·nate *vb* **dom·i·nat·ed; dom·i·nat·ing :** to have a commanding position or controlling power over
do·min·ion *n* **1 :** ruling or controlling power **:** SOVEREIGNTY **2 :** a territory under the control of a ruler **:** DOMAIN
dom·i·no *n, pl* **dom·i·noes** *or* **dom·i·nos :** one of a set of flat oblong dotted pieces used in playing a game (**dominoes**)
don *vb* **donned; don·ning :** to put on
do·nate *vb* **do·nat·ed; do·nat·ing :** to give as a way of helping people in need **:** CONTRIBUTE
do·na·tion *n* **:** something given to help those in need
done *past participle of* DO
don·key *n, pl* **donkeys :** an animal related to but smaller than the horse that has short hair in mane and tail and very large ears
do·nor *n* **:** a person who makes a donation
don't : do not
¹doo·dle *vb* **doo·dled; doo·dling :** to scribble, sketch, or make designs on paper often while thinking about something else
²doodle *n* **:** a scribble, design, or sketch done often while thinking about something else
¹doom *n* **1 :** a terrible or unhappy ending or happening **2 :** DEATH 1
²doom *vb* **doomed; doom·ing :** to make sure that something bad will happen
dooms·day *n* **:** the day the world ends or is destroyed
door *n* **1 :** a usually swinging or sliding frame or barrier by which an entrance (as into a house) is closed and opened **2 :** a part of a piece of furniture that swings or slides open or shut **3 :** DOORWAY
door·bell *n* **:** a bell or set of chimes that is rung usually by pushing a button beside an outside door
door·man *n, pl* **door·men :** a person whose job is to help people at the door of a building
door·step *n* **:** a step or a series of steps in front of an outside door
door·way *n* **:** the opening or passage that a door closes
do–ov·er *n* **:** a new attempt to do something after a previous attempt failed
dope *n* **1 :** an illegal drug **2 :** a stupid person **3 :** INFORMATION
dop·ey *adj* **dop·i·er; dop·i·est 1 :** lacking alertness and activity **:** SLUGGISH **2 :** STUPID 2
dorm *n* **:** DORMITORY
dor·mant *adj* **:** not active for the time being
dor·mer *n* **:** a window placed upright in a sloping roof or the structure containing it
dor·mi·to·ry *n, pl* **dor·mi·to·ries 1 :** a building at a school with rooms where students live **2 :** a large room for several people to sleep
dor·mouse *n, pl* **dor·mice :** a small European animal that resembles a mouse but has a bushy tail, lives mostly in trees, and is active at night
dor·sal *adj* **:** relating to or being on or near the surface of the body that in humans is the back but in most animals is the upper surface
do·ry *n, pl* **dories :** a boat with a flat bottom, high sides that flare out, and a sharp bow
¹dose *n* **:** a measured amount to be used at one time
²dose *vb* **dosed; dos·ing :** to give medicine to
¹dot *n* **1 :** a small point, mark, or spot **2 :** a certain point in time **3 :** a short click forming a letter or part of a letter (as in telegraphy)

²dot *vb* **dot·ted; dot·ting** : to mark with or as if with small spots
dote *vb* **dot·ed; dot·ing** : to give a lot of love or attention to
doth *present third person sing of do, archaic*
¹dou·ble *adj* **1 :** being twice as great or as many **2 :** made up of two parts or members **3 :** having two very different aspects **4 :** made for two **5 :** extra large in size or amount
²double *vb* **dou·bled; dou·bling 1 :** to make or become twice as great or as many : multiply by two **2 :** to fold usually in the middle **3 :** to bend over at the waist **4 :** CLENCH 2 **5 :** to turn sharply and go back over the same path **6 :** to have another use or job
³double *adv* **1 :** two times the amount **2 :** two together
⁴double *n* **1 :** something that is twice the usual size or amount **2 :** a hit in baseball that allows the batter to reach second base **3 :** someone or something that is very like another — **on the double :** very quickly
double bass *n* : an instrument of the violin family that is the largest member and has the deepest tone
dou·ble–cross *vb* **dou·ble–crossed; dou·ble–cross·ing** : BETRAY 2 — **dou·ble–cross·er** *n*
dou·ble·head·er *n* : two games played one right after the other on the same day
dou·ble–joint·ed *adj* : having a joint that permits unusual freedom of movement of the parts that are joined
double play *n* : a play in baseball by which two base runners are put out
dou·blet *n* : a close-fitting jacket worn by men in Europe especially in the 16th century
dou·ble–talk *n* : language that seems to make sense but is actually a mixture of sense and nonsense
dou·bly *adv* : to two times the amount or degree
¹doubt *vb* **doubt·ed; doubt·ing 1 :** to be uncertain about **2 :** to lack confidence in **3 :** to consider unlikely
²doubt *n* **1 :** a feeling of being uncertain **2 :** a reason for disbelief **3 :** the condition of being undecided **4 :** a lack of trust
doubt·ful *adj* **1 :** undecided in opinion **2 :** not likely to be true **3 :** not likely to be good **4 :** not certain in outcome — **doubt·ful·ly** *adv*
doubt·less *adv* **1 :** without doubt **2 :** in all probability
dough *n* **1 :** a thick mixture usually mainly of flour and liquid that is baked **2 :** MONEY 1
dough·nut *n* : a small ring of sweet dough fried in fat
dour *adj* : looking or being serious and unfriendly
douse *vb* **doused; dous·ing 1 :** to stick into water **2 :** to throw a liquid on **3 :** to put out : EXTINGUISH
¹dove *n* : a bird that is related to the pigeon but usually of somewhat smaller size
²dove *past of* DIVE
dowdy *adj* **dowd·i·er; dowd·i·est 1 :** not neatly or well dressed or cared for **2 :** not stylish
dow·el *n* : a pin or peg used for fastening together two pieces of wood
¹down *adv* **1 :** toward or in a lower position **2 :** to a lying or sitting position **3 :** toward or to the ground, floor, or bottom **4 :** below the horizon **5 :** to or toward the south **6 :** in or into the stomach **7 :** as a down payment **8 :** on paper **9 :** to a lower level or rate **10 :** to a weaker or worse condition **11 :** from a past time **12 :** to or in a state of less activity **13 :** in a way that limits movement
²down *prep* **1 :** from a higher to a lower point of something **2 :** along the course or path of
³down *vb* **downed; down·ing 1 :** to go or cause to go or come to the ground **2 :** EAT 1 **3 :** ¹DEFEAT 2
⁴down *adj* **1 :** in a low position **2 :** directed or going downward **3 :** at a lower level **4 :** having a lower score **5 :** SAD 1 **6 :** not working **7 :** finished or completed **8 :** learned completely
⁵down *n* : a low or falling period
⁶down *n* : a high area of land with low hills and no trees — usually used in pl.
⁷down *n* **1 :** soft fluffy feathers **2 :** small soft hairs
down·beat *n* : the first beat of a measure of music
down·cast *adj* **1 :** SAD 1 **2 :** directed down
down·fall *n* : a sudden fall (as from power, happiness, or a high position) or the cause of such a fall — **down·fall·en** *adj*
¹down·grade *n* : a downward slope (as of a road)
²downgrade *vb* **down·grad·ed; down·grad·ing** : to lower in grade, rank, position, or standing
down·heart·ed *adj* : SAD 1
¹down·hill *adv* **1 :** toward the bottom of a hill **2 :** toward a worse condition
²down·hill *adj* **1 :** sloping downward **2 :** having to do with skiing down mountains
down·load *vb* **down·load·ed; down·load·ing** : to transfer (data or files) from a large or remote computer to a smaller computer or other device
down payment *n* : a part of a price paid when something is bought with an agreement to pay the rest later

down·pour *n* : a heavy rain
[1]**down·right** *adv* : REALLY 2, VERY
[2]**downright** *adj* : [2]OUTRIGHT 1, ABSOLUTE
[1]**down·stairs** *adv* : down the stairs : on or to a lower floor
[2]**down·stairs** *adj* : situated on a lower floor or on the main or first floor
[3]**down·stairs** *n pl* : the lower floor of a building — usually used as singular
down·stream *adv* : in the direction a stream is flowing
[1]**down·town** *n* : the main or central part of a city or town
[2]**down·town** *adv* : to or toward the main or central part of a city or town
[1]**down·ward** *or* **down·wards** *adv* : from a higher place, amount, or level to a lower one
[2]**downward** *adj* : going or moving from a higher place, amount, or level to a lower one
down·wind *adv or adj* : in the direction the wind is blowing
downy *adj* **down·i·er; down·i·est** **1** : like small soft feathers **2** : covered or filled with small soft feathers or hairs
dow·ry *n, pl* **dowries** : money, goods, or property that in some cultures a woman gives to her husband in marriage
doz. *abbr* dozen
[1]**doze** *vb* **dozed; doz·ing** : to sleep lightly — **doze off** : to fall asleep
[2]**doze** *n* : a light sleep
doz·en *n, pl* **dozens** *or* **dozen** : a group of twelve
Dr. *abbr* doctor
drab *adj* **drab·ber; drab·best** **1** : not bright or interesting : DULL **2** : grayish brown in color — **drab·ly** *adv* — **drab·ness** *n*
[1]**draft** *n* **1** : a version of something written or drawn (as an essay, document, or plan) that has or will have more than one version **2** : a current of air **3** : a device to regulate an air supply (as in a fireplace) **4** : the act of pulling or hauling : the thing or amount pulled **5** : the act or an instance of drinking or inhaling : the portion drunk or inhaled at one time **6** : the act of drawing out liquid (as from a cask) : a portion of liquid drawn out **7** : the depth of water a ship needs in order to float **8** : the practice of ordering people into military service **9** : the practice of choosing someone to play on a professional sports team **10** : an order made by one person or organization to another to pay money to a third person or organization
[2]**draft** *adj* **1** : used for pulling loads **2** : not in final form **3** : ready to be drawn from a container
[3]**draft** *vb* **draft·ed; draft·ing** **1** : to write or draw a version of something (as an essay or plan) that usually needs more work **2** : to choose someone to do something **3** : to pick especially for required military service
drafty *adj* **draft·i·er; draft·i·est** : having usually cool air moving through
[1]**drag** *n* **1** : something used for pulling along (as a device used underwater to catch something) **2** : something without wheels (as a heavy sled for carrying loads) that is pulled along or over a surface **3** : something that slows down motion **4** : a dull or unpleasant event, person, or thing
[2]**drag** *vb* **dragged; drag·ging** **1** : to pull slowly or heavily **2** : to move with slowness or difficulty **3** : to move or cause to move along on the ground **4** : to bring by or as if by force **5** : to pass or cause to pass slowly **6** : to hang or lag behind **7** : to search or fish by pulling something (as a net) under water
drag·net *n* **1** : a net that is pulled along the bottom of a body of water in order to catch or find something **2** : a series of actions by police for catching a criminal
drag·on *n* : an imaginary animal usually pictured as a huge serpent or lizard with wings and large claws
drag·on·fly *n, pl* **drag·on·flies** : a large insect with a long slender body and four wings
drag race *n* : a race between vehicles to see who can increase speed most quickly over a short distance
[1]**drain** *vb* **drained; drain·ing** **1** : to remove (liquid) from something by letting it flow away or out **2** : to slowly make or become dry or empty **3** : to flow into, away from, or out of something **4** : to slowly disappear **5** : to tire out
[2]**drain** *n* **1** : something used to remove a liquid **2** : something that slowly empties of or uses up
drain·age *n* : the act or process of removing a liquid
drain·pipe *n* : a pipe for removing water
drake *n* : a male duck
dra·ma *n* **1** : a written work that tells a story through action and speech and is acted out : a usually serious play, movie, or television production **2** : the art or profession of creating or putting on plays **3** : an exciting or emotional situation or event
dra·mat·ic *adj* **1** : having to do with drama **2** : attracting attention **3** : sudden and extreme — **dra·mat·i·cal·ly** *adv*
dra·ma·tist *n* : PLAYWRIGHT
dra·ma·tize *vb* **dram·a·tized; dram·a·tiz·ing** **1** : to make into a play, movie, or other show **2** : to present in a way that attracts attention — **dra·ma·ti·za·tion** *n*
drank *past and past participle of* DRINK

[1]**drape** *vb* **draped; drap·ing** **1 :** to decorate or cover with or as if with folds of cloth **2 :** to arrange or hang in flowing lines
[2]**drape** *n, pl* **drapes :** DRAPERY 1
drap·ery *n, pl* **drap·er·ies** **1 :** long heavy curtains **2 :** a decorative fabric hung in loose folds
dras·tic *adj* **:** severe in effect **:** HARSH — **dras·ti·cal·ly** *adv*
draught *chiefly Brit spelling of* DRAFT
[1]**draw** *vb* **drew; drawn; draw·ing** **1 :** to cause to move by pulling **2 :** to create a picture of by making lines on a surface **3 :** to bring or pull out **4 :** to move in a particular direction **5 :** to bend (a bow) by pulling back the string **6 :** to move or go slowly or steadily **7 :** ATTRACT 2 **8 :** to get as a response **9 :** to bring or get from a source **10 :** INHALE 1 **11 :** to let air flow through **12 :** WITHDRAW **13 :** to take or get at random **14 :** to think of after considering information **15 :** to write out in proper form — **draw on** **1 :** to make use of something **2 :** to come closer — **draw out** **1 :** to make last longer **2 :** to cause to talk freely — **draw up** **1 :** to bring or come to a stop **2 :** to straighten up
[2]**draw** *n* **1 :** the act or the result of pulling out **2 :** a tie game or contest **3 :** something or someone that attracts people
draw·back *n* **:** an unwanted feature or characteristic
draw·bridge *n* **:** a bridge that moves up, down, or to the side to allow boats or vehicles to pass
draw·er *n* **1 :** a box that slides in and out of a piece of furniture and is used for storage **2 drawers** *pl* **:** UNDERPANTS
draw·ing *n* **1 :** a picture created by making lines on a surface **2 :** the act or art of creating a picture, plan, or sketch by making lines on a surface **3 :** an act or instance of picking something at random
drawing room *n* **:** a formal room for entertaining company
[1]**drawl** *vb* **drawled; drawl·ing :** to speak slowly with vowel sounds that are longer than usual
[2]**drawl** *n* **:** a way of speaking with vowel sounds that are longer than usual
drawn *adj* **:** looking very thin and tired especially from worry, pain, or illness
draw·string *n* **:** a string at the top of a bag or on clothing that can be pulled to close or tighten
[1]**dread** *vb* **dread·ed; dread·ing** **1 :** to fear or dislike greatly **2 :** to be very unwilling to face
[2]**dread** *n* **:** great fear especially of something that will or might happen
[3]**dread** *adj* **:** causing great fear or anxiety
dread·ful *adj* **1 :** causing fear **2 :** very unpleasant
dread·ful·ly *adv* **1 :** VERY **2 :** very badly
[1]**dream** *n* **1 :** a series of thoughts or visions that occur during sleep **2 :** [1]DAYDREAM **3 :** something very pleasing **4 :** a goal that is wished for
[2]**dream** *vb* **dreamed** *or* **dreamt; dream·ing** **1 :** to have a series of thoughts or visions while sleeping **2 :** to spend time having daydreams **3 :** to think of as happening or possible — **dream·er** *n* — **dream up :** to think of or invent
dreamy *adj* **dream·i·er; dream·i·est** **1 :** appearing to be daydreaming **2 :** seeming like a dream **3 :** quiet and relaxing — **dream·i·ly** *adv*
drea·ry *adj* **drea·ri·er; drea·ri·est :** dull and gloomy — **drea·ri·ly** *adv* — **drea·ri·ness** *n*
[1]**dredge** *vb* **dredged; dredg·ing :** to dig or gather with or as if with a device dragged along the bottom of a body of water — **dredg·er** *n*
[2]**dredge** *n* **1 :** a heavy iron frame with a net attached to be dragged along the bottom of a body of water **2 :** a machine or boat used in dragging along the bottom of a body of water **3 :** a machine for removing earth usually by buckets on an endless chain or by a suction tube
dregs *n pl* **1 :** solids that sink to the bottom of a liquid **2 :** the worst or most useless part
drench *vb* **drenched; drench·ing :** to make completely wet
[1]**dress** *vb* **dressed; dress·ing** **1 :** to put clothes on **2 :** to put on clothes in a particular way **3 :** to wear formal or fancy clothes **4 :** to apply medicine or bandages to **5 :** to trim or decorate for display **6 :** to prepare for cooking or eating — **dress up** **1 :** to put on formal or fancy clothes **2 :** to put on a costume
[2]**dress** *n* **1 :** a piece of clothing for a woman or girl that has a top part that covers the upper body and that is connected to a skirt covering the lower body **2 :** CLOTHING
[3]**dress** *adj* **:** proper for a formal event
[1]**dress·er** *n* **:** a piece of furniture that has drawers for storing clothes and that sometimes has a mirror
[2]**dresser** *n* **:** a person who dresses in a certain way
dress·ing *n* **1 :** a sauce put on a salad **2 :** a seasoned mixture used as a stuffing **3 :** material (as ointment or gauze) used to cover an injury **4 :** the act of putting on clothes
dressy *adj* **dress·i·er; dress·i·est** **1 :** requiring fancy clothes **2 :** proper for formal events

drew *past of* DRAW
[1]drib·ble *vb* **drib·bled; drib·bling** **1 :** to fall or let fall in small drops : TRICKLE **2 :** to let saliva or other liquid drip or trickle from the mouth **3 :** to move forward by bouncing, tapping, or kicking
[2]dribble *n* **1 :** a trickling flow **2 :** the act of moving a ball or puck forward by bouncing, kicking, or tapping it
drier *variant of* DRYER
[1]drift *n* **1 :** the slow movement of something carried by wind or water **2 :** a pile of something that has been blown by the wind **3 :** a course something appears to be taking **4 :** the meaning of something said or implied
[2]drift *vb* **drift·ed; drift·ing** **1 :** to move slowly on wind or water **2 :** to be piled up by wind or water **3 :** to move along or change without effort or purpose — **drift·er** *n*
drift·wood *n* : wood carried by water
[1]drill *vb* **drilled; drill·ing** **1 :** to make holes in with a drill **2 :** to teach by repeating a lesson or exercise again and again — **drill·er** *n*
[2]drill *n* **1 :** a tool for making holes in hard substances **2 :** the training of soldiers (as in marching) **3 :** instruction in a subject or physical training that is practiced repeatedly
[3]drill *n* : a special machine for making holes or furrows and planting seeds in them
[4]drill *vb* **drilled; drill·ing :** to sow seeds with or as if with a special machine
drily *variant of* DRYLY
[1]drink *vb* **drank; drunk; drink·ing** **1 :** to swallow liquid **2 :** to absorb a liquid **3 :** to drink alcoholic beverages **4 :** to take in through the senses — **drink·er** *n*
[2]drink *n* **1 :** a liquid safe for swallowing **2 :** an amount of liquid swallowed **3 :** alcoholic beverages
drink·able *adj* : suitable or safe for drinking
[1]drip *vb* **dripped; drip·ping** **1 :** to fall in drops **2 :** to let fall drops of liquid **3 :** to have or show a large amount of something
[2]drip *n* **1 :** the act of falling in drops **2 :** a drop of liquid that falls **3 :** the sound made by falling drops
[1]drive *vb* **drove; driv·en; driv·ing** **1 :** to direct the movement of **2 :** to go or carry in a vehicle **3 :** to move using force **4 :** to push in with force **5 :** to set or keep in motion or operation **6 :** to carry through **7 :** to force to work or to act **8 :** to bring into a particular condition — **driv·er** *n*
[2]drive *n* **1 :** a trip in a vehicle **2 :** DRIVEWAY **3 :** an often scenic public road **4 :** an organized effort to achieve a goal **5 :** a strong natural need or desire **6 :** energy and determination to succeed **7 :** an act of leading animals in a group to another place **8 :** the means for making a machine or machine part move **9 :** a device in a computer that can read information off and copy information onto disks or tape
drive–in *n* : a restaurant or theater that serves customers while they stay in their vehicles
drive–through *adj* : DRIVE-UP
drive–up *adj* : set up to allow customers to be served while they stay in their vehicles
drive·way *n* : a private road leading from the street to a house or garage
[1]driz·zle *n* : a fine misty rain
[2]drizzle *vb* **driz·zled; driz·zling :** to rain in very small drops
droid *n* : a mobile robot usually with a human form
droll *adj* **droller; droll·est :** having an odd or amusing quality
drom·e·dary *n, pl* **drom·e·dar·ies :** the camel of western Asia and northern Africa that has only one hump
[1]drone *n* : a male bee
[2]drone *vb* **droned; dron·ing :** to make or to speak with a low dull tone or hum
[3]drone *n* : a low dull tone or hum
[1]drool *vb* **drooled; drool·ing :** to let saliva drip from the mouth
[2]drool *n* : saliva that drips from the mouth
[1]droop *vb* **drooped; droop·ing** **1 :** to sink, bend, or hang down **2 :** to become sad or weak
[2]droop *n* : the condition of hanging or bending down
[1]drop *n* **1 :** a small amount of liquid that falls in a rounded shape **2 drops** *pl* : liquid medicine measured by drops **3 :** something (as a small round candy) that is shaped like a liquid drop **4 :** a small amount **5 :** the distance of a fall **6 :** a decrease in amount or quality **7 :** an act of delivering something : a place where something is left to be picked up
[2]drop *vb* **dropped; drop·ping** **1 :** to fall or let fall often by accident **2 :** to go down suddenly **3 :** to go or make lower **4 :** to become less or make less **5 :** LOSE 4 **6 :** DISAPPEAR 1 **7 :** to stop or let end **8 :** QUIT **9 :** to make a brief visit **10 :** to deliver with a quick stop **11 :** SEND 1 — **drop off :** to fall asleep
drop–down *adj* : PULL-DOWN
drop·let *n* : a tiny drop
drop·out *n* : a person who quits school or a training program
drop·per *n* : a short tube with a rubber bulb used to measure out liquids by drops
drought *n* : a long period of time during which there is very little or no rain
[1]drove *n* : a large group of animals or people moving or acting together

[2]**drove** *past of* DRIVE
drown *vb* **drowned; drown·ing** **1 :** to die or cause to die from being underwater and unable to breathe **2 :** to cover with a liquid **3 :** to overpower especially with noise **4 :** to make helpless or overwhelmed
[1]**drowse** *vb* **drowsed; drows·ing :** to sleep lightly
[2]**drowse** *n* **:** a light sleep **:** DOZE
drowsy *adj* **drows·i·er; drows·i·est** **1 :** ready to fall asleep **2 :** causing sleepiness — **drows·i·ly** *adv* — **drows·i·ness** *n*
drub *vb* **drubbed; drub·bing** **1 :** to beat severely **2 :** to defeat completely
drudge *n* **:** a person who does hard or dull work
drudg·ery *n, pl* **drudg·er·ies :** hard or dull work
[1]**drug** *n* **1 :** a substance used as a medicine or in making medicines **2 :** a substance (as cocaine or marijuana) that may harm or addict a user
[2]**drug** *vb* **drugged; drug·ging** **1 :** to poison with or as if with a drug **2 :** to make sleepy or unconscious with drugs
drug·gist *n* **:** a person who prepares and sells drugs and medicines **:** PHARMACIST
drug·store *n* **:** a retail store where medicines and often other items are sold **:** PHARMACY
[1]**drum** *n* **1 :** a musical instrument usually consisting of a metal or wooden round frame with flat ends covered by tightly stretched skin **2 :** a tapping sound **:** a sound of or like a drum **3 :** an object shaped like a cylinder
[2]**drum** *vb* **drummed; drum·ming** **1 :** to beat or play a drum **2 :** to make a tapping sound **:** make a sound like a drum **3 :** to beat or tap in a rhythmic way **4 :** to gather together or create by hard work **5 :** to drive or force by steady or repeated effort — **drum·mer** *n*
drum major *n* **:** the marching leader of a band or drum corps
drum ma·jor·ette *n* **:** a girl who is the marching leader of a band or drum corps
drum·stick *n* **1 :** a stick for beating a drum **2 :** the lower section of the leg of a bird eaten for food
[1]**drunk** *past participle of* DRINK
[2]**drunk** *adj* **drunk·er; drunk·est** **1 :** being so much under the influence of alcohol that normal thinking and acting become difficult or impossible **2 :** controlled by a strong feeling
[3]**drunk** *n* **:** DRUNKARD
drunk·ard *n* **:** a person who is often drunk
drunk·en *adj* **1 :** [2]DRUNK 1 **2 :** resulting from being drunk — **drunk·en·ly** *adv* — **drunk·en·ness** *n*
[1]**dry** *adj* **dri·er; dri·est** **1 :** not wet or moist **2 :** having little or no rain **3 :** not being in or under water **4 :** having little natural moisture **5 :** no longer liquid or sticky **6 :** containing no liquid **7 :** not giving milk **8 :** not producing desired results **9 :** not producing a wet substance from the body **10 :** funny but expressed in a serious way **11 :** UNINTERESTING **12 :** not sweet — **dry·ly** *or* **dri·ly** *adv* — **dry·ness** *n*
[2]**dry** *vb* **dried; dry·ing :** to remove or lose any moisture
dry cell *n* **:** a small cell producing electricity by means of chemicals in a sealed container
dry–clean *vb* **dry-cleaned; dry-clean·ing :** to clean (fabrics) with chemicals instead of water
dry cleaner *n* **:** a person whose business is cleaning fabrics with chemicals instead of water
dry cleaning *n* **1 :** the cleaning of fabrics with a substance other than water **2 :** something that has been cleaned by a dry cleaner
dry·er *also* **dri·er** *n* **:** a device for removing moisture by using heat or air
dry–erase board *n* **:** WHITEBOARD
dry ice *n* **:** solidified carbon dioxide used chiefly to keep something very cold
DST *abbr* daylight saving time
du·al *adj* **1 :** having two different parts or aspects **2 :** having two like parts
[1]**dub** *vb* **dubbed; dub·bing** **1 :** to make a knight of **2 :** [2]NAME 1, NICKNAME
[2]**dub** *vb* **dubbed; dub·bing :** to add (a different language or sound effects) to a film or broadcast
du·bi·ous *adj* **1 :** causing doubt **:** UNCERTAIN **2 :** feeling doubt **3 :** QUESTIONABLE 1 — **du·bi·ous·ly** *adv*
duch·ess *n* **1 :** the wife or widow of a duke **2 :** a woman who has the same rank as a duke
[1]**duck** *n* **:** a swimming bird that has a broad flat bill and is smaller than the related goose and swan
[2]**duck** *vb* **ducked; duck·ing** **1 :** to push under water for a moment **2 :** to lower the head or body suddenly **3 :** to avoid by moving quickly **4 :** to avoid a duty, question, or responsibility
duck·bill *n* **:** PLATYPUS
duck·ling *n* **:** a young duck
duct *n* **:** a pipe, tube, or vessel that carries something
duct tape *n* **:** a wide sticky usually silver tape made of cloth
dud *n* **1 :** a complete failure **2 :** a bomb or missile that fails to explode **3 duds** *pl* **:** CLOTHING
dude *n* **1 :** a person from the eastern United States in the West **2 :** [1]MAN 1, GUY
[1]**due** *adj* **1 :** required or expected to happen

or be done **2 :** owed or deserved **3 :** in a proper or necessary amount — **due to :** because of

[2]**due** *n* **1 :** something that should be given **2 dues** *pl* **:** a regular or legal charge or fee

[3]**due** *adv* **:** DIRECTLY 1

[1]**du·el** *n* **1 :** a fight between two persons especially that is fought by agreement with weapons in front of other people **2 :** a contest between two opponents

[2]**duel** *vb* **du·eled** *or* **du·elled; du·el·ing** *or* **du·el·ling :** to take part in an agreed-upon fight with weapons

du·et *n* **1 :** a piece of music for two performers **2 :** two people performing music together

dug *past and past participle of* DIG

dug·out *n* **1 :** a low shelter facing a baseball diamond and containing the players' bench **2 :** a shelter dug in a hillside or in the ground **3 :** a boat made by hollowing out a log

duke *n* **:** a man of the highest rank of the British nobility

[1]**dull** *adj* **dull·er; dull·est** **1 :** not sharp in edge or point **:** BLUNT **2 :** not shiny or bright **3 :** not interesting **:** BORING **4 :** not clear and ringing **5 :** not sharp or intense **6 :** slightly grayish **7 :** CLOUDY 1, OVERCAST **8 :** slow in understanding things **:** not smart **9 :** without energy or spirit **10 :** slow in action **:** SLUGGISH — **dull·ness** *n* — **dul·ly** *adv*

[2]**dull** *vb* **dulled; dull·ing :** to make or become less sharp, bright, or intense

du·ly *adv* **:** in a due or appropriate manner, time, or degree

dumb *adj* **dumb·er; dumb·est** **1 :** lacking the power of human speech **2** *often offensive* **:** lacking the ability to speak **3 :** temporarily unable to speak (as from shock or surprise) **4 :** STUPID 1, FOOLISH — **dumb·ly** *adv*

dumb·found *vb* **dumb·found·ed; dumb·found·ing :** to make speechless with surprise

dum·my *n, pl* **dummies** **1 :** something shaped like a human **2 :** a doll used in a ventriloquist's act **3 :** a stupid person

[1]**dump** *vb* **dumped; dump·ing** **1 :** to let fall in a heap **2 :** to get rid of

[2]**dump** *n* **1 :** a place for getting rid of trash **2 :** a place for storage of military materials or the materials stored **3 :** a messy or shabby place

dump·ling *n* **1 :** a small amount of dough cooked by boiling or steaming **2 :** a dessert of fruit wrapped in dough

dumps *n pl* **:** a sad mood

dumpy *adj* **dump·i·er; dump·i·est :** having a short and round body

dun *n* **:** a slightly brownish dark gray

dunce *n* **:** a stupid person

dune *n* **:** a hill or ridge of sand piled up by the wind

dung *n* **:** solid waste matter from an animal

dun·ga·ree *n* **1 :** a heavy cotton cloth **:** DENIM **2 dungarees** *pl* **:** clothes made of denim

dun·geon *n* **:** a dark usually underground prison

dunk *vb* **dunked; dunk·ing** **1 :** to dip into liquid **2 :** to jump and push the ball down through the basket in basketball

duo *n, pl* **du·os** **1 :** two people who are usually seen together **2 :** DUET

[1]**dupe** *n* **:** a person who has been or is easily deceived or cheated

[2]**dupe** *vb* **duped; dup·ing :** [2]TRICK

du·plex *n* **:** a house with two separate living spaces

[1]**du·pli·cate** *adj* **:** exactly the same as another

[2]**du·pli·cate** *vb* **du·pli·cat·ed; du·pli·cat·ing :** to make an exact copy of

[3]**du·pli·cate** *n* **:** a thing that is exactly like another

du·pli·ca·tion *n* **1 :** the act or process of copying **2 :** the state of being copied

du·ra·bil·i·ty *n* **:** ability to last or to stand hard or continued use

du·ra·ble *adj* **:** able to last a long time

du·ra·tion *n* **:** the time during which something exists or lasts

dur·ing *prep* **1 :** throughout the course of **2 :** at some point in the course of

dusk *n* **:** the time when the sky is getting dark at night

dusky *adj* **dusk·i·er; dusk·i·est** **1 :** somewhat dark in color **2 :** somewhat dark **:** DIM

[1]**dust** *n* **1 :** fine dry powdery particles (as of earth) **:** a fine powder that often builds up on furniture **2 :** a fine powder made from a particular substance or from something that has disintegrated **3 :** the surface of the ground

[2]**dust** *vb* **dust·ed; dust·ing** **1 :** to make free of dust **:** brush or wipe away dust **2 :** to sprinkle with or as if with fine particles — **dust·er** *n*

dust·pan *n* **:** a flat pan shaped like a shovel into which dirt from the floor is swept

dust storm *n* **:** a very strong wind carrying dust across a dry region

dusty *adj* **dust·i·er; dust·i·est** **1 :** filled or covered with dust **2 :** resembling dust

[1]**Dutch** *adj* **:** of or relating to the Netherlands, its people, or their language

[2]**Dutch** *n* **1 Dutch** *pl* **:** the people of the Netherlands **2 :** the language of the people of the Netherlands

du·ti·ful *adj* **:** doing or showing the willingness to do what is expected or required — **du·ti·ful·ly** *adv*

du·ty *n, pl* **duties** **1 :** something a person feels he or she ought to do because it is morally right **2 :** something a person is required to do by law **3 :** an action done as part of a job or position **4 :** the time during which a person must do his or her job **5 :** active military service **6 :** a tax especially on imports into a country

DVD *n, pl* **DVDs :** a plastic disk that is used to store information (as computer data or a movie) and is read using a laser

DVR *n, pl* **DVRs :** a machine that is used to make and watch recordings of television programs

[1]dwarf *n, pl* **dwarfs** *also* **dwarves** **1 :** a person, animal, or plant much smaller than normal size **2 :** a creature in legends that is usually pictured as a small person who is skilled at some craft

[2]dwarf *vb* **dwarfed; dwarf·ing :** to cause to appear smaller

[3]dwarf *adj* **:** of less than the usual size

dwarf planet *n* **:** an object in outer space similar to a planet but too small for its gravity to draw in other objects

dwell *vb* **dwelt** *or* **dwelled; dwell·ing** **1 :** to live in a place **:** RESIDE **2 :** to keep the attention directed — **dwell·er** *n*

dwell·ing *n* **:** a shelter in which a person or an animal lives

dwin·dle *vb* **dwin·dled; dwin·dling :** to make or become less or smaller

[1]dye *n* **:** a substance used to change the color of something

[2]dye *vb* **dyed; dye·ing :** to change the color of something using a substance

dying *present participle of* DIE

dy·nam·ic *adj* **:** always active, energetic, or changing

[1]dy·na·mite *n* **:** an explosive used in blasting

[2]dynamite *vb* **dy·na·mit·ed; dy·na·mit·ing :** to blow up with dynamite

dy·na·mo *n, pl* **dy·na·mos** **1 :** GENERATOR **2 :** an energetic person

dy·nas·ty *n, pl* **dy·nas·ties :** a series of rulers of the same family

dys·en·tery *n* **:** a disease marked especially by severe often bloody diarrhea

dys·lex·ia *n* **:** a learning disability in which a person usually has a problem in reading, spelling, and writing — **dys·lex·ic** *adj*

E

e *n, pl* **e's** *or* **es** *often cap* **1 :** the fifth letter of the English alphabet **2 :** a grade that shows a student's work is failing **3 :** a musical note referred to by the letter E

E *abbr* **1** east **2** eastern **3** excellent

ea. *abbr* each

[1]each *adj* **:** every one of two or more individuals considered separately

[2]each *pron* **:** each one

[3]each *adv* **:** to or for each **:** APIECE

each other *pron* **:** each of two or more in a shared action or relationship

ea·ger *adj* **:** very excited and interested — **ea·ger·ly** *adv* — **ea·ger·ness** *n*

ea·gle *n* **:** a large bird of prey noted for keen sight and powerful flight

ea·glet *n* **:** a young eagle

-ean — see -AN

[1]ear *n* **1 :** the organ of hearing and balance of vertebrates that in most mammals is made up of an outer part that collects sound, a middle part that carries sound, and an inner part that receives sound and sends nerve signals to the brain **2 :** the outer part of the ear **3 :** the sense of hearing **4 :** willing or sympathetic attention — **eared** *adj*

[2]ear *n* **:** the seed-bearing head of a cereal grass

ear·ache *n* **:** an ache or pain in the ear

ear·drum *n* **:** the membrane that separates the outer and middle parts of the ear and vibrates when sound waves strike it

earl *n* **:** a member of the British nobility who ranks below a marquess and above a viscount

[1]ear·ly *adv* **ear·li·er; ear·li·est** **1 :** at or near the beginning of a period of time **2 :** before the usual or expected time

[2]early *adj* **ear·li·er; ear·li·est :** occurring near the beginning or before the usual time

ear·muff *n* **:** one of a pair of coverings joined by a flexible band and worn to protect the ears from cold or noise

earn *vb* **earned; earn·ing** **1 :** to get for work done **2 :** to deserve as a result of labor or service

ear·nest *adj* **:** not light or playful — **ear·nest·ly** *adv* — **ear·nest·ness** *n*

earn·ings *n pl* **:** money received as wages or gained as profit

ear·phone *n* **:** a device that is worn over the opening of the ear or inserted into it and is used for listening to something

ear·ring *n* **:** an ornament worn on the ear

ear·shot *n* **:** the range within which a person's voice can be heard

earth *n* **1** *often cap* **:** the planet that we live on **2 :** land as distinguished from sea and air **3 :** ²SOIL 1

earth·en *adj* **:** made of earth or of baked clay

earth·en·ware *n* **:** things (as dishes) made of baked clay

earth·ly *adj* **1 :** having to do with or belonging to the earth **2 :** IMAGINABLE, POSSIBLE

earth·quake *n* **:** a shaking or trembling of a portion of the earth

earth·worm *n* **:** a worm that has a long body made up of similar segments and lives in damp soil

earthy *adj* **earth·i·er; earth·i·est 1 :** of or like earth **2 :** open and direct **3 :** not polite **:** CRUDE

ear·wax *n* **:** a yellowish brown waxy substance made by glands in the canal of the outer part of the ear

ear·wig *n* **:** an insect with long slender feelers and a part at the end of its body that pinches and is used for self-defense

¹**ease** *n* **1 :** freedom from pain or trouble **:** comfort of body or mind **2 :** lack of difficulty **3 :** freedom from any feeling of difficulty or embarrassment

²**ease** *vb* **eased; eas·ing 1 :** to free from discomfort or worry **:** RELIEVE **2 :** to make less tight **:** LOOSEN **3 :** to move very carefully

ea·sel *n* **:** a frame for supporting an artist's painting

eas·i·ly *adv* **1 :** without difficulty **2 :** without doubt **:** by far

¹**east** *n* **1 :** the direction of sunrise **:** the compass point opposite to west **2** *cap* **:** regions or countries east of a certain point

²**east** *adj* **:** placed toward, facing, or coming from the east

³**east** *adv* **:** to or toward the east

Eas·ter *n* **:** a Christian holy day that celebrates the Resurrection

east·er·ly *adv or adj* **1 :** toward the east **2 :** from the east

east·ern *adj* **1 :** lying toward or coming from the east **2** *often cap* **:** of, relating to, or like that of the East

east·ward *adv or adj* **:** toward the east

¹**easy** *adj* **eas·i·er; eas·i·est 1 :** not hard to do or get **:** not difficult **2 :** not hard to please **3 :** free from pain, trouble, or worry **4 :** COMFORTABLE 1 **5 :** showing ease **:** NATURAL

²**easy** *adv* **1 :** EASILY **2 :** slowly and carefully or calmly **3 :** without much punishment

eat *vb* **ate; eat·en; eat·ing 1 :** to chew and swallow food **2 :** to take a meal **3 :** to destroy as if by eating **:** CORRODE — **eat·er** *n*

eat·able *adj* **:** fit to be eaten **:** EDIBLE

eave *n* **:** the lower edge of a roof that sticks out past the wall — usually used in pl.

eaves·drop *vb* **eaves·dropped; eaves·drop·ping :** to listen secretly to private conversation

¹**ebb** *n* **1 :** the flowing out of the tide **2 :** a point reached after things have gotten worse

²**ebb** *vb* **ebbed; ebb·ing 1 :** to flow out or away **:** RECEDE **2 :** ¹DECLINE 2, WEAKEN

¹**eb·o·ny** *n, pl* **eb·o·nies :** a hard heavy blackish wood that comes from tropical trees

²**ebony** *adj* **1 :** made of or like ebony **2 :** very dark or black

e–book *n* **:** a book that is read on a computer, e-reader, or other electronic device

¹**ec·cen·tric** *adj* **1 :** acting or thinking in a strange way **2 :** not of the usual or normal kind

²**eccentric** *n* **:** a person who behaves strangely

¹**echo** *n, pl* **ech·oes :** the repetition of a sound caused by the reflection of sound waves

²**echo** *vb* **ech·oed; echo·ing 1 :** to send back or repeat a sound **2 :** to repeat another's words

éclair *n* **:** a long thin pastry filled with whipped cream or custard

¹**eclipse** *n* **1 :** a complete or partial hiding of the sun caused by the moon's passing between the sun and the earth **2 :** a darkening of the moon caused by its entering the shadow of the earth **3 :** the hiding of any celestial body by another

²**eclipse** *vb* **eclipsed; eclips·ing 1 :** to cause an eclipse of **2 :** to be or do much better than **:** OUTSHINE

eco–friend·ly *adj* **:** not harmful to the environment

eco·log·i·cal *adj* **:** of or relating to the science of ecology or the patterns of relationships between living things and their environment

ecol·o·gist *n* **:** a person specializing in ecology

ecol·o·gy *n* **1 :** a branch of science concerned with the relationships between living things and their environment **2 :** the pattern of relationships between living things and their environment

eco·nom·ic *adj* **1 :** of or relating to the study of economics **2 :** relating to or based on the making, selling, and using of goods and services

eco·nom·i·cal *adj* **1 :** using what is available carefully and without waste **:** FRUGAL **2 :** operating with little waste — **eco·nom·i·cal·ly** *adv*

eco·nom·ics *n pl* **:** the science concerned with the making, selling, and using of goods and services — used as singular or plural

econ·o·mize *vb* **econ·o·mized; econ·o·miz·ing 1 :** to be thrifty **2 :** to use less of **:** SAVE

econ·o·my *n, pl* **econ·o·mies 1 :** the way

in which goods and services are made, sold, and used in a country or area **2 :** the careful use of money and goods **:** THRIFT

eco·sys·tem *n* **:** the whole group of living and nonliving things that make up an environment and affect each other

ec·sta·sy *n, pl* **ec·sta·sies :** very great happiness or delight

ec·stat·ic *adj* **:** very happy or excited

ec·ze·ma *n* **:** a skin disease in which the skin is red and itchy and has scaly or crusty patches

[1]**-ed** *vb suffix or adj suffix* **1** — used to form the past participle of verbs **2 :** having **:** showing **3 :** having the characteristics of

[2]**-ed** *vb suffix* — used to form the past tense of verbs

[1]**ed·dy** *n, pl* **eddies :** a current of air or water running against the main current or in a circle

[2]**eddy** *vb* **ed·died; ed·dy·ing :** to move in a circle **:** to form an eddy

[1]**edge** *n* **1 :** the line where a surface ends **:** MARGIN, BORDER **2 :** the cutting side of a blade — **edged** *adj* — **on edge :** NERVOUS 2, TENSE

[2]**edge** *vb* **edged; edg·ing 1 :** to give a border to **2 :** to move slowly and gradually

edge·wise *adv* **:** SIDEWAYS 2

ed·i·ble *adj* **:** fit or safe to eat

edict *n* **:** a command or law given or made by an authority (as a ruler)

ed·i·fice *n* **:** a large or impressive building

ed·it *vb* **ed·it·ed; ed·it·ing 1 :** to correct, revise, and get ready for publication **:** collect and arrange material to be printed **2 :** to be in charge of the publication of something (as an encyclopedia or a newspaper) that is the work of many writers

edi·tion *n* **1 :** the form in which a book is published **2 :** the whole number of copies of a book, magazine, or newspaper published at one time **3 :** one of several issues of a newspaper for a single day

ed·i·tor *n* **:** a person whose job is to correct and revise writing so it can be published

[1]**ed·i·to·ri·al** *adj* **:** of or relating to an editor or editing

[2]**editorial** *n* **:** a newspaper or magazine article that gives the opinions of its editors or publishers

ed·u·cate *vb* **ed·u·cat·ed; ed·u·cat·ing 1 :** to provide schooling for **2 :** to develop the mind and morals of especially by formal instruction **:** TEACH **3 :** to provide with necessary information — **ed·u·ca·tor** *n*

ed·u·cat·ed *adj* **1 :** having an education and especially a good education **2 :** based on some knowledge

ed·u·ca·tion *n* **1 :** the act or process of teaching or of being taught **2 :** knowledge, skill, and development gained from study or training **3 :** the study of the methods and problems of teaching

ed·u·ca·tion·al *adj* **1 :** having to do with education **2 :** offering information or something of value in learning

[1]**-ee** *n suffix* **1 :** person who receives or benefits from a specified thing or action **2 :** person who does a specified thing

[2]**-ee** *n suffix* **1 :** a certain and especially a small kind of **2 :** one like or suggesting

eel *n* **:** a long fish that looks like a snake and has smooth slimy skin

-eer *n suffix* **:** person who is concerned with or conducts or produces as a profession

ee·rie *adj* **ee·ri·er; ee·ri·est :** causing fear and uneasiness **:** STRANGE

ef·face *vb* **ef·faced; ef·fac·ing :** to blot out completely

[1]**ef·fect** *n* **1 :** an event, condition, or state of affairs that is produced by a cause **:** INFLUENCE **2 :** the act of making a certain impression **3 :** EXECUTION 2, OPERATION **4 effects** *pl* **:** personal property or possessions **5 :** something created in film, television, or radio to imitate something real — **in effect :** in actual fact

[2]**effect** *vb* **ef·fect·ed; ef·fect·ing :** to make happen **:** bring about

ef·fec·tive *adj* **1 :** producing or able to produce a desired effect **2 :** IMPRESSIVE **3 :** being in operation — **ef·fec·tive·ly** *adv* — **ef·fec·tive·ness** *n*

ef·fec·tu·al *adj* **:** producing or able to produce a desired effect — **ef·fec·tu·al·ly** *adv*

ef·fi·cien·cy *n, pl* **ef·fi·cien·cies :** the ability to do something or produce something without waste

ef·fi·cient *adj* **:** capable of bringing about a desired result with little waste (as of time or energy) — **ef·fi·cient·ly** *adv*

ef·fort *n* **1 :** hard physical or mental work **:** EXERTION **2 :** a serious attempt **:** TRY **3 :** something produced by work

ef·fort·less *adj* **:** showing or needing little or no effort — **ef·fort·less·ly** *adv*

e.g. *abbr* for example — abbreviation for Latin *exempli gratia*, which means "for example"

[1]**egg** *n* **1** an oval or rounded body surrounded by a shell or membrane by which some animals (as birds, fish, insects, and reptiles) reproduce and from which the young hatches out **2 :** EGG CELL **3 :** the contents of the egg of a bird and especially a chicken that is eaten as food

[2]**egg** *vb* **egged; egg·ing :** to urge or encourage to do usually something foolish or dangerous

egg cell *n* **:** a female reproductive cell of animals and plants that can unite with a sperm cell to form a new individual

egg·nog *n* : a drink made of eggs beaten with sugar, milk or cream, and often alcoholic liquor
egg·plant *n* : an oval vegetable with a usually glossy purplish skin and white flesh
egg·shell *n* : the shell of an egg
egret *n* : a heron with usually white feathers
[1]**Egyp·tian** *adj* : of or relating to Egypt or the Egyptians
[2]**Egyptian** *n* **1** : a person who is born or lives in Egypt **2** : the language of the ancient Egyptians
ei·der *n* : a large duck of northern seas with very soft down
[1]**eight** *n* **1** : one more than seven : two times four : 8 **2** : the eighth in a set or series
[2]**eight** *adj* : being one more than seven
[1]**eigh·teen** *n* : one more than 17 : three times six : 18
[2]**eighteen** *adj* : being one more than 17
[1]**eigh·teenth** *adj* : coming right after 17th
[2]**eighteenth** *n* : number 18 in a series
[1]**eighth** *adj* : coming right after seventh
[2]**eighth** *n* **1** : number eight in a series **2** : one of eight equal parts
[1]**eight·i·eth** *adj* : coming right after 79th
[2]**eightieth** *n* : number 80 in a series
[1]**eighty** *adj* : eight times ten : 80
[2]**eighty** *n* : being eight times ten
[1]**ei·ther** *adj* **1** : [1]EACH **2** : being one or the other
[2]**either** *pron* : the one or the other
[3]**either** *conj* — used before words or phrases the last of which follows "or" to show that they are choices or possibilities
[4]**either** *adv* : ALSO — used after a negative statement
ejac·u·late *vb* **ejac·u·lat·ed; ejac·u·lat·ing** : EXCLAIM
eject *vb* **eject·ed; eject·ing** : to force or push out
eke out *vb* **eked out; ek·ing out** **1** : to get with great effort **2** : to add to bit by bit
[1]**elab·o·rate** *adj* : made or done with great care or much detail — **elab·o·rate·ly** *adv*
[2]**elab·o·rate** *vb* **elab·o·rat·ed; elab·o·rat·ing** **1** : to give more details about **2** : to work out in detail
elapse *vb* **elapsed; elaps·ing** : to slip past : go by
[1]**elas·tic** *adj* : capable of returning to original shape or size after being stretched, pressed, or squeezed together
[2]**elastic** *n* **1** : RUBBER BAND **2** : material that can be stretched
elas·tic·i·ty *n* : the quality or state of being easily stretched
elate *vb* **elat·ed; elat·ing** : to fill with joy or pride
ela·tion *n* : the quality or state of being filled with joy or pride
[1]**el·bow** *n* **1** : the joint or the region of the joint of the arm or of the same part of an animal's front legs **2** : a part (as of a pipe) bent like an elbow
[2]**elbow** *vb* **el·bowed; el·bow·ing** **1** : to jab with an elbow **2** : to push or force a way with or as if with the elbows
[1]**el·der** *n* : ELDERBERRY 1
[2]**elder** *adj* : being older than another person
[3]**elder** *n* **1** : a person who is older **2** : a person having authority because of age and experience **3** : an official in some churches
el·der·ber·ry *n, pl* **el·der·ber·ries** **1** : a shrub or small tree with clusters of small white flowers and a black or red berrylike fruit **2** : the fruit of the elderberry
el·der·ly *adj* : somewhat old
el·dest *adj* : being oldest of a group of people
[1]**elect** *vb* **elect·ed; elect·ing** : to select by vote **2** : to make a choice
[2]**elect** *adj* : chosen for office but not yet holding office
elec·tion *n* : an act of choosing or the fact of being chosen especially by vote
elec·tive *adj* : chosen or filled by election
electr- *or* **electro-** *prefix* **1** : electricity **2** : electric **3** : electric and
elec·tric *adj* **1** *or* **elec·tri·cal** : of or relating to electricity or its use **2** : heated, moved, made, or run by electricity **3** : giving off sounds through an electronic amplifier **4** : having a thrilling effect — **elec·tri·cal·ly** *adv*
electric eel *n* : a large South American eel-shaped fish with organs that can give an electric shock
elec·tri·cian *n* : a person who installs, operates, or repairs electrical equipment
elec·tric·i·ty *n* **1** : an important form of energy that is found in nature but that can be artificially produced by rubbing together two unlike things (as glass and silk), by the action of chemicals, or by means of a generator **2** : electric current
elec·tri·fy *vb* **elec·tri·fied; elec·tri·fy·ing** **1** : to charge with electricity **2** : to equip for use of or supply with electric power **3** : THRILL 1
elec·tro·cute *vb* **elec·tro·cut·ed; elec·tro·cut·ing** : to kill by an electric shock — **elec·tro·cu·tion** *n*
elec·trode *n* : a conductor (as a metal or carbon) used to make electrical contact with a part of an electrical circuit that is not metallic
elec·trol·y·sis *n* : the producing of chemical changes by passage of an electric current through a liquid
elec·tro·lyte *n* **1** : a substance (as an acid or salt) that when dissolved (as in water) con-

ducts an electric current **2 :** a substance (as sodium or calcium) that is an ion in the body regulating the flow of nutrients into and waste products out of cells

elec·tro·lyt·ic *adj* **:** of or relating to electrolysis or an electrolyte

elec·tro·mag·net *n* **:** a piece of iron encircled by a coil of wire through which an electric current is passed to magnetize the iron

elec·tro·mag·net·ic *adj* **:** of or relating to a magnetic field produced by an electric current

electromagnetic wave *n* **:** a wave (as a radio wave or wave of light) that travels at the speed of light and consists of a combined electric and magnetic effect

elec·tron *n* **:** a very small particle that has a negative charge of electricity and travels around the nucleus of an atom

elec·tron·ic *adj* **1 :** relating to or using the principles of electronics **2 :** operating by means of or using a computer — **elec·tron·i·cal·ly** *adv*

electronic mail *n* **:** [1]E-MAIL

elec·tron·ics *n* **:** a science that deals with the giving off, action, and effects of electrons in vacuums, gases, and semiconductors and with devices using such electrons

electron tube *n* **:** a device in which conduction of electricity by electrons takes place through a vacuum or a gas within a sealed container and which has various uses (as in radio and television)

el·e·gance *n* **1 :** gracefulness of style or movement **2 :** tasteful luxury

el·e·gant *adj* **:** showing good taste **:** having or showing beauty and refinement — **el·e·gant·ly** *adv*

el·e·ment *n* **1 :** any of more than 100 substances that cannot by ordinary chemical means be separated into different substances **2 :** one of the parts of which something is made up **3 elements** *pl* **:** the simplest principles of a subject of study **4 :** a member of a mathematical set **5 :** the state or place natural to or suited to a person or thing **6 elements** *pl* **:** the forces of nature

el·e·men·ta·ry *adj* **1 :** relating to the beginnings or simplest principles of a subject **2 :** relating to or teaching the basic subjects of education

el·e·phant *n* **:** a huge typically gray mammal of Africa or Asia with the nose drawn out into a long trunk and two large curved tusks

el·e·vate *vb* **el·e·vat·ed; el·e·vat·ing :** to lift up **:** RAISE

el·e·va·tion *n* **1 :** height especially above sea level **:** ALTITUDE **2 :** a raised place (as a hill) **3 :** the act of raising **:** the condition of being raised

el·e·va·tor *n* **1 :** a floor or little room that can be raised or lowered for carrying people or goods from one level to another **2 :** a device (as an endless belt) for raising material **3 :** GRAIN ELEVATOR

[1]**elev·en** *n* **1 :** one more than ten **:** 11 **2 :** the eleventh in a set or series

[2]**eleven** *adj* **:** being one more than ten

[1]**elev·enth** *adj* **:** coming right after tenth

[2]**eleventh** *n* **:** number eleven in a series

elf *n, pl* **elves :** an often mischievous fairy

elf·in *adj* **:** relating to elves

el·i·gi·ble *adj* **:** qualified to be chosen, to participate, or to receive

elim·i·nate *vb* **elim·i·nat·ed; elim·i·nat·ing :** to get rid of **:** do away with

elim·i·na·tion *n* **1 :** the act or process of excluding or getting rid of **2 :** a getting rid of waste from the body

elk *n* **1 :** a large deer of North America, Europe, and Asia with curved antlers having many branches **2 :** the moose of Europe and Asia

el·lipse *n* **:** a shape that looks like a flattened circle

el·lip·ti·cal *or* **el·lip·tic** *adj* **:** having the shape of an ellipse

elm *n* **:** a tall shade tree with a broad rather flat top and spreading branches

el·o·cu·tion *n* **:** the art of reading or speaking clearly and effectively in public

elon·gate *vb* **elon·gat·ed; elon·gat·ing :** to make or grow longer

elope *vb* **eloped; elop·ing :** to run away to be married — **elope·ment** *n*

el·o·quence *n* **1 :** speaking or writing that is forceful and convincing **2 :** the ability to speak or write with force and in a convincing way

el·o·quent *adj* **1 :** having or showing clear and forceful expression **2 :** clearly showing some feeling or meaning — **el·o·quent·ly** *adv*

[1]**else** *adv* **1 :** in a different way or place or at a different time **2 :** if the facts are or were different **:** if not

[2]**else** *adj* **1 :** being other and different **2 :** being in addition

else·where *adv* **:** in or to another place

elude *vb* **elud·ed; elud·ing :** to avoid or escape by being quick, skillful, or tricky

elu·sive *adj* **1 :** hard to find or capture **2 :** hard to understand or define

elves *pl of* ELF

em- — see EN-

[1]**e–mail** *or* **email** *n* **1 :** a system for sending messages between computers **2 :** a message sent electronically from one computer to another

[2]**e–mail** *or* **email** *vb* **e–mailed** *or* **emailed; e–mail·ing** *or* **email·ing :** to send e-mail or as e-mail

DICTIONARY

em·a·nate *vb* **em·a·nat·ed; em·a·nat·ing** **1 :** to come out from a source **2 :** to give off or out

eman·ci·pate *vb* **eman·ci·pat·ed; eman·ci·pat·ing :** to set free from control or slavery : LIBERATE — **eman·ci·pa·tor** *n*

eman·ci·pa·tion *n* **:** an act of setting someone free from control or slavery

em·balm *vb* **em·balmed; em·balm·ing :** to treat a dead body so as to preserve it from decay — **em·balm·er** *n*

em·bank·ment *n* **:** a raised bank or wall to carry a roadway or hold back water

em·bar·go *n, pl* **em·bar·goes :** an order of a government forbidding ships engaged in trade from leaving its ports

em·bark *vb* **em·barked; em·bark·ing** **1 :** to go on or put on board a ship or an airplane **2 :** to begin a project or task

em·bar·rass *vb* **em·bar·rassed; em·bar·rass·ing :** to cause to feel confused and foolish in front of other people

em·bar·rass·ment *n* **1 :** something that causes a person or group to feel foolish **2 :** the condition of feeling foolish in front of others

em·bas·sy *n, pl* **em·bas·sies** **1 :** a group of people led by an ambassador who represent their country in a foreign country **2 :** the building where an ambassador lives or works

em·bed *vb* **em·bed·ded; em·bed·ding :** to enclose in or as if in a surrounding substance

em·bel·lish *vb* **em·bel·lished; em·bel·lish·ing :** DECORATE 1 — **em·bel·lish·ment** *n*

em·ber *n* **:** a glowing piece of coal or wood in the ashes from a fire

em·bez·zle *vb* **em·bez·zled; em·bez·zling :** to steal (money or property) despite being entrusted to take care of it

em·bit·ter *vb* **em·bit·tered; em·bit·ter·ing :** to make sad and angry : make bitter

em·blem *n* **:** an object or an image used to suggest a thing that cannot be pictured

em·body *vb* **em·bod·ied; em·body·ing** **1 :** to give form to **2 :** to represent in visible form **3 :** to make something a body or system or part of a body or system

em·boss *vb* **em·bossed; em·boss·ing :** to decorate with a raised pattern or design

[1]**em·brace** *vb* **em·braced; em·brac·ing** **1 :** to hold in the arms : HUG **2 :** to surround on all sides **3 :** to accept readily or gladly **4 :** INCLUDE

[2]**embrace** *n* **:** an act of holding in the arms : HUG

em·broi·der *vb* **em·broi·dered; em·broi·der·ing** **1 :** to make with needlework **2 :** to decorate with needlework **3 :** to make more interesting by exaggerating or adding details

em·broi·dery *n, pl* **em·broi·der·ies** **1 :** needlework done to decorate cloth **2 :** the act or art of embroidering

em·bryo *n, pl* **em·bry·os** **1 :** an unborn human or animal in the earliest stages of growth when its basic structures are being formed **2 :** a tiny young plant inside a seed

[1]**em·er·ald** *n* **:** a gemstone of a rich green color

[2]**emerald** *adj* **:** brightly or richly green

emerge *vb* **emerged; emerg·ing** **1 :** to come out or into view **2 :** to become known

emer·gen·cy *n, pl* **emer·gen·cies :** an unexpected situation that requires immediate action

emergency room *n* **:** a room in a hospital with doctors, nurses, and medical equipment for treating people who need medical care immediately

em·ery *n, pl* **em·er·ies :** a mineral used as a powder for polishing and grinding

em·i·grant *n* **:** a person who leaves one country or region to live in another

em·i·grate *vb* **em·i·grat·ed; em·i·grat·ing :** to leave one country or region to live in another

em·i·gra·tion *n* **:** the act of leaving one region or country to live in another

em·i·nence *n* **1 :** the condition of being well-known and respected **2 :** a piece of high ground : HILL

em·i·nent *adj* **:** successful, well-known, and respected

em·is·sary *n, pl* **em·is·sar·ies :** a person sent on a mission to represent someone else

emis·sion *n* **1 :** the act of giving off **2 :** something that is given off

emit *vb* **emit·ted; emit·ting :** to send out from a source

emo·ji *n, pl* **emoji** *or* **emo·jis :** a small picture, symbol, or icon used in text messages, e-mail, and social media to express the writer's emotional state or to communicate a message playfully or briefly

emo·tion *n* **:** strong feeling (as anger, love, joy, or fear) often accompanied by a physical reaction

emo·tion·al *adj* **1 :** relating to a person's feelings **2 :** likely to show or express feelings **3 :** expressing strong feelings — **emo·tion·al·ly** *adv*

em·pa·thize *vb* **em·pa·thized; em·pa·thiz·ing :** to share the same feelings as another person : to feel empathy

em·pa·thy *n* **:** the understanding and sharing of the emotions and experiences of another person

em·per·or *n* **:** a man who rules an empire

em·pha·sis *n, pl* **em·pha·ses** **1 :** a forcefulness in the way something is said or written that gives it special attention or importance **2 :** special force given to one or more words or syllables in speaking or reading **3 :** special attention or importance given to something

em·pha·size *vb* **em·pha·sized; em·pha·siz·ing :** to give special attention or importance to

em·phat·ic *adj* **:** spoken or done forcefully — **em·phat·i·cal·ly** *adv*

em·phy·se·ma *n* **:** a disease in which the lungs become stretched and inefficient

em·pire *n* **1 :** a group of territories or peoples under one ruler **2 :** a country whose ruler is called an emperor

[1]**em·ploy** *vb* **em·ployed; em·ploy·ing 1 :** to give a job to **:** use the services of **2 :** to make use of

[2]**employ** *n* **:** the state of being hired for a job by

em·ploy·ee *n* **:** a person who is paid to work for another

em·ploy·er *n* **:** a person or business that pays others for their services

em·ploy·ment *n* **1 :** the act of using something **2 :** JOB 1, OCCUPATION **3 :** the act of hiring a person to do work

em·pow·er *vb* **em·pow·ered; em·pow·er·ing :** to give authority or legal power to

em·press *n* **1 :** a woman who rules an empire **2 :** the wife of an emperor

[1]**emp·ty** *adj* **emp·ti·er; emp·ti·est 1 :** containing nothing **2 :** not occupied or lived in **:** VACANT **3 :** not sincere or meaningful — **emp·ti·ness** *n*

[2]**empty** *vb* **emp·tied; emp·ty·ing 1 :** to remove the contents of **2 :** to remove all of (something) from a container **3 :** to become unoccupied **4 :** to flow into

emp·ty–hand·ed *adj* **1 :** not carrying or bringing anything **2 :** having gotten or gained nothing

EMT *n, pl* **EMTs** *or* **EMT's :** a person that is trained to give emergency medical care to a patient before and on the way to a hospital

emu *n* **:** a large fast-running Australian bird that cannot fly

em·u·late *vb* **em·u·lat·ed; em·u·lat·ing :** to try hard to be like or do better than **:** IMITATE

em·u·la·tion *n* **:** an attempt to be like or do better than others

emul·si·fy *vb* **emul·si·fied; emul·si·fy·ing :** to combine two liquids to make an emulsion

emul·sion *n* **:** two liquids mixed together so that tiny drops of one liquid are scattered throughout the other

en- *also* **em-** *prefix* **1 :** put or go into or onto **2 :** cause to be **3 :** provide with — in all senses usually *em-* before *b, m,* or *p*

[1]**-en** *also* **-n** *adj suffix* **:** made of **:** consisting of

[2]**-en** *vb suffix* **1 :** become or cause to be **2 :** cause or come to have

en·able *vb* **en·abled; en·abling :** to give strength, power, or ability to **:** make able

en·act *vb* **en·act·ed; en·act·ing 1 :** to perform or act out **2 :** to make into law — **en·act·ment** *n*

[1]**enam·el** *vb* **enam·eled** *or* **enam·elled; enam·el·ing** *or* **enam·el·ling :** to cover or decorate with a smooth hard glossy coating

[2]**enamel** *n* **1 :** a glassy substance used to coat the surface of metal, glass, and pottery **2 :** the hard outer surface of the teeth **3 :** a paint that dries to form a hard glossy coat

en·camp·ment *n* **1 :** the act of making a camp **2 :** [1]CAMP 1

en·case *vb* **en·cased; en·cas·ing :** to cover or surround **:** enclose in or as if in a case

-ence *n suffix* **1 :** action or process **2 :** quality or state

en·chant *vb* **en·chant·ed; en·chant·ing 1 :** to put under a spell by or as if by magic **:** BEWITCH **2 :** to please greatly **:** DELIGHT — **en·chant·ment** *n*

en·chant·ing *adj* **:** very attractive **:** CHARMING

en·chant·ress *n* **:** a woman who casts magic spells **:** WITCH, SORCERESS

en·cir·cle *vb* **en·cir·cled; en·cir·cling 1 :** to make a circle around **:** SURROUND **2 :** to go completely around

en·close *vb* **en·closed; en·clos·ing 1 :** to close in **:** SURROUND **2 :** to hold in **:** CONFINE **3 :** to put in the same package or envelope with something else

en·clo·sure *n* **1 :** the act of closing in or surrounding **2 :** a space that is closed in **3 :** the act of including with a letter or package **4 :** something included with a letter or package

en·com·pass *vb* **en·com·passed; en·com·pass·ing 1 :** to cover or surround **:** ENCIRCLE **2 :** INCLUDE

en·core *n* **1 :** a demand by an audience for a performance to continue or be repeated **2 :** a further appearance or performance given in response to applause

[1]**en·coun·ter** *vb* **en·coun·tered; en·coun·ter·ing 1 :** to meet face-to-face or by chance **2 :** to experience or face often unexpectedly

[2]**encounter** *n* **1 :** a meeting face-to-face and often by chance **2 :** an often unexpected experience

en·cour·age *vb* **en·cour·aged; en·cour·ag·ing 1 :** make more determined, hopeful, or confident **:** HEARTEN **2 :** to give help or support to **:** AID — **en·cour·ag·ing·ly** *adv*

en·cour·age·ment *n* **1 :** something that gives hope, determination, or confidence **2 :** the act of giving hope or confidence to

en·croach *vb* **en·croached; en·croach·ing 1 :** to take over the rights or property of another little by little or in secret **2 :** to go beyond the usual or proper limits

en·crust *vb* **en·crust·ed; en·crust·ing :** to cover with or as if with a crust

en·cum·ber *vb* **en·cum·bered; en·cum·ber·ing 1 :** to weigh down **:** BURDEN **2 :** to cause problems or delays for **:** HINDER

-en·cy *n suffix, pl* **-en·cies :** quality or state

en·cy·clo·pe·dia *n* **:** a book or a set of books containing information on all branches of learning in articles arranged alphabetically by subject

[1]**end** *n* **1 :** the part near the boundary of an area **2 :** the point where something stops or ceases to exist **3 :** the first or last part of a thing **4 :** DEATH 1, DESTRUCTION **5 :** [1]PURPOSE, GOAL **6 :** a player in football positioned at the end of the line of scrimmage **7 :** a part of an undertaking

[2]**end** *vb* **end·ed; end·ing :** to bring or come to an end **:** STOP, FINISH — **end up :** to reach or come to a place, condition, or situation unexpectedly

en·dan·ger *vb* **en·dan·gered; en·dan·ger·ing :** to expose to possible harm **:** RISK

en·dan·gered *adj* **:** close to becoming extinct **:** dying out

en·dear *vb* **en·deared; en·dear·ing :** to make beloved or admired

en·dear·ment *n* **:** a word or an act that shows love or affection

[1]**en·deav·or** *or Can and Brit* **endeavour** *vb* **en·deav·ored/endeavoured; en·deav·or·ing/endeavouring :** to make an effort **:** try hard

[2]**endeavor** *or Can and Brit* **endeavour** *n* **:** a serious effort or attempt

end·ing *n* **:** the final part **:** END

end·less *adj* **:** lasting or taking a long time — **end·less·ly** *adv*

en·do·crine gland *n* **:** any of several glands (as the thyroid or pituitary gland) that release hormones directly into the blood

en·dorse *vb* **en·dorsed; en·dors·ing 1 :** to show support or approval for **2 :** to sign the back of to receive payment — **en·dorse·ment** *n*

en·dow *vb* **en·dowed; en·dow·ing 1 :** to provide with money for support **2 :** to provide with something freely or naturally

en·dow·ment *n* **1 :** the act of providing money for support **2 :** money provided for support

end·point *n* **:** either of two points that mark the ends of a line segment or a point that marks the end of a ray

en·dur·ance *n* **:** the ability to put up with strain, suffering, or hardship

en·dure *vb* **en·dured; en·dur·ing 1 :** to continue to exist over a long time **:** LAST **2 :** to experience without giving in **3 :** to put up with

en·e·my *n, pl* **en·e·mies 1 :** a person who hates another **:** a person who attacks or tries to harm another **2 :** a country or group of people with which another country or group is at war or a person belonging to such a country or group **3 :** something that harms or threatens

en·er·get·ic *adj* **:** having or showing the ability to be active — **en·er·get·i·cal·ly** *adv*

en·er·gize *vb* **en·er·gized; en·er·giz·ing :** to give the ability to be active to **:** give energy to

en·er·gy *n, pl* **en·er·gies 1 :** ability to be active **:** strength of body or mind to do things or to work **2 :** strong action or effort **3 :** usable power or the resources (as oil) used to produce usable power

en·fold *vb* **en·fold·ed; en·fold·ing 1 :** to wrap up **2 :** [1]EMBRACE 1

en·force *vb* **en·forced; en·forc·ing 1 :** to make happen **2 :** to carry out or make effective — **en·force·ment** *n*

Eng. *abbr* **1** England **2** English

en·gage *vb* **en·gaged; en·gag·ing 1 :** to catch and keep fixed (as someone's attention) **2 :** to take part in or cause to take part in something **3 :** to enter into contest or battle with **4 :** to arrange for the services or use of **:** EMPLOY **5 :** MESH

en·gaged *adj* **1 :** busy with an activity **2 :** promised to be married

en·gage·ment *n* **1 :** the act of becoming engaged to be married **:** the state of being engaged to be married **2 :** EMPLOYMENT 3 **3 :** APPOINTMENT **4 :** a fight between armed forces **:** BATTLE

en·gag·ing *adj* **:** attractive or interesting

en·gine *n* **1 :** a mechanical tool or device **2 :** a machine for driving or operating something especially by using the energy of steam, gasoline, or oil **3 :** LOCOMOTIVE

[1]**en·gi·neer** *n* **1 :** a person who designs and builds machinery or technical equipment **:** a person who studies or works in a branch of engineering **2 :** a person who runs or is in charge of a railroad engine or other machinery or technical equipment

[2]**engineer** *vb* **en·gi·neered; en·gi·neer·ing 1 :** to plan, build, or manage as an engineer **2 :** to plan out in a skillful or clever way **:** CONTRIVE

en·gi·neer·ing *n* **:** the application of science to the goal of creating useful machines (as automobiles) or structures (as roads and dams)

[1]**En·glish** *adj* **:** of or relating to England, its people, or the English language

[2]**English** *n* **1 :** the language of England, the United States, and some other countries now or at one time under British rule **2 English**

pl : the people of England **3** : English language or literature as a subject in school

English horn *n* : a woodwind instrument that is similar to an oboe but is longer and has a deeper tone

en·grave *vb* **en·graved; en·grav·ing** **1** : to cut or carve (as letters or designs) on a hard surface **2** : to cut (as letters or designs) on or into **3** : to print from a cut surface — **en·grav·er** *n*

en·grav·ing *n* **1** : the art of cutting something especially into the surface of wood, stone, or metal **2** : a print made from a cut surface

en·gross *vb* **en·grossed; en·gross·ing** : to take the attention of completely

en·gulf *vb* **en·gulfed; en·gulf·ing** **1** : to flow over and cover or surround **2** : to be overwhelmed by

en·hance *vb* **en·hanced; en·hanc·ing** : to make greater or better

enig·ma *n* : someone or something that is hard to understand

en·joy *vb* **en·joyed; en·joy·ing** **1** : to get pleasure from **2** : to have the use or benefit of

en·joy·able *adj* : providing pleasure

en·joy·ment *n* **1** : the action or condition of getting pleasure or satisfaction from something **2** : something that gives pleasure

en·large *vb* **en·larged; en·larg·ing** : to make or grow larger : EXPAND

en·large·ment *n* **1** : an act of making or growing larger **2** : the state of having been made or having grown larger **3** : a larger copy of a photograph

en·light·en *vb* **en·light·ened; en·light·en·ing** : to give knowledge or understanding to

en·list *vb* **en·list·ed; en·list·ing** **1** : to join the armed forces as a volunteer **2** : to get the help of — **en·list·ment** *n*

en·list·ed *adj* : serving in the armed forces in a rank below a commissioned officer or warrant officer

en·liv·en *vb* **en·liv·ened; en·liv·en·ing** : to put life or spirit into

en·mi·ty *n, pl* **en·mi·ties** : hatred especially when shared : ILL WILL

enor·mous *adj* : unusually great in size, number, or degree — **enor·mous·ly** *adv*

[1]enough *adj* : equal to the needs or demands

[2]enough *adv* : in the amount necessary or to the degree necessary

[3]enough *pron* : a number or amount that provides what is needed

en·quire, en·quiry *chiefly Brit spelling of* INQUIRE, INQUIRY

en·rage *vb* **en·raged; en·rag·ing** : to fill with rage : ANGER

en·rich *vb* **en·riched; en·rich·ing** **1** : to make rich or richer **2** : to improve the quality of food by adding vitamins and minerals **3** : to make more fertile

en·roll *or chiefly Can and Brit* **enrol** *vb* **en·rolled; en·roll·ing** **1** : to include (as a name) on a roll or list **2** : to take in as a member **3** : to become a member : JOIN

en·roll·ment *or chiefly Can and Brit* **enrol·ment** *n* **1** : the act of becoming a member or being made a member **2** : the number of members

en route *adv* : on or along the way

en·sem·ble *n* : a group of people or things making up a complete unit

en·sign *n* **1** : a flag flown as the symbol of nationality **2** : a commissioned officer of the lowest rank in the navy or coast guard

en·slave *vb* **en·slaved; en·slav·ing** : to make a slave of

en·sue *vb* **en·sued; en·su·ing** : to come after in time or as a result : FOLLOW

en·sure *vb* **en·sured; en·sur·ing** : to make sure, certain, or safe : GUARANTEE

en·tan·gle *vb* **en·tan·gled; en·tan·gling** **1** : to make tangled or confused **2** : to catch in a tangle

en·ter *vb* **en·tered; en·ter·ing** **1** : to come or go in or into **2** : to stab into : PIERCE **3** : to put into a list or book : write down **4** : to put in or into **5** : to become a member of **6** : to become a participant in or take an interest in **7** : enroll in : begin attending

en·ter·prise *n* **1** : a project or undertaking that is difficult, complicated, or risky **2** : willingness to engage in daring or difficult action **3** : a business organization or activity

en·ter·pris·ing *adj* : bold and energetic in trying or experimenting

en·ter·tain *vb* **en·ter·tained; en·ter·tain·ing** **1** : to host a social event **2** : to have as a guest **3** : to perform for or provide amusement for **4** : to have in mind

en·ter·tain·er *n* : a person who performs for public entertainment

en·ter·tain·ment *n* **1** : the act of amusing or entertaining **2** : something (as a show) that is a form of amusement or recreation

en·thrall *vb* **en·thralled; en·thrall·ing** : to hold the attention of completely

en·throne *vb* **en·throned; en·thron·ing** **1** : to place on a throne **2** : to seat or put in a place to indicate authority or value

en·thu·si·asm *n* : strong feeling in favor of something

en·thu·si·ast *n* : a person who is very excited about or interested in something

en·thu·si·as·tic *adj* : feeling strong excitement about something : full of enthusiasm

en·thu·si·as·ti·cal·ly *adv* : with strong excitement

en·tice *vb* **en·ticed; en·tic·ing :** to attract by raising hope or desire : TEMPT
en·tire *adj* **:** complete in all parts or respects — **en·tire·ly** *adv*
en·tire·ty *n* **:** the whole or total amount
en·ti·tle *vb* **en·ti·tled; en·ti·tling 1 :** to give a title to **2 :** to give a right or claim to
en·trails *n pl* **:** the internal parts of an animal
¹en·trance *n* **1 :** the act of going in **2 :** a door, gate, or way for going in **3 :** permission to join, participate in, or attend
²en·trance *vb* **en·tranced; en·tranc·ing 1 :** to put into a trance **2 :** to fill with delight and wonder
en·trap *vb* **en·trapped; en·trap·ping :** to catch in or as if in a trap
en·treat *vb* **en·treat·ed; en·treat·ing :** to ask in a serious and urgent way
en·treaty *n, pl* **en·treat·ies :** a serious and urgent request
en·trust *vb* **en·trust·ed; en·trust·ing 1 :** to give care of something to **2 :** to give to another with confidence
en·try *n, pl* **en·tries 1 :** the act of going in : ENTRANCE **2 :** the right to go in or join **3 :** a place (as a hall or door) through which entrance is made **4 :** the act of making a written record of something **5 :** something written down as part of a list or a record **6 :** a person or thing taking part in a contest
en·twine *vb* **en·twined; en·twin·ing :** to twist or twine together or around
enu·mer·ate *vb* **enu·mer·at·ed; enu·mer·at·ing 1 :** ¹COUNT 1 **2 :** to name one after another : LIST
enun·ci·ate *vb* **enun·ci·at·ed; enun·ci·at·ing 1 :** to make known publicly **2 :** to pronounce words or parts of words
enun·ci·a·tion *n* **:** clearness of pronunciation
en·vel·op *vb* **en·vel·oped; en·vel·op·ing :** to put a covering completely around : wrap up or in
en·ve·lope *n* **:** a flat usually paper container (as for a letter)
en·vi·ous *adj* **:** feeling or showing unhappiness over someone else's good fortune and a desire to have the same — **en·vi·ous·ly** *adv*
en·vi·ron·ment *n* **1 :** a person's physical surroundings **2 :** the surrounding conditions or forces (as soil, climate, and living things) that influence a plant's or animal's characteristics and ability to survive **3 :** the social and cultural conditions that affect the life of a person or community
en·voy *n* **1 :** a representative sent by one government to another **2 :** MESSENGER
¹en·vy *n, pl* **envies 1 :** a feeling of unhappiness over another's good fortune together with a desire to have the same good fortune **2 :** a person or a thing that is envied
²envy *vb* **en·vied; en·vy·ing :** to feel unhappiness over the good fortune of (someone) and desire the same good fortune : feel envy toward or because of
en·zyme *n* **:** a substance produced by body cells that helps bring about or speed up bodily chemical activities (as the digestion of food) without being destroyed in so doing
eon *variant of* AEON
¹ep·ic *n* **:** a long poem that tells the story of a hero's deeds
²epic *adj* **1 :** telling a great and heroic story **2 :** heroic or impressive because of great size or effort
¹ep·i·dem·ic *n* **1 :** a rapidly spreading outbreak of disease **2 :** something harmful that spreads or develops rapidly
²epidemic *adj* **:** spreading widely and affecting many people at the same time
epi·der·mis *n* **1 :** a thin outer layer of skin covering the dermis **2 :** any of various thin outer layers of plants or animals
ep·i·lep·sy *n* **:** a disorder of the nervous system that causes people to have seizures
ep·i·neph·rine *n* **:** a hormone that causes blood vessels to narrow and the blood pressure to increase
ep·i·sode *n* **1 :** an event or one of a series of events that stands out clearly **2 :** one in a series of connected stories or performances
ep·i·taph *n* **:** a brief statement on a tombstone in memory of a dead person
ep·och *n* **:** a period that is important or memorable
¹equal *adj* **1 :** exactly the same in number, amount, degree, rank, or quality **2 :** the same for each person **3 :** having enough strength, ability, or means — **equal·ly** *adv*
²equal *vb* **equaled** *or* **equalled; equal·ing** *or* **equal·ling :** to be the same in number, amount, degree, rank, or quality as
³equal *n* **:** someone or something that is as good or valuable as another
equal·i·ty *n, pl* **equal·i·ties :** the condition or state of being the same in number, amount, degree, rank, or quality
equal·ize *vb* **equal·ized; equal·iz·ing :** to make even or equal
equa·tion *n* **1 :** a statement of the equality of two mathematical expressions **2 :** an expression representing a chemical reaction by means of chemical symbols
equa·tor *n* **:** an imaginary circle around the earth everywhere equally distant from the north pole and the south pole
equa·to·ri·al *adj* **:** relating to or lying near the equator
eques·tri·an *adj* **:** relating to the act of riding horses

equi·lat·er·al *adj* : having all sides or faces equal

equi·lib·ri·um *n* **1** : a state of balance between opposing forces or actions **2** : the normal balanced state of the body that is maintained by the inner part of the ear and allows a person or animal to stand or move without falling

equi·nox *n* : either of the two times each year (as in spring around March 21 and in fall around September 23) when the sun's center crosses the equator and day and night are everywhere of equal length

equip *vb* **equipped; equip·ping** : to provide with necessary supplies or features

equip·ment *n* : supplies or tools needed for a special purpose

1equiv·a·lent *adj* : alike or equal in number, value, or meaning

2equivalent *n* : something like or equal to something else in number, value, or meaning

1-er *adj suffix or adv suffix* — used to form the comparative degree of adjectives and adverbs of one syllable and of some adjectives and adverbs of two or more syllables

2-er *also* **-ier** *or* **-yer** *n suffix* **1** : a person whose work or business is connected with **2** : a person or thing belonging to or associated with **3** : a native of : resident of **4** : a person or thing that has **5** : a person or thing that produces **6** : a person or thing that performs a specified action **7** : a person or thing that is a suitable object of a specified action **8** : a person or thing that is

era *n* **1** : a period of time starting from some special date or event or known for a certain feature **2** : an important period of history

erad·i·cate *vb* **erad·i·cat·ed; erad·i·cat·ing** : to destroy completely

erase *vb* **erased; eras·ing** **1** : to cause to disappear by rubbing or scraping **2** : to remove marks from **3** : to remove recorded matter from — **eras·er** *n*

era·sure *n* **1** : an act of erasing **2** : something erased

1ere *prep* : 2BEFORE 2

2ere *conj* : 3BEFORE 3

e–read·er *n* : an electronic device used for reading e-books and similar material

1erect *adj* : straight up and down

2erect *vb* **erect·ed; erect·ing** **1** : to put up by fitting together materials or parts **2** : to set or place straight up — **erec·tor** *n*

er·mine *n* : a weasel of northern regions having a winter coat of white fur with a tail tipped in black

erode *vb* **erod·ed; erod·ing** : to wear away : destroy by wearing away

ero·sion *n* : the act of wearing away or eroding : the state of being eroded

err *vb* **erred; err·ing** : to make a mistake

er·rand *n* **1** : a short trip made to do or get something **2** : the purpose of a short trip

er·rant *adj* **1** : wandering in search of adventure **2** : straying from a proper course

er·rat·ic *adj* : not following a regular, usual, or expected course

er·ro·ne·ous *adj* : INCORRECT 1

er·ror *n* : a failure to be correct or accurate : MISTAKE

erupt *vb* **erupt·ed; erupt·ing** : to burst forth or cause to burst forth

erup·tion *n* : an act of bursting forth

-ery *n suffix, pl* **-er·ies** **1** : qualities considered as a group : character : -NESS **2** : art : practice **3** : place of doing, keeping, producing, or selling **4** : collection **5** : state or condition

1-es *n pl suffix* — used to form the plural of most nouns that end in *s, z, sh, ch,* or a final *y* that changes to *i* and of some nouns ending in *f* that changes to *v*

2-es *vb suffix* — used to form the third person singular present of most verbs that end in *s, z, sh, ch,* or a final *y* that changes to *i*

es·ca·la·tor *n* : a moving stairway for going from one floor of a building to another

es·ca·pade *n* : a daring or reckless adventure

1es·cape *vb* **es·caped; es·cap·ing** **1** : to get away : get free or clear **2** : to keep free of : AVOID **3** : to fail to be noticed or remembered by **4** : to leak out

2escape *n* **1** : the act of getting away **2** : a way of getting away

1es·cort *n* **1** : a person or group that accompanies someone to give protection or show courtesy **2** : the man who goes with a woman to a social event

2es·cort *vb* **es·cort·ed; es·cort·ing** : to accompany someone to protect or show courtesy

1-ese *adj suffix* : of, relating to, or coming from a certain place or country

2-ese *n suffix, pl* **-ese** **1** : native or resident of a specified place or country **2** : language of a particular place, country, or nationality

Es·ki·mo *n, pl* **Es·ki·mos** *now sometimes offensive, usually avoided in Canadian English* : a member of a group of native peoples of Alaska, northern Canada, Greenland, and eastern Siberia

ESL *abbr* English as a second language

esoph·a·gus *n, pl* **esoph·a·gi** : a muscular tube that leads from the mouth through the throat to the stomach

esp. *abbr* especially

es·pe·cial *adj* : more then usual : SPECIAL — **es·pe·cial·ly** *adv*

es·pi·o·nage *n* : the practice of spying : the use of spies

es·py *vb* **es·pied; es·py·ing** : to catch sight of

-ess *n suffix* : female
es·say *n* : a usually short piece of writing dealing with a subject from a personal point of view
es·say·ist *n* : a writer of essays
es·sence *n* **1** : the basic part of something **2** : a substance made from a plant or drug and having its special qualities **3** : [1]PERFUME 1
[1]**es·sen·tial** *adj* **1** : extremely important or necessary **2** : forming or belonging to the basic part of something — **es·sen·tial·ly** *adv*
[2]**essential** *n* : something that is basic or necessary
-est *adj suffix or adv suffix* — used to form the superlative of adjectives and adverbs of one syllable and of some adjectives and adverbs of two or more syllables
es·tab·lish *vb* **es·tab·lished; es·tab·lish·ing** **1** : to bring into being : FOUND **2** : to put beyond doubt : PROVE
es·tab·lish·ment *n* **1** : the act of founding or of proving **2** : a place where people live or do business
es·tate *n* **1** : the property of all kinds that a person leaves at death **2** : a mansion on a large piece of land **3** : [1]STATE 1
[1]**es·teem** *n* : respect and affection
[2]**esteem** *vb* **es·teemed; es·teem·ing** : to think favorably of
[1]**es·ti·mate** *vb* **es·ti·mat·ed; es·ti·mat·ing** : to give or form a general idea of (as the value, size, or cost of something)
[2]**es·ti·mate** *n* **1** : an opinion or judgment especially of the value or quality of something **2** : an approximation of the size or cost of something
es·ti·ma·tion *n* **1** : the act of making a judgment especially of value, size, or cost **2** : OPINION 2
es·tu·ary *n, pl* **es·tu·ar·ies** : an arm of the sea at the lower end of a river
et al. *abbr* and others — abbreviation for Latin *et alia*, which means "and others"
etc. *abbr* et cetera
et cet·era : and others of the same kind : and so forth : and so on
etch *vb* **etched; etch·ing** : to produce designs or figures on metal or glass by using acid to eat into the surface
etch·ing *n* **1** : the art or process of producing drawings or pictures by printing from etched plates **2** : a picture made from an etched plate
eter·nal *adj* **1** : lasting forever : having no beginning and no end **2** : continuing without interruption : seeming to last forever
eter·ni·ty *n, pl* **eter·ni·ties** **1** : time without end **2** : the state after death **3** : a period of time that seems endless
-eth — see -TH
ether *n* : a light flammable liquid used to dissolve fats and especially in the past as an anesthetic
ethe·re·al *adj* **1** : suggesting heaven or the heavens **2** : very delicate : AIRY
eth·i·cal *adj* **1** : involving questions of right and wrong : relating to ethics **2** : following accepted rules of behavior
eth·ics *n pl* **1** : a branch of philosophy dealing with what is morally right or wrong **2** : the rules of moral behavior governing an individual or a group — used as singular or plural
eth·nic *adj* : of or relating to groups of people with common characteristics and customs — **eth·ni·cal·ly** *adv*
et·i·quette *n* : the rules governing the proper way to behave or to do something
-ette *n suffix* **1** : little one **2** : female
et·y·mol·o·gy *n, pl* **et·y·mol·o·gies** : the history of a word shown by tracing it or its parts back to the earliest known forms and meanings both in its own language and any other language from which it may have been taken
eu·ca·lyp·tus *n, pl* **eu·ca·lyp·ti** *or* **eu·ca·lyp·tus·es** : a tree mainly of Australia that is widely grown for its timber, gums, and oils
eu·gle·na *n* : a tiny green single-celled organism that lives in freshwater and moves about by means of a flagellum
eu·ro *n, pl* **euros** : a coin or bill used by many countries of the European Union
[1]**Eu·ro·pe·an** *adj* : of or relating to Europe or the people of Europe
[2]**European** *n* : a native or resident of Europe
eu·ro·zone *n* : the geographical area made up of the countries that use the euro as the official currency
evac·u·ate *vb* **evac·u·at·ed; evac·u·at·ing** **1** : to leave or cause to leave a place of danger **2** : to make empty : empty out **3** : to discharge waste matter from the body
evade *vb* **evad·ed; evad·ing** : to get away from or avoid meeting directly
eval·u·ate *vb* **eval·u·at·ed; eval·u·at·ing** : to judge the value or condition of
eval·u·a·tion *n* : the act or result of judging the condition or value of
evan·ge·list *n* : a Christian preacher who tries to change or increase religious feelings
evap·o·rate *vb* **evap·o·rat·ed; evap·o·rat·ing** **1** : to change into vapor **2** : to remove some of the water from something (as by heating) **3** : to disappear without being seen to go
evap·o·ra·tion *n* : the process of changing from a liquid to a vapor
eve *n* **1** : EVENING **2** : the evening or day before a special day **3** : the period just before an important event

[1]**even** *adj* **1 :** having a flat, smooth, or level surface **2 :** being on the same line or level **3 :** staying the same over a period of time **4 :** equal in size, number, or amount **5 :** not giving an advantage to one side : FAIR **6 :** possible to divide by two — **even·ly** *adv* — **even·ness** *n*

[2]**even** *adv* **1** — used to stress a highly unlikely condition or instance **2 :** to a greater extent or degree : STILL **3 :** so much as **4 :** INDEED **5 :** at the very time

[3]**even** *vb* **evened; even·ing :** to make or become smooth or equal

eve·ning *n* **:** the final part of the day and early part of the night

evening star *n* **:** a bright planet (as Venus) seen in the western sky after sunset

event *n* **1 :** something important or notable that happens **2 :** a social occasion (as a party) **3 :** the fact of happening **4 :** a contest in a program of sports

event·ful *adj* **1 :** full of important happenings **2 :** very important

even·tu·al *adj* **:** coming at some later time — **even·tu·al·ly** *adv*

ev·er *adv* **1 :** at any time **2 :** in any way **3 :** ALWAYS 1

ev·er·glade *n* **:** a swampy grassland

[1]**ev·er·green** *n* **:** a plant (as a pine or a laurel) having leaves that stay green through more than one growing season

[2]**evergreen** *adj* **:** having leaves that stay green through more than one growing season

ev·er·last·ing *adj* **1 :** lasting forever : ETERNAL **2 :** going on for a long time

ev·ery *adj* **1 :** including each of a group or series without leaving out any **2 :** at regularly spaced times or distances

ev·ery·body *pron* **:** every person

ev·ery·day *adj* **:** used or suitable for every day : ORDINARY

ev·ery·one *pron* **:** every person

ev·ery·thing *pron* **:** all that exists or is important

ev·ery·where *adv* **:** in or to every place

evict *vb* **evict·ed; evict·ing :** to force (someone) to leave a place

ev·i·dence *n* **1 :** a sign which shows that something exists or is true : INDICATION **2 :** material presented to a court to help find the truth about something

ev·i·dent *adj* **:** clear to the sight or to the mind : PLAIN — **ev·i·dent·ly** *adv*

[1]**evil** *adj* **1 :** morally bad : WICKED **2 :** causing harm : tending to injure

[2]**evil** *n* **1 :** something that brings sorrow, trouble, or destruction **2 :** the fact of suffering or wrongdoing **3 :** bad behavior or moral state : WICKEDNESS

evoke *vb* **evoked; evok·ing :** to bring to mind

evo·lu·tion *n* **1 :** the theory that the various kinds of existing animals and plants have come from kinds that existed in the past **2 :** the process of development of an animal or a plant

evolve *vb* **evolved; evolv·ing :** to change or develop gradually

ewe *n* **:** a female sheep

ex- *prefix* **:** former

[1]**ex·act** *adj* **:** fully correct or precise : ACCURATE — **ex·act·ly** *adv* — **ex·act·ness** *n*

[2]**exact** *vb* **ex·act·ed; ex·act·ing :** to demand and get by force or threat

ex·act·ing *adj* **:** expecting a lot from a person

ex·ag·ger·ate *vb* **ex·ag·ger·at·ed; ex·ag·ger·at·ing :** to describe as larger or greater than what is true

ex·ag·ger·a·tion *n* **1 :** the act of describing as larger or greater than what is true **2 :** a statement that has been enlarged beyond what is true

ex·alt *vb* **ex·alt·ed; ex·alt·ing 1 :** to raise to a higher level **2 :** to praise highly

ex·am *n* **:** EXAMINATION

ex·am·i·na·tion *n* **1 :** the act of checking closely and carefully **2 :** a test given to determine progress, fitness, or knowledge

ex·am·ine *vb* **ex·am·ined; ex·am·in·ing 1 :** to look at or check carefully **2 :** to question closely

ex·am·ple *n* **1 :** something to be imitated : MODEL **2 :** a sample of something taken to show what the whole is like : INSTANCE **3 :** a problem to be solved to show how a rule works **4 :** something that is a warning to others

ex·as·per·ate *vb* **ex·as·per·at·ed; ex·as·per·at·ing :** to make angry

ex·as·per·a·tion *n* **:** extreme annoyance : ANGER

ex·ca·vate *vb* **ex·ca·vat·ed; ex·ca·vat·ing 1 :** to expose to view by digging away a covering **2 :** to hollow out : form a hole in **3 :** to make by hollowing out **4 :** to dig out and remove

ex·ca·va·tion *n* **1 :** the act of excavating **2 :** a hollow place formed by excavating

ex·ceed *vb* **ex·ceed·ed; ex·ceed·ing 1 :** to be greater than **2 :** to go or be beyond the limit of

ex·ceed·ing·ly *adv* **:** to a very great degree

ex·cel *vb* **ex·celled; ex·cel·ling :** to do better than others : SURPASS

ex·cel·lence *n* **:** high quality

ex·cel·lent *adj* **:** very good of its kind — **ex·cel·lent·ly** *adv*

[1]**ex·cept** *prep* **1 :** not including **2 :** other than : BUT

[2]**except** *conj* **:** if it were not for the fact that : ONLY

[3]**except** *vb* **ex·cept·ed; ex·cept·ing :** to leave out from a number or a whole : EXCLUDE

ex·cep·tion *n* **1 :** someone or something that is not included **2 :** a case to which a rule does not apply **3 :** an objection or a reason for objecting

ex·cep·tion·al *adj* **1 :** being unusual **2 :** better than average : SUPERIOR — **ex·cep·tion·al·ly** *adv*

[1]**ex·cess** *n* **1 :** a state of being more than enough **2 :** the amount by which something is or has too much

[2]**excess** *adj* **:** more than is usual or acceptable

ex·ces·sive *adj* **:** being too much — **ex·ces·sive·ly** *adv*

[1]**ex·change** *n* **1 :** an act of giving or taking of one thing in return for another : TRADE **2 :** a place where goods or services are exchanged **3 :** the act of giving and receiving between two groups

[2]**exchange** *vb* **ex·changed; ex·chang·ing :** to give or take one thing in return for another : TRADE, SWAP

ex·cit·able *adj* **:** easily excited

ex·cite *vb* **ex·cit·ed; ex·cit·ing 1 :** to stir up feeling in **2 :** to increase the activity of

ex·cit·ed *adj* **:** very enthusiastic and eager — **ex·ci·ted·ly** *adv*

ex·cite·ment *n* **1 :** something that stirs up feelings of great enthusiasm and interest **2 :** a feeling of great enthusiasm and interest : the state of being excited

ex·cit·ing *adj* **:** producing excitement

ex·claim *vb* **ex·claimed; ex·claim·ing :** to speak or cry out suddenly or with strong feeling

ex·cla·ma·tion *n* **:** a sharp or sudden cry or expression of strong feeling

exclamation point *n* **:** a punctuation mark ! used to show force in speaking or strong feeling

ex·clam·a·to·ry *adj* **:** containing or using exclamation

ex·clude *vb* **ex·clud·ed; ex·clud·ing :** to shut out : keep out

ex·clu·sion *n* **:** the act of shutting or keeping out : the state of being shut or kept out

ex·clu·sive *adj* **1 :** excluding or trying to exclude others **2 :** [4]SOLE 2 **3 :** ENTIRE, COMPLETE — **ex·clu·sive·ly** *adv*

ex·crete *vb* **ex·cret·ed; ex·cret·ing :** to separate and give off cellular waste matter from the body usually as urine or sweat

ex·cre·tion *n* **1 :** the act or process of separating and giving off cellular waste matter from the body **2 :** waste material given off from the body

ex·cre·to·ry *adj* **:** of or relating to excretion : used in excreting

ex·cur·sion *n* **1 :** a brief trip for pleasure **2 :** a trip at special reduced rates

ex·cus·able *adj* **:** possible to excuse

[1]**ex·cuse** *vb* **ex·cused; ex·cus·ing 1 :** to make apology for **2 :** to overlook or pardon as of little importance **3 :** to let off from doing something **4 :** to be an acceptable reason for

[2]**ex·cuse** *n* **1 :** a reason given for having done something wrong **2 :** something that is an acceptable reason for or justifies **3 :** a reason for doing something

ex·e·cute *vb* **ex·e·cut·ed; ex·e·cut·ing 1 :** to kill according to a legal order **2 :** to put into effect : CARRY OUT, PERFORM **3 :** to make according to a design

ex·e·cu·tion *n* **1 :** the act of killing someone as a legal penalty **2 :** the act of doing or performing something

[1]**ex·ec·u·tive** *adj* **1 :** fitted for or relating to the managing or directing of things **2 :** relating to the carrying out of the law and the conduct of public affairs

[2]**executive** *n* **1 :** a person who manages or directs **2 :** the executive branch of a government

ex·em·pli·fy *vb* **ex·em·pli·fied; ex·em·pli·fy·ing :** to serve as an example of

[1]**ex·empt** *adj* **:** free or released from some requirement that other persons must meet or deal with

[2]**exempt** *vb* **ex·empt·ed; ex·empt·ing :** to release from a requirement that others must meet

ex·emp·tion *n* **:** freedom from having to do something that other people are required to do

[1]**ex·er·cise** *n* **1 :** the act of putting into use, action, or practice **2 :** bodily activity for the sake of improving physical fitness **3 :** a school lesson or other task performed to develop skill : practice work : DRILL **4 exercises** *pl* **:** a program of songs, speeches, and announcements of awards and honors

[2]**exercise** *vb* **ex·er·cised; ex·er·cis·ing 1 :** to put into use : EXERT **2 :** to take part in bodily activity for the sake of improving physical fitness **3 :** to use again and again to train or develop

ex·ert *vb* **ex·ert·ed; ex·ert·ing 1 :** to put forth (as strength) : bring into use **2 :** to make an effort

ex·er·tion *n* **1 :** the act of putting into use **2 :** use of strength or ability

ex·hale *vb* **ex·haled; ex·hal·ing 1 :** to breathe out **2 :** to send forth : give off

[1]**ex·haust** *vb* **ex·haust·ed; ex·haust·ing 1 :** to tire out : FATIGUE **2 :** to use up completely **3 :** to try out all of

[2]**exhaust** *n* **1 :** the gas that escapes from an engine **2 :** a system of pipes through which exhaust escapes

ex·haus·tion *n* **1 :** the condition of being very tired **2 :** the act of using up completely

[1]**ex·hib·it** *vb* **ex·hib·it·ed; ex·hib·it·ing** **1 :** to show by outward signs : REVEAL **2 :** to put on display

[2]**exhibit** *n* **1 :** an article or collection shown in an exhibition **2 :** an object or document presented as evidence in a court of law

ex·hi·bi·tion *n* **1 :** the act of showing **2 :** a public showing (as of athletic skill or works of art)

ex·hil·a·rate *vb* **ex·hil·a·rat·ed; ex·hil·a·rat·ing :** to make cheerful or excited

ex·hort *vb* **ex·hort·ed; ex·hort·ing :** to try to influence by words or advice : urge strongly

[1]**ex·ile** *n* **1 :** the situation of a person who is forced to leave his or her own country **2 :** the period of time someone is forced to live away from his or her country **3 :** a person who is forced to leave his or her own country

[2]**exile** *vb* **ex·iled; ex·il·ing :** to force (someone) to leave his or her own country

ex·ist *vb* **ex·ist·ed; ex·ist·ing** **1 :** to have actual being : be real **2 :** to be found : OCCUR **3 :** to continue to live

ex·is·tence *n* **1 :** the fact or the condition of being or of being real **2 :** the state of being alive : LIFE

[1]**ex·it** *n* **1 :** the act of going out of or away from a place : DEPARTURE **2 :** a way of getting out of a place

[2]**exit** *vb* **ex·it·ed; ex·it·ing :** LEAVE 5, DEPART

ex·o·dus *n* **:** the departure of a large number of people at the same time

ex·or·bi·tant *adj* **:** more than what is fair, reasonable, or expected

exo·sphere *n* **:** the outermost region of the atmosphere

ex·ot·ic *adj* **1 :** very different, strange, or unusual **2 :** introduced from another country : not native

ex·pand *vb* **ex·pand·ed; ex·pand·ing** **1 :** to grow or increase in size, number, or amount **2 :** to open wide : UNFOLD **3 :** to take up or cause to take up more space **4 :** to speak or write about in greater detail

ex·panse *n* **:** a wide area or stretch

ex·pan·sion *n* **:** the act of growing or increasing : ENLARGEMENT

ex·pect *vb* **ex·pect·ed; ex·pect·ing** **1 :** to think that something probably will be or happen **2 :** to await the arrival of **3 :** to consider to be obliged **4 :** to consider reasonable, due, or necessary

ex·pec·tant *adj* **1 :** looking forward to or waiting for something **2 :** awaiting the birth of a child

ex·pec·ta·tion *n* **1 :** the state of looking forward to or waiting for something **2 :** something expected

ex·pe·di·ent *adj* **:** providing a quick and easy way to accomplish something — **ex·pe·di·ent·ly** *adv*

ex·pe·di·tion *n* **1 :** a journey for a particular purpose **2 :** a group of people traveling for exploration or adventure

ex·pel *vb* **ex·pelled; ex·pel·ling** **1 :** to force to leave **2 :** to force out

ex·pend *vb* **ex·pend·ed; ex·pend·ing** **1 :** to pay out : SPEND **2 :** to use up

ex·pen·di·ture *n* **1 :** the act of spending (as money, time, or energy) **2 :** something that is spent

ex·pense *n* **1 :** something spent or required to be spent : COST **2 :** a cause for spending

ex·pen·sive *adj* **:** COSTLY 1

[1]**ex·pe·ri·ence** *n* **1 :** the process of living through an event or events **2 :** the skill or knowledge gained by actually doing a thing **3 :** something that one has actually done or lived through

[2]**experience** *vb* **ex·pe·ri·enced; ex·pe·ri·enc·ing :** to undergo or live through : have experience of

ex·pe·ri·enced *adj* **:** made skillful or wise from having lived through or undergone something

[1]**ex·per·i·ment** *n* **:** a trial or test made to find out about something

[2]**ex·per·i·ment** *vb* **ex·per·i·ment·ed; ex·per·i·ment·ing :** to try or test a new way, idea, or activity : to make experiments

ex·per·i·men·tal *adj* **:** relating to, based on, or used for experiment

[1]**ex·pert** *adj* **:** showing special skill or knowledge gained from experience or training — **ex·pert·ly** *adv*

[2]**ex·pert** *n* **:** a person with special skill or knowledge of a subject

ex·per·tise *n* **:** the skill or knowledge of an expert

ex·pi·ra·tion *n* **1 :** the end of something that lasts for a certain period of time **2 :** the act of breathing out

ex·pire *vb* **ex·pired; ex·pir·ing** **1 :** to come to an end **2 :** [1]DIE 1 **3 :** to breathe out : EXHALE

ex·plain *vb* **ex·plained; ex·plain·ing** **1 :** to make clear : CLARIFY **2 :** to give the reasons for or cause of

ex·pla·na·tion *n* **1 :** the act or process of making clear or giving reasons for **2 :** a statement that makes something clear or gives reasons for something

ex·plan·a·to·ry *adj* **:** giving explanation

ex·plic·it *adj* **:** so clear in statement that there is no doubt about the meaning

ex·plode *vb* **ex·plod·ed; ex·plod·ing** **1 :** to burst or cause to burst with violence and noise **2 :** to suddenly show or say with great emotion

[1]**ex·ploit** *n* **:** an exciting or daring act

[2]**ex·ploit** *vb* **ex·ploit·ed; ex·ploit·ing** **1 :** to

get the value or use out of **2 :** to take unfair advantagc of
ex·plo·ra·tion *n* **:** the act or an instance of searching through or into
ex·plore *vb* **ex·plored; ex·plor·ing 1 :** to search through or into **:** study closely **2 :** to go into or through for purposes of discovery or adventure — **ex·plor·er** *n*
ex·plo·sion *n* **1 :** a sudden and noisy bursting (as of a bomb) **:** the act of exploding **2 :** a sudden outburst of feeling
[1]**ex·plo·sive** *adj* **1 :** able to cause explosion **2 :** tending to show anger easily **:** likely to explode — **ex·plo·sive·ly** *adv*
[2]**explosive** *n* **:** a substance that is used to cause an explosion
ex·po·nent *n* **:** a numeral written above and to the right of a number to show how many times the number is to be used as a factor
[1]**ex·port** *vb* **ex·port·ed; ex·port·ing :** to send a product to another country to sell it
[2]**ex·port** *n* **1 :** something that is sent to another country to be sold **2 :** the act of sending a product to another country to be sold
ex·pose *vb* **ex·posed; ex·pos·ing 1 :** to leave without protection, shelter, or care **:** subject to a harmful condition **2 :** to cause to be affected or influenced by something **3 :** to let light strike the photographic film or plate in taking a picture **4 :** to make known **:** REVEAL
ex·po·si·tion *n* **1 :** an explanation of something **2 :** a public exhibition
ex·po·sure *n* **1 :** the fact or condition of being subject to some effect or influence **2 :** the condition that results from being unprotected especially from severe weather (as extreme cold) **3 :** an act of making something public **4 :** the act of letting light strike a photographic film or the time during which light strikes a film **5 :** a section of a roll of film for one picture **6 :** position with respect to direction
ex·pound *vb* **ex·pound·ed; ex·pound·ing :** EXPLAIN 1, INTERPRET
[1]**ex·press** *vb* **ex·pressed; ex·press·ing 1 :** to make known especially in words **2 :** to represent by a sign or symbol **3 :** to send by a quick method of delivery
[2]**express** *adj* **1 :** clearly stated **2 :** of a certain sort **3 :** sent or traveling at high speed
[3]**express** *vb* **1 :** a system for the quick transportation of goods **2 :** a vehicle (as a train or elevator) run at special speed with few or no stops
ex·pres·sion *n* **1 :** the act or process of making known especially in words **2 :** a meaningful word or saying **3 :** the look on someone's face **4 :** a way of speaking, singing, or playing that shows mood or feeling
ex·pres·sive *adj* **1 :** showing emotions **:** full of expression **2 :** making something known — **ex·pres·sive·ly** *adv*
ex·press·ly *adv* **:** for the stated purpose **:** ESPECIALLY
ex·press·way *n* **:** a highway for rapid traffic
ex·pul·sion *n* **:** the act of forcing to leave **:** the state of being forced to leave
ex·qui·site *adj* **1 :** finely made or done **2 :** very pleasing (as through beauty) **3 :** INTENSE 1, EXTREME
ex·tend *vb* **ex·tend·ed; ex·tend·ing 1 :** to hold out **2 :** to stretch out or across something **3 :** to make longer **4 :** [1]STRETCH 2 **5 :** ENLARGE
ex·ten·sion *n* **1 :** the act of making something longer or greater **2 :** an increase in length or time **3 :** a part forming an addition or enlargement
ex·ten·sive *adj* **:** including or affecting many things
ex·tent *n* **1 :** the distance or range that is covered or affected by something **2 :** the point, degree, or limit to which something reaches or extends
[1]**ex·te·ri·or** *adj* **:** EXTERNAL
[2]**exterior** *n* **1 :** an external part or surface **2 :** the way someone appears
ex·ter·mi·nate *vb* **ex·ter·mi·nat·ed; ex·ter·mi·nat·ing :** to get rid of completely **:** wipe out — **ex·ter·mi·na·tion** *n*
ex·ter·nal *adj* **:** situated on or relating to the outside **:** OUTSIDE
ex·tinct *adj* **1 :** no longer active **2 :** no longer existing
ex·tinc·tion *n* **:** the state of being, becoming, or making extinct
ex·tin·guish *vb* **ex·tin·guished; ex·tin·guish·ing 1 :** to cause to stop burning **2 :** to cause to die out — **ex·tin·guish·er** *n*
ex·tol *vb* **ex·tolled; ex·tol·ling :** to praise highly **:** GLORIFY
[1]**ex·tra** *adj* **:** being more than what is usual, expected, or due
[2]**extra** *adv* **:** beyond the usual size, amount, or extent
[3]**extra** *n* **1 :** something additional **2 :** an added charge **3 :** a special edition of a newspaper **4 :** a person hired for a group scene (as in a movie)
extra- *prefix* **:** outside **:** beyond
[1]**ex·tract** *vb* **ex·tract·ed; ex·tract·ing 1 :** to remove by pulling **2 :** to get out by pressing, distilling, or by a chemical process **3 :** to choose and take out for separate use
[2]**ex·tract** *n* **1 :** a selection from a writing **2 :** a product obtained by pressing, distilling, or a chemical process
ex·trac·tion *n* **1 :** the act of pulling out **2 :** ORIGIN 2, DESCENT

ex·tra·cur·ric·u·lar *adj* **:** relating to activities (as athletics) that are offered by a school but are not part of the course of study

ex·traor·di·nary *adj* **:** so unusual as to be remarkable — **ex·traor·di·nari·ly** *adv*

ex·trav·a·gance *n* **1 :** the wasteful or careless spending of money **2 :** something that is wasteful especially of money **3 :** the quality or fact of being wasteful especially of money

ex·trav·a·gant *adj* **1 :** going beyond what is reasonable or suitable **2 :** wasteful especially of money — **ex·trav·a·gant·ly** *adv*

¹ex·treme *adj* **1 :** very great **2 :** farthest away **3 :** more demanding or dangerous than normal — **ex·treme·ly** *adv*

²extreme *n* **1 :** something as far as possible from a center or from its opposite **2 :** the greatest possible degree **:** MAXIMUM

ex·trem·i·ty *n, pl* **ex·trem·i·ties 1 :** the farthest limit, point, or part **2 :** an end part (as a foot) of a limb of the body **3 :** an extreme degree (as of emotion)

ex·tri·cate *vb* **ex·tri·cat·ed; ex·tri·cat·ing :** to free from a trap or difficulty

ex·u·ber·ant *adj* **:** filled with energy and enthusiasm — **ex·u·ber·ance** *n*

ex·ult *vb* **ex·ult·ed; ex·ult·ing :** to feel or show great happiness **:** REJOICE

ex·ul·tant *adj* **:** very happy and excited — **ex·ul·tant·ly** *adv*

-ey — see -Y

¹eye *n* **1 :** the organ of seeing that in vertebrates is a round organ filled with a jelly-like material, is located in a bony cavity in the skull, and has a lens which focuses light on the retina **2 :** the eye along with its surrounding parts (as the eyelids) **3 :** the colored surface of the iris **4 :** the ability to see **5 :** the ability to recognize or appreciate **6 :** ²GLANCE **7 :** close attention **:** WATCH **8 :** JUDGMENT 1 **9 :** something like or suggesting an eye **10 :** the center of something — **eyed** *adj* — **eye·less** *adj*

²eye *vb* **eyed; eye·ing** *or* **ey·ing :** to look at **:** watch closely

eye·ball *n* **:** the whole eye

eye·brow *n* **:** the arch or ridge over the eye **:** the hair on the ridge over the eye

eye·drop·per *n* **:** DROPPER

eye·glass *n* **1 :** a glass lens used to help a person to see clearly **2 eyeglasses** *pl* **:** GLASS 3

eye·lash *n* **:** one of the hairs that grow along the top of the eyelid

eye·let *n* **1 :** a small hole (as in cloth or leather) for a lace or rope **2 :** GROMMET

eye·lid *n* **:** the thin movable fold of skin and muscle that can be closed over the eyeball

eye·piece *n* **:** the lens or combination of lenses at the eye end of an optical instrument (as a microscope or telescope)

eye·sight *n* **:** ¹SIGHT 4, VISION

eye·sore *n* **:** something that looks ugly

eye·tooth *n, pl* **eye·teeth :** a canine tooth of the upper jaw

F

f *n, pl* **f's** *or* **fs** *often cap* **1 :** the sixth letter of the English alphabet **2 :** a grade that shows a student's work is failing **3 :** a musical note referred to by the letter F

f. *abbr* female

F *abbr* **1** Fahrenheit **2** false

fa *n* **:** the fourth note of the musical scale

fa·ble *n* **1 :** a story that is not true **2 :** a story in which animals speak and act like people and which is usually meant to teach a lesson

fab·ric *n* **1 :** CLOTH 1 **2 :** the basic structure

fab·u·lous *adj* **1 :** extremely good **2 :** very great in amount or size **3 :** told in or based on fable — **fab·u·lous·ly** *adv*

fa·cade *n* **:** the face or front of a building

¹face *n* **1 :** the front part of the head **2 :** an expression of the face **3 :** outward appearance **4 :** a funny or silly expression **5 :** an expression showing displeasure **6 :** ¹RESPECT 1 **7 :** a front, upper, or outer surface **8 :** one of the flat surfaces that bound a solid

²face *vb* **faced; fac·ing 1 :** to have the front or face toward **2 :** to cover the front or surface of **3 :** to oppose with determination

face–off *n* **1 :** a method of beginning play (as in hockey or lacrosse) in which the puck or ball is dropped between two opposing players **2 :** a clashing of forces or ideas

fac·et *n* **:** one of the small flat surfaces on a cut gem

fa·ce·tious *adj* **:** intended or trying to be funny — **fa·ce·tious·ly** *adv*

face–to–face *adv or adj* **:** within each other's presence

fa·cial *adj* **:** of or relating to the face

fa·cil·i·tate *vb* **fa·cil·i·tat·ed; fa·cil·i·tat·ing :** to make easier

fa·cil·i·ty *n, pl* **fa·cil·i·ties 1 :** something built for a particular purpose **2 :** something that makes an action, operation, or activity easier **3 :** ease in doing something

fac·sim·i·le *n, pl* **fac·sim·i·les 1 :** an exact copy **2 :** a system of sending and reproducing printed matter or pictures by means of signals sent over telephone lines

fact *n* **1 :** something that really exists or has occurred **2 :** a true piece of information — **in fact :** in truth : ACTUALLY

[1]**fac·tor** *n* **1 :** something that helps produce a result **2 :** any of the numbers that when multiplied together form a product

[2]**factor** *vb* **fac·tored; fac·tor·ing 1 :** to be considered in making a judgment **2 :** to find the factors of a number

fac·to·ry *n, pl* **fac·to·ries :** a place where products are manufactured

fac·tu·al *adj* **:** relating to or based on facts — **fac·tu·al·ly** *adv*

fac·ul·ty *n, pl* **fac·ul·ties 1 :** ability to do something : TALENT **2 :** one of the powers of the mind or body **3 :** the teachers in a school or college

fad *n* **:** something that is very popular for a short time

fade *vb* **fad·ed; fad·ing 1 :** to lose or cause to lose brightness of color **2 :** to dry up : WITHER **3 :** to grow dim or faint

Fahr·en·heit *adj* **:** relating to or having a temperature scale on which the boiling point of water is at 212 degrees above the zero of the scale and the freezing point is at 32 degrees above zero

[1]**fail** *vb* **failed; fail·ing 1 :** to be unsuccessful **2 :** to grade as not passing **3 :** to stop functioning **4 :** to be or become absent or not enough **5 :** to become bankrupt **6 :** [1]NEGLECT 2 **7 :** DISAPPOINT, DESERT **8 :** to lose strength : WEAKEN **9 :** to fall short **10 :** to die away

[2]**fail** *n* **:** FAILURE 2

fail·ing *n* **:** a weakness or flaw in a person's character, behavior, or ability

fail·ure *n* **1 :** a lack of success **2 :** the act of neglecting or forgetting to do or perform **3 :** an instance of not working properly **4 :** a loss of the ability to work normally **5 :** someone or something that has not succeeded **6 :** an instance of falling short **7 :** BANKRUPTCY

[1]**faint** *adj* **faint·er; faint·est 1 :** not clear or plain : DIM **2 :** weak or dizzy and likely to collapse **3 :** lacking strength — **faint·ly** *adv* — **faint·ness** *n*

[2]**faint** *vb* **faint·ed; faint·ing :** to suddenly lose consciousness

[3]**faint** *n* **:** an act or condition of suddenly losing consciousness

faint·heart·ed *adj* **:** COWARDLY 1

[1]**fair** *adj* **fair·er; fair·est 1 :** not favoring one over another **2 :** observing the rules **3 :** neither good nor bad **4 :** not stormy or cloudy **5 :** not dark **6 :** attractive in appearance : BEAUTIFUL **7 :** being within the foul lines — **fair·ness** *n*

[2]**fair** *adv* **:** according to the rules

[3]**fair** *n* **1 :** a large public event at which farm animals and products are shown and entertainment, amusements, and food are provided **2 :** an event at which people gather to buy, sell, or get information **3 :** a sale of articles for charity

fair·ground *n* **:** an area set aside for fairs, circuses, or exhibitions

fair·ly *adv* **1 :** in a just and proper manner **2 :** very close to **3 :** for the most part : RATHER

fair trade *n* **:** a movement that aims to help producers in developing countries get a fair price for their products in order to reduce poverty, improve working conditions, and protect the environment

fair·way *n* **:** the mowed part of a golf course between a tee and a green

[1]**fairy** *n, pl* **fair·ies :** an imaginary magical creature who has the form of a tiny human being

[2]**fairy** *adj* **:** relating to or like a fairy

fairy·land *n* **1 :** an imaginary place where fairies live **2 :** a beautiful or magical place

fairy tale *n* **:** a simple children's story about magical creatures

faith *n* **1 :** strong belief or trust **2 :** belief in God **3 :** a system of religious beliefs : RELIGION **4 :** loyalty to duty or to a person or thing

faith·ful *adj* **1 :** firm in devotion or support **2 :** RELIABLE **3 :** true to the facts : ACCURATE — **faith·ful·ly** *adv* — **faith·ful·ness** *n*

faith·less *adj* **:** not worthy of trust : DISLOYAL

[1]**fake** *adj* **:** not true or real

[2]**fake** *n* **:** a person or thing that is not really what is pretended

[3]**fake** *vb* **faked; fak·ing 1 :** [1]PRETEND 2 **2 :** to change or treat in a way that gives a false effect **3 :** to imitate in order to deceive

fal·con *n* **1 :** a hawk trained for use in hunting small game **2 :** any of several small hawks with long wings and swift flight

fal·con·ry *n* **:** the sport of hunting with a falcon

[1]**fall** *vb* **fell; fall·en; fall·ing 1 :** to come or go down freely by the force of gravity **2 :** to come as if by falling **3 :** to become lower (as in degree or value) **4 :** to topple from an upright position **5 :** to collapse wounded or

dead **6 :** to become captured **7 :** to occur at a certain time **8 :** to pass from one condition of body or mind to another — **fall back :** [2]RETREAT 1 — **fall short :** to fail to be as good or successful as expected

[2]**fall** *n* **1 :** the act or an instance of going or coming down by the force of gravity **2 :** AUTUMN **3 :** a thing or quantity that falls **4 :** a loss of greatness **:** DOWNFALL **5 :** WATERFALL — usually used in pl. **6 :** a decrease in size, amount, or value **7 :** the distance something falls

fal·la·cy *n, pl* **fal·la·cies 1 :** a false or mistaken idea **2 :** false reasoning

fall·out *n* **1 :** the usually radioactive particles falling through the atmosphere as a result of a nuclear explosion **2 :** the bad result of something

fal·low *adj* **:** not tilled or planted

fallow deer *n* **:** a small European deer with broad antlers and a pale yellowish coat spotted with white in summer

[1]**false** *adj* **fals·er; fals·est 1 :** not true, genuine, or honest **2 :** not faithful or loyal **3 :** not based on facts or sound judgment **4 :** CARELESS 2 — **false·ly** *adv*

[2]**false** *adv* **:** in a dishonest or misleading manner

false·hood *n* **1 :** [3]LIE **2 :** the habit of lying

fal·si·fy *vb* **fal·si·fied; fal·si·fy·ing :** to change in order to deceive

fal·si·ty *n, pl* **fal·si·ties 1 :** [3]LIE **2 :** the quality or state of being not true or genuine

fal·ter *vb* **fal·tered; fal·ter·ing 1 :** to move unsteadily **:** WAVER **2 :** to hesitate in speech **3 :** to hesitate in purpose or action

fame *n* **:** the fact or condition of being known or recognized by many people

famed *adj* **:** known widely and well **:** FAMOUS

fa·mil·ial *adj* **:** relating to or typical of a family

fa·mil·iar *adj* **1 :** often seen, heard, or experienced **2 :** closely acquainted **:** INTIMATE **3 :** having a good knowledge of **4 :** INFORMAL 1 **5 :** too friendly or bold

fa·mil·iar·i·ty *n, pl* **fa·mil·iar·i·ties 1 :** close friendship **:** INTIMACY **2 :** good knowledge of something **3 :** INFORMALITY

fa·mil·iar·ize *vb* **fa·mil·iar·ized; fa·mil·iar·iz·ing :** to make knowledgeable about

fam·i·ly *n, pl* **fam·i·lies 1 :** a social group made up of parents and their children **2 :** a group of people who come from the same ancestor **3 :** a group of people living together **:** HOUSEHOLD **4 :** a group of things sharing certain characteristics **5 :** a group of related living things (as plants or animals) that ranks above the genus and below the order in scientific classification

fam·ine *n* **:** a very great shortage of food that affects many people over a wide area

fam·ish *vb* **fam·ished; fam·ish·ing :** STARVE

fam·ished *adj* **:** very hungry

fa·mous *adj* **:** very well-known

fa·mous·ly *adv* **:** very well

[1]**fan** *n* **1 :** a machine or device that is used for producing a current of air **2 :** something having a semicircular shape — **fan·like** *adj*

[2]**fan** *vb* **fanned; fan·ning 1 :** to direct a current of air upon with a fan **2 :** to strike out in baseball

[3]**fan** *n* **:** an enthusiastic follower or admirer

[1]**fa·nat·ic** *adj* **:** very or overly enthusiastic or devoted

[2]**fanatic** *n* **:** a very enthusiastic supporter or admirer

fan·ci·ful *adj* **1 :** showing free use of the imagination **2 :** coming from imagination rather than reason — **fan·ci·ful·ly** *adv*

[1]**fan·cy** *adj* **fan·ci·er; fan·ci·est 1 :** not plain or ordinary **2 :** being above the average (as in quality or price) **3 :** done with great skill and grace — **fan·ci·ly** *adv* — **fan·ci·ness** *n*

[2]**fancy** *n, pl* **fan·cies 1 :** IMAGINATION 1 **2 :** LIKING **3 :** IDEA 2, NOTION

[3]**fancy** *vb* **fan·cied; fan·cy·ing 1 :** to have a liking for **2 :** IMAGINE 1

fang *n* **1 :** one of the long sharp teeth by which an animal seizes and holds its prey **2 :** one of the usually two long hollow or grooved teeth by which a poisonous snake injects its poison — **fanged** *adj*

fan·ny *n* **:** a person's buttocks **:** BACKSIDE

fan·tas·tic *adj* **1 :** produced by or like something produced by the imagination **2 :** extremely good **3 :** barely believable — **fan·tas·ti·cal·ly** *adv*

fan·ta·sy *n, pl* **fan·ta·sies 1 :** IMAGINATION 1 **2 :** something produced by the imagination

FAQ *abbr* frequently asked question, frequently asked questions — used to refer to a list of answers to typical questions that users of a website might ask

[1]**far** *adv* **far·ther** *or* **fur·ther; far·thest** *or* **fur·thest 1 :** at or to a great distance in space or time **2 :** to a great extent **:** MUCH **3 :** to or at a definite distance or point **4 :** to an advanced point — **by far :** by a great extent or degree

[2]**far** *adj* **far·ther** *or* **fur·ther; far·thest** *or* **fur·thest 1 :** very distant in space or time **2 :** the more distant of two **3 :** [1]LONG 2

far·away *adj* **1 :** [1]REMOTE 1, DISTANT **2 :** appearing as if lost in a daydream

farce *n* **:** something that is ridiculous

[1]**fare** *vb* **fared; far·ing :** to get along **:** SUCCEED

[2]**fare** *n* **1 :** the money a person pays to travel **2 :** a person paying a fare **3 :** FOOD 1

[1]**fare·well** *n* **:** [2]GOOD-BYE

[2]**fare·well** *adj* **:** relating to a time or act of leaving **:** FINAL

far·fetched *adj* : not likely to be true

[1]**farm** *n* **1 :** a piece of land used for raising crops or animals **2 :** an area of water where fish or shellfish are grown

[2]**farm** *vb* **farmed; farm·ing 1 :** to use for raising crops or animals **2 :** to work on or run a farm — **farm·er** *n*

farm·hand *n* : a farm worker

farm·ing *n* : the occupation or business of running a farm

farm·yard *n* : the yard around or enclosed by farm buildings

far–off *adj* : distant in time or space

far–reach·ing *adj* : having a wide range, influence, or effect

far·sight·ed *adj* **1 :** able to see distant things more clearly than near ones **2 :** able to judge how something will work out in the future — **far·sight·ed·ness** *n*

[1]**far·ther** *adv* **1 :** at or to a greater distance or more advanced point **2 :** more completely

[2]**farther** *adj* : more distant

[1]**far·thest** *adj* : most distant

[2]**farthest** *adv* **1 :** to or at the greatest distance in space or time **2 :** to the most advanced point

fas·ci·nate *vb* **fas·ci·nat·ed; fas·ci·nat·ing 1 :** to seize and hold the attention of **2 :** to attract greatly

fas·ci·nat·ing *adj* : extremely interesting or charming

fas·ci·na·tion *n* : a great interest in or attraction to something

fas·cism *n, often cap* : a political system headed by a dictator in which the government controls business and labor and opposition is not permitted

fas·cist *n, often cap* : a person who supports or practices fascism

[1]**fash·ion** *n* **1 :** the popular style of a thing at a certain time or among a certain group **2 :** MANNER 2, WAY

[2]**fashion** *vb* **fash·ioned; fash·ion·ing :** to give shape or form to

fash·ion·able *adj* : following the current fashion or style — **fash·ion·ably** *adv*

[1]**fast** *adj* **fast·er; fast·est 1 :** moving, operating, or acting quickly **2 :** taking a short time **3 :** indicating ahead of the correct time **4 :** firmly placed **5 :** not likely to fade **6 :** totally loyal

[2]**fast** *adv* **fast·er; fast·est 1 :** with great speed **2 :** to the full extent : SOUND **3 :** in a firm or fixed way

[3]**fast** *vb* **fast·ed; fast·ing 1 :** to go without eating **2 :** to eat in small amounts or only certain foods

[4]**fast** *n* **1 :** the act of going without food **2 :** a time when no food is eaten

fas·ten *vb* **fas·tened; fas·ten·ing 1 :** to attach or join by or as if by pinning, tying, or nailing **2 :** to make firm and secure **3 :** to become fixed or joined — **fas·ten·er** *n*

fas·ten·ing *n* : something that holds another thing shut or in the right position

fast food *n* : food that is prepared and served quickly — **fast–food** *adj*

fast–for·ward *vb* **fast–for·ward·ed; fast–for·ward·ing :** to advance a recording (as of music or video) at a faster rate than normal

fas·tid·i·ous *adj* : hard to please : very particular

[1]**fat** *adj* **fat·ter; fat·test 1 :** having much body fat **2 :** [1]THICK 1 **3 :** richly rewarding or profitable **4 :** swollen up — **fat·ness** *n*

[2]**fat** *n* **1 :** animal or plant tissue containing much greasy or oily material **2 :** any of numerous compounds of carbon, hydrogen, and oxygen that make up most of animal or plant fat and that are important to nutrition as sources of energy **3 :** a solid fat as distinguished from an oil **4 :** the best or richest part

fa·tal *adj* **1 :** causing death : MORTAL **2 :** causing ruin or failure — **fa·tal·ly** *adv*

fa·tal·i·ty *n, pl* **fa·tal·i·ties :** a death resulting from a disaster or accident

fate *n* **1 :** a power beyond human control that is believed to determine what happens : DESTINY **2 :** something that happens as though determined by fate : FORTUNE **3 :** final outcome

fate·ful *adj* : having serious results

[1]**fa·ther** *n* **1 :** a male parent **2** *cap* : GOD 1 **3 :** ANCESTOR 1 **4 :** a person who cares for another as a father might **5 :** a person who invents or begins something **6 :** PRIEST — used especially to address a priest or as a priest's title — **fa·ther·hood** *n* — **fa·ther·less** *adj*

[2]**father** *vb* **fa·thered; fa·ther·ing 1 :** to become the father of **2 :** to care for as a father **3 :** to be the founder, producer, or author of

fa·ther–in–law *n, pl* **fa·thers–in–law :** the father of a person's husband or wife

fa·ther·land *n* : the land of a person's birth

fa·ther·ly *adj* : of or like a father

[1]**fath·om** *n* : a unit of length equal to six feet (about 1.8 meters) used chiefly in measuring the depth of water

[2]**fathom** *vb* **fath·omed; fath·om·ing 1 :** to understand the reason for something **2 :** to measure the depth of water by means of a special line

[1]**fa·tigue** *n* **1 :** a state of being very tired **2 fa·tigues** *pl* : the uniform worn by members of the military for physical labor

[2]**fatigue** *vb* **fa·tigued; fa·tigu·ing :** to tire by work or exertion

fat·ten *vb* **fat·tened; fat·ten·ing :** to make or become fat

fat·ty *adj* **fat·ti·er; fat·ti·est :** containing or like fat
fau·cet *n* **:** a fixture for controlling the flow of a liquid (as from a pipe or cask)
fault *n* **1 :** a weakness in character **:** FAILING **2 :** responsibility for something wrong **3 :** FLAW, IMPERFECTION **4 :** a crack in the earth's crust along which movement occurs — **at fault :** responsible for something wrong
fault·less *adj* **:** [1]PERFECT 1
faulty *adj* **fault·i·er; fault·i·est :** having a fault, flaw, or weakness **:** IMPERFECT
faun *n* **:** a Roman god of country life represented as part goat and part man
fau·na *n* **:** the animal life typical of a region, period, or special environment
[1]**fa·vor** *or Can and Brit* **favour** *n* **1 :** an act of kindness **2 :** APPROVAL 1, LIKING **3 :** a preference for one side over another **4 :** a small gift or decorative item — **in favor of** *or Can and Brit* **in favour of 1 :** wanting or approving of **2 :** in support of
[2]**favor** *or Can and Brit* **favour** *vb* **fa·vored/favoured; fa·vor·ing/favouring 1 :** to prefer especially unfairly **2 :** to approve of **3 :** to present with **4 :** to make possible or easier **5 :** to look like
fa·vor·able *or Can and Brit* **favourable** *adj* **1 :** showing approval **2 :** tending to help — **fa·vor·ably** *or Can and Brit* **favourably** *adv*
[1]**fa·vor·ite** *or Can and Brit* **favourite** *n* **:** a person or a thing that is liked more than others
[2]**favorite** *or Can and Brit* **favourite** *adj* **:** most liked
fa·vor·it·ism *or Can and Brit* **favouritisn** *n* **:** the unfair treatment of some people better than others
fa·vour *Can and Brit spelling of* FAVOR
[1]**fawn** *n* **1 :** a young deer **2 :** a light grayish brown
[2]**fawn** *vb* **fawned; fawn·ing 1 :** to show affection — used especially of a dog **2 :** to try to win favor by acting as if someone is superior
[1]**fax** *n* **1 :** FACSIMILE 2 **2 :** a machine used to send or receive material by facsimile **3 :** something sent or received by facsimile
[2]**fax** *vb* **faxed; fax·ing :** to send material by facsimile
faze *vb* **fazed; faz·ing :** to cause to hesitate or feel fear
FBI *abbr* Federal Bureau of Investigation
[1]**fear** *vb* **feared; fear·ing :** to be afraid of **:** feel fear
[2]**fear** *n* **:** a strong unpleasant feeling caused by being aware of danger or expecting something bad to happen
fear·ful *adj* **1 :** causing fear **2 :** filled with fear **3 :** showing or caused by fear — **fear·ful·ly** *adv* — **fear·ful·ness** *n*
fear·less *adj* **:** not afraid **:** BRAVE — **fear·less·ly** *adv* — **fear·less·ness** *n*
fear·some *adj* **:** very frightening
fea·si·ble *adj* **:** possible to do or accomplish
[1]**feast** *n* **1 :** a fancy meal **2 :** a holy day observed by members of a religion
[2]**feast** *vb* **feast·ed; feast·ing 1 :** to eat well **2 :** [2]DELIGHT 1
feat *n* **:** an act showing courage, strength, or skill
[1]**feath·er** *n* **:** one of the light horny growths that make up the outer covering of a bird — **feath·ered** *adj*
[2]**feather** *vb* **feath·ered; feath·er·ing 1 :** to provide or decorate with feathers **2 :** to grow or form feathers
feath·ery *adj* **1 :** like a feather or tuft of feathers **2 :** covered with feathers
[1]**fea·ture** *n* **1 :** a part (as the nose or the mouth) of the face **2 :** something especially noticeable **3 :** MOVIE 1 **4 :** a special story in a newspaper or magazine
[2]**feature** *vb* **fea·tured; fea·tur·ing 1 :** to have as a characteristic **2 :** to give special prominence to **3 :** to play an important part
Feb. *abbr* February
Feb·ru·ary *n* **:** the second month of the year
fe·ces *n pl* **:** body waste that passes out from the intestine
fed·er·al *adj* **:** relating to a nation formed by the union of several parts
fed·er·a·tion *n* **:** a union of organizations or states
fee *n* **1 :** an amount of money that must be paid **2 :** a charge for services
fee·ble *adj* **fee·bler; fee·blest 1 :** lacking in strength or endurance **2 :** not effective or sufficient — **fee·ble·ness** *n* — **fee·bly** *adv*
[1]**feed** *vb* **fed; feed·ing 1 :** to give food to or give as food **2 :** to take food into the body **:** EAT **3 :** to supply with something necessary (as to growth or operation) — **feed·er** *n*
[2]**feed** *n* **:** food especially for livestock
feed·back *n* **:** helpful information or criticism given to someone to indicate what can be done to improve something
[1]**feel** *vb* **felt; feel·ing 1 :** to be aware of through physical contact **2 :** to examine or search for by touching **3 :** to be conscious of **4 :** to seem especially to the touch **5 :** to sense a physical, mental, or emotional state **6 :** to have sympathy **7 :** BELIEVE 4, THINK — **feel like :** to have an urge or desire to
[2]**feel** *n* **1 :** SENSATION 2, FEELING **2 :** the quality of something as learned through or as if through touch
feel·er *n* **:** a long flexible structure (as an insect's antenna) that is an organ of touch
feel·ing *n* **1 :** the sense by which a person knows whether things are hard or soft, hot

or cold, heavy or light **2 :** a sensation of temperature or pressure **3 :** a state of mind **4 feelings** *pl* **:** the state of a person's emotions **5 :** an opinion, belief, or expectation

feet *pl of* FOOT

feign *vb* **feigned; feign·ing :** [1]PRETEND 2

[1]**feint** *n* **:** a pretended blow or attack at one point or in one direction to take attention away from the point or direction the attack or blow is really coming from

[2]**feint** *vb* **feint·ed; feint·ing :** to make a feint

fe·lic·i·ty *n* **:** great happiness

[1]**fe·line** *adj* **1 :** of or relating to the domestic cat or a related animal (as a lion) **2 :** like or like that of a cat

[2]**feline** *n* **:** CAT

[1]**fell** *vb* **felled; fell·ing :** to cut or knock down

[2]**fell** *past of* FALL

[1]**fel·low** *n* **1 :** a male person **2 :** COMPANION 1, COMRADE

[2]**fellow** *adj* **:** belonging to the same group or class

fel·low·ship *n* **1 :** friendly relationship existing among persons **2 :** a group with similar interests

fel·on *n* **:** [2]CRIMINAL

fel·o·ny *n, pl* **fel·o·nies :** a very serious crime

[1]**felt** *n* **:** a soft heavy cloth made by rolling and pressing fibers together

[2]**felt** *past and past participle of* FEEL

fem. *abbr* feminine

[1]**fe·male** *adj* **1 :** of, relating to, or being the sex that bears young or lays eggs **2 :** having a pistil but no stamens **3 :** of or characteristic of women or girls

[2]**female** *n* **1 :** a woman or a girl **2 :** a person or animal that can bear young or lay eggs **3 :** a plant with a pistil but no stamens

fem·i·nine *adj* **1 :** [1]FEMALE 1 **2 :** [1]FEMALE 3

fem·i·nism *n* **1 :** the belief that women and men should have equal rights and opportunities **2 :** organized activity on behalf of women's rights and interests — **fem·i·nist** *n or adj*

fe·mur *n, pl* **fe·murs** *or* **fem·o·ra :** the long leg bone that extends from the hip to the knee

[1]**fence** *n* **:** a barrier (as of wood or wire) to prevent escape or entry or to mark a boundary

[2]**fence** *vb* **fenced; fenc·ing 1 :** to enclose with a fence **2 :** to fight with swords **:** to practice the sport of fencing — **fenc·er** *n*

fenc·ing *n* **:** the sport of having a pretended fight with blunted swords

fend *vb* **fend·ed; fend·ing 1 :** to drive away or repel **2 :** to get along without help

fend·er *n* **:** the part of a motor vehicle or bicycle that covers a wheel

fe·ral *adj* **:** having escaped from the care of people and become wild

[1]**fer·ment** *vb* **fer·ment·ed; fer·ment·ing :** to go through a chemical change that results in the production of alcohol

[2]**fer·ment** *n* **1 :** something (as yeast) that causes fermentation **2 :** an excited state

fer·men·ta·tion *n* **:** a chemical breaking down of a substance (as sugar) that is controlled by an enzyme, usually does not require oxygen, and typically results in the production of alcohol and carbon dioxide

fern *n* **:** a plant that produces spores instead of seeds and no flowers and whose leaves are usually divided into many parts — **fern·like** *adj*

fe·ro·cious *adj* **:** FIERCE 1, SAVAGE — **fe·ro·cious·ly** *adv*

fe·roc·i·ty *n, pl* **fe·roc·i·ties :** the quality or state of being fierce or savage

[1]**fer·ret** *n* **:** a domesticated animal with usually white or light brown or gray fur that originates from the European polecat

[2]**ferret** *vb* **fer·ret·ed; fer·ret·ing :** to find by eager searching

Fer·ris wheel *n* **:** an amusement park ride consisting of a large vertical wheel that is moved by a motor and has seats around its rim

[1]**fer·ry** *vb* **fer·ried; fer·ry·ing 1 :** to carry by boat over a body of water **2 :** to cross a body of water by a ferryboat **3 :** to transport for a short distance

[2]**ferry** *n, pl* **fer·ries 1 :** FERRYBOAT **2 :** a place where persons or things are ferried

fer·ry·boat *n* **:** a boat used to carry passengers, vehicles, or goods

fer·tile *adj* **1 :** producing many plants or crops **2 :** producing many ideas **3 :** capable of developing and growing

fer·til·i·ty *n* **:** the condition of being fertile

fer·til·iza·tion *n* **1 :** an act or process of making fertile **2 :** the joining of an egg cell and a sperm cell to form the first stage of an embryo

fer·til·ize *vb* **fer·til·ized; fer·til·iz·ing :** to make fertile or more fertile

fer·til·iz·er *n* **:** material added to soil to make it more fertile

fer·vent *adj* **:** felt very strongly — **fer·vent·ly** *adv*

fer·vor *n* **:** strong feeling or expression

fes·ter *vb* **fes·tered; fes·ter·ing :** to become painfully red and sore and usually full of pus

fes·ti·val *n* **1 :** a time or event of celebration **2 :** a program of cultural events or entertainment

fes·tive *adj* **1 :** having to do with a feast or festival **2 :** very merry and joyful

fes·tiv·i·ty *n, pl* **fes·tiv·i·ties 1 :** festive activity **2 :** celebration and enjoyment

[1]**fes·toon** *n* **:** a chain or strip hanging between two points as decoration

[2]**festoon** *vb* **fes·tooned; fes·toon·ing :** to hang or form festoons or other decorations on

fetch *vb* **fetched; fetch·ing** **1 :** to go after and bring back **2 :** to bring as a price : sell for
fetch·ing *adj* : very attractive
[1]**fet·ter** *n* **1 :** a chain for the feet **2 :** something that holds back : RESTRAINT
[2]**fetter** *vb* **fet·tered; fet·ter·ing** **1 :** to chain the feet of **2 :** to keep from moving or acting freely
fe·tus *n* : an animal not yet born or hatched but more developed than an embryo
[1]**feud** *n* : a long bitter quarrel between two people, families, or groups
[2]**feud** *vb* **feud·ed; feud·ing** : to carry on a long bitter quarrel
feu·dal *adj* : relating to feudalism
feu·dal·ism *n* : a social system existing in medieval Europe in which people worked and fought for nobles who gave them protection and land in return
fe·ver *n* **1 :** a body temperature that is higher than normal **2 :** a disease involving fever
fe·ver·ish *adj* **1 :** having a fever **2 :** characteristic of or relating to a fever **3 :** showing great emotion or activity : HECTIC — **fe·ver·ish·ly** *adv*
[1]**few** *pron* : not many people or things
[2]**few** *adj* **few·er; few·est** : not many but some
[3]**few** *n* : a small number of people or things
few·er *pron* : a smaller number
fez *n, pl* **fez·zes** : a round red felt hat that usually has a tassel but no brim
fi·an·cé *n* : a man who is engaged to be married
fi·an·cée *n* : a woman who engaged to be married
fi·as·co *n, pl* **fi·as·coes** : a complete failure
[1]**fib** *n* : a lie about something unimportant
[2]**fib** *vb* **fibbed; fib·bing** : to tell a lie about something unimportant — **fib·ber** *n*
fi·ber *or Can and Brit* **fibre** *n* **1 :** a thread or a structure or object resembling a thread **2** : plant material that cannot be digested
fi·ber·glass *or Can and Brit* **fibreglass** *n* : glass in the form of fibers used in various products (as filters and insulation)
fiber op·tics *or Can and Brit* **fibre optics** *n pl* : thin transparent fibers of glass or plastic that transmit light throughout their length
fi·brous *adj* : containing, made of, or like fibers
fib·u·la *n, pl* **fib·u·lae** *or* **fib·u·las** : the outer and smaller of the two bones between the knee and ankle
–fication *n suffix* : the act or process of or the result of
fick·le *adj* : changing often : not reliable — **fick·le·ness** *n*
fic·tion *n* **1 :** something told or written that is not fact **2 :** a made-up story **3 :** works of literature that are not true stories
fic·tion·al *adj* : not real or true : MADE-UP
fic·ti·tious *adj* : not real
[1]**fid·dle** *n* : VIOLIN
[2]**fiddle** *vb* **fid·dled; fid·dling** **1 :** to play on a fiddle **2 :** to move the hands or fingers restlessly **3 :** to spend time in aimless activity **4 :** to change or handle in a useless way **5 :** to handle in a harmful or foolish way : TAMPER — **fid·dler** *n*
fi·del·i·ty *n* **1 :** LOYALTY **2 :** ACCURACY
fidg·et *vb* **fidg·et·ed; fidg·et·ing** : to move in a restless or nervous way
fidg·ety *adj* : nervous and restless
fief *n* : an estate of land given to a vassal by a feudal lord
[1]**field** *n* **1 :** a piece of open, cleared, or cultivated land **2 :** a piece of land put to a special use or giving a special product **3 :** an area of activity or influence **4 :** a background on which something is drawn, painted, or mounted
[2]**field** *adj* : relating to a field
[3]**field** *vb* **field·ed; field·ing** : to catch or stop and throw a ball
field day *n* : a day of outdoor sports, activities, and athletic competitions
field·er *n* : a baseball player other than the pitcher or catcher on the team that is not at bat
field glasses *n pl* : binoculars without prisms
field goal *n* : a score in football made by kicking the ball through the goal during ordinary play
field hockey *n* : hockey played on a field
field trip *n* : a visit to a place (such as a museum) made by students to learn about something
fiend *n* **1 :** DEMON 1, DEVIL **2 :** a very wicked or cruel person **3 :** [2]FANATIC — **fiend·ish** *adj* — **fiend·ish·ly** *adv*
fierce *adj* **fierc·er; fierc·est** **1 :** likely to attack **2 :** having or showing very great energy or enthusiasm **3 :** wild or threatening in appearance **4 :** characterized by extreme force, intensity, or anger — **fierce·ly** *adv* — **fierce·ness** *n*
fi·ery *adj* **fi·er·i·er; fi·er·i·est** **1 :** marked by fire **2 :** hot or glowing like a fire **3 :** full of spirit **4 :** easily angered
fi·es·ta *n* : a celebration especially in Spain and Latin America that commemorates a saint
fife *n* : a small musical instrument like a flute that produces a shrill sound
[1]**fif·teen** *adj* : being one more than 14
[2]**fifteen** *n* : one more than 14 : three times five : 15
[1]**fif·teenth** *adj* : coming right after 14th
[2]**fifteenth** *n* : number 15 in a series
[1]**fifth** *adj* : coming right after fourth
[2]**fifth** *n* **1 :** number five in a series **2 :** one of five equal parts

[1]fif·ti·eth *adj* : coming right after 49th
[2]fiftieth *n* : number 50 in a series
[1]fif·ty *adj* : being five times ten
[2]fifty *n* : five times ten : 50
fig *n* : a sweet fruit that is oblong or shaped like a pear and is often eaten dried
[1]fight *vb* **fought; fight·ing** **1** : to struggle in battle or in physical combat **2** : to argue angrily : QUARREL **3** : to try hard **4** : to struggle against — **fight·er** *n*
[2]fight *n* **1** : a meeting in battle or in physical combat **2** : [1]QUARREL 1 **3** : strength or desire for fighting
fig·u·ra·tive *adj* : expressing one thing in terms normally used for another — **fig·u·ra·tive·ly** *adv*
[1]fig·ure *n* **1** : a symbol (as 1, 2, 3) that stands for a number : NUMERAL **2 figures** *pl* : ARITHMETIC 2 **3** : value or price expressed in figures **4** : the shape or outline of something or someone **5** : the shape of the body especially of a person **6** : an illustration in a printed text **7** : [1]PATTERN 1 **8** : a well-known or important person
[2]figure *vb* **fig·ured; fig·ur·ing** **1** : CALCULATE 1 **2** : BELIEVE 4, DECIDE — **figure on** **1** : to make plans based on **2** : to rely on **3** : to have in mind — **figure out** **1** : to discover or solve by thinking **2** : to find a solution for
fig·ure·head *n* **1** : a carved figure on the bow of a ship **2** : a person who is called the head of something but who has no real power
figure of speech *n, pl* **figures of speech** : an expression (as a simile or a metaphor) that uses words in other than a plain or literal way
fil·a·ment *n* **1** : a fine thread **2** : a fine wire (as in a light bulb) that is made to glow by the passage of an electric current **3** : the stalk of a plant stamen that bears the anther
fil·bert *n* : the hazel or its nut
filch *vb* **filched; filch·ing** : to steal in a sneaky way
[1]file *n* : a tool with sharp ridges or teeth for smoothing or rubbing down hard substances
[2]file *vb* **filed; fil·ing** : to rub, smooth, or cut away with a file
[3]file *vb* **filed; fil·ing** **1** : to arrange in an orderly way **2** : to enter or record officially
[4]file *n* **1** : a device (as a folder, case, or cabinet) for storing papers or records in an orderly way **2** : a collection of papers or records kept in a file **3** : a collection of data treated as a unit by a computer
[5]file *n* : a row of persons or things arranged one behind the other
[6]file *vb* **filed; fil·ing** : to walk in a row
fil·ial *adj* : relating to or suitable for a son or daughter
fil·i·gree *n* : decoration made of fine wire
Fil·i·pi·no *n* **1** : a person born or living in the Philippines **2** : the language of the Philippines
[1]fill *vb* **filled; fill·ing** **1** : to make or become full **2** : to use up all the space or time in **3** : to spread through **4** : to stop up : PLUG **5** : to do the duties of **6** : to hire a person for **7** : to supply according to directions **8** : to succeed in meeting or satisfying — **fill in** **1** : to insert information **2** : to provide information **3** : to take another's place — **fill out** **1** : to increase in size and fullness **2** : to complete by providing information
[2]fill *n* **1** : all that is wanted **2** : material for filling something
fill·er *n* : a material used for filling
fil·let *n* : a piece of boneless meat or fish
fill·ing *n* : a substance used to fill something else
filling station *n* : GAS STATION
fil·ly *n, pl* **fillies** : a young female horse
[1]film *n* **1** : a roll of material prepared for taking pictures **2** : MOVIE 1 **3** : a thin coating or layer
[2]film *vb* **filmed; film·ing** **1** : to make a movie **2** : to photograph on a film
filmy *adj* **film·i·er; film·i·est** : very thin and light
[1]fil·ter *n* **1** : a device or a mass of material (as sand or paper) with tiny openings through which a gas or liquid is passed to remove something **2** : a transparent material that absorbs light of some colors and is used for changing light (as in photography)
[2]filter *vb* **fil·tered; fil·ter·ing** **1** : to pass through a filter **2** : to remove by means of a filter
filth *n* : disgusting dirt
filthy *adj* **filth·i·er; filth·i·est** : extremely dirty — **filth·i·ness** *n*
fil·tra·tion *n* : the process of filtering
fin *n* **1** : any of the thin parts that stick out from the body of a water animal and especially a fish and are used in moving or guiding the body through the water **2** : something shaped like an animal's fin
[1]fi·nal *adj* **1** : coming or happening at the end **2** : not to be changed — **fi·nal·ly** *adv*
[2]final *n* **1** : the last match or game of a tournament **2** : a final examination in a course
fi·na·le *n* : the close or end of something (as a musical work)
fi·nal·i·ty *n* : the condition of being final or complete
fi·nal·ize *vb* **fi·nal·ized; fi·nal·iz·ing** : to put in a final or finished form
[1]fi·nance *n* **1 finances** *pl* : money available to a government, business, or individual **2** : the system that includes the circulation of money, the providing of banks and credit, and the making of investments

²finance *vb* **fi·nanced; fi·nanc·ing** : to provide money for
fi·nan·cial *adj* : having to do with money or finance — **fi·nan·cial·ly** *adv*
fin·an·cier *n* : a specialist in finance and especially in the financing of businesses
finch *n* : a songbird (as a sparrow, bunting, or canary) with a short bill used for eating seeds
¹find *vb* **found; find·ing** **1** : to come upon by chance **2** : to come upon or get by searching, study, or effort **3** : to make a decision about **4** : to know by experience **5** : to gain or regain the use of **6** : to become aware of being in a place, condition, or activity — **find·er** *n* — **find fault** : to criticize in an unfavorable way — **find out** : to learn by studying, watching, or searching
²find *n* : a usually valuable item or person found
find·ing *n* **1** : the decision of a court **2** : the results of an investigation
¹fine *n* : a sum of money to be paid as a punishment
²fine *vb* **fined; fin·ing** : to punish by requiring payment of a sum of money
³fine *adj* **fin·er; fin·est** **1** : very good in quality or appearance **2** : SATISFACTORY **3** : very small or thin **4** : made up of very small pieces — **fine·ly** *adv* — **fine·ness** *n*
⁴fine *adv* : very well
fin·ery *n, pl* **fin·er·ies** : stylish or showy clothes and jewelry
¹fin·ger *n* **1** : one of the five divisions of the end of the hand including the thumb **2** : something that resembles a finger **3** : the part of a glove into which a finger goes
²finger *vb* **fin·gered; fin·ger·ing** : to touch with the fingers : HANDLE
fin·ger·nail *n* : the hard covering at the end of a finger
¹fin·ger·print *n* : the unique pattern of marks made by pressing the tip of a finger on a surface
²fingerprint *vb* **fin·ger·print·ed; fin·ger·print·ing** : to obtain fingerprints in order to identify a person
fin·icky *adj* : very hard to please : FUSSY
¹fin·ish *vb* **fin·ished; fin·ish·ing** **1** : to bring or come to an end : COMPLETE **2** : to use up completely **3** : to end a competition in a certain position **4** : to put a final coat or surface on
²finish *n* **1** : ¹END 2, CONCLUSION **2** : the final treatment or coating of a surface or the appearance given by such a treatment
finish line *n* : a line marking the end of a racecourse
fi·nite *adj* : having definite limits
¹fink *n* **1** : a person who is disliked **2** : a person who tattles
²fink *vb* **finked; fink·ing** : to tell on : TATTLE
Finn *n* : a person born or living in Finland
finned *adj* : having fins
¹Finn·ish *adj* : relating to Finland, its people, or the Finnish language
²Finnish *n* : the language of the Finns
fiord *variant of* FJORD
fir *n* : a tall evergreen tree related to the pine that yields useful lumber
¹fire *n* **1** : the light and heat and especially the flame produced by burning **2** : fuel that is burning in a controlled setting (as in a fireplace) **3** : the destructive burning of something (as a building) **4** : the shooting of weapons **5** : ENTHUSIASM — **on fire** : actively burning — **under fire** **1** : exposed to the firing of enemy guns **2** : under attack
²fire *vb* **fired; fir·ing** **1** : ¹SHOOT 2 **2** : to dismiss from employment **3** : EXCITE 1, STIR **4** : to subject to great heat **5** : to set off : EXPLODE **6** : to set on fire
fire alarm *n* : an alarm sounded to signal that a fire has broken out
fire·arm *n* : a small weapon from which shot or a bullet is discharged by gunpowder
fire·crack·er *n* : a paper tube containing an explosive to be set off for amusement
fire drill *n* : a practice drill in getting out of a building in case of fire
fire engine *n* : a truck equipped to fight fires
fire escape *n* : a stairway that provides a way of escape from a building in case of fire
fire extinguisher *n* : a container filled with chemicals used to put out a fire
fire·fight·er *n* : a person whose job is to put out fires — **fire·fight·ing** *n*
fire·fly *n, pl* **fire·flies** : a small beetle producing a soft light
fire·house *n* : FIRE STATION
fire·man *n, pl* **fire·men** **1** : FIREFIGHTER **2** : a person who tends a fire
fire·place *n* : a structure with a hearth on which an open fire can be built (as for heating)
fire·proof *adj* : not easily burned : made safe against fire
fire·side *n* **1** : a place near the hearth **2** : ¹HOME 1
fire station *n* : a building housing fire engines and usually firefighters
fire wall *n* **1** : a wall constructed to prevent the spread of fire **2** *usu* **fire·wall** : computer hardware or software that prevents unauthorized access to private data (as on a company's local area network) by outside computer users (as of the Internet)
fire·wood *n* : wood cut for fuel
fire·work *n* **1** : a device that makes a display of light or noise by the burning of explosive or flammable materials **2 fireworks** *pl* : a display of fireworks

[1]**firm** *adj* **1 :** having a solid compact texture **2 :** STRONG 1, VIGOROUS **3 :** not likely to be changed **4 :** not easily moved or shaken **:** FAITHFUL **5 :** showing certainty or determination — **firm·ly** *adv* — **firm·ness** *n*

[2]**firm** *vb* **firmed; firm·ing** **1 :** to make or become hard or solid **2 :** to make more secure or strong **3 :** to put into final form

[3]**firm** *n* **:** BUSINESS 2

[1]**first** *adj* **:** coming before all others in time, order, or importance

[2]**first** *adv* **1 :** before any other **2 :** for the first time

[3]**first** *n* **1 :** number one in a series **2 :** something or someone that comes before all others **3 :** the winning place in a competition — **at first :** in the beginning

first aid *n* **:** care or treatment given to an ill or injured person in an emergency

first–class *adj* **1 :** relating to the best group in a classification **2 :** EXCELLENT

first·hand *adj or adv* **:** coming right from the original source

first lieutenant *n* **:** a commissioned officer in the army, air force, or marine corps ranking above a second lieutenant

first person *n* **:** a set of words or forms (as pronouns or verb forms) referring to the person speaking or writing them

first–rate *adj* **:** EXCELLENT

first re·spond·er *n* **:** a person (as a police officer or an EMT) who is responsible for going immediately to the scene of an accident or emergency to provide help

first sergeant *n* **1 :** a noncommissioned officer serving as the chief assistant to a military commander **2 :** a noncommissioned officer ranking above a sergeant first class in the army or above a gunnery sergeant in the marine corps

firth *n* **:** a narrow arm of the sea

[1]**fish** *n, pl* **fish** *or* **fish·es** **1 :** any of a large group of vertebrate animals that live in water, breathe with gills, and usually have fins and scales **2 :** an animal that lives in water — usually used in combination — **fish·like** *adj*

[2]**fish** *vb* **fished; fish·ing** **1 :** to catch or try to catch fish **2 :** to search for something by or as if by groping

fish·er·man *n, pl* **fish·er·men :** a person who fishes

fish·ery *n, pl* **fish·er·ies** **1 :** the business of catching, processing, and selling fish **2 :** a place for catching fish

fish·hook *n* **:** a hook used for catching fish

fishy *adj* **fish·i·er; fish·i·est** **1 :** of or like fish **2 :** causing doubt or suspicion **:** QUESTIONABLE

fis·sion *n* **1 :** a method of reproduction in which a living cell or body divides into two or more parts each of which grows into a whole new individual **2 :** the process of splitting an atomic nucleus with the release of large amounts of energy

fis·sure *n* **:** a narrow opening or crack

fist *n* **:** the hand with the fingers bent tight into the palm

fist bump *n* **:** a gesture in which two people bump their fists together (as in greeting or celebration) — **fist–bump** *vb*

[1]**fit** *adj* **fit·ter; fit·test** **1 :** good enough **:** suitable for **2 :** physically healthy **3 :** made ready — **fit·ness** *n*

[2]**fit** *n* **:** a sudden attack or outburst

[3]**fit** *vb* **fit·ted; fit·ting** **1 :** to be the right shape or size **2 :** to bring to the right shape or size **3 :** to find room or time for **4 :** to go into a particular place **5 :** to be suitable for or to **6 :** EQUIP

[4]**fit** *n* **:** the way something fits

fit·ful *adj* **:** not regular or steady — **fit·ful·ly** *adv*

[1]**fit·ting** *adj* **:** [1]APPROPRIATE, SUITABLE — **fit·ting·ly** *adv*

[2]**fitting** *n* **:** a small part that goes with something larger

[1]**five** *adj* **:** being one more than four

[2]**five** *n* **1 :** one more than four **:** 5 **2 :** the fifth in a set or series

[1]**fix** *vb* **fixed; fix·ing** **1 :** [1]REPAIR 1, MEND **2 :** to make firm or secure **3 :** to hold or direct steadily **4 :** to set definitely **:** ESTABLISH **5 :** to get ready **:** PREPARE **6 :** to cause to chemically change into an available and useful form — **fix·er** *n*

[2]**fix** *n* **1 :** an unpleasant or difficult position **2 :** something that solves a problem

fixed *adj* **1 :** not changing **:** SET **2 :** firmly placed — **fix·ed·ly** *adv*

fixed star *n* **:** a star so distant that its motion can be measured only by very careful observations over long periods

fix·ture *n* **:** something (as a light or sink) attached as a permanent part

[1]**fizz** *vb* **fizzed; fizz·ing :** to make a hissing or bubbling sound

[2]**fizz** *n* **1 :** a hissing or bubbling sound **2 :** a bubbling drink

fiz·zle *vb* **fiz·zled; fiz·zling :** to fail after a good start

fjord *or* **fiord** *n* **:** a narrow inlet of the sea between cliffs or steep slopes

FL *abbr* Florida

Fla. *abbr* Florida

flab·ber·gast *vb* **flab·ber·gast·ed; flab·ber·gast·ing :** to greatly surprise **:** ASTONISH

flab·by *adj* **flab·bi·er; flab·bi·est :** not hard and firm **:** SOFT — **flab·bi·ness** *n*

[1]**flag** *n* **:** a piece of cloth with a special design or color that is used as a symbol (as of a nation) or as a signal

²flag *vb* **flagged; flag·ging :** to signal to stop
³flag *vb* **flagged; flag·ging :** to become weak
fla·gel·lum *n, pl* **fla·gel·la :** a long whiplike structure that sticks out from a cell and by which some tiny organisms (as bacteria) move
flag·man *n, pl* **flag·men :** a person who signals with a flag
flag·on *n* **:** a container for liquids usually having a handle, spout, and lid
flag·pole *n* **:** a pole on which to raise a flag
fla·grant *adj* **:** so bad as to be impossible to overlook — **fla·grant·ly** *adv*
flag·ship *n* **:** the ship carrying the commander of a group of ships and flying a flag that tells the commander's rank
flag·staff *n, pl* **flag·staffs :** FLAGPOLE
¹flail *vb* **flailed; flail·ing 1 :** to wave the arms or legs wildly **2 :** to swing something with a violent motion
²flail *n* **:** a tool for threshing grain by hand
flair *n* **1 :** natural ability **2 :** ¹STYLE 4
¹flake *n* **:** a small thin flat piece
²flake *vb* **flaked; flak·ing :** to form or separate into small thin flat pieces
flaky *adj* **flak·i·er; flak·i·est :** tending to break apart into small thin flat pieces — **flak·i·ness** *n*
flam·boy·ant *adj* **:** having a noticeable or showy quality — **flam·boy·ant·ly** *adv*
¹flame *n* **1 :** the glowing gas that makes up part of a fire **2 :** a state of burning brightly **3 :** strongly felt emotion
²flame *vb* **flamed; flam·ing :** to burn with or as if with a flame
flame·throw·er *n* **:** a weapon that shoots a burning stream of fuel
fla·min·go *n, pl* **fla·min·gos** *or* **fla·min·goes :** a large pale pink to reddish waterbird with very long neck and legs and a broad bill bent downward at the end
flam·ma·ble *adj* **:** capable of being easily set on fire and of burning quickly
¹flank *n* **1 :** the area on the side of an animal between the ribs and the hip **2 :** ¹SIDE 3 **3 :** the right or left side of a formation (as of soldiers)
²flank *vb* **flanked; flank·ing 1 :** to be located at the side of **2 :** to attack or threaten the side of
flan·nel *n* **:** a soft cloth made of wool or cotton
¹flap *n* **1 :** something broad and flat or flexible that hangs loose **2 :** the motion or sound made by something broad and flexible (as a sail or wing) moving back and forth **3 :** an upset or worried state of mind
²flap *vb* **flapped; flap·ping :** to move with a beating or fluttering motion
flap·jack *n* **:** PANCAKE
¹flare *vb* **flared; flar·ing 1 :** to burn with an unsteady flame **2 :** to shine or burn suddenly or briefly **3 :** to become angry or active **4 :** to spread outward
²flare *n* **1 :** a sudden blaze of light **2 :** a blaze of light used to signal, light up something, or attract attention **3 :** a device or material used to produce a flare **4 :** a sudden outburst **5 :** a spreading outward **:** a part that spreads outward
¹flash *vb* **flashed; flash·ing 1 :** to shine or give off bright light suddenly **2 :** to appear quickly or suddenly **3 :** to come or pass very suddenly **4 :** to show briefly
²flash *n* **1 :** a sudden burst of or as if of light **2 :** a very short time
³flash *adj* **:** beginning suddenly and lasting only a short time
flash drive *n* **:** a small rectangular device that is designed to be plugged directly into a USB port on a computer and is often used for transferring files from one computer to another
flash·light *n* **:** a small portable electric light that runs on batteries
flash mob *n* **:** a group of people summoned (as by e-mail or text message) to a designated location at a specified time to perform an action (as singing or dancing) in public
flashy *adj* **flash·i·er; flash·i·est :** GAUDY, SHOWY
flask *n* **:** a container like a bottle with a flat or rounded body
¹flat *adj* **flat·ter; flat·test 1 :** having a smooth level surface **2 :** spread out on or along a surface **3 :** having a broad smooth surface and little thickness **4 :** very clear and definite **5 :** not changing in amount **6 :** not showing active business **7 :** ¹DULL 3 **8 :** having lost air **9 :** no longer having bubbles **10 :** lower than the true musical pitch **11 :** lower by a half step in music **12 :** not shiny — **flat·ly** *adv*
²flat *n* **1 :** a level area of land **:** PLAIN **2 :** a flat part or surface **3 :** a note or tone that is a half step lower than the note named **4 :** a sign ♭ meaning that the pitch of a musical note is to be lower by a half step **5 :** a tire that has lost air
³flat *adv* **1 :** on or against a flat surface **2 :** without any time more or less **:** EXACTLY **3 :** below the true musical pitch
flat·boat *n* **:** a large boat with a flat bottom and square ends
flat·car *n* **:** a railroad car without sides or a roof that is used to carry freight
flat·fish *n* **:** a fish (as the flounder) that has a flat body and swims on its side with both eyes on the upper side
flat–out *adj* **1 :** ²OUT-RIGHT 1 **2 :** greatest possible

flat out *adv* **1 :** in a very clear manner **2 :** at top speed
flat–pan·el *adj* **:** relating to a thin flat video display
flat·ten *vb* **flat·tened; flat·ten·ing :** to make or become flat
flat·ter *vb* **flat·tered; flat·ter·ing 1 :** to praise but not sincerely **2 :** to cause to feel pleased by showing respect or admiration **3 :** to show as favorably as possible **4 :** to make look more attractive — **flat·ter·er** *n*
flat·tery *n, pl* **flat·ter·ies :** praise that is not deserved or meant
flaunt *vb* **flaunt·ed; flaunt·ing 1 :** to wave or flutter in a showy way **2 :** to show in a way that attracts attention
[1]**fla·vor** *or Can and Brit* **flavour** *n* **1 :** the quality of something that affects the sense of taste **2 :** a substance added to food to give it a desired taste
[2]**flavor** *or Can and Brit* **flavour** *vb* **fla·vored/flavoured; fla·vor·ing/flavouring :** to give or add something to produce a taste — **fla·vored** *or Can and Brit* **flavoured** *adj*
fla·vor·ing *or Can and Brit* **flavouring** *n* **:** [1]FLAVOR 2
flaw *n* **:** a small fault or weakness — **flaw·less** *adj*
flax *n* **:** a plant with blue flowers that is grown for its fiber from which rope and linen is made and for its seed from which oil and livestock feed are obtained
flax·en *adj* **:** having a light yellow color
flax·seed *n* **:** the seed of flax from which linseed oil comes
flay *vb* **flayed; flay·ing 1 :** to strip off the skin or surface of **2 :** to beat severely
flea *n* **:** a small bloodsucking insect that has no wings and a hard body
[1]**fleck** *vb* **flecked; fleck·ing :** to mark with small streaks or spots
[2]**fleck** *n* **1 :** [1]SPOT 2, MARK **2 :** a small bit
fledg·ling *n* **:** a young bird that has just grown the feathers needed to fly
flee *vb* **fled; flee·ing :** to run away or away from
[1]**fleece** *n* **:** the woolly coat of an animal and especially a sheep
[2]**fleece** *vb* **fleeced; fleec·ing :** to rob or cheat by trickery
fleecy *adj* **fleec·i·er; fleec·i·est :** covered with, made of, or similar to fleece
[1]**fleet** *n* **1 :** a group of warships under one commander **2 :** a country's navy **3 :** a group of ships or vehicles that move together or are owned by one company
[2]**fleet** *adj* **fleet·er; fleet·est :** very swift — **fleet·ly** *adv*
fleet·ing *adj* **:** passing by quickly
flesh *n* **1 :** the soft parts of an animal's or person's body **2 :** the part of an animal that is eaten **:** MEAT **3 :** a soft edible plant part
fleshy *adj* **flesh·i·er; flesh·i·est 1 :** like or consisting of flesh **2 :** [1]FAT 1
flew *past of* FLY
flex *vb* **flexed; flex·ing 1 :** to bend especially again and again **2 :** to move or tense (a muscle)
flex·i·bil·i·ty *n* **:** the quality or state of being easy to bend
flex·i·ble *adj* **1 :** possible or easy to bend **2 :** easily changed
[1]**flick** *n* **:** a light snapping stroke
[2]**flick** *vb* **flicked; flick·ing :** to strike or move with a quick motion
[1]**flick·er** *vb* **flick·ered; flick·er·ing 1 :** to burn unsteadily **2 :** to appear briefly **3 :** to move quickly
[2]**flicker** *n* **1 :** a quick small movement **2 :** a quick movement of light
[3]**flicker** *n* **:** a large North American woodpecker
fli·er *or* **fly·er** *n* **1 :** a person or thing that flies **2** usually flyer **:** a printed sheet containing information or advertising that is given to many people
[1]**flight** *n* **1 :** an act of passing through the air by the use of wings **2 :** a passing through the air or space **3 :** a trip by an airplane or spacecraft **4 :** a group of similar things flying through the air together **5 :** an extraordinary display **6 :** a series of stairs from one level or floor to the next
[2]**flight** *n* **:** the act of running away
flight·less *adj* **:** unable to fly
flighty *adj* **flight·i·er; flight·i·est 1 :** easily excited or frightened **:** SKITTISH **2 :** not steady or serious
flim·sy *adj* **flim·si·er; flim·si·est :** not strong or solid
flinch *vb* **flinched; flinch·ing :** to draw back from or as if from pain or fear
[1]**fling** *vb* **flung; fling·ing 1 :** to throw hard or without care **2 :** to move forcefully
[2]**fling** *n* **1 :** an act of throwing hard or without care **2 :** a time of freedom for pleasure **3 :** a brief try
flint *n* **:** a very hard stone that produces a spark when struck by steel
flint·lock *n* **:** an old-fashioned firearm using a piece of flint for striking a spark to fire the charge
[1]**flip** *vb* **flipped; flip·ping :** to move or turn by or as if by tossing
[2]**flip** *n* **1 :** a quick turn, toss, or movement **2 :** a somersault in the air
flip·pant *adj* **:** not respectful or serious — **flip·pant·ly** *adv*
flip·per *n* **1 :** a broad flat limb (as of a seal or whale) used for swimming **2 :** a flat rub-

ber shoe with the front widened into a paddle for use in swimming

¹flirt *vb* **flirt·ed; flirt·ing :** to show a romantic interest in someone just for fun

²flirt *n* **:** a person who flirts a lot

flit *vb* **flit·ted; flit·ting :** to move, pass, or fly quickly from one place or thing to another

¹float *n* **1 :** something that rests in or on the surface of a liquid **2 :** an inflated support for a person in water **3 :** a light object that holds up the baited end of a fishing line **4 :** a platform anchored near a shore for the use of swimmers or boats **5 :** a structure that holds up an airplane in water **6 :** a soft drink with ice cream floating in it **7 :** a vehicle with a platform used to carry an exhibit in a parade

²float *vb* **float·ed; float·ing 1 :** to rest on the surface of a liquid **2 :** to be carried along by or as if by moving water or air **3 :** to cause to rest on or be carried by water

¹flock *n* **1 :** a group of animals living or kept together **2 :** a group someone watches over **3 :** a large number

²flock *vb* **flocked; flock·ing :** to gather or move in a crowd

floe *n* **:** a sheet or mass of floating ice

flog *vb* **flogged; flog·ging :** to beat severely with a rod or whip

¹flood *n* **1 :** a huge flow of water that rises and spreads over the land **2 :** the flowing in of the tide **3 :** a very large number or amount

²flood *vb* **flood·ed; flood·ing 1 :** to cover or become filled with water **2 :** to fill as if with a flood

flood·light *n* **:** a light that shines brightly over a wide area

flood·plain *n* **:** low flat land along a stream that is flooded when the stream overflows

flood·wa·ter *n* **:** the water of a flood

¹floor *n* **1 :** the part of a room on which people stand **2 :** the lower inside surface of a hollow structure **3 :** the area of ground at the bottom of something **4 :** a story of a building

²floor *vb* **floored; floor·ing 1 :** to cover or provide with a floor **2 :** to knock down

floor·ing *n* **1 :** ¹FLOOR 1 **2 :** material for floors

¹flop *vb* **flopped; flop·ping 1 :** to flap about **2 :** to drop or fall limply **3 :** ¹FAIL 1

²flop *n* **1 :** the act or sound of flapping about or falling limply **2 :** FAILURE 1

flop·py *adj* **flop·pi·er; flop·pi·est :** being soft and flexible

floppy disk *n* **:** a small flexible plastic disk with a magnetic coating on which computer data can be stored

flo·ra *n* **:** the plant life typical of a region, period, or special environment

flo·ral *adj* **:** of or relating to flowers

flor·id *adj* **1 :** very fancy or flowery in style **2 :** having a reddish color

flo·rist *n* **:** a person who sells flowers and houseplants

¹floss *n* **1 :** DENTAL FLOSS **2 :** soft thread used in embroidery **3 :** fluffy material full of fibers

²floss *vb* **flossed; floss·ing :** to use dental floss on

flo·til·la *n* **:** a fleet of usually small ships

¹flounce *vb* **flounced; flounc·ing 1 :** to move with exaggerated motions **2** *chiefly British* **:** to walk in a way that shows anger

²flounce *n* **:** a strip of fabric or ruffle attached by one edge — **flouncy** *adj*

¹floun·der *n* **:** a flatfish used for food

²flounder *vb* **floun·dered; floun·der·ing 1 :** to struggle to move or get footing **2 :** to behave or do something in a clumsy way

flour *n* **:** finely ground wheat or other food product

¹flour·ish *vb* **flour·ished; flour·ish·ing 1 :** to grow well **2 :** to do well **:** enjoy success **3 :** to make sweeping movements with

²flourish *n* **1 :** a fancy bit of decoration added to something **2 :** a sweeping motion

flout *vb* **flout·ed; flout·ing :** to ignore in an open and disrespectful way

¹flow *vb* **flowed; flow·ing 1 :** to move in or as if in a stream **2 :** to glide along smoothly **3 :** to hang loose and waving

²flow *n* **1 :** an act of moving in or as if in a stream **2 :** the rise of the tide **3 :** a smooth even movement **:** STREAM **4 :** an amount or mass of something moving in a stream

¹flow·er *n* **1 :** a plant part that produces seed **2 :** a small plant grown chiefly for its showy flowers **3 :** the state of bearing flowers **4 :** the best part or example — **flow·ered** *adj* — **flow·er·less** *adj*

²flower *vb* **flow·ered; flow·er·ing :** ²BLOOM 1

flower head *n* **:** a tight cluster of small flowers that are arranged so that the whole looks like a single flower

flowering plant *n* **:** a seed plant whose seeds are produced in the ovary of a flower

flow·ery *adj* **flow·er·i·er; flow·er·i·est 1 :** full of or covered with flowers **2 :** full of fancy words

flown *past participle of* FLY

flu *n* **1 :** INFLUENZA **2 :** any of several virus diseases something like a cold

fluc·tu·ate *vb* **fluc·tu·at·ed; fluc·tu·at·ing :** to change continually and especially up and down

flue *n* **:** an enclosed passage for smoke or air

flu·en·cy *n* **:** the ability to speak easily and well

flu·ent *adj* **1 :** able to speak easily and well **2 :** smooth and correct — **flu·ent·ly** *adv*

¹fluff *n* **:** something light and soft

²fluff *vb* **fluffed; fluff·ing :** to make or become fuller, lighter, or softer

fluffy *adj* **fluff·i·er; fluff·i·est** **1 :** having, covered with, or similar to down **2 :** being or looking light and soft

¹flu·id *adj* **1 :** capable of flowing like a liquid or gas **2 :** having a graceful or flowing style or appearance — **flu·id·ly** *adv*

²fluid *n* **:** something that tends to flow and take the shape of its container

fluid ounce *n* **:** a unit of liquid capacity equal to 1/16 of a pint (about 29.6 milliliters)

flung *past and past participle of* FLING

flunk *vb* **flunked; flunk·ing :** ¹FAIL 1

fluo·res·cent *adj* **1 :** giving out visible light when exposed to external radiation **2 :** producing visible light by means of a fluorescent coating **3 :** extremely bright or glowing

fluo·ri·date *vb* **fluo·ri·dat·ed; fluo·ri·dat·ing :** to add a fluoride to

fluo·ride *n* **:** a compound of fluorine

fluo·rine *n* **:** a yellowish flammable irritating gaseous chemical element

flur·ry *n, pl* **flurries** **1 :** a gust of wind **2 :** a brief light snowfall **3 :** a brief outburst

¹flush *vb* **flushed; flush·ing :** to cause to leave a hiding place

²flush *n* **1 :** an act of pouring water over or through **2 :** ²BLUSH 1

³flush *vb* **flushed; flush·ing** **1 :** ¹BLUSH 1 **2 :** to pour water over or through

⁴flush *adj* **:** even or level with another surface

⁵flush *adv* **:** so as to be even or level with another surface

¹flus·ter *vb* **flus·tered; flus·ter·ing :** to make nervous and confused **:** UPSET

²fluster *n* **:** a state of nervous confusion

flute *n* **:** a woodwind instrument in the form of a slender tube open at one end that is played by blowing across a hole near the closed end

¹flut·ter *vb* **flut·tered; flut·ter·ing** **1 :** to move the wings rapidly without flying or in making short flights **2 :** to move with a quick flapping motion **3 :** to move about excitedly

²flutter *n* **1 :** an act of moving or flapping quickly **2 :** a state of excitement

¹fly *vb* **flew; flown; fly·ing** **1 :** to move in or pass through the air with wings **2 :** to move through the air or before the wind **3 :** to float or cause to float, wave, or soar in the wind **4 :** to run away **:** FLEE **5 :** to pass or move swiftly **6 :** to operate or travel in an aircraft **7 :** to become suddenly emotional

²fly *n, pl* **flies** **1 :** a flap of material to cover a fastening in a garment **2 :** a layer of fabric that goes over the top of a tent **3 :** a baseball hit very high

³fly *n, pl* **flies** **1 :** a winged insect **2 :** any of a large group of mostly stout-bodied two-winged insects (as the housefly) **3 :** a fishhook made to look like an insect

fly·catch·er *n* **:** a small bird that eats flying insects

flyer *variant of* FLIER

flying fish *n* **:** a fish with large fins that let it jump from the water and move for a distance through the air

fly·way *n* **:** a route regularly followed by migratory birds

¹foal *n* **:** a young animal of the horse family especially when less than one year old

²foal *vb* **foaled; foal·ing :** to give birth to a baby horse

¹foam *n* **:** a mass of tiny bubbles that forms in or on the surface of a liquid

²foam *vb* **foamed; foam·ing :** to produce or form a mass of tiny bubbles

foamy *adj* **foam·i·er; foam·i·est :** covered with or looking like foam — **foam·i·ness** *n*

fo·cal *adj* **1 :** of, relating to, or having a focus **2 :** having central or great importance

¹fo·cus *n, pl* **fo·ci** *also* **fo·cus·es** **1 :** a point at which rays (as of light, heat, or sound) meet after being reflected or bent **:** the point at which an image is formed **2 :** the distance from a lens or mirror to a focus **3 :** an adjustment that gives clear vision **4 :** a center of activity or interest

²focus *vb* **fo·cused** *also* **fo·cussed; fo·cus·ing** *also* **fo·cus·sing** **1 :** to bring or come to a focus **2 :** to adjust the focus of **3 :** to direct or cause to direct at

fod·der *n* **:** coarse dry food (as cornstalks) for livestock

foe *n* **:** an enemy of a person or a country

¹fog *n* **1 :** tiny drops of water floating in the air at or near the ground **2 :** a confused state of mind

²fog *vb* **fogged; fog·ging :** to cover or become covered with tiny drops of water

fog·gy *adj* **fog·gi·er; fog·gi·est** **1 :** filled with fog **2 :** unsure or confused

fog·horn *n* **:** a loud horn sounded in foggy weather to give warning

foi·ble *n* **:** an unimportant weakness or failing

¹foil *vb* **foiled; foil·ing :** to prevent from achieving a goal

²foil *n* **:** a very thin sheet of metal

³foil *n* **:** a fencing sword having a light flexible blade with a blunt point

¹fold *n* **:** an enclosure for sheep

²fold *vb* **fold·ed; fold·ing** **1 :** to lay one part over or against another part **2 :** to clasp together **3 :** ¹EMBRACE 1

³fold *n* **1 :** an act or the result of laying one part over or against another **2 :** a part laid over another part **3 :** a bend produced in a rock layer by pressure

-fold *suffix* **1 :** multiplied by a specified number : times — used in adjectives and adverbs **2 :** having so many parts

fold·er *n* **1 :** a folded cover or large envelope for loose papers **2 :** a folded printed sheet **3 :** a part of a computer operating system used to organize files

fo·li·age *n* **:** the leaves of a plant

[1]folk *or* **folks** *n pl* **1 :** persons of a certain kind or group **2 folks** *pl* **:** people in general **3 folks** *pl* **:** family members and especially parents

[2]folk *adj* **:** created by the common people

folk·lore *n* **:** traditional customs, beliefs, stories, and sayings

folk·sing·er *n* **:** a person who sings songs (**folk songs**) created by and long sung among the common people

folk·tale *n* **:** a story made up and handed down by the common people

fol·low *vb* **fol·lowed; fol·low·ing** **1 :** to go or come after or behind **2 :** to come after in time or place **3 :** to go on the track of **4 :** to go along or beside **5 :** to be led or guided by : OBEY **6 :** to result from **7 :** to work in or at something as a way of life **8 :** to watch or pay attention to **9 :** UNDERSTAND **10 :** to sign up to see regularly the social media messages from someone or something (as a business) — **fol·low·er** *n* — **follow suit** **1 :** to play a card that belongs to the same group (as hearts) as the one first played **2 :** to do the same thing someone else has just done — **follow through** **:** to complete something started — **follow up** **:** to take additional similar or related action

[1]fol·low·ing *adj* **:** coming just after

[2]following *n* **:** a group of fans or supporters

[3]following *prep* **:** right after

fol·ly *n, pl* **follies** **1 :** lack of good sense **2 :** a foolish act or idea

fond *adj* **fond·er; fond·est** **1 :** having a liking or love **2 :** AFFECTIONATE, LOVING **3 :** strongly wished for — **fond·ly** *adv* — **fond·ness** *n*

fon·dle *vb* **fon·dled; fon·dling** **:** to touch or handle in a tender or loving manner

font *n* **1 :** a basin to hold water for baptism **2 :** SOURCE 1

food *n* **1 :** the material that people and animals eat : material containing carbohydrates, fats, proteins, and supplements (as minerals and vitamins) that is taken in by and used in the living body for growth and repair and as a source of energy for activities **2 :** inorganic substances (as nitrate and carbon dioxide) taken in by green plants and used to build organic nutrients **3 :** organic materials (as sugar and starch) formed by plants and used in their growth and activities **4 :** solid food as distinguished from drink

food bank *n* **:** an organization that collects donated food and gives it to needy people

food chain *n* **:** a sequence of organisms in which each depends on the next and usually lower member as a source of food

food·stuff *n* **:** a substance that is used as food

food web *n* **:** the whole group of interacting food chains in a community

[1]fool *n* **1 :** a person without good sense or judgment **2 :** JESTER

[2]fool *vb* **fooled; fool·ing** **1 :** to speak or act in a playful way or in fun : JOKE **2 :** [2]TRICK **3 :** to spend time in an aimless way **4 :** to play with or handle something carelessly

fool·har·dy *adj* **:** foolishly adventurous

fool·ish *adj* **:** showing or resulting from lack of good sense — **fool·ish·ly** *adv* — **fool·ish·ness** *n*

fool·proof *adj* **:** done, made, or planned so well that nothing can go wrong

[1]foot *n, pl* **feet** **1 :** the end part of the leg of an animal or person : the part of an animal on which it stands or moves **2 :** a unit of length equal to twelve inches (about .3 meter) **3 :** the lowest or end part of something — **on foot :** by walking

[2]foot *vb* **foot·ed; foot·ing** **1 :** [1]WALK 1 **2 :** [1]PAY 2

foot·ball *n* **1 :** a game played with an oval ball on a large field by two teams of eleven players that move the ball by kicking, passing, or running with it **2 :** the ball used in football

foot·ed *adj* **1 :** having a foot or feet **2 :** having such or so many feet

foot·fall *n* **:** the sound of a footstep

foot·hill *n* **:** a hill at the bottom of higher hills

foot·hold *n* **:** a place where the foot may be put (as for climbing)

foot·ing *n* **1 :** a firm position or placing of the feet **2 :** FOOTHOLD **3 :** position as compared to others **4 :** social relationship

foot·lights *n pl* **:** a row of lights set across the front of a stage floor

foot·man *n, pl* **foot·men** **:** a male servant who performs various duties (as letting visitors in and serving food)

foot·note *n* **:** a note at the bottom of a page

foot·path *n* **:** a path for walkers

foot·print *n* **:** a track left by a foot

foot·step *n* **1 :** a step of the foot **2 :** the distance covered by a step **3 :** FOOTPRINT **4 :** the sound of a foot taking a step **5 :** way of life or action

foot·stool *n* **:** a low stool for the feet

foot·work *n* **:** the skill with which the feet are moved

[1]for *prep* **1 :** by way of getting ready **2 :** toward the goal or purpose of **3 :** in order to reach **4 :** as being **5 :** because of **6** — used to show who or what is to receive something **7 :** in order to help, serve, or defend **8 :** directed at : AGAINST **9 :** in exchange as equal to **10 :** with regard to : CONCERNING **11 :** taking into account **12 :** through the period of **13 :** to a distance of **14 :** suitable to **15 :** in favor of **16 :** in place of or on behalf of **17 :** [2]AFTER 5

[2]**for** *conj* : BECAUSE

[1]**for·age** *n* : food (as grass) for browsing or grazing animals

[2]**forage** *vb* **for·aged; for·ag·ing** **1 :** to nibble or eat grass or other plants **2 :** [1]SEARCH 1

for·bear *vb* **for·bore; for·borne; for·bear·ing** **1 :** to hold back **2 :** to be patient when annoyed or troubled

for·bid *vb* **for·bade; for·bid·den; for·bid·ding :** to order not to do something

for·bid·ding *adj* : tending to frighten or discourage

[1]**force** *n* **1 :** power that has an effect on something **2 :** the state of existing and being enforced **3 :** a group of people available for a particular purpose **4 :** power or violence used on a person or thing **5 :** an influence (as a push or pull) that tends to produce a change in the speed or direction of motion of something

[2]**force** *vb* **forced; forc·ing** **1 :** to make someone or something do something **2 :** to get, make, or move by using physical power **3 :** to break open using physical power **4 :** to speed up the development of

force·ful *adj* : having much strength : VIGOROUS — **force·ful·ly** *adv* — **force·ful·ness** *n*

for·ceps *n, pl* **forceps** : an instrument for grasping, holding, or pulling on things especially in delicate operations (as by a jeweler or surgeon)

forc·ible *adj* **1 :** got, made, or done by physical power **2 :** showing a lot of strength or energy — **forc·ibly** *adv*

[1]**ford** *n* : a shallow place in a body of water that may be crossed by wading

[2]**ford** *vb* **ford·ed; ford·ing :** to cross by wading

[1]**fore** *adv* : in or toward the front

[2]**fore** *adj* : being or coming before in time, place, or order

[3]**fore** *n* : [1]FRONT 1

[4]**fore** *interj* — used by a golfer to warn someone within range of a hit ball

fore- *prefix* **1 :** earlier : beforehand **2 :** at the front : in front **3 :** front part of something specified

fore–and–aft *adj* : being in line with the length of a ship

fore·arm *n* : the part of the arm between the elbow and the wrist

fore·bear *n* : ANCESTOR 1

fore·bod·ing *n* : a feeling that something bad is going to happen

[1]**fore·cast** *vb* **forecast; fore·cast·ing** : to predict often after thought and study of available evidence — **fore·cast·er** *n*

[2]**forecast** *n* : a prediction of something in the future

fore·cas·tle *n* **1 :** the forward part of the upper deck of a ship **2 :** quarters for the crew in the forward part of a ship

fore·fa·ther *n* : ANCESTOR 1

fore·fin·ger *n* : INDEX FINGER

fore·foot *n, pl* **fore·feet** : one of the front feet of an animal with four feet

fore·front *n* : the most important part or position

forego *variant of* FORGO

fore·go·ing *adj* : going before : already mentioned

fore·gone conclusion *n* : something felt to be sure to happen

fore·ground *n* : the part of a picture or scene that seems to be nearest to and in front of the person looking at it

fore·hand *n* : a stroke in sports played with a racket made with the palm of the hand turned in the direction in which the hand is moving

fore·head *n* : the part of the face above the eyes

for·eign *adj* **1 :** located outside of a place or country and especially outside of a person's own country **2 :** belonging to a place or country other than the one under consideration **3 :** relating to or having to do with other nations **4 :** not normally belonging or wanted where found

for·eign·er *n* : a person who is from a foreign country

fore·leg *n* : a front leg of an animal

fore·limb *n* : an arm, fin, wing, or leg that is located toward the front of the body

fore·man *n, pl* **fore·men** : the leader of a group of workers

fore·mast *n* : the mast nearest the bow of the ship

[1]**fore·most** *adj* : first in time, place, or order : most important

[2]**foremost** *adv* : in the first place

fore·noon *n* : MORNING

fore·run·ner *n* : someone or something that comes before especially as a sign of the coming of another

fore·see *vb* **fore·saw; fore·seen; fore·see·ing** : to see or know about beforehand

fore·shad·ow *vb* **fore·shad·owed; fore·shad·ow·ing :** to give a hint of beforehand

fore·sight *n* **1 :** the ability to see what will or might happen in the future **2 :** care for the future : PRUDENCE

for·est *n* : a growth of trees and underbrush covering a large area — **for·est·ed** *adj*

fore·stall *vb* **fore·stalled; fore·stall·ing** : to keep out, interfere with, or prevent by steps taken in advance

forest ranger *n* : a person in charge of managing and protecting part of a public forest

for·est·ry *n* : the science and practice of caring for forests — **for·est·er** *n*

fore·tell *vb* **fore·told; fore·tell·ing** : to tell of a thing before it happens

fore·thought *n* : careful thinking or planning for the future

for·ev·er *adv* **1** : for a limitless time **2** : at all times

fore·warn *vb* **fore·warned; fore·warn·ing** : to warn in advance

forewent *past of* FORGO

fore·word *n* : PREFACE

[1]**for·feit** *vb* **for·feit·ed; for·feit·ing** : to lose or lose the right to as punishment for a fault, error, or crime

[2]**forfeit** *n* : something lost as punishment for a fault, error, or crime

[1]**forge** *vb* **forged; forg·ing** **1** : to shape and work metal by heating and hammering **2** : to bring into existence **3** : to produce something that is not genuine : COUNTERFEIT — **forg·er** *n*

[2]**forge** *n* : a furnace or a place with a furnace where metal is shaped by heating and hammering

[3]**forge** *vb* **forged; forg·ing** : to move forward slowly but steadily

forg·ery *n, pl* **forg·er·ies** **1** : the crime of falsely making or changing a written paper or signing someone else's name **2** : something that is falsely made or copied

for·get *vb* **for·got; for·got·ten** *or* **for·got; for·get·ting** **1** : to be unable to think of or remember **2** : to fail by accident to do (something) : OVERLOOK

for·get·ful *adj* : forgetting easily — **for·get·ful·ness** *n*

for·get–me–not *n* : a small low plant with bright blue flowers

for·give *vb* **for·gave; for·giv·en; for·giv·ing** : to stop feeling angry at or hurt by

for·give·ness *n* : the act of ending anger at

for·giv·ing *adj* : willing or ready to excuse an error or offense

for·go *also* **fore·go** *vb* **for·went** *also* **fore·went; for·gone** *also* **fore·gone; for·go·ing** *also* **fore·go·ing** : to give up the use or enjoyment of

[1]**fork** *n* **1** : an implement having a handle and two or more prongs for taking up (as in eating), pitching, or digging **2** : a forked part or tool **3** : the place where something divides or branches **4** : one of the parts into which something divides or branches

[2]**fork** *vb* **forked; fork·ing** **1** : to divide into branches **2** : to pitch or lift with a fork

forked *adj* : having one end divided into two or more branches

for·lorn *adj* : sad from being left alone — **for·lorn·ly** *adv*

[1]**form** *n* **1** : [1]SORT 1, KIND **2** : the shape and structure of something **3** : a printed sheet with blank spaces for information **4** : a way of doing something **5** : one of the different pronunciations, spellings, or inflections a word may have **6** : a mold in which concrete is placed to set

[2]**form** *vb* **formed; form·ing** **1** : to give form or shape to **2** : DEVELOP 5 **3** : to come or bring together in making **4** : to take shape : come into being

[1]**for·mal** *adj* **1** : following established form, custom, or rule **2** : acquired by attending classes in a school **3** : requiring proper clothing and manners **4** : suitable for a proper occasion — **for·mal·ly** *adv*

[2]**formal** *n* : a social gathering that requires proper clothing and behavior

for·mal·i·ty *n, pl* **for·mal·i·ties** **1** : the quality or state of being formal **2** : an established way of doing something

[1]**for·mat** *n* : the general organization or arrangement of something

[2]**format** *vb* **for·mat·ted; for·mat·ting** **1** : to organize or arrange in a certain way **2** : to prepare for storing computer data

for·ma·tion *n* **1** : a creation or development of something **2** : something that is formed or created **3** : an arrangement of something

for·mer *adj* : coming before in time

for·mer·ly *adv* : at an earlier time

for·mi·da·ble *adj* **1** : causing fear or awe **2** : offering serious difficulties **3** : large or impressive in size or extent — **for·mi·da·bly** *adv*

form·less *adj* : having no regular form or shape

for·mu·la *n* **1** : a direction giving amounts of the substances for the preparation of something (as a medicine) **2** : an established form or method **3** : a milk mixture or substitute for feeding a baby **4** : a general fact or rule expressed in symbols **5** : an expression in symbols giving the makeup of a substance

for·mu·late *vb* **for·mu·lat·ed; for·mu·lat·ing** : to create, invent, or produce by careful thought and effort

for·sake *vb* **for·sook; for·sak·en; for·sak·ing** : to give up or leave entirely

for·syth·ia *n* : a bush often grown for its bright yellow flowers that appear in early spring

fort *n* : a strong or fortified place

forte *n* : something in which a person shows special ability

forth *adv* **1 :** onward in time, place, or order **2 :** out into view
forth·com·ing *adj* **1 :** being about to appear **2 :** ready or available when needed
forth·right *adj* **:** going straight to the point clearly and firmly — **forth·right·ly** *adv*
forth·with *adv* **:** without delay **:** IMMEDIATELY
¹for·ti·eth *adj* **:** coming right after 39th
²fortieth *n* **:** number 40 in a series
for·ti·fi·ca·tion *n* **1 :** the act of making stronger or enriching **2 :** something built to strengthen or protect
for·ti·fy *vb* **for·ti·fied; for·ti·fy·ing** **1 :** to make strong **2 :** to add material to (something) to stengthen or improve it
for·ti·tude *n* **:** strength of mind that lets a person meet danger, pain, or hardship with courage
fort·night *n* **:** two weeks
for·tress *n* **:** a place that is protected against attack
for·tu·nate *adj* **1 :** bringing a good result **2 :** having good luck **:** LUCKY — **for·tu·nate·ly** *adv*
for·tune *n* **1 :** a large sum of money **2 :** what happens to a person **:** good or bad luck **3 :** what is to happen to one in the future **4 :** WEALTH
fortune cookie *n* **:** a thin cookie folded to contain a slip of paper on which is printed a fortune, proverb, or humorous statement
for·tune–tell·er *n* **:** a person who claims to foretell future events
¹for·ty *adj* **:** being four times ten
²forty *n* **:** four times ten **:** 40
for·ty–nin·er *n* **:** a person in the California gold rush of 1849
fo·rum *n* **1 :** the marketplace or public place of an ancient Roman city serving as the center for public business **2 :** a place or opportunity for discussion
¹for·ward *adj* **1 :** near, at, or belonging to the front part **2 :** moving, tending, or leading to a position in front **3 :** lacking proper modesty or reserve
²forward *or* **for·wards** *adv* **:** to or toward what is in front
³forward *vb* **for·ward·ed; for·ward·ing** **1 :** to send on or ahead **2 :** to help onward **:** ADVANCE
⁴forward *n* **:** a player at or near the front of his or her team or near the opponent's goal
fos·sil *n* **:** a trace or print or the remains of a plant or animal of a past age preserved in earth or rock
¹fos·ter *adj* **:** giving, receiving, or offering parental care even though not related by blood or legal ties
²foster *vb* **fos·tered; fos·ter·ing** **1 :** to give parental care to **2 :** to help the growth and development of
fought *past and past participle of* FIGHT
¹foul *adj* **foul·er; foul·est** **1 :** disgusting in looks, taste, or smell **2 :** full of or covered with something that pollutes **3 :** being vulgar or insulting **4 :** being wet and stormy **5 :** very unfair **6 :** very unpleasant or bad **7 :** breaking a rule in a game or sport **8 :** being outside the foul lines
²foul *n* **1 :** a ball in baseball that is batted outside the foul lines **2 :** an act of breaking the rules in a game or sport
³foul *vb* **fouled; foul·ing** **1 :** to make or become foul or filthy **2 :** to make a foul in a game
foul line *n* **:** either of two straight lines running from the rear corner of home plate through first and third base to the boundary of a baseball field
¹found *past and past participle of* FIND
²found *vb* **found·ed; found·ing** **:** to begin or create **:** ESTABLISH
foun·da·tion *n* **1 :** the support upon which something rests **2 :** the act of beginning or creating
¹found·er *n* **:** a person who creates or establishes something
²foun·der *vb* **foun·dered; foun·der·ing** **:** ¹SINK 1
found·ry *n, pl* **foundries** **:** a building or factory where metal goods are made
fount *n* **:** SOURCE 1
foun·tain *n* **1 :** an artificial stream or spray of water (as for drinking or ornament) or the device from which it comes **2 :** SOURCE 1 **3 :** a spring of water coming from the earth
fountain pen *n* **:** a pen with ink inside that is fed as needed to the writing point
¹four *adj* **:** being one more than three
²four *n* **1 :** one more than three **:** two times two **:** 4 **2 :** the fourth in a set or series
4x4 *also* **four–by–four** *n* **:** a four-wheel automotive vehicle (as a pickup) equipped with four-wheel drive
four·fold *adj* **:** being four times as great or as many
4–H *adj* **:** of or relating to a program in the U.S. that teaches farming skills and good citizenship to young people — **4–H'er** *also* **4–H·er** *n*
four·score *adj* **:** ²EIGHTY
four·some *n* **:** a group of four persons or things
¹four·teen *adj* **:** being one more than 13
²fourteen *n* **:** one more than 13 **:** two times seven **:** 14
¹four·teenth *adj* **:** coming right after 13th
²fourteenth *n* **:** number 14 in a series
¹fourth *adj* **:** coming right after third

²fourth *n* **1 :** number four in a series **2 :** one of four equal parts

Fourth of July *n* **:** INDEPENDENCE DAY

four–wheel drive *n* **:** an automotive drive mechanism that acts on all four wheels of the vehicle

fowl *n, pl* **fowl** *or* **fowls** **1 :** BIRD **2 :** a common domestic rooster or hen **3 :** the meat of a domestic fowl used as food

fox *n* **1 :** a wild animal closely related to the wolf that has a sharp snout, pointed ears, and a long bushy tail **2** *cap* **:** a member of an American Indian people formerly living in what is now Wisconsin

foxy *adj* **fox·i·er; fox·i·est :** very clever

foy·er *n* **1 :** a lobby especially in a theater **2 :** an entrance hall

fr. *abbr* from

Fr. *abbr* father

fra·cas *n* **:** a noisy quarrel **:** BRAWL

frack·ing *n* **:** the injection of fluid into shale beds at high pressure in order to free up petroleum resources (such as oil or natural gas) — **frack** *vb*

frac·tion *n* **1 :** a number (as 1/2, 2/3, 17/100) that indicates one or more equal parts of a whole or group and that may be considered as indicating also division of the number above the line by the number below the line **2 :** a part of a whole **:** FRAGMENT

frac·tion·al *adj* **1 :** of, relating to, or being a fraction **2 :** fairly small

¹frac·ture *n* **:** the result of breaking **:** damage or an injury caused by breaking

²fracture *vb* **frac·tured; frac·tur·ing :** ¹BREAK 2

frag·ile *adj* **:** easily broken or hurt **:** DELICATE

frag·ment *n* **:** a broken or incomplete part

fra·grance *n* **:** a sweet or pleasant smell

fra·grant *adj* **:** sweet or pleasant in smell — **fra·grant·ly** *adv*

frail *adj* **:** very delicate or weak

frail·ty *n, pl* **frailties** **1 :** the quality or state of being weak **2 :** a weakness of character

¹frame *vb* **framed; fram·ing** **1 :** to enclose in or as if in a frame **2 :** to express in words **3 :** to make appear guilty

²frame *n* **1 :** the structure of an animal and especially a human body **:** PHYSIQUE **2 :** an arrangement of parts that give form or support to something **3 :** an open case or structure for holding or enclosing something

³frame *adj* **:** having a wooden frame

frame of mind *n* **:** a particular state or mood

frame·work *n* **:** a basic supporting part or structure

franc *n* **:** any of various coins or bills used or once used in countries where French is widely spoken

Fran·co- *prefix* **1 :** French and **2 :** French

frank *adj* **:** free in or characterized by freedom in expressing feelings and opinions — **frank·ly** *adv* — **frank·ness** *n*

frank·furt·er *or* **frank·furt** *n* **:** a cooked sausage **:** HOT DOG

frank·in·cense *n* **:** a fragrant plant gum that is burned for its sweet smell

fran·tic *adj* **:** wildly excited

fran·ti·cal·ly *adv* **:** in a frantic way

fra·ter·nal *adj* **1 :** having to do with brothers **2 :** made up of members banded together like brothers

fraternal twin *n* **:** either of a pair of twins that are produced from different fertilized eggs and may not have the same sex or appearance

fra·ter·ni·ty *n, pl* **fra·ter·ni·ties** **:** a club of boys or men (as in a college)

fraud *n* **1 :** TRICKERY, DECEIT **2 :** an act of deceiving **:** TRICK **3 :** a person who pretends to be what he or she is not

fraud·u·lent *adj* **:** based on or done by deceit — **fraud·u·lent·ly** *adv*

fraught *adj* **:** full of some quality

¹fray *n* **:** ²FIGHT 1, BRAWL

²fray *vb* **frayed; fray·ing :** to wear into shreds

fraz·zle *n* **:** a tired or nervous condition

¹freak *n* **:** a strange, abnormal, or unusual person, thing, or event — **freak·ish** *adj* — **freaky** *adj*

²freak *adj* **:** not likely

¹freck·le *n* **:** a small brownish spot on the skin

²freckle *vb* **freck·led; freck·ling :** to mark or become marked with freckles or spots

¹free *adj* **fre·er; fre·est** **1 :** given without charge **2 :** having liberty **:** not being a slave or prisoner **3 :** not controlled by a harsh ruler or harsh laws **4 :** not physically held by something **5 :** not having or suffering from something unpleasant, unwanted, or painful **6 :** not held back by fear or uncertainty **:** OPEN **7 :** not blocked **:** CLEAR **8 :** not required to be doing something **9 :** not used or occupied **10 :** not combined — **free·ly** *adv*

²free *vb* **freed; free·ing :** to let go or set free **:** RELEASE

³free *adv* **1 :** in a free manner **:** FREELY **2 :** without charge

free·bie *or* **free·bee** *n* **:** something (as a theater ticket) given without charge

freed·man *n, pl* **freed·men** **:** a person freed from slavery

free·dom *n* **1 :** the condition of having liberty **2 :** ability to move or act as desired **3 :** release from something unpleasant **4 :** the quality of being very frank **:** CANDOR **5 :** a political right

DICTIONARY

free·hand *adj or adv* : done without mechanical aids
free·man *n, pl* **free·men** : a free person : a person who is not a slave
free·stand·ing *adj* : standing alone free of attachment or support
free·way *n* : an expressway that can be used without paying tolls
free will *n* : a person's own choice or decision
[1]**freeze** *vb* **froze; fro·zen; freez·ing** **1** : to harden into or be hardened into a solid (as ice) by loss of heat **2** : to be uncomfortably cold **3** : to damage by cold **4** : to clog or become clogged by ice **5** : to become completely still
[2]**freeze** *n* **1** : a period of freezing weather : cold weather **2** : the state of being frozen
freez·er *n* : a compartment or room used to freeze food or keep it frozen
freezing point *n* : the temperature at which a liquid becomes solid
[1]**freight** *n* **1** : goods or cargo carried by a ship, train, truck, or airplane **2** : the carrying (as by truck) of goods from one place to another **3** : the amount paid (as to a shipping company) for carrying goods **4** : a train that carries freight
[2]**freight** *vb* **frieght·ed; freight·ing** : to send by train, truck, airplane, or ship
freight·er *n* : a ship or airplane used to carry freight
[1]**French** *adj* : of or relating to France, its people, or the French language
[2]**French** *n* **1 French** *pl* : the people of France **2** : the language of the French people
french fry *n, often cap 1st F* : a strip of potato fried in deep fat
French horn *n* : a circular brass musical instrument with a large opening at one end and a mouthpiece shaped like a small funnel
fren·zied *adj* : very excited and upset
fren·zy *n, pl* **frenzies** : great and often wild or disorderly activity
fre·quen·cy *n, pl* **fre·quen·cies** **1** : frequent repetition **2** : rate of repetition
[1]**fre·quent** *vb* **fre·quent·ed; fre·quent·ing** : to visit often
[2]**fre·quent** *adj* : happening often — **fre·quent·ly** *adv*
fresh *adj* **fresh·er; fresh·est** **1** : not salt **2** : PURE 1, BRISK **3** : not frozen, canned, or pickled **4** : not stale, sour, or spoiled **5** : not dirty or rumpled **6** : [1]NEW 4 **7** : newly made or received **8** : rude and disrespectful — **fresh·ly** *adv* — **fresh·ness** *n*
fresh·en *vb* **fresh·ened; fresh·en·ing** : to make or become fresh
fresh·man *n, pl* **fresh·men** : a first year student in high school or college
fresh·wa·ter *adj* : relating to or living in fresh water
[1]**fret** *vb* **fret·ted; fret·ting** : [1]WORRY 3
[2]**fret** *n* : an irritated or worried state
fret·ful *adj* : irritated and worried — **fret·ful·ly** *adv*
Fri. *abbr* Friday
fri·ar *n* : a member of a Roman Catholic religious order for men
fric·tion *n* **1** : the rubbing of one thing against another **2** : resistance to motion between bodies in contact **3** : disagreement among persons or groups
Fri·day *n* : the sixth day of the week
[1]**friend** *n* **1** : a person who has a strong liking for and trust in another person **2** : a person who is not an enemy **3** : a person who helps or supports something — **friend·less** *adj*
[2]**friend** *vb* **friend·ed; friend·ing** : to include (someone) in a list of designated friends on a person's social networking site
friend·ly *adj* **friend·li·er; friend·li·est** **1** : having or showing the kindness and warmth of a friend **2** : being other than an enemy **3** : easy or suitable for — **friend·li·ness** *n*
friend·ship *n* **1** : the state of being friends **2** : a warm and kind feeling or attitude
frieze *n* : a band or stripe (as around a building) used as a decoration
frig·ate *n* **1** : a square-rigged warship **2** : a modern warship that is smaller than a destroyer
fright *n* **1** : sudden terror : great fear **2** : something that frightens or is ugly or shocking
fright·en *vb* **fright·ened; fright·en·ing** : to make afraid : TERRIFY — **fright·en·ing·ly** *adv*
fright·ful *adj* **1** : causing fear or alarm **2** : SHOCKING 1, OUTRAGEOUS — **fright·ful·ly** *adv*
frig·id *adj* **1** : freezing cold **2** : not friendly
frill *n* **1** : [2]RUFFLE **2** : something added mostly for show
frilly *adj* **frill·i·er; frill·i·est** : having ruffles
[1]**fringe** *n* **1** : a border or trimming made by or made to look like the loose ends of the cloth **2** : a narrow area along the edge
[2]**fringe** *vb* **fringed; fring·ing** **1** : to decorate with a fringe **2** : to go along or around
frisk *vb* **frisked; frisk·ing** **1** : to move around in a lively or playful way **2** : to search a person quickly for something that may be hidden
frisky *adj* **frisk·i·er; frisk·i·est** : PLAYFUL 1, LIVELY
[1]**frit·ter** *n* : a small amount of fried batter often containing fruit or meat
[2]**fritter** *vb* **frit·tered; frit·ter·ing** : to waste on unimportant things

fri·vol·i·ty *n, pl* **fri·vol·i·ties** : a lack of seriousness

friv·o·lous *adj* **1** : of little importance : TRIVIAL **2** : lacking in seriousness

frizzy *adj* **frizz·i·er; frizz·i·est** : very curly

fro *adv* : in a direction away

frock *n* : a woman's or girl's dress

frog *n* **1** : a tailless animal that is an amphibian with smooth moist skin and webbed feet that spends more of its time in water than the related toad **2** : an ornamental fastening for a garment

[1]**frol·ic** *vb* **frol·icked; frol·ick·ing** : to play about happily : ROMP

[2]**frolic** *n* : [1]FUN 1

frol·ic·some *adj* : very lively and playful

from *prep* **1** — used to show a starting point **2** — used to show a point of separation **3** — used to show a material, source, or cause

frond *n* : a large leaf (as of a palm or fern) or leaflike structure (as of a seaweed) with many divisions

[1]**front** *n* **1** : the forward part or surface **2** : a region in which active warfare is taking place **3** : the boundary between bodies of air at different temperatures — **in front of** : directly before or ahead of

[2]**front** *vb* **front·ed; front·ing** : [2]FACE 1

[3]**front** *adj* : situated at the front

fron·tal *adj* : of or directed at a front

[1]**fron·tier** *n* **1** : a border between two countries **2** : the edge of the settled part of a country

[2]**frontier** *adj* : of, living in, or situated in the frontier

fron·tiers·man *n, pl* **fron·tiers·men** : a person living on the frontier

[1]**frost** *n* **1** : a covering of tiny ice crystals on a cold surface formed from the water vapor in the air **2** : temperature cold enough to cause freezing

[2]**frost** *vb* **frost·ed; frost·ing** **1** : to cover with frosting **2** : to cover or become covered with frost

frost·bite *n* : slight freezing of a part of the body (as the feet or hands) or the damage to body tissues caused by such freezing

frost·ing *n* **1** : ICING **2** : a dull finish on glass

frosty *adj* **frost·i·er; frost·i·est** **1** : covered with frost **2** : cold enough to produce frost

[1]**froth** *n* : bubbles formed in or on liquids

[2]**froth** *vb* **frothed; froth·ing** : to produce or form bubbles in or on a liquid

frothy *adj* **froth·i·er; froth·i·est** : full of or made up of small bubbles

[1]**frown** *vb* **frowned; frown·ing** **1** : to have a serious facial expression (as in anger or thought) **2** : to look with disapproval

[2]**frown** *n* : a serious facial expression that shows anger, unhappiness, or deep thought

froze *past of* FREEZE

frozen *past participle of* FREEZE

fru·gal *adj* **1** : careful in spending or using supplies **2** : simple and without unnecessary things — **fru·gal·ly** *adv*

[1]**fruit** *n* **1** : a pulpy or juicy plant part (as rhubarb, a strawberry, or an orange) that is often eaten as a dessert and is distinguished from a vegetable **2** : a product of fertilization in a seed plant that consists of the ripened ovary of a flower with its included seeds **3** : [2]RESULT 1, PRODUCT — **fruit·ed** *adj*

[2]**fruit** *vb* **fruit·ed; fruit·ing** : to bear or cause to bear fruit

fruit·cake *n* : a rich cake containing nuts, dried or candied fruits, and spices

fruit·ful *adj* **1** : very productive **2** : bringing results — **fruit·ful·ly** *adv*

fruit·less *adj* **1** : not bearing fruit **2** : UNSUCCESSFUL — **fruit·less·ly** *adv*

fruity *adj* **fruit·i·er; fruit·i·est** : relating to or suggesting fruit

frus·trate *vb* **frus·trat·ed; frus·trat·ing** **1** : to cause to feel angry or discouraged **2** : to prevent from succeeding **3** : [1]DEFEAT 2

frus·trat·ing *adj* : causing feelings of disappointment and defeat

frus·tra·tion *n* : DISAPPOINTMENT 1, DEFEAT

[1]**fry** *vb* **fried; fry·ing** : to cook in fat

[2]**fry** *n, pl* **fries** : FRENCH FRY

[3]**fry** *n, pl* **fry** : a recently hatched or very young fish — usually used in pl.

ft. *abbr* **1** feet **2** foot **3** fort

fudge *n* : a soft creamy candy

[1]**fu·el** *n* : a substance (as oil or gasoline) that can be burned to produce heat or power

[2]**fuel** *vb* **fu·eled** *or Can and Brit* **fu·elled; fu·el·ing** *or Can and Brit* **fu·el·ling** : to supply with or take on fuel

[1]**fu·gi·tive** *adj* : running away or trying to escape

[2]**fugitive** *n* : a person who is running away

[1]**-ful** *adj suffix* **1** : full of **2** : characterized by **3** : having the qualities of **4** : tending or given to

[2]**-ful** *n suffix* : number or quantity that fills or would fill

ful·crum *n, pl* **fulcrums** *or* **ful·cra** : the support on which a lever turns in lifting something

ful·fill *or* **ful·fil** *vb* **ful·filled; ful·fill·ing** **1** : to make real **2** : SATISFY 4 — **ful·fill·ment** *n*

[1]**full** *adj* **1** : containing as much or as many as possible or normal **2** : [1]COMPLETE 1 **3** : not limited in any way **4** : plump and rounded in outline **5** : having much material — **full·ness** *n*

[2]**full** *adv* **1** : [2]VERY 1 **2** : COMPLETELY

³full *n* **1 :** the highest state, extent, or degree **2 :** the complete amount

full·back *n* **1 :** a football player who runs with the ball and blocks **2 :** a player in games like soccer and field hockey who is usually positioned near the goal

full–grown *adj* **:** having reached full growth or development

full moon *n* **:** the moon with its whole disk lighted

full–time *adj* **:** working or involving the full number of hours considered normal or standard

ful·ly *adv* **1 :** COMPLETELY **2 :** at least

¹fum·ble *vb* **fum·bled; fum·bling 1 :** to feel about for or handle something in a clumsy way **2 :** to lose hold of the ball in football

²fumble *n* **:** an act of losing hold of the ball in football

¹fume *n* **:** a disagreeable smoke, vapor, or gas — usually used in pl.

²fume *vb* **fumed; fum·ing 1 :** to give off a disagreeable smoke, vapor, or gas **2 :** to be angry **3 :** to say something in an angry way

¹fun *n* **1 :** someone or something that provides amusement or enjoyment **2 :** a good time **:** AMUSEMENT **3 :** words or actions to make someone or something an object of ridicule

²fun *adj* **1 :** providing fun **2 :** full of fun

¹func·tion *n* **1 :** the action for which a person or thing is designed or used **:** PURPOSE **2 :** a large important ceremony or social affair

²function *vb* **func·tioned; func·tion·ing :** to serve a certain purpose **:** WORK

function key *n* **:** any of a set of keys on a computer keyboard with special functions

fund *n* **1 :** a sum of money for a special purpose **2 funds** *pl* **:** available money **3 :** ¹STOCK 1, SUPPLY

¹fun·da·men·tal *adj* **:** being or forming a foundation **:** BASIC, ESSENTIAL — **fun·da·men·tal·ly** *adv*

²fundamental *n* **:** a basic part

fu·ner·al *n* **:** the ceremonies held for a dead person (as before burial)

fun·gal *or* **fun·gous** *adj* **:** of, relating to, or caused by a fungus

fun·gi·cide *n* **:** a substance used to kill fungi — **fun·gi·cid·al** *adj*

fun·gus *n, pl* **fun·gi** *also* **fun·gus·es :** any member of the kingdom of living things (as mushrooms, molds, and rusts) that have no chlorophyll, must live in or on plants, animals, or decaying material, and were formerly considered plants

funk *n* **:** a sad or worried state

fun·nel *n* **1 :** a utensil usually shaped like a hollow cone with a tube extending from the point and used to catch and direct a downward flow **2 :** a large pipe for the escape of smoke or for ventilation (as on a ship)

fun·nies *n pl* **:** comic strips or a section of a newspaper containing comic strips

¹fun·ny *adj* **fun·ni·er; fun·ni·est 1 :** causing laughter **:** full of humor **2 :** STRANGE 2

²funny *adv* **:** in an odd or peculiar way

fur *n* **1 :** the hairy coat of a mammal especially when fine, soft, and thick **2 :** a piece of the pelt of an animal **3 :** an article of clothing made with fur — **furred** *adj*

fu·ri·ous *adj* **1 :** very angry **2 :** very active or fast **3 :** very powerful or violent — **fu·ri·ous·ly** *adv*

furl *vb* **furled; furl·ing :** to wrap or roll close to or around something

fur·long *n* **:** a unit of length equal to 220 yards (about 201 meters)

fur·lough *n* **:** a leave of absence from duty

fur·nace *n* **:** an enclosed structure in which heat is produced (as for heating a house or melting metals)

fur·nish *vb* **fur·nished; fur·nish·ing 1 :** to provide with furniture **2 :** to provide with what is needed **3 :** to supply to someone or something

fur·nish·ings *n pl* **:** articles of furniture for a room or building

fur·ni·ture *n* **:** movable articles used to furnish a room

¹fur·row *n* **1 :** a trench made by or as if by a plow **2 :** a narrow groove **:** WRINKLE

²furrow *vb* **fur·rowed; fur·row·ing :** to make wrinkles or grooves in

fur·ry *adj* **fur·ri·er; fur·ri·est 1 :** covered with fur **2 :** like fur

¹fur·ther *adv* **1 :** ¹FARTHER 1 **2 :** ²BESIDES, ALSO **3 :** to a greater degree or extent

²further *vb* **fur·thered; fur·ther·ing :** to help forward **:** PROMOTE

³further *adj* **1 :** ²FARTHER **2 :** going or extending beyond **:** ADDITIONAL

fur·ther·more *adv* **:** MOREOVER

fur·thest *adv or adj* **:** FARTHEST

fur·tive *adj* **:** done in a sneaky or sly manner — **fur·tive·ly** *adv*

fu·ry *n, pl* **furies 1 :** violent anger **:** RAGE **2 :** wild and dangerous force

¹fuse *vb* **fused; fus·ing 1 :** to change into a liquid or to a plastic state by heat **2 :** to unite by or as if by melting together

²fuse *n* **:** a device having a metal wire or strip that melts and interrupts an electrical circuit when the current becomes too strong

³fuse *n* **1 :** a cord that is set afire to ignite an explosive by carrying fire to it **2 :** a device for setting off a bomb or torpedo

fu·se·lage *n* **:** the part of an airplane that holds the crew, passengers, and cargo

fu·sion *n* **1 :** an act of fusing or melting together **2 :** union by or as if by melting **3 :** union of atomic nuclei to form heavier nuclei resulting in the release of enormous quantities of energy

[1]fuss *n* **1 :** unnecessary activity or excitement often over something unimportant **2 :** [2]PROTEST 1 **3 :** a great show of interest

[2]fuss *vb* **fussed; fuss·ing :** to get excited or upset especially over something unimportant

fussy *adj* **fuss·i·er; fuss·i·est 1 :** inclined to complain or whine **2 :** hard to please **3 :** overly decorated and complicated

fu·tile *adj* **:** having no result or effect — **fu·tile·ly** *adv*

fu·til·i·ty *n* **:** the quality or state of being ineffective

[1]fu·ture *adj* **:** coming after the present

[2]future *n* **1 :** the period of time that is to come **2 :** the chance of future success

fuzz *n* **:** fine light hairs or fibers

fuzzy *adj* **fuzz·i·er; fuzz·i·est 1 :** covered with or looking like short fine hairs or fibers **2 :** not clear — **fuzz·i·ness** *n*

-fy *vb suffix* **-fied; -fy·ing 1 :** make **:** form into **2 :** provide with the characteristics of

G

g *n, pl* **g's** *or* **gs** *often cap* **1 :** the seventh letter of the English alphabet **2 :** the musical note referred to by the letter G **3 :** a unit of force equal to the force of gravity on a body

g. *abbr* gram

G *abbr* good

Ga., GA *abbr* Georgia

[1]gab *vb* **gabbed; gab·bing :** to talk in a relaxed way about unimportant things **:** CHAT

[2]gab *n* **:** talk about unimportant things

gab·ar·dine *n* **:** a firm cloth with a hard smooth finish

[1]gab·ble *vb* **gab·bled; gab·bling :** to talk in a fast or foolish way or in a way that is hard to understand

[2]gabble *n* **:** talk that is fast or foolish or hard to understand

gab·by *adj* **gab·bi·er; gab·bi·est :** fond of talking a lot **:** TALKATIVE

ga·ble *n* **:** the triangular part of an outside wall of a building formed by the sides of a sloping roof — **ga·bled** *adj*

gad *vb* **gad·ded; gad·ding :** to wander or roam from place to place

gad·about *n* **:** a person who goes to many different places for enjoyment

gad·fly *n, pl* **gad·flies 1 :** a large biting fly **2 :** a person who annoys others especially with constant criticism

gad·get *n* **:** a small useful device that is often interesting, unfamiliar, or unusual

[1]gag *vb* **gagged; gag·ging 1 :** to stop from speaking or crying out by or as if by covering or blocking the mouth **2 :** to vomit or feel like vomiting **3 :** CHOKE 2

[2]gag *n* **1 :** something covering or blocking the mouth especially to prevent speaking or crying out **2 :** something said or done to make other people laugh

gage *variant of* GAUGE

gag·gle *n* **1 :** a group of animals and especially a flock of geese **2 :** a group of people

gai·ety *n, pl* **gai·eties 1 :** happy and lively activity **:** MERRYMAKING **2 :** bright spirits or manner

gai·ly *adv* **1 :** in a merry or lively way **2 :** in a bright or showy way

[1]gain *n* **1 :** something valuable or desirable that is obtained or acquired **:** PROFIT **2 :** an increase in amount, size, or degree

[2]gain *vb* **gained; gain·ing 1 :** to get or win often by effort **2 :** to get or acquire in a natural or gradual way **3 :** to increase in **4 :** to get to **:** REACH **5 :** to get an advantage **:** PROFIT

gain·ful *adj* **:** producing gain **:** making money

gait *n* **:** a way of walking or running

gal. *abbr* gallon

[1]ga·la *n* **:** a large showy celebration

[2]gala *adj* **:** being or resembling a large showy celebration

ga·lac·tic *adj* **:** of or relating to a galaxy

gal·axy *n, pl* **gal·ax·ies 1 :** MILKY WAY GALAXY **2 :** one of the very large groups of stars, gas, and dust that make up the universe

gale *n* **1 :** a strong wind **2 :** a wind of from about 32 to 63 miles per hour (about 51 to 101 kilometers per hour) **3 :** an outburst of amusement

ga·le·na *n* **:** a bluish gray mineral that is the ore from which lead is obtained

[1]gall *n* **1 :** extreme boldness or rudeness **2 :** bile especially when obtained from an animal for use in the arts or medicine

²gall *n* **:** a sore spot (as on a horse's back) caused by rubbing

³gall *vb* **galled; gall·ing 1 :** to make sore by rubbing **2 :** to annoy or make angry

⁴gall *n* **:** an abnormal swelling or growth on a twig or leaf

gal·lant *adj* **1 :** showing courage **:** very brave **2 :** CHIVALROUS 2 **3 :** very polite to women **4 :** splendid or stately **5 :** showy in dress or in the way of acting — **gal·lant·ly** *adv*

gal·lant·ry *n* **1 :** courageous behavior **:** BRAVERY **2 :** polite attention shown to women

gall·blad·der *n* **:** a small sac in which bile from the liver is stored

gal·le·on *n* **:** a large sailing ship used by the Spanish from the 1400s to the 1700s

gal·lery *n, pl* **gal·ler·ies 1 :** a long narrow room or hall **2 :** an indoor structure (as in a theater or church) built out from one or more walls **3 :** a room or building in which people look at works of art **4 :** the highest balcony of seats in a theater or the people who sit there **5 :** a passage (as in wood) made by an animal and especially an insect

gal·ley *n, pl* **galleys 1 :** a large low ship of olden times moved by oars and sails **2 :** the kitchen especially of a ship or an airplane

gal·li·vant *vb* **gal·li·vant·ed; gal·li·vant·ing :** to travel from place to place doing things for pleasure

gal·lon *n* **:** a unit of liquid capacity equal to four quarts (about 3.8 liters)

¹gal·lop *vb* **gal·loped; gal·lop·ing 1 :** to run or cause to run at a gallop **2 :** to ride on a galloping horse

²gallop *n* **1 :** the fast springing way an animal with four feet and especially a horse runs when all four of its feet leave the ground at the same time **2 :** a ride or run on a galloping horse

gal·lows *n, pl* **gallows** *or* **gal·lows·es :** a structure from which criminals are hanged

ga·lore *adj* **:** in large amounts — used after the word it modifies

ga·losh *n* **:** a high shoe worn over another shoe to keep the foot dry especially in snow or wet weather — usually used in pl.

gal·va·nize *vb* **gal·va·nized; gal·va·niz·ing 1 :** to excite about something so that action is taken **2 :** to coat with zinc for protection

¹gam·ble *vb* **gam·bled; gam·bling 1 :** to play a game in which something (as money) can be won or lost **:** BET **2 :** to take a chance — **gam·bler** *n*

²gamble *n* **:** something that could produce a good or bad result **:** RISK

gam·bol *vb* **gam·boled** *or* **gam·bolled; gam·bol·ing** *or* **gam·bol·ling :** to run or play happily **:** FROLIC

¹game *n* **1 :** a contest or sport played according to rules with the players in direct opposition to each other **2 :** the manner of playing in a game or contest **3 :** playful activity **:** something done for amusement **4 :** animals hunted for sport or for food **5 :** the meat from animals hunted for food

²game *adj* **gam·er; gam·est 1 :** willing or ready to do something **2 :** full of spirit or eagerness **3 :** relating to or being animals that are hunted

game·keep·er *n* **:** a person in charge of the breeding and protection of game animals or birds on private land

game·ly *adv* **:** with spirit and courage

game pad *n* **:** a device having buttons and a joystick that is used for controlling images in video games

gam·ing *n* **:** the practice of gambling

gam·ma ray *n* **:** a ray that is like an X-ray but of higher energy and that is given off especially by a radioactive substance

gamy *adj* **gam·i·er; gam·i·est :** having the flavor or smell of meat from wild animals especially when slightly spoiled

¹gan·der *n* **:** a male goose

²gander *n* **:** a look or glance

gang *n* **1 :** a group of people working or going about together **2 :** a group of people acting together to do something illegal **3 :** a group of friends

gan·gli·on *n, pl* **gan·glia :** a mass of nerve cells especially outside the brain or spinal cord

gan·gly *adj* **gan·gli·er; gan·gli·est :** tall, thin, and awkward

gang·plank *n* **:** a movable bridge from a ship to the shore

gan·grene *n* **:** death of body tissue when the blood supply is cut off

gang·ster *n* **:** a member of a gang of criminals

gang up *vb* **ganged up; gang·ing up :** to join together as a group especially to attack, oppose, or criticize

gang·way *n* **1 :** a passage into, through, or out of an enclosed space **2 :** GANGPLANK

gan·net *n* **:** a large bird that eats fish and spends much time far from land

gan·try *n, pl* **gantries 1 :** a structure over railroad tracks for holding signals **2 :** a movable structure for preparing a rocket for launching

gap *n* **1 :** an opening made by a break or rupture **2 :** an opening between mountains **3 :** a hole or space where something is missing

¹gape *vb* **gaped; gap·ing 1 :** to stare with the mouth open in surprise or wonder **2 :** to open or part widely

²gape *n* **:** an act or instance of opening or staring with the mouth open

ga·rage *n* **1 :** a building or part of a building where vehicles are kept when not in use **2 :** a shop where vehicles are repaired

[1]garb *n* **:** style or kind of clothing

[2]garb *vb* **garbed; garb·ing :** CLOTHE 1

gar·bage *n* **1 :** material (as waste food) that has been thrown out **2 :** something that is worthless, useless, or untrue

gar·ble *vb* **gar·bled; gar·bling :** to change or twist the meaning or sound of

[1]gar·den *n* **1 :** a piece of ground in which fruits, flowers, or vegetables are grown **2 :** a public area for the showing of plants

[2]garden *vb* **gar·dened; gar·den·ing :** to make or work in a garden

gar·den·er *n* **:** a person who works in a garden especially for pay

gar·de·nia *n* **:** a large white or yellowish flower with a fragrant smell

gar·den–va·ri·ety *adj* **:** ORDINARY, COMMONPLACE

gar·gan·tuan *adj* **:** extremely large or great **:** HUGE

[1]gar·gle *vb* **gar·gled; gar·gling :** to rinse the throat with a liquid kept in motion by air forced through it from the lungs

[2]gargle *n* **1 :** a liquid used for rinsing the throat and mouth **2 :** a sound like that of gargling

gar·goyle *n* **:** a strange or frightening human or animal figure that sticks out from the roof of a building and often serves as a waterspout

gar·ish *adj* **:** too bright or showy **:** GAUDY — **gar·ish·ly** *adv*

[1]gar·land *n* **:** a wreath or rope of material (as leaves or flowers)

[2]garland *vb* **gar·land·ed; gar·land·ing :** to form into or decorate with a garland

gar·lic *n* **:** a plant related to the onion and grown for its bulbs that have a strong smell and taste and are used to flavor foods

gar·ment *n* **:** an article of clothing

gar·ner *vb* **gar·nered; gar·ner·ing 1 :** to collect or gather **2 :** to acquire or earn

gar·net *n* **:** a deep red mineral used as a gem

[1]gar·nish *vb* **gar·nished; gar·nish·ing :** to add decorations or seasoning (as to food)

[2]garnish *n* **:** something used to add decoration or flavoring (as to food)

gar·ret *n* **:** a room or unfinished part of a house just under the roof

[1]gar·ri·son *n* **1 :** a military camp, fort, or base **2 :** the soldiers stationed at a garrison

[2]garrison *vb* **gar·ri·soned; gar·ri·son·ing 1 :** to station troops in **2 :** to send (troops) to live in and defend

gar·ru·lous *adj* **:** very talkative

gar·ter *n* **:** a band worn to hold up a stocking or sock

garter snake *n* **:** any of numerous harmless American snakes with stripes along the back

[1]gas *n, pl* **gas·es 1 :** a substance (as oxygen or hydrogen) having no fixed shape and tending to expand without limit **2 :** NATURAL GAS **3 :** a gas or a mixture of gases used to make a person unconscious (as for an operation) **4 :** a substance that poisons the air or makes breathing difficult **5 :** GASOLINE **6 :** a gaseous product of digestion or the discomfort caused by it

[2]gas *vb* **gassed; gas·sing; gas·ses 1 :** to poison with gas **2 :** to supply with gas

gas·eous *adj* **1 :** having the form of gas **2 :** of or relating to gas

[1]gash *n* **:** a long deep cut

[2]gash *vb* **gashed; gash·ing :** to make a long deep cut in

gas mask *n* **:** a mask connected to a chemical air filter and used to protect the face and lungs from harmful gases

gas·o·line *n* **:** a flammable liquid made especially from natural gas found in the earth and from petroleum and used mostly as an automobile fuel

[1]gasp *vb* **gasped; gasp·ing 1 :** to breathe in suddenly and loudly with the mouth open because of surprise, shock, or pain **2 :** to breathe with difficulty **:** PANT **3 :** to utter with quick difficult breaths

[2]gasp *n* **1 :** the act of breathing in suddenly or with difficulty **2 :** something gasped

gas station *n* **:** a place for servicing motor vehicles especially with gasoline and oil

gas·tric juice *n* **:** an acid liquid made by the stomach that helps to digest food

gate *n* **1 :** an opening in a wall or fence **2 :** a part of a barrier (as a fence) that opens and closes like a door **3 :** a door, valve, or other device for controlling the flow of water or other fluids **4 :** an area at an airport where passengers arrive and leave

gate·house *n* **:** a small building near a gate

gate·keep·er *n* **:** a person who guards a gate

gate·way *n* **1 :** an opening for a gate **2 :** a passage into or out of a place or condition

[1]gath·er *vb* **gath·ered; gath·er·ing 1 :** to pick up and collect **2 :** to choose and collect **3 :** to come together in a group or around a center of attraction **4 :** to gain little by little **5 :** to bring or call forth (as strength or courage) from within **6 :** to get an idea **:** CONCLUDE **7 :** to draw together in or as if in folds

[2]gather *n* **:** the result of gathering cloth **:** PUCKER

gath·er·ing *n* **:** an occasion when people come together as a group

gaudy *adj* **gaud·i·er; gaud·i·est :** too bright and showy

[1]**gauge** *also* **gage** *n* **1 :** a measurement (as the distance between the rails of a railroad or the size of a shotgun barrel's inner diameter) according to some standard **2 :** an instrument for measuring, testing, or registering

[2]**gauge** *also* **gage** *vb* **gauged** *also* **gaged; gaug·ing** *also* **gag·ing 1 :** to measure exactly **2 :** to make a judgment about

gaunt *adj* **gaunt·er; gaunt·est :** very thin and bony (as from illness or hunger)

gaunt·let *n* **1 :** a glove made of small metal plates and worn with a suit of armor **2 :** a glove with a wide cuff that protects the wrist and part of the arm

gauze *n* **1 :** a thin fabric that allows light to pass through it **2 :** loosely woven cotton used as a bandage

gauzy *adj* **gauz·i·er; gauz·i·est :** thin and transparent like gauze

gave *past of* GIVE

gav·el *n* **:** a mallet with which the person in charge raps to get people's attention in a meeting or courtroom

gawk *vb* **gawked; gawk·ing :** to stare stupidly

gawky *adj* **gawk·i·er; gawk·i·est :** awkward and clumsy

gay *adj* **gay·er; gay·est 1 :** HAPPY **:** MERRY **2 :** cheerful and lively **3 :** brightly colored

[1]**gaze** *vb* **gazed; gaz·ing :** to fix the eyes in a long steady look

[2]**gaze** *n* **:** a long steady look

ga·ze·bo *n, pl* **ga·ze·bos :** a small building (as in a garden or park) that is usually open on the sides

ga·zelle *n* **:** a swift graceful antelope of Africa and Asia

ga·zette *n* **1 :** NEWSPAPER **2 :** a journal giving official information

gaz·et·teer *n* **:** a geographical dictionary

ga·zil·lion *n* **:** an extremely large number — **gazillion** *adj*

GB *abbr* gigabyte

[1]**gear** *n* **1 :** EQUIPMENT **2 :** a group of parts that has a specific function in a machine **3 :** a toothed wheel **:** COGWHEEL **4 :** the position the gears of a machine are in when they are ready to work **5 :** one of the adjustments in a motor vehicle that determine the direction of travel and the relative speed between the engine and the motion of the vehicle **6 :** working order or condition

[2]**gear** *vb* **geared; gear·ing 1 :** to make ready for operation **2 :** to be or make suitable

gear·shift *n* **:** a mechanism by which gears are connected and disconnected

gecko *n, pl* **geck·os** *or* **geck·oes :** a small tropical lizard that eats insects and is usually active at night

gee *interj* — used to show surprise, enthusiasm, or disappointment

geese *pl of* GOOSE

Gei·ger counter *n* **:** an instrument for detecting the presence of cosmic rays or radioactive substances

[1]**gel** *n* **:** a thick jellylike substance

[2]**gel** *vb* **gelled; gel·ling :** to change into a thick jellylike substance

gel·a·tin *n* **1 :** a gummy or sticky protein obtained by boiling animal tissues and used especially as food **2 :** an edible jelly made with gelatin

ge·lat·i·nous *adj* **:** resembling gelatin or jelly

gem *n* **1 :** a usually valuable stone cut and polished for jewelry **2 :** something prized as being beautiful or perfect

Gem·i·ni *n* **1 :** a constellation between Taurus and Cancer usually pictured as twins sitting together **2 :** the third sign of the zodiac or a person born under this sign

gem·stone *n* **:** a stone that when cut and polished can be used in jewelry

gen. *abbr* general

gen·der *n* **:** the state of being male or female **:** SEX

gene *n* **:** a unit of DNA that is usually located on a chromosome and that controls the development of one or more traits and is the basic unit by which genetic information is passed from parent to offspring

ge·ne·al·o·gy *n, pl* **ge·ne·al·o·gies 1 :** a line of ancestors of a person or family or a history of such a line of ancestors **2 :** the study of family lines of ancestors

genera *pl of* GENUS

[1]**gen·er·al** *adj* **1 :** having to do with the whole **:** applying to more than just a small area or group **2 :** not specific or detailed **3 :** involving or including many or most people **4 :** not specialized

[2]**general** *n* **:** a military officer ranking above a colonel — **in general :** for the most part

gen·er·al·iza·tion *n* **1 :** the act of forming conclusions from a small amount of information **2 :** a general statement **:** a conclusion based on only a small number of items or instances

gen·er·al·ize *vb* **gen·er·al·ized; gen·er·al·iz·ing :** to draw or state a general conclusion from a number of different items or instances

gen·er·al·ly *adv* **1 :** for the most part **2 :** in most cases **:** USUALLY

gen·er·ate *vb* **gen·er·at·ed; gen·er·at·ing :** to cause to come into being

gen·er·a·tion *n* **1 :** those being a single step in a line originating from one ancestor **2 :** a group of individuals born and living at about the same time **3 :** the act or process of producing or creating something

gen·er·a·tor *n* **:** a machine that produces electricity

gen·er·os·i·ty *n* **1 :** willingness to give or to share **2 :** an act of unselfish giving

gen·er·ous *adj* **1 :** freely giving or sharing **2 :** providing more than enough of what is needed **:** ABUNDANT — **gen·er·ous·ly** *adv*

ge·net·ic *adj* **:** of or relating to genes or genetics

genetic code *n* **:** the arrangement of chemical groups within the genes which specify particular kinds of amino acids used to make proteins

ge·net·i·cist *n* **:** a person specializing in genetics

ge·net·ics *n* **:** the scientific study of how the characteristics of living things are controlled by genes

ge·nial *adj* **:** cheerful and pleasant — **ge·nial·ly** *adv*

ge·nie *n* **:** a magic spirit believed to take human form and serve the person who calls it

gen·i·tal *adj* **:** of or relating to reproduction or the sexual organs

ge·nius *n* **1 :** a very smart or gifted person **2 :** great natural ability **3 :** a very clever or smart quality

gent *n* **:** [1]MAN 1, FELLOW

gen·teel *adj* **1 :** relating to the upper classes **2 :** having an elegant, tasteful, or polite quality

gen·tian *n* **:** a plant with smooth leaves and usually blue flowers

[1]**gen·tile** *n, often cap* **:** a person who is not Jewish

[2]**gentile** *adj, often cap* **:** of or relating to people who are not Jewish

gen·til·i·ty *n* **1 :** high social status **2 :** a quality of elegance and politeness

gen·tle *adj* **gen·tler; gen·tlest 1 :** having or showing a kind and quiet nature **:** not harsh, stern, or violent **2 :** not hard or forceful **3 :** not strong or harsh in quality or effect **4 :** not steep or sharp — **gen·tle·ness** *n*

gen·tle·folk *n pl* **:** GENTRY

gen·tle·man *n, pl* **gen·tle·men 1 :** a man with very good manners **2 :** a man of any social position — used especially in polite speech or when speaking to a group of men **3 :** a man of high social status — **gen·tle·man·ly** *adj*

gen·tle·wom·an *n, pl* **gen·tle·wom·en 1 :** a woman of good birth and position **2 :** a woman with very good manners **:** LADY

gen·tly *adv* **:** in a gentle manner

gen·try *n* **:** people of high social status

gen·u·flect *vb* **gen·u·flect·ed; gen·u·flect·ing :** to kneel on one knee and rise again as an act of deep respect (as in a church)

gen·u·ine *adj* **1 :** actual, real, or true **:** not false or fake **2 :** sincere and honest — **gen·u·ine·ly** *adv*

ge·nus *n, pl* **gen·era :** a group of related living things (as plants or animals) that ranks below the family in scientific classification and is made up of one or more species

geo- *prefix* **1 :** earth **:** soil **2 :** geographical

geo·cach·ing *n* **:** a game in which players use a GPS device to search for items hidden at given geographical coordinates

geo·chem·is·try *n* **:** a science that deals with the chemical composition of and chemical changes in the earth's crust

ge·ode *n* **:** a stone with a hollow space inside lined with crystals or mineral matter

geog. *abbr* **1** geographic **2** geographical **3** geography

geo·graph·ic *or* **geo·graph·i·cal** *adj* **:** of or relating to geography

ge·og·ra·phy *n* **1 :** a science that deals with the location of living and nonliving things on earth and the way they affect one another **2 :** the natural features of an area

geo·log·ic *or* **geo·log·i·cal** *adj* **:** of or relating to geology

ge·ol·o·gist *n* **:** a person specializing in geology

ge·ol·o·gy *n* **1 :** a science that deals with the history of the earth and its life especially as recorded in rocks **2 :** the geologic features (as mountains or plains) of an area

geo·mag·net·ic *adj* **:** of or relating to the magnetism of the earth

geo·met·ric *adj* **1 :** of or relating to geometry **2 :** consisting of points, lines, and angles

ge·om·e·try *n* **:** a branch of mathematics that deals with points, lines, angles, surfaces, and solids

ge·ra·ni·um *n* **:** a plant often grown for its bright flowers

ger·bil *n* **:** a small Old World desert animal that is a rodent and is often kept as a pet

germ *n* **1 :** a source from which something develops **2 :** a microorganism (as a bacterium) that causes disease **3 :** a bit of living matter (as a cell) capable of forming a new individual or one of its parts

[1]**Ger·man** *n* **1 :** a person born or living in Germany **2 :** the language spoken mainly in Germany, Austria, and parts of Switzerland

[2]**German** *adj* **:** of or relating to Germany, the Germans, or the German language

ger·ma·ni·um *n* **:** a white hard brittle element used as a semiconductor

German shepherd *n* **:** a large dog of German origin that is often used in police work and as a guide dog for the blind

germ cell *n* **:** a cell (as an egg or sperm cell) that contributes to the formation of a new individual

ger·mi·nate *vb* **ger·mi·nat·ed; ger·mi·nat·ing :** to begin to grow **:** SPROUT

ger·mi·na·tion *n* : a beginning of development (as of a seed)

ges·tic·u·late *vb* **ges·tic·u·lat·ed; ges·tic·u·lat·ing** : to make gestures especially when speaking

[1]**ges·ture** *n* **1** : a movement of the body (as the hands and arms) that expresses an idea or a feeling **2** : something said or done that shows a particular feeling

[2]**gesture** *vb* **ges·tured; ges·tur·ing** : to make or direct with a gesture

get *vb* **got; got** *or* **got·ten; get·ting** **1** : to gain possession of (as by receiving, earning, buying, or winning) **2** : to obtain by request or as a favor **3** : to come to have **4** : [1]CATCH 5 **5** : ARRIVE 1 **6** : GO 1, MOVE **7** : BECOME 1 **8** : to cause to be **9** : PREPARE 2 **10** : IRRITATE 1 **11** : [1]HIT 1 **12** : to find out by calculation **13** : to hear correctly **14** : UNDERSTAND 1 **15** : PERSUADE — **get ahead** : to achieve success (as in business) — **get along** **1** : to approach old age **2** : to stay friendly **3** : to manage with little — **get around** **1** : to become known by many people **2** : to avoid having to deal with **3** : to do or give attention to eventually — **get at** **1** : to reach with or as if with the hand **2** : to deal with **3** : to say or suggest in an indirect way — **get away** : to avoid being caught — **get away with** : to not be punished for — **get back at** : to get revenge on — **get by** **1** : to manage with little **2** : to do well enough to avoid failure — **get even** : to get revenge — **get into** : to become deeply interested in — **get it** : to receive punishment — **get off** **1** : to start out on a journey **2** : to escape punishment or harm — **get on** **1** : to approach old age **2** : to start or continue doing **3** : to stay friendly — **get out** **1** : [1]ESCAPE 1 **2** : to become known — **get over** **1** : to stop feeling unhappy about **2** : to recover from — **get up** **1** : to arise from bed **2** : [1]STAND 1 **3** : to find the ability — **get wind of** : to become aware of : hear about

get·away *n* **1** : [2]ESCAPE 1 **2** : a place suitable for vacation **3** : a usually short vacation

get–to·geth·er *n* : an informal social gathering

get·up *n* : [1]OUTFIT 1, COSTUME

gey·ser *n* : a spring that now and then shoots up hot water and steam

ghast·ly *adj* **ghast·li·er; ghast·li·est** **1** : very shocking or horrible **2** : like a ghost : PALE

ghet·to *n, pl* **ghettos** *or* **ghettoes** : a part of a city in which members of a particular group live in poor conditions

ghost *n* : the spirit of a dead person thought of as living in an unseen world or as appearing to living people

ghost·ly *adj* **ghost·li·er; ghost·li·est** : of, relating to, or like a ghost

ghost town *n* : a town where all the people have left

ghoul *n* **1** : an evil being of legend that robs graves and feeds on dead bodies **2** : someone whose activities suggest those of a ghoul : an evil or frightening person

GI *n* : a member of the United States armed forces

[1]**gi·ant** *n* **1** : an imaginary person of great size and strength **2** : a person or thing that is very large, successful, or powerful

[2]**giant** *adj* : much larger than ordinary : HUGE

giant panda *n* : PANDA 2

giant sequoia *n* : an evergreen tree of California that has needles for leaves and can sometimes grow to over 270 feet (about 82 meters) in height

gib·ber·ish *n* : confused meaningless talk

gib·bon *n* : a small tailless ape of southeastern Asia that has long arms and legs and lives mostly in trees

[1]**gibe** *or* **jibe** *vb* **gibed** *or* **jibed; gib·ing** *or* **jib·ing** : to speak or tease with words that are insulting or scornful : JEER

[2]**gibe** *or* **jibe** *n* : an insulting or scornful remark : JEER

gib·lets *n pl* : the edible inner organs (as the heart and liver) of a bird (as a turkey)

gid·dy *adj* **gid·di·er; gid·di·est** **1** : having a feeling of whirling or spinning about : DIZZY **2** : causing dizziness **3** : playful and silly **4** : feeling and showing great happiness and joy — **gid·di·ness** *n*

gift *n* **1** : a special ability : TALENT **2** : something given : PRESENT

gift card *n* : a card that is worth a certain amount of money and that is given to someone to buy something

gift·ed *adj* : having great natural ability

gig *n* **1** : a long light boat for a ship's captain **2** : a light carriage having two wheels and pulled by a horse

giga·byte *n* : a unit of computer information storage capacity equal to 1,073,741,824 bytes

gi·gan·tic *adj* : extremely large or great (as in size, weight, or strength)

[1]**gig·gle** *vb* **gig·gled; gig·gling** : to laugh with repeated short high sounds that sound childlike

[2]**giggle** *n* : a light silly laugh

Gi·la monster *n* : a large black and orange poisonous lizard of the southwestern United States

gild *vb* **gild·ed** *or* **gilt; gild·ing** : to cover with a thin coating of gold

[1]**gill** *n* : a unit of liquid capacity equal to a quarter of a pint (about 120 milliliters)

²gill *n* **:** an organ (as of a fish) for taking oxygen from water

¹gilt *n* **:** gold or something resembling gold applied to a surface

²gilt *n* **:** a young female pig

gim·let *n* **:** a small pointed tool for making holes

gim·mick *n* **:** a method or trick that is designed to get people's attention or to sell something

¹gin *n* **:** COTTON GIN

²gin *vb* **ginned; gin·ning :** to separate seeds from cotton in a cotton gin

³gin *n* **:** a strong alcoholic liquor flavored with juniper berries

gin·ger *n* **:** a hot spice obtained from the root of a tropical plant and used especially to season foods

ginger ale *n* **:** a soft drink flavored with ginger

gin·ger·bread *n* **:** a dark cake flavored with ginger and molasses

gin·ger·ly *adv* **:** with great caution or care

gin·ger·snap *n* **:** a thin hard cookie flavored with ginger

ging·ham *n* **:** a cotton cloth that is often plaid or checked

gi·nor·mous *adj* **:** extremely large

gi·raffe *n* **:** a spotted mammal of Africa with a very long neck that feeds mostly on the leaves of trees and is the tallest of living animals on land

gird *vb* **gird·ed** *or* **girt; gird·ing 1 :** to encircle or fasten with or as if with a belt or cord **2 :** to prepare for conflict or for some difficult task

gird·er *n* **:** a horizontal main supporting beam

¹gir·dle *n* **1 :** something (as a belt or sash) that encircles or binds **2 :** a tight undergarment worn below the waist by women

²girdle *vb* **gir·dled; gir·dling 1 :** to bind with or as if with a girdle, belt, or sash **:** ENCIRCLE **2 :** to strip a ring of bark from a tree trunk

girl *n* **1 :** a female child or young woman **2** *often offensive* **:** a female servant **3 :** GIRLFRIEND 2

girl·friend *n* **1 :** a female friend **2 :** a woman or girl involved in a romantic relationship

girl·hood *n* **:** the state or time of being a girl

girl·ish *adj* **:** relating to or having qualities often felt to be typical of girls

Girl Scout *n* **:** a member of the Girl Scouts of the United States of America

girth *n* **1 :** the measure or distance around something **2 :** a band put around the body of an animal to hold something (as a saddle) on its back

gist *n* **:** the main point of a matter

¹give *vb* **gave; giv·en; giv·ing 1 :** to hand over to be kept **:** PRESENT **2 :** to cause to have **3 :** to let someone or something have **4 :** to offer for consideration or acceptance **5 :** ²UTTER **6 :** FURNISH 2, PROVIDE **7 :** ¹PAY 1 **8 :** to deliver by some bodily action **9 :** to yield as a product **:** PRODUCE **10 :** to yield slightly — **give in :** to stop trying to fight — **give out 1 :** TELL 4 **2 :** to stop working — **give up 1 :** to let go of **2 :** QUIT — **give way 1 :** to break down **:** COLLAPSE **2 :** to be unable to resist

²give *n* **:** the ability to be bent or stretched

giv·en *adj* **1 :** being likely to have or do something **2 :** decided on beforehand

given name *n* **:** a first name

giz·zard *n* **:** a large muscular part of the digestive tract (as of a bird) in which food is churned and ground into small bits

gla·cial *adj* **1 :** of or relating to glaciers **2 :** very cold **3 :** very slow

gla·cier *n* **:** a large body of ice moving slowly down a slope or over a wide area of land

glad *adj* **glad·der; glad·dest 1 :** being happy and joyful **2 :** bringing or causing joy **3 :** very willing — **glad·ly** *adv* — **glad·ness** *n*

glad·den *vb* **glad·dened; glad·den·ing :** to make glad

glade *n* **:** a grassy open space in a forest

glad·i·a·tor *n* **:** a man in ancient Rome who took part in fights as public entertainment

glad·i·o·lus *n, pl* **glad·i·o·li** *or* **gladiolus** *also* **glad·i·o·lus·es :** a plant with long stiff pointed leaves and stalks of brightly colored flowers

glam·or·ous *adj* **:** very exciting and attractive

glam·our *n* **:** romantic, exciting, and often misleading attractiveness

¹glance *vb* **glanced; glanc·ing 1 :** to strike at an angle and fly off to one side **2 :** to give a quick look

²glance *n* **:** a quick look

gland *n* **:** a cluster of cells or an organ in the body that produces a substance (as saliva, sweat, or bile) to be used by the body or given off from it

glan·du·lar *adj* **:** of or relating to glands

¹glare *vb* **glared; glar·ing 1 :** to shine with a harsh bright light **2 :** to look fiercely or angrily

²glare *n* **1 :** a harsh bright light **2 :** a fierce or angry look

glar·ing *adj* **1 :** so bright as to be harsh **2 :** very noticeable

glass *n* **1 :** a hard brittle usually transparent substance commonly made from sand heated with chemicals **2 :** a drinking container made of glass **3 glasses** *pl* **:** a pair of glass or plastic lenses held in a frame and used to help a person see clearly or to protect the eyes **4 :** the contents of a glass

glass·blow·ing *n* **:** the art of shaping a mass of melted glass by blowing air into it through a tube
glass·ful *n* **:** the amount a glass will hold
glass·ware *n* **:** articles made of glass
glassy *adj* **glass·i·er; glass·i·est 1 :** smooth and shiny like glass **2 :** not shiny or bright
[1]**glaze** *vb* **glazed; glaz·ing 1 :** to cover with a smooth or glossy coating **2 :** to become dull
[2]**glaze** *n* **:** a glassy surface or coating
[1]**gleam** *n* **1 :** a faint, soft, or reflected light **2 :** a bright or shining look **3 :** a short or slight appearance
[2]**gleam** *vb* **gleamed; gleam·ing 1 :** to shine with a soft light **2 :** to give out gleams of light
glean *vb* **gleaned; glean·ing 1 :** to gather from a field what is left by the harvesters **2 :** to gather (as information) little by little with patient effort
glee *n* **:** great joy **:** DELIGHT — **glee·ful** *adj* — **glee·ful·ly** *adv*
glen *n* **:** a narrow hidden valley
glib *adj* **glib·ber; glib·best :** speaking or spoken carelessly and often insincerely — **glib·ly** *adv*
[1]**glide** *vb* **glid·ed; glid·ing :** to move with a smooth continuous motion
[2]**glide** *n* **:** the act or action of moving with a smooth continuous motion
glid·er *n* **:** an aircraft without an engine that glides on air currents
[1]**glim·mer** *vb* **glim·mered; glim·mer·ing :** to shine faintly and unsteadily
[2]**glimmer** *n* **1 :** a faint unsteady light **2 :** a faint suggestion **3 :** a small amount
[1]**glimpse** *vb* **glimpsed; glimps·ing :** to catch a quick view of
[2]**glimpse** *n* **:** a short hurried look
[1]**glint** *vb* **glint·ed; glint·ing :** to shine with tiny bright flashes
[2]**glint** *n* **:** a brief flash
glis·ten *vb* **glis·tened; glis·ten·ing :** to shine with a soft reflected light
glitch *n* **:** a usually minor problem
[1]**glit·ter** *vb* **glit·tered; glit·ter·ing :** to sparkle brightly
[2]**glitter** *n* **:** sparkling brightness — **glit·tery** *adj*
gloat *vb* **gloat·ed; gloat·ing :** to talk or think about something with mean or selfish satisfaction
glob·al *adj* **1 :** in or having to do with the whole earth **2 :** shaped like a globe
global warming *n* **:** a warming of the earth's atmosphere and oceans that is thought to be a result of air pollution
globe *n* **1 :** a round object **:** BALL, SPHERE **2 :** EARTH 1 **3 :** a round model of the earth used like a map
glob·ule *n* **:** a small round mass
glock·en·spiel *n* **:** a portable musical instrument with a series of metal bars played with hammers
gloom *n* **1 :** partial or complete darkness **2 :** a sad mood
gloomy *adj* **gloom·i·er; gloom·i·est 1 :** partly or completely dark **2 :** SAD 1, BLUE **3 :** causing feelings of sadness **4 :** not hopeful or promising — **gloom·i·ly** *adv*
glo·ri·fy *vb* **glo·ri·fied; glo·ri·fy·ing 1 :** to honor or praise as divine **:** WORSHIP **2 :** to give honor and praise to **3 :** to show in a way that looks good
glo·ri·ous *adj* **1 :** having or deserving praise or admiration **2 :** having great beauty or splendor **3 :** DELIGHTFUL — **glo·ri·ous·ly** *adv*
[1]**glo·ry** *n, pl* **glories 1 :** praise, honor, and admiration given to a person by others **2 :** something that brings honor, praise, or fame **3 :** BRILLIANCE, SPLENDOR
[2]**glory** *vb* **glo·ried; glo·ry·ing :** to rejoice proudly **:** be proud or boastful
[1]**gloss** *n* **1 :** brightness from a smooth surface **:** SHEEN **2 :** a falsely attractive surface appearance
[2]**gloss** *vb* **glossed; glos·sing 1 :** to shine the surface of **2 :** to explain as if unimportant
glos·sa·ry *n, pl* **glos·sa·ries :** a list that provides definitions for the difficult or unusual words used in a book
glossy *adj* **gloss·i·er; gloss·i·est :** smooth and shining on the surface
glove *n* **:** a covering for the hand having a separate section for each finger — **gloved** *adj*
[1]**glow** *vb* **glowed; glow·ing 1 :** to shine with or as if with great heat **2 :** to shine with steady light **3 :** to have a warm reddish color (as from exercise) **4 :** to look happy, excited, or healthy
[2]**glow** *n* **1 :** light such as comes from something that is very hot but not flaming **2 :** brightness or warmth of color **3 :** a feeling of physical warmth (as from exercise) **4 :** a warm and pleasant feeling
glow·er *vb* **glow·ered; glow·er·ing :** to stare angrily **:** SCOWL
glow·worm *n* **:** an insect or insect larva that gives off light
glu·cose *n* **:** a sugar in plant saps and fruits that is the usual form in which carbohydrate is taken in by the animal body and used as a source of energy
[1]**glue** *n* **:** a substance used to stick things tightly together — **glu·ey** *adj*
[2]**glue** *vb* **glued; glu·ing :** to stick with or as if with glue
glum *adj* **glum·mer; glum·mest :** gloomy and sad — **glum·ly** *adv*

[1]glut *vb* **glut·ted; glut·ting** **1 :** to make very full **2 :** to flood with goods so that supply is greater than demand

[2]glut *n* **:** too much of something

glu·ti·nous *adj* **:** like glue **:** STICKY

glut·ton *n* **:** a person or animal that overeats — **glut·ton·ous** *adj*

glut·tony *n, pl* **glut·ton·ies :** the act or habit of eating or drinking too much

gly·co·gen *n* **:** a white tasteless starchy substance that is the main form in which glucose is stored in the body

gm *abbr* gram

gnarled *adj* **:** being full of knots, twisted, and rugged

gnarly *adj* **gnarl·i·er; gnarl·i·est :** GNARLED

gnash *vb* **gnashed; gnash·ing :** to strike or grind (the teeth) together

gnat *n* **:** a very small two-winged fly

gnaw *vb* **gnawed; gnaw·ing :** to bite so as to wear away **:** bite or chew upon

gnome *n* **:** an imaginary dwarf believed to live inside the earth and guard treasure

gnu *n, pl* **gnu** *or* **gnus :** WILDEBEEST

go *vb* **went; gone; go·ing; goes** **1 :** to move or travel from one place to or toward another **2 :** to move away **:** LEAVE **3 :** to lead in a certain direction **4 :** to be sent **5 :** to become lost, used, or spent **6 :** to pass by **:** ELAPSE **7 :** to continue its course or action **:** RUN **8 :** to be able to fit in or through a space **9 :** to make its own special sound **10 :** to be suitable **:** MATCH **11 :** to reach some state — **go off 1 :** EXPLODE 1 **2 :** to begin to make a usual noise **3 :** to proceed as expected — **go on 1 :** to continue as time passes **2 :** to continue talking — **go out 1 :** to leave home **2 :** to stop burning — **go through :** [2]EXPERIENCE

[1]goad *n* **1 :** a pointed rod used to keep an animal moving **2 :** something that urges or forces someone to act

[2]goad *vb* **goad·ed; goad·ing :** to urge or force a person or an animal to act

goal *n* **1 :** [1]PURPOSE **2 :** an area or object into which a ball or puck must be driven in various games in order to score **3 :** a scoring of one or more points by driving a ball or puck into a goal **4 :** the point at which a race or journey is to end **5 :** an area to be reached safely in certain games

goal·ie *n* **:** GOALKEEPER

goal·keep·er *n* **:** a player who defends a goal

goal line *n* **:** a line that must be crossed to score a goal

goal·post *n* **:** one of two upright posts often with a crossbar that serve as the goal in various games

goal·tend·er *n* **:** GOALKEEPER

goat *n* **:** an animal that has hollow horns that curve backward, is related to the sheep, and is often raised for its milk, wool, and meat — **goat·like** *adj*

goa·tee *n* **:** a small beard trimmed to a point

goat·herd *n* **:** a person who tends goats

goat·skin *n* **:** the skin of a goat or leather made from it

gob *n* **:** [1]LUMP 1

[1]gob·ble *vb* **gob·bled; gob·bling :** to eat fast or greedily

[2]gobble *vb* **gob·bled; gob·bling :** to make the call of a turkey or a similar sound

[3]gobble *n* **:** the loud harsh call of a turkey

go–be·tween *n* **:** a person who acts as a messenger or peacemaker

gob·let *n* **:** a drinking glass with a foot and stem

gob·lin *n* **:** an ugly and often evil imaginary creature

god *n* **1** *cap* **:** the Being worshipped as the creator and ruler of the universe **2 :** a being believed to have more than human powers **3 :** an object worshipped as divine

god·child *n, pl* **god·chil·dren :** a person for whom another person acts as sponsor at baptism

god·daugh·ter *n* **:** a girl or woman for whom another person acts as sponsor at baptism

god·dess *n* **:** a female god

god·fa·ther *n* **:** a boy or man who is sponsor for someone at baptism

god·like *adj* **:** like or suitable for God or a god

god·ly *adj* **god·li·er; god·li·est :** DEVOUT 1, PIOUS

god·moth·er *n* **:** a girl or woman who is sponsor for someone at baptism

god·par·ent *n* **:** a sponsor at baptism

god·send *n* **:** some badly needed thing that comes unexpectedly

god·son *n* **:** a boy or man for whom another person acts as sponsor at baptism

God·speed *n* **:** a wish for success given to a person who is going away

goes *present third person sing of* GO

go–get·ter *n* **:** a person determined to succeed

gog·gle *vb* **gog·gled; gog·gling :** to stare with bulging or rolling eyes

gog·gles *n pl* **:** protective glasses set in a flexible frame (as of plastic) that fits snugly against the face

go·ings–on *n pl* **:** things that happen

goi·ter *n* **:** a swelling on the front of the neck caused by enlargement of the thyroid gland

gold *n* **1 :** a soft yellow metallic chemical element used especially in coins and jewelry **2 :** gold coins **3 :** a medal awarded as the first prize in a competition **4 :** a deep yellow

gold·en *adj* **1 :** like, made of, or containing gold **2 :** having the deep yellow color of gold **3** : very good or desirable **4** : very prosperous and happy

gold·en·rod *n* : a plant with tall stiff stems topped with clusters of tiny yellow flowers

gold·finch *n* **1** : a small European bird with a yellow patch on each wing **2** : a small mostly yellow American bird

gold·fish *n* : a small usually golden yellow or orange fish often kept in aquariums or ponds

gold·smith *n* : a person who makes or sells items of gold

golf *n* : a game played by hitting a small ball with special clubs into each of nine or 18 holes in as few strokes as possible

golf·er *n* : a person who plays golf

gon·do·la *n* **1** : a long narrow boat used in the canals of Venice, Italy **2** : a railroad freight car with no top **3** : an enclosure that hangs from a balloon or cable and carries passengers or instruments

[1]**gone** *past participle of* GO

[2]**gone** *adj* **1** : no longer present **2** : no longer existing **3** : [1]DEAD 1

gon·er *n* : someone or something with no chance of surviving or succeeding

gong *n* : a metallic disk that produces a harsh ringing tone when struck

[1]**good** *adj* **bet·ter; best** **1** : better than average **2** : SKILLFUL **3** : behaving well **4** : PLEASANT 1, ENJOYABLE **5** : HEALTHFUL **6** : of a favorable character or tendency **7** : suitable for a use : SATISFACTORY **8** : DESIRABLE 1, ATTRACTIVE **9** : showing good sense or judgment **10** : closely following a standard of what is correct or proper **11** : RELIABLE **12** : HELPFUL, KIND **13** : being honest and upright **14** : being at least the amount mentioned **15** : CONSIDERABLE — **as good as** : ALMOST

[2]**good** *n* **1** : WELFARE 1, BENEFIT **2** : the good part of a person or thing **3** : something right or good **4 goods** *pl* : products that are made for sale **5 goods** *pl* : personal property

[1]**good–bye** *or* **good–by** *interj* — used to express good wishes to someone who is leaving

[2]**good–bye** *or* **good–by** *n* : a remark made when someone is leaving

good–heart·ed *adj* : kind and generous — **good–heart·ed·ly** *adv*

good–hu·mored *adj* : GOOD-NATURED — **good–hu·mored·ly** *adv*

good·ly *adj* **good·li·er; good·li·est** **1** : of pleasing appearance **2** : LARGE, CONSIDERABLE

good–na·tured *adj* : having or showing a pleasant disposition — **good–na·tured·ly** *adv*

good·ness *n* **1** : the quality or state of being good **2** : excellence of morals and behavior

good–sized *adj* : fairly large

good–tem·pered *adj* : not easily angered or upset

good·will *n* : kind feelings or attitude

goody *n, pl* **good·ies** **1** : something especially good to eat **2** : something that is very attractive or desirable

goo·ey *adj* **goo·i·er; goo·i·est** : wet and sticky

[1]**goof** *n* **1** : a stupid or silly person **2** : [2]BLUNDER

[2]**goof** *vb* **goofed; goof·ing** **1** : to spend time foolishly **2** : to spend time doing silly or playful things **3** : to make a blunder

goofy *adj* **goof·i·er; goof·i·est** : [1]SILLY 1

goo·gle *vb* **goo·gled; goo·gling** : to use the Google search engine to obtain information about (someone or something) on the Internet

goose *n, pl* **geese** **1** : a waterbird with webbed feet that is related to the smaller duck and the larger swan **2** : a female goose **3** : the meat of a goose used as food

goose·ber·ry *n, pl* **goose·ber·ries** : the sour berry of a thorny bush related to the currant

goose bumps *n pl* : a roughness of the skin caused by cold, fear, or a sudden feeling of excitement

goose·flesh *n* : GOOSE BUMPS

goose pimples *n pl* : GOOSE BUMPS

go·pher *n* **1** : a burrowing animal that is about the size of a large rat and has strong claws on the forefeet and a large fur-lined pouch on the outside of each cheek **2** : a striped ground squirrel of North American prairies **3** : a burrowing land tortoise of the southern United States

[1]**gore** *n* **1** : blood from a wound or cut **2** : violence and bloodshed

[2]**gore** *vb* **gored; gor·ing** : to pierce or wound with a pointed object (as a horn or spear)

[1]**gorge** *n* : a narrow steep-walled canyon or part of a canyon

[2]**gorge** *vb* **gorged; gorg·ing** : to eat greedily

gor·geous *adj* : very beautiful — **gor·geous·ly** *adv* — **gor·geous·ness** *n*

go·ril·la *n* : a very large ape of the forests of central Africa that lives mostly on the ground

gory *adj* **gor·i·er; gor·i·est** **1** : covered with blood **2** : having or showing much violence and bloodshed

gos·ling *n* : a young goose

gos·pel *n* **1** *often cap* : the teachings of Jesus Christ and the apostles **2** : something told or accepted as being absolutely true

gos·sa·mer *n* : a film of cobwebs floating in the air

[1]**gos·sip** *n* **1** : a person who repeats stories about other people **2** : talk or rumors involving the personal lives of other people

[2]gossip *vb* **gos·siped; gos·sip·ing** : to talk about the personal lives of other people

got *past and past participle of* GET

gotten *past participle of* GET

[1]gouge *n* **1** : a chisel with a curved blade for scooping or cutting holes **2** : a hole or groove made by cutting or scraping

[2]gouge *vb* **gouged; goug·ing** : to make a hole or groove in something by cutting or scraping

gourd *n* : an inedible fruit with a hard rind and many seeds that grows on a vine, is related to the pumpkin and melon, and is often used for decoration or for making objects (as bowls)

gour·met *n* : a person who appreciates fine food and drink

gov. *abbr* governor

gov·ern *vb* **gov·erned; gov·ern·ing** **1** : [2]RULE 1 **2** : to influence the actions and conduct of : CONTROL **3** : to serve as a rule for

gov·ern·ess *n* : a woman who teaches and trains a child especially in a private home

gov·ern·ment *n* **1** : control and direction of public business (as of a city or a nation) **2** : a system of control : an established form of political rule **3** : the people making up a governing body

gov·ern·men·tal *adj* : of or relating to government or the government

gov·er·nor *n* : a person who governs and especially the elected head of a state of the United States

gov·er·nor·ship *n* **1** : the office or position of governor **2** : the term of office of a governor

govt. *abbr* government

gown *n* **1** : a dress suitable for special occasions **2** : a loose robe

GPS *n* : a navigation system that uses signals from satellites to determine the user's location and give directions to other places

[1]grab *vb* **grabbed; grab·bing** : to grasp or seize suddenly

[2]grab *n* : a sudden attempt to grasp or seize

[1]grace *n* **1** : a short prayer at a meal **2** : beauty and ease of movement **3** : pleasant, controlled, and polite behavior **4** : GOODWILL, FAVOR **5** : the condition of being in favor

[2]grace *vb* **graced; grac·ing** **1** : to do credit to : HONOR **2** : to make more attractive : ADORN

grace·ful *adj* : showing grace or beauty in form or action — **grace·ful·ly** *adv*

gra·cious *adj* **1** : being kind and courteous **2** : GRACEFUL — **gra·cious·ly** *adv* — **gra·cious·ness** *n*

grack·le *n* : a large blackbird with shiny feathers that show changeable green, purple, and bronze colors

[1]grade *n* **1** : a division of a school course representing a year's work **2** : the group of pupils in a school grade **3** : a mark or rating especially in school **4** : a position in a scale of rank, quality, or order **5** : a class of things that are of the same rank, quality, or order **6** : the degree of slope (as of a road)

[2]grade *vb* **grad·ed; grad·ing** **1** : to give a grade to as an indication of achievement **2** : to give a rating to **3** : to arrange in grades according to some quality **4** : to make level or evenly sloping

grad·er *n* **1** : a student in a specified grade **2** : a person who assigns grades **3** : a machine used for leveling earth

grade school *n* : a school including the first six or the first eight grades

grad·u·al *adj* : moving or happening by steps or degrees — **grad·u·al·ly** *adv*

[1]grad·u·ate *n* : a person who has completed the required course of study in a college or school

[2]grad·u·ate *vb* **grad·u·at·ed; grad·u·at·ing** : to finish a course of study : become a graduate

grad·u·a·tion *n* **1** : the act or process of finishing a course of study **2** : COMMENCEMENT 1

Graeco- — see GRECO-

graf·fi·ti *n* : writing or drawing made on a public structure without permission

[1]graft *n* **1** : a plant that has a twig or bud from another plant attached to it so they are joined and grow together **2** : something (as a piece of skin or a plant bud) that is joined to something similar so as to grow together **3** : something (as money or advantage) gotten in a dishonest way and especially by betraying a public trust

[2]graft *vb* **graft·ed; graft·ing** **1** : to attach a twig or bud from one plant to another plant so they are joined and grow together **2** : to join one thing to another as if by grafting **3** : to gain dishonestly — **graft·er** *n*

grain *n* **1** : the edible seed of some grasses (as wheat, corn, or oats) or a few other plants (as buckwheat) **2** : plants that produce grain **3** : a small hard particle **4** : a tiny amount **5** : a unit of weight equal to 0.0648 gram **6** : the arrangement of fibers in wood — **grained** *adj*

grain elevator *n* : a tall building for storing grain

gram *n* : a unit of mass in the metric system equal to 1/1000 kilogram

-gram *n suffix* : drawing : writing : record

gram·mar *n* **1** : the rules of how words are used in a language **2** : speech or writing judged according to the rules of grammar

gram·mat·i·cal *adj* : of, relating to, or following the rules of grammar — **gram·mat·i·cal·ly** *adv*

gra·na·ry *n, pl* **gra·na·ries** : a building in which grain is stored
grand *adj* **grand·er; grand·est** **1** : higher in rank than others **2** : great in size **3** : COMPREHENSIVE, INCLUSIVE **4** : IMPRESSIVE **5** : very good — **grand·ly** *adv*
grand·child *n, pl* **grand·chil·dren** : a child of a person's son or daughter
grand·daugh·ter *n* : a daughter of a person's son or daughter
gran·deur *n* : impressive greatness
grand·fa·ther *n* **1** : the father of someone's father or mother **2** : ANCESTOR
grandfather clock *n* : a tall clock standing directly on the floor
gran·di·ose *adj* : overly grand or exaggerated
grand·ma *n* : GRANDMOTHER 1
grand·moth·er *n* **1** : the mother of someone's father or mother **2** : a female ancestor
grand·pa *n* : GRANDFATHER 1
grand·par·ent *n* : a parent of someone's father or mother
grand·son *n* : a son of someone's son or daughter
grand·stand *n* : a usually roofed structure at a racecourse or stadium for spectators
gran·ite *n* : a very hard rock that is used for buildings and for monuments
gran·ny *n, pl* **gran·nies** : GRANDMOTHER 1
gra·no·la *n* : a mixture of oats and other ingredients (as raisins, coconut, or nuts) that is eaten especially for breakfast or as a snack
[1]**grant** *vb* **grant·ed; grant·ing** **1** : to agree to do, give, or allow **2** : to give as a favor or right **3** : to give legally or formally **4** : to admit to or agree with
[2]**grant** *n* **1** : the act of giving or agreeing to **2** : something given
grape *n* : a juicy berry that has a smooth green, dark red, or purple skin and grows in clusters on a woody vine (**grapevine**)
grape·fruit *n* : a large fruit with a yellow skin that is related to the orange and lemon
[1]**graph** *n* : a diagram that by means of dots and lines shows a system of relationships between things
[2]**graph** *vb* **graphed; graph·ing** : to show something using a graph
-graph *n suffix* **1** : something written **2** : instrument for making or sending records
[1]**graph·ic** *adj* **1** : being written, drawn, printed, or engraved **2** : described in very clear detail **3** : of or relating to the pictorial arts or to printing
[2]**graphic** *n* **1** : a picture, map, or graph used for illustration **2 graphics** *pl* : a pictorial image or series of images displayed on a computer screen
graphic novel *n* : a story that is presented in comic strips and is published as a book
graph·ite *n* : a soft black form of carbon used in making lead pencils and as a lubricant
-g·ra·phy *n suffix, pl* **-g·ra·phies** : writing or picturing in a special way, by a special means, or of a special thing
grapple *vb* **grap·pled; grap·pling** **1** : to seize or hold with an instrument (as a hook) **2** : to seize and struggle with another **3** : to deal with
[1]**grasp** *vb* **grasped; grasp·ing** **1** : to seize and hold with or as if with the hand **2** : to make the motion of seizing **3** : UNDERSTAND 1
[2]**grasp** *n* **1** : a grip of the hand **2** : [2]CONTROL 1, HOLD **3** : the power of seizing and holding : REACH **4** : [1]UNDERSTANDING 1
grasp·ing *adj* : GREEDY 1
grass *n* **1** : any of a large group of green plants with jointed stems, long slender leaves, and stalks of clustered flowers **2** : plants eaten by grazing animals **3** : land (as a lawn) covered with growing grass — **grass·like** *adj*
grass·hop·per *n* : a common leaping insect that feeds on plants
grass·land *n* : land covered with herbs (as grass and clover) rather than shrubs and trees
grassy *adj* **grass·i·er; grass·i·est** : like or covered with grass
[1]**grate** *vb* **grat·ed; grat·ing** **1** : to break into small pieces by rubbing against something rough **2** : to grind or rub against something with a harsh noise **3** : to have an irritating effect
[2]**grate** *n* **1** : a frame containing parallel or crossed bars (as in a window) **2** : a frame of iron bars to hold a fire
grate·ful *adj* **1** : feeling or showing thanks **2** : providing pleasure or comfort — **grate·ful·ly** *adv*
grat·er *n* : a device with a rough surface for grating
grat·i·fi·ca·tion *n* **1** : the act of giving pleasure or satisfaction to : the state of being pleased or satisfied **2** : something that pleases or satisfies
grat·i·fy *vb* **grat·i·fied; grat·i·fy·ing** **1** : to give pleasure or satisfaction to **2** : to do or give whatever is wanted by
grat·ing *n* : [2]GRATE 1
grat·i·tude *n* : a feeling of appreciation or thanks
[1]**grave** *n* : a hole in the ground for burying a dead body
[2]**grave** *adj* **grav·er; grav·est** **1** : very serious : IMPORTANT **2** : serious in appearance or manner — **grave·ly** *adv*
grav·el *n* : small pieces of rock and pebbles larger than grains of sand
grav·el·ly *adj* **1** : containing or made up of gravel **2** : sounding rough

grave·stone *n* : a monument on a grave

grave·yard *n* : CEMETERY

grav·i·tate *vb* **grav·i·tat·ed; grav·i·tat·ing** : to move or be drawn toward something

grav·i·ta·tion *n* **1** : GRAVITY 1 **2** : movement to or toward something

grav·i·ty *n, pl* **grav·i·ties** **1** : a force of attraction that tends to draw particles or bodies together **2** : the attraction of bodies by the force of gravity toward the center of the earth **3** : great seriousness

gra·vy *n, pl* **gravies** : a sauce made from the juice of cooked meat

¹gray *or chiefly Can and Brit* **grey** *adj* **gray·er/greyer; gray·est/greyest** **1** : of a color that is a blend of black and white **2** : having gray hair **3** : lacking cheer or brightness — **gray·ness** *or chiefly Can and Brit* **greyness** *n*

²gray *or chiefly Can and Brit* **grey** *n* : a color that is a blend of black and white

³gray *or chiefly Can and Brit* **grey** *vb* **grayed/greyed; gray·ing/greying** : to make or become gray

gray·ish *or chiefly Can and Brit* **greyish** *adj* : somewhat gray

¹graze *vb* **grazed; graz·ing** **1** : to eat grass **2** : to supply with grass or pasture

²graze *vb* **grazed; graz·ing** **1** : to rub lightly in passing : barely touch **2** : to scrape by rubbing against something

³graze *n* : a scrape or mark caused by scraping against something

¹grease *n* **1** : a substance obtained from animal fat by melting **2** : oily material **3** : a thick lubricant

²grease *vb* **greased; greas·ing** : to coat or lubricate with an oily material

grease·paint *n* : actors' makeup

greasy *adj* **greas·i·er; greas·i·est** **1** : covered with an oily material **2** : like or full of fat

great *adj* **great·er; great·est** **1** : very large in size : HUGE **2** : large in amount **3** : LONG 3 **4** : much beyond the ordinary **5** : IMPORTANT 1, DISTINGUISHED **6** : very talented or successful **7** : very good — **great·ly** *adv*

great–grand·child *n, pl* **great–grand·chil·dren** : a grandson (**great–grandson**) or granddaughter (**great–granddaughter**) of someone's son or daughter

great–grand·par·ent *n* : a grandfather (**great–grandfather**) or grandmother (**great–grandmother**) of someone's father or mother

grebe *n* : a swimming and diving bird related to the loons

Gre·cian *adj* : ²GREEK

Gre·co- *or* **Grae·co-** *prefix* **1** : Greece : Greeks **2** : Greek and

greed *n* : selfish desire for more than is needed

greedy *adj* **greed·i·er; greed·i·est** **1** : having or showing a selfish desire for more than is needed **2** : having a strong appetite for food or drink : very hungry **3** : very eager to have something — **greed·i·ly** *adv*

¹Greek *n* **1** : a person born or living in Greece **2** : the language of the Greeks

²Greek *adj* : of or relating to Greece, its people, or the Greek language

¹green *adj* **green·er; green·est** **1** : of the color of grass : colored green **2** : covered with green plant growth **3** : made of green plants or of the leafy parts of plants **4** : not ripe **5** : not fully processed, treated, or seasoned **6** : lacking training or experience **7** : JEALOUS 2 **8** : supporting the protection of or helping to protect the environment

²green *n* **1** : a color between blue and yellow : the color of growing grass **2** **greens** *pl* : leafy parts of plants used for food **3** : a grassy plain or plot

green bean *n* : a young long green pod of a bean plant eaten as a vegetable

green·ery *n, pl* **green·er·ies** : green plants or foliage

green·horn *n* : a person who is new at something

green·house *n* : a building with clear walls and roof (as of glass) for growing plants

greenhouse effect *n* : warming of the lower atmosphere of the earth that occurs when radiation from the sun is absorbed by the earth and then given off again and absorbed by carbon dioxide and water vapor in the atmosphere

green·ish *adj* : somewhat green

green thumb *n* : a talent for growing plants

greet *vb* **greet·ed; greet·ing** **1** : to speak to in a friendly polite way upon arrival : WELCOME **2** : to respond to in a certain way **3** : to present itself to — **greet·er** *n*

greet·ing *n* **1** : an expression of pleasure on meeting or seeing someone **2** : an expression of good wishes

gre·gar·i·ous *adj* **1** : enjoying the company of other people **2** : tending to live in a flock, herd, or community rather than alone

gre·nade *n* : a small bomb designed to be thrown by hand or fired (as by a rifle)

grew *past of* GROW

grey *chiefly Can and Brit spelling of* GRAY

grey·hound *n* : a tall swift dog with a smooth coat and good eyesight

grid *n* **1** : a network of horizontal and perpendicular lines (as for locating places on a map) **2** : a frame with bars running across it that is used to cover an opening **3** : a group of electrical conductors that form a network

grid·dle *n* : a flat surface or pan for cooking food

grid·iron *n* **1** : a grate for cooking food over a fire **2** : a football field

grief *n* **1** : very deep sorrow **2** : a cause of sorrow **3** : things that cause problems **4** : an unfortunate happening

griev·ance *n* : a reason for complaining

grieve *vb* **grieved; griev·ing** **1** : to feel or show grief **2** : to cause grief to

griev·ous *adj* **1** : causing suffering or pain **2** : SERIOUS 2, GRAVE

grif·fin *or* **grif·fon** *also* **gryph·on** *n* : an imaginary animal that is half eagle and half lion

[1]**grill** *vb* **grilled; grill·ing** **1** : to cook or be cooked on a frame of bars over fire **2** : to question intensely

[2]**grill** *n* **1** : a frame of bars on which food is cooked over a fire **2** : a cooking device equipped with a frame of bars **3** : a dish of grilled or broiled food **4** : a usually casual restaurant

grille *or* **grill** *n* : an often ornamental arrangement of bars forming a barrier or screen

grim *adj* **grim·mer; grim·mest** **1** : [1]SAVAGE 2, CRUEL **2** : harsh in action or appearance : STERN **3** : GLOOMY 3, DISMAL **4** : showing firmness and seriousness **5** : FRIGHTFUL 1 — **grim·ly** *adv*

[1]**gri·mace** *n* : a twisting of the face (as in disgust or pain)

[2]**grimace** *vb* **gri·maced; gri·mac·ing** : to twist the face

grime *n* : dirt rubbed into a surface

grimy *adj* **grim·i·er; grim·i·est** : [1]DIRTY 1

[1]**grin** *vb* **grinned; grin·ning** : to smile broadly showing teeth

[2]**grin** *n* : a broad smile that shows teeth

[1]**grind** *vb* **ground; grind·ing** **1** : to make or be made into powder or small pieces by rubbing **2** : to wear down, polish, or sharpen by friction **3** : to rub together with a scraping noise **4** : to operate or produce by or as if by turning a crank

[2]**grind** *n* **1** : an act of sharpening or reducing to powder **2** : steady hard work

grind·stone *n* : a flat round stone that turns to sharpen or shape things

[1]**grip** *vb* **gripped; grip·ping** **1** : to grab or hold tightly **2** : to hold the interest of

[2]**grip** *n* **1** : a strong grasp **2** : strength in holding : POWER **3** : UNDERSTANDING 1 **4** : SELF-CONTROL **5** : [1]HANDLE

[1]**gripe** *vb* **griped; grip·ing** : COMPLAIN

[2]**gripe** *n* : COMPLAINT 1

grippe *n* : a disease like or the same as influenza

gris·ly *adj* **gris·li·er; gris·li·est** : HORRIBLE 1, GRUESOME

grist *n* : grain to be ground or that is already ground

gris·tle *n* : CARTILAGE — **gris·tly** *adj*

grist·mill *n* : a mill for grinding grain

[1]**grit** *n* **1** : rough hard bits especially of sand **2** : strength of mind or spirit

[2]**grit** *vb* **grit·ted; grit·ting** : [1]GRIND 3, GRATE

grits *n pl* : coarsely ground hulled grain

grit·ty *adj* **grit·ti·er; grit·ti·est** **1** : containing or like rough hard bits especially of sand **2** : showing toughness and courage **3** : harshly realistic

griz·zled *adj* **1** : streaked or mixed with gray **2** : having gray hair

griz·zly bear *n* : a large powerful brown bear of western North America

[1]**groan** *vb* **groaned; groan·ing** **1** : to make or say with a moan **2** : to creak under a strain

[2]**groan** *n* : a low moaning sound

gro·cer *n* : a person who sells food and household supplies

gro·cery *n, pl* **gro·cer·ies** **1** *groceries pl* : food and household supplies sold at a store **2** : a store that sells food and household supplies

grog·gy *adj* **grog·gi·er; grog·gi·est** : weak, dazed, and unsteady

groin *n* : the fold or area where the abdomen joins the thigh

grom·met *n* : a metal or plastic ring to strengthen or protect a small hole

[1]**groom** *n* **1** : a man who has just been or is about to be married **2** : a person in charge of horses

[2]**groom** *vb* **groomed; groom·ing** **1** : to make neat and attractive **2** : to prepare for a purpose

[1]**groove** *n* **1** : a long narrow cut in a surface **2** : [1]ROUTINE 1

[2]**groove** *vb* **grooved; groov·ing** : to make a long narrow cut in

grope *vb* **groped; grop·ing** **1** : to move along by feeling with the hands **2** : to seek by or as if by feeling around

gros·beak *n* : a finch with a strong conical bill

[1]**gross** *adj* **gross·er; gross·est** **1** : noticeably bad : GLARING **2** : DISGUSTING **3** : consisting of a whole before anything is subtracted **4** : showing poor manners : VULGAR

[2]**gross** *n* : the whole before anything is deducted

[3]**gross** *n, pl* **gross** : twelve dozen

gro·tesque *adj* : unnatural in an odd or ugly way

grot·to *n, pl* **grot·toes** **1** : [1]CAVE, CAVERN **2** : an artificial structure like a cave

[1]**grouch** *n* : a person who is irritable or complains a lot

[2]**grouch** *vb* **grouched; grouch·ing** : COMPLAIN

grouchy *adj* **grouch·i·er; grouch·i·est** : tending to be irritable or to complain a lot

¹ground *n* **1 :** the surface of the earth **2 :** ²SOIL 1, EARTH **3 :** the bottom of a body of water **4 :** an area of land **5 :** an area used for some purpose **6 grounds** *pl* **:** the land around and belonging to a building **7 :** BACKGROUND 1 **8 :** a reason for a belief, action, or argument **9 :** an area of knowledge **10 :** a level of achievement or success **11 grounds** *pl* **:** material in a liquid that settles to the bottom

²ground *vb* **ground·ed; ground·ing 1 :** to provide a reason for **2 :** to instruct in basic knowledge or understanding **3 :** to run or cause to run aground **4 :** to connect electrically with the ground **5 :** to prevent (a plane or pilot) from flying **6 :** to prohibit from taking part in certain activities as punishment

³ground *past and past participle of* GRIND

ground·hog *n* **:** WOODCHUCK

ground·less *adj* **:** having no real reason

ground·work *n* **:** something upon which further work or progress is based

¹group *n* **1 :** a number of persons or things considered as a unit **2 :** a number of persons or things that are considered related in some way **3 :** a small band

²group *vb* **grouped; group·ing :** to arrange in, put into, or form a unit or group

¹grouse *n, pl* **grouse :** a brownish bird mostly of wooded areas that feeds especially on the ground and is sometimes hunted for food or sport

²grouse *vb* **groused; grous·ing :** COMPLAIN

grove *n* **:** a small forest or group of planted trees

grov·el *vb* **grov·eled** *or* **grov·elled; grov·el·ing** *or* **grov·el·ling 1 :** to kneel, lie, or crawl on the ground (as in fear) **2 :** to act toward someone in a weak or humble way

grow *vb* **grew; grown; grow·ing 1 :** to spring up and develop to maturity **2 :** to be able to live and develop **3 :** to be related in some way by reason of growing **4 :** ¹INCREASE, EXPAND **5 :** BECOME 1 **6 :** to cause to grow : RAISE — **grow·er** *n* — **grow on :** to become more appealing over time — **grow up :** to become an adult

growing pains *n pl* **:** pains that occur in the legs of growing children but have not been proven to be caused by growth

¹growl *vb* **growled; growl·ing 1 :** to make a deep threatening sound **2 :** to make a low rumbling noise **3 :** to complain or say in an angry way

²growl *n* **1 :** a deep threatening sound (as of an animal) **2 :** a grumbling or muttered complaint

grown *adj* **:** having reached full growth : MATURE

¹grown–up *adj* **:** ¹ADULT

²grown–up *n* **:** an adult person

growth *n* **1 :** a stage or condition in increasing, developing, or maturing **2 :** a natural process of increasing in size or developing **3 :** a gradual increase **4 :** something (as a covering of plants) produced by growing

¹grub *vb* **grubbed; grub·bing 1 :** to root out by digging **2 :** to work hard

²grub *n* **1 :** a soft thick wormlike larva (as of a beetle) **2 :** FOOD 1

grub·by *adj* **grub·bi·er; grub·bi·est :** ¹DIRTY 1

¹grudge *vb* **grudged; grudg·ing :** BEGRUDGE

²grudge *n* **:** a feeling of anger or dislike towards someone that lasts a long time

gru·el *n* **:** a thin porridge

gru·el·ing *or* **gru·el·ling** *adj* **:** calling for great effort

grue·some *adj* **:** causing horror or disgust

gruff *adj* **gruff·er; gruff·est :** rough in speech or manner — **gruff·ly** *adv*

¹grum·ble *vb* **grum·bled; grum·bling 1 :** to complain in a low voice **2 :** ¹RUMBLE

²grumble *n* **1 :** the act of complaining in a low voice **2 :** ²RUMBLE

grumpy *adj* **grump·i·er; grump·i·est :** GROUCHY, CROSS — **grump·i·ly** *adv*

¹grunt *vb* **grunt·ed; grunt·ing :** to make a short low sound

²grunt *n* **:** a short low sound (as of a pig)

gryphon *variant of* GRIFFIN

GSA *abbr* Girl Scouts of America

GSUSA *abbr* Girl Scouts of the United States of America

gt. *abbr* great

GU *abbr* Guam

¹guar·an·tee *n* **1 :** a promise that something will be or will happen as stated **2 :** something given as a promise of payment : SECURITY

²guarantee *vb* **guar·an·teed; guar·an·tee·ing 1 :** to make a promise about the condition or occurrence of something **2 :** to promise to be responsible for the debt or duty of another person

guar·an·tor *n* **:** a person who gives a guarantee

¹guard *n* **1 :** a person or a body of persons that guards against injury or danger **2 :** the act or duty of keeping watch **3 :** a device giving protection

²guard *vb* **guard·ed; guard·ing 1 :** to protect from danger : DEFEND **2 :** to watch over so as to prevent escape **3 :** to keep careful watch for in order to prevent

guard·ed *adj* **:** CAUTIOUS

guard·house *n* **1 :** a building used as a

headquarters by soldiers on guard duty **2** : a military jail

guard·ian *n* **1** : a person who guards or looks after something : CUSTODIAN **2** : a person who legally has the care of another person or of another person's property — **guard·ian·ship** *n*

guards·man *n, pl* **guards·men** : a member of a national guard, coast guard, or other similar military body

gua·va *n* : the sweet yellow fruit of a tropical American tree

gu·ber·na·to·ri·al *adj* : relating to a governor

guer·ril·la *or* **gue·ril·la** *n* : a member of a group carrying on warfare but not part of a regular army

[1]**guess** *vb* **guessed; guess·ing** **1** : to form an opinion or give an answer about from little or no information **2** : to solve correctly mainly by chance **3** : THINK 2, SUPPOSE — **guess·er** *n*

[2]**guess** *n* : an opinion or answer that is reached with little information or by chance

guess·work *n* : work done or results gotten by guessing

guest *n* **1** : a person invited to visit or stay in someone's home **2** : a person invited to a special place or event **3** : a customer at a hotel, motel, inn, or restaurant

[1]**guf·faw** *n* : a burst of loud laughter

[2]**guffaw** *vb* **guf·fawed; guf·faw·ing** : to laugh noisily

guid·ance *n* : help, instruction, or assistance

[1]**guide** *n* : someone or something (as a book) that leads, directs, or shows the right way

[2]**guide** *vb* **guid·ed; guid·ing** **1** : to show the way to **2** : to direct or control the course of **3** : [1]DIRECT 6, INSTRUCT

guide·book *n* : a book of information for travelers

guide dog *n* : a dog trained to lead a person who is blind

guide·line *n* : a rule about how something should be done

guide·post *n* : a post with signs giving directions for travelers

guide word *n* : either of the terms at the head of a page of an alphabetical reference work (as a dictionary) usually showing the first and last entries on the page

guild *n* : an association of people with common interests or aims

guile *n* : the use of clever and often dishonest methods

[1]**guil·lo·tine** *n* : a machine for cutting off a person's head with a heavy blade that slides down two grooved posts

[2]**guillotine** *vb* **guil·lo·tined; guil·lo·tin·ing** : to cut off a person's head with a guillotine

guilt *n* **1** : responsibility for having done something wrong and especially something against the law **2** : a feeling of shame or regret as a result of bad conduct — **guilt·less** *adj*

guilty *adj* **guilt·i·er; guilt·i·est** **1** : responsible for having done wrong **2** : suffering from or showing bad feelings about having done wrong — **guilt·i·ly** *adv*

guin·ea *n* : an old British gold coin

guinea fowl *n* : a dark gray African bird that is sometimes raised for food

guinea pig *n* : a small stocky South American animal that is a rodent with short ears and a very short tail and is often kept as a pet

guise *n* **1** : a style of dress **2** : outward appearance

gui·tar *n* : a musical instrument with six strings played by plucking or strumming

gulch *n* : a small narrow valley with steep sides

gulf *n* **1** : a part of an ocean or sea that extends into the land **2** : a deep split or gap in the earth **3** : a wide separation

gull *n* : a waterbird with webbed feet that is usually gray and white in color and has a thick strong bill

gul·let *n* : THROAT 2, ESOPHAGUS

gull·ible *adj* : easily fooled or cheated

gul·ly *n, pl* **gullies** : a trench worn in the earth by running water

[1]**gulp** *vb* **gulped; gulp·ing** **1** : to swallow in a hurry or in large amounts at a time **2** : to breathe in deeply **3** : to keep back as if by swallowing **4** : to say in a nervous way

[2]**gulp** *n* **1** : the act of swallowing or breathing deeply **2** : a large swallow

[1]**gum** *n* : the flesh at the roots of the teeth

[2]**gum** *n* **1** : CHEWING GUM **2** : a sticky substance obtained from plants that hardens on drying **3** : a substance like a plant gum (as in stickiness)

[3]**gum** *vb* **gummed; gum·ming** **1** : to smear, stick together, or clog with or as if with gum **2** : to cause not to work properly

gum·bo *n, pl* **gum·bos** : a rich soup usually thickened with okra

gum·drop *n* : a candy usually made from corn syrup and gelatin

gum·my *adj* **gum·mi·er; gum·mi·est** : consisting of or covered with gum or a sticky or chewy substance

gump·tion *n* : COURAGE

[1]**gun** *n* **1** : a weapon that fires bullets or shells **2** : CANNON **3** : something like a gun in shape or function **4** : a discharge of a gun

[2]**gun** *vb* **gunned; gun·ning** : to open the throttle of quickly so as to increase speed

gun·boat *n* : a small armed ship for use near a coast

gun·fire *n* : the firing of guns

gunk *n* : a dirty, greasy, or sticky substance — **gunky** *adj*

gun·man *n, pl* **gun·men** : a criminal armed with a gun

gun·ner *n* : a person who operates a gun

gun·nery *n* : the use of guns

gunnery sergeant *n* : a noncommissioned officer in the marines ranking above a staff sergeant

gun·pow·der *n* : an explosive powder used in guns and blasting

gun·shot *n* **1** : a shot from a gun **2** : the distance that can be reached by a gun

gun·wale *n* : the upper edge of a ship's side

gup·py *n, pl* **guppies** : a small tropical fish often kept as an aquarium fish

[1]**gur·gle** *vb* **gur·gled; gur·gling** **1** : to flow in a bubbling current **2** : to sound like a liquid flowing with a bubbling current

[2]**gurgle** *n* : a sound of or like liquid flowing with a bubbling current

[1]**gush** *vb* **gushed; gush·ing** **1** : to flow or pour out in large amounts **2** : to act or speak in a very affectionate or enthusiastic way

[2]**gush** *n* : a sudden free pouring out

gust *n* **1** : a sudden brief rush of wind **2** : a sudden outburst

gusty *adj* **gust·i·er; gust·i·est** : WINDY

[1]**gut** *n* **1** : the inner parts of an animal **2** : a person's stomach : BELLY **3** : the digestive tract or a part of it (as the intestine) **4** : the inner parts **5** : CATGUT **6** **guts** *pl* : COURAGE

[2]**gut** *vb* **gut·ted; gut·ting** **1** : to remove the inner organs from **2** : to destroy the inside of

gut·ter *n* **1** : a trough along the eaves of a house to catch and carry off water **2** : a low area (as at the side of a road) to carry off surface water

[1]**guy** *n* **1** : [1]FELLOW 1 **2** : PERSON 1

[2]**guy** *n* : a rope, chain, rod, or wire (**guy wire**) attached to something to steady it

guz·zle *vb* **guz·zled; guz·zling** : to drink greedily

gym *n* : GYMNASIUM

gym·na·si·um *n* : a room or building for sports events or exercise

gym·nast *n* : a person who is skilled in gymnastics

gym·nas·tic *adj* : of or relating to gymnastics

gym·nas·tics *n pl* : physical exercises for developing skill, strength, and control in the use of the body or a sport in which such exercises are performed — used as a singular

Gyp·sy *n, pl* **Gyp·sies** *sometimes offensive* : a member of a group of people coming from India to Europe long ago and living a wandering way of life

gypsy moth *n* : a moth whose caterpillar damages trees by eating the leaves

gy·rate *vb* **gy·rat·ed; gy·rat·ing** : to move back and forth with a circular motion — **gy·ra·tion** *n*

gy·ro·scope *n* : a wheel mounted to spin rapidly so that its axis is free to turn in various directions

H

h *n, pl* **h's** *or* **hs** *often cap* : the eighth letter of the English alphabet

ha *or* **hah** *interj* — used to show surprise or joy

hab·it *n* **1** : usual way of behaving **2** : clothing worn for a special purpose **3** : a way of acting or doing that has become fixed by being repeated often **4** : characteristic way of growing

hab·it·able *adj* : suitable or fit to live in

hab·i·tat *n* : the place where a plant or animal grows or lives in nature

hab·i·ta·tion *n* **1** : the act of living in a place **2** : a place to live

ha·bit·u·al *adj* **1** : occurring regularly or repeatedly : being or done by habit **2** : doing or acting by force of habit **3** : [1]REGULAR 2 — **ha·bit·u·al·ly** *adv*

ha·ci·en·da *n* : a large estate especially in a Spanish-speaking country

[1]**hack** *vb* **hacked; hack·ing** **1** : to cut with repeated chopping blows **2** : to cough in a short broken way **3** : to write computer programs for enjoyment **4** : to gain access to a computer illegally

[2]**hack** *n* : a short broken cough

[3]**hack** *n* **1** : a horse let out for hire or used for varied work **2** : a person who works for pay at a routine writing job **3** : a person who does work that is not good or original and especially a writer who is not very good

hack·er *n* **1** : HACK 3 **2** : an expert at programming and solving problems with a computer **3** : a person who illegally gains access to a computer system

hack·les *n pl* **:** hairs (as on the neck of a dog) that can be made to stand up
hack·ney *n, pl* **hack·neys :** a horse for ordinary riding or driving
hack·saw *n* **:** a saw with small teeth used for cutting hard materials (as metal)
had *past and past participle of* HAVE
had·dock *n, pl* **haddock** *or* **haddocks :** a fish of the northern Atlantic Ocean that is related to the cod and is often used for food
hadn't : had not
haf·ni·um *n* **:** a gray metallic chemical element
hag *n* **1 :** WITCH 1 **2 :** an ugly old woman
hag·gard *adj* **:** having a hungry, tired, or worried look
hag·gle *vb* **hag·gled; hag·gling :** to argue especially over a price — **hag·gler** *n*
hah *variant of* HA
ha–ha *interj* — used to show amusement or scorn
hai·ku *n, pl* **haiku :** a Japanese poem or form of poetry without rhyme having three lines with the first and last lines having five syllables and the middle having seven
[1]hail *n* **1 :** small lumps of ice and snow that fall from the clouds sometimes during thunderstorms **2 :** [1]VOLLEY 1
[2]hail *vb* **hailed; hail·ing 1 :** to fall as hail **2 :** to pour down like hail
[3]hail *vb* **hailed; hailing 1 :** GREET 1, WELCOME **2 :** to call out to — **hail from :** to come from
hail·stone *n* **:** a lump of hail
hail·storm *n* **:** a storm that brings hail
hair *n* **1 :** a threadlike growth from the skin of a person or animal **2 :** a covering or growth of hairs **3 :** something (as a growth on a leaf) like an animal hair **4 :** a very small distance or amount — **haired** *adj* — **hair·less** *adj* — **hair·like** *adj*
hair·cut *n* **:** the act, process, or result of cutting the hair
hair·do *n, pl* **hairdos :** a way of arranging a person's hair
hair·dress·er *n* **:** a person who styles or cuts hair — **hair·dress·ing** *n*
hair·pin *n* **:** a pin in the shape of a U for holding the hair in place
hair–rais·ing *adj* **:** causing terror, excitement, or great surprise
hair·style *n* **:** HAIRDO
hairy *adj* **hair·i·er; hair·i·est :** covered with hair — **hair·i·ness** *n*
ha·lal *adj* **1 :** fit for eating under Islamic law **2 :** selling or serving food fit for eating under Islamic law
[1]hale *adj* **:** strong and healthy
[2]hale *vb* **haled; hal·ing :** to force to go
[1]half *n, pl* **halves 1 :** one of two equal parts into which something can be divided **2 :** a part of something that is about equal to the remainder **3 :** one of a pair
[2]half *adj* **1 :** being one of two equal parts **2 :** amounting to about a half **:** PARTIAL
[3]half *adv* **1 :** to the extent of half **2 :** not completely
half·back *n* **1 :** a football player who runs with the ball and blocks **2 :** a player positioned behind the forward line in some games (as soccer)
half brother *n* **:** a brother by one parent only
half–dol·lar *n* **1 :** a coin representing 50 cents **2 :** the sum of 50 cents
half·heart·ed *adj* **:** lacking enthusiasm or interest — **half·heart·ed·ly** *adv*
half–knot *n* **:** a knot in which two rope ends are wrapped once around each other and which is used to start other knots
half–life *n, pl* **half–lives :** the time required for half of the atoms of a radioactive substance to change composition
half sister *n* **:** a sister by one parent only
half·time *n* **:** a period of rest between the halves of a game (as basketball)
[1]half·way *adv* **:** at or to half the distance
[2]halfway *adj* **1 :** midway between two points **2 :** PARTIAL 1
half–wit *n* **:** a very stupid person — **half–wit·ted** *adj*
hal·i·but *n, pl* **halibut** *or* **halibuts :** a very large saltwater flatfish often used for food
hall *n* **1 :** a passage in a building that leads to rooms **:** CORRIDOR **2 :** an entrance room **3 :** AUDITORIUM **4 :** a large building used for public purposes **5 :** a building or large room set apart for a special purpose
hal·le·lu·jah *interj* — used to express praise, joy, or thanks
hal·low *vb* **hal·lowed; hal·low·ing :** to set apart for holy purposes **:** treat as sacred
Hal·low·een *n* **:** October 31 celebrated especially by wearing costumes and trick-or-treating
hal·lu·ci·na·tion *n* **:** the seeing of objects or the experiencing of feelings that are not real but are usually the result of mental disorder or the effect of a drug
hal·lu·ci·no·gen *n* **:** a drug that causes hallucinations — **hal·lu·ci·no·gen·ic** *adj*
hall·way *n* **:** HALL 1, CORRIDOR
ha·lo *n, pl* **halos** *or* **haloes 1 :** a bright circle around the head of a person (as in a painting) that signifies holiness **2 :** a circle of light around the sun or moon caused by tiny ice crystals in the air
[1]halt *vb* **halt·ed; halt·ing 1 :** to stop or cause to stop marching or traveling **2 :** [2]END
[2]halt *n* **:** [1]END 2
hal·ter *n* **1 :** a set of straps placed around

an animal's head so the animal can be led or tied **2** : an article of clothing worn on a woman's upper body and held in place by straps around the neck and back

halve *vb* **halved; halv·ing** **1** : to divide into two equal parts **2** : to reduce to one half

halves *pl of* HALF

hal·yard *n* : a rope for raising or lowering a sail

ham *n* **1** : a cut of meat consisting of a thigh of pork **2** : an operator of an amateur radio station **3** : a showy performer

ham·burg·er *or* **ham·burg** *n* **1** : a sandwich made of a patty of ground beef in a split bun **2** : ground beef

ham·let *n* : a small village

[1]**ham·mer** *n* **1** : a tool consisting of a head fastened to a handle and used for pounding something (as a nail) **2** : something like a hammer in shape or action **3** : a heavy metal ball with a flexible handle thrown for distance in a track-and-field contest (**hammer throw**)

[2]**hammer** *vb* **ham·mered; ham·mer·ing** **1** : to strike with a hammer **2** : to fasten or build (as by nailing) with a hammer **3** : to hit something hard and repeatedly **4** : to beat hard — **hammer out** : to produce or bring about by persistent effort

ham·mer·head *n* : a shark that has a wide flattened head with the eyes spaced widely apart

ham·mock *n* : a swinging bed made of fabric or netting attached on either end to an upright object (as a tree)

[1]**ham·per** *vb* **ham·pered; ham·per·ing** : to keep from moving or acting freely

[2]**hamper** *n* : a large basket usually with a cover

ham·ster *n* : a stocky rodent with a short tail and large cheek pouches

[1]**hand** *n* **1** : the body part at the end of the human arm that includes the fingers and thumb **2** : a bodily structure (as the hind foot of an ape) like the human hand in function or form **3** : a pointer on a clock or watch **4** : [2]HELP 1, ASSISTANCE **5** : [2]CONTROL 1 **6** : one side of a problem **7** : an outburst of applause **8** : the cards held by a player in a card game **9** : a hired worker : LABORER **10** : a promise of marriage **11** : HANDWRITING **12** : ABILITY 1 **13** : a unit of measure equal to four inches (about ten centimeters) **14** : a part or share in doing something — **at hand** : near in time or place — **by hand** : without the use of automation : using the hands — **in hand** : in someone's possession or control — **on hand** **1** : available for use **2** : [3]PRESENT 2 — **out of hand** : out of control

[2]**hand** *vb* **hand·ed; hand·ing** : to give or pass with the hand

hand·bag *n* : a bag used for carrying money and small personal articles

hand·ball *n* : a game played by hitting a small ball against a wall or board with the hand

hand·bill *n* : a printed sheet (as of advertising) distributed by hand

hand·book *n* : a book of facts usually about one subject

hand·car *n* : a small railroad car that is made to move by hand or by a small motor

[1]**hand·cuff** *n* : a metal ring that can be locked around a person's wrist — usually used in pl.

[2]**handcuff** *vb* **hand·cuffed; hand·cuff·ing** : to put handcuffs on

hand·ed *adj* : using a particular hand or number of hands

hand·ful *n, pl* **handfuls** *or* **hands·ful** **1** : as much or as many as the hand will grasp **2** : a small amount or number

[1]**hand·i·cap** *n* **1** : a disadvantage that makes progress or success difficult **2** : a contest in which someone more skilled is given a disadvantage and someone less skilled is given an advantage **3** : the disadvantage or advantage given in a contest

[2]**handicap** *vb* **hand·i·capped; hand·i·capping** : to put at a disadvantage

hand·i·craft *n* **1** : an activity or craft (as weaving or pottery making) that requires skill with the hands **2** : an article made by skillful use of the hands

hand·i·ly *adv* : in a handy manner : EASILY

hand·i·work *n* : work done by the hands

hand·ker·chief *n, pl* **hand·ker·chiefs** : a small usually square piece of cloth used for wiping the face, nose, or eyes

[1]**han·dle** *n* : the part by which something (as a dish or tool) is picked up or held — **han·dled** *adj*

[2]**handle** *vb* **han·dled; han·dling** **1** : to touch, feel, hold, or move with the hand **2** : to manage or control especially with the hands **3** : MANAGE 1, DIRECT **4** : to deal with or act on **5** : to deal or trade in **6** : to put up with — **han·dler** *n*

han·dle·bars *n pl* : a bar (as on a bicycle) that has a handle at each end and is used for steering

hand·made *adj* : made by hand rather than by machine

hand–me–downs *n pl* : used clothes

hand·out *n* : something (as food, clothing, or money) given to a poor person

hand·rail *n* : a rail to be grasped by the hand for support

hands down *adv* : without question : EASILY

hand·shake *n* : a clasping of hands by two people (as in greeting)

DICTIONARY

hand·some *adj* **hand·som·er; hand·som·est** **1 :** having a pleasing and impressive appearance **2 :** CONSIDERABLE **3 :** more than enough — **hand·some·ly** *adv*

hand·spring *n* **:** a movement in which a person turns the body forward or backward in a full circle from a standing position and lands first on the hands and then on the feet

hand·stand *n* **:** an act of balancing on the hands with the body and legs straight up

hand–to–hand *adj* **:** involving bodily contact

hand·writ·ing *n* **:** a person's writing

handy *adj* **hand·i·er; hand·i·est** **1 :** very useful or helpful **2 :** within easy reach **3 :** clever or skillful especially with the hands

[1]**hang** *vb* **hung** *also* **hanged; hang·ing** **1 :** to fasten or be fastened to something without support from below **2 :** to kill or be killed by suspending (as from a gallows) by a rope tied around the neck **3 :** to cause to droop — **hang around** **1 :** to be or stay (somewhere) in an idle or casual way **2 :** to spend time in an idle or casual way — **hang on** **1 :** to hold or grip something tightly **2 :** to wait or stop briefly — **hang up** **1 :** to place on a hook or hanger **2 :** to end a telephone connection

[2]**hang** *n* **1 :** the way in which a thing hangs **2 :** skill to do something

han·gar *n* **:** a shelter for housing and repairing aircraft

hang·er *n* **:** a device on which something hangs

hang·man *n, pl* **hang·men** **:** a person who hangs criminals

hang·nail *n* **:** a bit of skin hanging loose at the side or base of a fingernail

hang·out *n* **:** a favorite place for spending time

han·ker *vb* **han·kered; han·ker·ing** **:** to have a great desire

han·som *n* **:** a light covered carriage that has two wheels and a driver's seat elevated at the rear

Ha·nuk·kah *also* **Cha·nu·kah** *n* **:** a Jewish holiday lasting eight days in November or December and marked by the lighting of candles

hap·haz·ard *adj* **:** marked by lack of plan, order, or direction — **hap·haz·ard·ly** *adv*

hap·less *adj* **:** [1]UNFORTUNATE 1

hap·pen *vb* **hap·pened; hap·pen·ing** **1 :** to take place **2 :** to occur or come about by chance **3 :** to do or be by chance **4 :** to come especially by way of injury or harm

hap·pen·ing *n* **:** something that occurs

hap·py *adj* **hap·pi·er; hap·pi·est** **1 :** feeling or showing pleasure **:** GLAD **2 :** enjoying one's condition **:** CONTENT **3 :** JOYFUL **4 :** FORTUNATE 1 **5 :** being suitable for something — **hap·pi·ly** *adv* — **hap·pi·ness** *n*

hap·py–go–lucky *adj* **:** free from care

ha·rangue *n* **:** a scolding speech or writing

ha·rass *vb* **ha·rassed; ha·rass·ing** **1 :** to annoy again and again **2 :** to make repeated attacks against an enemy — **ha·rass·ment** *n*

[1]**har·bor** *or Can and Brit* **harbour** *n* **1 :** a part of a body of water (as a sea or lake) so protected as to be a place of safety for ships **:** PORT **2 :** a place of safety and comfort **:** REFUGE

[2]**harbor** *or Can and Brit* **harbour** *vb* **har·bored/harboured; har·bor·ing/harbouring** **1 :** to give shelter to **2 :** to have or hold in the mind

[1]**hard** *adj* **hard·er; hard·est** **1 :** not easily cut, pierced, or divided **:** not soft **2 :** difficult to do or to understand **3 :** DILIGENT, ENERGETIC **4 :** difficult to put up with **:** SEVERE **5 :** sounding as the letter c in *cold* and the letter g in *geese* **6 :** carried on with steady and earnest effort **7 :** UNFEELING 2 **8 :** high in alcoholic content **9 :** containing substances that prevent lathering with soap — **hard·ness** *n*

[2]**hard** *adv* **hard·er; hard·est** **1 :** with great effort or energy **2 :** in a forceful way **3 :** with pain, bitterness, or resentment

hard copy *n* **:** a copy of information (as from computer storage) produced on paper in normal size

hard disk *n* **1 :** a rigid metal disk used to store computer data **2 :** HARD DRIVE

hard drive *n* **:** a data storage device of a computer containing one or more hard disks

hard·en *vb* **hard·ened; hard·en·ing** **1 :** to make or become hard or harder **2 :** to make or become hardy or strong **3 :** to make or become stubborn or unfeeling

hard·head·ed *adj* **1 :** STUBBORN 1 **2 :** using or showing good judgment

hard·heart·ed *adj* **:** showing or feeling no pity **:** UNFEELING

hard·ly *adv* **:** only just **:** BARELY

hard·ship *n* **:** something (as a loss or injury) that is hard to bear

hard·ware *n* **1 :** things (as tools, cutlery, or parts of machines) made of metal **2 :** equipment or parts used for a particular purpose

hard·wood *n* **1 :** the usually hard wood of a tree (as a maple or oak) with broad leaves as distinguished from the wood of a tree (as a pine) with leaves that are needles **2 :** a tree that produces hardwood

har·dy *adj* **har·di·er; har·di·est** **1 :** able to withstand weariness, hardship, or severe weather **2 :** BOLD 1, BRAVE — **har·di·ly** *adv* — **har·di·ness** *n*

hare *n* **:** a gnawing animal that resembles the

related rabbit but is usually larger and tends to live by itself

hare·brained *adj* **:** FOOLISH

hark *vb* **harked; hark·ing :** LISTEN 1 — **hark back :** to recall or cause to recall something earlier

[1]**harm** *n* **:** physical or mental damage **:** INJURY

[2]**harm** *vb* **harmed; harm·ing :** to cause hurt, injury, or damage to

harm·ful *adj* **:** causing or capable of causing harm **:** INJURIOUS — **harm·ful·ly** *adv*

harm·less *adj* **:** not harmful — **harm·less·ly** *adv*

har·mon·i·ca *n* **:** a small musical instrument held in the hand and played by the mouth

har·mo·ni·ous *adj* **1 :** showing agreement in action or feeling **2 :** combining so as to produce a pleasing result **3 :** having a pleasant sound — **har·mo·ni·ous·ly** *adv*

har·mo·nize *vb* **har·mo·nized; har·mo·niz·ing 1 :** to play or sing in harmony **2 :** to go together in a pleasing way **:** be in harmony

har·mo·ny *n, pl* **har·mo·nies 1 :** the playing of musical tones together in chords **2 :** a pleasing arrangement of parts **3 :** AGREEMENT 1, ACCORD

[1]**har·ness** *n* **:** the straps and fastenings placed on an animal so it can be controlled or prepared to pull a load

[2]**harness** *vb* **har·nessed; har·ness·ing 1 :** to put straps and fastenings on **2 :** to put to work **:** UTILIZE

[1]**harp** *n* **:** a musical instrument consisting of a triangular frame set with strings that are plucked by the fingers

[2]**harp** *vb* **harped; harp·ing :** to call attention to something over and over again

[1]**har·poon** *n* **:** a barbed spear used especially for hunting whales and large fish

[2]**harpoon** *vb* **har·pooned; har·poon·ing :** to strike with a barbed spear

harp·si·chord *n* **:** a keyboard instrument similar to a piano with strings that are plucked

[1]**har·row** *n* **:** a piece of farm equipment that has metal teeth or disks for breaking up and smoothing soil

[2]**harrow** *vb* **har·rowed; har·row·ing 1 :** to drag a harrow over (plowed ground) **2 :** [2]DISTRESS

har·row·ing *adj* **:** very distressing or painful

har·ry *vb* **har·ried; har·ry·ing :** HARASS

harsh *adj* **harsh·er; harsh·est 1 :** causing physical discomfort **2 :** having an unpleasant or harmful effect often because of great force or intensity **3 :** severe or cruel **:** not kind or lenient — **harsh·ly** *adv* — **harsh·ness** *n*

[1]**har·vest** *n* **1 :** the gathering of a crop **2 :** the season when crops are gathered **3 :** a ripe crop

[2]**harvest** *vb* **har·vest·ed; har·vest·ing 1 :** to gather in a crop **2 :** to gather or collect for use

har·vest·er *n* **1 :** a person who gathers crops or other natural products **2 :** a machine for harvesting field crops

has *present third person sing of* HAVE

[1]**hash** *n* **1 :** cooked meat and vegetables chopped together and browned **2 :** [1]MESS 1

[2]**hash** *vb* **hashed; hash·ing 1 :** to talk about **:** DISCUSS **2 :** to chop into small pieces

hash·tag *n* **:** a word or phrase that starts with the symbol # and that briefly indicates what a message (as a tweet) is about

hasn't : has not

hasp *n* **:** a fastener (as for a door) consisting of a hinged metal strap that fits over a metal loop and is held by a pin or padlock

[1]**has·sle** *n* **1 :** something that annoys or bothers **2 :** an argument or fight

[2]**hassle** *vb* **has·sled; has·sling :** to annoy continuously **:** HARASS

has·sock *n* **:** a firm stuffed cushion used as a seat or leg rest

haste *n* **1 :** quickness of motion or action **:** SPEED **2 :** hasty action

has·ten *vb* **has·tened; has·ten·ing :** to move or cause to move or act fast **:** HURRY

hasty *adj* **hast·i·er; hast·i·est 1 :** done or made in a hurry **2 :** made, done, or decided without proper care and thought — **hast·i·ly** *adv*

hat *n* **:** a covering for the head having a crown and usually a brim

[1]**hatch** *n* **1 :** an opening in the deck of a ship or in the floor or roof of a building **2 :** a small door or opening (as in an airplane) **3 :** the cover for such an opening

[2]**hatch** *vb* **hatched; hatch·ing 1 :** to come out of an egg **2 :** to break open and give forth young **3 :** to develop usually in secret

hatch·ery *n, pl* **hatch·er·ies :** a place for hatching eggs

hatch·et *n* **:** a small ax with a short handle

hatch·way *n* **:** a hatch usually having a ladder or stairs

[1]**hate** *n* **:** deep and bitter dislike

[2]**hate** *vb* **hat·ed; hat·ing :** to feel great dislike toward — **hate someone's guts :** to hate someone very much

hate·ful *adj* **1 :** full of hate **2 :** very bad or evil **:** causing or deserving hate

ha·tred *n* **:** [1]HATE

hat·ter *n* **:** a person who makes, sells, or cleans and repairs hats

haugh·ty *adj* **haugh·ti·er; haugh·ti·est :** having or showing a proud and superior attitude — **haugh·ti·ly** *adv* — **haugh·ti·ness** *n*

[1]**haul** *vb* **hauled; haul·ing 1 :** to pull or drag with effort **2 :** to transport in a vehicle

²haul *n* **1 :** the act of pulling or hauling **2 :** an amount collected **3 :** the distance or route traveled or over which a load is moved

haunch *n* **1 :** HINDQUARTER **2 :** the upper part of a person's thigh together with the back part of the hip

¹haunt *vb* **haunt·ed; haunt·ing 1 :** to visit or live in as a ghost **2 :** to visit often **3 :** to come to mind frequently

²haunt *n* **:** a place often visited

have *vb, past & past participle* **had;** *present participle* **hav·ing;** *present third person sing* **has 1 :** to hold or own **2 :** to possess as a characteristic **3 :** to eat or drink **4 :** to consist of or contain **5 :** to be affected by **6 :** to plan, organize, and run (an event) **7 :** to give birth to **8 :** to cause to be **9 :** to stand in some relationship to **10 :** to perform a function or engage in an activity **11 :** EXPERIENCE **12 :** to hold in the mind **13 :** OBTAIN, GAIN, GET **14 :** to cause to **15 :** ¹PERMIT 1 **16 :** ²TRICK **17** — used as a helping verb with the past participle of another verb **18 :** to be forced or feel obliged **19 :** ²EXERCISE 1, USE — **had better** *or* **had best :** would be wise to — **have to do with 1 :** to be about **2 :** to be involved in or responsible for

ha·ven *n* **:** a safe place

haven't : have not

hav·er·sack *n* **:** a bag worn over one shoulder for carrying supplies

hav·oc *n* **1 :** wide destruction **2 :** great confusion and lack of order

Ha·wai·ian *n* **1 :** a person born or living in Hawaii **2 :** the language of the Hawaiians

¹hawk *n* **:** a bird of prey that has a strong hooked bill and sharp curved claws and is smaller than most eagles

²hawk *vb* **hawked; hawk·ing :** to offer for sale by calling out — **hawk·er** *n*

³hawk *vb* **hawked; hawking :** to make a harsh coughing sound in clearing the throat

haw·ser *n* **:** a large rope for towing or tying up a ship

haw·thorn *n* **:** a thorny shrub or small tree with shiny leaves, white, pink, or red flowers, and small red fruits

¹hay *n* **:** any of various herbs (as grasses) cut and dried for use as food for animals

²hay *vb* **hayed; hay·ing :** to cut plants for hay

hay fever *n* **:** an allergy to pollen that is usually marked by sneezing, a runny or stuffed nose, and itchy and watering eyes

hay·loft *n* **:** a loft in a barn or stable for storing hay

hay·mow *n* **:** HAYLOFT

hay·stack *n* **:** a large pile of hay stored outdoors

hay·wire *adj* **1 :** working badly or in an odd way **2 :** emotionally or mentally out of control **:** CRAZY

¹haz·ard *n* **:** a source of danger

²hazard *vb* **haz·ard·ed; haz·ard·ing :** to offer something (such as a guess or an opinion) at the risk of being wrong

haz·ard·ous *adj* **:** DANGEROUS 1

haze *n* **:** fine dust, smoke, or fine particles of water in the air

ha·zel *n* **1 :** a shrub or small tree that bears an edible nut **2 :** a color that combines light brown with green and gray

ha·zel·nut *n* **:** the nut of a hazel

hazy *adj* **haz·i·er; haz·i·est 1 :** partly hidden or darkened by dust, smoke, or fine particles of water in the air **2 :** not clear in thought or meaning **:** VAGUE

H–bomb *n* **:** HYDROGEN BOMB

he *pron* **1 :** that male one **2 :** that person or one — used in a general way when the sex of the person is unknown

¹head *n* **1 :** the part of the body containing the brain, eyes, ears, nose, and mouth **2 :** ¹MIND 1 **3 :** control of the mind or feelings **4 :** the side of a coin or medal usually thought of as the front **5 :** DIRECTOR 1, LEADER **6 :** each person among a number **7** *pl* **head :** a unit of number **8 :** something like a head in position or use **9 :** the place where a stream begins **10 :** a tight mass of plant parts (as leaves or flowers) **11 :** a part of a machine, tool, or weapon that performs the main work **12 :** a place of leadership or honor **13 :** CLIMAX, CRISIS — **over someone's head :** beyond someone's understanding

²head *adj* **1 :** ²CHIEF 1 **2 :** located at the front **3 :** coming from in front

³head *vb* **head·ed; head·ing 1 :** to be the leader of **2 :** to go or cause to go in a certain direction **3 :** to be first or get in front of **4 :** to provide with or form a head

head·ache *n* **1 :** pain in the head **2 :** something that annoys or confuses

head·band *n* **:** a band worn on or around the head

head·board *n* **:** a vertical board at the head of a bed

head·dress *n* **:** a covering or ornament for the head

head·ed *adj* **:** having such a head or so many heads

head·first *adv* **:** with the head in front

head·gear *n* **:** something worn on the head

head·ing *n* **:** something (as a title or an address) at the top or beginning (as of a letter)

head·land *n* **:** a point of high land sticking out into the sea

head·light *n* **:** a light at the front of a vehicle

head·line *n* **:** a title of an article in a newspaper

¹head·long *adv* **1 :** HEADFIRST **2 :** without waiting to think things through
²headlong *adj* **1 :** ¹RASH, IMPULSIVE **2 :** plunging headfirst
head·mas·ter *n* **:** a man who heads the staff of a private school
head·mis·tress *n* **:** a woman who heads the staff of a private school
head–on *adv or adj* **:** with the front hitting or facing an object
head·phone *n* **:** an earphone held over the ear by a band worn on the head
head·quar·ters *n pl* **:** a place from which something is controlled or directed — used as singular or plural
head·stall *n* **:** an arrangement of straps or rope that fits around the head of an animal and forms part of a bridle or halter
head·stand *n* **:** the act of standing on the head with support from the hands
head start *n* **:** an advantage given at the beginning (as to a school child or a runner)
head·stone *n* **:** a stone that marks a grave
head·strong *adj* **:** very stubborn
head·wait·er *n* **:** the head of the staff of a restaurant
head·wa·ters *n pl* **:** the beginning and upper part of a stream
head·way *n* **1 :** movement in a forward direction (as of a ship) **2 :** ¹PROGRESS 2
heal *vb* **healed; heal·ing :** to make or become healthy or well again — **heal·er** *n*
health *n* **1 :** the condition of being free from illness or disease **2 :** the overall condition of the body
health·ful *adj* **:** good for the health
healthy *adj* **health·i·er; health·i·est 1 :** being sound and well **:** not sick **2 :** showing good health **3 :** aiding or building up health **4 :** rather large in extent or amount — **health·i·ly** *adv*
¹heap *n* **1 :** a large messy pile **2 :** a large number or amount
²heap *vb* **heaped; heap·ing 1 :** to make into a pile **:** throw or lay in a heap **2 :** to provide in large amounts **3 :** to fill to capacity
hear *vb* **heard; hear·ing 1 :** to take in through the ear **2 :** to have the power of hearing **3 :** to gain knowledge of by hearing **4 :** to listen to with care and attention — **hear·er** *n*
hear·ing *n* **1 :** the act or power of taking in sound through the ear **:** the sense by which a person hears **2 :** EARSHOT **3 :** a chance to be heard or known **4 :** a meeting at which arguments or testimony is heard
hearing aid *n* **:** an electronic device worn in or behind the ear of a person with poor hearing to make sounds louder
hear·ken *vb* **hear·kened; hear·ken·ing :** LISTEN 1
hear·say *n* **:** something heard from another **:** RUMOR
hearse *n* **:** a vehicle for carrying a dead person to the grave
heart *n* **1 :** a hollow muscular organ of the body that expands and contracts to move blood through the arteries and veins **2 :** something shaped like a heart **3 :** a part near the center or deep into the interior **4 :** the most essential part **5 :** human feelings **6 :** courage or enthusiasm — **by heart :** so as to be able to repeat from memory
heart·ache *n* **:** ¹SORROW 1
heart·beat *n* **:** a single contracting and expanding of the heart
heart·break *n* **:** very great or deep grief
heart·break·ing *adj* **:** causing great sorrow
heart·bro·ken *adj* **:** overcome by sorrow
heart·en *vb* **heart·ened; heart·en·ing :** to give new hope or courage to
heart·felt *adj* **:** deeply felt **:** SINCERE
hearth *n* **1 :** an area (as of brick) in front of a fireplace **2 :** the floor of a fireplace
hearth·stone *n* **:** a stone forming a hearth
heart·i·ly *adv* **1 :** with sincerity or enthusiasm **2 :** COMPLETELY
heart·less *adj* **:** UNFEELING 2, CRUEL
heart·sick *adj* **:** very sad
heart·wood *n* **:** the usually dark wood in the center of a tree
hearty *adj* **heart·i·er; heart·i·est 1 :** friendly and enthusiastic **2 :** strong, healthy, and active **3 :** having a good appetite **4 :** large and plentiful — **heart·i·ness** *n*
¹heat *vb* **heat·ed; heat·ing :** to make or become warm or hot
²heat *n* **1 :** a condition of being hot **:** WARMTH **2 :** hot weather **3 :** a form of energy that causes an object to rise in temperature **4 :** strength of feeling or force of action **5 :** a single race in a contest that includes two or more races
heat·ed *adj* **1 :** HOT 1 **2 :** ANGRY — **heat·ed·ly** *adv*
heat·er *n* **:** a device for heating
heath *n* **1 :** a low, woody, and often evergreen plant that grows chiefly on poor wet soil **2 :** a usually open level area of land on which heaths can grow
¹hea·then *adj* **1 :** relating to people who do not know about or worship the God of the Bible **2 :** UNCIVILIZED 1
²heathen *n, pl* **heathens** *or* **heathen 1 :** a person who does not know about and worship the God of the Bible **:** PAGAN **2 :** an uncivilized person
heath·er *n* **:** an evergreen heath of northern and mountainous areas with pink flowers and needlelike leaves
¹heave *vb* **heaved** *or* **hove; heav·ing 1 :** to

raise with an effort **2** : HURL, THROW **3** : to utter with an effort **4** : to rise and fall again and again **5** : to be thrown or raised up

[2]**heave** *n* **1** : an effort to lift or raise **2** : a forceful throw **3** : an upward motion (as of the chest in breathing or of waves in motion)

heav·en *n* **1** : SKY 1 — usually used in pl. **2** *often cap* : a place where good people are believed in some religions to be rewarded with eternal life after death **3** *cap* : GOD 1 **4** : a place or condition of complete happiness

heav·en·ly *adj* **1** : occurring or situated in the sky **2** : [1]DIVINE 1 **3** : entirely delightful

heavi·ly *adv* **1** : with or as if with weight **2** : in a slow and difficult way **3** : very much

heavy *adj* **heavi·er; heavi·est** **1** : having great weight **2** : unusually great in amount, force, or effect **3** : made with thick strong material **4** : dense and thick **5** : hard to put up with **6** : sad or troubled **7** : having little strength or energy — **heavi·ness** *n*

[1]**He·brew** *adj* : of or relating to the Hebrew peoples or the Hebrew language

[2]**Hebrew** *n* **1** : a member of any of a group of peoples of the ancient kingdom of Israel descended from Jacob of the Bible **2** : the language of the ancient Hebrews or a later form of it

hec·tic *adj* : filled with excitement, activity, or confusion

hecto- *prefix* : hundred

hec·to·me·ter *n* : a unit of length in the metric system equal to 100 meters

he'd : he had : he would

[1]**hedge** *n* : a fence or boundary made up of a thick growth of shrubs or low trees

[2]**hedge** *vb* **hedged; hedg·ing** **1** : to surround or protect with a thick growth of shrubs or low trees **2** : to avoid giving a direct or exact answer or promise

hedge·hog *n* **1** : a mammal of Europe, Asia, and Africa that eats insects, has sharp spines mixed with the hair on its back, and is able to roll itself up into a ball when threatened **2** : PORCUPINE

hedge·row *n* : a row of shrubs or trees around a field

[1]**heed** *vb* **heed·ed; heed·ing** : to pay attention to : MIND

[2]**heed** *n* : ATTENTION 1 — **heed·ful** *adj*

heed·less *adj* : not careful or attentive : CARELESS — **heed·less·ly** *adv*

[1]**heel** *n* **1** : the back part of the human foot behind the arch and below the ankle **2** : the part of an animal's limb corresponding to a person's heel **3** : a part (as of a stocking or shoe) that covers or supports the human heel **4** : one of the crusty ends of a loaf of bread **5** : a rear, low, or bottom part **6** : a mean selfish person

[2]**heel** *vb* **heeled; heel·ing** : to lean to one side

heft *vb* **heft·ed; heft·ing** : to lift something up

hefty *adj* **heft·i·er; heft·i·est** **1** : HEAVY 1 **2** : very forceful

heif·er *n* : a young cow

height *n* **1** : the distance from the bottom to the top of something standing upright **2** : distance upward **3** : the highest point or greatest degree

height·en *vb* **height·ened; height·en·ing** : to make greater : INCREASE

Heim·lich maneuver *n* : the use of upward pressure to the area directly above the navel of a choking person to force out an object blocking the trachea

heir *n* **1** : a person who inherits or has the right to inherit property after the death of its owner **2** : a person who has legal claim to a title or a throne when the person holding it dies

heir·ess *n* : a girl or a woman who is an heir

heir·loom *n* : a piece of personal property handed down in a family from one generation to another

held *past and past participle of* HOLD

he·li·cop·ter *n* : an aircraft supported in the air by horizontal propellers

he·li·port *n* : a place for a helicopter to land and take off

he·li·um *n* : a very light gaseous chemical element that is found in various natural gases, will not burn, and is used in balloons

hell *n* **1** : a place where evil people are believed in some religions to suffer after death **2** : a place or state of misery or wickedness

he'll : he shall : he will

hell·ish *adj* : extremely bad

hel·lo *interj* — used as a greeting or to express surprise

helm *n* **1** : a lever or wheel for steering a ship **2** : a position of control

hel·met *n* : a protective covering for the head

[1]**help** *vb* **helped; help·ing** **1** : to provide with what is useful in achieving an end **2** : to give relief from pain or disease **3** : PREVENT 1 **4** : [1]SERVE 1 — **help·er** *n*

[2]**help** *n* **1** : an act or instance of helping : AID **2** : the fact of being useful or helpful **3** : the ability to be helped **4** : a person or a thing that helps **5** : a body of hired helpers

help·ful *adj* : providing help — **help·ful·ly** *adv*

help·ing *n* : a serving of food

helping verb *n* : a verb (as *am, may,* or *will*) that is used with another verb to express person, number, mood, or tense

help·less *adj* : without help or defense — **help·less·ly** *adv* — **help·less·ness** *n*

hel·ter–skel·ter *adv* **1** : in a confused and reckless manner **2** : in great disorder

[1]hem *n* : a border of a cloth article made by folding back an edge and sewing it down
[2]hem *vb* **hemmed; hem·ming** **1** : to finish with or make a hem **2** : SURROUND 1
hemi- *prefix* : half
hemi·sphere *n* **1** : one of the halves of the earth as divided by the equator or by a meridian **2** : a half of a sphere **3** : either the left or the right half of the cerebrum — **hemi·spher·ic** *or* **hemi·spher·i·cal** *adj*
hem·lock *n* **1** : an evergreen tree related to the pine **2** : a poisonous plant with small white flowers and leaves divided into many parts
he·mo·glo·bin *n* : a protein of red blood cells that contains iron and carries oxygen from the lungs to the tissues and carbon dioxide from the tissues to the lungs
hem·or·rhage *n* : a large loss of blood
hemp *n* : a tall Asian plant grown for its tough woody fiber that is used especially in making rope and for its flowers and leaves that yield drugs (as marijuana)
hen *n* **1** : a female domestic fowl **2** : a female bird
hence *adv* **1** : from this place **2** : from this time **3** : as a result : THEREFORE
hence·forth *adv* : from this time on
hench·man *n, pl* **hench·men** : a trusted follower or supporter and especially one who performs unpleasant or illegal tasks
hep·a·ti·tis *n* : a disease which is caused by a virus and in which the liver is damaged and there is yellowing of the skin and fever
hepta- *or* **hept-** *prefix* : seven
hep·ta·gon *n* : a closed geometric figure having seven angles and seven sides
[1]her *adj* : relating to or belonging to a certain woman, girl, or female animal
[2]her *pron, objective case of* SHE
[1]her·ald *n* **1** : an official messenger **2** : a person who brings news or announces something
[2]herald *vb* **her·ald·ed; her·ald·ing** **1** : to give notice of : ANNOUNCE **2** : FORETELL
her·ald·ry *n* : the art or science of tracing and recording family history and creating coats of arms
herb *n* **1** : a plant with soft stems that die down at the end of the growing season **2** : a plant or plant part used in medicine or in seasoning foods
her·bi·vore *n* : an animal that feeds on plants
her·biv·o·rous *adj* : feeding on plants
[1]herd *n* : a number of animals of one kind kept or living together
[2]herd *vb* **herd·ed; herd·ing** : to gather and move as a group — **herd·er** *n*
herds·man *n, pl* **herds·men** : a person who owns or watches over a flock or herd
[1]here *adv* **1** : in or at this place **2** : at this time : happening now **3** : to or into this place : HITHER
[2]here *n* : this place
here·abouts *or* **here·about** *adv* : near or around this place
[1]here·af·ter *adv* **1** : after this **2** : in some future time or state
[2]hereafter *n* **1** : [2]FUTURE 1 **2** : life after death
here·by *adv* : by means of this
he·red·i·tary *adj* **1** : capable of being passed from parent to offspring **2** : received or passing from an ancestor to an heir
he·red·i·ty *n, pl* **he·red·i·ties** : the passing on of characteristics (as the color of the eyes or hair) from parents to offspring
here·in *adv* : in this
her·e·sy *n, pl* **her·e·sies** **1** : the holding of religious beliefs opposed to church doctrine : such a belief **2** : belief or opinion opposed to a generally accepted view
her·e·tic *n* : a person who believes or teaches something opposed to accepted beliefs (as of a church)
here·to·fore *adv* : up to this time
here·up·on *adv* : right after this
here·with *adv* : with this
her·i·tage *n* : the traditions, achievements, and beliefs that are part of the history of a group of people
her·mit *n* : a person who lives apart from others especially for religious reasons
hermit crab *n* : a small crab that lives in the empty shells of mollusks (as snails)
he·ro *n, pl* **heroes** **1** : a person admired for great deeds or fine qualities **2** : a person who shows great courage **3** : the chief male character in a story, play, or poem
he·ro·ic *adj* **1** : of or relating to heroism or heroes **2** : COURAGEOUS, DARING — **he·ro·ical·ly** *adv*
her·o·in *n* : a very harmful illegal drug that is highly addictive and is made from morphine
her·o·ine *n* **1** : a woman admired for great deeds or fine qualities **2** : the chief female character in a story, poem, or play
her·o·ism *n* **1** : behavior showing great courage especially for a noble purpose **2** : the qualities of a hero
her·on *n* : a wading bird that has long legs, a long neck, a long thin bill, and large wings
her·ring *n* : a fish of the northern Atlantic Ocean that is often used for food
hers *pron* : that which belongs to her
her·self *pron* : her own self
he's : he is : he has
hes·i·tan·cy *n* : the quality or state of being unwilling to do something because of doubt or nervousness

hes·i·tant *adj* **:** feeling or showing unwillingness to do something because of doubt or nervousness — **hes·i·tant·ly** *adv*

hes·i·tate *vb* **hes·i·tat·ed; hes·i·tat·ing 1 :** to pause before doing something **2 :** to be unwilling to do something because of doubt or nervousness — **hes·i·ta·tion** *n*

hew *vb* **hewed** *or* **hewn; hew·ing 1 :** to chop down **2 :** to shape by cutting with an ax

hex *n* **:** a harmful spell **:** JINX

hexa- *or* **hex-** *prefix* **:** six

hexa·gon *n* **:** a closed geometric figure having six angles and six sides — **hex·ag·o·nal** *adj*

hey *interj* — used to call attention or to express surprise or joy

hey·day *n* **:** the time of greatest strength, popularity, or success

hi *interj* — used especially as a greeting

HI *abbr* Hawaii

hi·ber·nate *vb* **hi·ber·nat·ed; hi·ber·nat·ing :** to pass all or part of the winter in an inactive state in which the body temperature drops and breathing slows — **hi·ber·na·tor** *n*

hi·ber·na·tion *n* **:** the act of passing all or part of the winter in an inactive state

[1]hic·cup *n* **:** a gulping sound caused by sudden movements of muscles active in breathing

[2]hiccup *vb* **hic·cuped** *also* **hic·cupped; hic·cup·ing** *also* **hic·cup·ping :** to make a gulping sound caused by sudden movements of muscles active in breathing

hick·o·ry *n, pl* **hick·o·ries :** a tall tree related to the walnuts that has strong tough wood and bears an edible nut (**hickory nut**) in a hard shell

[1]hide *vb* **hid; hid·den** *or* **hid; hid·ing 1 :** to put or stay out of sight **2 :** to keep secret **3 :** to screen from view

[2]hide *n* **:** the skin of an animal

hide–and–go–seek *n* **:** HIDE-AND-SEEK

hide–and–seek *n* **:** a game in which one player covers his or her eyes and after giving the others time to hide goes looking for them

hide·away *n* **:** [1]RETREAT 3, HIDEOUT

hid·eous *adj* **:** very ugly or disgusting **:** FRIGHTFUL — **hid·eous·ly** *adv*

hide·out *n* **:** a secret place for hiding (as from the police)

hi·ero·glyph·ic *n* **:** any of the symbols in the picture writing of ancient Egypt

hig·gle·dy–pig·gle·dy *adv or adj* **:** in a messy way **:** TOPSY-TURVY

[1]high *adj* **high·er; high·est 1 :** extending to a great distance above the ground **2 :** having a specified elevation **:** TALL **3 :** of greater degree, size, amount, or cost than average **4 :** having great force **5 :** pitched or sounding above some other sound **6 :** very serious **7 :** of the best quality **8 :** rich in quality

[2]high *adv* **higher; highest :** at or to a high place or degree

[3]high *n* **1 :** a high point or level **2 :** a region of high barometric pressure **3 :** the arrangement of gears in an automobile giving the highest speed of travel **4 :** the space overhead **:** SKY

high·brow *n* **:** a person of great learning or culture

high five *n* **:** a show of celebration by two people slapping each other's hands in the air

high–hand·ed *adj* **:** having or showing no regard for the rights, concerns, or feelings of others

high·land *n* **:** high or hilly country

[1]high·light *n* **:** a very interesting event or detail

[2]highlight *vb* **high·light·ed; high·light·ing 1 :** EMPHASIZE **2 :** to be an interesting event or detail **3 :** to mark with a highlighter **4 :** to cause (something on a computer screen) to be displayed in a way that stands out

high·light·er *n* **:** a pen with a wide felt tip and brightly colored ink for marking text on a page so that it stands out clearly

high·ly *adv* **1 :** to a high degree **:** very much **2 :** with much approval

high·ness *n* **1 :** the quality or state or being high **2** — used as a title for a person of very high rank

high–rise *adj* **:** having many stories

high school *n* **:** a school usually including the ninth to twelfth or tenth to twelfth grades

high seas *n pl* **:** the part of a sea or ocean that is away from land

high–spir·it·ed *adj* **:** LIVELY 1

high–strung *adj* **:** very sensitive or nervous

high tech *n* **:** technology involving the production or use of advanced or sophisticated devices — **high–tech** *adj*

high tide *n* **:** the tide when the water is at its greatest height

high·way *n* **:** a main road

high·way·man *n, pl* **high·way·men :** a man who robbed travelers on a road in past centuries

hi·jack *vb* **hi·jacked; hi·jack·ing 1 :** to stop and steal or steal from a moving vehicle **2 :** to take control of (an aircraft) by force — **high·jack·er** *n*

[1]hike *vb* **hiked; hik·ing :** to take a long walk especially for pleasure or exercise — **hik·er** *n*

[2]hike *n* **:** a long walk especially for pleasure or exercise

hi·lar·i·ous *adj* **:** very funny — **hi·lar·i·ous·ly** *adv*

hi·lar·i·ty *n* **:** noisy fun or laughter

hill *n* **1 :** a usually rounded elevation of land lower than a mountain **2 :** a surface that slopes **3 :** a heap or mound of something

hill·bil·ly *n, pl* **hill·bil·lies :** a person from a backwoods area

hill·ock *n* **:** a small hill

hill·side *n* **:** the part of a hill between the top and the foot

hill·top *n* **:** the highest part of a hill

hilly *adj* **hill·i·er; hill·i·est :** having many hills

hilt *n* **:** a handle especially of a sword or dagger

him *pron, objective case of* HE

him·self *pron* **:** his own self

hind *adj* **:** being at the end or back **:** REAR

hin·der *vb* **hin·dered; hin·der·ing :** to make slow or difficult

hind·quar·ter *n* **:** the back half of a side of the body or carcass of a four-footed animal

hin·drance *n* **:** someone or something that makes a situation more difficult

hind·sight *n* **:** understanding of something only after it has happened

Hin·du *n* **:** a person who follows Hinduism

Hin·du·ism *n* **:** a religion that originated in India, involves worship of many gods, and includes the belief in reincarnation

[1]hinge *n* **:** a jointed piece on which a door, gate, or lid turns or swings

[2]hinge *vb* **hinged; hing·ing 1 :** to attach by or provide with hinges **2 :** DEPEND 2

[1]hint *n* **1 :** information that helps a person guess an answer or do something more easily **2 :** a small amount **:** TRACE

[2]hint *vb* **hint·ed; hint·ing :** to suggest something without plainly asking or saying it

hin·ter·land *n* **:** a region far from cities

hip *n* **:** the part of the body that curves out below the waist on each side

hip–hop *n* **1 :** rap music **2 :** the culture associated with rap music

hip·pie *or* **hip·py** *n, pl* **hippies :** a usually young person who rejects the values and practices of society and opposes violence and war

hip·po *n, pl* **hip·pos :** HIPPOPOTAMUS

hip·po·pot·a·mus *n, pl* **hip·po·pot·a·mus·es** *or* **hip·po·pot·a·mi :** a large African animal with thick hairless brownish gray skin, a big head, and short legs that eats plants and spends most of its time in rivers

hire *vb* **hired; hir·ing 1 :** [1]EMPLOY 1 **2 :** to get the temporary use of in return for pay **3 :** to take a job

[1]his *adj* **:** relating to or belonging to a certain man, boy, or male animal

[2]his *pron* **:** that which belongs to him

[1]His·pan·ic *adj* **:** of or relating to people of Latin-American origin

[2]Hispanic *n* **:** a person of Latin-American origin

[1]hiss *vb* **hissed; hiss·ing 1 :** to make a sound like a long \s\ **2 :** to show dislike or disapproval by hissing **3 :** to say (something) in a loud or angry whisper

[2]hiss *n* **:** a sound like a long \s\ sometimes used as a sign of dislike or disapproval

hist. *abbr* **1** historian **2** historical **3** history

his·to·ri·an *n* **:** a person who studies or writes about history

his·tor·ic *adj* **:** famous in history

his·tor·i·cal *adj* **1 :** relating to or based on history **2 :** known to be true — **his·tor·i·cal·ly** *adv*

his·to·ry *n, pl* **his·to·ries 1 :** events of the past and especially those relating to a particular place or subject **2 :** a branch of knowledge that records and explains past events **3 :** a written report of past events **4 :** an established record of past events

[1]hit *vb* **hit; hit·ting 1 :** to strike or be struck by (someone or something) forcefully **2 :** to cause or allow (something) to come into contact with something **3 :** to affect or be affected by in a harmful or damaging way **4 :** OCCUR 1 **5 :** to come upon by chance **6 :** to arrive at — **hit·ter** *n*

[2]hit *n* **1 :** a blow striking an object aimed at **2 :** something very successful **3 :** a batted baseball that enables the batter to reach base safely **4 :** a match in a computer search

hit–and–run *adj* **:** being or involving a driver who does not stop after being in an automobile accident

[1]hitch *vb* **hitched; hitch·ing 1 :** to fasten by or as if by a hook or knot **2 :** HITCHHIKE **3 :** to pull or lift (something) with a quick movement

[2]hitch *n* **1 :** an unexpected stop or problem **2 :** a jerky movement or pull **3 :** a knot used for a temporary fastening

hitch·hike *vb* **hitch·hiked; hitch·hik·ing :** to travel by getting free rides in passing vehicles — **hitch·hik·er** *n*

hith·er *adv* **:** to this place

hith·er·to *adv* **:** up to this time

HIV *n* **:** a virus that causes AIDS by destroying large numbers of cells that help the human body fight infection

hive *n* **1 :** a container for housing honeybees **2 :** the usually aboveground nest of bees **3 :** a colony of bees **4 :** a place filled with busy people

hives *n pl* **:** an allergic condition in which the skin breaks out in large red itching patches

[1]hoard *n* **:** a supply usually of something of value stored away or hidden

[2]hoard *vb* **hoard·ed; hoard·ing :** to gather and store away — **hoard·er** *n*

hoarse *adj* **hoars·er; hoars·est** **1 :** harsh in sound **2 :** having a rough voice — **hoarse·ly** *adv* — **hoarse·ness** *n*

hoary *adj* **hoar·i·er; hoar·i·est** **1 :** very old **2 :** having gray or white hair

[1]**hoax** *vb* **hoaxed; hoax·ing :** to trick into thinking something is true or real when it isn't

[2]**hoax** *n* **1 :** an act meant to fool or deceive **2 :** something false passed off as real

[1]**hob·ble** *vb* **hob·bled; hob·bling :** to walk slowly and with difficulty

[2]**hobble** *n* **:** a slow and difficult way of walking

hob·by *n, pl* **hobbies :** an interest or activity engaged in for pleasure

hob·by·horse *n* **:** a stick that has an imitation horse's head and that a child pretends to ride

hob·gob·lin *n* **1 :** a mischievous elf **2 :** BOGEY 2

ho·bo *n, pl* **hoboes :** [1]VAGRANT

hock *n* **1 :** a small piece of meat from the leg of a pig **2 :** the part of the rear leg of a four-footed animal that is like a human ankle

hock·ey *n* **:** a game played on ice or in a field by two teams who try to drive a puck or ball through a goal by hitting it with a stick

hodge·podge *n* **:** a disorderly mixture

[1]**hoe** *n* **:** a tool with a long handle and a thin flat blade used for weeding and cultivating

[2]**hoe** *vb* **hoed; hoe·ing :** to weed or loosen the soil around plants with a hoe

[1]**hog** *n* **1 :** a usually large adult pig **2 :** a greedy or dirty person

[2]**hog** *vb* **hogged; hog·ging :** to take or use in a way that keeps others from having or using

ho·gan *n* **:** a Navajo Indian dwelling made of logs and mud with a door traditionally facing east

hog·gish *adj* **:** very selfish or greedy — **hog·gish·ly** *adv*

hogs·head *n* **1 :** a very large cask **2 :** a unit of liquid measure equal to 63 gallons (about 238 liters)

[1]**hoist** *vb* **hoist·ed; hoist·ing :** to lift up especially with a pulley

[2]**hoist** *n* **:** a device used for lifting heavy loads

[1]**hold** *vb* **held; hold·ing** **1 :** to have or keep a grip on **2 :** to take in and have within **:** CONTAIN **3 :** [1]SUPPORT 1 **4 :** to carry on by group action **5 :** to have as a position of responsibility **6 :** to continue in the same way or state **:** LAST **7 :** to remain fast or fastened **8 :** to have or keep possession or control of **9 :** to have in mind **10 :** to limit the movement or activity of **:** RESTRAIN **11 :** to continue in a condition or position **12 :** to continue moving on (a course) without change **13 :** to make accept a legal or moral duty **14 :** CONSIDER 3, REGARD — **hold·er** *n* — **hold out** **1 :** to continue to be present or exist **2 :** to refuse to yield or agree — **hold up** **1 :** [2]DELAY 2 **2 :** to rob while threatening with a weapon

[2]**hold** *n* **1 :** the act or way of holding **:** GRIP **2 :** a note or rest in music kept up longer than usual

[3]**hold** *n* **1 :** the part of a ship below the decks in which cargo is stored **2 :** the cargo compartment of an airplane

hold·up *n* **1 :** robbery by an armed robber **2 :** [1]DELAY

hole *n* **1 :** an opening into or through something **2 :** a hollowed out place **3 :** DEN 1, BURROW

hole up *vb* **holed up; hol·ing up :** to take shelter

hol·i·day *n* **1 :** a special day of celebration during which schools and businesses are often closed **2 :** VACATION

ho·li·ness *n* **1 :** the quality or state of being holy **2** — used as a title for persons of high religious position

[1]**hol·ler** *vb* **hol·lered; hol·ler·ing :** to cry out **:** SHOUT

[2]**holler** *n* **:** [2]SHOUT, CRY

[1]**hol·low** *adj* **hol·low·er; hol·low·est** **1 :** having a space inside **:** not solid **2 :** curved inward **:** SUNKEN **3 :** suggesting a sound made in an empty place **4 :** not sincere — **hol·low·ly** *adv*

[2]**hollow** *n* **1 :** a low spot in a surface **2 :** a small valley **3 :** an empty space within something

[3]**hollow** *vb* **hol·lowed; hol·low·ing :** to make or become hollow

hol·ly *n, pl* **hollies :** an evergreen tree or shrub that has shiny leaves with prickly edges and red berries

hol·ly·hock *n* **:** a plant with large rounded leaves and tall stalks of bright showy flowers

ho·lo·caust *n* **1 :** a complete destruction especially by fire **2** *often cap* **:** the killing of civilians and especially Jews by the Nazis during World War II

ho·lo·gram *n* **:** a three-dimensional picture made by laser light reflected onto a photographic substance without the use of a camera

hol·ster *n* **:** a usually leather case in which a pistol is carried or worn

ho·ly *adj* **ho·li·er; ho·li·est** **1 :** set apart for the service of God or of a divine being **:** SACRED **2 :** being a deity **3** — used in exclamations to indicate surprise or excitement

holy day *n* **:** a day set aside for special religious observance

hom- *or* **homo-** *prefix* : one and the same : similar : alike

hom•age *n* **1** : a feudal ceremony in which a person pledges loyalty to a lord and becomes a vassal **2** : [1]RESPECT 1

[1]**home** *n* **1** : the house or apartment where a person lives **2** : the place where a person was born or grew up **3** : HABITAT **4** : a place for the care of people unable to care for themselves **5** : a family living together **6** : [1]HOUSE 1 **7** : the goal or point to be reached in some games — **at home** : relaxed and comfortable

[2]**home** *adv* **1** : to or at home **2** : to the final place or limit

home•com•ing *n* : a return home

home•land *n* : the country a person comes from

home•less *adj* : having no home or permanent residence — **home•less•ness** *n*

home•like *adj* : like a home (as in comfort and kindly warmth)

home•ly *adj* **home•li•er; home•li•est** **1** : not pretty or handsome **2** : suggesting home life

home•made *adj* : made in the home

home•mak•er *n* : a person who manages a household especially as a spouse and a parent — **home•mak•ing** *n*

home page *n* : the page of a website that is seen first and that usually contains links to the other pages of the site

home plate *n* : the base that a baseball runner must touch to score

hom•er *n* : HOME RUN

home•room *n* : a classroom where students report at the start of each day

home run *n* : a hit in baseball that enables the batter to go around all the bases and score

home•school *vb* **home•schooled; home•school•ing** : to teach school subjects to at home

home•school•er *n* **1** : a person who teaches school subjects to children at home **2** : a child who is taught school subjects at home

home•sick *adj* : longing for home and family — **home•sick•ness** *n*

home•spun *adj* **1** : made at home **2** : made of a loosely woven fabric originally made from yarn spun at home **3** : not fancy : SIMPLE

[1]**home•stead** *n* **1** : a home and the land around it **2** : a piece of land gained from United States public lands by living on and farming it

[2]**homestead** *vb* **home•stead•ed; home•stead•ing** : to acquire or settle on public land for use as a homestead — **home•stead•er** *n*

home•town *n* : the city or town where a person was born or grew up

home•ward *or* **home•wards** *adv or adj* : toward home

home•work *n* : work (as school lessons) to be done at home

hom•ey *adj* **hom•i•er; hom•i•est** : HOMELIKE

ho•mi•cide *n* : a killing of one human being by another

hom•ing pigeon *n* : a racing pigeon trained to return home

hom•i•ny *n* : kernels of corn that have the outer covering removed by processing and that are eaten cooked as a cereal or vegetable

homo- — see HOM-

ho•mog•e•nize *vb* **ho•mog•e•nized; ho•mog•e•niz•ing** : to reduce the particles within a liquid (as milk or paint) to the same size and spread them evenly in the liquid

ho•mo•graph *n* : one of two or more words spelled alike but different in meaning or origin or pronunciation

hom•onym *n* **1** : HOMOPHONE **2** : HOMOGRAPH **3** : one of two or more words spelled and pronounced alike but different in meaning

ho•mo•phone *n* : one of two or more words pronounced alike but different in meaning or origin or spelling

hone *vb* **honed; hon•ing** : to sharpen with or as if with a fine abrasive stone

hon•est *adj* **1** : not engaging in or involving cheating, stealing, or lying **2** : not marked by lies or trickery : STRAIGHTFORWARD **3** : being just what is indicated : REAL, GENUINE

hon•est•ly *adv* **1** : without cheating or lying : in an honest manner **2** : in a real and sincere way **3** — used to stress the truth or sincerity of what is being said **4** — used to show annoyance or disapproval

hon•es•ty *n* : the quality or state of being truthful and fair

hon•ey *n* **1** : a sweet sticky material made by bees from the nectar of flowers and stored by them in a honeycomb for food **2** : [1]DARLING 1

hon•ey•bee *n* : a bee whose honey is used by people as food

hon•ey•comb *n* : a mass of wax cells built by honeybees in their nest to contain young bees and stores of honey

hon•ey•dew melon *n* : a pale melon with greenish sweet flesh and smooth skin

[1]**hon•ey•moon** *n* **1** : a trip taken by a recently married couple **2** : a period of harmony especially just after marriage

[2]**honeymoon** *vb* **hon•ey•mooned; hon•ey•moon•ing** : to go on a trip right after marrying — **hon•ey•moon•er** *n*

hon·ey·suck·le *n* **:** a climbing vine or a bush with fragrant white, yellow, or red flowers

[1]**honk** *vb* **honked; honk·ing :** to make a sound like the cry of a goose

[2]**honk** *n* **1 :** the cry of a goose **2 :** a loud sound like the cry of a goose

[1]**hon·or** *or Can and Brit* **honour** *n* **1 :** good character as judged by other people **:** REPUTATION **2 :** outward respect **:** RECOGNITION **3 :** PRIVILEGE **4** — used especially as a title for an official of high rank **5 :** a person whose character and accomplishments bring respect or fame **6 :** evidence or a symbol of great respect **7 :** high moral standards of behavior

[2]**honor** *or Can and Brit* **honour** *vb* **hon·ored/honoured; hon·or·ing/honouring** **1 :** [2]RESPECT 1 **2 :** to recognize and show admiration for publicly **3 :** to live up to or fulfill the requirements of

hon·or·able *or Can and Brit* **honourable** *adj* **1 :** bringing about or deserving honor **2 :** observing ideas of honor or reputation **3 :** having high moral standards of behavior **:** ETHICAL, UPRIGHT — **hon·or·ably** *or Can and Brit* **honourably** *adv*

hon·or·ary *adj* **:** given or done as an honor

hon·our *Can and Brit spelling of* HONOR

hood *n* **1 :** a covering for the head and neck and sometimes the face **2 :** the movable covering for an automobile engine **3 :** a cover that is used especially to protect or shield something — **hood·ed** *adj*

-hood *n suffix* **1 :** state **:** condition **:** quality **:** nature **2 :** instance of a specified state or quality **3 :** individuals sharing a specified state or character

hood·lum *n* **:** a tough and violent criminal **:** THUG

hood·wink *vb* **hood·winked; hood·wink·ing :** to mislead by trickery

hoof *n, pl* **hooves** *or* **hoofs** **1 :** a covering of tough material that protects the ends of the toes of some animals (as horses, oxen, or pigs) **2 :** a foot (as of a horse) covered by a hoof — **hoofed** *adj*

[1]**hook** *n* **1 :** a curved device (as a piece of bent metal) for catching, holding, or pulling something **2 :** something curved or bent like a hook — **by hook or by crook :** in any way **:** fairly or unfairly

[2]**hook** *vb* **hooked; hook·ing** **1 :** to bend in the shape of a hook **2 :** to catch or fasten with a hook **3 :** CONNECT 1

hooked *adj* **1 :** shaped like or provided with a hook **2 :** fascinated by or fond of something

hook·worm *n* **:** a small worm that lives in the intestines and makes people sick by sucking their blood

hooky *also* **hook·ey** *n* **:** TRUANT

hoop *n* **1 :** a circular figure or object **2 :** a circular band used for holding together the strips that make up the sides of a barrel or tub **3 :** a circle or series of circles of flexible material (as wire) used for holding a woman's skirt out from the body

hoo·ray *also* **hur·rah** *or* **hur·ray** *interj* — used to express joy, approval, or encouragement

[1]**hoot** *vb* **hoot·ed; hoot·ing** **1 :** to utter a loud shout or laugh **2 :** to make the noise of an owl or a similar cry **3 :** to express by hoots

[2]**hoot** *n* **1 :** the sound made by an owl **2 :** a loud laugh or shout **3 :** the least bit

[1]**hop** *vb* **hopped; hop·ping** **1 :** to move by short quick jumps **2 :** to jump on one foot **3 :** to jump over **4 :** to get on, in, or aboard by or as if by hopping **5 :** to make a quick trip especially by air

[2]**hop** *n* **1 :** a short quick jump especially on one leg **2 :** a short trip especially by air

[3]**hop** *n* **1 :** a twining vine whose greenish flowers look like small cones **2 hops** *pl* **:** the dried flowers of the hop plant used chiefly in making beer and ale

[1]**hope** *vb* **hoped; hop·ing :** to desire especially with expectation that the wish will be granted

[2]**hope** *n* **1 :** desire together with the expectation of getting what is wanted **2 :** a chance or likelihood for something desired **3 :** something wished for **4 :** someone or something that may be able to help

hope·ful *adj* **1 :** full of hope **2 :** giving hope **:** PROMISING — **hope·ful·ly** *adv*

hope·less *adj* **1 :** having no hope **2 :** offering no hope — **hope·less·ly** *adv* — **hope·less·ness** *n*

Ho·pi *n, pl* **Hopi** *or* **Ho·pis** **1 :** a member of an American Indian people of northeastern Arizona **2 :** the language of the Hopi people

hop·per *n* **1 :** someone or something that hops **2 :** an insect that moves by leaping **3 :** a container used for pouring material (as grain or coal) into a machine or a bin **4 :** a railroad car for materials that are transported in large quantities

hop·scotch *n* **:** a game in which a player tosses a stone into sections of a figure drawn on the ground and hops through the figure and back to pick up the stone

horde *n* **:** MULTITUDE, SWARM

ho·ri·zon *n* **1 :** the line where the earth or sea seems to meet the sky **2 :** the limit of a person's outlook or experience

[1]**hor·i·zon·tal** *adj* **:** lying flat or level **:** parallel to the horizon — **hor·i·zon·tal·ly** *adv*

[2]**horizontal** *n* **:** something (as a line or plane) that is parallel to the horizon

hor·mone *n* **:** any of various chemical substances produced by body cells and released especially into the blood and having a specific effect on cells or organs of the body usually at a distance from the place of origin

horn *n* **1 :** one of the hard bony growths on the head of many hoofed animals (as cattle, goats, or sheep) **2 :** the tough material of which horns and hooves are composed **3 :** a brass musical instrument (as a trumpet or French horn) **4 :** a usually electrical device that makes a noise like that of a horn **5 :** something shaped like or made from a horn **6 :** a musical or signaling instrument made from an animal's horn — **horned** *adj* — **horn·less** *adj*

horned toad *n* **:** a small harmless lizard with a wide flattened body like a toad and hard pointed growths on the skin

hor·net *n* **:** a large wasp that can give a severe sting

horn of plenty *n, pl* **horns of plenty :** CORNUCOPIA

horny *adj* **horn·i·er; horn·i·est 1 :** made of horn **2 :** hard and rough

horo·scope *n* **1 :** a diagram of the positions of the planets and signs of the zodiac used in astrology **2 :** a prediction based on astrology

hor·ren·dous *adj* **:** very bad

hor·ri·ble *adj* **1 :** causing horror **:** TERRIBLE **2 :** very unpleasant — **hor·ri·bly** *adv*

hor·rid *adj* **1 :** HORRIBLE **2 :** very unpleasant **:** DISGUSTING

hor·ri·fy *vb* **hor·ri·fied; hor·ri·fy·ing :** to cause to feel great fear, dread, or shock

hor·ror *n* **1 :** great fear, dread, or shock **2 :** a quality or thing that causes horror

horse *n* **1 :** a large hoofed animal that feeds especially on grasses and is used as a work animal and for riding **2 :** a frame that supports something (as wood while being cut) **3 :** a piece of gymnasium equipment used for vaulting exercises — **from the horse's mouth :** from the original source

¹horse·back *n* **:** the back of a horse

²horseback *adv* **:** on horseback

horse chestnut *n* **:** a shiny large brown nut that is unfit to eat and is the fruit of a tall tree native to Europe

horse·fly *n, pl* **horse·flies :** a large swift two-winged fly the females of which suck blood from animals

horse·hair *n* **1 :** the hair of a horse especially from the mane or tail **2 :** a cloth made from horsehair

horse·man *n, pl* **horse·men 1 :** a horseback rider **2 :** a person skilled in handling horses — **horse·man·ship** *n*

horse·play *n* **:** rough play

horse·pow·er *n* **:** a unit of power that equals the work done in lifting 550 pounds one foot in one second

horse·rad·ish *n* **:** a sharp-tasting relish made from the root of a tall white-flowered plant

horse·shoe *n* **1 :** a protective iron plate that is nailed to the rim of a horse's hoof **2 :** something shaped like a horseshoe **3 horseshoes** *pl* **:** a game in which horseshoes are tossed at a stake in the ground

horse·tail *n* **:** a primitive plant that produces spores and has small leaves resembling scales

horse·whip *vb* **horse·whipped; horse·whip·ping :** to beat severely with a whip made to be used on a horse

horse·wom·an *n, pl* **horse·wom·en :** a woman skilled in riding on horseback or in handling horses

hors·ey *also* **horsy** *adj* **hors·i·er; hors·i·est :** of or relating to horses or horsemen and horsewomen

¹hose *n, pl* **hose** *or* **hos·es 1** *pl hose* **:** STOCKING 1, SOCK **2 :** a flexible tube for carrying fluid

²hose *vb* **hosed; hos·ing :** to spray, water, or wash with a hose

ho·siery *n* **:** clothing (as stockings or socks) that is worn on the legs and feet

hos·pi·ta·ble *adj* **1 :** friendly and generous to guests and visitors **2 :** willing to deal with something new — **hos·pi·ta·bly** *adv*

hos·pi·tal *n* **:** a place where the sick and injured are given medical care

hos·pi·tal·i·ty *n* **:** friendly and generous treatment of guests

hos·pi·tal·ize *vb* **hos·pi·tal·ized; hos·pi·tal·iz·ing :** to place in a hospital for care and treatment — **hos·pi·tal·iza·tion** *n*

¹host *n* **1 :** a person who receives or entertains guests **2 :** a living animal or plant on or in which a parasite lives

²host *vb* **host·ed; host·ing :** to serve as host to or at

³host *n* **:** MULTITUDE

⁴host *n, often cap* **:** the bread used in Christian Communion

hos·tage *n* **:** a person who is captured by someone who demands that certain things be done before the captured person is freed

hos·tel *n* **:** a place providing inexpensive lodging usually for young travelers

host·ess *n* **:** a woman who receives or entertains guests

hos·tile *adj* **1 :** belonging to or relating to an enemy **2 :** UNFRIENDLY

hos·til·i·ty *n, pl* **hos·til·i·ties 1 :** an unfriendly or hostile state, attitude, or action **2** *hostilities pl* **:** acts of warfare

hot *adj* **hot·ter; hot·test 1 :** having a high temperature **2 :** having or causing the sensation of an uncomfortably high degree of body heat **3 :** having a spicy or peppery flavor **4 :** currently popular **5 :** close to something sought **6 :** easily excited **7 :** marked by or causing anger or strong feelings **8 :** very angry **9 :** recently stolen **10 :** recently made or received **11 :** RADIOACTIVE — **hot·ly** *adv* — **hot·ness** *n*

hot·cake *n* **:** PANCAKE

hot dog *n* **:** a frankfurter cooked and then served in a long split roll

ho·tel *n* **:** a place that provides lodging and meals for the public **:** INN

hot·head *n* **:** a person who is easily excited or angered — **hot·head·ed** *adj*

hot·house *n* **:** a heated building enclosed by glass for growing plants

hot·line *n* **:** a direct telephone line for getting help in an emergency

hot plate *n* **:** a small portable appliance for heating or cooking

hot rod *n* **:** an automobile rebuilt for high speed and fast acceleration

hot water *n* **:** a difficult or distressing situation

[1]**hound** *n* **:** a dog with drooping ears that is used in hunting and follows game by the sense of smell

[2]**hound** *vb* **hound·ed; hound·ing :** to hunt, chase, or annoy without ceasing

hour *n* **1 :** one of the 24 divisions of a day **:** 60 minutes **2 :** the time of day **3 :** a fixed or particular time **4 :** the distance that can be traveled in an hour

hour·glass *n* **:** a device for measuring time in which sand takes an hour to run from the upper into the lower part of a glass container

[1]**hour·ly** *adv* **:** at or during every hour

[2]**hourly** *adj* **1 :** occurring every hour **2 :** figured by the hour

[1]**house** *n, pl* **hous·es 1 :** a place built for people to live in **2 :** something (as a nest or den) used by an animal for shelter **3 :** a building in which something is kept **4 :** [1]HOUSEHOLD **5 :** a body of persons assembled to make the laws for a country **6 :** a business firm **7 :** the audience in a theater or concert hall **8 :** FAMILY 2 — **on the house :** free of charge

[2]**house** *vb* **housed; hous·ing 1 :** to provide with living quarters or shelter **2 :** CONTAIN 2

house·boat *n* **:** a roomy pleasure boat fitted for use as a place to live

house·boy *n* **:** a boy or man hired to do housework

house·fly *n, pl* **house·flies :** a two-winged fly that is common in houses and may carry disease germs

[1]**house·hold** *n* **:** all the people in a family or group who live together in one house

[2]**household** *adj* **1 :** of or relating to a house or a household **2 :** FAMILIAR 1

house·hold·er *n* **:** a person who lives in a dwelling alone or as the head of a household

house·hus·band *n* **:** a married man in charge of a household

house·keep·er *n* **:** a person employed to take care of a house

house·keep·ing *n* **:** the care and management of a house or the rooms of a hotel

house·maid *n* **:** a woman or girl hired to do housework

house·moth·er *n* **:** a woman who acts as hostess, supervisor, and often housekeeper in a residence for young people

House of Representatives *n* **:** the lower house of a legislature (as the United States Congress)

house·plant *n* **:** a plant grown or kept indoors

house·top *n* **:** [1]ROOF 1

house·warm·ing *n* **:** a party to celebrate moving into a new home

house·wife *n, pl* **house·wives :** a married woman in charge of a household

house·work *n* **:** the labor involved in housekeeping

hous·ing *n* **1 :** dwellings provided for a number of people **2 :** something that covers or protects

hove *past and past participle of* HEAVE

hov·el *n* **:** a small poorly built usually dirty house

hov·er *vb* **hov·ered; hov·er·ing 1 :** to fly or float in the air without moving far in any direction **2 :** to stay near a place

[1]**how** *adv* **1 :** in what way **:** by what means **2 :** for what reason **3 :** to what degree, number, or amount **4 :** in what state or condition — **how about :** what do you say to or think of — **how come :** [1]WHY — **how do you do :** HELLO

[2]**how** *conj* **:** in what manner or condition

how·ev·er *adv* **1 :** to whatever degree or extent **2 :** in whatever way **3 :** in spite of that

[1]**howl** *vb* **howled; howl·ing 1 :** to make a loud long mournful cry or sound **2 :** to cry out loudly (as with pain or amusement)

[2]**howl** *n* **1 :** a loud long mournful sound made by dogs and related animals (as wolves) **2 :** a long loud cry (as of distress, disappointment, or rage)

hr. *abbr* hour

H.S. *abbr* high school

ht. *abbr* height

HTML *n* **:** a computer language that is used to create pages on the World Wide Web that can include text, pictures, sound, video, and hyperlinks to other Web pages

hub *n* **1 :** the center of a wheel, propeller, or fan **2 :** a center of activity

hub·bub *n* : UPROAR

huck·le·ber·ry *n, pl* **huck·le·ber·ries** : a dark edible berry like a blueberry but with hard rather large seeds

huck·ster *n* : PEDDLER, HAWKER

[1]**hud·dle** *vb* **hud·dled; hud·dling** **1** : to crowd, push, or pile together **2** : to get together to talk something over **3** : to sit or lie in a curled or bent position

[2]**huddle** *n* **1** : a closely packed group **2** : a private meeting or conference **3** : a brief gathering of football players to hear instructions for the next play

hue *n* **1** : [1]COLOR 1 **2** : a shade of a color

[1]**huff** *vb* **huffed; huff·ing** **1** : to give off puffs (as of air or steam) **2** : to do or say in a way that shows anger

[2]**huff** *n* : a fit of anger or temper

huffy *adj* **huff·i·er; huff·i·est** : easily offended or angered — **huff·i·ly** *adv*

[1]**hug** *vb* **hugged; hug·ging** **1** : to clasp in the arms : EMBRACE **2** : to keep close to

[2]**hug** *n* : [2]EMBRACE

huge *adj* **hug·er; hug·est** : great in size or degree : VAST — **huge·ly** *adv*

hulk *n* **1** : a person or thing that is bulky or clumsy **2** : an abandoned wreck or shell of something (as a ship)

hulk·ing *adj* : very large or heavy

[1]**hull** *n* **1** : the outside covering of a fruit or seed **2** : the frame or body of a ship or boat

[2]**hull** *vb* **hulled; hull·ing** : to remove the outer covering of (a fruit or seed)

hul·la·ba·loo *n, pl* **hul·la·ba·loos** : a confused noise : UPROAR, COMMOTION

[1]**hum** *vb* **hummed; hum·ming** **1** : to utter a sound like a long \m\ **2** : to make the buzzing noise of a flying insect **3** : to make musical tones with closed lips **4** : to give forth a low murmur of sounds **5** : to be very busy or active

[2]**hum** *n* **1** : a low continuous noise **2** : musical tones voiced without words

[1]**hu·man** *adj* **1** : of, being, or characteristic of people as distinct from animals **2** : having the form or characteristics of people

[2]**human** *n* : HUMAN BEING — **hu·man·like** *adj*

human being *n* : a man, woman, or child : PERSON

hu·mane *adj* : having sympathy and consideration for people or animals — **hu·mane·ly** *adv*

[1]**hu·man·i·tar·i·an** *n* : a person who works to improve the lives and living conditions of other people

[2]**humanitarian** *adj* : relating to or characteristic of people who work to improve the lives and living conditions of other people

hu·man·i·ty *n, pl* **hu·man·i·ties** **1** : the quality or state of being human **2** : the human race **3** *humanities pl* : studies (as literature, history, and art) concerned primarily with human culture **4** : KINDNESS 1, SYMPATHY

hu·man·ly *adv* : within the range of human ability

[1]**hum·ble** *adj* **hum·bler; hum·blest** **1** : not regarding others as inferior : not overly proud : MODEST **2** : expressed in a way that does not show too much pride **3** : low in rank or condition — **hum·bly** *adv*

[2]**humble** *vb* **hum·bled; hum·bling** **1** : to make modest **2** : to easily and unexpectedly defeat

hum·bug *n* **1** : FRAUD 3 **2** : NONSENSE 1

hum·ding·er *n* : something striking or extraordinary

hum·drum *adj* : not interesting

hu·mer·us *n, pl* **humeri** : the long bone of the upper arm or forelimb that extends from the shoulder to the elbow

hu·mid *adj* : MOIST

hu·mid·i·fy *vb* **hu·mid·i·fied; hu·mid·i·fy·ing** : to make (as the air of a room) more moist — **hu·mid·i·fi·er** *n*

hu·mid·i·ty *n, pl* **hu·mid·i·ties** : the degree of wetness especially of the atmosphere

hu·mil·i·ate *vb* **hu·mil·i·at·ed; hu·mil·i·at·ing** : to cause (someone) to feel very ashamed or foolish

hu·mil·i·a·tion *n* **1** : the state of being made to feel ashamed or foolish **2** : an instance of being made to feel ashamed or foolish

hu·mil·i·ty *n* : the quality of being humble

hum·ming·bird *n* : a tiny brightly colored American bird whose wings make a humming sound in flight

hum·mock *n* : a rounded mound of earth : KNOLL

[1]**hu·mor** *or Can and Brit* **humour** *n* **1** : the amusing quality of something **2** : the ability to see or tell the amusing quality of things **3** : state of mind : MOOD — **hu·mor·less** *or Can and Brit* **humourless** *adj*

[2]**humor** *or Can and Brit* **humour** *vb* **hu·mored/humoured; hu·mor·ing/humouring** : to give in to the wishes of

hu·mor·ist *n* : a person who writes or talks in a humorous way

hu·mor·ous *adj* : full of humor : FUNNY — **hu·mor·ous·ly** *adv*

hu·mour *Can and Brit spelling of* HUMOR

hump *n* **1** : a rounded bulge or lump (as on the back of a camel) **2** : a difficult part (as of a task) — **humped** *adj*

hump·back *n* **1** : a humped or crooked back **2** : HUMPBACK WHALE — **hump·backed** *adj*

humpback whale *n* : a large whale that is black above and white below and has very long flippers

hu·mus *n* **:** the dark rich part of earth formed from decaying plant or animal material

[1]**hunch** *vb* **hunched; hunch·ing** **1 :** to bend the body into an arch or hump **2 :** to draw up close together or into an arch

[2]**hunch** *n* **:** a strong feeling about what will happen

hunch·back *n* **1 :** HUMPBACK 1 **2 :** a person with a humped or crooked back

[1]**hun·dred** *n* **1 :** ten times ten **:** 100 **2 :** a very large number

[2]**hundred** *adj* **:** being 100

[1]**hun·dredth** *adj* **:** coming right after 99th

[2]**hundredth** *n* **:** number 100 in a series

hung *past and past participle of* HANG

[1]**hun·ger** *n* **1 :** a desire or a need for food **2 :** a strong desire

[2]**hunger** *vb* **hun·gered; hun·ger·ing** **1 :** to feel a desire or need for food **2 :** to have a strong desire

hun·gry *adj* **hun·gri·er; hun·gri·est** **1 :** feeling or showing hunger **2 :** having a strong desire — **hun·gri·ly** *adv*

hunk *n* **:** a large lump or piece

hun·ker *vb* **hun·kered; hun·ker·ing** **:** [1]CROUCH — **hunker down :** to settle in for a long time

[1]**hunt** *vb* **hunt·ed; hunt·ing** **1 :** to chase after in order to capture or kill **2 :** to try to find — **hunting** *n*

[2]**hunt** *n* **1 :** an instance or the practice of chasing to capture or kill **2 :** an act of searching

hunt·er *n* **1 :** a person who hunts wild animals **2 :** a dog or horse used or trained for hunting **3 :** a person who searches for something

hunts·man *n, pl* **hunts·men** **:** HUNTER 1

[1]**hur·dle** *n* **1 :** a barrier to be jumped in a race **2 hurdles** *pl* **:** a race in which runners must jump over barriers **3 :** OBSTACLE

[2]**hurdle** *vb* **hur·dled; hur·dling** **1 :** to leap over while running **2 :** OVERCOME 1

hurl *vb* **hurled; hurl·ing** **:** to throw with force

hurrah, hurray *variants of* HOORAY

hur·ri·cane *n* **:** a tropical cyclone with winds of 74 miles (119 kilometers) per hour or greater usually accompanied by rain, thunder, and lightning

hur·ried *adj* **1 :** going or working with speed **:** FAST **2 :** done in a hurry — **hur·ried·ly** *adv*

[1]**hur·ry** *vb* **hur·ried; hur·ry·ing** **1 :** to carry or cause to go with haste **2 :** to move or act with haste **3 :** to speed up

[2]**hurry** *n* **:** a need to act or move more quickly than usual **:** RUSH

[1]**hurt** *vb* **hurt; hurt·ing** **1 :** to feel or cause pain **2 :** to do harm to **:** DAMAGE **3 :** to cause to be sad **4 :** to make poorer or more difficult

[2]**hurt** *n* **1 :** an injury or wound to the body **2 :** mental or emotional pain

[3]**hurt** *adj* **:** physically or emotionally injured

hurt·ful *adj* **:** causing injury or suffering

hur·tle *vb* **hur·tled; hur·tling** **:** to move or fall with great speed or force

[1]**hus·band** *n* **:** a married man

[2]**husband** *vb* **hus·band·ed; hus·band·ing** **:** to manage with thrift **:** use carefully

hus·band·ry *n* **1 :** the management or wise use of resources **:** THRIFT **2 :** the raising and management of plants or animals for food

[1]**hush** *vb* **hushed; hush·ing** **:** to make or become quiet, calm, or still **:** SOOTHE

[2]**hush** *n* **:** [1]QUIET

hush–hush *adj* **:** [1]SECRET 1, CONFIDENTIAL

[1]**husk** *n* **:** the outer covering of a fruit or seed

[2]**husk** *vb* **husked; husk·ing** **:** to remove the outer covering from (a fruit or seed) — **husk·er** *n*

[1]**hus·ky** *adj* **hus·ki·er; hus·ki·est** **:** HOARSE 2 — **hus·ki·ly** *adv* — **hus·ki·ness** *n*

[2]**husky** *n, pl* **huskies** **:** a strong dog with a thick coat often used to pull sleds in arctic regions

[3]**husky** *adj* **hus·ki·er; hus·ki·est** **1 :** STRONG 1, BURLY **2 :** larger than average — **hus·ki·ness** *n*

[1]**hus·tle** *vb* **hus·tled; hus·tling** **1 :** to push, crowd, or force forward roughly **2 :** to move or work rapidly and tirelessly

[2]**hustle** *n* **:** energetic activity

hut *n* **:** a small roughly made and often temporary dwelling

hutch *n* **1 :** a low cupboard usually having open shelves on top **2 :** a pen or coop for an animal

hy·a·cinth *n* **:** a plant often grown for its stalks of fragrant flowers shaped like bells

[1]**hy·brid** *n* **1 :** an animal or plant whose parents differ in some hereditary characteristic or belong to different groups (as breeds or species) **2 :** something that is of mixed origin or composition

[2]**hybrid** *adj* **:** of mixed origin **:** of or relating to a hybrid

hydr- *or* **hydro-** *prefix* **1 :** water **2 :** hydrogen

hy·drant *n* **:** a pipe with a spout through which water may be drawn

hy·drau·lic *adj* **1 :** operated, moved, or brought about by means of water **2 :** operated by liquid forced through a small hole or through a tube — **hy·drau·li·cal·ly** *adv*

hy·dro·car·bon *n* **:** a substance containing only carbon and hydrogen

hy·dro·chlo·ric acid *n* **:** a strong acid formed by dissolving in water a gas made up of hydrogen and chlorine

hy·dro·elec·tric *adj* **:** relating to or used in the making of electricity by waterpower

hy·dro·gen *n* : a colorless, odorless, and tasteless flammable gas that is the lightest of the chemical elements
hydrogen bomb *n* : a bomb whose great power is due to the sudden release of energy when the central portions of hydrogen atoms unite
hydrogen peroxide *n* : a liquid chemical containing hydrogen and oxygen and used for bleaching and as an antiseptic
hy·dro·plane *n* : a speedboat whose hull is completely or partly raised as it glides over water
hy·e·na *n* : a large doglike mammal of Asia and Africa that lives on flesh
hy·giene *n* **1** : a science that deals with the bringing about and keeping up of good health **2** : conditions or practices (as of cleanliness) necessary for health
hy·gien·ic *adj* : of, relating to, or leading toward health or hygiene
hy·gien·ist *n* : a person skilled in hygiene and especially in a specified branch of hygiene
hy·grom·e·ter *n* : an instrument for measuring the humidity of the air
hymn *n* : a song of praise especially to God
hym·nal *n* : a book of hymns
hyper- *prefix* : excessively
hy·per·ac·tive *adj* : extremely or overly active
hy·per·link *n* : an electronic link that allows a computer user to move directly from a marked place in a hypertext document to another in the same or a different document — **hyperlink** *vb*
hy·per·sen·si·tive *adj* : very sensitive
hy·per·ten·sion *n* : a medical condition marked by abnormally high blood pressure
hy·per·text *n* : an arrangement of the information in a computer database that allows the user to get other information by clicking on text displayed on the screen
hy·per·ven·ti·late *vb* **hy·per·ven·ti·lat·ed; hy·per·ven·ti·lat·ing** : to breathe very quickly and deeply
hy·pha *n, pl* **hy·phae** : one of the fine threads that make up the body of a fungus
¹hy·phen *n* : a mark - used to divide or to compound words or word elements
²hyphen *vb* **hy·phened; hy·phen·ing** : HYPHENATE
hy·phen·ate *vb* **hy·phen·at·ed; hy·phen·at·ing** : to connect or mark with a hyphen
hyp·no·sis *n* : a state which resembles sleep but is produced by a person who can then make suggestions to which the person in this state can respond
hyp·not·ic *adj* **1** : of or relating to hypnosis **2** : having an effect like that of hypnosis
hyp·no·tism *n* : the act or practice of producing a state like sleep in a person in which he or she will respond to suggestions made by the hypnotist
hyp·no·tist *n* : a person who hypnotizes others
hyp·no·tize *vb* **hyp·no·tized; hyp·no·tiz·ing** : to affect by or as if by hypnotism
hy·poc·ri·sy *n, pl* **hy·poc·ri·sies** : the quality of acting in a way that goes against claimed beliefs or feelings
hyp·o·crite *n* : a person who acts in a way that goes against what he or she claims to believe or feel — **hyp·o·crit·i·cal** *adj*
hy·po·der·mic needle *n* **1** : ¹NEEDLE 5 **2** : a small syringe used with a hollow needle to inject material (as a vaccine) into or beneath the skin
hypodermic syringe *n* : HYPODERMIC NEEDLE 2
hy·pot·e·nuse *n* : the side of a right triangle that is opposite the right angle
hy·poth·e·sis *n, pl* **hy·poth·e·ses** : something not proved but assumed to be true for purposes of argument or further study or investigation
hy·po·thet·i·cal *adj* **1** : involving or based on a hypothesis **2** : imagined as an example for further thought — **hy·po·thet·i·cal·ly** *adv*
hys·te·ria *n* : a state in which emotions (as fear or joy) are so strong that a person acts in an uncontrolled way
hys·ter·i·cal *adj* **1** : feeling or showing extreme and uncontrolled emotion **2** : very funny — **hys·ter·i·cal·ly** *adv*
hys·ter·ics *n pl* : an outburst of uncontrollable laughing or crying — used as singular or plural

I

i *n, pl* **i's** *or* **is** *often cap* **1 :** the ninth letter of the English alphabet **2 :** the number one in Roman numerals

I *pron* **:** the person speaking or writing

Ia., IA *abbr* Iowa

-ial *adj suffix* **:** [1]-AL

-ian — see -AN

ibex *n, pl* **ibex** *or* **ibex·es :** a wild goat that lives mostly in high mountains of Europe, Asia, and northeastern Africa and has large horns that curve backward

-ibility — see -ABILITY

ibis *n, pl* **ibis** *or* **ibis·es :** a tall bird related to the herons with long legs and a slender bill that curves down

-ible — see -ABLE

-ic *adj suffix* **1 :** of, relating to, or having the form of **:** being **2 :** coming from, consisting of, or containing **3 :** in the manner of **4 :** making use of **5 :** characterized by **:** exhibiting **6 :** affected with

-ical *adj suffix* **:** -IC

[1]ice *n* **1 :** frozen water **2 :** a sheet of frozen water **3 :** a substance like ice **4 :** a frozen dessert usually made with sweetened fruit juice

[2]ice *vb* **iced; ic·ing 1 :** to coat or become coated with ice **2 :** to chill with ice **3 :** to cover with icing

ice age *n* **:** a period of time during which much of the earth is covered with glaciers

ice·berg *n* **:** a large mass of ice that has broken away from a glacier and is floating in the ocean

ice·bound *adj* **:** surrounded or blocked by ice

ice·box *n* **:** REFRIGERATOR

ice·break·er *n* **1 :** a ship equipped to make and keep open a channel through ice **2 :** something said or done that helps people relax and begin talking in a social situation

ice cap *n* **:** a large more or less level glacier flowing outward in all directions from its center

ice–cold *adj* **:** very cold

ice cream *n* **:** a frozen food containing sweetened and flavored cream or butterfat

ice hockey *n* **:** hockey played on ice

ice–skate *vb* **ice–skat·ed; ice–skat·ing :** to skate on ice — **ice skat·er** *n*

ice skate *n* **:** a shoe with a special blade on the bottom that is used for skating on ice

ici·cle *n* **:** a hanging piece of ice formed from dripping water as it freezes

ic·ing *n* **:** a sweet coating for baked goods

icon *n* **1 :** a widely known symbol **2 :** a person who is very successful or admired **3 :** a religious image usually painted on a small wooden panel **4 :** a small picture or symbol on a computer display screen that represents an app, a function (as a command to save), or an object (as a file)

-ics *n pl suffix* **1 :** study **:** knowledge **:** skill **:** practice **2 :** characteristic actions or qualities

ICU *abbr* intensive care unit

icy *adj* **ic·i·er; ic·i·est 1 :** covered with, full of, or being ice **2 :** very cold **3 :** UNFRIENDLY — **ic·i·ly** *adv*

ID *abbr* **1** Idaho **2** identification

I'd : I had **:** I would

idea *n* **1 :** a thought or plan about what to do **2 :** something imagined or pictured in the mind **3 :** an understanding of something **4 :** a central meaning or purpose **5 :** an opinion or belief

[1]ide·al *adj* **:** having no flaw **:** PERFECT — **ide·al·ly** *adv*

[2]ideal *n* **1 :** a standard of perfection, beauty, or excellence **2 :** someone who deserves to be imitated or admired

iden·ti·cal *adj* **1 :** being one and the same **2 :** being exactly alike or equal — **iden·ti·cal·ly** *adv*

identical twin *n* **:** either one of a pair of twins of the same sex that come from a single fertilized egg and are physically similar

iden·ti·fi·ca·tion *n* **1 :** an act of finding out the identity of **2 :** something that shows or proves identity

iden·ti·fy *vb* **iden·ti·fied; iden·ti·fy·ing 1 :** to find out or show the identity of **2 :** to feel empathy for **3 :** to think of as joined or associated with

iden·ti·ty *n, pl* **iden·ti·ties 1 :** the set of qualities and beliefs that make one person or group different from others **:** INDIVIDUALITY **2 :** the fact of being the same person or thing as claimed **3 :** the fact or condition of being exactly alike **:** SAMENESS

id·i·o·cy *n, pl* **id·i·o·cies :** something very stupid or foolish

id·i·om *n* **:** an expression that cannot be understood from the meanings of its separate words but must be learned as a whole

id·i·o·syn·cra·sy *n, pl* **id·i·o·syn·cra·sies :** an unusual way of behaving or thinking that is characteristic of a person

id·i·ot *n* **:** a silly or foolish person

id·i·ot·ic *adj* **:** FOOLISH

[1]idle *adj* **idler; idlest 1 :** not working or in use **2 :** LAZY 1 **3 :** not based on anything real or serious — **idle·ness** *n* — **idly** *adv*

[2]**idle** *vb* **idled; idling** **1 :** to spend time doing nothing **2 :** to run without being connected for doing useful work

idol *n* **1 :** an image worshipped as a god **2 :** a much loved or admired person or thing

idol·ize *vb* **idol·ized; idol·iz·ing :** to love or admire greatly : make an idol of

i.e. *abbr* that is — abbreviation for Latin *id est,* which means "that is"

-ie *also* **-y** *n suffix, pl* **-ies :** little one

-ier — see [2]-ER

if *conj* **1 :** in the event that **2 :** WHETHER 1 **3** — used to introduce a wish

-ify *vb suffix* **-ified; -ify·ing :** -FY

ig·loo *n, pl* **igloos :** a house often made of blocks of snow and shaped like a dome

ig·ne·ous *adj* **:** formed by hardening of melted mineral material within the earth

ig·nite *vb* **ig·nit·ed; ig·nit·ing** **1 :** to set on fire : LIGHT **2 :** to catch fire

ig·ni·tion *n* **1 :** the act of causing something to start burning **2 :** the process or means (as an electric spark) of causing the fuel in an engine to burn so that the engine begins working **3 :** a device that is used to start a motor vehicle

ig·no·min·i·ous *adj* **:** DISGRACEFUL

ig·no·rance *n* **:** a lack of knowledge, understanding, or education : the state of being ignorant

ig·no·rant *adj* **1 :** having little or no knowledge : not educated **2 :** not knowing : UNAWARE **3 :** resulting from or showing lack of knowledge — **ig·no·rant·ly** *adv*

ig·nore *vb* **ig·nored; ig·nor·ing :** to pay no attention to

igua·na *n* **:** a large tropical American lizard with a ridge of tall scales along its back

IL *abbr* Illinois

il- — see IN-

[1]**ill** *adj* **worse; worst** **1 :** not in good health : SICK **2 :** not normal or sound **3 :** meant to do harm : EVIL **4 :** causing suffering or distress **5 :** not helpful **6 :** not kind or friendly **7 :** not right or proper

[2]**ill** *adv* **worse; worst** **1 :** with displeasure or anger **2 :** in a harsh or unkind way **3 :** SCARCELY 1, HARDLY **4 :** in a bad or faulty way

[3]**ill** *n* **1 :** the opposite of good **2 :** a sickness or disease **3 :** [2]TROUBLE 2

Ill. *abbr* Illinois

I'll : I shall : I will

il·le·gal *adj* **:** not allowed by the laws or rules — **il·le·gal·ly** *adv*

il·leg·i·ble *adj* **:** impossible or very hard to read — **il·leg·i·bly** *adv*

il·le·git·i·mate *adj* **:** not accepted by the law as rightful

il·lic·it *adj* **:** not permitted : UNLAWFUL

il·lit·er·a·cy *n* **:** the state or condition of being unable to read or write

[1]**il·lit·er·ate** *adj* **:** unable to read or write

[2]**illiterate** *n* **:** a person who is unable to read or write

ill–man·nered *adj* **:** not polite

ill–na·tured *adj* **:** having or showing an unfriendly nature

ill·ness *n* **1 :** an unhealthy condition of the body or mind **2 :** a specific sickness or disease

il·log·i·cal *adj* **:** not using or following good reasoning — **il·log·i·cal·ly** *adv*

ill–tem·pered *adj* **:** having or showing a bad temper

il·lu·mi·nate *vb* **il·lu·mi·nat·ed; il·lu·mi·nat·ing** **1 :** to supply with light : light up **2 :** to make clear : EXPLAIN

il·lu·mi·na·tion *n* **:** the action of lighting something : the state of being lighted

ill–use *vb* **ill–used; ill–us·ing :** to treat badly

il·lu·sion *n* **1 :** something that is false or unreal but seems to be true or real **2 :** a mistaken idea

il·lu·so·ry *adj* **:** based on something that is not true or real : DECEPTIVE

il·lus·trate *vb* **il·lus·trat·ed; il·lus·trat·ing** **1 :** to supply with pictures or diagrams meant to explain or decorate **2 :** to make clear by using examples **3 :** to serve as an example

il·lus·tra·tion *n* **1 :** a picture or diagram that explains or decorates **2 :** an example or instance used to make something clear **3 :** the action of illustrating : the condition of being illustrated

il·lus·tra·tive *adj* **:** serving as an example

il·lus·tra·tor *n* **:** an artist who makes illustrations (as for books)

il·lus·tri·ous *adj* **:** admired and respected because of greatness or achievement : EMINENT

ill will *n* **:** unfriendly feeling

IM *vb* **IM'd; IM'ing :** to communicate (with someone) by instant messaging

im- — see IN-

I'm : I am

im·age *n* **1 :** a picture or reflection of something produced by a device (as a mirror or lens) **2 :** someone who looks very much like another **3 :** the thought of how something looks **4 :** a representation (as a picture or statue) of something **5 :** an idea of what someone or something is like

im·ag·ery *n* **:** pictures or photographs of something

imag·in·able *adj* **:** possible to imagine

imag·i·nary *adj* **:** existing only in the imagination : not real

imag·i·na·tion *n* **1 :** the act, process, or power of forming a mental picture of something not present and especially of something one has not known or experienced **2 :** creative ability **3 :** a creation of the mind

imag·i·na·tive *adj* **1 :** relating to or showing imagination **2 :** having a lively imagination

imag·ine *vb* **imag·ined; imag·in·ing 1 :** to form a mental picture of **:** use the imagination **2 :** THINK 1

imag·in·ings *n pl* **:** products of the imagination

im·be·cile *n* **:** IDIOT, FOOL

im·i·tate *vb* **im·i·tat·ed; im·i·tat·ing 1 :** to follow as a pattern, model, or example **2 :** to be or appear like **:** RESEMBLE **3 :** to copy exactly **:** MIMIC

[1]**im·i·ta·tion** *n* **1 :** the act of copying someone or something **2 :** [1]COPY 1

[2]**imitation** *adj* **:** made to look like something else and especially something valuable

im·i·ta·tive *adj* **:** made or done to be like something or someone else

im·mac·u·late *adj* **1 :** perfectly clean **2 :** having no flaw or error — **im·mac·u·late·ly** *adv*

im·ma·te·ri·al *adj* **:** not important **:** INSIGNIFICANT

im·ma·ture *adj* **1 :** not yet fully grown or ripe **2 :** acting in or exhibiting a childish manner — **im·ma·ture·ly** *adv*

im·mea·sur·able *adj* **:** very great in size or amount — **im·mea·sur·ably** *adv*

im·me·di·ate *adj* **1 :** happening without any delay **2 :** occurring or existing now **3 :** having importance now **4 :** not far away in time or space **5 :** being next in line or nearest in relationship **6 :** having nothing between

im·me·di·ate·ly *adv* **1 :** with nothing between **2 :** right away

im·mense *adj* **:** very great in size or amount **:** HUGE — **im·mense·ly** *adv*

im·men·si·ty *n, pl* **im·men·si·ties :** extremely great size, amount, or extent

im·merse *vb* **im·mersed; im·mers·ing 1 :** to plunge into something (as a fluid) that surrounds or covers **2 :** to become completely involved with

im·mi·grant *n* **:** a person who comes to a country to live there

im·mi·grate *vb* **im·mi·grat·ed; im·mi·grat·ing :** to come into a foreign country to live

im·mi·gra·tion *n* **:** an act or instance of coming into a foreign country to live

im·mi·nent *adj* **:** being about to happen

im·mo·bile *adj* **:** unable to move or be moved

im·mo·bi·lize *vb* **im·mo·bi·lized; im·mo·bi·liz·ing :** to keep from moving **:** make immovable

im·mod·est *adj* **1 :** not proper in thought, conduct, or dress **2 :** being vain or showing vanity

im·mor·al *adj* **:** not following principles of right and wrong **:** WICKED, BAD

im·mo·ral·i·ty *n, pl* **im·mo·ral·i·ties :** the quality or state of being without principles of right and wrong

[1]**im·mor·tal** *adj* **:** living or lasting forever

[2]**immortal** *n* **1 :** a being that lives forever **:** a god or goddess **2 :** a person of lasting fame

im·mor·tal·i·ty *n* **1 :** the quality or state of living forever **:** endless life **2 :** lasting fame or glory

im·mov·able *adj* **1 :** impossible to move **:** firmly fixed in place **2 :** not able to be changed or persuaded

im·mune *adj* **1 :** having a high degree of resistance to an illness or disease **2 :** of, relating to, or involving the body's immune system **3 :** not influenced or affected by something **4 :** not subject to something **:** EXEMPT

immune system *n* **:** the system of the body that fights infection and disease and that includes especially the white blood cells and antibodies and the organs that produce them

im·mu·ni·ty *n, pl* **im·mu·ni·ties 1 :** freedom from an obligation or penalty to which others are subject **2 :** the power to resist infection whether natural or acquired (as by vaccination)

im·mu·ni·za·tion *n* **:** treatment (as with a vaccine) to produce immunity to a disease

im·mu·nize *vb* **im·mu·nized; im·mu·niz·ing :** to make immune especially by vaccination

imp *n* **1 :** a small demon **2 :** a mischievous child

[1]**im·pact** *n* **1 :** a striking of one body against another **:** COLLISION **2 :** a strong effect

[2]**im·pact** *vb* **im·pact·ed; im·pact·ing 1 :** to have a strong and often bad effect on **2 :** to hit with great force

im·pair *vb* **im·paired; im·pair·ing :** to make less (as in quantity, value, or strength) or worse **:** DAMAGE

im·pale *vb* **im·paled; im·pal·ing :** to pierce with something pointed

im·part *vb* **im·part·ed; im·part·ing 1 :** to give or grant from or as if from a supply **2 :** to make known

im·par·tial *adj* **:** not favoring one side over another **:** FAIR — **im·par·tial·ly** *adv*

im·par·tial·i·ty *n* **:** the quality or state of being fair and just

im·pass·able *adj* **:** impossible to pass, cross, or travel

im·pas·sioned *adj* **:** showing very strong feeling

im·pas·sive *adj* **:** not feeling or showing emotion — **im·pas·sive·ly** *adv*

im·pa·tience *n* **1 :** the quality of not wanting to put up with or wait for something or someone **:** lack of patience **2 :** restless or eager desire

im·pa·tient *adj* **1 :** not wanting to put up with or wait for something or someone **2 :** showing a lack of patience **3 :** restless and eager — **im·pa·tient·ly** *adv*

im·peach *vb* **im·peached; im·peach·ing :** to charge a public official formally with misconduct in office

im·pec·ca·ble *adj* **:** free from fault or error

im·pede *vb* **im·ped·ed; im·ped·ing :** to interfere with the movement or progress of

im·ped·i·ment *n* **1 :** something that interferes with movement or progress **2 :** a condition that makes it difficult to speak normally

im·pel *vb* **im·pelled; im·pel·ling :** to urge or force into action

im·pend·ing *adj* **:** happening or likely to happen soon

im·pen·e·tra·ble *adj* **1 :** impossible to pass through or see through **2 :** impossible to understand

im·per·a·tive *adj* **1 :** expressing a command, request, or strong encouragement **2 :** URGENT 1

im·per·cep·ti·ble *adj* **:** not noticeable by the senses or by the mind **:** very small or gradual — **im·per·cep·ti·bly** *adv*

im·per·fect *adj* **:** having a fault of some kind **:** not perfect — **im·per·fect·ly** *adv*

im·per·fec·tion *n* **1 :** the quality or state of having faults or defects **:** lack of perfection **2 :** a small flaw or fault

im·pe·ri·al *adj* **:** of or relating to an empire or its ruler

im·per·il *vb* **im·per·iled** *or* **im·per·illed; im·per·il·ing** *or* **im·per·il·ling :** to place in great danger

im·per·son·al *adj* **1 :** not caring about individual persons or their feelings **2 :** not showing or involving personal feelings

im·per·son·ate *vb* **im·per·son·at·ed; im·per·son·at·ing :** to pretend to be another person

im·per·son·a·tion *n* **:** the act of pretending to be another person

im·per·ti·nence *n* **:** the quality or state of being very rude or disrespectful

im·per·ti·nent *adj* **:** very rude **:** having or showing a lack of respect

im·per·turb·able *adj* **:** hard to disturb or upset **:** very calm

im·per·vi·ous *adj* **1 :** not letting something enter or pass through **2 :** not bothered or affected by something

im·pet·u·ous *adj* **:** acting or done quickly and without thought **:** IMPULSIVE

imp·ish *adj* **:** playful and mischievous — **imp·ish·ly** *adv*

im·pla·ca·ble *adj* **:** impossible to please, satisfy, or change

im·plant *vb* **im·plant·ed; im·plant·ing :** to set securely or deeply

[1]im·ple·ment *n* **:** an object (as a tool) intended for a certain use

[2]im·ple·ment *vb* **im·ple·ment·ed; im·ple·ment·ing :** to begin to do or use something

im·pli·cate *vb* **im·pli·cat·ed; im·pli·cat·ing :** to show to be connected or involved

im·pli·ca·tion *n* **1 :** the fact or state of being involved in or connected to something **2 :** a possible future effect or result **3 :** something that is suggested

im·plic·it *adj* **1 :** understood though not put clearly into words **2 :** not affected by doubt **:** ABSOLUTE — **im·plic·it·ly** *adv*

im·plore *vb* **im·plored; im·plor·ing :** to make a very serious or emotional request to or for — **im·plor·ing·ly** *adv*

im·ply *vb* **im·plied; im·ply·ing :** to express indirectly **:** suggest rather than say plainly

im·po·lite *adj* **:** not polite — **im·po·lite·ly** *adv*

[1]im·port *vb* **im·port·ed; im·port·ing :** to bring (as goods) into a country usually for selling

[2]im·port *n* **1 :** IMPORTANCE **2 :** something brought into a country

im·por·tance *n* **:** the quality or state of being important

im·por·tant *adj* **1 :** having serious meaning or worth **2 :** having power or authority — **im·por·tant·ly** *adv*

im·por·ta·tion *n* **:** the act or practice of bringing into a country

im·por·tune *vb* **im·por·tuned; im·por·tun·ing :** to beg or urge in a repeated or annoying way

im·pose *vb* **im·posed; im·pos·ing 1 :** to establish or apply as a charge or penalty **2 :** to force someone to accept or put up with **3 :** to ask for more than is fair or reasonable **:** take unfair advantage

im·pos·ing *adj* **:** impressive because of size, dignity, or magnificence

im·pos·si·bil·i·ty *n, pl* **im·pos·si·bil·i·ties 1 :** something that cannot be done or occur **2 :** the quality or state of being impossible

im·pos·si·ble *adj* **1 :** incapable of being or of occurring **:** not possible **2 :** very difficult **3 :** very bad or unpleasant — **im·pos·si·bly** *adv*

im·pos·tor *n* **:** a person who deceives others by pretending to be someone else

im·pos·ture *n* **:** the act of deceiving others by pretending to be someone else

im·po·tence *n* **:** the quality or state of lacking power or strength

im·po·tent *adj* **:** lacking in power, ability, or strength

im·pound *vb* **im·pound·ed; im·pound·ing :** to shut up in or as if in an enclosed place

im·pov·er·ish *vb* **im·pov·er·ished; im·pov·er·ish·ing 1 :** to make poor **2 :** to use up the strength or richness of

im·prac·ti·ca·ble *adj* : difficult to put into practice or use
im·prac·ti·cal *adj* **1** : not suitable for a situation : not practical **2** : not capable of dealing sensibly with matters that require action
im·pre·cise *adj* : not clear or exact
im·preg·na·ble *adj* : not able to be captured by attack : UNCONQUERABLE
im·press *vb* **im·pressed; im·press·ing** **1** : to produce by stamping, pressing, or printing **2** : to affect strongly or deeply and especially favorably **3** : to give a clear idea of
im·pres·sion *n* **1** : something (as a design) made by pressing or stamping a surface **2** : the effect that something or someone has on a person's thoughts or feelings **3** : an idea or belief that is usually uncertain **4** : an imitation of a famous person done for entertainment
im·pres·sion·able *adj* : easy to impress or influence
im·pres·sive *adj* : having the power to impress the mind or feelings especially in a positive way — **im·pres·sive·ly** *adv*
¹im·print *vb* **im·print·ed; im·print·ing** **1** : to make a mark by pressing agains a surface : STAMP **2** : to fix firmly in the mind or memory
²im·print *n* : a mark made by pressing against a surface
im·pris·on *vb* **im·pris·oned; im·pris·on·ing** : to put in prison
im·pris·on·ment *n* : the act of putting in prison : the state of being put or kept in prison
im·prob·a·bil·i·ty *n* : the quality or state of being unlikely
im·prob·a·ble *adj* : not likely : not probable — **im·prob·a·bly** *adv*
im·promp·tu *adj* : not prepared ahead of time : made or done without preparation
im·prop·er *adj* : not proper, right, or suitable — **im·prop·er·ly** *adv*
improper fraction *n* : a fraction whose numerator is equal to or larger than the denominator
im·prove *vb* **im·proved; im·prov·ing** : to make or become better
im·prove·ment *n* **1** : the act or process of making something better **2** : increased value or excellence **3** : an addition or change that makes something better or more valuable
im·pro·vi·sa·tion *n* **1** : the act or art of speaking or performing without practicing or preparing ahead of time **2** : something that is improvised
im·pro·vise *vb* **im·pro·vised; im·pro·vis·ing** **1** : to speak or perform without preparing ahead of time **2** : to make, invent, or arrange by using whatever is available
im·pu·dence *n* : behavior or speech that is bold and disrespectful
im·pu·dent *adj* : bold and disrespectful : very rude — **im·pu·dent·ly** *adv*
im·pulse *n* **1** : a force that starts a body into motion **2** : the motion produced by a starting force **3** : a strong sudden desire to do something **4** : NERVE IMPULSE
im·pul·sive *adj* **1** : acting or tending to act suddenly and without careful thought **2** : resulting from a sudden impulse — **im·pul·sive·ly** *adv*
im·pure *adj* **1** : not pure : UNCLEAN, DIRTY **2** : mixed with something else that is usually not as good
im·pu·ri·ty *n, pl* **im·pu·ri·ties** **1** : the quality or state of being impure **2** : something that is or makes something else impure
¹in *prep* **1** : located or positioned within **2** : INTO 1 **3** : DURING **4** : WITH 7 **5** — used to show a state or condition **6** — used to show manner or purpose **7** : INTO 2
²in *adv* **1** : to or toward the inside **2** : to or toward some particular place **3** : ¹NEAR 1 **4** : into the midst of something **5** : to or at its proper place **6** : on the inner side : WITHIN **7** : present and available for use — **in for** : sure to experience
³in *adj* **1** : being inside or within **2** : headed or bound inward **3** : FASHIONABLE
in. *abbr* inch
IN *abbr* Indiana
¹in- *or* **il-** *or* **im-** *or* **ir-** *prefix* : not : NON-, UN- — usually *il-* before *l*, *im-* before *b*, *m*, or *p*, *ir-* before *r* and *in-* before other sounds
²in- *or* **il-** *or* **im-** *or* **ir-** *prefix* **1** : in : within : into : toward : on — usually *il-* before *l*, *im-* before *b*, *m*, or *p*, *ir-* before *r*, and *in-* before other sounds **2** : EN- 2
in·abil·i·ty *n* : the condition of being unable to do something : lack of ability
in·ac·ces·si·bil·i·ty *n* : the quality or state of being hard or impossible to reach or get hold of
in·ac·ces·si·ble *adj* : hard or impossible to reach or get hold of
in·ac·cu·ra·cy *n, pl* **in·ac·cu·ra·cies** **1** : lack of correctness or exactness **2** : ERROR, MISTAKE
in·ac·cu·rate *adj* : not correct or exact — **in·ac·cu·rate·ly** *adv*
in·ac·tion *n* : lack of action or activity
in·ac·tive *adj* : not active or in use
in·ac·tiv·i·ty *n* : the state or condition of not acting or moving : lack of activity
in·ad·e·qua·cy *n, pl* **in·ad·e·qua·cies** : the condition of being not enough or not good enough
in·ad·e·quate *adj* : not enough or not good enough
in·ad·ver·tent *adj* : not intended or deliberate : ACCIDENTAL — **in·ad·ver·tent·ly** *adv*

in·ad·vis·able *adj* : not wise to do : not advisable
in·alien·able *adj* : impossible to take away or give up
inane *adj* : silly and pointless
in·an·i·mate *adj* : not living
in·ap·pro·pri·ate *adj* : not right or suited for some purpose or situation — **in·ap·pro·pri·ate·ly** *adv*
in·ar·tic·u·late *adj* **1** : not able to express ideas or feelings clearly and easily **2** : not understandable as spoken words
in·as·much as *conj* : considering that : BECAUSE
in·at·ten·tion *n* : failure to pay attention
in·at·ten·tive *adj* : not paying attention — **in·at·ten·tive·ly** *adv*
in·au·di·ble *adj* : impossible to hear — **in·au·di·bly** *adv*
in·au·gu·ral *adj* : occuring as part of an inauguration
in·au·gu·rate *vb* **in·au·gu·rat·ed; in·au·gu·rat·ing** **1** : to introduce into office with suitable ceremonies **2** : to celebrate the opening of **3** : to bring about the beginning of
in·au·gu·ra·tion *n* : an act or ceremony of introducing into office
in·born *adj* : existing from the time someone is born : natural or instinctive
in·breed *vb* **in·bred; in·breed·ing** : to breed with closely related individuals
inc. *abbr* **1** incomplete **2** incorporated
in·can·des·cent *adj* : white or glowing with great heat
incandescent lamp *n* : LIGHT BULB
in·ca·pa·ble *adj* : not able to do something
[1]**in·cense** *n* : material used to produce a strong and pleasant smell when burned
[2]**in·cense** *vb* **in·censed; in·cens·ing** : to make very angry
in·cen·tive *n* : something that makes a person try or work hard or harder
in·ces·sant *adj* : going on and on : not stopping or letting up — **in·ces·sant·ly** *adv*
[1]**inch** *n* : a unit of length equal to $^1/_{36}$ yard (2.54 centimeters)
[2]**inch** *vb* **inched; inch·ing** : to move a little bit at a time
inch·worm *n* : a small caterpillar that is a larva of moths and moves by bringing forward the hind part of the body and then extending forward the front part of the body
in·ci·dent *n* : an often unimportant happening that may form a part of a larger event
in·ci·den·tal *adj* : happening as an unimportant part of something else
in·ci·den·tal·ly *adv* **1** : as a matter of less interest or importance **2** — used to introduce a statement that provides additional information or changes the subject
in·cin·er·ate *vb* **in·cin·er·at·ed; in·cin·er·at·ing** : to burn to ashes
in·cin·er·a·tor *n* : a furnace or a container for burning waste materials
in·cise *vb* **in·cised; in·cis·ing** : to cut into : CARVE, ENGRAVE
in·ci·sion *n* : an act of cutting into something or the cut or wound that results
in·ci·sor *n* : a tooth (as any of the four front teeth of the human upper or lower jaw) for cutting
in·cite *vb* **in·cit·ed; in·cit·ing** : to stir up usually harmful or violent action or feeling
in·clem·ent *adj* : STORMY 1
in·cli·na·tion *n* **1** : an act or the action of bending or leaning **2** : a usually favorable feeling toward something **3** : [2]SLANT, TILT
[1]**in·cline** *vb* **in·clined; in·clin·ing** **1** : to cause to bend or lean **2** : [2]SLOPE, LEAN
[2]**in·cline** *n* : [1]SLOPE 2
in·clined *adj* **1** : having a desire **2** : having a tendency **3** : having a slope
in·clude *vb* **in·clud·ed; in·clud·ing** : to take in or have as part of a whole
in·clu·sion *n* **1** : an act taking in as part of a whole : the state of being taken in as part of a whole **2** : something taken in as part of a whole
in·clu·sive *adj* **1** : covering everything or all important points **2** : including the stated limits and all in between
in·cog·ni·to *adv or adj* : with someone's identity kept secret
in·co·her·ence *n* : the quality or state of not being connected in a clear or logical way
in·co·her·ent *adj* : not connected in a clear or logical way — **in·co·her·ent·ly** *adv*
in·come *n* : a gain usually measured in money that comes in from labor, business, or property
income tax *n* : a tax on the income of a person or business
in·com·ing *adj* : arriving at a destination
in·com·pa·ra·ble *adj* : better than any other — **in·com·pa·ra·bly** *adv*
in·com·pat·i·ble *adj* : not able to live or work together in harmony : not suited for each other — **in·com·pat·i·bly** *adv*
in·com·pe·tence *n* : the inability to do a good job
in·com·pe·tent *adj* : not able to do a good job — **in·com·pe·tent·ly** *adv*
in·com·plete *adj* : not finished : not complete — **in·com·plete·ly** *adv*
in·com·pre·hen·si·ble *adj* : impossible to understand — **in·com·pre·hen·si·bly** *adv*
in·con·ceiv·able *adj* : impossible to imagine or believe
in·con·gru·ous *adj* : not harmonious, suitable, or proper

DICTIONARY

in·con·sid·er·ate *adj* **:** careless of the rights or feelings of others

in·con·sis·ten·cy *n, pl* **in·con·sis·ten·cies** **1 :** the quality or state of not being in agreement or not being regular **2 :** something that is not in agreement or not regular

in·con·sis·tent *adj* **1 :** not being in agreement **2 :** not staying the same in thoughts or practices

in·con·spic·u·ous *adj* **:** not easily seen or noticed — **in·con·spic·u·ous·ly** *adv*

[1]**in·con·ve·nience** *n* **1 :** trouble or difficulty **:** lack of convenience **2 :** something that causes trouble or difficulty

[2]**inconvenience** *vb* **in·con·ve·nienced; in·con·ve·nienc·ing :** to cause difficulties for

in·con·ve·nient *adj* **:** causing trouble or difficulty **:** not convenient — **in·con·ve·nient·ly** *adv*

in·cor·po·rate *vb* **in·cor·po·rat·ed; in·cor·po·rat·ing** **1 :** to join or unite closely into a single mass or body **2 :** to make a corporation of

in·cor·rect *adj* **1 :** not accurate or true **:** not correct **:** WRONG **2 :** not proper — **in·cor·rect·ly** *adv*

[1]**in·crease** *vb* **in·creased; in·creas·ing :** to make or become greater

[2]**in·crease** *n* **:** an addition or enlargement in size, extent, or quantity

in·creas·ing·ly *adv* **:** more and more

in·cred·i·ble *adj* **1 :** too strange or unlikely to be believed **2 :** extremely or amazingly good, great, or large — **in·cred·i·bly** *adv*

in·cred·u·lous *adj* **:** feeling or showing disbelief **:** SKEPTICAL — **in·cred·u·lous·ly** *adv*

in·crim·i·nate *vb* **in·crim·i·nat·ed; in·crim·i·nat·ing :** to make (someone) appear guilty of or responsible for something

in·cu·bate *vb* **in·cu·bat·ed; in·cu·bat·ing** **1 :** to sit upon eggs to hatch them by warmth **2 :** to keep under conditions good for hatching or development

in·cu·ba·tion *n* **1 :** the act or process of incubating **2 :** the period of time between infection with germs and the appearance of symptoms of illness or disease

in·cu·ba·tor *n* **1 :** a device that provides enough heat to hatch eggs artificially **2 :** a device to help the growth of tiny newborn babies

in·cum·bent *n* **:** the holder of an office or position

in·cur *vb* **in·curred; in·cur·ring :** to experience as a result of a person's own actions

in·cur·able *adj* **:** impossible to cure — **in·cur·ably** *adv*

Ind. *abbr* **1** Indian **2** Indiana

in·debt·ed *adj* **:** being in debt **:** owing something — **in·debt·ed·ness** *n*

in·de·cen·cy *n, pl* **in·de·cen·cies** **1 :** offensive quality **:** lack of decency **2 :** an act or word that is offensive

in·de·cent *adj* **:** not decent **:** COARSE, VULGAR

in·de·ci·sion *n* **:** difficulty in making a decision

in·de·ci·sive *adj* **1 :** not decisive or final **2 :** finding it hard to make decisions — **in·de·ci·sive·ly** *adv*

in·deed *adv* **:** TRULY

in·de·fen·si·ble *adj* **:** impossible to defend

in·def·i·nite *adj* **1 :** not certain in amount or length **2 :** not clear in meaning or details — **in·def·i·nite·ly** *adv*

indefinite article *n* **:** either of the articles *a* or *an* used to show that the following noun refers to any person or thing of the kind named

in·del·i·ble *adj* **1 :** impossible to erase, remove, or blot out **2 :** making marks not easily removed — **in·del·i·bly** *adv*

in·del·i·cate *adj* **:** not polite or proper **:** COARSE — **in·del·i·cate·ly** *adv*

in·dent *vb* **in·dent·ed; in·dent·ing :** to set in from the margin

in·den·ta·tion *n* **1 :** a blank or empty space at the beginning of a written or printed line or paragraph **2 :** a cut or dent in something

in·de·pen·dence *n* **:** the quality or state of not being under the control of, reliant on, or connected with someone or something else

Independence Day *n* **:** July 4 observed by Americans as a legal holiday in honor of the adoption of the Declaration of Independence in 1776

[1]**in·de·pen·dent** *adj* **1 :** not under the control or rule of another **2 :** not connected with something else **:** SEPARATE **3 :** not depending on anyone else for money to live on **4 :** thinking freely **:** not looking to others for guidance — **in·de·pen·dent·ly** *adv*

[2]**independent** *n* **:** an independent person

in·de·scrib·able *adj* **:** impossible to describe — **in·de·scrib·ably** *adv*

in·de·struc·ti·ble *adj* **:** impossible to destroy

[1]**in·dex** *n, pl* **in·dex·es** *or* **in·di·ces** **1 :** a list of names or topics (as in a book) given in alphabetical order and showing where each is to be found **2 :** POINTER 1 **3 :** [1]SIGN 3, INDICATION

[2]**index** *vb* **in·dexed; in·dex·ing** **1 :** to provide (as a book) with an index **2 :** to list in an index

index finger *n* **:** the finger next to the thumb

[1]**In·di·an** *n* **1 :** a person born or living in India **2 :** AMERICAN INDIAN

[2]**Indian** *adj* **1 :** of or relating to India or its peoples **2 :** of or relating to the American Indians or their languages

Indian corn *n* **1 :** [1]CORN **2 :** corn that is of a variety having seeds of various colors (as reddish brown, dark purple, and yellow) and is typically used for ornamental purposes

Indian pipe *n* : a waxy white leafless woodland herb with a single drooping flower

Indian summer *n* : a period of mild weather in late autumn or early winter

in·di·cate *vb* **in·di·cat·ed; in·di·cat·ing** **1** : to point out or point to **2** : to state or express briefly

in·di·ca·tion *n* **1** : the act of pointing out or stating briefly **2** : something that points out or suggests something

in·dic·a·tive *adj* **1** : pointing out or showing something **2** : of or relating to the verb form that is used to state a fact that can be known or proved

in·di·ca·tor *n* **1** : a sign that shows or suggests the condition or existence of something **2** : a pointer on a dial or scale **3** : [1]DIAL 3, GAUGE

indices *pl of* INDEX

in·dict *vb* **in·dict·ed; in·dict·ing** : to formally charge with an offense or crime — **in·dict·ment** *n*

in·dif·fer·ence *n* : lack of interest or concern

in·dif·fer·ent *adj* **1** : not interested or concerned about something **2** : neither good nor bad — **in·dif·fer·ent·ly** *adv*

in·di·gest·ible *adj* : not capable of being broken down and used by the body as food : not easy to digest

in·di·ges·tion *n* : discomfort caused by slow or painful digestion

in·dig·nant *adj* : filled with or expressing anger caused by something unjust or unworthy — **in·dig·nant·ly** *adv*

in·dig·na·tion *n* : anger caused by something unjust or unworthy

in·dig·ni·ty *n, pl* **in·dig·ni·ties** **1** : an act that injures a person's dignity or self-respect **2** : treatment that shows a lack of respect

in·di·go *n, pl* **in·di·gos** *or* **in·di·goes** **1** : a blue dye made artificially or obtained especially formerly from plants (**indigo plants**) **2** : a deep purplish blue

in·di·rect *adj* **1** : not straight or direct **2** : not straightforward **3** : not having a plainly seen connection — **in·di·rect·ly** *adv* — **in·di·rect·ness** *n*

indirect object *n* : an object that represents the person or thing that receives what is being given or done

in·dis·creet *adj* : not having or showing good judgment : revealing things that should not be revealed — **in·dis·creet·ly** *adv*

in·dis·cre·tion *n* **1** : lack of good judgment or care in acting or saying things **2** : a thoughtless or careless act or remark

in·dis·crim·i·nate *adj* : not done in a careful way : wrongly causing widespread harm

in·dis·pens·able *adj* : extremely important or necessary : ESSENTIAL

in·dis·posed *adj* **1** : slightly ill **2** : not willing

in·dis·put·able *adj* : impossible to question or doubt — **in·dis·put·ably** *adv*

in·dis·tinct *adj* : not easily seen, heard, or recognized — **in·dis·tinct·ly** *adv*

in·dis·tin·guish·able *adj* : impossible to recognize as different

[1]**in·di·vid·u·al** *adj* **1** : relating to a single member of a group **2** : intended for one person **3** : [1]PARTICULAR 1, SEPARATE **4** : having a special quality : DISTINCTIVE — **in·di·vid·u·al·ly** *adv*

[2]**individual** *n* **1** : a single member of a group **2** : a single human being

in·di·vid·u·al·i·ty *n* : the qualities that make one person or thing different from all others

in·di·vis·i·ble *adj* : impossible to divide or separate — **in·di·vis·i·bly** *adv*

in·doc·tri·nate *vb* **in·doc·tri·nat·ed; in·doc·tri·nat·ing** : to teach especially the ideas, opinions, or beliefs of a certain group

in·do·lence *n* : the quality of being lazy

in·do·lent *adj* : LAZY 1, IDLE

in·dom·i·ta·ble *adj* : impossible to defeat

in·door *adj* : done, used, or belonging within a building

in·doors *adv* : in or into a building

in·du·bi·ta·ble *adj* : being beyond question or doubt — **in·du·bi·ta·bly** *adv*

in·duce *vb* **in·duced; in·duc·ing** **1** : to cause to do something **2** : to bring about **3** : to produce (as an electric current) by induction

in·duce·ment *n* : something that causes someone to do something

in·duct *vb* **in·duct·ed; in·duct·ing** **1** : to take in as a member of a military service **2** : to place in office **3** : to officially introduce (someone) as a member

in·duc·tion *n* **1** : the act or process of placing someone in a new job or position **2** : the production of an electrical or magnetic effect through the influence of a nearby magnet, electrical current, or electrically charged body

in·dulge *vb* **in·dulged; in·dulg·ing** **1** : to give in to the desires of **2** : to give in to a desire for something

in·dul·gence *n* **1** : the practice of allowing enjoyment of whatever is desired **2** : an act of doing what is desired **3** : something that a person enjoys or desires

in·dul·gent *adj* : feeling or showing a willingness to allow enjoyment of whatever is wanted : LENIENT — **in·dul·gent·ly** *adv*

in·dus·tri·al *adj* **1** : of, relating to, or engaged in industry **2** : having highly developed industries — **in·dus·tri·al·ly** *adv*

in·dus·tri·al·ist *n* : a person who owns or engages in the management of an industry

in·dus·tri·al·i·za·tion *n* : the process of developing industries : the state of having industry developed

in·dus·tri·al·ize *vb* **in·dus·tri·al·ized; in·dus·tri·al·iz·ing** : to develop industries

in·dus·tri·ous *adj* : working hard and steadily — **in·dus·tri·ous·ly** *adv*

in·dus·try *n, pl* **in·dus·tries** **1** : businesses that provide a certain product or service **2** : manufacturing activity **3** : the habit of working hard and steadily

-ine *adj suffix* : of, relating to, or like

in·ed·i·ble *adj* : not fit for eating

in·ef·fec·tive *adj* : not having the desired effect — **in·ef·fec·tive·ly** *adv*

in·ef·fec·tu·al *adj* : not producing the proper or desired effect — **in·ef·fec·tu·al·ly** *adv*

in·ef·fi·cien·cy *n, pl* **in·ef·fi·cien·cies** : the state or an instance of being ineffective or inefficient

in·ef·fi·cient *adj* **1** : not effective **2** : not capable of bringing about a desired result with little waste — **in·ef·fi·cient·ly** *adv*

in·elas·tic *adj* : not elastic

in·el·i·gi·ble *adj* : not qualified to be chosen or used

in·ept *adj* **1** : not suited to the occasion **2** : lacking in skill or ability — **in·ept·ly** *adv* — **in·ept·ness** *n*

in·equal·i·ty *n, pl* **in·equal·i·ties** : the quality of being unequal or uneven : lack of equality

in·ert *adj* : unable or slow to move or react — **in·ert·ness** *n*

in·er·tia *n* **1** : a property of matter by which it remains at rest or in motion in the same straight line unless acted upon by some external force **2** : a tendency not to move or change

in·es·cap·able *adj* : INEVITABLE

in·ev·i·ta·bil·i·ty *n* : the quality or state of being sure to happen

in·ev·i·ta·ble *adj* : sure to happen : CERTAIN — **in·ev·i·ta·bly** *adv*

in·ex·act *adj* : INACCURATE

in·ex·cus·able *adj* : not to be excused — **in·ex·cus·ably** *adv*

in·ex·haust·ible *adj* : plentiful enough not to give out or be used up

in·ex·o·ra·ble *adj* : RELENTLESS — **in·ex·o·ra·bly** *adv*

in·ex·pen·sive *adj* : [1]CHEAP 1

in·ex·pe·ri·ence *n* : lack of experience

in·ex·pe·ri·enced *adj* : having little or no experience

in·ex·pli·ca·ble *adj* : impossible to explain or account for — **in·ex·pli·ca·bly** *adv*

in·ex·press·ible *adj* : being beyond the power to express : INDESCRIBABLE — **in·ex·press·ibly** *adv*

in·fal·li·ble *adj* **1** : not capable of being wrong **2** : certain to succeed : SURE — **in·fal·li·bly** *adv*

in·fa·mous *adj* **1** : having an evil reputation **2** : [1]EVIL 1, BAD — **in·fa·mous·ly** *adv*

in·fa·my *n, pl* **in·fa·mies** **1** : an evil reputation **2** : an evil or terrible act

in·fan·cy *n, pl* **in·fan·cies** **1** : the first stage of a child's life : early childhood **2** : a beginning or early period of existence

[1]in·fant *n* **1** : a child in the first period of life : BABY **2** : [2]MINOR

[2]infant *adj* **1** : of or relating to infancy **2** : intended for young children

in·fan·tile *adj* : CHILDISH 2

in·fan·try *n, pl* **in·fan·tries** : a branch of an army composed of soldiers trained to fight on foot

in·fat·u·at·ed *adj* : having a foolish or very strong love or admiration

in·fat·u·a·tion *n* : the state of having a foolish or very strong love or admiration

in·fect *vb* **in·fect·ed; in·fect·ing** **1** : to pass on or introduce a germ, illness, or disease to : to cause sickness in **2** : to cause to share similar feelings

in·fec·tion *n* **1** : the act or process of passing on or introducing a germ, illness, or disease to : the state of being infected **2** : any disease caused by germs

in·fec·tious *adj* **1** : passing from one to another in the form of a germ **2** : easily spread to others

in·fer *vb* **in·ferred; in·fer·ring** **1** : to arrive at as a conclusion based on known facts **2** : [1]GUESS 1 **3** : [2]HINT, SUGGEST

in·fer·ence *n* **1** : the act or process of reaching a conclusion about something from known facts **2** : a conclusion or opinion reached based on known facts

[1]in·fe·ri·or *adj* **1** : situated lower down (as in place or importance) **2** : of little or less importance, value, or merit **3** : of poor quality

[2]inferior *n* : a less important person or thing

in·fe·ri·or·i·ty *n* **1** : the state of being of lower importance, value, or quality **2** : a sense of being less important or valuable

in·fer·nal *adj* **1** : very bad or unpleasant **2** : of or relating to hell

in·fer·tile *adj* : not fertile

in·fest *vb* **in·fest·ed; in·fest·ing** : to spread or swarm in or over in a harmful manner

in·fi·del *n* : a person who does not believe in a certain religion

in·field *n* **1** : the diamond-shaped part of a baseball field inside the bases and home plate **2** : the players in the infield

in·field·er *n* : a baseball player who plays in the infield

in·fi·nite *adj* **1** : having no limits of any kind **2** : seeming to be without limits — **in·fi·nite·ly** *adv*

in·fin·i·tes·i·mal *adj* : extremely small

in·fin·i·tive *n* : a verb form serving as a noun or as a modifier and at the same time taking objects and adverbial modifiers

in·fin·i·ty *n, pl* **in·fin·i·ties** **1** : the quality of being without limits **2** : a space, quantity, or period of time that is without limit

in·firm *adj* : weak or frail in body

in·fir·ma·ry *n, pl* **in·fir·ma·ries** : a place for the care and housing of sick people

in·fir·mi·ty *n, pl* **in·fir·mi·ties** : the condition of being weak or frail (as from age or illness)

in·flame *vb* **in·flamed; in·flam·ing** **1** : to make more active, excited, angry, or violent **2** : to cause to redden or grow hot (as from anger) **3** : to make or become sore, red, and swollen

in·flam·ma·ble *adj* **1** : FLAMMABLE **2** : easily inflamed : EXCITABLE

in·flam·ma·tion *n* : a bodily response to injury or disease in which heat, redness, and swelling are present

in·flam·ma·to·ry *adj* **1** : tending to excite anger or disorder **2** : causing or having inflammation

in·flat·able *adj* : possible to fill with air or gas

in·flate *vb* **in·flat·ed; in·flat·ing** **1** : to swell or fill with air or gas **2** : to cause to increase beyond proper limits

in·fla·tion *n* **1** : an act of filling with air or gas : the state of being filled with air or gas **2** : a continual rise in the price of goods and services

in·flect *vb* **in·flect·ed; in·flect·ing** **1** : to change a word by inflection **2** : to change the pitch of the voice

in·flec·tion *n* **1** : a change in the pitch of a person's voice **2** : a change in a word that shows a grammatical difference (as of number, person, or tense)

in·flex·i·ble *adj* **1** : not easily bent or twisted **2** : not easily influenced or persuaded **3** : not easily changed

in·flict *vb* **in·flict·ed; in·flict·ing** **1** : to give by or as if by striking **2** : to cause to be put up with

in·flo·res·cence *n* : the arrangement of flowers on a stalk

¹in·flu·ence *n* **1** : the act or power of causing an effect or change without use of direct force or authority **2** : a person or thing that has an indirect but usually important effect

²influence *vb* **in·flu·enced; in·flu·enc·ing** : to affect or change in an indirect but usually important way

in·flu·en·tial *adj* : having the power to cause change : having influence

in·flu·en·za *n* : a very contagious virus disease like a severe cold with fever

in·form *vb* **in·formed; in·form·ing** **1** : to let a person know something **2** : to give information so as to accuse or cause suspicion — **in·form·er** *n*

in·for·mal *adj* **1** : not requiring serious or formal behavior or dress **2** : suitable for ordinary or everyday use — **in·for·mal·ly** *adv*

in·for·mal·i·ty *n, pl* **in·for·mal·i·ties** : the quality or state of being informal

in·form·ant *n* : a person who gives information especially to accuse or cause suspicion about someone

in·for·ma·tion *n* : knowledge obtained from investigation, study, or instruction

information superhighway *n* : INTERNET

information technology *n* : the technology involved in the development, maintenance, and use of computer systems, software, and networks

in·for·ma·tive *adj* : giving knowledge or information : INSTRUCTIVE

in·frac·tion *n* : VIOLATION

in·fra·red *adj* : being, relating to, or producing rays like light but lying outside the visible spectrum at its red end

in·fre·quent *adj* **1** : seldom happening : RARE **2** : not placed, made, or done at frequent intervals — **in·fre·quent·ly** *adv*

in·fringe *vb* **in·fringed; in·fring·ing** **1** : to fail to obey or act in agreement with : VIOLATE **2** : to go further than is right or fair to another : ENCROACH — **in·fringe·ment** *n*

in·fu·ri·ate *vb* **in·fu·ri·at·ed; in·fu·ri·at·ing** : to make furious : ENRAGE

in·fuse *vb* **in·fused; in·fus·ing** **1** : to put in as if by pouring **2** : to steep without boiling — **in·fu·sion** *n*

¹-ing *n suffix* **1** : action or process **2** : product or result of an action or process **3** : something used in or connected with making or doing

²-ing *vb suffix or adj suffix* — used to form the present participle and sometimes to form adjectives that do not come from a verb

in·ge·nious *adj* : showing ingenuity : CLEVER — **in·ge·nious·ly** *adv*

in·ge·nu·ity *n, pl* **in·ge·nu·ities** : skill or cleverness in discovering, inventing, or planning

in·gen·u·ous *adj* : showing innocence and childlike honesty — **in·gen·u·ous·ly** *adv*

in·got *n* : a mass of metal cast into a shape that is easy to handle or store

in·gra·ti·ate *vb* **in·gra·ti·at·ed; in·gra·ti·at·ing** : to gain favor for by effort

in·gra·ti·at·ing *adj* **1** : PLEASING **2** : intended to gain someone's favor — **in·gra·ti·at·ing·ly** *adv*

in·grat·i·tude *n* : lack of gratitude

in·gre·di·ent *n* : one of the substances that make up a mixture

in·hab·it *vb* **in·hab·it·ed; in·hab·it·ing** : to live or dwell in

in·hab·i·tant *n* : a person or animal that lives in a place

in·ha·la·tion *n* : the act or an instance of breathing or drawing in by breathing

in·hale *vb* **in·haled; in·hal·ing** **1** : to draw in by breathing **2** : to breathe in

in·hal·er *n* : a device used for breathing medicine into the lungs

in·her·ent *adj* : belonging to or being a part of the nature of a person or thing — **in·her·ent·ly** *adv*

in·her·it *vb* **in·her·it·ed; in·her·it·ing** **1** : to get by legal right from a person at his or her death **2** : to get by heredity

in·her·i·tance *n* **1** : the act of getting by legal right from a person at his or her death or through heredity **2** : something gotten by legal right from a person at his or her death

in·hib·it *vb* **in·hib·it·ed; in·hib·it·ing** : to prevent or hold back from doing something

in·hos·pi·ta·ble *adj* : not friendly or generous : not showing hospitality — **in·hos·pi·ta·bly** *adv*

in·hu·man *adj* **1** : lacking pity or kindness **2** : unlike what might be expected by a human

in·hu·mane *adj* : not kind or humane

in·hu·man·i·ty *n, pl* **in·hu·man·i·ties** : a cruel act or attitude

in·iq·ui·ty *n, pl* **in·iq·ui·ties** : an evil or unfair act

¹ini·tial *n* **1** : the first letter of a name **2** : a large letter beginning a text or a paragraph

²initial *adj* : occurring at or marking the beginning — **ini·tial·ly** *adv*

³initial *vb* **ini·tialed** *or* **ini·tialled; ini·tial·ing** *or* **ini·tial·ling** : to mark with the first letter or letters of a name

ini·ti·ate *vb* **ini·ti·at·ed; ini·ti·at·ing** **1** : to set going : BEGIN **2** : to admit into a club by special ceremonies **3** : to teach (someone) the basic facts about something

ini·ti·a·tion *n* **1** : the act or an instance of initiating : the process of being initiated **2** : the ceremonies with which a person is admitted into a club

ini·tia·tive *n* **1** : a first step or movement **2** : energy shown in getting action started

in·ject *vb* **in·ject·ed; in·ject·ing** **1** : to force a fluid (as a medicine) into by using a special needle **2** : to introduce as something needed or additional

in·jec·tion *n* : an act or instance of forcing a fluid (as a medicine) into a part of the body by using a special needle

in·junc·tion *n* : a court order commanding or forbidding the doing of some act

in·jure *vb* **in·jured; in·jur·ing** : to cause pain or harm to

in·ju·ri·ous *adj* : causing injury or harm

in·ju·ry *n, pl* **in·ju·ries** **1** : hurt, damage, or loss suffered **2** : an act that damages or hurts

in·jus·tice *n* **1** : unfair treatment : violation of a person's rights **2** : an act of unfair treatment

ink *n* : a liquid material used for writing or printing

ink–jet *adj* : relating to or being a printer in which droplets of ink are sprayed onto the paper

in·kling *n* : a vague notion : HINT

ink·stand *n* : a small stand for holding ink and pens

ink·well *n* : a container for ink

inky *adj* **ink·i·er; ink·i·est** **1** : consisting of or like ink **2** : soiled with or as if with ink

in·laid *adj* **1** : set into a surface in a decorative pattern **2** : decorated with a design or material set into a surface

¹in·land *adj* : of or relating to the part of a country away from the coast

²inland *n* : the part of a country away from the coast or boundaries

³inland *adv* : into or toward the area away from a coast

in–law *n* : a relative by marriage and especially the mother or father of a person's husband or wife

¹in·lay *vb* **in·laid; in·lay·ing** : to set into a surface for decoration or strengthening

²in·lay *n* : inlaid work : material used in inlaying

in·let *n* **1** : a small or narrow bay **2** : an opening through which air, gas, or liquid can enter something

in–line skate *n* : a roller skate whose wheels are set in a line one behind the other

in·mate *n* : a person confined in an institution (as a hospital or prison)

in·most *adj* : INNERMOST

inn *n* : a house that provides a place to sleep and food for travelers

in·ner *adj* **1** : located farther in **2** : of or relating to the mind or spirit

inner ear *n* : the inner part of the ear that is located in a bony cavity and plays a key role in hearing and keeping the body properly balanced

in·ner·most *adj* : farthest inward

in·ning *n* : a division of a baseball game that consists of a turn at bat for each team

inn·keep·er *n* : the person who runs an inn

in·no·cence *n* **:** the quality or state of being free from sin or guilt

in·no·cent *adj* **1 :** free from sin **:** PURE **2 :** free from guilt or blame **3 :** free from evil influence or effect **:** HARMLESS — **in·no·cent·ly** *adv*

in·noc·u·ous *adj* **:** not harmful — **in·noc·u·ous·ly** *adv*

in·no·va·tion *n* **1 :** a new idea, method, or device **:** NOVELTY **2 :** the introduction of something new

in·nu·mer·a·ble *adj* **:** too many to be counted

in·oc·u·late *vb* **in·oc·u·lat·ed; in·oc·u·lat·ing :** to inject a material (as a vaccine) into to protect against or treat a disease

in·oc·u·la·tion *n* **:** an act or instance of injecting a material (as a vaccine) into to protect against or treat a disease

in·of·fen·sive *adj* **:** not likely to offend or bother anyone

in·op·por·tune *adj* **:** INCONVENIENT

¹in·put *n* **1 :** something (as power, a signal, or data) that is put into a machine or system **2 :** the point at which an input is made **3 :** the act of or process of putting in

²input *vb* **in·put·ted** *or* **input; in·put·ting :** to enter (as data) into a computer

in·quest *n* **:** an official investigation especially into the cause of a death

in·quire *or chiefly Brit* **enquire** *vb* **in·quired/enquired; in·quir·ing/enquiring 1 :** to ask or ask about **2 :** to make an investigation **3 :** to ask a question — **in·quir·er** *or chiefly Brit* **enquirer** *n* — **in·quir·ing·ly** *or chiefly Brit* **enquiringly** *adv*

in·qui·ry *or chiefly Brit* **enquiry** *n, pl* **in·qui·ries/enquiries 1 :** the act of asking a question or seeking information **2 :** a request for information **3 :** a thorough examination

in·quis·i·tive *adj* **1 :** in search of information **2 :** overly curious — **in·quis·i·tive·ly** *adv*

in·sane *adj* **1 :** not normal or healthy in mind **2 :** used by or for people who are insane **3 :** very foolish or unreasonable — **in·sane·ly** *adv*

in·san·i·ty *n* **:** the condition of being abnormal or unhealthy in mind

in·sa·tia·ble *adj* **:** impossible to satisfy

in·scribe *vb* **in·scribed; in·scrib·ing 1 :** to write, engrave, or print as a lasting record **2 :** to write, engrave, or print something on or in

in·scrip·tion *n* **:** words or a name inscribed on a surface

in·sect *n* **1 :** any of a group of small and often winged animals that are arthropods having six jointed legs and a body formed of a head, thorax, and abdomen **2 :** an animal (as a spider or a centipede) similar to the true insects — not used technically

in·sec·ti·cide *n* **:** a chemical used to kill insects

in·se·cure *adj* **1 :** not safe or secure **2 :** not confident

in·se·cu·ri·ty *n* **:** the quality or state of being not safe or not confident

in·sen·si·ble *adj* **1 :** not able to feel **2 :** not aware of or caring about something

in·sen·si·tive *adj* **1 :** lacking feeling **:** not sensitive **2 :** not caring or showing concern about the problems or feelings of others — **in·sen·si·tive·ly** *adv*

in·sen·si·tiv·i·ty *n* **:** lack of feeling

in·sep·a·ra·ble *adj* **:** impossible to separate

¹in·sert *vb* **in·sert·ed; in·sert·ing :** to put in or into

²in·sert *n* **:** something that is or is meant to be inserted

in·ser·tion *n* **1 :** the act or process of putting in or into **2 :** ²INSERT

¹in·set *n* **:** a smaller thing that is inserted into a larger thing

²inset *vb* **in·set** *or* **in·set·ted; in·set·ting :** ¹INSERT 2

¹in·side *n* **1 :** an inner side, surface, or space **:** INTERIOR **2 :** the inner parts of a person or animal — usually used in pl.

²inside *adv* **1 :** on the inner side **2 :** in or into the interior

³inside *adj* **1 :** relating to or being on or near the inside **2 :** relating or known to a certain few people

⁴inside *prep* **1 :** to or on the inside of **2 :** before the end of **:** WITHIN

inside out *adv* **1 :** in such a way that the inner surface becomes the outer **2 :** in or into a confused or disorganized state

in·sid·er *n* **:** a person having information not generally available

in·sight *n* **1 :** the ability to understand a person or a situation very clearly **2 :** the understanding of the truth of a situation

in·sig·nia *n, pl* **insignia** *or* **in·sig·ni·as :** an emblem of a certain office, authority, or honor

in·sig·nif·i·cance *n* **:** the quality or state of being unimportant

in·sig·nif·i·cant *adj* **:** not important — **in·sig·nif·i·cant·ly** *adv*

in·sin·cere *adj* **:** not expressing or showing true feelings **:** not sincere or honest — **in·sin·cere·ly** *adv*

in·sin·cer·i·ty *n* **:** lack of honesty in showing feelings

in·sin·u·ate *vb* **in·sin·u·at·ed; in·sin·u·at·ing 1 :** ²HINT, IMPLY **2 :** to bring or get in little by little or in a secret way

in·sip·id *adj* **1 :** having little taste or flavor **:** TASTELESS **2 :** not interesting or challenging **:** DULL

in·sist *vb* **in·sist·ed; in·sist·ing 1 :** to place

special stress or great importance **2 :** to make a demand
in·sis·tence *n* **:** the quality or state of being demanding about something
in·sis·tent *adj* **:** demanding that something happen or that someone act in a certain way — **in·sis·tent·ly** *adv*
in·so·lence *n* **:** lack of respect for rank or authority
in·so·lent *adj* **:** showing lack of respect for rank or authority — **in·so·lent·ly** *adv*
in·sol·u·ble *adj* **1 :** having no solution or explanation **2 :** difficult or impossible to dissolve
in·som·nia *n* **:** difficulty in sleeping
in·spect *vb* **in·spect·ed; in·spect·ing 1 :** to examine closely **2 :** to view and examine in an official way
in·spec·tion *n* **:** the act of examining closely or officially
in·spec·tor *n* **:** a person who makes inspections
in·spi·ra·tion *n* **1 :** the act or power of arousing the mind or the emotions **2 :** a clever idea **3 :** something that moves someone to act, create, or feel an emotion
in·spire *vb* **in·spired; in·spir·ing 1 :** to move or guide by divine influence **2 :** to move (someone) to act, create, or feel emotions **:** AROUSE **3 :** to cause something to occur or to be created or done
in·sta·bil·i·ty *n* **:** the quality or state of being unstable
in·stall *vb* **in·stalled; in·stall·ing 1 :** to put in office with ceremony **2 :** to put in place for use or service
in·stal·la·tion *n* **1 :** the act of putting something in place for use **:** the state of being put in place for use **2 :** something put in place for use
[1]in·stall·ment *n* **:** INSTALLATION 1
[2]installment *n* **:** one of several parts of something (as a book) presented over a period of time
in·stance *n* **1 :** a particular occurrence of something **:** EXAMPLE **2 :** a certain point or situation in a process or series of events
[1]in·stant *n* **:** a very short time **:** MOMENT
[2]instant *adj* **1 :** happening or done right away **2 :** partially prepared by the manufacturer to make final preparation easy
in·stan·ta·neous *adj* **:** happening or done very quickly **:** happening in an instant — **in·stan·ta·neous·ly** *adv*
in·stant·ly *adv* **:** without delay **:** IMMEDIATELY
instant mes·sag·ing *n* **:** a system for sending electronic messages immediately
in·stead *adv* **:** as a substitute
in·stead of *prep* **:** in place of **:** as a substitute for
in·step *n* **:** the arched middle part of the human foot between the ankle and the toes
in·sti·gate *vb* **in·sti·gat·ed; in·sti·gat·ing :** to cause to happen or begin
in·still *vb* **in·stilled; in·still·ing :** to put into the mind little by little
in·stinct *n* **1 :** an act or course of action in response to a stimulus that is automatic rather than learned **2 :** a way of knowing something without learning or thinking about it **3 :** a natural ability
in·stinc·tive *adj* **:** of or relating to instinct **:** resulting from instinct — **in·stinc·tive·ly** *adv*
[1]in·sti·tute *vb* **in·sti·tut·ed; in·sti·tut·ing 1 :** to begin or establish **2 :** to give a start to
[2]institute *n* **1 :** an organization for the promotion of a cause **2 :** a place for study usually in a special field
in·sti·tu·tion *n* **1 :** the beginning or establishment of something **2 :** an established custom, practice, or law **3 :** an established organization
in·struct *vb* **in·struct·ed; in·struct·ing 1 :** to give knowledge to **:** TEACH **2 :** to give information to **3 :** to give directions or commands to
in·struc·tion *n* **1 instructions** *pl* **:** a specific rule or command **2 instructions** *pl* **:** an outline of how something is to be done **3 :** the act or practice of teaching
in·struc·tive *adj* **:** helping to give knowledge or information
in·struc·tor *n* **:** TEACHER
in·stru·ment *n* **1 :** a tool or device for doing a particular kind of work **2 :** a device used to produce music **3 :** a way of getting something done **4 :** a legal document (as a deed) **5 :** a device that measures something (as altitude or temperature)
in·stru·men·tal *adj* **1 :** acting to get something done **2 :** relating to or done with an instrument **3 :** played on an instrument rather than sung
in·sub·or·di·nate *adj* **:** not obeying authority **:** DISOBEDIENT
in·sub·or·di·na·tion *n* **:** failure to obey authority
in·sub·stan·tial *adj* **:** not large or important
in·suf·fer·able *adj* **:** impossible to bear — **in·suf·fer·ably** *adv*
in·suf·fi·cient *adj* **:** not enough **:** not sufficient — **in·suf·fi·cient·ly** *adv*
in·su·late *vb* **in·su·lat·ed; in·su·lat·ing 1 :** to separate from others **:** ISOLATE **2 :** to separate a conductor of electricity, heat, or sound from other conductors by means of something that does not allow the passage of electricity, heat, or sound
in·su·la·tion *n* **1 :** material that is used to

stop the passage of electricity, heat, or sound from one conductor to another **2 :** the act of insulating : the state of being insulated

in·su·la·tor *n* **:** a material (as rubber or glass) that is a poor conductor of electricity, heat, or sound

in·su·lin *n* **:** a hormone made by the pancreas that helps the cells in the body take up glucose from the blood and that is used to treat diabetes

¹in·sult *vb* **in·sult·ed; in·sult·ing :** to treat or speak to with disrespect

²in·sult *n* **:** an act or statement showing disrespect

in·sur·ance *n* **1 :** an agreement by which a person pays a company and the company promises to pay money if the person becomes injured or dies or to pay for the value of property lost or damaged **2 :** the amount for which something is insured **3 :** the business of insuring persons or property

in·sure *vb* **in·sured; in·sur·ing 1 :** to give or get insurance on or for **2 :** to make certain — **in·sur·er** *n*

in·sur·gent *n* **:** a person who revolts : REBEL

in·sur·rec·tion *n* **:** an act or instance of rebelling against a government

in·tact *adj* **:** not broken or damaged : not touched especially by anything that harms

in·take *n* **1 :** the act of taking in **2 :** something taken in **3 :** a place where liquid or air is taken into something (as a pump)

in·tan·gi·ble *adj* **1 :** not capable of being touched **2 :** not having physical substance

in·te·ger *n* **:** a number that is a natural number (as 1, 2, or 3), the negative of a natural number (as –1, –2, –3), or 0

in·te·gral *adj* **:** very important and necessary : needed to make something complete

in·te·grate *vb* **in·te·grat·ed; in·te·grat·ing 1 :** to form into a whole : UNITE **2 :** to make a part of a larger unit **3 :** DESEGREGATE

integrated circuit *n* **:** a tiny group of electronic devices and their connections that is produced in or on a small slice of material (as silicon)

in·te·gra·tion *n* **1 :** the act or process of uniting different things **2 :** the practice of uniting people from different races in an attempt to give people equal rights

in·teg·ri·ty *n* **1 :** total honesty and sincerity **2 :** the condition of being free from damage or defect

in·tel·lect *n* **1 :** the ability to think and understand **2 :** a person with great powers of thinking and reasoning

¹in·tel·lec·tu·al *adj* **1 :** of or relating to thought or understanding **2 :** interested in serious study and thought **3 :** requiring study and thought — **in·tel·lec·tu·al·ly** *adv*

²intellectual *n* **:** a person who takes pleasure in serious study and thought

in·tel·li·gence *n* **1 :** the ability to learn and understand **2 :** secret information collected about an enemy or a possible enemy

in·tel·li·gent *adj* **1 :** having or showing serious thought and good judgment **2 :** able to learn and understand — **in·tel·li·gent·ly** *adv*

in·tel·li·gi·ble *adj* **:** possible to understand — **in·tel·li·gi·bly** *adv*

in·tem·per·ance *n* **:** lack of self-control (as in satisfying an appetite)

in·tem·per·ate *adj* **1 :** not moderate or mild **2 :** having or showing a lack of self-control (as in the use of alcoholic beverages)

in·tend *vb* **in·tend·ed; in·tend·ing :** to have in mind as a purpose or goal : PLAN

in·tense *adj* **1 :** very great in degree : EXTREME **2 :** done with great energy, enthusiasm, or effort **3 :** having very strong feelings — **in·tense·ly** *adv*

in·ten·si·fy *vb* **in·ten·si·fied; in·ten·si·fy·ing :** to make or become stronger or more extreme

in·ten·si·ty *n, pl* **in·ten·si·ties 1 :** strength or force **2 :** the degree or amount of a quality or condition

¹in·ten·sive *adj* **1 :** involving special effort or concentration **2 :** giving emphasis

²intensive *n* **:** a word that emphasizes or stresses something

intensive care *n* **:** constant observation and treatment of very ill patients in a special unit of a hospital

¹in·tent *n* **1 :** what someone plans to do or accomplish : PURPOSE **2 :** MEANING 2

²intent *adj* **1 :** showing concentration or great attention **2 :** showing great determination — **in·tent·ly** *adv*

in·ten·tion *n* **1 :** a determination to act in a particular way **2 :** an aim or plan

in·ten·tion·al *adj* **:** done in a deliberate way : not accidental — **in·ten·tion·al·ly** *adv*

in·ter *vb* **in·terred; in·ter·ring :** BURY 2

inter- *prefix* **1 :** between : among : together **2 :** mutual : mutually **3 :** located, occurring, or carried on between

in·ter·act *vb* **in·ter·act·ed; in·ter·act·ing 1 :** to talk or do things with other people **2 :** to act upon or together with something else

in·ter·ac·tion *n* **1 :** the act of talking or doing things with other people **2 :** the action or influence of things on one another

in·ter·ac·tive *adj* **:** designed to be used in a way that involves the frequent participation of a user — **in·ter·ac·tive·ly** *adv*

in·ter·cede *vb* **in·ter·ced·ed; in·ter·ced·ing 1 :** to try to help settle differences between unfriendly individuals or groups **2 :** to plead for the needs of someone else

in·ter·cept *vb* **in·ter·cept·ed; in·ter·cept·ing**

1 : to take, seize, or stop before reaching an intended destination **2 :** to catch (a football) passed by a member of the opposing team

[1]in·ter·change *vb* **in·ter·changed; in·ter·chang·ing :** to put each in the place of the other : EXCHANGE

[2]in·ter·change *n* **1 :** an act or instance of sharing or exchanging things **2 :** an area where highways meet and it is possibe to move from one to the other without stopping

in·ter·change·able *adj* **:** capable of being used in place of each other — **in·ter·change·ably** *adv*

in·ter·com *n* **:** a communication system with a microphone and loudspeaker at each end

in·ter·course *n* **:** dealings between persons or groups

in·ter·de·pen·dence *n* **:** the quality or state of depending on one another

in·ter·de·pen·dent *adj* **:** depending on one another

[1]in·ter·est *n* **1 :** a feeling of concern or curiosity about or desire to be involved with something **2 :** a quality that makes something more appealing or interesting **3 :** something that a person enjoys learning about or doing **4 :** something that provides help or benefit to a person or group **5 :** the money paid by a borrower for the use of borrowed money **6 :** the profit made on money that is invested **7 :** a right, title, or legal share in something **8 interests** *pl* **:** a group financially interested in an industry or business

[2]interest *vb* **in·ter·est·ed; in·ter·est·ing 1 :** to persuade to become involved in **2 :** to arouse and hold the concern, curiosity, or attention of

in·ter·est·ed *adj* **:** wanting to learn more about or become involved with something

in·ter·est·ing *adj* **:** holding the attention : not dull or boring — **in·ter·est·ing·ly** *adv*

in·ter·fere *vb* **in·ter·fered; in·ter·fer·ing 1 :** to get in the way of as an obstacle **2 :** to become involved in the concerns of others when such involvement is not wanted

in·ter·fer·ence *n* **1 :** something that gets in the way as an obstacle **2 :** involvement in the concerns of others when such involvement is not wanted

in·ter·im *n* **:** a period of time between events

[1]in·te·ri·or *adj* **1 :** being or occurring inside something : INNER **2 :** far from the border or shore : INLAND

[2]interior *n* **1 :** the inner part of something **2 :** the inland part

interj *abbr* interjection

in·ter·ject *vb* **in·ter·ject·ed; in·ter·ject·ing :** to put between or among other things

in·ter·jec·tion *n* **1 :** a word or cry (as "ouch") expressing sudden or strong feeling **2 :** the act of inserting or including something

in·ter·lace *vb* **in·ter·laced; in·ter·lac·ing :** to unite by or as if by lacing together

in·ter·lock *vb* **:** to connect or lock together

in·ter·lop·er *n* **:** a person present in a situation or place where he or she is not wanted

in·ter·lude *n* **1 :** a period of time or event that comes between others **2 :** an entertainment between the acts of a play **3 :** a musical composition between parts of a longer composition or of a drama

in·ter·mar·riage *n* **:** marriage between members of different groups

in·ter·mar·ry *vb* **in·ter·mar·ried; in·ter·mar·ry·ing :** to marry a member of a different group

in·ter·me·di·ary *n, pl* **in·ter·me·di·ar·ies :** GO-BETWEEN

[1]in·ter·me·di·ate *adj* **:** being or occurring in the middle of a series or between extremes — **in·ter·me·di·ate·ly** *adv*

[2]intermediate *n* **:** someone or something that is in the middle of a series or between extremes

in·ter·ment *n* **:** BURIAL

in·ter·mi·na·ble *adj* **:** having or seeming to have no end — **in·ter·mi·na·bly** *adv*

in·ter·min·gle *vb* **in·ter·min·gled; in·ter·min·gling :** to mix together

in·ter·mis·sion *n* **:** a pause or short break (as between acts of a play)

in·ter·mit·tent *adj* **:** starting, stopping, and starting again — **in·ter·mit·tent·ly** *adv*

[1]in·tern *vb* **in·terned; in·tern·ing :** to force to stay within a place (as a prison) especially during a war — **in·tern·ment** *n*

[2]in·tern *n* **:** a student or recent graduate in a special field of study (as medicine or teaching) who works for a period of time to gain practical experience — **in·tern·ship** *n*

in·ter·nal *adj* **1 :** being within something : INNER **2 :** occurring or located within the body **3 :** existing or occurring within a country — **in·ter·nal·ly** *adv*

in·ter·na·tion·al *adj* **1 :** involving two or more nations : occurring between nations **2 :** active or known in many nations — **in·ter·na·tion·al·ly** *adv*

In·ter·net *n* **:** a communications system that connects computers and databases all over the world

in·ter·pose *vb* **in·ter·posed; in·ter·pos·ing 1 :** to put between two or more things **2 :** to introduce between parts of a conversation

in·ter·pret *vb* **in·ter·pret·ed; in·ter·pret·ing 1 :** to explain the meaning of **2 :** to understand in a particular way **3 :** to bring out the meaning of

in·ter·pre·ta·tion *n* **1 :** the way something is explained or understood **2 :** a particular way of performing something (as a dramatic role)
in·ter·pret·er *n* **:** a person who turns spoken words of one language into a different language
in·ter·pre·tive *adj* **:** designed or serving to explain the meaning of something
in·ter·ra·cial *adj* **:** of or involving members of different races
in·ter·re·late *vb* **in·ter·re·lat·ed; in·ter·re·lat·ing :** to bring into or have a connection with each other
in·ter·ro·gate *vb* **in·ter·ro·gat·ed; in·ter·ro·gat·ing :** to question thoroughly
in·ter·ro·ga·tion *n* **:** the act of questioning thoroughly
in·ter·rog·a·tive *adj* **:** having the form or force of a question
in·ter·rupt *vb* **in·ter·rupt·ed; in·ter·rupt·ing 1 :** to stop or hinder by breaking in **2 :** to break the sameness or course of
in·ter·rup·tion *n* **:** an act of stopping or hindering by breaking in
in·ter·scho·las·tic *adj* **:** existing or carried on between schools
in·ter·sect *vb* **in·ter·sect·ed; in·ter·sect·ing :** to cut or divide by passing through or across **:** CROSS
in·ter·sec·tion *n* **1 :** the act or process of crossing or passing across **2 :** the place or point where two or more things (as streets) meet or cross each other **3 :** the set of mathematical elements common to two or more sets
in·ter·sperse *vb* **in·ter·spersed; in·ter·spers·ing 1 :** to put (something) here and there among other things **2 :** to put things at various places in or among
in·ter·state *adj* **:** existing or occurring between two or more states
in·ter·stel·lar *adj* **:** existing or taking place among the stars
in·ter·twine *vb* **in·ter·twined; in·ter·twin·ing :** to twist or weave together
in·ter·val *n* **1 :** a period of time between events or states **2 :** a space between things **3 :** the difference in pitch between two tones
in·ter·vene *vb* **in·ter·vened; in·ter·ven·ing 1 :** to come or occur between events, places, or points of time **2 :** to interfere with something so as to stop, settle, or change
in·ter·ven·tion *n* **:** the act or fact of taking action about something in order to have an effect on its outcome
¹in·ter·view *n* **1 :** a meeting at which people talk to each other in order to ask questions and get information **2 :** an account of an interview
²interview *vb* **in·ter·viewed; in·ter·view·ing :** to question and talk with to get information — **in·ter·view·er** *n*
in·ter·weave *vb* **in·ter·wove; in·ter·wo·ven; in·ter·weav·ing 1 :** to twist or weave together **2 :** to blend together
in·tes·ti·nal *adj* **:** of, relating to, or affecting the intestine
in·tes·tine *n* **:** the lower part of the digestive canal that is a long tube made up of the small intestine and large intestine and in which most of the digestion and absorption of food occurs and through which waste material passes to be discharged
in·ti·ma·cy *n, pl* **in·ti·ma·cies 1 :** a state marked by emotional closeness **2 :** a quality suggesting closeness or warmth **3 :** something that is very personal or private
¹in·ti·mate *vb* **in·ti·mat·ed; in·ti·mat·ing :** to say indirectly **:** hint at
²in·ti·mate *adj* **1 :** very personal or private **2 :** marked by very close association **3 :** suggesting closeness or warmth **:** COZY — **in·ti·mate·ly** *adv*
³in·ti·mate *n* **:** a very close and trusted friend
in·tim·i·date *vb* **in·tim·i·dat·ed; in·tim·i·dat·ing :** to frighten especially by threats
in·tim·i·da·tion *n* **:** the act of making frightened by or as if by threats
in·to *prep* **1 :** to the inside of **2 :** to the state, condition, position, or form of **3 :** so as to hit **:** AGAINST **4 :** in the direction of **5** — used to indicate division
in·tol·er·a·ble *adj* **:** UNBEARABLE — **in·tol·er·a·bly** *adv*
in·tol·er·ance *n* **1 :** the quality or state of being unable or unwilling to put up with **2 :** an unwillingness to grant rights to other people
in·tol·er·ant *adj* **1 :** not able or willing to put up with **2 :** not willing to grant rights to some people
in·to·na·tion *n* **:** the rise and fall in pitch of the voice in speech
in·tox·i·cate *vb* **in·tox·i·cat·ed; in·tox·i·cat·ing 1 :** to affect by alcohol or a drug especially so that normal thinking and acting becomes difficult or impossible **:** make drunk **2 :** to make wildly excited or enthusiastic
in·tox·i·ca·tion *n* **1 :** the condition of being drunk **2 :** an unhealthy state that is or is like a poisoning
in·tra·mu·ral *adj* **:** being or occurring within the limits of a school
intrans. *abbr* intransitive
in·tran·si·tive *adj* **:** not having or containing a direct object
in·trep·id *adj* **:** feeling no fear **:** BOLD
in·tri·ca·cy *n, pl* **in·tri·ca·cies 1 :** the quality or state of being complex or having many parts **2 :** something that is complex or has many parts

in·tri·cate *adj* **1 :** having many closely combined parts or elements **2 :** very difficult to follow or understand — **in·tri·cate·ly** *adv*

[1]in·trigue *vb* **in·trigued; in·trigu·ing 1 :** to arouse the interest or curiosity of **2 :** [2]PLOT 1, SCHEME

[2]in·trigue *n* **:** a secret and complex plot

in·tro·duce *vb* **in·tro·duced; in·tro·duc·ing 1 :** to cause to be acquainted : make known **2 :** to bring into practice or use **3 :** to make available for sale for the first time **4 :** to bring forward for discussion or consideration **5 :** to put in : INSERT

in·tro·duc·tion *n* **1 :** the part of a book that leads up to and explains what will be found in the main part **2 :** the act of causing a person to meet another person **3 :** the action of bringing into use, making available, or presenting for consideration or discussion **4 :** something introduced or added

in·tro·duc·to·ry *adj* **:** serving to introduce : PRELIMINARY

in·trude *vb* **in·trud·ed; in·trud·ing 1 :** to force in, into, or on especially where not right or proper **2 :** to come or go in without an invitation or right — **in·trud·er** *n*

in·tru·sion *n* **1 :** the act of going or forcing in without being wanted **2 :** something that goes in or interferes without being wanted

in·tu·i·tion *n* **1 :** the ability to know something without having proof **2 :** something known without proof

In·u·it *n, pl* **Inuit** *or* **In·u·its 1 :** a member of a group of native people of northern Canada, northern Alaska, and Greenland **2 :** any of the languages of the Inuit people

in·un·date *vb* **in·un·dat·ed; in·un·dat·ing :** to cover with or as if with a flood

in·vade *vb* **in·vad·ed; in·vad·ing 1 :** to enter by force to conquer or plunder **2 :** to show lack of respect for — **in·vad·er** *n*

[1]in·val·id *adj* **:** having no force or effect

[2]in·va·lid *n* **:** a person suffering from sickness or disability

in·val·i·date *vb* **in·val·i·dat·ed; in·val·i·dat·ing :** to weaken or destroy the effect of

in·valu·able *adj* **:** PRICELESS

in·vari·able *adj* **:** not changing or capable of change — **in·vari·ably** *adv*

in·va·sion *n* **:** an act of invading

in·vent *vb* **in·vent·ed; in·vent·ing 1 :** to create or produce for the first time **2 :** to think up : make up — **in·ven·tor** *n*

in·ven·tion *n* **1 :** an original device or process **2 :** [3]LIE **3 :** the act or process of inventing **4 :** the ability to think of new ideas

in·ven·tive *adj* **:** CREATIVE

[1]in·ven·to·ry *n, pl* **in·ven·to·ries 1 :** a supply of goods **2 :** a list of items (as goods on hand) **3 :** the act or process of making a list of items

[2]inventory *vb* **in·ven·to·ried; in·ven·to·ry·ing :** to make a complete list of

in·verse *adj* **1 :** opposite in order, nature, or effect **2 :** being a mathematical operation that is opposite in effect to another operation — **in·verse·ly** *adv*

in·vert *vb* **in·vert·ed; in·vert·ing 1 :** to turn inside out or upside down **2 :** to reverse the order or position of

[1]in·ver·te·brate *adj* **:** having no backbone

[2]invertebrate *n* **:** an animal (as a worm or a crab) that does not have a backbone

[1]in·vest *vb* **in·vest·ed; in·vest·ing :** to give power or authority to

[2]invest *vb* **in·vest·ed; in·vest·ing 1 :** to put out money in order to gain profit **2 :** to put out (as effort) in support of a usually worthy cause — **in·ves·tor** *n*

in·ves·ti·gate *vb* **in·ves·ti·gat·ed; in·ves·ti·gat·ing :** to study by close examination and questioning — **in·ves·ti·ga·tor** *n*

in·ves·ti·ga·tion *n* **:** the act or process of studying by close examination and questioning

in·vest·ment *n* **1 :** the act of putting out money in order to gain a profit **2 :** a sum of money invested **3 :** a property in which money is invested

in·vig·o·rate *vb* **in·vig·o·rat·ed; in·vig·o·rat·ing :** to give life and energy to

in·vin·ci·bil·i·ty *n* **:** the quality or state of being impossible to defeat

in·vin·ci·ble *adj* **:** impossible to defeat

in·vi·o·la·ble *adj* **1 :** too sacred to be broken or denied **2 :** impossible to harm or destroy by violence

in·vis·i·bil·i·ty *n* **:** the quality or state of being impossible to see

in·vis·i·ble *adj* **:** impossible to see — **in·vis·i·bly** *adv*

in·vi·ta·tion *n* **1 :** a written or spoken request for someone to go somewhere or do something **2 :** the act of inviting

in·vite *vb* **in·vit·ed; in·vit·ing 1 :** to ask (someone) to go somewhere or do something **2 :** [1]WELCOME 2 **3 :** to tend to bring on

in·vit·ing *adj* **:** ATTRACTIVE — **in·vit·ing·ly** *adv*

in·voice *n* **:** a list of goods shipped usually showing the price and the terms of sale

in·voke *vb* **in·voked; in·vok·ing 1 :** to ask for aid or protection (as in prayer) **2 :** to call forth by magic **3 :** to appeal to as an authority or for support

in·vol·un·tary *adj* **1 :** not done consciously **2 :** not done by choice — **in·vol·un·tari·ly** *adv*

in·volve *vb* **in·volved; in·volv·ing 1 :** to

draw into a situation : ENGAGE **2 :** to take part in **3 :** INCLUDE **4 :** to be accompanied by **5 :** to have or take the attention of completely — **in·volve·ment** *n*

in·volved *adj* **:** very complicated

in·vul·ner·a·ble *adj* **1 :** impossible to injure or damage **2 :** safe from attack

¹in·ward *adj* **1 :** toward the inside or center **2 :** of or concerning the mind or spirit

²inward *or* **in·wards** *adv* **1 :** toward the inside or center **2 :** toward the mind or spirit

in·ward·ly *adv* **1 :** in a way that is not openly shown or stated : PRIVATELY **2 :** on the inside

io·dine *n* **1 :** a chemical element found in seawater and seaweeds and used especially in medicine and photography **2 :** a solution of iodine in alcohol used to kill germs

io·dize *vb* **io·dized; io·diz·ing :** to add iodine to

ion *n* **:** an atom or group of atoms that carries an electric charge

-ion *n suffix* **1 :** act or process **2 :** result of an act or process **3 :** state or condition

ion·ize *vb* **ion·ized; ion·iz·ing :** to change into ions

ion·o·sphere *n* **:** the part of the earth's atmosphere beginning at an altitude of about 30 miles (50 kilometers) and extending outward that contains electrically charged particles

io·ta *n* **:** a tiny amount

IOU *n* **:** a written promise to pay a debt

-ious *adj suffix* **:** -OUS

IP address *n* **:** the numeric address of a computer on the Internet

IQ *n* **:** a number that represents a person's level of intelligence based on the score of a special test

ir- — see IN-

¹Iraqi *n, pl* **Iraqis :** a person born or living in Iraq

²Iraqi *adj* **:** of or relating to Iraq or its people

iras·ci·ble *adj* **:** easily angered

irate *adj* **:** ANGRY

ire *n* **:** ²ANGER, WRATH

ir·i·des·cence *n* **:** a shifting and constant change of colors producing rainbow effects

ir·i·des·cent *adj* **:** having iridescence

irid·i·um *n* **:** a hard brittle heavy metallic chemical element

iris *n* **1 :** the colored part around the pupil of an eye **2 :** a plant with long pointed leaves and large usually brightly colored flowers

¹Irish *adj* **:** of or relating to Ireland, its people, or the Irish language

²Irish *n* **1 Irish** *pl* **:** the people of Ireland **2 :** a language of Ireland

irk *vb* **irked; irk·ing :** ANNOY

irk·some *adj* **:** causing annoyance

¹iron *n* **1 :** a heavy silvery white metallic chemical element that rusts easily, is strongly attracted by magnets, occurs in meteorites and combined in minerals, and is necessary for transporting oxygen in the blood **2 :** a device that is heated and used for making cloth smooth **3 :** a device that is heated to perform a task **4 irons** *pl* **:** handcuffs or chains used to bind or to hinder movement

²iron *adj* **1 :** made of iron **2 :** strong and healthy **3 :** not giving in

³iron *vb* **ironed; iron·ing :** to press with a heated iron

iron·ic *also* **iron·i·cal** *adj* **:** relating to, containing, or showing irony — **iron·i·cal·ly** *adv*

iron·work *n* **1 :** things made of iron **2 iron·works** *pl* **:** a mill where iron or steel is smelted or heavy iron or steel products are made

iro·ny *n, pl* **iro·nies 1 :** the use of words that mean the opposite of what is really meant **2 :** a result opposite to what was expected

Ir·o·quois *n, pl* **Ir·o·quois :** a member of any of the peoples of an American Indian confederacy that existed originally in central New York state

ir·ra·di·ate *vb* **ir·ra·di·at·ed; ir·ra·di·at·ing 1 :** to cast rays of light on **2 :** to treat by exposure to radiation (as X-rays)

ir·ra·di·a·tion *n* **:** exposure to radiation

ir·ra·tio·nal *adj* **1 :** not able to reason **2 :** not based on reason — **ir·ra·tio·nal·ly** *adv*

ir·rec·on·cil·able *adj* **:** impossible to bring into agreement or harmony

ir·re·deem·able *adj* **:** impossible to save or help

ir·re·fut·able *adj* **:** impossible to prove wrong : INDISPUTABLE

ir·reg·u·lar *adj* **1 :** not following custom or rule **2 :** not following the usual manner of inflection **3 :** not straight, smooth, or even **4 :** not continuous or coming at set times — **ir·reg·u·lar·ly** *adv*

ir·reg·u·lar·i·ty *n, pl* **ir·reg·u·lar·i·ties 1 :** the quality or state of being unusual, uneven, or happening at different times **2 :** something that is unusual, uneven, or happening at different times

ir·rel·e·vance *n* **:** the quality or state of having no relation or importance to what is being considered

ir·rel·e·vant *adj* **:** having no importance or relation to what is being considered

ir·rep·a·ra·ble *adj* **:** impossible to get back or to make right — **ir·rep·a·ra·bly** *adv*

ir·re·place·able *adj* **:** too valuable or too rare to be replaced

ir·re·press·ible *adj* **:** impossible to repress or control

ir·re·proach·able *adj* : not deserving of criticism : without fault
ir·re·sist·ible *adj* : impossible to resist — **ir·re·sist·ibly** *adv*
ir·res·o·lute *adj* : uncertain how to act or proceed — **ir·res·o·lute·ly** *adv*
ir·re·spec·tive of *prep* : without regard to
ir·re·spon·si·bil·i·ty *n* : the quality or state of not being responsible
ir·re·spon·si·ble *adj* : having or showing little or no sense of responsibility — **ir·re·spon·si·bly** *adv*
ir·re·triev·able *adj* : impossible to get back — **ir·re·triev·ably** *adv*
ir·rev·er·ence *n* : lack of respect
ir·rev·er·ent *adj* : not respectful — **ir·rev·er·ent·ly** *adv*
ir·re·vers·i·ble *adj* : impossible to change back to a previous condition : impossible to reverse
ir·rev·o·ca·ble *adj* : impossible to take away or undo — **ir·rev·o·ca·bly** *adv*
ir·ri·gate *vb* **ir·ri·gat·ed; ir·ri·gat·ing** **1** : to supply (as land) with water by artificial means **2** : to clean with a flow of liquid
ir·ri·ga·tion *n* : an act or process of supplying with water or cleaning with a flow of liquid
ir·ri·ta·bil·i·ty *n* : the quality of easily becoming angry or annoyed
ir·ri·ta·ble *adj* : easily made angry or annoyed — **ir·ri·ta·bly** *adv*
ir·ri·tant *n* **1** : something that is annoying **2** : something that causes soreness or sensitivity
ir·ri·tate *vb* **ir·ri·tat·ed; ir·ri·tat·ing** **1** : ANNOY **2** : to make sensitive or sore
ir·ri·ta·tion *n* **1** : the act of making annoyed or sore and sensitive : the state of being annoyed or sore and sensitive **2** : IRRITANT 1
is *present third person sing of* BE
-ish *adj suffix* **1** : of, relating to, or being **2** : characteristic of **3** : somewhat **4** : about (as an age or a time)
Is·lam *n* : a religion based on belief in Allah as the only God and in Muhammad the prophet of God — **Is·lam·ic** *adj*
is·land *n* **1** : an area of land surrounded by water and smaller than a continent **2** : something like an island in its isolation
is·land·er *n* : a person who lives on an island
isle *n* : a usually small island
is·let *n* : a small island
-ism *n suffix* **1** : act : practice : process **2** : manner of action or behavior like that of a specified person or thing **3** : state : condition **4** : teachings : theory : system
isn't : is not
iso·bar *n* : a line on a map to indicate areas having the same atmospheric pressure
iso·late *vb* **iso·lat·ed; iso·lat·ing** : to place or keep apart from others
iso·la·tion *n* : the act of keeping apart from others : the condition of being kept apart from others
isos·ce·les triangle *n* : a triangle having two sides of equal length
ISP *abbr* Internet service provider
[1]Is·rae·li *adj* : of or relating to the country of Israel or its people
[2]Israeli *n* : a person born or living in the country of Israel
Is·ra·el·ite *n* : a person born or living in the ancient kingdom of Israel
is·su·ance *n* : the act of making something available or distributing something : the act of issuing
[1]is·sue *n* **1** : something that is discussed or disputed **2** : the version of a newspaper or magazine that is published at a particular time **3** : the action of going, coming, or flowing out **4** : OFFSPRING, PROGENY **5** : a giving off (as of blood) from the body **6** : the act of bringing out, offering, or making available
[2]issue *vb* **is·sued; is·su·ing** **1** : to go, come, or flow out **2** : to distribute officially **3** : to announce officially **4** : to send out for sale or circulation
-ist *n suffix* **1** : performer of a specified action : maker : producer **2** : a person who plays a specified musical instrument or operates a specified mechanical device **3** : a person who specializes in a specified art or science or skill **4** : a person who follows or favors a specified teaching, practice, system, or code of behavior
isth·mus *n* : a narrow strip of land separating two bodies of water and connecting two larger areas of land
[1]it *pron* **1** : the thing, act, or matter about which these words are spoken or written **2** : the whole situation **3** — used as a subject of a verb that expresses a condition or action without a doer
[2]it *n* : the player who has to do something special in a children's game
IT *abbr* information technology
ital. *abbr* **1** italic **2** italicized
[1]Ital·ian *n* **1** : a person born or living in Italy **2** : the language of the Italians
[2]Italian *adj* : of or relating to Italy, its people, or the Italian language
[1]ital·ic *adj* : of or relating to a type style with letters that slant to the right (as in "*italic* letters")
[2]italic *n* : a type style with letters that slant to the right : an italic letter or italic type
ital·i·cize *vb* **ital·i·cized; ital·i·ciz·ing** **1** : to print in italics **2** : UNDERLINE 1
[1]itch *vb* **itched; itch·ing** : to have or produce an unpleasant feeling that causes a desire to scratch
[2]itch *n* **1** : an unpleasant feeling that causes a desire to scratch **2** : a skin disorder in

which an itch is present **3 :** a restless usually constant desire
itchy *adj* **itch·i·er; itch·i·est :** having, feeling, or causing a desire to scratch
it'd : it had **:** it would
-ite *n suffix* **1 :** native **:** resident **2 :** descendant **3 :** adherent **:** follower
item *n* **1 :** a single thing in a list, account, or series **2 :** a brief piece of news
item·ize *vb* **item·ized; item·iz·ing :** to set down one by one **:** LIST
itin·er·ant *adj* **:** traveling from place to place
-itis *n suffix* **:** inflammation of
it'll : it shall **:** it will
its *adj* **:** relating to or belonging to it or itself
it's 1 : it is **2 :** it has
it·self *pron* **:** that identical one
-ity *n suffix, pl* **-ities :** quality **:** state **:** degree
I've : I have
-ive *adj suffix* **:** that does or tends to do a specified action
ivo·ry *n, pl* **ivo·ries 1 :** a hard creamy-white material that forms the tusks of mammals (as elephants) **2 :** a creamy white color
ivy *n, pl* **ivies 1 :** a climbing vine with evergreen leaves and black berries often found growing on buildings **2 :** a climbing plant that resembles ivy
-i·za·tion *n suffix* **:** action **:** process **:** state
-ize *vb suffix* **-ized; -iz·ing 1 :** cause to be or be like **:** form or cause to be formed into **2 :** cause to experience a specified action **3 :** saturate, treat, or combine with **4 :** treat like **5 :** engage in a specified activity

DICTIONARY

J

j *n, pl* **j's** *or* **js** *often cap* **:** the tenth letter of the English alphabet
¹jab *vb* **jabbed; jab·bing :** to poke quickly or suddenly with or as if with something sharp
²jab *n* **:** a quick or sudden poke
¹jab·ber *vb* **jab·bered; jab·ber·ing :** to talk too fast or not clearly enough to be understood
²jabber *n* **:** CHATTER
¹jack *n* **1 :** a device for lifting something heavy a short distance **2 :** a playing card with the picture of a young man **3 :** a small six-pointed usually metal object used in a children's game (**jacks**) **4 :** a socket used with a plug to connect one electric circuit with another
²jack *vb* **jacked; jack·ing :** to move or lift with a special device
jack·al *n* **:** a wild dog of Africa and Asia like but smaller than a wolf
jack·ass *n* **1 :** a donkey and especially a male donkey **2 :** a stupid person
jack·daw *n* **:** a black and gray European bird related to but smaller than a crow
jack·et *n* **1 :** a short coat **2 :** an outer cover or casing
jack–in–the–box *n, pl* **jack–in–the–box·es** *or* **jacks–in–the–box :** a small box out of which a toy figure springs when the lid is raised
jack–in–the–pul·pit *n, pl* **jack–in–the–pul·pits** *or* **jacks–in–the–pul·pit :** a plant that grows in moist shady woods and has a stalk of tiny yellowish flowers protected by a leaf bent over like a hood
¹jack·knife *n, pl* **jack·knives :** a knife that has a folding blade or blades and can be put in a pocket
²jackknife *vb* **jack·knifed; jack·knif·ing :** to double up like a jackknife
jack–of–all–trades *n, pl* **jacks–of–all–trades :** a person who can do several kinds of work fairly well
jack–o'–lan·tern *n* **:** a pumpkin with its insides scooped out and cut to look like a human face
jack·pot *n* **1 :** a large amount of money to be won **2 :** a large and often unexpected success or reward
jack·rab·bit *n* **:** a large hare of North America that has very long ears and long hind legs
jade *n* **:** a usually green mineral used for jewelry and carvings
jag·ged *adj* **:** having a sharply uneven edge or surface
jag·uar *n* **:** a large yellowish brown black-spotted animal of the cat family found chiefly from Mexico to Argentina
¹jail *n* **:** PRISON
²jail *vb* **jailed; jail·ing :** to shut up in or as if in a prison
jail·break *n* **:** escape from prison by force
jail·er *also* **jail·or** *n* **:** a person responsible for the operation of a prison
ja·lopy *n, pl* **ja·lop·ies :** a worn old automobile
¹jam *vb* **jammed; jam·ming 1 :** to crowd, squeeze, or wedge into a tight position **2 :** to put into action hard or suddenly **3 :** to hurt by pressure **4 :** to be or cause to be

stuck or unable to work because a part is wedged tight **5 :** to cause interference in (radio or television signals)

²jam *n* **:** a food made by boiling fruit with sugar until it is thick

³jam *n* **1 :** a crowded mass of people or things that blocks something **2 :** a difficult situation

jamb *n* **:** a vertical piece forming the side of an opening (as for a doorway)

jam·bo·ree *n* **1 :** a large party or celebration **2 :** a national or international camping assembly of Boy Scouts

Jan. *abbr* January

¹jan·gle *vb* **jan·gled; jan·gling :** to make or cause to make a sound like the harsh ringing of a bell

²jangle *n* **:** a harsh often ringing sound

jan·i·tor *n* **:** a person who takes care of a building (as a school)

Jan·u·ary *n* **:** the first month of the year

¹Jap·a·nese *adj* **:** of or relating to Japan, its people, or the Japanese language

²Japanese *n, pl* **Japanese 1 :** a person born or living in Japan **2 :** the language of the Japanese

Japanese beetle *n* **:** a small glossy green or brown Asian beetle now found in the United States that as a grub feeds on roots and as an adult eats leaves and fruits

¹jar *n* **1 :** a usually glass or pottery container with a wide mouth **2 :** the contents of a jar

²jar *vb* **jarred; jar·ring 1 :** to shake or cause to shake hard **2 :** to have a disagreeable effect

³jar *n* **1 :** ²JOLT 1 **2 :** ²SHOCK 1

jar·gon *n* **1 :** the special vocabulary of an activity or group **2 :** language that is not clear and is full of long words

jas·mine *n* **:** a usually climbing plant of warm regions with fragrant flowers

jas·per *n* **:** an opaque usually red, green, brown, or yellow stone used for making decorative objects

jaunt *n* **:** a short pleasure trip

jaun·ty *adj* **jaun·ti·er; jaun·ti·est :** lively in manner or appearance — **jaun·ti·ly** *adv* — **jaun·ti·ness** *n*

jav·e·lin *n* **1 :** a light spear **2 :** a slender rod thrown for distance in a track-and-field contest (**javelin throw**)

jaw *n* **1 :** either of an upper or lower bony structure that supports the soft parts of the mouth and usually bears teeth on its edge and of which the lower part is movable **2 :** a part of an invertebrate animal (as an insect) that resembles or does the work of a human jaw **3 :** one of a pair of moving parts that open and close for holding or crushing something

jaw·bone *n* **:** JAW 1

jay *n* **:** a usually blue bird related to the crow that has a loud call

jay·walk *vb* **jay·walked; jay·walk·ing :** to cross a street in a place or in a way that is against traffic regulations — **jay·walk·er** *n*

jazz *n* **:** a type of American music with lively rhythms and melodies that are often made up by musicians as they play

jeal·ous *adj* **1 :** feeling anger because of the belief that a loved one might be unfaithful **2 :** feeling a mean anger toward someone because he or she is more successful **3 :** CAREFUL 1, WATCHFUL — **jeal·ous·ly** *adv*

jeal·ou·sy *n, pl* **jeal·ou·sies 1 :** a feeling of unhappiness and anger caused by a belief that a loved one might be unfaithful **2 :** a feeling of unhappiness caused by wanting what someone else has

jeans *n pl* **:** pants made of denim

jeep *n* **:** a small motor vehicle used by the United States military for travel on rough surfaces

¹jeer *vb* **jeered; jeer·ing 1 :** to speak or cry out in scorn **2 :** to scorn or mock with taunts

²jeer *n* **:** a scornful remark or sound **:** TAUNT

Je·ho·vah *n* **:** GOD 1

jell *vb* **jelled; jell·ing 1 :** to become as firm as jelly **:** SET **2 :** to take shape

jel·lied *adj* **:** made into or as part of a jelly

jel·ly *n, pl* **jellies :** a soft springy food made from fruit juice boiled with sugar — **jel·ly·like** *adj*

jelly bean *n* **:** a chewy bean-shaped candy

jel·ly·fish *n* **:** a free-swimming sea animal related to the corals that has a nearly transparent jellylike body shaped like a saucer and tentacles with stinging cells

jen·net *n* **:** a female donkey

jeop·ar·dize *vb* **jeop·ar·dized; jeop·ar·diz·ing :** to put in danger

jeop·ar·dy *n* **:** DANGER 1

¹jerk *vb* **jerked; jerk·ing 1 :** to give a quick sharp pull or twist to **2 :** to move in a quick motion

²jerk *n* **1 :** a short quick pull or jolt **2 :** a foolish person

jer·kin *n* **:** a short sleeveless jacket

jerky *adj* **jerk·i·er; jerk·i·est :** moving with sudden starts and stops

jer·sey *n, pl* **jerseys 1 :** a knitted cloth (as of cotton) used mostly for making clothing **2 :** a shirt made of knitted fabric and especially one worn by a sports team

¹jest *n* **1 :** a comic act or remark **:** JOKE **2 :** a playful mood or manner

²jest *vb* **jest·ed; jest·ing :** to make comic remarks **:** JOKE

jest·er *n* **:** a person formerly kept in royal courts to amuse people

Je·sus *n* : JESUS CHRIST
Jesus Christ *n* : the founder of the Christian religion
[1]jet *n* **1** : a rush of liquid, gas, or vapor through a narrow opening or a nozzle **2** : JET AIRPLANE **3** : a nozzle for a rush of gas or liquid **4** : JET ENGINE
[2]jet *adj* : of a very dark black color
[3]jet *n* **1** : a black mineral that is often used for jewelry **2** : a very dark black
[4]jet *vb* **jet·ted; jet·ting** : to come forcefully from a narrow opening
jet airplane *n* : an airplane powered by a jet engine
jet engine *n* : an engine in which fuel burns to produce a rush of heated air and gases that shoot out from the rear and drive the engine forward
jet plane *n* : JET AIRPLANE
jet–pro·pelled *adj* : driven forward or onward by a jet engine
jet·sam *n* : goods thrown overboard to lighten a ship in danger of sinking
jet stream *n* : high-speed winds blowing from a westerly direction several miles above the earth's surface
jet·ti·son *vb* **jet·ti·soned; jet·ti·son·ing** : to throw out especially from a ship or an airplane
jet·ty *n, pl* **jetties** **1** : a pier built to change the path of the current or tide or to protect a harbor **2** : a landing wharf
Jew *n* : a person whose religion is Judaism or who is a descendant of the ancient Hebrews
jew·el *n* **1** : GEM 1 **2** : an ornament of precious metal often set with gemstones and worn on the body **3** : a person who is greatly admired
jew·el·er *or* **jew·el·ler** *n* : a person who makes or buys and sells jewelry and related articles (as silverware)
jew·el·ry *n* : ornamental pieces (as rings or necklaces) worn on the body
Jew·ish *adj* : of or relating to Jews or Judaism
jib *n* : a three-cornered sail extending forward from the foremast
[1]jibe *variant of* GIBE
[2]jibe *vb* **jibed; jib·ing** : to be in agreement
jif·fy *n, pl* **jiffies** : MOMENT 1
[1]jig *n* **1** : a lively dance **2** : music for a lively dance **3** : a dishonest act
[2]jig *vb* **jigged; jig·ging** **1** : to dance a jig **2** : to move with quick sudden motions
jig·gle *vb* **jig·gled; jig·gling** : to move or cause to move with quick little jerks
jig·saw *n* : a machine saw used to cut curved and irregular lines or openwork patterns
jigsaw puzzle *n* : a puzzle of many small pieces of a picture that must be fitted together
jim·my *vb* **jim·mied; jim·my·ing** : to force open with or as if with a short crowbar
jim·son·weed *n* : a poisonous weedy plant with bad-smelling leaves and large white or purple flowers
[1]jin·gle *vb* **jin·gled; jin·gling** : to make or cause to make a light clinking sound
[2]jingle *n* **1** : a light clinking sound **2** : a short catchy verse or song used to help sell a product
[1]jinx *n, pl* **jinx·es** : something or someone that brings bad luck
[2]jinx *vb* **jinxed; jinx·ing** : to bring bad luck to
jit·ters *n pl* : extreme nervousness
jit·tery *adj* **1** : very nervous **2** : showing nervousness
job *n* **1** : work done regularly for pay **2** : a special duty or function **3** : a piece of work usually done on order at an agreed rate **4** : something produced by or as if by work — **job·less** *adj*
jock *n* : ATHLETE
jock·ey *n, pl* **jockeys** **1** : a professional rider in a horse race **2** : OPERATOR 1
[1]jog *vb* **jogged; jog·ging** **1** : to go or cause to go at a slow run **2** : to run slowly (as for exercise) **3** : to give a slight shake or push to : NUDGE **4** : to make more alert — **jog·ger** *n*
[2]jog *n* **1** : a slow run **2** : a slight shake or push **3** : a slow jerky gait (as of a horse)
[3]jog *n* : a short change in direction
jog·gle *vb* **jog·gled; jog·gling** : to shake or cause to shake slightly
john·ny·cake *n* : a bread made of cornmeal, milk, flour, and eggs
join *vb* **joined; join·ing** **1** : to come into the company of **2** : to take part in a group activity **3** : to come, bring, or fasten together **4** : to become a member of **5** : to come or bring into close association **6** : to combine the elements of **7** : ADJOIN
[1]joint *n* **1** : a point where two bones of the skeleton come together usually in a way that allows motion **2** : a place where two things or parts are joined **3** : a part of a plant stem where a leaf or branch develops **4** : a business establishment — **joint·ed** *adj*
[2]joint *adj* **1** : joined together **2** : done by or shared by two or more — **joint·ly** *adv*
joist *n* : any of the small timbers or metal beams laid crosswise in a building to support a floor or ceiling
[1]joke *n* **1** : something said or done to cause laughter or amusement **2** : a very short story with a funny ending that is a surprise **3** : something not worthy of being taken seriously
[2]joke *vb* **joked; jok·ing** **1** : to say or do something to cause laughter or amusement **2** : to make funny remarks
jok·er *n* **1** : a person who says or does

things to make others laugh **2 :** an extra card used in some card games
jok·ing·ly *adv* **:** in a manner that is not meant to be taken seriously
jol·li·ty *n* **:** the state of being happy and cheerful
[1]**jol·ly** *adj* **jol·li·er; jol·li·est :** full of fun or joy
[2]**jolly** *adv* **:** [2]VERY 1
[1]**jolt** *vb* **jolt·ed; jolt·ing 1 :** to move or cause to move with a sudden jerky motion **2 :** to cause to be upset
[2]**jolt** *n* **1 :** an abrupt jerky and usually powerful blow or movement **2 :** a sudden shock or surprise
jon·quil *n* **:** a plant related to the daffodil but with fragrant yellow or white flowers with a short central tube
josh *vb* **joshed; josh·ing :** to make humorous remarks or tease in a good-natured way
jos·tle *vb* **jos·tled; jos·tling :** to push roughly
[1]**jot** *n* **:** the least bit
[2]**jot** *vb* **jot·ted; jot·ting :** to write briefly or in a hurry
jounce *vb* **jounced; jounc·ing :** to move, fall, or bounce so as to shake
jour·nal *n* **1 :** a brief record (as in a diary) of daily happenings **2 :** a magazine that reports on things of special interest to a particular group **3 :** a daily newspaper
jour·nal·ism *n* **1 :** the business of collecting and editing news (as for newspapers, radio, or television) **2 :** writing of general or popular interest
jour·nal·ist *n* **:** an editor or reporter of the news
[1]**jour·ney** *n, pl* **jour·neys :** an act of traveling from one place to another
[2]**journey** *vb* **jour·neyed; jour·ney·ing :** to travel to a distant place
jour·ney·man *n, pl* **jour·ney·men :** a worker who has learned a trade and usually works for another person by the day
[1]**joust** *vb* **joust·ed; joust·ing :** to take part in a combat on horseback with a lance
[2]**joust** *n* **:** a combat on horseback between two knights with lances
jo·vial *adj* **:** [1]JOLLY — **jo·vial·ly** *adv*
[1]**jowl** *n* **:** loose flesh hanging from the lower jaw, cheeks, and throat
[2]**jowl** *n* **1 :** an animal's jaw and especially the lower jaw **2 :** CHEEK 1
joy *n* **1 :** a feeling of pleasure or happiness that comes from success, good fortune, or a sense of well-being **2 :** something that gives pleasure or happiness
joy·ful *adj* **:** feeling, causing, or showing pleasure or happiness — **joy·ful·ly** *adv* — **joy·ful·ness** *n*
joy·ous *adj* **:** JOYFUL — **joy·ous·ly** *adv* — **joy·ous·ness** *n*
joy·stick *n* **:** a control lever (as for a computer display or an airplane) capable of motion in two or more directions
Jr. *abbr* junior
ju·bi·lant *adj* **:** expressing great joy especially with shouting **:** noisily happy
ju·bi·la·tion *n* **:** the act of rejoicing **:** the state of being noisily happy
ju·bi·lee *n* **1 :** a 50th anniversary **2 :** a time of celebration
Ju·da·ism *n* **:** a religion developed among the ancient Hebrews that stresses belief in one God and faithfulness to the laws of the Torah
[1]**judge** *vb* **judged; judg·ing 1 :** to form an opinion after careful consideration **2 :** to act with authority to reach a decision (as in a trial) **3 :** THINK 1 **4 :** to form an opinion of in comparison with others
[2]**judge** *n* **1 :** a public official whose duty is to decide questions brought before a court **2 :** a person appointed to decide in a contest or competition **3 :** a person with the experience to give a meaningful opinion **:** CRITIC
judg·ment *or chiefly Brit* **judge·ment** *n* **1 :** a decision or opinion (as of a court) given after careful consideration **2 :** an opinion or estimate formed by examining and comparing **3 :** the ability for reaching a decision after careful consideration
ju·di·cial *adj* **1 :** of courts or judges **2 :** ordered or done by a court — **ju·di·cial·ly** *adv*
ju·di·cious *adj* **:** having, using, or showing good judgment **:** WISE — **ju·di·cious·ly** *adv*
ju·do *n* **:** a sport developed in Japan in which opponents try to throw or pin each other to the ground
jug *n* **:** a large deep usually earthenware or glass container with a narrow mouth and a handle
jug·gle *vb* **jug·gled; jug·gling 1 :** to keep several things moving in the air at the same time **2 :** to work or do (several things) at the same time — **jug·gler** *n*
juice *n* **1 :** the liquid part that can be squeezed out of vegetables and fruit **2 :** the liquid part of meat
juicy *adj* **juic·i·er; juic·i·est :** having much liquid — **juic·i·ness** *n*
Ju·ly *n* **:** the seventh month of the year
[1]**jum·ble** *n* **:** a disorderly mass or pile
[2]**jumble** *vb* **jum·bled; jum·bling :** to mix in a confused mass
jum·bo *adj* **:** very large
[1]**jump** *vb* **jumped; jump·ing 1 :** to spring into the air **:** LEAP **2 :** to pass over or cause to pass over with or as if with a leap **3 :** to make a sudden movement **4 :** to make a sudden attack **5 :** to have or cause a sudden sharp increase **6 :** to make a hasty judgment — **jump the gun 1 :** to start in a race

before the starting signal **2 :** to do something before the proper time

²jump *n* **1 :** an act or instance of leaping **2 :** a sudden involuntary movement : START **3 :** a sharp sudden increase **4 :** an initial advantage

jump drive *n* **:** a small usually rectangular device used for storing and transferring computer data : FLASH DRIVE

jum·per *n* **1 :** someone or something that jumps **2 :** a sleeveless dress worn usually with a blouse

jumping jack *n* **:** an exercise in which a person who is standing jumps to a position with legs and arms spread out and then jumps back to the original position

jump·suit *n* **:** a one-piece garment consisting of a shirt with attached pants or shorts

jumpy *adj* **jump·i·er; jump·i·est :** NERVOUS 2

jun *abbr* junior

jun·co *n, pl* **juncos** *or* **juncoes :** a small mostly gray North American bird usually having a pink bill

junc·tion *n* **1 :** a place or point where two or more things meet **2 :** an act of joining

junc·ture *n* **:** an important or particular point or stage in a process or activity

June *n* **:** the sixth month of the year

jun·gle *n* **1 :** a thick or tangled growth of tropical plants **2 :** a large area of land usually in a tropical region covered with a thick tangled growth of plants

jungle gym *n* **:** a structure of bars for children to climb on

¹ju·nior *adj* **1 :** being younger — used to distinguish a son from a father with the same name **2 :** lower in rank **3 :** of or relating to students in the next-to-last year at a high school, college, or university

²junior *n* **1 :** a person who is younger or lower in rank than another **2 :** a student in the next-to-last year at a high school, college, or university

junior high school *n* **:** a school usually including seventh, eighth, and ninth grades

ju·ni·per *n* **:** an evergreen tree or shrub related to the pines but having tiny cones resembling berries

¹junk *n* **1 :** things that have been thrown away or are of little value or use **2 :** a poorly made product **3 :** something of little meaning, worth, or significance

²junk *vb* **junked; junk·ing :** to get rid of as worthless : SCRAP

³junk *n* **:** an Asian sailing boat that is high in the front

junk food *n* **:** food that is high in calories but low in nutritional content

junky *adj* **junk·i·er; junk·i·est :** of poor quality

Ju·pi·ter *n* **:** the planet that is fifth in order of distance from the sun and is the largest of the planets with a diameter of about 89,000 miles (140,000 kilometers)

ju·ror *n* **:** a member of a jury

ju·ry *n, pl* **juries 1 :** a group of citizens chosen to hear and decide the facts of a case in a court of law **2 :** a committee that judges and awards prizes (as at an exhibition)

¹just *adj* **1 :** being what is deserved **2 :** having a foundation in fact or reason : REASONABLE **3 :** agreeing with a standard of correctness **4 :** morally right or good — **just·ly** *adv*

²just *adv* **1 :** to an exact degree or in an exact manner **2 :** very recently **3 :** by a very small amount : with nothing to spare **4 :** by a very short distance **5 :** nothing other than **6 :** ²VERY 2

jus·tice *n* **1 :** fair treatment **2 :** ²JUDGE 1 **3 :** the process or result of using laws to fairly judge people accused of crimes **4 :** the quality of being fair or just

jus·ti·fi·ca·tion *n* **1 :** the act or an instance of proving to be just, right, or reasonable **2 :** sufficient reason to show that an action is correct or acceptable

jus·ti·fy *vb* **jus·ti·fied; jus·ti·fy·ing :** to prove or show to be just, right, or reasonable — **jus·ti·fi·able** *adj* — **jus·ti·fi·ably** *adv*

jut *vb* **jut·ted; jut·ting :** to extend or cause to extend above or beyond a surrounding area

jute *n* **:** a strong glossy fiber from a tropical plant used chiefly for making sacks and twine

¹ju·ve·nile *adj* **1 :** not fully grown or developed **2 :** of or designed for young people **3 :** having or showing a lack of emotional maturity

²juvenile *n* **:** a young person : YOUTH

K

k *n, pl* **k's** *or* **ks** *often cap* **1 :** the eleventh letter of the English alphabet **2 :** THOUSAND **3 :** KILOBYTE

kale *n* **:** a hardy cabbage with wrinkled leaves that do not form a head

ka·lei·do·scope *n* **1 :** a tube that contains bits of colored glass or plastic and two mirrors at one end and that shows many different patterns as it is turned **2 :** a changing pattern or scene

Kan. *abbr* Kansas

kan·ga·roo *n, pl* **kan·ga·roos :** a leaping mammal of Australia and nearby islands that feeds on plants and has long powerful hind legs, a thick tail used as a support in standing or walking, and in the female a pouch on the abdomen in which the young are carried

Kans. *abbr* Kansas

ka·o·lin *n* **:** a very pure white clay used in making porcelain

kar·a·o·ke *n* **:** a form of entertainment in which a device plays music to which a person sings along

kar·at *n* **:** a unit of fineness for gold

ka·ra·te *n* **:** an art of self-defense developed in Japan in which an attacker is defeated by kicks and punches

ka·ty·did *n* **:** a large green American grasshopper with males that make shrill noises

kay·ak *n* **:** a small boat that is pointed at both ends, holds one or two people, and is moved by a paddle with two blades

ka·zoo *n, pl* **ka·zoos :** a toy musical instrument which produces a buzzing tone when a person hums into the mouth hole

KB *abbr* kilobyte

keel *n* **:** a long heavy piece of wood or metal that runs along and usually sticks out from the center of the bottom of a ship

keel over *vb* **keeled over; keel·ing over :** to fall suddenly (as in a faint)

keen *adj* **1 :** having a fine edge or point **:** SHARP **2 :** having or showing mental sharpness **3 :** very sensitive (as in seeing, smelling, or hearing) **4 :** full of enthusiasm **:** EAGER **5 :** seeming to cut or sting — **keen·ly** *adv* — **keen·ness** *n*

¹keep *vb* **kept; keep·ing 1 :** to remain or cause to remain in a given place, situation, or condition **2 :** to put in a specified place for storage **3 :** PROTECT **4 :** to continue doing something **5 :** to continue to have in possession or power **6 :** to prevent from leaving **:** DETAIN **7 :** to hold back **8 :** to be faithful to **:** FULFILL **9 :** to act properly in relation to **10 :** to take care of **:** TEND **11 :** to have available for service or at one's disposal **12 :** to preserve a record in **13 :** to continue in an unspoiled condition **14 :** ¹REFRAIN — **keep an eye on :** ¹WATCH 3 — **keep up 1 :** to continue without interruption **2 :** to stay even with others (as in a race) **3 :** to stay well informed about something **4 :** MAINTAIN 2

²keep *n* **1 :** the strongest part of a castle in the Middle Ages **2 :** the necessities of life — **for keeps 1 :** with the understanding that a person or group may keep what is won **2 :** for a long time **:** PERMANENTLY

keep·er *n* **:** a person who watches, guards, or takes care of something

keep·ing *n* **1 :** watchful attention **:** CARE **2 :** a proper or fitting relationship **:** HARMONY

keep·sake *n* **:** something kept or given to be kept in memory of a person, place, or happening

keg *n* **1 :** a small barrel holding 30 gallons (about 114 liters) **2 :** the contents of a keg

kelp *n* **:** a large brown seaweed

ken·nel *n* **1 :** a shelter for a dog **2 :** a place where dogs or cats are bred or housed

kept *past and past participle of* KEEP

ker·chief *n, pl* **kerchiefs :** a square of cloth worn as a head covering or as a scarf

ker·nel *n* **1 :** the inner softer part of a seed, fruit stone, or nut **2 :** the whole grain or seed of a cereal plant **3 :** a very small amount

ker·o·sene *n* **:** a thin oil obtained from petroleum and used as a fuel and solvent

ketch *n* **:** a fore-and-aft rigged ship with two masts

ketch·up *also* **cat·sup** *n* **:** a thick seasoned sauce made from tomatoes

ket·tle *n* **1 :** a pot for boiling liquids **2 :** TEAKETTLE

ket·tle·drum *n* **:** a large brass or copper drum that has a rounded bottom and can be varied in pitch

¹key *n* **1 :** an instrument by which the bolt of a lock (as on a door) is turned or by which an engine is started **2 :** a device having the form or function of a key **3 :** the thing that is necessary or most important in doing something **4 :** something (as a map legend) that gives an explanation **:** SOLUTION **5 :** one of the levers with a flat surface that is pressed with a finger to activate a mechanism of a machine or instrument **6 :** a system of seven musical tones arranged in relation to a keynote from which the system is named

²key *vb* **keyed; key·ing 1 :** to regulate the

musical pitch of **2 :** to bring into harmony **3 :** to record or enter by operating the keys of a machine

[3]**key** *adj* **:** of great importance **:** most important

[4]**key** *n* **:** a low island or reef

key·board *n* **1 :** a row of keys by which a musical instrument (as a piano) is played **2 :** a portable electronic musical instrument with a row of keys like that of a piano **3 :** the whole arrangement of keys (as on a computer or typewriter)

key·hole *n* **:** a hole for receiving a key

key·note *n* **1 :** the first tone of a scale fundamental to harmony **2 :** the fundamental fact, idea, or mood

key·stone *n* **1 :** the wedge-shaped piece at the top of an arch that locks the other pieces in place **2 :** something on which other things depend for support

kg *abbr* kilogram

kha·ki *n* **1 :** a light yellowish brown cloth used especially for military uniforms **2 kha·kis** *pl* **:** a pair of pants made of khaki **3 :** a light yellowish brown

[1]**kick** *vb* **kicked; kick·ing 1 :** to hit with the foot **2 :** to move the legs forcefully **3 :** to put an end to — **kick·er** *n* — **kick off 1 :** to start play in a game (as in football or soccer) by kicking the ball **2 :** BEGIN 1

[2]**kick** *n* **1 :** a blow with the foot **2 :** the act of hitting a ball with the foot **3 :** a feeling or source of pleasure **4 :** a usually sudden strong interest

kick·ball *n* **:** a game similar to baseball played with a large rubber ball that is kicked instead of hit with a bat

kick·off *n* **:** a kick that puts the ball into play (as in football or soccer)

kick·stand *n* **:** a metal bar on a two-wheeled vehicle (as a bicycle) that is used to prop the vehicle up when it is not in use

[1]**kid** *n* **1 :** CHILD **2 :** a young goat or a related animal **3 :** the flesh, fur, or skin of a young goat or related animal or something (as leather) made from one of these

[2]**kid** *vb* **kid·ded; kid·ding 1 :** to deceive or trick as a joke **2 :** [1]TEASE — **kid·der** *n*

kid·nap *vb* **kid·napped; kid·nap·ping :** to carry away a person by force or by fraud and against his or her will — **kid·nap·per** *n*

kid·ney *n, pl* **kid·neys :** either of a pair of organs near the backbone that give off waste from the body in the form of urine and in humans are bean-shaped

kidney bean *n* **:** the large usually dark red edible seed of a bean plant

[1]**kill** *vb* **killed; kill·ing 1 :** to end the life of **2 :** to put an end to **3 :** to use up **4 :** [1]DEFEAT 2 **5 :** to cause to become very tired

[2]**kill** *n* **1 :** an act of taking the life of a person or animal **2 :** an animal whose life has been taken

kill·deer *n* **:** a grayish brown North American bird that has a high-pitched mournful call

[1]**kill·er** *n* **:** someone or something that takes the life of a person or animal

[2]**killer** *adj* **1 :** very impressive or effective **2 :** very difficult **3 :** causing death or ruin

killer whale *n* **:** a toothed whale that is mostly black above and white below and feeds especially on fish, squid, birds, and sea mammals (as seals)

kill·joy *n* **:** a person who spoils the pleasure of others

kiln *n* **:** a furnace or oven in which something (as pottery) is hardened, burned, or dried

ki·lo *n, pl* **kilos :** KILOGRAM

kilo- *prefix* **:** thousand

ki·lo·byte *n* **:** a unit of computer information storage equal to 1024 bytes

ki·lo·gram *n* **:** a metric unit of weight equal to 1000 grams

ki·lo·me·ter *or Can and Brit* **kilometre** *n* **:** a metric unit of length equal to 1000 meters

kilo·watt *n* **:** a unit of electrical power equal to 1000 watts

kilt *n* **:** a knee-length pleated skirt usually of tartan worn by men in Scotland

kil·ter *n* **:** proper condition

ki·mo·no *n, pl* **ki·mo·nos 1 :** a loose robe with wide sleeves that is traditionally worn with a broad sash as an outer garment by a Japanese person **2 :** a loose dressing gown worn chiefly by women

kin *n* **1 :** a person's relatives **2 :** KINSMAN

-kin *also* **-kins** *n suffix* **:** little

[1]**kind** *n* **:** a group of persons or things that belong together or have something in common

[2]**kind** *adj* **kind·er; kind·est 1 :** wanting or liking to do good and to bring happiness to others **:** CONSIDERATE **2 :** showing or growing out of gentleness or goodness of heart

kin·der·gar·ten *n* **:** a school or a class for very young children — **kin·der·gart·ner** *n*

kind·heart·ed *adj* **:** having or showing a kind and sympathetic nature

kin·dle *vb* **kin·dled; kin·dling 1 :** to set on fire **:** LIGHT **2 :** to stir up **:** EXCITE

kin·dling *n* **:** material that burns easily and is used for starting a fire

[1]**kind·ly** *adj* **kind·li·er; kind·li·est 1 :** [2]KIND 1 **2 :** pleasant or wholesome in nature — **kind·li·ness** *n*

[2]**kindly** *adv* **1 :** in a sympathetic manner **2 :** in a willing manner **3 :** in an appreciative manner **4 :** in an obliging manner

kind·ness *n* **1 :** the quality or state of being gentle and considerate **2 :** a kind deed **:** FAVOR

kind of *adv* **:** to a moderate degree **:** SOMEWHAT

[1]**kin·dred** *adj* **:** alike in nature or character

[2]**kindred** *n* **1 :** a group of related individuals **2 :** a person's relatives

ki·net·ic *adj* **:** relating to the motions of objects and the forces associated with them

kin·folk *n* **:** [2]KINDRED 2

king *n* **1 :** a male ruler of a country who usually inherits his position and rules for life **2 :** a person or thing that is better or more important than all others **3 :** the chief piece in the game of chess **4 :** a playing card bearing the picture of a king **5 :** a piece in checkers that has reached the opponent's back row

king·dom *n* **1 :** a country whose ruler is a king or queen **2 :** one of the three basic divisions (**animal kingdom, plant kingdom, mineral kingdom**) into which natural objects are commonly grouped **3 :** a group of related living things (as plants, animals, or bacteria) that ranks above the phylum and division in scientific classification and is the highest and broadest group

king·fish·er *n* **:** a crested bird with a short tail, long sharp bill, and bright feathers

king·let *n* **:** a small active bird especially of wooded areas

king·ly *adj* **1 :** suited to a king **2 :** of a king

king–size *or* **king–sized** *adj* **:** unusually large

kink *n* **1 :** a short tight twist or curl (as in a thread or hose) **2 :** [1]CRAMP 1 **3 :** an imperfection that makes something hard to use or work — **kinky** *adj*

-kins — see -KIN

kin·ship *n* **:** the quality or state of being related

kins·man *n, pl* **kins·men :** a relative usually by birth

kins·wom·an *n, pl* **kins·wom·en :** a woman who is a relative usually by birth

[1]**kiss** *vb* **kissed; kiss·ing 1 :** to touch with the lips as a mark of love or greeting **2 :** to touch gently or lightly

[2]**kiss** *n* **1 :** a loving touch with the lips **2 :** a gentle touch or contact

kiss·er *n* **1 :** a person who kisses **2 :** a person's face

[1]**kit** *n* **1 :** a set of articles for personal use **2 :** a set of tools or supplies **3 :** a set of parts to be put together

[2]**kit** *n* **:** a young fur-bearing animal

kitch·en *n* **:** a room in which food is prepared and cooking is done

kitch·en·ette *n* **:** a small kitchen

kitchen garden *n* **:** a piece of land where vegetables are grown for household use

kite *n* **1 :** a toy that consists of a light covered frame for flying in the air at the end of a long string **2 :** a small hawk with long narrow wings and deeply forked tail that feeds mostly on insects and small reptiles

kith *n* **:** familiar friends and neighbors or relatives

kit·ten *n* **:** a young cat — **kit·ten·ish** *adj*

kit·ty *n, pl* **kitties :** CAT 1, KITTEN

ki·wi *n* **1 :** a grayish-brown bird of New Zealand that is unable to fly **2 :** KIWIFRUIT

ki·wi·fruit *n* **:** the fruit of a Chinese vine having a fuzzy brown skin and slightly tart green flesh

klutz *n* **:** a clumsy person

km *abbr* kilometer

knack *n* **1 :** a natural ability **:** TALENT **2 :** a clever or skillful way of doing something

knap·sack *n* **:** a bag for carrying things on the shoulders or back

knave *n* **1 :** RASCAL 2 **2 :** [1]JACK 2

knead *vb* **knead·ed; knead·ing 1 :** to work and press into a mass with or as if with the hands **2 :** [2]MASSAGE — **knead·er** *n*

knee *n* **1 :** the joint or region in which the thigh and lower leg come together **2 :** the part of a garment covering the knee **3 :** [1]LAP

knee·cap *n* **:** a thick flat movable bone forming the front part of the knee

kneel *vb* **knelt** *or* **kneeled; kneel·ing :** to bend the knees and support the body on them

knell *n* **1 :** a stroke or sound of a bell especially when rung slowly for a death, funeral, or disaster **2 :** an indication of the end or failure of something

knew *past of* KNOW

knick·ers *n pl* **:** loose-fitting short pants gathered at the knee

knick·knack *n* **:** a small ornamental object

[1]**knife** *n, pl* **knives 1 :** a cutting instrument consisting of a sharp blade fastened to a handle **2 :** a cutting blade in a machine

[2]**knife** *vb* **knifes; knifed; knif·ing :** to stab, slash, or wound with a knife

[1]**knight** *n* **1 :** a warrior of the Middle Ages who fought on horseback, served a king, held a special military rank, and swore to behave in a noble way **2 :** a man honored for merit by a king or queen of England and ranking below a baronet **3 :** one of the pieces in the game of chess — **knight·ly** *adj*

[2]**knight** *vb* **knight·ed; knight·ing :** to honor a man for merit by granting him the title of knight

knight·hood *n* **:** the rank, dignity, or profession of a knight

knit *vb* **knit** *or* **knit·ted; knit·ting 1 :** to form a fabric or garment by interlacing yarn or thread in connected loops with needles (**knitting needles**) **2 :** [2]WRINKLE **3 :** to draw or come together closely as if knitted **:** unite firmly — **knit·ter** *n*

knob *n* **1 :** a small rounded handle **2 :** a

rounded switch on an electronic device **3** : a rounded lump **4** : a rounded hill

knob·by *adj* **knob·bi·er; knob·bi·est** **1** : covered with small rounded lumps **2** : forming rounded lumps

[1]**knock** *vb* **knocked; knock·ing** **1** : to strike in order to get someone's attention **2** : to bump against something without intending to **3** : to make a pounding noise **4** : to find fault with **5** : to hit forcefully — **knock down** **1** : to strike to the ground with or as if with a sharp blow **2** : to take apart — **knock off** : to stop doing something — **knock over** : to cause to fall

[2]**knock** *n* **1** : a pounding noise **2** : a sharp blow **3** : a difficult or painful experience

knock·er *n* : a device made like a hinge and fastened to a door for use in knocking

knock–kneed *adj* : having the legs curved inward at the knees

knoll *n* : a small round hill

[1]**knot** *n* **1** : a section of rope or string that has been tied together to form a lump or knob or to keep something secure **2** : [2]TANGLE 1 **3** : a painful or uncomfortable area in a body part **4** : a cluster of persons or things **5** : the inner end of a woody branch enclosed in a plant stem or a section of this in sawed lumber **6** : one nautical mile per hour (about two kilometers per hour)

[2]**knot** *vb* **knot·ted; knot·ting** **1** : to tie together in a way that cannot be easily untied **2** : to become tense or tight

knot·hole *n* : a hole in wood where a knot has come out

knot·ty *adj* **knot·ti·er; knot·ti·est** **1** : full of lumps, knobs, tangles, or hard spots **2** : DIFFICULT 3

know *vb* **knew; known; know·ing** **1** : to recognize the identity of **2** : to be aware of the truth of **3** : to have a practical understanding of **4** : to have information or knowledge **5** : to be or become aware **6** : to be acquainted or familiar with **7** : to have understanding of **8** : to recognize the nature of

know–how *n* : knowledge of how to get things done

know·ing *adj* **1** : having or showing special knowledge, information, or intelligence **2** : shrewdly and keenly alert — **know·ing·ly** *adv*

know–it–all *n* : a person who always claims to know everything

knowl·edge *n* **1** : understanding and skill gained by experience **2** : the state of being aware of something or of having information **3** : range of information or awareness **4** : something learned and kept in the mind : LEARNING

knowl·edge·able *adj* : having or showing understanding and skill gained through experience or education

known *adj* : generally recognized

knuck·le *n* : the rounded lump formed by the ends of two bones (as of a finger) where they come together in a joint

ko·ala *n* : a tailless Australian animal with thick fur and big hairy ears, sharp claws for climbing, and a pouch like the kangaroo's for carrying its young

kohl·ra·bi *n* : a cabbage that does not form a head but has a fleshy roundish edible stem

Ko·mo·do dragon *n* : a lizard of Indonesia that is the largest of all known lizards and may grow to be 10 feet (3 meters) long

kook *n* : a person who acts in a strange or insane way — **kooky** *adj*

kook·a·bur·ra *n* : an Australian bird that has a call resembling loud laughter

Ko·ran *n* : a book of sacred writings accepted by Muslims as revealed to Muhammad by Allah

[1]**Ko·re·an** *n* **1** : a person born or living in North Korea or South Korea **2** : the language of the Koreans

[2]**Korean** *adj* : of or relating to North Korea or South Korea, the Korean people, or their language

ko·sher *adj* **1** : accepted by Jewish law as fit for use **2** : selling or serving food that is accepted as fit for use according to Jewish law

krill *n* : tiny floating sea animals that resemble shrimp and are a chief food source of some whales

KS *abbr* Kansas

kud·zu *n* : a fast-growing Asian vine that is grown for hay and to control erosion and is often a serious weed in the southeastern United States

kum·quat *n* : a small citrus fruit that has a sweet rind and sour pulp and is used mostly in preserves

kung fu *n* : an art of self-defense without weapons that was developed in China

Kwan·zaa *n* : an African-American cultural festival held from December 26 to January 1

Ky., KY *abbr* Kentucky

L

l *n, pl* **l's** *or* **ls** *often cap* **1 :** the twelfth letter of the English alphabet **2 :** 50 in Roman numerals
L *abbr* **1** large **2** left **3** liter
la *n* **:** the sixth note of the musical scale
La., LA *abbr* Louisiana
lab *n* **:** LABORATORY
¹la·bel *n* **1 :** a slip (as of paper or cloth) attached to something to identify or describe it **2 :** a word or phrase that describes or names something or someone
²label *vb* **la·beled** *or* **la·belled; la·bel·ing** *or* **la·bel·ling 1 :** to put a word or words on (something) to identify or describe it **2 :** to name or describe with or as if with a label
¹la·bor *or Can and Brit* **labour** *n* **1 :** usually hard physical or mental effort **2 :** something that has to be done **:** TASK **3 :** work for which someone is paid **4 :** workers considered as a group **5 :** the process by which or time during which a woman gives birth
²labor *or Can and Brit* **labour** *vb* **la·bored/laboured; la·bor·ing/labouring 1 :** to work hard **:** TOIL **2 :** to move slowly and with great effort
lab·o·ra·to·ry *n, pl* **lab·o·ra·to·ries :** a room or building in which scientific experiments and tests are done
Labor Day *or Can* **Labour Day** *n* **:** the first Monday in September observed as a legal holiday in honor of working people
la·bored *or Can and Brit* **laboured** *adj* **:** produced or done with effort or difficulty
la·bor·er *or Can and Brit* **labourer** *n* **:** a person who does physical work for pay
la·bo·ri·ous *adj* **:** requiring much effort — **la·bo·ri·ous·ly** *adv*
labor union *or Can* **labour union** *n* **:** an organization of workers formed to help them get better pay and working conditions
la·bour *Can and Brit spelling of* LABOR
lab·y·rinth *n* **:** a place that has many confusing paths and passages
¹lace *vb* **laced; lac·ing :** to fasten or join with or as if with a cord or string
²lace *n* **1 :** a cord or string for pulling and holding together opposite edges (as of a shoe) **2 :** a very delicate fabric made with patterns of holes
lac·er·ate *vb* **lac·er·at·ed; lac·er·at·ing :** to injure by cutting or tearing deeply or roughly
lac·er·a·tion *n* **:** a deep or jagged cut or tear of the flesh
¹lack *vb* **lacked; lack·ing 1 :** to be missing **2 :** to need or be without something
²lack *n* **:** the fact or state of not having any or enough of something
¹lac·quer *n* **:** a material like varnish that dries quickly into a shiny layer (as on wood or metal)
²lacquer *vb* **lac·quered; lac·quer·ing :** to coat with lacquer
la·crosse *n* **:** a game played on a field using a long-handled stick with a shallow net for catching, throwing, and carrying the ball
lac·tose *n* **:** a sugar that is found in milk
lacy *adj* **lac·i·er; lac·i·est :** resembling or made of lace
lad *n* **:** BOY 1, YOUTH
lad·der *n* **:** a device used for climbing usually consisting of two long pieces of wood, rope, or metal joined at short distances by horizontal pieces on which a person may step
lad·die *n* **:** a young boy
lad·en *adj* **:** heavily loaded
¹la·dle *n* **:** a large and deep spoon with a long handle that is used especially for serving liquids
²ladle *vb* **la·dled; la·dling :** to take up and carry in a ladle
la·dy *n, pl* **la·dies 1 :** a woman of high social position **2 :** a woman or girl who behaves in a polite way **3 :** WOMAN 1 **4 :** WIFE **5 :** a British noblewoman — used as a title
la·dy·bird *n* **:** LADYBUG
la·dy·bug *n* **:** a small rounded beetle that is often brightly colored and spotted and feeds mostly on other insects (as aphids)
la·dy·like *adj* **:** suitable to a woman or girl who behaves in a polite way
la·dy·ship *n* **:** the rank of a lady — used as a title
lady's slipper *or* **lady slipper** *n* **:** a North American wild orchid with flowers resembling a slipper
¹lag *n* **:** a space of time between two events
²lag *vb* **lagged; lag·ging :** to move or advance slowly or more slowly than others
¹lag·gard *adj* **:** slow to act, move, or respond
²laggard *n* **:** a person who does not go or move as quickly as others
la·goon *n* **:** a shallow channel or pond near or connected to a larger body of water
laid *past and past participle of* LAY
lain *past participle of* LIE
lair *n* **:** the den or resting place of a wild animal
lake *n* **:** a large inland body of standing water
¹lamb *n* **1 :** a young sheep usually less than one year old **2 :** the meat of a lamb used as food
²lamb *vb* **lambed; lamb·ing :** to give birth to a lamb

lamb·kin *n* : a young lamb

[1]lame *adj* **lam·er; lam·est** **1** : not able to get around without pain or difficulty **2** : injured or sore so that walking or movement is painful or difficult **3** : not very convincing or effective — **lame·ly** *adv* — **lame·ness** *n*

[2]lame *vb* **lamed; lam·ing** : to make or become unable to get around without pain and difficulty

[1]la·ment *vb* **la·ment·ed; la·ment·ing** **1** : to mourn aloud : WAIL **2** : to express great sorrow or regret for

[2]lament *n* **1** : a crying out in great sorrow **2** : a sad song or poem

la·men·ta·ble *adj* : REGRETTABLE

lam·en·ta·tion *n* **1** : great sorrow **2** : an expression of great sorrow

lam·i·nat·ed *adj* : made of thin layers of material firmly joined together

lamp *n* : a device for producing light

lam·prey *n, pl* **lampreys** : a water animal that looks like an eel but has a sucking mouth with no jaws

[1]lance *n* : a weapon with a long handle and a sharp steel head used by knights on horseback

[2]lance *vb* **lanced; lanc·ing** : to cut open with a small sharp instrument

lance corporal *n* : an enlisted person in the marine corps ranking above a private first class

[1]land *n* **1** : the solid part of the surface of the earth **2** : an area of ground or soil of a particular kind **3** : a part of the earth's surface marked off by boundaries **4** : a country or nation **5** : the people of a country — **land·less** *adj*

[2]land *vb* **land·ed; land·ing** **1** : to go ashore or cause to go ashore from a ship **2** : to come down or bring down and settle on a surface **3** : to hit or come to a surface **4** : to be or cause to be in a particular place or condition **5** : to catch and bring in **6** : to succeed in getting

land·fill *n* **1** : a system of garbage and trash disposal in which waste is buried between layers of earth **2** : an area built up by such a landfill

land·hold·er *n* : LANDOWNER

land·ing *n* **1** : the act of returning to a surface after a flight or voyage **2** : a place for unloading or taking on passengers and cargo **3** : a level area at the top of a flight of stairs or between two flights of stairs

landing field *n* : a field where aircraft land and take off

landing strip *n* : AIRSTRIP

land·la·dy *n, pl* **land·la·dies** **1** : a woman who owns land or houses that she rents **2** : a woman who runs an inn or rooming house

land·locked *adj* **1** : shut in or nearly shut in by land **2** : kept from leaving fresh water by some barrier

land·lord *n* **1** : a person who owns land or houses and rents them to other people **2** : a person who runs an inn or rooming house

land·lub·ber *n* : a person who lives on land and knows little or nothing about the sea

land·mark *n* **1** : something (as a building, a large tree, or a statue) that is easy to see and can help a person find the way to a place near it **2** : a building of historical importance **3** : a very important event or achievement

land·mass *n* : a very large area of land

land mine *n* : a mine placed just below the surface of the ground and designed to be exploded by the weight of vehicles or troops passing over it

land·own·er *n* : a person who owns land

[1]land·scape *n* **1** : a picture of natural scenery **2** : the land that can be seen in one glance

[2]landscape *vb* **land·scaped; land·scap·ing** : to improve the natural beauty of a piece of land

land·slide *n* **1** : the sudden and rapid downward movement of a mass of rocks or earth on a steep slope **2** : the material that moves in a landslide **3** : the winning of an election by a very large number of votes

lane *n* **1** : a narrow path or road (usually between fences, hedges, or buildings) **2** : a special route (as for ships) **3** : a strip of road used for a single line of traffic **4** : a long narrow wooden floor used for bowling **5** : a narrow course of a track or swimming pool in which a competitor must stay during a race

lan·guage *n* **1** : the words and expressions used and understood by a large group of people **2** : spoken or written words of a particular kind **3** : a means of expressing ideas or feelings **4** : a formal system of signs and symbols that is used to carry information **5** : the special words used by a certain group or in a certain field **6** : the study of languages

lan·guid *adj* **1** : having very little strength, energy, or spirit **2** : having a slow and relaxed quality — **lan·guid·ly** *adv*

lan·guish *vb* **lan·guished; lan·guish·ing** **1** : to be or become weak, dull, or listless **2** : to continue for a long time without activity or progress in an unpleasant or unwanted situation

lank *adj* **lank·er; lank·est** **1** : not well filled out : THIN **2** : hanging straight and limp in an unattractive way

lanky *adj* **lank·i·er; lank·i·est** : very tall and thin

lan·tern *n* : a usually portable lamp with a protective covering

lan·yard *n* **1 :** a short rope or cord used as a fastening on ships **2 :** a cord worn around the neck to hold something (as a knife or whistle) **3 :** a strong cord with a hook at one end used in firing a cannon

¹lap *n* : the front part of a person between the hips and the knees when seated

²lap *vb* **lapped; lap·ping :** OVERLAP

³lap *n* **1 :** a part of something that overlaps another part **2 :** one time around or over a course (as of a racetrack or swimming pool) **3 :** a stage in a trip

⁴lap *vb* **lapped; lap·ping 1 :** to scoop up food or drink with the tongue **2 :** to splash gently

lap·dog *n* : a dog small enough to be held in a person's lap

la·pel *n* : the fold of the front of a coat or jacket below the collar

¹lapse *n* **1 :** a slight error usually caused by lack of attention or forgetfulness **2 :** a change that results in a worse condition **3 :** a passage of time

²lapse *vb* **lapsed; laps·ing 1 :** to slip, pass, or fall gradually **2 :** to come to an end **:** CEASE

lap·top *n* : a small portable computer that can run on battery power and has the main parts (as keyboard and display screen) combined into a single unit

lar·board *n* : ³PORT

lar·ce·ny *n, pl* **lar·ce·nies :** the unlawful taking of personal property without the owner's consent : THEFT

larch *n* : a tree related to the pine that sheds its needles each fall

lard *n* : a soft white fat from fatty tissue of the hog

lar·der *n* : a place where food is kept

large *adj* **larg·er; larg·est :** more than most others of a similar kind in amount or size **:** BIG — **large·ness** *n* — **at large 1 :** not captured or locked up **2 :** as a group or a whole **3 :** representing a whole state or district

large intestine *n* : the wide lower part of the intestine from which water is absorbed and in which feces are formed

large·ly *adv* : MOSTLY, CHIEFLY

lar·i·at *n* : a long light rope used to catch livestock or tie up grazing animals

¹lark *n* : a usually brownish bird of Europe and Asia that has a pleasant song

²lark *n* : something done for fun or adventure

lark·spur *n* : a tall plant that is often grown for its stalks of showy blue, purple, pink, or white flowers

lar·va *n, pl* **lar·vae 1 :** a young wingless form (as a grub or caterpillar) of many insects that hatches from an egg **2 :** an early form of an animal (as a frog) that at birth or hatching is very different from its parents

lar·yn·gi·tis *n* : swelling and irritation of the larynx in which the voice becomes hoarse or weak and the throat sore

lar·ynx *n, pl* **la·ryn·ges** *or* **lar·ynx·es :** the upper part of the trachea that contains the vocal cords

la·sa·gna *n* : layers of broad flat noodles baked with a sauce usually of tomatoes, cheese, and meat or vegetables

la·ser *n* : a device that produces a very powerful beam of light

laser printer *n* : a printer for computer output that produces high-quality images formed by a laser

¹lash *vb* **lashed; lash·ing 1 :** to hit with a whip **2 :** to move forcefully from side to side **3 :** to hit with force **4 :** to make a sudden and angry attack against

²lash *n* **1 :** a blow with a whip or switch **2 :** the flexible part of a whip **3 :** EYELASH

³lash *vb* **lashed; lashing :** to tie or tie down with a rope or chain

lash·ing *n* : something used for tying, wrapping, or fastening

lass *n* : GIRL 1

lass·ie *n* : a young girl

¹las·so *vb* **las·soed; las·so·ing :** to catch with a rope having a slipknot

²lasso *n, pl* **lassos** *or* **lassoes :** a rope with a slipknot that is used for catching animals

¹last *vb* **last·ed; last·ing 1 :** to go on **2 :** to stay in good condition **3 :** to be enough for the needs of **4 :** to be able to continue in a particular condition

²last *adv* **1 :** after any others in time or order **2 :** most recently

³last *adj* **1 :** following all the rest : FINAL **2 :** most recent **3 :** lowest in rank or position **4 :** most unlikely

⁴last *n* : a person or thing that is last — **at last** *or* **at long last :** after a long period of time : FINALLY

last·ing *adj* : continuing for a long while

last·ly *adv* : at the end

¹latch *n* : a movable piece that holds a door, gate, or window closed

²latch *vb* **latched; latch·ing :** to close or fasten with a latch

¹late *adj* **lat·er; lat·est 1 :** coming or occurring after the usual or proper time **2 :** coming or occurring toward the end **3 :** having died or recently left a certain position **4 :** RECENT 2 — **late·ness** *n*

²late *adv* **lat·er; lat·est 1 :** after the usual or proper time **2 :** near the end of something — **of late :** LATELY

late·com·er *n* : a person who arrives late
late·ly *adv* : not long ago : RECENTLY
la·tent *adj* : present but not visible or active
lat·er·al *adj* : being on or directed toward the side — **lat·er·al·ly** *adv*
la·tex *n* **1 :** a milky plant juice that is the source of rubber **2 :** a mixture of water and tiny particles of rubber or plastic used especially in paints
lath *n, pl* **laths :** a thin strip of wood used (as in a wall) as a base for plaster
lathe *n* : a machine in which a piece of material (as wood) is held and turned while being shaped by a tool
[1]**lath·er** *n* **1 :** the foam made by stirring soap and water together **2 :** foam from sweating (as on a horse)
[2]**lather** *vb* **lath·ered; lath·er·ing 1 :** to spread soapy foam over **2 :** to form a foam
[1]**Lat·in** *adj* **1 :** of or relating to the language of the ancient Romans **2 :** of or relating to the countries or people of Latin America
[2]**Latin** *n* **1 :** the language of the ancient Romans **2 :** a member of a people whose language and customs have descended from the ancient Romans **3 :** a person born or living in Latin America
La·ti·na *n* : a woman or girl born or living in Latin America or of Latin-American origin living in the United States
Lat·in–Amer·i·can *adj* : of or relating to Latin America or its people
Latin American *n* : a person born or living in Latin America
La·ti·no *n, pl* **Latinos :** a person born or living in Latin America or of Latin-American origin living in the United States
lat·i·tude *n* **1 :** the distance north or south of the equator measured in degrees **2 :** a region marked by its distance north or south of the equator **3 :** freedom to act or speak as desired
lat·ter *adj* **1 :** coming or occurring near the end **2 :** relating to or being the last thing or person mentioned
lat·tice *n* **1 :** a structure made of thin strips of wood or metal that cross each other **2 :** a window or gate having a lattice
[1]**laugh** *vb* **laughed; laugh·ing :** to show amusement, joy, or scorn by smiling and making sounds (as chuckling) in the throat
[2]**laugh** *n* : the act or sound of laughing
laugh·able *adj* : causing or likely to cause laughter or scorn — **laugh·ably** *adv*
laugh·ing·ly *adv* : with laughter
laugh·ing·stock *n* : a person or thing that is made fun of
laugh·ter *n* : the action or sound of laughing
[1]**launch** *vb* **launched; launch·ing 1 :** to throw or spring forward : HURL **2 :** to send off especially with force **3 :** to set afloat **4 :** to give a start to : BEGIN
[2]**launch** *n* : an act of launching
[3]**launch** *n* : a small open or partly covered motorboat
launch·pad *n* : a nonflammable platform from which a rocket can be launched
laun·der *vb* **laun·dered; laun·der·ing :** to wash or wash and iron clothes or household linens — **laun·der·er** *n*
laun·dry *n, pl* **laundries 1 :** clothes or household linens that need to be washed or that have been washed **2 :** a place where clothes and household linens are washed and dried
lau·rel *n* **1 :** a small evergreen European tree with shiny pointed leaves used in ancient times to crown victors (as in sports) **2 :** a tree or shrub (as the American **mountain laurel**) that resembles the European laurel **3 :** a crown of laurel used as a mark of honor
la·va *n* : melted rock coming from a volcano or after it has cooled and hardened
lav·a·to·ry *n, pl* **lav·a·to·ries 1 :** a small sink (as in a bathroom) **2 :** a room for washing that usually has a toilet **3 :** TOILET 3
lav·en·der *n* **1 :** a European mint with narrow leaves and stalks of small sweet-smelling pale violet flowers **2 :** a pale purple
[1]**lav·ish** *adj* **1 :** giving or involving a large amount **2 :** spent, produced, or given in large amounts — **lav·ish·ly** *adv*
[2]**lavish** *vb* **lav·ished; lav·ish·ing :** to spend, use, or give in large amounts
law *n* **1 :** a rule of conduct or action that a nation or a group of people agrees to follow **2 :** a whole collection of established rules **3 :** a rule or principle that always works the same way under the same conditions **4 :** a bill passed by a legislature **5 :** [2]POLICE 1 **6 :** the profession of a lawyer
law–abid·ing *adj* : obeying the law
law·break·er *n* : a person who breaks the law
law·ful *adj* **1 :** permitted by law **2 :** recognized by law — **law·ful·ly** *adv*
law·less *adj* **1 :** having no laws : not based on or controlled by law **2 :** uncontrolled by law : UNRULY — **law·less·ness** *n*
law·mak·er *n* : someone who takes part in writing and passing laws : LEGISLATOR — **law·mak·ing** *adj or n*
lawn *n* : ground (as around a house) covered with grass that is kept mowed
lawn mower *n* : a machine used to mow the grass on lawns
lawn tennis *n* : TENNIS
law·suit *n* : a process by which a dispute between people or organizations is decided in court

law·yer *n* **:** a person whose profession is to handle lawsuits for people or to give advice about legal rights and duties
lax *adj* **1 :** not firm or tight **:** LOOSE **2 :** not stern or strict — **lax·ness** *n*
¹lax·a·tive *adj* **:** tending to relieve constipation
²laxative *n* **:** a medicine that relieves constipation
¹lay *vb* **laid; lay·ing 1 :** to put or set down **2 :** to bring down (as with force) **3 :** to produce an egg **4 :** BURY 1 **5 :** to place in position on or along a surface **6 :** PREPARE 1, ARRANGE **7 :** to bring into contact with **8 :** to place a burden, charge, or penalty — **lay down :** to declare forcefully — **lay eyes on :** to catch sight of **:** SEE — **lay in :** to store for later use — **lay off 1 :** to stop employing often temporarily **2 :** to let alone — **lay out 1 :** to plan in detail **2 :** to arrange in a particular pattern or design **3 :** to explain in detail — **lay up 1 :** to store up **2 :** to disable or confine with illness or injury
²lay *n* **:** the way a thing lies in relation to something else
³lay *past of* LIE
¹lay·er *n* **1 :** one thickness of something laid over another **2 :** a person who lays something **3 :** a bird that lays eggs
²layer *vb* **lay·ered; lay·er·ing :** to form or arrange one thickness of something over another
lay·man *n, pl* **lay·men 1 :** a person who is not a member of the clergy **2 :** a person who is not a member of a certain profession
lay·out *n* **:** the design or arrangement of something
lay·per·son *n* **:** LAYMAN 1
laze *vb* **lazed; laz·ing :** to spend time relaxing
la·zy *adj* **la·zi·er; la·zi·est 1 :** not liking or willing to act or work **2 :** not having much activity **3 :** moving slowly **:** SLUGGISH — **la·zi·ly** *adv* — **la·zi·ness** *n*
lb *abbr* pound — abbreviation for Latin *libra,* which means "pound"
leach *vb* **leached; leach·ing :** to remove or remove from by the action of a liquid passing through a substance
¹lead *vb* **led; lead·ing 1 :** to guide on a way often by going ahead **2 :** to be at the head or front part of **3 :** to direct or guide the actions of **4 :** to be best, first, or ahead **5 :** to go through **:** LIVE **6 :** to reach or go in a certain direction
²lead *n* **1 :** position at the front **2 :** the amount or distance that a person or thing is ahead **3 :** the main role in a movie or play **4 :** something serving as an indication or clue **5 :** the first part of a news story
³lead *n* **1 :** a heavy soft gray metallic element that is easily bent and shaped **2 :** a long thin piece of graphite used in pencils **3 :** AMMUNITION
lead·en *adj* **1 :** made of lead **2 :** feeling heavy and difficult to move **3 :** of a dull gray color
lead·er *n* **:** someone or something that leads or is able to lead — **lead·er·ship** *n*
¹leaf *n, pl* **leaves 1 :** one of the usually flat green parts that grow from a plant stem and that functions mainly in making food by photosynthesis **2 :** FOLIAGE **3 :** a single sheet of a book containing a page on each side **4 :** a part that can be added to or removed from a table top — **leaf·less** *adj* — **leaf·like** *adj*
²leaf *vb* **leafed; leaf·ing 1 :** to grow leaves **2 :** to turn the pages of a book
leaf·let *n* **1 :** a printed and often folded sheet of paper that is usually given to people at no cost **2 :** one of the divisions of a leaf which is made up of two or more smaller parts **3 :** a young or small leaf
leaf·stalk *n* **:** a slender plant part that supports a leaf
leafy *adj* **leaf·i·er; leaf·i·est :** having, covered with, or resembling leaves
¹league *n* **1 :** a group of nations working together for a common purpose **2 :** an association of persons or groups with common interests or goals **3 :** an unofficial association or agreement **4 :** a class or category of a certain quality or type
²league *n* **:** any of several old units of distance from about 2.4 to 4.6 miles (3.9 to 7.4 kilometers)
¹leak *vb* **leaked; leak·ing 1 :** to enter or escape or let enter or escape through an opening usually by accident **2 :** to let a substance or light in or out through an opening **3 :** to make or become known
²leak *n* **1 :** a crack or hole that accidentally lets something pass in or out **2 :** the accidental or secret passing of information **3 :** an act or instance of leaking
leak·age *n* **:** the act or process of entering or escaping through a crack or hole **:** LEAK
leaky *adj* **leak·i·er; leak·i·est :** letting fluid in or out through a crack or hole
¹lean *vb* **leaned; lean·ing 1 :** to bend or tilt from an upright position **2 :** to bend and rest on **3 :** DEPEND 1 **4 :** to tend or move toward in opinion, taste, or desire
²lean *adj* **lean·er; lean·est 1 :** having too little flesh **:** SKINNY **2 :** having little body fat **3 :** containing very little fat **4 :** not large or plentiful — **lean·ness** *n*
lean–to *n, pl* **lean–tos 1 :** a building that has a roof with only one slope and is usually joined to another building **2 :** a rough

shelter that has a roof with only one slope and is held up by posts, rocks, or trees

[1]**leap** *vb* **leaped** *or* **leapt; leap·ing** **1** : to jump or cause to jump from a surface **2** : to move, act, or pass quickly — **leap·er** *n*

[2]**leap** *n* **1** : an act of springing up or over : JUMP **2** : a place that is jumped over or from **3** : the distance that is jumped

leap·frog *n* : a game in which one player bends down and another player leaps over the first player

leap year *n* : a year of 366 days with February 29 as the extra day

learn *vb* **learned** *also* **learnt; learn·ing** **1** : to get knowledge of or skill in by study, instruction, or experience **2** : MEMORIZE **3** : to become able through practice **4** : to come to realize and understand **5** : to find out **6** : to gain knowledge — **learn·er** *n*

learned *adj* : having or showing knowledge or learning

learn·ing *n* **1** : the act of a person who gains knowledge or skill **2** : knowledge or skill gained from teaching or study

learning disability *n* : any of various conditions (as dyslexia) that make learning difficult — **learning disabled** *adj*

[1]**lease** *n* **1** : an agreement by which a person exchanges property (as a car or house) for a period of time in return for payment or services **2** : a piece of property that is leased

[2]**lease** *vb* **leased; leas·ing** : to give or get the use of (property) in return for payment or services

[1]**leash** *n* : a line for holding or controlling an animal

[2]**leash** *vb* **leashed; leash·ing** : to put on a line for holding or controlling

[1]**least** *adj, superlative of* [1]LITTLE : smallest in size or degree

[2]**least** *n* : the smallest or lowest amount or degree — **at least** **1** : not less or fewer than **2** : in any case

[3]**least** *adv, superlative of* [2]LITTLE : in or to the smallest degree

least common denominator *n* : the least common multiple of the denominators of two or more fractions

least common multiple *n* : the smallest number that is a multiple of each of two or more numbers

leath·er *n* : animal skin that is prepared for use

leath·ery *adj* : like leather

[1]**leave** *vb* **left; leav·ing** **1** : to go away from **2** : to cause to remain behind on purpose or without meaning to **3** : to cause or allow to be or remain in a certain condition **4** : to cause to remain as a trace, mark, or sign **5** : to have as a remainder **6** : to allow to be under another's control **7** : to cause to be available **8** : to give by will **9** : to give up **10** : DELIVER 1

[2]**leave** *n* **1** : permitted absence from duty or work **2** : the act of going away and saying good-bye **3** : PERMISSION

leaved *adj* : having leaves

leav·en *vb* **leav·ened; leav·en·ing** : to cause to rise by adding something (as baking powder) that produces a gas

leaves *pl of* LEAF

leav·ings *n pl* : things remaining

[1]**lec·ture** *n* **1** : a talk or speech that teaches something **2** : a serious talk or scolding

[2]**lecture** *vb* **lec·tured; lec·tur·ing** **1** : to give a talk or speech that teaches something **2** : to give a serious or angry talk to — **lec·tur·er** *n*

led *past and past participle of* LEAD

LED *n* : an electronic device that emits light when power is supplied to it

ledge *n* **1** : a piece projecting from a top or an edge like a shelf **2** : a flat surface that sticks out from a wall of rock

[1]**lee** *n* **1** : a protecting shelter **2** : the side (as of a ship) sheltered from the wind

[2]**lee** *adj* : of or relating to the side sheltered from the wind

leech *n* **1** : a bloodsucking worm related to the earthworm **2** : a person who stays around other people and uses them for personal gain

leek *n* : a vegetable having leaves and thick stems which taste like a mild onion

[1]**leer** *vb* **leered; leer·ing** : to look with an unpleasant, mean, or eager glance

[2]**leer** *n* : an unpleasant, mean, or eager glance

leery *adj* : SUSPICIOUS 2, WARY

[1]**lee·ward** *n* : the side that is sheltered from the wind

[2]**leeward** *adj* : located on the side that is sheltered from the wind

[1]**left** *adj* **1** : located on the same side of the body as the heart **2** : located nearer to the left side of the body than to the right — **left** *adv*

[2]**left** *n* : the left side : a part or location on or toward the left side

[3]**left** *past and past participle of* LEAVE

left–hand *adj* **1** : located on the left side **2** : LEFT-HANDED

left–hand·ed *adj* **1** : using the left hand better or more easily than the right **2** : done or made with or for the left hand

left·over *n* : something (as food) left over

lefty *n, pl* **left·ies** : a left-handed person

leg *n* **1** : one of the limbs of an animal or person that support the body and are used in walking and running **2** : the part of the leg between the knee and the foot **3 :** something like a leg in shape or use **4 :** the part of a garment that covers the leg **5 :** a stage or part of a journey

leg·a·cy *n, pl* **leg·a·cies** **1 :** property (as money) left to a person by a will **2 :** something (as memories or knowledge) that comes from the past or a person of the past

le·gal *adj* **1 :** of or relating to law or lawyers **2 :** based on law **3 :** allowed by law or rules — **le·gal·ly** *adv*

le·gal·ize *vb* **le·gal·ized; le·gal·iz·ing :** to make allowable by law — **le·gal·iza·tion** *n*

leg·end *n* **1 :** an old story that is widely believed but cannot be proved to be true **2 :** a person or thing that is very famous for having special qualities or abilities **3 :** a list of symbols used (as on a map)

leg·end·ary *adj* **1 :** told about in legends **2 :** very famous because of special qualities or abilities

leg·ged *adj* **:** having legs especially of a certain kind or number

leg·ging *n* **:** an outer covering for the leg usually of cloth or leather

leg·i·ble *adj* **:** clear enough to be read — **leg·i·bly** *adv*

le·gion *n* **1 :** a group of from 3000 to 6000 soldiers that made up the chief army unit in ancient Rome **2 :** ARMY 1 **3 :** a very great number

leg·is·late *vb* **leg·is·lat·ed; leg·is·lat·ing :** to make laws

leg·is·la·tion *n* **1 :** the action of making laws **2 :** the laws that are made

leg·is·la·tive *adj* **1 :** having the power or authority to make laws **2 :** of or relating to the action or process by which laws are made

leg·is·la·tor *n* **:** a person who makes laws and is a member of a legislature

leg·is·la·ture *n* **:** a body of persons having the power to make and change laws

le·git·i·mate *adj* **1 :** accepted by the law as rightful **:** LAWFUL **2 :** being right or acceptable — **le·git·i·mate·ly** *adv*

leg·less *adj* **:** having no legs

le·gume *n* **:** any of a large group of plants (as peas, beans, and clover) with fruits that are pods which split into two parts and root nodules containing bacteria that fix nitrogen

lei·sure *n* **:** free time — **at leisure** *or* **at someone's leisure** **1 :** in a way that is not hurried **2 :** when there is free time available **3 :** not busy

lei·sure·ly *adj* **:** UNHURRIED

lem·on *n* **1 :** an oval yellow fruit with a sour juice that is related to the orange and grows on a small spiny tree **2 :** something unsatisfactory **:** DUD

lem·on·ade *n* **:** a drink made of lemon juice, sugar, and water

lend *vb* **lent; lend·ing** **1 :** ²LOAN **2 :** to give usually for a time **3 :** to add something that improves or makes more attractive — **lend·er** *n*

length *n* **1 :** the measured distance from one end to the other of the longer or longest side of an object **2 :** a measured distance **3 :** amount of time something takes **4 :** a piece of something that is long **5 :** the sound of a vowel or syllable as it is affected by the time needed to pronounce it — **at length** **1 :** very fully **2 :** at the end **:** FINALLY

length·en *vb* **length·ened; length·en·ing :** to make or become longer

length·ways *adv* **:** LENGTHWISE

length·wise *adj or adv* **:** in the direction of the length

lengthy *adj* **length·i·er; length·i·est :** very long

le·nient *adj* **:** being kind and patient **:** not strict — **le·nient·ly** *adv*

lens *n* **1 :** a clear curved piece of material (as glass) used to bend the rays of light to form an image **2 :** a clear part of the eye behind the pupil and iris that focuses rays of light on the retina to form clear images

len·til *n* **:** the flattened round edible seed of a plant originally of southwestern Asia

Leo *n* **1 :** a constellation between Cancer and Virgo imagined as a lion **2 :** the fifth sign of the zodiac or a person born under this sign

leop·ard *n* **:** a large animal of the cat family found in Asia and Africa that has a brownish buff coat with black spots and is an excellent climber

leop·ard·ess *n* **:** a female leopard

le·o·tard *n* **:** a tight one-piece garment worn by a dancer or acrobat

le·sion *n* **:** an abnormal spot or area of the body caused by sickness or injury

¹less *adj, comparative of* ¹LITTLE **1 :** being fewer **2 :** not so much **:** a smaller amount of

²less *adv, comparative of* ²LITTLE **:** not so much or so well

³less *n* **1 :** a smaller number or amount **2 :** something that is not as important

⁴less *prep* **:** ¹MINUS 1

-less *adj suffix* **1 :** not having **2 :** not able to be acted on or to act in a specified way

less·en *vb* **less·ened; less·en·ing :** to make or become fewer or smaller in amount

¹less·er *adj* **:** of smaller size or importance

²lesser *adv* **:** ²LESS

les·son *n* **1 :** something learned or taught **2 :** a single class or part of a course of instruction

lest *conj* **:** for fear that

let *vb* **let; let·ting** **1 :** to allow or permit to **2 :** to allow to go or pass **3 :** to cause to : MAKE **4 :** ²RENT 2 **5** — used as a warning — **let alone :** to leave undisturbed — **let down :** DISAPPOINT — **let go** **1 :** to relax or release a grip **2 :** to dismiss from employment **3 :** to fail to take care of — **let on :** to admit or reveal — **let up** **1 :** to slow down **2 :** ¹STOP 4, CEASE

-let *n suffix* **1 :** small one **2 :** something worn on

let·down *n* **:** DISAPPOINTMENT 2

let's : let us

¹let·ter *n* **1 :** one of the marks that are symbols for speech sounds in writing or print and that make up the alphabet **2 :** a written or printed communication (as one sent through the mail) **3 letters** *pl* **:** LITERATURE 2 **4 :** the strict or outward meaning **5 :** the initial of a school awarded to a student usually for athletic achievement

²letter *vb* **let·tered; let·ter·ing :** to mark with symbols for speech sounds

letter carrier *n* **:** a person who delivers mail

let·ter·head *n* **:** the name and address of an organization that is printed at the top of a piece of paper used as official stationery

let·ter·ing *n* **:** symbols for speech sounds written on something

let·tuce *n* **:** a garden plant that has large crisp leaves eaten especially in salads

leu·ke·mia *n* **:** a serious disease in which too many white blood cells are formed

le·vee *n* **:** a bank built along a river to prevent flooding

¹lev·el *n* **1 :** a horizontal line or surface usually at a named height **2 :** a step or stage in height, position, or rank **3 :** a device used (as by a carpenter) to find a horizontal line or surface

²level *vb* **lev·eled** *or* **lev·elled; lev·el·ing** *or* **lev·el·ling :** to make or become horizontal, flat, or even

³level *adj* **1 :** having a flat even surface **2 :** ¹HORIZONTAL **3 :** of the same height or rank **:** EVEN **4 :** steady and cool in judgment

¹le·ver *n* **1 :** a bar used to pry or move something **2 :** a stiff bar for lifting a weight at one point of its length by pressing or pulling at a second point while the bar turns on a support **3 :** a bar or rod used to run or adjust something

²lever *vb* **le·vered; le·ver·ing :** to raise or move with a bar

lev·i·tate *vb* **lev·i·tat·ed; lev·i·tat·ing :** to rise or make rise up in the air

¹levy *n, pl* **lev·ies :** something (as taxes) collected by authority of the law

²levy *vb* **lev·ied; levy·ing :** to collect legally

li·a·ble *adj* **1 :** LIKELY 1 **2 :** judged by law to be responsible for something **3 :** not sheltered or protected (as from danger or accident)

li·ar *n* **:** a person who tells lies

¹li·bel *n* **:** the publication of a false statement that hurts a person's reputation

²libel *vb* **li·beled** *or* **li·belled; li·bel·ing** *or* **li·bel·ling :** to hurt a person's reputation by publishing a false statement — **li·bel·er** *or* **li·bel·ler** *n*

lib·er·al *adj* **1 :** not stingy **:** GENEROUS **2 :** not strict **3 :** BROAD 4 — **lib·er·al·ly** *adv*

lib·er·ate *vb* **lib·er·at·ed; lib·er·at·ing :** to set free

lib·er·ty *n, pl* **lib·er·ties** **1 :** the state of being free **:** FREEDOM **2 :** freedom to do as desired **3 :** the state of not being busy **:** LEISURE **4 :** a political right **5 :** an action that is too free — **at liberty :** able to act or speak freely

Li·bra *n* **1 :** a constellation between Virgo and Scorpio imagined as a pair of scales **2 :** the seventh sign of the zodiac or a person born under this sign

li·brar·i·an *n* **:** a person in charge of a library

li·brary *n, pl* **li·brar·ies** **1 :** a place where literary or reference materials (as books, manuscripts, recordings, or films) are kept for use but are not for sale **2 :** a collection of literary or reference materials

lice *pl of* LOUSE

¹li·cense *or Can and Brit* **li·cence** *n* **1 :** permission to do something granted especially by qualified authority **2 :** a paper, card, or tag showing legal permission **3 :** freedom of action that is carried too far

²license *or chiefly Brit* **licence** *vb* **li·censed/li·cenced; li·cens·ing/li·cenc·ing :** to grant formal permission

li·chen *n* **:** a plantlike organism made up of an alga and a fungus growing together

¹lick *vb* **licked; lick·ing** **1 :** to pass the tongue over **2 :** to touch or pass over like a tongue **3 :** to hit again and again **:** BEAT **4 :** to get the better of **:** DEFEAT — **lick·ing** *n*

²lick *n* **1 :** the act of passing the tongue over **2 :** a small amount **3 :** a place (**salt lick**) where salt is found or provided for animals

lick·e·ty–split *adv* **:** at top speed

lic·o·rice *n* **1 :** the dried root of a European plant or a juice from it used in medicine and in candy **2 :** candy flavored with licorice

lid *n* **1 :** a movable cover **2 :** EYELID — **lid·ded** *adj* — **lid·less** *adj*

¹lie *vb* **lay; lain; ly·ing** **1 :** to stretch out or be stretched out **2 :** to be spread flat so as to cover **3 :** to be located or placed **4 :** to be or stay

²lie *vb* **lied; ly·ing :** to say something that is not true in order to deceive someone

³lie *n* **:** something said or done in the hope of deceiving **:** an untrue statement

liege *n* **:** a lord in the time of the Middle Ages

lieu·ten·ant *n* **1 :** an official who acts for a higher official **2 :** FIRST LIEUTENANT **3 :** SECOND LIEUTENANT **4 :** a commissioned officer in the navy or coast guard ranking above a lieutenant junior grade

lieutenant junior grade *n* **:** a commissioned officer in the navy or coast guard ranking above an ensign

life *n, pl* **lives 1 :** the state characterized by the ability to get and use energy, reproduce, grow, and respond to change **:** the quality that plants and animals lose when they die **2 :** the period during which a person or thing is alive or exists **3 :** all the experiences that make up the existence of a person **:** the course of existence **4 :** existence as a living being **5 :** a way of living **6 :** the time when something can be used or enjoyed **7 :** energy and spirit **8 :** BIOGRAPHY

life belt *n* **:** a life preserver worn like a belt

life·boat *n* **:** a sturdy boat (as one carried by a ship) for use in an emergency

life buoy *n* **:** a life preserver in the shape of a ring

life·guard *n* **:** a person employed at a beach or swimming pool to protect swimmers from drowning

life jacket *n* **:** a life preserver in the form of a vest

life·less *adj* **1 :** having no living things **2 :** dead or appearing to be dead **3 :** lacking spirit, interest, or energy

life·like *adj* **:** very like something that is alive

life·long *adj* **:** continuing through life

life preserver *n* **:** a device (as a life jacket or life buoy) designed to save a person from drowning by keeping the person afloat

life raft *n* **:** a small usually rubber boat for use by people forced into the water when a larger boat sinks

life·sav·er *n* **:** someone or something that provides greatly needed help

life–size *or* **life–sized** *adj* **:** of natural size **:** having the same size as the original

life·style *n* **:** the usual way of life of a person, group, or society

life·time *n* **:** LIFE 2

life vest *n* **:** LIFE JACKET

[1]**lift** *vb* **lift·ed; lift·ing 1 :** to raise from a lower to a higher position, rate, or amount **2 :** to rise from the ground **3 :** to move upward and disappear or become scattered

[2]**lift** *n* **1 :** the action or an instance of picking up and raising **2 :** an improved mood or condition **3 :** a ride in a vehicle **4** *chiefly British* **:** ELEVATOR 1 **5 :** an upward force (as on an airplane wing) that opposes the pull of gravity

lift·off *n* **:** a vertical takeoff (as by a rocket)

lig·a·ment *n* **:** a tough band of tissue that holds bones together or keeps an organ in place in the body

[1]**light** *n* **1 :** the bright form of energy given off by something (as the sun) that makes it possible to see **2 :** a source (as a lamp) of light **3 :** DAYLIGHT 1 **4 :** public knowledge **5 :** understanding that comes from information someone has provided

[2]**light** *adj* **light·er; light·est 1 :** having light **:** BRIGHT **2 :** not dark or deep in color

[3]**light** *vb* **lit** *or* **light·ed; light·ing 1 :** to make or become bright **2 :** to burn or cause to burn

[4]**light** *adj* **1 :** having little weight **:** not heavy **2 :** less in amount or force than usual **3 :** not hard to bear, do, pay, or digest **4 :** active in motion **5 :** free from care **:** HAPPY **6 :** not dense and thick **7 :** intended mainly to entertain — **light·ly** *adv* — **light·ness** *n*

[5]**light** *adv* **:** with little baggage

[6]**light** *vb* **lit** *or* **light·ed; light·ing 1 :** [2]PERCH, SETTLE **2 :** to come by chance

light bulb *n* **:** a lamp in which a glow is produced by the heating of a wire by an electric current

[1]**light·en** *vb* **light·ened; light·en·ing :** to make or become lighter, brighter, or clearer — **light·en·er** *n*

[2]**lighten** *vb* **lightened; lightening 1 :** to make or become less heavy **2 :** to make less sad or serious — **light·en·er** *n*

light·face *n* **:** a type having thin lines

light·heart·ed *adj* **:** free from worry — **light·heart·ed·ly** *adv* — **light·heart·ed·ness** *n*

light·house *n* **:** a tower that produces a powerful glow to guide sailors at night or in poor visibility

light·ing *n* **:** supply of light or of lights

light·ning *n* **:** the flashing of light caused by the passing of electricity from one cloud to another or between a cloud and the earth

lightning bug *n* **:** FIREFLY

light·weight *adj* **:** having less than the usual or expected weight

light–year *n* **:** a unit of length in astronomy equal to the distance that light travels in one year or about 5.88 trillion miles (9.46 trillion kilometers)

lik·able *or* **like·able** *adj* **:** having pleasant or attractive qualities **:** easily liked

[1]**like** *vb* **liked; lik·ing 1 :** ENJOY 1 **2 :** to feel toward **:** REGARD **3 :** CHOOSE 3, PREFER

[2]**like** *n* **:** LIKING, PREFERENCE

[3]**like** *adj* **:** SIMILAR, ALIKE

[4]**like** *prep* **1 :** similar or similarly to **2 :** typical of **3 :** likely to **4 :** such as **5 :** close to

[5]like *n* : [3]EQUAL, COUNTERPART
[6]like *conj* **1 :** AS IF **2 :** in the same way that : AS **3 :** such as
-like *adj suffix* : resembling or characteristic of
like·li·hood *n* : PROBABILITY 1
[1]like·ly *adj* **1 :** very possibly going to happen **2 :** seeming to be the truth : BELIEVABLE **3 :** giving hope of turning out well
[2]likely *adv* : without great doubt
lik·en *vb* **lik·ened; lik·en·ing :** to describe as similar to : COMPARE
like·ness *n* **1 :** the state of being similar : RESEMBLANCE **2 :** a picture of a person : PORTRAIT
like·wise *adv* **1 :** in similar manner **2 :** ALSO
lik·ing *n* : a feeling of being pleased with someone or something
li·lac *n* **1 :** a bush having clusters of fragrant pink, purple, or white flowers **2 :** a medium purple
lilt *vb* **lilt·ed; lilt·ing :** to sing or play in a lively cheerful manner
lily *n, pl* **lil·ies :** a plant (as the **Easter lily** or the **tiger lily**) that grows from a bulb and has a leafy stem and showy funnel-shaped flowers
lily of the valley *n, pl* **lilies of the valley :** a small plant related to the lilies that has usually two leaves and a stalk of fragrant flowers shaped like bells
li·ma bean *n* : the edible seed of a bean plant that is usually pale green or white
limb *n* **1 :** any of the paired parts (as an arm, wing, or leg) of an animal that stick out from the body and are used mostly in moving and grasping **2 :** a large branch of a tree — **limbed** *adj* — **limb·less** *adj*
[1]lim·ber *adj* : bending easily
[2]limber *vb* **lim·bered; lim·ber·ing :** to make or become limber
[1]lime *n* : a small greenish yellow fruit that is related to the lemon and orange
[2]lime *n* : a white substance made by heating limestone or shells and used in making plaster and cement and in farming
[3]lime *vb* **limed; lim·ing :** to treat or cover with a white substance made from limestone or shells
lime·light *n* : the center of public attention
lim·er·ick *n* : a funny poem with five lines
lime·stone *n* : a rock formed chiefly from animal remains (as shells or coral) that is used in building and gives lime when burned
[1]lim·it *n* **1 :** a point beyond which it is impossible to go **2 :** an amount or number that is the lowest or highest allowed **3 :** a boundary line
[2]limit *vb* **lim·it·ed; lim·it·ing :** to place a control on the size or extent of something
lim·i·ta·tion *n* **1 :** an act or instance of controlling the size or extent of something **2 :** something that controls size or extent
lim·it·ed *adj* : small in number
lim·it·less *adj* : having no boundaries : very numerous or large
lim·ou·sine *n* : a large luxurious automobile often driven by a chauffeur
[1]limp *vb* **limped; limp·ing :** to walk in a slow or uneven way because of an injury to a foot or leg
[2]limp *n* : a slow or uneven way of walking caused by an injury to a leg or foot
[3]limp *adj* : not firm or stiff — **limp·ly** *adv*
lim·pid *adj* : perfectly clear
lin·den *n* : a shade tree with heart-shaped leaves and drooping clusters of yellowish white flowers
[1]line *n* **1 :** a long thin cord or rope **2 :** a long narrow mark **3 :** an arrangement of people or things in a row **4 :** a row of letters, words, or musical notes across a page or column **5 :** the boundary or limit of a place **6 :** FAMILY 2 **7 :** a way of behaving or thinking **8 :** [1]OUTLINE 1, CONTOUR **9 :** an area of activity or interest **10 :** the position of military forces who are facing the enemy **11 :** a pipe carrying a fluid (as steam, water, or oil) **12 :** an outdoor wire carrying electricity or a telephone signal **13 lines** *pl* : the words of a part in a play **14 :** the path along which something moves or is directed **15 :** the track of a railway **16 :** AGREEMENT 1, HARMONY **17 :** a system of transportation **18 :** the football players whose positions are along the line of scrimmage **19 :** a geometric element produced by moving a point **20 :** a plan for making or doing something
[2]line *vb* **lined; lin·ing 1 :** to indicate with or draw a long narrow mark **2 :** to place or be placed in a row along — **line up 1 :** to gather or arrange in a row or rows **2 :** to put into alignment
[3]line *vb* **lined; lin·ing :** to cover the inner surface of
lin·eage *n* **1 :** the ancestors from whom a person is descended **2 :** people descended from the same ancestor
lin·ear *adj* **1 :** made up of, relating to, or like a line : STRAIGHT **2 :** involving a single dimension
lin·en *n* **1 :** smooth strong cloth or yarn made from flax **2 :** household articles (as tablecloths or sheets) or clothing that were once often made of linen
line of scrimmage *n* : an imaginary line in football parallel to the goal lines and running through the place where the ball is laid before each play begins
liner *n* : something that covers or is used to cover the inner surface of another thing

line segment *n* : SEGMENT 3
line-up *n* **1 :** a list of players taking part in a game (as baseball) **2 :** a row of persons arranged especially for police identification
-ling *n suffix* **1 :** one associated with **2 :** young, small, or minor one
lin·ger *vb* **lin·gered; lin·ger·ing 1 :** to be slow in leaving : DELAY **2 :** to continue to exist as time passes
lin·guist *n* **1 :** a person skilled in languages **2 :** a person who specializes in the study of human speech
lin·guis·tics *n* **:** the study of human speech including the nature, structure, and development of language or of a language or group of languages
lin·i·ment *n* **:** a liquid medicine rubbed on the skin to ease pain
lin·ing *n* **:** material that covers an inner surface
¹link *n* **1 :** a single ring of a chain **2 :** something that connects : CONNECTION **3 :** HYPERLINK
²link *vb* **linked; link·ing 1 :** to physically join or connect **2 :** to show or suggest a connection
linking verb *n* **:** an intransitive verb that connects a subject with a word or words in the predicate
li·no·leum *n* **:** a floor covering with a canvas back and a surface of hardened linseed oil and cork dust
lin·seed *n* **:** FLAXSEED
linseed oil *n* **:** a yellowish oil obtained from flaxseed
lint *n* **1 :** loose bits of thread **2 :** COTTON 1
lin·tel *n* **:** a horizontal piece or part across the top of an opening (as of a door) to carry the weight of the structure above it
li·on *n* **:** a large meat-eating animal of the cat family that has a brownish buff coat, a tufted tail, and in the male a shaggy mane and that lives in Africa and southern Asia
li·on·ess *n* **:** a female lion
lip *n* **1 :** either of the two folds of flesh that surround the mouth **2 :** the edge of a hollow container (as a jar) especially where it is slightly spread out **3 :** an edge (as of a wound) like or of flesh **4 :** an edge that sticks out — **lipped** *adj*
lip·stick *n* **:** a waxy solid colored cosmetic for the lips usually in stick form
liq·ue·fy *vb* **liq·ue·fied; liq·ue·fy·ing :** to make or become liquid
¹liq·uid *adj* **1 :** flowing freely like water **2 :** neither solid nor gaseous **3 :** clear and smooth or shining **4 :** made up of or easily changed into cash
²liquid *n* **:** a substance that flows freely like water
liq·uor *n* **:** a strong alcoholic beverage
¹lisp *vb* **lisped; lisp·ing :** to pronounce the sounds \s\ and \z\ as \th\ and \th\
²lisp *n* **:** the act or habit of pronouncing the sounds \s\ and \z\ as \th\ and \th\
¹list *n* **:** a series of items written, mentioned, or considered one following another
²list *vb* **list·ed; list·ing :** to put in a series of items
³list *vb* **listed; listing :** to lean to one side
⁴list *n* **:** a leaning over to one side
lis·ten *vb* **lis·tened; lis·ten·ing 1 :** to pay attention in order to hear **2 :** to hear and consider seriously — **lis·ten·er** *n*
list·less *adj* **:** too tired or too little interested to want to do things — **list·less·ly** *adv* — **list·less·ness** *n*
lit *past and past participle of* LIGHT
li·ter *or chiefly Can and Brit* **litre** *n* **:** a metric unit of liquid capacity equal to 1.057 quarts
lit·er·al *adj* **1 :** following the ordinary or usual meaning of the words **2 :** true to fact — **lit·er·al·ly** *adv* — **lit·er·al·ness** *n*
lit·er·ary *adj* **:** of or relating to literature
lit·er·ate *adj* **1 :** able to read and write **2 :** having gotten a good education
lit·er·a·ture *n* **1 :** written works considered as having high quality and ideas of lasting and widespread interest **2 :** written material
lithe *adj* **:** ¹LIMBER, SUPPLE
lith·o·sphere *n* **:** the outer part of the solid earth
lit·mus paper *n* **:** paper treated with coloring matter that turns red in the presence of an acid and blue in the presence of a base
li·tre *Can and Brit spelling of* LITER
¹lit·ter *n* **1 :** the young born to an animal at a single time **2 :** a messy collection of things scattered about : TRASH **3 :** material used to soak up the urine and feces of animals **4 :** a covered and curtained couch having poles and used for carrying a single passenger **5 :** a stretcher for carrying a sick or wounded person
²litter *vb* **lit·tered; lit·ter·ing 1 :** to throw or leave trash on the ground **2 :** to cover in an untidy way
lit·ter·bug *n* **:** a person who carelessly scatters trash in a public area
¹lit·tle *adj* **lit·tler** *or* **less; lit·tlest** *or* **least 1 :** small in size **2 :** small in quantity **3 :** ¹YOUNG 1 **4 :** short in duration or extent **5 :** small in importance **6 :** ¹NARROW 3
²little *adv* **less; least :** in a very small quantity or degree — **little by little :** by small steps or amounts : GRADUALLY
³little *n* **:** a small amount or quantity
Little Dipper *n* **:** a group of seven stars in the northern sky arranged in a form like a dipper with the North Star forming the tip of the handle

little finger *n* : the shortest finger of the hand farthest from the thumb

lit·ur·gy *n, pl* **lit·ur·gies** : a religious rite or body of rites — **li·tur·gi·cal** *adj*

[1]live *vb* **lived; liv·ing** **1** : to be alive **2** : to continue in life **3** : DWELL 1 **4** : to spend life — **live it up** : to live with great enthusiasm and excitement — **live up to** : to be good enough to satisfy expectations

[2]live *adj* **1** : having life : ALIVE **2** : broadcast at the time of production **3** : charged with an electric current **4** : burning usually without flame **5** : not exploded

live·li·hood *n* : [2]LIVING 3

live·long *adj* : during all of

live·ly *adj* **live·li·er; live·li·est** **1** : full of life : ACTIVE **2** : showing or resulting from active thought **3** : full of spirit or feeling : ANIMATED — **live·li·ness** *n*

liv·en *vb* **liv·ened; liv·en·ing** : to make or become lively — often used with *up*

live oak *n* : any of several American oaks that have evergreen leaves

liv·er *n* : a large gland in the body that has a rich blood supply, secretes bile, and helps in storing some nutrients and in forming some body wastes

liv·er·ied *adj* : wearing a special uniform

liv·er·wort *n* : a flowerless plant that resembles a moss

liv·ery *n, pl* **liv·er·ies** **1** : a special uniform worn by the servants of a wealthy household **2** : the business of keeping horses and vehicles for hire : a place (**livery stable**) that keeps horses and vehicles for hire

lives *pl of* LIFE

live·stock *n* : animals (as cows, horses, and pigs) kept or raised especially on a farm and for profit

live wire *n* : an alert active person

liv·id *adj* **1** : very angry **2** : pale as ashes **3** : discolored by bruising

[1]liv·ing *adj* **1** : not dead : ALIVE **2** : true to life

[2]living *n* **1** : the condition of being alive **2** : conduct or manner of life **3** : what a person has to have to meet basic needs

living room *n* : a room in a house for general family use

liz·ard *n* : a reptile with movable eyelids, ears that are outside the body, and usually four legs

lla·ma *n* : a South American hoofed animal that has a long neck, is related to the camel, and is sometimes used to carry loads and as a source of wool

lo *interj* — used to call attention or to show wonder or surprise

[1]load *n* **1** : something lifted up and carried : BURDEN **2** : the quantity of material put into a device at one time **3** : a large number or amount **4** : a mass or weight supported by something **5** : something that causes worry or sadness **6** : a charge for a firearm

[2]load *vb* **load·ed; load·ing** **1** : to put a load in or on **2** : to supply abundantly **3** : to put something into a device so it can be used — **load·er** *n*

[1]loaf *n, pl* **loaves** **1** : a usually oblong mass of bread **2** : a dish (as of meat) baked in an oblong form

[2]loaf *vb* **loafed; loaf·ing** : to spend time idly or lazily — **loaf·er** *n*

loam *n* : a soil having the appropriate amount of silt, clay, and sand for good plant growth

loamy *adj* **loam·i·er; loam·i·est** : made up of or like rich soil

[1]loan *n* **1** : money given with the understanding that it will be paid back **2** : something given for a time to a borrower **3** : permission to use something for a time

[2]loan *vb* **loaned; loan·ing** : to give to another for temporary use with the understanding that the same or a like thing will be returned

loath *also* **loth** *adj* : not willing

loathe *vb* **loathed; loath·ing** : to dislike greatly

loathing *n* : very great dislike

loath·some *adj* : very unpleasant

loaves *pl of* LOAF

[1]lob *vb* **lobbed; lob·bing** : to send (as a ball) in a high arc by hitting or throwing easily

[2]lob *n* : an act of throwing or hitting (as a ball) in a high arc

lob·by *n, pl* **lobbies** : a hall or entry especially when large enough to serve as a waiting room

lobe *n* : a rounded part — **lobed** *adj*

lob·ster *n* : a large edible sea animal that is a crustacean with five pairs of legs of which the first pair usually has large claws

[1]lo·cal *adj* : of, in, or relating to a particular place — **lo·cal·ly** *adv*

[2]local *n* **1** : a public vehicle (as a bus or train) that makes all or most stops on its run **2** : a branch (as of a lodge or labor union) in a particular place

local area network *n* : a computer network that covers a small area (as an office building or a home)

lo·cal·i·ty *n, pl* **lo·cal·i·ties** : a place and its surroundings

lo·cal·ize *vb* **lo·cal·ized; lo·cal·iz·ing** : to keep or be kept in a certain area

lo·cate *vb* **lo·cat·ed; lo·cat·ing** **1** : to find the position of **2** : to settle or establish in a particular place

lo·ca·tion *n* **1** : the act or process of establishing in or finding a particular place **2** : [1]PLACE 3, POSITION

[1]lock *n* : a small bunch of hair or of fiber (as cotton or wool)

²lock *n* **1 :** a fastening (as for a door) in which a bolt is operated (as by a key) **2 :** the device for exploding the charge or cartridge of a firearm **3 :** an enclosure (as in a canal) with gates at each end used in raising or lowering boats as they pass from level to level

³lock *vb* **locked; lock·ing 1 :** to fasten with or as if with a lock **2 :** to shut in or out by or as if by means of a lock **3 :** to make unable to move by linking parts together

lock·er *n* **:** a cabinet, compartment, or chest for personal use or for storing frozen food at a low temperature

locker room *n* **:** a room where sports players change clothes and store equipment in lockers

lock·et *n* **:** a small ornamental case usually worn on a chain

lock·jaw *n* **:** TETANUS

lock·smith *n* **:** a worker who makes or repairs locks

lock·up *n* **:** PRISON

lo·co·mo·tion *n* **:** the act or power of moving from place to place

lo·co·mo·tive *n* **:** a vehicle that moves under its own power and is used to haul cars on a railroad

lo·cust *n* **1 :** a grasshopper that moves in huge swarms and eats up the plants in its path **2 :** CICADA **3 :** a tree with hard wood, leaves with many leaflets, and drooping flower clusters

lode·stone *n* **:** a magnetic rock

¹lodge *vb* **lodged; lodg·ing 1 :** to provide a temporary living or sleeping space for **2 :** to use a place for living or sleeping **3 :** to become stuck or fixed **4 :** ³FILE 2

²lodge *n* **1 :** a house set apart for residence in a special season or by an employee on an estate **2 :** a den or resting place of an animal **3 :** the meeting place of a social organization

lodg·er *n* **:** a person who lives in a rented room in another's house

lodging *n* **1 :** a temporary living or sleeping place **2 lodgings** *pl* **:** a room or rooms in the house of another person rented as a place to live

loft *n* **1 :** an upper room or upper story of a building **2 :** a balcony in a church **3 :** an upper part of a barn

lofty *adj* **loft·i·er; loft·i·est 1 :** rising to a great height **2 :** of high rank or admirable quality **3 :** showing a proud and superior attitude — **loft·i·ly** *adv* — **loft·i·ness** *n*

¹log *n* **1 :** a large piece of a cut or fallen tree **2 :** a long piece of a tree trunk ready for sawing **3 :** the record of a ship's voyage or of an aircraft's flight **4 :** a record of performance, events, or daily activities

²log *vb* **logged; log·ging 1 :** to engage in cutting trees for timber **2 :** to make an official record of — **log on :** to connect to a computer or network

log·ger·head *n* **:** a very large sea turtle found in the warmer parts of the Atlantic Ocean

log·ic *n* **1 :** a proper or reasonable way of thinking about something **:** sound reasoning **2 :** a science that deals with the rules and processes used in sound thinking and reasoning

log·i·cal *adj* **1 :** according to a proper or reasonable way of thinking **2 :** according to what is reasonably expected — **log·i·cal·ly** *adv*

-logy *n suffix* **:** area of knowledge **:** science

loin *n* **1 :** the part of the body between the hip and the lower ribs **2 :** a piece of meat (as beef) from the loin of an animal

loi·ter *vb* **loi·tered; loi·ter·ing 1 :** to hang around somewhere for no good reason **2 :** to dawdle on the way to somewhere — **loi·ter·er** *n*

loll *vb* **lolled; loll·ing 1 :** to hang loosely **:** DROOP **2 :** to lie around lazily

lol·li·pop *or* **lol·ly·pop** *n* **:** a round piece of hard candy on the end of a stick

lone *adj* **1 :** having no companion **2 :** situated by itself

lone·ly *adj* **lone·li·er; lone·li·est 1 :** LONE 1 **2 :** not often visited **3 :** sad from being alone **:** LONESOME **4 :** producing sad feelings from being alone — **lone·li·ness** *n*

lone·some *adj* **1 :** sad from being without companions **2 :** not often visited or traveled over

¹long *adj* **lon·ger; lon·gest 1 :** of great length from end to end **:** not short **2 :** lasting for some time **:** not brief **3 :** being more than the usual length **4 :** having a stated length (as in distance or time) **5 :** of, relating to, or being one of the vowel sounds \ā, ē, ī, ō, ü\ and sometimes \ä\ and \ȯ\

²long *adv* **1 :** for or during a long time **2 :** for the whole length of **3 :** at a distant point of time

³long *n* **:** a long time

⁴long *vb* **longed; long·ing :** to wish for something very much

long division *n* **:** division in arithmetic that involves several steps that are written out

long·hand *n* **:** HANDWRITING

long·horn *n* **:** a cow with very long horns that was once common in the southwestern United States

long–horned *adj* **:** having long horns or antennae

long·house *n* **:** a long dwelling especially of the Iroquois for several families

long·ing *n* **:** an eager desire — **long·ing·ly** *adv*

lon·gi·tude *n* **:** distance measured in degrees east or west of an imaginary line that runs from the north pole to the south pole and passes through Greenwich, England

lon·gi·tu·di·nal *adj* **:** placed or running lengthwise — **lon·gi·tu·di·nal·ly** *adv*

long–lived *adj* **:** living or lasting for a long time

long–range *adj* **1 :** involving a long period of time **2 :** capable of traveling or being used over great distances

long–wind·ed *adj* **:** using or having too many words

[1]**look** *vb* **looked; look·ing 1 :** to use the power of vision **:** SEE **2 :** to direct the attention or eyes **3 :** SEEM 1 **4 :** to have an appearance that is suitable **5 :** [2]FACE 1 — **look after :** to take care of — **look down on :** to regard as bad or inferior — **look out :** to be careful — **look up 1 :** to search for in a reference book **2 :** to get better — **look up to :** RESPECT 1

[2]**look** *n* **1 :** an act of looking **2 :** the expression on a person's face or in a person's eyes **3 looks** *pl* **:** physical appearance **4 :** appearance that suggests what something is or means

looking glass *n* **:** [1]MIRROR 1

look·out *n* **1 :** a careful watch for something expected or feared **2 :** a high place from which a wide view is possible **3 :** a person who keeps watch

[1]**loom** *n* **:** a frame or machine for weaving cloth

[2]**loom** *vb* **loomed; loom·ing 1 :** to come into sight suddenly and often with a large, strange, or frightening appearance **2 :** to be about to happen

loon *n* **:** a large diving bird that eats fish and has a black head and a black back spotted with white

loonie *Can, n* **:** a Canadian one dollar coin

[1]**loop** *n* **1 :** an almost oval form produced when something flexible and thin (as a wire or a rope) crosses over itself **2 :** something (as a figure or bend) suggesting a flexible loop

[2]**loop** *vb* **looped; loop·ing 1 :** to make a circle or loop in **2 :** to form a circle or loop

loop·hole *n* **:** a way of avoiding something

[1]**loose** *adj* **loos·er; loos·est 1 :** not tightly fixed or fastened **2 :** not pulled tight **3 :** not tied up or shut in **4 :** not brought together in a bundle or binding **5 :** having parts that are not held or squeezed tightly together **6 :** not exact or precise — **loose·ly** *adv* — **loose·ness** *n*

[2]**loose** *vb* **loosed; loos·ing 1 :** to make less tight **2 :** to set free

loose–leaf *adj* **:** arranged so that pages can be put in or taken out

loos·en *vb* **loos·ened; loos·en·ing :** to make or become less tight or firmly fixed

[1]**loot** *n* **:** something stolen or taken by force

[2]**loot** *vb* **loot·ed; loot·ing :** [1]PLUNDER — **loot·er** *n*

[1]**lope** *n* **:** an effortless way of moving with long smooth steps

[2]**lope** *vb* **loped; lop·ing :** to go or run in an effortless way with long smooth steps

lop·sid·ed *adj* **:** uneven in position, size, or amount

[1]**lord** *n* **1 :** a person having power and authority over others **2** *cap* **:** GOD 1 **3** *cap* **:** JESUS CHRIST **4 :** a British nobleman or bishop — used as a title

[2]**lord** *vb* **lord·ed; lord·ing :** to act in a proud or bossy way toward others

lord·ship *n* **:** the rank or dignity of a lord — used as a title

lore *n* **:** common or traditional knowledge or belief

lose *vb* **lost; los·ing 1 :** to be unable to find or have at hand **2 :** to become deprived of **3 :** to become deprived of by death **4 :** to fail to use **:** WASTE **5 :** to fail to win **6 :** to fail to keep — **los·er** *n*

loss *n* **1 :** the act or fact of losing something **2 :** harm or distress that comes from losing something or someone **3 :** something that is lost **4 :** failure to win — **at a loss :** unsure of how to proceed

lost *adj* **1 :** unable to find the way **2 :** unable to be found **3 :** not used, won, or claimed **4 :** no longer possessed or known **5 :** fully occupied **6 :** not capable of succeeding

lot *n* **1 :** an object used in deciding something by chance or the use of such an object to decide something **2 :** FATE 2 **3 :** a piece or plot of land **4 :** a large number or amount

loth *variant of* LOATH

lo·tion *n* **:** a creamy liquid preparation used on the skin especially for healing or as a cosmetic

lot·tery *n, pl* **lot·ter·ies :** a way of raising money in which many tickets are sold and a few of these are drawn to win prizes

lo·tus *n* **:** any of various water lilies

[1]**loud** *adj* **1 :** not low, soft, or quiet in sound **:** NOISY **2 :** not quiet or calm in expression **3 :** too bright or showy to be pleasing — **loud·ly** *adv* — **loud·ness** *n*

[2]**loud** *adv* **:** in a loud manner

loud·speak·er *n* **:** an electronic device that makes sound louder

[1]**lounge** *vb* **lounged; loung·ing :** to stand, sit, or lie in a relaxed manner

[2]**lounge** *n* **1 :** a comfortable room where one can relax **2 :** a long chair or couch

louse *n, pl* **lice 1 :** a small, wingless, and usually flat insect that lives on the bodies of warm-blooded animals **2 :** an insect or related arthropod that resembles a body louse and feeds on plant juices or decaying matter

lousy *adj* **lous·i·er; lous·i·est** **1 :** BAD 1 **2 :** deserving disgust or contempt

lov·able *adj* **:** deserving to be loved **:** having attractive or appealing qualities

¹love *n* **1 :** strong and warm affection (as of a parent for a child) **2 :** a great liking **3 :** a beloved person

²love *vb* **loved; lov·ing** **1 :** to feel strong affection for **2 :** to like very much — **lov·er** *n*

love·ly *adj* **love·li·er; love·li·est** **1 :** very attractive or beautiful **2 :** very pleasing — **love·li·ness** *n*

lov·ing *adj* **:** feeling or showing love or great care — **lov·ing·ly** *adv*

¹low *vb* **lowed; low·ing :** to make the sound of a cow **:** MOO

²low *n* **:** the mooing of a cow

³low *adj* **low·er; low·est** **1 :** not high or tall **2 :** lying or going below the usual level **3 :** not loud **:** SOFT **4 :** deep in pitch **5 :** not cheerful **:** SAD **6 :** less than usual (as in quantity or value) **7 :** less than enough **8 :** not strong **9 :** not favorable **:** POOR — **low·ness** *n*

⁴low *n* **1 :** a point or level that is the least in degree, size, or amount **2 :** a region of reduced barometric pressure **3 :** the arrangement of gears in an automobile that gives the slowest speed of travel

⁵low *adv* **low·er; low·est :** so as to be low

¹low·er *adj* **1 :** located below another or others of the same kind **2 :** located toward the bottom part of something **3 :** placed below another or others in rank or order **4 :** less advanced or developed

²lower *vb* **low·ered; low·er·ing** **1 :** to move to a level or position that is below or less than an earlier one **2 :** to let or pull down **3 :** to make or become less (as in value, amount, or volume) **4 :** to reduce the height of

low·er·case *adj* **:** having the form a, b, c, rather than A, B, C — **lowercase** *n*

lowest common denominator *n* **:** LEAST COMMON DENOMINATOR

lowest common multiple *n* **:** LEAST COMMON MULTIPLE

low·land *n* **:** low flat country

lowly *adj* **low·li·er; low·li·est :** of low rank or importance: HUMBLE

loy·al *adj* **:** having or showing true and constant support for someone or something — **loy·al·ly** *adv*

loy·al·ty *n, pl* **loy·al·ties :** the quality or state of being true and constant in support of someone or something

loz·enge *n* **:** a small candy often containing medicine

LSD *n* **:** a dangerous drug that causes hallucinations

Lt. *abbr* lieutenant

ltd. *abbr* limited

lu·bri·cant *n* **:** something (as oil or grease) that makes a surface smooth or slippery

lu·bri·cate *vb* **lu·bri·cat·ed; lu·bri·cat·ing :** to apply oil or grease to in order to make smooth or slippery

lu·bri·ca·tion *n* **:** the act or process of making something smooth or slippery

lu·cid *adj* **1 :** having or showing the ability to think clearly **2 :** easily understood — **lu·cid·ly** *adv*

luck *n* **1 :** something that happens to a person by or as if by chance **2 :** the accidental way things happen **3 :** good fortune

luck·i·ly *adv* **:** by good luck

lucky *adj* **luck·i·er; luck·i·est** **1 :** helped by luck **:** FORTUNATE **2 :** happening because of good luck **3 :** thought of as bringing good luck

lu·di·crous *adj* **:** funny because of being ridiculous **:** ABSURD — **lu·di·crous·ly** *adv*

lug *vb* **lugged; lug·ging :** to pull or carry with great effort

lug·gage *n* **:** suitcases for a traveler's belongings **:** BAGGAGE

luke·warm *adj* **1 :** slightly warm **2 :** not very interested or eager

¹lull *vb* **lulled; lull·ing :** to make or become sleepy or less watchful

²lull *n* **:** a period of calm or inactivity

lul·la·by *n, pl* **lul·la·bies :** a song for helping a baby or child fall asleep

¹lum·ber *vb* **lum·bered; lum·ber·ing :** to move in a slow or awkward way

²lumber *n* **:** timber especially when sawed into boards

lum·ber·jack *n* **:** a person whose job is cutting down trees for wood

lum·ber·yard *n* **:** a place where lumber is kept for sale

lu·mi·nous *adj* **:** giving off light — **lu·mi·nous·ly** *adv*

¹lump *n* **1 :** a small piece or chunk **2 :** a swelling or growth **3 :** a tight feeling in the throat caused by emotion

²lump *vb* **lumped; lump·ing** **1 :** to group together **2 :** to form into lumps

³lump *adj* **:** not divided into parts

lumpy *adj* **lump·i·er; lump·i·est :** having or full of lumps

lu·nar *adj* **1 :** of or relating to the moon **2 :** measured by the revolutions of the moon

¹lu·na·tic *adj* **:** INSANE 1

²lunatic *n* **1 :** an insane person **2 :** a person who behaves very foolishly

¹lunch *n* **1 :** a light meal especially when eaten in the middle of the day **2 :** food prepared for lunch

²lunch *vb* **lunched; lunch·ing :** to eat lunch

lun·cheon *n* **1 :** [1]LUNCH 1 **2 :** a formal lunch
lunch·room *n* **:** a room (as in a school) where lunch may be eaten
lung *n* **:** either of two organs in the chest that are like bags and are the main breathing structure in animals that breathe air
[1]**lunge** *n* **:** a sudden movement forward
[2]**lunge** *vb* **lunged; lung·ing :** to move or reach forward in a sudden forceful way
lung·fish *n* **:** a fish that breathes with structures like lungs as well as with gills
lu·pine *n* **:** a plant related to the clovers that has tall spikes of showy flowers
[1]**lurch** *n* **:** a sudden swaying, tipping, or jerking movement
[2]**lurch** *vb* **lurched; lurch·ing :** to move with a sudden swaying, tipping, or jerking motion
[1]**lure** *n* **1 :** something that attracts or tempts **2 :** an artificial bait for catching fish
[2]**lure** *vb* **lured; lur·ing :** to tempt by offering pleasure or gain
lu·rid *adj* **1 :** causing shock or disgust **2 :** glowing with an overly bright color — **lu·rid·ly** *adv*
lurk *vb* **lurked; lurk·ing :** to hide in or about a place
lus·cious *adj* **1 :** having a delicious taste or smell **2 :** delightful to hear, see, or feel
lush *adj* **1 :** characterized by full and healthy growth **2 :** covered with a thick growth of healthy plants **3 :** LUXURIOUS 1 — **lush·ly** *adv* — **lush·ness** *n*
lust *n* **:** a strong longing
lus·ter *or Can and Brit* **lus·tre** *n* **:** the shiny quality of a surface that reflects light
lus·trous *adj* **:** having a shiny quality
lusty *adj* **lust·i·er; lust·i·est :** full of strength and energy
lute *n* **:** a musical instrument with a pear-shaped body and usually paired strings played with the fingers
lux·u·ri·ant *adj* **1 :** having heavy and thick growth **2 :** LUXURIOUS 1
lux·u·ri·ous *adj* **1 :** very fine and comfortable **:** having an appealing rich quality **2 :** feeling or showing a desire for fine and expensive things — **lux·u·ri·ous·ly** *adv*
lux·u·ry *n, pl* **lux·u·ries 1 :** very rich, pleasant, and comfortable surroundings **2 :** something desirable but expensive or hard to get **3 :** something adding to pleasure or comfort but not absolutely necessary
[1]**-ly** *adj suffix* **1 :** like **:** similar to **2 :** happening in each specified period of time **:** every
[2]**-ly** *adv suffix* **1 :** in a specified manner **2 :** from a specified point of view
lye *n* **:** a dangerous compound that is used in cleaning and in making soap
lying *present participle of* LIE
lymph *n* **:** a clear liquid like blood without the red blood cells that nourishes the tissues and carries off wastes
lym·phat·ic *adj* **:** relating to or carrying lymph
lymph node *n* **:** one of the small rounded bits of tissue in the body through which lymph passes to be filtered
lym·pho·cyte *n* **:** any of the white blood cells of the immune system that play a role in recognizing and destroying foreign cells, particles, or substances that have invaded the body
lynx *n, pl* **lynx** *or* **lynx·es :** any of several wildcats with rather long legs, a short tail, and often ears with tufts of long hairs at the tip
lyre *n* **:** a stringed musical instrument like a harp used by the ancient Greeks
[1]**lyr·ic** *n* **1 :** the words of a song — often used in pl. **2 :** a poem that expresses feelings in a way that is like a song
[2]**lyric** *adj* **:** expressing personal emotion in a way that is like a song

M

m *n, pl* **m's** *or* **ms** *often cap* **1 :** the 13th letter of the English alphabet **2 :** 1000 in Roman numerals
m. *abbr* **1** male **2** meter **3** mile
ma *n, often cap* **:** [1]MOTHER 1
MA *abbr* Massachusetts
ma'am *n* **:** MADAM
mac·ad·am *n* **:** a road surface made of small closely packed broken stone
ma·caque *n* **:** a monkey mostly found in Asia that often has a short tail
mac·a·ro·ni *n* **:** pasta in the shape of little curved tubes
ma·caw *n* **:** a large parrot of Central and South America with a long tail, a harsh voice, and bright feathers
[1]**mace** *n* **:** a spice made from the dried outer covering of the nutmeg

²mace *n* **1 :** a decorated pole carried by an official as a sign of authority **2 :** a heavy spiked club used as a medieval weapon
ma·chete *n* **:** a large heavy knife used for cutting sugarcane and underbrush and as a weapon
ma·chine *n* **1 :** a device with moving parts that does some desired work when it is provided with power **2 :** VEHICLE 2
machine gun *n* **:** a gun that fires bullets continuously and rapidly
ma·chin·ery *n* **1 :** a group of devices with moving parts that are used to perform specific jobs **2 :** the working parts of a device used to perform a particular job **3 :** the people and equipment by which something is done
machine shop *n* **:** a workshop in which metal articles are put together
ma·chin·ist *n* **:** a person who makes or works on machines
mack·er·el *n, pl* **mackerel** *or* **mackerels :** a fish of the North Atlantic that is green above with blue bars and silvery below and is often used as food
mack·i·naw *n* **:** a short heavy woolen coat
ma·cron *n* **:** a mark ¯ placed over a vowel to show that the vowel is long
mad *adj* **mad·der; mad·dest 1 :** ANGRY **2 :** INSANE 1 **3 :** done or made without thinking **4 :** INFATUATED **5 :** having rabies **6 :** marked by intense and often disorganized activity — **mad·ly** *adv* — **mad·ness** *n* — **like mad :** with a great amount of energy or speed
mad·am *n, pl* **mes·dames** — used without a name as a form of polite address to a woman
ma·dame *n, pl* **mes·dames** *or* **ma·dames** — used as a title that means *Mrs.* for a married woman who is not of an English-speaking nationality
mad·cap *adj* **:** RECKLESS, WILD
mad·den *vb* **mad·dened; mad·den·ing :** to make angry
mad·den·ing *adj* **:** very annoying
made *past and past participle of* MAKE
made–up *adj* **:** created from the imagination
mad·house *n* **:** a place or scene of complete confusion or noisy excitement
mad·man *n, pl* **mad·men :** a man who is or acts as if insane
mag·a·zine *n* **1 :** a publication issued at regular intervals (as weekly or monthly) **2 :** a storehouse or warehouse for military supplies **3 :** a container in a gun for holding cartridges
ma·gen·ta *n* **:** a deep purplish red
mag·got *n* **:** a legless grub that is the larva of a fly (as a housefly)
¹mag·ic *n* **1 :** the power to control natural forces possessed by certain persons (as wizards and witches) in folk tales and fiction **2 :** the art or skill of performing tricks or illusions for entertainment **3 :** a power that seems mysterious **4 :** something that charms
²magic *adj* **1 :** having or seeming to have the power to make impossible things happen **2 :** of or relating to the power to make impossible things happen **3 :** giving a feeling of enchantment
mag·i·cal *adj* **:** ²MAGIC
ma·gi·cian *n* **:** a person skilled in performing tricks or illusions
mag·is·trate *n* **1 :** a chief officer of government **2 :** a local official with some judicial power
mag·ma *n* **:** molten rock within the earth
mag·na·nim·i·ty *n* **:** the quality of being generous and noble
mag·nan·i·mous *adj* **:** generous and noble — **mag·nan·i·mous·ly** *adv*
mag·ne·sium *n* **:** a silvery white metallic chemical element that is lighter than aluminum and is used in lightweight alloys
mag·net *n* **:** a piece of material (as of iron, steel, or alloy) that is able to attract iron
mag·net·ic *adj* **1 :** acting like a magnet **2 :** of or relating to the earth's magnetism **3 :** having a great power to attract people
magnetic field *n* **:** the portion of space near a magnetic object within which magnetic forces can be detected
magnetic needle *n* **:** a narrow strip of magnetized steel that is free to swing around to show the direction of the earth's magnetism
magnetic pole *n* **1 :** either of the poles of a magnet **2 :** either of two small regions of the earth which are located near the north and south poles and toward which a compass needle points
magnetic tape *n* **:** a thin ribbon of plastic coated with a magnetic material on which information (as sound) may be stored
mag·ne·tism *n* **1 :** a magnet's power to attract **2 :** the power to attract others **:** personal charm
mag·ne·tize *vb* **mag·ne·tized; mag·ne·tiz·ing :** to cause to be magnetic
mag·nif·i·cence *n* **:** impressive beauty or greatness
mag·nif·i·cent *adj* **:** very beautiful or impressive — **mag·nif·i·cent·ly** *adv*
mag·ni·fy *vb* **mag·ni·fied; mag·ni·fy·ing 1 :** to enlarge in fact or appearance **2 :** to cause to seem greater or more important **:** EXAGGERATE
magnifying glass *n* **:** a lens that makes

something seen through it appear larger than it actually is

mag·ni·tude *n* **:** greatness of size or importance

mag·no·lia *n* **:** a tree or tall shrub having showy white, pink, yellow, or purple flowers that appear in early spring

mag·pie *n* **:** a noisy black-and-white bird related to the jays

Ma·hi·can *or* **Mo·hi·can** *n, pl* **Ma·hi·can** *or* **Ma·hi·cans** *or* **Mo·hi·can** *or* **Mo·hi·cans** **1 :** a member of an American Indian people of northeastern New York **2 :** the language of the Mahican people

ma·hog·a·ny *n, pl* **ma·hog·a·nies :** a strong reddish brown wood that is used especially for furniture and is obtained from several tropical trees

maid *n* **1 :** [1]MAIDEN **2 :** a female servant

[1]**maid·en** *n* **:** an unmarried girl or woman

[2]**maiden** *adj* **1 :** UNMARRIED **2 :** [1]FIRST

maid·en·hair fern *n* **:** a fern with slender stems and delicate feathery leaves

maiden name *n* **:** a woman's last name before she is married

maid of honor *n, pl* **maids of honor :** a woman who stands with the bride at a wedding

[1]**mail** *n* **1 :** letters and packages sent from one person to another through the post office **2 :** the system used for sending and delivering letters and packages **3 :** [1]E-MAIL 2

[2]**mail** *vb* **mailed; mail·ing :** to send letters and packages through the post office

[3]**mail** *n* **:** a fabric made of metal rings linked together and used as armor

mail·box *n* **1 :** a public box in which to place outgoing mail **2 :** a private box (as on a house) for the delivery of mail **3 :** a computer file in which e-mail is collected

mail carrier *n* **:** LETTER CARRIER

mail·man *n, pl* **mail·men :** LETTER CARRIER

maim *vb* **maimed; maim·ing :** to injure badly or cripple by violence

[1]**main** *adj* **:** first in size, rank, or importance **:** CHIEF — **main·ly** *adv*

[2]**main** *n* **1 :** the chief part **:** essential point **2 :** a principal line, tube, or pipe of a utility system **3 :** HIGH SEAS **4 :** physical strength **:** FORCE

main·land *n* **:** a continent or the largest part of a continent as distinguished from an offshore island or islands

main·mast *n* **:** the principal mast of a sailing ship

main·sail *n* **:** the principal sail on the mainmast

main·spring *n* **:** the principal spring in a mechanical device (as a watch or clock)

main·stay *n* **1 :** the large strong rope from the maintop of a ship usually to the foot of the foremast **2 :** a chief support

main·tain *vb* **main·tained; main·tain·ing** **1 :** to carry on **:** CONTINUE **2 :** to keep in a particular or desired state **3 :** to insist to be true **4 :** to provide for **:** SUPPORT

main·te·nance *n* **1 :** the act of keeping or providing for **:** the state of being kept or provided for **2 :** UPKEEP

main·top *n* **:** a platform around the head of a mainmast

maize *n* **:** [1]CORN

Maj. *abbr* major

ma·jes·tic *adj* **:** very impressive and beautiful or dignified — **ma·jes·ti·cal·ly** *adv*

maj·es·ty *n, pl* **maj·es·ties** **1** — used as a title for a king, queen, emperor, or empress **2 :** the quality or state of being impressive and dignified **3 :** royal dignity or authority

[1]**ma·jor** *adj* **1 :** great or greater in number, quantity, rank, or importance **2 :** of or relating to a musical scale of eight notes with half steps between the third and fourth and between the seventh and eighth notes and with whole steps between all the others

[2]**major** *n* **:** a commissioned officer in the army, air force, or marine corps ranking above a captain

ma·jor·i·ty *n, pl* **ma·jor·i·ties** **1 :** a number greater than half of a total **2 :** a group or party that makes up the greater part of a whole body of people **3 :** the amount by which a number is more than half the total **4 :** the age at which a person has the full rights of an adult

[1]**make** *vb* **made; mak·ing** **1 :** to form or put together out of material or parts **2 :** to cause to exist or occur **3 :** to prepare food or drink **4 :** to cause to be or become **5 :** COMPEL 1 **6 :** to arrange the blankets and sheets on (a bed) so that the mattress is covered **7 :** to combine to produce **8 :** GET 1, GAIN **9 :** [1]REACH 2 **10 :** [1]DO 1, PERFORM **11 :** to act so as to be — **mak·er** *n* — **make believe :** to act as if something known to be imaginary is real or true — **make fun of :** to cause to be the target of laughter in an unkind way — **make good :** FULFILL 1, COMPLETE — **make out** **1 :** to write out **2 :** UNDERSTAND 1 **3 :** IDENTIFY 1 **4 :** [1]FARE — **make up** **1 :** to create from the imagination **2 :** [2]FORM 3, COMPOSE **3 :** to do something to correct or repay a wrong **4 :** to become friendly again **5 :** to put on makeup **6 :** DECIDE

[2]**make** *n* **:** [1]BRAND 2

[1]**make–be·lieve** *n* **:** something that is imagined to be real or true

[2]**make–believe** *adj* **:** not real **:** IMAGINARY

DICTIONARY

make·shift *adj* : serving as a temporary substitute

make-up *n* **1** : any of various cosmetics (as lipstick or powder) **2** : the way the parts or elements of something are put together or joined **3** : materials used to change a performer's appearance (as for a play or movie)

mal- *prefix* **1** : bad : badly **2** : abnormal : abnormally

mal·ad·just·ed *adj* : not able to deal with other people in a normal or healthy way

mal·a·dy *n, pl* **mal·a·dies** : a disease or disorder of the body or mind

ma·lar·ia *n* : a serious disease with chills and fever that is spread by the bite of a mosquito

[1]**male** *n* **1** : a man or a boy **2** : a person or animal that produces germ cells (as sperm) that fertilize the eggs of a female **3** : a plant with stamens but no pistil

[2]**male** *adj* **1** : of, relating to, or being the sex that fertilizes the eggs of a female **2** : bearing stamens but no pistil **3** : of or characteristic of men or boys

ma·lev·o·lent *adj* : having or showing a desire to cause harm to another person

mal·for·ma·tion *n* : something that is badly or wrongly formed

mal·ice *n* : a desire to cause harm to another person

ma·li·cious *adj* : feeling or showing a desire to cause harm to another person — **ma·li·cious·ly** *adv*

[1]**ma·lign** *adj* : MALICIOUS

[2]**malign** *vb* **ma·ligned; ma·lign·ing** : to say evil things about : SLANDER

ma·lig·nant *adj* **1** : MALICIOUS **2** : likely to cause death : DEADLY — **ma·lig·nant·ly** *adv*

mall *n* **1** : a large building or group of buildings containing a variety of shops **2** : a public area for pedestrians

mal·lard *n* : a common wild duck of the northern hemisphere that is the ancestor of the domestic ducks

mal·lea·ble *adj* : capable of being extended or shaped with blows from a hammer

mal·let *n* **1** : a hammer with a barrel-shaped head of wood or other material **2** : a club with a short thick head and a long thin handle

mal·low *n* : a tall plant with usually large white, rose, or purplish flowers with five petals

mal·nu·tri·tion *n* : a condition of weakness and poor health that results from not eating enough food or from eating food without the proper nutrients

malt *n* **1** : grain and especially barley soaked in water until it has sprouted **2** : MALTED MILK

malt·ed milk *n* : a beverage made by dissolving a powder made from dried milk and cereals in milk

mal·treat *vb* **mal·treat·ed; mal·treat·ing** : to treat in a rough or unkind way : ABUSE

ma·ma *also* **mam·ma** *or* **mom·ma** *n* : [1]MOTHER 1

mam·mal *n* : a warm-blooded animal (as a dog, mouse, bear, whale, or human being) that has a backbone, feeds its young with milk produced by the mother, and has skin usually more or less covered with hair

[1]**mam·moth** *n* : a very large hairy extinct elephant with long tusks that curve upward

[2]**mammoth** *adj* : very large : HUGE

[1]**man** *n, pl* **men** **1** : an adult male human being **2** : a human being : PERSON **3** : the human race : MANKIND **4** : [1]HUSBAND **5** : an adult male servant or employee **6** : one of the pieces with which various games (as chess and checkers) are played **7** : a member of the group to which human beings belong including both modern humans and extinct related forms

[2]**man** *vb* **manned; man·ning** : to work at or do the work of operating

Man. *abbr* Manitoba

man·age *vb* **man·aged; man·ag·ing** **1** : to look after and make decisions about **2** : to succeed in doing : accomplish what is desired — **man·age·able** *adj*

man·age·ment *n* **1** : the act of looking after and making decisions about something **2** : the people who look after and make decisions about something

man·ag·er *n* **1** : a person who is in charge of a business or part of a business **2** : a person who directs the training and performance of a sports team

man·a·tee *n* : a mainly tropical water-dwelling mammal that eats plants and has a broad rounded tail

man·da·rin *n* **1** : a public official of the Chinese Empire **2** *cap* : the chief dialect of China

man·date *n* **1** : an order from a higher court to a lower court **2** : a command or instruction from an authority **3** : the instruction given by voters to their elected representatives

man·da·tory *adj* : required by law or by a command

man·di·ble *n* **1** : a lower jaw often with its soft parts **2** : either the upper or lower part of the bill of a bird **3** : either of a pair of mouth parts of some invertebrates (as an insect) that are usually used for biting

man·do·lin *n* : a musical instrument with four pairs of strings played by plucking

mane *n* : long heavy hair growing about the

neck and head of some animals (as a horse or lion) — **maned** *adj*

[1]**ma·neu·ver** *or Can and Brit* **manoeuvre** *n* **1 :** skillful action or management **2 :** a training exercise by armed forces **3 :** a planned movement of troops or ships

[2]**maneuver** *or Can and Brit* **manoeuvre** *vb* **ma·neu·vered/manoeuvred; ma·neu·ver·ing/manoeuvring 1 :** to guide skillfully **2 :** to move troops or ships where they are needed — **ma·neu·ver·abil·i·ty** *or Can and Brit* **manoeuvrability** *n* — **ma·neu·ver·able** *or Can and Brit* **manoeuvrable** *adj*

man·ga *n, pl* **manga** *also* **man·gas :** a Japanese comic book or graphic novel

man·ga·nese *n* **:** a grayish white brittle metallic chemical element that resembles iron

mange *n* **:** a contagious skin disease usually of domestic animals in which there is itching and loss of hair

man·ger *n* **:** an open box in which food for farm animals is placed

man·gle *vb* **man·gled; man·gling 1 :** to injure badly by cutting, tearing, or crushing **2 :** to spoil while making or performing

man·go *n, pl* **man·goes** *or* **man·gos :** a tropical fruit with yellowish red skin and juicy mildly tart yellow flesh

mangy *adj* **mang·i·er; mang·i·est 1 :** affected with mange **2 :** SHABBY 1 **3 :** SEEDY 2

man·hole *n* **:** a covered hole (as in a street) large enough to let a person pass through

man·hood *n* **1 :** the state of being an adult human male **2 :** qualities often associated with men **3 :** adult human males

ma·nia *n* **:** extreme enthusiasm

ma·ni·ac *n* **1 :** a person who is or behaves as if insane **2 :** a person who is extremely enthusiastic about something

[1]**man·i·cure** *n* **:** a treatment for the care of the hands and fingernails

[2]**manicure** *vb* **man·i·cured; man·i·cur·ing :** to give a beauty treatment to the hands and fingernails

man·i·cur·ist *n* **:** a person whose job is the treatment of hands and fingernails

[1]**man·i·fest** *adj* **:** easy to detect or recognize **:** OBVIOUS

[2]**manifest** *vb* **man·i·fest·ed; man·i·fest·ing :** to show plainly

man·i·fes·ta·tion *n* **1 :** the act of showing plainly **2 :** something that makes clear **:** EVIDENCE

man·i·fold *adj* **:** of many and various kinds

ma·nip·u·late *vb* **ma·nip·u·lat·ed; ma·nip·u·lat·ing 1 :** to operate, use, or move with the hands or by mechanical means **2 :** to manage skillfully and especially with intent to deceive

man·kind *n* **1 :** human beings **2 :** men as distinguished from women

man·ly *adj* **man·li·er; man·li·est :** having the qualities often associated with men — **man·li·ness** *n*

man–made *adj* **:** made by people rather than nature

man·na *n* **1 :** food which according to the Bible was supplied by a miracle to the Israelites in the wilderness **2 :** a usually sudden and unexpected source of pleasure or gain

man·ne·quin *n* **:** a form representing the human figure used especially for displaying clothes

man·ner *n* **1 :** the way something is done or happens **2 :** a way of acting **3 manners** *pl* **:** behavior toward or in the presence of other people **4 :** [1]SORT 1

man·nered *adj* **:** having manners of a specified kind

man·ner·ism *n* **:** a habit (as of looking or moving in a certain way) that occurs commonly in a person's behavior

man·ner·ly *adj* **:** showing good manners

ma·noeu·vre *Can and Brit spelling of* MANEUVER

man–of–war *n, pl* **men–of–war :** WARSHIP

man·or *n* **:** a large estate

man·sion *n* **:** a large fine house

man·slaugh·ter *n* **:** the unintentional but unlawful killing of a person

man·ta ray *n* **:** a very large ray of warm seas that has fins that resemble wings

man·tel *n* **:** a shelf above a fireplace

man·tel·piece *n* **1 :** a shelf above a fireplace along with side pieces **2 :** MANTEL

man·tis *n, pl* **man·tis·es** *also* **man·tes :** PRAYING MANTIS

man·tle *n* **1 :** a loose sleeveless outer garment **2 :** something that covers or wraps **3 :** the part of the earth's interior beneath the crust and above the central core **4 :** a fold of the body wall of a mollusk that produces the shell material

[1]**man·u·al** *adj* **1 :** of or relating to hard physical work **2 :** operated by the hands **3 :** of or with the hands — **man·u·al·ly** *adv*

[2]**manual** *n* **:** HANDBOOK

[1]**man·u·fac·ture** *vb* **man·u·fac·tured; man·u·fac·tur·ing 1 :** to make from raw materials by hand or machinery **2 :** to create using the imagination often in order to deceive — **man·u·fac·tur·er** *n*

[2]**manufacture** *n* **1 :** the making of products by hand or machinery **2 :** PRODUCTION 2

ma·nure *n* **:** material (as animal wastes) used to fertilize land

man·u·script *n* **1 :** a document written by hand especially before the development of printing **2 :** the original copy of a writer's work before it is printed

[1]**many** *adj* **more; most** **1 :** amounting to a large number **2 :** being one of a large but not definite number

[2]**many** *pron* **:** a large number of people or things

[3]**many** *n* **:** a large number

[1]**map** *n* **1 :** a picture or chart that shows the features of an area **2 :** a picture or chart of the sky showing the position of stars and planets

[2]**map** *vb* **mapped; map·ping** **1 :** to make a map of **2 :** to plan in detail

ma·ple *n* **:** a tree having deeply notched leaves and hard pale wood and including some whose sap is evaporated to a sweet syrup (**maple syrup**) and a brownish sugar (**maple sugar**)

Maple Leaf *n* **:** the national flag of Canada

mar *vb* **marred; mar·ring :** to ruin the beauty or perfection of **:** SPOIL

Mar. *abbr* March

ma·ra·ca *n* **:** a musical rhythm instrument made of a dried gourd with seeds or pebbles inside that is usually played in pairs by shaking

mar·a·thon *n* **1 :** a long-distance running race **2 :** a long hard contest

ma·raud *vb* **ma·raud·ed; ma·raud·ing :** to roam about and raid in search of things to steal — **ma·raud·er** *n*

mar·ble *n* **1 :** a type of limestone that is often polished and is used in architecture and sculpture **2 :** a little ball (as of glass) used in a children's game (**marbles**)

[1]**march** *vb* **marched; march·ing** **1 :** to move or cause to move along with a steady regular step especially with others **2 :** to make steady progress — **march·er** *n*

[2]**march** *n* **1 :** the action of moving along with a steady regular step especially with others **2 :** an organized walk by a large group of people to support or protest something **3 :** the distance covered in marching **4 :** a regular and organized way that soldiers walk **5 :** a musical piece in a lively rhythm with a strong beat that is suitable to march to

March *n* **:** the third month of the year

mar·chio·ness *n* **1 :** the wife or widow of a marquess **2 :** a woman who holds the rank of a marquess in her own right

mare *n* **:** an adult female horse or related animal (as a zebra or donkey)

mar·ga·rine *n* **:** a food product made usually from vegetable oils and skim milk and used as a spread or for cooking

mar·gin *n* **1 :** the part of a page or sheet outside the main body of print or writing **2 :** [1]BORDER 2 **3 :** an extra amount (as of time or money) allowed for use if needed **4 :** a measurement of difference

mari·gold *n* **:** a plant grown for its usually yellow, orange, or brownish red flowers

mar·i·jua·na *n* **:** dried leaves and flowers of the hemp plant smoked as a drug

ma·ri·na *n* **:** a dock or basin providing a place to anchor motorboats and yachts

[1]**ma·rine** *adj* **1 :** of or relating to the sea **2 :** of or relating to the navigation of the sea **:** NAUTICAL **3 :** of or relating to soldiers in the United States Marine Corps

[2]**marine** *n* **1 :** a soldier of the United States Marine Corps **2 :** the ships of a country

mar·i·ner *n* **:** SEAMAN 1, SAILOR

mar·i·o·nette *n* **:** a puppet moved by attached strings

mar·i·tal *adj* **:** of or relating to marriage

mar·i·time *adj* **1 :** of or relating to ocean navigation or trade **2 :** bordering on or living near the sea

[1]**mark** *n* **1 :** a blemish (as a scratch or stain) made on a surface **2 :** a written or printed symbol **3 :** something that shows that something else exists **:** SIGN, INDICATION **4 :** something aimed at **:** TARGET **5 :** a grade or score showing the quality of work or conduct **6 :** something designed or serving to record position **7 :** the starting line of a race

[2]**mark** *vb* **marked; mark·ing** **1 :** to indicate a location **2 :** to set apart by a line or boundary **3 :** to make a shape, symbol, or word on **4 :** to decide and show the value or quality of **:** GRADE **5 :** to be an important characteristic of **6 :** to take notice of — **mark·er** *n*

marked *adj* **1 :** having notes or information written on it **2 :** NOTICEABLE **3 :** showing identification

[1]**mar·ket** *n* **1 :** a public place where people gather to buy and sell things **2 :** a store where foods are sold to the public **3 :** a region in which something can be sold **4 :** an opportunity for selling something

[2]**market** *vb* **mar·ket·ed; mar·ket·ing :** to sell or promote the sale of

mar·ket·place *n* **:** a location where public sales are held

mark·ing *n* **1 :** a shape, symbol, or word on something **2 :** the arrangement or pattern of contrasting colors on an animal

marks·man *n, pl* **marks·men :** a person who shoots well — **marks·man·ship** *n*

mar·ma·lade *n* **:** a jam containing pieces of fruit and fruit rind

mar·mo·set *n* **:** a small monkey of South and Central America with soft fur and a bushy tail

mar·mot *n* **:** a stocky burrowing animal with short legs and a bushy tail that is related to the squirrels

[1]**ma·roon** *vb* **ma·rooned; ma·roon·ing :** to

abandon in a place that is difficult to escape from

[2]**maroon** *n* : a dark red

mar·quess *n* : a British nobleman ranking below a duke and above an earl

mar·quis *n* : MARQUESS

mar·quise *n* : MARCHIONESS

mar·riage *n* **1** : the state of being united in a legal relationship as spouses **2** : the act of getting married

mar·row *n* : BONE MARROW

mar·ry *vb* **mar·ried; mar·ry·ing** **1** : to take for husband or wife **2** : to become joined in marriage **3** : to join in marriage **4** : to give (as a child) in marriage

Mars *n* : the planet that is fourth in order of distance from the sun, is known for its redness, and has a diameter of about 4200 miles (6800 kilometers)

marsh *n* : an area of soft wet land with grasses and related plants

[1]**mar·shal** *n* **1** : a person who arranges and directs ceremonies **2** : an officer of the highest rank in some military forces **3** : a federal official having duties similar to those of a sheriff **4** : the head of a division of a city government

[2]**marshal** *vb* **mar·shaled** *or* **mar·shalled; mar·shal·ing** *or* **mar·shal·ling** : to arrange in order

marsh·mal·low *n* : a soft spongy sweet food made from corn syrup, sugar, and gelatin

marshy *adj* **marsh·i·er; marsh·i·est** : like or containing soft wet land

mar·su·pi·al *n* : a mammal (as a kangaroo or opossum) that does not develop a true placenta and usually has a pouch on the female's abdomen in which the young develop and are carried

mart *n* : a trading place : MARKET

mar·ten *n* : a slender animal related to the weasel that has soft gray or brown fur and often climbs trees

mar·tial *adj* : having to do with or suitable for war

martial art *n* : any of several forms of combat and self-defense (as karate or judo) that are widely practiced as sports

mar·tin *n* **1** : a European swallow with a forked tail **2** : any of several birds (as the North American **purple martin**) resembling or related to the true martin

Mar·tin Lu·ther King Day *n* : the third Monday in January observed as a legal holiday in the United States

[1]**mar·tyr** *n* : a person who suffers greatly or dies rather than give up his or her religion or principles

[2]**martyr** *vb* **mar·tyred; mar·tyr·ing** : to put to death for refusing to give up a belief

[1]**mar·vel** *n* : something that causes wonder or astonishment

[2]**marvel** *vb* **mar·veled** *or* **mar·velled; mar·vel·ing** *or* **mar·vel·ling** : to feel astonishment or wonder

mar·vel·ous *or chiefly Can and Brit* **mar·vel·lous** *adj* **1** : causing wonder or astonishment **2** : of the finest kind or quality — **mar·vel·ous·ly** *or chiefly Can and Brit* **marvellously** *adv*

masc. *abbr* masculine

mas·cot *n* : a person, animal, or object adopted as the symbol of a group (as a school or sports team) and believed to bring good luck

mas·cu·line *adj* **1** : of the male sex **2** : characteristic of or relating to men : MALE

[1]**mash** *vb* **mashed; mash·ing** : to make into a soft mass

[2]**mash** *n* **1** : a mixture of ground feeds used for feeding livestock **2** : a mass of something made soft by beating or crushing **3** : a wet mixture of crushed malt or grain used to make alcoholic drinks

[1]**mask** *n* **1** : a cover for the face or part of the face used for disguise or protection **2** : something that disguises or conceals

[2]**mask** *vb* **masked; mask·ing** : CONCEAL, DISGUISE

ma·son *n* : a person who builds or works with stone or brick

ma·son·ry *n, pl* **ma·son·ries** **1** : something built of stone or brick **2** : the work done using stone or brick **3** : the art, trade, or occupation of a mason

masque *n* : an old form of dramatic entertainment in which the actors wore masks

[1]**mas·quer·ade** *n* **1** : a party (as a dance) at which people wear masks and costumes **2** : the act of pretending to be something different

[2]**masquerade** *vb* **mas·quer·ad·ed; mas·quer·ad·ing** **1** : to wear a disguise **2** : to pretend to be something different : POSE — **mas·quer·ad·er** *n*

[1]**mass** *n* **1** : a large quantity or number **2** : an amount of something that holds or clings together **3** : large size : BULK **4** : the principal part : main body **5 masses** *pl* : the body of ordinary or common people

[2]**mass** *vb* **massed; mass·ing** : to collect into a large body

[3]**mass** *n, often cap* : a religious service in which communion is celebrated

Mass. *abbr* Massachusetts

[1]**mas·sa·cre** *n* : the violent and cruel killing of a large number of people

[2]**massacre** *vb* **mas·sa·cred; mas·sa·cring** : to kill a large number of people in a violent and cruel manner

[1]**mas·sage** *n* : a soothing treatment of the body done by rubbing, kneading, and tapping

[2]**massage** *vb* **mas·saged; mas·sag·ing** : to give a soothing treatment to (the body) by rubbing, stroking, or pressing with the hands

mas·sive *adj* : very large, heavy, and solid

mast *n* : a long pole that rises from the bottom of a ship and supports the sails and rigging — **mast·ed** *adj*

[1]**mas·ter** *n* **1** : someone having authority over another person, an animal, or a thing **2** : a male teacher **3** : an artist or performer of great skill **4** — used as a title for a young boy too young to be called *mister*

[2]**master** *vb* **mas·tered; mas·ter·ing** **1** : to get control of **2** : to become skillful at

mas·ter·ful *adj* **1** : tending to take control : displaying authority **2** : having or showing great skill

mas·ter·ly *adj* : showing exceptional knowledge or skill

mas·ter·piece *n* : something done or made with exceptional skill

master sergeant *n* : a noncommissioned officer in the army ranking above a sergeant first class or in the air force ranking above a technical sergeant or in the marines ranking above a gunnery sergeant

mas·tery *n* **1** : complete control **2** : a very high level of skill or knowledge

mast·head *n* : the top of a ship's mast

mas·ti·cate *vb* **mas·ti·cat·ed; mas·ti·cat·ing** : [1]CHEW

mas·tiff *n* : a very large powerful dog with a smooth coat

[1]**mat** *n* **1** : a piece of material used as a floor or seat covering or in front of a door to wipe the shoes on **2** : a decorative piece of material used under dishes or vases **3** : a pad or cushion for gymnastics or wrestling **4** : something made up of many tangled strands

[2]**mat** *vb* **mat·ted; mat·ting** : to form into a tangled mass

mat·a·dor *n* : a bullfighter who plays the most important human part in a bullfight

[1]**match** *n* **1** : a person or thing that is equal to or as good as another **2** : a contest between two individuals or teams **3** : a thing that is exactly like another thing **4** : two people or things that go well together **5** : MARRIAGE 1

[2]**match** *vb* **matched; match·ing** **1** : to be the same or suitable to one another **2** : to choose something that is the same as another or goes with it **3** : to place in competition **4** : to be as good as

[3]**match** *n* : a short slender piece of material tipped with a mixture that produces fire when scratched

match·book *n* : a small folder containing rows of paper matches

match·less *adj* : having no equal : better than any other of the same kind

[1]**mate** *n* **1** : COMPANION 1, COMRADE **2** *chiefly British* : [1]CHUM, FRIEND — often used as a familiar form of address **3** : either member of a breeding pair of animals **4** : an officer on a ship used to carry passengers or freight who ranks below the captain **5** : either member of a married couple **6** : either of two objects that go together

[2]**mate** *vb* **mat·ed; mat·ing** **1** : to join as married partners **2** : to come or bring together for breeding

[1]**ma·te·ri·al** *adj* **1** : of, relating to, or made of matter : PHYSICAL **2** : of or relating to a person's bodily needs or wants **3** : having real importance — **ma·teri·al·ly** *adv*

[2]**material** *n* **1** : the elements, substance, or parts of which something is made or can be made **2** : equipment needed for doing something

ma·te·ri·al·ize *vb* **ma·te·ri·al·ized; ma·te·ri·al·iz·ing** **1** : to appear suddenly **2** : to become actual fact **3** : to cause to take on a physical form

ma·ter·nal *adj* **1** : of or relating to a mother **2** : related through the mother — **ma·ter·nal·ly** *adv*

ma·ter·ni·ty *n* : the state of being a mother

math *n* : MATHEMATICS

math·e·mat·i·cal *adj* **1** : of or relating to numbers, quantities, measurements, and the relations between them : of or relating to mathematics **2** : [1]EXACT — **math·e·mat·i·cal·ly** *adv*

math·e·ma·ti·cian *n* : a specialist in mathematics

math·e·mat·ics *n* : the science that studies and explains numbers, quantities, measurements, and the relations between them

mat·i·nee *or* **mat·i·née** *n* : a musical or dramatic performance in the afternoon

ma·tri·arch *n* : a woman who is the head of a family, group, or state

mat·ri·mo·ni·al *adj* : of or relating to marriage

mat·ri·mo·ny *n* : MARRIAGE 1

ma·tron *n* **1** : a married woman usually of high social position **2** : a woman who is in charge of women or children (as in a school or police station)

[1]**mat·ter** *n* **1** : something to be dealt with or considered **2** : PROBLEM 2, DIFFICULTY **3** : the substance things are made of : something that takes up space and has weight **4** : material substance of a certain kind or function **5** : PUS **6** : a small quantity or amount — **as a matter of fact** : ACTUALLY — **no matter** : it makes no difference — **no**

matter what : regardless of the costs or consequences

²matter *vb* **mat·tered; mat·ter·ing** : to be of importance

mat·ter–of–fact *adj* : sticking to or concerned with fact and usually not showing emotion — **mat·ter–of–fact·ly** *adv*

mat·ting *n* : rough fabric used as a floor covering

mat·tress *n* : a springy pad for use on a bed

¹ma·ture *adj* **1** : fully grown or developed : ADULT, RIPE **2** : having or showing the qualities of an adult person

²mature *vb* **ma·tured; ma·tur·ing** : to reach full development

ma·tu·ri·ty *n* : the condition of being fully developed

¹maul *n* : a heavy hammer used especially for driving wedges or posts

²maul *vb* **mauled; maul·ing** **1** : to attack and injure by biting, cutting, or tearing flesh **2** : to handle roughly

mauve *n* : a medium purple, violet, or lilac

maxi- *prefix* : very long or large

max·il·la *n, pl* **max·il·lae** **1** : an upper jaw especially of a mammal **2** : either of the pair of mouth parts next behind the mandibles of an arthropod (as an insect or a crustacean)

max·im *n* : a short saying (as "live and let live") expressing a general truth or rule of conduct

max·i·mize *vb* **max·i·mized; max·i·miz·ing** : to increase (something) as much as possible

¹max·i·mum *n, pl* **max·i·ma** *or* **maximums** : the highest value : greatest amount

²maximum *adj* : as great as possible in amount or degree

³maximum *adv* : at the most

may *helping verb, past* **might;** *present sing & pl* **may** **1** : have permission to **2** : be in some degree likely to **3** — used to express a wish **4** — used to express purpose

May *n* : the fifth month of the year

may·be *adv* : possibly but not certainly

mayn't : may not

may·on·naise *n* : a creamy dressing usually made of egg yolk, oil, and vinegar or lemon juice

may·or *n* : an official elected to serve as head of a city, town, or borough

maze *n* : a confusing arrangement of paths or passages

MB *abbr* **1** Manitoba **2** megabyte

Md., MD *abbr* Maryland

M.D. *abbr* doctor of medicine

me *pron, objective case of* I

Me., ME *abbr* Maine

mead·ow *n* : usually moist and low grassland

mead·ow·lark *n* : a songbird that has brownish upper parts and a yellow breast

mea·ger *or Can and Brit* **mea·gre** *adj* **1** : not enough in quality or amount **2** : having little flesh : THIN

¹meal *n* **1** : the food eaten or prepared for eating at one time **2** : the act or time of eating

²meal *n* : coarsely ground seeds of a cereal grass and especially of corn

mealy *adj* **meal·i·er; meal·i·est** : soft, dry, and crumbly — **meal·i·ness** *n*

¹mean *vb* **meant; mean·ing** **1** : to represent or have as a definite explanation or idea : SIGNIFY **2** : to be an indication of **3** : to have in mind as a purpose : INTEND **4** : to intend for a particular use **5** : to have importance to

²mean *adj* **mean·er; mean·est** **1** : deliberately unkind **2** : STINGY 1 **3** : low in quality, worth, or dignity **4** : EXCELLENT — **mean·ly** *adv* — **mean·ness** *n*

³mean *adj* : occurring or being in a middle position : AVERAGE

⁴mean *n* **1** : a middle point or something (as a place, time, number, or rate) that falls at or near a middle point : MODERATION **2** : ARITHMETIC MEAN **3 means** *pl* : something that helps a person to get what he or she wants **4 means** *pl* : WEALTH 1 — **by all means** : CERTAINLY 1 — **by any means** : in any way — **by means of** : through the use of — **by no means** : certainly not

me·an·der *vb* **me·an·dered; me·an·der·ing** **1** : to follow a winding course **2** : to wander without a goal or purpose

mean·ing *n* **1** : the idea that is represented by a word, phrase, or statement **2** : the idea a person intends to express by something said or done **3** : the reason or explanation for something **4** : the quality of communicating something or of being important

mean·ing·ful *adj* : having a meaning or purpose — **mean·ing·ful·ly** *adv*

mean·ing·less *adj* : having no meaning or importance

mean–spir·it·ed *adj* : feeling or showing a cruel desire to cause harm or pain — **mean–spir·it·ed·ness** *n*

¹mean·time *n* **1** : the time between events or points of time **2** : a time during which more than one thing is being done

²meantime *adv* : in the time between events or points of time or during which more than one thing is being done

¹mean·while *n* : ¹MEANTIME

²meanwhile *adv* **1** : ²MEANTIME **2** : at the same time

mea·sles *n pl* **1** : a contagious disease in which there are fever and red spots on the skin **2** : any of several diseases (as

German measles) resembling true measles — used as singular or plural

mea·sly *adj* **mea·sli·er; mea·sli·est** : so small or unimportant as to be rejected with scorn

mea·sur·able *adj* : capable of having the size, extent, amount, or significance determined — **mea·sur·ably** *adv*

[1]**mea·sure** *n* **1** : EXTENT 2, DEGREE, AMOUNT **2** : the size, capacity, or quantity of something that has been determined **3** : something (as a yardstick or cup) used in determining size, capacity, or quantity **4** : a unit used in determining size, capacity, or quantity **5** : a system of determining size, capacity, or quantity **6** : the notes and rests between bar lines on a musical staff **7** : a way of accomplishing something — **for good measure** : as an extra

[2]**measure** *vb* **mea·sured; mea·sur·ing** **1** : to find out the size, extent, or amount of **2** : to separate out a fixed amount **3** : [1]ESTIMATE **4** : to bring into comparison **5** : to give a determination of size, capacity, or quantity : INDICATE **6** : to have as its size, capacity, or quantity — **measure up** : to satisfy needs or requirements

mea·sure·ment *n* **1** : the act of determining size, capacity, or quantity **2** : the extent, size, capacity, or amount of something as has been determined

meat *n* **1** : the flesh of an animal used as food — often does not include the flesh of fish or seafood **2** : solid food as distinguished from drink **3** : the part of something that can be eaten **4** : the most important part : SUBSTANCE — **meat·less** *adj*

meat·ball *n* : a small round lump of chopped or ground meat

me·chan·ic *n* : a person who makes or repairs machines

me·chan·i·cal *adj* **1** : of or relating to machinery **2** : made or operated by a machine **3** : done or produced as if by a machine — **me·chan·i·cal·ly** *adv*

me·chan·ics *n pl* **1** : a science dealing with the action of forces on objects **2** : the way something works or things are done — used as singular or plural

mech·a·nism *n* **1** : a piece of machinery **2** : the parts by which a machine operates **3** : the parts or steps that make up a process or activity

mech·a·nize *vb* **mech·a·nized; mech·a·niz·ing** **1** : to cause to be done by machines rather than humans or animals **2** : to equip with machinery

med·al *n* : a piece of metal often in the form of a coin with design and words in honor of a special event, a person, or an achievement

me·dal·lion *n* **1** : a large medal **2** : a decoration shaped like a large medal

med·dle *vb* **med·dled; med·dling** : to be overly interested or involved in someone else's business

med·dle·some *adj* : intruding in another person's business in an inconsiderate and annoying way

me·dia *n* : the system and organizations of communication through which information is spread to a large number of people — used as singular or plural

med·i·cal *adj* : of or relating to the science or practice of medicine or to the treatment of disease — **med·i·cal·ly** *adv*

med·i·cate *vb* **med·i·cat·ed; med·i·cat·ing** **1** : to treat with medicine **2** : to add medicinal material to

med·i·ca·tion *n* : MEDICINE 1

me·dic·i·nal *adj* : used or likely to prevent, cure, or relieve disease — **me·dic·i·nal·ly** *adv*

med·i·cine *n* **1** : something (as a pill or liquid) used to prevent, cure, or relieve a disease **2** : a science dealing with the prevention, cure, or relief of disease

medicine dropper *n* : DROPPER 2

medicine man *n* : a person especially among American Indian groups believed to have magic powers to cure illnesses and keep away evil spirits

me·di·eval *also* **me·di·ae·val** *adj* : of or relating to the Middle Ages

me·di·o·cre *adj* : neither good nor bad : ORDINARY

med·i·tate *vb* **med·i·tat·ed; med·i·tat·ing** **1** : to consider carefully : PLAN **2** : to spend time in quiet thinking : REFLECT

med·i·ta·tion *n* : the act or an instance of planning or thinking quietly

Med·i·ter·ra·nean *adj* : of or relating to the Mediterranean Sea or to the lands or peoples surrounding it

[1]**me·di·um** *n, pl* **me·di·ums** *or* **me·dia** **1** : something that is between or in the middle **2** : the thing by which or through which something is done **3** : the substance in which something lives or acts **4** *pl usually media* : a form or system of communication, information, or entertainment **5** : a person through whom other persons try to communicate with the spirits of the dead

[2]**medium** *adj* : intermediate in amount, quality, position, or degree

med·ley *n, pl* **medleys** **1** : MIXTURE 2, JUMBLE **2** : a musical selection made up of a series of different songs or parts of different compositions

me·dul·la ob·lon·ga·ta *n* : the part of the brain that joins the spinal cord and is concerned especially with control of involuntary activities (as breathing and beating of the heart) necessary for life

meek *adj* **meek·er; meek·est** : having or showing a quiet, gentle, and humble nature — **meek·ly** *adv* — **meek·ness** *n*

[1]**meet** *vb* **met; meet·ing** **1** : to get to know : become acquainted **2** : to come upon or across **3** : to be at a place to greet or keep an appointment **4** : to approach from the opposite direction **5** : to touch and join or cross **6** : to experience something **7** : to hold a gathering or assembly **8** : to be sensed by **9** : to deal with **10** : to fulfill the requirements of : SATISFY

[2]**meet** *n* : a meeting for sports competition

meet·ing *n* **1** : the act of persons or things that come together **2** : a gathering of people for a particular purpose

meet·ing·house *n* : a building used for public assembly and especially for Protestant worship

mega·byte *n* : a unit of computer information storage capacity equal to 1,048,576 bytes

mega·phone *n* : a device shaped like a cone that is used to direct the voice and increase its loudness

[1]**mel·an·choly** *adj* : SAD 1

[2]**melancholy** *n* : a sad or gloomy mood

[1]**mel·low** *adj* **1** : fully ripe or mature **2** : made mild by age **3** : being clear, full, and pure : not harsh **4** : very calm and relaxed — **mel·low·ness** *n*

[2]**mellow** *vb* **mel·lowed; mel·low·ing** : to make or become mild or relaxed especially over time

me·lod·ic *adj* : MELODIOUS

me·lo·di·ous *adj* : having a pleasant musical sound — **me·lo·di·ous·ly** *adv*

melo·dra·mat·ic *adj* : extremely or overly emotional

mel·o·dy *n, pl* **mel·o·dies** **1** : pleasing arrangement of sounds **2** : a series of musical notes or tones arranged in a definite pattern of pitch and rhythm **3** : the main part in a musical composition

mel·on *n* : a usually large fruit (as a watermelon or cantaloupe) that grows on a vine and has juicy sweet flesh and a hard rind

melt *vb* **melt·ed; melt·ing** **1** : to change from a solid to a liquid usually through the action of heat **2** : to grow less : DISAPPEAR **3** : to make or become gentle : SOFTEN **4** : to lose clear outline

melting point *n* : the temperature at which a solid melts

mem·ber *n* **1** : someone or something that is part of a group **2** : a part (as an arm or leg) of a person or animal **3** : a part of a structure

mem·ber·ship *n* **1** : the state or fact of belonging to a group **2** : the whole number of individuals that make up a group

mem·brane *n* : a thin soft flexible layer especially of animal or plant tissue

mem·bra·nous *adj* : made of or like membrane

me·men·to *n, pl* **me·men·tos** *or* **me·men·toes** : something that serves as a reminder

mem·o·ra·ble *adj* : worth remembering : not easily forgotten — **mem·o·ra·bly** *adv*

mem·o·ran·dum *n, pl* **mem·o·ran·dums** *or* **mem·o·ran·da** **1** : an informal report or message **2** : a written reminder

[1]**me·mo·ri·al** *n* : something by which the memory of a person or an event is kept alive : MONUMENT

[2]**memorial** *adj* : serving to honor the memory of a person or event

Memorial Day *n* : a legal holiday in remembrance of war dead observed on the last Monday in May in most states of the United States

mem·o·rize *vb* **mem·o·rized; mem·o·riz·ing** : to learn by heart

mem·o·ry *n, pl* **mem·o·ries** **1** : the power or process of remembering **2** : the store of things learned and kept in the mind **3** : the act of remembering and honoring **4** : something remembered **5** : the time within which past events are remembered **6** : a device or part in a computer which can receive and store information for use when wanted **7** : capacity for storing information

men *pl of* MAN

[1]**men·ace** *n* **1** : DANGER 2 **2** : an annoying person

[2]**menace** *vb* **men·aced; men·ac·ing** : to threaten harm to

me·nag·er·ie *n* : a collection of wild animals kept especially to be shown to the public

[1]**mend** *vb* **mend·ed; mend·ing** **1** : IMPROVE, CORRECT **2** : to put into good shape or working order again **3** : to improve in health : HEAL — **mend·er** *n*

[2]**mend** *n* : a place where something has been fixed so that it is usable again — **on the mend** : getting better

men·folk *or* **men·folks** *n pl* : the men of a family or community

men·ha·den *n, pl* **menhaden** : a fish of the Atlantic coast of the United States that is related to the herring and is a source of oil and fertilizer

me·nial *adj* : of or relating to boring or unpleasant work that does not require special skill

men–of–war *pl of* MAN-OF-WAR

me·no·rah *n* : a candle holder with seven or nine lights used in Jewish worship

men·stru·a·tion *n* : a discharge of bloody fluid from the uterus that usually happens each month

-ment *n suffix* **1 :** result, goal, or method of a specified action **2 :** action : process **3 :** place of a specified action **4 :** state : condition
men·tal *adj* **1 :** of or relating to the mind **2 :** done in the mind **3 :** intended for the care of persons affected by a disorder of the mind — **men·tal·ly** *adv*
men·tal·i·ty *n* **1 :** mental ability **2 :** a particular way of thinking : OUTLOOK
men·thol *n* **:** a white crystalline soothing substance from oils of mint
[1]**men·tion** *n* **:** a short statement calling attention to something or someone
[2]**mention** *vb* **men·tioned; men·tion·ing :** to refer to or speak about briefly
menu *n* **1 :** a list of dishes that may be ordered in a restaurant **2 :** the dishes or kinds of food served at a meal **3 :** a list shown on a computer screen from which a user can select an operation for the computer to perform
[1]**me·ow** *n* **:** the cry of a cat
[2]**meow** *vb* **me·owed; me·ow·ing :** to make the cry of a cat
mer·can·tile *adj* **:** of or relating to merchants or trade
[1]**mer·ce·nary** *n, pl* **mer·ce·nar·ies :** a soldier paid by a foreign country to fight in its army
[2]**mercenary** *adj* **1 :** doing something only for the pay or reward **2 :** greedy for money
mer·chan·dise *n* **:** goods that are bought and sold
mer·chant *n* **1 :** a person who buys and sells goods especially on a large scale or with foreign countries **2 :** STOREKEEPER 1
merchant marine *n* **1 :** the trading ships of a nation **2 :** the people who work in trading ships
mer·ci·ful *adj* **:** having or showing mercy or compassion — **mer·ci·ful·ly** *adv*
mer·ci·less *adj* **:** having no mercy or pity — **mer·ci·less·ly** *adv*
mer·cu·ry *n* **1 :** a heavy silvery white poisonous metallic chemical element that is liquid at ordinary temperatures **2 :** the column of mercury in a thermometer or barometer **3** *cap* **:** the planet that is nearest the sun and has a diameter of about 3000 miles (4700 kilometers)
mer·cy *n, pl* **mer·cies 1 :** kind and forgiving treatment of someone (as a wrongdoer or an opponent) **2 :** kindness or help given to an unfortunate person **3 :** a kind sympathetic disposition : willingness to forgive, spare, or help **4 :** a blessing as an act of divine love **5 :** a fortunate happening — **at the mercy of :** completely without protection from
mere *adj, superlative* **mer·est :** nothing more than
mere·ly *adv* **:** nothing else than : JUST
merge *vb* **merged; merg·ing :** to be or cause to be combined or blended into a single unit
merg·er *n* **:** the combination of two or more businesses into one
me·rid·i·an *n* **1 :** any imaginary semicircle on the earth's surface reaching from the north pole to the south pole **2 :** a representation of a meridian on a map or globe numbered according to degrees of longitude
me·ringue *n* **:** a light mixture of beaten egg whites and sugar used especially as a topping for pies or cakes
me·ri·no *n, pl* **me·ri·nos 1 :** a sheep of a breed that produces a heavy fleece of white fine wool **2 :** a fine wool and cotton yarn
[1]**mer·it** *n* **1 :** the condition or fact of deserving reward or punishment **2 :** [2]WORTH 1, VALUE **3 :** a quality worthy of praise : VIRTUE
[2]**merit** *vb* **mer·it·ed; mer·it·ing :** to be worthy of or have a right to
mer·i·to·ri·ous *adj* **:** deserving reward or honor : PRAISEWORTHY
mer·maid *n* **:** an imaginary sea creature usually shown with a woman's head and body and a fish's tail
mer·man *n, pl* **mer·men :** an imaginary sea creature usually shown with a man's head and body and a fish's tail
mer·ri·ment *n* **:** laughter and enjoyment
mer·ry *adj* **mer·ri·er; mer·ri·est 1 :** full of joy and good cheer **2 :** full of festive celebration and enjoyment — **mer·ri·ly** *adv*
mer·ry–go–round *n* **:** a round platform that spins and has seats and figures of animals on which people sit for a ride
mer·ry·mak·er *n* **:** a person taking part in joyful celebration
mer·ry·mak·ing *n* **:** fun and enjoyment : joyful celebration
me·sa *n* **:** a hill with a flat top and steep sides
mesdames *pl of* MADAM, MADAME *or* MRS.
[1]**mesh** *n* **1 :** a material of open texture with evenly spaced holes **2 :** one of the spaces formed by the threads of a net or the wires of a sieve or screen **3 :** the coming or fitting together (as of the teeth of two sets of gears)
[2]**mesh** *vb* **meshed; mesh·ing :** to fit or join together
mes·mer·ize *vb* **mes·mer·ized; mes·mer·iz·ing :** to hold the complete attention of : FASCINATE
Mes·o·zo·ic *n* **:** an era of geological history which extends from the Paleozoic to the Cenozoic and in which dinosaurs are present and the first birds, mammals, and flowering plants appear
mes·quite *n* **:** a spiny shrub or small tree of the southwestern United States and Mexico
[1]**mess** *n* **1 :** a dirty or untidy state **2 :** some-

thing in a dirty or untidy state **3 :** a difficult situation **4 :** a group of people (as military personnel) who regularly eat together **5 :** a place (as in the military) where meals are served

²mess *vb* **messed; mess·ing 1 :** to make dirty or untidy **2 :** to make mistakes in or mix up **3 :** to become confused or make an error **4 :** to use or do in an aimless way **5 :** to handle in a careless way **6 :** to deal with in a way that may cause anger or trouble

mes·sage *n* **1 :** the exchange of information in writing, in speech, or by signals **2 :** an underlying theme or idea

message board *n* **:** a public computer system on the Internet that allows people to read and leave messages for other users

mes·sen·ger *n* **:** a person who carries a message or does an errand

Messrs. *pl of* MR.

messy *adj* **mess·i·er; mess·i·est 1 :** not clean or tidy **2 :** causing or making a mess **3 :** not careful or precise — **mess·i·ness** *n*

met *past and past participle of* MEET

met·a·bol·ic *adj* **:** of or relating to metabolism

me·tab·o·lism *n* **:** the processes by which a living organism uses food to obtain energy and build tissue and disposes of waste material

met·al *n* **1 :** a substance (as gold, tin, copper, or bronze) that has a more or less shiny appearance, is a good conductor of electricity and heat, and usually can be made into a wire or hammered into a thin sheet **2 :** METTLE

me·tal·lic *adj* **1 :** relating to, being, or resembling a metal **2 :** containing or made of metal **3 :** having a harsh sound

met·al·lur·gi·cal *adj* **:** of or relating to metallurgy

met·al·lur·gy *n* **:** the science of obtaining metals from their ores and preparing them for use

meta·mor·phic *adj* **:** formed by the action of pressure, heat, and water that results in a more compact form

meta·mor·pho·sis *n, pl* **meta·mor·pho·ses 1 :** a great change in appearance or character **2 :** the process of great and usually rather sudden change in the form and habits of some animals during transformation from an immature stage (as a caterpillar or tadpole) to an adult stage (as a butterfly or frog)

met·a·phor *n* **:** a figure of speech comparing two unlike things without using *like* or *as*

mete *vb* **met·ed; met·ing :** to distribute as deserved

me·te·or *n* **:** one of the small pieces of matter in the solar system that enter the earth's atmosphere where friction may cause them to glow and form a streak of light

me·te·or·ic *adj* **1 :** of or relating to a meteor **2 :** like a meteor in speed or in sudden and temporary success

me·te·or·ite *n* **:** a meteor that reaches the surface of the earth

me·te·o·rol·o·gist *n* **:** a person who specializes in meteorology

me·te·o·rol·o·gy *n* **:** a science that deals with the atmosphere, weather, and weather forecasting

¹me·ter *or Can and Brit* **metre** *n* **1 :** a planned rhythm in poetry that is usually repeated **2 :** the repeated pattern of musical beats in a measure

²meter *or Can and Brit* **metre** *n* **:** a measure of length on which the metric system is based and which is equal to about 39.37 inches

³meter *n* **:** an instrument for measuring and sometimes recording the amount of something

-meter *n suffix* **:** instrument for measuring

meth·od *n* **1 :** a certain way of doing something **2 :** careful arrangement

me·thod·i·cal *adj* **1 :** done or arranged in a planned way **:** using a careful and orderly procedure **2 :** following a planned and orderly way of doing something especially out of habit — **me·thod·i·cal·ly** *adv*

me·tic·u·lous *adj* **:** showing extreme or excessive care in thinking about or dealing with small details

me·tre *Can and Brit spelling of* METER

met·ric *adj* **:** of, relating to, or based on the metric system

met·ri·cal *adj* **:** of or relating to poetic or musical meter

metric system *n* **:** a system of weights and measures in which the meter is the unit of length and the kilogram is the unit of weight

metric ton *n* **:** a unit of weight equal to 1000 kilograms

met·ro·nome *n* **:** a device that ticks in a regular pattern to help a musician play a piece of music at the proper speed

me·trop·o·lis *n* **1 :** the chief or capital city of a country, state, or region **2 :** a large or important city

met·ro·pol·i·tan *adj* **:** of, relating to, or like that of a large city

met·tle *n* **:** strength of spirit **:** COURAGE

¹mew *vb* **mewed; mew·ing :** to make a sound like a meow

²mew *n* **:** ¹MEOW

Mex. *abbr* **1** Mexican **2** Mexico

¹Mex·i·can *adj* **:** of or relating to Mexico or its people

²Mexican *n* **:** a person born or living in Mexico

mg *abbr* milligram
mi *n* : the third note of the musical scale
mi. *abbr* **1** mile **2** miles
MI *abbr* Michigan
mi·ca *n* : a mineral that easily breaks into very thin transparent sheets
mice *pl of* MOUSE
Mich. *abbr* Michigan
micr- *or* **micro-** *prefix* **1** : small : tiny **2** : millionth
mi·crobe *n* : a very tiny and often harmful living thing : MICROORGANISM
mi·cro·com·put·er *n* : PERSONAL COMPUTER
mi·cro·film *n* : a film on which something (as printing) is recorded in a much smaller size
mi·crom·e·ter *n* **1** : an instrument used with a telescope or microscope for measuring very small distances **2** : an instrument having a rod moved by fine screw threads and used for making exact measurements
mi·cro·or·gan·ism *n* : a living thing (as a bacterium) that can only be seen with a microscope
mi·cro·phone *n* : an instrument in which sound is changed into an electrical signal for transmitting or recording (as in radio or television)
mi·cro·pro·ces·sor *n* : a computer processor contained on an integrated-circuit chip
mi·cro·scope *n* : an instrument with one or more lenses used to help a person to see something very small by making it appear larger
mi·cro·scop·ic *adj* **1** : of, relating to, or conducted with the microscope **2** : so small as to be visible only through a microscope : very tiny — **mi·cro·scop·i·cal·ly** *adv*
[1]**mi·cro·wave** *n* **1** : a radio wave between one millimeter and one meter in wavelength **2** : MICROWAVE OVEN
[2]**microwave** *vb* **mi·cro·waved; mi·cro·wav·ing** : to cook or heat in a microwave oven
microwave oven *n* : an oven in which food is cooked by the heat produced as a result of penetration of the food by microwaves
[1]**mid** *adj* : being the part in the middle
[2]**mid** *prep* : AMID
mid·air *n* : a region in the air some distance above the ground
mid·day *n* : NOON
[1]**mid·dle** *adj* **1** : equally distant from the ends : CENTRAL **2** : being at neither extreme : halfway between two opposite states or conditions
[2]**middle** *n* : the part, point, or position that is equally distant from the ends or opposite sides : CENTER
middle age *n* : the period of life from about 45 to about 64 years of age — **mid·dle–aged** *adj*
Middle Ages *n pl* : the period of European history from about A.D. 500 to about 1500
middle class *n* : a social class between that of the wealthy and the poor
Middle English *n* : the English language of the 12th to 15th centuries
middle finger *n* : the long finger that is the middle one of the five fingers of the hand
middle school *n* : a school usually including grades five to eight or six to eight
midge *n* : a very small fly : GNAT
[1]**midg·et** *n, sometimes offensive* : a person who is much smaller than normal
[2]**midget** *adj* : much smaller than usual or normal
mid·night *n* : twelve o'clock at night
mid·rib *n* : the central vein of a leaf
mid·riff *n* : the middle part of the human body between the chest and the waist
mid·ship·man *n, pl* **mid·ship·men** : a person who is training to become an officer in the navy
[1]**midst** *n* **1** : the middle or central part **2** : a position among the members of a group **3** : the condition of being surrounded
[2]**midst** *prep* : AMID
mid·stream *n* : the part of a stream farthest from each bank
mid·sum·mer *n* **1** : the middle of summer **2** : the summer solstice
[1]**mid·way** *adv or adj* : in the middle of the way or distance : HALFWAY
[2]**mid·way** *n* : an area at a fair, carnival, or amusement park for food stands, games, and rides
mid·wife *n* : a woman who helps other women during childbirth
mid·win·ter *n* **1** : the middle of winter **2** : the winter solstice
mien *n* : a person's appearance or way of acting that shows mood or personality
[1]**might** *past of* MAY — used as a helping verb to show that something is possible but not likely
[2]**might** *n* : power that can be used (as by a person or group)
might·i·ly *adv* **1** : very forcefully **2** : very much
mightn't : might not
[1]**mighty** *adj* **might·i·er; might·i·est** **1** : having great power or strength **2** : done by or showing great power or strength **3** : great in size or effect
[2]**mighty** *adv* : [2]VERY 1
mi·grant *n* : a person or animal that migrates
mi·grate *vb* **mi·grat·ed; mi·grat·ing** **1** : to move from one country or region to another **2** : to pass from one region to another on a regular basis
mi·gra·tion *n* : the act or an instance of

moving from one place to another often on a regular basis
mi·gra·to·ry *adj* **1 :** moving from one place to another **2 :** of or relating to migration
mike *n* **:** MICROPHONE
mild *adj* **mild·er; mild·est 1 :** gentle in personality or behavior **2 :** not strong or harsh in action or effect **3 :** not sharp, spicy, or bitter **4 :** not extreme or severe — **mild·ly** *adv* — **mild·ness** *n*
[1]**mil·dew** *n* **1 :** a thin whitish growth produced by a fungus especially on decaying material or on living plants **2 :** a fungus producing mildew
[2]**mildew** *vb* **mil·dewed; mil·dew·ing :** to become affected with mildew
mile *n* **1 :** a measure of distance (**statute mile**) equal to 5280 feet (1609 meters) **2 :** a measure of distance (**geographical mile** or **nautical mile**) used in air and sea travel equal to about 6076 feet (1852 meters)
mile·age *n* **1 :** distance in miles **2 :** distance covered or traveled in miles **3 :** the average number of miles a car or truck will travel on a gallon of fuel **4 :** an amount of money given for traveling expenses at a certain rate per mile
mile·stone *n* **1 :** a stone by the side of a road showing the distance in miles to a given place **2 :** an important point in progress or development
[1]**mil·i·tary** *adj* **1 :** of or relating to soldiers, the army, or war **2 :** carried on by soldiers **:** supported by armed force
[2]**military** *n, pl* **military :** members of the armed forces
mi·li·tia *n* **:** a group of citizens with some military training who are called into service only in emergencies
[1]**milk** *n* **1 :** a whitish liquid produced and given off by the breasts or udder of a female mammal as food for her young **2 :** milk from an animal and especially a cow used as food by people **3 :** a liquid that looks like milk
[2]**milk** *vb* **milked; milk·ing :** to draw milk from (as by pressing)
milk·man *n, pl* **milk·men :** a person who sells or delivers milk
milk shake *n* **:** a drink made of milk, a flavoring syrup, and ice cream that is shaken or mixed thoroughly
milk tooth *n, pl* **milk teeth :** one of the first and temporary teeth of which humans grow 20
milk·weed *n* **:** a plant with milky juice and clusters of flowers
milky *adj* **milk·i·er; milk·i·est 1 :** like milk especially in color **2 :** containing or full of milk
Milky Way *n* **1 :** a broad band of light that stretches across the sky and is caused by the light of a very great number of faint stars **2 :** MILKY WAY GALAXY
Milky Way galaxy *n* **:** the galaxy of which the sun and the solar system are a part and which contains the stars that make up the Milky Way
[1]**mill** *n* **1 :** a building with machinery for grinding grain into flour **2 :** a machine or device that prepares a material for use by grinding or crushing **3 :** a factory using machines to make a product from raw material
[2]**mill** *vb* **milled; mill·ing 1 :** to subject to processing in a mill **2 :** to move about in a circle or in disorder
[3]**mill** *n* **:** one tenth of a cent
mil·len·ni·um *n, pl* **mil·len·nia** *or* **millenniums 1 :** a period of 1000 years **2 :** a 1000th anniversary or its celebration — **mil·len·ni·al** *adj*
mill·er *n* **:** a person who works in or runs a mill that grinds grain into flour
mil·let *n* **:** a grass with small whitish seeds that are used as food for people, livestock, and birds
milli- *prefix* **:** thousandth
mil·li·gram *n* **:** a unit of weight equal to 1/1000 gram
mil·li·li·ter *or Can and Brit* **millilitre** *n* **:** a unit of capacity equal to 1/1000 liter
mil·li·me·ter *or Can and Brit* **millimetre** *n* **:** a unit of length equal to 1/1000 meter
mil·li·ner *n* **:** a person who makes, decorates, or sells women's hats
[1]**mil·lion** *n* **1 :** one thousand thousands **:** 1,000,000 **2 :** a very large number
[2]**million** *adj* **1 :** being 1,000,000 **2 :** being very great in number
mil·lion·aire *n* **:** a person having a million dollars or more
[1]**mil·lionth** *adj* **:** being last in a series of a million
[2]**millionth** *n* **:** number 1,000,000 in a series
mil·li·pede *n* **:** an animal that is an arthropod with a long roundish body somewhat like that of a centipede but with two pairs of legs on most of its many body sections
mill·stone *n* **:** either of two large circular stones used for grinding grain
mime *n* **1 :** the art of showing a character or telling a story using body movements and gestures without words **2 :** a person who performs mime
mim·eo·graph *n* **:** a machine for making copies of typed, written, or drawn matter using a stencil
[1]**mim·ic** *n* **:** a person or animal that imitates something or someone
[2]**mimic** *vb* **mim·icked; mim·ick·ing 1 :** to imitate very closely **2 :** to make fun of by imitating

DICTIONARY

mim·ic·ry *n* : a type of protection from predators in which one animal resembles the coloring, form, or behavior of another animal that is harmful or bad-tasting
min. *abbr* minute
min·a·ret *n* : a tall slender tower of a mosque with a balcony from which the people are called to prayer
mince *vb* **minced; minc·ing** **1 :** to cut or chop into very small pieces **2 :** to act or speak in an unnaturally dainty way **3 :** to phrase comments in such a way as to not cause offense
mince·meat *n* : a finely chopped mixture (as of raisins, apples, spices, and sometimes meat) that is especially used in pies
¹mind *n* **1 :** the part of a person that thinks, reasons, feels, understands, and remembers **2 :** MEMORY 1 **3 :** INTENTION 1 **4 :** a person's view or opinion about something
²mind *vb* **mind·ed; mind·ing** **1 :** to pay attention to **2 :** OBEY 1 **3 :** to be bothered by **4 :** to object to : DISLIKE **5 :** to take charge of **6 :** to be careful about
mind·ed *adj* **1 :** having a particular kind of mind **2 :** greatly interested or concerned about something
mind·ful *adj* : keeping in mind : AWARE
mind·less *adj* : using or requiring little attention or thought
¹mine *pron* : that which belongs to me
²mine *n* **1 :** a pit or tunnel from which minerals (as coal, gold, or diamonds) are taken **2 :** an explosive device placed in the ground or water and set to explode when disturbed (as by an enemy soldier, vehicle, or ship) **3 :** a rich source of supply
³mine *vb* **mined; min·ing** **1 :** to dig or work in a mine **2 :** to obtain from a mine **3 :** to place explosive mines in or under — **min·er** *n*
¹min·er·al *n* **1 :** a naturally occurring solid substance (as diamond, gold, or quartz) that is not of plant or animal origin **2 :** a naturally occurring substance (as ore, coal, salt, or petroleum) obtained from the ground usually for humans to use
²mineral *adj* **1 :** of or relating to minerals **2 :** containing gases or mineral salts
mineral kingdom *n* : a basic group of natural objects that includes objects consisting of matter that does not come from plants and animals
min·gle *vb* **min·gled; min·gling** **1 :** to bring or combine together or with something else **2 :** to move among others within a group
mini- *prefix* : very short or small
¹min·i·a·ture *n* **1 :** a copy of something that is much smaller than the original **2 :** a very small portrait especially on ivory or metal
²miniature *adj* : very small : represented on a small scale
min·i·mize *vb* **min·i·mized; min·i·miz·ing :** to make as small as possible
¹min·i·mum *n, pl* **min·i·mums** *or* **min·i·ma** : the lowest value : the least amount
²minimum *adj* : being the least or lowest possible
min·ing *n* : the process or business of digging in mines to obtain minerals
¹min·is·ter *n* **1 :** a person who performs religious ceremonies especially in Protestant church services **2 :** a government official at the head of a section of government activities **3 :** a person who represents his or her government in a foreign country
²minister *vb* **min·is·tered; min·is·ter·ing :** to give help or care
min·is·try *n, pl* **min·is·tries** **1 :** the office or duties of a religious minister **2 :** a group of religious ministers : CLERGY **3 :** a section of a government headed by a minister
mink *n, pl* **mink** *or* **minks** **1 :** a small animal related to the weasel that has partly webbed feet, lives around water, and feeds on smaller animals (as frogs, crabs, and mice) **2 :** the soft thick usually brown fur of a mink
Minn. *abbr* Minnesota
min·now *n* **1 :** a small freshwater fish (as a shiner) related to the carp **2 :** a fish that looks like a true minnow
¹mi·nor *adj* **1 :** not great in size, importance, or seriousness **2 :** of or relating to a musical scale having the third tone lowered a half step
²minor *n* : a person too young to have the full rights of an adult
mi·nor·i·ty *n, pl* **mi·nor·i·ties** **1 :** the state of not being old enough to have the full rights of an adult **2 :** a number less than half of a total **3 :** a group that makes up a smaller part of a larger group **4 :** a part of a population that is in some ways (as in race or religion) different from others
min·strel *n* **1 :** a musical entertainer in the Middle Ages **2 :** a member of a group of entertainers who performed black American melodies and jokes with blackened faces in the 19th and early 20th centuries
¹mint *n* **1 :** a fragrant plant (as catnip or peppermint) with square stems **2 :** a piece of candy flavored with mint
²mint *n* **1 :** a place where coins are made from metals **2 :** a great amount especially of money
³mint *vb* **mint·ed; mint·ing :** to make coins out of metal : COIN
min·u·end *n* : a number from which another number is to be subtracted
min·u·et *n* : a slow graceful dance

[1]mi·nus *prep* **1 :** with the subtraction of **:** LESS **2 :** [1]WITHOUT 2

[2]minus *adj* **1 :** having a value that is below zero **2 :** located in the lower part of a range

mi·nus·cule *adj* **:** very small

minus sign *n* **:** a sign – used especially in mathematics to indicate subtraction (as in 8–6=2) or a quantity less than zero (as in –15°)

[1]min·ute *n* **1 :** a unit of time equal to 60 seconds **:** the 60th part of an hour **2 :** MOMENT 1 **3 :** one of 60 equal parts into which a degree can be divided for measuring angles **4 minutes** *pl* **:** a brief record of what was said and done during a meeting

[2]mi·nute *adj* **mi·nut·er; mi·nut·est 1 :** very small **:** TINY **2 :** marked by or paying attention to small details — **mi·nute·ly** *adv*

min·ute·man *n, pl* **min·ute·men :** a member of a group of armed men who favored independence of the American colonies and who were ready to fight at a minute's notice immediately before and during the American Revolution

mir·a·cle *n* **1 :** an extraordinary event taken as a sign of the power of God **2 :** something (as an event or accomplishment) that is very outstanding, unusual, or wonderful

mi·rac·u·lous *adj* **:** being or being like a miracle **:** very wonderful or amazing — **mi·rac·u·lous·ly** *adv*

mi·rage *n* **:** an illusion sometimes seen at sea, in the desert, or over hot pavement that looks like a pool of water or a mirror in which distant objects are glimpsed

[1]mire *n* **:** heavy deep mud

[2]mire *vb* **mired; mir·ing :** to stick or cause to become stuck in or as if in heavy deep mud

[1]mir·ror *n* **1 :** a piece of glass that reflects images **2 :** something that gives a true likeness or description

[2]mirror *vb* **mir·rored; mir·ror·ing :** to reflect in or as if in a mirror

mirth *n* **:** happiness and laughter **:** merry behavior

mis- *prefix* **1 :** in a way that is bad or wrong **2 :** bad **:** wrong **3 :** opposite or lack of

mis·ad·ven·ture *n* **:** an unfortunate or unpleasant event

mis·be·have *vb* **mis·be·haved; mis·be·hav·ing :** to behave badly

mis·cal·cu·late *vb* **mis·cal·cu·lat·ed; mis·cal·cu·lat·ing :** to make a mistake in figuring or estimating

mis·car·ry *vb* **mis·car·ried; mis·car·ry·ing :** to go wrong **:** FAIL

mis·cel·la·neous *adj* **:** consisting of many things of different sorts

mis·chief *n* **1 :** behavior or activity that annoys or bothers but is not meant to cause serious harm **2 :** injury or damage caused by a person

mis·chie·vous *adj* **1 :** causing or likely to cause minor injury or harm **2 :** showing a spirit of irresponsible fun or playfulness **3 :** harming or intended to do harm — **mis·chie·vous·ly** *adv*

mis·con·duct *n* **:** bad behavior

mis·count *vb* **mis·count·ed; mis·count·ing :** to incorrectly determine the total of

mis·cre·ant *n* **:** VILLAIN, RASCAL

mis·deed *n* **:** a bad action

mis·de·mean·or *n* **1 :** a crime less serious than a felony **2 :** MISDEED

mis·di·rect *vb* **mis·di·rect·ed; mis·di·rect·ing :** to send to the wrong place

mi·ser *n* **:** a stingy person who lives poorly in order to store away money

mis·er·a·ble *adj* **1 :** very unhappy or distressed **2 :** causing great discomfort **3 :** very unsatisfactory — **mis·er·a·bly** *adv*

mi·ser·ly *adj* **:** STINGY

mis·ery *n, pl* **mis·er·ies :** great suffering or unhappiness

mis·fit *n* **1 :** something that is the wrong shape or size or is inappropriate **2 :** a person who does not seem to belong in a particular group or situation

mis·for·tune *n* **1 :** bad luck **2 :** an unfortunate situation or event

mis·giv·ing *n* **:** a feeling of distrust or doubt especially about what is going to happen

mis·guid·ed *adj* **:** having or resulting from mistaken ideas or values

mis·hap *n* **:** an unfortunate accident

mis·judge *vb* **mis·judged; mis·judg·ing :** to make a wrong or unfair judgment or estimate of

mis·lay *vb* **mis·laid; mis·lay·ing :** to put in a place later forgotten **:** LOSE

mis·lead *vb* **mis·led; mis·lead·ing :** to cause (someone) to believe something that is not true

mis·place *vb* **mis·placed; mis·plac·ing 1 :** to put (something) where it doesn't belong **2 :** MISLAY

mis·print *n* **:** a mistake in a word that has been printed

mis·pro·nounce *vb* **mis·pro·nounced; mis·pro·nounc·ing :** to say or make the sounds of incorrectly

mis·pro·nun·ci·a·tion *n* **:** the act or state of saying or making the sounds of incorrectly

mis·read *vb* **mis·read; mis·read·ing 1 :** to incorrectly pronounce or understand something written **2 :** MISUNDERSTAND

mis·rep·re·sent *vb* **mis·rep·re·sent·ed; mis·rep·re·sent·ing :** to give a false or misleading idea of

[1]miss *vb* **missed; miss·ing 1 :** to fail to hit,

catch, reach, or get **2 :** [1]ESCAPE 2 **3 :** to fail to arrive in time for **4 :** to feel or notice the absence of **5 :** to fail to take **6 :** to fail to be present for **7 :** to fail to hear or see

[2]**miss** *n* **:** failure to hit or catch

[3]**miss** *n* **1** *cap* — used as a title before the name of an unmarried woman **2 :** young lady — used without a name as a form of polite address to a girl or young woman

Miss. *abbr* Mississippi

mis·shap·en *adj* **:** badly shaped

mis·sile *n* **:** an object (as a stone, arrow, bullet, or rocket) that is dropped, thrown, shot, or launched usually so as to strike something at a distance

miss·ing *adj* **1 :** [1]ABSENT 1 **2 :** LOST 4

mis·sion *n* **1 :** a task that is assigned or begun **2 :** a task that is regarded as a very important duty **3 :** a group of missionaries **4 :** a group of people sent by a government to represent it in a foreign country **5 :** a place where the work of missionaries is carried on

[1]**mis·sion·ary** *n, pl* **mis·sion·ar·ies :** a person sent to a place to spread a religious faith

[2]**missionary** *adj* **:** relating to efforts to gain new religious followers or to people sent to spread a religion

mis·sive *n* **:** [1]LETTER 2

mis·spell *vb* **mis·spelled; mis·spell·ing :** to spell in an incorrect way

mis·step *n* **1 :** a wrong movement **2 :** [2]MISTAKE 2, SLIP

[1]**mist** *n* **:** very tiny drops of water floating in the air or falling as fine rain

[2]**mist** *vb* **mist·ed; mist·ing 1 :** to cover or become covered with tiny drops of water **2 :** to become wet with tears **3 :** to rain very lightly

[1]**mis·take** *vb* **mis·took; mis·tak·en; mis·tak·ing 1 :** MISUNDERSTAND **2 :** to fail to recognize correctly

[2]**mistake** *n* **1 :** a wrong judgment or action **2 :** something that is incorrect

mis·tak·en *adj* **1 :** being in error **:** judging wrongly **2 :** [2]WRONG 2, INCORRECT — **mis·tak·en·ly** *adv*

mis·ter *n* **1** *cap* — used sometimes in writing instead of the usual *Mr.* **2 :** SIR 1

mis·tle·toe *n* **:** a plant with waxy white berries that grows on the branches and trunks of trees

mis·treat *vb* **mis·treat·ed; mis·treat·ing :** to handle, use, or act toward in a harsh way **:** ABUSE

mis·tress *n* **1 :** a female teacher **2 :** a woman who has control or authority over another person, an animal, or a thing

[1]**mis·trust** *n* **:** [1]DISTRUST

[2]**mistrust** *vb* **mis·trust·ed; mis·trust·ing 1 :** [2]DISTRUST, SUSPECT **2 :** to lack confidence in

misty *adj* **mist·i·er; mist·i·est 1 :** full of very tiny drops of water **2 :** clouded by tears **3 :** VAGUE 3, INDISTINCT — **mist·i·ly** *adv*

mis·un·der·stand *vb* **mis·un·der·stood; mis·un·der·stand·ing :** to fail to get the meaning of **:** fail to understand

mis·un·der·stand·ing *n* **1 :** a failure to get the meaning of **:** a failure to understand **2 :** ARGUMENT 1, QUARREL

[1]**mis·use** *vb* **mis·used; mis·us·ing 1 :** to put into action or service in a wrong way **2 :** [2]ABUSE 1, MISTREAT

[2]**mis·use** *n* **:** incorrect or improper handling

mite *n* **1 :** a tiny animal that is related to and resembles the spider and often lives as a parasite on plants and other animals **2 :** a very small person, thing, or amount — **a mite :** [2]SOMEWHAT

mi·to·chon·dri·on *n, pl* **mi·to·chon·dria :** one of the parts found in the cytoplasm of a cell outside the nucleus that provides the cell with energy released from the breakdown of nutrients

mi·to·sis *n, pl* **mi·to·ses :** a process of cell division in which two new nuclei are formed each containing the original number of chromosomes

mitt *n* **1 :** MITTEN **2 :** a baseball catcher's or first baseman's glove

mit·ten *n* **:** a covering for the hand having a separate division for the thumb only

[1]**mix** *vb* **mixed; mix·ing 1 :** to make into one thing by stirring together **:** BLEND **2 :** to become one thing through blending **3 :** to make by combining different things **4 :** to bring together **5 :** to feel or act friendly toward — **mix·er** *n* — **mix up 1 :** CONFUSE 1 **2 :** to put in the wrong place with other things **3 :** to involve or cause to be involved with a bad situation or group

[2]**mix** *n* **1 :** MIXTURE 2 **2 :** a prepared combination of ingredients for making a food

mixed *adj* **1 :** made up of two or more kinds **2 :** made up of both females and males **3 :** made up of parts that are very different from one another

mixed number *n* **:** a number (as $1\frac{2}{3}$) made up of a whole number and a fraction

mix·ture *n* **1 :** the act of combining **2 :** something combined or being combined **3 :** two or more substances combined together in such a way that each remains unchanged **4 :** a combination of different things

mix–up *n* **:** an instance of confusion

miz·zen *n* **1 :** a fore-and-aft sail set on the mizzenmast **2 :** MIZZENMAST

miz·zen·mast *n* **:** the mast behind or next behind the mainmast

ml *abbr* milliliter

mm *abbr* millimeter

MN *abbr* Minnesota
mo. *abbr* month
MO *abbr* Missouri
¹moan *n* **1 :** a long low sound showing pain or grief **2 :** a long low sound
²moan *vb* **moaned; moan·ing** **1 :** to utter a long low sound **2 :** COMPLAIN
moat *n* **:** a deep wide ditch around the walls of a castle or fort that is usually filled with water
¹mob *n* **1 :** a rowdy excited crowd **2 :** the people of a society who are poor and uneducated
²mob *vb* **mobbed; mob·bing** **:** to crowd about in an aggressive, excited, or annoying way
¹mo·bile *adj* **1 :** easily moved **:** MOVABLE **2 :** changing quickly in expression
²mo·bile *n* **:** an artistic structure whose parts can be moved especially by air currents
mobile phone *n* **:** CELL PHONE
mo·bi·lize *vb* **mo·bi·lized; mo·bi·liz·ing** **:** to assemble (as military forces) and make ready for action
moc·ca·sin *n* **1 :** a soft shoe with no heel and the sole and sides made of one piece **2 :** WATER MOCCASIN
¹mock *vb* **mocked; mock·ing** **1 :** to treat with scorn **:** RIDICULE **2 :** ²MIMIC 2
²mock *adj* **:** not real **:** MAKE-BELIEVE
mock·ery *n, pl* **mock·er·ies** **1 :** ¹RIDICULE **2 :** a bad imitation **:** FAKE
mock·ing·bird *n* **:** a songbird of the southern United States noted for its imitations of other birds
¹mode *n* **1 :** a particular form or variety of something **2 :** a way of doing something
²mode *n* **:** a popular fashion or style
¹mod·el *n* **1 :** a small but exact copy of a thing **2 :** a pattern or figure of something to be made **3 :** a person who sets a good example **4 :** a person who poses for an artist or photographer **5 :** a person who wears and displays garments that are for sale **6 :** a special type of a product
²model *adj* **1 :** worthy of being imitated **2 :** being a miniature copy
³model *vb* **mod·eled** *or Can and Brit* **mod·elled; mod·el·ing** *or Can and Brit* **mod·el·ling** **1 :** to plan or shape after a pattern **2 :** to make a model of **3 :** to act or serve as a model
mo·dem *n* **:** a device that changes electrical signals from one form to another and is used especially to send or receive computer data over a telephone line
¹mod·er·ate *adj* **1 :** neither too much nor too little **2 :** neither very good nor very bad **3 :** not expensive **:** REASONABLE **4 :** not extreme or excessive — **mod·er·ate·ly** *adv*
²mod·er·ate *vb* **mod·er·at·ed; mod·er·at·ing** **:** to make or become less extreme or severe
mod·er·a·tion *n* **1 :** the act of avoiding extreme behavior or belief **2 :** the condition of being reasonable and not extreme
mod·ern *adj* **1 :** of or characteristic of the present time or times not long past **2 :** of a style or way of thinking that is new and different **3 :** having a style that is newer and different from older, more traditional styles **4 :** of the period from about 1500 to the present
mod·ern·ize *vb* **mod·ern·ized; mod·ern·iz·ing** **:** to make or become new and different or suitable for the present time
mod·est *adj* **1 :** not overly proud or confident **:** not boastful **2 :** limited in size or amount **3 :** not showy **4 :** decent in thought, conduct, and dress — **mod·est·ly** *adv*
mod·es·ty *n* **:** the quality of being decent or not boastful
mod·i·fi·ca·tion *n* **1 :** the act or process of changing parts of something **2 :** a slightly changed form
mod·i·fi·er *n* **:** a word (as an adjective or adverb) used with another word to limit its meaning
mod·i·fy *vb* **mod·i·fied; mod·i·fy·ing** **1 :** to make changes in **2 :** to lower or reduce in amount or scale **3 :** to limit in meaning **:** QUALIFY
mod·ule *n* **:** a part of a space vehicle that can work alone
mo·hair *n* **:** a fabric or yarn made from the long silky hair of an Asian goat
Mo·hawk *n, pl* **Mohawk** *or* **Mo·hawks** **1 :** a member of an American Indian people of central New York **2 :** the language of the Mohawk people
Mo·he·gan *or* **Mo·hi·can** *n, pl* **Mo·he·gan** *or* **Mo·he·gans** *or* **Mohican** *or* **Mo·hi·cans** **:** a member of an American Indian people of southeastern Connecticut
moist *adj* **:** slightly wet **:** DAMP — **moist·ness** *n*
moist·en *vb* **moist·ened; moist·en·ing** **:** to make damp
mois·ture *n* **:** a small amount of liquid that makes something slightly wet
mo·lar *n* **:** a large tooth near the back of the mouth with a broad surface used for grinding
mo·las·ses *n* **:** a thick brown syrup that is made from raw sugar
¹mold *or Can and Brit* **mould** *n* **1 :** a hollow form in which something is shaped **2 :** something shaped in a mold
²mold *or Can and Brit* **mould** *vb* **mold·ed/moulded; mold·ing/moulding** **1 :** to work and press into shape **2 :** to shape in a hollow form **3 :** to influence or affect the character of

³mold *or Can and Brit* **mould** *n* **1 :** an often fuzzy surface growth of fungus on damp or decaying material **2 :** a fungus that forms mold

⁴mold *or Can and Brit* **mould** *vb* **mold·ed/moulded; mold·ing/moulding :** to become moldy

⁵mold *or Can and Brit* **mould** *n* **:** light rich crumbly earth that contains decaying material

mold·ing *or Can and Brit* **moulding** *n* **:** a strip of material having a design and used as a decoration (as on a wall or the edge of a table)

moldy *or Can and Brit* **mouldy** *adj* **mold·i·er/mouldier; mold·i·est/mouldiest :** covered with or containing mold

¹mole *n* **:** a small usually brown spot on the skin

²mole *n* **:** a small burrowing animal with soft fur and very small eyes

mo·lec·u·lar *adj* **:** of or relating to a molecule

mol·e·cule *n* **:** the smallest portion of a substance having the properties of the substance

mole·hill *n* **:** a little ridge of dirt pushed up by a mole as it burrows underground

mo·lest *vb* **mo·lest·ed; mo·lest·ing :** to disturb or injure by interfering

mol·li·fy *vb* **mol·li·fied; mol·li·fy·ing :** to soothe in temper or disposition

mol·lusk *n* **:** an animal (as a clam, snail, or octopus) that lives mostly in water and has a soft body usually enclosed in a shell containing calcium

molt *vb* **molt·ed; molt·ing :** to shed outer material (as hair, shell, or horns) that will be replaced by a new growth

mol·ten *adj* **:** melted especially by very great heat

mo·lyb·de·num *n* **:** a white metallic chemical element used in some steel to give greater strength and hardness

mom *n* **:** ¹MOTHER 1

mo·ment *n* **1 :** a very brief time **2 :** present time **3 :** IMPORTANCE

mo·men·tary *adj* **:** lasting only a very brief time — **mo·men·tar·i·ly** *adv*

mo·men·tous *adj* **:** very important

mo·men·tum *n* **:** the force that a moving body has because of its weight and motion

momma *variant of* MAMA

mom·my *n, pl* **mom·mies :** ¹MOTHER 1

Mon. *abbr* Monday

mon- *or* **mono-** *prefix* **:** one **:** single **:** alone

mon·arch *n* **1 :** a person who reigns over a kingdom or an empire **2 :** MONARCH BUTTERFLY

monarch butterfly *n* **:** a large orange and black American butterfly

mon·ar·chy *n, pl* **mon·ar·chies 1 :** a state or country having a king or queen **2 :** a form of government headed by a king or queen

mon·as·tery *n, pl* **mon·as·ter·ies :** a place where a community of monks lives and works

mo·nas·tic *adj* **:** of or relating to monks or monasteries

Mon·day *n* **:** the second day of the week

mo·ner·an *n* **:** any member of the kingdom of living things (as bacteria) consisting of a single simple cell that lacks a nucleus

mon·e·tary *adj* **:** of or relating to money

mon·ey *n, pl* **moneys** *or* **mon·ies 1 :** something (such as coins or bills) used to buy goods and services and to pay people for their work **2 :** a person's wealth

money order *n* **:** a piece of paper like a check that can be bought (as at a post office) and that orders payment of a sum of money printed on it to the person named

mon·goose *n, pl* **mon·goos·es :** a long thin furry animal with sharp claws that eats small animals (as snakes and mice), eggs, and fruit

¹mon·grel *n* **:** an animal of mixed or uncertain origin

²mongrel *adj* **:** of mixed or uncertain origin

¹mon·i·tor *n* **1 :** a video screen used for display **2 :** a student in a school picked for a special duty (as keeping order) **3 :** a person or thing that watches or checks something

²monitor *vb* **mon·i·tored; mon·i·tor·ing :** to watch or check for a special reason

monk *n* **:** a member of a religious group of men who promise to stay poor, obey the rules of their group, and not get married

¹mon·key *n, pl* **monkeys :** a furry animal of warm regions that has a long tail and that along with the apes is most closely related to humans

²monkey *vb* **mon·keyed; mon·key·ing 1 :** to spend time in an idle or aimless way **2 :** to handle secretly or in a careless or incorrect way

mon·key·shine *n* **:** PRANK — usually used in pl.

monkey wrench *n* **1 :** a wrench with one fixed and one adjustable jaw **2 :** something that disrupts

mono- — see MON-

mono·gram *n* **:** a design usually made by combining two or more of a person's initials

mono·plane *n* **:** an airplane with only one large wing that crosses the body

mo·nop·o·lize *vb* **mo·nop·o·lized; mo·nop·o·liz·ing :** to get or have complete control over

mo·nop·o·ly *n, pl* **mo·nop·o·lies 1 :** complete ownership or control of the entire supply of goods or a service in a certain market **2 :** a person or group having complete control over something **3 :** complete ownership or control of something

mono·syl·la·ble *n* **:** a word of one syllable

mo·not·o·nous *adj* **:** boring from always being the same — **mo·not·o·nous·ly** *adv*

mo·not·o·ny *n, pl* **mo·not·o·nies** : a boring lack of change
mon·soon *n* **1** : a wind in the Indian Ocean and southern Asia that blows from the southwest from April to October and from the northeast from October to April **2** : the rainy season that comes with the southwest monsoon
mon·ster *n* **1** : a strange or horrible creature **2** : something unusually large **3** : an extremely wicked or cruel person
mon·stros·i·ty *n, pl* **mon·stros·i·ties** : something that is large and ugly
mon·strous *adj* **1** : unusually large : ENORMOUS **2** : very bad or wrong **3** : having the qualities or appearance of a monster — **mon·strous·ly** *adv*
Mont. *abbr* Montana
month *n* : one of the twelve parts into which the year is divided
[1]**month·ly** *adj* **1** : happening, done, or published every month **2** : figured in terms of one month **3** : lasting a month — **monthly** *adv*
[2]**monthly** *n, pl* **monthlies** : a magazine published every month
mon·u·ment *n* **1** : a structure (as a building, stone, or statue) made to keep alive the memory of a person or event **2** : something that serves as a good reminder or example
[1]**moo** *vb* **mooed; moo·ing** : to make the sound of a cow : LOW
[2]**moo** *n, pl* **moos** : the low sound made by a cow
mooch *vb* **mooched; mooch·ing** : to get things from another person or live off the generosity of others without repayment — **mooch·er** *n*
[1]**mood** *n* : an emotional state of mind or feeling
[2]**mood** *n* : a set of forms of a verb that show whether the action or state expressed is to be thought of as a fact, a command, or a wish or possibility
moody *adj* **mood·i·er; mood·i·est** : often feeling or showing a gloomy or a bad frame of mind — **mood·i·ly** *adv* — **mood·i·ness** *n*
[1]**moon** *n* **1** : the natural celestial body that shines by reflecting light from the sun and revolves about the earth in about 29½ days **2** : SATELLITE 1
[2]**moon** *vb* **mooned; moon·ing** : [2]DAYDREAM
moon·beam *n* : a ray of light from the moon
moon·light *n* : the light of the moon
moon·lit *adj* : lighted by the moon
moon·shine *n* **1** : MOONLIGHT **2** : alcoholic liquor produced illegally
moon·stone *n* : a partly transparent shining stone used as a gem
[1]**moor** *n* : an area of open land that is too wet or too poor for farming
[2]**moor** *vb* **moored; moor·ing** : to fasten in place with cables, lines, or anchors
moor·ing *n* **1** : a place where a boat can be fastened so it will not float away **2** : a chain or line used to hold a boat in place
moor·land *n* : land consisting of ground that is too wet or too poor for farming
moose *n, pl* **moose** : a large animal with broad flattened antlers and humped shoulders that is related to the deer and lives in forests of Canada, the northern United States, Europe, and Asia
[1]**mop** *n* **1** : a tool for cleaning floors made of a bundle of cloth or yarn or a sponge fastened to a long handle **2** : something that looks like a cloth or yarn mop
[2]**mop** *vb* **mopped; mop·ping** : to wipe or clean with or as if with a mop
mope *vb* **moped; mop·ing** : to be in a dull and sad state of mind
mo·raine *n* : a pile of earth and stones left by a glacier
[1]**mor·al** *adj* **1** : concerned with or relating to what is right and wrong in human behavior **2** : able to teach a lesson of how people should behave **3** : [1]GOOD 13, VIRTUOUS **4** : able to tell right from wrong — **mor·al·ly** *adv*
[2]**moral** *n* **1** : the lesson to be learned from a story or experience **2 morals** *pl* : ways of behaving : moral conduct **3 morals** *pl* : teachings or rules of right behavior
mo·rale *n* : the condition of the mind or feelings (as in relation to enthusiasm, spirit, or hope) of an individual or group
mo·ral·i·ty *n, pl* **mo·ral·i·ties** **1** : the quality or fact of being in agreement with ideals of right behavior **2** : beliefs about what kind of behavior is good or bad
mo·rass *n* : MARSH, SWAMP
mo·ray eel *n* : an often brightly colored eel of warm seas with sharp teeth
mor·bid *adj* **1** : not healthy or normal **2** : having or showing an interest in unpleasant or gloomy things
[1]**more** *adj* **1** : greater in amount, number, or size **2** : [1]EXTRA, ADDITIONAL
[2]**more** *adv* **1** : in addition **2** : to a greater extent — often used with an adjective or adverb to form the comparative
[3]**more** *n* **1** : a greater amount or number **2** : an additional amount
more·over *adv* : in addition to what has been said : BESIDES
morn *n* : MORNING
morn·ing *n* : the early part of the day : the time from sunrise to noon
morning glory *n* : a vine that climbs by

DICTIONARY

twisting around something and has large trumpet-shaped flowers that close in bright sunshine

morning star *n* **:** a bright planet (as Venus) seen in the eastern sky before or at sunrise

mo·ron *n* **:** a stupid or foolish person

mo·rose *adj* **:** very serious, unhappy, and quiet

mor·phine *n* **:** a habit-forming drug made from opium and used to relieve pain

mor·row *n* **:** the next day

Morse code *n* **:** a system of sending messages that uses long and short sounds or dots and dashes to represent letters and numbers

mor·sel *n* **:** a small amount **:** a little piece (as of food)

[1]mor·tal *adj* **1 :** capable of causing death **2 :** certain to die **3 :** feeling great and lasting hatred **4 :** very great or overpowering **5 :** [1]HUMAN 1 — **mor·tal·ly** *adv*

[2]mortal *n* **:** a human being

[1]mor·tar *n* **1 :** a strong deep bowl in which substances are pounded or crushed with a pestle **2 :** a short light cannon used to shoot shells high into the air

[2]mortar *n* **:** a building material made of lime and cement mixed with sand and water that is spread between bricks or stones so as to hold them together when it hardens

[1]mort·gage *n* **1 :** a transfer of rights to a piece of property (as a house) that is usually in return for a loan of money and that is canceled when the loan is paid **2 :** the document recording such a transfer

[2]mortgage *vb* **mort·gaged; mort·gag·ing :** to transfer rights to a piece of property in return for a loan of money with the understanding that the rights end when the loan is paid

mor·ti·fy *vb* **mor·ti·fied; mor·ti·fy·ing :** to embarrass greatly

mo·sa·ic *n* **:** a decoration on a surface made by setting small pieces of glass, stone, or tile of different colors into another material to make patterns or pictures

Mos·lem *variant of* MUSLIM

mosque *n* **:** a building in which Muslims worship

mos·qui·to *n, pl* **mos·qui·toes :** a small fly the female of which punctures the skin of people and animals to suck their blood

moss *n* **1 :** a plant that has no flowers and grows as a small leafy stem in patches like cushions clinging to rocks, bark, or damp ground **2 :** a plant or plantlike organism (as a lichen) resembling moss

mossy *adj* **moss·i·er; moss·i·est :** like or covered with moss

[1]most *adj* **1 :** the majority of **:** almost all **2 :** greatest in amount or extent

[2]most *adv* **1 :** to the greatest or highest level or extent — often used with an adjective or adverb to form the superlative **2 :** VERY

[3]most *n* **:** the greatest amount, number, or part

most·ly *adv* **:** for the greatest part

mote *n* **:** a small particle **:** SPECK

mo·tel *n* **:** a building or group of buildings for travelers to stay in which the rooms are usually reached directly from an outdoor parking area

moth *n, pl* **moths :** an insect that usually flies at night and has mostly feathery antennae and stouter body, duller coloring, and smaller wings than the related butterflies

[1]moth·er *n* **1 :** a female parent **2 :** a nun in charge of a convent **3 :** [1]CAUSE 1, ORIGIN — **moth·er·hood** *n* — **moth·er·less** *adj*

[2]mother *adj* **1 :** of or having to do with a mother **2 :** being in a relation suggesting that of a mother to others

[3]mother *vb* **moth·ered; moth·er·ing :** to be or act as a mother to

moth·er·board *n* **:** the main circuit board especially of a small computer

moth·er–in–law *n, pl* **mothers–in–law :** the mother of someone's husband or wife

moth·er·ly *adj* **1 :** of or characteristic of a mother **2 :** like a mother

Mother Nature *n* **:** nature represented as a woman thought of as the guiding force behind natural events

moth·er–of–pearl *n* **:** a hard pearly material that lines the shell of some mollusks (as mussels) and is often used for ornamental objects and buttons

[1]mo·tion *n* **1 :** an act or process of changing place or position **:** MOVEMENT **2** a movement of the body or its parts **3 :** a formal plan or suggestion for action offered according to the rules of a meeting — **mo·tion·less** *adj*

[2]motion *vb* **mo·tioned; mo·tion·ing :** to direct or signal by a movement or sign

motion picture *n* **1 :** a series of pictures projected on a screen rapidly one after another so as to give the appearance of a continuous picture in which the objects move **2 :** MOVIE 1

mo·ti·vate *vb* **mo·ti·vat·ed; mo·ti·vat·ing :** to give or be a reason for doing something

[1]mo·tive *n* **:** a reason for doing something

[2]motive *adj* **:** causing motion

mot·ley *adj* **:** composed of various often unlike kinds or parts

[1]mo·tor *n* **:** a machine that produces motion or power for doing work

[2]motor *adj* **1 :** of, relating to, or designed for use in an automobile **2 :** equipped with or driven by a motor **3 :** causing or controlling movement

[3]motor *vb* **mo·tored; mo·tor·ing :** [1]DRIVE 2

mo·tor·bike *n* : a small usually lightweight motorcycle
mo·tor·boat *n* : an often small boat driven by a motor
mo·tor·cade *n* : a line of motor vehicles traveling as a group
mo·tor·car *n* : AUTOMOBILE
mo·tor·cy·cle *n* : a motorized vehicle for one or two passengers that has two wheels
mo·tor·ist *n* : a person who travels by automobile
mo·tor·ized *adj* **1** : having a motor **2** : using motor vehicles for transportation
motor scooter *n* : a motorized vehicle having two or three wheels like a child's scooter but having a seat
motor vehicle *n* : a motorized vehicle (as an automobile or motorcycle) not operated on rails
mot·tled *adj* : having spots or blotches of different colors
mot·to *n, pl* **mottoes** **1** : a phrase or word inscribed on something (as a coin or public building) to suggest its use or nature **2** : a short expression of a guiding rule of conduct
mould, moulding, mouldy *chiefly Can and Brit spelling of* MOLD, MOLDING, MOLDY
[1]**mound** *n* **1** : a small hill or heap of dirt or stones **2** : [1]HEAP 1, PILE **3** : the slightly raised ground on which a baseball pitcher stands
[2]**mound** *vb* **mound·ed; mound·ing** : to make a pile or heap of
[1]**mount** *n* : a high hill : MOUNTAIN — used especially before a proper name
[2]**mount** *vb* **mount·ed; mount·ing** **1** : to go up : CLIMB **2** : to get up onto something **3** : to increase rapidly in amount **4** : to prepare for use or display by fastening in position on a support **5** : to organize and carry out
[3]**mount** *n* **1** : a frame or support that holds something **2** : a horse used for riding
moun·tain *n* **1** : a raised area of land higher than a hill **2** : a great mass or huge number
moun·tain·eer *n* **1** : a person who lives in the mountains **2** : a mountain climber
mountain goat *n* : a goatlike animal of the mountains of western North America with a thick white coat and slightly curved black horns
mountain lion *n* : COUGAR
moun·tain·ous *adj* **1** : having many mountains **2** : like a mountain in size : HUGE
moun·tain·side *n* : the side of a mountain
moun·tain·top *n* : the highest part of a mountain
mount·ing *n* : a frame or support that holds something
mourn *vb* **mourned; mourn·ing** : to feel or show grief or sorrow especially over someone's death — **mourn·er** *n*
mourn·ful *adj* **1** : full of sorrow or sadness **2** : causing sorrow — **mourn·ful·ly** *adv* — **mourn·ful·ness** *n*
mourn·ing *n* **1** : the act of feeling or expressing sorrow **2** : an outward sign (as black clothes or an arm band) of grief for a person's death
mourning dove *n* : a dove of the United States named from its mournful cry
mouse *n, pl* **mice** **1** : a very small furry gnawing animal that is a rodent with a pointed snout and long slender tail **2** : a person without spirit or courage **3** *pl also* **mous·es** : a small movable device that is connected to a computer and used to move the cursor and select functions on the screen — **mouse·like** *adj*
mouse pad *n* : a thin flat pad (as of rubber) on which a computer mouse is used
mous·er *n* : a cat good at catching mice
moustache *chiefly Can and Brit spelling of* MUSTACHE
[1]**mouth** *n, pl* **mouths** **1** : the opening through which food passes into the body and which in humans is surrounded on the outside by the lips and contains the tongue and teeth **2** : an opening that is like a mouth **3** : the place where a stream enters a larger body of water
[2]**mouth** *vb* **mouthed; mouth·ing** **1** : to form with the lips without speaking **2** : to repeat without being sincere or without understanding
mouthed *adj* : having a mouth especially of a specified kind
mouth·ful *n* **1** : as much as the mouth will hold **2** : the amount put into the mouth at one time **3** : a word or phrase that is very long or difficult to say
mouth·piece *n* : the part put to, between, or near the lips
mov·able *or* **move·able** *adj* **1** : possible to move **2** : changing date from year to year
[1]**move** *vb* **moved; mov·ing** **1** : to go from one place to another **2** : to change the place or position of : SHIFT **3** : to set in motion **4** : to cause to act : PERSUADE **5** : to affect the feelings of **6** : to change position **7** : to change residence **8** : to suggest according to the rules in a meeting
[2]**move** *n* **1** : the action of changing position, place, or residence **2** : the act of moving a piece in a game **3** : the turn of a player to move **4** : an action taken to accomplish something
move·ment *n* **1** : the act or process of moving and especially changing place or position : an instance of moving **2** : a program or series of acts working toward a desired end **3** : a mechanical arrangement (as of

wheels) for causing a particular motion (as in a clock or watch) **4 :** a section of a longer piece of music **5 :** an emptying of waste matter from the bowels

mov·er *n* **:** a person or company that moves the belongings of others (as from one home to another)

mov·ie *n* **1 :** a story represented in motion pictures **2 :** a showing of a movie — often used in pl.

mov·ing *adj* **1 :** changing place or position **2 :** causing feelings of sadness or sympathy **3 :** used for transporting belongings from one place to another — **mov·ing·ly** *adv*

moving picture *n* **:** MOTION PICTURE 1

[1]**mow** *n* **:** the part of a barn where hay or straw is stored

[2]**mow** *vb* **mowed; mowed** *or* **mown; mow·ing 1 :** to cut down with a blade or machine **2 :** to cut the standing plant cover from **3 :** to cause to fall in a violent way — **mow·er** *n*

mpg *abbr* miles per gallon

mph *abbr* miles per hour

MP3 *n* **1 :** a computer format for creating sound files (as songs) that are much smaller than standard sound files **2 :** a computer file (as of a song) in the MP3 format

Mr. *n, pl* **Messrs.** — used as a title before a man's name

Mrs. *n, pl* **Mes·dames** — used as a title before a married woman's name

Ms. *n* — often used instead of *Miss* or *Mrs.*

MS *abbr* Mississippi

mt. *abbr* **1** mount **2** mountain

MT *abbr* Montana

[1]**much** *adj* **more; most 1 :** great in amount or extent **2 :** great in importance **3 :** more than enough

[2]**much** *adv* **more; most 1 :** to a great or high level or extent **2 :** just about **:** NEARLY

[3]**much** *n* **1 :** a great amount or part **2 :** something important or impressive

mu·ci·lage *n* **:** a water solution of a gum or similar substance used especially to stick things together

muck *n* **1 :** MUD, MIRE **2 :** soft moist barnyard manure **3 :** DIRT 2, FILTH

mu·cous *adj* **:** containing or producing mucus

mu·cus *n* **:** a slippery thick sticky substance that coats, protects, and moistens the linings of body passages and spaces (as of the nose, lungs, and intestines)

mud *n* **:** soft wet earth or dirt

[1]**mud·dle** *vb* **mud·dled; mud·dling 1 :** to be or cause to be confused or bewildered **2 :** to mix up in a confused manner **3 :** to think or proceed in a confused way

[2]**muddle** *n* **:** a state of confusion

[1]**mud·dy** *adj* **mud·di·er; mud·di·est 1 :** filled or covered with mud **2 :** looking like mud **3 :** not clear or bright **:** DULL **4 :** being mixed up

[2]**muddy** *vb* **mud·died; mud·dy·ing 1 :** to soil or stain with or as if with mud **2 :** to make cloudy or dull (as in color)

[1]**muff** *n* **:** a soft thick cover into which both hands can be placed to protect them from cold

[2]**muff** *vb* **muffed; muff·ing :** to make a mistake in doing or handling

muf·fin *n* **:** a bread made of batter containing eggs and baked in a small cup-shaped container

muf·fle *vb* **muf·fled; muf·fling 1 :** to deaden the sound of **2 :** to wrap up so as to hide or protect

muf·fler *n* **1 :** a scarf for the neck **2 :** a device to deaden the noise of an engine (as of an automobile)

mug *n* **:** a large drinking cup with a handle

mug·gy *adj* **mug·gi·er; mug·gi·est :** being very warm and humid — **mug·gi·ness** *n*

Mu·ham·mad *n* **:** the founder of Islam

mul·ber·ry *n, pl* **mul·ber·ries :** a tree that bears edible usually purple berries and has leaves on which silkworms can be fed

[1]**mulch** *n* **:** a material (as straw or bark) spread over the ground especially to protect the roots of plants from heat or cold, to keep soil moist, and to control weeds

[2]**mulch** *vb* **mulched; mulch·ing :** to cover with mulch

mule *n* **1 :** an animal that is an offspring of a donkey and a horse **2 :** a stubborn person

mul·ish *adj* **:** STUBBORN 1 — **mul·ish·ly** *adv*

mull *vb* **mulled; mull·ing :** to think about slowly and carefully **:** PONDER

mulled *adj* **:** mixed with sugar and spice and served warm

mul·let *n* **:** any of various chiefly saltwater fishes some mostly gray (**gray mullets**) and others red or golden (**red mullets**) that are often used as food

multi- *prefix* **1 :** many **:** much **2 :** more than two **3 :** many times over

mul·ti·col·ored *adj* **:** having, made up of, or including many colors

mul·ti·cul·tur·al *adj* **:** relating to or made up of several different cultures

mul·ti·me·dia *adj* **:** using or composed of more than one form of communication or expression

[1]**mul·ti·ple** *adj* **:** being or consisting of more than one

[2]**multiple** *n* **:** the number found by multiplying one number by another

mul·ti·pli·cand *n* **:** a number that is to be multiplied by another number

mul·ti·pli·ca·tion *n* **:** a short way of finding out what would be the result of adding one number the number of times indicated by a second number

mul·ti·pli·er *n* : a number by which another number is multiplied

mul·ti·ply *vb* **mul·ti·plied; mul·ti·ply·ing 1** : to increase in number : make or become more numerous **2** : to find the product of by means of multiplication

mul·ti·tude *n* : a great number of people or things

[1]**mum** *adj* : SILENT 4

[2]**mum** *chiefly Brit spelling of* MOM

[1]**mum·ble** *vb* **mum·bled; mum·bling** : to speak softly so that words are not clear

[2]**mumble** *n* : speech that is not clear enough to be understood

mum·my *n, pl* **mummies** : a dead body preserved for burial in the manner of the ancient Egyptians

mumps *n pl* : a contagious disease marked especially by fever and swelling of the glands around the lower jaw — used as singular or plural

munch *vb* **munched; munch·ing** : to eat or chew especially with a crunching sound

mu·nic·i·pal *adj* : of or relating to the government of a town or city

mu·nic·i·pal·i·ty *n, pl* **mu·nic·i·pal·i·ties** : a town or city having its own local government

mu·ni·tion *n* : military equipment and supplies for fighting : AMMUNITION

mural *n* : a usually large painting on a wall

[1]**mur·der** *n* : the intentional and unlawful killing of a human being

[2]**murder** *vb* **mur·dered; mur·der·ing 1** : to kill (someone) intentionally and unlawfully **2** : to spoil or ruin by performing or using badly — **mur·der·er** *n*

mur·der·ous *adj* **1** : intending or capable of causing murder : DEADLY **2** : very hard to bear or withstand

murk *n* : darkness or fog that is hard to see through

murky *adj* **murk·i·er; murk·i·est 1** : very dark or foggy **2** : CLOUDY 2 **3** : not clearly expressed or understood

[1]**mur·mur** *n* **1** : a low faint sound **2** : a quiet expression of an opinion or feeling

[2]**murmur** *vb* **mur·mured; mur·mur·ing 1** : to make a low faint sound **2** : to say in a voice too quiet to be heard clearly

mus·cle *n* **1** : a tissue of the body consisting of long cells that can contract and produce motion **2** : an organ of the body that is a mass of muscle tissue attached at either end (as to bones) so that it can make a body part move **3** : strength of the muscles

mus·cle–bound *adj* : having large muscles that do not move and stretch easily

mus·cu·lar *adj* **1** : of, relating to, or done by the muscles **2** : having large and strong muscles

muse *vb* **mused; mus·ing** : to think about carefully or thoroughly : PONDER

mu·se·um *n* : a building in which objects of interest or value are displayed

[1]**mush** *n* **1** : cornmeal boiled in water or milk **2** : something that is soft and wet and often shapeless

[2]**mush** *vb* **mushed; mush·ing** : to travel across snow with a sled pulled by dogs

[1]**mush·room** *n* : a part of a fungus that bears spores, grows above ground, and suggests an umbrella in shape

[2]**mushroom** *vb* **mush·roomed; mush·room·ing** : to appear or develop suddenly or increase rapidly

mushy *adj* **mush·i·er; mush·i·est 1** : soft and wet **2** : overly romantic or sentimental

mu·sic *n* **1** : an arrangement of sounds having melody, rhythm and usually harmony **2** : the art of producing pleasing or expressive combinations of tones especially with melody, rhythm, and usually harmony **3** : a musical composition set down on paper **4** : a pleasing sound

[1]**mu·si·cal** *adj* **1** : having to do with music or the writing or performing of music **2** : pleasing like music **3** : fond of or talented in music **4** : set to music — **mu·si·cal·ly** *adv*

[2]**musical** *n* : a movie or play that tells a story with both speaking and singing

music box *n* : a box that contains a mechanical device which uses gears like those of a clock to play a tune when the box is open

mu·si·cian *n* : a person who writes, sings, or plays music with skill and especially as a profession

musk *n* : a strong-smelling material that is used in perfumes and is obtained from a gland of an Asian deer (**musk deer**) or is prepared artificially

mus·ket *n* : a firearm that is loaded through the muzzle and that was once used by soldiers trained to fight on foot

mus·ke·teer *n* : a soldier armed with a musket

musk·mel·on *n* : a small round to oval melon (as a cantaloupe) with sweet usually green or orange flesh

musk ox *n* : a shaggy animal like an ox found in Greenland and northern North America

musk·rat *n, pl* **muskrat** *or* **musk·rats** : a North American animal that is a rodent living in or near water and having webbed hind feet, a long scaly tail, and glossy usually dark brown fur

musky *adj* **musk·i·er; musk·i·est** : having an odor of or resembling musk

Mus·lim *n* : a person whose religion is Islam

mus·lin *n* : a cotton fabric of plain weave

[1]**muss** *n* : a state of disorder : MESS

²muss *vb* **mussed; muss·ing** : to make messy or untidy

mus·sel *n* **1 :** a saltwater shellfish that has a long dark shell in two parts and is sometimes used as food **2 :** a freshwater clam of the United States with shells from which mother-of-pearl is obtained

¹must *helping verb, present and past all persons* **must** **1 :** to be commanded, requested, or urged to **2 :** to be required to **3 :** to be very likely to

²must *n* **:** something that is or seems to be required or necessary

mus·tache *or chiefly Can and Brit* **moustache** *n* **:** the hair growing on the human upper lip

mus·tang *n* **:** a small hardy wild horse of the western United States that is descended from horses brought in by the Spaniards

mus·tard *n* **:** a sharp-tasting yellow powder that is prepared from the seeds of a plant related to the cabbage and is used especially as a seasoning for foods

¹mus·ter *n* **1 :** a formal gathering of military troops for inspection **2 :** an act of careful examination or consideration to determine whether something is acceptable or good enough

²muster *vb* **mus·tered; mus·ter·ing** **1 :** to call together (as troops) for roll call or inspection **2 :** to bring into being or action

mustn't : must not

musty *adj* **must·i·er; must·i·est :** smelling of dampness, decay, or lack of fresh air

¹mu·tant *adj* **:** resulting from genetic mutation

²mutant *n* **:** a plant, animal, or microorganism resulting from genetic mutation

mu·tate *vb* **mu·tat·ed; mu·tat·ing** **:** to undergo genetic mutation

mu·ta·tion *n* **:** a change in a gene or the resulting new trait it produces in an individual

¹mute *adj* **mut·er; mut·est** **1 :** unable or unwilling to speak **2 :** felt or expressed without the use of words

²mute *n* **1 :** a person who cannot or does not speak **2 :** a device on a musical instrument that deadens, softens, or muffles its tone

³mute *vb* **mut·ed; mut·ing** **:** to soften or reduce the sound of

mu·ti·late *vb* **mu·ti·lat·ed; mu·ti·lat·ing** **1 :** to destroy or cut off a necessary part (as a limb) **:** MAIM **2 :** to ruin by damaging or changing

mu·ti·neer *n* **:** a person who takes part in a mutiny

mu·ti·nous *adj* **1 :** involved in turning against a person in charge (as the captain of a ship) **2 :** feeling or showing a desire to disobey

¹mu·ti·ny *n, pl* **mu·ti·nies** **1 :** a turning of a group (as of sailors) against a person in charge **2 :** refusal to obey those in charge

²mutiny *vb* **mu·ti·nied; mu·ti·ny·ing :** to try to take control away from a person in charge

mutt *n* **:** a dog that is a mix of usually undetermined breeds

mut·ter *vb* **mut·tered; mut·ter·ing** **1 :** to speak in a low voice with lips partly closed **2 :** to complain in a low voice **:** GRUMBLE

mut·ton *n* **:** the meat of an adult sheep

mu·tu·al *adj* **1 :** given and received in equal amount **2 :** having the same relation to one another **3 :** shared by two or more at the same time — **mu·tu·al·ly** *adv*

¹muz·zle *n* **1 :** the nose and mouth of an animal (as a dog) **2 :** a covering for the mouth of an animal to prevent it from biting or eating **3 :** the open end of a gun from which the bullet comes out when the gun is fired

²muzzle *vb* **muz·zled; muz·zling** **1 :** to put a muzzle on **2 :** to keep from free expression of ideas or opinions

my *adj* **:** belonging or relating to me or myself

my·nah *or* **my·na** *n* **:** an Asian bird that is related to the starling and can be trained to mimic words

¹myr·i·ad *n* **:** a very large number of things

²myriad *adj* **:** many in number **:** extremely numerous

myrrh *n* **:** a sticky brown fragrant material obtained from African and Arabian trees and used especially in perfumes or formerly in incense

myr·tle *n* **1 :** an evergreen shrub of southern Europe with fragrant flowers **2 :** ¹PERIWINKLE

my·self *pron* **:** my own self — **by myself :** ALONE

mys·te·ri·ous *adj* **:** strange, unknown, or hard to understand or explain — **mys·te·ri·ous·ly** *adv* — **mys·te·ri·ous·ness** *n*

mys·tery *n, pl* **mys·ter·ies** **1 :** something that has not been or cannot be explained **2 :** a piece of fiction about solving a crime

mys·tic *adj* **1 :** MYSTICAL **2 :** relating to magic **3 :** MYSTERIOUS

mys·ti·cal *adj* **:** having a spiritual meaning that is difficult to see or understand

mys·ti·fy *vb* **mys·ti·fied; mys·ti·fy·ing** **:** to confuse or bewilder completely

myth *n* **1 :** a story often describing the adventures of beings with more than human powers that attempts to explain mysterious events (as the changing of the seasons) or that explains a religious belief or practice **2 :** such stories as a group **3 :** a person or thing existing only in the imagination **4 :** a popular belief that is not true

myth·i·cal *adj* **1 :** based on or told of in a myth **2 :** IMAGINARY

my·thol·o·gy *n, pl* **my·thol·o·gies** **:** a collection of myths

N

n *n, pl* **n's** *or* **ns** *often cap* **:** the 14th letter of the English alphabet
n *abbr* noun
N *abbr* **1** north **2** northern
-n — see -EN
nab *vb* **nabbed; nab·bing :** [1]ARREST 1
na·cho *n, pl* **nachos :** a tortilla chip topped with melted cheese and often additional toppings
[1]**nag** *vb* **nagged; nag·ging 1 :** to annoy by repeated complaining, scolding, or urging **2 :** to annoy continually or again and again
[2]**nag** *n* **:** an old and usually worn-out horse
na·iad *n, pl* **na·iads** *or* **na·ia·des :** a nymph believed in ancient times to be living in lakes, rivers, and springs
[1]**nail** *n* **1 :** a tough covering protecting the upper end of each finger and toe **2 :** a slender pointed piece of metal driven into or through something for fastening
[2]**nail** *vb* **nailed; nail·ing :** to fasten with or as if with a nail
na·ive *or* **na·ïve** *adj* **na·iv·er; na·iv·est 1 :** lacking experience or knowledge **2 :** being simple and sincere — **na·ive·ly** *adv*
na·ked *adj* **1 :** having no clothes on **:** NUDE **2 :** lacking a usual or natural covering **3 :** not in its case or without a covering **4 :** stripped of anything misleading **:** PLAIN **5 :** not aided by an artificial device — **na·ked·ly** *adv* — **na·ked·ness** *n*
[1]**name** *n* **1 :** a word or combination of words by which a person or thing is known **2 :** REPUTATION 2 **3 :** a word or phrase used to describe and insult someone
[2]**name** *vb* **named; nam·ing 1 :** to choose a word or words by which something will be known **:** give a name to **2 :** to refer to by the word by which a person or thing is known **:** call by name **3 :** to appoint to a job of authority **4 :** to decide on **5 :** [2]MENTION **6 :** to choose to be
[3]**name** *adj* **:** well known because of wide distribution
name·less *adj* **1 :** having no name **2 :** not marked with a name **3 :** [1]UNKNOWN, ANONYMOUS **4 :** not to be described
name·ly *adv* **:** that is to say
name·sake *n* **:** a person who has the same name as someone else
nan·ny *n, pl* **nannies :** a child's nurse
nanny goat *n* **:** a female goat
[1]**nap** *n* **:** a short sleep especially during the day
[2]**nap** *vb* **napped; nap·ping 1 :** to sleep briefly especially during the day **2 :** to be unprepared
[3]**nap** *n* **:** a hairy or fluffy surface (as on cloth)
nape *n* **:** the back of the neck
naph·tha *n* **:** any of various usually flammable liquids prepared from coal or petroleum and used especially to dissolve substances
nap·kin *n* **:** a small piece of cloth or paper used when eating to wipe the lips or fingers and protect the clothes
nar·cis·sus *n, pl* **narcissus** *or* **nar·cis·sus·es** *or* **nar·cis·si :** a daffodil with flowers that have short trumpet-shaped tubes
[1]**nar·cot·ic** *n* **:** an addicting drug that in small doses dulls the senses, relieves pain, and brings on sleep but in larger doses has dangerous effects and that includes some (as morphine) that are used in medicine and others (as heroin) that are used illegally
[2]**narcotic** *adj* **:** of, relating to, or being a narcotic
nar·rate *vb* **nar·rat·ed; nar·rat·ing :** to tell in full detail — **nar·ra·tor** *n*
nar·ra·tion *n* **1 :** the act or process or an instance of telling in full detail **2 :** [1]NARRATIVE
[1]**nar·ra·tive** *n* **:** something (as a story) that is told in full detail
[2]**narrative** *adj* **:** having the form of a story
[1]**nar·row** *adj* **nar·row·er; nar·row·est 1 :** of slender width **2 :** limited in size or extent **3 :** not broad or open in mind or views **4 :** barely successful **:** CLOSE — **nar·row·ly** *adv* — **nar·row·ness** *n*
[2]**narrow** *vb* **nar·rowed; nar·row·ing 1 :** to make or become less wide **2 :** to limit in number **:** become fewer
[3]**narrow** *n* **:** a narrow passage connecting two bodies of water — usually used in pl.
nar·row–mind·ed *adj* **:** [1]NARROW 3, INTOLERANT — **nar·row–mind·ed·ly** *adv* — **nar·row–mind·ed·ness** *n*
nar·whal *n* **:** an arctic marine animal that is related to dolphins and whales and in the male has a long twisted ivory tusk
na·sal *adj* **1 :** of or relating to the nose **2 :** uttered with the nose passage open — **na·sal·ly** *adv*
nas·tur·tium *n* **:** an herb with roundish leaves and red, yellow, or white flowers
nas·ty *adj* **nas·ti·er; nas·ti·est 1 :** [2]MEAN 1 **2 :** very unpleasant **3 :** very serious **:** HARMFUL **4 :** very dirty **:** FILTHY **5 :** INDECENT — **nas·ti·ly** *adv* — **nas·ti·ness** *n*
na·tion *n* **1 :** COUNTRY 1 **2 :** a community of people made up of one or more nationalities usually with its own territory and government **3 :** NATIONALITY 3
[1]**na·tion·al** *adj* **:** of or relating to an entire country — **na·tion·al·ly** *adv*

²national *n* **:** a citizen of a particular country
National Guard *n* **:** a part of the United States military whose members are recruited by each state, equipped by the federal government, and can be used by either the state or the country
na·tion·al·ism *n* **:** devotion to the interests of a certain country and belief that it is better and more important than other countries
na·tion·al·ist *n* **:** a person who believes that his or her country is better and more important than other countries
na·tion·al·i·ty *n, pl* **na·tion·al·i·ties 1 :** the fact or state of belonging to a particular country **2 :** the state of being a separate country **3 :** a group of people having a common history, tradition, culture, or language
na·tion·al·ize *vb* **na·tion·al·ized; na·tion·al·iz·ing :** to place under government control
na·tion·wide *adj* **:** extending throughout an entire country
¹na·tive *adj* **1 :** born in a certain place or country **2 :** belonging to a person because of place of birth **3 :** living or growing naturally in a certain region **4 :** grown, produced, or coming from a certain place **5 :** NATURAL 3
²native *n* **1 :** a person who was born in or comes from a particular place **2 :** a kind of plant or animal that originally grew or lived in a particular place
Native American *n* **:** a member of any of the first groups of people to live in North and South America and especially in the United States
Na·tiv·i·ty *n, pl* **Na·tiv·i·ties :** the birth of Jesus Christ
nat·ty *adj* **nat·ti·er; nat·ti·est :** very neat, trim, and stylish — **nat·ti·ly** *adv*
nat·u·ral *adj* **1 :** found in or produced by nature **2 :** being or acting as expected **3 :** present or existing at birth **:** born in a person or animal **4 :** having qualities or skills without training or effort **5 :** occurring in the normal course of life **6 :** being simple and sincere **7 :** LIFELIKE **8 :** not raised or lowered in musical pitch using a sharp or flat
natural gas *n* **:** a flammable gas mixture from below the earth's surface that is used especially as a fuel
nat·u·ral·ist *n* **:** a person who studies nature and especially plants and animals as they live in nature
nat·u·ral·i·za·tion *n* **:** the act or process of making or becoming a citizen
nat·u·ral·ize *vb* **nat·u·ral·ized; nat·u·ral·iz·ing 1 :** to become or allow to become a citizen **2 :** to become or cause to become established as if native
nat·u·ral·ly *adv* **1 :** without anything added or changed **:** by natural character **2 :** in the normal or expected way **3 :** because of a quality present at birth **4 :** in a way that is relaxed and normal
natural number *n* **:** the number 1 or any number obtained by adding 1 to it one or more times
natural resource *n* **:** something (as water, a mineral, forest, or kind of animal) that is found in nature and is valuable to humans
na·ture *n* **1 :** the physical world and everything in it **2 :** natural scenery or surroundings **3 :** the basic character of a person or thing **4 :** natural feelings **:** DISPOSITION, TEMPERAMENT **5 :** ¹SORT 1, TYPE
¹naught *also* **nought** *pron* **:** ¹NOTHING 1
²naught *also* **nought** *n* **:** ZERO 1, CIPHER
naugh·ty *adj* **naugh·ti·er; naugh·ti·est :** behaving in a bad or improper way — **naugh·ti·ly** *adv* — **naugh·ti·ness** *n*
nau·sea *n* **1 :** a disturbed and unpleasant condition of the stomach **:** the feeling of being about to vomit **2 :** deep disgust **:** LOATHING
nau·se·ate *vb* **nau·se·at·ed; nau·se·at·ing :** to cause to feel nausea — **nau·se·at·ing** *adj* — **nau·se·at·ing·ly** *adv*
nau·seous *adj* **1 :** suffering from nausea **2 :** causing nausea
nau·ti·cal *adj* **:** of or relating to sailors, navigation, or ships
Na·va·jo *also* **Na·va·ho** *n, pl* **Na·va·jos** *also* **Na·va·hos 1 :** a member of an American Indian people of northern New Mexico and Arizona **2 :** the language of the Navajo people
na·val *adj* **:** of or relating to a navy or warships
nave *n* **:** the long central main part of a church
na·vel *n* **:** a hollow or bump in the middle of the stomach that marks the place where the umbilical cord was attached
nav·i·ga·ble *adj* **1 :** deep enough and wide enough to permit passage of ships **2 :** possible to steer — **nav·i·ga·bil·i·ty** *n*
nav·i·gate *vb* **nav·i·gat·ed; nav·i·gat·ing 1 :** to travel by water **2 :** to sail or travel over, on, or through **3 :** to steer a course in a ship or aircraft **4 :** to steer or direct the course of (as a boat) **5 :** to find information on the Internet or a website
nav·i·ga·tion *n* **1 :** the act or practice of steering, directing the course of, or finding a way through **2 :** the science of figuring out the position and course of a ship or aircraft — **nav·i·ga·tion·al** *adj*
nav·i·ga·tor *n* **:** an officer on a ship or aircraft responsible for directing its course
na·vy *n, pl* **navies 1 :** the complete military organization of a nation for warfare at sea **2 :** a dark blue

1nay *adv* : 1NO 2

2nay *n, pl* **nays** **1** : 3NO 2 **2** : 3NO 3

Na·zi *n* : a member of a political party controlling Germany from 1933 to 1945

NB *abbr* New Brunswick

NC *abbr* North Carolina

ND, N. Dak. *abbr* North Dakota

NE *abbr* **1** Nebraska **2** northeast

Ne·an·der·thal *or* **Ne·an·der·tal** *n* : an ancient human who lived 30,000 to 200,000 years ago

1near *adv* **near·er; near·est** **1** : at, within, or to a short distance or time **2** : ALMOST, NEARLY

2near *prep* : close to

3near *adj* **near·er; near·est** **1** : closely related or associated **2** : not far away in distance or time **3** : coming close : NARROW **4** : being the closer of two — **near·ness** *n*

4near *vb* **neared; near·ing** : to come near : APPROACH

near·by *adv or adj* : close at hand

near·ly *adv* **1** : in a close manner or relationship **2** : almost but not quite **3** : to the least extent

near·sight·ed *adj* : able to see things that are close more clearly than distant ones — **near·sight·ed·ness** *n*

neat *adj* **neat·er; neat·est** **1** : showing care and a concern for order **2** : skillful in a fascinating or entertaining way — **neat·ly** *adv* — **neat·ness** *n*

Neb., Nebr. *abbr* Nebraska

neb·u·la *n, pl* **neb·u·lae** *or* **neb·u·las** **1** : any of many clouds of gas or dust seen in the sky among the stars **2** : GALAXY 2

neb·u·lous *adj* : not clear : VAGUE

1nec·es·sary *adj* : needing to be had or done : ESSENTIAL — **nec·es·sar·i·ly** *adv*

2necessary *n, pl* **nec·es·sar·ies** : something that is needed

ne·ces·si·tate *vb* **ne·ces·si·tat·ed; ne·ces·si·tat·ing** : to make necessary : REQUIRE

ne·ces·si·ty *n, pl* **ne·ces·si·ties** **1** : the state of things that forces certain actions **2** : very great need **3** : the state of being in need : POVERTY **4** : something that is badly needed

neck *n* **1** : the part of the body between the head and the shoulders **2** : the section of a garment covering or nearest to the part connecting the head with the body **3** : something that is long and narrow or that connects two larger parts — **necked** *adj* — **neck and neck** : so nearly equal (as in a race or election) that one cannot be said to be ahead of the other

neck·er·chief *n, pl* **neck·er·chiefs** : a square of cloth worn folded around the neck like a scarf

neck·lace *n* : a piece of jewelry worn around the neck

neck·line *n* : the outline of the neck opening of a garment

neck·tie *n* : a narrow length of material worn under the collar and tied in front

nec·tar *n* : a sweet liquid produced by plants and used by bees in making honey

nec·tar·ine *n* : a peach with a smooth skin

née *or* **nee** *adj* — used to identify a woman by her maiden name

1need *vb* **need·ed; need·ing** **1** : to suffer from the lack of something important to life or health **2** : to be necessary **3** : to be without : REQUIRE

2need *n* **1** : something that must be done : OBLIGATION **2** : a lack of something necessary, useful, or desired **3** : something necessary or desired

need·ful *adj* : 1NECESSARY

1nee·dle *n* **1** : a small slender pointed usually steel tool used for sewing **2** : a slender pointed piece of metal or plastic (used for knitting) **3** : a leaf (as of a pine) shaped like a needle **4** : a pointer on a dial **5** : a slender hollow instrument that has a sharp point and by which material is put into or taken from the body through the skin — **nee·dle·like** *adj*

2needle *vb* **nee·dled; nee·dling** : 1TEASE, TAUNT

nee·dle·point *n* : embroidery done on canvas usually in simple even stitches across counted threads

need·less *adj* : UNNECESSARY — **need·less·ly** *adv*

nee·dle·work *n* **1** : things made by embroidery, knitting, or needlepoint **2** : the activity or art of making things by embroidery, knitting, or needlepoint

needn't : need not

needy *adj* **need·i·er; need·i·est** : very poor — **need·i·ness** *n*

ne'er *adv* : NEVER

ne'er–do–well *n* : a worthless person who will not work

1neg·a·tive *adj* **1** : emphasizing the bad side of a person, situation, or thing **2** : not positive **3** : less than zero and shown by a minus sign **4** : being the part toward which the electric current flows from the outside circuit **5** : of, being, or relating to electricity of which the electron is the unit and which is produced in a hard rubber rod that has been rubbed with wool **6** : having more electrons than protons — **neg·a·tive·ly** *adv* — **neg·a·tiv·i·ty** *n*

2negative *n* **1** : a part of something which is harmful or bad **2** : an expression (as the word *no*) that denies or says the opposite **3** : the side that argues or votes against something **4** : a photographic image on film from which a final picture is made

[1]**ne·glect** *vb* **ne·glect·ed; ne·glect·ing** **1 :** to fail to give the right amount of attention to **2 :** to fail to do or look after especially because of carelessness

[2]**neglect** *n* **1 :** lack of attention or care to something or someone **2 :** the state of not being looked after or given attention

ne·glect·ful *adj* **:** not looking after or giving attention to **:** NEGLIGENT

neg·li·gee *n* **:** a woman's loose robe made of thin material

neg·li·gence *n* **:** failure to take proper or normal care of something or someone

neg·li·gent *adj* **:** failing to take proper or normal care of something or someone — **neg·li·gent·ly** *adv*

neg·li·gi·ble *adj* **:** so small or unimportant as to deserve little or no attention

ne·go·tia·ble *adj* **1 :** able to be discussed in order to reach an agreement **2 :** able to be successfully dealt with or traveled over

ne·go·ti·ate *vb* **ne·go·ti·at·ed; ne·go·ti·at·ing** **1 :** to have a discussion with another in order to settle something **2 :** to arrange for by discussing **3 :** to be successful in getting around, through, or over — **ne·go·ti·a·tor** *n*

ne·go·ti·a·tion *n* **:** the act or process of having a discussion in order to reach an agreement

Ne·gro *n, pl* **Ne·groes** *sometimes offensive* **:** a member of a race of people native to Africa and classified according to certain physical characteristics (as dark skin)

[1]**neigh** *vb* **neighed; neigh·ing** **:** to make the long loud cry of a horse

[2]**neigh** *n* **:** the long loud cry of a horse

[1]**neigh·bor** *or Can and Brit* **neighbour** *n* **1 :** a person living near another **2 :** a person, animal, or thing located near some other person, animal, or thing

[2]**neighbor** *or Can and Brit* **neighbour** *vb* **neigh·bored/neighboured; neigh·bor·ing/neighbouring** **:** to be near or next to — **neigh·bor·ing** *or Can and Brit* **neighbouring** *adj*

neigh·bor·hood *or Can and Brit* **neighbourhood** *n* **1 :** a residential section of a city **2 :** the people living near one another **3 :** a place or region near **:** VICINITY **4 :** an amount, size, or range that is close to

neigh·bor·ly *or Can and Brit* **neighbourly** *adj* **:** familiar and helpful **:** FRIENDLY — **neigh·bor·li·ness** *or Can and Brit* **neighbourliness** *n*

[1]**nei·ther** *conj* **1 :** not either **2 :** also not

[2]**neither** *pron* **:** not the one and not the other

[3]**neither** *adj* **:** not either

ne·on *n* **:** a colorless gaseous chemical element found in very small amounts in the air and used in electric lamps

neo·phyte *n* **1 :** BEGINNER, NOVICE **2 :** a new convert

neph·ew *n* **:** a son of a person's brother or sister

Nep·tune *n* **:** the planet that is eighth in order of distance from the sun and has a diameter of about 31,000 miles (50,000 kilometers)

nep·tu·ni·um *n* **:** a radioactive chemical element similar to uranium

nerd *n* **1 :** a person who is socially awkward, unattractive, or not fashionable **2 :** a person who is extremely interested in technical or intellectual subjects — **nerdy** *adj*

nerve *n* **1 :** a bundle of nerve fibers that carries messages in the form of nerve impulses to or away from the brain and spinal cord **2 :** COURAGE, BOLDNESS **3 :** rude or disrespectful boldness **4 nerves** *pl* **:** feelings of worry **5 :** the sensitive soft inner part of a tooth — **nerve·less** *adj*

nerve cell *n* **:** a cell of the nervous system with fibers that carry nerve impulses

nerve fiber *n* **:** any of the threadlike extensions (as axons or dendrites) of a nerve cell that carry nerve impulses

nerve impulse *n* **:** an electrical signal carried by nerve cells which relays information from the body's sense organs to the brain and spinal cord or instructions from the brain and spinal cord to a body part (as a muscle or gland)

ner·vous *adj* **1 :** having or showing feelings of worry, fear, or anxiety **2 :** easily becoming worried, frightened, or anxious **3 :** of, relating to, or made up of nerves or nerve cells — **ner·vous·ly** *adv* — **ner·vous·ness** *n*

nervous system *n* **:** a system of the body that in vertebrates includes the brain, spinal cord, nerves, and sense organs and receives, interprets, and responds to stimuli from inside and outside the body

nervy *adj* **nerv·i·er; nerv·i·est** **1 :** showing calm courage **2 :** showing or acting with disrespectful boldness

-ness *n suffix* **:** state **:** condition

[1]**nest** *n* **1 :** a shelter made by an animal and especially a bird for its eggs and young **2 :** a place where some animals live and usually lay eggs **3 :** a cozy place **:** HOME **4 :** those living in a nest

[2]**nest** *vb* **nest·ed; nest·ing** **:** to build or live in a nest

nes·tle *vb* **nes·tled; nes·tling** **1 :** to lie close and snug **:** CUDDLE **2 :** to be located snugly or in a place not easily noticed

nest·ling *n* **:** a young bird not yet able to leave the nest

[1]**net** *n* **1 :** a device made of strands that weave in and out with open spaces between

and used to hold or catch something **2 :** a fabric made of strands of thread, cord, rope, or wire that weave in and out with much open space **3 :** the object placed between players in some games (as tennis) **4 :** the area that serves as the goal in some games (as soccer and hockey) **5** *often cap* **:** INTERNET **6 :** NETWORK 1 **7 :** something that traps and is difficult to escape from

²net *vb* **net·ted; net·ting 1 :** to cover with or as if with a net **2 :** to catch in or as if in a net

³net *adj* **:** remaining after all charges or expenses have been subtracted

⁴net *vb* **net·ted; net·ting :** to gain or produce as profit **:** CLEAR

net·book *n* **:** a small portable computer designed primarily for wireless Internet access

net·ting *n* **1 :** ¹NET 1 **2 :** ¹NET 2

net·tle *n* **:** a tall plant with hairs on the leaves that when touched can cause a painful skin rash

net·work *n* **1 :** an arrangement of things forming a pattern with spaces between **2 :** a system of computers and related devices connected by communications lines **3 :** a group of connected radio or television stations

neu·ron *n* **:** NERVE CELL

neu·ter *vb* **neu·tered; neu·ter·ing :** to remove the sex glands and especially the testes from **:** CASTRATE

¹neu·tral *n* **1 :** a person or group that does not favor either side in a quarrel, contest, or war **2 :** a grayish color or color that is not bright **3 :** a position of gears (as in the transmission of a motor vehicle) in which they are not in contact

²neutral *adj* **1 :** not favoring either side in a quarrel, contest, or war **2 :** of or relating to a country that doesn't favor either side in a dispute **3 :** not strong in opinion or feeling **4 :** having a color that is not bright **:** GRAYISH **5 :** neither acid nor basic **6 :** not electrically charged

neu·tral·i·ty *n* **:** the quality or state of not favoring one side or the other

neu·tral·i·za·tion *n* **:** the act or process of making chemically neutral **:** the state of being chemically neutral

neu·tral·ize *vb* **neu·tral·ized; neu·tral·iz·ing 1 :** to make chemically neutral **2 :** to make ineffective

neu·tron *n* **:** a particle that has a mass nearly equal to that of the proton but no electrical charge and that is present in all atomic nuclei except those of hydrogen

Nev. *abbr* Nevada

nev·er *adv* **1 :** not ever **:** at no time **2 :** not to any extent or in any way

nev·er·more *adv* **:** never again

nev·er·the·less *adv* **:** even so **:** HOWEVER

¹new *adj* **new·er; new·est 1 :** recently bought, acquired, or rented **2 :** taking the place of one that came before **3 :** recently discovered or learned **4 :** beginning as a repeating of a previous thing **5 :** being in a position, place, or state the first time **6 :** having recently come into existence **7 :** not used by anyone previously **8 :** not accustomed. — **new·ness** *n*

²new *adv* **:** NEWLY, RECENTLY

new·born *adj* **1 :** recently born **2 :** made new or strong again

new·com·er *n* **1 :** someone or something recently arrived **2 :** BEGINNER

new·el *n* **:** a post at the bottom or at a turn of a stairway

new·fan·gled *adj* **:** of the newest style **:** NOVEL

new·ly *adv* **:** not long ago **:** RECENTLY

new·ly·wed *n* **:** a person recently married

new moon *n* **1 :** the moon's phase when its dark side is toward the earth **2 :** the thin curved outline of the moon seen shortly after sunset for a few days after the new moon

news *n* **1 :** a report of recent events or unknown information **2 :** information or recent events reported in a newspaper or magazine or on a broadcast **3 :** a broadcast of information on recent events **4 :** an event that is interesting enough to be reported

news·boy *n* **:** a boy or man who delivers or sells newspapers

news·cast *n* **:** a radio or television broadcast of information on recent events

news·girl *n* **:** a girl or woman who delivers or sells newspapers

news·man *n, pl* **news·men :** a person who gathers or reports information on recent events

news·pa·per *n* **:** a paper that is printed and sold usually every day or weekly and that contains information on recent events, articles of opinion, features, and advertising

news·reel *n* **:** a short motion picture made in the past about events at that time

news·stand *n* **:** a place where newspapers and magazines are sold

news·wom·an *n, pl* **news·wom·en :** a woman who gathers or reports information on recent events

New World *n* **:** the lands in the western hemisphere and especially North and South America

newt *n* **:** a small salamander that lives mostly in water

New Year's Day *n* **:** January 1 observed as a legal holiday in many countries

¹next *adj* **:** coming just before or after

²next *adv* **1 :** in the nearest place, time, or order following **2 :** at the first time after this

³next *n* : a person or thing that immediately follows another person or thing
next–door *adj* : located in the next building, apartment, or room
next door *adv* : in or to the nearest building, apartment, or room
¹next to *prep* **1 :** BESIDE 1 **2 :** following right after
²next to *adv* : very nearly
Nez Percé *or* **Nez Perce** *pl* **Nez Percé** *or* **Nez Perc·és** *or* **Nez Perce** *or* **Nez Perc·es** **1 :** a member of an American Indian people of Idaho, Washington, and Oregon **2 :** the language of the Nez Percé people
NH *abbr* New Hampshire
nib *n* **1 :** a pointed object (as the bill of a bird) **2 :** the point of a pen
¹nib·ble *vb* **nib·bled; nib·bling :** to bite or chew gently or bit by bit
²nibble *n* : a very small amount
nice *adj* **nic·er; nic·est** **1 :** PLEASING, PLEASANT **2 :** kind, polite, and friendly **3 :** of good quality **4 :** done very well **5 :** well behaved — **nice·ly** *adv* — **nice·ness** *n*
ni·ce·ty *n, pl* **ni·ce·ties** **1 :** something dainty, delicate, or of especially good quality **2 :** a fine detail that is considered part of polite or proper behavior
niche *n* **1 :** an open hollow space in a wall (as for a statue) **2 :** a place, job, or use for which a person or a thing is best fitted
¹nick *n* **1 :** a small cut or chip in a surface **2 :** the last moment
²nick *vb* **nicked; nick·ing :** to make a small cut or chip in
nick·el *n* **1 :** a hard silvery white metallic chemical element that can be highly polished, resists weathering, and is used in alloys **2 :** a United States coin worth five cents
nick·er *vb* **nick·ered; nick·er·ing :** ¹NEIGH, WHINNY
¹nick·name *n* **1 :** a usually descriptive name used in addition to a person's given name **2 :** a familiar form of a proper name
²nickname *vb* **nick·named; nick·nam·ing :** to give a usually descriptive name to that is additional to a given name
nic·o·tine *n* : a poisonous substance found in small amounts in tobacco
niece *n* : a daughter of a person's brother or sister
nif·ty *adj* **nif·ti·er; nif·ti·est :** very unusual and attractive
nig·gling *adj* : PETTY 1
¹nigh *adv* **1 :** near in time or place **2 :** ALMOST, NEARLY
²nigh *adj* : ³CLOSE 1, NEAR
night *n* **1 :** the time between dusk and dawn when there is no sunlight **2 :** the early part of the night : NIGHTFALL **3 :** the darkness of night
night·club *n* : a place of entertainment open at night usually serving food and alcoholic beverages and having music for dancing
night crawl·er *n* : EARTHWORM
night·fall *n* : the coming of night
night·gown *n* : a loose garment worn in bed
night·hawk *n* : a bird that is active at twilight and feeds on insects caught in flight
night·in·gale *n* : a reddish brown European bird noted for the sweet song of the male usually heard at night
¹night·ly *adj* : happening or done at night or every night
²nightly *adv* : every night
night·mare *n* **1 :** a frightening dream **2 :** a horrible experience — **night·mar·ish** *adj*
night·shirt *n* : a long loose shirt worn in bed
night·stick *n* : a police officer's club
night·time *n* : NIGHT 1
nil *n* : nothing at all : ZERO
nim·ble *adj* **nim·bler; nim·blest** **1 :** quick and light in motion : AGILE **2 :** quick in understanding and learning : CLEVER — **nim·ble·ness** *n* — **nim·bly** *adv*
nim·bus *n, pl* **nim·bi** *or* **nim·bus·es :** a rain cloud
¹nine *adj* : being one more than eight
²nine *n* **1 :** one more than eight : three times three : 9 **2 :** the ninth in a set or series
¹nine·teen *adj* : being one more than 18
²nineteen *n* : one more than 18 : 19
¹nine·teenth *adj* : coming right after 18th
²nineteenth *n* : number 19 in a series
¹nine·ti·eth *adj* : coming right after 89th
²ninetieth *n* : number 90 in a series
¹nine·ty *adj* : being nine times ten
²ninety *n* : nine times ten : 90
nin·ja *n, pl* **ninja** *also* **nin·jas :** a person trained in ancient Japanese martial arts who works as a spy and assassin especially in the past
¹ninth *adj* : coming right after eighth
²ninth *n* **1 :** number nine in a series **2 :** one of nine equal parts
¹nip *vb* **nipped; nip·ping** **1 :** to bite or pinch lightly **2 :** to injure or make numb with cold **3 :** to remove or cut off by or as if by pinching **4 :** to move quickly — **nip (something) in the bud :** to stop (something) right away so it does not become a problem
²nip *n* : a light bite or pinch
³nip *n* : a small amount of liquor
nip and tuck *adj or adv* : so close that the lead shifts rapidly from one contestant to another
nip·ple *n* **1 :** the part of the breast or chest from which a baby or young animal sucks

milk **2 :** something (as the mouthpiece of a baby's bottle) like a nipple

nip·py *adj* **nip·pi·er; nip·pi·est :** CHILLY

nit *n* **:** the egg of a louse

ni·trate *n* **:** a substance that is made from or similar in composition to nitric acid

ni·tric acid *n* **:** a strong liquid acid that contains hydrogen, nitrogen, and oxygen and is used in making fertilizers, explosives, and dyes

ni·tro·gen *n* **:** a colorless odorless gaseous chemical element that makes up 78 percent of the atmosphere and forms a part of all living tissues

nitrogen cycle *n* **:** a continuous series of natural processes by which nitrogen passes from air to soil to living things and back into the air

nitrogen fix·a·tion *n* **:** the changing of nitrogen into an available and useful form especially by bacteria (**nitrogen–fixing bacteria**)

ni·tro·glyc·er·in *or* **ni·tro·glyc·er·ine** *n* **:** an oily liquid explosive from which dynamite is made

NJ *abbr* New Jersey

NL *abbr* Newfoundland and Labrador

NM, N. Mex. *abbr* New Mexico

[1]**no** *adv* **1 :** not at all **:** not any **2 :** not so — used to express disagreement or refusal **3** — used to express surprise, doubt, or disbelief

[2]**no** *adj* **1 :** not any **2 :** hardly any **:** very little **3 :** not a

[3]**no** *n, pl* **noes** *or* **nos 1 :** an act or instance of refusing or denying by the use of the word *no* **:** DENIAL **2 :** a vote or decision against something **3** *noes or nos pl* **:** persons voting against something

no. *abbr* **1** north **2** number

no·bil·i·ty *n, pl* **no·bil·i·ties 1 :** the quality or state of having a fine or admirable character **2 :** high social rank **3 :** the class or a group of people of high birth or rank

[1]**no·ble** *adj* **no·bler; no·blest 1 :** having or showing very fine or admirable qualities **2 :** of very high birth or rank **3 :** grand in appearance — **no·ble·ness** *n* — **no·bly** *adv*

[2]**noble** *n* **:** a person of high birth or rank

no·ble·man *n, pl* **no·ble·men :** a man of high birth or rank

no·ble·wom·an *n, pl* **no·ble·wom·en :** a woman of high birth or rank

[1]**no·body** *pron* **:** no person **:** not anybody

[2]**nobody** *n, pl* **no·bod·ies :** a person of no importance

noc·tur·nal *adj* **1 :** happening at night **2 :** active at night

[1]**nod** *vb* **nod·ded; nod·ding 1 :** to bend the head up and down one or more times **2 :** to move up and down **3 :** to tip the head in a certain direction — **nod off :** to fall asleep

[2]**nod** *n* **:** the action of bending the head up and down

node *n* **:** a thickened spot or part (as of a plant stem where a leaf develops)

nod·ule *n* **:** a small roundish lump or mass

no·el *n* **1 :** a Christmas carol **2** *cap* **:** the Christmas season

noes *pl of* NO

nog·gin *n* **:** a person's head

[1]**noise** *n* **1 :** a loud or unpleasant sound **2 :** [3]SOUND 1 — **noise·less** *adj* — **noise·less·ly** *adv*

[2]**noise** *vb* **noised; nois·ing :** to spread by rumor or report

noise·mak·er *n* **:** a device used to make noise especially at parties

noisy *adj* **nois·i·er; nois·i·est 1 :** making a lot of noise **2 :** full of noise — **nois·i·ly** *adv* — **nois·i·ness** *n*

[1]**no·mad** *n* **1 :** a member of a people having no permanent home but moving from place to place usually in search of food or to graze livestock **2 :** a person who moves often

[2]**nomad** *adj* **:** NOMADIC

no·mad·ic *adj* **1 :** characteristic of or being a nomad or group of nomads **2 :** roaming about from place to place

nom·i·nal *adj* **1 :** existing as something in name only **2 :** very small — **nom·i·nal·ly** *adv*

nom·i·nate *vb* **nom·i·nat·ed; nom·i·nat·ing :** to choose as a candidate for election, appointment, or honor

nom·i·na·tion *n* **:** the act or an instance of choosing as a candidate for election, appointment, or honor

nom·i·na·tive *adj* **:** being or belonging to the case of a noun or pronoun that is usually the subject of a verb

nom·i·nee *n* **:** someone or something that has been chosen as a candidate for election, appointment, or honor

non- *prefix* **:** not

non·cha·lance *n* **:** the state of being relaxed and free from concern or excitement

non·cha·lant *adj* **:** showing or having a relaxed manner free from concern or excitement — **non·cha·lant·ly** *adv*

non·com·bat·ant *n* **1 :** a member (as a chaplain) of the armed forces whose duties do not include fighting **2 :** a person who is not in the armed forces **:** CIVILIAN

non·com·mis·sioned officer *n* **:** an officer in the army, air force, or marine corps appointed from among the enlisted persons

non·com·mit·tal *adj* **:** not revealing thoughts or decisions

non·con·form·ist *n* **:** a person who does not

behave according to generally accepted standards or customs

non·de·script *adj* : having no special or interesting characteristics : not easily described

[1]**none** *pron* : not any : not one

[2]**none** *adv* **1** : not at all **2** : in no way

non·en·ti·ty *n, pl* **non·en·ti·ties** : someone or something of no importance

[1]**non·es·sen·tial** *adj* : not necessary

[2]**nonessential** *n* : something that is not necessary

none·the·less *adv* : NEVERTHELESS

non·fic·tion *n* : writing that is about facts or real events

non·flam·ma·ble *adj* : not easily set on fire

non·liv·ing *adj* : not living

non·par·ti·san *adj* : not supporting one party or side over another

non·per·ish·able *adj* : able to be stored for a long time without spoiling

non·plussed *adj* : so surprised or confused as to be at a loss as to what to say, think, or do

non·poi·son·ous *adj* : not poisonous

non·prof·it *adj* : not existing or done to make a profit

non·re·new·able *adj* : not restored or replaced by natural processes in a short period of time

[1]**non·res·i·dent** *adj* : not living in a certain place

[2]**nonresident** *n* : a person who does not live in a certain place

non·sec·tar·i·an *adj* : not limited to a particular religious group

non·sense *n* : foolish or meaningless words, ideas, or actions

non·sen·si·cal *adj* : making no sense : ABSURD

non·smok·er *n* : a person who does not smoke tobacco

non·smok·ing *adj* : reserved for the use of nonsmokers

non·stan·dard *adj* : different from or lower in quality than what is typical

non·stop *adv or adj* : without a stop

noo·dle *n* : a thin often flat strip of fresh or dried dough (as of flour and egg) that is usually boiled

nook *n* **1** : an inner corner **2** : a sheltered or hidden place

noon *n* : the middle of the day : twelve o'clock in the daytime

noon·day *n* : NOON, MIDDAY

no one *pron* : [1]NOBODY

noon·time *n* : NOON

noose *n* : a loop that passes through a knot at the end of a line so that it gets smaller when the other end of the line is pulled

nor *conj* : and not

norm *n* **1** : [1]AVERAGE 2 **2** : a common practice

[1]**nor·mal** *adj* **1** : of the regular or usual kind **2** : healthy in body or mind — **nor·mal·ly** *adv*

[2]**normal** *n* : the usual form, state, level, or amount : AVERAGE

nor·mal·cy *n* : NORMALITY

nor·mal·i·ty *n* : the quality or state of being of the regular or usual kind

Nor·man *n* **1** : one of the Scandinavians who conquered Normandy in the tenth century **2** : one of the people of mixed Norman and French ancestry who conquered England in 1066

Norse *n* **1** *pl* **Norse** : the people of Scandinavia **2** *pl* **Norse** : the people of Norway **3** : any of the languages of the Norse people

[1]**north** *adv* : to or toward the north

[2]**north** *adj* : placed toward, facing, or coming from the north

[3]**north** *n* **1** : the direction to the left of someone facing east : the compass point opposite to south **2** *cap* : regions or countries north of a point that is mentioned or understood

[1]**North American** *n* : a person born or living in North America

[2]**North American** *adj* : of or relating to North America or the North Americans

north·bound *adj* : going north

[1]**north·east** *adv* : to or toward the direction between north and east

[2]**northeast** *adj* : placed toward, facing, or coming from the northeast

[3]**northeast** *n* **1** : the direction between north and east **2** *cap* : regions or countries northeast of a point that is mentioned or understood

north·east·er·ly *adv or adj* **1** : from the northeast **2** : toward the northeast

north·east·ern *adj* **1** *often cap* : of, relating to, or like that of the Northeast **2** : lying toward or coming from the northeast

north·er·ly *adj or adv* **1** : from the north **2** : toward the north

north·ern *adj* **1** *often cap* : of, relating to, or like that of the North **2** : lying toward or coming from the north

northern lights *n pl* : AURORA BOREALIS

north·land *n, often cap* : land in the north : the north of a country or region

north pole *n* **1** *often cap N&P* : the most northern point of the earth : the northern end of the earth's axis **2** : the end of a magnet that points toward the north when the magnet is free to swing

North Star *n* : the star toward which the northern end of the earth's axis most closely points

north·ward *adv or adj* : toward the north
[1]**north·west** *adv* : to or toward the direction between north and west
[2]**northwest** *adj* : placed toward, facing, or coming from the northwest
[3]**northwest** *n* **1** : the direction between north and west **2** *cap* : regions or countries northwest of a point that is mentioned or understood
north·west·er·ly *adv or adj* **1** : from the northwest **2** : toward the northwest
north·west·ern *adj* **1** *often cap* : of, relating to, or like that of the Northwest **2** : lying toward or coming from the northwest
[1]**Nor·we·gian** *adj* : of or relating to Norway, its people, or the Norwegian language
[2]**Norwegian** *n* **1** : a person who is born or lives in Norway **2** : the language of the Norwegians
nos *pl of* NO
[1]**nose** *n* **1** : the part of the face or head that contains the nostrils **2** : the sense or organ of smell **3** : the front end or part of something **4** : an ability to discover — **nosed** *adj*
[2]**nose** *vb* **nosed; nos·ing** **1** : to search for or find by smelling **2** : to touch or rub with the nose : NUZZLE **3** : to search for especially in an unwelcome way : PRY **4** : to move ahead slowly or carefully
nose·bleed *n* : a bleeding at the nose
nose cone *n* : a protective cone forming the forward end of an airplane, rocket, or missile
nose·dive *n* **1** : a downward plunge (as of an airplane) **2** : a sudden sharp drop (as in prices)
nose–dive *vb* **nose–dived; nose–div·ing** : to plunge or drop suddenly or sharply
nos·tal·gia *n* : a longing for something past
nos·tal·gic *adj* : having, showing, or characterized by a longing for something past
nos·tril *n* : either of the outer openings of the nose through which people and many animals breathe
nosy *or* **nos·ey** *adj* **nos·i·er; nos·i·est** : wanting to know about someone else's business
not *adv* **1** — used to make a word or group of words negative **2** — used to stand for the negative of a group of words that comes before
[1]**no·ta·ble** *adj* **1** : deserving special notice : REMARKABLE **2** : very successful or respected : DISTINGUISHED — **no·ta·bly** *adv*
[2]**notable** *n* : a famous person
no·ta·rize *vb* **no·ta·rized; no·ta·riz·ing** : to sign as a notary public to show that a document is authentic
no·ta·ry public *n, pl* **notaries public** *or* **notary publics** : a public official who witnesses the making of a document (as a will) and signs it to show that it is authentic
no·ta·tion *n* **1** : the act of noting **2** : [2]NOTE 5 **3** : a system of signs, marks, or figures used to give a certain kind of information
[1]**notch** *n* **1** : a cut in the shape of a V in an edge or surface **2** : a narrow pass between mountains **3** : DEGREE 1, STEP
[2]**notch** *vb* **notched; notch·ing** : to make V-shaped cuts in
[1]**note** *vb* **not·ed; not·ing** **1** : to notice or observe with care **2** : to record in writing **3** : to make special mention of
[2]**note** *n* **1** : a musical sound : TONE **2** : a symbol in music that by its shape and position on the staff shows the pitch of a tone and the length of time it is to be held **3** : the musical call or song of a bird **4** : a quality that shows a feeling **5** : something written down often to aid the memory **6** : a printed comment in a book that helps explain part of the text **7** : DISTINCTION 3 **8** : a short written message or letter **9** : careful notice **10** : frame of mind : MOOD **11** : a piano key **12** : a written promise to pay a debt
note·book *n* : a book of blank pages for writing in
not·ed *adj* : well-known and highly regarded
note·wor·thy *adj* : worthy of attention : REMARKABLE
[1]**noth·ing** *pron* **1** : not anything : no thing **2** : someone or something of no interest, value, or importance
[2]**nothing** *adv* : not at all : in no way
[3]**nothing** *n* **1** : something that does not exist : empty space **2** : ZERO 1 **3** : someone or something of little or no worth or importance — **noth·ing·ness** *n* — **for nothing** **1** : for no reason **2** : for no money
[1]**no·tice** *n* **1** : WARNING, ANNOUNCEMENT **2** : an indication that an agreement will end at a specified time **3** : ATTENTION 1, HEED **4** : a written or printed announcement **5** : a short piece of writing that gives an opinion (as of a book or play)
[2]**notice** *vb* **no·ticed; no·tic·ing** : to become aware of : pay attention to
no·tice·able *adj* : deserving notice : likely to attract attention — **no·tice·ably** *adv*
no·ti·fi·ca·tion *n* **1** : the act or an instance of giving notice or information **2** : something written or printed that gives notice
no·ti·fy *vb* **no·ti·fied; no·ti·fy·ing** : to give notice to : INFORM
no·tion *n* **1** : IDEA 2 **2** : WHIM **3 notions** *pl* : small useful articles (as buttons, needles, and thread)
no·to·ri·e·ty *n* : the state of being widely known especially for some bad characteristic

no·to·ri·ous *adj* : widely known especially for some bad characteristic — **no·to·ri·ous·ly** *adv*

[1]**not·with·stand·ing** *prep* : in spite of

[2]**notwithstanding** *adv* : NEVERTHELESS

nou·gat *n* : a candy consisting of a sugar paste with nuts or fruit pieces

nought *variant of* NAUGHT

noun *n* : a word or phrase that is the name of something (as a person, place, or thing) and that is used in a sentence especially as subject or object of a verb or as object of a preposition

nour·ish *vb* **nour·ished; nour·ish·ing** : to cause to grow or live in a healthy state especially by providing with enough good food or nutrients — **nour·ish·ing** *adj*

nour·ish·ment *n* : something (as food) that causes growth or health

Nov. *abbr* November

[1]**nov·el** *adj* : new and different from what is already known

[2]**novel** *n* : a long story usually about imaginary characters and events

nov·el·ist *n* : a writer of novels

nov·el·ty *n, pl* **nov·el·ties** **1** : something new or unusual **2** : the quality or state of being new or unusual **3** : a small unusual ornament or toy

No·vem·ber *n* : the eleventh month of the year

nov·ice *n* **1** : a person who has no previous experience with something : BEGINNER **2** : a new member of a religious community who is preparing to take the vows of religion

[1]**now** *adv* **1** : at this time **2** : immediately before the present time **3** : in the time immediately to follow **4** — used to express command or introduce an important point **5** : SOMETIMES **6** : in the present circumstances **7** : at the time referred to — **now and then** : from time to time : OCCASIONALLY

[2]**now** *conj* : in view of the fact that : SINCE

[3]**now** *n* : the present time

now·a·days *adv* : at the present time

[1]**no·where** *adv* **1** : not in or at any place **2** : to no place **3** : not at all

[2]**nowhere** *n* : a place that does not exist

nox·ious *adj* : causing harm

noz·zle *n* : a short tube often used on the end of a hose or pipe to direct or speed up a flow of fluid

NS *abbr* Nova Scotia

NT *abbr* Northwest Territories

-n't *adv suffix* : not

NU *abbr* Nunavut

nub *n* **1** : a small rounded part that sticks out from something **2** : a small piece or end that remains after something has been removed or worn away

nub·by *adj* **nub·bi·er; nub·bi·est** : having small knobs or lumps

nu·cle·ar *adj* **1** : of, relating to, or being a nucleus (as of a cell) **2** : of or relating to the nucleus of the atom **3** : produced by a nuclear reaction **4** : of, relating to, or being a weapon whose destructive power comes from an uncontrolled nuclear reaction **5** : relating to or powered by nuclear energy

nu·cle·us *n, pl* **nu·clei** **1** : a usually round part of most cells that is enclosed in a double membrane, controls the activities of the cell, and contains the chromosomes **2** : the central part of an atom that comprises nearly all of the atomic mass and that consists of protons and neutrons **3** : a central point, group, or mass

nude *adj* **nud·er; nud·est** : not wearing clothes : NAKED

[1]**nudge** *vb* **nudged; nudg·ing** **1** : to touch or push gently **2** : to attract the attention of by touching or pushing gently (as with the elbow)

[2]**nudge** *n* : a slight push

nu·di·ty *n* : the state of having no clothes on

nug·get *n* **1** : a solid lump especially of precious metal **2** : a small usually rounded piece of food

nui·sance *n* : an annoying or troublesome person, thing, or situation

null *adj* : having no legal force : not binding

[1]**numb** *adj* **1** : unable to feel anything especially because of cold **2** : unable to think, feel, or react normally (as because of great fear, surprise, or sadness) — **numb·ly** *adv* — **numb·ness** *n*

[2]**numb** *vb* **numbed; numb·ing** : to make or become unable to feel pain or touch

[1]**num·ber** *n* **1** : the total of persons, things, or units taken together : AMOUNT **2** : a total that is not specified **3** : a unit belonging to a mathematical system and subject to its rules **4** : a word, symbol, or letter used to represent a mathematical number : NUMERAL **5** : a certain numeral for telling one person or thing from another or from others **6** : a quality of a word form that shows whether the word is singular or plural **7** : one of a series **8** : a song or dance usually that is part of a larger performance

[2]**number** *vb* **num·bered; num·ber·ing** **1** : [1]COUNT 1 **2** : INCLUDE **3** : to limit to a certain number **4** : to give a number to **5** : to add up to or have a total of

num·ber·less *adj* : too many to count

number line *n* : a line in which points are matched to numbers

nu·mer·al *n* : a symbol or group of symbols representing a number

nu·mer·a·tor *n* **:** the part of a fraction that is above the line

nu·mer·i·cal *adj* **:** of or relating to numbers **:** stated in numbers — **nu·mer·i·cal·ly** *adv*

nu·mer·ous *adj* **:** consisting of a large number **:** MANY

nun *n* **:** a woman belonging to a religious community and living according to vows

nun·nery *n, pl* **nun·ner·ies :** CONVENT

nup·tial *adj* **:** of or relating to marriage or a wedding

nup·tials *n pl* **:** WEDDING

[1]**nurse** *n* **1 :** a person skilled or trained in caring for sick or injured people **2 :** a woman employed for the care of a young child

[2]**nurse** *vb* **nursed; nurs·ing 1 :** to feed at the breast **:** SUCKLE **2 :** to take care of (as a young child or a sick person) **3 :** to treat with special care or attention

nurse·maid *n* **:** [1]NURSE 2

nurs·ery *n, pl* **nurs·er·ies 1 :** the room where a baby sleeps **2 :** a place where small children are temporarily cared for in their parent's absence **3 :** a place where plants (as trees or shrubs) are grown and usually sold

nursery rhyme *n* **:** a short rhyme for children that often tells a story

nursery school *n* **:** a school for children usually under five years old

[1]**nur·ture** *n* **1 :** the way a person or animal was raised **:** UPBRINGING **2 :** something (as food) that is essential to healthy growth and development

[2]**nurture** *vb* **nur·tured; nur·tur·ing 1 :** to provide with things (as food and protection) essential to healthy growth and development **2 :** to further the development of

nut *n* **1 :** a dry fruit or seed with a firm inner kernel and a hard shell **2 :** the often edible kernel of a nut **3 :** a small piece of metal with a hole through it that can be screwed onto a bolt for tightening or holding something **4 :** a foolish or crazy person **5 :** a person who is very interested in or enthusiastic about something — **nut·like** *adj*

nut·crack·er *n* **:** a device used for cracking the shells of nuts

nut·hatch *n* **:** a small bird that creeps on tree trunks and branches and eats insects

nut·meg *n* **:** a spice made from the ground seeds of a small tropical evergreen tree

nu·tri·ent *n* **:** a substance that is needed for healthy growth, development, and functioning

nu·tri·ment *n* **:** something that nourishes

nu·tri·tion *n* **:** the act or process of nourishing or being nourished **:** the processes by which a living thing takes in and uses nutrients

nu·tri·tion·al *adj* **:** relating to, providing, or involved in the proper intake of nutrients

nu·tri·tious *adj* **:** providing nutrients **:** NOURISHING

nu·tri·tive *adj* **1 :** NUTRITIONAL **2 :** NUTRITIOUS

nuts *adj* **1 :** enthusiastic about or interested in something **2 :** CRAZY 1

nut·shell *n* **:** the shell of a nut — **in a nutshell :** very briefly

nut·ty *adj* **nut·ti·er; nut·ti·est 1 :** not showing good sense **2 :** having a flavor like that of nuts

nuz·zle *vb* **nuz·zled; nuz·zling :** to push or rub with the nose

NV *abbr* Nevada

NW *abbr* northwest

NY *abbr* New York

ny·lon *n* **:** a strong man-made material used in the making of fabrics and plastics

nymph *n* **1 :** one of many goddesses in old legends represented as beautiful young women living in the mountains, forests, and waters **2 :** an immature insect that differs from the adult chiefly in being of smaller size and having undeveloped wings

O

o *n, pl* **o's** *or* **os** *often cap* **1 :** the 15th letter of the English alphabet **2 :** ZERO 1

O *variant of* OH

O. *abbr* Ohio

oaf *n* **:** a stupid or awkward person — **oaf·ish** *adj*

oak *n* **:** a tree or shrub that produces acorns and has tough wood much used for furniture and flooring

oak·en *adj* **:** made of oak

oar *n* **:** a long pole that is flat and wide at one end and that is used for rowing or steering a boat

oar·lock *n* **:** a usually U-shaped device for holding an oar in place

oars·man *n, pl* **oars·men :** a person who rows a boat

oa·sis *n, pl* **oa·ses :** a fertile or green spot in a desert

oat *n* **1 :** a cereal grass grown for its loose

clusters of seeds that are used for human food and animal feed **2 oats** *pl* : a crop or the seeds of the oat

oath *n, pl* **oaths** **1** : a solemn promise to tell the truth or do a specific thing **2** : an obscene or impolite word used to express anger or frustration

oat·meal *n* **1** : oat seeds that have had the outer covering removed and are ground into meal or flattened into flakes **2** : a hot cereal made from meal or flakes of oats

obe·di·ence *n* : the act of obeying : willingness to obey

obe·di·ent *adj* : willing to do as told by someone in authority : willing to obey — **obe·di·ent·ly** *adv*

obe·lisk *n* : a four-sided pillar that becomes narrower toward the top and ends in a pyramid

obese *adj* : very fat — **obe·si·ty** *n*

obey *vb* **obeyed; obey·ing** **1** : to follow the commands or guidance of **2** : to comply with : carry out

obit·u·ary *n, pl* **obit·u·ar·ies** : a notice of a person's death (as in a newspaper)

obj. *abbr* **1** object **2** objective

[1]**ob·ject** *n* **1** : something that may be seen or felt **2** : PURPOSE, AIM **3** : something that arouses feelings in an observer **4** : a noun or a term behaving like a noun that receives the action of a verb or completes the meaning of a preposition

[2]**ob·ject** *vb* **ob·ject·ed; ob·ject·ing** **1** : to offer or mention as a reason for a feeling of disapproval **2** : to oppose something firmly and usually with words

ob·jec·tion *n* **1** : an act of showing disapproval or great dislike **2** : a reason for or a feeling of disapproval

ob·jec·tion·able *adj* : arousing disapproval or great dislike : OFFENSIVE

[1]**ob·jec·tive** *adj* **1** : dealing with facts without allowing personal feelings to confuse them **2** : being or belonging to the case of a noun or pronoun that is an object of a transitive verb or a preposition **3** : being outside of the mind and independent of it — **ob·jec·tive·ly** *adv*

[2]**objective** *n* : PURPOSE, GOAL

ob·li·gate *vb* **ob·li·gat·ed; ob·li·gat·ing** : to make (someone) do something by law or because it is right

ob·li·ga·tion *n* **1** : something a person must do because of the demands of a promise or contract **2** : something a person feels he or she must do : DUTY **3** : a feeling of being indebted for an act of kindness

oblige *vb* **obliged; oblig·ing** **1** : [2]FORCE 1, COMPEL **2** : to do a favor for or do something as a favor **3** : to earn the gratitude of

oblig·ing *adj* : willing to do favors — **oblig·ing·ly** *adv*

oblique *adj* : having a slanting position or direction : neither perpendicular nor parallel — **oblique·ly** *adv*

oblit·er·ate *vb* **oblit·er·at·ed; oblit·er·at·ing** : to remove, destroy, or hide completely

obliv·i·on *n* **1** : the state of forgetting or having forgotten or of being unaware or unconscious **2** : the state of being forgotten

obliv·i·ous *adj* : not being conscious or aware — **obliv·i·ous·ly** *adv*

[1]**ob·long** *adj* : different from a square, circle, or sphere by being longer in one direction than the other

[2]**oblong** *n* : a figure or object that is larger in one direction than the other

ob·nox·ious *adj* : very disagreeable : HATEFUL — **ob·nox·ious·ly** *adv*

oboe *n* : a woodwind instrument with two reeds that is pitched higher than the bassoon and has a distinctive bright sound

ob·scene *adj* : very shocking to a person's sense of what is moral or decent

ob·scen·i·ty *n, pl* **ob·scen·i·ties** **1** : the quality or state of being shocking to a person's sense of what is moral or decent **2** : something that is shocking to a person's sense of what is moral or decent

[1]**ob·scure** *adj* **1** : not easy to see : FAINT **2** : hidden from view **3** : not easily understood or clearly expressed **4** : not outstanding or famous

[2]**obscure** *vb* **ob·scured; ob·scur·ing** : to make difficult to see or understand

ob·scu·ri·ty *n, pl* **ob·scu·ri·ties** **1** : the state of being difficult to see or understand **2** : the state of being unknown or forgotten **3** : something that is difficult to understand

ob·serv·able *adj* : NOTICEABLE — **ob·serv·ably** *adv*

ob·ser·vance *n* **1** : an established practice or ceremony **2** : an act of following a custom, rule, or law

ob·ser·vant *adj* : quick to take notice : WATCHFUL, ALERT — **ob·ser·vant·ly** *adv*

ob·ser·va·tion *n* **1** : an act or the power of seeing or taking notice of something **2** : the gathering of information by noting facts or occurrences **3** : an opinion formed or expressed after watching or noticing **4** : the fact of being watched and studied

ob·ser·va·to·ry *n, pl* **ob·ser·va·to·ries** : a place that has instruments for making observations (as of the stars)

ob·serve *vb* **ob·served; ob·serv·ing** **1** : to watch carefully **2** : to act in agreement with : OBEY **3** : CELEBRATE 1 **4** : [2]REMARK, SAY — **ob·serv·er** *n*

ob·sess *vb* **ob·sessed; ob·sess·ing** : to occupy the thoughts of completely or abnormally

ob·ses·sion *n* : a persistent abnormally strong interest in or concern about someone or something

ob·sid·i·an *n* : a smooth dark rock formed by the cooling of lava

ob·so·lete *adj* : no longer in use : OUT-OF-DATE

ob·sta·cle *n* : something that stands in the way or opposes : HINDRANCE

ob·sti·nate *adj* **1** : sticking stubbornly to an opinion or purpose **2** : difficult to deal with or get rid of — **ob·sti·nate·ly** *adv*

ob·struct *vb* **ob·struct·ed; ob·struct·ing** **1** : to block or make passage through difficult **2** : to be or come in the way of : HINDER **3** : to make (something) difficult to see

ob·struc·tion *n* **1** : an act of blocking or hindering : the state of having something that blocks or hinders **2** : something that gets in the way : OBSTACLE

ob·tain *vb* **ob·tained; ob·tain·ing** : to gain or get hold of with effort

ob·tain·able *adj* : possible to get

ob·tuse *adj* **1** : measuring more than a right angle **2** : not able to understand something obvious

ob·vi·ous *adj* : easily found, seen, or understood — **ob·vi·ous·ly** *adv* — **ob·vi·ous·ness** *n*

[1]oc·ca·sion *n* **1** : a special event **2** : the time of an event **3** : a suitable opportunity : a good chance

[2]occasion *vb* **oc·ca·sioned; oc·ca·sion·ing** : to bring about

oc·ca·sion·al *adj* : happening or met with now and then — **oc·ca·sion·al·ly** *adv*

oc·cu·pan·cy *n, pl* **oc·cu·pan·cies** : the act of using, living in, or taking possession of a place

oc·cu·pant *n* : a person who uses, lives in, or possesses a place

oc·cu·pa·tion *n* **1** : a person's business or profession **2** : the act of using or taking possession and control of a place

oc·cu·pa·tion·al *adj* : relating to a person's business or profession — **oc·cu·pa·tion·al·ly** *adv*

oc·cu·py *vb* **oc·cu·pied; oc·cu·py·ing** **1** : to fill up (an extent of time or space) **2** : to take up the attention or energies of **3** : to live in as an owner or tenant **4** : to take or hold possession of **5** : to perform the functions of

oc·cur *vb* **oc·curred; oc·cur·ring** **1** : to come by or as if by chance : HAPPEN **2** : to come into the mind **3** : to be found or met with : APPEAR

oc·cur·rence *n* **1** : something that happens **2** : the action or process of happening

ocean *n* **1** : the whole body of salt water that covers nearly three fourths of the earth **2** : one of the large bodies of water into which the larger body that covers the earth is divided

oce·an·ic *adj* : of or relating to the ocean

ocean·og·ra·phy *n* : a science that deals with the ocean

oce·lot *n* : a medium-sized American wildcat that is yellowish brown or grayish and blotched with black

o'·clock *adv* : according to the clock

Oct. *abbr* October

octa- *or* **octo-** *also* **oct-** *prefix* : eight

oc·ta·gon *n* : a flat geometric figure with eight angles and eight sides

oc·tag·o·nal *adj* : having eight sides

oc·tave *n* **1** : a space of eight steps between musical notes **2** : a tone or note that is eight steps above or below another note or tone

Oc·to·ber *n* : the tenth month of the year

oc·to·pus *n, pl* **oc·to·pus·es** *or* **oc·to·pi** : a marine animal that has a soft rounded body with eight long flexible arms about its base which have sucking disks able to seize and hold things (as prey)

oc·u·lar *adj* : of or relating to the eye or eyesight

odd *adj* **odd·er; odd·est** **1** : not usual or common : STRANGE **2** : not usual, expected, or planned **3** : not capable of being divided by two without leaving a remainder **4** : not one of a pair or a set **5** : being or having a number that cannot be divided by two without leaving a remainder **6** : some more than the number mentioned — **odd·ly** *adv* — **odd·ness** *n*

odd·ball *n* : a person who behaves strangely

odd·i·ty *n, pl* **odd·i·ties** **1** : something strange **2** : the quality or state of being strange

odds *n pl* **1** : a difference in favor of one thing over another **2** : conditions that make something difficult **3** : DISAGREEMENT 1

odds and ends *n pl* : things left over : miscellaneous things

ode *n* : a lyric poem that expresses a noble feeling with dignity

odi·ous *adj* : causing hatred or strong dislike : worthy of hatred

odom·e·ter *n* : an instrument for measuring the distance traveled (as by a vehicle)

odor *or Can and Brit* **odour** *n* : a particular smell — **odor·less** *or Can and Brit* **odour·less** *adj*

o'er *adv or prep* : OVER

of *prep* **1** — used to join an amount or a part with the whole which includes it **2** : belonging to, relating to, or connected with **3** : CONCERNING **4** : that is **5** : made from

6 : that has : WITH **7** — used to show what has been taken away **8** — used to indicate the reason for **9** : living in **10** : that involves **11** — used to indicate what an amount or number refers to **12** — used to indicate the point from which someone or something is located **13** — used to indicate the object affected by an action

[1]off *adv* **1** : from a place or position **2** : from a course : ASIDE **3** : so as not to be supported, covering or enclosing, or attached **4** : so as to be discontinued or finished **5** : away from work

[2]off *prep* **1** : away from the surface or top of **2** : at the expense of **3** : released or freed from **4** : below the usual level of **5** : away from

[3]off *adj* **1** : not operating or flowing **2** : not attached to or covering **3** : started on the way **4** : not taking place **5** : not correct : WRONG **6** : not as good as usual **7** : provided for **8** : small in degree : SLIGHT **9** : away from home or work

off. *abbr* office

of·fend *vb* **of·fend·ed; of·fend·ing** **1** : to hurt the feelings of or insult **2** : to do wrong

of·fend·er *n* : a person who does wrong

of·fense *or* **of·fence** *n* **1** : something done that hurts feelings or insults **2** : WRONGDOING, SIN **3** : the act of hurting feelings or insulting **4** : a team or the part of a team that attempts to score in a game **5** : an act of attacking : ASSAULT

[1]of·fen·sive *adj* **1** : causing displeasure or resentment **2** : of or relating to the attempt to score in a game or contest **3** : made for or relating to an attack — **of·fen·sive·ly** *adv* — **of·fen·sive·ness** *n*

[2]offensive *n* : [2]ATTACK 1 — **on the offensive** : in a situation that calls for opposing action

[1]of·fer *vb* **of·fered; of·fer·ing** **1** : to present (something) to be accepted or rejected **2** : to declare willingness **3** : to present for consideration : SUGGEST **4** : to make by effort **5** : to present as an act of worship

[2]offer *n* **1** : an act of presenting (something) to be accepted or rejected **2** : an act of declaring willingness **3** : a price suggested by someone prepared to buy : BID

of·fer·ing *n* **1** : something presented for acceptance **2** : a contribution to the support of a church **3** : a sacrifice given as part of worship

off·hand *adv or adj* : without previous thought or preparation

of·fice *n* **1** : a place where business is done or a service is supplied **2** : a special duty or position and especially one of authority in government

of·fice·hold·er *n* : a person who has been elected or appointed to a public position

of·fi·cer *n* **1** : a person given the responsibility of enforcing the law **2** : a person who holds a position of authority **3** : a person who holds a commission in the military

[1]of·fi·cial *n* : a person who holds a position of authority in an organization or government

[2]official *adj* **1** : relating to a position of authority **2** : having authority to perform a duty **3** : coming from or meeting the requirements of an authority **4** : proper for a person in office — **of·fi·cial·ly** *adv*

of·fi·ci·ate *vb* **of·fi·ci·at·ed; of·fi·ci·at·ing** **1** : to perform a ceremony or duty **2** : to act as an officer : PRESIDE

off·ing *n* : the near future or distance

off–lim·its *adj* : not to be entered or used

off–line *adj or adv* : not connected to or directly controlled by a computer system

off·set *vb* **offset; off·set·ting** : to make up for

off·shoot *n* : a branch of a main stem of a plant

[1]off·shore *adj* **1** : coming or moving away from the shore **2** : located off the shore

[2]off·shore *adv* : from the shore : at a distance from the shore

off·spring *n, pl* **offspring** *also* **off·springs** : the young of a person, animal, or plant

off·stage *adv or adj* : off or away from the stage

oft *adv* : OFTEN

of·ten *adv* : many times : FREQUENTLY

of·ten·times *adv* : OFTEN

ogle *vb* **ogled; ogling** : to look at in a way that suggests unusual interest or desire

ogre *n* **1** : an ugly giant of fairy tales and folklore who eats people **2** : a person or object that is frightening or causes strong feelings of dislike

oh *also* **O** *interj* **1** — used to express an emotion (as surprise or pain) **2** — used in direct address

OH *abbr* Ohio

[1]oil *n* **1** : any of numerous greasy usually liquid substances from plant, animal, or mineral sources that do not dissolve in water and are used especially as lubricants, fuels, and food **2** : PETROLEUM **3** : paint made of pigments and oil **4** : a painting done in oils

[2]oil *vb* **oiled; oil·ing** : to rub on or lubricate with a greasy substance

oil·cloth *n* : material treated with a greasy substance so as to be waterproof and used for shelf and table coverings

oily *adj* **oil·i·er; oil·i·est** : covered with or containing a greasy substance — **oil·i·ness** *n*

oint·ment *n* : a thick greasy medicine for use on the skin

Ojib·wa *or* **Ojib·way** *or* **Ojib·we** *n, pl* **Ojibwa** *or* **Ojib·was** *or* **Ojibway** *or* **Ojib·ways** *or*

Ojibwe *or* **Ojib·wes** **1 :** a member of an American Indian people originally of Michigan **2 :** the language of the Ojibwa people
[1]**OK** *or* **okay** *adv or adj* **:** all right
[2]**OK** *or* **okay** *n* **:** APPROVAL
[3]**OK** *or* **okay** *vb* **OK'd** *or* **okayed; OK'·ing** *or* **okay·ing :** APPROVE 2, AUTHORIZE
[4]**OK** *abbr* Oklahoma
oka·pi *n* **:** an animal of the African forests related to the giraffe
Okla. *abbr* Oklahoma
okra *n* **:** the green pods of a garden plant that are used as a vegetable especially in soups and stews
[1]**old** *adj* **1 :** having lived a long time **2 :** showing the effects of time or use **3 :** having existed for a specified length of time **4 :** dating from the distant past **:** ANCIENT **5 :** having lasted or been such for a long time **6 :** FORMER
[2]**old** *n* **:** a distant or earlier time
old·en *adj* **:** of an earlier period
Old English *n* **:** the language of England from the earliest documents in the seventh century to about 1100
old–fash·ioned *adj* **1 :** from or like that of an earlier time **2 :** using or preferring ways and traditions of the past
Old French *n* **:** the French language from the ninth to the thirteenth century
Old Glory *n* **:** the flag of the United States
old maid *n* **1 :** an elderly unmarried woman **2 :** a very neat fussy person **3 :** a card game in which cards are matched in pairs and the player holding the extra queen at the end loses
old–time *adj* **:** from or like that of an earlier or distant period
old–tim·er *n* **1 :** a person who has been part of an organization (as a business) for a long time **2 :** an old person
old–world *adj* **:** having old-fashioned charm
Old World *n* **:** the lands in the eastern hemisphere and especially Europe but not including Australia
ol·fac·to·ry *adj* **:** of or relating to smelling or the sense of smell
ol·ive *n* **1 :** the oily fruit of an evergreen tree that is eaten both ripe and unripe and is the source of an edible oil (**olive oil**) **2 :** a yellowish green color
Olym·pic *adj* **:** of or relating to the Olympic Games
Olympic Games *n pl* **:** a series of international athletic contests held as separate winter and summer events in a different country every four years
om·e·let *or* **om·e·lette** *n* **:** beaten eggs cooked without stirring until firm and folded in half often with a filling
omen *n* **:** a happening believed to be a sign or warning of a future event
om·i·nous *adj* **:** considered a sign of evil or trouble to come — **om·i·nous·ly** *adv*
omis·sion *n* **1 :** something left out **2 :** the act of leaving out **:** the state of being left out
omit *vb* **omit·ted; omit·ting** **1 :** to leave out **:** fail to include **2 :** to leave undone **:** NEGLECT
om·ni·bus *n, pl* **om·ni·bus·es :** BUS
om·nip·o·tent *adj* **:** having power or authority without limit **:** ALMIGHTY — **om·nip·o·tence** *n*
om·ni·vore *n* **:** an animal that feeds on plants and other animals
om·niv·o·rous *adj* **:** feeding on plants and animals
[1]**on** *prep* **1 :** in contact with and supported by **2** — used to indicate means of being carried **3** — used to indicate the location of something **4** — used to indicate the focus of a certain action **5 :** AGAINST 4 **6 :** near or connected with **7 :** [1]TO 1 **8 :** sometime during **9 :** in the state or process of **10 :** [2]ABOUT 3 **11 :** by means of
[2]**on** *adv* **1 :** into operation or a position allowing operation **2 :** in or into contact with a surface **3 :** forward in time, space, or action **4 :** from one to another
[3]**on** *adj* **1 :** being in operation **2 :** placed so as to allow operation **3 :** taking place **4 :** having been planned
ON *abbr* Ontario
[1]**once** *adv* **1 :** one time only **2 :** at some time in the past **:** FORMERLY **3 :** at any one time **:** EVER — **once and for all :** now and for the last time — **once in a while :** from time to time
[2]**once** *n* **:** one single time — **at once** **1 :** at the same time **2 :** IMMEDIATELY 2
[3]**once** *conj* **:** as soon as **:** WHEN
once–over *n* **:** a quick glance or examination
on·com·ing *adj* **:** coming nearer
[1]**one** *adj* **1 :** being a single unit or thing **2 :** being a certain unit or thing **3 :** being the same in kind or quality **4 :** not specified
[2]**one** *n* **1 :** the number denoting a single unit **:** 1 **2 :** the first in a set or series **3 :** a single person or thing
[3]**one** *pron* **1 :** a single member or individual **2 :** any person
one another *pron* **:** EACH OTHER
Onei·da *n, pl* **Oneida** *or* **Onei·das** **1 :** a member of an American Indian people originally of New York **2 :** the language of the Oneida people
oner·ous *adj* **:** being difficult and unpleasant to do or to deal with
one·self *pron* **:** a person's own self
one–sid·ed *adj* **1 :** done or occurring on one side only **2 :** having one side more

developed : LOPSIDED **3** : favoring or dominated by one side
one·time *adj* : FORMER
one–way *adj* : moving or allowing movement in one direction only
on·go·ing *adj* : being in progress or movement
on·ion *n* : the roundish edible bulb of a plant related to the lily that has a sharp odor and taste and is used as a vegetable and to season foods
on·line *adj or adv* : connected to, directly controlled by, or available through a computer system
on·look·er *n* : SPECTATOR
¹on·ly *adj* **1** : alone in or of a class or kind : SOLE **2** : best without doubt
²only *adv* **1** : no more than **2** : no one or nothing other than **3** : in no other situation, time, place, or condition except **4** : in the end **5** : as recently as
³only *conj* : except that
on·o·mato·poe·ia *n* : the forming of a word (as "buzz" or "hiss") in imitation of a natural sound
on·rush *n* : a strong fast movement forward
on·set *n* **1** : BEGINNING 1 **2** : ²ATTACK 1
on·slaught *n* : a violent attack
Ont. *abbr* Ontario
on·to *prep* : to a position on or against
¹on·ward *adv* : toward or at a point lying ahead in space or time : FORWARD
²onward *adj* : directed or moving forward
oo·dles *n pl* : a great quantity
¹ooze *n* : soft mud : SLIME
²ooze *vb* **oozed; ooz·ing** : to flow or leak out slowly
opal *n* : a mineral with soft changeable colors that is used as a gem
opaque *adj* **1** : not letting light through : not transparent **2** : not reflecting light : DULL
¹open *adj* **1** : not shut or blocked : not closed **2** : not sealed, locked, or fastened **3** : easy to enter, get through, or see **4** : ready to consider appeals or ideas **5** : not drawn together : spread out **6** : not enclosed or covered **7** : not secret : PUBLIC **8** : to be used, entered, or taken part in by all **9** : not decided or settled — **open·ly** *adv* — **open·ness** *n*
²open *vb* **opened; open·ing** **1** : to change or move from a shut condition **2** : to clear by or as if by removing something in the way **3** : to make or become ready for use **4** : to give access **5** : BEGIN 1, START — **open·er** *n*
³open *n* : space that is not enclosed or covered : OUTDOORS
open air *n* : space that is not enclosed or covered — **open–air** *adj*
open–and–shut *adj* : ¹PLAIN 3, OBVIOUS
open·heart·ed *adj* **1** : FRANK **2** : GENEROUS 1
open house *n* **1** : friendly and welcoming treatment to anyone who comes **2** : an event in which an organization (as a school) invites the public to visit
open·ing *n* **1** : a place that is not enclosed or covered : CLEARING **2** : an act of making or becoming ready for use **3** : BEGINNING **4** : ¹OCCASION 3 **5** : a job opportunity
open·work *n* : something made or work done so as to show spaces through the fabric or material
op·era *n* : a play in which the entire text is sung with orchestral accompaniment
op·er·ate *vb* **op·er·at·ed; op·er·at·ing** **1** : to work or cause to work in a proper or particular way **2** : MANAGE 1 **3** : to perform surgery : do an operation on
operating system *n* : a program or series of programs that controls the operation of a computer and directs the processing of the user's programs
op·er·a·tion *n* **1** : a set of actions for a particular purpose **2** : a medical procedure that involves cutting into a living body in order to repair or remove a damaged or diseased part **3** : the process of putting military forces into action **4** : the state of working or being able to work **5** : a method or manner of working **6** : a process (as addition or multiplication) of getting one mathematical expression from others according to a rule **7** : a single step performed by a computer in carrying out a program
op·er·a·tion·al *adj* : ready for use
op·er·a·tor *n* **1** : a person who manages or controls something **2** : a person in charge of a telephone switchboard **3** : a person who is skillful at achieving things by persuasion or deception
op·er·et·ta *n* : a funny play set to music with speaking, singing, and dancing scenes
opin·ion *n* **1** : a belief based on experience and on certain facts but not amounting to sure knowledge **2** : a judgment about a person or thing **3** : a statement by an expert after careful study
opin·ion·at·ed *adj* : having and expressing very strong ideas and opinions about things
opi·um *n* : a bitter brownish narcotic drug that is the dried juice of a poppy of Europe and Asia
opos·sum *n* : an American animal related to the kangaroo that has a long pointed snout, lives both on the ground and in trees, and is active at night
op·po·nent *n* : a person or thing that takes an opposite position in a contest, fight, or controversy

op·por·tu·ni·ty *n, pl* **op·por·tu·ni·ties** **1 :** a favorable combination of circumstances, time, and place **2 :** a chance for greater success
op·pose *vb* **op·posed; op·pos·ing** **1 :** to disagree with or disapprove of **2 :** to compete against **3 :** to provide contrast to **4 :** to offer resistance to **:** try to stop or defeat
[1]**op·po·site** *adj* **1 :** being at the other end, side, or corner **2 :** being as different as possible **3 :** being in a position to contrast with or cancel out
[2]**opposite** *n* **:** either of two persons or things that are as different as possible
[3]**opposite** *adv* **:** on the other side of someone or something **:** across from
[4]**opposite** *prep* **:** across from (someone or something)
op·po·si·tion *n* **1 :** the state of disagreeing with or disapproving of **2 :** the action of resisting **3 :** a group of people that disagree with, disapprove of, or resist someone or something
op·press *vb* **op·pressed; op·press·ing** **1 :** to control or rule in a harsh or cruel way **2 :** to cause to feel burdened in spirit — **op·press·or** *n*
op·pres·sion *n* **:** cruel or unjust use of power or authority
op·pres·sive *adj* **1 :** cruel or harsh without just cause **2 :** very unpleasant or uncomfortable — **op·pres·sive·ly** *adv*
op·tic *adj* **:** of or relating to seeing or the eye
op·ti·cal *adj* **1 :** relating to the science of optics **2 :** relating to seeing **:** VISUAL **3 :** involving the use of devices that are sensitive to light to get information for a computer
optical fiber *n* **:** a single fiber used in fiber optics
optical illusion *n* **:** something that looks different from what it actually is
op·ti·cian *n* **:** a person who prepares lenses for and sells eyeglasses
op·tics *n* **:** a science that deals with the nature and properties of light and the changes that it undergoes and produces
op·ti·mism *n* **:** a feeling or belief that good things will happen
op·ti·mist *n* **:** a person who habitually expects good things to happen
op·ti·mis·tic *adj* **:** expecting good things to happen **:** HOPEFUL — **op·ti·mis·ti·cal·ly** *adv*
op·ti·mum *adj* **:** most desirable or satisfactory
op·tion *n* **1 :** the power or right to choose **2 :** something that can be chosen **3 :** a right to buy or sell something at a specified price during a specified period
op·tion·al *adj* **:** left to choice **:** not required
op·tom·e·trist *n* **:** a person who examines the eyes and prescribes glasses or exercise to improve the eyesight
op·u·lent *adj* **:** having or showing much wealth
or *conj* — used between words or phrases that are choices
OR *abbr* Oregon
[1]**-or** *n suffix* **:** someone or something that does a specified thing
[2]**-or** *n suffix* **:** condition **:** activity
or·a·cle *n* **1 :** a person (as a priestess in ancient Greece) through whom a god is believed to speak **2 :** the place where a god speaks through a person **3 :** an answer given by a person through whom a god speaks
oral *adj* **1 :** [2]SPOKEN 1 **2 :** of, involving, or given by the mouth — **oral·ly** *adv*
or·ange *n* **1 :** a color between red and yellow **:** the color of a carrot **2 :** a sweet juicy citrus fruit with orange colored rind that grows on an evergreen tree with shining leaves and fragrant white flowers
orang·utan *n* **:** a large ape of Borneo and Sumatra that lives in trees, eats mostly fruit, leaves, and other plant matter, and has very long arms, long reddish brown hair, and a nearly hairless face
ora·tion *n* **:** an important speech given on a special occasion
or·a·tor *n* **:** a public speaker noted for skill and power in speaking
or·a·to·ry *n* **1 :** the art of making speeches **2 :** the style of language used in important speeches
orb *n* **:** something in the shape of a ball (as a planet or the eye)
[1]**or·bit** *n* **:** the path taken by one body circling around another body
[2]**orbit** *vb* **or·bit·ed; or·bit·ing** **1 :** to move in an orbit around **:** CIRCLE **2 :** to send up so as to move in an orbit
or·ca *n* **:** KILLER WHALE
or·chard *n* **:** a place where fruit trees are grown
or·ches·tra *n* **1 :** a group of musicians who perform instrumental music using mostly stringed instruments **2 :** the front part of the main floor in a theater — **or·ches·tral** *adj*
or·chid *n* **:** a plant with usually showy flowers with three petals of which the middle petal is enlarged and differs from the others in shape and color
or·dain *vb* **or·dained; or·dain·ing** **1 :** [2]DECREE **2 :** to make a person a Christian minister or priest by a special ceremony
or·deal *n* **:** a severe test or experience
[1]**or·der** *vb* **or·dered; or·der·ing** **1 :** to put into a particular grouping or sequence **:** ARRANGE **2 :** to give a command to or for

DICTIONARY

[2]**order** *n* **1 :** a certain rule or regulation : COMMAND **2 :** the arrangement of objects or events in space or time **3 :** the way something should be **4 :** the state of things when law or authority is obeyed **5 :** good working condition **6 :** a statement of what a person wants to buy **7 :** goods or items bought or sold **8 :** a group of people united (as by living under the same religious rules or by loyalty to common needs or duties) **9 orders** *pl* **:** the office of a person in the Christian ministry **10 :** a group of related living things (as plants or animals) that ranks above the family and below the class in scientific classification **11 :** a written direction to pay a sum of money — **in order that :** so that — **in order to :** for the purpose of

[1]**or·der·ly** *adj* **1 :** having a neat arrangement : TIDY **2 :** obeying commands or rules : well-behaved

[2]**orderly** *n, pl* **or·der·lies 1 :** a soldier who works for an officer especially to carry messages **2 :** a person who does cleaning and general work in a hospital

or·di·nal *n* **:** ORDINAL NUMBER

ordinal number *n* **:** a number that is used to show the place (as first, fifth, 22nd) taken by an element in a series

or·di·nance *n* **:** a law or regulation especially of a city or town

or·di·nar·i·ly *adv* **:** in the usual course of events : USUALLY

[1]**or·di·nary** *adj* **1 :** to be expected : NORMAL, USUAL **2 :** neither good nor bad : AVERAGE **3 :** not very good : MEDIOCRE

[2]**ordinary** *n* **:** the conditions or events that are usual or normal

ord·nance *n* **1 :** military supplies (as guns, ammunition, trucks, and tanks) **2 :** ARTILLERY 1

ore *n* **:** a mineral mined to obtain a substance (as gold) that it contains

Ore., Oreg. *abbr* Oregon

or·gan *n* **1 :** a musical instrument played by means of one or more keyboards and having pipes sounded by compressed air **2 :** a part of a person, plant, or animal that is specialized to perform a particular function **3 :** a way of getting something done

or·gan·ic *adj* **1 :** relating to or obtained from living things **2 :** relating to carbon compounds : containing carbon **3 :** being, involving, or producing food grown or made without the use of artificial chemicals

or·gan·ism *n* **:** a living thing made up of one or more cells and able to carry on the activities of life (as using energy, growing, or reproducing)

or·gan·ist *n* **:** a person who plays an organ

or·ga·ni·za·tion *n* **1 :** the act or process of arranging **2 :** the state or way of being arranged **3 :** a group of people united for a common purpose

or·ga·nize *vb* **or·ga·nized; or·ga·niz·ing 1 :** to arrange by effort and planning **2 :** to put in a certain order **3 :** to make separate parts into one united whole — **or·ga·niz·er** *n*

ori·ent *vb* **ori·ent·ed; ori·ent·ing 1 :** to set or arrange in a position especially so as to be lined up with certain points of the compass **2 :** to make familiar with an existing situation or environment **3 :** to direct toward the interests of a particular group — **ori·en·ta·tion** *n*

ori·en·tal *adj, often cap* **1** *sometimes offensive* **:** [1]ASIAN **2 :** relating to or from the region that includes the countries of eastern Asia (as China, Japan, South Korea, and North Korea)

ori·ga·mi *n* **:** the art of folding paper into three-dimensional figures or designs without cutting the paper or using glue

or·i·gin *n* **1 :** basic source or cause **2 :** a person's ancestry **3 :** the rise or beginning from a source

[1]**orig·i·nal** *adj* **1 :** of or relating to the source or beginning : FIRST **2 :** not copied from anything else : not translated : NEW **3 :** able to think up new things : CREATIVE — **orig·i·nal·ly** *adv*

[2]**original** *n* **:** something that is produced by an artist or writer and from which a copy or translation can be made

orig·i·nal·i·ty *n* **:** the quality or state of being creative or new and different

orig·i·nate *vb* **orig·i·nat·ed; orig·i·nat·ing 1 :** to bring into being : INVENT, INITIATE **2 :** to come into being — **orig·i·na·tor** *n*

ori·ole *n* **1 :** an American songbird related to the blackbird that has a bright orange and black male **2 :** a yellow and black bird of Europe and Asia related to the crow

[1]**or·na·ment** *n* **:** something that adds beauty : DECORATION

[2]**or·na·ment** *vb* **or·na·ment·ed; or·na·ment·ing :** DECORATE 1

[1]**or·na·men·tal** *adj* **:** serving to add beauty : DECORATIVE

[2]**ornamental** *n* **:** a plant grown for its beauty

or·na·men·ta·tion *n* **1 :** the act or process of decorating : the state of being decorated **2 :** something that adds beauty

or·nate *adj* **:** decorated in a fancy way — **or·nate·ly** *adv* — **or·nate·ness** *n*

or·nery *adj* **or·neri·er; or·neri·est :** becoming angry or annoyed easily

[1]**or·phan** *n* **:** a child whose parents are dead

[2]**orphan** *vb* **or·phaned; or·phan·ing :** to leave without parents : cause to become an orphan

or·phan·age *n* : a place where children who have lost their parents live and are cared for
or·tho·don·tist *n* : a dentist who adjusts badly placed or crooked teeth especially through the use of braces
or·tho·dox *adj* **1** : approved as measuring up to some standard : CONVENTIONAL **2** : closely following the established beliefs of a religion
[1]-ory *n suffix, pl* **-ories** : place of or for
[2]-ory *adj suffix* : of, relating to, or associated with
Osage *n, pl* **Osag·es** *or* **Osage** **1** : a member of an American Indian people of Missouri **2** : the language of the Osage people
os·cil·late *vb* **os·cil·lat·ed; os·cil·lat·ing** : to swing or move back and forth between two points
os·mo·sis *n* : a passing of material and especially water through a membrane (as of a living cell) that will not allow all kinds of molecules to pass
os·prey *n, pl* **ospreys** : a large hawk that feeds chiefly on fish
os·ten·si·ble *adj* : seeming to be true : APPARENT — **os·ten·si·bly** *adv*
os·ten·ta·tious *adj* : attracting or fond of attracting attention by showing off wealth or cleverness
os·tra·cize *vb* **os·tra·cized; os·tra·ciz·ing** : to shut out of a group
os·trich *n* : a very large bird of Africa that often weighs as much as 300 pounds (140 kilograms) and runs very fast but cannot fly
[1]oth·er *adj* **1** : being the one (as of two or more) left **2** : [1]SECOND 1 **3** : [1]EXTRA, ADDITIONAL **4** : different or separate from those already mentioned
[2]other *n* : a remaining or different one
[3]other *pron* : another thing
oth·er·wise *adv* **1** : in another way **2** : in different circumstances **3** : in other ways **4** : if not : or else
ot·ter *n* : a web-footed animal that lives mostly in the water, feeds on fish, and has dark brown fur
ouch *interj* — used especially to express sudden pain
ought *helping verb* **1** — used to show duty **2** — used to show what it would be wise to do **3** — used to show what is naturally expected **4** — used to show what is correct
oughtn't : ought not
ounce *n* **1** : a unit of weight equal to 1/16 pound (about 28 grams) **2** : a unit of liquid capacity equal to 1/16 pint (about 30 milliliters)
our *adj* : relating to or belonging to us : caused by, produced by, or participated in by us
ours *pron* : that which belongs to us
our·selves *pron* : our own selves
-ous *adj suffix* : full of : having : resembling
oust *vb* **oust·ed; oust·ing** : to force or drive out (as from office or from possession of something)
oust·er *n* : the act or an instance of forcing out or of being forced out
[1]out *adv* **1** : in a direction away from the inside, center, or surface **2** : away from home, business, or the usual or proper place **3** : so as to be used up, completed, or discontinued **4** : so as to be missing or moved from the usual or proper place **5** : in or into the open **6** : ALOUD **7** : beyond control or possession **8** : so as to be or make unsuccessful in reaching base in baseball
[2]out *prep* **1** : outward through **2** : outward on or along — **out of** **1** : from the inside to the outside of : not in **2** : beyond the limits or range of **3** : because of **4** : in a group of **5** : [1]WITHOUT 2 **6** : FROM 3
[3]out *adj* **1** : no longer in power or use **2** : no longer continuing or taking place **3** : not confined : not concealed or covered **4** : [1]ABSENT 1 **5** : located outside or at a distance **6** : being no longer at bat and not successful in reaching base **7** : no longer in fashion **8** : OUT-OF-BOUNDS
[4]out *n* : the act of causing a baseball player to be unsuccessful in reaching base
out- *prefix* : in a manner that goes beyond
out–and–out *adj* : THOROUGH 1, ABSOLUTE
out·board motor *n* : a small gasoline engine with an attached propeller that can be fastened to the back end of a small boat
out·break *n* : a sudden occurrence or increase of something
out·build·ing *n* : a building (as a shed or stable) separate from a main building
out·burst *n* **1** : a sudden expression of strong feeling **2** : a sudden increase of activity or growth
outcast *n* : a person who is not accepted by society
out·class *vb* **out·classed; out·class·ing** : to be or do much better than : SURPASS
out·come *n* : [2]RESULT 1
out·cry *n, pl* **out·cries** **1** : a loud and excited shout **2** : a strong protest
out·dat·ed *adj* : not modern or current
out·dis·tance *vb* **out·dis·tanced; out·dis·tanc·ing** : to go far ahead of (as in a race)
out·do *vb* **out·did; out·done; out·do·ing; out·does** : to do better than : SURPASS
out·door *adj* **1** : used, being, or done outside **2** : preferring to spend time in the open air
[1]out·doors *adv* : outside a building : in or into the open air

²outdoors *n* : the open air
out·er *adj* : located on the outside or farther out
out·er·most *adj* : farthest out
outer space *n* : the region beyond earth's atmosphere and especially beyond the solar system
out·field *n* : the part of a baseball field beyond the infield and between the foul lines
out·field·er *n* : a baseball player who plays in the outfield
¹out·fit *n* **1** : a set of clothing worn together **2** : the equipment for a special use **3** : a group of persons working together or associated in the same activity
²outfit *vb* **out·fit·ted; out·fit·ting** : to supply with equipment for a special purpose : EQUIP — **out·fit·ter** *n*
out·go *n, pl* **outgoes** : EXPENDITURE 2
out·go·ing *adj* **1** : FRIENDLY 1 **2** : leaving a place **3** : retiring from a place or position
out·grow *vb* **out·grew; out·grown; out·grow·ing** **1** : to grow too large or too old for **2** : to grow faster than
out·growth *n* : something that grows out of or develops from something else
out·ing *n* : a brief usually outdoor trip for pleasure
out·land·ish *adj* : very strange or unusual : BIZARRE
out·last *vb* **out·last·ed; out·last·ing** : to last longer than
¹out·law *n* : a person who has broken the law and is hiding or fleeing to avoid punishment
²outlaw *vb* **out·lawed; out·law·ing** : to make illegal
out·lay *n* : an amount of money spent
out·let *n* **1** : a place or opening for letting something out **2** : a way of releasing or expressing a feeling or impulse **3** : a device (as in a wall) into which the prongs of an electrical plug are inserted for making connection with an electrical circuit
¹out·line *n* **1** : a line that traces or forms the outer limits of an object or figure and shows its shape **2** : a drawing or picture or style of drawing in which only the outer edges of an object or figure are shown **3** : an often numbered or lettered list of the important parts of something (as an essay) **4** : a short treatment of a subject
²outline *vb* **out·lined; out·lin·ing** **1** : to draw or trace the outer edges of **2** : to list or describe the main features or parts of
out·live *vb* **out·lived; out·liv·ing** : to live or last longer than
out·look *n* **1** : a view from a certain place **2** : a way of thinking about or looking at things **3** : conditions that seem to lie ahead
out·ly·ing *adj* : being far from a central point : REMOTE
out·mod·ed *adj* : no longer in style or in use
out·num·ber *vb* **out·num·bered; out·num·ber·ing** : to be more than in number
out–of–bounds *adv or adj* : outside the limits of the playing area in a game or sport
out–of–date *adj* : not modern or current
out–of–doors *n* : ²OUTDOORS
out of doors *adv* : ¹OUTDOORS
out·post *n* **1** : a guard placed at a distance from a military force or camp **2** : the place occupied by such a guard **3** : an outlying settlement
out·pour·ing *n* : an act of expressing or giving freely
¹out·put *n* **1** : something produced **2** : the information produced by a computer
²output *vb* **out·put·ted** *or* **out·put; out·put·ting** : to produce something
¹out·rage *n* **1** : angry feelings caused by a hurtful, unjust, or insulting act **2** : an act that is hurtful or unjust or shows disrespect for a person's feelings
²outrage *vb* **out·raged; out·rag·ing** **1** : to cause to feel anger or strong resentment **2** : to cause to suffer great insult
out·ra·geous *adj* **1** : extremely annoying, insulting, or shameful **2** : very strange or unusual
¹out·right *adv* **1** : COMPLETELY **2** : without holding back **3** : quickly and entirely
²out·right *adj* **1** : complete and total : very clear or obvious **2** : done, made, or given with no restrictions or exceptions
out·run *vb* **out·ran; out·run; out·run·ning** : to run or move faster than
out·sell *vb* **out·sold; out·sell·ing** : to sell or be sold more than
out·set *n* : BEGINNING 1, START
out·shine *vb* **out·shone; out·shin·ing** **1** : to shine brighter than **2** : to do better than : OUTDO
¹out·side *n* **1** : an outer side or surface **2** : the greatest amount or limit : MOST
²outside *adj* **1** : of, relating to, or being on the outside **2** : not belonging to a place or group **3** : barely possible
³outside *adv* : ¹OUTDOORS
⁴outside *prep* **1** : on or to the outside of **2** : beyond the limits of
out·sid·er *n* : a person who does not belong to a particular group
out·size *adj* : unusually large
out·skirts *n pl* : the area that lies away from the center of a city or town
out·smart *vb* **out·smart·ed; out·smart·ing** : to beat or trick by being more clever than
out·spo·ken *adj* : talking in a free and honest way : BLUNT — **out·spo·ken·ly** *adv* — **out·spo·ken·ness** *n*
out·spread *adj* : spread out completely
out·stand·ing *adj* **1** : standing out espe-

cially because of excellence **2 :** UNPAID — **out·stand·ing·ly** *adv*
out·stay *vb* **out·stayed; out·stay·ing :** OVERSTAY
out·stretched *adj* **:** stretched out
out·strip *vb* **out·stripped; out·strip·ping 1 :** to go faster or farther than **2 :** to do better than
[1]**out·ward** *adj* **1 :** moving or turned toward the outside or away from a center **2 :** showing on the outside
[2]**outward** *or* **out·wards** *adv* **:** away from a center
out·ward·ly *adv* **:** on the outside **:** in outward appearance
out·weigh *vb* **out·weighed; out·weigh·ing :** to be greater than in weight or importance
out·wit *vb* **out·wit·ted; out·wit·ting :** OUTSMART
ova *pl of* OVUM
[1]**oval** *n* **:** something having the shape of an egg or ellipse
[2]**oval** *adj* **:** having the shape of an egg or ellipse **:** ELLIPTICAL
ova·ry *n, pl* **ova·ries 1 :** one of the usually two organs in the body of female animals in which eggs are produced **2 :** the larger rounded lower part of the pistil of a flower that contains the ovules in which the seeds are formed
ova·tion *n* **:** an expression of approval or enthusiasm made by clapping or cheering
ov·en *n* **:** a heated chamber (as in a stove) for baking, heating, or drying
[1]**over** *adv* **1 :** across a barrier or space **2 :** in a direction down or forward and down **3 :** across the brim **4 :** so as to bring the underside up **5 :** from one person or side to another **6 :** to someone's home **7 :** beyond a limit **8 :** more than needed **9 :** once more **:** AGAIN **10 :** [1]OVERNIGHT 1 — **over and over :** many times
[2]**over** *prep* **1 :** above in place **:** higher than **2 :** above in power or value **3 :** in front of **4 :** more than **5 :** down upon **6 :** all through or throughout **7 :** on or along the surface of **8 :** on or to the other side of **:** ACROSS **9 :** down from the top or edge of **10 :** having to do with
[3]**over** *adj* **1 :** being more than needed or expected **2 :** brought or come to an end
over- *prefix* **:** more than usual, normal, or proper
[1]**over·all** *adv* **:** as a whole **:** in most ways
[2]**overall** *adj* **:** including everyone or everything
over·alls *n pl* **:** loose pants usually with shoulder straps and a piece in front to cover the chest
over·bear·ing *adj* **:** acting in a proud or bossy way toward other people
over·board *adv* **1 :** over the side of a ship into the water **2 :** to extremes of enthusiasm
over·bur·den *vb* **over·bur·dened; over·bur·den·ing :** to burden too heavily
over·cast *adj* **:** covered with or darkened by clouds
over·charge *vb* **over·charged; over·charg·ing :** to charge too much money
over·coat *n* **:** a heavy coat worn over indoor clothing
over·come *vb* **over·came; overcome; over·com·ing 1 :** to win a victory over **:** CONQUER **2 :** to gain control of through great effort **3 :** to cause to lose physical ability or emotional control
over·crowd *vb* **over·crowd·ed; over·crowd·ing :** to cause to be too crowded
over·do *vb* **over·did; over·done; over·do·ing 1 :** to do too much of **2 :** to use too much of **3 :** to cook too long
over·dose *n* **:** too large a dose (as of a drug)
over·dress *vb* **over·dressed; over·dress·ing :** to dress in clothes too fancy for an occasion
over·due *adj* **1 :** not paid when due **2 :** delayed beyond an expected time **3 :** more than ready
over·eat *vb* **over·ate; over·eat·en; over·eat·ing :** to eat too much — **over·eat·er** *n*
over·es·ti·mate *vb* **over·es·ti·mat·ed; over·es·ti·mat·ing :** to estimate too highly
[1]**over·flow** *vb* **over·flowed; over·flow·ing 1 :** to flow over the top of **2 :** to flow over bounds **3 :** to fill or become filled beyond capacity **4 :** to fill a space up and spread beyond its limits
[2]**over·flow** *n* **1 :** a flowing over **2 :** something that flows over or fills a space and spreads beyond its limits
over·grown *adj* **1 :** grown too big **2 :** covered with plants that have grown in an uncontrolled way
[1]**over·hand** *adj* **:** made with the hand brought forward and down from above the shoulder
[2]**overhand** *adv* **:** with an overhand movement
[1]**over·hang** *vb* **over·hung; over·hang·ing :** to stick out or hang over
[2]**overhang** *n* **:** a part that overhangs
[1]**over·haul** *vb* **over·hauled; over·haul·ing 1 :** to examine thoroughly and make necessary repairs or improvements on **2 :** to catch up with **:** OVERTAKE
[2]**over·haul** *n* **:** an instance of overhauling
[1]**over·head** *adv* **:** above someone's head **:** in the sky or space above someone
[2]**over·head** *adj* **:** placed in the space above someone
[3]**over·head** *n* **:** the general expenses (as for rent or heat) of a business

over·hear *vb* **over·heard; over·hear·ing** : to hear something by accident without the speaker's knowledge

over·heat *vb* **over·heat·ed; over·heat·ing** : to heat too much : become too hot

over·joyed *adj* : filled with great joy

[1]**over·land** *adv* : by land rather than by water

[2]**overland** *adj* : going by land rather than by water

over·lap *vb* **over·lapped; over·lap·ping** : to place or be placed so that a part of one covers a part of another

[1]**over·lay** *vb* **over·laid; over·lay·ing** : to lay or spread over or across

[2]**over·lay** *n* : a usually thin covering that is laid over or across something

over·load *vb* **over·load·ed; over·load·ing** : to put too great a load on or in

over·look *vb* **over·looked; over·look·ing** **1** : to look down upon or provide a view of from above **2** : to fail to see : MISS **3** : to pay no attention to : IGNORE

over·ly *adv* : by too much : to an excessive degree

[1]**over·night** *adv* **1** : during or through the night **2** : very quickly or suddenly

[2]**overnight** *adj* **1** : done or lasting through the night **2** : staying for the night **3** : for use on short trips **4** : happening very quickly or suddenly

over·pass *n* **1** : a crossing (as of two highways or a highway and a railroad) at different levels usually by means of a bridge **2** : the upper level of an overpass

over·pop·u·la·tion *n* : the condition of having too many people living in a certain area

over·pow·er *vb* **over·pow·ered; over·pow·er·ing** **1** : to overcome by greater force : DEFEAT **2** : to affect by being too strong

over·rate *vb* **over·rat·ed; over·rat·ing** : to value or praise too highly

over·re·act *vb* **over·re·act·ed; over·re·act·ing** : to respond with an emotion that is too strong or an action that is extreme or unnecessary

over·ride *vb* **over·rode; over·rid·den; over·rid·ing** : to push aside as less important

over·ripe *adj* : passed beyond ripeness toward decay

over·rule *vb* **over·ruled; over·rul·ing** **1** : to decide against **2** : to set aside a decision or ruling made by someone having less authority

over·run *vb* **over·ran; overrun; over·run·ning** **1** : to take over and occupy by force **2** : to run or go past **3** : to spread over so as to cover

[1]**over·seas** *adv* : to or in a foreign country that is across the sea

[2]**overseas** *adj* : involving, occurring in, or intended for lands across the sea

over·see *vb* **over·saw; over·seen; over·see·ing** : to be in charge of : SUPERVISE

over·seer *n* : a person who supervises something

over·shad·ow *vb* **over·shad·owed; over·shad·ow·ing** **1** : to cast a shadow over : DARKEN **2** : to be or become more important than

over·shoe *n* : a shoe (as of rubber) worn over another for protection

over·shoot *vb* **over·shot; over·shoot·ing** : to miss by going beyond

over·sight *n* **1** : the act or duty of overseeing : watchful care **2** : an error or something forgotten through carelessness or haste

over·sim·pli·fy *vb* **over·sim·pli·fied; over·sim·pli·fy·ing** : to cause (something) to seem simpler than it is

over·size *or* **over·sized** *adj* : larger than the usual or normal size

over·sleep *vb* **over·slept; over·sleep·ing** : to sleep beyond the usual time or beyond the time set for getting up

over·state *vb* **over·stat·ed; over·stat·ing** : to put in too strong terms : EXAGGERATE

over·stay *vb* **over·stayed; over·stay·ing** : to stay beyond or longer than

over·step *vb* **over·stepped; over·step·ping** : to step over or beyond : EXCEED

over·sup·ply *n, pl* **over·sup·plies** : a supply that is too large

overt *adj* : not secret or hidden

over·take *vb* **over·took; over·tak·en; over·tak·ing** **1** : to catch up with and often pass **2** : to come upon or happen to suddenly or without warning

[1]**over·throw** *vb* **over·threw; over·thrown; over·throw·ing** **1** : OVERTURN 1 **2** : to cause the fall or end of : DESTROY

[2]**over·throw** *n* : an act of causing the fall or end of : the state of being overthrown : DEFEAT

over·time *n* **1** : time spent working that is more than one usually works in a day or a week **2** : extra time added to a game when the score is tied at the end of the normal playing time

over·ture *n* **1** : something first offered or suggested with the hope of reaching an agreement **2** : a piece of music played at the beginning of an opera or musical play

over·turn *vb* **over·turned; over·turn·ing** **1** : to turn over or upside down **2** : to reverse or cancel something previously decided or ordered

over·view *n* : a short explanation or description : SUMMARY

over·weight *adj* : weighing more than is normal, necessary, or allowed

over·whelm *vb* **over·whelmed; over·whelm-**

ing **1 :** to overcome completely (as with great force or emotion) **2 :** to cover over completely : SUBMERGE

over·whelm·ing *adj* **1 :** very great or strong **2 :** very difficult or confusing

[1]**over·work** *vb* **over·worked; over·work·ing** **1 :** to work or cause to work too much or too hard **2 :** to use too much or too often

[2]**overwork** *n* : too much work

over·wrought *adj* : very excited or upset

ovule *n* : a tiny structure in the ovary of a flower and on the scale of a cone that contains an egg cell and can develop into a seed following fertilization

ovum *n, pl* **ova** : EGG CELL

owe *vb* **owed; ow·ing** **1 :** to be obligated to pay, give, or return **2 :** to be in debt to **3 :** to have as a result

owing to *prep* : because of

owl *n* : a large bird with big head and eyes, hooked bill, and strong claws that is active at night and feeds on small animals — **owl·ish** *adj*

owl·et *n* : a young or small owl

[1]**own** *adj* — used to show the fact that something belongs to or relates to a particular person or thing and no other

[2]**own** *vb* **owned; own·ing** **1 :** to have or hold as property **2 :** to admit that something is true

own·er *n* : a person who owns something

own·er·ship *n* : the state or fact of owning something

ox *n, pl* **ox·en** *also* **ox** **1 :** one of our common domestic cattle or a closely related animal (as a yak) **2 :** an adult castrated male ox used especially for hauling loads

ox·bow *n* : a bend in a river in the shape of a U

ox·cart *n* : a cart pulled by oxen

ox·i·da·tion *n* : the process of oxidizing

ox·ide *n* : a compound of oxygen with another element or group of elements

ox·i·dize *vb* **ox·i·dized; ox·i·diz·ing** : to combine or become combined with oxygen

ox·y·gen *n* : a chemical element found in the air as a colorless odorless tasteless gas that is necessary for life

oys·ter *n* : a shellfish that lives on stony bottoms (**oyster beds**) in shallow seawater, has a rough grayish shell made up of two hinged parts, and is often used for food

oz. *abbr* **1** ounce **2** ounces

ozone *n* : a faintly blue form of oxygen that is present in the air in small quantities

ozone layer *n* : a layer of the earth's upper atmosphere that is characterized by high ozone content which blocks most of the sun's ultraviolet radiation from entering the lower atmosphere

P

p *n, pl* **p's** *or* **ps** *often cap* : the sixteenth letter of the English alphabet

p. *abbr* page

pa *n* : [1]FATHER 1

Pa., PA *abbr* Pennsylvania

[1]**pace** *n* **1 :** the speed of moving forward or ahead **2 :** the speed at which something is done or happens **3 :** a horse's gait in which the legs on the same side move at the same time **4 :** a single step or its length

[2]**pace** *vb* **paced; pac·ing** **1 :** to walk back and forth across **2 :** to walk with slow steps **3 :** to measure by steps **4 :** to set or regulate the speed at which something is done or happens

pa·cif·ic *adj* **1** *cap* **:** relating to the Pacific Ocean **2 :** [3]CALM 1, PEACEFUL **3 :** making peace : PEACEABLE

pac·i·fy *vb* **pac·i·fied; pac·i·fy·ing** : to make peaceful or quiet : CALM, SOOTHE

[1]**pack** *n* **1 :** a bundle arranged for carrying especially on the back of a person or animal **2 :** a group of like persons or things

[2]**pack** *vb* **packed; pack·ing** **1 :** to put into a container or bundle **2 :** to put things into **3 :** to crowd into so as to fill full : CRAM **4 :** to send away — **pack·er** *n*

pack·age *n* **1 :** a bundle made up for mailing or transporting **2 :** a container that covers or holds something **3 :** something that comes in a container

pack·et *n* : a small package

pact *n* : AGREEMENT 2, TREATY

[1]**pad** *n* **1 :** a tablet of writing or drawing paper **2 :** something soft used for protection or comfort : CUSHION **3 :** one of the cushioned parts of the underside of the feet of some animals **4 :** a floating leaf of a water plant (as a water lily) **5 :** a piece of material that holds ink used in inking rubber stamps

[2]**pad** *vb* **pad·ded; pad·ding** : to move with quiet steps

³pad *vb* **pad·ded; pad·ding** **1 :** to stuff or cover with soft material **2 :** to make longer by adding words
pad·ding *n* **:** soft material used to cover or line a surface
¹pad·dle *vb* **pad·dled; pad·dling** **1 :** to move or drive forward with an instrument like an oar or with short quick movements of hands and feet **2 :** to stir, mix, or beat with a paddle
²paddle *n* **1 :** an instrument like an oar used in moving and steering a small boat (as a canoe) **2 :** an implement having a broad flat end and used for beating, mixing, or hitting **3 :** one of the broad boards at the outer edge of a waterwheel or a paddle wheel
³paddle *vb* **paddled; paddling :** to move or splash about in the water
paddle wheel *n* **:** a wheel with broad boards near its outer edge used to make a boat move
pad·dock *n* **1 :** an enclosed area where animals are put to eat grass or to exercise **2 :** an enclosed area where racehorses are saddled and paraded
pad·dy *n, pl* **paddies :** wet land in which rice is grown
¹pad·lock *n* **:** a removable lock with a curved piece that snaps into a catch
²padlock *vb* **pad·locked; pad·lock·ing :** to fasten with a removable lock
¹pa·gan *n* **:** ²HEATHEN 1
²pagan *adj* **:** of or relating to heathens or their worship **:** HEATHEN
¹page *n* **1 :** one side of a printed or written sheet of paper **2 :** a large section of computer memory **3 :** the information found at a single World Wide Web address
²page *n* **1 :** a person employed (as by a hotel or the United States Congress) to carry messages or run errands **2 :** a boy being trained to be a knight in the Middle Ages
³page *vb* **paged; pag·ing :** to send for or contact someone by a public announcement or by using a pager
pag·eant *n* **1 :** a grand and fancy public ceremony and display **2 :** an entertainment made up of scenes based on history or legend **3 :** a contest in which a group of women or girls are judged
pag·er *n* **:** a small electronic device that beeps, vibrates, or flashes when it receives a signal
pa·go·da *n* **:** a tower of several stories built as a temple or memorial in eastern or southeastern Asia
paid *past and past participle of* PAY
pail *n* **1 :** a usually round container with a handle **:** BUCKET **2 :** PAILFUL
pail·ful *n, pl* **pail·fuls :** the amount a bucket holds
¹pain *n* **1 :** physical suffering that accompanies a bodily disorder (as a disease or an injury) **2 :** a very unpleasant feeling (as a prick or an ache) that is caused especially by something harmful **3 :** suffering of the mind or emotions **:** GRIEF **4 pains** *pl* **:** great care or effort **5 :** someone or something annoying — **pain·ful** *adj* — **pain·ful·ly** *adv* — **pain·less** *adj*
²pain *vb* **pained; pain·ing** **1 :** to cause physical or mental suffering in or to **2 :** to give or feel physical or mental suffering
pains·tak·ing *adj* **:** taking or showing great care — **pains·tak·ing·ly** *adv*
¹paint *vb* **paint·ed; paint·ing** **1 :** to cover a surface with or as if with paint **2 :** to make a picture or design by using paints **3 :** to describe clearly — **paint·er** *n*
²paint *n* **:** a mixture of coloring matter with a liquid that forms a dry coating when spread on a surface
paint·brush *n* **:** a tool with bristles that is used to apply paint
paint·ing *n* **1 :** a work of art made with paint **2 :** the art or occupation of creating pictures with paint
¹pair *n, pl* **pairs** *or* **pair** **1 :** two things that match or are meant to be used together **2 :** a thing having two similar parts that are connected **3 :** two people who are connected in some way or do something together
²pair *vb* **paired; pair·ing** **1 :** to put in or join in a group of two **2 :** to form a group of two **:** MATCH
Pai·ute *n* **1 :** a member of an American Indian people originally of Utah, Arizona, Nevada, and California **2 :** either of the two languages of the Paiute people
pa·ja·mas *or Can and Brit* **pyjamas** *n pl* **:** clothes usually consisting of pants and top that are worn for sleeping
pal *n* **:** a close friend
pal·ace *n* **1 :** the home of a ruler **2 :** a large or splendid house
pal·at·able *adj* **:** pleasant to the taste
pal·ate *n* **1 :** the top area of the inside of the mouth made up of a bony front part (**hard palate**) and a soft flexible back part (**soft palate**) **2 :** the sense of taste
¹pale *adj* **pal·er; pal·est** **1 :** having very light skin **2 :** having a lighter skin color than normal because of sickness or fear **3 :** not bright or brilliant **4 :** light in color or shade — **pale·ness** *n*
²pale *vb* **paled; pal·ing** **1 :** to lose color **2 :** to make or become less adequate, impressive, or intense
Pa·leo·zo·ic *n* **:** an era of geological history ending about 280 million years ago which

came before the Mesozoic and in which vertebrates and land plants first appeared

pal·ette *n* **1 :** a thin board or tablet on which a painter puts and mixes colors **2 :** the set of colors that an artist is using

pal·in·drome *n* **:** a word, phrase, sentence, or number that reads the same backward or forward

pal·i·sade *n* **1 :** a fence made of poles to protect against attack **2 :** a line of steep cliffs

¹pall *vb* **palled; pall·ing :** to become dull

²pall *n* **1 :** a heavy cloth covering for a coffin, hearse, or tomb **2 :** something that makes things gloomy or depressing

pall·bear·er *n* **:** a person who helps to carry the coffin at a funeral

pal·let *n* **1 :** a mattress of straw **2 :** a hard temporary bed

pal·lid *adj* **:** ¹PALE 1

pal·lor *n* **:** paleness of face

¹palm *n* **:** a tropical tree, shrub, or vine with a usually tall stem or trunk topped with large leaves that are shaped like feathers or fans

²palm *n* **1 :** the under part of the hand between the fingers and the wrist **2 :** a measure of length based on the width of a palm

³palm *vb* **palmed; palm·ing :** to hide in the hand — **palm off :** to get rid of or pass on in a dishonest way

pal·met·to *n, pl* **pal·met·tos** *or* **pal·met·toes :** a low-growing palm with leaves shaped like fans

pal·o·mi·no *n, pl* **pal·o·mi·nos :** a horse with a light golden coat and a cream or white mane and tail

pal·pi·tate *vb* **pal·pi·tat·ed; pal·pi·tat·ing :** ¹THROB 1

pal·sy *n* **1 :** PARALYSIS **2 :** an uncontrollable trembling of the body or a part of the body

pal·try *adj* **pal·tri·er; pal·tri·est :** of little amount, value, or importance

pam·pas *n pl* **:** wide treeless plains of South America

pam·per *vb* **pam·pered; pam·per·ing :** to treat (someone or something) with great care and attention

pam·phlet *n* **:** a short publication without a binding **:** BOOKLET

¹pan *n* **1 :** a usually shallow open container used for cooking **2 :** a shallow open tray or container

²pan *vb* **panned; pan·ning :** to wash earthy material so as to collect bits of metal (as gold) — **pan out :** to give a good result **:** SUCCEED

pan·cake *n* **:** a flat cake made of thin batter and cooked on both sides on a griddle

pan·cre·as *n* **:** a large gland near the stomach that produces insulin and a fluid (**pancreatic juice**) with enzymes that aid digestion

pan·cre·at·ic *adj* **:** of or relating to the pancreas

pan·da *n* **1 :** RED PANDA **2 :** a large black-and-white animal of central and western China that feeds mostly on the leaves and stems of the bamboo and is related to the bear

pan·de·mo·ni·um *n* **:** wild uproar

pane *n* **:** a sheet of glass (as in a window)

¹pan·el *n* **1 :** a usually rectangular section of something (as a door or a wall) **2 :** a piece of material (as plywood) made to form part of a surface (as of a wall) **3 :** a board into which instruments or controls are set **4 :** a group of people appointed for some service **5 :** a group of people taking part in a discussion or answering questions for an audience

²panel *vb* **pan·eled** *or* **pan·elled; pan·el·ing** *or* **pan·el·ling :** to cover or decorate with sections of material (as wood)

pan·el·ing *n* **:** sections of material (as wood) joined in a continuous surface and used to cover a wall or ceiling

pang *n* **:** a sudden sharp feeling of physical pain or emotion

¹pan·ic *n* **:** a sudden overpowering fear often without reasonable cause

²panic *vb* **pan·icked; pan·ick·ing :** to feel or cause to feel sudden overpowering fear

pan·icky *adj* **:** feeling or overcome with sudden fear

pan·o·rama *n* **:** a clear complete view in every direction

pan·sy *n, pl* **pansies :** a garden plant related to the violets that has large velvety colorful flowers

¹pant *vb* **pant·ed; pant·ing :** to breathe hard or quickly

²pant *n* **:** a hard or quick breath

pan·ta·loons *n pl* **:** PANTS

pan·ther *n* **1 :** LEOPARD **2 :** COUGAR **3 :** JAGUAR

pant·ie *or* **panty** *n, pl* **pant·ies :** a woman's or child's undergarment with short legs or no legs

¹pan·to·mime *n* **1 :** the act of showing or explaining something through movements of the body and face instead of by talking **2 :** a show in which a story is told by using expressions on the face and movements of the body instead of words

²pantomime *vb* **pan·to·mimed; pan·to·mim·ing :** to tell through movements rather than words

pan·try *n, pl* **pan·tries :** a small room where mainly food is kept

pants *n pl* **:** a piece of clothing usually reaching from the waist to the ankle and covering each leg separately

pa·pa *n* : [1]FATHER 1
papaw *variant of* PAWPAW
pa·pa·ya *n* : a yellow fruit that has a sweet flesh and many black seeds and grows on a tropical American tree
[1]**pa·per** *n* **1** : a material made from fibers (as of wood or cloth) and in the form of thin sheets or a sheet or piece of such material **2** : a piece of paper having something written or printed on it : DOCUMENT **3** : NEWSPAPER **4** : a piece of written schoolwork **5** : WALLPAPER
[2]**paper** *adj* : made of paper
[3]**paper** *vb* **pa·pered; pa·per·ing** : to cover with wallpaper
pa·per·back *n* : a book with a flexible paper binding
paper clip *n* : a piece of bent wire used to hold sheets of paper together
pa·per·work *n* : the documents that are a requirement for or a routine part of something
pa·pery *adj* : very thin or dry
pa·pier–mâ·ché *n* : material made of paper mixed with glue and other substances that hardens as it dries
pa·pri·ka *n* : a mild red spice made from dried peppers
pa·py·rus *n, pl* **pa·py·rus·es** *or* **pa·py·ri** **1** : a tall African plant related to the grasses that grows especially in Egypt **2** : a material like paper used by ancient people to write on
par *n* **1** : an equal level **2** : the score set for each hole of a golf course **3** : a usual or average level
par·a·ble *n* : a simple story that teaches a moral lesson
[1]**para·chute** *n* : a piece of equipment usually made of cloth and attached to someone or something for making a safe jump or drop from an airplane
[2]**parachute** *vb* **para·chut·ed; para·chut·ing** : to transport or come down by parachute
[1]**pa·rade** *n* **1** : a public celebration that includes people moving in order down a street by walking or riding in vehicles or on floats **2** : the formation of troops before an officer for inspection **3** : great show or display
[2]**parade** *vb* **pa·rad·ed; pa·rad·ing** **1** : to march in an orderly group **2** : to show off
par·a·dise *n* **1** : a place, state, or time of great beauty or happiness **2** : HEAVEN 2 **3** : the place where Adam and Eve first lived according to the Bible
par·a·dox *n* **1** : a statement that seems to say opposite things and yet is perhaps true **2** : a person or thing having qualities that seem to be opposite
par·af·fin *n* : a white waxy substance obtained from wood, coal, or petroleum and used in coating and sealing and in candles
para·graph *n* : a part of a piece of writing that is made up of one or more sentences and has to do with one topic or gives the words of one speaker
par·a·keet *n* : a small parrot that has a long tail and is sometimes kept as a caged bird
[1]**par·al·lel** *adj* : lying or moving in the same direction but always the same distance apart
[2]**parallel** *n* **1** : a line or surface that lies at or moves in the same direction as another but is always the same distance from it **2** : one of the imaginary circles on the earth's surface running in the same direction as the equator and marking latitude **3** : a way in which things are similar **4** : EQUAL
[3]**parallel** *vb* **par·al·leled; par·al·lel·ing** **1** : to move, run, or extend in the same direction with but always at the same distance from **2** : to be similar or equal to
par·al·lel·o·gram *n* : a plane figure with four sides whose opposite sides are parallel and equal
pa·ral·y·sis *n, pl* **pa·ral·y·ses** : loss of the ability to move all or part of the body (as from disease or injury)
par·a·lyze *vb* **par·a·lyzed; par·a·lyz·ing** **1** : to cause to be unable to move all or part of the body **2** : to destroy or decrease something's energy or ability to act
par·a·me·cium *n, pl* **par·a·me·cia** *also* **par·a·me·ciums** : a tiny living thing found in water that is a single cell shaped like a slipper and moves by means of cilia
para·med·ic *n* : a person specially trained to care for a patient before or during the trip to a hospital
par·a·mount *adj* : highest in importance or greatness
para·noid *adj* : having unreasonable feelings of suspicion, distrust, and persecution
par·a·pet *n* **1** : a low wall or fence at the edge of a platform, roof, or bridge **2** : a wall of earth or stone to protect soldiers
[1]**para·phrase** *vb* **para·phrased; para·phras·ing** : to give the meaning of in different words
[2]**paraphrase** *n* : a way of stating something again by giving the meaning in different words
para·pro·fes·sion·al *n* : a person trained to assist a professional person (as a teacher)
par·a·site *n* **1** : a living thing (as a flea, worm, or fungus) that lives in or on another living thing and gets food and sometimes shelter from it and usually causes harm to it **2** : a person who lives at the expense of another
par·a·sit·ic *adj* : relating to or having the habit of a parasite : caused by parasites
par·a·sol *n* : a light umbrella used as a protection against the sun
para·troop·er *n* : a soldier trained and equipped to parachute from an airplane

[1]par·cel *n* **1 :** PACKAGE 1 **2 :** a plot of land

[2]parcel *vb* **par·celed** *or* **par·celled; par·cel·ing** *or* **par·cel·ling :** to divide and give out by parts

parcel post *n* **:** a mail service that handles packages

parch *vb* **parched; parch·ing :** to dry or make dry from heat and lack of moisture

parch·ment *n* **1 :** the skin of a sheep or goat prepared so that it can be written on **2 :** strong tough paper used in baking and in wrapping food

[1]par·don *n* **1 :** forgiveness for wrong or rude behavior **2 :** the act of freeing from legal punishment

[2]pardon *vb* **par·doned; par·don·ing 1 :** to free from penalty for a fault or crime **2 :** to allow (a wrong act) to pass without punishment **:** FORGIVE

pare *vb* **pared; par·ing 1 :** to cut or shave off the outside or the ends of **2 :** to reduce as if by cutting

par·ent *n* **1 :** a father or mother of a child **2 :** an animal or plant that produces offspring

par·ent·age *n* **:** a line of ancestors

pa·ren·tal *adj* **:** of or as expected from a mother and father

pa·ren·the·sis *n, pl* **pa·ren·the·ses :** one of a pair of marks ( ) used to enclose a word or group of words or to group mathematical terms to be dealt with as a unit — **par·en·thet·i·cal** *adj*

par·ish *n* **1 :** a section of a church district under the care of a priest or minister **2 :** the people who attend a particular church **3 :** a division in the state of Louisiana that is similar to a county in other states

parish house *n* **:** a building for the educational and social activities of a church

pa·rish·io·ner *n* **:** a member of a particular church

[1]park *n* **1 :** an area of land set aside for recreation or for its beauty **2 :** an enclosed field for ball games

[2]park *vb* **parked; park·ing :** to stop a vehicle and leave it for a while

par·ka *n* **:** a very warm jacket with a hood

park·way *n* **:** a broad landscaped highway

[1]par·ley *n, pl* **parleys :** a discussion with an enemy

[2]parley *vb* **par·leyed; par·ley·ing :** to hold a discussion of terms with an enemy

par·lia·ment *n* **:** an assembly that is the highest legislative body of a country (as the United Kingdom)

par·lor *or Can and Brit* **parlour** *n* **1 :** a room for receiving guests and for conversation **2 :** a usually small place of business

pa·ro·chi·al school *n* **:** a private school that is run by a religious body

pa·role *n* **:** an early release of a prisoner

par·rot *n* **:** a brightly colored tropical bird that has a strong hooked bill and is sometimes trained to imitate human speech

[1]par·ry *vb* **par·ried; par·ry·ing 1 :** to turn aside an opponent's weapon or blow **2 :** to avoid by a skillful answer

[2]parry *n, pl* **par·ries :** an act or instance of skillfully avoiding something

pars·ley *n, pl* **pars·leys :** a garden plant that has small leaves used to season or decorate various foods

pars·nip *n* **:** the long white root of a garden plant that is cooked as a vegetable

par·son *n* **:** [1]MINISTER 1

par·son·age *n* **:** a house provided by a church for its pastor to live in

[1]part *n* **1 :** one of the sections into which something is divided **2 :** some of something **3 :** a general area **4 :** a piece of a machine **5 :** one of the sides or aspects **6 :** the role of a character in a play **7 :** a line along which the hair is divided **8 :** a person's share or duty **9 :** the music for a voice or instrument **10 :** a voice or instrument **11 :** a piece of a plant or animal body — **for the most part :** with few exceptions **:** on the whole

[2]part *vb* **part·ed; part·ing 1 :** to leave each other **2 :** to separate the hair by combing on each side of a line **3 :** to give up possession of **4 :** to hold apart **5 :** to come apart **6 :** to divide into parts

part. *abbr* participle

par·take *vb* **par·took; par·tak·en; par·tak·ing :** to take a share or part

par·tial *adj* **1 :** not complete **2 :** favoring one side of a question over another **3 :** fond or too fond of someone or something — **par·tial·ly** *adv*

par·ti·al·i·ty *n* **:** the quality or state of favoring one side over another

par·tic·i·pant *n* **:** a person who takes part in something

par·tic·i·pate *vb* **par·tic·i·pat·ed; par·tic·i·pat·ing :** to join with others in doing something

par·tic·i·pa·tion *n* **:** the act of joining with others in doing something

par·ti·ci·ple *n* **:** a form of a verb that is used to indicate a past or ongoing action and that can be used like an adjective

par·ti·cle *n* **:** a very small bit or amount of something

[1]par·tic·u·lar *adj* **1 :** relating to one person or thing **2 :** not usual **:** SPECIAL **3 :** having strong opinions about what is acceptable **4 :** being one of several **5 :** concerned about details — **par·tic·u·lar·ly** *adv* — **in particular 1 :** that can be specifically named **2 :** more specially than others **:** ESPECIALLY

[2]**particular** *n* : a single fact or detail
part·ing *n* : an act of leaving someone
par·ti·san *n* : a person who strongly supports something or someone — **par·ti·san·ship** *n*
[1]**par·ti·tion** *n* : a wall or screen that separates one area from another
[2]**partition** *vb* **par·ti·tioned; par·ti·tion·ing** : to divide into separate shares, parts, or areas
part·ly *adv* : somewhat but not completely
part·ner *n* **1** : a person who does or shares something with another **2** : either one of a married couple **3** : someone who plays with another person on the same side in a game **4** : one of two or more people who run a business together
part·ner·ship *n* : an arrangement in which people engage in an activity or business with one another or share something with each other
part of speech *n, pl* **parts of speech** : a class of words (as adjectives, adverbs, conjunctions, interjections, nouns, prepositions, pronouns, or verbs) identified according to the kinds of ideas they express and the work they do in a sentence
partook *past of* PARTAKE
par·tridge *n, pl* **partridge** *or* **par·tridg·es** : a plump grayish brown bird that lives mostly on the ground and is sometimes hunted for food or sport
part–time *adj* : involving fewer than the usual hours
par·ty *n, pl* **par·ties** **1** : a social gathering or the entertainment provided for it **2** : a person or group concerned in some action **3** : a group of people who take one side of a question or share a set of beliefs
[1]**pass** *vb* **passed; pass·ing** **1** : [1]MOVE 1, PROCEED **2** : to go away **3** : to go by or move past **4** : to go or allow to go across, over, or through **5** : to transfer or throw to another person **6** : to go successfully through an examination or inspection **7** : to cause or permit to elapse **8** : HAPPEN 1 **9** : to move from one place or condition to another **10** : to be or cause to be approved **11** : to be or cause to be identified or recognized **12** : [1]DIE 1 — **pass·er** *n* — **pass away** : [1]DIE 1 — **pass out** : to become unconscious : FAINT — **pass up** : to let go by : REFUSE
[2]**pass** *n* **1** : an opening or way for going along or through **2** : a gap in a mountain range
[3]**pass** *n* **1** : the act or an instance of moving **2** : the act or an instance of throwing or transferring (as a ball) to another person **3** : a written permit to go or come **4** : SITUATION 1
pass·able *adj* **1** : fit to be traveled on **2** : barely good enough — **pass·ably** *adv*
pas·sage *n* **1** : a space or path by which something or someone can go through **2** : a brief part of a speech or written work **3** : the act or process of going from one place or condition to another **4** : the act of approving a law **5** : a right or permission to go as a passenger
pas·sage·way *n* : a space, road, or way by which a person or thing may move
pas·sen·ger *n* : someone riding on or in a vehicle
passenger pigeon *n* : a North American wild pigeon once common but now extinct
pass·er·by *n, pl* **pass·ers·by** : someone who goes by
[1]**pass·ing** *adj* **1** : going by or past **2** : lasting only for a short time **3** : showing haste or lack of attention **4** : used for going past **5** : showing satisfactory work in a test or course of study
[2]**passing** *n* **1** : the act of going by or going away **2** : DEATH 1
pas·sion *n* **1** : a strong feeling or emotion **2** : an object of someone's love, liking, or desire **3** : strong liking or desire : LOVE
pas·sion·ate *adj* **1** : showing or affected by strong feeling **2** : easily caused to feel strong emotions — **pas·sion·ate·ly** *adv*
pas·sive *adj* **1** : not taking an active part **2** : showing that the person or thing represented by the subject is acted on by the verb **3** : offering no resistance — **pas·sive·ly** *adv*
Pass·over *n* : a Jewish holiday celebrated in March or April in honor of the freeing of the Hebrews from slavery in Egypt
pass·port *n* : a government document needed to enter or leave a country
pass·word *n* : a secret word, phrase, or group of numbers that a person must know to be allowed to enter a place or use a computer system
[1]**past** *adj* **1** : of or relating to a time that has gone by **2** : relating to a verb tense that expresses a time gone by **3** : no longer serving
[2]**past** *prep* **1** : [2]BEYOND 1 **2** : going close to and then beyond
[3]**past** *n* **1** : a former time **2** : life or history of a time gone by
[4]**past** *adv* : so as to pass by or beyond
pas·ta *n* **1** : a dough of flour, eggs, and water made in different shapes and dried or used fresh **2** : a dish of cooked pasta
[1]**paste** *n* **1** : a mixture of flour or starch and water used for sticking things together **2** : a soft smooth thick mixture
[2]**paste** *vb* **past·ed; past·ing** : to stick on or together with an adhesive mixture
paste·board *n* : CARDBOARD
[1]**pas·tel** *n* **1** : a soft pale color **2** : a crayon

made by mixing ground coloring matter with a watery solution of a gum **3 :** a drawing made with pastels

²pastel *adj* **1 :** made with pastels **2 :** light and pale in color

pas·teur·i·za·tion *n* **:** the process of heating a liquid to a temperature to kill germs and then rapidly cooling it

pas·teur·ize *vb* **pas·teur·ized; pas·teur·iz·ing :** to keep a liquid (as milk) for a time at a temperature high enough to kill many harmful germs and then cool it rapidly — **pas·teur·iz·er** *n*

pas·time *n* **:** something (as a hobby) that helps to make time pass pleasantly

pas·tor *n* **:** a minister or priest in charge of a church

pas·to·ral *adj* **1 :** of or relating to peaceful scenes of the countryside **2 :** of or relating to the pastor of a church

past participle *n* **:** a word that expresses completed action and is one of the principal parts of a verb

past·ry *n, pl* **past·ries 1 :** sweet baked goods (as pies) made mainly of flour and fat **2 :** a piece of sweet baked goods

past tense *n* **:** a verb tense used to express an action or state having already taken place or existed

pas·ture *n* **1 :** plants (as grass) for feeding grazing animals **2 :** land on which animals graze

¹pat *vb* **pat·ted; pat·ting :** to tap or stroke gently with the open hand

²pat *n* **1 :** a light tap with the open hand or a flat instrument **2 :** the sound of a pat or tap **3 :** a small flat piece (as of butter)

³pat *adj* **pat·ter; pat·test 1 :** learned perfectly **2 :** exactly suitable **3 :** not changing

pat. *abbr* patent

¹patch *n* **1 :** a piece of cloth used to mend or cover a torn or worn place **2 :** a small piece or area different from what is around it

²patch *vb* **patched; patch·ing :** to mend or cover with a piece of cloth — **patch up :** to resolve by agreement

patch·work *n* **1 :** pieces of cloth of different colors and shapes sewed together **2 :** something made up of different parts

pa·tel·la *n, pl* **pa·tel·lae** *or* **pa·tel·las :** KNEECAP

¹pat·ent *adj* **1 :** OBVIOUS, EVIDENT **2 :** relating to or concerned with patents

²pat·ent *n* **:** a document that gives the inventor of something the right to be the only one to make or sell the invention for a certain number of years

³pat·ent *vb* **pat·ent·ed; pat·ent·ing :** to obtain the legal right to be the only one to make or sell an invention

pa·ter·nal *adj* **1 :** of or like that of a father **:** FATHERLY **2 :** related through the father — **pa·ter·nal·ly** *adv*

path *n, pl* **paths 1 :** a track made by traveling on foot **2 :** the way or track in which something moves or in which something will be encountered **3 :** a way of life or thought

pa·thet·ic *adj* **:** causing feelings of pity, tenderness, or sorrow — **pa·thet·ic·al·ly** *adv*

path·way *n* **:** PATH 1

pa·tience *n* **:** the ability to remain calm when dealing with a difficult or annoying situation, task, or person

¹pa·tient *adj* **:** able to or showing the ability to remain calm when dealing with a difficult or annoying situation, task, or person — **pa·tient·ly** *adv*

²patient *n* **:** a person under medical care or treatment

pa·tio *n, pl* **pa·ti·os :** an open area next to a house that is usually paved

pa·tri·arch *n* **1 :** a man who heads a family, group, or government **2 :** a respected old man

pa·tri·ot *n* **:** a person who loves his or her country and strongly supports it

pa·tri·ot·ic *adj* **:** having or showing love that a person feels for his or her country

pa·tri·ot·ism *n* **:** love that a person feels for his or her country

¹pa·trol *n* **1 :** the action of going around an area to make sure that it is safe **2 :** a person or group going around an area to make sure that it is safe **3 :** a part of a Boy Scout or Girl Scout troop

²patrol *vb* **pa·trolled; pa·trol·ling :** to go around an area for the purpose of watching or protecting

pa·trol·man *n, pl* **pa·trol·men :** a police officer who has a regular beat

pa·tron *n* **1 :** a person who gives generous support or approval **2 :** CUSTOMER

pa·tron·age *n* **1 :** the help or business given by a supporter **2 :** a group of customers (as of a shop or theater) **3 :** the control by officials of giving out jobs, contracts, and favors

pa·tron·ize *vb* **pa·tron·ized; pa·tron·iz·ing 1 :** to act as a supporter of **2 :** to be a customer of **3 :** to treat (a person) as if he or she were not as good or less important

patron saint *n* **:** a saint to whom a church or society is dedicated

¹pat·ter *vb* **pat·tered; pat·ter·ing 1 :** to strike again and again with light blows **2 :** to run with quick light steps

²patter *n* **:** a series of quick light sounds

¹pat·tern *n* **1 :** the form or figures used in decoration **:** DESIGN **2 :** a model or guide for making something **3 :** the regular and repeated way in which something is done **4** : something worth copying : MODEL — **pat·terned** *adj*

[2]pattern *vb* **pat·terned; pat·tern·ing** **1** : to make or develop by following an example **2** : to have a design

pat·ty *n, pl* **pat·ties** : a small flat cake of chopped food

pau·per *n* : a very poor person

[1]pause *n* **1** : a temporary stop **2** : a sign 𝄐 above a musical note or rest to show that the note or rest is to be held longer

[2]pause *vb* **paused; paus·ing** : to stop for a time : make a temporary stop

pave *vb* **paved; pav·ing** : to make a hard surface on (as with concrete or asphalt) — **pave the way** : to make it easier for something to happen or for someone to do something

pave·ment *n* **1** : a hard surface of concrete or asphalt **2** : material used in making a hard surface

pa·vil·ion *n* **1** : a very large tent **2** : a building usually with open sides that is used as a place for entertainment or shelter in a park or garden

pav·ing *n* : PAVEMENT

[1]paw *n* : the foot of a four-footed animal (as a lion, dog, or cat) that has claws

[2]paw *vb* **pawed; paw·ing** **1** : to touch or hit with a paw **2** : to beat or scrape with a hoof **3** : to touch or handle in a clumsy or rude way

[1]pawn *n* **1** : the piece of least value in the game of chess **2** : a person who has little power and is controlled by a more powerful person or group

[2]pawn *vb* **pawned; pawn·ing** : to leave as a guarantee of repayment for a loan

pawn·bro·ker *n* : a person who lends money in exchange for personal property that can be sold if the money is not repaid

paw·paw *also* **pa·paw** *n* **1** : PAPAYA **2** : the greenish or yellow edible fruit of a North American tree with purple flowers

[1]pay *vb* **paid; pay·ing** **1** : to give (as money) in return for services received or for something bought **2** : to give money for (something owed) **3** : to get even with **4** : to give or offer freely **5** : to have a worthwhile result : be worth the effort or pains required — **pay·er** *n* — **pay off** **1** : to give all of what is owed **2** : to have a good result — **pay up** : to pay in full especially debts that are due

[2]pay *n* **1** : the act of giving money for something bought or used or for what is owed : PAYMENT **2** : SALARY

pay·able *adj* : that may, can, or must be paid

pay·check *n* : a check given or received as wages or salary

pay·ment *n* **1** : the act of giving money for something bought or for a service used **2** : money given to pay a debt

pay·roll *n* **1** : a list of persons who receive pay **2** : the amount of money necessary to pay the employees of a business

PC *n, pl* **PCs** *or* **PC's** : PERSONAL COMPUTER

PE *abbr* Prince Edward Island

pea *n, pl* **peas** **1** : a round green seed that is eaten as a vegetable and comes from the pods of a climbing garden plant **2** : a plant (as the sweet pea) resembling or related to the garden plant that produces peas

peace *n* **1** : freedom or a period of freedom from public disturbance or war **2** : a quiet and calm state of mind **3** : agreement and harmony among people **4** : an agreement to end a war

peace·able *adj* **1** : PEACEFUL 1 **2** : PEACEFUL 3

peace·ful *adj* **1** : not easily moved to argue or fight **2** : full of or enjoying quiet, calm, or freedom from disturbance **3** : not involving fighting — **peace·ful·ly** *adv* — **peace·ful·ness** *n*

peace·mak·er *n* : a person who settles an argument or stops a fight

peace pipe *n* : a decorated pipe of the American Indians used for certain ceremonies

peach *n* **1** : a fruit that is related to the plum and has a sweet juicy yellow or whitish pulp, hairy skin, and a large rough pit **2** : a pale yellowish pink color

pea·cock *n* : the male of a very large Asian pheasant that can lift up its very long colorful tail and spread it apart like a fan

peak *n* **1** : a prominent mountain **2** : the pointed top of a hill or mountain **3** : a sharp or pointed end **4** : the highest point of development

[1]peaked *adj* : having a point or a prominent end

[2]peak·ed *adj* : looking pale and sick

[1]peal *n* **1** : the sound of bells **2** : a loud sound : a series of loud sounds

[2]peal *vb* **pealed; peal·ing** : to make a loud sound and especially the sound of bells.

pea·nut *n* : a nutlike edible seed related to the pea that comes from the tough underground pods of a widely grown plant and that are eaten whole or crushed to form a spread (**peanut butter**) or produce oil for cooking (**peanut oil**)

pear *n* : a fruit with pale green or brownish skin and white sweet juicy flesh that is usually larger at the end opposite the stem

pearl *n* **1** : a smooth rounded shiny usually white body that is formed within the shell of some mollusks (as an oyster) usually around an irritating particle which has gotten into the shell **2 :** MOTHER-OF-PEARL **3 :** something like a pearl in shape, color, or value

pearly *adj* **pearl·i·er; pearl·i·est :** resembling a pearl in color, shape, or luster

peas·ant *n* **:** a farmer or farm worker of low social class

peat *n* **:** a blackish or dark brown material that is the remains of plants partly decayed in water and is dug and dried for use as fuel

peat moss *n* **:** a spongy brownish moss of wet areas that is often the chief plant making up peat

peb·ble *n* **:** a small rounded stone

pe·can *n* **:** an oval edible nut related to the walnut that usually has a thin shell and is the fruit of a tall tree of the central and southern United States

pec·ca·ry *n, pl* **pec·ca·ries :** a mostly tropical American animal that gathers in herds, is active at night, and looks like but is smaller than the related pig

1peck *vb* **pecked; peck·ing 1 :** to strike or pick up with the beak or a sharp instrument (as a pick) **2 :** to make by striking with the beak or a sharp instrument

2peck *n* **1 :** a unit of capacity equal to one quarter of a bushel **2 :** a great deal **:** a large quantity

3peck *n* **1 :** the act of striking with the bill or with a sharp instrument **2 :** a mark made by striking with the bill or with a sharp instrument

pe·cu·liar *adj* **1 :** of or limited to only one person, thing, or place **2 :** different from the usual **:** ODD — **pe·cu·liar·ly** *adv*

pe·cu·li·ar·i·ty *n, pl* **pe·cu·li·ar·i·ties 1 :** something odd or individual **2 :** the quality or state of being odd or individual

1ped·al *n* **:** a lever worked by the foot or feet

2pedal *vb* **ped·aled** *also* **ped·alled; ped·al·ing** *also* **ped·al·ling :** to use or work levers with a foot or feet

ped·dle *vb* **ped·dled; ped·dling :** to go about especially from house to house with goods for sale

ped·dler *also* **ped·lar** *n* **:** someone who goes about trying to sell things

ped·es·tal *n* **1 :** a support or foot of an upright structure (as a column, statue, or lamp) **2 :** a position of high regard

pe·des·tri·an *n* **:** a person who is walking

pe·di·a·tri·cian *n* **:** a doctor who specializes in the care of babies and children

ped·i·cure *n* **:** a treatment of the feet, toes, and toenails for beauty or comfort

ped·i·gree *n* **1 :** a table or list showing the line of ancestors of a person or animal **2 :** a line of ancestors

pe·dom·e·ter *n* **:** an instrument that measures the distance a person covers in walking

1peek *vb* **peeked; peek·ing 1 :** to look in a sneaky or cautious way **2 :** to take a quick glance

2peek *n* **:** a quick or sly look

1peel *vb* **peeled; peel·ing 1 :** to strip off the skin or bark of **2 :** to strip or tear off **3 :** to come off smoothly or in bits — **peel·er** *n*

2peel *n* **:** an outer covering and especially the skin of a fruit

1peep *vb* **peeped; peep·ing 1 :** to look through or as if through a small hole or a crack **:** PEEK **2 :** to look quickly **3 :** to show slightly

2peep *n* **1 :** a quick or sneaky look **2 :** the first appearance

3peep *vb* **peeped; peeping :** to make a short high sound such as a young bird makes — **peep·er** *n*

4peep *n* **:** a short high sound

1peer *vb* **peered; peer·ing 1 :** to look curiously or carefully **2 :** to come slightly into view **:** peep out

2peer *n* **1 :** a person of the same rank or kind **:** EQUAL **2 :** a member of one of the five ranks (duke, marquis, earl, viscount, and baron) of the British nobility

peer·less *adj* **:** having no equal

pee·vish *adj* **:** complaining a lot **:** IRRITABLE — **pee·vish·ly** *adv* — **pee·vish·ness** *n*

pee·wee *n* **:** someone or something that is small

1peg *n* **1 :** a small stick or rod (as of wood or metal) used especially to fasten things together or to hang things on **2 :** a piece driven into the ground to mark a boundary or to hold something **3 :** a level in approval or esteem

2peg *vb* **pegged; peg·ging 1 :** to mark or fasten with a small stick or rod driven into a surface **2 :** to work hard

PEI *abbr* Prince Edward Island

pel·i·can *n* **:** a large bird with webbed feet and a very large bill having a pouch on the lower part used to scoop in fish for food

pel·la·gra *n* **:** a disease caused by a diet containing too little protein and too little of a necessary vitamin

pel·let *n* **1 :** a little ball (as of food or medicine) **2 :** a piece of small shot **3 :** a wad of undigested material (as bones and fur) that was thrown up by a bird of prey (as an owl)

pell–mell *adv* **:** in a confused or hurried way

1pelt *n* **:** a skin of an animal especially with its fur or wool

2pelt *vb* **pelt·ed; pelt·ing 1 :** to hit with repeated blows **2 :** to repeatedly throw (something) at **3 :** to beat or pound against something again and again

pel·vis *n* **:** the bowl-shaped part of the skeleton that includes the hip bones and the lower bones of the backbone

DICTIONARY

[1]pen *n* **:** an instrument for writing with ink
[2]pen *vb* **penned; pen·ning :** to write especially with a pen
[3]pen *n* **:** a small enclosure especially for animals
[4]pen *vb* **penned; pen·ning :** to shut in a small enclosure
pe·nal *adj* **:** relating to or used for punishment
pe·nal·ize *vb* **pe·nal·ized; pe·nal·iz·ing :** to give a penalty to
pen·al·ty *n, pl* **pen·al·ties 1 :** punishment for doing something wrong **2 :** a disadvantage given for breaking a rule in a sport or game
pen·ance *n* **:** an act showing sorrow or regret for sin
pence *pl of* PENNY
[1]pen·cil *n* **:** a device for writing or drawing consisting of a stick of black or colored material enclosed in wood, plastic, or metal
[2]pencil *vb* **pen·ciled** *or* **pen·cilled; pen·cil·ing** *or* **pen·cil·ling :** to write, mark, or draw with a pencil
pen·dant *n* **:** a piece of jewelry hanging on a chain or cord that is worn around the neck
[1]pend·ing *prep* **:** while waiting for
[2]pending *adj* **:** not yet decided
pen·du·lum *n* **:** a weight hung from a point so as to swing freely back and forth under the action of gravity
pen·e·trate *vb* **pen·e·trat·ed; pen·e·trat·ing 1 :** to pass into or through **2 :** to see into or through
pen·e·tra·tion *n* **1 :** the act or process of piercing **2 :** keen understanding
pen·guin *n* **:** a short-legged seabird that cannot fly, uses its stiff wings for swimming, and is found in the colder regions of the southern hemisphere
pen·i·cil·lin *n* **:** an antibiotic that is produced by a mold and is used against disease-causing bacteria
pen·in·su·la *n* **:** a piece of land extending out into a body of water
pe·nis *n, pl* **pe·nis·es** *also* **pe·nes :** a male organ in mammals through which urine and sperm leave the body
pen·i·tence *n* **:** deep sadness that a person feels for his or her sins or faults
[1]pen·i·tent *adj* **:** feeling or showing sadness for a person's own sins or faults
[2]penitent *n* **:** a person who feels or shows sorrow for sins or faults
pen·i·ten·tia·ry *n, pl* **pen·i·ten·tia·ries :** PRISON
pen·knife *n, pl* **pen·knives :** a small jackknife
pen·man·ship *n* **:** style or quality of handwriting
Penn., Penna. *abbr* Pennsylvania
pen name *n* **:** a false name that an author uses on his or her work
pen·nant *n* **1 :** a narrow pointed flag used for identification, signaling, or decoration **2 :** a flag that serves as the emblem of a championship
pen·ni·less *adj* **:** very poor **:** having no money
pen·ny *n, pl* **pennies 1 :** CENT **2** *or pl* **pence :** a coin of the United Kingdom equal to 1/100 pound
pen pal *n* **:** a friend known only through letter writing
[1]pen·sion *n* **:** a sum paid regularly to a person who has retired from work
[2]pension *vb* **pen·sioned; pen·sion·ing :** to grant or give a regularly paid sum to (a person who has retired from work)
pen·sive *adj* **:** lost in serious or sad thought — **pen·sive·ly** *adv*
pent *adj* **:** kept inside **:** not released
penta- *or* **pent-** *prefix* **:** five
pen·ta·gon *n* **:** a flat geometric figure having five angles and five sides
pen·tath·lon *n* **:** an athletic contest in which each person participates in five different events
pent·house *n* **:** an apartment on the top floor or roof of a building
pe·on *n* **:** a person who does hard or dull work for very little money
pe·o·ny *n, pl* **pe·o·nies :** a plant that is widely grown for its large showy white, pink, or red flowers
[1]peo·ple *n, pl* **people** *or* **peoples 1 :** all persons considered together **2 :** a group of human beings who have something in common — often used in compounds instead of *persons* **3 :** a body of persons making up a race, tribe, or nation
[2]people *vb* **peo·pled; peo·pling 1 :** to fill with human beings or a certain type of human beings **2 :** to dwell on or in
[1]pep *n* **:** brisk energy or liveliness
[2]pep *vb* **pepped; pep·ping :** to make more lively or energetic
[1]pep·per *n* **1 :** a black or white spice that has a sharp flavor and comes from the dried ground-up fruit of an Indian climbing shrub **2 :** a usually green, red, or yellow vegetable that has a sharp or mildly sweet flavor and grows on a bushy garden plant
[2]pepper *vb* **pep·pered; pep·per·ing 1 :** to season with or as if with pepper **2 :** to hit with or as if with a shower of blows or objects
pep·per·mint *n* **1 :** a mint plant with small usually purple flowers that yields an oil used especially to flavor candies **2 :** a candy flavored with peppermint

pep·per·o·ni *n* : a spicy dry Italian sausage

pep·py *adj* **pep·pi·er; pep·pi·est** : full of brisk energy or liveliness

pep·sin *n* : an enzyme that starts the digestion of proteins in the stomach

per *prep* **1** : to or for each **2** : as directed by

per an·num *adv* : by the year : in or for each year : ANNUALLY

per cap·i·ta *adv or adj* : by or for each person

per·ceive *vb* **per·ceived; per·ceiv·ing** **1** : to become aware of through the senses and especially through sight **2** : to recognize or realize **3** : to think of as

1per·cent *adj or adv* : out of every hundred : measured by the number of units as compared with one hundred

2percent *n, pl* **percent** : a part or fraction of a whole expressed in hundredths

per·cent·age *n* **1** : a part of a whole expressed in hundredths **2** : a share of profits

per·cep·ti·ble *adj* : possible to detect

per·cep·tion *n* **1** : a judgment resulting from awareness or understanding **2** : the ability to understand (as meanings and ideas) **3** : understanding or awareness gained through the use of the senses

1perch *n* **1** : a place where birds roost **2** : a raised seat or position

2perch *vb* **perched; perch·ing** : to sit or rest on a raised seat or position

3perch *n, pl* **perch** *or* **perch·es** **1** : a common yellow and greenish brown fish of North America that is sometimes caught for food or sport **2** : any of various fish related to or resembling the North American perch

per·chance *adv* : PERHAPS

per·co·late *vb* **per·co·lat·ed; per·co·lat·ing** **1** : to trickle or cause to trickle through something porous : OOZE **2** : to prepare (coffee) by passing hot water through ground coffee beans again and again — **per·co·la·tion** *n* — **per·co·la·tor** *n*

per·cus·sion *n* : the musical instruments (as drums, cymbals, and maracas) that are played by striking or shaking

1pe·ren·ni·al *adj* **1** : present all through the year **2** : living from year to year **3** : never ending : CONSTANT **4** : happening again and again

2perennial *n* : a plant that lives from year to year

1per·fect *adj* **1** : having no mistake or flaw **2** : satisfying all requirements **3** : thoroughly skilled or trained : meeting the highest standards **4** : TOTAL 3 — **per·fect·ly** *adv*

2per·fect *vb* **per·fect·ed; per·fect·ing** : to improve (something) so that it has no flaws

per·fec·tion *n* **1** : a quality or condition that cannot be improved **2** : the act of improving something so that it has no flaws **3** : excellence or skill without flaw

per·fo·rate *vb* **per·fo·rat·ed; per·fo·rat·ing** : to make a hole or many holes through

per·form *vb* **per·formed; per·form·ing** **1** : to carry out : DO **2** : to do something needing special skill **3** : to give a public presentation for entertainment — **per·form·er** *n*

per·for·mance *n* **1** : the carrying out of an action **2** : a public entertainment

1per·fume *n* **1** : a liquid used to make a person smell nice **2** : a pleasant smell : FRAGRANCE

2per·fume *vb* **per·fumed; per·fum·ing** : to add a usually pleasant odor to

per·haps *adv* : possibly but not certainly : MAYBE

per·il *n* **1** : the state of being in great danger **2** : a cause or source of danger

per·il·ous *adj* : DANGEROUS 1 — **per·il·ous·ly** *adv*

pe·rim·e·ter *n* **1** : the whole outer boundary of a figure or area **2** : the length of the boundary of a figure

pe·ri·od *n* **1** : a punctuation mark . used chiefly to mark the end of a declarative sentence or an abbreviation **2** : a portion of time set apart by some quality **3** : a portion of time that forms a stage in history **4** : one of the divisions of a school day **5** : a single occurrence of menstruation

pe·ri·od·ic *adj* : occurring regularly over a period of time

1pe·ri·od·i·cal *adj* **1** : PERIODIC **2** : published regularly — **pe·ri·od·i·cal·ly** *adv*

2periodical *n* : something (as a magazine) published regularly (as every month)

peri·scope *n* : an instrument containing lenses and mirrors by which a person (as on a submarine) can get a view that would otherwise be blocked

per·ish *vb* **per·ished; per·ish·ing** : to become destroyed : DIE

per·ish·able *adj* : likely to spoil or decay

1per·i·win·kle *n* : an evergreen plant that spreads along the ground and has blue or white flowers

2periwinkle *n* : a small snail that lives along rocky seashores

perk *vb* **perked; perk·ing** **1** : to make or become more lively or cheerful **2** : to make fresher in appearance **3** : to lift in a quick, alert, or bold way

perky *adj* **perk·i·er; perk·i·est** : being lively and cheerful

per·ma·nence *n* : the quality or state of lasting forever or for a long time

per·ma·nent *adj* : lasting or meant to last for a long time : not temporary — **per·ma·nent·ly** *adv*

per·me·able *adj* **:** having pores or openings that let liquids or gases pass through

per·me·ate *vb* **per·me·at·ed; per·me·at·ing 1 :** to pass through something that has pores or small openings or is in a loose form **2 :** to spread throughout

per·mis·sion *n* **:** the approval of a person in authority

[1]**per·mit** *vb* **per·mit·ted; per·mit·ting 1 :** to allow to happen or do **:** give permission **2 :** to make possible **:** give an opportunity

[2]**per·mit** *n* **:** a statement of permission (as a license or pass)

per·ni·cious *adj* **:** causing great damage or harm

per·ox·ide *n* **:** HYDROGEN PEROXIDE

[1]**per·pen·dic·u·lar** *adj* **1 :** exactly vertical **2 :** being at right angles to a line or surface — **per·pen·dic·u·lar·ly** *adv*

[2]**perpendicular** *n* **:** a line, surface, or position at right angles to another line, surface, or position

per·pe·trate *vb* **per·pe·trat·ed; per·pe·trat·ing :** to bring about or carry out **:** COMMIT — **per·pe·tra·tor** *n*

per·pet·u·al *adj* **1 :** lasting forever or for a very long time **2 :** occurring continually **:** CONSTANT — **per·pet·u·al·ly** *adv*

per·pet·u·ate *vb* **per·pet·u·at·ed; per·pet·u·at·ing :** to cause to last a long time

per·plex *vb* **per·plexed; per·plex·ing :** to make unable to understand **:** CONFUSE

per·plexed *adj* **:** unable to understand something clearly or to think clearly

per·plex·i·ty *n, pl* **per·plex·i·ties 1 :** a puzzled or anxious state of mind **2 :** something that puzzles

per·se·cute *vb* **per·se·cut·ed; per·se·cut·ing :** to treat continually in a cruel and harmful way

per·se·cu·tion *n* **1 :** the act of continually treating in a cruel and harmful way **2 :** the state of being continually treated in a cruel and harmful way

per·se·ver·ance *n* **:** the act or power of continuing to do something in spite of difficulties

per·se·vere *vb* **per·se·vered; per·se·ver·ing :** to keep trying to do something in spite of difficulties

per·sim·mon *n* **:** an orange roundish sweet fruit that grows on a tree of the southeastern United States and Asia and may be very sour when unripe

per·sist *vb* **per·sist·ed; per·sist·ing 1 :** to keep on doing or saying something **:** continue stubbornly **2 :** to last on and on **:** continue to exist or occur

per·sist·ence *n* **1 :** the act or fact of stubbornly continuing to do something **2 :** the act or fact of continuing to exist longer than usual

per·sist·ent *adj* **:** continuing to act or exist longer than usual — **per·sist·ent·ly** *adv*

per·son *n* **1 :** a human being considered as an individual — sometimes used in compounds especially to avoid *man* in words that apply to both sexes **2 :** the body of a human being

per·son·able *adj* **:** pleasing in appearance or manner

per·son·age *n* **:** an important or famous person

per·son·al *adj* **1 :** of, relating to, or belonging to an individual human being **:** not public **:** not general **2 :** made or done by a particular individual and not by someone acting for him or her **3 :** of the body **4 :** relating to someone's private matters **5 :** intended for or given to one particular individual **6 :** relating to a particular individual or his or her qualities often in a way that is hurtful — **per·son·al·ly** *adv*

personal computer *n* **:** a computer designed for an individual user

per·son·al·i·ty *n, pl* **per·son·al·i·ties 1 :** the qualities (as moods or habits) that make one human being different from others **2 :** a human being's pleasing or interesting qualities **3 :** a famous person

personal pronoun *n* **:** a pronoun (as *I, you, it,* or *they*) used instead of a noun that names a definite person or thing

per·son·i·fy *vb* **per·son·i·fied; per·son·i·fy·ing :** to think of or represent as a person

per·son·nel *n* **:** a group of people employed in a business or an organization

per·spec·tive *n* **1 :** the angle or direction in which a person looks at an object **2 :** POINT OF VIEW **3 :** the ability to understand what is important and what isn't **4 :** an accurate rating of what is important and what isn't **5 :** the art of painting or drawing a scene so that objects in it seem to have their right shape and to be the right distance apart

per·spi·ra·tion *n* **1 :** the act or process of perspiring **2 :** salty liquid given off from skin glands

per·spire *vb* **per·spired; per·spir·ing :** to give off salty liquid through the skin

per·suade *vb* **per·suad·ed; per·suad·ing :** to win over to a belief or way of acting **:** CONVINCE

per·sua·sion *n* **1 :** the act of convincing **2 :** the power to convince **3 :** a way of believing **:** BELIEF

per·sua·sive *adj* **:** able or likely to convince — **per·sua·sive·ly** *adv* — **per·sua·sive·ness** *n*

pert *adj* **1 :** rude and disrespectful **:** FRESH **2 :** PERKY

per·tain *vb* **per·tained; per·tain·ing** **1 :** to relate to a person or thing **2 :** to belong to as a part, quality, or function

per·ti·nent *adj* **:** relating to the subject that is being thought about or discussed **:** RELEVANT

per·turb *vb* **per·turbed; per·turb·ing :** to disturb in mind **:** trouble greatly

pe·rus·al *n* **:** the act of reading or reading through carefully

pe·ruse *vb* **pe·rused; pe·rus·ing** **1 :** READ 1 **2 :** to read through carefully

per·vade *vb* **per·vad·ed; per·vad·ing :** to spread through all parts of **:** PERMEATE

per·verse *adj* **1 :** stubborn in being against what is right or sensible **2 :** wrong especially in a way that is strange or offensive

pes·ky *adj* **pesk·i·er; pesk·i·est :** TROUBLESOME 1

pe·so *n, pl* **pesos** **1 :** a bill or coin used in one of several Spanish-speaking countries of North and South America **2 :** a bill or coin used in the Philippines

pes·si·mism *n* **:** a feeling or belief that things are usually bad or that bad things will happen

pes·si·mist *n* **:** a person who habitually expects bad things to happen or thinks things are bad

pes·si·mis·tic *adj* **1 :** tending to think that bad things will happen **2 :** having the belief that evil is more common than good

pest *n* **1 :** NUISANCE **2 :** a plant or animal that is harmful to humans or property **3 :** PESTILENCE

pes·ter *vb* **pes·tered; pes·ter·ing :** to bother again and again

pes·ti·cide *n* **:** a substance used to destroy pests (as insects or weeds)

pes·ti·lence *n* **:** a contagious usually fatal disease that spreads quickly

pes·tle *n* **:** a tool shaped like a small club for crushing substances in a mortar

[1]**pet** *n* **1 :** a tame animal kept as a companion rather than for work **2 :** a person who is treated with special kindness or consideration

[2]**pet** *adj* **1 :** kept or treated as a pet **2 :** showing fondness **3 :** [2]FAVORITE

[3]**pet** *vb* **pet·ted; pet·ting :** to stroke or pat gently or lovingly

pet·al *n* **:** one of the often brightly colored leaflike outer parts of a flower

pet·i·ole *n* **:** the slender stem of a leaf

pe·tite *adj* **:** having a small trim figure

[1]**pe·ti·tion** *n* **1 :** an earnest appeal **2 :** a formal written request made to an authority

[2]**petition** *vb* **pe·ti·tioned; pe·ti·tion·ing :** to make an often formal request to or for — **pe·ti·tion·er** *n*

pe·trel *n* **:** a small seabird with long wings that flies far from land

pet·ri·fy *vb* **pet·ri·fied; pet·ri·fy·ing** **1 :** to change plant or animal matter into stone or something like stone **2 :** to frighten very much

pe·tro·leum *n* **:** a raw oil that is obtained from wells drilled in the ground and that is the source of gasoline, kerosene, and other oils used for fuel

pet·ti·coat *n* **:** a skirt worn under a dress or outer skirt

petting zoo *n* **:** a collection of farm animals or gentle exotic animals for children to pet and feed

pet·ty *adj* **pet·ti·er; pet·ti·est** **1 :** small and of no importance **2 :** showing or having a mean narrow-minded attitude — **pet·ti·ness** *n*

petty officer *n* **:** an officer in the navy or coast guard appointed from among the enlisted people

pet·u·lance *n* **:** an irritable temper

pet·u·lant *adj* **:** often in a bad mood **:** CROSS

pe·tu·nia *n* **:** a plant grown for its brightly colored flowers that are shaped like funnels

pew *n* **:** one of the benches with backs and sometimes doors set in rows in a church

pe·wee *n* **:** a small grayish or greenish brown bird that eats flying insects

pew·ter *n* **1 :** a dull gray metallic substance that contains mostly tin and that is used in making utensils (as pitchers and bowls) **2 :** utensils made of pewter

pg. *abbr* page

pH *n* **:** a measure of the acidity or alkalinity of a substance

phan·tom *n* **:** an image or figure that can be sensed (as with the eyes or ears) but that is not real

pha·raoh *n, often cap* **:** a ruler of ancient Egypt

phar·ma·cist *n* **:** a person whose job is preparing medicines according to a doctor's prescription

phar·ma·cy *n, pl* **phar·ma·cies :** a place where medicines are prepared and sold by a pharmacist **:** DRUGSTORE

phar·ynx *n, pl* **pha·ryn·ges** *also* **phar·ynx·es :** a tube extending from the back of the nasal passages and mouth to the esophagus that is the passage through which air passes to the larynx and food to the esophagus

phase *n* **1 :** a step or part in a series of events or actions **:** STAGE **2 :** the way that the moon or a planet looks to the eye at any time in its series of changes with respect to how it shines

pheas·ant *n* : a large brightly colored bird with a long tail that is related to the chicken and is sometimes hunted for food or sport

phe·nom·e·nal *adj* : very remarkable : EXTRAORDINARY

phe·nom·e·non *n, pl* **phe·nom·e·na** *or* **phe·nom·e·nons** **1** *pl phenomena* : an observable fact or event **2** : a rare or important fact or event **3** *pl phenomenons* : an extraordinary or exceptional person or thing

¹-phil *or* **-phile** *n suffix* : a person who loves or is strongly attracted to

²-phil *or* **-phile** *adj suffix* : having a fondness for or strong attraction to

phil·an·throp·ic *adj* : for or relating to the act of giving money and time to help needy people : CHARITABLE

phi·lan·thro·pist *n* : a person who gives generously to help other people

phi·lan·thro·py *n, pl* **phi·lan·thro·pies** **1** : desire and active effort to help other people **2** : something done or given to help needy people **3** : an organization giving or supported by charitable gifts

phil·o·den·dron *n* : a plant often grown for its showy usually shiny leaves

phi·los·o·pher *n* **1** : a person who studies ideas about knowledge, right and wrong, reasoning, and the value of things **2** : a person who takes misfortunes with calmness and courage

phil·o·soph·i·cal *also* **phil·o·soph·ic** *adj* **1** : of or relating to the study of basic ideas about knowledge, right and wrong, reasoning, and the value of things **2** : showing wisdom and calm when faced with misfortune — **phil·o·soph·i·cal·ly** *adv*

phi·los·o·phy *n, pl* **phi·los·o·phies** **1** : the study of the basic ideas about knowledge, right and wrong, reasoning, and the value of things **2** : a specific set of ideas of a person or a group **3** : a set of ideas about how to do something or how to live

phlox *n, pl* **phlox** *or* **phlox·es** : a plant grown for its showy clusters of usually white, pink, or purplish flowers

pho·bia *n* : an unreasonable, abnormal, and lasting fear of something

phoe·be *n* : a small grayish brown bird that eats flying insects

phoe·nix *n* : a legendary bird which was thought to live for 500 years, burn itself to death, and rise newborn from the ashes

phon- *or* **phono-** *prefix* : sound : voice : speech

¹phone *n* : ¹TELEPHONE

²phone *vb* **phoned; phon·ing** : ²TELEPHONE

pho·neme *n* : one of the smallest units of speech that distinguish one utterance from another

pho·net·ic *adj* : of or relating to spoken language or speech sounds

pho·nics *n* : a method of teaching beginners to read and pronounce words by learning the usual sound of letters, letter groups, and syllables

pho·no·graph *n* : an instrument that reproduces sounds recorded on a grooved disk

¹pho·ny *also* **pho·ney** *adj* **pho·ni·er; pho·ni·est** : not real or genuine

²phony *also* **phoney** *n, pl* **pho·nies** *also* **pho·neys** **1** : a person who is not sincere **2** : something that is not real or genuine

phos·pho·rus *n* : a white or yellowish waxlike chemical element that gives a faint glow in moist air

pho·to *n, pl* **photos** : ¹PHOTOGRAPH

¹pho·to·copy *n* : a copy of usually printed material made using a process in which an image is formed by the action of light on an electrically charged surface

²photocopy *vb* **pho·to·cop·ied; pho·to·copy·ing** : to make a photocopy of — **pho·to·copi·er** *n*

¹pho·to·graph *n* : a picture taken by a camera

²photograph *vb* **pho·to·graphed; pho·to·graph·ing** : to take a picture of with a camera — **pho·tog·ra·pher** *n*

pho·to·graph·ic *adj* : obtained by or used in photography

pho·tog·ra·phy *n* : the making of pictures by means of a camera that directs the image of an object onto a surface that is sensitive to light

pho·to·syn·the·sis *n* : the process by which green plants and a few other organisms (as some protists) form carbohydrates from carbon dioxide and water in the presence of light — **pho·to·syn·thet·ic** *adj*

¹phrase *n* **1** : a group of two or more words that express a single idea but do not form a complete sentence **2** : a brief expression that is commonly used

²phrase *vb* **phrased; phras·ing** : to express in words

phy·lum *n, pl* **phy·la** : a group of related living things (as animals or plants) that ranks above the class and below the kingdom in scientific classification

phys ed *n* : PHYSICAL EDUCATION

phys·i·cal *adj* **1** : of the body : BODILY **2** : existing in a form that can be touched or seen **3** : of or relating to physics — **phys·i·cal·ly** *adv*

physical education *n* : instruction in the care and development of the body

phy·si·cian *n* : a specialist in healing human disease : a doctor of medicine

phys·i·cist *n* : a person specializing in physics

phys·ics *n* : a science that deals with the facts about matter and motion and includes the subjects of mechanics, heat, light, electricity, sound, and the atomic nucleus

phys·i·o·log·i·cal *or* **phys·i·o·log·ic** *adj* : of or relating to the processes and activities that keep living things alive

phys·i·ol·o·gist *n* : a person specializing in physiology

phys·i·ol·o·gy *n* **1** : a branch of biology that deals with the processes and activities that keep living things alive **2** : the processes and activities by which a living thing or any part of it functions

phy·sique *n* : the size and shape of a person's body

pi *n, pl* **pis** **1** : the symbol π representing the ratio of the circumference of a circle to its diameter **2** : the ratio itself having a value of about 3.1416

pi·a·nist *n* : a person who plays the piano

pi·a·no *n, pl* **pianos** : a keyboard instrument having steel wire strings that make a sound when struck by hammers covered with felt

pic·co·lo *n, pl* **pic·co·los** : a high-pitched instrument resembling a small flute

[1]**pick** *vb* **picked; pick·ing** **1** : to gather one by one **2** : to remove bit by bit **3** : to remove unwanted material from between or inside **4** : CHOOSE 1, SELECT **5** : to walk along slowly and carefully **6** : to eat sparingly or in a finicky manner **7** : to steal from **8** : to start (a fight) with someone deliberately **9** : to pluck with the fingers or with a pick **10** : to unlock without a key — **pick·er** *n* — **pick on** : to single out for mean treatment — **pick up** **1** : to take hold of and lift **2** : to clean up : TIDY **3** : to stop for and take along **4** : LEARN 1 **5** : to get without great effort or by chance **6** : to get by buying **7** : to begin again after a temporary stop **8** : to bring within range of hearing **9** : to gain or get back speed or strength

[2]**pick** *n* **1** : a heavy tool with a wooden handle and a blade pointed at one or both ends for loosening or breaking up soil or rock **2** : a slender pointed instrument **3** : a thin piece of metal or plastic used to pluck the strings of a musical instrument **4** : the act or opportunity of choosing **5** : [1]CHOICE 3 **6** : the best ones

pick·ax *n* : [2]PICK 1

pick·er·el *n, pl* **pickerel** *or* **pick·er·els** : a freshwater fish that resembles but is smaller than the related pike

[1]**pick·et** *n* **1** : a pointed stake or slender post (as for making a fence) **2** : a soldier or a group of soldiers assigned to stand guard **3** : a person standing or marching near a place (as a factory or store) as part of a strike or protest

[2]**picket** *vb* **pick·et·ed; pick·et·ing** : to stand or march near a place as part of a strike or protest

[1]**pick·le** *n* **1** : a piece of food and especially a cucumber that has been preserved in a solution of salt water or vinegar **2** : a mixture of salt and water or vinegar for keeping foods : BRINE **3** : a difficult or very unpleasant situation

[2]**pickle** *vb* **pick·led; pick·ling** : to soak or keep in a solution of salt water or vinegar

pick·pock·et *n* : a thief who steals from pockets and purses

pick·up *n* : a light truck with an open body and low sides

picky *adj* **pick·i·er; pick·i·est** : hard to please

[1]**pic·nic** *n* **1** : an outdoor party with food taken along and eaten in the open **2** : a pleasant or carefree experience

[2]**picnic** *vb* **pic·nicked; pic·nick·ing** : to go on a picnic

pic·to·graph *n* **1** : an ancient or prehistoric drawing or painting on a rock wall **2** : a diagram showing information by means of pictures

pic·to·ri·al *adj* **1** : of or relating to pictures **2** : having or using pictures

[1]**pic·ture** *n* **1** : an image of something or someone formed on a surface (as by drawing, painting, printing, or photography) **2** : an idea of what someone or something might look like or be like **3** : a perfect example of something **4** : MOVIE 1 **5** : an image on the screen of a television set

[2]**picture** *vb* **pic·tured; pic·tur·ing** **1** : to show or represent in a drawing, painting, or photograph **2** : to form an idea or mental image of : IMAGINE **3** : to describe in a particular way

picture graph *n* : PICTOGRAPH 2

pic·tur·esque *adj* : suggesting a painted scene in being very pretty or charming

pie *n* : a food consisting of a pastry crust and a filling (as of fruit or meat)

pie·bald *adj* : spotted with two colors and especially black and white

[1]**piece** *n* **1** : a part cut, torn, or broken from something **2** : one of a group, set, or mass of things **3** : a portion marked off **4** : a single item or example **5** : a definite amount or size in which something is made or sold **6** : something made or written **7** : a movable object used in playing a board game **8** : [1]COIN 1 — **in one piece** : not broken, hurt, or damaged

[2]**piece** *vb* **pieced; piec·ing** : to join into a whole : connect the parts or pieces of

piece·meal *adv* : one piece at a time : little by little

pier *n* **1** : a support for a bridge **2** : a structure built out into the water as a place for boats to dock or for people to walk or to protect or form a harbor

pierce *vb* **pierced; pierc·ing** **1** : to make a hole in or through or as if in or through **2** : to force or make a way into or through

pierc·ing *adj* **1** : able to penetrate **2** : loud and high-pitched

pi·e·ty *n, pl* **pieties** : devotion to God : the state or fact of being pious

pig *n* **1** : a hoofed stout-bodied animal with a short tail and legs, thick bristly skin, and a long flattened snout **2** : a domestic pig developed from the wild boar and raised for meat **3** : a person who has a disagreeable or offensive habit or behavior (as being dirty, rude, or greedy) **4** : a metal cast (as of iron) poured directly from the smelting furnace into a mold

pi·geon *n* : a bird with a plump body, short legs, and smooth feathers and especially one that is a variety of the rock dove and is found in cities throughout the world

pi·geon–toed *adj* : having the toes and front of the foot turned inward

pig·gy·back *adv or adj* : on the back or shoulders

piggy bank *n* : a container for keeping coins that is often in the shape of a pig

pig·head·ed *adj* : very stubborn

pig·let *n* : a baby pig

pig·ment *n* **1** : a substance that gives color to other materials **2** : natural coloring matter in animals and plants

pig·pen *n* **1** : a place where pigs are kept **2** : a dirty or messy place

pig·sty *n* : PIGPEN

pig·tail *n* : a tight braid of hair

[1]**pike** *n, pl* **pike** *or* **pikes** : a long slender freshwater fish with a large mouth

[2]**pike** *n* : a long wooden pole with a steel point once used as a weapon by soldiers

[3]**pike** *n* : TURNPIKE, ROAD

[1]**pile** *n* : a large stake or pointed post (as of wood or steel) driven into the ground to support a foundation

[2]**pile** *n* **1** : a large number of things that are put one on top of another **2** : a great amount **3** : REACTOR

[3]**pile** *vb* **piled; pil·ing** **1** : to lay or place one on top of another : STACK **2** : to heap in large amounts **3** : to move or push forward in a crowd or group

[4]**pile** *n* : a soft surface of fine short raised threads or fibers

pil·fer *vb* **pil·fered; pil·fer·ing** : to steal small amounts or articles of small value

pil·grim *n* **1** : a person who travels to a holy place as an act of religious devotion **2** *cap* : one of the English colonists who founded the first permanent settlement in New England at Plymouth in 1620

pil·grim·age *n* : a journey made by a pilgrim

pil·ing *n* : a supporting structure made of large stakes or pointed posts driven into the ground

pill *n* : medicine or a food supplement in the form of a small rounded mass to be swallowed whole

[1]**pil·lage** *n* : the act of robbing by force especially during a war

[2]**pillage** *vb* **pil·laged; pil·lag·ing** : to rob by force especially during a war

pil·lar *n* **1** : a large post that supports something (as a roof) **2** : a single column built as a monument **3** : a supporting or important member or part **4** : something that resembles a column in shape

pil·lo·ry *n, pl* **pil·lo·ries** : a device once used for punishing someone in public consisting of a wooden frame with holes in which the head and hands can be locked

pil·low *n* : a bag filled with soft or springy material used as a cushion usually for the head of a person lying down

pil·low·case *n* : a removable covering for a pillow

[1]**pi·lot** *n* **1** : a person who flies an aircraft **2** : a person who steers a ship **3** : a person especially qualified to guide ships into and out of a port or in dangerous waters

[2]**pilot** *vb* **pi·lot·ed; pi·lot·ing** **1** : to fly (an airplane) **2** : to steer or guide (a boat)

pi·mien·to *also* **pi·men·to** *n, pl* **pi·mien·tos** *also* **pi·men·tos** : a mildly sweet pepper with thick flesh

pim·ple *n* : a small red swelling of the skin often containing pus — **pim·pled** *adj* — **pim·ply** *adj*

[1]**pin** *n* **1** : a small pointed piece of wire with a rounded head used especially for fastening pieces of cloth **2** : something (as an ornament or badge) fastened to the clothing by a pin **3** : a slender pointed piece (as of wood or metal) usually having the shape of a cylinder used to fasten articles together or in place **4** : one of ten pieces set up as the target in bowling

[2]**pin** *vb* **pinned; pin·ning** **1** : to fasten or join with a pin **2** : to prevent or be prevented from moving

pin·a·fore *n* : a sleeveless garment with a low neck worn as an apron or a dress

pi·ña·ta *n* : a decorated container filled with treats (as candy and toys) and hung up to be broken open by a blindfolded person with a stick

pin·cer *n* **1** **pincers** *pl* : a tool with two handles and two jaws for holding or gripping small objects **2** : a part (as the claw of a lobster) resembling a pair of pincers

[1]pinch *vb* **pinched; pinch·ing** **1** : to squeeze between the finger and thumb or between the jaws of an instrument **2** : to squeeze painfully **3** : to break off by squeezing with the thumb and fingers **4** : to cause to look thin or shrunken — **pinch pennies** : to be thrifty or stingy

[2]pinch *n* **1** : a time of emergency **2** : an act of squeezing skin between the thumb and fingers **3** : as much as may be picked up between the finger and the thumb : a very small amount

pinch hitter *n* **1** : a baseball player who is sent in to bat for another **2** : a person who does another's work in an emergency

pin·cush·ion *n* : a small cushion in which pins may be stuck when not in use

[1]pine *n* : an evergreen tree that has narrow needles for leaves, cones, and a wood that ranges from very soft to hard

[2]pine *vb* **pined; pin·ing** **1** : to become thin and weak because of sadness or worry **2** : to long for very much

pine·ap·ple *n* : a large fruit that grows on a tropical plant and has a thick skin and sweet juicy yellow flesh

pin·feath·er *n* : a new feather just breaking through the skin of a bird

pin·ion *vb* **pin·ioned; pin·ion·ing** **1** : to restrain by tying the arms to the body **2** : to tie up or hold tightly **3** : to prevent a bird from flying especially by cutting off the end of one wing

[1]pink *n* : a plant with narrow leaves that is grown for its showy pink, red, or white flowers

[2]pink *n* : a pale red color

[3]pink *adj* : colored a pale red

pink·eye *n* : a contagious infection that causes the eye and inner part of the eyelid to become red and sore

pin·kie *or* **pin·ky** : LITTLE FINGER

pink·ish *adj* : somewhat pink

pin·na·cle *n* **1** : the peak of a mountain **2** : the highest point of development or achievement **3** : a slender tower generally coming to a narrow point at the top

pin·point *vb* **pin·point·ed; pin·point·ing** : to locate or find out exactly

pint *n* : a unit of liquid capacity equal to one half quart or 16 ounces (about .47 liter)

pin·to *n, pl* **pintos** : a horse or pony that has patches of white and another color

pin·wheel *n* : a toy with fanlike blades at the end of a stick that spin in the wind

[1]pi·o·neer *n* **1** : a person who is one of the first to settle in an area **2** : a person who begins or helps develop something new and prepares the way for others to follow

[2]pioneer *vb* **pi·o·neered; pi·o·neer·ing** **1** : to explore or open up ways or regions for others to follow **2** : to begin something new or take part in the early development of something

pi·ous *adj* : showing devotion to God

[1]pipe *n* **1** : a long tube or hollow body for carrying a substance (as water, steam, or gas) **2** : a musical instrument or part of a musical instrument consisting of a tube (as of wood or metal) played by blowing or having air passed through it **3** : BAGPIPE — usually used in pl. **4** : a tube with a small bowl at one end for smoking tobacco or for blowing bubbles

[2]pipe *vb* **piped; pip·ing** **1** : to move by means of pipes **2** : to play on a pipe — **pip·er** *n* — **pipe down** : to stop talking or making noise — **pipe up** : to start talking : say something

pipe·line *n* : a line of connected pipes with pumps and control devices for carrying liquids or gases over a long distance

pip·ing *n* **1** : a quantity or system of pipes **2** : the music of a pipe **3** : a high-pitched sound or call **4** : a narrow fold of material used to decorate edges or seams

pique *vb* **piqued; piqu·ing** **1** : to stir up : EXCITE **2** : to make annoyed or angry

pi·ra·cy *n, pl* **pi·ra·cies** **1** : robbery of a ship at sea **2** : the use of another's work or invention without permission

pi·ra·nha *n* : a small South American freshwater fish that has very sharp teeth, often occurs in groups, and may attack human beings and animals in the water

pi·rate *n* : a robber of ships at sea : a person who commits piracy

pis *pl of* PI

Pi·sces *n* **1** : a constellation between Aquarius and Aries imagined as two fish **2** : the twelfth sign of the zodiac or a person born under this sign

pis·ta·chio *n, pl* **pis·ta·chios** : the greenish edible seed of a small Asian tree

pis·til *n* : the part in the center of a flower that is made up of the stigma, style, and ovary and produces the seed

pis·tol *n* : a small gun made to be aimed and fired with one hand

pis·ton *n* : a disk or short cylinder that slides back and forth inside a larger cylinder and is moved by steam in steam engines and by the explosion of fuel in automobiles

[1]pit *n* **1** : a cavity or hole in the ground usually made by digging **2** : an area set off from and often sunken below surrounding areas **3** : a small hole or dent on a surface **4 pits** *pl* : something very bad — **pit·ted** *adj*

[2]pit *vb* **pit·ted; pit·ting** **1** : to make small holes or dents in **2** : to set against another in a fight or contest

[3]**pit** *n* **:** a hard seed or stone of a fruit (as a peach or cherry)
[4]**pit** *vb* **pit·ted; pit·ting :** to remove the pit from
pi·ta *n* **:** a thin flat bread that can be opened to form a pocket for holding food
[1]**pitch** *vb* **pitched; pitch·ing 1 :** to set up and fix firmly in place **2 :** to throw usually toward a certain point **3 :** to throw a baseball or softball to a batter **4 :** to plunge or fall forward **5 :** [2]SLOPE, SLANT **6 :** to fix or set at a certain highness or lowness **7 :** to move in such a way that one end falls while the other end rises — **pitch in :** to contribute to a common task or goal
[2]**pitch** *n* **1 :** highness or lowness of sound **2 :** amount of slope **3 :** an up-and-down movement **4 :** the throw of a baseball or softball to a batter **5 :** the amount or level of something (as a feeling) — **pitched** *adj*
[3]**pitch** *n* **1 :** a dark sticky substance left over from distilling tar and used in making roofing paper, in waterproofing seams, and in paving **2 :** resin from various evergreen trees (as the pine)
pitch–black *adj* **:** extremely dark or black
pitch·blende *n* **:** a dark mineral that is a source of radium and uranium
pitch–dark *adj* **:** extremely dark
[1]**pitch·er** *n* **:** a container usually with a handle and a lip or spout used for holding and pouring out liquids
[2]**pitcher** *n* **:** the player who throws the ball to the batter in baseball or softball
pitch·fork *n* **:** a tool having a long handle and two or three metal prongs that is used especially for lifting and tossing hay or straw
pit·e·ous *adj* **:** PITIFUL — **pit·e·ous·ly** *adv*
pit·fall *n* **1 :** a covered or camouflaged pit used to capture animals or people **2 :** a danger or difficulty that is hidden or is not easily recognized
pith *n* **1 :** the loose spongy tissue forming the center of the stem in most plants **2 :** the important part
piti·able *adj* **:** PITIFUL
piti·ful *adj* **1 :** deserving or causing feelings of pity **2 :** deserving or causing a feeling of dislike or disgust by not being sufficient or good enough — **piti·ful·ly** *adv*
piti·less *adj* **:** having no pity **:** CRUEL
pi·tu·i·tary gland *n* **:** a gland at the base of the brain that produces several hormones of which one affects growth
[1]**pity** *n* **1 :** a feeling of sadness or sympathy for the suffering or unhappiness of others **2 :** something that causes regret or disappointment
[2]**pity** *vb* **pit·ied; pity·ing :** to feel sadness and sympathy for
[1]**piv·ot** *n* **1 :** a shaft or pin with a pointed end on which something turns **2 :** the action or an instance of turning around on a point
[2]**pivot** *vb* **piv·ot·ed; piv·ot·ing :** to turn on or as if on a pivot **:** turn around on a central point
pix·el *n* **:** any of the small parts that make up an image (as on a computer or television screen)
pix·ie *also* **pixy** *n, pl* **pix·ies :** a mischievous elf or fairy
piz·za *n* **:** a dish made of flattened bread dough topped usually with tomato sauce and cheese and often meat and vegetables and baked
pk. *abbr* **1** park **2** peck
pkg. *abbr* package
pl. *abbr* plural
plac·ard *n* **:** a large notice or poster for announcing or advertising something
pla·cate *vb* **pla·cat·ed; pla·cat·ing :** to calm the anger of
[1]**place** *n* **1 :** an available seat or space **:** ROOM **2 :** a region or space not specified **3 :** a particular portion of a surface **:** SPOT **4 :** a point in a speech or a piece of writing **5 :** a building or area used for a special purpose **6 :** a certain area or region of the world **7 :** a piece of land with a house on it **8 :** position in a scale or series in comparison with another or others **9 :** usual space or use **10 :** the position of a figure in a numeral **11 :** a public square **12 :** a short street
[2]**place** *vb* **placed; plac·ing 1 :** to put in or as if in a certain space or position **2 :** to give an order for **3 :** to appoint to a job or find a job for **4 :** to identify by connecting with a certain time, place, or happening
place·hold·er *n* **:** a symbol (as x, Δ, *) used in mathematics in the place of a numeral
place·kick *n* **:** a kick in football made with the ball held in place on the ground
pla·cen·ta *n* **:** the organ in most mammals by which the fetus is joined to the uterus of the mother and is nourished
place value *n* **:** the value of the location of a digit in a number
plac·id *adj* **:** calm and peaceful
pla·gia·rism *n* **:** an act of copying the ideas or words of another person without giving credit to that person
[1]**plague** *n* **1 :** something that causes much distress **2 :** a disease that causes death and spreads quickly to a large number of people **3 :** BUBONIC PLAGUE
[2]**plague** *vb* **plagued; plagu·ing 1 :** to affect with disease or trouble **2 :** to cause worry or distress to
plaid *n* **1 :** a pattern consisting of rectangles formed by crossed lines of various widths **2 :** TARTAN — **plaid** *adj*

[1]**plain** *adj* **plain·er; plain·est** **1 :** having no pattern or decoration **2 :** not handsome or beautiful **3 :** not hard to do or understand **4 :** without anything having been added **5 :** open and clear to the sight **6 :** FRANK **7 :** of common or average accomplishments or position **:** ORDINARY — **plain·ly** *adv* — **plain·ness** *n*

[2]**plain** *n* **:** a large area of level or rolling treeless land

[3]**plain** *adv* **:** without any question **:** to a complete degree

plain·tive *adj* **:** showing or suggesting sadness **:** MOURNFUL

[1]**plait** *n* **:** a flat braid (as of hair)

[2]**plait** *vb* **plait·ed; plait·ing** **1 :** [1]BRAID **2 :** to make by braiding

[1]**plan** *n* **1 :** a method or scheme of acting, doing, or arranging **2 :** a drawing or diagram showing the parts or outline of something

[2]**plan** *vb* **planned; plan·ning** **1 :** to form a diagram of or for **:** arrange the parts or details of ahead of time **2 :** to have in mind **:** INTEND

[1]**plane** *n* **1 :** AIRPLANE **2 :** a surface in which if any two points are chosen a straight line joining them lies completely in that surface **3 :** a level of thought, existence, or development **4 :** a level or flat surface

[2]**plane** *adj* **:** [1]HORIZONTAL, FLAT

[3]**plane** *n* **:** a tool that smooths wood by shaving off thin strips

[4]**plane** *vb* **planed; plan·ing** **1 :** to smooth or level off with a tool made for smoothing **2 :** to remove with or as if with a tool for smoothing wood

plan·et *n* **:** any large celestial body that orbits a star (as the sun)

plan·e·tar·i·um *n* **:** a building in which there is a device for projecting the images of celestial bodies on a ceiling shaped like a dome

plan·e·tary *adj* **1 :** of or relating to a planet **2 :** having a motion like that of a planet

plank *n* **:** a heavy thick board

plank·ton *n* **:** the tiny floating plants and animals of a body of water

[1]**plant** *vb* **plant·ed; plant·ing** **1 :** to place in the ground to grow **2 :** to fill with seeds or plants **3 :** to set firmly in the ground **4 :** to place firmly **5 :** to introduce as a thought or idea **6 :** to place (someone or something) secretly

[2]**plant** *n* **1 :** any member of the kingdom of many-celled mostly photosynthetic living things (as mosses, ferns, grasses, and trees) that lack a nervous system or sense organs and the ability to move about and that have cellulose cell walls **2 :** the buildings and equipment of an industrial business or an institution — **plant·like** *adj*

plan·tain *n* **:** the greenish fruit of a kind of banana plant that is eaten cooked and is larger, less sweet, and more starchy than the ordinary banana

plan·ta·tion *n* **1 :** a large area of land where crops are grown and harvested **2 :** a settlement in a new country or region

plant·er *n* **1 :** someone or something that plants crops **2 :** a person who owns or runs a plantation **3 :** a container in which plants are grown

plant kingdom *n* **:** a basic group of natural objects that includes all living and extinct plants

plant louse *n* **:** APHID

plaque *n* **1 :** a flat thin piece (as of metal) with writing on it that serves as a memorial of something **2 :** a sticky usually colorless thin film on the teeth that is formed by and contains bacteria

plas·ma *n* **:** the watery part of blood, lymph, or milk

[1]**plas·ter** *n* **:** a paste (as of lime, sand, and water) that hardens when it dries and is used for coating walls and ceilings

[2]**plaster** *vb* **plas·tered; plas·ter·ing** **1 :** to cover or smear with or as if with a paste used for coating **2 :** to paste or fasten on especially so as to cover

plaster of par·is *n, often cap 2nd P* **:** a white powder that mixes with water to form a paste that hardens quickly and is used for casts and molds

[1]**plas·tic** *adj* **1 :** made of plastic **2 :** capable of being molded or modeled

[2]**plastic** *n* **:** any of various manufactured materials that can be molded into objects or formed into films or fibers

[1]**plate** *n* **1 :** a shallow usually round dish **2 :** a main course of a meal **3 :** a thin flat piece of material **4 :** HOME PLATE **5 :** a piece of metal on which something is engraved or molded **6 :** an illustration often covering a full page of a book **7 :** a sheet of glass coated with a chemical sensitive to light for use in a camera

[2]**plate** *vb* **plat·ed; plat·ing** **:** to cover with a thin layer of metal (as gold or silver)

pla·teau *n, pl* **plateaus** *or* **pla·teaux** **:** a broad flat area of high land

plate·let *n* **:** one of the tiny colorless disk-shaped bodies of the blood that assist in blood clotting

plat·form *n* **1 :** a level usually raised surface **2 :** a raised floor or stage for performers or speakers **3 :** a statement of the beliefs and rules of conduct for which a group stands **4 :** an arrangement of computer components that uses a particular operating system

plat·i·num *n* : a heavy grayish white metallic chemical element

pla·toon *n* : a part of a military company usually made up of two or more squads

platoon sergeant *n* : a noncommissioned officer in the army ranking above a staff sergeant

plat·ter *n* : a large plate used especially for serving meat

platy·pus *n* : a small water-dwelling mammal of Australia that lays eggs and has webbed feet, dense fur, and a bill that resembles that of a duck

plau·si·ble *adj* : seeming to be reasonable — **plau·si·bly** *adv*

[1]**play** *vb* **played; play·ing** **1** : to do activities for enjoyment **2** : to take part in a game of **3** : to compete against in a game **4** : to produce music or sound with **5** : to perform the music of **6** : to act or present on the stage or screen **7** : PRETEND 1 **8** : to perform (as a trick) for fun **9** : [2]ACT 2, BEHAVE **10** : to handle something idly : TOY **11** : to affect something by performing a function **12** : to move swiftly or lightly

[2]**play** *n* **1** : a story performed on stage **2** : the action of or a particular action in a game **3** : exercise or activity for enjoyment **4** : a person's turn to take part in a game **5** : quick or light movement **6** : freedom of motion **7** : a way of acting : CONDUCT **8** : the state of being active

play·act·ing *n* : the performance of make-believe roles

play·er *n* **1** : a person who participates in a game **2** : a person who produces sound on a musical instrument **3** : a device that reproduces sounds or video images that have been recorded (as on magnetic tape or a hard drive)

play·ful *adj* **1** : full of energy and a desire for fun **2** : not serious : HUMOROUS — **play·ful·ly** *adv* — **play·ful·ness** *n*

play·ground *n* : an area used for games and playing

play·house *n* **1** : a small house for children to play in **2** : THEATER 1

playing card *n* : any of a set of cards marked to show rank and suit (**spades**, **hearts**, **diamonds**, or **clubs**) and used in playing various games

play·mate *n* : a friend with whom a child plays

play·off *n* : a game or series of games to determine a championship or to break a tie

play·pen *n* : a small enclosure in which a baby is placed to play

play·thing *n* : [1]TOY 1

play·wright *n* : a writer of plays

pla·za *n* : a public square in a city or town

plea *n* **1** : an earnest appeal **2** : something offered as a defense or excuse

plead *vb* **plead·ed** *or* **pled; plead·ing** **1** : to ask for in a serious and emotional way : BEG **2** : to offer as a defense, an excuse, or an apology **3** : to argue for or against : argue in court **4** : to answer to a criminal charge

pleas·ant *adj* **1** : giving pleasure : AGREEABLE **2** : having pleasing manners, behavior, or appearance — **pleas·ant·ly** *adv*

[1]**please** *vb* **pleased; pleas·ing** **1** : to make happy or satisfied **2** : to be willing : LIKE, CHOOSE

[2]**please** *adv* — used to show politeness or emphasis in requesting or accepting

pleas·ing *adj* : giving pleasure : AGREEABLE — **pleas·ing·ly** *adv*

plea·sur·able *adj* : PLEASANT 1

plea·sure *n* **1** : a feeling of enjoyment or satisfaction **2** : recreation or enjoyment **3** : something that pleases or delights **4** : a particular desire

[1]**pleat** *vb* **pleat·ed; pleat·ing** : to arrange in folds made by doubling material over on itself

[2]**pleat** *n* : a fold (as in cloth) made by doubling material over on itself

[1]**pledge** *n* **1** : a promise or agreement that must be kept **2** : something handed over to another to ensure that the giver will keep his or her promise or agreement **3** : a promise to give money

[2]**pledge** *vb* **pledged; pledg·ing** **1** : to promise to give **2** : to cause (someone) to promise something **3** : to give as assurance of a promise (as of repayment of a loan)

plen·ti·ful *adj* **1** : present in large numbers or amount : ABUNDANT **2** : giving or containing a large number or amount — **plen·ti·ful·ly** *adv*

plen·ty *n* : a full supply : more than enough

pleu·ri·sy *n* : a sore swollen state of the membrane that lines the chest often with fever, painful breathing, and coughing

plex·us *n, pl* **plex·us·es** : a network usually of nerves or blood vessels

pli·able *adj* **1** : possible to bend without breaking **2** : easily influenced

pli·ant *adj* : PLIABLE

pli·ers *n pl* : small pincers with long jaws used for bending or cutting wire or handling small things

plight *n* : a bad condition or state : PREDICAMENT

plod *vb* **plod·ded; plod·ding** : to move or travel slowly but steadily — **plod·der** *n*

[1]**plop** *vb* **plopped; plop·ping** **1** : to move with or make a sound like that of something dropping into water **2** : to sit or lie down heavily **3** : to place or drop heavily

²plop *n* : a sound like something dropping into water

¹plot *n* **1** : a secret usually evil scheme **2** : the plan or main story of a play or novel **3** : a small area of ground

²plot *vb* **plot·ted; plot·ting** **1** : to plan or scheme secretly usually to do something bad **2** : to make a plan of — **plot·ter** *n*

plough, ploughshare *chiefly Brit spelling of* PLOW, PLOWSHARE

plo·ver *n* : a small shorebird having a shorter and stouter bill than the related sandpiper

¹plow *or chiefly Brit* **plough** *n* **1** : a farm machine used to dig into, break up, and turn over soil **2** : a device (as a snowplow) used to spread or clear away matter on the ground

²plow *or chiefly Brit* **plough** *vb* **plowed/ploughed; plow·ing/ploughing** **1** : to dig into, break up, or turn over soil with a plow **2** : to move through or continue with force or determination

plow·share *or chiefly Brit* **ploughshare** *n* : the part of a plow that cuts into the earth

ploy *n, pl* **ploys** : a trick used to make someone do something or get an advantage

pls. *abbr* please

¹pluck *vb* **plucked; pluck·ing** **1** : to pull off : PICK **2** : to remove something (as a hair or feather) with a quick pull **3** : to seize and remove quickly : SNATCH **4** : to pull at (a string) and let go

²pluck *n* **1** : a sharp pull : TUG **2** : COURAGE, SPIRIT

plucky *adj* **pluck·i·er; pluck·i·est** : showing courage : BRAVE

¹plug *n* **1** : a device usually on a cord used to make an electrical connection by putting it into another part (as a socket) **2** : a piece (as of wood or metal) used to stop up or fill a hole

²plug *vb* **plugged; plug·ging** **1** : to connect to an electric circuit **2** : to stop or make tight with something that fills a hole **3** : to keep steadily at work or in action

plum *n* **1** : a fruit related to the peach and cherry that usually has smooth purple or reddish skin, sweet juicy flesh, and a stony pit **2** : a dark reddish purple **3** : a choice or desirable thing : PRIZE

plum·age *n* : the feathers of a bird

¹plumb *n* : a small weight attached to a line and used to show depth or a straight vertical line

²plumb *vb* **plumbed; plumb·ing** : to measure or test with a plumb

³plumb *adv* **1** : exactly straight up and down **2** : COMPLETELY

plumb·er *n* : a person who installs or repairs plumbing

plumb·ing *n* **1** : a system of pipes and fixtures for supplying and carrying off water in a building **2** : the installation or repair of part or all of such a system of pipes and fixtures

plume *n* **1** : a large or showy feather of a bird **2** : an ornamental feather or tuft of feathers (as on a hat) **3** : something shaped like a large feather — **plumed** *adj*

plum·met *vb* **plum·met·ed; plum·met·ing** : to fall straight down

¹plump *adj* **plumper; plumpest** : having a pleasingly full rounded shape — **plump·ness** *n*

²plump *vb* **plumped; plump·ing** **1** : to drop or fall heavily or suddenly **2** : to come out in favor of something

³plump *adv* : DIRECTLY 1

⁴plump *vb* **plumped; plump·ing** : to make or become rounded or filled out

¹plun·der *vb* **plun·dered; plun·der·ing** : to rob or steal especially openly and by force (as during war)

²plunder *n* : something stolen by force : LOOT

¹plunge *vb* **plunged; plung·ing** **1** : to leap or dive suddenly **2** : to thrust or force quickly **3** : to suddenly enter or cause to enter a certain situation or state **4** : to drop suddenly downward or forward and downward

²plunge *n* : a sudden dive, rush, or leap

plung·er *n* : a part that moves up and down usually inside a tube or cylinder to push something out

plunk *vb* **plunked; plunk·ing** **1** : to lie or sit down suddenly or heavily **2** : to drop or place heavily or carelessly **3** : to make a sound on (an instrument) by pulling the strings or keys

¹plu·ral *adj* : relating to or being a word form used to show more than one

²plural *n* : a form of a word used to show that more than one person or thing is meant

¹plus *adj* : falling high in a certain range

²plus *prep* : increased by : with the addition of

¹plush *adj* **plush·er; plush·est** **1** : made of a thick soft fabric **2** : very rich and fine

²plush *n* : a fabric like velvet

plus sign *n* : a sign + used in mathematics to show addition (as in 8+6=14) or a quantity greater than zero (as in +10°)

Plu·to *n* : a dwarf planet that orbits the sun at an average distance of 3.7 million miles (5.9 million kilometers) and has a diameter of about 1500 miles (2300 kilometers) and is often considered one of the planets

plu·to·ni·um *n* : a radioactive metallic chemical element formed from neptunium and used for releasing atomic energy

¹ply *vb* **plied; ply·ing** **1** : to use something

steadily or forcefully **2 :** to keep supplying **3 :** to work at

²ply *n, pl* **plies :** one of the folds, layers, or threads of which something (as yarn or plywood) is made up

ply·wood *n* **:** a strong board made by gluing together thin sheets of wood under heat and pressure

p.m., P.M. *abbr* afternoon — abbreviation for Latin *post meridiem*, which means "after noon"

pneu·mat·ic *adj* **1 :** moved or worked by the pressure of air **2 :** made to hold or be inflated with compressed air

pneu·mo·nia *n* **:** a serious illness affecting the lungs that is marked especially by fever, cough, and difficulty in breathing

P.O. *abbr* post office

¹poach *vb* **poached; poach·ing :** to cook slowly in liquid

²poach *vb* **poached; poaching :** to hunt or fish unlawfully

pock *n* **:** a small swelling like a pimple on the skin (as in smallpox) or the mark it leaves

¹pock·et *n* **1 :** a small bag sewn into a piece of clothing for carrying small articles **2 :** a place or thing that is different from the larger place or thing that it is part of **3 :** a condition of the air (as a down current) that causes an airplane to drop suddenly **4 :** a bag at the corner or side of a pool table

²pocket *vb* **pock·et·ed; pock·et·ing 1 :** to put something in a pocket **2 :** to keep often dishonestly

³pocket *adj* **:** POCKET-SIZE

pock·et·book *n* **1 :** HANDBAG **2 :** the amount of money that someone has to spend

pock·et·knife *n, pl* **pock·et·knives :** a small knife that has one or more blades that fold into the handle

pock·et–size *adj* **:** small enough to fit in a pocket

pock·mark *n* **1 :** the mark left by a pock **2 :** a small hole or dent — **pock·marked** *adj*

pod *n* **:** a fruit (as a pea or bean) that is dry when ripe and splits open to free its seeds

pod·cast *n* **:** a program (as of music or talk) available for download over the Internet

po·di·um *n* **1 :** a raised platform especially for the conductor of an orchestra **2 :** a stand with a slanted surface (as for holding papers or a book) that a person can stand behind or near when giving a speech

po·em *n* **:** a piece of writing often having figurative language and lines that have rhythm and sometimes rhyme

po·et *n* **:** a writer of poems

po·et·ic *or* **po·et·i·cal** *adj* **:** of, relating to, or like that of poets or poetry

po·et·ry *n* **1 :** writing that usually involves figurative language and lines that have rhythm and sometimes rhyme **:** VERSE **2 :** the writings of a poet

po·go stick *n* **:** a pole with a strong spring at the bottom and two rests for the feet on which a person stands and bounces

poin·set·tia *n* **:** a tropical plant with showy usually red leaves that grow like petals around its small greenish yellow flowers

¹point *n* **1 :** a separate or particular detail **:** ITEM **2 :** an individual quality **:** CHARACTERISTIC **3 :** the chief idea or meaning **4 :** PURPOSE, AIM **5 :** a geometric element that has a position but no dimensions and is pictured as a small dot **6 :** a particular place or position **7 :** a particular stage or moment **8 :** the usually sharp end (as of a sword, pin, or pencil) **9 :** a piece of land that sticks out **10 :** a dot in writing or printing **11 :** one of the 32 marks indicating direction on a compass **12 :** a unit of scoring in a game — **point·ed** *adj* — **pointy** *adj*

²point *vb* **point·ed; point·ing 1 :** to show the position or direction of something especially by extending a finger in a particular direction **2 :** to direct someone's attention to **3 :** ¹AIM 1, DIRECT **4 :** to give a sharp end to

point–blank *adv* **:** in a very clear and direct way

point·ed·ly *adv* **:** in a way that very clearly expresses a particular meaning or thought

point·er *n* **1 :** something that points or is used for pointing **2 :** a helpful hint **3 :** a large dog with long ears and short hair that is trained to direct its head and body in the direction of an animal that is being hunted

point·less *adj* **:** having no meaning or purpose

point of view *n, pl* **points of view :** a way of looking at or thinking about something

¹poise *vb* **poised; pois·ing 1 :** to hold or make steady by balancing **2 :** to remain in position without moving **3 :** to be or become ready for something

²poise *n* **1 :** the state of being balanced **2 :** a natural self-confident manner

¹poi·son *n* **:** a substance that by its chemical action can injure or kill a living thing

²poison *vb* **poi·soned; poi·son·ing 1 :** to injure or kill with poison **2 :** to put poison on or in

poison ivy *n* **1 :** a usually climbing plant that has leaves with three leaflets and can cause an itchy painful rash when touched **2 :** a skin rash caused by poison ivy

poison oak *n* **:** a bush related to poison ivy that can cause an itchy painful rash when touched

poi·son·ous *adj* : containing poison : having or causing an effect of poison

poison sumac *n* : a shrub or small tree related to poison ivy that can cause an itchy painful rash when touched

[1]**poke** *vb* **poked; pok·ing** **1 :** to push something usually thin or sharp into or at **2 :** to make by stabbing or piercing **3 :** to thrust or stick out or cause to thrust or stick out **4 :** to search through or look around often without purpose **5 :** to move slowly or lazily

[2]**poke** *n* : a quick push with something pointed

[1]**pok·er** *n* : a metal rod used for stirring a fire

[2]**po·ker** *n* : a card game in which players bet on the value of their cards

poky *or* **pok·ey** *adj* **pok·i·er; pok·i·est** **1 :** so slow as to be annoying **2 :** small and cramped

po·lar *adj* **1 :** of or relating to the north pole or south pole or nearby regions **2 :** coming from or being like a polar region **3 :** of or relating to a pole of a magnet

polar bear *n* : a large creamy-white bear of arctic regions

[1]**pole** *n* : a long straight thin piece of material (as wood or metal)

[2]**pole** *n* **1 :** either end of the imaginary line on which the earth or another planet turns **2 :** either of the two ends of a magnet

Pole *n* : a person born or living in Poland

pole·cat *n, pl* **pole·cats** *or* **polecat** **1 :** a brown or black European animal related to the weasel **2 :** SKUNK

pole vault *n* : a track-and-field event in which each athlete uses a pole to jump over a high bar

[1]**po·lice** *vb* **po·liced; po·lic·ing** : to keep order in or among

[2]**police** *n, pl* **police** **1 :** the department of government that keeps order and enforces law, investigates crimes, and makes arrests **2** *police pl* : members of a police force

police dog *n* : a dog trained to help police

po·lice·man *n, pl* **po·lice·men** : a man who is a police officer

police officer *n* : a member of a police force

po·lice·wom·an *n, pl* **po·lice·wom·en** : a woman who is a police officer

[1]**pol·i·cy** *n, pl* **pol·i·cies** : a set of guidelines or rules that determine a course of action

[2]**policy** *n, pl* **pol·i·cies** : a document that contains the agreement made by an insurance company with a person whose life or property is insured

po·lio *n* : a once common disease often affecting children and sometimes causing paralysis

po·lio·my·eli·tis *n* : POLIO

[1]**pol·ish** *vb* **pol·ished; pol·ish·ing** **1 :** to make smooth and shiny usually by rubbing **2 :** to improve in manners, condition, or style — **pol·ish·er** *n* — **polish off** : to finish completely

[2]**polish** *n* **1 :** a smooth and shiny surface **2 :** a substance for making a surface smooth and shiny **3 :** good manners : REFINEMENT

[1]**Pol·ish** *adj* : of or relating to Poland, the Poles, or Polish

[2]**Polish** *n* : the language of the Poles

po·lite *adj* **po·lit·er; po·lit·est** : showing courtesy or good manners — **po·lite·ly** *adv* — **po·lite·ness** *n*

po·lit·i·cal *adj* : relating to the government or the way government is carried on — **po·lit·i·cal·ly** *adv*

pol·i·ti·cian *n* : a person who is active in government usually as an elected official

pol·i·tics *n pl* **1 :** the activities, actions, and policies that are used to gain and hold power in a government or to influence a government **2 :** a person's opinions about the management of government — used as singular or plural

pol·ka *n* : a lively dance for couples or the music for it

pol·ka dot *n* : a dot in a pattern of evenly spaced dots (as on fabric)

[1]**poll** *n* **1 :** the casting or recording of the votes or opinions of a number of persons **2 :** the place where votes are cast — usually used in pl.

[2]**poll** *vb* **polled; poll·ing** : to question in order to get information or opinions about something

pol·lack *or* **pol·lock** *n, pl* **pollack** *or* **pollock** : either of two fishes of the northern Atlantic Ocean and the northern Pacific Ocean that are related to the cod and are often used for food

pol·len *n* : the very tiny grains produced by the stamens of a flower or special sacs of a male cone that fertilize the seeds and usually appear as fine yellow dust

pol·li·nate *vb* **pol·li·nat·ed; pol·li·nat·ing** : to transfer or carry pollen from a stamen to a pistil of a flower or from a male cone to a female cone

pol·li·na·tion *n* : the transfer of pollen from a stamen to a pistil of a flower or from a male cone to a female cone

pol·lut·ant *n* : a substance that makes something (as air or water) impure and often unsafe

pol·lute *vb* **pol·lut·ed; pol·lut·ing** : to spoil or make impure especially with waste made by humans — **pol·lut·er** *n*

pol·lu·tion *n* : the action of making something impure and often unsafe or unsuitable for use : the state of being polluted

pol·ly·wog *or* **pol·li·wog** *n* : TADPOLE
po·lo *n* : a game played by teams of players on horseback who use long-handled mallets to hit a wooden ball into a goal
poly- *prefix* : many : much : MULTI-
poly·es·ter *n* : a synthetic fiber used especially in clothing
poly·gon *n* : a flat geometric figure having three or more straight sides
poly·mer *n* : a chemical compound that is made of small molecules that are arranged in a simple repeating structure to form a larger molecule
pol·yp *n* : a small sea animal (as a coral) having a tubelike body closed and attached to something (as a rock) at one end and opening at the other with a mouth surrounded by tentacles
pome·gran·ate *n* : a reddish fruit that has a thick leathery skin and many seeds in a pulp of tart flavor and that grows on a tropical Asian tree
pom·mel *n* : a rounded knob on the handle of a sword or at the front of a saddle
pomp *n* : a show of wealth and splendor
pom–pom *n* **1** : a small fluffy ball used as decoration especially on clothing **2** : a usually brightly colored fluffy ball waved by cheerleaders
pomp·ous *adj* : having or showing an attitude of someone who thinks he or she is better than other people — **pomp·ous·ly** *adv*
pon·cho *n, pl* **ponchos** : a garment that is like a blanket with a hole in the middle for the head
pond *n* : a body of water usually smaller than a lake
pon·der *vb* **pon·dered; pon·der·ing** : to think over carefully
pon·der·ous *adj* **1** : very heavy **2** : slow or clumsy because of weight and size **3** : unpleasantly dull — **pon·der·ous·ly** *adv*
pon·toon *n* : a large hollow container filled with air and used to make something (as a boat, plane, or bridge) float
po·ny *n, pl* **ponies** : a small horse
pony express *n, often cap P & E* : a rapid postal system that operated across the western United States in 1860–61 by changing horses and riders along the way
po·ny·tail *n* : long hair that is pulled together and banded usually at the back of the head
poo·dle *n* : a small or medium-sized dog with a thick curly coat of solid color
[1]**pool** *n* **1** : a small deep body of usually fresh water **2** : something like a pool (as in shape or depth) **3** : a small body of standing liquid : PUDDLE **4** : SWIMMING POOL
[2]**pool** *n* **1** : a game of billiards played on a table with six pockets **2** : people, money, or things come together or put together for some purpose
[3]**pool** *vb* **pooled; pool·ing** : to contribute to a common fund or effort
pooped *adj* : very tired
poor *adj* **poor·er; poor·est** **1** : having little money or few possessions **2** : less than enough **3** : worthy of pity **4** : low in quality or condition : not satisfactory — **poor·ly** *adv*
[1]**pop** *vb* **popped; pop·ping** **1** : to burst or cause to burst with a short loud sound **2** : to cause to open suddenly **3** : to go, come, or appear suddenly or unexpectedly **4** : to put into or onto quickly or suddenly **5** : to stick out **6** : to shoot with a gun
[2]**pop** *n* **1** : a short loud sound **2** : SODA POP
pop·corn *n* **1** : corn whose kernels burst open when exposed to high heat to form white or yellowish puffy pieces **2** : the kernels after popping
pope *n, often cap* : the head of the Roman Catholic Church
pop·lar *n* : a tree that has rough bark and a white substance resembling cotton around its seeds
pop·py *n, pl* **poppies** : a plant with a hairy stem and showy usually red, yellow, or white flowers
pop·u·lace *n* **1** : the common people **2** : the people who live in a country or area : POPULATION
pop·u·lar *adj* **1** : of or relating to most of the people in a country or area **2** : enjoyed or approved by many people **3** : frequently encountered or widely accepted — **pop·u·lar·ly** *adv*
pop·u·lar·i·ty *n* : the quality or state of being liked, enjoyed, accepted, or practiced by a large number of people
pop·u·late *vb* **pop·u·lat·ed; pop·u·lat·ing** : to fill or provide with people, animals, or things
pop·u·la·tion *n* **1** : the whole number of people living in a country, city, or area **2** : a group of people or animals living in a certain place
pop·u·lous *adj* : having a large population
pop–up *n* : a window that appears suddenly on a computer screen often for advertising
por·ce·lain *n* : a hard white product of baked clay used especially for dishes, tile, and decorative objects
porch *n* : a covered entrance to a building usually with a separate roof
por·cu·pine *n* : a gnawing slow-moving animal that is a large rodent and has stiff sharp quills among its hairs
[1]**pore** *vb* **pored; por·ing** : to read with great attention : STUDY

²pore *n* **:** a tiny opening (as in the skin or in the soil)
pork *n* **:** the meat of a pig used for food
po·rous *adj* **1 :** full of small holes **2 :** capable of absorbing liquids
por·poise *n* **1 :** a small whale with teeth that resembles a dolphin but has a blunt rounded snout **2 :** DOLPHIN 1
por·ridge *n* **:** a soft food made by boiling partly ground grain or a vegetable (as peas) in water or milk until it thickens
¹port *n* **1 :** a town or city with a harbor where ships load or unload cargo **2 :** a place (as a harbor) where ships can find shelter from a storm
²port *n* **1 :** an opening (as in machinery) for gas, steam, or water to go in or out **2 :** PORTHOLE
³port *n* **:** the left side of a ship or airplane looking forward
por·ta·ble *adj* **:** easy or possible to carry or move about
por·tal *n* **:** a large or fancy door or gate
port·cul·lis *n* **:** a heavy iron gate that can be lowered to prevent entrance (as to a castle)
por·tend *vb* **por·tend·ed; por·tend·ing :** to give a sign or warning of beforehand
por·tent *n* **:** a sign or warning of something usually bad that is going to happen **:** OMEN
por·ten·tous *adj* **:** giving a sign or warning of something usually bad that is going to happen
por·ter *n* **1 :** a person whose job is to carry baggage (as at a hotel) **2 :** a person whose job is helping passengers on a train
port·fo·lio *n, pl* **port·fo·li·os 1 :** a flat case for carrying papers or drawings **2 :** a collection of art (as paintings) presented together in a folder
port·hole *n* **:** a small window in the side of a ship or airplane
por·ti·co *n, pl* **por·ti·coes** *or* **por·ti·cos :** a row of columns supporting a roof at the entrance of a building
¹por·tion *n* **1 :** a part or share of a whole **2 :** SERVING
²portion *vb* **por·tioned; por·tion·ing :** to divide into parts **:** DISTRIBUTE
port·ly *adj* **port·li·er; port·li·est :** having a round and heavy body **:** somewhat fat
por·trait *n* **:** a picture of a person usually showing the face
por·tray *vb* **por·trayed; por·tray·ing 1 :** to make a portrait of **2 :** to describe in words or words and images **3 :** to play the role of
por·tray·al *n* **:** the act or result of showing in a portrait or describing in words or images
¹Por·tu·guese *adj* **:** of or relating to Portugal, its people, or the Portuguese language
²Portuguese *n, pl* **Portuguese 1 :** a person born or living in Portugal **2 :** the language of Portugal and Brazil
¹pose *vb* **posed; pos·ing 1 :** to hold or cause to hold a special position of the body **2 :** to be or create **3 :** to ask (a question) **4 :** to pretend to be someone or something else
²pose *n* **1 :** a position of the body held for a special purpose **2 :** a pretended attitude
¹po·si·tion *n* **1 :** the way in which something or someone is placed or arranged **2 :** a way of looking at or considering things **3 :** the place where a person or thing is or should be **4 :** the situation that someone or something is in **5 :** the rank or role a person has in an organization or in society **6 :** JOB 1
²position *vb* **po·si·tioned; po·si·tion·ing :** to put in a particular place or arrangement
¹pos·i·tive *adj* **1 :** fully confident **:** CERTAIN **2 :** having a real or beneficial effect or result **3 :** beyond doubt **:** UNQUESTIONABLE **4 :** showing acceptance or approval **5 :** thinking of good qualities or possibilities **:** OPTIMISTIC **6 :** being greater than zero and often shown by a plus sign **7 :** being or relating to electricity of a kind that is produced in a glass rod rubbed with silk **8 :** having more protons than electrons **9 :** being the part from which the electric current flows to the external circuit **10 :** showing the presence of what is looked for or suspected to be present **11 :** relating to or having the form of an adjective or adverb that shows no degree of comparison — **pos·i·tive·ly** *adv*
²positive *n* **1 :** a good or useful feature or quality **2 :** the degree or a form of an adjective or adverb that shows no comparison
poss. *abbr* possessive
pos·se *n* **:** a group of people gathered together to make a search and especially in the past to search for a criminal
pos·sess *vb* **pos·sessed; pos·sess·ing 1 :** to have and hold as property **:** OWN **2 :** to have as a characteristic or quality **3 :** to enter into and control firmly — **pos·ses·sor** *n*
pos·ses·sion *n* **1 :** the act or state of possessing or holding as property **2 :** something that is held by someone as property
¹pos·ses·sive *adj* **1 :** being or belonging to the case of a noun or pronoun that shows possession **2 :** showing the desire to possess or control **:** unwilling to share
²possessive *n* **:** a word or form of a word that shows possession
pos·si·bil·i·ty *n, pl* **pos·si·bil·i·ties 1 :** a chance that something may or may not happen or exist **:** the state or fact of being possible **2 :** something that may happen
pos·si·ble *adj* **1 :** able to be done **2 :** able

to happen or exist **3 :** able or suited to be or to become

pos·si·bly *adv* **1 :** by any possibility **2 :** by nothing more than chance **:** PERHAPS

pos·sum *n* **:** OPOSSUM

[1]**post** *n* **:** a piece of material (as metal or wood) placed firmly in an upright position and used especially as a support or marker

[2]**post** *vb* **post·ed; post·ing** **1 :** to fasten (as a notice or sign) to a suitable place (as a wall or bulletin board) **2 :** to make known publicly as if by putting up a notice **3 :** to forbid persons from entering or using by putting up warning notices

[3]**post** *vb* **post·ed; post·ing** **1 :** to ride or travel quickly **2 :** to send by mail **3 :** to make aware of recent news about something

[4]**post** *n* **1 :** the place where a soldier or guard is stationed **2 :** a place where a body of troops is stationed **3 :** a place or office to which a person is appointed **4 :** TRADING POST

[5]**post** *vb* **post·ed; post·ing :** to station in a given place

post- *prefix* **:** after **:** later **:** following **:** behind

post·age *n* **:** a fee for sending a letter or package by mail

post·al *adj* **:** relating to the post office or the sending and delivery of mail

postal card *n* **1 :** a blank card with a postage stamp printed on it **2 :** POSTCARD 1

postal service *n* **:** a government department in charge of handling the mail

post·card *n* **1 :** a card on which a message may be sent by mail without an envelope and that often has a picture on one side **2 :** POSTAL CARD 1

post·er *n* **:** a usually large sheet with writing or pictures on it that is displayed as a notice, advertisement, or for decoration

pos·ter·i·ty *n* **:** all future generations

post·man *n, pl* **post·men :** LETTER CARRIER

post·mark *n* **:** a mark put on a piece of mail especially for canceling the postage stamp

post·mas·ter *n* **:** a person in charge of a post office

post·mis·tress *n* **:** a woman in charge of a post office

post office *n* **1 :** POSTAL SERVICE **2 :** a place where mail is received, handled, and sent out

post·paid *adv* **:** with postage paid by the sender

post·pone *vb* **post·poned; post·pon·ing :** to put off until a later time — **post·pone·ment** *n*

post·script *n* **:** a note added at the end of a letter, article, or book

pos·ture *n* **:** the way in which the body is positioned when sitting or standing **:** the general way of holding the body

po·sy *n, pl* **posies** **1 :** a small bunch of flowers **2 :** [1]FLOWER 1

[1]**pot** *n* **1 :** a deep usually rounded container **2 :** the amount a pot will hold

[2]**pot** *vb* **pot·ted; pot·ting :** to put or pack in a pot

pot·ash *n* **:** potassium or a compound of potassium

po·tas·si·um *n* **:** a silvery soft light metallic chemical element found especially in minerals

po·ta·to *n, pl* **po·ta·toes :** the thick edible usually rounded underground tuber of a widely grown South American plant that is eaten as a vegetable

potato chip *n* **:** a thin slice of potato fried crisp

po·tent *adj* **1 :** very effective **:** STRONG **2 :** having power or authority

[1]**po·ten·tial** *adj* **:** existing as a possibility **:** capable of becoming real — **po·ten·tial·ly** *adv*

[2]**potential** *n* **1 :** the chance or possibility that something will develop and become real **2 :** an ability or quality that can lead to success or excellence **:** PROMISE

pot·hole *n* **:** a deep round hole (as in a road)

po·tion *n* **:** a drink that is meant to have a special or magical effect on someone

pot·luck *n* **:** a meal to which people bring food to share

pot·ter *n* **:** a person who makes pottery

pot·tery *n, pl* **pot·ter·ies** **1 :** the art or craft of making objects (as dishes and vases) out of clay **2 :** objects made from clay that is shaped while moist and hardened by heat

pouch *n* **1 :** a small bag that can be closed (as with a string) **2 :** a bag for carrying goods or valuables **3 :** a pocket of folded skin especially for carrying the young (as on the abdomen of a kangaroo) or for carrying food (as in the cheek of a hamster) **4 :** a structure of the body in the form of a bag

poul·tice *n* **:** a soft and heated preparation usually containing medicine that is spread on cloth and placed on the skin to heal a sore or relieve pain

poul·try *n* **:** birds (as chickens, turkeys, ducks, and geese) raised for their meat or eggs

pounce *vb* **pounced; pounc·ing** **1 :** to suddenly jump toward and seize something with or as if with claws **2 :** to act, approach, or attack suddenly or without hesitation

[1]**pound** *n* **1 :** a measure of weight equal to sixteen ounces (about .45 kilogram) **2 :** any of several units of money (as of the United Kingdom or Egypt)

[2]**pound** *n* **:** a place where stray animals are kept

[3]**pound** *vb* **pound·ed; pound·ing** **1 :** to

crush or break into very small pieces by beating **2 :** to hit with force again and again **3 :** to move with heavy and loud steps **4 :** [1]THROB 1

pour *vb* **poured; pour·ing 1 :** to flow or cause to flow in or as if in a stream **2 :** to rain hard **3 :** to move or come continuously

[1]**pout** *vb* **pout·ed; pout·ing 1 :** to show displeasure by pushing out the lips **2 :** [1]SULK

[2]**pout** *n* **:** a facial expression that shows displeasure and is made by pushing out the lips

pov·er·ty *n* **:** the condition of being poor **:** lack of money or possessions

[1]**pow·der** *vb* **pow·dered; pow·der·ing 1 :** to sprinkle or cover with or as if with fine particles of something **2 :** to reduce or change to powder

[2]**powder** *n* **1 :** a dry substance made up of fine particles **2 :** something (as a food, medicine, or cosmetic) made in or changed to the form of a powder **3 :** GUNPOWDER

powder horn *n* **:** a cow or ox horn made into a container for carrying gunpowder

pow·dery *adj* **1 :** made of or like powder **2 :** easily crumbled **3 :** covered or sprinkled with or as if with powder

[1]**pow·er** *n* **1 :** possession of control, authority, or influence over others **2 :** a nation that has influence among other nations **3 :** the ability to act or produce an effect **4 :** the right to do something **5 :** physical might **:** STRENGTH **6 :** the number of times as shown by an exponent that a number is used as a factor to obtain a product **7 :** force or energy used to do work **8 :** the rate of speed at which work is done **9 :** the number of times an optical instrument (as a microscope) magnifies the object viewed

[2]**power** *vb* **pow·ered; pow·er·ing :** to supply with a form of energy

pow·er·ful *adj* **:** full of or having power, strength, or influence — **pow·er·ful·ly** *adv*

pow·er·house *n* **1 :** POWER PLANT **2 :** a person or thing having unusual strength or energy

pow·er·less *adj* **:** without power, strength, authority, or influence

power plant *n* **:** a building in which electric power is generated

pow·wow *n* **1 :** an American Indian ceremony or social gathering **2 :** a meeting for discussion

pp. *abbr* pages

PQ *abbr* Province of Quebec

pr. *abbr* pair

PR *abbr* Puerto Rico

prac·ti·ca·ble *adj* **:** possible to do or put into practice

prac·ti·cal *adj* **1 :** of or relating to real action rather than ideas or thought **2 :** capable of being put to use **:** reasonable to do or use **3 :** tending to act according to reason and logic

practical joke *n* **:** a joke involving an act rather than words **:** a trick played on someone — **practical joker** *n*

prac·ti·cal·ly *adv* **1 :** ALMOST **2 :** in a way that is reasonable or logical

[1]**prac·tice** *or Can and Brit* **practise** *vb* **prac·ticed/practised; prac·tic·ing/practising 1 :** to do or work at often so as to learn well or improve **2 :** to do or perform often or usually **3 :** to engage in or work at as a profession

[2]**practice** *n* **1 :** the act of doing something again and again in order to learn or improve **2 :** a regular event at which something is done again and again to increase skill **3 :** actual performance **:** USE **4 :** a usual way of doing something **5 :** continuous work in a profession

prai·rie *n* **:** a large area of level or rolling grassland

prairie chicken *n* **:** a grouse of the prairies of the central United States

prairie dog *n* **:** a burrowing animal of the prairies of the central and western United States that is related to the squirrel and lives in large colonies

prairie schooner *n* **:** a long covered wagon used by pioneers to cross the prairies

[1]**praise** *vb* **praised; prais·ing 1 :** to express approval of **2 :** to glorify (God or a saint)

[2]**praise** *n* **1 :** an expression of approval **2 :** [1]WORSHIP 1

praise·wor·thy *adj* **:** deserving praise

prance *vb* **pranced; pranc·ing 1 :** to move by taking high steps **2 :** to walk or move in a lively and proud way

prank *n* **:** a mischievous act **:** PRACTICAL JOKE

[1]**prat·tle** *vb* **prat·tled; prat·tling :** to talk a great deal about unimportant or uninteresting things

[2]**prattle** *n* **:** uninteresting or unimportant talk

pray *vb* **prayed; pray·ing 1 :** to speak to God especially to give thanks or ask for something **2 :** to hope or wish very much for **3 :** to ask earnestly **:** BEG

prayer *n* **1 :** words spoken to God **2 :** the act of praying to God **3 :** a strong hope or wish **4 :** a set form of words used in praying **5 :** a religious service that is mostly prayers

praying mantis *n* **:** a large usually green insect that feeds on other insects which are held in the raised front legs

pre- *prefix* **1 :** earlier than **:** before **2 :** beforehand **3 :** in front of **:** front

preach *vb* **preached; preach·ing 1 :** to give a sermon **2 :** to urge publicly

preach·er *n* **1 :** a person who gives sermons **2 :** [1]MINISTER 1
pre·am·ble *n* **:** an introduction (as to a law) that often gives the reasons for what follows
pre·car·i·ous *adj* **:** not safe, strong, or steady — **pre·car·i·ous·ly** *adv*
pre·cau·tion *n* **:** something done beforehand to prevent harm or trouble or bring about good results
pre·cede *vb* **pre·ced·ed; pre·ced·ing :** to be or go before in importance, position, or time
pre·ce·dent *n* **:** something that can be used as a rule or example to be followed in the future
pre·ced·ing *adj* **:** existing or happening before in time or place **:** PREVIOUS
pre·cinct *n* **1 :** any of the sections into which a town or city is divided for a particular purpose (as voting or police protection) **2 :** a surrounding or enclosed area
pre·cious *adj* **1 :** very valuable **2 :** greatly loved or valued
prec·i·pice *n* **:** a very steep side of a mountain or cliff
pre·cip·i·tate *vb* **pre·cip·i·tat·ed; pre·cip·i·tat·ing 1 :** to cause to happen suddenly or unexpectedly **2 :** to change from a vapor to a liquid or solid and fall as rain or snow **3 :** to separate from a solution
pre·cip·i·ta·tion *n* **:** water that falls to the earth as hail, mist, rain, sleet, or snow
pre·cise *adj* **1 :** exactly stated or explained **2 :** very exact **:** ACCURATE **3 :** being exactly the one mentioned or indicated and no other — **pre·cise·ly** *adv*
pre·ci·sion *n* **:** the quality or state of being precise or exact **:** ACCURACY
pre·co·cious *adj* **:** showing qualities or abilities of an adult at an unusually early age — **pre·co·cious·ly** *adv*
pred·a·tor *n* **:** an animal that lives mostly by killing and eating other animals
pred·a·to·ry *adj* **:** living by killing and eating other animals
pre·de·ces·sor *n* **:** a person who held a job or position before someone else
pre·dic·a·ment *n* **:** a bad situation
[1]**pred·i·cate** *n* **:** the part of a sentence or clause that tells what is said about the subject
[2]**predicate** *adj* **:** completing the meaning of a linking verb
pre·dict *vb* **pre·dict·ed; pre·dict·ing :** to say that (something) will or might happen in the future
pre·dic·tion *n* **1 :** an act of saying what will or might happen in the future **2 :** a statement about what will or might happen in the future
pre·dom·i·nance *n* **:** the quality or state of being greater than others in number, frequency, strength, influence, or authority
pre·dom·i·nant *adj* **:** greater than others in number, frequency, strength, influence, or authority
pre·dom·i·nate *vb* **pre·dom·i·nat·ed; pre·dom·i·nat·ing :** to be greater than others in number, frequency, strength, influence, or authority
preen *vb* **preened; preen·ing 1 :** to smooth and clean with the bill **2 :** to make a person's own appearance neat and tidy
pre·fab·ri·cat·ed *adj* **:** made of parts that are made at a factory and can be put together later
pref·ace *n* **:** a section at the beginning that introduces a book or a speech
pre·fer *vb* **pre·ferred; pre·fer·ring :** to like better than another or others
pref·er·a·ble *adj* **:** better or more desirable — **pref·er·a·bly** *adv*
pref·er·ence *n* **1 :** a choosing of or special liking for one person or thing rather than another or others **2 :** the power or chance to choose **:** CHOICE **3 :** a person or thing that is liked or wanted more than another
pre·fix *n* **:** a letter or group of letters that comes at the beginning of a word and has its own meaning
preg·nan·cy *n, pl* **preg·nan·cies :** the state of being pregnant
preg·nant *adj* **1 :** carrying one or more unborn offspring in the body **2 :** full of meaning
pre·hen·sile *adj* **:** capable of grasping something by wrapping around it
pre·his·tor·ic *adj* **:** relating to or existing in the time before written history began
[1]**prej·u·dice** *n* **1 :** a liking or dislike for one rather than another especially without good reason **2 :** a feeling of unfair dislike directed against an individual or a group because of some characteristic (as race or religion) **3 :** injury or damage to a person's rights
[2]**prejudice** *vb* **prej·u·diced; prej·u·dic·ing 1 :** to cause to have an unfair dislike of **2 :** to cause damage to (as a person's rights)
prej·u·diced *adj* **:** having or showing an unfair dislike of a person or group because of some characteristic (as race or religion)
[1]**pre·lim·i·nary** *n, pl* **pre·lim·i·nar·ies :** something that comes before the main or final part
[2]**preliminary** *adj* **:** coming before the main or full part
pre·lude *n* **1 :** something that comes before and prepares for the main or more important parts **2 :** a short piece of music played at the beginning of something (as an opera or church service)

pre·ma·ture *adj* : happening, coming, or done before the usual or proper time : too early — **pre·ma·ture·ly** *adv*

pre·med·i·tate *vb* **pre·med·i·tat·ed; pre·med·i·tat·ing** : to think about and plan beforehand

[1]**pre·mier** *adj* : first in importance, excellence, or rank

[2]**premier** *n* : PRIME MINISTER

[1]**pre·miere** *n* : a first showing or performance

[2]**premiere** *vb* **pre·miered; pre·mier·ing** : to have a first showing or performance

prem·ise *n* **1** : a statement or idea taken to be true and on which an argument or reasoning may be based **2 premises** *pl* : a piece of land with the buildings on it

pre·mi·um *n* **1** : a reward for a special act **2** : an amount above the regular or stated price **3** : the amount paid for a contract of insurance **4** : a high or extra value

pre·mo·lar *n* : a double-pointed tooth that comes between the canines and molars

pre·mo·ni·tion *n* : a feeling that something is going to happen

pre·oc·cu·pied *adj* : thinking about or worrying about one thing a great deal

prep *abbr* preposition

prep·a·ra·tion *n* **1** : the act or process of making or getting ready beforehand **2** : something done to make or get ready **3** : something made for a special purpose

pre·par·a·to·ry *adj* : preparing or serving to prepare for something

pre·pare *vb* **pre·pared; pre·par·ing** **1** : to make or get ready beforehand **2** : to put together the elements of

pre·pay *vb* **pre·paid; pre·pay·ing** : to pay or pay for beforehand

prep·o·si·tion *n* : a word or group of words that combines with a noun or pronoun to form a phrase that usually acts as an adverb, adjective, or noun

prep·o·si·tion·al *adj* : relating to or containing a preposition

pre·pos·ter·ous *adj* : making little or no sense : FOOLISH

pre·req·ui·site *n* : something that is needed beforehand : REQUIREMENT

pres. *abbr* **1** present **2** president

[1]**pre·school** *adj* : relating to the time in a child's life that comes before attendance at school

[2]**preschool** *n* : a school for children usually under five years old who are too young for kindergarten

pre·school·er *n* : a child of preschool age

pre·scribe *vb* **pre·scribed; pre·scrib·ing** **1** : to order or direct the use of as a remedy **2** : to lay down as a rule of action : ORDER

pre·scrip·tion *n* **1** : a written direction or order for the preparing and use of a medicine **2** : a medicine that is ordered by a doctor as a remedy

pres·ence *n* **1** : the fact or condition of being in a certain place **2** : position close to a person **3** : a person's appearance or manner

presence of mind *n* : ability to think clearly and act quickly in an emergency

[1]**pres·ent** *n* : something given : GIFT

[2]**pre·sent** *vb* **pre·sent·ed; pre·sent·ing** **1** : to give with ceremony **2** : to make a gift to **3** : to bring before the public **4** : to introduce one person to another **5** : to appear in a particular place **6** : to offer to view : SHOW, DISPLAY **7** : to come into or cause to come into being

[3]**pres·ent** *adj* **1** : not past or future : now going on **2** : being at a certain place and not elsewhere **3** : pointing out or relating to time that is not past or future

[4]**pres·ent** *n* : the time right now

pre·sent·able *adj* : having a satisfactory or pleasing appearance

pre·sen·ta·tion *n* **1** : an act of showing, describing, or explaining something to a group of people **2** : an act of giving a gift or award **3** : something given

pres·ent·ly *adv* **1** : before long : SOON **2** : at the present time : NOW

present participle *n* : the form of a verb that in English is formed with the suffix *-ing* and that expresses present action

present tense *n* : a verb tense that expresses action or state in the present time and is used of what is true at the time of speaking or is always true

pres·er·va·tion *n* : the effort of keeping from injury, loss, or decay

pre·ser·va·tive *n* : a substance added to food to keep it from spoiling

[1]**pre·serve** *vb* **pre·served; pre·serv·ing** **1** : to keep or save from injury, loss, or ruin : PROTECT **2** : to prepare (as by canning or pickling) fruits or vegetables to be kept for future use **3** : MAINTAIN 2, CONTINUE — **pre·serv·er** *n*

[2]**preserve** *n* **1** : fruit cooked in sugar or made into jam or jelly — often used in pl. **2** : an area where land and animals are protected

pre·side *vb* **pre·sid·ed; pre·sid·ing** : to be in charge

pres·i·den·cy *n, pl* **pres·i·den·cies** **1** : the office of president **2** : the term during which a president holds office

pres·i·dent *n* **1** : the head of the government and chief executive officer of a modern republic **2** : the chief officer of a company, organization, or society

pres·i·den·tial *adj* : of or relating to a president or the presidency

[1]press *vb* **pressed; press·ing 1 :** to push steadily against **2 :** to ask or urge strongly **3 :** to move forward forcefully **4 :** to squeeze so as to force out the juice or contents **5 :** to flatten out or smooth by bearing down upon especially by ironing

[2]press *n* **1 :** [2]CROWD 1, THRONG **2 :** a machine that uses pressure to shape, flatten, squeeze, or stamp **3 :** the act of pressing : PRESSURE **4 :** a printing or publishing business **5 :** the newspapers and magazines of a country **6 :** news reporters and broadcasters **7 :** PRINTING PRESS **8 :** CLOSET 2

press·ing *adj* : needing immediate attention

pres·sure *n* **1 :** the action of pushing steadily against **2 :** a force or influence that cannot be avoided **3 :** the force with which one body presses against another **4 :** the need to get things done

pres·tige *n* : importance or respect gained through success or excellence

pres·to *adv or adj* : suddenly as if by magic

pre·sum·ably *adv* : it seems likely : PROBABLY

pre·sume *vb* **pre·sumed; pre·sum·ing 1 :** to undertake without permission or good reason : DARE **2 :** to suppose to be true without proof

pre·sump·tion *n* **1 :** behavior or attitude going beyond what is proper **2 :** a strong reason for believing something to be so **3 :** something believed to be so but not proved

pre·sump·tu·ous *adj* : going beyond what is proper — **pre·sump·tu·ous·ly** *adv* — **pre·sump·tu·ous·ness** *n*

pre·teen *n* : a boy or girl who is 11 or 12 years old

pre·tend *vb* **pre·tend·ed; pre·tend·ing 1 :** to make believe **2 :** to put forward as true something that is not true — **pre·tend·er** *n*

pre·tense *or* **pre·tence** *n* **1 :** an act or appearance that looks real but is false **2 :** an effort to reach a certain condition or quality

pre·ten·tious *adj* : trying to appear better or more important than is really the case — **pre·ten·tious·ly** *adv* — **pre·ten·tious·ness** *n*

[1]pret·ty *adj* **pret·ti·er; pret·ti·est :** pleasing to the eye or ear especially because of being graceful or delicate — **pret·ti·ly** *adv* — **pret·ti·ness** *n*

[2]pretty *adv* : in some degree : FAIRLY

pret·zel *n* : a brown cracker that is salted and is often shaped like a loose knot

pre·vail *vb* **pre·vailed; pre·vail·ing 1 :** to succeed in convincing **2 :** to be or become usual, common, or widespread **3 :** to win against opposition

prev·a·lence *n* : the state of happening, being accepted, or being practiced often or over a wide area

prev·a·lent *adj* : accepted, practiced, or happening often or over a wide area

pre·vent *vb* **pre·vent·ed; pre·vent·ing 1 :** to keep from happening **2 :** to hold or keep back — **pre·vent·able** *adj*

pre·ven·tion *n* : the act or practice of keeping something from happening

pre·ven·tive *adj* : used for keeping something from happening

pre·view *n* : an instance of showing something (as a movie) before others get to see it

pre·vi·ous *adj* : going before in time or order : PRECEDING — **pre·vi·ous·ly** *adv*

[1]prey *n* **1 :** an animal that is hunted or killed by another animal for food **2 :** a person who is helpless and unable to escape attack : VICTIM

[2]prey *vb* **preyed; prey·ing 1 :** to hunt and kill for food **2 :** to have a harmful effect

[1]price *n* **1 :** the quantity of one thing given or asked for something else : the amount of money paid or to be paid **2 :** the cost at which something is gotten or done **3 :** a reward for the apprehension of a criminal

[2]price *vb* **priced; pric·ing 1 :** to determine the amount something costs **2 :** to find out how much something costs

price·less *adj* : more valuable than any amount of money : not to be bought for any amount of money

[1]prick *n* **1 :** an act of piercing with a small sharp point **2 :** a feeling of pain that accompanies a piercing of the skin with a sharp point **3 :** a sudden strong feeling

[2]prick *vb* **pricked; prick·ing 1 :** to point upward **2 :** to pierce slightly with a sharp point **3 :** to have or to cause a feeling of or as if of being pierced with a sharp point

prick·er *n* : [1]PRICKLE 1, THORN

[1]prick·le *n* **1 :** a small sharp point (as a thorn) **2 :** a slight stinging pain

[2]prickle *vb* **prick·led; prick·ling :** [2]PRICK 3

prick·ly *adj* **prick·li·er; prick·li·est 1 :** having small sharp points **2 :** having or causing slight stinging pain

prickly pear *n* : a cactus with flat branching spiny stems and a sweet fruit shaped like a pear

[1]pride *n* **1 :** a reasonable and justifiable feeling of being worthwhile : SELF-RESPECT **2 :** a feeling of being better than others **3 :** a sense of pleasure that comes from some act or possession **4 :** someone or something that makes someone proud

[2]pride *vb* **prid·ed; prid·ing :** to feel self-esteem

priest *n* : a person who has the authority to lead or perform religious ceremonies

priest·ess *n* : a woman who has the authority to lead or perform religious ceremonies

prim *adj* **prim·mer; prim·mest** : very formal and proper — **prim·ly** *adv*

pri·mar·i·ly *adv* : more than anything else : MAINLY

[1]**pri·ma·ry** *adj* **1** : first in time or development **2** : most important : MAIN **3** : not made or coming from something else : BASIC **4** : relating to or being the heaviest of three levels of stress in pronunciation

[2]**primary** *n, pl* **pri·ma·ries** : an election in which members of a political party nominate candidates for office

primary color *n* : one of the colors red, yellow, or blue which can be mixed together to make other colors

pri·mate *n* : any of a group of mammals that includes humans together with the apes and monkeys and a few related forms

[1]**prime** *n* : the period in life when a person is best in health, looks, or strength

[2]**prime** *adj* : first in importance, rank, or quality

[3]**prime** *vb* **primed; prim·ing** **1** : to put a first color or coating on (an unpainted surface) **2** : to put into working order by filling **3** : to make (someone or something) ready

prime minister *n* : the chief officer of the government in some countries

prime number *n* : a number (as 2, 3, or 5) that results in a whole number from division only when it is divided by itself or by 1

prim·er *n* **1** : a small book for teaching children to read **2** : a book or other writing that introduces a subject

pri·me·val *adj* : belonging to the earliest time : PRIMITIVE

prim·i·tive *adj* **1** : of or belonging to very early times **2** : of or belonging to an early stage of development

primp *vb* **primped; primp·ing** : to dress or arrange in a careful or fussy manner

prim·rose *n* : a small plant with large leaves and showy often yellow or pink flowers

prince *n* **1** : MONARCH 1 **2** : the son of a monarch **3** : a nobleman of very high or the highest rank

prince·ly *adj* **1** : suitable for a prince **2** : very large or impressive

prin·cess *n* : a daughter or granddaughter of a monarch : a female member of a royal family

[1]**prin·ci·pal** *adj* : highest in rank or importance : CHIEF — **prin·ci·pal·ly** *adv*

[2]**principal** *n* **1** : the head of a school **2** : a leading or most important person or thing **3** : a sum of money that is placed to earn interest, is owed as a debt, or is used as a fund

prin·ci·pal·i·ty *n, pl* **prin·ci·pal·i·ties** : a small territory that is ruled by a prince

principal parts *n pl* : the infinitive, the past tense, and the past and present participles of an English verb

prin·ci·ple *n* **1** : a general or basic truth on which other truths or theories can be based **2** : a rule of conduct based on beliefs of what is right and wrong **3** : a law or fact of nature which makes possible the working of a machine or device

[1]**print** *n* **1** : a mark made on the surface of something **2** : FOOTPRINT **3** : printed matter **4** : printed letters **5** : a picture, copy, or design taken from an engraving or photographic negative **6** : cloth upon which a design is stamped

[2]**print** *vb* **print·ed; print·ing** **1** : to write in separate letters **2** : PUBLISH 1 **3** : to make a copy of by pressing paper against an inked surface (as type or an engraving) **4** : to make a picture from a photographic negative — **print out** : to produce a paper copy of from a computer

print·er *n* **1** : a person or company whose business is making copies of text and images **2** : a machine that produces text and images on paper

print·ing *n* **1** : the art, practice, or business of making copies of text and images **2** : writing that uses separate letters

printing press *n* : a machine that makes copies of text and images

print·out *n* : a printed copy produced by a computer

[1]**pri·or** *n* : a monk who is head of a religious house

[2]**prior** *adj* **1** : being or happening before something else **2** : being more important than something else — **prior to** : [2]BEFORE 2

pri·or·ess *n, pl* **pri·or·ess·es** : a nun who is head of a religious house

pri·or·i·ty *n, pl* **pri·or·i·ties** : a condition of being more important than other things

pri·o·ry *n, pl* **pri·o·ries** : a religious house under the leadership of a prior or prioress

prism *n* : a transparent object that usually has three sides and bends light so that it breaks up into rainbow colors

pris·on *n* : a place where criminals are locked up

pris·on·er *n* : a person who has been captured or locked up

pri·va·cy *n* **1** : the state of being out of the sight and hearing of other people **2** : freedom from intrusion

[1]**pri·vate** *adj* **1** : having to do with or for the use of a single person or group : not public **2** : not holding any public office **3** : [1]SECRET 1 — **pri·vate·ly** *adv*

[2]**private** *n* : an enlisted person of the lowest

rank in the marine corps or of either of the two lowest ranks in the army

pri·va·teer *n* **1 :** a privately owned armed ship permitted by its government to make war on ships of an enemy country **2 :** a sailor on a privateer

private first class *n* **:** an enlisted person in the army or marine corps ranking above a private

priv·et *n* **:** a shrub with small white flowers that is often used for hedges

priv·i·lege *n* **1 :** a right or liberty granted as a favor or benefit especially to some and not others **2 :** an opportunity that is special and pleasant

priv·i·leged *adj* **:** having more things and a better chance in life than most people

privy *n, pl* **priv·ies :** a small building without plumbing used as a toilet

[1]**prize** *n* **1 :** something won or to be won in a contest **2 :** something unusually valuable or eagerly sought

[2]**prize** *adj* **1 :** outstanding of its kind **2 :** awarded as a prize **3 :** awarded a prize

[3]**prize** *vb* **prized; priz·ing :** to value highly **:** TREASURE

[4]**prize** *n* **:** something taken (as in war) by force especially at sea

prize·fight·er *n* **:** a professional boxer

[1]**pro** *n, pl* **pros :** an argument or evidence in favor of something

[2]**pro** *adv* **:** in favor of something

[3]**pro** *n or adj* **:** PROFESSIONAL

pro- *prefix* **:** approving **:** in favor of

prob·a·bil·i·ty *n, pl* **prob·a·bil·i·ties 1 :** the chance of happening **2 :** something likely **3 :** a measure of how likely a given event is

prob·a·ble *adj* **:** reasonably sure but not certain of happening or being true **:** LIKELY

prob·a·bly *adv* **:** very likely

pro·ba·tion *n* **1 :** the condition of being closely watched and evaluated for a period of time or the period of time during which this happens **2 :** the early release of a prisoner on certain conditions

[1]**probe** *n* **1 :** a slender instrument for examining a cavity (as a deep wound) **2 :** a careful investigation

[2]**probe** *vb* **probed; prob·ing 1 :** to examine with or as if with an instrument **2 :** to investigate thoroughly

prob·lem *n* **1 :** something to be worked out or solved **2 :** a person or thing that is hard to understand or deal with

pro·bos·cis *n* **:** a long flexible hollow body part (as the trunk of an elephant)

pro·ce·dure *n* **:** an action or series of actions for doing or accomplishing something

pro·ceed *vb* **pro·ceed·ed; pro·ceed·ing 1 :** to go forward or onward **:** ADVANCE **2 :** to begin and continue with an action or process **3 :** to go or act by an orderly method **4 :** to come from a source

pro·ceed·ings *n pl* **:** things that are said or done

pro·ceeds *n pl* **:** money or profit made

[1]**pro·cess** *n* **1 :** a series of actions, motions, or operations leading to some result **2 :** a series of changes that occur naturally

[2]**process** *vb* **pro·cessed; pro·cess·ing 1 :** to change by a special treatment **2 :** to take care of according to a routine **3 :** to take in and organize for use

pro·ces·sion *n* **:** a group of individuals moving along in an orderly often ceremonial way

pro·ces·sor *n* **1 :** a person or machine that changes something by a special treatment or takes care of something according to a routine **2 :** COMPUTER **3 :** the part of a computer that operates on data

pro·claim *vb* **pro·claimed; pro·claim·ing :** to announce publicly **:** DECLARE

proc·la·ma·tion *n* **1 :** the act of making something known publicly or officially **2 :** an official formal announcement

pro·cras·ti·nate *vb* **pro·cras·ti·nat·ed; pro·cras·ti·nat·ing :** to keep putting off something that should be done

pro·cure *vb* **pro·cured; pro·cur·ing :** OBTAIN

[1]**prod** *vb* **prod·ded; prod·ding 1 :** to poke with something **2 :** to stir or encourage a person or animal to action

[2]**prod** *n* **1 :** something used for stirring an animal to action **2 :** an act of poking **3 :** a sharp urging or reminder

[1]**prod·i·gal** *adj* **:** carelessly wasteful

[2]**prodigal** *n* **:** somebody who wastes money carelessly

prod·i·gy *n, pl* **prod·i·gies 1 :** an unusually talented child **2 :** an amazing event or action **:** WONDER

[1]**pro·duce** *vb* **pro·duced; pro·duc·ing 1 :** to bring forth **:** YIELD **2 :** [1]MANUFACTURE 1 **3 :** to bring to view **:** EXHIBIT **4 :** to prepare (as a play) for public presentation — **pro·duc·er** *n*

[2]**pro·duce** *n* **:** fresh fruits and vegetables

prod·uct *n* **1 :** the number resulting from the multiplication of two or more numbers **2 :** something resulting from manufacture, labor, thought, or growth

pro·duc·tion *n* **1 :** something prepared for public presentation **2 :** the act of manufacturing **3 :** the amount brought forth

pro·duc·tive *adj* **1 :** having the power to yield in large amounts **2 :** producing well

prof. *abbr* professor

[1]**pro·fane** *adj* **:** showing disrespect for God or holy things

²profane *vb* **pro·faned; pro·fan·ing :** to treat (something sacred) with great disrespect

pro·fan·i·ty *n, pl* **pro·fan·i·ties :** language that is offensive or disrespectful

pro·fess *vb* **pro·fessed; pro·fess·ing 1 :** to declare openly **2 :** PRETEND 2

pro·fes·sion *n* **1 :** an occupation (as medicine, law, or teaching) that is not mechanical or agricultural and that requires special education **2 :** an act of publicly declaring or claiming **3 :** the people working in an occupation

¹pro·fes·sion·al *adj* **1 :** relating to an occupation **:** of or as an expert **2 :** taking part in an activity (as a sport) in order to make money **3 :** participated in by people who are paid to compete **4 :** having or showing a quality appropriate in a profession — **pro·fes·sion·al·ly** *adv*

²professional *n* **1 :** a person who does a job that requires special education or skill **2 :** a person who is paid to participate in a sport or activity

pro·fes·sor *n* **:** a teacher especially of the highest rank at a college or university

prof·fer *vb* **prof·fered; prof·fer·ing :** ¹OFFER 1

pro·fi·cient *adj* **:** very good at doing something — **pro·fi·cient·ly** *adv*

pro·file *n* **1 :** something (as a head or a mountain) seen or drawn from the side **2 :** a level of activity that draws attention

¹prof·it *n* **1 :** the gain after all the expenses are subtracted from the total amount received **2 :** the gain or benefit from something — **prof·it·less** *adj*

²profit *vb* **prof·it·ed; prof·it·ing 1 :** to get some good out of something **:** GAIN **2 :** to be of use to (someone)

prof·it·able *adj* **:** producing a benefit or monetary gain — **prof·it·ably** *adv*

pro·found *adj* **1 :** having or showing great knowledge and understanding **2 :** very deeply felt — **pro·found·ly** *adv*

pro·fuse *adj* **:** very plentiful — **pro·fuse·ly** *adv*

pro·fu·sion *n* **:** a plentiful supply **:** PLENTY

prog·e·ny *n, pl* **prog·e·nies :** human descendants or animal offspring

¹pro·gram *n* **1 :** a brief statement or written outline (as of a concert, play, ceremony, or religious service) **2 :** PERFORMANCE 2 **3 :** a plan of action **4 :** a set of step-by-step instructions that tell a computer to do something with data

²program *vb* **pro·grammed; pro·gram·ming :** to give (a computer) a set of instructions **:** provide with a program

pro·gram·mer *n* **:** a person who creates and tests programs for computers

¹prog·ress *n* **1 :** the act of moving toward a goal **2 :** gradual improvement — **in progress :** happening at the present time

²pro·gress *vb* **pro·gressed; pro·gress·ing 1 :** to move forward in place or time **:** ADVANCE **2 :** to move toward a higher, better, or more advanced stage

pro·gres·sion *n* **1 :** the act of advancing or moving forward **2 :** a continuous and connected series (as of acts, events, or steps)

pro·gres·sive *adj* **1 :** of, relating to, or showing advancement **2 :** taking place gradually or step-by-step **3 :** favoring gradual political change and social improvement by action of the government — **pro·gres·sive·ly** *adv*

pro·hib·it *vb* **pro·hib·it·ed; pro·hib·it·ing 1 :** to forbid by authority **2 :** to make impossible

pro·hi·bi·tion *n* **1 :** the act of making something illegal or impossible **2 :** the forbidding by law of the sale or manufacture of alcoholic liquids for use as beverages

¹proj·ect *n* **1 :** a plan or scheme to do something **2 :** a task or problem in school that requires work over a period of time and is often displayed or presented **3 :** a group of houses or apartment buildings built according to a single plan

²pro·ject *vb* **pro·ject·ed; pro·ject·ing 1 :** to stick out **2 :** to cause to fall on a surface **3 :** to send or throw forward

pro·jec·tile *n* **:** something (as a bullet or rocket) thrown or shot especially from a weapon

pro·jec·tion *n* **1 :** something that sticks out **2 :** the act or process of causing to appear on a surface (as by means of motion pictures or slides)

pro·jec·tor *n* **:** a machine for producing images on a screen

pro·lif·ic *adj* **1 :** very inventive or productive **2 :** producing young or fruit in large numbers

pro·long *vb* **pro·longed; pro·long·ing :** to make longer than usual or expected

prom *n* **:** a usually formal dance given by a high school or college class

prom·e·nade *n* **1 :** a walk or ride for pleasure or to be seen **2 :** a place for walking

prom·i·nence *n* **1 :** the state of being important, famous, or noticeable **2 :** something (as a mountain) that is conspicuous

prom·i·nent *adj* **1 :** important or well-known **2 :** attracting attention (as by size or position) **:** CONSPICUOUS **3 :** sticking out beyond the surface — **prom·i·nent·ly** *adv*

¹prom·ise *n* **1 :** a statement by a person that he or she will do or not do something **2 :** a cause or ground for hope

²promise *vb* **prom·ised; prom·is·ing 1 :** to state that something will or will not be done **2 :** to give reason to expect

prom·is·ing *adj* : likely to turn out well or be good

prom·on·to·ry *n, pl* **prom·on·to·ries** : a high point of land sticking out into the sea

pro·mote *vb* **pro·mot·ed; pro·mot·ing** **1** : to move up in position or rank **2** : to help (something) to grow or develop

pro·mo·tion *n* **1** : the act of moving up in position or rank **2** : the act of helping something happen, develop, or increase

[1]**prompt** *vb* **prompt·ed; prompt·ing** **1** : to lead to do something **2** : to be the cause of **3** : to remind of something forgotten or poorly learned — **prompt·er** *n*

[2]**prompt** *adj* **prompt·er; prompt·est** **1** : quick and ready to act **2** : being on time : PUNCTUAL **3** : done at once : given without delay — **prompt·ly** *adv* — **prompt·ness** *n*

pron *abbr* pronoun

prone *adj* **1** : likely to be or act a certain way **2** : lying with the front of the body facing downward

prong *n* **1** : one of the sharp points of a fork **2** : a slender part that sticks out (as a point of an antler)

prong·horn *n* : an animal that resembles an antelope and lives mostly in the grasslands and deserts of western North America

pro·noun *n* : a word used as a substitute for a noun

pro·nounce *vb* **pro·nounced; pro·nounc·ing** **1** : to use the voice to make the sounds of **2** : to say correctly **3** : to state in an official or solemn way

pro·nounced *adj* : very noticeable

pro·nounce·ment *n* : an official or solemn statement

pro·nun·ci·a·tion *n* : the act or way of saying a word or words

[1]**proof** *n* **1** : evidence of truth or correctness **2** : a printing (as from type) prepared for study and correction **3** : a test print made from a photographic negative **4** : [1]TEST 2

[2]**proof** *adj* : able to keep out something that could be harmful — usually used in compounds

proof·read *vb* **proof·read; proof·read·ing** : to read over and fix mistakes in (written or printed matter) — **proof·read·er** *n*

[1]**prop** *vb* **propped; prop·ping** **1** : to keep from falling or slipping by providing a support under or against **2** : to give help, encouragement, or support to

[2]**prop** *n* : something that supports

[3]**prop** *n* : an object used by a performer or actor or used to create a certain effect in a play or movie

pro·pa·gan·da *n* : an organized spreading of often false ideas or the ideas spread in such a way

prop·a·gate *vb* **prop·a·gat·ed; prop·a·gat·ing** **1** : to have or cause to have offspring : MULTIPLY **2** : to cause (as an idea or belief) to spread out and affect a greater number or wider area

prop·a·ga·tion *n* : the act or process of causing to multiply or spread out

pro·pel *vb* **pro·pelled; pro·pel·ling** : to push or cause to move usually forward or onward

pro·pel·ler *n* : a device having a hub fitted with blades that is made to turn rapidly by an engine and that causes a ship, power boat, or airplane to move

pro·pen·si·ty *n* : a natural tendency to do or favor something

prop·er *adj* **1** : correct according to social or moral rules **2** : APPROPRIATE, SUITABLE **3** : strictly accurate : CORRECT **4** : referring to one individual only **5** : considered in its true or basic meaning

proper fraction *n* : a fraction in which the numerator is smaller than the denominator

prop·er·ly *adv* **1** : in a fit or suitable way **2** : according to fact

proper noun *n* : a noun that names a particular person, place, or thing

prop·er·ty *n, pl* **prop·er·ties** **1** : something (as land or money) that is owned **2** : a special quality of a thing

proph·e·cy *n, pl* **proph·e·cies** **1** : something foretold : PREDICTION **2** : the ability to predict what will happen in the future

proph·e·sy *vb* **proph·e·sied; proph·e·sy·ing** : FORETELL, PREDICT

proph·et *n* **1** : someone who declares publicly a message that he or she believes has come from God or a god **2** : a person who predicts the future

pro·phet·ic *adj* **1** : of or relating to a prophet or prophecy **2** : serving to foretell

pro·por·tion *n* **1** : the size, number, or amount of one thing or group of things as compared to that of another thing or group of things **2** : a balanced or pleasing arrangement **3** : a statement of the equality of two ratios (as $4/2 = 10/5$) **4** : a fair or just share **5** : size, shape, or extent of something

pro·por·tion·al *adj* : having a direct relationship to something in size, number, or amount — **pro·por·tion·al·ly** *adv*

pro·pos·al *n* **1** : an act of stating or putting forward something for consideration **2** : something suggested : PLAN **3** : an offer of marriage

pro·pose *vb* **pro·posed; pro·pos·ing** **1** : to make a suggestion to be thought over and talked about : SUGGEST **2** : to make plans : INTEND **3** : to make an offer of marriage **4** : to suggest (someone) for filling a place or position

prop·o·si·tion *n* **1 :** something suggested for discussion and thought **2 :** a statement to be proved, explained, or discussed

pro·pri·e·tor *n* **:** a person who owns something **:** OWNER

pro·pri·ety *n, pl* **pro·pri·eties** **1 :** correctness in manners or behavior **2 :** the quality or state of being proper **3** *proprieties pl* **:** the rules of correct behavior

pro·pul·sion *n* **1 :** the act or process of propelling **2 :** the force that moves something forward

pros *pl of* PRO

prose *n* **1 :** the ordinary language that people use in speaking or writing **2 :** writing without the repeating rhythm that is used in poetry

pros·e·cute *vb* **pros·e·cut·ed; pros·e·cut·ing** **1 :** to carry on a legal action against an accused person to prove his or her guilt **2 :** to follow up to the end **:** keep at

pros·e·cu·tion *n* **1 :** the act of carrying on a legal action against a person accused of a crime in court **2 :** the lawyers in a criminal case trying to prove that the accused person is guilty

pros·e·cu·tor *n* **:** a lawyer in a criminal case who tries to prove that the accused person is guilty

¹pros·pect *n* **1 :** something that is waited for or expected **:** POSSIBILITY **2 :** someone or something that is likely to be successful **:** a likely candidate **3 :** a wide view

²prospect *vb* **pros·pect·ed; pros·pect·ing** **:** to explore especially for mineral deposits

pro·spec·tive *adj* **1 :** likely to become **2 :** likely to come about

pros·pec·tor *n* **:** a person who explores a region in search of valuable minerals (as metals or oil)

pros·per *vb* **pros·pered; pros·per·ing** **1 :** to become successful usually by making money **2 :** ¹FLOURISH 1, THRIVE

pros·per·i·ty *n* **:** the state of being successful usually by making money

pros·per·ous *adj* **1 :** having or showing success or financial good fortune **2 :** strong and healthy in growth

¹pros·trate *adj* **1 :** lying with the face turned toward the ground **2 :** lacking strength or energy

²prostrate *vb* **pros·trat·ed; pros·trat·ing** **1 :** to lie on the ground with the face down **2 :** to bring to a weak and powerless condition

pro·tect *vb* **pro·tect·ed; pro·tect·ing** **:** keep from being harmed especially by covering or shielding **:** GUARD

pro·tec·tion *n* **1 :** the act of shielding from harm **:** the state of being shielded from harm **2 :** a person or thing that shields from harm

pro·tec·tive *adj* **:** giving or meant to keep from harm — **pro·tec·tive·ly** *adv* — **pro·tec·tive·ness** *n*

pro·tec·tor *n* **:** a person or thing that shields from harm or is intended to shield from harm

pro·tein *n* **:** a nutrient found in food (as meat, milk, eggs, and beans) that is made up of many amino acids joined together, is a necessary part of the diet, and is essential for normal cell structure and function

¹pro·test *vb* **pro·test·ed; pro·test·ing** **1 :** to complain strongly about **:** object to **2 :** to declare positively **:** ASSERT — **pro·test·er** *n*

²pro·test *n* **1 :** a complaint or objection against an idea, an act, or a way of doing things **2 :** an event in which people gather to show disapproval of something

¹Prot·es·tant *n* **:** a member of one of the Christian churches that separated from the Roman Catholic Church in the 16th century

²Protestant *adj* **:** of or relating to Protestants

pro·tist *n* **:** any member of the kingdom of mostly single-celled organisms (as protozoans and algae) that have a nucleus and sometimes form colonies

pro·ton *n* **:** a very small particle that exists in the nucleus of every atom and has a positive charge of electricity

pro·to·plasm *n* **:** the usually colorless and jellylike living part of cells

pro·to·zo·an *n* **:** a single-celled organism (as an amoeba or paramecium) that is a protist and is capable of movement

pro·tract *vb* **pro·tract·ed; pro·tract·ing** **:** to make longer **:** draw out in time or space

pro·trac·tor *n* **:** an instrument used for drawing and measuring angles

pro·trude *vb* **pro·trud·ed; pro·trud·ing** **:** to stick out or cause to stick out

proud *adj* **proud·er; proud·est** **1 :** having great self-respect or dignity **2 :** having a feeling of pleasure or satisfaction especially with a person's own achievements or with someone else's achievements **:** very pleased **3 :** having or showing a feeling of being better than others **:** HAUGHTY — **proud·ly** *adv*

prove *vb* **proved; proved** *or* **prov·en; prov·ing** **1 :** to show the truth or existence of something with facts **2 :** to turn out to be **3 :** to check the correctness of **4 :** to test by experiment or by a standard

prov·erb *n* **:** a short well-known saying containing a wise thought **:** MAXIM, ADAGE

pro·ver·bi·al *adj* **1 :** of a proverb **2 :** commonly spoken of — **pro·ver·bi·al·ly** *adv*

pro·vide *vb* **pro·vid·ed; pro·vid·ing** **1 :** to give something that is needed **2 :** to supply something **:** supply (someone) with something **3 :** to make as a condition — **pro·vid·er** *n*

pro·vid·ed *conj* : IF 1
prov·i·dence *n* **1** *often cap* : help or care from God or heaven **2** *cap* : God as the guide and protector of all human beings **3** : PRUDENCE, THRIFT
prov·ince *n* **1** : a part of a country having a government of its own (as one of the divisions of Canada) **2 provinces** *pl* : the part or parts of a country far from the capital or chief city **3** : an area of activity or authority
pro·vin·cial *adj* **1** : of, relating to, or coming from a province **2** : lacking in social graces or sophistication **3** : having narrow or limited concerns or interests
[1]**pro·vi·sion** *n* **1** : a stock or store of supplies and especially of food — usually used in pl. **2** : the act of supplying **3** : [1]CONDITION 2 **4** : something done beforehand
[2]**provision** *vb* **pro·vi·sioned; pro·vi·sion·ing** : to supply with things that are needed
prov·o·ca·tion *n* : something that causes anger or action
pro·voc·a·tive *adj* : serving or likely to cause a reaction (as interest, curiosity, or anger) — **pro·voc·a·tive·ly** *adv*
pro·voke *vb* **pro·voked; pro·vok·ing** **1** : to cause to become angry **2** : to bring about
prow *n* : the bow of a ship
prow·ess *n* **1** : great bravery especially in battle **2** : very great ability
prowl *vb* **prowled; prowl·ing** : to move about quietly and secretly in hunting or searching — **prowl·er** *n*
proxy *n, pl* **prox·ies** **1** : authority to act for another or a paper giving such authority **2** : a person with authority to act for another
prude *n* : a person who cares too much about proper speech and conduct — **prud·ish** *adj*
pru·dence *n* : careful good judgment that allows someone to avoid danger or risks
pru·dent *adj* : wise and careful in action or judgment — **pru·dent·ly** *adv*
[1]**prune** *n* : a dried plum
[2]**prune** *vb* **pruned; prun·ing** **1** : to cut off dead or unwanted parts of a bush or tree **2** : to cut out useless or unwanted parts (as unnecessary words in something written)
[1]**pry** *vb* **pried; pry·ing** **1** : to raise or open with a lever **2** : to get at with great difficulty
[2]**pry** *vb* **pried; pry·ing** : to be nosy about something
pry·ing *adj* : rudely nosy
P.S. *abbr* **1** postscript **2** public school
psalm *n* **1** : a sacred song or poem **2** *cap* : one of the hymns that make up the Old Testament Book of Psalms
psy·chi·a·trist *n* : a doctor specializing in psychiatry
psy·chi·a·try *n* : a branch of medicine dealing with problems of the mind, emotions, or behavior
psy·cho·log·i·cal *adj* : of or relating to psychology or the mind
psy·chol·o·gist *n* : a person specializing in psychology
psy·chol·o·gy *n* : the science that studies the mind and behavior
pt. *abbr* **1** pint **2** point
PTA *abbr* Parent-Teacher Association
ptero·dac·tyl *n* : a very large extinct flying reptile that lived at the same time as the dinosaurs
PTO *abbr* Parent-Teacher Organization
pub *n* : an establishment where alcoholic drinks are served
pu·ber·ty *n* : the age at or period during which the body of a boy or girl matures and becomes capable of reproducing
[1]**pub·lic** *adj* **1** : open to all **2** : of or relating to the people as a whole **3** : known to many people : not kept secret **4** : of, relating to, or working for a government or community **5** : WELL-KNOWN, PROMINENT — **pub·lic·ly** *adv*
[2]**public** *n* **1** : the people as a whole **2** : a group of people having common interests
pub·li·ca·tion *n* **1** : the act or process of producing (a printed work) and selling it to the public **2** : a printed work (as a book or magazine) made for sale or distribution
pub·lic·i·ty *n* **1** : attention that is given to someone or something by the media **2** : something that attracts the interest of the public
pub·li·cize *vb* **pub·li·cized; pub·li·ciz·ing** : to give publicity to
public school *n* : a free school paid for by taxes and run by a local government
pub·lish *vb* **pub·lished; pub·lish·ing** **1** : to bring printed works (as books) before the public usually for sale **2** : to print (as in a magazine or newspaper) **3** : to make widely known — **pub·lish·er** *n*
puck *n* : a rubber disk used in hockey
[1]**puck·er** *vb* **puck·ered; puck·er·ing** : to draw or cause to draw up into folds or wrinkles
[2]**pucker** *n* : a fold or wrinkle in a normally even surface
pud·ding *n* : a soft creamy dessert
pud·dle *n* : a very small pool of liquid
pudgy *adj* **pudg·i·er; pudg·i·est** : being short and plump : CHUBBY
pueb·lo *n, pl* **pueb·los** **1** : an American Indian village of Arizona or New Mexico made up of groups of stone or adobe houses with flat roofs **2** *cap* : a member of any of several American Indian peoples of Arizona or New Mexico
[1]**Puer·to Ri·can** *adj* : of or relating to Puerto Rico or Puerto Ricans

[2]Puerto Rican *n* : a person born or living in Puerto Rico

[1]puff *vb* **puffed; puff·ing** **1** : to breathe hard : PANT **2** : to send out small whiffs or clouds (as of smoke) **3** : to swell up or become swollen with or as if with air

[2]puff *n* **1** : a quick short instance of sending or letting out air, smoke, or steam **2** : a slight swelling **3** : a soft pad for putting powder on the skin **4** : a light pastry

puf·fin *n* : a black-and-white seabird that has a short thick neck and a large bill marked with several colors

puffy *adj* **puff·i·er; puff·i·est** **1** : somewhat swollen **2** : soft, light, and rounded **3** : BREATHLESS 1 **4** : blowing in puffs

pug *n* : a small muscular dog having a curled tail and a flattened face with wrinkles

pug nose *n* : a usually short nose turning up at the end

puke *vb* **puked; puk·ing** : [2]VOMIT

[1]pull *vb* **pulled; pull·ing** **1** : to use force on so as to cause movement toward the force **2** : to separate from a firm or a natural attachment **3** : [1]MOVE 1 **4** : to draw apart : TEAR, REND **5** : to move (something) up or down **6** : to operate by drawing toward **7** : to stretch repeatedly — **pull through** : to survive a difficult or dangerous period

[2]pull *n* **1** : the act or an instance of grasping and causing to move **2** : a device for making something move **3** : a force that draws one body toward another

pull–down *adj* : appearing on a computer screen below a selected item

pul·let *n* : a young hen

pul·ley *n, pl* **pulleys** : a wheel over which a belt, rope, or chain is pulled to lift or lower a heavy object

pull·over *n* : a garment (as a sweater) that is put on by being pulled over the head

pulp *n* **1** : the soft juicy or moist part of a fruit or vegetable **2** : the part of a fruit or vegetable that is left after the liquid has been squeezed from it **3** : a material prepared usually from wood or rags and used in making paper **4** : the soft sensitive tissue inside a tooth **5** : a seriously injured or damaged state

pul·pit *n* **1** : a raised place in which a clergyman stands while preaching or conducting a religious service **2** : the profession of preachers

pul·sate *vb* **pul·sat·ed; pul·sat·ing** : to have or show strong regular beats

pulse *n* **1** : a strong regular beating or throbbing **2** : the beat resulting from the regular widening of an artery in the body as blood flows through it

pul·ver·ize *vb* **pul·ver·ized; pul·ver·iz·ing** : to beat or grind into a powder or dust

pu·ma *n* : COUGAR

pum·ice *n* : a very light porous volcanic glass that is used in powder form for smoothing and polishing

pum·mel *vb* **pum·meled** *also* **pum·melled; pum·mel·ing** *also* **pum·mel·ling** : to strike again and again

[1]pump *n* : a device for raising, moving, or compressing liquids or gases

[2]pump *vb* **pumped; pump·ing** **1** : to raise, move, or compress by using a pump **2** : to fill by using a pump **3** : to draw, force, or drive onward in the manner of a pump **4** : to question again and again to find out something **5** : to move (something) up and down or in and out quickly and repeatedly **6** : to remove (a liquid or gas) from by using a pump

pum·per·nick·el *n* : a dark rye bread

pump·kin *n* : a large round orange fruit that grows on a vine, is related to the squash and cucumber, and is used for food or decoration

[1]pun *n* : a form of joking in which a person uses a word in two senses

[2]pun *vb* **punned; pun·ning** : to make a joke by using a word in two senses

[1]punch *vb* **punched; punch·ing** **1** : to strike with the fist **2** : to sharply press or poke **3** : to make (a hole) by pressing into or through something **4** : to make a hole in with a punch

[2]punch *n* : a drink usually containing different fruit juices

[3]punch *n* : a blow with or as if with the fist

[4]punch *n* : a tool for piercing, stamping, or cutting

punc·tu·al *adj* : arriving or acting at the right time : not late

punc·tu·ate *vb* **punc·tu·at·ed; punc·tu·at·ing** : to add punctuation marks to writing

punc·tu·a·tion *n* **1** : the act of adding punctuation marks to writing **2** : a system of using punctuation marks

punctuation mark *n* : any one of the marks (as a period, comma, or question mark) used in writing to make the meaning clear and separate parts (as clauses and sentences)

[1]punc·ture *n* **1** : an act of piercing with something pointed **2** : a hole or wound made by piercing with something pointed

[2]puncture *vb* **punc·tured; punc·tur·ing** **1** : to pierce with something pointed **2** : to weaken or damage as if by piercing a hole in

pun·gent *adj* : having a strong or sharp taste or smell — **pun·gent·ly** *adv*

pun·ish *vb* **pun·ished; pun·ish·ing** **1** : to make suffer for a fault or crime **2** : to make someone suffer for (as a crime)

pun·ish·able *adj* : deserving to be punished
pun·ish·ment *n* **1** : the act of making a wrongdoer suffer : the state or fact of being made to suffer for wrongdoing **2** : the penalty for a wrong or crime
punk *n* : a rude and violent young man
[1]**punt** *vb* **punt·ed; punt·ing** : to drop and kick a ball before it hits the ground — **punt·er** *n*
[2]**punt** *n* : an act or instance of dropping and kicking a ball before it hits the ground
pu·ny *adj* **pu·ni·er; pu·ni·est** **1** : small and weak in size or power **2** : not very impressive or effective
pup *n* **1** : PUPPY **2** : a young animal
pu·pa *n, pl* **pu·pae** *or* **pupas** : an insect (as a bee, moth, or beetle) in an intermediate inactive stage of its growth in which it is enclosed in a cocoon or case
[1]**pu·pil** *n* : a child in school or under the care of a teacher
[2]**pupil** *n* : the opening in the iris through which light enters the eye
pup·pet *n* **1** : a doll moved by hand or by strings or wires **2** : someone or something (as a government) whose acts are controlled by another
pup·py *n, pl* **puppies** : a young dog
[1]**pur·chase** *vb* **pur·chased; pur·chas·ing** : to get by paying money : BUY
[2]**purchase** *n* **1** : an act of buying **2** : something bought **3** : a firm hold or grasp or a safe place to stand
pure *adj* **pur·er; pur·est** **1** : not mixed with anything else : free from everything that might injure or lower the quality **2** : free from sin : INNOCENT, CHASTE **3** : nothing other than : ABSOLUTE — **pure·ly** *adv*
pure·bred *adj* : bred from ancestors of a single breed for many generations
[1]**purge** *vb* **purged; purg·ing** **1** : to get rid of **2** : to rid of unwanted things or people
[2]**purge** *n* **1** : an act or instance of ridding of what is unwanted **2** : the removal of members thought to be treacherous or disloyal
pu·ri·fi·ca·tion *n* : an act or instance of freeing from impurities or of being freed from impurities
pu·ri·fy *vb* **pu·ri·fied; pu·ri·fy·ing** : to make pure : free from impurities
pu·ri·tan *n* **1** *cap* : a member of a 16th and 17th century Protestant group in England and New England opposing formal customs of the Church of England **2** : a person who practices, preaches, or follows a stricter moral code than most people
pu·ri·ty *n* **1** : freedom from dirt or impurities **2** : freedom from sin or guilt
pur·ple *n* : a color between red and blue
pur·plish *adj* : somewhat purple
pur·pose *n* : something set up as a goal to be achieved : INTENTION, AIM — **on purpose** : PURPOSELY
pur·pose·ful *adj* : having a clear intention or aim — **pur·pose·ful·ly** *adv* — **pur·pose·ful·ness** *n*
pur·pose·ly *adv* : with a clear or known aim
[1]**purr** *vb* **purred; purr·ing** : to make the low murmuring sound of a contented cat or a similar sound
[2]**purr** *n* : the low murmuring sound of a contented cat or a similar sound
[1]**purse** *n* **1** : a bag or pouch for money **2** : HANDBAG **3** : the amount of money that a person, organization, or government has available for use **4** : a sum of money offered as a prize or collected as a present
[2]**purse** *vb* **pursed; purs·ing** : to form into a tight circle or line
pur·sue *vb* **pur·sued; pur·su·ing** **1** : to follow after in order to catch or destroy : CHASE **2** : to follow up or proceed with **3** : to try to get or do over a period of time — **pur·su·er** *n*
pur·suit *n* **1** : the act of chasing, following, or trying to obtain **2** : ACTIVITY 2, OCCUPATION
pus *n* : a thick yellowish substance that is produced when a part of the body or a wound becomes infected
[1]**push** *vb* **pushed; push·ing** **1** : to press against with force so as to drive or move away **2** : to force forward, downward, or outward **3** : to go or make go ahead **4** : to pressure to do something or work hard at something
[2]**push** *n* **1** : a sudden thrust : SHOVE **2** : a steady applying of force in a direction away from the body from which it comes
push button *n* : a small button or knob that when pushed operates something usually by closing an electric circuit
push·cart *n* : a cart pushed by hand
push·over *n* **1** : an opponent that is easy to defeat **2** : someone who is easy to persuade or influence **3** : something easily done
push–up *n* : an exercise performed while lying with the face down by raising and lowering the body with the straightening and bending of the arms
pushy *adj* **push·i·er; push·i·est** : too aggressive : FORWARD
pussy willow *n* : a willow with large furry flower clusters
put *vb* **put; put·ting** **1** : to place in or move into a particular position **2** : to bring into a specified state or condition **3** : to cause to undergo something **4** : to give expression to **5** : to devote to or urge to an activity **6** : to think of as worthy of : ATTRIBUTE **7**

: to begin a voyage — **put away** : to take in food and drink — **put down** **1** : to bring to an end by force **2** : CRITICIZE — **put forward** : PROPOSE 1 — **put in** **1** : to ask for **2** : to spend time in a place or activity — **put off** : to hold back to a later time : DEFER — **put on** **1** : to dress in **2** : PRETEND 2 **3** : [1]PRODUCE 4 — **put out** **1** : EXTINGUISH 1 **2** : IRRITATE 1, ANNOY **3** : [1]MAKE 1 **4** : to cause to be out (in baseball) **5** : to make use of — **put together** **1** : to create as a whole : CONSTRUCT **2** : to consider as a single unit — **put up** **1** : [1]BUILD 1 **2** : to make (as food) ready for later use **3** : to give or get shelter and often food **4** : to make by action or effort — **put up to** : to urge or cause to do something wrong or unexpected — **put up with** : to stand for : TOLERATE

put·out *n* : [4]OUT

pu·trid *adj* **1** : ROTTEN 1 **2** : coming from or suggesting something rotten

put·ter *vb* **put·tered; put·ter·ing** : to act or work without much purpose

[1]**put·ty** *n, pl* **putties** : a soft sticky substance that hardens as it dries and is used for holding glass in a window frame or filling holes

[2]**putty** *vb* **put·tied; put·ty·ing** : to seal up with putty

[1]**puz·zle** *vb* **puz·zled; puz·zling** **1** : CONFUSE 1, PERPLEX **2** : to solve by thought or by clever guessing

[2]**puzzle** *n* **1** : a question, problem, or device intended to test skill or cleverness **2** : JIGSAW PUZZLE **3** : something that perplexes : MYSTERY

puz·zle·ment *n* : the state of being perplexed

pyg·my *adj* : smaller than the usual size

pyjamas *Can and Brit spelling of* PAJAMAS

pyr·a·mid *n* **1** : a large structure built especially in ancient Egypt that usually has a square base and four triangular sides meeting at a point and that contains tombs **2** : a shape or structure with a polygon for its base and three or more triangles for its sides which meet to form the top

pyre *n* : a heap of wood for burning a dead body

py·thon *n* : a large nonpoisonous snake of Africa, Asia, and Australia that squeezes and suffocates its prey

Q

q *n, pl* **q's** *or* **qs** *often cap* : the 17th letter of the English alphabet

QC *abbr* Quebec

qt. *abbr* quart

[1]**quack** *vb* **quacked; quack·ing** : to make the cry of a duck

[2]**quack** *n* : a cry made by a duck

[3]**quack** *n* : a person who pretends to have medical knowledge and skill

[4]**quack** *adj* **1** : relating to or being a person who pretends to have medical knowledge and skill **2** : pretending to cure disease

quad·rant *n* **1** : one-fourth of a circle **2** : any of the four parts into which something is divided by two imaginary or real lines that intersect each other at right angles

quadri- *or* **quadr-** *or* **quadru-** *prefix* **1** : four **2** : fourth

quad·ri·lat·er·al *n* : a flat geometric figure of four sides and four angles

quad·ru·ped *n* : an animal having four feet

[1]**qua·dru·ple** *vb* **qua·dru·pled; qua·dru·pling** : to make or become four times as great or many

[2]**quadruple** *adj* **1** : having four units or parts **2** : being four times as great or as many

qua·dru·plet *n* : one of four offspring born at one birth

quag·mire *n* **1** : soft spongy wet ground that shakes or gives way under the foot **2** : a difficult situation

[1]**quail** *n, pl* **quail** *or* **quails** : a small plump bird (as a bobwhite) that feeds mostly on the ground and is sometimes hunted for food or sport

[2]**quail** *vb* **quailed; quail·ing** : to lose courage : draw back in fear

quaint *adj* **quaint·er; quaint·est** : pleasingly old-fashioned or unfamiliar — **quaint·ly** *adv* — **quaint·ness** *n*

[1]**quake** *vb* **quaked; quak·ing** **1** : to shake usually from shock or lack of stability **2** : to tremble or shudder usually from cold or fear

[2]**quake** *n* : EARTHQUAKE

qual·i·fi·ca·tion *n* **1** : a special skill, knowledge, or ability that makes someone suitable for a particular job or activity **2** : a condition or requirement that must be met **3** : something that is added to a statement to limit or change its meaning

qual·i·fy *vb* **qual·i·fied; qual·i·fy·ing** **1 :** to give the training, skill, or ability needed for a special purpose **2 :** to have or show the skill or ability needed for a special purpose or event **3 :** to narrow down or make less general in meaning

[1]**qual·i·ty** *n, pl* **qual·i·ties** **1 :** what sets a person or thing apart **:** CHARACTERISTIC **2 :** how good or bad something is **3 :** a high standard **:** EXCELLENCE

[2]**quality** *adj* **:** very good **:** EXCELLENT

qualm *n* **:** a feeling of doubt or uncertainty especially in matters of right and wrong

quan·da·ry *n, pl* **quan·da·ries** **:** a state of doubt or confusion

quan·ti·ty *n, pl* **quan·ti·ties** **1 :** [2]AMOUNT, NUMBER **2 :** a large number or amount

[1]**quar·an·tine** *n* **1 :** isolation of people, animals, or things (as plants) out of a certain area to prevent the spread of disease or pests **2 :** a period during which a person or animal with a contagious disease is isolated **3 :** a place (as a hospital) where a person or animal with a contagious disease is isolated

[2]**quarantine** *vb* **quar·an·tined; quar·an·tin·ing** **:** to put or hold in isolation to prevent the spread of disease or pests

[1]**quar·rel** *n* **1 :** an angry argument or disagreement **2 :** a cause of disagreement or complaint

[2]**quarrel** *vb* **quar·reled** *or* **quar·relled; quar·rel·ing** *or* **quar·rel·ling** **1 :** to argue angrily **2 :** to find fault

quar·rel·some *adj* **:** usually ready to disagree or argue

[1]**quar·ry** *n, pl* **quar·ries** **:** an animal or bird hunted as game or prey

[2]**quarry** *n, pl* **quar·ries** **:** an open pit usually for obtaining building stone, slate, or limestone

[3]**quarry** *vb* **quar·ried; quar·ry·ing** **1 :** to dig or take from or as if from a quarry **2 :** to make a quarry in

quart *n* **:** a measure of liquid capacity that equals two pints (about .95 liter)

[1]**quar·ter** *n* **1 :** one of four equal parts into which something can be divided **2 :** a United States coin worth 25 cents **3 :** someone or something (as a place, direction, or group) not clearly identified **4 :** a particular division or district of a city **5 quarters** *pl* **:** a dwelling place **6 :** MERCY 1

[2]**quarter** *vb* **quar·tered; quar·ter·ing** **1 :** to divide into four usually equal parts **2 :** to provide with lodgings or shelter

[3]**quarter** *adj* **:** consisting of or equal to one fourth of

quar·ter·back *n* **:** a football player who leads a team's attempts to score usually by passing the ball to other players

quarter horse *n* **:** a stocky muscular saddle horse capable of running fast for short distances

[1]**quar·ter·ly** *adv* **:** four times a year

[2]**quarterly** *adj* **:** coming or happening four times a year

[3]**quarterly** *n, pl* **quar·ter·lies** **:** a magazine published four times a year

quar·ter·mas·ter *n* **1 :** an army officer who provides clothing and supplies for troops **2 :** an officer of a ship (as in the navy) in charge of navigation

quar·tet *also* **quar·tette** *n* **1 :** a piece of music for four instruments or voices **2 :** a group of four singers or musicians who perform together **3 :** a group or set of four

quartz *n* **:** a common mineral often found in the form of colorless transparent crystals but sometimes (as in amethysts, agates, and jaspers) brightly colored

[1]**qua·ver** *vb* **qua·vered; qua·ver·ing** **:** to sound in shaky or unsteady tones

[2]**quaver** *n* **:** a sound that trembles or is unsteady

quay *n* **:** a structure built along the bank of a waterway (as a river) for use as a landing for loading and unloading boats

quea·sy *adj* **quea·si·er; quea·si·est** **1 :** somewhat nauseated **2 :** full of doubt **:** UNEASY — **quea·si·ness** *n*

queen *n* **1 :** a woman who rules a country or kingdom **2 :** the wife or widow of a king **3 :** a woman or girl who is highly respected or well-known within a field **4 :** the most powerful piece in the game of chess **5 :** a playing card bearing the figure of a queen **6 :** a fully developed adult female insect (as a bee or ant) that lays eggs — **queen·ly** *adj*

queer *adj* **queer·er; queer·est** **:** oddly unlike the usual or normal — **queer·ly** *adv*

quell *vb* **quelled; quell·ing** **1 :** to stop or end by force **2 :** [4]QUIET, CALM

quench *vb* **quenched; quench·ing** **1 :** to end by satisfying **2 :** to put out (as a fire)

quer·u·lous *adj* **:** having or showing a complaining attitude

[1]**que·ry** *n, pl* **queries** **:** [1]QUESTION 1

[2]**query** *vb* **que·ried; que·ry·ing** **1 :** to put as a question **2 :** to ask questions about especially in order to clear up a doubt **3 :** to ask questions of

que·so *n* **:** a sauce of melted cheese and chopped chili peppers

quest *n* **1 :** an effort to find or do something **2 :** a usually adventurous journey made in search of something

[1]**ques·tion** *n* **1 :** something asked **2 :** a topic discussed or argued about **3 :** OBJECTION 1 **4 :** doubt or uncertainty about something **5 :** POSSIBILITY 1, CHANCE

[2]**question** *vb* **ques·tioned; ques·tion·ing** **1**

: to ask questions of or about **2 :** to have or express doubts about
ques·tion·able *adj* **1 :** not certain or exact : DOUBTFUL **2 :** not believed to be true, sound, or proper
question mark *n* **:** a punctuation mark ? used chiefly at the end of a sentence to indicate a direct question
ques·tion·naire *n* **:** a set of questions to be asked of a number of people usually in order to gather information or opinions
[1]**queue** *n* **1 :** PIGTAIL **2 :** a waiting line
[2]**queue** *vb* **queued; queu·ing** *or* **queue·ing** : to form or wait in a line
[1]**quib·ble** *vb* **quib·bled; quib·bling :** to argue or complain about small and unimportant things
[2]**quibble** *n* **:** a small and usually unimportant complaint, criticism, or argument
[1]**quick** *adj* **quick·er; quick·est 1 :** done or taking place in a very short period of time **2 :** very swift : SPEEDY **3 :** fast in learning or understanding : mentally alert **4 :** easily stirred up — **quick·ly** *adv* — **quick·ness** *n*
[2]**quick** *n* **1 :** a very tender area of flesh (as under a fingernail) **2 :** someone's innermost feelings
[3]**quick** *adv* **quick·er; quick·est :** in a quick manner : FAST
quick·en *vb* **quick·ened; quick·en·ing 1** : to make or become faster : HASTEN **2 :** to make or become stronger or more active
quick·sand *n* **:** a deep area of loose sand mixed with water into which heavy objects sink
quick·sil·ver *n* **:** MERCURY 1
quick–tem·pered *adj* **:** easily made angry
[1]**qui·et** *n* **:** the quality or state of being calm or without noise
[2]**quiet** *adj* **qui·et·er; qui·et·est 1 :** free from noise or uproar **2 :** marked by little or no motion or activity : CALM **3 :** not disturbed : PEACEFUL **4 :** tending not to talk or show excitement much **5 :** not shown in an obvious way **6 :** away from public view : SECLUDED — **qui·et·ly** *adv* — **qui·et·ness** *n*
[3]**quiet** *adv* **:** in a quiet manner : QUIETLY
[4]**quiet** *vb* **qui·et·ed; qui·et·ing :** to make or become calmer or less noisy
quill *n* **1 :** a large stiff feather of a bird's wing or tail **2 :** the hollow tubelike part of a feather **3 :** a hollow sharp spine of a porcupine or hedgehog **4 :** a pen made from a feather
[1]**quilt** *n* **:** a bed cover made of two layers of cloth with a filling of wool, cotton, or down held together by patterned stitching
[2]**quilt** *vb* **quilt·ed; quilt·ing :** to stitch or sew together as in making a quilt
quince *n* **:** a hard sour yellow fruit that resembles an apple, grows on a shrubby Asian tree, and is used especially in jams and jellies
qui·nine *n* **:** a bitter drug obtained from cinchona bark and used to treat malaria
quin·tet *n* **1 :** a piece of music for five instruments or voices **2 :** a group of five singers or musicians who perform together **3 :** a group or set of five
quin·tu·plet *n* **1 :** one of five offspring born at one birth **2 :** a combination of five of a kind
quirk *n* **1 :** an odd or unusual characteristic or habit **2 :** something strange that happens by chance
quirky *adj* **quirk·i·er; quirk·i·est :** unusual especially in an interesting way
quit *vb* **quit; quit·ting :** to leave or stop doing something
quite *adv* **1 :** beyond question or doubt : COMPLETELY **2 :** to a considerable extent
quit·ter *n* **:** a person who gives up too easily
[1]**quiv·er** *n* **:** a case for carrying arrows
[2]**quiver** *vb* **quiv·ered; quiv·er·ing :** to move with a slight trembling motion
[3]**quiver** *n* **:** the act or instance of trembling
[1]**quiz** *n, pl* **quiz·zes :** a short test
[2]**quiz** *vb* **quizzed; quiz·zing :** to ask a lot of questions of
quiz·zi·cal *adj* **:** showing doubt, puzzlement or curiosity — **quiz·zi·cal·ly** *adv*
quoit *n* **:** a ring (as of rope) tossed at a peg in a game (**quoits**)
quo·rum *n* **:** the smallest number of people who must be present at a meeting in order for business to be carried on
quo·ta *n* **1 :** a limit on the number or amount of people or things that are allowed **2 :** a share assigned to each member of a group **3** : a specific amount or number of things that is expected to be achieved
quo·ta·tion *n* **:** material (as a sentence or passage from a book) that is repeated exactly by someone else
quotation mark *n* **:** one of a pair of punctuation marks " " or ' ' used chiefly to indicate the beginning and end of a quotation
[1]**quote** *vb* **quot·ed; quot·ing :** to repeat (someone else's words) exactly
[2]**quote** *n* **:** QUOTATION
quo·tient *n* **:** the number obtained by dividing one number by another

R

r *n, pl* **r's** *or* **rs** *often cap* **:** the 18th letter of the English alphabet
r. *abbr* right
R *abbr* regular
R. *abbr* rabbi
rab·bi *n, pl* **rab·bis :** a person educated in Jewish law and able to lead a Jewish congregation
rab·bit *n* **:** a short-tailed mammal that has soft fur and long ears and hind legs and digs burrows
rab·ble *n* **1 :** a crowd that is noisy and hard to control **:** MOB **2 :** a group of people looked down upon as ignorant and hard to handle
ra·bid *adj* **1 :** very angry **:** FURIOUS **2 :** having or expressing a very extreme opinion about or interest in something **3 :** affected with rabies — **ra·bid·ly** *adv*
ra·bies *n* **:** a deadly disease of the nervous system that affects animals and can be passed on to people by the bite of an infected animal
rac·coon *n* **:** a small North American animal that is mostly gray with black around the eyes, has a bushy tail with black rings, is active mostly at night, and eats small animals, fruits, eggs, and insects
[1]**race** *vb* **raced; rac·ing 1 :** to go, move, function, or drive at top speed **2 :** to take part in a contest of speed **3 :** to cause an engine of a motor vehicle in neutral to run fast
[2]**race** *n* **1 :** a contest of speed **2 :** a contest involving progress toward a goal **3 :** a strong or rapid current of water
[3]**race** *n* **1 :** any one of the groups that human beings can be divided into based on shared distinctive physical traits **2 :** a group of individuals who share a common culture or history **3 :** a major group of living things
race·course *n* **:** a place where races are held
race·horse *n* **:** a horse bred or kept for racing
rac·er *n* **1 :** a person, animal, or vehicle that participates in or is used for participation in races **2 :** a long slender active snake (as the blacksnake)
race·track *n* **:** a usually oval course on which races are run
ra·cial *adj* **:** of, relating to, or based on race — **ra·cial·ly** *adv*
rac·ism *n* **1 :** belief that certain races of people are by birth and nature superior to others **2 :** discrimination or hatred based on race
rac·ist *adj* **:** based on or showing racism — **racist** *n*
[1]**rack** *n* **:** a frame or stand for storing or displaying things
[2]**rack** *vb* **racked; rack·ing 1 :** to cause to suffer torture, pain, or sorrow **2 :** to force to think hard
[1]**rack·et** *n* **1 :** a loud confused noise **2 :** a dishonest scheme for obtaining money
[2]**racket** *or* **rac·quet** *n* **:** a piece of sports equipment consisting of a handle and a frame with strings stretched tightly across it
rack·e·teer *n* **:** a person who gets money or advantages by using force or threats
ra·dar *n* **:** a radio device for detecting the position of things in the distance and the direction of moving objects (as distant airplanes or ships)
ra·di·ance *n* **:** warm or vivid brightness
ra·di·ant *adj* **1 :** giving out or reflecting rays of light **2 :** glowing with love, confidence, or joy **3 :** transmitted by radiation
radiant energy *n* **:** energy sent out in the form of electromagnetic waves
ra·di·ate *vb* **ra·di·at·ed; ra·di·at·ing 1 :** to send out rays **:** SHINE **2 :** to come forth in the form of rays **3 :** to go out in a direct line from a center **4 :** to spread around from or as if from a center **5 :** to show very clearly
ra·di·a·tion *n* **1 :** the process of giving off energy in the form of waves or particles **2 :** something that is radiated (as light or X-rays)
ra·di·a·tor *n* **:** a device to heat air (as in a room) or to cool an object (as an automobile engine) by heating the surrounding air
[1]**rad·i·cal** *adj* **1 :** very new and different from the usual or ordinary **:** EXTREME **2 :** of or relating to people who favor rapid and sweeping changes in laws and government — **rad·i·cal·ly** *adv*
[2]**radical** *n* **:** a person who favors rapid and sweeping changes especially in laws and government
radii *pl of* RADIUS
[1]**ra·dio** *n, pl* **ra·di·os 1 :** the process that is used for sending or receiving signals by means of electromagnetic waves without a connecting wire **2 :** a device that receives signals sent by radio **3 :** programs that are broadcast by radio **4 :** a device used to both send and receive messages by radio **5 :** the radio broadcasting industry
[2]**radio** *adj* **1 :** of or relating to radio waves **2 :** of, relating to, or used in radio broadcasting
[3]**radio** *vb* **ra·di·oed; ra·di·o·ing :** to communicate or send a message to by radio
ra·dio·ac·tive *adj* **:** caused by or exhibiting radioactivity

ra·dio·ac·tiv·i·ty *n* **1 :** the giving off of rays of energy or particles by the breaking apart of atoms of certain elements (as uranium) **2 :** the rays or particles that are given off when atoms break apart

radio wave *n* **:** an electromagnetic wave used in radio, television, or radar communication

rad·ish *n* **:** a small roundish crisp root that has a sharp flavor and is usually eaten raw as a vegetable

ra·di·um *n* **:** a strongly radioactive element found in very small quantities in various minerals (as pitchblende) and used in the treatment of cancer

ra·di·us *n, pl* **ra·dii** **1 :** a straight line extending from the center of a circle to the outside edge or from the center of a sphere to the surface **2 :** an area that extends in all directions from a place **3 :** the bone on the thumb side of the arm between the wrist and the elbow

[1]raf·fle *n* **:** a contest for a prize in which people buy tickets and which is won by the person whose ticket is picked at a drawing

[2]raffle *vb* **raf·fled; raf·fl·ing :** to give (something) as a prize in a raffle

[1]raft *n* **:** a flat structure (as a group of logs fastened together) for support or transportation on water

[2]raft *n* **:** a large amount or number

raf·ter *n* **:** one of the usually sloping timbers that support a roof

rag *n* **1 :** a worn piece of cloth **2 rags** *pl* **:** shabby or very worn clothing

rag·a·muf·fin *n* **:** a poorly clothed and often dirty child

[1]rage *n* **1 :** very strong and uncontrolled anger **:** FURY **2 :** a fit of anger **3 :** violent action (as of wind or sea) **4 :** FAD

[2]rage *vb* **raged; rag·ing** **1 :** to feel or show extreme or uncontrolled anger **2 :** to continue out of control

rag·ged *adj* **1 :** having a rough or uneven edge or outline **2 :** very worn-out **:** TATTERED **3 :** wearing very worn-out clothes **4 :** done in an uneven way — **rag·ged·ly** *adv* — **rag·ged·ness** *n*

rag·gedy *adj* **1 :** RAGGED 2 **2 :** RAGGED 3

rag·tag *adj* **:** not well organized or put together

rag·time *n* **:** music that has a lively melody and a steady rhythm like a march

rag·weed *n* **:** a common weed with pollen that irritates the eyes and noses of some people

[1]raid *n* **:** a sudden attack or invasion

[2]raid *vb* **raid·ed; raid·ing** **1 :** to enter (a place) to look for something or someone or to steal or take something **2 :** to make a sudden attack — **raid·er** *n*

[1]rail *n* **1 :** a bar extending from one support to another and serving as a guard or barrier **2 :** a bar of steel forming a track for wheeled vehicles **3 :** RAILROAD 1

[2]rail *vb* **railed; rail·ing :** to provide with a railing

[3]rail *n* **:** a small or medium-sized wading bird related to the crane that has very long toes for walking on the soft mud of marshes

[4]rail *vb* **railed; rail·ing :** to scold or complain in harsh or bitter language

rail·ing *n* **1 :** a barrier (as a fence) made up of vertical bars and their supports **2 :** material for making rails

rail·lery *n* **:** an act or instance of making fun of someone in a good-natured way

rail·road *n* **1 :** a permanent road that has parallel steel rails that make a track for train cars **2 :** a company that owns and operates trains

rail·way *n* **:** RAILROAD 1

rai·ment *n* **:** CLOTHING

[1]rain *n* **1 :** water falling in drops from the clouds **2 :** a fall of water in drops from the clouds **3 :** rainy weather **4 :** a heavy fall of objects

[2]rain *vb* **rained; rain·ing** **1 :** to fall as water in drops from the clouds **2 :** to send down rain **3 :** to fall in large amounts **4 :** to give in large amounts — **rain cats and dogs** **:** POUR 2

rain·bow *n* **:** an arc of colors that appears in the sky opposite the sun and is caused by the sun shining through rain, mist, or spray

rain·coat *n* **:** a coat of waterproof or water-resistant material

rain·drop *n* **:** a drop of rain

rain·fall *n* **1 :** [1]RAIN 2 **2 :** amount of precipitation

rain forest *n* **:** a woodland with a high annual rainfall and very tall trees and that is often found in tropical regions

rain·proof *adj* **:** not letting in rain

rain·storm *n* **:** a storm of or with rain

rain·wa·ter *n* **:** water from rain

rainy *adj* **rain·i·er; rain·i·est :** having much rain

[1]raise *vb* **raised; rais·ing** **1 :** to cause to rise **:** LIFT **2 :** COLLECT 1 **3 :** to look after the growth and development of **:** GROW **4 :** to bring up a child **:** REAR **5 :** to bring to notice **6 :** [1]INCREASE **7 :** to make louder **8 :** to give life to **:** AROUSE **9 :** to set upright by lifting or building **10 :** PROMOTE 1, ELEVATE **11 :** to give rise to **:** PROVOKE **12 :** to make light and airy **13 :** to cause to form on the skin — **rais·er** *n*

[2]raise *n* **:** an increase in amount (as of pay)

rai·sin *n* **:** a sweet dried grape used for food

ra·ja *or* **ra·jah** *n* **:** an Indian prince

[1]rake *n* **:** a garden tool with a long handle and a bar with teeth or prongs at the end

²rake *vb* **raked; rak·ing** **1 :** to gather, loosen, or smooth thoroughly with or as if with a rake **2 :** to search through **3 :** to sweep the length of with gunfire
rak·ish *adj* **:** JAUNTY, DASHING
¹ral·ly *vb* **ral·lied; ral·ly·ing** **1 :** to bring or come together for a common purpose **2 :** to publicly support or oppose **3 :** to rouse from low spirits or weakness
²rally *n, pl* **rallies** **1 :** a sudden improvement in performance or condition **2 :** a big meeting held to rouse enthusiasm
¹ram *vb* **rammed; ram·ming** **1 :** to strike or strike against with violence **2 :** to force in, down, or together by driving or pressing **3 :** ²FORCE 2
²ram *n* **1 :** a male sheep **2 :** BATTERING RAM
RAM *n* **:** a computer memory that provides the main storage available to the user for programs and data
Ram·a·dan *n* **:** the ninth month of the Islamic calendar observed as sacred with fasting practiced daily from sunrise to sunset
¹ram·ble *vb* **ram·bled; ram·bling** **1 :** to go aimlessly from place to place **:** WANDER **2 :** to talk or write without a clear purpose or point **3 :** to grow or extend in many directions
²ramble *n* **:** a long stroll with no particular destination
ram·bunc·tious *adj* **:** not under control in a way that is playful or full of energy
ram·i·fi·ca·tion *n* **:** something that is the result of something else
ramp *n* **:** a sloping passage or roadway connecting different levels
ram·page *n* **:** a period or instance of violent action or behavior
ram·pant *adj* **:** existing or growing greatly and quickly
ram·part *n* **:** a broad bank or wall raised as a protective barrier
ram·rod *n* **:** a rod for forcing the charge down the barrel in a firearm that is loaded through the muzzle
ram·shack·le *adj* **:** ready to fall down
ran *past of* RUN
¹ranch *n* **1 :** a large farm for the raising of livestock (as cattle) **2 :** a farm devoted to a special crop
²ranch *vb* **ranched; ranch·ing** **:** to live or work on a large farm where livestock are raised — **ranch·er** *n*
ran·cid *adj* **:** having a strong disagreeable smell or taste from no longer being fresh
ran·cor *or Can and Brit* **rancour** *n* **:** deep hatred
ran·cor·ous *adj* **:** showing deep hatred
ran·dom *adj* **:** lacking a clear plan, purpose, or pattern — **ran·dom·ly** *adv* — **ran·dom·ness** *n*
ran·dom–ac·cess *adj* **:** permitting access to stored data in any order the user desires
random–access memory *n* **:** RAM
rang *past of* ³RING
¹range *n* **1 :** a series of things in a line **2 :** the distance over which someone or something can be seen, heard, or reached **3 :** a cooking stove **4 :** open land over which livestock may roam and feed **5 :** a variety of choices within a scale **6 :** the distance a gun will shoot **7 :** a place where shooting is practiced
²range *vb* **ranged; rang·ing** **1 :** to arrange in a particular place or order **2 :** to roam over or through **3 :** to come within an upper and a lower limit
rang·er *n* **1 :** FOREST RANGER **2 :** a soldier specially trained in close-range fighting and in raiding tactics
rangy *adj* **rang·i·er; rang·i·est :** tall and slender
¹rank *n* **1 :** ²ROW 1, SERIES **2 :** a line of soldiers standing side by side **3 ranks** *pl* **:** the body of enlisted persons in an army **4 :** position within a group **5 :** high social position **6 :** official grade or position
²rank *adj* **1 :** strong and active in growth **2 :** OUTRIGHT **3 :** having an unpleasant smell
³rank *vb* **ranked; rank·ing** **1 :** to take or have a certain position in a group **2 :** to arrange in a classification **3 :** to arrange in lines or in a formation
ran·kle *vb* **ran·kled; ran·kling** **:** to cause anger, irritation, or bitterness
ran·sack *vb* **ran·sacked; ran·sack·ing** **:** to search through in a way that causes disorder or damage
¹ran·som *n* **1 :** something paid or demanded for the freedom of a captured person **2 :** the act of freeing from captivity by paying a price
²ransom *vb* **ran·somed; ran·som·ing** **:** to free from captivity or punishment by paying a price
rant *vb* **rant·ed; rant·ing** **:** to talk loudly and wildly
¹rap *vb* **rapped; rap·ping** **:** to give a quick sharp blow
²rap *n* **1 :** a sharp blow or knock **2 :** the blame or punishment for something
³rap *vb* **rapped; rap·ping** **1 :** to talk freely and informally **2 :** to perform rap music
⁴rap *n* **1 :** an informal talk **:** CHAT **2 :** a type of music that usually has a fast rhythm and in which words are spoken instead of sung
ra·pa·cious *adj* **1 :** very greedy **2 :** PREDATORY — **ra·pa·cious·ly** *adv* — **ra·pa·cious·ness** *n*
¹rape *n* **:** a plant related to the mustard that is

grown for animals to graze on, for its seeds which are fed to birds, and as a source of oil

[2]**rape** *vb* **raped; rap·ing** : to have sexual intercourse with by force

[3]**rape** *n* : the crime of forcing someone to have sexual intercourse

rap·id *adj* : very fast — **rap·id·ly** *adv*

ra·pid·i·ty *n* : the quality or state of being rapid

rap·ids *n pl* : a part of a river where the current flows very fast usually over rocks

ra·pi·er *n* : a straight sword with a narrow blade having two sharp edges

rap·per *n* : a person who performs rap music

rap·port *n* : a friendly relationship

rapt *adj* : showing complete delight or interest

rap·tor *n* : BIRD OF PREY

rap·ture *n* : a strong feeling of joy, delight, or love

[1]**rare** *adj* **rar·er; rar·est** **1** : very uncommon **2** : very fine : EXCELLENT **3** : not thick or compact : THIN

[2]**rare** *adj* **rar·er; rar·est** : cooked so that the inside is still red

rare·ly *adv* : not often : SELDOM

rar·i·ty *n, pl* **rar·i·ties** **1** : the quality, state, or fact of being rare **2** : something that is uncommon

ras·cal *n* **1** : a usually young mischievous person **2** : a mean or dishonest person

[1]**rash** *adj* : done or made quickly and without thought of the likely result — **rash·ly** *adv* — **rash·ness** *n*

[2]**rash** *n* **1** : a breaking out of the skin with red spots (as from illness or an allergic reaction) **2** : a series of bad things that happen in a short time

[1]**rasp** *vb* **rasped; rasp·ing** **1** : to say with or make a harsh sound **2** : to rub with or as if with a rough object or substance

[2]**rasp** *n* **1** : a harsh sound or sensation **2** : a coarse file used for shaping or smoothing

rasp·ber·ry *n, pl* **rasp·ber·ries** : a sweet juicy red, black, or purple berry of a prickly plant

raspy *adj* : having a harsh sound

[1]**rat** *n* **1** : a gnawing animal with brown, black, white, or grayish fur that looks like but is larger than a mouse **2** : a person who betrays friends

[2]**rat** *vb* **rat·ted; rat·ting** : to betray a friend

[1]**rate** *n* **1** : a price or charge set according to a scale or standard **2** : the amount of something measured in units of something else or in comparison with others — **at any rate** : in any case

[2]**rate** *vb* **rat·ed; rat·ing** **1** : to be placed in comparison with others : RANK **2** : CONSIDER 3, REGARD **3** : to have a right to : DESERVE

rath·er *adv* **1** : [2]SOMEWHAT **2** : more willingly **3** : more correctly or truly **4** : INSTEAD

rat·i·fi·ca·tion *n* : the act or process of giving legal approval to

rat·i·fy *vb* **rat·i·fied; rat·i·fy·ing** : to give legal approval to (as by a vote)

rat·ing *n* : a position within a grading system

ra·tio *n, pl* **ra·tios** : the relationship in number or quantity between two or more things

[1]**ra·tion** *n* **1** : a food allowance for one day **2 rations** *pl* : [1]PROVISION 1 **3** : the amount each person is allowed by an authority

[2]**ration** *vb* **ra·tioned; ra·tion·ing** **1** : to control the amount an individual can use **2** : to use sparingly

ra·tio·nal *adj* **1** : having the ability to reason **2** : based on or showing reason — **ra·tio·nal·ly** *adv*

ra·tio·nale *n* : a basic explanation or reason for something

ra·tio·nal·ize *vb* **ra·tio·nal·ized; ra·tio·nal·iz·ing** : to find an excuse for something that seems reasonable or believable

rational number *n* : a number that can be expressed as a whole number or the quotient of two whole numbers

rat·ter *n* : a dog or cat that catches rats

[1]**rat·tle** *vb* **rat·tled; rat·tling** **1** : to make or cause to make a rapid series of short sharp sounds **2** : to move with a clatter **3** : to speak or say quickly or without stopping **4** : to disturb the calmness of : UPSET

[2]**rattle** *n* **1** : a series of short sharp sounds **2** : a toy that makes a rattling sound **3** : a part at the end of a rattlesnake's tail that makes a buzzing rattle when shaken

rat·tler *n* : RATTLESNAKE

rat·tle·snake *n* : a poisonous American snake with a rattle at the end of its tail

rat·ty *adj* **rat·ti·er; rat·ti·est** : in bad condition : SHABBY

rau·cous *adj* **1** : loud and harsh **2** : behaving in a rough and noisy way — **rau·cous·ly** *adv*

[1]**rav·age** *n* : destructive action or effect

[2]**ravage** *vb* **rav·aged; rav·ag·ing** : to attack or act upon with great violence

rave *vb* **raved; rav·ing** **1** : to talk wildly or as if crazy **2** : to talk with great enthusiasm

rav·el *vb* **rav·eled** *or* **rav·elled; rav·el·ing** *or* **rav·el·ling** : UNRAVEL 1

[1]**ra·ven** *n* : a large shiny black bird that is larger than the related crow

[2]**raven** *adj* : shiny and black like a raven's feathers

rav·en·ous *adj* : very hungry — **rav·en·ous·ly** *adv*

ra·vine *n* : a small narrow valley with steep sides that is larger than a gully and smaller than a canyon

rav·ish *vb* **rav·ished; rav·ish·ing** **1 :** to seize and take away by force **2 :** to fill with joy or delight

rav·ish·ing *adj* **:** very beautiful

raw *adj* **raw·er; raw·est** **1 :** not cooked **2 :** having the skin scraped or roughened **3 :** being in or nearly in the natural state **:** not treated or prepared **4 :** not trained or experienced **5 :** unpleasantly damp or cold **6 :** lacking a normal or usual finish — **raw·ness** *n*

raw·hide *n* **:** cattle skin before it has been made into leather

[1]**ray** *n* **1 :** one of the lines of light that appear to be given off by a bright object **2 :** a thin beam of radiant energy (as light) **3 :** light cast in rays **4 :** a tiny bit **:** PARTICLE **5 :** any of a group of lines that spread out from the same center **6 :** a straight line extending from a point in one direction only **7 :** a slender plant or animal structure

[2]**ray** *n* **:** a flat broad fish (as a skate or stingray) related to the shark that has its eyes on the top of its head and often winglike fins

ray·on *n* **:** a cloth made with fibers produced chemically from cellulose

raze *vb* **razed; raz·ing :** to destroy completely by knocking down or breaking to pieces **:** DEMOLISH

ra·zor *n* **:** a sharp cutting instrument used to shave off hair

razz *vb* **razzed; razz·ing :** to make fun of **:** TEASE

rd. *abbr* **1 :** road **2 :** rod

re *n* **:** the second note of the musical scale

re- *prefix* **1 :** again **2 :** back **:** backward

[1]**reach** *vb* **reached; reach·ing** **1 :** to extend the arm far enough to touch or grab **2 :** to arrive at **:** COME **3 :** to extend or stretch to **4 :** to communicate with **5 :** to grow, develop, or increase

[2]**reach** *n* **1 :** the distance within which something can be touched or grabbed **2 :** the act of stretching especially to take hold of something **3 :** the probability that something can be achieved **4 :** an unbroken stretch (as of a river) **5 :** ability to stretch (as an arm) so as to touch something

re·act *vb* **re·act·ed; re·act·ing** **1 :** to act or behave in response to something **2 :** to oppose a force or influence — usually used with *against* **3 :** to go through a chemical reaction

re·ac·tion *n* **1 :** behavior or attitude in response to something **2 :** a response of the body to a stimulus **3 :** a chemical change that is brought about by the action of one substance on another and results in a new substance being formed

re·ac·tor *n* **:** a device using atomic energy to produce heat

read *vb* **read; read·ing** **1 :** to understand language through written symbols for speech sounds **2 :** to speak aloud written or printed words **3 :** to learn from information provided in writing or printing **4 :** to discover something about by looking at certain characteristics or behavior **5 :** to show by letters or numbers **6 :** to explain what something is **7 :** to interpret stored data (as on a computer drive or optical disk)

read·able *adj* **:** able to be read easily

read·er *n* **1 :** a person who reads or has the ability to read **2 :** a book for learning or practicing reading

read·i·ly *adv* **1 :** quickly and easily **2 :** without hesitation or complaint

read·ing *n* **1 :** the act of reading **2 :** something read or available to be read **3 :** the number or fact shown on an instrument

read–only memory *n* **:** ROM

read·out *n* **1 :** information from an automatic device (as a computer) that is recorded (as on a disk) or presented in a form that can be seen **2 :** an electronic device that presents information in a form that can be seen

[1]**ready** *adj* **read·i·er; read·i·est** **1 :** prepared for use or action **2 :** likely to do something **3 :** WILLING 1 **4 :** needing or wanting something as soon as possible **5 :** showing ease and promptness **6 :** available right away **:** HANDY — **read·i·ness** *n*

[2]**ready** *vb* **read·ied; ready·ing :** to prepare for use or action

ready–made *adj* **:** made beforehand in large numbers

[1]**re·al** *adj* **1 :** not imaginary **:** ACTUAL **2 :** not artificial **:** GENUINE

[2]**real** *adv* **:** [2]VERY 1

real estate *n* **:** property consisting of buildings and land

re·al·ism *n* **:** willingness to face facts or to give in to what is necessary

re·al·is·tic *adj* **1 :** true to life or nature **2 :** ready to see things as they really are and to deal with them sensibly — **re·al·is·ti·cal·ly** *adv*

re·al·i·ty *n, pl* **re·al·i·ties** **1 :** the way things actually are **2 :** someone or something that is real or actually exists

re·al·i·za·tion *n* **1 :** the state of understanding or becoming aware of something **2 :** the act of accomplishing something planned or hoped for

re·al·ize *vb* **re·al·ized; re·al·iz·ing** **1 :** to be aware of **:** UNDERSTAND **2 :** to bring into being **:** ACCOMPLISH **3 :** to get as a result of effort **:** GAIN

re·al·ly *adv* **1 :** in fact **2 :** without question

realm *n* **1 :** KINGDOM 1 **2 :** field of activity or influence

real time *n* : the actual time during which something takes place — **real–time** *adj*
re·al·ty *n* : REAL ESTATE
ream *n* **1** : a quantity of paper that may equal 480, 500, or 516 sheets **2 reams** *pl* : a great amount
reap *vb* **reaped; reap·ing 1** : to cut (as grain) or clear (as a field) with a sickle, scythe, or machine **2** : [2]HARVEST 1 **3** : to get as a result
reap·er *n* : a worker or machine that harvests crops
re·ap·pear *vb* **re·ap·peared; re·ap·pear·ing** : to appear again after not being seen for a while
[1]**rear** *vb* **reared; rear·ing 1** : to rise up on the hind legs **2** : to bring up **3** : to rise high **4** : to take care of the breeding and raising of
[2]**rear** *n* **1** : the space or position at the back **2** : the part (as of an army) or area farthest from the enemy **3** : the human buttocks
[3]**rear** *adj* : being at the back
re·ar·range *vb* **re·ar·ranged; re·ar·rang·ing** : to arrange again usually in a different way
[1]**rea·son** *n* **1** : a statement given to explain a belief or an act **2** : a fact that makes something right or fair to do **3** : [1]CAUSE 1 **4** : the power to think and understand in a logical way **5** : a fair and sensible way of thinking about something
[2]**reason** *vb* **rea·soned; rea·son·ing 1** : to think in a logical way **2** : to talk with another in a sensible way so as to influence his or her actions or opinions **3** : to state or ask logically
rea·son·able *adj* **1** : fair and sensible **2** : not too expensive **3** : fairly or moderately good — **rea·son·able·ness** *n* — **rea·son·ably** *adv*
re·as·sure *vb* **re·as·sured; re·as·sur·ing** : to make (someone) feel less afraid, upset, or doubtful
re·as·sur·ance *n* : something that is said or done to make someone feel less afraid, upset, or doubtful
rebate *n* : the return of part of a payment or of an amount owed
[1]**reb·el** *n* **1** : a person who opposes or fights against a government **2** : a person who does not obey authority or follow usual standards
[2]**re·bel** *vb* **re·belled; re·bel·ling 1** : to be or fight against authority and especially the authority of a person's government **2** : to feel or show anger, strong dislike, or disapproval
[3]**reb·el** *adj* : opposing or fighting against a government or ruler
re·bel·lion *n* **1** : open opposition to authority **2** : an open fight by citizens against their government
re·bel·lious *adj* **1** : taking part in rebellion **2** : fighting against or refusing to obey authority — **re·bel·lious·ly** *adv* — **re·bel·lious·ness** *n*
re·birth *n* **1** : a period in which something becomes popular again **2** : a period of new life or growth
re·born *adj* : born again
[1]**re·bound** *vb* **re·bound·ed; re·bound·ing 1** : to bounce back after hitting something **2** : to get over a disappointment **3** : to catch a basketball after a player has thrown it at the basket and has not scored a point
[2]**re·bound** *n* **1** : the action of bouncing back after hitting something **2** : an immediate reaction to a loss or disappointment **3** : the act of catching a basketball after a player has thrown it at the basket and missed
[1]**re·buff** *vb* **re·buffed; re·buff·ing** : to refuse (something) in a sharp or rude way
[2]**rebuff** *n* : a sharp or rude refusal of something (as an offer)
re·build *vb* **re·built; re·build·ing 1** : to make important repairs to or changes in **2** : to construct again
[1]**re·buke** *vb* **re·buked; re·buk·ing** : to criticize severely
[2]**rebuke** *n* : an expression of strong disapproval
re·bus *n* : a riddle or puzzle made up of letters, pictures, and symbols whose names sound like the syllables and words of a phrase or sentence
re·but *vb* **re·but·ted; re·but·ting** : to prove to be wrong by argument or by proof
[1]**re·call** *vb* **re·called; re·call·ing 1** : to bring back to mind : REMEMBER **2** : to ask or order to come back
[2]**re·call** *n* **1** : the ability to remember or an instance of remembering **2** : a command to return
re·cap·ture *vb* **re·cap·tured; re·cap·tur·ing 1** : to regain possession of **2** : to experience again
rec'd. *abbr* received
re·cede *vb* **re·ced·ed; re·ced·ing 1** : to move back or away **2** : to become smaller or weaker
re·ceipt *n* **1** : a written statement saying that money or goods have been received **2** : RECIPE **3** : the act of receiving **4 receipts** *pl* : something received
re·ceive *vb* **re·ceived; re·ceiv·ing 1** : to take or get something that is given, paid, or sent **2** : [2]EXPERIENCE **3** : to accept as a visitor or member : WELCOME **4** : to change incoming radio waves into sounds or pictures
re·ceiv·er *n* **1** : a device for changing electricity or radio waves into light or sound **2** : a football player who catches passes thrown toward the opponent's goal

re·cent *adj* **1 :** of or relating to a time not long past **2 :** having lately appeared to come into being **:** NEW, FRESH — **re·cent·ly** *adv*

re·cep·ta·cle *n* **:** something used to receive and hold smaller objects

re·cep·tion *n* **1 :** the act or manner of welcoming **2 :** a social gathering to celebrate something or welcome someone **3 :** the ability to receive a radio or television broadcast **4 :** the act of catching a pass thrown toward the opponent's goal

re·cep·tion·ist *n* **:** an office employee who deals with callers or visitors

re·cep·tive *adj* **:** willing to consider new ideas

re·cep·tor *n* **:** a cell that receives a stimulus (as light or heat) and activates an associated nerve to send a message to the brain and that may be grouped into a sense organ (as a taste bud)

[1]re·cess *n* **1 :** a brief period for relaxation between work periods **2 :** a secret or hidden place **3 :** a hollow cut or built into a surface (as a wall) **4 :** a brief time off from the activity of a court

[2]recess *vb* **re·cessed; re·cess·ing 1 :** to put into a hollow space **2 :** to interrupt for or take a brief time off

re·ces·sion *n* **:** a period of reduced business activity

re·ces·sive *adj* **:** being or produced by a form of a gene whose effect can be hidden by a dominant gene and which can produce a noticeable effect only when two copies of the gene are present

rec·i·pe *n* **:** a set of instructions for making something (as a food dish) by combining various things

re·cip·i·ent *n* **:** someone who receives something

re·cip·ro·cal *n* **:** one of a pair of numbers (as 9 and $^1/_9$, $^2/_3$ and $^3/_2$) whose product is one

re·cit·al *n* **1 :** a public performance of music or dance given by one or more people **2 :** an act of describing something usually in great detail

rec·i·ta·tion *n* **1 :** the act or an instance of saying something out loud **2 :** the act of saying something in a particular order

re·cite *vb* **re·cit·ed; re·cit·ing 1 :** to repeat from memory **2 :** to tell about in detail

reck·less *adj* **:** showing lack of caution **:** engaging in wild careless behavior — **reck·less·ly** *adv* — **reck·less·ness** *n*

reck·on *vb* **reck·oned; reck·on·ing 1 :** to believe that something is true or possible **2 :** CALCULATE 1 **3 :** to regard or think of as **:** CONSIDER

re·claim *vb* **re·claimed; re·claim·ing 1 :** to get back (something that was lost or taken away) **2 :** to restore to an original state **3 :** to obtain from a waste product or by-product

rec·la·ma·tion *n* **:** the act or process of recovering **:** the state of being recovered

re·cline *vb* **re·clined; re·clin·ing 1 :** to lie down or sit back usually in a relaxed way **2 :** to lean backward

rec·og·ni·tion *n* **1 :** the act of knowing and remembering upon seeing **2 :** the act of accepting the existence, truth, or importance of something **3 :** special attention or notice

rec·og·nize *vb* **rec·og·nized; rec·og·niz·ing 1 :** to know and remember upon seeing **2 :** to be willing to accept **3 :** to take approving notice of

[1]re·coil *vb* **re·coiled; re·coil·ing 1 :** to draw back **2 :** to spring back to or as if to a starting position

[2]recoil *n* **:** a sudden backward movement or springing back (as of a gun just fired)

rec·ol·lect *vb* **rec·ol·lect·ed; rec·ol·lect·ing :** to call to mind **:** REMEMBER

rec·ol·lec·tion *n* **1 :** the act or power of remembering **:** MEMORY **2 :** something remembered

rec·om·mend *vb* **rec·om·mend·ed; rec·om·mend·ing 1 :** to present or support as worthy or fit **2 :** to make a suggestion **:** ADVISE **3 :** to make acceptable

rec·om·men·da·tion *n* **1 :** the act of presenting or supporting as worthy or fit **2 :** a thing or course of action suggested as suitable or appropriate **3 :** something (as a letter) that explains why a person is appropriate or qualified

[1]rec·om·pense *vb* **rec·om·pensed; rec·om·pens·ing :** to pay for or pay back

[2]recompense *n* **:** something given in return for damage or suffering

rec·on·cile *vb* **rec·on·ciled; rec·on·cil·ing 1 :** to make friendly again **2 :** to settle by agreement **:** ADJUST **3 :** to make agree **4 :** to cause to give in or accept

rec·on·cil·i·a·tion *n* **:** the act of becoming friendly again (as after a disagreement)

re·con·di·tion *vb* **re·con·di·tioned; re·con·di·tion·ing :** to restore to good condition

re·con·nais·sance *n* **:** a survey (as of enemy territory) to get information

re·con·sid·er *vb* **re·con·sid·ered; re·con·sid·er·ing :** to think carefully about again especially with the possibility of change or reversal

re·con·sid·er·a·tion *n* **:** the act of thinking carefully about again especially with the possibility of change or reversal

re·con·struct *vb* **re·con·struct·ed; re·con·struct·ing :** to make or form again **:** REBUILD

¹re·cord *vb* **re·cord·ed; re·cord·ing 1 :** to set down in writing **2 :** to show a measurement of **3 :** to change sound or visual images into a form (as on an optical disk or hard drive) that can be listened to or watched at a later time

²rec·ord *n* **1 :** something written to give proof of something or tell about past events **2 :** something that recalls or tells about past events **3 :** a performance or achievement that is the best of its kind **4 :** the known or recorded facts about a person or thing **5 :** something on which sound or visual images have been recorded — **of record** : made known in public documents — **on record :** published in official documents

³rec·ord *adj* **:** outstanding among other like things

re·cord·er *n* **1 :** a person or device that records **2 :** a musical instrument like a long hollow whistle with eight holes for the fingers

re·cord·ing *n* **:** ²RECORD 4

¹re·count *vb* **re·count·ed; re·count·ing :** to tell all about **:** NARRATE

²re·count *vb* **re·count·ed; re·count·ing :** to count again

³re·count *n* **:** a counting again (as of election votes)

re·course *n* **:** someone or something that can be turned to for help or protection

re·cov·er *vb* **re·cov·ered; re·cov·er·ing 1 :** to get back **:** REGAIN **2 :** to regain or return to a normal or usual state (as of health or composure **3 :** to make up for

re·cov·ery *n, pl* **re·cov·er·ies :** the act or process of regaining or returning to a normal or usual state

rec·re·a·tion *n* **:** something done for fun and relaxation

¹re·cruit *vb* **re·cruit·ed; re·cruit·ing 1 :** to enlist as a member of the armed forces **2** : to get the services of

²recruit *n* **1 :** a newly enlisted member of the armed forces **2 :** a newcomer to a group or field of activity

rect·an·gle *n* **:** a flat geometric four-sided figure with right angles and with opposite sides parallel

rect·an·gu·lar *adj* **:** shaped like a rectangle

rec·ti·fy *vb* **rec·ti·fied; rec·ti·fy·ing :** to set or make right

rec·tor *n* **:** PASTOR

rec·tum *n, pl* **rec·tums** *also* **rec·ta :** the last part of the large intestine

re·cu·per·ate *vb* **re·cu·per·at·ed; re·cu·per·at·ing :** to regain health or strength

re·cu·per·a·tion *n* **:** a recovery of health or strength

re·cur *vb* **re·curred; re·cur·ring :** to occur or appear again

re·cur·rence *n* **:** the state of occurring or appearing again or time after time

re·cur·rent *adj* **:** happening or appearing again and again

re·cy·cla·ble *adj* **:** able to be recycled

re·cy·cle *vb* **re·cy·cled; re·cy·cling :** to process (as paper, glass, or cans) in order to regain or reuse materials

¹red *adj* **red·der; red·dest 1 :** of the color of blood **:** colored red **2 :** flushed with emotion (as embarrassment) — **red·ness** *n*

²red *n* **1 :** the color of blood or of the ruby **2 :** something red in color

red·bird *n* **:** any of several birds (as a cardinal) with mostly red feathers

red blood cell *n* **:** a tiny reddish cell of the blood that contains hemoglobin and carries oxygen from the lungs to the tissues

red·breast *n* **:** a bird (as a robin) with a reddish breast

red cell *n* **:** RED BLOOD CELL

red·coat *n* **:** a British soldier especially in America during the Revolutionary War

red·den *vb* **red·dened; red·den·ing :** to make or become red

red·dish *adj* **:** somewhat red

re·deem *vb* **1 :** to make up for **2 :** to buy, get, or win back **3 :** to make good **:** FULFILL **4 :** to exchange for something of value **5 :** to free from sin — **re·deem·er** *n*

re·demp·tion *n* **1 :** the act of making up for **2 :** an exchange for something of value **3** : the act of saving from sin

red–hand·ed *adv or adj* **:** in the act of doing something wrong

red·head *n* **:** a person having reddish hair

red·head·ed *adj* **:** having reddish hair or a red head

red–hot *adj* **1 :** glowing red with heat **2 :** very active or successful **3 :** extremely popular

re·di·rect *vb* **re·di·rect·ed; re·di·rect·ing :** to change the course or direction of

re·dis·cov·er *vb* **re·dis·cov·ered; re·dis·cov·er·ing :** to discover again

red–let·ter *adj* **:** of special importance **:** MEMORABLE

re·do *vb* **re·did; re·done; re·do·ing :** to do over or again

re·dou·ble *vb* **re·dou·bled; re·dou·bling :** to greatly increase the size or amount of

red panda *n* **:** a long-tailed animal that is related to and resembles the raccoon, has long reddish brown fur, and is found from the Himalayas to southern China

re·dress *vb* **re·dressed; re·dress·ing :** to set right **:** REMEDY

red tape *n* **:** usually official rules and regulations that seem unnecessary and prevent things from being done quickly and easily

re·duce *vb* **re·duced; re·duc·ing 1 :** to make

smaller or less **2 :** to bring to a usually worse state **3 :** to lower in grade or rank **4 :** to change to a simpler form **5 :** to lose weight by dieting

re·duc·tion *n* **1 :** the act of making something smaller or less **:** the state of being made smaller or less **2 :** the amount by which something is made smaller or less

red·wood *n* **:** a very tall tree of California that bears cones and has light durable brownish red wood

reed *n* **1 :** a tall slender grass that grows in wet areas **2 :** a stem or a growth or mass of reeds **3 :** a thin flexible piece of cane, plastic, or metal fastened to the mouthpiece of an instrument (as a clarinet) or over an air opening in an instrument (as an accordion) and made to vibrate by an air current

reef *n* **:** a chain of rocks or coral or a ridge of sand at or near the surface of water

¹reek *n* **:** a strong or unpleasant smell

²reek *vb* **reeked; reek·ing :** to have a strong or unpleasant smell

¹reel *n* **1 :** a device that can be turned round and round to wind up something flexible **2 :** a quantity of something wound on a reel

²reel *vb* **reeled; reel·ing 1 :** to wind on a reel **2 :** to pull by the use of a reel — **reel off :** to say or recite rapidly or easily

³reel *vb* **reeled; reel·ing 1 :** to whirl or spin around **2 :** to be in a confused or dizzy state **3 :** to fall back suddenly (as after being hit) **4 :** to walk or move unsteadily **:** STAGGER

⁴reel *n* **:** a lively folk dance

re·elect *vb* **re·elect·ed; re·elect·ing :** to elect for another term

re·en·act *vb* **re·en·act·ed; re·en·act·ing :** to repeat the actions of (an earlier event)

re·en·ter *vb* **re·en·tered; re·en·ter·ing :** to enter again

re·es·tab·lish *vb* **re·es·tab·lished; re·es·tab·lish·ing :** to establish again **:** bring back into existence

ref *n* **:** ¹REFEREE 1

re·fer *vb* **re·ferred; re·fer·ring 1 :** to look at for information **2 :** to send or direct to some person or place for treatment, aid, information, or decision **3 :** to call attention **4 :** to mention (something) in talking or writing

¹ref·er·ee *n* **1 :** a sports official with final authority for conducting a game **2 :** a person who is asked to settle a disagreement

²referee *vb* **ref·er·eed; ref·er·ee·ing :** to act or be in charge of as referee

ref·er·ence *n* **1 :** the act of looking at or in something for information **2 :** a relation to or concern with something **3 :** the act or an instance of mentioning **4 :** a work (as a dictionary) that contains useful information **5 :** something that refers a reader to another source of information **6 :** a person who can be asked for information about another person's character or ability **7 :** a written statement about someone's character or ability

ref·er·en·dum *n, pl* **ref·er·en·da** *or* **ref·er·en·dums :** the practice of voting on an issue

¹re·fill *vb* **re·filled; re·fill·ing :** to fill or become filled again

²re·fill *n* **:** a new or fresh supply of something

re·fine *vb* **re·fined; re·fin·ing 1 :** to bring to a pure state **2 :** to make better **:** IMPROVE

re·fined *adj* **1 :** having or showing good taste or training **2 :** freed from impurities **:** PURE

re·fine·ment *n* **1 :** the act or process of improving something or bringing something to a pure state **2 :** excellence of manners or tastes **3 :** a small change meant to improve something

re·fin·ery *n, pl* **re·fin·er·ies :** a building and equipment where something (as oil or metal) is made pure and ready for use

re·fin·ish *vb* **re·fin·ished; re·fin·ish·ing :** to give (as furniture) a new surface

re·fit *vb* **re·fit·ted; re·fit·ting :** to make ready for use again

re·flect *vb* **re·flect·ed; re·flect·ing 1 :** to bend or throw back (waves of light, sound, or heat) **2 :** to give back an image or likeness of in the manner of a mirror **3 :** to make known **4 :** to cause to be thought of in a specified way or in a bad way **5 :** to think seriously and carefully about

re·flec·tion *n* **1 :** the return of light or sound waves from a surface **2 :** an image produced by or as if by a mirror **3 :** something that brings blame or disgrace **4 :** careful thought **5 :** an opinion formed or a remark made after careful thought

re·flec·tor *n* **:** a shiny surface for reflecting light or heat

re·flex *n* **1 :** an action or movement that is made automatically without thinking as a reaction to a stimulus **2 re·flex·es** *pl* **:** the natural ability to react quickly

re·for·est *vb* **re·for·est·ed; re·for·est·ing :** to renew forest growth by planting seeds or young trees

re·for·es·ta·tion *n* **:** the act of renewing forest growth by planting seeds or young trees

¹re·form *vb* **re·formed; re·form·ing 1 :** to make better or improve by removal of faults **2 :** to stop engaging in bad habits or behavior — **re·form·er** *n*

²reform *n* **:** the improvement of something by removing faults or problems

ref·or·ma·tion *n* **:** the act of changing something or someone for the better

re·fract *vb* **re·fract·ed; re·fract·ing :** to make (light) bend when it passes through at an angle

re·frac·tion *n* **:** the bending of a ray when it passes at an angle from one medium into another in which its speed is different (as when light passes from air into water)

re·frac·to·ry *adj* **1 :** resisting control or authority **:** STUBBORN **2 :** capable of enduring very high temperatures

¹re·frain *vb* **re·frained; re·frain·ing :** to keep from giving in to a desire or impulse

²refrain *n* **:** a phrase or verse repeated regularly in a poem or song

re·fresh *vb* **re·freshed; re·fresh·ing :** to bring back to an original state or normal condition (as by restoring energy or making more active) — **re·fresh·er** *n*

re·fresh·ment *n* **:** something (as food or drink) that refreshes — often used in pl.

re·frig·er·ate *vb* **re·frig·er·at·ed; re·frig·er·at·ing :** to make or keep cold or cool especially by placing in a refrigerator

re·frig·er·a·tor *n* **:** a device or room for keeping articles (as food) cool

re·fu·el *vb* **re·fu·eled; re·fu·el·ing :** to provide with or take on more fuel

ref·uge *n* **1 :** shelter or protection from danger or distress **2 :** a place that provides shelter or protection

ref·u·gee *n* **:** a person who flees for safety (as from war) usually to a foreign country

¹re·fund *vb* **re·fund·ed; re·fund·ing :** return (money) as repayment

²re·fund *n* **:** an amount of money that is returned as repayment

re·fus·al *n* **:** the act of showing unwillingness to do, give, or allow something

¹re·fuse *vb* **re·fused; re·fus·ing 1 :** to express unwillingness to accept **:** turn down (something) **2 :** to express or show unwillingness to do, give, or allow something

²ref·use *n* **:** TRASH 1, RUBBISH

re·fute *vb* **re·fut·ed; re·fut·ing :** to say or prove that something is wrong or untrue

reg. *abbr* **1** region **2** regular

re·gain *vb* **re·gained; re·gain·ing 1 :** to gain or get again **:** get back **2 :** to get back to **:** reach again

re·gal *adj* **:** relating to or suitable for a king or queen **:** ROYAL — **re·gal·ly** *adv*

re·gale *vb* **re·galed; re·gal·ing :** to give pleasure or amusement to

¹re·gard *n* **1 :** CONSIDERATION 2 **2 :** a feeling of respect **3 regards** *pl* **:** friendly greetings **4 :** a point to be considered **5 :** ²LOOK 1 — **in regard to :** in relation to — **with regard to :** in relation to

²regard *vb* **re·gard·ed; re·gard·ing 1 :** to think of in a particular way **:** CONSIDER **2 :** to look at **3 :** to give consideration to

re·gard·ing *prep* **:** relating to **:** ABOUT

re·gard·less *adv* **:** in spite of something that might be a problem

regardless of *prep* **:** in spite of

re·gat·ta *n* **:** a race or a series of races between sailboats, speedboats, or rowing boats

re·gen·er·ate *vb* **re·gen·er·at·ed; re·gen·er·at·ing :** to replace (as a lost or damaged body part) by new growth

re·gent *n* **:** a person who temporarily governs a kingdom in place of a monarch

re·gime *n* **1 :** a form or system of government **2 :** REGIMEN

reg·i·men *n* **:** a systematic course of action

reg·i·ment *n* **:** a military unit made up usually of a number of battalions

re·gion *n* **1 :** an area having no definite boundaries **2 :** a broad geographic area **3 :** VICINITY 2

re·gion·al *adj* **:** of, relating to, or characteristic of a certain geographic area

¹reg·is·ter *n* **1 :** an official list or book for keeping records of something **2 :** a mechanical device (as a cash register) that records items **3 :** a device for regulating ventilation or the flow of heated air from a furnace

²register *vb* **reg·is·tered; reg·is·ter·ing 1 :** to enter or enroll in an official list or book of public records **2 :** to record automatically **3 :** to show by expression and bodily movements **4 :** to make known officially and publicly **5 :** to be recognized or remembered **6 :** to get special protection for (something mailed) by paying extra postage

reg·is·tra·tion *n* **1 :** the act of entering on an official list **2 :** a document showing that something is registered

reg·is·try *n, pl* **reg·is·tries :** a place where registration takes place

¹re·gret *vb* **re·gret·ted; re·gret·ting :** to be sorry for

²regret *n* **1 :** sadness or disappointment caused especially by something beyond a person's control **2 :** an expression of sorrow or disappointment **3 regrets** *pl* **:** a note politely refusing to accept an invitation

re·gret·ful *adj* **:** feeling or showing regret — **re·gret·ful·ly** *adv*

re·gret·ta·ble *adj* **:** causing sorrow or disappointment — **re·gret·ta·bly** *adv*

re·group *vb* **re·grouped; re·group·ing :** to form into a new group

reg·u·lar *adj* **1 :** steady in practice or occurrence **:** happening on or as if on a schedule **2 :** following established usages or rules **3 :** ¹NORMAL 1 **4 :** following the usual manner of inflection **5 :** having all sides equal and all angles equal — **reg·u·lar·ly** *adv*

reg·u·lar·i·ty *n* **:** the quality or state of happening on or as if on a schedule

reg·u·late *vb* **reg·u·lat·ed; reg·u·lat·ing** **1 :** to bring under the control of authority : make rules concerning **2 :** to control the time, amount, degree, or rate of **3 :** to bring order or method to — **reg·u·la·tor** *n*

reg·u·la·tion *n* **1 :** a rule or law telling how something is to be done **2 :** the act of controlling or bringing under control

re·gur·gi·tate *vb* **re·gur·gi·tat·ed; re·gur·gi·tat·ing :** to bring food that has been swallowed back to and out of the mouth

re·hears·al *n* **:** a private performance or practice session in preparation for a public appearance

re·hearse *vb* **re·hearsed; re·hears·ing :** to practice in private in preparation for a public performance

[1]reign *n* **1 :** the authority or rule of a monarch **2 :** the time during which a monarch rules

[2]reign *vb* **reigned; reign·ing** **1 :** to rule as a monarch **2 :** to be usual or widespread **3 :** to be the best or most powerful

re·im·burse *vb* **re·im·bursed; re·im·burs·ing :** to pay back : REPAY — **re·im·burse·ment** *n*

[1]rein *n* **1 :** a line or strap that is attached at either end of the bit of a bridle and is used to control an animal — usually used in pl. **2 :** an influence that slows, limits, or holds back **3 :** controlling or guiding power

[2]rein *vb* **reined; rein·ing :** to check, control, or stop by or as if by reins

re·in·car·na·tion *n* **:** rebirth of the soul in a new body after death

rein·deer *n, pl* **reindeer :** CARIBOU

re·in·force *vb* **re·in·forced; re·in·forc·ing** **1 :** to strengthen with new supplies or more people **2 :** to strengthen by adding more material for support

re·in·force·ment *n* **1 :** people or things (as supplies) sent to help or support **2 :** the act of making something stronger or able to last longer

re·in·state *vb* **re·in·stat·ed; re·in·stat·ing :** to place again in a former position or condition — **re·in·state·ment** *n*

re·it·er·ate *vb* **re·it·er·at·ed; re·it·er·at·ing :** to repeat something said or done

[1]re·ject *vb* **re·ject·ed; re·ject·ing :** to refuse to accept, believe, or consider

[2]re·ject *n* **:** a person or thing not accepted as good enough for some purpose

re·jec·tion *n* **:** the act of not accepting, believing, or considering something : the state of being rejected

re·joice *vb* **re·joiced; re·joic·ing :** to feel or show joy or happiness

re·join *vb* **re·joined; re·join·ing** **1 :** to join again : return to **2 :** to reply often in a sharp or critical way

re·join·der *n* **:** [2]REPLY

re·kin·dle *vb* **re·kin·dled; re·kin·dling :** to cause to be active again

[1]re·lapse *n* **1 :** a return of illness after a period of improvement **2 :** a return to a former and undesirable state or condition

[2]re·lapse *vb* **re·lapsed; re·laps·ing :** to return to a former state or condition (as of illness or bad behavior) after a change for the better

re·late *vb* **re·lat·ed; re·lat·ing** **1 :** to give an account of : NARRATE **2 :** to show or have a relationship to or between : CONNECT

re·lat·ed *adj* **1 :** sharing some connection **2 :** connected by common ancestry or by marriage **3 :** connected by a usually distant common ancestor and typically sharing similar characteristics

re·la·tion *n* **1 :** CONNECTION 2, RELATIONSHIP **2 :** a related person : RELATIVE **3 :** REFERENCE 2, RESPECT **4 relations** *pl* **:** the interaction between two or more people, groups, or countries

re·la·tion·ship *n* **1 :** the state of being related or connected **2 :** connection by common ancestry or marriage **3 :** the state of interaction between two or more people, groups, or countries

[1]rel·a·tive *n* **:** a person connected with another by ancestry or marriage

[2]relative *adj* **1 :** existing in comparison to something else **2 :** RELEVANT — **rel·a·tive·ly** *adv*

re·lax *vb* **re·laxed; re·lax·ing** **1 :** to make or become loose or less tense **2 :** to make or become less severe or strict **3 :** to become calm and free from stress **4 :** to seek rest or enjoyment

re·lax·a·tion *n* **1 :** the act or fact of being or becoming rested, calm, or less tense or severe **2 :** a way of becoming rested or calm and free from stress

[1]re·lay *n* **1 :** a race between teams in which each team member covers a certain part of the course **2 :** the act of passing something from one person to the next **3 :** a fresh supply (as of horses or people) arranged to relieve others

[2]re·lay *vb* **re·layed; re·lay·ing :** to pass along by stages

[1]re·lease *vb* **re·leased; re·leas·ing** **1 :** to set free or let go of **2 :** to allow to escape **3 :** to relieve from a duty, responsibility, or burden **4 :** to give up or hand over to someone else **5 :** to permit to be published, sold, or shown

[2]release *n* **1 :** the act of setting free or letting go **2 :** the act of allowing something to escape **3 :** a discharge from an obligation or responsibility **4 :** relief or rescue from sorrow, suffering, or trouble **5 :** a device for holding or releasing a mechanism **6** : the act of making something available to the public **7** : something (as a new product or song) that is made available to the public

re·lent *vb* **re·lent·ed; re·lent·ing** **1** : to become less severe, harsh, or strict **2** : to give in after first resisting or refusing

re·lent·less *adj* : showing no lessening of severity, intensity, or strength — **re·lent·less·ly** *adv* — **re·lent·less·ness** *n*

rel·e·vance *n* : relation to the matter at hand

rel·e·vant *adj* : having something to do with the matter at hand

re·li·abil·i·ty *n* : the quality or state of being fit to be trusted or relied on

re·li·able *adj* : fit to be trusted or relied on: DEPENDABLE — **re·li·ably** *adv*

re·li·ance *n* : the act or state of depending on someone or something

rel·ic *n* **1** : something left behind after decay or disappearance **2** : an object that is considered holy because of its connection with a saint or martyr

re·lief *n* **1** : the feeling of happiness that occurs when something unpleasant or distressing stops or does not happen **2** : removal or lessening of something painful or troubling **3** : something that interrupts in a welcome way **4** : release from a post or from performance of a duty **5** : WELFARE 2 **6** : raising of figures or designs from the background **7** : elevations of a land surface

re·lieve *vb* **re·lieved; re·liev·ing** **1** : to free partly or wholly from a burden, pain, or distress **2** : to bring about the removal or lessening of **3** : to release from a post or duty **4** : to break the sameness of — **re·liev·er** *n*

re·li·gion *n* **1** : the belief in and worship of God or gods **2** : a system of religious beliefs and practices

re·li·gious *adj* **1** : believing in God or gods and following the practices of a religion **2** : of or relating to religion **3** : very devoted and faithful — **re·li·gious·ly** *adv*

re·lin·quish *vb* **re·lin·quished; re·lin·quish·ing** : to let go of : give up

[1]rel·ish *n* **1** : great enjoyment **2** : a highly seasoned food eaten with other food to add flavor

[2]relish *vb* **rel·ished; rel·ish·ing** **1** : to be pleased by : ENJOY **2** : to like the taste of

re·live *vb* **re·lived; re·liv·ing** : to experience again (as in the imagination)

re·luc·tance *n* : the quality or state of showing doubt or unwillingness

re·luc·tant *adj* : showing doubt or unwillingness — **re·luc·tant·ly** *adv*

re·ly *vb* **re·lied; re·ly·ing** : to trust in or depend on

re·main *vb* **re·mained; re·main·ing** **1** : to stay in the same place **2** : to stay after others have gone **3** : to continue to be **4** : to be left after others have been removed, subtracted, or destroyed **5** : to be something yet to be done or considered

re·main·der *n* **1** : a group or part that is left **2** : the number left after a subtraction **3** : the number left over from the dividend after division that is less than the divisor

re·mains *n pl* **1** : whatever is left over or behind **2** : a dead body

re·make *vb* **re·made; re·mak·ing** : to make again or in a different form

[1]re·mark *n* **1** : a brief comment **2 remarks** *pl* : a short speech

[2]remark *vb* **re·marked; re·mark·ing** : to make a comment : express as an observation

re·mark·able *adj* : worthy of being or likely to be noticed especially as being unusual — **re·mark·ably** *adv*

re·match *n* : a second meeting between the same contestants

re·me·di·al *adj* : intended to make something better

[1]rem·e·dy *n, pl* **rem·e·dies** **1** : a medicine or treatment that cures or relieves **2** : something that corrects a problem

[2]remedy *vb* **rem·e·died; rem·e·dy·ing** : to provide or serve as a cure or solution for

re·mem·ber *vb* **re·mem·bered; re·mem·ber·ing** **1** : to bring to mind or think of again **2** : to keep in mind **3** : to pass along greetings from

re·mem·brance *n* **1** : the act of thinking about again **2** : MEMORY 4 **3** : something that is done to honor the memory of a person or event **4** : something (as a souvenir) that brings to mind a past experience

Remembrance Day *Can and Brit n* **1** : November 11 set aside in commemoration of the end of hostilities in 1918 and 1945 and observed as a legal holiday in Canada **2** *or Brit* **Remembrance Sunday** : a Sunday that is usu. closest to November 11 and that in Great Britain is set aside in commemoration of the end of hostilities in 1918 and 1945

re·mind *vb* **re·mind·ed; re·mind·ing** : to cause to remember — **re·mind·er** *n*

rem·i·nisce *vb* **rem·i·nisced; rem·i·nisc·ing** : to talk or think about things in the past

rem·i·nis·cence *n* **1** : the act of recalling or telling of a past experience **2 reminiscences** *pl* : a story of a person's memorable experiences

rem·i·nis·cent *adj* : being a reminder of something else

re·miss *adj* : careless in the performance of work or duty

re·mis·sion *n* : a period of time during a serious illness when there are few or no symptoms

re·mit *vb* **re·mit·ted; re·mit·ting** **1 :** to send money (as in payment) **2 :** [2]PARDON 2
re·mit·tance *n* **:** money sent in payment
rem·nant *n* **:** something that remains or is left over
re·mod·el *vb* **re·mod·eled** *or* **re·mod·elled; re·mod·el·ing** *or* **re·mod·el·ling :** to change the structure or appearance of
re·mon·strate *vb* **re·mon·strat·ed; re·mon·strat·ing :** [1]PROTEST 1
re·morse *n* **:** deep regret for doing or saying something wrong — **re·morse·ful** *adj* — **re·morse·less** *adj*
[1]**re·mote** *adj* **re·mot·er; re·mot·est** **1 :** far off in place or time **2 :** SECLUDED 1 **3 :** small in degree **4 :** distant in manner **:** ALOOF **5 :** not closely connected or related — **re·mote·ly** *adv* — **re·mote·ness** *n*
[2]**remote** *n* **:** REMOTE CONTROL 1
remote control *n* **1 :** a device for controlling something from a distance **2 :** control (as by a radio signal) of operation from a distant point
re·mov·able *adj* **:** possible to be taken off or gotten rid of
re·mov·al *n* **:** the act of moving away or getting rid of **:** the fact of being moved away or gotten rid of
re·move *vb* **re·moved; re·mov·ing** **1 :** to move by lifting or taking off or away **2 :** to get rid of **3 :** to dismiss from a job or office
re·mov·er *n* **:** something (as a chemical) used in getting rid of a substance
re·nais·sance *n* **1** *cap* **:** the period of European history between the 14th and 17th centuries marked by a fresh interest in ancient art and literature and by the beginnings of modern science **2 :** the act of changing in a positive way **:** a period during which things are improving
re·name *vb* **re·named; re·nam·ing :** to give a new name to
rend *vb* **rent; rend·ing :** to tear apart by force
ren·der *vb* **ren·dered; ren·der·ing** **1 :** to cause to be or become **2 :** to furnish or give to another **3 :** to officially report **4 :** to obtain by heating **5 :** PERFORM 3
ren·dez·vous *n, pl* **ren·dez·vous** **1 :** a place agreed on for a meeting **2 :** a planned meeting
ren·di·tion *n* **:** an act or a result of performing
ren·e·gade *n* **1 :** a person who deserts a faith, cause, or party **2 :** a person who does not obey rules
re·nege *vb* **re·neged; re·neg·ing :** to go back on a promise or agreement
re·new *vb* **re·newed; re·new·ing** **1 :** to make or become new, fresh, or strong again **2 :** to make, do, or begin again **3 :** to put in a fresh supply of **4 :** to continue in force for a new period
re·new·able *adj* **:** capable of being replaced by natural processes
re·new·al *n* **1 :** the act of continuing in force for a new period **2 :** the state of being made new, fresh, or strong again **3 :** something renewed
re·nounce *vb* **re·nounced; re·nounc·ing** **1 :** to give up, abandon, or resign usually by a public declaration **2 :** to refuse to follow, obey, or recognize any longer
ren·o·vate *vb* **ren·o·vat·ed; ren·o·vat·ing :** to put in good condition again — **ren·o·va·tor** *n*
re·nown *n* **:** the state of being widely and favorably known
re·nowned *adj* **:** widely and favorably known
[1]**rent** *n* **:** money paid for the use of another's property — **for rent :** available for use at a price
[2]**rent** *vb* **rent·ed; rent·ing** **1 :** to pay money in exchange for the use of someone else's property **2 :** to give the possession and use of in return for for an agreed upon amount of money **3 :** to be available for use at a price
[3]**rent** *past and past participle of* REND
[1]**rent·al** *n* **:** an amount paid or collected as rent
[2]**rental** *adj* **:** relating to or available for rent
rent·er *n* **:** a person who pays money for the use of something (as a place to live)
re·open *vb* **re·opened; re·open·ing :** to open again
re·or·ga·nize *vb* **re·or·ga·nized; re·or·ga·niz·ing :** to organize differently
rep. *abbr* representative
[1]**re·pair** *vb* **re·paired; re·pair·ing** **1 :** to put back in good condition **:** FIX **2 :** to make up for
[2]**repair** *n* **1 :** the act or process of putting back in good condition **2 :** [1]CONDITION 4
rep·a·ra·tion *n* **1 :** the act of making up for a wrong **2 :** something paid by a country losing a war to the winner to make up for damages done in the war
re·past *n* **:** [1]MEAL
re·pay *vb* **re·paid; re·pay·ing** **1 :** to pay back **2 :** to do or give something in return
re·pay·ment *n* **:** the act or an instance of paying back
re·peal *vb* **re·pealed; re·peal·ing :** to do away with especially by legislative action
[1]**re·peat** *vb* **re·peat·ed; re·peat·ing** **1 :** to state or tell again **2 :** to say from memory **:** RECITE **3 :** to make or do again
[2]**repeat** *n* **1 :** the act of happening or being done again **2 :** something happening or being done again

re·peat·ed *adj* **:** done or happening again and again — **re·peat·ed·ly** *adv*
re·pel *vb* **re·pelled; re·pel·ling 1 :** to drive back **2 :** to push away **3 :** to keep out **:** RESIST **4 :** [2]DISGUST
re·pel·lent *n* **:** a substance used to keep off pests (as insects)
re·pent *vb* **re·pent·ed; re·pent·ing :** to acknowledge regret for having done something wrong
re·pen·tance *n* **:** the action or process of acknowledging regret for having done something wrong
re·pen·tant *adj* **:** feeling or showing regret for something said or done — **re·pen·tant·ly** *adv*
re·per·cus·sion *n* **:** a widespread, indirect, or unexpected effect of something said or done
rep·er·toire *n* **:** a list or supply of plays, operas, or pieces that a company or person is prepared to perform
rep·er·to·ry *n, pl* **rep·er·to·ries :** REPERTOIRE
rep·e·ti·tion *n* **1 :** the act or an instance of stating or doing again **2 :** something stated or done again
re·place *vb* **re·placed; re·plac·ing 1 :** to put back in a former or proper place **2 :** to take the place of **3 :** to put something new in the place of
re·place·ment *n* **1 :** the act of putting back, taking the place of, or substituting **:** the state of being put back or substituted **2 :** [1]SUBSTITUTE
re·plen·ish *vb* **re·plen·ished; re·plen·ish·ing :** to make full or complete once more
re·plete *adj* **:** well supplied
rep·li·ca *n* **:** a very exact copy
[1]**re·ply** *vb* **re·plied; re·ply·ing :** to say or do in answer **:** RESPOND
[2]**reply** *n, pl* **re·plies :** something said, written, or done in answer
[1]**re·port** *n* **1 :** a usually complete description or statement **2 :** a written or spoken statement that may or may not be true **3 :** REPUTATION 1 **4 :** an explosive noise
[2]**report** *vb* **re·port·ed; re·port·ing 1 :** to give a written or spoken description of something **2 :** to make known to the proper authorities **3 :** to complain about (someone) for misconduct **4 :** to make a statement that may or may not be true **5 :** to prepare or present an account of something (as for television or a newspaper) **6 :** to show up — **re·port·er** *n*
report card *n* **:** a written statement of a student's grades
[1]**re·pose** *vb* **re·posed; re·pos·ing :** to lay or lie at rest
[2]**repose** *n* **1 :** a state of resting **2 :** freedom from disturbance or excitement **:** CALM
rep·re·hen·si·ble *adj* **:** deserving criticism or condemnation
rep·re·sent *vb* **rep·re·sent·ed; rep·re·sent·ing 1 :** to present a picture, image, or likeness of **:** PORTRAY **2 :** to be a sign or symbol of **3 :** to act for or in place of
rep·re·sen·ta·tion *n* **1 :** one (as a picture or symbol) that is a sign or portrayal of something else **2 :** the act of doing something on behalf of another or others **:** the state of doing something on behalf of another or others (as in a legislative body)
[1]**rep·re·sen·ta·tive** *adj* **1 :** serving to portray **2 :** carried on by people elected to act for others **3 :** being a typical example of the thing mentioned
[2]**representative** *n* **1 :** a typical example (as of a group or class) **2 :** a person who acts for others (as in a legislature and especially in the House of Representatives of the United States or of a state)
re·press *vb* **re·pressed; re·press·ing :** to hold in check by or as if by pressure
[1]**re·prieve** *vb* **re·prieved; re·priev·ing 1 :** to delay something (as the punishment of a prisoner sentenced to die) **2 :** to give relief to
[2]**reprieve** *n* **1 :** the act of postponing something **2 :** a temporary relief
[1]**rep·ri·mand** *n* **:** a severe or formal criticism **:** CENSURE
[2]**reprimand** *vb* **rep·ri·mand·ed; rep·ri·mand·ing :** to criticize (a person) severely or formally
re·pri·sal *n* **:** an act in return for harm done by another **:** an act of revenge
[1]**re·proach** *vb* **re·proached; re·proach·ing :** to find fault with **:** BLAME
[2]**reproach** *n* **1 :** something that deserves blame or disgrace **2 :** an expression of disapproval — **re·proach·ful** *adj* — **re·proach·ful·ly** *adv*
re·pro·duce *vb* **re·pro·duced; re·pro·duc·ing 1 :** to produce another living thing of the same kind **2 :** to imitate closely **3 :** to make a copy of
re·pro·duc·tion *n* **1 :** the process by which living things produce offspring **2 :** the act or process of copying something **3 :** [1]COPY 1
re·pro·duc·tive *adj* **:** relating to or concerned with the production of offspring
re·proof *n* **:** blame or criticism for a fault
re·prove *vb* **re·proved; re·prov·ing :** to express blame or disapproval of **:** SCOLD
rep·tile *n* **:** a cold-blooded animal (as snake, lizard, turtle, or alligator) that breathes air and usually has the skin covered with scales or bony plates
re·pub·lic *n* **:** a country with elected representatives and an elected chief of state who is not a monarch and who is usually a president

[1]**re·pub·li·can** *n* **1 :** a person who favors a form of government having elected representatives **2** *cap* **:** a member of the Republican party of the United States
[2]**republican** *adj* **1 :** being a form of government having elected representatives **2 :** relating to a major political party in the United States that is associated with business interests and favors a limited government role in economic matters
re·pu·di·ate *vb* **re·pu·di·at·ed; re·pu·di·at·ing 1 :** to refuse to have anything to do with **2 :** to refuse to believe or approve of
[1]**re·pulse** *vb* **re·pulsed; re·puls·ing 1 :** to drive or beat back **:** REPEL **2 :** to reject in a rude or unfriendly way **:** SNUB **3 :** to cause dislike or disgust in
[2]**repulse** *n* **1 :** [2]REBUFF, SNUB **2 :** the action of driving back an attacker
re·pul·sive *adj* **:** causing disgust — **re·pul·sive·ly** *adv* — **re·pul·sive·ness** *n*
rep·u·ta·ble *adj* **:** having a good reputation
rep·u·ta·tion *n* **1 :** overall quality or character as seen or judged by people in general **2 :** notice by other people of some quality or ability
[1]**re·pute** *vb* **re·put·ed; re·put·ing :** CONSIDER 3
[2]**repute** *n* **1 :** REPUTATION 1 **2 :** good reputation **:** HONOR
[1]**re·quest** *n* **1 :** the act of asking for something **2 :** something asked for **3 :** the condition of being asked for
[2]**request** *vb* **re·quest·ed; re·quest·ing 1 :** to ask something of someone **2 :** to ask for
re·qui·em *n* **1 :** a mass for a dead person **2 :** a musical service or hymn in honor of dead people
re·quire *vb* **re·quired; re·quir·ing 1 :** to have a need for **2 :** [1]ORDER 2, COMMAND
re·quire·ment *n* **:** something that is necessary
[1]**req·ui·site** *adj* **:** needed for reaching a goal or achieving a purpose
[2]**requisite** *n* **:** REQUIREMENT
re·read *vb* **re·read; re·read·ing :** to read again
res. *abbr* residence
[1]**res·cue** *vb* **res·cued; res·cu·ing :** to free from danger **:** SAVE — **res·cu·er** *n*
[2]**rescue** *n* **:** an act of freeing someone or something from danger
[1]**re·search** *n* **:** careful study and investigation for the purpose of discovering and explaining new knowledge — **re·search·er** *n*
[2]**research** *vb* **re·searched; re·search·ing :** to search or investigate thoroughly
re·sem·blance *n* **:** the quality or state of being similar to another
re·sem·ble *vb* **re·sem·bled; re·sem·bling :** to be like or similar to
re·sent *vb* **re·sent·ed; re·sent·ing :** to feel annoyance or anger at
re·sent·ful *adj* **:** full of angry displeasure
re·sent·ment *n* **:** a feeling of angry displeasure at a real or imagined wrong, insult, or injury
res·er·va·tion *n* **1 :** an act of setting something aside for future use **2 :** an arrangement to have something (as seating in a restaurant) held for someone's use **3 :** something (as land) set aside for a special use **4 :** an area of land set aside for American Indians to live **5 :** something that limits
[1]**re·serve** *vb* **re·served; re·serv·ing 1 :** to arrange to have set aside and held for someone's use **2 :** to keep in store for special use **3 :** to keep from using until a future time **4 :** to hold over to a future time or place
[2]**reserve** *n* **1 reserves** *pl* **:** military forces held back or available for later use **2 :** an area of land set apart **3 :** caution in words and behavior **4 :** something stored for future use **5 :** an act of setting something aside for future use
re·served *adj* **1 :** cautious in words and actions **2 :** kept or set apart for future or special use
res·er·voir *n* **:** a place where something (as water) is kept in store for future use
re·set *vb* **re·set; re·set·ting :** to set again
re·side *vb* **re·sid·ed; re·sid·ing 1 :** to live permanently and continuously **:** DWELL **2 :** to have its place **:** EXIST
res·i·dence *n* **1 :** the act or fact of living in a place **2 :** a building used for a home **3 :** the time during which a person lives in a place
[1]**res·i·dent** *n* **:** a person who lives in a place
[2]**resident** *adj* **1 :** living in a place for some length of time **2 :** serving in a full-time position
res·i·den·tial *adj* **1 :** used as a residence or by residents **2 :** suitable for or containing residences
res·i·due *n* **:** whatever remains after a part is taken, set apart, or lost
re·sign *vb* **re·signed; re·sign·ing 1 :** to give up (a job or position) by a formal or official act **2 :** to prepare to accept something unpleasant
res·ig·na·tion *n* **1 :** an act of giving something up formally or officially **2 :** a letter or written statement that gives notice of giving something up **3 :** the feeling of a person who is prepared to accept something unpleasant
re·signed *adj* **:** showing acceptance of something unpleasant
res·in *n* **1 :** a yellowish or brownish substance obtained from the gum or sap of

some trees (as the pine) and used in varnishes and medicine **2 :** any of various manufactured products that are similar to natural resins in properties and are used especially as plastics

re·sist *vb* **re·sist·ed; re·sist·ing** **1 :** to fight against : OPPOSE **2 :** to avoid doing or having something **3 :** to withstand the force or effect of

re·sis·tance *n* **1 :** an act or instance of opposing **2 :** the ability to withstand the force or effect of **3 :** an opposing or slowing force **4 :** the opposition offered by a substance to the passage through it of an electric current

re·sis·tant *adj* **:** capable of withstanding the force or effect of

res·o·lute *adj* **:** firmly determined — **res·o·lute·ly** *adv*

res·o·lu·tion *n* **1 :** something decided on **2 :** firmness of purpose : DETERMINATION **3 :** the act of solving **4 :** the solution to a problem **5 :** a statement of the feelings, wishes, or decisions of a group

[1]**re·solve** *vb* **re·solved; re·solv·ing** **1 :** to find an answer to : SOLVE **2 :** to reach a firm decision about something **3 :** to decide by a formal resolution and vote

[2]**resolve** *n* **:** firmness of purpose : DETERMINATION

res·o·nance *n* **:** a long loud, clear, and deep quality of sound

res·o·nant *adj* **:** making a long loud, clear, and deep sound — **res·o·nant·ly** *adv*

[1]**re·sort** *n* **1 :** someone or something that is looked to for help **2 :** a place where people go on vacation

[2]**resort** *vb* **re·sort·ed; re·sort·ing** **:** to seek aid, relief, or advantage

re·sound *vb* **re·sound·ed; re·sound·ing** **1 :** to become filled with sound : REVERBERATE **2 :** to sound loudly

re·sound·ing *adj* **1 :** producing resonant sound **2 :** leaving no doubt

re·source *n* **1 resources** *pl* **:** a usable stock or supply (as of money or products) **2 :** NATURAL RESOURCE **3 :** the ability to meet and deal with situations

re·source·ful *adj* **:** clever in dealing with problems — **re·source·ful·ness** *n*

[1]**re·spect** *n* **1 :** high or special regard : ESTEEM **2 :** thoughtfulness or consideration **3 respects** *pl* **:** an expression of regard or courtesy **4 :** [1]DETAIL 2 **5 :** relation to or concern with something specified

[2]**respect** *vb* **re·spect·ed; re·spect·ing** **1 :** to consider worthy of high regard : ESTEEM **2 :** to pay attention to

re·spect·able *adj* **1 :** decent or correct in conduct : PROPER **2 :** fit to be seen : PRESENTABLE **3 :** deserving high regard **4 :** fair in size or quantity — **re·spect·ably** *adv*

re·spect·ful *adj* **:** showing high regard or courtesy — **re·spect·ful·ly** *adv*

re·spect·ing *prep* **:** CONCERNING

re·spec·tive *adj* **:** not the same or shared : SEPARATE — **re·spec·tive·ly** *adv*

res·pi·ra·tion *n* **1 :** the act or process of breathing : the inhaling of oxygen and the exhaling of carbon dioxide **2 :** the process by which cells use oxygen to break down sugar and obtain energy

res·pi·ra·tor *n* **1 :** a device covering the mouth or nose especially to prevent the breathing in of harmful substances (as dust or fumes) **2 :** a device used for helping a person to breathe

res·pi·ra·to·ry *adj* **:** of, relating to, or concerned with breathing or the parts of the body involved in breathing

respiratory system *n* **:** a system of the body used in breathing that in human beings consists of the nose, nasal passages, pharynx, larynx, trachea, bronchial tubes, and lungs

re·spire *vb* **re·spired; re·spir·ing** **:** BREATHE 1

res·pite *n* **1 :** a short delay **2 :** a period of rest or relief

re·splen·dent *adj* **:** shining brightly : SPLENDID — **re·splen·dent·ly** *adv*

re·spond *vb* **re·spond·ed; re·spond·ing** **1 :** to say something in return **2 :** to react in a way that shows some action was successful

re·sponse *n* **1 :** an act or instance of replying : ANSWER **2 :** words said or sung by the people or choir in a religious service **3 :** a reaction of a living being (as to a drug)

re·spon·si·bil·i·ty *n, pl* **re·spon·si·bil·i·ties** **1 :** the quality or state of being in charge of someone or something **2 :** the quality of being dependable **3 :** something or someone for which someone has charge

re·spon·si·ble *adj* **1 :** getting the credit or blame for acts or decisions **2 :** RELIABLE **3 :** needing a dependable person — **re·spon·si·bly** *adv*

re·spon·sive *adj* **1 :** showing interest **2 :** quick to respond in a sympathetic way — **re·spon·sive·ly** *adv* — **re·spon·sive·ness** *n*

[1]**rest** *vb* **rest·ed; rest·ing** **1 :** to relax, sleep, or refrain from taking part in work or an activity **2 :** to refrain from using for a short time **3 :** to sit or lie fixed or supported **4 :** DEPEND 2 **5 :** to lie dead **6 :** to fix or be fixed in trust or confidence

[2]**rest** *n* **:** something that is left over : REMAINDER

[3]**rest** *n* **1 :** a state of inactivity during which the body and mind become refreshed **2 :** freedom from activity or work **3 :** a state of not moving or not doing anything **4 :** a

place for stopping or refraining from activity **5 :** a silence in music **6 :** a symbol in music that stands for a certain period of silence in a measure **7 :** something used for support

res·tau·rant *n* **:** a public eating place

rest·ful *adj* **:** giving a feeling of peace or relaxation **:** QUIET

res·tive *adj* **:** showing impatience, nervousness, or discomfort

rest·less *adj* **1 :** not relaxed or calm **2 :** having or giving no rest — **rest·less·ly** *adv* — **rest·less·ness** *n*

res·to·ra·tion *n* **1 :** an act of returning something to its original condition **:** the result of having been returned to the original condition **2 :** something (as a building) that has been returned to its original condition

re·store *vb* **re·stored; re·stor·ing 1 :** to put or bring back to an earlier or original state **2 :** to put back into use or service **3 :** to give back

re·strain *vb* **re·strained; re·strain·ing 1 :** to keep from doing something **2 :** to keep back **:** CURB

re·straint *n* **1 :** the act of stopping or holding back **:** the state of being stopped or held back **2 :** a force or influence that stops or holds back **3 :** control over thoughts or feelings

re·strict *vb* **re·strict·ed; re·strict·ing :** to keep within bounds **:** set limits to

re·stric·tion *n* **1 :** something (as a law or rule) that limits **2 :** an act of limiting **:** the condition of being limited

re·stric·tive *adj* **:** serving or likely to keep within bounds

rest·room *n* **:** a room with a toilet and sink

[1]**re·sult** *vb* **re·sult·ed; re·sult·ing 1 :** to come about as an effect **2 :** to end as an effect

[2]**result** *n* **1 :** something that comes about as an effect or end **2 :** a good effect

re·sume *vb* **re·sumed; re·sum·ing 1 :** to begin again **2 :** to take or occupy again

re·sump·tion *n* **:** the act of starting again

res·ur·rect *vb* **res·ur·rect·ed; res·ur·rect·ing 1 :** to bring back to life **2 :** to bring to view or into use again

res·ur·rec·tion *n* **1 :** an instance of coming back into use or importance **2** *cap* **:** the rising of Jesus Christ from the dead **3** *often cap* **:** the act of rising again to life of all human dead before the final judgment

re·sus·ci·tate *vb* **re·sus·ci·tat·ed; re·sus·ci·tat·ing :** to bring back from apparent death or unconsciousness

re·sus·ci·ta·tion *n* **:** the act of bringing back from apparent death or unconsciousness

[1]**re·tail** *vb* **re·tailed; re·tail·ing :** to sell in small amounts to people for their own use — **re·tail·er** *n*

[2]**retail** *n* **:** the sale of products or goods in small amounts to people for their own use

[3]**retail** *adj* **:** relating to or engaged in selling products in small amounts to people for their own use

re·tain *vb* **re·tained; re·tain·ing 1 :** to keep or continue to use **2 :** to hold safe or unchanged

re·tal·i·ate *vb* **re·tal·i·at·ed; re·tal·i·at·ing :** to get revenge by returning like for like

re·tal·i·a·tion *n* **:** the act or an instance of getting revenge

re·tard *vb* **re·tard·ed; re·tard·ing :** to slow down **:** DELAY

retch *vb* **retched; retch·ing :** to vomit or try to vomit

re·ten·tion *n* **1 :** the act of continuing to possess, control, or hold **2 :** the power or ability to keep or hold something

ret·i·na *n, pl* **retinas** *also* **ret·i·nae :** the membrane that lines the back part of the eyeball, contains the rods and cones, and converts the images received by the lens into signals that are transmitted to the brain

re·tire *vb* **re·tired; re·tir·ing 1 :** to give up a job permanently **:** quit working **2 :** to go away especially to be alone **3 :** to go to bed **4 :** to withdraw from use or service **5 :** to get away from action or danger **:** RETREAT — **re·tire·ment** *n*

re·tired *adj* **:** not working at active duties or business

re·tir·ing *adj* **:** [1]SHY 2, RESERVED

[1]**re·tort** *vb* **re·tort·ed; re·tort·ing 1 :** to reply usually angrily or sharply **2 :** to reply with an argument against

[2]**retort** *n* **:** a quick, clever, or angry reply

re·trace *vb* **re·traced; re·trac·ing :** to go over once more

re·tract *vb* **re·tract·ed; re·tract·ing 1 :** to pull back or in **2 :** to take back (as an offer or statement) **:** WITHDRAW

[1]**re·treat** *n* **1 :** an act of going back or away especially from something dangerous, difficult, or disagreeable **2 :** a military signal for turning away from the enemy **3 :** a place of privacy or safety **4 :** a period of time in which a person goes away to pray, think quietly, or study

[2]**retreat** *vb* **re·treat·ed; re·treat·ing 1 :** to move back or away especially from something dangerous, difficult, or disagreeable **2 :** to go to a place of privacy or safety

ret·ri·bu·tion *n* **:** PUNISHMENT 1

re·trieve *vb* **re·trieved; re·triev·ing 1 :** to get and bring back **2 :** to find and bring back killed or wounded game

re·triev·er *n* **:** a dog that has a water-resistant coat and is skilled in retrieving game

ret·ro·spect *n* : a looking back on things past

1re·turn *vb* **re·turned; re·turn·ing 1 :** to come or go back again **2 :** to bring, give, send, or put back **3 :** REPAY 1 **4 :** to respond in the same way **5 :** to make an official report of **6 :** 1YIELD 4, PRODUCE

2return *n* **1 :** the act of coming or going back to a place or condition **2 :** RECURRENCE **3 :** the act of returning something (as to a former condition or owner) **4 :** something given in payment or exchange **5 :** a report of the results of voting **6 :** a statement of income to be taxed **7 :** the profit from labor, investment, or business

3return *adj* **1 :** happening or done for the second time **2 :** used for returning

re·tweet *vb* **re·tweet·ed; re·tweet·ing :** to post (as a message) again to the Twitter online message service — **retweet** *n*

re·union *n* **1 :** an act of coming or bringing together again after being apart **2 :** an organized gathering of people who have not been together for some time

re·unite *vb* **re·unit·ed; re·unit·ing :** to come or bring together again after being apart

re·use *vb* **re·used; re·us·ing :** to use again

rev *vb* **revved; rev·ving :** to increase the number of revolutions per minute of (a motor)

Rev. *abbr* reverend

re·veal *vb* **re·vealed; re·veals 1 :** to make known **2 :** to show clearly

rev·eil·le *n* : a signal sounded at about sunrise on a bugle to call soldiers or sailors to duty

1rev·el *vb* **rev·eled** *or* **rev·elled; rev·el·ing** *or* **rev·el·ling :** to take great pleasure

2revel *n* : a noisy or merry celebration

rev·e·la·tion *n* : a secret or surprising fact that is made known

rev·el·ry *n, pl* **rev·el·ries :** wild and noisy celebration

1re·venge *vb* **re·venged; re·veng·ing :** to cause harm or injury in return for

2revenge *n* **1 :** an act or instance of causing harm or injury in return for a wrong **2 :** a desire to cause harm or injury in return for a wrong **3 :** a chance for getting satisfaction

rev·e·nue *n* **1 :** money that is made by or paid to a business or organization **2 :** money collected by a government (as through taxes)

re·ver·ber·ate *vb* **re·ver·ber·at·ed; re·ver·ber·at·ing :** to continue in or as if in a series of echoes

re·vere *vb* **re·vered; re·ver·ing :** to have great respect for

rev·er·ence *n* : honor and respect often mixed with love and awe

rev·er·end *adj* **1 :** worthy of honor and respect **2** — used as a title for a member of the clergy

rev·er·ent *adj* : very respectful — **rev·er·ent·ly** *adv*

rev·er·ie *n, pl* **rev·er·ies :** the state of being lost in thought especially about pleasant things

re·ver·sal *n* : a change to an opposite or former state, condition, view, or direction

1re·verse *adj* **1 :** opposite to a previous, normal, or usual condition **2 :** opposite to the front

2reverse *vb* **re·versed; re·vers·ing 1 :** to turn completely around or upside down or inside out **2 :** to change the order or position of **3 :** to change or cause to change to an opposite or former state, condition, or view **4 :** to go or cause to go in the opposite direction

3reverse *n* **1 :** something opposite to something else : CONTRARY **2 :** an act or instance of changing to an opposite or former state, condition, view, or direction **3 :** the back part of something **4 :** a gear that reverses something

re·vert *vb* **re·vert·ed; re·vert·ing :** to come or go back

1re·view *n* **1 :** a look at or examination of **2 :** a piece of writing about the quality of something (as a book, performance, or product) **3 :** a fresh study of material studied before **4 :** a formal inspection of troops by officers of high rank or an important person

2review *vb* **re·viewed; re·view·ing 1 :** to look at or study again **2 :** to look at or examine carefully **3 :** to report on or evaluate the quality of **4 :** to make an official inspection of (as troops) — **re·view·er** *n*

re·vile *vb* **re·viled; re·vil·ing :** to speak to or about in an insulting way

re·vise *vb* **re·vised; re·vis·ing :** to make changes that correct or improve

re·viv·al *n* **1 :** a return of interest in **2 :** a new production of an older play or movie **3 :** a return of strength or importance **4 :** a meeting or series of meetings led by a preacher to stir up religious feelings or to make converts

re·vive *vb* **re·vived; re·viv·ing 1 :** to bring back or come back to life, consciousness, freshness, or activity **2 :** to bring back into use or popularity

re·voke *vb* **re·voked; re·vok·ing :** to take away or cancel

1re·volt *vb* **re·volt·ed; re·volt·ing 1 :** to rebel against a ruler or government **2 :** to be or cause to be disgusted or shocked

2revolt *n* : violent action against a ruler or government : REBELLION

rev·o·lu·tion *n* **1 :** the action by a celestial body of going round in a fixed course **2 :** a spinning motion around a center or axis : ROTATION **3 :** a single complete turn

DICTIONARY

(as of a wheel) **4 :** a sudden, extreme, or complete change (as in manner of living or working) **5 :** the overthrow of a ruler or government by violent action

rev·o·lu·tion·ary *adj* **1 :** relating to or involving rebellion against a ruler or government **2 :** being or bringing about a big or important change **3** *cap* **:** of or relating to the American Revolution

rev·o·lu·tion·ize *vb* **rev·o·lu·tion·ized; rev·o·lu·tion·iz·ing :** to change greatly or completely

re·volve *vb* **re·volved; re·volv·ing 1 :** to move in an orbit **2 :** ROTATE 1

re·volv·er *n* **:** a pistol having a revolving cylinder holding several bullets all of which may be shot without loading again

re·vue *n* **:** a show in a theater consisting usually of short and often funny sketches and songs

re·vul·sion *n* **:** a strong feeling of dislike or disgust

[1]**re·ward** *vb* **re·ward·ed; re·ward·ing 1 :** to give something (as money) to in return for a service or accomplishment **2 :** to give something in return for

[2]**reward** *n* **:** something (as money) given or offered in return for a service or accomplishment

re·wind *vb* **re·wound; re·wind·ing :** to reverse the winding or direction of play of

re·word *vb* **re·word·ed; re·word·ing :** to state in different words

re·write *vb* **re·wrote; re·writ·ten; re·writ·ing :** to write again especially in a different way

rhea *n* **:** a tall flightless South American bird that resembles but is smaller than the ostrich

rheu·mat·ic fever *n* **:** a serious disease especially of children that causes fever, pain and swelling of joints, and sometimes heart damage

rheu·ma·tism *n* **:** a condition in which muscles or joints are painful

rhine·stone *n* **:** a small imitation gem used in jewelry or for decoration

rhi·no *n, pl* **rhino** *or* **rhi·nos :** RHINOCEROS

rhi·noc·er·os *n, pl* **rhi·noc·er·os·es** *also* **rhinoceros :** a large plant-eating mammal of Africa and Asia with short legs, thick gray to brown skin with little hair, and one or two heavy upright horns on the snout

rho·do·den·dron *n* **:** a shrub with leathery evergreen leaves and showy clusters of flowers

rhom·bus *n* **:** a parallelogram whose sides are equal in length

rhu·barb *n* **:** the thick juicy pink or red stems of a garden plant that have a tart flavor and are used cooked especially in jams and desserts

[1]**rhyme** *n* **1 :** close similarity in the final sounds of two or more words or lines of writing **2 :** a piece of writing (as a poem) whose lines end in similar sounds

[2]**rhyme** *vb* **rhymed; rhym·ing 1 :** to end with the same sound **2 :** to have lines that end with the same sound **3 :** to cause lines or words to end with a similar sound

rhythm *n* **:** a regular repeated pattern of beats, sounds, activity, or movements

rhyth·mic *or* **rhyth·mi·cal** *adj* **:** having a regular repeated pattern of beats, sounds, activity, or movements — **rhyth·mi·cal·ly** *adv*

RI *abbr* Rhode Island

rib *n* **1 :** one of the curved bones of the chest that are joined to the backbone and help to stiffen the body wall and protect the organs **2 :** a piece of meat from an animal (as a cow or pig) that includes a rib and is used as food **3 :** something (as a piece of wire supporting the fabric of an umbrella) that is like a rib in shape or use **4 :** one of the parallel ridges in a knitted or woven fabric — **ribbed** *adj*

rib·bon *n* **1 :** a narrow strip of usually colorful fabric used especially for decoration or to tie things **2 :** a ribbon that is given as an award **3 :** TATTER 1, SHRED — usually used in pl.

rib cage *n* **:** the bony enclosing wall of the chest consisting of the ribs and their connecting parts

rice *n* **:** the small seeds of a tall cereal grass widely grown in warm wet regions that are the chief food in many parts of the world

rich *adj* **1 :** having a lot of money and possessions **:** WEALTHY **2 :** [1]VALUABLE 1, EXPENSIVE **3 :** well supplied **:** ABUNDANT **4 :** FERTILE 1 **5 :** containing much sugar, fat, or seasoning **6 :** deep and pleasing in color or tone — **rich·ly** *adv* — **rich·ness** *n*

rich·es *n pl* **:** things that make someone rich

rick·ets *n* **:** a disease especially of children in which the bones are soft and deformed and which is caused by lack of vitamin D

rick·ety *adj* **:** in poor condition and likely to break

rick·shaw *also* **rick·sha** *n* **:** a small carriage with two wheels that is pulled by one person and was used originally in Japan

ric·o·chet *vb* **ric·o·cheted; ric·o·chet·ing :** to bounce off at an angle

rid *vb* **rid** *also* **rid·ded; rid·ding :** to free from something **:** RELIEVE

[1]**rid·dle** *n* **1 :** a puzzling question to be solved or answered by guessing **2 :** someone or something that is hard to understand

[2]**riddle** *vb* **rid·dled; rid·dling 1 :** to pierce with many holes **2 :** to fill with something unpleasant or unwanted

[1]**ride** *vb* **rode; rid·den; rid·ing 1 :** to travel or move by sitting or standing on or in **2 :** to sit on and control so as to be carried

along **3 :** to be supported or carried on **4** : to travel over a surface **5 :** to endure without great harm or damage **6 :** DEPEND 2 — **rid·er** *n*

²ride *n* **1 :** a trip on horseback or by vehicle **2 :** a mechanical device (as a merry-go-round) that moves around while people sit or stand on it for entertainment **3 :** a way of getting from one place to another

ridge *n* **1 :** a range of hills or mountains or its upper part **2 :** a raised strip **3 :** the line made where two sloping surfaces come together — **ridged** *adj*

¹rid·i·cule *n* **:** the act of making fun of someone or something in a cruel or harsh way : mean or unkind comments or behavior

²ridicule *vb* **rid·i·culed; rid·i·cul·ing :** to make fun of in a cruel or harsh way

ri·dic·u·lous *adj* **:** causing or deserving ridicule : very silly or unreasonable — **ri·dic·u·lous·ly** *adv*

¹rif·fle *vb* **rif·fled; rif·fling 1 :** to move lightly **2 :** to look through quickly

²riffle *n* **1 :** a shallow area of a stream bed that causes ripples **2 :** ²RIPPLE 1

riff·raff *n* **:** a group of people who are not considered respectable or honest

¹ri·fle *vb* **ri·fled; ri·fling 1 :** to search through quickly and roughly often to steal something **2 :** ¹STEAL 1

²rifle *n* **:** a gun that has a long barrel with spiral grooves on its inside

rift *n* **1 :** an opening made by splitting or separation **2 :** a break in friendly relations

¹rig *vb* **rigged; rig·ging 1 :** to build or set up usually quickly and for temporary use **2 :** to provide (as a ship) with rigging **3** : CLOTHE 1, DRESS **4 :** to provide with gear

²rig *n* **1 :** the shape, number, and arrangement of sails and masts of a ship that sets it apart from other types of ships **2 :** equipment or machinery for a certain purpose

rig·ging *n* **:** lines and chains used on a ship to help support the masts and sails

¹right *adj* **1 :** following or in accordance with what is just, good, or proper **2 :** ACCURATE, CORRECT **3 :** SUITABLE, APPROPRIATE **4 :** located on the side of the body away from the heart **5 :** located nearer to the right side of the body than to the left **6** : being or meant to be the side on top, in front, or on the outside **7 :** in a normal or healthy state or condition **8 :** ¹STRAIGHT 1 — **right·ly** *adv* — **right·ness** *n*

²right *n* **1 :** the ideal of what is just, good, or proper **2 :** something to which a person has a just claim **3 :** the cause of truth or justice **4 :** the right side : a part or location that is on or toward the right side

³right *adv* **1 :** according to what is just, good, or proper **2 :** in the exact location, position, or moment : PRECISELY **3 :** in a direct line or course : STRAIGHT **4 :** according to truth or fact **5 :** in a suitable, proper, or desired way **6 :** all the way **7 :** without delay : IMMEDIATELY **8 :** on or to the right **9** : in a complete way — **right away :** without delay : IMMEDIATELY

⁴right *vb* **right·ed; right·ing 1 :** to make better or more just **2 :** to adjust or restore to a proper state or condition **3 :** to bring or bring back to an upright position **4 :** to become upright

right angle *n* **:** an angle formed by two lines that are perpendicular to each other : an angle of 90 degrees

righ·teous *adj* **1 :** doing or being what is just or proper **2 :** caused by an insult to what is believed to be just or proper — **righ·teous·ly** *adv* — **righ·teous·ness** *n*

right·ful *adj* **:** LAWFUL 2, PROPER — **right·ful·ly** *adv*

right–hand *adj* **1 :** located on the right side **2 :** RIGHT-HANDED 1 **3 :** relied on most of all

right–hand·ed *adj* **1 :** using the right hand better or more easily than the left **2 :** done or made with or for the right hand

right–of–way *n, pl* **rights–of–way 1 :** the legal right to pass over someone else's land **2 :** the right of some traffic to go before other traffic

right triangle *n* **:** a triangle having a right angle

righty *n, pl* **right·ies :** a right-handed person

rig·id *adj* **1 :** not flexible : STIFF **2 :** STRICT 2, SEVERE — **rig·id·ly** *adv*

rig·ma·role *n* **1 :** a long and usually meaningless or uninteresting story **2 :** a complicated and often unnecessary procedure

rig·or *or Can and Brit* **rigour** *n* **:** a harsh condition (as of discipline)

rig·or·ous *adj* **1 :** very strict **2 :** hard to endure because of extreme conditions : HARSH — **rig·or·ous·ly** *adv*

rile *vb* **riled; ril·ing :** to make angry

rill *n* **:** a very small stream

¹rim *n* **1 :** an outer edge especially of something curved **2 :** the part of a wheel that the tire is mounted on — **rimmed** *adj*

²rim *vb* **rimmed; rim·ming :** to form a rim around

rime *n* **:** ¹FROST 1

rind *n* **:** a tough outer layer

¹ring *n* **1 :** a circular band used for holding, fastening, or connecting **2 :** a circular band usually of precious metal worn especially on the finger as jewelry **3 :** something circular in shape **4 :** an often circular space for shows or contests **5 :** a group of people who work together for dishonest purposes **6 :** ANNUAL RING — **ringed** *adj*

[2]**ring** *vb* **ringed; ring·ing :** to place or form a ring around

[3]**ring** *vb* **rang; rung; ring·ing 1 :** to make or cause to make a clear vibrating sound **2 :** to announce by or as if by striking a bell **3 :** to sound loudly **4 :** to fill or be filled with the sound of something **5 :** to be filled with a humming sound **6 :** to seem to be a certain way **7 :** to call for especially by ringing a bell

[4]**ring** *n* **1 :** a clear sound made by or as if by vibrating metal **2 :** a continuous or repeating loud sound **3 :** something that suggests a certain quality **4 :** a telephone call

ring finger *n* **:** the third finger especially of the left hand when counting the index finger as the first

ring·lead·er *n* **:** a leader especially of a group of people who cause trouble

ring·let *n* **:** a long curl of hair

ring·tone *n* **:** a sound made by a cell phone to signal that a call is coming in

ring·worm *n* **:** a fungus infection that causes red ring-shaped patches to appear on the skin

rink *n* **:** a place for ice-skating or roller-skating

[1]**rinse** *vb* **rinsed; rins·ing 1 :** to wash lightly with water **2 :** to remove (something) with clean water

[2]**rinse** *n* **1 :** an act of washing with a liquid and especially with clean water **2 :** a liquid used for rinsing

[1]**ri·ot** *n* **1 :** violent and uncontrolled public behavior by a group of people **2 :** a colorful display **3 :** someone or something that is very funny

[2]**riot** *vb* **ri·ot·ed; ri·ot·ing :** to take part in violent and uncontrolled public behavior

[1]**rip** *vb* **ripped; rip·ping 1 :** to cut or tear open **:** split apart **2 :** to remove quickly (as by tearing) — **rip·per** *n*

[2]**rip** *n* **:** a usually long tear

ripe *adj* **rip·er; rip·est 1 :** fully grown and developed **2 :** of advanced years **3 :** [1]READY 1 — **ripe·ness** *n*

rip·en *vb* **rip·ened; rip·en·ing :** to make or become ripe

[1]**rip·ple** *vb* **rip·pled; rip·pling 1 :** to move or cause to move in small waves **2 :** to pass or spread over or through

[2]**ripple** *n* **1 :** a very small wave on the surface of a liquid **2 :** something that passes or spreads through

[1]**rise** *vb* **rose; ris·en; ris·ing 1 :** to get up from lying, kneeling, or sitting **2 :** to get up from sleeping in a bed **3 :** to go or move up **4 :** to swell in size or volume **5 :** to increase in amount or number **6 :** to become encouraged or grow stronger **7 :** to appear above the horizon **8 :** to gain a higher rank or position **9 :** to come into being **10 :** to successfully deal with a difficult situation **11 :** to return from death **12 :** to launch an attack or revolt — **ris·er** *n*

[2]**rise** *n* **1 :** an increase in amount, number, or volume **2 :** upward movement **3 :** the act of gaining a higher rank or position **4 :** BEGINNING 1, ORIGIN **5 :** an upward slope **6 :** a spot higher than surrounding ground **7 :** an angry reaction

[1]**risk** *n* **1 :** possibility of loss or injury **2 :** something or someone that may cause loss or injury

[2]**risk** *vb* **risked; risk·ing 1 :** to expose to danger **2 :** to take the risk or danger of

risky *adj* **risk·i·er; risk·i·est :** DANGEROUS 1

rite *n* **:** an act performed in a ceremony

rit·u·al *n* **:** a ceremony or series of acts that is always performed the same way

[1]**ri·val** *n* **:** someone or something that tries to defeat or be more successful than another

[2]**rival** *adj* **:** being equally good

[3]**rival** *vb* **ri·valed** *or* **ri·valled; ri·val·ing** *or* **ri·val·ling :** to be as good as or almost as good as

ri·val·ry *n, pl* **ri·val·ries :** the state of trying to defeat or be more successful than another **:** COMPETITION

riv·er *n* **1 :** a natural stream of water larger than a brook or creek **2 :** a large stream or flow

[1]**riv·et** *n* **:** a bolt with a head that is passed through two or more pieces and is hammered into place

[2]**rivet** *vb* **riv·et·ed; riv·et·ing 1 :** to fasten with rivets **2 :** to attract and hold (as someone's attention) completely **3 :** to make (someone) unable to move because of fear or shock

riv·u·let *n* **:** a small stream

RCMP *abbr* Royal Canadian Mounted Police

roach *n* **:** COCKROACH

road *n* **1 :** a hard flat surface for vehicles, persons, and animals to travel on **2 :** a way to achieve something

road·run·ner *n* **:** a long-tailed bird that is found in dry regions of the southwestern United States and is able to run very fast

road·side *n* **:** the strip of land beside a road

road·way *n* **:** the part of a road used by vehicles

roam *vb* **roamed; roam·ing :** to go from place to place with no fixed purpose or direction

[1]**roan** *adj* **:** of a dark color (as black or brown) mixed with white

[2]**roan** *n* **:** an animal (as a horse) with a dark-colored coat mixed with white

[1]**roar** *vb* **roared; roar·ing** **1 :** to make a long loud sound **2 :** to laugh loudly **3 :** to say loudly **4 :** to move with a loud noise
[2]**roar** *n* **:** a long shout, bellow, or loud noise
roar·ing *adj* **:** very active or strong
[1]**roast** *vb* **roast·ed; roast·ing** **1 :** to cook with dry heat (as in an oven) **2 :** to be or make very hot — **roast·er** *n*
[2]**roast** *adj* **:** cooked with dry heat
[3]**roast** *n* **1 :** a piece of meat suitable for cooking with dry heat **2 :** an outdoor party at which food is cooked over an open fire
rob *vb* **robbed; rob·bing** **1 :** to unlawfully take something away from a person or place in secrecy or by force, threat, or trickery **2 :** to keep from getting something due, expected, or desired — **rob·ber** *n*
rob·bery *n, pl* **rob·ber·ies :** the act or practice of taking something unlawfully
[1]**robe** *n* **1 :** a long loose or flowing garment **2 :** a loose garment worn especially after bathing or while relaxing at home
[2]**robe** *vb* **robed; rob·ing :** to dress especially in a robe
rob·in *n* **1 :** a large North American songbird with a grayish back and dull reddish breast **2 :** a small European songbird with an orange throat and breast
ro·bot *n* **1 :** a machine that looks and acts like a human being **2 :** a machine that can do the work of a person automatically or under the control of a computer
ro·bust *adj* **:** strong and healthy — **ro·bust·ly** *adv*
[1]**rock** *vb* **rocked; rock·ing** **1 :** to move gently back and forth or side to side **2 :** to cause (something) to shake violently
[2]**rock** *n* **1 :** solid mineral deposits **2 :** a mass of stone
[3]**rock** *n* **1 :** a rocking movement **2 :** popular music played on instruments that are amplified electronically
rock and roll *or* **rock 'n' roll** *n* **:** [3]ROCK 2
rock dove *n* **1 :** a bluish gray dove of Europe and Asia that nests on rocky cliffs **2 :** a variety of the rock dove that is now found in cities throughout the world
rock·er *n* **1 :** ROCKING CHAIR **2 :** a curving piece of wood or metal on which an object (as a cradle or rocking chair) rocks
[1]**rock·et** *n* **1 :** a firework that is driven through the air by the gases produced by a burning substance **2 :** a jet engine that is driven by gases produced by a burning substance **3 :** a bomb, missile, or vehicle that is driven by gases produced by a burning substance
[2]**rocket** *vb* **rock·et·ed; rock·et·ing** **1 :** to rise swiftly **2 :** to travel rapidly in or as if in a rocket
rock·ing chair *n* **:** a chair mounted on rockers
rocking horse *n* **:** a toy horse mounted on rockers
rock salt *n* **:** common salt in large crystals
rocky *adj* **rock·i·er; rock·i·est :** full of or consisting of rocks
rod *n* **1 :** a light flexible pole often with line and a reel attached used in fishing **2 :** a stick or bundle of twigs used in whipping a person **3 :** a straight slender stick or bar **4 :** a measure of length equal to $16^1/_2$ feet (about 5 meters) **5 :** a cell of the retina of the eye that is shaped like a rod and is sensitive to faint light
rode *past of* RIDE
ro·dent *n* **:** a usually small mammal (as a squirrel, rat, mouse, or beaver) with sharp front teeth used in gnawing
ro·deo *n, pl* **ro·de·os :** an exhibition that features cowboy skills (as riding and roping)
roe *n* **:** the eggs of a fish especially while still held together in a membrane
rogue *n* **1 :** a dishonest or evil person **2 :** a pleasantly mischievous person
rogu·ish *adj* **:** showing mischievousness — **rogu·ish·ly** *adv*
role *n* **1 :** a character assigned or taken on **2 :** a part played by an actor or singer **3 :** [1]FUNCTION 1
role model *n* **:** a person whose behavior in a certain function is imitated by others
[1]**roll** *vb* **rolled; roll·ing** **1 :** to move or cause to move by turning over and over on a surface **2 :** to shape or become shaped in rounded form **3 :** to sound with a full echoing tone or with a continuous beating sound **4 :** to flow in or as if in a continuous stream **5 :** to move or cause to move in a circular manner **6 :** to go by **:** PASS **7 :** to move with a side-to-side sway **8 :** to make smooth, even, or firm with a roller **9 :** to move on rollers or wheels — **roll around :** to happen again
[2]**roll** *n* **1 :** something or a quantity of something that is rolled up or rounded as if rolled **2 :** a small piece of baked bread dough **3 :** a writing that may be rolled up **:** SCROLL **4 :** an official list of names
[3]**roll** *n* **1 :** a sound produced by rapid strokes on a drum **2 :** a heavy echoing sound **3 :** a movement or action that involves turning over and over or circling around
roll·er *n* **1 :** a turning cylinder over or on which something is moved or which is used to press, shape, or smooth something **2 :** a rod on which something (as a map or hair) is rolled up **3 :** a small wheel **4 :** a long heavy wave on the sea

roller coaster *n* **:** an amusement park ride that is an elevated railway with sharp curves and steep slopes over which cars travel
roller–skate *vb* **roller–skat·ed; roller–skat·ing :** to ride on roller skates
roller skate *n* **:** a skate that has wheels instead of a runner
rolling pin *n* **:** a cylinder (as of wood) used to roll out dough
ROM *n* **:** a usually small computer memory that contains special-purpose information (as a program) which cannot be changed
[1]**Ro·man** *n* **1 :** a person born or living in Rome **2 :** a citizen of an ancient empire centered on Rome **3** *not cap* **:** upright letters or type
[2]**Roman** *adj* **1 :** of or relating to Rome or the Romans **2** *not cap* **:** of or relating to a type style with upright characters (as in "these letters")
Roman Catholic *adj* **:** belonging to or relating to the Christian church led by the pope
ro·mance *n* **1 :** an attraction or appeal to the emotions **2 :** a love story **3 :** a love affair **4 :** an old tale of knights and noble ladies **5 :** an adventure story
Ro·mance *adj* **:** relating to or being the languages (as French, Italian, and Spanish) that are descended from Latin
Roman numeral *n* **:** a numeral in a system of figures based on the ancient Roman system
ro·man·tic *adj* **1 :** stressing or appealing to the emotions or imagination **2 :** involving or showing feelings of love **3 :** not realistic **:** IMPRACTICAL **4 :** suitable for a love story — **ro·man·ti·cal·ly** *adv*
[1]**romp** *vb* **romped; romp·ing :** to play in a rough and noisy way
[2]**romp** *n* **:** rough and noisy play **:** FROLIC
romp·er *n* **:** a young child's one-piece garment having legs that can be unfastened around the inside — usually used in pl.
[1]**roof** *n, pl* **roofs 1 :** the upper covering part of a building **2 :** something like a roof in form, position, or purpose — **roofed** *adj*
[2]**roof** *vb* **roofed; roof·ing :** to cover with a roof
roof·ing *n* **:** material for a roof
[1]**rook** *n* **:** a crow of Europe and Asia that nests and sleeps in groups usually in the tops of trees
[2]**rook** *vb* **rooked; rook·ing :** [1]CHEAT 2, SWINDLE
[3]**rook** *n* **:** one of the pieces in the game of chess
rook·ie *n* **:** BEGINNER, RECRUIT
[1]**room** *n* **1 :** a divided part of the inside of a building **2 :** a bedroom in a home or hotel **3 :** the people in a room **4 :** available space **5 :** a suitable opportunity
[2]**room** *vb* **roomed; room·ing :** to provide with or live in lodgings
room·er *n* **:** LODGER
rooming house *n* **:** a house having furnished rooms for rent to lodgers
room·mate *n* **:** one of two or more people sharing a room or dwelling
roomy *adj* **room·i·er; room·i·est :** SPACIOUS — **room·i·ness** *n*
[1]**roost** *n* **:** a place where birds rest or sleep
[2]**roost** *vb* **roost·ed; roost·ing :** to settle down for rest or sleep
roost·er *n* **:** an adult male chicken
[1]**root** *n* **1 :** the leafless underground part of a plant that absorbs water and minerals, stores food, and holds the plant in place **2 :** the part of something by which it is attached **3 :** SOURCE 1 **4 :** the ancestors of a person or group of people **5 :** a special relationship **6 :** [1]CORE 3 **7 :** a word or part of a word from which other words are obtained by adding a prefix or suffix — **root·ed** *adj*
[2]**root** *vb* **root·ed; root·ing 1 :** to form or cause to form roots **2 :** to attach by or as if by roots — **root out :** to remove by or as if by pulling out the roots
[3]**root** *vb* **rooted; rooting :** to turn up or dig with or as if with the snout
[4]**root** *vb* **rooted; rooting :** to wish for the success of — **root·er** *n*
root beer *n* **:** a sweet drink flavored with extracts of roots and herbs
[1]**rope** *n* **1 :** a strong thick cord of strands (as of fiber or wire) twisted or braided together **2 :** a number of similar things held together on a string
[2]**rope** *vb* **roped; rop·ing 1 :** to bind, fasten, or tie with a cord **2 :** to set off or divide by a cord **3 :** [1]LASSO — **rop·er** *n*
ro·sa·ry *n, pl* **ro·sa·ries :** a string of beads used in counting prayers
[1]**rose** *past of* RISE
[2]**rose** *n* **1 :** a showy and usually fragrant white, yellow, pink, or red flower that grows on a prickly shrub **2 :** a medium pink
rose·mary *n* **:** a fragrant mint with needlelike leaves used as a seasoning in cooking
ro·sette *n* **:** a badge or ornament of ribbon gathered in the shape of a rose
rose·wood *n* **:** a reddish or purplish wood streaked with black that is used especially for making furniture and musical instruments
Rosh Ha·sha·nah *n* **:** the Jewish New Year observed as a religious holiday in September or October
ros·in *n* **:** a hard brittle yellow to dark red substance obtained especially from pine trees and used in varnishes and on violin bows
ros·ter *n* **:** an orderly list of people belonging to some group
ros·trum *n, pl* **ros·tra** *or* **rostrums :** a stage or platform for public speaking

rosy *adj* **ros·i·er; ros·i·est** **1 :** having a pink color **2 :** PROMISING, HOPEFUL
¹rot *vb* **rot·ted; rot·ting** **1 :** to undergo decay **2 :** to go to ruin
²rot *n* **1 :** the process of decaying **:** the state of being decayed **2 :** something that has decayed or is decaying
ro·ta·ry *adj* **1 :** turning on an axis like a wheel **2 :** having a rotating part
ro·tate *vb* **ro·tat·ed; ro·tat·ing** **1 :** to turn about an axis or a center **2 :** to go from one person to another or others in a cycle **3 :** to pass in a series
ro·ta·tion *n* **1 :** the act of turning about an axis **2 :** the system of growing different crops in the same field usually in a regular order
rote *n* **:** the act of repeating over and over often without attention to meaning
ro·tor *n* **1 :** the part of an electrical machine that turns **2 :** a system of spinning horizontal blades that support a helicopter in the air
rot·ten *adj* **1 :** having rotted **2 :** morally bad **3 :** of poor quality **4 :** very unpleasant
ro·tund *adj* **1 :** somewhat round **2 :** ¹PLUMP
rouge *n* **:** a cosmetic used to give a red color to cheeks or lips
¹rough *adj* **1 :** uneven in surface **2 :** having many bumps and jolts **3 :** not calm **4 :** being harsh or violent **5 :** difficult or unpleasant to deal with **6 :** coarse or rugged in nature or look **7 :** having a harsh sound **8 :** not complete or exact — **rough·ly** *adv* — **rough·ness** *n*
²rough *n* **1 :** uneven ground covered with high grass, brush, and stones **2 :** something in a crude or unfinished state
³rough *vb* **roughed; rough·ing** **1 :** to handle violently **:** BEAT **2 :** to make or shape coarsely or unevenly — **rough it :** to live without ordinary comforts
rough·age *n* **1 :** FIBER 2 **2 :** food (as bran) containing much indigestible material acting as fiber
rough·en *vb* **rough·ened; rough·en·ing :** to make or become rough
rough·neck *n* **:** a rough aggressive person
¹round *adj* **round·er; round·est** **1 :** having every part of the surface or circumference the same distance from the center **:** shaped like a circle or ball **2 :** shaped like a cylinder **3 :** ¹PLUMP **4 :** having curves rather than angles **5 :** ¹COMPLETE 1, FULL **6 :** nearly correct or exact **7 :** LARGE **8 :** moving in or forming a circle — **round·ish** *adj* — **round·ness** *n*
²round *adv* **:** ¹AROUND
³round *n* **1 :** a regularly covered route **2 :** something (as a circle or globe) that is round **3 :** one shot fired from a gun **4 :** a series or cycle of repeated actions or events **5 :** a song in which different singers sing the same melody and words one after another at intervals **6 :** a period of applause **7 :** an indirect path **8 :** ammunition for one shot **9 :** one of the parts into which a contest or game is divided **10 :** a cut of beef especially between the rump and the lower leg
⁴round *vb* **round·ed; round·ing** **1 :** to go or pass around **2 :** to express as a round number **3 :** to bring to completion **4 :** to make or become round — **round up** **1 :** to collect (as cattle) by circling in vehicles or on horseback and forcing them in **2 :** to gather in or bring together
⁵round *prep* **:** ²AROUND
round·about *adj* **:** not direct
round·house *n, pl* **round·hous·es :** a circular building where locomotives are kept or repaired
round trip *n* **:** a trip to a place and back usually over the same route
round·up *n* **1 :** the act of gathering together animals on the range by circling them in vehicles or on horseback and driving them in **2 :** the act of gathering together scattered persons or things **3 :** ²SUMMARY
round·worm *n* **:** a worm that has a round body with no segments and is sometimes a serious parasite of people and animals
rouse *vb* **roused; rous·ing** **1 :** ¹AWAKE 1 **2 :** to stir up **:** EXCITE
¹rout *vb* **rout·ed; rout·ing** **1 :** to cause to run away **2 :** to defeat completely
²rout *n* **1 :** an easy or lopsided defeat **2 :** wild confusion or disorderly retreat
¹route *n* **:** a regular, chosen, or assigned course of travel
²route *vb* **rout·ed; rout·ing :** to send or transport by a selected course
¹rou·tine *n* **1 :** a usual order and way of doing something **2 :** a series of things that are repeated as part of a performance
²routine *adj* **1 :** done very often **2 :** done or happening in a standard or usual way — **rou·tine·ly** *adv*
rove *vb* **roved; rov·ing :** to wander without definite plan or direction — **rov·er** *n*
¹row *vb* **rowed; row·ing** **1 :** to move a boat by using oars **2 :** to travel or carry in a rowboat
²row *n* **1 :** a series of persons or things lined up in an orderly arrangement **2 :** ¹WAY 1, STREET
³row *n* **:** noisy disturbance or quarrel
⁴row *n* **:** an act or instance of using oars to move a boat
row·boat *n* **:** a boat made to be moved by oars

[1]**row·dy** *adj* **row·di·er; row·di·est :** rough or noisy — **row·di·ness** *n*

[2]**rowdy** *n, pl* **rowdies :** a person who behaves coarsely or roughly

roy·al *adj* **1 :** of or relating to a king or queen : REGAL **2 :** fit for a king or queen — **roy·al·ly** *adv*

roy·al·ty *n, pl* **roy·al·ties 1 :** the status or power of a king or queen or his or her family **2 :** members of the royal family of a king or queen **3 :** a share of a product or profit (as of a mine) claimed by the owner for allowing another to use the property **4 :** payment made to the owner of a patent or copyright for the use of it

rpm *abbr* revolutions per minute

RR *abbr* railroad

RSS *n* **:** a computer document format that enables updates to websites to be easily distributed

R.S.V.P. *abbr* please reply — abbreviation for French *répondez s'il vous plaît,* which means "please reply"

rt. *abbr* right

rte. *abbr* route

[1]**rub** *vb* **rubbed; rub·bing 1 :** to move along the surface of something with pressure **2 :** to move back and forth against something in a way that causes pain or damage **3 :** to scour, polish, or smear by pressure and friction — **rub elbows with :** to meet and talk with in a friendly way — **rub in :** to keep reminding someone of (something unpleasant) — **rub off :** to come off a surface and often stick to another surface by rubbing — **rub the wrong way :** to cause to be angry : IRRITATE

[2]**rub** *n* **1 :** the act of rubbing **2 :** something that causes a problem

rub·ber *n* **1 :** an elastic substance obtained from the milky juice of some tropical plants **2 :** something (as an overshoe) made of rubber **3 :** something used in rubbing **4 :** a synthetic substance like rubber **5 :** a flat white rectangle on which a baseball pitcher stands

rubber band *n* **:** a continuous band made of rubber for holding things together : ELASTIC

rubber stamp *n* **:** a stamp with a printing face of rubber

rub·bery *adj* **:** weak, shaky, and unstable

rub·bish *n* **1 :** TRASH 1 **2 :** NONSENSE

rub·ble *n* **:** rough broken pieces of stone or brick from buildings

ru·ble *n* **:** a Russian coin or bill

ru·by *n, pl* **rubies 1 :** a gemstone of a deep red color **2 :** a deep purplish red

ruck·sack *n* **:** KNAPSACK

ruck·us *n* **:** a noisy disturbance or quarrel

rud·der *n* **:** a movable flat piece attached at the rear of a ship or aircraft for steering

rud·dy *adj* **rud·di·er; rud·di·est :** having a healthy reddish color

rude *adj* **rud·er; rud·est 1 :** IMPOLITE **2 :** not refined or cultured **3 :** roughly made — **rude·ly** *adv* — **rude·ness** *n*

ru·di·ment *n* **:** a basic principle

ru·di·men·ta·ry *adj* **1 :** ELEMENTARY, SIMPLE **2 :** not fully developed

rue *vb* **rued; ru·ing :** to feel sorrow or regret for

rue·ful *adj* **1 :** exciting pity or sympathy **2 :** MOURNFUL 1, REGRETFUL

ruff *n* **1 :** a large round collar of pleated fabric worn by men and women in the 16th and 17th centuries **2 :** a fringe of long hairs or feathers growing around or on the neck of an animal

ruf·fi·an *n* **:** a violent and cruel person

[1]**ruf·fle** *vb* **ruf·fled; ruf·fling 1 :** to move or lift so as to disturb the smoothness of **2 :** [2]TROUBLE 1, VEX

[2]**ruffle** *n* **:** a strip of fabric gathered or pleated on one edge

rug *n* **:** a piece of thick heavy fabric usually with a nap or pile used especially as a floor covering

rug·ged *adj* **1 :** having a rough uneven surface **2 :** STRONG 3, TOUGH **3 :** involving hardship — **rug·ged·ly** *adv* — **rug·ged·ness** *n*

[1]**ru·in** *vb* **ru·ined; ru·in·ing 1 :** to reduce to wreckage **2 :** to damage beyond repair **3 :** to have a very bad effect on the quality of (something) **4 :** [3]BANKRUPT

[2]**ruin** *n* **1 :** complete collapse or destruction **2 ruins** *pl* **:** the remains of something destroyed **3 :** the situation in which someone experiences loss of money, social status, or position — **in ruins :** nearly or completely destroyed

ru·in·ous *adj* **:** causing or likely to cause collapse or destruction — **ru·in·ous·ly** *adv*

[1]**rule** *n* **1 :** a guide or principle for conduct or action **2 :** an accepted or usual method, custom, or habit **3 :** the exercise of authority or control : GOVERNMENT **4 :** RULER 2

[2]**rule** *vb* **ruled; rul·ing 1 :** to exercise authority over : GOVERN **2 :** [1]CONTROL 1, DIRECT **3 :** to be supreme or outstanding in **4 :** to give or state as a considered decision **5 :** to mark with lines drawn along the straight edge of a ruler

rul·er *n* **1 :** a person (as a king or queen) having supreme power over a nation **2 :** a straight strip (as of plastic, wood, or metal) with a smooth edge that is marked off in units and used for measuring or as a guide in drawing straight lines

rul·ing *n* **:** an official decision (as by a judge)

rum *n* **:** an alcoholic liquor made from sugarcane or molasses

[1]**rum·ble** *vb* **rum·bled; rum·bling** : to make or move with a low heavy continuous sound

[2]**rumble** *n* : a low heavy rolling sound

ru·mi·nant *n* : a hoofed animal (as a cow or sheep) that chews its cud and has a stomach with usually four chambers — **ruminant** *adj*

ru·mi·nate *vb* **ru·mi·nat·ed; ru·mi·nat·ing** : to think carefully and deeply : MEDITATE

[1]**rum·mage** *vb* **rum·maged; rum·mag·ing** : to search especially by moving and looking through the contents of a place or container

[2]**rummage** *n* : a mixed up collection of different articles

rum·my *n* : a card game in which each player tries to lay down cards in groups of three or more

[1]**ru·mor** *or Can and Brit* **rumour** *n* : information or a story that is passed from one person to another but has not been proven to be true and has no known source

[2]**rumor** *or Can and Brit* **rumour** *vb* **rumored/rumoured; ru·mor·ing/rumouring** : to spread information or a story that has not been proven to be true

rump *n* **1** : the back part of an animal's body where the hips and thighs join **2** : a cut of beef between the loin and the round

rum·ple *vb* **rum·pled; rum·pling** : to make (something) messy or wrinkled

rum·pus *n* : a noisy disturbance or quarrel

[1]**run** *vb* **ran; run; run·ning** **1** : to go at a pace faster than a walk **2** : to go rapidly or hurriedly **3** : to take to flight **4** : to pass over, across, or through **5** : [2]FUNCTION **6** : to cause to function **7** : EXTEND 1 **8** : to move freely about **9** : [1]FLOW 1 **10** : to be in charge of : MANAGE **11** : to do something by or as if by running **12** : to take part in a race **13** : to move on or as if on wheels **14** : to go back and forth often according to a fixed schedule **15** : to migrate or move in schools **16** : to continue in force **17** : to pass into a specified condition **18** : to spread into another area **19** : to give off liquid **20** : to tend to develop a specified feature or quality **21** : to slip through or past **22** : to cause to penetrate **23** : to cause to go **24** : to take on **25** : to print or broadcast **26** : to be a candidate for office **27** : to occur again and again — **run away** : to leave home secretly without intending to return — **run into** : to meet by chance — **run off** : to leave in a hurry — **run out** **1** : to come to an end **2** : to become used up — **run out of** : to use up the available supply of — **run over** : [1]OVERFLOW 1

[2]**run** *n* **1** : an act or the action of running **2** : a score made in baseball by a base runner reaching home plate **3** : an enclosure for animals where they may feed and exercise **4** : the usual or normal kind **5** : a continuous series especially of similar things **6** : sudden heavy demands from depositors, creditors, or customers **7** : the quantity of work turned out in a continuous operation **8** : the distance covered in a period of continuous traveling **9** : a regular course or trip **10** : freedom of movement **11** : a way, track, or path frequented by animals **12** : [1]SLOPE 1 **13** : a spot in knitted fabric that has unraveled

[1]**run·away** *n* **1** : someone who leaves a place (as home) secretly without intending to return **2** : a horse that is running out of control

[2]**runaway** *adj* **1** : having left a place secretly with no intention of returning **2** : escaping from control

run–down *adj* **1** : in poor condition **2** : in poor health

[1]**rung** *past participle of* [3]RING

[2]**rung** *n* **1** : a rounded part placed as a crosspiece between the legs of a chair **2** : one of the crosspieces of a ladder

run–in *n* : an angry argument

run·ner *n* **1** : a person or animal that runs **2** : a thin piece or part on or in which something slides **3** : MESSENGER **4** : a slender creeping branch of a plant that roots at the end or at the joints to form new plants **5** : a long narrow carpet (as for a hall)

run·ner–up *n, pl* **run·ners–up** : the competitor in a contest who finishes second

run·ny *adj* **run·ni·er; run·ni·est** : giving off or likely to give off liquid

runt *n* : an unusually small person or animal

run·way *n* **1** : a path beaten by animals in going to and from feeding grounds **2** : a paved strip of ground on a landing field for the landing and takeoff of aircraft

ru·pee *n* : any of various coins (as of India or Pakistan)

[1]**rup·ture** *n* **1** : a break in peaceful or friendly relations **2** : a breaking or tearing apart of body tissue **3** : a crack or break in something

[2]**rupture** *vb* **rup·tured; rup·tur·ing** **1** : to part by violence : BREAK **2** : to produce a break or tear in **3** : to have or develop a break or tear

ru·ral *adj* : relating to the country, country people or life, or agriculture

ruse *n* : [1]TRICK 3, ARTIFICE

[1]**rush** *vb* **rushed; rush·ing** **1** : to move forward or act very quickly or in a way that shows eagerness or the need to hurry **2** : to perform in a short time or at high speed **3** : to make (someone) act quickly **4** : to bring (someone) to a place quickly **5** : [1]ATTACK 1, CHARGE

[2]**rush** *n* **1** : a quick strong forward motion

2 **:** a burst of activity or speed **3 :** an eager migration of people usually to a new place in search of wealth

[3]**rush** *n* **:** a grasslike marsh plant with hollow stems used in chair seats and mats

[4]**rush** *adj* **:** demanding special speed

[1]**Rus·sian** *adj* **:** of or relating to Russia, its people, or the Russian language

[2]**Russian** *n* **1 :** a person born or living in Russia **2 :** a language of the Russians

[1]**rust** *n* **1 :** a reddish coating formed on metal (as iron) when it is exposed especially to moist air **2 :** a plant disease caused by fungi that makes spots on plants **3 :** a fungus that causes a rust

[2]**rust** *vb* **rust·ed; rust·ing :** to make or become rusty

[1]**rus·tic** *adj* **1 :** relating to or suitable for the country **2 :** [1]PLAIN 7, SIMPLE **3 :** made from rough wood

[2]**rustic** *n* **:** a person living or raised in the country

[1]**rus·tle** *vb* **rus·tled; rus·tling 1 :** to make or cause to make a quick series of small sounds **2 :** to steal (as cattle) from the range — **rus·tler** *n*

[2]**rustle** *n* **:** a quick series of small sounds

rusty *adj* **rust·i·er; rust·i·est 1 :** affected by rust **2 :** less skilled and slow through lack of practice or use — **rust·i·ness** *n*

[1]**rut** *n* **1 :** a track worn by a wheel or by habitual passage **2 :** [1]ROUTINE 1

[2]**rut** *vb* **rut·ted; rut·ting :** to make a track in

ru·ta·ba·ga *n* **:** a turnip with a large yellow root

ruth·less *adj* **:** having no pity **:** CRUEL — **ruth·less·ly** *adv* — **ruth·less·ness** *n*

-ry *n suffix, pl* **-ries :** -ERY

rye *n* **:** a hardy cereal grass grown especially for its edible seeds that are used in flour and animal feeds

S

s *n, pl* **s's** *or* **ss** *often cap* **1 :** the 19th letter of the English alphabet **2 :** a grade rating a student's work as satisfactory

S *abbr* **1** satisfactory **2** small **3** south **4** southern

[1]**-s** *n pl suffix* — used to form the plural of most nouns that do not end in *s, z, sh, ch, x,* or *y* following a consonant and with or without an apostrophe to form the plural of abbreviations, numbers, letters, and symbols used as nouns

[2]**-s** *adv suffix* — used to form adverbs showing usual or repeated action or state

[3]**-s** *vb suffix* — used to form the third person singular present of most verbs that do not end in *s, z, sh, ch, x,* or *y* following a consonant

-'s *n suffix or pron suffix* — used to form the possessive of singular nouns, of plural nouns not ending in *s*, and of some pronouns

Sab·bath *n* **:** a day of the week that is regularly observed as a day of rest and worship

sa·ber *or* **sa·bre** *n* **:** a long sword with a curved blade

sa·ber–toothed cat *or Can and Brit* **sabre–toothed cat** *n* **:** SABER-TOOTHED TIGER

saber–toothed tiger *or Can and Brit* **sabre–toothed tiger** *n* **:** a very large extinct cat of prehistoric times with long sharp curved upper canine teeth

sa·ble *n* **1 :** the color black **2 :** a meat-eating animal of northern Europe and Asia that is related to the weasel and has soft brown fur

[1]**sab·o·tage** *n* **:** deliberate destruction of or damage to property

[2]**sabotage** *vb* **sab·o·taged; sab·o·tag·ing :** to damage or destroy on purpose **:** to engage in sabotage

sabre *Can and Brit spelling of* SABER

sac *n* **:** a part of a plant or animal resembling a bag and often containing a liquid or air — **sac·like** *adj*

sa·chem *n* **:** a North American Indian chief

[1]**sack** *n* **1 :** [1]BAG 1 **2 :** a sack and its contents

[2]**sack** *vb* **sacked; sack·ing 1 :** to put into a sack **2 :** to fire from a job or position

[3]**sack** *vb* **sacked; sack·ing :** to loot after capture **:** PLUNDER

sack·ing *n* **:** a strong rough cloth (as burlap) from which sacks are made

sac·ra·ment *n* **:** a Christian religious act or ceremony that is considered especially sacred

sa·cred *adj* **1 :** HOLY 1 **2 :** RELIGIOUS 2 **3 :** deserving to be respected and honored

[1]**sac·ri·fice** *n* **1 :** the act or ceremony of making an offering to God or a god especially on an altar **2 :** something offered as a religious act **3 :** an act of giving up something especially for the sake of someone or something

else **4 :** something given up especially for the sake of helping others

[2]sacrifice *vb* **sac·ri·ficed; sac·ri·fic·ing 1 :** to offer or kill as a religious act **2 :** to give up (something) especially for the sake of something or someone else

sad *adj* **sad·der; sad·dest 1 :** feeling or showing sorrow or unhappiness **2 :** causing sorrow or unhappiness — **sad·ly** *adv* — **sad·ness** *n*

sad·den *vb* **sad·dened; sad·den·ing :** to make or become sad

[1]sad·dle *n* **1 :** a padded and leather-covered seat for a rider on horseback **2 :** something like a saddle in shape, position, or use

[2]saddle *vb* **sad·dled; sad·dling 1 :** to put a saddle on **2 :** to put a load on **:** BURDEN

saddle horse *n* **:** a horse suited for or trained for riding

sa·fa·ri *n* **:** a trip to see or hunt animals especially in Africa

[1]safe *adj* **saf·er; saf·est 1 :** free or secure from harm or danger **2 :** giving protection or security against harm or danger **3 :** HARMLESS **4 :** unlikely to be wrong or cause disagreement **5 :** not likely to take risks **:** CAREFUL **6 :** successful in reaching a base in baseball — **safe·ly** *adv*

[2]safe *n* **:** a metal box with a lock that is used for keeping something (as money) safe

[1]safe·guard *n* **:** something that protects and gives safety

[2]safeguard *vb* **safe·guard·ed; safe·guard·ing :** to make or keep safe or secure

safe·keep·ing *n* **:** the act of keeping safe **:** protection from danger or loss

safe·ty *n* **:** freedom from danger or harm **:** the state of being safe

safety belt *n* **:** SEAT BELT

safety pin *n* **:** a pin that is bent back to form a spring and has a guard that covers the point

saf·fron *n* **1 :** an orange spice that is made from the dried stigmas of a crocus and is used to color or flavor foods **2 :** an orange to orange yellow

[1]sag *vb* **sagged; sag·ging 1 :** to sink, settle, or hang below the natural or right level **2 :** to become less firm or strong

[2]sag *n* **:** a part or area that sinks or hangs below the natural or right level

sa·ga *n* **1 :** a story of heroic deeds **2 :** a long and often complicated story

sa·ga·cious *adj* **:** quick and wise in understanding and judging

[1]sage *adj* **:** WISE — **sage·ly** *adv*

[2]sage *n* **:** a very wise person

[3]sage *n* **1 :** a mint with grayish green leaves used especially to flavor foods **2 :** SAGEBRUSH

sage·brush *n* **:** a plant of the western United States that grows as a low shrub and has a bitter juice and strong smell

sag·gy *adj* **:** hanging down too much **:** not firm

Sag·it·tar·i·us *n* **1 :** a constellation between Scorpio and Capricorn imagined as a centaur **2 :** the ninth sign of the zodiac or a person born under this sign

sa·gua·ro *n, pl* **sa·gua·ros :** a giant cactus of the southwestern United States and Mexico

said *past and past participle of* SAY

[1]sail *n* **1 :** a sheet of strong cloth (as canvas) used to catch enough wind to move boats through the water or over ice **2 :** the sails of a ship **3 :** a trip in a ship or boat moved especially by the wind

[2]sail *vb* **sailed; sail·ing 1 :** to travel on a boat moved especially by the wind **2 :** to travel on or by water **3 :** to control the motion of (a ship or boat) while traveling on water **4 :** to move or proceed in a quick and smooth way

sail·boat *n* **:** a boat equipped with sails

sail·fish *n* **:** a fish with a large fin like a sail on its back

sail·or *n* **:** a person who works on or controls a boat or ship as part of the crew

saint *n* **1 :** a good and holy person and especially one who in the Christian church is declared to be worthy of special honor **2 :** a person who is very good, helpful, or patient

Saint Ber·nard *n* **:** a very large powerful dog originally of the Swiss Alps and used in the past to find and help lost travelers

saint·ly *adj* **:** like a saint or like that of a saint — **saint·li·ness** *n*

sake *n* **1 :** PURPOSE **2 :** WELFARE 1, BENEFIT

sal·able *or* **sale·able** *adj* **:** good enough to sell

sal·ad *n* **1 :** a mixture of raw usually green leafy vegetables (as lettuce) combined with other vegetables (as tomato and cucumber) and served with a dressing **2 :** a mixture of small pieces of food (as meat, fish, pasta, fruit, or vegetables) usually combined with a dressing

sal·a·man·der *n* **:** a small animal with smooth moist skin that is related to the frog but looks like a lizard

sa·la·mi *n* **:** a large highly seasoned sausage of pork and beef that is usually eaten cold

sal·a·ry *n, pl* **sal·a·ries :** a fixed amount of money paid at regular times for work done

sale *n* **1 :** an exchange of goods or property for money **2 :** the state of being available for purchase **3 :** an event at which goods are sold at lowered prices

sales·clerk *n* **:** a person who works in a store selling goods

sales·man *n, pl* **sales·men :** a person who sells goods or services in a particular geographic area, in a store, or by telephone

sales·per·son *n* **:** SALESMAN

sales tax *n* **:** a tax paid by the buyer on goods bought

sales·wom·an *n, pl* **sales·wom·en :** a woman who sells goods or services in a particular geographic area, in a store, or by telephone

sa·li·va *n* **:** a watery fluid that moistens chewed food and contains enzymes which break down starch and that is secreted into the mouth from three pairs of glands near the mouth

sal·i·vary *adj* **:** of, relating to, or producing saliva

sal·low *adj* **:** slightly yellow in a way that does not look healthy

[1]**sal·ly** *n, pl* **sallies 1 :** a sudden attack especially by besieged soldiers **2 :** a clever and funny remark

[2]**sally** *vb* **sal·lied; sal·ly·ing 1 :** to rush out **2 :** to set out (as from home)

salm·on *n* **:** a fish with reddish or pinkish flesh that is often caught for sport or food and lives most of its life in the ocean but swims up rivers or streams as an adult to deposit or fertilize eggs

sa·lon *n* **:** a business that offers customers beauty treatments

sa·loon *n* **:** a place where alcoholic drinks are sold and drunk **:** BAR

sal·sa *n* **1 :** a spicy sauce of tomatoes, onions, and hot peppers **2 :** popular music of Latin American origin with characteristics of jazz and rock

[1]**salt** *n* **1 :** a colorless or white substance that consists of sodium and chlorine and is used in seasoning foods, preserving meats and fish, and in making soap and glass **2 :** a compound formed by the combination of an acid and a base or a metal

[2]**salt** *vb* **salt·ed; salt·ing :** to flavor or preserve with salt

[3]**salt** *adj* **:** containing salt **:** SALTY

salt·wa·ter *adj* **:** relating to or living in salt water

salty *adj* **salt·i·er; salt·i·est :** of, tasting of, or containing salt

sal·u·ta·tion *n* **1 :** an act or action of greeting **2 :** a word or phrase used as a greeting at the beginning of a letter

[1]**sa·lute** *vb* **sa·lut·ed; sa·lut·ing 1 :** to give a sign of respect to (as a military officer) especially by a movement of the right hand to the forehead **2 :** to show or express respect for **:** HONOR

[2]**salute** *n* **1 :** the position taken or the movement made when bringing the right hand to the forehead in a sign of respect (as for a military officer) **2 :** an act or ceremony that is a show of respect or honor

[1]**sal·vage** *n* **1 :** the act of saving a ship or its cargo **2 :** the saving or rescuing of possessions in danger of being lost (as from fire) **3 :** something that is saved (as from a wreck)

[2]**salvage** *vb* **sal·vaged; sal·vag·ing :** to recover (something usable) especially from wreckage or ruin

sal·va·tion *n* **1 :** the saving of a person from sin or evil **2 :** something that saves from danger or difficulty

[1]**salve** *n* **:** a healing or soothing ointment

[2]**salve** *vb* **salved; salv·ing :** to quiet or soothe with or as if with a salve

[1]**same** *adj* **1 :** not another **:** IDENTICAL **2 :** UNCHANGED **3 :** very much alike

[2]**same** *pron* **:** something identical with or like another

same·ness *n* **1 :** the quality or state of being identical or like another **2 :** MONOTONY

[1]**sam·ple** *n* **1 :** a part or piece that shows the quality or character of the whole **2 :** a small amount of something that is given to people to try

[2]**sample** *vb* **sam·pled; sam·pling :** to judge the quality or character of by trying or examining a small part or amount

san·a·to·ri·um *n, pl* **san·a·to·ri·ums** *or* **san·a·to·ria :** a place for the care and treatment usually of people recovering from illness or having a disease likely to last a long time

[1]**sanc·tion** *n* **1 :** official approval or permission **2 :** an action (as the ending of financial aid) taken by one or more nations to make another nation comply with a law or rule

[2]**sanction** *vb* **sanc·tioned; sanc·tion·ing :** to officially accept or allow

sanc·tu·ary *n, pl* **sanc·tu·ar·ies 1 :** a holy or sacred place **2 :** a building or room for religious worship **3 :** a place that provides safety or protection **4 :** the protection from danger or a difficult situation that is provided by a safe place

[1]**sand** *n* **1 :** loose material in grains produced by the natural breaking up of rocks **2 :** a soil made up mostly of sand

[2]**sand** *vb* **sand·ed; sand·ing 1 :** to sprinkle with sand **2 :** to smooth or clean with sandpaper — **sand·er** *n*

san·dal *n* **:** a shoe consisting of a sole that is held in place by straps

san·dal·wood *n* **:** the fragrant yellowish wood of an Asian tree

sand·bag *n* **:** a bag filled with sand and used as a weight (as on a balloon) or as part of a wall or dam

sand·bar *n* **:** a ridge of sand formed in water by tides or currents

sand·box *n* : a large low box for holding sand especially for children to play in
sand dollar *n* : a flat round sea urchin
sand·pa·per *n* : paper that has rough material (as sand) glued on one side and is used for smoothing and polishing
sand·pip·er *n* : a small shorebird with long slender legs and bill
sand·stone *n* : rock made of sand held together by a natural cement (as of calcium carbonate)
sand·storm *n* : a desert storm with strong wind that blows clouds of sand
¹sand·wich *n* : two or more slices of bread or a split roll with a filling (as meat or cheese) between them
²sandwich *vb* **sand·wiched; sand·wich·ing** : to fit in between two or more things or people
sandy *adj* **sand·i·er; sand·i·est** **1** : full of or covered with sand **2** : of a yellowish gray color
sane *adj* **san·er; san·est** **1** : having a healthy and sound mind **2** : very sensible
sang *past of* SING
san·i·tar·i·um *n, pl* **san·i·tar·i·ums** *or* **san·i·tar·ia** : SANATORIUM
san·i·tary *adj* **1** : relating to health or hygiene **2** : free from filth, infection, or other dangers to health
san·i·ta·tion *n* : the act or process of making or keeping things free from filth, infection, or other dangers to health
san·i·ty *n* : the state of having a healthy and sound mind
sank *past of* SINK
San·ta Claus *n* : the spirit of Christmas as represented by a plump jolly old man with a white beard who is dressed in a red suit and delivers presents to good children
¹sap *n* : a watery juice that circulates through a plant and carries food and nutrients
²sap *vb* **sapped; sap·ping** : to weaken or use up little by little
sap·ling *n* : a young tree
sap·phire *n* : a clear bright blue gemstone
sap·py *adj* **sap·pi·er; sap·pi·est** : sad or romantic in a foolish or exaggerated way
sap·wood *n* : young wood through which sap travels that is found just beneath the bark of a tree and is usually lighter in color than the heartwood
sar·casm *n* : the use of words that normally mean one thing to mean just the opposite usually to hurt someone's feelings or show scorn
sar·cas·tic *adj* **1** : showing sarcasm **2** : being in the habit of using sarcasm — **sar·cas·ti·cal·ly** *adv*
sar·dine *n* : a young or very small fish often preserved in oil and used for food
sa·ri *n* : a piece of clothing worn mainly by women of southern Asia that is a long light cloth wrapped around the body and head or shoulder
sar·sa·pa·ril·la *n* : a sweetened carbonated beverage that tastes somewhat like root beer
¹sash *n* : a broad band of cloth worn around the waist or over the shoulder
²sash *n* **1** : a frame for a pane of glass in a door or window **2** : the movable part of a window
Sask. *abbr* Saskatchewan
¹sass *n* : a rude or disrespectful reply
²sass *vb* **sassed; sass·ing** : to speak to in a rude or disrespectful way
sas·sa·fras *n* : a tall tree of eastern North America whose dried root bark was formerly used in medicine or as a flavoring
sassy *adj* **sass·i·er; sass·i·est** : having or showing a rude lack of respect
sat *past and past participle of* SIT
Sat. *abbr* Saturday
Sa·tan *n* : DEVIL 1
satch·el *n* : a small bag that often has a shoulder strap
sat·el·lite *n* **1** : a smaller body that revolves around a planet **2** : an object or vehicle sent out from the earth to revolve around the earth, moon, sun, or a planet
satellite dish *n* : a bowl-shaped antenna for receiving transmissions (as of television programs) from a satellite orbiting the earth
sat·in *n* : a cloth with a smooth shiny surface
sat·ire *n* **1** : humor that is used to make fun of and often show the weaknesses of someone or something **2** : something (as a book or movie) that uses satire
sat·is·fac·tion *n* **1** : a feeling of happiness or content with something : the condition of being satisfied **2** : something that makes a person happy, pleased, or content
sat·is·fac·to·ry *adj* : good enough for a particular purpose : causing satisfaction — **sat·is·fac·to·ri·ly** *adv*
sat·is·fy *vb* **sat·is·fied; sat·is·fy·ing** **1** : to make happy or contented **2** : to meet the needs of **3** : CONVINCE **4** : to do what has been agreed upon
sat·u·rate *vb* **sat·u·rat·ed; sat·u·rat·ing** : to soak completely
Sat·ur·day *n* : the seventh day of the week
Sat·urn *n* : the planet that is sixth in distance from the sun and has a diameter of about 75,000 miles (120,000 kilometers)
sauce *n* **1** : a usually thick liquid poured over or mixed with food **2** : boiled or canned fruit
sauce·pan *n* : a small deep cooking pan with a handle
sau·cer *n* : a small shallow dish often with a slightly lower center for holding a cup
saucy *adj* **sauc·i·er; sauc·i·est** **1** : being

rude and disrespectful : SASSY **2 :** stylish in dress or appearance — **sauc·i·ly** *adv*

sau·er·kraut *n* **:** finely cut cabbage soaked in a salty mixture

saun·ter *vb* **saun·tered; saun·ter·ing :** to walk in a slow relaxed way : STROLL

sau·sage *n* **1 :** spicy ground meat (as pork) usually stuffed in casings **2 :** a roll of sausage in a casing

[1]sav·age *adj* **1 :** not tamed : WILD **2 :** being cruel and brutal : FIERCE — **sav·age·ly** *adv*

[2]savage *n* **1 :** a person belonging to a group with a low level of civilization **2 :** a cruel or violent person

sav·age·ry *n, pl* **sav·age·ries 1 :** an uncivilized condition or character **2 :** an act of cruelty or violence

sa·van·na *also* **sa·van·nah** *n* **:** land of warm regions (as Africa) that is covered with grass and only a few shrubs and trees

[1]save *vb* **saved; sav·ing 1 :** to free or keep from danger or harm **2 :** to keep from being ruined : PRESERVE **3 :** to put aside for later use **4 :** to put aside money **5 :** to keep from being spent, wasted, or lost **6 :** to make unnecessary **7 :** to store data on a computer or on a storage device (as a flash drive)

[2]save *prep* **:** [1]EXCEPT 2

sav·ing *n* **1 :** something that is not spent, wasted, or lost **2 savings** *pl* **:** money put aside (as in a bank)

sav·ior *or Can and Brit* **sav·iour** *n* **1 :** a person who saves someone or something from danger or harm **2** *cap* **:** JESUS CHRIST

[1]sa·vor *or Can and Brit* **savour** *n* **:** the taste or smell of something

[2]savor *or Can and Brit* **savour** *vb* **sa·vored/savoured; sa·vor·ing/savouring 1 :** to taste or smell with pleasure **2 :** to delight in : ENJOY

sa·vo·ry *or Can and Brit* **savoury** *adj* **:** pleasing to the taste or smell

sav·vy *adj* **sav·vi·er; sav·vi·est :** having practical understanding or knowledge of something — **sav·vi·ly** *adv* — **sav·vi·ness** *n*

[1]saw *past of* SEE

[2]saw *n* **:** a tool or machine with a blade having sharp teeth that is used for cutting hard material (as wood or metal)

[3]saw *vb* **sawed; sawed** *or* **sawn; saw·ing :** to cut or shape with a saw

[4]saw *n* **:** a common saying : PROVERB

saw·dust *n* **:** tiny bits (as of wood) which fall from something being sawed

saw·horse *n* **:** a frame or rack on which wood is rested while being sawed

saw·mill *n* **:** a mill or factory having machinery for sawing logs

saw–toothed *adj* **:** having an edge or outline like the teeth of a saw

sax·o·phone *n* **:** a woodwind instrument usually in the form of a curved metal tube with keys used to change pitch and a mouthpiece with a single reed

[1]say *vb* **said; say·ing 1 :** to express in words **2 :** to state as an opinion or decision : DECLARE **3 :** [1]REPEAT 2, RECITE **4 :** INDICATE 2, SHOW **5 :** to consider as a possibility or example

[2]say *n* **1 :** an expression of opinion **2 :** the power to decide or help decide

say·ing *n* **:** PROVERB

SC *abbr* South Carolina

scab *n* **:** a crust mostly of hardened blood that forms over and protects a sore or wound as it heals

scab·bard *n* **:** a protective case or sheath for the blade of a sword or dagger

scab·by *adj* **scab·bi·er; scab·bi·est :** covered with scabs

sca·bies *n, pl* **scabies :** an itch or mange caused by mites living as parasites under the skin

scaf·fold *n* **1 :** a raised platform built as a support for workers and their tools and materials **2 :** a platform on which executions take place

scal·a·wag *or* **scal·ly·wag** *n* **:** RASCAL 1

[1]scald *vb* **scald·ed; scald·ing 1 :** to burn with or as if with hot liquid or steam **2 :** to bring to a temperature just below the boiling point

[2]scald *n* **:** an injury caused by burning with hot liquid or steam

scald·ing *adj* **:** very hot

[1]scale *n* **1 :** either pan of a balance or the balance itself **2 :** a device for weighing

[2]scale *n* **1 :** one of the small stiff plates that cover much of the body of some animals (as fish and snakes) **2 :** a thin layer or part suggesting a fish scale — **scaled** *adj* — **scale·less** *adj*

[3]scale *vb* **scaled; scal·ing 1 :** to remove the scales of **2 :** [2]FLAKE

[4]scale *vb* **scaled; scal·ing 1 :** to climb by or as if by a ladder **2 :** to regulate or set according to a standard — often used with *down* or *up*

[5]scale *n* **1 :** a series of musical tones going up or down in pitch in fixed steps **2 :** a series of spaces marked off by lines and used for measuring distances or amounts **3 :** a series of like things arranged in order (as according to size or degree) **4 :** the size of a picture, plan, or model of a thing compared to the size of the thing itself **5 :** a standard for measuring or judging **6 :** the size or extent of something especially in comparison to something else

[1]scal·lop *n* **1 :** an edible shellfish that is a mollusk with a ribbed shell in two parts **2 :** one of a series of half-circles that form a border on an edge (as of lace)

[2]scallop *vb* **scal·loped; scal·lop·ing** **1 :** to bake with crumbs, butter, and milk **2 :** to embroider, cut, or edge with half-circles

[1]scalp *n* **:** the part of the skin of the head usually covered with hair

[2]scalp *vb* **scalped; scalp·ing :** to remove the scalp from

scaly *adj* **scal·i·er; scal·i·est :** covered with scales or flakes

scamp *n* **:** RASCAL 1

[1]scam·per *vb* **scam·pered; scam·per·ing :** to run or move quickly and often playfully

[2]scamper *n* **:** a hurried and often playful run or movement

scan *vb* **scanned; scan·ning** **1 :** to examine or look over carefully **2 :** to look through or over quickly **3 :** to examine with a special device (as a scanner) especially to obtain information

scan·dal *n* **1 :** something that angers or shocks people because rules or standards of behavior are violated **2 :** talk that injures a person's good name

scan·dal·ous *adj* **1 :** containing shocking information **2 :** very bad or shocking

[1]Scan·di·na·vian *n* **:** a person born or living in Scandinavia

[2]Scandinavian *adj* **:** of or relating to Scandinavia or its people

scan·ner *n* **:** a device that converts a printed image (as text or a photograph) into a form a computer can display or alter

scant *adj* **1 :** barely enough **2 :** not quite to a full amount, degree, or extent

scanty *adj* **scant·i·er; scant·i·est :** barely enough **:** lacking in size or quantity

[1]scar *n* **1 :** a mark left on the skin after a wound heals **2 :** an ugly mark (as on furniture) showing damage **3 :** the lasting effect (as a feeling of sadness) of some unhappy experience

[2]scar *vb* **scarred; scar·ring** **1 :** to mark or become marked with a scar **2 :** to leave a lasting bad effect on

scar·ab *n* **:** a large dark beetle used in ancient Egypt as a symbol of eternal life

[1]scarce *adj* **scarc·er; scarc·est :** not plentiful

[2]scarce *adv* **:** HARDLY, SCARCELY

scarce·ly *adv* **1 :** only just **:** BARELY **2 :** certainly not

scar·ci·ty *n, pl* **scar·ci·ties :** a very small supply **:** the condition of being scarce

[1]scare *vb* **scared; scar·ing :** to become or cause to become frightened — **scare up :** to find or get with some difficulty

[2]scare *n* **1 :** a sudden feeling of fear **:** FRIGHT **2 :** a widespread state of alarm

scare·crow *n* **:** an object made to look like a person and set up to scare birds away from crops

scarf *n, pl* **scarves** *or* **scarfs** **1 :** a piece of cloth worn loosely on the shoulders, around the neck, or on the head **2 :** a long narrow strip of cloth used as a cover (as on a bureau)

[1]scar·let *n* **:** a bright red

[2]scarlet *adj* **:** colored bright red

scarlet fever *n* **:** a serious illness in which there is a sore throat, high fever, and red rash

scary *adj* **scar·i·er; scar·i·est :** causing fright

scat *vb* **scat·ted; scat·ting :** to go away quickly — often used as a command to frighten away an animal

scat·ter *vb* **scat·tered; scat·ter·ing** **1 :** to toss, sow, or place here and there **2 :** to separate or cause to separate and go in different ways

scat·ter·brain *n* **:** a person who is unable to concentrate or think clearly — **scat·ter·brained** *adj*

scav·enge *vb* **scav·enged; scav·eng·ing :** to search through and collect usable items especially from what has been thrown away

scav·en·ger *n* **1 :** a person who picks over junk or garbage for useful items **2 :** an animal (as a vulture) that feeds on dead or decaying material

scene *n* **1 :** a division of an act in a play **2 :** a single interesting or important happening in a play or story **3 :** the place of an event or action **4 :** a view or sight that resembles a picture **5 :** a display of anger or bad behavior

scen·ery *n* **1 :** the painted scenes used on a stage and the furnishings that go with them **2 :** pleasant outdoor scenes or views **3 :** a person's usual surroundings

sce·nic *adj* **1 :** having views of pleasant natural features **2 :** relating to stage scenery

[1]scent *n* **1 :** an odor that is given off by someone or something **2 :** power or sense of smell **3 :** a course followed in search or pursuit of something **4 :** [1]PERFUME 1

[2]scent *vb* **scent·ed; scent·ing** **1 :** to become aware of or follow through the sense of smell **2 :** to get a hint of **3 :** to fill with an odor **:** PERFUME

scep·ter *n* **:** a rod carried by a ruler as a sign of authority

[1]sched·ule *n* **1 :** a plan of things that need to be done and the times they will be done **2 :** a written or printed list of things and the time they will be done **3 :** a list of the times set for certain events **4 :** TIMETABLE

[2]schedule *vb* **sched·uled; sched·ul·ing :** to plan at a certain time

[1]scheme *n* **1 :** a secret plan **:** PLOT **2 :** a plan of something to be done **:** PROJECT **3 :** an organized design

[2]scheme *vb* **schemed; schem·ing :** to form a secret plan — **schem·er** *n*

schol·ar *n* **1 :** a student in a school **:** PUPIL **2 :** a person who knows a great deal about one or more subjects **:** a learned person

schol·ar·ly *adj* **:** like that of or suitable to learned persons

schol·ar·ship *n* **1 :** money given a student to help pay for further education **2 :** serious academic study or research of a subject

scho·las·tic *adj* **:** relating to schools, students, or education

[1]**school** *n* **1 :** a place for teaching and learning **2 :** a session of teaching and learning **3 :** SCHOOLHOUSE **4 :** the teachers and pupils of a school **5 :** a group of persons who share the same opinions and beliefs

[2]**school** *vb* **schooled; school·ing :** TEACH 2, TRAIN

[3]**school** *n* **:** a large number of one kind of fish or water animals swimming together

school·bag *n* **:** a bag for carrying schoolbooks

school·book *n* **:** TEXTBOOK

school·boy *n* **:** a boy who goes to school

school·girl *n* **:** a girl who goes to school

school·house *n, pl* **school·hous·es :** a building used as a place for teaching and learning

school·ing *n* **:** EDUCATION 1

school·mas·ter *n* **:** a man who is in charge of a school or teaches in a school

school·mate *n* **:** a fellow student

school·mis·tress *n* **:** a woman who is in charge of a school or teaches in a school

school·room *n* **:** CLASSROOM

school·teach·er *n* **:** a person who teaches in a school

school·work *n* **:** lessons done at school or assigned to be done at home

school·yard *n* **:** the playground of a school

schoo·ner *n* **:** a ship usually having two masts with the mainmast located toward the center and the shorter mast toward the front

schwa *n* **1 :** an unstressed vowel that is the usual sound of the first and last vowels of the English word *America* **2 :** the symbol ə commonly used for a schwa and sometimes also for a similarly pronounced stressed vowel (as in *cut*)

sci. *abbr* science

sci·ence *n* **1 :** knowledge about the natural world that is based on facts learned through experiments and observation **2 :** an area of study that deals with the natural world (as biology or physics) **3 :** a subject that is formally studied **4 :** something that can be studied and learned

science fiction *n* **:** made-up stories about the influence of real or imagined science on society or individuals

sci·en·tif·ic *adj* **1 :** relating to science or scientists **2 :** using or applying the methods of science — **sci·en·tif·i·cal·ly** *adv*

sci·en·tist *n* **:** a person who studies, specializes in, or investigates a field of science and does scientific work

scis·sors *n pl* **:** a cutting instrument with two blades fastened together so that the sharp edges slide against each other — used as singular or plural

scoff *vb* **scoffed; scoff·ing :** to show great disrespect with mocking laughter or behavior

[1]**scold** *vb* **scold·ed; scold·ing :** to find fault with or criticize in an angry way — **scold·ing** *n*

[2]**scold** *n* **:** a person who frequently criticizes and blames

[1]**scoop** *n* **1 :** the amount held by a scoop **2 :** a kitchen utensil resembling a deep spoon and used for digging into and lifting out a soft substance **3 :** a motion made with or as if with a scoop **4 :** a large deep shovel for digging, dipping, or shoveling

[2]**scoop** *vb* **scooped; scoop·ing 1 :** to take out or up with or as if with a dipping motion **2 :** to make something (as a hole) by creating a hollow place

scoot *vb* **scoot·ed; scoot·ing :** to go suddenly and quickly

scoot·er *n* **1 :** a vehicle consisting of a narrow rectangular base mounted between a front and a back wheel, guided by a handle attached to the front wheel, and moved by the rider pushing off with one foot **2 :** MOTOR SCOOTER

scope *n* **1 :** space or opportunity for action or thought **2 :** the area or amount covered, reached, or viewed

scorch *vb* **scorched; scorch·ing 1 :** to burn on the surface **2 :** to dry or shrivel with or as if with intense heat **3 :** to produce intense heat

[1]**score** *n* **1 :** a record of points made or lost (as in a game) **2 :** the number of points earned for correct answers on a test **3 :** a group of 20 things **:** TWENTY **4 :** harm done by someone and kept in mind for later response **5 :** DEBT 2 **6 :** a line (as a scratch) made with or as if with something sharp **7 :** [1]GROUND 8, REASON **8 :** the written or printed form of a musical composition — **score·less** *adj*

[2]**score** *vb* **scored; scor·ing 1 :** to make or cause to make a point or points in a game **2 :** to cut or mark with a line, scratch, or notch **3 :** ACHIEVE 1, WIN **4 :** [2]GRADE 1, MARK **5 :** to set down in an account **:** RECORD **6 :** to keep the score in a game

[1]**scorn** *n* **1 :** a strong feeling of disgust and anger **2 :** an expression of disgust and anger

²scorn *vb* **scorned; scorn·ing :** to show disgust and anger for

scorn·ful *adj* **:** feeling or showing disgust and anger — **scorn·ful·ly** *adv*

Scor·pio *n* **1 :** a constellation between Libra and Sagittarius imagined as a scorpion **2 :** the eighth sign of the zodiac or a person born under this sign

scor·pi·on *n* **:** an animal related to the spiders that has a long jointed body ending in a slender tail with a poisonous stinger at the end

Scot *n* **:** a person born or living in Scotland

¹Scotch *adj* **:** ¹SCOTTISH

²Scotch *n pl* **:** ²SCOTTISH

scot–free *adj* **:** completely free from duty, harm, or punishment

¹Scot·tish *adj* **:** of or relating to Scotland or the Scottish people

²Scottish *n pl* **:** the people of Scotland

scoun·drel *n* **:** a mean or wicked person

¹scour *vb* **scoured; scour·ing 1 :** to rub hard with a rough substance or object in order to clean **2 :** to free or clear from impurities by or as if by rubbing

²scour *vb* **scoured; scouring :** to go or move swiftly about, over, or through in search of something

¹scourge *n* **1 :** a cause of widespread or great suffering **2 :** ²WHIP 1

²scourge *vb* **scourged; scourg·ing 1 :** to cause trouble or suffering to **:** AFFLICT **2 :** to whip severely **:** FLOG

¹scout *vb* **scout·ed; scout·ing 1 :** to explore an area to find out information about it **2 :** to search an area for someone or something

²scout *n* **1 :** a person, group, boat, or plane that gathers information or searches an area **2** *often cap* **:** BOY SCOUT **3** *often cap* **:** GIRL SCOUT

scout·ing *n* **1 :** the activity of gathering information or searching an area **2** *often cap* **:** the general activities of Boy Scout and Girl Scout groups

scout·mas·ter *n* **:** the leader of a troop of Boy Scouts

scow *n* **:** a large boat with a flat bottom and square ends used chiefly for transporting bulk material (as ore, sand, or refuse)

¹scowl *vb* **scowled; scowl·ing 1 :** to make a look that shows anger **2 :** to say with an angry look

²scowl *n* **:** an angry look

scrag·gly *adj* **scrag·gli·er; scrag·gli·est :** of rough or uneven outline **:** UNKEMPT

scram *vb* **scrammed; scram·ming :** to go away at once — often used as a command

¹scram·ble *vb* **scram·bled; scram·bling 1 :** to move or climb quickly and if necessary on hands and knees **2 :** to cook the mixed whites and yolks of eggs by stirring them while frying **3 :** to put in the wrong order **4 :** to work hard to win or escape something

²scramble *n* **:** a disorderly rush

¹scrap *n* **1 :** a small bit **2 scraps** *pl* **:** pieces of leftover food **3 :** waste material (as metal) that can be made fit to use again

²scrap *vb* **scrapped; scrap·ping :** to abandon or throw away as worthless

³scrap *n* **:** ¹QUARREL 1, FIGHT

scrap·book *n* **:** a blank book in which clippings or pictures are kept

¹scrape *vb* **scraped; scrap·ing 1 :** to remove by repeated strokes with something sharp or rough **2 :** to clean or smooth by rubbing **3 :** to rub or cause to rub so as to make a harsh noise **4 :** to hurt or roughen by dragging against a rough surface **5 :** to get with difficulty and a little at a time

²scrape *n* **1 :** a sound, mark, or injury made by something being dragged or rubbed against something else **2 :** a difficult or unpleasant situation **3 :** the act of scraping

scrap·er *n* **:** a tool used to scrape something off a surface

¹scratch *vb* **scratched; scratch·ing 1 :** to scrape or rub lightly **2 :** to injure by scraping with something sharp **3 :** to make a scraping noise **4 :** to erase by scraping

²scratch *n* **:** a mark or injury made by scraping with something sharp

scratchy *adj* **scratch·i·er; scratch·i·est 1 :** likely to injure with something sharp **2 :** causing irritation **3 :** COARSE 1 **4 :** somewhat sore

¹scrawl *vb* **scrawled; scrawl·ing :** to write quickly and carelessly

²scrawl *n* **:** something written carelessly or without skill

scraw·ny *adj* **scraw·ni·er; scraw·ni·est :** poorly nourished **:** SKINNY

¹scream *vb* **screamed; scream·ing :** to cry out (as in fright) with a loud and high-pitched sound — **scream·er** *n*

²scream *n* **:** a long cry that is loud and high-pitched

¹screech *vb* **screeched; screech·ing 1 :** to make a high-pitched harsh sound **2 :** to utter with a high-pitched harsh sound **3 :** to cry out in a loud, high-pitched way (as in terror or pain) **4 :** to make a high-pitched harsh sound

²screech *n* **1 :** a high-pitched harsh cry **2 :** a high-pitched harsh sound

¹screen *n* **1 :** a frame that holds a usually wire netting and is used to let air in but keep pests (as insects) out **2 :** a curtain or wall used to hide or to protect **3 :** the flat surface on which movies are projected **4 :** the surface on which the image appears in an electronic display (as on a television set or computer terminal) **5 :** a network of wire set in a frame for separating finer parts from coarser parts (as of sand)

²screen *vb* **screened; screen·ing 1 :** to hide or protect with or as if with a curtain or wall **2 :** to separate or sift with a network of wire set in a frame **3 :** to look at carefully to select as suitable

screen saver *n* **:** a computer program that usually displays images on the screen of a computer that is on but not in use so as to prevent damage to the screen

¹screw *n* **1 :** a nail-shaped or rod-shaped piece of metal with a winding ridge around its length used for fastening and holding pieces together **2 :** the act of twisting **3 :** PROPELLER

²screw *vb* **screwed; screw·ing 1 :** to attach or fasten with a screw **2 :** to turn or twist on a winding ridge to attach **3 :** to twist out of shape **4 :** to increase in amount

screw·driv·er *n* **:** a tool for turning screws

screwy *adj* **screw·i·er; screw·i·est 1 :** oddly different and unfamiliar **2 :** CRAZY 1

¹scrib·ble *vb* **scrib·bled; scrib·bling :** to write quickly or carelessly — **scrib·bler** *n*

²scribble *n* **:** something written quickly or carelessly

scribe *n* **:** a person who copies writing (as in a book)

scrim·mage *n* **1 :** the action between two football teams when one attempts to move the ball down the field **2 :** a practice game between two teams or between two groups from the same team

script *n* **1 :** the written form of a play or movie or the lines to be said by a performer **2 :** HANDWRITING

scrip·ture *n* **1** *cap* **:** BIBLE 1 **2 :** writings sacred to a religious group

¹scroll *n* **:** a roll of paper or parchment on which something is written or engraved

²scroll *vb* **scrolled; scroll·ing :** to move words or images up or down a display screen as if by unrolling a scroll

¹scrub *vb* **scrubbed; scrub·bing :** to rub hard in washing

²scrub *n* **:** a thick growth of small or stunted shrubs or trees

³scrub *n* **:** the act, an instance, or a period of rubbing hard in washing

scrub·by *adj* **scrub·bi·er; scrub·bi·est :** covered with a thick growth of small or stunted shrubs or trees

scruff *n* **:** the loose skin on the back of the neck

scruffy *adj* **scruff·i·er; scruff·i·est :** dirty or shabby in appearance

scrump·tious *adj* **1 :** DELICIOUS **2 :** DELIGHTFUL

scrunch *vb* **scrunched; scrunch·ing 1 :** to cause (as facial features) to draw together **2 :** ¹CROUCH, HUNCH **3 :** to draw or squeeze together tightly **4 :** CRUMPLE 1 **5 :** ¹CRUSH 1

scru·ple *n* **1 :** a sense of right and wrong that keeps a person from doing something bad **2 :** a feeling of guilt from doing something bad

scru·pu·lous *adj* **:** careful in doing what is right and proper — **scru·pu·lous·ly** *adv*

scru·ti·nize *vb* **scru·ti·nized; scru·ti·niz·ing :** to examine very closely

scru·ti·ny *n* **:** a close inspection

scuba *n* **:** equipment used for breathing while swimming underwater

scuba diver *n* **:** a person who swims underwater with scuba gear

scuff *vb* **scuffed; scuff·ing 1 :** to scrape the feet while walking **2 :** to mark or scratch by scraping

¹scuf·fle *vb* **scuf·fled; scuf·fling 1 :** to fight briefly and not very seriously **2 :** SCUFF 1

²scuffle *n* **1 :** a short fight that is not very serious **2 :** the sound of shuffling

scull *n* **:** a boat driven by one or more pairs of short oars

sculpt *vb* **sculpt·ed; sculpt·ing :** ²SCULPTURE — **sculp·tor** *n*

¹sculp·ture *n* **1 :** the action or art of making statues by carving or chiseling (as in wood or stone), by modeling (as in clay), or by casting (as in melted metal) **2 :** a work of art produced by sculpture

²sculpture *vb* **sculp·tured; sculp·tur·ing :** to make (a work of art) by shaping (as stone, wood, or metal)

scum *n* **1 :** a film of matter that rises to the top of a boiling or fermenting liquid **2 :** a coating (as of algae) on the surface of still water **3 :** a loathsome person

¹scur·ry *vb* **scur·ried; scur·ry·ing :** to move quickly

²scurry *n, pl* **scur·ries :** the act of moving quickly

¹scur·vy *n* **:** a disease caused by a lack of vitamin C in which the teeth loosen, the gums soften, and there is bleeding under the skin

²scurvy *adj* **scur·vi·er; scur·vi·est :** ²MEAN 1, CONTEMPTIBLE

¹scut·tle *vb* **scut·tled; scut·tling :** to run rapidly from view

²scuttle *n* **:** a pail or bucket for carrying coal

³scuttle *n* **:** a small opening with a lid or cover (as in the deck of a ship)

⁴scuttle *vb* **scut·tled; scut·tling :** to sink (a ship) by cutting holes through the bottom or sides

scythe *n* : a tool with a curved blade on a long curved handle that is used to mow grass or grain by hand

SD, S. Dak. *abbr* South Dakota

SE *abbr* southeast

sea *n* **1 :** a body of salt water not as large as an ocean and often nearly surrounded by land **2 :** OCEAN 1 **3 :** rough water **4 :** something suggesting a sea's great size or depth

sea anemone *n* : a hollow sea animal that is related to the coral and has a cluster of tentacles around its mouth

sea·bird *n* : a bird (as a gull or puffin) that lives on or near the open ocean

sea·coast *n* : the shore of the sea

sea cucumber *n* : a sea animal that is related to the starfish and has a flexible muscular body shaped like a cucumber

[1]**sea·far·ing** *adj* : of or employed in sailing

[2]**seafaring** *n* : sailing on the sea as work or as recreation

sea·food *n* : saltwater fish and shellfish used as food

sea·go·ing *adj* : suitable or used for sea travel

sea·gull *n* : a gull that lives near the sea

sea horse *n* : a small fish with a head which looks like the head of a horse

[1]**seal** *n* **1 :** a sea mammal that swims with flippers, lives mostly in cold regions, bears young on land, feeds on fish and other sea animals (as squid), and is sometimes hunted for its fur, hide, or oil **2 :** the soft fur of a seal

[2]**seal** *n* **1 :** something that closes tightly **2 :** the condition of having a tight seal **3 :** an official mark stamped or pressed on something **4 :** a device with a cut or raised design or figure that can be stamped or pressed into wax or paper **5 :** a stamp that may be used to close a letter or package **6 :** something (as a pledge) that makes safe or secure

[3]**seal** *vb* **sealed; seal·ing 1 :** to close tightly or completely to prevent anyone or anything from moving in or out **2 :** to put an official mark on — **seal·er** *n*

sea level *n* : the surface of the sea halfway between the average high and low tides

sea lion *n* : a large seal of the Pacific Ocean

seal·skin *n* : [1]SEAL 2

seam *n* **1 :** the fold, line, or groove made by sewing together or joining two edges or two pieces of material **2 :** a layer in the ground of a mineral or metal

sea·man *n, pl* **sea·men 1 :** a person who helps in the handling of a ship at sea : SAILOR **2 :** an enlisted person in the navy or coast guard ranking above a seaman apprentice

seaman apprentice *n* : an enlisted person in the navy or coast guard ranking above a seaman recruit

seaman recruit *n* : an enlisted person of the lowest rank in the navy or coast guard

seam·stress *n* : a woman who sews especially for a living

sea·plane *n* : an airplane that can rise from and land on water

sea·port *n* : a port, harbor, or town within reach of seagoing ships

sear *vb* **seared; sear·ing 1 :** to burn, mark, or injure with or as if with sudden heat **2 :** to dry by or as if by heat : PARCH **3 :** to quickly cook the surface by high heat

[1]**search** *vb* **searched; search·ing 1 :** to go through or look around carefully and thoroughly in an effort to find something **2 :** to carefully look for someone or something **3 :** to look in the pockets or the clothing of (someone) for something hidden

[2]**search** *n* : an act or instance of looking for someone or something

search engine *n* : computer software used to search data (as text or a database) for requested information

search·light *n* : a lamp for sending a beam of bright light

sea·shell *n* : the shell of a sea animal

sea·shore *n* : the shore of a sea

sea·sick *adj* : sick in the stomach from the pitching or rolling of a ship — **sea·sick·ness** *n*

sea·side *n* : SEACOAST

[1]**sea·son** *n* **1 :** one of the four quarters into which a year is commonly divided **2 :** a period of time associated with something special

[2]**season** *vb* **sea·soned; sea·son·ing 1 :** to add flavor to (food) with spices and herbs **2 :** to make suitable for use (as by aging or drying)

sea·son·al *adj* : happening, available, or used at a certain season

sea·son·ing *n* : something added to food to give it more flavor

sea star *n* : STARFISH

[1]**seat** *n* **1 :** something (as a chair) used to sit in or on **2 :** the part of something on which a person sits **3 :** the place on or at which a person sits **4 :** a place that serves as a capital or center — **seat·ed** *adj*

[2]**seat** *vb* **seat·ed; seat·ing 1 :** to place in or on a seat **2 :** to have enough places to sit for

seat belt *n* : a strap (as in an automobile or airplane) designed to hold a person in a seat

sea urchin *n* : a small sea animal that is related to the starfish, lives on the sea bottom, and is enclosed in a roundish shell covered with spines that can move

sea·wall *n* : a bank or a wall to prevent sea waves from eroding the shore
sea·wa·ter *n* : water in or from the sea
sea·weed *n* : an alga (as a kelp) that grows in the sea
sea·wor·thy *adj* : fit or safe for a sea voyage
sec. *abbr* second
se·cede *vb* **se·ced·ed; se·ced·ing** : to end an association with an organization (as a country)
se·clud·ed *adj* **1** : hidden from sight **2** : living or kept away from others
se·clu·sion *n* : the condition of being hidden from sight or kept away from others
[1]**sec·ond** *adj* **1** : being next after the first in time or order **2** : next lower in rank, value, or importance than the first **3** : another of the same type
[2]**second** *n* **1** : a 60th part of a minute of time or of a degree **2** : MOMENT 1, INSTANT
[3]**second** *vb* **sec·ond·ed; sec·ond·ing** : to support a suggestion, motion, or nomination
[4]**second** *adv* : in the second place or rank
[5]**second** *n* : someone or something that is second
sec·ond·ary *adj* **1** : second in rank, value, or importance **2** : derived from or coming after something original or primary **3** : relating to secondary school **4** : relating to or being the second of three levels of stress in pronunciation
secondary school *n* : a school for students above elementary school level and below college level
sec·ond·hand *adj* **1** : not new : having had a previous owner **2** : selling used goods
second lieutenant *n* : a commissioned officer of the lowest rank in the army, air force, or marine corps
second person *n* : a set of words or forms (as pronouns or verb forms) referring to the person the speaker or writer is addressing
sec·ond–rate *adj* : of ordinary or second quality or value
se·cre·cy *n* **1** : the act of keeping things secret **2** : the quality or state of being secret or hidden
[1]**se·cret** *adj* **1** : hidden from the knowledge of others **2** : done, made, or working in a way that no other or only a few other people know about — **se·cret·ly** *adv*
[2]**secret** *n* : something kept or planned to be kept from others' knowledge
sec·re·tary *n, pl* **sec·re·tar·ies** **1** : a person who is employed to take care of records, letters, and routine work for another person **2** : an officer of a business corporation or society who is in charge of the letters and records and who keeps minutes of meetings **3** : a government official in charge of a department **4** : a writing desk with a top section for books
[1]**se·crete** *vb* **se·cret·ed; se·cret·ing** : to produce and give off as a secretion
[2]**secrete** *vb* **se·cret·ed; se·cret·ing** : to put in a hiding place
se·cre·tion *n* **1** : the act or process of giving off a substance **2** : a substance formed in and given off by a gland that usually performs a useful function in the body
se·cre·tive *adj* : tending to act in secret or keep secrets
sect *n* : a group within a religion which has a special set of teachings or a special way of doing things
[1]**sec·tion** *n* **1** : a division of a thing or place **2** : a part cut off or separated **3** : a part of a written work **4** : CROSS SECTION
[2]**section** *vb* **sec·tioned; sec·tion·ing** : to cut into parts
sec·tor *n* : a part of an area or of a sphere of activity
sec·u·lar *adj* **1** : not concerned with religion or the church **2** : not belonging to a religious order
[1]**se·cure** *adj* **se·cur·er; se·cur·est** **1** : free from danger or risk **2** : strong or firm enough to ensure safety **3** : free from worry or doubt : CONFIDENT **4** : [1]SURE 5, CERTAIN
[2]**secure** *vb* **se·cured; se·cur·ing** **1** : to make safe **2** : to fasten or put something in a place to keep it from coming loose **3** : to get hold of : ACQUIRE
se·cu·ri·ty *n, pl* **se·cu·ri·ties** **1** : the state of being safe : SAFETY **2** : freedom from worry or anxiety **3** : something given as a pledge of payment **4** : something (as a stock certificate) that is evidence of debt or ownership
se·dan *n* **1** : a closed automobile that has two or four doors and a permanent top and seats four or more people **2** : SEDAN CHAIR
sedan chair *n* : a chair made to hold one person and to be carried on two poles by two others
se·date *adj* : quiet and steady in manner or conduct — **se·date·ly** *adv*
sed·a·tive *n* : a medicine that calms or relaxes someone
sed·en·tary *adj* : doing much sitting : not physically active
sedge *n* : a plant that is like grass but has solid stems and grows in tufts in marshes
sed·i·ment *n* **1** : the material from a liquid that settles to the bottom **2** : material (as stones and sand) carried onto land or into water by water, wind, or a glacier
sed·i·men·ta·ry *adj* : relating to or formed from sediment
se·duce *vb* **se·duced; se·duc·ing** : to per-

suade (someone) to do something and especially to do something wrong

[1]see *vb* **saw; seen; see·ing** **1 :** to have the power of sight **2 :** to view with the eyes **3 :** to have experience of **4 :** to understand the meaning or importance of **5 :** to come to know **:** DISCOVER **6 :** to call on **:** VISIT **7 :** to form a mental picture of **8 :** to imagine as a possibility **9 :** to make sure **10 :** to attend to **11 :** to meet with **12 :** ACCOMPANY 1, ESCORT

[2]see *n* **1 :** the city in which a bishop's church is located **2 :** DIOCESE

[1]seed *n* **1 :** a tiny developing plant that is enclosed in a protective coat usually along with a supply of food and that is able to develop under suitable conditions into a plant like the one that produced it **2 :** a small structure (as a spore or a tiny dry fruit) other than a true seed by which a plant reproduces itself **3 :** the descendants of one individual **4 :** a source of development or growth **:** GERM — **seed·ed** *adj* — **seed·less** *adj*

[2]seed *vb* **seed·ed; seed·ing** **1 :** [2]SOW 2, PLANT **2 :** to produce or shed seeds **3 :** to take the seeds out of

seed·ling *n* **1 :** a young plant grown from seed **2 :** a young tree before it becomes a sapling

seed plant *n* **:** a plant that produces seed

seed·pod *n* **:** POD

seedy *adj* **seed·i·er; seed·i·est** **1 :** having or full of seeds **2 :** poor in condition or quality

seek *vb* **sought; seek·ing** **1 :** to try to find **2 :** to try to win or get **3 :** to make an attempt

seem *vb* **seemed; seem·ing** **1 :** to give the impression of being **:** APPEAR **2** — used to make a statement less forceful or more polite

seem·ing *adj* **:** APPARENT 3 — **seem·ing·ly** *adv*

seen *past participle of* SEE

seep *vb* **seeped; seep·ing** **:** to flow slowly through small openings

seer *n* **:** a person who predicts events

[1]see·saw *n* **1 :** a plank for children to play on that is balanced in the middle on a raised bar with one end going up while the other goes down **2 :** a situation in which something keeps changing from one state to another and back again

[2]seesaw *vb* **see·sawed; see·saw·ing** **:** to keep changing from one state to another and back again

seethe *vb* **seethed; seeth·ing** **1 :** to feel or show great excitement or emotion (as anger) **2 :** to move constantly and without order

seg·ment *n* **1 :** any of the parts into which a thing is divided or naturally separates **2 :** a part cut off from a figure (as a circle) by means of a line or plane **3 :** a part of a straight line included between two points

seg·re·gate *vb* **seg·re·gat·ed; seg·re·gat·ing** **:** to separate a race, class, or group from the rest of society

seg·re·ga·tion *n* **:** the practice or policy of separating a race, class, or group from the rest of society

seis·mo·graph *n* **:** a device that measures and records vibrations of the earth

seize *vb* **seized; seiz·ing** **1 :** to take possession of by or as if by force **2 :** to take hold of suddenly or with force **3 :** to take or use eagerly or quickly

sei·zure *n* **1 :** an act of taking suddenly or with force **:** the state of being taken suddenly or with force **2 :** an abnormal state in which a person usually experiences convulsions and may become unconscious

sel·dom *adv* **:** not often **:** RARELY

[1]se·lect *vb* **se·lect·ed; se·lect·ing** **:** to pick out from a group

[2]select *adj* **1 :** chosen to include the best or most suitable individuals **2 :** of special value or excellence

se·lec·tion *n* **1 :** the act or process of choosing **2 :** something that is chosen

se·lec·tive *adj* **:** careful to choose or include only the best or most suitable individuals

se·le·ni·um *n* **:** a gray powdery chemical element used chiefly in electronic devices

self *n, pl* **selves** **1 :** a person regarded as an individual apart from everyone else **2 :** a special side of a person's character

self- *prefix* **1 :** someone's or something's self **2 :** of or by someone's or something's self **3 :** to, with, for, or toward someone's or something's self

self–ad·dressed *adj* **:** addressed for return to the sender

self–cen·tered *adj* **:** SELFISH

self–con·fi·dence *n* **:** someone's confidence in himself or herself and in his or her own abilities

self–con·scious *adj* **:** feeling uncomfortably nervous or embarrassed when in the presence of or when being observed by other people — **self–con·scious·ly** *adv* — **self–con·scious·ness** *n*

self–con·trol *n* **:** someone's control over his or her own impulses, emotions, or actions

self–de·fense *n* **:** someone's act of defending himself or herself or his or her property

self–es·teem *n* **:** a feeling of satisfaction that someone has in himself or herself and his or her own abilities

self–ev·i·dent *adj* **:** clearly true and requiring no proof

self–gov·ern·ing *adj* **:** being governed by its own members or citizens

self–gov·ern·ment *n* : government by the people making up a group or community
self·ie *n* : a picture a person takes of himself or herself using a digital camera especially for posting on social media
self–im·por·tance *n* : an attitude showing that someone has an overly high opinion of his or her own importance
self–im·por·tant *adj* : having or showing the attitude of someone who has too high an opinion of his or her own importance : showing self-importance
self·ish *adj* : taking care of only a person's own needs and feelings without thought for others — **self·ish·ly** *adv* — **self·ish·ness** *n*
self·less *adj* : showing great concern for and willingness to give unselfishly to others — **self·less·ly** *adv* — **self·less·ness** *n*
self–pos·sessed *adj* : having or showing control of emotions or reactions
self–pro·pelled *adj* : containing within itself the means for its own movement
self–re·li·ance *n* : a feeling of trust that someone has in his or her own efforts and abilities
self–re·spect *n* : someone's proper regard for himself or herself as a human being
self–re·straint *n* : proper self-control over actions or emotions
self–righ·teous *adj* : having or showing the attitude of someone who strongly believes in the rightness of his or her own actions or opinions — **self–righ·teous·ness** *n*
self·same *adj* : exactly the same
self–ser·vice *adj* : allowing or requiring customers to serve themselves without help from workers
self–suf·fi·cient *adj* : able to live or function without the help of others
self–worth *n* : SELF-ESTEEM
sell *vb* **sold; sell·ing** **1** : to exchange in return for money or something else of value **2** : to make available for sale **3** : to be sold or priced — **sell·er** *n* — **sell out** **1** : to be bought until all are gone **2** : to betray a person or duty
selves *pl of* SELF
sem·a·phore *n* **1** : a device for sending signals that can be seen by the receiver **2** : a system of sending signals with two flags held one in each hand
sem·blance *n* : outward appearance
se·mes·ter *n* : either of two terms that make up a school year
semi- *prefix* **1** : half **2** : partly : not completely **3** : partial
semi·cir·cle *n* : half of a circle
semi·co·lon *n* : a punctuation mark ; that can be used to separate parts of a sentence which need clearer separation than would be shown by a comma, to separate main clauses which have no conjunction between, and to separate phrases and clauses containing commas
semi·con·duc·tor *n* : a solid substance that conducts electricity imperfectly
semi·fi·nal *n* : a match or game coming before the final round in a tournament
sem·i·nary *n, pl* **sem·i·nar·ies** **1** : a private school at or above the high school level **2** : a school for the training of priests, ministers, or rabbis
Sem·i·nole *n, pl* **Sem·i·noles** *or* **Seminole** : a member of an American Indian people of Florida and Oklahoma
semi·sol·id *adj* : having the qualities of both a solid and a liquid
Sen. *abbr* senate, senator
sen·ate *n* **1** *cap* : the upper house of a legislature (as the United States Congress) **2** : a governing body
sen·a·tor *n* : a member of a Senate
send *vb* **sent; send·ing** **1** : to cause to go **2** : to set in motion by physical force **3** : to cause to move in a particular direction or manner **4** : to cause someone to pass a message on or do an errand **5** : to give an order or request to come or go **6** : to bring into a certain condition — **send·er** *n*
Sen·e·ca *n, pl* **Seneca** *or* **Sen·e·cas** **1** : a member of an American Indian people of western New York **2** : the language of the Seneca people
[1]**se·nior** *n* **1** : a person older or higher in rank than someone else **2** : a student in the final year of high school or college **3** : an elderly person
[2]**senior** *adj* **1** : being older — often used to distinguish a father from a son with the same name **2** : higher in rank or office **3** : relating to students in the final year of high school or college
senior airman *n* : an enlisted person in the air force who ranks above airman first class but who has not been made sergeant
sen·sa·tion *n* **1** : awareness (as of noise or heat) or a mental process (as seeing or smelling) resulting from stimulation of a sense organ **2** : an indefinite awareness of a feeling or experience **3** : a state of excited interest or feeling **4** : a cause or object of excited interest
sen·sa·tion·al *adj* **1** : causing or meant to cause great interest **2** : very or unexpectedly excellent
[1]**sense** *n* **1** : a specialized function or mechanism (as sight, taste, or touch) of the body that involves the action and effect of a stimulus on a sense organ **2** : awareness arrived at through or as if through the senses **3** : a particular sensation or kind of sensation **4**

: the ability to make wise decisions **5** : an awareness or understanding of something **6** : a reason or excuse based on intelligence or good judgment **7** : a logical, sensible, or practical thing, act, or way of doing **8** : a meaning or one of a set of meanings a word, phrase, or story may have

²sense *vb* **sensed; sens·ing** : to be or become aware of

sense·less *adj* **1** : UNCONSCIOUS 2 **2** : STUPID 2 — **sense·less·ly** *adv*

sense organ *n* : a part of the body (as the eye or nose) that contains special cells that receive stimuli (as light) and activate associated nerves so that they carry impulses to the brain

sen·si·bil·i·ty *n, pl* **sen·si·bil·i·ties** **1** : the ability to receive or feel sensations **2** : the ability to feel and understand emotions

sen·si·ble *adj* **1** : showing or containing good sense or judgment **2** : designed for a practical purpose rather than for appearance **3** : capable of feeling or perceiving — **sen·si·bly** *adv*

sen·si·tive *adj* **1** : easily or strongly affected, impressed, or hurt **2** : likely to affect, impress, or hurt **3** : understanding of the feelings of others **4** : capable of responding to stimulation **5** : readily affected or changed often in an unpleasant or negative way — **sen·si·tive·ly** *adv*

sen·si·tiv·i·ty *n* **1** : an awareness and understanding of the feelings of others **2** : the ability to express thoughts and feelings

sen·so·ry *adj* : of or relating to sensation or the senses

sen·su·al *adj* : relating to the pleasing of the senses

sent *past and past participle of* SEND

¹sen·tence *n* **1** : a group of words that makes a statement, asks a question, or expresses a command, wish, or exclamation **2** : punishment set by a court **3** : a mathematical statement (as an equation) in words or symbols

²sentence *vb* **sen·tenced; sen·tenc·ing** : to set the punishment of

sen·ti·ment *n* **1** : a thought or attitude influenced by feeling **2** : OPINION 1 **3** : tender feelings of affection

sen·ti·men·tal *adj* **1** : influenced strongly by feelings of affection or yearning **2** : primarily affecting the emotions

sen·ti·nel *n* : SENTRY

sen·try *n, pl* **sentries** : a person (as a soldier) on duty as a guard

Sep. *abbr* September

se·pal *n* : one of the specialized leaves that form the calyx of a flower

¹sep·a·rate *vb* **sep·a·rat·ed; sep·a·rat·ing** **1** : to set or keep apart **2** : to make a distinction between **3** : to cease to be together : PART

²sep·a·rate *adj* **1** : set apart **2** : not shared : INDIVIDUAL **3** : existing independently from each other

sep·a·rate·ly *adv* : apart from others or another

sep·a·ra·tion *n* **1** : the act of setting or pulling apart : the state of being set or pulled apart **2** : a point or line at which something is divided **3** : a space between

Sept. *abbr* September

Sep·tem·ber *n* : the ninth month of the year

sep·tet *n* : a group or set of seven

sep·ul·chre *or* **sep·ul·cher** *n* : ¹GRAVE, TOMB

se·quel *n* **1** : a book or movie that continues a story begun in another **2** : an event that follows or comes afterward : RESULT

se·quence *n* **1** : the order in which things are or should be connected, related, or dated **2** : a group of things that come one after another

se·quin *n* : a bit of shiny metal or plastic used as an ornament usually on clothing

se·quoia *n* **1** : GIANT SEQUOIA **2** : REDWOOD

¹ser·e·nade *n* : music sung or played at night for a woman

²serenade *vb* **ser·e·nad·ed; ser·e·nad·ing** : to entertain (a woman) with music sung or played at night

se·rene *adj* **1** : being calm and quiet **2** : ¹CLEAR 2 — **se·rene·ly** *adv*

se·ren·i·ty *n* : the quality or state of being calm and peaceful

serf *n* : a servant or laborer of olden times who was treated as part of the land worked on and went along with the land if it was sold

serge *n* : a strong woolen cloth

ser·geant *n* **1** : a noncommissioned officer in the army or marine corps ranking above a corporal or in the air force ranking above an airman first class **2** : an officer in a police force

sergeant first class *n* : a noncommissioned officer in the army ranking above a staff sergeant

sergeant major *n* **1** : the chief noncommissioned officer at a military headquarters **2** : a noncommissioned officer in the marine corps ranking above a first sergeant

¹se·ri·al *adj* : arranged in or appearing in parts or numbers that follow a regular order

²serial *n* : a story appearing (as in a magazine or on television) in parts at regular intervals

se·ries *n, pl* **series** : a number of things or events arranged in order and connected by being alike in some way

se·ri·ous *adj* **1** : not joking or funny **2** : being such as to cause distress or harm **3** : thoughtful or quiet in appearance or man-

ner **4 :** requiring much thought or work — **se·ri·ous·ness** *n*
se·ri·ous·ly *adv* **1 :** in an earnest way **2 :** in a literal way **3 :** to a large degree or extent
ser·mon *n* **1 :** a speech usually by a priest, minister, or rabbi for the purpose of giving religious instruction **2 :** a serious talk to a person about his or her conduct
ser·pent *n* **:** a usually large snake
ser·pen·tine *adj* **:** winding or turning one way and another
se·rum *n* **:** the clear liquid part that can be separated from coagulated blood and contains antibodies
ser·vant *n* **:** a person hired to perform household or personal services
[1]**serve** *vb* **served; serv·ing** **1 :** to help people to food or drink or set out helpings of food or drink **2 :** to be of use **:** answer some purpose **3 :** to be a servant **4 :** to give the service and respect due **5 :** to be in prison for or during (a period of time) **6 :** to provide helpful services **7 :** to be enough for **8 :** to hold an office **:** perform a duty **9 :** to perform a term of service **10 :** to furnish with something needed or desired **11 :** to put the ball or shuttlecock in play (as in tennis, volleyball, or badminton) — **serve someone right :** to be deserved
[2]**serve** *n* **:** an act of putting the ball or shuttlecock in play (as in tennis, volleyball, or badminton)
[1]**ser·vice** *n* **1 :** [2]HELP 1, USE **2 :** a religious ceremony **3 :** the occupation or function of serving or working as a servant **4 :** the work or action of helping customers **5 :** a helpful or useful act **:** good turn **6 :** a set of dishes or silverware **7 :** an organization that provides something to the public **8 :** a nation's armed forces **9 :** an organization or business that supplies some public demand or provides maintenance and repair for something **10 :** [2]SERVE
[2]**service** *vb* **ser·viced; ser·vic·ing :** to work on in order to maintain or repair
ser·vice·able *adj* **1 :** USEFUL 1 **2 :** of adequate quality
ser·vice·man *n, pl* **ser·vice·men :** a man who is a member of the armed forces
service station *n* **:** GAS STATION
ser·vice·wom·an *n, pl* **ser·vice·wom·en :** a woman who is a member of the armed forces
ser·vile *adj* **1 :** of or suitable to a slave **2 :** very obedient and trying too hard to please
serv·ing *n* **:** a helping of food
ser·vi·tude *n* **:** the condition of being a slave or of having to obey another
ses·sion *n* **1 :** a meeting or period devoted to a particular activity **2 :** a single meeting (as of a court, lawmaking body, or school) **3 :** a whole series of meetings **4 :** the time during which a court, congress, or school meets
[1]**set** *vb* **set; set·ting** **1 :** to put or fix in a place or condition **2 :** to cause to be, become, or do **3 :** [1]START 4 **4 :** to fix or decide on **5 :** to furnish as a model **6 :** to adjust or put in order for use **7 :** to fix firmly **8 :** to pass below the horizon **:** go down **9 :** to begin some activity **10 :** to cause to sit **11 :** to arrange in a desired and especially a normal position **12 :** to become or cause to become firm or solid **13 :** to cover and warm eggs to hatch them **14 :** to locate the plot of (a story) **15 :** to provide (as words or verses) with music — **set aside :** to reserve for some purpose — **set eyes on :** to catch sight of **:** SEE — **set in :** to make its appearance **:** BEGIN — **set off** **1 :** to start a journey **2 :** EXPLODE 1 **3 :** to make noticeable **4 :** to cause to start — **set out** **1 :** to begin on a course or journey **2 :** to begin with a purpose — **set up** **1 :** to place or secure in position **2 :** to put in operation
[2]**set** *n* 1 **:** a number of persons or things of the same kind that belong together, are used together, or occur together **2 :** the act or action of going below the horizon **3 :** an electronic apparatus **4 :** a collection of mathematical elements **5 :** a group of tennis games that make up a match **6 :** the form or movement of the body or of its parts **7 :** an artificial setting for a scene of a play or motion picture
[3]**set** *adj* **1 :** fixed by authority **2 :** not very willing to change **3 :** [1]READY 1
set·back *n* **:** a slowing of progress **:** a temporary defeat
set·tee *n* **:** a long seat with a back
set·ter *n* **1 :** a large dog that has long hair and is used in hunting birds **2 :** one that sets
set·ting *n* **1 :** the act of one that sets **2 :** that in which something is set or mounted **3 :** the background (as time and place) of the action of a story or play
[1]**set·tle** *vb* **set·tled; set·tling** **1 :** to come to rest **2 :** to make a home **3 :** to make quiet **:** CALM **4 :** DECIDE 1 **5 :** to place so as to stay **6 :** to sink gradually to a lower level **7 :** to sink in a liquid **8 :** to give attention to **9 :** to fix by agreement **10 :** to put in order **11 :** to complete payment on **12 :** to bring to an end **13 :** to take up a stable life **14 :** to be content with
[2]**settle** *n* **:** a long wooden bench with arms and a high solid back
set·tle·ment *n* **1 :** a formal agreement that ends an argument or dispute **2 :** final payment (as of a bill) **3 :** the act or fact of establishing colonies **4 :** a place or region newly settled **5 :** a small village

set·tler *n* : a person who settles in a new region : COLONIST

[1]**sev·en** *adj* : being one more than six

[2]**seven** *n* **1** : one more than six : 7 **2** : the seventh in a set or series

[1]**sev·en·teen** *adj* : being one more than 16

[2]**seventeen** *n* : one more than 16 : 17

[1]**sev·en·teenth** *adj* : coming right after 16th

[2]**seventeenth** *n* : number 17 in a series

[1]**sev·enth** *adj* : coming right after sixth

[2]**seventh** *n* **1** : number seven in a series **2** : one of seven equal parts

[1]**sev·en·ti·eth** *adj* : coming right after 69th

[2]**seventieth** *n* : number 70 in a series

[1]**sev·en·ty** *adj* : being seven times ten

[2]**seventy** *n* : seven times ten : 70

sev·er *vb* **sev·ered; sev·er·ing** : to cut off

[1]**sev·er·al** *adj* **1** : consisting of more than two but not very many **2** : separate or distinct from others : DIFFERENT

[2]**several** *pron* : a small number : more than two but not many

se·vere *adj* **se·ver·er; se·ver·est** **1** : serious in feeling or manner **2** : hard to bear or deal with **3** : very strict : HARSH **4** : not having much decoration : PLAIN — **se·vere·ly** *adv*

se·ver·i·ty *n* : the quality or state of being severe

sew *vb* **sewed; sewn** *or* **sewed; sew·ing** **1** : to join or fasten by stitches **2** : to work with needle and thread

sew·age *n* : waste materials carried off by sewers

[1]**sew·er** *n* : a usually covered drain to carry off water and waste

[2]**sew·er** *n* : someone that sews

sew·er·age *n* **1** : the removal and disposal of waste materials by sewers **2** : a system of sewers

sew·ing *n* **1** : the act, method, or occupation of someone that works with needle and thread **2** : material being or to be worked with needle and thread

sex *n* **1** : either of two divisions into which many living things can be divided according to their roles in reproduction and which consist of males or females **2** : the state of being male or female **3** : sexual activity

sex·ism *n* : distinction and especially unjust distinction based on gender and made against one person or group (as women) in favor of another

sex·ist *adj* : based on or showing sexism — **sexist** *n*

sex·ton *n* : an official of a church who takes care of church buildings and property

sex·u·al *adj* **1** : of or relating to sex or the sexes **2** : of, relating to, or being the form of reproduction in which germ cells from two parents combine in fertilization to form a new individual — **sex·u·al·ly** *adv*

Sgt. *abbr* sergeant

shab·by *adj* **shab·bi·er; shab·bi·est** **1** : faded and worn from use or wear **2** : in poor condition : DILAPIDATED **3** : dressed in worn clothes **4** : not fair or generous — **shab·bi·ly** *adv* — **shab·bi·ness** *n*

shack *n* : HUT, SHANTY

[1]**shack·le** *n* **1** : a ring or band that prevents free use of the legs or arms **2** : something that prevents free action

[2]**shackle** *vb* **shack·led; shack·ling** **1** : to bind or fasten with a ring or band placed on the legs or arms **2** : to prevent free action

shad *n, pl* **shad** : a silvery ocean fish that swims up rivers to lay or fertilize eggs and is often used for food

[1]**shade** *n* **1** : space sheltered from light or heat and especially from the sun **2** : partial darkness **3** : something that blocks off or cuts down light **4** : the darkness or lightness of a color **5** : a very small difference or amount **6** : GHOST, SPIRIT **7** : the darkening of some objects in a painting or drawing to suggest that they are in shade

[2]**shade** *vb* **shad·ed; shad·ing** **1** : to shelter from light or heat **2** : to mark with or turn a darker color

[1]**shad·ow** *n* **1** : the dark figure cast on a surface by a body that is between the surface and the light **2** : [1]SHADE 2 **3** : PHANTOM **4** : a very little bit : TRACE **5** : something that causes a bad feeling **6** **shadows** *pl* : darkness caused by the setting of the sun

[2]**shadow** *vb* **shad·owed; shad·ow·ing** **1** : to cast a shadow upon **2** : to follow and watch closely especially in a secret way

shad·owy *adj* **1** : full of shade **2** : INDISTINCT

shady *adj* **shad·i·er; shad·i·est** **1** : sheltered from the sun's rays **2** : producing shade **3** : not right or honest

shaft *n* **1** : the long handle of a weapon, tool, or instrument **2** : one of two poles between which a horse is hitched to pull a wagon or carriage **3** : an arrow or its narrow stem **4** : a narrow beam of light **5** : a long narrow part or structure especially when round **6** : a mine opening made for finding or mining ore **7** : an opening or passage straight down through the floors of a building **8** : a bar to support rotating pieces of machinery or to give them motion

shag·gy *adj* **shag·gi·er; shag·gi·est** : covered with or made up of a long and tangled growth (as of hair)

[1]**shake** *vb* **shook; shak·en; shak·ing** **1** : to make or cause to make quick movements back and forth or up and down **2** : to tremble or make tremble : QUIVER **3** : to move from side to side **4** : to grasp and move

up and down **5 :** to get away from **6 :** to make less firm **:** WEAKEN **7 :** to cause to be, become, go, or move by or as if by using a quick back and forth motion

²shake *n* **:** a quick back and forth or up and down movement

shak·er *n* **:** a container used to mix the contents or sprinkle out some of the contents

shaky *adj* **shak·i·er; shak·i·est 1 :** characterized by quivering **:** not firm **2 :** likely to fail or be insufficient **:** UNSOUND — **shak·i·ly** *adv*

shale *n* **:** a rock with a fine grain formed from clay, mud, or silt

shall *helping verb, past* **should;** *present sing & pl* **shall 1 :** am or are going to or expecting to **:** WILL **2 :** is or are forced to **:** MUST

¹shal·low *adj* **shal·low·er; shal·low·est 1 :** not deep **2 :** taking in small amounts of air **3 :** showing little knowledge, thought, or feeling — **shal·low·ness** *n*

²shallow *n* **:** a shallow place in a body of water — usually used in pl.

¹sham *n* **1 :** something that deceives **:** HOAX **2 :** something that is claimed to be true or real but which is actually phony **3 :** a decorative covering for a pillow

²sham *adj* **:** not real **:** FALSE

³sham *vb* **shammed; sham·ming :** to act in a deceiving way

sham·ble *vb* **sham·bled; sham·bling :** to walk in an awkward unsteady way

sham·bles *n pl* **:** a place or scene of disorder or destruction — used as singular or plural

¹shame *n* **1 :** a painful emotion caused by having done something wrong or improper **2 :** ability to feel shame **3 :** ¹DISHONOR 1, DISGRACE **4 :** something that brings disgrace or causes painful emotion or strong regret

²shame *vb* **shamed; sham·ing 1 :** to make ashamed **2 :** ²DISHONOR **3 :** to force by causing to feel shame

shame·faced *adj* **:** seeming ashamed

shame·ful *adj* **:** bringing shame **:** DISGRACEFUL — **shame·ful·ly** *adv* — **shame·ful·ness** *n*

shame·less *adj* **:** having no shame — **shame·less·ly** *adv* — **shame·less·ness** *n*

¹sham·poo *n, pl* **sham·poos 1 :** a cleaner made for washing the hair **2 :** an act of washing the hair

²sham·poo *vb* **sham·pooed; sham·poo·ing :** to wash the hair and scalp

sham·rock *n* **:** a plant (as some clovers) that has leaves with three leaflets and is used as an emblem by the Irish

shank *n* **1 :** the part of the leg between the knee and ankle **2 :** a cut of meat from the usually upper part of the leg **3 :** the part of a tool that connects the working part with a part by which it is held or moved

shan't : shall not

shan·ty *n, pl* **shanties :** a small roughly built shelter or dwelling

¹shape *vb* **shaped; shap·ing 1 :** to give a certain form or shape to **2 :** to plan out **:** DEVISE **3 :** to have great influence on the development of — **shap·er** *n* — **shape up 1 :** to develop in a particular way **2 :** to improve in behavior or condition

²shape *n* **1 :** outward appearance **:** the form or outline of something **2 :** definite arrangement and form **3 :** ¹CONDITION 3 **4 :** a physically fit condition — **shaped** *adj*

shape·less *adj* **1 :** having no fixed or definite shape **2 :** lacking a pleasing or usual shape or form

shape·ly *adj* **shape·li·er; shape·li·est :** having a pleasing shape or form

shard *n* **:** a sharp piece or fragment of something

¹share *n* **1 :** a portion belonging to, due to, or contributed by one person **2 :** the part given or belonging to one of a group of people owning something together **3 :** any of the equal parts into which a property or corporation is divided

²share *vb* **shared; shar·ing 1 :** to divide and distribute in portions **2 :** to use, experience, or enjoy with others **3 :** to have or take a part in **4 :** to have in common

share·crop *vb* **share·cropped; share·crop·ping :** to farm another's land for a share of the crop or profit — **share·crop·per** *n*

¹shark *n* **:** a large usually gray saltwater fish that has sharp teeth and a skeleton of cartilage

²shark *n* **:** a person who cheats others out of money

¹sharp *adj* **sharp·er; sharp·est 1 :** having a thin edge or fine point (as for cutting or piercing) **2 :** brisk and cold **3 :** very smart **4 :** ATTENTIVE 1 **5 :** having very good ability to see or hear **6 :** ENERGETIC, BRISK **7 :** showing anger or disapproval **8 :** causing distress **:** SEVERE **9 :** strongly affecting the senses **10 :** ending in a point or edge **11 :** involving a sudden and quick change **12 :** clear in outline or detail **:** DISTINCT **13 :** raised in pitch by a half step **14 :** higher than true pitch **15 :** STYLISH — **sharp·ly** *adv* — **sharp·ness** *n*

²sharp *adv* **1 :** at an exact time **2 :** at a higher than true pitch **3 :** in a stylish way

³sharp *n* **1 :** a musical note or tone that is a half step higher than the note named **2 :** a sign ♯ that tells that a note is to be made higher by a half step

sharp·en *vb* **sharp·ened; sharp·en·ing :** to

make or become sharp or sharper — **sharp·en·er** *n*

shat·ter *vb* **shat·tered; shat·ter·ing** **1 :** to break or fall to pieces **2 :** to destroy or damage badly

[1]shave *vb* **shaved; shaved** *or* **shav·en; shav·ing** **1 :** to cut or trim off a thin layer of (as with a sharp blade) **2 :** to cut off very close to the skin **3 :** to make bare or smooth by cutting the hair from

[2]shave *n* **1 :** an act of making bare or smooth by cutting the hair from **2 :** a narrow escape

shav·ing *n* **:** a thin slice or strip sliced or trimmed off with a cutting tool

shawl *n* **:** a square or oblong piece of cloth used especially by women as a loose covering for the head or shoulders

she *pron* **:** that female one

sheaf *n, pl* **sheaves** **1 :** a bundle of stalks and ears of grain **2 :** a group of things fastened together

shear *vb* **sheared; sheared** *or* **shorn; shear·ing** **1 :** to cut the hair or wool from **:** CLIP **2 :** to cut or clip (as hair or wool) from something **3 :** to strip of as if by cutting **4 :** to cut or break sharply — **shear·er** *n*

shears *n pl* **:** a cutting tool like a pair of large scissors

sheath *n, pl* **sheaths** **1 :** a case for a blade (as of a knife) **2 :** a covering that surrounds and usually protects something

sheathe *vb* **sheathed; sheath·ing** **1 :** to put into a sheath **2 :** to cover with something that protects

sheath·ing *n* **:** material used as a protective covering

sheaves *pl of* SHEAF

[1]shed *vb* **shed; shed·ding** **1 :** to give off in drops **2 :** to get rid of **3 :** to give off or out **4 :** REPEL 3 **5 :** to lose or cast aside (a natural covering or part)

[2]shed *n* **:** a small simple building used especially for storage

she'd : she had **:** she would

sheen *n* **:** a bright or shining condition **:** LUSTER

sheep *n, pl* **sheep** **1 :** an animal related to the goat that is often raised for meat or for its wool and skin **2 :** a weak helpless person who is easily led

sheep·fold *n* **:** a pen or shelter for sheep

sheep·herd·er *n* **:** a person in charge of a flock of sheep

sheep·ish *adj* **1 :** like a sheep (as in being meek or shy) **2 :** feeling or showing embarrassment especially over being discovered having done something wrong or foolish — **sheep·ish·ly** *adv*

sheep·skin *n* **:** the skin of a sheep or leather prepared from it

sheer *adj* **sheer·er; sheer·est** **1 :** very thin or transparent **2 :** complete and total **:** ABSOLUTE **3 :** taken or acting apart from everything else **4 :** very steep

[1]sheet *n* **1 :** a large piece of cloth used to cover something and especially to cover a bed **2 :** a usually rectangular piece of paper **3 :** a broad continuous surface **4 :** something that is very thin as compared with its length and width

[2]sheet *n* **:** a rope or chain used to adjust the angle at which the sail of a boat is set to catch the wind

sheikh *or* **sheik** *n* **1 :** an Arab chief **2 :** a leader of a Muslim group

shek·el *n* **:** a bill or coin used in Israel

shelf *n, pl* **shelves** **1 :** a flat piece (as of wood or metal) set above a floor (as on a wall or in a bookcase) to hold things **2 :** a flat area (as of rock)

[1]shell *n* **1 :** a stiff hard covering of an animal (as a turtle, oyster, or crab) **2 :** the tough outer covering of an egg **3 :** the outer covering of a nut, fruit, or seed especially when hard or tough **4 :** something like a shell (as in shape, function, or material) **5 :** a narrow light racing boat rowed by one or more persons **6 :** a metal or paper case holding the explosive charge and the shot or object to be fired from a gun or cannon — **shelled** *adj*

[2]shell *vb* **shelled; shell·ing** **1 :** to remove the shell or outer covering of **2 :** to remove the kernels of grain from (as a cob of corn) **3 :** to shoot shells at or upon

she'll : she shall **:** she will

[1]shel·lac *n* **:** a varnish made from a material given off by an Asian insect dissolved usually in alcohol

[2]shellac *vb* **shel·lacked; shel·lack·ing** **:** to coat with shellac

shell·fish *n, pl* **shellfish** **:** an invertebrate animal (as a clam or lobster) that has a hard outer shell and lives in water

[1]shel·ter *n* **1 :** something that covers or protects **2 :** a place that provides food and housing to those in need **3 :** the condition of being protected

[2]shelter *vb* **shel·tered; shel·ter·ing** **1 :** to provide with a place that covers or protects **:** be a shelter for **2 :** to find and use a shelter for protection

shelve *vb* **shelved; shelv·ing** **1 :** to place or store on a shelf **2 :** to put off or aside **:** DEFER

shelves *pl of* SHELF

she·nan·i·gans *n pl* **:** funny or mischievous activity or behavior

[1]shep·herd *n* **:** a person who takes care of and guards a flock of sheep

[2]shepherd *vb* **shep·herded; shep·herd·ing**

1 : to take care of and guard a flock of sheep 2 : to gather, lead, or move in the manner of a shepherd

shep·herd·ess *n* : a woman who takes care of and guards a flock of sheep

sher·bet *n* : a frozen dessert made of sweetened fruit juice and milk

sher·iff *n* : the officer of a county who is in charge of enforcing the law

she's : she is : she has

Shet·land pony *n* : a small stocky horse with a heavy coat and short legs

[1]**shield** *n* **1** : a broad piece of armor carried (as by a soldier) for protection **2** : something that serves as a defense or protection

[2]**shield** *vb* **shield·ed; shield·ing** : to cover or screen (as from danger or harm) : provide with protection

[1]**shift** *vb* **shift·ed; shift·ing** **1** : to change or make a change in place, position, or direction **2** : to go through a change **3** : to change the arrangement of gears transmitting power (as in an automobile) **4** : to get along without help : FEND

[2]**shift** *n* **1** : a change in place, position, or direction **2** : a change in emphasis or attitude **3** : a group of workers who work together during a scheduled period of time **4** : the scheduled period of time during which one group of workers is working **5** : GEARSHIFT

shift·less *adj* : LAZY

shifty *adj* **shift·i·er; shift·i·est** : not worthy of trust : causing suspicion

shil·ling *n* : an old British coin equal to 1/20 pound

[1]**shim·mer** *vb* **shim·mered; shim·mer·ing** : to shine with a wavering light : GLIMMER

[2]**shimmer** *n* : a wavering light

shim·my *vb* **shim·mied; shim·my·ing** : to move the body from side to side

[1]**shin** *n* : the front part of the leg below the knee

[2]**shin** *vb* **shinned; shin·ning** : SHINNY

[1]**shine** *vb* **shone** *or* **shined; shin·ing** **1** : to give off light **2** : to be glossy : GLEAM **3** : to direct the light of **4** : to be outstanding **5** : to make bright by polishing

[2]**shine** *n* **1** : brightness from light given off or reflected **2** : fair weather : SUNSHINE **3** : [2]POLISH 1

shin·er *n* : a small silvery American freshwater fish

[1]**shin·gle** *n* **1** : a small thin piece of building material for laying in overlapping rows as a covering for the roof or sides of a building **2** : a small sign

[2]**shingle** *vb* **shin·gled; shin·gling** : to cover with shingles

shin·ny *vb* **shin·nied; shin·ny·ing** : to climb (as a pole) by grasping with arms and legs and moving upward by repeated jerks

Shin·to *n* : the traditional religion of Japan — **Shin·to** *adj* — **Shin·to·ism** *n*

shiny *adj* **shin·i·er; shin·i·est** : having a smooth bright appearance

[1]**ship** *n* **1** : a large boat designed for travel by sea **2** : AIRSHIP, AIRPLANE **3** : a vehicle for traveling beyond the earth's atmosphere

[2]**ship** *vb* **shipped; ship·ping** **1** : to cause to be transported **2** : to put or receive on board for transportation by water **3** : to send (someone) to a place **4** : to take into a ship or boat **5** : to sign on as a crew member on a ship

-ship *n suffix* **1** : state : condition : quality **2** : office : rank : profession **3** : skill **4** : something showing a quality or state of being **5** : someone having a specified rank

ship·board *n* **1** : a ship's side **2** : [1]SHIP 1

ship·ment *n* **1** : the act of shipping **2** : a package or goods shipped

ship·ping *n* **1** : the act or business of a person who ships goods **2** : a group of ships in one place or belonging to one port or country

ship·shape *adj* : being neat and orderly

[1]**ship·wreck** *n* **1** : a ruined or destroyed ship **2** : the loss or destruction of a ship

[2]**shipwreck** *vb* **ship·wrecked; ship·wreck·ing** **1** : to cause to experience destruction of a ship and usually be left stranded **2** : to ruin or destroy (a ship) by crashing ashore or sinking

ship·yard *n* : a place where ships are built or repaired

shirk *vb* **shirked; shirk·ing** : to avoid doing something especially because of laziness, fear, or dislike

shirt *n* : a piece of clothing for the upper part of the body usually with sleeves and often a collar

[1]**shiv·er** *vb* **shiv·ered; shiv·er·ing** : to shake slightly (as from cold or fear)

[2]**shiver** *n* : a small shaking movement of the body (as from cold or emotion)

[1]**shoal** *adj* **shoal·er; shoal·est** : [1]SHALLOW 1

[2]**shoal** *n* **1** : a place where a sea, lake, or river is shallow **2** : a mound or ridge of sand just below the surface of the water

[3]**shoal** *n* : [3]SCHOOL

[1]**shock** *n* : a bunch of sheaves of grain or stalks of corn set on end (as in a field)

[2]**shock** *n* **1** : a sudden strong unpleasant or upsetting feeling **2** : something that causes a sudden unpleasant or upsetting feeling **3** : a severe shake, jerk, or impact **4** : the effect of a charge of electricity passing through the body of a person or animal **5** : a serious bodily reaction that usually follows severe injury or large loss of blood

[3]shock *vb* **shocked; shock·ing** **1 :** to strike with surprise, horror, or disgust **2 :** to affect by a charge of electricity **3 :** to move to action especially by causing upset, surprise, or disgust

[4]shock *n* **:** a thick bushy mass

shock·ing *adj* **1 :** causing surprise, horror, or disgust **2 :** being intense or bright in color — **shock·ing·ly** *adv*

shod·dy *adj* **shod·di·er; shod·di·est :** poorly done or made — **shod·di·ness** *n*

[1]shoe *n* **1 :** an outer covering for the human foot usually having a thick and somewhat stiff sole and heel and a lighter upper part **2 :** HORSESHOE 1

[2]shoe *vb* **shod** *also* **shoed; shoe·ing :** to put a shoe or horseshoe on **:** furnish with shoes

shoe·horn *n* **:** a curved piece (as of metal) to help in sliding the heel of the foot into a shoe

shoe·lace *n* **:** a lace or string for fastening a shoe

shoe·mak·er *n* **:** a person who makes or repairs shoes

shoe·string *n* **:** SHOELACE

shone *past and past participle of* SHINE

shoo *vb* **shooed; shoo·ing :** to wave, scare, or send away — often used as a command

shook *past of* SHAKE

[1]shoot *vb* **shot; shoot·ing** **1 :** to let fly or cause to be driven forward with force **2 :** to cause a projectile (as a bullet) to be driven out of **3 :** to cause a weapon to discharge a projectile **4 :** to strike with a projectile from a bow or gun **5 :** to hit, throw, or kick (as a ball or puck) toward or into a goal **6 :** to score by shooting **7 :** [1]PLAY 2 **8 :** to thrust forward swiftly **9 :** to grow rapidly **10 :** to go, move, or pass rapidly **11 :** to direct at quickly and suddenly **12 :** to stream out suddenly **:** SPURT **13 :** to film or photograph **14 :** to pass swiftly along or through — **shoot·er** *n*

[2]shoot *n* **1 :** a stem or branch of a plant especially when young or just beginning to grow **2 :** a hunting party or trip

shooting star *n* **:** a meteor appearing as a temporary streak of light in the night sky

[1]shop *n* **1 :** a place where goods are sold **:** a usually small store **2 :** a worker's place of business **3 :** a place in which workers are doing a particular kind of work

[2]shop *vb* **shopped; shop·ping :** to visit stores or shops for the purpose of looking over and buying goods — **shop·per** *n*

shop·keep·er *n* **:** STOREKEEPER 1

shop·lift *vb* **shop·lift·ed; shop·lift·ing :** to steal merchandise on display in stores — **shop·lift·er** *n*

[1]shore *n* **:** the land along the edge of a body of water

[2]shore *vb* **shored; shor·ing :** to keep from sinking, sagging, or falling by placing a support under or against

shore·bird *n* **:** a bird (as a plover or sandpiper) that frequents the seashore

shore·line *n* **:** the line or strip of land where a body of water and the shore meet

shorn *past participle of* SHEAR

[1]short *adj* **short·er; short·est** **1 :** not long or tall **2 :** not great in distance **3 :** not lasting long **:** brief in time **4 :** cut down to a brief length **5 :** less than the usual or needed amount **6 :** having less than what is needed **:** not having enough **7 :** not reaching far enough **8 :** easily stirred up **9 :** rudely brief **10 :** of, relating to, or being one of the vowel sounds \ə, a, e, i, u̇\ and sometimes \ä\ and \ȯ\ — **short·ness** *n*

[2]short *adv* **1 :** with suddenness **2 :** to or at a point that is not as far as expected or desired

[3]short *n* **1 shorts** *pl* **:** pants that reach to or almost to the knees **2 shorts** *pl* **:** short underpants **3 :** something (as a movie) shorter than the usual or regular length **4 :** SHORT CIRCUIT

short·age *n* **:** a condition in which there is not enough of something needed **:** DEFICIT

short·cake *n* **:** a dessert made usually of rich biscuit dough baked and served with sweetened fruit

short circuit *n* **:** an electrical connection made between points in an electric circuit between which current does not normally flow

short·com·ing *n* **:** FAULT 1

short·cut *n* **:** a shorter, quicker, or easier way

short·en *vb* **short·ened; short·en·ing :** to make or become short or shorter

short·en·ing *n* **:** a fat used in baking especially to make pastry flaky

short·horn *n* **:** a cow of a short-horned breed of beef and dairy cattle developed in England

short–lived *adj* **:** living or lasting only a short time

short·ly *adv* **1 :** in or within a short time **:** SOON **2 :** in a brief way that shows anger or disapproval

short–sight·ed *adj* **1 :** made without thinking about what will happen in the future **2 :** NEARSIGHTED

short·stop *n* **:** a baseball infielder whose position is between second and third base

Sho·shone *or* **Sho·sho·ni** *n, pl* **Sho·shones** *or* **Shoshoni** **1 :** a member of a group of American Indian peoples originally of California, Idaho, Nevada, Utah, and Wyoming **2 :** the language of the Shoshones

[1]shot *n* **1 :** the act of shooting **2** *pl* **shot :** a bullet, ball, or pellet for a gun or cannon **3 :** ^{2}ATTEMPT, TRY **4 :** CHANCE **5 :** the flight of a projectile or the distance it travels **:** RANGE **6 :** a person who shoots **7 :** a heavy metal ball thrown for distance in a track-and-field contest (**shot put**) **8 :** an act of hitting, throwing, or kicking a ball or puck toward or into a goal **9 :** an injection of something (as medicine) into the body **10 :** PHOTOGRAPH

[2]**shot** *past and past participle of* SHOOT

shot·gun *n* **:** a gun with a long barrel used to fire shot at short range

should *past of* SHALL **1 :** ought to **2 :** happen to **3 —** used as a more polite or less assured form of *shall*

[1]**shoul·der** *n* **1 :** the part of the body of a person or animal where the arm or foreleg joins the body **2 :** the part of a piece of clothing that covers a person's shoulder **3 :** a part that resembles a person's shoulder in shape **4 :** the edge of a road

[2]**shoulder** *vb* **shoul·dered; shoul·der·ing 1 :** to push with the shoulder **2 :** to accept as a burden or duty

shoulder blade *n* **:** the flat triangular bone of the back of the shoulder

shouldn't : should not

[1]**shout** *vb* **shout·ed; shout·ing :** to make a sudden loud cry **2 :** to say in a loud voice

[2]**shout** *n* **:** a sudden loud cry

[1]**shove** *vb* **shoved; shov·ing 1 :** to push with steady force **2 :** to push along or away carelessly or rudely

[2]**shove** *n* **:** a forceful push

[1]**shov·el** *n* **1 :** a tool with a long handle and broad scoop used to lift and throw loose material (as dirt or snow) **2 :** as much as a shovel will hold

[2]**shovel** *vb* **shov·eled** *or* **shov·elled; shov·el·ing** *or* **shov·el·ling 1 :** to lift or throw with a shovel **2 :** to dig or clean out with a shovel **3 :** to move large amounts of into something quickly

[1]**show** *vb* **showed; shown** *or* **showed; show·ing 1 :** to place in sight **:** DISPLAY **2 :** REVEAL 2 **3 :** to make known **4 :** to give as appropriate treatment **5 :** TEACH 1, INSTRUCT **6 :** PROVE 1 **7 :** to lead to a place **:** DIRECT **8 :** to point out to **9 :** to be easily seen or noticed **— show off :** to make an obvious display of a person's own abilities or possessions in order to impress others **— show up :** APPEAR 3

[2]**show** *n* **1 :** a public performance intended to entertain people **2 :** a television or radio program **3 :** an event at which things of the same kind are put on display **4 :** a display to make known a feeling or quality **5 :** an appearance meant to deceive

show·boat *n* **:** a river steamboat used as a traveling theater

show·case *n* **:** a protective glass case in which things are displayed

[1]**show·er** *n* **1 :** a short fall of rain over a small area **2 :** a large number of things that fall, are given off, or happen at the same time **3 :** a bath in which water is sprayed on the body or a device for providing such a bath **4 :** a party where gifts are given especially to a woman who is about to be married or have a baby

[2]**shower** *vb* **show·ered; show·er·ing 1 :** to wet with fine spray or drops **2 :** to fall in or as if in a shower **3 :** to provide in great quantity **4 :** to bathe in a shower

show·man *n, pl* **show·men :** a person having a special skill for presenting something in a dramatic way

show–off *n* **:** a person who tries to impress other people with his or her abilities or possessions

showy *adj* **show·i·er; show·i·est 1 :** attracting attention **:** STRIKING **2 :** given to or being too much outward display **:** GAUDY

shrank *past of* SHRINK

shrap·nel *n* **:** small metal pieces that scatter outwards from an exploding bomb, shell, or mine

[1]**shred** *n* **1 :** a long narrow piece torn or cut off **:** STRIP **2 :** a small amount **:** BIT

[2]**shred** *vb* **shred·ded; shred·ding :** to cut or tear into small pieces

shrew *n* **1 :** a small mouselike animal with a long pointed snout and tiny eyes that lives mostly on insects and worms **2 :** an unpleasant bad-tempered woman

shrewd *adj* **shrewd·er; shrewd·est :** showing quick practical cleverness **— shrewd·ly** *adv* **— shrewd·ness** *n*

[1]**shriek** *vb* **shrieked; shriek·ing 1 :** to make a loud high-pitched cry **2 :** to say in a loud high-pitched voice

[2]**shriek** *n* **:** a loud high-pitched cry or sound

[1]**shrill** *vb* **shrilled; shrill·ing 1 :** to make a high-pitched usually piercing sound **2 :** to say in a loud high-pitched voice

[2]**shrill** *adj* **shrill·er; shrill·est :** having a high-pitched usually piercing sound **— shrill·ness** *n* **— shril·ly** *adv*

shrimp *n* **1 :** a small shellfish of the sea that is related to the crabs and lobsters and is often used for food **2** *often offensive* **:** a very small or unimportant person or thing

shrine *n* **1 :** a case or box for sacred relics (as the bones of saints) **2 :** a place connected with a holy person or event where people worship **3 :** a place that is considered sacred or regarded with great respect

shrink *vb* **shrank** *or* **shrunk; shrunk** *or*

shrunk·en; shrink·ing **1 :** to make or become smaller **2 :** to curl up or move back in or as if in fear or pain **3 :** to refrain from doing something especially because of difficulty or unpleasantness

shrink·age *n* **:** the amount by which something shrinks or becomes less

shriv·el *vb* **shriv·eled** *or* **shriv·elled; shriv·el·ing** *or* **shriv·el·ling :** to shrink and become dry and wrinkled

[1]shroud *n* **1 :** the cloth placed over or around a dead body **2 :** something that covers or hides

[2]shroud *vb* **shroud·ed; shroud·ing :** to cover or hide with or as if with a shroud

shrub *n* **:** a woody plant that has several stems and is smaller than most trees

shrub·bery *n, pl* **shrub·ber·ies :** a group of shrubs or an area where shrubs are growing

[1]shrug *vb* **shrugged; shrug·ging :** to raise and lower the shoulders usually to express doubt, uncertainty, or lack of interest

[2]shrug *n* **:** an act of raising and lowering the shoulders

[1]shuck *n* **:** a covering shell or husk

[2]shuck *vb* **shucked; shuck·ing :** to remove the shell or husk from

[1]shud·der *vb* **shud·dered; shud·der·ing 1 :** to tremble especially with fear or horror or from cold **2 :** to move or sound as if being shaken

[2]shudder *n* **:** an act or instance of trembling or shaking

[1]shuf·fle *vb* **shuf·fled; shuf·fling 1 :** to slide back and forth without lifting **2 :** to walk or move by sliding or dragging the feet **3 :** to mix up the order of (as playing cards) **4 :** to push or move about or from place to place

[2]shuffle *n* **1 :** a sliding or dragging walk **2 :** an act of mixing up or moving so as to change the order or position **3 :** a confusing jumble

shun *vb* **shunned; shun·ning :** to avoid purposely or by habit

shunt *vb* **shunt·ed; shunt·ing 1 :** to turn or move off to one side or out of the way **2 :** to switch (as a train) from one track to another

shut *vb* **shut; shut·ting 1 :** to close or become closed **2 :** to stop or cause to stop operation **3 :** to confine by or as if by enclosing or by blocking the way out **4 :** to close by bringing parts together — **shut out 1 :** to keep (something) from entering **2 :** to keep (an opponent) from scoring in a game — **shut up :** to stop talking

shut·out *n* **:** a game in which one side fails to score

shut·ter *n* **1 :** a usually movable cover for the outside of a window **2 :** a device in a camera that opens to let in light when a picture is taken

[1]shut·tle *n* **1 :** an instrument used in weaving to carry the thread back and forth from side to side through the threads that run lengthwise **2 :** a vehicle (as a bus or train) that goes back and forth over a short route **3 :** SPACE SHUTTLE

[2]shuttle *vb* **shut·tled; shut·tling :** to move or bring back and forth rapidly or often

shut·tle·cock *n* **:** a light cone-shaped object that is used in badminton

[1]shy *adj* **shi·er** *or* **shy·er; shi·est** *or* **shy·est 1 :** not feeling comfortable meeting and talking to people **2 :** easily frightened **:** TIMID **3 :** showing a dislike of attention **4 :** tending to avoid something or someone **5 :** having less than a full or an expected amount or number — **shy·ly** *adv* — **shy·ness** *n*

[2]shy *vb* **shied; shy·ing 1 :** to avoid or draw back in dislike or distaste **2 :** to move quickly to one side in fright

sib·ling *n* **:** a brother or sister

sick *adj* **sick·er; sick·est 1 :** affected with disease or illness **:** not well **2 :** of, relating to, or intended for use in or during illness **3 :** affected with or accompanied by nausea **4 :** badly upset by strong emotion **5 :** annoyed or bored of something from having too much of it **6 :** filled with disgust or anger

sick·bed *n* **:** a bed on which a sick person lies

sick·en *vb* **sick·ened; sick·en·ing 1 :** to make or become sick or ill **2 :** to cause to feel disgusted or angry

sick·en·ing *adj* **:** causing sickness or disgust — **sick·en·ing·ly** *adv*

sick·le *n* **:** a tool with a sharp curved blade and a short handle used especially to cut grass and grain

sick·ly *adj* **sick·li·er; sick·li·est 1 :** somewhat sick **:** often ailing **2 :** caused by or associated with ill health **3 :** SICKENING **4 :** appearing as if sick

sick·ness *n* **1 :** ill health **:** ILLNESS **2 :** a specific disease **3 :** NAUSEA 1

[1]side *n* **1 :** the right or left part of the body from the shoulder to the hip **2 :** a place, space, or direction away from or beyond a central point or line **3 :** a surface or line forming a border or face of an object **4 :** an outer surface or part of something considered as facing in a certain direction **5 :** either surface of a thin object **6 :** a place next to something or someone **7 :** an opinion or position viewed as opposite or different from another **8 :** a group of people involved in a competition, dispute, or war **9 :** a line of ancestors traced back from either parent

DICTIONARY

²side *adj* **1 :** of or located on the side **2 :** going toward or coming from the side **3 :** related to something in a minor or unimportant way **4 :** being in addition to a main portion
³side *vb* **sid·ed; sid·ing :** to agree with or support the opinions or actions of
side·arm *adv* **:** with the arm moving out to the side
side·board *n* **:** a piece of furniture for holding dishes, silverware, and table linen
side·burns *n pl* **:** hair growing on the side of the face in front of the ears
sid·ed *adj* **:** having sides often of a stated number or kind
side·line *n* **1 :** a line marking the side of a playing field or court **2 :** a business or a job done in addition to a person's regular occupation
¹side·long *adj* **:** made to one side or out of the corner of the eye
²sidelong *adv* **:** out of the corner of the eye
side·show *n* **:** a small show off to the side of a main show or exhibition (as of a circus)
side·step *vb* **side·stepped; side·step·ping 1 :** to take a sideways step **2 :** to avoid by a step to the side **3 :** to avoid answering or dealing with
side·track *vb* **side·tracked; side·track·ing :** to turn aside from a main purpose or direction
side·walk *n* **:** a usually paved walk at the side of a street or road
side·ways *adv or adj* **1 :** from one side **2 :** with one side forward **3 :** to one side
side·wise *adv or adj* **:** SIDEWAYS
sid·ing *n* **1 :** a short railroad track connected with the main track **2 :** material (as boards or metal pieces) used to cover the outside walls of frame buildings
si·dle *vb* **si·dled; si·dling :** to go or move with one side forward
siege *n* **:** the act of moving an army around a fortified place to capture it — **lay siege to :** to attack militarily
si·er·ra *n* **:** a range of mountains especially with jagged peaks
si·es·ta *n* **:** a nap or rest especially at midday
sieve *n* **:** a utensil with meshes or holes to separate finer particles from coarser ones or solids from liquids
sift *vb* **sift·ed; sift·ing 1 :** to pass or cause to pass through a sieve **2 :** to separate or separate out by or as if by passing through a sieve **3 :** to test or examine carefully — **sift·er** *n*
¹sigh *vb* **sighed; sigh·ing 1 :** to take or let out a long loud breath often as an expression of sadness or weariness **2 :** to make a sound like sighing **3 :** to say with a sigh
²sigh *n* **:** the act or a sound of taking or letting out a long loud breath
¹sight *n* **1 :** the function, process, or power of seeing **:** the sense by which a person or animal becomes aware of the position, form, and color of objects **2 :** the act of seeing **3 :** something that is seen **:** SPECTACLE **4 :** something that is worth seeing **5 :** something that is peculiar, funny, or messy **6 :** the presence of an object within the field of vision **7 :** the distance a person can see **8 :** a device (as a small metal bead on a gun barrel) that aids the eye in aiming or in finding the direction of an object
²sight *vb* **sight·ed; sight·ing 1 :** to get a look at **:** SEE **2 :** to look at through or as if through a device that aids the eye in aiming or in finding the direction of an object
sight·less *adj* **:** lacking sight **:** BLIND
sight·see *vb* **sight·saw; sight·see·ing :** to go about seeing places and things of interest — **sight·seer** *n*
¹sign *n* **1 :** a motion, action, or movement of the hand that means something **2 :** a public notice that advertises something or gives information **3 :** something that indicates what is present or is to come **4 :** a symbol (as + or ÷) indicating a mathematical operation **5 :** one of the twelve parts of the zodiac
²sign *vb* **signed; sign·ing 1 :** to put a signature on to show acceptance, agreement or responsibility **2 :** to communicate by using sign language **3 :** to represent or show by a motion, action, or movement **4 :** to make or place a sign on — **sign up :** to sign someone's name in order to get, do, or take something
¹sig·nal *n* **1 :** a sign, event, or word that serves to start some action **2 :** a sound, a movement of part of the body, or an object that gives warning or a command **3 :** a radio wave that transmits a message or effect (as in radio or television)
²signal *vb* **sig·naled** *or Can and Brit* **sig·nalled; sig·nal·ing** *or Can and Brit* **sig·nal·ling 1 :** to notify by a motion, action, movement, or sound **2 :** to communicate with motions, actions, movements, or sounds
³signal *adj* **1 :** unusually great **2 :** used for sending a message, warning, or command
sig·na·ture *n* **1 :** the name of a person written by that person **2 :** a sign or group of signs placed at the beginning of a staff in music to show the key (**key signature**) or the meter (**time signature**)
sign·board *n* **:** a board with a sign or notice on it
sig·nif·i·cance *n* **1 :** MEANING 2 **2 :** IMPORTANCE
sig·nif·i·cant *adj* **1 :** having a special or hid-

den meaning **2 :** IMPORTANT 1 **3 :** large enough to be noticed

sig·ni·fy *vb* **sig·ni·fied; sig·ni·fy·ing** **1 :** [1]MEAN 1, DENOTE **2 :** to show especially by a sign : make known **3 :** to have importance : MATTER

sign language *n* **:** a system of hand movements used for communication (as by people who are deaf)

sign·post *n* **:** a post with a sign (as for directing travelers)

Sikh·ism *n* **:** a religion that originated in India in the 16th century and involves worship of a single deity — **Sikh** *n*

si·lage *n* **:** fodder fermented (as in a silo) to produce a juicy feed for livestock

[1]**si·lence** *n* **1 :** the state of keeping or being silent **2 :** the state of there being no sound or noise : STILLNESS

[2]**silence** *vb* **si·lenced; si·lenc·ing** **1 :** to stop the noise or speech of : cause to be silent **2 :** SUPPRESS 1

si·lent *adj* **1 :** not speaking **2 :** not talkative **3 :** free from noise or sound : STILL **4 :** done or felt without being spoken **5 :** making no mention **6 :** not in operation **7 :** not pronounced **8 :** made without spoken dialogue — **si·lent·ly** *adv*

[1]**sil·hou·ette** *n* **1 :** [1]OUTLINE 1 **2 :** a drawing, picture, or portrait of the outline of a person or object filled in with a solid usually black color

[2]**silhouette** *vb* **sil·hou·ett·ed; sil·hou·ett·ing** **:** to represent by an outline : show against a light background

sil·i·con *n* **:** a chemical element that next to oxygen is the most common element in the earth's crust and is used especially in electronic devices

silk *n* **1 :** a fine fiber that is spun by many insect larvae usually to form their cocoon or by spiders to make their webs and that includes some kinds used for weaving cloth **2 :** thread, yarn, or fabric made from silk **3 :** the threadlike strands that are found over the kernels of an ear of corn

silk·en *adj* **1 :** made of or with silk **2 :** having a soft and smooth look or feel

silk·worm *n* **:** a yellowish caterpillar that is the larva of an Asian moth (**silk moth** or **silkworm moth**), is raised in captivity on mulberry leaves, and produces a strong silk that is the silk most used for thread or cloth

silky *adj* **silk·i·er; silk·i·est** **1 :** soft and smooth **2 :** agreeably smooth

sill *n* **1 :** a heavy horizontal piece (as of wood) that forms the bottom part of a window frame or a doorway **2 :** a horizontal supporting piece at the base of a structure

sil·ly *adj* **sil·li·er; sil·li·est** **1 :** having or showing a lack of common sense : FOOLISH **2 :** not serious or important **3 :** playful and lighthearted — **sil·li·ness** *n*

si·lo *n, pl* **silos :** a covered trench, pit, or especially a tall round building in which silage is made and stored

[1]**silt** *n* **1 :** particles of small size left as sediment from water **2 :** a soil made up mostly of silt and containing little clay

[2]**silt** *vb* **silt·ed; silt·ing** **:** to fill, cover, or block with silt

[1]**sil·ver** *n* **1 :** a soft white metallic chemical element that can be polished and is used for money, jewelry and ornaments, and table utensils **2 :** coin made of silver **3 :** SILVERWARE **4 :** a medal made of silver that is given to someone who wins second place in a contest **5 :** a medium gray

[2]**silver** *adj* **1 :** made of, coated with, or yielding the soft white metallic chemical element silver **2 :** having the medium gray color of silver

[3]**silver** *vb* **sil·vered; sil·ver·ing :** to coat with or as if with silver

sil·ver·smith *n* **:** a person who makes objects of silver

sil·ver·ware *n* **:** things (as knives, forks, and spoons) made of silver, silver-plated metal, or stainless steel

sil·very *adj* **:** shiny and medium gray

sim·i·lar *adj* **:** having qualities in common — **sim·i·lar·ly** *adv*

sim·i·lar·i·ty *n, pl* **sim·i·lar·i·ties :** the quality or state of being alike in some way or ways

sim·i·le *n* **:** a figure of speech comparing two unlike things using *like* or *as*

sim·mer *vb* **sim·mered; sim·mer·ing** **1 :** to cook gently at or just below the boiling point **2 :** to be on the point of bursting out with violence or anger

sim·per *vb* **sim·pered; sim·per·ing :** to smile or speak in a way that is not sincere or natural

sim·ple *adj* **sim·pler; sim·plest** **1 :** not hard to understand or solve **2 :** [1]EASY 1, STRAIGHTFORWARD **3 :** lacking in education, experience, or intelligence **4 :** not complex or fancy **5 :** INNOCENT 1, MODEST **6 :** not rich or important **7 :** ABSOLUTE 2

simple machine *n* **:** one of the fundamental devices that all machines were formerly thought to be made from

sim·ple·ton *n* **:** a foolish or stupid person

sim·plic·i·ty *n, pl* **sim·plic·i·ties** **1 :** the quality or state of being simple or plain and not complicated or difficult **2 :** SINCERITY **3 :** directness or clearness in speaking or writing

sim·pli·fy *vb* **sim·pli·fied; sim·pli·fy·ing :** to make simple or simpler : make easier

sim·ply *adv* **1 :** in a clear way **2 :** in a plain way **3 :** in a sincere and direct way **4 :** [2]ONLY 1, MERELY **5 :** in actual fact **:** REALLY, TRULY

si·mul·ta·neous *adj* **:** existing or taking place at the same time — **si·mul·ta·neous·ly** *adv*

[1]**sin** *n* **1 :** an action that breaks a religious law **2 :** an action that is or is felt to be bad

[2]**sin** *vb* **sinned; sin·ning :** to do something that breaks a religious law or is felt to be bad — **sin·ner** *n*

[1]**since** *adv* **1 :** from a definite past time until now **2 :** before the present time **:** AGO **3 :** after a time in the past

[2]**since** *conj* **1 :** in the period after **2 :** BECAUSE

[3]**since** *prep* **1 :** in the period after **2 :** continuously from

sin·cere *adj* **sin·cer·er; sin·cer·est 1 :** HONEST 1, STRAIGHTFORWARD **2 :** being what it seems to be **:** GENUINE — **sin·cere·ly** *adv*

sin·cer·i·ty *n* **:** freedom from fraud or deception **:** HONESTY

sin·ew *n* **:** TENDON

sin·ewy *adj* **1 :** STRONG 1, POWERFUL **2 :** full of tendons **:** TOUGH, STRINGY

sin·ful *adj* **:** being or full of sin **:** WICKED

sing *vb* **sang** *or* **sung; sung; sing·ing 1 :** to produce musical sounds with the voice **2 :** to express in musical tones **3 :** to make musical sounds **4 :** [1]CHANT 2 **5 :** to make a small high-pitched sound **6 :** to speak with enthusiasm **7 :** to do something with song — **sing·er** *n*

sing. *abbr* singular

singe *vb* **singed; singe·ing :** to burn lightly or on the surface **:** SCORCH

[1]**sin·gle** *adj* **1 :** being alone **:** being the only one **2 :** being a separate whole **:** INDIVIDUAL **3 :** not married **4 :** made up of or having only one **5 :** made for only one person

[2]**single** *vb* **sin·gled; sin·gling :** to select or distinguish (as one person or thing) from a number or group

[3]**single** *n* **1 :** a separate individual person or thing **2 :** a hit in baseball that enables the batter to reach first base

sin·gle–hand·ed *adj* **1 :** done or managed by one person or with one hand **2 :** working alone **:** lacking help — **single–handed** *adv* — **sin·gle–hand·ed·ly** *adv*

sin·gly *adv* **:** one by one **:** INDIVIDUALLY

sing·song *n* **:** a way of speaking in which the pitch of the voice rises and falls in a pattern — **singsong** *adj*

[1]**sin·gu·lar** *adj* **1 :** of, relating to, or being a word form used to show not more than one person or thing **2 :** [1]SUPERIOR 2, EXCEPTIONAL **3 :** of unusual quality **4 :** STRANGE 2, ODD

[2]**singular** *n* **:** a form of a word used to show that only one person or thing is meant

sin·is·ter *adj* **1 :** threatening evil, harm, or danger **2 :** [1]EVIL 1, CORRUPT

[1]**sink** *vb* **sank** *or* **sunk; sunk; sink·ing 1 :** to move or cause to move downward so as to be swallowed up **2 :** to fall or drop to a lower level **3 :** to penetrate or cause to penetrate **4 :** to go into or become absorbed **5 :** to become known or felt **6 :** to lessen in amount **7 :** to form by digging or boring **8 :** to spend (money) unwisely **9 :** to descend into a feeling of sadness or dread

[2]**sink** *n* **:** a wide bowl or basin attached to a wall or floor and having water faucets and a drain

sin·u·ous *adj* **:** having a wavy or winding form

si·nus *n* **:** any of several spaces in the skull mostly connected with the nostrils

Sioux *n, pl* **Sioux :** DAKOTA

[1]**sip** *vb* **sipped; sip·ping :** to take small drinks of

[2]**sip** *n* **1 :** the act of taking a small drink **2 :** a small amount taken by sipping

[1]**si·phon** *n* **1 :** a bent pipe or tube through which a liquid can be drawn by air pressure up and over the edge of a container **2 :** a tubelike part especially of a mollusk (as a clam) usually used to draw in or squirt out water

[2]**siphon** *vb* **si·phoned; si·phon·ing :** to draw off by or as if by a siphon

sir *n* **1** — used without a name as a form of polite address to a man **2** *cap* — used as a title before the given name of a knight or a baronet **3** *cap* — used without a name as a form of address at the beginning of a letter

[1]**sire** *n* **1** *often cap* **:** [1]FATHER 1 **2 :** the male parent of a domestic animal **3** — used in the past to address a man of rank (as a king)

[2]**sire** *vb* **sired; sir·ing :** to become the father of

si·ren *n* **:** a device that makes a loud warning sound

sir·loin *n* **:** a cut of beef taken from the part just in front of the rump

si·sal *n* **:** a long strong white fiber made from the leaves of a Mexican plant and used to make rope and twine

sis·sy *n, pl* **sis·sies** *usually offensive* **:** a fearful or cowardly person

sis·ter *n* **1 :** a female person or animal related to another person or animal by having one or both parents in common **2 :** a member of a religious society of women **:** NUN **3 :** a woman related to another by a common tie or interest — **sis·ter·ly** *adj*

sis·ter·hood *n* **1 :** the state of being a sister **2 :** women joined in a group

sis·ter–in–law *n, pl* **sis·ters–in–law** **1 :** the sister of someone's husband or wife **2 :** the wife of someone's brother or sister

sit *vb* **sat; sit·ting** **1 :** to rest upon the part of the body where the hips and legs join : to rest on the buttocks or hindquarters **2 :** to put the buttocks down on a surface **3 :** to cause to be seated **4 :** [2]PERCH **5 :** to be located or stay in a place or position **6 :** to provide seats for **7 :** to hold a place as a member of an official group **8 :** to hold a session **9 :** to pose for a portrait or photograph **10 :** BABYSIT

site *n* **1 :** the place where something (as a town or event) is found or took place **2 :** the space of ground a building rests upon **3 :** WEBSITE

sit·ter *n* **:** BABY-SITTER

sit·ting *n* **1 :** a period during which someone poses for a portrait or photograph **2 :** SESSION 2 **3 :** a time when a meal is served to a number of people

sitting room *n* **:** LIVING ROOM

sit·u·at·ed *adj* **1 :** having its place **2 :** being in such financial circumstances

sit·u·a·tion *n* **1 :** the combination of surrounding conditions **2 :** a state of affairs that is urgent or difficult **3 :** [1]PLACE 3 **4 :** position or place of employment : JOB

sit–up *n* **:** an exercise done by lying on the back and rising to a sitting position

[1]six *adj* **:** being one more than five

[2]six *n* **1 :** one more than five : two times three : 6 **2 :** the sixth in a set or series

six·pence *n* **1 :** the sum of six pence **2 :** an old British coin worth six pence

six–shoot·er *n* **:** a revolver having six chambers

[1]six·teen *adj* **:** being one more than 15

[2]sixteen *n* **:** one more than 15 : four times four : 16

[1]six·teenth *adj* **:** coming right after 15th

[2]sixteenth *n* **:** number 16 in a series

[1]sixth *adj* **:** coming right after fifth

[2]sixth *n* **1 :** number six in a series **2 :** one of six equal parts

[1]six·ti·eth *adj* **:** coming right after 59th

[2]sixtieth *n* **:** number 60 in a series

[1]six·ty *adj* **:** being six times ten

[2]sixty *n* **:** six times ten : 60

siz·able *or* **size·able** *adj* **:** fairly large

size *n* **1 :** the amount of space occupied by someone or something : how large or small someone or something is **2 :** the number or amount of people or things **3 :** one of a series of measures especially of manufactured articles (as clothing)

sized *adj* **:** having a specified size

siz·zle *vb* **siz·zled; siz·zling :** to make a hissing or sputtering noise in or as if in frying or burning

SK *abbr* Saskatchewan

[1]skate *vb* **skat·ed; skat·ing** **1 :** to glide along on skates **2 :** to slide or glide along — **skat·er** *n*

[2]skate *n* **1 :** a metal blade fitting the sole of the shoe or a shoe with a permanently attached metal blade used for gliding on ice **2 :** ROLLER SKATE

[3]skate *n* **:** a flat fish related to the sharks that has large and nearly triangular fins

[1]skate·board *n* **:** a short board mounted on small wheels that is used for coasting and often for performing athletic stunts

[2]skateboard *vb* **skate·board·ed; skate·board·ing :** to ride or perform stunts on a skateboard — **skate·board·er** *n*

skate park *n* **:** an outdoor area having structures and surfaces for roller-skating and skateboarding

skein *n* **:** a quantity of yarn or thread arranged in a loose coil

skel·e·tal *adj* **:** of or relating to a skeleton

skel·e·ton *n* **1 :** a firm structure or framework of a living thing that in vertebrates (as fish, birds, or humans) is typically made of bone and supports the soft tissues of the body and protects the internal organs **2 :** FRAMEWORK

skep·tic *n* **:** a person who has or shows doubt about something

skep·ti·cal *adj* **:** having or showing doubt

[1]sketch *n* **1 :** a rough outline or drawing showing the main features of something **2 :** a short written work (as a story or essay) **3 :** a short comic performance

[2]sketch *vb* **sketched; sketch·ing** **1 :** to make a drawing, rough draft, or outline of **2 :** to describe or outline (something) briefly

sketchy *adj* **sketch·i·er; sketch·i·est** **1 :** roughly outlined **2 :** lacking completeness or clearness

[1]ski *n, pl* **skis :** one of a pair of narrow strips fastened one on each foot and used in gliding over snow or water

[2]ski *vb* **skied; ski·ing :** to glide on skis — **ski·er** *n*

[1]skid *vb* **skid·ded; skid·ding** **1 :** [1]SLIDE 1, SLIP **2 :** to slide sideways **3 :** to roll or slide on a platform of logs, planks, or rails

[2]skid *n* **1 :** a platform of logs, planks, or rails used to support a heavy object while it is being moved or stored **2 :** the act of sliding

skiff *n* **:** a small light rowboat

ski·ing *n* **:** the art or sport of gliding and jumping on skis

skill *n* **1 :** ability that comes from training or practice **2 :** a developed or acquired ability

skilled *adj* **1 :** having skill **2 :** requiring skill and training

skil·let *n* : a frying pan
skill·ful *adj* **1** : having or showing ability : EXPERT **2** : done or made with ability — **skill·ful·ly** *adv*
skim *vb* **skimmed; skim·ming** **1** : to clean a liquid of scum or floating substance : remove (as cream or film) from the top part of a liquid **2** : to read or examine quickly and not thoroughly **3** : to skip (a stone) along the surface of water **4** : to pass swiftly or lightly over
skim milk *n* : milk from which the cream has been removed
skimp *vb* **skimped; skimp·ing** : to give too little or just enough attention or effort to or money for
skimpy *adj* **skimp·i·er; skimp·i·est** : very small in size or amount : SCANTY
¹skin *n* **1** : the usually flexible outer layer of an animal body that in vertebrate animals is made up of two layers of cells forming an inner dermis and an outer epidermis **2** : the hide of an animal **3** : an outer or surface layer — **skin·less** *adj* — **skinned** *adj*
²skin *vb* **skinned; skin·ning** **1** : to strip, scrape, or rub off the skin of **2** : to remove an outer layer from (as by peeling)
skin–dive *vb* **skin–dived; skin–div·ing** : to swim below the surface of water with a face mask and sometimes a portable breathing device — **skin diver** *n*
skin·ny *adj* **skin·ni·er; skin·ni·est** : very thin
¹skip *vb* **skipped; skip·ping** **1** : to move by taking short light steps and jumps **2** : to pass over or omit an item, space, or step **3** : to leap over lightly and nimbly **4** : to fail to attend or do **5** : to bound or cause to bound off one point after another : SKIM
²skip *n* **1** : a light bounding step **2** : a way of moving by hops and steps
skip·per *n* : the master of a ship and especially of a fishing, trading, or pleasure boat
¹skir·mish *n* **1** : a minor fight in war **2** : a minor argument
²skirmish *vb* **skir·mished; skir·mish·ing** : to take part in a fight or dispute
¹skirt *n* **1** : a piece of clothing or part of a piece of clothing worn by women or girls that hangs from the waist down **2** : a part or attachment serving as a rim, border, or edging
²skirt *vb* **skirt·ed; skirt·ing** **1** : ²BORDER 2 **2** : to go or pass around or about the outer edge of **3** : to avoid for fear of difficulty
skit *n* : a brief sketch in play form
skit·ter *vb* **skit·tered; skit·ter·ing** : to glide or skip lightly or quickly
skit·tish *adj* : easily frightened
skulk *vb* **skulked; skulk·ing** : to hide or move in a sly or sneaking way
skull *n* : the case of bone or cartilage that forms the skeleton of the head and face, encloses the brain, and supports the jaws
skunk *n* : a North American animal related to the weasels that has coarse black-and-white fur and can squirt out a fluid with a very unpleasant smell
sky *n, pl* **skies** **1** : the stretch of space over the earth **2** : ¹WEATHER, CLIMATE
sky·div·ing *n* : the sport of jumping from an airplane using a parachute
sky·lark *n* : a European lark noted for its song
sky·light *n* : a window or group of windows in a roof or ceiling
sky·line *n* **1** : the line where earth and sky seem to meet : HORIZON **2** : an outline against the sky
sky·scrap·er *n* : a very tall building
slab *n* : a flat thick piece or slice
¹slack *adj* **1** : CARELESS 2, NEGLIGENT **2** : not energetic : SLOW **3** : not tight or firm **4** : not busy or active
²slack *vb* **slacked; slack·ing** **1** : to make or become looser, slower, or less energetic **2** : to avoid work — **slack·er** *n*
³slack *n* **1** : a part (as of a rope or sail) that hangs loose without strain **2 slacks** *pl* : dressy pants **3** : a portion (as of work or resources) that is required but lacking **4** : additional relief from pressure — usually used with *cut*
slack·en *vb* **slack·ened; slack·en·ing** **1** : to make slower or less energetic **2** : to make less tight or firm
slag *n* : the waste left after the melting of ores and the separation of the metal from them
slain *past participle of* SLAY
slake *vb* **slaked; slak·ing** : QUENCH 1
¹slam *vb* **slammed; slam·ming** **1** : to shut with noisy force : BANG **2** : to strike or beat hard **3** : to put or place with force **4** : to criticize harshly
²slam *n* **1** : a severe blow **2** : the noise made by a violent act of closing : BANG
¹slan·der *vb* **slan·dered; slan·der·ing** : to make a false and damaging statement against
²slander *n* : a false statement that damages another person's reputation
slang *n* : very informal words used by a group of people
¹slant *vb* **slant·ed; slant·ing** : to turn or incline diagonally from a straight line or level : SLOPE
²slant *n* : a direction, line, or surface that is not level or straight up and down : SLOPE
³slant *adj* : not level or straight up and down
slant·wise *adv or adj* : at a slant : in a slanting position
¹slap *vb* **slapped; slap·ping** **1** : to strike with or as if with the open hand **2** : to make a sound like that of slapping **3** : to put, place, or throw with careless haste or force

²slap *n* **1 :** a quick sharp blow especially with the open hand **2 :** a noise like that made by a blow with the open hand

¹slash *vb* **slashed; slash·ing 1 :** to cut or strike at with sweeping blows **2 :** to reduce sharply

²slash *n* **1 :** an act of cutting or striking with sweeping strokes **2 :** a long cut or slit made with sweeping blows

slat *n* **:** a thin narrow strip of wood, plastic, or metal

slate *n* **1 :** a fine-grained usually bluish gray rock that splits into thin layers or plates and is used mostly for roofing and blackboards **2 :** a framed piece of slate used to write on

¹slaugh·ter *n* **1 :** the act of killing **2 :** the act of killing and preparing animals for food **3 :** destruction of many lives especially in battle

²slaughter *vb* **slaugh·tered; slaugh·ter·ing 1 :** ²BUTCHER 1 **2 :** ²MASSACRE

slaugh·ter·house *n, pl* **slaugh·ter·hous·es :** a building where animals are killed and prepared for food

Slav *n* **:** a native speaker of a Slavic language

¹slave *n* **1 :** a person who is owned by another person and can be sold at the owner's will **2 :** a person who is strongly influenced and controlled by something **3 :** DRUDGE

²slave *vb* **slaved; slav·ing :** to work very hard, for long hours, or under difficult conditions

slave·hold·er *n* **:** an owner of slaves

slav·ery *n* **1 :** the state of being owned by another person **:** BONDAGE **2 :** the custom or practice of owning slaves **3 :** hard tiring labor **:** DRUDGERY

Slav·ic *adj* **:** of, relating to, or characteristic of the Slavs or their languages

slav·ish *adj* **:** following, copying, or accepting something or someone without questioning

slay *vb* **slew; slain; slay·ing :** ¹KILL 1 — **slay·er** *n*

¹sled *n* **1 :** a vehicle on runners for carrying loads especially over snow **2 :** a small vehicle used mostly by children for sliding on snow and ice

²sled *vb* **sled·ded; sled·ding :** to ride or carry on a sled

sledge *n* **:** a strong heavy sled

sledge·ham·mer *n* **:** a large heavy hammer usually used with both hands

sleek *adj* **sleek·er; sleek·est 1 :** smooth and glossy as if polished **2 :** having a healthy well-groomed look **3 :** straight and smooth in design or shape **4 :** stylish and elegant

¹sleep *vb* **slept; sleep·ing :** to rest with eyes closed in a temporary state of inactivity **:** be or lie in a state of sleep

²sleep *n* **1 :** a natural temporary state of rest during which an individual becomes physically inactive and unaware of the surrounding environment and many bodily functions (as breathing) slow **2 :** an inactive state (as hibernation) like true sleep **3 :** DEATH 3 — **sleep·less** *adj* — **sleep·less·ness** *n*

sleep·er *n* **1 :** someone that sleeps **2 :** a railroad car with berths for sleeping

sleeping bag *n* **:** a large fabric bag that is warmly lined for sleeping outdoors or in a camp or tent

sleep·over *n* **:** an overnight stay at another's home

sleep·walk *vb* **sleep·walked; sleep·walk·ing :** to walk about while asleep — **sleep·walk·er** *n*

sleepy *adj* **sleep·i·er; sleep·i·est 1 :** ready to fall asleep **:** DROWSY **2 :** not active, noisy, or busy — **sleep·i·ness** *n*

¹sleet *n* **:** frozen or partly frozen rain

²sleet *vb* **sleet·ed; sleet·ing :** to shower sleet

sleeve *n* **1 :** the part of a piece of clothing covering the arm **2 :** a part that fits over or around something like a sleeve — **sleeved** *adj* — **sleeve·less** *adj* — **up someone's sleeve :** held secretly in reserve

sleigh *n* **:** an open usually horse-drawn vehicle with runners for use on snow or ice

sleight of hand *n* **:** skill and quickness in the use of the hands especially in doing magic tricks

slen·der *adj* **slen·der·er; slen·der·est 1 :** gracefully thin **2 :** narrow for its height or length **3 :** very little

slept *past and past participle of* SLEEP

slew *past of* SLAY

¹slice *vb* **sliced; slic·ing 1 :** to cut with or as if with a knife **2 :** to cut into thin flat pieces

²slice *n* **:** a thin flat piece cut from something

¹slick *vb* **slicked; slick·ing :** to make sleek or smooth

²slick *adj* **1 :** having a smooth surface **:** SLIPPERY **2 :** TRICKY **3 :** having skill and cleverness

slick·er *n* **:** a long loose raincoat

¹slide *vb* **slid; slid·ing 1 :** to move or cause to move smoothly over a surface **:** GLIDE **2 :** to move or pass smoothly and without much effort **3 :** to get gradually worse over time

²slide *n* **1 :** the act or motion of moving smoothly over a surface **2 :** a movement to a lower or worse condition **3 :** a surface down which a person or thing slides **4 :** a loosened mass that moves swiftly **:** AVALANCHE **5 :** a glass or plastic plate for holding an object to be examined under a microscope **6 :** a transparent picture that can be projected on a screen **7 :** something that operates or adjusts by sliding

slid·er *n* **1 :** one that slides **2 :** a very small sandwich of hamburger or other meat typically served on a bun

1slight *adj* **slight·er; slight·est 1 :** small of its kind or in amount **2 :** thin and delicate **3 :** not important **:** TRIVIAL **4 :** FLIMSY, FRAIL — **slight·ly** *adv*

2slight *vb* **slight·ed; slight·ing :** to treat without proper respect or courtesy

3slight *n* **1 :** an act or an instance of treating without proper respect or courtesy **2 :** an instance of being treated without proper respect or courtesy

1slim *adj* **slim·mer; slim·mest 1 :** SLENDER 1 **2 :** very small

2slim *vb* **slimmed; slim·ming :** to make or become slender

slime *n* **1 :** soft slippery mud **2 :** a soft slippery material (as on the skin of a slug or catfish)

slimy *adj* **slim·i·er; slim·i·est 1 :** having a slippery feel or look **2 :** covered with slime

1sling *vb* **slung; sling·ing 1 :** to throw with a sudden sweeping motion **:** FLING **2 :** to hurl with a sling

2sling *n* **1 :** a device (as a short strap with a string attached at each end) for hurling stones **2 :** a device (as a rope or chain) by which something is lifted or carried **3 :** a bandage hanging from the neck to hold up the arm or hand

3sling *vb* **slung; sling·ing 1 :** to put in or move or support with a sling **2 :** to hang from two points

sling·shot *n* **:** a forked stick with an elastic band attached for shooting small stones

slink *vb* **slunk; slink·ing :** to move or go by or as if by creeping especially so as not to be noticed (as in fear or shame)

1slip *vb* **slipped; slip·ping 1 :** to move easily and smoothly **2 :** to slide into or out of place or away from a support **3 :** to slide on a slippery surface so as to lose balance **4 :** to pass or let pass or escape without being noted, used, or done **5 :** to move into or out of a place without being noticed **6 :** to escape the attention or memory of **7 :** to put on or take off a piece of clothing quickly and easily **8 :** to make or become known by mistake **9 :** to go from one state or condition to an often worse one **10 :** to get away from — **slip up :** to make a mistake

2slip *n* **1 :** the act or an instance of sliding down or out of place **2 :** a secret or quick departure or escape **3 :** a small mistake **:** BLUNDER **4 :** a fall from some level or standard **:** DECLINE **5 :** a place for a ship between two piers **6 :** an undergarment for women made in dress or skirt length

3slip *n* **1 :** a usually small piece of paper and especially one used for some record **2 :** a long narrow piece of material

slip·cov·er *n* **:** a cover (as for a sofa or chair)

slip·knot *n* **:** a knot made by tying the end of a line around the line itself to form a loop so that the size of the loop may be changed by slipping the knot

slip·per *n* **:** a light low shoe that is easily slipped on the foot and is made to be worn indoors

slip·pery *adj* **slip·per·i·er; slip·per·i·est 1 :** having a surface smooth or wet enough to make holding onto or moving or standing on difficult **2 :** not to be trusted **:** TRICKY

slip·shod *adj* **:** very careless

1slit *n* **:** a long narrow cut or opening

2slit *vb* **slit; slit·ting :** to make a long narrow cut in **:** SLASH

slith·er *vb* **slith·ered; slith·er·ing :** 1GLIDE

slith·ery *adj* **:** having a slippery surface, texture, or quality

1sliv·er *n* **1 :** a long slender piece of something cut or torn off **:** SPLINTER **2 :** a small amount

2sliver *vb* **sliv·ered; sliv·er·ing :** to cut or form into long slender pieces

slob *n* **1 :** a sloppy or lazy person **2 :** an ordinary person

1slob·ber *vb* **slob·bered; slob·ber·ing :** to let saliva or liquid dribble from the mouth

2slobber *n* **:** dripping saliva

slo·gan *n* **:** a word or phrase used by a party, a group, or a business to attract attention

sloop *n* **:** a sailing boat with one mast and a fore-and-aft mainsail and jib

1slop *n* **1 :** thin tasteless drink or liquid food **2 :** food waste or gruel fed to animals **3 :** body waste **4 :** soft mud

2slop *vb* **slopped; slop·ping 1 :** to spill or spill something on or over **2 :** to feed slop to

1slope *n* **1 :** a piece of slanting ground (as a hillside) **2 :** upward or downward slant

2slope *vb* **sloped; slop·ing :** to take a slanting direction

slop·py *adj* **slop·pi·er; slop·pi·est 1 :** careless in work or in appearance **2 :** containing a lot of moisture **:** very wet

slosh *vb* **sloshed; slosh·ing 1 :** to walk with trouble through water, mud, or slush **2 :** to move with a splashing motion

1slot *n* **:** a narrow opening, groove, or passage

2slot *vb* **slot·ted; slot·ting :** to cut a narrow opening, groove, or passage in

sloth *n* **1 :** the quality or state of being lazy **2 :** an animal of Central and South America that hangs with its back downward and moves slowly along the branches of trees on whose leaves, twigs, and fruits it feeds

1slouch *n* **1 :** a lazy worthless person **2 :** a

way of standing, sitting, or walking with the head and shoulders bent forward

[2]slouch *vb* **slouched; slouch·ing :** to walk, stand, or sit lazily with the head and shoulders bent forward

slough *n* **:** a wet marshy or muddy place

slov·en·ly *adj* **1 :** personally untidy **2 :** very careless

[1]slow *adj* **slow·er; slow·est 1 :** moving, flowing, or going at less than the usual speed **2 :** taking more time than is expected or desired **3 :** not as smart or as quick to understand as most people **4 :** not active **5 :** indicating less than is correct **6 :** not easily aroused or excited — **slow·ly** *adv* — **slow·ness** *n*

[2]slow *vb* **slowed; slow·ing :** to go or make go less than the usual speed

[3]slow *adv* **slow·er; slow·est :** in a slow way

slow·poke *n* **:** a very slow person

sludge *n* **:** a soft muddy mass resulting from sewage treatment

[1]slug *n* **:** a wormlike animal living mostly on land and that is related to the snails but that has an undeveloped shell or no shell

[2]slug *n* **1 :** BULLET **2 :** a metal disk often used in place of a coin

[3]slug *n* **:** a hard blow especially with the fist

[4]slug *vb* **slugged; slug·ging :** to hit hard with the fist or with a bat

slug·gard *n* **:** a lazy person

slug·ger *n* **:** a boxer or baseball batter who hits hard

slug·gish *adj* **:** slow in movement or reaction — **slug·gish·ly** *adv*

[1]sluice *n* **1 :** a man-made channel for water with a gate for controlling its flow or changing its direction **2 :** a device for controlling the flow of water **3 :** a sloping trough for washing ore or for floating logs

[2]sluice *vb* **sluiced; sluic·ing 1 :** to wash in a stream of water running through a sluice **2 :** [3]FLUSH 2, DRENCH

slum *n* **:** a very poor crowded dirty section especially of a city

[1]slum·ber *vb* **slum·bered; slum·ber·ing :** [1]SLEEP 1

[2]slumber *n* **:** [2]SLEEP 1

[1]slump *vb* **slumped; slump·ing 1 :** to drop or slide down suddenly **:** COLLAPSE **2 :** [2]SLOUCH **3 :** to drop sharply

[2]slump *n* **:** a big or continued drop especially in prices, business, or performance

slung *past and past participle of* SLING

slunk *past and past participle of* SLINK

[1]slur *n* **:** an insulting remark

[2]slur *vb* **slurred; slur·ring :** to speak in a way that is difficult to understand

[3]slur *n* **:** a way of talking that is diffiuclt to understand

[1]slurp *vb* **slurped; slurp·ing :** to eat or drink noisily or with a sucking sound

[2]slurp *n* **:** a sucking sound made while eating and drinking

slush *n* **:** partly melted snow

slushy *adj* **slush·i·er; slush·i·est :** covered with or resembling partly melted snow

sly *adj* **sli·er** *or* **sly·er; sli·est** *or* **sly·est 1 :** both clever and tricky **2 :** tending to keep secrets and hide intentions **3 :** MISCHIEVOUS 2 — **sly·ly** *adv* — **sly·ness** *n* — **on the sly :** so as not to be seen or caught **:** SECRETLY

[1]smack *vb* **smacked; smack·ing 1 :** to make or give a noisy slap **2 :** to close and open the lips noisily especially in eating **3 :** to kiss usually loudly or hard

[2]smack *n* **1 :** a noisy slap or blow **2 :** a quick sharp noise made by the lips (as in enjoyment of some taste) **3 :** a loud kiss

[3]smack *adv* **:** in a square and sharp manner **:** DIRECTLY

[4]smack *vb* **smacked; smacking :** to have a flavor, trace, or suggestion

[5]smack *n* **:** a slight taste, trace, or touch of something

[1]small *adj* **small·er; small·est 1 :** little in size **2 :** few in numbers or members **3 :** little in amount **4 :** very young **5 :** not very much **6 :** UNIMPORTANT **7 :** operating on a limited scale **8 :** very soft and quiet **9 :** not generous **:** MEAN **10 :** made up of units of little worth **11 :** [1]HUMBLE 3, MODEST **12 :** lowered in pride **13 :** being letters that are not capitals — **small·ness** *n*

[2]small *n* **:** a part smaller and usually narrower than the rest

small intestine *n* **:** the long narrow upper part of the intestine in which food is mostly digested and from which digested food is absorbed into the body

small·pox *n* **:** a sometimes deadly disease in which fever and skin rash occur and which is believed to have been wiped out worldwide by vaccination

[1]smart *adj* **smart·er; smart·est 1 :** quick to learn or do **:** BRIGHT **2 :** showing good judgment **:** WISE **3 :** FRESH 8 **4 :** stylish and fashionable **5 :** BRISK, SPIRITED — **smart·ly** *adv* — **smart·ness** *n*

[2]smart *vb* **smart·ed; smart·ing 1 :** to cause or feel a sharp stinging pain **2 :** to be upset

[3]smart *n* **:** a stinging pain usually in one spot

smart al·eck *n* **:** a person who likes to show off in a clever but rude or annoying way

smart·phone *n* **:** a cell phone that includes additional software functions (as e-mail or an Internet browser)

[1]smash *n* **1 :** a violent blow **2 :** the action or sound of shattering or hitting violently **3 :** a striking success

DICTIONARY

²smash *vb* **smashed; smash·ing** **1 :** to break in pieces : SHATTER **2 :** to hit or move violently **3 :** to destroy completely

¹smear *vb* **smeared; smear·ing** **1 :** to spread or soil with something oily or sticky **2 :** to spread over a surface **3 :** to harm the reputation of (someone) with false statements

²smear *n* **:** a spot or streak made by or as if by an oily or sticky substance : SMUDGE

¹smell *vb* **smelled** *or* **smelt; smell·ing** **1 :** to become aware of the odor of by means of special cells located in the nose **2 :** to detect by means or use of the sense of smell **3 :** to have or give off an odor **4 :** to sense as if by smelling

²smell *n* **1 :** the sense by which a person or animal becomes aware of an odor **2 :** the sensation gotten through the sense of smell : ODOR, SCENT

smelly *adj* **smel·li·er; smel·li·est :** having an odor and especially a bad odor

¹smelt *n, pl* **smelts** *or* **smelt :** a small silvery fish that is sometimes used for food

²smelt *vb* **smelt·ed; smelt·ing :** to melt (as ore) in order to separate the metal : REFINE

¹smile *vb* **smiled; smil·ing** **1 :** make the corners of the mouth turn up in an expression of amusement or pleasure **2 :** to look with amusement or pleasure **3 :** to express by a smile

²smile *n* **:** an expression in which the corners of the mouth turn upward especially to show amusement or pleasure

smirk *vb* **smirked; smirk·ing :** to smile in an insincere manner — **smirk** *n*

smite *vb* **smote; smit·ten; smit·ing** **1 :** to strike hard especially with the hand or a weapon **2 :** to kill or injure

smith *n* **1 :** a worker in metals **2 :** BLACKSMITH

smith·er·eens *n pl* **:** small broken pieces

smithy *n, pl* **smith·ies :** the workshop of someone who works in metals and especially of a blacksmith

smock *n* **:** a loose outer garment worn especially for protection of clothing

smog *n* **:** a fog made heavier and thicker by the action of sunlight on polluted air

¹smoke *n* **1 :** the gas given off by burning materials (as coal, wood, or tobacco) made visible by particles of carbon floating in it **2 :** the act of drawing in and blowing out the fumes of burning tobacco

²smoke *vb* **smoked; smok·ing** **1 :** to give out smoke **2 :** to draw in and blow out the fumes of burning tobacco (as in a cigarette) **3 :** to expose (as meat) to the fumes of burning materials to give flavor and keep from spoiling — **smok·er** *n*

smoke de·tec·tor *n* **:** a device that sounds an alarm automatically when it detects smoke

smoke·house *n, pl* **smoke·hous·es :** a building where meat or fish is smoked

smoke·stack *n* **:** a large chimney or a pipe for carrying away smoke (as on a factory or ship)

smoky *adj* **smok·i·er; smok·i·est** **1 :** giving off smoke especially in large amounts **2 :** filled with or darkened by smoke **3 :** having a flavor, taste, or appearance of smoke

smol·der *or* **smoul·der** *vb* **smol·dered** *or* **smoul·dered; smol·der·ing** *or* **smoul·der·ing** **1 :** to burn slowly usually with smoke and without flame **2 :** to burn inwardly

¹smooth *adj* **smooth·er; smooth·est** **1 :** not rough or uneven in surface **2 :** not hairy **3 :** free from difficulties or things in the way **4 :** moving or progressing without breaks, sudden changes, or shifts **5 :** appearing to be friendly and flattering without really meaning it — **smooth·ly** *adv* — **smooth·ness** *n*

²smooth *vb* **smoothed; smooth·ing** **1 :** to remove bumps, lumps, or wrinkles : make smooth **2 :** to free from trouble or difficulty

smote *past of* SMITE

smoth·er *vb* **smoth·ered; smoth·er·ing** **1 :** to kill or injure by keeping from getting air or by exposing to smoke or fumes : SUFFOCATE **2 :** to become suffocated **3 :** to keep from growing or developing by or as if by covering **4 :** to keep from happening : SUPPRESS **5 :** to cover thickly

¹smudge *n* **1 :** a blurred spot or streak : SMEAR **2 :** a smoky fire (as to drive away mosquitoes)

²smudge *vb* **smudged; smudg·ing :** to soil or blur by rubbing or smearing

smug *adj* **smug·ger; smug·gest :** showing a superior attitude — **smug·ly** *adv*

smug·gle *vb* **smug·gled; smug·gling** **1 :** to export or import secretly and unlawfully **2 :** to take or bring secretly — **smug·gler** *n*

smut *n* **1 :** something (as a particle of soot) that soils or blackens **2 :** a destructive disease of plants (as cereal grasses) that is caused by a fungus **3 :** a fungus that causes smut

¹snack *n* **:** a small amount of food eaten between meals

²snack *vb* **snacked; snack·ing :** to eat a small amount of food between meals

¹snag *n* **1 :** a rough or broken part sticking out from something **2 :** an unexpected difficulty **3 :** a stump or stub of a tree branch especially when hidden under water

²snag *vb* **snagged; snag·ging** **1 :** to catch or damage on or as if on a part sticking up or out **2 :** to catch or capture by or as if by reaching out quickly and grabbing

snail *n* **:** a small slow-moving mollusk that

has a spiral shell into which it can draw itself for safety and that can live either on land or in water

[1]**snake** *n* **1 :** a limbless reptile that has a long body with scales and feeds usually on large insects or small animals and birds **2 :** a person who is mean or can't be trusted

[2]**snake** *vb* **snaked; snak·ing :** to crawl, wind, or move like a snake

snaky *adj* **snak·i·er; snak·i·est 1 :** of or like a snake **2 :** full of snakes

[1]**snap** *vb* **snapped; snap·ping 1 :** to break or break apart suddenly and often with a cracking noise **2 :** to grasp or grasp at something suddenly with the mouth or teeth **3 :** to speak or utter sharply or irritably **4 :** to make or cause to make a sharp or crackling sound **5 :** to close or fit in place with a quick movement **6 :** to put into or remove from a position suddenly or with a cracking sound **7 :** to act or be acted on with energy **8 :** to grasp at something eagerly **9 :** to get, take, or buy at once **10 :** to close by means of snaps or fasteners **11 :** to take a snapshot of **12 :** to make a short sharp sound by quickly moving the middle finger against the thumb

[2]**snap** *n* **1 :** a sudden short sharp sound **2 :** an act of moving the middle finger against the thumb to make a short sharp sound **3 :** something that is easy and presents no problems **4 :** a sudden change in weather **5 :** a catch or fastening that closes or locks with a click **6 :** SNAPSHOT **7 :** a short amount of time

[3]**snap** *adj* **1 :** made suddenly or without careful thought **2 :** closing with a click or by means of a device that snaps **3 :** very easy

snap·drag·on *n* **:** a garden plant with stalks of usually white, pink, red, or yellow flowers with two lips

snap·per *n* **1 :** SNAPPING TURTLE **2 :** an active fish of warm seas that is caught for sport and food

snap·ping tur·tle *n* **:** a large American turtle that catches its prey with a snap of the powerful jaws

snap·py *adj* **snap·pi·er; snap·pi·est 1 :** full of life **:** LIVELY **2 :** briskly cold **:** CHILLY **3 :** QUICK **4 :** STYLISH **5 :** clever and funny

snap·shot *n* **:** a photograph taken usually with an inexpensive hand-held camera

[1]**snare** *n* **1 :** a trap (as a noose) for catching small animals and birds **2 :** something that traps or deceives

[2]**snare** *vb* **snared; snar·ing :** to catch or entangle by or as if by use of a trap for catching small animals

snare drum *n* **:** a small drum with two heads that has strings stretched across its lower head to produce a rattling sound

[1]**snarl** *vb* **snarled; snarl·ing 1 :** to growl with a showing of teeth **2 :** to speak in an angry way

[2]**snarl** *n* **:** an angry growl

[3]**snarl** *n* **1 :** a tangle usually of hairs or thread **:** KNOT **2 :** a situation that makes movement difficult

[4]**snarl** *vb* **snarled; snarl·ing :** to get or become tangled

[1]**snatch** *vb* **snatched; snatch·ing :** to take hold of or try to take hold of something quickly or suddenly

[2]**snatch** *n* **1 :** something brief, hurried, or in small bits **2 :** an act of taking hold of something quickly **3 :** a brief period

[1]**sneak** *vb* **sneaked** *or* **snuck; sneak·ing :** to move, act, bring, put, or take in a sly or secret way

[2]**sneak** *n* **:** a person who acts in a sly or secret way

sneak·er *n* **:** a sports shoe with a rubber sole

sneaky *adj* **sneak·i·er; sneak·i·est :** behaving in a sly or secret way or showing that kind of behavior

[1]**sneer** *vb* **sneered; sneer·ing 1 :** to smile or laugh while making a face that shows disrespect **2 :** to speak or write in a disrespectful way

[2]**sneer** *n* **:** a disrespectful expression or remark

[1]**sneeze** *vb* **sneezed; sneez·ing :** to force the breath out in a sudden and noisy way

[2]**sneeze** *n* **:** an act or instance of sneezing

[1]**snick·er** *vb* **snick·ered; snick·er·ing :** to give a small and often mean or sly laugh

[2]**snicker** *n* **:** an act or sound of laughing in a mean or sly way

snick·er·doo·dle *n* **:** a cookie made with butter, sugar, and flour and that is rolled in cinnamon and sugar before baking

snide *adj* **:** unkind or insulting in an indirect way

[1]**sniff** *vb* **sniffed; sniff·ing 1 :** to smell by taking short breaths **2 :** to draw air into the nose in short breaths loud enough to be heard **3 :** to say with scorn

[2]**sniff** *n* **1 :** the act or sound of drawing air into the nose in short breaths (as to smell something) **2 :** an odor detected through the nose

snif·fle *vb* **snif·fled; snif·fling 1 :** to sniff repeatedly **2 :** to speak with sniffs

snif·fles *n pl* **:** a common cold in which the main symptom is a runny nose

[1]**snig·ger** *vb* **snig·gered; snig·ger·ing :** [1]SNICKER

[2]**snigger** *n* **:** [2]SNICKER

[1]**snip** *n* **1 :** a small piece that is clipped off **2 :** an act or sound of clipping

²snip *vb* **snipped; snip·ping :** to cut or cut off with or as if with shears or scissors

¹snipe *n, pl* **snipes** *or* **snipe :** a bird that lives in marshes and has a long straight bill

²snipe *vb* **sniped; snip·ing 1 :** to shoot from a hiding place (as at individual enemy soldiers) **2 :** to criticize someone in a harsh or unfair way — **snip·er** *n*

¹snitch *vb* **snitched; snitch·ing :** ¹STEAL 1

²snitch *vb* **snitched; snitching :** INFORM 2, TATTLE

³snitch *n, pl* **snitch·es :** TATTLETALE

snob *n* **:** a person who looks down on or avoids those felt to be less important

snob·bish *adj* **:** being or characteristic of a snob

snob·by *adj* **snob·bi·er; snob·bi·est :** SNOBBISH

¹snoop *vb* **snooped; snoop·ing :** to look or search especially in a sneaking or nosy way — **snoop·er** *n*

²snoop *n* **:** a person who looks or searches in a sneaky or nosy way

snoot *n* **:** ¹NOSE 1

snooty *adj* **snoot·i·er; snoot·i·est :** rude and arrogant especially to people from a lower class

¹snooze *vb* **snoozed; snooz·ing :** to take a nap

²snooze *n* **:** a short sleep **:** NAP

¹snore *vb* **snored; snor·ing :** to breathe with a rough hoarse noise while sleeping

²snore *n* **:** an act or sound of breathing with a rough hoarse noise while sleeping

¹snor·kel *n* **:** a tube used by swimmers for breathing with the head underwater

²snorkel *vb* **snor·keled** *or Can and Brit* **snorkelled; snor·kel·ing** *or Can and Brit* **snorkelling :** to swim underwater using a tube for breathing

¹snort *vb* **snort·ed; snort·ing 1 :** to force air through the nose with a rough harsh sound **2 :** to say something with anger or scorn

²snort *n* **:** an act of or the rough harsh sound made by forcing air through the nose

snot·ty *adj* **snot·ti·er; snot·ti·est :** rude and arrogant

snout *n* **1 :** the projecting part of an animal's face that includes the nose or nose and mouth **2 :** a usually large and ugly human nose

¹snow *n* **1 :** small white crystals of ice formed directly from the water vapor of the air **2 :** a mass of snowflakes fallen to earth

²snow *vb* **snowed; snow·ing :** to fall or cause to fall in or as snow

snow·ball *n* **:** a round mass of snow pressed or rolled together

snow·bank *n* **:** a mound or pile of snow that results from clearing pavement

snow–blind *adj* **:** having the eyes red and swollen and unable to see from the effect of glare reflected from snow

snow·blow·er *n* **:** a machine in which rotating parts pick up snow and throw it aside

snow·board *n* **:** a board like a wide ski ridden in a surfing position over snow — **snow·board·er** *n* — **snow·board·ing** *n*

snow·bound *adj* **:** shut in or blocked by snow

snow·drift *n* **:** a bank of drifted snow

snow·fall *n* **1 :** a fall of snow **2 :** the amount of snow that falls in a single storm or in a certain period

snow·flake *n* **:** a single snow crystal **:** a small mass of snow crystals

snow·man *n, pl* **snow·men :** snow shaped to look like a person

snow·mo·bile *n* **:** a small motor vehicle designed for travel on snow

snow·plow *n* **:** any of various devices used for clearing away snow

¹snow·shoe *n* **:** a light frame of wood strung with a net (as of rawhide) and worn under a shoe to prevent sinking into soft snow

²snowshoe *vb* **snow·shoed; snow·shoe·ing :** to walk with snowshoes

snow·storm *n* **:** a storm of falling snow

snow·suit *n* **:** a one-piece or two-piece warm outer garment for a child

snow thrower *n* **:** SNOWBLOWER

snowy *adj* **snow·i·er; snow·i·est 1 :** having or covered with snow **2 :** white like snow

¹snub *vb* **snubbed; snub·bing :** to ignore or treat rudely on purpose

²snub *n* **:** an act or an instance of ignoring or treating rudely on purpose

snub–nosed *adj* **:** having a stubby and usually slightly turned-up nose

snuck *past and past participle of* SNEAK

¹snuff *n* **:** powdered tobacco that is chewed, placed against the gums, or drawn in through the nostrils

²snuff *vb* **snuffed; snuff·ing :** to draw through or into the nose with force

³snuff *vb* **snuffed; snuffing 1 :** to cut or pinch off the burned end of the wick of a candle **2 :** to put an end to

¹snuf·fle *vb* **snuf·fled; snuf·fling :** to breathe noisily through a nose that is partly blocked

²snuffle *n* **:** the sound made in breathing through a nose that is partly blocked

snug *adj* **snug·ger; snug·gest 1 :** fitting closely and comfortably **2 :** COMFORTABLE 1, COZY **3 :** offering protection or a hiding place — **snug·ly** *adv*

snug·gle *vb* **snug·gled; snug·gling 1 :** to curl up comfortably or cozily **:** CUDDLE **2 :** to pull in close to someone

¹so *adv* **1 :** in the way indicated **2 :** in the same way **:** ALSO **3 :** ¹THEN 2 **4 :** to an indicated extent or way **5 :** to a great degree **:** VERY, EXTREMELY **6 :** to a definite but not specified amount **7 :** most certainly **:** INDEED **8 :** THEREFORE

²so *conj* **1 :** in order that **2 :** and therefore

³so *pron* **1 :** the same **:** THAT **2 :** approximately that

so. *abbr* south

¹soak *vb* **soaked; soak·ing 1 :** to lie covered with liquid **2 :** to place in a liquid to wet or as if to wet thoroughly **3 :** to make very wet **4 :** to enter or pass through something by or as if by tiny holes **:** PERMEATE **5 :** to draw in by or as if by absorption

²soak *n* **1 :** the act or process of letting something stay in a liquid for a long time to soften or clean it **2 :** a long bath

¹soap *n* **:** a substance that is used for washing

²soap *vb* **soaped; soap·ing :** to rub a cleaning substance over or into something

soap·stone *n* **:** a soft stone that has a soapy or greasy feeling

soapy *adj* **soap·i·er; soap·i·est 1 :** covered with soap **2 :** containing soap **3 :** like soap

soar *vb* **soared; soar·ing 1 :** to fly or glide through the air often at a great height **2 :** to increase quickly **3 :** to rise quickly **4 :** to rise to a great height

¹sob *vb* **sobbed; sob·bing 1 :** to cry noisily with short sudden breaths **2 :** to say while crying noisily

²sob *n* **:** an act or the sound of crying loudly with short sudden breaths

¹so·ber *adj* **1 :** not drinking too much **:** TEMPERATE **2 :** not drunk **3 :** having or showing a serious attitude **:** SOLEMN **4 :** having a plain color **5 :** carefully reasoned or considered **:** REALISTIC

²sober *vb* **so·bered; so·ber·ing 1 :** to make or become less drunk **2 :** to make or become serious or thoughtful

so–called *adj* **:** commonly or wrongly named

soc·cer *n* **:** a game played between two teams of eleven players in which a round inflated ball is moved toward a goal usually by kicking

so·cia·ble *adj* **1 :** liking to be around other people **:** FRIENDLY **2 :** involving or encouraging friendliness or pleasant companionship with other people

¹so·cial *adj* **1 :** enjoying other people **:** SOCIABLE **2 :** relating to interaction with other people especially for pleasure **3 :** of or relating to human beings as a group **4 :** living naturally in groups or communities **5 :** relating to or based on rank in a particular society — **so·cial·ly** *adv*

²social *n* **:** a friendly gathering usually for a special reason

so·cial·ism *n* **:** a social system or theory in which the government owns and controls the means of production (as factories) and distribution of goods

so·cial·ist *n* **:** a person who supports socialism

social media *n pl* **:** forms of electronic communication (as websites for social networking) through which users create online communities to share information, personal messages, and other content (as videos)

social networking *n* **:** the creation and maintenance of personal and business relationships especially online

social studies *n pl* **:** the studies (as civics, history, and geography) that deal with human relationships and the way society works

so·ci·ety *n, pl* **so·ci·et·ies 1 :** a community or group of people having common traditions, institutions, and interests **2 :** all of the people of the world **3 :** a group of persons with a common interest, belief, or purpose **4 :** friendly association with others

¹sock *n, pl* **socks :** a knitted or woven covering for the foot usually reaching past the ankle and sometimes to the knee

²sock *vb* **socked; sock·ing :** ¹HIT 1, PUNCH

³sock *n* **:** ³PUNCH

sock·et *n* **:** a small opening or hollow part that forms a holder for something

sod *n* **:** the upper layer of the soil that is filled with roots (as of grass)

so·da *n* **1 :** a powdery substance like salt used in washing and in making glass or soap **2 :** BAKING SODA **3 :** SODA WATER **4 :** SODA POP **5 :** a sweet drink made of soda water, flavoring, and often ice cream

soda pop *n* **:** a beverage containing soda water, flavoring, and a sweet syrup

soda water *n* **:** water with carbon dioxide added

sod·den *adj* **:** SOGGY

so·di·um *n* **:** a soft waxy silver-white chemical element occurring in nature in combined form (as in salt)

sodium bicarbonate *n* **:** BAKING SODA

sodium chlo·ride *n* **:** ¹SALT 1

so·fa *n* **:** a long upholstered seat usually with a back and arms

¹soft *adj* **soft·er; soft·est 1 :** not hard, solid, or firm **2 :** smooth or pleasant to touch **3 :** having a soothing or comfortable effect **:** not bright or glaring **4 :** quiet in pitch or volume **5 :** not strong or forceful **:** GENTLE **6 :** involving little work or effort **:** EASY **7 :** sounding like the *c* in *ace* and the *g* in *gem* **8 :** easily affected by emotions **:** sympathetic and kind **9 :** lacking in strength or fitness **10 :** free from substances that prevent lathering of soap **11 :** not containing alcohol — **soft·ness** *n*

²soft *adv* **softer; softest** : SOFTLY

soft·ball *n* **1** : a game like baseball played with a larger ball thrown underhand **2** : the ball used in softball

soft·en *vb* **soft·ened; soft·en·ing** **1** : to make or become soft or less firm **2** : to make or become gentler or less harsh — **soft·en·er** *n*

soft·ly *adv* : in a soft way : quietly or gently

soft·ware *n* : the programs and related information used by a computer

soft·wood *n* : the wood of a tree (as a pine or spruce) that has needles as distinguished from the wood of a tree (as a maple) with broad leaves

sog·gy *adj* **sog·gi·er; sog·gi·est** : heavy with water or moisture

¹soil *vb* **soiled; soil·ing** : to make or become dirty

²soil *n* **1** : the loose surface material of the earth in which plants grow **2** : COUNTRY 2, LAND — **soil·less** *adj*

¹so·journ *n* : a temporary stay

²sojourn *vb* **so·journed; so·journ·ing** : to stay as a temporary resident

sol *n* : the fifth note of the musical scale

so·lace *n* **1** : comfort in times of sorrow or worry **2** : something that gives comfort

so·lar *adj* **1** : of or relating to the sun **2** : measured by the earth's course around the sun **3** : produced or made to work by the action of the sun's light or heat

solar system *n* : the sun and the planets, asteroids, comets, and meteors that revolve around it

sold *past and past participle of* SELL

¹sol·der *n* : a metal or a mixture of metals used when melted to join or repair surfaces of metal

²solder *vb* **sol·dered; sol·der·ing** : to join together or repair with solder

sol·dier *n* : a person in military service and especially an enlisted person who is in the army

¹sole *n* **1** : the bottom of the foot **2** : the bottom of a shoe, slipper, or boot

²sole *vb* **soled; sol·ing** : to put a new sole on

³sole *n* : a flatfish that has a small mouth and small eyes set close together and is often used for food

⁴sole *adj* **1** : ¹SINGLE 1, ONLY **2** : limited or belonging only to the person or group mentioned

sole·ly *adv* **1** : without another involved : ALONE **2** : ²ONLY 2

sol·emn *adj* **1** : very serious or formal in manner, behavior, or expression **2** : done or made seriously and thoughtfully — **sol·emn·ly** *adv*

so·lem·ni·ty *n, pl* **so·lem·ni·ties** **1** : a serious or formal ceremony **2** : formal dignity

so·lic·it *vb* **so·lic·it·ed; so·lic·it·ing** **1** : to come to with a request or plea **2** : to try to get by asking or pleading

¹sol·id *adj* **1** : not hollow **2** : not loose or spongy : COMPACT **3** : neither liquid nor gaseous **4** : made firmly and well **5** : being without a break, interruption, or change **6** : UNANIMOUS 1 **7** : RELIABLE, DEPENDABLE **8** : of one material, kind, or color — **sol·id·ly** *adv*

²solid *n* **1** : something (as a cube) that has length, width, and thickness **2** : a substance that keeps its size and shape : a solid substance

so·lid·i·fy *vb* **so·lid·i·fied; so·lid·i·fy·ing** : to make or become solid

sol·i·taire *n* : a card game played by one person alone

sol·i·tary *adj* **1** : all alone : without anyone or anything else **2** : seldom visited : LONELY **3** : growing or living alone : not one of a group or cluster

sol·i·tude *n* : the quality or state of being alone or away from others : SECLUSION

¹so·lo *n, pl* **solos** **1** : a piece of music performed by one singer or musician **2** : an action done alone

²solo *adv or adj* : without another person : ALONE

³solo *vb* **so·loed; so·lo·ing** : to do something (as perform music or fly an airplane) alone or without an instructor

so·lo·ist *n* : a person who performs a solo

sol·stice *n* : the time of the year when the sun passes overhead the farthest north (**summer solstice**, about June 22) or south (**winter solstice**, about December 22) of the equator

sol·u·ble *adj* **1** : capable of being dissolved in liquid **2** : capable of being solved or explained

so·lu·tion *n* **1** : the act or process of solving **2** : an answer to a problem : EXPLANATION **3** : the act or process by which a solid, liquid, or gas is dissolved in a liquid **4** : a liquid in which something has been dissolved

solve *vb* **solved; solv·ing** : to find the answer to or a solution for

sol·vent *n* : a usually liquid substance in which other substances can be dissolved or dispersed

som·ber *or* **som·bre** *adj* **1** : very sad or serious **2** : being dark and gloomy : DULL

som·bre·ro *n, pl* **som·bre·ros** : a tall hat with a very wide brim worn especially in Mexico

¹some *adj* **1** : not known, named, or specified **2** : being one, a part, or an unspecified number of something **3** : being of an amount or number that is not mentioned

[2]**some** *pron* : a certain number or amount
[1]**-some** *adj suffix* : distinguished by a specified thing, quality, state, or action
[2]**-some** *n suffix* : group of so many members
[1]**some·body** *pron* : a person who is not known, named, or specified
[2]**somebody** *n, pl* **some·bod·ies** : a person of importance
some·day *adv* : at some future time
some·how *adv* : in a way that is not known or certain
some·one *pron* : a person who is not known, named, or specified
[1]**som·er·sault** *n* : a movement in which someone makes a complete turn by bringing the feet over the head
[2]**somersault** *vb* **som·er·sault·ed; som·er·sault·ing** : to perform a movement in which a person makes a complete turn by bringing the feet over the head
some·thing *pron* **1** : a thing that is not known or named **2** : a thing or amount that is clearly known but not named **3** : SOMEWHAT
some·time *adv* **1** : at a future time **2** : at a time not known or not specified
some·times *adv* : now and then : OCCASIONALLY
some·way *adv* : SOMEHOW
[1]**some·what** *pron* : some amount or extent
[2]**somewhat** *adv* : to some extent
some·where *adv* **1** : in, at, or to a place not known or named **2** : rather close to
son *n* **1** : a male child or offspring **2** : a man or boy closely associated with or thought of as a child of something (as a country, race, or religion)
so·nar *n* : a device for detecting objects underwater using reflected sound waves
so·na·ta *n* : a musical composition for one or two instruments consisting of three or four separate sections in different forms and keys
song *n* **1** : a short musical composition of words and music **2** : the act or art of singing **3** : a series of usually musical sounds produced by an animal and especially a bird **4** : a small amount
song·bird *n* : a bird that produces a series of usually musical sounds
son·ic *adj* : using, produced by, or relating to sound waves
sonic boom *n* : a sound like an explosion that is made by an aircraft traveling faster than the speed of sound
son–in–law *n, pl* **sons–in–law** : the husband of a person's daughter or son
son·ny *n, pl* **son·nies** : a young boy — used mostly by an older person to address a boy
so·no·rous *adj* : loud, deep, or rich in sound : RESONANT
soon *adv* **soon·er; soon·est** **1** : without delay : before long **2** : in a prompt way : QUICKLY **3** : before long **4** : [1]EARLY 2 **5** : by choice : WILLINGLY
soot *n* : a black powder formed when something is burned : the very fine powder that colors smoke
soothe *vb* **soothed; sooth·ing** **1** : to please by praise or attention **2** : RELIEVE 1 **3** : to calm down : COMFORT
sooth·say·er *n* : a person who claims to foretell events
sooty *adj* **soot·i·er; soot·i·est** **1** : covered with soot **2** : like soot in color
sop *vb* **sopped; sop·ping** **1** : to soak or dip in or as if in liquid **2** : to mop or soak up
so·phis·ti·cat·ed *adj* **1** : very complicated : COMPLEX **2** : having a lot of knowledge about the world especially through experience **3** : appealing to a person's intelligence
soph·o·more *n* : a student in his or her second year at a high school or college
so·pra·no *n, pl* **so·pra·nos** **1** : the highest part in harmony that has four parts **2** : the highest singing voice of women or boys **3** : a singer or an instrument having a soprano range or part
sor·cer·er *n* : a person who practices sorcery or witchcraft : WIZARD
sor·cer·ess *n* : a woman who practices sorcery or witchcraft : WITCH
sor·cery *n, pl* **sor·cer·ies** : the use of magic : WITCHCRAFT
sor·did *adj* **1** : very dirty : FILTHY **2** : of low moral quality
[1]**sore** *adj* **sor·er; sor·est** **1** : very painful or sensitive : TENDER **2** : hurt or red and swollen so as to be or seem painful **3** : causing emotional distress **4** : ANGRY — **sore·ly** *adv* — **sore·ness** *n*
[2]**sore** *n* : a sore or painful spot on the body usually with the skin broken or bruised and often with infection
sor·ghum *n* **1** : a tall grass that is grown for forage and grain **2** : a sweet syrup from the juice of sorghum stems
so·ror·i·ty *n, pl* **so·ror·i·ties** : a club of girls or women especially at a college
[1]**sor·rel** *n* **1** : a light reddish brown horse often with a white mane and tail **2** : a brownish orange to light brown
[2]**sorrel** *n* : any of several plants with sour juice
[1]**sor·row** *n* **1** : sadness felt after a loss (as of someone or something loved) **2** : a cause of grief or sadness **3** : a feeling of regret
[2]**sorrow** *vb* **sor·rowed; sor·row·ing** : to feel or express sorrow : GRIEVE
sor·row·ful *adj* **1** : full of or showing sadness **2** : causing sadness

sor·ry *adj* **sor·ri·er; sor·ri·est** **1** : feeling sorrow or regret **2** : causing sorrow, pity, or scorn : PITIFUL

[1]**sort** *n* **1** : a group of persons or things that have something in common : KIND **2** : PERSON 1, INDIVIDUAL **3** : general disposition : NATURE — **out of sorts** **1** : not feeling well **2** : easily angered : IRRITABLE

[2]**sort** *vb* **sort·ed; sort·ing** **1** : to separate and arrange according to kind or class **2** : [1]SEARCH 1

SOS *n* **1** : an international radio code distress signal used especially by ships and airplanes calling for help **2** : a call for help

[1]**so–so** *adv* : fairly well

[2]**so–so** *adj* : neither very good nor very bad

sought *past and past participle of* SEEK

soul *n* **1** : the spiritual part of a person believed to give life to the body **2** : the essential or most important part of something **3** : a person who leads or stirs others to action : LEADER **4** : a person's moral and emotional nature **5** : human being : PERSON **6** : a style of music expressing deep emotion that was created by African-Americans

[1]**sound** *adj* **1** : free from disease or weakness : HEALTHY **2** : solid and strong **3** : free from error **4** : showing good sense : WISE **5** : SEVERE 2 **6** : deep and undisturbed — **sound·ly** *adv* — **sound·ness** *n*

[2]**sound** *adv* : to the full extent

[3]**sound** *n* **1** : the sensation experienced through the sense of hearing : an instance or occurrence of this **2** : one of the noises that together make up human speech **3** : the suggestion carried or given by something heard or read **4** : hearing distance : EARSHOT — **sound·less** *adj* — **sound·less·ly** *adv*

[4]**sound** *vb* **sound·ed; sound·ing** **1** : to make or cause to make a sound or noise **2** : PRONOUNCE 1 **3** : to order, signal, or indicate by a sound **4** : to make known : PROCLAIM **5** : to make or give an impression especially when heard

[5]**sound** *n* : a long stretch of water that is wider than a strait and often connects two larger bodies of water or forms a channel between the mainland and an island

[6]**sound** *vb* **sounded; sounding** **1** : to measure the depth of (as by a weighted line dropped down from the surface) **2** : to try to find out the views or intentions of a person

sound·proof *adj* : capable of keeping sound from entering or escaping

sound wave *n* : a wave that is produced when a sound is made and is responsible for carrying the sound to the ear

soup *n* : a liquid food made by cooking vegetables, meat, or fish in a large amount of liquid

[1]**sour** *adj* **sour·er; sour·est** **1** : having an acid or tart taste **2** : having spoiled : not fresh **3** : suggesting decay **4** : not pleasant or friendly — **sour·ly** *adv* — **sour·ness** *n*

[2]**sour** *vb* **soured; sour·ing** **1** : to make or become acid or tart in taste (as by spoiling) **2** : to lose or cause to lose interest or enthusiasm **3** : to harm or damage

source *n* **1** : a cause or starting point **2** : the beginning of a stream of water **3** : someone or something that supplies information **4** : someone or something that provides what is needed

sou·sa·phone *n* : a large circular tuba designed to rest on the player's shoulder and used chiefly in marching bands

[1]**south** *adv* : to or toward the south

[2]**south** *adj* : placed toward, facing, or coming from the south

[3]**south** *n* **1** : the direction to the right of one facing east : the compass point opposite to north **2** *cap* : regions or countries south of a point that is mentioned or understood

[1]**South American** *n* : a person born or living in South America

[2]**South American** *adj* : of or relating to South America or the South American people

south·bound *adj* : going south

[1]**south·east** *adv* : to or toward the direction between south and east

[2]**southeast** *adj* : placed toward, facing, or coming from the southeast

[3]**southeast** *n* **1** : the direction between south and east **2** *cap* : regions or countries southeast of a point that is mentioned or understood

south·east·er·ly *adv or adj* **1** : from the southeast **2** : toward the southeast

south·east·ern *adj* **1** *often cap* : of, relating to, or like that of the Southeast **2** : lying toward or coming from the southeast

south·er·ly *adj or adv* **1** : from the south **2** : toward the south

south·ern *adj* **1** *often cap* : of, relating to, or like that of the South **2** : lying toward or coming from the south

south·paw *n* : a person (as a baseball pitcher) who is left-handed

south pole *n, often cap S&P* **1** : the most southern point of the earth : the southern end of the earth's axis **2** : the end of a magnet that points toward the south when the magnet is free to swing

south·ward *adv or adj* : toward the south

[1]**south·west** *adv* : to or toward the direction between south and west

[2]**southwest** *adj* : placed toward, facing, or coming from the southwest

[3]**southwest** *n* **1** : the direction between south and west **2** *cap* : regions or countries

southwest of a point that is mentioned or understood

south·west·er·ly *adv or adj* **1 :** from the southwest **2 :** toward the southwest

south·west·ern *adj* **1** *often cap* **:** of, relating to, or like that of the Southwest **2 :** lying toward or coming from the southwest

sou·ve·nir *n* **:** something that serves as a reminder

¹sov·er·eign *n* **1 :** a person (as a king or queen) having the highest power and authority **2 :** an old British gold coin

²sovereign *adj* **1 :** highest in power or authority **2 :** having independent authority **3 :** of the most important kind

sov·er·eign·ty *n, pl* **sov·er·eign·ties 1 :** supreme power especially over a political unit (as a country) **2 :** a country's independent authority and right of self-control

¹sow *n* **:** an adult female pig

²sow *vb* **sowed; sown** *or* **sowed; sow·ing 1 :** to plant or scatter (as seed) for growing **2 :** to cover with or as if with scattered seed for growing **3 :** to set in motion **:** cause to exist — **sow·er** *n*

sow bug *n* **:** WOOD LOUSE

soy·bean *n* **:** the edible seed of an Asian plant that is rich in protein

soy sauce *n* **:** a brown sauce made from soybeans and used especially in Chinese and Japanese cooking

¹space *n* **1 :** a part of a distance, area, or volume that can be measured **2 :** a certain place set apart or available **3 :** the area without limits in which all things exist and move **4 :** a period of time **5 :** the region beyond the earth's atmosphere **6 :** an empty place

²space *vb* **spaced; spac·ing :** to place or separate with some distance or time between

space·craft *n, pl* **spacecraft :** a vehicle for travel beyond the earth's atmosphere

space·ship *n* **:** SPACECRAFT

space shuttle *n* **:** a spacecraft designed to transport people and cargo between earth and space that can be used repeatedly

space station *n* **:** an artificial satellite designed to stay in orbit permanently and to be occupied by humans for long periods

space suit *n* **:** a suit that covers the entire body and is equipped to keep its wearer alive in space

spa·cious *adj* **:** having ample space

spade *n* **:** a digging tool with a long handle that has a flat blade which can be pushed into the ground with the foot

spa·ghet·ti *n* **:** pasta made in the shape of long thin strings

¹spam *n* **:** e-mail sent to a large number of addresses and usually containing advertising

²spam *vb* **spammed; spam·ming :** to send spam to — **spam·mer** *n*

¹span *n* **1 :** a limited portion of time **2 :** the spread (as of an arch or bridge) from one support to another **3 :** the width of something from one side to another

²span *vb* **spanned; span·ning 1 :** to reach or extend across **2 :** to continue over a period of time

span·gle *n* **:** SEQUIN

Span·iard *n* **:** a person born or living in Spain

span·iel *n* **:** a small or medium-sized dog with a thick wavy coat, long drooping ears, and usually short legs

¹Span·ish *adj* **:** of or relating to Spain, its people, or the Spanish language

²Spanish *n* **1 :** the language of Spain and the countries colonized by Spaniards **2 Spanish** *pl* **:** the people of Spain

spank *vb* **spanked; spank·ing :** to strike on the buttocks with the open hand

¹spank·ing *adj* **:** BRISK 1, LIVELY

²spanking *adv* **:** ¹VERY 1

¹spar *n* **:** a long rounded piece of wood or metal (as a mast) to which a sail is fastened

²spar *vb* **sparred; spar·ring 1 :** to box or make boxing movements with the fists for practice or for fun **2 :** to argue often in a playful way

¹spare *vb* **spared; spar·ing 1 :** to keep from being punished or harmed **:** show mercy to **2 :** to free from having to go through something difficult **3 :** to keep from using or spending **4 :** to give up especially as not really needed **5 :** to have left over

²spare *adj* **spar·er; spar·est 1 :** held in reserve (as for an emergency) **2 :** being over what is needed **3 :** somewhat thin **4 :** SCANTY

³spare *n* **1 :** a replacement or duplicate piece or part **2 :** the knocking down of all ten bowling pins with the first two balls

spare·ribs *n pl* **:** a cut of pork ribs

spar·ing *adj* **:** careful in the use of money or supplies — **spar·ing·ly** *adv*

¹spark *n* **1 :** a small bit of burning material **2 :** a hot glowing bit struck from a mass (as by steel on flint) **3 :** a short bright flash of electricity between two points **4 :** ²SPARKLE 1 **5 :** ¹TRACE 2

²spark *vb* **sparked; spark·ing 1 :** to give off or cause to give off small bits of burning material or short bright flashes of electricity **2 :** to set off

¹spar·kle *vb* **spar·kled; spar·kling 1 :** to give off small flashes of light **2 :** to be lively or bright

²sparkle *n* **1 :** a little flash of light **2 :** the quality of being bright or giving off small flashes of light

spar·kler *n* **:** a small firework that throws off very bright sparks as it burns

spark plug *n* **:** a device used in an engine to produce a spark that ignites a fuel mixture

spar·row *n* **:** a small songbird that has usually brownish or grayish feathers

sparrow hawk *n* **:** a small hawk

sparse *adj* **spars·er; spars·est :** not thickly grown or settled — **sparse·ly** *adv*

spasm *n* **1 :** a sudden uncontrolled and often painful tightening of muscles **2 :** a sudden, strong, and temporary effort, emotion, or outburst

spas·mod·ic *adj* **:** relating to or affected by spasm **:** involving spasms — **spas·mod·i·cal·ly** *adv*

¹spat *past and past participle of* SPIT

²spat *n* **:** a cloth or leather covering for the instep and ankle men once wore over shoes

³spat *n* **:** a brief unimportant quarrel

spa·tial *adj* **:** of or relating to space

¹spat·ter *vb* **spat·tered; spat·ter·ing 1 :** to splash with drops or small bits of something wet **2 :** to scatter by splashing

²spatter *n* **1 :** the act or sound of something splashing in drops **2 :** a drop or splash spattered on something **:** a spot or stain due to spattering

spat·u·la *n* **1 :** a tool resembling a knife with a broad flexible blade that is used mostly for spreading or mixing soft substances **2 :** a kitchen utensil with a long handle and a wide blade used for scraping batter from a bowl or for lifting and flipping food

¹spawn *vb* **spawned; spawn·ing :** to produce or deposit eggs

²spawn *n* **:** the eggs of a water animal (as an oyster or fish) that produces many small eggs

spay *vb* **spayed; spay·ing :** to remove the ovaries of (a female animal)

speak *vb* **spoke; spo·ken; speak·ing 1 :** to utter words **:** TALK **2 :** to utter in words **3 :** to mention in speech or writing **4 :** to use or be able to use in talking — **speak out :** to express an opinion openly — **speak up 1 :** to speak loudly and clearly **2 :** to express an opinion openly

speak·er *n* **1 :** a person who speaks **2 :** a person who conducts a meeting **3 :** LOUDSPEAKER

¹spear *n* **1 :** a weapon with a long straight handle and sharp head or blade used for throwing or jabbing **2 :** an instrument with a sharp point and curved hooks used in stabbing fish

²spear *vb* **speared; spear·ing :** to strike or pierce with or as if with a spear

³spear *n* **:** a usually young blade or sprout (as of grass)

¹spear·head *n* **1 :** the head or point of a spear **2 :** the person, thing, or group that is the leading force (as in a development or an attack)

²spearhead *vb* **spear·head·ed; spear·head·ing :** to serve as leader of

spear·mint *n* **:** a common mint used for flavoring

spe·cial *adj* **1 :** unusual and better in some way **:** EXTRAORDINARY **2 :** liked very well **3 :** different from others **:** UNIQUE **4 :** ¹EXTRA **5 :** meant for a particular purpose or occasion — **spe·cial·ly** *adv*

special education *n* **:** classes or instruction designed for students with special educational needs

spe·cial·ist *n* **1 :** a person who studies or works at a special occupation or branch of learning **2 :** an enlisted person in the army with a rank similar to that of corporal

spe·cial·ize *vb* **spe·cial·ized; spe·cial·iz·ing 1 :** to limit attention or energy to one business, subject, or study **2 :** to change and develop so as to be suited for some particular use or living conditions

spe·cial·ty *n, pl* **spe·cial·ties :** something for which a person or place is known

spe·cies *n, pl* **species 1 :** a group of similar living things that ranks below the genus in scientific classification and is made up of individuals able to produce offspring with one another **2 :** a class of things of the same kind and with the same name **:** KIND, SORT

spe·cif·ic *adj* **1 :** relating to or being an example of a certain kind of thing **2 :** relating to a particular individual or situation **3 :** clearly and exactly presented or stated — **spe·cif·ic·al·ly** *adv*

spec·i·fi·ca·tion *n* **1 :** the act or process of mentioning exactly and clearly **2 :** a single item exactly and clearly mentioned **3 :** a description of work to be done or materials to be used — often used in pl.

spec·i·fy *vb* **spec·i·fied; spec·i·fy·ing 1 :** to mention or name exactly and clearly **2 :** to include in a description of work to be done or materials to be used

spec·i·men *n* **1 :** something collected as a sample or for examination **2 :** a notable example of something **3 :** an example of a type of person

speck *n* **1 :** a small spot or blemish **2 :** a very small amount **:** BIT

¹speck·le *n* **:** a small mark (as of color)

²speckle *vb* **speck·led; speck·ling :** to mark or be marked with small spots

spec·ta·cle *n* **1 :** an unusual or impressive

public display (as a big parade) **2 spectacles** *pl* **:** EYEGLASSES **3 :** an object of curiosity or contempt

spec·tac·u·lar *adj* **:** STRIKING, SHOWY

spec·ta·tor *n* **:** a person who looks on (as at a sports event)

spec·ter *or* **spec·tre** *n* **1 :** GHOST **2 :** something that haunts or bothers the mind

spec·trum *n, pl* **spec·tra** *or* **spec·trums :** the group of different colors including red, orange, yellow, green, blue, indigo, and violet seen when light passes through a prism and falls on a surface or when sunlight is affected by drops of water (as in a rainbow)

spec·u·late *vb* **spec·u·lat·ed; spec·u·lat·ing 1 :** to think or wonder about something **2 :** to come up with ideas or theories about something **3 :** to engage in a risky but possibly very profitable business deal

spec·u·la·tion *n* **1 :** [2]GUESS **2 :** the taking of a big risk in business in hopes of making a big profit

SpEd, SPED *abbr* special education

speech *n* **1 :** the communication or expression of thoughts in spoken words **2 :** something that is spoken **:** STATEMENT **3 :** a public talk **4 :** a form of communication (as a language or dialect) used by a particular group **5 :** a way of speaking **6 :** the ability to speak

speech·less *adj* **:** unable to speak especially because of a strong emotion

[1]**speed** *n* **1 :** quickness in movement or action **2 :** rate of moving or doing

[2]**speed** *vb* **sped** *or* **speed·ed; speed·ing 1 :** to move or cause to move fast **:** HURRY **2 :** to go or drive at too high a rate of movement **3 :** to increase the rate of an action or movement — **speed up :** to move more quickly

speed·boat *n* **:** a motorboat designed to go fast

speed bump *n* **:** a low ridge built across a roadway (as in a parking lot) to limit vehicle speed

speed·om·e·ter *n* **:** an instrument that measures speed

speedy *adj* **speed·i·er; speed·i·est :** moving or taking place fast — **speed·i·ly** *adv*

[1]**spell** *vb* **spelled; spell·ing 1 :** to name, write, or print in order the letters of a word **2 :** to make up the letters of **3 :** to have (such) a spelling **4 :** to amount to **:** MEAN

[2]**spell** *n* **1 :** a spoken word or group of words believed to have magic power **:** CHARM **2 :** a very strong influence

[3]**spell** *n* **1 :** a short period of time **2 :** a stretch of a specified kind of weather **3 :** a period of bodily or mental distress or disorder **4 :** a person's turn at work or duty **5 :** a period spent in a job or occupation

[4]**spell** *vb* **spelled; spelling :** to take the place of for a time **:** RELIEVE

spell·bound *adj* **:** having the interest or attention held by or as if by magic power

spell–check·er *n* **:** a computer program that shows the user any words that might be incorrectly spelled

spell·er *n* **1 :** a person who spells words **2 :** a book with exercises for teaching spelling

spell·ing *n* **1 :** an exercise or the practice of forming words from letters **2 :** the letters composing a word

spend *vb* **spent; spend·ing 1 :** to use (money) to pay for something **2 :** to cause or allow (as time) to pass **3 :** to use wastefully **:** SQUANDER

spend·thrift *n* **:** a person who uses up money wastefully

spent *adj* **1 :** used up **2 :** drained of energy

sperm *n* **:** SPERM CELL

sperm cell *n* **:** a male reproductive cell of animals and plants that can unite with an egg cell to form a new individual cell

sperm whale *n* **:** a huge whale with a large head having a closed cavity that contains a mixture of wax and oil

spew *vb* **spewed; spew·ing :** to pour out

sphere *n* **1 :** an object (as the moon) shaped like a ball **2 :** a figure so shaped that every point on its surface is an equal distance from its center **3 :** a field of influence or activity

spher·i·cal *adj* **:** relating to or having the form of a sphere

sphinx *n* **:** a mythical figure of ancient Egypt having the body of a lion and the head of a man, a ram, or a hawk

[1]**spice** *n* **1 :** a seasoning (as pepper or nutmeg) that comes from a dried plant part and that is usually a powder or seed **2 :** something that adds interest

[2]**spice** *vb* **spiced; spic·ing :** to add something that gives flavor or interest

spick–and–span *or* **spic–and–span** *adj* **1 :** quite new and unused **2 :** very clean and neat

spicy *adj* **spic·i·er; spic·i·est 1 :** flavored with or containing spice **2 :** somewhat shocking or indecent — **spic·i·ness** *n*

spi·der *n* **1 :** a wingless animal that is somewhat like an insect but has eight legs instead of six and a body divided into two parts instead of three and that often spins threads of silk into webs for catching prey **2 :** a cast-iron frying pan

spi·der·web *n* **:** the silken web spun by most spiders and used as a resting place and a trap for prey

spig·ot *n* **1 :** a plug used to stop the vent in a barrel **2 :** FAUCET

[1]spike *n* **1 :** a very large nail **2 :** something pointed like a nail **3 :** one of the metal objects attached to the heel and sole of a shoe (as a baseball shoe) to prevent slipping

[2]spike *vb* **spiked; spik·ing 1 :** to fasten with large nails **2 :** to pierce or cut with or on a large nail **3 :** to hit or throw (a ball) sharply downward **4 :** to add alcohol or drugs to

[3]spike *n* **1 :** a tight mass of grain **2 :** a long usually rather narrow flower cluster in which the blossoms grow very close to a central stem

[1]spill *vb* **spilled** *also* **spilt; spill·ing 1 :** to cause or allow to fall, flow, or run out so as to be wasted or scattered **2 :** to flow or run out, over, or off and become wasted or scattered **3 :** to cause (blood) to flow by wounding **4 :** to make known

[2]spill *n* **1 :** an act of spilling **2 :** a fall especially from a horse or vehicle **3 :** something spilled

[1]spin *vb* **spun; spin·ning 1 :** to turn or cause to turn round and round rapidly **2 :** to make yarn or thread from (fibers) **3 :** to make (yarn or thread) from fibers **4 :** to form threads or a web or cocoon by giving off a sticky fluid that quickly hardens **5 :** to feel as if in a whirl **6 :** to make up and tell using the imagination **7 :** to move swiftly on wheels or in a vehicle **8 :** to make, shape, or produce by or as if by whirling — **spin·ner** *n*

[2]spin *n* **1 :** a rapid motion of turning around and around **2 :** a short trip in or on a wheeled vehicle

spin·ach *n* **:** a garden plant with usually large dark green leaves that are eaten cooked or raw as a vegetable

spi·nal *adj* **:** of, relating to, or located near the backbone or the spinal cord

spinal column *n* **:** BACKBONE 1

spinal cord *n* **:** a thick bundle of nerves that extends from the brain down through the cavity of the backbone and connects with nerves throughout the body to carry information to and from the brain

spin·dle *n* **1 :** a slender round rod or stick with narrowed ends by which thread is twisted in spinning and on which it is wound **2 :** something (as an axle or shaft) which has a slender round shape and on which something turns

spin·dly *adj* **:** being thin and long or tall and usually feeble or weak

spine *n* **1 :** BACKBONE 1 **2 :** a stiff pointed part growing from the surface of a plant or animal

spine·less *adj* **1 :** lacking spines **2 :** having no backbone **3 :** lacking spirit, courage, or determination

spin·et *n* **1 :** a harpsichord with one keyboard and only one string for each note **2 :** a small upright piano

spinning wheel *n* **:** a small machine driven by the hand or foot that is used to spin yarn or thread

spin·ster *n* **:** an unmarried woman past the usual age for marrying

spiny *adj* **spin·i·er; spin·i·est :** covered with spines

spiny lobster *n* **:** a sea animal that is related to and resembles the lobster

spi·ra·cle *n* **:** an opening on the body (as of an insect) used for breathing

[1]spi·ral *adj* **1 :** winding or circling around a center and gradually getting closer to or farther away from it **2 :** circling around a center like the thread of a screw

[2]spiral *n* **1 :** a single turn or coil in a spiral object **2 :** something having a form that winds or circles around a center

[3]spiral *vb* **spi·raled** *or* **spi·ralled; spi·ral·ing** *or* **spi·ral·ling :** to move in or as if in a winding or circular path

spire *n* **1 :** a pointed roof especially of a tower **2 :** STEEPLE

spi·rea *or* **spi·raea** *n* **:** a shrub related to the rose that bears clusters of small white or pink flowers

[1]spir·it *n* **1 :** [1]MOOD **2 :** a being (as a ghost) whose existence cannot be explained **3 :** a lively or brisk quality **4 :** a force within a human being thought to give the body life, energy, and power **:** SOUL **5 :** an attitude or feeling **6 :** PERSON 1 **7 :** an alcoholic liquor — usually used in pl. **8** *cap* **:** the active presence of God in human life **:** the third person of the Trinity **9 spirits** *pl* **:** a solution in alcohol **10 :** real meaning or intention — **spir·it·less** *adj*

[2]spirit *vb* **spir·it·ed; spir·it·ing :** to carry off secretly or mysteriously

spir·it·ed *adj* **:** full of courage or energy

[1]spir·i·tu·al *adj* **1 :** of, relating to, or consisting of spirit **:** not bodily or material **2 :** of or relating to sacred or religious matters — **spir·i·tu·al·ly** *adv*

[2]spiritual *n* **:** a religious folk song developed especially among black people of the southern United States

[1]spit *vb* **spit** *or* **spat; spit·ting 1 :** to force (saliva) from the mouth **2 :** to force (something) from the mouth **3 :** to express by or as if by spitting **4 :** to give off usually briskly **:** EMIT **5 :** to rain lightly or snow in flurries — **spit up :** [2]VOMIT

[2]spit *n* **1 :** SALIVA **2 :** a foamy material given off by some insects **3 :** perfect likeness

[3]spit *n* **1 :** a thin pointed rod for holding meat over a fire **2 :** a small point of land that runs out into a body of water

[1]spite *n* **:** dislike or hatred for another person with a wish to torment, anger, or defeat — **in spite of :** without being prevented by

[2]spite *vb* **spit·ed; spit·ing :** ANNOY, ANGER

spite·ful *adj* **:** filled with or showing spite **:** MALICIOUS — **spite·ful·ly** *adv*

spitting image *n* **:** IMAGE 2

spit·tle *n* **1 :** SALIVA **2 :** [2]SPIT 3

[1]splash *vb* **splashed; splash·ing 1 :** to hit (something liquid or sloppy) and cause to move and scatter roughly **2 :** to wet or soil by spattering with something wet (as water or mud) **3 :** to move or strike with a splashing sound **4 :** to spread or scatter like a splashed liquid

[2]splash *n* **1 :** material that has been hit and made to scatter **2 :** a spot or smear from or as if from liquid that has been hit and made to scatter **3 :** the sound or action of liquid that has been hit and made to scatter

[1]splat·ter *vb* **splat·tered; splat·ter·ing :** to splash against something in large drops

[2]splatter *n* **:** [2]SPLASH 2

spleen *n* **:** an organ near the stomach that destroys worn-out red blood cells and produces some of the white blood cells

splen·did *adj* **1 :** impressive in beauty, excellence, or magnificence **2 :** having or showing splendor **:** BRILLIANT **3 :** EXCELLENT — **splen·did·ly** *adv*

splen·dor *n* **1 :** great brightness **2 :** POMP, GLORY **3 :** an impressive feature

[1]splice *vb* **spliced; splic·ing 1 :** to unite (as two ropes) by weaving together **2 :** to unite (as rails or pieces of film) by connecting the ends together

[2]splice *n* **:** the process of joining or a joint made by weaving or connecting the ends together

splint *n* **1 :** a thin flexible strip of wood woven together with others in making a chair seat or basket **2 :** a rigid device for keeping a broken or displaced bone in place while it heals

[1]splin·ter *n* **:** a thin piece split or torn off lengthwise **:** SLIVER

[2]splinter *vb* **splin·tered; splin·ter·ing :** to break into slivers

[1]split *vb* **split; split·ting 1 :** to divide lengthwise or by layers **2 :** to separate into parts or groups **3 :** to burst or break apart or in pieces **4 :** to divide into shares or sections

[2]split *n* **1 :** a product or result of dividing, separating, or breaking apart **:** CRACK **2 :** the act or process of dividing, separating, or breaking apart **:** DIVISION **3 :** an action or position in which a person's legs are extended in a straight line and in opposite directions

[3]split *adj* **:** divided by or as if by splitting

splurge *vb* **splurged; splurg·ing :** to spend lavishly or give in to indulgence

splut·ter *vb* **splut·tered; splut·ter·ing 1 :** to make a noise as if spitting **2 :** to speak or say in haste or confusion

[1]spoil *vb* **spoiled** *or* **spoilt; spoil·ing 1 :** to damage the character of by allowing too many things or not correcting bad behavior **2 :** to damage badly **:** RUIN **3 :** to damage the quality or effect of **4 :** to decay or lose freshness, value, or usefulness by being kept too long

[2]spoil *n* **:** stolen goods **:** PLUNDER

spoil·age *n* **:** the process or result of the decay of food

spoil·er *n* **1 :** a person or thing that spoils something **2 :** a device (as on an airplane or automobile) that controls the flow of air and lift **3 :** information about the plot of a book, movie, or television show that when revealed spoils the surprise or suspense for a reader or viewer

[1]spoke *past of* SPEAK

[2]spoke *n* **:** one of the bars or rods extending from the hub of a wheel to the rim

[1]spoken *past participle of* SPEAK

[2]spo·ken *adj* **1 :** expressed in speech **:** ORAL **2 :** used in speaking **3 :** speaking in a specified manner

spokes·man *n, pl* **spokes·men :** a person who speaks for or represents someone or something

spokes·per·son *n* **:** SPOKESMAN

spokes·wom·an *n, pl* **spokes·wom·en :** a woman who speaks for or represents someone or something

[1]sponge *n* **1 :** a water animal that lives permanently attached to a solid surface (as the ocean bottom) and has a simple body of loosely connected cells with a skeleton supported by stiff fibers or hard particles **2 :** a piece of springy material that forms the skeleton of sponges or is manufactured and is used for cleaning **3 :** a pad of folded gauze used in surgery and medicine

[2]sponge *vb* **sponged; spong·ing 1 :** to clean or wipe with a sponge **2 :** to get something or live at the expense of another

spongy *adj* **spong·i·er; spong·i·est :** springy and absorbent

[1]spon·sor *n* **1 :** a person who takes the responsibility for some other person or thing **2 :** a person who represents someone being baptized and takes responsibility for his or her spiritual development **:** GODPARENT **3 :** a person or an organization that pays for or plans and carries out a project or activity **4 :** a person who gives money to someone participating in an event for charity **5 :** a person or an organization that pays the cost of a radio or television program — **spon·sor·ship** *n*

[2]**sponsor** *vb* **spon·sored; spon·sor·ing :** to act as sponsor for

spon·ta·ne·ous *adj* **1 :** done, said, or produced freely and naturally **2 :** acting or taking place without outside force or cause — **spon·ta·ne·ous·ly** *adv*

spontaneous combustion *n* **:** a bursting of material into flame from the heat produced within itself through chemical action

[1]**spook** *vb* **spooked; spook·ing :** to make or become frightened

[2]**spook** *n* **:** GHOST, SPECTER

spooky *adj* **spook·i·er; spook·i·est 1 :** scary and frightening **2 :** suggesting the presence of ghosts

spool *n* **:** a small cylinder which has a rim or ridge at each end and a hole from end to end for a pin or spindle and on which material (as thread, wire, or tape) is wound

[1]**spoon** *n* **:** an eating and cooking utensil consisting of a small shallow bowl with a handle

[2]**spoon** *vb* **spooned; spoon·ing :** to take up in or as if in a spoon

spoon·bill *n* **:** a wading bird having a bill which widens and flattens at the tip

spoon·ful *n, pl* **spoon·fuls** *also* **spoons·ful :** as much as a spoon can hold

spore *n* **:** a reproductive body that is produced by fungi and by some plants and microorganisms and consists of a single cell that is able to produce a new individual — **spored** *adj*

[1]**sport** *n* **1 :** physical activity (as running or an athletic game) engaged in for pleasure or exercise **2 :** a person who shows good sportsmanship **3 :** PASTIME, RECREATION **4 :** [1]FUN 3

[2]**sport** *vb* **sport·ed; sport·ing :** to wear in a way that attracts attention

sports·man *n, pl* **sports·men :** a person who engages in or is interested in sports and especially outdoor sports (as hunting and fishing)

sports·man·ship *n* **:** fair play, respect for opponents, and gracious behavior in winning or losing

sports medicine *n* **:** a field of medicine concerned with the prevention and treatment of injuries and disorders that are related to participation in sports

sports·wom·an *n, pl* **sports·wom·en :** a woman who engages in or is interested in sports and especially outdoor sports

sport–util·i·ty vehicle *n* **:** an automobile similar to a station wagon but built on a light truck frame

[1]**spot** *n* **1 :** a small part that is different from the main part **2 :** an area soiled or marked (as by dirt) **3 :** a particular place **4 :** POSITION 3 **5 :** FAULT — **spot·ted** *adj* — **on the spot 1 :** right away **2 :** at the place of action **3 :** in difficulty or danger

[2]**spot** *vb* **spot·ted; spot·ting 1 :** to mark or be marked with spots **2 :** to single out **:** IDENTIFY

spot·less *adj* **1 :** free from spot or blemish **2 :** perfectly clean or pure — **spot·less·ly** *adv*

[1]**spot·light** *n* **1 :** a spot of light used to show up a particular area, person, or thing (as on a stage) **2 :** public notice **3 :** a lamp used to direct a narrow strong beam of light on a small area

[2]**spotlight** *vb* **spot·light·ed** *or* **spot·lit; spot·light·ing 1 :** to light up with or as if with a spotlight **2 :** to bring to public attention

spotted owl *n* **:** a rare brown owl with white spots and dark stripes that is found from British Columbia to southern California and central Mexico

spot·ty *adj* **spot·ti·er; spot·ti·est 1 :** having spots **2 :** not always the same especially in quality

spouse *n* **:** a married person **:** HUSBAND, WIFE

[1]**spout** *vb* **spout·ed; spout·ing 1 :** to shoot out (liquid) with force **2 :** to speak with a long and quick flow of words so as to sound important **3 :** to flow out with force **:** SPURT

[2]**spout** *n* **1 :** a tube, pipe, or hole through which something (as rainwater) shoots out **2 :** a sudden strong stream of fluid

[1]**sprain** *n* **:** an injury that results from the sudden or severe twisting of a joint with stretching or tearing of ligaments

[2]**sprain** *vb* **sprained; sprain·ing :** to injure by a sudden or severe twist

sprang *past of* SPRING

[1]**sprawl** *vb* **sprawled; sprawl·ing 1 :** to lie or sit with arms and legs spread out **2 :** to spread out unevenly

[2]**sprawl** *n* **:** the act or posture of spreading out

[1]**spray** *vb* **sprayed; spray·ing 1 :** to scatter or let fall in a fine mist **2 :** to scatter fine mist on or into — **spray·er** *n*

[2]**spray** *n* **1 :** liquid flying in fine drops like water blown from a wave **2 :** a burst of fine mist **3 :** a device for scattering fine drops of liquid or mist

[3]**spray** *n* **:** a green or flowering branch or a usually flat arrangement of these

[1]**spread** *vb* **spread; spread·ing 1 :** to stretch out **:** EXTEND **2 :** to pass or cause to pass from person to person **3 :** to open or arrange over a larger area **4 :** to increase in size or occurrence **5 :** to scatter or be scattered **6 :** to give out over a period of time or among

a group **7 :** to put or have a layer of on a surface **8 :** to cover something with **9 :** to stretch or move apart **10 :** to prepare for a meal : SET

[2]**spread** *n* **1 :** the act or process of increasing in size, amount, or occurrence **2 :** the distance between two points that are farthest to each side **3 :** a noticeable display in a magazine or newspaper **4 :** a food to be put over the surface of bread or crackers **5 :** a very fine meal : FEAST **6 :** a cloth cover for a table or bed

spread·sheet *n* **:** an accounting program for a computer

spree *n* **:** an outburst of an activity

sprig *n* **:** a small shoot or twig

spright·ly *adj* **spright·li·er; spright·li·est** : full of spirit : LIVELY

[1]**spring** *vb* **sprang** *or* **sprung; sprung; spring·ing** **1 :** to move suddenly upward or forward : LEAP **2 :** to appear or grow quickly or suddenly **3 :** to have (a leak) appear **4** : to move quickly by or as if by stretching and springing back **5 :** to cause to operate suddenly **6 :** to come into being : ARISE

[2]**spring** *n* **1 :** the season between winter and summer including in the northern hemisphere usually the months of March, April, and May **2 :** a twisted or coiled strip of material (as metal) that recovers its original shape when it is released after being squeezed or stretched **3 :** the ability of something to return to its orginal shape when it is compressed or stretched **4 :** a source of supply (as of water coming up from the ground) **5 :** the act or an instance of leaping up or forward **6 :** a bouncy or lively quality

spring·board *n* **:** a flexible board usually fastened at one end and used for jumping high in the air in gymnastics or diving

spring peep·er *n* **:** a small frog that makes a high peeping sound heard mostly in spring

spring·time *n* **:** the season of spring

springy *adj* **spring·i·er; spring·i·est** **1 :** able to return to an original shape when twisted or stretched **2 :** having or showing a lively and energetic movement

[1]**sprin·kle** *vb* **sprin·kled; sprin·kling** **1 :** to scatter in drops or particles **2 :** to scatter over or in or among **3 :** to rain lightly — **sprin·kler** *n*

[2]**sprinkle** *n* **1 :** a light rain **2 :** SPRINKLING

sprin·kling *n* **:** a very small number or amount

[1]**sprint** *vb* **sprint·ed; sprint·ing** **:** to run at top speed especially for a short distance — **sprint·er** *n*

[2]**sprint** *n* **1 :** a short run at top speed **2 :** a race over a short distance

sprite *n* **:** ELF, FAIRY

sprock·et *n* **:** one of many points that stick up on the rim of a wheel (**sprocket wheel**) shaped so as to fit into the links of a chain

[1]**sprout** *vb* **sprout·ed; sprout·ing** **:** to produce or cause to produce new growth

[2]**sprout** *n* **:** a young stem of a plant especially when coming directly from a seed or root

[1]**spruce** *n* **:** an evergreen tree that has short needles for leaves, drooping cones, and light soft wood

[2]**spruce** *vb* **spruced; spruc·ing** **:** to make (someone or something) neat or stylish in appearance

[3]**spruce** *adj* **spruc·er; spruc·est** **:** neat or stylish in appearance — **spruce·ly** *adv*

sprung *past and past participle of* SPRING

spry *adj* **spri·er** *or* **spry·er; spri·est** *or* **spry·est** **:** LIVELY 1, ACTIVE

spun *past and past participle of* SPIN

spunk *n* **:** COURAGE, SPIRIT

spunky *adj* **spunk·i·er; spunk·i·est** **:** full of spirit and courage

[1]**spur** *n* **1 :** a pointed device fastened to the back of a rider's boot and used to urge a horse on **2 :** something that makes a person want to do something : INCENTIVE **3** : a mass of jagged rock coming out from the side of a mountain **4 :** a short section of railway track coming away from the main line **5 :** a usually short pointed growth or projecting part (as a spine on the leg of a rooster) — **spurred** *adj* — **on the spur of the moment** **:** without thinking for a long time — often used as an adjective

[2]**spur** *vb* **spurred; spur·ring** **1 :** to urge a horse on with spurs **2 :** INCITE

spurn *vb* **spurned; spurn·ing** **:** to reject with scorn

[1]**spurt** *vb* **spurt·ed; spurt·ing** **:** to pour out or make pour out suddenly

[2]**spurt** *n* **:** a sudden pouring out

[3]**spurt** *n* **:** a brief burst of increased effort, activity, or development

[1]**sput·ter** *vb* **sput·tered; sput·ter·ing** **1 :** to spit noisily from the mouth **2 :** to speak in a hasty or explosive way in confusion or excitement **3 :** to make explosive popping sounds

[2]**sputter** *n* **:** the act or sound of sputtering

[1]**spy** *vb* **spied; spy·ing** **1 :** to watch secretly **2 :** to catch sight of : SEE

[2]**spy** *n, pl* **spies** **1 :** a person who watches the movement or actions of others especially in secret **2 :** a person who tries secretly to get information especially about a country or organization for another country or organization

spy·glass *n* **:** a small telescope

squab *n* **:** a young pigeon especially when ready for use as food

[1]squab·ble *n* : a noisy quarrel usually over something unimportant

[2]squabble *vb* **squab·bled; squab·bling** : to quarrel noisily for little or no reason

squad *n* **1** : a small group of soldiers **2** : a small group working or playing together

squad car *n* : CRUISER 2

squad·ron *n* **1** : a group of soldiers, ships, or aircraft moving and working together **2** : a large group

squal·id *adj* : filthy or degraded from a lack of care or money

[1]squall *vb* **squalled; squall·ing** : to let out a harsh cry or scream

[2]squall *n* : a harsh cry

[3]squall *n* : a sudden strong gust of wind often with rain or snow

squal·or *n* : the quality or state of being squalid

squan·der *vb* **squan·dered; squan·der·ing** : to spend foolishly : WASTE

[1]square *n* **1** : a flat geometric figure that has four equal sides and four right angles **2** : something formed with four equal or roughly equal sides and four right angles **3** : the product of a number or amount multiplied by itself **4** : an open place or area where two or more streets meet **5** : a tool having at least one right angle and two or more straight edges used to mark or test right angles

[2]square *adj* **squar·er; squar·est** **1** : having four equal sides and four right angles **2** : being a unit of area consisting of a figure with four right angles and four sides of a given length **3** : having a specified length in each of two equal dimensions **4** : having outlines that suggest sharp corners rather than curves **5** : forming a right angle **6** : [1]JUST 4, FAIR **7** : not owing anything : EVEN **8** : large enough to satisfy — **square·ly** *adv*

[3]square *vb* **squared; squar·ing** **1** : to form with right angles, straight edges, and flat surfaces **2** : to make straight **3** : to multiply a number by itself **4** : AGREE 4 **5** : [2]BALANCE 2, SETTLE

[4]square *adv* : in a direct, firm, or honest way

square dance *n* : a dance for four couples who form the sides of a square

square knot *n* : a knot made of two half-knots tied in opposite directions that does not come untied easily

square–rigged *adj* : having the principal sails extended on yards fastened in a horizontal position to the masts at their center

square root *n* : a number that when multiplied by itself equals a specified number

[1]squash *vb* **squashed; squash·ing** : to beat or press into a soft or flat mass : CRUSH

[2]squash *n* : the fruit of a plant related to the gourd that comes in many varieties and is usually eaten as a vegetable

[1]squat *vb* **squat·ted; squat·ting** **1** : to crouch by bending the knees fully so as to sit on or close to the heels **2** : to settle without any right on land that someone else owns **3** : to settle on government land in order to become its owner

[2]squat *adj* **squat·ter; squat·test** **1** : low to the ground **2** : having a short thick body

[3]squat *n* : a position in which the knees are fully bent and the body sits on or close to the heels

[1]squawk *vb* **squawked; squawk·ing** **1** : to make a harsh short cry **2** : to complain or protest loudly or with strong feeling

[2]squawk *n* **1** : a harsh short cry **2** : a noisy complaint

[1]squeak *vb* **squeaked; squeak·ing** **1** : to make a short high-pitched cry or sound **2** : to barely get, win, or pass

[2]squeak *n* : a short high-pitched cry or sound

squeaky *adj* **squeak·i·er; squeak·i·est** : making or likely to make a short high-pitched cry or sound

[1]squeal *vb* **squealed; squeal·ing** **1** : to make a sharp long high-pitched cry or noise **2** : INFORM 2

[2]squeal *n* : a sharp high-pitched cry or noise

squea·mish *adj* : hesitant because of shock or disgust

[1]squeeze *vb* **squeezed; squeez·ing** **1** : to press together from the opposite sides or parts of : COMPRESS **2** : to get by squeezing **3** : to force or crowd in by compressing

[2]squeeze *n* : an act or instance of compressing

squid *n* : a sea mollusk that is related to the octopus and has a long thin soft body with eight short arms and two usually longer tentacles

[1]squint *vb* **squint·ed; squint·ing** **1** : to look or peer with the eyes partly closed **2** : to cause (an eye) to partly close

[2]squint *n* : the action or an instance of causing the eyes to partly close or of looking at something with the eyes partly closed

squire *n* **1** : a person who carries the shield or armor of a knight **2** : [1]ESCORT 1 **3** : an owner of a country estate

squirm *vb* **squirmed; squirm·ing** : to twist about because of nervousness or embarrassment or in an effort to move or escape

squir·rel *n* : a small gnawing animal that is a rodent usually with a bushy tail and soft fur and strong hind legs used especially for leaping among tree branches

[1]squirt *vb* **squirt·ed; squirt·ing** : to shoot out liquid in a thin stream : SPURT

²squirt *n* **:** a small powerful stream of liquid **:** JET

Sr. *abbr* **1** senior **2** sister

st. *abbr* state

St. *abbr* **1** saint **2** street

¹stab *n* **1 :** a wound produced by or as if by a pointed weapon **2 :** ²THRUST 1 **3 :** ²TRY, EFFORT

²stab *vb* **stabbed; stab·bing 1 :** to wound or pierce with or as if with a pointed weapon **2 :** ¹DRIVE 2, THRUST

sta·bil·i·ty *n, pl* **sta·bil·i·ties :** the condition of being reliable or unlikely to change suddenly or greatly

sta·bi·lize *vb* **sta·bi·lized; sta·bi·liz·ing :** to make or become unlikely to change suddenly or greatly — **sta·bi·liz·er** *n*

¹sta·ble *n* **:** a building in which horses are housed and cared for

²stable *vb* **sta·bled; sta·bling :** to put or keep in a stable

³stable *adj* **sta·bler; sta·blest 1 :** not easily changed or affected **2 :** not likely to change suddenly or greatly **3 :** LASTING

stac·ca·to *adj* **1 :** cut short so as not to sound connected **2 :** played or sung with breaks between notes

¹stack *n* **1 :** a neat pile of objects usually one on top of the other **2 :** a large number or amount **3 :** a large pile (as of hay) usually shaped like a cone **4 :** CHIMNEY 1, SMOKESTACK **5 :** a structure with shelves for storing books

²stack *vb* **stacked; stack·ing :** to arrange in or form a neat pile

sta·di·um *n, pl* **sta·di·ums** *or* **sta·dia :** a large usually outdoor structure with rows of seats for spectators at sports events

staff *n, pl* **staffs** *or* **staves 1 :** a pole, stick, rod, or bar used as a support or as a sign of authority **2** *pl staffs* **:** a group of persons serving as assistants to or employees under a chief **3 :** the five parallel lines with their four spaces on which music is written **4 :** something that is a source of strength **5** *pl staffs* **:** a group of military officers who plan and manage for a commanding officer

staff sergeant *n* **:** a noncommissioned officer in the army, air force, or marine corps ranking above a sergeant

stag *n* **:** an adult male deer

¹stage *n* **1 :** a raised floor (as for speaking or performing) **2 :** a step forward in a journey, a task, a process, or a development **:** PHASE **3 :** the theatrical profession or art **4 :** a place where something important happens **5 :** STAGECOACH

²stage *vb* **staged; stag·ing :** to produce or show to others on or as if on the stage

stage·coach *n* **:** a coach pulled by horses that runs on a schedule from place to place carrying passengers and mail

¹stag·ger *vb* **stag·gered; stag·ger·ing 1 :** to move or cause to move unsteadily from side to side as if about to fall **:** REEL **2 :** to cause or feel great surprise or shock **3 :** to arrange or be arranged in a zigzag but balanced way

²stagger *n* **:** a reeling or unsteady walk

stag·nant *adj* **1 :** not flowing **2 :** not active or brisk **:** DULL

stag·nate *vb* **stag·nat·ed; stag·nat·ing :** to be or become inactive or still

¹stain *vb* **stained; stain·ing 1 :** to soil or discolor especially in spots **2 :** to use something (as a dye) to change the color of **3 :** ¹CORRUPT 1 **4 :** ¹DISGRACE

²stain *n* **1 :** ¹SPOT 2, DISCOLORATION **2 :** a mark of guilt or disgrace **:** STIGMA **3 :** something (as a dye) used in staining — **stain·less** *adj*

stained glass *n* **:** pieces of colored glass used to make patterns in windows

stainless steel *n* **:** an alloy of steel and chromium that is resistant to stain, rust, and corrosion

stair *n* **1 :** a series of steps or flights of steps for going from one level to another — often used in pl. **2 :** one step of a stairway

stair·case *n* **:** a flight of steps with their supporting structure and railings

stair·way *n* **:** one or more flights of steps usually with connecting landings

¹stake *n* **1 :** a pointed piece (as of wood) that is driven into the ground as a marker or a support for something **2 :** a post to which a person is tied to be put to death by burning **3 :** something that is put up to be won or lost in gambling **4 :** the prize in a contest **5 :** ¹SHARE 1, INTEREST — **at stake :** in a position to be lost if something goes wrong

²stake *vb* **staked; stak·ing 1 :** ²BET 1 **2 :** to mark the limits of by stakes **3 :** to fasten or support (as plants) with stakes **4 :** to give money to in order to help (as with a project)

sta·lac·tite *n* **:** a deposit hanging from the roof or side of a cave in the shape of an icicle formed by the partial evaporation of dripping water containing minerals

sta·lag·mite *n* **:** a deposit like an upside down stalactite formed by the dripping of water containing minerals onto the floor of a cave

stale *adj* **stal·er; stal·est 1 :** having lost a good taste or quality through age **2 :** used or heard so often as to be dull **3 :** not so strong, energetic, or effective as before

¹stalk *n* **1 :** a plant stem especially when

DICTIONARY

not woody **2 :** a slender supporting structure — **stalked** *adj*

[2]**stalk** *vb* **stalked; stalk·ing** **1 :** to walk in a stiff or proud manner **2 :** to hunt slowly and quietly — **stalk·er** *n*

[1]**stall** *n* **1 :** a compartment for one animal in a stable or barn **2 :** a booth, stand, or counter where business may be carried on or articles may be displayed for sale **3 :** a seat in a church choir **:** a church pew **4 :** a small enclosed private compartment

[2]**stall** *vb* **stalled; stall·ing :** to distract attention or make excuses to gain time

[3]**stall** *vb* **stalled; stall·ing** **1 :** to stop or cause to stop usually by accident **2 :** to put or keep in a stall

stal·lion *n* **:** a male horse

stal·wart *adj* **:** STURDY 1, RESOLUTE

sta·men *n* **:** the part of a flower that produces pollen and is made up of an anther and a filament

stam·i·na *n* **:** the ability or strength to keep doing something for a long time

[1]**stam·mer** *vb* **stam·mered; stam·mer·ing** **:** to speak with involuntary stops and much repeating

[2]**stammer** *n* **:** an act or instance of speaking with involuntary stops and much repeating

[1]**stamp** *vb* **stamped; stamp·ing** **1 :** to bring the foot down hard and with noise **2 :** to put an end to by or as if by hitting with the bottom of the foot **3 :** to mark or cut out with a tool or device having a design **4 :** to attach a postage stamp to **5 :** CHARACTERIZE 1

[2]**stamp** *n* **1 :** a small piece of paper or a mark attached to something to show that a tax or fee has been paid **2 :** a device or instrument for marking with a design **3 :** the mark made by stamping **4 :** a sign of a special quality **5 :** the act of bringing the foot down hard

[1]**stam·pede** *n* **1 :** a wild rush or flight of frightened animals or people **2 :** a sudden foolish action or movement of a large number of people

[2]**stampede** *vb* **stam·ped·ed; stam·ped·ing** **1 :** to run or cause to run away in fright or panic **2 :** to act or cause to act together suddenly and without thought

stance *n* **:** way of standing **:** POSTURE

[1]**stand** *vb* **stood; stand·ing** **1 :** to be in or take an upright position on the feet **2 :** to take up or stay in a specified position or condition **3 :** to rest, remain, or set in a usually vertical position **4 :** to be in a specified place **5 :** to put up with **:** ENDURE **6 :** to have an opinion **7 :** to stay in effect **8 :** UNDERGO **9 :** to perform the duty of — **stand by** **1 :** to be or remain loyal or true to **2 :** to be present **3 :** to be or get ready to act — **stand for** **1 :** to be a symbol for **:** REPRESENT **2 :** to put up with **:** PERMIT — **stand out :** to be easily seen or recognized — **stand up** **1 :** to stay in good condition **2 :** to fail to keep an appointment with — **stand up for :** DEFEND 2 — **stand up to :** to face boldly

[2]**stand** *n* **1 :** a structure containing rows of seats for spectators of a sport or spectacle **2 :** a stall or booth often outdoors for a small business **3 :** [1]POSITION 2 **4 :** a group of plants growing near one another **5 :** an act of stopping or staying in one place **6 :** a halt for defense or resistance **7 :** a place or post which a person occupies **:** STATION **8 :** a small structure (as a rack or table) on or in which something may be placed **9 :** a raised area (as for speakers or performers)

[1]**stan·dard** *n* **1 :** something set up as a rule for measuring or as a model **2 :** the personal flag of the ruler of a state **3 :** an upright support **4 :** a figure used as a symbol by an organized body of people

[2]**standard** *adj* **1 :** used as or matching a model or rule to compare against **2 :** regularly and widely used **3 :** widely known and accepted to be of good and permanent value

stan·dard·ize *vb* **stan·dard·ized; stan·dard·iz·ing :** to make alike or matching a model

standard time *n* **:** the time established by law or by common usage over a region or country

[1]**stand·ing** *adj* **1 :** [1]ERECT **2 :** done while standing **3 :** not flowing **:** STAGNANT **4 :** remaining at the same level or amount until canceled **5 :** PERMANENT

[2]**standing** *n* **1 :** length of existence or service **2 :** [1]POSITION 5, STATUS

stand·point *n* **:** a way in which things are thought about **:** POINT OF VIEW

stand·still *n* **:** the condition of not being active or busy **:** STOP

stank *past of* STINK

stan·za *n* **:** a group of lines forming a division of a poem

[1]**sta·ple** *n* **1 :** a short thin wire with bent ends that is punched through papers and squeezed to hold them together or punched through thin material to fasten it to a surface **2 :** a piece of metal shaped like a U with sharp points to be driven into a surface to hold something (as a hook, rope, or wire)

[2]**staple** *vb* **sta·pled; sta·pling :** to fasten with staples

[3]**staple** *n* **1 :** a chief product of business or farming of a place **2 :** something that is used widely and often **3 :** the chief part of something

⁴staple *adj* **1 :** much used, needed, or enjoyed usually by many people **2 :** ¹PRINCIPAL, CHIEF
sta·pler *n* **:** a device that fastens using staples
¹star *n* **1 :** any of the celestial bodies except planets which are visible at night and look like fixed points of light **2 :** a figure or object with five or more points that represents or suggests a star in the sky **3 :** a very talented or popular performer **4 :** a planet that is believed in astrology to influence someone's life **5 :** the principal member of a theater or opera company
²star *vb* **starred; star·ring 1 :** to mark with a star or an asterisk as being special or very good **2 :** to present in the role of a star **3 :** to play the most important role **4 :** to perform in an outstanding manner
³star *adj* **1 :** being favored or very popular **2 :** being of outstanding excellence
star·board *n* **:** the right side of a ship or airplane looking forward
¹starch *n* **:** a white odorless tasteless substance that is the chief form in which carbohydrates are stored in plants, is an important component of many foods (as rice and bread), and has various uses (as for stiffening clothes)
²starch *vb* **starched; starch·ing :** to stiffen with starch
starchy *adj* **starch·i·er; starch·i·est :** like or containing starch
¹stare *vb* **stared; star·ing :** to look at hard and long often with wide-open eyes
²stare *n* **:** the act or an instance of looking at hard and long
star·fish *n* **:** a sea animal that usually has five arms that spread out from a central disk and feeds mostly on mollusks
¹stark *adj* **stark·er; stark·est 1 :** ¹BARREN 2, DESOLATE **2 :** clear and harsh **3 :** very obvious
²stark *adv* **:** COMPLETELY
star·light *n* **:** the light given by the stars
star·ling *n* **:** a dark brown or greenish black European bird that is now common in the United States
star·lit *adj* **:** lighted by the stars
star·ry *adj* **star·ri·er; star·ri·est 1 :** full of stars **2 :** shining like stars **3 :** having parts arranged like a star
Stars and Stripes *n pl* **:** the flag of the United States — used as singular
¹start *vb* **start·ed; start·ing 1 :** to begin an activity **2 :** to come or bring into being or action **3 :** to begin to move toward a particular place or in a particular direction **4 :** to cause to move, act, or operate **5 :** to give a sudden twitch or jerk (as in surprise) **6 :** to stick out or seem to stick out
²start *n* **1 :** a sudden twitching or jerking movement **2 :** a beginning of movement, action, or development **3 :** a brief act, movement, or effort **4 :** a place of beginning (as of a race)
start·er *n* **:** someone or something that starts something or causes something else to start
star·tle *vb* **star·tled; star·tling 1 :** to move or jump (as in surprise or fear) **2 :** to frighten suddenly but slightly
star·tling *adj* **:** causing a moment of fright or surprise
star·va·tion *n* **:** suffering or death caused by lack of food **:** the condition of being starved
starve *vb* **starved; starv·ing 1 :** to suffer or die or cause to suffer or die from lack of food **2 :** to suffer or cause to suffer from a lack of something other than food
¹stash *vb* **stashed; stash·ing :** to store in a usually secret place for future use
²stash *n* **:** an amount of something stored secretly for future use
¹state *n* **1 :** manner or condition of being **2 :** a body of people living in a certain territory under one government **:** the government of such a body of people **3 :** one of the divisions of a nation having a federal government
²state *vb* **stat·ed; stat·ing 1 :** to express especially in words **2 :** to set by rule, law, or authority
state·house *n* **:** the building where the legislature of a state meets
state·ly *adj* **state·li·er; state·li·est :** impressive in size or dignity — **state·li·ness** *n*
state·ment *n* **1 :** something written or said in a formal way **:** something stated **2 :** a brief record of a business account
state·room *n* **:** a private room on a ship or a train
states·man *n, pl* **states·men :** a usually wise, skilled, and respected government leader
¹stat·ic *n* **:** noise produced in a radio or television receiver by atmospheric or electrical disturbances
²static *adj* **1 :** showing little change or action **2 :** of or relating to charges of electricity (as those produced by friction) that do not flow
¹sta·tion *n* **1 :** a regular stopping place (as on a bus, train, or subway line) **:** DEPOT **2 :** a place for specialized observation or for a public service **3 :** a collection of or the place that contains radio or television equipment for transmitting or receiving **4 :** ¹POSITION 5, RANK **5 :** the place or position where a person or thing stands or is assigned to stand or remain **6 :** a post or area of duty
²station *vb* **sta·tioned; sta·tion·ing :** to assign to or set in a post or position **:** POST

sta·tion·ary *adj* **1 :** having been set in a certain place or post **:** IMMOBILE **2 :** not changing **:** STABLE
sta·tion·ery *n* **:** writing paper and envelopes
station wagon *n* **:** an automobile that is longer on the inside than a sedan and has one or more folding or removable seats but no separate luggage compartment
stat·ue *n* **:** an image or likeness (as of a person or animal) sculptured, modeled, or cast in a solid substance (as marble or bronze)
stat·ure *n* **1 :** a person's height **2 :** quality or fame gained (as by growth or development)
sta·tus *n* **1 :** position or rank of a person or thing **2 :** state of affairs **:** SITUATION
stat·ute *n* **:** LAW 4
staunch *adj* **staunch·er; staunch·est 1 :** strongly built **:** SUBSTANTIAL **2 :** LOYAL, STEADFAST — **staunch·ly** *adv*
[1]**stave** *n* **1 :** one of the narrow strips of wood or iron plates that form the sides, covering, or lining of something (as a barrel) **2 :** a wooden stick **:** STAFF
[2]**stave** *vb* **staved** *or* **stove; stav·ing 1 :** to break in the staves of **2 :** to smash a hole in — **stave off :** to keep away **:** ward off
staves *pl of* STAFF
[1]**stay** *vb* **stayed; stay·ing 1 :** to remain after others have gone **2 :** to continue unchanged **3 :** to stop going forward **:** PAUSE **4 :** to live for a while **5 :** to put a stop to **:** HALT
[2]**stay** *n* **1 :** a period of living in a place **2 :** the action of bringing to a stop **:** the state of being stopped
[3]**stay** *n* **:** a strong rope or wire used to steady or brace something (as a mast)
[4]**stay** *n* **1 :** [2]PROP, SUPPORT **2 :** a thin firm strip (as of steel or plastic) used to stiffen a garment (as a corset) or part of a garment (as a shirt collar)
[5]**stay** *vb* **stayed; staying :** to hold up
stead *n* **1 :** ADVANTAGE — used mostly in the phrase *stand someone in good stead* **2 :** the place usually taken or duty carried out by the person or thing mentioned
stead·fast *adj* **1 :** not changing **:** RESOLUTE **2 :** LOYAL — **stead·fast·ly** *adv* — **stead·fast·ness** *n*
[1]**steady** *adj* **steadi·er; steadi·est 1 :** firmly fixed in position **2 :** direct or sure in action **3 :** showing little change **4 :** not easily upset **5 :** RELIABLE — **stead·i·ly** *adv* — **stead·i·ness** *n*
[2]**steady** *vb* **stead·ied; steady·ing :** to make, keep, or become steady
steak *n* **1 :** a thick slice of meat and especially beef **2 :** a thick slice of a large fish (as salmon)
[1]**steal** *vb* **stole; sto·len; steal·ing 1 :** to take and carry away (something that belongs to another person) without permission and with the intention of keeping **2 :** to come or go quietly or secretly **3 :** to draw attention away from others **4 :** to take or get secretly or in a tricky way **5 :** to reach the next base safely in baseball by running to it when the ball has not been hit in play **6 :** to take (as a ball or puck) from another player **7 :** to take something from a situation
[2]**steal** *n* **1 :** the act or an instance of stealing **2 :** [1]BARGAIN 2
stealth *n* **:** sly or secret action
stealthy *adj* **stealth·i·er; stealth·i·est :** done in a sly or secret manner — **stealth·i·ly** *adv*
[1]**steam** *n* **1 :** the vapor into which water is changed when heated to the boiling point **2 :** steam or the heat or power produced by it when kept under pressure **3 :** the mist formed when water vapor cools **4 :** driving force **:** POWER
[2]**steam** *vb* **steamed; steam·ing 1 :** to give off steam or vapor **2 :** to rise or pass off as steam **3 :** to move or travel by or as if by the power of steam **4 :** to expose to steam (as for cooking)
steam·boat *n* **:** a boat powered by steam
steam engine *n* **:** an engine powered by steam
steam·er *n* **1 :** a ship powered by steam **2 :** a container in which something is steamed
steam·roll·er *n* **:** a machine that has wide heavy rollers for pressing down and smoothing roads
steam·ship *n* **:** STEAMER 1
steam shovel *n* **:** a power machine for digging
steamy *adj* **steam·i·er; steam·i·est 1 :** hot and humid **2 :** producing or covered with steam
steed *n* **:** a usually lively horse
[1]**steel** *n* **1 :** a hard and tough metal made by treating iron with great heat and mixing carbon with it **2 :** an item (as a sword) made of steel
[2]**steel** *vb* **steeled; steel·ing :** to fill with courage or determination
[3]**steel** *adj* **:** made of steel
steely *adj* **steel·i·er; steel·i·est :** like steel (as in hardness, strength, or color)
[1]**steep** *adj* **steep·er; steep·est 1 :** having a very sharp slope **:** almost straight up and down **2 :** too great or high — **steep·ly** *adv* — **steep·ness** *n*
[2]**steep** *vb* **steeped; steep·ing 1 :** to soak in a hot liquid **2 :** to fill with or involve deeply
stee·ple *n* **1 :** a tall pointed structure usually built on top of a church tower **2 :** a church tower
stee·ple·chase *n* **1 :** a horse race across coun-

try **2 :** a race on a course that has hedges, walls, and ditches to be crossed

[1]**steer** *vb* **steered; steer·ing** **1 :** to make a vehicle move in a particular direction **2 :** to guide or change the direction of something **3 :** to follow a course of action

[2]**steer** *n* **:** a castrated bull usually raised for beef

steering wheel *n* **:** a wheel that allows a driver to control the direction of a vehicle

stego·sau·rus *n* **:** a large plant-eating dinosaur with bony plates along its back and tail and with spikes at the end of the tail

[1]**stem** *n* **1 :** the main stalk of a plant that develops buds and shoots and usually grows above ground **2 :** a thin plant part (as a leafstalk) that supports another part **3 :** the bow of a ship **4 :** the basic part of a word to which prefixes or suffixes may be added **5 :** something like a stalk or shaft — **from stem to stern :** in or to every part **:** THOROUGHLY

[2]**stem** *vb* **stemmed; stem·ming** **1 :** to make progress against **2 :** to check or hold back the progress of

[3]**stem** *vb* **stemmed; stem·ming** **1 :** to develop as a consequence of **2 :** to come from **:** DERIVE **3 :** to remove the stem from

[4]**stem** *vb* **stemmed; stem·ming :** to stop or check by or as if by damming

stemmed *adj* **:** having a stem

[1]**sten·cil** *n* **1 :** a piece of material (as a sheet of paper or plastic) that has lettering or a design cut out and is used as a guide (as in painting or drawing) **2 :** a pattern, design, or print produced with a stencil

[2]**stencil** *vb* **sten·ciled** *or* **sten·cilled; sten·cil·ing** *or* **sten·cil·ling** **1 :** to mark or paint with a stencil **2 :** to produce with a stencil

[1]**step** *n* **1 :** a movement made by lifting one foot and putting it down in another spot **2 :** a rest or place for the foot in going up or down **:** STAIR **3 :** a combination of foot and body movements in a repeated pattern **4 :** manner of walking **5 :** FOOTPRINT **6 :** the sound of a footstep **7 :** the space passed over in one step **8 :** a short distance **9 :** the height of one stair **10 steps** *pl* **:** [1]COURSE 3 **11 :** one of a series of actions taken to achieve something **12 :** a stage in a process **13 :** a level, grade, or rank in a scale or series **14 :** the distance from one tone of a musical scale or one note on a musical staff to another that is one tone away (**half step**) or two tones away (**whole step**)

[2]**step** *vb* **stepped; step·ping** **1 :** to move in a particular way or direction by lifting one foot and putting it down in another spot **2 :** [1]DANCE 1 **3 :** to go on foot **:** WALK **4 :** to move quickly **5 :** to put or press the foot on or in **6 :** to come or move as if at a step by the foot **7 :** to measure by steps — **step up :** to increase the amount, speed, or intensity of

step–by–step *adj* **:** moving or happening by steps one after the other

step·fa·ther *n* **:** the husband of someone's parent when distinct from his or her natural or legal father

step·lad·der *n* **:** a light freestanding ladder with broad flat steps and a hinged frame

step·moth·er *n* **:** the wife of someone's parent when distinct from his or her natural or legal mother

steppe *n* **:** land that is dry, rather level, mostly treeless, and covered with grass in regions (as parts of Asia and southeastern Europe) with usually hot summers and cold winters

step·ping–stone *n* **1 :** a stone on which to step (as in crossing a stream) **2 :** something that helps in progress or advancement

-ster *n suffix* **1 :** someone who does or handles or operates **2 :** someone who makes or uses **3 :** someone who is associated with or takes part in **4 :** someone who is

ste·reo *n, pl* **ste·re·os :** a sound system that reproduces the effect of listening to the original sound — **stereo** *adj*

[1]**ste·reo·type** *n* **:** a fixed idea that many people have about a thing or a group that may often be untrue or only partly true

[2]**ste·reo·type** *vb* **ste·reo·typed; ste·reo·typ·ing :** to form a fixed and often untrue or only partly true idea about

ste·reo·typed *adj* **:** following a pattern or stereotype **:** lacking originality

ste·reo·typ·i·cal *adj* **:** based on or characteristic of a stereotype — **ste·reo·typ·i·cal·ly** *adv*

ster·ile *adj* **1 :** not able to produce fruit, crops, or offspring **:** not fertile **2 :** free from living germs

ster·il·ize *vb* **ster·il·ized; ster·il·iz·ing :** to make sterile and especially free from germs

[1]**ster·ling** *n* **1 :** British money **2 :** sterling silver **:** articles made from sterling silver

[2]**sterling** *adj* **1 :** of or relating to British sterling **2 :** being or made of a specific alloy that is mostly silver with a little copper **3 :** EXCELLENT

[1]**stern** *adj* **stern·er; stern·est** **1 :** hard and severe in nature or manner **:** very strict and serious **2 :** showing severe displeasure or disapproval **3 :** firm and not changeable — **stern·ly** *adv*

[2]**stern** *n* **:** the rear end of a boat

ster·num *n, pl* **ster·nums** *or* **ster·na :** BREASTBONE

ste·roid *n* **:** any of various chemical com-

DICTIONARY

pounds that include many hormones (as anabolic steroids)

stetho·scope *n* : a medical instrument used for listening to sounds produced in the body and especially those of the heart and lungs

[1]**stew** *n* **1 :** a dish of usually meat with vegetables prepared by slow boiling **2 :** a state of excitement, worry, or confusion

[2]**stew** *vb* **stewed; stew·ing 1 :** to boil slowly : SIMMER **2 :** to become excited or worried

stew·ard *n* **1 :** a manager of a very large home, an estate, or an organization **2 :** a person employed to manage the supply and distribution of food and look after the needs of passengers (as on an airplane or ship)

stew·ard·ess *n* : a woman who looks after passengers (as on an airplane or ship)

[1]**stick** *n* **1 :** a cut or broken branch or twig **2 :** a long thin piece of wood **3 :** WALKING STICK 1 **4 :** something like a stick in shape or use

[2]**stick** *vb* **stuck; stick·ing 1 :** to push into or through **2 :** to stab or pierce with something pointed **3 :** to put in place by or as if by pushing **4 :** to push out, up, into, or under **5 :** to put in a specified place or position **6 :** to remain in a place, situation, or environment **7 :** to halt the movement or action of **8 :** BAFFLE **9 :** to burden with something unpleasant **10 :** to fix or become fixed in place by or as if by gluing **11 :** to cling or cause to cling **12 :** to become blocked or jammed

stick·er *n* : something (as a slip of paper with glue on its back) that can be stuck to a surface

stick insect *n* : a wingless long-legged insect that has a long body resembling a stick

stick·le·back *n* : a small scaleless fish with sharp spines on its back

sticky *adj* **stick·i·er; stick·i·est 1 :** tending to cling like glue : ADHESIVE **2 :** coated with a substance that sticks to things **3 :** MUGGY, HUMID **4 :** tending to become blocked or jammed — **stick·i·ness** *n*

stiff *adj* **stiff·er; stiff·est 1 :** not easily bent **2 :** not easily moved **3 :** firm and not changeable **4 :** not friendly, relaxed, or graceful in manner **5 :** POWERFUL, STRONG **6 :** not flowing easily : THICK **7 :** SEVERE 3 **8** hard to do or deal with : DIFFICULT — **stiff·ly** *adv* — **stiff·ness** *n*

stiff·en *vb* **stiff·ened; stif·fen·ing 1 :** to make or become stiff or stiffer **2 :** to become tense and still

sti·fle *vb* **sti·fled; sti·fling 1 :** to cause or have difficulty in breathing **2 :** to keep in check by effort

stig·ma *n, pl* **stig·ma·ta** *or* **stig·mas 1 :** a mark of disgrace or dishonor **2 :** the upper part of the pistil of a flower which receives the pollen grains

stile *n* **1 :** a step or set of steps for crossing a fence or wall **2 :** TURNSTILE

sti·let·to *n, pl* **sti·let·tos** *or* **sti·let·toes :** a knife with a slender pointed blade

[1]**still** *adj* **1 :** having no motion **2 :** making no sound : QUIET **3 :** free from noise and commotion — **still·ness** *n*

[2]**still** *vb* **stilled; still·ing 1 :** to make or become motionless or silent **2 :** to calm or make less intense

[3]**still** *adv* **1 :** without motion **2 :** up to this or that time **3 :** NEVERTHELESS **4 :** [2]EVEN 2 **5 :** in addition

[4]**still** *n* : [1]QUIET, SILENCE

[5]**still** *n* : a device used in making alcoholic liquors

stilt *n* **1 :** one of a pair of tall poles each with a high step or loop for the support of a foot used to lift the person wearing them above the ground in walking **2 :** a stake or post used as one of the supports of a structure (as a building) above ground or water level

stilt·ed *adj* : not easy and natural

[1]**stim·u·lant** *n* **1 :** something (as a drug) that makes the body or one of its parts temporarily more active **2 :** STIMULUS 1

[2]**stimulant** *adj* : stimulating or tending to stimulate

stim·u·late *vb* **stim·u·lat·ed; stim·u·lat·ing 1 :** to make active or more active : AROUSE **2 :** to act on as a bodily stimulus or stimulant

stim·u·la·tion *n* : an act or result of making more active

stim·u·lus *n, pl* **stim·u·li 1 :** something that stirs or urges to action **2 :** an influence that acts usually from outside the body to partly change bodily activity (as by exciting a receptor or sense organ)

[1]**sting** *vb* **stung; sting·ing 1 :** to prick painfully usually with a sharp or poisonous stinger **2 :** to suffer or affect with sharp quick burning pain **3 :** to hurt emotionally

[2]**sting** *n* **1 :** an act of pricking painfully usually with a sharp or poisonous stinger **2 :** a wound or burning pain caused by the pricking of the skin with a stinger **3 :** emotional pain **4 :** STINGER

sting·er *n* : a sharp part of an animal (as a bee or scorpion) that is used to wound and often poison prey or an enemy

sting·ray *n* : a flat fish with a sharp stinging spine on its long thin tail

stin·gy *adj* **stin·gi·er; stin·gi·est 1 :** not generous **2 :** very small in amount — **stin·gi·ness** *n*

[1]**stink** *vb* **stank** *or* **stunk; stunk; stink·ing 1 :** to give off or cause to have a strong

unpleasant smell **2 :** to be very bad or unpleasant

[2]**stink** *n* **:** a strong unpleasant smell

stink·bug *n* **:** a bug that gives off a bad smell

stinky *adj* **stink·i·er; stink·i·est :** having a strong unpleasant smell

[1]**stint** *vb* **stint·ed; stint·ing :** to be stingy or sparing

[2]**stint** *n* **1 :** an amount of work given **2 :** a period of time spent at a particular activity

[1]**stir** *vb* **stirred; stir·ring 1 :** to make or cause to make a usually slight movement or change of position **2 :** to make active **3 :** to mix, dissolve, or move about by making a circular movement in **4 :** to cause to arise or take place

[2]**stir** *n* **1 :** a state of upset or activity **2 :** a slight movement **3 :** the act of making circular movements in

stir·ring *adj* **:** MOVING 2

stir·rup *n* **:** either of a pair of small light frames or loops often of metal hung by straps from a saddle and used as a support for the foot of a horseback rider

[1]**stitch** *n* **1 :** one in-and-out movement of a threaded needle in sewing or in closing a wound **:** a portion of thread left after one such movement **2 :** a single loop of thread or yarn around a tool (as a knitting needle or crochet hook) **3 :** a type or style of stitching **4 :** a sudden sharp pain especially in the side

[2]**stitch** *vb* **stitched; stitch·ing 1 :** to fasten or join by sewing **2 :** to make, mend, or decorate by or as if by sewing **3 :** SEW 2

[1]**stock** *n* **1 :** the whole supply or amount on hand **2 stocks** *pl* **:** a wooden frame with holes to hold the feet or the feet and hands once used to punish a wrongdoer publicly **3 :** the wooden part by which a rifle or shotgun is held against the shoulder during firing **4 :** the source from which others descend **:** ANCESTRY **5 :** farm animals **:** LIVESTOCK, CATTLE **6 :** a part ownership in a business that can be traded independently **7 :** liquid in which meat, fish, or vegetables have been simmered — **in stock :** on hand **:** in the store and available for purchase

[2]**stock** *vb* **stocked; stock·ing 1 :** to provide with or get supplies especially for future use **2 :** to get or keep a supply of

[3]**stock** *adj* **1 :** kept regularly in supply especially for sale **2 :** commonly used **:** STANDARD

stock·ade *n* **1 :** a line of strong posts set in the ground to form a defense **2 :** an enclosure usually formed by posts pounded into the ground

stock·bro·ker *n* **:** a person who handles orders to buy and sell stocks

stock·hold·er *n* **:** an owner of stock

stock·ing *n* **1 :** a close-fitting usually knit covering for the foot and leg **2 :** [1]SOCK

stock market *n* **:** a place where shares of stock are bought and sold

stocky *adj* **stock·i·er; stock·i·est :** short, broad, and sturdy in build

stock·yard *n* **:** a yard for keeping livestock about to be slaughtered or shipped

[1]**stole** *past of* STEAL

[2]**stole** *n* **:** a long wide scarf worn across the shoulders

stolen *past participle of* STEAL

stol·id *adj* **:** having or showing little or no feeling — **stol·id·ly** *adv*

[1]**stom·ach** *n* **1 :** the pouch into which food passes from the esophagus for mixing and digestion before passing to the small intestine **2 :** the part of the body that contains the stomach **:** ABDOMEN **3 :** [2]DESIRE 1, LIKING

[2]**stomach** *vb* **stom·ached; stom·ach·ing :** to bear patiently **:** put up with

stomp *vb* **stomped; stomp·ing :** to walk heavily or noisily **:** STAMP

[1]**stone** *n* **1 :** earth or mineral matter hardened in a mass **:** ROCK **2 :** a piece of rock coarser than gravel **3 :** GEM 1 **4 :** a stony mass that sometimes forms in certain organs of the body **5 :** the seed of a fruit (as a peach) in its hard case **6** *pl usually* **stone :** an English measure of weight equaling 14 pounds (about 6.3 kilograms)

[2]**stone** *vb* **stoned; ston·ing 1 :** to throw stones at **2 :** to remove the stony seeds of

[3]**stone** *adj* **:** relating to or made of stone

[4]**stone** *adv* **:** COMPLETELY, TOTALLY

Stone Age *n* **:** the oldest period in which human beings are known to have existed **:** the age during which stone tools were used

stony *adj* **ston·i·er; ston·i·est 1 :** full of stones **2 :** hard as or like stone **3 :** INSENSITIVE 1, UNFEELING

stood *past and past participle of* STAND

stool *n* **1 :** a seat without back or arms supported by three or four legs or by a central post **2 :** FOOTSTOOL **3 :** a mass of bodily waste discharged from the intestine

[1]**stoop** *vb* **stooped; stoop·ing 1 :** to bend down or over **2 :** to stand or walk with the head and shoulders bent forward **3 :** to do something that is petty, deceitful, or morally wrong

[2]**stoop** *n* **:** a forward bend of the head and shoulders

[3]**stoop** *n* **:** a porch, platform, or stairway at the entrance of a house or building

[1]**stop** *vb* **stopped; stop·ping 1 :** to cease moving especially temporarily or for a purpose **2 :** to halt the movement or progress

of **3 :** to keep from doing something **4 :** to come or bring (something) to an end **5 :** to cease operating or functioning **6 :** to close or block up or become closed or blocked up **:** PLUG **7 :** to take time

[2]stop *n* **1 :** [1]END 2, FINISH **2 :** the act of bringing or coming to a halt **:** the state of being stopped **3 :** a halt in a journey **:** STAY **4 :** a stopping place **5 :** something that delays, blocks, or brings to a halt **6 :** STOPPER, PLUG **7 :** a set of organ pipes of one tone quality **:** a control knob for such a set

stop·light *n* **1 :** TRAFFIC LIGHT **2 :** a light on the rear of a motor vehicle that goes on when the driver presses the brake pedal

stop·over *n* **:** a stop made during a journey

stop·page *n* **:** [2]STOP 2

stop·per *n* **:** something (as a cork or plug) used to close or block an opening

stop·watch *n* **:** a watch that can be started and stopped for exact timing (as of a race)

stor·age *n* **1 :** space or a place for putting things for future use or for safekeeping **2 :** the act of putting things somewhere especially for future use **:** the state of being stored

storage battery *n* **:** a battery that can be made capable of being used again by passing an electric current through it

[1]store *vb* **stored; stor·ing 1 :** to place or leave something in a location (as a warehouse, library, or computer memory) for later use, disposal, or safekeeping **2 :** to bring together or collect as a supply **3 :** to provide with what is needed **:** SUPPLY

[2]store *n* **1 :** a place where goods are sold **:** SHOP **2 :** a large quantity, supply, or number **3 stores** *pl* **:** something collected and kept for future use — **in store :** [1]READY 1

store·house *n, pl* **store·hous·es 1 :** a building for storing goods **2 :** a large supply or source

store·keep·er *n* **1 :** an owner or manager of a store or shop **2 :** a person in charge of supplies (as in a factory)

store·room *n* **:** a room for keeping things for future use

stork *n* **:** a large wading bird that has a long heavy bill and long legs and builds large nests usually in trees or on the top of roofs and poles

[1]storm *n* **1 :** a heavy fall of rain, snow, or sleet often with strong winds **2 :** a serious disturbance of any element of nature **3 :** a strong outburst **4 :** a violent attack on a defended position

[2]storm *vb* **stormed; storm·ing 1 :** to blow hard and rain, snow, or sleet heavily **2 :** to make a sudden mass attack against **3 :** to feel or express angry feelings **:** RAGE **4 :** to rush about violently or angrily

stormy *adj* **storm·i·er; storm·i·est 1 :** relating to or affected by a storm **2 :** displaying anger and strong emotions

[1]sto·ry *n, pl* **sto·ries 1 :** a report about incidents or events **:** ACCOUNT **2 :** a short often amusing tale **3 :** a fictional tale shorter than a novel **4 :** a widely told rumor **5 :** [3]LIE, FALSEHOOD

[2]sto·ry *also* **sto·rey** *n, pl* **sto·ries** *also* **storeys :** a set of rooms or an area making up one floor level of a building

stout *adj* **stout·er; stout·est 1 :** of strong character **:** BRAVE, DETERMINED **2 :** of a strong or lasting sort **:** STURDY, TOUGH **3 :** having a large body with much fat **4 :** wide and usually thick — **stout·ly** *adv* — **stout·ness** *n*

[1]stove *n* **:** a device usually of iron or steel that burns fuel or uses electricity to provide heat (as for cooking or heating)

[2]stove *past and past participle of* STAVE

stove·pipe *n* **1 :** a metal pipe to carry away smoke from a stove **2 :** a tall silk hat

stow *vb* **stowed; stow·ing 1 :** to put away **:** STORE **2 :** [2]LOAD 1 — **stow away :** to hide on a vehicle (as a ship) in order to travel without paying or being seen

stow·away *n* **:** a person who hides on a vehicle (as a ship) to travel without paying or being seen

strad·dle *vb* **strad·dled; strad·dling 1 :** to stand, sit, or walk with the legs spread wide apart **2 :** to stand, sit, or ride with a leg on either side of **3 :** to seem to favor two opposite sides of

strag·gle *vb* **strag·gled; strag·gling 1 :** to walk or move in a slow and disorderly way **2 :** to move away or spread out from others of the same kind — **strag·gler** *n*

strag·gly *adj* **strag·gli·er; strag·gli·est :** growing, hanging, or arranged in an untidy or scattered way

[1]straight *adj* **straight·er; straight·est 1 :** following the same direction throughout its length **:** not having curves, bends, or angles **2 :** being perfectly vertical or horizontal **3 :** following one after the other in order **4 :** not changing from an indicated pattern **5 :** not straying from what is right or honest **6 :** correctly ordered or arranged **7 :** [2]CORRECT 2 **8 :** not showing any feeling especially of amusement — **straight·ness** *n*

[2]straight *adv* **1 :** without delay or hesitation **2 :** in a direct and uninterrupted course **:** without turning or curving aside **3 :** in or into an upright position **4 :** without interruption **5 :** in a normal or correct way

straight·away *adv* : without delay : IMMEDIATELY
straight·en *vb* **straight·ened; straight·en·ing** **1** : to make or become straight **2** : to put in order
straight·for·ward *adj* : being clear and honest : FRANK — **straight·for·ward·ly** *adv*
straight·way *adv* : STRAIGHTAWAY
¹strain *n* **1** : a group of closely related living things that look similar but possess one or more unique characteristics **2** : a quality or disposition that runs through a family or group **3** : a small amount : TRACE **4** : MELODY 2, TUNE
²strain *vb* **strained; strain·ing** **1** : to stretch or be stretched, pulled, or used to the limit **2** : to stretch beyond a proper limit **3** : to try very hard : make a great effort **4** : to injure or be injured by too much or too hard use or effort **5** : to press or pass through a strainer : FILTER **6** : to pour off liquid from by using a strainer
³strain *n* **1** : great worry and concern or physical effort **2** : something that causes great worry and concern or physical effort **3** : bodily injury resulting from too much use or from a wrench or twist that stretches muscles and ligaments **4** : a force that pulls or stretches something to its limit : STRESS
strained *adj* **1** : showing the effects of worry and concern **2** : not easy or natural **3** : not friendly or relaxed
strain·er *n* : a device (as a screen, sieve, or filter) to hold back solid pieces while a liquid passes through
strait *n* **1** : a narrow channel connecting two bodies of water **2** : a situation of difficulty or distress — often used in pl.
¹strand *n* : the land bordering a body of water : SHORE, BEACH
²strand *vb* **strand·ed; strand·ing** **1** : to run, drive, or cause to drift from the water onto land **2** : to leave in a strange or unfavorable place especially without any way of leaving
³strand *n* **1** : one of the fibers, threads, strings, or wires twisted or braided to make a cord, rope, or cable **2** : something long or twisted like a rope
strange *adj* **strang·er; strang·est** **1** : UNFAMILIAR 1 **2** : different from what is usual, normal, or expected **3** : not relaxed : UNEASY — **strange·ly** *adv* — **strange·ness** *n*
strang·er *n* **1** : a person in a new or unfamiliar place **2** : a person whom another person does not know or has not met
stran·gle *vb* **stran·gled; stran·gling** **1** : to choke to death by squeezing the throat **2** : to die or suffer from or as if from being choked — **stran·gler** *n*
¹strap *n* : a narrow strip of flexible material used especially for fastening, holding together, or wrapping
²strap *vb* **strapped; strap·ping** **1** : to fasten with or attach by means of a strap **2** : to whip with a strap
strap·ping *adj* : strong and healthy
strat·a·gem *n* : a clever trick or plan
stra·te·gic *adj* **1** : relating to or showing the use of a plan or method to achieve a goal **2** : useful or important in military strategy
strat·e·gy *n, pl* **strat·e·gies** : a carefully developed plan or method for achieving a goal or the skill in developing and undertaking such a plan or method
strato·sphere *n* : an upper portion of the atmosphere extending from about 6 miles (10 kilometers) to 30 miles (50 kilometers) upward where temperature changes little and clouds rarely form
stra·tum *n, pl* **stra·ta** : ¹LAYER 1
stra·tus *n, pl* **stra·ti** : a cloud extending over a large area at an altitude of from 2000 to 7000 feet (600 to 2100 meters)
straw *n* **1** : dry plant stems (as of grain after threshing) **2** : a slender tube for sucking up a beverage
straw·ber·ry *n, pl* **straw·ber·ries** : the juicy edible usually red fruit of a low-growing plant with white flowers and long slender runners
¹stray *n* : a domestic animal (as a cat or dog) that is lost or has no home
²stray *vb* **strayed; stray·ing** **1** : to wander from a group or from the proper place : ROAM **2** : to go off from a direct or chosen route or the right course **3** : to become distracted from a topic or train of thought
³stray *adj* **1** : lost or having no home **2** : not in the proper or intended place **3** : occurring here and there : RANDOM
¹streak *n* **1** : a line or mark of a different color or texture from its background **2** : a narrow band of light **3** : an amount of a quality **4** : a short series of something — **streaked** *adj*
²streak *vb* **streaked; streak·ing** **1** : to make or have a line or mark of color in or on **2** : to move swiftly : RUSH
¹stream *n* **1** : a body of water (as a brook or river) flowing on the earth **2** : a flow of liquid or gas **3** : a steady series (as of words or events) following one another
²stream *vb* **streamed; stream·ing** **1** : to flow in or as if in a stream **2** : to give out a bodily fluid in large amounts **3** : to become wet with flowing liquid **4** : to trail out at full length **5** : to pour, enter, or arrive in large numbers **6** : to transfer (digital data, such as audio or video material) in a continuous stream

stream·er *n* **1 :** a flag that floats or moves in the wind **:** PENNANT **2 :** a long narrow strip (as of ribbon or paper) that is often hung for decoration **3 streamers** *pl* **:** AURORA BOREALIS

stream·lined *adj* **1 :** designed or constructed to make motion through water or air easier or as if for this purpose **2 :** made shorter, simpler, or more efficient

street *n* **1 :** a public road especially in a city, town, or village **2 :** the people living along a street

street·car *n* **:** a vehicle for carrying passengers that runs on rails and operates mostly on city streets

strength *n* **1 :** the quality or state of being physically strong **2 :** power to resist force **3 :** ability to produce an effect **4 :** degree of intensity **5 :** power as measured in numbers **6 :** a strong or positive quality **7 :** the inner courage or determination that allows a person to face and deal with difficulties

strength·en *vb* **strength·ened; strength·en·ing :** to make, grow, or become stronger or more powerful

stren·u·ous *adj* **1 :** showing or requiring much energy and effort **2 :** very active **:** ENERGETIC — **stren·u·ous·ly** *adv*

strep throat *n* **:** a sore throat that is accompanied by fever and caused by a bacterium

[1]**stress** *n* **1 :** a force that tends to change the shape of an object **2 :** something that causes physical or emotional tension **:** a state of tension resulting from a stress **3 :** special importance given to something **4 :** relative loudness or force of a part of a spoken word or a beat in music

[2]**stress** *vb* **stressed; stress·ing 1 :** to subject to excessive use or to forces that cause a change in shape **2 :** to cause or experience physical or emotional tension **3 :** to pronounce (part of a word) with relative loudness or force **4 :** to give special importance to **:** EMPHASIZE

stress mark *n* **:** a mark used to show what part or syllable of a written word should be stressed when spoken

[1]**stretch** *vb* **stretched; stretch·ing 1 :** to reach out **:** EXTEND, SPREAD **2 :** to pull or draw out in length or width or both **:** EXPAND, ENLARGE **3 :** to extend (as the body) in a flat position **4 :** to extend the body or limbs **5 :** to pull tight **6 :** to cause to reach or continue **7 :** EXAGGERATE **8 :** to become extended without breaking **9 :** to extend over a continuous period

[2]**stretch** *n* **1 :** the act of extending or drawing out beyond ordinary or normal limits **2 :** the ability to be pulled or drawn out in length or width or both **3 :** the act or an instance of stretching the body or one of its parts **4 :** a continuous extent in length, area, or time

stretch·er *n* **:** a device like a cot used for carrying sick or injured persons

strew *vb* **strewed; strewed** *or* **strewn; strew·ing 1 :** SCATTER 1 **2 :** to spread by scattering **3 :** to cover by or as if by scattering something

strick·en *adj* **1 :** showing the effect of disease, misfortune, or sorrow **2 :** hit or wounded by or as if by an object that was shot or thrown

strict *adj* **strict·er; strict·est 1 :** not to be avoided or ignored **:** requiring obedience **2 :** strongly enforcing rules and discipline **3 :** kept with great care **:** ABSOLUTE **4 :** carefully observing something (as a rule or principle) **5 :** EXACT 1, PRECISE — **strict·ly** *adv* — **strict·ness** *n*

[1]**stride** *vb* **strode; strid·den; strid·ing :** to walk or run with long even steps

[2]**stride** *n* **1 :** a long step or the distance covered by such a step **2 :** a step forward **:** ADVANCE **3 :** a way of walking

strife *n* **:** bitter and sometimes violent disagreement

[1]**strike** *vb* **struck; struck** *also* **strick·en; strik·ing 1 :** to touch, hit, or affect with force **2 :** to come into contact or collision with **3 :** to attack or seize suddenly **4 :** GO 1, PROCEED **5 :** to lower, take down, or take apart **6 :** to make known by sounding **:** cause to sound **7 :** to affect usually suddenly **8 :** to produce by or as if by a blow **9 :** to happen with damaging force or effect **10 :** to cause to ignite by scratching **11 :** to agree on the arrangements of **12 :** to make an impression on **13 :** to come to mind **14 :** to produce on a musical instrument **15 :** to remove or cancel with or as if with the stroke of a pen **16 :** to come upon **:** DISCOVER **17 :** to take on **:** ASSUME **18 :** to stop work in order to force an employer to meet demands regarding conditions of work **19 :** to produce by stamping — **strike out :** to be out in baseball by getting three strikes during a turn at bat — **strike up :** to cause to begin

[2]**strike** *n* **1 :** an act or instance of striking **2 :** a stopping of work by workers to force an employer to agree to demands **3 :** an unhelpful or undesirable characteristic **:** DISADVANTAGE **4 :** a baseball pitch that is not hit fair or that passes through a certain area over home plate (**strike zone**) without being hit and that counts against the batter **5 :** the knocking down of all the pins with the first ball in bowling **6 :** a discovery of a valuable mineral deposit **7 :** a military attack

strike·out *n* **:** an out in baseball that results

from a batter getting three strikes during a turn at bat

strik·ing *adj* : attracting attention : REMARKABLE — **strik·ing·ly** *adv*

[1]**string** *n* **1** : a thin cord used to bind, fasten, or tie **2** : something that resembles a string **3** : the gut, wire, or plastic cord of a musical instrument that vibrates to produce a tone when touched **4 strings** *pl* : the stringed instruments of an orchestra **5** : a group, series, or line of things threaded on a string or arranged as if strung together **6** : a series of events which follow each other in time **7 strings** *pl* : requirements that are connected with something

[2]**string** *vb* **strung; string·ing** **1** : to provide with strings **2** : [2]THREAD 4 **3** : to tie, hang, or fasten with string **4** : to set or stretch out in a line **5** : to remove the tough fibers of

string bass *n* : DOUBLE BASS

string bean *n* : a bean with a long slender pod that is cooked and eaten as a vegetable

stringed instrument *n* : a musical instrument (as a violin, guitar, or harp) sounded by plucking or striking or by drawing a bow across its tight strings

stringy *adj* **string·i·er; string·i·est** : containing, consisting of, or like string

[1]**strip** *vb* **stripped; strip·ping** **1** : to remove clothes : UNDRESS **2** : to remove a covering or surface layer from **3** : to make bare or clear **4** : to take away all duties, honors, or special rights **5** : to remove all the contents (as equipment or accessories) from **6** : to tear or damage the thread of (as a screw or bolt)

[2]**strip** *n* : a long narrow piece or area

[1]**stripe** *vb* **striped; strip·ing** : to make stripes on

[2]**stripe** *n* **1** : a line or long narrow section differing in color or appearance from the background **2** : a piece of material often with a special design worn (as on a sleeve) to show military rank or length of service

striped *adj* : having stripes

strive *vb* **strove; striv·en** *or* **strived; striv·ing** : to try very hard

strode *past of* STRIDE

[1]**stroke** *vb* **stroked; strok·ing** : to rub gently in one direction

[2]**stroke** *n* **1** : the act of striking : BLOW **2** : one of a series of repeated movements (as in swimming or rowing) **3** : a sudden serious illness caused by the breaking or blocking of an artery in the brain **4** : the sound of striking (as of a clock or bell) **5** : the hitting of a ball in a game (as golf or tennis) **6** : a sudden or unexpected example **7** : a single movement or the mark made by a single movement of a brush, pen, or tool **8** : a sudden action or process that results in something being struck **9** : effort by which something is done or the results of such effort

[1]**stroll** *vb* **strolled; stroll·ing** : to walk in a leisurely manner

[2]**stroll** *n* : a leisurely walk

stroll·er *n* : a small carriage in which a baby can sit and be pushed around

strong *adj* **stron·ger; stron·gest** **1** : having great power in the muscles **2** : HEALTHY 1 **3** : not easy to injure, overcome, or resist : SOLID **4** : ENTHUSIASTIC, ZEALOUS **5** : moving with speed and force **6** : having much of some quality : INTENSE **7** : having a great deal of power **8** : of a specified number **9** : PERSUASIVE **10** : well established : FIRM **11** : having a powerful action or effect **12** : very noticeable — **strong·ly** *adv*

strong·hold *n* : FORTRESS

strove *past of* STRIVE

struck *past and past participle of* STRIKE

struc·tur·al *adj* : relating to or affecting the way in which something is built

struc·ture *n* **1** : something built or arranged in a definite way **2** : the manner in which something is built, arranged, or organized

[1]**strug·gle** *vb* **strug·gled; strug·gling** **1** : to make a great effort to do or achieve something or to overcome someone or something **2** : to move with difficulty or with great effort

[2]**struggle** *n* **1** : a difficult or violent effort **2** : [2]FIGHT 1, CONTEST

strum *vb* **strummed; strum·ming** : to play on a stringed instrument by brushing the strings with the fingers

strung *past and past participle of* STRING

[1]**strut** *vb* **strut·ted; strut·ting** : to walk in a confident and proud way

[2]**strut** *n* **1** : a stiff proud step or walk **2** : a bar or brace used to resist pressure in the direction of its length

[1]**stub** *n* **1** : a short part remaining after the rest has been removed or used up **2** : a small part of a larger piece of printed paper (as a check or ticket) kept as a record of the purpose of the paper

[2]**stub** *vb* **stubbed; stub·bing** : to strike (as the toe) against an object

stub·ble *n* **1** : a short growth of beard **2** : the short ends of crops and especially cereal grasses remaining attached to the ground after harvest

stub·born *adj* **1** : refusing to change an opinion or course of action in spite of difficulty or urging **2** : PERSISTENT **3** : difficult to handle, manage, or treat — **stub·born·ly** *adv* — **stub·born·ness** *n*

stub·by *adj* **stub·bi·er; stub·bi·est** : short and thick like a stub

stuc·co *n, pl* **stuc·cos** *or* **stuc·coes** : a plaster for coating walls

stuck *past and past participle of* STICK

stuck–up *adj* : VAIN 2, CONCEITED

[1]**stud** *n* **1** : one of the smaller vertical supports in the walls of a building to which the wall materials are fastened **2** : a removable device like a button used for fastening or as an ornament **3** : one of the metal cleats used on a snow tire to provide a better grip **4** : a small piece of jewelry that is attached through a hole in part of a person's body

[2]**stud** *vb* **stud·ded; stud·ding** : to cover or be covered with many small items

stu·dent *n* : a person who studies especially in school : PUPIL

stu·dio *n, pl* **stu·di·os** **1** : the place where an artist, sculptor, or photographer works **2** : a place for the study of an art **3** : a place where movies are made **4** : a place from which radio or television programs are broadcast

stu·di·ous *adj* : very serious about studying — **stu·di·ous·ly** *adv*

[1]**study** *vb* **stud·ied; study·ing** **1** : to make an effort to learn about something by reading, investigating, or memorizing **2** : to give close attention to

[2]**study** *n, pl* **stud·ies** **1** : the act of making an effort to learn by reading, practicing, or memorizing **2** : a careful investigation or examination of something **3** : a room especially for study, reading, or writing

[1]**stuff** *n* **1** : materials, supplies, or equipment that people need or use **2** : writing, speech, sounds, actions, or ideas of little value **3** : something mentioned or understood but not named **4** : basic part of something : SUBSTANCE

[2]**stuff** *vb* **stuffed; stuff·ing** **1** : to force into something : THRUST **2** : to fill by packing or crowding things in : CRAM **3** : OVEREAT, GORGE **4** : to fill with a stuffing **5** : to block up : CONGEST

stuff·ing *n* **1** : a mixture (as of bread crumbs and seasonings) used to stuff a food (as meat or a vegetable) **2** : material used in filling up something

stuffy *adj* **stuff·i·er; stuff·i·est** **1** : needing fresh air **2** : stuffed or blocked up **3** : very formal and self-important

[1]**stum·ble** *vb* **stum·bled; stum·bling** **1** : to trip in walking, running, or dancing **2** : to walk unsteadily **3** : to speak or act in a clumsy manner **4** : to come unexpectedly or accidentally

[2]**stumble** *n* : an act or instance of tripping or walking unsteadily

[1]**stump** *n* **1** : the part of a tree that remains in the ground after the tree is cut down **2** : the part of something (as a tooth or a pencil) that remains after the rest has been removed, lost, or worn away : STUB

[2]**stump** *vb* **stumped; stump·ing** **1** : PERPLEX, BAFFLE **2** : to walk or walk over heavily, stiffly, or clumsily as if with a wooden leg

stun *vb* **stunned; stun·ning** **1** : to make dizzy or senseless by or as if by a blow **2** : to affect with shock or confusion : fill with disbelief

stung *past and past participle of* STING

stunk *past and past participle of* STINK

stun·ning *adj* **1** : able or likely to make a person senseless or confused **2** : unusually lovely or attractive : STRIKING

[1]**stunt** *n* **1** : an unusual or difficult performance or act **2** : something done for the purpose of gaining attention or publicity

[2]**stunt** *vb* **stunt·ed; stunt·ing** : to hold back the normal growth of

stu·pe·fy *vb* **stu·pe·fied; stu·pe·fy·ing** **1** : to make confused or unable to think clearly **2** : ASTONISH, ASTOUND

stu·pen·dous *adj* : amazing especially because of great size or height — **stu·pen·dous·ly** *adv*

stu·pid *adj* **stu·pid·er; stu·pid·est** **1** : not intelligent : slow in understanding **2** : not sensible : FOOLISH **3** : not interesting or worthwhile — **stu·pid·ly** *adv*

stu·pid·i·ty *n, pl* **stu·pid·i·ties** **1** : the quality or state of being foolish or slow in understanding **2** : a foolish thought, action, or remark

stu·por *n* : a condition of being not alert or able to think normally

stur·dy *adj* **stur·di·er; stur·di·est** **1** : firmly built or made **2** : strong and healthy in body : ROBUST **3** : RESOLUTE — **stur·di·ly** *adv* — **sturd·i·ness** *n*

stur·geon *n* : a large fish that has tough skin and rows of bony plates and is often used for food

[1]**stut·ter** *vb* **stut·tered; stut·ter·ing** : to speak or say with involuntary repetition or interruption of sounds

[2]**stutter** *n* : the act or an instance of speaking with involuntary repetition or interruption

[1]**sty** *n, pl* **sties** : PIGPEN

[2]**sty** *or* **stye** *n, pl* **sties** *or* **styes** : a painful red swelling on the edge of an eyelid

[1]**style** *n* **1** : a particular form or design of something **2** : a way of speaking or writing **3** : an individual way of behaving or doing something **4** : a method, manner, or quality that is felt to be very respectable, fashionable, or proper : FASHION **5** : an easy and graceful manner **6** : the narrow middle part of the pistil of a flower

[2]**style** *vb* **styled; styl·ing** **1** : to design and

make in a known or new style **2 :** to give a special shape to someone's hair **3 :** to identify by some descriptive term **:** CALL
styl·ish *adj* **:** having style **:** FASHIONABLE — **styl·ish·ly** *adv*
sty·lus *n, pl* **sty·li** *also* **sty·lus·es :** a pointed instrument used in ancient times for writing on wax tablets
[1]sub *n* **:** [1]SUBSTITUTE
[2]sub *vb* **subbed; sub·bing :** to act as a substitute
[3]sub *n* **:** SUBMARINE
sub- *prefix* **1 :** under **:** beneath **:** below **2 :** lower in importance or rank **:** lesser **3 :** division or part of
sub·di·vide *vb* **sub·di·vid·ed; sub·di·vid·ing 1 :** to divide the parts of into smaller parts **2 :** to divide (a piece of land) into lots on which houses will be built
sub·di·vi·sion *n* **1 :** the act of dividing into smaller parts **2 :** one of the parts into which something is subdivided
sub·due *vb* **sub·dued; sub·du·ing 1 :** to bring under control **2 :** to overcome in battle
sub·dued *adj* **:** lacking in liveliness, intensity, or strength
sub·head *n* **:** a heading under which one of the divisions of a subject is listed
sub·head·ing *n* **:** SUBHEAD
[1]sub·ject *n* **1 :** the person or thing discussed **:** TOPIC **2 :** an area of knowledge that is studied in school **3 :** a person who owes loyalty to a monarch or state **4 :** a person under the authority or control of another **5 :** the word or group of words about which the predicate makes a statement **6 :** a person or animal that is studied or experimented on
[2]subject *adj* **1 :** owing obedience or loyalty to another **2 :** possible or likely to be affected by **3 :** depending on
[3]sub·ject *vb* **sub·ject·ed; sub·ject·ing 1 :** to bring under control or rule **2 :** to cause to put up with
sub·jec·tive *adj* **:** based mainly on opinions or feelings rather than on facts
sub·lime *adj* **1 :** grand or noble in thought, expression, or manner **2 :** beautiful or impressive enough to arouse a feeling of admiration and wonder
sub·ma·rine *n* **:** a naval ship designed to operate underwater
sub·merge *vb* **sub·merged; sub·merg·ing 1 :** to put under or plunge into water **2 :** to cover or become covered with or as if with water
sub·mis·sion *n* **1 :** the act of putting forward something (as for consideration or comment) **2 :** the condition of being humble or obedient **3 :** the act of giving in to power or authority
sub·mis·sive *adj* **:** willing to give in to others — **sub·mis·sive·ly** *adv*
sub·mit *vb* **sub·mit·ted; sub·mit·ting 1 :** to leave to the judgment or approval of someone else **2 :** to yield to the authority, control, or choice of another **3 :** to put forward as an opinion, reason, or idea
[1]sub·or·di·nate *adj* **1 :** being in a lower class or rank **:** INFERIOR **2 :** yielding to or controlled by authority
[2]subordinate *n* **:** someone who has less power or authority than someone else
[3]sub·or·di·nate *vb* **sub·or·di·nat·ed; sub·or·di·nat·ing :** to treat as inferior in rank or importance
sub·scribe *vb* **sub·scribed; sub·scrib·ing 1 :** to place an order for a publication or service which is delivered over a stated period **2 :** to agree with or support — **sub·scrib·er** *n*
sub·scrip·tion *n* **:** an agreement to buy a publication or service for a stated period
sub·se·quent *adj* **:** following in time, order, or place — **sub·se·quent·ly** *adv*
sub·ser·vi·ent *adj* **:** SUBMISSIVE
sub·set *n* **:** a small division or portion
sub·side *vb* **sub·sid·ed; sub·sid·ing 1 :** to become less strong or intense **2 :** to become lower **:** SINK
sub·sist *vb* **sub·sist·ed; sub·sist·ing :** to continue living or being
sub·sis·tence *n* **:** the smallest amount (as of food and clothing) necessary to support life
sub·soil *n* **:** a layer of soil lying just under the topsoil
sub·stance *n* **1 :** material of a certain kind **2 :** the most basic or important part or quality **3 :** material belongings **:** WEALTH
sub·stan·dard *adj* **:** lower in quality than expected
sub·stan·tial *adj* **1 :** large in amount **2 :** IMPORTANT **3 :** firmly constructed **4 :** ABUNDANT **5 :** PROSPEROUS 1 **6 :** made up of or relating to substance **:** MATERIAL
[1]sub·sti·tute *n* **:** a person or thing that takes the place of another
[2]substitute *vb* **sub·sti·tut·ed; sub·sti·tut·ing 1 :** to put in the place of another **2 :** to take the place of another
sub·sti·tu·tion *n* **:** the act or process of putting in or taking the place of another
sub·ter·ra·nean *adj* **:** being, lying, or operating under the surface of the earth
sub·tle *adj* **sub·tler; sub·tlest 1 :** difficult to perceive **2 :** SHREWD, KEEN **3 :** DELICATE 1 — **sub·tly** *adv*
sub·top·ic *n* **:** a topic (as in a composition) that is a division of a main topic
sub·tract *vb* **sub·tract·ed; sub·tract·ing :** to

take away (as one part or number from another) : DEDUCT

sub·trac·tion *n* : the act or process of taking one number away from another

sub·urb *n* : a smaller community close to a city — **sub·ur·ban** *adj*

sub·way *n* : a usually electric underground railway

suc·ceed *vb* **suc·ceed·ed; suc·ceed·ing** **1** : to achieve a desired result : be successful **2** : to turn out well **3** : to come after : FOLLOW **4** : to come next after another person in office or position

suc·cess *n* **1** : satisfactory completion of something **2** : the gaining of wealth, respect, or fame **3** : a person or thing that succeeds

suc·cess·ful *adj* **1** : resulting or ending well or in success **2** : gaining or having gained success — **suc·cess·ful·ly** *adv*

suc·ces·sion *n* **1** : a series of people or things that follow one after another **2** : the order, act, or right of succeeding to a throne, title, or property

suc·ces·sive *adj* : following in order and without interruption — **suc·ces·sive·ly** *adv*

suc·ces·sor *n* : a person who succeeds to a throne, title, property, or office

suc·cor *n* : [2]HELP 1, RELIEF

suc·cu·lent *adj* : JUICY

suc·cumb *vb* **suc·cumbed; suc·cumb·ing** **1** : to yield to force or pressure **2** : [1]DIE 1

[1]such *adj* **1** : of a kind just specified or to be specified **2** : of the same class, type, or sort : SIMILAR **3** : so great : so remarkable

[2]such *pron* : that sort of person, thing, or group

suck *vb* **sucked; suck·ing** **1** : to draw something (as liquid or air) into the mouth **2** : to draw liquid from by action of the mouth **3** : to allow to dissolve gradually in the mouth **4** : to put (as a thumb) into the mouth and draw on as if drawing liquid **5** : to take in by or as if by absorption or suction

suck·er *n* **1** : a person easily fooled or cheated **2** : a part of an animal's body used for sucking or for clinging by suction **3** : LOLLIPOP **4** : a freshwater fish related to the carp that has thick soft lips for sucking in food **5** : a new stem from the roots or lower part of a plant **6** : SUCKLING

suck·le *vb* **suck·led; suck·ling** : to feed from the breast or udder

suck·ling *n* : a young mammal still sucking milk from its mother

su·crose *n* : a sweet usually crystalline substance found in many plants that is obtained especially from sugarcane and sugar beets for use in sweetening foods and beverages

suc·tion *n* **1** : the act or process of sucking **2** : the process of drawing something into a space (as in a pump) by removing air from the space **3** : the force caused by suction

sud·den *adj* **1** : happening or coming quickly and unexpectedly **2** : met with unexpectedly **3** : HASTY 2 — **sud·den·ly** *adv* — **sud·den·ness** *n* — **all of a sudden** : sooner than was expected : SUDDENLY

suds *n pl* **1** : soapy water especially when foamy **2** : the foam on soapy water

sue *vb* **sued; su·ing** : to seek justice or right by bringing legal action

suede *n* : leather tanned and rubbed so that it is soft and has a nap

su·et *n* : the hard fat around the kidneys in beef and mutton from which tallow is made

suf·fer *vb* **suf·fered; suf·fer·ing** **1** : to feel or endure pain, illness, or injury **2** : to experience something unpleasant **3** : to bear loss or damage **4** : to become worse **5** : [1]PERMIT 1 — **suf·fer·er** *n*

suf·fer·ing *n* : pain experienced during an injury or loss

suf·fice *vb* **suf·ficed; suf·fic·ing** : to satisfy a need : be enough

suf·fi·cient *adj* : enough to achieve a goal or fill a need — **suf·fi·cient·ly** *adv*

suf·fix *n* : a letter or group of letters that comes at the end of a word and has a meaning of its own

suf·fo·cate *vb* **suf·fo·cat·ed; suf·fo·cat·ing** **1** : to kill by stopping the breathing of or by depriving of oxygen to breathe **2** : to die from being unable to breathe **3** : to be or become choked or smothered **4** : to suffer from lack of fresh air

suf·fo·ca·tion *n* : the act of killing by or dying from lack of air : the state of being killed by lack of air

suf·frage *n* : the right to vote

[1]sug·ar *n* **1** : a sweet material that consists essentially of sucrose obtained from sugarcane or sugar beets, is typically colorless or white when pure, and is commonly used to sweeten foods and beverages **2** : any of numerous soluble and usually sweet carbohydrates (as glucose or sucrose) that occur naturally especially in plants

[2]sugar *vb* **su·gared; su·gar·ing** : to mix, cover, or sprinkle with sugar

sugar beet *n* : a large beet with white roots that is grown as a source of sugar

sug·ar·cane *n* : a tall strong grass with jointed stems widely raised in tropical regions for the sugar it yields

sugar maple *n* : a maple tree of the northeastern United States with hard strong wood and a sweet sap that is used to make maple syrup and maple sugar

sug·ary *adj* **1** : containing a lot of sugar **2** : too sweetly sentimental

sug·gest *vb* **sug·gest·ed; sug·gest·ing** **1** : to put (as a thought or desire) into a person's mind **2** : to recommend as being worthy of accepting or doing **3** : to call to mind through close connection or association

sug·ges·tion *n* **1** : a thought or plan that is offered or proposed **2** : the act or process of putting a thought in someone's mind **3** : [1]HINT 2

sug·ges·tive *adj* **1** : giving a hint **2** : full of suggestions **3** : suggesting something improper or indecent

sui·cide *n* **1** : the act of someone who kills himself or herself purposely **2** : a person who kills himself or herself purposely

[1]**suit** *n* **1** : a set of clothing having matching top and bottom pieces **2** : a set of clothes or protective coverings worn for a special purpose or under particular conditions **3** : an action in court to settle a disagreement or enforce a right or claim **4** : all the playing cards of one kind (as spades, hearts, diamonds, or clubs) in a pack

[2]**suit** *vb* **suit·ed; suit·ing** **1** : to be suitable or satisfactory **2** : to make suitable : ADAPT **3** : to be proper for or pleasing with **4** : to meet the needs or desires of

suit·able *adj* : being fit or right for a use or group — **suit·abil·i·ty** *n* — **suit·ably** *adv*

suit·case *n* : a flat rectangular traveling bag

suite *n* **1** : a number of connected rooms (as in a hotel) **2** : a set of matched furniture for a room

suit·or *n* : a man who tries to get a woman to marry him

sul·fur *also* **sul·phur** *n* : a yellow chemical element that is found widely in nature and is used in making chemicals and paper

sul·fu·rous *also* **sul·phu·rous** *adj* : containing or suggesting sulfur

[1]**sulk** *vb* **sulked; sulk·ing** : to be angry or irritable about something but childishly refuse to talk about it

[2]**sulk** *n* **1** : the state of a person who is sullenly silent or irritable **2** : a sulky mood

[1]**sulky** *adj* **sulk·i·er; sulk·i·est** **1** : angry or upset by something but refusing to discuss it **2** : often angry or upset

[2]**sulky** *n, pl* **sulk·ies** : a light vehicle with two wheels, a seat for the driver only, and usually no body

sul·len *adj* **1** : not sociable : SULKY **2** : GLOOMY 1, DREARY — **sul·len·ly** *adv*

sul·tan *n* : a ruler especially of a Muslim state

sul·ta·na *n* : the wife, mother, sister, or daughter of a sultan

sul·try *adj* **sul·tri·er; sul·tri·est** : very hot and humid

[1]**sum** *n* **1** : the result obtained by adding numbers **2** : a problem in arithmetic **3** : a quantity of money **4** : the whole amount

[2]**sum** *vb* **summed; sum·ming** : to find the total number of by adding or counting — **sum up** : to tell again in a few words : SUMMARIZE

su·mac *also* **su·mach** *n* : a tree, shrub, or woody vine that has leaves with many leaflets and loose clusters of red or white berries

sum·ma·rize *vb* **sum·ma·rized; sum·ma·riz·ing** : to tell in or reduce to a short statement of the main points

[1]**sum·ma·ry** *adj* **1** : expressing or covering the main points briefly : CONCISE **2** : done without delay

[2]**summary** *n, pl* **sum·ma·ries** : a short statement of the main points (as in a book or report)

[1]**sum·mer** *n* **1** : the season between spring and autumn which is in the northern hemisphere usually the months of June, July, and August **2** : one of the years of a person's lifetime

[2]**summer** *vb* **sum·mered; sum·mer·ing** : to pass the summer

sum·mer·time *n* : the summer season

sum·mery *adj* : relating to or typical of summer

sum·mit *n* : the highest point (as of a mountain) : TOP

sum·mon *vb* **sum·moned; sum·mon·ing** **1** : to call or send for : CONVENE **2** : to order to appear before a court of law **3** : to call into being : AROUSE

sum·mons *n, pl* **sum·mons·es** **1** : the act of calling or sending for **2** : a call by authority to appear at a place named or to attend to some duty **3** : a written order to appear in court

sump·tu·ous *adj* : very expensive or luxurious

[1]**sun** *n* **1** : the celestial body in our solar system whose light makes our day and around which the planets revolve **2** : SUNSHINE 1 **3** : an object in outer space like our sun

[2]**sun** *vb* **sunned; sun·ning** : to expose to or lie or sit in the rays of the sun

Sun. *abbr* Sunday

sun·bathe *vb* **sun·bathed; sun·bath·ing** : to sit or lie in the rays of the sun to get a tan

sun·beam *n* : a ray of sunlight

sun·block *n* : a preparation applied to the skin to prevent sunburn usually by blocking the sun's ultraviolet radiation

sun·bon·net *n* : a bonnet with a wide curving brim that shades the face and usually a ruffle at the back that protects the neck from the sun

[1]**sun·burn** *n* **:** a sore red state of the skin caused by too much sunlight

[2]**sunburn** *vb* **sun·burned** *or* **sun·burnt; sun·burn·ing :** to burn or discolor by exposure to the sun

sun·dae *n* **:** a serving of ice cream with a topping (as fruit, syrup, whipped cream, nuts, or bits of candy)

Sun·day *n* **:** the first day of the week

Sunday school *n* **:** a school held on Sunday in a church for religious education

sun·di·al *n* **:** a device that shows the time of day by the position of the shadow cast onto a marked plate by an object with a straight edge

sun·down *n* **:** SUNSET 2

sun·dries *n pl* **:** various small articles or items

sun·dry *adj* **:** more than one or two **:** VARIOUS

sun·fish *n, pl* **sunfish** *or* **sun·fish·es :** a small and brightly colored North American freshwater fish related to the perch

sun·flow·er *n* **:** a tall plant often grown for its large flower heads with brown center and yellow petals or for its edible oily seeds

sung *past and past participle of* SING

sun·glass·es *n pl* **:** glasses worn to protect the eyes from the sun

sunk *past and past participle of* SINK

sunk·en *adj* **1 :** fallen in **:** HOLLOW **2 :** lying at the bottom of a body of water **3 :** built or settled below the surrounding or normal level

sun·less *adj* **:** being without sunlight **:** DARK

sun·light *n* **:** SUNSHINE 1

sun·lit *adj* **:** lighted by the sun

sun·ny *adj* **sun·ni·er; sun·ni·est 1 :** bright with sunshine **2 :** MERRY 1, CHEERFUL

sun·rise *n* **1 :** the apparent rise of the sun above the horizon **2 :** the light and color of the rise of the sun above the horizon **3 :** the time at which the sun rises

sun·screen *n* **:** a preparation applied to the skin to prevent sunburn usually by chemically absorbing the sun's ultraviolet radiation

sun·set *n* **1 :** the apparent passing of the sun below the horizon **2 :** the light and color of the passing of the sun below the horizon **3 :** the time at which the sun sets

sun·shade *n* **:** something (as a parasol) used to protect from the sun's rays

sun·shine *n* **1 :** the sun's light or direct rays **:** the warmth and light given by the sun's rays **2 :** something that spreads warmth or happiness

sun·stroke *n* **:** an illness that is marked by high fever and weakness and is caused by exposure to too much sun

sun·tan *n* **:** a browning of skin from exposure to the sun

sun·up *n* **:** SUNRISE 2

sun·ward *adv or adj* **:** toward or facing the sun

sup *vb* **supped; sup·ping :** to eat the evening meal

su·per *adj* **1 :** very great **2 :** very good

super- *prefix* **1 :** more than **2 :** extremely **:** very

su·perb *adj* **:** outstandingly excellent, impressive, or beautiful

su·per·com·put·er *n* **:** a large very fast computer used especially for scientific computations

su·per·fi·cial *adj* **1 :** of or relating to the surface or appearance only **2 :** not thorough or complete — **su·per·fi·cial·ly** *adv*

su·per·flu·ous *adj* **:** going beyond what is enough or necessary **:** EXTRA

su·per·he·ro *n* **:** a fictional hero having extraordinary or superhuman powers

su·per·high·way *n* **:** an expressway for high-speed traffic

su·per·hu·man *adj* **:** going beyond normal human power, size, or ability

su·per·in·tend *vb* **su·per·in·tend·ed; su·per·in·tend·ing :** to have or exercise the charge of

su·per·in·ten·dent *n* **:** a person who looks after or manages something (as schools or a building)

[1]**su·pe·ri·or** *adj* **1 :** situated higher up **:** higher in rank, importance, numbers, or quality **2 :** excellent of its kind **:** BETTER **3 :** showing the feeling of being better or more important than others **:** ARROGANT

[2]**superior** *n* **1 :** a person who is higher than another in rank, importance, or quality **2 :** the head of a religious house or order

su·pe·ri·or·i·ty *n* **:** the state or fact of being better, more important, or higher in rank than others

[1]**su·per·la·tive** *adj* **1 :** being the form of an adjective or adverb that shows the greatest degree of comparison **2 :** better than all others **:** SUPREME

[2]**superlative** *n* **:** the superlative degree or a superlative form in a language

su·per·mar·ket *n* **:** a store selling foods and household items

su·per·nat·u·ral *adj* **:** of or relating to something beyond or outside of nature or the visible universe

su·per·sede *vb* **su·per·sed·ed; su·per·sed·ing :** to take the place or position of

su·per·son·ic *adj* **1 :** above the normal range of human hearing **2 :** having a speed from one to five times that of sound

su·per·sti·tion *n* **:** a belief or practice resulting from ignorance, fear of the unknown, or trust in magic or chance

su·per·sti·tious *adj* **:** showing or influenced by superstition

su·per·vise *vb* **su·per·vised; su·per·vis·ing** : to coordinate and direct the activities of
su·per·vi·sion *n* : the act of overseeing : MANAGEMENT
su·per·vi·sor *n* **1** : a person who is in charge of others **2** : an officer in charge of a unit or an operation of a business, government, or school
sup·per *n* **1** : the evening meal especially when dinner is eaten at midday **2** : refreshments served late in the evening especially at a social gathering
sup·plant *vb* **sup·plant·ed; sup·plant·ing** : to take the place of another
sup·ple *adj* **sup·pler; sup·plest** **1** : capable of bending or of being bent easily without stiffness, creases, or damage **2** : ADAPTABLE
[1]**sup·ple·ment** *n* : something that supplies what is needed or adds to something else
[2]**sup·ple·ment** *vb* **sup·ple·ment·ed; sup·ple·ment·ing** : to add to : COMPLETE
sup·ple·men·ta·ry *adj* : added to something else : ADDITIONAL
sup·pli·cate *vb* **sup·pli·cat·ed; sup·pli·cat·ing** : to ask or beg in a humble way : BESEECH
sup·pli·ca·tion *n* : the act of asking or begging in a humble way
[1]**sup·ply** *vb* **sup·plied; sup·ply·ing** **1** : to provide for : SATISFY **2** : to make available : FURNISH
[2]**supply** *n, pl* **sup·plies** **1** : the amount of something that is needed or can be gotten **2** : [2]STORE 3 **3** : the act or process of providing something
[1]**sup·port** *vb* **sup·port·ed; sup·port·ing** **1** : to hold up or in position : serve as a foundation or prop for **2** : to take sides with : FAVOR **3** : to provide evidence for : VERIFY **4** : to pay the costs of : MAINTAIN **5** : to keep going : SUSTAIN **6** : to provide help or encouragement to — **sup·port·er** *n*
[2]**support** *n* **1** : the act of supporting : the condition of being supported **2** : someone or something that supports
sup·pose *vb* **sup·posed; sup·pos·ing** **1** : to think of as true or as a fact for the sake of argument **2** : BELIEVE 2, THINK **3** : [1]GUESS 1
sup·posed *adj* **1** : forced, expected, or required **2** : believed or claimed to be true or real **3** : given permission — **sup·pos·ed·ly** *adv*
sup·press *vb* **sup·pressed; sup·press·ing** **1** : to put down (as by authority or force) : SUBDUE **2** : to hold back : REPRESS
sup·pres·sion *n* : an act or instance of putting down or holding back : the state of being put down or held back
su·prem·a·cy *n, pl* **su·prem·a·cies** : the highest rank, power, or authority
su·preme *adj* **1** : highest in rank, power, or authority **2** : highest in degree or quality **3** : most extreme or great — **su·preme·ly** *adv*
Supreme Being *n* : GOD 1
supreme court *n, often cap* : the highest court of law in the United States or in many of its states
[1]**sure** *adj* **sur·er; sur·est** **1** : having no doubt : CERTAIN **2** : true without question **3** : firmly established **4** : RELIABLE, TRUSTWORTHY **5** : bound to happen **6** : bound as if by fate
[2]**sure** *adv* **1** : SURELY 1 **2** : SURELY 2
sure·ly *adv* **1** : without doubt **2** : beyond question : REALLY **3** : with confidence : CONFIDENTLY
[1]**surf** *n* **1** : the waves of the sea that splash on the shore **2** : the sound, splash, and foam of breaking waves
[2]**surf** *vb* **surfed; surf·ing** **1** : to ride the incoming waves of the sea (as on a surfboard) **2** : to scan a wide range of offerings (as on television or the Internet) for something that is interesting or fills a need
[1]**sur·face** *n* **1** : the outside or any one side of an object **2** : the outside appearance
[2]**surface** *adj* : not deep or real
[3]**surface** *vb* **sur·faced; sur·fac·ing** **1** : to come to the surface **2** : to become obvious **3** : to give a new top layer to : make smooth (as by sanding or paving)
surf·board *n* : a long narrow board that floats and is ridden in surfing
surf·ing *n* : the sport of riding waves toward the shore usually while standing on a surfboard
[1]**surge** *vb* **surged; surg·ing** **1** : to rise suddenly and greatly **2** : to move suddenly and quickly in a particular direction
[2]**surge** *n* **1** : a rush like that of a wave **2** : a large wave
sur·geon *n* : a doctor who performs surgery
sur·gery *n, pl* **sur·ger·ies** : medical treatment (as of disease, injury, or physical abnormality) that involves cutting into the body usually to expose internal parts
sur·gi·cal *adj* : of, relating to, or associated with surgery or surgeons
sur·ly *adj* **sur·li·er; sur·li·est** : mean and rude : UNFRIENDLY
[1]**sur·mise** *n* : a thought or idea based on very little evidence : GUESS
[2]**surmise** *vb* **sur·mised; sur·mis·ing** : to form an idea on very little evidence : GUESS
sur·mount *vb* **sur·mount·ed; sur·mount·ing** **1** : OVERCOME 1 **2** : to get to the top of **3** : to be at the top of
sur·name *n* : the name that comes at the end of someone's full name
sur·pass *vb* **sur·passed; sur·pass·ing** **1** : to

be greater, better, or stronger than : EXCEED **2** : to go beyond the reach or powers of

[1]**sur·plus** *n* : an amount left over : EXCESS

[2]**surplus** *adj* : left over : EXTRA

[1]**sur·prise** *n* **1** : something that is unexpected **2** : ASTONISHMENT, AMAZEMENT **3** : an act or instance of coming upon without warning

[2]**surprise** *vb* **sur·prised; sur·pris·ing** **1** : to cause to feel wonder or amazement because of being unexpected **2** : to come upon without warning **3** : to attack without warning : capture by an unexpected attack

sur·pris·ing *adj* : causing astonishment : UNEXPECTED — **sur·pris·ing·ly** *adv*

[1]**sur·ren·der** *vb* **sur·ren·dered; sur·ren·der·ing** **1** : to give up after a struggle **2** : to let go of : RELINQUISH

[2]**surrender** *n* **1** : the act of giving up after a struggle **2** : the act of giving something over to the possession or control of someone else

sur·rey *n, pl* **surreys** : a pleasure carriage that has two wide seats and four wheels and is drawn by horses

sur·round *vb* **sur·round·ed; sur·round·ing** **1** : to enclose on all sides : ENCIRCLE **2** : to be closely related or connected to

sur·round·ings *n pl* : the circumstances, conditions, or things around an individual : ENVIRONMENT

[1]**sur·vey** *vb* **sur·veyed; sur·vey·ing** **1** : to look over : EXAMINE **2** : to find out the size, shape, or boundaries of (as a piece of land) **3** : to gather information from : ask questions of

[2]**sur·vey** *n, pl* **surveys** **1** : the action or an instance of gathering information or examining something **2** : something that is examined **3** : a history or description that covers a large subject briefly

sur·vey·ing *n* **1** : the act or occupation of a person who determines the size, shape, or boundaries of a piece of land **2** : a branch of mathematics that teaches how to measure the earth's surface and record these measurements accurately

sur·vey·or *n* : a person whose occupation is determining the size, shape, or boundries of pieces of land

sur·viv·al *n* : the continuation of life

sur·vive *vb* **sur·vived; sur·viv·ing** **1** : to remain alive : continue to exist **2** : to live or exist longer than or past the end of — **sur·vi·vor** *n*

sus·cep·ti·ble *adj* **1** : of such a nature as to permit **2** : having little resistance (as to infection or damage) **3** : easily affected or impressed by

[1]**sus·pect** *vb* **sus·pect·ed; sus·pect·ing** **1** : to suppose to be true or likely **2** : to have doubts of : DISTRUST **3** : to imagine to be guilty without proof

[2]**sus·pect** *n* : a person who is thought to be guilty of something

[3]**sus·pect** *adj* : thought of with suspicion

sus·pend *vb* **sus·pend·ed; sus·pend·ing** **1** : to force to give up some right or office for a time **2** : to hang especially so as to be free except at one point **3** : to stop or do away with for a time **4** : to stop operation or action for a time

sus·pend·er *n* : one of a pair of straps that are attached to pants or a skirt and go over the shoulders

sus·pense *n* : uncertainty, worry, or excitement in wondering about the result of something

sus·pen·sion *n* **1** : the act of stopping, removing, or making someone or something ineffective for a time **2** : the state of being stopped, removed, or made ineffective for a time **3** : the period during which someone or something is stopped, removed, or made ineffective **4** : the act of hanging : the state of being hung **5** : the system of springs that support the upper part of a vehicle on the axles

sus·pi·cion *n* **1** : an act or instance of suspecting or the state of being suspected **2** : a feeling that something is wrong : DOUBT

sus·pi·cious *adj* **1** : likely to arouse suspicion **2** : likely to distrust or be distrustful **3** : showing distrust

sus·tain *vb* **sus·tained; sus·tain·ing** **1** : to provide with what is needed **2** : to keep up the spirits of **3** : to keep up : PROLONG **4** : to hold up the weight of **5** : [2]EXPERIENCE **6** : to allow or uphold as true, legal, or fair

sus·te·nance *n* **1** : [2]LIVING 3, SUBSISTENCE **2** : the act of supplying with the necessities of life **3** : [2]SUPPORT 2

SUV *n, pl* **SUVs** : SPORT-UTILITY VEHICLE

SW *abbr* southwest

[1]**swab** *n* **1** : a yarn mop especially as used on a ship **2** : a wad of absorbent material usually wound around the end of a small stick and used for applying or removing material (as medicine or makeup)

[2]**swab** *vb* **swabbed; swab·bing** **1** : to clean with or as if with a mop **2** : to apply medication to with a wad of absorbent material

[1]**swag·ger** *vb* **swag·gered; swag·ger·ing** : to walk with a proud strut

[2]**swagger** *n* : an act or instance of walking with a proud strut

[1]**swal·low** *n* : a small bird that has long wings and a forked tail and feeds on insects caught while in flight

[2]**swallow** *vb* **swal·lowed; swal·low·ing** **1** : to

take into the stomach through the mouth and throat **2 :** to perform the actions used in swallowing something **3 :** to completely surround **:** ENGULF **4 :** to accept or believe without question **5 :** to keep from expressing or showing **:** REPRESS

[3]**swallow** *n* **1 :** an act of taking something into the stomach through the mouth and throat **:** an act of swallowing **2 :** an amount that can be swallowed at one time

swam *past of* SWIM

[1]**swamp** *n* **:** wet spongy land often partly covered with water

[2]**swamp** *vb* **swamped; swamp·ing** **1 :** to fill or cause to fill with water **:** sink after filling with water **2 :** OVERWHELM 1

swampy *adj* **swamp·i·er; swamp·i·est :** consisting of or like a swamp

swan *n* **:** a usually white waterbird that has a long neck and large body and is related to but larger than the goose

[1]**swap** *vb* **swapped; swap·ping :** to give in exchange **:** make an exchange **:** TRADE

[2]**swap** *n* **:** [1]EXCHANGE 1, TRADE

[1]**swarm** *n* **1 :** a large number of bees that leave a hive together to form a new colony elsewhere **2 :** a large number grouped together and usually in motion

[2]**swarm** *vb* **swarmed; swarm·ing** **1 :** to form a swarm and leave the hive **2 :** to move or gather in a large number **3 :** to be filled with a great number **:** TEEM

swar·thy *adj* **swar·thi·er; swar·thi·est :** having a dark complexion

[1]**swat** *vb* **swat·ted; swat·ting :** to hit with a quick hard blow

[2]**swat** *n* **:** a hard blow

swath *or* **swathe** *n, pl* **swaths** *or* **swathes** **1 :** an area of grass or grain that has been cut or mowed **2 :** a long broad strip or belt

[1]**sway** *vb* **swayed; sway·ing** **1 :** to swing slowly back and forth or from side to side **2 :** to change or cause to change between one point, position, or opinion and another

[2]**sway** *n* **1 :** the act of slowly swinging back and forth or from side to side **2 :** a controlling influence or force **:** RULE

swear *vb* **swore; sworn; swear·ing** **1 :** to use bad or vulgar language **:** CURSE **2 :** to make a statement or promise with sincerity or under oath **:** VOW **3 :** to give an oath to **4 :** to bind by an oath **5 :** to be or feel certain

[1]**sweat** *vb* **sweat** *or* **sweat·ed; sweat·ing** **1 :** to give off salty moisture through the pores of the skin **:** PERSPIRE **2 :** to collect moisture on the surface **3 :** to work hard enough to perspire

[2]**sweat** *n* **1 :** PERSPIRATION 2 **2 :** moisture coming from or collecting in drops on a surface **3 :** the condition of one perspiring

sweat·er *n* **:** a knitted or crocheted piece of clothing for the upper body

sweat gland *n* **:** a small gland of the skin that gives off perspiration

sweat·shirt *n* **:** a loose pullover or jacket without a collar and usually with long sleeves

sweaty *adj* **sweat·i·er; sweat·i·est :** wet with, stained by, or smelling of sweat

Swede *n* **:** a person born or living in Sweden

[1]**Swed·ish** *adj* **:** of or relating to Sweden, the Swedes, or Swedish

[2]**Swedish** *n* **:** the language of the Swedes

[1]**sweep** *vb* **swept; sweep·ing** **1 :** to remove with a broom or brush **2 :** to clean by removing loose dirt or small trash with a broom or brush **3 :** to move over or across swiftly often with force or destruction **4 :** to move or gather as if with a broom or brush **5 :** to move the eyes or an instrument through a wide curve **6 :** to touch a surface of quickly **7 :** to drive along with steady force **8 :** to become suddenly very popular throughout **9 :** to achieve a complete or easy victory — **sweep·er** *n*

[2]**sweep** *n* **1 :** a curving movement, course, or line **2 :** an act or instance of cleaning with a broom or brush **3 :** a wide stretch or curve of land **4 :** something that sweeps or works with a sweeping motion **5 :** a complete or easy victory **6 :** [1]RANGE 2, SCOPE **7 :** CHIMNEY SWEEP

[1]**sweep·ing** *adj* **1 :** moving or extending in a wide curve or over a wide area **2 :** EXTENSIVE

[2]**sweeping** *n* **1 :** an act of cleaning an area with a broom or brush **2 sweepings** *pl* **:** things collected by sweeping

sweep·stakes *n pl* **:** a contest in which money or prizes are given to winners picked by chance (as by drawing names) — used as singular or plural

[1]**sweet** *adj* **sweet·er; sweet·est** **1 :** containing or tasting of sugar **2 :** having a pleasant sound, smell, or appearance **3 :** very gentle, kind, or friendly **4 :** pleasing to the mind or feelings **:** AGREEABLE **5 :** much loved **:** DEAR **6 :** agreeable to oneself but not to others **7 :** not sour, stale, or spoiled **8 :** not salt or salted **9 :** having a mild taste **:** not sharp — **sweet·ly** *adv* — **sweet·ness** *n* — **sweet on :** in love with

[2]**sweet** *n* **1 :** something (as candy) that contains or tastes of sugar **2 :** [1]DARLING 1, DEAR

sweet corn *n* **:** corn with kernels rich in sugar that is cooked and eaten as a vegetable while young

sweet·en *vb* **sweet·ened; sweet·en·ing :** to make or become sweet or sweeter

DICTIONARY

sweet·en·ing *n* **1 :** the act or process of making sweet **2 :** something that sweetens
sweet·heart *n* **:** a person whom one loves
sweet·meat *n* **:** a food (as a piece of candy or candied fruit) rich in sugar
sweet pea *n* **:** a climbing plant that is grown for its fragrant flowers of many colors
sweet potato *n* **:** the large sweet edible root of a tropical vine that is cooked and eaten as a vegetable
1swell *vb* **swelled; swelled** *or* **swol·len; swell·ing** **1 :** to enlarge in an abnormal way usually by pressure from within or by growth **2 :** to grow or make bigger (as in size or value) **3 :** to stretch upward or outward **:** BULGE **4 :** to fill or become filled with emotion
2swell *n* **1 :** a gradual increase in size, value, or volume **2 :** a long rolling wave or series of waves in the open sea **3 :** the condition of bulging **4 :** a rounded elevation
3swell *adj* **:** EXCELLENT, FIRST-RATE
swell·ing *n* **:** a swollen lump or part
swel·ter *vb* **swel·tered; swel·ter·ing :** to suffer, sweat, or be faint from heat
swel·ter·ing *adj* **:** oppressively hot
swept *past and past participle of* SWEEP
1swerve *vb* **swerved; swerv·ing :** to turn aside suddenly from a straight line or course
2swerve *n* **:** an act or instance of turning aside suddenly
1swift *adj* **swift·er; swift·est** **1 :** moving or capable of moving with great speed **2 :** occurring suddenly — **swift·ly** *adv* — **swift·ness** *n*
2swift *adv* **:** in a swift manner
3swift *n* **:** a small usually black bird that is related to the hummingbirds but looks like a swallow
swig *n* **:** the amount drunk at one time **:** GULP
1swill *vb* **swilled; swill·ing :** to eat or drink greedily
2swill *n* **1 :** 1SLOP 2 **2 :** GARBAGE 1, REFUSE
1swim *vb* **swam; swum; swim·ming** **1 :** to move through or in water by moving arms, legs, fins, or tail **2 :** to cross by swimming **3 :** to float on or in or be covered with or as if with a liquid **4 :** to be dizzy **:** move or seem to move in a dizzying way — **swim·mer** *n*
2swim *n* **:** an act or period of swimming
swimming pool *n* **:** a tank (as of concrete or plastic) made for swimming
swim·suit *n* **:** a garment for swimming or bathing
1swin·dle *vb* **swin·dled; swin·dling :** to get money or property from dishonestly **:** CHEAT
2swindle *n* **:** an act or instance of getting money or property from someone dishonestly
swin·dler *n* **:** a person who swindles
swine *n, pl* **swine :** a wild or domestic pig
1swing *vb* **swung; swing·ing** **1 :** to move rapidly in a sweeping curve **2 :** to turn on a hinge or pivot **3 :** to move with a curving motion **4 :** to turn or move quickly in a particular direction **5 :** to move back and forth or from side to side while hanging from a fixed point **6 :** to move back and forth in or on a swing **7 :** to manage or handle successfully
2swing *n* **1 :** a seat usually hung by overhead ropes and used to move back and forth **2 :** an act of moving something (as a bat) rapidly in a sweeping curve **3 :** a sweeping movement, blow, or rhythm **4 :** the distance through which something sways to and fro **5 :** a style of jazz marked by lively rhythm and played mostly for dancing
1swipe *n* **:** a strong sweeping movement
2swipe *vb* **swiped; swip·ing** **1 :** 1STEAL 1 **2 :** to make a strong sweeping movement
1swirl *vb* **swirled; swirl·ing :** to move with a spinning or twisting motion
2swirl *n* **1 :** a spinning mass or motion **:** EDDY **2 :** busy movement or activity **3 :** a twisting shape or mark
1swish *vb* **swished; swish·ing :** to make, move, or strike with a soft sweeping or brushing sound
2swish *n* **1 :** a soft sweeping or brushing sound **2 :** a movement that produces a sweeping or brushing sound
1Swiss *n, pl* **Swiss :** a person born or living in Switzerland
2Swiss *adj* **:** of or relating to Switzerland or the Swiss
1switch *n* **1 :** a device for making, breaking, or changing the connections in an electrical circuit **2 :** a change from one thing to another **3 :** a narrow flexible whip, rod, or twig **4 :** an act of switching **5 :** a device for adjusting the rails of a track so that a train or streetcar may be turned from one track to another
2switch *vb* **switched; switch·ing** **1 :** to turn, shift, or change by operating a device that makes, breaks, or changes the connections in an electrical circuit **2 :** to move quickly from side to side **3 :** to make a shift or change **4 :** to strike with or as if with a whip, rod, or twig
switch·board *n* **:** a panel for controlling the operation of a number of electric circuits
1swiv·el *n* **:** a device joining two parts so that one or both can turn freely (as on a bolt or pin)
2swivel *vb* **swiv·eled** *or* **swiv·elled; swiv·el·ing** *or* **swiv·el·ling :** to turn on or as if on a swivel
swollen *past participle of* SWELL

[1]swoon *vb* **swooned; swoon·ing** : [2]FAINT
[2]swoon *n* : [3]FAINT
[1]swoop *vb* **swooped; swoop·ing** : to rush down or pounce suddenly
[2]swoop *n* : an act or instance of rushing down or pouncing suddenly
sword *n* : a weapon having a long blade usually with a sharp point and edge
sword·fish *n, pl* **swordfish** *or* **sword·fish·es** : a large ocean fish that has a long pointed bill formed by the bones of the upper jaw and is often used for food
swords·man *n, pl* **swords·men** : a person who fights with a sword
swore *past of* SWEAR
sworn *past participle of* SWEAR
swum *past participle of* SWIM
swung *past and past participle of* SWING
syc·a·more *n* **1** : a fig tree of Egypt and the Middle East **2** : a large tree of the United States with round hard fruits and bark that peels off in flakes
syl·lab·ic *adj* : relating to or being syllables
syl·lab·i·cate *vb* **syl·lab·i·cat·ed; syl·lab·i·cat·ing** : SYLLABIFY
syl·lab·i·ca·tion *n* : the forming of syllables : the dividing of words into syllables
syl·lab·i·fi·ca·tion *n* : SYLLABICATION
syl·lab·i·fy *vb* **syl·lab·i·fied; syl·lab·i·fy·ing** : to form or divide into syllables
syl·la·ble *n* **1** : a unit of spoken language that consists of one or more vowel sounds alone or with one or more consonant sounds coming before or following **2** : one or more letters (as *syl, la,* and *ble*) in a written word (as *syl*la*ble*) usually separated from the rest of the word by a centered dot or a hyphen and used as guides to the division of the word at the end of a line
sym·bol *n* **1** : something that stands for something else : EMBLEM **2** : a letter, character, or sign used instead of a word to represent a quantity, position, relationship, direction, or something to be done
sym·bol·ic *also* **sym·bol·i·cal** *adj* : of, relating to, or using symbols or symbolism
sym·bol·ism *n* **1** : the use of symbols to represent an idea or quality **2** : the meaning of a symbol
sym·bol·ize *vb* **sym·bol·ized; sym·bol·iz·ing** : to serve as a representation of
sym·met·ri·cal *or* **sym·met·ric** *adj* : having or showing symmetry
sym·me·try *n, pl* **sym·me·tries** : close agreement in size, shape, and position of parts that are on opposite sides of a dividing line or center : an arrangement involving regular and balanced proportions
sym·pa·thet·ic *adj* **1** : feeling or showing care or understanding **2** : feeling favorable — **sym·pa·thet·i·cal·ly** *adv*
sym·pa·thize *vb* **sym·pa·thized; sym·pa·thiz·ing** **1** : to feel or show pity or care and understanding for **2** : to be in favor of something
sym·pa·thy *n, pl* **sym·pa·thies** **1** : sorrow or pity for another **2** : readiness to favor or support **3** : a relationship between people or things in which whatever affects one similarly affects the other
sym·phon·ic *adj* : relating to a symphony
sym·pho·ny *n, pl* **sym·pho·nies** **1** : a usually long musical composition for a full orchestra **2** : a large orchestra of wind, string, and percussion instruments **3** : harmonious arrangement (as of sound or color)
symp·tom *n* **1** : a noticeable change in the body or its functions that indicates the presence of a disease or other disorder **2** : INDICATION 2, SIGN
syn. *abbr* synonym
syn·a·gogue *also* **syn·a·gog** *n* : a Jewish house of worship
syn·apse *n* : the point at which a nerve impulse passes from one nerve cell to another
syn·co·pa·tion *n* : an instance of temporarily accenting a normally weak beat in music to vary the rhythm
syn·o·nym *n* : a word having the same or almost the same meaning as another word in the same language
syn·on·y·mous *adj* : alike in meaning
syn·tax *n* : the way in which words are put together to form phrases, clauses, or sentences
syn·the·size *vb* **syn·the·sized; syn·the·siz·ing** : to produce from the combination of simpler materials
syn·thet·ic *adj* : produced artificially especially by chemical means : produced by human beings
sy·ringe *n* : a device used to force fluid into or withdraw it from the body or its cavities
syr·up *n* **1** : a thick sticky solution of sugar and water often containing flavoring or a medicine **2** : the juice of a fruit or plant with some of the water removed
sys·tem *n* **1** : a group of parts combined to form a whole that works or moves as a unit **2** : a body that functions as a whole **3** : a group of organs that together perform an important function in the body **4** : an orderly way of managing, controlling, organizing, or doing something
sys·tem·at·ic *adj* : using a system or a regular and orderly method — **sys·tem·at·i·cal·ly** *adv*
sys·tem·ic *adj* : of or relating to the body as a whole

T

t *n, pl* **t's** *or* **ts** *often cap* **:** the 20th letter of the English alphabet — **to a T :** just fine **:** EXACTLY

T *abbr* true

tab *n* **1 :** a short flap or tag attached to something for filing, pulling, or hanging **2 :** a careful watch

tab·by *n, pl* **tabbies :** a domestic cat with a striped and spotted coat

tab·er·na·cle *n* **1 :** a place of worship **2** *often cap* **:** a tent used as a place of worship by the ancient Israelites during their wanderings in the wilderness with Moses

[1]ta·ble *n* **1 :** a piece of furniture having a smooth flat top on legs **2 :** food to eat **3 :** the people around a table **4 :** short list **5 :** an arrangement in rows or columns for reference

[2]table *vb* **ta·bled; ta·bling 1 :** TABULATE **2 :** to put on a table

tab·leau *n, pl* **tab·leaux** *also* **tab·leaus :** a scene or event shown by a group of persons who remain still and silent

ta·ble·cloth *n* **:** a covering spread over a dining table before the places are set

ta·ble·land *n* **:** PLATEAU

ta·ble·spoon *n* **1 :** a large spoon used mostly for dishing up food **2 :** a unit of measure used in cooking equal to ½ fluid ounce (about 15 milliliters)

ta·ble·spoon·ful *n, pl* **tablespoonfuls** *also* **ta·ble·spoons·ful 1 :** as much as a tablespoon will hold **2 :** TABLESPOON 2

tab·let *n* **1 :** a thin flat slab used for writing, painting, or drawing **2 :** a number of sheets of writing paper glued together at one edge **3 :** a small usually round mass of material containing medicine **4 :** a mobile computing device that is flat like a pad of paper, that is usually controlled by touching the screen, and that is typically used for reading, watching videos, or accessing the Internet

table tennis *n* **:** a game played on a table by two or four players who use paddles to hit a small hollow plastic ball back and forth over a net

ta·ble·ware *n* **:** utensils (as of china, glass, or silver) for use at the table

tab·u·late *vb* **tab·u·lat·ed; tab·u·lat·ing :** to count and record in an orderly way

tac·it *adj* **:** understood or made known without being put into words — **tac·it·ly** *adv*

[1]tack *n* **1 :** a small nail with a sharp point and usually a broad flat head **2 :** the direction a ship is sailing as shown by the position the sails are set in **3 :** a course or method of action **4 :** a temporary stitch used in sewing

[2]tack *vb* **tacked; tack·ing 1 :** to fasten with tacks **2 :** to attach or join loosely or quickly **3 :** to change from one course to another in sailing **4 :** to follow a zigzag course

[1]tack·le *vb* **tack·led; tack·ling 1 :** to seize and throw (a person) to the ground **2 :** to begin working on

[2]tackle *n* **1 :** a set of special equipment **2 :** an arrangement of ropes and wheels for hoisting or pulling something heavy **3 :** an act of seizing and throwing a person to the ground **4 :** a football player positioned on the line of scrimmage

ta·co *n, pl* **tacos :** a corn tortilla usually folded and fried and filled with a spicy mixture (as of ground meat and cheese)

tact *n* **:** the ability to do or say things without offending other people

tact·ful *adj* **:** having or showing the ability to do or say things without offending other people — **tact·ful·ly** *adv* — **tact·ful·ness** *n*

tac·tic *n* **:** a planned action for some purpose

tac·tics *n pl* **1 :** the science and art of arranging and moving troops or warships for best use **2 :** a system or method for reaching a goal — used as singular or plural

tac·tile *adj* **:** relating to the sense of touch

tact·less *adj* **:** having or showing no tact — **tact·less·ly** *adv* — **tact·less·ness** *n*

tad·pole *n* **:** the larva of a frog or toad that has a long tail, breathes with gills, and lives in water

taf·fy *n, pl* **taffies :** a candy made usually of molasses or brown sugar boiled and pulled until soft

[1]tag *n* **:** a small flap or tab fixed or hanging on something

[2]tag *vb* **tagged; tag·ging 1 :** to follow closely and continually **2 :** to put a tab or label on — **tag along :** to follow another's lead in going from one place to another

[3]tag *n* **:** a game in which one player who is it chases the others and tries to touch one of them to make that person it

[4]tag *vb* **tagged; tag·ging 1 :** to touch in or as if in a game of tag **2 :** to touch a runner in baseball with the ball and cause the runner to be out

[1]tail *n* **1 :** the rear part of an animal or a usually slender flexible growth that extends from this part **2 :** something that in shape, appearance, or position is like an animal's tail **3 :** the back, last, or lower part of something **4 :** the side or end opposite the head — **tailed** *adj* — **tail·less** *adj*

²tail *vb* **tailed; tail·ing :** to follow closely to keep watch on

tail·gate *n* **:** a panel at the back end of a vehicle that can be lowered for loading and unloading

¹tai·lor *n* **:** a person whose business is making or making adjustments in clothes

²tailor *vb* **tai·lored; tai·lor·ing 1 :** to make or make adjustments in (clothes) **2 :** to change to fit a special need

tail·pipe *n* **:** the pipe carrying off the exhaust gases from the muffler of an engine in a car or truck

tail·spin *n* **:** a dive by an airplane turning in a circle

¹taint *vb* **taint·ed; taint·ing 1 :** to rot slightly **2 :** to affect slightly with something bad

²taint *n* **:** a trace of decay

¹take *vb* **took; tak·en; tak·ing 1 :** to get hold of **:** GRASP **2 :** to carry or go with from one place to another **3 :** to get control of **:** CAPTURE **4 :** to receive into the body **5 :** to get possession or use of **6 :** to begin to perform the responsibilities of **:** ASSUME **7 :** to do the action of **8 :** to use as a way of going from one place to another **9 :** REQUIRE 1 **10 :** to put up with **:** ENDURE **11 :** to come upon **12 :** to adopt or accept **13 :** WIN 2 **14 :** CHOOSE 1, SELECT **15 :** to sit in or on **16 :** to find out by testing or examining **17 :** to save in some permanent form **18 :** BELIEVE 2 **19 :** to be guided by **:** FOLLOW **20 :** to become affected suddenly **21 :** UNDERSTAND 4, INTERPRET **22 :** to react in a certain way **23 :** SUBTRACT **24 :** CONSIDER 1 **25 :** to have effect **:** be successful **26 :** to be formed or used with **27 :** CAPTIVATE, DELIGHT — **tak·er** *n* — **take advantage of 1 :** to make good use of **2 :** to treat (someone) unfairly — **take after :** RESEMBLE — **take back :** to try to cancel (as something said) — **take care :** to be careful — **take care of :** to do what is needed **:** look after — **take charge :** to assume care or control — **take effect 1 :** to go into existence or operation **2 :** to have an intended or expected result — **take for granted :** to assume as true, real, or expected — **take hold :** to become attached or established — **take in 1 :** to make smaller **2 :** to receive as a guest **3 :** to allow to join **4 :** to receive and do at home for pay **5 :** to have within its limits **6 :** to go to **7 :** to get the meaning of **8 :** ¹CHEAT 2 — **take off 1 :** to take away (a covering) **:** REMOVE **2 :** DEDUCT **3 :** to leave a surface in beginning a flight or leap — **take on 1 :** to begin (a task) or struggle against (an opponent) **2 :** to gain or show as or as if a part of oneself **3 :** ¹EMPLOY 2 **4 :** to make an unusual show of grief or anger — **take over :** to get control of — **take part :** to do or join in something together with others — **take place :** to come about or occur **:** HAPPEN — **take up 1 :** to get together from many sources **2 :** to start something for the first time or after a pause **3 :** to change by making tighter or shorter

²take *n* **1 :** the number or quantity of animals or fish killed, captured, or caught **2 :** money received

take·off *n* **1 :** an act or instance of leaving the ground (as by an airplane) **2 :** an imitation especially to mock the original **3 :** a spot at which something leaves the ground

talc *n* **:** a soft mineral that has a soapy feel and is used especially in making talcum powder

tal·cum powder *n* **:** a usually perfumed powder for the body made of talc

tale *n* **1 :** something told **2 :** a story about an imaginary event **3 :** ³LIE **4 :** a piece of harmful gossip

tal·ent *n* **1 :** unusual natural ability **2 :** a special often creative or artistic ability **3 :** a person of group of people having special ability — **tal·ent·ed** *adj*

tal·is·man *n, pl* **tal·is·mans :** a ring or stone carved with symbols and believed to have magical powers **:** CHARM

¹talk *vb* **talked; talk·ing 1 :** to express in speech **:** SPEAK **2 :** to speak about **:** DISCUSS **3 :** to cause or influence with words **4 :** to use a certain language **5 :** to exchange ideas by means of spoken words **:** CONVERSE **6 :** to pass on information other than by speaking **7 :** ²GOSSIP **8 :** to reveal secret information — **talk·er** *n* — **talk over :** DISCUSS 1

²talk *n* **1 :** the act or an instance of speaking with someone **2 :** a way of speaking **:** LANGUAGE **3 :** CONFERENCE **4 :** ¹RUMOR **5 :** the topic of comment or gossip **6 :** an informal address

talk·a·tive *adj* **:** fond of talking — **talk·a·tive·ness** *n*

talk·ing–to *n* **:** an often wordy scolding

¹tall *adj* **tall·er; tall·est 1 :** having unusually great height **2 :** of a stated height **3 :** made up — **tall·ness** *n*

²tall *adv* **:** so as to be or look tall

tal·low *n* **:** a white solid fat of cattle and sheep used mostly in making candles and soap

¹tal·ly *n, pl* **tallies 1 :** a recorded count **2 :** a score or point made (as in a game)

²tally *vb* **tal·lied; tal·ly·ing 1 :** to keep a

count of **2 :** to make a tally **:** SCORE **3 :** to match or agree **:** CORRESPOND

Tal·mud *n* **:** a collection of writings on Jewish law and custom and religious practice

tal·on *n* **:** the claw of a bird of prey — **tal·oned** *adj*

ta·ma·le *n* **:** seasoned ground meat rolled in cornmeal, wrapped in corn husks, and steamed

tam·bou·rine *n* **:** a small shallow drum with only one head and loose metal disks around the rim that is played by shaking or hitting with the hand

¹tame *adj* **tam·er; tam·est 1 :** changed from the wild state so as to become useful and obedient to people **:** DOMESTIC **2 :** not afraid of people **3 :** not interesting **:** DULL — **tame·ly** *adv*

²tame *vb* **tamed; tam·ing :** to make or become gentle or obedient — **tam·er** *n*

tamp *vb* **tamped; tamp·ing :** to press down or in by hitting lightly

tam·per *vb* **tam·pered; tam·per·ing :** to interfere or change in a secret or incorrect way

¹tan *vb* **tanned; tan·ning 1 :** to change animal hide into leather especially by soaking in a tannin solution **2 :** to make or become brown in color **3 :** ¹BEAT 1, THRASH

²tan *adj* **tan·ner; tan·nest :** of a light yellowish brown color

³tan *n* **1 :** a brown color given to the skin by the sun or wind **2 :** a light yellowish brown **:** the color of sand

tan·a·ger *n* **:** a brightly colored mostly tropical bird that feeds on insects and fruit

¹tan·dem *n* **1 :** a carriage pulled by horses hitched one behind the other **2 :** TANDEM BICYCLE

²tandem *adv* **:** one behind another

tandem bicycle *n* **:** a bicycle for two people sitting one behind the other

tang *n* **:** a sharp flavor or smell — **tangy** *adj*

tan·ger·ine *n* **:** a Chinese orange with a loose skin and sweet pulp

tan·gi·ble *adj* **1 :** possible to touch or handle **:** MATERIAL **2 :** easily seen or recognized — **tan·gi·bly** *adv*

¹tan·gle *vb* **tan·gled; tan·gling :** to twist or become twisted together into a mass that is hard to straighten out again

²tangle *n* **1 :** a mass that is twisted together and hard to straighten **2 :** a complicated or confused state

tank *n* **1 :** an often large container for a liquid **2 :** an enclosed combat vehicle that has heavy armor and guns and a tread which is an endless belt

tan·kard *n* **:** a tall cup with one handle and often a lid

tank·er *n* **:** a vehicle or ship with tanks for carrying a liquid

tan·ner *n* **:** a person who tans hides into leather

tan·nery *n, pl* **tan·ner·ies :** a place where hides are tanned

tan·nin *n* **:** a substance often made from oak bark or sumac and used in tanning animal hides, dyeing fabric and yarn, and making ink

tan·ta·lize *vb* **tan·ta·lized; tan·ta·liz·ing :** to tease or excite by or as if by showing, mentioning, or offering something desirable but keeping it out of reach

tan·trum *n* **:** an outburst of bad temper

Tao·ism *n* **:** a Chinese philosophy based on the writings of Lao-tzu that stresses living simply, honestly, and in harmony with nature — **Tao·ist** *n*

¹tap *vb* **tapped; tap·ping :** to hit lightly — **tap·per** *n*

²tap *n* **:** a light blow or its sound

³tap *n* **:** FAUCET, SPIGOT — **on tap :** coming up

⁴tap *vb* **tapped; tap·ping 1 :** to let out or cause to flow by making a hole or by pulling out a plug **2 :** to make a hole in to draw off a liquid **3 :** to draw from or upon **4 :** to connect into (a telephone wire) to listen secretly — **tap·per** *n*

tap–dance *vb* **tap–danced; tap–danc·ing :** to perform a tap dance — **tap–danc·er** *n*

tap dance *n* **:** a kind of dance featuring loud tapping sounds from shoes with metal plates on the heels and toes

¹tape *n* **1 :** a narrow strip of material that is sticky on one side and is used to stick one thing to another **2 :** MAGNETIC TAPE **3 :** ¹VIDEOTAPE 2 **4 :** TAPE RECORDING **5 :** a narrow band of cloth or plastic

²tape *vb* **taped; tap·ing 1 :** to fasten, cover, or hold up with sticky tape **2 :** to make a recording of

tape deck *n* **:** a device used to play back and often to record on magnetic tapes

tape measure *n* **:** a flexible piece of material marked off for measuring

¹ta·per *n* **1 :** a slender candle **2 :** a gradual lessening in thickness or width in a long object

²taper *vb* **ta·pered; ta·per·ing 1 :** to make or become gradually smaller toward one end **2 :** to grow gradually less and less

tape recorder *n* **:** a device for recording on and playing back magnetic tapes

tape recording *n* **:** a recording made on magnetic tape

tap·es·try *n, pl* **tap·es·tries :** a heavy cloth that has designs or pictures woven into it and is used especially as a wall hanging — **tap·es·tried** *adj*

tape·worm *n* : a worm with a long flat body that lives as a parasite in the intestines of people and animals
tap·i·o·ca *n* : small pieces of starch from roots of a tropical plant used especially in puddings
ta·pir *n* : a large hoofed plant-eating animal of tropical America and southeastern Asia that has short thick legs, a short tail, and a long flexible snout
tap·root *n* : a main root of a plant that grows straight down and gives off smaller side roots
taps *n pl* : the last bugle call at night blown as a signal to put out the lights — used as singular or plural
¹tar *n* **1** : a thick dark sticky liquid made from wood, coal, or peat **2** : a substance (as one formed by burning tobacco) that resembles tar
²tar *vb* **tarred; tar·ring** : to cover with or as if with tar
ta·ran·tu·la *n* : a large hairy spider of warm regions of North and South America whose bite may be painful but is usually not serious to humans except for a few South American species
tar·dy *adj* **tar·di·er; tar·di·est** : not on time : LATE — **tar·di·ness** *n*
tar·get *n* **1** : a mark or object to shoot at or attack **2** : a person or thing that is talked about, criticized, or laughed at **3** : a goal to be reached
tar·iff *n* **1** : a list of taxes placed by a government on goods coming into a country **2** : the tax or the rate of taxation set up in a tariff list
¹tar·nish *vb* **tar·nished; tar·nish·ing** **1** : to make or become dull, dim, or discolored **2** : to bring disgrace or ruin
²tarnish *n* : a surface coating formed during tarnishing
tarp *n* : TARPAULIN
tar·pau·lin *n* : a sheet of waterproof canvas
¹tar·ry *vb* **tar·ried; tar·ry·ing** **1** : to be slow in coming or going **2** : to stay in or at a place
²tar·ry *adj* : like or covered with tar
¹tart *adj* **tart·er; tart·est** **1** : pleasantly sharp or sour to the taste **2** : having an unkind quality — **tart·ly** *adv* — **tart·ness** *n*
²tart *n* : a small pie often with no top crust
tar·tan *n* : a woolen cloth with a plaid design originally made in Scotland
tar·tar *n* : a crust that forms on the teeth and consists of plaque that has become hardened by the deposit of calcium-containing salts
tar·tar sauce *or* **tar·tare sauce** *n* : a sauce made chiefly of mayonnaise and chopped pickles
task *n* : a piece of work that has been assigned, needs to be done, or presents a challenge
task bar *n* : a row of icons usually at the bottom of a computer screen showing programs that may be used by selecting their icons
tas·sel *n* **1** : a hanging ornament (as on clothing) made of a bunch of cords of the same length fastened at one end **2** : the male flower cluster on the top of some plants and especially corn
¹taste *vb* **tast·ed; tast·ing** **1** : to find out the flavor of something by taking a little into the mouth **2** : to have a certain flavor **3** : to recognize by the sense of taste **4** : to eat or drink usually in small amounts **5** : ²EXPERIENCE — **tast·er** *n*
²taste *n* **1** : the sense by which sweet, sour, bitter, or salty flavors are detected through sense organs (**taste buds**) in the tongue **2** : the quality of something recognized by the sense of taste or by this together with smell and touch : FLAVOR **3** : a small amount tasted **4** : a personal liking **5** : the ability to choose and enjoy what is good or beautiful **6** : a sample of what something is like
taste·ful *adj* : having or showing the ability to choose what is good, beautiful, or proper — **taste·ful·ly** *adv*
taste·less *adj* **1** : having little flavor **2** : lacking the ability to choose what is good, beautiful, or proper — **taste·less·ly** *adv*
tasty *adj* **tast·i·er; tast·i·est** : pleasing to the taste — **tast·i·ness** *n*
tat·ter *n* **1** : a part torn and left hanging : SHRED **2 tatters** *pl* : ragged clothing
tat·tered *adj* **1** : torn in or worn to shreds **2** : dressed in ragged clothes
tat·tle *vb* **tat·tled; tat·tling** : to tell on someone — **tat·tler** *n*
tat·tle·tale *n* : a person who tells on someone
¹tat·too *vb* **tat·tooed; tat·too·ing** : to mark the body with a picture or pattern by using a needle to put color under the skin
²tattoo *n, pl* **tat·toos** : a picture or design made by putting color under the skin
taught *past and past participle of* TEACH
¹taunt *n* : a mean insulting remark
²taunt *vb* **taunt·ed; taunt·ing** : to make fun of or say insulting things to
Tau·rus *n* **1** : a constellation between Aries and Gemini imagined as a bull **2** : the second sign of the zodiac or a person born under this sign
taut *adj* **taut·er; taut·est** **1** : tightly stretched **2** : very tense **3** : firm and not flabby — **taut·ly** *adv*
tav·ern *n* **1** : a place where beer and liquor are sold and drunk **2** : INN
taw·ny *adj* **taw·ni·er; taw·ni·est** : of a brownish orange color

[1]**tax** *n* : money collected by the government from people or businesses for public use

[2]**tax** *vb* **taxed; tax·ing** **1 :** to require to pay money to a government for public use **2 :** to cause a strain on

tax·able *adj* : subject to tax

tax·a·tion *n* **1 :** the action of taxing **2 :** money gotten from taxes

[1]**taxi** *n, pl* **tax·is :** TAXICAB

[2]**taxi** *vb* **tax·ied; taxi·ing** **1 :** to run an airplane slowly along the ground under its own power **2 :** to go by taxicab

taxi·cab *n* : a vehicle that carries passengers for a fare usually based on the distance traveled

taxi·der·my *n* : the practice or job of preparing, stuffing, and mounting the skins of animals

tax·on·o·my *n* : classification of living things (as plants and animals) using a system that is usually based on natural relationships

tax·pay·er *n* : a person who pays or is responsible for paying a tax

TB *n* : TUBERCULOSIS

T–ball *n* : baseball for young children in which the ball is batted from a tee rather than being pitched

tbs., **tbsp.** *abbr* tablespoon

tea *n* **1 :** the dried leaves and leaf buds of a shrub widely grown in eastern and southern Asia **2 :** a drink made by soaking tea in boiling water **3 :** refreshments often including tea served in late afternoon **4 :** a party at which tea is served **5 :** a drink or medicine made by soaking plant parts (as dried roots)

teach *vb* **taught; teach·ing** **1 :** to help in learning how to do something : show how **2 :** to guide the studies of **3 :** to give lessons in **4 :** to cause to know the unpleasant results of something

teach·er *n* : a person who passes on information or skill

teaching *n* **1 :** the duties or profession of a teacher **2 :** something taught

tea·cup *n* : a cup used with a saucer for hot drinks

teak *n* : the hard yellowish-brown wood of a tall Asian tree that resists decay

tea·ket·tle *n* : a covered pot that is used for boiling water and has a handle and spout

teal *n* : a small wild duck of America and Europe

[1]**team** *n* **1 :** a group of persons who work or play together **2 :** two or more animals used to pull the same vehicle or piece of machinery

[2]**team** *vb* **teamed; team·ing :** to form a team

team·mate *n* : a person who belongs to the same team as someone else

team·ster *n* : a worker who drives a team or a truck

team·work *n* : the work of a group of persons acting together

tea·pot *n* : a pot for making and serving tea

[1]**tear** *n* **1 :** a drop of the salty liquid that moistens the eyes and the inner eyelids and that flows from the eyes when someone is crying **2** *pl* **:** an act of crying

[2]**tear** *vb* **tore; torn; tear·ing** **1 :** to pull into two or more pieces by force **2 :** to wound or injure by or as if by tearing **:** LACERATE **3 :** to remove by force **4 :** to move powerfully or swiftly — **tear down :** to knock down and break into pieces

[3]**tear** *n* : damage from being torn

tear·drop *n* : [1]TEAR

tear·ful *adj* : flowing with, accompanied by, or causing tears — **tear·ful·ly** *adv*

[1]**tease** *vb* **teased; teas·ing** **1 :** to make fun of **2 :** to annoy again and again — **teas·er** *n*

[2]**tease** *n* **1 :** the act of making fun of or repeatedly bothering a person or animal **2 :** a person who makes fun of people usually in a friendly way

tea·spoon *n* **1 :** a small spoon used especially for stirring drinks **2 :** a unit of measure used in cooking equal to $^1/_6$ fluid ounce or $^1/_3$ tablespoon (about 5 milliliters)

tea·spoon·ful *n, pl* **teaspoonfuls** *also* **tea·spoons·ful** **1 :** as much as a teaspoon can hold **2 :** TEASPOON

teat *n* : NIPPLE 1 — used mostly of domestic animals

tech·ni·cal *adj* **1 :** having special knowledge especially of a mechanical or scientific subject **2 :** relating to a practical or scientific subject **3 :** according to a strict explanation of the rules or facts — **tech·ni·cal·ly** *adv*

tech·ni·cal·i·ty *n, pl* **tech·ni·cal·i·ties :** something that is understood only by a person with special training

tech·ni·cian *n* : a person skilled in the details or techniques of a subject, art, or job

tech·nique *n* **1 :** the way in which basic physical movements or skills are used **2 :** the ability to use basic physical movements and skills **3 :** a way of doing something using special knowledge or skill

tech·no·log·i·cal *adj* : of or relating to technology

tech·nol·o·gist *n* : a person who specializes in technology

tech·nol·o·gy *n, pl* **tech·nol·o·gies** **1 :** the use of science in solving problems (as in industry or engineering) **2 :** a method of or machine for doing something that is created by technology

ted·dy bear *n* : a stuffed toy bear

te·dious *adj* : tiring because of length or dullness — **te·dious·ly** *adv* — **te·dious·ness** *n*

tee *n* : a device (as a post or peg) on which a ball is placed to be hit or kicked in various sports

teem *vb* **teemed; teem·ing** : to be full of something

teen·age *or* **teen·aged** *adj* : being or relating to teenagers

teen·ag·er *n* : a person between the ages of 13 and 19

teens *n pl* : the years 13 through 19 in a person's life

tee·ny *adj* **tee·ni·er; tee·ni·est** : TINY

tee shirt *variant of* T-SHIRT

tee·ter *vb* **tee·tered; tee·ter·ing** : to move unsteadily back and forth or from side to side

tee·ter–tot·ter *n* : [1]SEESAW 1

teeth *pl of* TOOTH

teethe *vb* **teethed; teeth·ing** : to experience the growth of teeth through the gums

TEFL *abbr* teaching English as a foreign language

tele- *or* **tel-** *prefix* **1** : at a distance **2** : television **3** : using a telephone

tele·gram *n* : a message sent by telegraph

[1]**tele·graph** *n* : an electric device or system for sending messages by a code over connecting wires

[2]**telegraph** *vb* **tele·graphed; tele·graph·ing** **1** : to send by code over connecting wires **2** : to send a telegram to

tele·mar·ket·ing *n* : the act of selling goods or services by telephone

te·lep·a·thy *n* : a way of communicating thoughts directly from one mind to another without speech or signs

[1]**tele·phone** *n* : a device for transmitting and receiving sounds over long distances

[2]**telephone** *vb* **tele·phoned; tele·phon·ing** : to speak to by telephone

[1]**tele·scope** *n* : a piece of equipment shaped like a long tube that has lenses for viewing objects at a distance and especially for observing objects in outer space

[2]**telescope** *vb* **tele·scoped; tele·scop·ing** : to slide or force one part into another

tele·vise *vb* **tele·vised; tele·vis·ing** : to send (a program) by television

tele·vi·sion *n* **1** : an electronic system of sending images and sound over a wire or through space by devices that change light and sound into electrical signals and then change these back into light and sound **2** : a piece of equipment with a screen and speakers that reproduces images and sound **3** : programs that are broadcast by television

tell *vb* **told; tell·ing** **1** : to let a person know something : to give information to **2** : [1]ORDER 2 **3** : to find out by observing **4** : [1]SAY 1 **5** : to describe in detail **6** : to make known **7** : to bring the bad behavior of to the attention of an authority **8** : [1]COUNT 1 **9** : to have a noticeable result **10** : to act as evidence

tell·er *n* **1** : a person who tells stories : NARRATOR **2** : a bank employee who receives and pays out money **3** : a person who counts votes

tell·tale *adj* : indicating or giving evidence of something

[1]**temper** *n* **1** : characteristic state of feeling **2** : calmness of mind **3** : an angry mood **4** : a tendency to be easily angered **5** : the hardness or toughness of a substance (as metal)

[2]**temper** *vb* **tem·pered; tem·per·ing** **1** : to make less severe or extreme : SOFTEN **2** : to heat and cool a substance (as steel) until it is as hard, tough, or flexible as is wanted

tem·per·a·ment *n* : a person's attitude as it affects what he or she says or does

tem·per·a·men·tal *adj* **1** : likely to become angry or upset **2** : unpredictable in behavior or performance — **tem·per·a·men·tal·ly** *adv*

tem·per·ance *n* **1** : control over actions, thoughts, or feelings **2** : the use of little or no liquor

tem·per·ate *adj* **1** : keeping or held within limits : not extreme or excessive **2** : not drinking much liquor **3** : showing self-control **4** : having a mild climate that is not too hot or too cold

tem·per·a·ture *n* **1** : degree of hotness or coldness as measured on a scale **2** : abnormally high body heat : FEVER

tem·pest *n* **1** : a strong wind often accompanied by rain, hail, or snow **2** : UPROAR

tem·pes·tu·ous *adj* : very stormy

[1]**tem·ple** *n* : a building for worship

[2]**temple** *n* : the flattened space on either side of the forehead

tem·po *n, pl* **tem·pi** *or* **tempos** : the rate of speed at which a musical composition is played or sung

tem·po·rary *adj* : not permanent — **tem·po·rar·i·ly** *adv*

tempt *vb* **tempt·ed; tempt·ing** : to consider or cause to consider doing something wrong or unwise — **tempt·er** *n*

temp·ta·tion *n* **1** : the act of considering or causing to consider doing something wrong or unwise **2** : a strong desire **3** : something that causes a strong desire

[1]**ten** *adj* : being one more than nine

[2]**ten** *n* **1** : one more than nine : two times five : 10 **2** : the tenth in a set or series

te·na·cious *adj* **1** : PERSISTENT **2** : not easily pulled apart

te·nac·i·ty *n* : the quality or state of being persistent

¹ten·ant *n* : a person or business that rents property from its owner

²tenant *vb* **ten·ant·ed; ten·ant·ing** : to hold or live in as a renter

¹tend *vb* **tend·ed; tend·ing** **1** : to take care of **2** : to pay attention **3** : to manage the operation of

²tend *vb* **tended; tending** **1** : to be likely **2** : to move or turn in a certain direction

ten·den·cy *n, pl* **ten·den·cies** **1** : a leaning toward a particular kind of thought or action **2** : a way of doing something that is becoming more common : TREND

¹ten·der *adj* **ten·der·er; ten·der·est** **1** : not tough **2** : DELICATE 4 **3** : YOUNG 1 **4** : feeling or showing love **5** : very easily hurt — **ten·der·ly** *adv* — **ten·der·ness** *n*

²tender *vb* **ten·dered; ten·der·ing** **1** : to offer in payment **2** : to present for acceptance

³tender *n* **1** : ²OFFER 3 **2** : something (as money) that may be offered in payment

⁴tend·er *n* **1** : a boat that carries passengers or freight to a larger ship **2** : a car attached to a locomotive for carrying fuel or water

ten·der·heart·ed *adj* : easily affected with feelings of love, pity, or sorrow

ten·don *n* : a band of tough white fiber connecting a muscle to another part (as a bone)

ten·dril *n* **1** : a slender leafless winding stem by which some climbing plants attach themselves to a support **2** : something that winds like a plant's tendril

ten·e·ment *n* : a building divided into separate apartments for rent

Tenn. *abbr* Tennessee

ten·nis *n* : a game played on a level court by two or four players who use rackets to hit a ball back and forth across a low net dividing the court

ten·or *n* **1** : the next to the lowest part in harmony having four parts **2** : the highest male singing voice **3** : a singer or an instrument having a tenor range or part

¹tense *n* : a form of a verb used to show the time of the action or state

²tense *adj* **tens·er; tens·est** **1** : feeling or showing worry or nervousness : not relaxed **2** : marked by strain or uncertainty **3** : stretched tight — **tense·ly** *adv* — **tense·ness** *n*

³tense *vb* **tensed; tens·ing** **1** : to make or become worried or nervous **2** : to make (a muscle) hard and tight

ten·sion *n* **1** : the act of straining or stretching : the condition of being strained or stretched **2** : a state of worry or nervousness **3** : a state of unfriendliness

tent *n* : a portable shelter (as of canvas) stretched and supported by poles

ten·ta·cle *n* : one of the long thin flexible parts that stick out around the head or the mouth of an animal (as a jellyfish or sea anemone) and are used especially for feeling or grasping

ten·ta·tive *adj* **1** : not final **2** : showing caution or hesitation — **ten·ta·tive·ly** *adv*

tent caterpillar *n* : a caterpillar that lives in groups which spin a large silken web resembling a tent

tent city *n* : a group of many tents set up in an area to provide shelter (as for refugees or homeless people)

¹tenth *adj* : coming right after ninth

²tenth *n* **1** : number ten in a series **2** : one of ten equal parts

te·pee *n* : a tent shaped like a cone and used as a home by some American Indians

tep·id *adj* : LUKEWARM 1

¹term *n* **1** : a word or expression that has an exact meaning in some uses or is limited to a subject or field **2** : a period of time fixed especially by law or custom **3 terms** *pl* : conditions that limit the nature and scope of something (as a treaty or a will) **4 terms** *pl* : relationship between people **5** : any one of the numbers in a series **6** : the numerator or denominator of a fraction

²term *vb* **termed; term·ing** : to call by a particular name

¹ter·mi·nal *adj* : relating to or forming an end

²terminal *n* **1** : either end of a transportation line or a passenger or freight station located at it **2** : a device (as in a computer system) used to put in, receive, and display information **3** : a device at the end of a wire or on a machine for making an electrical connection

ter·mi·nate *vb* **ter·mi·nat·ed; ter·mi·nat·ing** : END, CLOSE

ter·mi·na·tion *n* **1** : the end of something **2** : the act of ending something

ter·mi·nus *n, pl* **ter·mi·ni** *or* **ter·mi·nus·es** **1** : an ending point **2** : the end of a travel route **3** : a station at the end of a travel route

ter·mite *n* : a chewing antlike insect of a light color that lives in large colonies and feeds on wood

tern *n* : a small slender seagull with black cap, white body, and narrow wings

¹ter·race *n* **1** : a level area next to a building **2** : a raised piece of land with the top leveled **3** : a row of houses on raised ground or a slope

²terrace *vb* **ter·raced; ter·rac·ing** : to form into a terrace or supply with terraces

ter·rain *n* : the features of the surface of a piece of land

ter·ra·pin *n* **:** a North American turtle that lives in or near fresh or somewhat salty water

ter·rar·i·um *n, pl* **ter·rar·ia** *or* **ter·rar·i·ums** **:** a usually glass container used for keeping plants or small animals (as turtles) indoors

ter·res·tri·al *adj* **1 :** relating to the earth or its people **2 :** living or growing on land

ter·ri·ble *adj* **1 :** very great in degree **2 :** very bad **3 :** causing great fear — **ter·ri·bly** *adv*

ter·ri·er *n* **:** a usually small dog originally used by hunters to force animals from their holes

ter·rif·ic *adj* **1 :** EXCELLENT **2 :** very unusual **:** EXTRAORDINARY **3 :** causing terror **:** TERRIBLE

ter·ri·fy *vb* **ter·ri·fied; ter·ri·fy·ing :** to cause (someone) to become very frightened

ter·ri·to·ri·al *adj* **1 :** of or relating to a territory **2 :** displaying behavior associated with defending an animal's territory

ter·ri·to·ry *n, pl* **ter·ri·to·ries 1 :** a geographical area belonging to or under the rule of a government **2 :** a part of the United States not included within any state but organized with a separate governing body **3 :** REGION 1, DISTRICT **4 :** an area that is occupied and defended by an animal or group of animals

ter·ror *n* **1 :** a state of great fear **2 :** a cause of great fear

ter·ror·ism *n* **:** the use of violence as a means of achieving a goal

ter·ror·ist *n* **:** someone who engages in terrorism

ter·ror·ize *vb* **ter·ror·ized; ter·ror·iz·ing 1 :** to fill with fear **2 :** to use terrorism against

terse *adj* **ters·er; ters·est :** being brief and to the point — **terse·ly** *adv*

¹test *n* **1 :** a set of questions or problems by which a person's knowledge, intelligence, or skills are measured **2 :** a means of finding out the nature, quality, or value of something

²test *vb* **test·ed; test·ing 1 :** to measure a person's knowledge, intelligence, or skills **2 :** to find out the nature, quality, or value of something

tes·ta·ment *n* **1 :** either of two main parts (**Old Testament** and **New Testament**) of the Bible **2 :** ²WILL 4

tes·ti·fy *vb* **tes·ti·fied; tes·ti·fy·ing :** to make a formal statement of something sworn to be true

tes·ti·mo·ny *n, pl* **tes·ti·mo·nies :** a statement made by a witness under oath especially in a court

tes·tis *n, pl* **tes·tes :** a male reproductive gland that produces sperm

test tube *n* **:** a plain tube of thin glass closed at one end and used especially in chemistry and biology

tet·a·nus *n* **:** a serious disease that is marked by spasms of the muscles especially of the jaws and that is caused by poison from a bacterium that usually enters the body through a wound

¹teth·er *vb* **teth·ered; teth·er·ing :** to fasten by a line that limits range of movement

²tether *n* **:** a line by which something is fastened so as to limit where it can go

Tex. *abbr* Texas

¹text *n* **1 :** the actual words of an author's work **2 :** the main body of printed or written matter on a page **3 :** TEXTBOOK **4 :** a passage from the Bible chosen as the subject of a sermon **5 :** TEXT MESSAGE

²text *vb* **:** to send a text message from one cell phone to another **:** to communicate by text messages — **text·er** *n*

text·book *n* **:** a book used in the study of a subject

tex·tile *n* **:** a woven or knit cloth

text message *n* **:** a short message sent electronically usually from one cell phone to another

tex·ture *n* **:** the structure, feel, and appearance of something

-th *or* **-eth** *adj suffix* — used to form numbers that show the place of something in a series

than *conj* **:** when compared to the way in which, the extent to which, or the degree to which

thank *vb* **thanked; thank·ing 1 :** to express gratitude to **2 :** to hold responsible

thank·ful *adj* **1 :** feeling or showing thanks **:** GRATEFUL **2 :** GLAD — **thank·ful·ly** *adv* — **thank·ful·ness** *n*

thank·less *adj* **1 :** UNGRATEFUL **2 :** not appreciated

thanks *n pl* **1 :** GRATITUDE **2 :** an expression of gratitude (as for something received) — **thanks to 1 :** with the help of **2 :** because of

thanks·giv·ing *n* **1** *cap* **:** THANKSGIVING DAY **2 :** a prayer or an expression of gratitude

Thanksgiving Day *n* **1 :** the fourth Thursday in November observed as a legal holiday in the US for giving thanks **2 :** the second Monday in October observed as a legal holiday in Canada for giving thanks

¹that *pron, pl* **those 1 :** the person or thing seen, mentioned, or understood **2 :** the time, action, or event mentioned **3 :** the one farther away **4 :** the one **:** the kind

²that *conj* **1** — used to introduce a clause that modifies a noun or adjective **2** — used to introduce a clause that modifies an adverb or adverbial expression **3** — used to

DICTIONARY

introduce a noun clause serving especially as the subject or object of a verb **4 :** ^{2}so 1 **5** — used to introduce a clause naming a result **6 :** BECAUSE

[3]**that** *adj, pl* **those** **1 :** being the one mentioned, indicated, or understood **2 :** being the one farther away

[4]**that** *pron* **1 :** WHO 2, WHOM, WHICH **2 :** in, on, or at which

[5]**that** *adv* **:** to the extent or degree shown (as by the hands)

[1]**thatch** *n* **:** a plant material (as straw) for use as roofing

[2]**thatch** *vb* **thatched; thatch·ing :** to cover (a roof) with straw or other plant material

[1]**thaw** *vb* **thawed; thaw·ing** **1 :** to melt or cause to melt **2 :** to grow less unfriendly or quiet in manner

[2]**thaw** *n* **1 :** a period of weather warm enough to melt ice and snow **2 :** the action, fact, or process of becoming less hostile or unfriendly

[1]**the** *definite article* **1 :** that or those mentioned, seen, or clearly understood **2 :** that or those near in space, time, or thought **3 :** ^{1}EACH **4 :** that or those considered best, most typical, or most worth singling out **5 :** any one typical of or standing for the entire class named **6 :** all those that are

[2]**the** *adv* **1 :** than before **2 :** to what extent **:** by how much **3 :** to that extent **:** by that much

the·ater *or chiefly Can and Brit* **the·atre** *n* **1 :** a building in which plays, motion pictures, or shows are presented **2 :** the art or profession of producing plays **3 :** plays or the performance of plays **4 :** a place or area where some important action is carried on

the·at·ri·cal *adj* **:** for or relating to the presentation of plays

thee *pron, objective case of* THOU

theft *n* **:** the act of stealing

their *adj* **:** of or relating to them or themselves especially as owners or as agents or objects of an action

theirs *pron* **:** that which belongs to them

them *pron, objective case of* THEY

theme *n* **1 :** a subject of a work of art, music, or literature **2 :** a specific quality, characteristic, or concern **3 :** a written exercise **:** ESSAY

theme park *n* **:** an amusement park in which the rides and buildings are based on a central subject

them·selves *pron* **:** their own selves

[1]**then** *adv* **1 :** at that time **2 :** soon after that **:** NEXT **3 :** in addition **:** BESIDES **4 :** in that case **5 :** as an expected result

[2]**then** *n* **:** that time

[3]**then** *adj* **:** existing or acting at that time

thence *adv* **1 :** from that place **2 :** from that fact

thence·forth *adv* **:** from that time on

the·ol·o·gy *n, pl* **the·ol·o·gies :** the study and explanation of religious faith, practice, and experience

the·o·ry *n, pl* **the·o·ries** **1 :** an idea or opinion that is presented as true **2 :** a general rule offered to explain a scientific phenomenon **3 :** the general rules followed in a science or an art

ther·a·peu·tic *adj* **:** MEDICINAL

ther·a·pist *n* **:** a person specializing in treating disorders or injuries of the body or mind especially in ways that do not involve drugs and surgery

ther·a·py *n, pl* **ther·a·pies :** treatment of a disorder or injury of the body or mind

[1]**there** *adv* **1 :** in or at that place **2 :** to or into that place **3 :** in that situation or way **4** — used to show satisfaction, soothing, or defiance **5** — used to attract attention

[2]**there** *pron* — used to introduce a sentence in which the subject comes after the verb

[3]**there** *n* **:** that place

there·abouts *also* **there·about** *adv* **1 :** near that place or time **2 :** near that number, degree, or amount

there·af·ter *adv* **:** after that

there·by *adv* **:** by that

there·fore *adv* **:** for that reason

there·in *adv* **:** in or into that place, time, or thing

there·of *adv* **:** of that or it

there·on *adv* **:** on that

there·to *adv* **:** to that

there·up·on *adv* **1 :** on that thing **2 :** for that reason **3 :** immediately after that **:** at once

there·with *adv* **:** with that

ther·mal *adj* **:** of, relating to, or caused by heat

ther·mom·e·ter *n* **:** an instrument for measuring temperature

ther·mos *n* **:** a container (as a bottle or jar) that has a vacuum between an inner and an outer wall and is used to keep liquids hot or cold for several hours

ther·mo·stat *n* **:** a device that automatically controls temperature

the·sau·rus *n, pl* **the·sau·ri** *or* **the·sau·rus·es :** a book of words and their synonyms

these *pl of* THIS

the·sis *n, pl* **the·ses** **1 :** a statement that a person wants to discuss or prove **2 :** an essay presenting results of original research

they *pron* **:** those individuals **:** those ones

they'd : they had **:** they would

they'll : they shall **:** they will

they're : they are

they've : they have

thi·a·mine *also* **thi·a·min** *n* : a type of vitamin B that is used by the body to convert carbohydrates into energy and to maintain normal nerve function

¹thick *adj* **thick·er; thick·est** **1** : having great size from one surface to its opposite **2** : closely packed together **3** : heavily built **4** : not flowing easily **5** : measuring a certain amount in the smallest of three dimensions **6** : producing speech that is hard to understand **7** : STUPID 1 **8** : occurring in large numbers : NUMEROUS **9** : having haze, fog, or mist **10** : too intense to see in — **thick·ly** *adv*

²thick *n* **1** : the most crowded or active part **2** : the part of greatest thickness

thick·en *vb* **thick·ened; thick·en·ing** : to make or become thick — **thick·en·er** *n*

thick·et *n* : a thick usually small patch of bushes or low trees

thick·ness *n* **1** : the quality or state of being thick **2** : the smallest of three dimensions

thick·set *adj* : STOCKY

thief *n, pl* **thieves** : a person who steals : ROBBER

thieve *vb* **thieved; thiev·ing** : ¹STEAL 1, ROB

thiev·ery *n* : THEFT

thigh *n* : the part of a leg between the hip and the knee

thim·ble *n* : a cap or cover used in sewing to protect the finger that pushes the needle

¹thin *adj* **thin·ner; thin·nest** **1** : having little body fat **2** : having little size from one surface to its opposite : not thick **3** : having the parts not close together **4** : flowing very easily **5** : having less than the usual number **6** : not very convincing **7** : somewhat weak or high **8** : having less oxygen than normal — **thin·ly** *adv* — **thin·ness** *n*

²thin *vb* **thinned; thin·ning** : to make or become smaller in thickness or number

thine *pron, archaic* : YOURS — used as singular or plural

thing *n* **1** : an act or matter that is or is to be done **2** : something that exists and can be talked about **3 things** *pl* : personal possessions **4** : ¹DETAIL 2 **5 things** *pl* : existing conditions and circumstance **6** : EVENT 1 **7** : ¹DEED 1, ACHIEVEMENT, ACT **8** : a piece of clothing **9** : what is needed or wanted **10** : an action or interest especially that someone enjoys very much **11** : ²INDIVIDUAL 1 **12** : a spoken or written observation or point

think *vb* **thought; think·ing** **1** : to have as an opinion or belief **2** : to form or have in the mind **3** : REMEMBER 1 **4** : to use the power of the mind to understand, find out, or decide **5** : to consider for some time : PONDER **6** : to invent something by thinking **7** : to hold a strong feeling **8** : to have as a plan **9** : to care about — **think·er** *n*

thin·ner *n* : a liquid used to thin paint

¹third *adj* : coming right after second

²third *n* **1** : number three in a series **2** : one of three equal parts

third person *n* : a set of words or forms (as pronouns or verb forms) referring to people or things that are not being addressed directly

¹thirst *n* **1** : a feeling of dryness in the mouth and throat that accompanies a need for liquids **2** : the bodily condition that produces thirst **3** : a strong desire

²thirst *vb* **thirst·ed; thirst·ing** **1** : to feel a need for liquids **2** : to have a strong desire

thirsty *adj* **thirst·i·er; thirst·i·est** **1** : feeling a need for liquids **2** : needing moisture **3** : having a strong desire : EAGER — **thirst·i·ly** *adv*

¹thir·teen *adj* : being one more than twelve

²thirteen *n* : one more than twelve : 13

¹thir·teenth *adj* : coming right after twelfth

²thirteenth *n* : number 13 in a series

¹thir·ti·eth *adj* : coming right after 29th

²thirtieth *n* : number 30 in a series

¹thir·ty *adj* : being three times ten

²thirty *n* : three times ten : 30

¹this *pron, pl* **these** **1** : the one nearer **2** : the person, thing, or idea that is present or near in place, time, or thought or that has just been mentioned

²this *adj, pl* **these** **1** : being the one present, near in place, time, or thought or that has just been mentioned **2** : being the one nearer

³this *adv* **1** : to the degree suggested by something in the present situation **2** : to the extent shown (as with the hands)

this·tle *n* : a prickly plant that has usually purplish often showy heads of flowers

thith·er *adv* : to that place : THERE

thong *n* **1** : a strip of leather used especially for fastening something **2** : a sandal held on by straps that run across the foot and between the big and second toe

tho·rax *n, pl* **tho·rax·es** *or* **tho·ra·ces** **1** : the part of the body of a mammal that lies between the neck and the abdomen and contains the heart and lungs **2** : the middle of the three main divisions of the body of an insect

thorn *n* **1** : a hard sharp leafless point on the stem or branch of a plant (as a rose bush) **2** : a bush or tree that has thorns

thorny *adj* **thorn·i·er; thorn·i·est** **1** : full of or covered with thorns **2** : full of difficulties

thor·ough *adj* **1** : being such to the fullest degree : COMPLETE **2** : careful about little things — **thor·ough·ly** *adv* — **thor·ough·ness** *n*

[1]**thor·ough·bred** *adj* **:** PUREBRED

[2]**thoroughbred** *n* **1** *cap* **:** a speedy horse of an English breed kept mainly for racing **2** **:** a purebred animal **3 :** a very educated or skilled person

thor·ough·fare *n* **1 :** a street or road open at both ends **2 :** a main road

thor·ough·go·ing *adj* **:** THOROUGH 1

those *pl of* THAT

thou *pron, archaic* **:** YOU

[1]**though** *conj* **:** ALTHOUGH

[2]**though** *adv* **:** HOWEVER 3, NEVERTHELESS

[1]**thought** *past and past participle of* THINK

[2]**thought** *n* **1 :** the act or process of thinking **2 :** something (as an idea or opinion) formed in the mind **3 :** serious attention

thought·ful *adj* **1 :** considerate of others **2 :** deep in thought **3 :** showing careful thinking — **thought·ful·ly** *adv* — **thought·ful·ness** *n*

thought·less *adj* **1 :** not considerate of others **2 :** not careful and alert **3 :** done without thinking — **thought·less·ly** *adv* — **thought·less·ness** *n*

[1]**thou·sand** *n* **1 :** ten times one hundred **:** 1000 **2 :** a very large number

[2]**thousand** *adj* **:** being 1000

[1]**thou·sandth** *adj* **:** coming right after 999th

[2]**thousandth** *n* **:** number 1000 in a series

thrash *vb* **thrashed; thrash·ing** **1 :** to beat very hard **2 :** to move about violently **3** **:** THRESH 1

thrash·er *n* **:** an American bird (as the common reddish brown **brown thrasher**) related to the mockingbird and noted for its song

[1]**thread** *n* **1 :** a thin fine cord formed by spinning and twisting short fibers into a continuous strand **2 :** a thin fine line or strand of something **3 :** the ridge or groove that winds around a screw **4 :** a train of thought that connects the parts of something (as an argument or story) — **thread·like** *adj*

[2]**thread** *vb* **thread·ed; thread·ing** **1 :** to put a thread in working position (as in a needle) **2 :** to pass something through another thing **3 :** to make a way through or between **4** **:** to put together on a thread **:** STRING

thread·bare *adj* **1 :** worn so much that the thread shows **:** SHABBY **2 :** not effective because of overuse

threat *n* **1 :** the act of showing an intention to do harm **2 :** someone or something that threatens

threat·en *vb* **threat·ened; threat·en·ing** **1** **:** to show an intention to do harm or something unwanted **2 :** to give warning of by an indication — **threat·en·ing·ly** *adv*

[1]**three** *adj* **:** being one more than two

[2]**three** *n* **1 :** one more than two **:** 3 **2 :** the third in a set or series

3–D *adj* **:** THREE-DIMENSIONAL 2

three–dimensional *adj* **1 :** relating to or having the three dimensions of length, width, and height **2 :** giving the appearance of depth or varying distances

three·fold *adj* **:** being three times as great or as many

three·score *adj* **:** [1]SIXTY

thresh *vb* **threshed; thresh·ing** **1 :** to separate the seed from a harvested plant by beating **2 :** THRASH 2

thresh·er *n* **:** THRESHING MACHINE

threshing machine *n* **:** a machine used to separate grain from harvested plants

thresh·old *n* **1 :** the sill of a door **2 :** a point or place of beginning or entering

threw *past of* THROW

thrice *adv* **:** three times

thrift *n* **:** careful management especially of money

thrifty *adj* **thrift·i·er; thrift·i·est** **:** carefully and wisely managing money

[1]**thrill** *vb* **thrilled; thrill·ing** **:** to have or cause to have a sudden feeling of excitement or pleasure — **thrill·er** *n*

[2]**thrill** *n* **1 :** a sudden strong feeling especially of excitement or happiness **2 :** something that produces a feeling of excitement

thrive *vb* **thrived** *or* **throve; thrived** *also* **thriv·en; thriv·ing** **:** to grow or develop very well **:** FLOURISH

throat *n* **1 :** the passage through the neck from the mouth to the stomach and lungs **2** **:** the front part of the neck on the outside

throaty *adj* **throat·i·er; throat·i·est** **:** uttered or produced in deep low tones

[1]**throb** *vb* **throbbed; throb·bing** **1 :** to feel repeated pangs of pain **2 :** to beat hard or fast **3 :** to beat or rotate in a normal way

[2]**throb** *n* **1 :** [2]BEAT 2, PULSE **2 :** pain that comes in repeated pangs

throne *n* **1 :** the chair used by a monarch or bishop for ceremonies **2 :** the position of king or queen

[1]**throng** *n* **:** a large group of people **:** CROWD

[2]**throng** *vb* **thronged; throng·ing** **:** [1]CROWD 4

[1]**throt·tle** *vb* **throt·tled; throt·tling** **1 :** to strangle or choke (someone) **2 :** to reduce the speed of (an engine) by closing the throttle valve

[2]**throttle** *n* **:** a valve or a lever that controls the valve for regulating the flow of steam or fuel in an engine

[1]**through** *prep* **1 :** into at one side and out at the other side of **2 :** from one side or end to another of **3 :** by way of **4 :** AMONG 1 **5** **:** by means of **6 :** over the whole of **7 :** dur-

ing the whole of **8 :** to and including **9 :** into and out of

[2]**through** *adv* **1 :** from one end or side to the other **2 :** from beginning to end **3 :** to completion **4 :** in or to every part

[3]**through** *adj* **1 :** having reached an end **2 :** allowing free or continuous passage **3 :** going from point of origin to destination without changes or transfers **4 :** coming from and going to points outside a local zone

[1]**through·out** *adv* **1 :** EVERYWHERE **2 :** from beginning to end

[2]**throughout** *prep* **1 :** in or to every part of **2 :** during the whole period of

throve *past of* THRIVE

[1]**throw** *vb* **threw; thrown; throw·ing 1 :** to send through the air with a quick forward motion of the arm **2 :** to put suddenly in a certain position or condition **3 :** to cause to fall **4 :** to put on or take off in a hurry **5 :** to move (the body or part of the body) in a certain way **6 :** to move (as a window or switch) to an open or closed position **7 :** to give by way of entertainment — **throw·er** *n* — **throw away 1 :** to get rid of **:** DISCARD **2 :** SQUANDER, WASTE — **throw out 1 :** to get rid of **2 :** to remove from a place, position, or participation **3 :** to give off **4 :** to cause to project **:** EXTEND — **throw up :** [2]VOMIT

[2]**throw** *n* **1 :** an act of causing something to move with a motion of the arm **2 :** the distance something is or may be sent with a motion of the arm

thrum *vb* **thrummed; thrum·ming :** to play a stringed instrument idly **:** STRUM

thrush *n* **:** a usually brown bird that has a spotted breast and a melodious song

[1]**thrust** *vb* **thrust; thrust·ing 1 :** to push with force **:** SHOVE **2 :** PIERCE 1, STAB **3 :** EXTEND **4 :** to press the acceptance of on someone

[2]**thrust** *n* **1 :** a push or jab with a pointed weapon **2 :** a military attack **3 :** a forward or upward push

thru·way *n* **:** EXPRESSWAY

Thu. *abbr* Thursday

[1]**thud** *n* **:** a dull sound **:** THUMP

[2]**thud** *vb* **thud·ded; thud·ding :** to move, strike, or pound so as to make a dull sound

thug *n* **:** a violent person or criminal

[1]**thumb** *n* **1 :** the short thick finger next to the forefinger **2 :** the part of a glove covering the thumb

[2]**thumb** *vb* **thumbed; thumb·ing 1 :** to turn the pages of quickly with the thumb **2 :** to seek or get (a ride) in a passing automobile by signaling with the thumb

thumb drive *n* **:** a small usually rectangular device used for storing and transferring computer data **:** FLASH DRIVE

thumb·tack *n* **:** a tack with a broad flat head for pressing into a board or wall with the thumb

[1]**thump** *vb* **thumped; thump·ing 1 :** to strike or beat with something thick or heavy so as to cause a dull sound **2 :** to beat hard **:** POUND

[2]**thump** *n* **1 :** a blow with something blunt or heavy **2 :** the sound made by or as if by a blow with something blunt or heavy

[1]**thun·der** *n* **1 :** the loud sound that follows a flash of lightning **2 :** a loud noise

[2]**thunder** *vb* **thun·dered; thun·der·ing 1 :** to produce thunder **2 :** to make a loud sound **3 :** [1]ROAR 1, SHOUT

thun·der·bolt *n* **:** a flash of lightning and the thunder that follows it

thun·der·cloud *n* **:** a dark storm cloud that produces lightning and thunder

thun·der·head *n* **:** a rounded mass of dark cloud with white edges often appearing before a thunderstorm

thun·der·show·er *n* **:** a shower with thunder and lightning

thun·der·storm *n* **:** a storm with thunder and lightning

thun·der·struck *adj* **:** stunned as if struck by a thunderbolt

Thur., Thurs. *abbr* Thursday

Thurs·day *n* **:** the fifth day of the week

thus *adv* **1 :** in this or that way **2 :** to this degree or extent **:** SO **3 :** because of this or that **:** THEREFORE

thwart *vb* **thwart·ed; thwart·ing :** to stop from happening or succeeding

thy *adj, archaic* **:** YOUR

thyme *n* **:** a mint with tiny fragrant leaves used especially in cooking

thy·roid *n* **:** a gland at the base of the neck that produces hormones which affect growth, development, and the rate at which the body uses energy

thy·self *pron, archaic* **:** YOURSELF

ti *n* **:** the seventh note of the musical scale

tib·ia *n, pl* **tib·i·ae** *also* **tib·i·as :** the inner and larger of the two bones between the knee and ankle

[1]**tick** *n* **1 :** a light rhythmic tap or beat (as of a clock) **2 :** a small mark used chiefly to draw attention to something or to check an item on a list

[2]**tick** *vb* **ticked; tick·ing 1 :** to make a light rhythmic tap or a series of light rhythmic taps **2 :** to mark, count, or announce by or as if by light rhythmic taps **3 :** [2]CHECK 4 **4 :** OPERATE 1, FUNCTION

[3]**tick** *n* **:** a tiny animal with eight legs that is related to the spider and attaches itself to

humans and animals from which it sucks blood

[1]**tick·et** *n* **1 :** a document or token showing that a fare or a fee for admission or participation has been paid **2 :** a summons or warning issued to a person who breaks a traffic law **3 :** a list of candidates for nomination or election **4 :** a slip or card recording a sale or giving information **5 :** the correct or desirable thing

[2]**ticket** *vb* **tick·et·ed; tick·et·ing** **1 :** to attach a tag to **:** LABEL **2 :** to give a traffic ticket to

[1]**tick·le** *vb* **tick·led; tick·ling** **1 :** to have a tingling or prickling sensation **2 :** to touch (a body part) lightly so as to cause laughter or jerky movements **3 :** to excite or stir up agreeably **4 :** AMUSE 2

[2]**tickle** *n* **:** a tingling or prickling sensation

tick·lish *adj* **1 :** sensitive to tickling **2 :** calling for careful handling

tid·al *adj* **:** of or relating to tides **:** flowing and ebbing like tides

tidal wave *n* **1 :** a very high sea wave that sometimes follows an earthquake **2 :** an unusual rise of water along a shore due to strong winds

tid·bit *n* **1 :** a small tasty piece of food **2 :** a small interesting but unimportant bit (as of news)

[1]**tide** *n* **1 :** the rising and falling of the surface of the ocean caused twice daily by the attraction of the sun and the moon **2 :** something that rises and falls or rushes in a mass

[2]**tide** *vb* **tid·ed; tid·ing** **:** to help to overcome or put up with a difficulty

tide pool *n* **:** a pool of salt water that is left behind when the tide goes out and in which small sea animals (as snails, crabs, and barnacles) are often found

tid·ings *n pl* **:** NEWS 4

[1]**ti·dy** *adj* **ti·di·er; ti·di·est** **1 :** well ordered and cared for **:** NEAT **2 :** LARGE, SUBSTANTIAL — **ti·di·ness** *n*

[2]**tidy** *vb* **ti·died; ti·dy·ing** **:** to make things neat

[1]**tie** *n* **1 :** NECKTIE **2 :** an equality in number (as of votes or scores) **3 :** a contest that ends with an equal score **4 :** one of the cross supports to which railroad rails are fastened **5 :** a connecting link **:** BOND **6 :** a line, ribbon, or cord used for fastening, joining, or closing **7 :** a part (as a beam or rod) holding two pieces together

[2]**tie** *vb* **tied; ty·ing** *or* **tie·ing** **1 :** to fasten, attach, or close by means of a tie **2 :** to form a knot or bow in **3 :** to bring together firmly **:** UNITE **4 :** to hold back from freedom of action **5 :** to make or have an equal score with in a contest

tier *n* **:** a row, rank, or layer usually arranged in a series one above the other

tiff *n* **:** a minor quarrel

ti·ger *n* **:** a large Asian meat-eating animal of the cat family that is light brown with black stripes

[1]**tight** *adj* **tight·er; tight·est** **1 :** very closely packed or compressed **2 :** fixed or held very firmly in place **3 :** fitting too closely **4 :** firmly stretched or drawn **:** TAUT **5 :** difficult to get through or out of **6 :** firm in control **7 :** STINGY 1 **8 :** low in supply **:** SCARCE **9 :** painfully or uncomfortably tense **10 :** barely allowing enough time — **tight·ly** *adv* — **tight·ness** *n*

[2]**tight** *adv* **1 :** in a firm, secure, or close manner **2 :** in a deep and uninterrupted manner **:** SOUNDLY

tight·en *vb* **tight·ened; tight·en·ing** **:** to make or become tight

tight·rope *n* **:** a rope or wire stretched tight on which an acrobat performs

tights *n pl* **:** a garment closely fitted to the body and covering it usually from the waist down

tight·wad *n* **:** a stingy person

ti·gress *n* **:** a female tiger

til·de *n* **:** a mark ˜ placed especially over the letter *n* (as in Spanish *señor*) to indicate a sound that is approximately \nyə\

[1]**tile** *n* **1 :** a thin piece of material (as plastic, stone, or clay) used for roofs, walls, floors, or drains **2 :** a small flat piece used in a game

[2]**tile** *vb* **tiled; til·ing** **:** to cover with tiles

[1]**till** *prep or conj* **:** UNTIL

[2]**till** *vb* **tilled; till·ing** **:** to work by plowing, sowing, and raising crops on

[3]**till** *n* **:** a drawer for money

till·age *n* **:** the practice of working land by plowing, sowing, and raising crops on

[1]**til·ler** *n* **:** a lever used to turn the rudder of a boat from side to side

[2]**tiller** *n* **:** someone or something that tills land

[1]**tilt** *vb* **tilt·ed; tilt·ing** **:** to move or shift so as to slant or tip

[2]**tilt** *n* **1 :** [2]SLANT **2 :** [1]SPEED 2

tim·ber *n* **1 :** wood suitable for building or for carpentry **2 :** a large squared piece of wood ready for use or forming part of a structure

tim·ber·land *n* **:** wooded land especially as a source of timber

tim·ber·line *n* **:** the upper limit beyond which trees do not grow (as on mountains)

[1]**time** *n* **1 :** a period during which an action, process, or condition exists or continues **2 :** a point or period when something occurs **:** OCCASION **3 :** one of a series of repeated instances or actions **4 :** a moment, hour, day, or year as shown by a clock or calendar **5 :** a set or usual moment or hour for

something to occur **6 :** a historical period **:** AGE **7 :** conditions of a period — usually used in pl. **8 times** *pl* **:** added quantities or examples **9 :** a person's experience during a certain period **10 :** a part of the day when a person is free to do as he or she pleases **11 :** rate of speed **:** TEMPO **12 :** a system of determining time **13 :** RHYTHM — **at times :** SOMETIMES — **for the time being :** for the present — **from time to time :** once in a while — **in time 1 :** soon enough **2 :** as time goes by **:** EVENTUALLY **3 :** at the correct speed in music — **time after time :** over and over again — **time and again :** over and over again

[2]**time** *vb* **timed; tim·ing 1 :** to arrange or set the point or rate at which something happens **2 :** to measure or record the point at which something happens, the length of the period it takes for something to happen, or the rate at which certain actions take place — **tim·er** *n*

time capsule *n* **:** a container holding records or objects representative of a current culture that is put in a safe place for discovery in the future

time·keep·er *n* **:** an official who keeps track of the time in a sports contest

time·less *adj* **:** not restricted to a certain historical period

time·ly *adj* **time·li·er; time·li·est 1 :** coming early or at the right time **2 :** especially suitable to the time

time–out *n* **1 :** a short period during a game in which play is stopped **2 :** a quiet period used as a way to discipline a child

time·piece *n* **:** a device (as a clock or watch) to measure the passing of time

times *prep* **:** multiplied by

time·ta·ble *n* **:** a table telling when something (as a bus or train) is scheduled to leave or arrive

time zone *n* **:** a geographic region within which the same standard time is used

tim·id *adj* **:** feeling or showing a lack of courage or self-confidence **:** SHY — **tim·id·ly** *adv* — **tim·id·ness** *n*

tim·ing *n* **:** the time when something happens or is done especially when it is thought of as having a good or bad effect on the result

tim·o·rous *adj* **:** easily frightened **:** FEARFUL — **tim·o·rous·ly** *adv*

tin *n* **1 :** a soft bluish white metallic chemical element used chiefly in combination with other metals or as a coating to protect other metals **2 :** something (as a can or sheet) made from tinplate

tin·der *n* **:** material that burns easily and can be used as kindling

tin·foil *n* **:** a thin metal sheeting usually of aluminum or an alloy of tin and lead

[1]**tinge** *n, pl* **ting·es :** a slight coloring, flavor, or quality

[2]**tinge** *vb* **tinged; tinge·ing :** to color or flavor slightly

[1]**tin·gle** *vb* **tin·gled; tin·gling :** to feel or cause a prickling or thrilling sensation

[2]**tingle** *n* **:** a prickling or thrilling sensation or condition

tin·ker *vb* **tin·kered; tin·ker·ing :** to repair or adjust something in an unskilled or experimental manner

[1]**tin·kle** *vb* **tin·kled; tin·kling :** to make or cause to make short high ringing or clinking sounds

[2]**tinkle** *n* **:** a short high ringing or clinking sound

tin·plate *n* **:** thin steel sheets covered with tin

tin·sel *n* **1 :** a thread or strip of metal or plastic used for decoration **2 :** something that seems attractive but is of little worth

tin·smith *n* **:** a worker in tin or sometimes other metals

[1]**tint** *n* **1 :** a slight or pale coloring **2 :** a shade of a color

[2]**tint** *vb* **tint·ed; tint·ing :** to give a tint to **:** COLOR

ti·ny *adj* **ti·ni·er; ti·ni·est :** very small

[1]**tip** *n* **1 :** the usually pointed end of something **2 :** a small piece or part serving as an end, cap, or point

[2]**tip** *vb* **tipped; tip·ping 1 :** to turn over **2 :** to bend from a straight position **:** SLANT **3 :** to raise and tilt forward

[3]**tip** *n* **:** a piece of useful or secret information

[4]**tip** *n* **:** a small sum of money given for a service

[5]**tip** *vb* **tipped; tip·ping :** to give a small sum of money for a service

[6]**tip** *vb* **tipped; tip·ping 1 :** to attach an end or point to **2 :** to cover or decorate the tip of

[1]**tip·toe** *n* **:** the position of being balanced on the balls of the feet and toes with the heels raised — usually used with *on*

[2]**tiptoe** *adv or adj* **:** on or as if on the balls of the feet and toes with the heels raised

[3]**tiptoe** *vb* **tip·toed; tip·toe·ing :** to walk on the balls of the feet and toes with the heels raised

[1]**tip·top** *adj* **:** EXCELLENT, FIRST-RATE

[2]**tiptop** *n* **:** the highest point

[1]**tire** *vb* **tired; tir·ing 1 :** to make or become weary **2 :** to lose or cause to lose patience or attention **:** BORE

[2]**tire** *n* **:** a rubber cushion that usually contains compressed air and fits around a wheel (as of an automobile)

tired *adj* **:** needing rest **:** WEARY

tire·less *adj* **:** never seeming to get tired — **tire·less·ly** *adv*

tire·some *adj* **:** causing boredom, annoyance, or impatience because of length or dullness

'tis : it is

tis·sue *n* **1 :** a fine lightweight fabric **2 :** a piece of soft absorbent paper **3 :** a mass or layer of cells usually of one kind that perform a special function and form the basic structural material of an animal or plant body

ti·tan·ic *adj* **:** enormous in size, force, or power

ti·tle *n* **1 :** the name given to something (as a book, song, or job) to identify or describe it **2 :** a word or group of words attached to a person's name to show an honor, rank, or office **3 :** a legal right to the ownership of property **4 :** CHAMPIONSHIP

tit·mouse *n, pl* **tit·mice :** a small active usually gray bird that feeds mostly on seeds and insects

¹tit·ter *vb* **tit·tered; tit·ter·ing :** to laugh in a quiet and nervous way

²titter *n* **:** a nervous laugh

Tlin·git *n, pl* **Tlingit** *or* **Tlin·gits 1 :** a member of a group of American Indian peoples of the islands and coast of southern Alaska **2 :** the language of the Tlingit people

TN *abbr* Tennessee

TNT *n* **:** an explosive used in artillery shells and bombs and in blasting

¹to *prep* **1 :** in the direction of **2 :** AGAINST 4, ON **3 :** as far as **4 :** so as to become or bring about **5 :** ²BEFORE 3 **6 :** ¹UNTIL **7 :** fitting or being a part of or response to **8 :** along with **9 :** in relation to or comparison with **10 :** in agreement with **11 :** within the limits of **12 :** contained, occurring, or included in **13** — used to show the one or ones that an action is directed toward **14 :** for no one except **15 :** into the action of **16** — used to mark an infinitive

²to *adv* **1 :** in a direction toward **2 :** to a conscious state

toad *n* **:** a tailless leaping animal that is an amphibian and differs from the related frog by having rough dry skin and by living mostly on land

toad·stool *n* **:** a mushroom especially when poisonous or unfit for food

¹toast *vb* **toast·ed; toast·ing 1 :** to make (food) crisp, hot, and brown by heat **2 :** to warm completely

²toast *n* **1 :** sliced bread made crisp, hot, and brown by heat **2 :** an act of drinking in honor of a person **3 :** a person in whose honor other people drink **4 :** a highly admired person

³toast *vb* **toast·ed; toast·ing :** to drink in honor of

toast·er *n* **:** an electrical appliance for making slices of bread crisp, hot, and brown

toasty *adj* **toast·i·er; toast·i·est :** comfortably warm

to·bac·co *n, pl* **to·bac·cos :** the usually large sticky leaves of a tall plant related to the potato that are dried and prepared for use in smoking or chewing or as snuff

to·bog·gan *n* **:** a long light sled made without runners and curved up at the front

¹to·day *adv* **1 :** on this day **2 :** at the present time

²today *n* **:** the present day, time, or age

tod·dler *n* **:** a small child

¹toe *n* **1 :** one of the separate parts of the front end of a foot **2 :** the front end or part of a foot or hoof **3 :** the front end of something worn on the foot — **toed** *adj*

²toe *vb* **toed; toe·ing :** to touch, reach, or kick with the toes

toe·nail *n* **:** the hard covering at the end of a toe

to·fu *n* **:** a soft food product prepared from soybeans

to·ga *n* **:** the loose outer garment worn in public by citizens of ancient Rome

to·geth·er *adv* **1 :** in or into one group, body, or place **2 :** in touch or in partnership with **3 :** with or near someone or something else **4 :** at one time **5 :** in or by combined effort **6 :** in or into agreement **7 :** considered as a whole **8 :** in or into contact **9 :** as a single unit or piece

¹toil *n* **:** long hard labor

²toil *vb* **toiled; toil·ing 1 :** to work hard and long **2 :** to go on with effort

toi·let *n* **1 :** a device for getting rid of body waste that consists usually of a bowl that is flushed with water **2 :** BATHROOM **3 :** the act or process of getting dressed and groomed

toilet paper *n* **:** a thin soft sanitary absorbent paper usually in a roll for bathroom use

to·ken *n* **1 :** an outer sign **:** PROOF **2 :** a piece like a coin that has a special use **3 :** an object used to suggest something that cannot be pictured **4 :** SOUVENIR **5 :** INDICATION 2

told *past and past participle of* TELL

tol·er·a·ble *adj* **1 :** capable of being put up with **2 :** fairly good — **tol·er·a·bly** *adv*

tol·er·ance *n* **1 :** ability to put up with something harmful, bad, or annoying **2 :** sympathy for or acceptance of feelings or habits which are different from someone's own

tol·er·ant *adj* **:** showing tolerance — **tol·er·ant·ly** *adv*

tol·er·ate *vb* **tol·er·at·ed; tol·er·at·ing 1 :** to allow something to be or to be done without making a move to stop it **2 :** to stand the action of

¹toll *n* **1 :** a tax paid for a privilege (as the use of a highway or bridge) **2 :** a charge paid for a service **3 :** the cost in life or health

²toll *vb* **tolled; toll·ing** **1 :** to announce or call by the sounding of a bell **2 :** to sound with slow strokes
³toll *n* **:** the sound of a bell ringing slowly
tom·a·hawk *n* **:** a light ax used as a weapon by North American Indians
to·ma·to *n, pl* **to·ma·toes :** the usually red juicy fruit of a plant related to the potato that is eaten raw or cooked as a vegetable
tomb *n* **1 :** ¹GRAVE **2 :** a house or burial chamber for dead people
tom·boy *n* **:** a girl who enjoys things that some people think are more suited to boys
tomb·stone *n* **:** GRAVESTONE
tom·cat *n* **:** a male cat
tome *n* **:** a big thick book
tom·fool·ery *n* **:** playful or foolish behavior
¹to·mor·row *adv* **:** on the day after today
²tomorrow *n* **:** the day after today
tom–tom *n* **:** a drum (as a traditional Asian, African, or American Indian drum) that is beaten with the hands
ton *n* **:** a measure of weight equal either to 2000 pounds (about 907 kilograms) (**short ton**) or 2240 pounds (about 1016 kilograms) (**long ton**) with the short ton being more frequently used in the United States and Canada
¹tone *n* **1 :** an individual way of speaking or writing especially when used to express an emotion **2 :** common character or quality **3 :** quality of spoken or musical sound **4 :** a sound on one pitch **5 :** a shade of color **6 :** a color that changes another **7 :** a healthy state of the body or any of its parts
²tone *vb* **toned; ton·ing :** to give a healthy state to **:** STRENGTHEN — **tone down :** to soften or blend in color, appearance, or sound
tongs *n pl* **:** a tool for taking hold of or lifting something that consists usually of two movable pieces joined at one end or in the middle
tongue *n* **1 :** a fleshy movable part of the mouth used in tasting, in taking and swallowing food, and by human beings in speaking **2 :** a particular way or quality of speaking **3 :** LANGUAGE 1 **4 :** something that is long and fastened at one end
tongue–tied *adj* **:** unable to speak clearly or freely (as from shyness)
ton·ic *n* **1 :** a medicine or preparation for improving the strength or health of mind or body **2 :** SODA POP — used mostly in New England **3 :** the first note of a scale
¹to·night *adv* **:** on this present night or the night following this present day
²tonight *n* **:** the present or the coming night
ton·nage *n* **1 :** ships in terms of the total number of tons that are or can be carried **2 :** total weight in tons shipped, carried, or mined
ton·sil *n* **:** either of a pair of masses of spongy tissue at the back of the mouth
ton·sil·li·tis *n* **:** a sore reddened state of the tonsils
too *adv* **1 :** in addition **:** ALSO **2 :** to a greater than wanted or needed degree **3 :** ¹VERY 1
took *past of* TAKE
¹tool *n* **1 :** an instrument (as a saw, file, knife, or wrench) used or worked by hand or machine to perform a task **2 :** something that helps to gain an end **3 :** a person used by another **:** DUPE
²tool *vb* **tooled; tool·ing** **1 :** to drive or ride in a vehicle **2 :** to shape, form, or finish with a tool **3 :** to equip a plant or industry with machines and tools for production
tool·box *n* **:** a box for storing or carrying tools
tool·shed *n* **:** a small building for storing tools
toon *or* **'toon** *n* **:** a comic strip or animated cartoon
toonie *Can n* **:** a Canadian two dollar coin
¹toot *vb* **toot·ed; toot·ing** **1 :** to sound a short blast (as on a horn) **2 :** to blow or sound an instrument (as a horn) especially in short blasts
²toot *n* **:** a short blast (as on a horn)
tooth *n, pl* **teeth** **1 :** one of the hard bony structures set in sockets on the jaws of most vertebrates and used especially to chew and bite **2 :** something like or suggesting an animal's tooth in shape, arrangement, or action **3 :** one of the projections around the rim of a wheel that fit between the projections on another part causing the other part to move as the wheel turns — **tooth·less** *adj*
tooth·ache *n* **:** pain in or near a tooth
tooth·brush *n* **:** a brush for cleaning the teeth
toothed *adj* **:** having or showing teeth especially of a particular kind
tooth·paste *n* **:** a paste for cleaning the teeth
tooth·pick *n* **:** a pointed instrument for removing bits of food caught between the teeth
tooth·some *adj* **:** pleasing to the taste **:** DELICIOUS
toothy *adj* **tooth·i·er; tooth·i·est :** having or showing many usually large teeth
¹top *n* **1 :** the highest point, level, or part of something **2 :** the upper end, edge, or surface **3 :** an upper piece, lid, or covering **4 :** the highest position **5 :** a garment worn on the upper part of the body **6 :** the stalk and leaves of a plant and especially of one with roots that are used for food
²top *vb* **topped; top·ping** **1 :** to cover with or be covered with **2 :** to go over the top of **3 :** to be better than or exceed **4 :** to remove or cut the top of

[3]**top** *adj* : relating to or being at the top
[4]**top** *n* : a child's toy with a tapering point on which it can be made to spin
to·paz *n* : a clear yellow crystal that is used as a gem
top·coat *n* : a lightweight overcoat
top·ic *n* : the subject of something that is being discussed or has been written or thought about
topic sentence *n* : a sentence that states the main thought of a paragraph
top·knot *n* : a tuft of feathers or hair on the top of the head
top·mast *n* : the second mast above a ship's deck
top·most *adj* : highest of all
top·ple *vb* **top·pled; top·pling** : to fall or cause to fall from an upright position
top·sail *n* **1** : the sail next above the lowest sail on a mast in a square-rigged ship **2** : the sail above the large sail on a mast in a ship with a fore-and-aft rig
top·soil *n* : the rich upper layer of soil in which plants have most of their roots
top·sy–tur·vy *adv or adj* **1** : upside down **2** : in complete disorder
toque *Can n* : a close-fitting knitted cap
To·rah *n* **1** : the Jewish Bible and especially the first five books of writings **2** : a scroll containing the first five books of the Jewish Bible that is used in religious services
torch *n* **1** : a flaming light that is made of something which burns brightly and that is usually carried in the hand **2** : something that gives light or guidance **3** : a portable device for producing a hot flame
tore *past of* TEAR
[1]**tor·ment** *vb* **tor·ment·ed; tor·ment·ing** **1** : to cause severe suffering of body or mind to **2** : VEX 1, HARASS
[2]**tor·ment** *n* **1** : extreme pain or distress of body or mind **2** : a cause of suffering in mind or body
torn *past participle of* TEAR
tor·na·do *n, pl* **tor·na·does** *or* **tor·na·dos** : a violent whirling wind accompanied by a cloud that is shaped like a funnel and moves overland in a narrow path
[1]**tor·pe·do** *n, pl* **tor·pe·does** : a long narrow self-propelled underwater weapon used for blowing up ships
[2]**torpedo** *vb* **tor·pe·doed; tor·pe·do·ing** : to hit with or destroy by a torpedo
tor·rent *n* **1** : a rushing stream of liquid **2** : a large amount of something especially that is released suddenly
tor·rid *adj* : very hot and usually dry
tor·so *n* : the human body except for the head, arms, and legs
tor·ti·lla *n* : a round flat bread made of corn or wheat flour and usually eaten hot with a filling
tor·toise *n* **1** : a usually large turtle that lives on land **2** : TURTLE
tor·toise·shell *n* **1** : a hard brown and yellow material that covers the shell of a sea tortoise used especially in the past for ornamental objects **2** : a brightly colored butterfly
tor·tu·ous *adj* : having many twists and turns
[1]**tor·ture** *n* **1** : the act of causing great pain especially to punish or to obtain a confession **2** : distress of body or mind
[2]**torture** *vb* **tor·tured; tor·tur·ing** **1** : to punish or force someone to do or say something by causing great pain **2** : to cause great suffering to — **tor·tur·er** *n*
[1]**toss** *vb* **tossed; toss·ing** **1** : to throw with a quick light motion **2** : to lift with a sudden motion **3** : to throw or swing back and forth or up and down **4** : to be thrown about rapidly **5** : to move about restlessly **6** : to stir or mix lightly
[2]**toss** *n* **1** : an act or instance of throwing something **2** : the act of lifting with a sudden motion
tot *n* : a young child
[1]**to·tal** *adj* **1** : being such to the fullest degree **2** : making up the whole **3** : of or relating to the whole of something **4** : making use of every means to do something — **to·tal·ly** *adv*
[2]**total** *n* : the entire number or amount counted : SUM
[3]**total** *vb* **to·taled** *or* **to·talled; to·tal·ing** *or* **to·tal·ling** **1** : to add up **2** : to amount to : NUMBER
tote *vb* **tot·ed; tot·ing** : CARRY 1, HAUL
to·tem *n* **1** : an object (as an animal or plant) serving as the emblem of a family or clan **2** : a carving or picture representing such an object
totem pole *n* : a usually wooden pole or pillar carved and painted with totems and set up by American Indian tribes of the northwest coast of North America
tot·ter *vb* **tot·tered; tot·ter·ing** **1** : to sway or rock as if about to fall **2** : to move unsteadily : STAGGER
tou·can *n* : a brightly colored tropical bird that has a very large beak and feeds mostly on fruit
[1]**touch** *vb* **touched; touch·ing** **1** : to feel or handle (as with the fingers) especially so as to be aware of **2** : to be or cause to be in contact with something **3** : to hit lightly **4** : [2]HARM **5** : to make use of **6** : to refer to in passing **7** : to affect the interest of **8** : to have an influence on **9** : to move emotionally
[2]**touch** *n* **1** : a light stroke or tap **2** : the act

or fact of touching or being touched **3 :** the special sense by which one is aware of light pressure **4 :** an impression gotten through the sense of touch **5 :** a state of contact or communication **6 :** a small amount : TRACE **7 :** a small detail

touch·down *n* **:** a score made in football by carrying or catching the ball over the opponent's goal line

touch·ing *adj* **:** causing a feeling of tenderness or pity

touch pad *n* **:** a flat surface on an electronic device (as a microwave oven) divided into several differently marked areas that are touched to make choices in controlling the device

touch screen *n* **:** a display screen (as for a computer) on which the user selects options by touching the screen

touch–tone *adj* **:** relating to or being a telephone with push buttons that produce tones corresponding to the numbers

touchy *adj* **touch·i·er; touch·i·est 1 :** easily hurt or insulted **2 :** calling for tact or careful handling

tough *adj* **tough·er; tough·est 1 :** strong or firm but flexible and not brittle **2 :** not easily chewed **3 :** physically or emotionally strong enough to put up with strain or hardship **4 :** very strict, firm, or determined **5 :** very difficult to do or deal with **6 :** LAWLESS 2 — **tough·ness** *n*

tough·en *vb* **tough·ened; tough·en·ing :** to make or become tough

¹tour *n* **1 :** a trip usually involving a series of stops and ending at the point where it started **2 :** a fixed period of duty

²tour *vb* **toured; tour·ing :** to make a tour of : travel as a tourist

tour·ist *n* **:** a person who travels for pleasure

tour·na·ment *n* **1 :** a series of contests played for a championship **2 :** a contest between knights wearing armor and fighting with blunted lances or swords

tour·ni·quet *n* **:** a device (as a bandage twisted tight) for stopping bleeding or blood flow

tou·sle *vb* **tou·sled; tou·sling :** to put into disorder by rough handling

¹tow *vb* **towed; tow·ing :** to draw or pull along behind

²tow *n* **:** an act or instance of drawing or pulling along behind : the fact or state of being drawn or pulled along behind

³tow *n* **:** short broken fiber of flax, hemp, or jute used for yarn, twine, or stuffing

to·ward *or* **to·wards** *prep* **1 :** in the direction of **2 :** along a course leading to **3 :** in regard to **4 :** so as to face **5 :** ²NEAR **6 :** as part of the payment for

tow·el *n* **:** a cloth or piece of absorbent paper for wiping or drying

¹tow·er *n* **:** a building or structure that is higher than its length or width, is higher than most of what surrounds it, and may stand by itself or be attached to a larger structure

²tower *vb* **tow·ered; tow·er·ing :** to reach or rise to a great height

tow·er·ing *adj* **1 :** rising high : TALL **2 :** very powerful or intense **3 :** going beyond proper bounds

tow·head *n* **:** a person having soft whitish hair

town *n* **1 :** a thickly settled area that is usually larger than a village but smaller than a city **2 :** the people of a town

town hall *n* **:** a public building used for offices and meetings of town government

town·ship *n* **1 :** a unit of local government in some northeastern and north central states **2 :** a division of territory in surveys of United States public lands containing 36 square miles (about 93 square kilometers)

tox·ic *adj* **:** containing, being, or caused by poisonous or dangerous material

tox·in *n* **:** a poison produced by a living thing (as an animal or bacterium)

¹toy *n* **1 :** something for a child to play with **2 :** something of little or no value **3 :** something small of its kind

²toy *vb* **toyed; toy·ing 1 :** to fidget or play with without thinking **2 :** to think about something briefly and not very seriously **3 :** to flirt with

¹trace *n* **1 :** a mark left by something that has passed or is past **2 :** a very small amount

²trace *vb* **traced; trac·ing 1 :** ²SKETCH 1 **2 :** to form (as letters) carefully **3 :** to copy (as a drawing) by following the lines as seen through a transparent sheet placed over the thing copied **4 :** to follow the footprints, track, or trail of **5 :** to study or follow the development of in detail **6 :** to follow something back to its cause or beginning

³trace *n* **:** either of the two straps, chains, or ropes of a harness that fasten a horse to a vehicle

tra·chea *n, pl* **tra·che·ae 1 :** a stiff-walled tube of the respiratory system that connects the pharynx with the lungs **2 :** a breathing tube of an insect that connects with the outside of the body and carries oxygen directly to the cells

trac·ing *n* **:** a copy of something traced from an original

¹track *n* **1 :** a mark left by something that has gone by **2 :** PATH 1, TRAIL **3 :** the rails of a railroad **4 :** a course laid out for racing **5 :** awareness of things or of the order in which things happen or ideas come **6 :** either of two endless metal belts on which a vehicle (as a tank) travels **7 :** track-and-field sports

²track *vb* **tracked; track·ing 1 :** to follow the marks or traces of : to search for someone or something **2 :** to bring indoors on the bottom of the shoes, feet, or paws

track–and–field *adj* **:** relating to or being sports events (as racing, throwing, and jumping contests) held on a running track and on the enclosed field

¹tract *n* **1 :** an indefinite stretch of land **2 :** a defined area of land **3 :** a system of body parts or organs that serve some special purpose

²tract *n* **:** a pamphlet of political or religious ideas and beliefs

trac·tion *n* **:** the force that causes a moving thing to slow down or to stick against the surface it is moving along

trac·tor *n* **1 :** a vehicle that has large rear wheels or moves on endless belts and is used especially for pulling farm implements **2 :** a short truck for hauling a trailer

¹trade *n* **1 :** the business or work in which a person takes part regularly **:** OCCUPATION **2 :** the business of buying and selling items **:** COMMERCE **3 :** an occupation requiring manual or mechanical skill **:** CRAFT **4 :** an act of trading **:** TRANSACTION **5 :** the persons working in a business or industry **6 :** a firm's customers

²trade *vb* **trad·ed; trad·ing 1 :** to give in exchange for something else **2 :** to take part in the exchange, purchase, or sale of goods **3 :** to deal regularly as a customer

trade·mark *n* **:** a device (as a word) that points clearly to the origin or ownership of merchandise to which it is applied and that is legally reserved for use only by the owner

trad·er *n* **1 :** a person who trades **2 :** a ship engaged in commerce

trades·man *n, pl* **trades·men 1 :** a person who runs a retail store **2 :** CRAFTSMAN 1

trades·peo·ple *n pl* **:** people engaged in occupations requiring manual or mechanical skill

trade wind *n* **:** a wind blowing steadily toward the equator from an easterly direction

trading post *n* **:** a store set up in a thinly settled region

tra·di·tion *n* **1 :** the handing down of information, beliefs, or customs from one generation to another **2 :** a belief or custom handed down from one generation to another

tra·di·tion·al *adj* **1 :** handed down from age to age **2 :** based on custom **:** CONVENTIONAL — **tra·di·tion·al·ly** *adv*

¹traf·fic *n* **1 :** the movement (as of vehicles or pedestrians) along a route **2 :** the people or goods carried by train, boat, or airplane or passing along a road, river, or air route **3 :** the business of carrying passengers or goods **4 :** the business of buying and selling **:** COMMERCE **5 :** exchange of information

²traffic *vb* **traf·ficked; traf·fick·ing :** ²TRADE 2

traffic light *n* **:** a visual signal (as a set of colored lights) for controlling the flow of vehicles

trag·e·dy *n, pl* **trag·e·dies 1 :** a disastrous event **2 :** a serious play that has a sad or disastrous ending

trag·ic *adj* **1 :** very unfortunate **2 :** of or relating to tragedy

¹trail *vb* **trailed; trail·ing 1 :** to drag or draw along behind **2 :** to become weak, soft, or less **3 :** to follow in the tracks of **:** PURSUE **4 :** to hang down, rest on, or creep over the ground **5 :** to lag behind

²trail *n* **1 :** a trace or mark left by something that has passed or been drawn along **2 :** a beaten path **3 :** a path marked through a forest or mountainous region

trail·er *n* **1 :** a platform or frame with wheels that is pulled behind a vehicle and used to transport things (as a boat) **2 :** a vehicle designed to serve wherever parked as a dwelling or a place of business **3 :** PREVIEW

¹train *n* **1 :** a connected series of railway cars usually hauled by a locomotive **2 :** a part of a gown that trails behind the wearer **3 :** a connected series **4 :** a moving line of persons, vehicles, or animals **5 :** the followers of an important person

²train *vb* **trained; train·ing 1 :** to give or receive instruction, discipline, or drill **2 :** to teach in an art, profession, or trade **3 :** to make ready (as by exercise) for a test of skill **4 :** to teach (an animal) to obey **5 :** to make (a plant) grow in a particular way usually by bending, trimming, or tying **6 :** to aim something at a target — **train·er** *n*

train·ing *n* **1 :** the course followed by a person or animal who trains or is being trained **2 :** the skill, knowledge, or experience acquired by a person or animal who has trained

training wheels *n pl* **:** a pair of small wheels connected to the rear axle of a bicycle to help a beginning rider keep balance

traipse *vb* **traipsed; traips·ing :** to walk or wander about

trait *n* **:** a quality that makes one person, animal, or thing different from another **:** CHARACTERISTIC

trai·tor *n* **1 :** a person who is not loyal or true to a friend, duty, cause, or belief or is false to a personal duty **2 :** a person who betrays his or her country : a person who commits treason

trai·tor·ous *adj* **1 :** guilty or capable of treason **2 :** amounting to treason

[1]**tramp** *vb* **tramped; tramp·ing 1 :** to travel or wander through on foot **2 :** to walk heavily

[2]**tramp** *n* **1 :** a person who wanders from place to place, has no home or job, and often lives by begging or stealing **2 :** the sounds made by the beat of marching feet **3 :** [2]HIKE

tram·ple *vb* **tram·pled; tram·pling 1 :** to tramp or tread heavily so as to bruise, crush, or injure something **2 :** to crush under the feet **3 :** to treat as if worthless or unimportant

tram·po·line *n* **:** a canvas sheet or web supported by springs in a metal frame used for springing and landing in acrobatic tumbling

trance *n* **1 :** a condition like sleep (as deep hypnosis) **2 :** a state of being so deeply absorbed in thought about something as to be unaware of anything else **3 :** STUPOR

tran·quil *adj* **:** very calm and quiet **:** PEACEFUL

tran·quil·iz·er *n* **:** a drug used to make someone calm and relaxed

tran·quil·li·ty *or* **tran·quil·i·ty** *n* **:** the state of being calm **:** QUIET

trans. *abbr* transitive

trans- *prefix* **1 :** on or to the other side of **:** across **:** beyond **2 :** so as to change or transfer

trans·act *vb* **trans·act·ed; trans·act·ing :** to carry on **:** MANAGE, CONDUCT

trans·ac·tion *n* **1 :** a business deal **2 transactions** *pl* **:** the record of the meeting of a club or organization

trans·at·lan·tic *adj* **:** crossing or being beyond the Atlantic Ocean

tran·scend *vb* **tran·scend·ed; tran·scend·ing 1 :** to rise above the limits of **2 :** to do better or more than

trans·con·ti·nen·tal *adj* **:** crossing, extending across, or being on the farther side of a continent

tran·scribe *vb* **tran·scribed; tran·scrib·ing :** to make a copy of

tran·script *n* **1 :** [1]COPY 1 **2 :** an official copy of a student's school record

[1]**trans·fer** *vb* **trans·ferred; trans·fer·ring 1 :** to move from one person or place to another **2 :** to pass or cause to pass from one person, place, or condition to another **3 :** to move to a different place, region, or job **4 :** to give over the possession or ownership of **5 :** to copy (as by printing) from one surface to another by contact **6 :** to change from one vehicle or transportation line to another

[2]**trans·fer** *n* **1 :** the act of giving over right, title, or interest in property to another person or other persons **2 :** an act or process of moving someone or something from one place to another **3 :** someone who has changed schools **4 :** a ticket allowing a passenger on a bus or train to continue the journey on another route without paying more fare

trans·fix *vb* **trans·fixed; trans·fix·ing :** to hold motionless by or as if by piercing through with a pointed weapon

trans·form *vb* **trans·formed; trans·form·ing :** to change completely

trans·for·ma·tion *n* **:** the act or process of changing completely **:** a complete change

trans·form·er *n* **:** a device for changing the voltage of an electric current

trans·fu·sion *n* **1 :** the process of passing a fluid (as blood) into a vein of a person or animal **2 :** the act of giving something a fresh supply

trans·gres·sion *n* **:** a violation of a command or law

[1]**tran·sient** *adj* **:** not lasting or staying long

[2]**transient** *n* **:** a person traveling about usually in search of work

tran·sis·tor *n* **:** a small solid electronic device used for controlling the flow of electricity

tran·sit *n* **1 :** the act of passing through or across **2 :** the act or method of carrying things from one place to another **3 :** local transportation of people in public vehicles **4 :** a surveyor's instrument for measuring angles

tran·si·tion *n* **:** an act or the process of passing from one state, stage, place, or subject to another **:** CHANGE

tran·si·tive *adj* **:** having or containing a direct object

trans·late *vb* **trans·lat·ed; trans·lat·ing 1 :** to turn from one language into another **2 :** to change from one form to another

trans·la·tion *n* **:** the act, process, or result of changing from one form or language into another

trans·lu·cent *adj* **:** not transparent but clear enough to allow rays of light to pass through

trans·mis·sion *n* **1 :** an act or process of transmitting, spreading, or passing along **2 :** the gears that pass power from the engine to the axle that gives motion to a motor vehicle

trans·mit *vb* **trans·mit·ted; trans·mit·ting 1 :** to transfer, pass, or spread from one person or place to another **2 :** to pass on by or as if by inheritance **3 :** to pass or cause to pass through space or through a material **4 :** to send out (a signal) by means of radio waves

trans·mit·ter *n* **1 :** someone or something that transmits something **2 :** the part of a telephone that includes the mouthpiece and a device that picks up sound waves and sends them over the wire **3 :** a device that sends out radio or television signals

tran·som *n* **1 :** a piece that lies crosswise in a structure (as in the frame of a window or of a door that has a window above it) **2 :** a window above a door or another window

trans·par·en·cy *n, pl* **trans·par·en·cies** **1 :** the quality or state of being transparent **2 :** a picture or design on glass or film that can be viewed by shining a light through it

trans·par·ent *adj* **1 :** clear enough or thin enough to be seen through **2 :** easily detected — **trans·par·ent·ly** *adv*

trans·pi·ra·tion *n* **:** the process by which plants give off water vapor through openings in their leaves

trans·pire *vb* **trans·pired; trans·pir·ing** **1 :** to come to pass **:** HAPPEN **2 :** to become known or apparent **3 :** to give off water vapor through openings in the leaves

[1]**trans·plant** *vb* **trans·plant·ed; trans·plant·ing** **1 :** to dig up and plant again in another soil or location **2 :** to remove from one place and settle or introduce elsewhere **3 :** to transfer (a body organ or tissue) from one part or individual to another

[2]**trans·plant** *n* **1 :** something or someone planted or moved elsewhere **2 :** the process or act of planting or moving elsewhere

[1]**trans·port** *vb* **trans·port·ed; trans·port·ing** **1 :** to carry from one place to another **2 :** to fill with delight

[2]**trans·port** *n* **1 :** the act of carrying from one place to another **:** TRANSPORTATION **2 :** a ship for carrying soldiers or military equipment **3 :** a vehicle used to carry people or goods from one place to another **4 :** a state of great joy or pleasure

trans·por·ta·tion *n* **1 :** an act, instance, or means of carrying people or goods from one place to another or of being carried from one place to another **2 :** public carrying of passengers or goods especially as a business

trans·pose *vb* **trans·posed; trans·pos·ing** **1 :** to change the position or order of **2 :** to write or perform in a different musical key

trans·verse *adj* **:** lying or being across **:** placed crosswise — **trans·verse·ly** *adv*

[1]**trap** *n* **1 :** a device for catching animals **2 :** something by which one is caught or stopped by surprise **3 :** a light one-horse carriage with springs **4 :** a device that allows something to pass through but keeps other things out

[2]**trap** *vb* **trapped; trap·ping** **1 :** to catch or be caught in a trap **2 :** to put or get in a place or position from which escape is not possible — **trap·per** *n*

trap·door *n* **:** a lifting or sliding door covering an opening in a floor or roof

tra·peze *n* **:** a short horizontal bar hung from two parallel ropes and used by acrobats

trap·e·zoid *n* **:** a flat geometric figure with four sides but with only two sides parallel

trap·pings *n pl* **1 :** ornamental covering especially for a horse **2 :** outward decoration or dress

trash *n* **1 :** something of little or no value that is thrown away **2 :** people who deserve little respect

[1]**trav·el** *vb* **trav·eled** *or Can and Brit* **trav·elled; trav·el·ing** *or Can and Brit* **trav·el·ling** **1 :** to journey from place to place or to a distant place **2 :** to get around **:** pass from one place to another **3 :** to journey through or over — **trav·el·er** *or Can and Brit* **trav·el·ler** *n*

[2]**travel** *n* **1 :** the act or a means of journeying from one place to another **2 :** [1]JOURNEY, TRIP — often used in pl. **3 :** the number journeying

tra·verse *vb* **tra·versed; tra·vers·ing** **:** to pass through, across, or over

[1]**trawl** *vb* **trawled; trawl·ing** **:** to fish or catch with a large net dragged along the sea bottom

[2]**trawl** *n* **:** a large net in the shape of a cone dragged along the sea bottom in fishing

trawl·er *n* **:** a boat used for fishing with a large net dragged along the sea bottom

tray *n* **:** an open container with a flat bottom and low rim for holding, carrying, or showing articles

treach·er·ous *adj* **1 :** not safe because of hidden dangers **2 :** not trustworthy **:** guilty of betrayal or likely to betray — **treach·er·ous·ly** *adv*

treach·ery *n, pl* **treach·er·ies** **1 :** the behavior of a person who betrays trust or faith **2 :** an act or instance of betraying trust or faith

[1]**tread** *vb* **trod; trod·den** *or* **trod; tread·ing** **1 :** to step or walk on or over **2 :** to beat or press with the feet **3 :** to move on foot **:** WALK — **tread water :** to keep the body upright in water and the head above water by moving the legs and arms

[2]**tread** *n* **1 :** the action, manner, or sound of stepping or walking **2 :** a mark made by a tire rolling over the ground **3 :** the part of something (as a shoe or tire) that touches a surface **4 :** the part of a step that is stepped on

trea·dle *n* **:** a device worked by the foot to drive a machine

tread·mill *n* **1 :** a device having an endless belt on which an individual walks or runs in place for exercise **2 :** a tiresome routine

trea·son *n* **:** the crime of trying or helping to overthrow the government of the criminal's own country or cause its defeat in war

[1]**trea·sure** *n* **1 :** wealth (as money or jewels)

stored up or held in reserve **2 :** something of great value

²treasure *vb* **trea·sured; trea·sur·ing :** to treat as precious : CHERISH

trea·sur·er *n* **:** a person (as an officer of a club or business) who has charge of the money

trea·sury *n, pl* **trea·sur·ies 1 :** a place in which money and valuable objects are kept **2 :** a place where money collected is kept and paid out **3** *cap* **:** a government department in charge of finances

¹treat *vb* **treat·ed; treat·ing 1 :** to handle, deal with, use, or act toward in a usually stated way **2 :** to pay for the food or entertainment of **3 :** to give medical or surgical care to : use medical care on **4 :** to expose to some action (as of a chemical)

²treat *n* **1 :** an often unexpected or unusual source of pleasure or amusement **2 :** a food that tastes very good and is not eaten very often **3 :** an instance of paying for someone's food or entertainment

treat·ment *n* **1 :** the act or manner of treating someone or something **2 :** medical or surgical care **3 :** a substance or method used in treating

trea·ty *n, pl* **trea·ties :** an agreement between two or more states or sovereigns

¹tre·ble *n* **1 :** the highest part in harmony having four parts : SOPRANO **2 :** an instrument having the highest range or part **3 :** a voice or sound that has a high pitch **4 :** the upper half of the musical pitch range

²treble *adj* **1 :** being three times the number or amount **2 :** relating to or having the range of a musical treble

³treble *vb* **tre·bled; tre·bling :** to make or become three times as much

¹tree *n* **1 :** a long-lived woody plant that has a single usually tall main stem with few or no branches on its lower part **2 :** a plant of treelike form **3 :** something shaped like a tree — **tree·less** *adj* — **tree·like** *adj*

²tree *vb* **treed; tree·ing :** to force to go up a tree

tree fern *n* **:** a tropical fern with a tall woody stalk and a crown of often feathery leaves

tree house *n* **:** a structure (as a playhouse) built among the branches of a tree

tree·top *n* **:** the highest part of a tree

tre·foil *n* **1 :** a clover or related plant having leaves with three leaflets **2 :** a fancy design with three leaflike parts

¹trek *vb* **trekked; trek·king :** to walk a long way with difficulty

²trek *n* **:** a slow or difficult journey

trel·lis *n* **:** a frame of lattice used especially as a screen or a support for climbing plants

¹trem·ble *vb* **trem·bled; trem·bling 1 :** to shake without control (as from fear or cold) : SHIVER **2 :** to move, sound, or happen as if shaken **3 :** to have strong fear or doubt

²tremble *n* **:** the act or a period of shaking

tre·men·dous *adj* **1 :** astonishingly large, strong, or great **2 :** very good or excellent — **tre·men·dous·ly** *adv*

trem·or *n* **1 :** a trembling or shaking especially from weakness or disease **2 :** a shaking motion of the earth during an earthquake

trem·u·lous *adj* **1 :** marked by trembling or shaking **2 :** FEARFUL 2, TIMID

trench *n* **:** a long narrow ditch

trend *n* **:** general direction taken in movement or change

trendy *adj* **trend·i·er; trend·i·est :** currently fashionable or popular

trep·i·da·tion *n* **:** a state of alarm or nervousness

¹tres·pass *n* **1 :** unlawful entry upon someone's land **2 :** ¹SIN, OFFENSE

²trespass *vb* **tres·passed; tres·pass·ing 1 :** to enter upon someone's land unlawfully **2 :** to do wrong : SIN — **tres·pass·er** *n*

tress *n* **:** a long lock of hair

tres·tle *n* **1 :** a braced frame consisting usually of a horizontal piece with spreading legs at each end that supports something (as the top of a table) **2 :** a structure of timbers or steel for supporting a road or railroad over a low place

T. rex *n* **:** TYRANNOSAUR

tri- *prefix* **:** three

tri·ad *n* **:** a chord made up usually of the first, third, and fifth notes of a scale

tri·al *n* **1 :** the hearing and judgment of something in court **2 :** a test of someone's ability to do or endure something **3 :** an experiment to test quality, value, or usefulness **4 :** the action or process of trying or testing

tri·an·gle *n* **1 :** a flat geometric figure that has three sides and three angles **2 :** something that has three sides and three angles **3 :** a musical instrument made of a steel rod bent in the shape of a triangle with one open angle

tri·an·gu·lar *adj* **1 :** having three angles, sides, or corners **2 :** of, relating to, or involving three parts or persons

trib·al *adj* **:** relating to a tribe

tribe *n* **1 :** a group of people including many families, clans, or generations **2 :** a group of people who are of the same kind or have the same occupation or interest

tribes·man *n, pl* **tribes·men :** a member of a tribe

trib·u·la·tion *n* **1 :** an experience that is hard to bear **2 :** distress or suffering resulting from cruel and unjust treatment or misfortune

tri·bu·nal *n* **:** a court of justice

trib·u·tary *n, pl* **trib·u·tar·ies :** a stream flowing into a larger stream or a lake

trib·ute *n* **1 :** something done, said, or given

to show respect, gratitude, or affection **2** : a payment made by one ruler or state to another especially to gain peace
tri·cer·a·tops *n, pl* **triceratops** : a large plant-eating dinosaur with three horns, a large bony crest around the neck, and hoofed toes
¹trick *n* **1** : an action intended to deceive or cheat **2** : a mischievous act : PRANK **3** : an action designed to puzzle or amuse **4** : a quick or clever way of doing something **5** : the cards played in one round of a game
²trick *vb* **tricked; trick·ing** : to deceive with tricks
³trick *adj* : relating to or involving actions intended to deceive or puzzle
trick·ery *n* : the use of actions intended to deceive or cheat
¹trick·le *vb* **trick·led; trick·ling** **1** : to run or fall in drops **2** : to flow in a thin slow stream **3** : to move slowly or in small numbers
²trickle *n* : a thin slow stream
trick or treat *n* : a children's Halloween practice of going around usually in costume asking for treats
trick·ster *n* : a person who uses tricks
tricky *adj* **trick·i·er; trick·i·est** **1** : requiring special care and skill **2** : likely to use tricks
tri·cy·cle *n* : a vehicle with three wheels that is usually moved by pedals
tri·dent *n* : a spear with three prongs
tried *past and past participle of* TRY
tried–and–true *adj* : found good or trustworthy through experience or testing
¹tri·fle *n* : something of little value or importance
²trifle *vb* **tri·fled; tri·fling** : to treat (someone or something) as unimportant
tri·fling *adj* **1** : not serious : FRIVOLOUS **2** : of little value
trig·ger *n* : the part of the lock of a gun that is pressed to release the hammer so that it will fire
¹trill *n* **1** : ¹WARBLE 1 **2** : the rapid vibration of one speech organ against another (as the tongue against the teeth) **3** : a quick movement back and forth between two musical tones one step apart
²trill *vb* **trilled; trill·ing** : to utter as or with a trill
tril·lion *n* : a thousand billions
tril·li·um *n* : a plant related to the lilies that has three leaves and a single flower with three petals and that blooms in the spring
¹trim *vb* **trimmed; trim·ming** **1** : to put decorations on : ADORN **2** : to make neat especially by cutting or clipping **3** : to free of unnecessary matter **4** : to adjust (as a sail) to a desired position — **trim·mer** *n*
²trim *adj* **trim·mer; trim·mest** : neat and compact in line or structure — **trim·ly** *adv*
³trim *n* **1** : material used for ornament or trimming **2** : the material (as wood, stone, or vinyl) in the finish of a building especially around doors and windows **3** : an act or instance of cutting or clipping
trim·ming *n* **1** : something that ornaments, seasons, or completes **2** : pieces trimmed from something
trin·ket *n* : a small object of little value
trio *n, pl* **tri·os** **1** : a group or set of three **2** : a group of three musicians who perform together
¹trip *vb* **tripped; trip·ping** **1** : to catch the foot against something so as to stumble : cause to stumble **2** : to make or cause to make a mistake **3** : to move (as in dancing) with light quick steps **4** : to release (as a spring) by moving a catch
²trip *n* **1** : an instance of traveling from one place to another **2** : a brief errand having a certain aim or being more or less regular **3** : the action of releasing something mechanically **4** : a device for releasing something by tripping a mechanism
tripe *n* : a part of the stomach of a cow used for food
¹tri·ple *vb* **tri·pled; tri·pling** : to make or become three times as great or as many
²triple *n* **1** : a sum, amount, or number that is three times as great **2** : a combination, group, or series of three **3** : a hit in baseball that lets the batter reach third base
³triple *adj* **1** : having three units or parts **2** : being three times as great or as many **3** : repeated three times
trip·let *n* **1** : a combination, set, or group of three **2** : one of three offspring born at one birth
tri·pod *n* **1** : something (as a container or stool) resting on three legs **2** : a stand (as for a camera) having three legs
trite *adj* **trit·er; trit·est** : so common that the newness and cleverness have worn off : STALE
¹tri·umph *n* **1** : the joy of victory or success **2** : an outstanding victory
²triumph *vb* **tri·umphed; tri·umph·ing** **1** : to celebrate victory or success in high spirits **2** : to gain victory : WIN
tri·um·phal *adj* : following or in celebration of victory
tri·um·phant *adj* **1** : VICTORIOUS, SUCCESSFUL **2** : rejoicing for or celebrating victory — **tri·um·phant·ly** *adv*
triv·ia *n* : interesting facts that are not well-known
triv·i·al *adj* : of little worth or importance
trod *past and past participle of* TREAD
trodden *past participle of* TREAD
¹troll *n* : a dwarf or giant of folklore living in caves or hills
²troll *vb* **trolled; troll·ing** **1** : to sing the parts

of (a song) in succession **2 :** to fish with a hook and line pulled along through the water

[3]**troll** *n* **:** a lure or a line with its lure and hook drawn through the water in fishing

trol·ley *n, pl* **trolleys 1 :** a passenger car that runs on tracks and gets its power through electricity **2 :** a wheeled cart

trom·bone *n* **:** a brass musical instrument made of a long bent tube that has a wide opening at one end and one section that slides in and out to make different tones

[1]**troop** *n* **1 :** a group of soldiers **2 troops** *pl* **:** armed forces **:** MILITARY **3 :** a group of beings or things **4 :** a unit of Boy Scouts or Girl Scouts under a leader

[2]**troop** *vb* **trooped; troop·ing :** to move or gather in groups

troop·er *n* **1 :** a soldier in a cavalry unit **2 :** a state police officer

tro·phy *n, pl* **trophies 1 :** something given to celebrate a victory or as an award for achievement **2 :** something taken in battle or conquest especially as a memorial

trop·ic *n* **1 :** either of two parallels of the earth's latitude of which one is about 23½ degrees north of the equator and the other about 23½ degrees south of the equator **2 tropics** *pl, often cap* **:** the region lying between the Tropic of Cancer and the Tropic of Capricorn

trop·i·cal *adj* **:** of, or occurring in the tropics

tropical fish *n* **:** a small often brightly colored fish kept in aquariums

tropical storm *n* **:** a storm that begins in the tropics with winds that are not as strong as those of a hurricane

[1]**trot** *n* **1 :** a gait of an animal with four feet that is faster than walking but slower than galloping and in which a front foot and the opposite hind foot move as a pair **2 :** a human jogging pace between a walk and a run

[2]**trot** *vb* **trot·ted; trot·ting 1 :** to ride, drive, go, or cause to go at a trot **2 :** to go along quickly **:** HURRY

[1]**trou·ble** *n* **1 :** something that causes worry or distress **:** MISFORTUNE **2 :** an instance of distress or disturbance **3 :** extra work or effort **4 :** ill health **:** AILMENT **5 :** failure to work normally

[2]**trouble** *vb* **trou·bled; trou·bling 1 :** to become or make worried or upset **2 :** to produce physical disorder in **:** AFFLICT **3 :** to put to inconvenience **4 :** to make an effort

trou·ble·some *adj* **1 :** giving distress or anxiety **2 :** difficult to deal with

trough *n* **1 :** a long shallow open container especially for water or feed for livestock **2 :** a channel for water **:** GUTTER **3 :** a long channel or hollow

trounce *vb* **trounced; trounc·ing 1 :** to beat severely **:** FLOG **2 :** to defeat thoroughly

troupe *n* **:** a group especially of performers who act or work together

trou·sers *n pl* **:** PANTS

trout *n, pl* **trout :** a freshwater fish related to the salmon that is often caught for food or sport

trow·el *n* **1 :** a small hand tool with a flat blade used for spreading and smoothing mortar or plaster **2 :** a small hand tool with a curved blade used by gardeners

tru·an·cy *n, pl* **tru·an·cies :** an act or an instance of staying out of school without permission

tru·ant *n* **1 :** a student who stays out of school without permission **2 :** a person who neglects his or her duty

truce *n* **:** an agreement between enemies or opponents to stop fighting for a certain period of time

[1]**truck** *n* **:** a vehicle (as a strong heavy wagon or motor vehicle) for carrying heavy articles or hauling a trailer

[2]**truck** *n* **:** close association

[3]**truck** *vb* **trucked; truck·ing :** to transport on or in a truck

trudge *vb* **trudged; trudg·ing :** to walk or march steadily and usually with much effort

[1]**true** *adj* **tru·er; tru·est 1 :** agreeing with the facts **:** ACCURATE **2 :** completely loyal **:** FAITHFUL **3 :** consistent or in accordance with **4 :** properly so called **:** GENUINE **5 :** placed or formed accurately **:** EXACT **6 :** being or holding by right **:** LEGITIMATE **7 :** fully realized or fulfilled

[2]**true** *adv* **1 :** in agreement with fact **:** TRUTHFULLY **2 :** in an accurate manner **:** ACCURATELY

[3]**true** *n* **:** the quality or state of being accurate (as in alignment)

[4]**true** *vb* **trued; true·ing** *also* **tru·ing :** to bring to exactly correct condition as to place, position, or shape

true–blue *adj* **:** very faithful

tru·ly *adv* **:** in a manner that is actual, genuine, honest, or without question

[1]**trum·pet** *n* **1 :** a brass musical instrument that consists of a tube formed into a long loop with a wide opening at one end and that has valves by which different tones are produced **2 :** something that is shaped like a trumpet

[2]**trumpet** *vb* **trum·pet·ed; trum·pet·ing 1 :** to blow a trumpet **2 :** to make a sound like that of a trumpet **3 :** to praise (something) loudly and publicly — **trum·pet·er** *n*

trun·dle *vb* **trun·dled; trun·dling :** to roll along **:** WHEEL

trundle bed *n* **:** a low bed on small wheels that can be rolled under a taller bed

trunk *n* **1 :** the thick main stem of a tree not including the branches and roots **2 :** a box or chest for holding clothes or other articles especially for traveling **3 :** the enclosed space in the rear of an automobile for carrying articles **4 :** the long round muscular nose of an elephant **5 trunks** *pl* **:** a swimsuit for a man or boy **6 :** the body of a person or animal not including the head, arms, and legs

[1]**truss** *vb* **trussed; truss·ing 1 :** to bind or tie firmly **2 :** to support, strengthen, or stiffen by a framework of beams

[2]**truss** *n* **:** a framework of beams or bars used in building and engineering

[1]**trust** *vb* **trust·ed; trust·ing 1 :** to rely on or on the truth of **:** BELIEVE **2 :** to place confidence in someone or something **3 :** to be confident **:** HOPE

[2]**trust** *n* **1 :** firm belief in the character, strength, or truth of someone or something **2 :** a person or thing in which confidence is placed **3 :** confident hope **4 :** a property interest held by one person or organization (as a bank) for the benefit of another **5 :** a combination of firms or corporations formed by a legal agreement and often held to reduce competition **6 :** an organization in which money is held or managed by someone for the benefit of another or others **7 :** responsibility for safety and well-being

trust·ee *n* **:** a person who has been given legal responsibility for someone else's property

trust·ful *adj* **:** full of trust — **trust·ful·ness** *n*

trust·ing *adj* **:** having or showing faith, confidence, or belief in someone or something

trust·wor·thy *adj* **:** deserving faith and confidence — **trust·wor·thi·ness** *n*

trusty *adj* **trust·i·er; trust·i·est :** worthy of being depended on

truth *n, pl* **truths 1 :** the body of real events or facts **2 :** the quality or state of being true **3 :** a true or accepted statement or idea — **in truth :** in actual fact **:** REALLY

truth·ful *adj* **:** telling or being in the habit of telling facts or making statements that are true — **truth·ful·ly** *adv* — **truth·ful·ness** *n*

[1]**try** *vb* **tried; try·ing 1 :** to make an effort or attempt at **2 :** to put to a test **3 :** to examine or investigate in a court of law **4 :** to conduct the trial of **5 :** to test to the limit — **try on :** to put on (a garment) to test the fit — **try out :** to compete to fill a part (as on an athletic team or in a play)

[2]**try** *n, pl* **tries :** an effort to do something **:** ATTEMPT

try·ing *adj* **:** hard to bear or put up with

try·out *n* **:** a test of the ability (as of an athlete or an actor) to fill a part or meet standards

T–shirt *also* **tee shirt** *n* **:** a shirt with short sleeves and no collar and usually made of cotton

tsp. *abbr* teaspoon

tsu·na·mi *n* **:** a large sea wave produced especially by an earthquake or volcanic eruption under the sea **:** TIDAL WAVE

Tu. *abbr* Tuesday

tub *n* **1 :** a wide low container **2 :** BATHTUB **3 :** an old or slow boat **4 :** the amount that a tub will hold

tu·ba *n* **:** a brass musical instrument of lowest pitch with an oval shape and valves for producing different tones

tub·by *adj* **tub·bi·er; tub·bi·est :** short and somewhat fat

tube *n* **1 :** a long hollow cylinder used especially to carry fluids **2 :** a long soft container whose contents (as toothpaste or glue) can be removed by squeezing **3 :** a slender channel within a plant or animal body **:** DUCT **4 :** a hollow cylinder of rubber inside a tire to hold air **5 :** ELECTRON TUBE **6 :** TELEVISION 2 — **tube·like** *adj*

tu·ber *n* **:** a short thick fleshy usually underground stem (as of a potato plant) having buds that can produce new plants

tu·ber·cu·lo·sis *n* **:** a serious disease that mostly affects the lungs and in which there is fever, cough, and difficulty in breathing

tu·bu·lar *adj* **1 :** having the form of or made up of a tube **2 :** made with tubes

[1]**tuck** *vb* **tucked; tuck·ing 1 :** to put or fit into a snug or safe place **2 :** to push in the edges of **3 :** to pull up into or as if into a fold **4 :** to cover by pushing in the edges of bedclothes **5 :** to eat or drink with obvious pleasure **6 :** to make stitched folds in

[2]**tuck** *n* **:** a fold stitched into cloth usually to alter it

tuck·er *vb* **tuck·ered; tuck·er·ing :** to cause to tire

Tue., Tues. *abbr* Tuesday

Tues·day *n* **:** the third day of the week

tuft *n* **1 :** a small bunch of long flexible things (as hairs or blades of grass) growing close together **2 :** [1]CLUMP 1 — **tuft·ed** *adj*

[1]**tug** *vb* **tugged; tug·ging 1 :** to pull hard **2 :** to move by pulling hard **:** DRAG **3 :** to tow with a tugboat

[2]**tug** *n* **1 :** an act of pulling hard **:** a hard pull **2 :** TUGBOAT **3 :** a strong pulling force **4 :** a struggle between two people or forces

tug·boat *n* **:** a small powerful boat used for towing ships

tug–of–war *n, pl* **tugs–of–war 1 :** a contest in which two teams pull against each other at opposite ends of a rope **2 :** a struggle to win

tu·ition *n* **:** money paid for instruction (as at a college)

tu·lip *n* **:** a plant related to the lily that grows from a bulb and has a large cup-shaped flower in early spring

[1]**tum·ble** *vb* **tum·bled; tum·bling 1 :** to fall suddenly and helplessly **2 :** to fall while rolling or bouncing **3 :** to move or go in a hurried or confused way **4 :** to toss together into a confused mass **5 :** to perform gymnastic feats of rolling and turning **6 :** to suffer a sudden downward turn or defeat

[2]**tumble** *n* **1 :** an act or instance of falling often while rolling or bouncing **2 :** a messy state or collection

tum·ble·down *adj* **:** DILAPIDATED

tum·bler *n* **1 :** a person (as an acrobat) who tumbles **2 :** a drinking glass **3 :** a movable part of a lock that must be adjusted (as by a key) before the lock will open

tum·ble·weed *n* **:** a plant that breaks away from its roots in autumn and tumbles about in the wind

tum·my *n, pl* **tummies 1 :** [1]STOMACH 1 **2 :** [1]STOMACH 2

tu·mor *or Can and Brit* **tumour** *n* **:** an abnormal growth of body tissue

tu·mult *n* **1 :** UPROAR **2 :** great confusion of mind

tu·mul·tu·ous *adj* **:** characterized by uproar

tu·na *n, pl* **tuna** *or* **tunas :** a large sea fish caught for food and sport

tun·dra *n* **:** a treeless plain of arctic regions having a permanently frozen layer below the surface of the soil

[1]**tune** *n* **1 :** a series of pleasing musical tones **:** MELODY **2 :** correct musical pitch or key **3 :** AGREEMENT 1, HARMONY **4 :** general attitude — **tune·ful** *adj*

[2]**tune** *vb* **tuned; tun·ing 1 :** to adjust a radio or television so that it receives clearly **2 :** to adjust in musical pitch **3 :** to come or bring into harmony **4 :** to put (as an engine) in good working order — often used with *up* — **tun·er** *n* — **tune out :** to ignore what is happening or being said

tung·sten *n* **:** a grayish-white hard metallic chemical element used especially for electrical parts (as for the fine wire in an electric light bulb) and to make alloys (as steel) harder

tu·nic *n* **1 :** a usually knee-length belted garment worn by ancient Greeks and Romans **2 :** a shirt or jacket reaching to or just below the hips

tuning fork *n* **:** a metal instrument that gives a fixed tone when struck and is useful for tuning musical instruments

[1]**tun·nel** *n* **:** a passage under the ground

[2]**tunnel** *vb* **tun·neled** *or* **tun·nelled; tun·nel·ing** *or* **tun·nel·ling :** to make a passage under the ground

tun·ny *n, pl* **tun·nies :** TUNA

tur·ban *n* **1 :** a head covering made of a long cloth wrapped around the head or around a cap **2 :** a woman's small soft hat with no brim

tur·bid *adj* **:** dark or discolored with sediment

tur·bine *n* **:** an engine whose central driving shaft is fitted with a series of winglike parts that are spun by the pressure of water, steam, or gas

tur·bu·lence *n* **:** irregular movements of air currents

tur·bu·lent *adj* **:** causing or being in a state of unrest, violence, or disturbance

tu·reen *n* **:** a deep bowl from which food (as soup) is served

turf *n* **1 :** the upper layer of soil bound into a thick mat by roots of grass and other plants **2 :** land covered with grass **3 :** an area that is or is felt to be under an individual's control

Turk *n* **:** a person born or living in Turkey

tur·key *n, pl* **turkeys :** a large North American bird related to the chicken and widely raised for food

[1]**Turk·ish** *adj* **:** of or relating to Turkey, the Turks, or Turkish

[2]**Turkish** *n* **:** the language of the Turks

tur·moil *n* **:** a very confused or disturbed state or condition

[1]**turn** *vb* **turned; turn·ing 1 :** to change in position usually by moving through an arc of a circle **2 :** to change course or direction **3 :** to move or direct toward or away from something **4 :** to become or cause to become a certain way **5 :** [1]CHANGE 1, TRANSFORM **6 :** to move or cause to move around a center **:** ROTATE **7 :** to twist so as to bring about a desired end **8 :** to go around **9 :** to reach or pass beyond **10 :** to become or make very unfriendly **11 :** to pass from one state to another **:** BECOME **12 :** EXECUTE 1, PERFORM **13 :** to set in another and especially an opposite direction **14 :** [1]WRENCH 2 **15 :** to think over **:** PONDER **16 :** [1]UPSET 2 **17 :** to make an appeal **18 :** to make or become spoiled **19 :** TRANSLATE 1 **20 :** to give a rounded form to (as on a lathe) — **turn down 1 :** to lower by using a control **2 :** [1]REFUSE 1, REJECT **3 :** to fold back or under — **turn off 1 :** to stop by using a control **2 :** to change direction — **turn on :** to make work by using a control — **turn out 1 :** to prove to be **2 :** to turn off — **turn over :** to give control or responsibility of to someone — **turn tail :** to turn so as to run away — **turn up 1 :** to be found or happen unexpectedly **2 :** to raise by or as if by using a control **3 :** ARRIVE 1

[2]**turn** *n* **1 :** the act of moving about a cen-

ter **2** : a change or changing of direction, course, or position **3** : a place at which something changes direction **4** : a period of action or activity : SPELL **5** : proper place in a waiting line or time in a schedule **6** : a change or changing of the general state or condition **7** : an act affecting another **8** : a short walk or ride **9** : a special purpose or need **10** : special quality **11** : the beginning of a new period of time **12** : a single circle or loop (as of rope passed around an object) **13** : natural or special skill — **at every turn** : all the time : CONSTANTLY, CONTINUOUSLY — **by turns** : one after another — **in turn** : one after the other in order — **to a turn** : precisely right

turn·about *n* : a change from one direction or one way of thinking or acting to the opposite

tur·nip *n* : the thick white or yellow root of a plant related to the cabbage that is cooked and eaten as a vegetable

turn·out *n* : a gathering of people for a special reason

turn·over *n* : a filled pastry with one half of the crust turned over the other

turn·pike *n* : a road that people must pay a toll to use

turn·stile *n* : a post having arms that turn around which is set at an entrance or exit so that people can pass through only on foot one by one

tur·pen·tine *n* : an oil made from resin and used as a solvent and as a paint thinner

tur·quoise *n* : a blue to greenish gray mineral used in jewelry

tur·ret *n* **1** : a little tower often at a corner of a building **2** : a low usually rotating structure (as in a tank, warship, or airplane) in which guns are mounted

tur·tle *n* : a reptile that lives on land, in water, or both and has a toothless horny beak and a shell of bony plates which covers the body and into which the head, legs, and tail can usually be drawn

tur·tle·dove *n* : a small wild pigeon that has a low soft cry

tur·tle·neck *n* **1** : a high turned-over collar **2** : a garment having a high turned-over collar

tusk *n* : a very long large tooth (as of an elephant or walrus) that sticks out when the mouth is closed and is used especially in digging and fighting

1tus·sle *n* **1** : a short fight or struggle **2** : a rough argument or a struggle against difficult odds

2tussle *vb* **tus·sled; tus·sling** **1** : to struggle roughly : SCUFFLE **2** : to argue or compete with

1tu·tor *n* : a teacher who works with an individual student

2tutor *vb* **tu·tored; tu·tor·ing** : to teach usually individually

tu·tu *n, pl* **tu·tus** : a short skirt that extends out and is worn by a ballerina

tux·e·do *n, pl* **tux·e·dos** *or* **tux·e·does** : a formal suit for a man

TV *n* : TELEVISION

twain *n* : 2TWO 1

1twang *n* **1** : a harsh quick ringing sound **2** : speech that seems to be produced by the nose as well as the mouth

2twang *vb* **twanged; twang·ing** : to sound or cause to sound with a harsh quick ringing noise

'twas : it was

1tweak *vb* **tweaked; tweak·ing** : to pinch and pull with a sudden jerk and twist

2tweak *n* : an act of pinching and pulling with a sudden jerk and twist

tweed *n* **1** : a rough woolen cloth **2** **tweeds** *pl* : clothing (as a suit) made of rough woolen cloth

tween *n* : a boy or girl who is 11 or 12 years old : PRETEEN

1tweet *n* **1** : a chirping note **2** : a post made on the Twitter online message service

2tweet *vb* **tweet·ed; tweet·ing** **1** : to make a chirping sound **2** : to post a message on the Twitter online message service

tweez·ers *n pl* : a small instrument that is used like pincers in grasping or pulling something

1twelfth *adj* : coming right after eleventh

2twelfth *n* : number twelve in a series

1twelve *adj* : being one more than eleven

2twelve *n* : one more than eleven : three times four : 12

twelve·month *n* : YEAR

1twen·ti·eth *adj* : coming right after 19th

2twentieth *n* : number 20 in a series

1twen·ty *adj* : being one more than 19

2twenty *n* : one more than 19 : four times five : 20

twice *adv* : two times

twid·dle *vb* **twid·dled; twid·dling** : 1TWIRL

twig *n* : a small shoot or branch

twi·light *n* **1** : the period or the light from the sky between full night and sunrise or between sunset and full night **2** : a period of decline

twill *n* : a way of weaving cloth that produces a pattern of diagonal lines

1twin *n* **1** : either of two offspring produced at one birth **2** : one of two persons or things closely related to or very like each other

2twin *adj* **1** : born with one other or as a pair at one birth **2** : made up of two similar, related, or connected members or parts **3** : being one of a pair

1twine *n* : a strong string of two or more strands twisted together

DICTIONARY

[2]**twine** *vb* **twined; twin·ing** **1 :** to twist together **2 :** to coil around a support
[1]**twinge** *n* **:** a sudden sharp stab (as of pain or emotion)
[2]**twinge** *vb* **twinged; twing·ing** *or* **twinge·ing :** to affect with or feel a sudden sharp pain or emotion
[1]**twin·kle** *vb* **twin·kled; twin·kling** **1 :** to shine or cause to shine with a flickering or sparkling light **2 :** to appear bright with amusement **3 :** to move or flutter rapidly
[2]**twinkle** *n* **1 :** [2]SPARKLE 1, FLICKER **2 :** a very short time
twin·kling *n* **:** [2]TWINKLE 2
[1]**twirl** *vb* **twirled; twirl·ing :** to turn or cause to turn rapidly — **twirl·er** *n*
[2]**twirl** *n* **:** an act of turning or causing to turn rapidly
[1]**twist** *vb* **twist·ed; twist·ing** **1 :** to turn a part of the body around **2 :** to follow a winding course **3 :** to form into an unnatural shape **:** CONTORT **4 :** to unite by winding one thread, strand, or wire around another **5 :** [2]TWINE 2 **6 :** to turn so as to sprain or hurt **7 :** to pull off, rotate, or break by a turning force **8 :** to turn (something) in a circular motion with the hand **9 :** to change the meaning of
[2]**twist** *n* **1 :** something that has been turned upon itself, coiled, or rotated **2 :** an act of turning with force, coiling, or rotating **:** the state of being turned with force, coiled, or rotated **3 :** a spiral turn or curve **4 :** a turn or development that is both surprising and strange **5 :** an act of changing the meaning
twist·er *n* **1 :** TORNADO **2 :** WATERSPOUT 2
[1]**twitch** *vb* **twitched; twitch·ing** **1 :** to move or cause to move with a slight trembling or jerky motion **:** QUIVER **2 :** to move or pull with a sudden motion **:** JERK
[2]**twitch** *n* **1 :** a slight tremble or jerk of a muscle or body part **2 :** a short sudden pull or jerk
[1]**twit·ter** *vb* **twit·tered; twit·ter·ing** **1 :** to make a series of chirping noises **2 :** to talk in a chattering fashion
[2]**twitter** *n* **1 :** the chirping of birds **2 :** a light chattering or laughing **3 :** a nervous upset state
[1]**two** *adj* **:** being one more than one
[2]**two** *n* **1 :** one more than one **:** 2 **2 :** the second in a set or series
two–dimensional *adj* **:** having the two dimensions of length and width
two–faced *adj* **:** saying different things to different people in order to gain their approval instead of speaking and behaving honestly
two·fold *adj* **:** being twice as great or as many
two–way *adj* **1 :** moving or acting or allowing movement or action in either direction **2 :** involving two persons or groups **3 :** made to send and receive messages
TX *abbr* Texas
ty·coon *n* **:** a very powerful and wealthy business person
tying *present participle of* TIE
[1]**type** *n* **1 :** a particular kind or group of things or people **:** VARIETY **2 :** a set of letters or figures that are used for printing or the letters or figures printed by them **3 :** the special qualities or characteristics by which members of a group are set apart from other groups
[2]**type** *vb* **typed; typ·ing** **1 :** to write with a keyboard (as on computer or typewriter) **2 :** to identify as belonging to a certain group
type·writ·er *n* **:** a machine that prints letters or figures when a person pushes its keys down
type·writ·ing *n* **1 :** the use of a typewriter **2 :** writing done with a typewriter
ty·phoid *n* **:** TYPHOID FEVER
typhoid fever *n* **:** a disease that spreads through contaminated food and water and in which there is fever, diarrhea, and great weakness
ty·phoon *n* **:** a tropical cyclone in the region of the Philippines or the China Sea
ty·phus *n* **:** a disease spread especially by body lice and in which there is high fever, delirium, severe headache, and a dark red rash
typ·i·cal *adj* **:** combining or showing the special characteristics of a group or kind — **typ·i·cal·ly** *adv*
typ·i·fy *vb* **typ·i·fied; typ·i·fy·ing** **1 :** REPRESENT 2 **2 :** to have the usual characteristics of **:** be a typical part of
typ·ist *n* **:** a person who uses a typewriter
ty·ran·ni·cal *adj* **:** relating to or like that of tyranny or a tyrant
ty·ran·no·saur *n* **:** a very large North American meat-eating dinosaur that had small forelegs and walked on its hind legs
ty·ran·no·sau·rus *n* **:** TYRANNOSAUR
tyr·an·ny *n, pl* **tyr·an·nies** **1 :** an act or the pattern of harsh, cruel, and unfair control over other people **2 :** a government in which all power is in the hands of a single ruler
ty·rant *n* **1 :** a ruler who has no legal limits on his or her power **2 :** a ruler who exercises total power harshly and cruelly **3 :** a person who uses authority or power harshly

U

u *n, pl* **u's** *or* **us** *often cap* **1 :** the 21st letter of the English alphabet **2 :** a grade rating a student's work as unsatisfactory

ud·der *n* **:** a large bag-shaped organ (as of a cow) enclosing two or more milk-producing glands each draining into a separate nipple on the lower surface

ugh *interj* — used to express disgust or horror

ug·ly *adj* **ug·li·er; ug·li·est** **1 :** unpleasant to look at **:** not attractive **2 :** [1]OFFENSIVE 3 **3 :** likely to cause bother or discomfort **:** TROUBLESOME **4 :** showing a mean or quarrelsome disposition — **ug·li·ness** *n*

UK *abbr* United Kingdom

uku·le·le *n* **:** a musical instrument like a small guitar with four strings

ul·cer *n* **:** a slow-healing open painful sore (as of the lining of the stomach) in which tissue breaks downs

ul·na *n, pl* **ul·nas** *or* **ul·nae** **:** the bone on the little-finger side of the arm between the wrist and elbow

ul·te·ri·or *adj* **:** kept hidden usually on purpose

[1]ul·ti·mate *adj* **1 :** last in a series **:** FINAL **2 :** most extreme **3 :** relating to or being the chief or most important — **ul·ti·mate·ly** *adv*

[2]ultimate *n* **1 :** something ultimate **2** *cap* **:** a game played on a rectangular field between two seven-player teams in which a plastic disc is thrown from player to player and in which a team scores by catching a throw in the opponent's end zone

ul·ti·ma·tum *n, pl* **ul·ti·ma·tums** *or* **ul·ti·ma·ta** **:** a final condition or demand that if rejected could end future negotiations and lead to forceful or undesirable action

ul·tra *adj* **:** [1]EXTREME 1

ultra- *prefix* **1 :** beyond in space **:** on the other side **2 :** beyond the limits of **:** SUPER- **3 :** beyond what is ordinary or proper

ul·tra·vi·o·let *adj* **:** relating to, producing, or being energy that is like light but has a slightly shorter wavelength and lies beyond the violet end of the spectrum

um·bil·i·cal cord *n* **:** a cord that contains blood vessels and connects a developing fetus with the placenta of the mother

um·brel·la *n* **:** a fabric covering stretched over a circular folding frame attached to a pole and used for protection against rain or sun

um·pire *n* **:** an official in a sport (as baseball) who enforces the rules

UN *abbr* United Nations

[1]un- *prefix* **1 :** not **:** IN-, NON- **2 :** opposite of **:** contrary to

[2]un- *prefix* **1 :** do the opposite of **:** DE-, DIS- **2 :** remove a specified thing from or free or release from **3 :** completely

un·able *adj* **:** not able

un·ac·cept·able *adj* **:** not pleasing or welcome **:** not acceptable

un·ac·count·able *adj* **:** not to be explained **:** STRANGE — **un·ac·count·ably** *adv*

un·ac·cus·tomed *adj* **:** not used to something

un·af·fect·ed *adj* **1 :** not influenced or changed **2 :** free from false behavior intended to impress others **:** GENUINE

un·afraid *adj* **:** not afraid

un·aid·ed *adj* **:** without help **:** not aided

un·al·loyed *adj* **:** PURE 1

unan·i·mous *adj* **1 :** having the same opinion **:** agreeing completely **2 :** agreed to by all

un·armed *adj* **:** having no weapons or armor

un·as·sum·ing *adj* **:** MODEST 1

un·at·trac·tive *adj* **:** not attractive **:** PLAIN

un·avoid·able *adj* **:** not preventable **:** INEVITABLE — **un·avoid·ably** *adv*

[1]un·aware *adv* **:** UNAWARES

[2]unaware *adj* **:** not having knowledge **:** not aware

un·awares *adv* **1 :** without warning **:** by surprise **2 :** without knowing **:** UNINTENTIONALLY

un·bear·able *adj* **:** seeming too great or too bad to put up with — **un·bear·ably** *adv*

un·be·com·ing *adj* **:** not suitable or proper **:** not becoming

un·be·knownst *also* **un·be·known** *adj* **:** happening without someone's knowledge **:** UNKNOWN

un·be·liev·able *adj* **1 :** too unlikely to be believed **2 :** very impressive or amazing — **un·be·liev·ably** *adv*

un·bi·ased *adj* **:** free from bias

un·bind *vb* **un·bound; un·bind·ing** **1 :** to remove a band from **:** UNTIE **2 :** to set free

un·born *adj* **:** not yet born

un·bound·ed *adj* **:** having no limits

un·break·able *adj* **:** not easily broken

un·bri·dled *adj* **:** not controlled or restrained

un·bro·ken *adj* **1 :** not damaged **:** WHOLE **2 :** not interrupted **:** CONTINUOUS **3 :** not tamed for use

un·buck·le *vb* **un·buck·led; un·buck·ling** **:** to unfasten the buckle of (as a belt)

un·bur·den *vb* **un·bur·dened; un·bur·den·ing** **:** to free from a burden and especially from something causing worry or unhappiness

un·but·ton *vb* **un·but·toned; un·but·ton·ing** **:** to unfasten the buttons of

un·called–for *adj* : not needed or wanted : not proper

un·can·ny *adj* **1 :** strange or unusual in a way that is surprising or mysterious **2 :** suggesting powers or abilities greater than normal — **un·can·ni·ly** *adv*

un·cer·tain *adj* **1 :** not exactly known or decided on **2 :** not sure **3 :** not known for sure **4 :** likely to change : not dependable — **un·cer·tain·ly** *adv*

un·cer·tain·ty *n, pl* **un·cer·tain·ties** **1 :** lack of certainty : DOUBT **2 :** something that is doubtful or unknown

un·change·able *adj* : not changing or capable of being changed

un·changed *adj* : not changed

un·chang·ing *adj* : not changing or able to change

un·char·ac·ter·is·tic *adj* : not typical or characteristic — **un·char·ac·ter·is·ti·cal·ly** *adv*

un·civ·il *adj* : IMPOLITE

un·civ·i·lized *adj* **1 :** having, relating to, or being like a culture that is not advanced **2 :** not having or showing good manners : RUDE

un·cle *n* **1 :** the brother of a person's father or mother **2 :** the husband of a person's aunt or uncle

un·clean *adj* **1 :** DIRTY 1, FILTHY **2 :** not pure and innocent **3 :** not allowed for use by religious law

un·clear *adj* : difficult to understand or make sense of

un·cleared *adj* : not cleared especially of trees or brush

un·clothed *adj* : not wearing or covered with clothes

un·com·fort·able *adj* **1 :** causing discomfort or uneasiness **2 :** feeling discomfort or uneasiness — **un·com·fort·ably** *adv*

un·com·mon *adj* **1 :** not often found or seen : UNUSUAL **2 :** not ordinary : REMARKABLE — **un·com·mon·ly** *adv*

un·com·pro·mis·ing *adj* : unwilling to give in even a little — **un·com·pro·mis·ing·ly** *adv*

un·con·cern *n* : lack of care or interest

un·con·cerned *adj* **1 :** free of worry **2 :** not involved or interested

un·con·di·tion·al *adj* : without any special exceptions — **un·con·di·tion·al·ly** *adv*

un·con·quer·able *adj* : not capable of being beaten or overcome

un·con·scious *adj* **1 :** not aware **2 :** having lost consciousness **3 :** not intentional or planned — **un·con·scious·ly** *adv* — **un·con·scious·ness** *n*

un·con·sti·tu·tion·al *adj* : not according to or agreeing with the constitution of a country or government

un·con·trol·la·ble *adj* : hard or impossible to control — **un·con·trol·la·bly** *adv*

un·con·trolled *adj* : not being controlled

un·co·op·er·a·tive *adj* : not showing a desire to act or work with others in a helpful way

un·couth *adj* : impolite in conduct or speech : CRUDE

un·cov·er *vb* **un·cov·ered; un·cov·er·ing** **1 :** to make known usually by investigation **2 :** to make visible by removing some covering **3 :** to remove the cover from

un·curl *vb* **un·curled; un·curl·ing** : to make or become straightened out from a curled position

un·cut *adj* **1 :** not cut down or cut into **2 :** not shaped by cutting

un·daunt·ed *adj* : not discouraged or afraid to continue

un·de·cid·ed *adj* **1 :** not yet settled or decided **2 :** not having decided : uncertain what to do

un·de·clared *adj* : not made known : not declared

un·de·feat·ed *adj* : having no losses

un·de·ni·able *adj* : clearly true : impossible to deny — **un·de·ni·ably** *adv*

[1]un·der *adv* **1 :** in or into a position below or beneath something **2 :** below some quantity or level

[2]under *prep* **1 :** lower than and topped or sheltered by **2 :** below the surface of **3 :** in or into such a position as to be covered or hidden by **4 :** commanded or guided by **5 :** controlled or managed by **6 :** affected or influenced by the action or effect of **7 :** within the division or grouping of **8 :** less or lower than (as in size, amount, or rank)

[3]under *adj* **1 :** lying or placed below or beneath **2 :** lower in position or authority — often used in combination

un·der·arm *n* : ARMPIT

un·der·brush *n* : shrubs and small trees growing among large trees

un·der·clothes *n pl* : UNDERWEAR

un·der·cooked *adj* : not cooked enough

un·der·cur·rent *n* **1 :** a flow of water that moves below the surface **2 :** a hidden feeling or tendency often different from the one openly shown

un·der·dog *n* : a person or team thought to have little chance of winning (as an election or a game)

un·der·foot *adv* **1 :** under the feet **2 :** close about a person's feet : in the way

un·der·gar·ment *n* : a garment to be worn under another

un·der·go *vb* **un·der·went; un·der·gone; un·der·go·ing** : to experience or endure (something)

[1]un·der·ground *adv* **1 :** below the surface of the earth **2 :** in or into hiding or secret operation

[2]**un·der·ground** *n* **1 :** SUBWAY **2 :** a secret political movement or group

[3]**un·der·ground** *adj* **1 :** located under the surface of the ground **2 :** done or happening secretly

un·der·growth *n* **:** low growth on the floor of a forest that includes shrubs, herbs, and saplings

[1]**un·der·hand** *adv* **:** with an upward movement of the hand or arm

[2]**underhand** *adj* **1 :** done in secret or so as to deceive **2 :** made with an upward movement of the hand or arm

un·der·hand·ed *adj* **:** [2]UNDERHAND 1

un·der·lie *vb* **un·der·lay; un·der·lain; un·der·ly·ing 1 :** to lie or be located under **2 :** to form the foundation of **:** SUPPORT

un·der·line *vb* **un·der·lined; un·der·lin·ing 1 :** to draw a line under **2 :** EMPHASIZE

un·der·mine *vb* **un·der·mined; un·der·min·ing 1 :** to dig out or wear away the supporting earth beneath **2 :** to weaken secretly or little by little

[1]**un·der·neath** *prep* **:** directly under

[2]**underneath** *adv* **1 :** below a surface or object **:** BENEATH **2 :** on the lower side

un·der·nour·ished *adj* **:** given too little food for proper health and growth

un·der·pants *n pl* **:** underwear worn on the lower part of the body

un·der·part *n* **:** a part lying on the lower side (as of a bird or mammal)

un·der·pass *n* **:** a road or passage that runs under something (as another road)

un·der·priv·i·leged *adj* **:** having fewer advantages than others especially because of being poor

un·der·rate *vb* **un·der·rat·ed; un·der·rat·ing :** to rate too low **:** UNDERVALUE

un·der·score *vb* **un·der·scored; un·der·scor·ing 1 :** UNDERLINE 1 **2 :** EMPHASIZE

un·der·sea *adj* **1 :** being or done under the sea or under the surface of the sea **2 :** used under the surface of the sea

un·der·shirt *n* **:** a collarless garment with or without sleeves that is worn as an undergarment

un·der·side *n* **:** the side or surface lying underneath

un·der·stand *vb* **un·der·stood; un·der·stand·ing 1 :** to get the meaning of **2 :** to know thoroughly **3 :** to have reason to believe **4 :** to take as meaning something not clearly made known **5 :** to have a sympathetic attitude **6 :** to accept as settled

un·der·stand·able *adj* **1 :** possible or easy to get or realize the meaning of **:** capable of being understood **2 :** normal and reasonable for a particular situation — **un·der·stand·ably** *adv*

[1]**un·der·stand·ing** *n* **1 :** ability to get the meaning of and judge **2 :** an agreement of opinion or feeling **3 :** a willingness to show kind or favorable feelings toward others **4 :** the particular way in which someone understands something

[2]**understanding** *adj* **:** having or showing kind or favorable feelings toward others **:** SYMPATHETIC

un·der·state·ment *n* **:** a statement that makes something seem smaller or less important or serious than it really is

un·der·study *n, pl* **un·der·stud·ies :** an actor who is prepared to take over another actor's part if necessary

un·der·take *vb* **un·der·took; un·der·tak·en; un·der·tak·ing 1 :** to plan or try to accomplish **2 :** to take on as a responsibility **:** AGREE

un·der·tak·er *n* **:** a person whose business is to prepare the dead for burial and to take charge of funerals

un·der·tak·ing *n* **:** an important or difficult task or project

un·der·tone *n* **1 :** a low or quiet voice **2 :** a partly hidden feeling or meaning

un·der·tow *n* **:** a current beneath the surface of the water that moves away from or along the shore while the surface water above it moves toward the shore

un·der·val·ue *vb* **un·der·val·ued; un·der·valu·ing :** to value below the real worth

[1]**un·der·wa·ter** *adj* **:** lying, growing, worn, performed, or operating below the surface of the water

[2]**un·der·wa·ter** *adv* **:** under the surface of the water

un·der·wear *n* **:** clothing worn next to the skin and under other clothing

un·der·weight *adj* **:** weighing less than what is normal, average, or necessary

underwent *past of* UNDERGO

un·der·world *n* **:** the world of crime

un·de·sir·able *adj* **:** having qualities that are not pleasing or wanted

un·de·vel·oped *adj* **1 :** not used for farming or building on **2 :** having few large industries and a simple economic system **3 :** not fully grown or matured

un·dig·ni·fied *adj* **:** lacking proper seriousness or self-control in behavior or appearance **:** not showing dignity

un·dis·cov·ered *adj* **:** not discovered

un·dis·put·ed *adj* **:** not disputed **:** UNQUESTIONABLE

un·dis·turbed *adj* **1 :** not moved, interrupted, or interfered with **2 :** not upset

un·di·vid·ed *adj* **:** complete or total

un·do *vb* **un·did; un·done; un·do·ing; un·does 1 :** UNTIE 2, UNFASTEN **2 :** to cancel

the effect of **:** REVERSE **3 :** to cause the ruin or failure of
un·do·ing *n* **:** a cause of ruin or failure
un·done *adj* **:** not done or finished
un·doubt·ed *adj* **:** definitely true or existing **:** not doubted
un·doubt·ed·ly *adv* **:** without doubt **:** SURELY
un·dress *vb* **un·dressed; un·dress·ing :** to remove the clothes or covering of
un·du·late *vb* **un·du·lat·ed; un·du·lat·ing :** to move in or as if in a wavy or flowing way
un·dy·ing *adj* **:** lasting forever **:** IMMORTAL
un·earth *vb* **un·earthed; un·earth·ing 1 :** to bring up from underground **:** dig up **2 :** to bring to light **:** UNCOVER
un·easy *adj* **un·eas·i·er; un·eas·i·est 1 :** not comfortable in manner **:** AWKWARD **2 :** showing or filled with worry **:** APPREHENSIVE — **un·eas·i·ly** *adv* — **un·eas·i·ness** *n*
un·ed·u·cat·ed *adj* **1 :** lacking in education and especially schooling **2 :** based on little or no knowledge or fact
un·em·ployed *adj* **:** having no job **:** not employed
un·em·ploy·ment *n* **1 :** the state of being out of work **2 :** the number of people who do not have jobs
un·end·ing *adj* **:** having no ending **:** ENDLESS
un·equal *adj* **1 :** not alike (as in size or value) **2 :** badly balanced or matched **3 :** not having the needed abilities — **un·equal·ly** *adv*
un·equaled *adj* **:** having no equal or match
un·even *adj* **1 :** ODD 2 **2 :** not level, straight, or smooth **3 :** IRREGULAR 4 **4 :** varying in quality **5 :** UNEQUAL 2 — **un·even·ly** *adv* — **un·even·ness** *n*
un·event·ful *adj* **:** having nothing exciting, interesting, or important happening **:** not eventful — **un·event·ful·ly** *adv*
un·ex·pect·ed *adj* **:** not expected **:** UNFORESEEN — **un·ex·pect·ed·ly** *adv*
un·fail·ing *adj* **:** not failing or likely to fail **:** CONSTANT — **un·fail·ing·ly** *adv*
un·fair *adj* **:** not fair, honest, or just — **un·fair·ly** *adv* — **un·fair·ness** *n*
un·faith·ful *adj* **:** not faithful **:** DISLOYAL
un·fa·mil·iar *adj* **1 :** not well known **:** STRANGE **2 :** lacking good knowledge of something
un·fas·ten *vb* **un·fas·tened; un·fas·ten·ing :** to make or become loose
un·fa·vor·able *adj* **1 :** expressing or showing disapproval **2 :** likely to make difficult or unpleasant — **un·fa·vor·ably** *adv*
un·feel·ing *adj* **:** having no kindness or sympathy **:** CRUEL
un·fin·ished *adj* **:** not finished
un·fit *adj* **1 :** not suitable **2 :** not qualified **3 :** physically unhealthy
un·fold *vb* **un·fold·ed; un·fold·ing 1 :** to open the folds of **:** open up **2 :** to lay open to view or understanding **:** REVEAL **3 :** to develop gradually
un·fol·low *vb* **un·fol·lowed; un·fol·low·ing :** to choose to no longer regularly see social media messages from someone or something (as a business)
un·fore·seen *adj* **:** not known beforehand **:** UNEXPECTED
un·for·get·ta·ble *adj* **:** not likely to be forgotten — **un·for·get·ta·bly** *adv*
un·for·giv·able *adj* **:** not to be forgiven or pardoned — **un·for·giv·ably** *adv*
un·for·tu·nate *adj* **1 :** not fortunate **:** UNLUCKY **2 :** accompanied by or resulting in bad luck **3 :** not proper or suitable — **un·for·tu·nate·ly** *adv*
un·found·ed *adj* **:** not based on facts or proof **:** GROUNDLESS
un·friend *vb* **un·friend·ed; un·friend·ing :** to remove (someone) from a list of designated friends on a person's social networking website
un·friend·ly *adj* **un·friend·li·er; un·friend·li·est 1 :** not friendly or kind **2 :** not agreeable **:** UNFAVORABLE
un·furl *vb* **un·furled; un·furl·ing :** to open out from a rolled or folded state
un·gain·ly *adj* **un·gain·li·er; un·gain·li·est :** CLUMSY 1, AWKWARD
un·god·ly *adj* **un·god·li·er; un·god·li·est 1 :** SINFUL, WICKED **2 :** not normal or bearable
un·gra·cious *adj* **:** not kind or polite
un·grate·ful *adj* **:** not feeling or showing thanks
un·gu·late *n* **:** a usually plant-eating animal (as a cow, horse, or sheep) with hooves
un·hap·py *adj* **un·hap·pi·er; un·hap·pi·est 1 :** not cheerful **:** SAD **2 :** not pleased or satisfied **3 :** full of or showing feelings of sadness or misery **4 :** not fortunate **:** UNLUCKY **5 :** not suitable **:** INAPPROPRIATE — **un·hap·pi·ly** *adv* — **un·hap·pi·ness** *n*
un·healthy *adj* **un·health·i·er; un·health·i·est 1 :** not good for someone's health **:** promoting a state of poor health **2 :** not in good health **:** SICKLY **3 :** HARMFUL, BAD — **un·health·i·ly** *adv*
un·heard *adj* **:** not heard
un·heard–of *adj* **:** not known before
un·hin·dered *adj* **:** not kept back **:** proceeding freely
un·hitch *vb* **un·hitched; un·hitch·ing :** to free from being hitched
un·ho·ly *adj* **un·ho·li·er; un·ho·li·est 1 :** not holy **:** WICKED **2 :** UNGODLY 2
un·hook *vb* **un·hooked; un·hook·ing 1 :** to remove from a hook **2 :** to unfasten the hooks of

un·horse *vb* **un·horsed; un·hors·ing** : to cause to fall from or as if from a horse
un·hur·ried *adj* : not in a rush
uni- *prefix* : one : single
uni·corn *n* : an imaginary animal that looks like a horse with one horn in the middle of the forehead
un·iden·ti·fi·able *adj* : impossible to identify : not recognizable
un·iden·ti·fied *adj* : having an identity that is not known or determined
uni·fi·ca·tion *n* : the act, process, or result of bringing or coming together into or as if into a single unit or group
[1]**uni·form** *adj* : always the same in form, manner, appearance, or degree throughout or over time — **uni·form·ly** *adv*
[2]**uniform** *n* : special clothing worn by members of a particular group (as an army)
uni·formed *adj* : dressed in uniform
uni·for·mi·ty *n, pl* **uni·for·mi·ties** : the quality or state of being the same in form, manner, appearance, or degree
uniform resource lo·ca·tor *n* : URL
uni·fy *vb* **uni·fied; uni·fy·ing** : to bring or come together into or as if into a single unit or group : UNITE
un·imag·in·able *adj* : not possible to imagine or understand
un·im·por·tant *adj* : not important
un·in·hab·it·ed *adj* : not lived in or on
un·in·tel·li·gi·ble *adj* : impossible to understand
un·in·ten·tion·al *adj* : not done on purpose : not intentional — **un·in·ten·tion·al·ly** *adv*
un·in·ter·est·ed *adj* : not interested
un·in·ter·est·ing *adj* : not attracting or keeping interest or attention
un·in·ter·rupt·ed *adj* : not interrupted : CONTINUOUS
un·in·vit·ed *adj* : not having been invited
union *n* **1** : an act or instance of uniting or joining two or more things into one **2** : something (as a nation) formed by a combining of parts or members **3** *cap* : the United States **4** *cap* : the group of states that supported the United States government in the American Civil War **5** : a device for connecting parts (as pipes) **6** : LABOR UNION
Union *adj* : relating to the group of states that supported the United States government in the American Civil War
union suit *n* : an undergarment with shirt and pants in one piece
unique *adj* **1** : being the only one of its kind **2** : very unusual : NOTABLE — **unique·ly** *adv* — **unique·ness** *n*
uni·son *n* : the state of being tuned or sounded at the same pitch or at an octave — **in unison 1** : in exact agreement **2** : at the same time
unit *n* **1** : a single thing, person, or group forming part of a whole **2** : the least whole number : ONE **3** : a fixed quantity (as of length, time, or value) used as a standard of measurement **4** : a part of a school course with a central theme
unite *vb* **unit·ed; unit·ing 1** : to put or come together to form a single unit **2** : to bind by legal or moral ties **3** : to join in action
unit·ed *adj* **1** : made one **2** : having the same goals, ideas, and principles
uni·ty *n, pl* **uni·ties 1** : the quality or state of being one **2** : the state of those who are in full agreement : HARMONY
uni·ver·sal *adj* **1** : including, covering, or taking in all or everything **2** : present or happening everywhere — **uni·ver·sal·ly** *adv*
universal resource lo·ca·tor *n* : URL
uni·verse *n* : all created things including the earth and celestial bodies viewed as making up one system
uni·ver·si·ty *n, pl* **uni·ver·si·ties** : an institution of higher learning that gives degrees in special fields and where research is performed
un·just *adj* : not just : UNFAIR — **un·just·ly** *adv*
un·kempt *adj* **1** : not combed **2** : not neat and orderly : UNTIDY
un·kind *adj* **un·kind·er; un·kind·est** : not kind or sympathetic — **un·kind·ly** *adv* — **un·kind·ness** *n*
[1]**un·known** *adj* : not known
[2]**unknown** *n* : one (as a quantity) that is unknown
un·lace *vb* **un·laced; un·lac·ing** : to undo the laces of
un·latch *vb* **unlatched; unlatching** : to open by lifting a latch
un·law·ful *adj* : not lawful : ILLEGAL — **un·law·ful·ly** *adv*
un·learned *adj* **1** : not educated **2** : not based on experience : INSTINCTIVE
un·leash *vb* **un·leashed; un·leash·ing** : to free from or as if from a leash
un·less *conj* : except on the condition that
un·lik·able *adj* : difficult to like
[1]**un·like** *prep* **1** : different from **2** : unusual for **3** : differently from
[2]**unlike** *adj* : DIFFERENT, UNEQUAL
un·like·ly *adj* **un·like·li·er; un·like·li·est 1** : not likely **2** : not promising
un·lim·it·ed *adj* **1** : having no restrictions or controls **2** : BOUNDLESS, INFINITE
un·load *vb* **un·load·ed; un·load·ing 1** : to take away or off : REMOVE **2** : to take a load from **3** : to get rid of or be freed from a load or burden
un·lock *vb* **un·locked; un·lock·ing 1** : to unfasten the lock of **2** : to make known
un·looked–for *adj* : not expected

un·loose *vb* **un·loosed; un·loos·ing** **1** : to make looser : RELAX **2** : to set free
un·lucky *adj* **un·luck·i·er; un·luck·i·est** **1** : not fortunate : having bad luck **2** : marked by bad luck or failure **3** : likely to bring misfortune **4** : causing distress or regret — **un·luck·i·ly** *adv*
un·man·age·able *adj* : hard or impossible to handle or control
un·man·ner·ly *adj* : not having or showing good manners
un·mar·ried *adj* : not married : SINGLE
un·mis·tak·able *adj* : impossible to mistake for anything else — **un·mis·tak·ably** *adv*
un·moved *adj* **1** : not being stirred by deep feelings or excitement **2** : staying in the same place or position
un·nat·u·ral *adj* **1** : different from what is found in nature or happens naturally **2** : different from what is usually considered normal behavior **3** : not genuine — **un·nat·u·ral·ly** *adv*
un·nec·es·sary *adj* : not needed — **un·nec·es·sar·i·ly** *adv*
un·nerve *vb* **un·nerved; un·nerv·ing** : to cause to lose confidence, courage, or self-control
un·no·tice·able *adj* : not easily noticed
un·num·bered *adj* **1** : not numbered **2** : INNUMERABLE
un·ob·served *adj* : not noticed
un·oc·cu·pied *adj* **1** : not being used, filled up, or lived in : EMPTY **2** : not busy
un·of·fi·cial *adj* : not official — **un·of·fi·cial·ly** *adv*
un·pack *vb* **un·packed; un·pack·ing** **1** : to separate and remove things that are packed **2** : to open and remove the contents of
un·paid *adj* : not paid
un·par·al·leled *adj* : having no counterpart or equal
un·pleas·ant *adj* : not pleasing or agreeable — **un·pleas·ant·ly** *adv* — **un·pleas·ant·ness** *n*
un·prec·e·dent·ed *adj* : not done or experienced before
un·pop·u·lar *adj* : not widely favored or approved
un·prof·it·able *adj* : not producing a profit
un·pre·dict·able *adj* : impossible to predict
un·prej·u·diced *adj* : not resulting from or having a bias for or against
un·pre·pared *adj* : not being or made ready
un·prin·ci·pled *adj* : not having or showing high moral principles
un·ques·tion·able *adj* : being beyond doubt — **un·ques·tion·ably** *adv*
un·ques·tion·ing *adj* : accepting without thinking or doubting
un·rav·el *vb* **un·rav·eled** *or* **un·rav·elled; un·rav·el·ing** *or* **un·rav·el·ling** **1** : to separate the threads of : UNTANGLE **2** : SOLVE
un·re·al *adj* : not actual or genuine
un·rea·son·able *adj* : not fair, sensible, appropriate, or moderate — **un·rea·son·ably** *adv*
un·re·lent·ing *adj* **1** : not giving in or softening in determination : STERN **2** : not letting up or weakening in energy or pace — **un·re·lent·ing·ly** *adv*
un·re·li·able *adj* : not worthy of trust
un·rest *n* : a disturbed or uneasy state
un·ripe *adj* : not ripe or mature
un·ri·valed *or* **un·ri·valled** *adj* : having no rival
un·roll *vb* **un·rolled; un·roll·ing** **1** : to unwind a roll of **2** : to become unrolled
un·ruf·fled *adj* **1** : not upset or disturbed **2** : [1]SMOOTH 4
un·ruly *adj* **un·rul·i·er; un·rul·i·est** : difficult to control — **un·rul·i·ness** *n*
un·safe *adj* : exposed or exposing to danger
un·san·i·tary *adj* : likely to cause sickness or disease : dirty or full of germs
un·sat·is·fac·to·ry *adj* : not what is needed or expected — **un·sat·is·fac·to·ri·ly** *adv*
un·sat·is·fied *adj* **1** : not fulfilled **2** : not pleased
un·scathed *adj* : completely without harm or injury
un·schooled *adj* : not trained or taught
un·sci·en·tif·ic *adj* : not using or applying the methods or principles of science : not scientific
un·scram·ble *vb* **un·scram·bled; un·scram·bling** : to make orderly or clear again
un·screw *vb* **un·screwed; un·screw·ing** **1** : to loosen or withdraw by turning **2** : to remove the screws from
un·scru·pu·lous *adj* : not having or showing regard for what is right and proper — **un·scru·pu·lous·ly** *adv*
un·seal *vb* **un·sealed; un·seal·ing** : to break or remove the seal of : OPEN
un·sea·son·able *adj* : happening or coming at the wrong time — **un·sea·son·ably** *adv*
un·sea·soned *adj* : not made ready or fit for use (as by the passage of time)
un·seat *vb* **un·seat·ed; un·seat·ing** **1** : to remove from a position of authority **2** : to cause to fall from a seat or saddle
un·seem·ly *adj* **un·seem·li·er; un·seem·li·est** : not polite or proper
un·seen *adj* : not seen : INVISIBLE
un·self·ish *adj* : not selfish — **un·self·ish·ly** *adv* — **un·self·ish·ness** *n*
un·set·tle *vb* **un·set·tled; un·set·tling** : to disturb the quiet or order of : UPSET
un·set·tled *adj* **1** : not staying the same **2** : feeling nervous, upset, or worried **3** : not finished or determined **4** : not paid **5** : not lived in by settlers
un·sheathe *vb* **un·sheathed; un·sheath·ing** : to draw from or as if from a sheath

un·sight·ly *adj* : not pleasant to look at : UGLY
un·skilled *adj* **1** : not having skill **2** : not needing skill
un·skill·ful *adj* : not skillful : not having skill — **un·skill·ful·ly** *adv*
un·sound *adj* **1** : not based on good reasoning or truth **2** : not firmly made or placed **3** : not healthy or in good condition **4** : being or having a mind that is not normal
un·speak·able *adj* **1** : impossible to express in words **2** : extremely bad — **un·speak·ably** *adv*
un·spec·i·fied *adj* : not mentioned or named
un·spoiled *adj* : not damaged or ruined
un·sta·ble *adj* : not stable
un·steady *adj* **un·stead·i·er; un·stead·i·est** : not steady : UNSTABLE — **un·stead·i·ly** *adv*
un·strap *vb* **un·strapped; un·strap·ping** : to remove or loosen a strap from
un·stressed *adj* : not accented
un·suc·cess·ful *adj* : not ending in or having gained success — **un·suc·cess·ful·ly** *adv*
un·suit·able *adj* : not fitting : INAPPROPRIATE
un·sup·port·ed *adj* **1** : not proved **2** : not held up
un·sur·passed *adj* : not exceeded (as in excellence)
un·sus·pect·ing *adj* : without suspicion
un·tan·gle *vb* **un·tan·gled; un·tan·gling** **1** : to remove a tangle from **2** : to straighten out
un·think·able *adj* : not to be thought of or considered as possible or reasonable
un·think·ing *adj* : not thinking about actions or words and how they will affect others
un·ti·dy *adj* **un·ti·di·er; un·ti·di·est** : not neat — **un·ti·di·ly** *adv* — **un·ti·di·ness** *n*
un·tie *vb* **un·tied; un·ty·ing** *or* **un·tie·ing** **1** : to undo the knots in **2** : to free from something that fastens or holds back
¹un·til *prep* : up to the time of
²until *conj* : up to the time that
un·time·ly *adj* **1** : happening or done before the expected, natural, or proper time **2** : coming at the wrong time
un·tir·ing *adj* : not becoming tired
un·to *prep* : ¹TO
un·told *adj* **1** : not told or made public **2** : too great or too numerous to be counted : VAST
un·touched *adj* **1** : not tasted **2** : not affected
un·to·ward *adj* : unexpected and unpleasant or improper
un·trou·bled *adj* : not troubled : free from worry
un·true *adj* **1** : not correct : FALSE **2** : not faithful : DISLOYAL
un·truth *n* **1** : the state of being false **2** : ³LIE
un·truth·ful *adj* : not containing or telling the truth : FALSE — **un·truth·ful·ly** *adv*
un·used *adj* **1** : not accustomed **2** : not having been used before **3** : not being used
un·usu·al *adj* : not done, found, used, experienced, or existing most of the time — **un·usu·al·ly** *adv*
un·veil *vb* **un·veiled; un·veil·ing** : to show or make known to the public for the first time
un·voiced *adj* : VOICELESS 2
un·want·ed *adj* : not desired or needed
un·wary *adj* **un·war·i·er; un·war·i·est** : easily fooled or surprised
un·washed *adj* : not having been washed : DIRTY
un·well *adj* : being in poor health
un·whole·some *adj* : not good for bodily, mental, or moral health
un·wieldy *adj* : hard to handle or control because of size or weight — **un·wield·i·ness** *n*
un·will·ing *adj* : not willing : RELUCTANT — **un·will·ing·ly** *adv* — **un·will·ing·ness** *n*
un·wind *vb* **un·wound; un·wind·ing** **1** : to uncoil a strand of **2** : RELAX 3
un·wise *adj* : FOOLISH — **un·wise·ly** *adv*
un·wor·thy *adj* **un·wor·thi·er; un·wor·thi·est** **1** : not deserving someone or something **2** : not appropriate for a particular kind of person or thing — **un·wor·thi·ness** *n*
un·wrap *vb* **un·wrapped; un·wrap·ping** : to remove the wrapping from
un·writ·ten *adj* : not in writing : followed by custom
un·yield·ing *adj* **1** : not soft or flexible : HARD **2** : showing or having firmness or determination
¹up *adv* **1** : in or to a high or higher place or position **2** : in or into a vertical position **3** : from beneath a surface (as ground or water) **4** : with greater force or to a greater level **5** : so as to make more active **6** : so as to appear or be present **7** : COMPLETELY **8** : so as to approach or be near **9** : from below the horizon **10** : out of bed **11** : in or into a better or more advanced state **12** : for consideration or discussion **13** : into the control of another **14** — used to show completeness **15** : so as to be closed **16** : in or into pieces **17** : to a stop **18** : into a working or usable state
²up *adj* **1** : risen above the horizon or ground **2** : being out of bed **3** : unusually high **4** : having been raised or built **5** : moving or going upward **6** : being busy and moving about **7** : well prepared **8** : happy or excited **9** : going on **10** : at an end **11** : well informed **12** : functioning correctly
³up *prep* **1** : to, toward, or at a higher point of **2** : to or toward the beginning of **3** : ¹ALONG 1 — **up to** **1** : as far as **2** : in accordance with **3** : to the limit of
⁴up *n* : a period or state of doing well

[5]**up** *vb* **upped; up·ping** **1 :** to act suddenly or surprisingly **2 :** to make or become higher

up–and–down *adj* **1 :** switching between upward and downward movement or action **2 :** PERPENDICULAR

[1]**up·beat** *n* **:** a beat in music that is not accented and especially one just before a downbeat

[2]**upbeat** *adj* **:** cheerful and positive

up·braid *vb* **up·braid·ed; up·braid·ing :** to criticize or scold severely

up·bring·ing *n* **:** the process of raising and training

up·com·ing *adj* **:** coming soon

[1]**up·date** *vb* **up·dat·ed; up·dat·ing** **1 :** to give or include the latest information **2 :** to make more modern

[2]**up·date** *n* **:** something that gives or includes the latest information

up·draft *n* **:** an upward movement of air

up·end *vb* **up·end·ed; up·end·ing :** to set, stand, or rise on end

up·grade *vb* **up·grad·ed; up·grad·ing** **1 :** to raise to a higher grade or position **2 :** to improve or replace old software or an old device

up·heav·al *n* **:** a period of great change or violent disorder

[1]**up·hill** *adv* **:** in an upward direction

[2]**up·hill** *adj* **1 :** going up **2 :** DIFFICULT 1

up·hold *vb* **up·held; up·hold·ing** **1 :** to give support to **2 :** to lift up

up·hol·ster *vb* **up·hol·stered; up·hol·ster·ing :** to provide with or as if with upholstery — **up·hol·ster·er** *n*

up·hol·stery *n, pl* **up·hol·ster·ies :** materials used to make a soft covering for a seat

up·keep *n* **:** the act or cost of keeping something in good condition

up·land *n* **:** high land usually far from a coast or sea

[1]**up·lift** *vb* **up·lift·ed; up·lift·ing** **1 :** to lift up **2 :** to make feel happy or hopeful

[2]**up·lift** *n* **:** an increase in happiness or hopefulness

up·load *vb* **up·load·ed; up·load·ing :** to transfer (data or files) to a large or remote computer from a smaller computer or other device

up·on *prep* **:** [1]ON

[1]**up·per** *adj* **1 :** higher in position or rank **2 :** farther inland

[2]**upper** *n* **:** something (as the parts of a shoe above the sole) that is upper

up·per·case *adj* **:** having the form A, B, C rather than a, b, c — **uppercase** *n*

upper hand *n* **:** ADVANTAGE 2

up·per·most *adj* **1 :** farthest up **2 :** being in the most important position

up·raise *vb* **up·raised; up·rais·ing :** to raise or lift up

[1]**up·right** *adj* **1 :** [1]VERTICAL **2 :** straight in posture **3 :** having or showing high moral standards — **up·right·ly** *adv*

[2]**upright** *adv* **:** in or into a vertical position

up·rise *vb* **up·rose; up·ris·en; up·ris·ing** **1 :** to rise to a higher position **2 :** to get up from sleeping or sitting

up·ris·ing *n* **:** REBELLION

up·roar *n* **:** a state of commotion, excitement, or violent disturbance

up·root *vb* **up·root·ed; up·root·ing** **1 :** to take out by or as if by pulling up by the roots **2 :** to take, send, or force away from a country or a traditional home

[1]**up·set** *vb* **up·set; up·set·ting** **1 :** to worry or make unhappy **2 :** to make somewhat ill **3 :** to force or be forced out of the usual position **:** OVERTURN **4 :** to cause confusion in **5 :** to defeat unexpectedly

[2]**up·set** *n* **1 :** an unexpected defeat **2 :** a feeling of illness in the stomach **3 :** a period of worry or unhappiness

[3]**up·set** *adj* **:** emotionally disturbed or unhappy

up·shot *n* **:** the final result

up·side–down *adj* **1 :** having the upper part underneath and the lower part on top **2 :** showing great confusion

up·side down *adv* **1 :** in such a way that the upper part is underneath and the lower part is on top **2 :** in or into great confusion

[1]**up·stairs** *adv* **:** up the stairs **:** on or to an upper floor

[2]**up·stairs** *adj* **:** being on or relating to an upper floor

[3]**up·stairs** *n* **:** the part of a building above the ground floor

up·stand·ing *adj* **:** HONEST 2

up·start *n* **:** a person who gains quick or unexpected success and shows off that success

up·stream *adv* **:** at or toward the beginning of a stream

up·swing *n* **:** a great increase or rise

up·tight *adj* **:** being tense, nervous, or uneasy

up–to–date *adj* **1 :** including the latest information **2 :** knowing, being, or making use of what is new or recent

up·town *adv* **:** to, toward, or in what is thought of as the upper part of a town or city

[1]**up·turn** *vb* **up·turned; up·turn·ing :** to turn upward or up or over

[2]**up·turn** *n* **:** an upward turning (as toward better conditions)

[1]**up·ward** *or* **up·wards** *adv* **1 :** in a direction from lower to higher **2 :** toward a higher or better state **3 :** toward a greater amount or a higher number or rate **4 :** toward the head

[2]**upward** *adj* **:** turned toward or being in a higher place or level — **up·ward·ly** *adv*

up·wind *adv or adj* **:** in the direction from which the wind is blowing

ura·ni·um *n* : a radioactive metallic chemical element used as a source of atomic energy
Ura·nus *n* : the planet that is seventh in order of distance from the sun and has a diameter of about 32,000 miles (51,000 kilometers)
ur·ban *adj* : of, relating to, or being a city
ur·chin *n* **1** : a mischievous or disrespectful youngster **2** : SEA URCHIN
-ure *suffix* **1** : act : process **2** : office : duty **3** : body performing an office or duty
urea *n* : a compound of nitrogen that is the chief solid substance dissolved in the urine of a mammal and is formed by the breaking down of protein
[1]**urge** *vb* **urged; urg·ing** **1** : to try to get (something) accepted : argue in favor of **2** : to try to convince **3** : [2]FORCE 1, DRIVE
[2]**urge** *n* : a strong desire
ur·gen·cy *n* : the quality or state of requiring immediate action or attention
ur·gent *adj* **1** : calling for immediate action **2** : having or showing a sense of requiring immediate action — **ur·gent·ly** *adv*
uri·nary *adj* : of or relating to urine or the parts of the body through which it passes
uri·nate *vb* **uri·nat·ed; uri·nat·ing** : to pass urine out of the body
uri·na·tion *n* : the act of urinating
urine *n* : the yellowish liquid produced by the kidneys and given off from the body as waste
URL *n* : the address of a computer or a document on the Internet
urn *n* **1** : a container usually in the form of a vase resting on a stand **2** : a closed container with a faucet used for serving a hot beverage
us *pron, objective case of* WE
US *abbr* United States
USA *abbr* United States of America
us·able *adj* : suitable or fit for use
us·age *n* **1** : usual way of doing things **2** : the way in which words and phrases are actually used **3** : the action of using : USE
USB *n* : a system for connecting a computer to another device (as a printer, keyboard, or mouse) by using a special kind of cord
[1]**use** *vb* **used; us·ing** **1** : to put into action or service : make use of **2** — used with *to* to show a former custom, fact, or state **3** : to take into the body **4** : to do something by means of **5** : to behave toward : TREAT — **us·er** *n* — **use up** : to make complete use of : EXHAUST
[2]**use** *n* **1** : the act of putting something into action or service **2** : the fact or state of being put into action or service **3** : way of putting into action or service **4** : the ability or power to put something into action or service **5** : the quality or state of being useful **6** : a reason or need to put into action or service **7** : LIKING
used *adj* **1** : SECONDHAND 1 **2** : having the habit of doing or putting up with something
use·ful *adj* **1** : capable of being put to use : USABLE **2** : helping to do or achieve something — **use·ful·ly** *adv* — **use·ful·ness** *n*
use·less *adj* : being of or having no use — **use·less·ly** *adv* — **use·less·ness** *n*
us·er–friend·ly *adj* : easy to learn, use, understand, or deal with — **user–friendliness** *n*
[1]**ush·er** *n* : a person who shows people to seats (as in a theater, at a game, or at a wedding)
[2]**usher** *vb* **ush·ered; ush·er·ing** **1** : to show or be shown to a place **2** : to come before as if to lead in or announce
usu. *abbr* **1** usual **2** usually
usu·al *adj* : done, found, used or existing most of the time — **usu·al·ly** *adv*
usurp *vb* **usurped; usurp·ing** : to take and hold unfairly or by force — **usurp·er** *n*
USVI *abbr* United States Virgin Islands
UT *abbr* Utah
uten·sil *n* **1** : a tool or container used in a home and especially a kitchen **2** : a useful tool
uter·us *n, pl* **uterus** *or* **uteri** : the organ of a female mammal in which the young develop before birth
util·i·ty *n, pl* **util·i·ties** **1** : the quality or state of being useful **2** : a business that supplies a public service (as electricity or gas) under special regulation by the government
uti·li·za·tion *n* : the action of making use of : the state of being used
uti·lize *vb* **uti·lized; uti·liz·ing** : to make use of especially for a certain job
[1]**ut·most** *adj* : of the greatest or highest degree or amount
[2]**utmost** *n* : the greatest or highest degree or amount
[1]**ut·ter** *adj* : in every way : TOTAL — **ut·ter·ly** *adv*
[2]**utter** *vb* **ut·tered; ut·ter·ing** **1** : to send forth as a sound **2** : to express in usually spoken words
ut·ter·ance *n* **1** : something said **2** : the act of saying something

V

v *n, pl* **v's** *or* **vs** *often cap* **1 :** the 22nd letter of the English alphabet **2 :** five in Roman numerals

v. *abbr* verb

Va., VA *abbr* Virginia

va·can·cy *n, pl* **va·can·cies** **1 :** something (as an office or hotel room) that is vacant **2 :** empty space **3 :** the state of being vacant

va·cant *adj* **1 :** not filled, used, or lived in **2 :** showing a lack of thought or expression **3 :** free from duties or care — **va·cant·ly** *adv*

va·cate *vb* **va·cat·ed; va·cat·ing :** to leave empty or not used

¹va·ca·tion *n* **1 :** a period during which activity (as of a school) is stopped for a time **2 :** a period spent away from home or business in travel or amusement

²vacation *vb* **va·ca·tioned; va·ca·tion·ing :** to take or spend a period away from home or business in travel or amusement — **va·ca·tion·er** *n*

vac·ci·nate *vb* **vac·ci·nat·ed; vac·ci·nat·ing :** to give a vaccine to usually by injection

vac·ci·na·tion *n* **:** the act of vaccinating

vac·cine *n* **:** a preparation containing usually killed or weakened microorganisms (as bacteria or viruses) that is given usually by injection to increase protection against a particular disease

vac·il·late *vb* **vac·il·lat·ed; vac·il·lat·ing :** to hesitate between courses or opinions **:** be unable to choose

¹vac·u·um *n, pl* **vac·u·ums** *or* **vac·ua** **1 :** a space completely empty of matter **2 :** a space from which most of the air has been removed (as by a pump) **3 :** VACUUM CLEANER

²vacuum *vb* **vac·u·umed; vac·u·um·ing :** to use a vacuum cleaner on

vacuum cleaner *n* **:** an electrical appliance for cleaning (as floors or rugs) by suction

¹vag·a·bond *adj* **:** moving from place to place without a fixed home

²vagabond *n* **:** a person who moves from place to place without a fixed home

va·gi·na *n* **:** a canal that leads from the uterus to the outside of the body

¹va·grant *n* **:** a person who has no steady job and wanders from place to place

²vagrant *adj* **1 :** wandering about from place to place **2 :** having no fixed course

vague *adj* **vagu·er; vagu·est** **1 :** not clearly expressed **2 :** not clearly understood or sensed **3 :** not clearly outlined — **vague·ly** *adv* — **vague·ness** *n*

vain *adj* **vain·er; vain·est** **1 :** having no success **2 :** having or showing the attitude of a person who thinks too highly of his or her looks or abilities — **vain·ly** *adv* — **in vain** **1 :** without success **2 :** in an unholy way

vale *n* **:** VALLEY

val·e·dic·to·ri·an *n* **:** a student usually of the highest standing in a class who gives the farewell speech at the graduation ceremonies

val·en·tine *n* **1 :** a greeting card or gift sent or given on Valentine's Day **2 :** a sweetheart given something as a sign of affection on Valentine's Day

Valentine's Day *n* **:** February 14 observed in honor of Saint Valentine and as a time for exchanging valentines

va·let *n* **1 :** a person who parks cars for guests (as at a restaurant) **2 :** a male servant or hotel employee who takes care of a man's clothes and does personal services

val·iant *adj* **1 :** boldly brave **2 :** done with courage **:** HEROIC — **val·iant·ly** *adv*

val·id *adj* **1 :** having legal force or effect **2 :** based on truth or fact — **val·id·ly** *adv*

val·i·date *vb* **val·i·dat·ed; val·i·dat·ing** **1 :** to have legal force or effect **2 :** to prove to be true, worthy, or justified

va·lid·i·ty *n* **:** the quality or state of being true or legally in force or effect

va·lise *n* **:** SUITCASE

val·ley *n, pl* **valleys :** an area of lowland between ranges of hills or mountains

val·or *or Can and Brit* **valour** *n* **:** COURAGE

val·or·ous *adj* **:** having or showing courage **:** BRAVE — **val·or·ous·ly** *adv*

¹valu·able *adj* **1 :** worth a large amount of money **2 :** of great use or service

²valuable *n* **:** a personal possession of great value

¹val·ue *n* **1 :** a fair return in goods, services, or money for something exchanged **2 :** worth in money **3 :** worth, usefulness, or importance in comparison with something else **4 :** a principle or quality that is valuable or desirable

²value *vb* **val·ued; val·u·ing** **1 :** to estimate the worth of **2 :** to think highly of

valve *n* **1 :** a structure in the body that temporarily closes to prevent passage of material or allow movement of a fluid in one direction only **2 :** a mechanical device by which the flow of liquid, gas, or loose material may be controlled by a movable part **3 :** a device on a brass musical instrument that changes the pitch of the tone **4 :** one of the separate pieces that make up the shell of some animals (as clams) and are often hinged

vam·pire *n* **:** the body of a dead person believed to come from the grave at night and suck the blood of sleeping people
vampire bat *n* **:** a bat of tropical America that feeds on the blood of birds and mammals
van *n* **:** a usually closed wagon or truck for moving goods or animals
va·na·di·um *n* **:** a metallic chemical element used in making a strong alloy of steel
van·dal *n* **:** a person who destroys or damages property on purpose
van·dal·ism *n* **:** intentional destruction of or damage to property
van·dal·ize *vb* **van·dal·ized; van·dal·iz·ing :** to destroy or damage property on purpose
vane *n* **1 :** WEATHER VANE **2 :** a flat or curved surface that turns around a center when moved by wind or water
van·guard *n* **1 :** the troops moving at the front of an army **2 :** FOREFRONT
va·nil·la *n* **:** a substance extracted from vanilla beans and used as a flavoring especially for sweet foods and beverages
vanilla bean *n* **:** the long pod of a tropical American orchid from which vanilla is extracted
van·ish *vb* **van·ished; van·ish·ing :** to pass from sight or existence **:** DISAPPEAR
van·i·ty *n, pl* **van·i·ties 1 :** the quality or fact of being vain **2 :** something that is vain **3 :** a small box for cosmetics
van·quish *vb* **van·quished; van·quish·ing :** OVERCOME 1
va·por *or Can and Brit* **vapour** *n* **1 :** fine bits (as of fog or smoke) floating in the air and clouding it **2 :** a substance in the form of a gas
va·por·ize *vb* **va·por·ized; va·por·iz·ing :** to turn from a liquid or solid into vapor — **va·por·iz·er** *n*
var. *abbr* variant
[1]**var·i·able** *adj* **1 :** able to change **:** likely to be changed **:** CHANGEABLE **2 :** having differences **3 :** different from what is normal or usual — **var·i·ably** *adv*
[2]**variable** *n* **1 :** something that changes or can be changed **2 :** PLACEHOLDER
[1]**var·i·ant** *adj* **:** differing from others of its kind or class
[2]**variant** *n* **1 :** one of two or more things that show slight differences **2 :** one of two or more different spellings or pronunciations of a word
var·i·a·tion *n* **1 :** a change in form, position, or condition **2 :** amount of change or difference **3 :** departure from what is usual to a group
var·ied *adj* **:** having many forms or types
var·ie·gat·ed *adj* **1 :** having patches, stripes, or marks of different colors **2 :** full of variety
va·ri·ety *n, pl* **va·ri·et·ies 1 :** a collection of different things **2 :** the quality or state of having different forms or types **3 :** something (as a plant or animal) that differs from others of the same general kind or of the group to which it belongs **4 :** entertainment made up of performances (as dances and songs) that follow one another and are not related
var·i·ous *adj* **1 :** of different kinds **2 :** different one from another **:** UNLIKE **3 :** made up of an indefinite number greater than one
[1]**var·nish** *n* **:** a liquid that is spread on a surface and dries into a hard coating
[2]**varnish** *vb* **var·nished; var·nish·ing :** to cover with or as if with a liquid that dries into a hard coating
var·si·ty *n, pl* **var·si·ties :** the main team that represents a school or club in contests
vary *vb* **var·ied; vary·ing 1 :** to make a partial change in **2 :** to make or be of different kinds **3 :** to show or undergo change **4 :** to differ from the usual members of a group
vas·cu·lar *adj* **:** of, relating to, containing, or being bodily vessels that carry fluid (as blood in an animal or sap in a plant)
vase *n* **:** an often round container of greater depth than width used chiefly for ornament or for flowers
vas·sal *n* **:** a person in the Middle Ages who received protection and land from a lord in return for loyalty and service
vast *adj* **:** very great in size or amount — **vast·ly** *adv* — **vast·ness** *n*
vat *n* **:** a large container (as a tub) especially for holding liquids in manufacturing processes
vaude·ville *n* **:** theatrical entertainment made up of songs, dances, and comic acts
[1]**vault** *n* **1 :** a room or compartment for storage or safekeeping **2 :** something like a vast ceiling **3 :** an arched structure of stone or concrete forming a ceiling or roof **4 :** a burial chamber
[2]**vault** *vb* **vault·ed; vault·ing :** to leap with the aid of the hands or a pole
[3]**vault** *n* **:** [2]LEAP
vb. *abbr* verb
VCR *n* **:** a device for recording (as television programs) on videocassettes and playing them back
veal *n* **:** the meat of a young calf used for food
vec·tor *n* **:** a living thing (as a mosquito, fly, or tick) that carries and passes on a disease-causing microorganism
vee·jay *n* **:** an announcer of a program (as on television) that features music videos
veer *vb* **veered; veer·ing :** to change direction

¹veg·e·ta·ble *adj* : containing or made from plants or parts of plants
²vegetable *n* **1** : a plant or plant part (as lettuce, broccoli, or peas) grown for use as food and eaten raw or cooked usually as part of a meal **2** : ²PLANT 1
veg·e·tar·i·an *n* : a person who does not eat meat
veg·e·ta·tion *n* : plant life or cover (as of an area)
veg·e·ta·tive *adj* : of, relating to, or functioning in nutrition and growth rather than reproduction
ve·he·mence *n* : the quality or state of being vehement
ve·he·ment *adj* **1** : showing great force or energy **2** : highly emotional **3** : expressed with force — **ve·he·ment·ly** *adv*
ve·hi·cle *n* **1** : something used to transport people or goods **2** : a means by which something is expressed, achieved, or shown
¹veil *n* **1** : a piece of cloth or net worn usually by women over the head and shoulders and sometimes over the face **2** : something that covers or hides like a veil
²veil *vb* **veiled; veil·ing** : to cover with or as if with a piece of cloth or net for the head and shoulders or face
vein *n* **1** : one of the blood vessels that carry the blood back to the heart **2** : a long narrow opening in rock filled with a specific mineral **3** : a streak of different color or texture (as in marble) **4** : a style of expression **5** : one of the bundles of fine tubes that make up the framework of a leaf and carry food, water, and nutrients in the plant **6** : one of the slender parts that stiffen and support the wing of an insect — **veined** *adj*
ve·loc·i·ty *n, pl* **ve·loc·i·ties** : quickness of motion : SPEED
¹vel·vet *n* : a fabric with short soft raised fibers
²velvet *adj* **1** : made of or covered with velvet **2** : VELVETY
vel·vety *adj* : soft and smooth
vend *vb* **vend·ed; vend·ing** : to sell or offer for sale — **ven·dor** *also* **vend·er** *n*
vending machine *n* : a machine for selling merchandise operated by putting money into a slot
ve·neer *n* : a layer of material that provides a finer surface or a stronger structure
ven·er·a·ble *adj* **1** : deserving to be venerated — often used as a religious title **2** : deserving honor or respect
ven·er·ate *vb* **ven·er·at·ed; ven·er·at·ing** **1** : to consider holy **2** : to show deep respect for
ven·er·a·tion *n* **1** : the act of showing respect for : the state of being shown respect **2** : a feeling of deep respect
ve·ne·tian blind *n* : a blind having thin horizontal slats that can be adjusted to keep out light or to let light come in between them
ven·geance *n* : harm done to someone usually as punishment in return for an injury or offense — **with a vengeance** **1** : with great force or effect **2** : to an extreme or excessive degree
venge·ful *adj* : wanting revenge
ven·i·son *n* : the meat of a deer used for food
Venn diagram *n* : a diagram that shows the relationship between two groups of things by means of overlapping circles
ven·om *n* : poison produced by an animal (as a snake or scorpion) and passed to a victim usually by biting or stinging
ven·om·ous *adj* : having or producing venom : POISONOUS
¹vent *vb* **vent·ed; vent·ing** **1** : to provide with an outlet **2** : to serve as an outlet for **3** : ³EXPRESS 1
²vent *n* **1** : an opening for the escape of a gas or liquid or for the relief of pressure **2** : an opportunity or means of release
ven·ti·late *vb* **ven·ti·lat·ed; ven·ti·lat·ing** **1** : to let in air and especially a current of fresh air **2** : to provide with fresh air **3** : to discuss freely and openly
ven·ti·la·tion *n* **1** : the act or process of ventilating **2** : a system or means of providing fresh air
ven·ti·la·tor *n* : a device for letting in fresh air or driving out bad or stale air
ven·tral *adj* : of, relating to, or being on or near the surface of the body that in human beings is the front but in most animals is the lower surface
ven·tri·cle *n* : the part of the heart from which blood passes into the arteries
ven·tril·o·quist *n* : a person skilled in speaking in such a way that the voice seems to come from a source other than the speaker
¹ven·ture *vb* **ven·tured; ven·tur·ing** **1** : to offer at the risk of being criticized **2** : to go ahead in spite of danger **3** : to face the risks and dangers of **4** : to expose to risk
²venture *n* **1** : a task or an act involving chance, risk, or danger **2** : a risky business deal
ven·ture·some *adj* **1** : tending to take risks **2** : involving risk
ven·tur·ous *adj* : VENTURESOME
Ve·nus *n* : the planet that is second in order of distance from the sun and has a diameter of about 7,500 miles (12,100 kilometers)
ve·ran·da *or* **ve·ran·dah** *n* : a long porch extending along one or more sides of a building
verb *n* : a word that expresses an act, occurrence, or state of being
ver·bal *adj* **1** : of, relating to, or consisting

of words **2** : spoken rather than written **3** : of, relating to, or formed from a verb — **ver·bal·ly** *adv*

ver·dant *adj* : green with growing plants

ver·dict *n* **1** : the decision reached by a jury **2** : JUDGMENT 2, OPINION

ver·dure *n* : green vegetation

[1]**verge** *n* **1** : THRESHOLD 2, BRINK **2** : something that borders, limits, or bounds : EDGE

[2]**verge** *vb* **verged; verg·ing** : to come near to being

ver·i·fi·ca·tion *n* : the act or process of confirming or checking the accuracy of : the state of being confirmed or having the accuracy of checked

ver·i·fy *vb* **ver·i·fied; ver·i·fy·ing** **1** : to prove to be true or correct : CONFIRM **2** : to check or test the accuracy of

ver·i·ta·ble *adj* : ACTUAL, TRUE — often used to emphasize similarity to something else

ver·min *n, pl* **vermin** : small common harmful or objectionable animals (as fleas or mice) that are difficult to get rid of

ver·nal *adj* : marking the beginning of spring

ver·sa·tile *adj* **1** : able to do many different kinds of things **2** : having many uses

ver·sa·til·i·ty *n* : the quality or state of having many uses or being able to do many different kinds of things

verse *n* **1** : a portion of a poem or song : STANZA **2** : writing in which words are arranged in a rhythmic pattern **3** : one of the short parts of a chapter in the Bible

versed *adj* : having knowledge or skill as a result of experience, study, or practice

ver·sion *n* **1** : an account or description from a certain point of view **2** : a translation especially of the Bible **3** : a form of a type or original

ver·sus *prep* : AGAINST 1

ver·te·bra *n, pl* **ver·te·brae** : one of the bony sections making up the backbone

[1]**ver·te·brate** *adj* : having vertebrae or a backbone

[2]**vertebrate** *n* : an animal (as a fish, amphibian, reptile, bird, or mammal) that has a backbone extending down the back of the body

ver·tex *n, pl* **ver·ti·ces** *also* **ver·tex·es** **1** : the point opposite to and farthest from the base of a geometrical figure **2** : the common endpoint of the sides of an angle

[1]**ver·ti·cal** *adj* : rising straight up and down from a level surface — **ver·ti·cal·ly** *adv*

[2]**vertical** *n* : something (as a line or plane) that rises straight up and down

ver·ti·go *n, pl* **ver·ti·goes** *or* **ver·ti·gos** : a feeling of dizziness

[1]**very** *adv* **1** : to a great degree : EXTREMELY **2** : in actual fact : TRULY

[2]**very** *adj* **1** : [2]EXACT, PRECISE **2** : exactly suitable or necessary **3** : MERE, BARE **4** : exactly the same

ves·pers *n pl, often cap* : a late afternoon or evening church service

ves·sel *n* **1** : a craft larger than a rowboat for navigation of the water **2** : a hollow utensil (as a cup or bowl) for holding something **3** : a tube (as an artery) in which a body fluid is contained and carried or circulated

[1]**vest** *n* : a sleeveless garment usually worn under a suit coat

[2]**vest** *vb* **vest·ed; vest·ing** **1** : to place or give into the possession or control of some person or authority **2** : to clothe in vestments

ves·ti·bule *n* : a hall or room between the outer door and the inside part of a building

ves·tige *n* : a tiny amount or visible sign of something lost or vanished : TRACE

ves·ti·gial *adj* : of, relating to, or being the last remaining amount or visible sign of something lost or vanished

vest·ment *n* : an outer garment especially for wear during ceremonies or by an official

[1]**vet** *n* : VETERINARIAN

[2]**vet** *n* : [1]VETERAN

[1]**vet·er·an** *n* **1** : a person who has had long experience **2** : a former member of the armed forces especially in war

[2]**veteran** *adj* : having gained skill through experience

vet·er·i·nar·i·an *n* : a doctor who gives medical treatment to animals

[1]**vet·er·i·nary** *adj* : of, relating to, specializing in, or being the medical care of animals

[2]**veterinary** *n, pl* **vet·er·i·nar·ies** : VETERINARIAN

Veterans Day *n* : a holiday observed on November 11 in the U.S. to honor veterans of the armed forces

[1]**ve·to** *n, pl* **vetoes** **1** : the act of forbidding something by a person in authority **2** : the power of a president, governor, or mayor to prevent something from becoming law

[2]**veto** *vb* **ve·toed; ve·to·ing** **1** : FORBID, PROHIBIT **2** : to prevent from becoming law by use of the power to do so

vex *vb* **vexed; vex·ing** **1** : to bring trouble, distress, or worry to **2** : to annoy by small irritations

vex·a·tion *n* **1** : the quality or state of being annoyed by small irritations **2** : the act of bringing trouble, distress, or worry to **3** : a cause of trouble or worry

VG *abbr* very good

v.i. *abbr* verb intransitive

VI *abbr* Virgin Islands

via *prep* : by way of

vi·a·ble *adj* **1** : capable of living or growing **2** : possible to use or apply

via·duct *n* : a bridge for carrying a road or railroad over something (as a gorge or highway)
vi·al *n* : a small container (as for medicines) that is usually made of glass or plastic
vi·brant *adj* : having or giving the sense of life, vigor, or action — **vi·brant·ly** *adv*
vi·brate *vb* **vi·brat·ed; vi·brat·ing** : to move or cause to move back and forth or from side to side very quickly
vi·bra·tion *n* **1** : a rapid motion (as of a stretched cord) back and forth **2** : the action of moving or causing to move back and forth or from side to side very quickly : the state of being swung back and forth **3** : a trembling motion
vic·ar *n* : a minister in charge of a church who serves under the authority of another minister
vi·car·i·ous *adj* : sharing in someone else's experiences through the use of imagination or sympathetic feelings — **vi·car·i·ous·ly** *adv* — **vi·car·i·ous·ness** *n*
vice *n* **1** : evil conduct or habits **2** : a moral fault or weakness
vice- *prefix* : one that takes the place of
vice pres·i·dent *n* : an official (as of a government) whose rank is next below that of the president and who takes the place of the president when necessary
vice ver·sa *adv* : with the order turned around
vi·cin·i·ty *n, pl* **vi·cin·i·ties** **1** : a surrounding area : NEIGHBORHOOD **2** : the state of being close
vi·cious *adj* **1** : very dangerous **2** : filled with or showing unkind feelings **3** : violent and cruel **4** : very severe — **vi·cious·ly** *adv* — **vi·cious·ness** *n*
vic·tim *n* **1** : a person who is cheated, fooled, or hurt by another **2** : an individual injured or killed (as by disease, violence, or disaster) **3** : a living being offered as a religious sacrifice
vic·tim·ize *vb* **vic·tim·ized; vic·tim·iz·ing** : to make a victim of
vic·tor *n* : WINNER, CONQUEROR
vic·to·ri·ous *adj* : having won a victory — **vic·to·ri·ous·ly** *adv*
vic·to·ry *n, pl* **vic·to·ries** **1** : the act of defeating an enemy or opponent **2** : success in a struggle against difficulties
vict·uals *n pl* : food and drink
vi·cu·ña *or* **vi·cu·na** *n* : an animal of the Andes that is related to the llama and has long soft woolly hair
[1]**vid·eo** *n* **1** : TELEVISION 1 **2** : the visual part of television **3** : [1]VIDEOTAPE 1 **4** : a recorded performance of a song
[2]**video** *adj* **1** : relating to or used in the sending or receiving of television images **2** : being, relating to, or involving images on a television screen or computer display
video camera *n* : a camera (as a camcorder) that records video and usually also audio
vid·eo·cas·sette *n* **1** : a case containing videotape for use with a VCR **2** : a recording (as of a movie) on a videocassette
videocassette recorder *n* : VCR
video game *n* : a game played with images on a video screen
[1]**vid·eo·tape** *n* **1** : a recording of visual images and sound (as of a television production) made on magnetic tape **2** : the magnetic tape used for such a recording
[2]**videotape** *vb* **vid·eo·taped; vid·eo·tap·ing** : to make a videotape of
videotape recorder *n* : a device for recording on videotape
vie *vb* **vied; vy·ing** : COMPETE
[1]**Viet·nam·ese** *n* **1** : a person born or living in Vietnam **2** : the language of the Vietnamese
[2]**Vietnamese** *adj* : of or relating to Vietnam, the Vietnamese people, or their language
[1]**view** *n* **1** : OPINION 1 **2** : all that can be seen from a certain place **3** : range of vision **4** : [1]PURPOSE **5** : a picture that represents something that can be seen
[2]**view** *vb* **viewed; view·ing** **1** : to look at carefully **2** : [1]SEE 1 **3** : [2]REGARD 5 — **view·er** *n*
view·find·er *n* : a device on a camera that shows the view to be included in the picture
view·point *n* : POINT OF VIEW, STANDPOINT
vig·il *n* : an act of keeping watch especially when sleep is usual
vig·i·lance *n* : the quality or state of staying alert especially to possible danger
vig·i·lant *adj* : alert especially to avoid danger
vig·i·lan·te *n* : a member of a group of volunteers who are not police but who decide on their own to stop crime and punish criminals
vig·or *or Can and Brit* **vigour** *n* **1** : strength or energy of body or mind **2** : active strength or force
vig·or·ous *adj* **1** : very healthy and strong **2** : done with force and energy — **vig·or·ous·ly** *adv*
Vi·king *n* : one of the Scandinavians who raided or invaded the coasts of Europe in the eighth to tenth centuries
vile *adj* **vil·er; vil·est** **1** : WICKED 1 **2** : very bad or unpleasant
vil·i·fy *vb* **vil·i·fied; vil·i·fy·ing** : to speak of harshly and often unfairly
vil·la *n* : a large house or estate usually in the country
vil·lage *n* **1** : a place where people live that is usually smaller than a town **2** : the people living in a village
vil·lag·er *n* : a person who lives in a village

vil·lain *n* **1 :** a wicked person **2 :** a character in a story or play who opposes the hero or heroine
vil·lain·ous *adj* **:** WICKED 1
vil·lainy *n, pl* **vil·lain·ies :** bad or evil behavior or actions
vil·lus *n, pl* **vil·li :** one of the tiny extensions shaped like fingers that line the small intestine and are active in absorbing nutrients
vim *n* **:** great energy and enthusiasm
vin·di·cate *vb* **vin·di·cat·ed; vin·di·cat·ing 1 :** to free from blame or guilt **2 :** to show to be true or correct
vin·dic·tive *adj* **1 :** likely to seek revenge **2 :** meant to be harmful
vine *n* **:** a plant whose stem requires support and which climbs by tendrils or twining or creeps along the ground — **vine·like** *adj*
vin·e·gar *n* **:** a sour liquid made from cider, wine, or malt and used to flavor or preserve foods
vine·yard *n* **:** a field of grapevines
[1]**vin·tage** *n* **1 :** the grapes grown or wine made during one season **2 :** the time when something started or was made
[2]**vintage** *adj* **1 :** produced in a particular year **2 :** of old and continuing interest, importance, or quality
vi·nyl *n* **:** a substance or product (as a fiber) made from an artificial plastic
[1]**vi·o·la** *n* **:** a garden plant that looks like but is smaller than a pansy
[2]**vi·o·la** *n* **:** a stringed musical instrument like a violin but slightly larger and lower in pitch
vi·o·late *vb* **vi·o·lat·ed; vi·o·lat·ing 1 :** to fail to keep **:** BREAK **2 :** to treat in a very disrespectful way **3 :** DISTURB 1 — **vi·o·la·tor** *n*
vi·o·la·tion *n* **:** an act or instance of violating something and especially a failure to do what is required or expected by a law, rule, or agreement
vi·o·lence *n* **1 :** the use of force to harm a person or damage property **2 :** great force or strength especially of a kind that involves destruction
vi·o·lent *adj* **1 :** showing very strong force **2 :** [1]EXTREME 1, INTENSE **3 :** using or likely to use harmful force **4 :** caused by force — **vi·o·lent·ly** *adv*
vi·o·let *n* **1 :** a wild or garden plant related to the pansies that has small often fragrant white, blue, purple, or yellow flowers **2 :** a bluish purple
vi·o·lin *n* **:** a stringed musical instrument with four strings that is usually held against the shoulder under the chin and played with a bow
vi·o·lin·ist *n* **:** a person who plays the violin
vi·per *n* **:** a poisonous heavy-bodied snake with long hollow fangs
vir·eo *n, pl* **vir·e·os :** a small songbird that eats insects and is olive-green or grayish in color
[1]**vir·gin** *n* **:** a person who has not had sexual intercourse
[2]**virgin** *adj* **:** not yet disturbed or changed by human activity
Vir·go *n* **1 :** a constellation between Leo and Libra imagined as a young woman **2 :** the sixth sign of the zodiac or a person born under this sign
vir·ile *adj* **:** having qualities generally associated with men
vir·tu·al *adj* **:** being in effect but not in fact or name **:** close to but not quite something — **vir·tu·al·ly** *adv*
virtual reality *n* **:** an artificial environment which is experienced through sights and sounds provided by a computer and in which a person's actions partly decide what happens in the environment
vir·tue *n* **1 :** morally good behavior or character **2 :** a good moral or desirable quality **3 :** the good result that comes from something — **by virtue of :** because of **:** through the force of
vir·tu·o·so *n, pl* **vir·tu·o·sos** *or* **vir·tu·o·si :** a person who is an outstanding performer especially in music
vir·tu·ous *adj* **:** morally good **:** having or showing virtue — **vir·tu·ous·ly** *adv*
vir·u·lent *adj* **:** spreading quickly and causing serious harm
vi·rus *n* **1 :** a disease-causing agent that is too tiny to be seen by the ordinary microscope, that may be a living organism or may be a very special kind of protein molecule, and that can only multiply when inside the cell of an organism **2 :** a disease caused by a virus **3 :** a usually hidden computer program that causes harm by making copies of itself and inserting them into other programs
vis·count *n* **:** a British nobleman ranking below an earl and above a baron
vis·count·ess *n* **1 :** the wife or widow of a viscount **2 :** a woman who holds the rank of a viscount in her own right
vise *n* **:** a device with two jaws that can be opened and closed by a screw or lever for holding or clamping work
vis·i·bil·i·ty *n* **:** the ability to see or be seen
vis·i·ble *adj* **1 :** capable of being seen **2 :** easily seen or understood **:** OBVIOUS — **vis·i·bly** *adv*
vi·sion *n* **1 :** the special sense by which the qualities of an object (as color) that make up its appearance are perceived through a process in which light rays entering the eye are transformed into signals that pass to the brain **2 :** the act or power of seeing **:** SIGHT **3 :** something dreamt or imagined **4 :** ex-

ceptional ability to know or believe what should happen or be done in the future

vi·sion·ary *n, pl* **vi·sion·ar·ies :** a person who has an exceptional ability to plan or have ideas for the future

[1]**vis·it** *vb* **vis·it·ed; vis·it·ing 1 :** to go to see for a particular purpose **2 :** to stay with for a time as a guest **3 :** to come to or upon

[2]**visit** *n* **1 :** an act of going to see a person, place, or thing for a particular purpose **2 :** a stay as a guest — **vis·i·tor** *n*

vi·sor *n* **1 :** the movable front upper piece of a helmet that is brought down to protect the face **2 :** a part (as on a cap) that sticks out to protect or shade the eyes

vis·ta *n* **:** a large and scenic view in the distance

vi·su·al *adj* **1 :** obtained by the use of sight **2 :** of, relating to, or used in seeing **3 :** appealing to the sense of sight — **vi·su·al·ly** *adv*

vi·su·al·ize *vb* **vi·su·al·ized; vi·su·al·iz·ing :** to see or form a mental image : IMAGINE

vi·tal *adj* **1 :** concerned with or necessary to the continuation of life **2 :** full of life and energy **3 :** very important — **vi·tal·ly** *adv*

vi·tal·i·ty *n, pl* **vi·tal·i·ties 1 :** capacity to live and develop **2 :** ENERGY 1, VIGOR

vi·tals *n pl* **:** the bodily organs (as the heart, lungs, and liver) that are needed to stay alive

vi·ta·min *n* **:** any of a group of substances that are found naturally in many foods, are necessary in small quantities for good health and normal development and functioning, and are designated by a capital letter and sometimes a number

vi·va·cious *adj* **:** full of energy and good spirits

vi·vac·i·ty *n* **:** the quality or state of being full of energy and good spirits

viv·id *adj* **1 :** producing strong mental images **2 :** very strong or bright **3 :** acting clearly and powerfully **4 :** seeming full of life and freshness — **viv·id·ly** *adv* — **viv·id·ness** *n*

vix·en *n* **:** a female fox

vo·cab·u·lary *n, pl* **vo·cab·u·lar·ies 1 :** a list or collection of words and their meanings **2 :** the words used in a language, by a group or individual, or in relation to a subject

vo·cal *adj* **1 :** uttered by the voice : ORAL **2 :** composed or arranged for or sung by the human voice **3 :** speaking freely or loudly : OUTSPOKEN **4 :** relating to or involved in producing the voice — **vo·cal·ly** *adv*

vocal cords *n pl* **:** a pair of folds of tissue that extend across the inside of the larynx and that produce the voice when air exhaled from the lungs causes them to tighten and vibrate

vo·cal·ist *n* **:** a person who sings : SINGER

vo·ca·tion *n* **1 :** a strong desire for a certain career or course of action **2 :** the work in which a person is regularly employed : OCCUPATION

vo·ca·tion·al *adj* **1 :** of, relating to, or concerned with an occupation **2 :** relating to or providing training in a skill or trade to be pursued as a career

vod·ka *n* **:** a colorless alcoholic liquor

vogue *n* **1 :** the quality or state of being popular at a certain time **2 :** something that is in fashion at a certain time

[1]**voice** *n* **1 :** sound that passes out of the mouth and throat of vertebrates and especially human beings and is produced mainly by the vibration of the vocal cords within the larynx (as in speaking or shouting) **2 :** musical sounds produced by singing **3 :** the power to use the voice **4 :** a sound similar to vocal sound **5 :** the right to express a wish, choice, or opinion **6 :** a means of expression

[2]**voice** *vb* **voiced; voic·ing :** to express in words

voice box *n* **:** LARYNX

voiced *adj* **1 :** having a voice of a specified kind **2 :** spoken with vibration of the vocal cords : not silent

voice·less *adj* **1 :** having no voice **2 :** spoken without vibration of the vocal cords

voice mail *n* **:** an electronic communication system in which spoken messages are recorded to be played back later

[1]**void** *adj* **1 :** containing nothing : EMPTY **2 :** being without : DEVOID **3 :** having no legal effect

[2]**void** *n* **:** empty space

vol. *abbr* **1** volume **2** volunteer

vol·a·tile *adj* **1 :** easily becoming a gas at a fairly low temperature **2 :** likely to change suddenly

vol·ca·nic *adj* **:** of, relating to, or produced by a volcano

vol·ca·no *n, pl* **vol·ca·noes** *or* **vol·ca·nos 1 :** an opening in the earth's crust from which hot or melted rock and steam erupt **2 :** a hill or mountain composed of material thrown out in a volcanic eruption

vole *n* **:** a small animal that is a rodent which looks like a fat mouse or rat and is sometimes harmful to crops

vo·li·tion *n* **:** the act or power of making choices or decisions without being influenced by other people : WILL

[1]**vol·ley** *n, pl* **volleys 1 :** a group of missiles (as arrows or bullets) passing through the air **2 :** the firing of many weapons (as rifles) at the same time **3 :** a bursting forth of many things at once **4 :** a hit or kick of the

ball while it is in the air before it touches the ground
[2]**volley** *vb* **vol·leyed; vol·ley·ing :** to hit an object (as a ball) while it is in the air before it touches the ground
vol·ley·ball *n* **1 :** a game played by two teams that hit a ball filled with air over a net without letting the ball touch the ground **2 :** the ball used in volleyball
volt *n* **:** a unit for measuring the force that moves an electric current
volt·age *n* **:** electric force measured in volts
vol·ume *n* **1 :** [1]BOOK 1 **2 :** one of a series of books that together form a complete work or collection **3 :** an amount of space that can be measured in cubic units **4 :** [2]AMOUNT **5 :** a large amount **6 :** the degree of loudness of a sound
vo·lu·mi·nous *adj* **1 :** of great size or amount **:** LARGE **2 :** [1]FULL 4
vol·un·tary *adj* **1 :** done, given, or acting of free choice **2 :** done or acting with no expectation of payment **3 :** relating to or controlled by the will — **vol·un·tar·i·ly** *adv*
[1]**vol·un·teer** *n* **:** a person who does something by free choice usually with no payment expected or given
[2]**volunteer** *adj* **:** relating to or done by volunteers
[3]**volunteer** *vb* **vol·un·teered; vol·un·teer·ing :** to offer or give without being asked or forced and usually with no expectation of payment
[1]**vom·it** *n* **:** material from the stomach brought up suddenly through the mouth
[2]**vomit** *vb* **vom·it·ed; vom·it·ing :** to bring up the contents of the stomach through the mouth
vo·ra·cious *adj* **1 :** very hungry **:** having a huge appetite **2 :** very eager — **vo·ra·cious·ly** *adv*
[1]**vote** *n* **1 :** a formal expression of opinion or choice (as by ballot in an election) **2 :** the decision reached by voting **3 :** the right to vote **4 :** the act or process of voting **5 :** a group of voters with some common interest or quality
[2]**vote** *vb* **vot·ed; vot·ing 1 :** to express a wish or choice by a vote **2 :** to elect, decide, pass, defeat, grant, or make legal by a vote **3 :** to declare by general agreement **4 :** to offer as a suggestion
vot·er *n* **:** a person who votes or who has the legal right to vote
vouch *vb* **vouched; vouch·ing :** to give a guarantee
vouch·safe *vb* **vouch·safed; vouch·saf·ing :** to give or grant as a special favor
[1]**vow** *n* **:** a solemn promise or statement
[2]**vow** *vb* **vowed; vow·ing :** to make a solemn promise **:** SWEAR
vow·el *n* **1 :** a speech sound (as \ə\, \ā\, or \ȯ\) produced without obstruction in the mouth **2 :** a letter (as *a, e, i, o, u*) representing a vowel
[1]**voy·age** *n* **:** a journey especially by water to a distant or unknown place
[2]**voyage** *vb* **voy·aged; voy·ag·ing :** to take a long trip usually by boat — **voy·ag·er** *n*
VP *abbr* vice president
vs. *abbr* versus
v.t. *abbr* verb transitive
Vt., VT *abbr* Vermont
vul·ca·nize *vb* **vul·ca·nized; vul·ca·niz·ing :** to treat rubber with chemicals in order to give it more strength or flexibility
vul·gar *adj* **1 :** having or showing poor taste or manners **:** COARSE **2 :** offensive in language or subject matter
vul·gar·i·ty *n, pl* **vul·gar·i·ties 1 :** the quality or state of having or showing poor taste or manners **2 :** rude or offensive language or behavior
vul·ner·a·ble *adj* **1 :** capable of being easily hurt or injured **2 :** open to attack or damage
vul·ture *n* **:** a large bird related to the hawks and eagles that has a head bare of feathers and feeds mostly on dead animals
vying *present participle of* VIE

W

w *n, pl* **w's** *or* **ws** *often cap* **:** the 23rd letter of the English alphabet
W *abbr* **1** west **2** western
WA *abbr* Washington
wacky *also* **whacky** *adj* **wack·i·er** *also* **whack·i·er; wack·i·est** *also* **whack·i·est :** CRAZY 2, INSANE
[1]**wad** *n* **1 :** a small mass or lump of soft material **2 :** a thick pile of folded money
[2]**wad** *vb* **wad·ded; wad·ding :** to crush or press into a small tight mass
[1]**wad·dle** *vb* **wad·dled; wad·dling :** to walk with short steps swaying like a duck
[2]**waddle** *n* **:** a way of walking by taking short steps and swaying from side to side
wade *vb* **wad·ed; wad·ing 1 :** to walk through something (as water, snow, or a crowd) that makes it hard to move **2 :** to

pass or cross by stepping through water **3** : to proceed with difficulty

wading bird *n* : a bird (as a heron) with long legs that wades in water in search of food

wa·fer *n* : a thin crisp cake or cracker

waf·fle *n* : a crisp cake of batter baked in a waffle iron and often indented with a pattern of small squares

waffle iron *n* : a cooking utensil with two hinged metal parts that come together for making waffles

[1]**waft** *vb* **waft·ed; waft·ing** : to move or be moved lightly by or as if by the action of waves or wind

[2]**waft** *n* : a slight breeze or puff of air

[1]**wag** *vb* **wagged; wag·ging** : to swing to and fro or from side to side

[2]**wag** *n* : a movement back and forth or from side to side

[3]**wag** *n* : a person full of jokes and humor

[1]**wage** *n* : payment for work done especially when figured by the hour or day

[2]**wage** *vb* **waged; wag·ing** : to engage in : carry on

[1]**wa·ger** *n* **1** : [1]BET 2 **2** : the act of betting

[2]**wager** *vb* **wa·gered; wa·ger·ing** : to bet on the result of a contest or question

wag·gish *adj* : showing or done in a spirit of harmless mischief

wag·gle *vb* **wag·gled; wag·gling** : to move backward and forward, from side to side, or up and down

wag·on *n* : a vehicle having four wheels and used for carrying goods

waif *n* : a homeless child

[1]**wail** *vb* **wailed; wail·ing** **1** : to make a long, loud cry of pain or grief **2** : to complain with a loud voice

[2]**wail** *n* : a long cry of grief or pain

wain·scot *n* : the bottom part of an inside wall especially when made of material different from the rest

wain·scot·ing *or* **wain·scot·ting** *n* : WAINSCOT

waist *n* **1** : the part of the body between the chest and the hips **2** : the part of a garment that fits around a person's waist

[1]**wait** *vb* **wait·ed; wait·ing** **1** : to stay in a place looking forward to something that is expected to happen **2** : to stop moving or doing something **3** : to remain not done or dealt with **4** : to serve food as a waiter or waitress

[2]**wait** *n* **1** : an act or period of waiting **2** : a hidden place from which a surprise attack can be made — usually used in the expression *lie in wait*

wait·er *n* : a person who serves food to people at tables

waiting room *n* : a room (as in a station or an office) for the use of people waiting

wait·ress *n* : a girl or woman who serves food to people at tables

waive *vb* **waived; waiv·ing** : to give up claim to

[1]**wake** *vb* **woke** *also* **waked; wo·ken** *or* **waked** *also* **woke; wak·ing** **1** : to arouse from sleep : AWAKE — often used with *up* **2** : to become alert or aware

[2]**wake** *n* : a watch held over the body of a dead person before burial

[3]**wake** *n* : a track or mark left by something moving especially in the water

wake·ful *adj* : not sleeping or able to sleep — **wake·ful·ness** *n*

wak·en *vb* **wak·ened; wak·en·ing** : [1]WAKE 1

[1]**walk** *vb* **walked; walk·ing** **1** : to move or cause to move along on foot at a natural slow pace **2** : to cover or pass over on foot **3** : to go with (a person or animal) by walking **4** : to go or cause to go to first base after four balls in baseball — **walk·er** *n* — **walk out** **1** : to leave suddenly and unexpectedly **2** : to go on strike

[2]**walk** *n* **1** : the act of moving along on foot at a natural slow pace **2** : a place or path for walking **3** : distance to be walked often measured in time required by a walker to cover **4** : way of walking **5** : an advance to first base after four balls in baseball **6** : position in life or the community **7** : a slow way of moving by a horse

walk·ie–talk·ie *n* : a small portable radio set for receiving and sending messages

walking stick *n* **1** : a stick used to maintain balance when walking **2** : STICK INSECT

walk·out *n* **1** : a labor strike **2** : the act of leaving a meeting or organization to show disapproval

[1]**wall** *n* **1** : one of the sides of a room or building **2** : a solid structure (as of stone) built to enclose or shut off a space **3** : something that separates one thing from another **4** : a layer of material enclosing space — **walled** *adj*

[2]**wall** *vb* **walled; wall·ing** : to build or have a wall in or around

wall·board *n* : a building material (as of wood pulp) made in large stiff sheets and used especially inside walls and ceilings

wal·let *n* : a small flat case for carrying paper money and personal papers

wall·eye *n* : a large North American freshwater fish that has large glassy eyes and is caught for food and sport

[1]**wal·lop** *vb* **wal·loped; wal·lop·ing** : to hit hard

[2]**wallop** *n* : a hard blow

[1]**wal·low** *vb* **wal·lowed; wal·low·ing** **1** : to roll about in or as if in deep mud **2** : to seem to want to be unhappy

²wallow *n* : a muddy or dust-filled area where animals roll about

wall·pa·per *n* : decorative paper for covering the walls of a room

wal·nut *n* : a wrinkled edible nut that comes from a tall tree with hard strong wood

wal·rus *n* : a large animal of northern seas that is related to the seal and has long ivory tusks, a tough wrinkled hide, and flippers used in swimming, diving, and moving about on land

¹waltz *n, pl* **waltz·es** : a dance in which couples glide to music having three beats to a measure

²waltz *vb* **waltzed; waltz·ing** : to dance a waltz

Wam·pa·noag *n, pl* **Wampanoag** *or* **Wam·pa·noags** : a member of an American Indian people of eastern Rhode Island and neighboring parts of Massachusetts

wam·pum *n* : beads made of shells and once used for money or ornament by North American Indians

wan *adj* **wan·ner; wan·nest** **1** : having a pale or sickly color **2** : showing little effort or energy — **wan·ly** *adv*

wand *n* : a slender rod

wan·der *vb* **wan·dered; wan·der·ing** **1** : to move about without a goal or purpose : RAMBLE **2** : to get off the right path or leave the right area : STRAY **3** : to lose concentration **4** : to follow a winding course — **wan·der·er** *n*

wane *vb* **waned; wan·ing** **1** : to grow smaller or less **2** : to grow shorter

¹want *vb* **want·ed; want·ing** **1** : to desire, wish, or long for something **2** : to feel or suffer the need of something **3** : to be without : LACK

²want *n* **1** : ²LACK 2, SHORTAGE **2** : the state of being very poor **3** : a wish for something : DESIRE

want·ing *adj* : falling below a standard, hope, or need

wan·ton *adj* **1** : not modest or proper : INDECENT **2** : showing no thought or care for the rights, feelings, or safety of others — **wan·ton·ly** *adv* — **wan·ton·ness** *n*

¹war *n* **1** : a state or period of fighting between states or nations **2** : a struggle between opposing forces or for a particular end

²war *vb* **warred; war·ring** : to engage in a series of battles

¹war·ble *n* **1** : low pleasing sounds that form a melody (as of a bird) **2** : the action of making low pleasing sounds that form a melody

²warble *vb* **war·bled; war·bling** : to sing a melody of low pleasing sounds

war·bler *n* **1** : an Old World bird related to the thrush and noted for its musical song **2** : a brightly colored American bird having a song that is usually weak and not musical

¹ward *n* **1** : a large room in a hospital where a number of patients often needing similar treatment are cared for **2** : one of the parts into which a town or city is divided for management **3** : a person under the protection of a guardian

²ward *vb* **ward·ed; ward·ing** : to avoid being hit or affected by

¹-ward *also* **-wards** *adj suffix* **1** : that moves, faces, or is pointed toward **2** : that is found in the direction of

²-ward *or* **-wards** *adv suffix* **1** : in a specified direction **2** : toward a specified place

war·den *n* **1** : a person who sees that certain laws are followed **2** : the chief official of a prison

ward·robe *n* **1** : a room or closet where clothes are kept **2** : the clothes a person owns

ware *n* **1** : manufactured articles or products of art or craft — often used in combination **2** : items (as dishes) of baked clay : POTTERY **3** : an article of merchandise

ware·house *n, pl* **ware·hous·es** : a building for storing goods and merchandise

war·fare *n* **1** : military fighting between enemies **2** : conflict between opposing forces or for a particular end

war·like *adj* **1** : fond of war **2** : fit for or characteristic of war

war·lock *n* : a man who practices witchcraft

¹warm *adj* **warm·er; warm·est** **1** : somewhat hot **2** : giving off a little heat **3** : making a person feel heat or experience no loss of body heat **4** : having a feeling of warmth **5** : showing strong feeling **6** : newly made : FRESH **7** : near the object sought **8** : of a color in the range yellow through orange to red — **warm·ly** *adv*

²warm *vb* **warmed; warm·ing** **1** : to make or become warm **2** : to give a feeling of warmth **3** : to become more interested than at first — **warm up** **1** : to exercise or practice lightly in preparation for more strenuous activity or a performance **2** : to run (as a motor) at slow speed before using

warm–blood·ed *adj* : able to keep up a relatively high constant body temperature that is independent of that of the surroundings

warmth *n* **1** : gentle heat **2** : strong feeling

warm–up *n* : the act or an instance of preparing for a performance or a more strenuous activity

warn *vb* **warned; warn·ing** **1** : to put on guard : CAUTION **2** : to notify especially in advance

warn·ing *n* **:** something that cautions of possible danger or trouble

¹warp *n* **1 :** the threads that go lengthwise in a loom and are crossed by the woof **2 :** a twist or curve that has developed in something once flat or straight

²warp *vb* **warped; warp·ing 1 :** to curve or twist out of shape **2 :** to cause to judge, choose, or act wrongly

¹war·rant *n* **1 :** a reason or cause for an opinion or action **2 :** a document giving legal power

²warrant *vb* **war·rant·ed; war·rant·ing 1 :** to be sure of or that **2 :** ²GUARANTEE 2 **3 :** to call for **:** JUSTIFY

warrant officer *n* **:** an officer in the armed forces in one of the grades between commissioned officers and noncommissioned officers

war·ren *n* **:** a place where rabbits live or are kept

war·rior *n* **:** a person who is or has been in warfare

war·ship *n* **:** a ship armed for combat

wart *n* **:** a small hard lump of thickened skin caused by a virus

wart·hog *n* **:** a wild African hog with pointed tusks and in the male thick growths of skin on the face which resemble warts

wary *adj* **war·i·er; war·i·est :** very cautious — **war·i·ly** *adv* — **war·i·ness** *n*

was *past first person & third person sing of* BE

¹wash *vb* **washed; wash·ing 1 :** to cleanse with water and usually a cleaning agent (as soap) **2 :** to wet completely with liquid **3 :** to flow along or overflow against **4 :** to remove or carry away by the action of water **5 :** to stand being cleansed without injury

²wash *n* **1 :** articles in the laundry **2 :** an act or instance of cleansing or of being cleansed **3 :** the flow, sound, or action of water **4 :** a backward flow of water (as made by the motion of a boat) **5 :** material carried or set down by water

Wash. *abbr* Washington

wash·able *adj* **:** capable of being cleansed without damage

wash·bowl *n* **:** a large bowl for water to wash the hands and face

wash·cloth *n* **:** a small towel for washing the face and body

wash·er *n* **1 :** WASHING MACHINE **2 :** a ring (as of metal) used to make something fit tightly or to prevent rubbing

washing machine *n* **:** a machine used for washing clothes and household linen

wash·out *n* **1 :** a place where earth has been washed away **2 :** a complete failure

wash·tub *n* **:** a tub for washing clothes or for soaking them before washing

wasn't : was not

wasp *n* **:** a winged insect related to the bee and ant that has a slender body with the abdomen attached by a narrow stalk and that in females and workers is capable of giving a very painful sting

wasp·ish *adj* **:** ³CROSS 3, IRRITABLE — **wasp·ish·ly** *adv*

¹waste *n* **1 :** the action of spending or using carelessly or uselessly **:** the state of being spent or used carelessly or uselessly **2 :** material left over or thrown away **3 :** material (as carbon dioxide in the lungs or urine in the kidneys) produced in and of no further use to the living body **4 :** a large area of barren land **:** WASTELAND

²waste *vb* **wast·ed; wast·ing 1 :** to spend or use carelessly or uselessly **2 :** to lose or cause to lose weight, strength, or energy **3 :** to bring to ruin

³waste *adj* **1 :** being wild and without people or crops **:** BARREN **2 :** of no further use

waste·bas·ket *n* **:** an open container for odds and ends to be thrown away

waste·ful *adj* **:** spending or using in a careless or foolish way — **waste·ful·ly** *adv* — **waste·ful·ness** *n*

waste·land *n* **:** land that is barren or not fit for crops

¹watch *vb* **watched; watch·ing 1 :** to keep in view **2 :** to be on the lookout **3 :** to take care of **:** TEND **4 :** to be careful of **5 :** to keep guard **6 :** to stay awake — **watch·er** *n* — **watch out :** to be aware of and ready for

²watch *n* **1 :** a small timepiece worn on the wrist or carried **2 :** close observation **3 :** ¹GUARD 2 **4 :** the time during which someone is on duty to guard or be on the lookout **5 :** an act of keeping awake to guard or protect

watch·dog *n* **:** a dog kept to guard property

watch·ful *adj* **:** ATTENTIVE 1, VIGILANT — **watch·ful·ly** *adv* — **watch·ful·ness** *n*

watch·man *n, pl* **watch·men :** a person whose job is to guard property at night or when the owners are away

watch·tow·er *n* **:** a tower for a guard or watchman

watch·word *n* **:** PASSWORD

¹wa·ter *n* **1 :** the liquid that comes from the clouds as rain and forms streams, lakes, and seas **2 :** a body of water or a part of a body of water

²water *vb* **wa·tered; wa·ter·ing 1 :** to wet or supply with water **2 :** to fill with liquid (as tears or saliva) **3 :** to add water to

wa·ter·bird *n* **:** a swimming or wading bird

water buffalo *n* **:** a buffalo of Asia with

large curving horns that is often used as a work animal

wa·ter·col·or *n* **1 :** a paint whose liquid part is water **2 :** a picture painted with watercolor **3 :** the art of painting with watercolor

wa·ter·course *n* **1 :** a channel in which water flows **2 :** a stream of water (as a river or brook)

wa·ter·cress *n* **:** a plant that grows in or near water and has sharp-tasting leaves used especially in salads

wa·ter·fall *n* **:** a fall of water from a height

water flea *n* **:** a tiny often brightly colored freshwater animal related to the crab and lobster

wa·ter·fowl *n* **1 :** a bird that is typically found in or near water **2 :** a swimming bird (as a duck or goose) often hunted as game

wa·ter·front *n* **:** land that borders on a body of water

water hyacinth *n* **:** a floating water plant that often clogs streams in the southern United States

water lily *n* **:** a water plant with rounded floating leaves and showy often fragrant flowers

wa·ter·line *n* **:** any of several lines marked on the outside of a ship that match the surface of the water when the ship floats evenly

wa·ter·logged *adj* **:** so filled or soaked with water as to be heavy or hard to manage

wa·ter·mark *n* **1 :** a mark that shows a level to which water has risen **2 :** a mark made in paper during manufacture that is visible when the paper is held up to the light

wa·ter·mel·on *n* **:** a large edible fruit with a hard rind and a sweet red juicy pulp

water moccasin *n* **:** a poisonous snake of the southern United States that lives in or near water

water park *n* **:** an amusement park with pools and wetted slides

wa·ter·pow·er *n* **:** the power of moving water used to run machinery

¹wa·ter·proof *adj* **:** not letting water through

²waterproof *vb* **wa·ter·proofed; wa·ter·proof·ing :** to make something resistant to letting water through

wa·ter·shed *n* **1 :** a dividing ridge (as a mountain range) separating one drainage area from others **2 :** the whole area that drains into a lake or river

wa·ter–ski *vb* **wa·ter–skied; wa·ter–ski·ing :** to ski on water while being pulled by a speedboat

water ski *n, pl* **water skis :** a ski used in water-skiing

wa·ter·spout *n* **1 :** a pipe for carrying off water from a roof **2 :** a slender cloud that is shaped like a funnel and extends down to a cloud of spray torn up from the surface of a body of water by a whirlwind

water strid·er *n* **:** a bug with long legs that skims over the surface of water

wa·ter·tight *adj* **:** so tight as to be waterproof

wa·ter·way *n* **:** a channel or a body of water by which ships can travel

wa·ter·wheel *n* **:** a wheel turned by a flow of water against it

wa·ter·works *n pl* **:** a system of dams, reservoirs, pumps, and pipes for supplying water (as to a city)

wa·tery *adj* **1 :** full of or giving out liquid **2 :** containing or giving out water or a thin liquid **3 :** like water especially in being thin, soggy, pale, or without flavor **4 :** lacking in strength or determination

watt *n* **:** a unit for measuring electric power

wat·tle *n* **:** a fleshy flap of skin that hangs usually from the neck (as of a bird)

¹wave *vb* **waved; wav·ing 1 :** to move (as the hand) to and fro as a signal or in greeting **2 :** to move (something) back and forth **3 :** to curve slightly **4 :** to flutter with a rolling movement

²wave *n* **1 :** a moving ridge on the surface of water **2 :** a waving motion **3 :** something that swells and dies away **4 :** a rolling movement passing along a surface or through the air **5 :** a curving shape or series of curving shapes **6 :** a sudden increase in something **7 :** a motion that is somewhat like a wave in water and transfers energy from point to point

wave·length *n* **:** the distance in the line of advance of a wave from any one point to the next similar point

wa·ver *vb* **wa·vered; wa·ver·ing 1 :** to be uncertain in opinion **2 :** to move unsteadily or to and fro **3 :** to give an unsteady sound

wavy *adj* **wav·i·er; wav·i·est :** like, having, or moving in waves — **wav·i·ness** *n*

¹wax *n* **1 :** a yellowish sticky substance made by bees and used in building the honeycomb **:** BEESWAX **2 :** a material (as paraffin) that resembles the wax made by bees (as by being soft and easily molded when warm)

²wax *vb* **waxed; wax·ing :** to treat or polish with wax

³wax *vb* **waxed; waxing 1 :** to grow larger or stronger **2 :** BECOME 1, GROW

wax bean *n* **:** a string bean with yellow waxy pods

wax·en *adj* **:** lacking vitality or animation

wax myrtle *n* **:** a shrub or small tree that has bluish gray waxy berries and is related to the bayberry

wax·wing *n* **:** a crested mostly brown bird having yellow on the tip of the tail and often a waxy substance on the tip of some wing feathers

waxy *adj* **wax·i·er; wax·i·est** **1 :** being like wax **2 :** made of or covered with wax **3 :** marked by smooth or shiny whiteness

[1]way *n* **1 :** the manner in which something is done or happens **2 :** the course traveled from one place to another : ROUTE **3 :** a noticeable point **4 :** [1]STATE 1 **5 :** distance in time or space **6 :** a special or personal manner of behaving **7 :** a talent for handling something **8 :** room to advance or pass **9 :** DIRECTION 3 **10 :** a track for travel : PATH, STREET **11 :** a course of action **12 :** personal choice as to situation or behavior : WISH **13 :** progress along a course **14 :** a particular place **15 :** CATEGORY, KIND — **by the way :** apart from that — **by way of** **1 :** for the purpose of **2 :** by the route through — **in someone's way** *also* **in the way :** in a position to hinder or obstruct — **out of the way** **1 :** in or to a place away from public view **2 :** done fully

[2]way *adv* **1 :** [1]FAR 1 **2 :** [1]FAR 2

way·far·er *n* **:** a traveler especially on foot

way·lay *vb* **way·laid; way·lay·ing :** to attack from hiding

-ways *adv suffix* **:** in such a way, direction, or manner

way·side *n* **:** the edge of a road — **by the wayside :** into a condition of neglect or disuse

way·ward *adj* **1 :** DISOBEDIENT **2 :** not following a rule or regular course of action

we *pron* **:** I and at least one other

We. *abbr* Wednesday

weak *adj* **1 :** lacking strength of body, mind, or spirit **2 :** not able to stand much strain or force **3 :** easily overcome **4 :** not able to function well **5 :** not rich in some usual or important element **6 :** lacking experience or skill **7 :** not loud or forceful **8 :** relating to or being the lightest of three levels of stress in pronunciation — **weakly** *adv*

weak·en *vb* **weak·ened; weak·en·ing :** to make or become weak or weaker

weak·ling *n* **:** a person or animal that lacks strength

weak·ness *n* **1 :** lack of strength **2 :** a weak point : FLAW **3 :** a special fondness or the object of a special fondness

wealth *n* **1 :** a large amount of money or possessions **2 :** a great amount or number

wealthy *adj* **wealth·i·er; wealth·i·est :** having a lot of money or possessions : RICH

wean *vb* **weaned; wean·ing** **1 :** to get a child or young animal used to food other than its mother's milk **2 :** to make someone stop desiring a thing he or she has been fond of

weap·on *n* **:** something (as a gun, knife, or club) to fight with

weap·on·ry *n* **:** a particular grouping of weapons

[1]wear *vb* **wore; worn; wear·ing** **1 :** to use as an article of clothing or decoration **2 :** to carry or use on the body **3 :** [1]SHOW 1 **4 :** to damage, waste, or produce by use or by scraping or rubbing **5 :** to make tired **6 :** to last through long use **7 :** to diminish or fail with the passing of time — **wear·er** *n* — **wear out** **1 :** to make useless by long or hard use **2 :** [1]TIRE 1

[2]wear *n* **1 :** the act of wearing : the state of being worn **2 :** clothing for a particular group or for a particular occasion **3 :** the result of wearing or use

wea·ri·some *adj* **:** TEDIOUS, DULL

[1]wea·ry *adj* **wea·ri·er; wea·ri·est** **1 :** having lost strength, energy, or freshness : TIRED **2 :** having lost patience, pleasure, or interest **3 :** causing a loss of strength or interest — **wea·ri·ly** *adv* — **wea·ri·ness** *n*

[2]weary *vb* **wea·ried; wea·ry·ing :** to make or become weary

wea·sel *n* **:** a small slender active animal related to the mink that feeds on small birds and animals (as mice)

[1]weath·er *n* **:** the state of the air and atmosphere in regard to how warm or cold, wet or dry, or clear or stormy it is

[2]weather *vb* **weath·ered; weath·er·ing** **1 :** to expose to the weather **2 :** to change (as in color or structure) by the action of the weather **3 :** to be able to last or come safely through

weath·er·man *n, pl* **weath·er·men :** a person who reports and forecasts the weather

weath·er·per·son *n* **:** WEATHERMAN

weather vane *n* **:** a movable device usually attached to a roof to show which way the wind is blowing

[1]weave *vb* **wove; wo·ven; weav·ing** **1 :** to move back and forth, up and down, or in and out **2 :** to form (as cloth) by lacing together strands of material **3 :** [1]SPIN 4 **4 :** to make by or as if by lacing parts together — **weav·er** *n*

[2]weave *n* **:** a method or pattern of lacing together strands of material

[1]web *n* **1 :** SPIDERWEB, COBWEB **2 :** a network of threads spun especially by the larvae of certain insects (as tent caterpillars) and usually serving as a nest or shelter **3 :** something that catches and holds like a spider's web **4 :** a complex pattern like something woven **5 :** a layer of skin or tissue that joins the toes of an animal (as a duck) **6** *cap* **:** WORLD WIDE WEB

[2]web *vb* **webbed; web·bing :** to join or surround with strands woven together

webbed *adj* **:** having or being toes joined by a layer of skin or tissue

web·cam *n* **:** a small video camera that is used to show live images on a website

web–foot·ed *adj* **:** having toes joined by a layer of skin or tissue

web page *n* **:** a page of written material and pictures that is shown on a website

web·site *or* **Web site** *n* **:** a group of World Wide Web pages usually containing links to each other and made available online by an individual, company, or organization

wed *vb* **wed·ded** *also* **wed; wed·ding** **1 :** MARRY **2 :** to connect closely

Wed. *abbr* Wednesday

we'd : we had **:** we should **:** we would

wed·ding *n* **:** a marriage ceremony

¹wedge *n* **1 :** a piece of wood or metal that tapers to a thin edge and is used for splitting logs or for tightening by being forced into a space **2 :** something with a triangular shape

²wedge *vb* **wedged; wedg·ing** **1 :** to crowd or squeeze in **2 :** to fasten, tighten, or separate with a triangular piece of wood or metal

wed·lock *n* **:** MARRIAGE 1

Wednes·day *n* **:** the fourth day of the week

wee *adj* **:** very small **:** TINY

¹weed *n* **:** a plant that tends to grow where not wanted and to crowd out more desirable plants

²weed *vb* **weed·ed; weed·ing** **1 :** to remove weeds from **2 :** to get rid of what is not wanted

weedy *adj* **weed·i·er; weed·i·est** **1 :** full of or consisting of weeds **2 :** like a weed especially in having strong rapid growth **3 :** very skinny

week *n* **1 :** seven days in a row especially beginning with Sunday and ending with Saturday **2 :** the working or school days that come between Sunday and Saturday

week·day *n* **:** a day of the week except Sunday or sometimes except Saturday and Sunday

week·end *n* **:** the period between the close of one work or school week and the beginning of the next

¹week·ly *adj* **1 :** happening, done, or produced every week **2 :** figured by the week

²weekly *n, pl* **weeklies** **:** a newspaper or magazine published every week

weep *vb* **wept; weep·ing** **:** to shed tears **:** CRY

weep·ing *adj* **:** having slender drooping branches

weeping willow *n* **:** a willow originally from Asia that has slender drooping branches

wee·vil *n* **:** a small beetle that has a long snout and often feeds on and is harmful to plants or plant products (as nuts, fruit, and grain)

weigh *vb* **weighed; weigh·ing** **1 :** to have weight or a specified weight **2 :** to find the weight of **3 :** to think about as if weighing **4 :** to lift an anchor before sailing — **weigh down :** to cause to bend down

¹weight *n* **1 :** the amount that something weighs **2 :** the force with which a body is pulled toward the earth **3 :** a unit (as a pound) for measuring weight **4 :** an object (as a piece of metal) of known weight for balancing a scale in weighing other objects **5 :** a heavy object used to hold or press down something **6 :** a heavy object lifted during exercise **7 :** ¹BURDEN 2 **8 :** strong influence

²weight *vb* **weight·ed; weight·ing** **1 :** to load or make heavy with a weight **2 :** to trouble with a burden

weight·less *adj* **1 :** having little or no weight **2 :** not affected by gravity

weighty *adj* **weight·i·er; weight·i·est** **1 :** having much weight **:** HEAVY **2 :** very important

weird *adj* **weird·er; weird·est :** very unusual **:** STRANGE

weirdo *n, pl* **weird·os :** a very strange person

¹wel·come *vb* **wel·comed; wel·com·ing** **1 :** to greet with friendship or courtesy **2 :** to receive or accept with pleasure

²welcome *adj* **1 :** greeted or received gladly **2 :** giving pleasure **:** PLEASING **3 :** willingly permitted to do, have, or enjoy something **4** — used in the phrase "You're welcome" as a reply to an expression of thanks

³welcome *n* **:** a friendly greeting

¹weld *vb* **weld·ed; weld·ing** **1 :** to join two pieces of metal or plastic by heating and allowing the edges to flow together **2 :** to be capable of being joined by heating and allowing the edges to flow together **3 :** to join closely — **weld·er** *n*

²weld *n* **:** a joint made by heating and allowing the edges to flow together

wel·fare *n* **1 :** the state of being or doing well especially in relation to happiness, well-being, or success **2 :** aid in the form of money or necessities for people in need

¹well *adv* **bet·ter; best** **1 :** in a skillful or expert manner **2 :** by as much as possible **:** COMPLETELY **3 :** in such a way as to be pleasing **:** as wanted **4 :** without trouble **5 :** in a thorough manner **6 :** in a familiar manner **7 :** by quite a lot **8 :** so as to be right **:** in a satisfactory way **9 :** in a complimentary or generous way **10 :** with reason or courtesy — **as well** **1 :** in addition **:** ALSO **2 :** with the same result

²well *interj* **1** — used to express surprise or doubt **2** — used to begin a conversation or remark or to continue one that was interrupted

³well *n* **1 :** a hole made in the earth to reach

a natural deposit (as of water, oil, or gas) **2** : a source of supply **3** : something like a deep hole

⁴well *adj* **1** : being in a satisfactory or good state **2** : free or recovered from ill health : HEALTHY **3** : FORTUNATE 1

⁵well *vb* **welled; well·ing** : to rise to the surface and flow out

we'll : we shall : we will

well–be·ing *n* : WELFARE 1

well–bred *adj* : having or showing good manners : POLITE

well–done *adj* **1** : done right **2** : cooked thoroughly

well–known *adj* : known by many people

well–nigh *adv* : ALMOST

well–off *adj* **1** : being in good condition or in a good situation **2** : WELL-TO-DO

well–to–do *adj* : having plenty of money and possessions

¹Welsh *adj* : of or relating to Wales or the people of Wales

²Welsh *n* : the people of Wales

welt *n* : a ridge raised on the skin (as by a blow)

wel·ter *n* : a confused jumble

wend *vb* **wend·ed; wend·ing** : to go from one place to another

went *past of* GO

wept *past and past participle of* WEEP

were *past second person sing, past pl, or past subjunctive of* BE

we're : we are

weren't : were not

were·wolf *n, pl* **were·wolves** : a person in folklore who is changed or is able to change into a wolf

¹west *adv* : to or toward the direction of sunset

²west *adj* : placed toward, facing, or coming from the direction of sunset

³west *n* **1** : the direction of sunset : the compass point opposite to east **2** *cap* : regions or countries west of a point that is mentioned or understood

west·bound *adj* : going west

west·er·ly *adj or adv* **1** : toward the west **2** : from the west

¹west·ern *adj* **1** *often cap* : of, relating to, or like that of the West **2** : lying toward or coming from the west

²western *n, often cap* : a story, film, or radio or television show about life in the western United States especially in the last part of the 19th century

west·ward *adv or adj* : toward the west

¹wet *adj* **wet·ter; wet·test** **1** : containing, covered with, or soaked with liquid (as water) **2** : RAINY **3** : not yet dry — **wet·ness** *n*

²wet *vb* **wet** *or* **wet·ted; wet·ting** : to make wet

³wet *n* : rainy weather : RAIN

we've : we have

¹whack *vb* **whacked; whack·ing** : to hit with a hard noisy blow

²whack *n* **1** : a hard noisy blow **2** : the sound of a hard noisy blow — **out of whack** : not in good working order or shape

whacky *variant of* WACKY

¹whale *n* : a very large sea mammal that has flippers and a flattened tail and breathes through an opening on the top of the head

²whale *vb* **whaled; whal·ing** : to hunt whales

whale·bone *n* : BALEEN

whal·er *n* : a person or ship that hunts whales

wharf *n, pl* **wharves** *also* **wharfs** : a structure built on the shore for loading and unloading ships

¹what *pron* **1** : which thing or things **2** : which sort of thing or person **3** : that which **4** — used to ask someone to repeat something **5** : ¹WHATEVER 1 — **what for** : ¹WHY — **what if** **1** : what would happen if **2** : what does it matter if

²what *adv* **1** : in what way : HOW **2** — used before one or more phrases that tell a cause

³what *adj* **1** — used to ask about the identity of a person, object, or matter **2** : how remarkable or surprising **3** : ²WHATEVER 1

¹what·ev·er *pron* **1** : anything or everything that **2** : no matter what **3** : what in the world

²whatever *adj* **1** : any and all : any. . . that **2** : of any kind at all

what·so·ev·er *pron or adj* : WHATEVER

wheat *n* : a cereal grain that grows in tight clusters on the tall stalks of a widely cultivated grass, that is typically made into fine white flour used mostly in breads, baked goods (as cakes and crackers), and pasta, and that is also used in animal feeds

wheat·en *adj* : containing or made from wheat

whee·dle *vb* **whee·dled; whee·dling** **1** : to get (someone) to think or act a certain way by flattering : COAX **2** : to gain or get by coaxing or flattering

¹wheel *n* **1** : a disk or circular frame that can turn on a central point **2** : something that is round **3** : STEERING WHEEL **4** : something having a wheel as its main part **5 wheels** *pl* : moving power : necessary parts — **wheeled** *adj*

²wheel *vb* **wheeled; wheel·ing** **1** : to carry or move on wheels or in a vehicle with wheels **2** : ROTATE 1 **3** : to change direction as if turning on a central point

wheel·bar·row *n* : a cart with two handles and usually one wheel for carrying small loads

wheel·chair *n* : a chair with wheels used especially by sick, injured, or disabled people to get about

[1]**wheeze** *vb* **wheezed; wheez·ing** **1** : to breathe with difficulty and usually with a whistling sound **2** : to make a whistling sound like someone having difficulty breathing

[2]**wheeze** *n* : a whistling sound like that made by someone having difficulty breathing

whelk *n* : a large sea snail that has a spiral shell and is sometimes used for food in Europe

whelp *n* : one of the young of an animal that eats flesh and especially of a dog

[1]**when** *adv* **1** : at what time **2** : the time at which **3** : at, in, or during which

[2]**when** *conj* **1** : at, during, or just after the time that **2** : in the event that : IF **3** : ALTHOUGH 1 **4** : the time at which

[3]**when** *pron* : what or which time

whence *adv* **1** : from what place, source, or cause **2** : from or out of which

when·ev·er *conj or adv* : at whatever time

[1]**where** *adv* **1** : at, in, or to what place **2** : at or in what way or direction

[2]**where** *conj* **1** : at, in, or to the place indicated **2** : every place that

[3]**where** *n* : what place, source, or cause

[1]**where·abouts** *adv* : near what place

[2]**whereabouts** *n pl* : the place where someone or something is — used as singular or plural

where·as *conj* **1** : since it is true that **2** : while just the opposite

where·by *adv* : by or through which

where·fore *adv* : [1]WHY

where·in *adv* **1** : in what way **2** : in which

where·of *conj* : of what : that of which

where·up·on *conj* : and then : at which time

[1]**wher·ev·er** *adv* **1** : where in the world **2** : any place at all

[2]**wherever** *conj* **1** : at, in, or to whatever place **2** : in any situation in which : at any time that

whet *vb* **whet·ted; whet·ting** **1** : to sharpen the edge of by rubbing on or with a stone **2** : to make (as the appetite) stronger

wheth·er *conj* **1** : if it is or was true that **2** : if it is or was better **3** — used to introduce two or more situations of which only one can occur

whet·stone *n* : a stone on which blades are sharpened

whew *n* : a sound almost like a whistle made as an exclamation chiefly to show amazement, discomfort, or relief

whey *n* : the watery part of milk that separates from the curd after the milk sours and thickens

[1]**which** *adj* : what certain one or ones

[2]**which** *pron* **1** : which one or ones **2** — used in place of the name of something other than people at the beginning of a clause

[1]**which·ev·er** *adj* : being whatever one or ones : no matter which

[2]**whichever** *pron* : whatever one or ones

[1]**whiff** *n* **1** : a small gust **2** : a small amount (as of a scent or a gas) that is breathed in **3** : HINT 2 **4** : STRIKEOUT

[2]**whiff** *vb* **whiffed; whiff·ing** **1** : to blow out or away in small amounts **2** : to breathe in an odor

[1]**while** *conj* **1** : during the time that **2** : ALTHOUGH 1

[2]**while** *n* **1** : a period of time **2** : time and effort used in doing something

[3]**while** *vb* **whiled; whil·ing** : to cause to pass especially in a pleasant way

whim *n* : a sudden wish or desire : a sudden change of mind

[1]**whim·per** *vb* **whim·pered; whim·per·ing** : to cry in low broken sounds : WHINE

[2]**whimper** *n* : a whining cry

whim·si·cal *adj* **1** : full of whims **2** : unusual in a playful or amusing way

[1]**whine** *vb* **whined; whin·ing** **1** : to make a high-pitched troubled cry or a similar sound **2** : to complain by or as if by whining

[2]**whine** *n* : a high-pitched troubled or complaining cry or sound

[1]**whin·ny** *vb* **whin·nied; whin·ny·ing** : to neigh usually in a low gentle way

[2]**whinny** *n, pl* **whinnies** : a low gentle neigh

[1]**whip** *vb* **whipped; whip·ping** **1** : to move, snatch, or jerk quickly or with force **2** : to hit with something long, thin, and flexible : LASH **3** : to defeat thoroughly **4** : to beat into foam **5** : to cause a strong emotion (as excitement) in **6** : to move back and forth in a lively way **7** : to make in a hurry

[2]**whip** *n* **1** : a long thin strip of material (as leather) used in punishing or urging on **2** : a dessert made by whipping some part of the mixture

whip·poor·will *n* : a bird of eastern North America that is active at night and has a loud call that sounds like its name

[1]**whir** *vb* **whirred; whir·ring** : to fly, operate, or turn rapidly with a buzzing sound

[2]**whir** *n* : a buzzing sound made by something spinning or operating quickly

[1]**whirl** *vb* **whirled; whirl·ing** **1** : to turn or move in circles rapidly **2** : to feel dizzy **3** : to move or carry around rapidly

[2]**whirl** *n* **1** : a rapid movement in circles **2** : something that is or seems to be moving in circles **3** : a state of busy movement : BUSTLE **4** : a brief or experimental try

whirl·pool *n* : a rapid swirl of water with a

low place in the center into which floating objects are drawn

whirl·wind *n* **:** a small windstorm in which the air turns rapidly in circles

[1]**whisk** *vb* **whisked; whisk·ing 1 :** to move suddenly and quickly **2 :** to brush with or as if with a whisk broom **3 :** to stir or beat with a whisk or fork

[2]**whisk** *n* **1 :** a quick sweeping or brushing motion **2 :** a kitchen utensil of wire used for whipping (as eggs or cream)

whisk broom *n* **:** a small broom with a short handle used for cleaning small areas or as a clothes brush

whis·ker *n* **1 whiskers** *pl* **:** the part of the beard that grows on the sides of the face and on the chin **2 :** one hair of the beard **3 :** a long bristle or hair growing near the mouth of an animal (as a cat)

whis·key *or* **whis·ky** *n, pl* **whis·keys** *or* **whis·kies :** a strong alcoholic drink usually made from grain (as of rye or barley)

[1]**whis·per** *vb* **whis·pered; whis·per·ing 1 :** to speak softly and quietly **2 :** to tell by speaking softly and quietly **3 :** to make a low rustling sound

[2]**whisper** *n* **1 :** a soft quiet way of speaking that can be heard only by people who are near **2 :** the act of speaking softly and quietly **3 :** something said softly and quietly **4 :** [1]HINT 1

[1]**whis·tle** *n* **1 :** a device by which a loud high-pitched sound is produced **2 :** a high-pitched sound (as that made by forcing the breath through puckered lips)

[2]**whistle** *vb* **whis·tled; whis·tling 1 :** to make a high-pitched sound by forcing the breath through the teeth or lips **2 :** to move, pass, or go with a high-pitched sound **3 :** to produce a high-pitched sound by forcing air or steam through a device **4 :** to express by forcing breath through the teeth or lips

whit *n* **:** a very small amount

[1]**white** *adj* **whit·er; whit·est 1 :** of the color of fresh snow **:** colored white **2 :** light or pale in color **3 :** pale gray **:** SILVERY **4 :** belonging to a race of people having light-colored skin **5 :** [1]BLANK 1 **6 :** not intended to cause harm **7 :** SNOWY 1 — **white·ness** *n*

[2]**white** *n* **1 :** the color of fresh snow **:** the opposite of black **2 :** the white part of something (as an egg) **3 :** white clothing **4 :** a person belonging to a race of people having light-colored skin

white blood cell *n* **:** one of the tiny colorless cells of the blood that help fight infection

white·board *n* **:** a large board with a smooth white surface that can be written on with special markers that can be erased

white·cap *n* **:** the top of a wave breaking into foam

white cell *n* **:** WHITE BLOOD CELL

white·fish *n* **:** a freshwater fish related to the trout that is greenish above and silvery below and is sometimes used for food

white flag *n* **:** a flag of plain white raised in asking for a truce or as a sign of surrender

whit·en *vb* **whit·ened; whit·en·ing :** to make or become white or whiter

white–tailed deer *n* **:** a common North American deer with the underside of the tail white

[1]**white·wash** *vb* **white·washed; white·wash·ing 1 :** to cover with a mixture that whitens **2 :** to try to hide the wrongdoing of

[2]**whitewash** *n* **:** a mixture (as of lime and water) for making a surface (as a wall) white

whith·er *adv* **:** to what place or situation

whit·ish *adj* **:** somewhat white

whit·tle *vb* **whit·tled; whit·tling 1 :** to cut or shave off chips from wood **:** shape by cutting or shaving off chips from wood **2 :** to reduce little by little

[1]**whiz** *or* **whizz** *vb* **whizzed; whiz·zing :** to move, pass, or fly rapidly with a buzzing sound

[2]**whiz** *or* **whizz** *n, pl* **whizz·es :** a buzzing sound

[3]**whiz** *n, pl* **whizzes :** WIZARD 2

who *pron* **1 :** what or which person or people **2** — used to stand for a person or people at the beginning of a clause

whoa *vb* — used as a command to an animal carrying a rider or pulling a load to stop

who·ev·er *pron* **:** whatever person

[1]**whole** *adj* **1 :** made up of all its parts **:** TOTAL, ENTIRE **2 :** all the **3 :** not cut up or ground **4 :** not scattered or divided **5 :** having all its proper parts **:** COMPLETE **6 :** completely healthy or sound — **whole·ness** *n*

[2]**whole** *n* **1 :** something that is full or complete **2 :** a sum of all the parts and elements — **on the whole 1 :** all things considered **2 :** in most cases

whole·heart·ed *adj* **:** not holding back — **whole·heart·ed·ly** *adv*

whole number *n* **:** a number that is zero or any of the natural numbers

[1]**whole·sale** *n* **:** the sale of goods in large quantities to dealers

[2]**wholesale** *adj* **1 :** of, relating to, or working at selling to dealers **2 :** done or happening on a large scale

[3]**wholesale** *vb* **whole·saled; whole·sal·ing :** to sell to dealers usually in large quantities — **whole·sal·er** *n*

whole·some *adj* **1 :** helping to improve or keep the body in good condition **2 :** healthy for the mind or morals — **whole·some·ness** *n*

whole wheat *adj* **:** made from or containing wheat kernels that were ground in their entirety

whol·ly *adv* **:** to the limit **:** COMPLETELY

whom *pron, objective case of* WHO

whom·ev·er *pron, objective case of* WHOEVER

¹whoop *vb* **whooped; whoop·ing 1 :** to shout or cheer loudly and strongly **2 :** to make the high-pitched gasping sound that follows a coughing attack in whooping cough

²whoop *n* **:** a loud strong shout or cheer

whooping cough *n* **:** a bacterial disease especially of children in which severe attacks of coughing are often followed by a high-pitched gasping intake of breath

whooping crane *n* **:** a large white nearly extinct North American crane that has a loud trumpeting call

¹whoosh *vb* **whooshed; whoosh·ing :** to pass or move along with a sound like that of something moving quickly

²whoosh *n, pl* **whoosh·es :** the sound created by something moving quickly

whop·per 1 : something huge of its kind **2 :** a big lie

whorl *n* **1 :** a row of parts (as leaves or petals) encircling a stem **2 :** something that whirls or winds

¹whose *adj* **:** of or relating to whom or which

²whose *pron* **:** that or those belonging to whom

¹why *adv* **:** for what cause or reason

²why *conj* **1 :** the cause or reason for which **2 :** for which

³why *interj* — used to express surprise, uncertainty, approval, disapproval, or impatience

WI *abbr* Wisconsin

wick *n* **:** a cord, strip, or ring of loosely woven material through which a liquid (as oil) is drawn to the top in a candle, lamp, or oil stove for burning

wick·ed *adj* **1 :** bad in behavior, moral state, or effect **:** EVIL **2 :** DANGEROUS 2 **3 :** of exceptional quality or degree — **wick·ed·ly** *adv* — **wick·ed·ness** *n*

¹wick·er *n* **1 :** a flexible twig (as of willow) used especially in making baskets or furniture **2 :** WICKERWORK

²wicker *adj* **:** made of wicker

wick·er·work *n* **:** something (as a basket or chair) made of wicker

wick·et *n* **1 :** an arch (as of wire) through which the ball is hit in the game of croquet **2 :** a small gate or door in or near a larger gate or door **3 :** a small window (as in a bank) through which business is conducted **4 :** either of the two sets of three rods topped by two crosspieces at which the ball is bowled in cricket

¹wide *adj* **wid·er; wid·est 1 :** having a large measure across **:** BROAD **2 :** opened as far as possible **3 :** covering a very large area **4 :** measured across or at right angles to length **5 :** not limited **:** having a large extent **6 :** to the side of **:** away from — **wide·ly** *adv* — **wide·ness** *n*

²wide *adv* **wid·er; wid·est 1 :** over a wide area **2 :** to the limit **:** COMPLETELY

wide–awake *adj* **1 :** fully awake **2 :** very alert

wid·en *vb* **wid·ened; wid·en·ing :** to make or become wide or wider

wide·spread *adj* **1 :** widely stretched out **2 :** widely scattered

¹wid·ow *n* **:** a woman whose spouse is dead

²widow *vb* **wid·owed; wid·ow·ing :** to make a widow or widower of

wid·ow·er *n* **:** a man whose spouse is dead

width *n* **1 :** the measurement of the shortest or shorter side of an object **:** BREADTH **2 :** a measured piece of something

wield *vb* **wield·ed; wield·ing 1 :** to use (as a tool) in an effective way **2 :** ²EXERCISE 1

wie·ner *n* **:** FRANKFURTER

wife *n, pl* **wives :** a married woman — **wife·ly** *adj*

Wi–Fi *certification mark* — used to certify that wireless computer networking devices operate together

wig *n* **:** a manufactured covering of natural or artificial hair for the head

¹wig·gle *vb* **wig·gled; wig·gling 1 :** to move up and down or from side to side with quick short motions **2 :** to proceed with twisting and turning movements

²wiggle *n* **:** a twisting turning motion

wig·gly *adj* **wig·gli·er; wig·gli·est 1 :** constantly moving with twisting turning motions **2 :** WAVY

wig·wam *n* **:** a cone-shaped tent formerly used as a house or shelter by some American Indians

¹wild *adj* **wild·er; wild·est 1 :** living in a state of nature and not under human control and care **:** not tame **2 :** growing or produced in nature **:** not cultivated by people **3 :** not civilized **:** SAVAGE **4 :** not kept under control **:** not restrained **5 :** made without knowledge **6 :** done without accuracy **7 :** going beyond what is usual **8 :** ENTHUSIASTIC — **wild·ly** *adv* — **wild·ness** *n*

²wild *n* **:** WILDERNESS

wild boar *n* **:** a wild pig of Europe and Asia that is the ancestor of the domestic pig

wild·cat *n* **:** a wild animal (as an ocelot or lynx) of the cat family that is of small or medium size

wil·de·beest *n* : a large African antelope with a head like that of an ox, curving horns, a short mane, and long tail
wil·der·ness *n* : an area in its natural state in which few or no people live
wild·fire *n* : an uncontrollable fire that destroys a wide area
wild·flower *n* : the flower of a wild plant or the plant bearing it
wild·life *n* : wild animals living in their natural environment
[1]**wile** *n* : a trick meant to trap or deceive
[2]**wile** *vb* **wiled; wil·ing** : [2]LURE
[1]**will** *helping verb, past* **would;** *present sing & pl* **will** **1** : wish to **2** : am, is, or are willing to **3** : am, is, or are determined to **4** : am, is, or are going to **5** : is or are commanded to **6** : is or are able to **7** : is or are likely or bound to
[2]**will** *n* **1** : a firm desire or determination **2** : the power to decide or control emotions or actions **3** : a particular person's decision or choice **4** : a legal paper in which a person states to whom his or her property is to be given after death
[3]**will** *vb* **willed; will·ing** **1** : to intend or order **2** : to bring to a certain condition by the power of the will **3** : to decide on by choice **4** : to leave by will
will·ful *or* **wil·ful** *adj* **1** : STUBBORN 1 **2** : INTENTIONAL — **will·ful·ly** *adv* — **will·ful·ness** *n*
wil·lies *n pl* : a fit of nervousness
will·ing *adj* **1** : feeling no objection **2** : not slow or lazy **3** : made, done, or given by choice : VOLUNTARY — **will·ing·ly** *adv* — **will·ing·ness** *n*
wil·low *n* : a tree or bush with narrow leaves, catkins for flowers, and tough flexible stems sometimes used in making baskets
will·pow·er *n* : strong determination
[1]**wilt** *vb* **wilt·ed; wilt·ing** **1** : to lose freshness and become limp **2** : to lose strength
[2]**wilt** *n* : a plant disease (as of tomatoes) in which wilting and browning of leaves leads to death of the plant
wily *adj* **wil·i·er; wil·i·est** : full of tricks : CRAFTY
[1]**win** *vb* **won; win·ning** **1** : to achieve the victory in a contest **2** : to obtain by victory **3** : to be the victor in **4** : to get by effort or skill : GAIN **5** : to ask and get the favor of — **win·ner** *n*
[2]**win** *n* : an act or instance of winning
wince *vb* **winced; winc·ing** : to draw back (as from pain)
winch *n* : a machine that has a roller on which rope is wound for pulling or lifting
[1]**wind** *n* **1** : a natural movement of the air **2** : power to breathe **3** : limited knowledge especially about something secret **4 winds** *pl* : wind instruments of a band or orchestra
[2]**wind** *vb* **wind·ed; wind·ing** : to cause to be out of breath
[3]**wind** *vb* **wound; wind·ing** **1** : to move in or be made up of a series of twists and turns **2** : to twist around **3** : to cover with something twisted around : WRAP **4** : to make the spring of tight — **wind up** **1** : to bring to an end : CONCLUDE **2** : to reach a place or situation that was not expected **3** : to swing the arm before pitching a baseball
wind·break *n* : something (as a growth of trees and shrubs) that reduces the force of the wind
wind·fall *n* **1** : something (as fruit from a tree) blown down by the wind **2** : an unexpected gift or gain
wind·ing *adj* **1** : having a course made up of a series of twists and turns **2** : having a curved or spiral form
wind instrument *n* : a musical instrument (as a clarinet, harmonica, or trumpet) sounded by the vibration of a stream of air and especially by the player's breath
wind·mill *n* : a mill or a machine (as for pumping water) worked by the wind turning sails or vanes at the top of a tower
win·dow *n* **1** : an opening in a wall to let in light and air **2** : the glass and frame that fill a window opening **3** : any of the areas into which a computer display may be divided and on which different types of information may be shown — **win·dow·less** *adj*
win·dow·pane *n* : a pane in a window
win·dow·sill *n* : SILL 1
wind·pipe *n* : TRACHEA 1
wind·proof *adj* : protecting from the wind
wind·shield *n* : a clear screen (as of glass) attached to the body of a vehicle (as a car) in front of the riders to protect them from the wind
wind·storm *n* : a storm with strong wind and little or no rain
wind·up *n* **1** : the last part of something : FINISH **2** : a swing of a baseball pitcher's arm before the pitch is thrown
[1]**wind·ward** *adj* : moving or placed toward the direction from which the wind is blowing
[2]**windward** *n* : the side or direction from which the wind is blowing
windy *adj* **wind·i·er; wind·i·est** : having much or strong wind
wine *n* **1** : an alcoholic beverage made from the fermented juice of grapes **2** : an alcoholic beverage made from the usually fermented juice of fruits (as peaches) other than grapes
win·ery *n, pl* **win·er·ies** : a place where wine is made

[1]**wing** *n* **1 :** one of the paired limbs or limb-like parts with which a bird, bat, or insect flies **2 :** something like a wing in appearance, use, or motion **3 :** a part (as of a building) that sticks out from the main part **4 :** a division of an organization **5 wings** *pl* **:** an area just off the stage of a theater — **wing·less** *adj* — **wing·like** *adj* — **on the wing :** in flight

[2]**wing** *vb* **winged; wing·ing** **1 :** to move by means of wings **:** FLY **2 :** [1]THROW 1

winged *adj* **:** having wings or winglike parts

wing·span *n* **:** the distance from the tip of one wing to the tip of the other wing

[1]**wink** *vb* **winked; wink·ing** **1 :** to close and open one eye quickly as a signal or hint **2 :** to close and open the eyelids quickly

[2]**wink** *n* **1 :** a hint or sign given by closing and opening one eye quickly **2 :** a brief period of sleep **3 :** an act of closing and opening usually one eye quickly **4 :** a very short time

[1]**win·ning** *n* **1 :** the act of a person or people who win **2 :** something won especially in gambling — often used in pl.

[2]**winning** *adj* **1 :** being someone or something that wins, has won, or wins often **2 :** tending to please or delight

win·now *vb* **win·nowed; win·now·ing** **1 :** to remove (as waste from grain) by a current of air **2 :** to sort or separate from a larger group

win·some *adj* **:** [2]WINNING 2

[1]**win·ter** *n* **1 :** the season between autumn and spring (as from December to March in the northern half of the earth) **2 :** one of the years of a person's life

[2]**winter** *vb* **win·tered; win·ter·ing** **1 :** to pass the winter **2 :** to keep, feed, or manage during the winter

win·ter·green *n* **:** a low evergreen plant with shiny leaves which produce an oil used in medicine and flavoring

win·ter·time *n* **:** the winter season

win·try *adj* **win·tri·er; win·tri·est** **1 :** marked by or characteristic of winter **2 :** not friendly **:** COLD

[1]**wipe** *vb* **wiped; wip·ing** **1 :** to clean or dry by rubbing **2 :** to remove by or as if by rubbing — **wip·er** *n* — **wipe out :** to destroy completely

[2]**wipe** *n* **:** an act of wiping **:** RUB

[1]**wire** *n* **1 :** metal in the form of a thread or slender rod **2 :** a number of strands grouped together and used to send or receive electrical signals **3 :** TELEGRAM

[2]**wire** *vb* **wired; wir·ing** **1 :** to provide or equip with wire **2 :** to bind with wire **3 :** to send or send word to by telegraph

[1]**wire·less** *adj* **:** relating to communication by electromagnetic waves but without connecting wires **:** RADIO

[2]**wireless** *n* **:** a computer, telephone, or network that uses radio waves to send and receive electronic signals

wiry *adj* **wir·i·er; wir·i·est** **1 :** being slender yet strong and muscular **2 :** coarse and stiff

Wis., Wisc. *abbr* Wisconsin

wis·dom *n* **1 :** knowledge or learning gained over time **2 :** good sense **3 :** a wise attitude, belief, or course of action

wisdom tooth *n* **:** the last tooth of the full set of teeth on each side of the upper and lower jaws

[1]**wise** *adj* **wis·er; wis·est** **1 :** having or showing good sense or good judgment **:** SENSIBLE **2 :** having knowledge or information **3 :** rude or insulting in speech — **wise·ly** *adv*

[2]**wise** *n* **:** MANNER 2, WAY — used in phrases such as *in any wise, in no wise,* or *in this wise*

-wise *adv suffix* **1 :** in the manner of **2 :** in the position or direction of **3 :** with regard to

wise·crack *n* **:** a clever and often insulting statement usually made in joking

[1]**wish** *vb* **wished; wish·ing** **1 :** to have a desire for **:** WANT **2 :** to form or express a desire concerning **3 :** to request by expressing a desire

[2]**wish** *n* **1 :** an act or instance of having or expressing a desire usually in the mind **2 :** something wanted **3 :** a desire for happiness or luck

wish·bone *n* **:** a bone in front of a bird's breastbone that is shaped like a V

wish·ful *adj* **:** having, showing, or based on a wish

wishy–washy *adj* **:** lacking spirit, courage, or determination **:** WEAK

wisp *n* **1 :** a thin piece or strand **2 :** a thin streak **3 :** a small amount of something

wispy *adj* **wisp·i·er; wisp·i·est :** being thin and light

wis·te·ria *also* **wis·tar·ia** *n* **:** a woody vine that is grown for its long clusters of violet, white, or pink flowers

wist·ful *adj* **:** feeling or showing a quiet longing especially for something in the past — **wist·ful·ly** *adv* — **wist·ful·ness** *n*

wit *n* **1 :** normal mental state — usually used in pl. **2 :** power to think, reason, or decide **3 :** clever and amusing comments, expressions, or talk **4 :** a talent for making clever and usually amusing comments **5 :** a person with a talent for making clever and amusing comments

witch *n* **1 :** a person and especially a woman believed to have magic powers **2 :** an ugly or mean old woman

witch·craft *n* **:** the use of sorcery or magic

witch doctor *n* : a person who uses magic to cure illness and fight off evil spirits

witch·ery *n, pl* **witch·er·ies** **1** : WITCHCRAFT **2** : power to charm or fascinate

witch ha·zel *n* **1** : a shrub with small yellow flowers in late fall or early spring **2** : a soothing alcoholic lotion made from the bark of the witch hazel

with *prep* **1** : in the company of **2** : by the use of **3** : having in or as part of it **4** : in regard to **5** : in possession of **6** : AGAINST 1 **7** : in shared relation to **8** : compared to **9** : in the opinion or judgment of **10** : so as to show **11** : as well as **12** : FROM 2 **13** : because of **14** : DESPITE **15** : if given **16** : at the time of or shortly after **17** : in support of **18** : in the direction of

with·draw *vb* **with·drew; with·drawn; with·draw·ing** **1** : to draw back : take away **2** : to take back (as something said or suggested) **3** : to go away especially for privacy or safety

with·draw·al *n* : an act or instance of withdrawing

with·er *vb* **with·ered; with·er·ing** : to shrivel or cause to shrivel from or as if from loss of moisture : WILT

with·ers *n pl* : the ridge between the shoulder bones of a horse

with·hold *vb* **with·held; with·hold·ing** : to refuse to give, grant, or allow

[1]**with·in** *adv* : [2]INSIDE

[2]**within** *prep* **1** : [4]INSIDE 1 **2** : not beyond the limits of **3** : before the end of

[1]**with·out** *prep* **1** : not accompanied by or showing **2** : completely lacking **3** : [4]OUTSIDE **4** : not using something

[2]**without** *adv* **1** : [3]OUTSIDE **2** : not having something

with·stand *vb* **with·stood; with·stand·ing** **1** : to hold out against **2** : to oppose (as an attack) successfully

wit·less *adj* : lacking in wit or intelligence

[1]**wit·ness** *n* **1** : a person who sees or otherwise has personal knowledge of something **2** : a person who gives testimony in court **3** : a person who is present at an action (as the signing of a will) so as to be able to say who did it **4** : TESTIMONY

[2]**witness** *vb* **wit·nessed; wit·ness·ing** **1** : to see or gain personal knowledge of something **2** : to act as a witness to **3** : to be or give proof of

wit·ted *adj* : having wit or understanding — used in combination

wit·ty *adj* **wit·ti·er; wit·ti·est** : having or showing cleverness

wives *pl of* WIFE

wiz·ard *n* **1** : SORCERER, MAGICIAN **2** : a very clever or skillful person

wiz·ard·ry *n* : the art or practice of a sorcerer

wk. *abbr* week

[1]**wob·ble** *vb* **wob·bled; wob·bling** : to move from side to side in a shaky manner — **wob·bly** *adj*

[2]**wobble** *n* : a rocking motion from side to side

woe *n* **1** : great sorrow, grief, or misfortune : TROUBLE **2** : something that causes a problem

woe·ful *adj* **1** : full of grief or misery **2** : bringing woe or misery **3** : very bad — **woe·ful·ly** *adv*

woke *past of* WAKE

woken *past participle of* WAKE

[1]**wolf** *n, pl* **wolves** **1** : a large bushy-tailed wild animal that resembles the related domestic dog, eats meat, and often lives and hunts in packs **2** : a crafty or fierce person — **wolf·ish** *adj*

[2]**wolf** *vb* **wolfed; wolf·ing** : to eat fast or greedily

wolf dog *n* **1** : WOLFHOUND **2** : the offspring of a wolf and a domestic dog

wolf·hound *n* : a large dog used especially in the past for hunting large animals

wol·fram *n* : TUNGSTEN

wol·ver·ine *n* : a mostly dark brown wild animal with shaggy fur that resembles a small bear but is related to the weasel, eats meat, and is found chiefly in the northern forests of North America

wolves *pl of* WOLF

wom·an *n, pl* **wom·en** **1** : an adult female person **2** : women considered as a group

wom·an·hood *n* **1** : the state of being a woman **2** : qualities often associated with women **3** : WOMAN 2

wom·an·kind *n* : WOMAN 2

wom·an·ly *adj* : having the qualities often associated with women

womb *n* : UTERUS

wom·en·folk *or* **wom·en·folks** *n pl* : women especially of one family or group

won *past and past participle of* WIN

[1]**won·der** *vb* **won·dered; won·der·ing** **1** : to be curious or have doubt **2** : to feel surprise or amazement

[2]**wonder** *n* **1** : something extraordinary : MARVEL **2** : a feeling (as of astonishment) caused by something extraordinary

won·der·ful *adj* **1** : causing marvel : MARVELOUS **2** : very good or fine — **won·der·ful·ly** *adv*

won·der·ing·ly *adv* : in or as if in astonishment

won·der·land *n* : a place of wonders or surprises

won·der·ment *n* : AMAZEMENT

won·drous *adj* : WONDERFUL 1

[1]**wont** *adj* : being in the habit of doing

[2]**wont** *n* : HABIT 3
won't : will not
woo *vb* **wooed; woo·ing** **1** : to try to gain the love of **2** : to try to gain
[1]**wood** *n* **1** : a thick growth of trees : a small forest — often used in pl. **2** : a hard fibrous material that makes up most of the substance of a tree or shrub beneath the bark and is often used as a building material or fuel
[2]**wood** *adj* **1** : WOODEN 1 **2** : used for or on wood **3** *or* **woods** : living or growing in woodland
wood·chuck *n* : a reddish brown burrowing animal that is a plant-eating rodent that hibernates during the winter : GROUNDHOG
wood·cock *n* : a brownish bird that has a long bill and feeds chiefly on earthworms
wood·cut·ter *n* : a person who cuts wood especially as an occupation
wood·ed *adj* : covered with trees
wood·en *adj* **1** : made of wood **2** : lacking spirit, ease, or charm
wood·land *n* : land covered with trees and shrubs : FOREST
wood·lot *n* : a small area of trees that is set aside to be used for firewood or to provide wood for building things
wood louse *n* : a tiny flat gray animal that is a crustacean usually found living under stones or bark
wood·peck·er *n* : a bird that climbs trees and drills holes in them with its bill in search of insects
wood·pile *n* : a pile of wood and especially firewood
wood·shed *n* : a shed for storing firewood
woods·man *n, pl* **woods·men** : a person who works in the forest and who is knowledgeable about trees and wood
woodsy *adj* **woods·i·er; woods·i·est** : being, located in, or suggesting woodland
wood·wind *n* : one of the group of wind instruments consisting of the flutes, oboes, clarinets, bassoons, and sometimes saxophones
wood·work *n* : work (as the edge around doorways) made of wood
wood·work·ing *n* : the art or process of shaping or working with wood
woody *adj* **wood·i·er; wood·i·est** **1** : having or covered with trees **2** : of or containing wood or wood fibers **3** : very much like wood
[1]**woof** *n* : a deep harsh sound made by a dog
[2]**woof** *vb* **woofed; woof·ing** : to make the deep harsh sound of a dog
[3]**woof** *n* **1** : the threads that cross the warp in weaving a fabric **2** : a woven fabric or its texture
wool *n* **1** : soft wavy or curly usually thick hair especially of the sheep **2** : a substance that looks like a mass of wavy hair **3** : a material (as yarn) made from wool
wool·en *or Can and Brit* **wool·len** *adj* **1** : made of wool **2** : producing cloth made of wool
wool·ly *adj* **wool·li·er; wool·li·est** : made of or resembling wool
woolly mammoth *n* : an extinct mammal that was a heavy-coated mammoth of cold northern regions
woo·zy *adj* **woo·zi·er; woo·zi·est** : slightly dizzy, nauseous, or weak
[1]**word** *n* **1** : a sound or combination of sounds that has meaning and is spoken by a human being **2** : a written or printed letter or letters standing for a spoken word **3** : a brief remark or conversation **4** : [2]COMMAND 2, ORDER **5** : NEWS **6** : [1]PROMISE 1 **7 words** *pl* : remarks said in anger or in a quarrel
[2]**word** *vb* **word·ed; word·ing** : to express in words : PHRASE
word·ing *n* : the way something is put into words
word processing *n* : the production of printed documents (as business letters) with automated and usually computerized equipment
word processor *n* **1** : a computer used for creating, storing, and printing text **2** : software designed to perform word processing
wordy *adj* **word·i·er; word·i·est** : using or containing many words or more words than are needed — **word·i·ness** *n*
wore *past of* WEAR
[1]**work** *n* **1** : the use of a person's physical or mental strength or ability in order to get something done or get some desired result **2** : OCCUPATION 1, EMPLOYMENT **3** : the place where someone works **4** : something that needs to be done or dealt with : TASK, JOB **5** : DEED 1, ACHIEVEMENT **6** : something produced by effort or hard work **7 works** *pl* : a place where industrial labor is done : PLANT, FACTORY **8 works** *pl* : the working or moving parts of a mechanical device **9** : the way someone performs labor : WORKMANSHIP **10 works** *pl* : everything possessed, available, or belonging
[2]**work** *vb* **worked** *or* **wrought; work·ing** **1** : to do something that involves physical or mental effort especially for money or because of a need instead of for pleasure : labor or cause to labor **2** : to have a job **3** : to perform or act or to cause to act as planned : OPERATE **4** : to force to do something that involves physical or mental effort **5** : to move or cause to move slowly or with

effort **6 :** to cause to happen **7 :** [1]MAKE 2, SHAPE **8 :** to make an effort especially for a long period **9 :** EXCITE 2, PROVOKE **10 :** to carry on an occupation in, through, or along — **work out 1 :** to invent or solve by effort **2 :** to go through an exercise routine

work·able *adj* **:** capable of being worked or done

work·bench *n* **:** a bench on which work is done (as by mechanics)

work·book *n* **:** a book made up of a series of problems or practice examples for a student to use as part of a course of study

worked up *adj* **:** emotionally excited and especially angry or upset

work·er *n* **1 :** a person who works **2 :** one of the members of a colony of bees, ants, wasps, or termites that do most of the work of the colony

work·ing *adj* **1 :** doing work especially for a living **2 :** relating to work **3 :** good enough to allow work or further work to be done

work·ing·man *n, pl* **work·ing·men :** a person who works for wages usually at manual labor

work·man *n, pl* **work·men 1 :** WORKINGMAN **2 :** a skilled worker (as a carpenter)

work·man·ship *n* **1 :** the art or skill of a workman **2 :** the quality of a piece of work

work·out *n* **:** an exercise or practice to test or improve ability or performance

work·shop *n* **:** a shop where work and especially skilled work is carried on

work·sta·tion *n* **1 :** an area with equipment for the performance of a particular task usually by one person **2 :** a computer usually connected to a larger network

world *n* **1 :** EARTH 3 **2 :** people in general **:** HUMANITY **3 :** a state of existence **4 :** a great number or amount **5 :** a part or section of the earth **6 :** an area of interest or activity

world·ly *adj* **world·li·er; world·li·est 1 :** of or relating to the affairs of life rather than with spiritual affairs **2 :** WORLDLY-WISE — **world·li·ness** *n*

world·ly–wise *adj* **:** aware of and having knowledge about the things and ways of this world

[1]**world·wide** *adj* **:** extending over or involving the entire world

[2]**worldwide** *adv* **:** throughout the world

World Wide Web *n* **:** a part of the Internet designed to allow easier navigation of the network through the use of text and graphics that link to other documents

[1]**worm** *n* **1 :** a usually long creeping or crawling animal (as a tapeworm) that has a soft body **2 :** EARTHWORM **3 :** a person hated or pitied **4 worms** *pl* **:** infection caused by parasitic worms living in the body — **worm·like** *adj*

[2]**worm** *vb* **wormed; worm·ing 1 :** to move slowly by creeping or wriggling **2 :** to get hold of or escape from by trickery **3 :** to rid of parasitic worms

wormy *adj* **worm·i·er; worm·i·est :** containing worms

worn *past participle of* WEAR

worn–out *adj* **1 :** useless from long or hard wear **2 :** very weary

wor·ri·some *adj* **1 :** worrying a lot **2 :** causing worry

[1]**wor·ry** *vb* **wor·ried; wor·ry·ing 1 :** to feel or express great concern **2 :** to make anxious or upset **3 :** to shake and tear with the teeth — **wor·ri·er** *n*

[2]**worry** *n, pl* **worries 1 :** concern about something that might happen **:** ANXIETY **2 :** a cause of great concern

[1]**worse** *adj, comparative of* BAD *or of* ILL **1 :** more bad or evil **2 :** being in poorer health **3 :** more unfavorable, difficult, or unpleasant **4 :** of poorer quality, value, or condition **5 :** less skillful **6 :** less happy **7 :** more faulty or unsuitable

[2]**worse** *n* **:** something worse

[3]**worse** *adv, comparative of* BADLY *or of* ILL **:** not as well **:** in a worse way

wors·en *vb* **wors·ened; wors·en·ing :** to get worse

[1]**wor·ship** *n* **1 :** deep respect toward God, a god, or a sacred object **2 :** too much respect or admiration

[2]**worship** *vb* **wor·shipped** *also* **wor·shiped; wor·ship·ping** *also* **wor·ship·ing 1 :** to honor or respect as a divine being **2 :** to regard with respect, honor, or devotion **3 :** to take part in worship or an act of worship — **wor·ship·per** *or* **wor·ship·er** *n*

[1]**worst** *adj, superlative of* BAD *or of* ILL **1 :** most bad, ill, or evil **2 :** most unfavorable, difficult, or unpleasant **3 :** least appropriate or acceptable **4 :** least skillful **5 :** most troubled

[2]**worst** *adv, superlative of* ILL *or of* BADLY **:** in the worst way possible

[3]**worst** *n* **:** a person or thing that is worst

[4]**worst** *vb* **worst·ed; worst·ing :** to get the better of **:** DEFEAT

wor·sted *n* **1 :** a smooth yarn spun from long fibers of wool **2 :** a fabric woven from a worsted yarn

[1]**worth** *prep* **1 :** equal in value to **2 :** having possessions or income equal to **3 :** deserving of **4 :** capable of

[2]**worth** *n* **1 :** the value or usefulness of something or someone **2 :** value as expressed in money or in amount of time something will last **3 :** EXCELLENCE 1

worth·less *adj* **1 :** lacking worth **2 :** USELESS

worth·while *adj* **:** being worth the time spent or effort used

wor·thy *adj* **wor·thi·er; wor·thi·est 1 :** having worth or excellence **2 :** having enough value or excellence — **wor·thi·ness** *n*

would *vb, past of* [1]WILL **1** — used as a helping verb to show that something might be likely or meant to happen under certain conditions **2** — used to describe what someone said, expected, or thought **3** — used as a politer form of *will* **4 :** prefers or prefer to **5 :** was or were going to **6 :** is or are able to **:** COULD **7 :** strongly desire **:** WISH

wouldn't : would not

[1]**wound** *n* **1 :** an injury that involves cutting or breaking of bodily tissue **2 :** an injury or hurt to a person's feelings or reputation

[2]**wound** *vb* **wound·ed; wound·ing 1 :** to hurt by cutting or breaking bodily tissue **2 :** to hurt the feelings or pride of

[3]**wound** *past and past participle of* WIND

wove *past of* WEAVE

woven *past participle of* WEAVE

[1]**wran·gle** *vb* **wran·gled; wran·gling 1 :** to argue angrily **2 :** to care for and herd livestock and especially horses

[2]**wrangle** *n* **:** [1]QUARREL 2

wran·gler *n* **1 :** a person who quarrels **2 :** a worker on a ranch who tends horses or cattle

[1]**wrap** *vb* **wrapped; wrap·ping 1 :** to cover by winding or folding **2 :** to enclose in a package **3 :** to wind or fold around **4 :** to involve the attention of completely — **wrap up 1 :** to bring to an end **2 :** to put on warm clothing

[2]**wrap** *n* **:** a warm loose outer garment (as a shawl, cape, or coat)

wrap·per *n* **1 :** a protective covering **2 :** a person who wraps merchandise **3 :** a garment that is worn wrapped about the body

wrap·ping *n* **:** something used to wrap something else **:** WRAPPER

wrath *n* **:** violent anger **:** RAGE

wrath·ful *adj* **1 :** full of wrath **2 :** showing wrath

wreak *vb* **wreaked; wreak·ing :** to bring down as or as if punishment

wreath *n, pl* **wreaths :** something twisted or woven into a circular shape

wreathe *vb* **wreathed; wreath·ing 1 :** to form into wreaths **2 :** to crown, decorate, or cover with or as if with a wreath

[1]**wreck** *n* **1 :** the remains (as of a ship or vehicle) after heavy damage usually by storm, collision, or fire **2 :** a person who is very tired, ill, worried, or unhappy **3 :** the action of damaging or destroying something **4 :** something in a state of ruin

[2]**wreck** *vb* **wrecked; wreck·ing 1 :** to damage or destroy by or as if by force or violence **2 :** to bring to ruin or an end **3 :** [2]SHIPWRECK 2

wreck·age *n* **1 :** the remains of a wreck **2 :** the act of wrecking **:** the state of being wrecked

wreck·er *n* **1 :** a truck for removing wrecked or broken-down vehicles **2 :** a person who wrecks something

wren *n* **:** a small brown songbird with a short tail that points upward

[1]**wrench** *vb* **wrenched; wrench·ing 1 :** to pull or twist with sudden sharp force **2 :** to injure by a sudden sharp twisting or straining

[2]**wrench** *n* **1 :** a tool used in turning nuts or bolts **2 :** a violent twist to one side or out of shape **3 :** an injury caused by twisting or straining **:** SPRAIN

wrest *vb* **wrest·ed; wrest·ing 1 :** to pull away by twisting or wringing **2 :** to obtain only by great and steady effort

[1]**wres·tle** *vb* **wres·tled; wres·tling 1 :** to fight by grasping and attempting to turn, trip, or throw down an opponent or to prevent the opponent from being able to move **2 :** to struggle to deal with — **wres·tler** *n*

[2]**wrestle** *n* **:** [2]STRUGGLE 1

wres·tling *n* **:** a sport in which two opponents wrestle each other

wretch *n* **1 :** a miserable unhappy person **2 :** a very bad person

wretch·ed *adj* **1 :** very unhappy or unfortunate **:** suffering greatly **2 :** causing misery or distress **3 :** of very poor quality **:** INFERIOR — **wretch·ed·ly** *adv* — **wretch·ed·ness** *n*

wrig·gle *vb* **wrig·gled; wrig·gling 1 :** to twist or move like a worm **:** SQUIRM, WIGGLE **2 :** to advance by twisting and turning

wrig·gler *n* **1 :** someone or something that squirms **2 :** a mosquito larva

wring *vb* **wrung; wring·ing 1 :** to twist or press so as to squeeze out moisture **2 :** to get by or as if by twisting or pressing **3 :** to twist with a forceful or violent motion **4 :** to affect as if by wringing **5 :** to twist (hands) together as a sign of anguish

wring·er *n* **:** a machine or device for squeezing liquid out of something (as laundry)

[1]**wrin·kle** *n* **1 :** a crease or small fold (as in the skin or in cloth) **2 :** a clever notion or trick **3 :** a surprise in a story or series of events

[2]**wrinkle** *vb* **wrin·kled; wrin·kling :** to develop or cause to develop creases or small folds

wrist *n* **:** the joint or the region of the joint between the hand and arm

wrist·band *n* **1 :** the part of a sleeve that goes around the wrist **2 :** a band that goes around the wrist (as for support or to absorb sweat)
wrist·watch *n* **:** a watch attached to a bracelet or strap and worn on the wrist
writ *n* **:** an order in writing signed by an officer of a court ordering someone to do or not to do something
write *vb* **wrote; writ·ten; writ·ing 1 :** to form letters or words with pen or pencil **2 :** to form the letters or the words of (as on paper) **3 :** to put down on paper **4 :** to make up and set down for others to read **5 :** to compose music **6 :** to communicate with someone by sending a letter
writ·er *n* **:** a person who writes especially as a business or occupation
writhe *vb* **writhed; writh·ing :** to twist and turn from side to side
writ·ing *n* **1 :** the act of a person who writes **2 :** HANDWRITING **3 :** something (as a letter or book) that is written
[1]**wrong** *adj* **1 :** not the one wanted or intended **2 :** not correct or true **:** FALSE **3 :** not right **:** SINFUL, EVIL **4 :** not satisfactory **:** causing unhappiness **5 :** not suitable **6 :** made so as to be placed down or under and not to be seen **7 :** not proper **8 :** not working correctly — **wrong·ly** *adv*
[2]**wrong** *n* **:** something (as an idea, rule, or action) that is not right
[3]**wrong** *adv* **:** in the wrong direction, manner, or way
[4]**wrong** *vb* **wronged; wrong·ing :** to treat badly or unfairly
wrong·do·er *n* **:** a person who does wrong and especially a moral wrong
wrong·do·ing *n* **:** bad behavior or action
wrong·ful *adj* **1 :** [1]WRONG 3, UNJUST **2 :** UNLAWFUL
wrote *past of* WRITE
[1]**wrought** *past and past participle of* WORK
[2]**wrought** *adj* **1 :** beaten into shape by tools **2 :** much too excited
wrung *past and past participle of* WRING
wry *adj* **wry·er; wry·est 1 :** funny in a clever or ironic way **2 :** expressing irony
wt. *abbr* weight
WV, W.Va. *abbr* West Virginia
www *abbr* World Wide Web
WY, Wyo. *abbr* Wyoming

X

x *n, pl* **x's** *or* **xs** *often cap* **1 :** the 24th letter of the English alphabet **2 :** ten in Roman numerals **3 :** an unknown quantity
X–ax·is *n* **:** the horizontal line on a coordinate graph
XL *abbr* extra large
Xmas *n* **:** CHRISTMAS
x–ray *vb* **x–rayed; x–ray·ing** *often cap X* **:** to examine, treat, or photograph with X–rays
X–ray *n* **1 :** a powerful invisible ray made up of very short waves that is somewhat similar to light and that is able to pass through some solids and acts on photographic film like light **2 :** a photograph taken by the use of X–rays
xy·lo·phone *n* **:** a musical instrument consisting of a series of wooden bars of different lengths that are struck by special mallets to produce musical notes

Y

y *n, pl* **y's** *or* **ys** *often cap* **:** the 25th letter of the English alphabet
[1]**-y** *also* **-ey** *adj suffix* **-i·er; -i·est 1 :** showing, full of, or made of **2 :** like **3 :** devoted to **:** enthusiastic about **4 :** tending to **5 :** somewhat **:** rather
[2]**-y** *n suffix, pl* **-ies 1 :** state **:** condition **:** quality **2 :** activity, place of business, or goods dealt with **3 :** whole body or group
[3]**-y** *n suffix, pl* **-ies :** occasion or example of a specified action
[4]**-y** — see -IE

yacht *n* : a small ship used for pleasure cruising or racing
yacht·ing *n* : the activity or recreation of racing or cruising in a yacht
yak *n* : a wild or domestic ox of the uplands of central Asia that has very long hair
yam *n* **1** : the starchy thick underground tuber of a climbing plant that is an important food in many tropical regions **2** : a sweet potato with a moist and usually orange flesh
[1]**yank** *n* : a strong sudden pull : JERK
[2]**yank** *vb* **yanked; yank·ing** : to pull suddenly or forcefully
Yan·kee *n* **1** : a person born or living in New England **2** : a person born or living in the northern United States **3** : a person born or living in the United States
[1]**yap** *vb* **yapped; yap·ping** **1** : to bark often continuously with quick high-pitched sounds **2** : to talk continuously and often loudly : CHATTER
[2]**yap** *n* : a quick high-pitched bark
[1]**yard** *n* **1** : an outdoor area next to a building that is often bordered (as by shrubs or fences) **2** : the grounds of a building **3** : a fenced area for livestock **4** : an area set aside for a business or activity **5** : a system of railroad tracks especially for keeping and repairing cars
[2]**yard** *n* **1** : a measure of length equal to three feet or 36 inches (about 0.91 meter) **2** : a long pole pointed toward the ends that holds up and spreads the top of a sail
yard·age *n* **1** : a total number of yards **2** : the length or size of something measured in yards
yard·arm *n* : either end of the yard of a square-rigged ship
yard·stick *n* **1** : a measuring stick a yard long **2** : a rule or standard by which something is measured or judged
yar·mul·ke *n* : a small round cap that is worn by some Jewish men and boys
yarn *n* **1** : a natural or manufactured fiber (as of cotton, wool, or rayon) formed as a continuous thread for use in knitting or weaving **2** : an interesting or exciting story
yaw *vb* **yawed; yaw·ing** : to turn suddenly from a straight course
yawl *n* : a sailboat having two masts with the shorter one behind the point where the stern enters the water
[1]**yawn** *vb* **yawned; yawn·ing** **1** : to open the mouth wide and take a deep breath usually as an involuntary reaction to being tired or bored **2** : to open wide
[2]**yawn** *n* : an opening of the mouth while taking a deep breath usually as an involuntary reaction to being tired or bored
y–ax·is *n* : the vertical line on a coordinate graph
yd. *abbr* yard
ye *pron* : YOU 1
[1]**yea** *adv* : [1]YES 1 — used when a person is voting aloud for something
[2]**yea** *n* **1** : a vote in favor of something **2** : a person casting a yea vote
year *n* **1** : the period of about 365¼ days required for the earth to make one complete trip around the sun **2** : a period of 365 days or in leap year 366 days beginning January 1 **3** : a fixed period of time **4** : the age of a person **5** : a long time
year·book *n* **1** : a book published once a year especially as a report or summary of a certain topic (as new discoveries in science) **2** : a publication that shows a school's current students and staff and the activities that took place during the school year
year·ling *n* : an animal that is between one and two years old
year·ly *adj* : occurring, made, or done every year : ANNUAL
yearn *vb* **yearned; yearn·ing** : to desire very much
yearn·ing *n* : an eager desire
year–round *adj* : active, present, or done throughout the entire year
yeast *n* **1** : a single-celled fungus that ferments sugar to produce alcohol and carbon dioxide **2** : a commercial product containing living yeast cells that is used in baking to make dough rise and in the making of alcoholic beverages (as wine)
[1]**yell** *vb* **yelled; yell·ing** : to speak, call, or cry out loudly (as in anger or to get someone's attention)
[2]**yell** *n* : a loud call or cry : SHOUT
[1]**yel·low** *adj* **1** : of the color of a lemon : colored yellow **2** : COWARDLY
[2]**yellow** *n* **1** : the color of a lemon **2** : something (as the yolk of an egg) yellow in color
[3]**yellow** *vb* **yel·lowed; yel·low·ing** : to turn yellow
yellow fever *n* : a disease carried by mosquitoes in parts of Africa and South America
yel·low·ish *adj* : somewhat yellow
yellow jacket *n* : a small wasp with yellow markings that usually nests in colonies in the ground and can sting repeatedly and painfully
[1]**yelp** *n* : a quick high-pitched bark or cry
[2]**yelp** *vb* **yelped; yelp·ing** : to make a quick high-pitched bark or cry
yen *n* : a strong desire : LONGING
yeo·man *n, pl* **yeo·men** **1** : a petty officer in the navy who works as a clerk **2** : a person who owns and cultivates a small farm
-yer — see [2]-ER
[1]**yes** *adv* **1** — used to express agreement

in answer to a question, request, or offer or with an earlier statement **2** — used to introduce a phrase with greater emphasis or clearness **3** — used to show uncertainty or polite interest **4** — used to indicate excitement

²yes *n* **:** a positive reply

¹yes·ter·day *adv* **:** on the day before today

²yesterday *n* **1 :** the day before today **2 :** the past in general

yes·ter·year *n* **:** a time in the past

¹yet *adv* **1 :** in addition **2 :** ²EVEN 4 **3 :** up to now **:** so far **4 :** at this time **5 :** up to the present **:** STILL **6 :** at some later time **7 :** NEVERTHELESS

²yet *conj* **:** in spite of the fact that

yew *n* **:** a tree or shrub with stiff needlelike evergreen leaves and seeds having a red juicy covering

Yid·dish *n* **:** a language related to German that was originally spoken by Jews of central and eastern Europe

¹yield *vb* **yield·ed; yield·ing 1 :** to give (something) over to the power or control or another **:** SURRENDER **2 :** to give in **3 :** to produce as a natural product **4 :** to produce or give back as interest or profit **5 :** to be productive **:** bring good results **6 :** to stop opposing or objecting to something **7 :** to give way under physical force so as to bend, stretch, or break **8 :** to allow another person or vehicle to go first

²yield *n* **1 :** the amount produced or returned **2 :** RETURN 5

¹yip *vb* **yipped; yip·ping :** ¹YAP 1

²yip *n* **:** ²YAP

YK *abbr* Yukon Territory

¹yo·del *vb* **yo·deled** *or* **yo·delled; yo·del·ing** *or* **yo·del·ling :** to sing or call with frequent sudden changes from the natural voice range to a higher range and back — **yo·del·er** *n*

²yodel *n* **:** a song or call made by yodeling

yo·gurt *n* **:** a thick soft food that is made of milk soured by the addition of bacteria and that is often flavored and sweetened

¹yoke *n* **1 :** a wooden bar or frame by which two work animals (as oxen) are harnessed at the heads or necks for drawing a plow or load **2 :** a frame fitted to a person's shoulders to carry a load in two equal parts **3 :** a clamp that holds or connects two parts **4** *pl usually* **yoke :** two animals yoked together **5 :** something that brings about pain, suffering, or a loss of freedom **6 :** SLAVERY 1 **7 :** a fitted or shaped piece at the shoulder of a garment or at the top of a skirt

²yoke *vb* **yoked; yok·ing 1 :** to put a yoke on **2 :** to attach a work animal to

yo·kel *n* **:** a person from a small town or the country who has little education or experience

yolk *n* **:** the yellow inner part of the egg of a bird or reptile containing stored food material for the developing young

Yom Kip·pur *n* **:** a Jewish holiday observed in September or October with fasting and prayer

¹yon *adj* **:** ²YONDER

²yon *adv* **1 :** ¹YONDER **2 :** THITHER

¹yon·der *adv* **:** at or in that place

²yonder *adj* **1 :** more distant **2 :** being at a distance within view

yore *n* **:** time long past

you *pron* **1 :** the person, thing, or group these words are spoken or written to **2 :** anyone at all

you'd : you had **:** you would

you'll : you shall **:** you will

¹young *adj* **youn·ger; youn·gest 1 :** being in the first or an early stage of life, growth, or development **2 :** lacking in experience **3 :** recently formed, produced, or come into being **:** NEW **4 :** YOUTHFUL 1

²young *n pl* **1 :** young people **2 :** immature or recently born offspring

youn·gest *n, pl* **youngest :** the least old member especially of a family

young·ster *n* **1 :** a young person **:** YOUTH **2 :** CHILD 3

your *adj* **1 :** relating to or belonging to you **2 :** by or from you **3 :** relating to people in general **4** — used before a title of honor in addressing a person

you're : you are

yours *pron* **:** that which belongs to you

your·self *pron, pl* **your·selves 1 :** your own self **2 :** your normal or healthy self

youth *n, pl* **youths 1 :** the time of life between being a child and an adult **2 :** a young man **3 :** young people **4 :** the quality or state of being young

youth·ful *adj* **1 :** belonging to, relating to, or characteristic of youth **2 :** not old or mature **3 :** having the appearance, spirit, or energy of youth — **youth·ful·ness** *n*

you've : you have

¹yowl *vb* **yowled; yowl·ing :** to utter a loud long cry (as of pain or suffering)

²yowl *n* **:** a loud long cry (as of pain or suffering)

yo–yo *n, pl* **yo–yos** *also* **yo–yoes :** a small round toy that has two flattened disks with a string attached to the center and that is made to fall and rise to the hand by unwinding and rewinding on the string

yr. *abbr* year

YT *abbr* Yukon Territory

yuc·ca *n* **:** a plant that grows in warm dry regions and has stiff pointed leaves at the base

DICTIONARY

and a tall stiff stalk of usually whitish flowers

yucky *adj* **yuck·i·er; yuck·i·est :** causing discomfort, disgust, or a strong feeling of dislike

yule *n, often cap* **:** CHRISTMAS

yule log *n, often cap Y* **:** a large log once put in the fireplace on Christmas Eve as the foundation of the fire

yule·tide *n, often cap* **:** the Christmas season

yum·my *adj* **yum·mi·er; yum·mi·est :** very pleasing especially to the taste

Z

z *n, pl* **z's** *or* **zs** *often cap* **:** the 26th letter of the English alphabet

za·ny *adj* **za·ni·er; za·ni·est :** very strange and silly

zap *vb* **zapped; zap·ping :** to hit with or as if with a jolt of electricity

zeal *n* **:** eager desire to get something done or see something succeed

zeal·ous *adj* **1 :** filled with or showing a strong and energetic desire to get something done or see something succeed **2 :** marked by passionate support for a person, cause, or ideal — **zeal·ous·ly** *adv*

ze·bra *n* **:** an African animal that is related to the horse and has a hide striped in black and white or black and buff

ze·bu *n* **:** an Asian domestic ox that has a large hump over the shoulders and loose skin with hanging folds

ze·nith *n* **1 :** the point in the sky directly overhead **2 :** the highest point or stage

zeph·yr *n* **:** a gentle breeze

zep·pe·lin *n* **:** an airship resembling a huge long balloon that has a metal frame and is driven through the air by engines carried on its underside

ze·ro *n, pl* **zeros** *or* **zeroes 1 :** the numerical symbol 0 meaning the absence of all size or quantity **2 :** the point on a scale (as on a thermometer) from which measurements are made **3 :** the temperature shown by the zero mark on a thermometer **4 :** a total lack of anything **:** NOTHING

zest *n* **1 :** a piece of the peel of a citrus fruit (as an orange or lemon) used to flavor foods **2 :** an enjoyable or exciting quality **3 :** keen enjoyment

1zig·zag *n* **1 :** one of a series of short sharp turns or angles in a line or course **2 :** a line, path, or pattern with a series of short sharp angles

2zigzag *adv* **:** in or by a line or course that has short sharp turns or angles

3zigzag *adj* **:** having short sharp turns or angles

4zigzag *vb* **zig·zagged; zig·zag·ging :** to form into or move along a line or course that has short sharp turns or angles

zil·lion *n* **:** an extremely large number

zinc *n* **:** a bluish white metal that tarnishes only slightly in moist air and is used mostly to make alloys and to give iron and steel a protective coating

1zing *n* **1 :** a high-pitched humming sound **2 :** a lively or energetic quality **3 :** a sharp or spicy flavor

2zing *vb* **zinged; zing·ing :** to move very quick with a high-pitched humming sound

zin·nia *n* **:** a garden plant grown for its long-lasting colorful flowers

1zip *vb* **zipped; zip·ping :** to move or act quickly and often with energy and enthusiasm

2zip *n* **:** energy and enthusiasm

3zip *vb* **zipped; zip·ping :** to close or open with a zipper

zip code *n* **:** a number that identifies each postal delivery area in the United States

zip line *n* **:** a cable that is hung along a slope and that has a pulley and harness attached for a rider

zip·per *n* **:** a fastener (as for a jacket) consisting of two rows of metal or plastic teeth and a sliding piece that closes an opening by bringing the teeth together — **zip·pered** *adj*

zip·py *adj* **zip·pi·er; zip·pi·est 1 :** SPEEDY **2 :** full of energy **:** LIVELY

zith·er *n* **:** a musical instrument with usually 30 to 40 strings that are plucked with the fingers or with a pick

zo·di·ac *n* **:** an imaginary belt in the sky that includes the paths of the planets and is divided into twelve constellations or signs each with a special name and symbol

zom·bie *also* **zom·bi** *n* **:** a person who is believed to have died and been brought back to life without speech or free will

1zone *n* **1 :** a region or area set off or characterized as different from surrounding or neighboring parts **2 :** one of the sections of an area created for or serving a particular use or purpose

²zone *vb* **zoned; zon·ing :** to divide into sections for different uses or purposes

zoo *n, pl* **zoos :** a place where living usually wild animals are kept for showing to the public

zoo·keep·er *n* **:** a person who cares for animals in a zoo

zoo·log·i·cal *adj* **:** of or relating to zoology

zoological garden *n* **:** ZOO

zoological park *n* **:** ZOO

zo·ol·o·gist *n* **:** a person who specializes in zoology

zo·ol·o·gy *n* **1 :** a branch of biology concerned with the study of animals and animal life **2 :** animal life (as of a region)

¹zoom *vb* **zoomed; zoom·ing 1 :** to move quickly often with a loud low hum or buzz **2 :** to move upward quickly

²zoom *n* **1 :** an act or process of moving quickly along or upwards **2 :** a loud low humming or buzzing sound

zuc·chi·ni *n* **:** a smooth cylinder-shaped green-skinned vegetable that is a type of squash

zwie·back *n* **:** a usually sweetened bread made with eggs that is baked and then sliced and toasted until dry and crisp

zy·gote *n* **:** the new cell formed when a sperm cell joins with an egg cell

THESAURUS

Using the Thesaurus

As with any thesaurus, the heart of the book is the list of **synonyms** (*Syn*), words that have the same essential meaning as the one you have in mind. Yet sometimes you may be looking for a word that means the same and sometimes looking for a word that is only similar to your word. Thus, at many entries you will find a list of **related words** (*Rel*), or near synonyms, words that may be close to your notion when an exact match is not quite right. And many times you may be thinking of a word with opposite meaning, and that is where a list of **antonyms** (*Ant*) will be helpful.

All of the entries in this book are in alphabetical order. Each thesaurus main entry contains a full list of at least two synonyms and often a list of antonyms, so no matter what word you start with, you will find its synonyms listed.

> **adjacent** • having a border in common *Syn* abutting, adjoining, bordering, contiguous, flanking, fringing, joining, juxtaposed, skirting, touching, verging *Rel* close, closest, immediate, near, nearby, nearest, neighboring, next, next-door, nigh *Ant* nonadjacent
>
> **contiguous** *Syn* ADJACENT, abutting, adjoining, bordering, flanking, fringing, joining, juxtaposed, skirting, touching, verging *Ant* nonadjacent

The word *contiguous*, in the synonym list at the principal entry **adjacent**, has its own entry with the same synonyms and antonyms.

A unique feature of this book not found in many thesauruses is the appearance of the **meaning core**, marked by a small raised black dot. The meaning core is a definition-like statement of the central meaning shared by all of the words in the synonym list. The main entry for the principal synonym of the list will contain the meaning core and often a list of related words as well (as at **adjacent** above). At a main entry for a synonym that is not the principal synonym, that principal synonym will be listed first, in SMALL CAPITALS, (as at **contiguous** above) and this tells you where to look if you want to read the meaning core for that list or to see if there are any listed related words.

Entry words ordinarily conform to normal dictionary practice: nouns are normally styled as singulars; verbs as infinitives. Homographs (words spelled the same but having a different part of speech) are given separate entries with a functional label, indicating whether noun (*n*), verb (*vb*), adjective (*adj*), preposition (*prep*), or conjunction (*conj*).

> **contrary** *adj* **1** • given to opposing or resisting wishes, commands, conditions, or circumstances *Syn* balky, froward, perverse, restive, wayward *Rel* headstrong, intractable, recalcitrant, refractory, unruly *Ant* complaisant, good-natured . . .
>
> **contrary** *n* *Syn* OPPOSITE, antipode, antithesis, antonym, contradictory, converse, counter, reverse

Whenever two homographs come together and have the same part of speech but have different origins, they are marked with a superscript homograph number and a part of speech label.

> **desert**[1] *n* *Syn* DUE, merit
>
> **desert**[2] *n* *Syn* WASTE, badlands, wilderness

Headwords that are synonyms and alphabetically close to each other are sometimes listed together.

summon, summons · to demand or request the presence or service of *Syn* call, cite, convene, convoke, muster *Rel* bid, command, enjoin, order

Parentheses enclose a particle or particles usually associated with a word. They may accompany a main entry word or a word in a list.

approve (of) · to have a favorable opinion of *Syn* accept, care (for), countenance, favor, OK (*or* okay), subscribe (to) *Rel* acclaim, applaud, laud, praise, salute *Ant* disapprove (of), discountenance, disfavor, frown (on *or* upon)

Parentheses also enclose material indicating a typical or, occasionally, a sole object of reference.

recant *Syn* ABJURE, forswear, renounce, retract *Ant* pledge (*allegiance, a vow*), elect (*a way of life, a means to an end*)

Spelling variants are labeled as such at the main entry or in lists.

specter *or* **spectre** *Syn* GHOST, apparition, bogey, phantasm, phantom, poltergeist, shade, shadow, spirit, spook, vision, wraith

adequate 1 · of a level of quality that meets one's needs or standards *Syn* acceptable, all right, decent, fine, OK (*or* okay), passable, respectable, satisfactory . . .

Plural usage is indicated in the spelling of the main entry or when necessary at a specific sense.

movie 1 · a story told by . . . *Syn* film, motion picture . . . **2 movies** *pl* · the art or business of making a movie *Syn* cinema, film, motion pictures . . .

A

A1 *Syn* EXCELLENT, bang-up, banner, capital, classic, crackerjack, dandy, divine, fabulous, fine, first-class, first-rate, grand, great, groovy, heavenly, jim-dandy, keen, marvelous (*or* marvellous), mean, neat, nifty, noble, par excellence, prime, sensational, splendid, stellar, sterling, superb, superior, superlative, supernal, swell, terrific, tip-top, top, top-notch, unsurpassed, wonderful *Ant* poor

aback *Syn* UNAWARES, suddenly, unaware, unexpectedly

abaft • toward or at the stern (of a vessel) *Syn* aft, astern *Rel* after, back, hind, hinder, posterior, rear *Ant* afore

abandon *n* • carefree freedom from constraint *Syn* abandonment, ease, lightheartedness, naturalness, spontaneity, unrestraint *Rel* ardor, enthusiasm, exuberance, fervor, spirit, warmth, zeal *Ant* constraint, restraint

abandon *vb* **1** • to quit absolutely *Syn* desert, forsake *Rel* cast, discard, junk, scrap *Ant* reclaim **2** *Syn* RELINQUISH, cede, leave, resign, surrender, waive, yield *Ant* keep

abandoned **1** • utterly depraved *Syn* dissolute, profligate, reprobate *Rel* debased, debauched, depraved, perverted *Ant* redeemed, regenerate **2** • left unoccupied or unused *Syn* derelict, deserted, disused, forgotten, forsaken, rejected, vacated *Rel* ignored, neglected, unattended, untended

abandonment *Syn* ABANDON, ease, lightheartedness, naturalness, spontaneity, unrestraint *Ant* constraint, restraint

abase • to lower in one's own estimation or in that of others *Syn* debase, degrade, demean, humble, humiliate *Rel* cower, cringe, fawn, toady, truckle *Ant* exalt, extol (*especially oneself*)

abash *Syn* EMBARRASS, discomfit, disconcert, faze, rattle *Ant* facilitate, relieve

abate **1** • to die down in force or intensity *Syn* ebb, subside, wane *Rel* decrease, diminish, dwindle *Ant* revive, rise **2** *Syn* DECREASE, diminish, dwindle, lessen, reduce *Ant* increase

abatement *Syn* DEDUCTION, discount, rebate

abbey *Syn* CLOISTER, convent, monastery, nunnery, priory

abbreviate *Syn* SHORTEN, abridge, curtail, retrench *Ant* elongate, extend, lengthen, prolong, protract

abdicate • to give up formally or definitely a position of trust, honor, or glory *Syn* renounce, resign *Rel* abandon, leave, relinquish, surrender *Ant* assume, usurp

abdomen *Syn* STOMACH, belly, gut, solar plexus, tummy

aberrant *Syn* DEVIANT, abnormal, anomalous, atypical, irregular, unnatural *Ant* natural, normal, regular, standard, typical

aberration **1** • mental disorder *Syn* alienation, derangement *Rel* dementia, insanity, lunacy *Ant* soundness (*of mind*) **2** *Syn* DEVIATION, deflection, divergence

abet *Syn* INCITE, foment, instigate *Ant* restrain

abettor **1** *Syn* ACCOMPLICE, accessory, cohort, confederate **2** *Syn* ALLY, backer, confederate, supporter, sympathizer

abeyance • a state of temporary inactivity *Syn* doldrums, dormancy, latency, quiescence, suspense, suspension *Rel* inaction, inertia, inertness, motionlessness *Ant* continuance, continuation

abeyant *Syn* LATENT, dormant, potential, quiescent *Ant* patent

abhor *Syn* HATE, abominate, detest, loathe *Ant* love

abhorrence • a feeling of extreme disgust or dislike *Syn* abomination, detestation, hate, hatred, loathing *Rel* distaste, repellency, repugnance *Ant* admiration, enjoyment

abhorrent **1** *Syn* HATEFUL, abominable, detestable, odious *Ant* lovable, sympathetic **2** *Syn* REPUGNANT, distasteful, invidious, obnoxious, repellent *Ant* congenial

abide **1** *Syn* BEAR (sense 2), brook, endure, stand, suffer, tolerate **2** *Syn* CONTINUE, endure, last, persist **3** *Syn* STAY, linger, remain, tarry, wait

ability • the physical or mental power to do something *Syn* capability, capacity, competence, competency, faculty *Rel* aptitude, aptness, endowment, facility, gift, knack, talent *Ant* disability, inability, incapability, incapacity, incompetence, incompetency, ineptitude, ineptness

abject *Syn* MEAN, ignoble, sordid

abjure • to abandon irrevocably and usually with solemnity or publicity *Syn* forswear, recant, renounce, retract *Rel* eschew, forbear, forgo *Ant* pledge (*allegiance, a vow*), elect (*a way of life, a means to an end*)

able *Syn* COMPETENT, capable, fit, good, qualified, suitable *Ant* incompetent, inept, poor, unfit, unqualified

abnegate *Syn* FORGO, eschew, forbear, sacrifice

abnegation *Syn* RENUNCIATION, self-abnegation, self-denial *Ant* indulgence, self-indulgence

abnormal *Syn* DEVIANT, aberrant, anomalous,

atypical, irregular, unnatural *Ant* natural, normal, regular, standard, typical

abode *Syn* HABITATION, domicile, dwelling, home, house, residence

abolish • to put an end to by formal action *Syn* abrogate, annul, cancel, dissolve, invalidate, negate, nullify, quash, repeal, rescind, void *Rel* countermand, override, overrule, overturn, veto

abominable *Syn* HATEFUL, abhorrent, detestable, odious *Ant* lovable, sympathetic

abominate *Syn* HATE, abhor, detest, loathe *Ant* love

abomination **1** • a person or thing from which one shrinks with intense dislike *Syn* anathema, bête noire, bugbear *Rel* annoyance, pest, plague *Ant* joy **2** *Syn* ABHORRENCE, detestation, hate, hatred, loathing *Ant* admiration, enjoyment

aboriginal *Syn* NATIVE, autochthonous, endemic, indigenous *Ant* alien, foreign

abortion *Syn* CANCELLATION, calling, calling off, dropping, recall, repeal, rescission, revocation *Ant* continuation

abortive *Syn* FUTILE, bootless, fruitless, vain *Ant* effective, effectual, efficacious, efficient, fruitful, productive, profitable, successful

abound *Syn* TEEM, overflow, swarm

abounding *Syn* RIFE, flush, fraught, replete, swarming, teeming, thick, thronging

about *prep* **1** • in reference to *Syn* concerning, regarding, respecting **2** *Syn* AROUND (sense 1), by, near, next to

about *adv* **1** *Syn* ALMOST, more or less, most, much, near, nearly, next to, nigh, practically, some, virtually, well-nigh **2** *Syn* AROUND (sense 2), over, round, through, throughout

above • to or in a higher place *Syn* aloft, over, overhead, skyward *Ant* below, beneath, under

aboveboard *Syn* STRAIGHTFORWARD, forthright *Ant* devious, indirect

abracadabra *Syn* GIBBERISH, hocus-pocus, mummery

abrade • to affect a surface by rubbing, scrapping, or wearing away *Syn* chafe, excoriate, fret, gall *Rel* grate, grind, rasp, scrape, scratch

abridge *Syn* SHORTEN, abbreviate, curtail, retrench *Ant* elongate, extend, lengthen, prolong, protract

abridgment • a condensation of a larger work *Syn* abstract, brief, conspectus, epitome, synopsis *Rel* compendium, digest, précis, sketch, syllabus *Ant* expansion

abrogate *Syn* ABOLISH, annul, cancel, dissolve, invalidate, negate, nullify, quash, repeal, rescind, void

abrupt **1** *Syn* PRECIPITATE, hasty, headlong, impetuous, sudden *Ant* deliberate **2** *Syn* STEEP, precipitous, sheer

abscess • a localized swollen area of infection containing pus *Syn* boil, carbuncle, furuncle, pimple, pustule

abscond *Syn* ESCAPE (sense 1), decamp, flee, fly

absence *Syn* LACK, dearth, defect, privation, want

absent *Syn* ABSTRACTED, absentminded, distraught, preoccupied *Ant* alert

absentminded *Syn* ABSTRACTED, absent, distraught, preoccupied *Ant* alert

absolute **1** • exercising power or authority without external restraint *Syn* arbitrary, autocratic, despotic, tyrannical, tyrannous *Rel* authoritarian, totalitarian *Ant* limited, restrained **2** *Syn* PURE, sheer, simple *Ant* adulterated, applied (*of science*), contaminated, polluted **3** *Syn* ULTIMATE, categorical

absolution *Syn* PARDON, amnesty, forgiveness, remission, remittal *Ant* penalty, punishment, retribution

absolve *Syn* EXCULPATE, acquit, exonerate, vindicate *Ant* accuse, inculpate

absorb **1** • to take (something) in so as to become imbued with it or to make it a part of one's being *Syn* assimilate, imbibe *Rel* impregnate, saturate, soak *Ant* exude, give out **2** *Syn* MONOPOLIZE, consume, engross

absorbed *Syn* INTENT, engrossed, rapt *Ant* distracted

absorbing *Syn* INTERESTING, arresting, engaging, engrossing, enthralling, fascinating, gripping, immersing, intriguing, involving, riveting *Ant* boring, drab, dry, dull, heavy, monotonous, tedious, uninteresting

abstain *Syn* REFRAIN, forbear

abstemiousness *Syn* TEMPERANCE, abstinence, continence, sobriety *Ant* excessiveness, immoderacy, intemperance, intemperateness

abstinence *Syn* TEMPERANCE, abstemiousness, continence, sobriety *Ant* excessiveness, immoderacy, intemperance, intemperateness

abstract *adj* **1** • having conceptual rather than concrete existence *Syn* ideal, transcendent, transcendental *Rel* general, generic, universal *Ant* concrete **2** • dealing with or expressing a quality or idea *Syn* conceptual, theoretical *Rel* conjectural, hypothetical, speculative *Ant* concrete

abstract *n* *Syn* ABRIDGMENT, brief, conspectus, epitome, synopsis *Ant* expansion

abstract *vb* **1** *Syn* DETACH, disengage *Ant* affix, attach **2** *Syn* SUMMARIZE, digest, encapsulate, epitomize, outline, recap, recapitulate, sum up, wrap up

abstracted • inattentive to what presently claims or demands consideration *Syn* absent, absentminded, distraught, preoccupied *Rel* engrossed, intent *Ant* alert

abstruse *Syn* RECONDITE, esoteric, occult

absurd *Syn* FOOLISH, preposterous, silly *Ant* sensible

abundant *Syn* PLENTIFUL, ample, copious, plenteous *Ant* scant, scanty

abuse *n* • vehemently expressed condemnation

or disapproval *Syn* billingsgate, invective, obloquy, scurrility, vituperation *Rel* animadversion, aspersion, reflection, stricture *Ant* adulation
abuse *vb* **1** • to use or treat a person or thing improperly or wrongfully *Syn* ill-treat, maltreat, mistreat, misuse, outrage *Rel* damage, harm, hurt, impair, injure, mar, spoil *Ant* honor, respect **2** *Syn* ATTACK (sense 2), assail, belabor, blast, castigate, excoriate, jump (on), lambaste (*or* lambast), scathe, slam, vituperate
abusive • coarse, insulting, and contemptuous in character or utterance *Syn* contumelious, opprobrious, scurrilous, vituperative *Rel* affronting, insulting, offending, outraging *Ant* complementary, respectful
abutment *Syn* BUTTRESS, pier
abutting *Syn* ADJACENT, adjoining, bordering, contiguous, flanking, fringing, joining, juxtaposed, skirting, touching, verging *Ant* nonadjacent
abysm *Syn* GULF, abyss, chasm
abysmal *Syn* DEEP, profound
abyss *Syn* GULF, abysm, chasm
academic **1** • of or relating to schooling or learning especially at an advanced level *Syn* educational, scholarly, scholastic *Rel* bookish, pedantic, professorial *Ant* nonacademic, unacademic **2** *Syn* PEDANTIC, bookish, scholastic **3** *Syn* THEORETICAL, speculative
accede *Syn* ASSENT, acquiesce, agree, consent, subscribe *Ant* dissent
accelerate *Syn* HURRY (sense 1), hasten, quicken, rush, speed (up), whisk *Ant* decelerate, retard, slow (down)
accent *n* **1** *Syn* EMPHASIS, accentuation, stress **2** *Syn* INFLECTION, intonation
accent *vb* *Syn* EMPHASIZE, accentuate, feature, highlight, play (up), point (up), stress, underline, underscore *Ant* play (down)
accentuate *Syn* EMPHASIZE, accent, feature, highlight, play (up), point (up), stress, underline, underscore *Ant* play (down)
accentuation *Syn* EMPHASIS, accent, stress
accept **1** *Syn* APPROVE (OF), care (for), countenance, favor, OK (*or* okay), subscribe (to) *Ant* disapprove (of), discountenance, disfavor, frown (on *or* upon) **2** *Syn* RECEIVE, admit, take
acceptability *Syn* SUFFICIENCY, adequacy, satisfactoriness *Ant* inadequacy, insufficiency
acceptable *Syn* ADEQUATE, all right, decent, fine, OK (*or* okay), passable, respectable, satisfactory, tolerable *Ant* deficient, inadequate, lacking, unacceptable, unsatisfactory, wanting
acceptation *Syn* MEANING, import, sense, significance, signification
accession *Syn* ADDITION, accretion, increment
accessory *n* **1** *Syn* ACCOMPLICE, abettor, cohort, confederate **2** *Syn* APPENDAGE, adjunct, appurtenance
accessory *adj* *Syn* AUXILIARY, adjuvant, ancillary, contributory, subservient, subsidiary
accident **1** • chance or a chance event bringing injury or loss *Syn* casualty, mishap *Rel* catastrophe, disaster **2** *Syn* CHANCE, fortune, hap, hazard, luck *Ant* law, principle
accidental • happening by chance *Syn* casual, chance, fluky, fortuitous, inadvertent, incidental, unintended, unintentional, unplanned, unpremeditated, unwitting *Rel* coincidental *Ant* deliberate, intended, intentional, planned, premeditated
acclaim **1** • to declare enthusiastic approval of *Syn* applaud, cheer, hail, laud, praise, salute, tout *Rel* ballyhoo *Ant* knock, pan, slam **2** *Syn* PRAISE, eulogize, extol, laud *Ant* blame
acclamation *Syn* APPLAUSE, cheering, cheers, ovation, plaudit(s), rave(s) *Ant* booing, hissing
acclimate *Syn* HARDEN (sense 2), acclimatize, season *Ant* soften
acclimatize *Syn* HARDEN (sense 2), acclimate, season *Ant* soften
accommodate **1** *Syn* ADAPT, adjust, conform, reconcile *Ant* unfit **2** *Syn* CONTAIN, hold **3** *Syn* OBLIGE, favor *Ant* disoblige
accompany • to go along with in order to provide assistance, protection, or companionship *Syn* attend, chaperone (*or* chaperon), convoy, escort, squire *Rel* associate, consort, pal (around), team (up)
accomplice • one associated with another in wrongdoing *Syn* abettor, accessory, cohort, confederate *Rel* collaborationist, collaborator, informant, informer
accomplish *Syn* PERFORM, achieve, discharge, effect, execute, fulfill
accomplished *Syn* CONSUMMATE, finished *Ant* crude
accomplishment **1** *Syn* ACQUIREMENT, acquisition, attainment **2** *Syn* FRUITION, achievement, actuality, attainment, consummation, fulfillment, realization *Ant* naught, nonfulfillment
accord *n* **1** *Syn* AGREEMENT, understanding **2** *Syn* HARMONY, concord, consonance *Ant* conflict
accord *vb* **1** *Syn* AGREE (sense 2), conform, correspond, harmonize, jibe, square, tally *Ant* differ (from) **2** *Syn* GRANT (sense 1), award, concede, vouchsafe
accordingly *Syn* THEREFORE, consequently, hence, so, then
accost *Syn* ADDRESS, greet, hail, salute
account *n* • a statement of actual events or conditions or of purported occurrences or conditions *Syn* chronicle, report, story, version
account *vb* **1** *Syn* CONSIDER (sense 2), deem, reckon, regard **2** *Syn* USE (sense 1), advantage, avail, profit, service

accountable *Syn* RESPONSIBLE, amenable, answerable, liable
account (for) *Syn* EXPLAIN (sense 2), explain away, rationalize
accoutre *or* **accouter** *Syn* FURNISH (sense 1), equip, fit (out), outfit, rig, supply *Ant* hold (back), keep (back), reserve, retain, withhold
accredit **1** *Syn* APPROVE, certify, endorse, sanction *Ant* disapprove **2** *Syn* ASCRIBE, assign, attribute, charge, credit, impute, refer **3** *Syn* AUTHORIZE, commission, license
accretion *Syn* ADDITION, accession, increment
accumulate **1** • to bring together so as to make a store or great quantity *Syn* amass, hoard *Rel* collect, gather *Ant* dissipate **2** *Syn* INCREASE (sense 2), appreciate, balloon, build (up), burgeon, enlarge, escalate, expand, mount, multiply, mushroom, proliferate, rise, snowball, swell, wax *Ant* contract, decrease, diminish, lessen, wane
accumulative *Syn* CUMULATIVE, additive, summative
accuracy *Syn* PRECISION, closeness, delicacy, exactitude, exactness, fineness, preciseness, rigorousness, veracity *Ant* coarseness, impreciseness, imprecision, inaccuracy, inexactness, roughness
accurate *Syn* CORRECT, exact, nice, precise, right *Ant* incorrect
accursed *Syn* EXECRABLE, cursed, damnable
accuse • to make a claim of wrongdoing against *Syn* charge, impeach, incriminate, indict *Rel* blame, castigate, censure, condemn, criticize, damn, denounce, fault, impugn, reproach, reprobate *Ant* absolve, acquit, clear, exculpate, exonerate, vindicate
accustom *Syn* HABITUATE, addict, inure
accustomed **1** • being in the habit or custom *Syn* given, habituated, used, wont *Rel* apt, inclined, liable, prone *Ant* unaccustomed, unused **2** *Syn* USUAL, customary, habitual, wonted
ace *Syn* EXPERT, adept, artist, authority, crackerjack, maestro, master, past master, scholar, shark, virtuoso, whiz, wizard *Ant* amateur
acerbity *Syn* ACRIMONY, asperity *Ant* suavity
ache *Syn* PAIN, pang, stitch, throe, twinge
achieve **1** *Syn* PERFORM, accomplish, discharge, effect, execute, fulfill **2** *Syn* REACH, attain, compass, gain
achievement **1** *Syn* FEAT, exploit **2** *Syn* FRUITION, accomplishment, actuality, attainment, consummation, fulfillment, realization *Ant* naught, nonfulfillment
acid *Syn* SOUR, acidulous, dry, tart
acidulous *Syn* SOUR, acid, dry, tart
acknowledge *Syn* ADMIT, agree, allow, concede, confess, grant, own (up) *Ant* deny
acknowledgment *Syn* CONFESSION, admission, avowal, concession
acme *Syn* SUMMIT, apex, apogee, climax, culmination, meridian, peak, pinnacle, zenith
acoustic *or* **acoustical** *Syn* AUDITORY, aural, auricular
acquaint *Syn* ENLIGHTEN (sense 1), advise, apprise, brief, clue, familiarize, fill in, inform, instruct, tell, wise (up)
acquaintance **1** • knowledge gained by personal experience *Syn* cognizance, familiarity *Rel* association, experience, exposure, intimacy, involvement *Ant* unfamiliarity **2** *Syn* FRIEND, confidant, intimate *Ant* foe
acquiesce *Syn* ASSENT, accede, agree, consent, subscribe *Ant* dissent
acquiescence *Syn* COMPLIANCE, resignation *Ant* forwardness
acquiescent **1** *Syn* COMPLIANT, resigned *Ant* forward **2** *Syn* PASSIVE, nonresistant, resigned, tolerant, tolerating, unresistant, unresisting, yielding *Ant* protesting, resistant, resisting, unyielding
acquire *Syn* EARN, attain, capture, carry, draw, gain, garner, get, land, make, obtain, procure, realize, secure, win *Ant* forfeit, lose
acquirement • a power or skill that is the fruit of exertion or effort *Syn* accomplishment, acquisition, attainment *Rel* achievement, feat
acquisition *Syn* ACQUIREMENT, accomplishment, attainment
acquisitive *Syn* COVETOUS, avaricious, grasping, greedy
acquisitiveness *Syn* GREED, avarice, avariciousness, avidity, covetousness, cupidity, greediness, rapaciousness, rapacity
acquit **1** *Syn* BEHAVE, comport, conduct, demean, deport, quit *Ant* misbehave **2** *Syn* EXCULPATE, absolve, exonerate, vindicate *Ant* accuse, inculpate
acrid *Syn* CAUSTIC, mordant, scathing *Ant* genial
acrimony • temper or language marked by irritation or some degree of anger or resentment *Syn* acerbity, asperity *Rel* bitterness *Ant* suavity
across • so as to intersect the length of something *Syn* athwart, crossways, crosswise
act *vb* **1** • to perform especially in an indicated way *Syn* behave, function, operate, react, work **2** • to assume the appearance or role of another person or character *Syn* impersonate, play **3** *Syn* SEEM, appear, look, make, sound
act *n* **1** *Syn* ACTION, deed **2** *Syn* FUNCTION, perform, serve, work
acting *Syn* TEMPORARY, ad interim, provisional *Ant* permanent
action **1** • something done or effected *Syn* act, deed *Rel* procedure, proceeding, process **2** *Syn* BATTLE, engagement **3** *Syn* SUIT, case, cause, lawsuit
activate **1** • to cause to function *Syn* actuate, crank (up), drive, move, propel, run, set off, spark, start, touch off, trigger, turn on *Rel* charge, electrify, energize, fire, fuel, gener-

ate, power, push *Ant* cut, deactivate, kill, shut off, turn off **2** *Syn* VITALIZE, energize *Ant* atrophy

active • at work or in effective action *Syn* dynamic, live, operative *Rel* agile, brisk, nimble *Ant* inactive

actor • one who, for the entertainment or edification of an audience, takes part in an exhibition simulating happenings in real life *Syn* impersonator, mime, mimic, mummer, performer, player, thespian, trouper

actual • existing in fact and not merely as a possibility *Syn* concrete, existent, factual, real, true, very *Rel* attested, authenticated, confirmed, demonstrated, established, proven, substantiated, validated, verified *Ant* conjectural, hypothetical, ideal, nonexistent, possible, potential, theoretical

actuality **1** *Syn* EXISTENCE, being *Ant* nonexistence **2** *Syn* FRUITION, accomplishment, achievement, attainment, consummation, fulfillment, realization *Ant* naught, nonfulfillment

actualize *Syn* REALIZE, embody, externalize, hypostatize, incarnate, materialize, objectify, reify

actuate *Syn* ACTIVATE, crank (up), drive, move, propel, run, set off, spark, start, touch off, trigger, turn on *Ant* cut, deactivate, kill, shut off, turn off

act up *Syn* CUT UP, clown (around), fool (around), horse (around), monkey (around), show off, skylark

acumen *Syn* DISCERNMENT, discrimination, insight, penetration, perception

acute **1** • of uncertain outcome *Syn* critical, crucial *Rel* climactic, culminating **2** *Syn* SHARP, keen *Ant* blunt, dull **3** *Syn* SHRILL, high-pitched, piping, screeching, shrieking, squeaking, squeaky, treble, whistling *Ant* bass, deep, low, throaty

ad *Syn* ANNOUNCEMENT, advertisement, bulletin, notice, notification, posting, release

adage *Syn* SAYING, aphorism, apothegm, epigram, maxim, motto, proverb, saw

adamant *Syn* OBSTINATE, adamantine, dogged, hard, hardened, hardheaded, hardhearted, headstrong, immovable, implacable, inflexible, mulish, obdurate, opinionated, ossified, pat, peevish, pertinacious, perverse, pigheaded, rigid, self-willed, stubborn, unbending, uncompromising, unrelenting, unyielding, willful (*or* wilful) *Ant* acquiescent, agreeable, amenable, compliant, complying, flexible, pliable, pliant, relenting, yielding

adamantine *Syn* OBSTINATE, adamant, dogged, hard, hardened, hardheaded, hardhearted, headstrong, immovable, implacable, inflexible, mulish, obdurate, opinionated, ossified, pat, peevish, pertinacious, perverse, pigheaded, rigid, self-willed, stubborn, unbending, uncompromising, unrelenting, unyielding, willful (*or* wilful) *Ant* acquiescent, agreeable, amenable, compliant, complying, flexible, pliable, pliant, relenting, yielding

adapt **1** • to bring into correspondence *Syn* accommodate, adjust, conform, reconcile *Rel* moderate, qualify, temper *Ant* unfit **2** *Syn* EDIT, compile, redact, revise, rewrite

adaptable *Syn* PLASTIC, ductile, malleable, pliable, pliant

add **1** • to combine (numbers) into a single sum *Syn* foot (up), sum, total *Rel* calculate, cast, cipher, compute, figure, reckon, tally **2** • to join (something) to a mass, quantity, or number so as to bring about an overall increase *Syn* adjoin, annex, append, tack (on) *Rel* affix, attach, fasten, fix, graft, hitch, tie *Ant* deduct, remove, subtract, take

added *Syn* ADDITIONAL, another, else, farther, further, more, other

addendum *Syn* APPENDIX, supplement

addict *n* **1** • a person who by habit and strong inclination indulges in something or the pursuit of something *Syn* devotee, habitué, votary **2** *Syn* FAN, aficionado, buff, bug, devotee, enthusiast, fanatic, fancier, fiend, freak, lover, maniac, nut

addict *vb* *Syn* HABITUATE, accustom, inure

addition • a thing that serves to increase another in size, amount, or content *Syn* accession, accretion, increment

additional • resulting in an increase in amount or number *Syn* added, another, else, farther, further, more, other *Rel* accessory, collateral, extraneous, side, supplemental, supplementary

additive *Syn* CUMULATIVE, accumulative, summative

addle *Syn* CONFUSE, befuddle, fuddle, muddle *Ant* enlighten

address *vb* **1** • to speak to or less often to write or make a sign to a person in recognition or in order to obtain recognition *Syn* accost, greet, hail, salute *Rel* converse, speak, talk **2** *Syn* DIRECT (sense 1), apply, devote *Ant* misdirect

address *n* **1** *Syn* SPEECH, harangue, homily, lecture, oration, sermon, talk **2** *Syn* TACT, poise, savoir faire *Ant* awkwardness

add (to) *Syn* INCREASE (sense 1), aggrandize, amplify, augment, boost, compound, enlarge, escalate, expand, extend, multiply, raise, swell, up *Ant* abate, contract, decrease, diminish, lessen, lower, reduce, subtract (from)

adduce • to bring forward by way of explanation, proof, illustration, or demonstration *Syn* advance, allege, cite *Rel* exemplify, illustrate

adept *n* *Syn* EXPERT, ace, artist, authority, crackerjack, maestro, master, past master, scholar, shark, virtuoso, whiz, wizard *Ant* amateur

adept *adj* *Syn* PROFICIENT, expert, masterly, skilled, skillful *Ant* amateur, amateurish, inexperienced, inexpert, unexperienced, unpracticed, unprofessional, unseasoned, unskilled, unskillful

adequacy *Syn* SUFFICIENCY, acceptability, satisfactoriness *Ant* inadequacy, insufficiency

adequate **1** • of a level of quality that meets one's needs or standards *Syn* acceptable, all right, decent, fine, OK (*or* okay), passable, respectable, satisfactory, tolerable *Rel* agreeable, bearable, endurable, sufferable *Ant* deficient, inadequate, lacking, unacceptable, unsatisfactory, wanting **2** *Syn* SUFFICIENT, competent, enough

adhere *Syn* STICK, cleave, cling, cohere

adherence *Syn* ADHESION, bonding

adherent *Syn* FOLLOWER, convert, disciple, partisan, pupil, votary *Ant* leader

adhesion • a physical sticking to as if by glue *Syn* adherence, bonding *Rel* agglutination, clumping, cohesion

adieu *Syn* GOOD-BYE, au revoir, bon voyage, farewell, Godspeed *Ant* hello

ad interim *Syn* TEMPORARY, acting, provisional *Ant* permanent

adjacent • having a border in common *Syn* abutting, adjoining, bordering, contiguous, flanking, fringing, joining, juxtaposed, skirting, touching, verging *Rel* close, closest, immediate, near, nearby, nearest, neighboring, next, next-door, nigh *Ant* nonadjacent

adjoin *Syn* ADD (SENSE 2), annex, append, tack (on) *Ant* deduct, remove, subtract, take

adjoining *Syn* ADJACENT, abutting, bordering, contiguous, flanking, fringing, joining, juxtaposed, skirting, touching, verging *Ant* nonadjacent

adjourn • to bring to a formal close for a period of time *Syn* recess, suspend *Rel* break off, discontinue, intermit, interrupt

adjudge *Syn* JUDGE, adjudicate, arbitrate

adjudicate *Syn* JUDGE, adjudge, arbitrate

adjunct *Syn* APPENDAGE, accessory, appurtenance

adjure *Syn* BEG, beseech, entreat, implore, importune, supplicate

adjust **1** • to set right or to rights *Syn* fix, regulate *Rel* correct, rectify *Ant* derange **2** *Syn* ADAPT, accommodate, conform, reconcile *Ant* unfit

adjutant *Syn* ASSISTANT, aid, aide, apprentice, coadjutor, deputy, helper, sidekick

adjuvant *Syn* AUXILIARY, accessory, ancillary, contributory, subservient, subsidiary

administer *Syn* ENFORCE, apply, execute, implement

administration *Syn* RULE (sense 2), authority, governance, government, jurisdiction, regime, regimen

administrator *Syn* EXECUTIVE, director, manager, superintendent, supervisor

admirable • deserving of high regard or great approval *Syn* commendable, creditable, laudable, meritorious, praiseworthy *Rel* awesome, distinctive, distinguished, excellent, honorable, noteworthy, noticeable, outstanding, reputable, worthy *Ant* censurable, discreditable, reprehensible

admiration **1** *Syn* REGARD, esteem, respect *Ant* despite **2** *Syn* WONDER (sense 2), amazement, awe, wonderment

admire *Syn* REGARD, esteem, respect *Ant* despise

admissible *Syn* PERMISSIBLE, allowable, licensable *Ant* banned, barred, forbidden, impermissible, inadmissible, interdicted, prohibited, proscribed

admission *Syn* CONFESSION, acknowledgment, avowal, concession

admit **1** • to accept the truth or existence of (something) usually reluctantly *Syn* acknowledge, agree, allow, concede, confess, grant, own (up) *Rel* disburden, unburden, unload *Ant* deny **2** *Syn* ENTER (sense 2), introduce **3** *Syn* RECEIVE, accept, take

admixture **1** • an added ingredient that destroys the purity or genuineness of a substance *Syn* adulterant, alloy *Rel* accretion, addition **2** *Syn* BLEND, amalgam, amalgamation, combination, composite, compound, fusion, intermixture, mix, mixture

admonish *Syn* REPROVE, chide, rebuke, reprimand, reproach

admonishing *Syn* CAUTIONARY, admonitory, cautioning, warning

admonition *Syn* WARNING, alarm, alert, caution, forewarning, notice

admonitory *Syn* CAUTIONARY, admonishing, cautioning, warning

ado *Syn* STIR, bustle, flurry, fuss, pother *Ant* tranquillity

adolescence *Syn* YOUTH, puberty, pubescence *Ant* age

adolescent **1** *Syn* CALLOW, green, immature, inexperienced, juvenile, puerile, raw, unfledged, unripe, unripened *Ant* adult, experienced, grown-up, mature, ripe **2** *Syn* CHILDISH, babyish, immature, infantile, juvenile, kiddish, puerile *Ant* adult, grown-up, mature **3** *Syn* YOUNG, immature, juvenile, youngish, youthful *Ant* adult, full-grown, mature, matured

adopt • to make one's own what in some fashion one owes to another *Syn* embrace, espouse *Rel* appropriate, arrogate, usurp *Ant* discard, repudiate

adorable *Syn* LOVABLE, darling, dear, disarming, endearing, precious, sweet, winning *Ant* abhorrent, abominable, detestable, hateful, odious, unlovable

adoration *Syn* REVERENCE (sense 1), veneration, worship

adore **1** *Syn* IDOLIZE, adulate, canonize, deify, dote (on), worship **2** *Syn* REVERE, reverence, venerate, worship *Ant* flout

adorn • to add something unessential in order to enhance the appearance *Syn* beautify, bedeck, deck, decorate, embellish, garnish, ornament *Rel* enhance, heighten, intensify *Ant* disfigure
adroit *Syn* CLEVER, cunning, ingenious
adroitness *Syn* DEXTERITY (sense 1), cleverness, finesse, sleight *Ant* awkwardness, clumsiness, gawkiness
adulate *Syn* IDOLIZE, adore, canonize, deify, dote (on), worship
adulation 1 *Syn* COMPLIMENT, flattery *Ant* taunt 2 *Syn* WORSHIP, deification, idolatry, idolization, worshipping
adult *Syn* MATURE, grown-up, matured, mellow, ripe *Ant* childish, immature
adulterant *Syn* ADMIXTURE, alloy
adulterate • to alter fraudulently especially for profit *Syn* doctor, load, sophisticate, weight *Rel* corrupt, debase, vitiate *Ant* refine
adulterated *Syn* IMPURE, alloyed, contaminated, dilute, diluted, polluted, tainted, thinned, weakened *Ant* pure, unadulterated, unalloyed, uncontaminated, undiluted, unpolluted, untainted
adumbrate *Syn* SUGGEST (sense 2), shadow *Ant* manifest
adumbration *Syn* SHADE, penumbra, shadow, umbra, umbrage
advance *n* 1 • an instance of notable progress in the development of knowledge, technology, or skill *Syn* advancement, breakthrough, enhancement, improvement, refinement *Rel* amelioration, boost, heightening, increase, melioration, strengthening, upgrade, uplift, upswing, uptrend, upturn *Ant* setback 2 • forward movement in time or place *Syn* advancement, furtherance, going, headway, march, onrush, passage, process, procession, progress, progression *Rel* current, drift, flow, flux, stream, way *Ant* recession, regression, retrogression 3 *Syn* OVERTURE, approach, bid, tender
advance *vb* 1 • to move or put ahead *Syn* forward, further, promote *Rel* aid, assist, help *Ant* check, retard 2 *Syn* ADDUCE, allege, cite
advanced 1 *Syn* LIBERAL (sense 2), progressive, radical *Ant* authoritarian 2 *Syn* PREMATURE, forward, precocious, untimely *Ant* matured
advancement 1 • the act of raising a person in grade, rank, or dignity, or the honor that comes to one who is so raised *Syn* elevation, preferment, promotion *Ant* degradation, reduction (*in rank or status*) 2 *Syn* ADVANCE (sense 1), breakthrough, enhancement, improvement, refinement *Ant* setback 3 *Syn* ADVANCE (sense 2), furtherance, going, headway, march, onrush, passage, process, procession, progress, progression *Ant* recession, regression, retrogression
advantage 1 • a factor or set of factors in a competition or rivalry giving one person or side a position of superiority over the other *Syn* allowance, edge, handicap, odds *Rel* preeminence, superlativeness *Ant* disadvantage, handicap 2 *Syn* USE (sense 1), account, avail, profit, service
advantageous *Syn* BENEFICIAL, favorable, helpful, profitable, salutary *Ant* disadvantageous, unfavorable, unhelpful
adventure *n* • an undertaking, an exploit, or an experience involving hazards and requiring boldness *Syn* enterprise, quest *Rel* achievement, exploit, feat
adventure *vb* *Syn* ENDANGER, compromise, gamble (with), hazard, imperil, jeopardize, menace, risk, venture
adventurous • courting danger or exposing oneself to danger in a greater degree than is required for courage *Syn* daredevil, daring, foolhardy, rash, reckless, venturesome *Rel* audacious, bold, brave, doughty, intrepid *Ant* cautious, unadventurous
adversary *Syn* ENEMY, antagonist, foe, opponent *Ant* friend
adverse 1 • so opposed as to cause interference and often harmful or fatal interference *Syn* antagonistic, counter, counteractive *Rel* harmful, hurtful, injurious *Ant* propitious 2 *Syn* HARMFUL, bad, baleful, baneful, damaging, deleterious, detrimental, evil, hurtful, ill, injurious, mischievous, noxious, pernicious, prejudicial *Ant* harmless, innocent, innocuous, inoffensive, safe
adversity *Syn* MISFORTUNE, knock, misadventure, mischance, mishap *Ant* fortune, luck
advert *Syn* REFER, allude
advertise *Syn* ANNOUNCE, blaze, broadcast, declare, enunciate, placard, post, proclaim, promulgate, publicize, publish, sound
advertisement 1 *Syn* ANNOUNCEMENT, ad, bulletin, notice, notification, posting, release 2 *Syn* DECLARATION, announcement, broadcasting, proclamation, promulgation, publication
advice • an opinion suggesting a wise or proper course of action *Syn* counsel, guidance *Rel* recommendation, suggestion
advisable *Syn* EXPEDIENT, desirable, judicious, politic, prudent, tactical, wise *Ant* imprudent, inadvisable, inexpedient, injudicious, unwise
advise 1 *Syn* ENLIGHTEN (sense 1), acquaint, apprise, brief, clue, familiarize, fill in, inform, instruct, tell, wise (up) 2 *Syn* INFORM (sense 2), apprise, notify
advised *Syn* DELIBERATE, considered, designed, premeditated, studied *Ant* casual
advocate *n* 1 *Syn* EXPONENT, apostle, backer, booster, champion, friend, promoter, proponent, supporter *Ant* adversary, antagonist, opponent 2 *Syn* LAWYER, attorney, barrister, counsel, counselor, solicitor

advocate *vb Syn* SUPPORT (sense 2), back, champion, uphold
aerial *Syn* AIRY, ethereal *Ant* substantial
aesthete • a person conspicuous for his enjoyment and appreciation of the beautiful, the exquisite, or the choice *Syn* connoisseur, dilettante
affable **1** *Syn* AMIABLE, agreeable, genial, good-natured, good-tempered, gracious, nice, sweet, well-disposed *Ant* disagreeable, ill-natured, ill-tempered, ungracious, unpleasant **2** *Syn* GRACIOUS, cordial, genial, sociable *Ant* ungracious
affair **1** • something done or dealt with *Syn* business, concern, matter, thing **2** *Syn* AMOUR, intrigue, liaison
affect[1] *vb* • to produce or to have an effect upon a person or upon a thing capable of a reaction *Syn* impress, influence, strike, sway, touch *Rel* actuate, drive, impel, move
affect[2] *vb Syn* ASSUME, counterfeit, feign, pretend, sham, simulate
affectation *Syn* POSE, air, mannerism
affecting *Syn* MOVING, emotional, impressive, poignant, stirring, touching *Ant* unemotional, unimpressive
affection **1** *Syn* ATTACHMENT, love *Ant* aversion **2** *Syn* FEELING, emotion, passion, sentiment
affectionate *Syn* LOVING, devoted, doting, fond *Ant* unloving
affiliated *Syn* RELATED, allied, cognate, kindred
affinity *Syn* ATTRACTION, sympathy
affirm *Syn* ASSERT, aver, avouch, avow, declare, predicate, profess, protest, warrant *Ant* controvert, deny
affix *Syn* FASTEN, attach, fix *Ant* loose, loosen, unfasten
afflatus *Syn* INSPIRATION, frenzy, fury
afflict • to cause persistent suffering to *Syn* agonize, bedevil, curse, harrow, martyr, persecute, plague, rack, torment, torture *Rel* assail, attack, beset, set upon
affliction *Syn* TRIAL, cross, tribulation, visitation
affluent *Syn* RICH, opulent, wealthy *Ant* poor
afford *Syn* GIVE, bestow, confer, donate, present
affray *n Syn* CONTEST, combat, conflict, fight, fray
affray *vb Syn* FRIGHTEN, affright, alarm, fright, scare, startle, terrify, terrorize *Ant* reassure
affright *Syn* FRIGHTEN, affray, alarm, fright, scare, startle, terrify, terrorize *Ant* reassure
affront *n Syn* INSULT, barb, dart, dig, epithet, indignity, name, offense (*or* offence), outrage, put-down, sarcasm, slight, slur
affront *vb Syn* OFFEND, insult, outrage
aficionado *Syn* FAN, addict, buff, bug, devotee, enthusiast, fanatic, fancier, fiend, freak, lover, maniac, nut
afield *Syn* WRONG, amiss, astray, awry *Ant* aright, right, well
afraid *Syn* FEARFUL (sense 1), apprehensive *Ant* fearless, intrepid
aft *Syn* ABAFT, astern *Ant* afore
after *adv* • following in time or place *Syn* afterward (*or* afterwards), later, subsequently, thereafter *Rel* next *Ant* before, beforehand, earlier, previously
after *prep* • subsequent to in time or order *Syn* behind, following *Rel* next *Ant* ahead of, before, ere, previous to, prior to
aftereffect *Syn* EFFECT, aftermath, consequence, event, issue, outcome, result, sequel, upshot *Ant* cause
aftermath *Syn* EFFECT, aftereffect, consequence, event, issue, outcome, result, sequel, upshot *Ant* cause
afterward *or* **afterwards** *Syn* AFTER, later, subsequently, thereafter *Ant* before, beforehand, earlier, previously
against • in or into contact with *Syn* on, upon *Rel* alongside, next, next to
age *n* **1** • the period in one's life when one is old in years and declining in body or mind or both *Syn* dotage, senescence, senility *Ant* youth **2** • a long or seemingly long period of time *Syn* aeon (*or* eon), cycle, eternity *Rel* infinity **3** • an extent of time associated with a particular person or thing *Syn* day, epoch, era, period, time *Rel* cycle, generation, year
age *vb Syn* MATURE, develop, ripen
aged *Syn* ELDERLY, aging, ancient, geriatric, long-lived, old, older, senior *Ant* young, youthful
agency *Syn* AGENT (sense 2), instrument, instrumentality, machinery, means, medium, organ, vehicle
agenda *Syn* PROGRAM, schedule, timetable
agent **1** • a person who acts or does business for another *Syn* attorney, commissary, delegate, deputy, envoy, factor, procurator, proxy, representative *Rel* ambassador, emissary, foreign minister, legate, minister **2** • something used to achieve an end *Syn* agency, instrument, instrumentality, machinery, means, medium, organ, vehicle *Rel* determinant, expedient, factor, influence, ingredient, mechanism, tool
agglomerate *Syn* AGGREGATE, agglomeration, aggregation, conglomerate, conglomeration *Ant* constituent
agglomeration *Syn* AGGREGATE, agglomerate, aggregation, conglomerate, conglomeration *Ant* constituent
aggrandize **1** *Syn* EXALT, dignify, ennoble, enshrine, glorify, magnify *Ant* abase, degrade, demean, humble, humiliate **2** *Syn* INCREASE (sense 1), add (to), amplify, augment, boost, compound, enlarge, escalate, expand, extend, multiply, raise, swell, up *Ant* abate,

contract, decrease, diminish, lessen, lower, reduce, subtract (from)

aggravate 1 *Syn* INTENSIFY, enhance, heighten *Ant* abate, allay, mitigate, temper 2 *Syn* IRRITATE, exasperate, nettle, peeve, provoke, rile

aggravating *Syn* ANNOYING, bothersome, disturbing, exasperating, frustrating, galling, irksome, irritating, maddening, nettling, peeving, pesty, rankling, riling, vexatious, vexing

aggregate 1 • a mass formed by parts or particles that are not merged into each other *Syn* agglomerate, agglomeration, aggregation, conglomerate, conglomeration *Rel* integrity, union, unity *Ant* constituent 2 *Syn* SUM, amount, number, quantity, total, whole

aggregation *Syn* AGGREGATE, agglomerate, agglomeration, conglomerate, conglomeration *Ant* constituent

aggression 1 *Syn* ATTACK (sense 2), assault, blitzkrieg, charge, descent, offense (*or* offence), offensive, onset, onslaught, raid, rush, strike 2 *Syn* BELLIGERENCE, aggressiveness, bellicosity, combativeness, contentiousness, disputatiousness, fight, militancy, pugnacity, scrappiness, truculence *Ant* pacifism

aggressive 1 • initiating hostile action in a struggle for supremacy *Syn* ATTACKING, offensive *Rel* encroaching, invading, trespassing *Ant* repelling, resisting 2 • conspicuously or obtrusively active or energetic *Syn* assertive, militant, pushing, pushy, self-assertive *Rel* energetic, strenuous, vigorous 3 *Syn* BELLIGERENT, argumentative, bellicose, combative, contentious, discordant, disputatious, gladiatorial, militant, pugnacious, quarrelsome, scrappy, truculent, warlike *Ant* nonbelligerent, pacific, peaceable, peaceful

aggressiveness *Syn* BELLIGERENCE, aggression, bellicosity, combativeness, contentiousness, disputatiousness, fight, militancy, pugnacity, scrappiness, truculence *Ant* pacifism

aggressor • one that starts armed conflict against another especially without reasonable cause *Syn* invader, raider *Rel* initiator, instigator

aggrieve *Syn* WRONG, oppress, persecute

agile • acting or moving with quickness and alacrity *Syn* brisk, nimble, spry *Rel* adroit, deft, dexterous *Ant* torpid

agility *Syn* DEXTERITY (sense 2), deftness, nimbleness, sleight, spryness *Ant* awkwardness, clumsiness, gawkiness

aging *Syn* ELDERLY, aged, ancient, geriatric, long-lived, old, older, senior *Ant* young, youthful

agitate 1 *Syn* DISCOMPOSE, disquiet, disturb, flurry, fluster, perturb, upset 2 *Syn* DISCUSS, argue, debate, dispute 3 *Syn* SHAKE (sense 2), convulse, rock

agitation *Syn* FRENZY, delirium, distraction, furor, furore, fury, hysteria, rage, rampage, uproar

agitator • a person who stirs up public feelings especially of discontent *Syn* demagogue, exciter, firebrand, fomenter, incendiary, inciter, instigator, rabble-rouser *Rel* advocate, alarmist, champion, demonstrator, exponent, extremist, insurgent, insurrectionist, marcher, objector, persuader, picketer, promoter, proponent, protester (*or* protestor), radical, rebel, reformer, revolter, revolutionary, revolutionist, subversive, supporter, troublemaker

agog *Syn* EAGER, anxious, athirst, avid, keen *Ant* listless

agonize 1 *Syn* AFFLICT, bedevil, curse, harrow, martyr, persecute, plague, rack, torment, torture 2 *Syn* WRITHE, squirm

agonizing *Syn* EXCRUCIATING, racking

agony *Syn* DISTRESS, dolor, misery, passion, suffering

agrarian *Syn* AGRICULTURAL, farming *Ant* nonagricultural

agree 1 • to come into or to be in harmony regarding a matter of opinion or a policy *Syn* coincide, concur *Rel* cooperate, unite *Ant* differ, disagree 2 • to exist or go together without conflict or incongruity *Syn* accord, conform, correspond, harmonize, jibe, square, tally *Ant* differ (from) 3 *Syn* ADMIT, acknowledge, allow, concede, confess, grant, own (up) *Ant* deny 4 *Syn* ASSENT, accede, acquiesce, consent, subscribe *Ant* dissent

agreeable 1 *Syn* AMIABLE, affable, genial, good-natured, good-tempered, gracious, nice, sweet, well-disposed *Ant* disagreeable, ill-natured, ill-tempered, ungracious, unpleasant 2 *Syn* PLEASANT, grateful, gratifying, pleasing, welcome *Ant* distasteful, harsh, unpleasant

agreement • a reconciliation of differences as to what should be done or not done *Syn* accord, understanding *Rel* cartel, concordat, contract, convention, entente, pact

agricultural • engaged in or concerned with agriculture *Syn* agrarian, farming *Rel* pastoral, rural *Ant* nonagricultural

agriculture • the science or the business of raising useful plants and animals *Syn* farming, husbandry

aground • resting on the shore or bottom of a body of water *Syn* beached, grounded, stranded *Rel* landed *Ant* afloat

ahead *Syn* ALONG, forth, forward, on, onward

ahead of *Syn* BEFORE, ere, of, previous to, prior to, to *Ant* after, following

aid *n* 1 *Syn* HELP, assistance 2 *Syn* ASSISTANT, adjutant, aide, apprentice, coadjutor, deputy, helper, sidekick

aid *vb* *Syn* HELP, assist *Ant* hinder

aide *Syn* ASSISTANT, adjutant, aid, apprentice, coadjutor, deputy, helper, sidekick

ail *Syn* TROUBLE, distress

ailment *Syn* DISEASE, complaint, condition, disorder, distemper, malady, syndrome
aim *vb* • to have as a controlling desire something beyond one's present power of attainment *Syn* aspire, pant *Rel* design, intend, propose, purpose
aim *n Syn* GOAL, ambition, aspiration, design, dream, end, intent, intention, mark, meaning, object, objective, plan, pretension, purpose, target, thing
aimlessly *Syn* HIT OR MISS, anyhow, anyway, anywise, desultorily, erratically, haphazard, haphazardly, helter-skelter, irregularly, randomly *Ant* methodically, systematically
air *n* **1** *Syn* AURA, atmosphere, climate, flavor, mood, note, temper **2** *Syn* MELODY, lay, song, strain, tune, warble **3** *Syn* POSE, affectation, mannerism
air *vb Syn* EXPRESS, broach, utter, vent, ventilate, voice *Ant* imply
airdrome *Syn* AIRPORT, airfield, airstrip, flying field, landing field, landing strip
airfield *Syn* AIRPORT, airdrome, airstrip, flying field, landing field, landing strip
airport • a place where airplanes take off and land *Syn* airdrome, airfield, airstrip, flying field, landing field, landing strip *Rel* air base, heliport
airstrip *Syn* AIRPORT, airdrome, airfield, flying field, landing field, landing strip
airy • as light and insubstantial as air *Syn* aerial, ethereal *Rel* rare, tenuous, thin *Ant* substantial
aisle *Syn* PASSAGE, arcade, cloister, corridor, gallery, hall, hallway, passageway
akin *Syn* ALIKE, analogous, comparable, correspondent, corresponding, like, matching, parallel, resembling, similar, such, suchlike *Ant* different, dissimilar, diverse, unlike
alacrity • cheerful readiness to do something *Syn* amenability, gameness, goodwill, willingness *Rel* celerity, quickness, rapidity, speed, speediness, swiftness
alarm *n* **1** *Syn* FEAR, consternation, dismay, dread, fright, horror, panic, terror, trepidation *Ant* fearlessness **2** *Syn* WARNING, admonition, alert, caution, forewarning, notice
alarm *vb Syn* FRIGHTEN, affray, affright, fright, scare, startle, terrify, terrorize *Ant* reassure
albeit *Syn* ALTHOUGH, howbeit, though, when, while
album *Syn* ANTHOLOGY, compilation, miscellany
alchemy *Syn* MAGIC, sorcery, thaumaturgy, witchcraft, witchery, wizardry
alcohol • a fermented or distilled beverage that can make a person drunk *Syn* booze, drink, grog, intoxicant, liquor, moonshine, spirits *Rel* ale, beer, brandy, gin, mead, mescal, rum, sake (*or* saki), table wine, tequila, vodka, whiskey (*or* whisky), wine
alcoholic *Syn* DRUNKARD, dipsomaniac, inebriate, soak, sot, tippler, toper, tosspot *Ant* teetotaler
alert *adj* **1** *Syn* INTELLIGENT, bright, brilliant, clever, knowing, quick-witted, smart *Ant* unintelligent **2** *Syn* WATCHFUL, vigilant, wide-awake
alert *n Syn* WARNING, admonition, alarm, caution, forewarning, notice
alert *vb Syn* WARN, caution, forewarn
alertness *Syn* VIGILANCE, attentiveness, lookout, surveillance, watch, watchfulness
alias *Syn* PSEUDONYM, incognito, nom de guerre, nom de plume, pen name
alibi **1** *Syn* APOLOGY, apologia, excuse, plea, pretext **2** *Syn* EXCUSE, defense, justification, plea, reason
alien *adj Syn* EXTRINSIC, extraneous, foreign *Ant* intrinsic
alien *n Syn* STRANGER, émigré, foreigner, immigrant, outlander, outsider
alienate **1** *Syn* ESTRANGE, disaffect, wean *Ant* reconcile **2** *Syn* TRANSFER, convey, deed
alienation **1** *Syn* ABERRATION, derangement *Ant* soundness (*of mind*) **2** *Syn* ESTRANGEMENT, disaffection, disgruntlement, souring *Ant* reconciliation
alight **1** • to come to rest after descending from the air *Syn* land, light, perch, roost, settle, touch down *Rel* belly-land, crash-land *Ant* take off **2** *Syn* DESCEND, dismount *Ant* ascend, climb
align *Syn* LINE, array, line up, range
alike • having qualities in common *Syn* akin, analogous, comparable, correspondent, corresponding, like, matching, parallel, resembling, similar, such, suchlike *Rel* commensurate, proportionate *Ant* different, dissimilar, diverse, unlike
alikeness *Syn* SIMILARITY, community, correspondence, likeness, parallelism, resemblance, similitude *Ant* dissimilarity, unlikeness
aliment *Syn* FOOD (sense 2), nourishment, nutriment, pabulum, pap, sustenance
alive **1** *Syn* AWARE, awake, cognizant, conscious, sensible *Ant* unaware **2** *Syn* CONSCIOUS, aware, cognizant, mindful, sensible, sentient *Ant* insensible, unaware, unconscious, unmindful **3** *Syn* LIVING, animate, animated, vital *Ant* lifeless
all *adj* **1** *Syn* WHOLE, entire, gross, total *Ant* partial **2** • including the entire membership of a group with no exceptions *Syn* each, every *Ant* no
all *adv Syn* APIECE, each, per capita
all-around **1** *Syn* VERSATILE, many-sided **2** *Syn* GENERAL (sense 2), bird's-eye, broad, nonspecific, overall *Ant* delineated, detailed, particularized, specific
allay *Syn* RELIEVE, alleviate, assuage, lighten, mitigate *Ant* alarm, embarrass, intensify

allege *Syn* ADDUCE, advance, cite
allegiance *Syn* FIDELITY, devotion, fealty, loyalty, piety *Ant* faithlessness, perfidy
allegory • a story intended to teach a basic truth or moral about life *Syn* fable, parable *Rel* morality play
allergic *Syn* ANTIPATHETIC, averse
alleviate *Syn* RELIEVE, allay, assuage, lighten, mitigate *Ant* alarm, embarrass, intensify
alliance • a chiefly political combination for a common object *Syn* coalition, confederacy, confederation, federation, fusion, league
allied *Syn* RELATED, affiliated, cognate, kindred
allocate *Syn* ALLOT, apportion, assign
allocation *Syn* APPROPRIATION, allotment, annuity, grant, subsidy
allot • to give as one's share, portion, role, or place *Syn* allocate, apportion, assign *Rel* deal, dispense, distribute, divide, dole
allotment *Syn* APPROPRIATION, allocation, annuity, grant, subsidy
all-out *Syn* EXHAUSTIVE, clean, complete, comprehensive, full-scale, out-and-out, thorough, thoroughgoing, total
allow **1** *Syn* ADMIT, acknowledge, agree, concede, confess, grant, own (up) *Ant* deny **2** *Syn* LET, leave, permit, suffer
allowable *Syn* PERMISSIBLE, admissible, licensable *Ant* banned, barred, forbidden, impermissible, inadmissible, interdicted, prohibited, proscribed
allowance **1** *Syn* ADVANTAGE, edge, handicap, odds *Ant* disadvantage, handicap **2** *Syn* PERMISSION, authorization, clearance, concurrence, consent, granting, leave, license (*or* licence), sanction, sufferance *Ant* interdiction, prohibition, proscription **3** *Syn* RATION, dole, pittance
alloy *Syn* ADMIXTURE, adulterant
alloyed *Syn* IMPURE, adulterated, contaminated, dilute, diluted, polluted, tainted, thinned, weakened *Ant* pure, unadulterated, unalloyed, uncontaminated, undiluted, unpolluted, untainted
all right *Syn* ADEQUATE, acceptable, decent, fine, OK (*or* okay), passable, respectable, satisfactory, tolerable *Ant* deficient, inadequate, lacking, unacceptable, unsatisfactory, wanting
allude **1** *Syn* HINT, imply, indicate, infer, insinuate, intimate, suggest **2** *Syn* REFER, advert
allure **1** *Syn* ATTRACT, bewitch, captivate, charm, enchant, fascinate *Ant* repel **2** *Syn* LURE, beguile, decoy, entice, lead on, seduce, tempt
alluring *Syn* ATTRACTIVE, bewitching, captivating, charming, enchanting, fascinating *Ant* forbidding, repellent
ally *n* **1** • someone associated with another to give assistance or moral support *Syn* abettor, backer, confederate, supporter, sympathizer *Rel* well-wisher **2** *Syn* PARTNER, colleague, confederate, copartner *Ant* rival
ally *vb* • to form or enter into an association that furthers the interests of its members *Syn* associate, band, club, confederate, conjoin, cooperate, federate, league, unite *Rel* collaborate, gang (up), team (up) *Ant* break up, disband
almost • very close to but not completely *Syn* about, more or less, most, much, near, nearly, next to, nigh, practically, some, virtually, well-nigh *Rel* appreciably, by and large, chiefly, largely, mainly, mostly
alms *Syn* CONTRIBUTION, benefaction, beneficence, charity, donation, philanthropy
aloft *Syn* ABOVE, over, overhead, skyward *Ant* below, beneath, under
alone **1** • isolated from others *Syn* desolate, forlorn, lone, lonely, lonesome, lorn, solitary *Rel* lone, single, sole, unique *Ant* accompanied **2** *Syn* ONLY, lone, singular, sole, solitary, special, unique
along • toward or at a point lying in advance in space or time *Syn* ahead, forth, forward, on, onward *Rel* before
aloof *Syn* INDIFFERENT, detached, disinterested, incurious, unconcerned, uninterested *Ant* avid
aloud • with one's normal voice speaking the words *Syn* audibly, out, out loud *Rel* clearly, discernibly, distinctly, distinguishably, perceptibly, plainly *Ant* inaudibly, silently, soundlessly
alp *Syn* MOUNTAIN, mesa, mount, peak, volcano
alpha *Syn* BEGINNING, birth, commencement, dawn, genesis, inception, incipiency, launch, morning, onset, outset, start, threshold *Ant* close, conclusion, end, ending
alter **1** *Syn* CHANGE (sense 1), make over, modify, recast, redo, refashion, remake, remodel, revamp, revise, rework, vary *Ant* fix, freeze, set, stabilize **2** *Syn* STERILIZE (sense 1), castrate, emasculate, geld, mutilate, spay *Ant* fertilize
alteration *Syn* CHANGE (sense 1), modification, variation *Ant* monotony, uniformity
altercation *Syn* QUARREL, bickering, spat, squabble, tiff, wrangle
alternate *Syn* INTERMITTENT, periodic, recurrent *Ant* continual, incessant
alternation *Syn* CHANGE (sense 2), mutation, permutation, vicissitude
alternative *Syn* CHOICE, election, option, preference, selection
although • in spite of the fact that *Syn* albeit, howbeit, though, when, while *Rel* but, whereas
altitude *Syn* HEIGHT, elevation
altogether *Syn* CHIEFLY, basically, by and large, generally, largely, mainly, mostly, over-

all, predominantly, primarily, principally, substantially
altruistic *Syn* CHARITABLE, benevolent, eleemosynary, humane, humanitarian, philanthropic *Ant* uncharitable
amalgam *Syn* BLEND, admixture, amalgamation, combination, composite, compound, fusion, intermixture, mix, mixture
amalgamate *Syn* MIX, blend, coalesce, commingle, fuse, merge, mingle
amalgamation **1** *Syn* BLEND, admixture, amalgam, combination, composite, compound, fusion, intermixture, mix, mixture **2** *Syn* CONSOLIDATION, merger *Ant* dissolution
amass *Syn* ACCUMULATE, hoard *Ant* dissipate
amateur *n* • a person who follows a pursuit without attaining proficiency or a professional status *Syn* dabbler, dilettante, tyro *Rel* apprentice, novice, probationer *Ant* expert, professional
amateur *adj* *Syn* AMATEURISH, dilettante, inexperienced, inexpert, nonprofessional, unprofessional, unskilled, unskillful *Ant* ace, adept, consummate, crackerjack, expert, master, masterful, masterly, professional, virtuoso
amateurish • lacking or showing a lack of expert skill *Syn* amateur, dilettante, inexperienced, inexpert, nonprofessional, unprofessional, unskilled, unskillful *Rel* primitive, self-taught, uninitiated, unprepared, unqualified, unschooled, untaught, untrained, untutored *Ant* ace, adept, consummate, crackerjack, expert, master, masterful, masterly, professional, virtuoso
amative *Syn* EROTIC, amatory, amorous, aphrodisiac
amatory *Syn* EROTIC, amative, amorous, aphrodisiac
amaze *Syn* SURPRISE (sense 2), astonish, astound, flabbergast
amazement *Syn* WONDER (sense 2), admiration, awe, wonderment
ambassador • a person sent on a mission to represent another *Syn* delegate, emissary, envoy, legate, minister, representative *Rel* agent, attaché, consul, deputy, diplomat, foreign minister, nuncio, procurator, proxy
ambiguous *Syn* OBSCURE, cryptic, dark, enigmatic, equivocal, vague *Ant* distinct, obvious
ambition *Syn* GOAL, aim, aspiration, design, dream, end, intent, intention, mark, meaning, object, objective, plan, pretension, purpose, target, thing
ambitious • straining or exceeding the capacity of their authors or executants *Syn* pretentious, utopian *Rel* audacious, bold, brave *Ant* modest
amble *Syn* SAUNTER, stroll
ambrosial *Syn* FRAGRANT, aromatic, perfumed, redolent, savory, scented, sweet *Ant* fetid, foul, malodorous, noisome, putrid, rancid, rank, reeking, reeky, smelly, stinking, stinky, strong
ambulant *Syn* ITINERANT, ambulatory, nomadic, peripatetic, vagrant
ambulatory *Syn* ITINERANT, ambulant, nomadic, peripatetic, vagrant
ambush *vb* *Syn* SURPRISE (sense 1), waylay
ameliorate *Syn* IMPROVE (sense 1), better, help *Ant* impair, worsen
amenability *Syn* ALACRITY, gameness, goodwill, willingness
amenable **1** *Syn* OBEDIENT, compliant, conformable, docile, law-abiding, submissive, tractable *Ant* contrary, disobedient, froward, insubordinate, intractable, rebellious, recalcitrant, refractory, unruly **2** *Syn* RESPONSIBLE, accountable, answerable, liable
amend *Syn* CORRECT, emend, rectify, redress, reform, remedy, revise
amends *Syn* REPARATION, indemnity, redress, restitution
amenity *Syn* COURTESY, attention, gallantry *Ant* discourtesy
amerce *Syn* PENALIZE, fine, mulct
American Indian • a member of any of the native peoples of the western hemisphere usually not including the Eskimos *Syn* Amerindian, Indian, Native American *Rel* mestizo
Amerindian *Syn* AMERICAN INDIAN, Indian, Native American
amiable • having an easygoing and pleasing manner especially in social situations *Syn* affable, agreeable, genial, good-natured, good-tempered, gracious, nice, sweet, well-disposed *Rel* amicable, cordial, friendly, neighborly *Ant* disagreeable, ill-natured, ill-tempered, ungracious, unpleasant
amicable • marked by or exhibiting goodwill or absence of antagonism *Syn* friendly, neighborly *Rel* pacific, peaceable, peaceful *Ant* antagonistic
amid *or* **amidst** *Syn* AMONG, mid, midst, through
amiss *Syn* WRONG, afield, astray, awry *Ant* aright, right, well
amity *Syn* FRIENDSHIP, comity, goodwill *Ant* animosity
amnesty *Syn* PARDON, absolution, forgiveness, remission, remittal *Ant* penalty, punishment, retribution
among • in or into the middle of *Syn* amid (*or* amidst), mid, midst, through *Rel* between, betwixt
amorous *Syn* EROTIC, amative, amatory, aphrodisiac
amorphous *Syn* FORMLESS, shapeless, unformed, unshaped, unstructured *Ant* formed, shaped, structured
amount **1** • a given or particular mass or aggregate of matter *Syn* measure, quantity, volume *Rel* body, portion **2** *Syn* SUM, aggregate, number, quantity, total, whole

amour • an instance of illicit sexual relationship *Syn* affair, intrigue, liaison
amour propre *Syn* CONCEIT, egoism, egotism, self-esteem, self-love *Ant* humility
ample **1** *Syn* PLENTIFUL, abundant, copious, plenteous *Ant* scant, scanty **2** *Syn* SPACIOUS, capacious, commodious
amplify **1** *Syn* EXPAND, dilate, distend, inflate, swell *Ant* abridge, circumscribe, contract **2** *Syn* INCREASE (sense 1), add (to), aggrandize, augment, boost, compound, enlarge, escalate, expand, extend, multiply, raise, swell, up *Ant* abate, contract, decrease, diminish, lessen, lower, reduce, subtract (from)
amplitude *Syn* EXPANSE, spread, stretch
amulet *Syn* FETISH, charm, talisman
amuse • to cause or enable one to pass one's time in pleasant or agreeable activity *Syn* divert, entertain, recreate *Rel* absorb, engross *Ant* bore
amusement • an agreeable activity or its effect *Syn* diversion, entertainment, recreation *Rel* absorption, engrossment *Ant* boredom
amusing *Syn* FUN, delightful, diverting, enjoyable, entertaining, pleasurable *Ant* boring, dull
anagogic *Syn* MYSTICAL, cabalistic, mystic
analgesic *Syn* ANODYNE, anesthetic *Ant* irritant, stimulant
analogous *Syn* ALIKE, akin, comparable, correspondent, corresponding, like, matching, parallel, resembling, similar, such, suchlike *Ant* different, dissimilar, diverse, unlike
analogue *Syn* PARALLEL, correlate, counterpart
analogy • a comparison between things essentially or generically different but strikingly alike in one or more pertinent aspects *Syn* metaphor, simile
analysis • separation of a whole into its fundamental elements or constituent parts *Syn* breakdown, dissection, resolution *Rel* division, separation *Ant* synthesis
analytical *Syn* LOGICAL, subtle *Ant* illogical
analyze • to identify and examine the basic elements or parts of (something) especially for discovering interrelationships *Syn* anatomize, assay, break down, dissect *Rel* assess, evaluate, examine, inspect, investigate, scrutinize
anarchic *Syn* LAWLESS, disorderly, lawbreaking, unruly *Ant* law-abiding, orderly
anarchy • a state in which there is widespread wrongdoing and disregard for rules and authority *Syn* chaos, lawlessness, misrule *Rel* commotion, tumult, uproar
anathema **1** *Syn* ABOMINATION, bête noire, bugbear *Ant* joy **2** *Syn* CURSE, imprecation, malediction *Ant* blessing
anathematize *Syn* EXECRATE, curse, damn, objurgate
anatomize *Syn* ANALYZE, assay, break down, dissect
anatomy *Syn* STRUCTURE, framework, skeleton
ancestor **1** • a person from whom one is descended *Syn* forebear, forefather, progenitor *Ant* descendant **2** • something belonging to an earlier time from which something else was later developed *Syn* antecedent, foregoer, forerunner, precursor, predecessor *Rel* archetype, model, original, prototype *Ant* descendant (*or* descendent)
ancestry • the line of ancestors from whom a person is descended *Syn* birth, blood, bloodline, breeding, descent, extraction, family tree, genealogy, line, lineage, origin, parentage, pedigree, stock, strain *Rel* heredity, succession *Ant* issue, posterity, progeny, seed
anchor *Syn* SECURE, moor, rivet
anchorite *Syn* RECLUSE, cenobite, eremite, hermit
ancient *adj Syn* ELDERLY, aged, aging, geriatric, long-lived, old, older, senior *Ant* young, youthful
ancient *n Syn* SENIOR CITIZEN, elder, golden-ager, oldster, old-timer *Ant* youngster, youth
ancillary *Syn* AUXILIARY, accessory, adjuvant, contributory, subservient, subsidiary
anecdote *Syn* STORY, narrative, tale, yarn
anemic *Syn* PALE (sense 2), bloodless
anesthetic *n Syn* ANODYNE, analgesic *Ant* irritant, stimulant
anesthetic *adj Syn* INSENSIBLE, impassible, insensitive *Ant* sensible (*to or of something*)
angel **1** *Syn* LAMB, dove, innocent, sheep *Ant* wolf **2** *Syn* SPONSOR, backer, guarantor, patron, surety
anger *n* • an intense emotional state of displeasure with someone or something *Syn* angriness, furor, fury, indignation, irateness, ire, outrage, rage, spleen, wrath, wrathfulness *Rel* aggravation, annoyance, exasperation, irritation, vexation *Ant* delight, pleasure
anger *vb* • to make angry *Syn* antagonize, enrage, incense, inflame, infuriate, madden, outrage, rankle, rile, roil *Rel* affront, aggravate, annoy, cross, exasperate, get, irritate, nettle, offend, peeve, pique, provoke, put out, ruffle, vex *Ant* delight, gratify, please
angered *Syn* ANGRY, apoplectic, enraged, foaming, fuming, furious, incensed, indignant, inflamed, infuriated, irate, ireful, mad, outraged, rabid, riled, roiled, sore, steaming, wrathful, wroth *Ant* delighted, pleased
angle **1** *Syn* PHASE, aspect, facet, side **2** *Syn* POINT OF VIEW, slant, standpoint, viewpoint
angriness *Syn* ANGER, furor, fury, indignation, irateness, ire, outrage, rage, spleen, wrath, wrathfulness *Ant* delight, pleasure
angry • feeling or showing anger *Syn* angered, apoplectic, enraged, foaming, fuming, furious, incensed, indignant, inflamed, infuriated, irate, ireful, mad, outraged, rabid,

riled, roiled, sore, steaming, wrathful, wroth *Rel* ranting, raving, stormy *Ant* delighted, pleased

anguish *Syn* SORROW, grief, heartache, heartbreak, regret, woe *Ant* joy

angular *Syn* LEAN, gaunt, lank, lanky, rawboned, scrawny, skinny, spare *Ant* fleshy

animadversion • a remark or statement that is an adverse criticism *Syn* aspersion, reflection, stricture *Rel* censure, criticism, reprehension *Ant* commendation

animadvert *Syn* REMARK, comment, commentate

animal *n* • one of the lower animals as distinguished from human beings *Syn* beast, brute, creature, critter *Rel* varmint, vermin

animal *adj Syn* CARNAL, fleshly, sensual *Ant* intellectual, spiritual

animate *vb* **1** • to give life, vigor, or spirit to *Syn* brace, energize, enliven, fire, invigorate, jazz (up), liven (up), pep (up), quicken, stimulate, vitalize, vivify *Rel* arouse, awake, awaken, raise, rouse, stir, wake (up) *Ant* damp, dampen, deaden, dull **2** *Syn* INFORM (sense 1), fire, inspire

animate *adj Syn* LIVING, alive, animated, vital *Ant* lifeless

animated **1** *Syn* LIVELY, gay, sprightly, vivacious *Ant* dull **2** *Syn* LIVING, alive, animate, vital *Ant* lifeless

animosity *Syn* ENMITY, animus, antagonism, antipathy, hostility, rancor *Ant* amity

animus *Syn* ENMITY, animosity, antagonism, antipathy, hostility, rancor *Ant* amity

annals *Syn* HISTORY, chronicle

annex *n* • an addition to a main (and often the original) building *Syn* ell, extension, wing *Rel* accretion, addition, increment

annex *vb Syn* ADD (sense 2), adjoin, append, tack (on) *Ant* deduct, remove, subtract, take

annihilation *Syn* DESTRUCTION, decimation, demolishment, demolition, desolation, devastation, extermination, extinction, havoc, loss, obliteration, ruin, ruination, wastage, wreckage *Ant* building, construction, erection, raising

announce • to make known openly or publicly *Syn* advertise, blaze, broadcast, declare, enunciate, placard, post, proclaim, promulgate, publicize, publish, sound *Rel* advise, apprise, inform, notify

announcement **1** • a published statement informing the public of a matter of general interest *Syn* ad, advertisement, bulletin, notice, notification, posting, release *Rel* advertising, ballyhoo, bill, billboard, boost, broadcast, broadside, buildup, campaign, circular, commercial, communication, dispatch, flier (*or* flyer), handbill, handout, message, newscast, placard, plug, poster, promotion, propaganda, publicity, report, sign, spot, telecast, word **2** *Syn* DECLARATION, advertisement, broadcasting, proclamation, promulgation, publication

annoy **1** • to disturb and nervously upset a person *Syn* bother, irk, vex *Rel* aggravate, exasperate, irritate, nettle, rile *Ant* soothe **2** *Syn* WORRY, harass, harry, pester, plague, tantalize, tease

annoying • causing annoyance *Syn* aggravating, bothersome, disturbing, exasperating, frustrating, galling, irksome, irritating, maddening, nettling, peeving, pesty, rankling, riling, vexatious, vexing *Rel* burdensome, discomforting, displeasing, disquieting, distressing, importunate, inconveniencing

annuity *Syn* APPROPRIATION, allocation, allotment, grant, subsidy

annul *Syn* ABOLISH, abrogate, cancel, dissolve, invalidate, negate, nullify, quash, repeal, rescind, void

anodyne • something used to relieve or prevent pain *Syn* analgesic, anesthetic

anoint *Syn* OIL, cream, grease, lubricate

anomalous **1** *Syn* DEVIANT, aberrant, abnormal, atypical, irregular, unnatural *Ant* natural, normal, regular, standard, typical **2** *Syn* IRREGULAR, unnatural *Ant* regular

anomaly *Syn* PARADOX, antinomy

anon *Syn* SHORTLY, momentarily, presently, soon

another *Syn* ADDITIONAL, added, else, farther, further, more, other

answer *n* **1** • something spoken or written by way of return to a question or demand *Syn* rejoinder, reply, response, retort *Rel* defense, justification, rebuttal, refutation, vindication **2** • something attained by mental effort and especially by computation *Syn* result, solution *Rel* conclusion, determination, explanation, finding

answer *vb* **1** • to say, write, or do something in response *Syn* rejoin, reply, respond, retort *Rel* acknowledge, recognize **2** *Syn* SATISFY (sense 2), fulfill, meet **3** *Syn* SOLVE, break, crack, dope (out), figure out, puzzle (out), resolve, riddle, unravel, work, work out

answerable **1** *Syn* RESPONSIBLE, accountable, amenable, liable **2** *Syn* SOLVABLE, explainable, explicable, resolvable, soluble *Ant* inexplicable, insoluble, unexplainable, unsolvable

antagonism *Syn* ENMITY, animosity, animus, antipathy, hostility, rancor *Ant* amity

antagonist *Syn* ENEMY, adversary, foe, opponent *Ant* friend

antagonistic *Syn* ADVERSE, counter, counteractive *Ant* propitious

antagonize **1** *Syn* ANGER, enrage, incense, inflame, infuriate, madden, outrage, rankle, rile, roil *Ant* delight, gratify, please **2** *Syn* RESIST, combat, conflict, contest, fight, oppose, withstand *Ant* abide, submit

ante *Syn* BET, pot, stake, wager

antecedent *n* **1** *Syn* CAUSE, determinant, occasion, reason **2** *Syn* ANCESTOR (sense 2), foregoer, forerunner, precursor, predecessor *Ant* descendant (*or* descendent)
antecedent *adj Syn* PREVIOUS, anterior, foregoing, precedent, preceding, prior *Ant* after, ensuing, following, subsequent, succeeding
anterior *Syn* PREVIOUS, antecedent, foregoing, precedent, preceding, prior *Ant* after, ensuing, following, subsequent, succeeding
anthology • a collection of writings *Syn* album, compilation, miscellany *Rel* archives
anthropoid • resembling humans *Syn* anthropomorphic, anthropomorphous
anthropomorphic *Syn* ANTHROPOID, anthropomorphous
anthropomorphous *Syn* ANTHROPOID, anthropomorphic
antic *adj Syn* FANTASTIC, bizarre, grotesque
antic *n Syn* PRANK, caper, dido, monkeyshine
anticipate **1** *Syn* FORESEE, apprehend, divine, foreknow **2** *Syn* PREVENT (sense 1), forestall
anticipation *Syn* PROSPECT, foretaste, outlook
antidote *Syn* CORRECTIVE, check, control
antinomy *Syn* PARADOX, anomaly
antipathetic • having a natural dislike for something *Syn* allergic, averse *Rel* adverse, antagonistic, disgusted, disinclined, hostile, intolerant, loath (*or* loth), nauseated, negative, opposed, opposing, reluctant, repelled, repulsed, resistant, resisting, revolted, shocked, squeamish, turned off, uncongenial, unfriendly, unsympathetic, unwilling
antipathy *Syn* ENMITY, animosity, animus, antagonism, hostility, rancor *Ant* amity
antipodal *Syn* OPPOSITE, antipodean, antithetical, antonymous, contradictory, contrary
antipode *Syn* OPPOSITE, antithesis, antonym, contradictory, contrary, converse, counter, reverse
antipodean *Syn* OPPOSITE, antipodal, antithetical, antonymous, contradictory, contrary
antiquated *Syn* OBSOLETE, archaic, dated, moth-eaten, outdated, outmoded, out-of-date, outworn, passé *Ant* new
antisocial *Syn* UNSOCIAL, asocial, nonsocial *Ant* social
antithesis *Syn* OPPOSITE, antipode, antonym, contradictory, contrary, converse, counter, reverse
antithetical *Syn* OPPOSITE, antipodal, antipodean, antonymous, contradictory, contrary
antonym *Syn* OPPOSITE, antipode, antithesis, contradictory, contrary, converse, counter, reverse
antonymous *Syn* OPPOSITE, antipodal, antipodean, antithetical, contradictory, contrary
anxiety *Syn* CARE, concern, solicitude, worry
anxious **1** *Syn* EAGER, agog, athirst, avid, keen *Ant* listless **2** *Syn* WORRIED, careful, concerned, solicitous
anyhow *Syn* HIT OR MISS, aimlessly, anyway, anywise, desultorily, erratically, haphazard, haphazardly, helter-skelter, irregularly, randomly *Ant* methodically, systematically
anyway *Syn* HIT OR MISS, aimlessly, anyhow, anywise, desultorily, erratically, haphazard, haphazardly, helter-skelter, irregularly, randomly *Ant* methodically, systematically
anywise **1** *Syn* AT ALL, ever **2** *Syn* HIT OR MISS, aimlessly, anyhow, anyway, desultorily, erratically, haphazard, haphazardly, helter-skelter, irregularly, randomly *Ant* methodically, systematically
apart • into parts or to pieces *Syn* asunder, piecemeal *Ant* together
apartment *Syn* ROOM (sense 1), chamber
apathetic *Syn* IMPASSIVE, phlegmatic, stoic, stolid *Ant* responsive
apathy **1** *Syn* IMPASSIVITY, phlegm, stoicism, stolidity **2** *Syn* INDIFFERENCE, casualness, disinterestedness, disregard, insouciance, nonchalance, unconcern *Ant* concern, interest, regard
ape *Syn* COPY, imitate, mimic, mock *Ant* originate
aperçu *Syn* COMPENDIUM, digest, pandect, précis, sketch, survey, syllabus
aperture • an opening allowing passage through or in and out *Syn* interstice, orifice *Rel* bore, perforation, prick, puncture
apex *Syn* SUMMIT, acme, apogee, climax, culmination, meridian, peak, pinnacle, zenith
aphorism *Syn* SAYING, adage, apothegm, epigram, maxim, motto, proverb, saw
aphrodisiac *Syn* EROTIC, amative, amatory, amorous
apiece **1** • for each one *Syn* all, each, per capita *Rel* apart, independently, individually, respectively, separately, singly **2** *Syn* EACH, individually, respectively, severally
aplomb **1** *Syn* CONFIDENCE, assurance, self-assurance, self-confidence, self-possession *Ant* diffidence **2** *Syn* EQUANIMITY, calmness, composure, coolheadedness, coolness, imperturbability, placidity, self-possession, serenity, tranquillity (*or* tranquility) *Ant* agitation, discomposure, perturbation
apocalypse *Syn* DISASTER, calamity, cataclysm, catastrophe
apocryphal *Syn* FICTITIOUS, fabulous, legendary, mythical *Ant* historical
apogee *Syn* SUMMIT, acme, apex, climax, culmination, meridian, peak, pinnacle, zenith
apologia *Syn* APOLOGY, alibi, excuse, plea, pretext
apology • the reason or reasons offered in explanation or defense of something (as an act, a policy, or a view) *Syn* alibi, apologia, excuse, plea, pretext *Rel* defense, justification, vindication
apoplectic *Syn* ANGRY, angered, enraged, foaming, fuming, furious, incensed, indig-

nant, inflamed, infuriated, irate, ireful, mad, outraged, rabid, riled, roiled, sore, steaming, wrathful, wroth *Ant* delighted, pleased

apostasy *Syn* DEFECTION, desertion

apostate *Syn* RENEGADE, backslider, recreant, turncoat *Ant* adherent, loyalist

apostle *Syn* EXPONENT, advocate, backer, booster, champion, friend, promoter, proponent, supporter *Ant* adversary, antagonist, opponent

apothecary *Syn* DRUGGIST, chemist, pharmacist

apothegm *Syn* SAYING, adage, aphorism, epigram, maxim, motto, proverb, saw

apotheosis *Syn* PARAGON, nonesuch, nonpareil

appall *Syn* DISMAY, daunt, horrify *Ant* cheer

appalling *Syn* FEARFUL (sense 2), awful, dreadful, frightful, horrible, horrific, shocking, terrible, terrific

appanage *Syn* RIGHT, birthright, perquisite, prerogative, privilege

apparatus **1** *Syn* EQUIPMENT, gear, machinery, matériel, outfit, paraphernalia, tackle **2** *Syn* MACHINE, engine, machinery, mechanism, motor

apparel *vb Syn* CLOTHE, array, attire, dress, robe *Ant* unclothe

apparel *n Syn* CLOTHES, attire, clothing, dress, raiment

apparent **1** • not actually being what appearance indicates *Syn* illusory, ostensible, seeming *Rel* false, wrong *Ant* real **2** *Syn* EVIDENT, clear, distinct, manifest, obvious, palpable, patent, plain **3** *Syn* VISIBLE, observable, seeable, visual *Ant* invisible, unseeable

apparently • to all outward appearances *Syn* evidently, ostensibly, presumably, seemingly, supposedly *Rel* externally, outwardly, visibly

apparition *Syn* GHOST, bogey, phantasm, phantom, poltergeist, shade, shadow, specter (*or* spectre), spirit, spook, vision, wraith

appeal *n Syn* PRAYER, petition, plea, suit

appeal *vb Syn* PRAY, petition, plead, sue

appear **1** • to come out into view *Syn* emerge, loom *Rel* arrive, come *Ant* disappear, vanish **2** *Syn* SEEM, act, look, make, sound

appearance • the outward show presented by a person or thing *Syn* aspect, look, semblance

appease *Syn* PACIFY, conciliate, disarm, mollify, placate, propitiate *Ant* anger, enrage, incense, infuriate, madden, outrage

appellation *Syn* NAME, denomination, designation, style, title

append *Syn* ADD (sense 2), adjoin, annex, tack (on) *Ant* deduct, remove, subtract, take

appendage • something regarded as additional and at the same time as subsidiary to another object *Syn* accessory, adjunct, appurtenance

appendix • additional matter subjoined to a book *Syn* addendum, supplement

apperception *Syn* RECOGNITION, assimilation, identification

appertain *Syn* BEAR (sense 3), apply, belong, pertain, relate

appetite **1** *Syn* DESIRE, lust, passion, urge *Ant* distaste **2** *Syn* LIKING, fancy, favor, fondness, like, love, partiality, preference, relish, shine, taste, use *Ant* aversion, disfavor, dislike, distaste, hatred, loathing

appetizing *Syn* PALATABLE, flavorsome, relishing, sapid, savory, tasty, toothsome *Ant* distasteful, unpalatable

applaud **1** • to demonstrate one's feeling, and especially one's approbation or joy, audibly and enthusiastically *Syn* cheer, root *Rel* acclaim, extol, praise *Ant* boo, hiss **2** *Syn* ACCLAIM, cheer, hail, laud, praise, salute, tout *Ant* knock, pan, slam **3** *Syn* COMMEND, compliment, recommend *Ant* admonish, censure

applause • enthusiastic and usually public expression of approval *Syn* acclamation, cheering, cheers, ovation, plaudit(s), rave(s) *Rel* clapping *Ant* booing, hissing

appliance **1** *Syn* GADGET, contraption, contrivance, gimmick, gizmo (*or* gismo), jigger **2** *Syn* IMPLEMENT, instrument, tool, utensil

applicable *Syn* PERTINENT, apposite, apropos, germane, material, pointed, relative, relevant *Ant* extraneous, immaterial, inapplicable, irrelevant, pointless

applicant *Syn* CANDIDATE, aspirant, campaigner, contender, hopeful, prospect, seeker

application *Syn* ATTENTION (sense 1), concentration, study *Ant* inattention

appliqué *Syn* OVERLAY, superimpose, superpose

apply **1** *Syn* BEAR (sense 3), appertain, belong, pertain, relate **2** *Syn* DIRECT (sense 1), address, devote *Ant* misdirect **3** *Syn* ENFORCE, administer, execute, implement **4** *Syn* EXERT, exercise, ply, put out, wield **5** *Syn* RESORT, go, refer, turn **6** *Syn* USE, avail, employ, utilize

appoint **1** • to decide upon (the time or date for an event) usually from a position of authority *Syn* designate, fix, name, set *Rel* adopt, assign, choose, determine, establish, opt (for), pick, pin down, prefer, select, settle, single (out), specify **2** • to pick (someone) by one's authority for a specific position or duty *Syn* assign, attach, commission, constitute, designate, detail, name *Rel* authorize, delegate, depute, deputize *Ant* discharge, dismiss, expel, fire

appointment *Syn* ENGAGEMENT, assignation, date, rendezvous, tryst

apportion **1** • to divide something carefully and distribute it among a number *Syn* parcel, portion, prorate, ration *Rel* accord, award, grant **2** *Syn* ALLOT, allocate, assign

apposite *Syn* PERTINENT, applicable, apropos, germane, material, pointed, relative, relevant *Ant* extraneous, immaterial, inapplicable, irrelevant, pointless

appraise *Syn* ESTIMATE (sense 1), assay, assess, evaluate, rate, value

appreciable *Syn* PERCEPTIBLE, detectable, discernible, distinguishable, palpable, sensible *Ant* impalpable, imperceptible, inappreciable, indistinguishable, insensible

appreciate **1** • to hold in high estimation *Syn* cherish, prize, treasure, value *Rel* admire, esteem, regard, respect *Ant* despise **2** *Syn* INCREASE (sense 2), accumulate, balloon, build (up), burgeon, enlarge, escalate, expand, mount, multiply, mushroom, proliferate, rise, snowball, swell, wax *Ant* contract, decrease, diminish, lessen, wane **3** *Syn* UNDERSTAND, comprehend

appreciation **1** *Syn* COMPREHENSION, apprehension, grasp, grip, perception, understanding **2** *Syn* THANKS, appreciativeness, gratefulness, gratitude, thankfulness *Ant* ingratitude, thanklessness, ungratefulness

appreciativeness *Syn* THANKS, appreciation, gratefulness, gratitude, thankfulness *Ant* ingratitude, thanklessness, ungratefulness

apprehend **1** *Syn* ARREST (sense 2), attach, detain **2** *Syn* FORESEE, anticipate, divine, foreknow

apprehension **1** *Syn* COMPREHENSION, appreciation, grasp, grip, perception, understanding **2** • fear (or an instance of it) that something is going wrong or will go wrong *Syn* foreboding, misgiving, presentiment *Rel* alarm, dread, fear, panic *Ant* confidence **3** *Syn* ARREST, attachment, detention

apprehensive *Syn* FEARFUL (sense 1), afraid *Ant* fearless, intrepid

apprentice *Syn* ASSISTANT, adjutant, aid, aide, coadjutor, deputy, helper, sidekick

apprise **1** *Syn* ENLIGHTEN (sense 1), acquaint, advise, brief, clue, familiarize, fill in, inform, instruct, tell, wise (up) **2** *Syn* INFORM (sense 2), advise, notify

approach *vb* **1** • to come or draw close (to) *Syn* approximate, near *Rel* accost, address **2** *Syn* MATCH, equal, rival, touch

approach *n* *Syn* OVERTURE, advance, bid, tender

approaching *Syn* FORTHCOMING, coming, imminent, impending, nearing, oncoming, pending, upcoming *Ant* late, recent

approbation *Syn* APPROVAL, blessing, favor, imprimatur, OK (*or* okay) *Ant* disapprobation, disapproval, disfavor

appropriate *vb* *Syn* ARROGATE, confiscate, preempt, usurp *Ant* renounce, yield

appropriate *adj* *Syn* FIT, apt, felicitous, fitting, happy, meet, proper, suitable *Ant* unfit

appropriately *Syn* PROPERLY, congruously, correctly, fittingly, happily, meetly, rightly, suitably *Ant* improperly, inappropriately, incongruously, incorrectly, unsuitably, wrongly

appropriateness • the quality or state of being especially suitable or fitting *Syn* aptness, felicitousness, fitness, fittingness, rightness, seemliness, suitability, suitableness *Rel* agreeableness, compatibility, congruity, harmoniousness *Ant* inappropriateness, inaptness, infelicity, unfitness

appropriation • a sum of money allotted for a specific use by official or formal action *Syn* allocation, allotment, annuity, grant, subsidy *Rel* advance, allowance, benefit, endowment, fund, stipend, trust

approval • an acceptance of something as satisfactory *Syn* approbation, blessing, favor, imprimatur, OK (*or* okay) *Rel* backing, endorsement, sanction, support *Ant* disapprobation, disapproval, disfavor

approve • to have or to express a favorable opinion of *Syn* accredit, certify, endorse, sanction *Rel* applaud, commend, compliment *Ant* disapprove

approve (of) • to have a favorable opinion of *Syn* accept, care (for), countenance, favor, OK (*or* okay), subscribe (to) *Rel* acclaim, applaud, laud, praise, salute *Ant* disapprove (of), discountenance, disfavor, frown (on *or* upon)

approximate *Syn* APPROACH, near

appurtenance *Syn* APPENDAGE, accessory, adjunct

apropos *Syn* PERTINENT, applicable, apposite, germane, material, pointed, relative, relevant *Ant* extraneous, immaterial, inapplicable, irrelevant, pointless

apt **1** *Syn* FIT, appropriate, felicitous, fitting, happy, meet, proper, suitable *Ant* unfit **2** *Syn* PRONE (sense 1), given, inclined, tending *Ant* erect **3** *Syn* QUICK, prompt, ready *Ant* sluggish

aptitude *Syn* GIFT (sense 2), bent, faculty, genius, knack, talent, turn

aptness *Syn* APPROPRIATENESS, felicitousness, fitness, fittingness, rightness, seemliness, suitability, suitableness *Ant* inappropriateness, inaptness, infelicity, unfitness

aqueduct *Syn* CHANNEL, canal, conduit, duct

arbiter **1** *Syn* JUDGE, arbitrator, referee, umpire **2** *Syn* MEDIATOR, arbitrator, conciliator, go-between, intercessor, intermediary, interposer, middleman, peacemaker

arbitrary *Syn* ABSOLUTE, autocratic, despotic, tyrannical, tyrannous *Ant* limited, restrained

arbitrate *Syn* JUDGE, adjudge, adjudicate

arbitrator **1** *Syn* JUDGE, arbiter, referee, umpire **2** *Syn* MEDIATOR, arbiter, conciliator, go-between, intercessor, intermediary, interposer, middleman, peacemaker

arc *Syn* CURVE, arch, bow

arcade *Syn* PASSAGE, aisle, cloister, corridor, gallery, hall, hallway, passageway

arcane *Syn* MYSTERIOUS, inscrutable
arch **1** *Syn* CURVE, arc, bow **2** *Syn* SAUCY, pert
archaic *Syn* OBSOLETE, antiquated, dated, moth-eaten, outdated, outmoded, out-of-date, outworn, passé
architect *Syn* ARTIST, artificer, artisan
archive *Syn* DOCUMENT, monument, record
arctic *Syn* COLD, chilly, cool, freezing, frigid, frosty, gelid, glacial, icy *Ant* hot
ardent *Syn* FERVENT, blazing, burning, charged, emotional, fervid, feverish, fiery, flaming, glowing, hot-blooded, impassioned, passionate, red-hot, vehement, warm, warm-blooded *Ant* cold, cool, dispassionate, impassive, unemotional
ardor *Syn* PASSION, enthusiasm, fervor, zeal
arduous *Syn* HARD, difficult *Ant* easy
area **1** • a distinguishable extent of surface and especially of the earth's surface *Syn* belt, region, tract, zone *Rel* district, locality **2** *Syn* REGION, demesne, field, zone **3** *Syn* SIZE, dimensions, extent, magnitude, volume
argot *Syn* TERMINOLOGY, cant, dialect, jargon, language, lingo, patois, patter, slang, vocabulary
argue **1** *Syn* DISCUSS, agitate, debate, dispute **2** *Syn* INDICATE, attest, bespeak, betoken, prove **3** *Syn* PERSUADE, convince, get, induce, move, prevail (on *or* upon), satisfy, talk (into), win (over)
argument **1** • a vigorous and often heated discussion of a moot question *Syn* controversy, dispute *Rel* argumentation, debate, disputation **2** *Syn* REASON (sense 1), ground, proof **3** *Syn* SUBJECT, leitmotiv, matter, motif, motive, subject matter, text, theme, topic
argumentation • the act or art of argument or an exercise of one's powers of argument *Syn* debate, dialectic, disputation, forensic *Rel* argument, controversy, dispute
argumentative *Syn* BELLIGERENT, aggressive, bellicose, combative, contentious, discordant, disputatious, gladiatorial, militant, pugnacious, quarrelsome, scrappy, truculent, warlike *Ant* nonbelligerent, pacific, peaceable, peaceful
arise **1** *Syn* ASCEND, climb, lift, mount, rise, soar, up, uprise, upsweep, upturn *Ant* decline, descend, dip, drop, fall (off) **2** *Syn* BEGIN (sense 1), commence, dawn, form, materialize, originate, set in, spring, start *Ant* cease, end, stop **3** *Syn* SPRING, derive, emanate, flow, issue, originate, proceed, rise, stem
aristocracy **1** • a body of persons who constitute a socially superior caste *Syn* county, elite, gentry, nobility, society *Ant* people, proletariat **2** *Syn* OLIGARCHY, plutocracy
aristocrat • a person of high birth or social station *Syn* GENTLEPERSON, noble, patrician *Ant* commoner, peasant, peon
arithmetic *Syn* CALCULATION, ciphering, computation, figures, figuring, reckoning
armistice *Syn* TRUCE, cease-fire, peace
armory • a place where military arms are stored *Syn* arsenal, depot, dump, magazine *Rel* fort, fortress, stronghold
army *Syn* MULTITUDE, host, legion
aroma *Syn* SMELL, odor, scent
aromatic **1** *Syn* FRAGRANT, ambrosial, perfumed, redolent, savory, scented, sweet *Ant* fetid, foul, malodorous, noisome, putrid, rancid, rank, reeking, reeky, smelly, stinking, stinky, strong **2** *Syn* ODOROUS, balmy, fragrant, redolent *Ant* malodorous, odorless
around **1** • close to *Syn* about, by, near, next to *Rel* alongside, beside **2** • in random positions within the boundaries of *Syn* about, over, round, through, throughout *Rel* on
arouse *Syn* STIR, awaken, rally, rouse, waken
arrange **1** *Syn* NEGOTIATE, concert **2** *Syn* ORDER, marshal, methodize, organize, systematize
arrant *Syn* OUTRIGHT, out-and-out, unmitigated
array *vb* **1** *Syn* CLOTHE, apparel, attire, dress, robe *Ant* unclothe **2** *Syn* LINE, align, line up, range
array *n* **1** *Syn* FINERY, best, bravery, caparison, feather, frippery, full dress, gaiety, regalia **2** *Syn* DISPLAY, parade, pomp
arrear *Syn* DEBT, debit, indebtedness, liability, obligation
arrest *n* • seizing and holding under restraint or in custody by authority of the law *Syn* apprehension, attachment, detention *Rel* seizing, seizure, taking
arrest *vb* **1** • to stop in midcourse *Syn* check, interrupt *Rel* interfere, interpose, intervene *Ant* activate, quicken **2** • to seize and hold under restraint or in custody by authority of the law *Syn* apprehend, attach, detain *Rel* seize, take
arresting **1** *Syn* INTERESTING, absorbing, engaging, engrossing, enthralling, fascinating, gripping, immersing, intriguing, involving, riveting *Ant* boring, drab, dry, dull, heavy, monotonous, tedious, uninteresting **2** *Syn* NOTICEABLE, conspicuous, outstanding, prominent, remarkable, salient, signal, striking
arrogance • an exaggerated sense of one's importance that shows itself in the making of excessive or unjustified claims *Syn* haughtiness, imperiousness, loftiness, lordliness, masterfulness, peremptoriness, pompousness, presumptuousness, pretense (*or* pretence), pretension, pretentiousness, self-importance, superciliousness, superiority *Rel* authoritativeness, bossiness, dominance, high-handedness *Ant* humility, modesty
arrogant **1** • having a feeling of superiority that shows itself in an overbearing attitude *Syn* cavalier, haughty, highfalutin,

high-handed, high-hat, imperious, important, lofty, lordly, masterful, overweening, peremptory, pompous, presumptuous, pretentious, supercilious, superior, uppish, uppity *Rel* authoritarian, bossy, dominant, dominating, domineering, magisterial, pontificating *Ant* humble, modest **2** *Syn* PROUD (sense 1), disdainful, haughty, insolent, lordly, overbearing, supercilious *Ant* ashamed, humble

arrogate • to seize or take over in a high-handed manner *Syn* appropriate, confiscate, preempt, usurp *Rel* grab, seize, take *Ant* renounce, yield

arsenal *Syn* ARMORY, depot, dump, magazine

arsonist • a person who deliberately and unlawfully sets fire to a building or other property *Syn* firebug, incendiary *Rel* igniter (*or* ignitor)

art **1** • the faculty of performing or executing expertly what is planned or devised *Syn* artifice, craft, cunning, skill **2** *Syn* TRADE, craft, handicraft, profession

artery *Syn* WAY, course, pass, passage, route

artful *Syn* SLY, crafty, cunning, foxy, guileful, insidious, tricky, wily

article **1** *Syn* ESSAY, composition, paper, theme **2** *Syn* PARAGRAPH, clause, count, plank, verse **3** *Syn* THING, object

articled *Syn* BOUND, bond, indentured

articulate *adj* • able to express oneself clearly and well *Syn* eloquent, fluent, well-spoken *Rel* facile, glib, smooth-tongued, voluble *Ant* inarticulate

articulate *vb* **1** • to form speech sounds *Syn* enunciate, pronounce **2** *Syn* PHRASE, clothe, couch, express, formulate, put, say, state, word

articulation *Syn* JOINT, suture

artifact *Syn* WORK (sense 3), opus, product, production

artifice **1** *Syn* ART, craft, cunning, skill **2** *Syn* TRICKERY, chicanery, hanky-panky, jugglery, legerdemain, subterfuge, wile **3** *Syn* TRICK, feint, gambit, maneuver, ploy, ruse, stratagem, wile

artificer **1** *Syn* ARTISAN, craftsman, handicrafter, tradesman **2** *Syn* ARTIST, architect, artisan

artificial **1** • not brought into being by nature but by human art or effort or by some process of manufacture *Syn* ersatz, factitious, synthetic *Rel* fabricated, fashioned, manufactured *Ant* natural **2** *Syn* IMITATION, bogus, factitious, fake, false, man-made, mimic, mock, sham, simulated, substitute, synthetic *Ant* genuine, natural, real **3** *Syn* INSINCERE, backhanded, double-dealing, feigned, hypocritical, left-handed, mealy, mealymouthed, two-faced, unctuous *Ant* genuine, heartfelt, honest, sincere, unfeigned

artisan **1** • a person whose occupation requires skill with the hands *Syn* artificer, craftsman, handicrafter, tradesman *Rel* artist, maker **2** *Syn* ARTIST, architect, artificer **3** *Syn* WORKER, craftsman, hand, handicraftsman, laborer, mechanic, operative, roustabout, workingman, workman *Ant* idler

artist **1** • one who makes something beautiful or useful or both *Syn* architect, artificer, artisan *Rel* craftsman, worker, workman **2** *Syn* EXPERT, ace, adept, authority, crackerjack, maestro, master, past master, scholar, shark, virtuoso, whiz, wizard *Ant* amateur

artless *Syn* NATURAL, ingenuous, naive, simple, unaffected, unsophisticated

artlessly *Syn* NATURALLY (sense 3), guilelessly, ingenuously, innocently, naively, sincerely, unaffectedly, unfeignedly, unpretentiously *Ant* affectedly, artificially, hypocritically, insincerely, pretentiously, unnaturally

as *Syn* BECAUSE, for, inasmuch as, since

ascend • to move or extend upward *Syn* arise, climb, lift, mount, rise, soar, up, uprise, upsweep, upturn *Rel* boost, elevate, raise, uplift, upraise *Ant* decline, descend, dip, drop, fall (off)

ascendancy *Syn* SUPREMACY, dominance, dominion, predominance, preeminence, sovereignty

ascertain *Syn* DISCOVER, determine, learn, unearth

ascetic *Syn* SEVERE, austere, stern *Ant* tender, tolerant

ascribe • to lay something (creditable, discreditable, or neutral) to the account of a person or thing *Syn* accredit, assign, attribute, charge, credit, impute, refer *Rel* affix, attach, fasten

aseptic *Syn* SANITARY, germfree, hygienic, sterile *Ant* insanitary, unhygienic, unsanitary

ash • the remains of combustible material after it has been destroyed by fire *Syn* cinders, clinkers, embers

ashamed **1** • acutely or manifestly conscious of embarrassment and humiliation *Syn* chagrined, mortified *Rel* abashed, discomfited, embarrassed *Ant* proud **2** *Syn* GUILTY, contrite, hangdog, penitent, remorseful, repentant, shamed, shamefaced *Ant* impenitent, remorseless, shameless, unashamed, unrepentant

ashen *Syn* PALE (sense 1), ashy, livid, pallid, wan *Ant* florid, flush, rubicund, ruddy, sanguine

ashy *Syn* PALE (sense 1), ashen, livid, pallid, wan *Ant* florid, flush, rubicund, ruddy, sanguine

asinine *Syn* SIMPLE, fatuous, foolish, silly *Ant* wise

ask **1** • to address a person in an attempt to elicit information *Syn* catechize, examine, inquire, interrogate, query, question, quiz **2** • to seek to obtain by making one's wants or desires known *Syn* request, solicit *Rel* appeal, petition, plead, pray, sue

askance • with distrust *Syn* distrustfully, doubtfully, doubtingly, dubiously, mistrustfully, skeptically, suspiciously *Rel* hesitantly, hesitatingly, incredulously, questioningly, quizzically, unbelievingly *Ant* trustfully, trustingly

askew *Syn* AWRY, aslant, cockeyed, crooked, listing, lopsided, oblique, skewed, slanted, slanting, slantwise, tilted, tipping, uneven *Ant* even, level, straight

aslant *Syn* AWRY, askew, cockeyed, crooked, listing, lopsided, oblique, skewed, slanted, slanting, slantwise, tilted, tipping, uneven *Ant* even, level, straight

asleep *Syn* NUMB, benumbed, dead, insensitive, numbed, unfeeling *Ant* feeling, sensitive

asocial *Syn* UNSOCIAL, antisocial, nonsocial *Ant* social

aspect **1** *Syn* APPEARANCE, look, semblance **2** *Syn* PHASE, angle, facet, side

asperity *Syn* ACRIMONY, acerbity *Ant* suavity

asperse *Syn* SLANDER, blacken, defame, libel, malign, smear, traduce, vilify

aspersion *Syn* ANIMADVERSION, reflection, stricture *Ant* commendation

asphyxiate *Syn* SUFFOCATE, choke, smother, stifle, strangle, throttle

aspirant *Syn* CANDIDATE, applicant, campaigner, contender, hopeful, prospect, seeker

aspiration *Syn* GOAL, aim, ambition, design, dream, end, intent, intention, mark, meaning, object, objective, plan, pretension, purpose, target, thing

aspire *Syn* AIM, pant

assail **1** *Syn* ATTACK (sense 1), assault, bombard, storm **2** *Syn* ATTACK (sense 2), abuse, belabor, blast, castigate, excoriate, jump (on), lambaste (*or* lambast), scathe, slam, vituperate

assassin • one who can be hired to murder *Syn* bravo, cutthroat, gunman *Rel* killer, murderer, slayer

assassinate *Syn* KILL, dispatch, execute, murder, slay

assault *vb* *Syn* ATTACK (sense 1), assail, bombard, storm

assault *n* **1** *Syn* ATTACK (sense 1), onset, onslaught **2** *Syn* ATTACK (sense 2), aggression, blitzkrieg, charge, descent, offense (*or* offence), offensive, onset, onslaught, raid, rush, strike

assay **1** *Syn* ANALYZE, anatomize, break down, dissect **2** *Syn* ATTEMPT, endeavor, essay, seek, strive, try **3** *Syn* ESTIMATE (sense 1), appraise, assess, evaluate, rate, value

assemblage *Syn* GATHERING, assembly, collection, congregation

assemble **1** *Syn* BUILD, construct, erect, fabricate, make, make up, piece, put up, raise, rear, set up *Ant* disassemble, dismantle, take down **2** *Syn* GATHER, collect, congregate

assembly *Syn* GATHERING, assemblage, collection, congregation

assent • concurrence with what someone else has stated or proposed *Syn* accede, acquiesce, agree, consent, subscribe *Rel* accept, receive *Ant* dissent

assert **1** • to state positively usually either in anticipation of denial or objection or in the face of it *Syn* affirm, aver, avouch, avow, declare, predicate, profess, protest, warrant *Rel* adduce, advance, allege, cite *Ant* controvert, deny **2** *Syn* MAINTAIN, defend, justify, vindicate

assertive *Syn* AGGRESSIVE (sense 1), militant, pushing, pushy, self-assertive

assess **1** *Syn* ESTIMATE (sense 1), appraise, assay, evaluate, rate, value **2** *Syn* IMPOSE, charge, exact, fine, lay, levy, put *Ant* remit

assessment *Syn* TAX, duty, imposition, impost, levy

assets *Syn* POSSESSIONS, belongings, effects, means, resources

assiduous *Syn* BUSY, diligent, industrious, sedulous *Ant* idle, unoccupied

assign **1** *Syn* ALLOT, allocate, apportion **2** *Syn* ASCRIBE, accredit, attribute, charge, credit, impute, refer **3** *Syn* PRESCRIBE, define **4** *Syn* APPOINT (sense 2), attach, commission, constitute, designate, detail, name *Ant* discharge, dismiss, expel, fire

assignation *Syn* ENGAGEMENT, appointment, date, rendezvous, tryst

assignment **1** *Syn* CHORE, duty, job, stint, task **2** *Syn* MISSION, charge, job, operation, post

assimilate **1** *Syn* ABSORB, imbibe *Ant* exude, give out **2** *Syn* EMBODY (sense 1), incorporate, integrate

assimilation *Syn* RECOGNITION, apperception, identification

assist *Syn* HELP, aid *Ant* hinder

assistance *Syn* HELP, aid

assistant • a person who helps a more skilled person *Syn* adjutant, aid, aide, apprentice, coadjutor, deputy, helper, sidekick *Rel* employee, hand, help, helpmate, helpmeet, hireling, laborer, mate, worker

associate *n* • a person frequently found in the company of another *Syn* companion, comrade, crony *Rel* ally, colleague, confederate, partner

associate *vb* **1** *Syn* ALLY, band, club, confederate, conjoin, cooperate, federate, league, unite *Ant* break up, disband **2** *Syn* JOIN, combine, conjoin, connect, link, relate, unite *Ant* disjoin, part **3** *Syn* SOCIALIZE, fraternize, hobnob, mingle, mix

association • a body of persons who unite in the pursuit of a common aim or object *Syn* club, order, society

assort • to arrange in systematic order or according to some definite method of arrangement or distribution *Syn* classify, pigeonhole, sort *Rel* arrange, methodize, order, systematize

assorted *Syn* MISCELLANEOUS, heterogeneous, motley, promiscuous
assuage *Syn* RELIEVE, allay, alleviate, lighten, mitigate *Ant* alarm, embarrass, intensify
assume **1** · to put on a false or deceptive appearance *Syn* affect, counterfeit, feign, pretend, sham, simulate *Rel* camouflage, cloak, disguise, dissemble, mask **2** *Syn* PRESUPPOSE, posit, postulate, premise, presume
assumption · something that is taken for granted or advanced as fact *Syn* posit, postulate, premise, presumption, presupposition *Rel* hypothesis, theory
assurance **1** *Syn* CERTAINTY, certitude, conviction *Ant* uncertainty **2** *Syn* CONFIDENCE, aplomb, self-assurance, self-confidence, self-possession *Ant* diffidence
assure *Syn* ENSURE, cinch, guarantee, guaranty, insure, secure
assured *Syn* CONFIDENT, presumptuous, sanguine, sure *Ant* apprehensive, diffident
astern *Syn* ABAFT, aft *Ant* afore
astonish *Syn* SURPRISE (sense 2), amaze, astound, flabbergast
astound *Syn* SURPRISE (sense 2), amaze, astonish, flabbergast
astral *Syn* STARRY, sidereal, stellar
astray *Syn* WRONG, afield, amiss, awry *Ant* aright, right, well
astute *Syn* SHREWD, perspicacious, sagacious
asunder *Syn* APART, piecemeal *Ant* together
asylum *Syn* SHELTER, cover, refuge, retreat, sanctuary
at all · in any way or respect *Syn* anywise, ever *Rel* somehow, someway
athirst *Syn* EAGER, agog, anxious, avid, keen *Ant* listless
athletic *Syn* MUSCULAR, brawny, burly, husky, sinewy
athletics · physical activities engaged in for exercise or play *Syn* games, sports
athwart *Syn* ACROSS, crossways, crosswise
atmosphere *Syn* AURA, air, climate, flavor, mood, note, temper
atom *Syn* PARTICLE, bit, iota, jot, mite, smidgen, tittle, whit
atomic *Syn* TINY, bitty, infinitesimal, microminiature, microscopic, miniature, minute, teeny, teeny-weeny, wee *Ant* astronomical, colossal, cosmic, elephantine, enormous, giant, gigantic, herculean, heroic, huge, immense, mammoth, massive, monster, monstrous, monumental, mountainous, prodigious, titanic, tremendous
atrabilious *Syn* MELANCHOLIC, hypochondriac, melancholy
atrocious *Syn* OUTRAGEOUS, heinous, monstrous
attach **1** *Syn* ARREST (sense 2), apprehend, detain **2** *Syn* FASTEN, affix, fix *Ant* loose, loosen, unfasten **3** *Syn* APPOINT (sense 2), assign, commission, constitute, designate, detail, name *Ant* discharge, dismiss, expel, fire
attachment **1** · the feeling which animates a person who is genuinely fond of someone or something *Syn* affection, love *Rel* devotedness, fondness *Ant* aversion **2** *Syn* ARREST, apprehension, detention
attack *n* **1** · an attempt made on another or on others to injure, destroy, or defame *Syn* assault, onset, onslaught *Rel* action, battle **2** · the act or action of setting upon with force or violence *Syn* aggression, assault, blitzkrieg, charge, descent, offense (*or* offence), offensive, onset, onslaught, raid, rush, strike *Rel* ambuscade, ambush **3** · a sudden experiencing of a physical or mental disorder *Syn* bout, case, fit, seizure, siege, spell *Rel* recurrence, relapse
attack *vb* **1** · to make an onslaught upon *Syn* assail, assault, bombard, storm *Rel* battle, contend, fight, war **2** · to criticize harshly and usually publicly *Syn* abuse, assail, belabor, blast, castigate, excoriate, jump (on), lambaste (*or* lambast), scathe, slam, vituperate *Rel* berate, harangue, harass, harry, revile, scold
attain **1** *Syn* EARN, acquire, capture, carry, draw, gain, garner, get, land, make, obtain, procure, realize, secure, win *Ant* forfeit, lose **2** *Syn* REACH, achieve, compass, gain
attainment **1** *Syn* ACQUIREMENT, accomplishment, acquisition **2** *Syn* FRUITION, accomplishment, achievement, actuality, consummation, fulfillment, realization *Ant* naught, nonfulfillment
attempt *n* · an effort to do or accomplish something *Syn* crack, endeavor, essay, fling, go, pass, shot, stab, trial, try, whack *Rel* bid, striving, struggle, throes, undertaking
attempt *vb* · to make an effort to do *Syn* assay, endeavor, essay, seek, strive, try *Rel* fight, strain, struggle, toil, trouble, work
attend **1** *Syn* ACCOMPANY, chaperone (*or* chaperon), convoy, escort, squire **2** *Syn* LISTEN, hark, hear, hearken, heed, mind *Ant* ignore, tune out **3** *Syn* TEND, mind, watch
attendant *Syn* ESCORT, companion, guard, guide
attention **1** · the direct focusing of the mind especially on something to be learned, worked out, or dealt with *Syn* application, concentration, study *Rel* assiduity, diligence, industriousness, sedulousness *Ant* inattention **2** · a state of being aware *Syn* awareness, cognizance, ear, eye, heed, notice, observance, observation *Rel* advisement, care, concern, consideration, regard, watch **3** *Syn* COURTESY, amenity, gallantry *Ant* discourtesy
attentiveness *Syn* VIGILANCE, alertness, lookout, surveillance, watch, watchfulness
attenuate *Syn* THIN, dilute, extenuate, rarefy *Ant* thicken

THESAURUS

attest 1 *Syn* CERTIFY, vouch, witness 2 *Syn* INDICATE, argue, bespeak, betoken, prove 3 *Syn* TESTIFY, depose, swear, witness
attire *vb Syn* CLOTHE, apparel, array, dress, robe *Ant* unclothe
attire *n Syn* CLOTHES, apparel, clothing, dress, raiment
attitude 1 *Syn* POSITION, stand 2 *Syn* POSTURE, pose
attorney 1 *Syn* AGENT (sense 1), commissary, delegate, deputy, envoy, factor, procurator, proxy, representative 2 *Syn* LAWYER, advocate, barrister, counsel, counselor, solicitor
attract • to draw another by exerting an irresistible or compelling influence *Syn* allure, bewitch, captivate, charm, enchant, fascinate *Rel* court, invite, solicit *Ant* repel
attraction • the relationship between persons or things that are involuntarily or naturally drawn together *Syn* affinity, sympathy
attractive 1 • drawing another by exerting a compelling influence *Syn* alluring, bewitching, captivating, charming, enchanting, fascinating *Rel* beautiful, bonny, comely, fair, lovely, pretty *Ant* forbidding, repellent 2 *Syn* BEAUTIFUL, beauteous, comely, cute, fair, gorgeous, handsome, knockout, lovely, pretty, ravishing, sightly, stunning, taking *Ant* homely, ill-favored, plain, ugly, unattractive, unbeautiful, unhandsome, unlovely, unpretty, unsightly
attribute *vb Syn* ASCRIBE, accredit, assign, charge, credit, impute, refer
attribute *n* 1 *Syn* CHARACTERISTIC, character, feature, mark, peculiarity, point, property, quality, trait 2 *Syn* SYMBOL, emblem, type
attrition *Syn* PENITENCE, compunction, contrition, remorse, repentance
attune *Syn* HARMONIZE, tune
atypical *Syn* DEVIANT, aberrant, abnormal, anomalous, irregular, unnatural *Ant* natural, normal, regular, standard, typical
audacious *Syn* BRAVE, bold, courageous, dauntless, doughty, fearless, intrepid, unafraid, undaunted, valiant, valorous *Ant* craven
audacity *Syn* EFFRONTERY, brashness, brass, brassiness, brazenness, cheek, cheekiness, chutzpah, gall, nerve, nerviness, pertness, presumption, presumptuousness, sauce, sauciness, temerity
audibly *Syn* ALOUD, out, out loud *Ant* inaudibly, silently, soundlessly
audit *n Syn* INSPECTION, check, checkup, examination, review, scan, scrutiny, survey
audit *vb Syn* SCRUTINIZE, examine, inspect, scan
auditory • of, relating to, or experienced through the sense of hearing *Syn* acoustic (*or* acoustical), aural, auricular *Rel* audible, clear, discernible, distinct, distinguishable, heard, perceptible
augment *Syn* INCREASE (sense 1), add (to), aggrandize, amplify, boost, compound, enlarge, escalate, expand, extend, multiply, raise, swell, up *Ant* abate, contract, decrease, diminish, lessen, lower, reduce, subtract (from)
augur *vb Syn* FORETELL, forebode, forecast, portend, predict, presage, prognosticate, prophesy
augur *n Syn* PROPHET, diviner, forecaster, foreseer, foreteller, fortune-teller, futurist, prognosticator, prophesier, seer, soothsayer
auguring *Syn* PREDICTION, cast, forecast, forecasting, foretelling, predicting, presaging, prognosis, prognosticating, prognostication, prophecy, soothsaying
augury *Syn* OMEN, auspice, boding, foreboding, foreshadowing, portent, prefiguring, presage
august 1 *Syn* DIGNIFIED, imposing, solemn, staid, stately *Ant* flighty, frivolous, giddy, goofy, silly, undignified 2 *Syn* GRAND, grandiose, imposing, magnificent, majestic, noble, stately
augustness *Syn* MAGNIFICENCE, brilliance, gloriousness, glory, grandeur, grandness, majesty, nobility, nobleness, resplendence, splendor, stateliness, stupendousness, sublimeness, superbness
auld lang syne *Syn* PAST, history, yesterday, yesteryear, yore
aura • a special quality or impression associated with something *Syn* air, atmosphere, climate, flavor, mood, note, temper *Rel* feel, feeling, sensation, sense, spirit
aural *Syn* AUDITORY, acoustic (*or* acoustical), auricular
aureate *Syn* RHETORICAL, bombastic, euphuistic, flowery, grandiloquent, magniloquent
au revoir *Syn* GOOD-BYE, adieu, bon voyage, farewell, Godspeed *Ant* hello
auricular *Syn* AUDITORY, acoustic (*or* acoustical), aural
auspice *Syn* OMEN, augury, boding, foreboding, foreshadowing, portent, prefiguring, presage
auspicious *Syn* FAVORABLE, benign, propitious *Ant* antagonistic, unfavorable
austere *Syn* SEVERE, ascetic, stern *Ant* tender, tolerant
autarchic *Syn* FREE, autarkic, autonomous, independent, sovereign *Ant* bond
autarchy *Syn* FREEDOM (sense 1), autarky, autonomy, independence, sovereignty *Ant* bondage
autarkic *Syn* FREE, autarchic, autonomous, independent, sovereign *Ant* bond
autarky *Syn* FREEDOM (sense 1), autarchy, autonomy, independence, sovereignty *Ant* bondage
authentic • being exactly as appears or is claimed *Syn* bona fide, genuine, veritable *Rel* authoritarian, dictatorial *Ant* spurious

authenticate *Syn* CONFIRM, corroborate, substantiate, validate, verify *Ant* contradict, deny
author *Syn* MAKER, creator
authoritarian **1** *Syn* BOSSY, autocratic, despotic, dictatorial, domineering, imperious, masterful, overbearing, peremptory, tyrannical, tyrannous **2** *Syn* DICTATORIAL, doctrinaire, dogmatic, magisterial
authority **1** *Syn* EXPERT, ace, adept, artist, crackerjack, maestro, master, past master, scholar, shark, virtuoso, whiz, wizard *Ant* amateur **2** *Syn* INFLUENCE, credit, prestige, weight **3** *Syn* RULE (sense 2), administration, governance, government, jurisdiction, regime, regimen
authorization *Syn* PERMISSION, allowance, clearance, concurrence, consent, granting, leave, license (*or* licence), sanction, sufferance *Ant* interdiction, prohibition, proscription
authorize • to invest with power or the right to act *Syn* accredit, commission, license *Rel* empower, enable
autobiography *Syn* BIOGRAPHY, confessions, life, memoir
autochthonous *Syn* NATIVE, aboriginal, endemic, indigenous *Ant* alien, foreign
autocrat *Syn* MONARCH, ruler, sovereign
autocratic **1** *Syn* ABSOLUTE, arbitrary, despotic, tyrannical, tyrannous *Ant* limited, restrained **2** *Syn* BOSSY, authoritarian, despotic, dictatorial, domineering, imperious, masterful, overbearing, peremptory, tyrannical, tyrannous
automatic *Syn* SPONTANEOUS, impulsive, instinctive, mechanical
autonomous *Syn* FREE, autarchic, autarkic, independent, sovereign *Ant* bond
autonomy *Syn* FREEDOM (sense 1), autarchy, autarky, independence, sovereignty *Ant* bondage
autopsy • examination of a dead body especially to find out the cause of death *Syn* postmortem, postmortem examination *Rel* dissection
auxiliary • supplying aid or support *Syn* accessory, adjuvant, ancillary, contributory, subservient, subsidiary *Rel* secondary, subordinate, tributary
avail *n* **1** *Syn* BENEFIT, profit *Ant* harm **2** *Syn* USE (sense 1), account, advantage, profit, service
avail *vb Syn* USE, apply, employ, utilize
avarice *Syn* GREED, acquisitiveness, avariciousness, avidity, covetousness, cupidity, greediness, rapaciousness, rapacity
avaricious *Syn* COVETOUS, acquisitive, grasping, greedy
avariciousness *Syn* GREED, acquisitiveness, avarice, avidity, covetousness, cupidity, greediness, rapaciousness, rapacity
avenge • to punish in kind the wrongdoer responsible *Syn* retaliate, revenge *Rel* castigate, chasten, chastise, discipline, penalize, punish, scourge
aver *Syn* ASSERT, affirm, avouch, avow, declare, predicate, profess, protest, warrant *Ant* controvert, deny
average **1** • what is typical of a group, class, or series *Syn* norm, normal, par, standard *Rel* golden mean, mean, median, middle **2** *Syn* MEDIUM, fair, indifferent, mediocre, middling, moderate, second-rate
averse **1** *Syn* ANTIPATHETIC, allergic **2** *Syn* DISINCLINED, hesitant, indisposed, loath, reluctant
aversion **1** *Syn* DISGUST, distaste, loathing, nausea, repugnance, repulsion, revulsion **2** *Syn* DISLIKE, disfavor, distaste *Ant* liking
avert **1** *Syn* PREVENT (sense 2), forestall, help, obviate, preclude **2** *Syn* TURN (sense 2), deflect, divert, sheer
avid *Syn* EAGER, agog, anxious, athirst, keen *Ant* listless
avidity *Syn* GREED, acquisitiveness, avarice, avariciousness, covetousness, cupidity, greediness, rapaciousness, rapacity
avoid *Syn* ESCAPE (sense 2), elude, eschew, evade, shun
avouch *Syn* ASSERT, affirm, aver, avow, declare, predicate, profess, protest, warrant *Ant* controvert, deny
avow *Syn* ASSERT, affirm, aver, avouch, declare, predicate, profess, protest, warrant *Ant* controvert, deny
avowal *Syn* CONFESSION, acknowledgment, admission, concession
await *Syn* EXPECT, hope, look *Ant* despair of
awake **1** *Syn* AWARE, alive, cognizant, conscious, sensible *Ant* unaware **2** *Syn* WAKEFUL, sleepless, wide-awake *Ant* asleep, dormant, dozing, napping, resting, sleeping, slumbering
awaken *Syn* STIR, arouse, rally, rouse, waken
award *n* • something given in recognition of achievement *Syn* decoration, distinction, honor, plume, premium, prize *Rel* badge, crown, cup, laurel, medal, order, ribbon, trophy
award *vb Syn* GRANT (sense 1), accord, concede, vouchsafe
aware **1** • having knowledge of something *Syn* alive, awake, cognizant, conscious, sensible *Rel* certain, positive, sure *Ant* unaware **2** *Syn* CONSCIOUS, alive, cognizant, mindful, sensible, sentient *Ant* insensible, unaware, unconscious, unmindful
awareness *Syn* ATTENTION (sense 2), cognizance, ear, eye, heed, notice, observance, observation
awe **1** *Syn* REVERENCE (sense 2), fear **2** *Syn* WONDER (sense 2), admiration, amazement, wonderment
awful *adj Syn* FEARFUL (sense 2), appalling, dreadful, frightful, horrible, horrific, shocking, terrible, terrific

awful *adv Syn* VERY, awfully, beastly, deadly, especially, exceedingly, extra, extremely, far, frightfully, full, greatly, heavily, highly, hugely, jolly, mightily, mighty, mortally, most, much, particularly, rattling, real, right, so, something, super, terribly, too, whacking *Ant* little, negligibly, nominally, slightly

awfully *Syn* VERY, awful, beastly, deadly, especially, exceedingly, extra, extremely, far, frightfully, full, greatly, heavily, highly, hugely, jolly, mightily, mighty, mortally, most, much, particularly, rattling, real, right, so, something, super, terribly, too, whacking *Ant* little, negligibly, nominally, slightly

awkward **1** • not marked by ease (as of performance, movement, or social conduct) *Syn* clumsy, gauche, inept, maladroit *Rel* rigid, stiff, wooden *Ant* deft, graceful, handy **2** *Syn* CUMBERSOME, clumsy, cranky, cumbrous, ungainly, unhandy, unwieldy *Ant* handy

awning *Syn* CANOPY, ceiling, roof, tent

awry *adj* • inclined or twisted to one side *Syn* askew, aslant, cockeyed, crooked, listing, lopsided, oblique, skewed, slanted, slanting, slantwise, tilted, tipping, uneven *Rel* asymmetrical (*or* asymmetric), contorted, disordered, distorted, irregular, unbalanced, unsymmetrical *Ant* even, level, straight

awry *adv Syn* WRONG, afield, amiss, astray *Ant* aright, right, well

axiom *Syn* PRINCIPLE, fundamental, law, theorem

B

babble *Syn* CHAT, blab, cackle, chatter, converse, gab, gabble, gas, jabber, jaw, palaver, patter, prate, prattle, rap, rattle, run on, talk, twitter, visit

babe *Syn* BABY, child, infant, newborn

babel **1** *Syn* DIN, clamor, hubbub, hullabaloo, pandemonium, racket, uproar *Ant* quiet **2** *Syn* MADHOUSE, bedlam, circus, hell

babushka *Syn* BANDANNA, handkerchief, kerchief, mantilla

baby *n* • a recently born person *Syn* babe, child, infant, newborn *Rel* cherub

baby *vb* • to treat with great or excessive care *Syn* coddle, dandle, mollycoddle, nurse, pamper, spoil *Rel* cater (to), humor, indulge *Ant* discipline

babyish *Syn* CHILDISH, adolescent, immature, infantile, juvenile, kiddish, puerile *Ant* adult, grown-up, mature

back *adj* • being at or in the part of something opposite the front part *Syn* hind, hindmost, posterior, rear, rearward *Ant* anterior, fore, forward, front

back *vb* **1** *Syn* RECEDE, retract, retreat, retrograde *Ant* advance, proceed **2** *Syn* SUPPORT (sense 2), advocate, champion, uphold

back *n Syn* SPINE, backbone, chine, vertebrae

backbiting *Syn* DETRACTION, calumny, scandal, slander

backbone **1** *Syn* SPINE, back, chine, vertebrae **2** *Syn* FORTITUDE, grit, guts, pluck, sand *Ant* pusillanimity

back down *Syn* RENEGE, back off, cop out

backdrop *Syn* BACKGROUND, environment, milieu, mise-en-scène, setting

backer **1** *Syn* ALLY, abettor, confederate, supporter, sympathizer **2** *Syn* EXPONENT, advocate, apostle, booster, champion, friend, promoter, proponent, supporter *Ant* adversary, antagonist, opponent **3** *Syn* SPONSOR, angel, guarantor, patron, surety

background • the place, time, and circumstances in which something occurs *Syn* backdrop, environment, milieu, mise-en-scène, setting

backhanded *Syn* INSINCERE, artificial, double-dealing, feigned, hypocritical, left-handed, mealy, mealymouthed, two-faced, unctuous *Ant* genuine, heartfelt, honest, sincere, unfeigned

back off *Syn* RENEGE, back down, cop out

backside *Syn* BUTTOCKS, bottom, breech, butt, fanny, hams, haunches, posterior, rear, rump, seat

backslide *Syn* LAPSE, relapse

backslider *Syn* RENEGADE, apostate, recreant, turncoat *Ant* adherent, loyalist

back talk • disrespectful or argumentative talk given in response to a command or request *Syn* cheek, impertinence, impudence, insolence, sass, sauce *Rel* comeback, rejoinder, retort, riposte, wisecrack

backup *Syn* SUBSTITUTE, pinch hitter, relief, replacement, reserve, stand-in, sub

backward • not moving or going ahead *Syn* regressive, retrograde, retrogressive *Rel* dilatory, laggard, slow *Ant* advanced

backwater *Syn* FRONTIER, backwoods, bush, hinterland, up-country

backwoods *Syn* FRONTIER, backwater, bush, hinterland, up-country

bad *adj* **1** • deviating from the dictates of moral law *Syn* evil, ill, naughty, wicked *Rel* iniquitous, vicious, villainous *Ant* good

2 • not measuring up to a standard of what is satisfactory *Syn* poor, wrong *Ant* good **3** *Syn* FAULTY, defective, flawed, imperfect *Ant* faultless, flawless, impeccable, perfect **4** *Syn* HARMFUL, adverse, baleful, baneful, damaging, deleterious, detrimental, evil, hurtful, ill, injurious, mischievous, noxious, pernicious, prejudicial *Ant* harmless, innocent, innocuous, inoffensive, safe **5** *Syn* SAD (sense 1), blue, brokenhearted, crestfallen, dejected, depressed, despondent, disconsolate, doleful, down, downcast, downhearted, droopy, forlorn, gloomy, glum, heartbroken, heartsick, heartsore, inconsolable, joyless, low, low-spirited, melancholy, miserable, mournful, saddened, sorrowful, sorry, unhappy, woebegone, woeful, wretched *Ant* blissful, buoyant, buoyed, cheerful, cheery, chipper, delighted, glad, gladdened, gladsome, gleeful, happy, joyful, joyous, jubilant, sunny, upbeat **6** *Syn* UNPLEASANT, disagreeable, displeasing, distasteful, nasty, rotten, sour, uncongenial, unlovely, unpleasing, unsatisfying, unwelcome *Ant* agreeable, congenial, good, grateful, gratifying, nice, palatable, pleasant, pleasing, pleasurable, satisfying, welcome

bad *n Syn* EVIL, evildoing, ill, immorality, iniquity, sin, villainy, wrong *Ant* good, morality, right, virtue

badge *Syn* SIGN (sense 1), mark, note, symptom, token

badger *Syn* BAIT, chivy, heckle, hector, hound, ride

badlands *Syn* WASTE, desert, wilderness

badly • in an unsatisfactory way *Syn* inadequately, poorly, unacceptably, unsatisfactorily *Rel* rottenly *Ant* acceptably, adequately, all right, fine, good, palatably, passably, so-so, tolerably

baffle *Syn* FRUSTRATE, balk, circumvent, foil, outwit, thwart *Ant* fulfill

bag *n* **1** • a container made of a flexible material and open or opening at the top *Syn* pouch, sack **2** *Syn* PURSE, handbag, pocketbook

bag *vb Syn* CATCH, capture, ensnare, entrap, snare, trap *Ant* miss

bail *vb Syn* DIP (sense 2), dish, ladle, scoop, spoon

bail *n Syn* GUARANTEE, bond, guaranty, security, surety

bailiwick *Syn* FIELD, domain, province, sphere, territory

bait • to persist in tormenting or harassing another *Syn* badger, chivy, heckle, hector, hound, ride *Rel* annoy, harass, harry, worry

bake *Syn* DRY, dehydrate, desiccate, parch *Ant* moisten, wet

balance *n* **1** • the stability or efficiency resulting from the equalization or exact adjustment of opposing forces *Syn* equilibrium, equipoise, poise, tension **2** *Syn* REMAINDER, leavings, remains, remnant, residue, residuum, rest **3** *Syn* SYMMETRY, harmony, proportion

balance *vb* **1** *Syn* COMPENSATE, counterbalance, counterpoise, countervail, offset **2** *Syn* EQUALIZE, equate, even, level **3** *Syn* STABILIZE, ballast, poise, steady, trim

balanced *Syn* SANE, clearheaded, lucid, normal, right, stable *Ant* crazed, crazy, demented, deranged, insane, lunatic, mad, maniacal, mental, unbalanced, unsound

bald *Syn* BARE, barren, naked, nude *Ant* covered

balderdash *Syn* NONSENSE, bull, bunk, drivel, gobbledygook, poppycock, rot, trash, twaddle

bale *Syn* BUNDLE, bunch, pack, package, packet, parcel

baleful **1** *Syn* DEADLY, deathly, fatal, fell, killer, lethal, mortal, murderous, pestilent, vital *Ant* healthful, healthy, nonfatal, nonlethal, wholesome **2** *Syn* HARMFUL, adverse, bad, baneful, damaging, deleterious, detrimental, evil, hurtful, ill, injurious, mischievous, noxious, pernicious, prejudicial *Ant* harmless, innocent, innocuous, inoffensive, safe **3** *Syn* OMINOUS, dire, foreboding, inauspicious, menacing, portentous, sinister, threatening **4** *Syn* SINISTER, malefic, maleficent, malign

balk **1** *Syn* DEMUR, boggle, jib, scruple, shy, stick, stickle, strain *Ant* accede **2** *Syn* FRUSTRATE, baffle, circumvent, foil, outwit, thwart *Ant* fulfill

balky **1** *Syn* CONTRARY, froward, perverse, restive, wayward *Ant* complaisant, good-natured **2** *Syn* DISOBEDIENT, contrary, defiant, froward, insubordinate, intractable, rebellious, recalcitrant, refractory, restive, ungovernable, unruly, untoward, wayward, willful (*or* wilful) *Ant* amenable, compliant, docile, obedient, tractable

ball *Syn* DANCE, cotillion, formal, hop, prom

ballast *Syn* STABILIZE, balance, poise, steady, trim

balloon *Syn* INCREASE (sense 2), accumulate, appreciate, build (up), burgeon, enlarge, escalate, expand, mount, multiply, mushroom, proliferate, rise, snowball, swell, wax *Ant* contract, decrease, diminish, lessen, wane

ballot *Syn* SUFFRAGE, franchise, vote

ballyhoo *Syn* PUBLICITY, promotion, propaganda

balmy **1** *Syn* CLEMENT, equable, gentle, mild, moderate, temperate *Ant* harsh, inclement, intemperate, severe **2** *Syn* ODOROUS, aromatic, fragrant, redolent *Ant* malodorous, odorless **3** *Syn* SOFT, bland, gentle, lenient, mild, smooth *Ant* hard, stern

balustrade *Syn* RAILING, banister, guardrail, rail

bamboozle *Syn* DUPE, befool, gull, hoax, hoodwink, trick

ban *n Syn* PROHIBITION (sense 2), embargo, interdict, interdiction, proscription, veto *Ant* prescription
ban *vb Syn* FORBID, bar, enjoin, interdict, outlaw, prohibit, proscribe *Ant* allow, let, permit, suffer
banal **1** *Syn* INSIPID, flat, inane, jejune, vapid, wishy-washy *Ant* sapid, zestful **2** *Syn* STALE, commonplace, hackney, hackneyed, moth-eaten, musty, stereotyped, threadbare, tired, trite *Ant* fresh, new, original
band *vb Syn* ALLY, associate, club, confederate, conjoin, cooperate, federate, league, unite *Ant* break up, disband
band *n* **1** *Syn* BOND, tie **2** *Syn* COMPANY, party, troop, troupe **3** *Syn* STRIP, fillet, ribbon, stripe
bandanna *or* **bandana** • a scarf worn on the head *Syn* babushka, handkerchief, kerchief, mantilla *Rel* shawl
bandwagon *Syn* CAMPAIGN, cause, crusade, drive, movement
bandy *Syn* EXCHANGE, interchange
bane *Syn* POISON, toxin, venom, virus
baneful *Syn* HARMFUL, adverse, bad, baleful, damaging, deleterious, detrimental, evil, hurtful, ill, injurious, mischievous, noxious, pernicious, prejudicial *Ant* harmless, innocent, innocuous, inoffensive, safe
bang *Syn* THRILL, exhilaration, kick, titillation
bangle *Syn* PENDANT, charm, lavalier
bang-up *Syn* EXCELLENT, A1, banner, capital, classic, crackerjack, dandy, divine, fabulous, fine, first-class, first-rate, grand, great, groovy, heavenly, jim-dandy, keen, marvelous (*or* marvellous), mean, neat, nifty, noble, par excellence, prime, sensational, splendid, stellar, sterling, superb, superior, superlative, supernal, swell, terrific, tip-top, top, top-notch, unsurpassed, wonderful *Ant* poor
banish • to remove by authority or force from a country, state, or sovereignty *Syn* deport, exile, expatriate, extradite, ostracize, transport *Rel* eject, expel, oust
banister *Syn* RAILING, balustrade, guardrail, rail
bank *n* **1** *Syn* HEAP, cock, mass, pile, shock, stack **2** *Syn* SHOAL, bar, reef **3** *Syn* SHORE, beach, coast, foreshore, littoral, strand
bank *vb* **1** *Syn* HEAP, cock, mass, pile, shock, stack **2** *Syn* RELY (ON), count, depend, reckon, trust
banner *adj Syn* EXCELLENT, A1, bang-up, capital, classic, crackerjack, dandy, divine, fabulous, fine, first-class, first-rate, grand, great, groovy, heavenly, jim-dandy, keen, marvelous (*or* marvellous), mean, neat, nifty, noble, par excellence, prime, sensational, splendid, stellar, sterling, superb, superior, superlative, supernal, swell, terrific, tip-top, top, top-notch, unsurpassed, wonderful *Ant* poor
banner *n Syn* FLAG, color, ensign, jack, pendant, pennant, pennon, standard, streamer
banning *Syn* PROHIBITION (sense 1), barring, enjoining, forbidding, interdicting, interdiction, outlawing, prohibiting, proscribing, proscription *Ant* prescription
banquet *Syn* DINNER, feast
banter *n* • good-natured teasing or exchanging of clever remarks *Syn* chaff, give-and-take, jesting, joshing, persiflage, raillery, repartee *Rel* barb, crack, dig, gag, jest, joke, quip, sally, wisecrack, witticism
banter *vb* **1** • to make fun of good-naturedly *Syn* chaff, jolly, josh, kid, rag, rib *Rel* deride, rally, ridicule, twit **2** *Syn* JOKE, fool, fun, jest, jive, josh, kid, quip, wisecrack
bar *n* **1** *Syn* ENCUMBRANCE, block, chain, clog, crimp, deterrent, drag, embarrassment, fetter, handicap, hindrance, hurdle, impediment, inhibition, interference, let, manacle, obstacle, obstruction, shackles, stop, stumbling block, trammel *Ant* aid, assistance, benefit, help **2** *Syn* BARROOM, café, groggery, grogshop, pub, saloon, tavern **3** *Syn* SHOAL, bank, reef
bar *vb* **1** *Syn* FORBID, ban, enjoin, interdict, outlaw, prohibit, proscribe *Ant* allow, let, permit, suffer **2** *Syn* HINDER, block, dam, impede, obstruct *Ant* further
barb *Syn* INSULT, affront, dart, dig, epithet, indignity, name, offense (*or* offence), outrage, put-down, sarcasm, slight, slur
barbarian • of, relating to, or characteristic of people that are not fully civilized *Syn* barbaric, barbarous, savage *Ant* civilized
barbaric *Syn* BARBARIAN, barbarous, savage *Ant* civilized
barbarism • a word or expression which offends against standards of correctness *Syn* corruption, impropriety, solecism, vernacularism, vulgarism
barbarity *Syn* CRUELTY, brutality, cruelness, heartlessness, inhumanity, sadism, savageness, savagery, viciousness, wantonness *Ant* benignity, compassion, good-heartedness, humanity, kindheartedness, kindness, sympathy
barbarous **1** *Syn* BARBARIAN, barbaric, savage *Ant* civilized **2** *Syn* FIERCE, cruel, fell, ferocious, inhuman, savage, truculent *Ant* mild, tame
bard *Syn* POET, minstrel, poetaster, rhymer, rhymester, troubadour, versifier
bare *adj* **1** • lacking naturally or conventionally appropriate covering or clothing *Syn* bald, barren, naked, nude *Rel* denuded, divested, stripped *Ant* covered **2** *Syn* MERE, very
bare *vb Syn* STRIP, denude, dismantle, divest *Ant* furnish, invest
barefaced *Syn* SHAMELESS, brash, brazen, impudent
bareness *Syn* VACANCY (sense 2), emptiness, vacuity *Ant* fullness

bargain *vb* • to talk over or dispute the terms of a purchase *Syn* chaffer, deal, dicker, haggle, horse-trade, negotiate, palter *Rel* argue, bicker, clash, quibble, squabble, wrangle
bargain *n Syn* CONTRACT, cartel, compact, concordat, convention, entente, pact, treaty
bark *vb* • to make the sound of or a sound suggestive of a dog *Syn* bay, growl, howl, snarl, yap, yelp *Rel* bawl, bellow, roar, vociferate
bark *n Syn* SKIN, hide, peel, pelt, rind
baroque *Syn* ORNATE, flamboyant, florid, rococo *Ant* austere, chaste
barrage • a rapid or overwhelming outpouring of many things at once *Syn* bombardment, cannonade, fusillade, hail, salvo, shower, storm, volley *Rel* broadside, burst, deluge, flood, flood tide, flush, gush, inundation, outburst, outflow, outpouring, overflow, spate, surge, torrent
barrel *n Syn* CASK, firkin, hogshead, keg, pipe, puncheon
barrel *vb Syn* HURRY (sense 2), bolt, bowl, breeze, career, course, dash, fly, hasten, hotfoot (it), hump, hurtle, hustle, pelt, race, rip, rocket, run, rush, rustle, scoot, scurry, scuttle, shoot, speed, step (along), tear, trot, whirl, whisk, zip, zoom *Ant* crawl, creep, poke
barren **1** *Syn* BARE, bald, naked, nude *Ant* covered **2** *Syn* STERILE, impotent, infertile, unfruitful *Ant* exuberant, fertile
barricade *Syn* BARRIER, fence, hedge, wall
barrier • a physical object that blocks the way *Syn* barricade, fence, hedge, wall *Rel* bar, encumbrance, handicap, hindrance, hurdle, impediment, obstacle, obstruction, roadblock, stop
barring *Syn* PROHIBITION (sense 1), banning, enjoining, forbidding, interdicting, interdiction, outlawing, prohibiting, proscribing, proscription *Ant* prescription
barrister *Syn* LAWYER, advocate, attorney, counsel, counselor, solicitor
barroom • a place of business where alcoholic beverages are sold to be consumed on the premises *Syn* bar, café, groggery, grogshop, pub, saloon, tavern *Rel* cabaret, dive, joint, nightclub, roadhouse, speakeasy
basal *Syn* FUNDAMENTAL, basic, radical, underlying
base *adj* • deserving of contempt because of the absence of higher values *Syn* low, vile *Rel* abject, ignoble, mean, sordid *Ant* noble
base *n* **1** • something on which another thing is reared or built or by which it is supported or fixed in place *Syn* basis, foundation, ground, groundwork *Ant* top **2** *Syn* CENTER (sense 2), capital, core, cynosure, eye, focus, heart, hub, mecca, nucleus, seat
base *vb* • to supply or to serve as a basis *Syn* found, ground, rest, stay *Rel* support, sustain
baseless • not justified or justifiable in any way *Syn* groundless, unfounded, unwarranted *Rel* false, wrong
bashful *Syn* SHY, coy, diffident, modest *Ant* obtrusive
basic **1** *Syn* ELEMENTARY, elemental, essential, fundamental, rudimentary, underlying *Ant* advanced **2** *Syn* FUNDAMENTAL, basal, radical, underlying
basically *Syn* CHIEFLY, altogether, by and large, generally, largely, mainly, mostly, overall, predominantly, primarily, principally, substantially
basis *Syn* BASE, foundation, ground, groundwork *Ant* top
baste *Syn* BEAT, belabor, buffet, pound, pummel, thrash
bastion *Syn* BULWARK, breastwork, parapet, rampart
bathe *Syn* WET, douse, drench, soak, souse, wash, water *Ant* dry
batter *Syn* MAIM, cripple, mangle, mutilate
battle *n* • a hostile meeting between opposing military forces *Syn* action, engagement *Rel* brush, encounter, skirmish
battle *vb Syn* CONTEND, fight, war
bauble *Syn* KNICKKNACK, curio, curiosity, gaud, gewgaw, novelty, ornamental, trinket
bawl *vb* **1** *Syn* ROAR, bellow, bluster, clamor, howl, ululate, vociferate **2** *Syn* SCOLD, berate, chew out, jaw, rail, rate, revile, tongue-lash, upbraid, vituperate, wig
bawl *n Syn* ROAR, bellow, bluster, ululation, vociferation
bay *vb Syn* BARK, growl, howl, snarl, yap, yelp
bay *n Syn* COMPARTMENT, cabin, cell, chamber, cubicle
bazaar *Syn* STORE, emporium, shop
be • to have actuality or reality *Syn* exist, live, subsist
beach *Syn* SHORE, bank, coast, foreshore, littoral, strand
beached *Syn* AGROUND, grounded, stranded *Ant* afloat
beak *Syn* BILL, neb, nib
beaming *Syn* BRIGHT, brilliant, effulgent, incandescent, lambent, lucent, luminous, lustrous, radiant, refulgent *Ant* dim, dull
bear *vb* **1** • to bring forth as products *Syn* produce, turn out, yield *Rel* breed, generate, propagate, reproduce **2** • to sustain something trying or painful *Syn* abide, brook, endure, stand, suffer, tolerate *Rel* accept, receive **3** • to have a connection especially logically *Syn* appertain, apply, belong, pertain, relate *Rel* affect, concern **4** *Syn* CARRY, convey, transmit, transport **5** *Syn* PRESS, bear down, crowd, jam, squeeze
bear *n Syn* GROUCH, complainer, crab, crank, croaker, curmudgeon, fusser, griper, grouser, growler, grumbler, grump, murmurer, mutterer, whiner

bearable • capable of being endured *Syn* endurable, sufferable, supportable, sustainable, tolerable *Rel* acceptable, allowable, livable, reasonable *Ant* insufferable, insupportable, intolerable, unbearable, unendurable, unsupportable

beard *Syn* FACE, brave, challenge, dare, defy *Ant* avoid

bear down *Syn* PRESS, bear, crowd, jam, squeeze

bearing • the way in which or the quality by which a person outwardly manifests personality *Syn* demeanor, deportment, mien, port, presence *Rel* attitude, pose, posture

beast *Syn* ANIMAL, brute, creature, critter

beastly *adj Syn* BRUTAL, bestial, brute, brutish, feral

beastly *adv Syn* VERY, awful, awfully, deadly, especially, exceedingly, extra, extremely, far, frightfully, full, greatly, heavily, highly, hugely, jolly, mightily, mighty, mortally, most, much, particularly, rattling, real, right, so, something, super, terribly, too, whacking *Ant* little, negligibly, nominally, slightly

beat *vb* **1** • to strike repeatedly *Syn* baste, belabor, buffet, pound, pummel, thrash *Rel* box, clout, cuff, hit, punch, slap, slug, smite, strike, swat **2** *Syn* CONQUER, defeat, lick, overcome, overthrow, reduce, rout, subdue, subjugate, surmount, vanquish **3** *Syn* PULSATE, palpitate, pulse, throb

beat *n* **1** *Syn* PULSATION, palpitation, pulse, throb **2** *Syn* RHYTHM, cadence, measure, meter

beatitude *Syn* HAPPINESS, blessedness, bliss, felicity *Ant* unhappiness

beau **1** *Syn* BOYFRIEND, fellow, man, swain **2** *Syn* FOP, buck, coxcomb, dandy, dude, exquisite

beau ideal *Syn* MODEL, example, exemplar, ideal, mirror, pattern, standard

beauteous *Syn* BEAUTIFUL, attractive, comely, cute, fair, gorgeous, handsome, knockout, lovely, pretty, ravishing, sightly, stunning, taking *Ant* homely, ill-favored, plain, ugly, unattractive, unbeautiful, unhandsome, unlovely, unpretty, unsightly

beautiful • very pleasing to look at *Syn* attractive, beauteous, comely, cute, fair, gorgeous, handsome, knockout, lovely, pretty, ravishing, sightly, stunning, taking *Rel* alluring, appealing, charming, dainty, delicate, delightful, elegant, exquisite, eye-catching, flawless, glamorous, glorious, perfect, personable, prepossessing, presentable, radiant, resplendent, splendid, statuesque, sublime, superb *Ant* homely, ill-favored, plain, ugly, unattractive, unbeautiful, unhandsome, unlovely, unpretty, unsightly

beautify *Syn* ADORN, bedeck, deck, decorate, embellish, garnish, ornament *Ant* disfigure

beauty *Syn* JIM-DANDY, corker, crackerjack, dandy, knockout, nifty, pip

because • for the reason that *Syn* as, for, inasmuch as, since

because of • as the result of *Syn* due to, owing to, through, with

beckon *Syn* MOTION, flag, gesture, signal, wave

becloud *Syn* OBSCURE, bedim, befog, cloud, darken, dim, eclipse, fog, obfuscate *Ant* illuminate, illumine

beclouded *Syn* OVERCAST, clouded, cloudy, dull, hazed, hazy, heavy, lowering, overclouded *Ant* clear, cloudless

become • to eventually have as a state or quality *Syn* come, get, go, grow, run, turn, wax *Rel* alter, change, metamorphose, modify, mutate, transfigure, transform, transmute

bedeck *Syn* ADORN, beautify, deck, decorate, embellish, garnish, ornament *Ant* disfigure

bedevil *Syn* AFFLICT, agonize, curse, harrow, martyr, persecute, plague, rack, torment, torture

bedim *Syn* OBSCURE, becloud, befog, cloud, darken, dim, eclipse, fog, obfuscate *Ant* illuminate, illumine

bedlam *Syn* MADHOUSE, babel, circus, hell

beef *Syn* COMPLAIN, bellyache, carp, crab, croak, fuss, gripe, grouse, growl, grumble, kick, moan, murmur, mutter, repine, squawk, wail, whine, yammer *Ant* rejoice

beetle *Syn* BULGE, jut, overhang, project, protrude, stick out

befall *Syn* HAPPEN, betide, chance, occur, transpire

befog *Syn* OBSCURE, becloud, bedim, cloud, darken, dim, eclipse, fog, obfuscate *Ant* illuminate, illumine

befool *Syn* DUPE, bamboozle, gull, hoax, hoodwink, trick

before • earlier than *Syn* ahead of, ere, of, previous to, prior to, to *Rel* till, until, up to *Ant* after, following

beforehand *Syn* EARLY, betimes, soon *Ant* late

befoul **1** *Syn* CONTAMINATE, defile, foul, poison, pollute, taint *Ant* decontaminate, purify **2** *Syn* DIRTY, begrime, besmirch, blacken, foul, grime, mire, muddy, smirch, smudge, soil, stain, sully *Ant* clean, cleanse

befuddle *Syn* CONFUSE, addle, fuddle, muddle *Ant* enlighten

beg • to ask or request urgently *Syn* adjure, beseech, entreat, implore, importune, supplicate *Rel* ask, request, solicit

beget *Syn* GENERATE, breed, engender, get, procreate, propagate, reproduce, sire

beggar • a person who lives by public begging *Syn* mendicant, panhandler *Rel* bum, drifter, hobo, tramp, vagabond, vagrant

beggarly *Syn* CONTEMPTIBLE, cheap, despicable, pitiable, scurvy, shabby, sorry *Ant* admirable, estimable, formidable

begin **1** • to come into existence *Syn* arise,

commence, dawn, form, materialize, originate, set in, spring, start *Rel* be, breathe, exist, live, subsist *Ant* cease, end, stop **2** • to take the first step in (a process or course of action) *Syn* commence, embark (on *or* upon), enter (into *or* upon), get off, kick off, launch, open, start, strike (into) *Rel* create, generate, inaugurate, initiate, innovate, invent, originate *Ant* conclude, end, finish, terminate

beginner • a person who is just starting out in a field of activity *Syn* colt, fledgling, freshman, greenhorn, neophyte, newbie, newcomer, novice, recruit, rookie, tenderfoot, tyro *Rel* amateur, apprentice, cub, dilettante, learner, probationer, student, trainee *Ant* old hand, old-timer, vet, veteran

beginning • the point at which something begins *Syn* alpha, birth, commencement, dawn, genesis, inception, incipiency, launch, morning, onset, outset, start, threshold *Rel* creation, inauguration, initiation, institution, origination *Ant* close, conclusion, end, ending

begrime *Syn* DIRTY, befoul, besmirch, blacken, foul, grime, mire, muddy, smirch, smudge, soil, stain, sully *Ant* clean, cleanse

begrudge *Syn* COVET, envy, grudge

beguile **1** *Syn* DECEIVE, betray, delude, double-cross, mislead *Ant* enlighten, undeceive **2** *Syn* LURE, allure, decoy, entice, lead on, seduce, tempt

behave **1** • to act or to cause oneself to do something in a certain way *Syn* acquit, comport, conduct, demean, deport, quit *Rel* bear, carry *Ant* misbehave **2** *Syn* ACT (sense 1), function, operate, react, work

behavior • one's actions in general or on a particular occasion *Syn* conduct, deportment *Rel* bearing, demeanor, mien

behemoth *Syn* GIANT, blockbuster, colossus, jumbo, leviathan, mammoth, monster, titan, whale, whopper *Ant* dwarf, midget, mini, miniature, peewee, pygmy, runt, shrimp

behest *Syn* COMMAND, bidding, dictate, injunction, mandate, order

behind *Syn* AFTER, following *Ant* ahead of, before, ere, previous to, prior to

behindhand *Syn* TARDY, late, overdue *Ant* prompt

behold *Syn* SEE (sense 1), contemplate, descry, discern, espy, note, notice, observe, perceive, remark, survey, view

beholder *Syn* SPECTATOR, bystander, eyewitness, kibitzer, looker-on, observer, onlooker, witness

being **1** *Syn* ENTITY, creature, individual, person **2** *Syn* EXISTENCE, actuality *Ant* nonexistence

belabor **1** *Syn* ATTACK (sense 2), abuse, assail, blast, castigate, excoriate, jump (on), lambaste (*or* lambast), scathe, slam, vituperate **2** *Syn* BEAT, baste, buffet, pound, pummel, thrash

belch **1** • to eject (gas) from the stomach by way of the mouth or matter from a containing cavity by way of an opening *Syn* burp, disgorge, regurgitate, spew, throw up, vomit *Rel* eject, expel **2** *Syn* ERUPT (sense 2), disgorge, eject, expel, jet, spew, spout, spurt

beleaguer *Syn* BESIEGE, blockade, invest

belie *Syn* MISREPRESENT, falsify, garble

belief **1** • the act of one who assents intellectually to something proposed or offered for acceptance as true or the state of mind of one who so assents *Syn* credence, credit, faith *Rel* assurance, certainty, certitude, conviction *Ant* disbelief, unbelief **2** *Syn* OPINION, conviction, persuasion, sentiment, view

believable *Syn* PLAUSIBLE, colorable, credible, specious

believe **1** • to have as an opinion *Syn* consider, deem, feel, figure, guess, hold, imagine, suppose, think *Rel* esteem, regard, view **2** • to regard as right or true *Syn* accept, credit, swallow, trust *Rel* account, accredit, understand *Ant* disbelieve, discredit, reject

belittle *Syn* DECRY, deprecate, derogate, detract, disparage, minimize *Ant* extol

bellicose *Syn* BELLIGERENT, aggressive, argumentative, combative, contentious, discordant, disputatious, gladiatorial, militant, pugnacious, quarrelsome, scrappy, truculent, warlike *Ant* nonbelligerent, pacific, peaceable, peaceful

bellicosity *Syn* BELLIGERENCE, aggression, aggressiveness, combativeness, contentiousness, disputatiousness, fight, militancy, pugnacity, scrappiness, truculence *Ant* pacifism

belligerence • an inclination to fight or quarrel *Syn* aggression, aggressiveness, bellicosity, combativeness, contentiousness, disputatiousness, fight, militancy, pugnacity, scrappiness, truculence *Rel* antagonism, fierceness, hostility, unfriendliness *Ant* pacifism

belligerent • feeling or displaying eagerness to fight *Syn* aggressive, argumentative, bellicose, combative, contentious, discordant, disputatious, gladiatorial, militant, pugnacious, quarrelsome, scrappy, truculent, warlike *Rel* antagonistic, fierce, hostile, hot-tempered *Ant* nonbelligerent, pacific, peaceable, peaceful

bellow *vb* *Syn* ROAR, bawl, bluster, clamor, howl, ululate, vociferate

bellow *n* *Syn* ROAR, bawl, bluster, ululation, vociferation

belly *Syn* STOMACH, abdomen, gut, solar plexus, tummy

bellyache *Syn* COMPLAIN, beef, carp, crab, croak, fuss, gripe, grouse, growl, grumble, kick, moan, murmur, mutter, repine, squawk, wail, whine, yammer *Ant* rejoice

belong *Syn* BEAR (sense 3), appertain, apply, pertain, relate

belongings *Syn* POSSESSIONS, assets, effects, means, resources

beloved *Syn* SWEETHEART, darling, dear, flame, honey, love, sweet
below • in a lower position relative to some other object or place *Syn* beneath, under, underneath *Ant* above
belt *Syn* AREA, region, tract, zone
bemoan *Syn* REGRET, deplore, lament, repent, rue
bemuse *Syn* DAZE, benumb, paralyze, petrify, stun, stupefy
bend *Syn* CURVE, twist
beneath *Syn* BELOW, under, underneath *Ant* above
benefaction *Syn* CONTRIBUTION, alms, beneficence, charity, donation, philanthropy
benefactor • one that helps another with gifts or money *Syn* donator, donor, patron *Rel* almsgiver, philanthropist
beneficence *Syn* CONTRIBUTION, alms, benefaction, charity, donation, philanthropy
beneficial • conferring benefits or promoting or contributing to personal or social well-being *Syn* advantageous, favorable, helpful, profitable, salutary *Rel* gratifying, rewarding, satisfying *Ant* disadvantageous, unfavorable, unhelpful
benefit • to do good or to be of advantage to someone *Syn* avail, profit *Rel* ameliorate, better, improve *Ant* harm
benevolent *Syn* CHARITABLE, altruistic, eleemosynary, humane, humanitarian, philanthropic *Ant* uncharitable
benighted *Syn* IGNORANT, dark, illiterate, nonliterate, simple, uneducated, uninstructed, unlearned, unlettered, unread, unschooled, untaught, untutored *Ant* educated, knowledgeable, literate, schooled
benign **1** *Syn* FAVORABLE, auspicious, propitious *Ant* antagonistic, unfavorable **2** *Syn* KIND, benignant, kindly *Ant* unkind
benignant *Syn* KIND, benign, kindly *Ant* unkind
bent *Syn* GIFT (sense 2), aptitude, faculty, genius, knack, talent, turn
benumb *Syn* DAZE, bemuse, paralyze, petrify, stun, stupefy
benumbed *Syn* NUMB, asleep, dead, insensitive, numbed, unfeeling *Ant* feeling, sensitive
bequeath *Syn* WILL, devise, leave, legate
berate *Syn* SCOLD, bawl, chew out, jaw, rail, rate, revile, tongue-lash, upbraid, vituperate, wig
berth **1** *Syn* ROOM (sense 2), clearance, elbow room, leeway, margin, play **2** *Syn* WHARF, dock, jetty, levee, pier, quay, slip
beseech *Syn* BEG, adjure, entreat, implore, importune, supplicate
beset *Syn* INFEST, overrun *Ant* disinfest
besiege • to surround (as a fortified place) with armed forces for the purpose of capturing or preventing commerce and communication *Syn* beleaguer, blockade, invest *Rel* barricade, block, cut off, dam, encircle
besmirch *Syn* DIRTY, befoul, begrime, blacken, foul, grime, mire, muddy, smirch, smudge, soil, stain, sully *Ant* clean, cleanse
besotted *Syn* FOND, infatuated, insensate
bespangled *Syn* SPOTTED, flecked, marbled, mottled, spangled, spattered, speckled, sprinkled, stippled
bespeak *Syn* INDICATE, argue, attest, betoken, prove
best **1** *Syn* ELITE, choice, cream, elect, fat, flower, pick, prime, upper crust **2** *Syn* FINERY, array, bravery, caparison, feather, frippery, full dress, gaiety, regalia
bestial *Syn* BRUTAL, beastly, brute, brutish, feral
bestow *Syn* GIVE, afford, confer, donate, present
bestrew *Syn* SCATTER (sense 2), dot, pepper, sow, spray, sprinkle, strew
bet *n* • something (as money) staked on a winner-take-all basis on the outcome of an uncertainty *Syn* ante, pot, stake, wager
bet *vb* • to risk (something) on the outcome of an uncertain event *Syn* gamble, go, lay, stake, wager *Rel* bid, offer
bête noire *Syn* ABOMINATION, anathema, bugbear *Ant* joy
bethink *Syn* REMEMBER, mind, recall, recollect, remind, reminisce *Ant* forget
betide *Syn* HAPPEN, befall, chance, occur, transpire
betimes *Syn* EARLY, beforehand, soon *Ant* late
betoken *Syn* INDICATE, argue, attest, bespeak, prove
betray **1** *Syn* DECEIVE, beguile, delude, double-cross, mislead *Ant* enlighten, undeceive **2** *Syn* REVEAL, disclose, discover, divulge, tell *Ant* conceal
betrayal • the act or fact of violating the trust or confidence of another *Syn* disloyalty, double cross, faithlessness, falseness, falsity, infidelity, perfidy, sellout, treachery, treason, unfaithfulness *Rel* abandonment, desertion
betrayer *Syn* TRAITOR, double-crosser, quisling, recreant, turncoat
betrothed • the person to whom one is engaged to be married *Syn* fiancé, fiancée, intended *Rel* admirer, beau, beloved, boyfriend, darling, dear, favorite, fellow, flame, girlfriend, honey, love, lover, steady, swain, sweet, sweetheart, valentine
better *adj* • more worthy or more pleasing than another or others *Syn* preferable, superior *Rel* choice, dainty, delicate
better *n* *Syn* SUPERIOR, elder, senior *Ant* inferior, subordinate, underling
better *vb* *Syn* IMPROVE (sense 1), ameliorate, help *Ant* impair, worsen
bettor *or* **better** • one that bets (as on the outcome of a contest or sports event) *Syn* gambler, wagerer *Rel* dicer

bewilder *Syn* PUZZLE, confound, distract, dumbfound, mystify, nonplus, perplex
bewitch *Syn* ATTRACT, allure, captivate, charm, enchant, fascinate *Ant* repel
bewitching *Syn* ATTRACTIVE, alluring, captivating, charming, enchanting, fascinating *Ant* forbidding, repellent
beyond *prep* **1** • on or to the farther side of *Syn* over, past *Rel* outside **2** • out of the reach or sphere of *Syn* outside, outside of, without *Rel* except *Ant* within
beyond *adv Syn* FARTHER, further
bias *n* **1** • an attitude that always favors one way of feeling or acting especially without considering any other possibilities *Syn* favor, one-sidedness, partiality, partisanship, prejudice *Rel* favoritism, nepotism *Ant* impartiality, neutrality, objectivity, open-mindedness **2** *Syn* PREDILECTION, partiality, prejudice, prepossession *Ant* aversion
bias *vb Syn* INCLINE, dispose, predispose *Ant* disincline, indispose
bickering *Syn* QUARREL, altercation, spat, squabble, tiff, wrangle
bid *vb* **1** *Syn* COMMAND, charge, direct, enjoin, instruct, order *Ant* comply, obey **2** *Syn* INVITE, court, solicit, woo
bid *n Syn* OVERTURE, advance, approach, tender
bidding *Syn* COMMAND, behest, dictate, injunction, mandate, order
big *Syn* LARGE, bulky, considerable, goodly, good-sized, grand, great, handsome, hefty, hulking, largish, outsize, oversize (*or* oversized), sizable (*or* sizeable), substantial, tidy, voluminous *Ant* little, puny, small, undersized
bigoted *Syn* INTOLERANT, narrow, narrow-minded, prejudiced, small-minded *Ant* broad-minded, liberal, open-minded, tolerant, unprejudiced
bill • the jaws of a bird together with their horny covering *Syn* beak, neb, nib
billingsgate *Syn* ABUSE, invective, obloquy, scurrility, vituperation *Ant* adulation
binary *Syn* DOUBLE, bipartite, dual, duplex, twin *Ant* single
biography • an account of the events and circumstances of a person's life *Syn* autobiography, confessions, life, memoir
biologic *Syn* DRUG, medicinal, pharmaceutical, simple
biotope *Syn* HABITAT, range, station
bipartite *Syn* DOUBLE, binary, dual, duplex, twin *Ant* single
bird's-eye *Syn* GENERAL (sense 2), all-around, broad, nonspecific, overall *Ant* delineated, detailed, particularized, specific
birth **1** *Syn* ANCESTRY, blood, bloodline, breeding, descent, extraction, family tree, genealogy, line, lineage, origin, parentage, pedigree, stock, strain *Ant* issue, posterity, progeny, seed **2** *Syn* BEGINNING, alpha, commencement, dawn, genesis, inception, incipiency, launch, morning, onset, outset, start, threshold *Ant* close, conclusion, end, ending
birthright **1** *Syn* HERITAGE, inheritance, patrimony **2** *Syn* RIGHT, appanage, perquisite, prerogative, privilege
bit *Syn* PARTICLE, atom, iota, jot, mite, smidgen, tittle, whit
bite *vb* • to attack with or as if with the teeth *Syn* champ, gnash, gnaw *Rel* consume, devour, eat
bite *n Syn* CHILL, bitterness, bleakness, chilliness, nip, rawness, sharpness
biting *Syn* INCISIVE, clear-cut, crisp, cutting, trenchant
bitterness *Syn* CHILL, bite, bleakness, chilliness, nip, rawness, sharpness
bitty *Syn* TINY, atomic, infinitesimal, microminiature, microscopic, miniature, minute, teeny, teeny-weeny, wee *Ant* astronomical, colossal, cosmic, elephantine, enormous, giant, gigantic, herculean, heroic, huge, immense, mammoth, massive, monster, monstrous, monumental, mountainous, prodigious, titanic, tremendous
bizarre *Syn* FANTASTIC, antic, grotesque
blab **1** *Syn* CHAT, babble, cackle, chatter, converse, gab, gabble, gas, jabber, jaw, palaver, patter, prate, prattle, rap, rattle, run on, talk, twitter, visit **2** *Syn* GOSSIP, tattle
blackball *Syn* EXCLUDE, debar, disbar, eliminate, rule out, shut out, suspend *Ant* admit, include
blacken **1** *Syn* DIRTY, befoul, begrime, besmirch, foul, grime, mire, muddy, smirch, smudge, soil, stain, sully *Ant* clean, cleanse **2** *Syn* SLANDER, asperse, defame, libel, malign, smear, traduce, vilify
blackguard *Syn* VILLAIN, knave, miscreant, rapscallion, rascal, rogue, scamp, scoundrel
blackout *Syn* FAINT, coma, insensibility, knockout, swoon
black out *Syn* FAINT, pass out, swoon *Ant* come around, come round, come to, revive
blame *n* • responsibility for misdeed or delinquency *Syn* culpability, fault, guilt *Rel* accountability, answerability, responsibility
blame *vb Syn* CRITICIZE, censure, condemn, denounce, reprehend, reprobate
blameworthy • deserving reproach and punishment for a wrong, sinful, or criminal act, practice, or condition *Syn* culpable, guilty *Ant* blameless
blanch *Syn* WHITEN, bleach, blench, decolorize, dull, fade, pale, wash out *Ant* blacken, darken, deepen
bland *Syn* SOFT, balmy, gentle, lenient, mild, smooth *Ant* hard, stern
blandish *Syn* COAX, blarney, cajole, soft-soap, wheedle
blank *adj Syn* EMPTY, vacant, vacuous, void *Ant* full

blank *n Syn* VACANCY (sense 1), blankness, emptiness, vacuity, void *Ant* fullness
blanket *Syn* GENERAL (sense 1), common, generic, global, overall, universal *Ant* individual, particular
blankness *Syn* VACANCY (sense 1), blank, emptiness, vacuity, void *Ant* fullness
blarney *Syn* COAX, blandish, cajole, soft-soap, wheedle
blasphemous *Syn* IMPIOUS, profane, sacrilegious *Ant* pious, reverent
blasphemy **1** • impious or irreverent speech *Syn* cursing, profanity, swearing *Rel* affront, indignity, insult *Ant* adoration **2** *Syn* PROFANATION, desecration, sacrilege
blast *n* • severe, sudden, or surprising ruin or injury *Syn* blight, nip *Rel* destruction
blast *vb* **1** • to ruin or to injure severely, suddenly, or surprisingly *Syn* blight, nip *Rel* destroy **2** *Syn* ATTACK (sense 2), abuse, assail, belabor, castigate, excoriate, jump (on), lambaste (*or* lambast), scathe, slam, vituperate
blatant **1** *Syn* EGREGIOUS, conspicuous, flagrant, glaring, gross, obvious, patent, pronounced, rank, striking **2** *Syn* VOCIFEROUS, boisterous, clamorous, obstreperous, strident
blaze *n* • brightly burning light or fire *Syn* flame, flare, glare, glow *Rel* fire, firing, igniting, ignition, kindling
blaze *vb* **1** • to burn or appear to burn brightly *Syn* flame, flare, glare, glow *Rel* illuminate, illumine, light **2** *Syn* ANNOUNCE, advertise, broadcast, declare, enunciate, placard, post, proclaim, promulgate, publicize, publish, sound
blazing *Syn* FERVENT, ardent, burning, charged, emotional, fervid, feverish, fiery, flaming, glowing, hot-blooded, impassioned, passionate, red-hot, vehement, warm, warm-blooded *Ant* cold, cool, dispassionate, impassive, unemotional
bleach *Syn* WHITEN, blanch, blench, decolorize, dull, fade, pale, wash out *Ant* blacken, darken, deepen
bleak *Syn* DISMAL, cheerless, desolate, dispiriting, dreary
bleakness *Syn* CHILL, bite, bitterness, chilliness, nip, rawness, sharpness
bleed **1** *Syn* EXUDE, ooze, percolate, seep, strain, sweat, weep **2** *Syn* FLEECE, cheat, chisel, cozen, defraud, hustle, mulct, rook, shortchange, skin, squeeze, stick, sting, swindle, victimize
blemish • something that spoils the appearance or completeness of a thing *Syn* defect, deformity, disfigurement, fault, flaw, imperfection, mark, pockmark, scar *Rel* abnormality, distortion, irregularity, malformation
blench **1** *Syn* RECOIL, flinch, quail, shrink, wince *Ant* confront, defy **2** *Syn* WHITEN, blanch, bleach, decolorize, dull, fade, pale, wash out *Ant* blacken, darken, deepen
blend *n* • a distinct entity formed by the combining of two or more different things *Syn* admixture, amalgam, amalgamation, combination, composite, compound, fusion, intermixture, mix, mixture *Rel* coalescence, concoction, incorporation, intermingling, mingling
blend *vb Syn* MIX, amalgamate, coalesce, commingle, fuse, merge, mingle
blessed *Syn* HOLY (sense 2), consecrated, hallowed, sacred, sacrosant, sanctified *Ant* unconsecrated, unhallowed
blessedness **1** *Syn* HOLINESS, devoutness, godliness, piety, piousness, sainthood, saintliness, saintship, sanctity *Ant* godlessness, impiety, ungodliness, unholiness **2** *Syn* HAPPINESS, beatitude, bliss, felicity *Ant* unhappiness
blessing **1** *Syn* APPROVAL, approbation, favor, imprimatur, OK (*or* okay) *Ant* disapprobation, disapproval, disfavor **2** *Syn* CONSECRATION, hallowing, sanctification
blight *n Syn* BLAST, nip
blight *vb Syn* BLAST, nip
blind • lacking the power of sight *Syn* eyeless, sightless, stone blind *Rel* unobservant, unobserving *Ant* sighted
bliss *Syn* HAPPINESS, beatitude, blessedness, felicity *Ant* unhappiness
blithe *Syn* CHEERFUL (sense 1), blithesome, bright, buoyant, cheery, chipper, gay, gladsome, lightsome, sunny, upbeat *Ant* dour, gloomy, glum, morose, saturnine, sulky, sullen
blithesome **1** *Syn* CHEERFUL (sense 1), blithe, bright, buoyant, cheery, chipper, gay, gladsome, lightsome, sunny, upbeat *Ant* dour, gloomy, glum, morose, saturnine, sulky, sullen **2** *Syn* MERRY, festive, gay, gleeful, jocose, jocund, jolly, jovial, laughing, mirthful, sunny
blitzkrieg *Syn* ATTACK (sense 2), aggression, assault, charge, descent, offense (*or* offence), offensive, onset, onslaught, raid, rush, strike
bloc **1** *Syn* COMBINATION, combine, faction, party, ring **2** *Syn* FACTION, body, coalition, party, sect, set, side, wing
block *n Syn* ENCUMBRANCE, bar, chain, clog, crimp, deterrent, drag, embarrassment, fetter, handicap, hindrance, hurdle, impediment, inhibition, interference, let, manacle, obstacle, obstruction, shackles, stop, stumbling block, trammel *Ant* aid, assistance, benefit, help
block *vb Syn* HINDER, bar, dam, impede, obstruct *Ant* further
blockade *Syn* BESIEGE, beleaguer, invest
blockbuster *Syn* GIANT, behemoth, colossus, jumbo, leviathan, mammoth, monster, titan, whale, whopper *Ant* dwarf, midget, mini, miniature, peewee, pygmy, runt, shrimp
blond *or* **blonde** • of a pale yellow or yellowish brown color *Syn* fair, flaxen, golden,

sandy, straw, tawny *Rel* gold, light, white *Ant* dark

blood *Syn* ANCESTRY, birth, bloodline, breeding, descent, extraction, family tree, genealogy, line, lineage, origin, parentage, pedigree, stock, strain *Ant* issue, posterity, progeny, seed

bloodless *Syn* PALE (sense 2), anemic

bloodline *Syn* ANCESTRY, birth, blood, breeding, descent, extraction, family tree, genealogy, line, lineage, origin, parentage, pedigree, stock, strain *Ant* issue, posterity, progeny, seed

bloodthirsty • eager for or marked by the shedding of blood, extreme violence, or killing *Syn* bloody, homicidal, murdering, murderous, sanguinary, sanguine *Rel* barbaric, barbarous, cruel, heartless, inhumane, sadistic, savage, vicious, wanton

bloody **1** • affected by or involving the shedding of blood *Syn* gory, sanguinary, sanguine, sanguineous **2** *Syn* BLOODTHIRSTY, homicidal, murdering, murderous, sanguinary, sanguine

bloom *n Syn* BLOSSOM, blow, flower

bloom *vb* **1** *Syn* BLOSSOM, blow, flower **2** *Syn* BLUSH, color, crimson, flush, glow, redden

blossom *n* • the period or state of florescence of a seed plant *Syn* bloom, blow, flower

blossom *vb* • to become florescent *Syn* bloom, blow, flower

blot *Syn* STIGMA, brand, stain

blotch *Syn* SPOT, dapple, dot, fleck, freckle, marble, mottle, pepper, speck, speckle, splotch, sprinkle, stipple

blot out *Syn* ERASE, cancel, delete, efface, expunge, obliterate

blow *vb Syn* BLOSSOM, bloom, flower

blow *n Syn* BLOSSOM, bloom, flower

blowsy *Syn* SLATTERNLY, dowdy, frowzy

blubber *Syn* CRY, keen, wail, weep, whimper

blue *Syn* SAD (sense 1), bad, brokenhearted, crestfallen, dejected, depressed, despondent, disconsolate, doleful, down, downcast, downhearted, droopy, forlorn, gloomy, glum, heartbroken, heartsick, heartsore, inconsolable, joyless, low, low-spirited, melancholy, miserable, mournful, saddened, sorrowful, sorry, unhappy, woebegone, woeful, wretched *Ant* blissful, buoyant, buoyed, cheerful, cheery, chipper, delighted, glad, gladdened, gladsome, gleeful, happy, joyful, joyous, jubilant, sunny, upbeat

bluejacket *Syn* MARINER, gob, sailor, seaman, tar

blueprint *n Syn* SKETCH, delineate, diagram, draft, outline, plot, trace

blueprint *vb Syn* SKETCH, delineation, diagram, draft, outline, plot, tracing

blues *Syn* SADNESS, dejection, depression, desolation, despondency, disconsolateness, dispiritedness, doldrums, downheartedness, dreariness, dumps, forlornness, gloom, gloominess, heartsickness, joylessness, melancholy, mopes, oppression, unhappiness *Ant* bliss, blissfulness, ecstasy, elatedness, elation, euphoria, exhilaration, exuberance, exultation, felicity, gladness, gladsomeness, happiness, heaven, intoxication, joy, joyfulness, joyousness, jubilation, rapture, rapturousness

bluff • abrupt and unceremonious in speech or manner *Syn* blunt, brusque, crusty, curt, gruff *Rel* hearty, sincere *Ant* smooth, suave

blunder *n Syn* ERROR, bull, faux pas, howler, lapse, mistake, slip

blunder *vb Syn* STUMBLE, bumble, flounder, galumph, lollop, lumber, lurch, trip

blunt **1** *Syn* BLUFF, brusque, crusty, curt, gruff *Ant* smooth, suave **2** *Syn* DULL (sense 1), obtuse *Ant* lively

blurb *Syn* CRITICISM, critique, puff, review

blush • to develop a rosy facial color (as from excitement or embarrassment) *Syn* bloom, color, crimson, flush, glow, redden *Rel* rouge

bluster *vb* **1** *Syn* RANT, fulminate, rave, spout **2** *Syn* ROAR, bawl, bellow, clamor, howl, ululate, vociferate

bluster *n Syn* ROAR, bawl, bellow, ululation, vociferation

board *Syn* HARBOR, entertain, house, lodge, shelter

boarder *Syn* TENANT, lodger, renter, roomer *Ant* landlord

boast • to give vent in speech to one's pride in oneself or something intimately connected with oneself *Syn* brag, crow, gasconade, vaunt *Rel* flaunt, parade, show *Ant* depreciate (*oneself, one's accomplishments*)

boat • a floating structure designed to carry persons or goods over water *Syn* craft, ship, vessel

bob *Syn* CLIP, crop, curtail, cut, cut back, dock, lop (off), nip, pare, prune, shave, shear, snip, trim

bobble *Syn* BOTCH, bungle, butcher, flub, foozle, foul up, fumble, louse up, mangle, mess (up), muff, murder

bodily • of or relating to the human body *Syn* corporal, corporeal, physical, somatic *Rel* animal, carnal, fleshly, sensual

boding *Syn* OMEN, augury, auspice, foreboding, foreshadowing, portent, prefiguring, presage

body **1** • the dead physical substance of a human being or animal *Syn* cadaver, carcass, corpse **2** *Syn* FACTION, bloc, coalition, party, sect, set, side, wing

bog *Syn* SWAMP, fen, marsh, marshland, mire, morass, muskeg, slough, swampland

bogey *Syn* GHOST, apparition, phantasm, phantom, poltergeist, shade, shadow, specter (*or* spectre), spirit, spook, vision, wraith

boggle *Syn* DEMUR, balk, jib, scruple, shy, stick, stickle, strain *Ant* accede

bogus **1** *Syn* COUNTERFEIT, fake, phony, pinchbeck, pseudo, sham, spurious *Ant* bona fide, genuine **2** *Syn* IMITATION, artificial, factitious, fake, false, man-made, mimic, mock, sham, simulated, substitute, synthetic *Ant* genuine, natural, real

boil *vb* • to prepare (as food) in a liquid heated to the point where it emits considerable steam *Syn* parboil, seethe, simmer, stew

boil *n Syn* ABSCESS, carbuncle, furuncle, pimple, pustule

boisterous **1** • being rough or noisy in a high-spirited way *Syn* knockabout, rambunctious, raucous, rowdy *Rel* rampageous, riotous, stormy, tempestuous, turbulent, violent *Ant* orderly **2** *Syn* VOCIFEROUS, blatant, clamorous, obstreperous, strident

bold *Syn* BRAVE, audacious, courageous, dauntless, doughty, fearless, intrepid, unafraid, undaunted, valiant, valorous *Ant* craven

bolster *Syn* SUPPORT (sense 1), brace, buttress, prop, sustain

bolt *Syn* HURRY (sense 2), barrel, bowl, breeze, career, course, dash, fly, hasten, hotfoot (it), hump, hurtle, hustle, pelt, race, rip, rocket, run, rush, rustle, scoot, scurry, scuttle, shoot, speed, step (along), tear, trot, whirl, whisk, zip, zoom *Ant* crawl, creep, poke

bombard *Syn* ATTACK (sense 1), assail, assault, storm

bombardment *Syn* BARRAGE, cannonade, fusillade, hail, salvo, shower, storm, volley

bombast • speech or writing characterized by high-flown pomposity or pretentiousness of language disproportionate to the thought or subject matter *Syn* fustian, rant, rhapsody, rodomontade *Rel* grandiloquence, magniloquence, rhetoric

bombastic *Syn* RHETORICAL, aureate, euphuistic, flowery, grandiloquent, magniloquent

bona fide *Syn* AUTHENTIC, genuine, veritable *Ant* spurious

bond *n* **1** • something which serves to bind or bring two or more things firmly together *Syn* band, tie **2** *Syn* GUARANTEE, bail, guaranty, security, surety

bond *adj Syn* BOUND, articled, indentured

bonding *Syn* ADHESION, adherence

bondman *Syn* SLAVE (sense 1), bondsman, chattel, thrall *Ant* freeman

bondsman *Syn* SLAVE (sense 1), bondman, chattel, thrall *Ant* freeman

bonus • something given in addition to what is ordinarily expected or owed *Syn* dividend, extra, gratuity, gravy, lagniappe, perquisite, tip *Rel* fillip

bon vivant *Syn* EPICURE, gastronome, glutton, gourmand, gourmet

bon voyage *Syn* GOOD-BYE, adieu, au revoir, farewell, Godspeed *Ant* hello

booby *Syn* FOOL (sense 2), goose, half-wit, jackass, lunatic, nincompoop, ninny, nitwit, nut, simpleton, turkey, yo-yo

bookish **1** • suggestive of the vocabulary used in books *Syn* erudite, learned, literary *Rel* academic, pedantic, scholastic *Ant* colloquial, nonliterary **2** *Syn* PEDANTIC, academic, scholastic

boon *adj Syn* CONVIVIAL, companionable, extroverted, gregarious, outgoing, sociable, social *Ant* antisocial, introverted, reclusive, unsociable

boon *n Syn* GIFT (sense 1), favor, gratuity, largess, present

boorish *Syn* CLOWNISH, churlish, cloddish, loutish, uncouth *Ant* civil, courteous, courtly, cultivated, genteel, gentlemanly, ladylike, polished, polite, refined, well-bred

boost **1** *Syn* INCREASE (sense 1), add (to), aggrandize, amplify, augment, compound, enlarge, escalate, expand, extend, multiply, raise, swell, up *Ant* abate, contract, decrease, diminish, lessen, lower, reduce, subtract (from) **2** *Syn* LIFT, elevate, heave, hoist, raise, rear *Ant* lower

booster *Syn* EXPONENT, advocate, apostle, backer, champion, friend, promoter, proponent, supporter *Ant* adversary, antagonist, opponent

bootleg *Syn* SMUGGLED, contraband

bootless *Syn* FUTILE, abortive, fruitless, vain *Ant* effective, effectual, efficacious, efficient, fruitful, productive, profitable, successful

bootlicker *Syn* PARASITE, favorite, hanger-on, leech, lickspittle, sponge, sponger, sycophant, toady

booty *Syn* SPOIL, loot, plunder, prize, swag

booze *Syn* ALCOHOL, drink, grog, intoxicant, liquor, moonshine, spirits

border *n* • the line or relatively narrow space which marks the limit or outermost bound of something *Syn* brim, brink, edge, margin, rim, verge *Rel* bound, confine, end, limit

border *vb* • to serve as a border for *Syn* bound, fringe, margin, rim, skirt *Rel* edge, hem, trim

bordering *Syn* ADJACENT, abutting, adjoining, contiguous, flanking, fringing, joining, juxtaposed, skirting, touching, verging *Ant* nonadjacent

bore *Syn* PERFORATE, drill, prick, punch, puncture

boredom *Syn* TEDIUM, doldrums, ennui

boring • causing weariness, restlessness, or lack of interest *Syn* drab, dreary, dry, dull, flat, heavy, humdrum, jading, leaden, monotonous, pedestrian, ponderous, stodgy, stuffy, stupid, tame, tedious, tiresome, tiring, unanimated, uninteresting, wearisome, weary, wearying *Rel* undramatic, unentertaining, uneventful, unexciting, uninspiring, unnewsworthy, unrewarding, unsatisfying, unsensational, unspectacular *Ant* absorbing,

engaging, engrossing, gripping, interesting, intriguing, involving
boss • the person (as an employer or supervisor) who tells people and especially workers what to do *Syn* captain, chief, foreman, head, headman, helmsman, kingpin, leader, master, taskmaster *Rel* administrator, commander, director, executive, general, manager, overseer, principal, standard-bearer, straw boss, superintendent, superior, supervisor
bossy • fond of ordering people around *Syn* authoritarian, autocratic, despotic, dictatorial, domineering, imperious, masterful, overbearing, peremptory, tyrannical, tyrannous *Rel* arrogant, disdainful, haughty, lofty, lordly, proud, supercilious, superior
botch • to make or do (something) in a clumsy or unskillful way *Syn* bobble, bungle, butcher, flub, foozle, foul up, fumble, louse up, mangle, mess (up), muff, murder *Rel* blunder, goof (up), gum (up)
bother *vb Syn* ANNOY, irk, vex *Ant* soothe
bother *n Syn* COMMOTION, bustle, clatter, disturbance, furor, furore, fuss, hubbub, hullabaloo, hurly-burly, pandemonium, pother, row, ruckus, ruction, rumpus, shindy, squall, stew, stir, storm, to-do, tumult, turmoil, uproar, welter, whirl
bothersome *Syn* ANNOYING, aggravating, disturbing, exasperating, frustrating, galling, irksome, irritating, maddening, nettling, peeving, pesty, rankling, riling, vexatious, vexing
bottom *Syn* BUTTOCKS, backside, breech, butt, fanny, hams, haunches, posterior, rear, rump, seat
bough *Syn* SHOOT, branch, limb
bounce *Syn* DISMISS, cashier, discharge, drop, fire, sack
bound *adj* • obliged to serve a master or in a clearly defined capacity for a certain number of years by the terms of a contract or mutual agreement *Syn* articled, bond, indentured
bound *n* **1** *Syn* BORDER, fringe, margin, rim, skirt **2** *Syn* JUMP, leap, spring, vault
bound *vb* **1** *Syn* JUMP, leap, spring, vault **2** *Syn* LIMIT, confine, end, term **3** *Syn* SKIP, curvet, hop, lollop, lope, ricochet
boundless *Syn* INFINITE, endless, illimitable, immeasurable, indefinite, limitless, measureless, unbounded, unfathomable, unlimited *Ant* bounded, circumscribed, confined, definite, finite, limited, restricted
bounteous *Syn* LIBERAL (sense 1), bountiful, generous, handsome, munificent, openhanded *Ant* close
bountiful *Syn* LIBERAL (sense 1), bounteous, generous, handsome, munificent, openhanded *Ant* close
bouquet *Syn* FRAGRANCE, incense, perfume, redolence *Ant* stench, stink
bout **1** *Syn* ATTACK (sense 3), case, fit, seizure, siege, spell **2** *Syn* SPELL, go, shift, stint, tour, trick, turn
bow *n Syn* CURVE, arc, arch
bow *vb* **1** *Syn* FLEX, buckle, crook *Ant* extend **2** *Syn* YIELD, capitulate, cave, defer, relent, submit, succumb
bowl *Syn* HURRY (sense 2), barrel, bolt, breeze, career, course, dash, fly, hasten, hotfoot (it), hump, hurtle, hustle, pelt, race, rip, rocket, run, rush, rustle, scoot, scurry, scuttle, shoot, speed, step (along), tear, trot, whirl, whisk, zip, zoom *Ant* crawl, creep, poke
box *n Syn* CHEST, caddy, case, casket, locker, trunk
box *vb Syn* STRIKE, clout, cuff, hit, punch, slap, slog, slug, smite, swat
boy • a male person who has not yet reached adulthood *Syn* lad, laddie, nipper, shaver, sonny, stripling, tad *Rel* adolescent, juvenile, kid, minor, moppet, teenager, youngster, youth
boyfriend • a male romantic companion *Syn* beau, fellow, man, swain *Rel* admirer, crush, steady
brace *vb* **1** *Syn* ANIMATE, energize, enliven, fire, invigorate, jazz (up), liven (up), pep (up), quicken, stimulate, vitalize, vivify *Ant* damp, dampen, deaden, dull **2** *Syn* SUPPORT (sense 1), bolster, buttress, prop, sustain
brace *n* **1** *Syn* COUPLE, pair, yoke **2** *Syn* PAIR, couple, duo, twain, twosome
bracing *Syn* TONIC, invigorating, refreshing, restorative, reviving, stimulating, stimulative, vitalizing
brag *Syn* BOAST, crow, gasconade, vaunt *Ant* depreciate (*oneself, one's accomplishments*)
braid *n* • a length of something formed of three or more strands woven together *Syn* lace, lacing, plait *Rel* pigtail, rickrack (*or* ricrac), stripe
braid *vb* **1** • to form into a braid *Syn* plait, pleat *Rel* interlace, interweave, weave **2** *Syn* WEAVE, crochet, knit, plait, tat
brain *Syn* MIND, intellect, intelligence, psyche, soul, wit
brake *vb Syn* SLOW, decelerate, retard *Ant* accelerate, hasten, hurry, quicken, rush, speed (up), step up
brake *n Syn* THICKET, brushwood, chaparral, coppice, copse, covert
branch *Syn* SHOOT, bough, limb
brand *vb Syn* MARK, label, stamp, tag, ticket
brand *n* **1** *Syn* MARK, label, stamp, tag, ticket **2** *Syn* STIGMA, blot, stain
brandish *Syn* SWING (sense 1), flourish, shake, thrash, wave
brash *Syn* SHAMELESS, barefaced, brazen, impudent
brashness *Syn* EFFRONTERY, audacity, brass, brassiness, brazenness, cheek, cheekiness, chutzpah, gall, nerve, nerviness, pertness, presumption, presumptuousness, sauce, sauciness, temerity

brass *Syn* EFFRONTERY, audacity, brashness, brassiness, brazenness, cheek, cheekiness, chutzpah, gall, nerve, nerviness, pertness, presumption, presumptuousness, sauce, sauciness, temerity

brassiness *Syn* EFFRONTERY, audacity, brashness, brass, brazenness, cheek, cheekiness, chutzpah, gall, nerve, nerviness, pertness, presumption, presumptuousness, sauce, sauciness, temerity

brave *adj* • having or showing no fear when faced with something dangerous, difficult, or unknown *Syn* audacious, bold, courageous, dauntless, doughty, fearless, intrepid, unafraid, undaunted, valiant, valorous *Rel* adventurous, daredevil, daring, venturesome *Ant* craven

brave *vb Syn* FACE, beard, challenge, dare, defy *Ant* avoid

bravery **1** *Syn* COURAGE, courageousness, daring, dauntlessness, doughtiness, fearlessness, gallantry, greatheartedness, guts, hardihood, heart, heroism, intrepidity, intrepidness, nerve, stoutness, valor *Ant* cowardice, cowardliness, cravenness, dastardliness, spinelessness, yellowness **2** *Syn* FINERY, array, best, caparison, feather, frippery, full dress, gaiety, regalia

bravo *Syn* ASSASSIN, cutthroat, gunman

brawl • a noisy fight or quarrel *Syn* broil, fracas, melee, row, rumpus, scrap *Rel* affray, conflict, contest, fight, fray

brawny *Syn* MUSCULAR, athletic, burly, husky, sinewy

brazen *Syn* SHAMELESS, barefaced, brash, impudent

brazenness *Syn* EFFRONTERY, audacity, brashness, brass, brassiness, cheek, cheekiness, chutzpah, gall, nerve, nerviness, pertness, presumption, presumptuousness, sauce, sauciness, temerity

breach **1** • the act or the offense of failing to keep the law or to do what the law, duty, or obligation requires *Syn* contravention, infraction, infringement, transgression, trespass, violation *Ant* observance **2** • a pulling apart in relations or in connections *Syn* break, rent, rift, rupture, schism, split *Rel* division, separation, severance

bread *Syn* LIVING, bread and butter, keep, livelihood, maintenance, subsistence, support, sustenance

bread and butter *Syn* LIVING, bread, keep, livelihood, maintenance, subsistence, support, sustenance

break *n* **1** • a lapse in continuity *Syn* gap, hiatus, interim, interruption, interval, lacuna *Rel* division, separation, severance **2** *Syn* OPPORTUNITY, chance, occasion, time **3** *Syn* PAUSE, breath, breather, interruption, lull, recess **4** *Syn* BREACH, rent, rift, rupture, schism, split

break *vb* **1** • to come apart or cause to come apart *Syn* burst, bust, crack, shatter, shiver, snap *Rel* crumble, decay, disintegrate *Ant* cleave (*together*), keep (*of laws*) **2** *Syn* SOLVE, answer, crack, dope (out), figure out, puzzle (out), resolve, riddle, unravel, work, work out

breakdown *Syn* ANALYSIS, dissection, resolution *Ant* synthesis

break down *Syn* ANALYZE, anatomize, assay, dissect

break out *Syn* ERUPT (sense 1), burst (forth), explode, flame, flare (up)

breakthrough *Syn* ADVANCE (sense 1), advancement, enhancement, improvement, refinement *Ant* setback

breastwork *Syn* BULWARK, bastion, parapet, rampart

breath *Syn* PAUSE, break, breather, interruption, lull, recess

breather *Syn* PAUSE, break, breath, interruption, lull, recess

breech *Syn* BUTTOCKS, backside, bottom, butt, fanny, hams, haunches, posterior, rear, rump, seat

breed *vb Syn* GENERATE, beget, engender, get, procreate, propagate, reproduce, sire

breed *n Syn* VARIETY (sense 2), clone, cultivar, race, stock, strain, subspecies

breeding **1** *Syn* ANCESTRY, birth, blood, bloodline, descent, extraction, family tree, genealogy, line, lineage, origin, parentage, pedigree, stock, strain *Ant* issue, posterity, progeny, seed **2** *Syn* CULTURE, cultivation, refinement

breeze *n Syn* CINCH, child's play, duck soup, picnic, pushover, snap *Ant* chore, headache, labor

breeze *vb Syn* HURRY (sense 2), barrel, bolt, bowl, career, course, dash, fly, hasten, hotfoot (it), hump, hurtle, hustle, pelt, race, rip, rocket, run, rush, rustle, scoot, scurry, scuttle, shoot, speed, step (along), tear, trot, whirl, whisk, zip, zoom *Ant* crawl, creep, poke

bribable *Syn* VENAL, corruptible, purchasable *Ant* incorruptible, uncorruptible

bridle **1** *Syn* RESTRAIN, check, curb, inhibit *Syn* RESTRAIN, bridle, check, curb, inhibit *Ant* abandon (*oneself*), activate, impel, incite **2** *Syn* STRUT, bristle, swagger

brief *n Syn* ABRIDGMENT, abstract, conspectus, epitome, synopsis *Ant* expansion

brief *vb Syn* ENLIGHTEN (sense 1), acquaint, advise, apprise, clue, familiarize, fill in, inform, instruct, tell, wise (up)

briefly *Syn* SUCCINCTLY, compactly, concisely, crisply, laconically, pithily, summarily, tersely *Ant* diffusely, long-windedly, verbosely, wordily

brig *Syn* JAIL, guardroom, hoosegow, jug, lockup, pen, penitentiary, prison, stockade

bright **1** • actually or seemingly shining or

glowing with light *Syn* beaming, brilliant, effulgent, incandescent, lambent, lucent, luminous, lustrous, radiant, refulgent *Rel* enlightened, illuminated, illumined, lighted, lightened *Ant* dim, dull **2** *Syn* CHEERFUL (sense 1), blithe, blithesome, buoyant, cheery, chipper, gay, gladsome, lightsome, sunny, upbeat *Ant* dour, gloomy, glum, morose, saturnine, sulky, sullen **3** *Syn* CHEERFUL (sense 2), cheering, cheery, gay, glad *Ant* bleak, cheerless, dark, depressing, dismal, dreary, gloomy, gray **4** *Syn* INTELLIGENT, alert, brilliant, clever, knowing, quick-witted, smart *Ant* unintelligent

brilliance *Syn* MAGNIFICENCE, augustness, gloriousness, glory, grandeur, grandness, majesty, nobility, nobleness, resplendence, splendor, stateliness, stupendousness, sublimeness, superbness

brilliant **1** *Syn* BRIGHT, beaming, effulgent, incandescent, lambent, lucent, luminous, lustrous, radiant, refulgent *Ant* dim, dull **2** *Syn* INTELLIGENT, alert, bright, clever, knowing, quick-witted, smart *Ant* unintelligent

brim *Syn* BORDER, brink, edge, margin, rim, verge

bring • to convey from one place to another *Syn* fetch, take *Rel* bear, carry, convey *Ant* remove, withdraw

bring about *Syn* EFFECT, cause, create, effectuate, engender, generate, induce, make, produce, prompt, result (in), spawn, work, yield

brink *Syn* BORDER, brim, edge, margin, rim, verge

brisk *Syn* AGILE, nimble, spry *Ant* torpid

bristle *Syn* STRUT, bridle, swagger

bristly *Syn* HAIRY (sense 1), fleecy, furry, hirsute, rough, shaggy, unshorn, woolly *Ant* bald, furless, hairless, shorn, smooth

brittle *Syn* FRAGILE, crisp, frangible, friable, short *Ant* tough

broach *Syn* EXPRESS, air, utter, vent, ventilate, voice *Ant* imply

broad **1** • having horizontal extent *Syn* deep, wide *Rel* extended, extensive *Ant* narrow **2** *Syn* EXTENSIVE, expansive, extended, far-flung, far-reaching, wide, widespread *Ant* narrow **3** *Syn* GENERAL (sense 2), all-around, bird's-eye, nonspecific, overall *Ant* delineated, detailed, particularized, specific

broadcast **1** *Syn* ANNOUNCE, advertise, blaze, declare, enunciate, placard, post, proclaim, promulgate, publicize, publish, sound **2** *Syn* STREW, scatter, sow, straw

broadcasting *Syn* DECLARATION, advertisement, announcement, proclamation, promulgation, publication

broadside *Syn* SIDEWAYS, edgewise, sidewise

Brobdingnagian *Syn* HUGE, colossal, cyclopean, elephantine, enormous, gargantuan, giant, gigantean, gigantic, Herculean, immense, mammoth, titanic, vast *Ant* bitty, diminutive, microscopic (*or* microscopical), midget, miniature, minute, pocket, pygmy, teeny, teeny-weeny, tiny, wee

broil *Syn* BRAWL, fracas, melee, row, rumpus, scrap

brokenhearted *Syn* SAD (sense 1), bad, blue, crestfallen, dejected, depressed, despondent, disconsolate, doleful, down, downcast, downhearted, droopy, forlorn, gloomy, glum, heartbroken, heartsick, heartsore, inconsolable, joyless, low, low-spirited, melancholy, miserable, mournful, saddened, sorrowful, sorry, unhappy, woebegone, woeful, wretched *Ant* blissful, buoyant, buoyed, cheerful, cheery, chipper, delighted, glad, gladdened, gladsome, gleeful, happy, joyful, joyous, jubilant, sunny, upbeat

bromide *Syn* COMMONPLACE, cliché, platitude, truism

brook *Syn* BEAR (sense 2), abide, endure, stand, suffer, tolerate

browbeat *Syn* INTIMIDATE, bulldoze, bully, cow

brownie *Syn* FAIRY, elf, fay, pixie (*also* pixy), sprite

bruise *vb Syn* CRUSH (sense 1), macerate, mash, smash, squash

bruise *n Syn* WOUND, contusion, lesion, trauma, traumatism

bruit (about) *Syn* RUMOR, circulate, noise (about), whisper

brush *vb* • to touch lightly in passing *Syn* glance, graze, shave, skim *Rel* contact, touch

brush *n Syn* ENCOUNTER, skirmish

brushwood *Syn* THICKET, brake, chaparral, coppice, copse, covert

brusque *Syn* BLUFF, blunt, crusty, curt, gruff *Ant* smooth, suave

brutal • characteristic of an animal in nature, action, or instinct *Syn* beastly, bestial, brute, brutish, feral *Rel* animal, carnal, fleshly, sensual

brutality *Syn* CRUELTY, barbarity, cruelness, heartlessness, inhumanity, sadism, savageness, savagery, viciousness, wantonness *Ant* benignity, compassion, good-heartedness, humanity, kindheartedness, kindness, sympathy

brute *n Syn* ANIMAL, beast, creature, critter

brute *adj Syn* BRUTAL, beastly, bestial, brutish, feral

brutish *Syn* BRUTAL, beastly, bestial, brute, feral

buccaneer *Syn* PIRATE, corsair, freebooter, privateer

buck *Syn* FOP, beau, coxcomb, dandy, dude, exquisite

buckaroo *Syn* COWBOY, cowhand, cowman, cowpoke, cowpuncher

buckle *Syn* FLEX, bow, crook *Ant* extend

bucolic *Syn* RURAL, pastoral, rustic *Ant* urban

buff *n Syn* FAN, addict, aficionado, bug, devotee, enthusiast, fanatic, fancier, fiend, freak, lover, maniac, nut
buff *vb Syn* POLISH, burnish, dress, gloss, grind, rub, shine, smooth
buffed *Syn* GLOSSY, burnished, glistening, lustrous, polished, rubbed, satin, satiny, sleek *Ant* dim, dull, flat, lusterless, matte
buffer *Syn* CUSHION, gentle, soften
buffet *vb Syn* BEAT, baste, belabor, pound, pummel, thrash
buffet *n Syn* CABINET, closet, cupboard, hutch, locker, sideboard
bug *Syn* FAN, addict, aficionado, buff, devotee, enthusiast, fanatic, fancier, fiend, freak, lover, maniac, nut
bugbear *Syn* ABOMINATION, anathema, bête noire *Ant* joy
build *vb* • to form by putting together parts or materials *Syn* assemble, construct, erect, fabricate, make, make up, piece, put up, raise, rear, set up *Rel* fashion, forge, frame, manufacture, mold, produce, shape *Ant* disassemble, dismantle, take down
build *n Syn* PHYSIQUE, constitution, habit
building • something built as a dwelling, shelter, or place for human activity *Syn* edifice, structure *Rel* construction, erection
build (up) *Syn* INCREASE (sense 2), accumulate, appreciate, balloon, burgeon, enlarge, escalate, expand, mount, multiply, mushroom, proliferate, rise, snowball, swell, wax *Ant* contract, decrease, diminish, lessen, wane
bulge *vb* • to extend outward beyond the usual and normal line *Syn* beetle, jut, overhang, project, protrude, stick out *Rel* dilate, distend, expand, swell
bulge *n Syn* PROJECTION, protrusion, protuberance
bulk • a body of usually material substance that constitutes a thing or unit *Syn* mass, volume *Rel* figure, form, shape
bulky **1** *Syn* LARGE, big, considerable, goodly, good-sized, grand, great, handsome, hefty, hulking, largish, outsize, oversize (*or* oversized), sizable (*or* sizeable), substantial, tidy, voluminous *Ant* little, puny, small, undersized **2** *Syn* MASSIVE, massy, monumental, substantial
bull **1** *Syn* ERROR, blunder, faux pas, howler, lapse, mistake, slip **2** *Syn* NONSENSE, balderdash, bunk, drivel, gobbledygook, poppycock, rot, trash, twaddle
bulldoze *Syn* INTIMIDATE, browbeat, bully, cow
bulletin *Syn* ANNOUNCEMENT, ad, advertisement, notice, notification, posting, release
bully *Syn* INTIMIDATE, browbeat, bulldoze, cow
bulwark • an aboveground defensive structure that forms part of a fortification *Syn* bastion, breastwork, parapet, rampart *Rel* citadel, fort, fortress, stronghold
bum *Syn* VAGABOND, hobo, tramp, truant, vagrant
bumble *Syn* STUMBLE, blunder, flounder, galumph, lollop, lumber, lurch, trip
bummer *Syn* DISAPPOINTMENT (sense 2), letdown
bump • to come or cause to come into violent contact or close or direct opposition *Syn* clash, collide, conflict *Rel* hit, smite, strike
bumpkin *Syn* HICK, clodhopper, countryman, provincial, rustic, yokel *Ant* cosmopolitan, sophisticate
bunch **1** *Syn* BUNDLE, bale, pack, package, packet, parcel **2** *Syn* GROUP, cluster, lot, parcel
bundle • things done up for storage, sale, or carriage *Syn* bale, bunch, pack, package, packet, parcel *Rel* assemblage, collection, gathering
bungle *Syn* BOTCH, bobble, butcher, flub, foozle, foul up, fumble, louse up, mangle, mess (up), muff, murder
bunk *Syn* NONSENSE, balderdash, bull, drivel, gobbledygook, poppycock, rot, trash, twaddle
buoyant *Syn* CHEERFUL (sense 1), blithe, blithesome, bright, cheery, chipper, gay, gladsome, lightsome, sunny, upbeat *Ant* dour, gloomy, glum, morose, saturnine, sulky, sullen
buoyant *Syn* ELASTIC (sense 2), effervescent, expansive, resilient, volatile *Ant* depressed
burden *vb* • to lay a heavy load upon or to lie like a heavy load upon a person or thing *Syn* charge, cumber, encumber, lade, load, saddle, tax, weigh, weight *Rel* depress, oppress, weigh
burden *n* **1** *Syn* LOAD, cargo, freight, lading **2** *Syn* OBLIGATION, charge, commitment, duty, need, responsibility **3** *Syn* SUBSTANCE, core, gist, pith, purport
burdensome *Syn* ONEROUS, exacting, oppressive
bureaucrat • a worker in a government agency *Syn* functionary, public servant *Rel* clerk, officeholder, official
burg *Syn* CITY, megalopolis, metropolis, municipality, town
burgeon *Syn* INCREASE (sense 2), accumulate, appreciate, balloon, build (up), enlarge, escalate, expand, mount, multiply, mushroom, proliferate, rise, snowball, swell, wax *Ant* contract, decrease, diminish, lessen, wane
burglar *Syn* THIEF, larcener, larcenist, robber
burglarize *Syn* ROB, loot, plunder, rifle
burglary *Syn* THEFT, larceny, robbery
burlesque *n Syn* CARICATURE, parody, travesty
burlesque *vb Syn* CARICATURE, parody, travesty
burly *Syn* MUSCULAR, athletic, brawny, husky, sinewy
burn • to injure by exposure to fire or intense heat *Syn* char, scorch, sear, singe *Rel* fire, ignite, kindle, light
burning *Syn* FERVENT, ardent, blazing,

charged, emotional, fervid, feverish, fiery, flaming, glowing, hot-blooded, impassioned, passionate, red-hot, vehement, warm, warm-blooded *Ant* cold, cool, dispassionate, impassive, unemotional

burnish *Syn* POLISH, buff, dress, gloss, grind, rub, shine, smooth

burnished *Syn* GLOSSY, buffed, glistening, lustrous, polished, rubbed, satin, satiny, sleek *Ant* dim, dull, flat, lusterless, matte

burnout *Syn* FATIGUE, collapse, exhaustion, lassitude, prostration, tiredness, weariness *Ant* refreshment, rejuvenation, revitalization

burp *Syn* BELCH, disgorge, regurgitate, spew, throw up, vomit

burst *vb Syn* BREAK, bust, crack, shatter, shiver, snap *Ant* cleave (*together*), keep (*of laws*)

burst *n Syn* OUTBREAK, flare, flare-up, flash, flicker, flurry, flutter, outburst, spurt

burst (forth) *Syn* ERUPT (sense 1), break out, explode, flame, flare (up)

bury *Syn* HIDE, cache, conceal, ensconce, screen, secrete

bush *Syn* FRONTIER, backwater, backwoods, hinterland, up-country

business **1** • one of the forms or branches of human endeavor which have for their objective the supplying of commodities *Syn* commerce, industry, trade, traffic **2** *Syn* WORK (sense 2), calling, employment, occupation, pursuit **3** *Syn* AFFAIR, concern, matter, thing

bust *Syn* BREAK, burst, crack, shatter, shiver, snap *Ant* cleave (*together*), keep (*of laws*)

bustle **1** *Syn* COMMOTION, bother, clatter, disturbance, furor, furore, fuss, hubbub, hullabaloo, hurly-burly, pandemonium, pother, row, ruckus, ruction, rumpus, shindy, squall, stew, stir, storm, to-do, tumult, turmoil, uproar, welter, whirl **2** *Syn* STIR, ado, flurry, fuss, pother *Ant* tranquillity

busy • actively engaged or occupied in work or in accomplishing a purpose or intention *Syn* assiduous, diligent, industrious, sedulous *Rel* absorbed, engrossed, intent *Ant* idle, unoccupied

busybody • a person who meddles in the affairs of others *Syn* interferer, interloper, intruder, kibitzer, meddler *Rel* peeper, peeping Tom, snoop, snooper, spy

butcher **1** *Syn* BOTCH, bobble, bungle, flub, foozle, foul up, fumble, louse up, mangle, mess (up), muff, murder **2** *Syn* MASSACRE, mow (down), slaughter

butchery *Syn* MASSACRE, carnage, pogrom, slaughter

butt **1** *Syn* BUTTOCKS, backside, bottom, breech, fanny, hams, haunches, posterior, rear, rump, seat **2** *Syn* LAUGHINGSTOCK, mark, mock, mockery, target

butt in *Syn* INTERFERE, intrude, meddle, mess, nose, obtrude, poke, pry, snoop

buttocks • the part of the body upon which someone sits *Syn* backside, bottom, breech, butt, fanny, hams, haunches, posterior, rear, rump, seat

buttress *n* • auxiliary structures designed to serve as a prop, shore, or support for a wall (as of a building) *Syn* abutment, pier

buttress *vb Syn* SUPPORT (sense 1), bolster, brace, prop, sustain

buy • to get possession of (something) by giving money in exchange for *Syn* pick up, purchase, take *Rel* acquire, get, obtain, procure, secure

by **1** • using as a means of approach or action *Syn* through, with **2** *Syn* AROUND (sense 1), about, near, next to

by and large *Syn* CHIEFLY, altogether, basically, generally, largely, mainly, mostly, overall, predominantly, primarily, principally, substantially

bygone *Syn* EXTINCT, dead, defunct, departed, expired, gone, vanished *Ant* alive, existent, existing, extant, living

bylaw *Syn* RULE (sense 1), ground rule, regulation

by-product *Syn* DERIVATIVE, offshoot, outgrowth, spin-off *Ant* origin, root, source

bystander *Syn* SPECTATOR, beholder, eyewitness, kibitzer, looker-on, observer, onlooker, witness

byword *Syn* CATCHWORD, shibboleth, slogan

C

cabal *Syn* PLOT, conspiracy, intrigue, machination

cabalistic *Syn* MYSTICAL, anagogic, mystic

cabin **1** *Syn* COMPARTMENT, bay, cell, chamber, cubicle **2** *Syn* SHACK, camp, hovel, hut, hutch, shanty

cabinet • a storage case typically having doors and shelves *Syn* buffet, closet, cupboard, hutch, locker, sideboard *Rel* bookcase, secretary

cable *Syn* CORD, lace, lacing, line, rope, string, wire

cache *vb* **1** *Syn* HIDE, bury, conceal, ensconce, screen, secrete **2** *Syn* HOARD, lay away, lay up, put by, salt away, squirrel (away), stash, stockpile, store, stow

cache *n Syn* STORE, deposit, hoard, reserve

cackle *Syn* CHAT, babble, blab, chatter, converse, gab, gabble, gas, jabber, jaw, palaver, patter, prate, prattle, rap, rattle, run on, talk, twitter, visit

cadaver *Syn* BODY, carcass, corpse

cadaverous *Syn* HAGGARD, careworn, pinched, wasted, worn

caddy *Syn* CHEST, box, case, casket, locker, trunk

cadence *Syn* RHYTHM, beat, measure, meter

café **1** *Syn* BARROOM, bar, groggery, grogshop, pub, saloon, tavern **2** *Syn* RESTAURANT, diner, grill

cage *Syn* ENCLOSE, coop, corral, envelop, fence, pen, wall

cajole *Syn* COAX, blandish, blarney, soft-soap, wheedle

cake *Syn* HARDEN (sense 1), indurate, petrify, solidify *Ant* soften

calamitous *Syn* UNLUCKY, disastrous, hapless, ill-fated, ill-starred, luckless, unfortunate *Ant* fortunate, happy, lucky

calamity *Syn* DISASTER, apocalypse, cataclysm, catastrophe

calculate **1** • to determine something (as cost, speed, or quantity) by mathematical processes *Syn* compute, estimate, reckon *Rel* consider, study, weigh **2** *Syn* ESTIMATE (sense 2), call, conjecture, figure, gauge, guess, judge, make, place, put, reckon, suppose

calculating *Syn* CAUTIOUS, chary, circumspect, wary *Ant* adventurous, temerarious

calculation **1** • the act or process of performing mathematical operations to find a value *Syn* arithmetic, ciphering, computation, figures, figuring, reckoning *Rel* mathematics **2** *Syn* CAUTION, chariness, circumspection, wariness *Ant* adventurousness, temerity

caliber *Syn* QUALITY (sense 2), stature

call *vb* **1** *Syn* ESTIMATE (sense 2), calculate, conjecture, figure, gauge, guess, judge, make, place, put, reckon, suppose **2** *Syn* SUMMON, cite, convene, convoke, muster

call *n Syn* VISIT, visitation

caller *Syn* VISITOR, guest, visitant

calling **1** *Syn* CANCELLATION, abortion, calling off, dropping, recall, repeal, rescission, revocation *Ant* continuation **2** *Syn* OCCUPATION, employment, line, profession, trade, vocation, work **3** *Syn* WORK (sense 2), business, employment, occupation, pursuit

calling off *Syn* CANCELLATION, abortion, calling, dropping, recall, repeal, rescission, revocation *Ant* continuation

callous *Syn* HARDENED, indurated *Ant* softened

callow **1** • lacking in adult experience or maturity *Syn* adolescent, green, immature, inexperienced, juvenile, puerile, raw, unfledged, unripe, unripened *Rel* babyish, childish, infantile *Ant* adult, experienced, grown-up, mature, ripe **2** *Syn* RUDE (sense 1), crude, green, raw, rough, uncouth *Ant* civil, urbane

calm *adj* • quiet and free from all that disturbs or excites *Syn* halcyon, peaceful, placid, serene, tranquil *Rel* noiseless, quiet, still, stilly *Ant* agitated, stormy

calm *n* • a state of freedom from storm or disturbance *Syn* calmness, hush, peace, peacefulness, placidity, quiet, quietness, quietude, repose, restfulness, sereneness, serenity, still, stillness, tranquillity (*or* tranquility) *Rel* lull, pause, respite *Ant* bustle, commotion, hubbub, hurly-burly, pandemonium, tumult, turmoil, uproar

calm *vb* • to relieve or to bring to an end whatever distresses, agitates, or disturbs *Syn* compose, lull, quiet, quieten, settle, soothe, still, tranquilize *Rel* allay, alleviate, assuage, mitigate, relieve *Ant* agitate, arouse

calmness **1** *Syn* CALM, hush, peace, peacefulness, placidity, quiet, quietness, quietude, repose, restfulness, sereneness, serenity, still, stillness, tranquillity (*or* tranquility) *Ant* bustle, commotion, hubbub, hurly-burly, pandemonium, tumult, turmoil, uproar **2** *Syn* EQUANIMITY, aplomb, composure, coolheadedness, coolness, imperturbability, placidity, self-possession, serenity, tranquillity (*or* tranquility) *Ant* agitation, discomposure, perturbation

calumny *Syn* DETRACTION, backbiting, scandal, slander

camaraderie *Syn* COMPANIONSHIP, company, comradeship, fellowship, society

camouflage *Syn* DISGUISE, cloak, dissemble, mask

camp *Syn* SHACK, cabin, hovel, hut, hutch, shanty

campaign • a series of activities undertaken to achieve a goal *Syn* bandwagon, cause, crusade, drive, movement *Rel* attack, march, offensive

campaigner *Syn* CANDIDATE, applicant, aspirant, contender, hopeful, prospect, seeker

camper • a motor vehicle that is specially equipped for living while traveling *Syn* caravan, mobile home, motor home, trailer *Rel* van

canal *Syn* CHANNEL, aqueduct, conduit, duct

cancel **1** *Syn* ABOLISH, abrogate, annul, dissolve, invalidate, negate, nullify, quash, repeal, rescind, void **2** *Syn* ERASE, blot out, delete, efface, expunge, obliterate

cancellation • the act of putting an end to something planned or previously agreed to *Syn* abortion, calling, calling off, dropping, recall, repeal, rescission, revocation *Rel* annulment, invalidation, neutralization, nullification *Ant* continuation

candid *Syn* FRANK, open, plain *Ant* reticent
candidate • one who seeks an office, honor, position, or award *Syn* applicant, aspirant, campaigner, contender, hopeful, prospect, seeker *Rel* competitor, contestant, entrant
candor • the free expression of one's true feelings and opinions *Syn* directness, forthrightness, frankness, openheartedness, openness, plainness, straightforwardness *Rel* earnestness, sincerity, sobriety *Ant* dissembling, pretense (*or* pretence)
cannonade *Syn* BARRAGE, bombardment, fusillade, hail, salvo, shower, storm, volley
canon *Syn* LAW, ordinance, precept, regulation, rule, statute
canonize *Syn* IDOLIZE, adore, adulate, deify, dote (on), worship
canopy • a raised covering over something for decoration or protection *Syn* awning, ceiling, roof, tent *Rel* screen, shade, shelter, shield, sunshade
cant **1** *Syn* HYPOCRISY, dissembling, dissimulation, insincerity, piousness, sanctimoniousness *Ant* genuineness, sincerity **2** *Syn* TERMINOLOGY, argot, dialect, jargon, language, lingo, patois, patter, slang, vocabulary
canvass • to go around and approach (people) with a request for opinions or information *Syn* poll, solicit, survey *Rel* interrogate, interview, question
canyon • a narrow opening between hillsides or mountains that can be used for passage *Syn* defile, flume, gap, gorge, gulch, gulf, notch, pass, ravine *Rel* abyss, chasm, cirque, cleft, crevasse, crevice, fissure
capability *Syn* ABILITY, capacity, competence, competency, faculty *Ant* disability, inability, incapability, incapacity, incompetence, incompetency, ineptitude, ineptness
capable *Syn* COMPETENT, able, fit, good, qualified, suitable *Ant* incompetent, inept, poor, unfit, unqualified
capacious *Syn* SPACIOUS, ample, commodious
capacity **1** *Syn* ABILITY, capability, competence, competency, faculty *Ant* disability, inability, incapability, incapacity, incompetence, incompetency, ineptitude, ineptness **2** *Syn* ROLE, function, job, part, place, position, purpose, task, work
caparison *Syn* FINERY, array, best, bravery, feather, frippery, full dress, gaiety, regalia
caper *Syn* PRANK, antic, dido, monkeyshine
capital *n* *Syn* CENTER (sense 2), base, core, cynosure, eye, focus, heart, hub, mecca, nucleus, seat
capital *adj* **1** *Syn* CHIEF, foremost, leading, main, principal *Ant* subordinate **2** *Syn* EXCELLENT, A1, bang-up, banner, classic, crackerjack, dandy, divine, fabulous, fine, first-class, first-rate, grand, great, groovy, heavenly, jim-dandy, keen, marvelous (*or* marvellous), mean, neat, nifty, noble, par excellence, prime, sensational, splendid, stellar, sterling, superb, superior, superlative, supernal, swell, terrific, tip-top, top, top-notch, unsurpassed, wonderful *Ant* poor
capitulate *Syn* YIELD, bow, cave, defer, relent, submit, succumb
capitulation *Syn* SURRENDER, submission
caprice *Syn* WHIM, fancy, freak, notion, vagary, whimsy
capricious **1** *Syn* INCONSTANT, fickle, mercurial, unstable *Ant* constant **2** *Syn* WHIMSICAL, freakish, impulsive
capsize *Syn* OVERTURN, overthrow, subvert, upset
capsule *Syn* PILL, lozenge, tablet
captain *Syn* BOSS, chief, foreman, head, headman, helmsman, kingpin, leader, master, taskmaster
caption *Syn* INSCRIPTION, legend
captious *Syn* CRITICAL, carping, caviling, censorious, faultfinding, hypercritical *Ant* uncritical
captivate *Syn* ATTRACT, allure, bewitch, charm, enchant, fascinate *Ant* repel
captivating *Syn* ATTRACTIVE, alluring, bewitching, charming, enchanting, fascinating *Ant* forbidding, repellent
capture **1** *Syn* CATCH, bag, ensnare, entrap, snare, trap *Ant* miss **2** *Syn* EARN, acquire, attain, carry, draw, gain, garner, get, land, make, obtain, procure, realize, secure, win *Ant* forfeit, lose
caravan *Syn* CAMPER, mobile home, motor home, trailer
carbon copy *Syn* COPY, duplicate, duplication, facsimile, imitation, reduplication, replica, replication, reproduction *Ant* original
carbuncle *Syn* ABSCESS, boil, furuncle, pimple, pustule
carcass *Syn* BODY, cadaver, corpse
cardinal *Syn* ESSENTIAL, fundamental, vital
care **1** • a troubled or engrossed state of mind or the thing that causes this *Syn* anxiety, concern, solicitude, worry *Rel* effort, exertion, pains, trouble **2** *Syn* CUSTODY, guardianship, keeping, safekeeping, trust, ward
career *Syn* HURRY (sense 2), barrel, bolt, bowl, breeze, course, dash, fly, hasten, hotfoot (it), hump, hurtle, hustle, pelt, race, rip, rocket, run, rush, rustle, scoot, scurry, scuttle, shoot, speed, step (along), tear, trot, whirl, whisk, zip, zoom *Ant* crawl, creep, poke
care (for) *Syn* APPROVE (OF), accept, countenance, favor, OK (*or* okay), subscribe (to) *Ant* disapprove (of), discountenance, disfavor, frown (on *or* upon)
carefree • having or showing a lack of concern or seriousness *Syn* careless, cavalier, devil-may-care, easygoing, gay, happy-go-lucky, insouciant, lighthearted, unconcerned *Rel* breezy, nonchalant *Ant* careworn

careful **1** • marked by close attention to details or care in execution or performance *Syn* meticulous, punctilious, punctual, scrupulous *Rel* cautious, circumspect, wary *Ant* careless **2** *Syn* WORRIED, anxious, concerned, solicitous

careless **1** • showing lack of concern or attention *Syn* heedless, inadvertent, thoughtless *Rel* lax, neglectful, negligent, remiss, slack *Ant* careful **2** *Syn* CAREFREE, cavalier, devil-may-care, easygoing, gay, happy-go-lucky, insouciant, lighthearted, unconcerned *Ant* careworn **3** *Syn* NEGLIGENT, derelict, lax, neglectful, neglecting, remiss, slack *Ant* attentive, careful, conscientious

caress • to show affection or love by touching or handling *Syn* cosset, cuddle, dandle, fondle, pet *Rel* coquet, dally, flirt, toy, trifle

careworn *Syn* HAGGARD, cadaverous, pinched, wasted, worn

cargo *Syn* LOAD, burden, freight, lading

caricature *n* **1** • a grotesque or bizarre imitation of something *Syn* burlesque, parody, travesty *Rel* humor, sarcasm, satire, wit **2** *Syn* EXAGGERATION, coloring, elaboration, embellishment, embroidering, hyperbole, magnification, overstatement, padding, stretching *Ant* understatement

caricature *vb* • to make a grotesque or bizarre imitation of something *Syn* burlesque, parody, travesty *Rel* ape, copy, imitate, mimic, mock

carnage *Syn* MASSACRE, butchery, pogrom, slaughter

carnal • characterized by physical rather than intellectual or spiritual orientation *Syn* animal, fleshly, sensual *Rel* bodily, corporal, corporeal, physical, somatic *Ant* intellectual, spiritual

carnival *Syn* FESTIVAL, celebration, festivity, fete (*or* fête), fiesta, gala, jubilee

carol *Syn* SING, chant, descant, hymn, intone, trill, troll, warble

carp **1** *Syn* COMPLAIN, beef, bellyache, crab, croak, fuss, gripe, grouse, growl, grumble, kick, moan, murmur, mutter, repine, squawk, wail, whine, yammer *Ant* rejoice **2** *Syn* QUIBBLE, cavil, fuss, nitpick

carper *Syn* CRITIC, castigator, caviler (*or* caviller), censurer, faultfinder, nitpicker, railer, scold

carping *Syn* CRITICAL, captious, caviling, censorious, faultfinding, hypercritical *Ant* uncritical

carry **1** • to be the agent or the means whereby something or someone is moved from one place to another *Syn* bear, convey, transmit, transport *Rel* bring, fetch, take **2** *Syn* EARN, acquire, attain, capture, draw, gain, garner, get, land, make, obtain, procure, realize, secure, win *Ant* forfeit, lose

carry away *Syn* ENTRANCE, enrapture, enthrall (*or* enthral), overjoy, ravish, transport

carry on *Syn* PERSEVERE, persist

cartel **1** • a number of businesses or enterprises united for commercial advantage *Syn* combination, combine, syndicate, trust *Rel* chain, conglomerate, multinational **2** *Syn* CONTRACT, bargain, compact, concordat, convention, entente, pact, treaty **3** *Syn* MONOPOLY, corner, pool, syndicate, trust

carve **1** • to cut an outline or a shape out of or into some substance *Syn* chisel, engrave, etch, incise, sculpt, sculpture *Rel* fashion, form, make, shape **2** *Syn* CUT, chop, hew, slash, slit

cascade *Syn* WATERFALL, cataract, fall(s)

case **1** *Syn* ATTACK (sense 3), bout, fit, seizure, siege, spell **2** *Syn* CHEST, box, caddy, casket, locker, trunk **3** *Syn* EXAMPLE, exemplar, illustration, instance, representative, sample, specimen **4** *Syn* SUIT, action, cause, lawsuit

casement *Syn* WINDOW, oriel

cash *Syn* MONEY, coin, coinage, currency, legal tender, specie

cashier *Syn* DISMISS, bounce, discharge, drop, fire, sack

cask • an enclosed wooden vessel for holding beverages *Syn* barrel, firkin, hogshead, keg, pipe, puncheon *Rel* tub, vat

casket *Syn* CHEST, box, caddy, case, locker, trunk

cast *vb* **1** *Syn* DISCARD, junk, molt, scrap, shed, slough **2** *Syn* THROW, fling, hurl, pitch, sling, toss

cast *n* *Syn* PREDICTION, auguring, forecast, forecasting, foretelling, predicting, presaging, prognosis, prognosticating, prognostication, prophecy, soothsaying

castaway *Syn* OUTCAST, derelict, pariah, reprobate, untouchable

castigate **1** *Syn* ATTACK (sense 2), abuse, assail, belabor, blast, excoriate, jump (on), lambaste (*or* lambast), scathe, slam, vituperate **2** *Syn* PUNISH, chasten, chastise, correct, discipline *Ant* excuse, pardon

castigating *Syn* PUNITIVE, chastening, chastising, correcting, correctional, corrective, disciplinary, disciplining, penal, penalizing

castigator *Syn* CRITIC, carper, caviler (*or* caviller), censurer, faultfinder, nitpicker, railer, scold

castle *Syn* MANSION, château, countryseat, estate, hacienda, hall, manor, manor house, palace, villa

castrate *Syn* STERILIZE (sense 1), alter, emasculate, geld, mutilate, spay *Ant* fertilize

casual **1** *Syn* ACCIDENTAL, chance, fluky, fortuitous, inadvertent, incidental, unintended, unintentional, unplanned, unpremeditated, unwitting *Ant* deliberate, intended, intentional, planned, premeditated **2** *Syn* FITFUL, choppy, discontinuous, erratic, intermittent, irregular, occasional, spasmodic, sporadic, spotty, unsteady *Ant* constant, continuous, regular, steady **3** *Syn* RANDOM, chance, chancy, desultory, haphazard, happy-go-lucky, hit-or-miss *Ant* methodical, nonrandom, orderly, systematic

casualness *Syn* INDIFFERENCE, apathy, disinterestedness, disregard, insouciance, nonchalance, unconcern *Ant* concern, interest, regard

casualty *Syn* ACCIDENT, mishap

cataclysm **1** *Syn* CONVULSION, paroxysm, storm, tempest, tumult, upheaval, uproar **2** *Syn* DISASTER, apocalypse, calamity, catastrophe

cataclysmal *or* **cataclysmic** *Syn* CONVULSIVE, stormy, tempestuous, tumultuous

catalog *n Syn* LIST, inventory, register, roll, roster, schedule, table

catalog *vb Syn* RECORD, enroll, list, register

cataract **1** *Syn* FLOOD, deluge, inundation, spate, torrent **2** *Syn* WATERFALL, cascade, fall(s)

catastrophe *Syn* DISASTER, apocalypse, calamity, cataclysm

catch • to come to possess or control by or as if by seizing *Syn* bag, capture, ensnare, entrap, snare, trap *Rel* clutch, grab, grasp, seize, snatch, take *Ant* miss

catching *Syn* INFECTIOUS (sense 1), communicable, contagious

catchword • a phrase that catches the eye or the ear and is repeated so often that it becomes a formula *Syn* byword, shibboleth, slogan *Rel* caption, inscription, legend

catechize *Syn* ASK (sense 1), examine, inquire, interrogate, query, question, quiz

categorical **1** *Syn* EXPLICIT, definite, express, specific *Ant* ambiguous **2** *Syn* ULTIMATE, absolute

cater • to furnish with what satisfies the appetite or desires *Syn* pander, purvey *Rel* accouter, appoint, equip, furnish

catholic *Syn* UNIVERSAL (sense 1), cosmic, cosmopolitan, ecumenical *Ant* particular

catnap *Syn* SLEEP, doze, drowse, nap, slumber, snooze

cause *n* **1** • that (as a person, fact, or condition) which is responsible for an effect *Syn* antecedent, determinant, occasion, reason *Rel* goad, impulse, incentive, inducement, motive, spring, spur **2** *Syn* CAMPAIGN, bandwagon, crusade, drive, movement **3** *Syn* SUIT, action, case, lawsuit

cause *vb Syn* EFFECT, bring about, create, effectuate, engender, generate, induce, make, produce, prompt, result (in), spawn, work, yield

caustic • stingingly incisive *Syn* acrid, mordant, scathing *Rel* biting, cutting, incisive, trenchant *Ant* genial

caution *n* **1** • careful prudence especially in reducing or avoiding risk or danger *Syn* calculation, chariness, circumspection, wariness *Rel* alertness, vigilance, watchfulness *Ant* adventurousness, temerity **2** *Syn* WARNING, admonition, alarm, alert, forewarning, notice

caution *vb Syn* WARN, alert, forewarn

cautionary • serving as or offering a warning *Syn* admonishing, admonitory, cautioning, warning *Rel* didactic, moralistic, moralizing

cautioning *Syn* CAUTIONARY, admonishing, admonitory, warning

cautious • prudently watchful and discreet in the face of danger or risk *Syn* calculating, chary, circumspect, wary *Rel* alert, vigilant, watchful *Ant* adventurous, temerarious

cavalcade *Syn* PROCESSION, cortege, motorcade, parade

cavalier **1** *Syn* ARROGANT, haughty, highfalutin, high-handed, high-hat, imperious, important, lofty, lordly, masterful, overweening, peremptory, pompous, presumptuous, pretentious, supercilious, superior, uppish, uppity *Ant* humble, modest **2** *Syn* CAREFREE, careless, devil-may-care, easygoing, gay, happy-go-lucky, insouciant, lighthearted, unconcerned *Ant* careworn

cave *Syn* YIELD, bow, capitulate, defer, relent, submit, succumb

cavil *Syn* QUIBBLE, carp, fuss, nitpick

caviler *or* **caviller** *Syn* CRITIC, carper, castigator, censurer, faultfinder, nitpicker, railer, scold

caviling *Syn* CRITICAL, captious, carping, censorious, faultfinding, hypercritical *Ant* uncritical

cavity *Syn* HOLE, hollow, pocket, vacuum, void

cease *Syn* STOP, desist, discontinue, quit

cease-fire *Syn* TRUCE, armistice, peace

cede *Syn* RELINQUISH, abandon, leave, resign, surrender, waive, yield *Ant* keep

ceiling *Syn* CANOPY, awning, roof, tent

celebrate *Syn* KEEP (sense 1), commemorate, observe, solemnize *Ant* break

celebrated *Syn* FAMOUS, famed, noted, notorious, prominent, renowned, star, well-known *Ant* anonymous, obscure, unknown

celebration *Syn* FESTIVAL, carnival, festivity, fete (*or* fête), fiesta, gala, jubilee

celebrity *Syn* FAME, éclat, glory, honor, notoriety, renown, reputation, repute *Ant* infamy, obscurity

celestial • of, relating to, or suggesting heaven *Syn* Elysian, empyreal, empyrean, heavenly, supernal *Rel* ethereal, supernatural, transcendent, transcendental, unearthly, unworldly *Ant* hellish, infernal

cell *Syn* COMPARTMENT, bay, cabin, chamber, cubicle

cenobite *Syn* RECLUSE, anchorite, eremite, hermit

censorious *Syn* CRITICAL, captious, carping, caviling, faultfinding, hypercritical *Ant* uncritical
censure *n* • an often public or formal expression of disapproval *Syn* condemnation, denunciation, rebuke, reprimand, reproach, reproof, stricture *Rel* admonishment, admonition, castigation, chastisement, punishment *Ant* citation, commendation, endorsement
censure *vb Syn* CRITICIZE, blame, condemn, denounce, reprehend, reprobate
censurer *Syn* CRITIC, carper, castigator, caviler (*or* caviller), faultfinder, nitpicker, railer, scold
center *n* **1** • an area or point that is an equal distance from all points along an edge or outer surface *Syn* core, middle, midpoint, midst *Rel* inside, interior *Ant* perimeter, periphery **2** • a thing or place that is of greatest importance to an activity or interest *Syn* base, capital, core, cynosure, eye, focus, heart, hub, mecca, nucleus, seat *Rel* focus, headquarters
center *vb* • to draw to or fix upon a center *Syn* centralize, concentrate, focus *Rel* depend, hang, hinge, turn
central • dominant or most important *Syn* focal, pivotal *Rel* dominant, paramount, predominant, preponderant
centralize *Syn* CENTER, concentrate, focus
cerebral *Syn* MENTAL, intellectual, intelligent, psychic
ceremonial *adj* • characterized or marked by attention to the forms, procedures, and details prescribed as right, proper, or requisite *Syn* ceremonious, conventional, formal, solemn *Rel* liturgical, ritualistic
ceremonial *n Syn* FORM (sense 2), ceremony, formality, liturgy, rite, ritual
ceremonious *Syn* CEREMONIAL, conventional, formal, solemn
ceremony *Syn* FORM (sense 2), ceremonial, formality, liturgy, rite, ritual
certain **1** • bound to follow in obedience to the laws of nature or of thought *Syn* inevitable, necessary *Ant* probable, supposed **2** *Syn* INEVITABLE, inescapable, necessary, sure, unavoidable *Ant* avoidable, escapable, uncertain, unsure **3** *Syn* SURE, cocksure, positive *Ant* unsure
certainty • a state of mind in which one is free from doubt *Syn* assurance, certitude, conviction *Rel* belief, credence, faith *Ant* uncertainty
certify **1** • to testify to the truth or genuineness of something *Syn* attest, vouch, witness *Rel* assert, aver, avouch, avow, profess **2** *Syn* APPROVE, accredit, endorse, sanction *Ant* disapprove
certitude *Syn* CERTAINTY, assurance, conviction *Ant* uncertainty
chafe *Syn* ABRADE, excoriate, fret, gall
chaff *n Syn* BANTER, give-and-take, jesting, joshing, persiflage, raillery, repartee
chaff *vb* **1** *Syn* BANTER, jolly, josh, kid, rag, rib **2** *Syn* TEASE, jive, josh, kid, rally, razz, rib, ride, roast
chaffer *Syn* BARGAIN, deal, dicker, haggle, horse-trade, negotiate, palter
chagrined *Syn* ASHAMED, mortified *Ant* proud
chain **1** *Syn* ENCUMBRANCE, bar, block, clog, crimp, deterrent, drag, embarrassment, fetter, handicap, hindrance, hurdle, impediment, inhibition, interference, let, manacle, obstacle, obstruction, shackles, stop, stumbling block, trammel *Ant* aid, assistance, benefit, help **2** *Syn* SUCCESSION, progression, sequence, series, string, train
challenge *vb* **1** • to invite (someone) to take part in a contest or to perform a feat *Syn* dare, defy, stump *Rel* beard, brave, brazen, breast, confront, face, outbrave **2** *Syn* FACE, beard, brave, dare, defy *Ant* avoid
challenge *n Syn* OBJECTION, complaint, demur, expostulation, fuss, protest, question, remonstrance
challenger *Syn* COMPETITOR, competition, contender, contestant, rival
chamber **1** *Syn* COMPARTMENT, bay, cabin, cell, cubicle **2** *Syn* ROOM (sense 1), apartment
champ *Syn* BITE, gnash, gnaw
champion *n* **1** *Syn* EXPONENT, advocate, apostle, backer, booster, friend, promoter, proponent, supporter *Ant* adversary, antagonist, opponent **2** *Syn* VICTOR, conqueror, vanquisher, winner
champion *vb Syn* SUPPORT (sense 2), advocate, back, uphold
chance *n* **1** • something that happens without an apparent or determinable cause or as a result of unpredictable forces *Syn* accident, fortune, hap, hazard, luck *Rel* contingency, emergency, exigency, juncture, pass *Ant* law, principle **2** *Syn* OPPORTUNITY, break, occasion, time **3** *Syn* PROBABILITY, odds, percentage
chance *adj* **1** *Syn* ACCIDENTAL, casual, fluky, fortuitous, inadvertent, incidental, unintended, unintentional, unplanned, unpremeditated, unwitting *Ant* deliberate, intended, intentional, planned, premeditated **2** *Syn* RANDOM, casual, chancy, desultory, haphazard, happy-go-lucky, hit-or-miss *Ant* methodical, nonrandom, orderly, systematic
chance *vb Syn* HAPPEN, befall, betide, occur, transpire
chance (upon) *Syn* HAPPEN (on *or* upon), encounter, find, hit (upon), meet, stumble (on *or* onto)
chancy *Syn* RANDOM, casual, chance, desultory, haphazard, happy-go-lucky, hit-or-miss *Ant* methodical, nonrandom, orderly, systematic

change *n* **1** • a making different *Syn* alteration, modification, variation *Rel* diversity, variety *Ant* monotony, uniformity **2** • a result of a making different *Syn* alternation, mutation, permutation, vicissitude *Rel* conversion, metamorphosis, transformation, transmogrification, transmutation

change *vb* **1** • to make different in some way *Syn* alter, make over, modify, recast, redo, refashion, remake, remodel, revamp, revise, rework, vary *Rel* deform, metamorphose, mutate *Ant* fix, freeze, set, stabilize **2** • to pass from one form, state, or level to another *Syn* fluctuate, mutate, shift, vary *Rel* metamorphose, transmute *Ant* stabilize **3** • to give up (something) and take something else in return *Syn* commute, exchange, shift, substitute, swap, switch, trade *Rel* interchange

changeable • having or showing a marked capacity for changes or a marked tendency to alter under slight provocation *Syn* changeful, mutable, protean, variable *Rel* capricious, fickle, inconstant, mercurial, unstable *Ant* stable, unchangeable

changeful *Syn* CHANGEABLE, mutable, protean, variable *Ant* stable, unchangeable

channel *n* **1** • something through which a fluid (as water) is led or flows *Syn* aqueduct, canal, conduit, duct *Rel* pass, passage, way **2** *Syn* STRAIT, narrows, passage, sound

channel *vb* • to cause to move to a central point or along a restricted pathway *Syn* channelize, conduct, direct, funnel, pipe, siphon *Rel* carry, convey, transmit

channelize *Syn* CHANNEL, conduct, direct, funnel, pipe, siphon

chant *Syn* SING, carol, descant, hymn, intone, trill, troll, warble

chaos **1** *Syn* ANARCHY, lawlessness, misrule **2** *Syn* CONFUSION, clutter, disarray, disorder, jumble, muddle, snarl

chaotic *Syn* MESSY, cluttered, confused, disarranged, disarrayed, disheveled (*or* dishevelled), disordered, disorderly, higgledy-piggledy, hugger-mugger, jumbled, littered, messed, muddled, mussed, mussy, pell-mell, rumpled, sloppy, topsy-turvy, tousled, tumbled, unkempt, untidy, upside-down *Ant* neat, ordered, orderly, organized, shipshape, snug, tidied, tidy, trim

chaparral *Syn* THICKET, brake, brushwood, coppice, copse, covert

chaperone *or* **chaperon** *Syn* ACCOMPANY, attend, convoy, escort, squire

char *Syn* BURN, scorch, sear, singe

character **1** • an arbitrary or conventional device that is used in writing and in printing, but is neither a word nor a phrase nor a picture *Syn* mark, sign, symbol **2** *Syn* CHARACTERISTIC, attribute, feature, mark, peculiarity, point, property, quality, trait **3** *Syn* CREDENTIAL, recommendation, reference, testimonial **4** *Syn* DISPOSITION, complexion, individuality, personality, temper, temperament **5** *Syn* ECCENTRIC, codger, crackbrain, crackpot, crank, kook, nut, oddball, screwball, weirdo **6** *Syn* TYPE, description, ilk, kidney, kind, nature, sort, stripe

characteristic *adj* • being or revealing a quality specific or identifying to an individual or group *Syn* distinctive, individual, peculiar *Rel* especial, particular, special, specific

characteristic *n* • something that sets apart an individual from others of the same kind *Syn* attribute, character, feature, mark, peculiarity, point, property, quality, trait *Rel* badge, indication, sign

characterize • to be a peculiar or significant quality or feature of something *Syn* distinguish, mark, qualify *Rel* demarcate, differentiate, distinguish

charge *vb* **1** *Syn* ACCUSE, impeach, incriminate, indict *Ant* absolve, acquit, clear, exculpate, exonerate, vindicate **2** *Syn* ASCRIBE, accredit, assign, attribute, credit, impute, refer **3** *Syn* BURDEN, cumber, encumber, lade, load, saddle, tax, weigh, weight **4** *Syn* COMMAND, bid, direct, enjoin, instruct, order *Ant* comply, obey **5** *Syn* IMPOSE, assess, exact, fine, lay, levy, put *Ant* remit

charge *n* **1** *Syn* ATTACK (sense 2), aggression, assault, blitzkrieg, descent, offense (*or* offence), offensive, onset, onslaught, raid, rush, strike **2** *Syn* MISSION, assignment, job, operation, post **3** *Syn* OBLIGATION, burden, commitment, duty, need, responsibility **4** *Syn* PRICE, cost, expense **5** • a formal claim of criminal wrongdoing against a person *Syn* complaint, count, indictment, rap *Rel* accusation, allegation

charged *Syn* FERVENT, ardent, blazing, burning, emotional, fervid, feverish, fiery, flaming, glowing, hot-blooded, impassioned, passionate, red-hot, vehement, warm, warm-blooded *Ant* cold, cool, dispassionate, impassive, unemotional

chariness *Syn* CAUTION, calculation, circumspection, wariness *Ant* adventurousness, temerity

charitable • having or showing interest in or being concerned with the welfare of others *Syn* altruistic, benevolent, eleemosynary, humane, humanitarian, philanthropic *Rel* bounteous, bountiful, generous, liberal, munificent, openhanded *Ant* uncharitable

charity **1** *Syn* CONTRIBUTION, alms, benefaction, beneficence, donation, philanthropy **2** *Syn* MERCY, clemency, grace, lenity

charlatan *Syn* IMPOSTOR, faker, mountebank, quack

charley horse *Syn* CRAMP, crick, spasm

charm *vb Syn* ATTRACT, allure, bewitch, captivate, enchant, fascinate *Ant* repel

charm *n* **1** *Syn* FETISH, amulet, talisman **2** *Syn* PENDANT, bangle, lavalier
charmer *Syn* MAGICIAN (sense 1), conjurer (*or* conjuror), enchanter, necromancer, sorcerer, voodoo, witch, wizard
charming *Syn* ATTRACTIVE, alluring, bewitching, captivating, enchanting, fascinating *Ant* forbidding, repellent
chart *n* • a stylized or symbolic depiction of something incapable of direct verbal or pictorial representation *Syn* graph, map *Rel* design, plan, plot, project, scheme
chart *vb* • to make a representation of something with a chart *Syn* graph, map
charter *Syn* HIRE, lease, let, rent
chary *Syn* CAUTIOUS, calculating, circumspect, wary *Ant* adventurous, temerarious
chase *Syn* PURSUIT, chasing, dogging, following, hounding, pursuing, shadowing, tagging, tailing, tracing, tracking, trailing
chasing *Syn* PURSUIT, chase, dogging, following, hounding, pursuing, shadowing, tagging, tailing, tracing, tracking, trailing
chasm *Syn* GULF, abysm, abyss
chaste • free from all taint of what is lewd or salacious *Syn* decent, modest, pure *Rel* ethical, moral, righteous, virtuous *Ant* bizarre (*of style, effect*), immoral, lewd, wanton
chasten *Syn* PUNISH, castigate, chastise, correct, discipline *Ant* excuse, pardon
chasteness *Syn* CHASTITY, modesty, purity *Ant* immodesty, impurity, unchastity
chastening *Syn* PUNITIVE, castigating, chastising, correcting, correctional, corrective, disciplinary, disciplining, penal, penalizing
chastise *Syn* PUNISH, castigate, chasten, correct, discipline *Ant* excuse, pardon
chastising *Syn* PUNITIVE, castigating, chastening, correcting, correctional, corrective, disciplinary, disciplining, penal, penalizing
chastity • the quality or state of being morally pure *Syn* chasteness, modesty, purity *Rel* goodness, righteousness, virtuousness *Ant* immodesty, impurity, unchastity
chat *n* • friendly, informal conversation or an instance of this *Syn* chatter, chitchat, gabfest, gossip, palaver, rap, small talk, table talk, talk, tête-à-tête *Rel* colloquy, conference, discourse, parley, powwow, symposium
chat *vb* • to engage in casual or rambling conversation *Syn* babble, blab, cackle, chatter, converse, gab, gabble, gas, jabber, jaw, palaver, patter, prate, prattle, rap, rattle, run on, talk, twitter, visit *Rel* gossip, tattle
château *Syn* MANSION, castle, countryseat, estate, hacienda, hall, manor, manor house, palace, villa
chattel *Syn* SLAVE (sense 1), bondman, bondsman, thrall *Ant* freeman
chatter *vb* *Syn* CHAT, babble, blab, cackle, converse, gab, gabble, gas, jabber, jaw, palaver, patter, prate, prattle, rap, rattle, run on, talk, twitter, visit
chatter *n* *Syn* CHAT, chitchat, gabfest, gossip, palaver, rap, small talk, table talk, talk, tête-à-tête
cheap *Syn* CONTEMPTIBLE, beggarly, despicable, pitiable, scurvy, shabby, sorry *Ant* admirable, estimable, formidable
cheat *Syn* FLEECE, bleed, chisel, cozen, defraud, hustle, mulct, rook, shortchange, skin, squeeze, stick, sting, swindle, victimize
check *vb* **1** *Syn* ARREST (sense 1), interrupt *Ant* activate, quicken **2** *Syn* RESTRAIN, bridle, curb, inhibit *Ant* abandon (*oneself*), activate, impel, incite
check *n* **1** *Syn* CORRECTIVE, antidote, control **2** *Syn* INSPECTION, audit, checkup, examination, review, scan, scrutiny, survey **3** *Syn* RESTRICTION, condition, constraint, curb, fetter, limitation, restraint
checked *Syn* VARIEGATED, checkered, dappled, motley, parti-colored, piebald, pied, skewbald
checkered *Syn* VARIEGATED, checked, dappled, motley, parti-colored, piebald, pied, skewbald
checkup *Syn* INSPECTION, audit, check, examination, review, scan, scrutiny, survey
cheek **1** *Syn* BACK TALK, impertinence, impudence, insolence, sass, sauce **2** *Syn* EFFRONTERY, audacity, brashness, brass, brassiness, brazenness, cheekiness, chutzpah, gall, nerve, nerviness, pertness, presumption, presumptuousness, sauce, sauciness, temerity
cheekiness *Syn* EFFRONTERY, audacity, brashness, brass, brassiness, brazenness, cheek, chutzpah, gall, nerve, nerviness, pertness, presumption, presumptuousness, sauce, sauciness, temerity
cheep *vb* *Syn* CHIRP, chirrup, chitter, peep, tweet, twitter
cheep *n* *Syn* CHIRP, chirrup, chitter, peep, tweet, twitter
cheer **1** *Syn* ACCLAIM, applaud, hail, laud, praise, salute, tout *Ant* knock, pan, slam **2** *Syn* APPLAUD, root *Ant* boo, hiss **3** *Syn* ENCOURAGE, embolden, hearten, inspirit, nerve, steel *Ant* discourage
cheerful **1** • having or showing a good mood or disposition *Syn* blithe, blithesome, bright, buoyant, cheery, chipper, gay, gladsome, lightsome, sunny, upbeat *Rel* hopeful, optimistic, sanguine *Ant* dour, gloomy, glum, morose, saturnine, sulky, sullen **2** • serving to lift one's spirits *Syn* bright, cheering, cheery, gay, glad *Rel* gladdening, heartening, heartwarming *Ant* bleak, cheerless, dark, depressing, dismal, dreary, gloomy, gray **3** *Syn* GLAD, happy, joyful, joyous, lighthearted *Ant* sad
cheering *n* *Syn* APPLAUSE, acclamation,

cheers, ovation, plaudit(s), rave(s) *Ant* booing, hissing

cheering *adj* **1** *Syn* CHEERFUL (sense 2), bright, cheery, gay, glad *Ant* bleak, cheerless, dark, depressing, dismal, dreary, gloomy, gray **2** *Syn* HEARTWARMING, comforting, encouraging, fulfilling, gladdening, gratifying, heartening, rewarding, satisfying *Ant* depressing, discouraging, disheartening, dispiriting

cheerless *Syn* DISMAL, bleak, desolate, dispiriting, dreary

cheers *Syn* APPLAUSE, acclamation, cheering, ovation, plaudit(s), rave(s) *Ant* booing, hissing

cheery **1** *Syn* CHEERFUL (sense 1), blithe, blithesome, bright, buoyant, chipper, gay, gladsome, lightsome, sunny, upbeat *Ant* dour, gloomy, glum, morose, saturnine, sulky, sullen **2** *Syn* CHEERFUL (sense 2), bright, cheering, gay, glad *Ant* bleak, cheerless, dark, depressing, dismal, dreary, gloomy, gray

cheeseparing *Syn* STINGY, close, closefisted, miserly, niggardly, parsimonious, penny-pinching, penurious, tight, tightfisted *Ant* generous

chemist *Syn* DRUGGIST, apothecary, pharmacist

cherish **1** *Syn* APPRECIATE, prize, treasure, value *Ant* despise **2** *Syn* NURSE, cultivate, foster, nurture

chest • a covered rectangular container for storing or transporting things *Syn* box, caddy, case, casket, locker, trunk *Rel* crate

chesterfield *Syn* COUCH, davenport, divan, lounge, settee, sofa

chew out *Syn* SCOLD, bawl, berate, jaw, rail, rate, revile, tongue-lash, upbraid, vituperate, wig

chic *Syn* STYLISH, dashing, fashionable, modish, smart

chicane *Syn* DECEPTION, chicanery, double-dealing, fraud, trickery

chicanery **1** *Syn* DECEPTION, chicane, double-dealing, fraud, trickery **2** *Syn* TRICKERY, artifice, hanky-panky, jugglery, legerdemain, subterfuge, wile

chicken *adj* *Syn* COWARDLY, chickenhearted, craven, dastardly, lily-livered, pusillanimous, recreant, spineless, unheroic, yellow *Ant* brave, courageous, daring, dauntless, doughty, fearless, gallant, greathearted, gutsy, hardy, heroic, intrepid, lionhearted, stalwart, stout, stouthearted, valiant, valorous

chicken *n* *Syn* COWARD, craven, dastard, poltroon, recreant *Ant* hero, stalwart, valiant

chickenhearted *Syn* COWARDLY, chicken, craven, dastardly, lily-livered, pusillanimous, recreant, spineless, unheroic, yellow *Ant* brave, courageous, daring, dauntless, doughty, fearless, gallant, greathearted, gutsy, hardy, heroic, intrepid, lionhearted, stalwart, stout, stouthearted, valiant, valorous

chide *Syn* REPROVE, admonish, rebuke, reprimand, reproach

chief *adj* • first in importance or in standing *Syn* capital, foremost, leading, main, principal *Rel* dominant, paramount, predominant, preponderant, preponderating, sovereign *Ant* subordinate

chief *n* **1** • the person in whom resides authority or ruling power *Syn* chieftain, head, headman, leader, master *Rel* governor, ruler **2** *Syn* BOSS, captain, foreman, head, headman, helmsman, kingpin, leader, master, taskmaster **3** *Syn* HEAD, commanding, first, foremost, high, lead, leading, managing, preeminent, premier, presiding, primary, prime, principal, supreme

chiefly **1** • for the most part *Syn* altogether, basically, by and large, generally, largely, mainly, mostly, overall, predominantly, primarily, principally, substantially *Rel* nearly, practically, virtually **2** *Syn* LARGELY, generally, greatly, mainly, mostly, principally

chieftain *Syn* CHIEF, head, headman, leader, master

child *Syn* BABY, babe, infant, newborn

childish • having or showing the annoying qualities (as silliness) associated with children *Syn* adolescent, babyish, immature, infantile, juvenile, kiddish, puerile *Rel* boyish, girlish *Ant* adult, grown-up, mature

child's play **1** *Syn* CINCH, breeze, duck soup, picnic, pushover, snap *Ant* chore, headache, labor **2** *Syn* TRIFLE, frippery, nothing, triviality

chill • an uncomfortable degree of coolness *Syn* bite, bitterness, bleakness, chilliness, nip, rawness, sharpness *Rel* briskness, crispness

chilliness *Syn* CHILL, bite, bitterness, bleakness, nip, rawness, sharpness

chilly *Syn* COLD, arctic, cool, freezing, frigid, frosty, gelid, glacial, icy *Ant* hot

chimerical *Syn* IMAGINARY, fanciful, fantastic, quixotic, visionary *Ant* actual, real

chine *Syn* SPINE, back, backbone, vertebrae

chink *Syn* CRACK, cleft, cranny, crevasse, crevice, fissure

chipper *Syn* CHEERFUL (sense 1), blithe, blithesome, bright, buoyant, cheery, gay, gladsome, lightsome, sunny, upbeat *Ant* dour, gloomy, glum, morose, saturnine, sulky, sullen

chirp *n* • the little sounds characteristic of small animals or sounds that suggest such small animal sounds *Syn* cheep, chirrup, chitter, peep, tweet, twitter

chirp *vb* • to make a short, sharp, and usually repetitive sound *Syn* cheep, chirrup, chitter, peep, tweet, twitter

chirrup *n* *Syn* CHIRP, cheep, chitter, peep, tweet, twitter

chirrup *vb* *Syn* CHIRP, cheep, chitter, peep, tweet, twitter

chisel 1 *Syn* CARVE, engrave, etch, incise, sculpt, sculpture 2 *Syn* FLEECE, bleed, cheat, cozen, defraud, hustle, mulct, rook, shortchange, skin, squeeze, stick, sting, swindle, victimize
chitchat *Syn* CHAT, chatter, gabfest, gossip, palaver, rap, small talk, table talk, talk, tête-à-tête
chitter *n* *Syn* CHIRP, cheep, chirrup, peep, tweet, twitter
chitter *vb* *Syn* CHIRP, cheep, chirrup, peep, tweet, twitter
chivalrous *Syn* CIVIL, courteous, courtly, gallant, polite *Ant* rude, uncivil
chivy *Syn* BAIT, badger, heckle, hector, hound, ride
choice *adj* • having qualities that appeal to a fine or highly refined taste *Syn* dainty, delicate, elegant, exquisite, rare, recherché *Rel* incomparable, peerless, preeminent, superlative, supreme, surpassing *Ant* indifferent, medium
choice *n* 1 • the act or opportunity of choosing or the thing chosen *Syn* alternative, election, option, preference, selection 2 *Syn* ELITE, best, cream, elect, fat, flower, pick, prime, upper crust
choke *Syn* SUFFOCATE, asphyxiate, smother, stifle, strangle, throttle
choleric *Syn* IRASCIBLE, cranky, cross, splenetic, testy, touchy
choose • to fix upon one of a number of things as the one to be taken, accepted, or adopted *Syn* cull, elect, opt, pick, prefer, select, single *Rel* adopt, embrace, espouse *Ant* eschew, reject
choosy *or* **choosey** *Syn* SELECTIVE, particular, picky *Ant* nonselective
chop 1 • to cut into small pieces *Syn* dice, hash, mince *Rel* chip, grind, mash, puree, slice 2 *Syn* CUT, carve, hew, slash, slit
choppy *Syn* FITFUL, casual, discontinuous, erratic, intermittent, irregular, occasional, spasmodic, sporadic, spotty, unsteady *Ant* constant, continuous, regular, steady
chore • a piece of work that needs to be done regularly *Syn* assignment, duty, job, stint, task *Rel* endeavor, enterprise, project, undertaking
chow *Syn* MEAL, feed, mess, repast, table
chronic *Syn* INVETERATE, confirmed, deep-rooted, deep-seated
chronicle 1 *Syn* ACCOUNT, report, story, version 2 *Syn* HISTORY, annals
chthonian *Syn* INFERNAL, chthonic, Hadean, hellish, stygian, Tartarean *Ant* supernal
chthonic *Syn* INFERNAL, chthonian, Hadean, hellish, stygian, Tartarean *Ant* supernal
chubby *Syn* FLESHY, corpulent, fat, obese, plump, portly, rotund, stout *Ant* scrawny, skinny
chummy *Syn* FAMILIAR, close, confidential, intimate, thick *Ant* aloof
chump *Syn* DUPE, gull, pigeon, sap, sucker, tool
chunky *Syn* STOCKY, dumpy, squat, stubby, thick, thickset
church *Syn* RELIGION, communion, creed, denomination, faith, persuasion, sect
churlish *Syn* CLOWNISH, boorish, cloddish, loutish, uncouth *Ant* civil, courteous, courtly, cultivated, genteel, gentlemanly, ladylike, polished, polite, refined, well-bred
chutzpah *Syn* EFFRONTERY, audacity, brashness, brass, brassiness, brazenness, cheek, cheekiness, gall, nerve, nerviness, pertness, presumption, presumptuousness, sauce, sauciness, temerity
cinch *n* • something that is easy to do *Syn* breeze, child's play, duck soup, picnic, pushover, snap *Rel* nothing *Ant* chore, headache, labor
cinch *vb* *Syn* ENSURE, assure, guarantee, guaranty, insure, secure
cinders *Syn* ASH, clinkers, embers
cinema *Syn* MOVIE (sense 2), film, motion pictures, pictures, screen
ciphering *Syn* CALCULATION, arithmetic, computation, figures, figuring, reckoning
circle 1 *Syn* SURROUND, compass, encircle, encompass, environ, gird, girdle, hem, ring 2 *Syn* TURN (sense 1), eddy, gyrate, pirouette, revolve, rotate, spin, swirl, twirl, wheel, whirl
circuit *Syn* CIRCUMFERENCE, compass, perimeter, periphery
circuitous *Syn* INDIRECT, roundabout *Ant* direct, forthright, straightforward
circulate 1 *Syn* RUMOR, bruit (about), noise (about), whisper 2 *Syn* SPREAD, diffuse, disseminate, propagate, radiate
circumference • a continuous line enclosing an area or space *Syn* circuit, compass, perimeter, periphery *Rel* contour, outline
circumlocution *Syn* VERBIAGE, periphrasis, pleonasm, redundancy, tautology
circumscribe *Syn* LIMIT, confine, restrict *Ant* widen
circumspect *Syn* CAUTIOUS, calculating, chary, wary *Ant* adventurous, temerarious
circumspection *Syn* CAUTION, calculation, chariness, wariness *Ant* adventurousness, temerity
circumstance *Syn* OCCURRENCE, episode, event, incident
circumstantial • dealing with a matter fully and usually point by point *Syn* detailed, itemized, minute, particular, particularized *Rel* accurate, correct, exact, nice, precise *Ant* abridged, summary
circumvent *Syn* FRUSTRATE, baffle, balk, foil, outwit, thwart *Ant* fulfill
circus *Syn* MADHOUSE, babel, bedlam, hell
citadel *Syn* FORT, fastness, fortress, stronghold

citation *Syn* ENCOMIUM, eulogy, panegyric, tribute
cite **1** *Syn* ADDUCE, advance, allege **2** *Syn* QUOTE, repeat **3** *Syn* SUMMON, call, convene, convoke, muster
citizen • a person who is regarded as a member of a sovereign state, entitled to its protection, and subject to its laws *Syn* national, subject *Ant* alien
city • a thickly settled and highly populated area *Syn* burg, megalopolis, metropolis, municipality, town *Rel* borough
civil • observant of the forms required by good breeding *Syn* chivalrous, courteous, courtly, gallant, polite *Rel* amiable, complaisant, obliging *Ant* rude, uncivil
civility *Syn* POLITENESS, courteousness, courtesy, gentility, graciousness, mannerliness *Ant* discourteousness, discourtesy, impoliteness, incivility, rudeness, ungraciousness
civilized *Syn* CULTIVATED, cultured, genteel, polished, refined *Ant* philistine, uncivilized, uncultured, unpolished, unrefined
claim *n* • an actual or alleged right to demand something as one's possession, quality, power, or prerogative *Syn* pretense, pretension, title *Rel* affirmation, assertion, declaration, protestation
claim *vb* *Syn* DEMAND, exact, require
clamor *n* *Syn* DIN, babel, hubbub, hullabaloo, pandemonium, racket, uproar *Ant* quiet
clamor *vb* *Syn* ROAR, bawl, bellow, bluster, howl, ululate, vociferate
clamorous *Syn* VOCIFEROUS, blatant, boisterous, obstreperous, strident
clam up *Syn* SHUT UP, hush, quiet (down) *Ant* speak, talk
clandestine *Syn* SECRET, covert, furtive, stealthy, surreptitious, underhand, underhanded
clarify *Syn* EXPLAIN (sense 1), clear (up), construe, demonstrate, elucidate, explicate, expound, illuminate, illustrate, interpret, spell out *Ant* obscure
clash *vb* *Syn* BUMP, collide, conflict
clash *n* *Syn* IMPACT, collision, concussion, impingement, jar, jolt, percussion, shock
class *n* *Syn* ELEGANCE, elegancy, grace, gracefulness, handsomeness, majesty, refinement, stateliness
class *vb* • to order a number of things according to a scale or to place a thing in its due order *Syn* gradate, grade, graduate, rank, rate *Rel* divide, part, separate
classic *Syn* EXCELLENT, A1, bang-up, banner, capital, crackerjack, dandy, divine, fabulous, fine, first-class, first-rate, grand, great, groovy, heavenly, jim-dandy, keen, marvelous (*or* marvellous), mean, neat, nifty, noble, par excellence, prime, sensational, splendid, stellar, sterling, superb, superior, superlative, supernal, swell, terrific, tip-top, top, top-notch, unsurpassed, wonderful *Ant* poor
classify *Syn* ASSORT, pigeonhole, sort
clatter *Syn* COMMOTION, bother, bustle, disturbance, furor, furore, fuss, hubbub, hullabaloo, hurly-burly, pandemonium, pother, row, ruckus, ruction, rumpus, shindy, squall, stew, stir, storm, to-do, tumult, turmoil, uproar, welter, whirl
clause *Syn* PARAGRAPH, article, count, plank, verse
clean *adj* *Syn* EXHAUSTIVE, all-out, complete, comprehensive, full-scale, out-and-out, thorough, thoroughgoing, total
clean (out) *Syn* DEPLETE, consume, drain, exhaust, expend, spend, use up *Ant* renew, replace
clear *adj* **1** • having the property of being literally or figuratively seen through *Syn* diaphanous, limpid, lucid, pellucid, translucent, transparent *Rel* bright, luminous *Ant* confused, turbid **2** • quickly and easily understood *Syn* lucid, perspicuous *Rel* definite, explicit, express *Ant* abstruse, unintelligible **3** *Syn* EVIDENT, apparent, distinct, manifest, obvious, palpable, patent, plain
clear *vb* **1** *Syn* RID, disabuse, purge, unburden **2** *Syn* EMPTY, evacuate, vacate, void *Ant* fill, load
clearance **1** *Syn* PERMISSION, allowance, authorization, concurrence, consent, granting, leave, license (*or* licence), sanction, sufferance *Ant* interdiction, prohibition, proscription **2** *Syn* ROOM (sense 2), berth, elbow room, leeway, margin, play
clear-cut *Syn* INCISIVE, biting, crisp, cutting, trenchant
clearheaded *Syn* SANE, balanced, lucid, normal, right, stable *Ant* crazed, crazy, demented, deranged, insane, lunatic, mad, maniacal, mental, unbalanced, unsound
clear (up) *Syn* EXPLAIN (sense 1), clarify, construe, demonstrate, elucidate, explicate, expound, illuminate, illustrate, interpret, spell out *Ant* obscure
cleave[1] *vb* *Syn* STICK, adhere, cling, cohere
cleave[2] *vb* *Syn* TEAR, rend, rip, rive, split
cleft *Syn* CRACK, chink, cranny, crevasse, crevice, fissure
clemency **1** *Syn* FORBEARANCE, indulgence, leniency, mercifulness, tolerance *Ant* anger, vindictiveness **2** *Syn* MERCY, charity, grace, lenity
clement **1** • marked by temperatures that are neither too high nor too low *Syn* balmy, equable, gentle, mild, moderate, temperate *Rel* clear, cloudless, fair, rainless, sunny, sunshiny *Ant* harsh, inclement, intemperate, severe **2** *Syn* FORBEARING, indulgent, lenient, merciful, tolerant *Ant* unrelenting
clemently *Syn* FORBEARINGLY, indulgently, leniently, mercifully, tolerantly
clever **1** • having or showing a high degree of practical intelligence or skill in contriv-

ance *Syn* adroit, cunning, ingenious *Rel* deft, dexterous, handy **2** *Syn* INTELLIGENT, alert, bright, brilliant, knowing, quick-witted, smart *Ant* unintelligent

cleverness *Syn* DEXTERITY (sense 1), adroitness, finesse, sleight *Ant* awkwardness, clumsiness, gawkiness

cliché *Syn* COMMONPLACE, bromide, platitude, truism

climate *Syn* AURA, air, atmosphere, flavor, mood, note, temper

climax **1** *Syn* SUMMIT, acme, apex, apogee, culmination, meridian, peak, pinnacle, zenith **2** *Syn* TURNING POINT, landmark, milestone

climb *Syn* ASCEND, arise, lift, mount, rise, soar, up, uprise, upsweep, upturn *Ant* decline, descend, dip, drop, fall (off)

cling *Syn* STICK, adhere, cleave, cohere

clinkers *Syn* ASH, cinders, embers

clip • to make (as hair) shorter with or as if with the use of shears *Syn* bob, crop, curtail, cut, cut back, dock, lop (off), nip, pare, prune, shave, shear, snip, trim *Rel* manicure, mow

cloak *Syn* DISGUISE, camouflage, dissemble, mask

clod *Syn* OAF, gawk, hulk, lout, lubber, lug

cloddish *Syn* CLOWNISH, boorish, churlish, loutish, uncouth *Ant* civil, courteous, courtly, cultivated, genteel, gentlemanly, ladylike, polished, polite, refined, well-bred

clodhopper *Syn* HICK, bumpkin, countryman, provincial, rustic, yokel *Ant* cosmopolitan, sophisticate

clog *n* *Syn* ENCUMBRANCE, bar, block, chain, crimp, deterrent, drag, embarrassment, fetter, handicap, hindrance, hurdle, impediment, inhibition, interference, let, manacle, obstacle, obstruction, shackles, stop, stumbling block, trammel *Ant* aid, assistance, benefit, help

clog *vb* *Syn* HAMPER, fetter, hog-tie, manacle, shackle, trammel *Ant* assist (*persons*), expedite (*work, projects*)

cloister **1** • a place of retirement from the world for members of a religious community *Syn* abbey, convent, monastery, nunnery, priory **2** *Syn* PASSAGE, aisle, arcade, corridor, gallery, hall, hallway, passageway

cloistered *Syn* SECLUDED, covert, isolated, quiet, remote, retired, secret, sheltered

clone *Syn* VARIETY (sense 2), breed, cultivar, race, stock, strain, subspecies

close *adj* **1** • not far (as in place, time, or relationship) from the point, position, or relation that is indicated or understood *Syn* near, nearby, nigh *Rel* abutting, adjacent, adjoining, contiguous *Ant* remote, remotely **2** • having constituent parts that are massed tightly together *Syn* compact, dense, thick *Rel* compressed, condensed, constricted *Ant* open **3** *Syn* FAMILIAR, chummy, confidential, intimate, thick *Ant* aloof **4** *Syn* SILENT (sense 1), close-lipped, closemouthed, reserved, reticent, secretive, taciturn, tight-lipped, uncommunicative *Ant* talkative **5** *Syn* SECRETIVE, closemouthed, dark, reticent, uncommunicative *Ant* communicative, open **6** *Syn* STINGY, cheeseparing, closefisted, miserly, niggardly, parsimonious, penny-pinching, penurious, tight, tightfisted *Ant* generous

close *n* *Syn* FINALE, closing, conclusion, consummation, end, ending, finis, finish, windup *Ant* beginning, dawn, opening, start

closefisted *Syn* STINGY, cheeseparing, close, miserly, niggardly, parsimonious, penny-pinching, penurious, tight, tightfisted *Ant* generous

close-lipped *Syn* SILENT (sense 1), close, closemouthed, reserved, reticent, secretive, taciturn, tight-lipped, uncommunicative *Ant* talkative

closemouthed **1** *Syn* SECRETIVE, close, dark, reticent, uncommunicative *Ant* communicative, open **2** *Syn* SILENT (sense 1), close, close-lipped, reserved, reticent, secretive, taciturn, tight-lipped, uncommunicative *Ant* talkative

closeness **1** *Syn* PRECISION, accuracy, delicacy, exactitude, exactness, fineness, preciseness, rigorousness, veracity *Ant* coarseness, impreciseness, imprecision, inaccuracy, inexactness, roughness **2** *Syn* PROXIMITY, contiguity, immediacy, nearness *Ant* distance, remoteness

closet *Syn* CABINET, buffet, cupboard, hutch, locker, sideboard

closing *Syn* FINALE, close, conclusion, consummation, end, ending, finis, finish, windup *Ant* beginning, dawn, opening, start

clot *Syn* COAGULATE, congeal, curdle, jell, jelly, set

clothe **1** • to cover with or as if with garments *Syn* apparel, array, attire, dress, robe *Ant* unclothe **2** *Syn* PHRASE, articulate, couch, express, formulate, put, say, state, word

clothes • a person's garments considered collectively *Syn* apparel, attire, clothing, dress, raiment

clothing *Syn* CLOTHES, apparel, attire, dress, raiment

cloud *Syn* OBSCURE, becloud, bedim, befog, darken, dim, eclipse, fog, obfuscate *Ant* illuminate, illumine

cloudburst *Syn* RAIN (sense 1), deluge, downpour, rainfall, rainstorm, storm, wet

clouded *Syn* OVERCAST, beclouded, cloudy, dull, hazed, hazy, heavy, lowering, overclouded *Ant* clear, cloudless

cloudy *Syn* OVERCAST, beclouded, clouded, dull, hazed, hazy, heavy, lowering, overclouded *Ant* clear, cloudless

clout *Syn* STRIKE, box, cuff, hit, punch, slap, slog, slug, smite, swat

clown (around) *Syn* CUT UP, act up, fool

(around), horse (around), monkey (around), show off, skylark
clowning *Syn* HORSEPLAY, foolery, high jinks, horsing (around), monkeying, monkeyshines, roughhouse, roughhousing, shenanigans, skylarking, tomfoolery
clownish • having or showing crudely insensitive or impolite manners *Syn* boorish, churlish, cloddish, loutish, uncouth *Rel* coarse, ill-bred, uncultivated, unpolished, unrefined *Ant* civil, courteous, courtly, cultivated, genteel, gentlemanly, ladylike, polished, polite, refined, well-bred
cloy *Syn* SATIATE, glut, gorge, pall, sate, surfeit
club *vb* *Syn* ALLY, associate, band, confederate, conjoin, cooperate, federate, league, unite *Ant* break up, disband
club *n* *Syn* ASSOCIATION, order, society
clue *Syn* ENLIGHTEN (sense 1), acquaint, advise, apprise, brief, familiarize, fill in, inform, instruct, tell, wise (up)
clumsy **1** *Syn* AWKWARD, gauche, inept, maladroit *Ant* deft, graceful, handy **2** *Syn* CUMBERSOME, awkward, cranky, cumbrous, ungainly, unhandy, unwieldy *Ant* handy
cluster *Syn* GROUP, bunch, lot, parcel
clutch **1** *Syn* HOLD, grasp, grip **2** *Syn* TAKE, grab, grasp, seize, snatch
clutter *Syn* CONFUSION, chaos, disarray, disorder, jumble, muddle, snarl
cluttered *Syn* MESSY, chaotic, confused, disarranged, disarrayed, disheveled (*or* dishevelled), disordered, disorderly, higgledy-piggledy, hugger-mugger, jumbled, littered, messed, muddled, mussed, mussy, pell-mell, rumpled, sloppy, topsy-turvy, tousled, tumbled, unkempt, untidy, upside-down *Ant* neat, ordered, orderly, organized, shipshape, snug, tidied, tidy, trim
coadjutor *Syn* ASSISTANT, adjutant, aid, aide, apprentice, deputy, helper, sidekick
coagulate • to alter by chemical reaction from a liquid to a more or less firm jelly *Syn* clot, congeal, curdle, jell, jelly, set *Rel* harden, solidify
coalesce *Syn* MIX, amalgamate, blend, commingle, fuse, merge, mingle
coalition **1** *Syn* ALLIANCE, confederacy, confederation, federation, fusion, league **2** *Syn* FACTION, bloc, body, party, sect, set, side, wing
coarse • offensive to good taste or morals *Syn* gross, obscene, ribald, vulgar *Rel* callow, crude, green, raw, rough, rude, uncouth *Ant* fine, refined
coast *n* *Syn* SHORE, bank, beach, foreshore, littoral, strand
coast *vb* *Syn* SLIDE, glide, glissade, skid, slip, slither, toboggan
coax • to get (someone) to do something by gentle urging, special attention, or flattery *Syn* blandish, blarney, cajole, soft-soap, wheedle *Rel* adulate, flatter, overpraise
cock *n* *Syn* HEAP, bank, mass, pile, shock, stack
cock *vb* *Syn* HEAP, bank, mass, pile, shock, stack
cockeyed *Syn* AWRY, askew, aslant, crooked, listing, lopsided, oblique, skewed, slanted, slanting, slantwise, tilted, tipping, uneven *Ant* even, level, straight
cocksure *Syn* SURE, certain, positive *Ant* unsure
coddle *Syn* BABY, dandle, mollycoddle, nurse, pamper, spoil *Ant* abuse, ill-treat, ill-use, maltreat, mishandle, mistreat, misuse
codger *Syn* ECCENTRIC, character, crackbrain, crackpot, crank, kook, nut, oddball, screwball, weirdo
coerce *Syn* FORCE, compel, constrain, oblige
coercion *Syn* FORCE, compulsion, constraint, duress, restraint, violence
coetaneous *Syn* CONTEMPORARY, coeval, coincident, concomitant, concurrent, contemporaneous, simultaneous, synchronous
coeval *Syn* CONTEMPORARY, coetaneous, coincident, concomitant, concurrent, contemporaneous, simultaneous, synchronous
cogent • having the power to persuade *Syn* compelling, conclusive, convincing, decisive, effective, forceful, persuasive, satisfying, strong, telling *Rel* sound, valid, well-founded *Ant* inconclusive, indecisive, ineffective, unconvincing
cogitate *Syn* THINK (sense 2), deliberate, reason, reflect, speculate
cognate *Syn* RELATED, affiliated, allied, kindred
cognizance **1** *Syn* ACQUAINTANCE, familiarity *Ant* unfamiliarity **2** *Syn* ATTENTION (sense 2), awareness, ear, eye, heed, notice, observance, observation
cognizant **1** *Syn* AWARE, alive, awake, conscious, sensible *Ant* unaware **2** *Syn* CONSCIOUS, alive, aware, mindful, sensible, sentient *Ant* insensible, unaware, unconscious, unmindful
cohere *Syn* STICK, adhere, cleave, cling
cohort *Syn* ACCOMPLICE, abettor, accessory, confederate
coil *Syn* WIND, curl, entwine, twine, twist, wreathe
coiling *Syn* SPIRAL, corkscrew, helical, screwlike, winding
coin *Syn* MONEY, cash, coinage, currency, legal tender, specie
coinage *Syn* MONEY, cash, coin, currency, legal tender, specie
coincide *Syn* AGREE (sense 1), concur *Ant* differ, disagree
coincident *Syn* CONTEMPORARY, coetaneous, coeval, concomitant, concurrent, contemporaneous, simultaneous, synchronous
cold • having a temperature below that which

is normal or comfortable *Syn* arctic, chilly, cool, freezing, frigid, frosty, gelid, glacial, icy *Ant* hot
collapse *Syn* FATIGUE, burnout, exhaustion, lassitude, prostration, tiredness, weariness *Ant* refreshment, rejuvenation, revitalization
collate *Syn* COMPARE, contrast
collateral *Syn* SUBORDINATE, dependent, secondary, subject, tributary *Ant* chief, dominant, leading
collation *Syn* COMPARISON, contrast, parallel
colleague *Syn* PARTNER, ally, confederate, copartner *Ant* rival
collect *Syn* GATHER, assemble, congregate
collected *Syn* COOL, composed, imperturbable, nonchalant, unflappable, unruffled *Ant* agitated, ardent
collection *Syn* GATHERING, assemblage, assembly, congregation
collide *Syn* BUMP, clash, conflict
collision *Syn* IMPACT, clash, concussion, impingement, jar, jolt, percussion, shock
color *n* **1** • a property or attribute of a visible thing recognizable only when rays of light fall upon it and serving to distinguish things otherwise visually identical (as shape or size) *Syn* hue, shade, tinge, tint, tone **2** *Syn* PIGMENT, coloring, dye, dyestuff, stain, tincture **3** *Syn* FLAG, banner, ensign, jack, pendant, pennant, pennon, standard, streamer
color *vb* *Syn* BLUSH, bloom, crimson, flush, glow, redden
colorable *Syn* PLAUSIBLE, believable, credible, specious
colorful • marked by a variety of usually vivid colors *Syn* motley, multicolored, polychromatic, polychrome, varicolored, variegated *Rel* brave, bright, brilliant, gay *Ant* colorless, monochromatic, solid
coloring **1** *Syn* EXAGGERATION, caricature, elaboration, embellishment, embroidering, hyperbole, magnification, overstatement, padding, stretching *Ant* understatement **2** *Syn* PIGMENT, color, dye, dyestuff, stain, tincture
colorless • lacking an addition of color *Syn* uncolored, undyed, unpainted, unstained, white *Rel* clear, limpid, liquid, lucent, pellucid, transparent *Ant* colored, dyed, painted, stained, tinged, tinted
colossal *Syn* HUGE, Brobdingnagian, cyclopean, elephantine, enormous, gargantuan, giant, gigantean, gigantic, Herculean, immense, mammoth, titanic, vast *Ant* bitty, diminutive, microscopic (*or* microscopical), midget, miniature, minute, pocket, pygmy, teeny, teeny-weeny, tiny, wee
colossus *Syn* GIANT, behemoth, blockbuster, jumbo, leviathan, mammoth, monster, titan, whale, whopper *Ant* dwarf, midget, mini, miniature, peewee, pygmy, runt, shrimp
colt *Syn* BEGINNER, fledgling, freshman, greenhorn, neophyte, newbie, newcomer, novice, recruit, rookie, tenderfoot, tyro *Ant* old hand, old-timer, vet, veteran
column *Syn* PILLAR, pilaster
coma *Syn* FAINT, blackout, insensibility, knockout, swoon
comatose *Syn* LETHARGIC, sluggish, torpid *Ant* energetic, vigorous
comb *Syn* SEEK, ferret out, hunt, ransack, rummage, scour, search
combat *n* *Syn* CONTEST, affray, conflict, fight, fray
combat *vb* *Syn* RESIST, antagonize, conflict, contest, fight, oppose, withstand *Ant* abide, submit
combative *Syn* BELLIGERENT, aggressive, argumentative, bellicose, contentious, discordant, disputatious, gladiatorial, militant, pugnacious, quarrelsome, scrappy, truculent, warlike *Ant* nonbelligerent, pacific, peaceable, peaceful
combativeness *Syn* BELLIGERENCE, aggression, aggressiveness, bellicosity, contentiousness, disputatiousness, fight, militancy, pugnacity, scrappiness, truculence *Ant* pacifism
combination **1** • a union, either of individuals or of organized interests, for mutual support in obtaining common political or private ends *Syn* bloc, combine, faction, party, ring *Rel* cartel, corner, monopoly, pool, syndicate, trust **2** *Syn* BLEND, admixture, amalgam, amalgamation, composite, compound, fusion, intermixture, mix, mixture **3** *Syn* CARTEL, combine, syndicate, trust
combine *n* **1** *Syn* CARTEL, combination, syndicate, trust **2** *Syn* COMBINATION, bloc, faction, party, ring
combine *vb* **1** *Syn* JOIN, associate, conjoin, connect, link, relate, unite *Ant* disjoin, part **2** *Syn* UNITE, concur, conjoin, cooperate *Ant* part
combustible • showing a tendency to catch or be set on fire *Syn* flammable, incendiary, inflammable, inflammatory *Rel* burnable
come *Syn* BECOME, get, go, grow, run, turn, wax
come around *Syn* COME TO, come round, revive
comedown • a loss of status *Syn* decline, descent, down, downfall, fall *Rel* breakdown, collapse, crash, meltdown, ruin, undoing *Ant* aggrandizement, ascent, exaltation, rise, up
comedy • humorous entertainment *Syn* farce, humor, slapstick *Rel* burlesque, parody, satire
comely *Syn* BEAUTIFUL, attractive, beauteous, cute, fair, gorgeous, handsome, knockout, lovely, pretty, ravishing, sightly, stunning, taking *Ant* homely, ill-favored, plain, ugly, unattractive, unbeautiful, unhandsome, unlovely, unpretty, unsightly
come round *Syn* COME TO, come around, revive

comestibles *Syn* FOOD (sense 1), feed, fodder, forage, provender, provisions, viands, victuals
come to • to gain consciousness again *Syn* come around, come round, revive *Rel* pull through, rally, recover
comfort *vb* • to give or offer a person help or assistance in relieving his suffering or sorrow *Syn* console, solace *Rel* delight, gladden, please, rejoice *Ant* afflict, bother
comfort *n Syn* REST, ease, leisure, relaxation, repose
comfortable • enjoying or providing condition or circumstances which make for one's contentment and security *Syn* cozy, easy, restful, snug *Rel* comforting, consoling, solacing *Ant* miserable, uncomfortable
comforting *Syn* HEARTWARMING, cheering, encouraging, fulfilling, gladdening, gratifying, heartening, rewarding, satisfying *Ant* depressing, discouraging, disheartening, dispiriting
comic *Syn* LAUGHABLE, comical, droll, farcical, funny, ludicrous, ridiculous, risible
comical *Syn* LAUGHABLE, comic, droll, farcical, funny, ludicrous, ridiculous, risible
coming *Syn* FORTHCOMING, approaching, imminent, impending, nearing, oncoming, pending, upcoming *Ant* late, recent
comity *Syn* FRIENDSHIP, amity, goodwill *Ant* animosity
command *n* • a direction that must or should be obeyed *Syn* behest, bidding, dictate, injunction, mandate, order *Rel* charge, charging, direction, instruction
command *vb* • to issue orders to someone to give, get, or do something *Syn* bid, charge, direct, enjoin, instruct, order *Rel* conduct, control, direct, manage *Ant* comply, obey
commanding *Syn* HEAD, chief, first, foremost, high, lead, leading, managing, preeminent, premier, presiding, primary, prime, principal, supreme
commemorate *Syn* KEEP (sense 1), celebrate, observe, solemnize *Ant* break
commemorative *Syn* MEMORIAL, keepsake, memento, monument, remembrance, reminder, souvenir, token
commence **1** *Syn* BEGIN (sense 1), arise, dawn, form, materialize, originate, set in, spring, start *Ant* cease, end, stop **2** *Syn* BEGIN (sense 2), embark (on *or* upon), enter (into *or* upon), get off, kick off, launch, open, start, strike (into) *Ant* conclude, end, finish, terminate
commencement *Syn* BEGINNING, alpha, birth, dawn, genesis, inception, incipiency, launch, morning, onset, outset, start, threshold *Ant* close, conclusion, end, ending
commend • to voice or otherwise manifest to others one's warm approval *Syn* applaud, compliment, recommend *Rel* acclaim, eulogize, extol, laud, praise *Ant* admonish, censure
commendable *Syn* ADMIRABLE, creditable, laudable, meritorious, praiseworthy *Ant* censurable, discreditable, reprehensible
commensurable *Syn* PROPORTIONAL, commensurate, proportionate
commensurate *Syn* PROPORTIONAL, commensurable, proportionate
comment *vb Syn* REMARK, animadvert, commentate
comment *n Syn* REMARK, commentary, note, obiter dictum, observation
commentary *Syn* REMARK, comment, note, obiter dictum, observation
commentate *Syn* REMARK, animadvert, comment
commerce **1** • the buying and selling of goods especially on a large scale and between different places *Syn* business, marketplace, trade, traffic *Rel* free trade **2** *Syn* BUSINESS, industry, trade, traffic
commercial • fit or likely to be sold especially on a large scale *Syn* marketable, salable (*or* saleable) *Rel* mass-produced, wholesale *Ant* noncommercial, nonsalable, uncommercial, unmarketable, unsalable
commingle *Syn* MIX, amalgamate, blend, coalesce, fuse, merge, mingle
commiseration *Syn* SYMPATHY, compassion, condolence, empathy, pity, ruth
commissary *Syn* AGENT (sense 1), attorney, delegate, deputy, envoy, factor, procurator, proxy, representative
commission **1** *Syn* AUTHORIZE, accredit, license **2** *Syn* APPOINT (sense 2), assign, attach, constitute, designate, detail, name *Ant* discharge, dismiss, expel, fire
commit • to assign to a person or place for some definite end or purpose (as custody or safekeeping) *Syn* confide, consign, entrust, relegate *Rel* move, remove, shift, transfer
commitment *Syn* OBLIGATION, burden, charge, duty, need, responsibility
commodious *Syn* SPACIOUS, ample, capacious
common **1** • generally met with and not in any way special, strange, or unusual *Syn* familiar, ordinary, popular, vulgar *Rel* current, prevailing, prevalent, rife *Ant* exceptional, uncommon **2** *Syn* GENERAL (sense 1), blanket, generic, global, overall, universal *Ant* individual, particular **3** *Syn* RECIPROCAL (sense 1), mutual
commonly *Syn* NATURALLY (sense 1), generally, normally, ordinarily, typically, usually *Ant* abnormally, atypically, extraordinarily, uncommonly, unusually
commonplace *n* • an idea or expression lacking in originality or freshness *Syn* bromide, cliché, platitude, truism *Rel* expression, idiom, locution, phrase

commonplace *adj Syn* STALE, banal, hackney, hackneyed, moth-eaten, musty, stereotyped, threadbare, tired, trite *Ant* fresh, new, original
common sense **1** • the ability to make intelligent decisions especially in everyday matters *Syn* discreetness, discretion, horse sense, levelheadedness, prudence, sense, sensibleness, wisdom, wit *Rel* street smarts *Ant* imprudence, indiscretion **2** *Syn* SENSE, good sense, gumption, horse sense, judgment, wisdom
commonwealth *Syn* NATION, country, land, sovereignty, state
commotion • a state of noisy, confused activity *Syn* bother, bustle, clatter, disturbance, furor, furore, fuss, hubbub, hullabaloo, hurly-burly, pandemonium, pother, row, ruckus, ruction, rumpus, shindy, squall, stew, stir, storm, to-do, tumult, turmoil, uproar, welter, whirl *Rel* cacophony, clamor, din, howl, hue and cry, noise, outcry, racket, roar
communicable *Syn* INFECTIOUS (sense 1), catching, contagious
communicate • to cause (something) to pass from one to another *Syn* convey, impart, spread, transfer, transfuse, transmit *Rel* deliver, hand over, surrender, turn over
communion **1** *Syn* RAPPORT, fellowship, rapprochement **2** *Syn* RELIGION, church, creed, denomination, faith, persuasion, sect
community *Syn* SIMILARITY, alikeness, correspondence, likeness, parallelism, resemblance, similitude *Ant* dissimilarity, unlikeness
commute *Syn* CHANGE (sense 3), exchange, shift, substitute, swap, switch, trade
compact *vb* • to bring or gather together the parts, particles, elements, or units of a thing so as to form a close mass or an integral whole *Syn* concentrate, consolidate, unify *Rel* compress, condense, contract
compact *adj Syn* CLOSE (sense 2), dense, thick *Ant* open
compact *n Syn* CONTRACT, bargain, cartel, concordat, convention, entente, pact, treaty
compactly *Syn* SUCCINCTLY, briefly, concisely, crisply, laconically, pithily, summarily, tersely *Ant* diffusely, long-windedly, verbosely, wordily
companion **1** *Syn* ASSOCIATE, comrade, crony **2** *Syn* ESCORT, attendant, guard, guide
companionable *Syn* CONVIVIAL, boon, extroverted, gregarious, outgoing, sociable, social *Ant* antisocial, introverted, reclusive, unsociable
companionship • the feeling of closeness and friendship that exists between companions *Syn* camaraderie, company, comradeship, fellowship, society *Rel* amity, benevolence, cordiality, friendliness, friendship, goodwill, kindliness
company **1** • a group of persons who are associated in a joint endeavor or who are assembled for a common end *Syn* band, party, troop, troupe *Rel* circle, clique, coterie, set **2** *Syn* COMPANIONSHIP, camaraderie, comradeship, fellowship, society
comparable *Syn* ALIKE, akin, analogous, correspondent, corresponding, like, matching, parallel, resembling, similar, such, suchlike *Ant* different, dissimilar, diverse, unlike
compare • to set two or more things side by side in order to show likenesses and differences *Syn* collate, contrast *Rel* approach, equal, match, rival, touch
comparison • a setting of things side by side so as to discover or exhibit their likenesses and differences *Syn* collation, contrast, parallel *Rel* affinity, analogy, likeness, resemblance, similarity, similitude
compartment • one of the parts into which an enclosed space is divided *Syn* bay, cabin, cell, chamber, cubicle *Rel* cubbyhole, pigeonhole
compass *n* **1** *Syn* CIRCUMFERENCE, circuit, perimeter, periphery **2** *Syn* RANGE, gamut, horizon, ken, orbit, purview, radius, reach, scope, sweep
compass *vb* **1** *Syn* REACH, achieve, attain, gain **2** *Syn* SURROUND, circle, encircle, encompass, environ, gird, girdle, hem, ring
compassion *Syn* SYMPATHY, commiseration, condolence, empathy, pity, ruth
compassionate *Syn* TENDER, responsive, sympathetic, warm, warmhearted *Ant* callous, severe
compatible **1** *Syn* CONSISTENT, conformable (to), congruous, consonant, correspondent (with *or* to), harmonious, nonconflicting *Ant* conflicting, incompatible, incongruous, inconsistent, inharmonious, unharmonious **2** *Syn* CONSONANT, congenial, congruous, consistent, sympathetic *Ant* dissonant (*in music*), inconstant
compel *Syn* FORCE, coerce, constrain, oblige
compelling *Syn* COGENT, conclusive, convincing, decisive, effective, forceful, persuasive, satisfying, strong, telling *Ant* inconclusive, indecisive, ineffective, unconvincing
compendious **1** *Syn* CONCISE, laconic, pithy, succinct, summary, terse *Ant* redundant **2** *Syn* ENCYCLOPEDIC, complete, comprehensive, full, global, inclusive, in-depth, omnibus, panoramic, universal
compendium • a condensed treatment of a subject *Syn* aperçu, digest, pandect, précis, sketch, survey, syllabus *Rel* abridgement, abstract, brief, conspectus, epitome
compensate **1** • to make up for or to undo the effects of *Syn* balance, counterbalance, counterpoise, countervail, offset *Rel* counteract, negative, neutralize **2** *Syn* PAY, indemnify, recompense, reimburse, remunerate, repay, satisfy

compete 1 • to strive to gain the mastery or upper hand *Syn* contend, contest *Rel* battle, fight 2 *Syn* RIVAL, emulate, vie

competence *Syn* ABILITY, capability, capacity, competency, faculty *Ant* disability, inability, incapability, incapacity, incompetence, incompetency, ineptitude, ineptness

competency *Syn* ABILITY, capability, capacity, competence, faculty *Ant* disability, inability, incapability, incapacity, incompetence, incompetency, ineptitude, ineptness

competent 1 • having the required skills for an acceptable level of performance *Syn* able, capable, fit, good, qualified, suitable *Rel* accomplished, ace, adept, experienced, expert, master, masterful, masterly, practiced (*or* practised), prepared, proficient, schooled, seasoned, skilled, skillful, trained, veteran *Ant* incompetent, inept, poor, unfit, unqualified 2 *Syn* SUFFICIENT, adequate, enough

competition *Syn* COMPETITOR, challenger, contender, contestant, rival

competitor • one who strives for the same thing as another *Syn* challenger, competition, contender, contestant, rival *Rel* finalist, semifinalist

compilation *Syn* ANTHOLOGY, album, miscellany

compile *Syn* EDIT, adapt, redact, revise, rewrite

complacence • an often unjustified feeling of being pleased with oneself or with one's situation or achievements *Syn* complacency, conceit, conceitedness, ego, egotism, pompousness, pride, pridefulness, self-admiration, self-conceit, self-esteem, self-importance, self-satisfaction, smugness, vaingloriousness, vainglory, vainness, vanity *Rel* assurance, confidence, self-assurance, self-confidence *Ant* humbleness, humility, modesty

complacency *Syn* COMPLACENCE, conceit, conceitedness, ego, egotism, pompousness, pride, pridefulness, self-admiration, self-conceit, self-esteem, self-importance, self-satisfaction, smugness, vaingloriousness, vainglory, vainness, vanity *Ant* humbleness, humility, modesty

complacent 1 • feeling or showing an often excessive or unjustified satisfaction in one's possessions, attainments, accomplishments, or virtues *Syn* priggish, self-complacent, self-satisfied, smug *Rel* assured, confident, self-assured, self-confident, self-possessed 2 *Syn* CONCEITED, egoistic, egotistic (*or* egotistical), important, overweening, pompous, prideful, proud, self-conceited, self-important, self-satisfied, smug, stuck-up, vain, vainglorious *Ant* humble, modest

complain • to express dissatisfaction, pain, or resentment usually tiresomely *Syn* beef, bellyache, carp, crab, croak, fuss, gripe, grouse, growl, grumble, kick, moan, murmur, mutter, repine, squawk, wail, whine, yammer *Rel* object (to), protest, quarrel (with) *Ant* rejoice

complainer *Syn* GROUCH, bear, crab, crank, croaker, curmudgeon, fusser, griper, grouser, growler, grumbler, grump, murmurer, mutterer, whiner

complaint 1 *Syn* DISEASE, ailment, condition, disorder, distemper, malady, syndrome *Syn* OBJECTION, complaint, demur, expostulation, fuss, protest, question, remonstrance 2 *Syn* OBJECTION, challenge, demur, expostulation, fuss, protest, question, remonstrance 3 *Syn* CHARGE, count, indictment, rap

complemental *Syn* RECIPROCAL (sense 2), complementary, convertible, correlative, corresponding

complementary *Syn* RECIPROCAL (sense 2), complemental, convertible, correlative, corresponding

complete *vb Syn* CONCLUDE (sense 1), conclude, end, finish, terminate

complete *adj* 1 *Syn* ENCYCLOPEDIC, compendious, comprehensive, full, global, inclusive, in-depth, omnibus, panoramic, universal 2 *Syn* EXHAUSTIVE, all-out, clean, comprehensive, full-scale, out-and-out, thorough, thoroughgoing, total 3 *Syn* FULL, plenary, replete *Ant* empty

complex *adj* • having parts or elements that are more or less confusingly interrelated *Syn* complicated, intricate, involved, knotty *Rel* amalgamated, blended, fused, merged, mingled, mixed *Ant* simple

complex *n Syn* SYSTEM, network, organism, scheme *Ant* chaos

complexion *Syn* DISPOSITION, character, individuality, personality, temper, temperament

compliance • passive or weak agreement to what is asked or demanded *Syn* acquiescence, resignation *Rel* amenableness, docility, obedience, tractableness *Ant* forwardness

compliant 1 • manifesting acceptance (as of another's will or something disagreeable) *Syn* acquiescent, resigned *Rel* amenable, docile, obedient, tractable *Ant* forward 2 *Syn* OBEDIENT, amenable, conformable, docile, law-abiding, submissive, tractable *Ant* contrary, disobedient, froward, insubordinate, intractable, rebellious, recalcitrant, refractory, unruly

complicated *Syn* COMPLEX, intricate, involved, knotty *Ant* simple

compliment *n* • praise addressed directly to a person *Syn* adulation, flattery *Rel* encomium, eulogy, panegyric, tribute *Ant* taunt

compliment *vb Syn* COMMEND, applaud, recommend *Ant* admonish, censure

compliments • best wishes *Syn* congratulations, felicitations, greetings, regards, respects *Rel* approval, blessing, endorsement

comply *Syn* OBEY, mind *Ant* command, order

component *Syn* ELEMENT, constituent, factor, ingredient *Ant* composite, compound (*in science*)
comport *Syn* BEHAVE, acquit, conduct, demean, deport, quit *Ant* misbehave
compose *Syn* CALM, lull, quiet, quieten, settle, soothe, still, tranquilize *Ant* agitate, arouse
composed *Syn* COOL, collected, imperturbable, nonchalant, unflappable, unruffled *Ant* agitated, ardent
composite *Syn* BLEND, admixture, amalgam, amalgamation, combination, compound, fusion, intermixture, mix, mixture
composition *Syn* ESSAY, article, paper, theme
composure *Syn* EQUANIMITY, aplomb, calmness, coolheadedness, coolness, imperturbability, placidity, self-possession, serenity, tranquillity (*or* tranquility) *Ant* agitation, discomposure, perturbation
compound **1** *Syn* BLEND, admixture, amalgam, amalgamation, combination, composite, fusion, intermixture, mix, mixture **2** *Syn* INCREASE (sense 1), add (to), aggrandize, amplify, augment, boost, enlarge, escalate, expand, extend, multiply, raise, swell, up *Ant* abate, contract, decrease, diminish, lessen, lower, reduce, subtract (from)
comprehend **1** *Syn* INCLUDE, embrace, imply, involve, subsume *Ant* exclude **2** *Syn* UNDERSTAND, appreciate
comprehension • the knowledge gained from the process of coming to know or understand something *Syn* appreciation, apprehension, grasp, grip, perception, understanding *Rel* absorption, assimilation, uptake
comprehensive **1** *Syn* ENCYCLOPEDIC, compendious, complete, full, global, inclusive, in-depth, omnibus, panoramic, universal **2** *Syn* EXHAUSTIVE, all-out, clean, complete, full-scale, out-and-out, thorough, thoroughgoing, total
compress *Syn* CONTRACT, condense, constrict, deflate, shrink *Ant* expand
compromise *Syn* ENDANGER, adventure, gamble (with), hazard, imperil, jeopardize, menace, risk, venture
compulsion *Syn* FORCE, coercion, constraint, duress, restraint, violence
compulsive • caused by or suggestive of an irresistible urge *Syn* impulsive, obsessive *Rel* irrepressible, uncontrollable
compulsory *Syn* MANDATORY, forced, imperative, incumbent, involuntary, necessary, nonelective, obligatory, peremptory, required *Ant* elective, optional, voluntary
compunction **1** *Syn* PENITENCE, attrition, contrition, remorse, repentance **2** *Syn* QUALM, misgiving, scruple
computation *Syn* CALCULATION, arithmetic, ciphering, figures, figuring, reckoning
compute *Syn* CALCULATE, estimate, reckon
comrade *Syn* ASSOCIATE, companion, crony
comradeship *Syn* COMPANIONSHIP, camaraderie, company, fellowship, society
conation *Syn* WILL, volition
concave *Syn* HOLLOW, dented, depressed, indented, recessed, sunken *Ant* bulging, convex, protruding, protuberant
conceal *Syn* HIDE, bury, cache, ensconce, screen, secrete
concede **1** *Syn* ADMIT, acknowledge, agree, allow, confess, grant, own (up) *Ant* deny **2** *Syn* GRANT (sense 1), accord, award, vouchsafe
conceit **1** • an attitude of regarding oneself with favor *Syn* amour propre, egoism, egotism, self-esteem, self-love *Rel* pride, vainglory, vanity *Ant* humility **2** *Syn* COMPLACENCE, complacency, conceitedness, ego, egotism, pompousness, pride, pridefulness, self-admiration, self-conceit, self-esteem, self-importance, self-satisfaction, smugness, vaingloriousness, vainglory, vainness, vanity *Ant* humbleness, humility, modesty
conceited • having too high an opinion of oneself *Syn* complacent, egoistic, egotistic (*or* egotistical), important, overweening, pompous, prideful, proud, self-conceited, self-important, self-satisfied, smug, stuck-up, vain, vainglorious *Rel* boastful, braggart, bragging *Ant* humble, modest
conceitedness *Syn* COMPLACENCE, complacency, conceit, ego, egotism, pompousness, pride, pridefulness, self-admiration, self-conceit, self-esteem, self-importance, self-satisfaction, smugness, vaingloriousness, vainglory, vainness, vanity *Ant* humbleness, humility, modesty
conceivably *Syn* PERHAPS, maybe, mayhap, perchance, possibly
conceive *Syn* THINK (sense 1), envisage, envision, fancy, imagine, realize
concentrate **1** *Syn* CENTER, centralize, focus **2** *Syn* COMPACT, consolidate, unify
concentration *Syn* ATTENTION (sense 1), application, study *Ant* inattention
concept *Syn* IDEA, conception, impression, notion, thought
conception *Syn* IDEA, concept, impression, notion, thought
conceptual *Syn* ABSTRACT (sense 2), theoretical *Ant* concrete
concern **1** *Syn* AFFAIR, business, matter, thing **2** *Syn* CARE, anxiety, solicitude, worry
concerned *Syn* WORRIED, anxious, careful, solicitous
concerning *Syn* ABOUT, regarding, respecting
concert *Syn* NEGOTIATE, arrange
concession *Syn* CONFESSION, acknowledgment, admission, avowal
conciliate *Syn* PACIFY, appease, disarm, mollify, placate, propitiate *Ant* anger, enrage, incense, infuriate, madden, outrage
conciliator *Syn* MEDIATOR, arbiter, arbitrator,

go-between, intercessor, intermediary, interposer, middleman, peacemaker
concise • presented with or given to brevity of expression *Syn* compendious, laconic, pithy, succinct, summary, terse *Rel* compressed, condensed *Ant* redundant
concisely *Syn* SUCCINCTLY, briefly, compactly, crisply, laconically, pithily, summarily, tersely *Ant* diffusely, long-windedly, verbosely, wordily
conclude **1** • to bring to a natural or appropriate close *Syn* complete, end, finish, terminate **2** *Syn* INFER, deduce, gather, judge
concluding *Syn* LAST, eventual, final, latest, terminal, ultimate *Ant* first
conclusion **1** *Syn* FINALE, close, closing, consummation, end, ending, finis, finish, windup *Ant* beginning, dawn, opening, start **2** *Syn* INFERENCE (sense 1), deduction, judgment
conclusive **1** • having or manifesting qualities that bring something to a finish or end *Syn* decisive, definitive, determinative *Rel* cogent, compelling, convincing, telling, valid *Ant* inconclusive **2** *Syn* COGENT, compelling, convincing, decisive, effective, forceful, persuasive, satisfying, strong, telling *Ant* inconclusive, indecisive, ineffective, unconvincing
concoct **1** *Syn* CONTRIVE, devise, frame, invent **2** *Syn* INVENT, contrive, cook (up), devise, fabricate, make up, manufacture, think (up)
concomitant *Syn* CONTEMPORARY, coetaneous, coeval, coincident, concurrent, contemporaneous, simultaneous, synchronous
concord *Syn* HARMONY, accord, consonance *Ant* conflict
concordat *Syn* CONTRACT, bargain, cartel, compact, convention, entente, pact, treaty
concourse *Syn* JUNCTION, confluence
concrete *Syn* ACTUAL, existent, factual, real, true, very *Ant* conjectural, hypothetical, ideal, nonexistent, possible, potential, theoretical
concur **1** *Syn* AGREE (sense 1), coincide *Ant* differ, disagree **2** *Syn* UNITE, combine, conjoin, cooperate *Ant* part
concurrence *Syn* PERMISSION, allowance, authorization, clearance, consent, granting, leave, license (*or* licence), sanction, sufferance *Ant* interdiction, prohibition, proscription
concurrent *Syn* CONTEMPORARY, coetaneous, coeval, coincident, concomitant, contemporaneous, simultaneous, synchronous
concussion *Syn* IMPACT, clash, collision, impingement, jar, jolt, percussion, shock
condemn **1** *Syn* CRITICIZE, blame, censure, denounce, reprehend, reprobate **2** *Syn* SENTENCE, damn, doom, proscribe
condemnation *Syn* CENSURE, denunciation, rebuke, reprimand, reproach, reproof, stricture *Ant* citation, commendation, endorsement
condense *Syn* CONTRACT, compress, constrict, deflate, shrink *Ant* expand
condescend *Syn* STOOP, deign
condign *Syn* DUE, rightful
condition *n* **1** • something that limits or qualifies an agreement or offer *Syn* provision, proviso, reservation, stipulation, strings, terms *Rel* prerequisite, requirement, requisite **2** *Syn* DISEASE, ailment, complaint, disorder, distemper, malady, syndrome **3** *Syn* RESTRICTION, check, constraint, curb, fetter, limitation, restraint **4** *Syn* STATE, mode, posture, situation, status
condition *vb Syn* PREPARE, fit, qualify, ready
conditional *Syn* DEPENDENT, contingent, relative *Ant* absolute, infinite, original
condolence *Syn* SYMPATHY, commiseration, compassion, empathy, pity, ruth
condone *Syn* EXCUSE, forgive, pardon, remit *Ant* punish
conduct *vb* **1** • to use one's skill, authority, or other powers in order to lead, guide, command, or dominate persons or things *Syn* control, direct, manage *Rel* oversee, supervise **2** *Syn* BEHAVE, acquit, comport, demean, deport, quit *Ant* misbehave **3** *Syn* CHANNEL, channelize, direct, funnel, pipe, siphon
conduct *n Syn* BEHAVIOR, deportment
conduit *Syn* CHANNEL, aqueduct, canal, duct
confederacy *Syn* ALLIANCE, coalition, confederation, federation, fusion, league
confederate *n* **1** *Syn* ACCOMPLICE, abettor, accessory, cohort **2** *Syn* ALLY, abettor, backer, supporter, sympathizer **3** *Syn* PARTNER, ally, colleague, copartner *Ant* rival
confederate *vb Syn* ALLY, associate, band, club, conjoin, cooperate, federate, league, unite *Ant* break up, disband
confederation *Syn* ALLIANCE, coalition, confederacy, federation, fusion, league
confer **1** • to give the ownership or benefit of (something) formally or publicly *Syn* accord, award, grant *Rel* bestow, contribute, donate, give, present **2** *Syn* GIVE, afford, bestow, donate, present
confess *Syn* ADMIT, acknowledge, agree, allow, concede, grant, own (up) *Ant* deny
confession • an open declaration of something (as a fault or the commission of an offense) about oneself *Syn* acknowledgment, admission, avowal, concession *Rel* allowance
confessions *Syn* BIOGRAPHY, autobiography, life, memoir
confidant *Syn* FRIEND, acquaintance, intimate *Ant* foe
confide *Syn* COMMIT, consign, entrust, relegate
confidence **1** • a feeling or showing of adequacy or reliance on oneself and one's powers *Syn* aplomb, assurance, self-assurance,

self-confidence, self-possession *Rel* courage, mettle, resolution, spirit, tenacity *Ant* diffidence **2** *Syn* TRUST, dependence, faith, reliance *Ant* mistrust

confident • not inhibited by doubts, fears, or a sense of inferiority *Syn* assured, presumptuous, sanguine, sure *Rel* bold, brave, courageous, dauntless, fearless, intrepid, unafraid, undaunted, valiant *Ant* apprehensive, diffident

confidential *Syn* FAMILIAR, chummy, close, intimate, thick *Ant* aloof

configuration *Syn* FORM (sense 1), conformation, figure, shape

confine *n Syn* LIMIT, bound, end, term

confine *vb Syn* LIMIT, circumscribe, restrict *Ant* widen

confirm • to attest to the truth, genuineness, accuracy, or validity of something *Syn* authenticate, corroborate, substantiate, validate, verify *Rel* back, support, uphold *Ant* contradict, deny

confirmed *Syn* INVETERATE, chronic, deep-rooted, deep-seated

confiscate *Syn* ARROGATE, appropriate, preempt, usurp *Ant* renounce, yield

conflagration *Syn* FIRE, holocaust

conflict *vb* **1** *Syn* BUMP, clash, collide **2** *Syn* RESIST, antagonize, combat, contest, fight, oppose, withstand *Ant* abide, submit

conflict *n* **1** *Syn* CONTEST, affray, combat, fight, fray **2** *Syn* DISCORD, contention, difference, dissension, schism, strife, variance

confluence *Syn* JUNCTION, concourse

conform **1** *Syn* ADAPT, accommodate, adjust, reconcile *Ant* unfit **2** *Syn* AGREE (sense 2), accord, correspond, harmonize, jibe, square, tally *Ant* differ (from)

conformable **1** *Syn* OBEDIENT, amenable, compliant, docile, law-abiding, submissive, tractable *Ant* contrary, disobedient, froward, insubordinate, intractable, rebellious, recalcitrant, refractory, unruly **2** *Syn* CONSISTENT, compatible, congruous, consonant, correspondent (with *or* to), harmonious, nonconflicting *Ant* conflicting, incompatible, incongruous, inconsistent, inharmonious, unharmonious

conformation *Syn* FORM (sense 1), configuration, figure, shape

confound **1** *Syn* MISTAKE, confuse *Ant* recognize **2** *Syn* PUZZLE, bewilder, distract, dumbfound, mystify, nonplus, perplex

confront *Syn* MEET, encounter, face *Ant* avoid

confuse **1** • to make unclear in mind or purpose *Syn* addle, befuddle, fuddle, muddle *Rel* bewilder, confound, mystify, perplex, puzzle *Ant* enlighten **2** *Syn* DISORDER, derange, disarrange, disarray, discompose, dishevel, dislocate, disorganize, disrupt, disturb, hash, jumble, mess (up), mix (up), muddle, muss, rumple, scramble, shuffle, tousle, tumble, upset *Ant* arrange, array, draw up, marshal, order, organize, range, regulate, straighten (up), tidy **3** *Syn* MISTAKE, confound *Ant* recognize

confused *Syn* MESSY, chaotic, cluttered, disarranged, disarrayed, disheveled (*or* dishevelled), disordered, disorderly, higgledy-piggledy, hugger-mugger, jumbled, littered, messed, muddled, mussed, mussy, pell-mell, rumpled, sloppy, topsy-turvy, tousled, tumbled, unkempt, untidy, upside-down *Ant* neat, ordered, orderly, organized, shipshape, snug, tidied, tidy, trim

confusion • a condition in which things are not in their normal or proper places or relationships *Syn* chaos, clutter, disarray, disorder, jumble, muddle, snarl *Rel* derangement, disarrangement, disorganization, disturbance

confute *Syn* DISPROVE, controvert, rebut, refute *Ant* demonstrate, prove

congeal *Syn* COAGULATE, clot, curdle, jell, jelly, set

congenial *Syn* CONSONANT, compatible, congruous, consistent, sympathetic *Ant* dissonant (*in music*), inconstant

congenital *Syn* INNATE, hereditary, inborn, inbred, inherited *Ant* acquired

conglomerate *Syn* AGGREGATE, agglomerate, agglomeration, aggregation, conglomeration *Ant* constituent

conglomeration *Syn* AGGREGATE, agglomerate, agglomeration, aggregation, conglomerate *Ant* constituent

congratulations *Syn* COMPLIMENTS, felicitations, greetings, regards, respects

congregate *Syn* GATHER, assemble, collect

congregation *Syn* GATHERING, assemblage, assembly, collection

congruous **1** *Syn* CONSISTENT, compatible, conformable (to), consonant, correspondent (with *or* to), harmonious, nonconflicting *Ant* conflicting, incompatible, incongruous, inconsistent, inharmonious, unharmonious **2** *Syn* CONSONANT, compatible, congenial, consistent, sympathetic *Ant* dissonant (*in music*), inconstant

congruously *Syn* PROPERLY, appropriately, correctly, fittingly, happily, meetly, rightly, suitably *Ant* improperly, inappropriately, incongruously, incorrectly, unsuitably, wrongly

conjectural *Syn* SUPPOSED, hypothetical, purported, putative, reputed, suppositious, supposititious *Ant* certain

conjecture *n* • an opinion or judgment based on little or no evidence *Syn* guess, supposition, surmise *Rel* hypothesis, theory, thesis

conjecture *vb Syn* ESTIMATE (sense 2), calculate, call, figure, gauge, guess, judge, make, place, put, reckon, suppose

conjoin **1** *Syn* ALLY, associate, band, club, confederate, cooperate, federate, league, unite *Ant* break up, disband **2** *Syn* JOIN, associate, combine, connect, link, relate, unite *Ant* disjoin, part **3** *Syn* UNITE, combine, concur, cooperate *Ant* part

conjugal *Syn* MARITAL, connubial, married, matrimonial, nuptial, wedded

conjurer *or* **conjuror** **1** *Syn* MAGICIAN (sense 1), charmer, enchanter, necromancer, sorcerer, voodoo, witch, wizard **2** *Syn* MAGICIAN (sense 2), prestidigitator, trickster

connect *Syn* JOIN, associate, combine, conjoin, link, relate, unite *Ant* disjoin, part

connoisseur *Syn* AESTHETE, dilettante

connubial *Syn* MARITAL, conjugal, married, matrimonial, nuptial, wedded

conquer • to get the better of or to bring into subjection by force or strategy *Syn* beat, defeat, lick, overcome, overthrow, reduce, rout, subdue, subjugate, surmount, vanquish *Rel* baffle, balk, circumvent, foil, frustrate, outwit, thwart

conqueror *Syn* VICTOR, champion, vanquisher, winner

conquest *Syn* VICTORY, triumph *Ant* defeat

conscientious *Syn* UPRIGHT, honest, honorable, just, scrupulous

conscious **1** • having specified facts or feelings actively impressed on the mind *Syn* alive, aware, cognizant, mindful, sensible, sentient *Rel* attentive, heedful, observant, regardful, vigilant, watchful *Ant* insensible, unaware, unconscious, unmindful **2** *Syn* AWARE, alive, awake, cognizant, sensible *Ant* unaware

consciously *Syn* INTENTIONALLY, deliberately, designedly, knowingly, purposefully, purposely, willfully, wittingly *Ant* inadvertently, unconsciously, unintentionally, unknowingly, unwittingly

consecrate *Syn* DEVOTE, dedicate, hallow

consecrated *Syn* HOLY (sense 2), blessed, hallowed, sacred, sacrosanct, sanctified *Ant* unconsecrated, unhallowed

consecration • the act of making something holy through religious ritual *Syn* blessing, hallowing, sanctification *Rel* dedication

consecutive • following one after the other in order *Syn* sequent, sequential, serial, successive *Rel* ensuing, following, succeeding *Ant* inconsecutive

consent **1** *Syn* ASSENT, accede, acquiesce, agree, subscribe *Ant* dissent **2** *Syn* PERMISSION, allowance, authorization, clearance, concurrence, granting, leave, license (*or* licence), sanction, sufferance *Ant* interdiction, prohibition, proscription

consequence **1** *Syn* EFFECT, aftereffect, aftermath, event, issue, outcome, result, sequel, upshot *Ant* cause **2** *Syn* IMPORTANCE, import, moment, significance, weight *Ant* unimportance

consequently *Syn* THEREFORE, accordingly, hence, so, then

conservative • tending to favor established ideas, conditions, or institutions *Syn* orthodox, traditional *Rel* hidebound, old-fashioned, reactionary *Ant* liberal, nontraditional, progressive

conserve *Syn* SAVE, preserve *Ant* consume, spend

consider **1** • to give serious thought to *Syn* contemplate, excogitate, study, weigh *Rel* meditate, muse, ponder, ruminate **2** • to come to view, judge, or classify *Syn* account, deem, reckon, regard *Rel* conceive, fancy, imagine, think **3** *Syn* BELIEVE (sense 1), deem, feel, figure, guess, hold, imagine, suppose, think *Ant* disbelieve, discredit, reject

considerable *Syn* LARGE, big, bulky, goodly, good-sized, grand, great, handsome, hefty, hulking, largish, outsize, oversize (*or* oversized), sizable (*or* sizeable), substantial, tidy, voluminous *Ant* little, puny, small, undersized

considered *Syn* DELIBERATE, advised, designed, premeditated, studied *Ant* casual

consign *Syn* COMMIT, confide, entrust, relegate

consistent **1** • not having or showing any apparent conflict *Syn* compatible, conformable (to), congruous, consonant, correspondent (with *or* to), harmonious, nonconflicting *Rel* appropriate, fitting, meet, suitable *Ant* conflicting, incompatible, incongruous, inconsistent, inharmonious, unharmonious **2** *Syn* CONSONANT, compatible, congenial, congruous, sympathetic *Ant* dissonant (*in music*), inconstant

console *Syn* COMFORT, solace *Ant* afflict, bother

consolidate *Syn* COMPACT, concentrate, unify

consolidation • a union of two or more business corporations *Syn* amalgamation, merger *Ant* dissolution

consonance *Syn* HARMONY, accord, concord *Ant* conflict

consonant **1** • conforming (as to a pattern, standard, or relationship) without discord or difficulty *Syn* compatible, congenial, congruous, consistent, sympathetic *Rel* accordant, according, agreeable, agreeing, conformable, conforming, harmonious, harmonizing *Ant* dissonant (*in music*), inconstant **2** *Syn* CONSISTENT, compatible, conformable (to), congruous, correspondent (with *or* to), harmonious, nonconflicting *Ant* conflicting, incompatible, incongruous, inconsistent, inharmonious, unharmonious

consort *Syn* SPOUSE, mate, partner

conspectus *Syn* ABRIDGMENT, abstract, brief, epitome, synopsis *Ant* expansion

conspicuous **1** *Syn* EGREGIOUS, blatant, flagrant, glaring, gross, obvious, patent, pronounced, rank, striking **2** *Syn* NOTICEABLE, arresting, outstanding, prominent, remarkable, salient, signal, striking

conspiracy *Syn* PLOT, cabal, intrigue, machination

conspire *Syn* PLOT, contrive, intrigue, machinate, scheme

constant **1** *Syn* CONTINUAL, continuous, incessant, perennial, perpetual, unremitting *Ant* intermittent **2** *Syn* FAITHFUL, devoted, devout, fast, good, loyal, pious, staunch (*or* stanch), steadfast, steady, true, true-blue *Ant* disloyal, faithless, false, fickle, inconstant, perfidious, recreant, traitorous, treacherous, unfaithful, untrue **3** *Syn* STEADY, equable, even, uniform *Ant* jumpy, nervous, unsteady

consternation *Syn* FEAR, alarm, dismay, dread, fright, horror, panic, terror, trepidation *Ant* fearlessness

constituent *Syn* ELEMENT, component, factor, ingredient *Ant* composite, compound (*in science*)

constitute *Syn* APPOINT (sense 2), assign, attach, commission, designate, detail, name *Ant* discharge, dismiss, expel, fire

constitution *Syn* PHYSIQUE, build, habit

constitutional *adj Syn* INHERENT, essential, ingrained, intrinsic *Ant* adventitious

constitutional *n Syn* WALK, perambulation, ramble, range, saunter, stroll, turn

constitutionally *Syn* NATURALLY (sense 2), inherently, innately, intrinsically *Ant* affectedly, artificially, hypocritically, insincerely, pretentiously, unnaturally

constrain *Syn* FORCE, coerce, compel, oblige

constraint **1** *Syn* FORCE, coercion, compulsion, duress, restraint, violence **2** *Syn* RESTRICTION, check, condition, curb, fetter, limitation, restraint

constrict *Syn* CONTRACT, compress, condense, deflate, shrink *Ant* expand

construct *Syn* BUILD, assemble, erect, fabricate, make, make up, piece, put up, raise, rear, set up *Ant* disassemble, dismantle, take down

construe *Syn* EXPLAIN (sense 1), clarify, clear (up), demonstrate, elucidate, explicate, expound, illuminate, illustrate, interpret, spell out *Ant* obscure

consume **1** *Syn* DEPLETE, clean (out), drain, exhaust, expend, spend, use up *Ant* renew, replace **2** *Syn* EAT, devour, ingest, swallow **3** *Syn* MONOPOLIZE, absorb, engross **4** *Syn* WASTE, dissipate, fritter, squander *Ant* conserve, save

consummate • brought to completion or perfection *Syn* accomplished, finished *Rel* entire, intact, perfect, whole *Ant* crude

consummation **1** *Syn* FINALE, close, closing, conclusion, end, ending, finis, finish, windup *Ant* beginning, dawn, opening, start **2** *Syn* FRUITION, accomplishment, achievement, actuality, attainment, fulfillment, realization *Ant* naught, nonfulfillment

contagious *Syn* INFECTIOUS (sense 1), catching, communicable

contain • to have or be capable of having within *Syn* accommodate, hold *Rel* admit, receive, take

container • something into which a liquid or smaller objects can be put for storage or transportation *Syn* holder, receptacle, vessel *Rel* cartridge

contaminate • to make unfit for use by the addition of something harmful or undesirable *Syn* befoul, defile, foul, poison, pollute, taint *Rel* infect *Ant* decontaminate, purify

contaminated *Syn* IMPURE, adulterated, alloyed, dilute, diluted, polluted, tainted, thinned, weakened *Ant* pure, unadulterated, unalloyed, uncontaminated, undiluted, unpolluted, untainted

contemn *Syn* DESPISE, disdain, scorn, scout *Ant* appreciate

contemplate **1** *Syn* CONSIDER (sense 1), excogitate, study, weigh **2** *Syn* SEE (sense 1), behold, descry, discern, espy, note, notice, observe, perceive, remark, survey, view

contemplative **1** • given to or marked by long, quiet thinking *Syn* meditative, melancholy, pensive, reflective, ruminant, thoughtful *Rel* introspective, retrospective *Ant* unreflective **2** *Syn* THOUGHTFUL (sense 1), meditative, pensive, reflective, speculative *Ant* thoughtless

contemporaneous *Syn* CONTEMPORARY, coetaneous, coeval, coincident, concomitant, concurrent, simultaneous, synchronous

contemporary **1** • existing, living, or occurring at the same time *Syn* coetaneous, coeval, coincident, concomitant, concurrent, contemporaneous, simultaneous, synchronous *Rel* existing, living, subsisting **2** *Syn* MODERN, current, hot, mod, modernistic, new, newfangled, new-fashioned, present-day, red-hot, space-age, ultramodern, up-to-date *Ant* antiquated, archaic, dated, fusty, musty, noncontemporary, oldfangled, old-fashioned, old-time, out-of-date, passé

contempt • open dislike for someone or something considered unworthy of one's concern or respect *Syn* despite, despitefulness, disdain, scorn *Rel* abhorrence, abomination, execration, hate, hatred, loathing *Ant* admiration, esteem, regard, respect

contemptible • arousing or deserving scorn or disdain *Syn* beggarly, cheap, despicable, pitiable, scurvy, shabby, sorry *Rel* abhorrent, abominable, detestable, hateful, odious *Ant* admirable, estimable, formidable

contend **1** • to strive in opposition to someone or something *Syn* battle, fight, war *Rel* altercate, quarrel, squabble, wrangle **2** *Syn* COMPETE, contest

contender **1** *Syn* CANDIDATE, applicant, aspirant, campaigner, hopeful, prospect, seeker **2** *Syn* COMPETITOR, challenger, competition, contestant, rival

content • feeling that one's needs or desires have been met *Syn* contented, gratified, happy, pleased, satisfied *Rel* delighted, glad, joyful, joyous, jubilant *Ant* discontent, discontented, displeased, dissatisfied, malcontent, unhappy

contented *Syn* CONTENT, gratified, happy, pleased, satisfied *Ant* discontent, discontented, displeased, dissatisfied, malcontent, unhappy

contention *Syn* DISCORD, conflict, difference, dissension, schism, strife, variance

contentious *Syn* BELLIGERENT, aggressive, argumentative, bellicose, combative, discordant, disputatious, gladiatorial, militant, pugnacious, quarrelsome, scrappy, truculent, warlike *Ant* nonbelligerent, pacific, peaceable, peaceful

contentiousness *Syn* BELLIGERENCE, aggression, aggressiveness, bellicosity, combativeness, disputatiousness, fight, militancy, pugnacity, scrappiness, truculence *Ant* pacifism

contest *n* • a battle between opposing forces for supremacy, for power, or for possessions *Syn* affray, combat, conflict, fight, fray *Rel* brush, encounter, skirmish

contest *vb* **1** *Syn* COMPETE, contend **2** *Syn* RESIST, antagonize, combat, conflict, fight, oppose, withstand *Ant* abide, submit

contestant *Syn* COMPETITOR, challenger, competition, contender, rival

contiguity *Syn* PROXIMITY, closeness, immediacy, nearness *Ant* distance, remoteness

contiguous *Syn* ADJACENT, abutting, adjoining, bordering, flanking, fringing, joining, juxtaposed, skirting, touching, verging *Ant* nonadjacent

continence *Syn* TEMPERANCE, abstemiousness, abstinence, sobriety *Ant* excessiveness, immoderacy, intemperance, intemperateness

continent *Syn* SOBER, temperate, unimpassioned *Ant* drunk, excited

contingency *Syn* JUNCTURE, crisis, emergency, exigency, pass, pinch, strait

contingent *Syn* DEPENDENT, conditional, relative *Ant* absolute, infinite, original

continual • characterized by continued occurrence or recurrence over a relatively long period of time *Syn* constant, continuous, incessant, perennial, perpetual, unremitting *Rel* endless, everlasting, interminable, unceasing *Ant* intermittent

continuance *Syn* CONTINUATION, duration, endurance, persistence, subsistence *Ant* ending, termination

continuation • uninterrupted or lasting existence *Syn* continuance, duration, endurance, persistence, subsistence *Rel* elongation, extension, lengthening, prolongation *Ant* ending, termination

continue **1** • to remain indefinitely in existence or in a given condition or course *Syn* abide, endure, last, persist *Rel* remain, stay **2** *Syn* RESUME, renew, reopen, restart

continuous *Syn* CONTINUAL, constant, incessant, perennial, perpetual, unremitting *Ant* intermittent

contort *Syn* DEFORM, distort, warp

contour *Syn* OUTLINE, profile, silhouette, skyline

contraband *Syn* SMUGGLED, bootleg

contract *n* **1** • an agreement reached after negotiation and ending in an exchange of promises between the parties concerned *Syn* bargain, cartel, compact, concordat, convention, entente, pact, treaty **2** *Syn* PROMISE, covenant, engage, pledge, plight

contract *vb* • to decrease in bulk, volume, or content *Syn* compress, condense, constrict, deflate, shrink *Rel* decrease, diminish, dwindle, reduce *Ant* expand

contradict *Syn* DENY, contravene, gainsay, impugn, negative, traverse *Ant* concede, confirm

contradiction *Syn* DENIAL (sense 2), disallowance, disavowal, disclaimer, negation, rejection, repudiation *Ant* acknowledgment, admission, avowal, confirmation

contradictory *adj* *Syn* OPPOSITE, antipodal, antipodean, antithetical, antonymous, contrary

contradictory *n* *Syn* OPPOSITE, antipode, antithesis, antonym, contrary, converse, counter, reverse

contraption **1** *Syn* DEVICE, contrivance, gadget **2** *Syn* GADGET, appliance, contrivance, gimmick, gizmo (*or* gismo), jigger

contrariness *Syn* DISOBEDIENCE, defiance, frowardness, insubordination, intractability, rebelliousness, recalcitrance, refractoriness, unruliness, willfulness *Ant* amenability, compliance, docility, obedience

contrary *adj* **1** • given to opposing or resisting wishes, commands, conditions, or circumstances *Syn* balky, froward, perverse, restive, wayward *Rel* headstrong, intractable, recalcitrant, refractory, unruly *Ant* complaisant, good-natured **2** *Syn* DISOBEDIENT, balky, defiant, froward, insubordinate, intractable, rebellious, recalcitrant, refractory, restive, ungovernable, unruly, untoward, wayward, willful (*or* wilful) *Ant* amenable, compliant, docile, obedient, tractable **3** *Syn* OPPOSITE, antipodal, antipodean, antithetical, antonymous, contradictory

contrary *n* *Syn* OPPOSITE, antipode, antithesis, antonym, contradictory, converse, counter, reverse

contrast *vb* *Syn* COMPARE, collate

contrast *n* *Syn* COMPARISON, collation, parallel

contravene *Syn* DENY, contradict, gainsay, impugn, negative, traverse *Ant* concede, confirm

contravention *Syn* BREACH (sense 1), infraction, infringement, transgression, trespass, violation
contribution • a gift of money or its equivalent to a charity, humanitarian cause, or public institution *Syn* alms, benefaction, beneficence, charity, donation, philanthropy *Rel* offering, tithe
contributory *Syn* AUXILIARY, accessory, adjuvant, ancillary, subservient, subsidiary
contrite *Syn* GUILTY, ashamed, hangdog, penitent, remorseful, repentant, shamed, shamefaced *Ant* impenitent, remorseless, shameless, unashamed, unrepentant
contrition *Syn* PENITENCE, attrition, compunction, remorse, repentance
contrivance **1** *Syn* DEVICE, contraption, gadget **2** *Syn* GADGET, appliance, contraption, gimmick, gizmo (*or* gismo), jigger
contrive **1** *Syn* ENGINEER, finagle, finesse, frame, machinate, maneuver, manipulate, mastermind, negotiate, wangle **2** *Syn* INVENT, concoct, cook (up), devise, fabricate, make up, manufacture, think (up) **3** *Syn* PLOT, conspire, intrigue, machinate, scheme
control *vb Syn* CONDUCT, direct, manage
control *n Syn* CORRECTIVE, antidote, check
controversy *Syn* ARGUMENT, dispute
controvert *Syn* DISPROVE, confute, rebut, refute *Ant* demonstrate, prove
contumacious *Syn* INSUBORDINATE, factious, mutinous, rebellious, seditious
contumelious *Syn* ABUSIVE, opprobrious, scurrilous, vituperative *Ant* complementary, respectful
contusion *Syn* WOUND, bruise, lesion, trauma, traumatism
conundrum *Syn* MYSTERY, enigma, problem, puzzle, riddle
convalesce **1** • to become healthy and strong again after illness or weakness *Syn* gain, heal, mend, rally, recover, recuperate, snap back *Rel* come around, come round, come to, improve, pick up, revive **2** *Syn* IMPROVE (sense 2), gain, recover, recuperate
convenance *Syn* FORM (sense 3), convention, usage
convene *Syn* SUMMON, call, cite, convoke, muster
convent *Syn* CLOISTER, abbey, monastery, nunnery, priory
convention **1** *Syn* CONTRACT, bargain, cartel, compact, concordat, entente, pact, treaty **2** *Syn* FORM (sense 3), convenance, usage
conventional *Syn* CEREMONIAL, ceremonious, formal, solemn
converse *vb* **1** *Syn* CHAT, babble, blab, cackle, chatter, gab, gabble, gas, jabber, jaw, palaver, patter, prate, prattle, rap, rattle, run on, talk, twitter, visit **2** *Syn* SPEAK, talk
converse *n Syn* OPPOSITE, antipode, antithesis, antonym, contradictory, contrary, counter, reverse
conversion *Syn* TRANSFORMATION, metamorphosis, transfiguration, transmogrification, transmutation
convert *n Syn* FOLLOWER, adherent, disciple, partisan, pupil, votary *Ant* leader
convert *vb* **1** • to change in form, appearance, or use *Syn* make over, metamorphose, transfigure, transform *Rel* adjust, alter, modify **2** *Syn* TRANSFORM, metamorphose, transfigure, transmogrify, transmute
convertible *Syn* RECIPROCAL (sense 2), complemental, complementary, correlative, corresponding
convey **1** *Syn* CARRY, bear, transmit, transport **2** *Syn* COMMUNICATE, impart, spread, transfer, transfuse, transmit **3** *Syn* TRANSFER, alienate, deed
convict *Syn* CRIMINAL, culprit, delinquent, felon, malefactor
conviction **1** *Syn* CERTAINTY, assurance, certitude *Ant* uncertainty **2** *Syn* OPINION, belief, persuasion, sentiment, view
convince *Syn* PERSUADE, argue, get, induce, move, prevail (on *or* upon), satisfy, talk (into), win (over)
convincing *Syn* COGENT, compelling, conclusive, decisive, effective, forceful, persuasive, satisfying, strong, telling *Ant* inconclusive, indecisive, ineffective, unconvincing
convivial • likely to seek or enjoy the company of others *Syn* boon, companionable, extroverted, gregarious, outgoing, sociable, social *Rel* cordial, friendly, hospitable *Ant* antisocial, introverted, reclusive, unsociable
convoke *Syn* SUMMON, call, cite, convene, muster
convoy *Syn* ACCOMPANY, attend, chaperone (*or* chaperon), escort, squire
convulse *Syn* SHAKE (sense 2), agitate, rock
convulsion **1** • a violent disturbance (as of the political or social order) *Syn* cataclysm, paroxysm, storm, tempest, tumult, upheaval, uproar *Rel* overthrow, overturn, revolution, subversion, upset **2** *Syn* FIT, paroxysm, spasm
convulsive • marked by sudden or violent disturbance *Syn* cataclysmal (*or* cataclysmic), stormy, tempestuous, tumultuous *Rel* fitful, spasmodic, sporadic
cook (up) *Syn* INVENT, concoct, contrive, devise, fabricate, make up, manufacture, think (up)
cool **1** • showing or seeming to show freedom from agitation or excitement *Syn* collected, composed, imperturbable, nonchalant, unflappable, unruffled *Rel* calm, placid, serene, tranquil *Ant* agitated, ardent **2** *Syn* COLD, arctic, chilly, freezing, frigid, frosty, gelid, glacial, icy *Ant* hot
coolheadedness *Syn* EQUANIMITY, aplomb, calmness, composure, coolness, imperturb-

ability, placidity, self-possession, serenity, tranquillity (*or* tranquility) *Ant* agitation, discomposure, perturbation

coolness *Syn* EQUANIMITY, aplomb, calmness, composure, coolheadedness, imperturbability, placidity, self-possession, serenity, tranquillity (*or* tranquility) *Ant* agitation, discomposure, perturbation

coop *Syn* ENCLOSE, cage, corral, envelop, fence, pen, wall

cooperate **1** *Syn* ALLY, associate, band, club, confederate, conjoin, federate, league, unite *Ant* break up, disband **2** *Syn* UNITE, combine, concur, conjoin *Ant* part

coordinate *Syn* EQUAL, counterpart, equivalent, fellow, like, match, parallel, peer, rival

cop *Syn* STEAL, filch, lift, pilfer, pinch, purloin, snitch, swipe

copartner *Syn* PARTNER, ally, colleague, confederate *Ant* rival

copious *Syn* PLENTIFUL, abundant, ample, plenteous *Ant* scant, scanty

cop out *Syn* RENEGE, back down, back off

coppice *Syn* THICKET, brake, brushwood, chaparral, copse, covert

copse *Syn* THICKET, brake, brushwood, chaparral, coppice, covert

copy *n* • something that is made to look exactly like something else *Syn* carbon copy, duplicate, duplication, facsimile, imitation, reduplication, replica, replication, reproduction *Rel* counterfeit, dummy, fake, forgery, image, impression, imprint, likeness, mock-up, phony, print, re-creation, reconstruction, semblance, shadow, sham, simulation *Ant* original

copy *vb* • to make something like an already existing thing in form, appearance, or obvious or salient characteristics *Syn* ape, imitate, mimic, mock *Ant* originate

cord • a length of braided, flexible material that is used for tying or connecting things *Syn* cable, lace, lacing, line, rope, string, wire *Rel* guy, lanyard, stay

cordial *Syn* GRACIOUS, affable, genial, sociable *Ant* ungracious

core **1** *Syn* CENTER (sense 1), middle, midpoint, midst *Ant* perimeter, periphery **2** *Syn* CENTER (sense 2), base, capital, cynosure, eye, focus, heart, hub, mecca, nucleus, seat **3** *Syn* CRUX, gist, heart, nub, pith, pivot **4** *Syn* SUBSTANCE, burden, gist, pith, purport

corker *Syn* JIM-DANDY, beauty, crackerjack, dandy, knockout, nifty, pip

corkscrew *Syn* SPIRAL, coiling, helical, screwlike, winding

corner *Syn* MONOPOLY, cartel, pool, syndicate, trust

corny • appealing to the emotions in an obvious and tiresome way *Syn* maudlin, mawkish, mushy, saccharine, sappy, schmaltzy, sentimental, sloppy, sugarcoated, sugary *Rel* dreamy, moonstruck, nostalgic *Ant* unsentimental

corporal *Syn* BODILY, corporeal, physical, somatic

corporeal **1** *Syn* BODILY, corporal, physical, somatic **2** *Syn* MATERIAL, objective, phenomenal, physical, sensible *Ant* immaterial

corpse *Syn* BODY, cadaver, carcass

corpulent *Syn* FLESHY, chubby, fat, obese, plump, portly, rotund, stout *Ant* scrawny, skinny

corral *Syn* ENCLOSE, cage, coop, envelop, fence, pen, wall

correct *adj* • conforming to standard, fact, or truth *Syn* accurate, exact, nice, precise, right *Rel* faultless, flawless, impeccable *Ant* incorrect

correct *vb* **1** • to set or make right something which is wrong *Syn* amend, emend, rectify, redress, reform, remedy, revise *Rel* ameliorate, better, improve **2** *Syn* PUNISH, castigate, chasten, chastise, discipline *Ant* excuse, pardon

correctable *Syn* REMEDIABLE, fixable, rectifiable, repairable, reparable *Ant* incorrigible, irremediable, irreparable

correcting *Syn* PUNITIVE, castigating, chastening, chastising, correctional, corrective, disciplinary, disciplining, penal, penalizing

correctional *Syn* PUNITIVE, castigating, chastening, chastising, correcting, corrective, disciplinary, disciplining, penal, penalizing

corrective *n* • something which serves to keep another thing in its desired place or condition *Syn* antidote, check, control

corrective *adj* **1** *Syn* CURATIVE, remedial, restorative, sanative **2** *Syn* PUNITIVE, castigating, chastening, chastising, correcting, correctional, disciplinary, disciplining, penal, penalizing

correctly *Syn* PROPERLY, appropriately, congruously, fittingly, happily, meetly, rightly, suitably *Ant* improperly, inappropriately, incongruously, incorrectly, unsuitably, wrongly

correlate *Syn* PARALLEL, analogue, counterpart

correlative *Syn* RECIPROCAL (sense 2), complemental, complementary, convertible, corresponding

correspond *Syn* AGREE (sense 2), accord, conform, harmonize, jibe, square, tally *Ant* differ (from)

correspondence *Syn* SIMILARITY, alikeness, community, likeness, parallelism, resemblance, similitude *Ant* dissimilarity, unlikeness

correspondent *adj* **1** *Syn* ALIKE, akin, analogous, comparable, corresponding, like, matching, parallel, resembling, similar, such, suchlike *Ant* different, dissimilar, diverse, unlike **2** *Syn* CONSISTENT, compatible, conformable (to), congruous, consonant, harmonious, nonconflicting *Ant* conflicting, incompatible, incongruous, inconsistent, inharmonious, unharmonious

correspondent *n Syn* REPORTER, journalist

corresponding **1** *Syn* ALIKE, akin, analogous, comparable, correspondent, like, matching, parallel, resembling, similar, such, suchlike *Ant* different, dissimilar, diverse, unlike **2** *Syn* RECIPROCAL (sense 2), complemental, complementary, convertible, correlative

corridor *Syn* PASSAGE, aisle, arcade, cloister, gallery, hall, hallway, passageway

corroborate *Syn* CONFIRM, authenticate, substantiate, validate, verify *Ant* contradict, deny

corrupt *adj* **1** • having or showing lowered moral character or standards *Syn* debased, debauched, decadent, degenerate, degraded, demoralized, depraved, dissipated, dissolute, perverse, perverted, reprobate, warped *Rel* crooked, cutthroat, dishonest, unethical, unprincipled, unscrupulous *Ant* uncorrupted **2** *Syn* VICIOUS, degenerate, flagitious, infamous, iniquitous, nefarious, villainous *Ant* virtuous

corrupt *vb Syn* DEBASE, debauch, deprave, pervert, vitiate *Ant* amend (*morals, character*), elevate (*taste, way of life*)

corrupted *Syn* DEBASED, debauched, depraved, perverted, vitiated

corruptible *Syn* VENAL, bribable, purchasable *Ant* incorruptible, uncorruptible

corruption *Syn* BARBARISM, impropriety, solecism, vernacularism, vulgarism

corsair *Syn* PIRATE, buccaneer, freebooter, privateer

cortege *Syn* PROCESSION, cavalcade, motorcade, parade

coruscate *Syn* FLASH, glance, gleam, glint, glisten, glitter, scintillate, sparkle, twinkle

cosmic *Syn* UNIVERSAL (sense 1), catholic, cosmopolitan, ecumenical *Ant* particular

cosmopolitan *n* • a person with the outlook, experience, and manners thought to be typical of big city dwellers *Syn* metropolitan, sophisticate *Rel* urbanite *Ant* bumpkin, hick, provincial, rustic, yokel

cosmopolitan *adj* **1** *Syn* UNIVERSAL (sense 1), catholic, cosmic, ecumenical *Ant* particular **2** *Syn* WORLDLY-WISE, smart, sophisticated, worldly *Ant* ingenuous, innocent, naive, unsophisticated, unworldly, wide-eyed

cosset *Syn* CARESS, cuddle, dandle, fondle, pet

cost *Syn* PRICE, charge, expense

costly • having a high value or valuation, especially in terms of money *Syn* dear, expensive, invaluable, precious, priceless, valuable *Rel* excessive, exorbitant, extravagant *Ant* cheap

cotillion *Syn* DANCE, ball, formal, hop, prom

couch *n* • a long upholstered piece of furniture designed for several sitters *Syn* chesterfield, davenport, divan, lounge, settee, sofa *Rel* love seat

couch *vb Syn* PHRASE, articulate, clothe, express, formulate, put, say, state, word

counsel **1** *Syn* ADVICE, guidance **2** *Syn* LAWYER, advocate, attorney, barrister, counselor, solicitor

counselor *Syn* LAWYER, advocate, attorney, barrister, counsel, solicitor

count *vb* **1** • to ascertain the total of units in a collection by noting one after another *Syn* enumerate, number, tell *Rel* calculate, compute, estimate, reckon **2** *Syn* MATTER, import, mean, signify, weigh **3** *Syn* RELY (ON), bank, depend, reckon, trust

count *n* **1** *Syn* CHARGE, complaint, indictment, rap **2** *Syn* PARAGRAPH, article, clause, plank, verse

countenance *vb* **1** *Syn* APPROVE (OF), accept, care (for), favor, OK (*or* okay), subscribe (to) *Ant* disapprove (of), discountenance, disfavor, frown (on *or* upon) **2** *Syn* FAVOR, encourage *Ant* disapprove

countenance *n Syn* FACE, mug, physiognomy, puss, visage

counter *adj Syn* ADVERSE, antagonistic, counteractive *Ant* propitious

counter *n Syn* OPPOSITE, antipode, antithesis, antonym, contradictory, contrary, converse, reverse

counteract *Syn* NEUTRALIZE, negative

counteractive *Syn* ADVERSE, antagonistic, counter *Ant* propitious

counterbalance *Syn* COMPENSATE, balance, counterpoise, countervail, offset

counterfeit *adj* • being an imitation intended to mislead or deceive *Syn* bogus, fake, phony, pinchbeck, pseudo, sham, spurious *Rel* feigned, pretended, simulated *Ant* bona fide, genuine

counterfeit *vb Syn* ASSUME, affect, feign, pretend, sham, simulate

counterpart **1** *Syn* EQUAL, coordinate, equivalent, fellow, like, match, parallel, peer, rival **2** *Syn* PARALLEL, analogue, correlate

counterpoise *Syn* COMPENSATE, balance, counterbalance, countervail, offset

countervail *Syn* COMPENSATE, balance, counterbalance, counterpoise, offset

countless • too many to be counted *Syn* innumerable, numberless, uncountable, uncounted, unnumbered, untold *Rel* endless, infinite, unlimited, vast *Ant* countable

country *Syn* NATION, commonwealth, land, sovereignty, state

countryman *Syn* HICK, bumpkin, clodhopper, provincial, rustic, yokel *Ant* cosmopolitan, sophisticate

countryseat *Syn* MANSION, castle, château, estate, hacienda, hall, manor, manor house, palace, villa

county *Syn* ARISTOCRACY, elite, gentry, nobility, society *Ant* people, proletariat
coup *Syn* REBELLION, insurrection, mutiny, putsch, revolt, revolution, uprising
couple **1** • two things of the same kind *Syn* brace, pair, yoke **2** *Syn* PAIR, brace, duo, twain, twosome
courage • strength of mind to carry on in spite of danger *Syn* bravery, courageousness, daring, dauntlessness, doughtiness, fearlessness, gallantry, greatheartedness, guts, hardihood, heart, heroism, intrepidity, intrepidness, nerve, stoutness, valor *Rel* backbone, fiber, fortitude, grit, gumption, mettle, pluck, spunk *Ant* cowardice, cowardliness, cravenness, dastardliness, spinelessness, yellowness
courageous *Syn* BRAVE, audacious, bold, dauntless, doughty, fearless, intrepid, unafraid, undaunted, valiant, valorous *Ant* craven
courageousness *Syn* COURAGE, bravery, daring, dauntlessness, doughtiness, fearlessness, gallantry, greatheartedness, guts, hardihood, heart, heroism, intrepidity, intrepidness, nerve, stoutness, valor *Ant* cowardice, cowardliness, cravenness, dastardliness, spinelessness, yellowness
course *vb Syn* HURRY (sense 2), barrel, bolt, bowl, breeze, career, dash, fly, hasten, hotfoot (it), hump, hurtle, hustle, pelt, race, rip, rocket, run, rush, rustle, scoot, scurry, scuttle, shoot, speed, step (along), tear, trot, whirl, whisk, zip, zoom *Ant* crawl, creep, poke
course *n Syn* WAY, artery, pass, passage, route
court *Syn* INVITE, bid, solicit, woo
courteous *Syn* CIVIL, chivalrous, courtly, gallant, polite *Ant* rude, uncivil
courteousness *Syn* POLITENESS, civility, courtesy, gentility, graciousness, mannerliness *Ant* discourteousness, discourtesy, impoliteness, incivility, rudeness, ungraciousness
courtesy **1** • a manner or an act which promotes agreeable or pleasant social relations *Syn* amenity, attention, gallantry *Rel* affability, cordiality, geniality, graciousness *Ant* discourtesy **2** *Syn* POLITENESS, civility, courteousness, gentility, graciousness, mannerliness *Ant* discourteousness, discourtesy, impoliteness, incivility, rudeness, ungraciousness
courtly *Syn* CIVIL, chivalrous, courteous, gallant, polite *Ant* rude, uncivil
covenant *Syn* PROMISE, contract, engage, pledge, plight
cover *vb* **1** • to put or place or to be put or placed over or around *Syn* envelop, overspread, shroud, veil, wrap *Rel* conceal, hide, screen *Ant* bare **2** *Syn* TRAVERSE, crisscross, cross, cut (across), follow, go, pass (over), proceed (along), travel
cover *n Syn* SHELTER, asylum, refuge, retreat, sanctuary
covert *adj* **1** *Syn* SECLUDED, cloistered, isolated, quiet, remote, retired, secret, sheltered **2** *Syn* SECRET, clandestine, furtive, stealthy, surreptitious, underhand, underhanded
covert *n Syn* THICKET, brake, brushwood, chaparral, coppice, copse
covet **1** • to desire selfishly to have something for one's own *Syn* begrudge, envy, grudge **2** *Syn* DESIRE, crave, want, wish
covetous **1** • having or manifesting a strong desire for especially material possessions *Syn* acquisitive, avaricious, grasping, greedy *Rel* envious, jealous **2** *Syn* ENVIOUS, invidious, jaundiced, jealous, resentful
covetousness *Syn* GREED, acquisitiveness, avarice, avariciousness, avidity, cupidity, greediness, rapaciousness, rapacity
cow *Syn* INTIMIDATE, browbeat, bulldoze, bully
coward • a person who shows a shameful lack of courage in the face of danger *Syn* chicken, craven, dastard, poltroon, recreant *Rel* defeatist, quitter *Ant* hero, stalwart, valiant
cowardly • having or showing a shameful lack of courage *Syn* chicken, chickenhearted, craven, dastardly, lily-livered, pusillanimous, recreant, spineless, unheroic, yellow *Rel* diffident, fainthearted, fearful, timid, timorous *Ant* brave, courageous, daring, dauntless, doughty, fearless, gallant, greathearted, gutsy, hardy, heroic, intrepid, lionhearted, stalwart, stout, stouthearted, valiant, valorous
cowboy • a man who tends cattle or horses at a ranch or on the range *Syn* buckaroo, cowhand, cowman, cowpoke, cowpuncher *Rel* cowgirl
cower *Syn* FAWN, cringe, toady, truckle *Ant* domineer
cowhand *Syn* COWBOY, buckaroo, cowman, cowpoke, cowpuncher
cowman *Syn* COWBOY, buckaroo, cowhand, cowpoke, cowpuncher
cowpoke *Syn* COWBOY, buckaroo, cowhand, cowman, cowpuncher
cowpuncher *Syn* COWBOY, buckaroo, cowhand, cowman, cowpoke
coxcomb *Syn* FOP, beau, buck, dandy, dude, exquisite
coy *Syn* SHY, bashful, diffident, modest *Ant* obtrusive
cozen *Syn* FLEECE, bleed, cheat, chisel, defraud, hustle, mulct, rook, shortchange, skin, squeeze, stick, sting, swindle, victimize
cozy *Syn* COMFORTABLE, easy, restful, snug *Ant* miserable, uncomfortable
crab *vb Syn* COMPLAIN, beef, bellyache, carp, croak, fuss, gripe, grouse, growl, grumble, kick, moan, murmur, mutter, repine, squawk, wail, whine, yammer *Ant* rejoice
crab *n Syn* GROUCH, bear, complainer, crank, croaker, curmudgeon, fusser, griper, grouser,

growler, grumbler, grump, murmurer, mutterer, whiner

crabbed *Syn* SULLEN, dour, gloomy, glum, morose, saturnine, sulky, surly

crack *n* **1** • an opening, break, or discontinuity made by or as if by splitting or rupture *Syn* chink, cleft, cranny, crevasse, crevice, fissure *Rel* breach, rent, rift, split **2** *Syn* JOKE, gag, jape, jest, quip, wisecrack, witticism **3** *Syn* ATTEMPT, endeavor, essay, fling, go, pass, shot, stab, trial, try, whack

crack *vb* **1** *Syn* BREAK, burst, bust, shatter, shiver, snap *Ant* cleave (*together*), keep (*of laws*) **2** *Syn* SOLVE, answer, break, dope (out), figure out, puzzle (out), resolve, riddle, unravel, work, work out

crackbrain *Syn* ECCENTRIC, character, codger, crackpot, crank, kook, nut, oddball, screwball, weirdo

crackerjack *adj Syn* EXCELLENT, A1, bang-up, banner, capital, classic, dandy, divine, fabulous, fine, first-class, first-rate, grand, great, groovy, heavenly, jim-dandy, keen, marvelous (*or* marvellous), mean, neat, nifty, noble, par excellence, prime, sensational, splendid, stellar, sterling, superb, superior, superlative, supernal, swell, terrific, tip-top, top, top-notch, unsurpassed, wonderful *Ant* poor

crackerjack *n* **1** *Syn* EXPERT, ace, adept, artist, authority, maestro, master, past master, scholar, shark, virtuoso, whiz, wizard *Ant* amateur **2** *Syn* JIM-DANDY, beauty, corker, dandy, knockout, nifty, pip

crackpot *Syn* ECCENTRIC, character, codger, crackbrain, crank, kook, nut, oddball, screwball, weirdo

craft **1** *Syn* ART, artifice, cunning, skill **2** *Syn* TRADE, art, handicraft, profession **3** *Syn* BOAT, ship, vessel

craftsman **1** *Syn* ARTISAN, artificer, handicrafter, tradesman **2** *Syn* WORKER, artisan, hand, handicraftsman, laborer, mechanic, operative, roustabout, workingman, workman *Ant* idler

crafty *Syn* SLY, artful, cunning, foxy, guileful, insidious, tricky, wily

cram *Syn* PACK, crowd, ram, stuff, tamp

cramp • a painful sudden tightening of a muscle *Syn* charley horse, crick, spasm *Rel* contraction, jerk, stitch, twinge, twitch

crank **1** *Syn* ECCENTRIC, character, codger, crackbrain, crackpot, kook, nut, oddball, screwball, weirdo **2** *Syn* GROUCH, bear, complainer, crab, croaker, curmudgeon, fusser, griper, grouser, growler, grumbler, grump, murmurer, mutterer, whiner

crank (up) *Syn* ACTIVATE, actuate, drive, move, propel, run, set off, spark, start, touch off, trigger, turn on *Ant* cut, deactivate, kill, shut off, turn off

cranky **1** *Syn* CUMBERSOME, awkward, clumsy, cumbrous, ungainly, unhandy, unwieldy *Ant* handy **2** *Syn* IRASCIBLE, choleric, cross, splenetic, testy, touchy

cranny *Syn* CRACK, chink, cleft, crevasse, crevice, fissure

crass *Syn* STUPID, dense, dull, dumb, slow *Ant* intelligent

crave *Syn* DESIRE, covet, want, wish

craven *adj Syn* COWARDLY, chicken, chickenhearted, dastardly, lily-livered, pusillanimous, recreant, spineless, unheroic, yellow *Ant* brave, courageous, daring, dauntless, doughty, fearless, gallant, greathearted, gutsy, hardy, heroic, intrepid, lionhearted, stalwart, stout, stouthearted, valiant, valorous

craven *n Syn* COWARD, chicken, dastard, poltroon, recreant, *Ant* hero, stalwart, valiant

craze *Syn* FASHION, cry, dernier cri, fad, mode, rage, style, vogue

crazed *Syn* INSANE, crazy, demented, deranged, lunatic, mad, maniac, non compos mentis *Ant* sane

crazy *Syn* INSANE, crazed, demented, deranged, lunatic, mad, maniac, non compos mentis *Ant* sane

cream *n Syn* ELITE, best, choice, elect, fat, flower, pick, prime, upper crust

cream *vb Syn* OIL, anoint, grease, lubricate

create **1** *Syn* EFFECT, bring about, cause, effectuate, engender, generate, induce, make, produce, prompt, result (in), spawn, work, yield **2** *Syn* FOUND, establish, institute, organize

creator *Syn* MAKER, author

creature **1** *Syn* ANIMAL, beast, brute, critter **2** *Syn* ENTITY, being, individual, person

credence *Syn* BELIEF, credit, faith *Ant* disbelief, unbelief

credential • something presented by one person to another in proof that he is what or who he claims to be *Syn* character, recommendation, reference, testimonial *Rel* accreditation, certification, endorsement, sanction

credible *Syn* PLAUSIBLE, believable, colorable, specious

credit *vb Syn* ASCRIBE, accredit, assign, attribute, charge, impute, refer

credit *n* **1** *Syn* BELIEF, credence, faith *Ant* disbelief, unbelief **2** *Syn* INFLUENCE, authority, prestige, weight

creditable *Syn* ADMIRABLE, commendable, laudable, meritorious, praiseworthy *Ant* censurable, discreditable, reprehensible

credulity • readiness to believe the claims of others without sufficient evidence *Syn* credulousness, gullibility, naivete *Rel* artlessness, simplicity, unsophistication *Ant* incredulity, skepticism

credulousness *Syn* CREDULITY, gullibility, naivete *Ant* incredulity, skepticism

creed *Syn* RELIGION, church, communion, denomination, faith, persuasion, sect
creepy *Syn* EERIE, haunting, spooky, uncanny, unearthly, weird
crestfallen *Syn* SAD (sense 1), bad, blue, brokenhearted, dejected, depressed, despondent, disconsolate, doleful, down, downcast, downhearted, droopy, forlorn, gloomy, glum, heartbroken, heartsick, heartsore, inconsolable, joyless, low, low-spirited, melancholy, miserable, mournful, saddened, sorrowful, sorry, unhappy, woebegone, woeful, wretched *Ant* blissful, buoyant, buoyed, cheerful, cheery, chipper, delighted, glad, gladdened, gladsome, gleeful, happy, joyful, joyous, jubilant, sunny, upbeat
crevasse *Syn* CRACK, chink, cleft, cranny, crevice, fissure
crevice *Syn* CRACK, chink, cleft, cranny, crevasse, fissure
crick *Syn* CRAMP, charley horse, spasm
crime *Syn* OFFENSE (sense 2), scandal, sin, vice
criminal • one who has committed a usually serious offense especially against the law *Syn* convict, culprit, delinquent, felon, malefactor *Rel* offender, sinner
crimp *Syn* ENCUMBRANCE, bar, block, chain, clog, deterrent, drag, embarrassment, fetter, handicap, hindrance, hurdle, impediment, inhibition, interference, let, manacle, obstacle, obstruction, shackles, stop, stumbling block, trammel *Ant* aid, assistance, benefit, help
crimson *Syn* BLUSH, bloom, color, flush, glow, redden
cringe *Syn* FAWN, cower, toady, truckle *Ant* domineer
cripple *Syn* MAIM, batter, mangle, mutilate
crisis *Syn* JUNCTURE, contingency, emergency, exigency, pass, pinch, strait
crisp **1** *Syn* FRAGILE, brittle, frangible, friable, short *Ant* tough **2** *Syn* INCISIVE, biting, clear-cut, cutting, trenchant
crisply *Syn* SUCCINCTLY, briefly, compactly, concisely, laconically, pithily, summarily, tersely *Ant* diffusely, long-windedly, verbosely, wordily
crisscross *Syn* TRAVERSE, cover, cross, cut (across), follow, go, pass (over), proceed (along), travel
criterion *Syn* STANDARD, gauge, touchstone, yardstick
critic • a person given to harsh judgments and to finding faults *Syn* carper, castigator, caviler (*or* caviller), censurer, faultfinder, nitpicker, railer, scold *Rel* belittler, derider, detractor
critical **1** • exhibiting the spirit of one who detects and points out faults or defects *Syn* captious, carping, caviling, censorious, faultfinding, hypercritical *Rel* judicious *Ant* uncritical **2** *Syn* ACUTE, crucial **3** *Syn* CRUCIAL, key, pivotal, vital
criticism • a discourse presenting one's conclusions after examining a work of art and especially of literature *Syn* blurb, critique, puff, review
criticize • to find fault with someone or something openly, often publicly, and with varying degrees of severity *Syn* blame, censure, condemn, denounce, reprehend, reprobate *Rel* examine, inspect, scan, scrutinize
critique *Syn* CRITICISM, blurb, puff, review
critter *Syn* ANIMAL, beast, brute, creature
croak *Syn* COMPLAIN, beef, bellyache, carp, crab, fuss, gripe, grouse, growl, grumble, kick, moan, murmur, mutter, repine, squawk, wail, whine, yammer *Ant* rejoice
croaker *Syn* GROUCH, bear, complainer, crab, crank, curmudgeon, fusser, griper, grouser, growler, grumbler, grump, murmurer, mutterer, whiner
crochet *Syn* WEAVE, braid, knit, plait, tat
crony *Syn* ASSOCIATE, companion, comrade
crook *Syn* FLEX, bow, buckle *Ant* extend
crooked **1** • not straight or straightforward *Syn* devious, oblique *Rel* askew, awry *Ant* straight **2** *Syn* AWRY, askew, aslant, cockeyed, listing, lopsided, oblique, skewed, slanted, slanting, slantwise, tilted, tipping, uneven *Ant* even, level, straight
crop *Syn* CLIP, bob, curtail, cut, cut back, dock, lop (off), nip, pare, prune, shave, shear, snip, trim
cross *adj* *Syn* IRASCIBLE, choleric, cranky, splenetic, testy, touchy
cross *vb* *Syn* TRAVERSE, cover, crisscross, cut (across), follow, go, pass (over), proceed (along), travel
cross *n* *Syn* TRIAL, affliction, tribulation, visitation
crossways *Syn* ACROSS, athwart, crosswise
crosswise *Syn* ACROSS, athwart, crossways
crow *Syn* BOAST, brag, gasconade, vaunt *Ant* depreciate (*oneself, one's accomplishments*)
crowd *n* • a more or less closely assembled multitude usually of persons *Syn* crush, horde, mob, press, rout, throng *Rel* army, host, legion, multitude
crowd *vb* **1** *Syn* PACK, cram, ram, stuff, tamp **2** *Syn* PRESS, bear, bear down, jam, squeeze
crucial **1** • of the greatest possible importance *Syn* critical, key, pivotal, vital *Rel* decisive, life-and-death **2** *Syn* ACUTE, critical
crude *Syn* RUDE (sense 1), callow, green, raw, rough, uncouth *Ant* civil, urbane
cruel *Syn* FIERCE, barbarous, fell, ferocious, inhuman, savage, truculent *Ant* mild, tame
cruelness *Syn* CRUELTY, barbarity, brutality, heartlessness, inhumanity, sadism, savageness, savagery, viciousness, wantonness *Ant* benignity, compassion, good-heartedness, humanity, kindheartedness, kindness, sympathy
cruelty • the willful infliction of pain and suffering on others *Syn* barbarity, brutality, cru-

elness, heartlessness, inhumanity, sadism, savageness, savagery, viciousness, wantonness *Rel* mercilessness, ruthlessness *Ant* benignity, compassion, good-heartedness, humanity, kindheartedness, kindness, sympathy
cruise *Syn* JOURNEY, excursion, expedition, jaunt, pilgrimage, tour, trip, voyage
crumble **1** *Syn* DECAY, decompose, disintegrate, putrefy, rot, spoil **2** *Syn* DETERIORATE, decay, decline, degenerate, descend, ebb, rot, sink, worsen *Ant* ameliorate, improve, meliorate
crusade *Syn* CAMPAIGN, bandwagon, cause, drive, movement
crusader *Syn* ZEALOT, fanatic, militant, partisan
crush *vb* **1** • to reduce or be reduced to a pulpy or broken mass *Syn* bruise, macerate, mash, smash, squash *Rel* crowd, jam, press, squeeze **2** • to bring to an end by destroying or defeating *Syn* extinguish, quash, quell, quench, suppress *Rel* demolish, destroy
crush *n Syn* CROWD, horde, mob, press, rout, throng
crusty *Syn* BLUFF, blunt, brusque, curt, gruff *Ant* smooth, suave
crux • the central part or aspect of something under consideration *Syn* core, gist, heart, nub, pith, pivot *Rel* course, direction, drift, tenor
cry *vb* • to show grief, pain, or distress by tears and usually inarticulate utterances *Syn* blubber, keen, wail, weep, whimper *Rel* bemoan, bewail, deplore, lament
cry *n* **1** *Syn* FASHION, craze, dernier cri, fad, mode, rage, style, vogue **2** *Syn* SLOGAN, shibboleth, watchword
crying *Syn* PRESSING, exigent, imperative, importunate, insistent, instant, urgent
cryptic *Syn* OBSCURE, ambiguous, dark, enigmatic, equivocal, vague *Ant* distinct, obvious
cubicle *Syn* COMPARTMENT, bay, cabin, cell, chamber
cuddle *Syn* CARESS, cosset, dandle, fondle, pet
cuff *Syn* STRIKE, box, clout, hit, punch, slap, slog, slug, smite, swat
cull *Syn* CHOOSE, elect, opt, pick, prefer, select, single *Ant* eschew, reject
culmination *Syn* SUMMIT, acme, apex, apogee, climax, meridian, peak, pinnacle, zenith
culpability *Syn* BLAME, fault, guilt
culpable *Syn* BLAMEWORTHY, guilty *Ant* blameless
culprit *Syn* CRIMINAL, convict, delinquent, felon, malefactor
cultivar *Syn* VARIETY (sense 2), breed, clone, race, stock, strain, subspecies
cultivate *Syn* NURSE, cherish, foster, nurture
cultivated • having or showing a taste for the fine arts and gracious living *Syn* civilized, cultured, genteel, polished, refined *Rel* cerebral, highbrow, intellectual *Ant* philistine, uncivilized, uncultured, unpolished, unrefined
cultivation *Syn* CULTURE, breeding, refinement
culture • enlightenment and excellence of taste acquired by intellectual and aesthetic training *Syn* breeding, cultivation, refinement
cultured *Syn* CULTIVATED, civilized, genteel, polished, refined *Ant* philistine, uncivilized, uncultured, unpolished, unrefined
cumber *Syn* BURDEN, charge, encumber, lade, load, saddle, tax, weigh, weight
cumbersome **1** • difficult to use or operate especially because of size, weight, or design *Syn* awkward, clumsy, cranky, cumbrous, ungainly, unhandy, unwieldy *Rel* uncontrollable, unmanageable *Ant* handy **2** *Syn* HEAVY, cumbrous, hefty, ponderous, weighty *Ant* light
cumbrous **1** *Syn* CUMBERSOME, awkward, clumsy, cranky, ungainly, unhandy, unwieldy *Ant* handy **2** *Syn* HEAVY, cumbersome, hefty, ponderous, weighty *Ant* light
cumulative • increasing or produced by the addition of like or assimilable things *Syn* accumulative, additive, summative *Rel* accumulated, amassed
cunning *n* **1** *Syn* ART, artifice, craft, skill **2** *Syn* DECEIT, dissimulation, duplicity, guile
cunning *adj* **1** *Syn* CLEVER, adroit, ingenious **2** *Syn* SLY, artful, crafty, foxy, guileful, insidious, tricky, wily
cupboard *Syn* CABINET, buffet, closet, hutch, locker, sideboard
cupidity *Syn* GREED, acquisitiveness, avarice, avariciousness, avidity, covetousness, greediness, rapaciousness, rapacity
curative • returning or tending to return to a state of normalcy or health *Syn* corrective, remedial, restorative, sanative *Rel* curing, healing, remedying
curb *vb Syn* RESTRAIN, bridle, check, inhibit *Ant* abandon (*oneself*), activate, impel, incite
curb *n Syn* RESTRICTION, check, condition, constraint, fetter, limitation, restraint
curdle *Syn* COAGULATE, clot, congeal, jell, jelly, set
cure *vb* • to rectify an unhealthy or undesirable condition especially by some specific treatment *Syn* heal, remedy
cure *n Syn* REMEDY, medicament, medication, medicine, physic, specific
curio *Syn* KNICKKNACK, bauble, curiosity, gaud, gewgaw, novelty, ornamental, trinket
curiosity *Syn* KNICKKNACK, bauble, curio, gaud, gewgaw, novelty, ornamental, trinket
curious **1** • interested in what is not one's personal or proper concern *Syn* inquisitive, nosy, prying, snoopy *Rel* interfering, intermeddling, meddling, tampering *Ant* incurious, uninterested **2** *Syn* STRANGE, eccentric, erratic, odd, outlandish, peculiar, quaint, queer, singular, unique *Ant* familiar

curl *Syn* WIND, coil, entwine, twine, twist, wreathe
curmudgeon *Syn* GROUCH, bear, complainer, crab, crank, croaker, fusser, griper, grouser, growler, grumbler, grump, murmurer, mutterer, whiner
currency *Syn* MONEY, cash, coin, coinage, legal tender, specie
current *n Syn* FLOW, flood, flux, stream, tide
current *adj* **1** *Syn* MODERN, contemporary, hot, mod, modernistic, new, newfangled, new-fashioned, present-day, red-hot, space-age, ultramodern, up-to-date *Ant* antiquated, archaic, dated, fusty, musty, noncontemporary, old-fangled, old-fashioned, old-time, out-of-date, passé **2** *Syn* PRESENT, extant, ongoing, present-day *Ant* ago, future, past **3** *Syn* PREVAILING, prevalent, rife
curse *n* • a denunciation that conveys a wish or threat of evil *Syn* anathema, imprecation, malediction *Rel* execration, objurgation *Ant* blessing
curse *vb* **1** *Syn* AFFLICT, agonize, bedevil, harrow, martyr, persecute, plague, rack, torment, torture **2** *Syn* EXECRATE, anathematize, damn, objurgate
cursed *Syn* EXECRABLE, accursed, damnable
cursing *Syn* BLASPHEMY, profanity, swearing *Ant* adoration
cursory *Syn* SUPERFICIAL, shallow, uncritical *Ant* deep, profound
curt *Syn* BLUFF, blunt, brusque, crusty, gruff *Ant* smooth, suave
curtail **1** *Syn* CLIP, bob, crop, cut, cut back, dock, lop (off), nip, pare, prune, shave, shear, snip, trim **2** *Syn* SHORTEN, abbreviate, abridge, retrench *Ant* elongate, extend, lengthen, prolong, protract
curve *n* • a line or something which follows a line that is neither straight nor angular but rounded *Syn* arc, arch, bow *Rel* circuit, circumference, compass
curve *vb* • to swerve or cause to swerve from a straight line or course *Syn* bend, twist *Rel* deflect, divert, turn
curvet *Syn* SKIP, bound, hop, lollop, lope, ricochet
cushion • to lessen the shock of *Syn* buffer, gentle, soften *Rel* baffle, dampen, deaden, dull
custodian *Syn* PROTECTOR, defender, guard, protection
custody • responsibility for the safety and well-being of someone or something *Syn* care, guardianship, keeping, safekeeping, trust, ward *Rel* control, governorship, management, superintendence, supervision
custom *Syn* HABIT, fashion, pattern, practice, trick, way, wont
customary *Syn* USUAL, accustomed, habitual, wonted
cut **1** • to penetrate and divide something with a sharp-bladed tool or instrument *Syn* carve, chop, hew, slash, slit *Rel* cleave, rive, split, tear **2** *Syn* CLIP, bob, crop, curtail, cut back, dock, lop (off), nip, pare, prune, shave, shear, snip, trim
cut (across) *Syn* TRAVERSE, cover, crisscross, cross, follow, go, pass (over), proceed (along), travel
cut back *Syn* CLIP, bob, crop, curtail, cut, dock, lop (off), nip, pare, prune, shave, shear, snip, trim
cute *Syn* BEAUTIFUL, attractive, beauteous, comely, fair, gorgeous, handsome, knockout, lovely, pretty, ravishing, sightly, stunning, taking *Ant* homely, ill-favored, plain, ugly, unattractive, unbeautiful, unhandsome, unlovely, unpretty, unsightly
cutthroat *n Syn* ASSASSIN, bravo, gunman
cutthroat *adj Syn* UNPRINCIPLED, immoral, Machiavellian, unconscionable, unethical, unmoral, unscrupulous *Ant* ethical, moral, principled, scrupulous
cutting *Syn* INCISIVE, biting, clear-cut, crisp, trenchant
cut up • to engage in attention-getting playful or boisterous behavior *Syn* act up, clown (around), fool (around), horse (around), monkey (around), show off, skylark *Rel* carry on, misbehave
cyclone *Syn* TORNADO, twister
cyclopean *Syn* HUGE, Brobdingnagian, colossal, elephantine, enormous, gargantuan, giant, gigantean, gigantic, Herculean, immense, mammoth, titanic, vast *Ant* bitty, diminutive, microscopic (*or* microscopical), midget, miniature, minute, pocket, pygmy, teeny, teeny-weeny, tiny, wee
cynical • deeply and often contemptuously distrustful *Syn* misanthropic, pessimistic *Rel* flouting, girding, scoffing, sneering
cynosure *Syn* CENTER (sense 2), base, capital, core, eye, focus, heart, hub, mecca, nucleus, seat

D

dabbler *Syn* AMATEUR, dilettante, tyro *Ant* expert, professional
daily *adj* • occurring, done, produced, or appearing every day *Syn* day-to-day, diurnal *Rel* alternate, cyclical, intermittent, periodic, recurrent, recurring, regular
dainty **1** *Syn* CHOICE, delicate, elegant, exquisite, rare, recherché *Ant* indifferent, medium **2** *Syn* NICE, fastidious, finical, finicking, finicky, fussy, particular, pernickety, persnickety, squeamish
dais *Syn* PLATFORM, podium, rostrum, stage, stand
dally *Syn* FLIRT, frivol, trifle
dam *n* • a bank of earth constructed to control water *Syn* dike, embankment, levee *Rel* breakwater, jetty, seawall
dam *vb* *Syn* HINDER, bar, block, impede, obstruct *Ant* further
damage *vb* *Syn* INJURE, harm, hurt, impair, mar, spoil *Ant* aid
damage *n* *Syn* INJURY, harm, hurt, mischief
damages *Syn* FINE, forfeit, forfeiture, mulct, penalty
damaging *Syn* HARMFUL, adverse, bad, baleful, baneful, deleterious, detrimental, evil, hurtful, ill, injurious, mischievous, noxious, pernicious, prejudicial *Ant* harmless, innocent, innocuous, inoffensive, safe
dame *Syn* GENTLEWOMAN, lady, noblewoman
damn **1** *Syn* EXECRATE, anathematize, curse, objurgate **2** *Syn* SENTENCE, condemn, doom, proscribe
damnable *Syn* EXECRABLE, accursed, cursed
damp *Syn* WET, dank, humid, moist *Ant* dry
dance • a social gathering for dancing *Syn* ball, cotillion, formal, hop, prom *Rel* blowout, celebration, event, festival, festivity, fete (*or* fête), gala, masquerade, mixer, party, reception, shindig, soiree (*or* soirée)
dandle **1** *Syn* BABY, coddle, mollycoddle, nurse, pamper, spoil *Ant* abuse, ill-treat, ill-use, maltreat, mishandle, mistreat, misuse **2** *Syn* CARESS, cosset, cuddle, fondle, pet
dandy *adj* *Syn* EXCELLENT, A1, bang-up, banner, capital, classic, crackerjack, divine, fabulous, fine, first-class, first-rate, grand, great, groovy, heavenly, jim-dandy, keen, marvelous (*or* marvellous), mean, neat, nifty, noble, par excellence, prime, sensational, splendid, stellar, sterling, superb, superior, superlative, supernal, swell, terrific, tip-top, top, top-notch, unsurpassed, wonderful *Ant* poor
dandy *n* **1** *Syn* FOP, beau, buck, coxcomb, dude, exquisite **2** *Syn* JIM-DANDY, beauty, corker, crackerjack, knockout, nifty, pip
danger **1** • something that may cause injury or harm *Syn* hazard, menace, peril, pitfall, risk, threat, trouble *Rel* snare, trap **2** • the state of not being protected from injury, harm, or evil *Syn* distress, endangerment, imperilment, jeopardy, peril, risk, trouble *Rel* exposure, liability, vulnerability *Ant* safeness, safety, security
dangerous • attended by or involving the possibility of loss, evil, injury, or harm *Syn* hazardous, perilous, precarious, risky *Rel* insecure, unsafe *Ant* safe, secure
dangle *Syn* HANG, sling, suspend
dank *Syn* WET, damp, humid, moist *Ant* dry
dapple *Syn* SPOT, blotch, dot, fleck, freckle, marble, mottle, pepper, speck, speckle, splotch, sprinkle, stipple
dappled *Syn* VARIEGATED, checked, checkered, motley, parti-colored, piebald, pied, skewbald
dare **1** *Syn* CHALLENGE, defy, stump **2** *Syn* FACE, beard, brave, challenge, defy *Ant* avoid
daredevil *Syn* ADVENTUROUS, daring, foolhardy, rash, reckless, venturesome *Ant* cautious, unadventurous
daring *adj* *Syn* ADVENTUROUS, daredevil, foolhardy, rash, reckless, venturesome *Ant* cautious, unadventurous
daring *n* *Syn* COURAGE, bravery, courageousness, dauntlessness, doughtiness, fearlessness, gallantry, greatheartedness, guts, hardihood, heart, heroism, intrepidity, intrepidness, nerve, stoutness, valor *Ant* cowardice, cowardliness, cravenness, dastardliness, spinelessness, yellowness
dark **1** • deficient in light *Syn* dim, dusky, gloomy, murky, obscure *Ant* light **2** *Syn* IGNORANT, benighted, illiterate, nonliterate, simple, uneducated, uninstructed, unlearned, unlettered, unread, unschooled, untaught, untutored *Ant* educated, knowledgeable, literate, schooled **3** *Syn* OBSCURE, ambiguous, cryptic, enigmatic, equivocal, vague *Ant* distinct, obvious **4** *Syn* SECRETIVE, close, closemouthed, reticent, uncommunicative *Ant* communicative, open
darken *Syn* OBSCURE, becloud, bedim, befog, cloud, dim, eclipse, fog, obfuscate *Ant* illuminate, illumine
darling *n* **1** *Syn* FAVORITE, minion, pet, preference **2** *Syn* SWEETHEART, beloved, dear, flame, honey, love, sweet
darling *adj* *Syn* LOVABLE, adorable, dear, disarming, endearing, precious, sweet, winning *Ant* abhorrent, abominable, detestable, hateful, odious, unlovable
dart *vb* *Syn* FLY, float, sail, scud, shoot, skim

dart *n Syn* INSULT, affront, barb, dig, epithet, indignity, name, offense (*or* offence), outrage, put-down, sarcasm, slight, slur
dash *vb Syn* HURRY (sense 2), barrel, bolt, bowl, breeze, career, course, fly, hasten, hotfoot (it), hump, hurtle, hustle, pelt, race, rip, rocket, run, rush, rustle, scoot, scurry, scuttle, shoot, speed, step (along), tear, trot, whirl, whisk, zip, zoom *Ant* crawl, creep, poke
dash *n* **1** *Syn* TOUCH, shade, smack, soupçon, spice, strain, streak, suggestion, suspicion, tincture, tinge, vein **2** *Syn* VIGOR, drive, élan, esprit, punch, spirit, verve, vim
dashing *Syn* STYLISH, chic, fashionable, modish, smart
dashingly *Syn* SMARTLY, nattily, sharply, sprucely *Ant* sloppily, slovenly
dastard *Syn* COWARD, chicken, craven, poltroon, recreant *Ant* hero, stalwart, valiant
dastardly *Syn* COWARDLY, chicken, chickenhearted, craven, lily-livered, pusillanimous, recreant, spineless, unheroic, yellow *Ant* brave, courageous, daring, dauntless, doughty, fearless, gallant, greathearted, gutsy, hardy, heroic, intrepid, lionhearted, stalwart, stout, stouthearted, valiant, valorous
date *Syn* ENGAGEMENT, appointment, assignation, rendezvous, tryst
dated *Syn* OBSOLETE, antiquated, archaic, moth-eaten, outdated, out-of-date, outmoded, outworn, passé
datum *Syn* FACT, detail, nicety, particular, particularity, point
daunt **1** *Syn* DISCOURAGE (sense 1), demoralize, dishearten, dismay, dispirit, unnerve *Ant* embolden, encourage, hearten, nerve, steel **2** *Syn* DISMAY, appall, horrify *Ant* cheer
dauntless *Syn* BRAVE, audacious, bold, courageous, doughty, fearless, intrepid, unafraid, undaunted, valiant, valorous *Ant* craven
dauntlessness *Syn* COURAGE, bravery, courageousness, daring, doughtiness, fearlessness, gallantry, greatheartedness, guts, hardihood, heart, heroism, intrepidity, intrepidness, nerve, stoutness, valor *Ant* cowardice, cowardliness, cravenness, dastardliness, spinelessness, yellowness
davenport *Syn* COUCH, chesterfield, divan, lounge, settee, sofa
dawdle *Syn* DELAY (sense 2), lag, loiter, procrastinate *Ant* hasten, hurry
dawn *n Syn* BEGINNING, alpha, birth, commencement, genesis, inception, incipiency, launch, morning, onset, outset, start, threshold *Ant* close, conclusion, end, ending
dawn *vb Syn* BEGIN (sense 1), arise, commence, form, materialize, originate, set in, spring, start *Ant* cease, end, stop
day *Syn* AGE (sense 3), epoch, era, period, time
daydream *Syn* FANCY, dream, fantasy, nightmare, phantasm, phantasy, vision *Ant* reality
daydreaming *Syn* REVERIE, study, trance, woolgathering
day-to-day *Syn* DAILY, diurnal
daze *vb* • to dull or deaden the powers of the mind through some disturbing experience or influence *Syn* bemuse, benumb, paralyze, petrify, stun, stupefy *Rel* bewilder, confound, mystify, puzzle
daze *n Syn* HAZE (sense 2), fog, muddle, spin
dazzled *Syn* GIDDY, dizzy, swimming, vertiginous
dead **1** • devoid of life *Syn* deceased, defunct, departed, inanimate, late, lifeless *Rel* alive **2** *Syn* EXTINCT, bygone, defunct, departed, expired, gone, vanished *Ant* alive, existent, existing, extant, living **3** *Syn* NUMB, asleep, benumbed, insensitive, numbed, unfeeling *Ant* feeling, sensitive
deadlock *Syn* DRAW, stalemate, standoff, tie
deadly *adj* • likely to cause or capable of causing death *Syn* baleful, deathly, fatal, fell, killer, lethal, mortal, murderous, pestilent, vital *Rel* baneful, destructive, harmful, noxious, pernicious *Ant* healthful, healthy, nonfatal, nonlethal, wholesome
deadly *adv Syn* VERY, awful, awfully, beastly, especially, exceedingly, extra, extremely, far, frightfully, full, greatly, heavily, highly, hugely, jolly, mightily, mighty, mortally, most, much, particularly, rattling, real, right, so, something, super, terribly, too, whacking *Ant* little, negligibly, nominally, slightly
deal *n Syn* SALE, trade, transaction
deal *vb* **1** *Syn* BARGAIN, chaffer, dicker, haggle, horse-trade, negotiate, palter **2** *Syn* DISTRIBUTE, dispense, divide, dole *Ant* amass, collect **3** *Syn* TREAT, handle **4** *Syn* MARKET, merchandise, put up, retail, sell, vend *Ant* buy, purchase
dealer *Syn* MERCHANT, merchandiser, trader, tradesman, trafficker
dear *adj* **1** *Syn* COSTLY, expensive, invaluable, precious, priceless, valuable *Ant* cheap **2** *Syn* LOVABLE, adorable, darling, disarming, endearing, precious, sweet, winning *Ant* abhorrent, abominable, detestable, hateful, odious, unlovable
dear *n Syn* SWEETHEART, beloved, darling, flame, honey, love, sweet
dearth **1** *Syn* DEFICIENCY, deficit, failure, famine, inadequacy, insufficiency, lack, paucity, poverty, scantiness, scarceness, scarcity, shortage, want *Ant* abundance, adequacy, amplitude, plenitude, plenty, sufficiency **2** *Syn* LACK, absence, defect, privation, want
death • the end or the ending of life *Syn* decease, demise, passing *Ant* life
deathless *Syn* IMMORTAL, undying, unfading *Ant* mortal
deathly *Syn* DEADLY, baleful, fatal, fell, killer, lethal, mortal, murderous, pestilent, vital

Ant healthful, healthy, nonfatal, nonlethal, wholesome

debar *Syn* EXCLUDE, blackball, disbar, eliminate, rule out, shut out, suspend *Ant* admit, include

debase 1 • to cause a person or thing to become impaired and lowered in quality or character *Syn* corrupt, debauch, deprave, pervert, vitiate *Rel* contaminate, defile, pollute, taint *Ant* amend (*morals, character*), elevate (*taste, way of life*) **2** *Syn* ABASE, degrade, demean, humble, humiliate *Ant* exalt, extol (*especially oneself*)

debased 1 • being lowered in quality or character *Syn* corrupted, debauched, depraved, perverted, vitiated *Rel* decadent, degenerate, degenerated, deteriorated **2** *Syn* CORRUPT, debauched, decadent, degenerate, degraded, demoralized, depraved, dissipated, dissolute, perverse, perverted, reprobate, warped *Ant* uncorrupted

debate *n Syn* ARGUMENTATION, dialectic, disputation, forensic

debate *vb Syn* DISCUSS, agitate, argue, dispute

debauch *Syn* DEBASE, corrupt, deprave, pervert, vitiate *Ant* amend (*morals, character*), elevate (*taste, way of life*)

debauched 1 *Syn* CORRUPT, debased, decadent, degenerate, degraded, demoralized, depraved, dissipated, dissolute, perverse, perverted, reprobate, warped *Ant* uncorrupted **2** *Syn* DEBASED, corrupted, depraved, perverted, vitiated

debilitate *Syn* WEAKEN, enervate, enfeeble, sap, soften *Ant* strengthen

debit *Syn* DEBT, arrear, indebtedness, liability, obligation

debonair *Syn* SUAVE, smooth, sophisticated, urbane *Ant* boorish, churlish, clownish, loutish, uncouth

debris *Syn* REFUSE, garbage, offal, rubbish, trash, waste

debt • something, and especially a sum of money, that is owed *Syn* arrear, debit, indebtedness, liability, obligation

decadence *Syn* DETERIORATION, declension, decline, degeneration, devolution *Ant* amelioration, improvement

decadent *Syn* CORRUPT, debased, debauched, degenerate, degraded, demoralized, depraved, dissipated, dissolute, perverse, perverted, reprobate, warped *Ant* uncorrupted

decamp *Syn* ESCAPE (sense 1), abscond, flee, fly

decay 1 • to undergo or to cause to undergo destructive changes *Syn* crumble, decompose, disintegrate, putrefy, rot, spoil *Rel* debilitate, enfeeble, sap, undermine, weaken **2** *Syn* DETERIORATE, crumble, decline, degenerate, descend, ebb, rot, sink, worsen *Ant* ameliorate, improve, meliorate

decease *Syn* DEATH, demise, passing *Ant* life

deceased *Syn* DEAD, defunct, departed, inanimate, late, lifeless

deceit • the act or practice of imposing upon the credulity of others by dishonesty, fraud, or trickery *Syn* cunning, dissimulation, duplicity, guile *Rel* chicane, chicanery, deception, double-dealing, fraud, trickery

deceive • to lead astray or into evil or to frustrate by underhandedness or craft *Syn* beguile, betray, delude, double-cross, mislead *Rel* cheat, cozen, defraud, overreach *Ant* enlighten, undeceive

decelerate *Syn* SLOW, brake, retard *Ant* accelerate, hasten, hurry, quicken, rush, speed (up), step up

decency *Syn* DECORUM, dignity, etiquette, propriety *Ant* indecorum, license

decent 1 *Syn* ADEQUATE, acceptable, all right, fine, OK (*or* okay), passable, respectable, satisfactory, tolerable *Ant* deficient, inadequate, lacking, unacceptable, unsatisfactory, wanting **2** *Syn* CHASTE, modest, pure *Ant* bizarre (*of style, effect*), immoral, lewd, wanton **3** *Syn* DECOROUS, nice, proper, seemly *Ant* blatant, indecorous

deception • the act or practice of deliberately deceiving *Syn* chicane, chicanery, double-dealing, fraud, trickery *Rel* cunning, deceit, dissimulation, duplicity, guile

deceptive *Syn* MISLEADING, delusive, delusory

decide • to come or to cause to come to a conclusion *Syn* determine, resolve, rule, settle *Rel* conclude, gather, judge

decided • free from any doubt, wavering, or ambiguity *Syn* decisive, determined, resolved *Rel* definite, definitive

decimation *Syn* DESTRUCTION, annihilation, demolishment, demolition, desolation, devastation, extermination, extinction, havoc, loss, obliteration, ruin, ruination, wastage, wreckage *Ant* building, construction, erection, raising

decisive 1 *Syn* COGENT, compelling, conclusive, convincing, effective, forceful, persuasive, satisfying, strong, telling *Ant* inconclusive, indecisive, ineffective, unconvincing **2** *Syn* CONCLUSIVE, definitive, determinative *Ant* inconclusive **3** *Syn* DECIDED, determined, resolved

deck *Syn* ADORN, beautify, bedeck, decorate, embellish, garnish, ornament *Ant* disfigure

declaration • the act of making known openly or publicly *Syn* advertisement, announcement, broadcasting, proclamation, promulgation, publication

declare 1 *Syn* ANNOUNCE, advertise, blaze, broadcast, enunciate, placard, post, proclaim, promulgate, publicize, publish, sound **2** *Syn* ASSERT, affirm, aver, avouch, avow, predicate, profess, protest, warrant *Ant* controvert, deny

declass *Syn* DEGRADE, demote, disrate, reduce *Ant* elevate
declension *Syn* DETERIORATION, decadence, decline, degeneration, devolution *Ant* amelioration, improvement
decline *vb* **1** • to turn away by not accepting, receiving, or considering *Syn* refuse, reject, repudiate, spurn *Rel* balk, boggle, demur, jib, scruple, shy, stick, stickle *Ant* accept **2** *Syn* DETERIORATE, crumble, decay, degenerate, descend, ebb, rot, sink, worsen *Ant* ameliorate, improve, meliorate
decline *n* **1** *Syn* COMEDOWN, descent, down, downfall, fall *Ant* aggrandizement, ascent, exaltation, rise, up **2** *Syn* DETERIORATION, decadence, declension, degeneration, devolution *Ant* amelioration, improvement
decolorize *Syn* WHITEN, blanch, bleach, blench, dull, fade, pale, wash out *Ant* blacken, darken, deepen
decompose *Syn* DECAY, crumble, disintegrate, putrefy, rot, spoil
decorate *Syn* ADORN, beautify, bedeck, deck, embellish, garnish, ornament *Ant* disfigure
decoration *Syn* AWARD, distinction, honor, plume, premium, prize
decorous • conforming to an accepted standard of what is right or fitting or is regarded as good form *Syn* decent, nice, proper, seemly *Rel* ceremonial, ceremonious, conventional, formal *Ant* blatant, indecorous
decorticate *Syn* SKIN, flay, pare, peel
decorum • the quality or character of rightness, fitness, or honorableness in behavior or conduct *Syn* decency, dignity, etiquette, propriety *Rel* ceremoniousness, conventionality, formality *Ant* indecorum, license
decoy *Syn* LURE, allure, beguile, entice, lead on, seduce, tempt
decrease • to make or grow less especially gradually *Syn* abate, diminish, dwindle, lessen, reduce *Rel* abbreviate, abridge, curtail, retrench, shorten *Ant* increase
decree *Syn* DICTATE, impose, ordain, prescribe
decrepit *Syn* WEAK, feeble, fragile, frail, infirm *Ant* strong
decry • to indicate one's low opinion of something *Syn* belittle, deprecate, derogate, detract, disparage, minimize *Rel* disapprove *Ant* extol
dedicate *Syn* DEVOTE, consecrate, hallow
deduce *Syn* INFER, conclude, gather, judge
deducible *Syn* DEDUCTIVE, derivable, inferable, reasoned
deduction **1** • an amount subtracted from a gross sum *Syn* abatement, discount, rebate **2** *Syn* INFERENCE (sense 1), conclusion, judgment
deductive • being or provable by reasoning in which the conclusion follows necessarily from given information *Syn* deducible, derivable, inferable, reasoned *Rel* conjectural, hypothetical, purported, supposed, suppositional
deed *n* *Syn* ACTION, act
deed *vb* *Syn* TRANSFER, alienate, convey
deem **1** *Syn* BELIEVE (sense 1), consider, feel, figure, guess, hold, imagine, suppose, think *Ant* disbelieve, discredit, reject **2** *Syn* CONSIDER (sense 2), account, reckon, regard
deep *adj* **1** • having great extension downward or inward *Syn* abysmal, profound **2** *Syn* BROAD, wide *Ant* narrow
deep *n* *Syn* THICK, depth, height, middle, midst
deep-rooted *Syn* INVETERATE, chronic, confirmed, deep-seated
deep-seated *Syn* INVETERATE, chronic, confirmed, deep-rooted
defamatory *Syn* LIBELOUS, scandalous, slanderous
defame *Syn* SLANDER, asperse, blacken, libel, malign, smear, traduce, vilify
default *Syn* FAILURE, dereliction, miscarriage, neglect
defeat *Syn* CONQUER, beat, lick, overcome, overthrow, reduce, rout, subdue, subjugate, surmount, vanquish
defect **1** *Syn* BLEMISH, deformity, disfigurement, fault, flaw, imperfection, mark, pockmark, scar **2** *Syn* LACK, absence, dearth, privation, want
defection • conscious abandonment of allegiance or duty *Syn* apostasy, desertion *Rel* alienation, disaffection, estrangement
defective *Syn* FAULTY, bad, flawed, imperfect *Ant* faultless, flawless, impeccable, perfect
defend **1** • to keep secure from danger or against attack *Syn* guard, protect, safeguard, shield *Rel* avert, prevent, ward *Ant* attack, combat **2** *Syn* MAINTAIN, assert, justify, vindicate
defendable *Syn* TENABLE, defensible, justifiable, maintainable, supportable, sustainable *Ant* indefensible, insupportable, unjustifiable, untenable
defender *Syn* PROTECTOR, custodian, guard, protection
defense *Syn* EXCUSE, alibi, justification, plea, reason
defensible *Syn* TENABLE, defendable, justifiable, maintainable, supportable, sustainable *Ant* indefensible, insupportable, unjustifiable, untenable
defer **1** *Syn* POSTPONE, delay, hold off (on), hold up, put off, shelve **2** *Syn* YIELD, bow, capitulate, cave, relent, submit, succumb
deference *Syn* HONOR, homage, obeisance, reverence
deferential *Syn* RESPECTFUL, dutiful, regardful *Ant* disrespectful
defiance **1** *Syn* DISOBEDIENCE, contrariness, frowardness, insubordination, intractability, rebelliousness, recalcitrance, refractoriness, unruliness, willfulness *Ant* amenability,

compliance, docility, obedience **2** *Syn* RESISTANCE, opposition *Ant* acquiescence

defiant *Syn* DISOBEDIENT, balky, contrary, froward, insubordinate, intractable, rebellious, recalcitrant, refractory, restive, ungovernable, unruly, untoward, wayward, willful (*or* wilful) *Ant* amenable, compliant, docile, obedient, tractable

deficiency **1** • a falling short of an essential or desirable amount or number *Syn* dearth, deficit, failure, famine, inadequacy, insufficiency, lack, paucity, poverty, scantiness, scarceness, scarcity, shortage, want *Rel* absence, omission *Ant* abundance, adequacy, amplitude, plenitude, plenty, sufficiency **2** *Syn* IMPERFECTION, fault, shortcoming *Ant* perfection

deficit *Syn* DEFICIENCY, dearth, failure, famine, inadequacy, insufficiency, lack, paucity, poverty, scantiness, scarceness, scarcity, shortage, want *Ant* abundance, adequacy, amplitude, plenitude, plenty, sufficiency

defile *n Syn* CANYON, flume, gap, gorge, gulch, gulf, notch, pass, ravine

defile *vb* **1** *Syn* CONTAMINATE, befoul, foul, poison, pollute, taint *Ant* decontaminate, purify **2** *Syn* DESECRATE, profane, violate

define *Syn* PRESCRIBE, assign

definite *Syn* EXPLICIT, categorical, express, specific *Ant* ambiguous

definitive *Syn* CONCLUSIVE, decisive, determinative *Ant* inconclusive

deflate *Syn* CONTRACT, compress, condense, constrict, shrink *Ant* expand

deflect *Syn* TURN (sense 2), avert, divert, sheer

deflection *Syn* DEVIATION, aberration, divergence

deform • to mar or spoil by or as if by twisting *Syn* contort, distort, warp *Rel* batter, cripple, maim, mangle, mutilate

deformity *Syn* BLEMISH, defect, disfigurement, fault, flaw, imperfection, mark, pockmark, scar

defraud *Syn* FLEECE, bleed, cheat, chisel, cozen, hustle, mulct, rook, shortchange, skin, squeeze, stick, sting, swindle, victimize

deftness *Syn* DEXTERITY (sense 2), agility, nimbleness, sleight, spryness *Ant* awkwardness, clumsiness, gawkiness

defunct **1** *Syn* DEAD, deceased, departed, inanimate, late, lifeless **2** *Syn* EXTINCT, bygone, dead, departed, expired, gone, vanished *Ant* alive, existent, existing, extant, living

defy **1** *Syn* CHALLENGE, dare, stump **2** *Syn* FACE, beard, brave, challenge, dare *Ant* avoid

degenerate *adj* **1** *Syn* CORRUPT, debased, debauched, decadent, degraded, demoralized, depraved, dissipated, dissolute, perverse, perverted, reprobate, warped *Ant* uncorrupted **2** *Syn* VICIOUS, corrupt, flagitious, infamous, iniquitous, nefarious, villainous *Ant* virtuous

degenerate *vb Syn* DETERIORATE, crumble, decay, decline, descend, ebb, rot, sink, worsen *Ant* ameliorate, improve, meliorate

degeneration *Syn* DETERIORATION, decadence, declension, decline, devolution *Ant* amelioration, improvement

degrade **1** • to lower in station, rank, or grade *Syn* declass, demote, disrate, reduce *Rel* abase, debase, humble, humiliate *Ant* elevate **2** *Syn* ABASE, debase, demean, humble, humiliate *Ant* exalt, extol (*especially oneself*)

degraded *Syn* CORRUPT, debased, debauched, decadent, degenerate, demoralized, depraved, dissipated, dissolute, perverse, perverted, reprobate, warped *Ant* uncorrupted

dehydrate *Syn* DRY, bake, desiccate, parch *Ant* moisten, wet

deification *Syn* WORSHIP, adulation, idolatry, idolization, worshipping

deify *Syn* IDOLIZE, adore, adulate, canonize, dote (on), worship

deign *Syn* STOOP, condescend

dejected *Syn* SAD (sense 1), bad, blue, brokenhearted, crestfallen, depressed, despondent, disconsolate, doleful, down, downcast, downhearted, droopy, forlorn, gloomy, glum, heartbroken, heartsick, heartsore, inconsolable, joyless, low, low-spirited, melancholy, miserable, mournful, saddened, sorrowful, sorry, unhappy, woebegone, woeful, wretched *Ant* blissful, buoyant, buoyed, cheerful, cheery, chipper, delighted, glad, gladdened, gladsome, gleeful, happy, joyful, joyous, jubilant, sunny, upbeat

dejection *Syn* SADNESS, blues, depression, desolation, despondency, disconsolateness, dispiritedness, doldrums, downheartedness, dreariness, dumps, forlornness, gloom, gloominess, heartsickness, joylessness, melancholy, mopes, oppression, unhappiness *Ant* bliss, blissfulness, ecstasy, elatedness, elation, euphoria, exhilaration, exuberance, exultation, felicity, gladness, gladsomeness, happiness, heaven, intoxication, joy, joyfulness, joyousness, jubilation, rapture, rapturousness

delay *n* • an instance or period of being prevented from going about one's business *Syn* detainment, holdup, wait *Rel* deferment, postponement

delay *vb* **1** • to cause to be late or behind in movement or progress *Syn* detain, retard, slacken, slow *Rel* block, hinder, impede, obstruct *Ant* expedite, hasten **2** • to move or act slowly so that progress is hindered or work remains undone or unfinished *Syn* dawdle, lag, loiter, procrastinate *Rel* linger, stay, tarry, wait *Ant* hasten, hurry **3** *Syn* POSTPONE, defer, hold off (on), hold up, put off, shelve

delectable *Syn* DELIGHTFUL, delicious, luscious *Ant* boring, distressing, horrid
delectation *Syn* PLEASURE, delight, enjoyment, fruition, joy *Ant* anger, displeasure, vexation
delegate 1 • a person who stands in place of another or others *Syn* deputy, representative 2 *Syn* AGENT (sense 1), attorney, commissary, deputy, envoy, factor, procurator, proxy, representative 3 *Syn* AMBASSADOR, emissary, envoy, legate, minister, representative
delete *Syn* ERASE, blot out, cancel, efface, expunge, obliterate
deleterious *Syn* HARMFUL, adverse, bad, baleful, baneful, damaging, detrimental, evil, hurtful, ill, injurious, mischievous, noxious, pernicious, prejudicial *Ant* harmless, innocent, innocuous, inoffensive, safe
deliberate *adj* 1 • arrived at after due thought *Syn* advised, considered, designed, premeditated, studied *Rel* planned, projected, schemed *Ant* casual 2 *Syn* VOLUNTARY, intentional, willful, willing *Ant* instinctive, involuntary 3 *Syn* SLOW, dilatory, laggard, leisurely *Ant* fast
deliberate *vb* *Syn* THINK (sense 2), cogitate, reason, reflect, speculate
deliberately *Syn* INTENTIONALLY, consciously, designedly, knowingly, purposefully, purposely, willfully, wittingly *Ant* inadvertently, unconsciously, unintentionally, unknowingly, unwittingly
delicacy *Syn* PRECISION, accuracy, closeness, exactitude, exactness, fineness, preciseness, rigorousness, veracity *Ant* coarseness, impreciseness, imprecision, inaccuracy, inexactness, roughness
delicate *Syn* CHOICE, dainty, elegant, exquisite, rare, recherché *Ant* indifferent, medium
delicious *Syn* DELIGHTFUL, delectable, luscious *Ant* boring, distressing, horrid
delight *vb* *Syn* PLEASE, gladden, gratify, regale, rejoice, tickle *Ant* anger, displease, vex
delight *n* *Syn* PLEASURE, delectation, enjoyment, fruition, joy *Ant* anger, displeasure, vexation
delightful 1 • highly pleasing to the senses or to aesthetic taste *Syn* delectable, delicious, luscious *Rel* alluring, attractive, charming, enchanting, fascinating *Ant* boring, distressing, horrid 2 *Syn* FUN, amusing, diverting, enjoyable, entertaining, pleasurable *Ant* boring, dull
delineate 1 *Syn* REPRESENT, depict, limn, picture, portray 2 *Syn* SKETCH, blueprint, diagram, draft, outline, plot, trace
delineation *Syn* SKETCH, blueprint, diagram, draft, outline, plot, tracing
delinquent *Syn* CRIMINAL, convict, culprit, felon, malefactor
deliquesce *Syn* LIQUEFY, fuse, melt, thaw
delirious *Syn* FURIOUS, frantic, frenetic, frenzied, rabid, wild
delirium 1 *Syn* FRENZY, agitation, distraction, furor, furore, fury, hysteria, rage, rampage, uproar 2 *Syn* MANIA, frenzy, hysteria
deliver 1 *Syn* RESCUE, ransom, reclaim, redeem, save 2 *Syn* FURNISH (sense 2), feed, give, hand, hand over, provide, supply *Ant* hold (back), keep (back), reserve, retain, withhold
deliverer *Syn* SAVIOR, redeemer, rescuer, saver
delude *Syn* DECEIVE, beguile, betray, double-cross, mislead *Ant* enlighten, undeceive
deluge *n* 1 *Syn* FLOOD, cataract, inundation, spate, torrent 2 *Syn* RAIN (sense 1), cloudburst, downpour, rainfall, rainstorm, storm, wet
deluge *vb* *Syn* FLOOD, drown, engulf, inundate, overflow, overwhelm, submerge, submerse, swamp *Ant* drain
delusion • something which is believed to be or is accepted as being true or real but which is actually false or unreal *Syn* hallucination, illusion, mirage *Rel* chicane, chicanery, deception, trickery
delusive *Syn* MISLEADING, deceptive, delusory
delusory *Syn* MISLEADING, deceptive, delusive
deluxe *Syn* LUXURIOUS, lavish, luxuriant, opulent, palatial, plush, sumptuous *Ant* ascetic, austere, humble, Spartan
delve *Syn* DIG, excavate, grub, spade
delve (into) *Syn* EXPLORE, dig (into), inquire (into), investigate, look (into), probe, research
demagogue *Syn* AGITATOR, exciter, firebrand, fomenter, incendiary, inciter, instigator, rabble-rouser
demand • to ask or call for something as due or as necessary or as strongly desired *Syn* claim, exact, require *Rel* ask, request, solicit
demarcate *Syn* DISTINGUISH, differentiate, discriminate *Ant* confound
demean 1 *Syn* ABASE, debase, degrade, humble, humiliate *Ant* exalt, extol (*especially oneself*) 2 *Syn* BEHAVE, acquit, comport, conduct, deport, quit *Ant* misbehave
demeanor *Syn* BEARING, deportment, mien, port, presence
demented *Syn* INSANE, crazed, crazy, deranged, lunatic, mad, maniac, non compos mentis *Ant* sane
demesne *Syn* REGION, area, field, zone
demise *Syn* DEATH, decease, passing *Ant* life
democratic • of, relating to, or favoring political democracy *Syn* popular, republican, self-governing, self-ruling *Rel* representative *Ant* undemocratic
demolish *Syn* DESTROY, raze
demolishment *Syn* DESTRUCTION, annihilation, decimation, demolition, desolation, devastation, extermination, extinction, havoc,

loss, obliteration, ruin, ruination, wastage, wreckage *Ant* building, construction, erection, raising
demolition *Syn* DESTRUCTION, annihilation, decimation, demolishment, desolation, devastation, extermination, extinction, havoc, loss, obliteration, ruin, ruination, wastage, wreckage *Ant* building, construction, erection, raising
demon *or* **daemon** • an evil spirit *Syn* devil, fiend, ghoul, imp, incubus *Rel* apparition, bogey, brownie, dwarf, elf, faerie, fairy, familiar, fay, ghost, gnome, goblin, gremlin, hobgoblin, leprechaun, monster, ogre, phantasm, phantom, pixie, poltergeist, puck, shade, shadow, specter (*or* spectre), spirit, spook, sprite, troll, vision, wraith
demoniac *Syn* FIENDISH, demonic, devilish, diabolic, diabolical
demonic *Syn* FIENDISH, demoniac, devilish, diabolic, diabolical
demonstrate **1** *Syn* EXPLAIN (sense 1), clarify, clear (up), construe, elucidate, explicate, expound, illuminate, illustrate, interpret, spell out *Ant* obscure **2** *Syn* PROVE, test, try *Ant* disprove **3** *Syn* SHOW (sense 1), evidence, evince, manifest *Ant* disguise
demonstration *Syn* PROOF, test, trial
demonstrative • showing feeling freely *Syn* effusive, emotional, uninhibited, unreserved, unrestrained *Rel* dramatic, histrionic, melodramatic, theatrical *Ant* inhibited, reserved, restrained, undemonstrative, unemotional
demoralize *Syn* DISCOURAGE (sense 1), daunt, dishearten, dismay, dispirit, unnerve *Ant* embolden, encourage, hearten, nerve, steel
demoralized *Syn* CORRUPT, debased, debauched, decadent, degenerate, degraded, depraved, dissipated, dissolute, perverse, perverted, reprobate, warped *Ant* uncorrupted
demote *Syn* DEGRADE, declass, disrate, reduce *Ant* elevate
demur *vb* • to hesitate or show reluctance because of difficulties in the way *Syn* balk, boggle, jib, scruple, shy, stick, stickle, strain *Rel* falter, hesitate, vacillate, waver *Ant* accede
demur *n* *Syn* OBJECTION, challenge, complaint, expostulation, fuss, protest, question, remonstrance
denial **1** • an unwillingness to grant something asked for *Syn* disallowance, nay, no, refusal, rejection *Rel* decline, rebuff, repudiation *Ant* allowance, grant **2** • a refusal to confirm the truth of a statement *Syn* contradiction, disallowance, disavowal, disclaimer, negation, rejection, repudiation *Rel* disproof, rebuttal, refutation *Ant* acknowledgment, admission, avowal, confirmation
denizen *Syn* INHABITANT, dweller, habitant, occupant, resident, resider *Ant* transient
denomination **1** *Syn* NAME, appellation, designation, style, title **2** *Syn* RELIGION, church, communion, creed, faith, persuasion, sect
denote *Syn* MEAN, import, signify
denounce *Syn* CRITICIZE, blame, censure, condemn, reprehend, reprobate
dense **1** *Syn* CLOSE (sense 2), compact, thick *Ant* open **2** *Syn* STUPID, crass, dull, dumb, slow *Ant* intelligent
dented *Syn* HOLLOW, concave, depressed, indented, recessed, sunken *Ant* bulging, convex, protruding, protuberant
denude *Syn* STRIP, bare, dismantle, divest *Ant* furnish, invest
denunciation *Syn* CENSURE, condemnation, rebuke, reprimand, reproach, reproof, stricture *Ant* citation, commendation, endorsement
deny • to refuse to accept as true or valid *Syn* contradict, contravene, gainsay, impugn, negative, traverse *Rel* decline, refuse, reject, repudiate *Ant* concede, confirm
depart **1** *Syn* GO, leave, quit, retire, withdraw *Ant* come **2** *Syn* SWERVE, deviate, digress, diverge, veer
departed **1** *Syn* DEAD, deceased, defunct, inanimate, late, lifeless **2** *Syn* EXTINCT, bygone, dead, defunct, expired, gone, vanished *Ant* alive, existent, existing, extant, living
depend **1** • to rest or to be contingent upon something uncertain, variable, or indeterminable *Syn* hang, hinge, turn **2** • to place reliance or trust *Syn* count, lean, reckon, rely *Rel* commit, confide, entrust, trust **3** *Syn* RELY (ON), bank, count, reckon, trust
dependable • worthy of one's trust *Syn* good, reliable, responsible, safe, solid, steady, sure, tried, tried-and-true, true, trustworthy, trusty *Rel* attested, authenticated, blameless, confirmed, constant, devoted, effective, faithful, fast, firm, honest, infallible, irreproachable, loyal, proven, sincere, single-minded, sound, staunch (*or* stanch), steadfast, strong, telling, unerring, unimpeachable, unquestionable, valid, validated, verified *Ant* irresponsible, undependable, unreliable, untrustworthy
dependence *Syn* TRUST, confidence, faith, reliance *Ant* mistrust
dependent **1** • determined or conditioned by another *Syn* conditional, contingent, relative *Rel* exposed, liable, open, subject, susceptible *Ant* absolute, infinite, original **2** *Syn* SUBORDINATE, collateral, secondary, subject, tributary *Ant* chief, dominant, leading
depict *Syn* REPRESENT, delineate, limn, picture, portray
deplete • to make complete use of *Syn* clean (out), consume, drain, exhaust, expend, spend, use up *Rel* decrease, diminish, lessen, reduce *Ant* renew, replace
deplorable *Syn* REGRETTABLE, distressful, distressing, grievous, heartbreaking, heartrending, lamentable, unfortunate, woeful

deplore *Syn* REGRET, bemoan, lament, repent, rue

deport 1 *Syn* BANISH, exile, expatriate, extradite, ostracize, transport 2 *Syn* BEHAVE, acquit, comport, conduct, demean, quit *Ant* misbehave

deportment 1 *Syn* BEARING, demeanor, mien, port, presence 2 *Syn* BEHAVIOR, conduct

depose *Syn* TESTIFY, attest, swear, witness

deposit 1 • matter which settles to the bottom of a liquid *Syn* dregs, grounds, lees, precipitate, sediment 2 *Syn* STORE, cache, hoard, reserve

depository *Syn* STOREHOUSE, depot, magazine, repository, storage, stowage, warehouse

depot 1 *Syn* ARMORY, arsenal, dump, magazine 2 *Syn* STOREHOUSE, depository, magazine, repository, storage, stowage, warehouse

deprave *Syn* DEBASE, corrupt, debauch, pervert, vitiate *Ant* amend (*morals, character*), elevate (*taste, way of life*)

depraved 1 *Syn* CORRUPT, debased, debauched, decadent, degenerate, degraded, demoralized, dissipated, dissolute, perverse, perverted, reprobate, warped *Ant* uncorrupted 2 *Syn* DEBASED, corrupted, debauched, perverted, vitiated

deprecate 1 *Syn* DECRY, belittle, derogate, detract, disparage, minimize *Ant* extol 2 *Syn* DISAPPROVE (OF), discountenance, disfavor, dislike, frown (on), reprove *Ant* approve, favor, like

depreciative *Syn* DEROGATORY, depreciatory, disparaging, pejorative, slighting

depreciatory *Syn* DEROGATORY, depreciative, disparaging, pejorative, slighting

depress • to lower in spirit or mood *Syn* oppress, weigh *Rel* ail, distress, trouble *Ant* cheer, elate

depressed 1 *Syn* HOLLOW, concave, dented, indented, recessed, sunken *Ant* bulging, convex, protruding, protuberant 2 *Syn* SAD (sense 1), bad, blue, brokenhearted, crestfallen, dejected, despondent, disconsolate, doleful, down, downcast, downhearted, droopy, forlorn, gloomy, glum, heartbroken, heartsick, heartsore, inconsolable, joyless, low, low-spirited, melancholy, miserable, mournful, saddened, sorrowful, sorry, unhappy, woebegone, woeful, wretched *Ant* blissful, buoyant, buoyed, cheerful, cheery, chipper, delighted, glad, gladdened, gladsome, gleeful, happy, joyful, joyous, jubilant, sunny, upbeat

depressing *Syn* SAD (sense 2), dismal, drear, dreary, heartbreaking, heartrending, melancholy, pathetic, saddening, sorry, tearful, teary *Ant* cheering, cheery, glad, happy

depression *Syn* SADNESS, blues, dejection, desolation, despondency, disconsolateness, dispiritedness, doldrums, downheartedness, dreariness, dumps, forlornness, gloom, gloominess, heartsickness, joylessness, melancholy, mopes, oppression, unhappiness *Ant* bliss, blissfulness, ecstasy, elatedness, elation, euphoria, exhilaration, exuberance, exultation, felicity, gladness, gladsomeness, happiness, heaven, intoxication, joy, joyfulness, joyousness, jubilation, rapture, rapturousness

deprived • kept from having the necessities of life or a healthful environment *Syn* disadvantaged, underprivileged *Rel* impoverished, needy, poor *Ant* privileged

depth *Syn* THICK, deep, height, middle, midst

deputy 1 *Syn* AGENT (sense 1), attorney, commissary, delegate, envoy, factor, procurator, proxy, representative 2 *Syn* DELEGATE, representative 3 *Syn* ASSISTANT, adjutant, aid, aide, apprentice, coadjutor, helper, sidekick

deracinate *Syn* EXTERMINATE, eradicate, extirpate, uproot, wipe

derange *Syn* DISORDER, confuse, disarrange, disarray, discompose, dishevel, dislocate, disorganize, disrupt, disturb, hash, jumble, mess (up), mix (up), muddle, muss, rumple, scramble, shuffle, tousle, tumble, upset *Ant* arrange, array, draw up, marshal, order, organize, range, regulate, straighten (up), tidy

deranged *Syn* INSANE, crazed, crazy, demented, lunatic, mad, maniac, non compos mentis *Ant* sane

derangement *Syn* ABERRATION, alienation *Ant* soundness (*of mind*)

derelict *adj* 1 *Syn* ABANDONED (sense 2), deserted, disused, forgotten, forsaken, rejected, vacated 2 *Syn* NEGLIGENT, careless, lax, neglectful, neglecting, remiss, slack *Ant* attentive, careful, conscientious

derelict *n* *Syn* OUTCAST, castaway, pariah, reprobate, untouchable

dereliction *Syn* FAILURE, default, miscarriage, neglect

deride *Syn* RIDICULE, mock, rally, taunt, twit

derivable *Syn* DEDUCTIVE, deducible, inferable, reasoned

derivative • something that naturally develops or is developed from something else *Syn* by-product, offshoot, outgrowth, spin-off *Rel* aftereffect, aftermath, consequence, copy, descendant (*or* descendent), duplicate, facsimile, replica, reproduction, result, side effect *Ant* origin, root, source

derive *Syn* SPRING, arise, emanate, flow, issue, originate, proceed, rise, stem

dernier cri *Syn* FASHION, craze, cry, fad, mode, rage, style, vogue

derogate *Syn* DECRY, belittle, deprecate, detract, disparage, minimize *Ant* extol

derogatory • designed or tending to belittle *Syn* depreciative, depreciatory, disparaging, pejorative, slighting *Rel* belittling, decrying, minimizing

descant 1 *Syn* DISCOURSE, dilate, expatiate 2 *Syn* SING, carol, chant, hymn, intone, trill, troll, warble

descend 1 • to get or come down from a height *Syn* alight, dismount *Ant* ascend, climb 2 *Syn* DETERIORATE, crumble, decay, decline, degenerate, ebb, rot, sink, worsen *Ant* ameliorate, improve, meliorate

descendants *Syn* OFFSPRING, issue, posterity, progeny, young

descent 1 *Syn* ANCESTRY, birth, blood, bloodline, breeding, extraction, family tree, genealogy, line, lineage, origin, parentage, pedigree, stock, strain *Ant* issue, posterity, progeny, seed 2 *Syn* ATTACK (sense 2), aggression, assault, blitzkrieg, charge, offense (*or* offence), offensive, onset, onslaught, raid, rush, strike 3 *Syn* COMEDOWN, decline, down, downfall, fall *Ant* aggrandizement, ascent, exaltation, rise, up

describe *Syn* RELATE, narrate, recite, recount, rehearse, report, state

description *Syn* TYPE, character, ilk, kidney, kind, nature, sort, stripe

descry *Syn* SEE (sense 1), behold, contemplate, discern, espy, note, notice, observe, perceive, remark, survey, view

desecrate • to treat (a sacred place or object) shamefully or with great disrespect *Syn* defile, profane, violate *Rel* blaspheme, curse, swear

desecration *Syn* PROFANATION, blasphemy, sacrilege

desert *vb* *Syn* ABANDON, forsake *Ant* reclaim

desert[1] *n* *Syn* DUE, merit

desert[2] *n* *Syn* WASTE, badlands, wilderness

deserted *Syn* ABANDONED (sense 2), derelict, disused, forgotten, forsaken, rejected, vacated

desertion *Syn* DEFECTION, apostasy

deserve • to be or become worthy of *Syn* earn, merit, rate *Rel* gain, get, win

deserving *Syn* WORTHY, good, meritorious *Ant* no-good, undeserving, valueless, worthless

desiccate *Syn* DRY, bake, dehydrate, parch *Ant* moisten, wet

design *n* 1 *Syn* FIGURE, device, motif, pattern 2 *Syn* GOAL, aim, ambition, aspiration, dream, end, intent, intention, mark, meaning, object, objective, plan, pretension, purpose, target, thing 3 *Syn* PLAN, plot, project, scheme

design *vb* 1 *Syn* INTEND, mean, propose, purpose 2 *Syn* PLAN, plot, project, scheme

designate 1 *Syn* APPOINT (sense 1), fix, name, set 2 *Syn* APPOINT (sense 2), assign, attach, commission, constitute, detail, name *Ant* discharge, dismiss, expel, fire

designation *Syn* NAME, appellation, denomination, style, title

designed *Syn* DELIBERATE, advised, considered, premeditated, studied *Ant* casual

designedly *Syn* INTENTIONALLY, consciously, deliberately, knowingly, purposefully, purposely, willfully, wittingly *Ant* inadvertently, unconsciously, unintentionally, unknowingly, unwittingly

desirable *Syn* EXPEDIENT, advisable, judicious, politic, prudent, tactical, wise *Ant* imprudent, inadvisable, inexpedient, injudicious, unwise

desire *n* • a longing for something that promises enjoyment or satisfaction *Syn* appetite, lust, passion, urge *Rel* hankering, hunger, hungering, longing, pining, thirst, thirsting, yearning *Ant* distaste

desire *vb* • to have a longing for something *Syn* covet, crave, want, wish *Rel* hanker, hunger, long, pine, thirst, yearn

desist *Syn* STOP, cease, discontinue, quit

desolate 1 *Syn* ALONE, forlorn, lone, lonely, lonesome, lorn, solitary *Ant* accompanied 2 *Syn* DISMAL, bleak, cheerless, dispiriting, dreary

desolation 1 *Syn* DESTRUCTION, annihilation, decimation, demolishment, demolition, devastation, extermination, extinction, havoc, loss, obliteration, ruin, ruination, wastage, wreckage *Ant* building, construction, erection, raising 2 *Syn* SADNESS, blues, dejection, depression, despondency, disconsolateness, dispiritedness, doldrums, downheartedness, dreariness, dumps, forlornness, gloom, gloominess, heartsickness, joylessness, melancholy, mopes, oppression, unhappiness *Ant* bliss, blissfulness, ecstasy, elatedness, elation, euphoria, exhilaration, exuberance, exultation, felicity, gladness, gladsomeness, happiness, heaven, intoxication, joy, joyfulness, joyousness, jubilation, rapture, rapturousness

despair *Syn* DESPONDENCY, desperation, forlornness, hopelessness *Ant* lightheartedness

despairing *Syn* DESPONDENT, desperate, forlorn, hopeless *Ant* lighthearted

desperate *Syn* DESPONDENT, despairing, forlorn, hopeless *Ant* lighthearted

desperation *Syn* DESPONDENCY, despair, forlornness, hopelessness *Ant* lightheartedness

despicable *Syn* CONTEMPTIBLE, beggarly, cheap, pitiable, scurvy, shabby, sorry *Ant* admirable, estimable, formidable

despise 1 • to regard as beneath one's notice and as unworthy of attention or interest *Syn* contemn, disdain, scorn, scout *Rel* abhor, abominate, detest, hate, loathe *Ant* appreciate 2 *Syn* SCORN (sense 1), disregard, flout *Ant* honor, respect

despite *n* 1 • the feeling or attitude of despising *Syn* contempt, disdain, scorn 2 *Syn* CONTEMPT, despitefulness, disdain, scorn *Ant* admiration, esteem, regard, respect 3 *Syn* MALICE, grudge, ill will, malevolence, malignancy, malignity, spite, spleen *Ant* charity

despite *prep Syn* NOTWITHSTANDING, in spite of

despitefulness *Syn* CONTEMPT, despite, disdain, scorn *Ant* admiration, esteem, regard, respect

despoil *Syn* RAVAGE, devastate, pillage, sack, spoliate, waste

despondency **1** • the state or feeling of having lost hope *Syn* despair, desperation, forlornness, hopelessness *Rel* blues, dejection, depression, dumps, melancholia, melancholy, sadness *Ant* lightheartedness **2** *Syn* SADNESS, blues, dejection, depression, desolation, disconsolateness, dispiritedness, doldrums, downheartedness, dreariness, dumps, forlornness, gloom, gloominess, heartsickness, joylessness, melancholy, mopes, oppression, unhappiness *Ant* bliss, blissfulness, ecstasy, elatedness, elation, euphoria, exhilaration, exuberance, exultation, felicity, gladness, gladsomeness, happiness, heaven, intoxication, joy, joyfulness, joyousness, jubilation, rapture, rapturousness

despondent **1** • having lost all or nearly all hope *Syn* despairing, desperate, forlorn, hopeless *Rel* grieving, mourning, sorrowing *Ant* lighthearted **2** *Syn* SAD (sense 1), bad, blue, brokenhearted, crestfallen, dejected, depressed, disconsolate, doleful, down, downcast, downhearted, droopy, forlorn, gloomy, glum, heartbroken, heartsick, heartsore, inconsolable, joyless, low, low-spirited, melancholy, miserable, mournful, saddened, sorrowful, sorry, unhappy, woebegone, woeful, wretched *Ant* blissful, buoyant, buoyed, cheerful, cheery, chipper, delighted, glad, gladdened, gladsome, gleeful, happy, joyful, joyous, jubilant, sunny, upbeat

despotic **1** *Syn* ABSOLUTE, arbitrary, autocratic, tyrannical, tyrannous *Ant* limited, restrained **2** *Syn* BOSSY, authoritarian, autocratic, dictatorial, domineering, imperious, masterful, overbearing, peremptory, tyrannical, tyrannous

destiny *Syn* FATE, doom, lot, portion

destitute **1** *Syn* DEVOID, void **2** *Syn* POOR, impecunious, indigent, necessitous, needy, penniless, poverty-stricken *Ant* rich

destitution *Syn* POVERTY, indigence, penury, privation, want *Ant* riches

destroy • to bring to ruin *Syn* demolish, raze *Rel* dilapidate, ruin, wreck

destruction • the state or fact of being rendered nonexistent, physically unsound, or useless *Syn* annihilation, decimation, demolishment, demolition, desolation, devastation, extermination, extinction, havoc, loss, obliteration, ruin, ruination, wastage, wreckage *Rel* depredation, despoilment, despoliation *Ant* building, construction, erection, raising

desultorily *Syn* HIT OR MISS, aimlessly, anyhow, anyway, anywise, erratically, haphazard, haphazardly, helter-skelter, irregularly, randomly *Ant* methodically, systematically

desultory *Syn* RANDOM, casual, chance, chancy, haphazard, happy-go-lucky, hit-or-miss *Ant* methodical, nonrandom, orderly, systematic

detach • to remove one thing from another with which it is in union or association *Syn* abstract, disengage *Rel* divorce, part, separate, sever, sunder *Ant* affix, attach

detached *Syn* INDIFFERENT, aloof, disinterested, incurious, unconcerned, uninterested *Ant* avid

detachment • lack of favoritism toward one side or another *Syn* disinterestedness, impartiality, neutrality, objectivity *Rel* equitableness, fairness *Ant* bias, favor, favoritism, one-sidedness, partiality, partisanship, prejudice

detail *n* **1** *Syn* FACT, datum, nicety, particular, particularity, point **2** *Syn* ITEM, particular **3** *Syn* PART, division, fraction, fragment, member, parcel, piece, portion, section, sector, segment *Ant* whole

detail *vb Syn* APPOINT (sense 2), assign, attach, commission, constitute, designate, detail, name *Ant* discharge, dismiss, expel, fire

detailed *Syn* CIRCUMSTANTIAL, itemized, minute, particular, particularized *Ant* abridged, summary

detain **1** *Syn* ARREST (sense 2), apprehend, attach **2** *Syn* DELAY (sense 1), retard, slacken, slow *Ant* expedite, hasten **3** *Syn* KEEP (sense 2), hold back, keep back, keep out, reserve, retain, withhold *Ant* relinquish

detainment *Syn* DELAY, holdup, wait

detectable *Syn* PERCEPTIBLE, appreciable, discernible, distinguishable, palpable, sensible *Ant* impalpable, imperceptible, inappreciable, indistinguishable, insensible

detention *Syn* ARREST, apprehension, attachment

deter *Syn* DISCOURAGE (sense 2), dissuade, inhibit *Ant* encourage, persuade

deteriorate • to become worse or of less value *Syn* crumble, decay, decline, degenerate, descend, ebb, rot, sink, worsen *Rel* recede, wane *Ant* ameliorate, improve, meliorate

deterioration • a falling from a higher to a lower level in quality, character, or vitality *Syn* decadence, declension, decline, degeneration, devolution *Rel* impairment, spoiling *Ant* amelioration, improvement

determinant *Syn* CAUSE, antecedent, occasion, reason

determinative *Syn* CONCLUSIVE, decisive, definitive *Ant* inconclusive

determine **1** *Syn* DECIDE, resolve, rule, settle **2** *Syn* DISCOVER, ascertain, learn, unearth

determined *Syn* DECIDED, decisive, resolved

deterrent *Syn* ENCUMBRANCE, bar, block, chain, clog, crimp, drag, embarrassment, fetter, handicap, hindrance, hurdle, impediment, inhibition, interference, let, manacle, obstacle, obstruction, shackles, stop, stumbling block, trammel *Ant* aid, assistance, benefit, help

detest *Syn* HATE, abhor, abominate, loathe *Ant* love

detestable *Syn* HATEFUL, abhorrent, abominable, odious *Ant* lovable, sympathetic

detestation *Syn* ABHORRENCE, abomination, hate, hatred, loathing *Ant* admiration, enjoyment

detract *Syn* DECRY, belittle, deprecate, derogate, disparage, minimize *Ant* extol

detraction • the expression of damaging or malicious opinions *Syn* backbiting, calumny, scandal, slander *Rel* damage, harm, hurt, injury

detrimental *Syn* HARMFUL, adverse, bad, baleful, baneful, damaging, deleterious, evil, hurtful, ill, injurious, mischievous, noxious, pernicious, prejudicial *Ant* harmless, innocent, innocuous, inoffensive, safe

devastate *Syn* RAVAGE, despoil, pillage, sack, spoliate, waste

devastation *Syn* DESTRUCTION, annihilation, decimation, demolishment, demolition, desolation, extermination, extinction, havoc, loss, obliteration, ruin, ruination, wastage, wreckage *Ant* building, construction, erection, raising

develop **1** *Syn* MATURE, age, ripen **2** *Syn* UNFOLD, elaborate, evolve, perfect

deviant • departing from some accepted standard of what is normal *Syn* aberrant, abnormal, anomalous, atypical, irregular, unnatural *Rel* extraordinary, preternatural *Ant* natural, normal, regular, standard, typical

deviate *Syn* SWERVE, depart, digress, diverge, veer

deviation • departure from a straight course or procedure or from a norm or standard *Syn* aberration, deflection, divergence

device **1** • something usually of a mechanical character that performs a function or effects a desired end *Syn* contraption, contrivance, gadget *Rel* appliance, implement, instrument, tool, utensil **2** *Syn* FIGURE, design, motif, pattern

devil *Syn* DEMON, fiend, ghoul, imp, incubus

devilish *Syn* FIENDISH, demoniac, demonic, diabolic, diabolical

devil-may-care *Syn* CAREFREE, careless, cavalier, easygoing, gay, happy-go-lucky, insouciant, lighthearted, unconcerned *Ant* careworn

devious *Syn* CROOKED, oblique *Ant* straight

devise **1** *Syn* INVENT, concoct, contrive, cook (up), fabricate, make up, manufacture, think (up) **2** *Syn* WILL, bequeath, leave, legate

devoid • showing a want or lack *Syn* destitute, void *Rel* bare, barren

devolution *Syn* DETERIORATION, decadence, declension, decline, degeneration *Ant* amelioration, improvement

devote **1** • to set apart for a particular and often a better or higher use or end *Syn* consecrate, dedicate, hallow *Rel* commit, confide, consign, entrust **2** *Syn* DIRECT (sense 1), address, apply *Ant* misdirect

devoted **1** *Syn* FAITHFUL, constant, devout, fast, good, loyal, pious, staunch (*or* stanch), steadfast, steady, true, true-blue *Ant* disloyal, faithless, false, fickle, inconstant, perfidious, recreant, traitorous, treacherous, unfaithful, untrue **2** *Syn* LOVING, affectionate, doting, fond *Ant* unloving

devotee **1** *Syn* ADDICT, habitué, votary **2** *Syn* FAN, addict, aficionado, buff, bug, enthusiast, fanatic, fancier, fiend, freak, lover, maniac, nut

devotion *Syn* FIDELITY, allegiance, fealty, loyalty, piety *Ant* faithlessness, perfidy

devour *Syn* EAT, consume, ingest, swallow

devout **1** *Syn* HOLY (sense 1), godly, pious, religious, sainted, saintly *Ant* faithless, godless, impious, irreligious, ungodly, unholy **2** *Syn* FAITHFUL, constant, devoted, fast, good, loyal, pious, staunch (*or* stanch), steadfast, steady, true, true-blue *Ant* disloyal, faithless, false, fickle, inconstant, perfidious, recreant, traitorous, treacherous, unfaithful, untrue

devoutness *Syn* HOLINESS, blessedness, godliness, piety, piousness, sainthood, saintliness, saintship, sanctity *Ant* godlessness, impiety, ungodliness, unholiness

dexterity **1** • mental skill or quickness *Syn* adroitness, cleverness, finesse, sleight *Rel* ability, prowess, talent **2** • ease and grace in physical activity *Syn* agility, deftness, nimbleness, sleight, spryness *Rel* coordination *Ant* awkwardness, clumsiness, gawkiness **3** *Syn* READINESS, ease, facility

diabolic *Syn* FIENDISH, demoniac, demonic, devilish, diabolical

diabolical *Syn* FIENDISH, demoniac, demonic, devilish, diabolic

diagram *vb Syn* SKETCH, blueprint, delineate, draft, outline, plot, trace

diagram *n Syn* SKETCH, blueprint, delineation, draft, outline, plot, tracing

dialect **1** *Syn* LANGUAGE (sense 1), idiom, speech, tongue **2** *Syn* TERMINOLOGY, argot, cant, jargon, language, lingo, patois, patter, slang, vocabulary

dialectic *Syn* ARGUMENTATION, debate, disputation, forensic

diaphanous *Syn* CLEAR (sense 1), limpid, lucid, pellucid, translucent, transparent *Ant* confused, turbid

diatribe *Syn* TIRADE, jeremiad, philippic *Ant* eulogy

dice *Syn* CHOP, hash, mince

dicker *Syn* BARGAIN, chaffer, deal, haggle, horse-trade, negotiate, palter

dictate *vb* • to lay down expressly something to be followed, observed, obeyed, or accepted *Syn* decree, impose, ordain, prescribe *Rel* control, direct, manage

dictate *n* *Syn* COMMAND, behest, bidding, injunction, mandate, order

dictatorial **1** • imposing one's will or opinions on others *Syn* authoritarian, doctrinaire, dogmatic, magisterial *Rel* domineering, imperative, imperious, masterful, peremptory **2** *Syn* BOSSY, authoritarian, autocratic, despotic, domineering, imperious, masterful, overbearing, peremptory, tyrannical, tyrannous

diction *Syn* LANGUAGE (sense 2), phraseology, phrasing, style, vocabulary

dido *Syn* PRANK, antic, caper, monkeyshine

differ • to be unlike or out of harmony *Syn* disagree, dissent, vary *Rel* depart, deviate, diverge *Ant* agree

difference **1** *Syn* DISCORD, conflict, contention, dissension, schism, strife, variance **2** *Syn* DISSIMILARITY, distinction, divergence, divergency, unlikeness *Ant* similarity

different • unlike in kind or character *Syn* disparate, divergent, diverse, various *Rel* distinct, separate, several *Ant* alike, identical, same

differentiate *Syn* DISTINGUISH, demarcate, discriminate *Ant* confound

difficult *Syn* HARD, arduous *Ant* easy

difficulty • something which demands effort and endurance if it is to be overcome or one's end achieved *Syn* hardship, rigor, vicissitude *Rel* impediment, obstacle, obstruction, snag

diffident *Syn* SHY, bashful, coy, modest *Ant* obtrusive

diffuse *vb* *Syn* SPREAD, circulate, disseminate, propagate, radiate

diffuse *adj* *Syn* WORDY, prolix, redundant, verbose *Ant* compact, concise, crisp, pithy, succinct, terse

dig *vb* • to loosen and turn over or remove (as soil) with or as if with a spade *Syn* delve, excavate, grub, spade *Rel* enter, penetrate, pierce, probe

dig *n* *Syn* INSULT, affront, barb, dart, epithet, indignity, name, offense (*or* offence), outrage, put-down, sarcasm, slight, slur

digest *n* *Syn* COMPENDIUM, aperçu, pandect, précis, sketch, survey, syllabus

digest *vb* *Syn* SUMMARIZE, abstract, encapsulate, epitomize, outline, recap, recapitulate, sum up, wrap up

dig (into) *Syn* EXPLORE, delve (into), inquire (into), investigate, look (into), probe, research

digit *Syn* NUMBER, figure, integer, numeral

dignified • having or showing a serious and reserved manner *Syn* august, imposing, solemn, staid, stately *Rel* decorous, formal, proper, seemly *Ant* flighty, frivolous, giddy, goofy, silly, undignified

dignify **1** • to enhance the status of or raise in human estimation *Syn* ennoble, glorify, honor *Rel* elevate, lift, raise **2** *Syn* EXALT, aggrandize, ennoble, enshrine, glorify, magnify *Ant* abase, degrade, demean, humble, humiliate

dignity *Syn* DECORUM, decency, etiquette, propriety *Ant* indecorum, license

digress *Syn* SWERVE, depart, deviate, diverge, veer

digression • a departure from a subject or theme *Syn* divagation, episode, excursus

dike *Syn* DAM, embankment, levee

dilapidate *Syn* RUIN, wreck

dilapidated *Syn* SHABBY, dingy, faded, seedy, threadbare

dilate **1** *Syn* DISCOURSE, descant, expatiate **2** *Syn* EXPAND, amplify, distend, inflate, swell *Ant* abridge, circumscribe, contract

dilatory *Syn* SLOW, deliberate, laggard, leisurely *Ant* fast

dilemma *Syn* PREDICAMENT, fix, jam, pickle, plight, quandary, scrape

dilettante *n* **1** *Syn* AESTHETE, connoisseur **2** *Syn* AMATEUR, dabbler, tyro *Ant* expert, professional

dilettante *adj* *Syn* AMATEURISH, amateur, inexperienced, inexpert, nonprofessional, unprofessional, unskilled, unskillful *Ant* ace, adept, consummate, crackerjack, expert, master, masterful, masterly, professional, virtuoso

diligent *Syn* BUSY, assiduous, industrious, sedulous *Ant* idle, unoccupied

dilute **1** *Syn* IMPURE, adulterated, alloyed, contaminated, diluted, polluted, tainted, thinned, weakened *Ant* pure, unadulterated, unalloyed, uncontaminated, undiluted, unpolluted, untainted **2** *Syn* THIN, attenuate, extenuate, rarefy *Ant* thicken

diluted *Syn* IMPURE, adulterated, alloyed, contaminated, dilute, polluted, tainted, thinned, weakened *Ant* pure, unadulterated, unalloyed, uncontaminated, undiluted, unpolluted, untainted

dim *adj* *Syn* DARK, dusky, gloomy, murky, obscure *Ant* light

dim *vb* *Syn* OBSCURE, becloud, bedim, befog, cloud, darken, eclipse, fog, obfuscate *Ant* illuminate, illumine

dimensions *Syn* SIZE, area, extent, magnitude, volume

diminish *Syn* DECREASE, abate, dwindle, lessen, reduce *Ant* increase

din • a disturbing or confusing welter of sounds *Syn* babel, clamor, hubbub, hullabaloo, pandemonium, racket, uproar *Rel* blatancy, boisterousness, clamorousness, stridency *Ant* quiet

diner *Syn* RESTAURANT, café, grill

dingy *Syn* SHABBY, dilapidated, faded, seedy, threadbare

dinner • a usually elaborate meal served to guests or to a group often to mark an occasion or honor an individual *Syn* banquet, feast

dip **1** • to plunge a person or thing into or as if into liquid *Syn* duck, dunk, immerse, souse, submerge **2** • to remove a liquid or a loose or soft substance from a container by means of an implement shaped to hold liquid *Syn* bail, dish, ladle, scoop, spoon

dipsomaniac *Syn* DRUNKARD, alcoholic, inebriate, soak, sot, tippler, toper, tosspot *Ant* teetotaler

dire *Syn* OMINOUS, baleful, foreboding, inauspicious, menacing, portentous, sinister, threatening

direct **1** • to turn or bend one's attention or efforts toward a certain object or objective *Syn* address, apply, devote *Rel* bend **2** • to turn something toward its appointed or intended mark or goal *Syn* aim, lay, level, point, train *Rel* engineer, guide, lead, pilot, steer *Ant* misdirect **3** *Syn* CHANNEL, channelize, conduct, funnel, pipe, siphon **4** *Syn* COMMAND, bid, charge, enjoin, instruct, order *Ant* comply, obey **5** *Syn* CONDUCT, control, manage

directly *Syn* PRESENTLY, shortly, soon

directness *Syn* CANDOR, forthrightness, frankness, openheartedness, openness, plainness, straightforwardness *Ant* dissembling, pretense (*or* pretence)

director *Syn* EXECUTIVE, administrator, manager, superintendent, supervisor

dirty *adj* • conspicuously unclean or impure *Syn* filthy, foul, nasty, squalid *Ant* clean

dirty *vb* • to make dirty *Syn* befoul, begrime, besmirch, blacken, foul, grime, mire, muddy, smirch, smudge, soil, stain, sully *Rel* contaminate, defile, pollute, taint *Ant* clean, cleanse

disabuse *Syn* RID, clear, purge, unburden

disadvantage • a feature of someone or something that creates difficulty for achieving success *Syn* drawback, handicap, liability, minus, penalty, strike *Rel* stranglehold *Ant* advantage, asset, edge, plus

disadvantaged *Syn* DEPRIVED, underprivileged *Ant* privileged

disaffect *Syn* ESTRANGE, alienate, wean *Ant* reconcile

disaffection *Syn* ESTRANGEMENT, alienation, disgruntlement, souring *Ant* reconciliation

disagree *Syn* DIFFER, dissent, vary *Ant* agree

disagreeable *Syn* UNPLEASANT, bad, displeasing, distasteful, nasty, rotten, sour, uncongenial, unlovely, unpleasing, unsatisfying, unwelcome *Ant* agreeable, congenial, good, grateful, gratifying, nice, palatable, pleasant, pleasing, pleasurable, satisfying, welcome

disallow *Syn* DISCLAIM, disavow, disown, repudiate *Ant* claim

disallowance **1** *Syn* DENIAL (sense 1), nay, no, refusal, rejection *Ant* allowance, grant **2** *Syn* DENIAL (sense 2), contradiction, disavowal, disclaimer, negation, rejection, repudiation *Ant* acknowledgment, admission, avowal, confirmation

disappear *Syn* VANISH, evanesce, evaporate, fade *Ant* appear, loom

disappointment **1** • the emotion felt when one's expectations are not met *Syn* dismay, dissatisfaction, frustration, letdown *Rel* disenchantment, disillusionment *Ant* contentment, gratification, satisfaction **2** • something that disappoints *Syn* bummer, letdown *Rel* anticlimax, failure, fiasco, fizzle

disapprove (of) • to hold an unfavorable opinion of *Syn* deprecate, discountenance, disfavor, dislike, frown (on), reprove *Rel* blame, censure, condemn, criticize, denounce, reprehend, reprobate *Ant* approve, favor, like

disarm *Syn* PACIFY, appease, conciliate, mollify, placate, propitiate *Ant* anger, enrage, incense, infuriate, madden, outrage

disarming *Syn* LOVABLE, adorable, darling, dear, endearing, precious, sweet, winning *Ant* abhorrent, abominable, detestable, hateful, odious, unlovable

disarrange *Syn* DISORDER, confuse, derange, disarray, discompose, dishevel, dislocate, disorganize, disrupt, disturb, hash, jumble, mess (up), mix (up), muddle, muss, rumple, scramble, shuffle, tousle, tumble, upset *Ant* arrange, array, draw up, marshal, order, organize, range, regulate, straighten (up), tidy

disarranged *Syn* MESSY, chaotic, cluttered, confused, disarrayed, disheveled (*or* dishevelled), disordered, disorderly, higgledy-piggledy, hugger-mugger, jumbled, littered, messed, muddled, mussed, mussy, pell-mell, rumpled, sloppy, topsy-turvy, tousled, tumbled, unkempt, untidy, upside-down *Ant* neat, ordered, orderly, organized, shipshape, snug, tidied, tidy, trim

disarray *n* *Syn* CONFUSION, chaos, clutter, disorder, jumble, muddle, snarl

disarray *vb* *Syn* DISORDER, confuse, derange, disarrange, discompose, dishevel, dislocate, disorganize, disrupt, disturb, hash, jumble, mess (up), mix (up), muddle, muss, rumple, scramble, shuffle, tousle, tumble, upset *Ant* arrange, array, draw up, marshal, order, organize, range, regulate, straighten (up), tidy

disarrayed *Syn* MESSY, chaotic, cluttered, confused, disarranged, disheveled (*or* dishevelled), disordered, disorderly, higgledy-piggledy, hugger-mugger, jumbled, littered, messed, muddled, mussed, mussy, pell-mell, rumpled, sloppy, topsy-turvy, tousled, tumbled, unkempt, untidy, upside-down *Ant* neat, ordered, orderly, organized, shipshape, snug, tidied, tidy, trim

disaster • an event bringing great damage, loss, or destruction *Syn* apocalypse, calamity, cataclysm, catastrophe *Rel* accident, casualty, mishap

disastrous *Syn* UNLUCKY, calamitous, hapless, ill-fated, ill-starred, luckless, unfortunate *Ant* fortunate, happy, lucky

disavow *Syn* DISCLAIM, disallow, disown, repudiate *Ant* claim

disavowal *Syn* DENIAL (sense 2), contradiction, disallowance, disclaimer, negation, rejection, repudiation *Ant* acknowledgment, admission, avowal, confirmation

disbar *Syn* EXCLUDE, blackball, debar, eliminate, rule out, shut out, suspend *Ant* admit, include

disbelief *Syn* UNBELIEF, incredulity *Ant* belief

disbeliever *Syn* SKEPTIC, doubter, questioner, unbeliever

disburse *Syn* SPEND, expend *Ant* save

discard • to get rid of *Syn* cast, junk, molt, scrap, shed, slough *Rel* abandon, desert, forsake

discern *Syn* SEE (sense 1), behold, contemplate, descry, espy, note, notice, observe, perceive, remark, survey, view

discernible *Syn* PERCEPTIBLE, appreciable, detectable, distinguishable, palpable, sensible *Ant* impalpable, imperceptible, inappreciable, indistinguishable, insensible

discernment • a power to see what is not evident to the average mind *Syn* acumen, discrimination, insight, penetration, perception *Rel* intuition, reason, understanding

discharge **1** *Syn* DISMISS, bounce, cashier, drop, fire, sack **2** *Syn* FREE, emancipate, liberate, manumit, release **3** *Syn* PERFORM, accomplish, achieve, effect, execute, fulfill

disciple *Syn* FOLLOWER, adherent, convert, partisan, pupil, votary *Ant* leader

disciplinary *Syn* PUNITIVE, castigating, chastening, chastising, correcting, correctional, corrective, disciplining, penal, penalizing

discipline *n Syn* MORALE, esprit de corps

discipline *vb* **1** *Syn* PUNISH, castigate, chasten, chastise, correct *Ant* excuse, pardon **2** *Syn* TEACH, educate, instruct, school, train

disciplining *Syn* PUNITIVE, castigating, chastening, chastising, correcting, correctional, corrective, disciplinary, penal, penalizing

disclaim • to refuse to admit, accept, or approve *Syn* disallow, disavow, disown, repudiate *Rel* contradict, deny, gainsay, traverse *Ant* claim

disclaimer *Syn* DENIAL (sense 2), contradiction, disallowance, disavowal, negation, rejection, repudiation *Ant* acknowledgment, admission, avowal, confirmation

disclose *Syn* REVEAL, betray, discover, divulge, tell *Ant* conceal

disclosure *Syn* REVELATION (sense 2), divulgence, exposure

discomfit *Syn* EMBARRASS, abash, disconcert, faze, rattle *Ant* facilitate, relieve

discomforting *Syn* TROUBLESOME, discomposing, disquieting, distressing, disturbing, perturbing, troubling, troublous, unsettling, upsetting, worrisome *Ant* reassuring, untroublesome

discommode *Syn* INCONVENIENCE, disoblige, disturb, incommode, trouble *Ant* accommodate, oblige

discompose **1** • to excite one so as to destroy one's capacity for clear or collected thought or prompt action *Syn* agitate, disquiet, disturb, flurry, fluster, perturb, upset *Rel* discomfit, disconcert, embarrass, faze, rattle **2** *Syn* DISORDER, confuse, derange, disarrange, disarray, dishevel, dislocate, disorganize, disrupt, disturb, hash, jumble, mess (up), mix (up), muddle, muss, rumple, scramble, shuffle, tousle, tumble, upset *Ant* arrange, array, draw up, marshal, order, organize, range, regulate, straighten (up), tidy

discomposing *Syn* TROUBLESOME, discomforting, disquieting, distressing, disturbing, perturbing, troubling, troublous, unsettling, upsetting, worrisome *Ant* reassuring, untroublesome

disconcert *Syn* EMBARRASS, abash, discomfit, faze, rattle *Ant* facilitate, relieve

disconsolate *Syn* SAD (sense 1), bad, blue, brokenhearted, crestfallen, dejected, depressed, despondent, doleful, down, downcast, downhearted, droopy, forlorn, gloomy, glum, heartbroken, heartsick, heartsore, inconsolable, joyless, low, low-spirited, melancholy, miserable, mournful, saddened, sorrowful, sorry, unhappy, woebegone, woeful, wretched *Ant* blissful, buoyant, buoyed, cheerful, cheery, chipper, delighted, glad, gladdened, gladsome, gleeful, happy, joyful, joyous, jubilant, sunny, upbeat

disconsolateness *Syn* SADNESS, blues, dejection, depression, desolation, despondency, dispiritedness, doldrums, downheartedness, dreariness, dumps, forlornness, gloom, gloominess, heartsickness, joylessness, melancholy, mopes, oppression, unhappiness *Ant* bliss, blissfulness, ecstasy, elatedness, elation, euphoria, exhilaration, exuberance, exultation, felicity, gladness, gladsomeness, happiness, heaven, intoxication, joy, joyfulness, joyousness, jubilation, rapture, rapturousness

discontinue *Syn* STOP, cease, desist, quit

discontinuous *Syn* FITFUL, casual, choppy, erratic, intermittent, irregular, occasional, spasmodic, sporadic, spotty, unsteady *Ant* constant, continuous, regular, steady

discord • a state or condition marked by disagreement and lack of harmony *Syn* conflict, contention, difference, dissension, schism, strife, variance *Rel* discrepancy, incompatibility, incongruity, inconsistency, inconsonance, uncongeniality

discordant **1** *Syn* BELLIGERENT, aggressive, argumentative, bellicose, combative, contentious, disputatious, gladiatorial, militant, pugnacious, quarrelsome, scrappy, truculent, warlike *Ant* nonbelligerent, pacific, peaceable, peaceful **2** *Syn* INCONSONANT, discrepant, incompatible, incongruous, inconsistent, uncongenial, unsympathetic *Ant* consonant

discount *Syn* DEDUCTION, abatement, rebate

discountenance *Syn* DISAPPROVE (OF), deprecate, disfavor, dislike, frown (on), reprove *Ant* approve, favor, like

discourage **1** • to lessen the courage or confidence of *Syn* daunt, demoralize, dishearten, dismay, dispirit, unnerve *Rel* browbeat, bully, cow, intimidate *Ant* embolden, encourage, hearten, nerve, steel **2** • to steer (a person) from an activity or course of action *Syn* deter, dissuade, inhibit *Rel* divert *Ant* encourage, persuade

discourse *n* • a systematic, serious, and often learned exposition of a subject or topic *Syn* disquisition, dissertation, monograph, thesis, treatise *Rel* article, essay, paper

discourse *vb* • to talk or sometimes write especially formally and at length upon a subject *Syn* descant, dilate, expatiate *Rel* argue, discuss, dispute

discourteous *Syn* IMPOLITE, ill-bred, ill-mannered, impertinent, inconsiderate, rude, thoughtless, uncalled-for, uncivil, ungracious, unmannerly *Ant* civil, considerate, courteous, genteel, gracious, mannerly, polite, thoughtful, well-bred

discover **1** • to find out something not previously known *Syn* ascertain, determine, learn, unearth *Rel* discern, espy, observe, perceive **2** *Syn* REVEAL, betray, disclose, divulge, tell *Ant* conceal

discreet *Syn* PRUDENT, foresighted, forethoughtful, provident

discreetness *Syn* COMMON SENSE, discretion, horse sense, levelheadedness, prudence, sense, sensibleness, wisdom, wit *Ant* imprudence, indiscretion

discrepant *Syn* INCONSONANT, discordant, incompatible, incongruous, inconsistent, uncongenial, unsympathetic *Ant* consonant

discrete *Syn* DISTINCT, separate, several

discretion **1** *Syn* COMMON SENSE, discreetness, horse sense, levelheadedness, prudence, sense, sensibleness, wisdom, wit *Ant* imprudence, indiscretion **2** *Syn* PRUDENCE, foresight, forethought, providence

discretionary *Syn* OPTIONAL, elective, voluntary *Ant* compulsory, mandatory, nonelective, obligatory, required

discriminate *Syn* DISTINGUISH, demarcate, differentiate *Ant* confound

discrimination *Syn* DISCERNMENT, acumen, insight, penetration, perception

discuss • to exchange views about something in order to arrive at the truth or to convince others *Syn* agitate, argue, debate, dispute *Rel* elucidate, explain, explicate, expound, interpret

disdain *n* *Syn* CONTEMPT, despite, despitefulness, scorn *Ant* admiration, esteem, regard, respect

disdain *vb* *Syn* DESPISE, contemn, scorn, scout *Ant* appreciate

disdainful *Syn* PROUD (sense 1), arrogant, haughty, insolent, lordly, overbearing, supercilious *Ant* ashamed, humble

disease • an impairment of the normal state of the living body that interferes with normal bodily functions *Syn* ailment, complaint, condition, disorder, distemper, malady, syndrome

diseased *Syn* UNWHOLESOME, morbid, pathological, sickly *Ant* wholesome

disembarrass *Syn* EXTRICATE, disencumber, disentangle, untangle

disencumber *Syn* EXTRICATE, disembarrass, disentangle, untangle

disengage *Syn* DETACH, abstract *Ant* affix, attach

disentangle *Syn* EXTRICATE, disembarrass, disencumber, untangle

disfavor *vb* *Syn* DISAPPROVE (OF), deprecate, discountenance, dislike, frown (on), reprove *Ant* approve, favor, like

disfavor *n* *Syn* DISLIKE, aversion, distaste *Ant* liking

disfigurement *Syn* BLEMISH, defect, deformity, fault, flaw, imperfection, mark, pockmark, scar

disgorge **1** *Syn* BELCH, burp, regurgitate, spew, throw up, vomit **2** *Syn* ERUPT (sense 2), belch, eject, expel, jet, spew, spout, spurt

disgrace • the state of suffering loss of esteem and of enduring reproach *Syn* dishonor, disrepute, ignominy, infamy, obloquy, odium, opprobrium, shame *Rel* abasement, debasement, degradation, humbling, humiliation *Ant* esteem, respect

disgruntlement *Syn* ESTRANGEMENT, alienation, disaffection, souring *Ant* reconciliation

disguise • to alter so as to hide the true appearance or character of *Syn* camouflage, cloak, dissemble, mask *Rel* conceal, hide

disgust *n* • a dislike so strong as to cause stomach upset or queasiness *Syn* aversion, distaste, loathing, nausea, repugnance, repulsion, revulsion *Rel* abhorrence, abomination, execration, hate, hatred

disgust *vb* • to cause to feel disgust *Syn* nauseate, repel, repulse, revolt, sicken, turn off *Rel* displease, distress

dish *Syn* DIP (sense 2), bail, ladle, scoop, spoon

dishearten *Syn* DISCOURAGE (sense 1), daunt, demoralize, dismay, dispirit, unnerve *Ant* embolden, encourage, hearten, nerve, steel

dishevel *Syn* DISORDER, confuse, derange, disarrange, disarray, discompose, dislocate, disorganize, disrupt, disturb, hash, jumble, mess (up), mix (up), muddle, muss, rumple, scramble, shuffle, tousle, tumble, upset *Ant* arrange, array, draw up, marshal, order, organize, range, regulate, straighten (up), tidy

disheveled **1** *Syn* SLIPSHOD, sloppy, slovenly, unkempt **2** *Syn* MESSY, chaotic, cluttered, confused, disarranged, disarrayed, disordered, disorderly, higgledy-piggledy, hugger-mugger, jumbled, littered, messed, muddled, mussed, mussy, pell-mell, rumpled, sloppy, topsy-turvy, tousled, tumbled, unkempt, untidy, upside-down *Ant* neat, ordered, orderly, organized, shipshape, snug, tidied, tidy, trim

dishonor *Syn* DISGRACE, disrepute, ignominy, infamy, obloquy, odium, opprobrium, shame *Ant* esteem, respect

disinclination *Syn* RELUCTANCE, hesitance, hesitancy, unwillingness *Ant* inclination, willingness

disinclined • lacking the will or the desire to do something *Syn* averse, hesitant, indisposed, loath, reluctant *Rel* antipathetic, unsympathetic

disinfect *Syn* STERILIZE (sense 2), fumigate, sanitize

disintegrate *Syn* DECAY, crumble, decompose, putrefy, rot, spoil

disinterested *Syn* INDIFFERENT, aloof, detached, incurious, unconcerned, uninterested *Ant* avid

disinterestedness **1** *Syn* DETACHMENT, impartiality, neutrality, objectivity *Ant* bias, favor, favoritism, one-sidedness, partiality, partisanship, prejudice **2** *Syn* INDIFFERENCE, apathy, casualness, disregard, insouciance, nonchalance, unconcern *Ant* concern, interest, regard

dislike *n* • a feeling of aversion or disapproval *Syn* aversion, disfavor, distaste *Rel* detestation, hate, hatred *Ant* liking

dislike *vb* *Syn* DISAPPROVE (OF), deprecate, discountenance, disfavor, frown (on), reprove *Ant* approve, favor, like

dislocate *Syn* DISORDER, confuse, derange, disarrange, disarray, discompose, dishevel, disorganize, disrupt, disturb, hash, jumble, mess (up), mix (up), muddle, muss, rumple, scramble, shuffle, tousle, tumble, upset *Ant* arrange, array, draw up, marshal, order, organize, range, regulate, straighten (up), tidy

disloyal *Syn* FAITHLESS, false, perfidious, traitorous, treacherous *Ant* faithful

disloyalty *Syn* BETRAYAL, double cross, faithlessness, falseness, falsity, infidelity, perfidy, sellout, treachery, treason, unfaithfulness

dismal **1** • devoid of all that makes for cheer or comfort *Syn* bleak, cheerless, desolate, dispiriting, dreary *Rel* dark, gloomy, murky **2** *Syn* SAD (sense 2), depressing, drear, dreary, heartbreaking, heartrending, melancholy, pathetic, saddening, sorry, tearful, teary *Ant* cheering, cheery, glad, happy

dismantle *Syn* STRIP, bare, denude, divest *Ant* furnish, invest

dismay *vb* **1** • to unnerve and check by arousing fear, apprehension, or aversion *Syn* appall, daunt, horrify *Rel* bewilder, confound, dumbfound, mystify, nonplus, perplex, puzzle *Ant* cheer **2** *Syn* DISCOURAGE (sense 1), daunt, demoralize, dishearten, dispirit, unnerve *Ant* embolden, encourage, hearten, nerve, steel

dismay *n* **1** *Syn* DISAPPOINTMENT (sense 1), dissatisfaction, frustration, letdown *Ant* contentment, gratification, satisfaction **2** *Syn* FEAR, alarm, consternation, dread, fright, horror, panic, terror, trepidation *Ant* fearlessness

dismiss • to let go from one's employ or service *Syn* bounce, cashier, discharge, drop, fire, sack

dismount *Syn* DESCEND, alight *Ant* ascend, climb

disobedience • refusal to obey *Syn* contrariness, defiance, frowardness, insubordination, intractability, rebelliousness, recalcitrance, refractoriness, unruliness, willfulness *Rel* disrespect, impudence, insolence, rudeness *Ant* amenability, compliance, docility, obedience

disobedient • given to resisting authority or another's control *Syn* balky, contrary, defiant, froward, insubordinate, intractable, rebellious, recalcitrant, refractory, restive, ungovernable, unruly, untoward, wayward, willful (*or* wilful) *Rel* insurgent, mutinous *Ant* amenable, compliant, docile, obedient, tractable

disoblige *Syn* INCONVENIENCE, discommode, disturb, incommode, trouble *Ant* accommodate, oblige

disorder *vb* • to undo the proper order or arrangement of *Syn* confuse, derange, disarrange, disarray, discompose, dishevel, dislocate, disorganize, disrupt, disturb, hash, jumble, mess (up), mix (up), muddle, muss, rumple, scramble, shuffle, tousle, tumble, upset *Rel* embroil, entangle, snarl, tangle *Ant* arrange, array, draw up, marshal, order, organize, range, regulate, straighten (up), tidy

disorder *n* **1** *Syn* CONFUSION, chaos, clutter, disarray, jumble, muddle, snarl **2** *Syn* DISEASE, ailment, complaint, condition, distemper, malady, syndrome

disordered *Syn* MESSY, chaotic, cluttered, confused, disarranged, disarrayed, disheveled (*or* dishevelled), disorderly, higgledy-piggledy, hugger-mugger, jumbled, littered, messed, muddled, mussed, mussy, pell-mell, rumpled, sloppy, topsy-turvy, tousled, tumbled, unkempt, untidy, upside-down *Ant* neat, ordered, orderly, organized, shipshape, snug, tidied, tidy, trim

disorderly 1 *Syn* LAWLESS, anarchic, lawbreaking, unruly *Ant* law-abiding, orderly 2 *Syn* MESSY, chaotic, cluttered, confused, disarranged, disarrayed, disheveled (*or* dishevelled), disordered, higgledy-piggledy, hugger-mugger, jumbled, littered, messed, muddled, mussed, mussy, pell-mell, rumpled, sloppy, topsy-turvy, tousled, tumbled, unkempt, untidy, upside-down *Ant* neat, ordered, orderly, organized, shipshape, snug, tidied, tidy, trim
disorganize *Syn* DISORDER, confuse, derange, disarrange, disarray, discompose, dishevel, dislocate, disrupt, disturb, hash, jumble, mess (up), mix (up), muddle, muss, rumple, scramble, shuffle, tousle, tumble, upset *Ant* arrange, array, draw up, marshal, order, organize, range, regulate, straighten (up), tidy
disown *Syn* DISCLAIM, disallow, disavow, repudiate *Ant* claim
disparage *Syn* DECRY, belittle, deprecate, derogate, detract, minimize *Ant* extol
disparaging *Syn* DEROGATORY, depreciative, depreciatory, pejorative, slighting
disparate *Syn* DIFFERENT, divergent, diverse, various *Ant* alike, identical, same
dispassionate *Syn* FAIR, equitable, impartial, just, objective, unbiased, uncolored *Ant* unfair
dispatch *n* 1 *Syn* HASTE, expedition, hurry, speed *Ant* deliberation 2 *Syn* LETTER, epistle, memorandum, message, missive, note, report
dispatch *vb* 1 *Syn* KILL, assassinate, execute, murder, slay 2 *Syn* SEND, forward, remit, route, ship, transmit *Ant* accept, receive
dispel *Syn* SCATTER (sense 1), disperse, dissipate
dispensable *Syn* UNNECESSARY, gratuitous, needless, nonessential, uncalled-for, unessential, unwarranted *Ant* essential, indispensable, necessary, needed, needful, required
dispense *Syn* DISTRIBUTE, deal, divide, dole *Ant* amass, collect
disperse *Syn* SCATTER (sense 1), dispel, dissipate
dispirit *Syn* DISCOURAGE (sense 1), daunt, demoralize, dishearten, dismay, unnerve *Ant* embolden, encourage, hearten, nerve, steel
dispiritedness *Syn* SADNESS, blues, dejection, depression, desolation, despondency, disconsolateness, doldrums, downheartedness, dreariness, dumps, forlornness, gloom, gloominess, heartsickness, joylessness, melancholy, mopes, oppression, unhappiness *Ant* bliss, blissfulness, ecstasy, elatedness, elation, euphoria, exhilaration, exuberance, exultation, felicity, gladness, gladsomeness, happiness, heaven, intoxication, joy, joyfulness, joyousness, jubilation, rapture, rapturousness
dispiriting *Syn* DISMAL, bleak, cheerless, desolate, dreary
displace *Syn* REPLACE, supersede, supplant
display *n* • a striking or spectacular show or exhibition for the sake of effect *Syn* array, parade, pomp *Rel* ostentation, ostentatiousness, pretension, pretentiousness, show, showiness
display *vb Syn* SHOW (sense 2), exhibit, expose, flaunt, parade *Ant* disguise
displeasing *Syn* UNPLEASANT, bad, disagreeable, distasteful, nasty, rotten, sour, uncongenial, unlovely, unpleasing, unsatisfying, unwelcome *Ant* agreeable, congenial, good, grateful, gratifying, nice, palatable, pleasant, pleasing, pleasurable, satisfying, welcome
disport *n Syn* PLAY, frolic, gambol, rollick, romp, sport *Ant* work
disport *vb Syn* PLAY, frolic, gambol, rollick, romp, sport
dispose *Syn* INCLINE, bias, predispose *Ant* disincline, indispose
disposition • the prevailing and dominant quality or qualities which distinguish or identify a person or group *Syn* character, complexion, individuality, personality, temper, temperament
disprove • to show by presenting evidence that something is not true *Syn* confute, controvert, rebut, refute *Rel* contravene, impugn, negative, traverse *Ant* demonstrate, prove
disputation *Syn* ARGUMENTATION, debate, dialectic, forensic
disputatious *Syn* BELLIGERENT, aggressive, argumentative, bellicose, combative, contentious, discordant, gladiatorial, militant, pugnacious, quarrelsome, scrappy, truculent, warlike *Ant* nonbelligerent, pacific, peaceable, peaceful
disputatiousness *Syn* BELLIGERENCE, aggression, aggressiveness, bellicosity, combativeness, contentiousness, fight, militancy, pugnacity, scrappiness, truculence *Ant* pacifism
dispute *n Syn* ARGUMENT, controversy
dispute *vb Syn* DISCUSS, agitate, argue, debate
disquiet *vb Syn* DISCOMPOSE, agitate, disturb, flurry, fluster, perturb, upset
disquiet *n Syn* UNREST, ferment, restiveness, restlessness, turmoil, uneasiness *Ant* calm, ease, peace, quiet
disquieting *Syn* TROUBLESOME, discomforting, discomposing, distressing, disturbing, perturbing, troubling, troublous, unsettling, upsetting, worrisome *Ant* reassuring, untroublesome
disquisition *Syn* DISCOURSE, dissertation, monograph, thesis, treatise
disrate *Syn* DEGRADE, declass, demote, reduce *Ant* elevate
disregard *n Syn* INDIFFERENCE, apathy, casualness, disinterestedness, insouciance, nonchalance, unconcern *Ant* concern, interest, regard
disregard *vb* 1 *Syn* NEGLECT, forget, ignore, omit, overlook, slight *Ant* cherish 2 *Syn*

SCORN (sense 1), despise, flout *Ant* honor, respect

disrepute *Syn* DISGRACE, dishonor, ignominy, infamy, obloquy, odium, opprobrium, shame *Ant* esteem, respect

disrupt *Syn* DISORDER, confuse, derange, disarrange, disarray, discompose, dishevel, dislocate, disorganize, disturb, hash, jumble, mess (up), mix (up), muddle, muss, rumple, scramble, shuffle, tousle, tumble, upset *Ant* arrange, array, draw up, marshal, order, organize, range, regulate, straighten (up), tidy

dissatisfaction *Syn* DISAPPOINTMENT (sense 1), dismay, frustration, letdown *Ant* contentment, gratification, satisfaction

dissect *Syn* ANALYZE, anatomize, assay, break down

dissection *Syn* ANALYSIS, breakdown, resolution *Ant* synthesis

dissemble *Syn* DISGUISE, camouflage, cloak, mask

dissembling *Syn* HYPOCRISY, cant, dissimulation, insincerity, piousness, sanctimoniousness *Ant* genuineness, sincerity

disseminate *Syn* SPREAD, circulate, diffuse, propagate, radiate

dissension *Syn* DISCORD, conflict, contention, difference, schism, strife, variance

dissent *vb Syn* DIFFER, disagree, vary *Ant* agree

dissent *n Syn* HERESY, dissidence, heterodoxy, nonconformity *Ant* conformity, orthodoxy

dissenter *Syn* HERETIC, dissident, nonconformist *Ant* conformer, conformist

dissertation *Syn* DISCOURSE, disquisition, monograph, thesis, treatise

disservice • unfair or inadequate treatment of someone or something or an instance of this *Syn* injury, injustice, raw deal, wrong *Rel* insult, offense, outrage *Ant* justice

dissidence *Syn* HERESY, dissent, heterodoxy, nonconformity *Ant* conformity, orthodoxy

dissimilarity • lack of agreement or correspondence or an instance of this *Syn* difference, distinction, divergence, divergency, unlikeness *Rel* disparity, diversity *Ant* similarity

dissimulation **1** *Syn* DECEIT, cunning, duplicity, guile **2** *Syn* HYPOCRISY, cant, dissembling, insincerity, piousness, sanctimoniousness *Ant* genuineness, sincerity

dissipate **1** *Syn* SCATTER (sense 1), dispel, disperse **2** *Syn* WASTE, consume, fritter, squander *Ant* conserve, save

dissipated *Syn* CORRUPT, debased, debauched, decadent, degenerate, degraded, demoralized, depraved, dissolute, perverse, perverted, reprobate, warped *Ant* uncorrupted

dissolute **1** *Syn* ABANDONED (sense 1), profligate, reprobate *Ant* redeemed, regenerate **2** *Syn* CORRUPT, debased, debauched, decadent, degenerate, degraded, demoralized, depraved, dissipated, perverse, perverted, reprobate, warped *Ant* uncorrupted

dissolve *Syn* ABOLISH, abrogate, annul, cancel, invalidate, negate, nullify, quash, repeal, rescind, void

dissuade *Syn* DISCOURAGE (sense 2), deter, inhibit *Ant* encourage, persuade

distant • not close in space, time, or relationship *Syn* far, faraway, far-off, remote, removed

distaste **1** *Syn* DISGUST, aversion, loathing, nausea, repugnance, repulsion, revulsion **2** *Syn* DISLIKE, aversion, disfavor *Ant* liking

distasteful **1** *Syn* REPUGNANT, abhorrent, invidious, obnoxious, repellent *Ant* congenial **2** *Syn* UNPLEASANT, bad, disagreeable, displeasing, nasty, rotten, sour, uncongenial, unlovely, unpleasing, unsatisfying, unwelcome *Ant* agreeable, congenial, good, grateful, gratifying, nice, palatable, pleasant, pleasing, pleasurable, satisfying, welcome

distemper *Syn* DISEASE, ailment, complaint, condition, disorder, malady, syndrome

distend *Syn* EXPAND, amplify, dilate, inflate, swell *Ant* abridge, circumscribe, contract

distinct **1** • capable of being distinguished as differing *Syn* discrete, separate, several *Rel* distinctive, individual, peculiar **2** *Syn* EVIDENT, apparent, clear, manifest, obvious, palpable, patent, plain

distinction **1** *Syn* AWARD, decoration, honor, plume, premium, prize **2** *Syn* DISSIMILARITY, difference, divergence, divergency, unlikeness *Ant* similarity **3** *Syn* EXCELLENCE, excellency, merit, value, virtue *Ant* deficiency

distinctive *Syn* CHARACTERISTIC, individual, peculiar

distinguish **1** • to recognize the differences between *Syn* demarcate, differentiate, discriminate *Rel* divide, part, separate *Ant* confound **2** *Syn* CHARACTERIZE, mark, qualify

distinguishable *Syn* PERCEPTIBLE, appreciable, detectable, discernible, palpable, sensible *Ant* impalpable, imperceptible, inappreciable, indistinguishable, insensible

distinguished *Syn* EMINENT, illustrious, noble, notable, noteworthy, outstanding, preeminent, prestigious, signal, star, superior

distort *Syn* DEFORM, contort, warp

distract *Syn* PUZZLE, bewilder, confound, dumbfound, mystify, nonplus, perplex

distraction *Syn* FRENZY, agitation, delirium, furor, furore, fury, hysteria, rage, rampage, uproar

distraught *Syn* ABSTRACTED, absent, absent-minded, preoccupied *Ant* alert

distress *n* **1** • the state of being in great trouble or in mental or physical anguish *Syn* agony, dolor, misery, passion, suffering *Rel* affliction, trial, tribulation **2** *Syn* DANGER (sense 2), endangerment, imperilment, jeopardy, peril, risk, trouble *Ant* safeness, safety, security

distress *vb Syn* TROUBLE, ail
distressful *Syn* REGRETTABLE, deplorable, distressing, grievous, heartbreaking, heart-rending, lamentable, unfortunate, woeful
distressing **1** *Syn* REGRETTABLE, deplorable, distressful, grievous, heartbreaking, heartrending, lamentable, unfortunate, woeful **2** *Syn* TROUBLESOME, discomforting, discomposing, disquieting, disturbing, perturbing, troubling, troublous, unsettling, upsetting, worrisome *Ant* reassuring, untroublesome
distribute • to give out, usually in shares, to each member of a group *Syn* deal, dispense, divide, dole *Rel* allocate, allot, apportion, assign *Ant* amass, collect
district *Syn* LOCALITY, neighborhood, vicinity
distrust *vb* • to have no trust or confidence in *Syn* doubt, mistrust, question, suspect *Rel* disbelieve, discount, discredit, negate *Ant* trust
distrust *n Syn* DOUBT, distrustfulness, incertitude, misgiving, mistrust, mistrustfulness, skepticism, suspicion, uncertainty *Ant* assurance, belief, certainty, certitude, confidence, conviction, sureness, surety, trust
distrustfully *Syn* ASKANCE, doubtfully, doubtingly, dubiously, mistrustfully, skeptically, suspiciously *Ant* trustfully, trustingly
distrustfulness *Syn* DOUBT, distrust, incertitude, misgiving, mistrust, mistrustfulness, skepticism, suspicion, uncertainty *Ant* assurance, belief, certainty, certitude, confidence, conviction, sureness, surety, trust
disturb **1** *Syn* DISCOMPOSE, agitate, disquiet, flurry, fluster, perturb, upset **2** *Syn* DISORDER, confuse, derange, disarrange, disarray, discompose, dishevel, dislocate, disorganize, disrupt, hash, jumble, mess (up), mix (up), muddle, muss, rumple, scramble, shuffle, tousle, tumble, upset *Ant* arrange, array, draw up, marshal, order, organize, range, regulate, straighten (up), tidy **3** *Syn* INCONVENIENCE, discommode, disoblige, incommode, trouble *Ant* accommodate, oblige
disturbance *Syn* COMMOTION, bother, bustle, clatter, furor, furore, fuss, hubbub, hullabaloo, hurly-burly, pandemonium, pother, row, ruckus, ruction, rumpus, shindy, squall, stew, stir, storm, to-do, tumult, turmoil, uproar, welter, whirl
disturbing **1** *Syn* ANNOYING, aggravating, bothersome, exasperating, frustrating, galling, irksome, irritating, maddening, nettling, peeving, pesty, rankling, riling, vexatious, vexing **2** *Syn* TROUBLESOME, discomforting, discomposing, disquieting, distressing, perturbing, troubling, troublous, unsettling, upsetting, worrisome *Ant* reassuring, untroublesome
disused *Syn* ABANDONED (sense 2), derelict, deserted, forgotten, forsaken, rejected, vacated
dither *Syn* SHAKE (sense 1), quake, quaver, quiver, shimmy, shiver, shudder, teeter, totter, tremble, wobble
diurnal *Syn* DAILY, day-to-day
divagation *Syn* DIGRESSION, episode, excursus
divan *Syn* COUCH, chesterfield, davenport, lounge, settee, sofa
dive *Syn* PLUNGE, pitch
diverge *Syn* SWERVE, depart, deviate, digress, veer
divergence **1** *Syn* DEVIATION, aberration, deflection **2** *Syn* DISSIMILARITY, difference, distinction, divergency, unlikeness *Ant* similarity
divergency *Syn* DISSIMILARITY, difference, distinction, divergence, unlikeness *Ant* similarity
divergent *Syn* DIFFERENT, disparate, diverse, various *Ant* alike, identical, same
divers *Syn* MANY, multifarious, numerous, several, sundry, various *Ant* few
diverse *Syn* DIFFERENT, disparate, divergent, various *Ant* alike, identical, same
diversion *Syn* AMUSEMENT, entertainment, recreation *Ant* boredom
divert **1** *Syn* AMUSE, entertain, recreate *Ant* bore **2** *Syn* TURN (sense 2), avert, deflect, sheer
diverting *Syn* FUN, amusing, delightful, enjoyable, entertaining, pleasurable *Ant* boring, dull
divest *Syn* STRIP, bare, denude, dismantle *Ant* furnish, invest
divide **1** *Syn* DISTRIBUTE, deal, dispense, dole *Ant* amass, collect **2** *Syn* SEPARATE, divorce, part, sever, sunder *Ant* combine
dividend *Syn* BONUS, extra, gratuity, gravy, lagniappe, perquisite, tip
divine *adj Syn* EXCELLENT, A1, bang-up, banner, capital, classic, crackerjack, dandy, fabulous, fine, first-class, first-rate, grand, great, groovy, heavenly, jim-dandy, keen, marvelous (*or* marvellous), mean, neat, nifty, noble, par excellence, prime, sensational, splendid, stellar, sterling, superb, superior, superlative, supernal, swell, terrific, tip-top, top, top-notch, unsurpassed, wonderful *Ant* poor
divine *vb Syn* FORESEE, anticipate, apprehend, foreknow
diviner *Syn* PROPHET, augur, forecaster, foreseer, foreteller, fortune-teller, futurist, prognosticator, prophesier, seer, soothsayer
division *Syn* PART, detail, fraction, fragment, member, parcel, piece, portion, section, sector, segment *Ant* whole
divorce *Syn* SEPARATE, divide, part, sever, sunder *Ant* combine
divulge *Syn* REVEAL, betray, disclose, discover, tell *Ant* conceal
divulgence *Syn* REVELATION (sense 2), disclosure, exposure

dizzy *Syn* GIDDY, dazzled, swimming, vertiginous
docile *Syn* OBEDIENT, amenable, compliant, conformable, law-abiding, submissive, tractable *Ant* contrary, disobedient, froward, insubordinate, intractable, rebellious, recalcitrant, refractory, unruly
dock *vb Syn* CLIP, bob, crop, curtail, cut, cut back, lop (off), nip, pare, prune, shave, shear, snip, trim
dock *n Syn* WHARF, berth, jetty, levee, pier, quay, slip
doctor *Syn* ADULTERATE, load, sophisticate, weight *Ant* refine
doctrinaire *Syn* DICTATORIAL, authoritarian, dogmatic, magisterial
doctrine • a principle accepted as valid and authoritative *Syn* dogma, tenet *Rel* instruction, teaching
document **1** • something preserved and serving as evidence (as of an event, a situation, or the culture of the period) *Syn* archive, monument, record *Rel* evidence, testimony **2** *Syn* PAPER, instrument
dodge • to avoid or evade by some maneuver or shift *Syn* duck, fence, malinger, parry, shirk, sidestep *Rel* avoid, elude, escape, evade *Ant* face
dogged **1** *Syn* OBSTINATE, adamant, adamantine, hard, hardened, hardheaded, hardhearted, headstrong, immovable, implacable, inflexible, mulish, obdurate, opinionated, ossified, pat, peevish, pertinacious, perverse, pigheaded, rigid, self-willed, stubborn, unbending, uncompromising, unrelenting, unyielding, willful (*or* wilful) *Ant* acquiescent, agreeable, amenable, compliant, complying, flexible, pliable, pliant, relenting, yielding **2** *Syn* PERSISTENT, insistent, patient, persevering, pertinacious, tenacious
dogging *Syn* PURSUIT, chase, chasing, following, hounding, pursuing, shadowing, tagging, tailing, tracing, tracking, trailing
dogma *Syn* DOCTRINE, tenet
dogmatic *Syn* DICTATORIAL, authoritarian, doctrinaire, magisterial
doldrums **1** *Syn* ABEYANCE, dormancy, latency, quiescence, suspense, suspension *Ant* continuance, continuation **2** *Syn* SADNESS, blues, dejection, depression, desolation, despondency, disconsolateness, dispiritedness, downheartedness, dreariness, dumps, forlornness, gloom, gloominess, heartsickness, joylessness, melancholy, mopes, oppression, unhappiness *Ant* bliss, blissfulness, ecstasy, elatedness, elation, euphoria, exhilaration, exuberance, exultation, felicity, gladness, gladsomeness, happiness, heaven, intoxication, joy, joyfulness, joyousness, jubilation, rapture, rapturousness **3** *Syn* TEDIUM, boredom, ennui
dole *vb Syn* DISTRIBUTE, deal, dispense, divide *Ant* amass, collect
dole *n Syn* RATION, allowance, pittance
doleful **1** *Syn* MELANCHOLY, dolorous, lugubrious, plaintive, rueful **2** *Syn* SAD (sense 1), bad, blue, brokenhearted, crestfallen, dejected, depressed, despondent, disconsolate, down, downcast, downhearted, droopy, forlorn, gloomy, glum, heartbroken, heartsick, heartsore, inconsolable, joyless, low, low-spirited, melancholy, miserable, mournful, saddened, sorrowful, sorry, unhappy, woebegone, woeful, wretched *Ant* blissful, buoyant, buoyed, cheerful, cheery, chipper, delighted, glad, gladdened, gladsome, gleeful, happy, joyful, joyous, jubilant, sunny, upbeat
dolor *Syn* DISTRESS, agony, misery, passion, suffering
dolorous *Syn* MELANCHOLY, doleful, lugubrious, plaintive, rueful
domain *Syn* FIELD, bailiwick, province, sphere, territory
domestic *Syn* SERVANT, flunky, lackey, menial, retainer, steward *Ant* master
domicile *Syn* HABITATION, abode, dwelling, home, house, residence
dominance *Syn* SUPREMACY, ascendancy, dominion, predominance, preeminence, sovereignty
dominant • superior to all others in power, influence, position, or rank *Syn* paramount, predominant, preponderant, preponderating, sovereign *Rel* prevailing, prevalent *Ant* subordinate
domineering **1** *Syn* BOSSY, authoritarian, autocratic, despotic, dictatorial, imperious, masterful, overbearing, peremptory, tyrannical, tyrannous **2** *Syn* MASTERFUL, imperative, imperious, peremptory
dominion *Syn* SUPREMACY, ascendancy, dominance, predominance, preeminence, sovereignty
donate *Syn* GIVE, afford, bestow, confer, present
donation *Syn* CONTRIBUTION, alms, benefaction, beneficence, charity, philanthropy
donator *Syn* BENEFACTOR, donor, patron
donor *Syn* BENEFACTOR, donator, patron
doom *n Syn* FATE, destiny, lot, portion
doom *vb Syn* SENTENCE, condemn, damn, proscribe
door • an entrance to a place *Syn* doorway, gate, gateway, portal, postern *Rel* access, entrance, entrée, entry, ingress
doorway *Syn* DOOR, gate, gateway, portal, postern
dope (out) *Syn* SOLVE, answer, break, crack, figure out, puzzle (out), resolve, riddle, unravel, work, work out
dormancy *Syn* ABEYANCE, doldrums, latency, quiescence, suspense, suspension *Ant* continuance, continuation
dormant *Syn* LATENT, abeyant, potential, quiescent *Ant* patent

dot **1** *Syn* SCATTER (sense 2), bestrew, pepper, sow, spray, sprinkle, strew **2** *Syn* SPOT, blotch, dapple, fleck, freckle, marble, mottle, pepper, speck, speckle, splotch, sprinkle, stipple

dotage *Syn* AGE (sense 1), senescence, senility

dote *Syn* LIKE, enjoy, fancy, love, relish *Ant* dislike

dote (on) *Syn* IDOLIZE, adore, adulate, canonize, deify, worship

doting *Syn* LOVING, affectionate, devoted, fond *Ant* unloving

double • consisting of two members or parts that are usually joined *Syn* binary, bipartite, dual, duplex, twin *Rel* mated, paired *Ant* single

double cross *Syn* BETRAYAL, disloyalty, faithlessness, falseness, falsity, infidelity, perfidy, sellout, treachery, treason, unfaithfulness

double-cross *Syn* DECEIVE, beguile, betray, delude, mislead *Ant* enlighten, undeceive

double-crosser *Syn* TRAITOR, betrayer, quisling, recreant, turncoat

double-dealing *n* *Syn* DECEPTION, chicane, chicanery, fraud, trickery

double-dealing *adj* *Syn* INSINCERE, artificial, backhanded, feigned, hypocritical, left-handed, mealy, mealymouthed, two-faced, unctuous *Ant* genuine, heartfelt, honest, sincere, unfeigned

doubt *n* • a feeling or attitude that one does not know the truth, truthfulness, or trustworthiness of someone or something *Syn* distrust, distrustfulness, incertitude, misgiving, mistrust, mistrustfulness, skepticism, suspicion, uncertainty *Rel* disbelief, incredulity, unbelief *Ant* assurance, belief, certainty, certitude, confidence, conviction, sureness, surety, trust

doubt *vb* *Syn* DISTRUST, mistrust, question, suspect *Ant* trust

doubter *Syn* SKEPTIC, disbeliever, questioner, unbeliever

doubtful **1** • not affording assurance of the worth, soundness, success, or certainty of something or someone *Syn* dubious, problematic, questionable *Rel* distrustful, distrusting, mistrustful, mistrusting *Ant* cocksure, positive **2** *Syn* IMPROBABLE, dubious, far-fetched, flimsy, questionable, unapt, unlikely *Ant* likely, probable

doubtfully *Syn* ASKANCE, distrustfully, doubtingly, dubiously, mistrustfully, skeptically, suspiciously *Ant* trustfully, trustingly

doubtingly *Syn* ASKANCE, distrustfully, doubtfully, dubiously, mistrustfully, skeptically, suspiciously *Ant* trustfully, trustingly

doubtless *Syn* PROBABLY, likely, presumably *Ant* improbably

doughtiness *Syn* COURAGE, bravery, courageousness, daring, dauntlessness, fearlessness, gallantry, greatheartedness, guts, hardihood, heart, heroism, intrepidity, intrepidness, nerve, stoutness, valor *Ant* cowardice, cowardliness, cravenness, dastardliness, spinelessness, yellowness

doughty *Syn* BRAVE, audacious, bold, courageous, dauntless, fearless, intrepid, unafraid, undaunted, valiant, valorous *Ant* craven

dour *Syn* SULLEN, crabbed, gloomy, glum, morose, saturnine, sulky, surly

douse *Syn* WET, bathe, drench, soak, souse, wash, water *Ant* dry

dove *Syn* LAMB, angel, innocent, sheep *Ant* wolf

dowdily *Syn* SLOPPILY, slovenly, unstylishly *Ant* nattily, sharply, smartly, sprucely

dowdy *Syn* SLATTERNLY, blowsy, frowzy

dower • to furnish or provide with a gift *Syn* endow, endue *Rel* accouter, appoint, equip, furnish, outfit

down *n* **1** *Syn* COMEDOWN, decline, descent, downfall, fall *Ant* aggrandizement, ascent, exaltation, rise, up **2** *Syn* PLAIN, grassland, prairie, savanna, steppe, tundra, veld (*or* veldt)

down *adj* *Syn* SAD (sense 1), bad, blue, brokenhearted, crestfallen, dejected, depressed, despondent, disconsolate, doleful, downcast, downhearted, droopy, forlorn, gloomy, glum, heartbroken, heartsick, heartsore, inconsolable, joyless, low, low-spirited, melancholy, miserable, mournful, saddened, sorrowful, sorry, unhappy, woebegone, woeful, wretched *Ant* blissful, buoyant, buoyed, cheerful, cheery, chipper, delighted, glad, gladdened, gladsome, gleeful, happy, joyful, joyous, jubilant, sunny, upbeat

downcast *Syn* SAD (sense 1), bad, blue, brokenhearted, crestfallen, dejected, depressed, despondent, disconsolate, doleful, down, downhearted, droopy, forlorn, gloomy, glum, heartbroken, heartsick, heartsore, inconsolable, joyless, low, low-spirited, melancholy, miserable, mournful, saddened, sorrowful, sorry, unhappy, woebegone, woeful, wretched *Ant* blissful, buoyant, buoyed, cheerful, cheery, chipper, delighted, glad, gladdened, gladsome, gleeful, happy, joyful, joyous, jubilant, sunny, upbeat

downfall *Syn* COMEDOWN, decline, descent, down, fall *Ant* aggrandizement, ascent, exaltation, rise, up

downhearted *Syn* SAD (sense 1), bad, blue, brokenhearted, crestfallen, dejected, depressed, despondent, disconsolate, doleful, down, downcast, droopy, forlorn, gloomy, glum, heartbroken, heartsick, heartsore, inconsolable, joyless, low, low-spirited, melancholy, miserable, mournful, saddened, sorrowful, sorry, unhappy, woebegone, woeful, wretched *Ant* blissful, buoyant, buoyed, cheerful, cheery, chipper, delighted, glad, gladdened, gladsome, gleeful, happy, joyful, joyous, jubilant, sunny, upbeat

downheartedness *Syn* SADNESS, blues, dejection, depression, desolation, despondency, disconsolateness, dispiritedness, doldrums, dreariness, dumps, forlornness, gloom, gloominess, heartsickness, joylessness, melancholy, mopes, oppression, unhappiness *Ant* bliss, blissfulness, ecstasy, elatedness, elation, euphoria, exhilaration, exuberance, exultation, felicity, gladness, gladsomeness, happiness, heaven, intoxication, joy, joyfulness, joyousness, jubilation, rapture, rapturousness

downpour *Syn* RAIN (sense 1), cloudburst, deluge, rainfall, rainstorm, storm, wet

doze *Syn* SLEEP, catnap, drowse, nap, slumber, snooze

drab *Syn* BORING, dreary, dry, dull, flat, heavy, humdrum, jading, leaden, monotonous, pedestrian, ponderous, stodgy, stuffy, stupid, tame, tedious, tiresome, tiring, unanimated, uninteresting, wearisome, weary, wearying *Ant* absorbing, engaging, engrossing, gripping, interesting, intriguing, involving

draft *vb Syn* SKETCH, blueprint, delineate, diagram, outline, plot, trace

draft *n Syn* SKETCH, blueprint, delineation, diagram, outline, plot, tracing

drag *n Syn* ENCUMBRANCE, bar, block, chain, clog, crimp, deterrent, embarrassment, fetter, handicap, hindrance, hurdle, impediment, inhibition, interference, let, manacle, obstacle, obstruction, shackles, stop, stumbling block, trammel *Ant* aid, assistance, benefit, help

drag *vb Syn* PULL, draw, hale, haul, tow, tug

drain *Syn* DEPLETE, clean (out), consume, exhaust, expend, spend, use up *Ant* renew, replace

dramatic • of, relating to, or suggestive of plays, or the performance of a play *Syn* dramaturgic, histrionic, melodramatic, theatrical

dramaturgic *Syn* DRAMATIC, histrionic, melodramatic, theatrical

draw *n* • an indecisive ending to a contest or competition *Syn* deadlock, stalemate, standoff, tie

draw *vb* **1** *Syn* EARN, acquire, attain, capture, carry, gain, garner, get, land, make, obtain, procure, realize, secure, win *Ant* forfeit, lose **2** *Syn* PULL, drag, hale, haul, tow, tug

drawback *Syn* DISADVANTAGE, handicap, liability, minus, penalty, strike *Ant* advantage, asset, edge, plus

dread *Syn* FEAR, alarm, consternation, dismay, fright, horror, panic, terror, trepidation *Ant* fearlessness

dreadful *Syn* FEARFUL (sense 2), appalling, awful, frightful, horrible, horrific, shocking, terrible, terrific

dream **1** *Syn* FANCY, daydream, fantasy, nightmare, phantasm, phantasy, vision *Ant* reality **2** *Syn* GOAL, aim, ambition, aspiration, design, end, intent, intention, mark, meaning, object, objective, plan, pretension, purpose, target, thing

dreamer *Syn* IDEALIST, romantic, romanticist, utopian, visionary *Ant* pragmatist, realist

drear *Syn* SAD (sense 2), depressing, dismal, dreary, heartbreaking, heartrending, melancholy, pathetic, saddening, sorry, tearful, teary *Ant* cheering, cheery, glad, happy

dreariness *Syn* SADNESS, blues, dejection, depression, desolation, despondency, disconsolateness, dispiritedness, doldrums, downheartedness, dumps, forlornness, gloom, gloominess, heartsickness, joylessness, melancholy, mopes, oppression, unhappiness *Ant* bliss, blissfulness, ecstasy, elatedness, elation, euphoria, exhilaration, exuberance, exultation, felicity, gladness, gladsomeness, happiness, heaven, intoxication, joy, joyfulness, joyousness, jubilation, rapture, rapturousness

dreary **1** *Syn* BORING, drab, dry, dull, flat, heavy, humdrum, jading, leaden, monotonous, pedestrian, ponderous, stodgy, stuffy, stupid, tame, tedious, tiresome, tiring, unanimated, uninteresting, wearisome, weary, wearying *Ant* absorbing, engaging, engrossing, gripping, interesting, intriguing, involving **2** *Syn* DISMAL, bleak, cheerless, desolate, dispiriting **3** *Syn* SAD (sense 2), depressing, dismal, drear, heartbreaking, heartrending, melancholy, pathetic, saddening, sorry, tearful, teary *Ant* cheering, cheery, glad, happy

dregs *Syn* DEPOSIT, grounds, lees, precipitate, sediment

drench **1** *Syn* SOAK, impregnate, saturate, sop, steep, waterlog **2** *Syn* WET, bathe, douse, soak, souse, wash, water *Ant* dry

dress *adj* • relating to or suitable for wearing to an event requiring elegant dress and manners *Syn* dressy, formal *Rel* costume *Ant* casual, informal, sporty

dress *vb* **1** *Syn* CLOTHE, apparel, array, attire, robe *Ant* unclothe **2** *Syn* POLISH, buff, burnish, gloss, grind, rub, shine, smooth

dress *n Syn* CLOTHES, apparel, attire, clothing, raiment

dressy *Syn* DRESS, formal *Ant* casual, informal, sporty

drift *Syn* TENDENCY, tenor, trend

drifter *Syn* NOMAD, gadabout, rambler, roamer, rover, stroller, vagabond, wanderer, wayfarer

drill **1** *Syn* PERFORATE, bore, prick, punch, puncture **2** *Syn* PRACTICE, exercise

drink *Syn* ALCOHOL, booze, grog, intoxicant, liquor, moonshine, spirits

drive *vb Syn* ACTIVATE, actuate, crank (up), move, propel, run, set off, spark, start, touch off, trigger, turn on *Ant* cut, deactivate, kill, shut off, turn off

drive *n* **1** *Syn* CAMPAIGN, bandwagon, cause, crusade, movement **2** *Syn* VIGOR, dash, élan, esprit, punch, spirit, verve, vim

drivel *Syn* NONSENSE, balderdash, bull, bunk, gobbledygook, poppycock, rot, trash, twaddle

droll *Syn* LAUGHABLE, comic, comical, farcical, funny, ludicrous, ridiculous, risible

drone *Syn* LAZYBONES, idler, loafer, slouch, slug, sluggard *Ant* doer, go-getter, hummer, hustler, rustler, self-starter

droop • to become literally or figuratively limp through loss of vigor or freshness *Syn* flag, sag, wilt *Rel* drop, fall, sink, slump, subside

droopy *Syn* SAD (sense 1), bad, blue, brokenhearted, crestfallen, dejected, depressed, despondent, disconsolate, doleful, down, downcast, downhearted, forlorn, gloomy, glum, heartbroken, heartsick, heartsore, inconsolable, joyless, low, low-spirited, melancholy, miserable, mournful, saddened, sorrowful, sorry, unhappy, woebegone, woeful, wretched *Ant* blissful, buoyant, buoyed, cheerful, cheery, chipper, delighted, glad, gladdened, gladsome, gleeful, happy, joyful, joyous, jubilant, sunny, upbeat

drop **1** *Syn* DISMISS, bounce, cashier, discharge, fire, sack **2** *Syn* FALL, sink, slump, subside *Ant* rise

dropping *Syn* CANCELLATION, abortion, calling, calling off, recall, repeal, rescission, revocation *Ant* continuation

drown *Syn* FLOOD, deluge, engulf, inundate, overflow, overwhelm, submerge, submerse, swamp *Ant* drain

drowse *Syn* SLEEP, catnap, doze, nap, slumber, snooze

drowsiness *Syn* SLEEPINESS, somnolence *Ant* insomnia, sleeplessness, wakefulness

drowsy *Syn* SLEEPY, slumberous, somnolent

drudge *n* *Syn* SLAVE (sense 2), drudger, grubber, laborer, peon, plugger, slogger, toiler, worker *Ant* freeman

drudge *vb* *Syn* LABOR, endeavor, grub, hump, hustle, moil, peg (away), plod, plow, plug, slave, slog, strain, strive, struggle, sweat, toil, travail, work *Ant* dabble, fiddle (around), fool (around), mess (around), putter (around)

drudger *Syn* SLAVE (sense 2), drudge, grubber, laborer, peon, plugger, slogger, toiler, worker *Ant* freeman

drudgery *Syn* WORK (sense 1), grind, labor, toil, travail *Ant* fun, play

drug • a substance used by itself or in a mixture for the treatment or in the diagnosis of disease *Syn* biologic, medicinal, pharmaceutical, simple *Rel* cure, medicament, medication, medicine, physic, remedy, specific

druggist • one who deals in medicinal drugs *Syn* apothecary, chemist, pharmacist

drunk • having the faculties impaired by alcohol *Syn* drunken, inebriated, intoxicated, tight, tipsy *Rel* befuddled, confused, fuddled *Ant* sober

drunkard • one who is habitually drunk *Syn* alcoholic, dipsomaniac, inebriate, soak, sot, tippler, toper, tosspot *Ant* teetotaler

drunken *Syn* DRUNK, inebriated, intoxicated, tight, tipsy *Ant* sober

dry *vb* • to treat or to affect so as to deprive of moisture *Syn* bake, dehydrate, desiccate, parch *Rel* deplete, drain, exhaust *Ant* moisten, wet

dry *adj* **1** *Syn* BORING, drab, dreary, dull, flat, heavy, humdrum, jading, leaden, monotonous, pedestrian, ponderous, stodgy, stuffy, stupid, tame, tedious, tiresome, tiring, unanimated, uninteresting, wearisome, weary, wearying *Ant* absorbing, engaging, engrossing, gripping, interesting, intriguing, involving **2** *Syn* SOUR, acid, acidulous, tart

dry run *Syn* REHEARSAL, practice, trial

dual *Syn* DOUBLE, binary, bipartite, duplex, twin *Ant* single

dubious **1** *Syn* DOUBTFUL, problematic, questionable *Ant* cocksure, positive **2** *Syn* IMPROBABLE, doubtful, far-fetched, flimsy, questionable, unapt, unlikely *Ant* likely, probable

dubiously *Syn* ASKANCE, distrustfully, doubtfully, doubtingly, mistrustfully, skeptically, suspiciously *Ant* trustfully, trustingly

duck **1** *Syn* DIP (sense 1), dunk, immerse, souse, submerge **2** *Syn* DODGE, fence, malinger, parry, shirk, sidestep *Ant* face

duck soup *Syn* CINCH, breeze, child's play, picnic, pushover, snap *Ant* chore, headache, labor

duct *Syn* CHANNEL, aqueduct, canal, conduit

ductile *Syn* PLASTIC, adaptable, malleable, pliable, pliant

dude **1** *Syn* FOP, beau, buck, coxcomb, dandy, exquisite **2** *Syn* MAN (sense 1), fellow, gent, gentleman, guy, male

dudgeon *Syn* OFFENSE (sense 1), huff, pique, resentment, umbrage

due *adj* • being in accordance with what is just and appropriate *Syn* condign, rightful *Rel* appropriate, fit, fitting, meet, proper, suitable

due *n* • what is justly owed to a person (sometimes a thing), especially as a recompense or compensation *Syn* desert, merit *Rel* compensation, payment, recompense, recompensing, repayment, satisfaction

due to *Syn* BECAUSE OF, owing to, through, with

dulcet *Syn* SWEET, engaging, winning, winsome *Ant* bitter, sour

dull *adj* **1** • lacking sharpness of edge or point *Syn* blunt, obtuse *Ant* feeling, poignant (*sensation, reaction*), sharp **2** *Syn* BORING, drab, dreary, dry, flat, heavy, humdrum, jading, leaden, monotonous, pedestrian, ponderous, stodgy, stuffy, stupid, tame, tedious, tiresome, tiring, unanimated, uninteresting, wearisome, weary, wearying *Ant* absorbing, engaging, engrossing, gripping, interesting, intriguing, involving **3** *Syn* OVERCAST, beclouded, clouded, cloudy, hazed, hazy, heavy, lowering, overclouded *Ant* clear, cloudless **4** *Syn* STUPID, crass, dense, dumb, slow *Ant* intelligent

dull *vb Syn* WHITEN, blanch, bleach, blench, decolorize, fade, pale, wash out *Ant* blacken, darken, deepen

dumb **1** *Syn* SILENT (sense 3), mum, mute, speechless, uncommunicative, wordless **2** *Syn* STUPID, crass, dense, dull, slow *Ant* intelligent

dumbfound *Syn* PUZZLE, bewilder, confound, distract, mystify, nonplus, perplex

dump *Syn* ARMORY, arsenal, depot, magazine

dumps *Syn* SADNESS, blues, dejection, depression, desolation, despondency, disconsolateness, dispiritedness, doldrums, downheartedness, dreariness, forlornness, gloom, gloominess, heartsickness, joylessness, melancholy, mopes, oppression, unhappiness *Ant* bliss, blissfulness, ecstasy, elatedness, elation, euphoria, exhilaration, exuberance, exultation, felicity, gladness, gladsomeness, happiness, heaven, intoxication, joy, joyfulness, joyousness, jubilation, rapture, rapturousness

dumpy *Syn* STOCKY, chunky, squat, stubby, thick, thickset

dunk *Syn* DIP (sense 1), duck, immerse, souse, submerge

duo *Syn* PAIR, brace, couple, twain, twosome

dupe *n* • one who is easily deceived or cheated *Syn* chump, gull, pigeon, sap, sucker, tool *Rel* victim

dupe *vb* • mean to delude by underhanded means or methods *Syn* bamboozle, befool, gull, hoax, hoodwink, trick *Rel* beguile, betray, deceive, delude, double-cross, mislead

duplex *Syn* DOUBLE, binary, bipartite, dual, twin *Ant* single

duplicate *Syn* COPY, carbon copy, duplication, facsimile, imitation, reduplication, replica, replication, reproduction *Ant* original

duplication *Syn* COPY, carbon copy, duplicate, facsimile, imitation, reduplication, replica, replication, reproduction *Ant* original

duplicity *Syn* DECEIT, cunning, dissimulation, guile

durable *Syn* LASTING, perdurable, permanent, perpetual, stable *Ant* fleeting

duration *Syn* CONTINUATION, continuance, endurance, persistence, subsistence *Ant* ending, termination

duress *Syn* FORCE, coercion, compulsion, constraint, restraint, violence

dusky *Syn* DARK, dim, gloomy, murky, obscure *Ant* light

dutiful *Syn* RESPECTFUL, deferential, regardful *Ant* disrespectful

duty **1** *Syn* CHORE, assignment, job, stint, task **2** *Syn* FUNCTION, office, province **3** *Syn* OBLIGATION, burden, charge, commitment, need, responsibility **4** *Syn* TAX, assessment, imposition, impost, levy

dwarf • a living thing much smaller than others of its kind *Syn* midget, pygmy, runt

dwell *Syn* RESIDE, live, lodge, put up, sojourn, stay, stop

dweller *Syn* INHABITANT, denizen, habitant, occupant, resident, resider *Ant* transient

dwelling *Syn* HABITATION, abode, domicile, home, house, residence

dwindle *Syn* DECREASE, abate, diminish, lessen, reduce *Ant* increase

dye *Syn* PIGMENT, color, coloring, dyestuff, stain, tincture

dyestuff *Syn* PIGMENT, color, coloring, dye, stain, tincture

dynamic *Syn* ACTIVE, live, operative *Ant* inactive

E

each *adv* **1** • by, for, or to every one of the many *Syn* apiece, individually, respectively, severally **2** *Syn* APIECE, all, per capita

each *adj Syn* ALL, every *Ant* no

eager • moved by a strong and urgent desire or interest *Syn* agog, anxious, athirst, avid, keen *Rel* coveting, craving, desiring *Ant* listless

ear *Syn* ATTENTION (sense 2), awareness, cognizance, eye, heed, notice, observance, observation

early • at or nearly at the beginning of a specified or implied period of time *Syn* beforehand, betimes, soon *Ant* late

earn **1** • to receive as return for effort *Syn* acquire, attain, capture, carry, draw, gain, garner, get, land, make, obtain, procure, realize, secure, win *Rel* clear, net *Ant* forfeit, lose **2** *Syn* DESERVE, merit, rate

earnest *n Syn* PLEDGE, hostage, pawn, token

earnest *adj Syn* SERIOUS, grave, sedate, sober, solemn, somber, staid *Ant* flippant, light

earnestness • a mental state free of jesting or

trifling *Syn* gravity, intentness, seriousness, soberness, sobriety, solemnity *Rel* deliberation, determination, firmness, purposefulness, resolve *Ant* frivolity, levity, lightheartedness

earsplitting *Syn* LOUD, hoarse, raucous, stentorian, stertorous, strident *Ant* low, low-pitched

earth • the entire area or extent of space in which human beings think of themselves as living and acting *Syn* globe, planet, world *Rel* cosmos, macrocosm, universe

earthly • of, belonging to, or characteristic of the earth or life on earth *Syn* earthy, mundane, sublunary, terrestrial, worldly *Rel* profane, secular, temporal

earthy *Syn* EARTHLY, mundane, sublunary, terrestrial, worldly

ease *n* **1** *Syn* ABANDON, abandonment, lightheartedness, naturalness, spontaneity, unrestraint *Ant* constraint, restraint **2** *Syn* READINESS, dexterity, facility **3** *Syn* REST, comfort, leisure, relaxation, repose

ease *vb Syn* SLACKEN, loosen, relax, slack *Ant* strain, stretch, tense, tighten

easily • without difficulty *Syn* effortlessly, facilely, fluently, freely, handily, lightly, painlessly, readily, smoothly *Rel* ably, adeptly, adroitly, competently, dexterously, efficiently, expertly, proficiently, skillfully *Ant* arduously, laboriously

easy **1** • causing or involving little or no difficulty *Syn* effortless, facile, light, simple, smooth *Ant* hard **2** *Syn* COMFORTABLE, cozy, restful, snug *Ant* miserable, uncomfortable

easygoing *Syn* CAREFREE, careless, cavalier, devil-may-care, gay, happy-go-lucky, insouciant, lighthearted, unconcerned *Ant* careworn

eat • to take food into the stomach through the mouth *Syn* consume, devour, ingest, swallow *Rel* bite, champ, gnaw

ebb **1** *Syn* ABATE, subside, wane *Ant* revive, rise **2** *Syn* DETERIORATE, crumble, decay, decline, degenerate, descend, rot, sink, worsen *Ant* ameliorate, improve, meliorate

eccentric *n* • a person of odd or whimsical habits *Syn* character, codger, crackbrain, crackpot, crank, kook, nut, oddball, screwball, weirdo *Rel* bohemian, maverick, nonconformist

eccentric *adj Syn* STRANGE, curious, erratic, odd, outlandish, peculiar, quaint, queer, singular, unique *Ant* familiar

echelon *Syn* LINE, file, rank, row, tier

echo *Syn* REPEAT (sense 2), parrot, quote

éclat *Syn* FAME, celebrity, glory, honor, notoriety, renown, reputation, repute *Ant* infamy, obscurity

eclipse *Syn* OBSCURE, becloud, bedim, befog, cloud, darken, dim, fog, obfuscate *Ant* illuminate, illumine

economical *Syn* FRUGAL, economizing, provident, scrimping, sparing, thrifty *Ant* prodigal, wasteful

economize • to avoid unnecessary waste or expense *Syn* save, scrimp, skimp *Rel* conserve, husband, manage *Ant* waste

economizing *Syn* FRUGAL, economical, provident, scrimping, sparing, thrifty *Ant* prodigal, wasteful

economy • careful management of material resources *Syn* frugality, husbandry, providence, scrimping, skimping, thrift *Rel* conservation, saving *Ant* wastefulness

ecstasy • a state of overwhelming usually pleasurable emotion *Syn* elation, euphoria, exhilaration, heaven, intoxication, paradise, rapture, rhapsody, transport *Rel* exaltation *Ant* depression

ecstatic • experiencing or marked by overwhelming usually pleasurable emotion *Syn* elated, enraptured, entranced, euphoric, exhilarated, intoxicated, rapturous, rhapsodic *Rel* exultant, jubilant, triumphant *Ant* depressed

ecumenical *Syn* UNIVERSAL (sense 1), catholic, cosmic, cosmopolitan *Ant* particular

eddy *n* • a swirling mass especially of water *Syn* maelstrom, vortex, whirlpool

eddy *vb Syn* TURN (sense 1), circle, gyrate, pirouette, revolve, rotate, spin, swirl, twirl, wheel, whirl

edge *n* **1** *Syn* ADVANTAGE, allowance, handicap, odds *Ant* disadvantage, handicap **2** *Syn* BORDER, brim, brink, margin, rim, verge

edge *vb Syn* SHARPEN, grind, hone, strop, whet *Ant* blunt, dull

edgewise *Syn* SIDEWAYS, broadside, sidewise

edifice *Syn* BUILDING, structure

edify *Syn* ENLIGHTEN (sense 1), educate, nurture

edit • to prepare material for publication *Syn* adapt, compile, redact, revise, rewrite *Rel* fabricate, fashion, form, make

edition • the total number of copies of the same work printed during a stretch of time *Syn* impression, printing, reissue, reprinting

educate **1** *Syn* ENLIGHTEN (sense 1), edify, nurture **2** *Syn* TEACH, discipline, instruct, school, train

educated • having or displaying advanced knowledge or education *Syn* erudite, knowledgeable, learned, literate, scholarly, well-read *Rel* civilized, cultivated, cultured *Ant* ignorant, illiterate, uneducated

education **1** • the act or process of imparting knowledge or skills to another *Syn* instruction, schooling, teaching, training, tutelage, tutoring *Rel* coaching, conditioning, cultivation, preparation, readying **2** • the understanding and information gained from being educated *Syn* erudition, knowledge, learnedness, learning, scholarship, science *Rel* culture, edification, enlightenment

educational *Syn* ACADEMIC, scholarly, scholastic *Ant* nonacademic, unacademic
educator *Syn* TEACHER, instructor, pedagogue, preceptor, schoolteacher
educe • to bring or draw out what is hidden, latent, or reserved *Syn* elicit, evoke, extort, extract *Rel* drag, draw, pull
eerie • fearfully and mysteriously strange or fantastic *Syn* creepy, haunting, spooky, uncanny, unearthly, weird *Rel* ghostly, spectral
efface *Syn* ERASE, blot out, cancel, delete, expunge, obliterate
effect *n* • a condition, situation, or occurrence ascribable to a cause *Syn* aftereffect, aftermath, consequence, event, issue, outcome, result, sequel, upshot *Ant* cause
effect *vb* **1** • to be the cause of (a situation, action, or state of mind) *Syn* bring about, cause, create, effectuate, engender, generate, induce, make, produce, prompt, result (in), spawn, work, yield *Rel* decide, determine **2** *Syn* PERFORM, accomplish, achieve, discharge, execute, fulfill
effective **1** • producing or capable of producing a result *Syn* effectual, efficacious, efficient *Rel* forceful, forcible, potent, powerful *Ant* futile, ineffective **2** *Syn* COGENT, compelling, conclusive, convincing, decisive, forceful, persuasive, satisfying, strong, telling *Ant* inconclusive, indecisive, ineffective, unconvincing
effects *Syn* POSSESSIONS, assets, belongings, means, resources
effectual *Syn* EFFECTIVE, efficacious, efficient *Ant* futile, ineffective
effectuate *Syn* EFFECT, bring about, cause, create, engender, generate, induce, make, produce, prompt, result (in), spawn, work, yield
effeminate • of or relating to a man characterized by qualities traditionally associated with women *Syn* effete, epicene
effervescent *Syn* ELASTIC (sense 2), buoyant, expansive, resilient, volatile *Ant* depressed
effete *Syn* EFFEMINATE, epicene
efficacious *Syn* EFFECTIVE, effectual, efficient *Ant* futile, ineffective
efficient *Syn* EFFECTIVE, effectual, efficacious *Ant* futile, ineffective
effigy *Syn* IMAGE, icon, mask, photograph, portrait, statue
effort • the active use or expenditure of physical or mental power to produce a desired result *Syn* exertion, pains, trouble *Rel* labor, toil, travail, work *Ant* ease
effortless *Syn* EASY, facile, light, simple, smooth *Ant* hard
effortlessly *Syn* EASILY, facilely, fluently, freely, handily, lightly, painlessly, readily, smoothly *Ant* arduously, laboriously
effrontery • shameless boldness *Syn* audacity, brashness, brass, brassiness, brazenness, cheek, cheekiness, chutzpah, gall, nerve, nerviness, pertness, presumption, presumptuousness, sauce, sauciness, temerity *Rel* arrogance, assurance, cockiness, confidence, overconfidence, sanguinity, self-assurance, self-confidence
effulgent *Syn* BRIGHT, beaming, brilliant, incandescent, lambent, lucent, luminous, lustrous, radiant, refulgent *Ant* dim, dull
effusive *Syn* DEMONSTRATIVE, emotional, uninhibited, unreserved, unrestrained *Ant* inhibited, reserved, restrained, undemonstrative, unemotional
egg (on) *Syn* URGE, encourage, exhort, goad, press, prod, prompt
ego *Syn* COMPLACENCE, complacency, conceit, conceitedness, egotism, pompousness, pride, pridefulness, self-admiration, self-conceit, self-esteem, self-importance, self-satisfaction, smugness, vaingloriousness, vainglory, vainness, vanity *Ant* humbleness, humility, modesty
egocentric • overly concerned with one's own desires, needs, or interests *Syn* egoistic, egotistic (*or* egotistical), self-centered, selfish, self-seeking *Rel* complacent, conceited, self-conceited, self-directed, self-important, self-indulgent, self-satisfied, smug, vain *Ant* selfless
egoism *Syn* CONCEIT, amour propre, egotism, self-esteem, self-love *Ant* humility
egoistic **1** *Syn* CONCEITED, complacent, egotistic (*or* egotistical), important, overweening, pompous, prideful, proud, self-conceited, self-important, self-satisfied, smug, stuck-up, vain, vainglorious *Ant* humble, modest **2** *Syn* EGOCENTRIC, egotistic (*or* egotistical), self-centered, selfish, self-seeking *Ant* selfless
egotism **1** *Syn* COMPLACENCE, complacency, conceit, conceitedness, ego, pompousness, pride, pridefulness, self-admiration, self-conceit, self-esteem, self-importance, self-satisfaction, smugness, vaingloriousness, vainglory, vainness, vanity *Ant* humbleness, humility, modesty **2** *Syn* CONCEIT, amour propre, egoism, self-esteem, self-love *Ant* humility
egotistic *or* **egotistical** **1** *Syn* CONCEITED, complacent, egoistic, important, overweening, pompous, prideful, proud, self-conceited, self-important, self-satisfied, smug, stuck-up, vain, vainglorious *Ant* humble, modest **2** *Syn* EGOCENTRIC, egoistic, self-centered, selfish, self-seeking *Ant* selfless
egregious • very noticeable especially for being incorrect or bad *Syn* blatant, conspicuous, flagrant, glaring, gross, obvious, patent, pronounced, rank, striking *Rel* clear, distinct, evident, notable, outstanding, plain, salient
eject *Syn* ERUPT (sense 2), belch, disgorge, expel, jet, spew, spout, spurt
elaborate *Syn* UNFOLD, develop, evolve, perfect
elaboration *Syn* EXAGGERATION, caricature,

coloring, embellishment, embroidering, hyperbole, magnification, overstatement, padding, stretching *Ant* understatement

élan *Syn* VIGOR, dash, drive, esprit, punch, spirit, verve, vim

elapse *Syn* PASS, expire, pass away

elastic **1** • able to endure strain without being permanently affected or injured *Syn* flexible, resilient, springy, supple *Rel* ductile, pliable, pliant *Ant* rigid **2** • able to recover quickly from depression and maintain high spirits *Syn* buoyant, effervescent, expansive, resilient, volatile *Rel* high-spirited, mettlesome, spirited *Ant* depressed

elate • to fill with great joy *Syn* elevate, enrapture, exhilarate, overjoy, transport *Rel* excite, inspire, stimulate, uplift *Ant* depress

elated *Syn* ECSTATIC, enraptured, entranced, euphoric, exhilarated, intoxicated, rapturous, rhapsodic *Ant* depressed

elation *Syn* ECSTASY, euphoria, exhilaration, heaven, intoxication, paradise, rapture, rhapsody, transport *Ant* depression

elbow room *Syn* ROOM (sense 2), berth, clearance, leeway, margin, play

elder **1** *Syn* SENIOR CITIZEN, ancient, golden-ager, oldster, old-timer *Ant* youngster, youth **2** *Syn* SUPERIOR, better, senior *Ant* inferior, subordinate, underling

elderly • being of advanced years and especially past middle age *Syn* aged, aging, ancient, geriatric, long-lived, old, older, senior *Rel* adult, grown-up, mature, middle-aged *Ant* young, youthful

elect *vb* *Syn* CHOOSE, cull, opt, pick, prefer, select, single *Ant* eschew, reject

elect *n* *Syn* ELITE, best, choice, cream, fat, flower, pick, prime, upper crust

elect *adj* *Syn* SELECT, exclusive, picked *Ant* indiscriminate

election *Syn* CHOICE, alternative, option, preference, selection

elective *Syn* OPTIONAL, discretionary, voluntary *Ant* compulsory, mandatory, nonelective, obligatory, required

electrify *Syn* THRILL, enthuse

eleemosynary *Syn* CHARITABLE, altruistic, benevolent, humane, humanitarian, philanthropic *Ant* uncharitable

elegance • dignified or restrained beauty of form, appearance, or style *Syn* class, elegancy, grace, gracefulness, handsomeness, majesty, refinement, stateliness *Rel* grandeur, lavishness, luxuriousness, magnificence, ornateness, richness, splendor

elegancy *Syn* ELEGANCE, class, grace, gracefulness, handsomeness, majesty, refinement, stateliness

elegant *Syn* CHOICE, dainty, delicate, exquisite, rare, recherché *Ant* indifferent, medium

element • one of the parts of a compound or complex whole *Syn* component, constituent, factor, ingredient *Rel* fundamental, principle *Ant* composite, compound (*in science*)

elemental *Syn* ELEMENTARY, basic, essential, fundamental, rudimentary, underlying *Ant* advanced

elementary • of or relating to the simplest facts or theories of a subject *Syn* basic, elemental, essential, fundamental, rudimentary, underlying *Rel* primal, primary, prime *Ant* advanced

elephantine *Syn* HUGE, Brobdingnagian, colossal, cyclopean, enormous, gargantuan, giant, gigantean, gigantic, Herculean, immense, mammoth, titanic, vast *Ant* bitty, diminutive, microscopic (*or* microscopical), midget, miniature, minute, pocket, pygmy, teeny, teeny-weeny, tiny, wee

elevate **1** *Syn* ELATE, enrapture, exhilarate, overjoy, transport *Ant* depress **2** *Syn* LIFT, boost, heave, hoist, raise, rear *Ant* lower

elevation **1** *Syn* ADVANCEMENT, preferment, promotion *Ant* degradation, reduction (*in rank or status*) **2** *Syn* HEIGHT, altitude

elf *Syn* FAIRY, brownie, fay, pixie (*also* pixy), sprite

elicit *Syn* EDUCE, evoke, extort, extract

eliminate *Syn* EXCLUDE, blackball, debar, disbar, rule out, shut out, suspend *Ant* admit, include

elite **1** • individuals carefully selected as being the best of a class *Syn* best, choice, cream, elect, fat, flower, pick, prime, upper crust *Rel* aristocracy, (the) establishment, gentry, nobility, society, (the) top, upper class **2** *Syn* ARISTOCRACY, county, gentry, nobility, society *Ant* people, proletariat

ell *Syn* ANNEX, extension, wing

elongate *Syn* EXTEND, lengthen, prolong, protract *Ant* abridge, shorten

elongated *Syn* LONG (sense 1), extended, king-size (*or* king-sized), lengthy *Ant* brief, short

eloquent **1** *Syn* ARTICULATE, fluent, well-spoken *Ant* inarticulate **2** *Syn* EXPRESSIVE, meaning, meaningful, pregnant, revealing, significant, suggestive

else *Syn* ADDITIONAL, added, another, farther, further, more, other

elucidate *Syn* EXPLAIN (sense 1), clarify, clear (up), construe, demonstrate, explicate, expound, illuminate, illustrate, interpret, spell out *Ant* obscure

elude *Syn* ESCAPE (sense 2), avoid, eschew, evade, shun

Elysian *Syn* CELESTIAL, empyreal, empyrean, heavenly, supernal *Ant* hellish, infernal

emanate *Syn* SPRING, arise, derive, flow, issue, originate, proceed, rise, stem

emancipate *Syn* FREE, discharge, liberate, manumit, release

emasculate *Syn* STERILIZE (sense 1), alter, castrate, geld, mutilate, spay *Ant* fertilize

embankment *Syn* DAM, dike, levee
embargo *Syn* PROHIBITION (sense 2), ban, interdict, interdiction, proscription, veto *Ant* prescription
embark (on *or* **upon)** *Syn* BEGIN (sense 2), commence, enter (into *or* upon), get off, kick off, launch, open, start, strike (into) *Ant* conclude, end, finish, terminate
embarrass • to distress by confusing or confounding *Syn* abash, discomfit, disconcert, faze, rattle *Rel* discompose, disturb, flurry, fluster, perturb *Ant* facilitate, relieve
embarrassment *Syn* ENCUMBRANCE, bar, block, chain, clog, crimp, deterrent, drag, fetter, handicap, hindrance, hurdle, impediment, inhibition, interference, let, manacle, obstacle, obstruction, shackles, stop, stumbling block, trammel *Ant* aid, assistance, benefit, help
embellish *Syn* ADORN, beautify, bedeck, deck, decorate, garnish, ornament *Ant* disfigure
embellishment *Syn* EXAGGERATION, caricature, coloring, elaboration, embroidering, hyperbole, magnification, overstatement, padding, stretching *Ant* understatement
embers *Syn* ASH, cinders, clinkers
emblem *Syn* SYMBOL, attribute, type
embodiment • a visible representation of something abstract (as a quality) *Syn* epitome, incarnation, manifestation, personification *Rel* exemplification, incorporation, substantiation
embody **1** • to make a part of a body or system *Syn* assimilate, incorporate, integrate *Rel* amalgamate, blend, combine, commingle, fuse, intermingle, merge, mingle **2** • to represent in visible form *Syn* epitomize, incarnate, manifest, materialize, personalize, personify, substantiate *Rel* actualize, realize **3** *Syn* REALIZE, actualize, externalize, hypostatize, incarnate, materialize, objectify, reify
embolden *Syn* ENCOURAGE, cheer, hearten, inspirit, nerve, steel *Ant* discourage
embrace **1** *Syn* ADOPT, espouse *Ant* discard, repudiate **2** *Syn* INCLUDE, comprehend, imply, involve, subsume *Ant* exclude
embroidering *Syn* EXAGGERATION, caricature, coloring, elaboration, embellishment, hyperbole, magnification, overstatement, padding, stretching *Ant* understatement
emend *Syn* CORRECT, amend, rectify, redress, reform, remedy, revise
emerge *Syn* APPEAR, loom *Ant* disappear, vanish
emergency *Syn* JUNCTURE, contingency, crisis, exigency, pass, pinch, strait
emigrant • a person who leaves one country in order to settle in another *Syn* immigrant, migrant *Rel* alien, emigré, exile, expatriate, foreigner, fugitive, refugee
emigrate *Syn* MIGRATE, immigrate
émigré *Syn* STRANGER, alien, foreigner, immigrant, outlander, outsider
eminent • standing above others in rank, importance, or achievement *Syn* distinguished, illustrious, noble, notable, noteworthy, outstanding, preeminent, prestigious, signal, star, superior *Rel* celebrated, famed, famous, glorious, honored, renowned, reputable
emissary *Syn* AMBASSADOR, delegate, envoy, legate, minister, representative
emolument *Syn* WAGE, fee, hire, pay, salary, stipend
emotion *Syn* FEELING, affection, passion, sentiment
emotional **1** *Syn* DEMONSTRATIVE, effusive, uninhibited, unreserved, unrestrained *Ant* inhibited, reserved, restrained, undemonstrative, unemotional **2** *Syn* FERVENT, ardent, blazing, burning, charged, fervid, feverish, fiery, flaming, glowing, hot-blooded, impassioned, passionate, red-hot, vehement, warm, warm-blooded *Ant* cold, cool, dispassionate, impassive, unemotional **3** *Syn* MOVING, affecting, impressive, poignant, stirring, touching *Ant* unemotional, unimpressive
empathy *Syn* SYMPATHY, commiseration, compassion, condolence, pity, ruth
emphasis • exerted force or special stress that gives impressiveness or importance to something *Syn* accent, accentuation, stress
emphasize • to indicate the importance of by giving prominent display *Syn* accent, accentuate, feature, highlight, play (up), point (up), stress, underline, underscore *Rel* focus, identify, pinpoint, spotlight *Ant* play (down)
employ *Syn* USE, apply, avail, utilize
employment **1** *Syn* OCCUPATION, calling, line, profession, trade, vocation, work **2** *Syn* WORK (sense 2), business, calling, occupation, pursuit
emporium *Syn* STORE, bazaar, shop
emptiness **1** *Syn* VACANCY (sense 1), blank, blankness, vacuity, void *Ant* fullness **2** *Syn* VACANCY (sense 2), bareness, vacuity *Ant* fullness
empty *adj* **1** • lacking the contents that could or should be present *Syn* blank, vacant, vacuous, void *Rel* destitute, devoid, void *Ant* full **2** *Syn* MEANINGLESS, inane, pointless, senseless *Ant* meaningful **3** *Syn* VAIN, hollow, idle, nugatory, otiose
empty *vb* • to remove the contents of *Syn* clear, evacuate, vacate, void *Rel* deplete, drain, eliminate, exhaust *Ant* fill, load
empyreal *Syn* CELESTIAL, Elysian, empyrean, heavenly, supernal *Ant* hellish, infernal
empyrean *Syn* CELESTIAL, Elysian, empyreal, heavenly, supernal *Ant* hellish, infernal
emulate *Syn* RIVAL, compete, vie
enact • to put into effect through legislative or authoritative action *Syn* lay down, legislate, make, pass *Rel* bring about, effect *Ant* repeal, rescind, revoke
encapsulate *Syn* SUMMARIZE, abstract, digest,

epitomize, outline, recap, recapitulate, sum up, wrap up
enchant *Syn* ATTRACT, allure, bewitch, captivate, charm, fascinate *Ant* repel
enchanter *Syn* MAGICIAN (sense 1), charmer, conjurer (*or* conjuror), necromancer, sorcerer, voodoo, witch, wizard
enchanting *Syn* ATTRACTIVE, alluring, bewitching, captivating, charming, fascinating *Ant* forbidding, repellent
enchantress *Syn* SIREN, seductress, temptress
encircle *Syn* SURROUND, circle, compass, encompass, environ, gird, girdle, hem, ring
enclose • to shut in or confine by or as if by barriers *Syn* cage, coop, corral, envelop, fence, pen, wall *Rel* circumscribe, confine, limit, restrict
encomium • a more or less formal and public expression of praise *Syn* citation, eulogy, panegyric, tribute *Rel* extollation, extolling, laudation, lauding, praise, praising
encompass *Syn* SURROUND, circle, compass, encircle, environ, gird, girdle, hem, ring
encounter *n* • a sudden, hostile, and usually brief confrontation or dispute between factions or persons *Syn* brush, skirmish *Rel* battle, engagement
encounter *vb* **1** *Syn* HAPPEN (on *or* upon), chance (upon), find, hit (upon), meet, stumble (on *or* onto) **2** *Syn* MEET, confront, face *Ant* avoid
encourage **1** • to fill with courage or strength of purpose especially in preparation for a hard task *Syn* cheer, embolden, hearten, inspirit, nerve, steel *Rel* excite, galvanize, pique, provoke, quicken, stimulate *Ant* discourage **2** *Syn* FAVOR, countenance *Ant* disapprove **3** *Syn* URGE, egg (on), exhort, goad, press, prod, prompt
encouraging *Syn* HEARTWARMING, cheering, comforting, fulfilling, gladdening, gratifying, heartening, rewarding, satisfying *Ant* depressing, discouraging, disheartening, dispiriting
encroach *Syn* TRESPASS, entrench, infringe, invade
encumber *Syn* BURDEN, charge, cumber, lade, load, saddle, tax, weigh, weight
encumbrance • something that makes movement or progress more difficult *Syn* bar, block, chain, clog, crimp, deterrent, drag, embarrassment, fetter, handicap, hindrance, hurdle, impediment, inhibition, interference, let, manacle, obstacle, obstruction, shackles, stop, stumbling block, trammel *Rel* catch, hitch, rub, snag *Ant* aid, assistance, benefit, help
encyclopedic • covering everything or all important points *Syn* compendious, complete, comprehensive, full, global, inclusive, in-depth, omnibus, panoramic, universal *Rel* broad, catholic, extensive, far-reaching, general, overall, sweeping, vast, wide
end *n* **1** • the point at which something ceases *Syn* ending, termination, terminus *Rel* close, closing, completion, concluding, conclusion, finish, finishing *Ant* beginning **2** *Syn* FINALE, close, closing, conclusion, consummation, ending, finis, finish, windup *Ant* beginning, dawn, opening, start **3** *Syn* GOAL, aim, ambition, aspiration, design, dream, intent, intention, mark, meaning, object, objective, plan, pretension, purpose, target, thing
end *vb* **1** *Syn* CONCLUDE (sense 1), complete, finish, terminate **2** *Syn* LIMIT, bound, confine, term
endanger • to place in danger *Syn* adventure, compromise, gamble (with), hazard, imperil, jeopardize, menace, risk, venture *Rel* intimidate, threaten
endangerment *Syn* DANGER (sense 2), distress, imperilment, jeopardy, peril, risk, trouble *Ant* safeness, safety, security
endearing *Syn* LOVABLE, adorable, darling, dear, disarming, precious, sweet, winning *Ant* abhorrent, abominable, detestable, hateful, odious, unlovable
endeavor *vb* **1** *Syn* ATTEMPT, assay, essay, seek, strive, try **2** *Syn* LABOR, drudge, grub, hump, hustle, moil, peg (away), plod, plow, plug, slave, slog, strain, strive, struggle, sweat, toil, travail, work *Ant* dabble, fiddle (around), fool (around), mess (around), putter (around)
endeavor *n* *Syn* ATTEMPT, crack, essay, fling, go, pass, shot, stab, trial, try, whack
endemic *Syn* NATIVE, aboriginal, autochthonous, indigenous *Ant* alien, foreign
ending **1** *Syn* END, termination, terminus *Ant* beginning **2** *Syn* FINALE, close, closing, conclusion, consummation, end, finis, finish, windup *Ant* beginning, dawn, opening, start
endless **1** *Syn* EVERLASTING, interminable, unceasing *Ant* transitory **2** *Syn* INFINITE, boundless, illimitable, immeasurable, indefinite, limitless, measureless, unbounded, unfathomable, unlimited *Ant* bounded, circumscribed, confined, definite, finite, limited, restricted
endorse *Syn* APPROVE, accredit, certify, sanction *Ant* disapprove
endow *Syn* DOWER, endue
endue *Syn* DOWER, endow
endurable *Syn* BEARABLE, sufferable, supportable, sustainable, tolerable *Ant* insufferable, insupportable, intolerable, unbearable, unendurable, unsupportable
endurance *Syn* CONTINUATION, continuance, duration, persistence, subsistence *Ant* ending, termination
endure **1** *Syn* BEAR (sense 2), abide, brook, stand, suffer, tolerate **2** *Syn* CONTINUE, abide, last, persist
enemy • one that is hostile toward another *Syn* adversary, antagonist, foe, opponent *Rel* archenemy *Ant* friend

energetic *Syn* VIGOROUS, lusty, nervous, strenuous *Ant* languorous, lethargic
energize **1** *Syn* ANIMATE, brace, enliven, fire, invigorate, jazz (up), liven (up), pep (up), quicken, stimulate, vitalize, vivify *Ant* damp, dampen, deaden, dull **2** *Syn* STRENGTHEN, fortify, invigorate, reinforce *Ant* weaken **3** *Syn* VITALIZE, activate *Ant* atrophy
energy *Syn* POWER (sense 1), force, might, puissance, strength *Ant* impotence
enervate *Syn* WEAKEN, debilitate, enfeeble, sap, soften *Ant* strengthen
enervated *Syn* LISTLESS, lackadaisical, languid, languishing, languorous, limp, spiritless *Ant* ambitious, animated, energetic, enterprising, motivated
enfeeble *Syn* WEAKEN, debilitate, enervate, sap, soften *Ant* strengthen
enforce • to carry out effectively *Syn* administer, apply, execute, implement *Rel* effect, effectuate
engage *Syn* PROMISE, contract, covenant, pledge, plight
engagement **1** • a promise to be in an agreed place at a specified time, usually for a particular purpose *Syn* appointment, assignation, date, rendezvous, tryst **2** *Syn* BATTLE, action
engaging **1** *Syn* INTERESTING, absorbing, arresting, engrossing, enthralling, fascinating, gripping, immersing, intriguing, involving, riveting *Ant* boring, drab, dry, dull, heavy, monotonous, tedious, uninteresting **2** *Syn* SWEET, dulcet, winning, winsome *Ant* bitter, sour
engender **1** *Syn* EFFECT, bring about, cause, create, effectuate, generate, induce, make, produce, prompt, result (in), spawn, work, yield **2** *Syn* GENERATE, beget, breed, get, procreate, propagate, reproduce, sire
engine *Syn* MACHINE, apparatus, machinery, mechanism, motor
engineer **1** • to plan out usually with subtle skill or care *Syn* contrive, finagle, finesse, frame, machinate, maneuver, manipulate, mastermind, negotiate, wangle *Rel* intrigue, plot, scheme **2** *Syn* GUIDE, lead, pilot, steer *Ant* misguide
engrave *Syn* CARVE, chisel, etch, incise, sculpt, sculpture
engross *Syn* MONOPOLIZE, absorb, consume
engrossed *Syn* INTENT, absorbed, rapt *Ant* distracted
engrossing *Syn* INTERESTING, absorbing, arresting, engaging, enthralling, fascinating, gripping, immersing, intriguing, involving, riveting *Ant* boring, drab, dry, dull, heavy, monotonous, tedious, uninteresting
engulf *Syn* FLOOD, deluge, drown, inundate, overflow, overwhelm, submerge, submerse, swamp *Ant* drain
enhance *Syn* INTENSIFY, aggravate, heighten *Ant* abate, allay, mitigate, temper
enhancement *Syn* ADVANCE (sense 1), advancement, breakthrough, improvement, refinement *Ant* setback
enigma *Syn* MYSTERY, conundrum, problem, puzzle, riddle
enigmatic *Syn* OBSCURE, ambiguous, cryptic, dark, equivocal, vague *Ant* distinct, obvious
enjoin **1** *Syn* COMMAND, bid, charge, direct, instruct, order *Ant* comply, obey **2** *Syn* FORBID, ban, bar, interdict, outlaw, prohibit, proscribe *Ant* allow, let, permit, suffer
enjoining *Syn* PROHIBITION (sense 1), banning, barring, forbidding, interdicting, interdiction, outlawing, prohibiting, proscribing, proscription *Ant* prescription
enjoy **1** *Syn* HAVE, hold, own, possess **2** *Syn* LIKE, dote, fancy, love, relish *Ant* dislike
enjoyable *Syn* FUN, amusing, delightful, diverting, entertaining, pleasurable *Ant* boring, dull
enjoyment *Syn* PLEASURE, delectation, delight, fruition, joy *Ant* anger, displeasure, vexation
enlarge **1** *Syn* INCREASE (sense 1), add (to), aggrandize, amplify, augment, boost, compound, escalate, expand, extend, multiply, raise, swell, up *Ant* abate, contract, decrease, diminish, lessen, lower, reduce, subtract (from) **2** *Syn* INCREASE (sense 2), accumulate, appreciate, balloon, build (up), burgeon, escalate, expand, mount, multiply, mushroom, proliferate, rise, snowball, swell, wax *Ant* contract, decrease, diminish, lessen, wane
enlighten **1** • to give information to *Syn* acquaint, advise, apprise, brief, clue, familiarize, fill in, inform, instruct, tell, wise (up) *Rel* clarify, clear (up), construe, elucidate, explain, explicate, expound, illuminate, illustrate, interpret, spell out **2** • to provide (someone) with moral or spiritual understanding *Syn* edify, educate, nurture *Rel* elevate, ennoble, lift, uplift **3** *Syn* ILLUMINATE, illustrate, light, lighten *Ant* darken, obscure
enliven *Syn* ANIMATE, brace, energize, fire, invigorate, jazz (up), liven (up), pep (up), quicken, stimulate, vitalize, vivify *Ant* damp, dampen, deaden, dull
enmesh *Syn* ENTANGLE, ensnare, entrap, mesh, snare, tangle, trap *Ant* disentangle
enmity • deep-seated dislike or ill will or a manifestation of such a feeling *Syn* animosity, animus, antagonism, antipathy, hostility, rancor *Rel* abhorrence, detestation, hate, hatred, loathing *Ant* amity
ennoble **1** *Syn* DIGNIFY, glorify, honor **2** *Syn* EXALT, aggrandize, dignify, enshrine, glorify, magnify *Ant* abase, degrade, demean, humble, humiliate
ennui *Syn* TEDIUM, boredom, doldrums
enormous *Syn* HUGE, Brobdingnagian, colossal, cyclopean, elephantine, gargantuan, gi-

ant, gigantean, gigantic, Herculean, immense, mammoth, titanic, vast *Ant* bitty, diminutive, microscopic (*or* microscopical), midget, miniature, minute, pocket, pygmy, teeny, teeny-weeny, tiny, wee

enough *Syn* SUFFICIENT, adequate, competent

enrage *Syn* ANGER, antagonize, incense, inflame, infuriate, madden, outrage, rankle, rile, roil *Ant* delight, gratify, please

enraged *Syn* ANGRY, angered, apoplectic, foaming, fuming, furious, incensed, indignant, inflamed, infuriated, irate, ireful, mad, outraged, rabid, riled, roiled, sore, steaming, wrathful, wroth *Ant* delighted, pleased

enrapture **1** *Syn* ELATE, elevate, exhilarate, overjoy, transport *Ant* depress **2** *Syn* ENTRANCE, carry away, enthrall (*or* enthral), overjoy, ravish, transport

enraptured *Syn* ECSTATIC, elated, entranced, euphoric, exhilarated, intoxicated, rapturous, rhapsodic *Ant* depressed

enroll *Syn* RECORD, catalog, list, register

ensconce *Syn* HIDE, bury, cache, conceal, screen, secrete

enshrine *Syn* EXALT, aggrandize, dignify, ennoble, glorify, magnify *Ant* abase, degrade, demean, humble, humiliate

ensign *Syn* FLAG, banner, color, jack, pendant, pennant, pennon, standard, streamer

ensnare **1** *Syn* CATCH, bag, capture, entrap, snare, trap *Ant* miss **2** *Syn* ENTANGLE, enmesh, entrap, mesh, snare, tangle, trap *Ant* disentangle

ensue *Syn* FOLLOW (sense 1), succeed, supervene *Ant* forsake (*a teacher or teachings*), precede

ensure • to make sure, certain, or safe *Syn* assure, cinch, guarantee, guaranty, insure, secure *Rel* attest, certify, vouch, warrant, witness

entangle • to catch or hold as if in a net *Syn* enmesh, ensnare, entrap, mesh, snare, tangle, trap *Rel* bag, capture, collar *Ant* disentangle

entente *Syn* CONTRACT, bargain, cartel, compact, concordat, convention, pact, treaty

enter **1** • to make way into something so as to reach or pass through the interior *Syn* penetrate, pierce, probe *Rel* encroach, entrench, invade, trespass *Ant* issue from **2** • to cause or permit to go in or get in *Syn* admit, introduce *Rel* insert, insinuate, intercalate, interpolate, introduce

enter (into *or* **upon)** *Syn* BEGIN (sense 2), commence, embark (on *or* upon), get off, kick off, launch, open, start, strike (into) *Ant* conclude, end, finish, terminate

enterprise *Syn* ADVENTURE, quest

entertain **1** *Syn* AMUSE, divert, recreate *Ant* bore **2** *Syn* HARBOR, board, house, lodge, shelter

entertaining *Syn* FUN, amusing, delightful, diverting, enjoyable, pleasurable *Ant* boring, dull

entertainment *Syn* AMUSEMENT, diversion, recreation *Ant* boredom

enthrall *or* **enthral** *Syn* ENTRANCE, carry away, enrapture, overjoy, ravish, transport

enthralling *Syn* INTERESTING, absorbing, arresting, engaging, engrossing, fascinating, gripping, immersing, intriguing, involving, riveting *Ant* boring, drab, dry, dull, heavy, monotonous, tedious, uninteresting

enthuse **1** *Syn* GUSH (sense 2), fuss, rave, rhapsodize, slobber **2** *Syn* THRILL, electrify

enthusiasm *Syn* PASSION, ardor, fervor, zeal

enthusiast **1** • a person who manifests excessive ardor, fervor, or devotion in an attachment to some cause, idea, party, or church *Syn* fanatic, zealot *Rel* addict, devotee, votary **2** *Syn* FAN, addict, aficionado, buff, bug, devotee, fanatic, fancier, fiend, freak, lover, maniac, nut

entice *Syn* LURE, allure, beguile, decoy, lead on, seduce, tempt

entire **1** *Syn* PERFECT, intact, whole *Ant* imperfect **2** *Syn* WHOLE, all, gross, total *Ant* partial

entity • one that has real and independent existence *Syn* being, creature, individual, person

entrance • to fill with overwhelming emotion (as wonder or delight) *Syn* carry away, enrapture, enthrall (*or* enthral), overjoy, ravish, transport *Rel* delight, gladden, gratify, please, satisfy

entranced *Syn* ECSTATIC, elated, enraptured, euphoric, exhilarated, intoxicated, rapturous, rhapsodic *Ant* depressed

entrap **1** *Syn* CATCH, bag, capture, ensnare, snare, trap *Ant* miss **2** *Syn* ENTANGLE, enmesh, ensnare, mesh, snare, tangle, trap *Ant* disentangle

entreat *Syn* BEG, adjure, beseech, implore, importune, supplicate

entrench *Syn* TRESPASS, encroach, infringe, invade

entrust *Syn* COMMIT, confide, consign, relegate

entwine *Syn* WIND, coil, curl, twine, twist, wreathe

enumerate *Syn* COUNT, number, tell

enunciate **1** *Syn* ANNOUNCE, advertise, blaze, broadcast, declare, placard, post, proclaim, promulgate, publicize, publish, sound **2** *Syn* ARTICULATE, pronounce

envelop **1** *Syn* COVER, overspread, shroud, veil, wrap *Ant* bare **2** *Syn* ENCLOSE, cage, coop, corral, fence, pen, wall

envious • having or showing mean resentment of another's possessions or advantages *Syn* covetous, invidious, jaundiced, jealous, resentful *Rel* begrudging, grudging

environ *Syn* SURROUND, circle, compass, encircle, encompass, gird, girdle, hem, ring

environment *Syn* BACKGROUND, backdrop, milieu, mise-en-scène, setting

envisage *Syn* THINK (sense 1), conceive, envision, fancy, imagine, realize
envision *Syn* THINK (sense 1), conceive, envisage, fancy, imagine, realize
envoy **1** *Syn* AGENT (sense 1), attorney, commissary, delegate, deputy, factor, procurator, proxy, representative **2** *Syn* AMBASSADOR, delegate, emissary, legate, minister, representative
envy *Syn* COVET, begrudge, grudge
ephemeral *Syn* MOMENTARY, evanescent, flash, fleeting, fugitive, impermanent, passing, short-lived, temporary, transient, transitory *Ant* enduring, eternal, everlasting, lasting, long-lived, permanent, perpetual
epicene *Syn* EFFEMINATE, effete
epicure • one who takes great pleasure in eating and drinking *Syn* bon vivant, gastronome, glutton, gourmand, gourmet *Rel* aesthete, connoisseur, dilettante
epicurean *Syn* SENSUOUS, luxurious, sybaritic, voluptuous
epigram *Syn* SAYING, adage, aphorism, apothegm, maxim, motto, proverb, saw
episode **1** *Syn* DIGRESSION, divagation, excursus **2** *Syn* OCCURRENCE, circumstance, event, incident
epistle *Syn* LETTER, dispatch, memorandum, message, missive, note, report
epithet *Syn* INSULT, affront, barb, dart, dig, indignity, name, offense (*or* offence), outrage, put-down, sarcasm, slight, slur
epitome **1** *Syn* ABRIDGMENT, abstract, brief, conspectus, synopsis *Ant* expansion **2** *Syn* EMBODIMENT, incarnation, manifestation, personification
epitomize **1** *Syn* EMBODY (sense 2), incarnate, manifest, materialize, personalize, personify, substantiate **2** *Syn* SUMMARIZE, abstract, digest, encapsulate, outline, recap, recapitulate, sum up, wrap up
epoch *Syn* AGE (sense 3), day, era, period, time
equable **1** *Syn* CLEMENT, balmy, gentle, mild, moderate, temperate *Ant* harsh, inclement, intemperate, severe **2** *Syn* STEADY, constant, even, uniform *Ant* jumpy, nervous, unsteady
equal *n* • one that is equal to another in status, achievement, or value *Syn* coordinate, counterpart, equivalent, fellow, like, match, parallel, peer, rival *Rel* analogue (*or* analog), associate, colleague, companion, competitor, double, mate, partner, twin
equal *vb Syn* MATCH, approach, rival, touch
equal *adj Syn* SAME, equivalent, identic, identical, selfsame, tantamount, very *Ant* different
equalize • to make equal in amount, degree, or status *Syn* balance, equate, even, level *Rel* accommodate, adjust, compensate, fit
equanimity • evenness of emotions or temper *Syn* aplomb, calmness, composure, coolheadedness, coolness, imperturbability, placidity, self-possession, serenity, tranquillity (*or* tranquility) *Rel* assurance, confidence, poise, self-assurance, self-confidence *Ant* agitation, discomposure, perturbation
equate *Syn* EQUALIZE, balance, even, level
equilibrium *Syn* BALANCE, equipoise, poise, tension
equip *Syn* FURNISH (sense 1), accoutre (*or* accouter), fit (out), outfit, rig, supply *Ant* hold (back), keep (back), reserve, retain, withhold
equipment • items needed for the performance of a task or useful in effecting a given end *Syn* apparatus, gear, machinery, matériel, outfit, paraphernalia, tackle
equipoise *Syn* BALANCE, equilibrium, poise, tension
equitable *Syn* FAIR, dispassionate, impartial, just, objective, unbiased, uncolored *Ant* unfair
equivalent *n Syn* EQUAL, coordinate, counterpart, fellow, like, match, parallel, peer, rival
equivalent *adj Syn* SAME, equal, identic, identical, selfsame, tantamount, very *Ant* different
equivocal *Syn* OBSCURE, ambiguous, cryptic, dark, enigmatic, vague *Ant* distinct, obvious
equivocate *Syn* LIE, fib, palter, prevaricate
era *Syn* AGE (sense 3), day, epoch, period, time
eradicate *Syn* EXTERMINATE, deracinate, extirpate, uproot, wipe
erase • to strike, rub, or scrape out something so that it no longer has effect or existence *Syn* blot out, cancel, delete, efface, expunge, obliterate *Rel* annul, negate, nullify
ere *Syn* BEFORE, ahead of, of, previous to, prior to, to *Ant* after, following
erect *adj* • rising straight up *Syn* perpendicular, plumb, raised, standing, upright, upstanding, vertical *Rel* elevated, lifted, upended, upraised *Ant* flat, recumbent
erect *vb Syn* BUILD, assemble, construct, fabricate, make, make up, piece, put up, raise, rear, set up *Ant* disassemble, dismantle, take down
eremite *Syn* RECLUSE, anchorite, cenobite, hermit
erotic • of, devoted to, affected by, or tending to arouse sexual love or desire *Syn* amative, amatory, amorous, aphrodisiac *Rel* ardent, fervent, fervid, impassioned, passionate, perfervid
erratic **1** *Syn* FITFUL, casual, choppy, discontinuous, intermittent, irregular, occasional, spasmodic, sporadic, spotty, unsteady *Ant* constant, continuous, regular, steady **2** *Syn* STRANGE, curious, eccentric, odd, outlandish, peculiar, quaint, queer, singular, unique *Ant* familiar
erratically *Syn* HIT OR MISS, aimlessly, anyhow,

anyway, anywise, desultorily, haphazard, haphazardly, helter-skelter, irregularly, randomly *Ant* methodically, systematically

erroneousness *Syn* FALLACY (sense 2), fallaciousness, falseness, falsity, untruth *Ant* truth

error **1** • something (as an act, statement, or belief) that departs from what is or is generally held to be acceptable *Syn* blunder, bull, faux pas, howler, lapse, mistake, slip **2** *Syn* FALLACY (sense 1), falsehood, falsity, illusion, misconception, myth, old wives' tale, untruth *Ant* truth, verity

errorless *Syn* IMPECCABLE, faultless, flawless

ersatz *Syn* ARTIFICIAL, factitious, synthetic *Ant* natural

erstwhile *Syn* FORMER, late, old, onetime, past, sometime, whilom

erudite **1** *Syn* BOOKISH, learned, literary *Ant* colloquial, nonliterary **2** *Syn* EDUCATED, knowledgeable, learned, literate, scholarly, well-read *Ant* ignorant, illiterate, uneducated **3** *Syn* LEARNED, scholarly

erudition **1** *Syn* EDUCATION (sense 2), knowledge, learnedness, learning, scholarship, science **2** *Syn* KNOWLEDGE, information, learning, lore, scholarship, science *Ant* ignorance

erupt **1** • to develop suddenly and violently *Syn* break out, burst (forth), explode, flame, flare (up) *Rel* burgeon, mushroom, snowball **2** • to throw out or off (something from within) often violently *Syn* belch, disgorge, eject, expel, jet, spew, spout, spurt *Rel* gush, pour, stream, surge

escalate **1** *Syn* INCREASE (sense 1), add (to), aggrandize, amplify, augment, boost, compound, enlarge, expand, extend, multiply, raise, swell, up *Ant* abate, contract, decrease, diminish, lessen, lower, reduce, subtract (from) **2** *Syn* INCREASE (sense 2), accumulate, appreciate, balloon, build (up), burgeon, enlarge, expand, mount, multiply, mushroom, proliferate, rise, snowball, swell, wax *Ant* contract, decrease, diminish, lessen, wane

escape **1** • to run away especially from something that limits one's freedom or threatens one's well-being *Syn* abscond, decamp, flee, fly **2** • to get away or keep away from what one does not wish to incur, endure, or encounter *Syn* avoid, elude, eschew, evade, shun

eschew **1** *Syn* ESCAPE (sense 2), avoid, elude, evade, shun **2** *Syn* FORGO, abnegate, forbear, sacrifice

escort *n* • one that accompanies another for protection, guidance, or as a courtesy *Syn* attendant, companion, guard, guide *Rel* chaperone (*or* chaperon), conductor, leader, pilot, shadow, sidekick, squire

escort *vb Syn* ACCOMPANY, attend, chaperone (*or* chaperon), convoy, squire

esoteric *Syn* RECONDITE, abstruse, occult

especial *Syn* SPECIAL, individual, particular, specific

especially *Syn* VERY, awful, awfully, beastly, deadly, exceedingly, extra, extremely, far, frightfully, full, greatly, heavily, highly, hugely, jolly, mightily, mighty, mortally, most, much, particularly, rattling, real, right, so, something, super, terribly, too, whacking *Ant* little, negligibly, nominally, slightly

espousal *Syn* MARRIAGE, matrimony, nuptial, wedding, wedlock

espouse *Syn* ADOPT, embrace *Ant* discard, repudiate

esprit *Syn* VIGOR, dash, drive, élan, punch, spirit, verve, vim

esprit de corps *Syn* MORALE, discipline

espy *Syn* SEE (sense 1), behold, contemplate, descry, discern, note, notice, observe, perceive, remark, survey, view

essay *n* **1** • a relatively brief discourse written for others' reading or consideration *Syn* article, composition, paper, theme **2** *Syn* ATTEMPT, crack, endeavor, fling, go, pass, shot, stab, trial, try, whack

essay *vb Syn* ATTEMPT, assay, endeavor, seek, strive, try

essential **1** • so important as to be indispensable *Syn* cardinal, fundamental, vital *Rel* basal, basic, underlying **2** *Syn* ELEMENTARY, basic, elemental, fundamental, rudimentary, underlying *Ant* advanced **3** *Syn* INHERENT, constitutional, ingrained, intrinsic *Ant* adventitious **4** *Syn* NEEDFUL, indispensable, necessary, requisite

establish **1** *Syn* FOUND, create, institute, organize **2** *Syn* SET, fix, settle

estate *Syn* MANSION, castle, château, countryseat, hacienda, hall, manor, manor house, palace, villa

esteem *n Syn* REGARD, admiration, respect *Ant* despite

esteem *vb Syn* REGARD, admire, respect *Ant* despise

estimate **1** • to judge a thing with respect to its worth *Syn* appraise, assay, assess, evaluate, rate, value *Rel* adjudge, adjudicate, judge **2** • to decide the size, amount, number, or distance of (something) without actual measurement *Syn* calculate, call, conjecture, figure, gauge, guess, judge, make, place, put, reckon, suppose **3** *Syn* CALCULATE, compute, reckon

estrange • to cause one to break a bond or tie of affection or loyalty *Syn* alienate, disaffect, wean *Rel* divide, divorce, part, separate, sever, sunder *Ant* reconcile

estrangement • the loss of friendship or affection *Syn* alienation, disaffection, disgruntlement, souring *Rel* antagonism, embitterment, envenoming *Ant* reconciliation

etch *Syn* CARVE, chisel, engrave, incise, sculpt, sculpture

ethereal *Syn* AIRY, aerial *Ant* substantial
ethical *Syn* MORAL, noble, righteous, virtuous
ethics • the code of good conduct for an individual or group *Syn* morality, morals, principles, standards *Rel* customs, etiquette, manners, mores
etiquette *Syn* DECORUM, decency, dignity, propriety *Ant* indecorum, license
eulogize *Syn* PRAISE, acclaim, extol, laud *Ant* blame
eulogy *Syn* ENCOMIUM, citation, panegyric, tribute
euphoria *Syn* ECSTASY, elation, exhilaration, heaven, intoxication, paradise, rapture, rhapsody, transport *Ant* depression
euphoric *Syn* ECSTATIC, elated, enraptured, entranced, exhilarated, intoxicated, rapturous, rhapsodic *Ant* depressed
euphuistic *Syn* RHETORICAL, aureate, bombastic, flowery, grandiloquent, magniloquent
evacuate *Syn* EMPTY, clear, vacate, void *Ant* fill, load
evade *Syn* ESCAPE (sense 2), avoid, elude, eschew, shun
evaluate *Syn* ESTIMATE (sense 1), appraise, assay, assess, rate, value
evanesce *Syn* VANISH, disappear, evaporate, fade *Ant* appear, loom
evanescent *Syn* MOMENTARY, ephemeral, flash, fleeting, fugitive, impermanent, passing, short-lived, temporary, transient, transitory *Ant* enduring, eternal, everlasting, lasting, long-lived, permanent, perpetual
evaporate *Syn* VANISH, disappear, evanesce, fade *Ant* appear, loom
even *vb Syn* EQUALIZE, balance, equate, level
even *adj* **1** *Syn* LEVEL, flat, flush, plain, plane, smooth **2** *Syn* STEADY, constant, equable, uniform *Ant* jumpy, nervous, unsteady
event **1** *Syn* EFFECT, aftereffect, aftermath, consequence, issue, outcome, result, sequel, upshot *Ant* cause **2** *Syn* OCCURRENCE, circumstance, episode, incident
eventual *Syn* LAST, concluding, final, latest, terminal, ultimate *Ant* first
ever *Syn* AT ALL, anywise
everlasting • continuing on and on without end *Syn* endless, interminable, unceasing *Rel* boundless, eternal, infinite *Ant* transitory
every *Syn* ALL, each *Ant* no
evidence *Syn* SHOW (sense 1), demonstrate, evince, manifest *Ant* disguise
evident • readily perceived or apprehended *Syn* apparent, clear, distinct, manifest, obvious, palpable, patent, plain *Rel* appreciable, perceptible, ponderable, sensible, tangible
evidently *Syn* APPARENTLY, ostensibly, presumably, seemingly, supposedly
evil *n* • that which is morally unacceptable *Syn* bad, evildoing, ill, immorality, iniquity, sin, villainy, wrong *Rel* atrociousness, badness, evilness, heinousness, nefariousness, sinfulness, vileness, wickedness *Ant* good, morality, right, virtue
evil *adj* **1** *Syn* BAD (sense 1), ill, naughty, wicked *Ant* good **2** *Syn* HARMFUL, adverse, bad, baleful, baneful, damaging, deleterious, detrimental, hurtful, ill, injurious, mischievous, noxious, pernicious, prejudicial *Ant* harmless, innocent, innocuous, inoffensive, safe
evildoing *Syn* EVIL, bad, ill, immorality, iniquity, sin, villainy, wrong *Ant* good, morality, right, virtue
evince *Syn* SHOW (sense 1), demonstrate, evidence, manifest *Ant* disguise
evoke *Syn* EDUCE, elicit, extort, extract
evolve *Syn* UNFOLD, develop, elaborate, perfect
exact *adj Syn* CORRECT, accurate, nice, precise, right *Ant* incorrect
exact *vb* **1** *Syn* DEMAND, claim, require **2** *Syn* IMPOSE, assess, charge, fine, lay, levy, put *Ant* remit
exacting *Syn* ONEROUS, burdensome, oppressive
exactitude *Syn* PRECISION, accuracy, closeness, delicacy, exactness, fineness, preciseness, rigorousness, veracity *Ant* coarseness, impreciseness, imprecision, inaccuracy, inexactness, roughness
exactly *Syn* STRICTLY, precisely, rigidly, rigorously *Ant* imprecisely, inexactly, loosely
exactness *Syn* PRECISION, accuracy, closeness, delicacy, exactitude, fineness, preciseness, rigorousness, veracity *Ant* coarseness, impreciseness, imprecision, inaccuracy, inexactness, roughness
exaggerate *Syn* OVERSTATE, overdo, overdraw, put on *Ant* understate
exaggeration • the representation of something in terms that go beyond the facts *Syn* caricature, coloring, elaboration, embellishment, embroidering, hyperbole, magnification, overstatement, padding, stretching *Rel* amplification, enhancement *Ant* understatement
exalt • to enhance the status of *Syn* aggrandize, dignify, ennoble, enshrine, glorify, magnify *Rel* boost, elevate, lift, promote, raise, upgrade, uplift *Ant* abase, degrade, demean, humble, humiliate
examination *Syn* INSPECTION, audit, check, checkup, review, scan, scrutiny, survey
examine **1** *Syn* ASK (sense 1), catechize, inquire, interrogate, query, question, quiz **2** *Syn* SCRUTINIZE, audit, inspect, scan
example **1** • one of a group or collection that shows what the whole is like *Syn* case, exemplar, illustration, instance, representative, sample, specimen *Rel* cross section **2** *Syn* MODEL, beau ideal, exemplar, ideal, mirror, pattern, standard

exasperate *Syn* IRRITATE, aggravate, nettle, peeve, provoke, rile
exasperating *Syn* ANNOYING, aggravating, bothersome, disturbing, frustrating, galling, irksome, irritating, maddening, nettling, peeving, pesty, rankling, riling, vexatious, vexing
excavate *Syn* DIG, delve, grub, spade
exceed • to go or to be beyond a stated or implied limit, measure, or degree *Syn* excel, outdo, outstrip, surpass, transcend
exceedingly *Syn* VERY, awful, awfully, beastly, deadly, especially, extra, extremely, far, frightfully, full, greatly, heavily, highly, hugely, jolly, mightily, mighty, mortally, most, much, particularly, rattling, real, right, so, something, super, terribly, too, whacking *Ant* little, negligibly, nominally, slightly
excel *Syn* EXCEED, outdo, outstrip, surpass, transcend
excellence • a quality that gives something special worth *Syn* distinction, excellency, merit, value, virtue *Rel* advantage, edge, superiority *Ant* deficiency
excellency *Syn* EXCELLENCE, distinction, merit, value, virtue *Ant* deficiency
excellent • of the very best kind *Syn* A1, bang-up, banner, capital, classic, crackerjack, dandy, divine, fabulous, fine, first-class, first-rate, grand, great, groovy, heavenly, jim-dandy, keen, marvelous (*or* marvellous), mean, neat, nifty, noble, par excellence, prime, sensational, splendid, stellar, sterling, superb, superior, superlative, supernal, swell, terrific, tip-top, top, top-notch, unsurpassed, wonderful *Rel* OK, acceptable, adequate, all right, decent, good, passable, satisfactory, tolerable *Ant* poor
exceptionable *Syn* OBJECTIONABLE, unacceptable, undesirable, unwanted, unwelcome
exceptional • being out of the ordinary *Syn* extraordinary, phenomenal, unusual, unwonted *Rel* conspicuous, noticeable, outstanding, prominent, remarkable, salient, signal *Ant* average, common
excess • the state or an instance of going beyond what is usual, proper, or needed *Syn* fat, overabundance, overage, overflow, overkill, overmuch, oversupply, superabundance, superfluity, surfeit, surplus *Rel* abundance, bounty, plentitude, plenty, profusion, sufficiency *Ant* deficiency, deficit, insufficiency
excessive • going beyond a normal or acceptable limit *Syn* exorbitant, extravagant, extreme, immoderate, inordinate *Rel* extra, spare, superfluous, supernumerary, surplus *Ant* deficient
exchange 1 • to give and receive reciprocally *Syn* bandy, interchange 2 *Syn* CHANGE (sense 3), commute, shift, substitute, swap, switch, trade
excitable • easily excited by nature *Syn* flighty, fluttery, high-strung, jittery, jumpy, nervous, skittish, spooky *Rel* hot-blooded, mercurial, temperamental, unstable, volatile, volcanic *Ant* unflappable
excitant *Syn* STIMULUS, impetus, incitement, stimulant
excite *Syn* PROVOKE, galvanize, pique, quicken, stimulate
exciter *Syn* AGITATOR, demagogue, firebrand, fomenter, incendiary, inciter, instigator, rabble-rouser
exciting *Syn* PROVOCATIVE, inciting, instigating, piquing, provoking, stimulating
exclude • to prevent the participation, consideration, or inclusion of *Syn* blackball, debar, disbar, eliminate, rule out, shut out, suspend *Rel* bar, block, hinder *Ant* admit, include
exclusive *Syn* SELECT, elect, picked *Ant* indiscriminate
excogitate *Syn* CONSIDER (sense 1), contemplate, study, weigh
excoriate 1 *Syn* ABRADE, chafe, fret, gall 2 *Syn* ATTACK (sense 2), abuse, assail, belabor, blast, castigate, jump (on), lambaste (*or* lambast), scathe, slam, vituperate
excruciating • intensely or unbearably painful *Syn* agonizing, racking *Rel* tormenting, torturing
exculpate • to free from alleged fault or guilt *Syn* absolve, acquit, exonerate, vindicate *Rel* explain, justify, rationalize *Ant* accuse, inculpate
excursion *Syn* JOURNEY, cruise, expedition, jaunt, pilgrimage, tour, trip, voyage
excursus *Syn* DIGRESSION, divagation, episode
excusable *Syn* VENIAL, forgivable, pardonable, remittable *Ant* inexcusable, mortal, unforgivable, unpardonable
excuse *n* 1 • an explanation that frees one from fault or blame *Syn* alibi, defense, justification, plea, reason *Rel* acknowledgment, apology, atonement, confession, cop-out, guise, out, pretense (*or* pretence), pretext, rationale, rationalization 2 *Syn* APOLOGY, alibi, apologia, plea, pretext
excuse *vb* • to exact neither punishment nor redress for or from *Syn* condone, forgive, pardon, remit *Rel* account, explain, justify, rationalize *Ant* punish
execrable • so odious as to be utterly detestable *Syn* accursed, cursed, damnable *Rel* atrocious, heinous, monstrous, outrageous
execrate • to denounce violently *Syn* anathematize, curse, damn, objurgate *Rel* censure, condemn, denounce, reprehend, reprobate
execute 1 *Syn* ENFORCE, administer, apply, implement 2 *Syn* KILL, assassinate, dispatch, murder, slay 3 *Syn* PERFORM, accomplish, achieve, discharge, effect, fulfill
executive • a person who manages or directs

Syn administrator, director, manager, superintendent, supervisor *Rel* officer, official
exemplar 1 *Syn* EXAMPLE, case, illustration, instance, representative, sample, specimen 2 *Syn* MODEL, beau ideal, example, ideal, mirror, pattern, standard
exercise *n* • repeated activity or exertion *Syn* drill, practice *Rel* act, action, deed
exercise *vb* *Syn* EXERT, apply, ply, put out, wield
exert • to bring to bear especially forcefully or effectively *Syn* apply, exercise, ply, put out, wield *Rel* employ, use, utilize
exertion *Syn* EFFORT, pains, trouble *Ant* ease
exhaust 1 *Syn* DEPLETE, clean (out), consume, drain, expend, spend, use up *Ant* renew, replace 2 *Syn* TIRE, fatigue, jade, tucker, weary
exhaustion *Syn* FATIGUE, burnout, collapse, lassitude, prostration, tiredness, weariness *Ant* refreshment, rejuvenation, revitalization
exhaustive • trying all possibilities *Syn* all-out, clean, complete, comprehensive, full-scale, out-and-out, thorough, thoroughgoing, total *Rel* broad, extensive, far-reaching, in-depth, wide
exhibit *n* *Syn* EXHIBITION, exposition, fair, show
exhibit *vb* *Syn* SHOW (sense 2), display, expose, flaunt, parade *Ant* disguise
exhibition • a public display of objects of interest *Syn* exhibit, exposition, fair, show
exhilarate *Syn* ELATE, elevate, enrapture, overjoy, transport *Ant* depress
exhilarated *Syn* ECSTATIC, elated, enraptured, entranced, euphoric, intoxicated, rapturous, rhapsodic *Ant* depressed
exhilaration 1 *Syn* ECSTASY, elation, euphoria, heaven, intoxication, paradise, rapture, rhapsody, transport *Ant* depression 2 *Syn* THRILL, bang, kick, titillation
exhort *Syn* URGE, egg (on), encourage, goad, press, prod, prompt
exigency 1 *Syn* JUNCTURE, contingency, crisis, emergency, pass, pinch, strait 2 *Syn* NEED, necessity
exigent *Syn* PRESSING, crying, imperative, importunate, insistent, instant, urgent
exiguous *Syn* MEAGER, scant, scanty, scrimpy, skimpy, spare, sparse *Ant* ample, copious
exile *Syn* BANISH, deport, expatriate, extradite, ostracize, transport
exist *Syn* BE, live, subsist
existence • the state or fact of having independent reality *Syn* actuality, being *Rel* condition, situation, state, status *Ant* nonexistence
existent *Syn* ACTUAL, concrete, factual, real, true, very *Ant* conjectural, hypothetical, ideal, nonexistent, possible, potential, theoretical
exonerate *Syn* EXCULPATE, absolve, acquit, vindicate *Ant* accuse, inculpate
exorbitant *Syn* EXCESSIVE, extravagant, extreme, immoderate, inordinate *Ant* deficient
exordium *Syn* INTRODUCTION, foreword, preamble, preface, prelude, prologue
exotic • excitingly or mysteriously unusual *Syn* fantastic, glamorous, marvelous (*or* marvellous), outlandish, romantic, strange *Rel* colorful, picturesque, quaint
expand 1 • to increase or become increased in size, bulk, or volume *Syn* amplify, dilate, distend, inflate, swell *Rel* augment, enlarge, increase *Ant* abridge, circumscribe, contract 2 *Syn* INCREASE (sense 1), add (to), aggrandize, amplify, augment, boost, compound, enlarge, escalate, extend, multiply, raise, swell, up *Ant* abate, contract, decrease, diminish, lessen, lower, reduce, subtract (from) 3 *Syn* INCREASE (sense 2), accumulate, appreciate, balloon, build (up), burgeon, enlarge, escalate, mount, multiply, mushroom, proliferate, rise, snowball, swell, wax *Ant* contract, decrease, diminish, lessen, wane
expanse • a significantly large area or range *Syn* amplitude, spread, stretch *Rel* compass, orbit, range, reach, scope, sweep
expansive 1 *Syn* ELASTIC (sense 2), buoyant, effervescent, resilient, volatile *Ant* depressed 2 *Syn* EXTENSIVE, broad, extended, far-flung, far-reaching, wide, widespread *Ant* narrow
expatiate *Syn* DISCOURSE, descant, dilate
expatriate *Syn* BANISH, deport, exile, extradite, ostracize, transport
expect • to anticipate in the mind *Syn* await, hope, look *Rel* anticipate, apprehend, divine, foreknow, foresee *Ant* despair of
expedient *adj* • suitable for bringing about a desired result under the circumstances *Syn* advisable, desirable, judicious, politic, prudent, tactical, wise *Rel* advantageous, beneficial, profitable *Ant* imprudent, inadvisable, inexpedient, injudicious, unwise
expedient *n* *Syn* RESOURCE, makeshift, resort, shift, stopgap, substitute, surrogate
expedition 1 *Syn* HASTE, dispatch, hurry, speed *Ant* deliberation 2 *Syn* JOURNEY, cruise, excursion, jaunt, pilgrimage, tour, trip, voyage
expeditious *Syn* FAST, fleet, hasty, quick, rapid, speedy, swift *Ant* slow
expel *Syn* ERUPT (sense 2), belch, disgorge, eject, jet, spew, spout, spurt
expend 1 *Syn* DEPLETE, clean (out), consume, drain, exhaust, spend, use up *Ant* renew, replace 2 *Syn* SPEND, disburse *Ant* save
expense *Syn* PRICE, charge, cost
expensive *Syn* COSTLY, dear, invaluable, precious, priceless, valuable *Ant* cheap
expensively *Syn* HIGH, extravagantly, grandly, lavishly, luxuriously, opulently, richly, sumptuously *Ant* austerely, humbly, modestly, plainly, simply

experience • to pass through the process of actually coming to know or to feel *Syn* suffer, sustain, undergo *Rel* behold, perceive, see, survey, view

expert *n* • a person with a high level of knowledge or skill in a field *Syn* ace, adept, artist, authority, crackerjack, maestro, master, past master, scholar, shark, virtuoso, whiz, wizard *Rel* pro, professional *Ant* amateur

expert *adj Syn* PROFICIENT, adept, masterly, skilled, skillful *Ant* amateur, amateurish, inexperienced, inexpert, unexperienced, unpracticed, unprofessional, unseasoned, unskilled, unskillful

expire *Syn* PASS, elapse, pass away

expired *Syn* EXTINCT, bygone, dead, defunct, departed, gone, vanished *Ant* alive, existent, existing, extant, living

explain **1** • to make the meaning of something understood or more comprehensible *Syn* clarify, clear (up), construe, demonstrate, elucidate, explicate, expound, illuminate, illustrate, interpret, spell out *Rel* decipher, decode *Ant* obscure **2** • to give the reason for or cause of *Syn* account (for), explain away, rationalize *Rel* condone, excuse, forgive, justify

explainable *Syn* SOLVABLE, answerable, explicable, resolvable, soluble *Ant* inexplicable, insoluble, unexplainable, unsolvable

explain away *Syn* EXPLAIN (sense 2), account (for), rationalize

explicable *Syn* SOLVABLE, answerable, explainable, resolvable, soluble *Ant* inexplicable, insoluble, unexplainable, unsolvable

explicate *Syn* EXPLAIN (sense 1), clarify, clear (up), construe, demonstrate, elucidate, expound, illuminate, illustrate, interpret, spell out *Ant* obscure

explicit • characterized by full precise expression and meaning that is perfectly clear *Syn* categorical, definite, express, specific *Rel* accurate, exact, precise *Ant* ambiguous

explode *Syn* ERUPT (sense 1), break out, burst (forth), flame, flare (up)

exploit *Syn* FEAT, achievement

explore • to search through or into *Syn* delve (into), dig (into), inquire (into), investigate, look (into), probe, research *Rel* examine, inspect, sift, study, view

exponent • a person who actively supports or favors a cause *Syn* advocate, apostle, backer, booster, champion, friend, promoter, proponent, supporter *Rel* loyalist, partisan, stalwart *Ant* adversary, antagonist, opponent

expose *Syn* SHOW (sense 2), display, exhibit, flaunt, parade *Ant* disguise

exposé *Syn* EXPOSITION, exposure

exposed *Syn* LIABLE, open, prone, sensitive, subject, susceptible *Ant* exempt, immune

exposition **1** • a setting forth or laying open of a thing or things hitherto not known or fully understood *Syn* exposé, exposure **2** *Syn* EXHIBITION, exhibit, fair, show

expostulate *Syn* OBJECT, kick, protest, remonstrate *Ant* acquiesce

expostulation *Syn* OBJECTION, challenge, complaint, demur, fuss, protest, question, remonstrance

exposure **1** *Syn* EXPOSITION, exposé **2** *Syn* REVELATION (sense 2), disclosure, divulgence

expound *Syn* EXPLAIN (sense 1), clarify, clear (up), construe, demonstrate, elucidate, explicate, illuminate, illustrate, interpret, spell out *Ant* obscure

express *vb* **1** • to let out what one feels or thinks *Syn* air, broach, utter, vent, ventilate, voice *Rel* speak, talk *Ant* imply **2** *Syn* PHRASE, articulate, clothe, couch, formulate, put, say, state, word

express *adj Syn* EXPLICIT, categorical, definite, specific *Ant* ambiguous

expression *Syn* PHRASE, idiom, locution

expressive • clearly conveying a special meaning (as one's mood) *Syn* eloquent, meaning, meaningful, pregnant, revealing, significant, suggestive *Rel* evocative, flavorful, graphic, pictorial, redolent, reminiscent, rich, sententious, vivid, weighty

expunge *Syn* ERASE, blot out, cancel, delete, efface, obliterate

exquisite *adj* **1** *Syn* CHOICE, dainty, delicate, elegant, rare, recherché *Ant* indifferent, medium **2** *Syn* INTENSE, fierce, vehement, violent *Ant* subdued

exquisite *n Syn* FOP, beau, buck, coxcomb, dandy, dude

extant *Syn* PRESENT, current, ongoing, present-day *Ant* ago, future, past

extemporaneous • composed, devised, or done at the moment rather than beforehand *Syn* extemporary, extempore, impromptu, improvised, offhand, unpremeditated *Rel* impulsive, spontaneous

extemporary *Syn* EXTEMPORANEOUS, extempore, impromptu, improvised, offhand, unpremeditated

extempore *Syn* EXTEMPORANEOUS, extemporary, impromptu, improvised, offhand, unpremeditated

extend **1** • to make or become longer *Syn* elongate, lengthen, prolong, protract *Rel* augment, enlarge, increase *Ant* abridge, shorten **2** *Syn* INCREASE (sense 1), add (to), aggrandize, amplify, augment, boost, compound, enlarge, escalate, expand, multiply, raise, swell, up *Ant* abate, contract, decrease, diminish, lessen, lower, reduce, subtract (from)

extended **1** *Syn* EXTENSIVE, broad, expansive, far-flung, far-reaching, wide, widespread *Ant* narrow **2** *Syn* LONG (sense 1), elongated, king-size (*or* king-sized), lengthy *Ant* brief, short **3** *Syn* LONG (sense 2), far, great, lengthy, long-lived, long-range, long-term, marathon *Ant* brief, short, short-lived, short-range, short-term

extension *Syn* ANNEX, ell, wing

extensive • having considerable extent *Syn* broad, expansive, extended, far-flung, far-reaching, wide, widespread *Rel* comprehensive, general, global, inclusive *Ant* narrow

extent *Syn* SIZE, area, dimensions, magnitude, volume

extenuate **1** *Syn* PALLIATE, gloss, gloze, whiten, whitewash **2** *Syn* THIN, attenuate, dilute, rarefy *Ant* thicken

exterior *Syn* OUTER, external, outside, outward *Ant* inner

exterminate • to destroy utterly *Syn* deracinate, eradicate, extirpate, uproot, wipe *Rel* abate, abolish, annihilate, extinguish

extermination *Syn* DESTRUCTION, annihilation, decimation, demolishment, demolition, desolation, devastation, extinction, havoc, loss, obliteration, ruin, ruination, wastage, wreckage *Ant* building, construction, erection, raising

external *Syn* OUTER, exterior, outside, outward *Ant* inner

externalize *Syn* REALIZE, actualize, embody, hypostatize, incarnate, materialize, objectify, reify

extinct • no longer existing *Syn* bygone, dead, defunct, departed, expired, gone, vanished *Rel* nonexistent *Ant* alive, existent, existing, extant, living

extinction *Syn* DESTRUCTION, annihilation, decimation, demolishment, demolition, desolation, devastation, extermination, havoc, loss, obliteration, ruin, ruination, wastage, wreckage *Ant* building, construction, erection, raising

extinguish *Syn* CRUSH (sense 2), quash, quell, quench, suppress

extirpate *Syn* EXTERMINATE, deracinate, eradicate, uproot, wipe

extol *Syn* PRAISE, acclaim, eulogize, laud *Ant* blame

extort *Syn* EDUCE, elicit, evoke, extract

extra *n Syn* BONUS, dividend, gratuity, gravy, lagniappe, perquisite, tip

extra *adj Syn* SUPERFLUOUS, spare, supernumerary, surplus

extra *adv Syn* VERY, awful, awfully, beastly, deadly, especially, exceedingly, extremely, far, frightfully, full, greatly, heavily, highly, hugely, jolly, mightily, mighty, mortally, most, much, particularly, rattling, real, right, so, something, super, terribly, too, whacking *Ant* little, negligibly, nominally, slightly

extract *Syn* EDUCE, elicit, evoke, extort

extraction *Syn* ANCESTRY, birth, blood, bloodline, breeding, descent, family tree, genealogy, line, lineage, origin, parentage, pedigree, stock, strain *Ant* issue, posterity, progeny, seed

extradite *Syn* BANISH, deport, exile, expatriate, ostracize, transport

extraneous **1** *Syn* EXTRINSIC, alien, foreign *Ant* intrinsic **2** *Syn* IRRELEVANT, immaterial, inapplicable *Ant* applicable, apposite, apropos, germane, material, pertinent, relevant

extraordinary *Syn* EXCEPTIONAL, phenomenal, unusual, unwonted *Ant* average, common

extravagant **1** *Syn* EXCESSIVE, exorbitant, extreme, immoderate, inordinate *Ant* deficient **2** *Syn* PRODIGAL, profligate, spendthrift, squandering, thriftless, unthrifty, wasteful *Ant* conserving, economical, economizing, frugal, scrimping, skimping, thrifty

extravagantly *Syn* HIGH, expensively, grandly, lavishly, luxuriously, opulently, richly, sumptuously *Ant* austerely, humbly, modestly, plainly, simply

extreme *Syn* EXCESSIVE, exorbitant, extravagant, immoderate, inordinate *Ant* deficient

extremely *Syn* VERY, awful, awfully, beastly, deadly, especially, exceedingly, extra, far, frightfully, full, greatly, heavily, highly, hugely, jolly, mightily, mighty, mortally, most, much, particularly, rattling, real, right, so, something, super, terribly, too, whacking *Ant* little, negligibly, nominally, slightly

extremist *Syn* RADICAL, revolutionary, revolutionist *Ant* moderate

extricate • to free or release from what binds or holds back *Syn* disembarrass, disencumber, disentangle, untangle *Rel* abstract, detach, disengage

extrinsic • external to a thing, its essential nature, or its original character *Syn* alien, extraneous, foreign *Rel* exterior, external, outer, outside, outward *Ant* intrinsic

extroverted *Syn* CONVIVIAL, boon, companionable, gregarious, outgoing, sociable, social *Ant* antisocial, introverted, reclusive, unsociable

exuberant *Syn* PROFUSE, lavish, lush, luxuriant, prodigal *Ant* scant, scanty, spare

exude • to flow forth slowly through small openings *Syn* bleed, ooze, percolate, seep, strain, sweat, weep *Rel* dribble, drip, trickle

exultant • having or expressing feelings of joy or triumph *Syn* exulting, glorying, jubilant, rejoicing, triumphant *Rel* ecstatic, elated, euphoric

exulting *Syn* EXULTANT, glorying, jubilant, rejoicing, triumphant

eye **1** *Syn* ATTENTION (sense 2), awareness, cognizance, ear, heed, notice, observance, observation **2** *Syn* CENTER (sense 2), base, capital, core, cynosure, focus, heart, hub, mecca, nucleus, seat

eyeless *Syn* BLIND, sightless, stone blind *Ant* sighted

eyewitness *Syn* SPECTATOR, beholder, bystander, kibitzer, looker-on, observer, onlooker, witness

F

fable **1** *Syn* ALLEGORY, parable **2** *Syn* FICTION, fabrication, figment
fabricate **1** *Syn* BUILD, assemble, construct, erect, make, make up, piece, put up, raise, rear, set up *Ant* disassemble, dismantle, take down **2** *Syn* INVENT, concoct, contrive, cook (up), devise, make up, manufacture, think (up) **3** *Syn* MAKE, fashion, forge, form, manufacture, shape
fabrication *Syn* FICTION, fable, figment
fabulous **1** *Syn* EXCELLENT, A1, bang-up, banner, capital, classic, crackerjack, dandy, divine, fine, first-class, first-rate, grand, great, groovy, heavenly, jim-dandy, keen, marvelous (*or* marvellous), mean, neat, nifty, noble, par excellence, prime, sensational, splendid, stellar, sterling, superb, superior, superlative, supernal, swell, terrific, tip-top, top, top-notch, unsurpassed, wonderful *Ant* poor **2** *Syn* FICTITIOUS, apocryphal, legendary, mythical *Ant* historical
face *n* **1** • the front part of a human or sometimes animal head including the mouth, nose, eyes, forehead, and cheeks *Syn* countenance, mug, physiognomy, puss, visage **2** *Syn* GRIMACE, frown, lower, mouth, pout, scowl
face *vb* **1** • to confront with courage or boldness *Syn* beard, brave, challenge, dare, defy *Rel* confront, encounter, meet *Ant* avoid **2** *Syn* MEET, confront, encounter *Ant* avoid
facet *Syn* PHASE, angle, aspect, side
facetious **1** *Syn* FLIPPANT, flip, pert, smart, smart-alecky (*or* smart-aleck) *Ant* earnest, sincere **2** *Syn* WITTY, humorous, jocose, jocular
facetiousness *Syn* FRIVOLITY, flightiness, flippancy, frivolousness, levity, light-headedness, lightness
facile *Syn* EASY, effortless, light, simple, smooth *Ant* hard
facilely *Syn* EASILY, effortlessly, fluently, freely, handily, lightly, painlessly, readily, smoothly *Ant* arduously, laboriously
facility *Syn* READINESS, dexterity, ease
facsimile *Syn* COPY, carbon copy, duplicate, duplication, imitation, reduplication, replica, replication, reproduction *Ant* original
fact • a single piece of information *Syn* datum, detail, nicety, particular, particularity, point *Rel* article, item
faction **1** • a group of people acting together within a larger group *Syn* bloc, body, coalition, party, sect, set, side, wing *Rel* crew, gang, pack, team **2** *Syn* COMBINATION, bloc, combine, party, ring
factious *Syn* INSUBORDINATE, contumacious, mutinous, rebellious, seditious
factitious **1** *Syn* ARTIFICIAL, ersatz, synthetic *Ant* natural **2** *Syn* IMITATION, artificial, bogus, fake, false, man-made, mimic, mock, sham, simulated, substitute, synthetic *Ant* genuine, natural, real
factor **1** *Syn* AGENT (sense 1), attorney, commissary, delegate, deputy, envoy, procurator, proxy, representative **2** *Syn* ELEMENT, component, constituent, ingredient *Ant* composite, compound (*in science*)
factual *Syn* ACTUAL, concrete, existent, real, true, very *Ant* conjectural, hypothetical, ideal, nonexistent, possible, potential, theoretical
faculty **1** *Syn* ABILITY, capability, capacity, competence, competency *Ant* disability, inability, incapability, incapacity, incompetence, incompetency, ineptitude, ineptness **2** *Syn* GIFT (sense 2), aptitude, bent, genius, knack, talent, turn **3** *Syn* POWER (sense 2), function
fad *Syn* FASHION, craze, cry, dernier cri, mode, rage, style, vogue
fade **1** *Syn* VANISH, disappear, evanesce, evaporate *Ant* appear, loom **2** *Syn* WHITEN, blanch, bleach, blench, decolorize, dull, pale, wash out *Ant* blacken, darken, deepen
faded *Syn* SHABBY, dilapidated, dingy, seedy, threadbare
failing *Syn* FAULT, foible, frailty, vice *Ant* merit
failure **1** • an omission on the part of someone or something of what is expected or required *Syn* default, dereliction, miscarriage, neglect *Rel* failing, fault **2** *Syn* DEFICIENCY, dearth, deficit, famine, inadequacy, insufficiency, lack, paucity, poverty, scantiness, scarceness, scarcity, shortage, want *Ant* abundance, adequacy, amplitude, plenitude, plenty, sufficiency
faineant *Syn* LAZY, indolent, slothful *Ant* industrious
faint *n* • a temporary or permanent state of unconsciousness *Syn* blackout, coma, insensibility, knockout, swoon *Rel* daze, stupor, trance
faint *vb* • to lose consciousness *Syn* black out, pass out, swoon *Rel* break down, collapse *Ant* come around, come round, come to, revive
faintheartedness *Syn* TIMIDITY, timidness, timorousness *Ant* audaciousness, audacity, boldness, guts, nerve
fair *adj* **1** • characterized by honesty, justice, and freedom from improper influence *Syn* dispassionate, equitable, impartial, just, objective, unbiased, uncolored *Rel* detached,

disinterested, indifferent *Ant* unfair **2** *Syn* BEAUTIFUL, attractive, beauteous, comely, cute, gorgeous, handsome, knockout, lovely, pretty, ravishing, sightly, stunning, taking *Ant* homely, ill-favored, plain, ugly, unattractive, unbeautiful, unhandsome, unlovely, unpretty, unsightly **3** *Syn* BLOND, flaxen, golden, sandy, straw, tawny *Ant* dark **4** *Syn* MEDIUM, average, indifferent, mediocre, middling, moderate, second-rate

fair *n Syn* EXHIBITION, exhibit, exposition, show

fairy • an imaginary being usually having a small human form and magical powers *Syn* BROWNIE, elf, fay, pixie (*also* pixy), sprite *Rel* dwarf, gnome, goblin, gremlin, hobgoblin, imp, leprechaun, troll

faith **1** *Syn* BELIEF, credence, credit *Ant* disbelief, unbelief **2** *Syn* RELIGION, church, communion, creed, denomination, persuasion, sect **3** *Syn* TRUST, confidence, dependence, reliance *Ant* mistrust

faithful • firm in one's allegiance to someone or something *Syn* constant, devoted, devout, fast, good, loyal, pious, staunch (*or* stanch), steadfast, steady, true, true-blue *Rel* dependable, dutiful, reliable, tried, trustworthy *Ant* disloyal, faithless, false, fickle, inconstant, perfidious, recreant, traitorous, treacherous, unfaithful, untrue

faithless • not true to allegiance or duty *Syn* disloyal, false, perfidious, traitorous, treacherous *Rel* capricious, fickle, inconstant, unstable *Ant* faithful

faithlessness *Syn* BETRAYAL, disloyalty, double cross, falseness, falsity, infidelity, perfidy, sellout, treachery, treason, unfaithfulness

fake **1** *Syn* COUNTERFEIT, bogus, phony, pinchbeck, pseudo, sham, spurious *Ant* bona fide, genuine **2** *Syn* IMITATION, artificial, bogus, factitious, false, man-made, mimic, mock, sham, simulated, substitute, synthetic *Ant* genuine, natural, real

faker *Syn* IMPOSTOR, charlatan, mountebank, quack

fall *vb* • to go or to let go downward freely *Syn* drop, sink, slump, subside *Rel* alight, descend, dismount *Ant* rise

fall *n Syn* COMEDOWN, decline, descent, down, downfall *Ant* aggrandizement, ascent, exaltation, rise, up

fallacious *Syn* ILLOGICAL, invalid, irrational, nonrational, unreasonable, unreasoning, unsound, weak *Ant* logical, rational, reasonable, sound, valid

fallaciousness *Syn* FALLACY (sense 2), erroneousness, falseness, falsity, untruth *Ant* truth

fallacy **1** • a false idea or belief *Syn* error, falsehood, falsity, illusion, misconception, myth, old wives' tale, untruth *Rel* superstition *Ant* truth, verity **2** • the quality or state of being false *Syn* erroneousness, fallaciousness, falseness, falsity, untruth *Rel* speciousness, spuriousness *Ant* truth

fall(s) *Syn* WATERFALL, cascade, cataract

false **1** *Syn* FAITHLESS, disloyal, perfidious, traitorous, treacherous *Ant* faithful **2** *Syn* IMITATION, artificial, bogus, factitious, fake, man-made, mimic, mock, sham, simulated, substitute, synthetic *Ant* genuine, natural, real

falsehood **1** *Syn* FALLACY (sense 1), error, falsity, illusion, misconception, myth, old wives' tale, untruth *Ant* truth, verity **2** *Syn* LIE, fib, misrepresentation, story, untruth *Ant* truth

falseness **1** *Syn* BETRAYAL, disloyalty, double cross, faithlessness, falsity, infidelity, perfidy, sellout, treachery, treason, unfaithfulness **2** *Syn* FALLACY (sense 2), erroneousness, fallaciousness, falsity, untruth *Ant* truth

falsify *Syn* MISREPRESENT, belie, garble

falsity **1** *Syn* BETRAYAL, disloyalty, double cross, faithlessness, falseness, infidelity, perfidy, sellout, treachery, treason, unfaithfulness **2** *Syn* FALLACY (sense 1), error, falsehood, illusion, misconception, myth, old wives' tale, untruth *Ant* truth, verity **3** *Syn* FALLACY (sense 2), erroneousness, fallaciousness, falseness, untruth *Ant* truth

falter *Syn* HESITATE, vacillate, waver *Ant* dive (in), plunge (in)

faltering *Syn* HESITATION, hesitance, hesitancy, indecision, irresolution, shilly-shallying, vacillation, wavering, wobbling

fame • the state of being widely known for one's deeds *Syn* celebrity, éclat, glory, honor, notoriety, renown, reputation, repute *Rel* acclaim, acclamation, applause *Ant* infamy, obscurity

famed *Syn* FAMOUS, celebrated, noted, notorious, prominent, renowned, star, well-known *Ant* anonymous, obscure, unknown

familiar **1** • near to one another because of frequent association or shared interests *Syn* chummy, close, confidential, intimate, thick *Rel* amicable, friendly, neighborly *Ant* aloof **2** *Syn* COMMON, ordinary, popular, vulgar *Ant* exceptional, uncommon

familiarity **1** *Syn* ACQUAINTANCE, cognizance *Ant* unfamiliarity **2** *Syn* IMPROPRIETY (sense 1), gaffe, indiscretion, solecism *Ant* amenity, civility, courtesy, formality, gesture

familiarize *Syn* ENLIGHTEN (sense 1), acquaint, advise, apprise, brief, clue, fill in, inform, instruct, tell, wise (up)

family tree *Syn* ANCESTRY, birth, blood, bloodline, breeding, descent, extraction, genealogy, line, lineage, origin, parentage, pedigree, stock, strain *Ant* issue, posterity, progeny, seed

famine *Syn* DEFICIENCY, dearth, deficit, failure, inadequacy, insufficiency, lack, paucity, poverty, scantiness, scarceness, scarcity, shortage, want *Ant* abundance, adequacy, amplitude, plenitude, plenty, sufficiency

famous • widely known *Syn* celebrated, famed, noted, notorious, prominent, renowned, star, well-known *Rel* fabled, fabulous, legendary *Ant* anonymous, obscure, unknown

fan • a person with a strong and habitual liking for something *Syn* addict, aficionado, buff, bug, devotee, enthusiast, fanatic, fancier, fiend, freak, lover, maniac, nut *Rel* groupie

fanatic **1** *Syn* ENTHUSIAST, zealot **2** *Syn* FAN, addict, aficionado, buff, bug, devotee, enthusiast, fancier, fiend, freak, lover, maniac, nut **3** *Syn* ZEALOT, crusader, militant, partisan

fancier *Syn* FAN, addict, aficionado, buff, bug, devotee, enthusiast, fanatic, fiend, freak, lover, maniac, nut

fanciful *Syn* IMAGINARY, chimerical, fantastic, quixotic, visionary *Ant* actual, real

fancy *n* **1** • a vivid idea or image present in the mind but having no concrete or objective reality *Syn* daydream, dream, fantasy, nightmare, phantasm, phantasy, vision *Rel* fable, fabrication, fiction, figment *Ant* reality **2** *Syn* IMAGINATION, fantasy **3** *Syn* LIKING, appetite, favor, fondness, like, love, partiality, preference, relish, shine, taste, use *Ant* aversion, disfavor, dislike, distaste, hatred, loathing **4** *Syn* WHIM, caprice, freak, notion, vagary, whimsy

fancy *vb* **1** *Syn* LIKE, dote, enjoy, love, relish *Ant* dislike **2** *Syn* THINK (sense 1), conceive, envisage, envision, imagine, realize

fanny *Syn* BUTTOCKS, backside, bottom, breech, butt, hams, haunches, posterior, rear, rump, seat

fantastic **1** • conceived or made without reference to reality *Syn* antic, bizarre, grotesque *Rel* conceived, fancied, imagined **2** *Syn* EXOTIC, glamorous, marvelous (*or* marvellous), outlandish, romantic, strange **3** *Syn* IMAGINARY, chimerical, fanciful, quixotic, visionary *Ant* actual, real

fantasy **1** *Syn* FANCY, daydream, dream, nightmare, phantasm, phantasy, vision *Ant* reality **2** *Syn* IMAGINATION, fancy

far *adj* **1** *Syn* DISTANT, faraway, far-off, remote, removed **2** *Syn* LONG (sense 2), extended, great, lengthy, long-lived, long-range, long-term, marathon *Ant* brief, short, short-lived, short-range, short-term

far *adv* *Syn* VERY, awful, awfully, beastly, deadly, especially, exceedingly, extra, extremely, frightfully, full, greatly, heavily, highly, hugely, jolly, mightily, mighty, mortally, most, much, particularly, rattling, real, right, so, something, super, terribly, too, whacking *Ant* little, negligibly, nominally, slightly

faraway *Syn* DISTANT, far, far-off, remote, removed

farce *Syn* COMEDY, humor, slapstick

farcical *Syn* LAUGHABLE, comic, comical, droll, funny, ludicrous, ridiculous, risible

farewell *Syn* GOOD-BYE, adieu, au revoir, bon voyage, Godspeed *Ant* hello

far-fetched *Syn* IMPROBABLE, doubtful, dubious, flimsy, questionable, unapt, unlikely *Ant* likely, probable

far-flung *Syn* EXTENSIVE, broad, expansive, extended, far-reaching, wide, widespread *Ant* narrow

farming *adj* *Syn* AGRICULTURAL, agrarian *Ant* nonagricultural

farming *n* *Syn* AGRICULTURE, husbandry

far-off *Syn* DISTANT, far, faraway, remote, removed

far-reaching *Syn* EXTENSIVE, broad, expansive, extended, far-flung, wide, widespread *Ant* narrow

farther *adv* • at or to a greater distance or more avanced point *Syn* beyond, further

farther *adj* *Syn* ADDITIONAL, added, another, else, further, more, other

fascinate *Syn* ATTRACT, allure, bewitch, captivate, charm, enchant *Ant* repel

fascinating **1** *Syn* ATTRACTIVE, alluring, bewitching, captivating, charming, enchanting *Ant* forbidding, repellent **2** *Syn* INTERESTING, absorbing, arresting, engaging, engrossing, enthralling, gripping, immersing, intriguing, involving, riveting *Ant* boring, drab, dry, dull, heavy, monotonous, tedious, uninteresting

fashion *n* **1** • the prevailing or accepted custom *Syn* craze, cry, dernier cri, fad, mode, rage, style, vogue *Rel* drift, tendency, trend **2** *Syn* HABIT, custom, pattern, practice, trick, way, wont **3** *Syn* METHOD, manner, mode, system, way

fashion *vb* *Syn* MAKE, fabricate, forge, form, manufacture, shape

fashionable *Syn* STYLISH, chic, dashing, modish, smart

fashionableness *Syn* POPULARITY, favor, hotness, modishness, vogue *Ant* disfavor, unpopularity

fast **1** • moving, proceeding, or acting with great celerity *Syn* expeditious, fleet, hasty, quick, rapid, speedy, swift *Ant* slow **2** *Syn* FAITHFUL, constant, devoted, devout, good, loyal, pious, staunch (*or* stanch), steadfast, steady, true, true-blue *Ant* disloyal, faithless, false, fickle, inconstant, perfidious, recreant, traitorous, treacherous, unfaithful, untrue

fasten • to cause one thing to hold to another *Syn* affix, attach, fix *Rel* anchor, moor, rivet, secure *Ant* loose, loosen, unfasten

fastidious *Syn* NICE, dainty, finical, finicking, finicky, fussy, particular, pernickety, persnickety, squeamish
fastness *Syn* FORT, citadel, fortress, stronghold
fat *n* **1** *Syn* ELITE, best, choice, cream, elect, flower, pick, prime, upper crust **2** *Syn* EXCESS, overabundance, overage, overflow, overkill, overmuch, oversupply, superabundance, superfluity, surfeit, surplus *Ant* deficiency, deficit, insufficiency
fat *adj* **1** *Syn* FERTILE, fecund, fruitful, luxuriant, productive, prolific, rich *Ant* barren, infertile, sterile, unfruitful, unproductive **2** *Syn* FLESHY, chubby, corpulent, obese, plump, portly, rotund, stout *Ant* scrawny, skinny
fatal *Syn* DEADLY, baleful, deathly, fell, killer, lethal, mortal, murderous, pestilent, vital *Ant* healthful, healthy, nonfatal, nonlethal, wholesome
fate • whatever is destined or inevitably decreed for one *Syn* destiny, doom, lot, portion *Rel* consequence, effect, issue, outcome, result, upshot
fathom • to measure depth typically with a weighted line *Syn* plumb, sound
fatigue *n* • a complete depletion of energy or strength *Syn* burnout, collapse, exhaustion, lassitude, prostration, tiredness, weariness *Rel* debilitation, enervation, faintness, feebleness, weakness *Ant* refreshment, rejuvenation, revitalization
fatigue *vb* *Syn* TIRE, exhaust, jade, tucker, weary
fatuous *Syn* SIMPLE, asinine, foolish, silly *Ant* wise
fault **1** • an imperfection in character or an ingrained moral weakness *Syn* failing, foible, frailty, vice *Rel* infirmity, weakness *Ant* merit **2** *Syn* BLAME, culpability, guilt **3** *Syn* BLEMISH, defect, deformity, disfigurement, flaw, imperfection, mark, pockmark, scar **4** *Syn* IMPERFECTION, deficiency, shortcoming *Ant* perfection
faultfinder *Syn* CRITIC, carper, castigator, caviler (*or* caviller), censurer, nitpicker, railer, scold
faultfinding *Syn* CRITICAL, captious, carping, caviling, censorious, hypercritical *Ant* uncritical
faultless *Syn* IMPECCABLE, errorless, flawless
faulty • having a fault *Syn* bad, defective, flawed, imperfect *Rel* fallible *Ant* faultless, flawless, impeccable, perfect
faux pas *Syn* ERROR, blunder, bull, howler, lapse, mistake, slip
favor *vb* **1** • to give the support of one's approval to *Syn* countenance, encourage *Rel* approve, endorse *Ant* disapprove **2** *Syn* APPROVE (OF), accept, care (for), countenance, OK (*or* okay), subscribe (to) *Ant* disapprove (of), discountenance, disfavor, frown (on *or* upon) **3** *Syn* OBLIGE, accommodate *Ant* disoblige
favor *n* **1** *Syn* APPROVAL, approbation, blessing, imprimatur, OK (*or* okay) *Ant* disapprobation, disapproval, disfavor **2** *Syn* BIAS, one-sidedness, partiality, partisanship, prejudice *Ant* impartiality, neutrality, objectivity, open-mindedness **3** *Syn* GIFT (sense 1), boon, gratuity, largess, present **4** *Syn* LIKING, appetite, fancy, fondness, like, love, partiality, preference, relish, shine, taste, use *Ant* aversion, disfavor, dislike, distaste, hatred, loathing **5** *Syn* POPULARITY, fashionableness, hotness, modishness, vogue *Ant* disfavor, unpopularity
favorable **1** • being of good omen or presaging a happy or successful outcome *Syn* auspicious, benign, propitious *Rel* advantageous, beneficial, profitable *Ant* antagonistic, unfavorable **2** *Syn* BENEFICIAL, advantageous, helpful, profitable, salutary *Ant* disadvantageous, unfavorable, unhelpful
favorite **1** • a person or thing that is preferred over others *Syn* darling, minion, pet, preference *Rel* beloved, dear **2** *Syn* PARASITE, bootlicker, hanger-on, leech, lickspittle, sponge, sponger, sycophant, toady
fawn • to behave abjectly before a superior *Syn* cower, cringe, toady, truckle *Rel* blandish, cajole, coax, wheedle *Ant* domineer
fawner *Syn* SYCOPHANT, flunky, toady
fay *Syn* FAIRY, brownie, elf, pixie (*also* pixy), sprite
faze *Syn* EMBARRASS, abash, discomfit, disconcert, rattle *Ant* facilitate, relieve
fealty *Syn* FIDELITY, allegiance, devotion, loyalty, piety *Ant* faithlessness, perfidy
fear **1** • agitation or dismay which overcomes one in the anticipation or in the presence of danger *Syn* alarm, consternation, dismay, dread, fright, horror, panic, terror, trepidation *Rel* apprehension, foreboding, misgiving, presentiment *Ant* fearlessness **2** *Syn* REVERENCE (sense 2), awe
fearful **1** • inspired or moved by fear *Syn* afraid, apprehensive *Rel* timid, timorous *Ant* fearless, intrepid **2** • causing fear *Syn* appalling, awful, dreadful, frightful, horrible, horrific, shocking, terrible, terrific *Rel* alarming, frightening, terrifying
fearless *Syn* BRAVE, audacious, bold, courageous, dauntless, doughty, intrepid, unafraid, undaunted, valiant, valorous *Ant* craven
fearlessness *Syn* COURAGE, bravery, courageousness, daring, dauntlessness, doughtiness, gallantry, greatheartedness, guts, hardihood, heart, heroism, intrepidity, intrepidness, nerve, stoutness, valor *Ant* cowardice, cowardliness, cravenness, dastardliness, spinelessness, yellowness
feasible *Syn* POSSIBLE, practicable

feast *Syn* DINNER, banquet
feat • a remarkable deed or performance *Syn* achievement, exploit *Rel* act, action, deed
feather *Syn* FINERY, array, best, bravery, caparison, frippery, full dress, gaiety, regalia
feature *n Syn* CHARACTERISTIC, attribute, character, mark, peculiarity, point, property, quality, trait
feature *vb Syn* EMPHASIZE, accent, accentuate, highlight, play (up), point (up), stress, underline, underscore *Ant* play (down)
fecund *Syn* FERTILE, fat, fruitful, luxuriant, productive, prolific, rich *Ant* barren, infertile, sterile, unfruitful, unproductive
fecundity *Syn* FERTILITY, fruitfulness, prolificacy *Ant* infertility, sterility
federate *Syn* ALLY, associate, band, club, confederate, conjoin, cooperate, league, unite *Ant* break up, disband
federation *Syn* ALLIANCE, coalition, confederacy, confederation, fusion, league
fee *Syn* WAGE, emolument, hire, pay, salary, stipend
feeble *Syn* WEAK, decrepit, fragile, frail, infirm *Ant* strong
feed *vb* **1** • to provide the food that one needs or desires *Syn* graze, nourish, pasture *Rel* cherish, foster, nurse, nurture *Ant* starve **2** *Syn* FURNISH (sense 2), deliver, give, hand, hand over, provide, supply *Ant* hold (back), keep (back), reserve, retain, withhold
feed *n* **1** *Syn* FOOD (sense 1), comestibles, fodder, forage, provender, provisions, viands, victuals **2** *Syn* MEAL, chow, mess, repast, table
feel **1** *Syn* BELIEVE (sense 1), consider, deem, figure, guess, hold, imagine, suppose, think *Ant* disbelieve, discredit, reject **2** *Syn* TOUCH, handle, palpate, paw
feeling **1** • subjective response or reaction *Syn* affection, emotion, passion, sentiment *Rel* affecting, affection, impressing, impression, touching **2** *Syn* SENSATION (sense 2), sense, sensibility
feign *Syn* ASSUME, affect, counterfeit, pretend, sham, simulate
feigned *Syn* INSINCERE, artificial, backhanded, double-dealing, hypocritical, left-handed, mealy, mealymouthed, two-faced, unctuous *Ant* genuine, heartfelt, honest, sincere, unfeigned
feint *Syn* TRICK, artifice, gambit, maneuver, ploy, ruse, stratagem, wile
felicitations *Syn* COMPLIMENTS, congratulations, greetings, regards, respects
felicitous *Syn* FIT, appropriate, apt, fitting, happy, meet, proper, suitable *Ant* unfit
felicitousness *Syn* APPROPRIATENESS, aptness, fitness, fittingness, rightness, seemliness, suitability, suitableness *Ant* inappropriateness, inaptness, infelicity, unfitness
felicity *Syn* HAPPINESS, beatitude, blessedness, bliss *Ant* unhappiness
fell **1** *Syn* DEADLY, baleful, deathly, fatal, killer, lethal, mortal, murderous, pestilent, vital *Ant* healthful, healthy, nonfatal, nonlethal, wholesome **2** *Syn* FIERCE, barbarous, cruel, ferocious, inhuman, savage, truculent *Ant* mild, tame
fellow **1** *Syn* BOYFRIEND, beau, man, swain **2** *Syn* EQUAL, coordinate, counterpart, equivalent, like, match, parallel, peer, rival **3** *Syn* MAN, dude, gent, gentleman, guy, male
fellowship **1** *Syn* COMPANIONSHIP, camaraderie, company, comradeship, society **2** *Syn* RAPPORT, communion, rapprochement
felon *Syn* CRIMINAL, convict, culprit, delinquent, malefactor
female *adj* • of, relating to, or marked by qualities traditionally associated with women *Syn* feminine, ladylike, womanish, womanlike, womanly *Ant* male
female *n Syn* WOMAN (sense 1), lady
feminine *Syn* FEMALE, ladylike, womanish, womanlike, womanly *Ant* male
fen *Syn* SWAMP, bog, marsh, marshland, mire, morass, muskeg, slough, swampland
fence *n Syn* BARRIER, barricade, hedge, wall
fence *vb* **1** *Syn* DODGE, duck, malinger, parry, shirk, sidestep *Ant* face **2** *Syn* ENCLOSE, cage, coop, corral, envelop, pen, wall
feral *Syn* BRUTAL, beastly, bestial, brute, brutish
ferment *Syn* UNREST, disquiet, restiveness, restlessness, turmoil, uneasiness *Ant* calm, ease, peace, quiet
ferocious *Syn* FIERCE, barbarous, cruel, fell, inhuman, savage, truculent *Ant* mild, tame
ferret out *Syn* SEEK, comb, hunt, ransack, rummage, scour, search
fertile • producing abundantly *Syn* fat, fecund, fruitful, luxuriant, productive, prolific, rich *Rel* bearing, producing, yielding *Ant* barren, infertile, sterile, unfruitful, unproductive
fertility • the quality or state of being fertile *Syn* fecundity, fruitfulness, prolificacy *Ant* infertility, sterility
fervent • having or expressing great depth of feeling *Syn* ardent, blazing, burning, charged, emotional, fervid, feverish, fiery, flaming, glowing, hot-blooded, impassioned, passionate, red-hot, vehement, warm, warm-blooded *Rel* gushing, maudlin, mawkish, mushy, sentimental *Ant* cold, cool, dispassionate, impassive, unemotional
fervid *Syn* FERVENT, ardent, blazing, burning, charged, emotional, feverish, fiery, flaming, glowing, hot-blooded, impassioned, passionate, red-hot, vehement, warm, warm-blooded *Ant* cold, cool, dispassionate, impassive, unemotional
fervor *Syn* PASSION, ardor, enthusiasm, zeal
festival • a time or program of special events

and entertainment in honor of something *Syn* carnival, celebration, festivity, fete (*or* fête), fiesta, gala, jubilee *Rel* jamboree, jollification, merrymaking, revel, revelry

festive *Syn* MERRY, blithesome, gay, gleeful, jocose, jocund, jolly, jovial, laughing, mirthful, sunny

festivity *Syn* FESTIVAL, carnival, celebration, fete (*or* fête), fiesta, gala, jubilee

fetch *Syn* BRING, take *Ant* remove, withdraw

fete *or* **fête** *Syn* FESTIVAL, carnival, celebration, festivity, fiesta, gala, jubilee

fetid *Syn* MALODOROUS, fusty, musty, noisome, putrid, rancid, rank, stinking *Ant* odorous

fetish • an object believed to be endowed with the virtue of averting evil or of bringing good fortune *Syn* amulet, charm, talisman

fetter *n* **1** *Syn* ENCUMBRANCE, bar, block, chain, clog, crimp, deterrent, drag, embarrassment, handicap, hindrance, hurdle, impediment, inhibition, interference, let, manacle, obstacle, obstruction, shackles, stop, stumbling block, trammel *Ant* aid, assistance, benefit, help **2** *Syn* RESTRICTION, check, condition, constraint, curb, limitation, restraint

fetter *vb Syn* HAMPER, clog, hog-tie, manacle, shackle, trammel *Ant* assist (*persons*), expedite (*work, projects*)

feverish *Syn* FERVENT, ardent, blazing, burning, charged, emotional, fervid, fiery, flaming, glowing, hot-blooded, impassioned, passionate, red-hot, vehement, warm, warm-blooded *Ant* cold, cool, dispassionate, impassive, unemotional

fiancé *Syn* BETROTHED, fiancée, intended

fiancée *Syn* BETROTHED, fiancé, intended

fib *vb Syn* LIE, equivocate, palter, prevaricate

fib *n Syn* LIE, falsehood, misrepresentation, story, untruth *Ant* truth

fickle *Syn* INCONSTANT, capricious, mercurial, unstable *Ant* constant

fiction • a story, account, explanation, or conception which is an invention of the human mind *Syn* fable, fabrication, figment *Rel* anecdote, narrative, story, tale, yarn

fictitious • having the character of something invented or imagined as opposed to something true or genuine *Syn* apocryphal, fabulous, legendary, mythical *Rel* created, invented *Ant* historical

fidelity • faithfulness to something to which one is bound by a pledge or duty *Syn* allegiance, devotion, fealty, loyalty, piety *Rel* constancy, faithfulness, staunchness, steadfastness *Ant* faithlessness, perfidy

fidgety *Syn* IMPATIENT, jittery, jumpy, nervous, restive, restless, uneasy, unquiet *Ant* patient

field **1** • a limited area of knowledge or endeavor to which pursuits, activities, and interests are confined *Syn* bailiwick, domain, province, sphere, territory *Rel* bounds, confines, limits **2** *Syn* REGION, area, demesne, zone

fiend **1** *Syn* DEMON, devil, ghoul, imp, incubus **2** *Syn* FAN, addict, aficionado, buff, bug, devotee, enthusiast, fanatic, fancier, freak, lover, maniac, nut

fiendish • having or manifesting qualities associated with devils, demons, and fiends *Syn* demoniac, demonic, devilish, diabolic, diabolical *Rel* hellish, infernal

fierce **1** • displaying fury or malignity in looks or actions *Syn* barbarous, cruel, fell, ferocious, inhuman, savage, truculent *Rel* menacing, threatening *Ant* mild, tame **2** *Syn* INTENSE, exquisite, vehement, violent *Ant* subdued

fiery **1** *Syn* FERVENT, ardent, blazing, burning, charged, emotional, fervid, feverish, flaming, glowing, hot-blooded, impassioned, passionate, red-hot, vehement, warm, warm-blooded *Ant* cold, cool, dispassionate, impassive, unemotional **2** *Syn* SPIRITED, gingery, high-spirited, mettlesome, peppery, spunky *Ant* spiritless

fiesta *Syn* FESTIVAL, carnival, celebration, festivity, fete (*or* fête), gala, jubilee

fight *n* **1** *Syn* BELLIGERENCE, aggression, aggressiveness, bellicosity, combativeness, contentiousness, disputatiousness, militancy, pugnacity, scrappiness, truculence *Ant* pacifism **2** *Syn* CONTEST, affray, combat, conflict, fray

fight *vb* **1** *Syn* CONTEND, battle, war **2** *Syn* RESIST, antagonize, combat, conflict, contest, oppose, withstand *Ant* abide, submit

figment *Syn* FICTION, fable, fabrication

figure *n* **1** • a unit in a decorative composition (as in fabric) *Syn* design, device, motif, pattern **2** *Syn* FORM (sense 1), configuration, conformation, shape **3** *Syn* NUMBER, digit, integer, numeral

figure *vb* **1** *Syn* BELIEVE (sense 1), consider, deem, feel, guess, hold, imagine, suppose, think *Ant* disbelieve, discredit, reject **2** *Syn* ESTIMATE (sense 2), calculate, call, conjecture, gauge, guess, judge, make, place, put, reckon, suppose

figure out *Syn* SOLVE, answer, break, crack, dope (out), puzzle (out), resolve, riddle, unravel, work, work out

figures *Syn* CALCULATION, arithmetic, ciphering, computation, figuring, reckoning

figuring *Syn* CALCULATION, arithmetic, ciphering, computation, figures, reckoning

filch *Syn* STEAL, cop, lift, pilfer, pinch, purloin, snitch, swipe

file *Syn* LINE, echelon, rank, row, tier

fillet *Syn* STRIP, band, ribbon, stripe

fill in *Syn* ENLIGHTEN (sense 1), acquaint, advise, apprise, brief, clue, familiarize, inform, instruct, tell, wise (up)

film **1** *Syn* MOVIE (sense 1), motion picture, moving picture, picture **2** *Syn* MOVIE (sense 2), cinema, motion pictures, pictures, screen

filthy *Syn* DIRTY, foul, nasty, squalid *Ant* clean

finagle *Syn* ENGINEER, contrive, finesse, frame, machinate, maneuver, manipulate, mastermind, negotiate, wangle

final *Syn* LAST, concluding, eventual, latest, terminal, ultimate *Ant* first

finale • the last part of a process or action *Syn* close, closing, conclusion, consummation, end, ending, finis, finish, windup *Rel* apex, climax, crescendo, culmination, peak, summit, zenith *Ant* beginning, dawn, opening, start

financial • of or relating to the possession, making, borrowing, lending, or expenditure of money *Syn* fiscal, monetary, pecuniary

find *Syn* HAPPEN (on *or* upon), chance (upon), encounter, hit (upon), meet, stumble (on *or* onto)

fine *n* • a sum of money to be paid as a punishment *Syn* damages, forfeit, forfeiture, mulct, penalty *Rel* reparations

fine *adj* **1** *Syn* ADEQUATE, acceptable, all right, decent, OK (*or* okay), passable, respectable, satisfactory, tolerable *Ant* deficient, inadequate, lacking, unacceptable, unsatisfactory, wanting **2** *Syn* EXCELLENT, A1, bang-up, banner, capital, classic, crackerjack, dandy, divine, fabulous, first-class, first-rate, grand, great, groovy, heavenly, jim-dandy, keen, marvelous (*or* marvellous), mean, neat, nifty, noble, par excellence, prime, sensational, splendid, stellar, sterling, superb, superior, superlative, supernal, swell, terrific, tip-top, top, top-notch, unsurpassed, wonderful *Ant* poor

fine *vb* **1** *Syn* IMPOSE, assess, charge, exact, lay, levy, put *Ant* remit **2** *Syn* PENALIZE, amerce, mulct

fineness *Syn* PRECISION, accuracy, closeness, delicacy, exactitude, exactness, preciseness, rigorousness, veracity *Ant* coarseness, impreciseness, imprecision, inaccuracy, inexactness, roughness

finery • dressy clothing *Syn* array, best, bravery, caparison, feather, frippery, full dress, gaiety, regalia *Rel* apparel, attire, costume, duds, raiment

finesse *n* *Syn* DEXTERITY (sense 1), adroitness, cleverness, sleight *Ant* awkwardness, clumsiness, gawkiness

finesse *vb* *Syn* ENGINEER, contrive, finagle, frame, machinate, maneuver, manipulate, mastermind, negotiate, wangle

finical *Syn* NICE, dainty, fastidious, finicking, finicky, fussy, particular, pernickety, persnickety, squeamish

finicking *Syn* NICE, dainty, fastidious, finical, finicky, fussy, particular, pernickety, persnickety, squeamish

finicky *Syn* NICE, dainty, fastidious, finical, finicking, fussy, particular, pernickety, persnickety, squeamish

finis *Syn* FINALE, close, closing, conclusion, consummation, end, ending, finish, windup *Ant* beginning, dawn, opening, start

finish *vb* *Syn* CONCLUDE (sense 1), complete, end, terminate

finish *n* *Syn* FINALE, close, closing, conclusion, consummation, end, ending, finis, windup *Ant* beginning, dawn, opening, start

finished *Syn* CONSUMMATE, accomplished *Ant* crude

fire *n* • a destructive burning *Syn* conflagration, holocaust *Rel* blaze, flame, flare, glare

fire *vb* **1** *Syn* ANIMATE, brace, energize, enliven, invigorate, jazz (up), liven (up), pep (up), quicken, stimulate, vitalize, vivify *Ant* damp, dampen, deaden, dull **2** *Syn* DISMISS, bounce, cashier, discharge, drop, sack **3** *Syn* INFORM (sense 1), animate, inspire **4** *Syn* LIGHT, ignite, kindle

firebrand *Syn* AGITATOR, demagogue, exciter, fomenter, incendiary, inciter, instigator, rabble-rouser

firebug *Syn* ARSONIST, incendiary

firkin *Syn* CASK, barrel, hogshead, keg, pipe, puncheon

firm • having a texture or consistency that resists deformation by external force *Syn* hard, solid *Rel* close, compact, dense, thick *Ant* flabby, loose

first *Syn* HEAD, chief, commanding, foremost, high, lead, leading, managing, preeminent, premier, presiding, primary, prime, principal, supreme

first-class *Syn* EXCELLENT, A1, bang-up, banner, capital, classic, crackerjack, dandy, divine, fabulous, fine, first-rate, grand, great, groovy, heavenly, jim-dandy, keen, marvelous (*or* marvellous), mean, neat, nifty, noble, par excellence, prime, sensational, splendid, stellar, sterling, superb, superior, superlative, supernal, swell, terrific, tip-top, top, top-notch, unsurpassed, wonderful *Ant* poor

first-rate *Syn* EXCELLENT, A1, bang-up, banner, capital, classic, crackerjack, dandy, divine, fabulous, fine, first-class, grand, great, groovy, heavenly, jim-dandy, keen, marvelous (*or* marvellous), mean, neat, nifty, noble, par excellence, prime, sensational, splendid, stellar, sterling, superb, superior, superlative, supernal, swell, terrific, tip-top, top, top-notch, unsurpassed, wonderful *Ant* poor

fiscal *Syn* FINANCIAL, monetary, pecuniary

fissure *Syn* CRACK, chink, cleft, cranny, crevasse, crevice

fit *adj* **1** • right with respect to some end, need, use, or circumstances *Syn* appropriate, apt, felicitous, fitting, happy, meet, proper, suitable *Rel* adaptable, adapted, adjustable, adjusted, conformable, conformed *Ant* unfit **2** *Syn* COMPETENT, able, capable, good, qualified, suitable *Ant* incompetent, inept, poor, unfit, unqualified

fit *n* **1** • an episode of bodily or mental disorder or excess *Syn* convulsion, paroxysm, spasm **2** *Syn* ATTACK (sense 3), bout, case, seizure, siege, spell

fit *vb Syn* PREPARE, condition, qualify, ready

fitful • lacking in steadiness or regularity of occurrence *Syn* casual, choppy, discontinuous, erratic, intermittent, irregular, occasional, spasmodic, sporadic, spotty, unsteady *Rel* convulsive, sudden, violent *Ant* constant, continuous, regular, steady

fitness **1** *Syn* APPROPRIATENESS, aptness, felicitousness, fittingness, rightness, seemliness, suitability, suitableness *Ant* inappropriateness, inaptness, infelicity, unfitness **2** *Syn* HEALTH, healthiness, heartiness, robustness, soundness, wellness, wholeness, wholesomeness *Ant* illness, sickness, unhealthiness, unsoundness

fit (out) *Syn* FURNISH (sense 1), accoutre (*or* accouter), equip, outfit, rig, supply *Ant* hold (back), keep (back), reserve, retain, withhold

fitting *Syn* FIT, appropriate, apt, felicitous, happy, meet, proper, suitable *Ant* unfit

fittingly *Syn* PROPERLY, appropriately, congruously, correctly, happily, meetly, rightly, suitably *Ant* improperly, inappropriately, incongruously, incorrectly, unsuitably, wrongly

fittingness *Syn* APPROPRIATENESS, aptness, felicitousness, fitness, rightness, seemliness, suitability, suitableness *Ant* inappropriateness, inaptness, infelicity, unfitness

fix *vb* **1** *Syn* ADJUST, regulate *Ant* derange **2** *Syn* APPOINT (sense 1), designate, name, set *Ant* discharge, dismiss, expel, fire **3** *Syn* FASTEN, affix, attach *Ant* loose, loosen, unfasten **4** *Syn* SET, establish, settle

fix *n Syn* PREDICAMENT, dilemma, jam, pickle, plight, quandary, scrape

fixable *Syn* REMEDIABLE, correctable, rectifiable, repairable, reparable *Ant* incorrigible, irremediable, irreparable

flabbergast *Syn* SURPRISE (sense 2), amaze, astonish, astound

flabby *Syn* LIMP, flaccid, flimsy, floppy, sleazy

flaccid *Syn* LIMP, flabby, flimsy, floppy, sleazy

flag *n* • a piece of fabric that is used as a symbol (as of a nation) or as a signaling device *Syn* banner, color, ensign, jack, pendant, pennant, pennon, standard, streamer

flag *vb* **1** *Syn* DROOP, sag, wilt **2** *Syn* MOTION, beckon, gesture, signal, wave

flagitious *Syn* VICIOUS, corrupt, degenerate, infamous, iniquitous, nefarious, villainous *Ant* virtuous

flagrant **1** • bad or objectionable *Syn* glaring, gross, rank *Rel* atrocious, heinous, monstrous, outrageous **2** *Syn* EGREGIOUS, blatant, conspicuous, glaring, gross, obvious, patent, pronounced, rank, striking

flair *Syn* LEANING, penchant, proclivity, propensity *Ant* distaste

flamboyance *Syn* OSTENTATION, flashiness, garishness, gaudiness, glitz, ostentatiousness, pretentiousness, showiness, swank *Ant* austerity, plainness, severity

flamboyant **1** *Syn* GAUDY, flashy, garish, glitzy, loud, ostentatious, splashy, swank (*or* swanky), tawdry *Ant* conservative, quiet, understated **2** *Syn* ORNATE, baroque, florid, rococo *Ant* austere, chaste

flame *n* **1** *Syn* BLAZE, flare, glare, glow **2** *Syn* SWEETHEART, beloved, darling, dear, honey, love, sweet

flame *vb* **1** *Syn* BLAZE, flare, glare, glow **2** *Syn* ERUPT (sense 1), break out, burst (forth), explode, flare (up)

flaming *Syn* FERVENT, ardent, blazing, burning, charged, emotional, fervid, feverish, fiery, glowing, hot-blooded, impassioned, passionate, red-hot, vehement, warm, warm-blooded *Ant* cold, cool, dispassionate, impassive, unemotional

flammable *Syn* COMBUSTIBLE, incendiary, inflammable, inflammatory

flanking *Syn* ADJACENT, abutting, adjoining, bordering, contiguous, fringing, joining, juxtaposed, skirting, touching, verging *Ant* nonadjacent

flapjack *Syn* PANCAKE, griddle cake, hotcake, slapjack

flare *vb Syn* BLAZE, flame, glare, glow

flare *n* **1** *Syn* BLAZE, flame, glare, glow **2** *Syn* OUTBREAK, burst, flare-up, flash, flicker, flurry, flutter, outburst, spurt

flare (up) *Syn* ERUPT (sense 1), break out, burst (forth), explode, flame

flare-up *Syn* OUTBREAK, burst, flare, flash, flicker, flurry, flutter, outburst, spurt

flash *vb* • to shoot forth light (as in rays or sparks) *Syn* coruscate, glance, gleam, glint, glisten, glitter, scintillate, sparkle, twinkle *Rel* dart, fly, shoot

flash *n* **1** *Syn* INSTANT, jiffy, minute, moment, second, shake, split second, trice, twinkle, twinkling, wink **2** *Syn* OUTBREAK, burst, flare, flare-up, flicker, flurry, flutter, outburst, spurt

flash *adj Syn* MOMENTARY, ephemeral, evanescent, fleeting, fugitive, impermanent, passing, short-lived, temporary, transient, transitory *Ant* enduring, eternal, everlasting, lasting, long-lived, permanent, perpetual

flashiness *Syn* OSTENTATION, flamboyance, garishness, gaudiness, glitz, ostentatiousness, pretentiousness, showiness, swank *Ant* austerity, plainness, severity

flashy *Syn* GAUDY, flamboyant, garish, glitzy, loud, ostentatious, splashy, swank (*or* swanky), tawdry *Ant* conservative, quiet, understated

flat **1** *Syn* BORING, drab, dreary, dry, dull, heavy, humdrum, jading, leaden, monotonous, pedestrian, ponderous, stodgy, stuffy, stupid, tame, tedious, tiresome, tiring, unanimated, uninteresting, wearisome, weary, wearying *Ant* absorbing, engaging, engrossing, gripping, interesting, intriguing, involving **2** *Syn* INSIPID, banal, inane, jejune, vapid, wishy-washy *Ant* sapid, zestful **3** *Syn* LEVEL, even, flush, plain, plane, smooth

flattery *Syn* COMPLIMENT, adulation *Ant* taunt

flatulent *Syn* INFLATED, tumid, turgid *Ant* pithy

flaunt *Syn* SHOW (sense 2), display, exhibit, expose, parade *Ant* disguise

flavor **1** *Syn* AURA, air, atmosphere, climate, mood, note, temper **2** *Syn* TASTE (sense 1), relish, savor, smack, tang *Ant* antipathy

flavorsome *Syn* PALATABLE, appetizing, relishing, sapid, savory, tasty, toothsome *Ant* distasteful, unpalatable

flaw *Syn* BLEMISH, defect, deformity, disfigurement, fault, imperfection, mark, pockmark, scar

flawed *Syn* FAULTY, bad, defective, imperfect *Ant* faultless, flawless, impeccable, perfect

flawless *Syn* IMPECCABLE, errorless, faultless

flaxen *Syn* BLOND, fair, golden, sandy, straw, tawny *Ant* dark

flay *Syn* SKIN, decorticate, pare, peel

fleck *Syn* SPOT, blotch, dapple, dot, freckle, marble, mottle, pepper, speck, speckle, splotch, sprinkle, stipple

flecked *Syn* SPOTTED, bespangled, marbled, mottled, spangled, spattered, speckled, sprinkled, stippled

fledgling *Syn* BEGINNER, colt, freshman, greenhorn, neophyte, newbie, newcomer, novice, recruit, rookie, tenderfoot, tyro *Ant* old hand, old-timer, vet, veteran

flee *Syn* ESCAPE (sense 1), abscond, decamp, fly

fleece • to rob by the use of trickery or threats *Syn* bleed, cheat, chisel, cozen, defraud, hustle, mulct, rook, shortchange, skin, squeeze, stick, sting, swindle, victimize *Rel* extort, wrench, wrest, wring

fleecy *Syn* HAIRY (sense 1), bristly, furry, hirsute, rough, shaggy, unshorn, woolly *Ant* bald, furless, hairless, shorn, smooth

fleer *Syn* SCOFF, flout, gibe, gird, jeer, sneer

fleet *Syn* FAST, expeditious, hasty, quick, rapid, speedy, swift *Ant* slow

fleeting *Syn* MOMENTARY, ephemeral, evanescent, flash, fugitive, impermanent, passing, short-lived, temporary, transient, transitory *Ant* enduring, eternal, everlasting, lasting, long-lived, permanent, perpetual

fleshly *Syn* CARNAL, animal, sensual *Ant* intellectual, spiritual

fleshy • thick and heavy in body because of superfluous fat *Syn* chubby, corpulent, fat, obese, plump, portly, rotund, stout *Rel* brawny, burly, husky, muscular *Ant* scrawny, skinny

flex • to bend *Syn* bow, buckle, crook *Rel* bend, curve, twist *Ant* extend

flexible **1** *Syn* ELASTIC (sense 1), resilient, springy, supple *Ant* rigid **2** *Syn* WILLOWY, limber, lissome, lithe, pliable, pliant, supple *Ant* inflexible, rigid, stiff

flexuous *Syn* WINDING, serpentine, sinuous, tortuous *Ant* straight

flicker *vb Syn* FLIT, flitter, flutter, hover

flicker *n Syn* OUTBREAK, burst, flare, flare-up, flash, flurry, flutter, outburst, spurt

flightiness **1** *Syn* FRIVOLITY, facetiousness, flippancy, frivolousness, levity, light-headedness, lightness **2** *Syn* LIGHTNESS, flippancy, frivolity, levity, light-mindedness, volatility *Ant* seriousness

flighty *Syn* EXCITABLE, fluttery, high-strung, jittery, jumpy, nervous, skittish, spooky *Ant* unflappable

flimsy **1** *Syn* IMPROBABLE, doubtful, dubious, far-fetched, questionable, unapt, unlikely *Ant* likely, probable **2** *Syn* LIMP, flabby, flaccid, floppy, sleazy

flinch *Syn* RECOIL, blench, quail, shrink, wince *Ant* confront, defy

fling *n Syn* ATTEMPT, crack, endeavor, essay, go, pass, shot, stab, trial, try, whack

fling *vb Syn* THROW, cast, hurl, pitch, sling, toss

flip *Syn* FLIPPANT, facetious, pert, smart, smart-alecky (*or* smart-aleck) *Ant* earnest, sincere

flippancy **1** *Syn* FRIVOLITY, facetiousness, flightiness, frivolousness, levity, light-headedness, lightness **2** *Syn* LIGHTNESS, flightiness, frivolity, levity, light-mindedness, volatility *Ant* seriousness

flippant • making light of something usually regarded as serious or sacred *Syn* facetious, flip, pert, smart, smart-alecky (*or* smart-aleck) *Rel* flighty, frivolous *Ant* earnest, sincere

flirt • to show a liking for someone just for fun *Syn* dally, frivol, trifle *Rel* josh, kid, put on, razz, rib, tease

flit • to move or fly briskly, irregularly, and usually intermittently *Syn* flicker, flitter, flutter, hover *Rel* dart, float, fly, scud, skim

flitter *Syn* FLIT, flicker, flutter, hover

float *Syn* FLY, dart, sail, scud, shoot, skim

flood *n* **1** • a great or overwhelming flow of or as if of water *Syn* cataract, deluge, inundation, spate, torrent *Rel* current, flow, stream, tide **2** *Syn* FLOW, current, flux, stream, tide

flood *vb* • to cover or become filled with a flood *Syn* deluge, drown, engulf, inundate, overflow, overwhelm, submerge, submerse, swamp *Rel* overcome, overrun *Ant* drain

floppy *Syn* LIMP, flabby, flaccid, flimsy, sleazy

florid *Syn* ORNATE, baroque, flamboyant, rococo *Ant* austere, chaste

flounder *Syn* STUMBLE, blunder, bumble, galumph, lollop, lumber, lurch, trip

flourish **1** *Syn* SUCCEED, prosper, thrive *Ant* attempt, fail **2** *Syn* SWING (sense 1), brandish, shake, thrash, wave

flout **1** *Syn* SCOFF, fleer, gibe, gird, jeer, sneer **2** *Syn* SCORN (sense 1), despise, disregard *Ant* honor, respect

flow *n* • something suggestive of running water *Syn* current, flood, flux, stream, tide *Rel* progression, sequence, series, succession

flow *vb* *Syn* SPRING, arise, derive, emanate, issue, originate, proceed, rise, stem

flower *n* **1** *Syn* BLOSSOM, bloom, blow **2** *Syn* ELITE, best, choice, cream, elect, fat, pick, prime, upper crust

flower *vb* *Syn* BLOSSOM, bloom, blow

flowery *Syn* RHETORICAL, aureate, bombastic, euphuistic, grandiloquent, magniloquent

flub *Syn* BOTCH, bobble, bungle, butcher, foozle, foul up, fumble, louse up, mangle, mess (up), muff, murder

fluctuate **1** *Syn* CHANGE (sense 2), mutate, shift, vary *Ant* stabilize **2** *Syn* SWING (sense 2), oscillate, pendulate, sway, undulate, vibrate, waver

fluent *Syn* ARTICULATE, eloquent, well-spoken *Ant* inarticulate

fluently *Syn* EASILY, effortlessly, facilely, freely, handily, lightly, painlessly, readily, smoothly *Ant* arduously, laboriously

fluky *Syn* ACCIDENTAL, casual, chance, fortuitous, inadvertent, incidental, unintended, unintentional, unplanned, unpremeditated, unwitting *Ant* deliberate, intended, intentional, planned, premeditated

flume *Syn* CANYON, defile, gap, gorge, gulch, gulf, notch, pass, ravine

flunky **1** *Syn* SERVANT, domestic, lackey, menial, retainer, steward *Ant* master **2** *Syn* SYCOPHANT, fawner, toady

flurry *vb* *Syn* DISCOMPOSE, agitate, disquiet, disturb, fluster, perturb, upset

flurry *n* **1** *Syn* OUTBREAK, burst, flare, flare-up, flash, flicker, flutter, outburst, spurt **2** *Syn* STIR, ado, bustle, fuss, pother *Ant* tranquillity

flush *vb* *Syn* BLUSH, bloom, color, crimson, glow, redden

flush *adj* **1** *Syn* LEVEL, even, flat, plain, plane, smooth **2** *Syn* RIFE, abounding, fraught, replete, swarming, teeming, thick, thronging

fluster *Syn* DISCOMPOSE, agitate, disquiet, disturb, flurry, perturb, upset

flutter *vb* *Syn* FLIT, flicker, flitter, hover

flutter *n* *Syn* OUTBREAK, burst, flare, flare-up, flash, flicker, flurry, outburst, spurt

fluttery *Syn* EXCITABLE, flighty, high-strung, jittery, jumpy, nervous, skittish, spooky *Ant* unflappable

flux *Syn* FLOW, current, flood, stream, tide

fly **1** • to pass lightly or quickly over or above a surface *Syn* dart, float, sail, scud, shoot, skim *Rel* flicker, flit, flitter, flutter, hover **2** *Syn* ESCAPE (sense 1), abscond, decamp, flee **3** *Syn* HURRY (sense 2), barrel, bolt, bowl, breeze, career, course, dash, hasten, hotfoot (it), hump, hurtle, hustle, pelt, race, rip, rocket, run, rush, rustle, scoot, scurry, scuttle, shoot, speed, step (along), tear, trot, whirl, whisk, zip, zoom *Ant* crawl, creep, poke

flying field *Syn* AIRPORT, airdrome, airfield, airstrip, landing field, landing strip

foam • a mass of bubbles gathering in or on the surface of a liquid or something as insubstantial as such a mass *Syn* froth, lather, scum, spume, suds, yeast

foaming *Syn* ANGRY, angered, apoplectic, enraged, fuming, furious, incensed, indignant, inflamed, infuriated, irate, ireful, mad, outraged, rabid, riled, roiled, sore, steaming, wrathful, wroth *Ant* delighted, pleased

focal *Syn* CENTRAL, pivotal

focus *vb* *Syn* CENTER, centralize, concentrate

focus *n* *Syn* CENTER (sense 2), base, capital, core, cynosure, eye, heart, hub, mecca, nucleus, seat

fodder *Syn* FOOD (sense 1), comestibles, feed, forage, provender, provisions, viands, victuals

foe *Syn* ENEMY, adversary, antagonist, opponent *Ant* friend

fog *n* **1** *Syn* HAZE (sense 1), mist, murk, reek, smog, soup **2** *Syn* HAZE (sense 2), daze, muddle, spin

fog *vb* *Syn* OBSCURE, becloud, bedim, befog, cloud, darken, dim, eclipse, obfuscate *Ant* illuminate, illumine

foible *Syn* FAULT, failing, frailty, vice *Ant* merit

foil *Syn* FRUSTRATE, baffle, balk, circumvent, outwit, thwart *Ant* fulfill

folklore • the body of customs, beliefs, stories, and sayings associated with a people, thing, or place *Syn* legend, lore, myth, mythology, tradition *Rel* information, knowledge, wisdom

follow **1** • to come after in time *Syn* ensue, succeed, supervene **2** • to go after or on the trail of *Syn* chase, pursue, tag, tail, trail *Rel* accompany, attend, convoy *Ant* forsake (*a teacher or* *teachings*), precede **3** *Syn* TRAVERSE, cover, crisscross, cross, cut (across), go, pass (over), proceed (along), travel

follower • one who follows the teachings of another *Syn* adherent, convert, disciple, partisan, pupil, votary *Rel* devotee, flunky, hanger-on, henchman, lackey, satellite, stooge, sycophant, toady, yes-man *Ant* leader

following *prep Syn* AFTER, behind *Ant* ahead of, before, ere, previous to, prior to

following *n Syn* PURSUIT, chase, chasing, dogging, hounding, pursuing, shadowing, tagging, tailing, tracing, tracking, trailing

foment *Syn* INCITE, abet, instigate *Ant* restrain

fomenter *Syn* AGITATOR, demagogue, exciter, firebrand, incendiary, inciter, instigator, rabble-rouser

fond **1** • made blindly or stupidly foolish *Syn* besotted, infatuated, insensate *Rel* asinine, fatuous, foolish, silly, simple **2** *Syn* LOVING, affectionate, devoted, doting *Ant* unloving

fondle *Syn* CARESS, cosset, cuddle, dandle, pet

fondness *Syn* LIKING, appetite, fancy, favor, like, love, partiality, preference, relish, shine, taste, use *Ant* aversion, disfavor, dislike, distaste, hatred, loathing

food **1** • things that are edible for human beings or animals *Syn* comestibles, feed, fodder, forage, provender, provisions, viands, victuals **2** • material which feeds and supports the mind or the spirit *Syn* aliment, nourishment, nutriment, pabulum, pap, sustenance

fool *n* **1** • a person formerly kept in a royal or noble household to amuse with jests and pranks *Syn* jester, motley *Rel* buffoon, clown, comedian, comedienne, comic, cutup, harlequin, zany **2** • a person who lacks good sense or judgment *Syn* booby, goose, halfwit, jackass, lunatic, nincompoop, ninny, nitwit, nut, simpleton, turkey, yo-yo *Rel* daredevil

fool *vb Syn* JOKE, banter, fun, jest, jive, josh, kid, quip, wisecrack

fool (around) *Syn* CUT UP, act up, clown (around), horse (around), monkey (around), show off, skylark

foolery *Syn* HORSEPLAY, clowning, high jinks, horsing (around), monkeying, monkeyshines, roughhouse, roughhousing, shenanigans, skylarking, tomfoolery

foolhardy *Syn* ADVENTUROUS, daredevil, daring, rash, reckless, venturesome *Ant* cautious, unadventurous

foolish **1** • felt to be ridiculous because not exhibiting good sense *Syn* absurd, preposterous, silly *Rel* laughable, ludicrous, ridiculous *Ant* sensible **2** *Syn* SIMPLE, asinine, fatuous, silly *Ant* wise

foot (it) *Syn* WALK, hoof (it), leg (it), pad, step, traipse, tread

foot (up) *Syn* ADD (sense 1), sum, total *Ant* deduct, remove, subtract, take

foozle *Syn* BOTCH, bobble, bungle, butcher, flub, foul up, fumble, louse up, mangle, mess (up), muff, murder

fop • a man who is conspicuously fashionable or elegant in dress or manners *Syn* beau, buck, coxcomb, dandy, dude, exquisite

for *Syn* BECAUSE, as, inasmuch as, since

forage *Syn* FOOD (sense 1), comestibles, feed, fodder, provender, provisions, viands, victuals

forbear **1** *Syn* FORGO, abnegate, eschew, sacrifice **2** *Syn* REFRAIN, abstain

forbearance **1** • a disinclination to be severe or rigorous *Syn* clemency, indulgence, leniency, mercifulness, tolerance *Rel* longanimity, long-suffering, patience *Ant* anger, vindictiveness **2** *Syn* PATIENCE, longanimity, long-suffering, resignation *Ant* impatience

forbearing • disinclined by nature, disposition, or circumstances to be severe or rigorous *Syn* clement, indulgent, lenient, merciful, tolerant *Rel* gentle, mild, soft *Ant* unrelenting

forbearingly • in a forbearing manner *Syn* clemently, indulgently, leniently, mercifully, tolerantly

forbid • to order not to do or use or to be done or used *Syn* ban, bar, enjoin, interdict, outlaw, prohibit, proscribe *Rel* deter, discourage, dissuade *Ant* allow, let, permit, suffer

forbidding *Syn* PROHIBITION (sense 1), banning, barring, enjoining, interdicting, interdiction, outlawing, prohibiting, proscribing, proscription *Ant* prescription

force *n* **1** • the exercise of power in order to impose one's will on a person or to have one's will with a thing *Syn* coercion, compulsion, constraint, duress, restraint, violence *Rel* fierceness, intensity, vehemence **2** *Syn* POWER (sense 1), energy, might, puissance, strength *Ant* impotence

force *vb* • to cause a person or thing to yield to pressure *Syn* coerce, compel, constrain, oblige *Rel* drive, impel, move

forced **1** • produced or kept up through effort *Syn* labored, strained *Rel* coerced, compelled, constrained **2** *Syn* MANDATORY, compulsory, imperative, incumbent, involuntary, necessary, nonelective, obligatory, peremptory, required *Ant* elective, optional, voluntary

forceful **1** *Syn* COGENT, compelling, conclusive, convincing, decisive, effective, persuasive, satisfying, strong, telling *Ant* inconclusive, indecisive, ineffective, unconvincing **2** *Syn* POWERFUL, forcible, potent, puissant *Ant* inefficacious, powerless

forcible *Syn* POWERFUL, forceful, potent, puissant *Ant* inefficacious, powerless

forebear *Syn* ANCESTOR (sense 1), forefather, progenitor *Ant* descendant (*or* descendent)
forebode *Syn* FORETELL, augur, forecast, portend, predict, presage, prognosticate, prophesy
foreboding *n* **1** *Syn* OMEN, augury, auspice, boding, foreshadowing, portent, prefiguring, presage **2** *Syn* PREMONITION, presage, presentiment
foreboding *adj Syn* OMINOUS, baleful, dire, inauspicious, menacing, portentous, sinister, threatening
forecast *vb Syn* FORETELL, augur, forebode, portend, predict, presage, prognosticate, prophesy
forecast *n Syn* PREDICTION, auguring, cast, forecasting, foretelling, predicting, presaging, prognosis, prognosticating, prognostication, prophecy, soothsaying
forecaster *Syn* PROPHET, augur, diviner, foreseer, foreteller, fortune-teller, futurist, prognosticator, prophesier, seer, soothsayer
forecasting *Syn* PREDICTION, auguring, cast, forecast, foretelling, predicting, presaging, prognosis, prognosticating, prognostication, prophecy, soothsaying
forefather *Syn* ANCESTOR (sense 1), forebear, progenitor *Ant* descendant (*or* descendent)
foregoer *Syn* ANCESTOR (sense 2), antecedent, forerunner, precursor, predecessor *Ant* descendant (*or* descendent)
foregoing *Syn* PREVIOUS, antecedent, anterior, precedent, preceding, prior *Ant* after, ensuing, following, subsequent, succeeding
foreign *Syn* EXTRINSIC, alien, extraneous *Ant* intrinsic
foreigner *Syn* STRANGER, alien, émigré, immigrant, outlander, outsider
foreknow *Syn* FORESEE, anticipate, apprehend, divine
foreknowledge *Syn* FORESIGHT (sense 1), prescience *Ant* improvidence, shortsightedness
foreman *Syn* BOSS, captain, chief, head, headman, helmsman, kingpin, leader, master, taskmaster
foremost **1** *Syn* CHIEF, capital, leading, main, principal *Ant* subordinate **2** *Syn* HEAD, chief, commanding, first, high, lead, leading, managing, preeminent, premier, presiding, primary, prime, principal, supreme
forensic *Syn* ARGUMENTATION, debate, dialectic, disputation
forerunner **1** • one that goes before or in some way announces the coming of another *Syn* harbinger, herald, precursor *Rel* anticipator **2** *Syn* ANCESTOR (sense 2), antecedent, foregoer, precursor, predecessor *Ant* descendant (*or* descendent)
foresee • to know or expect in advance that something will happen or come into existence or be made manifest *Syn* anticipate, apprehend, divine, foreknow *Rel* forecast, foretell, predict, prognosticate, prophesy
foreseer *Syn* PROPHET, augur, diviner, forecaster, foreteller, fortune-teller, futurist, prognosticator, prophesier, seer, soothsayer
foreshadowing *Syn* OMEN, augury, auspice, boding, foreboding, portent, prefiguring, presage
foreshore *Syn* SHORE, bank, beach, coast, littoral, strand
foresight **1** • the special ability to see or know about events before they actually occur *Syn* foreknowledge, prescience *Rel* premonition, presentiment **2** • concern or preparation for the future *Syn* farsightedness, foresightedness, forethought, prescience, providence *Rel* precaution, premeditation *Ant* improvidence, shortsightedness **3** *Syn* PRUDENCE, discretion, forethought, providence
foresighted *Syn* PRUDENT, discreet, forethoughtful, provident
forestall **1** *Syn* PREVENT (sense 1), anticipate **2** *Syn* PREVENT (sense 2), avert, help, obviate, preclude
foretaste *Syn* PROSPECT, anticipation, outlook
foretell • to tell something before it happens through special knowledge or occult power *Syn* augur, forebode, forecast, portend, predict, presage, prognosticate, prophesy *Rel* anticipate, apprehend, divine, foreknow, foresee
foreteller *Syn* PROPHET, augur, diviner, forecaster, foreseer, fortune-teller, futurist, prognosticator, prophesier, seer, soothsayer
foretelling *Syn* PREDICTION, auguring, cast, forecast, forecasting, predicting, presaging, prognosis, prognosticating, prognostication, prophecy, soothsaying
forethought *Syn* PRUDENCE, discretion, foresight, providence
forethoughtful *Syn* PRUDENT, discreet, foresighted, provident
forewarn *Syn* WARN, alert, caution
forewarning *Syn* WARNING, admonition, alarm, alert, caution, notice
foreword *Syn* INTRODUCTION, exordium, preamble, preface, prelude, prologue
forfeit *Syn* FINE, damages, forfeiture, mulct, penalty
forfeiture *Syn* FINE, damages, forfeit, mulct, penalty
forge *Syn* MAKE, fabricate, fashion, form, manufacture, shape
forget *Syn* NEGLECT, disregard, ignore, omit, overlook, slight *Ant* cherish
forgetful • losing or letting go from one's mind something once known or learned *Syn* oblivious, unmindful *Rel* lax, neglectful, negligent, remiss, slack
forgivable *Syn* VENIAL, excusable, pardonable,

remittable *Ant* inexcusable, mortal, unforgivable, unpardonable

forgive *Syn* EXCUSE, condone, pardon, remit *Ant* punish

forgiveness *Syn* PARDON, absolution, amnesty, remission, remittal *Ant* penalty, punishment, retribution

forgo • to deny oneself something for the sake of an end *Syn* abnegate, eschew, forbear, sacrifice *Rel* abandon, relinquish, surrender, waive

forgotten *Syn* ABANDONED (sense 2), derelict, deserted, disused, forsaken, rejected, vacated

forlorn **1** *Syn* ALONE, desolate, lone, lonely, lonesome, lorn, solitary *Ant* accompanied **2** *Syn* DESPONDENT, despairing, desperate, hopeless *Ant* lighthearted **3** *Syn* SAD (sense 1), bad, blue, brokenhearted, crestfallen, dejected, depressed, despondent, disconsolate, doleful, down, downcast, downhearted, droopy, gloomy, glum, heartbroken, heartsick, heartsore, inconsolable, joyless, low, low-spirited, melancholy, miserable, mournful, saddened, sorrowful, sorry, unhappy, woebegone, woeful, wretched *Ant* blissful, buoyant, buoyed, cheerful, cheery, chipper, delighted, glad, gladdened, gladsome, gleeful, happy, joyful, joyous, jubilant, sunny, upbeat

forlornness **1** *Syn* DESPONDENCY, despair, desperation, hopelessness *Ant* lightheartedness **2** *Syn* SADNESS, blues, dejection, depression, desolation, despondency, disconsolateness, dispiritedness, doldrums, downheartedness, dreariness, dumps, gloom, gloominess, heartsickness, joylessness, melancholy, mopes, oppression, unhappiness *Ant* bliss, blissfulness, ecstasy, elatedness, elation, euphoria, exhilaration, exuberance, exultation, felicity, gladness, gladsomeness, happiness, heaven, intoxication, joy, joyfulness, joyousness, jubilation, rapture, rapturousness

form *n* **1** • outward appearance of something as distinguished from the substance of which it is made *Syn* configuration, conformation, figure, shape *Rel* contour, outline, profile, silhouette **2** • conduct regulated by an external control (as custom or a formal protocol of procedure) *Syn* ceremonial, ceremony, formality, liturgy, rite, ritual *Rel* procedure, proceeding, process **3** • a fixed or accepted way of doing or sometimes of expressing something *Syn* convenance, convention, usage

form *vb* **1** *Syn* BEGIN (sense 1), arise, commence, dawn, materialize, originate, set in, spring, start *Ant* cease, end, stop **2** *Syn* MAKE, fabricate, fashion, forge, manufacture, shape

formal *adj* **1** *Syn* CEREMONIAL, ceremonious, conventional, solemn **2** *Syn* DRESS, dressy *Ant* casual, informal, sporty

formal *n* *Syn* DANCE, ball, cotillion, hop, prom

formality *Syn* FORM (sense 2), ceremonial, ceremony, liturgy, rite, ritual

formalize *Syn* STANDARDIZE, homogenize, normalize, regularize

former • having been such at some previous time *Syn* erstwhile, late, old, onetime, past, sometime, whilom *Rel* bygone, dead, extinct

formless • having no definite or recognizable form *Syn* amorphous, shapeless, unformed, unshaped, unstructured *Rel* characterless, featureless, nondescript *Ant* formed, shaped, structured

formulate *Syn* PHRASE, articulate, clothe, couch, express, put, say, state, word

forsake *Syn* ABANDON, desert *Ant* reclaim

forsaken *Syn* ABANDONED (sense 2), derelict, deserted, disused, forgotten, rejected, vacated

forswear *Syn* ABJURE, recant, renounce, retract *Ant* pledge (*allegiance, a vow*), elect (*a way of life, a means to an end*)

fort • a structure or place offering resistance to a hostile force *Syn* citadel, fastness, fortress, stronghold

forth **1** *Syn* ALONG, ahead, forward, on, onward **2** *Syn* ONWARD, forward

forthcoming • being soon to appear or take place *Syn* approaching, coming, imminent, impending, nearing, oncoming, pending, upcoming *Rel* future *Ant* late, recent

forthright *Syn* STRAIGHTFORWARD, aboveboard *Ant* devious, indirect

forthrightness *Syn* CANDOR, directness, frankness, openheartedness, openness, plainness, straightforwardness *Ant* dissembling, pretense (*or* pretence)

fortify *Syn* STRENGTHEN, energize, invigorate, reinforce *Ant* weaken

fortitude • a quality of character combining courage and staying power *Syn* backbone, grit, guts, pluck, sand *Rel* courage, mettle, resolution, spirit, tenacity *Ant* pusillanimity

fortress *Syn* FORT, citadel, fastness, stronghold

fortuitous *Syn* ACCIDENTAL, casual, chance, fluky, inadvertent, incidental, unintended, unintentional, unplanned, unpremeditated, unwitting *Ant* deliberate, intended, intentional, planned, premeditated

fortunate *Syn* LUCKY, happy, providential *Ant* unlucky

fortune *Syn* CHANCE, accident, hap, hazard, luck *Ant* law, principle

fortune-teller *Syn* PROPHET, augur, diviner, forecaster, foreseer, foreteller, futurist, prognosticator, prophesier, seer, soothsayer

forward *vb* **1** *Syn* ADVANCE (sense 1), further, promote *Ant* check, retard **2** *Syn* SEND, dispatch, remit, route, ship, transmit *Ant* accept, receive

forward *adv* **1** *Syn* ALONG, ahead, forth, on, onward (*or* onwards) **2** *Syn* ONWARD, forth
forward *adj Syn* PREMATURE, advanced, precocious, untimely *Ant* matured
foster *Syn* NURSE, cherish, cultivate, nurture
foul *vb* **1** *Syn* CONTAMINATE, befoul, defile, poison, pollute, taint *Ant* decontaminate, purify **2** *Syn* DIRTY, befoul, begrime, besmirch, blacken, grime, mire, muddy, smirch, smudge, soil, stain, sully *Ant* clean, cleanse
foul *adj Syn* DIRTY, filthy, nasty, squalid *Ant* clean
foul up *Syn* BOTCH, bobble, bungle, butcher, flub, foozle, fumble, louse up, mangle, mess (up), muff, murder
found **1** • to set going or to bring into existence *Syn* create, establish, institute, organize *Rel* begin, commence, inaugurate, initiate, start **2** *Syn* BASE, ground, rest, stay
foundation *Syn* BASE, basis, ground, groundwork *Ant* top
foxy *Syn* SLY, artful, crafty, cunning, guileful, insidious, tricky, wily
fracas *Syn* BRAWL, broil, melee, row, rumpus, scrap
fraction *Syn* PART, detail, division, fragment, member, parcel, piece, portion, section, sector, segment *Ant* whole
fractious *Syn* IRRITABLE, fretful, huffy, peevish, pettish, petulant, querulous, snappish, waspish *Ant* easygoing
fragile **1** • easily broken *Syn* brittle, crisp, frangible, friable, short *Ant* tough **2** *Syn* WEAK, decrepit, feeble, frail, infirm *Ant* strong
fragment *Syn* PART, detail, division, fraction, member, parcel, piece, portion, section, sector, segment *Ant* whole
fragrance • a sweet or pleasant odor *Syn* bouquet, incense, perfume, redolence *Rel* aroma, odor, scent, smell *Ant* stench, stink
fragrant **1** • having a pleasant smell *Syn* ambrosial, aromatic, perfumed, redolent, savory, scented, sweet *Rel* flowery, fruity, pungent, spicy *Ant* fetid, foul, malodorous, noisome, putrid, rancid, rank, reeking, reeky, smelly, stinking, stinky, strong **2** *Syn* ODOROUS, aromatic, balmy, redolent *Ant* malodorous, odorless
frail *Syn* WEAK, decrepit, feeble, fragile, infirm *Ant* strong
frailty *Syn* FAULT, failing, foible, vice *Ant* merit
frame *Syn* ENGINEER, contrive, finagle, finesse, machinate, maneuver, manipulate, mastermind, negotiate, wangle
framework *Syn* STRUCTURE, anatomy, skeleton
franchise *Syn* SUFFRAGE, ballot, vote
frangible *Syn* FRAGILE, brittle, crisp, friable, short *Ant* tough
frank • marked by free, forthright, and sincere expression *Syn* candid, open, plain *Rel* ingenuous, naive, natural, simple, unsophisticated *Ant* reticent
frankness *Syn* CANDOR, directness, forthrightness, openheartedness, openness, plainness, straightforwardness *Ant* dissembling, pretense (*or* pretence)
frantic *Syn* FURIOUS, delirious, frenetic, frenzied, rabid, wild
fraternize *Syn* SOCIALIZE, associate, hobnob, mingle, mix
fraud *Syn* DECEPTION, chicane, chicanery, double-dealing, trickery
fraught *Syn* RIFE, abounding, flush, replete, swarming, teeming, thick, thronging
fray *Syn* CONTEST, affray, combat, conflict, fight
freak **1** *Syn* FAN, addict, aficionado, buff, bug, devotee, enthusiast, fanatic, fancier, fiend, lover, maniac, nut **2** *Syn* WHIM, caprice, fancy, notion, vagary, whimsy
freakish *Syn* WHIMSICAL, capricious, impulsive
freckle *Syn* SPOT, blotch, dapple, dot, fleck, marble, mottle, pepper, speck, speckle, splotch, sprinkle, stipple
free *adj* • not subject to the rule or control of another *Syn* autarchic, autarkic, autonomous, independent, sovereign *Rel* delivered, emancipated, enfranchised, freed, liberated, released *Ant* bond
free *vb* • to relieve from constraint or restraint *Syn* discharge, emancipate, liberate, manumit, release *Rel* deliver, enfranchise
freebooter *Syn* PIRATE, buccaneer, corsair, privateer
freedom **1** • the state or condition of not being subject to external rule or control *Syn* autarchy, autarky, autonomy, independence, sovereignty *Rel* delivery, emancipation, enfranchisement, liberation, manumission, release *Ant* bondage **2** • the power or condition of acting without compulsion *Syn* liberty, license *Rel* exemption, immunity *Ant* necessity
freely *Syn* EASILY, effortlessly, facilely, fluently, handily, lightly, painlessly, readily, smoothly *Ant* arduously, laboriously
freezing *Syn* COLD, arctic, chilly, cool, frigid, frosty, gelid, glacial, icy *Ant* hot
freight *Syn* LOAD, burden, cargo, lading
frenetic *Syn* FURIOUS, delirious, frantic, frenzied, rabid, wild
frenzied *Syn* FURIOUS, delirious, frantic, frenetic, rabid, wild
frenzy **1** • a state of wildly excited activity or emotion *Syn* agitation, delirium, distraction, furor, furore, fury, hysteria, rage, rampage, uproar *Rel* chaos, confusion, disorder, turmoil **2** *Syn* INSPIRATION, afflatus, fury **3** *Syn* MANIA, delirium, hysteria
frequently *Syn* OFTEN, oft, oftentimes
fresh *Syn* NEW, modern, modernistic, new-

fangled, new-fashioned, novel, original *Ant* old

freshman *Syn* BEGINNER, colt, fledgling, greenhorn, neophyte, newbie, newcomer, novice, recruit, rookie, tenderfoot, tyro *Ant* old hand, old-timer, vet, veteran

fret *Syn* ABRADE, chafe, excoriate, gall

fretful *Syn* IRRITABLE, fractious, huffy, peevish, pettish, petulant, querulous, snappish, waspish *Ant* easygoing

friable *Syn* FRAGILE, brittle, crisp, frangible, short *Ant* tough

friar *Syn* RELIGIOUS, monk, nun

friend **1** • a person, and especially one not related by blood, with whom one is on good and usually familiar terms *Syn* acquaintance, confidant, intimate *Rel* associate, companion, comrade, crony *Ant* foe **2** *Syn* EXPONENT, advocate, apostle, backer, booster, champion, promoter, proponent, supporter *Ant* adversary, antagonist, opponent

friendly *Syn* AMICABLE, neighborly *Ant* antagonistic

friendship • the relation existing between persons, communities, states, or peoples that are in accord and in sympathy with each other *Syn* amity, comity, goodwill *Rel* affinity, attraction, sympathy *Ant* animosity

fright *n Syn* FEAR, alarm, consternation, dismay, dread, horror, panic, terror, trepidation *Ant* fearlessness

fright *vb Syn* FRIGHTEN, affray, affright, alarm, scare, startle, terrify, terrorize *Ant* reassure

frighten • to strike or to fill with fear or dread *Syn* affray, affright, alarm, fright, scare, startle, terrify, terrorize *Rel* appall, daunt, dismay, horrify *Ant* reassure

frightful *Syn* FEARFUL (sense 2), appalling, awful, dreadful, horrible, horrific, shocking, terrible, terrific

frightfully *Syn* VERY, awful, awfully, beastly, deadly, especially, exceedingly, extra, extremely, far, full, greatly, heavily, highly, hugely, jolly, mightily, mighty, mortally, most, much, particularly, rattling, real, right, so, something, super, terribly, too, whacking *Ant* little, negligibly, nominally, slightly

frigid *Syn* COLD, arctic, chilly, cool, freezing, frosty, gelid, glacial, icy *Ant* hot

fringe *Syn* BORDER, bound, margin, rim, skirt

fringing *Syn* ADJACENT, abutting, adjoining, bordering, contiguous, flanking, joining, juxtaposed, skirting, touching, verging *Ant* nonadjacent

frippery **1** *Syn* FINERY, array, best, bravery, caparison, feather, full dress, gaiety, regalia **2** *Syn* TRIFLE, child's play, nothing, triviality

fritter *Syn* WASTE, consume, dissipate, squander *Ant* conserve, save

frivol *Syn* FLIRT, dally, trifle

frivolity **1** • a lack of seriousness often at an improper time *Syn* facetiousness, flightiness, flippancy, frivolousness, levity, light-headedness, lightness *Rel* cheerfulness, gaiety, glee, high-spiritedness, lightheartedness, merriment, mirth **2** *Syn* LIGHTNESS, flightiness, flippancy, levity, light-mindedness, volatility *Ant* seriousness

frivolous *Syn* UNIMPORTANT, inconsequential, inconsiderable, insignificant, little, minor, minute, negligible, slight, small, small-fry, trifling, trivial *Ant* big, consequential, eventful, important, major, material, meaningful, momentous, significant, substantial, weighty

frivolousness *Syn* FRIVOLITY, facetiousness, flightiness, flippancy, levity, light-headedness, lightness

frolic *n Syn* PLAY, disport, gambol, rollick, romp, sport *Ant* work

frolic *vb Syn* PLAY, disport, gambol, rollick, romp, sport

frolicsome *Syn* PLAYFUL, impish, mischievous, roguish, sportive, waggish

frontier • a rural region that forms the edge of the settled or developed part of a country *Syn* backwater, backwoods, bush, hinterland, upcountry *Rel* country, countryside, sticks

frosty *Syn* COLD, arctic, chilly, cool, freezing, frigid, gelid, glacial, icy *Ant* hot

froth *Syn* FOAM, lather, scum, spume, suds, yeast

froward **1** *Syn* CONTRARY, balky, perverse, restive, wayward *Ant* complaisant, good-natured **2** *Syn* DISOBEDIENT, balky, contrary, defiant, insubordinate, intractable, rebellious, recalcitrant, refractory, restive, ungovernable, unruly, untoward, wayward, willful (*or* wilful) *Ant* amenable, compliant, docile, obedient, tractable **3** *Syn* UNCONTROLLABLE, headstrong, intractable, recalcitrant, refractory, ungovernable, unmanageable, unruly, untoward, wayward, willful (*or* wilful) *Ant* controllable, governable, tractable

frowardness *Syn* DISOBEDIENCE, contrariness, defiance, insubordination, intractability, rebelliousness, recalcitrance, refractoriness, unruliness, willfulness *Ant* amenability, compliance, docility, obedience

frown *vb* • to look with anger or disapproval *Syn* glare, gloom, glower, lower, scowl *Rel* gape, gaze, ogle, stare *Ant* beam, smile

frown *n Syn* GRIMACE, face, lower, mouth, pout, scowl

frown (on) *Syn* DISAPPROVE (OF), deprecate, discountenance, disfavor, dislike, reprove *Ant* approve, favor, like

frowzy *Syn* SLATTERNLY, blowsy, dowdy

frugal • careful in the management of money or resources *Syn* economical, economizing, provident, scrimping, sparing, thrifty *Rel* conserving, preserving, saving *Ant* prodigal, wasteful

frugality *Syn* ECONOMY, husbandry, providence, scrimping, skimping, thrift *Ant* wastefulness

fruitful *Syn* FERTILE, fat, fecund, luxuriant, productive, prolific, rich *Ant* barren, infertile, sterile, unfruitful, unproductive

fruitfulness *Syn* FERTILITY, fecundity, prolificacy *Ant* infertility, sterility

fruition **1** • the state of being actual or complete *Syn* accomplishment, achievement, actuality, attainment, consummation, fulfillment, realization *Ant* naught, nonfulfillment **2** *Syn* PLEASURE, delectation, delight, enjoyment, joy *Ant* anger, displeasure, vexation

fruitless *Syn* FUTILE, abortive, bootless, vain *Ant* effective, effectual, efficacious, efficient, fruitful, productive, profitable, successful

frustrate • to come between a person and his or her aim or desire or to defeat another's plan *Syn* baffle, balk, circumvent, foil, outwit, thwart *Rel* counteract, negative, neutralize *Ant* fulfill

frustrating *Syn* ANNOYING, aggravating, bothersome, disturbing, exasperating, galling, irksome, irritating, maddening, nettling, peeving, pesty, rankling, riling, vexatious, vexing

frustration *Syn* DISAPPOINTMENT (sense 1), dismay, dissatisfaction, letdown *Ant* contentment, gratification, satisfaction

fuddle *Syn* CONFUSE, addle, befuddle, muddle *Ant* enlighten

fugitive *Syn* MOMENTARY, ephemeral, evanescent, flash, fleeting, impermanent, passing, short-lived, temporary, transient, transitory *Ant* enduring, eternal, everlasting, lasting, long-lived, permanent, perpetual

fulfill **1** *Syn* PERFORM, accomplish, achieve, discharge, effect, execute **2** *Syn* SATISFY (sense 2), answer, meet

fulfilling *Syn* HEARTWARMING, cheering, comforting, encouraging, gladdening, gratifying, heartening, rewarding, satisfying *Ant* depressing, discouraging, disheartening, dispiriting

fulfillment *Syn* FRUITION, accomplishment, achievement, actuality, attainment, consummation, realization *Ant* naught, nonfulfillment

full *adj* **1** • containing all that is wanted or needed or possible *Syn* complete, plenary, replete *Rel* comprehending, comprehensive, including, inclusive *Ant* empty **2** *Syn* ENCYCLOPEDIC, compendious, complete, comprehensive, global, inclusive, in-depth, omnibus, panoramic, universal

full *adv* *Syn* VERY, awful, awfully, beastly, deadly, especially, exceedingly, extra, extremely, far, frightfully, greatly, heavily, highly, hugely, jolly, mightily, mighty, mortally, most, much, particularly, rattling, real, right, so, something, super, terribly, too, whacking *Ant* little, negligibly, nominally, slightly

full dress *Syn* FINERY, array, best, bravery, caparison, feather, frippery, gaiety, regalia

full-scale *Syn* EXHAUSTIVE, all-out, clean, complete, comprehensive, out-and-out, thorough, thoroughgoing, total

fulminate *Syn* RANT, bluster, rave, spout

fumble *Syn* BOTCH, bobble, bungle, butcher, flub, foozle, foul up, louse up, mangle, mess (up), muff, murder

fumigate *Syn* STERILIZE (sense 2), disinfect, sanitize

fuming *Syn* ANGRY, angered, apoplectic, enraged, foaming, furious, incensed, indignant, inflamed, infuriated, irate, ireful, mad, outraged, rabid, riled, roiled, sore, steaming, wrathful, wroth *Ant* delighted, pleased

fun *adj* • providing amusement or enjoyment *Syn* amusing, delightful, diverting, enjoyable, entertaining, pleasurable *Rel* agreeable, beguiling, pleasant *Ant* boring, dull

fun *n* • action or speech that is intended to amuse or arouse laughter *Syn* game, jest, play, sport *Rel* amusement, diversion, entertainment, recreation

fun *vb* *Syn* JOKE, banter, fool, jest, jive, josh, kid, quip, wisecrack

function *n* **1** • acts or operations expected of a person or thing *Syn* duty, office, province *Rel* end, goal, intention, object, objective, purpose **2** *Syn* POWER (sense 2), faculty **3** *Syn* ROLE, capacity, job, part, place, position, purpose, task, work

function *vb* **1** • to have a certain purpose *Syn* act, perform, serve, work *Rel* operate, run **2** *Syn* ACT (sense 1), behave, operate, react, work

functionary *Syn* BUREAUCRAT, public servant

fundamental *adj* **1** • forming or affecting the groundwork, roots, or lowest part of something *Syn* basal, basic, radical, underlying *Rel* primal, primary, prime, primordial **2** *Syn* ELEMENTARY, basic, elemental, essential, rudimentary, underlying *Ant* advanced **3** *Syn* ESSENTIAL, cardinal, vital

fundamental *n* *Syn* PRINCIPLE, axiom, law, theorem

funnel *Syn* CHANNEL, channelize, conduct, direct, pipe, siphon

funny *Syn* LAUGHABLE, comic, comical, droll, farcical, ludicrous, ridiculous, risible

furious **1** • marked by uncontrollable excitement especially under the stress of a powerful emotion *Syn* delirious, frantic, frenetic, frenzied, rabid, wild *Rel* excited, provoked, stimulated **2** *Syn* ANGRY, angered, apoplectic, enraged, foaming, fuming, incensed, indignant, inflamed, infuriated, irate, ireful, mad, outraged, rabid, riled, roiled, sore, steaming, wrathful, wroth *Ant* delighted, pleased

furnish **1** • to provide (someone) with what is needed for a task or activity *Syn* accoutre (*or* accouter), equip, fit (out), outfit, rig, supply *Rel* stock, store **2** • to put (something) into the possession of someone for use or consumption *Syn* deliver, feed, give, hand, hand over, provide, supply *Rel* administer, dispense, distribute, dole (out), mete (out), parcel (out) *Ant* hold (back), keep (back), reserve, retain, withhold

furor **1** *Syn* ANGER, angriness, fury, indignation, irateness, ire, outrage, rage, spleen, wrath, wrathfulness *Ant* delight, pleasure **2** *Syn* COMMOTION, bother, bustle, clatter, disturbance, furore, fuss, hubbub, hullabaloo, hurly-burly, pandemonium, pother, row, ruckus, ruction, rumpus, shindy, squall, stew, stir, storm, to-do, tumult, turmoil, uproar, welter, whirl **3** *Syn* FRENZY, agitation, delirium, distraction, furore, fury, hysteria, rage, rampage, uproar

furore **1** *Syn* COMMOTION, bother, bustle, clatter, disturbance, furor, fuss, hubbub, hullabaloo, hurly-burly, pandemonium, pother, row, ruckus, ruction, rumpus, shindy, squall, stew, stir, storm, to-do, tumult, turmoil, uproar, welter, whirl **2** *Syn* FRENZY, agitation, delirium, distraction, furor, fury, hysteria, rage, rampage, uproar

furry **1** *Syn* HAIRY (sense 1), bristly, fleecy, hirsute, rough, shaggy, unshorn, woolly *Ant* bald, furless, hairless, shorn, smooth **2** *Syn* HAIRY (sense 2), fuzzy, rough, shaggy, woolly

further *adj Syn* ADDITIONAL, added, another, else, farther, more, other

further *vb Syn* ADVANCE (sense 1), forward, promote *Ant* check, retard

further *adv Syn* FARTHER, beyond

furtherance *Syn* ADVANCE (sense 2), advancement, going, headway, march, onrush, passage, process, procession, progress, progression *Ant* recession, regression, retrogression

furtive *Syn* SECRET, clandestine, covert, stealthy, surreptitious, underhand, underhanded

furuncle *Syn* ABSCESS, boil, carbuncle, pimple, pustule

fury **1** *Syn* ANGER, angriness, furor, indignation, irateness, ire, outrage, rage, spleen, wrath, wrathfulness *Ant* delight, pleasure **2** *Syn* FRENZY, agitation, delirium, distraction, furor, furore, hysteria, rage, rampage, uproar **3** *Syn* INSPIRATION, afflatus, frenzy

fuse **1** *Syn* LIQUEFY, deliquesce, melt, thaw **2** *Syn* MIX, amalgamate, blend, coalesce, commingle, merge, mingle

fusillade *Syn* BARRAGE, bombardment, cannonade, hail, salvo, shower, storm, volley

fusion **1** *Syn* ALLIANCE, coalition, confederacy, confederation, federation, league **2** *Syn* BLEND, admixture, amalgam, amalgamation, combination, composite, compound, intermixture, mix, mixture

fuss *n* **1** *Syn* COMMOTION, bother, bustle, clatter, disturbance, furor, furore, hubbub, hullabaloo, hurly-burly, pandemonium, pother, row, ruckus, ruction, rumpus, shindy, squall, stew, stir, storm, to-do, tumult, turmoil, uproar, welter, whirl **2** *Syn* STIR, ado, bustle, flurry, pother *Ant* tranquillity **3** *Syn* OBJECTION, challenge, complaint, demur, expostulation, protest, question, remonstrance

fuss *vb* **1** *Syn* COMPLAIN, beef, bellyache, carp, crab, croak, gripe, grouse, growl, grumble, kick, moan, murmur, mutter, repine, squawk, wail, whine, yammer *Ant* rejoice **2** *Syn* GUSH (sense 2), enthuse, rave, rhapsodize, slobber **3** *Syn* QUIBBLE, carp, cavil, nitpick

fusser *Syn* GROUCH, bear, complainer, crab, crank, croaker, curmudgeon, griper, grouser, growler, grumbler, grump, murmurer, mutterer, whiner

fussy *Syn* NICE, dainty, fastidious, finical, finicking, finicky, particular, pernickety, persnickety, squeamish

fustian *Syn* BOMBAST, rant, rhapsody, rodomontade

fusty *Syn* MALODOROUS, fetid, musty, noisome, putrid, rancid, rank, stinking *Ant* odorous

futile • barren of result *Syn* abortive, bootless, fruitless, vain *Rel* idle, nugatory, otiose, vain *Ant* effective, effectual, efficacious, efficient, fruitful, productive, profitable, successful

futurist *Syn* PROPHET, augur, diviner, forecaster, foreseer, foreteller, fortune-teller, prognosticator, prophesier, seer, soothsayer

fuzzy *Syn* HAIRY (sense 2), furry, rough, shaggy, woolly

G

gab *Syn* CHAT, babble, blab, cackle, chatter, converse, gabble, gas, jabber, jaw, palaver, patter, prate, prattle, rap, rattle, run on, talk, twitter, visit
gabble *Syn* CHAT, babble, blab, cackle, chatter, converse, gab, gas, jabber, jaw, palaver, patter, prate, prattle, rap, rattle, run on, talk, twitter, visit
gabfest *Syn* CHAT, chatter, chitchat, gossip, palaver, rap, small talk, table talk, talk, tête-à-tête
gad *Syn* WANDER, gallivant, meander, prowl, ramble, range, roam, rove, stray, traipse
gadabout *Syn* NOMAD, drifter, rambler, roamer, rover, stroller, vagabond, wanderer, wayfarer
gadget **1** • an interesting and often novel device with a practical use *Syn* appliance, contraption, contrivance, gimmick, gizmo (*or* gismo), jigger *Rel* implement, instrument, tool, utensil **2** *Syn* DEVICE, contraption, contrivance
gaffe *Syn* IMPROPRIETY (sense 1), familiarity, indiscretion, solecism *Ant* amenity, civility, courtesy, formality, gesture
gag *Syn* JOKE, crack, jape, jest, quip, wisecrack, witticism
gaiety *Syn* FINERY, array, best, bravery, caparison, feather, frippery, full dress, regalia
gain **1** *Syn* CONVALESCE, heal, mend, rally, recover, recuperate, snap back **2** *Syn* EARN, acquire, attain, capture, carry, draw, garner, get, land, make, obtain, procure, realize, secure, win *Ant* forfeit, lose **3** *Syn* GET, obtain, procure, secure, win **4** *Syn* IMPROVE (sense 2), convalesce, recover, recuperate **5** *Syn* REACH, achieve, attain, compass
gainful *Syn* PAYING, lucrative, profitable, remunerative
gainsay *Syn* DENY, contradict, contravene, impugn, negative, traverse *Ant* concede, confirm
gal *Syn* GIRLFRIEND, lady, woman
gala *Syn* FESTIVAL, carnival, celebration, festivity, fete (*or* fête), fiesta, jubilee
gall *vb Syn* ABRADE, chafe, excoriate, fret
gall *n Syn* EFFRONTERY, audacity, brashness, brass, brassiness, brazenness, cheek, cheekiness, chutzpah, nerve, nerviness, pertness, presumption, presumptuousness, sauce, sauciness, temerity
gallant *Syn* CIVIL, chivalrous, courteous, courtly, polite *Ant* rude, uncivil
gallantry **1** *Syn* COURAGE, bravery, courageousness, daring, dauntlessness, doughtiness, fearlessness, greatheartedness, guts, hardihood, heart, heroism, intrepidity, intrepidness, nerve, stoutness, valor *Ant* cowardice, cowardliness, cravenness, dastardliness, spinelessness, yellowness **2** *Syn* COURTESY, amenity, attention *Ant* discourtesy **3** *Syn* HEROISM, prowess, valor
gallery *Syn* PASSAGE, aisle, arcade, cloister, corridor, hall, hallway, passageway
galling *Syn* ANNOYING, aggravating, bothersome, disturbing, exasperating, frustrating, irksome, irritating, maddening, nettling, peeving, pesty, rankling, riling, vexatious, vexing
gallivant *Syn* WANDER, gad, meander, prowl, ramble, range, roam, rove, stray, traipse
galumph *Syn* STUMBLE, blunder, bumble, flounder, lollop, lumber, lurch, trip
galvanize *Syn* PROVOKE, excite, pique, quicken, stimulate
gambit *Syn* TRICK, artifice, feint, maneuver, ploy, ruse, stratagem, wile
gamble *Syn* BET, go, lay, stake, wager
gambler *Syn* BETTOR, wagerer
gamble (with) *Syn* ENDANGER, adventure, compromise, hazard, imperil, jeopardize, menace, risk, venture
gambol *n Syn* PLAY, disport, frolic, rollick, romp, sport *Ant* work
gambol *vb Syn* PLAY, disport, frolic, rollick, romp, sport
game *Syn* FUN, jest, play, sport
gameness *Syn* ALACRITY, amenability, goodwill, willingness
games *Syn* ATHLETICS, sports
gamut *Syn* RANGE, compass, horizon, ken, orbit, purview, radius, reach, scope, sweep
gangling *Syn* LANKY, gangly, rangy, spindling, spindly
gangly *Syn* LANKY, gangling, rangy, spindling, spindly
gap **1** *Syn* BREAK, hiatus, interim, interruption, interval, lacuna **2** *Syn* CANYON, defile, flume, gorge, gulch, gulf, notch, pass, ravine
gape **1** • to look long and hard in wonder or surprise *Syn* gawk, gaze, goggle, peer, rubberneck, stare *Rel* glare, gloat, glower **2** *Syn* GAZE, glare, gloat, peer, stare
garbage *Syn* REFUSE, debris, offal, rubbish, trash, waste
garble *Syn* MISREPRESENT, belie, falsify
gargantuan *Syn* HUGE, Brobdingnagian, colossal, cyclopean, elephantine, enormous, giant, gigantean, gigantic, herculean, immense, mammoth, titanic, vast *Ant* bitty, diminutive, microscopic (*or* microscopical), midget, miniature, minute, pocket, pygmy, teeny, teeny-weeny, tiny, wee

garish *Syn* GAUDY, flamboyant, flashy, glitzy, loud, ostentatious, splashy, swank (*or* swanky), tawdry *Ant* conservative, quiet, understated

garishness *Syn* OSTENTATION, flamboyance, flashiness, gaudiness, glitz, ostentatiousness, pretentiousness, showiness, swank *Ant* austerity, plainness, severity

garner **1** *Syn* EARN, acquire, attain, capture, carry, draw, gain, get, land, make, obtain, procure, realize, secure, win *Ant* forfeit, lose **2** *Syn* REAP, gather, glean, harvest

garnish *Syn* ADORN, beautify, bedeck, deck, decorate, embellish, ornament *Ant* disfigure

garrulity *Syn* TALKATIVENESS, garrulousness, glibness, loquaciousness, loquacity, volubility *Ant* silence

garrulous *Syn* TALKATIVE, glib, loquacious, voluble *Ant* closemouthed, laconic, reserved, reticent, taciturn, tight-lipped

garrulousness *Syn* TALKATIVENESS, garrulity, glibness, loquaciousness, loquacity, volubility *Ant* silence

gas *Syn* CHAT, babble, blab, cackle, chatter, converse, gab, gabble, jabber, jaw, palaver, patter, prate, prattle, rap, rattle, run on, talk, twitter, visit

gasconade *Syn* BOAST, brag, crow, vaunt *Ant* depreciate (*oneself, one's accomplishments*)

gastronome *Syn* EPICURE, bon vivant, glutton, gourmand, gourmet

gate *Syn* DOOR, doorway, gateway, portal, postern

gateway *Syn* DOOR, doorway, gate, portal, postern

gather **1** • to come or bring together *Syn* assemble, collect, congregate *Rel* accumulate, amass, hoard **2** *Syn* INFER, conclude, deduce, judge **3** *Syn* REAP, garner, glean, harvest

gathering • a number of individuals come or brought together *Syn* assemblage, assembly, collection, congregation *Rel* crowd, crush, horde, mob, press, rout, throng

gauche *Syn* AWKWARD, clumsy, inept, maladroit *Ant* deft, graceful, handy

gaud *Syn* KNICKKNACK, bauble, curio, curiosity, gewgaw, novelty, ornamental, trinket

gaudiness *Syn* OSTENTATION, flamboyance, flashiness, garishness, glitz, ostentatiousness, pretentiousness, showiness, swank *Ant* austerity, plainness, severity

gaudy • excessively showy *Syn* flamboyant, flashy, garish, glitzy, loud, ostentatious, splashy, swank (*or* swanky), tawdry *Rel* meretricious, pretentious *Ant* conservative, quiet, understated

gauge *n Syn* STANDARD, criterion, touchstone, yardstick

gauge *vb Syn* ESTIMATE (sense 2), calculate, call, conjecture, figure, guess, judge, make, place, put, reckon, suppose

gaunt *Syn* LEAN, angular, lank, lanky, rawboned, scrawny, skinny, spare *Ant* fleshy

gawk *vb Syn* GAPE, gaze, goggle, peer, rubberneck, stare

gawk *n Syn* OAF, clod, hulk, lout, lubber, lug

gay **1** *Syn* CAREFREE, careless, cavalier, devil-may-care, easygoing, happy-go-lucky, insouciant, lighthearted, unconcerned *Ant* careworn **2** *Syn* CHEERFUL (sense 1), blithe, blithesome, bright, buoyant, cheery, chipper, gladsome, lightsome, sunny, upbeat *Ant* dour, gloomy, glum, morose, saturnine, sulky, sullen **3** *Syn* CHEERFUL (sense 2), bright, cheering, cheery, glad *Ant* bleak, cheerless, dark, depressing, dismal, dreary, gloomy, gray **4** *Syn* LIVELY, animated, sprightly, vivacious *Ant* dull **5** *Syn* MERRY, blithesome, festive, gleeful, jocose, jocund, jolly, jovial, laughing, mirthful, sunny

gaze **1** • to look at long and attentively *Syn* gape, glare, gloat, peer, stare *Rel* look, see, watch **2** *Syn* GAPE, gawk, goggle, peer, rubberneck, stare

gear *Syn* EQUIPMENT, apparatus, machinery, matériel, outfit, paraphernalia, tackle

geld *Syn* STERILIZE (sense 1), alter, castrate, emasculate, mutilate, spay *Ant* fertilize

gelid *Syn* COLD, arctic, chilly, cool, freezing, frigid, frosty, glacial, icy *Ant* hot

genealogy *Syn* ANCESTRY, birth, blood, bloodline, breeding, descent, extraction, family tree, line, lineage, origin, parentage, pedigree, stock, strain *Ant* issue, posterity, progeny, seed

general **1** • belonging or relating to the whole *Syn* blanket, common, generic, global, overall, universal *Rel* broad, collective, comprehensive, extensive, pervasive, sweeping, ubiquitous, wholesale, wide, widespread *Ant* individual, particular **2** • relating to the main elements and not to specific details *Syn* all-around, bird's-eye, broad, nonspecific, overall *Rel* comprehensive, inclusive *Ant* delineated, detailed, particularized, specific

generally **1** *Syn* CHIEFLY, altogether, basically, by and large, largely, mainly, mostly, overall, predominantly, primarily, principally, substantially **2** *Syn* LARGELY, chiefly, greatly, mainly, mostly, principally **3** *Syn* NATURALLY (sense 1), commonly, normally, ordinarily, typically, usually *Ant* abnormally, atypically, extraordinarily, uncommonly, unusually

generate **1** • to give life or origin to or to bring into existence by or as if by natural processes *Syn* beget, breed, engender, get, procreate, propagate, reproduce, sire *Rel* bear, produce, yield **2** *Syn* EFFECT, bring about, cause, create, effectuate, engender, induce, make, produce, prompt, result (in), spawn, work, yield

generic *Syn* GENERAL (sense 1), blanket,

common, global, overall, universal *Ant* individual, particular

generous *Syn* LIBERAL (sense 1), bounteous, bountiful, handsome, munificent, openhanded *Ant* close

genesis *Syn* BEGINNING, alpha, birth, commencement, dawn, inception, incipiency, launch, morning, onset, outset, start, threshold *Ant* close, conclusion, end, ending

genial **1** *Syn* AMIABLE, affable, agreeable, good-natured, good-tempered, gracious, nice, sweet, well-disposed *Ant* disagreeable, ill-natured, ill-tempered, ungracious, unpleasant **2** *Syn* GRACIOUS, affable, cordial, sociable *Ant* ungracious

genius *Syn* GIFT (sense 2), aptitude, bent, faculty, knack, talent, turn

gent *Syn* MAN (sense 1), dude, fellow, gentleman, guy, male

genteel *Syn* CULTIVATED, civilized, cultured, polished, refined *Ant* philistine, uncivilized, uncultured, unpolished, unrefined

gentility *Syn* POLITENESS, civility, courteousness, courtesy, graciousness, mannerliness *Ant* discourteousness, discourtesy, impoliteness, incivility, rudeness, ungraciousness

gentle *adj* **1** *Syn* CLEMENT, balmy, equable, mild, moderate, temperate *Ant* harsh, inclement, intemperate, severe **2** *Syn* SOFT, balmy, bland, lenient, mild, smooth *Ant* hard, stern

gentle *vb Syn* CUSHION, buffer, soften

gentleman **1** • a man of high birth or social position *Syn* lord, nobleman **2** *Syn* MAN, dude, fellow, gent, guy, male

gentleperson *Syn* ARISTOCRAT, noble, patrician

gentlewoman • a woman of high birth or social position *Syn* dame, lady, noblewoman

gentry *Syn* ARISTOCRACY, county, elite, nobility, society *Ant* people, proletariat

genuine *Syn* AUTHENTIC, bona fide, veritable *Ant* spurious

geriatric *Syn* ELDERLY, aged, aging, ancient, long-lived, old, older, senior *Ant* young, youthful

germane *Syn* PERTINENT, applicable, apposite, apropos, material, pointed, relative, relevant *Ant* extraneous, immaterial, inapplicable, irrelevant, pointless

germfree *Syn* SANITARY, aseptic, hygienic, sterile *Ant* insanitary, unhygienic, unsanitary

gesture *Syn* MOTION, beckon, flag, signal, wave

get **1** • to come into possession of *Syn* gain, obtain, procure, secure, win *Rel* bring, fetch **2** *Syn* BECOME, come, go, grow, run, turn, wax **3** *Syn* EARN, acquire, attain, capture, carry, draw, gain, garner, land, make, obtain, procure, realize, secure, win *Ant* forfeit, lose **4** *Syn* GENERATE, beget, breed, engender, procreate, propagate, reproduce, sire **5** *Syn* PERSUADE, argue, convince, induce, move, prevail (on *or* upon), satisfy, talk (into), win (over)

get off *Syn* BEGIN (sense 2), commence, embark (on *or* upon), enter (into *or* upon), kick off, launch, open, start, strike (into) *Ant* conclude, end, finish, terminate

gewgaw *Syn* KNICKKNACK, bauble, curio, curiosity, gaud, novelty, ornamental, trinket

ghastly • horrifying and repellent in appearance or aspect *Syn* grim, grisly, gruesome, lurid, macabre *Rel* deadly, deathly

ghost • the soul of a dead person thought of especially as appearing to living people *Syn* apparition, bogey, phantasm, phantom, poltergeist, shade, shadow, specter (*or* spectre), spirit, spook, vision, wraith *Rel* banshee, demon (*or* daemon), familiar (*or* familiar spirit), genie, imp, incubus, puck, vampire, zombie

ghoul *Syn* DEMON, devil, fiend, imp, incubus

giant *n* • something that is unusually large and powerful *Syn* behemoth, blockbuster, colossus, jumbo, leviathan, mammoth, monster, titan, whale, whopper *Rel* amazon *Ant* dwarf, midget, mini, miniature, peewee, pygmy, runt, shrimp

giant *adj Syn* HUGE, Brobdingnagian, colossal, cyclopean, elephantine, enormous, gargantuan, gigantean, gigantic, Herculean, immense, mammoth, titanic, vast *Ant* bitty, diminutive, microscopic (*or* microscopical), midget, miniature, minute, pocket, pygmy, teeny, teeny-weeny, tiny, wee

gibberish • speech or actions that are esoteric in nature and suggest the magical, strange, or unknown *Syn* abracadabra, hocus-pocus, mummery

gibe *Syn* SCOFF, fleer, flout, gird, jeer, sneer

giddy • affected by a sensation of being whirled about or around *Syn* dazzled, dizzy, swimming, vertiginous *Rel* reeling, whirling

gift **1** • something, often of value but not necessarily material, given freely to another for his benefit or pleasure *Syn* boon, favor, gratuity, largess, present *Rel* alms, benefaction, contribution, donation **2** • a special ability or a capacity for a definite kind of activity or achievement *Syn* aptitude, bent, faculty, genius, knack, talent, turn *Rel* dowry, endowment

gigantean *Syn* HUGE, Brobdingnagian, colossal, cyclopean, elephantine, enormous, gargantuan, giant, gigantic, Herculean, immense, mammoth, titanic, vast *Ant* bitty, diminutive, microscopic (*or* microscopical), midget, miniature, minute, pocket, pygmy, teeny, teeny-weeny, tiny, wee

gigantic *Syn* HUGE, Brobdingnagian, colossal, cyclopean, elephantine, enormous, gargantuan, giant, gigantean, Herculean, immense, mammoth, titanic, vast *Ant* bitty, diminutive, microscopic (*or* microscopical), midget, miniature, minute, pocket, pygmy, teeny, teeny-weeny, tiny, wee

gimmick *Syn* GADGET, appliance, contraption, contrivance, gizmo (*or* gismo), jigger

gingery *Syn* SPIRITED, fiery, high-spirited, mettlesome, peppery, spunky *Ant* spiritless

gird **1** *Syn* SCOFF, fleer, flout, gibe, jeer, sneer **2** *Syn* SURROUND, circle, compass, encircle, encompass, environ, girdle, hem, ring

girdle *Syn* SURROUND, circle, compass, encircle, encompass, environ, gird, hem, ring

girl • a female person who has not yet reached adulthood *Syn* lass, lassie, miss, missy *Rel* adolescent, juvenile, kid, minor, moppet, teenager, youngster

girlfriend • a female romantic companion *Syn* gal, lady, woman *Rel* beloved, darling, sweetheart

gist **1** *Syn* CRUX, core, heart, nub, pith, pivot **2** *Syn* SUBSTANCE, burden, core, pith, purport

give **1** • to convey something or make something over or available to another *Syn* afford, bestow, confer, donate, present *Rel* accord, award, concede, grant, vouchsafe **2** *Syn* FURNISH (sense 2), deliver, feed, hand, hand over, provide, supply *Ant* hold (back), keep (back), reserve, retain, withhold

give-and-take *Syn* BANTER, chaff, jesting, joshing, persiflage, raillery, repartee

given **1** *Syn* ACCUSTOMED, habituated, used, wont *Ant* unaccustomed, unused **2** *Syn* PRONE (sense 1), apt, inclined, tending *Ant* erect

gizmo *or* **gismo** *Syn* GADGET, appliance, contraption, contrivance, gimmick, jigger

glacial *Syn* COLD, arctic, chilly, cool, freezing, frigid, frosty, gelid, icy *Ant* hot

glad **1** • characterized by or expressing the mood of one who is pleased or delighted *Syn* cheerful, happy, joyful, joyous, lighthearted *Rel* delighted, gratified, pleased, rejoiced, tickled *Ant* sad **2** *Syn* CHEERFUL (sense 2), bright, cheering, cheery, gay *Ant* bleak, cheerless, dark, depressing, dismal, dreary, gloomy, gray

gladden *Syn* PLEASE, delight, gratify, regale, rejoice, tickle *Ant* anger, displease, vex

gladdening *Syn* HEARTWARMING, cheering, comforting, encouraging, fulfilling, gratifying, heartening, rewarding, satisfying *Ant* depressing, discouraging, disheartening, dispiriting

gladiatorial *Syn* BELLIGERENT, aggressive, argumentative, bellicose, combative, contentious, discordant, disputatious, militant, pugnacious, quarrelsome, scrappy, truculent, warlike *Ant* nonbelligerent, pacific, peaceable, peaceful

gladsome *Syn* CHEERFUL (sense 1), blithe, blithesome, bright, buoyant, cheery, chipper, gay, lightsome, sunny, upbeat *Ant* dour, gloomy, glum, morose, saturnine, sulky, sullen

glamorize *Syn* IDEALIZE, glorify, romanticize

glamorous *Syn* EXOTIC, fantastic, marvelous (*or* marvellous), outlandish, romantic, strange

glance **1** *Syn* BRUSH, graze, shave, skim **2** *Syn* FLASH, coruscate, gleam, glint, glisten, glitter, scintillate, sparkle, twinkle **3** *Syn* LOOK, glimpse, peek, peep, sight, view

glare *n* *Syn* BLAZE, flame, flare, glow

glare *vb* **1** *Syn* BLAZE, flame, flare, glow **2** *Syn* FROWN, gloom, glower, lower, scowl *Ant* beam, smile **3** *Syn* GAZE, gape, gloat, peer, stare

glaring **1** *Syn* EGREGIOUS, blatant, conspicuous, flagrant, gross, obvious, patent, pronounced, rank, striking **2** *Syn* FLAGRANT, gross, rank

glaze *Syn* LUSTER, gloss, sheen

gleam *Syn* FLASH, coruscate, glance, glint, glisten, glitter, scintillate, sparkle, twinkle

glean *Syn* REAP, garner, gather, harvest

glee *Syn* MIRTH, hilarity, jollity

gleeful *Syn* MERRY, blithesome, festive, gay, jocose, jocund, jolly, jovial, laughing, mirthful, sunny

glib *Syn* TALKATIVE, garrulous, loquacious, voluble *Ant* closemouthed, laconic, reserved, reticent, taciturn, tight-lipped

glibness *Syn* TALKATIVENESS, garrulity, garrulousness, loquaciousness, loquacity, volubility *Ant* silence

glide *Syn* SLIDE, coast, glissade, skid, slip, slither, toboggan

glimpse *Syn* LOOK, glance, peek, peep, sight, view

glint *Syn* FLASH, coruscate, glance, gleam, glisten, glitter, scintillate, sparkle, twinkle

glissade *Syn* SLIDE, coast, glide, skid, slip, slither, toboggan

glisten *Syn* FLASH, coruscate, glance, gleam, glint, glitter, scintillate, sparkle, twinkle

glistening *Syn* GLOSSY, buffed, burnished, lustrous, polished, rubbed, satin, satiny, sleek *Ant* dim, dull, flat, lusterless, matte

glitter *Syn* FLASH, coruscate, glance, gleam, glint, glisten, scintillate, sparkle, twinkle

glitz *Syn* OSTENTATION, flamboyance, flashiness, garishness, gaudiness, ostentatiousness, pretentiousness, showiness, swank *Ant* austerity, plainness, severity

glitzy *Syn* GAUDY, flamboyant, flashy, garish, loud, ostentatious, splashy, swank (*or* swanky), tawdry *Ant* conservative, quiet, understated

gloat *Syn* GAZE, gape, glare, peer, stare

global **1** *Syn* ENCYCLOPEDIC, compendious, complete, comprehensive, full, inclusive, in-depth, omnibus, panoramic, universal **2** *Syn* GENERAL (sense 1), blanket, common, generic, overall, universal *Ant* individual, particular

globe *Syn* EARTH, planet, world

gloom *vb Syn* FROWN, glare, glower, lower, scowl *Ant* beam, smile

gloom *n Syn* SADNESS, blues, dejection, depression, desolation, despondency, disconsolateness, dispiritedness, doldrums, downheartedness, dreariness, dumps, forlornness, gloominess, heartsickness, joylessness, melancholy, mopes, oppression, unhappiness *Ant* bliss, blissfulness, ecstasy, elatedness, elation, euphoria, exhilaration, exuberance, exultation, felicity, gladness, gladsomeness, happiness, heaven, intoxication, joy, joyfulness, joyousness, jubilation, rapture, rapturousness

gloominess *Syn* SADNESS, blues, dejection, depression, desolation, despondency, disconsolateness, dispiritedness, doldrums, downheartedness, dreariness, dumps, forlornness, gloom, heartsickness, joylessness, melancholy, mopes, oppression, unhappiness *Ant* bliss, blissfulness, ecstasy, elatedness, elation, euphoria, exhilaration, exuberance, exultation, felicity, gladness, gladsomeness, happiness, heaven, intoxication, joy, joyfulness, joyousness, jubilation, rapture, rapturousness

gloomy **1** *Syn* DARK, dim, dusky, murky, obscure *Ant* light **2** *Syn* SAD (sense 1), bad, blue, brokenhearted, crestfallen, dejected, depressed, despondent, disconsolate, doleful, down, downcast, downhearted, droopy, forlorn, glum, heartbroken, heartsick, heartsore, inconsolable, joyless, low, low-spirited, melancholy, miserable, mournful, saddened, sorrowful, sorry, unhappy, woebegone, woeful, wretched *Ant* blissful, buoyant, buoyed, cheerful, cheery, chipper, delighted, glad, gladdened, gladsome, gleeful, happy, joyful, joyous, jubilant, sunny, upbeat **3** *Syn* SULLEN, crabbed, dour, glum, morose, saturnine, sulky, surly

glorify **1** *Syn* DIGNIFY, ennoble, honor **2** *Syn* EXALT, aggrandize, dignify, ennoble, enshrine, magnify *Ant* abase, degrade, demean, humble, humiliate **3** *Syn* IDEALIZE, glamorize, romanticize

glorious *Syn* SPLENDID, gorgeous, resplendent, sublime, superb

gloriousness *Syn* MAGNIFICENCE, augustness, brilliance, glory, grandeur, grandness, majesty, nobility, nobleness, resplendence, splendor, stateliness, stupendousness, sublimeness, superbness

glory **1** *Syn* FAME, celebrity, éclat, honor, notoriety, renown, reputation, repute *Ant* infamy, obscurity **2** *Syn* MAGNIFICENCE, augustness, brilliance, gloriousness, grandeur, grandness, majesty, nobility, nobleness, resplendence, splendor, stateliness, stupendousness, sublimeness, superbness

glorying *Syn* EXULTANT, exulting, jubilant, rejoicing, triumphant

gloss *n Syn* LUSTER, glaze, sheen

gloss *vb* **1** *Syn* PALLIATE, extenuate, gloze, whiten, whitewash **2** *Syn* POLISH, buff, burnish, dress, grind, rub, shine, smooth

glossy **1** • having a shiny surface or finish *Syn* buffed, burnished, glistening, lustrous, polished, rubbed, satin, satiny, sleek *Rel* silken, silky, slick, slippery *Ant* dim, dull, flat, lusterless, matte **2** *Syn* SLEEK, satiny, silken, silky, slick, velvety

glow *n Syn* BLAZE, flame, flare, glare

glow *vb* **1** *Syn* BLAZE, flame, flare, glare **2** *Syn* BLUSH, bloom, color, crimson, flush, redden

glower *Syn* FROWN, glare, gloom, lower, scowl *Ant* beam, smile

glowing *Syn* FERVENT, ardent, blazing, burning, charged, emotional, fervid, feverish, fiery, flaming, hot-blooded, impassioned, passionate, red-hot, vehement, warm, warm-blooded *Ant* cold, cool, dispassionate, impassive, unemotional

gloze *Syn* PALLIATE, extenuate, gloss, whiten, whitewash

glum **1** *Syn* SAD (sense 1), bad, blue, brokenhearted, crestfallen, dejected, depressed, despondent, disconsolate, doleful, down, downcast, downhearted, droopy, forlorn, gloomy, heartbroken, heartsick, heartsore, inconsolable, joyless, low, low-spirited, melancholy, miserable, mournful, saddened, sorrowful, sorry, unhappy, woebegone, woeful, wretched *Ant* blissful, buoyant, buoyed, cheerful, cheery, chipper, delighted, glad, gladdened, gladsome, gleeful, happy, joyful, joyous, jubilant, sunny, upbeat **2** *Syn* SULLEN, crabbed, dour, gloomy, morose, saturnine, sulky, surly

glut *Syn* SATIATE, cloy, gorge, pall, sate, surfeit

glutton **1** • one who eats greedily or too much *Syn* gorger, gormandizer, gourmand, hog, overeater, stuffer, swiller *Rel* feaster, trencherman **2** *Syn* EPICURE, bon vivant, gastronome, glutton, gourmet

gluttonous *Syn* VORACIOUS, rapacious, ravening, ravenous

gnash *Syn* BITE, champ, gnaw

gnaw *Syn* BITE, champ, gnash

go *vb* **1** • to move out of or away from where one is *Syn* depart, leave, quit, retire, withdraw *Rel* abscond, decamp, escape, flee, fly *Ant* come **2** *Syn* BET, gamble, lay, stake, wager **3** *Syn* BECOME, come, get, grow, run, turn, wax **4** *Syn* RESORT, apply, refer, turn **5** *Syn* TRAVERSE, cover, crisscross, cross, cut (across), follow, pass (over), proceed (along), travel

go *n* **1** *Syn* ATTEMPT, crack, endeavor, essay, fling, pass, shot, stab, trial, try, whack **2** *Syn* SPELL, bout, shift, stint, tour, trick, turn

goad *n Syn* MOTIVE, impulse, incentive, inducement, spring, spur

goad *vb Syn* URGE, egg (on), encourage, exhort, press, prod, prompt
goal • something that one hopes or intends to accomplish *Syn* aim, ambition, aspiration, design, dream, end, intent, intention, mark, meaning, object, objective, plan, pretension, purpose, target, thing *Rel* plot, project, scheme
gob *Syn* MARINER, bluejacket, sailor, seaman, tar
gobbledygook *Syn* NONSENSE, balderdash, bull, bunk, drivel, poppycock, rot, trash, twaddle
go-between *Syn* MEDIATOR, arbiter, arbitrator, conciliator, intercessor, intermediary, interposer, middleman, peacemaker
godless *Syn* IRRELIGIOUS, nonreligious, ungodly, unreligious *Ant* religious
godliness *Syn* HOLINESS, blessedness, devoutness, piety, piousness, sainthood, saintliness, saintship, sanctity *Ant* godlessness, impiety, ungodliness, unholiness
godly *Syn* HOLY (sense 1), devout, pious, religious, sainted, saintly *Ant* faithless, godless, impious, irreligious, ungodly, unholy
Godspeed *Syn* GOOD-BYE, adieu, au revoir, bon voyage, farewell *Ant* hello
goggle *Syn* GAPE, gawk, gaze, peer, rubberneck, stare
going *Syn* ADVANCE (sense 2), advancement, furtherance, headway, march, onrush, passage, process, procession, progress, progression *Ant* recession, regression, retrogression
golden *Syn* BLOND, fair, flaxen, sandy, straw, tawny *Ant* dark
golden-ager *Syn* SENIOR CITIZEN, ancient, elder, oldster, old-timer *Ant* youngster, youth
gone *Syn* EXTINCT, bygone, dead, defunct, departed, expired, vanished *Ant* alive, existent, existing, extant, living
good **1** *Syn* COMPETENT, able, capable, fit, qualified, suitable *Ant* incompetent, inept, poor, unfit, unqualified **2** *Syn* DEPENDABLE, reliable, responsible, safe, solid, steady, sure, tried, tried-and-true, true, trustworthy, trusty *Ant* irresponsible, undependable, unreliable, untrustworthy **3** *Syn* FAITHFUL, constant, devoted, devout, fast, loyal, pious, staunch (*or* stanch), steadfast, steady, true, true-blue *Ant* disloyal, faithless, false, fickle, inconstant, perfidious, recreant, traitorous, treacherous, unfaithful, untrue **4** *Syn* WORTHY, deserving, meritorious *Ant* no-good, undeserving, valueless, worthless
good-bye *or* **good-by** • an expression of good wishes at parting *Syn* adieu, au revoir, bon voyage, farewell, Godspeed *Rel* leave-taking, send-off *Ant* hello
goodly *Syn* LARGE, big, bulky, considerable, good-sized, grand, great, handsome, hefty, hulking, largish, outsize, oversize (*or* oversized), sizable (*or* sizeable), substantial, tidy, voluminous *Ant* little, puny, small, undersized
good-natured *Syn* AMIABLE, affable, agreeable, genial, good-tempered, gracious, nice, sweet, well-disposed *Ant* disagreeable, ill-natured, ill-tempered, ungracious, unpleasant
goodness • moral excellence *Syn* morality, rectitude, virtue *Rel* nobility, righteousness, virtuousness *Ant* badness, evil
good sense *Syn* SENSE, common sense, gumption, horse sense, judgment, wisdom
good-sized *Syn* LARGE, big, bulky, considerable, goodly, grand, great, handsome, hefty, hulking, largish, outsize, oversize (*or* oversized), sizable (*or* sizeable), substantial, tidy, voluminous *Ant* little, puny, small, undersized
good-tempered *Syn* AMIABLE, affable, agreeable, genial, good-natured, gracious, nice, sweet, well-disposed *Ant* disagreeable, ill-natured, ill-tempered, ungracious, unpleasant
goodwill **1** *Syn* ALACRITY, amenability, gameness, willingness **2** *Syn* FRIENDSHIP, amity, comity *Ant* animosity
goose *Syn* FOOL (sense 2), booby, half-wit, jackass, lunatic, nincompoop, ninny, nitwit, nut, simpleton, turkey, yo-yo
gorge *n Syn* CANYON, defile, flume, gap, gulch, gulf, notch, pass, ravine
gorge *vb Syn* SATIATE, cloy, glut, pall, sate, surfeit
gorgeous **1** *Syn* BEAUTIFUL, attractive, beauteous, comely, cute, fair, handsome, knockout, lovely, pretty, ravishing, sightly, stunning, taking *Ant* homely, ill-favored, plain, ugly, unattractive, unbeautiful, unhandsome, unlovely, unpretty, unsightly **2** *Syn* SPLENDID, glorious, resplendent, sublime, superb
gorger *Syn* GLUTTON, gormandizer, gourmand, hog, overeater, stuffer, swiller
gormandizer *Syn* GLUTTON, gorger, gourmand, hog, overeater, stuffer, swiller
gory *Syn* BLOODY, sanguinary, sanguine, sanguineous
gossip *vb* • to disclose something, often of questionable veracity, that is better kept to oneself *Syn* blab, tattle
gossip *n* **1** *Syn* CHAT, chatter, chitchat, gabfest, palaver, rap, small talk, table talk, talk, tête-à-tête **2** *Syn* REPORT, hearsay, rumor
gourmand **1** *Syn* EPICURE, bon vivant, gastronome, glutton, gourmet **2** *Syn* GLUTTON, gorger, gormandizer, hog, overeater, stuffer, swiller
gourmet *Syn* EPICURE, bon vivant, gastronome, glutton, gourmand
governance *Syn* RULE (sense 2), administration, authority, government, jurisdiction, regime, regimen
government *Syn* RULE (sense 2), administration, authority, governance, jurisdiction, regime, regimen

grab *Syn* TAKE, clutch, grasp, seize, snatch
grace **1** *Syn* ELEGANCE, class, elegancy, gracefulness, handsomeness, majesty, refinement, stateliness **2** *Syn* MERCY, charity, clemency, lenity
gracefulness *Syn* ELEGANCE, class, elegancy, grace, handsomeness, majesty, refinement, stateliness
graceless *Syn* INAPPROPRIATE, improper, inapt, incongruous, incorrect, indecorous, inept, infelicitous, unapt, unbecoming, unfit, unhappy, unseemly, unsuitable, wrong *Ant* appropriate, becoming, befitting, correct, decorous, felicitous, fit, fitting, genteel, happy, meet, proper, right, seemly, suitable
gracious **1** • marked by kindly courtesy *Syn* affable, cordial, genial, sociable *Rel* amiable, complaisant, obliging *Ant* ungracious **2** *Syn* AMIABLE, affable, agreeable, genial, good-natured, good-tempered, nice, sweet, well-disposed *Ant* disagreeable, ill-natured, ill-tempered, ungracious, unpleasant
graciousness *Syn* POLITENESS, civility, courteousness, courtesy, gentility, mannerliness *Ant* discourteousness, discourtesy, impoliteness, incivility, rudeness, ungraciousness
gradate *Syn* CLASS, grade, graduate, rank, rate
gradation • difference or variation between two things that are nearly alike *Syn* nuance, shade *Rel* difference, dissimilarity, distinction, divergence
gradational *Syn* GRADUAL, incremental, phased, piecemeal, step-by-step *Ant* sudden
grade *Syn* CLASS, gradate, graduate, rank, rate
gradual • proceeding or changing by steps or degrees *Syn* gradational, incremental, phased, piecemeal, step-by-step *Rel* progressive, stepped, tapered *Ant* sudden
graduate *Syn* CLASS, gradate, grade, rank, rate
grand **1** • large, handsome, dignified, and impressive *Syn* august, grandiose, imposing, magnificent, majestic, noble, stately *Rel* luxurious, opulent, sumptuous **2** *Syn* EXCELLENT, A1, bang-up, banner, capital, classic, crackerjack, dandy, divine, fabulous, fine, first-class, first-rate, great, groovy, heavenly, jim-dandy, keen, marvelous (*or* marvellous), mean, neat, nifty, noble, par excellence, prime, sensational, splendid, stellar, sterling, superb, superior, superlative, supernal, swell, terrific, tip-top, top, top-notch, unsurpassed, wonderful *Ant* poor **3** *Syn* LARGE, big, bulky, considerable, goodly, good-sized, great, handsome, hefty, hulking, largish, outsize, oversize (*or* oversized), sizable (*or* sizeable), substantial, tidy, voluminous *Ant* little, puny, small, undersized
grandeur *Syn* MAGNIFICENCE, augustness, brilliance, gloriousness, glory, grandness, majesty, nobility, nobleness, resplendence, splendor, stateliness, stupendousness, sublimeness, superbness
grandiloquent *Syn* RHETORICAL, aureate, bombastic, euphuistic, flowery, magniloquent
grandiose *Syn* GRAND, august, imposing, magnificent, majestic, noble, stately
grandly *Syn* HIGH, expensively, extravagantly, lavishly, luxuriously, opulently, richly, sumptuously *Ant* austerely, humbly, modestly, plainly, simply
grandness *Syn* MAGNIFICENCE, augustness, brilliance, gloriousness, glory, grandeur, majesty, nobility, nobleness, resplendence, splendor, stateliness, stupendousness, sublimeness, superbness
grant *vb* **1** • to give as a favor or as a right *Syn* accord, award, concede, vouchsafe *Rel* bestow, confer, donate, give, present **2** *Syn* ADMIT, acknowledge, agree, allow, concede, confess, own (up) *Ant* deny
grant *n* *Syn* APPROPRIATION, allocation, allotment, annuity, subsidy
granting *Syn* PERMISSION, allowance, authorization, clearance, concurrence, consent, leave, license (*or* licence), sanction, sufferance *Ant* interdiction, prohibition, proscription
graph *n* *Syn* CHART, map
graph *vb* *Syn* CHART, map
graphic • giving a clear visual impression especially in words *Syn* pictorial, picturesque, vivid *Rel* clear, lucid, perspicuous
grapple *Syn* WRESTLE, scuffle, tussle
grasp *n* **1** *Syn* COMPREHENSION, appreciation, apprehension, grip, perception, understanding **2** *Syn* HOLD, clutch, grip
grasp *vb* *Syn* TAKE, clutch, grab, seize, snatch
grasping *Syn* COVETOUS, acquisitive, avaricious, greedy
grassland *Syn* PLAIN, down, prairie, savanna, steppe, tundra, veld (*or* veldt)
grate *Syn* SCRAPE, grind, rasp, scratch
grateful *Syn* PLEASANT, agreeable, gratifying, pleasing, welcome *Ant* distasteful, harsh, unpleasant
gratefulness *Syn* THANKS, appreciation, appreciativeness, gratitude, thankfulness *Ant* ingratitude, thanklessness, ungratefulness
gratified *Syn* CONTENT, contented, happy, pleased, satisfied *Ant* discontent, discontented, displeased, dissatisfied, malcontent, unhappy
gratify *Syn* PLEASE, delight, gladden, regale, rejoice, tickle *Ant* anger, displease, vex
gratifying **1** *Syn* HEARTWARMING, cheering, comforting, encouraging, fulfilling, gladdening, heartening, rewarding, satisfying *Ant* depressing, discouraging, disheartening, dispiriting **2** *Syn* PLEASANT, agreeable, gratifying, pleasing, welcome *Ant* distasteful, harsh, unpleasant
gratitude *Syn* THANKS, appreciation, appreciativeness, gratefulness, thankfulness *Ant* ingratitude, thanklessness, ungratefulness

gratuitous **1** *Syn* SUPEREROGATORY, uncalled-for, wanton **2** *Syn* UNNECESSARY, dispensable, needless, nonessential, uncalled-for, unessential, unwarranted *Ant* essential, indispensable, necessary, needed, needful, required

gratuity **1** *Syn* BONUS, dividend, extra, gravy, lagniappe, perquisite, tip **2** *Syn* GIFT (sense 1), boon, favor, largess, present

grave *Syn* SERIOUS, earnest, sedate, sober, solemn, somber, staid *Ant* flippant, light

gravity *Syn* EARNESTNESS, intentness, seriousness, soberness, sobriety, solemnity *Ant* frivolity, levity, lightheartedness

gravy *Syn* BONUS, dividend, extra, gratuity, lagniappe, perquisite, tip

graze **1** *Syn* BRUSH, glance, shave, skim **2** *Syn* FEED, nourish, pasture *Ant* starve

grease *Syn* OIL, anoint, cream, lubricate

great **1** *Syn* EXCELLENT, A1, bang-up, banner, capital, classic, crackerjack, dandy, divine, fabulous, fine, first-class, first-rate, grand, groovy, heavenly, jim-dandy, keen, marvelous (*or* marvellous), mean, neat, nifty, noble, par excellence, prime, sensational, splendid, stellar, sterling, superb, superior, superlative, supernal, swell, terrific, tip-top, top, top-notch, unsurpassed, wonderful *Ant* poor **2** *Syn* LARGE, big, bulky, considerable, goodly, good-sized, grand, handsome, hefty, hulking, largish, outsize, oversize (*or* oversized), sizable (*or* sizeable), substantial, tidy, voluminous *Ant* little, puny, small, undersized **3** *Syn* LONG (sense 2), extended, far, lengthy, long-lived, long-range, long-term, marathon *Ant* brief, short, short-lived, short-range, short-term

greatheartedness *Syn* COURAGE, bravery, courageousness, daring, dauntlessness, doughtiness, fearlessness, gallantry, guts, hardihood, heart, heroism, intrepidity, intrepidness, nerve, stoutness, valor *Ant* cowardice, cowardliness, cravenness, dastardliness, spinelessness, yellowness

greatly **1** *Syn* LARGELY, chiefly, generally, mainly, mostly, principally **2** *Syn* VERY, awful, awfully, beastly, deadly, especially, exceedingly, extra, extremely, far, frightfully, full, heavily, highly, hugely, jolly, mightily, mighty, mortally, most, much, particularly, rattling, real, right, so, something, super, terribly, too, whacking *Ant* little, negligibly, nominally, slightly

greed • an intense selfish desire for wealth or possessions *Syn* acquisitiveness, avarice, avariciousness, avidity, covetousness, cupidity, greediness, rapaciousness, rapacity *Rel* materialism, possessiveness

greediness *Syn* GREED, acquisitiveness, avarice, avariciousness, avidity, covetousness, cupidity, rapaciousness, rapacity

greedy *Syn* COVETOUS, acquisitive, avaricious, grasping

green **1** *Syn* CALLOW, adolescent, immature, inexperienced, juvenile, puerile, raw, unfledged, unripe, unripened *Ant* adult, experienced, grown-up, mature, ripe **2** *Syn* RUDE (sense 1), callow, crude, raw, rough, uncouth *Ant* civil, urbane

greenhorn *Syn* BEGINNER, colt, fledgling, freshman, neophyte, newbie, newcomer, novice, recruit, rookie, tenderfoot, tyro *Ant* old hand, old-timer, vet, veteran

greet *Syn* ADDRESS, accost, hail, salute

greetings *Syn* COMPLIMENTS, congratulations, felicitations, regards, respects

gregarious *Syn* CONVIVIAL, boon, companionable, extroverted, outgoing, sociable, social *Ant* antisocial, introverted, reclusive, unsociable

griddle cake *Syn* PANCAKE, flapjack, hotcake, slapjack

grief *Syn* SORROW, anguish, heartache, heartbreak, regret, woe *Ant* joy

grieve • to feel or express sorrow or grief *Syn* mourn, sorrow *Rel* bear, endure, suffer *Ant* rejoice

grievous *Syn* REGRETTABLE, deplorable, distressful, distressing, heartbreaking, heartrending, lamentable, unfortunate, woeful

grill *Syn* RESTAURANT, café, diner

grim **1** • being extremely obdurate or firm in action or purpose *Syn* implacable, merciless, relentless, unrelenting *Rel* adamant, inexorable, inflexible, obdurate *Ant* lenient **2** *Syn* GHASTLY, grisly, gruesome, lurid, macabre

grimace • a twisting of the facial features in disgust or disapproval *Syn* face, frown, lower, mouth, pout, scowl *Rel* flinch, squinch, wince

grime *Syn* DIRTY, befoul, begrime, besmirch, blacken, foul, mire, muddy, smirch, smudge, soil, stain, sully *Ant* clean, cleanse

grin *n* *Syn* SMILE, simper, smirk *Ant* frown

grin *vb* *Syn* SMILE, simper, smirk *Ant* frown

grind *vb* **1** *Syn* POLISH, buff, burnish, dress, gloss, rub, shine, smooth **2** *Syn* SCRAPE, grate, rasp, scratch **3** *Syn* SHARPEN, edge, hone, strop, whet *Ant* blunt, dull

grind *n* *Syn* WORK (sense 1), drudgery, labor, toil, travail *Ant* play

grip **1** *Syn* COMPREHENSION, appreciation, apprehension, grasp, grip, understanding **2** *Syn* HOLD, clutch, grasp

gripe *Syn* COMPLAIN, beef, bellyache, carp, crab, croak, fuss, grouse, growl, grumble, kick, moan, murmur, mutter, repine, squawk, wail, whine, yammer *Ant* rejoice

griper *Syn* GROUCH, bear, complainer, crab, crank, croaker, curmudgeon, fusser, grouser, growler, grumbler, grump, murmurer, mutterer, whiner

gripping *Syn* INTERESTING, absorbing, arresting, engaging, engrossing, enthralling, fascinating, immersing, intriguing, involving,

riveting *Ant* boring, drab, dry, dull, heavy, monotonous, tedious, uninteresting
grisly *Syn* GHASTLY, grim, gruesome, lurid, macabre
grit *Syn* FORTITUDE, backbone, guts, pluck, sand *Ant* pusillanimity
groan *n* **1** *Syn* LAMENT, howl, keen, lamentation, moan, plaint, wail *Ant* exultation, rejoicing **2** *Syn* SIGH, moan, sob
groan *vb* *Syn* SIGH, moan, sob
grog *Syn* ALCOHOL, booze, drink, intoxicant, liquor, moonshine, spirits
groggery *Syn* BARROOM, bar, café, grogshop, pub, saloon, tavern
grogshop *Syn* BARROOM, bar, café, groggery, pub, saloon, tavern
groovy *Syn* EXCELLENT, A1, bang-up, banner, capital, classic, crackerjack, dandy, divine, fabulous, fine, first-class, first-rate, grand, great, heavenly, jim-dandy, keen, marvelous (*or* marvellous), mean, neat, nifty, noble, par excellence, prime, sensational, splendid, stellar, sterling, superb, superior, superlative, supernal, swell, terrific, tip-top, top, top-notch, unsurpassed, wonderful *Ant* poor
gross **1** *Syn* COARSE, obscene, ribald, vulgar *Ant* fine, refined **2** *Syn* EGREGIOUS, blatant, conspicuous, flagrant, glaring, obvious, patent, pronounced, rank, striking **3** *Syn* FLAGRANT, glaring, rank **4** *Syn* WHOLE, all, entire, total *Ant* partial
grotesque *Syn* FANTASTIC, antic, bizarre
grouch • an irritable and complaining person *Syn* bear, complainer, crab, crank, croaker, curmudgeon, fusser, griper, grouser, growler, grumbler, grump, murmurer, mutterer, whiner *Rel* fulminator, malcontent, sorehead
ground *n* **1** *Syn* BASE, basis, foundation, groundwork *Ant* top **2** *Syn* REASON (sense 1), argument, proof
ground *vb* *Syn* BASE, found, rest, stay
grounded *Syn* AGROUND, beached, stranded *Ant* afloat
groundless **1** • having no basis in reason or fact *Syn* invalid, nonvalid, unfounded, ungrounded, unreasonable, unsubstantiated, unsupported, unwarranted *Rel* illogical, irrational, nonlogical, unconscionable, unsound *Ant* good, hard, just, justified, reasonable, reasoned, substantiated, valid, well-founded **2** *Syn* BASELESS, unfounded, unwarranted
ground rule *Syn* RULE (sense 1), bylaw, regulation
grounds *Syn* DEPOSIT, dregs, lees, precipitate, sediment
groundwork *Syn* BASE, basis, foundation, ground *Ant* top
group • a collection or assemblage of persons or things *Syn* bunch, cluster, lot, parcel *Rel* band, company, party, troop, troupe
grouse *Syn* COMPLAIN, beef, bellyache, carp, crab, croak, fuss, gripe, growl, grumble, kick, moan, murmur, mutter, repine, squawk, wail, whine, yammer *Ant* rejoice
grouser *Syn* GROUCH, bear, complainer, crab, crank, croaker, curmudgeon, fusser, griper, growler, grumbler, grump, murmurer, mutterer, whiner
grovel *Syn* WALLOW, welter
grow *Syn* BECOME, come, get, go, run, turn, wax
growl **1** *Syn* BARK, bay, howl, snarl, yap, yelp **2** *Syn* COMPLAIN, beef, bellyache, carp, crab, croak, fuss, gripe, grouse, grumble, kick, moan, murmur, mutter, repine, squawk, wail, whine, yammer *Ant* rejoice
growler *Syn* GROUCH, bear, complainer, crab, crank, croaker, curmudgeon, fusser, griper, grouser, grumbler, grump, murmurer, mutterer, whiner
grown-up *Syn* MATURE, adult, matured, mellow, ripe *Ant* childish, immature
grub **1** *Syn* DIG, delve, excavate, spade **2** *Syn* LABOR, drudge, endeavor, hump, hustle, moil, peg (away), plod, plow, plug, slave, slog, strain, strive, struggle, sweat, toil, travail, work *Ant* dabble, fiddle (around), fool (around), mess (around), putter (around)
grubber *Syn* SLAVE (sense 2), drudge, drudger, laborer, peon, plugger, slogger, toiler, worker *Ant* freeman
grudge *vb* *Syn* COVET, begrudge, envy
grudge *n* *Syn* MALICE, despite, ill will, malevolence, malignancy, malignity, spite, spleen *Ant* charity
gruesome *Syn* GHASTLY, grim, grisly, lurid, macabre
gruff *Syn* BLUFF, blunt, brusque, crusty, curt *Ant* smooth, suave
grumble *Syn* COMPLAIN, beef, bellyache, carp, crab, croak, fuss, gripe, grouse, growl, kick, moan, murmur, mutter, repine, squawk, wail, whine, yammer *Ant* rejoice
grumbler *Syn* GROUCH, bear, complainer, crab, crank, croaker, curmudgeon, fusser, griper, grouser, growler, grump, murmurer, mutterer, whiner
grump *Syn* GROUCH, bear, complainer, crab, crank, croaker, curmudgeon, fusser, griper, grouser, growler, grumbler, murmurer, mutterer, whiner
guarantee *n* • an assurance for the fulfillment of a condition or a person who provides such assurance *Syn* bail, bond, guaranty, security, surety *Rel* earnest, pledge, token
guarantee *vb* *Syn* ENSURE, assure, cinch, guaranty, insure, secure
guarantor *Syn* SPONSOR, angel, backer, patron, surety
guaranty *vb* *Syn* ENSURE, assure, cinch, guarantee, insure, secure
guaranty *n* *Syn* GUARANTEE, bail, bond, security, surety
guard *vb* *Syn* DEFEND, protect, safeguard, shield *Ant* attack, combat

guard *n* **1** *Syn* ESCORT, attendant, companion, guide **2** *Syn* PROTECTOR, custodian, defender, protection
guardianship *Syn* CUSTODY, care, keeping, safekeeping, trust, ward
guardrail *Syn* RAILING, balustrade, banister, rail
guardroom *Syn* JAIL, brig, hoosegow, jug, lockup, pen, penitentiary, prison, stockade
guess *vb* **1** *Syn* BELIEVE (sense 1), consider, deem, feel, figure, hold, imagine, suppose, think *Ant* disbelieve, discredit, reject **2** *Syn* ESTIMATE (sense 2), calculate, call, conjecture, figure, gauge, judge, make, place, put, reckon, suppose
guess *n Syn* CONJECTURE, supposition, surmise
guest *Syn* VISITOR, caller, visitant
guidance *Syn* ADVICE, counsel
guide *vb* • to put or lead on a course or into the way to be followed *Syn* engineer, lead, pilot, steer *Rel* accompany, chaperon, conduct, convoy, escort *Ant* misguide
guide *n Syn* ESCORT, attendant, companion, guard
guile *Syn* DECEIT, cunning, dissimulation, duplicity
guileful *Syn* SLY, artful, crafty, cunning, foxy, insidious, tricky, wily
guilelessly *Syn* NATURALLY (sense 3), artlessly, ingenuously, innocently, naively, sincerely, unaffectedly, unfeignedly, unpretentiously *Ant* affectedly, artificially, hypocritically, insincerely, pretentiously, unnaturally
guilt *Syn* BLAME, culpability, fault
guilty **1** • suffering from or expressive of a feeling of responsibility for wrongdoing *Syn* ashamed, contrite, hangdog, penitent, remorseful, repentant, shamed, shamefaced *Rel* apologetic, sorry *Ant* impenitent, remorseless, shameless, unashamed, unrepentant **2** *Syn* BLAMEWORTHY, culpable *Ant* blameless
gulch *Syn* CANYON, defile, flume, gap, gorge, gulf, notch, pass, ravine
gulf **1** • a hollow place of vast width and depth *Syn* abysm, abyss, chasm **2** *Syn* CANYON, defile, flume, gap, gorge, gulch, notch, pass, ravine
gull *vb Syn* DUPE, bamboozle, befool, hoax, hoodwink, trick
gull *n Syn* DUPE, chump, pigeon, sap, sucker, tool
gullibility *Syn* CREDULITY, credulousness, naivete *Ant* incredulity, skepticism
gumption **1** *Syn* COMMON SENSE, discreetness, discretion, horse sense, levelheadedness, prudence, sense, sensibleness, wisdom, wit *Ant* imprudence, indiscretion **2** *Syn* SENSE, common sense, good sense, horse sense, judgment, wisdom
gunman *Syn* ASSASSIN, bravo, cutthroat
gush **1** • to flow out in great quantities or with force *Syn* jet, pour, rush, spew, spout, spurt, squirt *Rel* cascade, issue, roll, run, stream *Ant* dribble, drip, drop, trickle **2** • to make an exaggerated display of affection or enthusiasm *Syn* enthuse, fuss, rave, rhapsodize, slobber *Rel* dote (on), fawn **3** *Syn* POUR, sluice, stream
gut *Syn* STOMACH, abdomen, belly, solar plexus, tummy
guts **1** *Syn* COURAGE, bravery, courageousness, daring, dauntlessness, doughtiness, fearlessness, gallantry, greatheartedness, hardihood, heart, heroism, intrepidity, intrepidness, nerve, stoutness, valor *Ant* cowardice, cowardliness, cravenness, dastardliness, spinelessness, yellowness **2** *Syn* FORTITUDE, backbone, grit, pluck, sand *Ant* pusillanimity
guy *Syn* MAN (sense 1), dude, fellow, gent, gentleman, male
gyrate *Syn* TURN (sense 1), circle, eddy, pirouette, revolve, rotate, spin, swirl, twirl, wheel, whirl

H

habit **1** • a usual manner of behaving or doing *Syn* custom, fashion, pattern, practice, trick, way, wont *Rel* addiction **2** *Syn* PHYSIQUE, build, constitution
habitant *Syn* INHABITANT, denizen, dweller, occupant, resident, resider *Ant* transient
habitat • the place in which a particular kind of organism lives or grows *Syn* biotope, range, station
habitation • the place where one lives *Syn* abode, domicile, dwelling, home, house, residence
habitual *Syn* USUAL, accustomed, customary, wonted
habituate • to make used to something *Syn* accustom, addict, inure *Rel* discipline, school, teach, train
habituated *Syn* ACCUSTOMED, given, used, wont *Ant* unaccustomed, unused
habitué *Syn* ADDICT, devotee, votary
hacienda *Syn* MANSION, castle, château, countryseat, estate, hall, manor, manor house, palace, villa
hack *Syn* MERCENARY, hireling

hackney *Syn* STALE, banal, commonplace, hackneyed, moth-eaten, musty, stereotyped, threadbare, tired, trite *Ant* fresh, new, original

hackneyed *Syn* STALE, banal, commonplace, hackney, moth-eaten, musty, stereotyped, threadbare, tired, trite *Ant* fresh, new, original

Hadean *Syn* INFERNAL, chthonian, chthonic, hellish, stygian, Tartarean *Ant* supernal

haggard • thin and drawn by or as if by worry, fatigue, hunger, or illness *Syn* cadaverous, careworn, pinched, wasted, worn *Rel* gaunt, lean, scrawny, skinny

haggle *Syn* BARGAIN, chaffer, deal, dicker, horse-trade, negotiate, palter

hail *vb* **1** *Syn* ACCLAIM, applaud, cheer, laud, praise, salute, tout *Ant* knock, pan, slam **2** *Syn* ADDRESS, accost, greet, salute

hail *n* **1** *Syn* BARRAGE, bombardment, cannonade, fusillade, salvo, shower, storm, volley **2** *Syn* RAIN (sense 2), shower, storm

hairy **1** • covered with or as if with hair *Syn* bristly, fleecy, furry, hirsute, rough, shaggy, unshorn, woolly *Rel* bearded, mustachioed, whiskered *Ant* bald, furless, hairless, shorn, smooth **2** • made of or resembling hair *Syn* furry, fuzzy, rough, shaggy, woolly *Rel* downy, fluffy, nappy

halcyon *Syn* CALM, peaceful, placid, serene, tranquil *Ant* agitated, stormy

hale *adj* *Syn* HEALTHY, robust, sound, well, wholesome *Ant* unhealthy

hale *vb* *Syn* PULL, drag, draw, haul, tow, tug

halfway *Syn* MIDDLE, intermediary, intermediate, medial, median, medium, mid, middlemost, midmost, midway *Ant* extreme, farthermost, farthest, furthermost, furthest, outermost, outmost, remotest, utmost

half-wit *Syn* FOOL (sense 2), booby, goose, jackass, lunatic, nincompoop, ninny, nitwit, nut, simpleton, turkey, yo-yo

hall **1** *Syn* MANSION, castle, château, countryseat, estate, hacienda, manor, manor house, palace, villa **2** *Syn* PASSAGE, aisle, arcade, cloister, corridor, gallery, hallway, passageway

hallow *Syn* DEVOTE, consecrate, dedicate

hallowed *Syn* HOLY (sense 2), blessed, consecrated, sacred, sacrosanct, sanctified *Ant* unconsecrated, unhallowed

hallowing *Syn* CONSECRATION, blessing, sanctification

hallucination *Syn* DELUSION, illusion, mirage

hallway *Syn* PASSAGE, aisle, arcade, cloister, corridor, gallery, hall, passageway

hamper • to hinder or impede in moving, progressing, or acting freely *Syn* clog, fetter, hog-tie, manacle, shackle, trammel *Rel* bar, block, hinder, impede, obstruct *Ant* assist (*persons*), expedite (*work, projects*)

hams *Syn* BUTTOCKS, backside, bottom, breech, butt, fanny, haunches, posterior, rear, rump, seat

hand *n* *Syn* WORKER, artisan, craftsman, handicraftsman, laborer, mechanic, operative, roustabout, workingman, workman *Ant* idler

hand *vb* *Syn* FURNISH (sense 2), deliver, feed, give, hand over, provide, supply *Ant* hold (back), keep (back), reserve, retain, withhold

handbag *Syn* PURSE, bag, pocketbook

handicap **1** *Syn* ADVANTAGE, allowance, edge, odds *Ant* disadvantage, handicap **2** *Syn* DISADVANTAGE, drawback, liability, minus, penalty, strike *Ant* advantage, asset, edge, plus **3** *Syn* ENCUMBRANCE, bar, block, chain, clog, crimp, deterrent, drag, embarrassment, fetter, hindrance, hurdle, impediment, inhibition, interference, let, manacle, obstacle, obstruction, shackles, stop, stumbling block, trammel *Ant* aid, assistance, benefit, help

handicraft *Syn* TRADE, art, craft, profession

handicrafter *Syn* ARTISAN, artificer, craftsman, tradesman

handicraftsman *Syn* WORKER, artisan, craftsman, hand, laborer, mechanic, operative, roustabout, workingman, workman *Ant* idler

handily *Syn* EASILY, effortlessly, facilely, fluently, freely, lightly, painlessly, readily, smoothly *Ant* arduously, laboriously

handkerchief *Syn* BANDANNA, babushka, kerchief, mantilla

handle **1** • to deal with or manage usually with dexterity or efficiency *Syn* manipulate, ply, swing, wield *Rel* brandish, flourish, shake, swing, wave **2** *Syn* TOUCH, feel, palpate, paw **3** *Syn* TREAT, deal

hand over *Syn* FURNISH (sense 2), deliver, feed, give, hand, provide, supply *Ant* hold (back), keep (back), reserve, retain, withhold

handsome **1** *Syn* BEAUTIFUL, attractive, beauteous, comely, cute, fair, gorgeous, knockout, lovely, pretty, ravishing, sightly, stunning, taking *Ant* homely, ill-favored, plain, ugly, unattractive, unbeautiful, unhandsome, unlovely, unpretty, unsightly **2** *Syn* LARGE, big, bulky, considerable, goodly, good-sized, grand, great, hefty, hulking, largish, outsize, oversize (*or* oversized), sizable (*or* sizeable), substantial, tidy, voluminous *Ant* little, puny, small, undersized **3** *Syn* LIBERAL (sense 1), bounteous, bountiful, generous, munificent, openhanded *Ant* close

handsomeness *Syn* ELEGANCE, class, elegancy, grace, gracefulness, majesty, refinement, stateliness

hang **1** • to place or be placed so as to be supported at one point or side usually at the top *Syn* dangle, sling, suspend *Rel* adhere, cling, stick **2** *Syn* DEPEND (sense 1), hinge, turn

hangdog *Syn* GUILTY, ashamed, contrite,

penitent, remorseful, repentant, shamed, shamefaced *Ant* impenitent, remorseless, shameless, unashamed, unrepentant

hanger-on *Syn* PARASITE, bootlicker, favorite, leech, lickspittle, sponge, sponger, sycophant, toady

hangout • a place for spending time or for socializing *Syn* haunt, rendezvous, resort *Rel* camp, canteen, club, clubhouse, den, harbor, haven, nest, refuge, retreat

hanker *Syn* LONG, hunger, pine, thirst, yearn

hanky-panky *Syn* TRICKERY, artifice, chicanery, jugglery, legerdemain, subterfuge, wile

hap *Syn* CHANCE, accident, fortune, hazard, luck *Ant* law, principle

haphazard *adv Syn* HIT OR MISS, aimlessly, anyhow, anyway, anywise, desultorily, erratically, haphazardly, helter-skelter, irregularly, randomly *Ant* methodically, systematically

haphazard *adj Syn* RANDOM, casual, chance, chancy, desultory, happy-go-lucky, hit-or-miss *Ant* methodical, nonrandom, orderly, systematic

haphazardly *Syn* HIT OR MISS, aimlessly, anyhow, anyway, anywise, desultorily, erratically, haphazard, helter-skelter, irregularly, randomly *Ant* methodically, systematically

hapless *Syn* UNLUCKY, calamitous, disastrous, ill-fated, ill-starred, luckless, unfortunate *Ant* fortunate, happy, lucky

happen • to come to pass or to come about *Syn* befall, betide, chance, occur, transpire

happen (on *or* upon) • to come upon unexpectedly or by chance *Syn* chance (upon), encounter, find, hit (upon), meet, stumble (on *or* onto) *Rel* confront, face

happily *Syn* PROPERLY, appropriately, congruously, correctly, fittingly, meetly, rightly, suitably *Ant* improperly, inappropriately, incongruously, incorrectly, unsuitably, wrongly

happiness • a state of well-being or pleasurable satisfaction *Syn* beatitude, blessedness, bliss, felicity *Rel* content, contentedness, satisfaction, satisfiedness *Ant* unhappiness

happy **1** *Syn* CONTENT, contented, gratified, pleased, satisfied *Ant* discontent, discontented, displeased, dissatisfied, malcontent, unhappy **2** *Syn* FIT, appropriate, apt, felicitous, fitting, meet, proper, suitable *Ant* unfit **3** *Syn* GLAD, cheerful, joyful, joyous, lighthearted *Ant* sad **4** *Syn* LUCKY, fortunate, providential *Ant* unlucky

happy-go-lucky **1** *Syn* CAREFREE, careless, cavalier, devil-may-care, easygoing, gay, insouciant, lighthearted, unconcerned *Ant* careworn **2** *Syn* RANDOM, casual, chance, chancy, desultory, haphazard, hit-or-miss *Ant* methodical, nonrandom, orderly, systematic

harangue *Syn* SPEECH, address, homily, lecture, oration, sermon, talk

harass *Syn* WORRY, annoy, harry, pester, plague, tantalize, tease

harbinger *Syn* FORERUNNER, herald, precursor

harbor *n* • a place where seacraft may ride secure *Syn* haven, port

harbor *vb* • to provide with shelter or refuge *Syn* board, entertain, house, lodge, shelter *Rel* cherish, foster, nurse, nurture

hard **1** • demanding great toil or effort *Syn* arduous, difficult *Rel* burdensome, exacting, onerous, oppressive *Ant* easy **2** *Syn* FIRM, solid *Ant* flabby, loose **3** *Syn* OBSTINATE, adamant, adamantine, dogged, hardened, hardheaded, hardhearted, headstrong, immovable, implacable, inflexible, mulish, obdurate, opinionated, ossified, pat, peevish, pertinacious, perverse, pigheaded, rigid, self-willed, stubborn, unbending, uncompromising, unrelenting, unyielding, willful (*or* wilful) *Ant* acquiescent, agreeable, amenable, compliant, complying, flexible, pliable, pliant, relenting, yielding

harden **1** • to make or to become physically hard or solid *Syn* cake, indurate, petrify, solidify *Rel* compact, concentrate, consolidate *Ant* soften **2** • to make proof against hardship, strain, or exposure *Syn* acclimate, acclimatize, season *Rel* accustom, habituate, inure *Ant* soften

hardened **1** • grown or become hard *Syn* callous, indurated *Rel* compacted, concentrated, consolidated *Ant* softened **2** *Syn* OBSTINATE, adamant, adamantine, dogged, hard, hardheaded, hardhearted, headstrong, immovable, implacable, inflexible, mulish, obdurate, opinionated, ossified, pat, peevish, pertinacious, perverse, pigheaded, rigid, self-willed, stubborn, unbending, uncompromising, unrelenting, unyielding, willful (*or* wilful) *Ant* acquiescent, agreeable, amenable, compliant, complying, flexible, pliable, pliant, relenting, yielding

hardheaded *Syn* OBSTINATE, adamant, adamantine, dogged, hard, hardened, hardhearted, headstrong, immovable, implacable, inflexible, mulish, obdurate, opinionated, ossified, pat, peevish, pertinacious, perverse, pigheaded, rigid, self-willed, stubborn, unbending, uncompromising, unrelenting, unyielding, willful (*or* wilful) *Ant* acquiescent, agreeable, amenable, compliant, complying, flexible, pliable, pliant, relenting, yielding

hardhearted *Syn* OBSTINATE, adamant, adamantine, dogged, hard, hardened, hardheaded, headstrong, immovable, implacable, inflexible, mulish, obdurate, opinionated, ossified, pat, peevish, pertinacious, perverse, pigheaded, rigid, self-willed, stubborn, unbending, uncompromising, unrelenting, unyielding, willful (*or* wilful) *Ant* acquiescent, agreeable, amenable, compliant, complying, flexible, pliable, pliant, relenting, yielding

hardihood *Syn* COURAGE, bravery, courageousness, daring, dauntlessness, doughtiness, fearlessness, gallantry, greatheartedness, guts, heart, heroism, intrepidity, intrepidness, nerve, stoutness, valor *Ant* cowardice, cowardliness, cravenness, dastardliness, spinelessness, yellowness

hardness *Syn* SEVERITY, harshness, inflexibility, rigidity, rigidness, rigorousness, sternness, strictness *Ant* flexibility, gentleness, laxness, mildness

hardship *Syn* DIFFICULTY, rigor, vicissitude

hark *Syn* LISTEN, attend, hear, hearken, heed, mind *Ant* ignore, tune out

harm *vb Syn* INJURE, damage, hurt, impair, mar, spoil *Ant* aid

harm *n Syn* INJURY, damage, hurt, mischief

harmful • causing or capable of causing harm *Syn* adverse, bad, baleful, baneful, damaging, deleterious, detrimental, evil, hurtful, ill, injurious, mischievous, noxious, pernicious, prejudicial *Rel* hostile, inimical, unfriendly *Ant* harmless, innocent, innocuous, inoffensive, safe

harmless • not having hurtful or injurious qualities *Syn* innocent, innocuous, inoffensive, unoffending *Ant* harmful

harmonious *Syn* CONSISTENT, compatible, conformable (to), congruous, consonant, correspondent (with *or* to), nonconflicting *Ant* conflicting, incompatible, incongruous, inconsistent, inharmonious, unharmonious

harmonize **1** • to bring into consonance or accord *Syn* attune, tune *Rel* adapt, adjust, reconcile **2** *Syn* AGREE (sense 2), accord, conform, correspond, jibe, square, tally *Ant* differ (from)

harmony **1** • the effect produced when different things come together without clashing or disagreement *Syn* accord, concord, consonance *Rel* articulation, concatenation, integration *Ant* conflict **2** *Syn* SYMMETRY, balance, proportion

harrow *Syn* AFFLICT, agonize, bedevil, curse, martyr, persecute, plague, rack, torment, torture

harry *Syn* WORRY, annoy, harass, pester, plague, tantalize, tease

harsh *Syn* ROUGH, rugged, scabrous, uneven *Ant* smooth

harshness *Syn* SEVERITY, hardness, inflexibility, rigidity, rigidness, rigorousness, sternness, strictness *Ant* flexibility, gentleness, laxness, mildness

harvest *Syn* REAP, garner, gather, glean

hash **1** *Syn* CHOP, dice, mince **2** *Syn* DISORDER, confuse, derange, disarrange, disarray, discompose, dishevel, dislocate, disorganize, disrupt, disturb, jumble, mess (up), mix (up), muddle, muss, rumple, scramble, shuffle, tousle, tumble, upset *Ant* arrange, array, draw up, marshal, order, organize, range, regulate, straighten (up), tidy

haste • rapidity of motion or action *Syn* dispatch, expedition, hurry, speed *Rel* alacrity, celerity, legerity *Ant* deliberation

hasten **1** *Syn* HURRY (sense 1), accelerate, quicken, rush, speed (up), whisk *Ant* decelerate, retard, slow (down) **2** *Syn* HURRY (sense 2), barrel, bolt, bowl, breeze, career, course, dash, fly, hotfoot (it), hump, hurtle, hustle, pelt, race, rip, rocket, run, rush, rustle, scoot, scurry, scuttle, shoot, speed, step (along), tear, trot, whirl, whisk, zip, zoom *Ant* crawl, creep, poke

hasty **1** *Syn* FAST, expeditious, fleet, quick, rapid, speedy, swift *Ant* slow **2** *Syn* PRECIPITATE, abrupt, headlong, impetuous, sudden *Ant* deliberate

hate *vb* • to feel extreme enmity or dislike *Syn* abhor, abominate, detest, loathe *Rel* contemn, despise, disdain, scorn *Ant* love

hate *n Syn* ABHORRENCE, abomination, detestation, hatred, loathing *Ant* admiration, enjoyment

hateful • deserving of or arousing hate *Syn* abhorrent, abominable, detestable, odious *Rel* antipathetic, averse, unsympathetic *Ant* lovable, sympathetic

hatred *Syn* ABHORRENCE, abomination, detestation, hate, loathing *Ant* admiration, enjoyment

haughtiness *Syn* ARROGANCE, imperiousness, loftiness, lordliness, masterfulness, peremptoriness, pompousness, presumptuousness, pretense (*or* pretence), pretension, pretentiousness, self-importance, superciliousness, superiority *Ant* humility, modesty

haughty **1** *Syn* ARROGANT, cavalier, highfalutin, high-handed, high-hat, imperious, important, lofty, lordly, masterful, overweening, peremptory, pompous, presumptuous, pretentious, supercilious, superior, uppish, uppity *Ant* humble, modest **2** *Syn* PROUD (sense 1), arrogant, disdainful, insolent, lordly, overbearing, supercilious *Ant* ashamed, humble

haul *Syn* PULL, drag, draw, hale, tow, tug

haunches *Syn* BUTTOCKS, backside, bottom, breech, butt, fanny, hams, posterior, rear, rump, seat

haunt *Syn* HANGOUT, rendezvous, resort

haunting *Syn* EERIE, creepy, spooky, uncanny, unearthly, weird

have • to keep, control, or experience as one's own *Syn* enjoy, hold, own, possess

haven *Syn* HARBOR, port

have (to) *Syn* NEED (sense 1), must, ought (to), shall, should *Ant* have, hold

havoc *Syn* DESTRUCTION, annihilation, decimation, demolishment, demolition, desolation, devastation, extermination, extinction, loss, obliteration, ruin, ruination, wastage, wreckage *Ant* building, construction, erection, raising

hazard *n* **1** *Syn* CHANCE, accident, fortune, hap, luck *Ant* law, principle **2** *Syn* DANGER (sense 1), menace, peril, pitfall, risk, threat, trouble *Ant* safeness, safety, security

hazard *vb* *Syn* ENDANGER, adventure, compromise, gamble (with), imperil, jeopardize, menace, risk, venture

hazardous *Syn* DANGEROUS, perilous, precarious, risky *Ant* safe, secure

haze **1** • an atmospheric condition in which suspended particles in the air rob it of its transparency *Syn* fog, mist, murk, reek, smog, soup *Rel* cloud, fume, miasma, smoke, steam **2** • a state of mental confusion *Syn* daze, fog, muddle, spin *Rel* reverie, stupor, trance

hazed *Syn* OVERCAST, beclouded, clouded, cloudy, dull, hazy, heavy, lowering, overclouded *Ant* clear, cloudless

hazy *Syn* OVERCAST, beclouded, clouded, cloudy, dull, hazed, heavy, lowering, overclouded *Ant* clear, cloudless

head *adj* • highest in rank or authority *Syn* chief, commanding, first, foremost, high, lead, leading, managing, preeminent, premier, presiding, primary, prime, principal, supreme *Rel* high-level, senior

head *n* **1** *Syn* BOSS, captain, chief, foreman, headman, helmsman, kingpin, leader, master, taskmaster **2** *Syn* CHIEF, chieftain, headman, leader, master

headlong *Syn* PRECIPITATE, abrupt, hasty, impetuous, sudden *Ant* deliberate

headman **1** *Syn* BOSS, captain, chief, foreman, head, helmsman, kingpin, leader, master, taskmaster **2** *Syn* CHIEF, chieftain, head, leader, master

headstrong **1** *Syn* OBSTINATE, adamant, adamantine, dogged, hard, hardened, hardheaded, hardhearted, immovable, implacable, inflexible, mulish, obdurate, opinionated, ossified, pat, peevish, pertinacious, perverse, pigheaded, rigid, self-willed, stubborn, unbending, uncompromising, unrelenting, unyielding, willful (*or* wilful) *Ant* acquiescent, agreeable, amenable, compliant, complying, flexible, pliable, pliant, relenting, yielding **2** *Syn* UNCONTROLLABLE, froward, intractable, recalcitrant, refractory, ungovernable, unmanageable, unruly, untoward, wayward, willful (*or* wilful) *Ant* controllable, governable, tractable **3** *Syn* UNRULY, intractable, recalcitrant, refractory, ungovernable, willful *Ant* docile, tractable

headway **1** *Syn* ADVANCE (sense 2), advancement, furtherance, going, march, onrush, passage, process, procession, progress, progression *Ant* recession, regression, retrogression **2** *Syn* SPEED, impetus, momentum, pace, velocity

heal **1** *Syn* CONVALESCE, gain, mend, rally, recover, recuperate, snap back **2** *Syn* CURE, remedy

health • the condition of being sound in body *Syn* fitness, healthiness, heartiness, robustness, soundness, wellness, wholeness, wholesomeness *Rel* fettle, shape *Ant* illness, sickness, unhealthiness, unsoundness

healthful • conducive or beneficial to the health or soundness of body or mind *Syn* healthy, hygienic, salubrious, salutary, sanitary, wholesome *Rel* advantageous, beneficial, profitable

healthiness *Syn* HEALTH, fitness, heartiness, robustness, soundness, wellness, wholeness, wholesomeness *Ant* illness, sickness, unhealthiness, unsoundness

healthy **1** • having or manifesting health of mind or body or indicative of such health *Syn* hale, robust, sound, well, wholesome *Rel* energetic, lusty, vigorous *Ant* unhealthy **2** *Syn* HEALTHFUL, hygienic, salubrious, salutary, sanitary, wholesome

heap *n* • a quantity of things brought together into a more or less compact group *Syn* bank, cock, mass, pile, shock, stack *Rel* aggregate, aggregation, conglomerate, conglomeration

heap *vb* • to bring a number of things together into a more or less compact group or collection *Syn* bank, cock, mass, pile, shock, stack *Rel* accumulate, amass, hoard

hear *Syn* LISTEN, attend, hark, hearken, heed, mind *Ant* ignore, tune out

hearken *Syn* LISTEN, attend, hark, hear, heed, mind *Ant* ignore, tune out

hearsay *Syn* REPORT, gossip, rumor

heart **1** *Syn* CENTER (sense 2), base, capital, core, cynosure, eye, focus, hub, mecca, nucleus, seat **2** *Syn* COURAGE, bravery, courageousness, daring, dauntlessness, doughtiness, fearlessness, gallantry, greatheartedness, guts, hardihood, heroism, intrepidity, intrepidness, nerve, stoutness, valor *Ant* cowardice, cowardliness, cravenness, dastardliness, spinelessness, yellowness **3** *Syn* CRUX, core, gist, nub, pith, pivot

heartache *Syn* SORROW, anguish, grief, heartbreak, regret, woe *Ant* joy

heartbreak *Syn* SORROW, anguish, grief, heartache, regret, woe *Ant* joy

heartbreaking **1** *Syn* REGRETTABLE, deplorable, distressful, distressing, grievous, heartrending, lamentable, unfortunate, woeful **2** *Syn* SAD (sense 2), depressing, dismal, drear, dreary, heartrending, melancholy, pathetic, saddening, sorry, tearful, teary *Ant* cheering, cheery, glad, happy

heartbroken *Syn* SAD (sense 1), bad, blue, brokenhearted, crestfallen, dejected, depressed, despondent, disconsolate, doleful, down, downcast, downhearted, droopy, forlorn, gloomy, glum, heartsick, heartsore, inconsolable, joyless, low, low-spirited, melancholy, miserable, mournful, saddened, sorrowful, sorry, unhappy, woebegone, woeful, wretched *Ant* blissful, buoyant, buoyed, cheerful, cheery, chipper, delighted, glad, gladdened, gladsome, gleeful, happy, joyful, joyous, jubilant, sunny, upbeat

hearten *Syn* ENCOURAGE, cheer, embolden, inspirit, nerve, steel *Ant* discourage

heartening *Syn* HEARTWARMING, cheering, comforting, encouraging, fulfilling, gladdening, gratifying, rewarding, satisfying *Ant* depressing, discouraging, disheartening, dispiriting

heartfelt *Syn* SINCERE, hearty, unfeigned, wholehearted, whole-souled *Ant* insincere

heartiness *Syn* HEALTH, fitness, healthiness, robustness, soundness, wellness, wholeness, wholesomeness *Ant* illness, sickness, unhealthiness, unsoundness

heartlessness *Syn* CRUELTY, barbarity, brutality, cruelness, inhumanity, sadism, savageness, savagery, viciousness, wantonness *Ant* benignity, compassion, good-heartedness, humanity, kindheartedness, kindness, sympathy

heartrending **1** *Syn* REGRETTABLE, deplorable, distressful, distressing, grievous, heartbreaking, lamentable, unfortunate, woeful **2** *Syn* SAD (sense 2), depressing, dismal, drear, dreary, heartbreaking, melancholy, pathetic, saddening, sorry, tearful, teary *Ant* cheering, cheery, glad, happy

heartsick *Syn* SAD (sense 1), bad, blue, brokenhearted, crestfallen, dejected, depressed, despondent, disconsolate, doleful, down, downcast, downhearted, droopy, forlorn, gloomy, glum, heartbroken, heartsore, inconsolable, joyless, low, low-spirited, melancholy, miserable, mournful, saddened, sorrowful, sorry, unhappy, woebegone, woeful, wretched *Ant* blissful, buoyant, buoyed, cheerful, cheery, chipper, delighted, glad, gladdened, gladsome, gleeful, happy, joyful, joyous, jubilant, sunny, upbeat

heartsickness *Syn* SADNESS, blues, dejection, depression, desolation, despondency, disconsolateness, dispiritedness, doldrums, downheartedness, dreariness, dumps, forlornness, gloom, gloominess, joylessness, melancholy, mopes, oppression, unhappiness *Ant* bliss, blissfulness, ecstasy, elatedness, elation, euphoria, exhilaration, exuberance, exultation, felicity, gladness, gladsomeness, happiness, heaven, intoxication, joy, joyfulness, joyousness, jubilation, rapture, rapturousness

heartsore *Syn* SAD (sense 1), bad, blue, brokenhearted, crestfallen, dejected, depressed, despondent, disconsolate, doleful, down, downcast, downhearted, droopy, forlorn, gloomy, glum, heartbroken, heartsick, inconsolable, joyless, low, low-spirited, melancholy, miserable, mournful, saddened, sorrowful, sorry, unhappy, woebegone, woeful, wretched *Ant* blissful, buoyant, buoyed, cheerful, cheery, chipper, delighted, glad, gladdened, gladsome, gleeful, happy, joyful, joyous, jubilant, sunny, upbeat

heartwarming • making one feel good inside *Syn* cheering, comforting, encouraging, fulfilling, gladdening, gratifying, heartening, rewarding, satisfying *Rel* affecting, inspiring, moving, poignant, stirring, touching *Ant* depressing, discouraging, disheartening, dispiriting

hearty *Syn* SINCERE, heartfelt, unfeigned, wholehearted, whole-souled *Ant* insincere

heave *Syn* LIFT, boost, elevate, hoist, raise, rear *Ant* lower

heaven *Syn* ECSTASY, elation, euphoria, exhilaration, intoxication, paradise, rapture, rhapsody, transport *Ant* depression

heavenly **1** *Syn* CELESTIAL, Elysian, empyreal, empyrean, supernal *Ant* hellish, infernal **2** *Syn* EXCELLENT, A1, bang-up, banner, capital, classic, crackerjack, dandy, divine, fabulous, fine, first-class, first-rate, grand, great, groovy, jim-dandy, keen, marvelous (*or* marvellous), mean, neat, nifty, noble, par excellence, prime, sensational, splendid, stellar, sterling, superb, superior, superlative, supernal, swell, terrific, tip-top, top, top-notch, unsurpassed, wonderful *Ant* poor

heavily *Syn* VERY, awful, awfully, beastly, deadly, especially, exceedingly, extra, extremely, far, frightfully, full, greatly, highly, hugely, jolly, mightily, mighty, mortally, most, much, particularly, rattling, real, right, so, something, super, terribly, too, whacking *Ant* little, negligibly, nominally, slightly

heavy **1** • having great weight *Syn* cumbersome, cumbrous, hefty, ponderous, weighty *Rel* firm, hard, solid *Ant* light **2** *Syn* BORING, drab, dreary, dry, dull, flat, humdrum, jading, leaden, monotonous, pedestrian, ponderous, stodgy, stuffy, stupid, tame, tedious, tiresome, tiring, unanimated, uninteresting, wearisome, weary, wearying *Ant* absorbing, engaging, engrossing, gripping, interesting, intriguing, involving **3** *Syn* OVERCAST, beclouded, clouded, cloudy, dull, hazed, hazy, lowering, overclouded *Ant* clear, cloudless

heckle *Syn* BAIT, badger, chivy, hector, hound, ride

hector *Syn* BAIT, badger, chivy, heckle, hound, ride

hedge *Syn* BARRIER, barricade, fence, wall

heed *n Syn* ATTENTION (sense 2), awareness, cognizance, ear, eye, notice, observance, observation

heed *vb Syn* LISTEN, attend, hark, hear, hearken, mind *Ant* ignore, tune out

heedless *Syn* CARELESS, inadvertent, thoughtless *Ant* careful
hefty **1** *Syn* HEAVY, cumbersome, cumbrous, ponderous, weighty *Ant* light **2** *Syn* LARGE, big, bulky, considerable, goodly, good-sized, grand, great, handsome, hulking, largish, outsize, oversize (*or* oversized), sizable (*or* sizeable), substantial, tidy, voluminous *Ant* little, puny, small, undersized
height **1** • the distance a thing rises above the level on which it stands *Syn* altitude, elevation **2** *Syn* THICK, deep, depth, middle, midst
heighten *Syn* INTENSIFY, aggravate, enhance *Ant* abate, allay, mitigate, temper
heinous *Syn* OUTRAGEOUS, atrocious, monstrous
helical *Syn* SPIRAL, coiling, corkscrew, screwlike, winding
hell *Syn* MADHOUSE, babel, bedlam, circus
hellish *Syn* INFERNAL, chthonian, chthonic, Hadean, stygian, Tartarean *Ant* supernal
helmsman *Syn* BOSS, captain, chief, foreman, head, headman, kingpin, leader, master, taskmaster
help *n* • an act or instance of giving what will benefit or assist *Syn* aid, assistance *Rel* cooperation, union, uniting
help *vb* **1** • to give assistance or support *Syn* aid, assist *Rel* back, champion, support, uphold *Ant* hinder **2** *Syn* IMPROVE (sense 1), ameliorate, better *Ant* impair, worsen **3** *Syn* PREVENT (sense 2), avert, forestall, obviate, preclude
helper *Syn* ASSISTANT, adjutant, aid, aide, apprentice, coadjutor, deputy, sidekick
helpful *Syn* BENEFICIAL, advantageous, favorable, profitable, salutary *Ant* disadvantageous, unfavorable, unhelpful
helpless *Syn* POWERLESS, impotent, weak *Ant* mighty, potent, powerful, puissant, strong
helter-skelter *Syn* HIT OR MISS, aimlessly, anyhow, anyway, anywise, desultorily, erratically, haphazard, haphazardly, irregularly, randomly *Ant* methodically, systematically
hem *Syn* SURROUND, circle, compass, encircle, encompass, environ, gird, girdle, ring
hence *Syn* THEREFORE, accordingly, consequently, so, then
herald *Syn* FORERUNNER (sense 1), harbinger, precursor
Herculean *Syn* HUGE, Brobdingnagian, colossal, cyclopean, elephantine, enormous, gargantuan, giant, gigantean, gigantic, immense, mammoth, titanic, vast *Ant* bitty, diminutive, microscopic (*or* microscopical), midget, miniature, minute, pocket, pygmy, teeny, teeny-weeny, tiny, wee
hereditary *Syn* INNATE, congenital, inborn, inbred, inherited *Ant* acquired
heresy • departure from a generally accepted theory, opinion, or practice *Syn* dissent, dissidence, heterodoxy, nonconformity *Rel* error, fallacy, falsehood, misbelief, misconception, myth *Ant* conformity, orthodoxy
heretic • one who believes, teaches, or advocates something opposed to accepted beliefs *Syn* dissenter, dissident, nonconformist *Rel* apostate, defector, renegade, schismatic, separationist, separatist *Ant* conformer, conformist
heritage • something which one receives or is entitled to receive by succession *Syn* birthright, inheritance, patrimony
hermit *Syn* RECLUSE, anchorite, cenobite, eremite
heroism **1** • conspicuous courage or bravery *Syn* gallantry, prowess, valor *Rel* bravery, dauntlessness, doughtiness, intrepidity **2** *Syn* COURAGE, bravery, courageousness, daring, dauntlessness, doughtiness, fearlessness, gallantry, greatheartedness, guts, hardihood, heart, intrepidity, intrepidness, nerve, stoutness, valor *Ant* cowardice, cowardliness, cravenness, dastardliness, spinelessness, yellowness
hesitance **1** *Syn* HESITATION, faltering, hesitancy, indecision, irresolution, shilly-shallying, vacillation, wavering, wobbling **2** *Syn* RELUCTANCE, disinclination, hesitancy, unwillingness *Ant* inclination, willingness
hesitancy **1** *Syn* HESITATION, faltering, hesitance, indecision, irresolution, shilly-shallying, vacillation, wavering, wobbling **2** *Syn* RELUCTANCE, disinclination, hesitance, unwillingness *Ant* inclination, willingness
hesitant *Syn* DISINCLINED, averse, indisposed, loath, reluctant
hesitate • to show irresolution or uncertainty *Syn* falter, vacillate, waver *Rel* balk, boggle, demur, scruple, shy, stick, stickle *Ant* dive (in), plunge (in)
hesitation • the act or an instance of pausing because of uncertainty about the right course of action *Syn* faltering, hesitance, hesitancy, indecision, irresolution, shilly-shallying, vacillation, wavering, wobbling *Rel* delay, hawing, procrastination, waiting
heterodoxy *Syn* HERESY, dissent, dissidence, nonconformity *Ant* conformity, orthodoxy
heterogeneous *Syn* MISCELLANEOUS, assorted, motley, promiscuous
hew *Syn* CUT, carve, chop, slash, slit
hiatus *Syn* BREAK, gap, interim, interruption, interval, lacuna
hick • an awkward or simple person especially from a small town or the country *Syn* bumpkin, clodhopper, countryman, provincial, rustic, yokel *Rel* boor, clod, gawk, lout, oaf *Ant* cosmopolitan, sophisticate
hide *vb* • to withdraw or to withhold from sight or observation *Syn* bury, cache, conceal, ensconce, screen, secrete *Rel* camouflage, cloak, disguise, dissemble, mask

hide *n* *Syn* SKIN, bark, peel, pelt, rind
hideous *Syn* UGLY, ill-favored, unsightly *Ant* beautiful
higgledy-piggledy *Syn* MESSY, chaotic, cluttered, confused, disarranged, disarrayed, disheveled (*or* dishevelled), disordered, disorderly, hugger-mugger, jumbled, littered, messed, muddled, mussed, mussy, pell-mell, rumpled, sloppy, topsy-turvy, tousled, tumbled, unkempt, untidy, upside-down *Ant* neat, ordered, orderly, organized, shipshape, snug, tidied, tidy, trim
high **1** • having a relatively great upward extension *Syn* lofty, tall *Rel* elevated, lifted, raised, reared *Ant* low **2** • in a luxurious manner *Syn* expensively, extravagantly, grandly, lavishly, luxuriously, opulently, richly, sumptuously *Rel* imposingly, impressively, magnificently, splendidly *Ant* austerely, humbly, modestly, plainly, simply **3** *Syn* HEAD, chief, commanding, first, foremost, lead, leading, managing, preeminent, premier, presiding, primary, prime, principal, supreme
highfalutin *Syn* ARROGANT, cavalier, haughty, high-handed, high-hat, imperious, important, lofty, lordly, masterful, overweening, peremptory, pompous, presumptuous, pretentious, supercilious, superior, uppish, uppity *Ant* humble, modest
high-handed *Syn* ARROGANT, cavalier, haughty, highfalutin, high-hat, imperious, important, lofty, lordly, masterful, overweening, peremptory, pompous, presumptuous, pretentious, supercilious, superior, uppish, uppity *Ant* humble, modest
high-hat *Syn* ARROGANT, cavalier, haughty, highfalutin, high-handed, imperious, important, lofty, lordly, masterful, overweening, peremptory, pompous, presumptuous, pretentious, supercilious, superior, uppish, uppity *Ant* humble, modest
high jinks *Syn* HORSEPLAY, clowning, foolery, horsing (around), monkeying, monkeyshines, roughhouse, roughhousing, shenanigans, skylarking, tomfoolery
highlight *Syn* EMPHASIZE, accent, accentuate, feature, play (up), point (up), stress, underline, underscore *Ant* play (down)
highly *Syn* VERY, awful, awfully, beastly, deadly, especially, exceedingly, extra, extremely, far, frightfully, full, greatly, heavily, hugely, jolly, mightily, mighty, mortally, most, much, particularly, rattling, real, right, so, something, super, terribly, too, whacking *Ant* little, negligibly, nominally, slightly
high-pitched *Syn* SHRILL, acute, piping, screeching, shrieking, squeaking, squeaky, treble, whistling *Ant* bass, deep, low, throaty
high-spirited *Syn* SPIRITED, fiery, gingery, mettlesome, peppery, spunky *Ant* spiritless
high-strung *Syn* EXCITABLE, flighty, fluttery, jittery, jumpy, nervous, skittish, spooky *Ant* unflappable
hilarity *Syn* MIRTH, glee, jollity
hind *Syn* BACK, hindmost, posterior, rear, rearward *Ant* anterior, fore, forward, front
hinder • to put obstacles in the way *Syn* bar, block, dam, impede, obstruct *Rel* arrest, check, interrupt *Ant* further
hindmost *Syn* BACK, hind, posterior, rear, rearward *Ant* anterior, fore, forward, front
hindrance *Syn* ENCUMBRANCE, bar, block, chain, clog, crimp, deterrent, drag, embarrassment, fetter, handicap, hurdle, impediment, inhibition, interference, let, manacle, obstacle, obstruction, shackles, stop, stumbling block, trammel *Ant* aid, assistance, benefit, help
hinge *Syn* DEPEND (sense 1), hang, turn
hint • to convey an idea indirectly *Syn* allude, imply, indicate, infer, insinuate, intimate, suggest *Rel* advert, mention, point, refer, signal, signify
hinterland *Syn* FRONTIER, backwater, backwoods, bush, up-country
hire *vb* • to take or engage something or grant the use of something for a stipulated price or rate *Syn* charter, lease, let, rent *Rel* get, obtain, procure, secure
hire *n* *Syn* WAGE, emolument, fee, pay, salary, stipend
hireling *Syn* MERCENARY, hack
hirsute *Syn* HAIRY (sense 1), bristly, fleecy, furry, rough, shaggy, unshorn, woolly *Ant* bald, furless, hairless, shorn, smooth
history **1** • a chronological record of events *Syn* annals, chronicle **2** *Syn* PAST, auld lang syne, yesterday, yesteryear, yore
histrionic *Syn* DRAMATIC, dramaturgic, melodramatic, theatrical
hit *Syn* STRIKE, box, clout, cuff, punch, slap, slog, slug, smite, swat
hit or miss • without definite aim, direction, rule, or method *Syn* aimlessly, anyhow, anyway, anywise, desultorily, erratically, haphazard, haphazardly, helter-skelter, irregularly, randomly *Rel* capriciously, carelessly, casually, indiscriminately, informally, offhand, offhandedly, promiscuously, whimsically *Ant* methodically, systematically
hit-or-miss *Syn* RANDOM, casual, chance, chancy, desultory, haphazard, happy-go-lucky *Ant* methodical, nonrandom, orderly, systematic
hit (upon) *Syn* HAPPEN (on *or* upon), chance (upon), encounter, find, meet, stumble (on *or* onto)
hoard *vb* **1** • to put (something of future use or value) in a safe or secret place *Syn* cache, lay away, lay up, put by, salt away, squirrel (away), stash, stockpile, store, stow *Rel* accumulate, acquire, amass, assemble, collect, concentrate, garner, gather, round up, scrape

(together) **2** *Syn* ACCUMULATE, amass *Ant* dissipate
hoard *n Syn* STORE, cache, deposit, reserve
hoarse *Syn* LOUD, earsplitting, raucous, stentorian, stertorous, strident *Ant* low, low-pitched
hoax *Syn* DUPE, bamboozle, befool, gull, hoodwink, trick
hobnob *Syn* SOCIALIZE, associate, fraternize, mingle, mix
hobo *Syn* VAGABOND, bum, tramp, truant, vagrant
hocus-pocus *Syn* GIBBERISH, abracadabra, mummery
hog *Syn* GLUTTON, gorger, gormandizer, gourmand, overeater, stuffer, swiller
hogshead *Syn* CASK, barrel, firkin, keg, pipe, puncheon
hog-tie *Syn* HAMPER, clog, fetter, manacle, shackle, trammel *Ant* assist (*persons*), expedite (*work, projects*)
hoist *Syn* LIFT, boost, elevate, heave, raise, rear *Ant* lower
hold *n* • the act or manner of grasping or holding *Syn* clutch, grasp, grip *Rel* ownership, possession
hold *vb* **1** *Syn* BELIEVE (sense 1), consider, deem, feel, figure, guess, imagine, suppose, think *Ant* disbelieve, discredit, reject **2** *Syn* CONTAIN, accommodate **3** *Syn* HAVE, enjoy, own, possess
hold back *Syn* KEEP (sense 2), detain, keep back, keep out, reserve, retain, withhold *Ant* relinquish
holder **1** *Syn* CONTAINER, receptacle, vessel **2** *Syn* PROPRIETOR, owner, possessor
hold off (on) *Syn* POSTPONE, defer, delay, hold up, put off, shelve
holdup *Syn* DELAY, detainment, wait
hold up *Syn* POSTPONE, defer, delay, hold off (on), put off, shelve
hole • a space within the substance of a body or mass *Syn* cavity, hollow, pocket, vacuum, void *Rel* aperture, interstice, orifice
holiness • the quality or state of being spiritually pure or virtuous *Syn* blessedness, devoutness, godliness, piety, piousness, sainthood, saintliness, saintship, sanctity *Rel* asceticism, devotion, morality, prayerfulness, religiousness, spirituality *Ant* godlessness, impiety, ungodliness, unholiness
holler *n Syn* SHOUT, scream, screech, shriek, squeal, whoop, yell
holler *vb Syn* SHOUT, scream, screech, shriek, squeal, whoop, yell
hollow *adj* **1** • curved inward *Syn* concave, dented, depressed, indented, recessed, sunken *Rel* alveolar, cavernous, cuplike, cupped *Ant* bulging, convex, protruding, protuberant **2** *Syn* VAIN, empty, idle, nugatory, otiose
hollow *n Syn* HOLE, cavity, pocket, vacuum, void
holocaust *Syn* FIRE, conflagration
holy **1** • showing devotion to God and to a life of virtue *Syn* devout, godly, pious, religious, sainted, saintly *Rel* ascetic, prayerful, reverent, reverential, spiritual, worshipful *Ant* faithless, godless, impious, irreligious, ungodly, unholy **2** • set apart or worthy of veneration by association with God *Syn* blessed, consecrated, hallowed, sacred, sacrosanct, sanctified *Rel* adored, enshrined, glorified, revered, venerated, worshipped *Ant* unconsecrated, unhallowed
homage *Syn* HONOR, deference, obeisance, reverence
home *Syn* HABITATION, abode, domicile, dwelling, house, residence
homely *Syn* PLAIN, simple, unpretentious *Ant* lovely
homicidal *Syn* BLOODTHIRSTY, bloody, murdering, murderous, sanguinary, sanguine
homily *Syn* SPEECH, address, harangue, lecture, oration, sermon, talk
homogenize *Syn* STANDARDIZE, formalize, normalize, regularize
hone *Syn* SHARPEN, edge, grind, strop, whet *Ant* blunt, dull
honest **1** *Syn* TRUTHFUL, veracious *Ant* dishonest, fibbing, lying, mendacious, prevaricating, untruthful **2** *Syn* UPRIGHT, conscientious, honorable, just, scrupulous
honesty • uprightness as evidenced in character and actions *Syn* honor, integrity, probity *Rel* truth, veracity, verity *Ant* dishonesty
honey *Syn* SWEETHEART, beloved, darling, dear, flame, love, sweet
honor *n* **1** • respect or esteem shown one as his or her due or claimed by one as a right *Syn* deference, homage, obeisance, reverence *Rel* acknowledgment, recognition **2** *Syn* AWARD, decoration, distinction, plume, premium, prize **3** *Syn* FAME, celebrity, éclat, glory, notoriety, renown, reputation, repute *Ant* infamy, obscurity **4** *Syn* HONESTY, integrity, probity *Ant* dishonesty
honor *vb Syn* DIGNIFY, ennoble, glorify
honorable *Syn* UPRIGHT, conscientious, honest, just, scrupulous
hoodwink *Syn* DUPE, bamboozle, befool, gull, hoax, trick
hoof (it) *Syn* WALK, foot (it), leg (it), pad, step, traipse, tread
hoosegow *Syn* JAIL, brig, guardroom, jug, lockup, pen, penitentiary, prison, stockade
hop *n Syn* DANCE, ball, cotillion, formal, prom
hop *vb Syn* SKIP, bound, curvet, lollop, lope, ricochet
hope *Syn* EXPECT, await, look *Ant* despair of
hopeful *adj* • having or showing confidence that the end or outcome will be favorable *Syn*

optimistic, roseate, rose-colored *Rel* awaiting, expecting, hoping *Ant* despairing, hopeless

hopeful *n Syn* CANDIDATE, applicant, aspirant, campaigner, contender, prospect, seeker

hopeless **1** *Syn* DESPONDENT, despairing, desperate, forlorn *Ant* lighthearted **2** *Syn* IMPOSSIBLE, unachievable, unattainable, unsolvable *Ant* achievable, attainable, doable, feasible, possible, realizable, workable

hopelessness *Syn* DESPONDENCY, despair, desperation, forlornness *Ant* lightheartedness

horde *Syn* CROWD, crush, mob, press, rout, throng

horizon *Syn* RANGE, compass, gamut, ken, orbit, purview, radius, reach, scope, sweep

horrendous *Syn* HORRIBLE, horrid, horrific *Ant* fascinating

horrible **1** • inspiring horror or abhorrence *Syn* horrendous, horrid, horrific *Rel* abhorrent, abominable, detestable, hateful *Ant* fascinating **2** *Syn* FEARFUL (sense 2), appalling, awful, dreadful, frightful, horrific, shocking, terrible, terrific

horrid *Syn* HORRIBLE, horrendous, horrific *Ant* fascinating

horrific **1** *Syn* FEARFUL (sense 2), appalling, awful, dreadful, frightful, horrible, shocking, terrible, terrific **2** *Syn* HORRIBLE, horrendous, horrid *Ant* fascinating

horrify *Syn* DISMAY, appall, daunt *Ant* cheer

horror *Syn* FEAR, alarm, consternation, dismay, dread, fright, panic, terror, trepidation *Ant* fearlessness

horse (around) *Syn* CUT UP, act up, clown (around), fool (around), monkey (around), show off, skylark

horseplay • wildly playful or mischievous behavior *Syn* clowning, foolery, high jinks, horsing (around), monkeying, monkeyshines, roughhouse, roughhousing, shenanigans, skylarking, tomfoolery *Rel* buffoonery, clownishness, foolishness, funning, jesting, joking, nonsense, waggery

horse sense **1** *Syn* COMMON SENSE, discreetness, discretion, gumption, levelheadedness, prudence, sense, sensibleness, wisdom, wit *Ant* imprudence, indiscretion **2** *Syn* SENSE, common sense, good sense, gumption, judgment, wisdom

horse-trade *Syn* BARGAIN, chaffer, deal, dicker, haggle, negotiate, palter

horsing (around) *Syn* HORSEPLAY, clowning, foolery, high jinks, monkeying, monkeyshines, roughhouse, roughhousing, shenanigans, skylarking, tomfoolery

host *Syn* MULTITUDE, army, legion

hostage *Syn* PLEDGE, earnest, pawn, token

hostility *Syn* ENMITY, animosity, animus, antagonism, antipathy, rancor *Ant* amity

hot *Syn* MODERN, contemporary, current, mod, modernistic, new, newfangled, newfashioned, present-day, red-hot, space-age, ultramodern, up-to-date *Ant* antiquated, archaic, dated, fusty, musty, noncontemporary, oldfangled, old-fashioned, old-time, out-of-date, passé

hot-blooded *Syn* FERVENT, ardent, blazing, burning, charged, emotional, fervid, feverish, fiery, flaming, glowing, impassioned, passionate, red-hot, vehement, warm, warm-blooded *Ant* cold, cool, dispassionate, impassive, unemotional

hotcake *Syn* PANCAKE, flapjack, griddle cake, slapjack

hotfoot (it) *Syn* HURRY (sense 2), barrel, bolt, bowl, breeze, career, course, dash, fly, hasten, hump, hurtle, hustle, pelt, race, rip, rocket, run, rush, rustle, scoot, scurry, scuttle, shoot, speed, step (along), tear, trot, whirl, whisk, zip, zoom *Ant* crawl, creep, poke

hotness *Syn* POPULARITY, fashionableness, favor, modishness, vogue *Ant* disfavor, unpopularity

hound *Syn* BAIT, badger, chivy, heckle, hector, ride

hounding *Syn* PURSUIT, chase, chasing, dogging, following, pursuing, shadowing, tagging, tailing, tracing, tracking, trailing

house *n Syn* HABITATION, abode, domicile, dwelling, home, residence

house *vb Syn* HARBOR, board, entertain, lodge, shelter

hovel *Syn* SHACK, cabin, camp, hut, hutch, shanty

hover *Syn* FLIT, flicker, flitter, flutter

howbeit *Syn* ALTHOUGH, albeit, though, when, while

howl *vb* **1** *Syn* BARK, bay, growl, snarl, yap, yelp **2** *Syn* ROAR, bawl, bellow, bluster, clamor, ululate, vociferate **3** *Syn* SCREAM, screech, shriek, shrill, squall, squeal, yell, yelp

howl *n Syn* LAMENT, groan, keen, lamentation, moan, plaint, wail *Ant* exultation, rejoicing

howler *Syn* ERROR, blunder, bull, faux pas, lapse, mistake, slip

hub *Syn* CENTER (sense 2), base, capital, core, cynosure, eye, focus, heart, mecca, nucleus, seat

hubbub **1** *Syn* COMMOTION, bother, bustle, clatter, disturbance, furor, furore, fuss, hullabaloo, hurly-burly, pandemonium, pother, row, ruckus, ruction, rumpus, shindy, squall, stew, stir, storm, to-do, tumult, turmoil, uproar, welter, whirl **2** *Syn* DIN, babel, clamor, hullabaloo, pandemonium, racket, uproar *Ant* quiet

hue *Syn* COLOR, shade, tinge, tint, tone

huff *Syn* OFFENSE (sense 1), dudgeon, pique, resentment, umbrage

huffy *Syn* IRRITABLE, fractious, fretful, peevish, pettish, petulant, querulous, snappish, waspish *Ant* easygoing

huge • exceedingly or excessively large *Syn* Brobdingnagian, colossal, cyclopean, elephantine, enormous, gargantuan, giant, gigantean, gigantic, Herculean, immense, mammoth, titanic, vast *Rel* monstrous, monumental, prodigious, stupendous, tremendous *Ant* bitty, diminutive, microscopic (*or* microscopical), midget, miniature, minute, pocket, pygmy, teeny, teeny-weeny, tiny, wee

hugely *Syn* VERY, awful, awfully, beastly, deadly, especially, exceedingly, extra, extremely, far, frightfully, full, greatly, heavily, highly, jolly, mightily, mighty, mortally, most, much, particularly, rattling, real, right, so, something, super, terribly, too, whacking *Ant* little, negligibly, nominally, slightly

hugger-mugger *Syn* MESSY, chaotic, cluttered, confused, disarranged, disarrayed, disheveled (*or* dishevelled), disordered, disorderly, higgledy-piggledy, jumbled, littered, messed, muddled, mussed, mussy, pell-mell, rumpled, sloppy, topsy-turvy, tousled, tumbled, unkempt, untidy, upside-down *Ant* neat, ordered, orderly, organized, shipshape, snug, tidied, tidy, trim

hulk *Syn* OAF, clod, gawk, lout, lubber, lug

hulking *Syn* LARGE, big, bulky, considerable, goodly, good-sized, grand, great, handsome, hefty, largish, outsize, oversize (*or* oversized), sizable (*or* sizeable), substantial, tidy, voluminous *Ant* little, puny, small, undersized

hullabaloo **1** *Syn* COMMOTION, bother, bustle, clatter, disturbance, furor, furore, fuss, hubbub, hurly-burly, pandemonium, pother, row, ruckus, ruction, rumpus, shindy, squall, stew, stir, storm, to-do, tumult, turmoil, uproar, welter, whirl **2** *Syn* DIN, babel, clamor, hubbub, pandemonium, racket, uproar *Ant* quiet

humane *Syn* CHARITABLE, altruistic, benevolent, eleemosynary, humanitarian, philanthropic *Ant* uncharitable

humanitarian *Syn* CHARITABLE, altruistic, benevolent, eleemosynary, humane, philanthropic *Ant* uncharitable

humble *adj* • lacking all signs of pride, aggressiveness, or self-assertiveness *Syn* lowly, meek, modest *Rel* subdued, submissive, tame

humble *vb Syn* abase, debase, degrade, demean, humiliate *Ant* exalt, extol (*especially oneself*)

humdrum *Syn* BORING, drab, dreary, dry, dull, flat, heavy, jading, leaden, monotonous, pedestrian, ponderous, stodgy, stuffy, stupid, tame, tedious, tiresome, tiring, unanimated, uninteresting, wearisome, weary, wearying *Ant* absorbing, engaging, engrossing, gripping, interesting, intriguing, involving

humid *Syn* WET, damp, dank, moist *Ant* dry

humiliate *Syn* ABASE, debase, degrade, demean, humble *Ant* exalt, extol (*especially oneself*)

humor **1** *Syn* COMEDY, farce, slapstick **2** *Syn* MOOD, temper, vein **3** *Syn* WIT, irony, repartee, sarcasm, satire

humorous *Syn* WITTY, facetious, jocose, jocular

hump **1** *Syn* HURRY (sense 2), barrel, bolt, bowl, breeze, career, course, dash, fly, hasten, hotfoot (it), hurtle, hustle, pelt, race, rip, rocket, run, rush, rustle, scoot, scurry, scuttle, shoot, speed, step (along), tear, trot, whirl, whisk, zip, zoom *Ant* crawl, creep, poke **2** *Syn* LABOR, drudge, endeavor, grub, hustle, moil, peg (away), plod, plow, plug, slave, slog, strain, strive, struggle, sweat, toil, travail, work *Ant* dabble, fiddle (around), fool (around), mess (around), putter (around)

hunger *Syn* LONG, hanker, pine, thirst, yearn

hunt *Syn* SEEK, comb, ferret out, ransack, rummage, scour, search

hurdle *Syn* ENCUMBRANCE, bar, block, chain, clog, crimp, deterrent, drag, embarrassment, fetter, handicap, hindrance, impediment, inhibition, interference, let, manacle, obstacle, obstruction, shackles, stop, stumbling block, trammel *Ant* aid, assistance, benefit, help

hurl *Syn* THROW, cast, fling, pitch, sling, toss

hurly-burly *Syn* COMMOTION, bother, bustle, clatter, disturbance, furor, furore, fuss, hubbub, hullabaloo, pandemonium, pother, row, ruckus, ruction, rumpus, shindy, squall, stew, stir, storm, to-do, tumult, turmoil, uproar, welter, whirl

hurricane • a violent rotating storm originating in the tropics and often moving into temperate latitudes *Syn* tropical storm, typhoon *Rel* whirlwind, whirly

hurry *vb* **1** • to cause to move or proceed fast or faster *Syn* accelerate, hasten, quicken, rush, speed (up), whisk *Rel* drive, goad, prod, propel, push, race, spur, stir, urge *Ant* decelerate, retard, slow (down) **2** • to proceed or move quickly *Syn* barrel, bolt, bowl, breeze, career, course, dash, fly, hasten, hotfoot (it), hump, hurtle, hustle, pelt, race, rip, rocket, run, rush, rustle, scoot, scurry, scuttle, shoot, speed, step (along), tear, trot, whirl, whisk, zip, zoom *Rel* dart, flit, scamper, scud, scuffle *Ant* crawl, creep, poke

hurry *n Syn* HASTE, dispatch, expedition, speed *Ant* deliberation

hurt *vb Syn* INJURE, damage, harm, impair, mar, spoil *Ant* aid

hurt *n Syn* INJURY, damage, harm, mischief

hurtful *Syn* HARMFUL, adverse, bad, baleful, baneful, damaging, deleterious, detrimental, evil, ill, injurious, mischievous, noxious, pernicious, prejudicial *Ant* harmless, innocent, innocuous, inoffensive, safe

hurtle *Syn* HURRY (sense 2), barrel, bolt, bowl, breeze, career, course, dash, fly, hasten, hotfoot (it), hump, hustle, pelt, race, rip, rocket, run, rush, rustle, scoot, scurry, scuttle, shoot, speed, step (along), tear, trot, whirl, whisk, zip, zoom *Ant* crawl, creep, poke

husbandry **1** *Syn* AGRICULTURE, farming **2** *Syn* ECONOMY, frugality, providence, scrimping, skimping, thrift *Ant* wastefulness

hush *n* **1** *Syn* CALM, calmness, peace, peacefulness, placidity, quiet, quietness, quietude, repose, restfulness, sereneness, serenity, still, stillness, tranquillity (*or* tranquility) *Ant* bustle, commotion, hubbub, hurly-burly, pandemonium, tumult, turmoil, uproar **2** *Syn* SILENCE, quiet, quietness, quietude, still, stillness *Ant* noise, sound

hush *vb Syn* SHUT UP, clam up, quiet (down) *Ant* speak, talk

hushed *Syn* SILENT (sense 2), muted, noiseless, quiet, quieted, soundless, still *Ant* noisy, unquiet

husky *Syn* MUSCULAR, athletic, brawny, burly, sinewy

hustle **1** *Syn* FLEECE, bleed, cheat, chisel, cozen, defraud, mulct, rook, shortchange, skin, squeeze, stick, sting, swindle, victimize **2** *Syn* HURRY (sense 2), barrel, bolt, bowl, breeze, career, course, dash, fly, hasten, hotfoot (it), hump, hurtle, pelt, race, rip, rocket, run, rush, rustle, scoot, scurry, scuttle, shoot, speed, step (along), tear, trot, whirl, whisk, zip, zoom *Ant* crawl, creep, poke **3** *Syn* LABOR, drudge, endeavor, fag, grub, hump, moil, peg (away), plod, plow, plug, slave, slog, strain, strive, struggle, sweat, toil, travail, work *Ant* dabble, fiddle (around), fool (around), mess (around), putter (around)

hut *Syn* SHACK, cabin, camp, hovel, hutch, shanty

hutch **1** *Syn* CABINET, buffet, closet, cupboard, locker, sideboard **2** *Syn* SHACK, cabin, camp, hovel, hut, shanty

hygienic **1** *Syn* HEALTHFUL, healthy, salubrious, salutary, sanitary, wholesome **2** *Syn* SANITARY, aseptic, germfree, sterile *Ant* insanitary, unhygienic, unsanitary

hymn *Syn* SING, carol, chant, descant, intone, trill, troll, warble

hyperbole *Syn* EXAGGERATION, caricature, coloring, elaboration, embellishment, embroidering, magnification, overstatement, padding, stretching *Ant* understatement

hypercritical *Syn* CRITICAL, captious, carping, caviling, censorious, faultfinding *Ant* uncritical

hypochondriac *Syn* MELANCHOLIC, atrabilious, melancholy

hypocrisy • the pretending of having virtues, principles, or beliefs that one in fact does not have *Syn* cant, dissembling, dissimulation, insincerity, piousness, sanctimoniousness *Rel* deception, deceptiveness, dishonesty, falsity, pretense, pretension, pretentiousness, self-righteousness, self-satisfaction *Ant* genuineness, sincerity

hypocritical *Syn* INSINCERE, double-dealing, feigned, left-handed, mealy, mealymouthed, two-faced, unctuous *Ant* genuine, heartfelt, honest, sincere, unfeigned

hypostatize *Syn* REALIZE, actualize, embody, externalize, incarnate, materialize, objectify, reify

hypothesis *Syn* THEORY, proposition, supposition

hypothetical *Syn* SUPPOSED, conjectural, purported, putative, reputed, suppositious, supposititious *Ant* certain

hysteria **1** *Syn* FRENZY, agitation, delirium, distraction, furor, furore, fury, rage, rampage, uproar **2** *Syn* MANIA, delirium, frenzy

I

icon *Syn* IMAGE, effigy, mask, photograph, portrait, statue

iconoclast *Syn* REBEL, insurgent

icy *Syn* COLD, arctic, chilly, cool, freezing, frigid, frosty, gelid, glacial *Ant* hot

idea • what exists in the mind as a representation as of something comprehended or as a formulation as of a plan *Syn* concept, conception, impression, notion, thought *Rel* belief, conviction, opinion, sentiment, view

ideal *adj Syn* ABSTRACT (sense 1), transcendent, transcendental *Ant* concrete

ideal *n Syn* MODEL, beau, example, exemplar, ideal, mirror, pattern, standard

idealist • one whose conduct is guided more by the image of perfection than by the real world *Syn* dreamer, romantic, romanticist, utopian, visionary *Rel* sentimentalist *Ant* pragmatist, realist

idealize • to represent or think of as better

than reality *Syn* glamorize, glorify, romanticize *Rel* daydream, imagine, romance, theorize, vision

identic *Syn* SAME, equal, equivalent, identical, selfsame, tantamount, very *Ant* different

identical *Syn* SAME, equal, equivalent, identic, selfsame, tantamount, very *Ant* different

identification *Syn* RECOGNITION, apperception, assimilation

idiom **1** *Syn* LANGUAGE (sense 1), dialect, speech, tongue **2** *Syn* PHRASE, expression, locution

idle *vb* • to spend time not in work but in idleness *Syn* laze, loaf, loll, lounge *Rel* relax, repose, rest

idle *adj* **1** *Syn* INACTIVE, inert, passive, supine *Ant* active, live **2** *Syn* VAIN, empty, hollow, nugatory, otiose

idler *Syn* LAZYBONES, drone, loafer, slouch, slug, sluggard *Ant* doer, go-getter, hummer, hustler, rustler, self-starter

idolatry *Syn* WORSHIP, adulation, deification, idolization, worshipping

idolization *Syn* WORSHIP, adulation, deification, idolatry, worshipping

idolize • to love or admire too much *Syn* adore, adulate, canonize, deify, dote (on), worship *Rel* appreciate, cherish, esteem, prize, treasure, value

ignite *Syn* LIGHT, fire, kindle

ignoble *Syn* MEAN, abject, sordid

ignominy *Syn* DISGRACE, dishonor, disrepute, ignominy, infamy, obloquy, odium, opprobrium, shame *Ant* esteem, respect

ignorant • lacking in education or the knowledge gained from books *Syn* benighted, dark, illiterate, nonliterate, simple, uneducated, uninstructed, unlearned, unlettered, unread, unschooled, untaught, untutored *Rel* lowbrow, uncultivated, uncultured *Ant* educated, knowledgeable, literate, schooled

ignore *Syn* NEGLECT, disregard, forget, omit, overlook, slight *Ant* cherish

ilk *Syn* TYPE, character, description, kidney, kind, nature, sort, stripe

ill **1** *Syn* BAD (sense 1), evil, naughty, wicked *Ant* good **2** *Syn* EVIL, bad, evildoing, immorality, iniquity, sin, villainy, wrong *Ant* good, morality, right, virtue **3** *Syn* HARMFUL, adverse, bad, baleful, baneful, damaging, deleterious, detrimental, evil, hurtful, injurious, mischievous, noxious, pernicious, prejudicial *Ant* harmless, innocent, innocuous, inoffensive, safe

ill-advised *Syn* INDISCREET, imprudent, inadvisable, injudicious, tactless, unadvisable, unwise *Ant* advisable, discreet, judicious, prudent, tactful, wise

ill-bred *Syn* IMPOLITE, discourteous, ill-mannered, impertinent, inconsiderate, rude, thoughtless, uncalled-for, uncivil, ungracious, unmannerly *Ant* civil, considerate, courteous, genteel, gracious, mannerly, polite, thoughtful, well-bred

illegal *Syn* UNLAWFUL, illegitimate, illicit *Ant* lawful

illegitimate *Syn* UNLAWFUL, illegal, illicit *Ant* lawful

ill-fated *Syn* UNLUCKY, calamitous, disastrous, hapless, ill-starred, luckless, unfortunate *Ant* fortunate, happy, lucky

ill-favored *Syn* UGLY, hideous, unsightly *Ant* beautiful

illicit *Syn* UNLAWFUL, illegal, illegitimate *Ant* lawful

illimitable *Syn* INFINITE, boundless, endless, immeasurable, indefinite, limitless, measureless, unbounded, unfathomable, unlimited *Ant* bounded, circumscribed, confined, definite, finite, limited, restricted

illiterate *Syn* IGNORANT, benighted, dark, nonliterate, simple, uneducated, uninstructed, unlearned, unlettered, unread, unschooled, untaught, untutored *Ant* educated, knowledgeable, literate, schooled

ill-mannered *Syn* IMPOLITE, discourteous, ill-bred, impertinent, inconsiderate, rude, thoughtless, uncalled-for, uncivil, ungracious, unmannerly *Ant* civil, considerate, courteous, genteel, gracious, mannerly, polite, thoughtful, well-bred

illogical • not using or following good reasoning *Syn* fallacious, invalid, irrational, nonrational, unreasonable, unreasoning, unsound, weak *Rel* misleading, specious *Ant* logical, rational, reasonable, sound, valid

ill-starred *Syn* UNLUCKY, calamitous, disastrous, hapless, ill-fated, luckless, unfortunate *Ant* fortunate, happy, lucky

ill-treat *Syn* ABUSE, maltreat, mistreat, misuse, outrage *Ant* honor, respect

illuminate, illumine **1** • to fill with or to throw light upon *Syn* enlighten, illustrate, light, lighten *Rel* fire, kindle *Ant* darken, obscure **2** *Syn* EXPLAIN (sense 1), clarify, clear (up), construe, demonstrate, elucidate, explicate, expound, illustrate, interpret, spell out *Ant* obscure

illusion **1** *Syn* DELUSION, hallucination, mirage **2** *Syn* FALLACY (sense 1), error, falsehood, falsity, misconception, myth, old wives' tale, untruth *Ant* truth, verity

illusory *Syn* APPARENT, ostensible, seeming *Ant* real

illustrate **1** *Syn* EXPLAIN (sense 1), clarify, clear (up), construe, demonstrate, elucidate, explicate, expound, illuminate, interpret, spell out *Ant* obscure **2** *Syn* ILLUMINATE, enlighten, light, lighten *Ant* darken, obscure

illustration *Syn* EXAMPLE, case, exemplar, instance, representative, sample, specimen

illustrious *Syn* EMINENT, distinguished, noble, notable, noteworthy, outstanding, preeminent, prestigious, signal, star, superior

ill will *Syn* MALICE, despite, grudge, malevolence, malignancy, malignity, spite, spleen *Ant* charity

image **1** • a lifelike representation especially of a living being *Syn* effigy, icon, mask, photograph, portrait, statue *Rel* copy, duplicate, facsimile, replica, reproduction **2** *Syn* SENSATION (sense 1), percept, sense-datum, sensum

imaginary • unreal or unbelievable or conceiving such unreal or unbelievable things *Syn* chimerical, fanciful, fantastic, quixotic, visionary *Rel* apocryphal, fabulous, fictitious, legendary, mythical *Ant* actual, real

imagination • the power or function of the mind by which mental images of things are formed or the exercise of that power *Syn* fancy, fantasy *Rel* creation, invention

imagine **1** *Syn* BELIEVE (sense 1), consider, deem, feel, figure, guess, hold, suppose, think *Ant* disbelieve, discredit, reject **2** *Syn* THINK (sense 1), conceive, envisage, envision, fancy, realize

imbibe *Syn* ABSORB, assimilate *Ant* exude, give out

imbue *Syn* INFUSE, ingrain, inoculate, leaven, suffuse

imitate *Syn* COPY, ape, mimic, mock *Ant* originate

imitation • being such in appearance only and made with or manufactured from usually cheaper materials *Syn* artificial, bogus, factitious, fake, false, man-made, mimic, mock, sham, simulated, substitute, synthetic *Rel* adulterated, affected, concocted, counterfeit, cultured, deceptive, doctored, dummy, fabricated, feigned, forged, fraudulent, fudged, juggled, manipulated, manufactured, misleading, phony, pseudo, spurious, tampered (with), unauthentic *Ant* genuine, natural, real

imitation *n Syn* COPY, carbon copy, duplicate, duplication, facsimile, reduplication, replica, replication, reproduction *Ant* original

immaterial **1** • not composed of matter *Syn* incorporeal, spiritual *Ant* material **2** *Syn* IRRELEVANT, extraneous, inapplicable *Ant* applicable, apposite, apropos, germane, material, pertinent, relevant

immature **1** • not fully developed *Syn* unmatured, unmellow, unripe *Rel* callow, crude, green, rude *Ant* mature **2** *Syn* CALLOW, adolescent, green, inexperienced, juvenile, puerile, raw, unfledged, unripe, unripened *Ant* adult, experienced, grown-up, mature, ripe **3** *Syn* CHILDISH, adolescent, babyish, infantile, juvenile, kiddish, puerile *Ant* adult, grown-up, mature **4** *Syn* YOUNG, adolescent, juvenile, youngish, youthful *Ant* adult, full-grown, mature, matured

immeasurable *Syn* INFINITE, boundless, endless, illimitable, indefinite, limitless, measureless, unbounded, unfathomable, unlimited *Ant* bounded, circumscribed, confined, definite, finite, limited, restricted

immediacy *Syn* PROXIMITY, closeness, contiguity, nearness *Ant* distance, remoteness

immense *Syn* HUGE, Brobdingnagian, colossal, cyclopean, elephantine, enormous, gargantuan, giant, gigantean, gigantic, Herculean, mammoth, titanic, vast *Ant* bitty, diminutive, microscopic (*or* microscopical), midget, miniature, minute, pocket, pygmy, teeny, teeny-weeny, tiny, wee

immerse *Syn* DIP (sense 1), duck, dunk, souse, submerge

immersing *Syn* INTERESTING, absorbing, arresting, engaging, engrossing, enthralling, fascinating, gripping, intriguing, involving, riveting *Ant* boring, drab, dry, dull, heavy, monotonous, tedious, uninteresting

immigrant **1** *Syn* EMIGRANT, migrant **2** *Syn* STRANGER, alien, émigré, foreigner, outlander, outsider

immigrate *Syn* MIGRATE, emigrate

imminent *Syn* FORTHCOMING, approaching, coming, impending, nearing, oncoming, pending, upcoming *Ant* late, recent

immobile *Syn* IMMOVABLE, immotive *Ant* movable

immoderate *Syn* EXCESSIVE, exorbitant, extravagant, extreme, inordinate *Ant* deficient

immoral *Syn* UNPRINCIPLED, cutthroat, Machiavellian, unconscionable, unethical, unmoral, unscrupulous *Ant* ethical, moral, principled, scrupulous

immorality *Syn* EVIL, bad, evildoing, ill, iniquity, sin, villainy, wrong *Ant* good, morality, right, virtue

immortal • not subject to death or decay *Syn* deathless, undying, unfading *Rel* endless, everlasting *Ant* mortal

immotive *Syn* IMMOVABLE, immobile *Ant* movable

immovable **1** • incapable of moving or being moved *Syn* immobile, immotive *Ant* movable **2** *Syn* OBSTINATE, adamant, adamantine, dogged, hard, hardened, hardheaded, hardhearted, headstrong, implacable, inflexible, mulish, obdurate, opinionated, ossified, pat, peevish, pertinacious, perverse, pigheaded, rigid, self-willed, stubborn, unbending, uncompromising, unrelenting, unyielding, willful (*or* wilful) *Ant* acquiescent, agreeable, amenable, compliant, complying, flexible, pliable, pliant, relenting, yielding

immure *Syn* IMPRISON, incarcerate, intern, jail

imp *Syn* DEMON, devil, fiend, ghoul, incubus

impact • a forcible or enforced contact between two or more things *Syn* clash, collision, concussion, impingement, jar, jolt, percussion, shock *Rel* hit, hitting, slap, slapping, smiting, striking, stroke

impair *Syn* INJURE, damage, harm, hurt, mar, spoil *Ant* aid

impalpable *Syn* IMPERCEPTIBLE, inappreciable, indistinguishable, insensible *Ant* appreciable, discernible, palpable, perceptible, sensible

impart *Syn* COMMUNICATE, convey, spread, transfer, transfuse, transmit

impartial *Syn* FAIR, dispassionate, equitable, just, objective, unbiased, uncolored *Ant* unfair

impartiality *Syn* DETACHMENT, disinterestedness, neutrality, objectivity *Ant* bias, favor, favoritism, one-sidedness, partiality, partisanship, prejudice

impassable • not allowing passage *Syn* impenetrable, impermeable, impervious *Ant* passable

impassible *Syn* INSENSIBLE, anesthetic, insensitive *Ant* sensible (*to or of something*)

impassioned *Syn* FERVENT, ardent, blazing, burning, charged, emotional, fervid, feverish, fiery, flaming, glowing, hot-blooded, passionate, red-hot, vehement, warm, warm-blooded *Ant* cold, cool, dispassionate, impassive, unemotional

impassive • unresponsive to what might normally excite interest or emotion *Syn* apathetic, phlegmatic, stoic, stolid *Rel* collected, composed, cool, imperturbable *Ant* responsive

impassivity, **impassiveness** • unresponsiveness to something that might normally excite interest or emotion *Syn* apathy, phlegm, stoicism, stolidity

impatient • manifesting signs of unrest or an inability to keep still or quiet *Syn* fidgety, jittery, jumpy, nervous, restive, restless, uneasy, unquiet *Rel* fretful, irritable, querulous, snappish, waspish *Ant* patient

impeach *Syn* ACCUSE, charge, incriminate, indict *Ant* absolve, acquit, clear, exculpate, exonerate, vindicate

impeccable • absolutely correct and beyond criticism *Syn* errorless, faultless, flawless *Rel* inerrant, infallible, unerring

impecunious *Syn* POOR, destitute, indigent, necessitous, needy, penniless, poverty-stricken *Ant* rich

impede *Syn* HINDER, bar, block, dam, obstruct *Ant* further

impediment *Syn* ENCUMBRANCE, bar, block, chain, clog, crimp, deterrent, drag, embarrassment, fetter, handicap, hindrance, hurdle, inhibition, interference, let, manacle, obstacle, obstruction, shackles, stop, stumbling block, trammel *Ant* aid, assistance, benefit, help

impending *Syn* FORTHCOMING, approaching, coming, imminent, nearing, oncoming, pending, upcoming *Ant* late, recent

impenetrable **1** *Syn* IMPASSABLE, impermeable, impervious *Ant* passable **2** *Syn* INCOMPREHENSIBLE, unfathomable, unintelligible *Ant* fathomable, intelligible, understandable

impenetrate *Syn* PERMEATE, impregnate, interpenetrate, penetrate, pervade, saturate

impenitent *Syn* REMORSELESS, unrepentant *Ant* contrite, guilty, penitent, regretful, remorseful, repentant, sorry

imperative **1** *Syn* MANDATORY, compulsory, forced, incumbent, involuntary, necessary, nonelective, obligatory, peremptory, required *Ant* elective, optional, voluntary **2** *Syn* MASTERFUL, domineering, imperious, peremptory **3** *Syn* PRESSING, crying, exigent, importunate, insistent, instant, urgent

imperceptible • not perceptible by a sense or by the mind *Syn* impalpable, inappreciable, indistinguishable, insensible *Rel* inaudible, intangible, invisible *Ant* appreciable, discernible, palpable, perceptible, sensible

imperfect *Syn* FAULTY, bad, defective, flawed *Ant* faultless, flawless, impeccable, perfect

imperfection **1** • an instance of failure to reach a standard of excellence or perfection *Syn* deficiency, fault, shortcoming *Rel* dereliction, failure, neglect *Ant* perfection **2** *Syn* BLEMISH, defect, deformity, disfigurement, fault, flaw, mark, pockmark, scar

imperial *Syn* KINGLY, princely, queenly, regal, royal

imperil *Syn* ENDANGER, adventure, compromise, gamble (with), hazard, jeopardize, menace, risk, venture

imperilment *Syn* DANGER (sense 2), distress, endangerment, jeopardy, peril, risk, trouble *Ant* safeness, safety, security

imperious **1** *Syn* ARROGANT, cavalier, haughty, highfalutin, high-handed, high-hat, important, lofty, lordly, masterful, overweening, peremptory, pompous, presumptuous, pretentious, supercilious, superior, uppish, uppity *Ant* humble, modest **2** *Syn* BOSSY, authoritarian, autocratic, despotic, dictatorial, domineering, masterful, overbearing, peremptory, tyrannical, tyrannous **3** *Syn* MASTERFUL, domineering, imperative, peremptory

imperiousness *Syn* ARROGANCE, haughtiness, loftiness, lordliness, masterfulness, peremptoriness, pompousness, presumptuousness, pretense (*or* pretence), pretension, pretentiousness, self-importance, superciliousness, superiority *Ant* humility, modesty

impermanent *Syn* MOMENTARY, ephemeral, evanescent, flash, fleeting, fugitive, passing, short-lived, temporary, transient, transitory *Ant* enduring, eternal, everlasting, lasting, long-lived, permanent, perpetual

impermeable *Syn* IMPASSABLE, impenetrable, impervious *Ant* passable

impersonate *Syn* ACT (sense 2), play

impersonator *Syn* ACTOR, mime, mimic, mummer, performer, player, thespian, trouper

impertinence *Syn* BACK TALK, cheek, impudence, insolence, sass, sauce

impertinent *Syn* IMPOLITE, discourteous, ill-bred, ill-mannered, inconsiderate, rude, thoughtless, uncalled-for, uncivil, ungracious, unmannerly *Ant* civil, considerate, courteous, genteel, gracious, mannerly, polite, thoughtful, well-bred

imperturbability *Syn* EQUANIMITY, aplomb, calmness, composure, coolheadedness, coolness, placidity, self-possession, serenity, tranquillity (*or* tranquility) *Ant* agitation, discomposure, perturbation

imperturbable **1** *Syn* COOL, collected, composed, nonchalant, unflappable, unruffled *Ant* agitated, ardent **2** *Syn* UNFLAPPABLE, nerveless, unshakable *Ant* perturbable, shakable

impervious *Syn* IMPASSABLE, impenetrable, impermeable *Ant* passable

impetuous *Syn* PRECIPITATE, abrupt, hasty, headlong, sudden *Ant* deliberate

impetus **1** *Syn* SPEED, headway, momentum, pace, velocity **2** *Syn* STIMULUS, excitant, incitement, stimulant

impingement *Syn* IMPACT, clash, collision, concussion, jar, jolt, percussion, shock

impious • lacking in reverence for what is sacred or divine *Syn* blasphemous, profane, sacrilegious *Rel* flagitious, iniquitous, nefarious *Ant* pious, reverent

impish *Syn* PLAYFUL, frolicsome, mischievous, roguish, sportive, waggish

implacable **1** *Syn* GRIM, merciless, relentless, unrelenting *Ant* lenient **2** *Syn* OBSTINATE, adamant, adamantine, dogged, hard, hardened, hardheaded, hardhearted, headstrong, immovable, inflexible, mulish, obdurate, opinionated, ossified, pat, peevish, pertinacious, perverse, pigheaded, rigid, self-willed, stubborn, unbending, uncompromising, unrelenting, unyielding, willful (*or* wilful) *Ant* acquiescent, agreeable, amenable, compliant, complying, flexible, pliable, pliant, relenting, yielding

implant • to introduce into the mind *Syn* inculcate, instill *Rel* imbue, infuse, ingrain, inoculate, leaven

implement *n* • a relatively simple device for performing work *Syn* appliance, instrument, tool, utensil *Rel* apparatus, machine, mechanism

implement *vb* *Syn* ENFORCE, administer, apply, execute

implicit • understood although not put into words *Syn* implied, tacit, unexpressed, unspoken, unvoiced, wordless *Rel* inferred *Ant* explicit, express, expressed, spoken, stated

implied *Syn* IMPLICIT, tacit, unexpressed, unspoken, unvoiced, wordless *Ant* explicit, express, expressed, spoken, stated

implore *Syn* BEG, adjure, beseech, entreat, importune, supplicate

imply **1** *Syn* HINT, allude, indicate, infer, insinuate, intimate, suggest **2** *Syn* INCLUDE, comprehend, embrace, involve, subsume *Ant* exclude

impolite • showing a lack of manners or consideration for others *Syn* discourteous, ill-bred, ill-mannered, impertinent, inconsiderate, rude, thoughtless, uncivil, ungracious, unmannerly *Rel* audacious, bold, bold-faced, brash, brassy, disrespectful, impudent, insolent, saucy, shameless *Ant* civil, considerate, courteous, genteel, gracious, mannerly, polite, thoughtful, well-bred

import *n* **1** *Syn* IMPORTANCE, consequence, moment, significance, weight *Ant* unimportance **2** *Syn* MEANING, acceptation, sense, significance, signification

import *vb* **1** *Syn* MATTER, count, mean, signify, weigh **2** *Syn* MEAN, denote, signify

importance • the quality or state of being of notable worth or influence *Syn* consequence, import, moment, significance, weight *Rel* conspicuousness, prominence, saliency *Ant* unimportance

important **1** *Syn* ARROGANT, cavalier, haughty, highfalutin, high-handed, high-hat, imperious, lofty, lordly, masterful, overweening, peremptory, pompous, presumptuous, pretentious, supercilious, superior, uppish, uppity *Ant* humble, modest **2** *Syn* CONCEITED, complacent, egoistic, egotistic (*or* egotistical), overweening, pompous, prideful, proud, self-conceited, self-important, self-satisfied, smug, stuck-up, vain, vainglorious *Ant* humble, modest

importunate *Syn* PRESSING, crying, exigent, imperative, insistent, instant, urgent

importune *Syn* BEG, adjure, beseech, entreat, implore, supplicate

impose **1** • to establish or apply as a charge or penalty *Syn* assess, charge, exact, fine, lay, levy, put *Rel* dock, mulct, penalize, tax *Ant* remit **2** *Syn* DICTATE, decree, ordain, prescribe

imposing **1** *Syn* DIGNIFIED, august, solemn, staid, stately *Ant* flighty, frivolous, giddy, goofy, silly, undignified **2** *Syn* GRAND, august, grandiose, magnificent, majestic, noble, stately

imposition *Syn* TAX, assessment, duty, impost, levy

impossible • incapable of being solved or accomplished *Syn* hopeless, unachievable, unattainable, unsolvable *Rel* impracticable, impractical *Ant* achievable, attainable, doable, feasible, possible, realizable, workable

impost *Syn* TAX, assessment, duty, imposition, levy

impostor • a person who fraudulently pretends to be someone or something else *Syn* charlatan, faker, mountebank, quack *Rel* cheat, fake, fraud, humbug, imposture

impotence *Syn* INABILITY, inadequacy, incapability, incapacity, incompetence, ineptitude, powerlessness *Ant* ability, adequacy, capability, capacity, competence, potency

impotent **1** *Syn* POWERLESS, helpless, weak *Ant* mighty, potent, powerful, puissant, strong **2** *Syn* STERILE, barren, infertile, unfruitful *Ant* exuberant, fertile

impracticable *Syn* IMPRACTICAL, inoperable, nonpractical, unusable, unworkable, useless *Ant* applicable, feasible, functional, operable, operational, practicable, practical, usable, useful, workable

impractical • not capable of being put to use or account *Syn* impracticable, inoperable, nonpractical, unusable, unworkable, useless *Rel* unsuitable *Ant* applicable, feasible, functional, operable, operational, practicable, practical, usable, useful, workable

imprecation *Syn* CURSE, anathema, malediction *Ant* blessing

impregnable *Syn* INVINCIBLE, indomitable, inexpugnable, invulnerable, unassailable, unconquerable

impregnate **1** *Syn* PERMEATE, impenetrate, interpenetrate, penetrate, pervade, saturate **2** *Syn* SOAK, drench, saturate, sop, steep, waterlog

impress *vb Syn* AFFECT, influence, strike, sway, touch

impress *n Syn* IMPRESSION, imprint, print, stamp

impressible *Syn* SENTIENT, impressionable, responsive, sensitive, susceptible

impression **1** • the perceptible trace or traces left by pressure *Syn* impress, imprint, print, stamp *Rel* trace, track, vestige **2** *Syn* EDITION, printing, reissue, reprinting **3** *Syn* IDEA, concept, conception, notion, thought

impressionable *Syn* SENTIENT, impressible, responsive, sensitive, susceptible

impressive *Syn* MOVING, affecting, emotional, poignant, stirring, touching *Ant* unemotional, unimpressive

imprimatur *Syn* APPROVAL, approbation, blessing, favor, OK (*or* okay) *Ant* disapprobation, disapproval, disfavor

imprint *Syn* IMPRESSION, impress, print, stamp

imprison • to confine closely so that escape is impossible or unlikely *Syn* immure, incarcerate, intern, jail *Rel* circumscribe, confine, limit, restrict

improbable • not likely to be true or to occur *Syn* doubtful, dubious, far-fetched, flimsy, questionable, unapt, unlikely *Rel* implausible, impossible, inconceivable, incredible, last, unbelievable, unthinkable *Ant* likely, probable

impromptu *Syn* EXTEMPORANEOUS, extemporary, extempore, improvised, offhand, unpremeditated

improper **1** *Syn* INAPPROPRIATE, graceless, inapt, incongruous, incorrect, indecorous, inept, infelicitous, unapt, unbecoming, unfit, unhappy, unseemly, unsuitable, wrong *Ant* appropriate, becoming, befitting, correct, decorous, felicitous, fit, fitting, genteel, happy, meet, proper, right, seemly, suitable **2** *Syn* UNFIT, inappropriate, inapt, infelicitous, unfitting, unhappy, unsuitable *Ant* fit

impropriety **1** • a socially improper or unsuitable act or remark *Syn* familiarity, gaffe, indiscretion, solecism *Rel* blunder, error, flub, fumble, goof, lapse, miscue, misstep, mistake, slip, slipup, stumble *Ant* amenity, civility, courtesy, formality, gesture **2** • the quality or state of not being socially proper *Syn* inappropriateness, incorrectness, indecency, unfitness *Rel* coarseness, crudeness *Ant* appropriateness, correctness, decency, decorousness, fitness, propriety, rightness, seemliness, suitability **3** *Syn* BARBARISM, corruption, solecism, vernacularism, vulgarism

improve **1** • to make more acceptable or bring nearer to some standard *Syn* ameliorate, better, help *Rel* benefit, profit *Ant* impair, worsen **2** • to grow or become better (as in health or well-being) *Syn* convalesce, gain, recover, recuperate

improvement *Syn* ADVANCE (sense 1), advancement, breakthrough, enhancement, refinement *Ant* setback

improvised *Syn* EXTEMPORANEOUS, extemporary, extempore, impromptu, offhand, unpremeditated

imprudent *Syn* INDISCREET, ill-advised, inadvisable, injudicious, tactless, unadvisable, unwise *Ant* advisable, discreet, judicious, prudent, tactful, wise

impudence *Syn* BACK TALK, cheek, impertinence, insolence, sass, sauce

impudent *Syn* SHAMELESS, barefaced, brash, brazen

impugn *Syn* DENY, contradict, contravene, gainsay, negative, traverse *Ant* concede, confirm

impulse *Syn* MOTIVE, goad, incentive, inducement, spring, spur

impulsive **1** *Syn* COMPULSIVE, obsessive **2** *Syn* SPONTANEOUS, automatic, instinctive, mechanical **3** *Syn* WHIMSICAL, capricious, freakish

impure • containing foreign or lower-grade substances *Syn* adulterated, alloyed, contaminated, dilute, diluted, polluted, tainted, thinned, weakened *Rel* befouled, besmirched, corrupted, debased, defiled, dirtied, fouled, soiled, spoiled, sullied *Ant* pure, unadulterated, unalloyed, uncontaminated, undiluted, unpolluted, untainted

impute *Syn* ASCRIBE, accredit, assign, attribute, charge, credit, refer

inability • the lack of sufficient ability, power, or means *Syn* impotence, inadequacy, incapability, incapacity, incompetence, ineptitude, powerlessness *Rel* inaptitude *Ant* ability, adequacy, capability, capacity, competence, potency

inactive • not engaged in work or activity *Syn* idle, inert, passive, supine *Rel* abeyant, dormant, latent, potential, quiescent *Ant* active, live

inadequacy **1** *Syn* DEFICIENCY, dearth, deficit, failure, famine, insufficiency, lack, paucity, poverty, scantiness, scarceness, scarcity, shortage, want *Ant* abundance, adequacy, amplitude, plenitude, plenty, sufficiency **2** *Syn* INABILITY, impotence, incapability, incapacity, incompetence, ineptitude, powerlessness *Ant* ability, adequacy, capability, capacity, competence, potency

inadequately *Syn* BADLY, poorly, unacceptably, unsatisfactorily *Ant* acceptably, adequately, all right, fine, good, palatably, passably, so-so, tolerably

inadvertent **1** *Syn* ACCIDENTAL, casual, chance, fluky, fortuitous, incidental, unintended, unintentional, unplanned, unpremeditated, unwitting *Ant* deliberate, intended, intentional, planned, premeditated **2** *Syn* CARELESS, heedless, thoughtless *Ant* careful

inadvisable *Syn* INDISCREET, ill-advised, imprudent, injudicious, tactless, unadvisable, unwise *Ant* advisable, discreet, judicious, prudent, tactful, wise

inane **1** *Syn* INSIPID, banal, flat, jejune, vapid, wishy-washy *Ant* sapid, zestful **2** *Syn* MEANINGLESS, empty, pointless, senseless *Ant* meaningful

inanimate *Syn* DEAD, deceased, defunct, departed, late, lifeless

inapplicable *Syn* IRRELEVANT, extraneous, immaterial *Ant* applicable, apposite, apropos, germane, material, pertinent, relevant

inappreciable *Syn* IMPERCEPTIBLE, impalpable, indistinguishable, insensible *Ant* appreciable, discernible, palpable, perceptible, sensible

inappropriate **1** • not appropriate for a particular occasion or situation *Syn* graceless, improper, inapt, incongruous, incorrect, indecorous, inept, infelicitous, unapt, unbecoming, unfit, unhappy, unseemly, unsuitable, wrong *Rel* inopportune, unfortunate, unseasonable, untimely *Ant* appropriate, becoming, befitting, correct, decorous, felicitous, fit, fitting, genteel, happy, meet, proper, right, seemly, suitable **2** *Syn* UNFIT, improper, inapt, infelicitous, unfitting, unhappy, unsuitable *Ant* fit

inappropriateness *Syn* IMPROPRIETY (sense 2), incorrectness, indecency, unfitness *Ant* appropriateness, correctness, decency, decorousness, fitness, propriety, rightness, seemliness, suitability

inapt **1** *Syn* INAPPROPRIATE, graceless, improper, incongruous, incorrect, indecorous, inept, infelicitous, unapt, unbecoming, unfit, unhappy, unseemly, unsuitable, wrong *Ant* appropriate, becoming, befitting, correct, decorous, felicitous, fit, fitting, genteel, happy, meet, proper, right, seemly, suitable **2** *Syn* UNFIT, improper, inappropriate, infelicitous, unfitting, unhappy, unsuitable *Ant* fit

inarticulate *Syn* MUTE, speechless, voiceless

inasmuch as *Syn* BECAUSE, as, for, since

inaugurate *Syn* INITIATE, induct, install, invest

inauspicious *Syn* OMINOUS, baleful, dire, foreboding, menacing, portentous, sinister, threatening

inborn *Syn* INNATE, congenital, hereditary, inbred, inherited *Ant* acquired

inbred *Syn* INNATE, congenital, hereditary, inborn, inherited *Ant* acquired

incandescent *Syn* BRIGHT, beaming, brilliant, effulgent, lambent, lucent, luminous, lustrous, radiant, refulgent *Ant* dim, dull

incapability *Syn* INABILITY, impotence, inadequacy, incapacity, incompetence, ineptitude, powerlessness *Ant* ability, adequacy, capability, capacity, competence, potency

incapable *Syn* INCOMPETENT, inept, inexpert, unfit, unqualified, unskilled, unskillful *Ant* able, capable, competent, expert, fit, qualified, skilled, skillful

incapacity *Syn* INABILITY, impotence, inadequacy, incapability, incompetence, ineptitude, powerlessness *Ant* ability, adequacy, capability, capacity, competence, potency

incarcerate *Syn* IMPRISON, immure, intern, jail

incarnate **1** *Syn* EMBODY (sense 2), epitomize, manifest, materialize, personalize, personify, substantiate **2** *Syn* REALIZE, actualize, embody, externalize, hypostatize, materialize, objectify, reify

incarnation *Syn* EMBODIMENT, epitome, manifestation, personification

incendiary *n* **1** *Syn* AGITATOR, demagogue, exciter, firebrand, fomenter, inciter, instigator, rabble-rouser **2** *Syn* ARSONIST, firebug

incendiary *adj* *Syn* COMBUSTIBLE, flammable, inflammable, inflammatory

incense **1** *Syn* ANGER, antagonize, enrage, inflame, infuriate, madden, outrage, rankle, rile, roil *Ant* delight, gratify, please **2** *Syn* FRAGRANCE, bouquet, perfume, redolence *Ant* stench, stink

incensed *Syn* ANGRY, angered, apoplectic, enraged, foaming, fuming, furious, indignant, inflamed, infuriated, irate, ireful, mad, outraged, rabid, riled, roiled, sore, steaming, wrathful, wroth *Ant* delighted, pleased

incentive *Syn* MOTIVE, goad, impulse, inducement, spring, spur

inception **1** *Syn* BEGINNING, alpha, birth, commencement, dawn, genesis, incipiency, launch, morning, onset, outset, start, threshold *Ant* close, conclusion, end, ending **2** *Syn* ORIGIN, prime mover, provenance, provenience, root, source

incertitude *Syn* DOUBT, distrust, distrustfulness, misgiving, mistrust, mistrustfulness, skepticism, suspicion, uncertainty *Ant* assurance, belief, certainty, certitude, confidence, conviction, sureness, surety, trust

incessant *Syn* CONTINUAL, constant, continuous, perennial, perpetual, unremitting *Ant* intermittent

incident *Syn* OCCURRENCE, circumstance, episode, event

incidental *Syn* ACCIDENTAL, casual, chance, fluky, fortuitous, inadvertent, unintended, unintentional, unplanned, unpremeditated, unwitting *Ant* deliberate, intended, intentional, planned, premeditated

incipiency *Syn* BEGINNING, alpha, birth, commencement, dawn, genesis, inception, launch, morning, onset, outset, start, threshold *Ant* close, conclusion, end, ending

incise *Syn* CARVE, chisel, engrave, etch, sculpt, sculpture

incisive • having, manifesting, or suggesting a keen alertness of mind *Syn* biting, clear-cut, crisp, cutting, trenchant *Rel* concise, laconic, succinct, terse

incite • to spur to action *Syn* abet, foment, instigate *Rel* excite, galvanize, pique, provoke, stimulate *Ant* restrain

incitement *Syn* STIMULUS, excitant, impetus, stimulant

inciter *Syn* AGITATOR, demagogue, exciter, firebrand, fomenter, incendiary, instigator, rabble-rouser

inciting *Syn* PROVOCATIVE, exciting, instigating, piquing, provoking, stimulating

incline **1** • to influence one to have or to take an attitude toward something *Syn* bias, dispose, predispose *Rel* affect, influence, sway *Ant* disincline, indispose **2** *Syn* SLANT, lean, slope

inclined *Syn* PRONE (sense 1), apt, given, tending *Ant* erect

include • to contain within as part of the whole *Syn* comprehend, embrace, imply, involve, subsume *Rel* accommodate, contain, hold *Ant* exclude

inclusive *Syn* ENCYCLOPEDIC, compendious, complete, comprehensive, full, global, in-depth, omnibus, panoramic, universal

incognito *Syn* PSEUDONYM, alias, nom de guerre, nom de plume, pen name

incommode *Syn* INCONVENIENCE, discommode, disoblige, disturb, trouble *Ant* accommodate, oblige

incomparable *Syn* SUPREME, peerless, preeminent, superlative, surpassing, transcendent

incompatible *Syn* INCONSONANT, discordant, discrepant, incongruous, inconsistent, uncongenial, unsympathetic *Ant* consonant

incompetence *Syn* INABILITY, impotence, inadequacy, incapability, incapacity, ineptitude, powerlessness *Ant* ability, adequacy, capability, capacity, competence, potency

incompetent • lacking qualities (as knowledge, skill, or ability) required to do a job *Syn* incapable, inept, inexpert, unfit, unqualified, unskilled, unskillful *Rel* ineffective, ineffectual, inefficient *Ant* able, capable, competent, expert, fit, qualified, skilled, skillful

incompletely *Syn* PARTLY, part, partially *Ant* completely, entirely, totally, wholly

incomprehensible • impossible to understand *Syn* impenetrable, unfathomable, unintelligible *Rel* abstruse, baffling, bewildering, confounding, confusing, cryptic, enigmatic, esoteric, inscrutable, mysterious, mystifying, obscure, perplexing, puzzling, recondite, unanswerable, unknowable *Ant* fathomable, intelligible, understandable

incongruous **1** *Syn* INAPPROPRIATE, graceless, improper, inapt, incorrect, indecorous, inept, infelicitous, unapt, unbecoming, unfit, unhappy, unseemly, unsuitable, wrong *Ant* appropriate, becoming, befitting, correct, decorous, felicitous, fit, fitting, genteel, happy, meet, proper, right, seemly, suitable **2** *Syn* INCONSONANT, discordant, discrepant, incompatible, inconsistent, uncongenial, unsympathetic *Ant* consonant

inconsequential *Syn* UNIMPORTANT, frivolous, inconsiderable, insignificant, little, minor, minute, negligible, slight, small, small-fry, trifling, trivial *Ant* big, consequential, eventful, important, major, material, meaningful, momentous, significant, substantial, weighty

inconsiderable *Syn* UNIMPORTANT, frivolous, inconsequential, insignificant, little, minor, minute, negligible, slight, small, small-fry, trifling, trivial *Ant* big, consequential, eventful, important, major, material, meaningful, momentous, significant, substantial, weighty

inconsiderate *Syn* IMPOLITE, discourteous, ill-bred, ill-mannered, impertinent, rude, thoughtless, uncalled-for, uncivil, ungracious, unmannerly *Ant* civil, considerate, courteous, genteel, gracious, mannerly, polite, thoughtful, well-bred

inconsistent *Syn* INCONSONANT, discordant, discrepant, incompatible, incongruous, uncongenial, unsympathetic *Ant* consonant

inconsolable *Syn* SAD (sense 1), bad, blue, brokenhearted, crestfallen, dejected, depressed, despondent, disconsolate, doleful, down, downcast, downhearted, droopy, forlorn, gloomy, glum, heartbroken, heartsick, heartsore, joyless, low, low-spirited, melancholy, miserable, mournful, saddened, sorrowful, sorry, unhappy, woebegone, woeful, wretched *Ant* blissful, buoyant, buoyed, cheerful, cheery, chipper, delighted, glad, gladdened, gladsome, gleeful, happy, joyful, joyous, jubilant, sunny, upbeat

inconsonant • not in agreement with or not agreeable to *Syn* discordant, discrepant, incompatible, incongruous, inconsistent, uncongenial, unsympathetic *Ant* consonant

inconspicuous *Syn* UNOBTRUSIVE, unnoticeable *Ant* conspicuous, noticeable

inconstant • lacking firmness or steadiness (as in purpose or devotion) *Syn* capricious, fickle, mercurial, unstable *Rel* changeable, changeful, mutable, protean, variable *Ant* constant

incontestable *Syn* IRREFUTABLE, incontrovertible, indisputable, indubitable, unanswerable, undeniable, unquestionable *Ant* answerable, debatable, disputable, questionable

incontrovertible *Syn* IRREFUTABLE, incontestable, indisputable, indubitable, unanswerable, undeniable, unquestionable *Ant* answerable, debatable, disputable, questionable

inconvenience • to cause discomfort to or trouble for *Syn* discommode, disoblige, disturb, incommode, trouble *Rel* burden, encumber, saddle, weigh *Ant* accommodate, oblige

incorporate *Syn* EMBODY (sense 1), assimilate, integrate

incorporeal *Syn* IMMATERIAL, spiritual *Ant* material

incorrect *Syn* INAPPROPRIATE, graceless, improper, inapt, incongruous, indecorous, inept, infelicitous, unapt, unbecoming, unfit, unhappy, unseemly, unsuitable, wrong *Ant* appropriate, becoming, befitting, correct, decorous, felicitous, fit, fitting, genteel, happy, meet, proper, right, seemly, suitable

incorrectness *Syn* IMPROPRIETY (sense 2), inappropriateness, indecency, unfitness *Ant* appropriateness, correctness, decency, decorousness, fitness, propriety, rightness, seemliness, suitability

increase **1** • to make greater in size, amount, or number *Syn* add (to), aggrandize, amplify, augment, boost, compound, enlarge, escalate, expand, extend, multiply, raise, swell, up *Rel* skyrocket *Ant* abate, contract, decrease, diminish, lessen, lower, reduce, subtract (from) **2** • to become greater in extent, volume, amount, or number *Syn* accumulate, appreciate, balloon, build (up), burgeon, enlarge, escalate, expand, mount, multiply, mushroom, proliferate, rise, snowball, swell, wax *Rel* rocket, skyrocket *Ant* contract, decrease, diminish, lessen, wane

incredulity *Syn* UNBELIEF, disbelief *Ant* belief

increment *Syn* ADDITION, accession, accretion

incremental *Syn* GRADUAL, gradational, phased, piecemeal, step-by-step *Ant* sudden

incriminate *Syn* ACCUSE, charge, impeach, indict *Ant* absolve, acquit, clear, exculpate, exonerate, vindicate

incubus *Syn* DEMON, devil, fiend, ghoul, imp

inculcate *Syn* IMPLANT, instill

incumbent *Syn* MANDATORY, compulsory, forced, imperative, involuntary, necessary, nonelective, obligatory, peremptory, required *Ant* elective, optional, voluntary

incurious *Syn* INDIFFERENT, aloof, detached, disinterested, unconcerned, uninterested *Ant* avid

incursion *Syn* INVASION, inroad, raid

indebtedness *Syn* DEBT, arrear, debit, liability, obligation

indecency *Syn* IMPROPRIETY (sense 2), inappropriateness, incorrectness, unfitness *Ant* appropriateness, correctness, decency, decorousness, fitness, propriety, rightness, seemliness, suitability

indecision *Syn* HESITATION, faltering, hesitance, hesitancy, irresolution, shilly-shallying, vacillation, wavering, wobbling

indecorous *Syn* INAPPROPRIATE, graceless, improper, inapt, incongruous, incorrect, inept, infelicitous, unapt, unbecoming, unfit, unhappy, unseemly, unsuitable, wrong *Ant* appropriate, becoming, befitting, correct, decorous, felicitous, fit, fitting, genteel, happy, meet, proper, right, seemly, suitable

indefatigable • capable of prolonged and arduous effort *Syn* tireless, unflagging, untiring, unwearied, unwearying, weariless *Rel* assiduous, busy, diligent, industrious, sedulous

indefensible *Syn* INEXCUSABLE, unforgivable, unjustifiable, unpardonable, unwarrantable *Ant* defensible, excusable, forgivable, justifiable, pardonable

indefinable *Syn* UNUTTERABLE, indescribable, ineffable, inexpressible, unspeakable

indefinite *Syn* INFINITE, boundless, endless, illimitable, immeasurable, limitless, measureless, unbounded, unfathomable, unlimited *Ant* bounded, circumscribed, confined, definite, finite, limited, restricted

indemnify *Syn* PAY, compensate, recompense, reimburse, remunerate, repay, satisfy

indemnity *Syn* REPARATION, amends, redress, restitution

indented *Syn* HOLLOW, concave, dented, depressed, recessed, sunken *Ant* bulging, convex, protruding, protuberant

indentured *Syn* BOUND, articled, bond

independence *Syn* FREEDOM (sense 1), autarchy, autarky, autonomy, sovereignty *Ant* bondage

independent **1** *Syn* FREE, autarchic, autarkic, autonomous, sovereign *Ant* bond **2** *Syn* SELF-SUFFICIENT, self-reliant, self-supporting *Ant* dependent, reliant

in-depth *Syn* ENCYCLOPEDIC, compendious, complete, comprehensive, full, global, inclusive, omnibus, panoramic, universal

indescribable *Syn* UNUTTERABLE, indefinable, ineffable, inexpressible, unspeakable

Indian *Syn* AMERICAN INDIAN, Amerindian, Native American

indicate **1** • to give evidence of or to serve as ground for a valid or reasonable inference *Syn* argue, attest, bespeak, betoken, prove *Rel* hint, intimate, suggest **2** *Syn* HINT, allude, imply, infer, insinuate, intimate, suggest

indict *Syn* ACCUSE, charge, impeach, incriminate *Ant* absolve, acquit, clear, exculpate, exonerate, vindicate

indictment *Syn* CHARGE, complaint, count, rap

indifference • lack of interest or concern *Syn* apathy, casualness, disinterestedness, disregard, insouciance, nonchalance, unconcern *Rel* halfheartedness, lukewarmness *Ant* concern, interest, regard

indifferent **1** • not showing or feeling interest *Syn* aloof, detached, disinterested, incurious, unconcerned, uninterested *Rel* dispassionate, fair, impartial, unbiased *Ant* avid **2** *Syn* MEDIUM, average, fair, mediocre, middling, moderate, second-rate

indigence *Syn* POVERTY, destitution, penury, privation, want *Ant* riches

indigenous *Syn* NATIVE, aboriginal, autochthonous, endemic *Ant* alien, foreign

indigent *Syn* POOR, destitute, impecunious, necessitous, needy, penniless, poverty-stricken *Ant* rich

indignant *Syn* ANGRY, angered, apoplectic, enraged, foaming, fuming, furious, incensed, inflamed, infuriated, irate, ireful, mad, outraged, rabid, riled, roiled, sore, steaming, wrathful, wroth *Ant* delighted, pleased

indignation *Syn* ANGER, angriness, furor, fury, irateness, ire, outrage, rage, spleen, wrath, wrathfulness *Ant* delight, pleasure

indignity *Syn* INSULT, affront, barb, dart, dig, epithet, name, offense (*or* offence), outrage, put-down, sarcasm, slight, slur

indirect • deviating from a direct line or straightforward course *Syn* circuitous, roundabout *Rel* crooked, devious, oblique *Ant* direct, forthright, straightforward

indiscreet • showing poor judgment especially in personal relationships or social situations *Syn* ill-advised, imprudent, inadvisable, injudicious, tactless, unadvisable, unwise *Rel* dumb, idiotic, moronic, stupid *Ant* advisable, discreet, judicious, prudent, tactful, wise

indiscretion *Syn* IMPROPRIETY (sense 1), familiarity, gaffe, solecism *Ant* amenity, civility, courtesy, formality, gesture

indiscriminate • including all or nearly all within the range of choice, operation, or effectiveness *Syn* sweeping, wholesale *Rel* assorted, heterogeneous, miscellaneous, motley, promiscuous *Ant* discriminating, selective

indispensable *Syn* NEEDFUL, essential, necessary, requisite

indisposed *Syn* DISINCLINED, averse, hesitant, loath, reluctant

indisputable *Syn* IRREFUTABLE, incontestable, incontrovertible, indubitable, unanswerable, undeniable, unquestionable *Ant* answerable, debatable, disputable, questionable

indistinguishable *Syn* IMPERCEPTIBLE, impalpable, inappreciable, insensible *Ant* appreciable, discernible, palpable, perceptible, sensible

individual *adj* **1** *Syn* CHARACTERISTIC, distinctive, peculiar **2** *Syn* SPECIAL, especial, particular, specific

individual *n* *Syn* ENTITY, being, creature, person

individuality *Syn* DISPOSITION, character, complexion, personality, temper, temperament

individually *Syn* EACH, apiece, respectively, severally

indolent *Syn* LAZY, faineant, slothful *Ant* industrious

indomitable *Syn* INVINCIBLE, impregnable, inexpugnable, invulnerable, unassailable, unconquerable

indubitable *Syn* IRREFUTABLE, incontestable, incontrovertible, indisputable, unanswerable, undeniable, unquestionable *Ant* answerable, debatable, disputable, questionable

induce **1** *Syn* EFFECT, bring about, cause, create, effectuate, engender, generate, make, produce, prompt, result (in), spawn, work, yield **2** *Syn* PERSUADE, argue, convince, get, move, prevail (on *or* upon), satisfy, talk (into), win (over)

inducement *Syn* MOTIVE, goad, impulse, incentive, spring, spur

induct *Syn* INITIATE, inaugurate, install, invest

indulgence *Syn* FORBEARANCE, clemency, leniency, mercifulness, tolerance *Ant* anger, vindictiveness

indulgent *Syn* FORBEARING, clement, lenient, merciful, tolerant *Ant* unrelenting

indulgently *Syn* FORBEARINGLY, clemently, leniently, mercifully, tolerantly

indurate *Syn* HARDEN (sense 1), cake, petrify, solidify *Ant* soften

indurated *Syn* HARDENED, callous *Ant* softened

industrious *Syn* BUSY, assiduous, diligent, sedulous *Ant* idle, unoccupied

industry *Syn* BUSINESS, commerce, trade, traffic
inebriate *Syn* DRUNKARD, alcoholic, dipsomaniac, soak, sot, tippler, toper, tosspot *Ant* teetotaler
inebriated *Syn* DRUNK, drunken, intoxicated, tight, tipsy *Ant* sober
ineffable *Syn* UNUTTERABLE, indefinable, indescribable, inexpressible, unspeakable
ineffective • not producing or incapable of producing an intended result *Syn* ineffectual, inefficacious, inefficient *Rel* abortive, bootless, fruitless, futile, vain *Ant* effective
ineffectual *Syn* INEFFECTIVE, inefficacious, inefficient *Ant* effective
inefficacious *Syn* INEFFECTIVE, ineffectual, inefficient *Ant* effective
inefficient *Syn* INEFFECTIVE, ineffectual, inefficacious *Ant* effective
inept **1** *Syn* AWKWARD, clumsy, gauche, maladroit *Ant* deft, graceful, handy **2** *Syn* INAPPROPRIATE, graceless, improper, inapt, incongruous, incorrect, indecorous, infelicitous, unapt, unbecoming, unfit, unhappy, unseemly, unsuitable, wrong *Ant* appropriate, becoming, befitting, correct, decorous, felicitous, fit, fitting, genteel, happy, meet, proper, right, seemly, suitable **3** *Syn* INCOMPETENT, incapable, inexpert, unfit, unqualified, unskilled, unskillful *Ant* able, capable, competent, expert, fit, qualified, skilled, skillful
ineptitude *Syn* INABILITY, impotence, inadequacy, incapability, incapacity, incompetence, powerlessness *Ant* ability, adequacy, capability, capacity, competence, potency
inerrable *Syn* INFALLIBLE, inerrant, unerring *Ant* fallible
inerrant *Syn* INFALLIBLE, inerrable, unerring *Ant* fallible
inert *Syn* INACTIVE, idle, passive, supine *Ant* active, live
inescapable *Syn* INEVITABLE, certain, necessary, sure, unavoidable *Ant* avoidable, escapable, uncertain, unsure
inevitable **1** • impossible to avoid or evade *Syn* certain, inescapable, necessary, sure, unavoidable *Rel* decided, definite, settled *Ant* avoidable, escapable, uncertain, unsure **2** *Syn* CERTAIN, necessary *Ant* probable, supposed
inexcusable • too bad to be excused or justified *Syn* indefensible, unforgivable, unjustifiable, unpardonable, unwarrantable *Rel* insufferable, insupportable, intolerable, unbearable, unendurable *Ant* defensible, excusable, forgivable, justifiable, pardonable
inexperienced **1** *Syn* AMATEURISH, amateur, dilettante, inexpert, nonprofessional, unprofessional, unskilled, unskillful *Ant* ace, adept, consummate, crackerjack, expert, master, masterful, masterly, professional, virtuoso **2** *Syn* CALLOW, adolescent, green, immature, juvenile, puerile, raw, unfledged, unripe, unripened *Ant* adult, experienced, grown-up, mature, ripe
inexpert **1** *Syn* AMATEURISH, amateur, dilettante, inexperienced, nonprofessional, unprofessional, unskilled, unskillful *Ant* ace, adept, consummate, crackerjack, expert, master, masterful, masterly, professional, virtuoso **2** *Syn* INCOMPETENT, incapable, inept, unfit, unqualified, unskilled, unskillful *Ant* able, capable, competent, expert, fit, qualified, skilled, skillful
inexpressible *Syn* UNUTTERABLE, indefinable, indescribable, ineffable, unspeakable
inexpugnable *Syn* INVINCIBLE, impregnable, indomitable, invulnerable, unassailable, unconquerable
infallible • incapable of making mistakes or errors *Syn* inerrable, inerrant, unerring *Rel* certain, inevitable, necessary *Ant* fallible
infamous *Syn* VICIOUS, corrupt, degenerate, flagitious, iniquitous, nefarious, villainous *Ant* virtuous
infamy *Syn* DISGRACE, dishonor, disrepute, ignominy, obloquy, odium, opprobrium, shame *Ant* esteem, respect
infant *Syn* BABY, babe, child, newborn
infantile *Syn* CHILDISH, adolescent, babyish, immature, juvenile, kiddish, puerile *Ant* adult, grown-up, mature
infatuated *Syn* FOND, besotted, insensate
infectious • transmissible by infection *Syn* catching, communicable, contagious *Rel* mephitic, pestilent, pestilential, poisonous, toxic, virulent
infelicitous **1** *Syn* INAPPROPRIATE, graceless, improper, inapt, incongruous, incorrect, indecorous, inept, unapt, unbecoming, unfit, unhappy, unseemly, unsuitable, wrong *Ant* appropriate, becoming, befitting, correct, decorous, felicitous, fit, fitting, genteel, happy, meet, proper, right, seemly, suitable **2** *Syn* UNFIT, improper, inappropriate, inapt, unfitting, unhappy, unsuitable *Ant* fit
infer **1** • to arrive at by reasoning from evidence or from premises *Syn* conclude, deduce, gather, judge *Rel* reason, speculate, think **2** *Syn* HINT, allude, imply, indicate, insinuate, intimate, suggest
inferable *Syn* DEDUCTIVE, deducible, derivable, reasoned
inference • the deriving of a conclusion by reasoning *Syn* conclusion, deduction, judgment
inferior *n Syn* UNDERLING, junior, subordinate *Ant* senior, superior
inferior *adj Syn* LESSER, junior, less, lower, minor, smaller, subordinate, under *Ant* greater, higher, major, more, primary, prime, senior, superior
infernal • of or relating to a nether world of the dead *Syn* chthonian, chthonic, Hadean,

hellish, stygian, Tartarean *Rel* demoniac, devilish, diabolical, fiendish *Ant* supernal

infertile *Syn* STERILE, barren, impotent, unfruitful *Ant* exuberant, fertile

infest • to spread or swarm over in a troublesome manner *Syn* beset, overrun *Rel* abound, swarm, teem *Ant* disinfest

infidelity *Syn* BETRAYAL, disloyalty, double cross, faithlessness, falseness, falsity, perfidy, sellout, treachery, treason, unfaithfulness

infinite • being or seeming to be without limits *Syn* boundless, endless, illimitable, immeasurable, indefinite, limitless, measureless, unbounded, unfathomable, unlimited *Rel* abysmal, bottomless *Ant* bounded, circumscribed, confined, definite, finite, limited, restricted

infinitesimal *Syn* TINY, atomic, bitty, microminiature, microscopic, miniature, minute, teeny, teeny-weeny, wee *Ant* astronomical, colossal, cosmic, elephantine, enormous, giant, gigantic, herculean, heroic, huge, immense, mammoth, massive, monster, monstrous, monumental, mountainous, prodigious, titanic, tremendous

infirm *Syn* WEAK, decrepit, feeble, fragile, frail *Ant* strong

inflame *Syn* ANGER, antagonize, enrage, incense, infuriate, madden, outrage, rankle, rile, roil *Ant* delight, gratify, please

inflamed *Syn* ANGRY, angered, apoplectic, enraged, foaming, fuming, furious, incensed, indignant, infuriated, irate, ireful, mad, outraged, rabid, riled, roiled, sore, steaming, wrathful, wroth *Ant* delighted, pleased

inflammable *Syn* COMBUSTIBLE, flammable, incendiary, inflammatory

inflammatory *Syn* COMBUSTIBLE, flammable, incendiary, inflammable

inflate *Syn* EXPAND, amplify, dilate, distend, swell *Ant* abridge, circumscribe, contract

inflated • swollen with or as if with something insubstantial *Syn* flatulent, tumid, turgid *Rel* aureate, bombastic, flowery, grandiloquent, magniloquent, rhetorical *Ant* pithy

inflection • a particular manner of employing the sounds of the voice in speech *Syn* accent, intonation *Rel* articulation, enunciation, pronunciation

inflexibility *Syn* SEVERITY, hardness, harshness, rigidity, rigidness, rigorousness, sternness, strictness *Ant* flexibility, gentleness, laxness, mildness

inflexible **1** *Syn* OBSTINATE, adamant, adamantine, dogged, hard, hardened, hardheaded, hardhearted, headstrong, immovable, implacable, mulish, obdurate, opinionated, ossified, pat, peevish, pertinacious, perverse, pigheaded, rigid, self-willed, stubborn, unbending, uncompromising, unrelenting, unyielding, willful (*or* wilful) *Ant* acquiescent, agreeable, amenable, compliant, complying, flexible, pliable, pliant, relenting, yielding **2** *Syn* STIFF, rigid, stark, tense, wooden *Ant* relaxed, supple

influence *n* • power exerted over the minds or behavior of others *Syn* authority, credit, prestige, weight *Rel* actuation, drive, driving, impelling, impulsion

influence *vb* *Syn* AFFECT, impress, strike, sway, touch

inform **1** • to stimulate (as mental powers) to higher or more intense activity *Syn* animate, fire, inspire *Rel* imbue, infuse, inoculate, leaven **2** • to make one aware of something *Syn* acquaint, advise, apprise, notify *Rel* communicate, impart **3** *Syn* ENLIGHTEN (sense 1), advise, apprise, brief, clue, familiarize, fill in, instruct, tell, wise (up)

information **1** *Syn* KNOWLEDGE, erudition, learning, lore, scholarship, science *Ant* ignorance **2** *Syn* NEWS, intelligence, item, story, tidings, word

infraction *Syn* BREACH (sense 1), contravention, infringement, transgression, trespass, violation

infrequent • not common or abundant *Syn* occasional, rare, scarce, sporadic, uncommon *Rel* exceptional *Ant* frequent

infrequently *Syn* SELDOM, little, rarely *Ant* frequently, often

infringe *Syn* TRESPASS, encroach, entrench, invade

infringement *Syn* BREACH (sense 1), contravention, infraction, transgression, trespass, violation

infuriate *Syn* ANGER, antagonize, enrage, incense, inflame, madden, outrage, rankle, rile, roil *Ant* delight, gratify, please

infuriated *Syn* ANGRY, angered, apoplectic, enraged, foaming, fuming, furious, incensed, indignant, inflamed, irate, ireful, mad, outraged, rabid, riled, roiled, sore, steaming, wrathful, wroth *Ant* delighted, pleased

infuse • to introduce one thing into another so as to affect it throughout *Syn* imbue, ingrain, inoculate, leaven, suffuse *Rel* impenetrate, impregnate, permeate, pervade, saturate

ingeminate *Syn* REPEAT (sense 1), iterate, reiterate

ingenious *Syn* CLEVER, adroit, cunning

ingenuous *Syn* NATURAL, artless, naive, simple, unaffected, unsophisticated

ingenuously *Syn* NATURALLY (sense 3), artlessly, guilelessly, innocently, naively, sincerely, unaffectedly, unfeignedly, unpretentiously *Ant* affectedly, artificially, hypocritically, insincerely, pretentiously, unnaturally

ingest *Syn* EAT, consume, devour, swallow

ingrain *Syn* INFUSE, imbue, inoculate, leaven, suffuse

ingrained *Syn* INHERENT, constitutional, essential, intrinsic *Ant* adventitious

ingredient *Syn* ELEMENT, component, constituent, factor *Ant* composite, compound (*in science*)

inhabitant • one who lives permanently in a place *Syn* denizen, dweller, habitant, occupant, resident, resider *Rel* aborigine, native *Ant* transient

inherent • being a part, element, or quality of a thing's inmost being *Syn* constitutional, essential, ingrained, intrinsic *Rel* congenital, inborn, inbred, innate *Ant* adventitious

inherently *Syn* NATURALLY (sense 2), constitutionally, innately, intrinsically *Ant* affectedly, artificially, hypocritically, insincerely, pretentiously, unnaturally

inheritance *Syn* HERITAGE, birthright, patrimony

inherited *Syn* INNATE, congenital, hereditary, inborn, inbred *Ant* acquired

inhibit **1** *Syn* DISCOURAGE (sense 2), deter, dissuade *Ant* encourage, persuade **2** *Syn* RESTRAIN, bridle, check, curb *Ant* abandon (*oneself*), activate, impel, incite

inhibition *Syn* ENCUMBRANCE, bar, block, chain, clog, crimp, deterrent, drag, embarrassment, fetter, handicap, hindrance, hurdle, impediment, interference, let, manacle, obstacle, obstruction, shackles, stop, stumbling block, trammel *Ant* aid, assistance, benefit, help

inhuman *Syn* FIERCE, barbarous, cruel, fell, ferocious, savage, truculent *Ant* mild, tame

inhumanity *Syn* CRUELTY, barbarity, brutality, cruelness, heartlessness, sadism, savageness, savagery, viciousness, wantonness *Ant* benignity, compassion, good-heartedness, humanity, kindheartedness, kindness, sympathy

iniquitous *Syn* VICIOUS, corrupt, degenerate, flagitious, infamous, nefarious, villainous *Ant* virtuous

iniquity *Syn* EVIL, bad, evildoing, ill, immorality, sin, villainy, wrong *Ant* good, morality, right, virtue

initial • marking a beginning or constituting a start *Syn* original, primordial *Rel* beginning, commencing, starting *Ant* final

initiate • to put through the formalities for becoming a member or an official *Syn* inaugurate, induct, install, invest *Rel* admit, enter, introduce

initiative *Syn* MANDATE, plebiscite, referendum

injudicious *Syn* INDISCREET, ill-advised, imprudent, inadvisable, tactless, unadvisable, unwise *Ant* advisable, discreet, judicious, prudent, tactful, wise

injunction *Syn* COMMAND, behest, bidding, dictate, mandate, order

injure • to deplete the soundness, strength, effectiveness, or perfection of something *Syn* damage, harm, hurt, impair, mar, spoil *Rel* deface, disfigure *Ant* aid

injurious *Syn* HARMFUL, adverse, bad, baleful, baneful, damaging, deleterious, detrimental, evil, hurtful, ill, mischievous, noxious, pernicious, prejudicial *Ant* harmless, innocent, innocuous, inoffensive, safe

injury **1** • the act or the result of inflicting something that causes loss or pain *Syn* damage, harm, hurt, mischief *Rel* agony, distress, misery, suffering **2** *Syn* DISSERVICE, injustice, raw deal, wrong *Ant* justice

injustice *Syn* DISSERVICE, injury, raw deal, wrong *Ant* justice

innate • not acquired after birth *Syn* congenital, hereditary, inborn, inbred, inherited *Rel* constitutional, essential, ingrained, inherent, intrinsic *Ant* acquired

innately *Syn* NATURALLY (sense 2), constitutionally, inherently, intrinsically *Ant* affectedly, artificially, hypocritically, insincerely, pretentiously, unnaturally

inner • situated further in *Syn* inside, interior, internal, intestine, inward *Rel* central, focal, middle, nuclear *Ant* outer

innocent *adj* *Syn* HARMLESS, innocuous, inoffensive, unoffending *Ant* harmful

innocent *n* *Syn* LAMB. angel, dove, sheep *Ant* wolf

innocently *Syn* NATURALLY (sense 3), artlessly, guilelessly, ingenuously, naively, sincerely, unaffectedly, unfeignedly, unpretentiously *Ant* affectedly, artificially, hypocritically, insincerely, pretentiously, unnaturally

innocuous *Syn* HARMLESS, innocent, inoffensive, unoffending *Ant* harmful

innumerable *Syn* COUNTLESS, numberless, uncountable, uncounted, unnumbered, untold *Ant* countable

inoculate *Syn* INFUSE, imbue, ingrain, leaven, suffuse

inoffensive *Syn* HARMLESS, innocent, innocuous, unoffending *Ant* harmful

inoperable *Syn* IMPRACTICAL, impracticable, nonpractical, unusable, unworkable, useless *Ant* applicable, feasible, functional, operable, operational, practicable, practical, usable, useful, workable

inordinate *Syn* EXCESSIVE, exorbitant, extravagant, extreme, immoderate *Ant* deficient

inquest *Syn* INQUIRY, inquisition, investigation, probe, research

inquire *Syn* ASK (sense 1), catechize, examine, interrogate, query, question, quiz

inquire (into) *Syn* EXPLORE, delve (into), dig (into), investigate, look (into), probe, research

inquiry • a search for truth, knowledge, or information *Syn* inquest, inquisition, investi-

gation, probe, research *Rel* catechizing, interrogation, questioning
inquisition *Syn* INQUIRY, inquest, investigation, probe, research
inquisitive *Syn* CURIOUS, nosy, prying, snoopy *Ant* incurious, uninterested
inroad *Syn* INVASION, incursion, raid
insane • afflicted by or manifesting unsoundness of mind or an inability to control one's rational processes *Syn* crazed, crazy, demented, deranged, lunatic, mad, maniac, non compos mentis *Rel* irrational, unreasonable *Ant* sane
insanity • a deranged state of mind or serious mental disorder *Syn* lunacy, mania, psychosis *Rel* aberration, alienation, derangement *Ant* sanity
inscription • something written, printed, or engraved (as on a coin or a medal or under or over a picture) to indicate or describe the purpose or the nature of the thing *Syn* caption, legend
inscrutable *Syn* MYSTERIOUS, arcane
insensate *Syn* FOND, besotted, infatuated
insensibility *Syn* FAINT, blackout, coma, knockout, swoon
insensible **1** • unresponsive to stimuli or to external influences *Syn* anesthetic, impassible, insensitive *Rel* blunt, dull, obtuse *Ant* sensible (*to or of something*) **2** *Syn* IMPERCEPTIBLE, impalpable, inappreciable, indistinguishable *Ant* appreciable, discernible, palpable, perceptible, sensible
insensitive **1** *Syn* INSENSIBLE, anesthetic, impassible *Ant* sensible (*to or of something*) **2** *Syn* NUMB, asleep, benumbed, dead, numbed, unfeeling *Ant* feeling, sensitive
insert *Syn* INTRODUCE, insinuate, intercalate, interject, interpolate, interpose *Ant* abstract, withdraw
inside *Syn* INNER, interior, internal, intestine, inward *Ant* outer
insidious *Syn* SLY, artful, crafty, cunning, foxy, guileful, tricky, wily
insight *Syn* DISCERNMENT, acumen, discrimination, penetration, perception
insignificant *Syn* UNIMPORTANT, frivolous, inconsequential, inconsiderable, little, minor, minute, negligible, slight, small, small-fry, trifling, trivial *Ant* big, consequential, eventful, important, major, material, meaningful, momentous, significant, substantial, weighty
insincere • not being or expressing what one appears to be or express *Syn* artificial, backhanded, double-dealing, feigned, hypocritical, left-handed, mealy, mealymouthed, two-faced, unctuous *Rel* empty, hollow, meaningless *Ant* genuine, heartfelt, honest, sincere, unfeigned
insincerity *Syn* HYPOCRISY, cant, dissembling, dissimulation, piousness, sanctimoniousness *Ant* genuineness, sincerity
insinuate **1** *Syn* HINT, allude, imply, indicate, infer, intimate, suggest **2** *Syn* INTRODUCE, insert, intercalate, interject, interpolate, interpose *Ant* abstract, withdraw
insipid • devoid of qualities that make for spirit and character *Syn* banal, flat, inane, jejune, vapid, wishy-washy *Rel* rare, slight, tenuous, thin *Ant* sapid, zestful
insistent **1** *Syn* PERSISTENT, dogged, patient, persevering, pertinacious, tenacious **2** *Syn* PRESSING, crying, exigent, imperative, importunate, instant, urgent
insolence *Syn* BACK TALK, cheek, impertinence, impudence, sass, sauce
insolent *Syn* PROUD (sense 1), arrogant, disdainful, haughty, lordly, overbearing, supercilious *Ant* ashamed, humble
insouciance *Syn* INDIFFERENCE, apathy, casualness, disinterestedness, disregard, nonchalance, unconcern *Ant* concern, interest, regard
insouciant *Syn* CAREFREE, careless, cavalier, devil-may-care, easygoing, gay, happy-go-lucky, lighthearted, unconcerned *Ant* careworn
inspect *Syn* SCRUTINIZE, audit, examine, scan
inspection • a close look at or over someone or something in order to judge condition *Syn* audit, check, checkup, examination, review, scan, scrutiny, survey *Rel* analysis, dissection
inspiration • a divine or seemingly divine imparting of knowledge or power *Syn* afflatus, frenzy, fury *Rel* enlightenment, illumination
inspire *Syn* INFORM (sense 1), animate, fire
inspirit *Syn* ENCOURAGE, cheer, embolden, hearten, nerve, steel *Ant* discourage
in spite of *Syn* NOTWITHSTANDING, despite
install *Syn* INITIATE, inaugurate, induct, invest
instance *n* *Syn* EXAMPLE, case, exemplar, illustration, representative, sample, specimen
instance *vb* *Syn* MENTION, name, specify
instant *n* • a very small space of time *Syn* flash, jiffy, minute, moment, second, shake, split second, trice, twinkle, twinkling, wink *Rel* microsecond, nanosecond
instant *adj* *Syn* PRESSING, crying, exigent, imperative, importunate, insistent, urgent
instigate *Syn* INCITE, abet, foment *Ant* restrain
instigating *Syn* PROVOCATIVE, exciting, inciting, piquing, provoking, stimulating
instigator *Syn* AGITATOR, demagogue, exciter, firebrand, fomenter, incendiary, inciter, rabble-rouser
instill *Syn* IMPLANT, inculcate
instinctive *Syn* SPONTANEOUS, automatic, impulsive, mechanical
institute *Syn* FOUND, create, establish, organize
instruct **1** *Syn* COMMAND, bid, charge, di-

rect, enjoin, order *Ant* comply, obey **2** *Syn* ENLIGHTEN (sense 1), acquaint, advise, apprise, brief, clue, familiarize, fill in, inform, tell, wise (up) **3** *Syn* TEACH, discipline, educate, school, train

instruction *Syn* EDUCATION (sense 1), schooling, teaching, training, tutelage, tutoring

instructor *Syn* TEACHER, educator, pedagogue, preceptor, schoolteacher

instrument **1** *Syn* AGENT (sense 2), agency, instrumentality, machinery, means, medium, organ, vehicle **2** *Syn* IMPLEMENT, appliance, tool, utensil

instrument *Syn* PAPER, document

instrumentality *Syn* AGENT (sense 2), agency, instrument, machinery, means, medium, organ, vehicle

insubordinate **1** • unwilling to submit to authority *Syn* contumacious, factious, mutinous, rebellious, seditious *Rel* intractable, recalcitrant, refractory, ungovernable, unruly **2** *Syn* DISOBEDIENT, balky, contrary, defiant, froward, intractable, rebellious, recalcitrant, refractory, restive, ungovernable, unruly, untoward, wayward, willful (*or* wilful) *Ant* amenable, compliant, docile, obedient, tractable

insubordination *Syn* DISOBEDIENCE, contrariness, defiance, frowardness, intractability, rebelliousness, recalcitrance, refractoriness, unruliness, willfulness *Ant* amenability, compliance, docility, obedience

insufferable *Syn* UNBEARABLE, insupportable, intolerable, unendurable, unsupportable *Ant* endurable, sufferable, supportable, tolerable

insufficiency *Syn* DEFICIENCY, dearth, deficit, failure, famine, inadequacy, lack, paucity, poverty, scantiness, scarceness, scarcity, shortage, want *Ant* abundance, adequacy, amplitude, plenitude, plenty, sufficiency

insular • having the narrow and limited outlook characteristic of geographic isolation *Syn* local, parochial, provincial, small-town *Rel* insulated, isolated, secluded

insulate *Syn* ISOLATE, seclude, segregate, sequester

insulation *Syn* ISOLATION, secludedness, seclusion, segregation, separateness, sequestration, solitariness, solitude

insult *n* • an act or expression showing scorn and usually intended to hurt another's feelings *Syn* affront, barb, dart, dig, epithet, indignity, name, offense (*or* offence), outrage, put-down, sarcasm, slight, slur *Rel* abuse, attack, criticism, disapproval, disgrace, dishonor, gibe (*or* jibe), invective, jeer, opprobrium, shame, slam, sneer, taunt, torment, torture, vituperation

insult *vb Syn* OFFEND, affront, outrage

insupportable *Syn* UNBEARABLE, insufferable, intolerable, unendurable, unsupportable *Ant* endurable, sufferable, supportable, tolerable

insure *Syn* ENSURE, assure, cinch, guarantee, guaranty, secure

insurgent *Syn* REBEL, iconoclast

insurrection *Syn* REBELLION, coup, mutiny, putsch, revolt, revolution, uprising

intact *Syn* PERFECT, entire, whole *Ant* imperfect

integer *Syn* NUMBER, digit, figure, numeral

integrate *Syn* EMBODY (sense 1), assimilate, incorporate

integrity **1** *Syn* HONESTY, honor, probity *Ant* dishonesty **2** *Syn* UNITY, solidarity, union

intellect *Syn* MIND, brain, intelligence, psyche, soul, wit

intellectual *Syn* MENTAL, cerebral, intelligent, psychic

intelligence **1** *Syn* MIND, brain, intellect, psyche, soul, wit **2** *Syn* NEWS, information, item, story, tidings, word

intelligent **1** • mentally quick or keen *Syn* alert, bright, brilliant, clever, knowing, quick-witted, smart *Rel* acute, keen, sharp *Ant* unintelligent **2** *Syn* MENTAL, cerebral, intellectual, psychic

intend • to have in mind as a purpose or goal *Syn* design, mean, propose, purpose *Rel* aim, aspire

intended *Syn* BETROTHED, fiancé, fiancée

intense • extreme in degree, power, or effect *Syn* exquisite, fierce, vehement, violent *Rel* aggravated, enhanced, heightened, intensified *Ant* subdued

intensify • to increase markedly in degree or measure *Syn* aggravate, enhance, heighten *Rel* accent, accentuate, emphasize, stress *Ant* abate, allay, mitigate, temper

intent *adj* • having one's mind or attention deeply fixed *Syn* absorbed, engrossed, rapt *Rel* attending, attentive, minding, watching *Ant* distracted

intent *n Syn* GOAL, aim, ambition, aspiration, design, dream, end, intention, mark, meaning, object, objective, plan, pretension, purpose, target, thing

intention • what one intends to accomplish or attain *Syn* aim, design, end, goal, intent, object, objective, purpose *Rel* plan, project, scheme

intentional *Syn* VOLUNTARY, deliberate, willful, willing *Ant* instinctive, involuntary

intentionally • with full awareness of what one is doing *Syn* consciously, deliberately, designedly, knowingly, purposefully, purposely, willfully, wittingly *Rel* calculatingly, studiedly *Ant* inadvertently, unconsciously, unintentionally, unknowingly, unwittingly

intentness *Syn* EARNESTNESS, gravity, seriousness, soberness, sobriety, solemnity *Ant* frivolity, levity, lightheartedness

intercalate *Syn* INTRODUCE, insert, insinuate, interject, interpolate, interpose *Ant* abstract, withdraw
intercede *Syn* INTERVENE, interpose, mediate
intercessor *Syn* MEDIATOR, arbiter, arbitrator, conciliator, go-between, intermediary, interposer, middleman, peacemaker
interchange *Syn* EXCHANGE, bandy
interdict *vb Syn* FORBID, ban, bar, enjoin, outlaw, prohibit, proscribe *Ant* allow, let, permit, suffer
interdict *n Syn* PROHIBITION (sense 2), ban, embargo, interdiction, proscription, veto *Ant* prescription
interdicting *Syn* PROHIBITION (sense 1), banning, barring, enjoining, forbidding, interdiction, outlawing, prohibiting, proscribing, proscription *Ant* prescription
interdiction **1** *Syn* PROHIBITION (sense 1), banning, barring, enjoining, forbidding, interdicting, outlawing, prohibiting, proscribing, proscription *Ant* prescription **2** *Syn* PROHIBITION (sense 2), ban, embargo, interdict, proscription, veto *Ant* prescription
interesting • holding the attention or provoking interest *Syn* absorbing, arresting, engaging, engrossing, enthralling, fascinating, gripping, immersing, intriguing, involving, riveting *Rel* breathtaking, electric, electrifying, exciting, exhilarating, galvanizing, inspiring, rousing, stimulating, stirring, thrilling *Ant* boring, drab, dry, dull, heavy, monotonous, tedious, uninteresting
interfere • to interest oneself in what is not one's concern *Syn* butt in, intrude, meddle, mess, nose, obtrude, poke, pry, snoop *Rel* intercede, interpose, intervene
interference *Syn* ENCUMBRANCE, bar, block, chain, clog, crimp, deterrent, drag, embarrassment, fetter, handicap, hindrance, hurdle, impediment, inhibition, let, manacle, obstacle, obstruction, shackles, stop, stumbling block, trammel *Ant* aid, assistance, benefit, help
interferer *Syn* BUSYBODY, interloper, intruder, kibitzer, meddler
interfering *Syn* INTRUSIVE, intruding, meddlesome, meddling, nosy (*or* nosey), obtrusive, officious, presumptuous, prying, snoopy *Ant* unobtrusive
interim *Syn* BREAK, gap, hiatus, interruption, interval, lacuna
interior *Syn* INNER, inside, internal, intestine, inward *Ant* outer
interject *Syn* INTRODUCE, insert, insinuate, intercalate, interpolate, interpose *Ant* abstract, withdraw
interloper *Syn* BUSYBODY, interferer, intruder, kibitzer, meddler
intermediary *Syn* MEDIATOR, arbiter, arbitrator, conciliator, go-between, intercessor, interposer, middleman, peacemaker
intermediary *Syn* MIDDLE, halfway, intermediate, medial, median, medium, mid, middlemost, midmost, midway *Ant* extreme, farthermost, farthest, furthermost, furthest, outermost, outmost, remotest, utmost
intermediate *Syn* MIDDLE, halfway, intermediary, medial, median, medium, mid, middlemost, midmost, midway *Ant* extreme, farthermost, farthest, furthermost, furthest, outermost, outmost, remotest, utmost
interminable *Syn* EVERLASTING, endless, unceasing *Ant* transitory
intermittent **1** • occurring or appearing in interrupted sequence *Syn* alternate, periodic, recurrent *Rel* arrested, checked, interrupted *Ant* continual, incessant **2** *Syn* FITFUL, casual, choppy, discontinuous, erratic, irregular, occasional, spasmodic, sporadic, spotty, unsteady *Ant* constant, continuous, regular, steady
intermixture *Syn* BLEND, admixture, amalgam, amalgamation, combination, composite, compound, fusion, mix, mixture
intern *Syn* IMPRISON, immure, incarcerate, jail
internal *Syn* INNER, inside, interior, intestine, inward *Ant* outer
interpenetrate *Syn* PERMEATE, impenetrate, impregnate, penetrate, pervade, saturate
interpolate *Syn* INTRODUCE, insert, insinuate, intercalate, interject, interpose *Ant* abstract, withdraw
interpose **1** *Syn* INTERVENE, intercede, mediate **2** *Syn* INTRODUCE, insert, insinuate, intercalate, interject, interpolate *Ant* abstract, withdraw
interposer *Syn* MEDIATOR, arbiter, arbitrator, conciliator, go-between, intercessor, intermediary, middleman, peacemaker
interpret *Syn* EXPLAIN (sense 1), clarify, clear (up), construe, demonstrate, elucidate, explicate, expound, illuminate, illustrate, spell out *Ant* obscure
interrogate *Syn* ASK (sense 1), catechize, examine, inquire, query, question, quiz
interrupt *Syn* ARREST (sense 1), check *Ant* activate, quicken
interruption **1** *Syn* BREAK, gap, hiatus, interim, interval, lacuna **2** *Syn* PAUSE, break, breath, breather, lull, recess
interstice *Syn* APERTURE, orifice
interval *Syn* BREAK, gap, hiatus, interim, interruption, lacuna
intervene • to act as a go-between for opposing sides *Syn* intercede, interpose, mediate *Rel* butt in, interfere, intrude, meddle, obtrude, pry, snoop
intestine *Syn* INNER, inside, interior, internal, inward *Ant* outer
intimate *adj Syn* FAMILIAR, chummy, close, confidential, thick *Ant* aloof
intimate *n Syn* FRIEND, acquaintance, confidant *Ant* foe

intimate *vb Syn* HINT, allude, imply, indicate, infer, insinuate, suggest

intimidate • to frighten into submission *Syn* browbeat, bulldoze, bully, cow *Rel* frighten, terrify, terrorize

intolerable *Syn* UNBEARABLE, insufferable, insupportable, unendurable, unsupportable *Ant* endurable, sufferable, supportable, tolerable

intolerant • unwilling to grant other people social rights or to accept other viewpoints *Syn* bigoted, narrow, narrow-minded, prejudiced, small-minded *Rel* conservative, hidebound, old-fashioned, reactionary *Ant* broad-minded, liberal, open-minded, tolerant, unprejudiced

intonation *Syn* INFLECTION, accent

intone *Syn* SING, carol, chant, descant, hymn, trill, troll, warble

intoxicant *Syn* ALCOHOL, booze, drink, grog, liquor, moonshine, spirits

intoxicated **1** *Syn* DRUNK, drunken, inebriated, tight, tipsy *Ant* sober **2** *Syn* ECSTATIC, elated, enraptured, entranced, euphoric, exhilarated, rapturous, rhapsodic *Ant* depressed

intoxication *Syn* ECSTASY, elation, euphoria, exhilaration, heaven, paradise, rapture, rhapsody, transport *Ant* depression

intractability *Syn* DISOBEDIENCE, contrariness, defiance, frowardness, insubordination, rebelliousness, recalcitrance, refractoriness, unruliness, willfulness *Ant* amenability, compliance, docility, obedience

intractable **1** *Syn* DISOBEDIENT, balky, contrary, defiant, froward, insubordinate, rebellious, recalcitrant, refractory, restive, ungovernable, unruly, untoward, wayward, willful (*or* wilful) *Ant* amenable, compliant, docile, obedient, tractable **2** *Syn* UNCONTROLLABLE, froward, headstrong, recalcitrant, refractory, ungovernable, unmanageable, unruly, untoward, wayward, willful (*or* wilful) *Ant* controllable, governable, tractable **3** *Syn* UNRULY, headstrong, recalcitrant, refractory, ungovernable, willful *Ant* docile, tractable

intrepid *Syn* BRAVE, audacious, bold, courageous, dauntless, doughty, fearless, unafraid, undaunted, valiant, valorous *Ant* craven

intrepidity *Syn* COURAGE, bravery, courageousness, daring, dauntlessness, doughtiness, fearlessness, gallantry, greatheartedness, guts, hardihood, heart, heroism, intrepidness, nerve, stoutness, valor *Ant* cowardice, cowardliness, cravenness, dastardliness, spinelessness, yellowness

intrepidness *Syn* COURAGE, bravery, courageousness, daring, dauntlessness, doughtiness, fearlessness, gallantry, greatheartedness, guts, hardihood, heart, heroism, intrepidity, nerve, stoutness, valor *Ant* cowardice, cowardliness, cravenness, dastardliness, spinelessness, yellowness

intricate *Syn* COMPLEX, complicated, involved, knotty *Ant* simple

intrigue *n* **1** *Syn* AMOUR, affair, liaison **2** *Syn* PLOT, cabal, conspiracy, machination

intrigue *vb Syn* PLOT, conspire, contrive, machinate, scheme

intriguing *Syn* INTERESTING, absorbing, arresting, engaging, engrossing, enthralling, fascinating, gripping, immersing, involving, riveting *Ant* boring, drab, dry, dull, heavy, monotonous, tedious, uninteresting

intrinsic *Syn* INHERENT, constitutional, essential, ingrained *Ant* adventitious

intrinsically *Syn* NATURALLY (sense 2), constitutionally, inherently, innately *Ant* affectedly, artificially, hypocritically, insincerely, pretentiously, unnaturally

introduce **1** • to put among or between others *Syn* insert, insinuate, intercalate, interject, interpolate, interpose *Ant* abstract, withdraw **2** *Syn* ENTER (sense 2), admit

introduction • something that serves as a preliminary or antecedent *Syn* exordium, foreword, preamble, preface, prelude, prologue

introductory *Syn* PRELIMINARY, prefatory, preparatory

intrude *Syn* INTERFERE, butt in, meddle, mess, nose, obtrude, poke, pry, snoop

intruder *Syn* BUSYBODY, interferer, interloper, kibitzer, meddler

intruding *Syn* INTRUSIVE, interfering, meddlesome, meddling, nosy (*or* nosey), obtrusive, officious, presumptuous, prying, snoopy *Ant* unobtrusive

intrusive • thrusting oneself where one is not welcome or invited *Syn* interfering, intruding, meddlesome, meddling, nosy (*or* nosey), obtrusive, officious, presumptuous, prying, snoopy *Rel* bold, brazen, impertinent, impudent, insolent, rude *Ant* unobtrusive

intuition *Syn* REASON (sense 2), understanding

inundate *Syn* FLOOD, deluge, drown, engulf, overflow, overwhelm, submerge, submerse, swamp *Ant* drain

inundation *Syn* FLOOD, cataract, deluge, spate, torrent

inure *Syn* HABITUATE, accustom, addict

invade *Syn* TRESPASS, encroach, entrench, infringe

invader *Syn* AGGRESSOR, raider

invalid **1** *Syn* GROUNDLESS, nonvalid, unfounded, ungrounded, unreasonable, unsubstantiated, unsupported, unwarranted *Ant* good, hard, just, justified, reasonable, reasoned, substantiated, valid, well-founded **2** *Syn* ILLOGICAL, fallacious, irrational, nonrational, unreasonable, unreasoning, unsound, weak *Ant* logical, rational, reasonable, sound, valid

invalidate *Syn* ABOLISH, abrogate, annul, cancel, dissolve, negate, nullify, quash, repeal, rescind, void

invaluable *Syn* COSTLY, dear, expensive, precious, priceless, valuable *Ant* cheap

invariant *Syn* UNIFORM, steady, unchanging, undeviating, unvarying, unwavering *Ant* changing, deviating, varying

invasion • a hostile entrance into the territory of another *Syn* incursion, inroad, raid *Rel* aggression, attack, offense, offensive

invective *Syn* ABUSE, billingsgate, obloquy, scurrility, vituperation *Ant* adulation

invent • to create or think of by clever use of the imagination *Syn* concoct, contrive, cook (up), devise, fabricate, make up, manufacture, think (up) *Rel* coin, contrive, create, design, hatch, produce

inventory *Syn* LIST, catalog, register, roll, roster, schedule, table

invert *Syn* REVERSE, transpose

invest **1** *Syn* BESIEGE, beleaguer, blockade **2** *Syn* INITIATE, inaugurate, induct, install

investigate *Syn* EXPLORE, delve (into), dig (into), inquire (into), look (into), probe, research

investigation *Syn* INQUIRY, inquest, inquisition, probe, research

inveterate • so firmly established that change is almost impossible *Syn* chronic, confirmed, deep-rooted, deep-seated *Rel* accustomed, addicted, habituated

invidious **1** *Syn* ENVIOUS, covetous, jaundiced, jealous, resentful **2** *Syn* REPUGNANT, abhorrent, distasteful, obnoxious, repellent *Ant* congenial

invigorate **1** *Syn* ANIMATE, brace, energize, enliven, fire, jazz (up), liven (up), pep (up), quicken, stimulate, vitalize, vivify *Ant* damp, dampen, deaden, dull **2** *Syn* STRENGTHEN, energize, fortify, reinforce *Ant* weaken

invigorating *Syn* TONIC, bracing, refreshing, restorative, reviving, stimulating, stimulative, vitalizing

invincible • incapable of being conquered *Syn* impregnable, indomitable, inexpugnable, invulnerable, unassailable, unconquerable *Rel* dauntless, intrepid, undaunted

inviolable *Syn* SACRED, inviolate, sacrosanct

inviolate *Syn* SACRED, inviolable, sacrosanct

invite • to request the presence or participation of *Syn* bid, court, solicit, woo *Rel* ask, request

involuntary *Syn* MANDATORY, compulsory, forced, imperative, incumbent, necessary, nonelective, obligatory, peremptory, required *Ant* elective, optional, voluntary

involve *Syn* INCLUDE, comprehend, embrace, imply, subsume *Ant* exclude

involved *Syn* COMPLEX, complicated, intricate, knotty *Ant* simple

involving *Syn* INTERESTING, absorbing, arresting, engaging, engrossing, enthralling, fascinating, gripping, immersing, intriguing, riveting *Ant* boring, drab, dry, dull, heavy, monotonous, tedious, uninteresting

invulnerable *Syn* INVINCIBLE, impregnable, indomitable, inexpugnable, unassailable, unconquerable

inward *Syn* INNER, inside, interior, internal, intestine *Ant* outer

iota *Syn* PARTICLE, atom, bit, jot, mite, smidgen, tittle, whit

irascible • easily aroused to anger *Syn* choleric, cranky, cross, splenetic, testy, touchy *Rel* fractious, huffy, irritable, peevish, petulant, querulous, snappish, waspish

irate *Syn* ANGRY, angered, apoplectic, enraged, foaming, fuming, furious, incensed, indignant, inflamed, infuriated, ireful, mad, outraged, rabid, riled, roiled, sore, steaming, wrathful, wroth *Ant* delighted, pleased

irateness *Syn* ANGER, angriness, furor, fury, indignation, ire, outrage, rage, spleen, wrath, wrathfulness *Ant* delight, pleasure

ire *Syn* ANGER, angriness, furor, fury, indignation, irateness, outrage, rage, spleen, wrath, wrathfulness *Ant* delight, pleasure

ireful *Syn* ANGRY, angered, apoplectic, enraged, foaming, fuming, furious, incensed, indignant, inflamed, infuriated, irate, mad, outraged, rabid, riled, roiled, sore, steaming, wrathful, wroth *Ant* delighted, pleased

irenic *Syn* PACIFIC, pacifist, pacifistic, peaceable, peaceful *Ant* bellicose

iridescent *Syn* PRISMATIC, opalescent, opaline

irk *Syn* ANNOY, bother, vex *Ant* soothe

irksome *Syn* ANNOYING, aggravating, bothersome, disturbing, exasperating, frustrating, galling, irritating, maddening, nettling, peeving, pesty, rankling, riling, vexatious, vexing

ironic *Syn* SARCASTIC, sardonic, satiric

irony *Syn* WIT, humor, repartee, sarcasm, satire

irrational *Syn* ILLOGICAL, fallacious, invalid, nonrational, unreasonable, unreasoning, unsound, weak *Ant* logical, rational, reasonable, sound, valid

irrefutable • not capable of being challenged or proved wrong *Syn* incontestable, incontrovertible, indisputable, indubitable, unanswerable, undeniable, unquestionable *Rel* certain, definite, positive, sure *Ant* answerable, debatable, disputable, questionable

irregular **1** • not conforming to rule, law, or custom *Syn* anomalous, unnatural *Rel* aberrant, abnormal, atypical *Ant* regular **2** *Syn* DEVIANT, aberrant, abnormal, anomalous, atypical, unnatural *Ant* natural, normal, regular, standard, typical **3** *Syn* FITFUL, casual, choppy, discontinuous, erratic, intermittent, occasional, spasmodic, sporadic, spotty, unsteady *Ant* constant, continuous, regular, steady

irregularly *Syn* HIT OR MISS, aimlessly, anyhow, anyway, anywise, desultorily, erratically, haphazard, haphazardly, helter-skelter, randomly *Ant* methodically, systematically
irrelevant • not having anything to do with the matter at hand *Syn* extraneous, immaterial, inapplicable *Rel* inconsequential, insignificant, unimportant *Ant* applicable, apposite, apropos, germane, material, pertinent, relevant
irreligious • lacking religious emotions, doctrines, or practices *Syn* godless, nonreligious, ungodly, unreligious *Rel* blasphemous, impious, profane, sacrilegious *Ant* religious
irresolution *Syn* HESITATION, faltering, hesitance, hesitancy, indecision, shilly-shallying, vacillation, wavering, wobbling
irritable • easily exasperated *Syn* fractious, fretful, huffy, peevish, pettish, petulant, querulous, snappish, waspish *Rel* choleric, cranky, cross, irascible, splenetic, testy, touchy *Ant* easygoing
irritate • to excite a feeling of anger or annoyance *Syn* aggravate, exasperate, nettle, peeve, provoke, rile *Rel* annoy, bother, irk, vex
irritating *Syn* ANNOYING, aggravating, bothersome, disturbing, exasperating, frustrating, galling, irksome, maddening, nettling, peeving, pesty, rankling, riling, vexatious, vexing
isolate • to set apart from others *Syn* insulate, seclude, segregate, sequester *Rel* abstract, detach, disengage
isolated *Syn* SECLUDED, cloistered, covert, quiet, remote, retired, secret, sheltered
isolation • the state of being alone or kept apart from others *Syn* insulation, secludedness, seclusion, segregation, separateness, sequestration, solitariness, solitude *Rel* loneliness, lonesomeness
issue *n* **1** *Syn* EFFECT, aftereffect, aftermath, consequence, event, outcome, result, sequel, upshot *Ant* cause **2** *Syn* OFFSPRING, descendants, posterity, progeny, young
issue *vb Syn* SPRING, arise, derive, emanate, flow, originate, proceed, rise, stem
item **1** • one of the distinct parts of a whole *Syn* detail, particular *Rel* article, object, thing **2** *Syn* NEWS, information, intelligence, story, tidings, word
itemized *Syn* CIRCUMSTANTIAL, detailed, minute, particular, particularized *Ant* abridged, summary
iterate *Syn* REPEAT (sense 1), ingeminate, reiterate
itinerant • traveling from place to place *Syn* ambulant, ambulatory, nomadic, peripatetic, vagrant *Rel* rambling, ranging, roaming, roving, straying, wandering

J

jabber *Syn* CHAT, babble, blab, cackle, chatter, converse, gab, gabble, gas, jaw, palaver, patter, prate, prattle, rap, rattle, run on, talk, twitter, visit
jack *Syn* FLAG, banner, color, ensign, pendant, pennant, pennon, standard, streamer
jackass *Syn* FOOL (sense 2), booby, goose, half-wit, lunatic, nincompoop, ninny, nitwit, nut, simpleton, turkey, yo-yo
jade *Syn* TIRE, exhaust, fatigue, tucker, weary
jading *Syn* BORING, drab, dreary, dry, dull, flat, heavy, humdrum, leaden, monotonous, pedestrian, ponderous, stodgy, stuffy, stupid, tame, tedious, tiresome, tiring, unanimated, uninteresting, wearisome, weary, wearying *Ant* absorbing, engaging, engrossing, gripping, interesting, intriguing, involving
jail *n* • a place of confinement for persons held in lawful custody *Syn* brig, guardroom, hoosegow, jug, lockup, pen, penitentiary, prison, stockade *Rel* bull pen
jail *vb Syn* IMPRISON, immure, incarcerate, intern
jam *n Syn* PREDICAMENT, dilemma, fix, pickle, plight, quandary, scrape
jam *vb Syn* PRESS, bear, bear down, crowd, squeeze
jape *Syn* JOKE, crack, gag, jest, quip, wisecrack, witticism
jar *Syn* IMPACT, clash, collision, concussion, impingement, jolt, percussion, shock
jargon *Syn* TERMINOLOGY, argot, cant, dialect, language, lingo, patois, patter, slang, vocabulary
jaundiced *Syn* ENVIOUS, covetous, invidious, jealous, resentful
jaunt *Syn* JOURNEY, cruise, excursion, expedition, pilgrimage, tour, trip, voyage
jaw **1** *Syn* CHAT, babble, blab, cackle, chatter, converse, gab, gabble, gas, jabber, palaver, patter, prate, prattle, rap, rattle, run on, talk, twitter, visit **2** *Syn* SCOLD, bawl, berate, chew out, rail, rate, revile, tongue-lash, upbraid, vituperate, wig
jazz (up) *Syn* ANIMATE, brace, energize, enliven, fire, invigorate, liven (up), pep (up), quicken, stimulate, vitalize, vivify *Ant* damp, dampen, deaden, dull
jealous *Syn* ENVIOUS, covetous, invidious, jaundiced, resentful

jeer *Syn* SCOFF, fleer, flout, gibe, gird, sneer
jejune *Syn* INSIPID, banal, flat, inane, vapid, wishy-washy *Ant* sapid, zestful
jell *Syn* COAGULATE, clot, congeal, curdle, jelly, set
jelly *Syn* COAGULATE, clot, congeal, curdle, jell, set
jeopardize *Syn* ENDANGER, adventure, compromise, gamble (with), hazard, imperil, menace, risk, venture
jeopardy *Syn* DANGER (sense 2), distress, endangerment, imperilment, peril, risk, trouble *Ant* safeness, safety, security
jeremiad *Syn* TIRADE, diatribe, philippic *Ant* eulogy
jerk • to make a sudden sharp quick movement *Syn* snap, twitch, yank *Rel* drag, pull
jest *n* **1** *Syn* FUN, game, play, sport **2** *Syn* JOKE, crack, gag, jape, quip, wisecrack, witticism
jest *vb* *Syn* JOKE, banter, fool, fun, jive, josh, kid, quip, wisecrack
jester *Syn* FOOL (sense 1), motley
jesting *Syn* BANTER, chaff, give-and-take, joshing, persiflage, raillery, repartee
jet **1** *Syn* ERUPT (sense 2), belch, disgorge, eject, expel, spew, spout, spurt **2** *Syn* GUSH (sense 1), pour, rush, spew, spout, spurt, squirt *Ant* dribble, drip, drop, trickle
jetty *Syn* WHARF, berth, dock, levee, pier, quay, slip
jib *Syn* DEMUR, balk, boggle, scruple, shy, stick, stickle, strain *Ant* accede
jibe *Syn* AGREE (sense 2), accord, conform, correspond, harmonize, square, tally *Ant* differ (from)
jiffy *Syn* INSTANT, flash, minute, moment, second, shake, split second, trice, twinkle, twinkling, wink
jigger *Syn* GADGET, appliance, contraption, contrivance, gimmick, gizmo (*or* gismo)
jim-dandy *adj* *Syn* EXCELLENT, A1, bang-up, banner, capital, classic, crackerjack, dandy, divine, fabulous, fine, first-class, first-rate, grand, great, groovy, heavenly, keen, marvelous (*or* marvellous), mean, neat, nifty, noble, par excellence, prime, sensational, splendid, stellar, sterling, superb, superior, superlative, supernal, swell, terrific, tip-top, top, top-notch, unsurpassed, wonderful *Ant* poor
jim-dandy *n* • something very good of its kind *Syn* beauty, corker, crackerjack, dandy, knockout, nifty, pip *Rel* marvel, wonder
jittery **1** *Syn* EXCITABLE, flighty, fluttery, high-strung, jumpy, nervous, skittish, spooky *Ant* unflappable **2** *Syn* IMPATIENT, fidgety, jumpy, nervous, restive, restless, uneasy, unquiet *Ant* patient
jive **1** *Syn* JOKE, banter, fool, fun, jest, josh, kid, quip, wisecrack **2** *Syn* TEASE, chaff, josh, kid, rally, razz, rib, ride, roast
job **1** *Syn* CHORE, assignment, duty, stint, task **2** *Syn* MISSION, assignment, charge, operation, post **3** *Syn* ROLE, capacity, function, part, place, position, purpose, task, work
jocose **1** *Syn* MERRY, blithesome, festive, gay, gleeful, jocund, jolly, jovial, laughing, mirthful, sunny **2** *Syn* WITTY, facetious, humorous, jocular
jocular *Syn* WITTY, facetious, humorous, jocose
jocund *Syn* MERRY, blithesome, festive, gay, gleeful, jocose, jolly, jovial, laughing, mirthful, sunny
jog *n* *Syn* POKE, nudge, prod
jog *vb* *Syn* POKE, nudge, prod
join • to bring or come together into some manner of union *Syn* associate, combine, conjoin, connect, link, relate, unite *Rel* concur, cooperate *Ant* disjoin, part
joining *Syn* ADJACENT, abutting, adjoining, bordering, contiguous, flanking, fringing, juxtaposed, skirting, touching, verging *Ant* nonadjacent
joint • a place where two or more things are united *Syn* articulation, suture
joke *n* • something said or done to provoke laughter *Syn* crack, gag, jape, jest, quip, wisecrack, witticism *Rel* antic, caper, dido, monkeyshine, prank
joke *vb* • to make jokes *Syn* banter, fool, fun, jest, jive, josh, kid, quip, wisecrack *Rel* chaff, mock, rally, razz, rib, ridicule, tease
jollity *Syn* MIRTH, glee, hilarity
jolly *vb* *Syn* BANTER, chaff, josh, kid, rag, rib
jolly *adj* *Syn* MERRY, blithesome, festive, gay, gleeful, jocose, jocund, jovial, laughing, mirthful, sunny
jolly *adv* *Syn* VERY, awful, awfully, beastly, deadly, especially, exceedingly, extra, extremely, far, frightfully, full, greatly, heavily, highly, hugely, mightily, mighty, mortally, most, much, particularly, rattling, real, right, so, something, super, terribly, too, whacking *Ant* little, negligibly, nominally, slightly
jolt *Syn* IMPACT, clash, collision, concussion, impingement, jar, percussion, shock
josh **1** *Syn* BANTER, chaff, jolly, kid, rag, rib **2** *Syn* JOKE, banter, fool, fun, jest, jive, kid, quip, wisecrack **3** *Syn* TEASE, chaff, jive, kid, rally, razz, rib, ride, roast
joshing *Syn* BANTER, chaff, give-and-take, jesting, persiflage, raillery, repartee
jot *Syn* PARTICLE, atom, bit, iota, mite, smidgen, tittle, whit
journal • a publication that appears at regular intervals *Syn* magazine, newspaper, organ, periodical, review
journalist *Syn* REPORTER, correspondent
journey • travel or a passage from one place to another *Syn* cruise, excursion, expedition, jaunt, pilgrimage, tour, trip, voyage
jovial *Syn* MERRY, blithesome, festive, gay,

gleeful, jocose, jocund, jolly, laughing, mirthful, sunny

joy *Syn* PLEASURE, delectation, delight, enjoyment, fruition *Ant* anger, displeasure, vexation

joyful *Syn* GLAD, cheerful, happy, joyous, lighthearted *Ant* sad

joyless *Syn* SAD (sense 1), bad, blue, brokenhearted, crestfallen, dejected, depressed, despondent, disconsolate, doleful, down, downcast, downhearted, droopy, forlorn, gloomy, glum, heartbroken, heartsick, heartsore, inconsolable, low, low-spirited, melancholy, miserable, mournful, saddened, sorrowful, sorry, unhappy, woebegone, woeful, wretched *Ant* blissful, buoyant, buoyed, cheerful, cheery, chipper, delighted, glad, gladdened, gladsome, gleeful, happy, joyful, joyous, jubilant, sunny, upbeat

joylessness *Syn* SADNESS, blues, dejection, depression, desolation, despondency, disconsolateness, dispiritedness, doldrums, downheartedness, dreariness, dumps, forlornness, gloom, gloominess, heartsickness, melancholy, mopes, oppression, unhappiness *Ant* bliss, blissfulness, ecstasy, elatedness, elation, euphoria, exhilaration, exuberance, exultation, felicity, gladness, gladsomeness, happiness, heaven, intoxication, joy, joyfulness, joyousness, jubilation, rapture, rapturousness

joyous *Syn* GLAD, cheerful, happy, joyful, lighthearted *Ant* sad

jubilant *Syn* EXULTANT, exulting, glorying, rejoicing, triumphant

jubilee *Syn* FESTIVAL, carnival, celebration, festivity, fete (*or* fête), fiesta, gala

judge *n* • a person who impartially decides unsettled questions or controversial issues *Syn* arbiter, arbitrator, referee, umpire

judge *vb* **1** • to decide something in dispute or controversy upon its merits and upon evidence *Syn* adjudge, adjudicate, arbitrate *Rel* decide, determine, rule, settle **2** *Syn* ESTIMATE (sense 2), calculate, call, conjecture, figure, gauge, guess, make, place, put, reckon, suppose **3** *Syn* INFER, conclude, deduce, gather

judgment **1** *Syn* INFERENCE (sense 1), conclusion, deduction **2** *Syn* SENSE, common sense, good sense, gumption, horse sense, wisdom

judicious **1** *Syn* EXPEDIENT, advisable, desirable, politic, prudent, tactical, wise *Ant* imprudent, inadvisable, inexpedient, injudicious, unwise **2** *Syn* WISE, prudent, sage, sane, sapient, sensible *Ant* simple

jug *Syn* JAIL, brig, guardroom, hoosegow, lockup, pen, penitentiary, prison, stockade

jugglery *Syn* TRICKERY, artifice, chicanery, hanky-panky, legerdemain, subterfuge, wile

jumble *n* *Syn* CONFUSION, chaos, clutter, disarray, disorder, muddle, snarl

jumble *vb* *Syn* DISORDER, confuse, derange, disarrange, disarray, discompose, dishevel, dislocate, disorganize, disrupt, disturb, hash, mess (up), mix (up), muddle, muss, rumple, scramble, shuffle, tousle, tumble, upset *Ant* arrange, array, draw up, marshal, order, organize, range, regulate, straighten (up), tidy

jumbled *Syn* MESSY, chaotic, cluttered, confused, disarranged, disarrayed, disheveled (*or* dishevelled), disordered, disorderly, higgledy-piggledy, hugger-mugger, littered, messed, muddled, mussed, mussy, pell-mell, rumpled, sloppy, topsy-turvy, tousled, tumbled, unkempt, untidy, upside-down *Ant* neat, ordered, orderly, organized, shipshape, snug, tidied, tidy, trim

jumbo *Syn* GIANT, behemoth, blockbuster, colossus, leviathan, mammoth, monster, titan, whale, whopper *Ant* dwarf, midget, mini, miniature, peewee, pygmy, runt, shrimp

jump *n* • a sudden move through space *Syn* bound, leap, spring, vault

jump *vb* • to move suddenly through space by or as if by muscular action *Syn* bound, leap, spring, vault

jump (on) *Syn* ATTACK (sense 2), abuse, assail, belabor, blast, castigate, excoriate, lambaste (*or* lambast), scathe, slam, vituperate

jumpy **1** *Syn* EXCITABLE, flighty, fluttery, high-strung, jittery, nervous, skittish, spooky *Ant* unflappable **2** *Syn* IMPATIENT, fidgety, jittery, nervous, restive, restless, uneasy, unquiet *Ant* patient

junction • the act, state, or place of meeting or uniting *Syn* concourse, confluence

juncture • a critical or crucial time or state of affairs *Syn* contingency, crisis, emergency, exigency, pass, pinch, strait *Rel* condition, posture, situation, state, status

junior *adj* *Syn* LESSER, inferior, less, lower, minor, smaller, subordinate, under *Ant* greater, higher, major, more, primary, prime, senior, superior

junior *n* *Syn* UNDERLING, inferior, subordinate *Ant* senior, superior

junk *Syn* DISCARD, cast, molt, scrap, shed, slough

jurisdiction *Syn* RULE (sense 2), administration, authority, governance, government, regime, regimen

just **1** *Syn* FAIR, dispassionate, equitable, impartial, objective, unbiased, uncolored *Ant* unfair **2** *Syn* UPRIGHT, conscientious, honest, honorable, scrupulous

justifiable *Syn* TENABLE, defendable, defensible, maintainable, supportable, sustainable *Ant* indefensible, insupportable, unjustifiable, untenable

justification *Syn* EXCUSE, alibi, defense, plea, reason

justify *Syn* MAINTAIN, assert, defend, vindicate

jut *Syn* BULGE, beetle, overhang, project, protrude, stick out

juvenile **1** *Syn* CALLOW, adolescent, green, immature, inexperienced, puerile, raw, unfledged, unripe, unripened *Ant* adult, experienced, grown-up, mature, ripe **2** *Syn* CHILDISH, adolescent, babyish, immature, infantile, kiddish, puerile *Ant* adult, grown-up, mature **3** *Syn* YOUNG, adolescent, immature, youngish, youthful *Ant* adult, full-grown, mature, matured

juxtaposed *Syn* ADJACENT, abutting, adjoining, bordering, contiguous, flanking, fringing, joining, skirting, touching, verging *Ant* nonadjacent

K

keen *vb Syn* CRY, blubber, wail, weep, whimper

keen *adj* **1** *Syn* EAGER, agog, anxious, athirst, avid *Ant* listless **2** *Syn* EXCELLENT, A1, bang-up, banner, capital, classic, crackerjack, dandy, divine, fabulous, fine, first-class, first-rate, grand, great, groovy, heavenly, jim-dandy, marvelous (*or* marvellous), mean, neat, nifty, noble, par excellence, prime, sensational, splendid, stellar, sterling, superb, superior, superlative, supernal, swell, terrific, tip-top, top, top-notch, unsurpassed, wonderful *Ant* poor **3** *Syn* SHARP, acute *Ant* blunt, dull

keen *n Syn* LAMENT, groan, howl, lamentation, moan, plaint, wail *Ant* exultation, rejoicing

keep *vb* **1** • to notice or honor a day, occasion, or deed *Syn* celebrate, commemorate, observe, solemnize *Rel* regard, respect *Ant* break **2** • to hold in one's possession or under one's control *Syn* detain, hold back, keep back, keep out, reserve, retain, withhold *Rel* conserve, preserve, save *Ant* relinquish

keep *n Syn* LIVING, bread, bread and butter, livelihood, maintenance, subsistence, support, sustenance

keep back *Syn* KEEP (sense 2), detain, hold back, keep out, reserve, retain, withhold *Ant* relinquish

keeping *Syn* CUSTODY, care, guardianship, safekeeping, trust, ward

keep out *Syn* KEEP (sense 2), detain, hold back, keep back, reserve, retain, withhold *Ant* relinquish

keepsake *Syn* MEMORIAL, commemorative, memento, monument, remembrance, reminder, souvenir, token

keg *Syn* CASK, barrel, firkin, hogshead, pipe, puncheon

ken *Syn* RANGE, compass, gamut, horizon, orbit, purview, radius, reach, scope, sweep

kerchief *Syn* BANDANNA, babushka, handkerchief, mantilla

key *Syn* CRUCIAL, critical, pivotal, vital

kibitzer **1** *Syn* BUSYBODY, interferer, interloper, intruder, meddler **2** *Syn* SPECTATOR, beholder, bystander, eyewitness, looker-on, observer, onlooker, witness

kick *vb* **1** *Syn* COMPLAIN, beef, bellyache, carp, crab, croak, fuss, gripe, grouse, growl, grumble, moan, murmur, mutter, repine, squawk, wail, whine, yammer *Ant* rejoice **2** *Syn* OBJECT, expostulate, protest, remonstrate *Ant* acquiesce

kick *n Syn* THRILL, bang, exhilaration, titillation

kick off *Syn* BEGIN (sense 2), commence, embark (on *or* upon), enter (into *or* upon), get off, launch, open, start, strike (into) *Ant* conclude, end, finish, terminate

kid **1** *Syn* BANTER, chaff, jolly, josh, rag, rib **2** *Syn* JOKE, banter, fool, fun, jest, jive, josh, quip, wisecrack **3** *Syn* TEASE, chaff, jive, josh, rally, razz, rib, ride, roast

kiddish *Syn* CHILDISH, adolescent, babyish, immature, infantile, juvenile, puerile *Ant* adult, grown-up, mature

kidney *Syn* TYPE, character, description, ilk, kind, nature, sort, stripe

kill • to deprive of life *Syn* assassinate, dispatch, execute, murder, slay

killer *Syn* DEADLY, baleful, deathly, fatal, fell, lethal, mortal, murderous, pestilent, vital *Ant* healthful, healthy, nonfatal, nonlethal, wholesome

kin *Syn* RELATIVE, kinsman, relation

kind *adj* • showing or having a gentle considerate nature *Syn* benign, benignant, kindly *Rel* altruistic, benevolent, charitable, eleemosynary, humane, humanitarian, philanthropic *Ant* unkind

kind *n Syn* TYPE, character, description, ilk, kidney, nature, sort, stripe

kindle *Syn* LIGHT, fire, ignite

kindly *Syn* KIND, benign, benignant *Ant* unkind

kindred *Syn* RELATED, affiliated, allied, cognate

kingly • of, relating to, or befitting one who occupies a throne *Syn* imperial, princely, queenly, regal, royal

kingpin *Syn* BOSS, captain, chief, foreman, head, headman, helmsman, leader, master, taskmaster
king-size *or* **king-sized** *Syn* LONG (sense 1), elongated, extended, lengthy *Ant* brief, short
kinsman *Syn* RELATIVE, kin, relation
knack *Syn* GIFT (sense 2), aptitude, bent, faculty, genius, talent, turn
knave *Syn* VILLAIN, blackguard, miscreant, rapscallion, rascal, rogue, scamp, scoundrel
knickknack • a small object displayed for its attractiveness or interest *Syn* bauble, curio, curiosity, gaud, gewgaw, novelty, ornamental, trinket *Rel* bric-a-brac, trumpery
knit *Syn* WEAVE, braid, crochet, plait, tat
knock *n* **1** *Syn* MISFORTUNE, adversity, misadventure, mischance, mishap *Ant* fortune, luck **2** *Syn* TAP, rap, thud, thump
knock *vb Syn* TAP, rap, thud, thump
knockabout *Syn* BOISTEROUS, rambunctious, raucous, rowdy *Ant* orderly
knockout *adj Syn* BEAUTIFUL, attractive, beauteous, comely, cute, fair, gorgeous, handsome, lovely, pretty, ravishing, sightly, stunning, taking *Ant* homely, ill-favored, plain, ugly, unattractive, unbeautiful, unhandsome, unlovely, unpretty, unsightly
knockout *n* **1** *Syn* FAINT, blackout, coma, insensibility, swoon **2** *Syn* JIM-DANDY, beauty, corker, crackerjack, dandy, nifty, pip
knotty *Syn* COMPLEX, complicated, intricate, involved *Ant* simple
knowing *Syn* INTELLIGENT, alert, bright, brilliant, clever, quick-witted, smart *Ant* unintelligent
knowingly *Syn* INTENTIONALLY, consciously, deliberately, designedly, purposefully, purposely, willfully, wittingly *Ant* inadvertently, unconsciously, unintentionally, unknowingly, unwittingly
knowledge **1** • what is or can be known by an individual or by mankind *Syn* erudition, information, learning, lore, scholarship, science *Ant* ignorance **2** *Syn* EDUCATION (sense 2), erudition, learnedness, learning, scholarship, science
knowledgeable *Syn* EDUCATED, erudite, learned, literate, scholarly, well-read *Ant* ignorant, illiterate, uneducated
kook *Syn* ECCENTRIC, character, codger, crackbrain, crackpot, crank, nut, oddball, screwball, weirdo

L

label *n Syn* MARK, brand, stamp, tag, ticket
label *vb Syn* MARK, brand, stamp, tag, ticket
labor *vb* • to devote serious and sustained effort *Syn* drudge, endeavor, grub, hump, hustle, moil, peg (away), plod, plow, plug, slave, slog, strain, strive, struggle, sweat, toil, travail, work *Rel* apply (oneself), attempt, buckle (down), hammer (away), pitch in *Ant* dabble, fiddle (around), fool (around), mess (around), putter (around)
labor *n Syn* WORK (sense 1), drudgery, grind, toil, travail *Ant* play
labored *Syn* FORCED, strained
laborer **1** *Syn* SLAVE (sense 2), drudge, drudger, grubber, peon, plugger, slogger, toiler, worker *Ant* freeman **2** *Syn* WORKER, artisan, craftsman, hand, handicraftsman, mechanic, operative, roustabout, workingman, workman *Ant* idler
lace **1** *Syn* BRAID, lacing, plait **2** *Syn* CORD, cable, lacing, line, rope, string, wire
lacing **1** *Syn* BRAID, lace, plait **2** *Syn* CORD, cable, lace, line, rope, string, wire
lack *n* **1** • the fact or state of being wanting or deficient *Syn* absence, dearth, defect, privation, want *Rel* exigency, necessity, need **2** *Syn* DEFICIENCY, dearth, deficit, failure, famine, inadequacy, insufficiency, paucity, poverty, scantiness, scarceness, scarcity, shortage, want *Ant* abundance, adequacy, amplitude, plenitude, plenty, sufficiency
lack *vb* • to be without something and especially something essential or greatly needed *Syn* need, require, want
lackadaisical *Syn* LISTLESS, enervated, languid, languishing, languorous, limp, spiritless *Ant* ambitious, animated, energetic, enterprising, motivated
lackey *Syn* SERVANT, domestic, flunky, menial, retainer, steward *Ant* master
laconic *Syn* CONCISE, compendious, pithy, succinct, summary, terse *Ant* redundant
laconically *Syn* SUCCINCTLY, briefly, compactly, concisely, crisply, pithily, summarily, tersely *Ant* diffusely, long-windedly, verbosely, wordily
lacuna *Syn* BREAK, gap, hiatus, interim, interruption, interval
lad *Syn* BOY, laddie, nipper, shaver, sonny, stripling, tad, youth
laddie *Syn* BOY, lad, nipper, shaver, sonny, stripling, tad, youth
lade *Syn* BURDEN, charge, cumber, encumber, load, saddle, tax, weigh, weight
lading *Syn* LOAD, burden, cargo, freight
ladle *Syn* DIP (sense 2), bail, dish, scoop, spoon

lady 1 *Syn* WOMAN, female 2 *Syn* GIRLFRIEND, gal, woman 3 *Syn* GENTLEWOMAN, dame, noblewoman
ladylike *Syn* FEMALE, feminine, womanish, womanlike, womanly *Ant* male
lag *Syn* DELAY (sense 2), dawdle, loiter, procrastinate *Ant* hasten, hurry
laggard *Syn* SLOW, deliberate, dilatory, leisurely *Ant* fast
laggardly *Syn* SLOW, leisurely, slowly, sluggishly, tardily *Ant* apace, briskly, fast, fleetly, full tilt, hastily, quick, quickly, rapidly, snappily, speedily, swift, swiftly
lagniappe *Syn* BONUS, dividend, extra, gratuity, gravy, perquisite, tip
lamb • an innocent or gentle person *Syn* angel, dove, innocent, sheep *Rel* cherub, saint *Ant* wolf
lambaste *or* **lambast** *Syn* ATTACK (sense 2), abuse, assail, belabor, blast, castigate, excoriate, jump (on), scathe, slam, vituperate
lambent *Syn* BRIGHT, beaming, brilliant, effulgent, incandescent, lucent, luminous, lustrous, radiant, refulgent *Ant* dim, dull
lament *n* • a crying out in grief *Syn* groan, howl, keen, lamentation, moan, plaint, wail *Rel* grieving, mourning, weeping *Ant* exultation, rejoicing
lament *vb* *Syn* REGRET, bemoan, deplore, repent, rue
lamentable *Syn* REGRETTABLE, deplorable, distressful, distressing, grievous, heartbreaking, heartrending, unfortunate, woeful
lamentation *Syn* LAMENT, groan, howl, keen, moan, plaint, wail *Ant* exultation, rejoicing
land *vb* 1 *Syn* ALIGHT, light, perch, roost, settle, touch down *Ant* take off 2 *Syn* EARN, acquire, attain, capture, carry, draw, gain, garner, get, make, obtain, procure, realize, secure, win *Ant* forfeit, lose
land *n* *Syn* NATION, commonwealth, country, sovereignty, state
landing field *Syn* AIRPORT, airdrome, airfield, airstrip, flying field, landing strip
landing strip *Syn* AIRPORT, airdrome, airfield, airstrip, flying field, landing field
landmark *Syn* TURNING POINT, climax, milestone
language 1 • a body or system of words and phrases used by a large community or by a people, a nation, or a group of nations *Syn* dialect, idiom, speech, tongue *Rel* argot, cant, jargon, lingo, patois, slang, vernacular 2 • oral or written expression or a quality of such expression that is dependent on the variety, arrangement, or expressiveness of words *Syn* diction, phraseology, phrasing, style, vocabulary 3 *Syn* TERMINOLOGY, argot, cant, dialect, jargon, lingo, patois, patter, slang, vocabulary
languid *Syn* LISTLESS, enervated, lackadaisical, languishing, languorous, limp, spiritless *Ant* ambitious, animated, energetic, enterprising, motivated
languishing *Syn* LISTLESS, enervated, lackadaisical, languid, languorous, limp, spiritless *Ant* ambitious, animated, energetic, enterprising, motivated
languor *Syn* LETHARGY, lassitude, stupor, torpidity, torpor *Ant* vigor
languorous *Syn* LISTLESS, enervated, lackadaisical, languid, languishing, limp, spiritless *Ant* ambitious, animated, energetic, enterprising, motivated
lank *Syn* LEAN, angular, gaunt, lanky, rawboned, scrawny, skinny, spare *Ant* fleshy
lanky 1 • being tall, thin and usually loose-jointed *Syn* gangling, gangly, rangy, spindling, spindly *Rel* angular, bony, gaunt, lank, rawboned, scrawny, skinny 2 *Syn* LEAN, angular, gaunt, lank, rawboned, scrawny, skinny, spare *Ant* fleshy
lap *Syn* OVERLAP, overlay, overlie, overspread
lapse *vb* • to fall from a better or higher state into a lower or poorer one *Syn* backslide, relapse *Rel* return, revert
lapse *n* *Syn* ERROR, blunder, bull, faux pas, howler, mistake, slip
larcener *Syn* THIEF, burglar, larcenist, robber
larcenist *Syn* THIEF, burglar, larcener, robber
larceny *Syn* THEFT, burglary, robbery
large • of a size greater than average of its kind *Syn* big, bulky, considerable, goodly, good-sized, grand, great, handsome, hefty, hulking, largish, outsize, oversize (*or* oversized), sizable (*or* sizeable), substantial, tidy, voluminous *Rel* abundant, ample, appreciable, astronomical, bumper, capacious, cavernous, colossal, commodious, copious, enormous, excessive, exorbitant, extravagant, extreme, fat, gigantic, gross, heroic, huge, immense, immoderate, inordinate, jumbo, king-size (*or* king-sized), major, mammoth, massive, monolithic, monstrous, monumental, plentiful, prodigious, roomy, spacious, staggering, stupendous, super, thick, tremendous, vast, vasty, whacking, whopping *Ant* little, puny, small, undersized
largely 1 • in a reasonably inclusive manner *Syn* chiefly, generally, greatly, mainly, mostly, principally 2 *Syn* CHIEFLY, altogether, basically, by and large, generally, mainly, mostly, overall, predominantly, primarily, principally, substantially
largess *Syn* GIFT (sense 1), boon, favor, gratuity, present
largish *Syn* LARGE, big, bulky, considerable, goodly, good-sized, grand, great, handsome, hefty, hulking, outsize, oversize (*or* oversized), sizable (*or* sizeable), substantial, tidy, voluminous *Ant* little, puny, small, undersized
lascivious *Syn* LICENTIOUS, lecherous, lewd, libertine, libidinous, lustful, wanton *Ant* continent

lass *Syn* GIRL, lassie, miss, missy
lassie *Syn* GIRL, lass, miss, missy
lassitude **1** *Syn* FATIGUE, burnout, collapse, exhaustion, prostration, tiredness, weariness *Ant* refreshment, rejuvenation, revitalization **2** *Syn* LETHARGY, languor, stupor, torpidity, torpor *Ant* vigor
last *adj* • following all others as in time, order, or importance *Syn* concluding, eventual, final, latest, terminal, ultimate *Ant* first
last *vb Syn* CONTINUE, abide, endure, persist
lasting • enduring so long as to seem fixed or established *Syn* durable, perdurable, permanent, perpetual, stable *Rel* abiding, continuing, enduring, persistent, persisting *Ant* fleeting
late **1** *Syn* DEAD, deceased, defunct, departed, inanimate, lifeless **2** *Syn* FORMER, erstwhile, old, onetime, past, sometime, whilom **3** *Syn* TARDY, behindhand, overdue *Ant* prompt
latency *Syn* ABEYANCE, doldrums, dormancy, quiescence, suspense, suspension *Ant* continuance, continuation
latent • not now showing signs of activity or existence *Syn* abeyant, dormant, potential, quiescent *Rel* concealed, hidden *Ant* patent
later *Syn* AFTER, afterward (*or* afterwards), subsequently, thereafter *Ant* before, beforehand, earlier, previously
latest *Syn* LAST, concluding, eventual, final, terminal, ultimate *Ant* first
lather *Syn* FOAM, froth, scum, spume, suds, yeast
laud **1** *Syn* ACCLAIM, applaud, cheer, hail, praise, salute, tout *Ant* knock, pan, slam **2** *Syn* PRAISE, acclaim, eulogize, extol *Ant* blame
laudable *Syn* ADMIRABLE, commendable, creditable, meritorious, praiseworthy *Ant* censurable, discreditable, reprehensible
laughable • provoking laughter or mirth *Syn* comic, comical, droll, farcical, funny, ludicrous, ridiculous, risible *Rel* amusing, diverting, entertaining
laughing *Syn* MERRY, blithesome, festive, gay, gleeful, jocose, jocund, jolly, jovial, mirthful, sunny
laughingstock • a person or thing that is made fun of *Syn* butt, mark, mock, mockery, target *Rel* chump, dupe, fall guy, fool, gull, monkey, pigeon, sap, sucker, victim
launch *n Syn* BEGINNING, alpha, birth, commencement, dawn, genesis, inception, incipiency, morning, onset, outset, start, threshold *Ant* close, conclusion, end, ending
launch *vb Syn* BEGIN (sense 2), commence, embark (on *or* upon), enter (into *or* upon), get off, kick off, open, start, strike (into) *Ant* conclude, end, finish, terminate
lavalier *Syn* PENDANT, bangle, charm
lavish **1** *Syn* LUXURIOUS, deluxe, luxuriant, opulent, palatial, plush, sumptuous *Ant* ascetic, austere, humble, Spartan **2** *Syn* PROFUSE, exuberant, lush, luxuriant, prodigal *Ant* scant, scanty, spare
lavishly *Syn* HIGH, expensively, extravagantly, grandly, luxuriously, opulently, richly, sumptuously *Ant* austerely, humbly, modestly, plainly, simply
law **1** • a principle governing action or procedure *Syn* canon, ordinance, precept, regulation, rule, statute *Rel* command, dictate, mandate **2** *Syn* PRINCIPLE, axiom, fundamental, theorem
law-abiding *Syn* OBEDIENT, amenable, compliant, conformable, docile, submissive, tractable *Ant* contrary, disobedient, froward, insubordinate, intractable, rebellious, recalcitrant, refractory, unruly
lawbreaking *Syn* LAWLESS, anarchic, disorderly, unruly *Ant* law-abiding, orderly
lawful • being in accordance with law *Syn* legal, legitimate, licit *Rel* condign, due, rightful *Ant* unlawful
lawless • not restrained by or under the control of legal authority *Syn* anarchic, disorderly, lawbreaking, unruly *Rel* defiant, insubordinate, mutinous, rebellious, refractory, riotous *Ant* law-abiding, orderly
lawlessness *Syn* ANARCHY, chaos, misrule
lawsuit *Syn* SUIT, action, case, cause
lawyer • a person authorized to practice law in the courts or to serve clients in the capacity of legal agent or adviser *Syn* advocate, attorney, barrister, counsel, counselor, solicitor
lax **1** *Syn* LOOSE, relaxed, slack *Ant* strict, tight **2** *Syn* NEGLIGENT, careless, derelict, neglectful, neglecting, remiss, slack *Ant* attentive, careful, conscientious
lay *vb* **1** *Syn* BET, gamble, go, stake, wager **2** *Syn* IMPOSE, assess, charge, exact, fine, levy, put *Ant* remit
lay *n Syn* MELODY, air, song, strain, tune, warble
lay *adj Syn* PROFANE, secular, temporal *Ant* sacred
lay away *Syn* HOARD, cache, lay up, put by, salt away, squirrel (away), stash, stockpile, store, stow
lay down *Syn* ENACT, legislate, make, pass *Ant* repeal, rescind, revoke
lay up *Syn* HOARD, cache, lay away, put by, salt away, squirrel (away), stash, stockpile, store, stow
laze *Syn* IDLE, loaf, loll, lounge
lazy • not easily aroused to activity *Syn* faineant, indolent, slothful *Rel* idle, inactive, inert, passive, supine *Ant* industrious
lazybones • a lazy person *Syn* drone, idler, loafer, slouch, slug, sluggard *Rel* bum, ne'er-do-well *Ant* doer, go-getter, hummer, hustler, rustler, self-starter
lead *vb Syn* GUIDE, engineer, pilot, steer *Ant* misguide

lead *adj Syn* HEAD, chief, commanding, first, foremost, high, leading, managing, preeminent, premier, presiding, primary, prime, principal, supreme

leaden *Syn* BORING, drab, dreary, dry, dull, flat, heavy, humdrum, jading, monotonous, pedestrian, ponderous, stodgy, stuffy, stupid, tame, tedious, tiresome, tiring, unanimated, uninteresting, wearisome, weary, wearying *Ant* absorbing, engaging, engrossing, gripping, interesting, intriguing, involving

leader **1** *Syn* BOSS, captain, chief, foreman, head, headman, helmsman, kingpin, master, taskmaster **2** *Syn* CHIEF, chieftain, head, headman, master

leading **1** *Syn* CHIEF, capital, foremost, main, principal *Ant* subordinate **2** *Syn* HEAD, chief, commanding, first, foremost, high, lead, managing, preeminent, premier, presiding, primary, prime, principal, supreme

lead on *Syn* LURE, allure, beguile, decoy, entice, seduce, tempt

league *n Syn* ALLIANCE, coalition, confederacy, confederation, federation, fusion

league *vb Syn* ALLY, associate, band, club, confederate, conjoin, cooperate, federate, unite *Ant* break up, disband

lean *adj* • thin because of an absence of excess flesh *Syn* angular, gaunt, lank, lanky, rawboned, scrawny, skinny, spare *Rel* slender, slight, slim, thin *Ant* fleshy

lean *vb Syn* SLANT, incline, slope

leaning • a strong instinct or liking for something *Syn* flair, penchant, proclivity, propensity *Rel* bias, partiality, predilection, prejudice, prepossession *Ant* distaste

leap *vb Syn* JUMP, bound, spring, vault

leap *n Syn* JUMP, bound, spring, vault

learn *Syn* DISCOVER, ascertain, determine, unearth

learned **1** • possessing or manifesting unusually wide and deep knowledge *Syn* erudite, scholarly *Rel* cultivated, cultured **2** *Syn* BOOKISH, erudite, literary *Ant* colloquial, nonliterary **3** *Syn* EDUCATED, erudite, knowledgeable, literate, scholarly, well-read *Ant* ignorant, illiterate, uneducated

learnedness *Syn* EDUCATION (sense 2), erudition, knowledge, learning, scholarship, science

learning **1** *Syn* EDUCATION (sense 2), erudition, knowledge, learnedness, scholarship, science **2** *Syn* KNOWLEDGE, erudition, information, lore, scholarship, science *Ant* ignorance

lease *Syn* HIRE, charter, let, rent

least *Syn* MINIMAL, littlest, lowest, minimum, slightest *Ant* full, greatest, largest, maximum, top, topmost, utmost

leave *vb* **1** *Syn* GO, depart, quit, retire, withdraw *Ant* come **2** *Syn* LET, allow, permit, suffer **3** *Syn* RELINQUISH, abandon, cede, resign, surrender, waive, yield *Ant* keep **4** *Syn* WILL, bequeath, devise, legate

leave *n Syn* PERMISSION, allowance, authorization, clearance, concurrence, consent, granting, license (*or* licence), sanction, sufferance *Ant* interdiction, prohibition, proscription

leaven *Syn* INFUSE, imbue, ingrain, inoculate, suffuse

leavings *Syn* REMAINDER, balance, remains, remnant, residue, residuum, rest

lecherous *Syn* LICENTIOUS, lascivious, lewd, libertine, libidinous, lustful, wanton *Ant* continent

lecture *Syn* SPEECH, address, harangue, homily, oration, sermon, talk

leech *Syn* PARASITE, bootlicker, favorite, hanger-on, lickspittle, sponge, sponger, sycophant, toady

lees *Syn* DEPOSIT, dregs, grounds, precipitate, sediment

leeway *Syn* ROOM (sense 2), berth, clearance, elbow room, margin, play

left-handed *Syn* INSINCERE, artificial, backhanded, double-dealing, feigned, hypocritical, mealy, mealymouthed, two-faced, unctuous *Ant* genuine, heartfelt, honest, sincere, unfeigned

legal *Syn* LAWFUL, legitimate, licit *Ant* unlawful

legal tender *Syn* MONEY, cash, coin, coinage, currency, specie

legate *n Syn* AMBASSADOR, delegate, emissary, envoy, minister, representative

legate *vb Syn* WILL, bequeath, devise, leave

legend **1** *Syn* FOLKLORE, lore, myth, mythology, tradition **2** *Syn* INSCRIPTION, caption **3** *Syn* MYTH, saga

legendary *Syn* FICTITIOUS, apocryphal, fabulous, mythical *Ant* historical

legerdemain *Syn* TRICKERY, artifice, chicanery, hanky-panky, jugglery, subterfuge, wile

legion *Syn* MULTITUDE, army, host

legislate *Syn* ENACT, lay down, make, pass *Ant* repeal, rescind, revoke

leg (it) *Syn* WALK, foot (it), hoof (it), pad, step, traipse, tread

legitimate *Syn* LAWFUL, legal, licit *Ant* unlawful

leisure *Syn* REST, comfort, ease, relaxation, repose

leisurely *adj Syn* SLOW, deliberate, dilatory, laggard *Ant* fast

leisurely *adv Syn* SLOW, laggardly, slowly, sluggishly, tardily *Ant* apace, briskly, fast, fleetly, full tilt, hastily, quick, quickly, rapidly, snappily, speedily, swift, swiftly

leitmotiv *Syn* SUBJECT, argument, matter, motif, motive, subject matter, text, theme, topic

lengthen *Syn* EXTEND, elongate, prolong, protract *Ant* abridge, shorten

lengthy **1** *Syn* LONG (sense 1), elongated, extended, king-size (*or* king-sized) *Ant* brief, short **2** *Syn* LONG (sense 2), extended, far, great, long-lived, long-range, long-term, marathon *Ant* brief, short, short-lived, short-range, short-term

leniency *Syn* FORBEARANCE, clemency, indulgence, mercifulness, tolerance *Ant* anger, vindictiveness

lenient **1** *Syn* FORBEARING, clement, indulgent, merciful, tolerant *Ant* unrelenting **2** *Syn* SOFT, balmy, bland, gentle, mild, smooth *Ant* hard, stern

leniently *Syn* FORBEARINGLY, clemently, indulgently, mercifully, tolerantly

lenity *Syn* MERCY, charity, clemency, grace

lesion *Syn* WOUND, bruise, contusion, trauma, traumatism

less *Syn* LESSER, inferior, junior, lower, minor, smaller, subordinate, under *Ant* greater, higher, major, more, primary, prime, senior, superior

lessen *Syn* DECREASE, abate, diminish, dwindle, reduce *Ant* increase

lesser • having not so great importance or rank as another *Syn* inferior, junior, less, lower, minor, smaller, subordinate, under *Rel* little, mean, small *Ant* greater, higher, major, more, primary, prime, senior, superior

let *vb* **1** • to neither forbid nor prevent *Syn* allow, leave, permit, suffer *Rel* accredit, approve, certify, endorse, sanction **2** *Syn* HIRE, charter, lease, rent

let *n* *Syn* ENCUMBRANCE, bar, block, chain, clog, crimp, deterrent, drag, embarrassment, fetter, handicap, hindrance, hurdle, impediment, inhibition, interference, manacle, obstacle, obstruction, shackles, stop, stumbling block, trammel *Ant* aid, assistance, benefit, help

letdown **1** *Syn* DISAPPOINTMENT (sense 1), dismay, dissatisfaction, frustration *Ant* contentment, gratification, satisfaction **2** *Syn* DISAPPOINTMENT (sense 2), bummer

lethal *Syn* DEADLY, baleful, deathly, fatal, fell, killer, mortal, murderous, pestilent, vital *Ant* healthful, healthy, nonfatal, nonlethal, wholesome

lethargic • deficient in alertness or activity *Syn* comatose, sluggish, torpid *Rel* idle, inactive, inert, passive, supine *Ant* energetic, vigorous

lethargy • physical or mental inertness *Syn* languor, lassitude, stupor, torpidity, torpor *Rel* comatoseness, sluggishness *Ant* vigor

letter • a direct or personal written or printed message addressed to a person or organization *Syn* dispatch, epistle, memorandum, message, missive, note, report

levee **1** *Syn* DAM, dike, embankment **2** *Syn* WHARF, berth, dock, jetty, pier, quay, slip

level *adj* • having a surface without bends, curves, or irregularities *Syn* even, flat, flush, plain, plane, smooth *Rel* akin, alike, identical, like, parallel, similar, uniform

level *vb* *Syn* EQUALIZE, balance, equate, even

levelheadedness *Syn* COMMON SENSE, discreetness, discretion, horse sense, prudence, sense, sensibleness, wisdom, wit *Ant* imprudence, indiscretion

leviathan *Syn* GIANT, behemoth, blockbuster, colossus, jumbo, mammoth, monster, titan, whale, whopper *Ant* dwarf, midget, mini, miniature, peewee, pygmy, runt, shrimp

levity **1** *Syn* FRIVOLITY, facetiousness, flightiness, flippancy, frivolousness, lightheadedness, lightness **2** *Syn* LIGHTNESS, flightiness, flippancy, frivolity, light-mindedness, volatility *Ant* seriousness

levy *vb* *Syn* IMPOSE, assess, charge, exact, fine, lay, put *Ant* remit

levy *n* *Syn* TAX, assessment, duty, imposition, impost

lewd *Syn* LICENTIOUS, lascivious, lecherous, libertine, libidinous, lustful, wanton *Ant* continent

liability **1** *Syn* DEBT, arrear, debit, indebtedness, obligation **2** *Syn* DISADVANTAGE, drawback, handicap, minus, penalty, strike *Ant* advantage, asset, edge, plus

liable **1** • being by nature or through circumstances likely to experience something adverse *Syn* exposed, open, prone, sensitive, subject, susceptible *Ant* exempt, immune **2** *Syn* RESPONSIBLE, accountable, amenable, answerable

liaison *Syn* AMOUR, affair, intrigue

libel *Syn* SLANDER, asperse, blacken, defame, malign, smear, traduce, vilify

libelous *or* **libellous** • causing or intended to cause unjust injury to a person's good name *Syn* defamatory, scandalous, slanderous *Rel* erroneous, false, inaccurate, incorrect, inexact, invalid, off, unsound, untrue, wrong

liberal **1** • giving or given freely and unstintingly *Syn* bounteous, bountiful, generous, handsome, munificent, openhanded *Rel* exuberant, lavish, prodigal, profuse *Ant* close **2** • not bound by what is orthodox, established, or traditional *Syn* advanced, progressive, radical *Rel* forbearing, indulgent, lenient, tolerant *Ant* authoritarian

liberate *Syn* FREE, discharge, emancipate, manumit, release

libertine *Syn* LICENTIOUS, lascivious, lecherous, lewd, libidinous, lustful, wanton *Ant* continent

liberty *Syn* FREEDOM (sense 2), license *Ant* necessity

libidinous *Syn* LICENTIOUS, lascivious, lecherous, lewd, libertine, lustful, wanton *Ant* continent

licensable *Syn* PERMISSIBLE, admissible, allowable *Ant* banned, barred, forbidden, impermissible, inadmissible, interdicted, prohibited, proscribed

license *vb Syn* AUTHORIZE, accredit, commission

license *n* **1** *Syn* FREEDOM (sense 2), liberty *Ant* necessity **2** *Syn* PERMISSION, allowance, authorization, clearance, concurrence, consent, granting, leave, sanction, sufferance *Ant* interdiction, prohibition, proscription

licentious • lacking moral restraint especially in a disregarding of sexual restraints *Syn* lascivious, lecherous, lewd, libertine, libidinous, lustful, wanton *Rel* abandoned, dissolute, profligate, reprobate *Ant* continent

licit *Syn* LAWFUL, legal, legitimate *Ant* unlawful

lick *Syn* CONQUER, beat, defeat, overcome, overthrow, reduce, rout, subdue, subjugate, surmount, vanquish

lickspittle *Syn* PARASITE, bootlicker, favorite, hanger-on, leech, sponge, sponger, sycophant, toady

lie *n* • a statement or declaration that is not true *Syn* falsehood, fib, misrepresentation, story, untruth *Rel* equivocation, fib, fibbing, prevarication *Ant* truth

lie *vb* • to tell an untruth *Syn* equivocate, fib, palter, prevaricate *Rel* beguile, deceive, delude, mislead

life *Syn* BIOGRAPHY, autobiography, confessions, memoir

lifeless *Syn* DEAD, deceased, defunct, departed, inanimate, late

lift **1** • to move from a lower to a higher place or position *Syn* boost, elevate, heave, hoist, raise, rear *Rel* arise, ascend, levitate, mount, rise, rocket, soar, surge, tower *Ant* lower **2** *Syn* ASCEND, arise, climb, mount, rise, soar, up, uprise, upsweep, upturn *Ant* decline, descend, dip, drop, fall (off) **3** *Syn* STEAL, cop, filch, pilfer, pinch, purloin, snitch, swipe

light *vb* **1** • to cause something to start burning *Syn* fire, ignite, kindle **2** *Syn* ALIGHT, land, perch, roost, settle, touch down *Ant* take off **3** *Syn* ILLUMINATE, enlighten, illustrate, lighten *Ant* darken, obscure

light *adj Syn* EASY, effortless, facile, simple, smooth *Ant* hard

lighten **1** *Syn* ILLUMINATE, enlighten, illustrate, light *Ant* darken, obscure **2** *Syn* RELIEVE, allay, alleviate, assuage, mitigate *Ant* alarm, embarrass, intensify

light-headedness *Syn* FRIVOLITY, facetiousness, flightiness, flippancy, frivolousness, levity, lightness

lighthearted **1** *Syn* CAREFREE, careless, cavalier, devil-may-care, easygoing, gay, happy-go-lucky, insouciant, unconcerned *Ant* careworn **2** *Syn* GLAD, cheerful, happy, joyful, joyous *Ant* sad

lightheartedness *Syn* ABANDON, abandonment, ease, naturalness, spontaneity, unrestraint *Ant* constraint, restraint

lightly *Syn* EASILY, effortlessly, facilely, fluently, freely, handily, painlessly, readily, smoothly *Ant* arduously, laboriously

light-mindedness *Syn* LIGHTNESS, flightiness, flippancy, frivolity, levity, volatility *Ant* seriousness

lightness **1** • gaiety or indifference where seriousness and attention are called for *Syn* flightiness, flippancy, frivolity, levity, light-mindedness, volatility *Rel* buoyancy, effervescence, elasticity, expansiveness, resiliency *Ant* seriousness **2** *Syn* FRIVOLITY, facetiousness, flightiness, flippancy, frivolousness, levity, light-headedness

lightsome *Syn* CHEERFUL (sense 1), blithe, blithesome, bright, buoyant, cheery, chipper, gay, gladsome, sunny, upbeat *Ant* dour, gloomy, glum, morose, saturnine, sulky, sullen

like *vb* • to feel attraction toward or take pleasure in *Syn* dote, enjoy, fancy, love, relish *Rel* choose, elect, prefer, select *Ant* dislike

like *adj* **1** *Syn* ALIKE, akin, analogous, comparable, correspondent, corresponding, matching, parallel, resembling, similar, such, suchlike *Ant* different, dissimilar, diverse, unlike **2** *Syn* EQUAL, coordinate, counterpart, equivalent, fellow, match, parallel, peer, rival

like *n Syn* LIKING, appetite, fancy, favor, fondness, love, partiality, preference, relish, shine, taste, use *Ant* aversion, disfavor, dislike, distaste, hatred, loathing

likely *adj Syn* PROBABLE, possible *Ant* certain, improbable

likely *adv Syn* PROBABLY, doubtless, presumably *Ant* improbably

likeness *n Syn* SIMILARITY, alikeness, community, correspondence, parallelism, resemblance, similitude *Ant* dissimilarity, unlikeness

liking • positive regard for something *Syn* appetite, fancy, favor, fondness, like, love, partiality, preference, relish, shine, taste, use *Rel* craving, desire, longing, thirst, yen *Ant* aversion, disfavor, dislike, distaste, hatred, loathing

lily-livered *Syn* COWARDLY, chicken, chickenhearted, craven, dastardly, pusillanimous, recreant, spineless, unheroic, yellow *Ant* brave, courageous, daring, dauntless, doughty, fearless, gallant, greathearted, gutsy, hardy, heroic, intrepid, lionhearted, stalwart, stout, stouthearted, valiant, valorous

limb *Syn* SHOOT, bough, branch

limber **1** *Syn* SUPPLE, lissome, lithe, lithesome **2** *Syn* WILLOWY, flexible, lissome, lithe, pliable, pliant, supple *Ant* inflexible, rigid, stiff

limit *n* • a material or immaterial point beyond which something does not or cannot extend

Syn bound, confine, end, term *Rel* circumscription, confinement, limitation, restriction
limit *vb* • to set bounds for *Syn* circumscribe, confine, restrict *Rel* assign, define, prescribe *Ant* widen
limitation *Syn* RESTRICTION, check, condition, constraint, curb, fetter, restraint
limitless *Syn* INFINITE, boundless, endless, illimitable, immeasurable, indefinite, measureless, unbounded, unfathomable, unlimited *Ant* bounded, circumscribed, confined, definite, finite, limited, restricted
limn *Syn* REPRESENT, delineate, depict, picture, portray
limp **1** • deficient in firmness of texture, substance, or structure *Syn* flabby, flaccid, flimsy, floppy, sleazy *Rel* lax, loose, relaxed, slack **2** *Syn* LISTLESS, enervated, lackadaisical, languid, languishing, languorous, spiritless *Ant* ambitious, animated, energetic, enterprising, motivated
limpid *Syn* CLEAR (sense 1), diaphanous, lucid, pellucid, translucent, transparent *Ant* confused, turbid
line *n* **1** • a series of things arranged in continuous or uniform order *Syn* echelon, file, rank, row, tier *Rel* chain, progression, sequence, series, succession **2** *Syn* ANCESTRY, birth, blood, bloodline, breeding, descent, extraction, family tree, genealogy, lineage, origin, parentage, pedigree, stock, strain *Ant* issue, posterity, progeny, seed **3** *Syn* CORD, cable, lace, lacing, rope, string, wire **4** *Syn* OCCUPATION, calling, employment, profession, trade, vocation, work
line *vb* • to arrange in a line or in lines *Syn* align, array, line up, range *Rel* arrange, marshal, order
lineage *Syn* ANCESTRY, birth, blood, bloodline, breeding, descent, extraction, family tree, genealogy, line, origin, parentage, pedigree, stock, strain *Ant* issue, posterity, progeny, seed
line up *Syn* LINE, align, array, range
linger *Syn* STAY, abide, remain, tarry, wait
lingo *Syn* TERMINOLOGY, argot, cant, dialect, jargon, language, patois, patter, slang, vocabulary
link *Syn* JOIN, associate, combine, conjoin, connect, relate, unite *Ant* disjoin, part
liquefy • to convert or to become converted to a liquid state *Syn* deliquesce, fuse, melt, thaw
liquor *Syn* ALCOHOL, booze, drink, grog, intoxicant, moonshine, spirits
lissome **1** *Syn* SUPPLE, limber, lithe, lithesome **2** *Syn* WILLOWY, flexible, limber, lithe, pliable, pliant, supple *Ant* inflexible, rigid, stiff
list *n* • a series of items (as names) written down or printed as a memorandum or record *Syn* catalog, inventory, register, roll, roster, schedule, table
list *vb* *Syn* RECORD, catalog, enroll, register
listen • to pay attention especially through the act of hearing *Syn* attend, hark, hear, hearken, heed, mind *Ant* ignore, tune out
listing *Syn* AWRY, askew, aslant, cockeyed, crooked, lopsided, oblique, skewed, slanted, slanting, slantwise, tilted, tipping, uneven *Ant* even, level, straight
listless • lacking bodily energy or motivation *Syn* enervated, lackadaisical, languid, languishing, languorous, limp, spiritless *Rel* indolent, lazy, slothful *Ant* ambitious, animated, energetic, enterprising, motivated
literary *Syn* BOOKISH, erudite, learned *Ant* colloquial, nonliterary
literate *Syn* EDUCATED, erudite, knowledgeable, learned, scholarly, well-read *Ant* ignorant, illiterate, uneducated
lithe **1** *Syn* SUPPLE, limber, lissome, lithesome **2** *Syn* WILLOWY, flexible, limber, lissome, pliable, pliant, supple *Ant* inflexible, rigid, stiff
lithesome *Syn* SUPPLE, limber, lissome, lithe
littered *Syn* MESSY, chaotic, cluttered, confused, disarranged, disarrayed, disheveled (*or* dishevelled), disordered, disorderly, higgledy-piggledy, hugger-mugger, jumbled, messed, muddled, mussed, mussy, pell-mell, rumpled, sloppy, topsy-turvy, tousled, tumbled, unkempt, untidy, upside-down *Ant* neat, ordered, orderly, organized, shipshape, snug, tidied, tidy, trim
little *adv* *Syn* SELDOM, infrequently, rarely *Ant* frequently, often
little *adj* *Syn* UNIMPORTANT, frivolous, inconsequential, inconsiderable, insignificant, minor, minute, negligible, slight, small, small-fry, trifling, trivial *Ant* big, consequential, eventful, important, major, material, meaningful, momentous, significant, substantial, weighty
littlest *Syn* MINIMAL, least, lowest, minimum, slightest *Ant* full, greatest, largest, maximum, top, topmost, utmost
littoral *Syn* SHORE, bank, beach, coast, foreshore, strand
liturgy *Syn* FORM (sense 2), ceremonial, ceremony, formality, rite, ritual
live *adj* *Syn* ACTIVE, dynamic, operative *Ant* inactive
live *vb* **1** *Syn* BE, exist, subsist **2** *Syn* RESIDE, dwell, lodge, put up, sojourn, stay, stop
livelihood *Syn* LIVING, bread, bread and butter, keep, maintenance, subsistence, support, sustenance
lively • keenly alive and spirited *Syn* animated, gay, sprightly, vivacious *Rel* agile, brisk, nimble, spry *Ant* dull
liven (up) *Syn* ANIMATE, brace, energize, enliven, fire, invigorate, jazz (up), pep (up), quicken, stimulate, vitalize, vivify *Ant* damp, dampen, deaden, dull

livid *Syn* PALE (sense 1), ashen, ashy, pallid, wan *Ant* florid, flush, rubicund, ruddy, sanguine
living *adj* • having or showing life *Syn* alive, animate, animated, vital *Rel* being, existing, subsisting *Ant* lifeless
living *n* • supplies or resources needed to live *Syn* bread, bread and butter, keep, livelihood, maintenance, subsistence, support, sustenance
load *n* • something which is carried, conveyed, or transported from one place to another *Syn* burden, cargo, freight, lading
load *vb* **1** *Syn* ADULTERATE, doctor, sophisticate, weight *Ant* refine **2** *Syn* BURDEN, charge, cumber, encumber, lade, saddle, tax, weigh, weight
loaf *Syn* IDLE, laze, loll, lounge
loafer *Syn* LAZYBONES, drone, idler, slouch, slug, sluggard *Ant* doer, go-getter, hummer, hustler, rustler, self-starter
loath *Syn* DISINCLINED, averse, hesitant, indisposed, reluctant
loathe *Syn* HATE, abhor, abominate, detest *Ant* love
loathing **1** *Syn* ABHORRENCE, abomination, detestation, hate, hatred *Ant* admiration, enjoyment **2** *Syn* DISGUST, aversion, distaste, nausea, repugnance, repulsion, revulsion
loathsome *Syn* OFFENSIVE, repugnant, repulsive, revolting
local *Syn* INSULAR, parochial, provincial, small-town
locality • a more or less definitely circumscribed place or region *Syn* district, neighborhood, vicinity *Rel* area, belt, region, tract, zone
location *Syn* PLACE, position, site, situation, spot, station
locker **1** *Syn* CABINET, buffet, closet, cupboard, hutch, sideboard **2** *Syn* CHEST, box, caddy, case, casket, trunk
lockup *Syn* JAIL, brig, guardroom, hoosegow, jug, pen, penitentiary, prison, stockade
locomotion *Syn* MOTION, move, movement, stir
locution *Syn* PHRASE, expression, idiom
lodge **1** *Syn* HARBOR, board, entertain, house, shelter **2** *Syn* RESIDE, dwell, live, put up, sojourn, stay, stop
lodger *Syn* TENANT, boarder, renter, roomer *Ant* landlord
loftiness *Syn* ARROGANCE, haughtiness, imperiousness, lordliness, masterfulness, peremptoriness, pompousness, presumptuousness, pretense (*or* pretence), pretension, pretentiousness, self-importance, superciliousness, superiority *Ant* humility, modesty
lofty **1** *Syn* ARROGANT, cavalier, haughty, highfalutin, high-handed, high-hat, imperious, important, lordly, masterful, overweening, peremptory, pompous, presumptuous, pretentious, supercilious, superior, uppish, uppity *Ant* humble, modest **2** *Syn* HIGH, tall *Ant* low
logical • having or showing skill in thinking or reasoning *Syn* analytical, subtle *Rel* cogent, compelling, convincing, sound, telling, valid *Ant* illogical
logistic *Syn* STRATEGIC, tactical
logistics *Syn* STRATEGY, tactics
loiter *Syn* DELAY (sense 2), dawdle, lag, procrastinate *Ant* hasten, hurry
loll *Syn* IDLE, laze, loaf, lounge
lollop **1** *Syn* SKIP, bound, curvet, hop, lope, ricochet **2** *Syn* STUMBLE, blunder, bumble, flounder, galumph, lumber, lurch, trip
lone **1** *Syn* ALONE, desolate, forlorn, lonely, lonesome, lorn, solitary *Ant* accompanied **2** *Syn* ONLY, alone, singular, sole, solitary, special, unique **3** *Syn* SINGLE, particular, separate, sole, solitary, unique *Ant* accompanied, conjugal, supported
lonely *Syn* ALONE, desolate, forlorn, lone, lonesome, lorn, solitary *Ant* accompanied
lonesome *Syn* ALONE, desolate, forlorn, lone, lonely, lorn, solitary *Ant* accompanied
long *adj* **1** • of great extent from end to end *Syn* elongated, extended, king-size (*or* king-sized), lengthy *Rel* extensive, far-reaching, longish, outstretched *Ant* brief, short **2** • lasting for a considerable time *Syn* extended, far, great, lengthy, long-lived, long-range, long-term, marathon *Rel* endless, everlasting, interminable, persistent *Ant* brief, short, short-lived, short-range, short-term
long *vb* • to have a strong desire for something *Syn* hanker, hunger, pine, thirst, yearn *Rel* covet, crave, desire, want, wish
longanimity *Syn* PATIENCE, forbearance, long-suffering, resignation *Ant* impatience
long-lived **1** *Syn* ELDERLY, aged, aging, ancient, geriatric, old, older, senior *Ant* young, youthful **2** *Syn* LONG (sense 2), extended, far, great, lengthy, long-range, long-term, marathon *Ant* brief, short, short-lived, short-range, short-term
long-range *Syn* LONG (sense 2), extended, far, great, lengthy, long-lived, long-term, marathon *Ant* brief, short, short-lived, short-range, short-term
long-suffering *Syn* PATIENCE, forbearance, longanimity, resignation *Ant* impatience
long-term *Syn* LONG (sense 2), extended, far, great, lengthy, long-lived, long-range, marathon *Ant* brief, short, short-lived, short-range, short-term
look *n* **1** • the directing of one's eyes in order to see *Syn* glance, glimpse, peek, peep, sight, view *Rel* gaze, gazing, stare, staring **2** *Syn* APPEARANCE, aspect, semblance
look *vb* **1** *Syn* EXPECT, await, hope *Ant* despair of **2** *Syn* SEEM, act, appear, make, sound **3** *Syn* SEE (sense 2), watch
looker-on *Syn* SPECTATOR, beholder, by-

stander, eyewitness, kibitzer, observer, onlooker, witness
look (into) *Syn* EXPLORE, delve (into), dig (into), inquire (into), investigate, probe, research
lookout *Syn* VIGILANCE, alertness, attentiveness, surveillance, watch, watchfulness
loom *Syn* APPEAR, emerge *Ant* disappear, vanish
loose • not tightly bound, held, restrained, or stretched *Syn* lax, relaxed, slack *Rel* flabby, flaccid, flimsy, limp *Ant* strict, tight
loosen *Syn* SLACKEN, ease, relax, slack *Ant* strain, stretch, tense, tighten
loot **1** *Syn* ROB, burglarize, plunder, rifle **2** *Syn* SPOIL, booty, plunder, prize, swag
lope *Syn* SKIP, bound, curvet, hop, lollop, ricochet
lop (off) *Syn* CLIP, bob, crop, curtail, cut, cut back, dock, nip, pare, prune, shave, shear, snip, trim
lopsided *Syn* AWRY, askew, aslant, cockeyed, crooked, listing, oblique, skewed, slanted, slanting, slantwise, tilted, tipping, uneven *Ant* even, level, straight
loquacious *Syn* TALKATIVE, garrulous, glib, voluble *Ant* closemouthed, laconic, reserved, reticent, taciturn, tight-lipped
loquaciousness *Syn* TALKATIVENESS, garrulity, garrulousness, glibness, loquacity, volubility *Ant* silence
loquacity *Syn* TALKATIVENESS, garrulity, garrulousness, glibness, loquaciousness, volubility *Ant* silence
lord *Syn* GENTLEMAN, nobleman
lordliness *Syn* ARROGANCE, haughtiness, imperiousness, loftiness, masterfulness, peremptoriness, pompousness, presumptuousness, pretense (*or* pretence), pretension, pretentiousness, self-importance, superciliousness, superiority *Ant* humility, modesty
lordly **1** *Syn* ARROGANT, cavalier, haughty, highfalutin, high-handed, high-hat, imperious, important, lofty, masterful, overweening, peremptory, pompous, presumptuous, pretentious, supercilious, superior, uppish, uppity *Ant* humble, modest **2** *Syn* PROUD (sense 1), arrogant, disdainful, haughty, insolent, overbearing, supercilious *Ant* ashamed, humble
lore **1** *Syn* FOLKLORE, legend, myth, mythology, tradition **2** *Syn* KNOWLEDGE, erudition, information, learning, scholarship, science *Ant* ignorance
lorn *Syn* ALONE, desolate, forlorn, lone, lonely, lonesome, solitary *Ant* accompanied
loss *Syn* DESTRUCTION, annihilation, decimation, demolishment, demolition, desolation, devastation, extermination, extinction, havoc, obliteration, ruin, ruination, wastage, wreckage *Ant* building, construction, erection, raising
lot **1** *Syn* FATE, destiny, doom, portion **2** *Syn* GROUP, bunch, cluster, parcel
loud **1** • marked by intensity or volume of sound *Syn* earsplitting, hoarse, raucous, stentorian, stertorous, strident *Ant* low, low-pitched **2** *Syn* GAUDY, flamboyant, flashy, garish, glitzy, ostentatious, splashy, swank (*or* swanky), tawdry *Ant* conservative, quiet, understated
lounge *n* *Syn* COUCH, chesterfield, davenport, divan, settee, sofa
lounge *vb* *Syn* IDLE, laze, loaf, loll
louse up *Syn* BOTCH, bobble, bungle, butcher, flub, foozle, foul up, fumble, mangle, mess (up), muff, murder
lout *Syn* OAF, clod, gawk, hulk, lubber, lug
loutish *Syn* CLOWNISH, boorish, churlish, cloddish, uncouth *Ant* civil, courteous, courtly, cultivated, genteel, gentlemanly, ladylike, polished, polite, refined, well-bred
lovable • having qualities that tend to make one loved *Syn* adorable, darling, dear, disarming, endearing, precious, sweet, winning *Rel* embraceable, kissable *Ant* abhorrent, abominable, detestable, hateful, odious, unlovable
love *vb* *Syn* LIKE, dote, enjoy, fancy, relish *Ant* dislike
love *n* **1** *Syn* ATTACHMENT, affection *Ant* aversion **2** *Syn* LIKING, appetite, fancy, favor, fondness, like, partiality, preference, relish, shine, taste, use *Ant* aversion, disfavor, dislike, distaste, hatred, loathing **3** *Syn* SWEETHEART, beloved, darling, dear, flame, honey, sweet
lovely *Syn* BEAUTIFUL, attractive, beauteous, comely, cute, fair, gorgeous, handsome, knockout, pretty, ravishing, sightly, stunning, taking *Ant* homely, ill-favored, plain, ugly, unattractive, unbeautiful, unhandsome, unlovely, unpretty, unsightly
lover *Syn* FAN, addict, aficionado, buff, bug, devotee, enthusiast, fanatic, fancier, fiend, freak, maniac, nut
loving • feeling or expressing love *Syn* affectionate, devoted, doting, fond *Rel* amatory, amorous, erotic *Ant* unloving
low **1** *Syn* BASE, vile *Ant* noble **2** *Syn* SAD (sense 1), bad, blue, brokenhearted, crestfallen, dejected, depressed, despondent, disconsolate, doleful, down, downcast, downhearted, droopy, forlorn, gloomy, glum, heartbroken, heartsick, heartsore, inconsolable, joyless, low-spirited, melancholy, miserable, mournful, saddened, sorrowful, sorry, unhappy, woebegone, woeful, wretched *Ant* blissful, buoyant, buoyed, cheerful, cheery, chipper, delighted, glad, gladdened, gladsome, gleeful, happy, joyful, joyous, jubilant, sunny, upbeat
lower *adj* *Syn* LESSER, inferior, junior, less, minor, smaller, subordinate, under *Ant* greater, higher, major, more, primary, prime, senior, superior
lower *vb* *Syn* FROWN, glare, gloom, glower, scowl *Ant* beam, smile

lower *n Syn* GRIMACE, face, frown, mouth, pout, scowl
lowering *Syn* OVERCAST, beclouded, clouded, cloudy, dull, hazed, hazy, heavy, overclouded *Ant* clear, cloudless
lowest *Syn* MINIMAL, least, littlest, minimum, slightest *Ant* full, greatest, largest, maximum, top, topmost, utmost
lowly *Syn* HUMBLE, meek, modest
low-spirited *Syn* SAD (sense 1), bad, blue, brokenhearted, crestfallen, dejected, depressed, despondent, disconsolate, doleful, down, downcast, downhearted, droopy, forlorn, gloomy, glum, heartbroken, heartsick, heartsore, inconsolable, joyless, low, melancholy, miserable, mournful, saddened, sorrowful, sorry, unhappy, woebegone, woeful, wretched *Ant* blissful, buoyant, buoyed, cheerful, cheery, chipper, delighted, glad, gladdened, gladsome, gleeful, happy, joyful, joyous, jubilant, sunny, upbeat
loyal *Syn* FAITHFUL, constant, devoted, devout, fast, good, pious, staunch (*or* stanch), steadfast, steady, true, true-blue *Ant* disloyal, faithless, false, fickle, inconstant, perfidious, recreant, traitorous, treacherous, unfaithful, untrue
loyalty *Syn* FIDELITY, allegiance, devotion, fealty, piety *Ant* faithlessness, perfidy
lozenge *Syn* PILL, capsule, tablet
lubber *Syn* OAF, clod, gawk, hulk, lout, lug
lubricate *Syn* OIL, anoint, cream, grease
lucent *Syn* BRIGHT, beaming, brilliant, effulgent, incandescent, lambent, luminous, lustrous, radiant, refulgent *Ant* dim, dull
lucid **1** *Syn* CLEAR (sense 1), diaphanous, limpid, pellucid, translucent, transparent *Ant* confused, turbid **2** *Syn* CLEAR (sense 2), perspicuous *Ant* abstruse, unintelligible **3** *Syn* SANE, balanced, clearheaded, normal, right, stable *Ant* crazed, crazy, demented, deranged, insane, lunatic, mad, maniacal, mental, unbalanced, unsound
luck *Syn* CHANCE, accident, fortune, hap, hazard *Ant* law, principle
luckless *Syn* UNLUCKY, calamitous, disastrous, hapless, ill-fated, ill-starred, unfortunate *Ant* fortunate, happy, lucky
lucky • meeting with unforeseen success *Syn* fortunate, happy, providential *Rel* auspicious, benign, favorable, propitious *Ant* unlucky
lucrative *Syn* PAYING, gainful, profitable, remunerative
ludicrous *Syn* LAUGHABLE, comic, comical, droll, farcical, funny, ridiculous, risible
lug *Syn* OAF, clod, gawk, hulk, lout, lubber
lugubrious *Syn* MELANCHOLY, doleful, dolorous, plaintive, rueful
lull *vb Syn* CALM, compose, quiet, quieten, settle, soothe, still, tranquilize *Ant* agitate, arouse
lull *n Syn* PAUSE, break, breath, breather, interruption, recess
lumber *Syn* STUMBLE, blunder, bumble, flounder, galumph, lollop, lurch, trip
luminous *Syn* BRIGHT, beaming, brilliant, effulgent, incandescent, lambent, lucent, lustrous, radiant, refulgent *Ant* dim, dull
lunacy *Syn* INSANITY, mania, psychosis *Ant* sanity
lunatic *n Syn* FOOL (sense 2), booby, goose, half-wit, jackass, nincompoop, ninny, nitwit, nut, simpleton, turkey, yo-yo
lunatic *adj Syn* INSANE, crazed, crazy, demented, deranged, mad, maniac, non compos mentis *Ant* sane
lurch *Syn* STUMBLE, blunder, bumble, flounder, galumph, lollop, lumber, trip
lure • to lead away from a usual or proper course by offering some pleasure or advantage *Syn* allure, beguile, decoy, entice, lead on, seduce, tempt *Rel* inveigle, persuade, rope (in), snow
lurid *Syn* GHASTLY, grim, grisly, gruesome, macabre
lurk • to behave so as to escape attention *Syn* skulk, slink, sneak *Rel* conceal, hide, secrete
luscious *Syn* DELIGHTFUL, delectable, delicious *Ant* boring, distressing, horrid
lush *Syn* PROFUSE, exuberant, lavish, luxuriant, prodigal *Ant* scant, scanty, spare
lust *Syn* DESIRE, appetite, passion, urge *Ant* distaste
luster • the quality or condition of shining by reflected light *Syn* glaze, gloss, sheen *Rel* iridescence, opalescence
lustful *Syn* LICENTIOUS, lascivious, lecherous, lewd, libertine, libidinous, wanton *Ant* continent
lustrous **1** *Syn* BRIGHT, beaming, brilliant, effulgent, incandescent, lambent, lucent, luminous, radiant, refulgent *Ant* dim, dull **2** *Syn* GLOSSY, buffed, burnished, glistening, polished, rubbed, satin, satiny, sleek *Ant* dim, dull, flat, lusterless, matte
lusty *Syn* VIGOROUS, energetic, nervous, strenuous *Ant* languorous, lethargic
luxuriant **1** *Syn* FERTILE, fat, fecund, fruitful, productive, prolific, rich *Ant* barren, infertile, sterile, unfruitful, unproductive **2** *Syn* LUXURIOUS, deluxe, lavish, opulent, palatial, plush, sumptuous *Ant* ascetic, austere, humble, Spartan **3** *Syn* PROFUSE, exuberant, lavish, lush, prodigal *Ant* scant, scanty, spare
luxurious **1** • showing obvious signs of wealth and comfort *Syn* deluxe, lavish, luxuriant, opulent, palatial, plush, sumptuous *Rel* costly, expensive *Ant* ascetic, austere, humble, Spartan **2** *Syn* SENSUOUS, epicurean, sybaritic, voluptuous
luxuriously *Syn* HIGH, expensively, extravagantly, grandly, lavishly, opulently, richly, sumptuously *Ant* austerely, humbly, modestly, plainly, simply
lyric *Syn* POEM, song, verse

M

macabre *Syn* GHASTLY, grim, grisly, gruesome, lurid
macerate *Syn* CRUSH (sense 1), bruise, mash, smash, squash
Machiavellian *Syn* UNPRINCIPLED, cutthroat, immoral, unconscionable, unethical, unmoral, unscrupulous *Ant* ethical, moral, principled, scrupulous
machinate **1** *Syn* ENGINEER, contrive, finagle, finesse, frame, maneuver, manipulate, mastermind, negotiate, wangle **2** *Syn* PLOT, conspire, contrive, intrigue, scheme
machination *Syn* PLOT, cabal, conspiracy, intrigue
machine • a device or system by which energy can be converted into useful work *Syn* apparatus, engine, machinery, mechanism, motor *Rel* contraption, contrivance, device, gadget
machinery **1** *Syn* AGENT (sense 2), agency, instrument, instrumentality, means, medium, organ, vehicle **2** *Syn* EQUIPMENT, apparatus, gear, matériel, outfit, paraphernalia, tackle **3** *Syn* MACHINE, apparatus, engine, mechanism, motor
mad **1** *Syn* ANGRY, angered, apoplectic, enraged, foaming, fuming, furious, incensed, indignant, inflamed, infuriated, irate, ireful, outraged, rabid, riled, roiled, sore, steaming, wrathful, wroth *Ant* delighted, pleased **2** *Syn* INSANE, crazed, crazy, demented, deranged, lunatic, maniac, non compos mentis *Ant* sane
madden *Syn* ANGER, antagonize, enrage, incense, inflame, infuriate, outrage, rankle, rile, roil *Ant* delight, gratify, please
maddening *Syn* ANNOYING, aggravating, bothersome, disturbing, exasperating, frustrating, galling, irksome, irritating, nettling, peeving, pesty, rankling, riling, vexatious, vexing
madhouse • a place of uproar or confusion *Syn* babel, bedlam, circus, hell *Rel* commotion, havoc, pandemonium, racket, ruckus, tumult, turmoil
maelstrom *Syn* EDDY, vortex, whirlpool
maestro *Syn* EXPERT, ace, adept, artist, authority, crackerjack, master, past master, scholar, shark, virtuoso, whiz, wizard *Ant* amateur
magazine **1** *Syn* ARMORY, arsenal, depot, dump **2** *Syn* STOREHOUSE, depository, depot, repository, storage, stowage, warehouse **3** *Syn* JOURNAL, newspaper, organ, periodical, review
magic • the use of means (as charms or spells) believed to have supernatural power over natural forces *Syn* alchemy, sorcery, thaumaturgy, witchcraft, witchery, wizardry
magician **1** • a person skilled in using supernatural forces *Syn* charmer, conjurer (*or* conjuror), enchanter, necromancer, sorcerer, voodoo, witch, wizard *Rel* enchantress, hag, hex, sorceress, warlock **2** • one who practices tricks and illusions for entertainment *Syn* conjurer (*or* conjuror), prestidigitator, trickster *Rel* charmer, enchanter, enchantress
magisterial *Syn* DICTATORIAL, authoritarian, doctrinaire, dogmatic
magnification *Syn* EXAGGERATION, caricature, coloring, elaboration, embellishment, embroidering, hyperbole, overstatement, padding, stretching *Ant* understatement
magnificence • impressiveness of beauty on a large scale *Syn* augustness, brilliance, gloriousness, glory, grandeur, grandness, majesty, nobility, nobleness, resplendence, splendor, stateliness, stupendousness, sublimeness, superbness *Rel* awesomeness, marvelousness, wondrousness
magnificent *Syn* GRAND, august, grandiose, imposing, majestic, noble, stately
magnify *Syn* EXALT, aggrandize, dignify, ennoble, enshrine, glorify *Ant* abase, degrade, demean, humble, humiliate
magniloquent *Syn* RHETORICAL, aureate, bombastic, euphuistic, flowery, grandiloquent
magnitude *Syn* SIZE, area, dimensions, extent, volume
maim • to injure so severely as to cause lasting damage *Syn* batter, cripple, mangle, mutilate *Rel* damage, injure, mar, spoil
main *Syn* CHIEF, capital, foremost, leading, principal *Ant* subordinate
mainly **1** *Syn* CHIEFLY, altogether, basically, by and large, generally, largely, mostly, overall, predominantly, primarily, principally, substantially **2** *Syn* LARGELY, chiefly, generally, greatly, mostly, principally
maintain • to uphold as true, right, just, or reasonable *Syn* assert, defend, justify, vindicate *Rel* affirm, aver, avouch, avow, declare, profess, protest
maintainable *Syn* TENABLE, defendable, defensible, justifiable, supportable, sustainable *Ant* indefensible, insupportable, unjustifiable, untenable
maintenance *Syn* LIVING, bread, bread and butter, keep, livelihood, subsistence, support, sustenance
majestic *Syn* GRAND, august, grandiose, imposing, magnificent, noble, stately
majesty **1** *Syn* ELEGANCE, class, elegancy, grace, gracefulness, handsomeness, refine-

ment, stateliness **2** *Syn* MAGNIFICENCE, augustness, brilliance, gloriousness, glory, grandeur, grandness, nobility, nobleness, resplendence, splendor, stateliness, stupendousness, sublimeness, superbness

make **1** • to bring something into being by forming, shaping, combining, or altering materials *Syn* fabricate, fashion, forge, form, manufacture, shape *Rel* bear, produce, turn out, yield **2** *Syn* BUILD, assemble, construct, erect, fabricate, make up, piece, put up, raise, rear, set up *Ant* disassemble, dismantle, take down **3** *Syn* EARN, acquire, attain, capture, carry, draw, gain, garner, get, land, obtain, procure, realize, secure, win *Ant* forfeit, lose **4** *Syn* EFFECT, bring about, cause, create, effectuate, engender, generate, induce, produce, prompt, result (in), spawn, work, yield **5** *Syn* ENACT, lay down, legislate, pass *Ant* repeal, rescind, revoke **6** *Syn* ESTIMATE (sense 2), calculate, call, conjecture, figure, gauge, guess, judge, place, put, reckon, suppose **7** *Syn* SEEM, act, appear, look, sound

make-believe *Syn* PRETENSE, pretension

make over **1** *Syn* CHANGE (sense 1), alter, modify, recast, redo, refashion, remake, remodel, revamp, revise, rework, vary *Ant* fix, freeze, set, stabilize **2** *Syn* CONVERT, metamorphose, transfigure, transform

maker • one who brings something into being or existence *Syn* author, creator

makeshift *Syn* RESOURCE, expedient, resort, shift, stopgap, substitute, surrogate

make up **1** *Syn* BUILD, assemble, construct, erect, fabricate, make, piece, put up, raise, rear, set up *Ant* disassemble, dismantle, take down **2** *Syn* INVENT, concoct, contrive, cook (up), devise, fabricate, manufacture, think (up)

maladroit *Syn* AWKWARD, clumsy, gauche, inept *Ant* deft, graceful, handy

malady *Syn* DISEASE, ailment, complaint, condition, disorder, distemper, syndrome

male *adj* • of, relating to, or marked by qualities traditionally associated with men *Syn* manful, manlike, manly, mannish, masculine, virile *Ant* female

male *n* *Syn* MAN, dude, fellow, gent, gentleman, guy

malediction *Syn* CURSE, anathema, imprecation *Ant* blessing

malefactor *Syn* CRIMINAL, convict, culprit, delinquent, felon

malefic *Syn* SINISTER, baleful, maleficent, malign

maleficent *Syn* SINISTER, baleful, malefic, malign

malevolence *Syn* MALICE, despite, grudge, ill will, malignancy, malignity, spite, spleen *Ant* charity

malevolent *Syn* MALICIOUS, malign, malignant, spiteful

malfeasance *Syn* MISCONDUCT, misbehavior, misdoing, wrongdoing

malice • the desire to see another experience pain, injury, or distress *Syn* despite, grudge, ill will, malevolence, malignancy, malignity, spite, spleen *Rel* maliciousness, spitefulness *Ant* charity

malicious • having, showing, or indicative of intense often vicious ill will *Syn* malevolent, malign, malignant, spiteful *Rel* poisonous, venomous

malign *adj* **1** *Syn* MALICIOUS, malevolent, malignant, spiteful **2** *Syn* SINISTER, baleful, malefic, maleficent

malign *vb* *Syn* SLANDER, asperse, blacken, defame, libel, smear, traduce, vilify

malignancy *Syn* MALICE, despite, grudge, ill will, malevolence, malignity, spite, spleen *Ant* charity

malignant *Syn* MALICIOUS, malevolent, malign, spiteful

malignity *Syn* MALICE, despite, grudge, ill will, malevolence, malignancy, spite, spleen *Ant* charity

malinger *Syn* DODGE, duck, fence, parry, shirk, sidestep *Ant* face

malleable *Syn* PLASTIC, adaptable, ductile, pliable, pliant

malodorous • having an unpleasant smell *Syn* fetid, fusty, musty, noisome, putrid, rancid, rank, stinking *Ant* odorous

maltreat *Syn* ABUSE, ill-treat, mistreat, misuse, outrage *Ant* honor, respect

mammoth **1** *Syn* GIANT, behemoth, blockbuster, colossus, jumbo, leviathan, monster, titan, whale, whopper *Ant* dwarf, midget, mini, miniature, peewee, pygmy, runt, shrimp **2** *Syn* HUGE, Brobdingnagian, colossal, cyclopean, elephantine, enormous, gargantuan, giant, gigantean, gigantic, Herculean, immense, titanic, vast *Ant* bitty, diminutive, microscopic (*or* microscopical), midget, miniature, minute, pocket, pygmy, teeny, teeny-weeny, tiny, wee

man **1** • an adult male human being *Syn* dude, fellow, gent, gentleman, guy, male **2** *Syn* BOYFRIEND, beau, fellow, swain

manacle *n* *Syn* ENCUMBRANCE, bar, block, chain, clog, crimp, deterrent, drag, embarrassment, fetter, handicap, hindrance, hurdle, impediment, inhibition, interference, let, obstacle, obstruction, shackles, stop, stumbling block, trammel *Ant* aid, assistance, benefit, help

manacle *vb* *Syn* HAMPER, clog, fetter, hog-tie, shackle, trammel *Ant* assist (*persons*), expedite (*work, projects*)

manage *Syn* CONDUCT, control, direct

manager *Syn* EXECUTIVE, administrator, director, superintendent, supervisor

managing *Syn* HEAD, chief, commanding, first, foremost, high, lead, leading, preeminent, premier, presiding, primary, prime, principal, supreme

mandate 1 • an authorization to take a political action given to a representative *Syn* initiative, plebiscite, referendum 2 *Syn* COMMAND, behest, bidding, dictate, injunction, order

mandatory • forcing one's compliance or participation by or as if by law *Syn* compulsory, forced, imperative, incumbent, involuntary, necessary, nonelective, obligatory, peremptory, required *Rel* all-important, essential, indispensable, needed, requisite *Ant* elective, optional, voluntary

maneuver *vb Syn* ENGINEER, contrive, finagle, finesse, frame, machinate, manipulate, mastermind, negotiate, wangle

maneuver *n Syn* TRICK, artifice, feint, gambit, ploy, ruse, stratagem, wile

manful *Syn* MALE, manlike, manly, mannish, masculine, virile *Ant* female

mangle 1 *Syn* BOTCH, bobble, bungle, butcher, flub, foozle, foul up, fumble, louse up, mess (up), muff, murder 2 *Syn* MAIM, batter, cripple, mutilate

manhood *Syn* VIRILITY, manliness, masculinity *Ant* femininity

mania 1 • a state of mind in which there is loss of control over emotional, nervous, or mental processes *Syn* delirium, frenzy, hysteria *Rel* dejection, depression, melancholia, melancholy, sadness 2 *Syn* INSANITY, lunacy, psychosis *Ant* sanity

maniac *n Syn* FAN, addict, aficionado, buff, bug, devotee, enthusiast, fanatic, fancier, fiend, freak, lover, nut

maniac *adj Syn* INSANE, crazed, crazy, demented, deranged, lunatic, mad, non compos mentis *Ant* sane

manifest *vb* 1 *Syn* EMBODY (sense 2), epitomize, incarnate, materialize, personalize, personify, substantiate 2 *Syn* SHOW (sense 1), demonstrate, evidence, evince *Ant* disguise

manifest *adj Syn* EVIDENT, apparent, clear, distinct, obvious, palpable, patent, plain

manifestation *Syn* EMBODIMENT, epitome, incarnation, personification

manipulate 1 *Syn* ENGINEER, contrive, finagle, finesse, frame, machinate, maneuver, mastermind, negotiate, wangle 2 *Syn* HANDLE, ply, swing, wield

manlike *Syn* MALE, manful, manly, mannish, masculine, virile *Ant* female

manliness *Syn* VIRILITY, manhood, masculinity *Ant* femininity

manly *Syn* MALE, manful, manlike, mannish, masculine, virile *Ant* female

man-made *Syn* IMITATION, artificial, bogus, factitious, fake, false, mimic, mock, sham, simulated, substitute, synthetic *Ant* genuine, natural, real

manner *Syn* METHOD, fashion, mode, system, way

mannerism *Syn* POSE, affectation, air

mannerliness *Syn* POLITENESS, civility, courteousness, courtesy, gentility, graciousness *Ant* discourteousness, discourtesy, impoliteness, incivility, rudeness, ungraciousness

mannish *Syn* MALE, manful, manlike, manly, masculine, virile *Ant* female

manor *Syn* MANSION, castle, château, countryseat, estate, hacienda, hall, manor house, palace, villa

manor house *Syn* MANSION, castle, château, countryseat, estate, hacienda, hall, manor, palace, villa

mansion • a large impressive residence *Syn* castle, château, countryseat, estate, hacienda, hall, manor, manor house, palace, villa *Rel* showplace

mantilla *Syn* BANDANNA, babushka, handkerchief, kerchief

manufacture 1 *Syn* INVENT, concoct, contrive, cook (up), devise, fabricate, make up, think (up) 2 *Syn* MAKE, fabricate, fashion, forge, form, shape

manumit *Syn* FREE, discharge, emancipate, liberate, release

many • amounting to or being one at a large indefinite number *Syn* divers, multifarious, numerous, several, sundry, various *Ant* few

many-sided *Syn* VERSATILE, all-around

map *n Syn* CHART, graph

map *vb Syn* CHART, graph

mar *Syn* INJURE, damage, harm, hurt, impair, spoil *Ant* aid

marathon *Syn* LONG (sense 2), extended, far, great, lengthy, long-lived, long-range, long-term *Ant* brief, short, short-lived, short-range, short-term

marble *Syn* SPOT, blotch, dapple, dot, fleck, freckle, mottle, pepper, speck, speckle, splotch, sprinkle, stipple

marbled *Syn* SPOTTED, bespangled, flecked, spangled, spattered, speckled, sprinkled, stippled

march *Syn* ADVANCE (sense 2), advancement, furtherance, going, headway, onrush, passage, process, procession, progress, progression *Ant* recession, regression, retrogression

margin *vb Syn* BORDER, bound, fringe, rim, skirt

margin *n* 1 *Syn* BORDER, brim, brink, edge, rim, verge 2 *Syn* ROOM (sense 2), berth, clearance, elbow room, leeway, play

marine 1 • of or relating to the sea *Syn* maritime, oceanic, pelagic *Rel* abyssal, deep-sea, deepwater, saltwater 2 • of or relating to the navigation of the sea *Syn* maritime, nautical, naval

mariner • a person engaged in sailing or handling a ship *Syn* bluejacket, gob, sailor, seaman, tar

marital • of or relating to marriage *Syn* conjugal, connubial, married, matrimonial, nuptial, wedded *Rel* espoused, matched, mated

maritime **1** *Syn* MARINE (sense 1), oceanic, pelagic **2** *Syn* MARINE (sense 2), nautical, naval

mark *n* **1** • a symbol or device used for identification or indication of ownership *Syn* brand, label, stamp, tag, ticket **2** *Syn* BLEMISH, defect, deformity, disfigurement, fault, flaw, imperfection, pockmark, scar **3** *Syn* CHARACTERISTIC, attribute, character, feature, peculiarity, point, property, quality, trait **4** *Syn* CHARACTER, sign, symbol **5** *Syn* GOAL, aim, ambition, aspiration, design, dream, end, intent, intention, meaning, object, objective, plan, pretension, purpose, target, thing **6** *Syn* LAUGHINGSTOCK, butt, mock, mockery, target **7** *Syn* SIGN (sense 1), badge, note, symptom, token

mark *vb* **1** • to affix, attach, or impress something which serves for identification *Syn* brand, label, stamp, tag, ticket *Rel* impress, imprint, print **2** *Syn* CHARACTERIZE, distinguish, qualify

market • to offer for sale to the public *Syn* deal (in), merchandise, put up, retail, sell, vend *Rel* wholesale *Ant* buy, purchase

marketable *Syn* COMMERCIAL, salable (*or* saleable) *Ant* noncommercial, nonsalable, uncommercial, unmarketable, unsalable

marriage • acts by which two people are joined as spouses or the state of being joined as spouses *Syn* espousal, matrimony, nuptial, wedding, wedlock

married *Syn* MARITAL, conjugal, connubial, matrimonial, nuptial, wedded

marsh *Syn* SWAMP, bog, fen, marshland, mire, morass, muskeg, slough, swampland

marshal *Syn* ORDER, arrange, methodize, organize, systematize

marshland *Syn* SWAMP, bog, fen, marsh, mire, morass, muskeg, slough, swampland

martial • of, relating to, or suited for war or a warrior *Syn* military, warlike *Rel* bellicose, belligerent, combative, pugnacious

martyr *Syn* AFFLICT, agonize, bedevil, curse, harrow, persecute, plague, rack, torment, torture

marvel *Syn* WONDER (sense 1), miracle, phenomenon, prodigy

marvelous *or* **marvellous** **1** *Syn* EXCELLENT, A1, bang-up, banner, capital, classic, crackerjack, dandy, divine, fabulous, fine, first-class, first-rate, grand, great, groovy, heavenly, jim-dandy, keen, mean, neat, nifty, noble, par excellence, prime, sensational, splendid, stellar, sterling, superb, superior, superlative, supernal, swell, terrific, tip-top, top, top-notch, unsurpassed, wonderful *Ant* poor **2** *Syn* EXOTIC, fantastic, glamorous, outlandish, romantic, strange

masculine *Syn* MALE, manful, manlike, manly, mannish, virile *Ant* female

masculinity *Syn* VIRILITY, manhood, manliness *Ant* femininity

mash *Syn* CRUSH (sense 1), bruise, macerate, smash, squash

mask *vb* *Syn* DISGUISE, camouflage, cloak, dissemble

mask *n* *Syn* IMAGE, effigy, icon, photograph, portrait, statue

mass *n* **1** *Syn* BULK, volume **2** *Syn* HEAP, bank, cock, pile, shock, stack

mass *vb* *Syn* HEAP, bank, cock, pile, shock, stack

massacre *n* • the act or an instance of killing a number of usually helpless or unresisting human beings under circumstances of atrocity or cruelty *Syn* butchery, carnage, pogrom, slaughter *Rel* assassination, killing, murder, murdering, slaying

massacre *vb* • to kill on a large scale *Syn* butcher, mow (down), slaughter *Rel* assassinate, execute, murder, slay

massive • impressively large or heavy *Syn* bulky, massy, monumental, substantial *Rel* heavy, ponderous, weighty

massy *Syn* MASSIVE, bulky, monumental, substantial

master **1** *Syn* BOSS, captain, chief, foreman, head, headman, helmsman, kingpin, leader, taskmaster **2** *Syn* CHIEF, chieftain, head, headman, leader **3** *Syn* EXPERT, ace, adept, artist, authority, crackerjack, maestro, past master, scholar, shark, virtuoso, whiz, wizard *Ant* amateur

masterful **1** • tending to impose one's will on others *Syn* DICTATORIAL, domineering, imperative, imperious, peremptory *Rel* authoritarian, doctrinaire, dogmatic, magisterial, oracular **2** *Syn* ARROGANT, cavalier, haughty, highfalutin, high-handed, high-hat, imperious, important, lofty, lordly, overweening, peremptory, pompous, presumptuous, pretentious, supercilious, superior, uppish, uppity *Ant* humble, modest **3** *Syn* BOSSY, authoritarian, autocratic, despotic, dictatorial, domineering, imperious, overbearing, peremptory, tyrannical, tyrannous

masterfulness *Syn* ARROGANCE, haughtiness, imperiousness, loftiness, lordliness, peremptoriness, pompousness, presumptuousness, pretense (*or* pretence), pretension, pretentiousness, self-importance, superciliousness, superiority *Ant* humility, modesty

masterly *Syn* PROFICIENT, adept, expert, skilled, skillful *Ant* amateur, amateurish, inexperienced, inexpert, unexperienced, unpracticed, unprofessional, unseasoned, unskilled, unskillful

mastermind *Syn* ENGINEER, contrive, finagle, finesse, frame, machinate, maneuver, manipulate, negotiate, wangle

match *vb* • to come up to or nearly up to the level or standard of *Syn* approach, equal, rival, touch *Rel* accord, agree, conform, correspond, harmonize, square
match *n Syn* EQUAL, coordinate, counterpart, equivalent, fellow, like, parallel, peer, rival
matching *Syn* ALIKE, akin, analogous, comparable, correspondent, corresponding, like, parallel, resembling, similar, such, suchlike *Ant* different, dissimilar, diverse, unlike
mate *Syn* SPOUSE, consort, partner
material *adj* **1** • of or belonging to actuality *Syn* corporeal, objective, phenomenal, physical, sensible *Rel* animal, carnal, fleshly, sensual *Ant* immaterial **2** *Syn* PERTINENT, applicable, apposite, apropos, germane, pointed, relative, relevant *Ant* extraneous, immaterial, inapplicable, irrelevant, pointless
material *n Syn* MATTER, stuff, substance
materialize **1** *Syn* BEGIN (sense 1), arise, commence, dawn, form, originate, set in, spring, start *Ant* cease, end, stop **2** *Syn* EMBODY (sense 2), epitomize, incarnate, manifest, personalize, personify, substantiate **3** *Syn* REALIZE, actualize, embody, externalize, hypostatize, incarnate, objectify, reify
matériel *Syn* EQUIPMENT, apparatus, gear, machinery, outfit, paraphernalia, tackle
matrimonial *Syn* MARITAL, conjugal, connubial, married, nuptial, wedded
matrimony *Syn* MARRIAGE, espousal, nuptial, wedding, wedlock
matter *n* **1** • what goes into the makeup or forms the being of a thing whether physical or not *Syn* material, stuff, substance **2** *Syn* AFFAIR, business, concern, thing **3** *Syn* SUBJECT, argument, leitmotiv, motif, motive, subject matter, text, theme, topic
matter *vb* • to be of importance *Syn* count, import, mean, signify, weigh *Rel* affect, influence, sway
matter-of-fact *Syn* PROSAIC, prosy
mature *adj* • having attained the normal peak of natural growth and development *Syn* adult, grown-up, matured, mellow, ripe *Ant* childish, immature
mature *vb* • to become fully developed or ripe *Syn* age, develop, ripen *Rel* acclimate, acclimatize, harden, season
matured *Syn* MATURE, adult, grown-up, mellow, ripe *Ant* childish, immature
maudlin **1** *Syn* CORNY, mawkish, mushy, saccharine, sappy, schmaltzy, sentimental, sloppy, sugarcoated, sugary *Ant* unsentimental **2** *Syn* SENTIMENTAL, mawkish, mushy, romantic, slushy, soppy
mawkish **1** *Syn* CORNY, maudlin, mushy, saccharine, sappy, schmaltzy, sentimental, sloppy, sugarcoated, sugary *Ant* unsentimental **2** *Syn* SENTIMENTAL, maudlin, mushy, romantic, slushy, soppy
maxim *Syn* SAYING, adage, aphorism, apothegm, epigram, motto, proverb, saw
maybe *Syn* PERHAPS, conceivably, mayhap, perchance, possibly
mayhap *Syn* PERHAPS, conceivably, maybe, perchance, possibly
meager • falling short of what is normal, necessary, or desirable *Syn* exiguous, scant, scanty, scrimpy, skimpy, spare, sparse *Rel* rare, slender, slight, slim, tenuous, thin *Ant* ample, copious
meal • food eaten or prepared for eating at one time *Syn* chow, feed, mess, repast, table *Rel* board
mealy *Syn* INSINCERE, artificial, backhanded, double-dealing, feigned, hypocritical, left-handed, mealymouthed, two-faced, unctuous *Ant* genuine, heartfelt, honest, sincere, unfeigned
mealymouthed *Syn* INSINCERE, artificial, backhanded, double-dealing, feigned, hypocritical, left-handed, mealy, two-faced, unctuous *Ant* genuine, heartfelt, honest, sincere, unfeigned
mean *adj* **1** • being below the normal standards of human decency and dignity *Syn* abject, ignoble, sordid *Rel* base, low, vile **2** *Syn* EXCELLENT, A1, bang-up, banner, capital, classic, crackerjack, dandy, divine, fabulous, fine, first-class, first-rate, grand, great, groovy, heavenly, jim-dandy, keen, marvelous (*or* marvellous), neat, nifty, noble, par excellence, prime, sensational, splendid, stellar, sterling, superb, superior, superlative, supernal, swell, terrific, tip-top, top, top-notch, unsurpassed, wonderful *Ant* poor
mean *vb* **1** • to convey (as an idea) to the mind *Syn* denote, import, signify *Rel* bear, carry, convey, transmit **2** *Syn* INTEND, design, propose, purpose **3** *Syn* MATTER, count, import, signify, weigh
meander *Syn* WANDER, gad, gallivant, prowl, ramble, range, roam, rove, stray, traipse
meaning *n* **1** • the idea that something conveys to the mind *Syn* acceptation, import, sense, significance, signification *Rel* hint, hinting, implication, intimation, suggestion **2** *Syn* GOAL, aim, ambition, aspiration, design, dream, end, intent, intention, mark, object, objective, plan, pretension, purpose, target, thing
meaning *adj Syn* EXPRESSIVE, eloquent, meaningful, pregnant, revealing, significant, suggestive
meaningful *Syn* EXPRESSIVE, eloquent, meaning, pregnant, revealing, significant, suggestive
meaningless • having no meaning *Syn* empty, inane, pointless, senseless *Rel* insignificant, trivial, unimportant *Ant* meaningful
means **1** • one by which work is accomplished or an end effected *Syn* agency, agent,

channel, instrument, instrumentality, medium, organ, vehicle *Rel* fashion, manner, method, mode, system, way **2** *Syn* AGENT (sense 2), agency, instrument, instrumentality, machinery, medium, organ, vehicle

means *Syn* POSSESSIONS, assets, belongings, effects, resources

measly *Syn* PETTY, paltry, picayune, picayunish, puny, trifling, trivial *Ant* gross, important, momentous

measure **1** *Syn* AMOUNT, quantity, volume **2** *Syn* RHYTHM, beat, cadence, meter

measureless *Syn* INFINITE, boundless, endless, illimitable, immeasurable, indefinite, limitless, unbounded, unfathomable, unlimited *Ant* bounded, circumscribed, confined, definite, finite, limited, restricted

mecca *Syn* CENTER (sense 2), base, capital, core, cynosure, eye, focus, heart, hub, nucleus, seat

mechanic *Syn* WORKER, artisan, craftsman, hand, handicraftsman, laborer, operative, roustabout, workingman, workman *Ant* idler

mechanical *Syn* SPONTANEOUS, automatic, impulsive, instinctive

mechanism *Syn* MACHINE, apparatus, engine, machinery, motor

meddle *Syn* INTERFERE, butt in, intrude, mess, nose, obtrude, poke, pry, snoop

meddler *Syn* BUSYBODY, interferer, interloper, intruder, kibitzer

meddlesome *Syn* INTRUSIVE, interfering, intruding, meddling, nosy (*or* nosey), obtrusive, officious, presumptuous, prying, snoopy *Ant* unobtrusive

meddling *Syn* INTRUSIVE, interfering, intruding, meddlesome, nosy (*or* nosey), obtrusive, officious, presumptuous, prying, snoopy *Ant* unobtrusive

medial *Syn* MIDDLE, halfway, intermediary, intermediate, median, medium, mid, middlemost, midmost, midway *Ant* extreme, farthermost, farthest, furthermost, furthest, outermost, outmost, remotest, utmost

median *Syn* MIDDLE, halfway, intermediary, intermediate, medial, medium, mid, middlemost, midmost, midway *Ant* extreme, farthermost, farthest, furthermost, furthest, outermost, outmost, remotest, utmost

mediate *Syn* INTERVENE, intercede, interpose

mediator • one who works with opposing sides in order to bring about an agreement *Syn* arbiter, arbitrator, conciliator, go-between, intercessor, intermediary, interposer, middleman, peacemaker *Rel* moderator

medicament *Syn* REMEDY, cure, medication, medicine, physic, specific

medication *Syn* REMEDY, cure, medicament, medicine, physic, specific

medicinal *Syn* DRUG, biologic, pharmaceutical, simple

medicine *Syn* REMEDY, cure, medicament, medication, physic, specific

mediocre *Syn* MEDIUM, average, fair, indifferent, middling, moderate, second-rate

meditate *Syn* PONDER, muse, ruminate

meditative **1** *Syn* CONTEMPLATIVE, melancholy, pensive, reflective, ruminant, thoughtful *Ant* unreflective **2** *Syn* THOUGHTFUL (sense 1), contemplative, pensive, reflective, speculative *Ant* thoughtless

medium *adj* **1** • about midway between the extremes of a scale, measurement, or evaluation *Syn* average, fair, indifferent, mediocre, middling, moderate, second-rate *Rel* average, mean, median, par **2** *Syn* MIDDLE, halfway, intermediary, intermediate, medial, median, mid, middlemost, midmost, midway *Ant* extreme, farthermost, farthest, furthermost, furthest, outermost, outmost, remotest, utmost

medium *n* *Syn* AGENT (sense 2), agency, instrument, instrumentality, machinery, means, organ, vehicle

meek *Syn* HUMBLE, lowly, modest

meet *vb* **1** • to come together face-to-face or as if face-to-face *Syn* confront, encounter, face *Rel* accost, address, greet, salute *Ant* avoid **2** *Syn* HAPPEN (on *or* upon), chance (upon), encounter, find, hit (upon), stumble (on *or* onto)

meet *adj* **1** *Syn* FIT, appropriate, apt, felicitous, fitting, happy, proper, suitable *Ant* unfit **2** *Syn* SATISFY (sense 2), answer, fulfill

meetly *Syn* PROPERLY, appropriately, congruously, correctly, fittingly, happily, rightly, suitably *Ant* improperly, inappropriately, incongruously, incorrectly, unsuitably, wrongly

megalopolis *Syn* CITY, burg, metropolis, municipality, town

melancholic • gloomy or depressed especially as a manifestation of one's temperament or state of health *Syn* atrabilious, hypochondriac, melancholy *Rel* despairing, desperate, despondent, forlorn, hopeless

melancholy *adj* **1** • expressing or suggesting sorrow or mourning *Syn* doleful, dolorous, lugubrious, plaintive, rueful *Rel* moving, pathetic, poignant, touching **2** *Syn* CONTEMPLATIVE, meditative, pensive, reflective, ruminant, thoughtful *Ant* unreflective **3** *Syn* MELANCHOLIC, atrabilious, hypochondriac **4** *Syn* SAD (sense 1), bad, blue, brokenhearted, crestfallen, dejected, depressed, despondent, disconsolate, doleful, down, downcast, downhearted, droopy, forlorn, gloomy, glum, heartbroken, heartsick, heartsore, inconsolable, joyless, low, low-spirited, miserable, mournful, saddened, sorrowful, sorry, unhappy, woebegone, woeful, wretched *Ant* blissful, buoyant, buoyed, cheerful, cheery, chipper, delighted, glad, gladdened, gladsome, gleeful, happy, joyful, joyous, jubilant, sunny, upbeat **5** *Syn* SAD (sense 2), depressing, dismal, drear, dreary, heartbreaking, heartrending, pathetic, saddening, sorry, tearful, teary *Ant* cheering, cheery, glad, happy

melancholy *n Syn* SADNESS, blues, dejection, depression, desolation, despondency, disconsolateness, dispiritedness, doldrums, downheartedness, dreariness, dumps, forlornness, gloom, gloominess, heartsickness, joylessness, mopes, oppression, unhappiness *Ant* bliss, blissfulness, ecstasy, elatedness, elation, euphoria, exhilaration, exuberance, exultation, felicity, gladness, gladsomeness, happiness, heaven, intoxication, joy, joyfulness, joyousness, jubilation, rapture, rapturousness

melee *Syn* BRAWL, broil, fracas, row, rumpus, scrap

mellow *Syn* MATURE, adult, grown-up, matured, ripe *Ant* childish, immature

melodramatic *Syn* DRAMATIC, dramaturgic, histrionic, theatrical

melody • a rhythmic series of musical tones arranged to give a pleasing effect *Syn* air, lay, song, strain, tune, warble *Rel* descant

melt *Syn* LIQUEFY, deliquesce, fuse, thaw

member *Syn* PART, detail, division, fraction, fragment, parcel, piece, portion, section, sector, segment *Ant* whole

memento *Syn* MEMORIAL, commemorative, keepsake, monument, remembrance, reminder, souvenir, token

memoir *Syn* BIOGRAPHY, autobiography, confessions, life

memorable *Syn* NOTEWORTHY, notable

memorandum *Syn* LETTER, dispatch, epistle, message, missive, note, report

memorial • something that serves to keep alive the memory of a person or event *Syn* commemorative, keepsake, memento, monument, remembrance, reminder, souvenir, token *Rel* memorabilia

memory • the capacity for or the act of remembering or the thing remembered *Syn* mind, recollection, remembrance, reminiscence, souvenir *Rel* brain, intellect, intelligence, soul, wit *Ant* oblivion

menace *n Syn* DANGER (sense 1), hazard, peril, pitfall, risk, threat, trouble *Ant* safeness, safety, security

menace *vb Syn* ENDANGER, adventure, compromise, gamble (with), hazard, imperil, jeopardize, risk, venture

menacing *Syn* OMINOUS, baleful, dire, foreboding, inauspicious, portentous, sinister, threatening

mend **1** • to put into good order something that is injured, damaged, or defective *Syn* patch, rebuild, repair *Rel* ameliorate, better, help, improve **2** *Syn* CONVALESCE, gain, heal, rally, recover, recuperate, snap back

mendicant *Syn* BEGGAR, panhandler

menial *n Syn* SERVANT, domestic, flunky, lackey, retainer, steward *Ant* master

menial *adj Syn* SUBSERVIENT, obsequious, servile, slavish *Ant* domineering, overbearing

mental • of or relating to the mind *Syn* cerebral, intellectual, intelligent, psychic

mention • to refer to someone or something in a clear unmistakable manner *Syn* instance, name, specify *Rel* advert, allude, refer

mephitic *Syn* POISONOUS, miasmal, miasmatic, miasmic, pestilent, pestilential, toxic, venomous, virulent *Ant* nonpoisonous, nontoxic, nonvenomous

mercenary • one who serves merely for pay or sordid advantage *Syn* hack, hireling *Rel* abject, ignoble, mean, sordid

merchandise *Syn* MARKET, deal (in), put up, retail, sell, vend *Ant* buy, purchase

merchandiser *Syn* MERCHANT, dealer, trader, tradesman, trafficker

merchant • a buyer and seller of goods for profit *Syn* dealer, merchandiser, trader, tradesman, trafficker *Rel* businessman

merciful *Syn* FORBEARING, clement, indulgent, lenient, tolerant *Ant* unrelenting

mercifully *Syn* FORBEARINGLY, clemently, indulgently, leniently, tolerantly

mercifulness *Syn* FORBEARANCE, clemency, indulgence, leniency, tolerance *Ant* anger, vindictiveness

merciless *Syn* GRIM, implacable, relentless, unrelenting *Ant* lenient

mercurial *Syn* INCONSTANT, capricious, fickle, unstable *Ant* constant

mercy • a disposition to show compassion or kindness *Syn* charity, clemency, grace, lenity *Rel* commiseration, compassion, pity, ruth, sympathy

mere • being as stated with nothing more added or extra *Syn* bare, very

merge *Syn* MIX, amalgamate, blend, coalesce, commingle, fuse, mingle

merger *Syn* CONSOLIDATION, amalgamation *Ant* dissolution

meridian *Syn* SUMMIT, acme, apex, apogee, climax, culmination, peak, pinnacle, zenith

merit *vb Syn* DESERVE, earn, rate

merit *n* **1** *Syn* DUE, desert **2** *Syn* EXCELLENCE, distinction, excellency, value, virtue *Ant* deficiency

meritorious **1** *Syn* ADMIRABLE, commendable, creditable, laudable, praiseworthy *Ant* censurable, discreditable, reprehensible **2** *Syn* WORTHY, deserving, good *Ant* no-good, undeserving, valueless, worthless

merry • indicative of or marked by high spirits or good humor *Syn* blithesome, festive, gay, gleeful, jocose, jocund, jolly, jovial, laughing, mirthful, sunny *Rel* amused, beaming, chuckling, giggling, smiling

mesa *Syn* MOUNTAIN, alp, mount, peak, volcano

mesh *Syn* ENTANGLE, enmesh, ensnare, entrap, snare, tangle, trap *Ant* disentangle
mess *vb Syn* INTERFERE, butt in, intrude, meddle, nose, obtrude, poke, pry, snoop
mess *n Syn* MEAL, chow, feed, repast, table
message *Syn* LETTER, dispatch, epistle, memorandum, missive, note, report
messed *Syn* MESSY, chaotic, cluttered, confused, disarranged, disarrayed, disheveled (*or* dishevelled), disordered, disorderly, higgledy-piggledy, hugger-mugger, jumbled, littered, muddled, mussed, mussy, pell-mell, rumpled, sloppy, topsy-turvy, tousled, tumbled, unkempt, untidy, upside-down *Ant* neat, ordered, orderly, organized, shipshape, snug, tidied, tidy, trim
mess (up) **1** *Syn* BOTCH, bobble, bungle, butcher, flub, foozle, foul up, fumble, louse up, mangle, muff, murder **2** *Syn* DISORDER, confuse, derange, disarrange, disarray, discompose, dishevel, dislocate, disorganize, disrupt, disturb, hash, jumble, mix (up), muddle, muss, rumple, scramble, shuffle, tousle, tumble, upset *Ant* arrange, array, draw up, marshal, order, organize, range, regulate, straighten (up), tidy
messy • lacking in order, neatness, and often cleanliness *Syn* chaotic, cluttered, confused, disarranged, disarrayed, disheveled (*or* dishevelled), disordered, disorderly, higgledy-piggledy, hugger-mugger, jumbled, littered, messed, muddled, mussed, mussy, pell-mell, rumpled, sloppy, topsy-turvy, tousled, tumbled, unkempt, untidy, upside-down *Rel* besmirched, blackened, dingy, dirty, filthy, foul, grimy, grubby, grungy, mucky, nasty, soiled, spotted, squalid, stained, sullied, unclean, uncleanly *Ant* neat, ordered, orderly, organized, shipshape, snug, tidied, tidy, trim
metamorphose **1** *Syn* CONVERT, make over, transfigure, transform **2** *Syn* TRANSFORM, convert, transfigure, transmogrify, transmute
metamorphosis *Syn* TRANSFORMATION, conversion, transfiguration, transmogrification, transmutation
metaphor *Syn* ANALOGY, simile
metaphrase *Syn* TRANSLATION, paraphrase, version
meter *Syn* RHYTHM, beat, cadence, measure
method • the means taken or procedure followed in achieving an end *Syn* fashion, manner, mode, system, way *Rel* procedure, proceeding, process
methodical *Syn* ORDERLY, regular, systematic *Ant* chaotic, disorderly
methodize *Syn* ORDER, arrange, marshal, organize, systematize
meticulous *Syn* CAREFUL, punctilious, punctual, scrupulous *Ant* careless
metropolis *Syn* CITY, burg, megalopolis, municipality, town
metropolitan *Syn* COSMOPOLITAN, sophisticate *Ant* bumpkin, hick, provincial, rustic, yokel
mettlesome *Syn* SPIRITED, fiery, gingery, high-spirited, peppery, spunky *Ant* spiritless
miasmal *Syn* POISONOUS, mephitic, miasmatic, miasmic, pestilent, pestilential, toxic, venomous, virulent *Ant* nonpoisonous, nontoxic, nonvenomous
miasmatic *Syn* POISONOUS, mephitic, miasmal, miasmic, pestilent, pestilential, toxic, venomous, virulent *Ant* nonpoisonous, nontoxic, nonvenomous
miasmic *Syn* POISONOUS, mephitic, miasmal, miasmatic, pestilent, pestilential, toxic, venomous, virulent *Ant* nonpoisonous, nontoxic, nonvenomous
microminiature *Syn* TINY, atomic, bitty, infinitesimal, microscopic, miniature, minute, teeny, teeny-weeny, wee *Ant* astronomical, colossal, cosmic, elephantine, enormous, giant, gigantic, herculean, heroic, huge, immense, mammoth, massive, monster, monstrous, monumental, mountainous, prodigious, titanic, tremendous
microscopic *Syn* TINY, atomic, bitty, infinitesimal, microminiature, miniature, minute, teeny, teeny-weeny, wee *Ant* astronomical, colossal, cosmic, elephantine, enormous, giant, gigantic, herculean, heroic, huge, immense, mammoth, massive, monster, monstrous, monumental, mountainous, prodigious, titanic, tremendous
mid *prep Syn* AMONG, amid (*or* amidst), midst, through
mid *adj Syn* MIDDLE, halfway, intermediary, intermediate, medial, median, medium, middlemost, midmost, midway *Ant* extreme, farthermost, farthest, furthermost, furthest, outermost, outmost, remotest, utmost
middle *adj* • occupying a position equally distant from the ends or extremes *Syn* halfway, intermediary, intermediate, medial, median, medium, mid, middlemost, midmost, midway *Rel* equidistant *Ant* extreme, farthermost, farthest, furthermost, furthest, outermost, outmost, remotest, utmost
middle *n* **1** *Syn* CENTER (sense 1), core, midpoint, midst *Ant* perimeter, periphery **2** *Syn* THICK, deep, depth, height, midst
middleman *Syn* MEDIATOR, arbiter, arbitrator, conciliator, go-between, intercessor, intermediary, interposer, peacemaker
middlemost *Syn* MIDDLE, halfway, intermediary, intermediate, medial, median, medium, mid, midmost, midway *Ant* extreme, farthermost, farthest, furthermost, furthest, outermost, outmost, remotest, utmost
middling *Syn* MEDIUM, average, fair, indifferent, mediocre, moderate, second-rate
midget *Syn* DWARF, pygmy, runt
midmost *Syn* MIDDLE, halfway, intermediary, intermediate, medial, median, medium, mid,

middlemost, midway *Ant* extreme, farthermost, farthest, furthermost, furthest, outermost, outmost, remotest, utmost
midpoint *Syn* CENTER (sense 1), core, middle, midst *Ant* perimeter, periphery
midst *prep Syn* AMONG, amid (*or* amidst), mid, through
midst *n* **1** *Syn* CENTER (sense 1), core, middle, midpoint *Ant* perimeter, periphery **2** *Syn* THICK, deep, depth, height, middle
midway *Syn* MIDDLE, halfway, intermediary, intermediate, medial, median, medium, mid, middlemost, midmost *Ant* extreme, farthermost, farthest, furthermost, furthest, outermost, outmost, remotest, utmost
mien *Syn* BEARING, demeanor, deportment, port, presence
might *Syn* POWER (sense 1), energy, force, puissance, strength *Ant* impotence
mightily *Syn* VERY, awful, awfully, beastly, deadly, especially, exceedingly, extra, extremely, far, frightfully, full, greatly, heavily, highly, hugely, jolly, mighty, mortally, most, much, particularly, rattling, real, right, so, something, super, terribly, too, whacking *Ant* little, negligibly, nominally, slightly
mighty *Syn* VERY, awful, awfully, beastly, deadly, especially, exceedingly, extra, extremely, far, frightfully, full, greatly, heavily, highly, hugely, jolly, mightily, mortally, most, much, particularly, rattling, real, right, so, something, super, terribly, too, whacking *Ant* little, negligibly, nominally, slightly
migrant *Syn* EMIGRANT, immigrant
migrate • to move from one country, place, or locality to another *Syn* emigrate, immigrate
mild **1** *Syn* CLEMENT, balmy, equable, gentle, moderate, temperate *Ant* harsh, inclement, intemperate, severe **2** *Syn* SOFT, balmy, bland, gentle, lenient, smooth *Ant* hard, stern
milestone *Syn* TURNING POINT, climax, landmark
milieu *Syn* BACKGROUND, backdrop, environment, mise-en-scène, setting
militancy *Syn* BELLIGERENCE, aggression, aggressiveness, bellicosity, combativeness, contentiousness, disputatiousness, fight, pugnacity, scrappiness, truculence *Ant* pacifism
militant *n Syn* ZEALOT, crusader, fanatic, partisan
militant *adj* **1** *Syn* BELLIGERENT, aggressive, argumentative, bellicose, combative, contentious, discordant, disputatious, gladiatorial, pugnacious, quarrelsome, scrappy, truculent, warlike *Ant* nonbelligerent, pacific, peaceable, peaceful **2** *Syn* AGGRESSIVE (sense 1), assertive, pushing, pushy, self-assertive
military *Syn* MARTIAL, warlike
mime *Syn* ACTOR, impersonator, mimic, mummer, performer, player, thespian, trouper
mimic *n Syn* ACTOR, impersonator, mime, mummer, performer, player, thespian, trouper
mimic *vb Syn* COPY, ape, imitate, mock *Ant* originate
mimic *adj Syn* IMITATION, artificial, bogus, factitious, fake, false, man-made, mock, sham, simulated, substitute, synthetic *Ant* genuine, natural, real
mince *Syn* CHOP, dice, hash
mind *n* **1** • the element or complex of elements in an individual that feels, perceives, thinks, wills, and especially reasons *Syn* brain, intellect, intelligence, psyche, soul, wit *Rel* faculty, function, power **2** *Syn* MEMORY, recollection, remembrance, reminiscence, souvenir *Ant* oblivion
mind *vb* **1** *Syn* LISTEN, attend, hark, hear, hearken, heed *Ant* ignore, tune out **2** *Syn* OBEY, comply *Ant* command, order **3** *Syn* REMEMBER, bethink, recall, recollect, remind, reminisce *Ant* forget **4** *Syn* TEND, attend, watch
mindful *Syn* CONSCIOUS, alive, aware, cognizant, sensible, sentient *Ant* insensible, unaware, unconscious, unmindful
mingle **1** *Syn* MIX, amalgamate, blend, coalesce, commingle, fuse, merge **2** *Syn* SOCIALIZE, associate, fraternize, hobnob, mix
miniature *Syn* TINY, atomic, bitty, infinitesimal, microminiature, microscopic, minute, teeny, teeny-weeny, wee *Ant* astronomical, colossal, cosmic, elephantine, enormous, giant, gigantic, herculean, heroic, huge, immense, mammoth, massive, monster, monstrous, monumental, mountainous, prodigious, titanic, tremendous
minimal • being the least in amount, number, or size possible *Syn* least, littlest, lowest, minimum, slightest *Rel* fewer, lesser, low, slight, small, smaller *Ant* full, greatest, largest, maximum, top, topmost, utmost
minimize *Syn* DECRY, belittle, deprecate, derogate, detract, disparage *Ant* extol
minimum *Syn* MINIMAL, least, littlest, lowest, slightest *Ant* full, greatest, largest, maximum, top, topmost, utmost
minion *Syn* FAVORITE, pet, preference
minister *Syn* AMBASSADOR, delegate, emissary, envoy, legate, representative
minor **1** *Syn* LESSER, inferior, junior, less, lower, smaller, subordinate, under *Ant* greater, higher, major, more, primary, prime, senior, superior **2** *Syn* UNIMPORTANT, frivolous, inconsequential, inconsiderable, insignificant, little, minute, negligible, slight, small, small-fry, trifling, trivial *Ant* big, consequential, eventful, important, major, material, meaningful, momentous, significant, substantial, weighty
minstrel *Syn* POET, bard, poetaster, rhymer, rhymester, troubadour, versifier
minus *Syn* DISADVANTAGE, drawback, handi-

cap, liability, penalty, strike *Ant* advantage, asset, edge, plus

minute *adj* **1** *Syn* CIRCUMSTANTIAL, detailed, itemized, particular, particularized *Ant* abridged, summary **2** *Syn* TINY, atomic, bitty, infinitesimal, microminiature, microscopic, miniature, teeny, teeny-weeny, wee *Ant* astronomical, colossal, cosmic, elephantine, enormous, giant, gigantic, herculean, heroic, huge, immense, mammoth, massive, monster, monstrous, monumental, mountainous, prodigious, titanic, tremendous **3** *Syn* UNIMPORTANT, frivolous, inconsequential, inconsiderable, insignificant, little, minor, negligible, slight, small, small-fry, trifling, trivial *Ant* big, consequential, eventful, important, major, material, meaningful, momentous, significant, substantial, weighty

minute *n Syn* INSTANT, flash, jiffy, moment, second, shake, split second, trice, twinkle, twinkling, wink

miracle *Syn* WONDER (sense 1), marvel, phenomenon, prodigy

miraculous *Syn* SUPERNATURAL, preternatural, superhuman, supranatural

mirage *Syn* DELUSION, hallucination, illusion

mire *vb Syn* DIRTY, befoul, begrime, besmirch, blacken, foul, grime, muddy, smirch, smudge, soil, stain, sully *Ant* clean, cleanse

mire *n Syn* SWAMP, bog, fen, marsh, marshland, morass, muskeg, slough, swampland

mirror *Syn* MODEL, beau ideal, example, exemplar, ideal, pattern, standard

mirth • a mood or temper characterized by joy and high spirits and usually manifested in laughter and merrymaking *Syn* glee, hilarity, jollity *Rel* cheer, cheerfulness, gladness, happiness, joyfulness, lightheartedness

mirthful *Syn* MERRY, blithesome, festive, gay, gleeful, jocose, jocund, jolly, jovial, laughing, sunny

misadventure *Syn* MISFORTUNE, adversity, knock, mischance, mishap *Ant* fortune, luck

misanthropic *Syn* CYNICAL, pessimistic

misapprehend *Syn* MISUNDERSTAND, misconstrue, misinterpret, misread, miss, mistake *Ant* apprehend, catch, comprehend, conceive, fathom, grasp, know, make out, penetrate, perceive, savvy, see, seize, take in, understand

misbehavior *Syn* MISCONDUCT, malfeasance, misdoing, wrongdoing

miscalculate • to make an incorrect judgment regarding *Syn* misconceive, misjudge, mistake *Rel* misconstrue, misinterpret, misunderstand

miscarriage *Syn* FAILURE, default, dereliction, neglect

miscellaneous • consisting of diverse things or members *Syn* assorted, heterogeneous, motley, promiscuous *Rel* different, disparate, divergent, diverse, various

miscellany *Syn* ANTHOLOGY, album, compilation

mischance *Syn* MISFORTUNE, adversity, knock, misadventure, mishap *Ant* fortune, luck

mischief *Syn* INJURY, damage, harm, hurt

mischievous **1** *Syn* HARMFUL, adverse, bad, baleful, baneful, damaging, deleterious, detrimental, evil, hurtful, ill, injurious, noxious, pernicious, prejudicial *Ant* harmless, innocent, innocuous, inoffensive, safe **2** *Syn* PLAYFUL, frolicsome, impish, roguish, sportive, waggish

misconceive *Syn* MISCALCULATE, misjudge, mistake

misconception *Syn* FALLACY (sense 1), error, falsehood, falsity, illusion, myth, old wives' tale, untruth *Ant* truth, verity

misconduct • improper or illegal behavior *Syn* malfeasance, misbehavior, misdoing, wrongdoing *Rel* malefaction, misdeed, sin, wrong

misconstrue *Syn* MISUNDERSTAND, misapprehend, misinterpret, misread, miss, mistake *Ant* apprehend, catch, comprehend, conceive, fathom, grasp, know, make out, penetrate, perceive, savvy, see, seize, take in, understand

miscreant *Syn* VILLAIN, blackguard, knave, rapscallion, rascal, rogue, scamp, scoundrel

misdoing *Syn* MISCONDUCT, malfeasance, misbehavior, wrongdoing

mise-en-scène *Syn* BACKGROUND, backdrop, environment, milieu, setting

miserable *Syn* SAD (sense 1), bad, blue, brokenhearted, crestfallen, dejected, depressed, despondent, disconsolate, doleful, down, downcast, downhearted, droopy, forlorn, gloomy, glum, heartbroken, heartsick, heartsore, inconsolable, joyless, low, low-spirited, melancholy, mournful, saddened, sorrowful, sorry, unhappy, woebegone, woeful, wretched *Ant* blissful, buoyant, buoyed, cheerful, cheery, chipper, delighted, glad, gladdened, gladsome, gleeful, happy, joyful, joyous, jubilant, sunny, upbeat

miserly *Syn* STINGY, cheeseparing, close, closefisted, niggardly, parsimonious, penny-pinching, penurious, tight, tightfisted *Ant* generous

misery *Syn* DISTRESS, agony, dolor, passion, suffering

misfortune • bad luck or an example of this *Syn* adversity, knock, misadventure, mischance, mishap *Rel* calamity, cataclysm, catastrophe, disaster *Ant* fortune, luck

misgiving **1** *Syn* DOUBT, distrust, distrustfulness, incertitude, mistrust, mistrustfulness, skepticism, suspicion, uncertainty *Ant* assurance, belief, certainty, certitude, confidence, conviction, sureness, surety, trust **2** *Syn* QUALM, compunction, scruple

mishap **1** *Syn* ACCIDENT, casualty **2** *Syn* MISFORTUNE, adversity, knock, misadventure, mischance *Ant* fortune, luck
misinterpret *Syn* MISUNDERSTAND, misapprehend, misconstrue, misread, miss, mistake *Ant* apprehend, catch, comprehend, conceive, fathom, grasp, know, make out, penetrate, perceive, savvy, see, seize, take in, understand
misjudge *Syn* MISCALCULATE, misconceive, mistake
mislead *Syn* DECEIVE, beguile, betray, delude, double-cross *Ant* enlighten, undeceive
misleading • having an appearance or character that leads one astray or into error *Syn* deceptive, delusive, delusory *Rel* casuistical, fallacious, sophistical
misread *Syn* MISUNDERSTAND, misapprehend, misconstrue, misinterpret, miss, mistake *Ant* apprehend, catch, comprehend, conceive, fathom, grasp, know, make out, penetrate, perceive, savvy, see, seize, take in, understand
misrepresent • to give a false or misleading representation of usually with an intent to deceive *Syn* belie, falsify, garble *Rel* camouflage, cloak, disguise, dissemble, mask
misrepresentation *Syn* LIE, falsehood, fib, story, untruth *Ant* truth
misrule *Syn* ANARCHY, chaos, lawlessness
miss *vb* *Syn* MISUNDERSTAND, misapprehend, misconstrue, misinterpret, misread, mistake *Ant* apprehend, catch, comprehend, conceive, fathom, grasp, know, make out, penetrate, perceive, savvy, see, seize, take in, understand
miss *n* *Syn* GIRL, lass, lassie, missy
mission • a specific task with which a person or group is charged *Syn* assignment, charge, job, operation, post *Rel* burden, chore, duty, need, obligation, requirement, responsibility
missive *Syn* LETTER, dispatch, epistle, memorandum, message, note, report
missy *Syn* GIRL, lass, lassy, miss
mist *Syn* HAZE (sense 1), fog, murk, reek, smog, soup
mistake *vb* **1** • to take one thing to be another *Syn* confound, confuse *Rel* addle, muddle *Ant* recognize **2** *Syn* MISCALCULATE, misconceive, misjudge **3** *Syn* MISUNDERSTAND, misapprehend, misconstrue, misinterpret, misread, miss *Ant* apprehend, catch, comprehend, conceive, fathom, grasp, know, make out, penetrate, perceive, savvy, see, seize, take in, understand
mistake *n* *Syn* ERROR, blunder, bull, faux pas, howler, lapse, slip
mistreat *Syn* ABUSE, ill-treat, maltreat, misuse, outrage *Ant* honor, respect
mistrust *vb* *Syn* DISTRUST, doubt, question, suspect *Ant* trust
mistrust *n* *Syn* DOUBT, distrust, distrustfulness, incertitude, misgiving, mistrustfulness, skepticism, suspicion, uncertainty *Ant* assurance, belief, certainty, certitude, confidence, conviction, sureness, surety, trust
mistrustfully *Syn* ASKANCE, distrustfully, doubtfully, doubtingly, dubiously, skeptically, suspiciously *Ant* trustfully, trustingly
mistrustfulness *Syn* DOUBT, distrust, distrustfulness, incertitude, misgiving, mistrust, skepticism, suspicion, uncertainty *Ant* assurance, belief, certainty, certitude, confidence, conviction, sureness, surety, trust
misunderstand • to fail to understand the true or actual meaning of *Syn* misapprehend, misconstrue, misinterpret, misread, miss, mistake *Rel* misconceive *Ant* apprehend, catch, comprehend, conceive, fathom, grasp, know, make out, penetrate, perceive, savvy, see, seize, take in, understand
misuse *Syn* ABUSE, ill-treat, maltreat, mistreat, outrage *Ant* honor, respect
mite *Syn* PARTICLE, atom, bit, iota, jot, smidgen, tittle, whit
mitigate *Syn* RELIEVE, allay, alleviate, assuage, lighten *Ant* alarm, embarrass, intensify
mix *vb* **1** • to combine or be combined into a more or less uniform whole *Syn* amalgamate, blend, coalesce, commingle, fuse, merge, mingle *Rel* combine, conjoin, join, unite **2** *Syn* SOCIALIZE, associate, fraternize, hobnob, mingle
mix *n* *Syn* BLEND, admixture, amalgam, amalgamation, combination, composite, compound, fusion, intermixture, mixture
mixture *Syn* BLEND, admixture, amalgam, amalgamation, combination, composite, compound, fusion, intermixture, mix
mix (up) *Syn* DISORDER, confuse, derange, disarrange, disarray, discompose, dishevel, dislocate, disorganize, disrupt, disturb, hash, jumble, mess (up), muddle, muss, rumple, scramble, shuffle, tousle, tumble, upset *Ant* arrange, array, draw up, marshal, order, organize, range, regulate, straighten (up), tidy
moan *vb* **1** *Syn* COMPLAIN, beef, bellyache, carp, crab, croak, fuss, gripe, grouse, growl, grumble, kick, murmur, mutter, repine, squawk, wail, whine, yammer *Ant* rejoice **2** *Syn* SIGH, groan, sob
moan *n* **1** *Syn* LAMENT, groan, howl, keen, lamentation, plaint, wail *Ant* exultation, rejoicing **2** *Syn* SIGH, groan, sob
mob *Syn* CROWD, crush, horde, press, rout, throng
mobile *Syn* MOVABLE, motive *Ant* immovable, stationary
mobile home *Syn* CAMPER, caravan, motor home, trailer
mock *vb* **1** *Syn* COPY, ape, imitate, mimic *Ant* originate **2** *Syn* RIDICULE, deride, rally, taunt, twit

mock *adj Syn* IMITATION, artificial, bogus, factitious, fake, false, man-made, mimic, sham, simulated, substitute, synthetic *Ant* genuine, natural, real
mock *n Syn* LAUGHINGSTOCK, butt, mark, mockery, target
mockery *Syn* LAUGHINGSTOCK, butt, mark, mock, target
mod *Syn* MODERN, contemporary, current, hot, modernistic, new, newfangled, new-fashioned, present-day, red-hot, space-age, ultramodern, up-to-date *Ant* antiquated, archaic, dated, fusty, musty, noncontemporary, oldfangled, old-fashioned, old-time, out-of-date, passé
mode **1** *Syn* FASHION, craze, cry, dernier cri, fad, rage, style, vogue **2** *Syn* METHOD, fashion, manner, system, way **3** *Syn* STATE, condition, posture, situation, status
model • someone or something set before one for guidance or imitation *Syn* beau ideal, example, exemplar, ideal, mirror, pattern, standard *Rel* criterion, gauge, standard, touchstone
moderate *vb* • to modify something so as to avoid an extreme or to keep within bounds *Syn* qualify, temper *Rel* abate, decrease, diminish, lessen, reduce
moderate *adj* **1** *Syn* CLEMENT, balmy, equable, gentle, mild, temperate *Ant* harsh, inclement, intemperate, severe **2** *Syn* MEDIUM, average, fair, indifferent, mediocre, middling, second-rate
modern **1** • being or involving the latest methods, concepts, information, or styles *Syn* contemporary, current, hot, mod, modernistic, new, newfangled, new-fashioned, present-day, red-hot, space-age, ultramodern, up-to-date *Rel* fashionable, in, modish, stylish *Ant* antiquated, archaic, dated, fusty, musty, noncontemporary, oldfangled, old-fashioned, old-time, out-of-date, passé **2** *Syn* NEW, fresh, modernistic, newfangled, new-fashioned, novel, original *Ant* old
modernistic **1** *Syn* MODERN, contemporary, current, hot, mod, new, newfangled, new-fashioned, present-day, red-hot, space-age, ultramodern, up-to-date *Ant* antiquated, archaic, dated, fusty, musty, noncontemporary, oldfangled, old-fashioned, old-time, out-of-date, passé **2** *Syn* NEW, fresh, modern, newfangled, new-fashioned, novel, original *Ant* old
modest **1** *Syn* CHASTE, decent, pure *Ant* bizarre (*of style, effect*), immoral, lewd, wanton **2** *Syn* HUMBLE, lowly, meek **3** *Syn* SHY, bashful, coy, diffident *Ant* obtrusive
modesty *Syn* CHASTITY, chasteness, purity *Ant* immodesty, impurity, unchastity
modification *Syn* CHANGE (sense 1), alteration, variation *Ant* monotony, uniformity
modify *Syn* CHANGE (sense 1), alter, make over, recast, redo, refashion, remake, remodel, revamp, revise, rework, vary *Ant* fix, freeze, set, stabilize
modish *Syn* STYLISH, chic, dashing, fashionable, smart
modishness *Syn* POPULARITY, fashionableness, favor, hotness, vogue *Ant* disfavor, unpopularity
moil *Syn* LABOR, drudge, endeavor, grub, hump, hustle, peg (away), plod, plow, plug, slave, slog, strain, strive, struggle, sweat, toil, travail, work *Ant* dabble, fiddle (around), fool (around), mess (around), putter (around)
moist *Syn* WET, damp, dank, humid *Ant* dry
mollify *Syn* PACIFY, appease, conciliate, disarm, placate, propitiate *Ant* anger, enrage, incense, infuriate, madden, outrage
mollycoddle *Syn* BABY, coddle, dandle, nurse, pamper, spoil *Ant* abuse, ill-treat, ill-use, maltreat, mishandle, mistreat, misuse
molt *Syn* DISCARD, cast, junk, scrap, shed, slough
moment **1** *Syn* IMPORTANCE, consequence, import, significance, weight *Ant* unimportance **2** *Syn* INSTANT, flash, jiffy, minute, second, shake, split second, trice, twinkle, twinkling, wink
momentarily *Syn* SHORTLY, anon, presently, soon
momentary • lasting only for a short time *Syn* ephemeral, evanescent, flash, fleeting, fugitive, impermanent, passing, short-lived, temporary, transient, transitory *Rel* brief, short *Ant* enduring, eternal, everlasting, lasting, long-lived, permanent, perpetual
momentum *Syn* SPEED, headway, impetus, pace, velocity
monarch • one who rules over a people with a sole, supreme, and usually hereditary authority *Syn* autocrat, ruler, sovereign *Rel* authoritarian, czar, despot, dictator, emperor, empress, kaiser, king, lord, mogul, overlord, potentate, prince, queen, royalty, satrap, sultan, tyrant
monastery *Syn* CLOISTER, abbey, convent, nunnery, priory
monetary *Syn* FINANCIAL, fiscal, pecuniary
money • something (as pieces of stamped metal or paper certificates) customarily and legally used as a medium of exchange *Syn* cash, coin, coinage, currency, legal tender, specie
monk *Syn* RELIGIOUS, friar, nun
monkey (around) *Syn* CUT UP, act up, clown (around), fool (around), horse (around), show off, skylark
monkeying *Syn* HORSEPLAY, clowning, foolery, high jinks, horsing (around), monkeyshines, roughhouse, roughhousing, shenanigans, skylarking, tomfoolery
monkeyshine *Syn* PRANK, antic, caper, dido
monkeyshines *Syn* HORSEPLAY, clowning,

foolery, high jinks, horsing (around), monkeying, roughhouse, roughhousing, shenanigans, skylarking, tomfoolery

monograph *Syn* DISCOURSE, disquisition, dissertation, thesis, treatise

monopolize • to take up completely *Syn* absorb, consume, engross *Rel* have, hold, own, possess

monopoly • exclusive possession or control *Syn* cartel, corner, pool, syndicate, trust

monotonous *Syn* BORING, drab, dreary, dry, dull, flat, heavy, humdrum, jading, leaden, pedestrian, ponderous, stodgy, stuffy, stupid, tame, tedious, tiresome, tiring, unanimated, uninteresting, wearisome, weary, wearying *Ant* absorbing, engaging, engrossing, gripping, interesting, intriguing

monster *Syn* GIANT, behemoth, blockbuster, colossus, jumbo, leviathan, mammoth, titan, whale, whopper *Ant* dwarf, midget, mini, miniature, peewee, pygmy, runt, shrimp

monstrous **1** • extremely impressive *Syn* monumental, prodigious, stupendous, tremendous *Rel* colossal, enormous, gigantic, huge, immense, mammoth, vast **2** *Syn* OUTRAGEOUS, atrocious, heinous

monument **1** *Syn* DOCUMENT, archive, record **2** *Syn* MEMORIAL, commemorative, keepsake, memento, remembrance, reminder, souvenir, token

monumental **1** *Syn* MASSIVE, bulky, massy, substantial **2** *Syn* MONSTROUS, prodigious, stupendous, tremendous

mood **1** • a state of mind in which an emotion or set of emotions gains ascendancy *Syn* humor, temper, vein *Rel* character, disposition, individuality, personality, temperament **2** *Syn* AURA, air, atmosphere, climate, flavor, note, temper

moonshine *Syn* ALCOHOL, booze, drink, grog, intoxicant, liquor, spirits

moor *Syn* SECURE, anchor, rivet

mope *Syn* SULK, pout

mopes *Syn* SADNESS, blues, dejection, depression, desolation, despondency, disconsolateness, dispiritedness, doldrums, downheartedness, dreariness, dumps, forlornness, gloom, gloominess, heartsickness, joylessness, melancholy, oppression, unhappiness *Ant* bliss, blissfulness, ecstasy, elatedness, elation, euphoria, exhilaration, exuberance, exultation, felicity, gladness, gladsomeness, happiness, heaven, intoxication, joy, joyfulness, joyousness, jubilation, rapture, rapturousness

moral • conforming to a standard of what is right and good *Syn* ethical, noble, righteous, virtuous *Rel* good, right

morale • a sense of common purpose or dedication with respect to a group *Syn* discipline, esprit de corps *Rel* drive, spirit, vigor

morality **1** *Syn* ETHICS, morals, principles, standards **2** *Syn* GOODNESS, rectitude, virtue *Ant* badness, evil

morally *Syn* VIRTUALLY, practically

morals *Syn* ETHICS, morality, principles, standards

morass *Syn* SWAMP, bog, fen, marsh, marshland, mire, muskeg, slough, swampland

morbid *Syn* UNWHOLESOME, diseased, pathological, sickly *Ant* wholesome

mordant *Syn* CAUSTIC, acrid, scathing *Ant* genial

more *Syn* ADDITIONAL, added, another, else, farther, further, other

more or less *Syn* ALMOST, about, most, much, near, nearly, next to, nigh, practically, some, virtually, well-nigh

morning *Syn* BEGINNING, alpha, birth, commencement, dawn, genesis, inception, incipiency, launch, onset, outset, start, threshold *Ant* close, conclusion, end, ending

morose *Syn* SULLEN, crabbed, dour, gloomy, glum, saturnine, sulky, surly

mortal *Syn* DEADLY, baleful, deathly, fatal, fell, killer, lethal, murderous, pestilent, vital *Ant* healthful, healthy, nonfatal, nonlethal, wholesome

mortally *Syn* VERY, awful, awfully, beastly, deadly, especially, exceedingly, extra, extremely, far, frightfully, full, greatly, heavily, highly, hugely, jolly, mightily, mighty, most, much, particularly, rattling, real, right, so, something, super, terribly, too, whacking *Ant* little, negligibly, nominally, slightly

mortified *Syn* ASHAMED, chagrined *Ant* proud

most **1** *Syn* ALMOST, about, more or less, much, near, nearly, next to, nigh, practically, some, virtually, well-nigh **2** *Syn* VERY, awful, awfully, beastly, deadly, especially, exceedingly, extra, extremely, far, frightfully, full, greatly, heavily, highly, hugely, jolly, mightily, mighty, mortally, much, particularly, rattling, real, right, so, something, super, terribly, too, whacking *Ant* little, negligibly, nominally, slightly

mostly **1** *Syn* CHIEFLY, altogether, basically, by and large, generally, largely, mainly, overall, predominantly, primarily, principally, substantially **2** *Syn* LARGELY, chiefly, generally, greatly, mainly, principally

moth-eaten *Syn* OBSOLETE, antiquated, archaic, dated, outdated, out-of-date, outmoded, outworn, passé

moth-eaten *Syn* STALE, banal, commonplace, hackney, hackneyed, musty, stereotyped, threadbare, tired, trite *Ant* fresh, new, original

motif **1** *Syn* FIGURE, design, device, pattern **2** *Syn* SUBJECT, argument, leitmotiv, matter, motive, subject matter, text, theme, topic

motion *n* • the act or an instance of moving *Syn* locomotion, move, movement, stir *Rel* headway, impetus, momentum, pace, speed, velocity

motion *vb* • to direct or notify by a movement or gesture *Syn* beckon, flag, gesture, signal, wave *Rel* gesticulate, pantomime, sign

motion picture *Syn* MOVIE (sense 1), film, moving picture, picture

motion pictures *Syn* MOVIE (sense 2), cinema, film, pictures, screen

motive *n* **1** • a stimulus to action *Syn* goad, impulse, incentive, inducement, spring, spur *Rel* antecedent, cause, determinant, reason **2** *Syn* SUBJECT, argument, leitmotiv, matter, motif, subject matter, text, theme, topic

motive *adj Syn* MOVABLE, mobile *Ant* immovable, stationary

motley *adj* **1** *Syn* COLORFUL, multicolored, polychromatic, polychrome, varicolored, variegated *Ant* colorless, monochromatic, solid **2** *Syn* MISCELLANEOUS, assorted, heterogeneous, promiscuous **3** *Syn* VARIEGATED, checked, checkered, dappled, parti-colored, piebald, pied, skewbald

motley *n Syn* FOOL (sense 1), jester

motor *Syn* MACHINE, apparatus, engine, machinery, mechanism

motorcade *Syn* PROCESSION, cavalcade, cortege, parade

motor home *Syn* CAMPER, caravan, mobile home, trailer

mottle *Syn* SPOT, blotch, dapple, dot, fleck, freckle, marble, pepper, speck, speckle, splotch, sprinkle, stipple

mottled *Syn* SPOTTED, bespangled, flecked, marbled, spangled, spattered, speckled, sprinkled, stippled

motto *Syn* SAYING, adage, aphorism, apothegm, epigram, maxim, proverb, saw

mount *vb* **1** *Syn* ASCEND, arise, climb, lift, rise, soar, up, uprise, upsweep, upturn *Ant* decline, descend, dip, drop, fall (off) **2** *Syn* INCREASE (sense 2), accumulate, appreciate, balloon, build (up), burgeon, enlarge, escalate, expand, multiply, mushroom, proliferate, rise, snowball, swell, wax *Ant* contract, decrease, diminish, lessen, wane

mount *n Syn* MOUNTAIN, alp, mesa, peak, volcano

mountain • a relatively steep and high elevation of land *Syn* alp, mesa, mount, peak, volcano *Rel* altitude, elevation, height

mountebank *Syn* IMPOSTOR, charlatan, faker, quack

mourn *Syn* GRIEVE, sorrow *Ant* rejoice

mournful *Syn* SAD (sense 1), bad, blue, brokenhearted, crestfallen, dejected, depressed, despondent, disconsolate, doleful, down, downcast, downhearted, droopy, forlorn, gloomy, glum, heartbroken, heartsick, heartsore, inconsolable, joyless, low, low-spirited, melancholy, miserable, saddened, sorrowful, sorry, unhappy, woebegone, woeful, wretched *Ant* blissful, buoyant, buoyed, cheerful, cheery, chipper, delighted, glad, gladdened, gladsome, gleeful, happy, joyful, joyous, jubilant, sunny, upbeat

mouth *Syn* GRIMACE, face, frown, lower, pout, scowl

movable • capable of moving or of being moved *Syn* mobile, motive *Rel* changeable, changeful, mutable, variable *Ant* immovable, stationary

move *vb* **1** • to change or to cause to change from one place to another *Syn* remove, shift, transfer *Rel* displace, replace, supersede, supplant **2** *Syn* ACTIVATE, actuate, crank (up), drive, propel, run, set off, spark, start, touch off, trigger, turn on *Ant* cut, deactivate, kill, shut off, turn off **3** *Syn* PERSUADE, argue, convince, get, induce, prevail (on *or* upon), satisfy, talk (into), win (over)

move *n Syn* MOTION, locomotion, movement, stir

movement **1** *Syn* CAMPAIGN, bandwagon, cause, crusade, drive **2** *Syn* MOTION, locomotion, move, stir

movie **1** • a story told by means of a series of continuously projected pictures and a sound track *Syn* film, motion picture, moving picture, picture *Rel* animated cartoon, cartoon, docudrama, documentary, feature **2 movies** *pl* • the art or business of making a movie *Syn* cinema, film, motion pictures, pictures, screen *Rel* show business

moving • having the power to affect the feelings or sympathies *Syn* affecting, emotional, impressive, poignant, stirring, touching *Rel* eloquent, expressive, meaningful, significant *Ant* unemotional, unimpressive

moving picture *Syn* MOVIE (sense 1), film, motion picture, picture

mow (down) *Syn* MASSACRE, butcher, slaughter

much **1** *Syn* ALMOST, about, more or less, most, near, nearly, next to, nigh, practically, some, virtually, well-nigh **2** *Syn* VERY, awful, awfully, beastly, deadly, especially, exceedingly, extra, extremely, far, frightfully, full, greatly, heavily, highly, hugely, jolly, mightily, mighty, mortally, most, particularly, rattling, real, right, so, something, super, terribly, too, whacking *Ant* little, negligibly, nominally, slightly

muddle *vb* **1** *Syn* CONFUSE, addle, befuddle, fuddle *Ant* enlighten **2** *Syn* DISORDER, confuse, derange, disarrange, disarray, discompose, dishevel, dislocate, disorganize, disrupt, disturb, hash, jumble, mess (up), mix (up), muss, rumple, scramble, shuffle, tousle, tumble, upset *Ant* arrange, array, draw up, marshal, order, organize, range, regulate, straighten (up), tidy

muddle *n* **1** *Syn* CONFUSION, chaos, clutter, disarray, disorder, jumble, snarl **2** *Syn* HAZE (sense 2), daze, fog, spin

muddled *Syn* MESSY, chaotic, cluttered, confused, disarranged, disarrayed, disheveled (*or* dishevelled), disordered, disorderly, higgledy-piggledy, hugger-mugger, jumbled, littered, messed, mussed, mussy, pell-mell, rumpled, sloppy, topsy-turvy, tousled, tumbled, unkempt, untidy, upside-down *Ant* neat, ordered, orderly, organized, shipshape, snug, tidied, tidy, trim

muddy **1** *Syn* DIRTY, befoul, begrime, besmirch, blacken, foul, grime, mire, smirch, smudge, soil, stain, sully *Ant* clean, cleanse **2** *Syn* TURBID, roily *Ant* clear, limpid

muff *Syn* BOTCH, bobble, bungle, butcher, flub, foozle, foul up, fumble, louse up, mangle, mess (up), murder

mug *Syn* FACE, countenance, physiognomy, puss, visage

mulct *n Syn* FINE, damages, forfeit, forfeiture, penalty

mulct *vb* **1** *Syn* FLEECE, bleed, cheat, chisel, cozen, defraud, hustle, rook, shortchange, skin, squeeze, stick, sting, swindle, victimize **2** *Syn* PENALIZE, amerce, fine

mulish *Syn* OBSTINATE, adamant, adamantine, dogged, hard, hardened, hardheaded, hardhearted, headstrong, immovable, implacable, inflexible, obdurate, opinionated, ossified, pat, peevish, pertinacious, perverse, pigheaded, rigid, self-willed, stubborn, unbending, uncompromising, unrelenting, unyielding, willful (*or* wilful) *Ant* acquiescent, agreeable, amenable, compliant, complying, flexible, pliable, pliant, relenting, yielding

multicolored *Syn* COLORFUL, motley, polychromatic, polychrome, varicolored, variegated *Ant* colorless, monochromatic, solid

multifarious *Syn* MANY, divers, numerous, several, sundry, various *Ant* few

multiply **1** *Syn* INCREASE (sense 1), add (to), aggrandize, amplify, augment, boost, compound, enlarge, escalate, expand, extend, raise, swell, up *Ant* abate, contract, decrease, diminish, lessen, lower, reduce, subtract (from) **2** *Syn* INCREASE (sense 2), accumulate, appreciate, balloon, build (up), burgeon, enlarge, escalate, expand, mount, mushroom, proliferate, rise, snowball, swell, wax *Ant* contract, decrease, diminish, lessen, wane

multitude • a very large number of individuals or things *Syn* army, host, legion *Rel* crowd, crush, horde, mob, press, throng

mum *Syn* SILENT (sense 3), dumb, mute, speechless, uncommunicative, wordless *Ant* communicative, speaking, talking

mummer *Syn* ACTOR, impersonator, mime, mimic, performer, player, thespian, trouper

mummery *Syn* GIBBERISH, abracadabra, hocus-pocus

mundane *Syn* EARTHLY, earthy, sublunary, terrestrial, worldly

municipality *Syn* CITY, burg, megalopolis, metropolis, town

munificent *Syn* LIBERAL (sense 1), bounteous, bountiful, generous, handsome, openhanded *Ant* close

murder **1** *Syn* KILL, assassinate, dispatch, execute, slay **2** *Syn* BOTCH, bobble, bungle, butcher, flub, foozle, foul up, fumble, louse up, mangle, mess (up), muff

murdering *Syn* BLOODTHIRSTY, bloody, homicidal, murderous, sanguinary, sanguine

murderous **1** *Syn* BLOODTHIRSTY, bloody, homicidal, murdering, sanguinary, sanguine **2** *Syn* DEADLY, baleful, deathly, fatal, fell, killer, lethal, mortal, pestilent, vital *Ant* healthful, healthy, nonfatal, nonlethal, wholesome

murk *Syn* HAZE (sense 1), fog, mist, reek, smog, soup

murky *Syn* DARK, dim, dusky, gloomy, obscure *Ant* light

murmur *Syn* COMPLAIN, beef, bellyache, carp, crab, croak, fuss, gripe, grouse, growl, grumble, kick, moan, mutter, repine, squawk, wail, whine, yammer *Ant* rejoice

murmurer *Syn* GROUCH, bear, complainer, crab, crank, croaker, curmudgeon, fusser, griper, grouser, growler, grumbler, grump, mutterer, whiner

muscular • strong and powerful in build or action *Syn* athletic, brawny, burly, husky, sinewy *Rel* hale, healthy, robust, sound

muse *Syn* PONDER, meditate, ruminate

mushroom *Syn* INCREASE (sense 2), accumulate, appreciate, balloon, build (up), burgeon, enlarge, escalate, expand, mount, multiply, proliferate, rise, snowball, swell, wax *Ant* contract, decrease, diminish, lessen, wane

mushy **1** *Syn* CORNY, maudlin, mawkish, saccharine, sappy, schmaltzy, sentimental, sloppy, sugarcoated, sugary *Ant* unsentimental **2** *Syn* SENTIMENTAL, maudlin, mawkish, romantic, slushy, soppy

muskeg *Syn* SWAMP, bog, fen, marsh, marshland, mire, morass, slough, swampland

muss *Syn* DISORDER, confuse, derange, disarrange, disarray, discompose, dishevel, dislocate, disorganize, disrupt, disturb, hash, jumble, mess (up), mix (up), muddle, rumple, scramble, shuffle, tousle, tumble, upset *Ant* arrange, array, ray, up, marshal, order, organize, range, regulate, straighten (up), tidy

mussed *Syn* MESSY, chaotic, cluttered, confused, disarranged, disarrayed, disheveled (*or* dishevelled), disordered, disorderly, higgledy-piggledy, hugger-mugger, jumbled, littered, messed, muddled, mussy, pell-mell, rumpled, sloppy, topsy-turvy, tousled, tumbled, unkempt, untidy, upside-down *Ant* neat, ordered, orderly, organized, shipshape, snug, tidied, tidy, trim

mussy *Syn* MESSY, chaotic, cluttered, confused, disarranged, disarrayed, disheveled (*or* dishevelled), disordered, disorderly, higgledy-piggledy, hugger-mugger, jumbled, littered, messed, muddled, mussed, pell-mell, rumpled, sloppy, topsy-turvy, tousled, tumbled, unkempt, untidy, upside-down *Ant* neat, ordered, orderly, organized, shipshape, snug, tidied, tidy, trim

must *Syn* NEED (sense 1), have (to), ought (to), shall, should *Ant* have, hold

muster *Syn* SUMMON, call, cite, convene, convoke

musty **1** *Syn* MALODOROUS, fetid, fusty, noisome, putrid, rancid, rank, stinking *Ant* odorous **2** *Syn* STALE, banal, commonplace, hackney, hackneyed, moth-eaten, stereotyped, threadbare, tired, trite *Ant* fresh, new, original

mutable *Syn* CHANGEABLE, changeful, protean, variable *Ant* stable, unchangeable

mutate *Syn* CHANGE (sense 2), fluctuate, shift, vary *Ant* stabilize

mutation *Syn* CHANGE (sense 2), alternation, permutation, vicissitude

mute **1** • unable to speak *Syn* inarticulate, speechless, voiceless *Rel* mum, nonspeaking, quiet, silent, wordless **2** *Syn* SILENT (sense 3), dumb, mum, speechless, uncommunicative, wordless

muted *Syn* SILENT (sense 2), hushed, noiseless, quiet, quieted, soundless, still *Ant* noisy, unquiet

mutilate **1** *Syn* MAIM, batter, cripple, mangle **2** *Syn* STERILIZE (sense 1), alter, castrate, emasculate, geld, spay *Ant* fertilize

mutinous *Syn* INSUBORDINATE, contumacious, factious, rebellious, seditious

mutiny *Syn* REBELLION, coup, insurrection, putsch, revolt, revolution, uprising

mutter *Syn* COMPLAIN, beef, bellyache, carp, crab, croak, fuss, gripe, grouse, growl, grumble, kick, moan, murmur, repine, squawk, wail, whine, yammer

mutterer *Syn* GROUCH, bear, complainer, crab, crank, croaker, curmudgeon, fusser, griper, grouser, growler, grumbler, grump, murmurer, whiner

mutual *Syn* RECIPROCAL (sense 1), common

mysterious • being beyond one's power to discover, understand, or explain *Syn* arcane, inscrutable *Rel* abstruse, esoteric, occult, recondite

mystery • something which baffles or perplexes *Syn* conundrum, enigma, problem, puzzle, riddle

mystic *Syn* MYSTICAL, anagogic, cabalistic

mystical • having a spiritual meaning or reality that is neither apparent to the senses nor obvious to the intelligence *Syn* anagogic, cabalistic, mystic *Rel* abysmal, deep, profound

mystify *Syn* PUZZLE, bewilder, confound, distract, dumbfound, nonplus, perplex

myth **1** • a traditional story of ostensibly historical content whose origin has been lost *Syn* legend, saga *Rel* fable, fabrication, fiction, figment **2** *Syn* FALLACY (sense 1), error, falsehood, falsity, illusion, misconception, old wives' tale, untruth *Ant* truth, verity **3** *Syn* FOLKLORE, legend, lore, mythology, tradition

mythical *Syn* FICTITIOUS, apocryphal, fabulous, legendary *Ant* historical

mythology *Syn* FOLKLORE, legend, lore, myth, tradition

N

naive *Syn* NATURAL, artless, ingenuous, simple, unaffected, unsophisticated

naively *Syn* NATURALLY (sense 3), artlessly, guilelessly, ingenuously, innocently, sincerely, unaffectedly, unfeignedly, unpretentiously *Ant* affectedly, artificially, hypocritically, insincerely, pretentiously, unnaturally

naivete *Syn* CREDULITY, credulousness, gullibility *Ant* incredulity, skepticism

naked *Syn* BARE, bald, barren, nude *Ant* covered

name *n* **1** • the word or combination of words by which something is called and by means of which it can be distinguished or identified *Syn* appellation, denomination, designation, style, title **2** *Syn* INSULT, affront, barb, dart, dig, epithet, indignity, offense (*or* offence), outrage, put-down, sarcasm, slight, slur

name *vb* **1** *Syn* APPOINT (sense 1), designate, fix, set *Ant* discharge, dismiss, expel, fire **2** *Syn* MENTION, instance, specify **3** *Syn* APPOINT (sense 2), assign, attach, commission, constitute, designate, detail *Ant* discharge, dismiss, expel, fire

nap *Syn* SLEEP, catnap, doze, drowse, slumber, snooze

narrate *Syn* RELATE, describe, recite, recount, rehearse, report, state

narrative *Syn* STORY, anecdote, tale, yarn

narrow *Syn* INTOLERANT, bigoted, narrow-

minded, prejudiced, small-minded *Ant* broad-minded, liberal, open-minded, tolerant, unprejudiced
narrow-minded *Syn* INTOLERANT, bigoted, narrow, prejudiced, small-minded *Ant* broad-minded, liberal, open-minded, tolerant, unprejudiced
narrows *Syn* STRAIT, channel, passage, sound
nasty **1** *Syn* DIRTY, filthy, foul, squalid *Ant* clean **2** *Syn* UNPLEASANT, bad, disagreeable, displeasing, distasteful, rotten, sour, uncongenial, unlovely, unpleasing, unsatisfying, unwelcome *Ant* agreeable, congenial, good, grateful, gratifying, nice, palatable, pleasant, pleasing, pleasurable, satisfying, welcome
nation • a body of people composed of one or more nationalities usually with its own territory and government *Syn* commonwealth, country, land, sovereignty, state *Rel* city-state
national *Syn* CITIZEN, subject *Ant* alien
native • belonging to a particular place by birth or origin *Syn* aboriginal, autochthonous, endemic, indigenous *Ant* alien, foreign
Native American *Syn* AMERICAN INDIAN, Amerindian, Indian
nattily *Syn* SMARTLY, dashingly, sharply, sprucely *Ant* sloppily, slovenly
natural **1** • free from pretension or calculation *Syn* artless, ingenuous, naive, simple, unaffected, unsophisticated *Rel* impulsive, instinctive, spontaneous **2** *Syn* REGULAR, normal, typical *Ant* irregular
naturally **1** • according to the usual course of things *Syn* commonly, generally, normally, ordinarily, typically, usually *Rel* customarily, habitually, regularly, routinely *Ant* abnormally, atypically, extraordinarily, uncommonly, unusually **2** • by natural character or ability *Syn* constitutionally, inherently, innately, intrinsically *Rel* elementally, essentially, fundamentally **3** • without any attempt to impress by deception or exaggeration *Syn* artlessly, guilelessly, ingenuously, innocently, naively, sincerely, unaffectedly, unfeignedly, unpretentiously *Rel* genuinely, honestly, simply, truly *Ant* affectedly, artificially, hypocritically, insincerely, pretentiously, unnaturally
naturalness *Syn* ABANDON, abandonment, ease, lightheartedness, spontaneity, unrestraint *Ant* constraint, restraint
nature *Syn* TYPE, character, description, ilk, kidney, kind, sort, stripe
naughty *Syn* BAD (sense 1), evil, ill, wicked *Ant* good
nausea *Syn* DISGUST, aversion, distaste, loathing, repugnance, repulsion, revulsion
nauseate *Syn* DISGUST, repel, repulse, revolt, sicken, turn off
nautical *Syn* MARINE (sense 2), maritime, naval
naval *Syn* MARINE (sense 2), maritime, nautical
nay *Syn* DENIAL (sense 1), disallowance, no, refusal, rejection *Ant* allowance, grant
near *adv Syn* ALMOST, about, more or less, most, much, nearly, next to, nigh, practically, some, virtually, well-nigh
near *adj Syn* CLOSE (sense 1), nearby, nigh *Ant* remote
near *n Syn* APPROACH, approximate
near *prep Syn* AROUND (sense 1), about, by, next to
nearby *Syn* CLOSE (sense 1), near, nigh *Ant* remote, remotely
nearing *Syn* FORTHCOMING, approaching, coming, imminent, impending, oncoming, pending, upcoming *Ant* late, recent
nearly *Syn* ALMOST, about, more or less, most, much, near, next to, nigh, practically, some, virtually, well-nigh
nearness *Syn* PROXIMITY, closeness, contiguity, immediacy *Ant* distance, remoteness
neat **1** • manifesting care and orderliness *Syn* shipshape, snug, spick-and-span, tidy, trig, trim *Rel* clean, cleanly *Ant* filthy **2** *Syn* EXCELLENT, A1, bang-up, banner, capital, classic, crackerjack, dandy, divine, fabulous, fine, first-class, first-rate, grand, great, groovy, heavenly, jim-dandy, keen, marvelous (*or* marvellous), mean, nifty, noble, par excellence, prime, sensational, splendid, stellar, sterling, superb, superior, superlative, supernal, swell, terrific, tip-top, top, top-notch, unsurpassed, wonderful *Ant* poor
neb *Syn* BILL, beak, nib
necessary **1** *Syn* CERTAIN, inevitable *Ant* probable, supposed **2** *Syn* INEVITABLE, certain, inescapable, sure, unavoidable *Ant* avoidable, escapable, uncertain, unsure **3** *Syn* MANDATORY, compulsory, forced, imperative, incumbent, involuntary, nonelective, obligatory, peremptory, required *Ant* elective, optional, voluntary **4** *Syn* NEEDFUL, essential, indispensable, requisite
necessitous *Syn* POOR, destitute, impecunious, indigent, needy, penniless, poverty-stricken *Ant* rich
necessity *Syn* NEED, exigency
necromancer *Syn* MAGICIAN (sense 1), charmer, conjurer (*or* conjuror), enchanter, sorcerer, voodoo, witch, wizard
need *n* **1** • a pressing lack of something essential *Syn* exigency, necessity *Rel* pressure, strain, stress **2** *Syn* OBLIGATION, burden, charge, commitment, duty, responsibility
need *vb* **1** • to be under necessity or obligation to *Syn* have (to), must, ought (to), shall, should *Rel* will **2** • to have as a requirement *Syn* demand, necessitate, require, take, want, warrant *Rel* entail, involve *Ant* have, hold **3** *Syn* LACK, require, want
needful • required for supply or relief *Syn*

essential, indispensable, necessary, requisite *Rel* lacked, needed, required, wanted

needless *Syn* UNNECESSARY, dispensable, gratuitous, nonessential, uncalled-for, unessential, unwarranted *Ant* essential, indispensable, necessary, needed, needful, required

needy *Syn* POOR, destitute, impecunious, indigent, necessitous, penniless, poverty-stricken *Ant* rich

nefarious *Syn* VICIOUS, corrupt, degenerate, flagitious, infamous, iniquitous, villainous *Ant* virtuous

negate *Syn* ABOLISH, abrogate, annul, cancel, dissolve, invalidate, nullify, quash, repeal, rescind, void

negation *Syn* DENIAL (sense 2), contradiction, disallowance, disavowal, disclaimer, rejection, repudiation *Ant* acknowledgment, admission, avowal, confirmation

negative **1** *Syn* DENY, contradict, contravene, gainsay, impugn, traverse *Ant* concede, confirm **2** *Syn* NEUTRALIZE, counteract

neglect *vb* • to pass over without giving due attention *Syn* disregard, forget, ignore, omit, overlook, slight *Ant* cherish

neglect *n Syn* FAILURE, default, dereliction, miscarriage

neglectful *Syn* NEGLIGENT, careless, derelict, lax, neglecting, remiss, slack *Ant* attentive, careful, conscientious

neglecting *Syn* NEGLIGENT, careless, derelict, lax, neglectful, remiss, slack *Ant* attentive, careful, conscientious

negligent • failing to give proper care and attention *Syn* careless, derelict, lax, neglectful, neglecting, remiss, slack *Rel* heedless, incautious, irresponsible, reckless, wild *Ant* attentive, careful, conscientious

negligible *Syn* UNIMPORTANT, frivolous, inconsequential, inconsiderable, insignificant, little, minor, minute, slight, small, small-fry, trifling, trivial *Ant* big, consequential, eventful, important, major, material, meaningful, momentous, significant, substantial, weighty

negotiate **1** • to bring about by mutual agreement *Syn* arrange, concert **2** *Syn* BARGAIN, chaffer, deal, dicker, haggle, horse-trade, palter **3** *Syn* ENGINEER, contrive, finagle, finesse, frame, machinate, maneuver, manipulate, mastermind, wangle

neighborhood *Syn* LOCALITY, district, vicinity

neighborly *Syn* AMICABLE, friendly *Ant* antagonistic

neophyte *Syn* BEGINNER, colt, fledgling, freshman, greenhorn, newbie, newcomer, novice, recruit, rookie, tenderfoot, tyro *Ant* old hand, old-timer, vet, veteran

nerve *n* **1** *Syn* COURAGE, bravery, courageousness, daring, dauntlessness, doughtiness, fearlessness, gallantry, greatheartedness, guts, hardihood, heart, heroism, intrepidity, intrepidness, stoutness, valor *Ant* cowardice, cowardliness, cravenness, dastardliness, spinelessness, yellowness **2** *Syn* EFFRONTERY, audacity, brashness, brass, brassiness, brazenness, cheek, cheekiness, chutzpah, gall, nerviness, pertness, presumption, presumptuousness, sauce, sauciness, temerity

nerve *vb Syn* ENCOURAGE, cheer, embolden, hearten, inspirit, steel *Ant* discourage

nerveless *Syn* UNFLAPPABLE, imperturbable, unshakable *Ant* perturbable, shakable

nerviness *Syn* EFFRONTERY, audacity, brashness, brass, brassiness, brazenness, cheek, cheekiness, chutzpah, gall, nerve, pertness, presumption, presumptuousness, sauce, sauciness, temerity

nervous **1** *Syn* EXCITABLE, flighty, fluttery, high-strung, jittery, jumpy, skittish, spooky *Ant* unflappable **2** *Syn* IMPATIENT, fidgety, jittery, jumpy, restive, restless, uneasy, unquiet *Ant* patient **3** *Syn* VIGOROUS, energetic, lusty, strenuous *Ant* languorous, lethargic

nettle *Syn* IRRITATE, aggravate, exasperate, peeve, provoke, rile

nettling *Syn* ANNOYING, aggravating, bothersome, disturbing, exasperating, frustrating, galling, irksome, irritating, maddening, peeving, pesty, rankling, riling, vexatious, vexing

network *Syn* SYSTEM, complex, organism, scheme *Ant* chaos

neutrality *Syn* DETACHMENT, disinterestedness, impartiality, objectivity *Ant* bias, favor, favoritism, one-sidedness, partiality, partisanship, prejudice

neutralize • to make inoperative or ineffective usually by means of an opposite force, influence, or effect *Syn* counteract, negative *Rel* compensate, counterbalance, counterpoise, countervail

new **1** • having recently come into existence or use *Syn* fresh, modern, modernistic, newfangled, new-fashioned, novel, original *Ant* old **2** *Syn* MODERN, contemporary, current, hot, mod, modernistic, newfangled, new-fashioned, present-day, red-hot, space-age, ultramodern, up-to-date *Ant* antiquated, archaic, dated, fusty, musty, noncontemporary, oldfangled, old-fashioned, old-time, out-of-date, passé

newbie *Syn* BEGINNER, colt, fledgling, freshman, greenhorn, neophyte, newcomer, novice, recruit, rookie, tenderfoot, tyro *Ant* old hand, old-timer, vet, veteran

newborn *Syn* BABY, babe, child, infant

newcomer *Syn* BEGINNER, colt, fledgling, freshman, greenhorn, neophyte, newbie, novice, recruit, rookie, tenderfoot, tyro *Ant* old hand, old-timer, vet, veteran

newfangled **1** *Syn* MODERN, contemporary, current, hot, mod, modernistic, new, new-fashioned, present-day, red-hot, space-age, ultramodern, up-to-date *Ant* antiquated, archaic, dated, fusty, musty, noncontemporary, oldfangled, old-fashioned, old-time, out-of-date, passé **2** *Syn* NEW, fresh, modern, modernistic, new-fashioned, novel, original *Ant* old

new-fashioned *Syn* NEW, fresh, modern, modernistic, newfangled, novel, original *Ant* old

news • a report of recent events or facts not previously known *Syn* information, intelligence, item, story, tidings, word *Rel* announcement, communication, message

newspaper *Syn* JOURNAL, magazine, organ, periodical, review

next to *adv Syn* ALMOST, about, more or less, most, much, near, nearly, nigh, practically, some, virtually, well-nigh

next to *prep Syn* AROUND (sense 1), about, by, near

nib *Syn* BILL, beak, neb

nice **1** • having or displaying exacting standards *Syn* dainty, fastidious, finical, finicking, finicky, fussy, particular, pernickety, persnickety, squeamish *Rel* judicious, sage, sapient, wise **2** *Syn* AMIABLE, affable, agreeable, genial, good-natured, good-tempered, gracious, sweet, well-disposed *Ant* disagreeable, ill-natured, ill-tempered, ungracious, unpleasant **3** *Syn* CORRECT, accurate, exact, precise, right *Ant* incorrect **4** *Syn* DECOROUS, decent, proper, seemly *Ant* blatant, indecorous

nicety *Syn* FACT, datum, detail, particular, particularity, point

nifty *adj Syn* EXCELLENT, A1, bang-up, banner, capital, classic, crackerjack, dandy, divine, fabulous, fine, first-class, first-rate, grand, great, groovy, heavenly, jim-dandy, keen, marvelous (*or* marvellous), mean, neat, noble, par excellence, prime, sensational, splendid, stellar, sterling, superb, superior, superlative, supernal, swell, terrific, tip-top, top, top-notch, unsurpassed, wonderful *Ant* poor

nifty *n Syn* JIM-DANDY, beauty, corker, crackerjack, dandy, knockout, pip

niggardly *Syn* STINGY, cheeseparing, close, closefisted, miserly, parsimonious, penny-pinching, penurious, tight, tightfisted *Ant* generous

nigh *adv Syn* ALMOST, about, more or less, most, much, near, nearly, next to, practically, some, virtually, well-nigh

nigh *adj Syn* CLOSE (sense 1), near, nearby *Ant* remote

night *Syn* NIGHTLY, nocturnal *Ant* daily

nightly • of, relating to, or associated with the night *Syn* night, nocturnal *Ant* daily

nightmare *Syn* FANCY, daydream, dream, fantasy, phantasm, phantasy, vision *Ant* reality

nimble *Syn* AGILE, brisk, spry *Ant* torpid

nimbleness *Syn* DEXTERITY (sense 2), agility, deftness, sleight, spryness *Ant* awkwardness, clumsiness, gawkiness

nincompoop *Syn* FOOL (sense 2), booby, goose, half-wit, jackass, lunatic, ninny, nitwit, nut, simpleton, turkey, yo-yo

ninny *Syn* FOOL (sense 2), booby, goose, half-wit, jackass, lunatic, nincompoop, nitwit, nut, simpleton, turkey, yo-yo

nip *vb* **1** *Syn* BLAST, blight **2** *Syn* CLIP, bob, crop, curtail, cut, cut back, dock, lop (off), pare, prune, shave, shear, snip, trim

nip *n* **1** *Syn* BLAST, blight **2** *Syn* CHILL, bite, bitterness, bleakness, chilliness, rawness, sharpness

nipper *Syn* BOY, lad, laddie, shaver, sonny, stripling, tad, youth

nitpick *Syn* QUIBBLE, carp, cavil, fuss

nitpicker *Syn* CRITIC, carper, castigator, caviler (*or* caviller), censurer, faultfinder, railer, scold

nitwit *Syn* FOOL (sense 2), booby, goose, half-wit, jackass, lunatic, nincompoop, ninny, simpleton, turkey, yo-yo

no *Syn* DENIAL (sense 1), disallowance, nay, refusal, rejection *Ant* allowance, grant

nobility **1** *Syn* ARISTOCRACY, county, elite, gentry, society *Ant* people, proletariat **2** *Syn* MAGNIFICENCE, augustness, brilliance, gloriousness, glory, grandeur, grandness, majesty, nobleness, resplendence, splendor, stateliness, stupendousness, sublimeness, superbness

noble *adj* **1** *Syn* EMINENT, distinguished, illustrious, notable, noteworthy, outstanding, preeminent, prestigious, signal, star, superior **2** *Syn* EXCELLENT, A1, bang-up, banner, capital, classic, crackerjack, dandy, divine, fabulous, fine, first-class, first-rate, grand, great, groovy, heavenly, jim-dandy, keen, marvelous (*or* marvellous), mean, neat, nifty, par excellence, prime, sensational, splendid, stellar, sterling, superb, superior, superlative, supernal, swell, terrific, tip-top, top, top-notch, unsurpassed, wonderful *Ant* poor **3** *Syn* GRAND, august, grandiose, imposing, magnificent, majestic, stately **4** *Syn* MORAL, ethical, righteous, virtuous

noble *n Syn* ARISTOCRAT, gentleperson, patrician

nobleman *n Syn* GENTLEMAN, lord

nobleness *Syn* MAGNIFICENCE, augustness, brilliance, gloriousness, glory, grandeur, grandness, majesty, nobility, resplendence, splendor, stateliness, stupendousness, sublimeness, superbness

noblewoman *Syn* GENTLEWOMAN, dame, lady

nocturnal *Syn* NIGHTLY, night *Ant* daily

noise (about) *Syn* RUMOR, bruit (about), circulate, whisper

noiseless **1** *Syn* SILENT (sense 2), hushed,

muted, quiet, quieted, soundless, still *Ant* noisy, unquiet **2** *Syn* STILL, quiet, silent, stilly *Ant* noisy, stirring

noisome *Syn* MALODOROUS, fetid, fusty, musty, putrid, rancid, rank, stinking

nomad • a person who roams about without a fixed route or destination *Syn* drifter, gadabout, rambler, roamer, rover, stroller, vagabond, wanderer, wayfarer *Rel* laggard, straggler

nomadic *Syn* ITINERANT, ambulant, ambulatory, peripatetic, vagrant

nom de guerre *Syn* PSEUDONYM, alias, incognito, nom de plume, pen name

nom de plume *Syn* PSEUDONYM, alias, incognito, nom de guerre, pen name

nonchalance *Syn* INDIFFERENCE, apathy, casualness, disinterestedness, disregard, insouciance, unconcern *Ant* concern, interest, regard

nonchalant *Syn* COOL, collected, composed, imperturbable, unflappable, unruffled *Ant* agitated, ardent

non compos mentis *Syn* INSANE, crazed, crazy, demented, deranged, lunatic, mad, maniac *Ant* sane

nonconflicting *Syn* CONSISTENT, compatible, conformable (to), congruous, consonant, correspondent (with *or* to), harmonious *Ant* conflicting, incompatible, incongruous, inconsistent, inharmonious, unharmonious

nonconformist *Syn* HERETIC, dissenter, dissident *Ant* conformer, conformist

nonconformity *Syn* HERESY, dissent, dissidence, heterodoxy *Ant* conformity, orthodoxy

nonelective *Syn* MANDATORY, compulsory, forced, imperative, incumbent, involuntary, necessary, obligatory, peremptory, required *Ant* elective, optional, voluntary

nonessential *Syn* UNNECESSARY, dispensable, gratuitous, needless, uncalled-for, unessential, unwarranted *Ant* essential, indispensable, necessary, needed, needful, required

nonesuch *Syn* PARAGON, apotheosis, nonpareil

nonliterate *Syn* IGNORANT, benighted, dark, illiterate, simple, uneducated, uninstructed, unlearned, unlettered, unread, unschooled, untaught, untutored *Ant* educated, knowledgeable, literate, schooled

nonpareil *Syn* PARAGON, apotheosis, nonesuch

nonplus *Syn* PUZZLE, bewilder, confound, distract, dumbfound, mystify, perplex

nonpractical *Syn* IMPRACTICAL, impracticable, inoperable, unusable, unworkable, useless *Ant* applicable, feasible, functional, operable, operational, practicable, practical, usable, useful, workable

nonprofessional *Syn* AMATEURISH, amateur, dilettante, inexperienced, inexpert, unprofessional, unskilled, unskillful *Ant* ace, adept, consummate, crackerjack, expert, master, masterful, masterly, professional, virtuoso

nonrational *Syn* ILLOGICAL, fallacious, invalid, irrational, unreasonable, unreasoning, unsound, weak *Ant* logical, rational, reasonable, sound, valid

nonreligious *Syn* IRRELIGIOUS, godless, ungodly, unreligious *Ant* religious

nonresistant *Syn* PASSIVE, acquiescent, resigned, tolerant, tolerating, unresistant, unresisting, yielding *Ant* protesting, resistant, resisting, unyielding

nonsense • something said or proposed that seems senseless or absurd *Syn* balderdash, bull, bunk, drivel, gobbledygook, poppycock, rot, trash, twaddle *Rel* absurdity, foolishness, preposterousness, silliness

nonsocial *Syn* UNSOCIAL, antisocial, asocial *Ant* social

nonspecific *Syn* GENERAL (sense 2), all-around, bird's-eye, broad, overall *Ant* delineated, detailed, particularized, specific

nonvalid *Syn* GROUNDLESS, invalid, unfounded, ungrounded, unreasonable, unsubstantiated, unsupported, unwarranted *Ant* good, hard, just, justified, reasonable, reasoned, substantiated, valid, well-founded

norm *Syn* AVERAGE, normal, par, standard

normal **1** *Syn* AVERAGE, norm, par, standard **2** *Syn* REGULAR, natural, typical *Ant* irregular **3** *Syn* SANE, balanced, clearheaded, lucid, right, stable *Ant* crazed, crazy, demented, deranged, insane, lunatic, mad, maniacal, mental, unbalanced, unsound

normalize *Syn* STANDARDIZE, formalize, homogenize, regularize

normally *Syn* NATURALLY (sense 1), commonly, generally, ordinarily, typically, usually *Ant* abnormally, atypically, extraordinarily, uncommonly, unusually

nose *Syn* INTERFERE, butt in, intrude, meddle, mess, obtrude, poke, pry, snoop

nosy **1** *Syn* CURIOUS, inquisitive, prying, snoopy *Ant* incurious, uninterested **2** *Syn* INTRUSIVE, interfering, intruding, meddlesome, meddling, obtrusive, officious, presumptuous, prying, snoopy *Ant* unobtrusive

notable **1** *Syn* EMINENT, distinguished, illustrious, noble, noteworthy, outstanding, preeminent, prestigious, signal, star, superior **2** *Syn* NOTEWORTHY, memorable

notch *Syn* CANYON, defile, flume, gap, gorge, gulch, gulf, pass, ravine

note *n* **1** *Syn* AURA, air, atmosphere, climate, flavor, mood, temper **2** *Syn* LETTER, dispatch, epistle, memorandum, message, missive, report **3** *Syn* REMARK, comment, commentary, obiter dictum, observation **4** *Syn* SIGN (sense 1), badge, mark, symptom, token

note *vb Syn* SEE (sense 1), behold, contemplate, descry, discern, espy, notice, observe, perceive, remark, survey, view
noted *Syn* FAMOUS, celebrated, famed, notorious, prominent, renowned, star, well-known *Ant* anonymous, obscure, unknown
noteworthy **1** • having some quality that attracts one's attention *Syn* memorable, notable *Rel* conspicuous, noticeable, prominent, remarkable **2** *Syn* EMINENT, distinguished, illustrious, noble, notable, outstanding, preeminent, prestigious, signal, star, superior
nothing *Syn* TRIFLE, child's play, frippery, triviality
notice *n* **1** *Syn* ANNOUNCEMENT, ad, advertisement, bulletin, notification, posting, release **2** *Syn* ATTENTION (sense 2), awareness, cognizance, ear, eye, heed, observance, observation **3** *Syn* WARNING, admonition, alarm, alert, caution, forewarning
notice *vb* **1** *Syn* SEE (sense 1), behold, contemplate, descry, discern, espy, note, observe, perceive, remark, survey, view
noticeable • attracting notice or attention *Syn* arresting, conspicuous, outstanding, prominent, remarkable, salient, signal, striking *Rel* evident, manifest, obvious, palpable, patent
notification *Syn* ANNOUNCEMENT, ad, advertisement, bulletin, notice, posting, release
notify *Syn* INFORM (sense 2), advise, apprise
notion **1** *Syn* IDEA, concept, conception, impression, thought **2** *Syn* WHIM, caprice, fancy, freak, vagary, whimsy
notoriety *Syn* FAME, celebrity, éclat, glory, honor, renown, reputation, repute *Ant* infamy, obscurity
notorious *Syn* FAMOUS, celebrated, famed, noted, prominent, renowned, star, well-known *Ant* anonymous, obscure, unknown
notwithstanding • without being prevented or obstructed by *Syn* despite, in spite of
nourish *Syn* FEED, graze, pasture *Ant* starve
nourishing *Syn* NUTRITIOUS, nutrient, nutritional, nutritive *Ant* nonnutritious
nourishment *Syn* FOOD (sense 2), aliment, nutriment, pabulum, pap, sustenance
novel *Syn* NEW, fresh, modern, modernistic, newfangled, new-fashioned, original *Ant* old
novelty *Syn* KNICKKNACK, bauble, curio, curiosity, gaud, gewgaw, ornamental, trinket
novice *Syn* BEGINNER, colt, fledgling, freshman, greenhorn, neophyte, newbie, newcomer, recruit, rookie, tenderfoot, tyro *Ant* old hand, old-timer, vet, veteran
noxious *Syn* HARMFUL, adverse, bad, baleful, baneful, damaging, deleterious, detrimental, evil, hurtful, ill, injurious, mischievous, pernicious, prejudicial *Ant* harmless, innocent, innocuous, inoffensive, safe
nuance *Syn* GRADATION, shade
nub *Syn* CRUX, core, gist, heart, pith, pivot
nucleus *Syn* CENTER (sense 2), base, capital, core, cynosure, eye, focus, heart, hub, mecca, seat
nude *Syn* BARE, bald, barren, naked *Ant* covered
nudge *n Syn* POKE, jog, prod
nudge *vb Syn* POKE, jog, prod
nugatory *Syn* VAIN, empty, hollow, idle, otiose
nullify *Syn* ABOLISH, abrogate, annul, cancel, dissolve, invalidate, negate, quash, repeal, rescind, void
numb • lacking in sensation or feeling *Syn* asleep, benumbed, dead, insensitive, numbed, unfeeling *Rel* chilled, nipped *Ant* feeling, sensitive
numbed *Syn* NUMB, asleep, benumbed, dead, insensitive, unfeeling *Ant* feeling, sensitive
number *n* **1** • a character by which an arithmetical value is designated *Syn* digit, figure, integer, numeral **2** *Syn* SUM, aggregate, amount, quantity, total, whole
number *vb Syn* COUNT, enumerate, tell
numberless *Syn* COUNTLESS, innumerable, uncountable, uncounted, unnumbered, untold *Ant* countable
numeral *Syn* NUMBER, digit, figure, integer
numerous *Syn* MANY, divers, multifarious, several, sundry, various *Ant* few
nun *Syn* RELIGIOUS, friar, monk
nunnery *Syn* CLOISTER, abbey, convent, monastery, priory
nuptial *adj Syn* MARITAL, conjugal, connubial, married, matrimonial, wedded
nuptial *n Syn* MARRIAGE, espousal, matrimony, wedding, wedlock
nurse **1** • to promote the growth, development, or progress of *Syn* cherish, cultivate, foster, nurture *Rel* feed, nourish **2** *Syn* BABY, coddle, dandle, mollycoddle, pamper, spoil *Ant* abuse, ill-treat, ill-use, maltreat, mishandle, mistreat, misuse
nurture **1** *Syn* ENLIGHTEN (sense 1), edify, educate **2** *Syn* NURSE, cherish, cultivate, foster
nut **1** *Syn* ECCENTRIC, character, codger, crackbrain, crackpot, crank, kook, oddball, screwball, weirdo **2** *Syn* FAN, addict, aficionado, buff, bug, devotee, enthusiast, fanatic, fancier, fiend, freak, lover, maniac **3** *Syn* FOOL (sense 2), booby, goose, half-wit, jackass, lunatic, nincompoop, ninny, nitwit, simpleton, turkey, yo-yo
nutrient *Syn* NUTRITIOUS, nourishing, nutritional, nutritive *Ant* nonnutritious
nutriment *Syn* FOOD (sense 2), aliment, nourishment, pabulum, pap, sustenance
nutritional *Syn* NUTRITIOUS, nourishing, nutrient, nutritive *Ant* nonnutritious
nutritious • providing the substances necessary for health and bodily growth *Syn* nourishing, nutrient, nutritional, nutritive *Rel* dietary, dietetic *Ant* nonnutritious
nutritive *Syn* NUTRITIOUS, nourishing, nutrient, nutritional *Ant* nonnutritious

O

oaf • a big clumsy often slow-witted person *Syn* clod, gawk, hulk, lout, lubber, lug *Rel* chump, loser, schlemiel, turkey

oath *Syn* PROMISE, pledge, troth, vow, word

obdurate *Syn* OBSTINATE, adamant, adamantine, dogged, hard, hardened, hardheaded, hardhearted, headstrong, immovable, implacable, inflexible, mulish, opinionated, ossified, pat, peevish, pertinacious, perverse, pigheaded, rigid, self-willed, stubborn, unbending, uncompromising, unrelenting, unyielding, willful (*or* wilful) *Ant* acquiescent, agreeable, amenable, compliant, complying, flexible, pliable, pliant, relenting, yielding

obedient • readily giving in to the command or authority of another *Syn* amenable, compliant, conformable, docile, law-abiding, submissive, tractable *Rel* acquiescent, agreeable, amiable, obliging *Ant* contrary, disobedient, froward, insubordinate, intractable, rebellious, recalcitrant, refractory, unruly

obeisance *Syn* HONOR, deference, homage, reverence

obese *Syn* FLESHY, chubby, corpulent, fat, plump, portly, rotund, stout *Ant* scrawny, skinny

obey • to follow the wish, direction, or command of another *Syn* comply, mind *Rel* bow, defer, submit, succumb, yield *Ant* command, order

obfuscate *Syn* OBSCURE, becloud, bedim, befog, cloud, darken, dim, eclipse, fog *Ant* illuminate, illumine

obiter dictum *Syn* REMARK, comment, commentary, note, observation

object *vb* • to oppose by arguing against *Syn* expostulate, kick, protest, remonstrate *Rel* balk, boggle, demur, jib, scruple, shy, stick, stickle *Ant* acquiesce

object *n* **1** *Syn* GOAL, aim, ambition, aspiration, design, dream, end, intent, intention, mark, meaning, objective, plan, pretension, purpose, target, thing **2** *Syn* THING, article

objectify *Syn* REALIZE, actualize, embody, externalize, hypostatize, incarnate, materialize, reify

objection *n* • a feeling or declaration of disapproval or dissent *Syn* challenge, complaint, demur, expostulation, fuss, protest, question, remonstrance *Rel* compunction, doubt, misgiving, qualm, scruple

objectionable • arousing or likely to arouse objection *Syn* exceptionable, unacceptable, undesirable, unwanted, unwelcome

objective *adj* **1** *Syn* FAIR, dispassionate, equitable, impartial, just, unbiased, uncolored *Ant* unfair **2** *Syn* MATERIAL, corporeal, phenomenal, physical, sensible *Ant* immaterial

objective *n* *Syn* GOAL, aim, ambition, aspiration, design, dream, end, intent, intention, mark, meaning, object, plan, pretension, purpose, target, thing

objectivity *Syn* DETACHMENT, disinterestedness, impartiality, neutrality *Ant* bias, favor, favoritism, one-sidedness, partiality, partisanship, prejudice

objurgate *Syn* EXECRATE, anathematize, curse, damn

obligation **1** • something one must do because of prior agreement *Syn* burden, charge, commitment, duty, need, responsibility *Rel* pledge, promise **2** *Syn* DEBT, arrear, debit, indebtedness, liability

obligatory *Syn* MANDATORY, compulsory, forced, imperative, incumbent, involuntary, necessary, nonelective, peremptory, required *Ant* elective, optional, voluntary

oblige **1** • to do a service or courtesy *Syn* accommodate, favor *Rel* gratify, please *Ant* disoblige **2** *Syn* FORCE, coerce, compel, constrain

oblique **1** *Syn* AWRY, askew, aslant, cockeyed, crooked, listing, lopsided, skewed, slanted, slanting, slantwise, tilted, tipping, uneven *Ant* even, level, straight **2** *Syn* CROOKED, devious *Ant* straight

obliterate *Syn* ERASE, blot out, cancel, delete, efface, expunge

obliteration *Syn* DESTRUCTION, annihilation, decimation, demolishment, demolition, desolation, devastation, extermination, extinction, havoc, loss, ruin, ruination, wastage, wreckage *Ant* building, construction, erection, raising

oblivious *Syn* FORGETFUL, unmindful

obloquy **1** *Syn* ABUSE, billingsgate, invective, scurrility, vituperation *Ant* adulation **2** *Syn* DISGRACE, dishonor, disrepute, ignominy, infamy, odium, opprobrium, shame *Ant* esteem, respect

obnoxious *Syn* REPUGNANT, abhorrent, distasteful, invidious, repellent *Ant* congenial

obscene *Syn* COARSE, gross, ribald, vulgar *Ant* fine, refined

obscure *adj* **1** • not clearly understandable *Syn* ambiguous, cryptic, dark, enigmatic, equivocal, vague *Rel* abstruse, esoteric, occult, recondite *Ant* distinct, obvious **2** *Syn* DARK, dim, dusky, gloomy, murky *Ant* light

obscure *vb* • to make dark, dim, or indistinct *Syn* becloud, bedim, befog, cloud, darken, dim, eclipse, fog, obfuscate *Rel* conceal, hide, screen *Ant* illuminate, illumine

obsequious *Syn* SUBSERVIENT, menial, servile, slavish *Ant* domineering, overbearing
observable *Syn* VISIBLE, apparent, seeable, visual *Ant* invisible, unseeable
observance *Syn* ATTENTION (sense 2), awareness, cognizance, ear, eye, heed, notice, observation
observation **1** *Syn* ATTENTION (sense 2), awareness, cognizance, ear, eye, heed, notice, observance **2** *Syn* REMARK, comment, commentary, note, obiter dictum
observe **1** *Syn* KEEP (sense 1), celebrate, commemorate, solemnize *Ant* break **2** *Syn* SEE (sense 1), behold, contemplate, descry, discern, espy, note, notice, perceive, remark, survey, view
observer *Syn* SPECTATOR, beholder, bystander, eyewitness, kibitzer, looker-on, onlooker, witness
obsessive *Syn* COMPULSIVE, impulsive
obsolete • having passed its time of use or usefulness *Syn* antiquated, archaic, dated, moth-eaten, outdated, out-of-date, outmoded, outworn, passé *Rel* aging, obsolescent
obstacle *Syn* ENCUMBRANCE, bar, block, chain, clog, crimp, deterrent, drag, embarrassment, fetter, handicap, hindrance, hurdle, impediment, inhibition, interference, let, manacle, obstruction, shackles, stop, stumbling block, trammel *Ant* aid, assistance, benefit, help
obstinate • sticking to an opinion, purpose, or course of action in spite of reason, arguments, or persuasion *Syn* adamant, adamantine, dogged, hard, hardened, hardheaded, hardhearted, headstrong, immovable, implacable, inflexible, mulish, obdurate, opinionated, ossified, pat, peevish, pertinacious, perverse, pigheaded, rigid, self-willed, stubborn, unbending, uncompromising, unrelenting, unyielding, willful (*or* wilful) *Rel* hidebound, narrow-minded *Ant* acquiescent, agreeable, amenable, compliant, complying, flexible, pliable, pliant, relenting, yielding
obstreperous *Syn* VOCIFEROUS, blatant, boisterous, clamorous, strident
obstruct *Syn* HINDER, bar, block, dam, impede *Ant* further
obstruction *Syn* ENCUMBRANCE, bar, block, chain, clog, crimp, deterrent, drag, embarrassment, fetter, handicap, hindrance, hurdle, impediment, inhibition, interference, let, manacle, obstacle, shackles, stop, stumbling block, trammel *Ant* aid, assistance, benefit, help
obtain **1** *Syn* EARN, acquire, attain, capture, carry, draw, gain, garner, get, land, make, procure, realize, secure, win *Ant* forfeit, lose **2** *Syn* GET, gain, procure, secure, win
obtrude *Syn* INTERFERE, butt in, intrude, meddle, mess, nose, poke, pry, snoop
obtrusive *Syn* INTRUSIVE, interfering, intruding, meddlesome, meddling, nosy (*or* nosey), officious, presumptuous, prying, snoopy *Ant* unobtrusive
obtuse *Syn* DULL (sense 1), blunt *Ant* lively
obviate *Syn* PREVENT (sense 2), avert, forestall, help, preclude
obvious **1** *Syn* EGREGIOUS, blatant, conspicuous, flagrant, glaring, gross, patent, pronounced, rank, striking **2** *Syn* EVIDENT, apparent, clear, distinct, manifest, palpable, patent, plain
occasion **1** *Syn* CAUSE, antecedent, determinant, reason **2** *Syn* OPPORTUNITY, break, chance, time
occasional **1** *Syn* FITFUL, casual, choppy, discontinuous, erratic, intermittent, irregular, spasmodic, sporadic, spotty, unsteady *Ant* constant, continuous, regular, steady **2** *Syn* INFREQUENT, rare, scarce, sporadic, uncommon *Ant* frequent
occult *Syn* RECONDITE, abstruse, esoteric
occupant *Syn* INHABITANT, denizen, dweller, habitant, resident, resider *Ant* transient
occupation **1** • the activity by which one regularly makes a living *Syn* calling, employment, line, profession, trade, vocation, work *Rel* racket **2** *Syn* WORK (sense 2), business, calling, employment, pursuit
occur *Syn* HAPPEN, befall, betide, chance, transpire
occurrence • something that happens or takes place *Syn* circumstance, episode, event, incident *Rel* appearance, emergence
oceanic *Syn* MARINE (sense 1), maritime, pelagic
odd *Syn* STRANGE, curious, eccentric, erratic, outlandish, peculiar, quaint, queer, singular, unique *Ant* familiar
oddball *Syn* ECCENTRIC, character, codger, crackbrain, crackpot, crank, kook, nut, screwball, weirdo
odds **1** *Syn* ADVANTAGE, allowance, edge, handicap *Ant* disadvantage, handicap **2** *Syn* PROBABILITY, chance, percentage
odious *Syn* HATEFUL, abhorrent, abominable, detestable *Ant* lovable, sympathetic
odium *Syn* DISGRACE, dishonor, disrepute, ignominy, infamy, obloquy, opprobrium, shame *Ant* esteem, respect
odor *Syn* SMELL, aroma, scent
odorous • emitting and diffusing scent *Syn* aromatic, balmy, fragrant, redolent *Ant* malodorous, odorless
of *Syn* BEFORE, ahead, ere, of, previous to, prior to, to *Ant* after, following
offal *Syn* REFUSE, debris, garbage, rubbish, trash, waste
offend • to cause hurt feelings or deep resentment *Syn* affront, insult, outrage *Rel* annoy, bother, irk, vex
offense **1** • an emotional response to a slight or indignity *Syn* dudgeon, huff, pique, re-

sentment, umbrage *Rel* affront, indignity, insult **2** • a transgression of law *Syn* crime, scandal, sin, vice *Rel* grievance, injury, injustice, wrong **3** *Syn* ATTACK (sense 2), aggression, assault, blitzkrieg, charge, descent, offensive, onset, onslaught, raid, rush, strike **4** *Syn* INSULT, affront, barb, dart, dig, epithet, indignity, name, outrage, put-down, sarcasm, slight, slur

offensive *adj* • utterly distasteful or unpleasant to the senses or sensibilities *Syn* loathsome, repugnant, repulsive, revolting *Rel* abhorrent, distasteful, invidious, obnoxious, repellent

offensive *n Syn* ATTACK (sense 2), aggression, assault, blitzkrieg, charge, descent, offense (*or* offence), onset, onslaught, raid, rush, strike

offer *vb* • to put something before another for acceptance or consideration *Syn* prefer, present, proffer, tender *Rel* bestow, confer, give

offer *n Syn* PROPOSAL, proffer, proposition, suggestion

offhand *Syn* EXTEMPORANEOUS, extemporary, extempore, impromptu, improvised, unpremeditated

office *Syn* FUNCTION, duty, province

officious *Syn* INTRUSIVE, interfering, intruding, meddlesome, meddling, nosy (*or* nosey), snoopy *Ant* unobtrusive

offset *Syn* COMPENSATE, balance, counterbalance, counterpoise, countervail

offshoot *Syn* DERIVATIVE, by-product, outgrowth, spin-off *Ant* origin, root, source

offspring • those who follow in direct parental line *Syn* descendants, issue, posterity, progeny, young

oft *Syn* OFTEN, frequently, oftentimes

often • many times *Syn* frequently, oft, oftentimes

oftentimes *Syn* OFTEN, frequently, oft

oil • to smear, rub over, or lubricate with oil or an oily substance *Syn* anoint, cream, grease, lubricate

OK *or* **okay** *adj Syn* ADEQUATE, acceptable, all right, decent, fine, passable, respectable, satisfactory, tolerable *Ant* deficient, inadequate, lacking, unacceptable, unsatisfactory, wanting

OK *or* **okay** *n Syn* APPROVAL, approbation, blessing, favor, imprimatur *Ant* disapproval, disfavor

OK *or* **okay** *vb Syn* APPROVE (OF), accept, care (for), countenance, favor, subscribe (to) *Ant* disapprove (of), discountenance, disfavor, frown (on *or* upon)

old **1** *Syn* ELDERLY, aged, aging, ancient, geriatric, long-lived, older, senior *Ant* young, youthful **2** *Syn* FORMER, erstwhile, late, onetime, past, sometime, whilom

older *Syn* ELDERLY, aged, aging, ancient, geriatric, long-lived, old, senior *Ant* young, youthful

oldster *Syn* SENIOR CITIZEN, ancient, elder, golden-ager, old-timer *Ant* youngster, youth

old-timer *Syn* SENIOR CITIZEN, ancient, elder, golden-ager, oldster *Ant* youngster, youth

old wives' tale *Syn* FALLACY (sense 1), error, falsehood, falsity, illusion, misconception, myth, untruth *Ant* truth, verity

oligarchy • government by, or a state governed by, the few *Syn* aristocracy, plutocracy

omen • something believed to be a sign or warning of a future event *Syn* augury, auspice, boding, foreboding, foreshadowing, portent, prefiguring, presage *Rel* forerunner, harbinger, herald, precursor

ominous • being or showing a sign of evil or calamity to come *Syn* baleful, dire, foreboding, inauspicious, menacing, portentous, sinister, threatening *Rel* dark, gloomy

omit *Syn* NEGLECT, disregard, forget, ignore, overlook, slight *Ant* cherish

omnibus *Syn* ENCYCLOPEDIC, compendious, complete, comprehensive, full, global, inclusive, in-depth, panoramic, universal

on *prep Syn* AGAINST, upon

on *adv Syn* ALONG, ahead, forth, forward, onward

oncoming *Syn* FORTHCOMING, approaching, coming, imminent, impending, nearing, pending, upcoming *Ant* late, recent

onerous • imposing great hardship or strain *Syn* burdensome, exacting, oppressive *Rel* cumbersome, cumbrous, heavy, hefty, ponderous, weighty

one-sidedness *Syn* BIAS, favor, partiality, partisanship, prejudice *Ant* impartiality, neutrality, objectivity, open-mindedness

onetime *Syn* FORMER, erstwhile, late, old, past, sometime, whilom

ongoing *Syn* PRESENT, current, extant, present-day *Ant* ago, future, past

onlooker *Syn* SPECTATOR, beholder, bystander, eyewitness, kibitzer, looker-on, observer, witness

only • being the one or ones of a class with no other members *Syn* alone, lone, singular, sole, solitary, special, unique *Rel* solo, unaccompanied, unattended

onrush *Syn* ADVANCE (sense 2), advancement, furtherance, going, headway, march, passage, process, procession, progress, progression *Ant* recession, regression, retrogression

onset **1** *Syn* ATTACK (sense 1), assault, onslaught **2** *Syn* ATTACK (sense 2), aggression, assault, blitzkrieg, charge, descent, offense (*or* offence), offensive, onslaught, raid, rush, strike **3** *Syn* BEGINNING, alpha, birth, commencement, dawn, genesis, inception, incipiency, launch, morning, outset, start, threshold *Ant* close, conclusion, end, ending

onslaught 1 *Syn* ATTACK (sense 1), assault, onset 2 *Syn* ATTACK (sense 2), aggression, assault, blitzkrieg, charge, descent, offense (*or* offence), offensive, onset, raid, rush, strike
onward 1 • toward or at a point lying ahead in space or time *Syn* forth, forward 2 *Syn* ALONG, ahead, forth, forward, on
ooze *Syn* EXUDE, bleed, percolate, seep, strain, sweat, weep
opalescent *Syn* PRISMATIC, iridescent, opaline
opaline *Syn* PRISMATIC, iridescent, opalescent
open *vb Syn* BEGIN (sense 2), commence, embark (on *or* upon), enter (into *or* upon), get off, kick off, launch, start, strike (into) *Ant* conclude, end, finish, terminate
open *adj* 1 *Syn* FRANK, candid, plain *Ant* reticent *Syn* LIABLE, exposed, prone, sensitive, subject, susceptible *Ant* exempt, immune
open-air *Syn* OUTDOOR, out-of-door (*or* out-of-doors) *Ant* indoor
openhanded *Syn* LIBERAL (sense 1), bounteous, bountiful, generous, handsome, munificent *Ant* close
openheartedness *Syn* CANDOR, directness, forthrightness, frankness, openness, plainness, straightforwardness *Ant* dissembling, pretense (*or* pretence)
openness *Syn* CANDOR, directness, forthrightness, frankness, openheartedness, plainness, straightforwardness *Ant* dissembling, pretense (*or* pretence)
operate *Syn* ACT (sense 1), behave, function, react, work
operation *Syn* MISSION, assignment, charge, job, post
operative *adj Syn* ACTIVE, dynamic, live *Ant* inactive
operative *n Syn* WORKER, artisan, craftsman, hand, handicraftsman, laborer, mechanic, roustabout, workingman, workman *Ant* idler
opinion • a judgment one holds as true *Syn* belief, conviction, persuasion, sentiment, view *Rel* concept, conception, idea, impression, notion, thought
opinionated *Syn* OBSTINATE, adamant, adamantine, dogged, hard, hardened, hardheaded, hardhearted, headstrong, immovable, implacable, inflexible, mulish, obdurate, ossified, pat, peevish, pertinacious, perverse, pigheaded, rigid, self-willed, stubborn, unbending, uncompromising, unrelenting, unyielding, willful (*or* wilful) *Ant* acquiescent, agreeable, amenable, compliant, complying, flexible, pliable, pliant, relenting, yielding
opponent *Syn* ENEMY, adversary, antagonist, foe *Ant* friend
opportune *Syn* SEASONABLE, pat, timely, well-timed *Ant* unseasonable
opportunity • a state of affairs or a combination of circumstances favorable to some end *Syn* break, chance, occasion, time *Rel* contingency, emergency, juncture, pass
oppose *Syn* RESIST, antagonize, combat, conflict, contest, fight, withstand *Ant* abide, submit
opposite *adj* • so far apart as to be or to seem irreconcilable *Syn* antipodal, antipodean, antithetical, antonymous, contradictory, contrary *Rel* converse, reverse
opposite *n* • something that is exactly opposed or contrary *Syn* antipode, antithesis, antonym, contradictory, contrary, converse, counter, reverse
opposition *Syn* RESISTANCE, defiance *Ant* acquiescence
oppress 1 *Syn* DEPRESS, weigh *Ant* cheer, elate 2 *Syn* WRONG, aggrieve, persecute
oppression *Syn* SADNESS, blues, dejection, depression, desolation, despondency, disconsolateness, dispiritedness, doldrums, downheartedness, dreariness, dumps, forlornness, gloom, gloominess, heartsickness, joylessness, melancholy, mopes, unhappiness *Ant* bliss, blissfulness, ecstasy, elatedness, elation, euphoria, exhilaration, exuberance, exultation, felicity, gladness, gladsomeness, happiness, heaven, intoxication, joy, joyfulness, joyousness, jubilation, rapture, rapturousness
oppressive *Syn* ONEROUS, burdensome, exacting
opprobrious *Syn* ABUSIVE, contumelious, scurrilous, vituperative *Ant* complementary, respectful
opprobrium *Syn* DISGRACE, dishonor, disrepute, ignominy, infamy, obloquy, odium, shame *Ant* esteem, respect
opt *Syn* CHOOSE, cull, elect, pick, prefer, select, single *Ant* eschew, reject
optimistic *Syn* HOPEFUL, roseate, rose-colored *Ant* despairing, hopeless
option *Syn* CHOICE, alternative, election, preference, selection
optional • subject to one's freedom of choice *Syn* discretionary, elective, voluntary *Rel* alternative, chosen *Ant* compulsory, mandatory, nonelective, obligatory, required
opulent 1 *Syn* LUXURIOUS, deluxe, lavish, luxuriant, palatial, plush, sumptuous *Ant* ascetic, austere, humble, Spartan 2 *Syn* RICH, affluent, wealthy *Ant* poor
opulently *Syn* HIGH, expensively, extravagantly, grandly, lavishly, luxuriously, richly, sumptuously *Ant* austerely, humbly, modestly, plainly, simply
opus *Syn* WORK (sense 3), artifact, product, production
oral 1 *Syn* VERBAL, spoken, unwritten *Ant* written 2 *Syn* VOCAL (sense 1), uttered, voiced *Ant* nonvocal
oration *Syn* SPEECH, address, harangue, homily, lecture, sermon, talk

orbit *Syn* RANGE, compass, gamut, horizon, ken, purview, radius, reach, scope, sweep
ordain *Syn* DICTATE, decree, impose, prescribe
order *vb* **1** • to put persons or things into their proper places in relation to each other *Syn* arrange, marshal, methodize, organize, systematize *Rel* adjust, regulate **2** *Syn* COMMAND, bid, charge, direct, enjoin, instruct *Ant* comply, obey
order *n* **1** *Syn* ASSOCIATION, club, society **2** *Syn* COMMAND, behest, bidding, dictate, injunction, mandate
orderly • following a set arrangement, design, or pattern *Syn* methodical, regular, systematic *Rel* neat, spick-and-span, tidy, trim *Ant* chaotic, disorderly
ordinance *Syn* LAW, canon, precept, regulation, rule, statute
ordinarily *Syn* NATURALLY (sense 1), commonly, generally, normally, typically, usually *Ant* abnormally, atypically, extraordinarily, uncommonly, unusually
ordinary *Syn* COMMON, familiar, popular, vulgar *Ant* exceptional, uncommon
organ **1** *Syn* AGENT (sense 2), agency, instrument, instrumentality, machinery, means, medium, vehicle **2** *Syn* JOURNAL, magazine, newspaper, periodical, review
organism *Syn* SYSTEM, complex, network, scheme *Ant* chaos
organize **1** *Syn* FOUND, create, establish, institute **2** *Syn* ORDER, arrange, marshal, methodize, systematize
oriel *Syn* WINDOW, casement
orifice *Syn* APERTURE, interstice
origin **1** • the point at which something begins its course or its existence *Syn* inception, prime mover, provenance, provenience, root, source *Rel* beginning, commencement, initiation, starting **2** *Syn* ANCESTRY, birth, blood, bloodline, breeding, descent, extraction, family tree, genealogy, line, lineage, parentage, pedigree, stock, strain *Ant* issue, posterity, progeny, seed
original **1** *Syn* INITIAL, primordial *Ant* final **2** *Syn* NEW, fresh, modern, modernistic, newfangled, new-fashioned, novel *Ant* old
originate **1** *Syn* BEGIN (sense 1), arise, commence, dawn, form, materialize, set in, spring, start *Ant* cease, end, stop **2** *Syn* SPRING, arise, derive, emanate, flow, issue, proceed, rise, stem
ornament *Syn* ADORN, beautify, bedeck, deck, decorate, embellish, garnish *Ant* disfigure
ornamental *Syn* KNICKKNACK, bauble, curio, curiosity, gaud, gewgaw, novelty, trinket
ornate • elaborately and often pretentiously decorated or designed *Syn* baroque, flamboyant, florid, rococo *Rel* adorned, decorated, embellished, ornamented *Ant* austere, chaste
orotund *Syn* RESONANT, resounding, ringing, sonorous, vibrant
orthodox *Syn* CONSERVATIVE, traditional *Ant* liberal, nontraditional, progressive
oscillate *Syn* SWING (sense 2), fluctuate, pendulate, sway, undulate, vibrate, waver
ossified *Syn* OBSTINATE, adamant, adamantine, dogged, hard, hardened, hardheaded, hardhearted, headstrong, immovable, implacable, inflexible, mulish, obdurate, opinionated, pat, peevish, pertinacious, perverse, pigheaded, rigid, self-willed, stubborn, unbending, uncompromising, unrelenting, unyielding, willful (*or* wilful) *Ant* acquiescent, agreeable, amenable, compliant, complying, flexible, pliable, pliant, relenting, yielding
ostensible *Syn* APPARENT, illusory, seeming *Ant* real
ostensibly *Syn* APPARENTLY, evidently, presumably, seemingly, supposedly
ostentation • excessive or unnecessary display *Syn* flamboyance, flashiness, garishness, gaudiness, glitz, ostentatiousness, pretentiousness, showiness, swank *Rel* extravaganza, pageant, parade, show *Ant* austerity, plainness, severity
ostentatious **1** *Syn* GAUDY, flamboyant, flashy, garish, glitzy, loud, splashy, swank (*or* swanky), tawdry *Ant* conservative, quiet, understated **2** *Syn* SHOWY, pretentious
ostentatiousness *Syn* OSTENTATION, flamboyance, flashiness, garishness, gaudiness, glitz, pretentiousness, showiness, swank *Ant* austerity, plainness, severity
ostracize *Syn* BANISH, deport, exile, expatriate, extradite, transport
other *Syn* ADDITIONAL, added, another, else, farther, further, more
otiose *Syn* VAIN, empty, hollow, idle, nugatory
ought (to) *Syn* NEED (sense 1), have (to), must, shall, should *Ant* have, hold
out **1** *Syn* ALOUD, audibly, out loud *Ant* inaudibly, silently, soundlessly **2** *Syn* OUTDOORS, outside *Ant* indoors
out-and-out **1** *Syn* EXHAUSTIVE, all-out, clean, complete, comprehensive, full-scale, thorough, thoroughgoing, total **2** *Syn* OUTRIGHT, arrant, unmitigated
outbreak • a sudden and usually temporary growth of activity *Syn* burst, flare, flare-up, flash, flicker, flurry, flutter, outburst, spurt *Rel* binge, jag, spree
outburst *Syn* OUTBREAK, burst, flare, flare-up, flash, flicker, flurry, flutter, spurt
outcast • one that is cast out or refused acceptance by society *Syn* castaway, derelict, pariah, reprobate, untouchable *Rel* hobo, tramp, vagabond, vagrant
outcome *Syn* EFFECT, aftereffect, aftermath, consequence, event, issue, result, sequel, upshot *Ant* cause

outdated *Syn* OBSOLETE, antiquated, archaic, dated, moth-eaten, out-of-date, outmoded, outworn, passé
outdo *Syn* EXCEED, excel, outstrip, surpass, transcend
outdoor • of, relating to, or held in the open air *Syn* open-air, out-of-door (*or* out-of-doors) *Rel* airy *Ant* indoor
outdoors • in or into the open air *Syn* out, outside *Rel* without *Ant* indoors
outer • being or located outside something *Syn* exterior, external, outside, outward *Rel* alien, extraneous, extrinsic, foreign *Ant* inner
outfit *n Syn* EQUIPMENT, apparatus, gear, machinery, matériel, paraphernalia, tackle
outfit *vb Syn* FURNISH (sense 1), accoutre (*or* accouter), equip, fit (out), rig, supply *Ant* hold (back), keep (back), reserve, retain, withhold
outgoing *Syn* CONVIVIAL, boon, companionable, extroverted, gregarious, sociable, social *Ant* antisocial, introverted, reclusive, unsociable
outgrowth *Syn* DERIVATIVE, by-product, offshoot, spin-off *Ant* origin, root, source
outlander *Syn* STRANGER, alien, émigré, foreigner, immigrant, outsider
outlandish **1** *Syn* EXOTIC, fantastic, glamorous, marvelous (*or* marvellous), romantic, strange **2** *Syn* STRANGE, curious, eccentric, erratic, odd, peculiar, quaint, queer, singular, unique *Ant* familiar
outlast *Syn* OUTLIVE, survive
outlaw *Syn* FORBID, ban, bar, enjoin, interdict, prohibit, proscribe *Ant* allow, let, permit, suffer
outlawing *Syn* PROHIBITION (sense 1), banning, barring, enjoining, forbidding, interdicting, interdiction, prohibiting, proscribing, proscription *Ant* prescription
outline *n* **1** • the line that bounds and gives form to something *Syn* contour, profile, silhouette, skyline *Rel* configuration, conformation, figure, form, shape **2** *Syn* SKETCH, blueprint, delineation, diagram, draft, plot, tracing
outline *vb* **1** *Syn* SKETCH, blueprint, delineate, diagram, draft, plot, trace **2** *Syn* SUMMARIZE, abstract, digest, encapsulate, epitomize, recap, recapitulate, sum up, wrap up
outlive • to remain in existence longer than *Syn* outlast, survive *Rel* abide, continue, endure, persist
outlook *Syn* PROSPECT, anticipation, foretaste
out loud *Syn* ALOUD, audibly, out *Ant* inaudibly, silently, soundlessly
outmoded *Syn* OBSOLETE, antiquated, archaic, dated, moth-eaten, outdated, out-of-date, outworn, passé
out-of-date *Syn* OBSOLETE, antiquated, archaic, dated, moth-eaten, outdated, outmoded, outworn, passé
out-of-door *or* **out-of-doors** *Syn* OUTDOOR, open-air *Ant* indoor
outrage *vb* **1** *Syn* ABUSE, ill-treat, maltreat, mistreat, misuse *Ant* honor, respect **2** *Syn* ANGER, antagonize, enrage, incense, inflame, infuriate, madden, rankle, rile, roil *Ant* delight, gratify, please **3** *Syn* OFFEND, affront, insult
outrage *n* **1** *Syn* ANGER, angriness, furor, fury, indignation, irateness, ire, rage, spleen, wrath, wrathfulness *Ant* delight, pleasure **2** *Syn* INSULT, affront, barb, dart, dig, epithet, indignity, name, offense (*or* offence), put-down, sarcasm, slight, slur
outraged *Syn* ANGRY, angered, apoplectic, enraged, foaming, fuming, furious, incensed, indignant, inflamed, infuriated, irate, ireful, mad, rabid, riled, roiled, sore, steaming, wrathful, wroth *Ant* delighted, pleased
outrageous • enormously or flagrantly bad or horrible *Syn* atrocious, heinous, monstrous *Rel* flagrant, glaring, gross, rank
outrank *Syn* OUTWEIGH, overbalance, overshadow, overweigh
outright • being exactly what is stated *Syn* arrant, out-and-out, unmitigated
outset *Syn* BEGINNING, alpha, birth, commencement, dawn, genesis, inception, incipiency, launch, morning, onset, start, threshold *Ant* close, conclusion, end, ending
outside *adv Syn* OUTDOORS, out *Ant* indoors
outside *adj Syn* OUTER, exterior, external, outward *Ant* inner
outside *prep Syn* BEYOND (sense 2), outside of, without *Ant* within
outside of *Syn* BEYOND (sense 2), outside, without *Ant* within
outsider *Syn* STRANGER, alien, émigré, foreigner, immigrant, outlander
outsize *Syn* LARGE, big, bulky, considerable, goodly, good-sized, grand, great, handsome, hefty, hulking, largish, oversize (*or* oversized), sizable (*or* sizeable), substantial, tidy, voluminous *Ant* little, puny, small, undersized
outstanding **1** *Syn* EMINENT, distinguished, illustrious, noble, notable, noteworthy, preeminent, prestigious, signal, star, superior **2** *Syn* NOTICEABLE, arresting, conspicuous, prominent, remarkable, salient, signal, striking
outstrip *Syn* EXCEED, excel, outdo, surpass, transcend
outward *Syn* OUTER, exterior, external, outside *Ant* inner
outweigh • to be greater in importance than *Syn* outrank, overbalance, overshadow, overweigh *Rel* count, import, matter, mean, signify, weigh
outwit *Syn* FRUSTRATE, baffle, balk, circumvent, foil, thwart *Ant* fulfill
outworn *Syn* OBSOLETE, antiquated, archaic,

dated, moth-eaten, outdated, out-of-date, outmoded, passé
ovation *Syn* APPLAUSE, acclamation, cheering, cheers, plaudit(s), rave(s) *Ant* booing, hissing
over *adv Syn* ABOVE, aloft, overhead, skyward *Ant* below, beneath, under
over *prep* **1** *Syn* AROUND (sense 2), about, round, through, throughout **2** *Syn* BEYOND (sense 1), past *Ant* within
overabundance *Syn* EXCESS, fat, overage, overflow, overkill, overmuch, oversupply, superabundance, superfluity, surfeit, surplus *Ant* deficiency, deficit, insufficiency
overage *Syn* EXCESS, fat, overabundance, overflow, overkill, overmuch, oversupply, superabundance, superfluity, surfeit, surplus *Ant* deficiency, deficit, insufficiency
overall *adv Syn* CHIEFLY, altogether, basically, by and large, generally, largely, mainly, mostly, predominantly, primarily, principally, substantially
overall *adj* **1** *Syn* GENERAL (sense 1), blanket, common, generic, global, universal *Ant* individual, particular **2** *Syn* GENERAL (sense 2), all-around, bird's-eye, broad, nonspecific *Ant* delineated, detailed, particularized, specific
overbalance *Syn* OUTWEIGH, outrank, overshadow, overweigh
overbearing **1** *Syn* BOSSY, authoritarian, autocratic, despotic, dictatorial, domineering, imperious, masterful, peremptory, tyrannical, tyrannous **2** *Syn* PROUD (sense 1), arrogant, disdainful, haughty, insolent, lordly, supercilious *Ant* ashamed, humble
overcast • covered over by clouds *Syn* beclouded, clouded, cloudy, dull, hazed, hazy, heavy, lowering, overclouded *Rel* bedimmed, befogged, blackened, darkened, darksome, dim, dimmed, dulled, dusky, misty, murky, obscure, obscured, overshadowed *Ant* clear, cloudless
overclouded *Syn* OVERCAST, beclouded, clouded, cloudy, dull, hazed, hazy, heavy, lowering *Ant* clear, cloudless
overcome *Syn* CONQUER, beat, defeat, lick, overthrow, reduce, rout, subdue, subjugate, surmount, vanquish
overdo *Syn* OVERSTATE, exaggerate, overdraw, put on *Ant* understate
overdraw *Syn* OVERSTATE, exaggerate, overdo, put on *Ant* understate
overdue *Syn* TARDY, behindhand, late *Ant* prompt
overeater *Syn* GLUTTON, gorger, gormandizer, gourmand, hog, stuffer, swiller
overflow *n* **1** *Syn* EXCESS, fat, overabundance, overage, overkill, overmuch, oversupply, superabundance, superfluity, surfeit, surplus *Ant* deficiency, deficit, insufficiency **2** *Syn* FLOOD, deluge, drown, engulf, inundate, overwhelm, submerge, submerse, swamp *Ant* drain
overflow *vb Syn* TEEM, abound, swarm
overhang *Syn* BULGE, beetle, jut, project, protrude, stick out
overhead *Syn* ABOVE, aloft, over, skyward *Ant* below, beneath, under
overjoy **1** *Syn* ELATE, elevate, enrapture, exhilarate, transport *Ant* depress **2** *Syn* ENTRANCE, carry away, enrapture, enthrall (*or* enthral), ravish, transport
overkill *Syn* EXCESS, fat, overabundance, overage, overflow, overmuch, oversupply, superabundance, superfluity, surfeit, surplus *Ant* deficiency, deficit, insufficiency
overlap • to lie over parts of one another *Syn* lap, overlay, overlie, overspread *Rel* shingle
overlay **1** • to lay or spread over or across *Syn* appliqué, superimpose, superpose **2** *Syn* OVERLAP, lap, overlie, overspread
overlie *Syn* OVERLAP, lap, overlay, overspread
overlook *Syn* NEGLECT, disregard, forget, ignore, omit, slight *Ant* cherish
overmuch *Syn* EXCESS, fat, overabundance, overage, overflow, overkill, oversupply, superabundance, superfluity, surfeit, surplus *Ant* deficiency, deficit, insufficiency
overrun *Syn* INFEST, beset *Ant* disinfest
overshadow *Syn* OUTWEIGH, outrank, overbalance, overweigh
oversight • the function or duty of watching or guarding for the sake of proper control or direction *Syn* supervision, surveillance *Rel* control, controlling, direction, management
oversize *or* **oversized** *Syn* LARGE, big, bulky, considerable, goodly, good-sized, grand, great, handsome, hefty, hulking, largish, outsize, sizable (*or* sizeable), substantial, tidy, voluminous *Ant* little, puny, small, undersized
overspread **1** *Syn* COVER, envelop, shroud, veil, wrap *Ant* bare **2** *Syn* OVERLAP, lap, overlay, overlie
overstate • to describe or express in too strong terms *Syn* exaggerate, overdo, overdraw, put on *Rel* color, elaborate, embellish, embroider, magnify, pad, stretch *Ant* understate
overstatement *Syn* EXAGGERATION, caricature, coloring, elaboration, embellishment, embroidering, hyperbole, magnification, padding, stretching *Ant* understatement
oversupply *Syn* EXCESS, fat, overabundance, overage, overflow, overkill, overmuch, superabundance, superfluity, surfeit, surplus *Ant* deficiency, deficit, insufficiency
overthrow **1** *Syn* CONQUER, beat, defeat, lick, overcome, reduce, rout, subdue, subjugate, surmount, vanquish **2** *Syn* OVERTURN, capsize, subvert, upset
overture • an action taken to win the favor or approval of another person or party *Syn* ad-

vance, approach, bid, tender *Rel* proposal, proposition
overturn • to turn from an upright or proper position *Syn* capsize, overthrow, subvert, upset *Rel* invert, reverse, transpose
overweening **1** *Syn* ARROGANT, cavalier, haughty, highfalutin, high-handed, high-hat, imperious, important, lofty, lordly, masterful, peremptory, pompous, presumptuous, pretentious, supercilious, superior, uppish, uppity *Ant* humble, modest **2** *Syn* CONCEITED, complacent, egoistic, egotistic (*or* egotistical), important, pompous, prideful, proud, self-conceited, self-important, self-satisfied, smug, stuck-up, vain, vainglorious *Ant* humble, modest
overweigh *Syn* OUTWEIGH, outrank, overbalance, overshadow
overwhelm *Syn* FLOOD, deluge, drown, engulf, inundate, overflow, submerge, submerse, swamp *Ant* drain
owing to *Syn* BECAUSE OF, due to, through, with
own *Syn* HAVE, enjoy, hold, possess
owner *Syn* PROPRIETOR, holder, possessor
own (up) *Syn* ADMIT, acknowledge, agree, allow, concede, confess, grant *Ant* deny

P

pabulum *Syn* FOOD (sense 2), aliment, nourishment, nutriment, pap, sustenance
pace *Syn* SPEED, headway, impetus, momentum, velocity
pacific • affording or promoting peace *Syn* irenic, pacifist, pacifistic, peaceable, peaceful *Rel* calm, placid, serene, tranquil *Ant* bellicose
pacifist *Syn* PACIFIC, irenic, pacifistic, peaceable, peaceful *Ant* bellicose
pacifistic *Syn* PACIFIC, irenic, pacifist, peaceable, peaceful *Ant* bellicose
pacify • to lessen the anger or agitation of *Syn* appease, conciliate, disarm, mollify, placate, propitiate *Rel* calm, comfort, console, content, quiet, soothe *Ant* anger, enrage, incense, infuriate, madden, outrage
pack *vb* • to fill a limited space with more than is practicable or fitting *Syn* cram, crowd, ram, stuff, tamp *Rel* compact, consolidate
pack *n* *Syn* BUNDLE, bale, bunch, package, packet, parcel
package *Syn* BUNDLE, bale, bunch, pack, packet, parcel
packet *Syn* BUNDLE, bale, bunch, pack, package, parcel
pact *Syn* CONTRACT, bargain, cartel, compact, concordat, convention, entente, treaty
pad *Syn* WALK, foot (it), hoof (it), leg (it), step, traipse, tread
padding *Syn* EXAGGERATION, caricature, coloring, elaboration, embellishment, embroidering, hyperbole, magnification, overstatement, stretching *Ant* understatement
pain • a bodily sensation that causes acute discomfort or suffering *Syn* ache, pang, stitch, throe, twinge *Rel* agony, distress, passion, suffering
painlessly *Syn* EASILY, effortlessly, facilely, fluently, freely, handily, lightly, readily, smoothly *Ant* arduously, laboriously
pains *Syn* EFFORT, exertion, trouble *Ant* ease
pair **1** • two things of the same or similar kind that match or are considered together *Syn* brace, couple, duo, twain, twosome *Rel* span, yoke **2** *Syn* COUPLE, brace, yoke
palace *Syn* MANSION, castle, château, countryseat, estate, hacienda, hall, manor, manor house, villa
palatable • agreeable or pleasant to the taste *Syn* appetizing, flavorsome, relishing, sapid, savory, tasty, toothsome *Rel* delectable, delicious, delightful, luscious *Ant* distasteful, unpalatable
palatial *Syn* LUXURIOUS, deluxe, lavish, luxuriant, opulent, plush, sumptuous *Ant* ascetic, austere, humble, Spartan
palaver *vb* *Syn* CHAT, babble, blab, cackle, chatter, converse, gab, gabble, gas, jabber, jaw, patter, prate, prattle, rap, rattle, run on, talk, twitter, visit
palaver *n* *Syn* CHAT, chatter, chitchat, gabfest, gossip, rap, small talk, table talk, talk, tête-à-tête
pale *adj* **1** • deficient in color or in intensity of color *Syn* ashen, ashy, livid, pallid, wan *Rel* ghastly, macabre *Ant* florid, flush, rubicund, ruddy, sanguine **2** • being weak and thin in substance or in vital qualities *Syn* anemic, bloodless *Rel* inane, insipid, jejune, wishy-washy
pale *vb* *Syn* WHITEN, blanch, bleach, blench, decolorize, dull, fade, wash out *Ant* blacken, darken, deepen
pall *Syn* SATIATE, cloy, glut, gorge, sate, surfeit
palliate • to give a speciously fine appearance to what is base, evil, or erroneous *Syn* extenuate, gloss, gloze, whiten, whitewash *Rel* alleviate, lighten, mitigate, relieve
pallid *Syn* PALE (sense 1), ashen, ashy, livid,

wan *Ant* florid, flush, rubicund, ruddy, sanguine

palpable **1** *Syn* EVIDENT, apparent, clear, distinct, manifest, obvious, patent, plain **2** *Syn* PERCEPTIBLE, appreciable, detectable, discernible, distinguishable, sensible *Ant* impalpable, imperceptible, inappreciable, indistinguishable, insensible **3** *Syn* TANGIBLE, touchable *Ant* impalpable, intangible

palpate *Syn* TOUCH, feel, handle, paw

palpitate *Syn* PULSATE, beat, pulse, throb

palpitation *Syn* PULSATION, beat, pulse, throb

palter **1** *Syn* BARGAIN, chaffer, deal, dicker, haggle, horse-trade, negotiate **2** *Syn* LIE, equivocate, fib, prevaricate

paltry *Syn* PETTY, measly, picayune, picayunish, puny, trifling, trivial *Ant* gross, important, momentous

pamper *Syn* BABY, coddle, dandle, mollycoddle, nurse, spoil *Ant* abuse, ill-treat, ill-use, maltreat, mishandle, mistreat, misuse

pancake • a flat cake made from thin batter and cooked on both sides (as on a griddle) *Syn* flapjack, griddle cake, hotcake, slapjack *Rel* crepe (*or* crêpe), waffle

pandect *Syn* COMPENDIUM, aperçu, précis, sketch, survey, syllabus

pandemonium **1** *Syn* COMMOTION, bother, bustle, clatter, disturbance, furor, furore, fuss, hubbub, hullabaloo, hurly-burly, pother, row, ruckus, ruction, rumpus, shindy, squall, stew, stir, storm, to-do, tumult, turmoil, uproar, welter, whirl **2** *Syn* DIN, babel, clamor, hubbub, hullabaloo, racket, uproar *Ant* quiet

pander *Syn* CATER, purvey

panegyric *Syn* ENCOMIUM, citation, eulogy, tribute

pang *Syn* PAIN, ache, stitch, throe, twinge

panhandler *Syn* BEGGAR, mendicant

panic *Syn* FEAR, alarm, consternation, dismay, dread, fright, horror, terror, trepidation *Ant* fearlessness

panoramic *Syn* ENCYCLOPEDIC, compendious, complete, comprehensive, full, global, inclusive, in-depth, omnibus, universal

pant *Syn* AIM, aspire

pap *Syn* FOOD (sense 2), aliment, nourishment, nutriment, pabulum, sustenance

paper **1** • a written or printed statement that is of value as a source of information or proof of a right, contention, or claim *Syn* document, instrument **2** *Syn* ESSAY, article, composition, theme

par *Syn* AVERAGE, norm, normal, standard

parable *Syn* ALLEGORY, fable

parade *n* **1** *Syn* DISPLAY, array, pomp **2** *Syn* PROCESSION, cavalcade, cortege, motorcade

parade *vb* *Syn* SHOW (sense 2), display, exhibit, expose, flaunt *Ant* disguise

paradise *Syn* ECSTASY, elation, euphoria, exhilaration, heaven, intoxication, rapture, rhapsody, transport *Ant* depression

paradox • an expression or revelation of an inner or inherent contradiction *Syn* anomaly, antinomy

paragon • a model of excellence or perfection *Syn* apotheosis, nonesuch, nonpareil

paragraph • one of the several and individually distinct statements of a discourse or instrument, each of which deals with a particular point or item *Syn* article, clause, count, plank, verse

parallel *n* **1** • one that corresponds to or closely resembles another *Syn* analogue, correlate, counterpart **2** *Syn* COMPARISON, collation, contrast **3** *Syn* EQUAL, coordinate, counterpart, equivalent, fellow, like, match, peer, rival

parallel *adj* *Syn* ALIKE, akin, analogous, comparable, correspondent, corresponding, like, matching, resembling, similar, such, suchlike *Ant* different, dissimilar, diverse, unlike

parallelism *Syn* SIMILARITY, alikeness, community, correspondence, likeness, resemblance, similitude *Ant* dissimilarity, unlikeness

paralyze *Syn* DAZE, bemuse, benumb, petrify, stun, stupefy

paramount *Syn* DOMINANT, predominant, preponderant, preponderating, sovereign *Ant* subordinate

parapet *Syn* BULWARK, bastion, breastwork, rampart

paraphernalia *Syn* EQUIPMENT, apparatus, gear, machinery, matériel, outfit, tackle

paraphrase *vb* • to express something (as a text or statement) in different words *Syn* rephrase, restate, reword, translate *Rel* summarize *Ant* quote

paraphrase *n* *Syn* TRANSLATION, metaphrase, version

parasite • a usually obsequious flatterer or self-seeker *Syn* bootlicker, favorite, hanger-on, leech, lickspittle, sponge, sponger, sycophant, toady *Rel* cringer, fawner, truckler

parboil *Syn* BOIL, seethe, simmer, stew

parcel *vb* *Syn* APPORTION, portion, prorate, ration

parcel *n* **1** *Syn* BUNDLE, bale, bunch, pack, package, packet **2** *Syn* GROUP, bunch, cluster, lot **3** *Syn* PART, detail, division, fraction, fragment, member, piece, portion, section, sector, segment *Ant* whole

parch *Syn* DRY, bake, dehydrate, desiccate *Ant* moisten, wet

pardon *n* • release from the guilt or penalty of an offense *Syn* absolution, amnesty, forgiveness, remission, remittal *Ant* penalty, punishment, retribution

pardon *vb* *Syn* EXCUSE, condone, forgive, remit *Ant* punish

pardonable *Syn* VENIAL, excusable, forgivable, remittable *Ant* inexcusable, mortal, unforgivable, unpardonable

pare 1 *Syn* CLIP, bob, crop, curtail, cut, cut back, dock, lop (off), nip, prune, shave, shear, snip, trim 2 *Syn* SKIN, decorticate, flay, peel

parentage *Syn* ANCESTRY, birth, blood, bloodline, breeding, descent, extraction, family tree, genealogy, line, lineage, origin, pedigree, stock, strain *Ant* issue, posterity, progeny, seed

par excellence *Syn* EXCELLENT, A1, bang-up, banner, capital, classic, crackerjack, dandy, divine, fabulous, fine, first-class, first-rate, grand, great, groovy, heavenly, jim-dandy, keen, marvelous (*or* marvellous), mean, neat, nifty, noble, prime, sensational, splendid, stellar, sterling, superb, superior, superlative, supernal, swell, terrific, tip-top, top, top-notch, unsurpassed, wonderful *Ant* poor

pariah *Syn* OUTCAST, castaway, derelict, reprobate, untouchable

parochial *Syn* INSULAR, local, provincial, small-town

parody *n Syn* CARICATURE, burlesque, travesty

parody *vb Syn* CARICATURE, burlesque, travesty

paroxysm 1 *Syn* CONVULSION, cataclysm, storm, tempest, tumult, upheaval, uproar 2 *Syn* FIT, convulsion, spasm

parrot *Syn* REPEAT (sense 2), echo, quote

parry *Syn* DODGE, duck, fence, malinger, shirk, sidestep *Ant* face

parsimonious *Syn* STINGY, cheeseparing, close, closefisted, miserly, niggardly, penny-pinching, penurious, tight, tightfisted *Ant* generous

part *n* 1 • something less than the whole *Syn* detail, division, fraction, fragment, member, parcel, piece, portion, section, sector, segment *Ant* whole 2 *Syn* ROLE, capacity, function, job, place, position, purpose, task, work

part *adv Syn* PARTLY, incompletely, partially *Ant* completely, entirely, totally, wholly

part *vb Syn* SEPARATE, divide, divorce, sever, sunder *Ant* combine

partake *Syn* SHARE, participate

partaker *Syn* PARTICIPANT, participator, party, sharer *Ant* nonparticipant

partiality 1 *Syn* BIAS, favor, one-sidedness, partisanship, prejudice *Ant* impartiality, neutrality, objectivity, open-mindedness 2 *Syn* LIKING, appetite, fancy, favor, fondness, like, love, preference, relish, shine, taste, use *Ant* aversion, disfavor, dislike, distaste, hatred, loathing 3 *Syn* PREDILECTION, bias, prejudice, prepossession *Ant* aversion

partially *Syn* PARTLY, incompletely, part *Ant* completely, entirely, totally, wholly

participant • one who takes part in something *Syn* partaker, participator, party, sharer *Rel* actor *Ant* nonparticipant

participate *Syn* SHARE, partake

participator *Syn* PARTICIPANT, partaker, party, sharer *Ant* nonparticipant

particle • a tiny or insignificant amount, part, or piece *Syn* atom, bit, iota, jot, mite, smidgen, tittle, whit

parti-colored *Syn* VARIEGATED, checked, checkered, dappled, motley, piebald, pied, skewbald

particular *adj* 1 *Syn* CIRCUMSTANTIAL, detailed, itemized, minute, particularized *Ant* abridged, summary 2 *Syn* NICE, dainty, fastidious, finical, finicking, finicky, fussy, pernickety, persnickety, squeamish 3 *Syn* SELECTIVE, choosy (*or* choosey), picky *Ant* nonselective 4 *Syn* SINGLE, lone, separate, sole, solitary, unique *Ant* accompanied, conjugal, supported 5 *Syn* SPECIAL, especial, individual, specific

particular *n* 1 *Syn* FACT, datum, detail, nicety, particularity, point 2 *Syn* ITEM, detail

particularity *Syn* FACT, datum, detail, nicety, particular, point

particularized *Syn* CIRCUMSTANTIAL, detailed, itemized, minute, particular *Ant* abridged, summary

particularly *Syn* VERY, awful, awfully, beastly, deadly, especially, exceedingly, extra, extremely, far, frightfully, full, greatly, heavily, highly, hugely, jolly, mightily, mighty, mortally, most, much, rattling, real, right, so, something, super, terribly, too, whacking *Ant* little, negligibly, nominally, slightly

partisan 1 *Syn* FOLLOWER, adherent, convert, disciple, pupil, votary *Ant* leader 2 *Syn* ZEALOT, crusader, fanatic, militant

partisanship *Syn* BIAS, favor, one-sidedness, partiality, prejudice *Ant* impartiality, neutrality, objectivity, open-mindedness

partly • in some measure or degree *Syn* incompletely, part, partially *Rel* in part *Ant* completely, entirely, totally, wholly

partner 1 • one associated in action with another *Syn* ally, colleague, confederate, copartner *Ant* rival 2 *Syn* SPOUSE, consort, mate

party 1 *Syn* COMBINATION, bloc, combine, faction, ring 2 *Syn* COMPANY, band, troop, troupe 3 *Syn* FACTION, bloc, body, coalition, sect, set, side, wing 4 *Syn* PARTICIPANT, partaker, participator, sharer *Ant* nonparticipant

pass *vb* 1 • move or come to a termination or end *Syn* elapse, expire, pass away *Rel* depart, go, leave, quit, withdraw 2 *Syn* ENACT, lay down, legislate, make *Ant* repeal, rescind, revoke

pass *n* 1 *Syn* ATTEMPT, crack, endeavor, essay, fling, go, shot, stab, trial, try, whack 2 *Syn* CANYON, defile, flume, gap, gorge, gulch, gulf, notch, ravine 3 *Syn* JUNCTURE, contingency, crisis, emergency, exigency, pinch, strait **4** *Syn* WAY, artery, course, passage, route

passable *Syn* ADEQUATE, acceptable, all right, decent, fine, OK (*or* okay), respectable, satisfactory, tolerable *Ant* deficient, inadequate, lacking, unacceptable, unsatisfactory, wanting

passage **1** • a typically long narrow way connecting parts of a building *Syn* aisle, arcade, cloister, corridor, gallery, hall, hallway, passageway **2** *Syn* ADVANCE (sense 2), advancement, furtherance, going, headway, march, onrush, process, procession, progress, progression *Ant* recession, regression, retrogression **3** *Syn* STRAIT, channel, narrows, sound **4** *Syn* WAY, artery, course, pass, route

passageway *Syn* PASSAGE, aisle, arcade, cloister, corridor, gallery, hall, hallway

pass away *Syn* PASS, elapse, expire

passé *Syn* OBSOLETE, antiquated, archaic, dated, moth-eaten, outdated, out-of-date, outmoded, outworn

passing *n Syn* DEATH, decease, demise *Ant* life

passing *adj Syn* MOMENTARY, ephemeral, evanescent, flash, fleeting, fugitive, impermanent, short-lived, temporary, transient, transitory *Ant* enduring, eternal, everlasting, lasting, long-lived, permanent, perpetual

passion **1** • intense emotion compelling action *Syn* ardor, enthusiasm, fervor, zeal *Rel* ecstasy, rapture, transport **2** *Syn* DESIRE, appetite, lust, urge *Ant* distaste **3** *Syn* DISTRESS, agony, dolor, misery, suffering **4** *Syn* FEELING, affection, emotion, sentiment

passionate *Syn* FERVENT, ardent, blazing, burning, charged, emotional, fervid, feverish, fiery, flaming, glowing, hot-blooded, impassioned, red-hot, vehement, warm, warm-blooded *Ant* cold, cool, dispassionate, impassive, unemotional

passive **1** • receiving or enduring without offering resistance *Syn* acquiescent, nonresistant, resigned, tolerant, tolerating, unresistant, unresisting, yielding *Rel* forbearing, long-suffering, patient, uncomplaining *Ant* protesting, resistant, resisting, unyielding **2** *Syn* INACTIVE, idle, inert, supine *Ant* active, live

pass out *Syn* FAINT, black out, swoon *Ant* come around, come round, come to, revive

pass (over) *Syn* TRAVERSE, cover, crisscross, cross, cut (across), follow, go, proceed (along), travel

past *n* • the events or experience of former times *Syn* auld lang syne, history, yesterday, yesteryear, yore *Rel* bygone

past *prep Syn* BEYOND (sense 1), over *Ant* within

past *adj Syn* FORMER, erstwhile, late, old, onetime, sometime, whilom

past master *Syn* EXPERT, ace, adept, artist, authority, crackerjack, maestro, master, scholar, shark, virtuoso, whiz, wizard *Ant* amateur

pastoral *Syn* RURAL, bucolic, rustic *Ant* urban

pasture *Syn* FEED, graze, nourish *Ant* starve

pat **1** *Syn* OBSTINATE, adamant, adamantine, dogged, hard, hardened, hardheaded, hardhearted, headstrong, immovable, implacable, inflexible, mulish, obdurate, opinionated, ossified, peevish, pertinacious, perverse, pigheaded, rigid, self-willed, stubborn, unbending, uncompromising, unrelenting, unyielding, willful (*or* wilful) *Ant* acquiescent, agreeable, amenable, compliant, complying, flexible, pliable, pliant, relenting, yielding **2** *Syn* SEASONABLE, opportune, timely, well-timed *Ant* unseasonable

patch *Syn* MEND, rebuild, repair

patent **1** *Syn* EGREGIOUS, blatant, conspicuous, flagrant, glaring, gross, obvious, pronounced, rank, striking **2** *Syn* EVIDENT, apparent, clear, distinct, manifest, obvious, palpable, plain

pathetic *Syn* SAD (sense 2), depressing, dismal, drear, dreary, heartbreaking, heartrending, melancholy, saddening, sorry, tearful, teary *Ant* cheering, cheery, glad, happy

pathological *Syn* UNWHOLESOME, diseased, morbid, sickly *Ant* wholesome

patience • the power or capacity to endure without complaint something difficult or disagreeable *Syn* forbearance, longanimity, long-suffering, resignation *Rel* perseverance, persistence *Ant* impatience

patient *Syn* PERSISTENT, dogged, insistent, persevering, pertinacious, tenacious

patois *Syn* TERMINOLOGY, argot, cant, dialect, jargon, language, lingo, patter, slang, vocabulary

patrician *Syn* ARISTOCRAT, gentleperson, noble

patrimony *Syn* HERITAGE, birthright, inheritance

patron **1** *Syn* BENEFACTOR, donator, donor **2** *Syn* SPONSOR, angel, backer, guarantor, surety

patter *vb Syn* CHAT, babble, blab, cackle, chatter, converse, gab, gabble, gas, jabber, jaw, palaver, prate, prattle, rap, rattle, run on, talk, twitter, visit

patter *n Syn* TERMINOLOGY, argot, cant, dialect, jargon, language, lingo, patois, slang, vocabulary

pattern **1** *Syn* HABIT, custom, fashion, practice, trick, way, wont **2** *Syn* MODEL, beau ideal, example, exemplar, ideal, mirror, standard **3** *Syn* FIGURE, design, device, motif

paucity *Syn* DEFICIENCY, dearth, deficit, failure, famine, inadequacy, insufficiency, lack, poverty, scantiness, scarceness, scarcity, shortage, want *Ant* abundance, adequacy, amplitude, plenitude, plenty, sufficiency

pause • a momentary halt in an activity *Syn* break, breath, breather, interruption, lull, recess *Rel* time-out

paw *Syn* TOUCH, feel, handle, palpate

pawn *Syn* PLEDGE, earnest, hostage, token

pay *vb* • to give money or its equivalent in return for something *Syn* compensate, indemnify, recompense, reimburse, remunerate, repay, satisfy

pay *n Syn* WAGE, emolument, fee, hire, salary, stipend

paying • yielding a profit *Syn* gainful, lucrative, profitable, remunerative

peace **1** *Syn* CALM, calmness, hush, peacefulness, placidity, quiet, quietness, quietude, repose, restfulness, sereneness, serenity, still, stillness, tranquillity (*or* tranquility) *Ant* bustle, commotion, hubbub, hurly-burly, pandemonium, tumult, turmoil, uproar **2** *Syn* TRUCE, armistice, cease-fire

peaceable *Syn* PACIFIC, irenic, pacifist, pacifistic, peaceful *Ant* bellicose

peaceful **1** *Syn* CALM, halcyon, placid, serene, tranquil *Ant* agitated, stormy **2** *Syn* PACIFIC, irenic, pacifist, pacifistic, peaceable *Ant* bellicose

peacefulness *Syn* CALM, calmness, hush, peace, placidity, quiet, quietness, quietude, repose, restfulness, sereneness, serenity, still, stillness, tranquillity (*or* tranquility) *Ant* bustle, commotion, hubbub, hurly-burly, pandemonium, tumult, turmoil, uproar

peacemaker *Syn* MEDIATOR, arbiter, arbitrator, conciliator, go-between, intercessor, intermediary, interposer, middleman

peak **1** *Syn* MOUNTAIN, alp, mesa, mount, volcano **2** *Syn* SUMMIT, acme, apex, apogee, climax, culmination, meridian, pinnacle, zenith

peculiar **1** *Syn* CHARACTERISTIC, distinctive, individual **2** *Syn* STRANGE, curious, eccentric, erratic, odd, outlandish, quaint, queer, singular, unique *Ant* familiar

peculiarity *Syn* CHARACTERISTIC, attribute, character, feature, mark, point, property, quality, trait

pecuniary *Syn* FINANCIAL, fiscal, monetary

pedagogue *Syn* TEACHER, educator, instructor, preceptor, schoolteacher

pedantic • too narrowly concerned with scholarly matters *Syn* academic, bookish, scholastic *Rel* erudite, learned

pedestrian *Syn* BORING, drab, dreary, dry, dull, flat, heavy, humdrum, jading, leaden, monotonous, ponderous, stodgy, stuffy, stupid, tame, tedious, tiresome, tiring, unanimated, uninteresting, wearisome, weary, wearying *Ant* absorbing, engaging, engrossing, gripping, interesting, intriguing, involving

pedigree *Syn* ANCESTRY, birth, blood, bloodline, breeding, descent, extraction, family tree, genealogy, line, lineage, origin, parentage, stock, strain *Ant* issue, posterity, progeny, seed

peek *Syn* LOOK, glance, glimpse, peep, sight, view

peel *n Syn* SKIN, bark, hide, pelt, rind

peel *vb Syn* SKIN, decorticate, flay, pare

peep *vb Syn* CHIRP, cheep, chirrup, chitter, tweet, twitter

peep *n* **1** *Syn* CHIRP, cheep, chirrup, chitter, tweet, twitter **2** *Syn* LOOK, glance, glimpse, peek, sight, view

peer *n Syn* EQUAL, coordinate, counterpart, equivalent, fellow, like, match, parallel, rival

peer *vb* **1** *Syn* GAPE, gawk, gaze, goggle, rubberneck, stare **2** *Syn* GAZE, gape, glare, gloat, stare

peerless *Syn* SUPREME, incomparable, preeminent, superlative, surpassing, transcendent

peeve *Syn* IRRITATE, aggravate, exasperate, nettle, provoke, rile

peeving *Syn* ANNOYING, aggravating, bothersome, disturbing, exasperating, frustrating, galling, irksome, irritating, maddening, nettling, pesty, rankling, riling, vexatious, vexing

peevish **1** *Syn* IRRITABLE, fractious, fretful, huffy, pettish, petulant, querulous, snappish, waspish *Ant* easygoing **2** *Syn* OBSTINATE, adamant, adamantine, dogged, hard, hardened, hardheaded, hardhearted, headstrong, immovable, implacable, inflexible, mulish, obdurate, opinionated, ossified, pat, pertinacious, perverse, pigheaded, rigid, self-willed, stubborn, unbending, uncompromising, unrelenting, unyielding, willful (*or* wilful) *Ant* acquiescent, agreeable, amenable, compliant, complying, flexible, pliable, pliant, relenting, yielding

peg (away) *Syn* LABOR, drudge, endeavor, grub, hump, hustle, moil, plod, plow, plug, slave, slog, strain, strive, struggle, sweat, toil, travail, work *Ant* dabble, fiddle (around), fool (around), mess (around), putter (around)

pejorative *Syn* DEROGATORY, depreciative, depreciatory, disparaging, slighting

pelagic *Syn* MARINE (sense 1), maritime, oceanic

pell-mell *Syn* MESSY, chaotic, cluttered, confused, disarranged, disarrayed, disheveled (*or* dishevelled), disordered, disorderly, higgledy-piggledy, hugger-mugger, jumbled, littered, messed, muddled, mussed, mussy, rumpled, sloppy, topsy-turvy, tousled, tumbled, unkempt, untidy, upside-down *Ant* neat, ordered, orderly, organized, shipshape, snug, tidied, tidy, trim

pellucid *Syn* CLEAR (sense 1), diaphanous, limpid, lucid, translucent, transparent *Ant* confused, turbid

pelt *vb Syn* HURRY (sense 2), barrel, bolt, bowl, breeze, career, course, dash, fly, hasten, hotfoot (it), hump, hurtle, hustle, race, rip, rocket, run, rush, rustle, scoot, scurry, scuttle, shoot, speed, step (along), tear, trot, whirl, whisk, zip, zoom *Ant* crawl, creep, poke

pelt *n Syn* SKIN, bark, hide, peel, rind

pen *vb Syn* ENCLOSE, cage, coop, corral, envelop, fence, wall

pen *n Syn* JAIL, brig, guardroom, hoosegow, jug, lockup, penitentiary, prison, stockade

penal *Syn* PUNITIVE, castigating, chastening, chastising, correcting, correctional, corrective, disciplinary, disciplining, penalizing

penalize • to inflict a penalty on *Syn* amerce, fine, mulct *Rel* chasten, correct, discipline, punish

penalizing *Syn* PUNITIVE, castigating, chastening, chastising, correcting, correctional, corrective, disciplinary, disciplining, penal

penalty **1** *Syn* DISADVANTAGE, drawback, handicap, liability, minus, strike *Ant* advantage, asset, edge, plus **2** *Syn* FINE, damages, forfeit, forfeiture, mulct

penchant *Syn* LEANING, flair, proclivity, propensity *Ant* distaste

pendant **1** • an ornament worn on a chain around the neck or wrist *Syn* bangle, charm, lavalier *Rel* locket, teardrop **2** *Syn* FLAG, banner, color, ensign, jack, pennant, pennon, standard, streamer

pendent *Syn* SUSPENDED, pendulous

pending *Syn* FORTHCOMING, approaching, coming, imminent, impending, nearing, oncoming, upcoming *Ant* late, recent

pendulate *Syn* SWING (sense 2), fluctuate, oscillate, sway, undulate, vibrate, waver

pendulous *Syn* SUSPENDED, pendent

penetrate **1** *Syn* ENTER (sense 1), pierce, probe *Ant* issue from **2** *Syn* PERMEATE, impenetrate, impregnate, interpenetrate, pervade, saturate

penetration *Syn* DISCERNMENT, acumen, discrimination, insight, perception

penitence • regret for sin or wrongdoing *Syn* attrition, compunction, contrition, remorse, repentance *Rel* anguish, regret, sorrow

penitent *Syn* GUILTY, ashamed, contrite, hangdog, remorseful, repentant, shamed, shamefaced *Ant* impenitent, remorseless, shameless, unashamed, unrepentant

penitentiary *Syn* JAIL, brig, guardroom, hoosegow, jug, lockup, pen, prison, stockade

pen name *Syn* PSEUDONYM, alias, incognito, nom de guerre, nom de plume

pennant *Syn* FLAG, banner, color, ensign, jack, pendant, pennon, standard, streamer

penniless *Syn* POOR, destitute, impecunious, indigent, necessitous, needy, poverty-stricken *Ant* rich

pennon *Syn* FLAG, banner, color, ensign, jack, pendant, pennant, standard, streamer

penny-pinching *Syn* STINGY, cheeseparing, close, closefisted, miserly, niggardly, parsimonious, penurious, tight, tightfisted *Ant* generous

pensive **1** *Syn* CONTEMPLATIVE, meditative, melancholy, reflective, ruminant, thoughtful *Ant* unreflective **2** *Syn* THOUGHTFUL (sense 1), contemplative, meditative, reflective, speculative *Ant* thoughtless

penumbra *Syn* SHADE, adumbration, shadow, umbra, umbrage

penurious *Syn* STINGY, cheeseparing, close, closefisted, miserly, niggardly, parsimonious, penny-pinching, tight, tightfisted *Ant* generous

penury *Syn* POVERTY, destitution, indigence, privation, want *Ant* riches

peon *Syn* SLAVE (sense 2), drudge, drudger, grubber, laborer, plugger, slogger, toiler, worker *Ant* freeman

pepper **1** *Syn* SCATTER (sense 2), bestrew, dot, sow, spray, sprinkle, strew **2** *Syn* SPOT, blotch, dapple, dot, fleck, freckle, marble, mottle, speck, speckle, splotch, sprinkle, stipple

peppery *Syn* SPIRITED, fiery, gingery, high-spirited, mettlesome, spunky *Ant* spiritless

pep (up) *Syn* ANIMATE, brace, energize, enliven, fire, invigorate, jazz (up), liven (up), quicken, stimulate, vitalize, vivify *Ant* damp, dampen, deaden, dull

perambulation *Syn* WALK, constitutional, ramble, range, saunter, stroll, turn

per capita *Syn* APIECE, all, each

perceive *Syn* SEE (sense 1), behold, contemplate, descry, discern, espy, note, notice, observe, remark, survey, view

percentage *Syn* PROBABILITY, chance, odds

percept *Syn* SENSATION (sense 1), image, sense-datum, sensum

perceptible • able to be perceived by a sense or by the mind *Syn* appreciable, detectable, discernible, distinguishable, palpable, sensible *Rel* audible, observable, tangible, visible *Ant* impalpable, imperceptible, inappreciable, indistinguishable, insensible

perception **1** *Syn* COMPREHENSION, appreciation, apprehension, grasp, grip, understanding **2** *Syn* DISCERNMENT, acumen, discrimination, insight, penetration

perch *Syn* ALIGHT, land, light, roost, settle, touch down *Ant* take off

perchance *Syn* PERHAPS, conceivably, maybe, mayhap, possibly

percolate *Syn* EXUDE, bleed, ooze, seep, strain, sweat, weep

percussion *Syn* IMPACT, clash, collision, concussion, impingement, jar, jolt, shock

perdurable *Syn* LASTING, durable, permanent, perpetual, stable *Ant* fleeting

peremptoriness *Syn* ARROGANCE, haughtiness, imperiousness, loftiness, lordliness, masterfulness, pompousness, presumptuousness, pretense (*or* pretence), pretension, pretentiousness, self-importance, superciliousness, superiority *Ant* humility, modesty

peremptory **1** *Syn* ARROGANT, cavalier, haughty, highfalutin, high-handed, high-hat, imperious, important, lofty, lordly, masterful, overweening, pompous, presumptuous, pretentious, supercilious, superior, uppish, uppity *Ant* humble, modest **2** *Syn* BOSSY, authoritarian, autocratic, despotic, dictatorial, domineering, imperious, masterful, overbearing, tyrannical, tyrannous **3** *Syn* MANDATORY, compulsory, forced, imperative, incumbent, involuntary, necessary, nonelective, obligatory, required *Ant* elective, optional, voluntary **4** *Syn* MASTERFUL, domineering, imperative, imperious

perennial *Syn* CONTINUAL, constant, continuous, incessant, perpetual, unremitting *Ant* intermittent

perfect *n* • not lacking or faulty in any particular *Syn* entire, intact, whole *Rel* absolute, pure, sheer, simple *Ant* imperfect

perfect *vb* *Syn* UNFOLD, develop, elaborate, evolve

perfidious *Syn* FAITHLESS, disloyal, false, traitorous, treacherous *Ant* faithful

perfidy *Syn* BETRAYAL, disloyalty, double cross, faithlessness, falseness, falsity, infidelity, sellout, treachery, treason, unfaithfulness

perforate • to pierce through so as to leave a hole *Syn* bore, drill, prick, punch, puncture *Rel* enter, penetrate, pierce, probe

perform **1** • to carry out or into effect *Syn* accomplish, achieve, discharge, effect, execute, fulfill *Rel* attain, compass, gain, reach **2** *Syn* FUNCTION, act, serve, work

performer *Syn* ACTOR, impersonator, mime, mimic, mummer, player, thespian, trouper

perfume *Syn* FRAGRANCE, bouquet, incense, redolence *Ant* stench, stink

perfumed *Syn* FRAGRANT, ambrosial, aromatic, redolent, savory, scented, sweet *Ant* fetid, foul, malodorous, noisome, putrid, rancid, rank, reeking, reeky, smelly, stinking, stinky, strong

perhaps • it is possible *Syn* conceivably, maybe, mayhap, perchance, possibly *Rel* likely, probably

peril **1** *Syn* DANGER (sense 1), hazard, menace, pitfall, risk, threat, trouble *Ant* safeness, safety, security **2** *Syn* DANGER (sense 2), distress, endangerment, imperilment, jeopardy, risk, trouble *Ant* safeness, safety, security

perilous *Syn* DANGEROUS, hazardous, precarious, risky *Ant* safe, secure

perimeter *Syn* CIRCUMFERENCE, circuit, compass, periphery

period *Syn* AGE (sense 3), day, epoch, era, time

periodic *Syn* INTERMITTENT, alternate, recurrent *Ant* continual, incessant

periodical *Syn* JOURNAL, magazine, newspaper, organ, review

peripatetic *Syn* ITINERANT, ambulant, ambulatory, nomadic, vagrant

periphery *Syn* CIRCUMFERENCE, circuit, compass, perimeter

periphrasis *Syn* VERBIAGE, circumlocution, pleonasm, redundancy, tautology

permanent *Syn* LASTING, durable, perdurable, perpetual, stable *Ant* fleeting

permeate • to pass or cause to pass through every part of a thing *Syn* impenetrate, impregnate, interpenetrate, penetrate, pervade, saturate *Rel* imbue, infuse, ingrain

permissible • that may be permitted *Syn* admissible, allowable, licensable *Rel* acceptable, bearable, endurable, tolerable *Ant* banned, barred, forbidden, impermissible, inadmissible, interdicted, prohibited, proscribed

permission • the approval by someone in authority for the doing of something *Syn* allowance, authorization, clearance, concurrence, consent, granting, leave, license (*or* licence), sanction, sufferance *Rel* imprimatur, seal, signature, stamp *Ant* interdiction, prohibition, proscription

permit *Syn* LET, allow, leave, suffer

permutation *Syn* CHANGE (sense 2), alternation, mutation, vicissitude

pernicious *Syn* HARMFUL, adverse, bad, baleful, baneful, damaging, deleterious, detrimental, evil, hurtful, ill, injurious, mischievous, noxious, prejudicial *Ant* harmless, innocent, innocuous, inoffensive, safe

pernickety *Syn* NICE, dainty, fastidious, finical, finicking, finicky, fussy, particular, persnickety, squeamish

perpendicular **1** *Syn* ERECT, plumb, raised, standing, upright, upstanding, vertical *Ant* flat, recumbent **2** *Syn* VERTICAL, plumb *Ant* horizontal

perpetual **1** *Syn* CONTINUAL, constant, continuous, incessant, perennial, unremitting *Ant* intermittent **2** *Syn* LASTING, durable, perdurable, permanent, stable *Ant* fleeting

perplex *Syn* PUZZLE, bewilder, confound, distract, dumbfound, mystify, nonplus

perquisite **1** *Syn* BONUS, dividend, extra, gratuity, gravy, lagniappe, tip **2** *Syn* RIGHT, appanage, birthright, prerogative, privilege

persecute **1** *Syn* AFFLICT, agonize, bedevil, curse, harrow, martyr, plague, rack, torment, torture **2** *Syn* WRONG, aggrieve, oppress

persevere • to continue despite difficulties, opposition, or discouragement *Syn* carry on, persist *Rel* hang on

persevering *Syn* PERSISTENT, dogged, insistent, patient, pertinacious, tenacious

persiflage *Syn* BANTER, chaff, give-and-take, jesting, joshing, raillery, repartee

persist **1** *Syn* CONTINUE, abide, endure, last **2** *Syn* PERSEVERE, carry on

persistence *Syn* CONTINUATION, continuance, duration, endurance, subsistence *Ant* ending, termination

persistent • continuing despite difficulties, opposition, or discouragement *Syn* dogged, insistent, patient, persevering, pertinacious, tenacious *Rel* assured, certain, dedicated, determined, firm, intent, positive, resolute, resolved, single-minded, sure

persnickety *Syn* NICE, dainty, fastidious, finical, finicking, finicky, fussy, particular, pernickety, squeamish

person *Syn* ENTITY, being, creature, individual

personality *Syn* DISPOSITION, character, complexion, individuality, temper, temperament

personalize *Syn* EMBODY (sense 2), epitomize, incarnate, manifest, materialize, personify, substantiate

personification *Syn* EMBODIMENT, epitome, incarnation, manifestation

personify *Syn* EMBODY (sense 2), epitomize, incarnate, manifest, materialize, personalize, substantiate

perspicacious *Syn* SHREWD, astute, sagacious

perspicuous *Syn* CLEAR (sense 2), lucid *Ant* abstruse, unintelligible

persuade • to cause (someone) to agree with a belief or course of action by using arguments or earnest request *Syn* argue, convince, get, induce, move, prevail (on *or* upon), satisfy, talk (into), win (over) *Rel* cajole, coax, exhort, urge

persuasion **1** *Syn* OPINION, belief, conviction, sentiment, view **2** *Syn* RELIGION, church, communion, creed, denomination, faith, sect

persuasive *Syn* COGENT, compelling, conclusive, convincing, decisive, effective, forceful, satisfying, strong, telling *Ant* inconclusive, indecisive, ineffective, unconvincing

pert **1** *Syn* FLIPPANT, facetious, flip, smart, smart-alecky (*or* smart-aleck) *Ant* earnest, sincere **2** *Syn* SAUCY, arch

pertain *Syn* BEAR (sense 3), appertain, apply, belong, relate

pertinacious **1** *Syn* OBSTINATE, adamant, adamantine, dogged, hard, hardened, hardheaded, hardhearted, headstrong, immovable, implacable, inflexible, mulish, obdurate, opinionated, ossified, pat, peevish, perverse, pigheaded, rigid, self-willed, stubborn, unbending, uncompromising, unrelenting, unyielding, willful (*or* wilful) *Ant* acquiescent, agreeable, amenable, compliant, complying, flexible, pliable, pliant, relenting, yielding **2** *Syn* PERSISTENT, dogged, insistent, patient, persevering, tenacious

pertinent • having to do with the matter at hand *Syn* applicable, apposite, apropos, germane, material, pointed, relative, relevant *Rel* appropriate, apt, fit, fitting, suitable *Ant* extraneous, immaterial, inapplicable, irrelevant, pointless

pertness *Syn* EFFRONTERY, audacity, brashness, brass, brassiness, brazenness, cheek, cheekiness, chutzpah, gall, nerve, nerviness, presumption, presumptuousness, sauce, sauciness, temerity

perturb *Syn* DISCOMPOSE, agitate, disquiet, disturb, flurry, fluster, upset

perturbing *Syn* TROUBLESOME, discomforting, discomposing, disquieting, distressing, disturbing, troubling, troublous, unsettling, upsetting, worrisome *Ant* reassuring, untroublesome

pervade *Syn* PERMEATE, impenetrate, impregnate, interpenetrate, penetrate, saturate

perverse **1** *Syn* CORRUPT, debased, debauched, decadent, degenerate, degraded, demoralized, depraved, dissipated, dissolute, perverted, reprobate, warped *Ant* uncorrupted **2** *Syn* OBSTINATE, adamant, adamantine, dogged, hard, hardened, hardheaded, hardhearted, headstrong, immovable, implacable, inflexible, mulish, obdurate, opinionated, ossified, pat, peevish, pertinacious, pigheaded, rigid, self-willed, stubborn, unbending, uncompromising, unrelenting, unyielding, willful (*or* wilful) *Ant* acquiescent, agreeable, amenable, compliant, complying, flexible, pliable, pliant, relenting, yielding **3** *Syn* CONTRARY, balky, froward, perverse, restive, wayward *Ant* complaisant, good-natured

pervert *Syn* DEBASE, corrupt, debauch, deprave, vitiate *Ant* amend (*morals, character*), elevate (*taste, way of life*)

perverted **1** *Syn* CORRUPT, debased, debauched, decadent, degenerate, degraded, demoralized, depraved, dissipated, dissolute, perverse, reprobate, warped *Ant* uncorrupted **2** *Syn* DEBASED, corrupted, debauched, depraved, vitiated

pessimistic *Syn* CYNICAL, misanthropic

pester *Syn* WORRY, annoy, harass, harry, plague, tantalize, tease

pestilent **1** *Syn* DEADLY, baleful, deathly, fatal, fell, killer, lethal, mortal, murderous, vital *Ant* healthful, healthy, nonfatal, nonlethal, wholesome **2** *Syn* POISONOUS, mephitic, miasmal, miasmatic, miasmic, pestilential, toxic, venomous, virulent *Ant* nonpoisonous, nontoxic, nonvenomous

pestilential *Syn* POISONOUS, mephitic, miasmal, miasmatic, miasmic, pestilent, toxic, venomous, virulent *Ant* nonpoisonous, nontoxic, nonvenomous

pesty *Syn* ANNOYING, aggravating, bothersome, disturbing, exasperating, frustrating, galling, irksome, irritating, maddening, net-

tling, peeving, rankling, riling, vexatious, vexing
pet *vb Syn* CARESS, cosset, cuddle, dandle, fondle
pet *n Syn* FAVORITE, darling, minion, preference
petition *n Syn* PRAYER, appeal, plea, suit
petition *vb Syn* PRAY, appeal, plead, sue
petitioner *Syn* SUPPLICANT, pleader, solicitor, suitor, suppliant
petrify **1** *Syn* DAZE, bemuse, benumb, paralyze, stun, stupefy **2** *Syn* HARDEN (sense 1), cake, indurate, solidify *Ant* soften
pettish *Syn* IRRITABLE, fractious, fretful, huffy, peevish, petulant, querulous, snappish, waspish *Ant* easygoing
petty • being often contemptibly insignificant or unimportant *Syn* measly, paltry, picayune, picayunish, puny, trifling, trivial *Rel* diminutive, little, minute, small *Ant* gross, important, momentous
petulant *Syn* IRRITABLE, fractious, fretful, huffy, peevish, pettish, querulous, snappish, waspish *Ant* easygoing
phantasm **1** *Syn* FANCY, daydream, dream, fantasy, nightmare, phantasy, vision *Ant* reality **2** *Syn* GHOST, apparition, bogey, phantom, poltergeist, shade, shadow, specter (*or* spectre), spirit, spook, vision, wraith
phantasy *Syn* FANCY, daydream, dream, fantasy, nightmare, phantasm, vision *Ant* reality
phantom *Syn* GHOST, apparition, bogey, phantasm, poltergeist, shade, shadow, specter (*or* spectre), spirit, spook, vision, wraith
pharmaceutical *Syn* DRUG, biologic, medicinal, simple
pharmacist *Syn* DRUGGIST, apothecary, chemist
phase • one of the possible ways of viewing or being presented to view *Syn* angle, aspect, facet, side *Rel* condition, posture, situation, state
phased *Syn* GRADUAL, gradational, incremental, piecemeal, step-by-step *Ant* sudden
phenomenal **1** *Syn* EXCEPTIONAL, extraordinary, unusual, unwonted *Ant* average, common **2** *Syn* MATERIAL, corporeal, objective, physical, sensible *Ant* immaterial
phenomenon *Syn* WONDER (sense 1), marvel, miracle, prodigy
philanthropic *Syn* CHARITABLE, altruistic, benevolent, eleemosynary, humane, humanitarian *Ant* uncharitable
philanthropy *Syn* CONTRIBUTION, alms, benefaction, beneficence, charity, donation
philippic *Syn* TIRADE, diatribe, jeremiad *Ant* eulogy
phlegm *Syn* IMPASSIVITY, apathy, stoicism, stolidity
phlegmatic *Syn* IMPASSIVE, apathetic, stoic, stolid *Ant* responsive
phony *Syn* COUNTERFEIT, bogus, fake, pinchbeck, pseudo, sham, spurious *Ant* bona fide, genuine
photograph *Syn* IMAGE, effigy, icon, mask, portrait, statue
phrase *n* • a group of words which, taken together, express a notion and may be used as a part of a sentence *Syn* expression, idiom, locution
phrase *vb* • to convey in appropriate or telling terms *Syn* articulate, clothe, couch, express, formulate, put, say, state, word *Rel* craft, frame
phraseology *Syn* LANGUAGE (sense 2), diction, phrasing, style, vocabulary
phrasing *Syn* LANGUAGE (sense 2), diction, phraseology, style, vocabulary
physic *Syn* REMEDY, cure, medicament, medication, medicine, specific
physical **1** *Syn* BODILY, corporal, corporeal, somatic **2** *Syn* MATERIAL, corporeal, objective, phenomenal, sensible
physiognomy *Syn* FACE, countenance, mug, puss, visage
physique • bodily makeup or type *Syn* build, constitution, habit *Rel* body
picayune *Syn* PETTY, measly, paltry, picayunish, puny, trifling, trivial *Ant* gross, important, momentous
picayunish *Syn* PETTY, measly, paltry, picayune, puny, trifling, trivial *Ant* gross, important, momentous
pick *vb Syn* CHOOSE, cull, elect, opt, prefer, select, single *Ant* eschew, reject
pick *n Syn* ELITE, best, choice, cream, elect, fat, flower, prime, upper crust
picked *Syn* SELECT, elect, exclusive *Ant* indiscriminate
pickle *Syn* PREDICAMENT, dilemma, fix, jam, plight, quandary, scrape
pick up *Syn* BUY, purchase, take
picky *Syn* SELECTIVE, choosy (*or* choosey), particular *Ant* nonselective
picnic *Syn* CINCH, breeze, child's play, duck soup, pushover, snap *Ant* chore, headache, labor
pictorial *Syn* GRAPHIC, picturesque, vivid
picture *n Syn* MOVIE (sense 1), film, motion, moving picture, picture
picture *vb Syn* REPRESENT, delineate, depict, limn, portray
pictures *Syn* MOVIE (sense 2), cinema, film, motion, pictures, screen
picturesque *Syn* GRAPHIC, pictorial, vivid
piebald *Syn* VARIEGATED, checked, checkered, dappled, motley, parti-colored, pied, skewbald
piece *vb Syn* BUILD, assemble, construct, erect, fabricate, make, make up, put up, raise, rear, set up *Ant* disassemble, dismantle, take down
piece *n Syn* PART, detail, division, fraction, fragment, member, parcel, portion, section, sector, segment *Ant* whole

piecemeal 1 *Syn* APART, asunder *Ant* together 2 *Syn* GRADUAL, gradational, incremental, phased, step-by-step *Ant* sudden
pied *Syn* VARIEGATED, checked, checkered, dappled, motley, parti-colored, piebald, skewbald
pier 1 *Syn* BUTTRESS, abutment 2 *Syn* WHARF, berth, dock, jetty, levee, quay, slip
pierce *Syn* ENTER (sense 1), penetrate, probe *Ant* issue from
piety 1 *Syn* FIDELITY, allegiance, devotion, fealty, loyalty *Ant* faithlessness, perfidy 2 *Syn* HOLINESS, blessedness, devoutness, godliness, piousness, sainthood, saintliness, saintship, sanctity *Ant* godlessness, impiety, ungodliness, unholiness
pigeon *Syn* DUPE, chump, gull, sap, sucker, tool
pigeonhole *Syn* ASSORT, classify, sort
pigheaded *Syn* OBSTINATE, adamant, adamantine, dogged, hard, hardened, hardheaded, hardhearted, headstrong, immovable, implacable, inflexible, mulish, obdurate, opinionated, ossified, pat, peevish, pertinacious, perverse, rigid, self-willed, stubborn, unbending, uncompromising, unrelenting, unyielding, willful (*or* wilful) *Ant* acquiescent, agreeable, amenable, compliant, complying, flexible, pliable, pliant, relenting, yielding
pigment • a substance used to color other materials *Syn* color, coloring, dye, dyestuff, stain, tincture *Rel* cast, hue, shade, tinge, tint, tone
pilaster *Syn* PILLAR, column
pile *vb* *Syn* HEAP, bank, cock, mass, shock, stack
pile *n* *Syn* HEAP, bank, cock, mass, shock, stack
pilfer *Syn* STEAL, cop, filch, lift, pinch, purloin, snitch, swipe
pilgrimage *Syn* JOURNEY, cruise, excursion, expedition, jaunt, tour, trip, voyage
pill • a small mass containing medicine to be taken orally *Syn* capsule, lozenge, tablet *Rel* drug, medication, pharmaceutical, specific
pillage *Syn* RAVAGE, despoil, devastate, sack, spoliate, waste
pillar • a firm upright support for a superstructure *Syn* column, pilaster
pilot *Syn* GUIDE, engineer, lead, steer *Ant* misguide
pimple *Syn* ABSCESS, boil, carbuncle, furuncle, pustule
pinch *n* *Syn* JUNCTURE, contingency, crisis, emergency, exigency, pass, strait
pinch *vb* *Syn* STEAL, cop, filch, lift, pilfer, purloin, snitch, swipe
pinchbeck *Syn* COUNTERFEIT, bogus, fake, phony, pseudo, sham, spurious *Ant* bona fide, genuine
pinched *Syn* HAGGARD, cadaverous, careworn, wasted, worn
pinch hitter *Syn* SUBSTITUTE, backup, relief, replacement, reserve, stand-in, sub
pine *Syn* LONG, hanker, hunger, thirst, yearn
pinnacle *Syn* SUMMIT, acme, apex, apogee, climax, culmination, meridian, peak, zenith
pious 1 *Syn* HOLY (sense 1), devout, godly, religious, sainted, saintly *Ant* faithless, godless, impious, irreligious, ungodly, unholy 2 *Syn* FAITHFUL, constant, devoted, fast, good, loyal, staunch (*or* stanch), steadfast, steady, true, true-blue *Ant* disloyal, faithless, false, fickle, inconstant, perfidious, recreant, traitorous, treacherous, unfaithful, untrue
piousness *Syn* HOLINESS, blessedness, devoutness, godliness, piety, sainthood, saintliness, saintship, sanctity *Ant* godlessness, impiety, ungodliness, unholiness
piousness *Syn* HYPOCRISY, cant, dissembling, dissimulation, insincerity, sanctimoniousness *Ant* genuineness, sincerity
pip *Syn* JIM-DANDY, beauty, corker, crackerjack, dandy, knockout, nifty
pipe *n* *Syn* CASK, barrel, firkin, hogshead, keg, puncheon
pipe *vb* *Syn* CHANNEL, channelize, conduct, direct, funnel, siphon
piping *Syn* SHRILL, acute, high-pitched, screeching, shrieking, squeaking, squeaky, treble, whistling *Ant* bass, deep, low, throaty
piquant *Syn* PUNGENT, poignant, racy, snappy, spicy *Ant* bland
pique *n* *Syn* OFFENSE (sense 1), dudgeon, huff, resentment, umbrage
pique *vb* 1 *Syn* PRIDE, plume, preen 2 *Syn* PROVOKE, excite, galvanize, quicken, stimulate
piquing *Syn* PROVOCATIVE, exciting, inciting, instigating, provoking, stimulating
pirate • a robber on the high seas *Syn* buccaneer, corsair, freebooter, privateer
pirouette *Syn* TURN (sense 1), circle, eddy, gyrate, revolve, rotate, spin, swirl, twirl, wheel, whirl
pitch 1 *Syn* PLUNGE, dive 2 *Syn* THROW, cast, fling, hurl, sling, toss
piteous *Syn* PITIFUL, pitiable *Ant* cruel
pitfall *Syn* DANGER (sense 1), hazard, menace, peril, risk, threat, trouble *Ant* safeness, safety, security
pith 1 *Syn* CRUX, core, gist, heart, nub, pivot 2 *Syn* SUBSTANCE, burden, core, gist, purport
pithily *Syn* SUCCINCTLY, briefly, compactly, concisely, crisply, laconically, summarily, tersely *Ant* diffusely, long-windedly, verbosely, wordily
pithy *Syn* CONCISE, compendious, laconic, succinct, summary, terse *Ant* redundant
pitiable 1 *Syn* CONTEMPTIBLE, beggarly, cheap, despicable, scurvy, shabby, sorry *Ant* admirable, estimable, formidable 2 *Syn* PITIFUL, piteous *Ant* cruel
pitiful • arousing or deserving pity *Syn* pite-

ous, pitiable *Rel* affecting, moving, pathetic, touching *Ant* cruel

pittance *Syn* RATION, allowance, dole

pity *Syn* SYMPATHY, commiseration, compassion, condolence, empathy, ruth

pivot *Syn* CRUX, core, gist, heart, nub, pith

pivotal **1** *Syn* CENTRAL, focal **2** *Syn* CRUCIAL, critical, key, vital

pixie *also* **pixy** *Syn* FAIRY, brownie, elf, fay, sprite

placard *Syn* ANNOUNCE, advertise, blaze, broadcast, declare, enunciate, post, proclaim, promulgate, publicize, publish, sound

placate *Syn* PACIFY, appease, conciliate, disarm, mollify, propitiate *Ant* anger, enrage, incense, infuriate, madden, outrage

place *n* **1** • the portion of space occupied by or chosen for something *Syn* location, position, site, situation, spot, station *Rel* district, locality, vicinity **2** *Syn* ROLE, capacity, function, job, part, position, purpose, task, work

place *vb* *Syn* ESTIMATE (sense 2), calculate, call, conjecture, figure, gauge, guess, judge, make, put, reckon, suppose

placid *Syn* CALM, halcyon, peaceful, serene, tranquil *Ant* agitated, stormy

placidity **1** *Syn* CALM, calmness, hush, peace, peacefulness, quiet, quietness, quietude, repose, restfulness, sereneness, serenity, still, stillness, tranquillity (*or* tranquility) *Ant* bustle, commotion, hubbub, hurly-burly, pandemonium, tumult, turmoil, uproar **2** *Syn* EQUANIMITY, aplomb, calmness, composure, coolheadedness, coolness, imperturbability, self-possession, serenity, tranquillity (*or* tranquility) *Ant* agitation, discomposure, perturbation

plague **1** *Syn* AFFLICT, agonize, bedevil, curse, harrow, martyr, persecute, rack, torment, torture **2** *Syn* WORRY, annoy, harass, harry, pester, tantalize, tease

plain *adj* **1** • free from all ostentation or superficial embellishment *Syn* homely, simple, unpretentious *Rel* hideous, ill-favored, ugly, unsightly *Ant* lovely **2** *Syn* EVIDENT, apparent, clear, distinct, manifest, obvious, palpable, patent **3** *Syn* FRANK, candid, open *Ant* reticent **4** *Syn* LEVEL, even, flat, flush, plane, smooth

plain *n* • a broad area of level or rolling treeless country *Syn* down, grassland, prairie, savanna, steppe, tundra, veld (*or* veldt) *Rel* pampas

plainness *Syn* CANDOR, directness, forthrightness, frankness, openheartedness, openness, straightforwardness *Ant* dissembling, pretense (*or* pretence)

plaint *Syn* LAMENT, groan, howl, keen, lamentation, moan, wail *Ant* exultation, rejoicing

plaintive *Syn* MELANCHOLY, doleful, dolorous, lugubrious, rueful

plait *n* *Syn* BRAID, lace, lacing

plait *vb* **1** *Syn* BRAID, pleat **2** *Syn* WEAVE, braid, crochet, knit, tat

plan *n* **1** • a method devised for making or doing something or achieving an end *Syn* design, plot, project, scheme *Rel* intent, intention, purpose **2** *Syn* GOAL, aim, ambition, aspiration, design, dream, end, intent, intention, mark, meaning, object, objective, pretension, purpose, target, thing

plan *vb* • to formulate a plan for arranging, realizing, or achieving something *Syn* design, plot, project, scheme *Rel* intend, propose, purpose

plane *Syn* LEVEL, even, flat, flush, plain, smooth

planet *Syn* EARTH, globe, world

plank *Syn* PARAGRAPH, article, clause, count, verse

plastic • susceptible of being modified in form or nature *Syn* adaptable, ductile, malleable, pliable, pliant *Rel* elastic, flexible, resilient, supple

platform • a level usually raised surface *Syn* dais, podium, rostrum, stage, stand *Rel* altar, pulpit

platitude *Syn* COMMONPLACE, bromide, cliché, truism

plaudit(s) *Syn* APPLAUSE, acclamation, cheering, cheers, ovation, rave(s) *Ant* booing, hissing

plausible • appearing worthy of belief *Syn* believable, colorable, credible, specious *Rel* bland, diplomatic, politic, smooth, suave

play *n* **1** • activity engaged in for amusement *Syn* disport, frolic, gambol, rollick, romp, sport *Rel* delectation, delight, enjoyment, pleasure *Ant* work **2** *Syn* FUN, game, jest, sport **3** *Syn* ROOM (sense 2), berth, clearance, elbow room, leeway, margin

play *vb* **1** • to engage in an activity for amusement or recreation *Syn* disport, frolic, gambol, rollick, romp, sport *Rel* amuse, divert, entertain, recreate **2** *Syn* ACT (sense 2), impersonate

player *Syn* ACTOR, impersonator, mime, mimic, mummer, performer, thespian, trouper

playful • given to or characterized by play, jests, or tricks *Syn* frolicsome, impish, mischievous, roguish, sportive, waggish *Rel* gay, lively, sprightly

play (up) *Syn* EMPHASIZE, accent, accentuate, feature, highlight, point (up), stress, underline, underscore *Ant* play (down)

plea **1** *Syn* APOLOGY, alibi, apologia, excuse, pretext **2** *Syn* EXCUSE, alibi, defense, justification, reason **3** *Syn* PRAYER, appeal, petition, suit

plead *Syn* PRAY, appeal, petition, sue

pleader *Syn* SUPPLICANT, petitioner, solicitor, suitor, suppliant

pleasant • highly acceptable to the mind or the senses *Syn* agreeable, grateful, gratifying, pleasing, welcome *Rel* alluring, attractive, charming *Ant* distasteful, harsh, unpleasant

please • to give or be a source of pleasure to *Syn* delight, gladden, gratify, regale, rejoice, tickle *Rel* content, satisfy *Ant* anger, displease, vex

pleased *Syn* CONTENT, contented, gratified, happy, satisfied *Ant* discontent, discontented, displeased, dissatisfied, malcontent, unhappy

pleasing *Syn* PLEASANT, agreeable, grateful, gratifying, welcome *Ant* distasteful, harsh, unpleasant

pleasurable *Syn* FUN, amusing, delightful, diverting, enjoyable, entertaining *Ant* boring, dull

pleasure • the agreeable emotion accompanying the expectation, acquisition, or possession of something good or greatly desired *Syn* delectation, delight, enjoyment, fruition, joy *Rel* bliss, felicity, happiness *Ant* anger, displeasure, vexation

pleat *Syn* BRAID, plait

plebiscite *Syn* MANDATE, initiative, referendum

pledge **1** • something given or held as a sign of another's good faith or intentions *Syn* earnest, hostage, pawn, token *Rel* bail, bond, guarantee, guaranty, security, surety **2** *Syn* PROMISE, contract, covenant, engage, plight **3** *Syn* PROMISE, oath, troth, vow, word

plenary *Syn* FULL, complete, replete *Ant* empty

plenteous *Syn* PLENTIFUL, abundant, ample, copious *Ant* scant, scanty

plentiful • being more than enough without being excessive *Syn* abundant, ample, copious, plenteous *Rel* fruitful, prolific *Ant* scant, scanty

pleonasm *Syn* VERBIAGE, circumlocution, periphrasis, redundancy, tautology

pliable **1** *Syn* PLASTIC, adaptable, ductile, malleable, pliant **2** *Syn* WILLOWY, flexible, limber, lissome, lithe, pliant, supple *Ant* inflexible, rigid, stiff

pliant **1** *Syn* PLASTIC, adaptable, ductile, malleable, pliable **2** *Syn* WILLOWY, flexible, limber, lissome, lithe, pliable, supple *Ant* inflexible, rigid, stiff

plight **1** *Syn* PREDICAMENT, dilemma, fix, jam, pickle, quandary, scrape **2** *Syn* PROMISE, contract, covenant, engage, pledge

plod *Syn* LABOR, drudge, endeavor, grub, hump, hustle, moil, peg (away), plow, plug, slave, slog, strain, strive, struggle, sweat, toil, travail, work *Ant* dabble, fiddle (around), fool (around), mess (around), putter (around)

plot *n* **1** • a plan secretly devised to accomplish an evil or treacherous end *Syn* cabal, conspiracy, intrigue, machination *Rel* contraption, contrivance, device **2** *Syn* PLAN, design, project, scheme **3** *Syn* SKETCH, blueprint, delineation, diagram, draft, outline, tracing

plot *vb* **1** • to engage in a secret plan to accomplish evil or unlawful ends *Syn* conspire, contrive, intrigue, machinate, scheme *Rel* brew, concoct, cook (up), hatch **2** *Syn* PLAN, design, project, scheme **3** *Syn* SKETCH, blueprint, delineate, diagram, draft, outline, trace

plow *Syn* LABOR, drudge, endeavor, grub, hump, hustle, moil, peg (away), plod, plug, slave, slog, strain, strive, struggle, sweat, toil, travail, work *Ant* dabble, fiddle (around), fool (around), mess (around), putter (around)

ploy *Syn* TRICK, artifice, feint, gambit, maneuver, ruse, stratagem, wile

pluck *Syn* FORTITUDE, backbone, grit, guts, sand *Ant* pusillanimity

plug *Syn* LABOR, drudge, endeavor, grub, hump, hustle, moil, peg (away), plod, plow, slave, slog, strain, strive, struggle, sweat, toil, travail, work *Ant* dabble, fiddle (around), fool (around), mess (around), putter (around)

plugger *Syn* SLAVE (sense 2), drudge, drudger, grubber, laborer, peon, slogger, toiler, worker *Ant* freeman

plumb *n* **1** *Syn* ERECT, perpendicular, raised, standing, upright, upstanding, vertical *Ant* flat, recumbent **2** *Syn* VERTICAL, perpendicular *Ant* horizontal

plumb *vb* *Syn* FATHOM, sound

plume *n* *Syn* AWARD, decoration, distinction, honor, premium, prize

plume *vb* *Syn* PRIDE, pique, preen

plump *Syn* FLESHY, chubby, corpulent, fat, obese, portly, rotund, stout *Ant* scrawny, skinny

plunder *vb* *Syn* ROB, burglarize, loot, rifle

plunder *n* *Syn* SPOIL, booty, loot, prize, swag

plunge • to thrust or cast oneself or something into or as if into deep water *Syn* dive, pitch *Rel* dip, immerse, submerge

plush *Syn* LUXURIOUS, deluxe, lavish, luxuriant, opulent, palatial, sumptuous *Ant* ascetic, austere, humble, Spartan

plutocracy *Syn* OLIGARCHY, aristocracy

ply **1** *Syn* EXERT, apply, exercise, put out, wield **2** *Syn* HANDLE, manipulate, swing, wield

pocket *Syn* HOLE, cavity, hollow, vacuum, void

pocketbook *Syn* PURSE, bag, handbag

pockmark *Syn* BLEMISH, defect, deformity, disfigurement, fault, flaw, imperfection, mark, scar

podium *Syn* PLATFORM, dais, rostrum, stage, stand

poem • a composition using rhythm and often rhyme to create a lyrical effect *Syn* lyric, song, verse *Rel* English sonnet, ballad, blank verse, elegy, epic, epigram, free verse, haiku, jingle, lament, lay, limerick, minstrelsy, ode, poesy, poetry, psalm, rhyme, sonnet

poet • a writer of verse *Syn* bard, minstrel, poetaster, rhymer, rhymester, troubadour, versifier *Rel* author, creator, maker

poetaster *Syn* POET, bard, minstrel, rhymer, rhymester, troubadour, versifier

pogrom *Syn* MASSACRE, butchery, carnage, slaughter

poignant **1** *Syn* MOVING, affecting, emotional, impressive, stirring, touching *Ant* unemotional, unimpressive **2** *Syn* PUNGENT, piquant, racy, snappy, spicy *Ant* bland

point **1** *Syn* CHARACTERISTIC, attribute, character, feature, mark, peculiarity, property, quality, trait **2** *Syn* FACT, datum, detail, nicety, particular, particularity

pointed *Syn* PERTINENT, applicable, apposite, apropos, germane, material, relative, relevant *Ant* extraneous, immaterial, inapplicable, irrelevant, pointless

pointless *Syn* MEANINGLESS, empty, inane, senseless *Ant* meaningful

point of view • a position from which something is considered or evaluated *Syn* angle, slant, standpoint, viewpoint *Rel* attitude, position, stand

point (up) *Syn* EMPHASIZE, accent, accentuate, feature, highlight, play (up), stress, underline, underscore *Ant* play (down)

poise *n* **1** *Syn* BALANCE, equilibrium, equipoise, tension **2** *Syn* TACT, address, savoir faire *Ant* awkwardness

poise *vb* *Syn* STABILIZE, balance, ballast, steady, trim

poison *n* • something that harms, interferes with, or destroys the activity, progress, or welfare of something else *Syn* bane, toxin, venom, virus

poison *vb* *Syn* CONTAMINATE, befoul, defile, foul, pollute, taint *Ant* decontaminate, purify

poisonous • having the properties or effects of poison *Syn* mephitic, miasmal, miasmatic, miasmic, pestilent, pestilential, toxic, venomous, virulent *Rel* deadly, fatal, lethal, mortal *Ant* nonpoisonous, nontoxic, nonvenomous

poke *n* • a quick thrust with or as if with the hand *Syn* jog, nudge, prod

poke *vb* **1** • to thrust something into so as to stir up, urge on, or attract attention *Syn* jog, nudge, prod *Rel* push, shove, thrust **2** *Syn* INTERFERE, butt in, intrude, meddle, mess, nose, obtrude, pry, snoop

polish • to make smooth or glossy usually by repeatedly applying surface pressure *Syn* buff, burnish, dress, gloss, grind, rub, shine, smooth *Rel* sleek, slick

polished **1** *Syn* CULTIVATED, civilized, cultured, genteel, refined *Ant* philistine, uncivilized, uncultured, unpolished, unrefined **2** *Syn* GLOSSY, buffed, burnished, glistening, lustrous, rubbed, satin, satiny, sleek *Ant* dim, dull, flat, lusterless, matte

polite *Syn* CIVIL, chivalrous, courteous, courtly, gallant *Ant* rude, uncivil

politeness • speech or behavior that is a sign of good breeding *Syn* civility, courteousness, courtesy, gentility, graciousness, mannerliness *Rel* attentiveness, consideration, thoughtfulness *Ant* discourteousness, discourtesy, impoliteness, incivility, rudeness, ungraciousness

politic *Syn* EXPEDIENT, advisable, desirable, judicious, prudent, tactical, wise *Ant* imprudent, inadvisable, inexpedient, injudicious, unwise

politician • a person engaged in the art or science of government *Syn* politico, statesman

politico *Syn* POLITICIAN, statesman

poll *Syn* CANVASS, solicit, survey

pollute *Syn* CONTAMINATE, befoul, defile, foul, poison, taint *Ant* decontaminate, purify

polluted *Syn* IMPURE, adulterated, alloyed, contaminated, dilute, diluted, tainted, thinned, weakened *Ant* pure, unadulterated, unalloyed, uncontaminated, undiluted, unpolluted, untainted

poltergeist *Syn* GHOST, apparition, bogey, phantasm, phantom, shade, shadow, specter (*or* spectre), spirit, spook, vision, wraith

poltroon *Syn* COWARD, chicken, craven, dastard, recreant *Ant* hero, stalwart, valiant

polychromatic *Syn* COLORFUL, motley, multicolored, polychrome, varicolored, variegated *Ant* colorless, monochromatic, solid

polychrome *Syn* COLORFUL, motley, multicolored, polychromatic, varicolored, variegated *Ant* colorless, monochromatic, solid

pomp *Syn* DISPLAY, array, parade

pompous **1** *Syn* ARROGANT, cavalier, haughty, highfalutin, high-handed, high-hat, imperious, important, lofty, lordly, masterful, overweening, peremptory, presumptuous, pretentious, supercilious, superior, uppish, uppity *Ant* humble, modest **2** *Syn* CONCEITED, complacent, egoistic, egotistic (*or* egotistical), important, overweening, prideful, proud, self-conceited, self-important, self-satisfied, smug, stuck-up, vain, vainglorious *Ant* humble, modest

pompousness **1** *Syn* ARROGANCE, haughtiness, imperiousness, loftiness, lordliness, masterfulness, peremptoriness, presumptuousness, pretense (*or* pretence), pretension, pretentiousness, self-importance, superciliousness, superiority *Ant* humility, modesty **2** *Syn* COMPLACENCE, complacency, conceit, conceitedness, ego, egotism, pride, pridefulness, self-admiration, self-conceit, self-esteem, self-importance, self-satisfaction, smugness, vaingloriousness, vainglory, vainness, vanity *Ant* humbleness, humility, modesty

ponder • to consider or examine attentively or deliberately *Syn* meditate, muse, ruminate *Rel* consider, contemplate, weigh

ponderous **1** *Syn* BORING, drab, dreary, dry, dull, flat, heavy, humdrum, jading, leaden, monotonous, pedestrian, stodgy, stuffy, stupid, tame, tedious, tiresome, tiring, unanimated, uninteresting, wearisome, weary, wearying *Ant* absorbing, engaging, engrossing, gripping, interesting, intriguing, involving **2** *Syn* HEAVY, cumbersome, cumbrous, hefty, weighty *Ant* light

pool *Syn* MONOPOLY, cartel, corner, syndicate, trust

poor **1** • lacking money or material possessions *Syn* destitute, impecunious, indigent, necessitous, needy, penniless, poverty-stricken *Ant* rich **2** *Syn* BAD (sense 2), wrong *Ant* good

poorly *Syn* BADLY, inadequately, unacceptably, unsatisfactorily *Ant* acceptably, adequately, all right, fine, good, palatably, passably, so-so, tolerably

poppycock *Syn* NONSENSE, balderdash, bull, bunk, drivel, gobbledygook, rot, trash, twaddle

popular **1** *Syn* COMMON, familiar, ordinary, vulgar *Ant* exceptional, uncommon **2** *Syn* DEMOCRATIC, republican, self-governing, self-ruling *Ant* undemocratic

popularity • the state of enjoying widespread approval *Syn* fashionableness, favor, hotness, modishness, vogue *Rel* craze, fad, mode, rage, style, trend *Ant* disfavor, unpopularity

port[1] *n Syn* BEARING, demeanor, deportment, mien, presence

port[2] *n Syn* HARBOR, haven

portal *Syn* DOOR, doorway, gate, gateway, postern

portend *Syn* FORETELL, augur, forebode, forecast, predict, presage, prognosticate, prophesy

portent *Syn* OMEN, augury, auspice, boding, foreboding, foreshadowing, prefiguring, presage

portentous *Syn* OMINOUS, baleful, dire, foreboding, inauspicious, menacing, sinister, threatening

portion *vb Syn* APPORTION, parcel, prorate, ration

portion *n* **1** *Syn* FATE, destiny, doom, lot **2** *Syn* PART, detail, division, fraction, fragment, member, parcel, piece, section, sector, segment *Ant* whole

portly *Syn* FLESHY, chubby, corpulent, fat, obese, plump, rotund, stout *Ant* scrawny, skinny

portrait *Syn* IMAGE, effigy, icon, mask, photograph, statue

portray *Syn* REPRESENT, delineate, depict, limn, picture

pose *n* **1** • an adopted way of speaking or behaving *Syn* affectation, air, mannerism **2** *Syn* POSTURE, attitude

pose *vb Syn* PROPOSE, propound

posit *n Syn* ASSUMPTION, postulate, premise, presumption, presupposition

posit *vb Syn* PRESUPPOSE, assume, postulate, premise, presume

position **1** • a firmly held point of view or way of regarding something *Syn* attitude, stand *Rel* angle, point of view, slant, standpoint, viewpoint **2** *Syn* PLACE, location, site, situation, spot, station **3** *Syn* ROLE, capacity, function, job, part, place, purpose, task, work

positive *Syn* SURE, certain, cocksure *Ant* unsure

possess *Syn* HAVE, enjoy, hold, own

possessions • all the items that taken together constitute a person's or group's property or wealth *Syn* assets, belongings, effects, means, resources

possessor *Syn* PROPRIETOR, holder, owner

possible **1** • capable of being realized *Syn* feasible, practicable *Rel* practical **2** *Syn* PROBABLE, likely *Ant* certain, improbable

possibly *Syn* PERHAPS, conceivably, maybe, mayhap, perchance

post *vb Syn* ANNOUNCE, advertise, blaze, broadcast, declare, enunciate, placard, proclaim, promulgate, publicize, publish, sound

post *n Syn* MISSION, assignment, charge, job, operation

posterior **1** *Syn* BACK, hind, hindmost, rear, rearward *Ant* anterior, fore, forward, front **2** *Syn* BUTTOCKS, backside, bottom, breech, butt, fanny, hams, haunches, rear, rump, seat

posterity *Syn* OFFSPRING, descendants, issue, progeny, young

postern *Syn* DOOR, doorway, gate, gateway, portal

posting *Syn* ANNOUNCEMENT, ad, advertisement, bulletin, notice, notification, release

postmortem *Syn* AUTOPSY, postmortem examination

postmortem examination *Syn* AUTOPSY, postmortem

postpone • to assign to a later time *Syn* defer, delay, hold off (on), hold up, put off, shelve *Rel* suspend

postulate *n Syn* ASSUMPTION, posit, premise, presumption, presupposition

postulate *vb Syn* PRESUPPOSE, assume, posit, premise, presume

posture **1** • the position or bearing of the body *Syn* attitude, pose *Rel* bearing, deportment, mien **2** *Syn* STATE, condition, mode, situation, status

pot *Syn* BET, ante, stake, wager

potent *Syn* POWERFUL, forceful, forcible, puissant *Ant* inefficacious, powerless

potential *Syn* LATENT, abeyant, dormant, quiescent *Ant* patent

pother **1** *Syn* COMMOTION, bother, bustle,

clatter, disturbance, furor, furore, fuss, hubbub, hullabaloo, hurly-burly, pandemonium, row, ruckus, ruction, rumpus, shindy, squall, stew, stir, storm, to-do, tumult, turmoil, uproar, welter, whirl **2** *Syn* STIR, ado, bustle, flurry, fuss *Ant* tranquillity

pouch *Syn* BAG, sack

pound *Syn* BEAT, baste, belabor, buffet, pummel, thrash

pour **1** • to send forth or come forth abundantly *Syn* gush, sluice, stream *Rel* appear, emerge **2** *Syn* GUSH (sense 1), jet, rush, spew, spout, spurt, squirt *Ant* dribble, drip, drop, trickle

pout *n Syn* GRIMACE, face, frown, lower, mouth, scowl

pout *vb Syn* SULK, mope

poverty **1** • the state of one with insufficient resources *Syn* destitution, indigence, penury, privation, want *Rel* exigency, necessity, need *Ant* riches **2** *Syn* DEFICIENCY, dearth, deficit, failure, famine, inadequacy, insufficiency, lack, paucity, scantiness, scarceness, scarcity, shortage, want *Ant* abundance, adequacy, amplitude, plenitude, plenty, sufficiency

poverty-stricken *Syn* POOR, destitute, impecunious, indigent, necessitous, needy, penniless *Ant* rich

power **1** • the ability to exert effort *Syn* energy, force, might, puissance, strength *Rel* ability, capability, capacity *Ant* impotence **2** • the ability of a living being to perform in a given way or a capacity for a particular kind of performance *Syn* faculty, function

powerful • having or manifesting power to effect great or striking results *Syn* forceful, forcible, potent, puissant *Rel* able, capable, competent *Ant* inefficacious, powerless

powerless • unable to act or achieve one's purpose *Syn* helpless, impotent, weak *Rel* incapable, incompetent, ineffective, ineffectual, inept, unfit, useless *Ant* mighty, potent, powerful, puissant, strong

powerlessness *Syn* INABILITY, impotence, inadequacy, incapability, incapacity, incompetence, ineptitude *Ant* ability, adequacy, capability, capacity, competence, potency

practicable *Syn* POSSIBLE, feasible

practically **1** *Syn* ALMOST, about, more or less, most, much, near, nearly, next to, nigh, some, virtually, well-nigh **2** *Syn* VIRTUALLY, morally

practice *vb* • to perform or cause one to perform an act or series of acts repeatedly in order to master or strengthen a skill or ability *Syn* drill, exercise *Rel* execute, fulfill, perform

practice *n* **1** *Syn* EXERCISE, drill **2** *Syn* HABIT, custom, fashion, pattern, trick, way, wont **3** *Syn* REHEARSAL, dry run, trial

prairie *Syn* PLAIN, down, grassland, savanna, steppe, tundra, veld (*or* veldt)

praise **1** • to express approval of or esteem for *Syn* acclaim, eulogize, extol, laud *Rel* applaud, commend, compliment *Ant* blame **2** *Syn* ACCLAIM, applaud, cheer, hail, laud, salute, tout *Ant* knock, pan, slam

praiseworthy *Syn* ADMIRABLE, commendable, creditable, laudable, meritorious *Ant* censurable, discreditable, reprehensible

prank • a playful or mischievous act intended as a joke *Syn* caper, antic, monkeyshine, dido *Rel* frolic, gambol, play, rollick, sport

prate *Syn* CHAT, babble, blab, cackle, chatter, converse, gab, gabble, gas, jabber, jaw, palaver, patter, prattle, rap, rattle, run on, talk, twitter, visit

prattle *Syn* CHAT, babble, blab, cackle, chatter, converse, gab, gabble, gas, jabber, jaw, palaver, patter, prate, rap, rattle, run on, talk, twitter, visit

pray • to request or make a request for in a humble, beseeching manner *Syn* appeal, petition, plead, sue *Rel* beg, beseech, entreat, implore, supplicate

prayer • an earnest and usually a formal request for something *Syn* appeal, petition, plea, suit *Rel* begging, beseeching, entreaty, imploring, supplication

preamble *Syn* INTRODUCTION, exordium, foreword, preface, prelude, prologue

precarious *Syn* DANGEROUS, hazardous, perilous, risky *Ant* safe, secure

precedent *Syn* PREVIOUS, antecedent, anterior, foregoing, preceding, prior *Ant* after, ensuing, following, subsequent, succeeding

preceding *Syn* PREVIOUS, antecedent, anterior, foregoing, precedent, prior *Ant* after, ensuing, following, subsequent, succeeding

precept *Syn* LAW, canon, ordinance, regulation, rule, statute

preceptor *Syn* TEACHER, educator, instructor, pedagogue, schoolteacher

precious **1** *Syn* COSTLY, dear, expensive, invaluable, priceless, valuable *Ant* cheap **2** *Syn* LOVABLE, adorable, darling, dear, disarming, endearing, sweet, winning *Ant* abhorrent, abominable, detestable, hateful, odious, unlovable

precipitate *adj* • showing undue haste or unexpectedness *Syn* abrupt, hasty, headlong, impetuous, sudden *Rel* headstrong, refractory, willful *Ant* deliberate

precipitate *n Syn* DEPOSIT, dregs, grounds, lees, sediment

precipitous *Syn* STEEP, abrupt, sheer

précis *Syn* COMPENDIUM, aperçu, digest, pandect, sketch, survey, syllabus

precise *Syn* CORRECT, accurate, exact, nice, right *Ant* incorrect

precisely *Syn* STRICTLY, exactly, rigidly, rigorously *Ant* imprecisely, inexactly, loosely

preciseness *Syn* PRECISION, accuracy, closeness, delicacy, exactitude, exactness, fineness, rigorousness, veracity *Ant* coarseness, impreciseness, imprecision, inaccuracy, inexactness, roughness

precision • the quality or state of being very accurate *Syn* accuracy, closeness, delicacy, exactitude, exactness, fineness, preciseness, rigorousness, veracity *Rel* correctness, rightness, strictness, truth *Ant* coarseness, impreciseness, imprecision, inaccuracy, inexactness, roughness

preclude *Syn* PREVENT (sense 2), avert, forestall, help, obviate

precocious *Syn* PREMATURE, advanced, forward, untimely *Ant* matured

precursor **1** *Syn* FORERUNNER, harbinger, herald **2** *Syn* ANCESTOR (sense 2), antecedent, foregoer, forerunner, predecessor *Ant* descendant (*or* descendent)

predecessor *Syn* ANCESTOR (sense 2), antecedent, foregoer, forerunner, precursor *Ant* descendant (*or* descendent)

predicament • a difficult, perplexing, or trying situation *Syn* dilemma, fix, jam, pickle, plight, quandary, scrape *Rel* condition, posture, situation, state

predicate *Syn* ASSERT, affirm, aver, avouch, avow, declare, profess, protest, warrant *Ant* controvert, deny

predict *Syn* FORETELL, augur, forebode, forecast, portend, presage, prognosticate, prophesy

predicting *Syn* PREDICTION, auguring, cast, forecast, forecasting, foretelling, presaging, prognosis, prognosticating, prognostication, prophecy, soothsaying

prediction • a declaration that something will happen in the future *Syn* auguring, cast, forecast, forecasting, foretelling, predicting, presaging, prognosis, prognosticating, prognostication, prophecy, soothsaying *Rel* augury, omen, portent, sign

predilection • an attitude of mind that predisposes one to favor something *Syn* bias, partiality, prejudice, prepossession *Rel* flair, leaning, proclivity, propensity *Ant* aversion

predispose *Syn* INCLINE, bias, dispose *Ant* disincline, indispose

predominance *Syn* SUPREMACY, ascendancy, dominance, dominion, preeminence, sovereignty

predominant *Syn* DOMINANT, paramount, preponderant, preponderating, sovereign *Ant* subordinate

predominantly *Syn* CHIEFLY, altogether, basically, by and large, generally, largely, mainly, mostly, overall, primarily, principally, substantially

preeminence *Syn* SUPREMACY, ascendancy, dominance, dominion, predominance, sovereignty

preeminent **1** *Syn* EMINENT, distinguished, illustrious, noble, notable, noteworthy, outstanding, prestigious, signal, star, superior **2** *Syn* HEAD, chief, commanding, first, foremost, high, lead, leading, managing, premier, presiding, primary, prime, principal, supreme **3** *Syn* SUPREME, incomparable, peerless, superlative, surpassing, transcendent

preempt *Syn* ARROGATE, appropriate, confiscate, usurp *Ant* renounce, yield

preen *Syn* PRIDE, pique, plume

preface *Syn* INTRODUCTION, exordium, foreword, preamble, prelude, prologue

prefatory *Syn* PRELIMINARY, introductory, preparatory

prefer **1** *Syn* CHOOSE, cull, elect, opt, pick, select, single *Ant* eschew, reject **2** *Syn* OFFER, present, proffer, tender

preferable *Syn* BETTER, superior

preference **1** *Syn* CHOICE, alternative, election, option, selection **2** *Syn* FAVORITE, darling, minion, pet **3** *Syn* LIKING, appetite, fancy, favor, fondness, like, love, partiality, relish, shine, taste, use *Ant* aversion, disfavor, dislike, distaste, hatred, loathing

preferment *Syn* ADVANCEMENT, elevation, promotion *Ant* degradation, reduction (*in rank or status*)

prefiguring *Syn* OMEN, augury, auspice, boding, foreboding, foreshadowing, portent, presage

pregnant *Syn* EXPRESSIVE, eloquent, meaning, meaningful, revealing, significant, suggestive

prejudice **1** *Syn* BIAS, favor, one-sidedness, partiality, partisanship *Ant* impartiality, neutrality, objectivity, open-mindedness **2** *Syn* PREDILECTION, bias, partiality, prepossession *Ant* aversion

prejudiced *Syn* INTOLERANT, bigoted, narrow, narrow-minded, small-minded *Ant* broad-minded, liberal, open-minded, tolerant, unprejudiced

prejudicial *Syn* HARMFUL, adverse, bad, baleful, baneful, damaging, deleterious, detrimental, evil, hurtful, ill, injurious, mischievous, noxious, pernicious *Ant* harmless, innocent, innocuous, inoffensive, safe

preliminary • serving to make ready the way for something that follows *Syn* introductory, prefatory, preparatory *Rel* primal, primary

prelude *Syn* INTRODUCTION, exordium, foreword, preamble, preface, prologue

premature • unduly early in coming, happening, or developing *Syn* advanced, forward, precocious, untimely *Rel* immature, unmatured, unmellow, unripe *Ant* matured

premeditated *Syn* DELIBERATE, advised, considered, designed, studied *Ant* casual

premier *Syn* HEAD, chief, commanding, first, foremost, high, lead, leading, managing, preeminent, presiding, primary, prime, principal, supreme

premise *n* *Syn* ASSUMPTION, posit, postulate, presumption, presupposition
premise *vb* *Syn* PRESUPPOSE, assume, posit, postulate, presume
premium *Syn* AWARD, decoration, distinction, honor, plume, prize
premonition • a feeling that something bad will happen *Syn* foreboding, presage, presentiment *Rel* anticipation, foreknowledge
preoccupied *Syn* ABSTRACTED, absent, absentminded, distraught *Ant* alert
preparatory *Syn* PRELIMINARY, introductory, prefatory
prepare • to make ready beforehand usually for some purpose, use, or activity *Syn* condition, fit, qualify, ready *Rel* furnish, provide, supply
preponderant *Syn* DOMINANT, paramount, predominant, preponderating, sovereign *Ant* subordinate
preponderating *Syn* DOMINANT, paramount, predominant, preponderant, sovereign *Ant* subordinate
prepossession *Syn* PREDILECTION, bias, partiality, prejudice *Ant* aversion
preposterous *Syn* FOOLISH, absurd, silly *Ant* sensible
prerequisite *Syn* REQUIREMENT, requisite
prerogative *Syn* RIGHT, appanage, birthright, perquisite, privilege
presage *vb* *Syn* FORETELL, augur, forebode, forecast, portend, predict, prognosticate, prophesy
presage *n* **1** *Syn* OMEN, augury, auspice, boding, foreboding, foreshadowing, portent, prefiguring **2** *Syn* PREMONITION, foreboding, presentiment
presaging *Syn* PREDICTION, auguring, cast, forecast, forecasting, foretelling, predicting, prognosis, prognosticating, prognostication, prophecy, soothsaying
prescience *Syn* FORESIGHT (sense 1), foreknowledge *Ant* improvidence, shortsightedness
prescribe **1** • to fix arbitrarily or authoritatively for the sake of order or of a clear understanding *Syn* assign, define *Rel* establish, fix, set, settle **2** *Syn* DICTATE, decree, impose, ordain
prescription *Syn* RECEIPT, recipe
presence *Syn* BEARING, demeanor, deportment, mien, port
present *adj* • existing or in progress right now *Syn* current, extant, ongoing, present-day *Rel* contemporary, mod, modern, new, newfangled, new-fashioned, now, recent, red-hot, space-age, ultramodern, up-to-date *Ant* ago, future, past
present *n* *Syn* GIFT (sense 1), boon, favor, gratuity, largess
present *vb* **1** *Syn* GIVE, afford, bestow, confer, donate **2** *Syn* OFFER, prefer, proffer, tender
present-day **1** *Syn* MODERN, contemporary, current, hot, mod, modernistic, newfangled, new, new-fashioned, red-hot, space-age, ultramodern, up-to-date *Ant* antiquated, archaic, dated, fusty, musty, noncontemporary, oldfangled, old-fashioned, old-time, out-of-date, passé **2** *Syn* PRESENT, current, extant, ongoing *Ant* ago, future, past
presentiment *Syn* PREMONITION, foreboding, presage
presently **1** • without undue time lapse *Syn* directly, shortly, soon **2** *Syn* SHORTLY, anon, momentarily, soon
preserve *Syn* SAVE, conserve *Ant* consume, spend
presiding *Syn* HEAD, chief, commanding, first, foremost, high, lead, leading, managing, preeminent, premier, primary, prime, principal, supreme
press *vb* **1** • to act upon through steady pushing or thrusting force exerted in contact *Syn* bear, bear down, crowd, jam, squeeze *Rel* propel, push, shove, thrust **2** *Syn* URGE, egg (on), encourage, exhort, goad, prod, prompt
press *n* *Syn* CROWD, crush, horde, mob, rout, throng
pressing • demanding or claiming especially immediate attention *Syn* crying, exigent, imperative, importunate, insistent, instant, urgent *Rel* direct, immediate
pressure *Syn* STRESS, strain, tension
prestidigitator *Syn* MAGICIAN (sense 2), conjurer (*or* conjuror), trickster
prestige *Syn* INFLUENCE, authority, credit, weight
prestigious *Syn* EMINENT, distinguished, illustrious, noble, notable, noteworthy, outstanding, preeminent, signal, star, superior
presumably **1** *Syn* APPARENTLY, evidently, ostensibly, seemingly, supposedly **2** *Syn* PROBABLY, doubtless, likely *Ant* improbably
presume *Syn* PRESUPPOSE, assume, posit, postulate, premise
presumption **1** *Syn* ASSUMPTION, posit, postulate, premise, presupposition **2** *Syn* EFFRONTERY, audacity, brashness, brass, brassiness, brazenness, cheek, cheekiness, chutzpah, gall, nerve, nerviness, pertness, presumptuousness, sauce, sauciness, temerity
presumptuous **1** *Syn* ARROGANT, cavalier, haughty, highfalutin, high-handed, high-hat, imperious, important, lofty, lordly, masterful, overweening, peremptory, pompous, pretentious, supercilious, superior, uppish, uppity *Ant* humble, modest **2** *Syn* CONFIDENT, assured, sanguine, sure *Ant* apprehensive, diffident **3** *Syn* INTRUSIVE, interfering, intruding, meddlesome, meddling, nosy (*or* nosey), obtrusive, officious, prying, snoopy *Ant* unobtrusive

presumptuousness 1 *Syn* ARROGANCE, haughtiness, imperiousness, loftiness, lordliness, masterfulness, peremptoriness, pompousness, pretense (*or* pretence), pretension, pretentiousness, self-importance, superciliousness, superiority *Ant* humility, modesty **2** *Syn* EFFRONTERY, audacity, brashness, brass, brassiness, brazenness, cheek, cheekiness, chutzpah, gall, nerve, nerviness, pertness, presumption, sauce, sauciness, temerity

presuppose • to take something for granted or as true or existent especially as a basis for action or reasoning *Syn* assume, posit, postulate, premise, presume *Rel* conjecture, guess, surmise

presupposition *Syn* ASSUMPTION, posit, postulate, premise, presumption

pretend *Syn* ASSUME, affect, counterfeit, feign, sham, simulate

pretense 1 • the offering of something false as real or true *Syn* make-believe, pretension *Rel* deceit, deception, fake, fraud, humbug, imposture, sham **2** *Syn* CLAIM, pretension, title **3** *Syn* ARROGANCE, haughtiness, imperiousness, loftiness, lordliness, masterfulness, peremptoriness, pompousness, presumptuousness, pretension, pretentiousness, self-importance, superciliousness, superiority *Ant* humility, modesty

pretension 1 *Syn* ARROGANCE, haughtiness, imperiousness, loftiness, lordliness, masterfulness, peremptoriness, pompousness, presumptuousness, pretense (*or* pretence), pretentiousness, self-importance, superciliousness, superiority *Ant* humility, modesty **2** *Syn* CLAIM, pretense, title **3** *Syn* GOAL, aim, ambition, aspiration, design, dream, end, intent, intention, mark, meaning, object, objective, plan, purpose, target, thing **4** *Syn* PRETENSE, make-believe

pretentious 1 *Syn* AMBITIOUS (sense 2), utopian *Ant* modest **2** *Syn* ARROGANT, cavalier, haughty, highfalutin, high-handed, high-hat, imperious, important, lofty, lordly, masterful, overweening, peremptory, pompous, presumptuous, supercilious, superior, uppish, uppity *Ant* humble, modest **3** *Syn* SHOWY, ostentatious

pretentiousness 1 *Syn* ARROGANCE, haughtiness, imperiousness, loftiness, lordliness, masterfulness, peremptoriness, pompousness, presumptuousness, pretense (*or* pretence), pretension, self-importance, superciliousness, superiority *Ant* humility, modesty **2** *Syn* OSTENTATION, flamboyance, flashiness, garishness, gaudiness, glitz, ostentatiousness, showiness, swank *Ant* austerity, plainness, severity

preternatural *Syn* SUPERNATURAL, miraculous, superhuman, supranatural

pretext *Syn* APOLOGY, alibi, apologia, excuse, plea

pretty *Syn* BEAUTIFUL, attractive, beauteous, comely, cute, fair, gorgeous, handsome, knockout, lovely, ravishing, sightly, stunning, taking *Ant* homely, ill-favored, plain, ugly, unattractive, unbeautiful, unhandsome, unlovely, unpretty, unsightly

prevailing • general (as in circulation, acceptance, or use) in a given place or at a given time *Syn* current, prevalent, rife *Rel* dominant, predominant, preponderant

prevail (on *or* upon) *Syn* PERSUADE, argue, convince, get, induce, move, satisfy, talk (into), win (over)

prevalent *Syn* PREVAILING, current, rife

prevaricate *Syn* LIE, equivocate, fib, palter

prevent 1 • to deal with beforehand *Syn* anticipate, forestall *Rel* baffle, balk, foil, frustrate, thwart **2** • to stop from advancing or occurring *Syn* avert, forestall, help, obviate, preclude *Rel* anticipate, provide

previous • going before another in time or order *Syn* antecedent, anterior, foregoing, precedent, preceding, prior *Rel* advance, early, premature *Ant* after, ensuing, following, subsequent, succeeding

previous to *Syn* BEFORE, ahead of, ere, of, prior to, to *Ant* after, following

prey *Syn* VICTIM, quarry

price • the quantity of one thing that is exchanged or demanded in barter or sale for another *Syn* charge, cost, expense

priceless *Syn* COSTLY, dear, expensive, invaluable, precious, valuable *Ant* cheap

prick *Syn* PERFORATE, bore, drill, punch, puncture

pride *n* 1 • an attitude of inordinate self-esteem or superiority *Syn* vainglory, vanity *Rel* arrogance, disdain, disdainfulness, haughtiness, insolence, superciliousness *Ant* humility, shame **2** *Syn* COMPLACENCE, complacency, conceit, conceitedness, ego, egotism, pompousness, pridefulness, self-admiration, self-conceit, self-esteem, self-importance, self-satisfaction, smugness, vaingloriousness, vainglory, vainness, vanity *Ant* humbleness, humility, modesty

pride *vb* • to congratulate oneself because of something one is, has, or has done or achieved *Syn* pique, plume, preen *Rel* boast, brag, crow, gasconade, vaunt

prideful *Syn* CONCEITED, complacent, egoistic, egotistic (*or* egotistical), important, overweening, pompous, proud, self-conceited, self-important, self-satisfied, smug, stuck-up, vain, vainglorious *Ant* humble, modest

pridefulness *Syn* COMPLACENCE, complacency, conceit, conceitedness, ego, egotism, pompousness, pride, self-admiration, self-conceit, self-esteem, self-importance, self-satisfaction, smugness, vaingloriousness, vainglory, vainness, vanity *Ant* humbleness, humility, modesty

priggish 1 *Syn* COMPLACENT, self-complacent, self-satisfied, smug 2 *Syn* PRIM, prissy, prudish, puritanical, straitlaced, stuffy

prim • excessively concerned with what one regards as proper or right *Syn* priggish, prissy, prudish, puritanical, straitlaced, stuffy *Rel* correct, nice, precise

primal *Syn* PRIMARY, prime, primeval, primitive, primordial, pristine

primarily *Syn* CHIEFLY, altogether, basically, by and large, generally, largely, mainly, mostly, overall, predominantly, principally, substantially

primary 1 • first in some respect (as order, character, or importance) *Syn* primal, prime, primeval, primitive, primordial, pristine *Rel* beginning, commencing, initial, initiating, starting 2 *Syn* HEAD, chief, commanding, first, foremost, high, lead, leading, managing, preeminent, premier, presiding, prime, principal, supreme

prime *n Syn* ELITE, best, choice, cream, elect, fat, flower, pick, upper crust

prime *adj* 1 *Syn* EXCELLENT, A1, bang-up, banner, capital, classic, crackerjack, dandy, divine, fabulous, fine, first-class, first-rate, grand, great, groovy, heavenly, jim-dandy, keen, marvelous (*or* marvellous), mean, neat, nifty, noble, par excellence, sensational, splendid, stellar, sterling, superb, superior, superlative, supernal, swell, terrific, tiptop, top, top-notch, unsurpassed, wonderful *Ant* poor 2 *Syn* HEAD, chief, commanding, first, foremost, high, lead, leading, managing, preeminent, premier, presiding, primary, principal, supreme 3 *Syn* PRIMARY, primal, primeval, primitive, primordial, pristine

prime mover *Syn* ORIGIN, inception, provenance, provenience, root, source

primeval *Syn* PRIMARY, primal, prime, primitive, primordial, pristine

primitive *Syn* PRIMARY, primal, prime, primeval, primordial, pristine

primordial 1 *Syn* INITIAL, original *Ant* final 2 *Syn* PRIMARY, primal, prime, primeval, primitive, pristine

princely *Syn* KINGLY, imperial, queenly, regal, royal

principal 1 *Syn* CHIEF, capital, foremost, leading, main *Ant* subordinate 2 *Syn* HEAD, chief, commanding, first, foremost, high, lead, leading, managing, preeminent, premier, presiding, primary, prime, supreme

principally 1 *Syn* CHIEFLY, altogether, basically, by and large, generally, largely, mainly, mostly, overall, predominantly, primarily, substantially 2 *Syn* LARGELY, chiefly, generally, greatly, mainly, mostly

principle • a comprehensive and fundamental rule, doctrine, or assumption *Syn* axiom, fundamental, law, theorem *Rel* basis, foundation, ground

principles *Syn* ETHICS, morality, morals, standards

print *Syn* IMPRESSION, impress, imprint, stamp

printing *Syn* EDITION, impression, reissue, reprinting

prior *Syn* PREVIOUS, antecedent, anterior, foregoing, precedent, preceding *Ant* after, ensuing, following, subsequent, succeeding

prior to *Syn* BEFORE, ahead of, ere, of, previous to, to *Ant* after, following

priory *Syn* CLOISTER, abbey, convent, monastery, nunnery

prismatic • marked by or displaying a variety of colors *Syn* iridescent, opalescent, opaline

prison *Syn* JAIL, brig, guardroom, hoosegow, jug, lockup, pen, penitentiary, stockade

prissy *Syn* PRIM, priggish, prudish, puritanical, straitlaced, stuffy

pristine *Syn* PRIMARY, primal, prime, primeval, primitive, primordial

privateer *Syn* PIRATE, buccaneer, corsair, freebooter

privation 1 *Syn* LACK, absence, dearth, defect, want 2 *Syn* POVERTY, destitution, indigence, penury, want *Ant* riches

privilege *Syn* RIGHT, appanage, birthright, perquisite, prerogative

prize *vb Syn* APPRECIATE, cherish, treasure, value *Ant* despise

prize *n* 1 *Syn* AWARD, decoration, distinction, honor, plume, premium 2 *Syn* SPOIL, booty, loot, plunder, swag

probability • a measure of how often an event will occur instead of another *Syn* chance, odds, percentage *Rel* outlook, prospect

probable • almost sure to be or to become true or real *Syn* likely, possible *Rel* believable, colorable, credible, plausible *Ant* certain, improbable

probably • without much doubt *Syn* doubtless, likely, presumably *Rel* mayhap, perchance, perhaps, possibly *Ant* improbably

probe *vb* 1 *Syn* ENTER (sense 1), penetrate, pierce *Ant* issue from 2 *Syn* EXPLORE, delve (into), dig (into), inquire (into), investigate, look (into), research

probe *n Syn* INQUIRY, inquest, inquisition, investigation, research

probity *Syn* HONESTY, honor, integrity *Ant* dishonesty

problem *Syn* MYSTERY, conundrum, enigma, puzzle, riddle

problematic *Syn* DOUBTFUL, dubious, questionable *Ant* cocksure, positive

procedure *Syn* PROCESS, proceeding

proceed *Syn* SPRING, arise, derive, emanate, flow, issue, originate, rise, stem

proceed (along) *Syn* TRAVERSE, cover, crisscross, cross, cut (across), follow, go, pass (over), travel

proceeding *Syn* PROCESS, procedure

process 1 • the series of actions, operations,

or motions involved in the accomplishment of an end *Syn* procedure, proceeding *Rel* advance, progress **2** *Syn* ADVANCE (sense 2), advancement, furtherance, going, headway, march, onrush, passage, procession, progress, progression *Ant* recession, regression, retrogression

procession **1** • a body (as of persons and vehicles) moving along in a usually ceremonial order *Syn* cavalcade, cortege, motorcade, parade *Rel* sequence, succession, train **2** *Syn* ADVANCE (sense 2), advancement, furtherance, going, headway, march, onrush, passage, process, progress, progression *Ant* recession, regression, retrogression

proclaim *Syn* ANNOUNCE, advertise, blaze, broadcast, declare, enunciate, placard, post, promulgate, publicize, publish, sound

proclamation *Syn* DECLARATION, advertisement, announcement, broadcasting, promulgation, publication

proclivity *Syn* LEANING, flair, penchant, propensity *Ant* distaste

procrastinate *Syn* DELAY (sense 2), dawdle, lag, loiter *Ant* hasten, hurry

procreate *Syn* GENERATE, beget, breed, engender, get, propagate, reproduce, sire

procurator *Syn* AGENT (sense 1), attorney, commissary, delegate, deputy, envoy, factor, proxy, representative

procure **1** *Syn* EARN, acquire, attain, capture, carry, draw, gain, garner, get, land, make, obtain, realize, secure, win *Ant* forfeit, lose **2** *Syn* GET, gain, obtain, secure, win

prod *n* *Syn* POKE, jog, nudge

prod *vb* **1** *Syn* POKE, jog, nudge **2** *Syn* URGE, egg (on), encourage, exhort, goad, press, prompt

prodigal *adj* **1** • given to spending money freely or foolishly *Syn* extravagant, profligate, spendthrift, squandering, thriftless, unthrifty, wasteful *Rel* improvident, myopic, shortsighted *Ant* conserving, economical, economizing, frugal, scrimping, skimping, thrifty **2** *Syn* PROFUSE, exuberant, lavish, lush, luxuriant *Ant* scant, scanty, spare

prodigal *n* • someone who carelessly spends money *Syn* profligate, spender, spendthrift, squanderer, waster, wastrel *Ant* economizer

prodigious *Syn* MONSTROUS, monumental, stupendous, tremendous

prodigy *Syn* WONDER (sense 1), marvel, miracle, phenomenon

produce *vb* **1** *Syn* BEAR (sense 1), turn out, yield **2** *Syn* EFFECT, bring about, cause, create, effectuate, engender, generate, induce, make, prompt, result (in), spawn, work, yield

produce *n* *Syn* PRODUCT, production

product **1** • something produced by physical labor or intellectual effort *Syn* produce, production **2** *Syn* WORK (sense 3), artifact, opus, production

production **1** *Syn* PRODUCT, produce **2** *Syn* WORK (sense 3), artifact, opus, product

productive *Syn* FERTILE, fat, fecund, fruitful, luxuriant, prolific, rich *Ant* barren, infertile, sterile, unfruitful, unproductive

profanation • a violation or a misuse of something normally held sacred *Syn* blasphemy, desecration, sacrilege *Rel* contamination, defilement, pollution

profane *adj* **1** • not concerned with religion or religious purposes *Syn* lay, secular, temporal *Rel* earthly, mundane, terrestrial, worldly *Ant* sacred **2** *Syn* IMPIOUS, blasphemous, sacrilegious *Ant* pious, reverent

profane *vb* *Syn* DESECRATE, defile, violate

profanity *Syn* BLASPHEMY, cursing, swearing *Ant* adoration

profess *Syn* ASSERT, affirm, aver, avouch, avow, declare, predicate, protest, warrant *Ant* controvert, deny

profession **1** *Syn* OCCUPATION, calling, employment, line, trade, vocation, work **2** *Syn* TRADE, art, craft, handicraft

proffer *vb* *Syn* OFFER, prefer, present, tender

proffer *n* *Syn* PROPOSAL, offer, proposition, suggestion

proficient • having great knowledge and experience in a trade or profession *Syn* adept, expert, masterly, skilled, skillful *Rel* effective, effectual, efficient *Ant* amateur, amateurish, inexperienced, inexpert, unexperienced, unpracticed, unprofessional, unseasoned, unskilled, unskillful

profile *Syn* OUTLINE, contour, silhouette, skyline

profit *vb* *Syn* BENEFIT, avail *Ant* harm

profit *n* *Syn* USE (sense 1), account, advantage, avail, service

profitable **1** *Syn* BENEFICIAL, advantageous, favorable, helpful, salutary *Ant* disadvantageous, unfavorable, unhelpful **2** *Syn* PAYING, gainful, lucrative, remunerative

profligate *adj* **1** *Syn* ABANDONED (sense 1), dissolute, reprobate *Ant* redeemed, regenerate **2** *Syn* PRODIGAL, extravagant, spendthrift, squandering, thriftless, unthrifty, wasteful *Ant* conserving, economical, economizing, frugal, scrimping, skimping, thrifty

profligate *n* *Syn* PRODIGAL, spender, spendthrift, squanderer, waster, wastrel *Ant* economizer

profound *Syn* DEEP, abysmal

profuse • giving or given out in great abundance *Syn* exuberant, lavish, lush, luxuriant, prodigal *Rel* abundant, copious, plentiful *Ant* scant, scanty, spare

progenitor *Syn* ANCESTOR (sense 1), forebear, forefather *Ant* descendant (*or* descendent)

progeny *Syn* OFFSPRING, descendants, issue, posterity, young

prognosis *Syn* PREDICTION, auguring, cast, forecast, forecasting, foretelling, predicting,

presaging, prognosticating, prognostication, prophecy, soothsaying
prognosticate *Syn* FORETELL, augur, forebode, forecast, portend, predict, presage, prophesy
prognosticating *Syn* PREDICTION, auguring, cast, forecast, forecasting, foretelling, predicting, presaging, prognosis, prognostication, prophecy, soothsaying
prognostication *Syn* PREDICTION, auguring, cast, forecast, forecasting, foretelling, predicting, presaging, prognosis, prognosticating, prophecy, soothsaying
prognosticator *Syn* PROPHET, augur, diviner, forecaster, foreseer, foreteller, fortune-teller, futurist, prophesier, seer, soothsayer
program • a formulated plan listing things to be done or to take place especially in chronological order *Syn* agenda, schedule, timetable
progress *Syn* ADVANCE (sense 2), advancement, furtherance, going, headway, march, onrush, passage, process, procession, progression *Ant* recession, regression, retrogression
progression **1** *Syn* ADVANCE (sense 2), advancement, furtherance, going, headway, march, onrush, passage, process, procession, progress *Ant* recession, regression, retrogression **2** *Syn* SUCCESSION, chain, sequence, series, string, train
progressive *Syn* LIBERAL (sense 2), advanced, radical *Ant* authoritarian
prohibit *Syn* FORBID, ban, bar, enjoin, interdict, outlaw, proscribe *Ant* allow, let, permit, suffer
prohibiting *Syn* PROHIBITION (sense 1), banning, barring, enjoining, forbidding, interdicting, interdiction, outlawing, proscribing, proscription *Ant* prescription
prohibition **1** • the act of ordering that something not be done or used *Syn* banning, barring, enjoining, forbidding, interdicting, interdiction, outlawing, prohibiting, proscribing, proscription *Rel* bidding, charging, decreeing, dictation, direction, instruction **2** • an order that something not be done or used *Syn* ban, embargo, interdict, interdiction, proscription, veto *Rel* constraint, denial, deterrent, disallowance, discouragement, inhibition, injunction, limitation, negation, objection, protest, refusal, rejection, repression, restraint, restriction, suppression, taboo *Ant* prescription
project *vb* **1** *Syn* BULGE, beetle, jut, overhang, protrude, stick out **2** *Syn* PLAN, design, plot, scheme
project *n* *Syn* PLAN, design, plot, scheme
projection • an extension beyond the normal line or surface *Syn* bulge, protrusion, protuberance
proliferate *Syn* INCREASE (sense 2), accumulate, appreciate, balloon, build (up), burgeon, enlarge, escalate, expand, mount, multiply, mushroom, rise, snowball, swell, wax *Ant* contract, decrease, diminish, lessen, wane
prolific *Syn* FERTILE, fat, fecund, fruitful, luxuriant, productive, rich *Ant* barren, infertile, sterile, unfruitful, unproductive
prolificacy *Syn* FERTILITY, fecundity, fruitfulness *Ant* infertility, sterility
prolix *Syn* WORDY, diffuse, redundant, verbose *Ant* compact, concise, crisp, pithy, succinct, terse
prologue *Syn* INTRODUCTION, exordium, foreword, preamble, preface, prelude
prolong *Syn* EXTEND, elongate, lengthen, protract *Ant* abridge, shorten
prom *Syn* DANCE, ball, cotillion, formal, hop
prominent **1** *Syn* FAMOUS, celebrated, famed, noted, notorious, renowned, star, well-known *Ant* anonymous, obscure, unknown **2** *Syn* NOTICEABLE, arresting, conspicuous, outstanding, remarkable, salient, signal, striking
promiscuous *Syn* MISCELLANEOUS, assorted, heterogeneous, motley
promise *n* • a person's solemn declaration that he or she will do or not do something *Syn* oath, pledge, troth, vow, word *Rel* appointment, arrangement, commitment, engagement
promise *vb* • to give one's word to do, bring about, or provide *Syn* contract, covenant, engage, pledge, plight *Rel* accede, agree, assent, consent
promote *Syn* ADVANCE (sense 1), forward, further *Ant* check, retard
promoter *Syn* EXPONENT, advocate, apostle, backer, booster, champion, friend, proponent, supporter *Ant* adversary, antagonist, opponent
promotion **1** *Syn* ADVANCEMENT, elevation, preferment *Ant* degradation, reduction (*in rank or status*) **2** *Syn* PUBLICITY, ballyhoo, propaganda
prompt *vb* **1** *Syn* EFFECT, bring about, cause, create, effectuate, engender, generate, induce, make, produce, result (in), spawn, work, yield **2** *Syn* URGE, egg (on), encourage, exhort, goad, press, prod
prompt *adj* *Syn* QUICK, apt, ready *Ant* sluggish
promulgate *Syn* ANNOUNCE, advertise, blaze, broadcast, declare, enunciate, placard, post, proclaim, publicize, publish, sound
promulgation *Syn* DECLARATION, advertisement, announcement, broadcasting, proclamation, publication
prone **1** • having a tendency to be or act in a certain way *Syn* apt, given, inclined, tending *Rel* choosing, preferring **2** • lying down *Syn* couchant, dormant, prostrate, recumbent, supine *Rel* flat, level *Ant* erect **3** *Syn* LIABLE, exposed, open, sensitive, subject, susceptible *Ant* exempt, immune

pronounce *Syn* ARTICULATE, enunciate
pronounced *Syn* EGREGIOUS, blatant, conspicuous, flagrant, glaring, gross, obvious, patent, rank, striking
proof **1** • something that serves as evidence compelling the acceptance of a truth or fact *Syn* demonstration, test, trial **2** *Syn* REASON (sense 1), argument, ground
prop *Syn* SUPPORT (sense 1), bolster, brace, buttress, sustain
propaganda *Syn* PUBLICITY, ballyhoo, promotion
propagate **1** *Syn* GENERATE, beget, breed, engender, get, procreate, reproduce, sire **2** *Syn* SPREAD, circulate, diffuse, disseminate, radiate
propel **1** *Syn* ACTIVATE, actuate, crank (up), drive, move, run, set off, spark, start, touch off, trigger, turn on *Ant* cut, deactivate, kill, shut off, turn off **2** *Syn* PUSH, shove, thrust
propensity *Syn* LEANING, flair, penchant, proclivity *Ant* distaste
proper **1** *Syn* DECOROUS, decent, nice, seemly *Ant* blatant, indecorous **2** *Syn* FIT, appropriate, apt, felicitous, fitting, happy, meet, suitable *Ant* unfit
properly • in a manner suitable for the occasion or purpose *Syn* appropriately, congruously, correctly, fittingly, happily, meetly, rightly, suitably *Rel* well *Ant* improperly, inappropriately, incongruously, incorrectly, unsuitably, wrongly
property *Syn* CHARACTERISTIC, attribute, character, feature, mark, peculiarity, point, quality, trait
prophecy **1** *Syn* PREDICTION, auguring, cast, forecast, forecasting, foretelling, predicting, presaging, prognosis, prognosticating, prognostication, soothsaying **2** *Syn* REVELATION (sense 1), vision
prophesier *Syn* PROPHET, augur, diviner, forecaster, foreseer, foreteller, fortune-teller, futurist, prognosticator, seer, soothsayer
prophesy *Syn* FORETELL, augur, forebode, forecast, portend, predict, presage, prognosticate
prophet • one who predicts future events or developments *Syn* augur, diviner, forecaster, foreseer, foreteller, fortune-teller, futurist, prognosticator, prophesier, seer, soothsayer *Rel* prophetess
propitiate *Syn* PACIFY, appease, conciliate, disarm, mollify, placate *Ant* anger, enrage, incense, infuriate, madden, outrage
propitious *Syn* FAVORABLE, auspicious, benign *Ant* antagonistic, unfavorable
proponent *Syn* EXPONENT, advocate, apostle, backer, booster, champion, friend, promoter, supporter *Ant* adversary, antagonist, opponent
proportion *Syn* SYMMETRY, balance, harmony
proportional • corresponding in size, degree, or intensity *Syn* commensurable, commensurate, proportionate *Rel* correlative, corresponding, reciprocal
proportionate *Syn* PROPORTIONAL, commensurable, commensurate
proposal • something which is presented for consideration *Syn* offer, proffer, proposition, suggestion *Rel* feeler, overture
propose **1** • to set before the mind for consideration *Syn* pose, propound *Rel* state **2** *Syn* INTEND, design, mean, purpose
proposition **1** *Syn* PROPOSAL, offer, proffer, suggestion **2** *Syn* THEORY, hypothesis, supposition
propound *Syn* PROPOSE, pose
proprietor • one who has a legal or rightful claim to ownership *Syn* holder, owner, possessor *Rel* homeowner, landowner
propriety *Syn* DECORUM, decency, dignity, etiquette *Ant* indecorum, license
prorate *Syn* APPORTION, parcel, portion, ration
prosaic • having a plain, practical, everyday character or quality *Syn* matter-of-fact, prosy *Rel* practicable, practical
proscribe **1** *Syn* FORBID, ban, bar, enjoin, interdict, outlaw, prohibit *Ant* allow, let, permit, suffer **2** *Syn* SENTENCE, condemn, damn, doom
proscribing *Syn* PROHIBITION (sense 1), banning, barring, enjoining, forbidding, interdicting, interdiction, outlawing, prohibiting, proscription *Ant* prescription
proscription **1** *Syn* PROHIBITION (sense 1), banning, barring, enjoining, forbidding, interdicting, interdiction, outlawing, prohibiting, proscribing *Ant* prescription **2** *Syn* PROHIBITION (sense 2), ban, embargo, interdict, interdiction, veto *Ant* prescription
prospect **1** • an advance realization of something to come *Syn* anticipation, foretaste, outlook *Rel* expectation, hope **2** *Syn* CANDIDATE, applicant, aspirant, campaigner, contender, hopeful, seeker
prosper *Syn* SUCCEED, flourish, thrive *Ant* attempt, fail
prostration *Syn* FATIGUE, burnout, collapse, exhaustion, lassitude, tiredness, weariness *Ant* refreshment, rejuvenation, revitalization
prosy *Syn* PROSAIC, matter-of-fact
protean *Syn* CHANGEABLE, changeful, mutable, variable *Ant* stable, unchangeable
protect *Syn* DEFEND, guard, safeguard, shield *Ant* attack, combat
protection **1** *Syn* PROTECTOR, custodian, defender, guard **2** *Syn* SAFETY, safeness, security *Ant* danger, distress, endangerment, imperilment, jeopardy, peril, trouble
protector • someone that protects *Syn* custodian, defender, guard, protection *Rel* bodyguard, champion
protest *vb* **1** *Syn* ASSERT, affirm, aver,

avouch, avow, declare, predicate, profess, warrant *Ant* controvert, deny **2** *Syn* OBJECT, expostulate, kick, remonstrate *Ant* acquiesce
protest *n* *Syn* OBJECTION, challenge, complaint, demur, expostulation, fuss, question, remonstrance
protract *Syn* EXTEND, elongate, lengthen, prolong *Ant* abridge, shorten
protrude *Syn* BULGE, beetle, jut, overhang, project, stick out
protrusion *Syn* PROJECTION, bulge, protuberance
protuberance *Syn* PROJECTION, bulge, protrusion
proud **1** • showing scorn for inferiors *Syn* arrogant, disdainful, haughty, insolent, lordly, overbearing, supercilious *Rel* contemptuous, scornful *Ant* ashamed, humble **2** • having or exhibiting undue or excessive pride especially in one's appearance or achievements *Syn* vain, vainglorious *Rel* aggrandized, exalted, magnified *Ant* ashamed, humble **3** *Syn* CONCEITED, complacent, egoistic, egotistic (*or* egotistical), important, overweening, pompous, prideful, self-conceited, self-important, self-satisfied, smug, stuck-up, vain, vainglorious *Ant* humble, modest
prove **1** • to establish a point by appropriate objective means *Syn* demonstrate, test, try *Rel* confirm, corroborate, substantiate, verify *Ant* disprove **2** *Syn* INDICATE, argue, attest, bespeak, betoken
provenance *Syn* ORIGIN, inception, prime mover, provenience, root, source
provender *Syn* FOOD (sense 1), comestibles, feed, fodder, forage, provisions, viands, victuals
provenience *Syn* ORIGIN, inception, prime mover, provenance, root, source
proverb *Syn* SAYING, adage, aphorism, apothegm, epigram, maxim, motto, saw
provide *Syn* FURNISH (sense 2), deliver, feed, give, hand, hand over, supply *Ant* hold (back), keep (back), reserve, retain, withhold
providence **1** *Syn* ECONOMY, frugality, husbandry, scrimping, skimping, thrift *Ant* wastefulness **2** *Syn* PRUDENCE, discretion, foresight, forethought
provident **1** *Syn* FRUGAL, economical, economizing, scrimping, sparing, thrifty *Ant* prodigal, wasteful **2** *Syn* PRUDENT, discreet, foresighted, forethoughtful
providential *Syn* LUCKY, fortunate, happy *Ant* unlucky
province **1** *Syn* FIELD, bailiwick, domain, sphere, territory **2** *Syn* FUNCTION, duty, office
provincial *n* *Syn* HICK, bumpkin, clodhopper, countryman, rustic, yokel *Ant* cosmopolitan, sophisticate
provincial *adj* *Syn* INSULAR, local, parochial, small-town
provision *Syn* CONDITION, proviso, reservation, stipulation, strings, terms
provisional *Syn* TEMPORARY, acting, ad interim *Ant* permanent
provisions *Syn* FOOD (sense 1), comestibles, feed, fodder, forage, provender, viands, victuals
proviso *Syn* CONDITION, provision, reservation, stipulation, strings, terms
provocative • serving or likely to arouse a strong reaction *Syn* exciting, inciting, instigating, piquing, provoking, stimulating *Rel* explosive, fiery, incendiary, inflammatory, triggering
provoke **1** • to arouse as if pricking *Syn* excite, galvanize, pique, quicken, stimulate *Rel* arouse, rouse, stir **2** *Syn* IRRITATE, aggravate, exasperate, nettle, peeve, rile
provoking *Syn* PROVOCATIVE, exciting, inciting, instigating, piquing, stimulating
prowess *Syn* HEROISM, gallantry, valor
prowl *Syn* WANDER, gad, gallivant, meander, ramble, range, roam, rove, stray, traipse
proximity • the state or condition of being near *Syn* closeness, contiguity, immediacy, nearness *Rel* abutment, juxtaposition *Ant* distance, remoteness
proxy *Syn* AGENT (sense 1), attorney, commissary, delegate, deputy, envoy, factor, procurator, representative
prudence **1** good sense or shrewdness in the management of affairs *Syn* discretion, foresight, forethought, providence *Rel* calculation, caution, circumspection **2** *Syn* COMMON SENSE, discreetness, discretion, horse sense, levelheadedness, sense, sensibleness, wisdom, wit *Ant* imprudence, indiscretion
prudent **1** • making provision for the future *Syn* discreet, foresighted, forethoughtful, provident *Rel* calculating, cautious, circumspect, wary **2** *Syn* EXPEDIENT, advisable, desirable, judicious, politic, tactical, wise *Ant* imprudent, inadvisable, inexpedient, injudicious, unwise **3** *Syn* WISE, judicious, sage, sane, sapient, sensible *Ant* simple
prudish *Syn* PRIM, priggish, prissy, puritanical, straitlaced, stuffy
prune *Syn* CLIP, bob, crop, curtail, cut, cut back, dock, lop (off), nip, pare, shave, shear, snip, trim
pry *Syn* INTERFERE, butt in, intrude, meddle, mess, nose, obtrude, poke, snoop
prying **1** *Syn* CURIOUS, inquisitive, nosy, snoopy *Ant* incurious, uninterested **2** *Syn* INTRUSIVE, interfering, intruding, meddlesome, meddling, nosy (*or* nosey), obtrusive, officious, presumptuous, snoopy *Ant* unobtrusive
pseudo *Syn* COUNTERFEIT, bogus, fake, phony, pinchbeck, sham, spurious *Ant* bona fide, genuine

pseudonym • a fictitious or assumed name *Syn* alias, incognito, nom de guerre, nom de plume, pen name

psyche *Syn* MIND, brain, intellect, intelligence, soul, wit

psychic *Syn* MENTAL, cerebral, intellectual, intelligent

psychosis *Syn* INSANITY, lunacy, mania *Ant* sanity

pub *Syn* BARROOM, bar, café, groggery, grogshop, saloon, tavern

puberty *Syn* YOUTH, adolescence, pubescence *Ant* age

pubescence *Syn* YOUTH, adolescence, puberty *Ant* age

publication *Syn* DECLARATION, advertisement, announcement, broadcasting, proclamation, promulgation

publicity • an act or device designed to attract public interest and to mold public opinion *Syn* ballyhoo, promotion, propaganda *Rel* advertisement, announcement, broadcasting, promulgation, publication

publicize *Syn* ANNOUNCE, advertise, blaze, broadcast, declare, enunciate, placard, post, proclaim, promulgate, publish, sound

public servant *Syn* BUREAUCRAT, functionary

publish *Syn* ANNOUNCE, advertise, blaze, broadcast, declare, enunciate, placard, post, proclaim, promulgate, publicize, sound

puerile **1** *Syn* CALLOW, adolescent, green, immature, inexperienced, juvenile, raw, unfledged, unripe, unripened *Ant* adult, experienced, grown-up, mature, ripe **2** *Syn* CHILDISH, adolescent, babyish, immature, infantile, juvenile, kiddish *Ant* adult, grown-up, mature

puff *Syn* CRITICISM, blurb, critique, review

pugnacious *Syn* BELLIGERENT, aggressive, argumentative, bellicose, combative, contentious, discordant, disputatious, gladiatorial, militant, quarrelsome, scrappy, truculent, warlike *Ant* nonbelligerent, pacific, peaceable, peaceful

pugnacity *Syn* BELLIGERENCE, aggression, aggressiveness, bellicosity, combativeness, contentiousness, disputatiousness, fight, militancy, scrappiness, truculence *Ant* pacifism

puissance *Syn* POWER (sense 1), energy, force, might, strength *Ant* impotence

puissant *Syn* POWERFUL, forceful, forcible, potent *Ant* inefficacious, powerless

pull • to cause to move toward or after an applied force *Syn* drag, draw, hale, haul, tow, tug

pulsate • to course or move with or as if with rhythmic strokes *Syn* beat, palpitate, pulse, throb *Rel* fluctuate, oscillate, swing, vibrate, waver

pulsation • a rhythmical movement or one single step in recurring rhythmic steps *Syn* beat, palpitation, pulse, throb

pulse *vb Syn* PULSATE, beat, palpitate, throb

pulse *n Syn* PULSATION, beat, palpitation, throb

pummel *Syn* BEAT, baste, belabor, buffet, pound, thrash

punch *vb* **1** *Syn* PERFORATE, bore, drill, prick, puncture **2** *Syn* STRIKE, box, clout, cuff, hit, slap, slog, slug, smite, swat

punch *n Syn* VIGOR, dash, drive, élan, esprit, spirit, verve, vim

puncheon *Syn* CASK, barrel, firkin, hogshead, keg, pipe

punctilious *Syn* CAREFUL, meticulous, punctual, scrupulous *Ant* careless

punctual *Syn* CAREFUL, meticulous, punctilious, scrupulous *Ant* careless

puncture *Syn* PERFORATE, bore, drill, prick, punch

pungent • sharp and stimulating to the mind or the senses *Syn* piquant, poignant, racy, snappy, spicy *Rel* biting, cutting, incisive, trenchant *Ant* bland

punish • to inflict a penalty on in requital for wrongdoing *Syn* castigate, chasten, chastise, correct, discipline *Rel* amerce, fine, mulct, penalize *Ant* excuse, pardon

punitive • inflicting, involving, or serving as punishment *Syn* castigating, chastening, chastising, correcting, correctional, corrective, disciplinary, disciplining, penal, penalizing *Rel* retaliatory, retributive, retributory, revengeful

puny *Syn* PETTY, measly, paltry, picayune, picayunish, trifling, trivial *Ant* gross, important, momentous

pupil **1** *Syn* STUDENT, scholar **2** *Syn* FOLLOWER, adherent, convert, disciple, partisan, votary *Ant* leader

purchasable *Syn* VENAL, bribable, corruptible *Ant* incorruptible, uncorruptible

purchase *Syn* BUY, pick up, take

pure **1** • containing nothing that does not properly belong *Syn* absolute, sheer, simple *Rel* elemental, elementary *Ant* adulterated, applied (*of science*), contaminated, polluted **2** *Syn* CHASTE, decent, modest *Ant* bizarre (*of style, effect*), immoral, lewd, wanton

purge *Syn* RID, clear, disabuse, unburden

puritanical *Syn* PRIM, priggish, prissy, prudish, straitlaced, stuffy

purity *Syn* CHASTITY, chasteness, modesty *Ant* immodesty, impurity, unchastity

purloin *Syn* STEAL, cop, filch, lift, pilfer, pinch, snitch, swipe

purport *Syn* SUBSTANCE, burden, core, gist, pith

purported *Syn* SUPPOSED, conjectural, hypothetical, putative, reputed, suppositious, supposititious *Ant* certain

purpose *n* **1** *Syn* GOAL, aim, ambition, aspiration, design, dream, end, intent, intention, mark, meaning, object, objective, plan, pre-

tension, target, thing **2** *Syn* ROLE, capacity, function, job, part, place, position, task, work
purpose *vb Syn* INTEND, design, mean, propose
purposefully *Syn* INTENTIONALLY, consciously, deliberately, designedly, knowingly, purposely, willfully, wittingly *Ant* inadvertently, unconsciously, unintentionally, unknowingly, unwittingly
purposely *Syn* INTENTIONALLY, consciously, deliberately, designedly, knowingly, purposefully, willfully, wittingly *Ant* inadvertently, unconsciously, unintentionally, unknowingly, unwittingly
purse • a container for carrying money and small personal items *Syn* bag, handbag, pocketbook *Rel* billfold, wallet
pursuing *Syn* PURSUIT, chase, chasing, dogging, following, hounding, shadowing, tagging, tailing, tracing, tracking, trailing
pursuit **1** • the act of going after or in the tracks of another *Syn* chase, chasing, dogging, following, hounding, pursuing, shadowing, tagging, tailing, tracing, tracking, trailing *Rel* tagging along **2** *Syn* WORK (sense 2), business, calling, employment, occupation
purvey *Syn* CATER, pander
purview *Syn* RANGE, compass, gamut, horizon, ken, orbit, radius, reach, scope, sweep
push • to press against with force so as to cause to move ahead or aside *Syn* propel, shove, thrust *Rel* drive, impel, move
pushing *Syn* AGGRESSIVE (sense 1), assertive, militant, pushy, self-assertive
pushover *Syn* CINCH, breeze, child's play, duck soup, picnic, snap *Ant* chore, headache, labor
pushy *Syn* AGGRESSIVE (sense 1), assertive, militant, pushing, self-assertive
pusillanimous *Syn* COWARDLY, chicken, chickenhearted, craven, dastardly, lily-livered, recreant, spineless, unheroic, yellow *Ant* brave, courageous, daring, dauntless, doughty, fearless, gallant, greathearted, gutsy, hardy, heroic, intrepid, lionhearted, stalwart, stout, stouthearted, valiant, valorous
puss *Syn* FACE, countenance, mug, physiognomy, visage
pustule *Syn* ABSCESS, boil, carbuncle, furuncle, pimple
put **1** *Syn* ESTIMATE (sense 2), calculate, call, conjecture, figure, gauge, guess, judge, make, place, reckon, suppose **2** *Syn* IMPOSE, assess, charge, exact, fine, lay, levy *Ant* remit **3** *Syn* PHRASE, articulate, clothe, couch, express, formulate, say, state, word
putative *Syn* SUPPOSED, conjectural, hypothetical, purported, reputed, suppositious, supposititious *Ant* certain
put by *Syn* HOARD, cache, lay away, lay up, salt away, squirrel (away), stash, stockpile, store, stow
put-down *Syn* INSULT, affront, barb, dart, dig, epithet, indignity, name, offense (*or* offence), outrage, sarcasm, slight, slur
put off *Syn* POSTPONE, defer, delay, hold off (on), hold up, shelve
put on *Syn* OVERSTATE, exaggerate, overdo, overdraw *Ant* understate
put out *Syn* EXERT, apply, exercise, ply, wield
putrefy *Syn* DECAY, crumble, decompose, disintegrate, rot, spoil
putrid *Syn* MALODOROUS, fetid, fusty, musty, noisome, rancid, rank, stinking *Ant* odorous
putsch *Syn* REBELLION, coup, insurrection, mutiny, revolt, revolution, uprising
put up **1** *Syn* BUILD, assemble, construct, erect, fabricate, make, make up, piece, raise, rear, set up *Ant* disassemble, dismantle, take down **2** *Syn* MARKET, deal (in), merchandise, retail, sell, vend *Ant* buy, purchase **3** *Syn* RESIDE, dwell, live, lodge, sojourn, stay, stop
puzzle *vb* **1** • to baffle and disturb mentally *Syn* bewilder, confound, distract, dumbfound, mystify, nonplus, perplex *Rel* amaze, astound, flabbergast, surprise **2** *Syn* SOLVE, answer, break, crack, dope (out), figure out, resolve, riddle, unravel, work, work out
puzzle *n Syn* MYSTERY, conundrum, enigma, problem, riddle
pygmy *Syn* DWARF, midget, runt

Q

quack *Syn* IMPOSTOR, charlatan, faker, mountebank
quail *Syn* RECOIL, blench, flinch, shrink, wince *Ant* confront, defy
quaint *Syn* STRANGE, curious, eccentric, erratic, odd, outlandish, peculiar, queer, singular, unique *Ant* familiar
quake *Syn* SHAKE (sense 1), dither, quaver, quiver, shimmy, shiver, shudder, teeter, totter, tremble, wobble
qualified *Syn* COMPETENT, able, capable, fit, good, qualified, suitable *Ant* incompetent, inept, poor, unfit, unqualified
qualify **1** *Syn* CHARACTERIZE, distinguish, mark **2** *Syn* MODERATE, temper **3** *Syn* PREPARE, condition, fit, ready

quality 1 • a usually high level of merit or superiority *Syn* caliber, stature *Rel* excellence, virtue 2 *Syn* CHARACTERISTIC, attribute, character, feature, mark, peculiarity, point, property, trait

qualm • an uneasy feeling about the rightness of what one is doing or going to do *Syn* compunction, misgiving, scruple *Rel* conscience

quandary *Syn* PREDICAMENT, dilemma, fix, jam, pickle, plight, scrape

quantity 1 *Syn* AMOUNT, measure, volume 2 *Syn* SUM, aggregate, amount, number, total, whole

quarrel • a usually verbal dispute marked by anger or discord *Syn* altercation, bickering, spat, squabble, tiff, wrangle *Rel* brawl, broil, fracas, melee, row, rumpus, scrap

quarrelsome *Syn* BELLIGERENT, aggressive, argumentative, bellicose, combative, contentious, discordant, disputatious, gladiatorial, militant, pugnacious, scrappy, truculent, warlike *Ant* nonbelligerent, pacific, peaceable, peaceful

quarry *Syn* VICTIM, prey

quash 1 *Syn* ABOLISH, abrogate, annul, cancel, dissolve, invalidate, negate, nullify, repeal, rescind, void 2 *Syn* CRUSH (sense 2), extinguish, quell, quench, suppress

quaver *Syn* SHAKE (sense 1), dither, quake, quiver, shimmy, shiver, shudder, teeter, totter, tremble, wobble

quay *Syn* WHARF, berth, dock, jetty, levee, pier, slip

queenly *Syn* KINGLY, imperial, princely, regal, royal

queer *Syn* STRANGE, curious, eccentric, erratic, odd, outlandish, peculiar, quaint, singular, unique *Ant* familiar

quell *Syn* CRUSH (sense 2), extinguish, quash, quench, suppress

quench *Syn* CRUSH (sense 2), extinguish, quash, quell, suppress

querulous *Syn* IRRITABLE, fractious, fretful, huffy, peevish, pettish, petulant, snappish, waspish *Ant* easygoing

query *Syn* ASK (sense 1), catechize, examine, inquire, interrogate, question, quiz

quest *Syn* ADVENTURE, enterprise

question *vb* 1 *Syn* ASK (sense 1), catechize, examine, inquire, interrogate, query, quiz 2 *Syn* DISTRUST, doubt, mistrust, suspect *Ant* trust

question *n* *Syn* OBJECTION, challenge, complaint, demur, expostulation, fuss, protest, remonstrance

questionable 1 *Syn* DOUBTFUL, dubious, problematic *Ant* cocksure, positive 2 *Syn* IMPROBABLE, doubtful, dubious, farfetched, flimsy, unapt, unlikely *Ant* likely, probable

questioner *Syn* SKEPTIC, disbeliever, doubter, unbeliever

quibble • to make often peevish criticisms or objections about matters that are minor, unimportant, or irrelevant *Syn* carp, cavil, fuss, nitpick *Rel* criticize, fault

quick 1 • able to respond without delay or hesitation or indicative of such ability *Syn* apt, prompt, ready *Rel* clever, intelligent, quick-witted, smart *Ant* sluggish 2 *Syn* FAST, expeditious, fleet, hasty, rapid, speedy, swift *Ant* slow

quicken 1 *Syn* ANIMATE, brace, energize, enliven, fire, invigorate, jazz (up), liven (up), pep (up), stimulate, vitalize, vivify *Ant* damp, dampen, deaden, dull 2 *Syn* HURRY (sense 1), accelerate, hasten, rush, speed (up), whisk *Ant* decelerate, retard, slow (down) 3 *Syn* PROVOKE, excite, galvanize, pique, stimulate

quick-witted *Syn* INTELLIGENT, alert, bright, brilliant, clever, knowing, smart *Ant* unintelligent

quiescence *Syn* ABEYANCE, doldrums, dormancy, latency, suspense, suspension *Ant* continuance, continuation

quiescent *Syn* LATENT, abeyant, dormant, potential *Ant* patent

quiet *n* 1 *Syn* CALM, calmness, hush, peace, peacefulness, placidity, quietness, quietude, repose, restfulness, sereneness, serenity, still, stillness, tranquillity (*or* tranquility) *Ant* bustle, commotion, hubbub, hurly-burly, pandemonium, tumult, turmoil, uproar 2 *Syn* SILENCE, hush, quietness, quietude, still, stillness *Ant* noise, sound

quiet *vb* *Syn* CALM, compose, lull, quieten, settle, soothe, still, tranquilize *Ant* agitate, arouse

quiet *adj* 1 *Syn* SECLUDED, cloistered, covert, isolated, remote, retired, secret, sheltered 2 *Syn* SILENT (sense 2), hushed, muted, noiseless, quieted, soundless, still *Ant* noisy, unquiet 3 *Syn* STILL, noiseless, silent, stilly *Ant* noisy, stirring

quiet (down) *Syn* SHUT UP, clam up, hush *Ant* speak, talk

quieted *Syn* SILENT (sense 2), hushed, muted, noiseless, quiet, soundless, still *Ant* noisy, unquiet

quieten *Syn* CALM, compose, lull, quiet, settle, soothe, still, tranquilize *Ant* agitate, arouse

quietness 1 *Syn* CALM, calmness, hush, peace, peacefulness, placidity, quiet, quietude, repose, restfulness, sereneness, serenity, still, stillness, tranquillity (*or* tranquility) *Ant* bustle, commotion, hubbub, hurly-burly, pandemonium, tumult, turmoil, uproar 2 *Syn* SILENCE, hush, quiet, quietude, still, stillness *Ant* noise, sound

quietude 1 *Syn* CALM, calmness, hush, peace, peacefulness, placidity, quiet, quietness, repose, restfulness, sereneness, serenity, still, stillness, tranquillity (*or* tranquility) 2 *Syn* SILENCE, hush, quiet, quietness, still, stillness *Ant* noise, sound

quip *vb Syn* JOKE, banter, fool, fun, jest, jive, josh, kid, wisecrack

quip *n Syn* JOKE, crack, gag, jape, jest, wisecrack, witticism

quisling *Syn* TRAITOR, betrayer, double-crosser, recreant, turncoat

quit **1** *Syn* BEHAVE, acquit, comport, conduct, demean, deport *Ant* misbehave **2** *Syn* GO, depart, leave, retire, withdraw *Ant* come **3** *Syn* STOP, cease, desist, discontinue

quiver *Syn* SHAKE (sense 1), dither, quake, quaver, shimmy, shiver, shudder, teeter, totter, tremble, wobble

quixotic *Syn* IMAGINARY, chimerical, fanciful, fantastic, visionary *Ant* actual, real

quiz *Syn* ASK (sense 1), catechize, examine, inquire, interrogate, query, question

quote **1** • to speak or write again something already said or written by another *Syn* cite, repeat *Rel* adduce, advance, allege **2** *Syn* REPEAT (sense 2), echo, parrot

R

rabble-rouser *Syn* AGITATOR, demagogue, exciter, firebrand, fomenter, incendiary, inciter, instigator

rabid **1** *Syn* ANGRY, angered, apoplectic, enraged, foaming, fuming, furious, incensed, indignant, inflamed, infuriated, irate, ireful, mad, outraged, riled, roiled, sore, steaming, wrathful, wroth *Ant* delighted, pleased **2** *Syn* FURIOUS, delirious, frantic, frenetic, frenzied, wild

race *vb Syn* HURRY (sense 2), barrel, bolt, bowl, breeze, career, course, dash, fly, hasten, hotfoot (it), hump, hurtle, hustle, pelt, rip, rocket, run, rush, rustle, scoot, scurry, scuttle, shoot, speed, step (along), tear, trot, whirl, whisk, zip, zoom *Ant* crawl, creep, poke

race *n Syn* VARIETY (sense 2), breed, clone, cultivar, stock, strain, subspecies

rack *Syn* AFFLICT, agonize, bedevil, curse, harrow, martyr, persecute, plague, torment, torture

racket *Syn* DIN, babel, clamor, hubbub, hullabaloo, pandemonium, uproar *Ant* quiet

racking *Syn* EXCRUCIATING, agonizing

racy *Syn* PUNGENT, piquant, poignant, snappy, spicy *Ant* bland

radiant *Syn* BRIGHT, beaming, brilliant, effulgent, incandescent, lambent, lucent, luminous, lustrous, refulgent *Ant* dim, dull

radiate *Syn* SPREAD, circulate, diffuse, disseminate, propagate

radical *n* • a person who favors rapid and sweeping changes especially in laws and methods of government *Syn* extremist, revolutionary, revolutionist *Ant* moderate

radical *adj* **1** *Syn* FUNDAMENTAL, basal, basic, underlying **2** *Syn* LIBERAL (sense 2), advanced, progressive *Ant* authoritarian

radius *Syn* RANGE, compass, gamut, horizon, ken, orbit, purview, reach, scope, sweep

rag *Syn* BANTER, chaff, jolly, josh, kid, rib

rage **1** *Syn* ANGER, angriness, furor, fury, indignation, irateness, ire, outrage, spleen, wrath, wrathfulness *Ant* delight, pleasure **2** *Syn* FASHION, craze, cry, dernier cri, fad, mode, style, vogue **3** *Syn* FRENZY, agitation, delirium, distraction, furor, furore, fury, hysteria, rampage, uproar

raid **1** *Syn* ATTACK (sense 2), aggression, assault, blitzkrieg, charge, descent, offense (*or* offence), offensive, onset, onslaught, rush, strike **2** *Syn* INVASION, incursion, inroad

raider *Syn* AGGRESSOR, invader

rail *n Syn* RAILING, balustrade, banister, guardrail

rail *vb Syn* SCOLD, bawl, berate, chew out, jaw, rate, revile, tongue-lash, upbraid, vituperate, wig

railer *Syn* CRITIC, carper, castigator, caviler (*or* caviller), censurer, faultfinder, nitpicker, scold

railing • a protective barrier consisting of a horizontal bar and its supports *Syn* balustrade, banister, guardrail, rail *Rel* handrail

raillery *Syn* BANTER, chaff, give-and-take, jesting, joshing, persiflage, repartee

raiment *Syn* CLOTHES, apparel, attire, clothing, dress

rain **1** • a steady falling of water from the sky in significant quantity *Syn* cloudburst, deluge, downpour, rainfall, rainstorm, storm, wet *Rel* precipitation, shower **2** • a heavy fall of objects *Syn* hail, shower, storm *Rel* barrage, broadside, cannonade, fusillade, salvo, volley

rainfall *Syn* RAIN (sense 1), cloudburst, deluge, downpour, rainstorm, storm, wet

rainstorm *Syn* RAIN (sense 1), cloudburst, deluge, downpour, rainfall, storm, wet

raise **1** *Syn* BUILD, assemble, construct, erect, fabricate, make, make up, piece, put up, rear, set up *Ant* disassemble, dismantle, take down **2** *Syn* INCREASE (sense 1), add (to), aggrandize, amplify, augment, boost, compound, enlarge, escalate, expand, extend, multiply, swell, up *Ant* abate, contract, decrease, diminish, lessen, lower, reduce, subtract (from) **3** *Syn* LIFT, boost, elevate, heave, hoist, rear *Ant* lower

raised *Syn* ERECT, perpendicular, plumb, standing, upright, upstanding, vertical *Ant* flat, recumbent

rally[1] *vb* **1** *Syn* CONVALESCE, gain, heal, mend, recover, recuperate, snap back **2** *Syn* STIR, arouse, awaken, rouse, waken

rally[2] *vb* **1** *Syn* RIDICULE, deride, mock, taunt, twit **2** *Syn* TEASE, chaff, jive, josh, kid, razz, rib, ride, roast

ram *Syn* PACK, cram, crowd, stuff, tamp

ramble **1** *Syn* WALK, constitutional, perambulation, range, saunter, stroll, turn **2** *Syn* WANDER, gad, gallivant, meander, prowl, range, roam, rove, stray, traipse

rambler *Syn* NOMAD, drifter, gadabout, roamer, rover, stroller, vagabond, wanderer, wayfarer

rambunctious *Syn* BOISTEROUS, knockabout, raucous, rowdy *Ant* orderly

rampage *Syn* FRENZY, agitation, delirium, distraction, furor, furore, fury, hysteria, rage, uproar

rampart *Syn* BULWARK, bastion, breastwork, parapet

rancid *Syn* MALODOROUS, fetid, fusty, musty, noisome, putrid, rank, stinking *Ant* odorous

rancor *Syn* ENMITY, animosity, animus, antagonism, antipathy, hostility *Ant* amity

random • determined by accident rather than by design *Syn* casual, chance, chancy, desultory, haphazard, happy-go-lucky, hit-or-miss *Rel* accidental, casual, fortuitous *Ant* methodical, nonrandom, orderly, systematic

randomly *Syn* HIT OR MISS, aimlessly, anyhow, anyway, anywise, desultorily, erratically, haphazard, haphazardly, helter-skelter, irregularly *Ant* methodically, systematically

range *n* **1** • the extent that lies within the powers of something to cover or control *Syn* compass, gamut, horizon, ken, orbit, purview, radius, reach, scope, sweep *Rel* area, extent **2** *Syn* HABITAT, biotope, station **3** *Syn* WALK, constitutional, perambulation, ramble, saunter, stroll, turn

range *vb* **1** *Syn* LINE, align, array, line up **2** *Syn* WANDER, gad, gallivant, meander, prowl, ramble, roam, rove, stray, traipse

rangy *Syn* LANKY, gangling, gangly, spindling, spindly

rank *vb Syn* CLASS, gradate, grade, graduate, rate

rank *adj* **1** *Syn* EGREGIOUS, blatant, conspicuous, flagrant, glaring, gross, obvious, patent, pronounced, striking **2** *Syn* FLAGRANT, glaring, gross **3** *Syn* MALODOROUS, fetid, fusty, musty, noisome, putrid, rancid, stinking *Ant* odorous

rank *n Syn* LINE, echelon, file, row, tier

rankle *Syn* ANGER, antagonize, enrage, incense, inflame, infuriate, madden, outrage, rile, roil *Ant* delight, gratify, please

rankling *Syn* ANNOYING, aggravating, bothersome, disturbing, exasperating, frustrating, galling, irksome, irritating, maddening, nettling, peeving, pesty, riling, vexatious, vexing

ransack *Syn* SEEK, comb, ferret out, hunt, rummage, scour, search

ransom *Syn* RESCUE, deliver, reclaim, redeem, save

rant *vb* • to talk loudly and wildly *Syn* bluster, fulminate, rave, spout *Rel* sound off, speak out, speak up

rant *n Syn* BOMBAST, fustian, rhapsody, rodomontade

rap *vb* **1** *Syn* CHAT, babble, blab, cackle, chatter, converse, gab, gabble, gas, jabber, jaw, palaver, patter, prate, prattle, rattle, run on, talk, twitter, visit **2** *Syn* TAP, knock, thud, thump

rap *n* **1** *Syn* CHAT, chatter, chitchat, gabfest, gossip, palaver, small talk, table talk, talk, tête-à-tête **2** *Syn* TAP, knock, thud, thump **3** *Syn* CHARGE, complaint, count, indictment

rapacious *Syn* VORACIOUS, gluttonous, ravening, ravenous

rapaciousness *Syn* GREED, acquisitiveness, avarice, avariciousness, avidity, covetousness, cupidity, greediness, rapacity

rapacity *Syn* GREED, acquisitiveness, avarice, avariciousness, avidity, covetousness, cupidity, greediness, rapaciousness

rapid *Syn* FAST, expeditious, fleet, hasty, quick, speedy, swift *Ant* slow

rapport • a friendly relationship marked by ready communication and mutual understanding *Syn* communion, fellowship, rapprochement *Rel* accord, agreement, concord, harmony

rapprochement *Syn* RAPPORT, communion, fellowship

rapscallion *Syn* VILLAIN, blackguard, knave, miscreant, rascal, rogue, scamp, scoundrel

rapt *Syn* INTENT, absorbed, engrossed *Ant* distracted

rapture *Syn* ECSTASY, elation, euphoria, exhilaration, heaven, intoxication, paradise, rhapsody, transport *Ant* depression

rapturous *Syn* ECSTATIC, elated, enraptured, entranced, euphoric, exhilarated, intoxicated, rhapsodic *Ant* depressed

rare **1** *Syn* CHOICE, dainty, delicate, elegant, exquisite, recherché *Ant* indifferent, medium **2** *Syn* INFREQUENT, occasional, scarce, sporadic, uncommon *Ant* frequent **3** *Syn* THIN, slender, slight, slim, tenuous *Ant* thick

rarefy *Syn* THIN, attenuate, dilute, extenuate *Ant* thicken

rarely *Syn* SELDOM, infrequently, little *Ant* frequently, often

rascal *Syn* VILLAIN, blackguard, knave, miscreant, rapscallion, rogue, scamp, scoundrel

rash *Syn* ADVENTUROUS, daredevil, daring, foolhardy, reckless, venturesome *Ant* cautious, unadventurous

rasp *Syn* SCRAPE, grate, grind, scratch

rate[1] *vb* **1** *Syn* CLASS, gradate, grade, graduate, rank **2** *Syn* DESERVE, earn, merit **3** *Syn* ESTIMATE (sense 1), appraise, assay, assess, evaluate, value

rate[2] *vb Syn* SCOLD, bawl, berate, chew out, jaw, rail, revile, tongue-lash, upbraid, vituperate, wig

ration *n* • an amount allotted or made available especially from a limited supply *Syn* allowance, dole, pittance *Rel* apportionment, portion, portioning

ration *vb Syn* APPORTION, parcel, portion, prorate

rationalize *Syn* EXPLAIN (sense 2), account (for), explain away

rattle **1** *Syn* CHAT, babble, blab, cackle, chatter, converse, gab, gabble, gas, jabber, jaw, palaver, patter, prate, prattle, rap, talk, twitter, visit **2** *Syn* EMBARRASS, abash, discomfit, disconcert, faze *Ant* facilitate, relieve

rattling *Syn* VERY, awful, awfully, beastly, deadly, especially, exceedingly, extra, extremely, far, frightfully, full, greatly, heavily, highly, hugely, jolly, mightily, mighty, mortally, most, much, particularly, real, right, so, something, super, terribly, too, whacking *Ant* little, negligibly, nominally, slightly

raucous **1** *Syn* BOISTEROUS, knockabout, rambunctious, rowdy *Ant* orderly **2** *Syn* LOUD, earsplitting, hoarse, stentorian, stertorous, strident *Ant* low, low-pitched

ravage • to lay waste by plundering or destroying *Syn* despoil, devastate, pillage, sack, spoliate, waste *Rel* demolish, destroy, raze

rave **1** *Syn* GUSH (sense 2), enthuse, fuss, rhapsodize, slobber **2** *Syn* RANT, bluster, fulminate, spout

ravening *Syn* VORACIOUS, gluttonous, rapacious, ravenous

ravenous *Syn* VORACIOUS, gluttonous, rapacious, ravening

rave(s) *Syn* APPLAUSE, acclamation, cheering, cheers, ovation, plaudit(s) *Ant* booing, hissing

ravine *Syn* CANYON, defile, flume, gap, gorge, gulch, gulf, notch, pass

ravish *Syn* ENTRANCE, carry away, enrapture, enthrall (*or* enthral), overjoy, transport

ravishing *Syn* BEAUTIFUL, attractive, beauteous, comely, cute, fair, gorgeous, handsome, knockout, lovely, pretty, sightly, stunning, taking *Ant* homely, ill-favored, plain, ugly, unattractive, unbeautiful, unhandsome, unlovely, unpretty, unsightly

raw **1** *Syn* CALLOW, adolescent, green, immature, inexperienced, juvenile, puerile, unfledged, unripe, unripened *Ant* adult, experienced, grown-up, mature, ripe **2** *Syn* RUDE (sense 1), callow, crude, green, rough, uncouth *Ant* civil, urbane

rawboned *Syn* LEAN, angular, gaunt, lank, lanky, scrawny, skinny, spare *Ant* fleshy

raw deal *Syn* DISSERVICE, injury, injustice, wrong *Ant* justice

rawness *Syn* CHILL, bite, bitterness, bleakness, chilliness, nip, sharpness

raze *Syn* DESTROY, demolish

razz *Syn* TEASE, chaff, jive, josh, kid, rally, rib, ride, roast

reach *vb* • to arrive at a point by effort or work *Syn* achieve, attain, compass, gain *Rel* accomplish, effect, execute, fulfill, perform

reach *n Syn* RANGE, compass, gamut, horizon, ken, orbit, purview, radius, scope, sweep

react *Syn* ACT (sense 1), behave, function, operate, work

readdress *Syn* RECONSIDER, reanalyze, reconceive, reevaluate, reexamine, rethink, review, reweigh

readily *Syn* EASILY, effortlessly, facilely, fluently, freely, handily, lightly, painlessly, smoothly *Ant* arduously, laboriously

readiness • the power of doing something without evidence of effort *Syn* dexterity, ease, facility *Rel* aptness, promptness, quickness

ready *vb Syn* PREPARE, condition, fit, qualify

ready *adj Syn* QUICK, apt, prompt *Ant* sluggish

real *adj Syn* ACTUAL, concrete, existent, factual, true, very *Ant* conjectural, hypothetical, ideal, nonexistent, possible, potential, theoretical

real *adv Syn* VERY, awful, awfully, beastly, deadly, especially, exceedingly, extra, extremely, far, frightfully, full, greatly, heavily, highly, hugely, jolly, mightily, mighty, mortally, most, much, particularly, rattling, right, so, something, super, terribly, too, whacking *Ant* little, negligibly, nominally, slightly

realization *Syn* FRUITION, accomplishment, achievement, actuality, attainment, consummation, fulfillment *Ant* naught, nonfulfillment

realize **1** • to bring into concrete existence something that has existed as an abstraction or a conception or a possibility *Syn* actualize, embody, externalize, hypostatize, incarnate, materialize, objectify, reify *Rel* accomplish, achieve, effect, execute, fulfill, perform **2** *Syn* EARN, acquire, attain, capture, carry, draw, gain, garner, get, land, make, obtain, procure, secure, win *Ant* forfeit, lose **3** *Syn* THINK (sense 1), conceive, envisage, envision, fancy, imagine

reanalyze *Syn* RECONSIDER, readdress, reconceive, reevaluate, reexamine, rethink, review, reweigh
reanimation *Syn* REVIVAL, rebirth, regeneration, rejuvenation, renewal, resurgence, resurrection, resuscitation, revitalization
reap • to do the work of collecting ripened crops *Syn* garner, gather, glean, harvest *Rel* assemble, collect
rear *n* **1** *Syn* BACK, hind, hindmost, posterior, rearward *Ant* anterior, fore, forward, front **2** *Syn* BUTTOCKS, backside, bottom, breech, butt, fanny, hams, haunches, posterior, rump, seat
rear *vb* **1** *Syn* BUILD, assemble, construct, erect, fabricate, make, make up, piece, put up, raise, set up *Ant* disassemble, dismantle, take down **2** *Syn* LIFT, boost, elevate, heave, hoist, raise *Ant* lower
rearward *Syn* BACK, hind, hindmost, posterior, rear *Ant* anterior, fore, forward, front
reason *n* **1** • a point or points that support something open to question *Syn* argument, ground, proof *Rel* explanation, justification, rationalization **2** • the power of the mind by which people attain truth or knowledge *Syn* intuition, understanding *Rel* brain, intellect, intelligence, mind **3** *Syn* CAUSE, antecedent, determinant, occasion **4** *Syn* EXCUSE, alibi, defense, justification, plea
reason *vb Syn* THINK (sense 2), cogitate, deliberate, reflect, speculate
reasoned *Syn* DEDUCTIVE, deducible, derivable, inferable
rebate *Syn* DEDUCTION, abatement, discount
rebel • one who rises up against constituted authority or the established order *Syn* iconoclast, insurgent *Rel* adversary, antagonist, opponent
rebellion • an outbreak against authority *Syn* coup, insurrection, mutiny, putsch, revolt, revolution, uprising *Rel* sedition, treason
rebellious **1** *Syn* DISOBEDIENT, balky, contrary, defiant, froward, insubordinate, intractable, recalcitrant, refractory, restive, ungovernable, unruly, untoward, wayward, willful (*or* wilful) *Ant* amenable, compliant, docile, obedient, tractable **2** *Syn* INSUBORDINATE, contumacious, factious, mutinous, seditious
rebelliousness *Syn* DISOBEDIENCE, contrariness, defiance, frowardness, insubordination, intractability, recalcitrance, refractoriness, unruliness, willfulness *Ant* amenability, compliance, docility, obedience
rebirth *Syn* REVIVAL, reanimation, regeneration, rejuvenation, renewal, resurgence, resurrection, resuscitation, revitalization
rebound • to spring back to an original position or shape *Syn* recoil, repercuss, resile, reverberate *Rel* bound, ricochet, skip
rebuild *Syn* MEND, patch, repair
rebuke **1** *Syn* CENSURE, condemnation, denunciation, reprimand, reproach, reproof, stricture *Ant* citation, commendation, endorsement **2** *Syn* REPROVE, admonish, chide, reprimand, reproach
rebut *Syn* DISPROVE, confute, controvert, refute *Ant* demonstrate, prove
recalcitrance *Syn* DISOBEDIENCE, contrariness, defiance, frowardness, insubordination, intractability, rebelliousness, refractoriness, unruliness, willfulness *Ant* amenability, compliance, docility, obedience
recalcitrant **1** *Syn* DISOBEDIENT, balky, contrary, defiant, froward, insubordinate, intractable, rebellious, refractory, restive, ungovernable, unruly, untoward, wayward, willful (*or* wilful) *Ant* amenable, compliant, docile, obedient, tractable **2** *Syn* UNCONTROLLABLE, froward, headstrong, intractable, refractory, ungovernable, unmanageable, unruly, untoward, wayward, willful (*or* wilful) *Ant* controllable, governable, tractable **3** *Syn* UNRULY, headstrong, intractable, refractory, ungovernable, willful *Ant* docile, tractable
recall *n Syn* CANCELLATION, abortion, calling, calling off, dropping, repeal, rescission, revocation *Ant* continuation
recall *vb* **1** *Syn* REMEMBER, bethink, mind, recollect, remind, reminisce *Ant* forget **2** *Syn* REVOKE, repeal, rescind, reverse
recant *Syn* ABJURE, forswear, renounce, retract *Ant* pledge (*allegiance, a vow*), elect (*a way of life, a means to an end*)
recap *Syn* SUMMARIZE, abstract, digest, encapsulate, epitomize, outline, recapitulate, sum up, wrap up
recapitulate *Syn* SUMMARIZE, abstract, digest, encapsulate, epitomize, outline, recap, sum up, wrap up
recast *Syn* CHANGE (sense 1), alter, make over, modify, redo, refashion, remake, remodel, revamp, revise, rework, vary *Ant* fix, freeze, set, stabilize
recede • to move backward *Syn* back, retract, retreat, retrograde *Rel* depart, retire, withdraw *Ant* advance, proceed
receipt • a formula or set of directions for the compounding of ingredients especially in cookery and medicine *Syn* prescription, recipe
receive • to bring and accept into one's possession, one's presence, a group, or the mind *Syn* accept, admit, take *Rel* enter, penetrate
receptacle *Syn* CONTAINER, holder, vessel
recess **1** *Syn* ADJOURN, suspend **2** *Syn* PAUSE, break, breath, breather, interruption, lull
recessed *Syn* HOLLOW, concave, dented, depressed, indented, sunken *Ant* bulging, convex, protruding, protuberant
recherché *Syn* CHOICE, dainty, delicate, elegant, exquisite, rare *Ant* indifferent, medium

recipe *Syn* RECEIPT, prescription
reciprocal **1** • shared, felt, or shown by both sides concerned *Syn* common, mutual *Rel* partaken, participated, shared **2** • like, equivalent, or similarly related to each other (as in kind, quality, or value) *Syn* complemental, complementary, convertible, correlative, corresponding *Rel* equivalent, identical, same
reciprocate • to give back usually in kind or in quantity *Syn* requite, retaliate, return *Rel* exchange, interchange
recite *Syn* RELATE, describe, narrate, recount, rehearse, report, state
reckless *Syn* ADVENTUROUS, daredevil, daring, foolhardy, rash, venturesome *Ant* cautious, unadventurous
reckon **1** *Syn* CALCULATE, compute, estimate **2** *Syn* CONSIDER (sense 2), account, deem, regard **3** *Syn* ESTIMATE (sense 2), calculate, call, conjecture, figure, gauge, guess, judge, make, place, put, suppose **4** *Syn* RELY (ON), bank, count, depend, trust
reckoning *Syn* CALCULATION, arithmetic, ciphering, computation, figures, figuring
reclaim *Syn* RESCUE, deliver, ransom, redeem, save
recluse • a person who leads a secluded or solitary life *Syn* anchorite, cenobite, eremite, hermit
recognition • a learning process that relates a perception of something new to knowledge already possessed *Syn* apperception, assimilation, identification
recoil **1** • to draw back in fear or distaste *Syn* blench, flinch, quail, shrink, wince *Rel* falter, hesitate, waver *Ant* confront, defy **2** *Syn* REBOUND, repercuss, resile, reverberate
recollect *Syn* REMEMBER, bethink, mind, recall, remind, reminisce *Ant* forget
recollection *Syn* MEMORY, mind, remembrance, reminiscence, souvenir *Ant* oblivion
recommend *Syn* COMMEND, applaud, compliment *Ant* admonish, censure
recommendation *Syn* CREDENTIAL, character, reference, testimonial
recompense *Syn* PAY, compensate, indemnify, reimburse, remunerate, repay, satisfy
reconceive *Syn* RECONSIDER, readdress, reanalyze, reevaluate, reexamine, rethink, review, reweigh
reconcile *Syn* ADAPT, accommodate, adjust, conform *Ant* unfit
recondite • beyond the reach of the average intelligence *Syn* abstruse, esoteric, occult *Rel* erudite, learned, scholarly
reconsider • to consider again especially with the possibility of change or reversal *Syn* readdress, reanalyze, reconceive, reevaluate, reexamine, rethink, review, reweigh *Rel* reappraise, reassess
record *vb* **1** • to set down in writing usually for the purpose of written evidence or official record of *Syn* catalog, enroll, list, register *Rel* admit, enter, introduce **2** *Syn* RELATE, describe, narrate, recite, rehearse, report, state
record *n* *Syn* DOCUMENT, archive, monument
recount *Syn* RELATE, describe, narrate, recite, rehearse, report, state
recoup *Syn* RECOVER, recruit, regain, retrieve
recover **1** • to get back again *Syn* recoup, recruit, regain, retrieve *Rel* reclaim, redeem, rescue **2** *Syn* CONVALESCE, gain, heal, mend, rally, recuperate, snap back **3** *Syn* IMPROVE (sense 2), convalesce, gain, recuperate
recreant *adj* *Syn* COWARDLY, chicken, chickenhearted, craven, dastardly, lily-livered, pusillanimous, spineless, unheroic, yellow *Ant* brave, courageous, daring, dauntless, doughty, fearless, gallant, greathearted, gutsy, hardy, heroic, intrepid, lionhearted, stalwart, stout, stouthearted, valiant, valorous
recreant *n* **1** *Syn* COWARD, chicken, craven, dastard, poltroon *Ant* hero, stalwart, valiant **2** *Syn* RENEGADE, apostate, backslider, turncoat *Ant* adherent, loyalist **3** *Syn* TRAITOR, betrayer, double-crosser, quisling, turncoat
recreate *Syn* AMUSE, divert, entertain *Ant* bore
recreation *Syn* AMUSEMENT, diversion, entertainment *Ant* boredom
recrudesce *Syn* RETURN, recur, revert
recrudescence *Syn* RETURN, recurrence, reversion
recruit *n* *Syn* BEGINNER, colt, fledgling, freshman, greenhorn, neophyte, newbie, newcomer, novice, rookie, tenderfoot, tyro *Ant* old hand, old-timer, vet, veteran
recruit *vb* *Syn* RECOVER, recoup, regain, retrieve
rectifiable *Syn* REMEDIABLE, correctable, fixable, repairable, reparable *Ant* incorrigible, irremediable, irreparable
rectify *Syn* CORRECT, amend, emend, redress, reform, remedy, revise
rectitude *Syn* GOODNESS, morality, virtue *Ant* badness, evil
recuperate **1** *Syn* CONVALESCE, gain, heal, mend, rally, recover, snap back **2** *Syn* IMPROVE (sense 2), convalesce, gain, recover
recur *Syn* RETURN, recrudesce, revert
recurrence *Syn* RETURN, recrudescence, reversion
recurrent *Syn* INTERMITTENT, alternate, periodic *Ant* continual, incessant
redact *Syn* EDIT, adapt, compile, revise, rewrite
redden *Syn* BLUSH, bloom, color, crimson, flush, glow
redeem *Syn* RESCUE, deliver, ransom, reclaim, save
redeemer *Syn* SAVIOR, deliverer, rescuer, saver
red-hot **1** *Syn* FERVENT, ardent, blazing,

burning, charged, emotional, fervid, feverish, fiery, flaming, glowing, hot-blooded, impassioned, passionate, vehement, warm, warm-blooded *Ant* cold, cool, dispassionate, impassive, unemotional **2** *Syn* MODERN, contemporary, current, hot, mod, modernistic, new, newfangled, new-fashioned, present-day, space-age, ultramodern, up-to-date *Ant* antiquated, archaic, dated, fusty, musty, noncontemporary, oldfangled, old-fashioned, old-time, out-of-date, passé

redo *Syn* CHANGE (sense 1), alter, make over, modify, recast, refashion, remake, remodel, revamp, revise, rework, vary *Ant* fix, freeze, set, stabilize

redolence *Syn* FRAGRANCE, bouquet, incense, perfume *Ant* stench, stink

redolent **1** *Syn* FRAGRANT, ambrosial, aromatic, perfumed, savory, scented, sweet *Ant* fetid, foul, malodorous, noisome, putrid, rancid, rank, reeking, reeky, smelly, stinking, stinky, strong **2** *Syn* ODOROUS, aromatic, balmy, fragrant *Ant* malodorous, odorless

redress *vb Syn* CORRECT, amend, emend, rectify, reform, remedy, revise

redress *n Syn* REPARATION, amends, indemnity, restitution

reduce **1** *Syn* CONQUER, beat, defeat, lick, overcome, overthrow, rout, subdue, subjugate, surmount, vanquish **2** *Syn* DECREASE, abate, diminish, dwindle, lessen *Ant* increase **3** *Syn* DEGRADE, declass, demote, disrate *Ant* elevate

redundancy *Syn* VERBIAGE, circumlocution, periphrasis, pleonasm, tautology

redundant *Syn* WORDY, diffuse, prolix, verbose *Ant* compact, concise, crisp, pithy, succinct, terse

reduplication *Syn* COPY, carbon copy, duplicate, duplication, facsimile, imitation, replica, replication, reproduction *Ant* original

reef *Syn* SHOAL, bank, bar

reek *Syn* HAZE (sense 1), fog, mist, murk, smog, soup

reel • to move uncertainly or uncontrollably or unsteadily (as from weakness or intoxication) *Syn* stagger, totter, whirl *Rel* revolve, rotate, spin, turn

reevaluate *Syn* RECONSIDER, readdress, reanalyze, reconceive, reexamine, rethink, review, reweigh

reexamine *Syn* RECONSIDER, readdress, reanalyze, reconceive, reevaluate, rethink, review, reweigh

refashion *Syn* CHANGE (sense 1), alter, make over, modify, recast, redo, remake, remodel, revamp, revise, rework, vary *Ant* fix, freeze, set, stabilize

refer **1** • to call or direct attention to something *Syn* advert, allude *Rel* insert, interpolate, introduce **2** *Syn* ASCRIBE, accredit, assign, attribute, charge, credit, impute **3** *Syn* RESORT, apply, go, turn

referee *Syn* JUDGE, arbiter, arbitrator, umpire

reference *Syn* CREDENTIAL, character, recommendation, testimonial

referendum *Syn* MANDATE, initiative, plebiscite

refined *Syn* CULTIVATED, civilized, cultured, genteel, polished *Ant* philistine, uncivilized, uncultured, unpolished, unrefined

refinement **1** *Syn* ADVANCE (sense 1), advancement, breakthrough, enhancement, improvement *Ant* setback **2** *Syn* CULTURE, breeding, cultivation **3** *Syn* ELEGANCE, class, elegancy, grace, gracefulness, handsomeness, majesty, stateliness

reflect *Syn* THINK (sense 2), cogitate, deliberate, reason, speculate

reflection *Syn* ANIMADVERSION, aspersion, stricture *Ant* commendation

reflective **1** *Syn* CONTEMPLATIVE, meditative, melancholy, pensive, ruminant, thoughtful *Ant* unreflective **2** *Syn* THOUGHTFUL (sense 1), contemplative, meditative, pensive, speculative *Ant* thoughtless

reform *Syn* CORRECT, amend, emend, rectify, redress, remedy, revise

refractoriness *Syn* DISOBEDIENCE, contrariness, defiance, frowardness, insubordination, intractability, rebelliousness, recalcitrance, unruliness, willfulness *Ant* amenability, compliance, docility, obedience

refractory **1** *Syn* DISOBEDIENT, balky, contrary, defiant, froward, insubordinate, intractable, rebellious, recalcitrant, restive, ungovernable, unruly, untoward, wayward, willful (*or* wilful) *Ant* amenable, compliant, docile, obedient, tractable **2** *Syn* UNCONTROLLABLE, froward, headstrong, intractable, recalcitrant, ungovernable, unmanageable, unruly, untoward, wayward, willful (*or* wilful) *Ant* controllable, governable, tractable **3** *Syn* UNRULY, headstrong, intractable, recalcitrant, ungovernable, willful *Ant* docile, tractable

refrain • to hold oneself back from doing or indulging in *Syn* abstain, forbear *Rel* arrest, check, interrupt

refresh *Syn* RENEW, refurbish, rejuvenate, renovate, restore

refreshing *Syn* TONIC, bracing, invigorating, restorative, reviving, stimulating, stimulative, vitalizing

refuge *Syn* SHELTER, asylum, cover, retreat, sanctuary

refulgent *Syn* BRIGHT, beaming, brilliant, effulgent, incandescent, lambent, lucent, luminous, lustrous, radiant *Ant* dim, dull

refund *Syn* REPAY, reimburse

refurbish *Syn* RENEW, refresh, rejuvenate, renovate, restore

refusal *Syn* DENIAL (sense 1), disallowance, nay, no, rejection *Ant* allowance, grant

refuse *n* • matter that is regarded as worthless

and fit only for throwing away *Syn* debris, garbage, offal, rubbish, trash, waste
refuse *vb Syn* DECLINE, reject, repudiate, spurn *Ant* accept
refute *Syn* DISPROVE, confute, controvert, rebut *Ant* demonstrate, prove
regain *Syn* RECOVER, recoup, recruit, retrieve
regal *Syn* KINGLY, imperial, princely, queenly, royal
regale *Syn* PLEASE, delight, gladden, gratify, rejoice, tickle *Ant* anger, displease, vex
regalia *Syn* FINERY, array, best, bravery, caparison, feather, frippery, full dress, gaiety
regard *n* • a feeling of deferential approval and liking *Syn* respect, esteem, admiration *Rel* deference, homage, honor, reverence *Ant* despite
regard *vb* **1** • to recognize the worth of a person or thing *Syn* admire, esteem, respect *Rel* appreciate, cherish, prize, treasure, value *Ant* despise **2** *Syn* CONSIDER (sense 2), account, deem, reckon
regardful *Syn* RESPECTFUL, deferential, dutiful *Ant* disrespectful
regarding *Syn* ABOUT, concerning, respecting
regards *Syn* COMPLIMENTS, congratulations, felicitations, greetings, respects
regeneration *Syn* REVIVAL, reanimation, rebirth, rejuvenation, renewal, resurgence, resurrection, resuscitation, revitalization
regime *Syn* RULE (sense 2), administration, authority, governance, government, jurisdiction, regimen
regimen *Syn* RULE (sense 2), administration, authority, governance, government, jurisdiction, regime
region **1** • a part or portion having no fixed boundaries *Syn* area, demesne, field, zone *Rel* section **2** *Syn* AREA, belt, tract, zone
register *n Syn* LIST, catalog, inventory, roll, roster, schedule, table
register *vb Syn* RECORD, catalog, enroll, list
regress • to go back to a previous and usually lower state or level *Syn* retrogress, revert *Rel* backslide, lapse, relapse *Ant* advance, develop, evolve, progress
regression • the act or an instance of going back to an earlier and lower level especially of intelligence or behavior *Syn* retrogression, reversion *Rel* backslide, lapse, relapse *Ant* advancement, development, evolution, progression
regressive *Syn* BACKWARD, retrograde, retrogressive *Ant* advanced
regret *vb* • to feel sorry or dissatisfied about *Syn* bemoan, deplore, lament, repent, rue *Rel* bewail, grieve (for), mourn, sorrow (for)
regret *n Syn* SORROW, anguish, grief, heartache, heartbreak, woe *Ant* joy
regrettable • of a kind to cause great distress *Syn* deplorable, distressful, distressing, grievous, heartbreaking, heartrending, lamentable, unfortunate, woeful *Rel* affecting, moving, poignant, touching
regular **1** • being of the sort or kind that is expected as usual, ordinary, or average *Syn* natural, normal, typical *Rel* customary, habitual, usual *Ant* irregular **2** *Syn* ORDERLY, methodical, systematic *Ant* chaotic, disorderly
regularize *Syn* STANDARDIZE, formalize, homogenize, normalize
regulate *Syn* ADJUST, fix *Ant* derange
regulation **1** *Syn* LAW, canon, ordinance, precept, rule, statute **2** *Syn* RULE (sense 1), bylaw, ground rule
regurgitate *Syn* BELCH, burp, disgorge, spew, throw up, vomit
rehearsal • a private performance or session in preparation for a public appearance *Syn* dry run, practice, trial *Rel* dress rehearsal
rehearse *Syn* RELATE, describe, narrate, recite, recount, report, state
reify *Syn* REALIZE, actualize, embody, externalize, hypostatize, incarnate, materialize, objectify
reimburse **1** *Syn* PAY, compensate, indemnify, recompense, remunerate, repay, satisfy **2** *Syn* REPAY, refund
reinforce *Syn* STRENGTHEN, energize, fortify, invigorate *Ant* weaken
reissue *Syn* EDITION, impression, printing, reprinting
reiterate *Syn* REPEAT (sense 1), ingeminate, iterate
reject *Syn* DECLINE, refuse, repudiate, spurn *Ant* accept
rejected *Syn* ABANDONED (sense 2), derelict, deserted, disused, forgotten, forsaken, vacated
rejection **1** *Syn* DENIAL, disallowance, nay, no, refusal *Ant* allowance, grant **2** *Syn* DENIAL (sense 2), contradiction, disallowance, disavowal, disclaimer, negation, repudiation *Ant* acknowledgment, admission, avowal, confirmation
rejoice *Syn* PLEASE, delight, gladden, gratify, regale, tickle *Ant* anger, displease, vex
rejoicing *Syn* EXULTANT, exulting, glorying, jubilant, triumphant
rejoin *Syn* ANSWER, reply, respond, retort
rejoinder *Syn* ANSWER (sense 1), reply, response, retort
rejuvenate *Syn* RENEW, refresh, refurbish, renovate, restore
rejuvenation *Syn* REVIVAL, reanimation, rebirth, regeneration, renewal, resurgence, resurrection, resuscitation, revitalization
relapse *Syn* LAPSE, backslide
relate **1** • to tell orally or in writing the details or circumstances of a situation *Syn* describe, narrate, recite, recount, rehearse, report, state *Rel* disclose, divulge, reveal, tell **2** *Syn* BEAR (sense 3), appertain, apply, belong, pertain **3** *Syn* JOIN, associate, com-

bine, conjoin, connect, link, unite *Ant* disjoin, part

related • connected by or as if by family ties *Syn* affiliated, allied, cognate, kindred *Rel* associated, connected

relation *Syn* RELATIVE, kin, kinsman

relative *n* • a person connected with another by blood or marriage *Syn* kin, kinsman, relation *Rel* in-law

relative *adj* **1** *Syn* DEPENDENT, conditional, contingent *Ant* absolute, infinite, original **2** *Syn* PERTINENT, applicable, apposite, apropos, germane, material, pointed *Ant* extraneous, immaterial, inapplicable, irrelevant, pointless

relax *Syn* SLACKEN, ease, loosen, slack *Ant* strain, stretch, tense, tighten

relaxation *Syn* REST, comfort, ease, leisure, repose

relaxed *Syn* LOOSE, lax, slack *Ant* strict, tight

release *n Syn* ANNOUNCEMENT, ad, advertisement, bulletin, notice, notification, posting

release *vb Syn* FREE, discharge, emancipate, liberate, manumit

relegate *Syn* COMMIT (sense 1), confide, consign, entrust

relent *Syn* YIELD, bow, capitulate, cave, defer, submit, succumb

relentless *Syn* GRIM, implacable, merciless, unrelenting *Ant* lenient

relevant *Syn* PERTINENT, applicable, apposite, apropos, germane, material, pointed, relative *Ant* extraneous, immaterial, inapplicable, irrelevant, pointless

reliable *Syn* DEPENDABLE, good, responsible, safe, solid, steady, sure, tried, tried-and-true, true, trustworthy, trusty *Ant* irresponsible, undependable, unreliable, untrustworthy

reliance *Syn* TRUST, confidence, dependence, faith *Ant* mistrust

relic *Syn* VESTIGE, shadow, trace

relief *Syn* SUBSTITUTE, backup, pinch hitter, replacement, reserve, stand-in, sub

relieve • to make something more tolerable or less grievous *Syn* allay, alleviate, assuage, lighten, mitigate *Rel* comfort, console, solace *Ant* alarm, embarrass, intensify

religion • a system of religious belief or the body of persons who accept such a system *Syn* church, communion, creed, denomination, faith, persuasion, sect

religious *n* • a member of a religious order usually bound by monastic vows of poverty, chastity, and obedience *Syn* friar, monk, nun

religious *adj Syn* HOLY (sense 1), devout, godly, pious, sainted, saintly *Ant* faithless, godless, impious, irreligious, ungodly, unholy

relinquish • to give up completely *Syn* abandon, cede, leave, resign, surrender, waive, yield *Rel* abdicate, renounce *Ant* keep

relish *vb Syn* LIKE, dote, enjoy, fancy, love *Ant* dislike

relish *n* **1** *Syn* LIKING, appetite, fancy, favor, fondness, like, love, partiality, preference, shine, taste, use *Ant* aversion, disfavor, dislike, distaste, hatred, loathing **2** *Syn* TASTE (sense 1), flavor, savor, smack, tang *Ant* antipathy

relishing *Syn* PALATABLE, appetizing, flavorsome, sapid, savory, tasty, toothsome *Ant* distasteful, unpalatable

reluctance • a lack of willingness or desire to do or accept something *Syn* disinclination, hesitance, hesitancy, unwillingness *Rel* faltering, hesitation, indecision, irresolution, shilly-shallying, staggering, vacillation, wavering *Ant* inclination, willingness

reluctant *Syn* DISINCLINED, averse, hesitant, indisposed, loath

rely (on) *or* **rely upon** • to have or place full confidence *Syn* bank, count, depend, reckon, trust *Rel* commit, confide, entrust

remain *Syn* STAY, abide, linger, tarry, wait

remainder • a remaining or left-over group, part, or trace *Syn* balance, leavings, remains, remnant, residue, residuum, rest

remains *Syn* REMAINDER, balance, leavings, remnant, residue, residuum, rest

remake *Syn* CHANGE (sense 1), alter, make over, modify, recast, redo, refashion, remodel, revamp, revise, rework, vary *Ant* fix, freeze, set, stabilize

remark *n* • an expression of opinion or judgment *Syn* comment, commentary, note, obiter dictum, observation

remark *vb* **1** • to make observations and pass judgment thereon *Syn* animadvert, comment, commentate **2** *Syn* SEE (sense 1), behold, contemplate, descry, discern, espy, note, notice, observe, perceive, survey, view

remarkable *Syn* NOTICEABLE, arresting, conspicuous, outstanding, prominent, salient, signal, striking

remediable • capable of being corrected *Syn* correctable, fixable, rectifiable, repairable, reparable *Rel* amendable, improvable, resolvable *Ant* incorrigible, irremediable, irreparable

remedial *Syn* CURATIVE, corrective, restorative, sanative

remedy *n* • something prescribed or used for the treatment of disease *Syn* cure, medicament, medication, medicine, physic, specific

remedy *vb* **1** *Syn* CORRECT, amend, emend, rectify, redress, reform, revise **2** *Syn* CURE, heal

remember • to bring an image or idea from the past into the mind *Syn* bethink, mind, recall, recollect, remind, reminisce *Ant* forget

remembrance **1** *Syn* MEMORIAL, commemorative, keepsake, memento, monument, reminder, souvenir, token **2** *Syn* MEMORY, mind, recollection, reminiscence, souvenir *Ant* oblivion

remind *Syn* REMEMBER, bethink, mind, recall, recollect, reminisce *Ant* forget

reminder *Syn* MEMORIAL, commemorative, keepsake, memento, monument, remembrance, souvenir, token

reminisce *Syn* REMEMBER, bethink, mind, recall, recollect, remind *Ant* forget

reminiscence *Syn* MEMORY, mind, recollection, remembrance, souvenir *Ant* oblivion

remiss *Syn* NEGLIGENT, careless, derelict, lax, neglectful, neglecting, slack *Ant* attentive, careful, conscientious

remission *Syn* PARDON, absolution, amnesty, forgiveness, remittal *Ant* penalty, punishment, retribution

remit **1** *Syn* EXCUSE, condone, forgive, pardon *Ant* punish **2** *Syn* SEND, dispatch, forward, route, ship, transmit *Ant* accept, receive

remittable *Syn* VENIAL, excusable, forgivable, pardonable *Ant* inexcusable, mortal, unforgivable, unpardonable

remittal *Syn* PARDON, absolution, amnesty, forgiveness, remission *Ant* penalty, punishment, retribution

remnant *Syn* REMAINDER, balance, leavings, remains, residue, residuum, rest

remodel *Syn* CHANGE (sense 1), alter, make over, modify, recast, redo, refashion, remake, revamp, revise, rework, vary *Ant* fix, freeze, set, stabilize

remonstrance *Syn* OBJECTION, challenge, complaint, demur, expostulation, fuss, protest, question

remonstrate *Syn* OBJECT, expostulate, kick, protest *Ant* acquiesce

remorse *Syn* PENITENCE, attrition, compunction, contrition, repentance

remorseful *Syn* GUILTY, ashamed, contrite, hangdog, penitent, repentant, shamed, shamefaced *Ant* impenitent, remorseless, shameless, unashamed, unrepentant

remorseless • not sorry for having done wrong *Syn* impenitent, unrepentant *Rel* compassionless, cruel, merciless, pitiless, ruthless, unmerciful *Ant* contrite, guilty, penitent, regretful, remorseful, repentant, sorry

remote **1** *Syn* DISTANT, far, faraway, far-off, removed **2** *Syn* SECLUDED, cloistered, covert, isolated, quiet, retired, secret, sheltered

remove *Syn* MOVE (sense 2), shift, transfer

removed *Syn* DISTANT, far, faraway, far-off, remote

remunerate *Syn* PAY, compensate, indemnify, recompense, reimburse, repay, satisfy

remunerative *Syn* PAYING, gainful, lucrative, profitable

rend *Syn* TEAR, cleave, rip, rive, split

rendezvous **1** *Syn* ENGAGEMENT, appointment, assignation, date, tryst **2** *Syn* HANGOUT, haunt, resort

renegade • a person who forsakes his or her faith, party, cause, or allegiance and aligns with another *Syn* apostate, backslider, recreant, turncoat *Rel* iconoclast, insurgent, rebel *Ant* adherent, loyalist

renege • to break a promise or agreement *Syn* back down, back off, cop out *Rel* chicken (out)

renew **1** • to make like new *Syn* refresh, refurbish, rejuvenate, renovate, restore *Rel* mend, rebuild, repair **2** *Syn* RESUME, continue, reopen, restart

renewal *Syn* REVIVAL, reanimation, rebirth, regeneration, rejuvenation, resurgence, resurrection, resuscitation, revitalization

renounce **1** *Syn* ABDICATE, resign *Ant* assume, usurp **2** *Syn* ABJURE, forswear, recant, retract *Ant* pledge (*allegiance, a vow*), elect (*a way of life, a means to an end*)

renovate *Syn* RENEW, refresh, refurbish, rejuvenate, restore

renown *Syn* FAME, celebrity, éclat, glory, honor, notoriety, reputation, repute *Ant* infamy, obscurity

renowned *Syn* FAMOUS, celebrated, famed, noted, notorious, prominent, star, well-known *Ant* anonymous, obscure, unknown

rent **1** *Syn* HIRE, charter, lease, let **2** *Syn* BREACH, break, rift, rupture, schism, split

renter *Syn* TENANT, boarder, lodger, roomer *Ant* landlord

renunciation • voluntary surrender or putting aside of something desired or desirable *Syn* abnegation, self-abnegation, self-denial *Rel* eschewing, forbearing, forgoing, sacrifice, sacrificing *Ant* indulgence, self-indulgence

reopen *Syn* RESUME, continue, renew, restart

repair *Syn* MEND, patch, rebuild

repairable *Syn* REMEDIABLE, correctable, fixable, rectifiable, reparable *Ant* incorrigible, irremediable, irreparable

reparable *Syn* REMEDIABLE, correctable, fixable, rectifiable, repairable *Ant* incorrigible, irremediable, irreparable

reparation • a return for something lost or suffered, usually through the fault of another *Syn* amends, indemnity, redress, restitution *Rel* atonement, expiation

repartee **1** *Syn* BANTER, chaff, give-and-take, jesting, joshing, persiflage, raillery **2** *Syn* WIT, humor, irony, sarcasm, satire

repast *Syn* MEAL, chow, feed, mess, table

repay **1** • to make a return payment to *Syn* refund, reimburse *Rel* quit, satisfy, settle **2** *Syn* PAY, compensate, indemnify, recompense, reimburse, remunerate, satisfy

repeal *vb* **1** *Syn* ABOLISH, abrogate, annul, cancel, dissolve, invalidate, negate, nullify, quash, rescind, void **2** *Syn* REVOKE, recall, rescind, reverse

repeal *n* *Syn* CANCELLATION, abortion, calling, calling off, dropping, recall, rescission, revocation *Ant* continuation

repeat 1 • to say or do again *Syn* ingeminate, iterate, reiterate *Rel* recrudesce, recur, return, revert 2 • to say after another *Syn* echo, parrot, quote *Rel* mouth 3 *Syn* QUOTE, cite

repel *Syn* DISGUST, nauseate, repulse, revolt, sicken, turn off

repellent *Syn* REPUGNANT, abhorrent, distasteful, invidious, obnoxious *Ant* congenial

repent *Syn* REGRET, bemoan, deplore, lament, rue

repentance *Syn* PENITENCE, attrition, compunction, contrition, remorse

repentant *Syn* GUILTY, ashamed, contrite, hangdog, penitent, remorseful, shamed, shamefaced *Ant* impenitent, remorseless, shameless, unashamed, unrepentant

repercuss *Syn* REBOUND, recoil, resile, reverberate

rephrase *Syn* PARAPHRASE, restate, reword, translate *Ant* quote

repine *Syn* COMPLAIN, beef, bellyache, carp, crab, croak, fuss, gripe, grouse, growl, grumble, kick, moan, murmur, mutter, squawk, wail, whine, yammer *Ant* rejoice

replace • to put out of a usual or proper place or into the place of another *Syn* displace, supersede, supplant *Rel* renew, restore

replacement *Syn* SUBSTITUTE, backup, pinch hitter, relief, reserve, stand-in, sub

replete *Syn* FULL, complete, plenary *Ant* empty

replete *Syn* RIFE, abounding, flush, fraught, swarming, teeming, thick, thronging

replica *Syn* COPY, carbon copy, duplicate, duplication, facsimile, imitation, reduplication, replication, reproduction *Ant* original

replication *Syn* COPY, carbon copy, duplicate, duplication, facsimile, imitation, reduplication, replica, reproduction *Ant* original

reply *vb Syn* ANSWER, rejoin, respond, retort

reply *n Syn* ANSWER (sense 1), rejoinder, response, retort

report *n* 1 • common talk or an instance of it that spreads rapidly *Syn* gossip, hearsay, rumor *Rel* conversation, conversing, speaking, speech, talk, talking 2 *Syn* ACCOUNT, chronicle, story, version 3 *Syn* LETTER, dispatch, epistle, memorandum, message, missive, note

report *vb Syn* RELATE, describe, narrate, recite, recount, rehearse, state

reporter • a person employed by a newspaper, magazine, or radio or television station to gather, write, or report news *Syn* correspondent, journalist *Rel* announcer, broadcaster, newscaster, newsman, newspaperman

repose 1 *Syn* CALM, calmness, hush, peace, peacefulness, placidity, quiet, quietness, quietude, restfulness, sereneness, serenity, still, stillness, tranquillity (*or* tranquility) *Ant* bustle, commotion, hubbub, hurly-burly, pandemonium, tumult, turmoil, uproar 2 *Syn* REST, comfort, ease, leisure, relaxation

repository *Syn* STOREHOUSE, depository, depot, magazine, storage, stowage, warehouse

reprehend *Syn* CRITICIZE, blame, censure, condemn, denounce, reprobate

represent • to present an image or lifelike imitation of (as in art) *Syn* delineate, depict, limn, picture, portray *Rel* display, exhibit, show

representative 1 *Syn* AGENT (sense 1), attorney, commissary, delegate, deputy, envoy, factor, procurator, proxy 2 *Syn* AMBASSADOR, delegate, emissary, envoy, legate, minister 3 *Syn* DELEGATE, deputy 4 *Syn* EXAMPLE, case, exemplar, illustration, instance, sample, specimen

reprimand 1 *Syn* CENSURE, condemnation, denunciation, rebuke, reproach, reproof, stricture *Ant* citation, commendation, endorsement 2 *Syn* REPROVE, admonish, chide, rebuke, reproach

reprinting *Syn* EDITION, impression, printing, reissue

reprisal *Syn* RETALIATION, retribution, revenge, vengeance

reproach *n* 1 *Syn* CENSURE, condemnation, denunciation, rebuke, reprimand, reproof, stricture *Ant* citation, commendation, endorsement 2 *Syn* REPROVE, admonish, chide, rebuke, reprimand

reprobate *adj* 1 *Syn* ABANDONED (sense 1), dissolute, profligate *Ant* redeemed, regenerate 2 *Syn* CORRUPT, debased, debauched, decadent, degenerate, degraded, demoralized, depraved, dissipated, dissolute, perverse, perverted, warped *Ant* uncorrupted

reprobate *vb Syn* CRITICIZE, blame, censure, condemn, denounce, reprehend

reprobate *n Syn* OUTCAST, castaway, derelict, pariah, untouchable

reproduce *Syn* GENERATE, beget, breed, engender, get, procreate, propagate, sire

reproduction *Syn* COPY, carbon copy, duplicate, duplication, facsimile, imitation, reduplication, replica, replication *Ant* original

reproof *Syn* CENSURE, condemnation, denunciation, rebuke, reprimand, reproach, stricture *Ant* citation, commendation, endorsement

reprove 1 • to criticize adversely *Syn* admonish, chide, rebuke, reprimand, reproach *Rel* censure, criticize, reprehend, reprobate 2 *Syn* DISAPPROVE (OF), deprecate, discountenance, disfavor, dislike, frown (on) *Ant* approve, favor, like

republican *Syn* DEMOCRATIC, popular, self-governing, self-ruling *Ant* undemocratic

repudiate 1 *Syn* DECLINE, refuse, reject, spurn *Ant* accept 2 *Syn* DISCLAIM, disallow, disavow, disown *Ant* claim

repudiation *Syn* DENIAL (sense 2), contradiction, disallowance, disavowal, disclaimer,

negation, rejection *Ant* acknowledgment, admission, avowal, confirmation
repugnance *Syn* DISGUST, aversion, distaste, loathing, nausea, repulsion, revulsion
repugnant **1** • so alien or unlikable as to arouse antagonism and aversion *Syn* abhorrent, distasteful, invidious, obnoxious, repellent *Rel* alien, extraneous, extrinsic, foreign *Ant* congenial **2** *Syn* OFFENSIVE, loathsome, repulsive, revolting
repulse *Syn* DISGUST, turn off
repulsion *Syn* DISGUST, aversion, distaste, loathing, nausea, repugnance, revulsion
repulsive *Syn* OFFENSIVE, loathsome, repugnant, revolting
reputation *Syn* FAME, celebrity, éclat, glory, honor, notoriety, renown, repute *Ant* infamy, obscurity
repute *Syn* FAME, celebrity, éclat, glory, honor, notoriety, renown, reputation *Ant* infamy, obscurity
reputed *Syn* SUPPOSED, conjectural, hypothetical, purported, putative, suppositious, supposititious *Ant* certain
request *Syn* ASK, solicit
require **1** *Syn* DEMAND, claim, exact **2** *Syn* LACK, need, want
required *Syn* MANDATORY, compulsory, forced, imperative, incumbent, involuntary, necessary, nonelective, obligatory, peremptory *Ant* elective, optional, voluntary
requirement • something essential to the existence or occurrence of something else *Syn* prerequisite, requisite
requisite *adj* *Syn* NEEDFUL, essential, indispensable, necessary
requisite *n* *Syn* REQUIREMENT, prerequisite
requite *Syn* RECIPROCATE, retaliate, return
rescind **1** *Syn* ABOLISH, abrogate, annul, cancel, dissolve, invalidate, negate, nullify, quash, repeal, void **2** *Syn* REVOKE, recall, repeal, reverse
rescission *Syn* CANCELLATION, abortion, calling, calling off, dropping, recall, repeal, revocation *Ant* continuation
rescue • to set free from confinement or danger *Syn* deliver, ransom, reclaim, redeem, save *Rel* emancipate, free, liberate, manumit, release
rescuer *Syn* SAVIOR, deliverer, redeemer, saver
research *vb* *Syn* EXPLORE, delve (into), dig (into), inquire (into), investigate, look (into), probe
research *n* *Syn* INQUIRY, inquest, inquisition, investigation, probe
resemblance *Syn* SIMILARITY, alikeness, community, correspondence, likeness, parallelism, similitude *Ant* dissimilarity, unlikeness
resembling *Syn* ALIKE, akin, analogous, comparable, correspondent, corresponding, like, matching, parallel, similar, such, suchlike *Ant* different, dissimilar, diverse, unlike
resentful *Syn* ENVIOUS, covetous, invidious, jaundiced, jealous
resentment *Syn* OFFENSE (sense 1), dudgeon, huff, pique, umbrage
reservation *Syn* CONDITION, provision, proviso, stipulation, strings, terms
reserve *vb* *Syn* KEEP (sense 2), detain, hold back, keep back, keep out, retain, withhold *Ant* relinquish
reserve *n* **1** *Syn* SUBSTITUTE, backup, pinch hitter, relief, replacement, stand-in, sub **1** *Syn* STORE, cache, deposit, hoard
reserved *Syn* SILENT (sense 1), close, close-lipped, closemouthed, reticent, secretive, taciturn, tight-lipped, uncommunicative *Ant* talkative
reside • to have as one's habitation or domicile *Syn* dwell, live, lodge, put up, sojourn, stay, stop *Rel* abide, remain
residence *Syn* HABITATION, abode, domicile, dwelling, home, house
resident *Syn* INHABITANT, denizen, dweller, habitant, occupant, resider *Ant* transient
resider *Syn* INHABITANT, denizen, dweller, habitant, occupant, resident *Ant* transient
residue *Syn* REMAINDER, balance, leavings, remains, remnant, residuum, rest
residuum *Syn* REMAINDER, balance, leavings, remains, remnant, residue, rest
resign **1** *Syn* ABDICATE, renounce *Ant* assume, usurp **2** *Syn* RELINQUISH, abandon, cede, leave, surrender, waive, yield *Ant* keep
resignation **1** *Syn* COMPLIANCE, acquiescence *Ant* forwardness **2** *Syn* PATIENCE, forbearance, longanimity, long-suffering *Ant* impatience
resigned **1** *Syn* COMPLIANT, acquiescent *Ant* forward **2** *Syn* PASSIVE, acquiescent, nonresistant, tolerant, tolerating, unresistant, unresisting, yielding *Ant* protesting, resistant, resisting, unyielding
resile *Syn* REBOUND, recoil, repercuss, reverberate
resilient **1** *Syn* ELASTIC (sense 1), flexible, springy, supple *Ant* rigid **2** *Syn* ELASTIC (sense 2), buoyant, effervescent, expansive, volatile *Ant* depressed
resist • to stand firm against a person or influence *Syn* antagonize, combat, conflict, contest, fight, oppose, withstand *Rel* assail, assault, attack *Ant* abide, submit
resistance • the inclination to resist *Syn* defiance, opposition *Rel* demur, objection, protest, remonstrance *Ant* acquiescence
resolution *Syn* ANALYSIS, breakdown, dissection *Ant* synthesis
resolvable *Syn* SOLVABLE, answerable, explainable, explicable, soluble *Ant* inexplicable, insoluble, unexplainable, unsolvable
resolve **1** *Syn* DECIDE, determine, rule, settle

2 *Syn* SOLVE, answer, break, crack, dope (out), figure out, puzzle (out), riddle, unravel, work, work out

resolved *Syn* DECIDED, decisive, determined

resonant • marked by conspicuously full and rich sounds or tones (as of speech or music) *Syn* orotund, resounding, ringing, sonorous, vibrant *Rel* full, replete

resort *vb* • to betake oneself or to have recourse when in need of help or relief *Syn* apply, go, refer, turn *Rel* address, devote, direct

resort *n* **1** *Syn* HANGOUT, haunt, rendezvous **2** *Syn* RESOURCE, expedient, makeshift, shift, stopgap, substitute, surrogate

resounding *Syn* RESONANT, orotund, ringing, sonorous, vibrant

resource • something one turns to in the absence of the usual means or source of supply *Syn* expedient, makeshift, resort, shift, stopgap, substitute, surrogate *Rel* contraption, contrivance, device

resources *Syn* POSSESSIONS, assets, belongings, effects, means

respect *n* *Syn* REGARD, admiration, esteem *Ant* despite

respect *vb* *Syn* REGARD, admire, esteem *Ant* despise

respectable *Syn* ADEQUATE, acceptable, all right, decent, fine, OK (*or* okay), passable, satisfactory, tolerable *Ant* deficient, inadequate, lacking, unacceptable, unsatisfactory, wanting

respectful • marked by or showing proper regard for another's higher status *Syn* deferential, dutiful, regardful *Rel* reverent, reverential, venerating, worshipful *Ant* disrespectful

respecting *Syn* ABOUT, concerning, regarding

respectively *Syn* EACH, apiece, individually, severally

respects *Syn* COMPLIMENTS, congratulations, felicitations, greetings, regards

resplendence *Syn* MAGNIFICENCE, augustness, brilliance, gloriousness, glory, grandeur, grandness, majesty, nobility, nobleness, splendor, stateliness, stupendousness, sublimeness, superbness

resplendent *Syn* SPLENDID, glorious, gorgeous, sublime, superb

respond *Syn* ANSWER, rejoin, reply, retort

response *Syn* ANSWER (sense 1), rejoinder, reply, retort

responsibility *Syn* OBLIGATION, burden, charge, commitment, duty, need

responsible **1** • subject to being held to account *Syn* accountable, amenable, answerable, liable *Rel* exposed, open, subject **2** *Syn* DEPENDABLE, good, reliable, safe, solid, steady, sure, tried, tried-and-true, true, trustworthy, trusty *Ant* irresponsible, undependable, unreliable, untrustworthy

responsive **1** *Syn* SENTIENT, impressible, impressionable, sensitive, susceptible **2** *Syn* TENDER, compassionate, sympathetic, warm, warmhearted *Ant* callous, severe

rest *n* **1** • freedom from toil or strain *Syn* comfort, ease, leisure, relaxation, repose *Rel* deferring, intermission, intermitting, suspending, suspension **2** *Syn* REMAINDER, balance, leavings, remains, remnant, residue, residuum

rest *vb* *Syn* BASE, found, ground, stay

restart *Syn* RESUME, continue, renew, reopen

restate *Syn* PARAPHRASE, rephrase, reword, translate *Ant* quote

restaurant • a public establishment where meals are served to paying customers for consumption on the premises *Syn* café, diner, grill *Rel* cafeteria, coffeehouse, garden, luncheonette, lunchroom, snack bar, tearoom

restful *Syn* COMFORTABLE, cozy, easy, snug *Ant* miserable, uncomfortable

restfulness *Syn* CALM, calmness, hush, peace, peacefulness, placidity, quiet, quietness, quietude, repose, sereneness, serenity, still, stillness, tranquillity (*or* tranquility) *Ant* bustle, commotion, hubbub, hurly-burly, pandemonium, tumult, turmoil, uproar

restitution *Syn* REPARATION, amends, indemnity, redress

restive **1** *Syn* CONTRARY, balky, froward, perverse, wayward *Ant* complaisant, good-natured **2** *Syn* DISOBEDIENT, balky, contrary, defiant, froward, insubordinate, intractable, rebellious, recalcitrant, refractory, ungovernable, unruly, untoward, wayward, willful (*or* wilful) *Ant* amenable, compliant, docile, obedient, tractable **3** *Syn* IMPATIENT, fidgety, jittery, jumpy, nervous, restless, uneasy, unquiet *Ant* patient

restiveness *Syn* UNREST, disquiet, ferment, restlessness, turmoil, uneasiness *Ant* calm, ease, peace, quiet

restless *Syn* IMPATIENT, fidgety, jittery, jumpy, nervous, restive, uneasy, unquiet *Ant* patient

restlessness *Syn* UNREST, disquiet, ferment, restiveness, turmoil, uneasiness *Ant* calm, ease, peace, quiet

restorative **1** *Syn* CURATIVE, corrective, remedial, sanative **2** *Syn* TONIC, bracing, invigorating, refreshing, reviving, stimulating, stimulative, vitalizing

restore **1** • to help or cause to regain signs of life and vigor *Syn* resuscitate, revive, revivify *Rel* cure, heal, remedy **2** *Syn* RENEW, refresh, refurbish, rejuvenate, renovate

restrain • to hold back from or control in doing something *Syn* bridle, check, curb, inhibit *Rel* arrest, interrupt *Ant* abandon (*oneself*), activate, impel, incite

restraint **1** *Syn* FORCE, coercion, compulsion, constraint, duress, violence **2** *Syn* RESTRICTION, check, condition, constraint, curb, fetter, limitation

restrict *Syn* LIMIT, circumscribe, confine *Ant* widen
restriction • something that limits one's freedom of action or choice *Syn* check, condition, constraint, curb, fetter, limitation, restraint *Rel* stipulation, strings
result 1 *Syn* ANSWER (sense 2), solution 2 *Syn* EFFECT, aftereffect, aftermath, consequence, event, issue, outcome, sequel, upshot *Ant* cause
result (in) *Syn* EFFECT, bring about, cause, create, effectuate, engender, generate, induce, make, produce, prompt, spawn, work, yield
resume • to begin again or return to after an interruption *Syn* continue, renew, reopen, restart *Rel* resuscitate, revive
resurgence *Syn* REVIVAL, reanimation, rebirth, regeneration, rejuvenation, renewal, resurrection, resuscitation, revitalization
resurrection *Syn* REVIVAL, reanimation, rebirth, regeneration, rejuvenation, renewal, resurgence, resuscitation, revitalization
resuscitate *Syn* RESTORE, revive, revivify
resuscitation *Syn* REVIVAL, reanimation, rebirth, regeneration, rejuvenation, renewal, resurgence, resurrection, revitalization
retail *Syn* MARKET, deal (in), merchandise, put up, sell, vend *Ant* buy, purchase
retain *Syn* KEEP (sense 2), detain, hold back, keep back, keep out, reserve, withhold *Ant* relinquish
retainer *Syn* SERVANT, domestic, flunky, lackey, menial, steward *Ant* master
retaliate 1 *Syn* RECIPROCATE, requite, return 2 *Syn* AVENGE, revenge
retaliation • the act of inflicting or the intent to inflict injury in return for injury *Syn* reprisal, retribution, revenge, vengeance *Rel* correcting, correction, discipline, disciplining, punishment
retard 1 *Syn* DELAY (sense 1), detain, slacken, slow *Ant* expedite, hasten 2 *Syn* SLOW, brake, decelerate *Ant* accelerate, hasten, hurry, quicken, rush, speed (up), step up
rethink *Syn* RECONSIDER, readdress, reanalyze, reconceive, reevaluate, reexamine, review, reweigh
reticent 1 *Syn* SECRETIVE, close, closemouthed, dark, uncommunicative *Ant* communicative, open 2 *Syn* SILENT (sense 1), close, close-lipped, closemouthed, reserved, secretive, taciturn, tight-lipped, uncommunicative *Ant* talkative
retire *Syn* GO, depart, leave, quit, withdraw *Ant* come
retired *Syn* SECLUDED, cloistered, covert, isolated, quiet, remote, secret, sheltered
retort *vb Syn* ANSWER, rejoin, reply, respond
retort *n Syn* ANSWER (sense 1), rejoinder, reply, response
retract 1 *Syn* ABJURE, forswear, recant, renounce *Ant* pledge (*allegiance, a vow*), elect (*a way of life, a means to an end*) 2 *Syn* RECEDE, back, retreat, retreat, retrograde *Ant* advance, proceed
retreat *vb Syn* RECEDE, back, retract, retrograde *Ant* advance, proceed
retreat *n Syn* SHELTER, asylum, cover, refuge, sanctuary
retrench *Syn* SHORTEN, abbreviate, abridge, curtail *Ant* elongate, extend, lengthen, prolong, protract
retribution *Syn* RETALIATION, reprisal, revenge, vengeance
retrieve *Syn* RECOVER, recoup, recruit, regain
retrograde *adj Syn* BACKWARD, regressive, retrogressive *Ant* advanced
retrograde *vb Syn* RECEDE, back, retract, retreat *Ant* advance, proceed
retrogress *Syn* REGRESS, revert *Ant* advance, develop, evolve, progress
retrogression *Syn* REGRESSION, reversion *Ant* advancement, development, evolution, progression
retrogressive *Syn* BACKWARD, regressive, retrograde *Ant* advanced
return *n* • the act of coming back to or from a place or condition *Syn* recrudescence, recurrence, reversion
return *vb* 1 • to go or come back (as to a person, place, or condition) *Syn* recrudesce, recur, revert *Rel* advert 2 *Syn* RECIPROCATE, requite, retaliate
revamp *Syn* CHANGE (sense 1), alter, make over, modify, recast, redo, refashion, remake, remodel, revise, rework, vary *Ant* fix, freeze, set, stabilize
reveal • to make known what has been or should be concealed *Syn* betray, disclose, discover, divulge, tell *Rel* communicate, impart *Ant* conceal
revealing *Syn* EXPRESSIVE, eloquent, meaning, meaningful, pregnant, significant, suggestive
revelation 1 • disclosure or something disclosed by or as if by divine or preternatural means *Syn* prophecy, vision *Ant* adumbration 2 • the act or an instance of making known something previously unknown or concealed *Syn* disclosure, divulgence, exposure *Rel* bombshell, surprise
revenge *vb Syn* AVENGE, retaliate
revenge *n Syn* RETALIATION, reprisal, retribution, vengeance
revengeful *Syn* VINDICTIVE, vengeful
reverberate *Syn* REBOUND, recoil, repercuss, resile
revere • to honor and admire profoundly and respectfully *Syn* adore, reverence, venerate, worship *Rel* admire, esteem, regard, respect *Ant* flout
reverence *n* 1 • a feeling of worshipful respect *Syn* adoration, veneration, worship *Rel* ardor, fervor, passion, zeal 2 • the emotion

inspired by what arouses one's deep respect or veneration *Syn* awe, fear **3** *Syn* HONOR, deference, homage, obeisance

reverence *vb Syn* REVERE, adore, venerate, worship *Ant* flout

reverie • the state of being lost in thought *Syn* daydreaming, study, trance, woolgathering *Rel* contemplation, meditation, musing

reverse *vb* **1** • to change to the opposite position *Syn* invert, transpose *Rel* capsize, overturn, upset **2** *Syn* REVOKE, recall, repeal, rescind

reverse *n Syn* OPPOSITE, antipode, antithesis, antonym, contradictory, contrary, converse, counter

reversion **1** *Syn* REGRESSION, retrogression *Ant* advancement, development, evolution, progression **2** *Syn* RETURN, recrudescence, recurrence

revert **1** *Syn* REGRESS, retrogress *Ant* advance, develop, evolve, progress **2** *Syn* RETURN, recrudesce, recur

review *n* **1** *Syn* CRITICISM, blurb, critique, puff **2** *Syn* INSPECTION, audit, check, checkup, examination, scan, scrutiny, survey **3** *Syn* JOURNAL, magazine, newspaper, organ, periodical

review *vb Syn* RECONSIDER, readdress, reanalyze, reconceive, reevaluate, reexamine, rethink, reweigh

revile *Syn* SCOLD, bawl, berate, chew out, jaw, rail, rate, tongue-lash, upbraid, vituperate, wig

revise **1** *Syn* CHANGE (sense 1), alter, make over, modify, recast, redo, refashion, remake, remodel, revamp, rework, vary *Ant* fix, freeze, set, stabilize **2** *Syn* CORRECT, amend, emend, rectify, redress, reform, remedy **3** *Syn* EDIT, adapt, compile, redact, rewrite

revitalization *Syn* REVIVAL, reanimation, rebirth, regeneration, rejuvenation, renewal, resurgence, resurrection, resuscitation

revival • the act or an instance of bringing something back to life, public attention, or vigorous activity *Syn* reanimation, rebirth, regeneration, rejuvenation, renewal, resurgence, resurrection, resuscitation, revitalization *Rel* renaissance, renascence

revive **1** *Syn* COME TO, come around, come round **2** *Syn* RESTORE, resuscitate, revivify

revivify *Syn* RESTORE, resuscitate, revive

reviving *Syn* TONIC, bracing, invigorating, refreshing, restorative, stimulating, stimulative, vitalizing

revocation *Syn* CANCELLATION, abortion, calling, calling off, dropping, recall, repeal, rescission *Ant* continuation

revoke • to annul by recalling or taking back *Syn* recall, repeal, rescind, reverse *Rel* abrogate, annul, void

revolt *vb Syn* DISGUST, nauseate, repel, repulse, sicken, turn off

revolt *n Syn* REBELLION, coup, insurrection, mutiny, putsch, revolution, uprising

revolting *Syn* OFFENSIVE, loathsome, repugnant, repulsive

revolution *Syn* REBELLION, coup, insurrection, mutiny, putsch, revolt, uprising

revolutionary *Syn* RADICAL, extremist, revolutionist *Ant* moderate

revolutionist *Syn* RADICAL, extremist, revolutionary *Ant* moderate

revolve *Syn* TURN (sense 1), circle, eddy, gyrate, pirouette, rotate, spin, swirl, twirl, wheel, whirl

revulsion *Syn* DISGUST, aversion, distaste, loathing, nausea, repugnance, repulsion

rewarding *Syn* HEARTWARMING, cheering, comforting, encouraging, fulfilling, gladdening, gratifying, heartening, satisfying *Ant* depressing, discouraging, disheartening, dispiriting

reweigh *Syn* RECONSIDER, readdress, reanalyze, reconceive, reevaluate, reexamine, rethink, review

reword *Syn* PARAPHRASE, rephrase, restate, translate *Ant* quote

rework *Syn* CHANGE (sense 1), alter, make over, modify, recast, redo, refashion, remake, remodel, revamp, revise, vary *Ant* fix, freeze, set, stabilize

rewrite *Syn* EDIT, adapt, compile, redact, revise

rhapsodic *Syn* ECSTATIC, elated, enraptured, entranced, euphoric, exhilarated, intoxicated, rapturous *Ant* depressed

rhapsodize *Syn* GUSH (sense 2), enthuse, fuss, rave, slobber

rhapsody **1** *Syn* BOMBAST, fustian, rant, rodomontade **2** *Syn* ECSTASY, elation, euphoria, exhilaration, heaven, intoxication, paradise, rapture, transport *Ant* depression

rhetorical • emphasizing style often at the expense of thought *Syn* aureate, bombastic, euphuistic, flowery, grandiloquent, magniloquent *Rel* articulate, eloquent, fluent, glib, vocal, voluble

rhymer *Syn* POET, bard, minstrel, poetaster, rhymester, troubadour, versifier

rhymester *Syn* POET, bard, minstrel, poetaster, rhymer, troubadour, versifier

rhythm • the recurrent pattern formed by a series of sounds having a regular rise and fall in intensity *Syn* beat, cadence, measure, meter *Rel* accent, accentuation, emphasis, stress

rib **1** *Syn* BANTER, chaff, jolly, josh, kid, rag **2** *Syn* TEASE, chaff, jive, josh, kid, rally, razz, ride, roast

ribald *Syn* COARSE, gross, obscene, vulgar *Ant* fine, refined

ribbon *Syn* STRIP, band, fillet, stripe

rich **1** • having goods, property, and money in abundance *Syn* affluent, opulent, wealthy *Ant* poor **2** *Syn* FERTILE, fat, fecund, fruitful, luxuriant, productive, prolific *Ant* barren, infertile, sterile, unfruitful, unproductive

richly *Syn* HIGH, expensively, extravagantly, grandly, lavishly, luxuriously, opulently, sumptuously *Ant* austerely, humbly, modestly, plainly, simply

ricochet *Syn* SKIP, bound, curvet, hop, lollop, lope

rid • to set a person or thing free of something that encumbers *Syn* clear, disabuse, purge, unburden *Rel* free, liberate, release

riddle *n Syn* MYSTERY, conundrum, enigma, problem, puzzle

riddle *vb Syn* SOLVE, answer, break, crack, dope (out), figure out, puzzle (out), resolve, unravel, work, work out

ride **1** *Syn* BAIT, badger, chivy, heckle, hector, hound **2** *Syn* TEASE, chaff, jive, josh, kid, rally, razz, rib, roast

ridicule • to make an object of laughter of *Syn* deride, mock, rally, taunt, twit *Rel* flout, gibe, jeer, scoff

ridiculous *Syn* LAUGHABLE, comic, comical, droll, farcical, funny, ludicrous, risible

rife **1** • possessing or covered with great numbers or amounts of something specified *Syn* abounding, flush, fraught, replete, swarming, teeming, thick, thronging *Rel* alive, animated, astir, brimming, bulging, bursting, bustling, busy, buzzing, chockfull (*or* chockful), clogged, congested, crammed, crowded, fat, filled, full, humming, jam-packed, jammed, lively, loaded, overcrowded, overfilled, overflowing, overfull, overloaded, overstuffed, packed, saturated, stuffed, surfeited **2** *Syn* PREVAILING, current, prevalent

rifle *Syn* ROB, burglarize, loot, plunder

rift *Syn* BREACH, break, rent, rupture, schism, split

rig *Syn* FURNISH (sense 1), accoutre (*or* accouter), equip, fit (out), outfit, supply *Ant* hold (back), keep (back), reserve, retain, withhold

right *n* • something to which one has a just claim *Syn* appanage, birthright, perquisite, prerogative, privilege *Rel* claim, title

right *adj* **1** *Syn* CORRECT, accurate, exact, nice, precise *Ant* incorrect **2** *Syn* SANE, balanced, clearheaded, lucid, normal, stable *Ant* crazed, crazy, demented, deranged, insane, lunatic, mad, maniacal, mental, unbalanced, unsound

right *adv Syn* VERY, awful, awfully, beastly, deadly, especially, exceedingly, extra, extremely, far, frightfully, full, greatly, heavily, highly, hugely, jolly, mightily, mighty, mortally, most, much, particularly, rattling, real, so, something, super, terribly, too, whacking *Ant* little, negligibly, nominally, slightly

righteous *Syn* MORAL, ethical, noble, virtuous

rightful *Syn* DUE, condign

rightly *Syn* PROPERLY, appropriately, congruously, correctly, fittingly, happily, meetly, suitably *Ant* improperly, inappropriately, incongruously, incorrectly, unsuitably, wrongly

rightness *Syn* APPROPRIATENESS, aptness, felicitousness, fitness, fittingness, seemliness, suitability, suitableness *Ant* inappropriateness, inaptness, infelicity, unfitness

rigid **1** • extremely severe or stern *Syn* rigorous, strict, stringent *Rel* adamant, adamantine, inexorable, inflexible, obdurate *Ant* lax **2** *Syn* OBSTINATE, adamant, adamantine, dogged, hard, hardened, hardheaded, hardhearted, headstrong, immovable, implacable, inflexible, mulish, obdurate, opinionated, ossified, pat, peevish, pertinacious, perverse, pigheaded, self-willed, stubborn, unbending, uncompromising, unrelenting, unyielding, willful (*or* wilful) *Ant* acquiescent, agreeable, amenable, compliant, complying, flexible, pliable, pliant, relenting, yielding **3** *Syn* STIFF, inflexible, stark, tense, wooden *Ant* relaxed, supple

rigidity *Syn* SEVERITY, hardness, harshness, inflexibility, rigidness, rigorousness, sternness, strictness *Ant* flexibility, gentleness, laxness, mildness

rigidly *Syn* STRICTLY, exactly, precisely, rigorously *Ant* imprecisely, inexactly, loosely

rigidness *Syn* SEVERITY, hardness, harshness, inflexibility, rigidity, rigorousness, sternness, strictness *Ant* flexibility, gentleness, laxness, mildness

rigor *Syn* DIFFICULTY, hardship, vicissitude

rigorous *Syn* RIGID, strict, stringent *Ant* lax

rigorously *Syn* STRICTLY, exactly, precisely, rigidly *Ant* imprecisely, inexactly, loosely

rigorousness **1** *Syn* PRECISION, accuracy, closeness, delicacy, exactitude, exactness, fineness, preciseness, veracity *Ant* coarseness, impreciseness, imprecision, inaccuracy, inexactness, roughness **2** *Syn* SEVERITY, hardness, harshness, inflexibility, rigidity, rigidness, sternness, strictness *Ant* flexibility, gentleness, laxness, mildness

rile **1** *Syn* ANGER, antagonize, enrage, incense, inflame, infuriate, madden, outrage, rankle, roil *Ant* delight, gratify, please **2** *Syn* IRRITATE, aggravate, exasperate, nettle, peeve, provoke

riled *Syn* ANGRY, angered, apoplectic, enraged, foaming, fuming, furious, incensed, indignant, inflamed, infuriated, irate, ireful, mad, outraged, rabid, roiled, sore, steaming, wrathful, wroth *Ant* delighted, pleased

riling *Syn* ANNOYING, aggravating, bothersome, disturbing, exasperating, frustrating, galling, irksome, irritating, maddening, nettling, peeving, pesty, rankling, vexatious, vexing

rim *vb Syn* BORDER, bound, fringe, margin, skirt

rim *n Syn* BORDER, brim, brink, edge, margin, verge
rind *Syn* SKIN, bark, hide, peel, pelt
ring *n Syn* COMBINATION, bloc, combine, faction, party
ring *vb Syn* SURROUND, circle, compass, encircle, encompass, environ, gird, girdle, hem
ringing *Syn* RESONANT, orotund, resounding, sonorous, vibrant
rip **1** *Syn* HURRY (sense 2), barrel, bolt, bowl, breeze, career, course, dash, fly, hasten, hotfoot (it), hump, hurtle, hustle, pelt, race, rocket, run, rush, rustle, scoot, scurry, scuttle, shoot, speed, step (along), tear, trot, whirl, whisk, zip, zoom *Ant* crawl, creep, poke **2** *Syn* TEAR, cleave, rend, rive, split
ripe *Syn* MATURE, adult, grown-up, matured, mellow *Ant* childish, immature
ripen *Syn* MATURE, age, develop
rise **1** *Syn* ASCEND, arise, climb, lift, mount, soar, up, uprise, upsweep, upturn *Ant* decline, descend, dip, drop, fall (off) **2** *Syn* INCREASE (sense 2), accumulate, appreciate, balloon, build (up), burgeon, enlarge, escalate, expand, mount, multiply, mushroom, proliferate, snowball, swell, wax *Ant* contract, decrease, diminish, lessen, wane **3** *Syn* SPRING, arise, derive, emanate, flow, issue, originate, proceed, stem
risible *Syn* LAUGHABLE, comic, comical, droll, farcical, funny, ludicrous, ridiculous
risk *n* **1** *Syn* DANGER (sense 1), hazard, menace, peril, pitfall, threat, trouble *Ant* safeness, safety, security **2** *Syn* DANGER (sense 2), distress, endangerment, imperilment, jeopardy, peril, trouble *Ant* safeness, safety, security
risk *vb Syn* ENDANGER, adventure, compromise, gamble (with), hazard, imperil, jeopardize, menace, venture
risky *Syn* DANGEROUS, hazardous, perilous, precarious *Ant* safe, secure
rite *Syn* FORM (sense 2), ceremonial, ceremony, formality, liturgy, ritual
ritual *Syn* FORM (sense 2), ceremonial, ceremony, formality, liturgy, rite
rival *vb* **1** • to strive to equal or surpass *Syn* compete, emulate, vie *Rel* attempt, strive, struggle, try **2** *Syn* MATCH, approach, equal, touch
rival *n* **1** *Syn* COMPETITOR, challenger, competition, contender, contestant **2** *Syn* EQUAL, coordinate, counterpart, equivalent, fellow, like, match, parallel, peer
rive *Syn* TEAR, cleave, rend, rip, split
rivet *Syn* SECURE, anchor, moor
riveting *Syn* INTERESTING, absorbing, arresting, engaging, engrossing, enthralling, fascinating, gripping, immersing, intriguing, involving *Ant* boring, drab, dry, dull, heavy, monotonous, tedious, uninteresting
roam *Syn* WANDER, gad, gallivant, meander, prowl, ramble, range, rove, stray, traipse
roamer *Syn* NOMAD, drifter, gadabout, rambler, rover, stroller, vagabond, wanderer, wayfarer
roar *n* • a very loud and often a continuous noise *Syn* bawl, bellow, bluster, ululation, vociferation
roar *vb* • to make a very loud and often a continuous or protracted noise *Syn* bawl, bellow, bluster, clamor, howl, ululate, vociferate *Rel* rebound, repercuss, reverberate
roast *Syn* TEASE, chaff, jive, josh, kid, rally, razz, rib, ride
rob • to take possessions unlawfully *Syn* burglarize, loot, plunder, rifle *Rel* filch, lift, pilfer, purloin, steal
robber *Syn* THIEF, burglar, larcener, larcenist
robbery *Syn* THEFT, burglary, larceny
robe *Syn* CLOTHE, apparel, array, attire, dress *Ant* unclothe
robust *Syn* HEALTHY, hale, sound, well, wholesome *Ant* unhealthy
robustness *Syn* HEALTH, fitness, healthiness, heartiness, soundness, wellness, wholeness, wholesomeness *Ant* illness, sickness, unhealthiness, unsoundness
rock *Syn* SHAKE (sense 2), agitate, convulse
rocket *Syn* HURRY (sense 2), barrel, bolt, bowl, breeze, career, course, dash, fly, hasten, hotfoot (it), hump, hurtle, hustle, pelt, race, rip, run, rush, rustle, scoot, scurry, scuttle, shoot, speed, step (along), tear, trot, whirl, whisk, zip, zoom *Ant* crawl, creep, poke
rococo *Syn* ORNATE, baroque, flamboyant, florid *Ant* austere, chaste
rodomontade *Syn* BOMBAST, fustian, rant, rhapsody
rogue *Syn* VILLAIN, blackguard, knave, miscreant, rapscallion, rascal, scamp, scoundrel
roguish *Syn* PLAYFUL, frolicsome, impish, mischievous, sportive, waggish
roil *Syn* ANGER, antagonize, enrage, incense, inflame, infuriate, madden, outrage, rankle, rile *Ant* delight, gratify, please
roiled *Syn* ANGRY, angered, apoplectic, enraged, foaming, fuming, furious, incensed, indignant, inflamed, infuriated, irate, ireful, mad, outraged, rabid, riled, sore, steaming, wrathful, wroth *Ant* delighted, pleased
roily *Syn* TURBID, muddy *Ant* clear, limpid
role • the action for which a person or thing is specially fitted or used or for which a thing exists *Syn* capacity, function, job, part, place, position, purpose, task, work *Rel* affair, business, concern, involvement, participation
roll *Syn* LIST, catalog, inventory, register, roster, schedule, table
rollick *vb Syn* PLAY, disport, frolic, gambol, romp, sport *Ant* work
rollick *n Syn* PLAY, disport, frolic, gambol, romp, sport

romantic *adj* **1** *Syn* EXOTIC, fantastic, glamorous, marvelous (*or* marvellous), outlandish, strange **2** *Syn* SENTIMENTAL, maudlin, mawkish, mushy, slushy, soppy
romantic *n Syn* IDEALIST, dreamer, romanticist, utopian, visionary *Ant* pragmatist, realist
romanticist *Syn* IDEALIST, dreamer, romantic, utopian, visionary *Ant* pragmatist, realist
romanticize *Syn* IDEALIZE, glamorize, glorify
romp *n Syn* PLAY, disport, frolic, gambol, rollick, sport *Ant* work
romp *vb Syn* PLAY, disport, frolic, gambol, rollick, sport
roof *Syn* CANOPY, awning, ceiling, tent
rook *Syn* FLEECE, bleed, cheat, chisel, cozen, defraud, hustle, mulct, shortchange, skin, squeeze, stick, sting, swindle, victimize
rookie *Syn* BEGINNER, colt, fledgling, freshman, greenhorn, neophyte, newbie, newcomer, novice, recruit, tenderfoot, tyro *Ant* old hand, old-timer, vet, veteran
room **1** • space in a building enclosed or set apart by a partition *Syn* apartment, chamber **2** • enough space or range for free movement *Syn* berth, clearance, elbow room, leeway, margin, play
roomer *Syn* TENANT, boarder, lodger, renter *Ant* landlord
roost *Syn* ALIGHT, land, light, perch, settle, touch down *Ant* take off
root *vb Syn* APPLAUD, cheer *Ant* boo, hiss
root *n Syn* ORIGIN, inception, prime mover, provenance, provenience, source
rope *Syn* CORD, cable, lace, lacing, line, string, wire
roseate *Syn* HOPEFUL, optimistic, rose-colored *Ant* despairing, hopeless
rose-colored *Syn* HOPEFUL, optimistic, roseate *Ant* despairing, hopeless
roster *Syn* LIST, catalog, inventory, register, roll, schedule, table
rostrum *Syn* PLATFORM, dais, podium, stage, stand
rot *vb* **1** *Syn* DECAY, crumble, decompose, disintegrate, putrefy, spoil **2** *Syn* DETERIORATE, crumble, decay, decline, degenerate, descend, ebb, sink, worsen *Ant* ameliorate, improve, meliorate
rot *n Syn* NONSENSE, balderdash, bull, bunk, drivel, gobbledygook, poppycock, trash, twaddle
rotate *Syn* TURN (sense 1), circle, eddy, gyrate, pirouette, revolve, spin, swirl, twirl, wheel, whirl
rotten *Syn* UNPLEASANT, bad, disagreeable, displeasing, distasteful, nasty, sour, uncongenial, unlovely, unpleasing, unsatisfying, unwelcome *Ant* agreeable, congenial, good, grateful, gratifying, nice, palatable, pleasant, pleasing, pleasurable, satisfying, welcome
rotund *Syn* FLESHY, chubby, corpulent, fat, obese, plump, portly, stout *Ant* scrawny, skinny
rough **1** • not smooth or even *Syn* harsh, rugged, scabrous, uneven *Rel* firm, hard, solid *Ant* smooth **2** *Syn* HAIRY (sense 1), bristly, fleecy, furry, hirsute, shaggy, unshorn, woolly *Ant* bald, furless, hairless, shorn, smooth **3** *Syn* HAIRY (sense 2), furry, fuzzy, shaggy, woolly **4** *Syn* RUDE (sense 1), callow, crude, green, raw, uncouth *Ant* civil, urbane
roughhouse *Syn* HORSEPLAY, clowning, foolery, high jinks, horsing (around), monkeying, monkeyshines, roughhousing, shenanigans, skylarking, tomfoolery
roughhousing *Syn* HORSEPLAY, clowning, foolery, high jinks, horsing (around), monkeying, monkeyshines, roughhouse, shenanigans, skylarking, tomfoolery
round *Syn* AROUND (sense 2), about, over, through, throughout
roundabout *Syn* INDIRECT, circuitous *Ant* direct, forthright, straightforward
rouse *Syn* STIR, arouse, awaken, rally, waken
roustabout *Syn* WORKER, artisan, craftsman, hand, handicraftsman, laborer, mechanic, operative, workingman, workman *Ant* idler
rout *vb Syn* CONQUER, beat, defeat, lick, overcome, overthrow, reduce, subdue, subjugate, surmount, vanquish
rout *n Syn* CROWD, crush, horde, mob, press, throng
route *vb Syn* SEND, dispatch, forward, remit, ship, transmit *Ant* accept, receive
route *n Syn* WAY, artery, course, pass, passage
rove *Syn* WANDER, gad, gallivant, meander, prowl, ramble, range, roam, stray, traipse
rover *Syn* NOMAD, drifter, gadabout, rambler, roamer, stroller, vagabond, wanderer, wayfarer
row **1** *Syn* BRAWL, broil, fracas, melee, rumpus, scrap **2** *Syn* COMMOTION, bother, bustle, clatter, disturbance, furor, furore, fuss, hubbub, hullabaloo, hurly-burly, pandemonium, pother, ruckus, ruction, rumpus, shindy, squall, stew, stir, storm, to-do, tumult, turmoil, uproar, welter, whirl **3** *Syn* LINE, echelon, file, rank, tier
rowdy *Syn* BOISTEROUS, knockabout, rambunctious, raucous *Ant* orderly
royal *Syn* KINGLY, imperial, princely, queenly, regal
rub *Syn* POLISH, buff, burnish, dress, gloss, grind, shine, smooth
rubbed *Syn* GLOSSY, buffed, burnished, glistening, lustrous, polished, satin, satiny, sleek *Ant* dim, dull, flat, lusterless, matte
rubberneck *Syn* GAPE, gawk, gaze, goggle, peer, stare
rubbish *Syn* REFUSE, debris, garbage, offal, trash, waste
ruckus *Syn* COMMOTION, bother, bustle, clatter, disturbance, furor, furore, fuss, hub-

bub, hullabaloo, hurly-burly, pandemonium, pother, row, ruction, rumpus, shindy, squall, stew, stir, storm, to-do, tumult, turmoil, uproar, welter, whirl

ruction *Syn* COMMOTION, bother, bustle, clatter, disturbance, furor, furore, fuss, hubbub, hullabaloo, hurly-burly, pandemonium, pother, row, ruckus, rumpus, shindy, squall, stew, stir, storm, to-do, tumult, turmoil, uproar, welter, whirl

rude **1** • lacking in social refinement *Syn* callow, crude, green, raw, rough, uncouth *Rel* boorish, churlish, clownish, loutish **2** *Syn* IMPOLITE, discourteous, ill-bred, ill-mannered, impertinent, inconsiderate, thoughtless, uncalled-for, uncivil, ungracious, unmannerly *Ant* civil, considerate, courteous, genteel, gracious, mannerly, polite, thoughtful, well-bred

rudimentary *Syn* ELEMENTARY, basic, elemental, essential, fundamental, underlying *Ant* advanced

rue *Syn* REGRET, bemoan, deplore, lament, repent

rueful *Syn* MELANCHOLY, doleful, dolorous, lugubrious, plaintive

rugged *Syn* ROUGH, harsh, scabrous, uneven *Ant* smooth

ruin *vb* • to subject to forces that are destructive of soundness, worth, or usefulness *Syn* dilapidate, wreck *Rel* demolish, destroy, raze

ruin *n* *Syn* DESTRUCTION, annihilation, decimation, demolishment, demolition, desolation, devastation, extermination, extinction, havoc, loss, obliteration, ruination, wastage, wreckage *Ant* building, construction, erection, raising

ruination *Syn* DESTRUCTION, annihilation, decimation, demolishment, demolition, desolation, devastation, extermination, extinction, havoc, loss, obliteration, ruin, wastage, wreckage *Ant* building, construction, erection, raising

rule *n* **1** • a statement spelling out the proper procedure or conduct for an activity *Syn* bylaw, ground rule, regulation *Rel* code, constitution, decalogue **2** • lawful control over the affairs of a political unit (as a nation) *Syn* administration, authority, governance, government, jurisdiction, regime, regimen *Rel* reign **3** *Syn* LAW, canon, ordinance, precept, regulation, statute

rule *vb* *Syn* DECIDE, determine, resolve, settle

rule out *Syn* EXCLUDE, blackball, debar, disbar, eliminate, shut out, suspend *Ant* admit, include

ruler *Syn* MONARCH, autocrat, sovereign

ruminant *Syn* CONTEMPLATIVE, meditative, melancholy, pensive, reflective, thoughtful *Ant* unreflective

ruminate *Syn* PONDER, meditate, muse

rummage *Syn* SEEK, comb, ferret out, hunt, ransack, scour, search

rumor *vb* • to make (as a piece of information) the subject of common talk without any authority or confirmation of accuracy *Syn* bruit (about), circulate, noise (about), whisper *Rel* bandy (about), blab, gossip

rumor *n* *Syn* REPORT, gossip, hearsay

rump *Syn* BUTTOCKS, backside, bottom, breech, butt, fanny, hams, haunches, posterior, rear, seat

rumple *Syn* DISORDER, confuse, derange, disarrange, disarray, discompose, dishevel, dislocate, disorganize, disrupt, disturb, hash, jumble, mess (up), mix (up), muddle, muss, scramble, shuffle, tousle, tumble, upset *Ant* arrange, array, draw up, marshal, order, organize, range, regulate, straighten (up), tidy

rumpled *Syn* MESSY, chaotic, cluttered, confused, disarranged, disarrayed, disheveled (*or* dishevelled), disordered, disorderly, higgledy-piggledy, hugger-mugger, jumbled, littered, messed, muddled, mussed, mussy, pell-mell, sloppy, topsy-turvy, tousled, tumbled, unkempt, untidy, upside-down *Ant* neat, ordered, orderly, organized, shipshape, snug, tidied, tidy, trim

rumpus **1** *Syn* BRAWL, broil, fracas, melee, row, scrap **2** *Syn* COMMOTION, bother, bustle, clatter, disturbance, furor, furore, fuss, hubbub, hullabaloo, hurly-burly, pandemonium, pother, row, ruckus, ruction, shindy, squall, stew, stir, storm, to-do, tumult, turmoil, uproar, welter, whirl

run **1** *Syn* ACTIVATE, actuate, crank (up), drive, move, propel, set off, spark, start, touch off, trigger, turn on *Ant* cut, deactivate, kill, shut off, turn off **2** *Syn* BECOME, come, get, go, grow, turn, wax **3** *Syn* HURRY (sense 2), barrel, bolt, bowl, breeze, career, course, dash, fly, hasten, hotfoot (it), hump, hurtle, hustle, pelt, race, rip, rocket, rush, rustle, scoot, scurry, scuttle, shoot, speed, step (along), tear, trot, whirl, whisk, zip, zoom *Ant* crawl, creep, poke

run on *Syn* CHAT, babble, blab, cackle, chatter, converse, gab, gabble, gas, jabber, jaw, palaver, patter, prate, prattle, rap, rattle, talk, twitter, visit

runt *Syn* DWARF, midget, pygmy

rupture *Syn* BREACH, break, rent, rift, schism, split

rural • relating to or characteristic of the country *Syn* bucolic, pastoral, rustic *Ant* urban

ruse *Syn* TRICK, artifice, feint, gambit, maneuver, ploy, stratagem, wile

rush *vb* **1** *Syn* GUSH (sense 1), jet, pour, spew, spout, spurt, squirt *Ant* dribble, drip, drop, trickle **2** *Syn* HURRY (sense 1), accelerate, hasten, quicken, speed (up), whisk

Ant decelerate, retard, slow (down) **3** *Syn* HURRY (sense 2), barrel, bolt, bowl, breeze, career, course, dash, fly, hasten, hotfoot (it), hump, hurtle, hustle, pelt, race, rip, rocket, run, rustle, scoot, scurry, scuttle, shoot, speed, step (along), tear, trot, whirl, whisk, zip, zoom *Ant* crawl, creep, poke

rush *n Syn* ATTACK (sense 2), aggression, assault, blitzkrieg, charge, descent, offense (*or* offence), offensive, onset, onslaught, raid, strike

rustic *n Syn* HICK, bumpkin, clodhopper, countryman, provincial, yokel *Ant* cosmopolitan, sophisticate

rustic *adj Syn* RURAL, bucolic, pastoral *Ant* urban

rustle *Syn* HURRY (sense 2), barrel, bolt, bowl, breeze, career, course, dash, fly, hasten, hotfoot (it), hump, hurtle, hustle, pelt, race, rip, rocket, run, rush, scoot, scurry, scuttle, shoot, speed, step (along), tear, trot, whirl, whisk, zip, zoom *Ant* crawl, creep, poke

ruth *Syn* SYMPATHY, commiseration, compassion, condolence, empathy, pity

S

saccharine *Syn* CORNY, maudlin, mawkish, mushy, sappy, schmaltzy, sentimental, sloppy, sugarcoated, sugary *Ant* unsentimental

sack *n Syn* BAG, pouch

sack *vb* **1** *Syn* DISMISS, bounce, cashier, discharge, drop, fire **2** *Syn* RAVAGE, despoil, devastate, pillage, spoliate, waste

sacred **1** • protected (as by law, custom, or human respect) against abuse *Syn* inviolable, inviolate, sacrosanct *Rel* defended, guarded, protected, shielded **2** *Syn* HOLY (sense 2), blessed, consecrated, hallowed, sacrosanct, sanctified *Ant* unconsecrated, unhallowed

sacrifice *Syn* FORGO, abnegate, eschew, forbear

sacrilege *Syn* PROFANATION, blasphemy, desecration

sacrilegious *Syn* IMPIOUS, blasphemous, profane *Ant* pious, reverent

sacrosanct **1** *Syn* SACRED, inviolable, inviolate **2** *Syn* HOLY (sense 2), blessed, consecrated, hallowed, sacred, sanctified *Ant* unconsecrated, unhallowed

sad **1** • feeling unhappiness *Syn* bad, blue, brokenhearted, crestfallen, dejected, depressed, despondent, disconsolate, doleful, down, downcast, downhearted, droopy, forlorn, gloomy, glum, heartbroken, heartsick, heartsore, inconsolable, joyless, low, low-spirited, melancholy, miserable, mournful, saddened, sorrowful, sorry, unhappy, woebegone, woeful, wretched *Rel* aggrieved, distressed, troubled *Ant* blissful, buoyant, buoyed, cheerful, cheery, chipper, delighted, glad, gladdened, gladsome, gleeful, happy, joyful, joyous, jubilant, sunny, upbeat **2** • causing unhappiness *Syn* depressing, dismal, drear, dreary, heartbreaking, heartrending, melancholy, pathetic, saddening, sorry, tearful, teary *Rel* discomforting, discomposing, disquieting, distressing, disturbing, perturbing *Ant* cheering, cheery, glad, happy

saddened *Syn* SAD (sense 1), bad, blue, brokenhearted, crestfallen, dejected, depressed, despondent, disconsolate, doleful, down, downcast, downhearted, droopy, forlorn, gloomy, glum, heartbroken, heartsick, heartsore, inconsolable, joyless, low, low-spirited, melancholy, miserable, mournful, sorrowful, sorry, unhappy, woebegone, woeful, wretched *Ant* blissful, buoyant, buoyed, cheerful, cheery, chipper, delighted, glad, gladdened, gladsome, gleeful, happy, joyful, joyous, jubilant, sunny, upbeat

saddening *Syn* SAD (sense 2), depressing, dismal, drear, dreary, heartbreaking, heartrending, melancholy, pathetic, sorry, tearful, teary *Ant* cheering, cheery, glad, happy

saddle *Syn* BURDEN, charge, cumber, encumber, lade, load, tax, weigh, weight

sadism *Syn* CRUELTY, barbarity, brutality, cruelness, heartlessness, inhumanity, savageness, savagery, viciousness, wantonness *Ant* benignity, compassion, good-heartedness, humanity, kindheartedness, kindness, sympathy

sadness • a state or spell of low spirits *Syn* blues, dejection, depression, desolation, despondency, disconsolateness, dispiritedness, doldrums, downheartedness, dreariness, dumps, forlornness, gloom, gloominess, heartsickness, joylessness, melancholy, mopes, oppression, unhappiness *Rel* melancholia, self-pity *Ant* bliss, blissfulness, ecstasy, elatedness, elation, euphoria, exhilaration, exuberance, exultation, felicity, gladness, gladsomeness, happiness, heaven, intoxication, joy, joyfulness, joyousness, jubilation, rapture, rapturousness

safe *Syn* DEPENDABLE, good, reliable, responsible, solid, steady, sure, tried, tried-and-true,

true, trustworthy, trusty *Ant* irresponsible, undependable, unreliable, untrustworthy
safeguard *Syn* DEFEND, guard, protect, shield *Ant* attack, combat
safekeeping *Syn* CUSTODY, care, guardianship, keeping, trust, ward
safeness *Syn* SAFETY, protection, security *Ant* danger, distress, endangerment, imperilment, jeopardy, peril, trouble
safety • the state of not being exposed to danger *Syn* safeness, security *Rel* aegis, defense, guardianship, ward *Ant* danger, distress, endangerment, imperilment, jeopardy, peril, trouble
sag *Syn* DROOP, flag, wilt
saga *Syn* MYTH, legend
sagacious *Syn* SHREWD, astute, perspicacious
sage *Syn* WISE, judicious, prudent, sane, sapient, sensible *Ant* simple
sail *Syn* FLY, dart, float, scud, shoot, skim
sailor *Syn* MARINER, bluejacket, gob, seaman, tar
sainted *Syn* HOLY (sense 1), devout, godly, pious, religious, saintly *Ant* faithless, godless, impious, irreligious, ungodly, unholy
sainthood *Syn* HOLINESS, blessedness, devoutness, godliness, piety, piousness, saintliness, saintship, sanctity *Ant* godlessness, impiety, ungodliness, unholiness
saintliness *Syn* HOLINESS, blessedness, devoutness, godliness, piety, piousness, sainthood, saintship, sanctity *Ant* godlessness, impiety, ungodliness, unholiness
saintly *Syn* HOLY (sense 1), devout, godly, pious, religious, sainted *Ant* faithless, godless, impious, irreligious, ungodly, unholy
saintship *Syn* HOLINESS, blessedness, devoutness, godliness, piety, piousness, sainthood, saintliness, sanctity *Ant* godlessness, impiety, ungodliness, unholiness
salable *or* **saleable** *Syn* COMMERCIAL, marketable *Ant* noncommercial, nonsalable, uncommercial, unmarketable, unsalable
salary *Syn* WAGE, emolument, fee, hire, pay, stipend
sale • the transfer of ownership of something from one person to another for a price *Syn* deal, trade, transaction *Rel* auction
salient *Syn* NOTICEABLE, arresting, conspicuous, outstanding, prominent, remarkable, signal, striking
saloon *Syn* BARROOM, bar, café, groggery, grogshop, pub, tavern
salt away *Syn* HOARD, cache, lay away, lay up, put by, squirrel (away), stash, stockpile, store, stow
salubrious *Syn* HEALTHFUL, healthy, hygienic, salutary, sanitary, wholesome
salutary **1** *Syn* BENEFICIAL, advantageous, favorable, helpful, profitable *Ant* disadvantageous, unfavorable, unhelpful **2** *Syn* HEALTHFUL, healthy, hygienic, salubrious, sanitary, wholesome
salute **1** *Syn* ACCLAIM, applaud, cheer, hail, laud, praise, tout *Ant* knock, pan, slam **2** *Syn* ADDRESS, accost, greet, hail
salvo *Syn* BARRAGE, bombardment, cannonade, fusillade, hail, shower, storm, volley
same • not different or not differing from one another *Syn* equivalent, identic, identical, selfsame, tantamount, very *Rel* akin, alike, like, parallel, uniform *Ant* different
sample *Syn* EXAMPLE, case, exemplar, illustration, instance, representative, specimen
sanative *Syn* CURATIVE, corrective, remedial, restorative
sanctification *Syn* CONSECRATION, blessing, hallowing
sanctified *Syn* HOLY (sense 1), blessed, consecrated, hallowed, sacred, sacrosanct *Ant* unconsecrated, unhallowed
sanctimoniousness *Syn* HYPOCRISY, cant, dissembling, dissimulation, insincerity, piousness *Ant* genuineness, sincerity
sanction *vb* *Syn* APPROVE, accredit, certify, endorse *Ant* disapprove
sanction *n* *Syn* PERMISSION, allowance, authorization, clearance, concurrence, consent, granting, leave, license (*or* licence), sufferance *Ant* interdiction, prohibition, proscription
sanctity *Syn* HOLINESS, blessedness, devoutness, godliness, piety, piousness, sainthood, saintliness, saintship *Ant* godlessness, impiety, ungodliness, unholiness
sanctuary *Syn* SHELTER, asylum, cover, refuge, retreat
sand *Syn* FORTITUDE, backbone, grit, guts, pluck *Ant* pusillanimity
sandy *Syn* BLOND, fair, flaxen, golden, straw, tawny *Ant* dark
sane **1** • having full use of one's mind and control over one's actions *Syn* balanced, clearheaded, lucid, normal, right, stable *Rel* clear, logical, rational, reasonable *Ant* crazed, crazy, demented, deranged, insane, lunatic, mad, maniacal, mental, unbalanced, unsound **2** *Syn* WISE, judicious, prudent, sage, sapient, sensible *Ant* simple
sanguinary **1** *Syn* BLOODTHIRSTY, bloody, homicidal, murdering, murderous, sanguine **2** *Syn* BLOODY, gory, sanguine, sanguineous
sanguine **1** *Syn* BLOODTHIRSTY, bloody, homicidal, murdering, murderous, sanguinary **2** *Syn* BLOODY, gory, sanguinary, sanguineous **3** *Syn* CONFIDENT, assured, presumptuous, sure *Ant* apprehensive, diffident
sanguineous *Syn* BLOODY, gory, sanguinary, sanguine
sanitary **1** • free from filth, infection, or dangers to health *Syn* aseptic, germfree, hygienic, sterile *Rel* antibacterial, antiseptic, germicidal *Ant* insanitary, unhygienic, unsanitary **2** *Syn* HEALTHFUL, healthy, hygienic, salubrious, salutary, wholesome

sanitize *Syn* STERILIZE (sense 2), disinfect, fumigate
sap *n Syn* DUPE, chump, gull, pigeon, sucker, tool
sap *vb Syn* WEAKEN, debilitate, enervate, enfeeble, soften *Ant* strengthen
sapid *Syn* PALATABLE, appetizing, flavorsome, relishing, savory, tasty, toothsome *Ant* distasteful, unpalatable
sapient *Syn* WISE, judicious, prudent, sage, sane, sensible *Ant* simple
sappy *Syn* CORNY, maudlin, mawkish, mushy, saccharine, schmaltzy, sentimental, sloppy, sugarcoated, sugary *Ant* unsentimental
sarcasm **1** *Syn* INSULT, affront, barb, dart, dig, epithet, indignity, name, offense (*or* offence), outrage, put-down, slight, slur **2** *Syn* WIT, humor, irony, repartee, satire
sarcastic • marked by bitterness and a power or will to cut or sting *Syn* ironic, sardonic, satiric *Rel* biting, cutting, trenchant
sardonic *Syn* SARCASTIC, ironic, satiric
sass *Syn* BACK TALK, cheek, impertinence, impudence, insolence, sauce
sate *Syn* SATIATE, cloy, glut, gorge, pall, surfeit
satiate • to fill to repletion *Syn* cloy, glut, gorge, pall, sate, surfeit *Rel* content, satisfy
satin *Syn* GLOSSY, buffed, burnished, glistening, lustrous, polished, rubbed, satiny, sleek *Ant* dim, dull, flat, lusterless, matte
satiny **1** *Syn* GLOSSY, buffed, burnished, glistening, lustrous, polished, rubbed, satin, sleek *Ant* dim, dull, flat, lusterless, matte **2** *Syn* SLEEK, glossy, silken, silky, slick, velvety
satire *Syn* WIT, humor, irony, repartee, sarcasm
satiric *Syn* SARCASTIC, ironic, sardonic
satisfactoriness *Syn* SUFFICIENCY, acceptability, adequacy *Ant* inadequacy, insufficiency
satisfactory *Syn* ADEQUATE, acceptable, all right, decent, fine, OK (*or* okay), passable, respectable, tolerable *Ant* deficient, inadequate, lacking, unacceptable, unsatisfactory, wanting
satisfied *Syn* CONTENT, contented, gratified, happy, pleased *Ant* discontent, discontented, displeased, dissatisfied, malcontent, unhappy
satisfy **1** • to measure up to a set of criteria or requirements *Syn* answer, fulfill, meet *Rel* demonstrate, prove, test, try **2** *Syn* PAY, compensate, indemnify, recompense, reimburse, remunerate, repay **3** *Syn* PERSUADE, argue, convince, get, induce, move, prevail (on *or* upon), talk (into), win (over)
satisfying **1** *Syn* COGENT, compelling, conclusive, convincing, decisive, effective, forceful, persuasive, strong, telling *Ant* inconclusive, indecisive, ineffective, unconvincing **2** *Syn* HEARTWARMING, cheering, comforting, encouraging, fulfilling, gladdening, gratifying, heartening, rewarding *Ant* depressing, discouraging, disheartening, dispiriting
saturate **1** *Syn* PERMEATE, impenetrate, impregnate, interpenetrate, penetrate, pervade **2** *Syn* SOAK, drench, impregnate, sop, steep, waterlog
saturnine *Syn* SULLEN, crabbed, dour, gloomy, glum, morose, sulky, surly
sauce **1** *Syn* BACK TALK, cheek, impertinence, impudence, insolence, sass **2** *Syn* EFFRONTERY, audacity, brashness, brass, brassiness, brazenness, cheek, cheekiness, chutzpah, gall, nerve, nerviness, pertness, presumption, presumptuousness, sauciness, temerity
sauciness *Syn* EFFRONTERY, audacity, brashness, brass, brassiness, brazenness, cheek, cheekiness, chutzpah, gall, nerve, nerviness, pertness, presumption, presumptuousness, sauce, temerity
saucy • flippant and bold in manner or attitude *Syn* arch, pert *Rel* flippant, frivolous, light-minded, volatile
saunter *vb* • to walk slowly in an idle or aimless manner *Syn* amble, stroll
saunter *n Syn* WALK, constitutional, perambulation, ramble, range, stroll, turn
savage **1** *Syn* BARBARIAN, barbaric, barbarous *Ant* civilized **2** *Syn* FIERCE, barbarous, cruel, fell, ferocious, inhuman, truculent *Ant* mild, tame
savageness *Syn* CRUELTY, barbarity, brutality, cruelness, heartlessness, inhumanity, sadism, savagery, viciousness, wantonness *Ant* benignity, compassion, good-heartedness, humanity, kindheartedness, kindness, sympathy
savagery *Syn* CRUELTY, barbarity, brutality, cruelness, heartlessness, inhumanity, sadism, savageness, viciousness, wantonness *Ant* benignity, compassion, good-heartedness, humanity, kindheartedness, kindness, sympathy
savanna *Syn* PLAIN, down, grassland, prairie, steppe, tundra, veld (*or* veldt)
save **1** • to keep secure or maintain intact from injury, decay, or loss *Syn* conserve, preserve *Rel* enjoy, have, hold, own, possess *Ant* consume, spend **2** *Syn* ECONOMIZE, scrimp, skimp *Ant* waste **3** *Syn* RESCUE, deliver, ransom, reclaim, redeem
saver *Syn* SAVIOR, deliverer, redeemer, rescuer
savior *or* **saviour** • one that saves from danger or destruction *Syn* deliverer, redeemer, rescuer, saver *Rel* custodian, defender, guard, guardian, keeper, lookout, protector, sentinel, sentry, warden, warder, watch, watchman
savoir faire *Syn* TACT, address, poise *Ant* awkwardness
savor *Syn* TASTE (sense 1), flavor, relish, smack, tang *Ant* antipathy

savory 1 *Syn* FRAGRANT, ambrosial, aromatic, perfumed, redolent, scented, sweet *Ant* fetid, foul, malodorous, noisome, putrid, rancid, rank, reeking, reeky, smelly, stinking, stinky, strong 2 *Syn* PALATABLE, appetizing, flavorsome, relishing, sapid, tasty, toothsome *Ant* distasteful, unpalatable

saw *Syn* SAYING, adage, aphorism, apothegm, epigram, maxim, motto, proverb

say 1 • to express in words *Syn* state, tell, utter *Rel* articulate, enunciate, pronounce 2 *Syn* PHRASE, articulate, clothe, couch, express, formulate, put, state, word

saying • an often repeated statement that usually is brief and expresses a common observation or general truth *Syn* adage, aphorism, apothegm, epigram, maxim, motto, proverb, saw

scabrous *Syn* ROUGH, harsh, rugged, uneven *Ant* smooth

scamp *Syn* VILLAIN, blackguard, knave, miscreant, rapscallion, rascal, rogue, scoundrel

scamper *Syn* SCUTTLE, scurry, skedaddle, sprint

scan *n Syn* INSPECTION, audit, check, checkup, examination, review, scrutiny, survey

scan *vb Syn* SCRUTINIZE, audit, examine, inspect

scandal 1 *Syn* DETRACTION, backbiting, calumny, slander 2 *Syn* OFFENSE (sense 2), crime, sin, vice

scandalous *Syn* LIBELOUS, defamatory, slanderous

scant *Syn* MEAGER, exiguous, scanty, scrimpy, skimpy, spare, sparse *Ant* ample, copious

scantiness *Syn* DEFICIENCY, dearth, deficit, failure, famine, inadequacy, insufficiency, lack, paucity, poverty, scarceness, scarcity, shortage, want *Ant* abundance, adequacy, amplitude, plenitude, plenty, sufficiency

scanty *Syn* MEAGER, exiguous, scant, scrimpy, skimpy, spare, sparse *Ant* ample, copious

scar *Syn* BLEMISH, defect, deformity, disfigurement, fault, flaw, imperfection, mark, pockmark

scarce *Syn* INFREQUENT, occasional, rare, sporadic, uncommon *Ant* frequent

scarceness *Syn* DEFICIENCY, dearth, deficit, failure, famine, inadequacy, insufficiency, lack, paucity, poverty, scantiness, scarcity, shortage, want *Ant* abundance, adequacy, amplitude, plenitude, plenty, sufficiency

scarcity *Syn* DEFICIENCY, dearth, deficit, failure, famine, inadequacy, insufficiency, lack, paucity, poverty, scantiness, scarceness, shortage, want *Ant* abundance, adequacy, amplitude, plenitude, plenty, sufficiency

scare *Syn* FRIGHTEN, affray, affright, alarm, fright, startle, terrify, terrorize *Ant* reassure

scathe *Syn* ATTACK (sense 2), abuse, assail, belabor, blast, castigate, excoriate, jump (on), lambaste (*or* lambast), slam, vituperate

scathing *Syn* CAUSTIC, acrid, mordant *Ant* genial

scatter 1 • to cause to separate or break up *Syn* dispel, disperse, dissipate *Rel* cast, fling, throw, toss 2 • to cover by or as if by scattering something over or on *Syn* bestrew, dot, pepper, sow, spray, sprinkle, strew *Rel* blanket, dust 3 *Syn* STREW, broadcast, sow, straw

scent *Syn* SMELL, aroma, odor

scented *Syn* FRAGRANT, ambrosial, aromatic, perfumed, redolent, savory, sweet *Ant* fetid, foul, malodorous, noisome, putrid, rancid, rank, reeking, reeky, smelly, stinking, stinky, strong

schedule 1 *Syn* LIST, catalog, inventory, register, roll, roster, table 2 *Syn* PROGRAM, agenda, timetable

scheme *n* 1 *Syn* PLAN, design, plot, project 2 *Syn* SYSTEM, complex, network, organism *Ant* chaos

scheme *vb* 1 *Syn* PLAN, design, plot, project 2 *Syn* PLOT, conspire, contrive, intrigue, machinate

schism 1 *Syn* DISCORD, conflict, contention, difference, dissension, strife, variance 2 *Syn* BREACH, break, rent, rift, rupture, split

schismatic *Syn* HERETIC, dissenter, nonconformist, sectarian, sectary *Ant* conformer, conformist

schmaltzy *Syn* CORNY, maudlin, mawkish, mushy, saccharine, sappy, sentimental, sloppy, sugarcoated, sugary *Ant* unsentimental

scholar 1 *Syn* EXPERT, ace, adept, artist, authority, crackerjack, maestro, master, past master, shark, virtuoso, whiz, wizard *Ant* amateur 2 *Syn* STUDENT, pupil

scholarly 1 *Syn* ACADEMIC, educational, scholastic *Ant* nonacademic, unacademic 2 *Syn* EDUCATED, erudite, knowledgeable, learned, literate, well-read *Ant* ignorant, illiterate, uneducated 3 *Syn* LEARNED, erudite

scholarship 1 *Syn* EDUCATION (sense 2), erudition, knowledge, learnedness, learning, science 2 *Syn* KNOWLEDGE, erudition, information, learning, lore, science *Ant* ignorance

scholastic 1 *Syn* ACADEMIC, educational, scholarly *Ant* nonacademic, unacademic 2 *Syn* PEDANTIC, academic, bookish

school *Syn* TEACH, discipline, educate, instruct, train

schooling *Syn* EDUCATION (sense 1), instruction, teaching, training, tutelage, tutoring

schoolteacher *Syn* TEACHER, educator, instructor, pedagogue, preceptor

science 1 *Syn* EDUCATION (sense 2), erudition, knowledge, learnedness, learning, scholarship 2 *Syn* KNOWLEDGE, erudition, information, learning, lore, scholarship *Ant* ignorance

scintillate *Syn* FLASH, coruscate, glance, gleam, glint, glisten, glitter, sparkle, twinkle

scoff • to show one's contempt in derision or mockery *Syn* fleer, flout, gibe, gird, jeer, sneer *Rel* deride, mock, ridicule, taunt
scold *vb* • to reproach angrily and abusively *Syn* bawl, berate, chew out, jaw, rail, rate, revile, tongue-lash, upbraid, vituperate, wig *Rel* blame, censure, criticize, reprehend, reprobate
scold *n Syn* CRITIC, carper, castigator, caviler (*or* caviller), censurer, faultfinder, nitpicker, railer
scoop *Syn* DIP (sense 2), bail, dish, ladle, spoon
scoot *Syn* HURRY (sense 2), barrel, bolt, bowl, breeze, career, course, dash, fly, hasten, hotfoot (it), hump, hurtle, hustle, pelt, race, rip, rocket, run, rush, rustle, scurry, scuttle, shoot, speed, step (along), tear, trot, whirl, whisk, zip, zoom *Ant* crawl, creep, poke
scope *Syn* RANGE, compass, gamut, horizon, ken, orbit, purview, radius, reach, sweep
scorch *Syn* BURN, char, sear, singe
scorn *vb* **1** • to ignore in a disrespectful manner *Syn* despise, disregard, flout *Rel* dismiss, forget, ignore, neglect, overlook, overpass, pass over, slight, slur (over) **2** • to show contempt for *Syn* disdain, high-hat, slight, sniff (at), snub *Rel* scout *Ant* honor, respect **3** *Syn* DESPISE, contemn, disdain, scout *Ant* appreciate
scorn *n Syn* CONTEMPT, despite, despitefulness, disdain *Ant* admiration, esteem, regard, respect
scoundrel *Syn* VILLAIN, blackguard, knave, miscreant, rapscallion, rascal, rogue, scamp
scour *Syn* SEEK, comb, ferret out, hunt, ransack, rummage, search
scout *Syn* DESPISE, contemn, disdain, scorn *Ant* appreciate
scowl *vb Syn* FROWN, glare, gloom, glower, lower *Ant* beam, smile
scowl *n Syn* GRIMACE, face, frown, lower, mouth, pout
scramble *Syn* DISORDER, confuse, derange, disarrange, disarray, discompose, dishevel, dislocate, disorganize, disrupt, disturb, hash, jumble, mess (up), mix (up), muddle, muss, rumple, shuffle, tousle, tumble, upset *Ant* arrange, array, draw up, marshal, order, organize, range, regulate, straighten (up), tidy
scrap *Syn* DISCARD, cast, junk, molt, shed, slough
scrape *vb* • to rub or slide against something that is harsh, rough, or sharp *Syn* grate, grind, rasp, scratch
scrape *n* **1** *Syn* PREDICAMENT, dilemma, fix, jam, pickle, plight, quandary **2** *Syn* BRAWL, broil, fracas, melee, row, rumpus
scrappiness *Syn* BELLIGERENCE, aggression, aggressiveness, bellicosity, combativeness, contentiousness, disputatiousness, fight, militancy, pugnacity, truculence *Ant* pacifism
scrappy *Syn* BELLIGERENT, aggressive, argumentative, bellicose, combative, contentious, discordant, disputatious, gladiatorial, militant, pugnacious, quarrelsome, truculent, warlike *Ant* nonbelligerent, pacific, peaceable, peaceful
scratch *Syn* SCRAPE, grate, grind, rasp
scrawny *Syn* LEAN, angular, gaunt, lank, lanky, rawboned, skinny, spare *Ant* fleshy
scream *vb* **1** • to cry out loudly and emotionally *Syn* howl, screech, shriek, shrill, squall, squeal, yell, yelp *Rel* bawl, bay, call, caterwaul, cry, holler, keen, shout, squawk, vociferate, wail, yawp (*or* yaup), yowl **2** *Syn* SHOUT, holler, screech, shriek, squeal, whoop, yell
scream *n Syn* SHOUT, holler, screech, shriek, squeal, whoop, yell
screech *vb* **1** *Syn* SCREAM, howl, shriek, shrill, squall, squeal, yell, yelp **2** *Syn* SHOUT, holler, scream, shriek, squeal, whoop, yell
screech *n Syn* SHOUT, holler, scream, shriek, squeal, whoop, yell
screeching *Syn* SHRILL, acute, high-pitched, piping, shrieking, squeaking, squeaky, treble, whistling *Ant* bass, deep, low, throaty
screen *vb Syn* HIDE, bury, cache, conceal, ensconce, secrete
screen *n Syn* MOVIE (sense 2), cinema, film, motion pictures, pictures
screwball *Syn* ECCENTRIC, character, codger, crackbrain, crackpot, crank, kook, nut, oddball, weirdo
screwlike *Syn* SPIRAL, coiling, corkscrew, helical, winding
scrimp *Syn* ECONOMIZE, save, skimp *Ant* waste
scrimping *n Syn* ECONOMY, frugality, husbandry, providence, skimping, thrift *Ant* wastefulness
scrimping *adj Syn* FRUGAL, economical, economizing, provident, sparing, thrifty *Ant* prodigal, wasteful
scrimpy *Syn* MEAGER, exiguous, scant, scanty, skimpy, spare, sparse *Ant* ample, copious
scruple *vb Syn* DEMUR, balk, boggle, jib, shy, stick, stickle, strain *Ant* accede
scruple *n Syn* QUALM, compunction, misgiving
scrupulous **1** *Syn* CAREFUL, meticulous, punctilious, punctual *Ant* careless **2** *Syn* UPRIGHT, conscientious, honest, honorable, just
scrutinize • to look at or over *Syn* audit, examine, inspect, scan *Rel* consider, study, weigh
scrutiny *Syn* INSPECTION, audit, check, checkup, examination, review, scan, survey
scud *Syn* FLY, dart, float, sail, shoot, skim
scuffle *Syn* WRESTLE, grapple, tussle
sculpt *Syn* CARVE, chisel, engrave, etch, incise, sculpture

sculpture *Syn* CARVE, chisel, engrave, etch, incise, sculpt
scum *Syn* FOAM, froth, lather, spume, suds, yeast
scurrility *Syn* ABUSE, billingsgate, invective, obloquy, vituperation *Ant* adulation
scurrilous *Syn* ABUSIVE, contumelious, opprobrious, vituperative *Ant* complementary, respectful
scurry **1** *Syn* HURRY (sense 2), barrel, bolt, bowl, breeze, career, course, dash, fly, hasten, hotfoot (it), hump, hurtle, hustle, pelt, race, rip, rocket, run, rush, rustle, scoot, scuttle, shoot, speed, step (along), tear, trot, whirl, whisk, zip, zoom *Ant* crawl, creep, poke **2** *Syn* SCUTTLE, scamper, skedaddle, sprint
scurvy *Syn* CONTEMPTIBLE, beggarly, cheap, despicable, pitiable, shabby, sorry *Ant* admirable, estimable, formidable
scuttle **1** • to move with or as if with short brisk steps *Syn* scamper, scurry, skedaddle, sprint *Rel* charge, dash, rush, shoot, tear **2** *Syn* HURRY (sense 2), barrel, bolt, bowl, breeze, career, course, dash, fly, hasten, hotfoot (it), hump, hurtle, hustle, pelt, race, rip, rocket, run, rush, rustle, scoot, scurry, shoot, speed, step (along), tear, trot, whirl, whisk, zip, zoom *Ant* crawl, creep, poke
seaman *Syn* MARINER, bluejacket, gob, sailor, tar
sear *Syn* BURN, char, scorch, singe
search *Syn* SEEK, comb, ferret out, hunt, ransack, rummage, scour
season *Syn* HARDEN (sense 2), acclimate, acclimatize *Ant* soften
seasonable • done or occurring at a good, suitable, or proper time *Syn* opportune, pat, timely, well-timed *Rel* apposite, apropos, pertinent, relevant *Ant* unseasonable
seat **1** *Syn* BUTTOCKS, backside, bottom, breech, butt, fanny, hams, haunches, posterior, rear, rump **2** *Syn* CENTER (sense 2), base, capital, core, cynosure, eye, focus, heart, hub, mecca, nucleus
seclude *Syn* ISOLATE, insulate, segregate, sequester
secluded • hidden from view *Syn* cloistered, covert, isolated, quiet, remote, retired, secret, sheltered *Rel* lonely, reclusive, solitary
secludedness *Syn* ISOLATION, insulation, seclusion, segregation, separateness, sequestration, solitariness, solitude
seclusion *Syn* ISOLATION, insulation, secludedness, segregation, separateness, sequestration, solitariness, solitude
second *Syn* INSTANT, flash, jiffy, minute, moment, shake, split second, trice, twinkle, twinkling, wink
secondary *Syn* SUBORDINATE, collateral, dependent, subject, tributary *Ant* chief, dominant, leading
second-rate *Syn* MEDIUM, average, fair, indifferent, mediocre, middling, moderate
secret **1** • done without attracting observation *Syn* clandestine, covert, furtive, stealthy, surreptitious, underhand, underhanded *Rel* arcane, inscrutable, mysterious **2** *Syn* SECLUDED, cloistered, covert, isolated, quiet, remote, retired, sheltered
secrete *Syn* HIDE, bury, cache, conceal, ensconce, screen
secretive **1** • given to keeping one's activities hidden from public observation or knowledge *Syn* close, closemouthed, dark, reticent, uncommunicative *Rel* quiet, reserved, silent, taciturn, tight-lipped *Ant* communicative, open **2** *Syn* SILENT (sense 1), close, close-lipped, closemouthed, reserved, reticent, taciturn, tight-lipped, uncommunicative *Ant* talkative
sect **1** *Syn* FACTION, bloc, body, coalition, party, set, side, wing **2** *Syn* RELIGION, church, communion, creed, denomination, faith, persuasion
section *Syn* PART, detail, division, fraction, fragment, member, parcel, piece, portion, sector, segment *Ant* whole
sector *Syn* PART, detail, division, fraction, fragment, member, parcel, piece, portion, section, segment *Ant* whole
secular *Syn* PROFANE, lay, temporal *Ant* sacred
secure **1** • to fasten or fix firmly *Syn* anchor, moor, rivet *Rel* establish, fix, set, settle **2** *Syn* EARN, acquire, attain, capture, carry, draw, gain, garner, get, land, make, obtain, procure, realize, win *Ant* forfeit, lose **3** *Syn* ENSURE, assure, cinch, guarantee, guaranty, insure **4** *Syn* GET, gain, obtain, procure, win
security **1** *Syn* GUARANTEE, bail, bond, guaranty, surety **2** *Syn* SAFETY, protection, safeness *Ant* danger, distress, endangerment, imperilment, jeopardy, peril, trouble
sedate *Syn* SERIOUS, earnest, grave, sober, solemn, somber, staid *Ant* flippant, light
sediment *Syn* DEPOSIT, dregs, grounds, lees, precipitate
seditious *Syn* INSUBORDINATE, contumacious, factious, mutinous, rebellious
seduce *Syn* LURE, allure, beguile, decoy, entice, lead on, tempt
seductress *Syn* SIREN, enchantress, temptress
sedulous *Syn* BUSY, assiduous, diligent, industrious *Ant* idle, unoccupied
see **1** • to take cognizance of by physical or mental vision *Syn* behold, contemplate, descry, discern, espy, note, notice, observe, perceive, remark, survey, view *Rel* examine, inspect, scan, scrutinize **2** • to perceive something by means of the eyes *Syn* look, watch *Rel* gape, gaze, glare, stare
seeable *Syn* VISIBLE, apparent, observable, visual *Ant* invisible, unseeable

seedy *Syn* SHABBY, dilapidated, dingy, faded, threadbare
seek **1** • to look for *Syn* comb, ferret out, hunt, ransack, rummage, scour, search *Rel* ask, inquire, interrogate, question **2** *Syn* ATTEMPT, assay, endeavor, essay, strive, try
seeker *Syn* CANDIDATE, applicant, aspirant, campaigner, contender, hopeful, prospect
seem • to give the impression of being *Syn* act, appear, look, make, sound *Rel* dissemble, pretend
seeming *Syn* APPARENT, illusory, ostensible *Ant* real
seemingly *Syn* APPARENTLY, evidently, ostensibly, presumably, supposedly
seemliness *Syn* APPROPRIATENESS, aptness, felicitousness, fitness, fittingness, rightness, suitability, suitableness *Ant* inappropriateness, inaptness, infelicity, unfitness
seemly *Syn* DECOROUS, decent, nice, proper *Ant* blatant, indecorous
seep *Syn* EXUDE, bleed, ooze, percolate, strain, sweat, weep
seer *Syn* PROPHET, augur, diviner, forecaster, foreseer, foreteller, fortune-teller, futurist, prognosticator, prophesier, soothsayer
seethe *Syn* BOIL, parboil, simmer, stew
segment *Syn* PART, detail, division, fraction, fragment, member, parcel, piece, portion, section, sector *Ant* whole
segregate *Syn* ISOLATE, insulate, seclude, sequester
segregation *Syn* ISOLATION, insulation, secludedness, seclusion, separateness, sequestration, solitariness, solitude
seize *Syn* TAKE, clutch, grab, grasp, snatch
seizure *Syn* ATTACK (sense 3), bout, case, fit, siege, spell
seldom • not often *Syn* infrequently, little, rarely *Rel* ne'er, never *Ant* frequently, often
select *adj* • chosen from a number or group by fitness, superiority, or preference *Syn* elect, exclusive, picked *Rel* choice, dainty, delicate, exquisite, rare, recherché *Ant* indiscriminate
select *vb* *Syn* CHOOSE, cull, elect, opt, pick, prefer, single *Ant* eschew, reject
selection *Syn* CHOICE, alternative, election, option, preference
selective • tending to select carefully *Syn* choosy (*or* choosey), particular, picky *Rel* fastidious, finicky, fussy *Ant* nonselective
self-abnegation *Syn* RENUNCIATION, abnegation, self-denial *Ant* indulgence, self-indulgence
self-admiration *Syn* COMPLACENCE, complacency, conceit, conceitedness, ego, egotism, pompousness, pride, pridefulness, self-conceit, self-esteem, self-importance, self-satisfaction, smugness, vaingloriousness, vainglory, vainness, vanity *Ant* humbleness, humility, modesty
self-assertive *Syn* AGGRESSIVE (sense 1), assertive, militant, pushing, pushy
self-assurance *Syn* CONFIDENCE, aplomb, assurance, self-confidence, self-possession *Ant* diffidence
self-centered *Syn* EGOCENTRIC, egoistic, egotistic (*or* egotistical), selfish, self-seeking *Ant* selfless
self-complacent *Syn* COMPLACENT, priggish, self-satisfied, smug
self-conceit *Syn* COMPLACENCE, complacency, conceit, conceitedness, ego, egotism, pompousness, pride, pridefulness, self-admiration, self-esteem, self-importance, self-satisfaction, smugness, vaingloriousness, vainglory, vainness, vanity *Ant* humbleness, humility, modesty
self-conceited *Syn* CONCEITED, complacent, egoistic, egotistic (*or* egotistical), important, overweening, pompous, prideful, proud, self-important, self-satisfied, smug, stuck-up, vain, vainglorious *Ant* humble, modest
self-confidence *Syn* CONFIDENCE, aplomb, assurance, self-assurance, self-possession *Ant* diffidence
self-denial *Syn* RENUNCIATION, abnegation, self-abnegation *Ant* indulgence, self-indulgence
self-esteem **1** *Syn* COMPLACENCE, complacency, conceit, conceitedness, ego, egotism, pompousness, pride, pridefulness, self-admiration, self-conceit, self-importance, self-satisfaction, smugness, vaingloriousness, vainglory, vainness, vanity *Ant* humbleness, humility, modesty **2** *Syn* CONCEIT, amour propre, egoism, egotism, self-love *Ant* humility
self-governing *Syn* DEMOCRATIC, popular, republican, self-ruling *Ant* undemocratic
self-importance *Syn* ARROGANCE, haughtiness, imperiousness, loftiness, lordliness, masterfulness, peremptoriness, pompousness, presumptuousness, pretense (*or* pretence), pretension, pretentiousness, superciliousness, superiority *Ant* humility, modesty
self-importance *Syn* COMPLACENCE, complacency, conceit, conceitedness, ego, egotism, pompousness, pride, pridefulness, self-admiration, self-conceit, self-esteem, self-satisfaction, smugness, vaingloriousness, vainglory, vainness, vanity *Ant* humbleness, humility, modesty
self-important *Syn* CONCEITED, complacent, egoistic, egotistic (*or* egotistical), important, overweening, pompous, prideful, proud, self-conceited, self-satisfied, smug, stuck-up, vain, vainglorious *Ant* humble, modest
selfish *Syn* EGOCENTRIC, egoistic, egotistic (*or* egotistical), self-centered, self-seeking *Ant* selfless
self-love *Syn* CONCEIT, amour propre, egoism, egotism, self-esteem *Ant* humility

self-possession 1 *Syn* CONFIDENCE, aplomb, assurance, self-assurance, self-confidence *Ant* diffidence 2 *Syn* EQUANIMITY, aplomb, calmness, composure, coolheadedness, coolness, imperturbability, placidity, serenity, tranquillity (*or* tranquility) *Ant* agitation, discomposure, perturbation
self-reliant *Syn* SELF-SUFFICIENT, independent, self-supporting *Ant* dependent, reliant
self-ruling *Syn* DEMOCRATIC, popular, republican, self-governing *Ant* undemocratic
selfsame *Syn* SAME, equal, equivalent, identic, identical, tantamount, very *Ant* different
self-satisfaction *Syn* COMPLACENCE, complacency, conceit, conceitedness, ego, egotism, pompousness, pride, pridefulness, self-admiration, self-conceit, self-esteem, self-importance, smugness, vaingloriousness, vainglory, vainness, vanity *Ant* humbleness, humility, modesty
self-satisfied 1 *Syn* COMPLACENT, priggish, self-complacent, smug 2 *Syn* CONCEITED, complacent, egoistic, egotistic (*or* egotistical), important, overweening, pompous, prideful, proud, self-conceited, self-important, smug, stuck-up, vain, vainglorious *Ant* humble, modest
self-seeking *Syn* EGOCENTRIC, egoistic, egotistic (*or* egotistical), self-centered, selfish *Ant* selfless
self-sufficient • able to take care of oneself without outside help *Syn* independent, self-reliant, self-supporting *Rel* potent, powerful, resilient, strong *Ant* dependent, reliant
self-supporting *Syn* SELF-SUFFICIENT, independent, self-reliant *Ant* dependent, reliant
self-willed *Syn* OBSTINATE, adamant, adamantine, dogged, hard, hardened, hardheaded, hardhearted, headstrong, immovable, implacable, inflexible, mulish, obdurate, opinionated, ossified, pat, peevish, pertinacious, perverse, pigheaded, rigid, stubborn, unbending, uncompromising, unrelenting, unyielding, willful (*or* wilful) *Ant* acquiescent, agreeable, amenable, compliant, complying, flexible, pliable, pliant, relenting, yielding
sell *Syn* MARKET, deal (in), merchandise, put up, retail, vend *Ant* buy, purchase
sellout *Syn* BETRAYAL, disloyalty, double cross, faithlessness, falseness, falsity, infidelity, perfidy, treachery, treason, unfaithfulness
semblance *Syn* APPEARANCE, aspect, look
send • to cause to go or be taken from one place, person or condition to another *Syn* dispatch, forward, remit, route, ship, transmit *Rel* quicken, speed *Ant* accept, receive
senescence *Syn* AGE (sense 1), dotage, senility
senility *Syn* AGE (sense 1), dotage, senescence
senior *adj Syn* ELDERLY, aged, aging, ancient, geriatric, long-lived, old, older *Ant* young, youthful
senior *n Syn* SUPERIOR, better, elder *Ant* inferior, subordinate, underling
senior citizen • a person of advanced years *Syn* ancient, elder, golden-ager, oldster, old-timer *Rel* senior *Ant* youngster, youth
sensation 1 • awareness (as of heat or pain) due to stimulation of a sense organ *Syn* image, percept, sense-datum, sensum *Rel* impress, impression, print, stamp 2 • the power to respond or an act of responding to stimuli *Syn* feeling, sense, sensibility *Rel* palpability, palpableness, perceptibility, perceptibleness, ponderability, ponderableness, tangibility, tangibleness
sensational *Syn* EXCELLENT, A1, bang-up, banner, capital, classic, crackerjack, dandy, divine, fabulous, fine, first-class, first-rate, grand, great, groovy, heavenly, jim-dandy, keen, marvelous (*or* marvellous), mean, neat, nifty, noble, par excellence, prime, splendid, stellar, sterling, superb, superior, superlative, supernal, swell, terrific, tip-top, top, top-notch, unsurpassed, wonderful *Ant* poor
sense 1 • the ability to reach intelligent conclusions *Syn* common sense, good sense, gumption, horse sense, judgment, wisdom *Rel* discretion, foresight, prudence 2 *Syn* COMMON SENSE, discreetness, discretion, horse sense, levelheadedness, prudence, sense, sensibleness, wisdom, wit *Ant* imprudence, indiscretion 3 *Syn* MEANING, acceptation, import, significance, signification 4 *Syn* SENSATION (sense 2), feeling, sensibility
sense-datum *Syn* SENSATION (sense 1), image, percept, sensum
senseless *Syn* MEANINGLESS, empty, inane, pointless *Ant* meaningful
sensibility *Syn* SENSATION (sense 2), feeling, sense
sensible 1 *Syn* AWARE, alive, awake, cognizant, conscious *Ant* unaware 2 *Syn* CONSCIOUS, alive, aware, cognizant, mindful, sentient *Ant* insensible, unaware, unconscious, unmindful 3 *Syn* MATERIAL, corporeal, objective, phenomenal, physical *Ant* immaterial 4 *Syn* PERCEPTIBLE, appreciable, detectable, discernible, distinguishable, palpable *Ant* impalpable, imperceptible, inappreciable, indistinguishable, insensible 5 *Syn* WISE, judicious, prudent, sage, sane, sapient *Ant* simple
sensibleness *Syn* COMMON SENSE, discreetness, discretion, horse sense, levelheadedness, prudence, sense, wisdom, wit *Ant* imprudence, indiscretion
sensitive 1 *Syn* LIABLE, exposed, open, prone, subject, susceptible *Ant* exempt, immune 2 *Syn* SENTIENT, impressible, impressionable, responsive, susceptible

sensual *Syn* CARNAL, animal, fleshly *Ant* intellectual, spiritual

sensum *Syn* SENSATION (sense 1), image, percept, sense-datum

sensuous • relating to or providing pleasure through gratification of the senses *Syn* epicurean, luxurious, sybaritic, voluptuous *Rel* imaginal, sensational

sentence • to decree the fate or punishment of one adjudged guilty, unworthy, or unfit *Syn* condemn, damn, doom, proscribe *Rel* adjudge, adjudicate, judge

sentient **1** • readily affected by external stimuli *Syn* impressible, impressionable, responsive, sensitive, susceptible **2** *Syn* CONSCIOUS, alive, aware, cognizant, mindful, sensible *Ant* insensible, unaware, unconscious, unmindful

sentiment **1** *Syn* FEELING, affection, emotion, passion **2** *Syn* OPINION, belief, conviction, persuasion, view

sentimental **1** • unduly or affectedly emotional *Syn* maudlin, mawkish, mushy, romantic, slushy, soppy *Rel* affectionate, emotional, feeling, passionate **2** *Syn* CORNY, maudlin, mawkish, mushy, saccharine, sappy, schmaltzy, sloppy, sugarcoated, sugary *Ant* unsentimental

separate *vb* • to become or cause to become disunited or disjoined *Syn* divide, divorce, part, sever, sunder *Rel* cleave, rend, rive, split, tear *Ant* combine

separate *adj* **1** *Syn* DISTINCT, discrete, several **2** *Syn* SINGLE, lone, particular, sole, solitary, unique *Ant* accompanied, conjugal, supported

separateness *Syn* ISOLATION, insulation, secludedness, seclusion, segregation, sequestration, solitariness, solitude

sequel *Syn* EFFECT, aftereffect, aftermath, consequence, event, issue, outcome, result, upshot *Ant* cause

sequence *Syn* SUCCESSION, chain, progression, series, string, train

sequent *Syn* CONSECUTIVE, sequential, serial, successive *Ant* inconsecutive

sequential *Syn* CONSECUTIVE, sequent, serial, successive *Ant* inconsecutive

sequester *Syn* ISOLATE, insulate, seclude, segregate

sequestration *Syn* ISOLATION, insulation, secludedness, seclusion, segregation, separateness, solitariness, solitude

serene *Syn* CALM, halcyon, peaceful, placid, tranquil *Ant* agitated, stormy

sereneness *Syn* CALM, calmness, hush, peace, peacefulness, placidity, quiet, quietness, quietude, repose, restfulness, serenity, still, stillness, tranquillity (*or* tranquility) *Ant* bustle, commotion, hubbub, hurly-burly, pandemonium, tumult, turmoil, uproar

serenity **1** *Syn* CALM, calmness, hush, peace, peacefulness, placidity, quiet, quietness, quietude, repose, restfulness, sereneness, still, stillness, tranquillity (*or* tranquility) *Ant* bustle, commotion, hubbub, hurly-burly, pandemonium, tumult, turmoil, uproar **2** *Syn* EQUANIMITY, aplomb, calmness, composure, coolheadedness, coolness, imperturbability, placidity, self-possession, tranquillity (*or* tranquility) *Ant* agitation, discomposure, perturbation

serial *Syn* CONSECUTIVE, sequent, sequential, successive *Ant* inconsecutive

series *Syn* SUCCESSION, chain, progression, sequence, string, train

serious • not light or frivolous (as in disposition, appearance, or manner) *Syn* earnest, grave, sedate, sober, solemn, somber, staid *Rel* ascetic, austere, severe, stern *Ant* flippant, light

seriousness *Syn* EARNESTNESS, gravity, intentness, soberness, sobriety, solemnity *Ant* frivolity, levity, lightheartedness

sermon *Syn* SPEECH, address, harangue, homily, lecture, oration, talk

serpentine *Syn* WINDING, flexuous, sinuous, tortuous *Ant* straight

servant • a person hired to perform household or personal services *Syn* domestic, flunky, lackey, menial, retainer, steward *Rel* butler, footman, handmaiden, houseboy, maid, maidservant, majordomo, man, manservant, servitor, valet, woman *Ant* master

serve *Syn* FUNCTION, act, perform, work

service *Syn* USE (sense 1), account, advantage, avail, profit

servile *Syn* SUBSERVIENT, menial, obsequious, slavish *Ant* domineering, overbearing

set *vb* **1** • to position (something) in a specified place *Syn* establish, fix, settle *Rel* implant **2** *Syn* APPOINT (sense 1), designate, fix, name *Ant* discharge, dismiss, expel, fire **3** *Syn* COAGULATE, clot, congeal, curdle, jell, jelly

set *n* *Syn* FACTION, bloc, body, coalition, party, sect, side, wing

set in *Syn* BEGIN (sense 1), arise, commence, dawn, form, materialize, originate, spring, start *Ant* cease, end, stop

set off *Syn* ACTIVATE, actuate, crank (up), drive, move, propel, run, spark, start, touch off, trigger, turn on *Ant* cut, deactivate, kill, shut off, turn off

settee *Syn* COUCH, chesterfield, davenport, divan, lounge, sofa

setting *Syn* BACKGROUND, backdrop, environment, milieu, mise-en-scène

settle **1** *Syn* ALIGHT, land, light, perch, roost, touch down *Ant* take off **2** *Syn* CALM, compose, lull, quiet, quieten, soothe, still, tranquilize *Ant* agitate, arouse **3** *Syn* DECIDE, determine, resolve, rule **4** *Syn* SET, establish, fix

set up *Syn* BUILD, assemble, construct, erect, fabricate, make, make up, piece, put up, raise, rear *Ant* disassemble, dismantle, take down

sever *Syn* SEPARATE, divide, divorce, part, sunder *Ant* combine

several **1** *Syn* DISTINCT, discrete, separate **2** *Syn* MANY, divers, multifarious, numerous, sundry, various *Ant* few

severally *Syn* EACH, apiece, individually, respectively

severe • given to or marked by strict discipline and firm restraint *Syn* ascetic, austere, stern *Rel* burdensome, exacting, onerous, oppressive *Ant* tender, tolerant

severity • the quality or state of being demanding or unyielding (as in discipline or criticism) *Syn* hardness, harshness, inflexibility, rigidity, rigidness, rigorousness, sternness, strictness *Rel* hardheartedness, implacability, obduracy *Ant* flexibility, gentleness, laxness, mildness

shabby **1** being ill-kept and showing signs of wear and tear *Syn* dilapidated, dingy, faded, seedy, threadbare *Rel* haggard, worn **2** *Syn* CONTEMPTIBLE, beggarly, cheap, despicable, pitiable, scurvy, sorry *Ant* admirable, estimable, formidable

shack • a small, simply constructed, and often temporary dwelling *Syn* cabin, camp, hovel, hut, hutch, shanty *Rel* lean-to, shed

shackle *Syn* HAMPER, clog, fetter, hog-tie, manacle, trammel *Ant* assist (*persons*), expedite (*work, projects*)

shackles *Syn* ENCUMBRANCE, bar, block, chain, clog, crimp, deterrent, drag, embarrassment, fetter, handicap, hindrance, hurdle, impediment, inhibition, interference, let, manacle, obstacle, obstruction, stop, stumbling block, trammel *Ant* aid, assistance, benefit, help

shade **1** • comparative darkness or obscurity due to interception of light rays *Syn* adumbration, penumbra, shadow, umbra, umbrage *Rel* darkness, dimness, obscurity **2** *Syn* COLOR, hue, tinge, tint, tone **3** *Syn* GHOST, apparition, bogey, phantasm, phantom, poltergeist, shadow, specter (*or* spectre), spirit, spook, vision, wraith **4** *Syn* GRADATION, nuance **5** *Syn* TOUCH, dash, smack, soupçon, spice, strain, streak, suggestion, suspicion, tincture, tinge, vein

shadow *n* **1** *Syn* GHOST, apparition, bogey, phantasm, phantom, poltergeist, shade, specter (*or* spectre), spirit, spook, vision, wraith **2** *Syn* SHADE, adumbration, penumbra, umbra, umbrage **3** *Syn* VESTIGE, relic, trace

shadow *vb* *Syn* SUGGEST (sense 2), adumbrate *Ant* manifest

shadowing *Syn* PURSUIT, chase, chasing, dogging, following, hounding, pursuing, tagging, tailing, tracing, tracking, trailing

shaggy **1** *Syn* HAIRY (sense 1), bristly, fleecy, furry, hirsute, rough, woolly *Ant* bald, furless, hairless, shorn, smooth **2** *Syn* HAIRY (sense 2), furry, fuzzy, rough, woolly

shake *vb* **1** • to exhibit vibratory, wavering, or oscillating movement often as an evidence of instability *Syn* dither, quake, quaver, quiver, shimmy, shiver, shudder, teeter, totter, tremble, wobble *Rel* fluctuate, oscillate, sway, swing, vibrate, waver **2** • to move up and down or to and fro with some violence *Syn* agitate, convulse, rock *Rel* drive, impel, move **3** *Syn* SWING (sense 1), brandish, flourish, thrash, wave

shake *n* *Syn* INSTANT, flash, jiffy, minute, moment, second, split second, trice, twinkle, twinkling, wink

shall *Syn* NEED (sense 1), have (to), must, ought (to), should *Ant* have, hold

shallow *Syn* SUPERFICIAL, cursory, uncritical *Ant* deep, profound

sham *vb* *Syn* ASSUME, affect, counterfeit, feign, pretend, simulate

sham *adj* **1** *Syn* COUNTERFEIT, bogus, fake, phony, pinchbeck, pseudo, spurious *Ant* bona fide, genuine **2** *Syn* IMITATION, artificial, bogus, factitious, fake, false, man-made, mimic, mock, simulated, substitute, synthetic *Ant* genuine, natural, real

shame *Syn* DISGRACE, dishonor, disrepute, ignominy, infamy, obloquy, odium, opprobrium *Ant* esteem, respect

shamed *Syn* GUILTY, ashamed, contrite, hangdog, penitent, remorseful, repentant, shamefaced *Ant* impenitent, remorseless, shameless, unashamed, unrepentant

shamefaced *Syn* GUILTY, ashamed, contrite, hangdog, penitent, remorseful, repentant, shamed *Ant* impenitent, remorseless, shameless, unashamed, unrepentant

shameless • characterized by or exhibiting boldness and a lack of shame *Syn* barefaced, brash, brazen, impudent *Rel* abandoned, dissolute, profligate

shanty *Syn* SHACK, cabin, camp, hovel, hut, hutch

shape **1** *Syn* FORM (sense 1), configuration, conformation, figure **2** *Syn* MAKE, fabricate, fashion, forge, form, manufacture

shapeless *Syn* FORMLESS, amorphous, unformed, unshaped, unstructured *Ant* formed, shaped, structured

share • to have, get, or use in common with another or others *Syn* partake, participate *Rel* communicate, impart

sharer *Syn* PARTICIPANT, partaker, participator, party *Ant* nonparticipant

shark *Syn* EXPERT, ace, adept, artist, authority, crackerjack, maestro, master, past master, scholar, virtuoso, whiz, wizard *Ant* amateur

sharp • having or showing alert competence and clear understanding *Syn* acute, keen *Rel* biting, cutting, incisive, trenchant *Ant* blunt, dull

sharpen • to make sharp or sharper *Syn* edge, grind, hone, strop, whet *Rel* file *Ant* blunt, dull

sharply *Syn* SMARTLY, dashingly, nattily, sprucely *Ant* sloppily, slovenly

sharpness *Syn* CHILL, bite, bitterness, bleakness, chilliness, nip, rawness

shatter *Syn* BREAK, burst, bust, crack, shiver, snap *Ant* cleave (*together*), keep (*of laws*)

shave **1** *Syn* BRUSH, glance, graze, skim **2** *Syn* CLIP, bob, crop, curtail, cut, cut back, dock, lop (off), nip, pare, prune, shear, snip, trim

shaver *Syn* BOY, lad, laddie, nipper, sonny, stripling, tad, youth

shear *Syn* CLIP, bob, crop, curtail, cut, cut back, dock, lop (off), nip, pare, prune, shave, snip, trim

shed *Syn* DISCARD, cast, junk, molt, scrap, slough

sheen *Syn* LUSTER, glaze, gloss

sheep *Syn* LAMB, angel, dove, innocent *Ant* wolf

sheer *adj* **1** *Syn* PURE, absolute, simple *Ant* adulterated, applied (*of science*), contaminated, polluted **2** *Syn* STEEP, abrupt, precipitous

sheer *vb Syn* TURN (sense 2), avert, deflect, divert

shelter *n* • something that covers or affords protection *Syn* asylum, cover, refuge, retreat, sanctuary *Rel* protection, safeguard, safeguarding

shelter *vb Syn* HARBOR, board, entertain, house, lodge

sheltered *Syn* SECLUDED, cloistered, covert, isolated, quiet, remote, retired, secret

shelve *Syn* POSTPONE, defer, delay, hold off (on), hold up, put off

shenanigans *Syn* HORSEPLAY, clowning, foolery, high jinks, horsing (around), monkeying, monkeyshines, roughhouse, roughhousing, skylarking, tomfoolery

shibboleth **1** *Syn* CATCHWORD, byword, slogan **2** *Syn* SLOGAN, cry, watchword

shield *Syn* DEFEND, guard, protect, safeguard *Ant* attack, combat

shift *vb* **1** *Syn* CHANGE (sense 2), fluctuate, mutate, vary *Ant* stabilize **2** *Syn* CHANGE (sense 3), commute, exchange, substitute, swap, switch, trade **3** *Syn* MOVE (sense 2), remove, transfer

shift *n* **1** *Syn* RESOURCE, expedient, makeshift, resort, stopgap, substitute, surrogate **2** *Syn* SPELL, bout, go, stint, tour, trick, turn

shilly-shallying *Syn* HESITATION, faltering, hesitance, hesitancy, indecision, irresolution, vacillation, wavering, wobbling

shimmy *Syn* SHAKE (sense 1), dither, quake, quaver, quiver, shiver, shudder, teeter, totter, tremble, wobble

shindy *Syn* COMMOTION, bother, bustle, clatter, disturbance, furor, furore, fuss, hubbub, hullabaloo, hurly-burly, pandemonium, pother, row, ruckus, ruction, rumpus, squall, stew, stir, storm, to-do, tumult, turmoil, uproar, welter, whirl

shine *n Syn* LIKING, appetite, fancy, favor, fondness, like, love, partiality, preference, relish, taste, use *Ant* aversion, disfavor, dislike, distaste, hatred, loathing

shine *vb Syn* POLISH, buff, burnish, dress, gloss, grind, rub, smooth

ship *n Syn* BOAT, craft, vessel

ship *vb Syn* SEND, dispatch, forward, remit, route, transmit *Ant* accept, receive

shipshape *Syn* NEAT, snug, spick-and-span, tidy, trig, trim *Ant* filthy

shirk *Syn* DODGE, duck, fence, malinger, parry, sidestep *Ant* face

shiver **1** *Syn* BREAK, burst, bust, crack, shatter, snap *Ant* cleave (*together*), keep (*of laws*) **2** *Syn* SHAKE (sense 1), dither, quake, quaver, quiver, shimmy, shudder, teeter, totter, tremble, wobble

shoal • a shallow place in a body of water *Syn* bank, bar, reef

shock *vb Syn* HEAP, bank, cock, mass, pile, stack

shock *n* **1** *Syn* HEAP, bank, cock, mass, pile, stack **2** *Syn* IMPACT, clash, collision, concussion, impingement, jar, jolt, percussion

shocking *Syn* FEARFUL (sense 2), appalling, awful, dreadful, frightful, horrible, horrific, terrible, terrific

shoot *n* • a branch or a part of a plant that is an outgrowth from a main stem *Syn* bough, branch, limb

shoot *vb* **1** *Syn* FLY, dart, float, sail, scud, skim **2** *Syn* HURRY (sense 2), barrel, bolt, bowl, breeze, career, course, dash, fly, hasten, hotfoot (it), hump, hurtle, hustle, pelt, race, rip, rocket, run, rush, rustle, scoot, scurry, scuttle, speed, step (along), tear, trot, whirl, whisk, zip, zoom *Ant* crawl, creep, poke

shop *Syn* STORE, bazaar, emporium

shore • land bordering a usually large body of water *Syn* bank, beach, coast, foreshore, littoral, strand

short *Syn* FRAGILE, brittle, crisp, frangible, friable *Ant* tough

shortage *Syn* DEFICIENCY, dearth, deficit, failure, famine, inadequacy, insufficiency, lack, paucity, poverty, scantiness, scarceness, scarcity, want *Ant* abundance, adequacy, amplitude, plenitude, plenty, sufficiency

shortchange *Syn* FLEECE, bleed, cheat, chisel, cozen, defraud, hustle, mulct, rook, skin, squeeze, stick, sting, swindle, victimize

shortcoming *Syn* IMPERFECTION, deficiency, fault *Ant* perfection

shorten • to reduce in extent *Syn* abbreviate, abridge, curtail, retrench *Rel* decrease, diminish, lessen, reduce *Ant* elongate, extend, lengthen, prolong, protract

short-lived *Syn* MOMENTARY, ephemeral, evanescent, flash, fleeting, fugitive, impermanent, passing, temporary, transient, transitory *Ant* enduring, eternal, everlasting, lasting, long-lived, permanent, perpetual

shortly **1** • at or within a short time *Syn* anon, momentarily, presently, soon *Rel* directly, forthwith, immediately, instantly, now, promptly, pronto, right away, right now, straightaway **2** *Syn* PRESENTLY, directly, soon

shot *Syn* ATTEMPT, crack, endeavor, essay, fling, go, pass, stab, trial, try, whack

should *Syn* NEED (sense 1), have (to), must, ought (to), shall *Ant* have, hold

shout *n* • a sudden loud cry *Syn* holler, scream, screech, shriek, squeal, whoop, yell *Rel* bawl, bellow, clamor, roar, vociferation

shout *vb* • to utter a sudden loud cry (as to attract attention) *Syn* holler, scream, screech, shriek, squeal, whoop, yell *Rel* bawl, bellow, howl, roar

shove *Syn* PUSH, propel, thrust

show *vb* **1** • to reveal outwardly or make apparent *Syn* demonstrate, evidence, evince, manifest *Rel* disclose, discover, reveal **2** • to present so as to invite notice or attention *Syn* display, exhibit, expose, flaunt, parade *Rel* argue, attest, bespeak, betoken, indicate, prove *Ant* disguise

show *n* *Syn* EXHIBITION, exhibit, exposition, fair

shower *n* *Syn* BARRAGE, bombardment, cannonade, fusillade, hail, salvo, storm, volley

shower *vb* *Syn* RAIN (sense 2), hail, storm

showiness *Syn* OSTENTATION, flamboyance, flashiness, garishness, gaudiness, glitz, ostentatiousness, pretentiousness, swank *Ant* austerity, plainness, severity

show off *Syn* CUT UP, act up, clown (around), fool (around), horse (around), monkey (around), skylark

showy • given to excess outward display *Syn* ostentatious, pretentious *Rel* flashy, garish, gaudy, meretricious, tawdry

shrewd • acute in perception and sound in judgment *Syn* astute, perspicacious, sagacious *Rel* clever, intelligent, knowing, quick-witted, smart

shriek *vb* **1** *Syn* SCREAM, howl, screech, shrill, squall, squeal, yell, yelp **2** *Syn* SHOUT, holler, scream, screech, squeal, whoop, yell

shriek *n* *Syn* SHOUT, holler, scream, screech, squeal, whoop, yell

shrieking *Syn* SHRILL, acute, high-pitched, piping, screeching, squeaking, squeaky, treble, whistling *Ant* bass, deep, low, throaty

shrill *adj* • having a high musical pitch or range *Syn* acute, high-pitched, piping, screeching, shrieking, squeaking, squeaky, treble, whistling *Rel* peeping, thin, tinny *Ant* bass, deep, low, throaty

shrill *vb* *Syn* SCREAM, howl, screech, shriek, squeal, yell, yelp

shrink **1** *Syn* CONTRACT, compress, condense, constrict, deflate *Ant* expand **2** *Syn* RECOIL, blench, flinch, quail, wince *Ant* confront, defy

shrivel *Syn* WITHER, wizen

shroud *Syn* COVER, envelop, overspread, veil, wrap *Ant* bare

shudder *Syn* SHAKE (sense 1), dither, quake, quaver, quiver, shimmy, shiver, teeter, totter, tremble, wobble

shuffle *Syn* DISORDER, confuse, derange, disarrange, disarray, discompose, dishevel, dislocate, disorganize, disrupt, disturb, hash, jumble, mess (up), mix (up), muddle, muss, rumple, scramble, tousle, tumble, upset *Ant* arrange, array, draw up, marshal, order, organize, range, regulate, straighten (up), tidy

shun *Syn* ESCAPE (sense 2), avoid, elude, eschew, evade

shut out *Syn* EXCLUDE, blackball, debar, disbar, eliminate, rule out, suspend *Ant* admit, include

shut up • to stop talking *Syn* clam up, hush, quiet (down) *Rel* calm (down), cool (down), settle (down) *Ant* speak, talk

shy *adj* • not inclined to be forward *Syn* bashful, coy, diffident, modest *Rel* timid, timorous *Ant* obtrusive

shy *vb* *Syn* DEMUR, balk, boggle, jib, scruple, stick, stickle, strain *Ant* accede

sicken *Syn* DISGUST, nauseate, repel, repulse, revolt, turn off

sickly *Syn* UNWHOLESOME, diseased, morbid, pathological *Ant* wholesome

side **1** *Syn* FACTION, bloc, body, coalition, party, sect, set, wing **2** *Syn* PHASE, angle, aspect, facet

sideboard *Syn* CABINET, buffet, closet, cupboard, hutch, locker

sidekick *Syn* ASSISTANT, adjutant, aid, aide, apprentice, coadjutor, deputy, helper

sidereal *Syn* STARRY, astral, stellar

sidestep *Syn* DODGE, duck, fence, malinger, parry, shirk *Ant* face

sideways • with one side faced forward *Syn* broadside, edgewise, sidewise *Rel* aslant, indirectly, obliquely

sidewise *Syn* SIDEWAYS, broadside, edgewise

siege *Syn* ATTACK (sense 3), bout, case, fit, seizure, spell

sigh *n* • a usually inarticulate sound indicating mental or physical pain or distress *Syn* groan, moan, sob *Rel* grief, regret, sorrow

sigh *vb* • to let out a deep audible breath (as in weariness or sorrow) *Syn* groan, moan, sob *Rel* bemoan, bewail, deplore, lament

sight *Syn* LOOK, glance, glimpse, peek, peep, view

sightless *Syn* BLIND, eyeless, stone blind *Ant* sighted

sightly *Syn* BEAUTIFUL, attractive, beauteous, comely, cute, fair, gorgeous, handsome, knockout, lovely, pretty, ravishing, stunning, taking *Ant* homely, ill-favored, plain, ugly, unattractive, unbeautiful, unhandsome, unlovely, unpretty, unsightly

sign **1** • a discernible indication of what is not itself directly perceptible *Syn* badge, mark, note, symptom, token *Rel* attestation, attesting, betokening, indication **2** *Syn* CHARACTER, mark, symbol

signal *adj* **1** *Syn* EMINENT, distinguished, illustrious, noble, notable, noteworthy, outstanding, preeminent, prestigious, star, superior **2** *Syn* NOTICEABLE, arresting, conspicuous, outstanding, prominent, remarkable, salient, striking

signal *vb* *Syn* MOTION, beckon, flag, gesture, wave

significance **1** *Syn* IMPORTANCE, consequence, import, moment, weight *Ant* unimportance **2** *Syn* MEANING, acceptation, import, sense, signification

significant *Syn* EXPRESSIVE, eloquent, meaning, meaningful, pregnant, revealing, suggestive

signification *Syn* MEANING, acceptation, import, sense, significance

signify **1** *Syn* MATTER, count, import, mean, weigh **2** *Syn* MEAN, denote, import

silence • the near or complete absence of sound *Syn* hush, quiet, quietness, quietude, still, stillness *Rel* calm, lull, peacefulness, tranquility *Ant* noise, sound

silent **1** • showing restraint in speaking *Syn* close, close-lipped, closemouthed, reserved, reticent, secretive, taciturn, tight-lipped, uncommunicative *Rel* checked, curbed, inhibited, restrained *Ant* talkative **2** • mostly or entirely without sound *Syn* hushed, muted, noiseless, quiet, quieted, soundless, still *Rel* peaceful, tranquil *Ant* noisy, unquiet **3** • deliberately refraining from speech *Syn* dumb, mum, mute, speechless, uncommunicative, wordless *Rel* inarticulate, tongue-tied *Ant* communicative, speaking, talking **4** *Syn* STILL, quiet, stilly *Ant* noisy, stirring

silhouette *Syn* OUTLINE, contour, profile, skyline

silken *Syn* SLEEK, glossy, satiny, silky, slick, velvety

silky *Syn* SLEEK, glossy, satiny, silken, slick, velvety

silly **1** *Syn* FOOLISH, absurd, preposterous *Ant* sensible **2** *Syn* SIMPLE, asinine, fatuous, foolish *Ant* wise

similar *Syn* ALIKE, akin, analogous, comparable, correspondent, corresponding, like, matching, parallel, resembling, such, suchlike *Ant* different, dissimilar, diverse, unlike

similarity • the quality or state of having many qualities in common *Syn* alikeness, community, correspondence, likeness, parallelism, resemblance, similitude *Rel* analogousness *Ant* dissimilarity, unlikeness

simile *Syn* ANALOGY, metaphor

similitude *Syn* SIMILARITY, alikeness, community, correspondence, likeness, parallelism, resemblance *Ant* dissimilarity, unlikeness

simmer *Syn* BOIL, parboil, seethe, stew

simper *n* *Syn* SMILE, grin, smirk *Ant* frown

simper *vb* *Syn* SMILE, grin, smirk *Ant* frown

simple *adj* **1** • actually or apparently deficient in intelligence *Syn* asinine, fatuous, foolish, silly *Rel* childish, childlike *Ant* wise **2** *Syn* EASY, effortless, facile, light, smooth *Ant* hard **3** *Syn* IGNORANT, benighted, dark, illiterate, nonliterate, uneducated, uninstructed, unlearned, unlettered, unread, unschooled, untaught, untutored *Ant* educated, knowledgeable, literate, schooled **4** *Syn* NATURAL, artless, ingenuous, naive, unaffected, unsophisticated **5** *Syn* PLAIN, homely, unpretentious *Ant* lovely **6** *Syn* PURE, absolute, sheer *Ant* adulterated, applied (*of science*), contaminated, polluted

simple *n* *Syn* DRUG, biologic, medicinal, pharmaceutical

simpleton *Syn* FOOL (sense 2), booby, goose, half-wit, jackass, lunatic, nincompoop, ninny, nitwit, nut, turkey, yo-yo

simulate *Syn* ASSUME, affect, counterfeit, feign, pretend, sham

simulated *Syn* IMITATION, artificial, bogus, factitious, fake, false, man-made, mimic, mock, sham, substitute, synthetic *Ant* genuine, natural, real

simultaneous *Syn* CONTEMPORARY, coetaneous, coeval, coincident, concomitant, concurrent, contemporaneous, synchronous

sin **1** *Syn* EVIL, bad, evildoing, ill, immorality, iniquity, villainy, wrong *Ant* good, morality, right, virtue **2** *Syn* OFFENSE (sense 2), crime, scandal, vice

since *Syn* BECAUSE, as, for, inasmuch as

sincere • genuine in feeling *Syn* heartfelt, hearty, unfeigned, wholehearted, whole-souled *Rel* candid, frank, open, plain *Ant* insincere

sincerely *Syn* NATURALLY (sense 3), artlessly, guilelessly, ingenuously, innocently, naively, unaffectedly, unfeignedly, unpretentiously *Ant* affectedly, artificially, hypocritically, insincerely, pretentiously, unnaturally

sinewy *Syn* MUSCULAR, athletic, brawny, burly, husky

sing • to produce musical tones by or as if by means of the voice *Syn* carol, chant, descant, hymn, intone, trill, troll, warble

singe *Syn* BURN, char, scorch, sear
single *adj* **1** • one as distinguished from two or more or all others *Syn* lone, particular, separate, sole, solitary, unique *Rel* especial, individual, special, specific *Ant* accompanied, conjugal, supported **2** *Syn* UNMARRIED, celibate, maiden, virgin
single *vb Syn* CHOOSE, cull, elect, opt, pick, prefer, select *Ant* eschew, reject
singular *adj* **1** *Syn* ONLY, alone, lone, solitary, special, unique **2** *Syn* STRANGE, curious, eccentric, erratic, odd, outlandish, peculiar, quaint, queer, unique *Ant* familiar
sinister **1** • seriously threatening evil or disaster *Syn* baleful, malefic, maleficent, malign *Rel* fateful, inauspicious, ominous, portentous, unpropitious **2** *Syn* OMINOUS, baleful, dire, foreboding, inauspicious, menacing, portentous, threatening
sink **1** *Syn* DETERIORATE, crumble, decay, decline, degenerate, descend, ebb, rot, worsen *Ant* ameliorate, improve, meliorate **2** *Syn* FALL, drop, slump, subside *Ant* rise
sinuous *Syn* WINDING, flexuous, serpentine, tortuous *Ant* straight
siphon *Syn* CHANNEL, channelize, direct, funnel, pipe
sire *Syn* GENERATE, beget, breed, engender, get, procreate, propagate, reproduce
siren • a woman whom men find irresistibly attractive *Syn* enchantress, seductress, temptress *Rel* charmer, seducer
sissy *Syn* COWARD, chicken, craven, dastard, poltroon, recreant *Ant* hero, stalwart, valiant
site *Syn* PLACE, location, position, situation, spot, station
situation **1** *Syn* PLACE, location, position, site, spot, station **2** *Syn* STATE, condition, mode, posture, status
sizable *or* **sizeable** *Syn* LARGE, big, bulky, considerable, goodly, good-sized, grand, great, handsome, hefty, hulking, largish, outsize, oversize (*or* oversized), substantial, tidy, voluminous *Ant* little, puny, small, undersized
size • the amount of measurable space or area occupied by a thing *Syn* area, dimensions, extent, magnitude, volume *Rel* amplitude, expanse, spread, stretch
skedaddle *Syn* SCUTTLE, scamper, scurry, sprint
skeleton *Syn* STRUCTURE, anatomy, framework
skeptic • a person who is always ready to doubt or question the truth or existence of something *Syn* disbeliever, doubter, questioner, unbeliever *Rel* cynic, misanthrope, pessimist
skeptically *Syn* ASKANCE, distrustfully, doubtfully, doubtingly, dubiously, mistrustfully, suspiciously *Ant* trustfully, trustingly
skepticism *Syn* DOUBT, distrust, distrustfulness, incertitude, misgiving, mistrust, mistrustfulness, suspicion, uncertainty *Ant* assurance, belief, certainty, certitude, confidence, conviction, sureness, surety, trust
sketch *n* **1** • a rough drawing representing the chief features of an object or scene *Syn* blueprint, delineation, diagram, draft, outline, plot, tracing *Rel* design, plan, project, scheme **2** *Syn* COMPENDIUM, aperçu, digest, pandect, précis, survey, syllabus
sketch *vb* • to make a sketch, rough draft, or outline of *Syn* blueprint, delineate, diagram, draft, outline, plot, trace *Rel* design, plan, project, scheme
skewbald *Syn* VARIEGATED, checked, checkered, dappled, motley, parti-colored, piebald, pied
skewed *Syn* AWRY, askew, aslant, cockeyed, crooked, listing, lopsided, oblique, slanted, slanting, slantwise, tilted, tipping, uneven *Ant* even, level, straight
skid *Syn* SLIDE, coast, glide, glissade, slip, slither, toboggan
skill *Syn* ART, artifice, craft, cunning
skilled *Syn* PROFICIENT, adept, expert, masterly, skillful *Ant* amateur, amateurish, inexperienced, inexpert, unexperienced, unpracticed, unprofessional, unseasoned, unskilled, unskillful
skillful *Syn* PROFICIENT, adept, expert, masterly, skilled *Ant* amateur, amateurish, inexperienced, inexpert, unexperienced, unpracticed, unprofessional, unseasoned, unskilled, unskillful
skim **1** *Syn* BRUSH, glance, graze, shave **2** *Syn* FLY, dart, float, sail, scud, shoot
skimp *Syn* ECONOMIZE, save, scrimp *Ant* waste
skimping *Syn* ECONOMY, frugality, husbandry, providence, scrimping, thrift *Ant* wastefulness
skimpy *Syn* MEAGER, exiguous, scant, scanty, scrimpy, spare, sparse *Ant* ample, copious
skin *n* • an outer or surface layer especially the outer limiting layer of an animal body *Syn* bark, hide, peel, pelt, rind
skin *vb* **1** • to remove the surface, skin, or thin outer covering of *Syn* decorticate, flay, pare, peel **2** *Syn* FLEECE, bleed, cheat, chisel, cozen, defraud, hustle, mulct, rook, shortchange, squeeze, stick, sting, swindle, victimize
skinny *Syn* LEAN, angular, gaunt, lank, lanky, rawboned, scrawny, spare *Ant* fleshy
skip • to move or advance with successive springs or leaps *Syn* bound, curvet, hop, lollop, lope, ricochet
skirmish *Syn* ENCOUNTER, brush
skirt *Syn* BORDER, bound, fringe, margin, rim
skirting *Syn* ADJACENT, abutting, adjoining, bordering, contiguous, flanking, fringing, joining, juxtaposed, touching, verging *Ant* nonadjacent

skittish *Syn* EXCITABLE, flighty, fluttery, highstrung, jittery, jumpy, nervous, spooky *Ant* unflappable
skulk *Syn* LURK, slink, sneak
skylark *Syn* CUT UP, act up, clown (around), fool (around), horse (around), monkey (around), show off
skylarking *Syn* HORSEPLAY, clowning, foolery, high jinks, horsing (around), monkeying, monkeyshines, roughhouse, roughhousing, shenanigans, tomfoolery
skyline *Syn* OUTLINE, contour, profile, silhouette
skyward *Syn* ABOVE, aloft, over, overhead *Ant* below, beneath, under
slack *adj* **1** *Syn* LOOSE, lax, relaxed *Ant* strict, tight **2** *Syn* NEGLIGENT, careless, derelict, lax, neglectful, neglecting, remiss *Ant* attentive, careful, conscientious
slack *vb Syn* SLACKEN, ease, loosen, relax *Ant* strain, stretch, tense, tighten
slacken **1** • to make less taut *Syn* ease, loosen, relax, slack *Rel* detach, free, unbind, undo, unfasten, untie *Ant* strain, stretch, tense, tighten **2** *Syn* DELAY (sense 1), detain, retard, slow *Ant* expedite, hasten
slam *Syn* ATTACK (sense 2), abuse, assail, belabor, blast, castigate, excoriate, jump (on), lambaste (*or* lambast), scathe, vituperate
slander *vb* • to make untrue and harmful statements about *Syn* asperse, blacken, defame, libel, malign, smear, traduce, vilify *Rel* belittle, detract, disparage
slander *n Syn* DETRACTION, backbiting, calumny, scandal
slanderous *Syn* LIBELOUS, defamatory, scandalous
slang *Syn* TERMINOLOGY, argot, cant, dialect, jargon, language, lingo, patois, patter, vocabulary
slant *vb* • to set or be set at an angle *Syn* incline, lean, slope *Rel* deviate, diverge, swerve, veer
slant *n Syn* POINT OF VIEW, angle, standpoint, viewpoint
slanted *Syn* AWRY, askew, aslant, cockeyed, crooked, listing, lopsided, oblique, skewed, slanting, slantwise, tilted, tipping, uneven *Ant* even, level, straight
slanting *Syn* AWRY, askew, aslant, cockeyed, crooked, listing, lopsided, oblique, skewed, slanted, slantwise, tilted, tipping, uneven *Ant* even, level, straight
slantwise *Syn* AWRY, askew, aslant, cockeyed, crooked, listing, lopsided, oblique, skewed, slanted, slanting, tilted, tipping, uneven *Ant* even, level, straight
slap *Syn* STRIKE, box, clout, cuff, hit, punch, slog, slug, smite, swat
slapjack *Syn* PANCAKE, flapjack, griddle cake, hotcake
slapstick *Syn* COMEDY, farce, humor
slash *Syn* CUT, carve, chop, hew, slit
slatternly • being habitually untidy and very dirty especially in dress or appearance *Syn* blowsy, dowdy, frowzy *Rel* disheveled, slipshod, sloppy, slovenly, unkempt
slaughter *vb Syn* MASSACRE, butcher, mow (down)
slaughter *n Syn* MASSACRE, butchery, carnage, pogrom
slave *n* **1** • a person who is considered the property of another person *Syn* bondman, bondsman, chattel, thrall *Rel* domestic, drudge, lackey, menial, servant *Ant* freeman **2** • a person who does very hard or dull work *Syn* drudge, drudger, grubber, laborer, peon, plugger, slogger, toiler, worker *Rel* workhorse
slave *vb Syn* LABOR, drudge, endeavor, grub, hump, hustle, moil, peg (away), plod, plow, plug, slog, strain, strive, struggle, sweat, toil, travail, work *Ant* dabble, fiddle (around), fool (around), mess (around), putter (around)
slavish *Syn* SUBSERVIENT, menial, obsequious, servile *Ant* domineering, overbearing
slay *Syn* KILL, assassinate, dispatch, execute, murder
sleazy *Syn* LIMP, flabby, flaccid, flimsy, floppy
sleek **1** • having a smooth bright surface or appearance *Syn* glossy, satiny, silken, silky, slick, velvety *Rel* bright, brilliant, lustrous **2** *Syn* GLOSSY, buffed, burnished, glistening, lustrous, polished, rubbed, satin, satiny *Ant* dim, dull, flat, lusterless, matte
sleep • to take rest by a suspension of consciousness *Syn* catnap, doze, drowse, nap, slumber, snooze *Rel* relax, repose, rest
sleepiness • the quality or state of desiring or needing sleep *Syn* drowsiness, somnolence *Rel* lassitude, lethargy, sluggishness, torpor *Ant* insomnia, sleeplessness, wakefulness
sleepless *Syn* WAKEFUL, awake, wide-awake *Ant* asleep, dormant, dozing, napping, resting, sleeping, slumbering
sleepy • affected by or inducing of a desire to sleep *Syn* drowsy, slumberous, somnolent *Rel* comatose, lethargic, sluggish
sleight **1** *Syn* DEXTERITY (sense 1), adroitness, cleverness, finesse *Ant* awkwardness, clumsiness, gawkiness **2** *Syn* DEXTERITY (sense 2), agility, deftness, nimbleness, spryness *Ant* awkwardness, clumsiness, gawkiness
slender *Syn* THIN, rare, slight, slim, tenuous *Ant* thick
slick *Syn* SLEEK, glossy, satiny, silken, silky, velvety
slide • to go or progress with a smooth continuous motion *Syn* coast, glide, glissade, skid, slip, slither, toboggan
slight *n Syn* INSULT, affront, barb, dart, dig,

epithet, indignity, name, offense (*or* offence), outrage, put-down, sarcasm, slur

slight *vb Syn* NEGLECT, disregard, forget, ignore, omit, overlook *Ant* cherish

slight *adj* **1** *Syn* THIN, rare, slender, slim, tenuous *Ant* thick **2** *Syn* UNIMPORTANT, frivolous, inconsequential, inconsiderable, insignificant, little, minor, minute, negligible, small, small-fry, trifling, trivial *Ant* big, consequential, eventful, important, major, material, meaningful, momentous, significant, substantial, weighty

slightest *Syn* MINIMAL, least, littlest, lowest, minimum *Ant* full, greatest, largest, maximum, top, topmost, utmost

slighting *Syn* DEROGATORY, depreciative, depreciatory, disparaging, pejorative

slim *Syn* THIN, rare, slender, slight, tenuous *Ant* thick

sling **1** *Syn* HANG, dangle, suspend **2** *Syn* THROW, cast, fling, hurl, pitch, toss

slink *Syn* LURK, skulk, sneak

slip *n* **1** *Syn* ERROR, blunder, bull, faux pas, howler, lapse, mistake **2** *Syn* WHARF, berth, dock, jetty, levee, pier, quay

slip *vb Syn* SLIDE, coast, glide, glissade, skid, slither, toboggan

slipshod • negligent of or marked by lack of neatness and order especially in appearance or dress *Syn* disheveled, sloppy, slovenly, unkempt *Rel* lax, neglectful, negligent, remiss, slack

slit *Syn* CUT, carve, chop, hew, slash

slither *Syn* SLIDE, coast, glide, glissade, skid, slip, toboggan

slobber *Syn* GUSH (sense 2), enthuse, fuss, rave, rhapsodize

slog **1** *Syn* LABOR, drudge, endeavor, grub, hump, hustle, moil, peg (away), plod, plow, plug, slave, strain, strive, struggle, sweat, toil, travail, work *Ant* dabble, fiddle (around), fool (around), mess (around), putter (around) **2** *Syn* STRIKE, box, clout, cuff, hit, punch, slap, slug, smite, swat

slogan **1** an attention-getting word or phrase used to publicize something (as a campaign or product) *Syn* cry, shibboleth, watchword *Rel* tag line **2** *Syn* CATCHWORD, byword, shibboleth

slogger *Syn* SLAVE (sense 2), drudge, drudger, grubber, laborer, peon, plugger, toiler, worker *Ant* freeman

slope *Syn* SLANT, incline, lean

sloppily • in a careless or unfashionable manner *Syn* dowdily, slovenly, unstylishly *Rel* slatternly *Ant* nattily, sharply, smartly, sprucely

sloppy **1** *Syn* CORNY, maudlin, mawkish, mushy, saccharine, sappy, schmaltzy, sentimental, sugarcoated, sugary *Ant* unsentimental **2** *Syn* MESSY, chaotic, cluttered, confused, disarranged, disarrayed, disheveled (*or* dishevelled), disordered, disorderly, higgledy-piggledy, hugger-mugger, jumbled, littered, messed, muddled, mussed, mussy, pell-mell, rumpled, topsy-turvy, tousled, tumbled, unkempt, untidy, upside-down *Ant* neat, ordered, orderly, organized, shipshape, snug, tidied, tidy, trim **3** *Syn* SLIPSHOD, disheveled, slovenly, unkempt

slothful *Syn* LAZY, faineant, indolent *Ant* industrious

slouch *Syn* LAZYBONES, drone, idler, loafer, slug, sluggard *Ant* doer, go-getter, hummer, hustler, rustler, self-starter

slough *vb Syn* DISCARD, cast, junk, molt, scrap, shed

slough *n Syn* SWAMP, bog, fen, marsh, marshland, mire, morass, muskeg, swampland

slovenly *adj Syn* SLIPSHOD, disheveled, sloppy, unkempt

slovenly *adv Syn* SLOPPILY, dowdily, unstylishly *Ant* nattily, sharply, smartly, sprucely

slow *adj* **1** • moving, flowing, or proceeding at less than the usual, desirable, or required speed *Syn* deliberate, dilatory, laggard, leisurely *Ant* fast **2** *Syn* STUPID, crass, dense, dull, dumb *Ant* intelligent

slow *adv* • at a pace that is less than usual, desirable, or expected *Syn* laggardly, leisurely, slowly, sluggishly, tardily *Rel* carefully, cautiously, deliberately, purposefully *Ant* apace, briskly, fast, fleetly, full tilt, hastily, quick, quickly, rapidly, snappily, speedily, swift, swiftly

slow *vb* **1** • to cause to move or proceed at a less rapid pace *Syn* brake, decelerate, retard *Rel* halt, stop *Ant* accelerate, hasten, hurry, quicken, rush, speed (up), step up **2** *Syn* DELAY (sense 1), detain, retard, slacken *Ant* expedite, hasten

slowly *Syn* SLOW, laggardly, leisurely, sluggishly, tardily *Ant* apace, briskly, fast, fleetly, full tilt, hastily, quick, quickly, rapidly, snappily, speedily, swift, swiftly

slug *n Syn* LAZYBONES, drone, idler, loafer, slouch, sluggard *Ant* doer, go-getter, hummer, hustler, rustler, self-starter

slug *vb Syn* STRIKE, box, clout, cuff, hit, punch, slap, slog, smite, swat

sluggard *Syn* LAZYBONES, drone, idler, loafer, slouch, slug *Ant* doer, go-getter, hummer, hustler, rustler, self-starter

sluggish *Syn* LETHARGIC, comatose, torpid *Ant* energetic, vigorous

sluggishly *Syn* SLOW, laggardly, leisurely, slowly, tardily *Ant* apace, briskly, fast, fleetly, full tilt, hastily, quick, quickly, rapidly, snappily, speedily, swift, swiftly

sluice *Syn* POUR, gush, stream

slumber *Syn* SLEEP, catnap, doze, drowse, nap, snooze

slumberous *Syn* SLEEPY, drowsy, somnolent

slump *Syn* FALL, drop, sink, subside *Ant* rise

slur *Syn* INSULT, affront, barb, dart, dig, epithet, indignity, name, offense (*or* offence), outrage, put-down, sarcasm, slight

slushy *Syn* SENTIMENTAL, maudlin, mawkish, mushy, romantic, soppy

sly • attaining or seeking to attain one's ends by devious means *Syn* artful, crafty, cunning, foxy, guileful, insidious, tricky, wily *Rel* clandestine, covert, furtive, secret, stealthy

smack **1** *Syn* TASTE (sense 1), flavor, relish, savor, tang *Ant* antipathy **2** *Syn* TOUCH, dash, shade, soupçon, spice, strain, streak, suggestion, suspicion, tincture, tinge, vein

small *Syn* UNIMPORTANT, frivolous, inconsequential, inconsiderable, insignificant, little, minor, minute, negligible, slight, small-fry, trifling, trivial *Ant* big, consequential, eventful, important, major, material, meaningful, momentous, significant, substantial, weighty

smaller *Syn* LESSER, inferior, junior, less, lower, minor, subordinate, under *Ant* greater, higher, major, more, primary, prime, senior, superior

small-fry *Syn* UNIMPORTANT, frivolous, inconsequential, inconsiderable, insignificant, little, minor, minute, negligible, slight, small, trifling, trivial *Ant* big, consequential, eventful, important, major, material, meaningful, momentous, significant, substantial, weighty

small-minded *Syn* INTOLERANT, bigoted, narrow, narrow-minded, prejudiced *Ant* broad-minded, liberal, open-minded, tolerant, unprejudiced

small talk *Syn* CHAT, chatter, chitchat, gabfest, gossip, palaver, rap, table talk, talk, tête-à-tête

small-town *Syn* INSULAR, local, parochial, provincial

smart **1** *Syn* FLIPPANT, facetious, flip, pert, smart-alecky (*or* smart-aleck) *Ant* earnest, sincere **2** *Syn* INTELLIGENT, alert, bright, brilliant, clever, knowing, quick-witted *Ant* unintelligent **3** *Syn* STYLISH, chic, dashing, fashionable, modish **4** *Syn* WORLDLY-WISE, cosmopolitan, sophisticated, worldly *Ant* ingenuous, innocent, naive, unsophisticated, unworldly, wide-eyed

smart aleck • a person who likes to show off in a clever but annoying way *Syn* smarty (*or* smartie), wise guy, wiseacre *Rel* know-it-all

smart-alecky *or* **smart-aleck** *Syn* FLIPPANT, facetious, flip, pert, smart *Ant* earnest, sincere

smartly • in a strikingly neat and trim manner *Syn* dashingly, nattily, sharply, sprucely *Rel* neatly, orderly, tidily, trimly *Ant* sloppily, slovenly

smarty *or* **smartie** *Syn* SMART ALECK, wise guy, wiseacre

smash *Syn* CRUSH (sense 1), bruise, macerate, mash, squash

smear *Syn* SLANDER, asperse, blacken, defame, libel, malign, traduce, vilify

smell • the quality that makes a thing perceptible to the olfactory sense *Syn* aroma, odor, scent *Rel* bouquet, fragrance, incense, perfume, redolence

smidgen *Syn* PARTICLE, atom, bit, iota, jot, mite, tittle, whit

smile *n* • a facial expression in which the lips curve slightly upward especially in expression of pleasure or amusement *Syn* grin, simper, smirk *Ant* frown

smile *vb* • to have, produce, or exhibit a smile *Syn* grin, simper, smirk *Ant* frown

smirch *Syn* DIRTY, befoul, begrime, besmirch, blacken, foul, grime, mire, muddy, smudge, soil, stain, sully *Ant* clean, cleanse

smirk *n* *Syn* SMILE, grin, simper *Ant* frown

smirk *vb* *Syn* SMILE, grin, simper

smite *Syn* STRIKE, box, clout, cuff, hit, punch, slap, slog, slug, swat

smog *Syn* HAZE (sense 1), fog, mist, murk, reek, soup

smooth *adj* **1** *Syn* EASY, effortless, facile, light, simple *Ant* hard **2** *Syn* SOFT, balmy, bland, gentle, lenient, mild *Ant* hard, stern **3** *Syn* SUAVE, debonair, sophisticated, urbane *Ant* boorish, churlish, clownish, loutish, uncouth **4** *Syn* LEVEL, even, flat, flush, plain, plane

smooth *vb* *Syn* POLISH, buff, burnish, dress, gloss, grind, rub, shine

smoothly *Syn* EASILY, effortlessly, facilely, fluently, freely, handily, lightly, painlessly, readily *Ant* arduously, laboriously

smother *Syn* SUFFOCATE, asphyxiate, choke, stifle, strangle, throttle

smudge *Syn* DIRTY, befoul, begrime, besmirch, blacken, foul, grime, mire, muddy, smirch, soil, stain, sully *Ant* clean, cleanse

smug **1** *Syn* COMPLACENT, priggish, self-complacent, self-satisfied **2** *Syn* CONCEITED, complacent, egoistic, egotistic (*or* egotistical), important, overweening, pompous, prideful, proud, self-conceited, self-important, self-satisfied, stuck-up, vain, vainglorious *Ant* humble, modest

smuggled • imported or exported secretly and in violation of the law *Syn* bootleg, contraband

smugness *Syn* COMPLACENCE, complacency, conceit, conceitedness, ego, egotism, pompousness, pride, pridefulness, self-admiration, self-conceit, self-esteem, self-importance, self-satisfaction, vaingloriousness, vainglory, vainness, vanity *Ant* humbleness, humility, modesty

snap *vb* **1** *Syn* BREAK, burst, bust, crack, shatter, shiver *Ant* cleave (*together*), keep (*of laws*) **2** *Syn* JERK, twitch, yank

snap *n* *Syn* CINCH, breeze, child's play, duck soup, picnic, pushover *Ant* chore, headache, labor

snap back *Syn* CONVALESCE, gain, heal, mend, rally, recover, recuperate

snappish *Syn* IRRITABLE, fractious, fretful, huffy, peevish, pettish, petulant, querulous, waspish *Ant* easygoing
snappy *Syn* PUNGENT, piquant, poignant, racy, spicy *Ant* bland
snare **1** *Syn* CATCH, bag, capture, ensnare, entrap, trap *Ant* miss **2** *Syn* ENTANGLE, enmesh, ensnare, entrap, mesh, tangle, trap *Ant* disentangle
snarl *vb Syn* BARK, bay, growl, howl, yap, yelp
snarl *n Syn* CONFUSION, chaos, clutter, disarray, disorder, jumble, muddle
snatch *Syn* TAKE, clutch, grab, grasp, seize
sneak *Syn* LURK, skulk, slink
sneer *Syn* SCOFF, fleer, flout, gibe, gird, jeer
snip *Syn* CLIP, bob, crop, curtail, cut, cut back, dock, lop (off), nip, pare, prune, shave, shear, trim
snitch *Syn* STEAL, cop, filch, lift, pilfer, pinch, purloin, swipe
snoop *Syn* INTERFERE, butt in, intrude, meddle, mess, nose, obtrude, poke, pry
snoopy **1** *Syn* CURIOUS, inquisitive, nosy, prying *Ant* incurious, uninterested **2** *Syn* INTRUSIVE, interfering, intruding, meddlesome, meddling, nosy (*or* nosey), obtrusive, officious, presumptuous, prying *Ant* unobtrusive
snooze *Syn* SLEEP, catnap, doze, drowse, nap, slumber
snowball *Syn* INCREASE (sense 2), accumulate, appreciate, balloon, build (up), burgeon, enlarge, escalate, expand, mount, multiply, mushroom, proliferate, rise, swell, wax *Ant* contract, decrease, diminish, lessen, wane
snug **1** *Syn* COMFORTABLE, cozy, easy, restful *Ant* miserable, uncomfortable **2** *Syn* NEAT, shipshape, spick-and-span, tidy, trig, trim *Ant* filthy
so **1** *Syn* THEREFORE, accordingly, consequently, hence, then **2** *Syn* VERY, awful, awfully, beastly, deadly, especially, exceedingly, extra, extremely, far, frightfully, full, greatly, heavily, highly, hugely, jolly, mightily, mighty, mortally, most, much, particularly, rattling, real, right, something, super, terribly, too, whacking *Ant* little, negligibly, nominally, slightly
soak *vb* **1** • to permeate or be permeated with a liquid *Syn* drench, impregnate, saturate, sop, steep, waterlog *Rel* dip, immerse, submerge **2** *Syn* WET, bathe, douse, drench, souse, wash, water *Ant* dry
soak *n Syn* DRUNKARD, alcoholic, dipsomaniac, inebriate, sot, tippler, toper, tosspot *Ant* teetotaler
soar *Syn* ASCEND, arise, climb, lift, mount, rise, up, uprise, upsweep, upturn *Ant* decline, descend, dip, drop, fall (off)
sob *vb Syn* SIGH, groan, moan
sob *n Syn* SIGH, groan, moan
sober **1** • having or exhibiting self-control and avoiding extremes of behavior *Syn* continent, temperate, unimpassioned *Rel* abstaining, forbearing *Ant* drunk, excited **2** *Syn* SERIOUS, earnest, grave, sedate, solemn, somber, staid *Ant* flippant, light
soberness *Syn* EARNESTNESS, gravity, intentness, seriousness, sobriety, solemnity *Ant* frivolity, levity, lightheartedness
sobriety **1** *Syn* EARNESTNESS, gravity, intentness, seriousness, soberness, solemnity *Ant* frivolity, levity, lightheartedness **2** *Syn* TEMPERANCE, abstemiousness, abstinence, continence *Ant* excessiveness, immoderacy, intemperance, intemperateness
sociable **1** *Syn* CONVIVIAL, boon, companionable, extroverted, gregarious, outgoing, social *Ant* antisocial, introverted, reclusive, unsociable **2** *Syn* GRACIOUS, affable, cordial, genial *Ant* ungracious
social *Syn* CONVIVIAL, boon, companionable, extroverted, gregarious, outgoing, sociable *Ant* antisocial, introverted, reclusive, unsociable
socialize • to take part in social activities *Syn* associate, fraternize, hobnob, mingle, mix
society **1** *Syn* ARISTOCRACY, county, elite, gentry, nobility *Ant* people, proletariat **2** *Syn* ASSOCIATION, club, order **3** *Syn* COMPANIONSHIP, camaraderie, company, comradeship, fellowship
sofa *Syn* COUCH, chesterfield, davenport, divan, lounge, settee
soft • free from all harshness, roughness, or intensity *Syn* balmy, bland, gentle, lenient, mild, smooth *Rel* moderated, tempered *Ant* hard, stern
soften **1** *Syn* CUSHION, buffer, gentle **2** *Syn* WEAKEN, debilitate, enervate, enfeeble, sap
soft-soap *Syn* COAX, blandish, blarney, cajole, wheedle
soil *Syn* DIRTY, befoul, begrime, besmirch, blacken, foul, grime, mire, muddy, smirch, smudge, stain, sully *Ant* clean, cleanse
sojourn *Syn* RESIDE, dwell, live, lodge, put up, stay, stop
solace *Syn* COMFORT, console *Ant* afflict, bother
solar plexus *Syn* STOMACH, abdomen, belly, gut, tummy
sole **1** *Syn* ONLY, alone, lone, singular, solitary, special, unique **2** *Syn* SINGLE, lone, particular, separate, solitary, unique *Ant* accompanied, conjugal, supported
solecism **1** *Syn* BARBARISM, corruption, impropriety, vernacularism, vulgarism **2** *Syn* IMPROPRIETY (sense 1), familiarity, gaffe, indiscretion *Ant* amenity, civility, courtesy, formality, gesture
solemn **1** *Syn* CEREMONIAL, ceremonious, conventional, formal **2** *Syn* DIGNIFIED, august, imposing, staid, stately *Ant* flighty, frivolous, giddy, goofy, silly, undignified **3**

Syn SERIOUS, earnest, grave, sedate, sober, somber, staid *Ant* flippant, light

solemnity *Syn* EARNESTNESS, gravity, intentness, seriousness, soberness, sobriety *Ant* frivolity, levity, lightheartedness

solemnize *Syn* KEEP (sense 1), celebrate, commemorate, observe *Ant* break

solicit **1** *Syn* CANVASS, poll, survey **2** *Syn* INVITE, bid, court, woo **3** *Syn* ASK, request

solicitor **1** *Syn* LAWYER, advocate, attorney, barrister, counsel, counselor **2** *Syn* SUPPLICANT, petitioner, pleader, suitor, suppliant

solicitous *Syn* WORRIED, anxious, careful, concerned

solicitude *Syn* CARE, anxiety, concern, worry

solid **1** *Syn* DEPENDABLE, good, reliable, responsible, safe, steady, sure, tried, tried-and-true, true, trustworthy, trusty *Ant* irresponsible, undependable, unreliable, untrustworthy **2** *Syn* FIRM, hard *Ant* flabby, loose

solidarity *Syn* UNITY, integrity, union

solidify *Syn* HARDEN (sense 1), cake, indurate, petrify *Ant* soften

solitariness *Syn* ISOLATION, insulation, secludedness, seclusion, segregation, separateness, sequestration, solitude

solitary **1** *Syn* ALONE, desolate, forlorn, lone, lonely, lonesome, lorn *Ant* accompanied **2** *Syn* ONLY, alone, lone, singular, sole, special, unique **3** *Syn* SINGLE, lone, particular, separate, sole, unique *Ant* accompanied, conjugal, supported

solitude *Syn* ISOLATION, insulation, secludedness, seclusion, segregation, separateness, sequestration, solitariness

soluble *Syn* SOLVABLE, answerable, explainable, explicable, resolvable *Ant* inexplicable, insoluble, unexplainable, unsolvable

solution *Syn* ANSWER (sense 2), result

solvable • capable of having the reason for or cause of determined *Syn* answerable, explainable, explicable, resolvable, soluble *Rel* analyzable, decipherable *Ant* inexplicable, insoluble, unexplainable, unsolvable

solve • to find an answer for through reasoning *Syn* answer, break, crack, dope (out), figure out, puzzle (out), resolve, riddle, unravel, work, work out *Rel* clear (up), iron out, straighten (out), unscramble, untangle, untie

somatic *Syn* BODILY, corporal, corporeal, physical

somber *Syn* SERIOUS, earnest, grave, sedate, sober, solemn, staid *Ant* flippant, light

some *Syn* ALMOST, about, more or less, most, much, near, nearly, next to, nigh, practically, virtually, well-nigh

something *Syn* VERY, awful, awfully, beastly, deadly, especially, exceedingly, extra, extremely, far, frightfully, full, greatly, heavily, highly, hugely, jolly, mightily, mighty, mortally, most, much, particularly, rattling, real, right, so, super, terribly, too, whacking *Ant* little, negligibly, nominally, slightly

sometime *Syn* FORMER, erstwhile, late, old, onetime, past, whilom

somnolence *Syn* SLEEPINESS, drowsiness *Ant* insomnia, sleeplessness, wakefulness

somnolent *Syn* SLEEPY, drowsy, slumberous

song **1** *Syn* MELODY, air, lay, strain, tune, warble **2** *Syn* POEM, lyric, verse

sonny *Syn* BOY, lad, laddie, nipper, shaver, stripling, tad, youth

sonorous *Syn* RESONANT, orotund, resounding, ringing, vibrant

soon **1** *Syn* EARLY, beforehand, betimes *Ant* late **2** *Syn* PRESENTLY, directly, shortly **3** *Syn* SHORTLY, anon, momentarily, presently

soothe *Syn* CALM, compose, lull, quiet, quieten, settle, still, tranquilize *Ant* agitate, arouse

soothsayer *Syn* PROPHET, augur, diviner, forecaster, foreseer, foreteller, fortune-teller, futurist, prognosticator, prophesier, seer

soothsaying *Syn* PREDICTION, auguring, cast, forecast, forecasting, foretelling, predicting, presaging, prognosis, prognosticating, prognostication, prophecy

sop *Syn* SOAK, drench, impregnate, saturate, steep, waterlog

sophisticate *vb* *Syn* ADULTERATE, doctor, load, weight *Ant* refine

sophisticate *n* *Syn* COSMOPOLITAN, metropolitan *Ant* bumpkin, hick, provincial, rustic, yokel

sophisticated **1** *Syn* SUAVE, debonair, smooth, urbane *Ant* boorish, churlish, clownish, loutish, uncouth **2** *Syn* WORLDLY-WISE, cosmopolitan, smart, worldly *Ant* ingenuous, innocent, naive, unsophisticated, unworldly, wide-eyed

soppy *Syn* SENTIMENTAL, maudlin, mawkish, mushy, romantic, slushy

sorcerer *Syn* MAGICIAN (sense 1), charmer, conjurer (*or* conjuror), enchanter, necromancer, voodoo, witch, wizard

sorcery *Syn* MAGIC, alchemy, thaumaturgy, witchcraft, witchery, wizardry

sordid *Syn* MEAN, abject, ignoble

sore *Syn* ANGRY, angered, apoplectic, enraged, foaming, fuming, furious, incensed, indignant, inflamed, infuriated, irate, ireful, mad, outraged, rabid, riled, roiled, steaming, wrathful, wroth *Ant* delighted, pleased

sorrow *n* • distress of mind *Syn* anguish, grief, heartache, heartbreak, regret, woe *Rel* grieving, mourning *Ant* joy

sorrow *vb* *Syn* GRIEVE, mourn *Ant* rejoice

sorrowful *Syn* SAD (sense 1), bad, blue, brokenhearted, crestfallen, dejected, depressed, despondent, disconsolate, doleful, down, downcast, downhearted, droopy, forlorn, gloomy, glum, heartbroken, heartsick, heartsore, inconsolable, joyless, low, low-spirited, melancholy, miserable, mournful, saddened, sorry, unhappy, woebegone, woeful, wretched *Ant* blissful, buoyant, buoyed, cheerful, cheery, chipper, delighted, glad, gladdened, gladsome, gleeful, happy, joyful, joyous, jubilant, sunny, upbeat

sorry **1** *Syn* CONTEMPTIBLE, beggarly, cheap, despicable, pitiable, scurvy, shabby *Ant* admirable, estimable, formidable **2** *Syn* SAD (sense 1), bad, blue, brokenhearted, crestfallen, dejected, depressed, despondent, disconsolate, doleful, down, downcast, downhearted, droopy, forlorn, gloomy, glum, heartbroken, heartsick, heartsore, inconsolable, joyless, low, low-spirited, melancholy, miserable, mournful, saddened, sorrowful, unhappy, woebegone, woeful, wretched *Ant* blissful, buoyant, buoyed, cheerful, cheery, chipper, delighted, glad, gladdened, gladsome, gleeful, happy, joyful, joyous, jubilant, sunny, upbeat **3** *Syn* SAD (sense 2), depressing, dismal, drear, dreary, heartbreaking, heartrending, melancholy, pathetic, saddening, tearful, teary *Ant* cheering, cheery, glad, happy

sort *vb Syn* ASSORT, classify, pigeonhole

sort *n Syn* TYPE, character, description, ilk, kidney, kind, nature, stripe

sot *Syn* DRUNKARD, alcoholic, dipsomaniac, inebriate, soak, tippler, toper, tosspot *Ant* teetotaler

soul *Syn* MIND, brain, intellect, intelligence, psyche, wit

sound *vb* **1** *Syn* ANNOUNCE, advertise, blaze, broadcast, declare, enunciate, placard, post, proclaim, promulgate, publicize, publish **2** *Syn* FATHOM, plumb **3** *Syn* SEEM, act, appear, look, make

sound *adj Syn* HEALTHY, hale, robust, well, wholesome *Ant* unhealthy

sound *n Syn* STRAIT, channel, narrows, passage

soundless *Syn* SILENT (sense 2), hushed, muted, noiseless, quiet, quieted, still

soundness *Syn* HEALTH, fitness, healthiness, heartiness, robustness, wellness, wholeness, wholesomeness *Ant* illness, sickness, unhealthiness, unsoundness

sound off *Syn* SPEAK UP, speak out, spout (off)

soup *Syn* HAZE (sense 1), fog, mist, murk, reek, smog

soupçon *Syn* TOUCH, dash, shade, smack, spice, strain, streak, suggestion, suspicion, tincture, tinge, vein

sour **1** • having a taste devoid of sweetness *Syn* acid, acidulous, dry, tart *Rel* acrid, bitter **2** *Syn* UNPLEASANT, bad, disagreeable, displeasing, distasteful, nasty, rotten, uncongenial, unlovely, unpleasing, unsatisfying, unwelcome *Ant* agreeable, congenial, good, grateful, gratifying, nice, palatable, pleasant, pleasing, pleasurable, satisfying, welcome

source *Syn* ORIGIN, inception, prime mover, provenance, provenience, root

souring *Syn* ESTRANGEMENT, disaffection, disgruntlement *Ant* reconciliation

souse **1** *Syn* DIP (sense 1), duck, dunk, immerse, submerge **2** *Syn* WET, bathe, douse, drench, soak, wash, water *Ant* dry

souvenir **1** *Syn* MEMORIAL, commemorative, keepsake, memento, monument, remembrance, reminder, token **2** *Syn* MEMORY, mind, recollection, remembrance, reminiscence *Ant* oblivion

sovereign *adj* **1** *Syn* DOMINANT, paramount, predominant, preponderant, preponderating *Ant* subordinate **2** *Syn* FREE, autarchic, autarkic, autonomous, independent *Ant* bond

sovereign *n Syn* MONARCH, autocrat, ruler

sovereignty **1** *Syn* FREEDOM (sense 1), autarchy, autarky, autonomy, independence *Ant* bondage **2** *Syn* NATION, commonwealth, country, land, state **3** *Syn* SUPREMACY, ascendancy, dominance, dominion, preeminence

sow **1** *Syn* SCATTER (sense 2), bestrew, dot, pepper, spray, sprinkle, strew **2** *Syn* STREW, broadcast, scatter, straw

space-age *Syn* MODERN, contemporary, current, hot, mod, modernistic, new, newfangled, new-fashioned, present-day, red-hot, ultramodern, up-to-date *Ant* antiquated, archaic, dated, fusty, musty, noncontemporary, oldfangled, old-fashioned, old-time, out-of-date, passé

spacious • larger in extent or capacity than the average *Syn* ample, capacious, commodious *Rel* enormous, huge, immense, vast

spade *Syn* DIG, delve, excavate, grub

spangled *Syn* SPOTTED, bespangled, flecked, marbled, mottled, spattered, speckled, sprinkled, stippled

spare **1** *Syn* LEAN, angular, gaunt, lank, lanky, rawboned, scrawny, skinny *Ant* fleshy **2** *Syn* MEAGER, exiguous, scant, scanty, scrimpy, skimpy, sparse *Ant* ample, copious **3** *Syn* SUPERFLUOUS, extra, supernumerary, surplus

sparing *Syn* FRUGAL, economical, economizing, provident, scrimping, thrifty *Ant* prodigal, wasteful

spark *Syn* ACTIVATE, actuate, crank (up), drive, move, propel, run, set off, start, touch off, trigger, turn on *Ant* cut, deactivate, kill, shut off, turn off

sparkle *Syn* FLASH, coruscate, glance, gleam, glint, glisten, glitter, scintillate, twinkle

sparse *Syn* MEAGER, exiguous, scant, scanty, scrimpy, skimpy, spare *Ant* ample, copious

spasm **1** *Syn* CRAMP, charley horse, crick **2** *Syn* FIT, convulsion, paroxysm

spasmodic *Syn* FITFUL, casual, choppy, discontinuous, erratic, intermittent, irregular, occasional, sporadic, spotty, unsteady *Ant* constant, continuous, regular, steady

spat *Syn* QUARREL, altercation, bickering, squabble, tiff, wrangle

spate *Syn* FLOOD, cataract, deluge, inundation, torrent

spattered *Syn* SPOTTED, bespangled, flecked, marbled, mottled, spangled, speckled, sprinkled, stippled

spawn *Syn* EFFECT, bring about, cause, create, effectuate, engender, generate, induce, make, produce, prompt, result (in), work, yield

spay *Syn* STERILIZE (sense 1), alter, castrate, emasculate, geld, mutilate *Ant* fertilize

speak • to articulate words so as to express thoughts *Syn* converse, talk *Rel* articulate, enunciate, pronounce

speak out *Syn* SPEAK UP, sound off, spout (off)

speak up • to voice one's opinions freely with force *Syn* sound off, speak out, spout (off) *Rel* bawl, call, cry, holler, shout, sing (out), vociferate, yell

special **1** of or relating to one thing or class *Syn* especial, individual, particular, specific *Rel* characteristic, distinctive, peculiar **2** *Syn* ONLY, alone, lone, singular, sole, solitary, unique

specie *Syn* MONEY, cash, coin, coinage, currency, legal tender

specific *adj* **1** *Syn* EXPLICIT, categorical, definite, express *Ant* ambiguous **2** *Syn* SPECIAL, especial, individual, particular

specific *n* *Syn* REMEDY, cure, medicament, medication, medicine, physic

specify *Syn* MENTION, instance, name

specimen *Syn* EXAMPLE, case, exemplar, illustration, instance, representative, sample

specious *Syn* PLAUSIBLE, believable, colorable, credible

speck *Syn* SPOT, blotch, dapple, dot, fleck, freckle, marble, mottle, pepper, speckle, splotch, sprinkle, stipple

speckle *Syn* SPOT, blotch, dapple, dot, fleck, freckle, marble, mottle, pepper, speck, splotch, sprinkle, stipple

speckled *Syn* SPOTTED, bespangled, flecked, marbled, mottled, spangled, spattered, sprinkled, stippled

spectator • one who looks on or watches *Syn* beholder, bystander, eyewitness, kibitzer, looker-on, observer, onlooker, witness

specter *or* **spectre** *Syn* GHOST, apparition, bogey, phantasm, phantom, poltergeist, shade, shadow, spirit, spook, vision, wraith

speculate *Syn* THINK (sense 2), cogitate, deliberate, reason, reflect

speculative **1** *Syn* THEORETICAL, academic **2** *Syn* THOUGHTFUL (sense 1), contemplative, meditative, pensive, reflective *Ant* thoughtless

speech **1** • a usually formal discourse delivered to an audience *Syn* address, harangue, homily, lecture, oration, sermon, talk **2** *Syn* LANGUAGE (sense 1), dialect, idiom, tongue

speechless **1** *Syn* MUTE, inarticulate, voiceless **2** *Syn* SILENT (sense 3), dumb, mum, mute, uncommunicative, wordless

speed *n* **1** • rate of motion, performance, or action *Syn* headway, impetus, momentum, pace, velocity **2** *Syn* HASTE, dispatch, expedition, hurry *Ant* deliberation

speed *vb* *Syn* HURRY (sense 2), barrel, bolt, bowl, breeze, career, course, dash, fly, hasten, hotfoot (it), hump, hurtle, hustle, pelt, race, rip, rocket, run, rush, rustle, scoot, scurry, scuttle, shoot, step (along), tear, trot, whirl, whisk, zip, zoom *Ant* crawl, creep, poke

speed (up) *Syn* HURRY (sense 1), accelerate, hasten, quicken, rush, whisk *Ant* decelerate, retard, slow (down)

speedy *Syn* FAST, expeditious, fleet, hasty, quick, rapid, swift *Ant* slow

spell **1** • a limited period or amount of activity *Syn* bout, go, shift, stint, tour, trick, turn *Rel* period **2** *Syn* ATTACK (sense 3), bout, case, fit, seizure, siege

spell out *Syn* EXPLAIN (sense 1), clarify, clear (up), construe, demonstrate, elucidate, explicate, expound, illuminate, illustrate, interpret *Ant* obscure

spend **1** • to use up or pay out *Syn* disburse, expend *Rel* deal, dispense, distribute, divide, dole *Ant* save **2** *Syn* DEPLETE, clean (out), consume, drain, exhaust, expend, use up *Ant* renew, replace

spender *Syn* PRODIGAL, profligate, spendthrift, squanderer, waster, wastrel *Ant* economizer

spendthrift *adj* *Syn* PRODIGAL, extravagant, profligate, squandering, thriftless, unthrifty, wasteful *Ant* conserving, economical, economizing, frugal, scrimping, skimping, thrifty

spendthrift *n* *Syn* PRODIGAL, profligate, spender, squanderer, waster, wastrel *Ant* economizer

spew **1** *Syn* BELCH, burp, disgorge, regurgitate, throw up, vomit **2** *Syn* ERUPT (sense 2), belch, disgorge, eject, expel, jet, spout, spurt **3** *Syn* GUSH (sense 1), jet, pour, rush, spout, spurt, squirt *Ant* dribble, drip, drop, trickle

sphere *Syn* FIELD, bailiwick, domain, province, territory

spice *Syn* TOUCH, dash, shade, smack, soupçon, strain, streak, suggestion, suspicion, tincture, tinge, vein

spick-and-span *Syn* NEAT, shipshape, snug, tidy, trig, trim *Ant* filthy

spicy *Syn* PUNGENT, piquant, poignant, racy, snappy *Ant* bland

spin *n* *Syn* HAZE (sense 2), daze, fog, muddle

spin *vb Syn* TURN (sense 1), circle, eddy, gyrate, pirouette, revolve, rotate, swirl, twirl, wheel, whirl
spindling *Syn* LANKY, gangling, gangly, rangy, spindly
spindly *Syn* LANKY, gangling, gangly, rangy, spindling
spine • the articulated column of bones that is the central and axial feature of a vertebrate skeleton *Syn* back, backbone, chine, vertebrae
spineless *Syn* COWARDLY, chicken, chickenhearted, craven, dastardly, lily-livered, pusillanimous, recreant, unheroic, yellow *Ant* brave, courageous, daring, dauntless, doughty, fearless, gallant, greathearted, gutsy, hardy, heroic, intrepid, lionhearted, stalwart, stout, stouthearted, valiant, valorous
spin-off *Syn* DERIVATIVE, by-product, offshoot, outgrowth *Ant* origin, root, source
spiral • turning around an axis like the thread of a screw *Syn* coiling, corkscrew, helical, screwlike, winding *Rel* curling, curving, twisting
spirit **1** *Syn* GHOST, apparition, bogey, phantasm, phantom, poltergeist, shade, shadow, specter (*or* spectre), spook, vision, wraith **2** *Syn* VIGOR, dash, drive, élan, esprit, punch, verve, vim
spirited • full of energy, animation, or courage *Syn* fiery, gingery, high-spirited, mettlesome, peppery, spunky *Rel* audacious, bold, brave, courageous, intrepid, valiant *Ant* spiritless
spiritless *Syn* LISTLESS, enervated, lackadaisical, languid, languishing, languorous, limp *Ant* ambitious, animated, energetic, enterprising, motivated
spirits *Syn* ALCOHOL, booze, drink, grog, intoxicant, liquor, moonshine
spiritual *Syn* IMMATERIAL, incorporeal *Ant* material
spite *Syn* MALICE, despite, grudge, ill will, malevolence, malignancy, malignity, spleen *Ant* charity
spiteful *Syn* MALICIOUS, malevolent, malign, malignant
splashy *Syn* GAUDY, flamboyant, flashy, garish, glitzy, loud, ostentatious, swank (*or* swanky), tawdry *Ant* conservative, quiet, understated
spleen **1** *Syn* ANGER, angriness, furor, fury, indignation, irateness, ire, outrage, rage, wrath, wrathfulness *Ant* delight, pleasure **2** *Syn* MALICE, despite, grudge, ill will, malevolence, malignancy, malignity, spite *Ant* charity
splendid **1** • extraordinarily or transcendently impressive *Syn* glorious, gorgeous, resplendent, sublime, superb *Rel* bright, brilliant, effulgent, luminous, radiant **2** *Syn* EXCELLENT, A1, bang-up, banner, capital, classic, crackerjack, dandy, divine, fabulous, fine, first-class, first-rate, grand, great, groovy, heavenly, jim-dandy, keen, marvelous (*or* marvellous), mean, neat, nifty, noble, par excellence, prime, sensational, stellar, sterling, superb, superior, superlative, supernal, swell, terrific, tip-top, top, top-notch, unsurpassed, wonderful *Ant* poor
splendor *Syn* MAGNIFICENCE, augustness, brilliance, gloriousness, glory, grandeur, grandness, majesty, nobility, nobleness, resplendence, stateliness, stupendousness, sublimeness, superbness
splenetic *Syn* IRASCIBLE, choleric, cranky, cross, testy, touchy
split *vb Syn* TEAR, cleave, rend, rip, rive
split *n Syn* BREACH, break, rent, rift, rupture, schism
split second *Syn* INSTANT, flash, jiffy, minute, moment, second, shake, trice, twinkle, twinkling, wink
splotch *Syn* SPOT, blotch, dapple, dot, fleck, freckle, marble, mottle, pepper, speck, speckle, sprinkle, stipple
spoil *n* • something taken from another by force or craft *Syn* booty, loot, plunder, prize, swag *Rel* burglary, larceny, robbery, theft
spoil *vb* **1** *Syn* BABY, coddle, dandle, mollycoddle, nurse, pamper *Ant* abuse, ill-treat, ill-use, maltreat, mishandle, mistreat, misuse **2** *Syn* DECAY, crumble, decompose, disintegrate, putrefy, rot **3** *Syn* INJURE, damage, harm, hurt, impair, mar *Ant* aid
spoken *Syn* VERBAL, oral, unwritten *Ant* written
spoliate *Syn* RAVAGE, despoil, devastate, pillage, sack, waste
sponge *Syn* PARASITE, bootlicker, favorite, hanger-on, leech, lickspittle, sponger, sycophant, toady
sponger *Syn* PARASITE, bootlicker, favorite, hanger-on, leech, lickspittle, sponge, sycophant, toady
sponsor • one who assumes responsibility for some other person or thing *Syn* angel, backer, guarantor, patron, surety *Rel* advocate, advocator, champion, support, supporter, upholder
spontaneity *Syn* ABANDON, abandonment, ease, lightheartedness, naturalness, unrestraint *Ant* constraint, restraint
spontaneous • acting or activated without deliberation *Syn* automatic, impulsive, instinctive, mechanical *Rel* extemporaneous, extempore, impromptu, improvised, offhand, unpremeditated
spook *Syn* GHOST, apparition, bogey, phantasm, phantom, poltergeist, shade, shadow, specter (*or* spectre), spirit, vision, wraith
spooky **1** *Syn* EERIE, creepy, haunting, uncanny, unearthly, weird **2** *Syn* EXCITABLE, flighty, fluttery, high-strung, jittery, jumpy, nervous, skittish *Ant* unflappable

spoon *Syn* DIP (sense 2), bail, dish, ladle, scoop
sporadic **1** *Syn* FITFUL, casual, choppy, discontinuous, erratic, intermittent, irregular, occasional, spasmodic, spotty, unsteady *Ant* constant, continuous, regular, steady **2** *Syn* INFREQUENT, occasional, rare, scarce, uncommon *Ant* frequent
sport *n* **1** *Syn* FUN, game, jest, play **2** *Syn* PLAY, disport, frolic, gambol, rollick, romp
sport *vb* *Syn* PLAY, disport, frolic, gambol, rollick, romp *Ant* work
sportive *Syn* PLAYFUL, frolicsome, impish, mischievous, roguish, waggish
sports *Syn* ATHLETICS, games
spot *vb* • to mark with small spots especially unevenly *Syn* blotch, dapple, dot, fleck, freckle, marble, mottle, pepper, speck, speckle, splotch, sprinkle, stipple *Rel* blot, dye, stain
spot *n* *Syn* PLACE, location, position, site, situation, station
spotted • marked with spots or streaks *Syn* bespangled, flecked, marbled, mottled, spangled, spattered, speckled, sprinkled, stippled
spotty *Syn* FITFUL, casual, choppy, discontinuous, erratic, intermittent, irregular, occasional, spasmodic, sporadic, unsteady *Ant* constant, continuous, regular, steady
spouse • the person to whom another is married *Syn* consort, mate, partner *Rel* husband, man, old man
spout **1** *Syn* ERUPT (sense 2), belch, disgorge, eject, expel, jet, spew, spurt **2** *Syn* GUSH (sense 1), jet, pour, rush, spew, spurt, squirt *Ant* dribble, drip, drop, trickle **3** *Syn* RANT, bluster, fulminate, rave
spout (off) *Syn* SPEAK UP, sound off, speak out
spray *Syn* SCATTER (sense 2), bestrew, dot, pepper, sow, sprinkle, strew
spread *vb* **1** • to extend or cause to extend over an area or space *Syn* circulate, diffuse, disseminate, propagate, radiate *Rel* deal, dispense, distribute **2** *Syn* COMMUNICATE, convey, impart, transfer, transfuse, transmit
spread *n* *Syn* EXPANSE, amplitude, stretch
sprightly *Syn* LIVELY, animated, gay, vivacious *Ant* dull
spring *vb* **1** • to come up or out of something into existence *Syn* arise, derive, emanate, flow, issue, originate, proceed, rise, stem *Rel* appear, emerge, loom **2** *Syn* BEGIN (sense 1), arise, commence, dawn, form, materialize, originate, set in, start *Ant* cease, end, stop **3** *Syn* JUMP, bound, leap, vault
spring *n* **1** *Syn* JUMP, bound, leap, vault **2** *Syn* MOTIVE, goad, impulse, incentive, inducement, spur
springy *Syn* ELASTIC (sense 1), flexible, resilient, supple *Ant* rigid
sprinkle **1** *Syn* SCATTER (sense 2), bestrew, dot, pepper, sow, spray, strew **2** *Syn* SPOT, blotch, dapple, dot, fleck, freckle, marble, mottle, pepper, speck, speckle, splotch, stipple
sprinkled *Syn* SPOTTED, bespangled, flecked, marbled, mottled, spangled, spattered, speckled, stippled
sprint *Syn* SCUTTLE, scamper, scurry, skedaddle
sprite *Syn* FAIRY, brownie, elf, fay, pixie (*also* pixy)
sprucely *Syn* SMARTLY, dashingly, nattily, sharply *Ant* sloppily, slovenly
spry *Syn* AGILE, brisk, nimble *Ant* torpid
spryness *Syn* DEXTERITY (sense 2), agility, deftness, nimbleness, sleight *Ant* awkwardness, clumsiness, gawkiness
spume *Syn* FOAM, froth, lather, scum, suds, yeast
spunky *Syn* SPIRITED, fiery, gingery, high-spirited, mettlesome, peppery *Ant* spiritless
spur *Syn* MOTIVE, goad, impulse, incentive, inducement, spring
spurious *Syn* COUNTERFEIT, bogus, fake, phony, pinchbeck, pseudo, sham *Ant* bona fide, genuine
spurn *Syn* DECLINE, refuse, reject, repudiate *Ant* accept
spurt *vb* **1** *Syn* ERUPT (sense 2), belch, disgorge, eject, expel, jet, spew, spout **2** *Syn* GUSH (sense 1), jet, pour, rush, spew, spout, squirt *Ant* dribble, drip, drop, trickle
spurt *n* *Syn* OUTBREAK, burst, flare, flare-up, flash, flicker, flurry, flutter, outburst
squabble *Syn* QUARREL, altercation, bickering, spat, tiff, wrangle
squalid *Syn* DIRTY, filthy, foul, nasty *Ant* clean
squall *n* *Syn* COMMOTION, bother, bustle, clatter, disturbance, furor, furore, fuss, hubbub, hullabaloo, hurly-burly, pandemonium, pother, row, ruckus, ruction, rumpus, shindy, stew, stir, storm, to-do, tumult, turmoil, uproar, welter, whirl
squall *vb* *Syn* SCREAM, howl, screech, shriek, shrill, squeal, yell, yelp
squander *Syn* WASTE, consume, dissipate, fritter *Ant* conserve, save
squanderer *Syn* PRODIGAL, profligate, spender, spendthrift, waster, wastrel *Ant* economizer
squandering *Syn* PRODIGAL, extravagant, profligate, spendthrift, thriftless, unthrifty, wasteful *Ant* conserving, economical, economizing, frugal, scrimping, skimping, thrifty
square *Syn* AGREE (sense 2), accord, conform, correspond, harmonize, jibe, tally *Ant* differ (from)
squash *Syn* CRUSH (sense 1), bruise, macerate, mash, smash
squat *Syn* STOCKY, chunky, dumpy, stubby, thick, thickset

squawk *Syn* COMPLAIN, beef, bellyache, carp, crab, croak, fuss, gripe, grouse, growl, grumble, kick, moan, murmur, mutter, repine, wail, whine, yammer *Ant* rejoice

squeaking *Syn* SHRILL, acute, high-pitched, piping, screeching, shrieking, squeaky, treble, whistling *Ant* bass, deep, low, throaty

squeaky *Syn* SHRILL, acute, high-pitched, piping, screeching, shrieking, squeaking, treble, whistling *Ant* bass, deep, low, throaty

squeal *vb* **1** *Syn* SCREAM, howl, screech, shriek, shrill, squall, yell, yelp **2** *Syn* SHOUT, holler, scream, screech, shriek, whoop, yell

squeal *n Syn* SHOUT, holler, scream, screech, shriek, whoop, yell

squeamish *Syn* NICE, dainty, fastidious, finical, finicking, finicky, fussy, particular, pernickety, persnickety

squeeze **1** *Syn* FLEECE, bleed, cheat, chisel, cozen, defraud, hustle, mulct, rook, shortchange, skin, stick, sting, swindle, victimize **2** *Syn* PRESS, bear, bear down, crowd, jam

squire *Syn* ACCOMPANY, attend, chaperone (*or* chaperon), convoy, escort

squirm *Syn* WRITHE, agonize

squirrel (away) *Syn* HOARD, cache, lay away, lay up, put by, salt away, stash, stockpile, store, stow

squirt *Syn* GUSH (sense 1), jet, pour, rush, spew, spout, spurt *Ant* dribble, drip, drop, trickle

stab *Syn* ATTEMPT, crack, endeavor, essay, fling, go, pass, shot, trial, try, whack

stabilize • to make or become stable, steadfast, or firm *Syn* balance, ballast, poise, steady, trim *Rel* adjust, fix, regulate

stable **1** *Syn* LASTING, durable, perdurable, permanent, perpetual *Ant* fleeting **2** *Syn* SANE, balanced, clearheaded, lucid, normal, right *Ant* crazed, crazy, demented, deranged, insane, lunatic, mad, maniacal, mental, unbalanced, unsound

stack *n Syn* HEAP, bank, cock, mass, pile, shock

stack *vb Syn* HEAP, bank, cock, mass, pile, shock

stage *Syn* PLATFORM, dais, podium, rostrum, stand

stagger *Syn* REEL, totter, whirl

staid **1** *Syn* DIGNIFIED, august, imposing, solemn, stately *Ant* flighty, frivolous, giddy, goofy, silly, undignified **2** *Syn* SERIOUS, earnest, grave, sedate, sober, solemn, somber *Ant* flippant, light

stain *vb Syn* DIRTY, befoul, begrime, besmirch, blacken, foul, grime, mire, muddy, smirch, smudge, soil, sully *Ant* clean, cleanse

stain *n* **1** *Syn* PIGMENT, color, coloring, dye, dyestuff, tincture **2** *Syn* STIGMA, blot, brand

stake *n Syn* BET, ante, pot, wager

stake *vb Syn* BET, gamble, go, lay, wager

stale • used or heard so often as to be dull *Syn* banal, commonplace, hackney, hackneyed, moth-eaten, musty, stereotyped, threadbare, tired, trite *Rel* canned, unimaginative, uninspired, unoriginal *Ant* fresh, new, original

stalemate *Syn* DRAW, deadlock, standoff, tie

stalwart *Syn* STRONG, stout, sturdy, tenacious, tough *Ant* weak

stamp *n* **1** *Syn* IMPRESSION, impress, imprint, print **2** *Syn* MARK, brand, label, tag, ticket

stamp *vb* **1** *Syn* MARK, brand, label, tag, ticket **2** *Syn* TRAMPLE, stomp, tramp, tromp

stand *vb Syn* BEAR (sense 2), abide, brook, endure, suffer, tolerate

stand *n* **1** *Syn* PLATFORM, dais, podium, rostrum, stage **2** *Syn* POSITION, attitude

standard **1** • a means of determining what a thing should be *Syn* criterion, gauge, touchstone, yardstick *Rel* average, mean, median, norm, par **2** *Syn* AVERAGE, norm, normal, par **3** *Syn* FLAG, banner, color, ensign, jack, pendant, pennant, pennon, streamer **4** *Syn* MODEL, beau ideal, example, exemplar, ideal, mirror, pattern

standardize • to make agree with a single established standard or model *Syn* formalize, homogenize, normalize, regularize *Rel* codify, organize, systematize

standards *Syn* ETHICS, morality, morals, principles

stand-in *Syn* SUBSTITUTE, backup, pinch hitter, relief, replacement, reserve, sub

standing *Syn* ERECT, perpendicular, plumb, raised, upright, upstanding, vertical *Ant* flat, recumbent

standoff *Syn* DRAW, deadlock, stalemate, tie

standpoint *Syn* POINT OF VIEW, angle, slant, viewpoint

star **1** *Syn* EMINENT, distinguished, illustrious, noble, notable, noteworthy, outstanding, preeminent, prestigious, signal, superior **2** *Syn* FAMOUS, celebrated, famed, noted, notorious, prominent, renowned, well-known *Ant* anonymous, obscure, unknown

stare **1** *Syn* GAPE, gawk, gaze, goggle, peer, rubberneck **2** *Syn* GAZE, gape, glare, gloat, peer

stark *Syn* STIFF, inflexible, rigid, tense, wooden *Ant* relaxed, supple

starry • of, relating to, or suggestive of a star or group of stars *Syn* astral, sidereal, stellar

start *vb* **1** *Syn* ACTIVATE, actuate, crank (up), drive, move, propel, run, set off, spark, touch off, trigger, turn on *Ant* cut, deactivate, kill, shut off, turn off **2** *Syn* BEGIN (sense 1), arise, commence, dawn, form, materialize, originate, set in, spring *Ant* cease, end, stop **3** *Syn* BEGIN (sense 2), commence, embark (on *or* upon), enter (into *or* upon), get off, kick off, launch, open, strike (into) *Ant* conclude, end, finish, terminate

start *n Syn* BEGINNING, alpha, birth, commencement, dawn, genesis, inception, incipiency, launch, morning, onset, outset, threshold *Ant* close, conclusion, end, ending
startle *Syn* FRIGHTEN, affray, affright, alarm, fright, scare, terrify, terrorize *Ant* reassure
stash *Syn* HOARD, cache, lay away, lay up, put by, salt away, squirrel (away), stockpile, store, stow
state *n* **1** • the way in which one manifests existence or the circumstances under which one exists or by which one is given distinctive character *Syn* condition, mode, posture, situation, status *Rel* aspect, phase **2** *Syn* NATION, commonwealth, country, land, sovereignty
state *vb* **1** *Syn* PHRASE, articulate, clothe, couch, express, formulate, put, say, word **2** *Syn* RELATE, describe, narrate, recite, recount, rehearse, report **3** *Syn* SAY, tell, utter
stateliness **1** *Syn* ELEGANCE, class, elegancy, grace, gracefulness, handsomeness, majesty, refinement **2** *Syn* MAGNIFICENCE, augustness, brilliance, gloriousness, glory, grandeur, grandness, majesty, nobility, nobleness, resplendence, splendor, stupendousness, sublimeness, superbness
stately **1** *Syn* DIGNIFIED, august, imposing, solemn, staid *Ant* flighty, frivolous, giddy, goofy, silly, undignified **2** *Syn* GRAND, august, grandiose, imposing, magnificent, majestic, noble
statesman *Syn* POLITICIAN, politico
station **1** *Syn* HABITAT, biotope, range **2** *Syn* PLACE, location, position, site, situation, spot
statue *Syn* IMAGE, effigy, mask, photograph, portrait
stature *Syn* QUALITY (sense 2), caliber
status *Syn* STATE, condition, mode, posture, situation
statute *Syn* LAW, canon, ordinance, precept, regulation, rule
staunch *or* **stanch** *Syn* FAITHFUL, constant, devoted, devout, fast, good, loyal, pious, steadfast, steady, true, true-blue *Ant* disloyal, faithless, false, fickle, inconstant, perfidious, recreant, traitorous, treacherous, unfaithful, untrue
stay **1** • to continue to be in one place for a noticeable time *Syn* abide, linger, remain, tarry, wait *Rel* delay, lag, loiter, procrastinate **2** *Syn* BASE, found, ground, rest **3** *Syn* RESIDE, dwell, live, lodge, put up, sojourn, stop
steadfast *Syn* FAITHFUL, constant, devoted, devout, fast, good, loyal, pious, staunch (*or* stanch), steady, true, true-blue *Ant* disloyal, faithless, false, fickle, inconstant, perfidious, recreant, traitorous, treacherous, unfaithful, untrue
steady *adj* **1** • not varying throughout a course or extent *Syn* constant, equable, even, uniform *Rel* durable, lasting, perdurable, perpetual, stable *Ant* jumpy, nervous, unsteady **2** *Syn* DEPENDABLE, good, reliable, responsible, safe, solid, sure, tried, tried-and-true, true, trustworthy, trusty *Ant* irresponsible, undependable, unreliable, untrustworthy **3** *Syn* FAITHFUL, constant, devoted, devout, fast, good, loyal, pious, staunch (*or* stanch), steadfast, true, true-blue *Ant* disloyal, faithless, false, fickle, inconstant, perfidious, recreant, traitorous, treacherous, unfaithful, untrue **4** *Syn* UNIFORM, invariant, unchanging, undeviating, unvarying, unwavering *Ant* changing, deviating, varying
steady *vb Syn* STABILIZE, balance, ballast, poise, trim
steal • to take from another without right or without detection *Syn* cop, filch, lift, pilfer, pinch, purloin, snitch, swipe *Rel* burglarize, loot, plunder, rifle, rob
stealthy *Syn* SECRET, clandestine, covert, furtive, surreptitious, underhand, underhanded
steaming *Syn* ANGRY, angered, apoplectic, enraged, foaming, fuming, furious, incensed, indignant, inflamed, infuriated, irate, ireful, mad, outraged, rabid, riled, roiled, sore, wrathful, wroth *Ant* delighted, pleased
steel *Syn* ENCOURAGE, cheer, embolden, hearten, inspirit, nerve *Ant* discourage
steep *adj* • having an incline approaching the perpendicular *Syn* abrupt, precipitous, sheer *Rel* elevated, lifted, raised
steep *vb Syn* SOAK, drench, impregnate, saturate, sop, waterlog
steer *Syn* GUIDE, engineer, lead, pilot *Ant* misguide
stellar **1** *Syn* EXCELLENT, A1, bang-up, banner, capital, classic, crackerjack, dandy, divine, fabulous, fine, first-class, first-rate, grand, great, groovy, heavenly, jim-dandy, keen, marvelous (*or* marvellous), mean, neat, nifty, noble, par excellence, prime, sensational, splendid, sterling, superb, superior, superlative, supernal, swell, terrific, tip-top, top, top-notch, unsurpassed, wonderful *Ant* poor **2** *Syn* STARRY, astral, sidereal
stem *Syn* SPRING, arise, derive, emanate, flow, issue, originate, proceed, rise
stentorian *Syn* LOUD, earsplitting, hoarse, raucous, stertorous, strident *Ant* low, low-pitched
step *Syn* WALK, foot (it), hoof (it), leg (it), pad, traipse, tread
step (along) *Syn* HURRY (sense 2), barrel, bolt, bowl, breeze, career, course, dash, fly, hasten, hotfoot (it), hump, hurtle, hustle, pelt, race, rip, rocket, run, rush, rustle, scoot, scurry, scuttle, shoot, speed, tear, trot, whirl, whisk, zip, zoom *Ant* crawl, creep, poke
step-by-step *Syn* GRADUAL, gradational, incremental, phased, piecemeal *Ant* sudden
steppe *Syn* PLAIN, down, grassland, prairie, savanna, tundra, veld (*or* veldt)

stereotyped *Syn* STALE, banal, commonplace, hackney, hackneyed, moth-eaten, musty, threadbare, tired, trite *Ant* fresh, new, original

sterile **1** • not able to bear fruit, crops, or offspring *Syn* barren, impotent, infertile, unfruitful *Rel* bald, bare, naked *Ant* exuberant, fertile **2** *Syn* SANITARY, aseptic, germfree, hygienic *Ant* insanitary, unhygienic, unsanitary

sterilize **1** • to make incapable of producing offspring *Syn* alter, castrate, emasculate, geld, mutilate, spay *Ant* fertilize **2** • to free from living microorganisms *Syn* disinfect, fumigate, sanitize

sterling *Syn* EXCELLENT, A1, bang-up, banner, capital, classic, crackerjack, dandy, divine, fabulous, fine, first-class, first-rate, grand, great, groovy, heavenly, jim-dandy, keen, marvelous (*or* marvellous), mean, neat, nifty, noble, par excellence, prime, sensational, splendid, stellar, superb, superior, superlative, supernal, swell, terrific, tip-top, top, top-notch, unsurpassed, wonderful *Ant* poor

stern *Syn* SEVERE, ascetic, austere *Ant* tender, tolerant

sternness *Syn* SEVERITY, hardness, harshness, inflexibility, rigidity, rigidness, rigorousness, strictness *Ant* flexibility, gentleness, laxness, mildness

stertorous *Syn* LOUD, earsplitting, hoarse, raucous, stentorian, strident *Ant* low, low-pitched

stew *vb Syn* BOIL, parboil, seethe, simmer

stew *n Syn* COMMOTION, bother, bustle, clatter, disturbance, furor, furore, fuss, hubbub, hullabaloo, hurly-burly, pandemonium, pother, row, ruckus, ruction, rumpus, shindy, squall, stir, storm, to-do, tumult, turmoil, uproar, welter, whirl

steward *Syn* SERVANT, domestic, flunky, lackey, menial, retainer *Ant* master

stick **1** • to become or cause to become closely and firmly attached *Syn* adhere, cleave, cling, cohere *Rel* bind, tie **2** *Syn* DEMUR, balk, boggle, jib, scruple, shy, stickle, strain *Ant* accede **3** *Syn* FLEECE, bleed, cheat, chisel, cozen, defraud, hustle, mulct, rook, shortchange, skin, squeeze, sting, swindle, victimize

stickle *Syn* DEMUR, balk, boggle, jib, scruple, shy, stick, strain *Ant* accede

stick out *Syn* BULGE, beetle, jut, overhang, project, protrude

stiff • difficult to bend *Syn* inflexible, rigid, stark, tense, wooden *Rel* stout, strong, tenacious, tough *Ant* relaxed, supple

stifle *Syn* SUFFOCATE, asphyxiate, choke, smother, strangle, throttle

stigma • a mark of shame or discredit *Syn* blot, brand, stain *Rel* disgrace, dishonor, odium, opprobrium, shame

still *adj* **1** • making no stir or noise *Syn* noiseless, quiet, silent, stilly *Rel* calm, peaceful, placid, serene, tranquil *Ant* noisy, stirring **2** *Syn* SILENT (sense 2), hushed, muted, noiseless, quiet, quieted, soundless *Ant* noisy, unquiet

still *n* **1** *Syn* CALM, calmness, hush, peace, peace, peacefulness, placidity, quiet, quietness, quietude, repose, restfulness, sereneness, serenity, stillness, tranquillity (*or* tranquility) *Ant* bustle, commotion, hubbub, hurly-burly, pandemonium, tumult, turmoil, uproar **2** *Syn* SILENCE, hush, quiet, quietness, quietude, stillness *Ant* noise, sound

still *vb Syn* CALM, compose, lull, quiet, quieten, settle, soothe, tranquilize *Ant* agitate, arouse

stillness **1** *Syn* CALM, calmness, hush, peace, peacefulness, placidity, quiet, quietness, quietude, repose, restfulness, sereneness, serenity, still, tranquillity (*or* tranquility) *Ant* bustle, commotion, hubbub, hurly-burly, pandemonium, tumult, turmoil, uproar **2** *Syn* SILENCE, hush, quiet, quietness, quietude, still *Ant* noise, sound

stilly *Syn* STILL, noiseless, quiet, silent *Ant* noisy, stirring

stimulant *Syn* STIMULUS, excitant, impetus, incitement

stimulate **1** *Syn* ANIMATE, brace, energize, enliven, fire, invigorate, jazz (up), liven (up), pep (up), quicken, vitalize, vivify *Ant* damp, dampen, deaden, dull **2** *Syn* PROVOKE, excite, galvanize, pique, quicken

stimulating **1** *Syn* PROVOCATIVE, exciting, inciting, instigating, piquing, provoking **2** *Syn* TONIC, bracing, invigorating, refreshing, restorative, reviving, stimulative, vitalizing

stimulative *Syn* TONIC, bracing, invigorating, refreshing, restorative, reviving, stimulating, vitalizing

stimulus • something that rouses or incites to activity *Syn* excitant, impetus, incitement, stimulant *Rel* goad, incentive, inducement, motive, spur

sting *Syn* FLEECE, bleed, cheat, chisel, cozen, defraud, hustle, mulct, rook, shortchange, skin, squeeze, stick, swindle, victimize

stingy • being unwilling or showing unwillingness to share with others *Syn* cheeseparing, close, closefisted, miserly, niggardly, parsimonious, penny-pinching, penurious, tight, tightfisted *Rel* ignoble, mean, sordid *Ant* generous

stinking *Syn* MALODOROUS, fetid, fusty, musty, noisome, putrid, rancid, rank *Ant* odorous

stint **1** *Syn* CHORE, assignment, duty, job, task **2** *Syn* SPELL, bout, go, shift, tour, trick, turn

stipend *Syn* WAGE, emolument, fee, hire, pay, salary

stipple *Syn* SPOT, blotch, dapple, dot, fleck, freckle, marble, mottle, pepper, speck, speckle, splotch, sprinkle

stippled *Syn* SPOTTED, bespangled, flecked, marbled, mottled, spangled, spattered, speckled, sprinkled

stipulation *Syn* CONDITION, provision, proviso, reservation, strings, terms

stir *n* **1** • signs of excited activity, hurry, or commotion *Syn* ado, bustle, flurry, fuss, pother *Rel* agitation, disquiet, disquieting, disturbance *Ant* tranquillity **2** *Syn* COMMOTION, bother, bustle, clatter, disturbance, furor, furore, fuss, hubbub, hullabaloo, hurly-burly, pandemonium, pother, row, ruckus, ruction, rumpus, shindy, squall, stew, storm, to-do, tumult, turmoil, uproar, welter, whirl **3** *Syn* MOTION, locomotion, move, movement

stir *vb* • to cause to shift from quiescence or torpor into activity *Syn* arouse, awaken, rally, rouse, waken *Rel* excite, galvanize, provoke, quicken, stimulate

stirring *Syn* MOVING, affecting, emotional, impressive, poignant, touching *Ant* unemotional, unimpressive

stitch *Syn* PAIN, ache, pang, throe, twinge

stock **1** *Syn* ANCESTRY, birth, blood, bloodline, breeding, descent, extraction, family tree, genealogy, line, lineage, origin, parentage, pedigree, strain *Ant* issue, posterity, progeny, seed **2** *Syn* VARIETY (sense 2), breed, clone, cultivar, race, strain, subspecies

stockade *Syn* JAIL, brig, guardroom, hoosegow, jug, lockup, pen, penitentiary, prison

stockpile *Syn* HOARD, cache, lay away, lay up, put by, salt away, squirrel (away), stash, store, stow

stocky • compact, sturdy, and relatively thick in build *Syn* chunky, dumpy, squat, stubby, thick, thickset

stodgy *Syn* BORING, drab, dreary, dry, dull, flat, heavy, humdrum, jading, leaden, monotonous, pedestrian, ponderous, stuffy, stupid, tame, tedious, tiresome, tiring, unanimated, uninteresting, wearisome, weary, wearying *Ant* absorbing, engaging, engrossing, gripping, interesting, intriguing, involving

stoic *Syn* IMPASSIVE, apathetic, phlegmatic, stolid *Ant* responsive

stoicism *Syn* IMPASSIVITY, apathy, phlegm, stolidity

stolid *Syn* IMPASSIVE, apathetic, phlegmatic, stoic *Ant* responsive

stolidity *Syn* IMPASSIVITY, apathy, phlegm, stoicism

stomach • the part of the body between the chest and the pelvis *Syn* abdomen, belly, gut, solar plexus, tummy *Rel* middle, midriff, waist

stomp *Syn* TRAMPLE, stamp, tramp, tromp

stone blind *Syn* BLIND, eyeless, sightless *Ant* sighted

stoop • to descend from one's real or pretended level of dignity *Syn* condescend, deign *Rel* abase, demean, humble

stop *vb* **1** • to suspend or cause to suspend activity *Syn* cease, desist, discontinue, quit *Rel* arrest, check, interrupt **2** *Syn* RESIDE, dwell, live, lodge, put up, sojourn, stay

stop *n* *Syn* ENCUMBRANCE, bar, block, chain, clog, crimp, deterrent, drag, embarrassment, fetter, handicap, hindrance, hurdle, impediment, inhibition, interference, let, manacle, obstacle, obstruction, shackles, stumbling block, trammel *Ant* aid, assistance, benefit, help

stopgap *Syn* RESOURCE, expedient, makeshift, resort, shift, substitute, surrogate

storage *Syn* STOREHOUSE, depository, depot, magazine, repository, stowage, warehouse

store *vb* *Syn* HOARD, cache, lay away, lay up, put by, salt away, squirrel (away), stash, stockpile, stow

store *n* **1** • a collection of things kept available for future use or need *Syn* cache, deposit, hoard, reserve *Rel* budget, fund, nest egg, pool, reservoir, stock, stockpile, supply; accumulation, assemblage, collection, gathering **2** • an establishment where goods are sold to consumers *Syn* bazaar, emporium, shop *Rel* boutique, market, marketplace, outlet

storehouse • a building for storing goods *Syn* depository, depot, magazine, repository, storage, stowage, warehouse *Rel* cache, stockroom, storeroom

storm *vb* *Syn* ATTACK (sense 1), assail, assault, bombard

storm *n* **1** *Syn* BARRAGE, bombardment, cannonade, fusillade, hail, salvo, shower, volley **2** *Syn* COMMOTION, bother, bustle, clatter, disturbance, furor, furore, fuss, hubbub, hullabaloo, hurly-burly, pandemonium, pother, row, ruckus, ruction, rumpus, shindy, squall, stew, stir, to-do, tumult, turmoil, uproar, welter, whirl **3** *Syn* CONVULSION, cataclysm, paroxysm, tempest, tumult, upheaval, uproar **4** *Syn* RAIN (sense 1), cloudburst, deluge, downpour, rainfall, rainstorm, wet **5** *Syn* RAIN (sense 2), hail, shower

stormy *Syn* CONVULSIVE, cataclysmal (*or* cataclysmic), tempestuous, tumultuous

story **1** • a recital of happenings less elaborate than a novel *Syn* anecdote, narrative, tale, yarn *Rel* description, narration **2** *Syn* ACCOUNT, chronicle, report, version **3** *Syn* LIE, falsehood, fib, misrepresentation, untruth *Ant* truth **4** *Syn* NEWS, information, intelligence, item, tidings, word

stout **1** *Syn* FLESHY, chubby, corpulent, fat, obese, plump, portly, rotund *Ant* scrawny, skinny **2** *Syn* STRONG, stalwart, sturdy, tenacious, tough *Ant* weak

stoutness *Syn* COURAGE, bravery, courageousness, daring, dauntlessness, doughtiness, fearlessness, gallantry, greatheartedness, guts, hardihood, heart, heroism, intrepidity, intrepidness, nerve, valor *Ant* cowardice, cowardliness, cravenness, dastardliness, spinelessness, yellowness

stow *Syn* HOARD, cache, lay away, lay up, put by, salt away, squirrel (away), stash, stockpile, store

stowage *Syn* STOREHOUSE, depository, depot, magazine, repository, storage, warehouse

straighten • to cause to follow a line that is without bends or curls *Syn* unbend, uncurl *Rel* uncoil, unwind *Ant* bend, crook, curl, curve

straightforward • free from all that is dishonest or secretive *Syn* aboveboard, forthright *Rel* honest, honorable, just, upright *Ant* devious, indirect

straightforwardness *Syn* CANDOR, directness, forthrightness, frankness, openheartedness, openness, plainness *Ant* dissembling, pretense (*or* pretence)

strain *n* **1** *Syn* ANCESTRY, birth, blood, bloodline, breeding, descent, extraction, family tree, genealogy, line, lineage, origin, parentage, pedigree, stock *Ant* issue, posterity, progeny, seed **2** *Syn* MELODY, air, lay, song, tune, warble **3** *Syn* STRESS, pressure, tension **4** *Syn* TOUCH, dash, shade, smack, soupçon, spice, streak, suggestion, suspicion, tincture, tinge, vein **5** *Syn* VARIETY (sense 2), breed, clone, cultivar, race, stock, subspecies

strain *vb* **1** *Syn* DEMUR, balk, boggle, jib, scruple, shy, stick, stickle *Ant* accede **2** *Syn* EXUDE, bleed, ooze, percolate, seep, sweat, weep **3** *Syn* LABOR, drudge, endeavor, grub, hump, hustle, moil, peg (away), plod, plow, plug, slave, slog, strive, struggle, sweat, toil, travail, work *Ant* dabble, fiddle (around), fool (around), mess (around), putter (around)

strained *Syn* FORCED, labored

strait **1** • a comparatively narrow stretch of water connecting two larger bodies of water *Syn* channel, narrows, passage, sound **2** *Syn* JUNCTURE, contingency, crisis, emergency, exigency, pass, pinch

straitlaced *Syn* PRIM, priggish, prissy, prudish, puritanical, stuffy

strand *Syn* SHORE, bank, beach, coast, foreshore, littoral

stranded *Syn* AGROUND, beached, grounded *Ant* afloat

strange **1** • departing from what is ordinary, usual, and to be expected *Syn* curious, eccentric, erratic, odd, outlandish, peculiar, quaint, queer, singular, unique *Rel* aberrant, abnormal, atypical *Ant* familiar **2** *Syn* EXOTIC, fantastic, glamorous, marvelous (*or* marvellous), outlandish, romantic

stranger • a nonresident or an unknown person in a community *Syn* alien, émigré, foreigner, immigrant, outlander, outsider

strangle *Syn* SUFFOCATE, asphyxiate, choke, smother, stifle, throttle

stratagem *Syn* TRICK, artifice, feint, gambit, maneuver, ploy, ruse, wile

strategic • of, relating to, or marked by strategy *Syn* logistic, tactical

strategy • the art of devising or employing plans toward a usually military goal *Syn* logistics, tactics

straw *adj* *Syn* BLOND, fair, flaxen, golden, sandy, tawny *Ant* dark

straw *vb* *Syn* STREW, broadcast, scatter, sow

stray *Syn* WANDER, gad, gallivant, meander, prowl, ramble, range, roam, rove, traipse

streak *Syn* TOUCH, dash, shade, smack, soupçon, spice, strain, suggestion, suspicion, tincture, tinge, vein

stream *n* *Syn* FLOW, current, flood, flux, tide

stream *vb* *Syn* POUR, gush, sluice

streamer *Syn* FLAG, banner, color, ensign, jack, pendant, pennant, pennon, standard

strength *Syn* POWER (sense 1), energy, force, might, puissance *Ant* impotence

strengthen • to make strong or stronger *Syn* energize, fortify, invigorate, reinforce *Rel* cheer, embolden, encourage, hearten, inspirit, nerve, steel *Ant* weaken

strenuous *Syn* VIGOROUS, energetic, lusty, nervous *Ant* languorous, lethargic

stress *n* **1** • the action or effect of force exerted within or upon a thing *Syn* pressure, strain, tension **2** *Syn* EMPHASIS, accent, accentuation

stress *vb* *Syn* EMPHASIZE, accentuate, feature, highlight, play (up), point (up), underline, underscore *Ant* play (down)

stretch *Syn* EXPANSE, amplitude, spread

stretching *Syn* EXAGGERATION, caricature, coloring, elaboration, embellishment, embroidering, hyperbole, magnification, overstatement, padding *Ant* understatement

strew **1** • to throw loosely or at intervals *Syn* broadcast, scatter, sow, straw *Rel* disseminate, spread **2** *Syn* SCATTER (sense 2), bestrew, dot, pepper, sow, spray, sprinkle

strict *Syn* RIGID, rigorous, stringent *Ant* lax

strictly • without any relaxation of standards or precision *Syn* exactly, precisely, rigidly, rigorously *Rel* carefully, conscientiously, meticulously, scrupulously *Ant* imprecisely, inexactly, loosely

strictness *Syn* SEVERITY, hardness, harshness, inflexibility, rigidity, rigidness, rigorousness, sternness *Ant* flexibility, gentleness, laxness, mildness

stricture **1** *Syn* ANIMADVERSION, aspersion, reflection *Ant* commendation **2** *Syn* CENSURE, condemnation, denunciation, rebuke, reprimand, reproach, reproof *Ant* citation, commendation, endorsement

strident 1 *Syn* LOUD, earsplitting, hoarse, raucous, stentorian, stertorous *Ant* low, low-pitched 2 *Syn* VOCIFEROUS, blatant, boisterous, clamorous, obstreperous

strife *Syn* DISCORD, conflict, contention, difference, dissension, schism, variance

strike *vb* 1 • to deliver (a blow) in a strong, vigorous manner *Syn* box, clout, cuff, hit, punch, slap, slog, slug, smite, swat *Rel* baste, beat, belabor, buffet, pound, pummel, thrash 2 *Syn* AFFECT, impress, influence, sway, touch 3 *Syn* BEGIN (sense 2), commence, embark (on *or* upon), enter (into *or* upon), get off, kick off, launch, open, start *Ant* conclude, end, finish, terminate

strike *n* 1 *Syn* ATTACK (sense 2), aggression, assault, blitzkrieg, charge, descent, offense (*or* offence), offensive, onset, onslaught, raid, rush 2 *Syn* DISADVANTAGE, drawback, handicap, liability, minus, penalty *Ant* advantage, asset, edge, plus

striking 1 *Syn* EGREGIOUS, blatant, conspicuous, flagrant, glaring, gross, obvious, patent, pronounced, rank 2 *Syn* NOTICEABLE, arresting, conspicuous, outstanding, prominent, remarkable, salient, signal

string 1 *Syn* CORD, cable, lace, lacing, line, rope, wire 2 *Syn* SUCCESSION, chain, progression, sequence, series, train

stringent *Syn* RIGID, rigorous, strict *Ant* lax

strings *Syn* CONDITION, provision, proviso, reservation, stipulation, terms

strip *n* • long narrow piece or area *Syn* band, fillet, ribbon, stripe

strip *vb* • to remove what clothes, furnishes, or invests a person or thing *Syn* bare, denude, dismantle, divest *Rel* despoil, devastate, ravage, spoliate, waste *Ant* furnish, invest

stripe 1 *Syn* STRIP, band, fillet, ribbon 2 *Syn* TYPE, character, description, ilk, kidney, kind, nature, sort

stripling *Syn* BOY, lad, laddie, nipper, shaver, sonny, tad, youth

strive 1 *Syn* ATTEMPT, assay, endeavor, essay, seek, try 2 *Syn* LABOR, drudge, endeavor, grub, hump, hustle, moil, peg (away), plod, plow, plug, slave, slog, strain, struggle, sweat, toil, travail, work *Ant* dabble, fiddle (around), fool (around), mess (around), putter (around)

stroll *vb* *Syn* SAUNTER, amble

stroll *n* *Syn* WALK, constitutional, perambulation, ramble, range, saunter, turn

stroller *Syn* NOMAD, drifter, gadabout, rambler, roamer, rover, vagabond, wanderer, wayfarer

strong 1 • showing power to resist or to endure *Syn* stalwart, stout, sturdy, tenacious, tough *Rel* energetic, lusty, vigorous *Ant* weak 2 *Syn* COGENT, compelling, conclusive, convincing, decisive, effective, forceful, persuasive, satisfying, telling *Ant* inconclusive, indecisive, ineffective, unconvincing

stronghold *Syn* FORT, citadel, fastness, fortress

strop *Syn* SHARPEN, edge, grind, hone, whet *Ant* blunt, dull

structure 1 • something made up of interdependent parts in a definite pattern of organization *Syn* anatomy, framework, skeleton *Rel* articulation, concatenation, integration 2 *Syn* BUILDING, edifice

struggle *Syn* LABOR, drudge, endeavor, grub, hump, hustle, moil, peg (away), plod, plow, plug, slave, slog, strain, strive, sweat, toil, travail, work *Ant* dabble, fiddle (around), fool (around), mess (around), putter (around)

strut • to walk with an air of pomposity or affected dignity *Syn* bridle, bristle, swagger *Rel* exhibit, expose, flaunt, parade, show

stubborn *Syn* OBSTINATE, adamant, adamantine, dogged, hard, hardened, hardheaded, hardhearted, headstrong, immovable, implacable, inflexible, mulish, obdurate, opinionated, ossified, pat, peevish, pertinacious, perverse, pigheaded, rigid, self-willed, unbending, uncompromising, unrelenting, unyielding, willful (*or* wilful) *Ant* acquiescent, agreeable, amenable, compliant, complying, flexible, pliable, pliant, relenting, yielding

stubby *Syn* STOCKY, chunky, dumpy, squat, thick, thickset

stuck-up *Syn* CONCEITED, complacent, egoistic, egotistic (*or* egotistical), important, overweening, pompous, prideful, proud, self-conceited, self-important, self-satisfied, smug, vain, vainglorious *Ant* humble, modest

student *Syn* pupil, scholar *Rel* schoolboy, schoolchild, schoolgirl

studied *Syn* DELIBERATE, advised, considered, designed, premeditated *Ant* casual

study *n* 1 *Syn* ATTENTION (sense 1), application, concentration *Ant* inattention 2 *Syn* REVERIE, daydreaming, trance, woolgathering

study *vb* *Syn* CONSIDER (sense 1), contemplate, excogitate, weigh

stuff *n* *Syn* MATTER, material, substance

stuff *vb* *Syn* PACK, cram, crowd, ram, tamp

stuffer *Syn* GLUTTON, gorger, gormandizer, gourmand, hog, overeater, swiller

stuffy 1 *Syn* BORING, drab, dreary, dry, dull, flat, heavy, humdrum, jading, leaden, monotonous, pedestrian, ponderous, stodgy, stupid, tame, tedious, tiresome, tiring, unanimated, uninteresting, wearisome, weary, wearying *Ant* absorbing, engaging, engrossing, gripping, interesting, intriguing, involving 2 *Syn* PRIM, priggish, prissy, prudish, puritanical, straitlaced

stumble • to move so clumsily or unsteadily as to fall or nearly fall *Syn* blunder, bumble,

flounder, galumph, lollop, lumber, lurch, trip *Rel* reel, stagger, totter
stumble (on *or* onto) *Syn* HAPPEN (on *or* upon), chance (upon), encounter, find, hit (upon), meet
stumbling block *Syn* ENCUMBRANCE, bar, block, chain, clog, crimp, deterrent, drag, embarrassment, fetter, handicap, hindrance, hurdle, impediment, inhibition, interference, let, manacle, obstacle, obstruction, shackles, stop, trammel *Ant* aid, assistance, benefit, help
stump *Syn* CHALLENGE, dare, defy
stun *Syn* DAZE, bemuse, benumb, paralyze, petrify, stupefy
stunning *Syn* BEAUTIFUL, attractive, beauteous, comely, cute, fair, gorgeous, handsome, knockout, lovely, pretty, ravishing, sightly, taking *Ant* homely, ill-favored, plain, ugly, unattractive, unbeautiful, unhandsome, unlovely, unpretty, unsightly
stupefy *Syn* DAZE, bemuse, benumb, paralyze, petrify, stun
stupendous *Syn* MONSTROUS, monumental, prodigious, tremendous
stupendousness *Syn* MAGNIFICENCE, augustness, brilliance, gloriousness, glory, grandeur, grandness, majesty, nobility, nobleness, resplendence, splendor, stateliness, sublimeness, superbness
stupid **1** • lacking in power to absorb ideas or impressions *Syn* crass, dense, dull, dumb, slow *Rel* asinine, fatuous, foolish, silly, simple *Ant* intelligent **2** *Syn* BORING, drab, dreary, dry, dull, flat, heavy, humdrum, jading, leaden, monotonous, pedestrian, ponderous, stodgy, stuffy, tame, tedious, tiresome, tiring, unanimated, uninteresting, wearisome, weary, wearying *Ant* absorbing, engaging, engrossing, gripping, interesting, intriguing, involving
stupor *Syn* LETHARGY, languor, lassitude, torpidity, torpor *Ant* vigor
sturdy *Syn* STRONG, stalwart, stout, tenacious, tough *Ant* weak
stygian *Syn* INFERNAL, chthonian, chthonic, Hadean, hellish, Tartarean *Ant* supernal
style **1** *Syn* FASHION, craze, cry, dernier cri, fad, mode, rage, vogue **2** *Syn* LANGUAGE (sense 2), diction, phraseology, phrasing, vocabulary **3** *Syn* NAME, appellation, denomination, designation, title
stylish • conforming to current fashion *Syn* chic, dashing, fashionable, modish, smart *Rel* modernistic, new, newfangled, new-fashioned, novel
suave • having or showing very polished and worldly manners *Syn* debonair, smooth, sophisticated, urbane *Rel* glib, slick, unctuous *Ant* boorish, churlish, clownish, loutish, uncouth
sub *Syn* SUBSTITUTE, backup, pinch hitter, relief, replacement, reserve, stand-in
subdue *Syn* CONQUER, beat, defeat, lick, overcome, overthrow, reduce, rout, subjugate, surmount, vanquish
subdued *Syn* TAME, submissive *Ant* fierce
subject *n* **1** • the basic idea or the principal object of attention in a discourse or artistic composition *Syn* argument, leitmotiv, matter, motif, motive, subject matter, text, theme, topic **2** *Syn* CITIZEN, national *Ant* alien
subject *adj* **1** *Syn* LIABLE, exposed, open, prone, sensitive, susceptible *Ant* exempt, immune **2** *Syn* SUBORDINATE, collateral, dependent, secondary, tributary *Ant* chief, dominant, leading
subject matter *Syn* SUBJECT, argument, leitmotiv, matter, motif, motive, text, theme, topic
subjugate *Syn* CONQUER, beat, defeat, lick, overcome, overthrow, reduce, rout, subdue, surmount, vanquish
sublime *Syn* SPLENDID, glorious, gorgeous, resplendent, superb
sublimeness *Syn* MAGNIFICENCE, augustness, brilliance, gloriousness, glory, grandeur, grandness, majesty, nobility, nobleness, resplendence, splendor, stateliness, stupendousness, superbness
sublunary *Syn* EARTHLY, earthy, mundane, terrestrial, worldly
submerge **1** *Syn* DIP (sense 1), duck, dunk, immerse, souse **2** *Syn* FLOOD, deluge, drown, engulf, inundate, overflow, overwhelm, submerse, swamp *Ant* drain
submerse *Syn* FLOOD, deluge, drown, engulf, inundate, overflow, overwhelm, submerge, swamp *Ant* drain
submission *Syn* SURRENDER, capitulation
submissive **1** *Syn* OBEDIENT, amenable, compliant, conformable, docile, law-abiding, tractable *Ant* contrary, disobedient, froward, insubordinate, intractable, rebellious, recalcitrant, refractory, unruly **2** *Syn* TAME, subdued *Ant* fierce
submit *Syn* YIELD, bow, capitulate, cave, defer, relent, succumb
subordinate *adj* **1** • placed in or occupying a lower class, rank, or status *Syn* collateral, dependent, secondary, subject, tributary *Rel* adjuvant, auxiliary, contributory, subservient, subsidiary *Ant* chief, dominant, leading **2** *Syn* LESSER, inferior, junior, less, lower, minor, smaller, under *Ant* greater, higher, major, more, primary, prime, senior, superior
subordinate *n* *Syn* UNDERLING, inferior, junior *Ant* senior, superior
subscribe *Syn* ASSENT, accede, acquiesce, agree, consent *Ant* dissent
subscribe (to) *Syn* APPROVE (OF), accept, care (for), countenance, favor, OK (*or* okay)

Ant disapprove (of), discountenance, disfavor, frown (on *or* upon)
subsequently *Syn* AFTER, afterward (*or* afterwards), later, thereafter *Ant* before, beforehand, earlier, previously
subservient **1** • showing or characterized by extreme compliance or abject obedience *Syn* menial, obsequious, servile, slavish *Rel* cowering, cringing, fawning, truckling *Ant* domineering, overbearing **2** *Syn* AUXILIARY, accessory, adjuvant, ancillary, contributory, subsidiary
subside **1** *Syn* ABATE, ebb, wane *Ant* revive, rise **2** *Syn* FALL, drop, sink, slump *Ant* rise
subsidiary *Syn* AUXILIARY, accessory, adjuvant, ancillary, contributory, subservient
subsidy *Syn* APPROPRIATION, allocation, allotment, annuity, grant
subsist *Syn* BE, exist, live
subsistence **1** *Syn* CONTINUATION, continuance, duration, endurance, persistence *Ant* ending, termination **2** *Syn* LIVING, bread, bread and butter, keep, livelihood, maintenance, support, sustenance
subspecies *Syn* VARIETY (sense 2), breed, clone, cultivar, race, stock, strain
substance **1** • the inner significance or central meaning of something written or said *Syn* burden, core, gist, pith, purport *Rel* center, focus, heart, nucleus **2** *Syn* MATTER, material, stuff
substantial **1** *Syn* LARGE, big, bulky, considerable, goodly, good-sized, grand, great, handsome, hefty, hulking, largish, outsize, oversize (*or* oversized), sizable (*or* sizeable), tidy, voluminous *Ant* little, puny, small, undersized **2** *Syn* MASSIVE, bulky, massy, monumental
substantially *Syn* CHIEFLY, altogether, basically, by and large, generally, largely, mainly, mostly, overall, predominantly, primarily, principally
substantiate **1** *Syn* CONFIRM, authenticate, corroborate, validate, verify *Ant* contradict, deny **2** *Syn* EMBODY (sense 2), epitomize, incarnate, manifest, materialize, personalize, personify
substitute *n* **1** • a person or thing that takes the place of another *Syn* backup, pinch hitter, relief, replacement, reserve, stand-in, sub *Rel* alternate, understudy **2** *Syn* RESOURCE, expedient, makeshift, resort, shift, stopgap, surrogate
substitute *vb* *Syn* CHANGE (sense 3), commute, exchange, shift, swap, switch, trade
substitute *adj* *Syn* IMITATION, artificial, bogus, factitious, fake, false, man-made, mimic, mock, sham, simulated, synthetic *Ant* genuine, natural, real
subsume *Syn* INCLUDE, comprehend, embrace, imply, involve *Ant* exclude
subterfuge *Syn* TRICKERY, artifice, chicanery, hanky-panky, jugglery, legerdemain, wile
subtle *Syn* LOGICAL, analytical *Ant* illogical
subvert *Syn* OVERTURN, capsize, overthrow, upset
succeed **1** • to attain or be attaining a desired end *Syn* flourish, prosper, thrive *Rel* achieve, attain, gain, reach *Ant* attempt, fail **2** *Syn* FOLLOW (sense 1), ensue, supervene *Ant* forsake (*a teacher or teachings*), precede
succession • a number of things that follow each other in some order *Syn* chain, progression, sequence, series, string, train *Rel* consecutiveness, successiveness
successive *Syn* CONSECUTIVE, sequent, sequential, serial *Ant* inconsecutive
succinct *Syn* CONCISE, compendious, laconic, pithy, summary, terse *Ant* redundant
succinctly • in a few words *Syn* briefly, compactly, concisely, crisply, laconically, pithily, summarily, tersely *Rel* aphoristically *Ant* diffusely, long-windedly, verbosely, wordily
succumb *Syn* YIELD, bow, capitulate, cave, defer, relent, submit
such *Syn* ALIKE, akin, analogous, comparable, correspondent, corresponding, like, matching, parallel, resembling, similar, suchlike *Ant* different, dissimilar, diverse, unlike
suchlike *Syn* ALIKE, akin, analogous, comparable, correspondent, corresponding, like, matching, parallel, resembling, similar, such *Ant* different, dissimilar, diverse, unlike
sucker *Syn* DUPE, chump, gull, pigeon, sap, tool
sudden *Syn* PRECIPITATE, abrupt, hasty, headlong, impetuous *Ant* deliberate
suddenly *Syn* UNAWARES, aback, unaware, unexpectedly
suds *Syn* FOAM, froth, lather, scum, spume, yeast
sue *Syn* PRAY, appeal, petition, plead
suffer **1** *Syn* BEAR (sense 2), abide, brook, endure, stand, tolerate **2** *Syn* EXPERIENCE, sustain, undergo **3** *Syn* LET, allow, leave, permit
sufferable *Syn* BEARABLE, endurable, supportable, sustainable, tolerable *Ant* insufferable, insupportable, intolerable, unbearable, unendurable, unsupportable
sufferance *Syn* PERMISSION, allowance, authorization, clearance, concurrence, consent, granting, leave, license (*or* licence), sanction *Ant* interdiction, prohibition, proscription
suffering *Syn* DISTRESS, agony, dolor, misery, passion
sufficiency • the quality or state of meeting one's needs adequately *Syn* acceptability, adequacy, satisfactoriness *Rel* appropriateness, correctness, fitness, goodness, properness, rightness, seemliness, suitability, suitableness *Ant* inadequacy, insufficiency
sufficient • being what is necessary or desirable *Syn* adequate, competent, enough
suffocate • to stop the respiration of *Syn* as-

phyxiate, choke, smother, stifle, strangle, throttle

suffrage • the right, privilege, or power of expressing one's choice or wish (as in an election or in the determination of policy) *Syn* ballot, franchise, vote

suffuse *Syn* INFUSE, imbue, ingrain, inoculate, leaven

sugarcoated *Syn* CORNY, maudlin, mawkish, mushy, saccharine, sappy, schmaltzy, sentimental, sloppy, sugary *Ant* unsentimental

sugary *Syn* CORNY, maudlin, mawkish, mushy, saccharine, sappy, schmaltzy, sentimental, sloppy, sugarcoated *Ant* unsentimental

suggest **1** • to call to mind by thought, through close connection, or by association *Syn* adumbrate, shadow *Ant* manifest **2** *Syn* HINT, allude, imply, indicate, infer, insinuate, intimate

suggestion **1** *Syn* PROPOSAL, offer, proffer, proposition **2** *Syn* TOUCH, dash, shade, smack, soupçon, spice, strain, streak, suspicion, tincture, tinge, vein

suggestive *Syn* EXPRESSIVE, eloquent, meaning, meaningful, pregnant, revealing, significant

suit **1** • a legal proceeding instituted for the sake of demanding justice or enforcing a right *Syn* action, case, cause, lawsuit **2** *Syn* PRAYER, appeal, petition, plea

suitability *Syn* APPROPRIATENESS, aptness, felicitousness, fitness, fittingness, rightness, seemliness, suitableness *Ant* inappropriateness, inaptness, infelicity, unfitness

suitable **1** *Syn* COMPETENT, able, capable, fit, good, qualified *Ant* incompetent, inept, poor, unfit, unqualified **2** *Syn* FIT, appropriate, apt, felicitous, fitting, happy, meet, proper *Ant* unfit

suitableness *Syn* APPROPRIATENESS, aptness, felicitousness, fitness, fittingness, rightness, seemliness, suitability *Ant* inappropriateness, inaptness, infelicity, unfitness

suitably *Syn* PROPERLY, appropriately, congruously, correctly, fittingly, happily, meetly, rightly *Ant* improperly, inappropriately, incongruously, incorrectly, unsuitably, wrongly

suitor *Syn* SUPPLICANT, petitioner, pleader, solicitor, suppliant

sulk • to silently go about in a bad mood *Syn* mope, pout *Rel* brood, dwell (on), mull (over), muse (over), ponder

sulky *Syn* SULLEN, crabbed, dour, gloomy, glum, morose, saturnine, surly

sullen • showing a forbidding or disagreeable mood *Syn* crabbed, dour, gloomy, glum, morose, saturnine, sulky, surly *Rel* frowning, glowering, lowering, scowling

sully *Syn* DIRTY, befoul, begrime, besmirch, blacken, foul, grime, mire, muddy, smirch, smudge, soil, stain *Ant* clean, cleanse

sum *n* • the result of simple addition of all the numbers or particulars in a given group *Syn* aggregate, amount, number, quantity, total, whole

sum *vb Syn* ADD (sense 1), foot (up), total *Ant* deduct, remove, subtract, take

summarily *Syn* SUCCINCTLY, briefly, compactly, concisely, crisply, laconically, pithily, tersely *Ant* diffusely, long-windedly, verbosely, wordily

summarize • to make into a short statement of the main points (as of a report) *Syn* abstract, digest, encapsulate, epitomize, outline, recap, recapitulate, sum up, wrap up *Rel* abridge, condense, curtail, shorten

summary *Syn* CONCISE, compendious, laconic, pithy, succinct, terse *Ant* redundant

summative *Syn* CUMULATIVE, accumulative, additive

summit • the highest point attained or attainable *Syn* acme, apex, apogee, climax, culmination, meridian, peak, pinnacle, zenith

summon, summons • to demand or request the presence or service of *Syn* call, cite, convene, convoke, muster *Rel* bid, command, enjoin, order

sumptuous *Syn* LUXURIOUS, deluxe, lavish, luxuriant, opulent, palatial, plush *Ant* ascetic, austere, humble, Spartan

sumptuously *Syn* HIGH, expensively, extravagantly, grandly, lavishly, luxuriously, opulently, richly *Ant* austerely, humbly, modestly, plainly, simply

sum up *Syn* SUMMARIZE, abstract, digest, encapsulate, epitomize, outline, recap, recapitulate, wrap up

sunder *Syn* SEPARATE, divide, divorce, part, sever *Ant* combine

sundry *Syn* MANY, divers, multifarious, numerous, several, various *Ant* few

sunken *Syn* HOLLOW, concave, dented, depressed, indented, recessed *Ant* bulging, convex, protruding, protuberant

sunny **1** *Syn* CHEERFUL (sense 1), blithe, blithesome, bright, buoyant, cheery, chipper, gay, gladsome, lightsome, upbeat *Ant* dour, gloomy, glum, morose, saturnine, sulky, sullen **2** *Syn* MERRY, blithesome, festive, gay, gleeful, jocose, jocund, jolly, jovial, laughing, mirthful

super *Syn* VERY, awful, awfully, beastly, deadly, especially, exceedingly, extra, extremely, far, frightfully, full, greatly, heavily, highly, hugely, jolly, mightily, mighty, mortally, most, much, particularly, rattling, real, right, so, something, terribly, too, whacking *Ant* little, negligibly, nominally, slightly

superabundance *Syn* EXCESS, fat, overabundance, overage, overflow, overkill, overmuch, oversupply, superfluity, surfeit, surplus *Ant* deficiency, deficit, insufficiency

superb **1** *Syn* EXCELLENT, A1, bang-up,

banner, capital, classic, crackerjack, dandy, divine, fabulous, fine, first-class, first-rate, grand, great, groovy, heavenly, jim-dandy, keen, marvelous (*or* marvellous), mean, neat, nifty, noble, par excellence, prime, sensational, splendid, stellar, sterling, superior, superlative, supernal, swell, terrific, tip-top, top, top-notch, unsurpassed, wonderful *Ant* poor **2** *Syn* SPLENDID, glorious, gorgeous, resplendent, sublime

superbness *Syn* MAGNIFICENCE, augustness, brilliance, gloriousness, glory, grandeur, grandness, majesty, nobility, nobleness, resplendence, splendor, stateliness, stupendousness, sublimeness

supercilious **1** *Syn* ARROGANT, cavalier, haughty, highfalutin, high-handed, high-hat, imperious, important, lofty, lordly, masterful, overweening, peremptory, pompous, presumptuous, pretentious, superior, uppish, uppity *Ant* humble, modest **2** *Syn* PROUD (sense 1), arrogant, disdainful, haughty, insolent, lordly, overbearing *Ant* ashamed, humble

superciliousness *Syn* ARROGANCE, haughtiness, imperiousness, loftiness, lordliness, masterfulness, peremptoriness, pompousness, presumptuousness, pretense (*or* pretence), pretension, pretentiousness, self-importance, superiority *Ant* humility, modesty

supererogatory • given or done without compulsion, need, or warrant *Syn* gratuitous, uncalled-for, wanton *Rel* autonomous, free, independent

superficial • lacking in depth or solidity *Syn* cursory, shallow, uncritical *Ant* deep, profound

superfluity *Syn* EXCESS, fat, overabundance, overage, overflow, overkill, overmuch, oversupply, superabundance, surfeit, surplus *Ant* deficiency, deficit, insufficiency

superfluous • exceeding what is needed or necessary *Syn* extra, spare, supernumerary, surplus *Rel* gratuitous, supererogatory, uncalled-for, wanton

superhuman *Syn* SUPERNATURAL, miraculous, preternatural, supranatural

superimpose *Syn* OVERLAY, appliqué, superpose

superintendent *Syn* EXECUTIVE, administrator, director, manager, supervisor

superior *n* • one who is above another in rank, station, or office *Syn* better, elder, senior *Rel* boss, chief, head, leader, master *Ant* inferior, subordinate, underling

superior *adj* **1** *Syn* ARROGANT, cavalier, haughty, highfalutin, high-handed, high-hat, imperious, important, lofty, lordly, masterful, overweening, peremptory, pompous, presumptuous, pretentious, supercilious, uppish, uppity *Ant* humble, modest **2** *Syn* BETTER, preferable **3** *Syn* EMINENT, distinguished, illustrious, noble, notable, noteworthy, outstanding, preeminent, prestigious, signal, star **4** *Syn* EXCELLENT, A1, bang-up, banner, capital, classic, crackerjack, dandy, divine, fabulous, fine, first-class, first-rate, grand, great, groovy, heavenly, jim-dandy, keen, marvelous (*or* marvellous), mean, neat, nifty, noble, par excellence, prime, sensational, splendid, stellar, sterling, superb, superlative, supernal, swell, terrific, tip-top, top, top-notch, unsurpassed, wonderful *Ant* poor

superiority *Syn* ARROGANCE, haughtiness, imperiousness, loftiness, lordliness, masterfulness, peremptoriness, pompousness, presumptuousness, pretense (*or* pretence), pretension, pretentiousness, self-importance, superciliousness *Ant* humility, modesty

superlative **1** *Syn* EXCELLENT, A1, bang-up, banner, capital, classic, crackerjack, dandy, divine, fabulous, fine, first-class, first-rate, grand, great, groovy, heavenly, jim-dandy, keen, marvelous (*or* marvellous), mean, neat, nifty, noble, par excellence, prime, sensational, splendid, stellar, sterling, superb, superior, supernal, swell, terrific, tip-top, top, top-notch, unsurpassed, wonderful *Ant* poor **2** *Syn* SUPREME, incomparable, peerless, preeminent, surpassing, transcendent

supernal **1** *Syn* CELESTIAL, Elysian, empyreal, empyrean, heavenly *Ant* hellish, infernal **2** *Syn* EXCELLENT, A1, bang-up, banner, capital, classic, crackerjack, dandy, divine, fabulous, fine, first-class, first-rate, grand, great, groovy, heavenly, jim-dandy, keen, marvelous (*or* marvellous), mean, neat, nifty, noble, par excellence, prime, sensational, splendid, stellar, sterling, superb, superior, superlative, swell, terrific, tip-top, top, top-notch, unsurpassed, wonderful *Ant* poor

supernatural • of or relating to an order of existence beyond the visible observable universe *Syn* miraculous, preternatural, superhuman, supranatural *Rel* blessed, divine, holy, sacred, spiritual

supernumerary *Syn* SUPERFLUOUS, extra, spare, surplus

superpose *Syn* OVERLAY, appliqué, superimpose

supersede *Syn* REPLACE, displace, supplant

supervene *Syn* FOLLOW (sense 1), ensue, succeed *Ant* forsake (*a teacher or teachings*), precede

supervision *Syn* OVERSIGHT, surveillance

supervisor *Syn* EXECUTIVE, administrator, director, manager, superintendent

supine *Syn* INACTIVE, idle, inert, passive *Ant* active, live

supplant *Syn* REPLACE, displace, supersede

supple **1** • able to bend or twist with ease and grace *Syn* limber, lissome, lithe, lithesome *Rel* elegant, graceful **2** *Syn* ELASTIC (sense 1), flexible, resilient, springy *Ant* rigid

3 *Syn* WILLOWY, flexible, limber, lissome, lithe, pliable, pliant *Ant* inflexible, rigid, stiff

supplement *Syn* APPENDIX, addendum

suppliant *Syn* SUPPLICANT, petitioner, pleader, solicitor, suitor

supplicant • one who asks earnestly for a favor or gift *Syn* petitioner, pleader, solicitor, suitor, suppliant *Rel* beggar, mendicant, panhandler

supplicate *Syn* BEG, adjure, beseech, entreat, implore, importune

supply **1** *Syn* FURNISH (sense 1), accoutre (*or* accouter), equip, fit (out), outfit, rig *Ant* hold (back), keep (back), reserve, retain, withhold **2** *Syn* FURNISH (sense 2), deliver, feed, give, hand, hand over, provide *Ant* hold (back), keep (back), reserve, retain, withhold

support *vb* **1** • to hold up in position by serving as a foundation or base for *Syn* bolster, brace, buttress, prop, sustain *Rel* bear, carry, convey **2** • to favor actively one that meets opposition *Syn* advocate, back, champion, uphold *Rel* approve, endorse, sanction

support *n* *Syn* LIVING, bread, bread and butter, keep, livelihood, maintenance, subsistence, sustenance

supportable **1** *Syn* BEARABLE, endurable, sufferable, sustainable, tolerable *Ant* insufferable, insupportable, intolerable, unbearable, unendurable, unsupportable **2** *Syn* TENABLE, defendable, defensible, justifiable, maintainable, sustainable *Ant* indefensible, insupportable, unjustifiable, untenable

supporter **1** *Syn* ALLY, abettor, backer, confederate, sympathizer **2** *Syn* EXPONENT, advocate, apostle, backer, booster, champion, friend, promoter, proponent *Ant* adversary, antagonist, opponent

suppose **1** *Syn* BELIEVE (sense 1), consider, deem, feel, figure, guess, hold, imagine, think *Ant* disbelieve, discredit, reject **2** *Syn* ESTIMATE (sense 2), calculate, call, conjecture, figure, gauge, guess, judge, make, place, put, reckon

supposed • accepted or advanced as true or real on the basis of less than conclusive evidence *Syn* conjectural, hypothetical, purported, putative, reputed, suppositious, supposititious *Rel* assumed, postulated, presumed, presupposed *Ant* certain

supposedly *Syn* APPARENTLY, evidently, ostensibly, presumably, seemingly

supposition **1** *Syn* CONJECTURE, guess, surmise **2** *Syn* THEORY, hypothesis, proposition

suppositious *Syn* SUPPOSED, conjectural, hypothetical, purported, putative, reputed, supposititious *Ant* certain

supposititious *Syn* SUPPOSED, conjectural, hypothetical, purported, putative, reputed, suppositious *Ant* certain

suppress *Syn* CRUSH (sense 2), extinguish, quash, quell, quench

supranatural *Syn* SUPERNATURAL, miraculous, preternatural, superhuman

supremacy • controlling power or influence over others *Syn* ascendancy, dominance, dominion, predominance, preeminence, sovereignty *Rel* authority, command, control, mastery

supreme **1** • developed to the utmost and not exceeded by any other in degree, quality, or intensity *Syn* incomparable, peerless, preeminent, superlative, surpassing, transcendent **2** *Syn* HEAD, chief, commanding, first, foremost, high, lead, leading, managing, preeminent, premier, presiding, primary, prime, principal

sure **1** • having no doubt or uncertainty *Syn* certain, cocksure, positive *Rel* decided, decisive *Ant* unsure **2** *Syn* CONFIDENT, assured, presumptuous, sanguine *Ant* apprehensive, diffident **3** *Syn* DEPENDABLE, good, reliable, responsible, safe, solid, steady, tried, tried-and-true, true, trustworthy, trusty *Ant* irresponsible, undependable, unreliable, untrustworthy **4** *Syn* INEVITABLE, certain, inescapable, necessary, unavoidable *Ant* avoidable, escapable, uncertain, unsure

surety **1** *Syn* GUARANTEE, bail, bond, guaranty, security **2** *Syn* SPONSOR, angel, backer, guarantor, patron

surfeit *n* *Syn* EXCESS, fat, overabundance, overage, overflow, overkill, overmuch, oversupply, superabundance, superfluity, surplus *Ant* deficit, insufficiency

surfeit *vb* *Syn* SATIATE, cloy, glut, gorge, pall, sate

surly *Syn* SULLEN, crabbed, dour, gloomy, glum, morose, saturnine, sulky

surmise *Syn* CONJECTURE, guess, supposition

surmount *Syn* CONQUER, beat, defeat, lick, overcome, overthrow, reduce, rout, subdue, subjugate, vanquish

surpass *Syn* EXCEED, excel, outdo, outstrip, transcend

surpassing *Syn* SUPREME, incomparable, peerless, preeminent, superlative, transcendent

surplus **1** *Syn* EXCESS, fat, overabundance, overage, overflow, overkill, overmuch, oversupply, superabundance, superfluity, surfeit *Ant* deficiency, deficit, insufficiency **2** *Syn* SUPERFLUOUS, extra, spare, supernumerary

surprise **1** • to attack unawares *Syn* ambush, waylay *Rel* capture, catch **2** • to impress forcibly through unexpectedness *Syn* amaze, astonish, astound, flabbergast *Rel* alarm, frighten, scare, startle

surrender *n* • the yielding of one's person, forces, or possessions to another *Syn* capitulation, submission

surrender *vb* *Syn* RELINQUISH, abandon, cede, leave, resign, waive, yield *Ant* keep

surreptitious *Syn* SECRET, clandestine, covert, furtive, stealthy, underhand, underhanded

surrogate *Syn* RESOURCE, expedient, makeshift, resort, shift, stopgap, substitute

surround • to close in or as if in a ring about something *Syn* circle, compass, encircle, encompass, environ, gird, girdle, hem, ring *Rel* enclose, envelop, fence, wall

surveillance **1** *Syn* OVERSIGHT, supervision **2** *Syn* VIGILANCE, alertness, attentiveness, lookout, watch, watchfulness

survey *vb* **1** *Syn* CANVASS, poll, solicit **2** *Syn* SEE (sense 1), behold, contemplate, descry, discern, espy, note, notice, observe, perceive, remark, view

survey *n* **1** *Syn* COMPENDIUM, aperçu, digest, pandect, précis, sketch, syllabus **2** *Syn* INSPECTION, audit, check, checkup, examination, review, scan, scrutiny

survive *Syn* OUTLIVE, outlast

susceptible **1** *Syn* LIABLE, exposed, open, prone, sensitive, subject *Ant* exempt, immune **2** *Syn* SENTIENT, impressible, impressionable, responsive, sensitive

suspect *Syn* DISTRUST, doubt, mistrust, question *Ant* trust

suspend **1** *Syn* ADJOURN, recess **2** *Syn* EXCLUDE, blackball, debar, disbar, eliminate, rule out, shut out *Ant* admit, include **3** *Syn* HANG, dangle, sling

suspended • hanging from or remaining in place as if hanging from a support *Syn* pendent, pendulous

suspense *Syn* ABEYANCE, doldrums, dormancy, latency, quiescence, suspension *Ant* continuance, continuation

suspension *Syn* ABEYANCE, doldrums, dormancy, latency, quiescence, suspense *Ant* continuance, continuation

suspicion **1** *Syn* DOUBT, distrust, distrustfulness, incertitude, misgiving, mistrust, mistrustfulness, skepticism, uncertainty *Ant* assurance, belief, certainty, certitude, confidence, conviction, sureness, surety, trust **2** *Syn* TOUCH, dash, shade, smack, soupçon, spice, strain, streak, suggestion, tincture, tinge, vein

suspiciously *Syn* ASKANCE, distrustfully, doubtfully, doubtingly, dubiously, mistrustfully, skeptically *Ant* trustfully, trustingly

sustain **1** *Syn* EXPERIENCE, suffer, undergo **2** *Syn* SUPPORT (sense 1), bolster, brace, buttress, prop

sustainable **1** *Syn* BEARABLE, endurable, sufferable, supportable, tolerable *Ant* insufferable, insupportable, intolerable, unbearable, unendurable, unsupportable **2** *Syn* TENABLE, defendable, defensible, justifiable, maintainable, supportable *Ant* indefensible, insupportable, unjustifiable, untenable

sustenance **1** *Syn* FOOD (sense 2), aliment, nourishment, nutriment, pabulum, pap **2** *Syn* LIVING, bread, bread and butter, keep, livelihood, maintenance, subsistence, support

suture *Syn* JOINT, articulation

swag *Syn* SPOIL, booty, loot, plunder, prize

swagger *Syn* STRUT, bridle, bristle

swain *Syn* BOYFRIEND, beau, fellow, man

swallow *Syn* EAT, consume, devour, ingest

swamp *n* • spongy land saturated or partially covered with water *Syn* bog, fen, marsh, marshland, mire, morass, muskeg, slough, swampland *Rel* quagmire

swamp *vb* *Syn* FLOOD, deluge, drown, engulf, inundate, overflow, overwhelm, submerge, submerse *Ant* drain

swampland *Syn* SWAMP, bog, fen, marsh, marshland, mire, morass, muskeg, slough

swank *n* *Syn* OSTENTATION, flamboyance, flashiness, garishness, gaudiness, glitz, ostentatiousness, pretentiousness, showiness *Ant* austerity, plainness, severity

swank *or* **swanky** *n* *Syn* GAUDY, flamboyant, flashy, garish, glitzy, loud, ostentatious, splashy, tawdry *Ant* conservative, quiet, understated

swap *Syn* CHANGE (sense 3), commute, exchange, shift, substitute, switch, trade

swarm *Syn* TEEM, abound, overflow

swarming *Syn* RIFE, abounding, flush, fraught, replete, teeming, thick, thronging

swat *Syn* STRIKE, box, clout, cuff, hit, punch, slap, slog, slug, smite

sway **1** *Syn* AFFECT, impress, influence, strike, touch **2** *Syn* SWING (sense 2), fluctuate, oscillate, pendulate, undulate, vibrate, waver

swear *Syn* TESTIFY, attest, depose, witness

swearing *Syn* BLASPHEMY, cursing, profanity *Ant* adoration

sweat **1** *Syn* EXUDE, bleed, ooze, percolate, seep, strain, weep **2** *Syn* LABOR, drudge, endeavor, grub, hump, hustle, moil, peg (away), plod, plow, plug, slave, slog, strain, strive, struggle, toil, travail, work *Ant* dabble, fiddle (around), fool (around), mess (around), putter (around)

sweep *Syn* RANGE, compass, gamut, horizon, ken, orbit, purview, radius, reach, scope

sweeping *Syn* INDISCRIMINATE, wholesale *Ant* discriminating, selective

sweet *adj* **1** • distinctly pleasing or charming *Syn* dulcet, engaging, winning, winsome *Rel* agreeable, grateful, gratifying, pleasant, pleasing, welcome *Ant* bitter, sour **2** *Syn* AMIABLE, affable, agreeable, genial, good-natured, good-tempered, gracious, nice, well-disposed *Ant* disagreeable, ill-natured, ill-tempered, ungracious, unpleasant **3** *Syn* FRAGRANT, ambrosial, aromatic, perfumed, redolent, savory, scented *Ant* fetid, foul, malodorous, noisome, putrid, rancid, rank, reeking, reeky, smelly, stinking, stinky, strong **4** *Syn* LOVABLE, darling, dear, disarming,

endearing, precious, winning *Ant* abhorrent, abominable, detestable, hateful, odious, unlovable
sweet *n Syn* SWEETHEART, beloved, darling, dear, flame, honey, love
sweetheart • a person with whom one is in love *Syn* beloved, darling, dear, flame, honey, love, sweet *Rel* beau, boyfriend, fellow, lover, man, swain
swell *adj Syn* EXCELLENT, A1, bang-up, banner, capital, classic, crackerjack, dandy, divine, fabulous, fine, first-class, first-rate, grand, great, groovy, heavenly, jim-dandy, keen, marvelous (*or* marvellous), mean, neat, nifty, noble, par excellence, prime, sensational, splendid, stellar, sterling, superb, superior, superlative, supernal, terrific, tip-top, top, top-notch, unsurpassed, wonderful *Ant* poor
swell *vb* **1** *Syn* EXPAND, amplify, dilate, distend, inflate *Ant* abridge, circumscribe, contract **2** *Syn* INCREASE (sense 1), add (to), aggrandize, amplify, augment, boost, compound, enlarge, escalate, expand, extend, multiply, raise, up *Ant* abate, contract, decrease, diminish, lessen, lower, reduce, subtract (from) **3** *Syn* INCREASE (sense 2), accumulate, appreciate, balloon, build (up), burgeon, enlarge, escalate, expand, mount, multiply, mushroom, proliferate, rise, snowball, wax *Ant* contract, decrease, diminish, lessen, wane
swerve • to turn aside from a straight course *Syn* depart, deviate, digress, diverge, veer *Rel* avert, deflect, divert, sheer, turn
swift *Syn* FAST, expeditious, fleet, hasty, quick, rapid, speedy *Ant* slow
swiller *Syn* GLUTTON, gorger, gormandizer, gourmand, hog, overeater, stuffer
swimming *Syn* GIDDY, dazzled, dizzy, vertiginous
swindle *Syn* FLEECE, bleed, cheat, chisel, cozen, defraud, hustle, mulct, rook, shortchange, skin, squeeze, stick, sting, victimize
swing **1** • to wield or cause to move to and fro or up and down *Syn* brandish, flourish, shake, thrash, wave *Rel* display, exhibit, flaunt, parade, show **2** • to move from one direction to its opposite *Syn* fluctuate, oscillate, pendulate, sway, undulate, vibrate, waver *Rel* gyrate, revolve, rotate, spin, turn, wheel, whirl **3** *Syn* HANDLE, manipulate, ply, wield
swipe *Syn* STEAL, cop, filch, lift, pilfer, pinch, purloin, snitch
swirl *Syn* TURN (sense 1), circle, eddy, gyrate, pirouette, revolve, rotate, spin, twirl, wheel, whirl
switch *Syn* CHANGE (sense 3), commute, exchange, shift, substitute, swap, trade
swoon *n Syn* FAINT, blackout, coma, insensibility, knockout
swoon *vb Syn* FAINT, black out, pass out *Ant* come around, come round, come to, revive
sybaritic *Syn* SENSUOUS, epicurean, luxurious, voluptuous
sycophant **1** • a person who flatters another in order to get ahead *Syn* fawner, flunky, toady *Rel* yes-man **2** *Syn* PARASITE, bootlicker, favorite, hanger-on, leech, lickspittle, sponge, sponger, toady
syllabus *Syn* COMPENDIUM, aperçu, digest, pandect, précis, sketch, survey
symbol **1** • something concrete that represents or suggests another thing that cannot in itself be pictured *Syn* attribute, emblem, type *Rel* badge, mark, sign, token **2** *Syn* CHARACTER, mark, sign
symmetry • beauty of form or arrangement arising from balanced proportions *Syn* balance, harmony, proportion
sympathetic **1** *Syn* CONSONANT, compatible, congenial, congruous, consistent *Ant* dissonant (*in music*), inconstant **2** *Syn* TENDER, compassionate, responsive, warm, warmhearted *Ant* callous, severe
sympathizer *Syn* ALLY, abettor, backer, confederate, supporter
sympathy **1** • the act or capacity for sharing in the interests and especially in the painful experiences of another *Syn* commiseration, compassion, condolence, empathy, pity, ruth *Rel* responsiveness, tenderness, warmheartedness, warmth **2** *Syn* ATTRACTION, affinity
symptom *Syn* SIGN (sense 1), badge, mark, note, token
synchronous *Syn* CONTEMPORARY, coetaneous, coeval, coincident, concomitant, concurrent, contemporaneous, simultaneous
syndicate **1** *Syn* CARTEL, combination, combine, trust **2** *Syn* MONOPOLY, cartel, corner, pool, trust
syndrome *Syn* DISEASE, ailment, complaint, condition, disorder, distemper, malady
synopsis *Syn* ABRIDGMENT, abstract, brief, conspectus, epitome *Ant* expansion
synthetic **1** *Syn* ARTIFICIAL, ersatz, factitious *Ant* natural **2** *Syn* IMITATION, artificial, bogus, factitious, fake, false, man-made, mimic, mock, sham, simulated, substitute *Ant* genuine, natural, real
system **1** • an organized integrated whole made up of diverse but interrelated and interdependent parts *Syn* complex, network, organism, scheme *Ant* chaos **2** *Syn* METHOD, fashion, manner, mode, way
systematic *Syn* ORDERLY, methodical, regular *Ant* chaotic, disorderly
systematize *Syn* ORDER, arrange, marshal, methodize, organize

T

table **1** *Syn* LIST, catalog, inventory, register, roll, roster, schedule **2** *Syn* MEAL, chow, feed, mess, repast
tablet *Syn* PILL, capsule, lozenge
table talk *Syn* CHAT, chatter, chitchat, gabfest, gossip, palaver, rap, small talk, talk, tête-à-tête
tacit *Syn* IMPLICIT, implied, unexpressed, unspoken, unvoiced, wordless *Ant* explicit, express, expressed, spoken, stated
taciturn *Syn* SILENT (sense 1), close, close-lipped, closemouthed, reserved, reticent, secretive, tight-lipped, uncommunicative *Ant* talkative
tackle *Syn* EQUIPMENT, apparatus, gear, machinery, matériel, outfit, paraphernalia
tack (on) *Syn* ADD (sense 2), adjoin, annex, append *Ant* deduct, remove, subtract, take
tact • skill and grace in dealing with others *Syn* address, poise, savoir faire *Rel* diplomacy, policy, suavity, urbanity *Ant* awkwardness
tactical **1** *Syn* EXPEDIENT, advisable, desirable, judicious, politic, prudent, wise *Ant* imprudent, inadvisable, inexpedient, injudicious, unwise **2** *Syn* STRATEGIC, logistic
tactics *Syn* STRATEGY, logistics
tactless *Syn* INDISCREET, ill-advised, imprudent, inadvisable, injudicious, unadvisable, unwise *Ant* advisable, discreet, judicious, prudent, tactful, wise
tad *Syn* BOY, lad, laddie, nipper, shaver, sonny, stripling, youth
tag *n* *Syn* MARK, brand, label, stamp, ticket
tag *vb* *Syn* MARK, brand, label, stamp, ticket
tagging *Syn* PURSUIT, chase, chasing, dogging, following, hounding, pursuing, shadowing, tailing, tracing, tracking, trailing
tailing *Syn* PURSUIT, chase, chasing, dogging, following, hounding, pursuing, shadowing, tagging, tracing, tracking, trailing
taint *Syn* CONTAMINATE, befoul, defile, foul, poison, pollute *Ant* decontaminate, purify
tainted *Syn* IMPURE, adulterated, alloyed, contaminated, dilute, diluted, polluted, thinned, weakened *Ant* pure, unadulterated, unalloyed, uncontaminated, undiluted, unpolluted, untainted
take **1** • to get hold of by or as if by catching up with the hand *Syn* clutch, grab, grasp, seize, snatch *Rel* have, hold, own, possess **2** *Syn* BRING, fetch *Ant* remove, withdraw **3** *Syn* BUY, pick up, purchase **4** *Syn* RECEIVE, accept, admit
taking *Syn* BEAUTIFUL, attractive, beauteous, comely, cute, fair, gorgeous, handsome, knockout, lovely, pretty, ravishing, sightly, stunning *Ant* homely, ill-favored, plain, ugly, unattractive, unbeautiful, unhandsome, unlovely, unpretty, unsightly
tale *Syn* STORY, anecdote, narrative, yarn
talent *Syn* GIFT (sense 2), aptitude, bent, faculty, genius, knack, turn
talisman *Syn* FETISH, amulet, charm
talk *vb* **1** *Syn* CHAT, babble, blab, cackle, chatter, converse, gab, gabble, gas, jabber, jaw, palaver, patter, prate, prattle, rap, rattle, run on, twitter, visit **2** *Syn* SPEAK, converse
talk *n* **1** *Syn* CHAT, chatter, chitchat, gabfest, gossip, palaver, rap, small, table talk, talk, tête-à-tête **2** *Syn* SPEECH, address, harangue, homily, lecture, oration, sermon
talkative • given to talk or talking *Syn* garrulous, glib, loquacious, voluble *Rel* articulate, eloquent, fluent, vocal *Ant* closemouthed, laconic, reserved, reticent, taciturn, tight-lipped
talkativeness • the inclination to talk or to talking *Syn* garrulity, garrulousness, glibness, loquaciousness, loquacity, volubility *Rel* articulateness, eloquence, fluency *Ant* silence
talk (into) *Syn* PERSUADE, argue, convince, get, induce, move, prevail (on *or* upon), satisfy, win (over)
tall *Syn* HIGH, lofty *Ant* low
tally *Syn* AGREE (sense 2), accord, conform, correspond, harmonize, jibe, square *Ant* differ (from)
tame **1** • made docile and tractable *Syn* subdued, submissive *Rel* amenable, biddable, docile, obedient, tractable *Ant* fierce **2** *Syn* BORING, drab, dreary, dry, dull, flat, heavy, humdrum, jading, leaden, monotonous, pedestrian, ponderous, stodgy, stuffy, stupid, tedious, tiresome, tiring, unanimated, uninteresting, wearisome, weary, wearying *Ant* absorbing, engaging, engrossing, gripping, interesting, intriguing, involving
tamp *Syn* PACK, cram, crowd, ram, stuff
tang *Syn* TASTE (sense 1), flavor, relish, savor, smack *Ant* antipathy
tangible • capable of being perceived by the sense of touch *Syn* palpable, touchable *Rel* tactile *Ant* impalpable, intangible
tangle *Syn* ENTANGLE, enmesh, ensnare, entrap, mesh, snare, trap *Ant* disentangle
tantalize *Syn* WORRY, annoy, harass, harry, pester, plague, tease
tantamount *Syn* SAME, equal, equivalent, identic, identical, selfsame, very *Ant* different
tap *n* • a light usually audible blow or the sound made by such a blow *Syn* knock, rap, thud, thump

tap *vb* • to strike or hit audibly *Syn* knock, rap, thud, thump *Rel* smite, strike

tar *Syn* MARINER, bluejacket, gob, sailor, seaman

tardily *Syn* SLOW, laggardly, leisurely, slowly, sluggishly *Ant* apace, briskly, fast, fleetly, full tilt, hastily, quick, quickly, rapidly, snappily, speedily, swift, swiftly

tardy • not arriving, occurring, or done at the set, due, or expected time *Syn* behindhand, late, overdue *Rel* dilatory, laggard, slow *Ant* prompt

target **1** *Syn* GOAL, aim, ambition, aspiration, design, dream, end, intent, intention, mark, meaning, object, objective, plan, pretension, purpose, thing **2** *Syn* LAUGHINGSTOCK, butt, mark, mock, mockery

tarry *Syn* STAY, abide, linger, remain, wait

tart *Syn* SOUR, acid, acidulous, dry

Tartarean *Syn* INFERNAL, chthonian, chthonic, Hadean, hellish, stygian *Ant* supernal

task **1** *Syn* CHORE, assignment, duty, job, stint **2** *Syn* ROLE, capacity, function, job, part, place, position, purpose, work

taskmaster *Syn* BOSS, captain, chief, foreman, head, headman, helmsman, kingpin, leader, master

taste **1** • the property of a substance which makes it perceptible to the gustatory sense *Syn* flavor, relish, savor, smack, tang **2** • a liking for or enjoyment of something because of the pleasure it gives *Syn* gusto, palate, relish, zest *Rel* partiality, predilection, prepossession *Ant* antipathy **3** *Syn* LIKING, appetite, fancy, favor, fondness, like, love, partiality, preference, relish, shine, use *Ant* aversion, disfavor, dislike, distaste, hatred, loathing

tasty *Syn* PALATABLE, appetizing, flavorsome, relishing, sapid, savory, toothsome *Ant* distasteful, unpalatable

tat *Syn* WEAVE, braid, crochet, knit, plait

tattle *Syn* GOSSIP, blab

taunt *Syn* RIDICULE, deride, mock, rally, twit

taut *Syn* TIGHT, tense *Ant* loose

tautology *Syn* VERBIAGE, circumlocution, periphrasis, pleonasm, redundancy

tavern *Syn* BARROOM, bar, café, groggery, grogshop, pub, saloon

tawdry *Syn* GAUDY, flamboyant, flashy, garish, glitzy, loud, ostentatious, splashy, swank (*or* swanky) *Ant* conservative, quiet, understated

tawny *Syn* BLOND, fair, flaxen, golden, sandy, straw *Ant* dark

tax *n* • a charge usually of money collected by the government from people or businesses for public use *Syn* assessment, duty, imposition, impost, levy *Rel* custom(s), excise, income tax, poll tax, sales tax, tariff, toll, tribute, withholding tax

tax *vb* *Syn* BURDEN, charge, cumber, encumber, lade, load, saddle, weigh, weight

teach • to cause to acquire knowledge or skill *Syn* discipline, educate, instruct, school, train *Rel* communicate, impart

teacher • a person whose occupation is to give formal instruction in a school *Syn* educator, instructor, pedagogue, preceptor, schoolteacher *Rel* headmaster, master, schoolmaster

teaching *Syn* EDUCATION (sense 1), instruction, schooling, training, tutelage, tutoring

tear **1** • to separate forcibly *Syn* cleave, rend, rip, rive, split *Rel* cut, slash, slit **2** *Syn* HURRY (sense 2), barrel, bolt, bowl, breeze, career, course, dash, fly, hasten, hotfoot (it), hump, hurtle, hustle, pelt, race, rip, rocket, run, rush, rustle, scoot, scurry, scuttle, shoot, speed, step (along), trot, whirl, whisk, zip, zoom *Ant* crawl, creep, poke

tearful *Syn* SAD (sense 2), depressing, dismal, drear, dreary, heartbreaking, heartrending, melancholy, pathetic, saddening, sorry, teary *Ant* cheering, cheery, glad, happy

teary *Syn* SAD (sense 2), depressing, dismal, drear, dreary, heartbreaking, heartrending, melancholy, pathetic, saddening, sorry, tearful *Ant* cheering, cheery, glad, happy

tease **1** • to make fun of in a good-natured way *Syn* chaff, jive, josh, kid, rally, razz, rib, ride, roast *Rel* banter, joke **2** *Syn* WORRY, annoy, harass, harry, pester, plague, tantalize

tedious *Syn* BORING, drab, dreary, dry, dull, flat, heavy, humdrum, jading, leaden, monotonous, pedestrian, ponderous, stodgy, stuffy, stupid, tame, tiresome, tiring, unanimated, uninteresting, wearisome, weary, wearying *Ant* absorbing, engaging, engrossing, gripping, interesting, intriguing, involving

tedium • a state of dissatisfaction and weariness *Syn* boredom, doldrums, ennui *Rel* irksomeness, tediousness, tiresomeness, wearisomeness

teem • to be present in large quantity *Syn* abound, overflow, swarm *Rel* bear, produce, turn out, yield

teeming *Syn* RIFE, abounding, flush, fraught, replete, swarming, thick, thronging

teeny *Syn* TINY, atomic, bitty, infinitesimal, microminiature, microscopic, miniature, minute, teeny-weeny, wee *Ant* astronomical, colossal, cosmic, elephantine, enormous, giant, gigantic, herculean, heroic, huge, immense, mammoth, massive, monster, monstrous, monumental, mountainous, prodigious, titanic, tremendous

teeny-weeny *Syn* TINY, atomic, bitty, infinitesimal, microminiature, microscopic, miniature, minute, teeny, wee *Ant* astronomical, colossal, cosmic, elephantine, enormous, giant, gigantic, herculean, heroic, huge, immense, mammoth, massive, monster, monstrous, monumental, mountainous, prodigious, titanic, tremendous

teeter *Syn* SHAKE (sense 1), dither, quake, quaver, quiver, shimmy, shiver, shudder, totter, tremble, wobble

tell **1** *Syn* COUNT, enumerate, number **2** *Syn* ENLIGHTEN (sense 1), acquaint, advise, apprise, brief, clue, familiarize, fill in, inform, instruct, wise (up) **3** *Syn* REVEAL, betray, disclose, discover, divulge *Ant* conceal **4** *Syn* SAY, state, utter

telling *Syn* COGENT, compelling, conclusive, convincing, decisive, effective, forceful, persuasive, satisfying, strong *Ant* inconclusive, indecisive, ineffective, unconvincing

temerity *Syn* EFFRONTERY, audacity, brashness, brass, brassiness, brazenness, cheek, cheekiness, chutzpah, gall, nerve, nerviness, pertness, presumption, presumptuousness, sauce, sauciness

temper *n* **1** *Syn* AURA, air, atmosphere, climate, flavor, mood, note **2** *Syn* DISPOSITION, character, complexion, individuality, personality, temperament **3** *Syn* MOOD, humor, vein

temper *vb Syn* MODERATE, qualify

temperament *Syn* DISPOSITION, character, complexion, individuality, personality, temper

temperance • self-restraint in the gratification of appetites or passions *Syn* abstinence, abstemiousness, continence, sobriety *Rel* eschewal, forbearance, forbearing, forgoing, sacrifice, sacrificing *Ant* excessiveness, immoderacy, intemperance, intemperateness

temperate **1** *Syn* CLEMENT, balmy, equable, gentle, mild, moderate *Ant* harsh, inclement, intemperate, severe **2** *Syn* SOBER, continent, unimpassioned *Ant* drunk, excited

tempest *Syn* CONVULSION, cataclysm, paroxysm, storm, tumult, upheaval, uproar

tempestuous *Syn* CONVULSIVE, cataclysmal (*or* cataclysmic), stormy, tumultuous

temporal *Syn* PROFANE, lay, secular *Ant* sacred

temporary **1** • lasting, continuing, or serving for a limited time *Syn* acting, ad interim, provisional *Ant* permanent **2** *Syn* MOMENTARY, ephemeral, evanescent, flash, fleeting, fugitive, impermanent, passing, short-lived, transient, transitory *Ant* enduring, eternal, everlasting, lasting, long-lived, permanent, perpetual

tempt *Syn* LURE, allure, beguile, decoy, entice, lead on, seduce

temptress *Syn* SIREN, enchantress, seductress

tenable • capable of being defended with good reasoning against verbal attack *Syn* defendable, defensible, justifiable, maintainable, supportable, sustainable *Rel* rational, reasonable, sensible *Ant* indefensible, insupportable, unjustifiable, untenable

tenacious **1** *Syn* PERSISTENT, dogged, insistent, patient, persevering, pertinacious **2** *Syn* STRONG, stalwart, stout, sturdy, tough *Ant* weak

tenant • one who rents a room or apartment in another's house *Syn* boarder, lodger, renter, roomer *Rel* roommate *Ant* landlord

tend • to supervise or take charge of *Syn* attend, mind, watch *Rel* defend, guard, protect, safeguard, shield

tendency • movement in a particular direction *Syn* drift, tenor, trend *Rel* leaning, penchant, proclivity, propensity

tender *adj* • showing or expressing interest in another *Syn* compassionate, responsive, sympathetic, warm, warmhearted *Rel* gentle, lenient, mild, soft *Ant* callous, severe

tender *vb Syn* OFFER, prefer, present, proffer

tender *n Syn* OVERTURE, advance, approach, bid

tenderfoot *Syn* BEGINNER, colt, fledgling, freshman, greenhorn, neophyte, newbie, newcomer, novice, recruit, rookie, tyro *Ant* old hand, old-timer, vet, veteran

tending *Syn* PRONE (sense 1), apt, given, inclined

tenet *Syn* DOCTRINE, dogma

tenor *Syn* TENDENCY, drift, trend

tense **1** *Syn* STIFF, inflexible, rigid, stark, wooden *Ant* relaxed, supple **2** *Syn* TIGHT, taut *Ant* loose

tension **1** *Syn* BALANCE, equilibrium, equipoise, poise **2** *Syn* STRESS, pressure, strain

tent *Syn* CANOPY, awning, ceiling, roof

tenuous *Syn* THIN, rare, slender, slight, slim *Ant* thick

term **1** *Syn* LIMIT, bound, confine, end **2** *Syn* WORD, vocable

terminal *Syn* LAST, concluding, eventual, final, latest, ultimate *Ant* first

terminate *Syn* CONCLUDE (sense 1), complete, end, finish

termination *Syn* END, ending, terminus *Ant* beginning

terminology • the special terms or expressions of a particular group or field *Syn* argot, cant, dialect, jargon, language, lingo, patois, patter, slang, vocabulary *Rel* colloquialism, idiom, localism, parlance, pidgin, provincialism, regionalism, speech, vernacular

terminus *Syn* END, ending, termination *Ant* beginning

terms *Syn* CONDITION, provision, proviso, reservation, stipulation, strings

terrestrial *Syn* EARTHLY, earthy, mundane, sublunary, worldly

terrible *Syn* FEARFUL (sense 2), appalling, awful, dreadful, frightful, horrible, horrific, shocking, terrific

terribly *Syn* VERY, awful, awfully, beastly, deadly, especially, exceedingly, extra, extremely, far, frightfully, full, greatly, heavily, highly, hugely, jolly, mightily, mighty, mortally, most, much, particularly, rattling, real, right, so, something, super, too, whacking *Ant* little, negligibly, nominally, slightly

terrific **1** *Syn* EXCELLENT, A1, bang-up, banner, capital, classic, crackerjack, dandy, divine, fabulous, fine, first-class, first-rate, grand, great, groovy, heavenly, jim-dandy, keen, marvelous (*or* marvellous), mean, neat, nifty, noble, par excellence, prime, sensational, splendid, stellar, sterling, superb, superior, superlative, supernal, swell, tip-top, top, top-notch, unsurpassed, wonderful *Ant* poor **2** *Syn* FEARFUL (sense 2), appalling, awful, dreadful, frightful, horrible, horrific, shocking, terrible

terrify *Syn* FRIGHTEN, affray, affright, alarm, fright, scare, startle, terrorize *Ant* reassure

territory *Syn* FIELD, bailiwick, domain, province, sphere

terror *Syn* FEAR, alarm, consternation, dismay, dread, fright, horror, panic, trepidation *Ant* fearlessness

terrorize *Syn* FRIGHTEN, affray, affright, alarm, fright, scare, startle, terrify *Ant* reassure

terse *Syn* CONCISE, compendious, laconic, pithy, succinct, summary *Ant* redundant

tersely *Syn* SUCCINCTLY, briefly, compactly, concisely, crisply, laconically, pithily, summarily *Ant* diffusely, long-windedly, verbosely, wordily

test *n Syn* PROOF, demonstration, trial

test *vb Syn* PROVE, demonstrate, try *Ant* disprove

testify • to make a solemn declaration under oath for the purpose of establishing a fact *Syn* attest, depose, swear, witness *Rel* vouch

testimonial *Syn* CREDENTIAL, character, recommendation, reference

testy *Syn* IRASCIBLE, choleric, cranky, cross, splenetic, touchy

tête-à-tête *Syn* CHAT, chatter, chitchat, gabfest, gossip, palaver, rap, small talk, table talk, talk

text *Syn* SUBJECT, argument, leitmotiv, matter, motif, motive, subject matter, theme, topic

thankfulness *Syn* THANKS, appreciation, appreciativeness, gratefulness, gratitude *Ant* ingratitude, thanklessness, ungratefulness

thankless • not showing gratitude *Syn* unappreciative, ungrateful *Rel* rude, thoughtless, ungracious *Ant* appreciative, grateful, obliged, thankful

thanks • acknowledgment of having received something good from another *Syn* appreciation, appreciativeness, gratefulness, gratitude, thankfulness *Rel* thanksgiving *Ant* ingratitude, thanklessness, ungratefulness

thaumaturgy *Syn* MAGIC, alchemy, sorcery, witchcraft, witchery, wizardry

thaw *Syn* LIQUEFY, deliquesce, fuse, melt

theatrical *Syn* DRAMATIC, dramaturgic, histrionic, melodramatic

theft • an unlawful taking of property especially personal property stolen from its rightful owner *Syn* burglary, larceny, robbery

theme **1** *Syn* ESSAY, article, composition, paper **2** *Syn* SUBJECT, argument, leitmotiv, matter, motif, motive, subject matter, text, topic

then *Syn* THEREFORE, accordingly, consequently, hence, so

theorem *Syn* PRINCIPLE, axiom, fundamental, law

theoretical **1** • concerned principally with abstractions and theories *Syn* academic, speculative *Rel* conjectural, hypothetical, supposed **2** *Syn* ABSTRACT (sense 2), conceptual *Ant* concrete

theory • an idea that is the starting point for making a case or conducting an investigation *Syn* hypothesis, proposition, supposition *Rel* assumption, concession, premise, presumption, presupposition

thereafter *Syn* AFTER, afterward (*or* afterwards), later, subsequently *Ant* before, beforehand, earlier, previously

therefore • for this or that reason *Syn* accordingly, consequently, hence, so, then

thesis *Syn* DISCOURSE, disquisition, dissertation, monograph, treatise

thespian *Syn* ACTOR, impersonator, mime, mimic, mummer, performer, player, trouper

thick *n* • the most intense or characteristic phase of something *Syn* deep, depth, height, middle, midst *Rel* center, heart

thick *adj* **1** *Syn* CLOSE (sense 2), compact, dense *Ant* open **2** *Syn* FAMILIAR, chummy, close, confidential, intimate *Ant* aloof **3** *Syn* RIFE, abounding, flush, fraught, replete, swarming, teeming, thronging **4** *Syn* STOCKY, chunky, dumpy, squat, stubby, thickset

thicket • a thick patch of shrubbery, small trees, or underbrush *Syn* brake, brushwood, chaparral, coppice, copse, covert *Rel* canebrake

thickset *Syn* STOCKY, chunky, dumpy, squat, stubby, thick

thief • one that steals especially stealthily or secretly *Syn* burglar, larcener, larcenist, robber

thin *adj* • not thick, broad, abundant, or dense *Syn* rare, slender, slight, slim, tenuous *Rel* gaunt, lank, lanky, lean, spare *Ant* thick

thin *vb* • to make thin or thinner or less dense *Syn* attenuate, dilute, extenuate, rarefy *Rel* decrease, diminish, lessen, reduce *Ant* thicken

thing **1** • whatever is apprehended as having actual, distinct, and demonstrable existence *Syn* article, object *Rel* detail, item, particular

2 *Syn* AFFAIR, business, concern, matter 3 *Syn* GOAL, aim, ambition, aspiration, design, dream, end, intent, intention, mark, meaning, object, objective, plan, pretension, purpose, target

think 1 • to form an idea of *Syn* conceive, envisage, envision, fancy, imagine, realize *Rel* consider, contemplate, study, weigh 2 • to use one's powers of conception, judgment, or inference *Syn* cogitate, deliberate, reason, reflect, speculate *Rel* meditate, muse, ponder, ruminate 3 *Syn* BELIEVE (sense 1), consider, deem, feel, figure, guess, hold, imagine, suppose *Ant* disbelieve, discredit, reject

think (up) *Syn* INVENT, concoct, contrive, cook (up), devise, fabricate, make up, manufacture

thinned *Syn* IMPURE, adulterated, alloyed, contaminated, dilute, diluted, polluted, tainted, weakened *Ant* pure, unadulterated, unalloyed, uncontaminated, undiluted, unpolluted, untainted

thirst *Syn* LONG, hanker, hunger, pine, yearn

thorough *Syn* EXHAUSTIVE, comprehensive, full-scale, out-and-out, thoroughgoing, total

thoroughgoing *Syn* EXHAUSTIVE, all-out, clean, complete, comprehensive, full-scale, out-and-out, thorough, total

though *Syn* ALTHOUGH, albeit, howbeit, when, while

thought *Syn* IDEA, concept, conception, impression, notion

thoughtful 1 • characterized by or exhibiting the power to think *Syn* contemplative, meditative, pensive, reflective, speculative *Rel* earnest, grave, serious, sober 2 • mindful of others *Syn* attentive, considerate *Rel* anxious, careful, concerned, solicitous *Ant* thoughtless 3 *Syn* CONTEMPLATIVE, meditative, melancholy, pensive, reflective, ruminant *Ant* unreflective

thoughtless 1 *Syn* CARELESS, heedless, inadvertent *Ant* careful 2 *Syn* IMPOLITE, discourteous, ill-bred, ill-mannered, impertinent, inconsiderate, rude, uncalled-for, uncivil, ungracious, unmannerly *Ant* civil, considerate, courteous, genteel, gracious, mannerly, polite, thoughtful, well-bred

thrall *Syn* SLAVE (sense 1), bondman, bondsman, chattel *Ant* freeman

thrash 1 *Syn* BEAT, baste, belabor, buffet, pound, pummel 2 *Syn* SWING (sense 1), brandish, flourish, shake, wave

threadbare 1 *Syn* SHABBY, dilapidated, dingy, faded, seedy 2 *Syn* STALE, banal, commonplace, hackney, hackneyed, moth-eaten, musty, stereotyped, tired, trite *Ant* fresh, new, original

threat *Syn* DANGER (sense 1), hazard, menace, peril, pitfall, risk, trouble *Ant* safeness, safety, security

threatening *Syn* OMINOUS, baleful, dire, foreboding, inauspicious, menacing, portentous, sinister

threshold *Syn* BEGINNING, alpha, birth, commencement, dawn, genesis, inception, incipiency, launch, morning, onset, outset, start *Ant* close, conclusion, end, ending

thrift *Syn* ECONOMY, frugality, husbandry, providence, scrimping, skimping *Ant* wastefulness

thriftless *Syn* PRODIGAL, extravagant, profligate, spendthrift, squandering, unthrifty, wasteful *Ant* conserving, economical, economizing, frugal, scrimping, skimping, thrifty

thrifty *Syn* FRUGAL, economical, economizing, provident, scrimping, sparing *Ant* prodigal, wasteful

thrill *n* • a pleasurably intense stimulation of the feelings *Syn* bang, exhilaration, kick, titillation *Rel* arousal, electrification, intoxication, stimulation

thrill *vb* • to excite with emotions that provoke pleasurable sensations or to be so excited *Syn* electrify, enthuse *Rel* excite, galvanize, provoke, quicken, stimulate

thrive *Syn* SUCCEED, flourish, prosper *Ant* attempt, fail

throb *vb Syn* PULSATE, beat, palpitate, pulse

throb *n Syn* PULSATION, beat, palpitation, pulse

throe *Syn* PAIN, ache, pang, stitch, twinge

throng *Syn* CROWD, crush, horde, mob, press, rout

thronging *Syn* RIFE, abounding, flush, fraught, replete, swarming, teeming, thick

throttle *Syn* SUFFOCATE, asphyxiate, choke, smother, stifle, strangle

through 1 *Syn* AMONG, amid (*or* amidst), mid, midst 2 *Syn* BECAUSE OF, due to, owing to, with 3 *Syn* AROUND (sense 2), about, over, round, throughout 4 *Syn* BY, with

throughout *Syn* AROUND (sense 2), about, over, round, through

throw • to cause to move swiftly through space by a propulsive movement or a propelling force *Syn* cast, fling, hurl, pitch, sling, toss *Rel* drive, impel

throw up *Syn* BELCH, burp, disgorge, regurgitate, spew, vomit

thrust *Syn* PUSH, propel, shove

thud *n Syn* TAP, knock, rap, thump

thud *vb Syn* TAP, knock, rap, thump

thump *n Syn* TAP, knock, rap, thud

thump *vb Syn* TAP, knock, rap, thud

thwart *Syn* FRUSTRATE, baffle, balk, circumvent, foil, outwit *Ant* fulfill

ticket *n Syn* MARK, brand, label, stamp, tag

ticket *vb Syn* MARK, brand, label, stamp, tag

tickle *Syn* PLEASE, delight, gladden, gratify, regale, rejoice *Ant* anger, displease, vex

tide *Syn* FLOW, current, flood, flux, stream

tidings *Syn* NEWS, information, intelligence, item, story, word

tidy **1** *Syn* LARGE, big, bulky, considerable, goodly, good-sized, grand, great, handsome, hefty, hulking, largish, outsize, oversize (*or* oversized), sizable (*or* sizeable), substantial, voluminous *Ant* little, puny, small, undersized **2** *Syn* NEAT, shipshape, snug, spick-and-span, trig, trim *Ant* filthy

tie **1** *Syn* BOND, band **2** *Syn* DRAW, deadlock, stalemate, standoff

tier *Syn* LINE, echelon, file, rank, row

tiff *Syn* QUARREL, altercation, bickering, spat, squabble, wrangle

tight **1** • fitting, drawn, or stretched so that there is no slackness or looseness *Syn* taut, tense *Rel* rigid, strict, stringent *Ant* loose **2** *Syn* DRUNK, drunken, inebriated, intoxicated, tipsy *Ant* sober **3** *Syn* STINGY, cheeseparing, close, closefisted, miserly, niggardly, parsimonious, penny-pinching, penurious, tightfisted

tightfisted *Syn* STINGY, cheeseparing, close, closefisted, miserly, niggardly, parsimonious, penny-pinching, penurious, tight *Ant* generous

tight-lipped *Syn* SILENT (sense 1), close, close-lipped, closemouthed, reserved, reticent, secretive, taciturn, uncommunicative *Ant* talkative

tilted *Syn* AWRY, askew, aslant, cockeyed, crooked, listing, lopsided, oblique, skewed, slanted, slanting, slantwise, tipping, uneven *Ant* even, level, straight

time **1** *Syn* AGE (sense 3), day, epoch, era, period **2** *Syn* OPPORTUNITY, break, chance, occasion

timely *Syn* SEASONABLE, opportune, pat, well-timed *Ant* unseasonable

timetable *Syn* PROGRAM, agenda, schedule

timidity • lack of willingness to assert oneself and take risks *Syn* faintheartedness, timidness, timorousness *Rel* bashfulness, constraint, embarrassment, inhibition, restraint, shyness, skittishness *Ant* audaciousness, audacity, boldness, guts, nerve

timidness *Syn* TIMIDITY, faintheartedness, timorousness *Ant* audaciousness, audacity, boldness, guts, nerve

timorousness *Syn* TIMIDITY, faintheartedness, timidness *Ant* audaciousness, audacity, boldness, guts, nerve

tincture **1** *Syn* PIGMENT, color, coloring, dye, dyestuff, stain **2** *Syn* TOUCH, dash, shade, smack, soupçon, spice, strain, streak, suggestion, suspicion, tinge, vein

tinge **1** *Syn* COLOR, hue, shade, tint, tone **2** *Syn* TOUCH, dash, shade, smack, soupçon, spice, strain, streak, suggestion, suspicion, tincture, vein

tint *Syn* COLOR, hue, shade, tinge, tone

tiny • very small in size *Syn* atomic, bitty, infinitesimal, microminiature, microscopic, miniature, minute, teeny, teeny-weeny, wee *Rel* diminutive, dinky, dwarf, dwarfish, insignificant, little, midget, model, petite, pint-size (*or* pint-sized), pocket, pocket-size, puny, pygmy, scrubby, small, smallish, undersized *Ant* astronomical, colossal, cosmic, elephantine, enormous, giant, gigantic, herculean, heroic, huge, immense, mammoth, massive, monster, monstrous, monumental, mountainous, prodigious, titanic, tremendous

tip *Syn* BONUS, dividend, extra, gratuity, gravy, lagniappe, perquisite

tipping *Syn* AWRY, askew, aslant, cockeyed, crooked, listing, lopsided, oblique, skewed, slanted, slanting, slantwise, tilted, uneven *Ant* even, level, straight

tippler *Syn* DRUNKARD, alcoholic, dipsomaniac, inebriate, soak, sot, toper, tosspot *Ant* teetotaler

tipsy *Syn* DRUNK, drunken, inebriated, intoxicated, tight *Ant* sober

tip-top *Syn* EXCELLENT, A1, bang-up, banner, capital, classic, crackerjack, dandy, divine, fabulous, fine, first-class, first-rate, grand, great, groovy, heavenly, jim-dandy, keen, marvelous (*or* marvellous), mean, neat, nifty, noble, par excellence, prime, sensational, splendid, stellar, sterling, superb, superior, superlative, supernal, swell, terrific, top, top-notch, unsurpassed, wonderful *Ant* poor

tirade • a violent, often long-winded, and usually denunciatory speech or writing *Syn* diatribe, jeremiad, philippic *Rel* harangue, oration, speech *Ant* eulogy

tire • to make or become unable or unwilling to continue (as from a loss of physical strength or endurance) *Syn* exhaust, fatigue, jade, tucker, weary *Rel* annoy, bother, irk, vex

tired *Syn* STALE, banal, commonplace, hackney, hackneyed, moth-eaten, musty, stereotyped, threadbare, trite *Ant* fresh, new, original

tiredness *Syn* FATIGUE, burnout, collapse, exhaustion, lassitude, prostration, weariness *Ant* refreshment, rejuvenation, revitalization

tireless *Syn* INDEFATIGABLE, unflagging, untiring, unwearied, unwearying, weariless

tiresome *Syn* BORING, drab, dreary, dry, dull, flat, heavy, humdrum, jading, leaden, monotonous, pedestrian, ponderous, stodgy, stuffy, stupid, tame, tedious, tiring, unanimated, uninteresting, wearisome, weary, wearying *Ant* absorbing, engaging, engrossing, gripping, interesting, intriguing, involving

tiring *Syn* BORING, drab, dreary, dry, dull, flat, heavy, humdrum, jading, leaden, monotonous, pedestrian, ponderous, stodgy, stuffy, stupid, tame, tedious, tiresome, unanimated, uninteresting, wearisome, weary, wearying

Ant absorbing, engaging, engrossing, gripping, interesting, intriguing, involving

titan *Syn* GIANT, behemoth, blockbuster, colossus, jumbo, leviathan, mammoth, monster, whale, whopper *Ant* dwarf, midget, mini, miniature, peewee, pygmy, runt, shrimp

titanic *Syn* HUGE, Brobdingnagian, colossal, cyclopean, elephantine, enormous, gargantuan, giant, gigantean, gigantic, Herculean, immense, mammoth, vast *Ant* bitty, diminutive, microscopic (*or* microscopical), midget, miniature, minute, pocket, pygmy, teeny, teeny-weeny, tiny, wee

titillation *Syn* THRILL, bang, exhilaration, kick

title **1** *Syn* CLAIM, pretense, pretension **2** *Syn* NAME, appellation, denomination, designation, style

tittle *Syn* PARTICLE, atom, bit, iota, jot, mite, smidgen, whit

to *Syn* BEFORE, ahead of, ere, of, previous, prior to, to *Ant* after, following

toady *vb Syn* FAWN, cower, cringe, truckle *Ant* domineer

toady *n* **1** *Syn* PARASITE, bootlicker, favorite, hanger-on, leech, lickspittle, sponge, sponger, sycophant **2** *Syn* SYCOPHANT, fawner, flunky

toboggan *Syn* SLIDE, coast, glide, glissade, skid, slip, slither

to-do *Syn* COMMOTION, bother, bustle, clatter, disturbance, furor, furore, fuss, hubbub, hullabaloo, hurly-burly, pandemonium, pother, row, ruckus, ruction, rumpus, shindy, squall, stew, stir, storm, tumult, turmoil, uproar, welter, whirl

toil *vb Syn* LABOR, drudge, endeavor, grub, hump, hustle, moil, peg (away), plod, plow, plug, slave, slog, strain, strive, struggle, sweat, travail, work *Ant* dabble, fiddle (around), fool (around), mess (around), putter (around)

toil *n Syn* WORK (sense 1), drudgery, grind, labor, travail *Ant* play

toiler *Syn* SLAVE (sense 2), drudge, drudger, grubber, laborer, peon, plugger, slogger, worker *Ant* freeman

token **1** *Syn* MEMORIAL, commemorative, keepsake, memento, monument, remembrance, reminder, souvenir **2** *Syn* PLEDGE, earnest, hostage, pawn **3** *Syn* SIGN (sense 1), badge, mark, note, symptom

tolerable **1** *Syn* ADEQUATE, acceptable, all right, decent, fine, OK (*or* okay), passable, respectable, satisfactory *Ant* deficient, inadequate, lacking, unacceptable, unsatisfactory, wanting **2** *Syn* BEARABLE, endurable, sufferable, supportable, sustainable *Ant* insufferable, insupportable, intolerable, unbearable, unendurable, unsupportable

tolerance *Syn* FORBEARANCE, clemency, indulgence, leniency, mercifulness *Ant* anger, vindictiveness

tolerant **1** *Syn* FORBEARING, clement, indulgent, lenient, merciful *Ant* unrelenting **2** *Syn* PASSIVE, acquiescent, nonresistant, resigned, tolerating, unresistant, unresisting, yielding *Ant* protesting, resistant, resisting, unyielding

tolerantly *Syn* FORBEARINGLY, clemently, indulgently, leniently, mercifully

tolerate *Syn* BEAR (sense 2), abide, brook, endure, stand, suffer

tolerating *Syn* PASSIVE, acquiescent, nonresistant, resigned, tolerant, unresistant, unresisting, yielding *Ant* protesting, resistant, resisting, unyielding

tomfoolery *Syn* HORSEPLAY, clowning, foolery, high jinks, horsing (around), monkeying, monkeyshines, roughhouse, roughhousing, shenanigans, skylarking

tone *Syn* COLOR, hue, shade, tinge, tint

tongue *Syn* LANGUAGE (sense 1), dialect, idiom, speech

tongue-lash *Syn* SCOLD, bawl, berate, chew out, jaw, rail, rate, revile, upbraid, vituperate, wig

tonic • having a renewing effect on the state of the body or mind *Syn* bracing, invigorating, refreshing, restorative, reviving, stimulating, stimulative, vitalizing *Rel* conditioning, strengthening

too *Syn* VERY, awful, awfully, beastly, deadly, especially, exceedingly, extra, extremely, far, frightfully, full, greatly, heavily, highly, hugely, jolly, mightily, mighty, mortally, most, much, particularly, rattling, real, right, so, something, super, terribly, whacking *Ant* little, negligibly, nominally, slightly

tool **1** *Syn* DUPE, chump, gull, pigeon, sap, sucker **2** *Syn* IMPLEMENT, appliance, instrument, utensil

toothsome *Syn* PALATABLE, appetizing, flavorsome, relishing, sapid, savory, tasty *Ant* distasteful, unpalatable

top *Syn* EXCELLENT, A1, bang-up, banner, capital, classic, crackerjack, dandy, divine, fabulous, fine, first-class, first-rate, grand, great, groovy, heavenly, jim-dandy, keen, marvelous (*or* marvellous), mean, neat, nifty, noble, par excellence, prime, sensational, splendid, stellar, sterling, superb, superior, superlative, supernal, swell, terrific, tip-top, top-notch, unsurpassed, wonderful *Ant* poor

toper *Syn* DRUNKARD, alcoholic, dipsomaniac, inebriate, soak, sot, tippler, tosspot *Ant* teetotaler

topic *Syn* SUBJECT, argument, leitmotiv, matter, motif, motive, subject matter, text, theme

top-notch *Syn* EXCELLENT, A1, bang-up, banner, capital, classic, crackerjack, dandy, divine, fabulous, fine, first-class, first-rate, grand, great, groovy, heavenly, jim-dandy, keen, marvelous (*or* marvellous), mean, neat, nifty, noble, par excellence, prime, sensational, splendid, stellar, sterling, superb, superior, superlative, supernal, swell, terrific, tip-top, top, unsurpassed, wonderful *Ant* poor

topsy-turvy *Syn* MESSY, chaotic, cluttered, confused, disarranged, disarrayed, disheveled (*or* dishevelled), disordered, disorderly, higgledy-piggledy, hugger-mugger, jumbled, littered, messed, muddled, mussed, mussy, pell-mell, rumpled, sloppy, tousled, tumbled, unkempt, untidy, upside-down *Ant* neat, ordered, orderly, organized, shipshape, snug, tidied, tidy, trim

torment *Syn* AFFLICT, agonize, bedevil, curse, harrow, martyr, persecute, plague, rack, torture

tornado • a violent whirling wind accompanied by a funnel-shaped cloud *Syn* cyclone, twister *Rel* whirlwind, whirly

torpid *Syn* LETHARGIC, comatose, sluggish *Ant* energetic, vigorous

torpidity *Syn* LETHARGY, languor, lassitude, stupor, torpor *Ant* vigor

torpor *Syn* LETHARGY, languor, lassitude, stupor, torpidity *Ant* vigor

torrent *Syn* FLOOD, cataract, deluge, inundation, spate

tortuous *Syn* WINDING, flexuous, serpentine, sinuous *Ant* straight

torture *Syn* AFFLICT, agonize, bedevil, devil, harrow, martyr, persecute, plague, rack, torment

toss *Syn* THROW, cast, fling, hurl, pitch, sling

tosspot *Syn* DRUNKARD, alcoholic, dipsomaniac, inebriate, soak, sot, tippler, toper *Ant* teetotaler

total *vb Syn* ADD (sense 1), foot (up), sum *Ant* deduct, remove, subtract, take

total *adj* **1** *Syn* EXHAUSTIVE, all-out, clean, complete, comprehensive, full-scale, out-and-out, thorough, thoroughgoing **2** *Syn* WHOLE, all, entire, gross *Ant* partial

total *n Syn* SUM, aggregate, amount, number, quantity, whole

totter **1** *Syn* REEL, stagger, whirl **2** *Syn* SHAKE (sense 1), dither, quake, quaver, quiver, shimmy, shiver, shudder, teeter, tremble, wobble

touch *n* • a very small amount or perceptible trace of something added *Syn* dash, shade, smack, soupçon, spice, strain, streak, suggestion, suspicion, tincture, tinge, vein *Rel* trace, vestige

touch *vb* **1** • to probe with a sensitive part of the body (as a finger) so as to get or produce a sensation often in the course of examining or exploring *Syn* feel, handle, palpate, paw *Rel* examine, inspect, scrutinize **2** *Syn* AFFECT, impress, influence, strike, sway **3** *Syn* MATCH, approach, equal, rival

touchable *Syn* TANGIBLE, palpable *Ant* impalpable, intangible

touch down *Syn* ALIGHT, land, light, perch, roost, settle *Ant* take off

touching **1** *Syn* ADJACENT, abutting, adjoining, bordering, contiguous, flanking, fringing, joining, juxtaposed, skirting, verging *Ant* nonadjacent **2** *Syn* MOVING, affecting, emotional, impressive, poignant, stirring *Ant* unemotional, unimpressive

touch off *Syn* ACTIVATE, actuate, crank (up), drive, move, propel, run, set off, spark, start, trigger, turn on *Ant* cut, deactivate, kill, shut off, turn off

touchstone *Syn* STANDARD, criterion, gauge, yardstick

touchy *Syn* IRASCIBLE, choleric, cranky, cross, splenetic, testy

tough *Syn* STRONG, stalwart, stout, sturdy, tenacious *Ant* weak

tour **1** *Syn* JOURNEY, cruise, excursion, expedition, jaunt, pilgrimage, trip, voyage **2** *Syn* SPELL, bout, go, shift, stint, trick, turn

tousle *Syn* DISORDER, confuse, derange, disarrange, disarray, discompose, dishevel, dislocate, disorganize, disrupt, disturb, hash, jumble, mess (up), mix (up), muddle, muss, rumple, scramble, shuffle, tumble, upset *Ant* arrange, array, draw up, marshal, order, organize, range, regulate, straighten (up), tidy

tousled *Syn* MESSY, chaotic, cluttered, confused, disarranged, disarrayed, disheveled (*or* dishevelled), disordered, disorderly, higgledy-piggledy, hugger-mugger, jumbled, littered, messed, muddled, mussed, mussy, pell-mell, rumpled, sloppy, topsy-turvy, tumbled, unkempt, untidy, upside-down *Ant* neat, ordered, orderly, organized, shipshape, snug, tidied, tidy, trim

tout *Syn* ACCLAIM, applaud, cheer, hail, laud, praise, salute *Ant* knock, pan, slam

tow *Syn* PULL, drag, draw, hale, haul, tug

town *Syn* CITY, burg, megalopolis, metropolis, municipality

toxic *Syn* POISONOUS, mephitic, miasmal, miasmatic, miasmic, pestilent, pestilential, venomous, virulent *Ant* nonpoisonous, nontoxic, nonvenomous

toxin *Syn* POISON, bane, venom, virus

trace *vb Syn* SKETCH, blueprint, delineate, diagram, draft, outline, plot

trace *n Syn* VESTIGE, relic, shadow

tracing **1** *Syn* PURSUIT, chase, chasing, dogging, following, hounding, pursuing, shadowing, tagging, tailing, tracking, trailing **2** *Syn* SKETCH, blueprint, delineation, diagram, draft, outline, plot

tracking *Syn* PURSUIT, chase, chasing, dogging, following, hounding, pursuing, shadowing, tagging, tailing, tracing, trailing

tract *Syn* AREA, belt, region, zone

tractable *Syn* OBEDIENT, amenable, compliant, conformable, docile, law-abiding, submissive *Ant* contrary, disobedient, froward, insubordinate, intractable, rebellious, recalcitrant, refractory, unruly

trade *n* **1** • a pursuit followed as an occupation or means of livelihood and requiring technical knowledge and skill *Syn* art, craft, handicraft, profession *Rel* employment, occupation, pursuit, work **2** *Syn* BUSINESS, commerce, industry, traffic **3** *Syn* OCCUPATION, calling, employment, line, profession, vocation, work **4** *Syn* SALE, deal, transaction

trade *vb Syn* CHANGE (sense 3), commute, exchange, shift, substitute, swap, switch

trader *Syn* MERCHANT, dealer, merchandiser, tradesman, trafficker

tradesman **1** *Syn* ARTISAN, artificer, craftsman, handicrafter **2** *Syn* MERCHANT, dealer, merchandiser, trader, trafficker

tradition *Syn* FOLKLORE, legend, lore, myth, mythology

traditional *Syn* CONSERVATIVE, orthodox *Ant* liberal, nontraditional, progressive

traduce *Syn* SLANDER, asperse, blacken, defame, libel, malign, smear, vilify

traffic *Syn* BUSINESS, commerce, industry, trade

trafficker *Syn* MERCHANT, dealer, merchandiser, trader, tradesman

trailer *Syn* CAMPER, caravan, mobile home, motor home

trailing *Syn* PURSUIT, chase, chasing, dogging, following, hounding, pursuing, shadowing, tagging, tailing, tracing, tracking

train *n Syn* SUCCESSION, chain, progression, sequence, series, string

train *vb Syn* TEACH, discipline, educate, instruct, school

training *Syn* EDUCATION (sense 1), instruction, schooling, teaching, tutelage, tutoring

traipse **1** *Syn* WALK, foot (it), hoof (it), leg (it), pad, step, tread **2** *Syn* WANDER, gad, gallivant, meander, prowl, ramble, range, roam, rove, stray

trait *Syn* CHARACTERISTIC, attribute, character, feature, mark, peculiarity, point, property, quality

traitor • one who betrays a trust or an allegiance *Syn* betrayer, double-crosser, quisling, recreant, turncoat *Rel* collaborationist, collaborator, subversive

traitorous *Syn* FAITHLESS, disloyal, false, perfidious, treacherous *Ant* faithful

trammel *n Syn* ENCUMBRANCE, bar, block, chain, clog, crimp, deterrent, drag, embarrassment, fetter, handicap, hindrance, hurdle, impediment, inhibition, interference, let, manacle, obstacle, obstruction, shackles, stop, stumbling block *Ant* aid, assistance, benefit, help

trammel *vb Syn* HAMPER, clog, fetter, hog-tie, manacle, shackle *Ant* assist (*persons*), expedite (*work, projects*)

tramp *vb Syn* TRAMPLE, stamp, stomp, tromp

tramp *n Syn* VAGABOND, bum, hobo, truant, vagrant

trample • to tread on heavily so as to crush or injure *Syn* stamp, stomp, tramp, tromp *Rel* override, run down, run over, step (on)

trance *Syn* REVERIE, daydreaming, study, woolgathering

tranquil *Syn* CALM, halcyon, peaceful, placid, serene *Ant* agitated, stormy

tranquilize *Syn* CALM, compose, lull, quiet, quieten, settle, soothe, still *Ant* agitate, arouse

tranquillity *or* **tranquility** **1** *Syn* CALM, calmness, hush, peace, peacefulness, placidity, quiet, quietness, quietude, repose, restfulness, sereneness, serenity, still, stillness *Ant* bustle, commotion, hubbub, hurly-burly, pandemonium, tumult, turmoil, uproar **2** *Syn* EQUANIMITY, aplomb, calmness, composure, coolheadedness, coolness, imperturbability, placidity, self-possession, serenity *Ant* agitation, discomposure, perturbation

transaction *Syn* SALE, deal, trade

transcend *Syn* EXCEED, excel, outdo, outstrip, surpass

transcendent **1** *Syn* ABSTRACT (sense 1), ideal, transcendental *Ant* concrete **2** *Syn* SUPREME, incomparable, peerless, preeminent, superlative, surpassing

transcendental *Syn* ABSTRACT (sense 1), ideal, transcendent *Ant* concrete

transfer **1** • to shift title or possession from one owner to another *Syn* alienate, convey, deed **2** *Syn* COMMUNICATE, convey, impart, spread, transfuse, transmit **3** *Syn* MOVE (sense 2), remove, shift

transfiguration *Syn* TRANSFORMATION, conversion, metamorphosis, transmogrification, transmutation

transfigure **1** *Syn* CONVERT, make over, metamorphose, transform **2** *Syn* TRANSFORM, convert, metamorphose, transmogrify, transmute

transform **1** • to change a thing into a different thing *Syn* convert, metamorphose, transfigure, transmogrify, transmute *Rel* alter, change, modify, vary **2** *Syn* CONVERT, make over, metamorphose, transfigure

transformation • a change of one thing into another different thing *Syn* conversion, metamorphosis, transfiguration, transmutation *Rel* alteration, change, modification, variation

transfuse *Syn* COMMUNICATE, convey, impart, spread, transfer, transmit

transgression *Syn* BREACH (sense 1), contravention, infraction, infringement, trespass, violation

transient *Syn* MOMENTARY, ephemeral, evanescent, flash, fleeting, fugitive, impermanent, passing, short-lived, temporary, transitory *Ant* enduring, eternal, everlasting, lasting, long-lived, permanent, perpetual

transitory *Syn* MOMENTARY, ephemeral, evanescent, flash, fleeting, fugitive, impermanent, passing, short-lived, temporary, transient *Ant* eternal, everlasting, lasting, long-lived, permanent, perpetual

translate *Syn* PARAPHRASE, rephrase, restate, reword *Ant* quote

translation • a restating often in a simpler language of something previously stated or written *Syn* metaphrase, paraphrase, version

translucent *Syn* CLEAR (sense 1), diaphanous, limpid, lucid, pellucid, transparent *Ant* confused, turbid

transmit **1** *Syn* CARRY, bear, convey, transport **2** *Syn* COMMUNICATE, convey, impart, spread, transfer, transfuse **3** *Syn* SEND, dispatch, forward, remit, route, ship *Ant* accept, receive

transmogrification *Syn* TRANSFORMATION, conversion, metamorphosis, transfiguration, transmutation

transmogrify *Syn* TRANSFORM, convert, metamorphose, transfigure, transmute

transmutation *Syn* TRANSFORMATION, conversion, metamorphosis, transfiguration

transmute *Syn* TRANSFORM, convert, metamorphose, transfigure, transmogrify

transparent *Syn* CLEAR (sense 1), diaphanous, limpid, lucid, pellucid, translucent *Ant* confused, turbid

transpire *Syn* HAPPEN, befall, betide, chance, occur

transport *vb* **1** • to carry away by strong and usually pleasurable emotion *Syn* enrapture, entrance, ravish *Rel* excite, provoke, quicken, stimulate **2** *Syn* BANISH, deport, exile, expatriate, extradite, ostracize **3** *Syn* CARRY, bear, convey, transmit **4** *Syn* ELATE, elevate, enrapture, exhilarate, overjoy *Ant* depress **5** *Syn* ENTRANCE, carry away, enrapture, enthrall (*or* enthral), overjoy, ravish

transport *n* *Syn* ECSTASY, elation, euphoria, exhilaration, heaven, intoxication, paradise, rapture, rhapsody *Ant* depression

transpose *Syn* REVERSE, invert

trap **1** *Syn* CATCH, bag, capture, ensnare, entrap, snare *Ant* miss **2** *Syn* ENTANGLE, enmesh, ensnare, entrap, mesh, snare, tangle *Ant* disentangle

trash **1** *Syn* NONSENSE, balderdash, bull, bunk, drivel, gobbledygook, poppycock, rot, twaddle **2** *Syn* REFUSE, debris, garbage, offal, rubbish, waste

trauma *Syn* WOUND, bruise, contusion, lesion, traumatism

traumatism *Syn* WOUND, bruise, contusion, lesion, trauma

travail *vb* *Syn* LABOR, drudge, endeavor, grub, hump, hustle, moil, peg (away), plod, plow, plug, slave, slog, strain, strive, struggle, sweat, toil, work *Ant* dabble, fiddle (around), fool (around), mess (around), putter (around)

travail *n* *Syn* WORK (sense 1), drudgery, grind, labor, toil *Ant* play

travel *Syn* TRAVERSE, cover, crisscross, cross, cut (across), follow, go, pass (over), proceed (along)

traverse **1** • to make one's way through, across, or over *Syn* cover, crisscross, cross, cut (across), follow, go, pass (over), proceed (along), travel *Rel* hike, tread, walk **2** *Syn* DENY, contradict, contravene, gainsay, impugn, negative *Ant* concede, confirm

travesty *n* *Syn* CARICATURE, burlesque, parody

travesty *vb* *Syn* CARICATURE, burlesque, parody

treacherous *Syn* FAITHLESS, disloyal, false, perfidious, traitorous *Ant* faithful

treachery *Syn* BETRAYAL, disloyalty, double cross, faithlessness, falseness, falsity, infidelity, perfidy, sellout, treason, unfaithfulness

tread *Syn* WALK, foot (it), hoof (it), leg (it), pad, step, traipse

treason *Syn* BETRAYAL, disloyalty, double cross, faithlessness, falseness, falsity, infidelity, perfidy, sellout, treachery, unfaithfulness

treasure *Syn* APPRECIATE, cherish, prize, value *Ant* despise

treat • to have to do with or behave toward (a person or thing) in a specified manner *Syn* deal, handle *Rel* conduct, manage

treatise *Syn* DISCOURSE, disquisition, dissertation, monograph, thesis

treaty *Syn* CONTRACT, bargain, cartel, compact, concordat, convention, entente, pact

treble *Syn* SHRILL, acute, high-pitched, piping, screeching, shrieking, squeaking, squeaky, whistling *Ant* bass, deep, low, throaty

tremble *Syn* SHAKE (sense 1), dither, quake, quaver, quiver, shimmy, shiver, shudder, teeter, totter, wobble

tremendous *Syn* MONSTROUS, monumental, prodigious, stupendous

trenchant *Syn* INCISIVE, biting, clear-cut, crisp, cutting

trend *Syn* TENDENCY, drift, tenor

trepidation *Syn* FEAR, alarm, consternation, dismay, dread, fright, horror, panic, terror *Ant* fearlessness

trespass *vb* • to make inroads upon the property, territory, or rights of another *Syn* encroach, entrench, infringe, invade *Rel* butt in, interlope, intrude, obtrude

trespass *n* *Syn* BREACH (sense 1), contravention, infraction, infringement, transgression, violation

trial **1** • the state or fact of being tested (as by suffering) *Syn* affliction, cross, tribulation, visitation *Rel* agony, distress, misery, suffering **2** *Syn* ATTEMPT, crack, endeavor, essay, fling, go, pass, shot, stab, try, whack **3** *Syn* PROOF, demonstration, test **4** *Syn* REHEARSAL, dry run, practice

tribulation *Syn* TRIAL, affliction, cross, visitation

tributary *Syn* SUBORDINATE, collateral, dependent, secondary, subject *Ant* chief, dominant, leading

tribute *Syn* ENCOMIUM, citation, eulogy, panegyric

trice *Syn* INSTANT, flash, jiffy, minute, moment, second, shake, split second, twinkle, twinkling, wink

trick *n* **1** • an indirect means to gain an end *Syn* artifice, feint, gambit, maneuver, ploy, ruse, stratagem, wile *Rel* cheat, counterfeit, deceit, deception, fake, fraud, humbug, imposture **2** *Syn* HABIT, custom, fashion, pattern, practice, way, wont **3** *Syn* SPELL, bout, go, shift, stint, tour, turn

trick *vb Syn* DUPE, bamboozle, befool, gull, hoax, hoodwink

trickery **1** • the use of clever underhanded actions to achieve an end *Syn* artifice, chicanery, hanky-panky, jugglery, legerdemain, subterfuge, wile *Rel* artfulness, caginess, craftiness, cunning, deviousness, foxiness, shadiness, sharpness, shiftiness, slickness, slipperiness, slyness, sneakiness, treachery, underhandedness, wiliness **2** *Syn* DECEPTION, chicane, chicanery, double-dealing, fraud

trickster *Syn* MAGICIAN (sense 2), conjurer (*or* conjuror), prestidigitator

tricky *Syn* SLY, artful, crafty, cunning, foxy, guileful, insidious, wily

tried *Syn* DEPENDABLE, good, reliable, responsible, safe, solid, steady, sure, tried-and-true, true, trustworthy, trusty *Ant* irresponsible, undependable, unreliable, untrustworthy

tried-and-true *Syn* DEPENDABLE, good, reliable, responsible, safe, solid, steady, sure, tried, true, trustworthy, trusty *Ant* irresponsible, undependable, unreliable, untrustworthy

trifle *n* • something of little importance *Syn* child's play, frippery, nothing, triviality *Rel* naught, nothingness, smoke, zero

trifle *vb Syn* FLIRT, dally, frivol

trifling **1** *Syn* PETTY, measly, paltry, picayune, picayunish, puny, trivial *Ant* gross, important, momentous **2** *Syn* UNIMPORTANT, frivolous, inconsequential, inconsiderable, insignificant, little, minor, minute, negligible, slight, small, small-fry, trivial *Ant* big, consequential, eventful, important, major, material, meaningful, momentous, significant, substantial, weighty

trig *Syn* NEAT, shipshape, snug, spick-and-span, tidy, trim *Ant* filthy

trigger *Syn* ACTIVATE, actuate, crank (up), drive, move, propel, run, set off, spark, start, touch off, turn on *Ant* cut, deactivate, kill, shut off, turn off

trill *Syn* SING, carol, chant, descant, hymn, intone, troll, warble

trim *vb* **1** *Syn* CLIP, bob, crop, curtail, cut, cut back, dock, lop (off), nip, pare, prune, shave, shear, snip **2** *Syn* STABILIZE, balance, ballast, poise, steady

trim *adj Syn* NEAT, shipshape, snug, spick-and-span, tidy, trig *Ant* filthy

trinket *Syn* KNICKKNACK, bauble, curio, curiosity, gaud, gewgaw, novelty, ornamental

trip *n Syn* JOURNEY, cruise, excursion, expedition, jaunt, pilgrimage, tour, voyage

trip *vb Syn* STUMBLE, blunder, bumble, flounder, galumph, lollop, lumber, lurch

trite *Syn* STALE, banal, commonplace, hackney, hackneyed, moth-eaten, musty, stereotyped, threadbare, tired *Ant* fresh, new, original

triumph *Syn* VICTORY, conquest *Ant* defeat

triumphant *Syn* EXULTANT, exulting, glorying, jubilant, rejoicing

trivial **1** *Syn* PETTY, measly, paltry, picayune, picayunish, puny, trifling *Ant* gross, important, momentous **2** *Syn* UNIMPORTANT, frivolous, inconsequential, inconsiderable, insignificant, little, minor, minute, negligible, slight, small, small-fry, trifling *Ant* big, consequential, eventful, important, major, material, meaningful, momentous, significant, substantial, weighty

triviality *Syn* TRIFLE, child's play, frippery, nothing

troll *Syn* SING, carol, chant, descant, hymn, intone, trill, warble

tromp *Syn* TRAMPLE, stamp, stomp, tramp

troop *Syn* COMPANY, band, party, troupe

tropical storm *Syn* HURRICANE, typhoon

trot *Syn* HURRY (sense 2), barrel, bolt, bowl, breeze, career, course, dash, fly, hasten, hotfoot (it), hump, hurtle, hustle, pelt, race, rip, rocket, run, rush, rustle, scoot, scurry, scuttle, shoot, speed, step (along), tear, whirl, whisk, zip, zoom *Ant* crawl, creep, poke

troth *Syn* PROMISE, oath, pledge, vow, word

troubadour *Syn* POET, bard, minstrel, poetaster, rhymer, rhymester, versifier

trouble *vb* **1** • to cause to be uneasy or upset *Syn* ail, distress *Rel* agitate, discompose, disquiet, disturb, perturb, upset **2** *Syn* INCONVENIENCE, discommode, disoblige, disturb, incommode *Ant* accommodate, oblige

trouble *n* **1** *Syn* DANGER (sense 1), hazard, menace, peril, pitfall, risk, threat *Ant* safeness, safety, security **2** *Syn* EFFORT, exertion, pains *Ant* ease **3** *Syn* DANGER (sense 2), distress, endangerment, imperilment, jeopardy, peril, risk *Ant* safeness, safety, security

troublesome • causing worry or anxiety *Syn*

discomforting, discomposing, disquieting, distressing, disturbing, perturbing, troubling, troublous, unsettling, upsetting, worrisome *Rel* daunting, demoralizing, discomfiting, disconcerting, discouraging, disheartening, dismaying, dispiriting *Ant* reassuring, untroublesome

troubling *Syn* TROUBLESOME, discomforting, discomposing, disquieting, distressing, disturbing, perturbing, troublous, unsettling, upsetting, worrisome *Ant* reassuring, untroublesome

troublous *Syn* TROUBLESOME, discomforting, discomposing, disquieting, distressing, disturbing, perturbing, troubling, unsettling, upsetting, worrisome *Ant* reassuring, untroublesome

troupe *Syn* COMPANY, band, party, troop

trouper *Syn* ACTOR, impersonator, mime, mimic, mummer, performer, player, thespian

truant *Syn* VAGABOND, bum, hobo, tramp, vagrant

truce • a suspension of or an agreement for suspending hostilities *Syn* armistice, cease-fire, peace

truckle *Syn* FAWN, cower, cringe, toady *Ant* domineer

truculence *Syn* BELLIGERENCE, aggression, aggressiveness, bellicosity, combativeness, contentiousness, disputatiousness, fight, militancy, pugnacity, scrappiness *Ant* pacifism

truculent **1** *Syn* BELLIGERENT, aggressive, argumentative, bellicose, combative, contentious, discordant, disputatious, gladiatorial, militant, pugnacious, quarrelsome, scrappy, warlike *Ant* nonbelligerent, pacific, peaceable, peaceful **2** *Syn* FIERCE, barbarous, cruel, fell, ferocious, inhuman, savage *Ant* mild, tame

true **1** *Syn* ACTUAL, concrete, existent, factual, real, very *Ant* conjectural, hypothetical, ideal, nonexistent, possible, potential, theoretical **2** *Syn* DEPENDABLE, good, reliable, responsible, safe, solid, steady, sure, tried, trustworthy, trusty *Ant* irresponsible, undependable, unreliable, untrustworthy **3** *Syn* FAITHFUL, constant, devoted, devout, fast, good, loyal, pious, staunch (*or* stanch), steadfast, steady, true-blue *Ant* disloyal, faithless, false, fickle, inconstant, perfidious, recreant, traitorous, treacherous, unfaithful, untrue

true-blue *Syn* FAITHFUL, constant, devoted, devout, fast, good, loyal, pious, staunch (*or* stanch), steadfast, steady, true *Ant* disloyal, faithless, false, fickle, inconstant, perfidious, recreant, traitorous, treacherous, unfaithful, untrue

truism *Syn* COMMONPLACE, bromide, cliché, platitude

trunk *Syn* CHEST, box, caddy, case, casket, locker

trust *vb* **1** • assured reliance on the character, ability, strength, or truth of someone or something *Syn* confidence, dependence, faith, reliance *Rel* assurance, certainty, certitude, conviction *Ant* mistrust **2** *Syn* CARTEL, combination, combine, syndicate **3** *Syn* CUSTODY, care, guardianship, keeping, safekeeping, ward **4** *Syn* MONOPOLY, cartel, corner, pool, syndicate

trust *n* *Syn* RELY (ON), bank, count, depend, reckon

trustworthy *Syn* DEPENDABLE, good, reliable, responsible, safe, solid, steady, sure, tried, tried-and-true, true, trusty *Ant* irresponsible, undependable, unreliable, untrustworthy

trusty *Syn* DEPENDABLE, good, reliable, responsible, safe, solid, steady, sure, tried, tried-and-true, true, trustworthy *Ant* irresponsible, undependable, unreliable, untrustworthy

truth • the quality or state of keeping close to fact and avoiding distortion or misrepresentation *Syn* veracity, verisimilitude, verity *Rel* correctness, exactness, precision, rightness *Ant* falsehood, lie, untruth

truthful • being in the habit of telling the truth *Syn* honest, veracious *Rel* candid, frank, open, plainspoken *Ant* dishonest, fibbing, lying, mendacious, prevaricating, untruthful

try *vb* **1** *Syn* ATTEMPT, assay, endeavor, essay, seek, strive **2** *Syn* PROVE, demonstrate, test *Ant* disprove

try *n* *Syn* ATTEMPT, crack, endeavor, essay, fling, go, pass, shot, stab, trial, whack

tryst *Syn* ENGAGEMENT, appointment, assignation, date, rendezvous

tucker *Syn* TIRE, exhaust, fatigue, jade, weary

tug *Syn* PULL, drag, draw, hale, haul, tow

tumble *Syn* DISORDER, confuse, derange, disarrange, disarray, discompose, dishevel, dislocate, disorganize, disrupt, disturb, hash, jumble, mess (up), mix (up), muddle, muss, rumple, scramble, shuffle, tousle, upset *Ant* arrange, array, draw up, marshal, order, organize, range, regulate, straighten (up), tidy

tumbled *Syn* MESSY, chaotic, cluttered, confused, disarranged, disarrayed, disheveled (*or* dishevelled), disordered, disorderly, higgledy-piggledy, hugger-mugger, jumbled, littered, messed, muddled, mussed, mussy, pell-mell, rumpled, sloppy, topsy-turvy, tousled, unkempt, untidy, upside-down *Ant* neat, ordered, orderly, organized, shipshape, snug, tidied, tidy, trim

tumid *Syn* INFLATED, flatulent, turgid *Ant* pithy

tummy *Syn* STOMACH, abdomen, belly, gut, solar plexus

tumult **1** *Syn* COMMOTION, bother, bustle, clatter, disturbance, furor, furore, fuss, hubbub, hullabaloo, hurly-burly, pandemonium, pother, row, ruckus, ruction, rumpus, shindy, squall, stew, stir, storm, to-do, turmoil, uproar, welter, whirl **2** *Syn* CONVULSION, cataclysm, paroxysm, storm, tempest, upheaval, uproar

tumultuous *Syn* CONVULSIVE, cataclysmal (*or* cataclysmic), stormy, tempestuous

tundra *Syn* PLAIN, down, grassland, prairie, savanna, steppe, veld (*or* veldt)

tune *vb Syn* HARMONIZE, attune

tune *n Syn* MELODY, air, lay, song, strain, warble

turbid • not clear or translucent but clouded with or as if with sediment *Syn* muddy, roily *Rel* dark, murky, obscure *Ant* clear, limpid

turgid *Syn* INFLATED, flatulent, tumid *Ant* pithy

turkey *Syn* FOOL (sense 2), booby, goose, half-wit, jackass, lunatic, nincompoop, ninny, nitwit, nut, simpleton, yo-yo

turmoil **1** *Syn* COMMOTION, bother, bustle, clatter, disturbance, furor, furore, fuss, hubbub, hullabaloo, hurly-burly, pandemonium, pother, row, ruckus, ruction, rumpus, shindy, squall, stew, stir, storm, to-do, tumult, uproar, welter, whirl **2** *Syn* UNREST, disquiet, ferment, restiveness, restlessness, uneasiness *Ant* calm, ease, peace, quiet

turn *vb* **1** • to move or cause to move in a curved or circular path on or as if on an axis *Syn* circle, eddy, gyrate, pirouette, revolve, rotate, spin, swirl, twirl, wheel, whirl *Rel* fluctuate, oscillate, pendulate, swing, undulate, vibrate **2** • to change or cause to change course or direction *Syn* avert, deflect, divert, sheer *Rel* depart, deviate, digress, diverge, swerve, veer **3** *Syn* BECOME, come, get, go, grow, run, wax **4** *Syn* DEPEND (sense 1), hang, hinge **5** *Syn* RESORT, apply, go, refer

turn *n* **1** *Syn* GIFT (sense 2), aptitude, bent, faculty, genius, knack, talent **2** *Syn* SPELL, bout, go, shift, stint, tour, trick **3** *Syn* WALK, constitutional, perambulation, ramble, range, saunter, stroll

turncoat **1** *Syn* RENEGADE, apostate, backslider, recreant *Ant* adherent, loyalist **2** *Syn* TRAITOR, betrayer, double-crosser, quisling, recreant

turning point • a point in a chain of events at which an important change (as in one's fortunes) occurs *Syn* climax, landmark, milestone *Rel* break, clincher, highlight

turn off *Syn* DISGUST, nauseate, repel, repulse, revolt, sicken

turn on *Syn* ACTIVATE, actuate, crank (up), drive, move, propel, run, set off, spark, start, touch off, trigger *Ant* cut, deactivate, kill, shut off, turn off

turn out *Syn* BEAR (sense 1), produce, yield

tussle *Syn* WRESTLE, grapple, scuffle

tutelage *Syn* EDUCATION (sense 1), instruction, schooling, teaching, training, tutoring

tutoring *Syn* EDUCATION (sense 1), instruction, schooling, teaching, training, tutelage

twaddle *Syn* NONSENSE, balderdash, bull, bunk, drivel, gobbledygook, poppycock, rot, trash

twain *Syn* PAIR, brace, couple, duo, twosome

tweet *vb Syn* CHIRP, cheep, chirrup, chitter, peep, twitter

tweet *n Syn* CHIRP, cheep, chirrup, chitter, peep, twitter

twin *Syn* DOUBLE, binary, bipartite, dual, duplex *Ant* single

twine *Syn* WIND, coil, curl, entwine, twist, wreathe

twinge *Syn* PAIN, ache, pang, stitch, throe

twinkle *vb Syn* FLASH, coruscate, glance, gleam, glint, glisten, glitter, scintillate, sparkle

twinkle *n Syn* INSTANT, flash, jiffy, minute, moment, second, shake, split second, trice, twinkling, wink

twinkling *Syn* INSTANT, flash, jiffy, minute, moment, second, shake, split second, trice, twinkle, wink

twirl *Syn* TURN (sense 1), circle, eddy, gyrate, pirouette, revolve, rotate, spin, swirl, wheel, whirl

twist **1** *Syn* CURVE, bend **2** *Syn* WIND, coil, curl, entwine, twine, wreathe

twister *Syn* TORNADO, cyclone

twit *Syn* RIDICULE, deride, mock, rally, taunt

twitch *Syn* JERK, snap, yank

twitter *vb* **1** *Syn* CHAT, babble, blab, cackle, chatter, converse, gab, gabble, gas, jabber, jaw, palaver, patter, prate, prattle, rap, rattle, run on, talk, visit **2** *Syn* CHIRP, cheep, chirrup, chitter, peep, tweet

twitter *n Syn* CHIRP, cheep, chirrup, chitter, peep, tweet

two-faced *Syn* INSINCERE, artificial, backhanded, double-dealing, feigned, hypocritical, left-handed, mealy, mealymouthed, unctuous *Ant* genuine, heartfelt, honest, sincere, unfeigned

twosome *Syn* PAIR, brace, couple, duo, twain

type **1** • a number of individuals thought of as a group because of a common quality or qualities *Syn* character, description, ilk, kidney, kind, nature, sort, stripe *Rel* example, exemplar, model, pattern **2** *Syn* SYMBOL, attribute, emblem

typhoon *Syn* HURRICANE, tropical storm

typical *Syn* REGULAR, natural, normal *Ant* irregular

typically *Syn* NATURALLY (sense 1), commonly, generally, normally, ordinarily, usually *Ant* abnormally, atypically, extraordinarily, uncommonly, unusually

tyrannical **1** *Syn* ABSOLUTE, arbitrary, autocratic, despotic, tyrannous *Ant* limited, restrained **2** *Syn* BOSSY, authoritarian, autocratic, despotic, dictatorial, domineering, imperious, masterful, overbearing, peremptory, tyrannous

tyrannous **1** *Syn* ABSOLUTE, arbitrary, autocratic, despotic, tyrannical *Ant* limited, restrained **2** *Syn* BOSSY, authoritarian, autocratic, despotic, dictatorial, domineering, imperious, masterful, overbearing, peremptory, tyrannical

tyro **1** *Syn* AMATEUR, dabbler, dilettante *Ant* expert, professional **2** *Syn* BEGINNER, colt, fledgling, freshman, greenhorn, neophyte, newbie, newcomer, novice, recruit, rookie, tenderfoot *Ant* old hand, old-timer, vet, veteran

U

ugly • unpleasing to the sight *Syn* hideous, ill-favored, unsightly *Rel* homely, plain *Ant* beautiful

ultimate **1** • being so fundamental as to represent the extreme limit of actual or possible knowledge *Syn* absolute, categorical **2** *Syn* LAST, concluding, eventual, final, latest, terminal *Ant* first

ultramodern *Syn* MODERN, contemporary, current, hot, mod, modernistic, new, newfangled, new-fashioned, present-day, red-hot, space-age, up-to-date *Ant* antiquated, archaic, dated, fusty, musty, noncontemporary, oldfangled, old-fashioned, old-time, out-of-date, passé

ululate *Syn* ROAR, bawl, bellow, bluster, clamor, howl, vociferate

ululation *Syn* ROAR, bawl, bellow, bluster, vociferation

umbra *Syn* SHADE, adumbration, penumbra, shadow, umbrage

umbrage **1** *Syn* OFFENSE (sense 1), dudgeon, huff, pique, resentment **2** *Syn* SHADE, adumbration, penumbra, shadow, umbra

umpire *Syn* JUDGE, arbiter, arbitrator, referee

unabashed • not embarrassed or ashamed *Syn* unashamed, unblushing, unembarrassed *Rel* prideful, proud *Ant* abashed, ashamed, embarrassed, shamefaced, sheepish

unacceptable *Syn* OBJECTIONABLE, exceptionable, undesirable, unwanted, unwelcome

unacceptably *Syn* BADLY, inadequately, poorly, unsatisfactorily *Ant* acceptably, adequately, all right, fine, good, palatably, passably, so-so, tolerably

unachievable *Syn* IMPOSSIBLE, hopeless, unattainable, unsolvable *Ant* achievable, attainable, doable, feasible, possible, realizable, workable

unadvisable *Syn* INDISCREET, ill-advised, imprudent, inadvisable, injudicious, tactless, unwise *Ant* advisable, discreet, judicious, prudent, tactful, wise

unaffected *Syn* NATURAL, artless, ingenuous, naive, simple, unsophisticated

unaffectedly *Syn* NATURALLY (sense 3), artlessly, guilelessly, ingenuously, innocently, naively, sincerely, unpretentiously *Ant* affectedly, artificially, hypocritically, insincerely, pretentiously, unnaturally

unafraid *Syn* BRAVE, audacious, bold, courageous, dauntless, doughty, fearless, intrepid, undaunted, valiant, valorous *Ant* craven

unanimated *Syn* BORING, drab, dreary, dry, dull, flat, heavy, humdrum, jading, leaden, monotonous, pedestrian, ponderous, stodgy, stuffy, stupid, tame, tedious, tiresome, tiring, uninteresting, wearisome, weary, wearying *Ant* absorbing, engaging, engrossing, gripping, interesting, intriguing, involving

unanswerable *Syn* IRREFUTABLE, incontestable, incontrovertible, indisputable, indubitable, undeniable, unquestionable *Ant* answerable, debatable, disputable, questionable

unanticipated *Syn* UNEXPECTED, unforeseen, unlooked-for *Ant* anticipated, expected, foreseen

unappreciative *Syn* THANKLESS, ungrateful *Ant* appreciative, grateful, obliged, thankful

unapt **1** *Syn* IMPROBABLE, doubtful, dubious, far-fetched, flimsy, questionable, unlikely *Ant* likely, probable **2** *Syn* INAPPROPRIATE, graceless, improper, inapt, incongruous, incorrect, indecorous, inept, infelicitous, unbecoming, unfit, unhappy, unseemly, unsuitable, wrong *Ant* appropriate, becoming, befitting, correct, decorous, felicitous, fit, fitting, genteel, happy, meet, proper, right, seemly, suitable

unashamed *Syn* UNABASHED, unblushing, unembarrassed *Ant* abashed, ashamed, embarrassed, shamefaced, sheepish

unassailable *Syn* INVINCIBLE, impregnable, indomitable, inexpugnable, invulnerable, unconquerable

unattached *Syn* UNMARRIED, single, unwed *Ant* espoused, married

unattainable *Syn* IMPOSSIBLE, hopeless, unachievable, unsolvable *Ant* achievable, attainable, doable, feasible, possible, realizable, workable

unavoidable *Syn* INEVITABLE, certain, inescapable, necessary, sure *Ant* avoidable, escapable, uncertain, unsure

unaware *Syn* UNAWARES, aback, suddenly, unexpectedly

unawares • without warning *Syn* aback, suddenly, unaware, unexpectedly *Rel* abruptly, short

unbearable • more than can be put up with *Syn* insufferable, insupportable, intolerable, unendurable, unsupportable *Rel* unacceptable *Ant* endurable, sufferable, supportable, tolerable

unbecoming *Syn* INAPPROPRIATE, graceless, improper, inapt, incongruous, incorrect, indecorous, inept, infelicitous, unapt, unfit, unhappy, unseemly, unsuitable, wrong *Ant* appropriate, becoming, befitting, correct, decorous, felicitous, fit, fitting, genteel, happy, meet, proper, right, seemly, suitable

unbelief • the attitude or state of mind of one who does not believe *Syn* disbelief, incredulity *Rel* doubt, dubiety, dubiosity, skepticism, uncertainty *Ant* belief

unbeliever *Syn* SKEPTIC, disbeliever, doubter, questioner

unbend *Syn* STRAIGHTEN, uncurl *Ant* bend, crook, curl, curve

unbending *Syn* OBSTINATE, adamant, adamantine, dogged, hard, hardened, hardheaded, hardhearted, headstrong, immovable, implacable, inflexible, mulish, obdurate, opinionated, ossified, pat, peevish, pertinacious, perverse, pigheaded, rigid, self-willed, stubborn, uncompromising, unrelenting, unyielding, willful (*or* wilful) *Ant* acquiescent, agreeable, amenable, compliant, complying, flexible, pliable, pliant, relenting, yielding

unbiased *Syn* FAIR, dispassionate, equitable, impartial, just, objective, uncolored *Ant* unfair

unblushing *Syn* UNABASHED, unashamed, unembarrassed *Ant* abashed, ashamed, embarrassed, shamefaced, sheepish

unbounded *Syn* INFINITE, boundless, endless, illimitable, immeasurable, indefinite, limitless, measureless, unfathomable, unlimited *Ant* bounded, circumscribed, confined, definite, finite, limited, restricted

unburden *Syn* RID, clear, disabuse, purge

uncalled-for **1** *Syn* IMPOLITE, discourteous, ill-bred, ill-mannered, impertinent, inconsiderate, rude, thoughtless, uncivil, ungracious, unmannerly *Ant* civil, considerate, courteous, genteel, gracious, mannerly, polite, thoughtful, well-bred **2** *Syn* UNNECESSARY, dispensable, gratuitous, needless, nonessential, unessential, unwarranted *Ant* essential, indispensable, necessary, needed, needful, required

uncanny *Syn* EERIE, creepy, haunting, spooky, unearthly, weird

unceasing *Syn* EVERLASTING, endless, interminable *Ant* transitory

uncertainty *Syn* DOUBT, distrust, distrustfulness, incertitude, misgiving, mistrust, mistrustfulness, skepticism, suspicion *Ant* assurance, belief, certainty, certitude, confidence, conviction, sureness, surety, trust

unchanging *Syn* UNIFORM, invariant, steady, undeviating, unvarying, unwavering *Ant* changing, deviating, varying

uncivil *Syn* IMPOLITE, discourteous, ill-bred, ill-mannered, impertinent, inconsiderate, rude, thoughtless, uncalled-for, ungracious, unmannerly *Ant* civil, considerate, courteous, genteel, gracious, mannerly, polite, thoughtful, well-bred

uncolored **1** *Syn* COLORLESS, undyed, unpainted, unstained, white *Ant* colored, dyed, painted, stained, tinged, tinted **2** *Syn* FAIR, dispassionate, equitable, impartial, just, objective, unbiased *Ant* unfair

uncommon *Syn* INFREQUENT, occasional, rare, scarce, sporadic *Ant* frequent

uncommunicative **1** *Syn* SECRETIVE, close, closemouthed, dark, reticent *Ant* communicative, open **2** *Syn* SILENT (sense 1), close, close-lipped, closemouthed, reserved, reticent, secretive, taciturn, tight-lipped *Ant* talkative **3** *Syn* SILENT (sense 3), dumb, mum, mute, speechless, wordless *Ant* communicative, speaking, talking

uncompromising *Syn* OBSTINATE, adamant, adamantine, dogged, hard, hardened, hardheaded, hardhearted, headstrong, immovable, implacable, inflexible, mulish, obdurate, opinionated, ossified, pat, peevish, pertinacious, perverse, pigheaded, rigid, self-willed, stubborn, unbending, unrelenting, unyielding, willful (*or* wilful) *Ant* acquiescent, agreeable, amenable, compliant, complying, flexible, pliable, pliant, relenting, yielding

unconcern *Syn* INDIFFERENCE, apathy, casualness, disinterestedness, disregard, insouciance, nonchalance *Ant* concern, interest, regard

unconcerned **1** *Syn* CAREFREE, careless, cavalier, devil-may-care, easygoing, gay, happy-go-lucky, insouciant, lighthearted *Ant* careworn **2** *Syn* INDIFFERENT, aloof, detached, disinterested, incurious, uninterested *Ant* avid

uncongenial **1** *Syn* INCONSONANT, discordant, discrepant, incompatible, incongruous, inconsistent, unsympathetic *Ant* consonant **2** *Syn* UNPLEASANT, bad, disagreeable, displeasing, distasteful, nasty, rotten, sour, unlovely, unpleasing, unsatisfying, unwelcome *Ant* agreeable, congenial, good, grateful, gratifying, nice, palatable, pleasant, pleasing, pleasurable, satisfying, welcome

unconquerable *Syn* INVINCIBLE, impregnable, indomitable, inexpugnable, invulnerable, unassailable

unconscionable *Syn* UNPRINCIPLED, cutthroat, immoral, Machiavellian, unethical, unmoral, unscrupulous *Ant* ethical, moral, principled, scrupulous

uncontrollable • given to resisting control or discipline by others *Syn* froward, headstrong, intractable, recalcitrant, refractory, ungovernable, unmanageable, unruly, untoward, wayward, willful (*or* wilful) *Rel* contrary, incorrigible, obstinate, perverse, self-willed, stubborn *Ant* controllable, governable, tractable

uncountable *Syn* COUNTLESS, innumerable, numberless, uncounted, unnumbered, untold *Ant* countable

uncounted *Syn* COUNTLESS, innumerable, numberless, uncountable, unnumbered, untold *Ant* countable

uncouth **1** *Syn* CLOWNISH, boorish, churlish, cloddish, loutish *Ant* civil, courteous, courtly, cultivated, genteel, gentlemanly, ladylike, polished, polite, refined, well-bred **2** *Syn* RUDE (sense 1), callow, crude, green, raw, rough *Ant* civil, urbane

uncritical *Syn* SUPERFICIAL, cursory, shallow *Ant* deep, profound

unctuous *Syn* INSINCERE, artificial, backhanded, double-dealing, feigned, hypocritical, left-handed, mealy, mealymouthed, two-faced *Ant* genuine, heartfelt, honest, sincere, unfeigned

uncurl *Syn* STRAIGHTEN, unbend *Ant* bend, crook, curl, curve

undaunted *Syn* BRAVE, audacious, bold, courageous, dauntless, doughty, fearless, intrepid, unafraid, valiant, valorous *Ant* craven

undeniable *Syn* IRREFUTABLE, incontestable, incontrovertible, indisputable, indubitable, unanswerable, unquestionable *Ant* answerable, debatable, disputable, questionable

under **1** *Syn* BELOW, beneath, underneath *Ant* above **2** *Syn* LESSER, inferior, junior, less, lower, minor, smaller, subordinate *Ant* greater, higher, major, more, primary, prime, senior, superior

undergo *Syn* EXPERIENCE, suffer, sustain

underhand *Syn* SECRET, clandestine, covert, furtive, stealthy, surreptitious, underhanded

underhanded *Syn* SECRET, clandestine, covert, furtive, stealthy, surreptitious, underhand

underline *Syn* EMPHASIZE, accent, accentuate, feature, highlight, play (up), point (up), stress, underscore *Ant* play (down)

underling • one who is of lower rank and typically under the authority of another *Syn* inferior, junior, subordinate *Rel* attendant, follower, retainer *Ant* senior, superior

underlying **1** *Syn* ELEMENTARY, basic, elemental, essential, fundamental, rudimentary *Ant* advanced **2** *Syn* FUNDAMENTAL, basal, basic, radical

underneath *Syn* BELOW, beneath, under *Ant* above

underprivileged *Syn* DEPRIVED, disadvantaged *Ant* privileged

underscore *Syn* EMPHASIZE, accent, accentuate, feature, highlight, play (up), point (up), stress, underline *Ant* play (down)

understand • to have a clear or complete idea of *Syn* appreciate, comprehend *Rel* conceive, envisage, envision, realize, think

understanding **1** *Syn* AGREEMENT, accord **2** *Syn* COMPREHENSION, appreciation, apprehension, grasp, grip, perception **3** *Syn* REASON (sense 2), intuition

undesirable *Syn* OBJECTIONABLE, exceptionable, unacceptable, unwanted, unwelcome

undeviating *Syn* UNIFORM, invariant, steady, unchanging, unvarying, unwavering *Ant* changing, deviating, varying

undulate *Syn* SWING (sense 2), fluctuate, oscillate, pendulate, sway, vibrate, waver

undyed *Syn* COLORLESS, uncolored, unpainted, unstained, white *Ant* colored, dyed, painted, stained, tinged, tinted

undying *Syn* IMMORTAL, deathless, unfading *Ant* mortal

unearth *Syn* DISCOVER, ascertain, determine, learn

unearthly *Syn* EERIE, creepy, haunting, spooky, uncanny, weird

uneasiness *Syn* UNREST, disquiet, ferment, restiveness, restlessness, turmoil *Ant* calm, ease, peace, quiet

uneasy *Syn* IMPATIENT, fidgety, jittery, jumpy, nervous, restive, restless, unquiet *Ant* patient

uneducated *Syn* IGNORANT, benighted, dark, illiterate, nonliterate, simple, uninstructed, unlearned, unlettered, unread, unschooled, untaught, untutored *Ant* educated, knowledged

unembarrassed *Syn* UNABASHED, unashamed, unblushing *Ant* abashed, ashamed, embarrassed, shamefaced, sheepish

unendurable *Syn* UNBEARABLE, insufferable, insupportable, intolerable, unsupportable *Ant* endurable, sufferable, supportable, tolerable

unerring *Syn* INFALLIBLE, inerrable, inerrant *Ant* fallible

unessential *Syn* UNNECESSARY, dispensable, gratuitous, needless, nonessential, uncalled-for, unwarranted *Ant* essential, indispensable, necessary, needed, needful, required

unethical *Syn* UNPRINCIPLED, cutthroat, immoral, Machiavellian, unconscionable, unmoral, unscrupulous *Ant* ethical, moral, principled, scrupulous

uneven **1** *Syn* AWRY, askew, aslant, cockeyed, crooked, listing, lopsided, oblique, skewed, slanted, slanting, slantwise, tilted, tipping *Ant* even, level, straight **2** *Syn* ROUGH, harsh, rugged, scabrous *Ant* smooth

unexpected • not expected *Syn* unanticipated, unforeseen, unlooked-for *Rel* unintended, unplanned *Ant* anticipated, expected, foreseen

unexpectedly *Syn* UNAWARES, aback, suddenly, unaware

unexpressed *Syn* IMPLICIT, implied, tacit, unspoken, unvoiced, wordless *Ant* explicit, express, expressed, spoken, stated

unfading *Syn* IMMORTAL, deathless, undying *Ant* mortal

unfaithfulness *Syn* BETRAYAL, disloyalty, double cross, faithlessness, falseness, falsity, infidelity, perfidy, sellout, treachery, treason

unfathomable **1** *Syn* INCOMPREHENSIBLE, impenetrable, unintelligible *Ant* fathomable, intelligible, understandable **2** *Syn* INFINITE, boundless, endless, illimitable, immeasurable, indefinite, limitless, measureless, unbounded, unlimited *Ant* bounded, circumscribed, confined, definite, finite, limited, restricted

unfeeling *Syn* NUMB, asleep, benumbed, dead, insensitive, numbed *Ant* feeling, sensitive

unfeigned *Syn* SINCERE, heartfelt, hearty, wholehearted, whole-souled *Ant* insincere

unfeignedly *Syn* NATURALLY (sense 3), artlessly, guilelessly, ingenuously, innocently, naively, sincerely, unaffectedly, unpretentiously *Ant* affectedly, artificially, hypocritically, insincerely, pretentiously, unnaturally

unfit **1** • not adapted or appropriate to a particular end or purpose *Syn* improper, inappropriate, inapt, infelicitous, unfitting, unhappy, unsuitable *Ant* fit **2** *Syn* INAPPROPRIATE, graceless, improper, inapt, incongruous, incorrect, indecorous, inept, infelicitous, unapt, unbecoming, unhappy, unseemly, unsuitable, wrong *Ant* appropriate, becoming, befitting, correct, decorous, felicitous, fit, fitting, genteel, happy, meet, proper, right, seemly, suitable **3** *Syn* INCOMPETENT, incapable, inept, inexpert, unqualified, unskilled, unskillful *Ant* able, capable, competent, expert, fit, qualified, skilled, skillful

unfitness *Syn* IMPROPRIETY (sense 2), inappropriateness, incorrectness, indecency *Ant* appropriateness, correctness, decency, decorousness, fitness, propriety, rightness, seemliness, suitability

unfitting *Syn* UNFIT, improper, inappropriate, inapt, infelicitous, unhappy, unsuitable *Ant* fit

unflagging *Syn* INDEFATIGABLE, tireless, untiring, unwearied, unwearying, weariless

unflappable **1** • not easily panicked or upset *Syn* imperturbable, nerveless, unshakable *Rel* calm, collected, composed, cool, coolheaded, nonchalant, placid, self-possessed, serene, tranquil, undisturbed, unperturbed, unruffled, unshaken, untroubled, unworried *Ant* perturbable, shakable **2** *Syn* COOL, collected, composed, imperturbable, nonchalant, unruffled *Ant* agitated, ardent

unfledged *Syn* CALLOW, adolescent, green, immature, inexperienced, juvenile, puerile, raw, unripe, unripened *Ant* adult, experienced, grown-up, mature, ripe

unfold • to disclose by degrees to the sight or understanding *Syn* develop, elaborate, evolve, perfect *Rel* demonstrate, evidence, evince, manifest, show

unforeseen *Syn* UNEXPECTED, unanticipated, unlooked-for *Ant* anticipated, expected, foreseen

unforgivable *Syn* INEXCUSABLE, indefensible, unjustifiable, unpardonable, unwarrantable *Ant* defensible, excusable, forgivable, justifiable, pardonable

unformed *Syn* FORMLESS, amorphous, shapeless, unshaped, unstructured *Ant* formed, shaped, structured

unfortunate **1** *Syn* REGRETTABLE, deplorable, distressful, distressing, grievous, heartbreaking, heartrending, lamentable, woeful **2** *Syn* UNLUCKY, calamitous, disastrous, hapless, ill-fated, ill-starred, luckless *Ant* fortunate, happy, lucky

unfounded **1** *Syn* BASELESS, groundless, unwarranted **2** *Syn* GROUNDLESS, invalid, nonvalid, ungrounded, unreasonable, unsubstantiated, unsupported, unwarranted *Ant* good, hard, just, justified, reasonable, reasoned, substantiated, valid, well-founded

unfruitful *Syn* STERILE, barren, impotent, infertile *Ant* exuberant, fertile

ungainly *Syn* CUMBERSOME, awkward, clumsy, cranky, cumbrous, unhandy, unwieldy *Ant* handy

ungodly *Syn* IRRELIGIOUS, godless, nonreligious, unreligious *Ant* religious

ungovernable **1** *Syn* DISOBEDIENT, balky, contrary, defiant, froward, insubordinate, intractable, rebellious, recalcitrant, refractory, restive, unruly, untoward, wayward, willful (*or* wilful) *Ant* amenable, compliant, docile, obedient, tractable **2** *Syn* UNCONTROLLABLE, froward, headstrong, intractable, recalcitrant, refractory, unmanageable, unruly, untoward, wayward, willful (*or* wilful) *Ant* controllable, governable, tractable **3** *Syn* UNRULY, headstrong, intractable, recalcitrant, refractory, willful *Ant* docile, tractable

ungracious *Syn* IMPOLITE, discourteous, ill-bred, ill-mannered, impertinent, inconsiderate, rude, thoughtless, uncalled-for, uncivil, ungracious, unmannerly *Ant* civil, considerate, courteous, genteel, gracious, mannerly, polite, thoughtful, well-bred

ungrateful *Syn* THANKLESS, unappreciative *Ant* appreciative, grateful, obliged, thankful

ungrounded *Syn* GROUNDLESS, invalid, nonvalid, unfounded, unreasonable, unsubstantiated, unsupported, unwarranted *Ant* good, hard, just, justified, reasonable, reasoned, substantiated, valid, well-founded

unhandy *Syn* CUMBERSOME, awkward, clumsy, cranky, cumbrous, ungainly, unwieldy *Ant* handy

unhappiness *Syn* SADNESS, blues, dejection, depression, desolation, despondency, disconsolateness, dispiritedness, doldrums, downheartedness, dreariness, dumps, forlornness, gloom, gloominess, heartsickness, joylessness, melancholy, mopes, oppression *Ant* bliss, blissfulness, ecstasy, elatedness, elation, euphoria, exhilaration, exuberance, exultation, felicity, gladness, gladsomeness, happiness, heaven, intoxication, joy, joyfulness, joyousness, jubilation, rapture, rapturousness

unhappy **1** *Syn* INAPPROPRIATE, graceless, improper, inapt, incongruous, incorrect, indecorous, inept, infelicitous, unapt, unbecoming, unfit, unseemly, unsuitable, wrong *Ant* appropriate, becoming, befitting, correct, decorous, felicitous, fit, fitting, genteel, happy, meet, proper, right, seemly, suitable **2** *Syn* SAD (sense 1), bad, blue, brokenhearted, crestfallen, dejected, depressed, despondent, disconsolate, doleful, down, downcast, downhearted, droopy, forlorn, gloomy, glum, heartbroken, heartsick, heartsore, inconsolable, joyless, low, low-spirited, melancholy, miserable, mournful, saddened, sorrowful, sorry, woebegone, woeful, wretched *Ant* blissful, buoyant, buoyed, cheerful, cheery, chipper, delighted, glad, gladdened, gladsome, gleeful, happy, joyful, joyous, jubilant, sunny, upbeat **3** *Syn* UNFIT, improper, inappropriate, inapt, infelicitous, unfitting, unsuitable *Ant* fit

unheroic *Syn* COWARDLY, chicken, chickenhearted, craven, dastardly, lily-livered, pusillanimous, recreant, spineless, yellow *Ant* brave, courageous, daring, dauntless, doughty, fearless, gallant, greathearted, gutsy, hardy, heroic, intrepid, lionhearted, stalwart, stout, stouthearted, valiant, valorous

uniform **1** • not varying *Syn* invariant, steady, unchanging, undeviating, unvarying, unwavering *Rel* immutable, invariable, unalterable, unchangeable *Ant* changing, deviating, varying **2** *Syn* STEADY, constant, equable, even *Ant* jumpy, nervous, unsteady

unify *Syn* COMPACT, concentrate, consolidate

unimpassioned *Syn* SOBER, continent, temperate *Ant* drunk, excited

unimportant • lacking importance *Syn* frivolous, inconsequential, inconsiderable, insignificant, little, minor, minute, negligible, slight, small, small-fry, trifling, trivial *Rel* jerkwater, one-horse *Ant* big, consequential, eventful, important, major, material, meaningful, momentous, significant, substantial, weighty

uninhibited *Syn* DEMONSTRATIVE, effusive, emotional, unreserved, unrestrained *Ant* inhibited, reserved, restrained, undemonstrative, unemotional

uninstructed *Syn* IGNORANT, benighted, dark, illiterate, nonliterate, simple, uneducated, unlearned, unlettered, unread, unschooled, untaught, untutored *Ant* educated, knowledgeable, literate, schooled

unintelligible *Syn* INCOMPREHENSIBLE, impenetrable, unfathomable *Ant* fathomable, intelligible, understandable

unintended *Syn* ACCIDENTAL, casual, chance, fluky, fortuitous, inadvertent, incidental, unintentional, unplanned, unpremeditated, unwitting *Ant* deliberate, intended, intentional, planned, premeditated

unintentional *Syn* ACCIDENTAL, casual, chance, fluky, fortuitous, inadvertent, incidental, unintended, unplanned, unpremeditated, unwitting *Ant* deliberate, intended, intentional, planned, premeditated

uninterested *Syn* INDIFFERENT, aloof, detached, disinterested, incurious, unconcerned *Ant* avid

uninteresting *Syn* BORING, drab, dreary, dry, dull, flat, heavy, humdrum, jading, leaden, monotonous, pedestrian, ponderous, stodgy, stuffy, stupid, tame, tedious, tiresome, tiring, unanimated, wearisome, weary, wearying *Ant* absorbing, engaging, engrossing, gripping, interesting, intriguing, involving

union *Syn* UNITY, integrity, solidarity

unique **1** *Syn* ONLY, alone, lone, singular, sole, solitary, special **2** *Syn* SINGLE, lone, particular, separate, sole, solitary *Ant* accompanied, conjugal, supported **3** *Syn* STRANGE, curious, eccentric, erratic, odd, outlandish, peculiar, quaint, queer, singular *Ant* familiar

unite **1** • to join forces or act in concert *Syn* combine, concur, conjoin, cooperate *Rel* coalesce, commingle, fuse, mingle *Ant* part **2** *Syn* ALLY, associate, band, club, confederate, conjoin, cooperate, federate, league *Ant* break up, disband **3** *Syn* JOIN, associate, combine, conjoin, connect, link, relate *Ant* disjoin, part

unity • the character of a thing that is a whole composed of many parts *Syn* integrity, solidarity, union *Rel* assimilation, embodiment, identification, incorporation

universal **1** • present or significant throughout the world *Syn* catholic, cosmic, cosmopolitan, ecumenical *Rel* earthly, mundane, terrestrial, worldly **2** • of, belonging, or relating to all or the whole *Syn* common, general, generic *Ant* particular **3** *Syn* EN-

CYCLOPEDIC, compendious, complete, comprehensive, full, global, inclusive, in-depth, omnibus, panoramic **4** *Syn* GENERAL (sense 1), blanket, common, generic, global, overall *Ant* individual, particular

unjustifiable *Syn* INEXCUSABLE, indefensible, unforgivable, unpardonable, unwarrantable *Ant* defensible, excusable, forgivable, justifiable, pardonable

unkempt **1** *Syn* MESSY, chaotic, cluttered, confused, disarranged, disarrayed, disheveled (*or* dishevelled), disordered, disorderly, higgledy-piggledy, hugger-mugger, jumbled, littered, messed, muddled, mussed, mussy, pell-mell, rumpled, sloppy, topsy-turvy, tousled, tumbled, untidy, upside-down *Ant* neat, ordered, orderly, organized, shipshape, snug, tidied, tidy, trim **2** *Syn* SLIPSHOD, disheveled, sloppy, slovenly

unlawful • contrary to or prohibited by the law *Syn* illegal, illegitimate, illicit *Rel* flagitious, iniquitous, nefarious *Ant* lawful

unlearned *Syn* IGNORANT, benighted, dark, illiterate, nonliterate, simple, uneducated, uninstructed, unlettered, unread, unschooled, untaught, untutored *Ant* educated, knowledgeable, literate, schooled

unlettered *Syn* IGNORANT, benighted, dark, illiterate, nonliterate, simple, uneducated, uninstructed, unlearned, unread, unschooled, untaught, untutored *Ant* educated, knowledgeable, literate, schooled

unlikely *Syn* IMPROBABLE, doubtful, dubious, far-fetched, flimsy, questionable, unapt *Ant* likely, probable

unlikeness *Syn* DISSIMILARITY, difference, distinction, divergence, divergency *Ant* similarity

unlimited *Syn* INFINITE, boundless, endless, illimitable, immeasurable, indefinite, limitless, measureless, unbounded, unfathomable *Ant* bounded, circumscribed, confined, definite, finite, limited, restricted

unlooked-for *Syn* UNEXPECTED, unanticipated, unforeseen *Ant* anticipated, expected, foreseen

unlovely *Syn* UNPLEASANT, bad, disagreeable, displeasing, distasteful, nasty, rotten, sour, uncongenial, unpleasing, unsatisfying, unwelcome *Ant* agreeable, congenial, good, grateful, gratifying, nice, palatable, pleasant, pleasing, pleasurable, satisfying, welcome

unlucky • involving or suffering misfortune that results from chance *Syn* calamitous, disastrous, hapless, ill-fated, ill-starred, luckless, unfortunate *Rel* awkward, inept *Ant* fortunate, happy, lucky

unmanageable *Syn* UNCONTROLLABLE, froward, headstrong, intractable, recalcitrant, refractory, ungovernable, unruly, untoward, wayward, willful (*or* wilful) *Ant* controllable, governable, tractable

unmannerly *Syn* IMPOLITE, discourteous, ill-bred, ill-mannered, impertinent, inconsiderate, rude, thoughtless, uncalled-for, uncivil, ungracious *Ant* civil, considerate, courteous, genteel, gracious, mannerly, polite, thoughtful, well-bred

unmarried • being without a spouse *Syn* single, unattached, unwed *Ant* espoused, married

unmatured *Syn* IMMATURE, unmellow, unripe *Ant* mature

unmellow *Syn* IMMATURE, unmatured, unripe *Ant* mature

unmindful *Syn* FORGETFUL, oblivious

unmitigated *Syn* OUTRIGHT, arrant, out-and-out

unmoral *Syn* UNPRINCIPLED, cutthroat, immoral, Machiavellian, unconscionable, unethical, unscrupulous *Ant* ethical, moral, principled, scrupulous

unnatural **1** *Syn* DEVIANT, aberrant, abnormal, anomalous, atypical, irregular *Ant* natural, normal, regular, standard, typical **2** *Syn* IRREGULAR, anomalous *Ant* regular

unnecessary • not needed by the circumstances or to accomplish an end *Syn* dispensable, gratuitous, needless, nonessential, uncalled-for, unessential, unwarranted *Rel* discretionary, elective, optional *Ant* essential, indispensable, necessary, needed, needful, required

unnerve *Syn* DISCOURAGE (sense 1), daunt, demoralize, dishearten, dismay, dispirit *Ant* embolden, encourage, hearten, nerve, steel

unnoticeable *Syn* UNOBTRUSIVE, inconspicuous *Ant* conspicuous, noticeable

unnumbered *Syn* COUNTLESS, innumerable, numberless, uncountable, uncounted, untold *Ant* countable

unobtrusive • not readily seen or noticed *Syn* inconspicuous, unnoticeable *Rel* unnoticed *Ant* conspicuous, noticeable

unoffending *Syn* HARMLESS, innocent, innocuous, inoffensive *Ant* harmful

unpainted *Syn* COLORLESS, uncolored, undyed, unstained, white *Ant* colored, dyed, painted, stained, tinged, tinted

unpardonable *Syn* INEXCUSABLE, indefensible, unforgivable, unjustifiable, unwarrantable *Ant* defensible, excusable, forgivable, justifiable, pardonable

unplanned *Syn* ACCIDENTAL, casual, chance, fluky, fortuitous, inadvertent, incidental, unintended, unintentional, unpremeditated, unwitting *Ant* deliberate, intended, intentional, planned, premeditated

unpleasant • not giving pleasure to the mind or senses *Syn* bad, disagreeable, displeasing, distasteful, nasty, rotten, sour, uncongenial, unlovely, unpleasing, unsatisfying, unwelcome *Rel* abhorrent, abominable, annoying, appalling, awful, beastly, disgusting, dreadful, foul, galling, hideous, horrendous, horrible, horrid, invidious, irritating, loathsome, noisome, obnoxious, obscene, odious, repellent, repugnant, repulsive, revolting, scandalous, shocking, sickening, ugly, vexing, villainous *Ant* agreeable, congenial, good, grateful, gratifying, nice, palatable, pleasant, pleasing, pleasurable, satisfying, welcome

unpleasing *Syn* UNPLEASANT, bad, disagreeable, displeasing, distasteful, nasty, rotten, sour, uncongenial, unlovely, unsatisfying, unwelcome *Ant* agreeable, congenial, good, grateful, gratifying, nice, palatable, pleasant, pleasing, pleasurable, satisfying, welcome

unpremeditated **1** *Syn* ACCIDENTAL, casual, chance, fluky, fortuitous, inadvertent, incidental, unintended, unintentional, unplanned, unwitting *Ant* deliberate, intended, intentional, planned, premeditated **2** *Syn* EXTEMPORANEOUS, extemporary, extempore, impromptu, improvised, offhand *Ant* premeditated

unpretentious *Syn* PLAIN, homely, simple *Ant* lovely

unpretentiously *Syn* NATURALLY (sense 3), artlessly, guilelessly, ingenuously, innocently, naively, sincerely, unaffectedly, unfeignedly *Ant* affectedly, artificially, hypocritically, insincerely, pretentiously, unnaturally

unprincipled • not guided by or showing a concern for what is right *Syn* cutthroat, immoral, Machiavellian, unconscionable, unethical, unmoral, unscrupulous *Rel* calculating, intriguing, opportunistic, scheming *Ant* ethical, moral, principled, scrupulous

unprofessional *Syn* AMATEURISH, amateur, dilettante, inexperienced, inexpert, nonprofessional, unskilled, unskillful *Ant* ace, adept, consummate, crackerjack, expert, master, masterful, masterly, professional, virtuoso

unqualified *Syn* INCOMPETENT, incapable, inept, inexpert, unfit, unskilled, unskillful *Ant* able, capable, competent, expert, fit, qualified, skilled, skillful

unquestionable *Syn* IRREFUTABLE, incontestable, incontrovertible, indisputable, indubitable, unanswerable, undeniable *Ant* answerable, debatable, disputable, questionable

unquiet *Syn* IMPATIENT, fidgety, jittery, jumpy, nervous, restive, restless, uneasy *Ant* patient

unravel *Syn* SOLVE, answer, break, crack, dope (out), figure out, puzzle (out), resolve, riddle, work, work out

unread *Syn* IGNORANT, benighted, dark, illiterate, nonliterate, simple, uneducated, uninstructed, unlearned, unlettered, unschooled, untaught, untutored *Ant* educated, knowledgeable, literate, schooled

unreasonable **1** *Syn* GROUNDLESS, invalid, nonvalid, unfounded, ungrounded, unsubstantiated, unsupported, unwarranted *Ant* good, hard, just, justified, reasonable, reasoned, substantiated, valid, well-founded **2** *Syn* ILLOGICAL, fallacious, invalid, irrational, nonrational, unreasoning, unsound, weak *Ant* logical, rational, reasonable, sound, valid

unreasoning *Syn* ILLOGICAL, fallacious, invalid, irrational, nonrational, unreasonable, unsound, weak *Ant* logical, rational, reasonable, sound, valid

unrelenting **1** *Syn* GRIM, implacable, merciless, relentless *Ant* lenient **2** *Syn* OBSTINATE, adamant, adamantine, dogged, hard, hardened, hardheaded, hardhearted, headstrong, immovable, implacable, inflexible, mulish, obdurate, opinionated, ossified, pat, peevish, pertinacious, perverse, pigheaded, rigid, self-willed, stubborn, unbending, uncompromising, unyielding, willful (*or* wilful) *Ant* acquiescent, agreeable, amenable, compliant, complying, flexible, pliable, pliant, relenting, yielding

unreligious *Syn* IRRELIGIOUS, godless, nonreligious, ungodly *Ant* religious

unremitting *Syn* CONTINUAL, constant, continuous, incessant, perennial, perpetual *Ant* intermittent

unrepentant *Syn* REMORSELESS, impenitent *Ant* contrite, guilty, penitent, regretful, remorseful, repentant, sorry

unreserved *Syn* DEMONSTRATIVE, effusive, emotional, uninhibited, unrestrained *Ant* inhibited, reserved, restrained, undemonstrative, unemotional

unresistant *Syn* PASSIVE, acquiescent, nonresistant, resigned, tolerant, tolerating, unresisting, yielding *Ant* protesting, resistant, resisting, unyielding

unresisting *Syn* PASSIVE, acquiescent, nonresistant, resigned, tolerant, tolerating, unresistant, yielding *Ant* protesting, resistant, resisting, unyielding

unrest • a disturbed or uneasy state *Syn* disquiet, ferment, restiveness, restlessness, turmoil, uneasiness *Rel* fidgets *Ant* calm, ease, peace, quiet

unrestrained *Syn* DEMONSTRATIVE, effusive, emotional, uninhibited, unreserved *Ant* inhibited, reserved, restrained, undemonstrative, unemotional

unrestraint *Syn* ABANDON, abandonment, ease, lightheartedness, naturalness, spontaneity *Ant* constraint, restraint

unripe **1** *Syn* CALLOW, adolescent, green, immature, inexperienced, juvenile, puerile, raw, unfledged, unripened *Ant* adult, experienced, grown-up, mature, ripe **2** *Syn* IMMATURE, unmatured, unmellow *Ant* mature

unripened *Syn* CALLOW, adolescent, green, immature, inexperienced, juvenile, puerile,

raw, unfledged, unripe *Ant* adult, experienced, grown-up, mature, ripe
unruffled *Syn* COOL, collected, composed, imperturbable, nonchalant, unflappable *Ant* agitated, ardent
unruliness *Syn* DISOBEDIENCE, contrariness, defiance, frowardness, insubordination, intractability, rebelliousness, recalcitrance, refractoriness, willfulness *Ant* amenability, compliance, docility, obedience
unruly **1** • not submissive to government or control *Syn* headstrong, intractable, recalcitrant, refractory, ungovernable, willful *Rel* contumacious, insubordinate, rebellious *Ant* docile, tractable **2** *Syn* DISOBEDIENT, balky, contrary, defiant, froward, insubordinate, intractable, rebellious, recalcitrant, refractory, restive, ungovernable, untoward, wayward, willful (*or* wilful) *Ant* amenable, compliant, docile, obedient, tractable **3** *Syn* LAWLESS, anarchic, disorderly, lawbreaking *Ant* law-abiding, orderly **4** *Syn* UNCONTROLLABLE, froward, headstrong, intractable, recalcitrant, refractory, ungovernable, unmanageable, unruly, untoward, wayward, willful (*or* wilful) *Ant* controllable, governable, tractable
unsatisfactorily *Syn* BADLY, inadequately, poorly, unacceptably *Ant* acceptably, adequately, all right, fine, good, palatably, passably, so-so, tolerably
unsatisfying *Syn* UNPLEASANT, bad, disagreeable, displeasing, distasteful, nasty, rotten, sour, uncongenial, unlovely, unpleasing, unwelcome *Ant* agreeable, congenial, good, grateful, gratifying, nice, palatable, pleasant, pleasing, pleasurable, satisfying, welcome
unschooled *Syn* IGNORANT, benighted, dark, illiterate, nonliterate, simple, uneducated, uninstructed, unlearned, unlettered, unread, untaught, untutored *Ant* educated, knowledgeable, literate, schooled
unscrupulous *Syn* UNPRINCIPLED, cutthroat, immoral, Machiavellian, unconscionable, unethical, unmoral *Ant* ethical, moral, principled, scrupulous
unseemly *Syn* INAPPROPRIATE, graceless, improper, inapt, incongruous, incorrect, indecorous, inept, infelicitous, unapt, unbecoming, unfit, unhappy, unsuitable, wrong *Ant* appropriate, becoming, befitting, correct, decorous, felicitous, fit, fitting, genteel, happy, meet, proper, right, seemly, suitable
unsettling *Syn* TROUBLESOME, discomforting, discomposing, disquieting, distressing, disturbing, perturbing, troubling, troublous, upsetting, worrisome *Ant* reassuring, untroublesome
unshakable *Syn* UNFLAPPABLE, imperturbable, nerveless *Ant* perturbable, shakable
unshaped *Syn* FORMLESS, amorphous, shapeless, unformed, unstructured *Ant* formed, shaped, structured
unshorn *Syn* HAIRY (sense 1), bristly, fleecy, furry, hirsute, rough, shaggy, woolly *Ant* bald, furless, hairless, shorn, smooth
unsightly *Syn* UGLY, hideous, ill-favored *Ant* beautiful
unskilled **1** *Syn* AMATEURISH, amateur, dilettante, inexperienced, inexpert, nonprofessional, unprofessional, unskillful *Ant* ace, adept, consummate, crackerjack, expert, master, masterful, masterly, professional, virtuoso **2** *Syn* INCOMPETENT, incapable, inept, inexpert, unfit, unqualified, unskillful *Ant* able, capable, competent, expert, fit, qualified, skilled, skillful
unskillful **1** *Syn* AMATEURISH, amateur, dilettante, inexperienced, inexpert, nonprofessional, unprofessional, unskilled *Ant* ace, adept, consummate, crackerjack, expert, master, masterful, masterly, professional, virtuoso **2** *Syn* INCOMPETENT, incapable, inept, inexpert, unfit, unqualified, unskilled *Ant* able, capable, competent, expert, fit, qualified, skilled, skillful
unsocial • disliking or avoiding the company of others *Syn* antisocial, asocial, nonsocial *Ant* social
unsolvable *Syn* IMPOSSIBLE, hopeless, unachievable, unattainable *Ant* achievable, attainable, doable, feasible, possible, realizable, workable
unsophisticated *Syn* NATURAL, artless, ingenuous, naive, simple, unaffected
unsound *Syn* ILLOGICAL, fallacious, invalid, irrational, nonrational, unreasonable, unreasoning, weak *Ant* logical, rational, reasonable, sound, valid
unspeakable *Syn* UNUTTERABLE, indefinable, indescribable, ineffable, inexpressible
unspoken *Syn* IMPLICIT, implied, tacit, unexpressed, unvoiced, wordless *Ant* explicit, express, expressed, spoken, stated
unstable *Syn* INCONSTANT, capricious, fickle, mercurial *Ant* constant
unstained *Syn* COLORLESS, uncolored, undyed, unpainted, white *Ant* colored, dyed, painted, stained, tinged, tinted
unsteady *Syn* FITFUL, casual, choppy, discontinuous, erratic, intermittent, irregular, occasional, spasmodic, sporadic, spotty *Ant* constant, continuous, regular, steady
unstructured *Syn* FORMLESS, amorphous, shapeless, unformed, unshaped *Ant* formed, shaped, structured
unstylishly *Syn* SLOPPILY, dowdily, slovenly *Ant* nattily, sharply, smartly, sprucely
unsubstantiated *Syn* GROUNDLESS, invalid, nonvalid, unfounded, ungrounded, unreasonable, unsupported, unwarranted *Ant* good, hard, just, justified, reasonable, reasoned, substantiated, valid, well-founded
unsuitable **1** *Syn* INAPPROPRIATE, graceless, improper, inapt, incongruous, incorrect,

indecorous, inept, infelicitous, unapt, unbecoming, unfit, unhappy, unseemly, wrong *Ant* appropriate, becoming, befitting, correct, decorous, felicitous, fit, fitting, genteel, happy, meet, proper, right, seemly, suitable **2** *Syn* UNFIT, improper, inappropriate, inapt, infelicitous, unfitting, unhappy *Ant* fit

unsupportable *Syn* UNBEARABLE, insufferable, insupportable, intolerable, unendurable *Ant* endurable, sufferable, supportable, tolerable

unsupported *Syn* GROUNDLESS, invalid, nonvalid, unfounded, ungrounded, unreasonable, unsubstantiated, unwarranted *Ant* good, hard, just, justified, reasonable, reasoned, substantiated, valid, well-founded

unsurpassed *Syn* EXCELLENT, A1, bang-up, banner, capital, classic, crackerjack, dandy, divine, fabulous, fine, first-class, first-rate, grand, great, groovy, heavenly, jim-dandy, keen, marvelous (*or* marvellous), mean, neat, nifty, noble, par excellence, prime, sensational, splendid, stellar, sterling, superb, superior, superlative, supernal, swell, terrific, tip-top, top, top-notch, wonderful *Ant* poor

unsympathetic *Syn* INCONSONANT, discordant, discrepant, incompatible, incongruous, inconsistent, uncongenial *Ant* consonant

untangle *Syn* EXTRICATE, disembarrass, disencumber, disentangle

untaught *Syn* IGNORANT, benighted, dark, illiterate, nonliterate, simple, uneducated, uninstructed, unlearned, unlettered, unread, unschooled, untutored *Ant* educated, knowledgeable, literate, schooled

unthrifty *Syn* PRODIGAL, extravagant, profligate, spendthrift, squandering, thriftless, wasteful *Ant* conserving, economical, economizing, frugal, scrimping, skimping, thrifty

untidy *Syn* MESSY, chaotic, cluttered, confused, disarranged, disarrayed, disheveled (*or* dishevelled), disordered, disorderly, higgledy-piggledy, hugger-mugger, jumbled, littered, messed, muddled, mussed, mussy, pell-mell, rumpled, sloppy, topsy-turvy, tousled, tumbled, unkempt, upside-down *Ant* neat, ordered, orderly, organized, shipshape, snug, tidied, tidy, trim

untimely *Syn* PREMATURE, advanced, forward, precocious *Ant* matured

untiring *Syn* INDEFATIGABLE, tireless, unflagging, unwearied, unwearying, weariless

untold *Syn* COUNTLESS, innumerable, numberless, uncountable, uncounted, unnumbered *Ant* countable

untouchable *Syn* OUTCAST, derelict, pariah, reprobate

untoward **1** *Syn* DISOBEDIENT, balky, contrary, defiant, froward, insubordinate, intractable, rebellious, recalcitrant, refractory, restive, ungovernable, unruly, wayward, willful (*or* wilful) *Ant* amenable, compliant, docile, obedient, tractable **2** *Syn* UNCONTROLLABLE, froward, headstrong, intractable, recalcitrant, refractory, ungovernable, unmanageable, unruly, wayward, willful (*or* wilful) *Ant* controllable, governable, tractable

untruth **1** *Syn* FALLACY (sense 1), error, falsehood, falsity, illusion, misconception, myth, old wives' tale *Ant* truth, verity **2** *Syn* FALLACY (sense 2), erroneousness, fallaciousness, falseness, falsity *Ant* truth **3** *Syn* LIE, falsehood, fib, misrepresentation, story *Ant* truth

untutored *Syn* IGNORANT, benighted, dark, illiterate, nonliterate, simple, uneducated, uninstructed, unlearned, unlettered, unread, unschooled, untaught *Ant* educated, knowledgeable, literate, schooled

unusable *Syn* IMPRACTICAL, impracticable, inoperable, nonpractical, unworkable, useless *Ant* applicable, feasible, functional, operable, operational, practicable, practical, usable, useful, workable

unusual *Syn* EXCEPTIONAL, extraordinary, phenomenal, unwonted *Ant* average, common

unutterable • not capable of being put into words *Syn* indefinable, indescribable, ineffable, inexpressible, unspeakable

unvarying *Syn* UNIFORM, invariant, steady, unchanging, undeviating, unwavering *Ant* changing, deviating, varying

unvoiced *Syn* IMPLICIT, implied, tacit, unexpressed, unspoken, wordless *Ant* explicit, express, expressed, spoken, stated

unwanted *Syn* OBJECTIONABLE, exceptionable, unacceptable, undesirable, unwelcome

unwarrantable *Syn* INEXCUSABLE, indefensible, unforgivable, unjustifiable, unpardonable *Ant* defensible, excusable, forgivable, justifiable, pardonable

unwarranted **1** *Syn* BASELESS, groundless, unfounded **2** *Syn* GROUNDLESS, invalid, nonvalid, unfounded, ungrounded, unreasonable, unsubstantiated, unsupported *Ant* good, hard, just, justified, reasonable, reasoned, substantiated, valid, well-founded **3** *Syn* UNNECESSARY, dispensable, gratuitous, needless, nonessential, uncalled-for, unessential *Ant* essential, indispensable, necessary, needed, needful, required

unwavering *Syn* UNIFORM, invariant, steady, unchanging, undeviating, unvarying *Ant* changing, deviating, varying

unwearied *Syn* INDEFATIGABLE, tireless, unflagging, untiring, unwearying, weariless

unwearying *Syn* INDEFATIGABLE, tireless, unflagging, untiring, unwearied, weariless

unwed *Syn* UNMARRIED, single, unattached *Ant* espoused, married

unwelcome **1** *Syn* OBJECTIONABLE, exceptionable, unacceptable, undesirable, unwanted **2** *Syn* UNPLEASANT, bad, disagreeable, displeasing, distasteful, nasty, rotten, sour, uncongenial, unlovely, unpleasing, unsatisfying *Ant* agreeable, congenial, good, grateful, gratifying, nice, palatable, pleasant, pleasing, pleasurable, satisfying, welcome

unwholesome • detrimental to physical, mental, or moral well-being *Syn* diseased, morbid, pathological, sickly *Rel* baneful, deleterious, detrimental, noxious, pernicious *Ant* wholesome

unwieldy *Syn* CUMBERSOME, awkward, clumsy, cranky, cumbrous, ungainly, unhandy *Ant* handy

unwillingness *Syn* RELUCTANCE, disinclination, hesitance, hesitancy *Ant* inclination, willingness

unwise *Syn* INDISCREET, ill-advised, imprudent, inadvisable, injudicious, tactless, unadvisable *Ant* advisable, discreet, judicious, prudent, tactful, wise

unwitting *Syn* ACCIDENTAL, casual, chance, fluky, fortuitous, inadvertent, incidental, unintended, unintentional, unplanned, unpremeditated *Ant* deliberate, intended, intentional, planned, premeditated

unwonted *Syn* EXCEPTIONAL, extraordinary, phenomenal, unusual *Ant* average, common

unworkable *Syn* IMPRACTICAL, impracticable, inoperable, nonpractical, unusable, useless *Ant* applicable, feasible, functional, operable, operational, practicable, practical, usable, useful, workable

unwritten *Syn* VERBAL, oral, spoken *Ant* written

unyielding *Syn* OBSTINATE, adamant, adamantine, dogged, hard, hardened, hardheaded, hardhearted, headstrong, immovable, implacable, inflexible, mulish, obdurate, opinionated, ossified, pat, peevish, pertinacious, perverse, pigheaded, rigid, self-willed, stubborn, unbending, uncompromising, unrelenting, willful (*or* wilful) *Ant* acquiescent, agreeable, amenable, compliant, complying, flexible, pliable, pliant, relenting, yielding

up **1** *Syn* ASCEND, arise, climb, lift, mount, rise, soar, uprise, upsweep, upturn *Ant* decline, descend, dip, drop, fall (off) **2** *Syn* INCREASE (sense 1), add (to), aggrandize, amplify, augment, boost, compound, enlarge, escalate, expand, extend, multiply, raise, swell *Ant* abate, contract, decrease, diminish, lessen, lower, reduce, subtract (from)

upbeat *Syn* CHEERFUL (sense 1), blithe, blithesome, bright, buoyant, cheery, chipper, gay, gladsome, lightsome, sunny *Ant* dour, gloomy, glum, morose, saturnine, sulky, sullen

upbraid *Syn* SCOLD, bawl, berate, chew out, jaw, rail, rate, revile, tongue-lash, vituperate, wig

upcoming *Syn* FORTHCOMING, approaching, coming, imminent, impending, nearing, oncoming, pending *Ant* late, recent

up-country *Syn* FRONTIER, backwater, backwoods, bush, hinterland

upheaval *Syn* CONVULSION, cataclysm, paroxysm, storm, tempest, tumult, uproar

uphold *Syn* SUPPORT (sense 2), advocate, back, champion

upon *Syn* AGAINST, on

upper crust *Syn* ELITE, best, choice, cream, elect, fat, flower, pick, prime

uppish *Syn* ARROGANT, cavalier, haughty, highfalutin, high-handed, high-hat, imperious, important, lofty, lordly, masterful, overweening, peremptory, pompous, presumptuous, pretentious, supercilious, superior, uppity *Ant* humble, modest

uppity *Syn* ARROGANT, cavalier, haughty, highfalutin, high-handed, high-hat, imperious, important, lofty, lordly, masterful, overweening, peremptory, pompous, presumptuous, pretentious, supercilious, superior, uppish *Ant* humble, modest

upright **1** • having or showing a strict regard for what is morally right *Syn* conscientious, honest, honorable, just, scrupulous *Rel* ethical, righteous, virtuous **2** *Syn* ERECT, perpendicular, plumb, raised, standing, upstanding, vertical *Ant* flat, recumbent

uprise *Syn* ASCEND, arise, climb, lift, mount, rise, soar, up, upsweep, upturn *Ant* decline, descend, dip, drop, fall (off)

uprising *Syn* REBELLION, coup, insurrection, mutiny, putsch, revolt, revolution

uproar **1** *Syn* COMMOTION, bother, bustle, clatter, disturbance, furor, furore, fuss, hubbub, hullabaloo, hurly-burly, pandemonium, pother, row, ruckus, ruction, rumpus, shindy, squall, stew, stir, storm, to-do, tumult, turmoil, welter, whirl **2** *Syn* CONVULSION, cataclysm, paroxysm, storm, tempest, tumult, upheaval **3** *Syn* DIN, babel, clamor, hubbub, hullabaloo, pandemonium, racket *Ant* quiet **4** *Syn* FRENZY, agitation, delirium, distraction, furor, furore, fury, hysteria, rage, rampage

uproot *Syn* EXTERMINATE, deracinate, eradicate, extirpate, wipe

upset *vb* *Syn* DISCOMPOSE, agitate, disquiet, disturb, flurry, fluster, perturb

upset *n* *Syn* DISORDER, confuse, derange, disarrange, disarray, discompose, dishevel, dislocate, disorganize, disrupt, disturb, hash, jumble, mess (up), mix (up), muddle, muss, rumple, scramble, shuffle, tousle, tumble *Ant* arrange, array, draw up, marshal, order, organize, range, regulate, straighten (up), tidy

upset *Syn* OVERTURN, capsize, overthrow, subvert

upsetting *Syn* TROUBLESOME, discomforting, discomposing, disquieting, distressing, disturbing, perturbing, troubling, troublous, unsettling, worrisome *Ant* reassuring, untroublesome

upshot *Syn* EFFECT, aftereffect, aftermath, consequence, event, issue, outcome, result, sequel *Ant* cause

upside-down *Syn* MESSY, chaotic, cluttered, confused, disarranged, disarrayed, disheveled (*or* dishevelled), disordered, disorderly, higgledy-piggledy, hugger-mugger, jumbled, littered, messed, muddled, mussed, mussy, pell-mell, rumpled, sloppy, topsy-turvy, tousled, tumbled, unkempt, untidy *Ant* neat, ordered, orderly, organized, shipshape, snug, tidied, tidy, trim

upstanding *Syn* ERECT, perpendicular, plumb, raised, standing, upright, vertical *Ant* flat, recumbent

upsweep *Syn* ASCEND, arise, climb, lift, mount, rise, soar, up, uprise, upturn *Ant* decline, descend, dip, drop, fall (off)

up-to-date *Syn* MODERN, contemporary, current, hot, mod, modernistic, new, newfangled, new-fashioned, present-day, red-hot, space-age, ultramodern *Ant* antiquated, archaic, dated, fusty, musty, noncontemporary, oldfangled, old-fashioned, old-time, out-of-date, passé

upturn *Syn* ASCEND, arise, climb, lift, mount, rise, soar, up, uprise, upsweep *Ant* decline, descend, dip, drop, fall (off)

urbane *Syn* SUAVE, debonair, smooth, sophisticated *Ant* boorish, churlish, clownish, loutish, uncouth

urge *vb* • to try to persuade (someone) through earnest appeals to follow a course of action *Syn* egg (on), encourage, exhort, goad, press, prod, prompt *Rel* drive, propel, spur, stimulate

urge *n Syn* DESIRE, appetite, lust, passion *Ant* distaste

urgent *Syn* PRESSING, crying, exigent, imperative, importunate, insistent, instant

usage *Syn* FORM (sense 3), convenance, convention

use *n* **1** • a useful or valuable end, result, or purpose *Syn* account, advantage, avail, profit, service *Rel* benefit **2** • a capacity for serving an end or purpose *Syn* usefulness, utility *Rel* applicability, pertinence, relevance **3** *Syn* LIKING, appetite, fancy, favor, fondness, like, love, partiality, preference, relish, shine, taste *Ant* aversion, disfavor, dislike, distaste, hatred, loathing

use *vb* • to put into service especially to attain an end *Syn* apply, avail, employ, utilize *Rel* handle, manipulate, ply, wield

used *Syn* ACCUSTOMED, given, habituated, wont *Ant* unaccustomed, unused

usefulness *Syn* USE (sense 2), utility

useless *Syn* IMPRACTICAL, impracticable, inoperable, nonpractical, unusable, unworkable *Ant* applicable, feasible, functional, operable, operational, practicable, practical, usable, useful, workable

use up *Syn* DEPLETE, clean (out), consume, drain, exhaust, expend, spend *Ant* renew, replace

usual • familiar through frequent or regular repetition *Syn* accustomed, customary, habitual, wont, wonted *Rel* natural, normal, regular, typical

usually *Syn* NATURALLY (sense 1), commonly, generally, normally, ordinarily, typically *Ant* abnormally, atypically, extraordinarily, uncommonly, unusually

usurp *Syn* ARROGATE, appropriate, confiscate, preempt *Ant* renounce, yield

utensil *Syn* IMPLEMENT, appliance, instrument, tool

utility *Syn* USE (sense 2), usefulness

utilize *Syn* USE, apply, avail, employ

utopian *adj Syn* AMBITIOUS (sense 2), pretentious *Ant* modest

utopian *n Syn* IDEALIST, dreamer, romantic, romanticist, visionary

utter **1** *Syn* EXPRESS, air, broach, vent, ventilate, voice *Ant* imply **2** *Syn* SAY, state, tell

uttered *Syn* VOCAL (sense 1), oral, voiced *Ant* nonvocal

V

vacancy **1** • empty space *Syn* blank, blankness, emptiness, vacuity, void *Rel* nothingness **2** • the quality or state of being empty *Syn* bareness, emptiness, vacuity *Rel* hollowness *Ant* fullness

vacant *Syn* EMPTY, blank, vacuous, void *Ant* full

vacate *Syn* EMPTY, clear, evacuate, void *Ant* fill, load

vacated *Syn* ABANDONED (sense 2), derelict, deserted, disused, forgotten, forsaken, rejected

vacillate *Syn* HESITATE, falter, waver *Ant* dive (in), plunge (in)

vacillation *Syn* HESITATION, faltering, hesitance, hesitancy, indecision, irresolution, shilly-shallying, wavering, wobbling

vacuity **1** *Syn* VACANCY (sense 1), blank,

blankness, emptiness, void *Ant* fullness **2** *Syn* VACANCY (sense 2), bareness, emptiness *Ant* fullness

vacuous *Syn* EMPTY, blank, vacant, void *Ant* full

vacuum *Syn* HOLE, cavity, hollow, pocket, void

vagabond **1** • a person who wanders at will or as a habit *Syn* bum, hobo, tramp, truant, vagrant *Rel* roamer, rover, wanderer **2** *Syn* NOMAD, drifter, gadabout, rambler, roamer, rover, stroller, wanderer, wayfarer

vagary *Syn* WHIM, caprice, fancy, freak, notion, whimsy

vagrant *adj Syn* ITINERANT, ambulant, ambulatory, nomadic, peripatetic

vagrant *n Syn* VAGABOND, bum, hobo, tramp, truant

vague *Syn* OBSCURE, ambiguous, cryptic, dark, enigmatic, equivocal *Ant* distinct, obvious

vain **1** • being without worth or significance *Syn* empty, hollow, idle, nugatory, otiose **2** *Syn* CONCEITED, complacent, egoistic, egotistic (*or* egotistical), important, overweening, pompous, prideful, proud, self-conceited, self-important, self-satisfied, smug, stuck-up, vainglorious *Ant* humble, modest **3** *Syn* FUTILE, abortive, bootless, fruitless *Ant* effective, effectual, efficacious, efficient, fruitful, productive, profitable, successful **4** *Syn* PROUD (sense 2), vainglorious *Ant* ashamed, humble

vainglorious **1** *Syn* CONCEITED, complacent, egoistic, egotistic (*or* egotistical), important, overweening, pompous, prideful, proud, self-conceited, self-important, self-satisfied, smug, stuck-up, vain *Ant* humble, modest **2** *Syn* PROUD (sense 2), vain *Ant* ashamed, humble

vaingloriousness *Syn* COMPLACENCE, complacency, conceit, conceitedness, ego, egotism, pompousness, pride, pridefulness, self-admiration, self-conceit, self-esteem, self-importance, self-satisfaction, smugness, vainglory, vainness, vanity *Ant* humbleness, humility, modesty

vainglory **1** *Syn* COMPLACENCE, complacency, conceit, conceitedness, ego, egotism, pompousness, pride, pridefulness, self-admiration, self-conceit, self-esteem, self-importance, self-satisfaction, smugness, vaingloriousness, vainness, vanity *Ant* humbleness, humility, modesty **2** *Syn* PRIDE, vanity *Ant* humility, shame

vainness *Syn* COMPLACENCE, complacency, conceit, conceitedness, ego, egotism, pompousness, pride, pridefulness, self-admiration, self-conceit, self-esteem, self-importance, self-satisfaction, smugness, vaingloriousness, vainglory, vanity *Ant* humbleness, humility, modesty

valiant *Syn* BRAVE, audacious, bold, courageous, dauntless, doughty, fearless, intrepid, unafraid, undaunted, valorous *Ant* craven

validate *Syn* CONFIRM, authenticate, corroborate, substantiate, verify *Ant* contradict, deny

valor **1** *Syn* COURAGE, bravery, courageousness, daring, dauntlessness, doughtiness, fearlessness, gallantry, greatheartedness, guts, hardihood, heart, heroism, intrepidity, intrepidness, nerve, stoutness *Ant* cowardice, cowardliness, cravenness, dastardliness, spinelessness, yellowness **2** *Syn* HEROISM, gallantry, prowess

valorous *Syn* BRAVE, audacious, bold, courageous, dauntless, doughty, fearless, intrepid, unafraid, undaunted, valiant *Ant* craven

valuable *Syn* COSTLY, dear, expensive, invaluable, precious, priceless *Ant* cheap

value *vb* **1** *Syn* APPRECIATE, cherish, prize, treasure *Ant* despise **2** *Syn* ESTIMATE (sense 1), appraise, assay, assess, evaluate, rate

value *adj Syn* EXCELLENCE, distinction, excellency, merit, virtue *Ant* deficiency

vanish • to pass from view or out of existence *Syn* disappear, evanesce, evaporate, fade *Rel* escape, flee, fly *Ant* appear, loom

vanished *Syn* EXTINCT, bygone, dead, defunct, departed, expired, gone *Ant* alive, existent, existing, extant, living

vanity **1** *Syn* COMPLACENCE, complacency, conceit, conceitedness, ego, egotism, pompousness, pride, pridefulness, self-admiration, self-conceit, self-esteem, self-importance, self-satisfaction, smugness, vaingloriousness, vainglory, vainness *Ant* humbleness, humility, modesty **2** *Syn* PRIDE, vainglory *Ant* humility, shame

vanquish *Syn* CONQUER, beat, defeat, lick, overcome, overthrow, reduce, rout, subdue, subjugate, surmount

vanquisher *Syn* VICTOR, champion, conqueror, winner

vapid *Syn* INSIPID, banal, flat, inane, jejune, wishy-washy *Ant* sapid, zestful

variable *Syn* CHANGEABLE, changeful, mutable, protean *Ant* stable, unchangeable

variance *Syn* DISCORD, conflict, contention, difference, dissension, schism, strife

variation *Syn* CHANGE (sense 1), alteration, modification *Ant* monotony, uniformity

varicolored *Syn* COLORFUL, motley, multicolored, polychromatic, polychrome, variegated *Ant* colorless, monochromatic, solid

variegated **1** • having a pattern involving different colors or shades of color *Syn* checked, checkered, dappled, motley, particolored, piebald, pied, skewbald *Rel* flecked, marbled, mottled, spattered, spotted, stippled **2** *Syn* COLORFUL, motley, multicolored, polychromatic, polychrome, varicolored *Ant* colorless, monochromatic, solid

variety • a group of related plants or animals

narrower in scope than a species *Syn* breed, clone, cultivar, race, stock, strain, subspecies

various **1** *Syn* DIFFERENT, disparate, divergent, diverse *Ant* alike, identical, same **2** *Syn* MANY, divers, multifarious, numerous, several, sundry *Ant* few

vary **1** *Syn* CHANGE (sense 1), alter, make over, modify, recast, redo, refashion, remake, remodel, revamp, revise, rework *Ant* fix, freeze, set, stabilize **2** *Syn* CHANGE (sense 2), fluctuate, mutate, shift *Ant* stabilize **3** *Syn* DIFFER, disagree, dissent *Ant* agree

vast *Syn* HUGE, Brobdingnagian, colossal, cyclopean, elephantine, enormous, gargantuan, giant, gigantean, gigantic, Herculean, immense, mammoth, titanic *Ant* bitty, diminutive, microscopic (*or* microscopical), midget, miniature, minute, pocket, pygmy, teeny, teeny-weeny, tiny, wee

vault *vb Syn* JUMP, bound, leap, spring

vault *n Syn* JUMP, bound, leap, spring

vaunt *Syn* BOAST, brag, crow, gasconade *Ant* depreciate (*oneself, one's accomplishments*)

veer *Syn* SWERVE, depart, deviate, digress, diverge

vehement **1** *Syn* FERVENT, ardent, blazing, burning, charged, emotional, fervid, feverish, fiery, flaming, glowing, hot-blooded, impassioned, passionate, red-hot, warm, warm-blooded *Ant* cold, cool, dispassionate, impassive, unemotional **2** *Syn* INTENSE, exquisite, fierce, violent *Ant* subdued

vehicle *Syn* AGENT (sense 2), agency, instrument, instrumentality, machinery, means, medium, organ

veil *Syn* COVER, envelop, overspread, shroud, wrap *Ant* bare

vein **1** *Syn* MOOD, humor, temper **2** *Syn* TOUCH, dash, shade, smack, soupçon, spice, strain, streak, suggestion, suspicion, tincture, tinge

veld *or* **veldt** *Syn* PLAIN, down, grassland, prairie, savanna, steppe, tundra

velocity *Syn* SPEED, headway, impetus, momentum, pace

velvety *Syn* SLEEK, glossy, satiny, silken, silky, slick

venal • open to improper influence and especially bribery *Syn* bribable, corruptible, purchasable *Rel* hack, mercenary *Ant* incorruptible, uncorruptible

vend *Syn* MARKET, deal (in), merchandise, put up, retail, sell *Ant* buy, purchase

venerate *Syn* REVERE, adore, reverence, worship *Ant* flout

veneration *Syn* REVERENCE (sense 1), adoration, worship

vengeance *Syn* RETALIATION, reprisal, retribution, revenge

vengeful *Syn* VINDICTIVE, revengeful

venial • worthy of forgiveness *Syn* excusable, forgivable, pardonable, remittable *Rel* justifiable, redeemable *Ant* inexcusable, mortal, unforgivable, unpardonable

venom *Syn* POISON, bane, toxin, virus

venomous *Syn* POISONOUS, mephitic, miasmal, miasmatic, miasmic, pestilent, pestilential, toxic, virulent *Ant* nonpoisonous, nontoxic, nonvenomous

vent *Syn* EXPRESS, air, broach, utter, ventilate, voice *Ant* imply

ventilate *Syn* EXPRESS, air, broach, utter, vent, voice *Ant* imply

venture *Syn* ENDANGER, adventure, compromise, gamble (with), hazard, imperil, jeopardize, menace, risk

venturesome *Syn* ADVENTUROUS, daredevil, daring, foolhardy, rash, reckless *Ant* cautious, unadventurous

veracious *Syn* TRUTHFUL, honest *Ant* dishonest, fibbing, lying, mendacious, prevaricating, untruthful

veracity **1** *Syn* PRECISION, accuracy, closeness, delicacy, exactitude, exactness, fineness, preciseness, rigorousness *Ant* coarseness, impreciseness, imprecision, inaccuracy, inexactness, roughness **2** *Syn* TRUTH, verisimilitude, verity *Ant* falsehood, lie, untruth

verbal • made or carried on through speaking rather than in writing *Syn* oral, spoken, unwritten *Rel* implicit, informal *Ant* written

verbiage • an excess of words usually of little or obscure content *Syn* circumlocution, periphrasis, pleonasm, redundancy, tautology *Rel* diffuseness, prolixity, verboseness, wordiness

verbose *Syn* WORDY, diffuse, prolix, redundant *Ant* compact, concise, crisp, pithy, succinct, terse

verge *Syn* BORDER, brim, brink, edge, margin, rim

verging *Syn* ADJACENT, abutting, adjoining, bordering, contiguous, flanking, fringing, joining, juxtaposed, skirting, touching *Ant* nonadjacent

verify *Syn* CONFIRM, authenticate, corroborate, substantiate, validate *Ant* contradict, deny

verisimilitude *Syn* TRUTH, veracity, verity *Ant* falsehood, lie, untruth

veritable *Syn* AUTHENTIC, bona fide, genuine *Ant* spurious

verity *Syn* TRUTH, veracity, verisimilitude *Ant* falsehood, lie, untruth

vernacularism *Syn* BARBARISM, corruption, impropriety, solecism, vulgarism

versatile • having a wide range of skills or abilities or many different uses *Syn* all-around, many-sided *Rel* gifted, talented

verse **1** *Syn* PARAGRAPH, article, clause, count, plank **2** *Syn* POEM, lyric, song

versifier *Syn* POET, bard, minstrel, poetaster, rhymer, rhymester, troubadour
version **1** *Syn* ACCOUNT, chronicle, report, story **2** *Syn* TRANSLATION, metaphrase, paraphrase
vertebrae *Syn* SPINE, back, backbone, chine
vertical **1** • being at right angles to a base line *Syn* perpendicular, plumb *Ant* horizontal **2** *Syn* ERECT, perpendicular, plumb, raised, standing, upright, upstanding *Ant* flat, recumbent
vertiginous *Syn* GIDDY, dazzled, dizzy, swimming
verve *Syn* VIGOR, dash, drive, élan, esprit, punch, spirit, vim
very *adv* • to a great degree *Syn* awful, awfully, beastly, deadly, especially, exceedingly, extra, extremely, far, frightfully, full, greatly, heavily, highly, hugely, jolly, mightily, mighty, mortally, most, much, particularly, rattling, real, right, so, something, super, terribly, too, whacking *Rel* completely, entirely, purely, thoroughly, totally, utterly *Ant* little, negligibly, nominally, slightly
very *adj* **1** *Syn* ACTUAL, concrete, existent, factual, real, true *Ant* conjectural, hypothetical, ideal, nonexistent, possible, potential, theoretical **2** *Syn* MERE, bare **3** *Syn* SAME, equal, equivalent, identic, identical, selfsame, tantamount *Ant* different
vessel **1** *Syn* BOAT, craft, ship **2** *Syn* CONTAINER, holder, receptacle
vestige • a tiny often physical indication of something lost or vanished *Syn* relic, shadow, trace *Rel* memento, remembrance, reminder
veto *Syn* PROHIBITION (sense 2), ban, embargo, interdict, interdiction, proscription *Ant* prescription
vex *Syn* ANNOY, bother, irk *Ant* soothe
vexatious *Syn* ANNOYING, aggravating, bothersome, disturbing, exasperating, frustrating, galling, irksome, irritating, maddening, nettling, peeving, pesty, rankling, riling, vexing
vexing *Syn* ANNOYING, aggravating, bothersome, disturbing, exasperating, frustrating, galling, irksome, irritating, maddening, nettling, peeving, pesty, rankling, riling, vexatious
viands *Syn* FOOD (sense 1), comestibles, feed, fodder, forage, provender, provisions, victuals
vibrant *Syn* RESONANT, orotund, resounding, ringing, sonorous
vibrate *Syn* SWING (sense 2), fluctuate, oscillate, pendulate, sway, undulate, waver
vice **1** *Syn* FAULT, failing, foible, frailty *Ant* merit **2** *Syn* OFFENSE (sense 2), crime, scandal, sin
vicinity *Syn* LOCALITY, district, neighborhood
vicious • highly reprehensible or offensive in character, nature, or conduct *Syn* corrupt, degenerate, flagitious, infamous, iniquitous, nefarious, villainous *Rel* debased, debauched, depraved, perverted *Ant* virtuous
viciousness *Syn* CRUELTY, barbarity, brutality, cruelness, heartlessness, inhumanity, sadism, savageness, savagery, wantonness *Ant* benignity, compassion, good-heartedness, humanity, kindheartedness, kindness, sympathy
vicissitude **1** *Syn* CHANGE (sense 2), alternation, mutation, permutation **2** *Syn* DIFFICULTY, hardship, rigor
victim • one killed or injured for the ends of the one who kills or injures *Syn* prey, quarry
victimize *Syn* FLEECE, bleed, cheat, chisel, cozen, defraud, hustle, mulct, rook, shortchange, skin, squeeze, stick, sting, swindle
victor • one that defeats an enemy or opponent *Syn* champion, conqueror, vanquisher, winner
victory • a successful outcome in a contest or struggle *Syn* conquest, triumph *Rel* gaining, winning *Ant* defeat
victuals *Syn* FOOD (sense 1), comestibles, feed, fodder, forage, provender, provisions, viands
vie *Syn* RIVAL, compete, emulate
view *vb* **1** *Syn* LOOK, glance, glimpse, peek, peep, sight **2** *Syn* SEE (sense 1), behold, contemplate, descry, discern, espy, note, notice, observe, perceive, remark, survey
view *n* *Syn* OPINION, belief, conviction, persuasion, sentiment
viewpoint *Syn* POINT OF VIEW, angle, slant, standpoint
vigilance • the act or state of being constantly attentive and responsive to signs of opportunity, activity, or danger *Syn* alertness, attentiveness, lookout, surveillance, watch, watchfulness *Rel* aliveness, awareness, consciousness, sensitivity
vigilant *Syn* WATCHFUL, alert, wide-awake
vigor • a quality of force, forcefulness, or energy *Syn* dash, drive, élan, esprit, punch, spirit, verve, vim *Rel* energy, force, might, power, strength
vigorous • having or showing great vitality and force *Syn* energetic, lusty, nervous, strenuous *Rel* manful, manly, virile *Ant* languorous, lethargic
vile *Syn* BASE, low *Ant* noble
vilify *Syn* SLANDER, asperse, blacken, defame, libel, malign, smear, traduce
villa *Syn* MANSION, castle, château, countryseat, estate, hacienda, hall, manor, manor house, palace
villain • a low, mean, reprehensible person utterly lacking in principles *Syn* blackguard, knave, miscreant, rapscallion, rascal, rogue, scamp, scoundrel *Rel* offender, sinner
villainous *Syn* VICIOUS, corrupt, degenerate,

flagitious, infamous, iniquitous, nefarious *Ant* virtuous

villainy *Syn* EVIL, bad, evildoing, ill, immorality, iniquity, sin, wrong *Ant* good, morality, right, virtue

vim *Syn* VIGOR, dash, drive, élan, esprit, punch, spirit, verve

vindicate **1** *Syn* EXCULPATE, absolve, acquit, exonerate *Ant* accuse, inculpate **2** *Syn* MAINTAIN, assert, defend, justify

vindictive • showing or motivated by a desire for vengeance *Syn* revengeful, vengeful *Rel* grim, implacable, merciless, relentless, unrelenting

violate *Syn* DESECRATE, defile, profane

violation *Syn* BREACH (sense 1), contravention, infraction, infringement, transgression, trespass

violence *Syn* FORCE, coercion, compulsion, constraint, duress, restraint

violent *Syn* INTENSE, exquisite, fierce, vehement *Ant* subdued

virile *Syn* MALE, manful, manlike, manly, mannish, masculine *Ant* female

virility • the set of qualities considered appropriate for or characteristic of men *Syn* manhood, manliness, masculinity *Rel* maleness *Ant* femininity

virtually **1** • not absolutely or actually, yet so nearly so that the difference is negligible *Syn* morally, practically **2** *Syn* ALMOST, about, more or less, most, much, near, nearly, next to, nigh, practically, some, well-nigh

virtue **1** *Syn* EXCELLENCE, distinction, excellency, merit, value *Ant* deficiency **2** *Syn* GOODNESS, morality, rectitude *Ant* badness, evil

virtuoso *Syn* EXPERT, ace, adept, artist, authority, crackerjack, maestro, master, past master, scholar, shark, whiz, wizard *Ant* amateur

virtuous *Syn* MORAL, ethical, noble, righteous

virulent *Syn* POISONOUS, mephitic, miasmal, miasmatic, miasmic, pestilent, pestilential, toxic, venomous *Ant* nonpoisonous, nontoxic, nonvenomous

virus *Syn* POISON, bane, toxin, venom

visage *Syn* FACE, countenance, mug, physiognomy, puss

visible • capable of being seen *Syn* apparent, observable, seeable, visual *Rel* external, outer, outward *Ant* invisible, unseeable

vision **1** *Syn* FANCY, daydream, dream, fantasy, nightmare, phantasm, phantasy *Ant* reality **2** *Syn* GHOST, apparition, bogey, phantasm, phantom, poltergeist, shade, shadow, specter (*or* spectre), spirit, spook, wraith **3** *Syn* REVELATION (sense 1), prophecy

visionary *adj* *Syn* IDEALIST, dreamer, romantic, romanticist, utopian *Ant* pragmatist, realist

visionary *n* *Syn* IMAGINARY, chimerical, fanciful, fantastic, quixotic *Ant* actual, real

visit *n* • a usually brief stay with another as an act of friendship or courtesy *Syn* call, visitation

visit *vb* *Syn* CHAT, babble, blab, cackle, chatter, converse, gab, gabble, gas, jabber, jaw, palaver, patter, prate, prattle, rap, rattle, run on, talk, twitter

visitant *Syn* VISITOR, caller, guest

visitation **1** *Syn* TRIAL, affliction, cross, tribulation **2** *Syn* VISIT, call

visitor • one who visits another *Syn* caller, guest, visitant

visual *Syn* VISIBLE, apparent, observable, seeable *Ant* invisible, unseeable

vital **1** *Syn* CRUCIAL, critical, key, pivotal **2** *Syn* DEADLY, baleful, deathly, fatal, fell, killer, lethal, mortal, murderous, pestilent *Ant* healthful, healthy, nonfatal, nonlethal, wholesome **3** *Syn* ESSENTIAL, cardinal, fundamental **4** *Syn* LIVING, alive, animate, animated *Ant* lifeless

vitalize **1** • to arouse to activity, animation, or life *Syn* activate, energize *Rel* animate, enliven, quicken, vivify *Ant* atrophy **2** *Syn* ANIMATE, brace, energize, enliven, fire, invigorate, jazz (up), liven (up), pep (up), quicken, stimulate, vivify *Ant* damp, dampen, deaden, dull

vitalizing *Syn* TONIC, bracing, invigorating, refreshing, restorative, reviving, stimulating, stimulative

vitiate *Syn* DEBASE, corrupt, debauch, deprave, pervert *Ant* amend (*morals, character*), elevate (*taste, way of life*)

vitiated *Syn* DEBASED, corrupted, debauched, depraved, perverted

vituperate **1** *Syn* ATTACK (sense 2), abuse, assail, belabor, blast, castigate, excoriate, jump (on), lambaste (*or* lambast), scathe, slam **2** *Syn* SCOLD, bawl, berate, chew out, jaw, rail, rate, revile, tongue-lash, upbraid, wig

vituperation *Syn* ABUSE, billingsgate, invective, obloquy, scurrility *Ant* adulation

vituperative *Syn* ABUSIVE, contumelious, opprobrious, scurrilous *Ant* complementary, respectful

vivacious *Syn* LIVELY, animated, gay, sprightly *Ant* dull

vivid *Syn* GRAPHIC, pictorial, picturesque

vivify *Syn* ANIMATE, brace, energize, enliven, fire, invigorate, jazz (up), liven (up), pep (up), quicken, stimulate, vitalize *Ant* damp, dampen, deaden, dull

vocable *Syn* WORD, term

vocabulary **1** *Syn* LANGUAGE (sense 2), diction, phraseology, phrasing, style **2** *Syn* TERMINOLOGY, argot, cant, dialect, jargon, language, lingo, patois, patter, slang

vocal • uttered by the voice or having to do with such utterance *Syn* oral, uttered, voiced *Rel* articulate, articulated, spoken *Ant* nonvocal

vocation *Syn* OCCUPATION, calling, employment, line, profession, trade, work

vociferate *Syn* ROAR, bawl, bellow, bluster, clamor, howl, ululate

vociferation *Syn* ROAR, bawl, bellow, bluster, ululation

vociferous • so loud or insistent as to compel attention *Syn* blatant, boisterous, clamorous, obstreperous, strident *Rel* noisy, sounding

vogue **1** *Syn* FASHION, craze, cry, dernier cri, fad, mode, rage, style **2** *Syn* POPULARITY, fashionableness, favor, hotness, modishness *Ant* disfavor, unpopularity

voice *Syn* EXPRESS, air, broach, utter, vent, ventilate *Ant* imply

voiced *Syn* VOCAL (sense 1), oral, uttered *Ant* nonvocal

voiceless *Syn* MUTE, inarticulate, speechless

void *vb* **1** *Syn* ABOLISH, abrogate, annul, cancel, dissolve, invalidate, negate, nullify, quash, repeal, rescind **2** *Syn* EMPTY, clear, evacuate, vacate *Ant* fill, load

void *adj* **1** *Syn* DEVOID, destitute **2** *Syn* EMPTY, blank, vacant, vacuous *Ant* full

void *n* **1** *Syn* HOLE, cavity, hollow, pocket, vacuum **2** *Syn* VACANCY (sense 1), blank, blankness, emptiness, vacuity *Ant* fullness

volatile *Syn* ELASTIC (sense 2), buoyant, effervescent, expansive, resilient *Ant* depressed

volatility *Syn* LIGHTNESS, flightiness, flippancy, frivolity, levity, light-mindedness *Ant* seriousness

volcano *Syn* MOUNTAIN, alp, mesa, mount, peak

volition *Syn* WILL, conation

volley *Syn* BARRAGE, bombardment, cannonade, fusillade, hail, salvo, shower, storm

volubility *Syn* TALKATIVENESS, garrulity, garrulousness, glibness, loquaciousness, loquacity *Ant* silence

voluble *Syn* TALKATIVE, garrulous, glib, loquacious *Ant* closemouthed, laconic, reserved, reticent, taciturn, tight-lipped

volume **1** *Syn* AMOUNT, measure, quantity **2** *Syn* BULK, mass **3** *Syn* SIZE, area, dimensions, extent, magnitude

voluminous *Syn* LARGE, big, bulky, considerable, goodly, good-sized, grand, great, handsome, hefty, hulking, largish, outsize, oversize (*or* oversized), sizable (*or* sizeable), substantial, tidy *Ant* little, puny, small, undersized

voluntary **1** • done or brought about of one's own will *Syn* deliberate, intentional, willful, willing *Rel* chosen, elected, opted *Ant* instinctive, involuntary **2** *Syn* OPTIONAL, discretionary, elective *Ant* compulsory, mandatory, nonelective, obligatory, required

voluptuous *Syn* SENSUOUS, epicurean, luxurious, sybaritic

vomit *Syn* BELCH, burp, disgorge, regurgitate, spew, throw up

voodoo *Syn* MAGICIAN (sense 1), charmer, conjurer (*or* conjuror), enchanter, necromancer, sorcerer, witch, wizard

voracious • excessively greedy *Syn* gluttonous, rapacious, ravening, ravenous *Rel* acquisitive, covetous, grasping, greedy

vortex *Syn* EDDY, maelstrom, whirlpool

votary **1** *Syn* ADDICT, devotee, habitué **2** *Syn* FOLLOWER, adherent, convert, disciple, partisan, pupil *Ant* leader

vote *Syn* SUFFRAGE, ballot, franchise

vouch *Syn* CERTIFY, attest, witness

vouchsafe *Syn* GRANT (sense 1), accord, award, concede

vow *Syn* PROMISE, oath, pledge, troth, word

voyage *Syn* JOURNEY, cruise, excursion, expedition, jaunt, pilgrimage, tour, trip

vulgar **1** *Syn* COARSE, gross, obscene, ribald *Ant* fine, refined **2** *Syn* COMMON, familiar, ordinary, popular *Ant* exceptional, uncommon

vulgarism *Syn* BARBARISM, corruption, impropriety, solecism, vernacularism

W

wage, wages • the price paid a person for his or her labor or services *Syn* emolument, fee, hire, pay, salary, stipend *Rel* recompense, recompensing, remuneration

wager *n* *Syn* BET, ante, pot, stake

wager *vb* *Syn* BET, gamble, go, lay, stake

wagerer *Syn* BETTOR, gambler

waggish *Syn* PLAYFUL, frolicsome, impish, mischievous, roguish, sportive

wail *vb* **1** *Syn* COMPLAIN, beef, bellyache, carp, crab, croak, fuss, gripe, grouse, growl, grumble, kick, moan, murmur, mutter, repine, squawk, whine, yammer **2** *Syn* CRY, blubber, keen, weep, whimper

wail *n* *Syn* LAMENT, groan, howl, keen, lamentation, moan, plaint *Ant* exultation, rejoicing

wait *n* *Syn* DELAY, detainment, holdup

wait *vb Syn* STAY, abide, linger, remain, tarry
waive *Syn* RELINQUISH, abandon, cede, leave, resign, surrender, yield *Ant* keep
wakeful • not sleeping or able to sleep *Syn* awake, sleepless, wide-awake *Rel* aroused, awakened, roused, wakened *Ant* asleep, dormant, dozing, napping, resting, sleeping, slumbering
waken *Syn* STIR, arouse, awaken, rally, rouse
walk *n* • a relaxed journey on foot for exercise or pleasure *Syn* constitutional, perambulation, ramble, range, saunter, stroll, turn *Rel* parade, promenade
walk *vb* • to go on foot *Syn* foot (it), hoof (it), leg (it), pad, step, traipse, tread *Rel* parade, promenade
wall *n Syn* BARRIER, barricade, fence, hedge
wall *vb Syn* ENCLOSE, cage, coop, corral, envelop, fence, pen
wallow • to move clumsily and in a debased or pitable condition *Syn* grovel, welter *Rel* crawl, creep
wan *Syn* PALE (sense 1), ashen, ashy, livid, pallid *Ant* florid, flush, rubicund, ruddy, sanguine
wander • to move about from place to place more or less aimlessly and without a plan *Syn* gad, gallivant, meander, prowl, ramble, range, roam, rove, stray, traipse
wanderer *Syn* NOMAD, drifter, gadabout, rambler, roamer, rover, stroller, vagabond, wayfarer
wane *Syn* ABATE, ebb, subside *Ant* revive, rise
wangle *Syn* ENGINEER, contrive, finagle, finesse, frame, machinate, maneuver, manipulate, mastermind, negotiate
want *n* **1** *Syn* DEFICIENCY, dearth, deficit, failure, famine, inadequacy, insufficiency, lack, paucity, poverty, scantiness, scarceness, scarcity, shortage *Ant* abundance, adequacy, amplitude, plenitude, plenty, sufficiency **2** *Syn* LACK, absence, dearth, defect, privation **3** *Syn* POVERTY, destitution, indigence, penury, privation *Ant* riches
want *vb* **1** *Syn* DESIRE, covet, crave, wish **2** *Syn* LACK, need, require
wanton **1** *Syn* LICENTIOUS, lascivious, lecherous, lewd, libertine, libidinous, lustful *Ant* continent **2** *Syn* SUPEREROGATORY, gratuitous, uncalled-for
wantonness *Syn* CRUELTY, barbarity, brutality, cruelness, heartlessness, inhumanity, sadism, savageness, savagery, viciousness *Ant* benignity, compassion, good-heartedness, humanity, kindheartedness, kindness, sympathy
war *Syn* CONTEND, battle, fight
warble *n Syn* MELODY, air, lay, song, strain, tune
warble *vb Syn* SING, carol, chant, descant, hymn, intone, trill, troll
ward *Syn* CUSTODY, care, guardianship, keeping, safekeeping, trust
warehouse *Syn* STOREHOUSE, depository, depot, magazine, repository, storage, stowage
wariness *Syn* CAUTION, calculation, chariness, circumspection *Ant* adventurousness, temerity
warlike **1** *Syn* BELLIGERENT, aggressive, argumentative, bellicose, combative, contentious, discordant, disputatious, gladiatorial, militant, pugnacious, quarrelsome, scrappy, truculent *Ant* nonbelligerent, pacific, peaceable, peaceful **2** *Syn* MARTIAL, military
warm **1** *Syn* FERVENT, ardent, blazing, burning, charged, emotional, fervid, feverish, fiery, flaming, glowing, hot-blooded, impassioned, passionate, red-hot, vehement, warm-blooded *Ant* cold, cool, dispassionate, impassive, unemotional **2** *Syn* TENDER, compassionate, responsive, sympathetic, warmhearted *Ant* callous, severe
warm-blooded *Syn* FERVENT, ardent, blazing, burning, charged, emotional, fervid, feverish, fiery, flaming, glowing, hot-blooded, impassioned, passionate, red-hot, vehement, warm *Ant* cold, cool, dispassionate, impassive, unemotional
warmhearted *Syn* TENDER, compassionate, responsive, sympathetic, warm *Ant* callous, severe
warn • to let one know of approaching danger or risk *Syn* alert, caution, forewarn *Rel* advise, apprise, inform, notify
warning *n* • the act or an instance of telling beforehand of danger or risk *Syn* admonition, alarm, alert, caution, forewarning, notice *Rel* auguring, augury, forecasting, foretelling, predicting, prediction, presaging, prognosticating, prophecy, prophesying
warning *adj Syn* CAUTIONARY, admonishing, admonitory, cautioning
warp *Syn* DEFORM, contort, distort
warped *Syn* CORRUPT, debased, debauched, decadent, degenerate, degraded, demoralized, depraved, dissipated, dissolute, perverse, perverted, reprobate *Ant* uncorrupted
warrant *Syn* ASSERT, affirm, aver, avouch, avow, declare, predicate, profess, protest *Ant* controvert, deny
wary *Syn* CAUTIOUS, calculating, chary, circumspect *Ant* adventurous, temerarious
wash *Syn* WET, bathe, douse, drench, soak, souse, water *Ant* dry
wash out *Syn* WHITEN, blanch, bleach, blench, decolorize, dull, fade, pale *Ant* blacken, darken, deepen
waspish *Syn* IRRITABLE, fractious, fretful, huffy, peevish, pettish, petulant, querulous, snappish *Ant* easygoing
wastage *Syn* DESTRUCTION, annihilation, decimation, demolishment, demolition, desolation, devastation, extermination, extinc-

tion, havoc, loss, obliteration, ruin, ruination, wreckage *Ant* building, construction, erection, raising

waste *n* **1** • an area of the earth unsuitable for cultivation or general habitation *Syn* badlands, desert, wilderness **2** *Syn* REFUSE, debris, garbage, offal, rubbish, trash

waste *vb* **1** • to spend or expend freely and usually foolishly or futilely *Syn* consume, dissipate, fritter, squander *Rel* disburse, expend, spend *Ant* conserve, save **2** *Syn* RAVAGE, despoil, devastate, pillage, sack, spoliate

wasted *Syn* HAGGARD, cadaverous, careworn, pinched, worn

wasteful *Syn* PRODIGAL, extravagant, profligate, spendthrift, squandering, thriftless, unthrifty *Ant* conserving, economical, economizing, frugal, scrimping, skimping, thrifty

waster *Syn* PRODIGAL, profligate, spender, spendthrift, squanderer, wastrel *Ant* economizer

wastrel *Syn* PRODIGAL, profligate, spender, spendthrift, squanderer, waster *Ant* economizer

watch *vb* **1** *Syn* SEE (sense 2), look **2** *Syn* TEND, attend, mind

watch *n* *Syn* VIGILANCE, alertness, attentiveness, lookout, surveillance, watchfulness

watchful • on the lookout especially for danger or for opportunities *Syn* alert, vigilant, wide-awake *Rel* cautious, chary, circumspect, wary

watchfulness *Syn* VIGILANCE, alertness, attentiveness, lookout, surveillance, watch

watchword *Syn* SLOGAN, cry, shibboleth

water *Syn* WET, bathe, douse, drench, soak, souse, wash *Ant* dry

waterfall • a fall of water usually from a great height *Syn* cascade, cataract, fall(s) *Rel* rapid(s), white water

waterlog *Syn* SOAK, drench, impregnate, saturate, sop, steep

wave **1** *Syn* MOTION, beckon, flag, gesture, signal **2** *Syn* SWING (sense 1), brandish, flourish, shake, thrash

waver **1** *Syn* HESITATE, falter, vacillate *Ant* dive (in), plunge (in) **2** *Syn* SWING (sense 2), fluctuate, oscillate, pendulate, sway, undulate, vibrate

wavering *Syn* HESITATION, faltering, hesitance, hesitancy, indecision, irresolution, shilly-shallying, vacillation, wobbling

wax **1** *Syn* BECOME, come, get, go, grow, run, turn **2** *Syn* INCREASE (sense 2), accumulate, appreciate, balloon, build (up), burgeon, enlarge, escalate, expand, mount, multiply, mushroom, proliferate, rise, snowball, swell *Ant* contract, decrease, diminish, lessen, wane

way **1** • a track or path traversed in going from one place to another *Syn* artery, course, pass, passage, route **2** *Syn* HABIT, custom, fashion, pattern, practice, trick, wont **3** *Syn* METHOD, fashion, manner, mode, system

wayfarer *Syn* NOMAD, drifter, gadabout, rambler, roamer, rover, stroller, vagabond, wanderer

waylay *Syn* SURPRISE (sense 1), ambush

wayward **1** *Syn* CONTRARY, balky, froward, perverse, restive *Ant* complaisant, good-natured **2** *Syn* DISOBEDIENT, balky, contrary, defiant, froward, insubordinate, intractable, rebellious, recalcitrant, refractory, restive, ungovernable, unruly, untoward, willful (*or* wilful) *Ant* amenable, compliant, docile, obedient, tractable **3** *Syn* UNCONTROLLABLE, froward, headstrong, intractable, recalcitrant, refractory, ungovernable, unmanageable, unruly, untoward, willful (*or* wilful) *Ant* controllable, governable, tractable

weak **1** • lacking physical, mental, or moral strength *Syn* decrepit, feeble, fragile, frail, infirm *Rel* debilitated, enfeebled, weakened *Ant* strong **2** *Syn* ILLOGICAL, fallacious, invalid, irrational, nonrational, unreasonable, unreasoning, unsound *Ant* logical, rational, reasonable, sound, valid **3** *Syn* POWERLESS, helpless, impotent *Ant* mighty, potent, powerful, puissant, strong

weaken • to diminish the strength or vigor of *Syn* debilitate, enervate, enfeeble, sap, soften *Rel* cripple, disable, emasculate, unman, unnerve *Ant* strengthen

weakened *Syn* IMPURE, adulterated, alloyed, contaminated, dilute, diluted, polluted, tainted, thinned *Ant* pure, unadulterated, unalloyed, uncontaminated, undiluted, unpolluted, untainted

wealthy *Syn* RICH, affluent, opulent *Ant* poor

wean *Syn* ESTRANGE, alienate, disaffect *Ant* reconcile

weariless *Syn* INDEFATIGABLE, tireless, unflagging, untiring, unwearied, unwearying

weariness *Syn* FATIGUE, burnout, collapse, exhaustion, lassitude, prostration, tiredness *Ant* refreshment, rejuvenation, revitalization

wearisome *Syn* BORING, drab, dreary, dry, dull, flat, heavy, humdrum, jading, leaden, monotonous, pedestrian, ponderous, stodgy, stuffy, stupid, tame, tedious, tiresome, tiring, unanimated, uninteresting, weary, wearying *Ant* absorbing, engaging, engrossing, gripping, interesting, intriguing, involving

weary *adj* *Syn* BORING, drab, dreary, dry, dull, flat, heavy, humdrum, jading, leaden, monotonous, pedestrian, ponderous, stodgy, stuffy, stupid, tame, tedious, tiresome, tiring, unanimated, uninteresting, wearisome, wearying *Ant* absorbing, engaging, engrossing, gripping, interesting, intriguing, involving

weary *vb* *Syn* TIRE, exhaust, fatigue, jade, tucker

wearying *Syn* BORING, drab, dreary, dry, dull,

flat, heavy, humdrum, jading, leaden, monotonous, pedestrian, ponderous, stodgy, stuffy, stupid, tame, tedious, tiresome, tiring, unanimated, uninteresting, wearisome, weary

weave • to make a textile or to form an article by interlacing threads or strands of material *Syn* braid, crochet, knit, plait, tat

wedded *Syn* MARITAL, conjugal, connubial, married, matrimonial, nuptial

wedding *Syn* MARRIAGE, espousal, matrimony, nuptial, wedlock

wedlock *Syn* MARRIAGE, espousal, matrimony, nuptial, wedding

wee *Syn* TINY, atomic, bitty, infinitesimal, microminiature, microscopic, miniature, minute, teeny, teeny-weeny *Ant* astronomical, colossal, cosmic, elephantine, enormous, giant, gigantic, herculean, heroic, huge, immense, mammoth, massive, monster, monstrous, monumental, mountainous, prodigious, titanic, tremendous

weep **1** *Syn* CRY, blubber, keen, wail, whimper **2** *Syn* EXUDE, bleed, ooze, percolate, seep, strain, sweat

weigh **1** *Syn* BURDEN, charge, cumber, encumber, lade, load, saddle, tax, weight **2** *Syn* CONSIDER (sense 1), contemplate, excogitate, study **3** *Syn* DEPRESS, oppress *Ant* cheer, elate **4** *Syn* MATTER, count, import, mean, signify

weight *vb* **1** *Syn* ADULTERATE, doctor, load, sophisticate *Ant* refine **2** *Syn* BURDEN, charge, cumber, encumber, lade, load, saddle, tax, weigh

weight *n* **1** *Syn* IMPORTANCE, consequence, import, moment, significance *Ant* unimportance **2** *Syn* INFLUENCE, authority, credit, prestige

weighty *Syn* HEAVY, cumbersome, cumbrous, hefty, ponderous *Ant* light

weird *Syn* EERIE, creepy, haunting, spooky, uncanny, unearthly

weirdo *Syn* ECCENTRIC, character, codger, crackbrain, crackpot, crank, kook, nut, oddball, screwball

welcome *Syn* PLEASANT, agreeable, grateful, gratifying, pleasing *Ant* distasteful, harsh, unpleasant

well *Syn* HEALTHY, hale, robust, sound, wholesome *Ant* unhealthy

well-disposed *Syn* AMIABLE, affable, agreeable, genial, good-natured, good-tempered, gracious, nice, sweet *Ant* disagreeable, ill-natured, ill-tempered, ungracious, unpleasant

well-known *Syn* FAMOUS, celebrated, famed, noted, notorious, prominent, renowned, star *Ant* anonymous, obscure, unknown

wellness *Syn* HEALTH, fitness, healthiness, heartiness, robustness, soundness, wholeness, wholesomeness *Ant* illness, sickness, unhealthiness, unsoundness

well-nigh *Syn* ALMOST, about, more or less, most, much, near, nearly, next to, nigh, practically, some, virtually

well-read *Syn* EDUCATED, erudite, knowledgeable, learned, literate, scholarly *Ant* ignorant, illiterate, uneducated

well-spoken *Syn* ARTICULATE, eloquent, fluent *Ant* inarticulate

well-timed *Syn* SEASONABLE, opportune, pat, timely *Ant* unseasonable

welter *n* *Syn* COMMOTION, bother, bustle, clatter, disturbance, furor, furore, fuss, hubbub, hullabaloo, hurly-burly, pandemonium, pother, row, ruckus, ruction, rumpus, shindy, squall, stew, stir, storm, to-do, tumult, turmoil, uproar, whirl

welter *vb* *Syn* WALLOW, grovel

wet *adj* • covered or more or less soaked with liquid *Syn* damp, dank, humid, moist *Rel* drenched, saturated, soaked, waterlogged *Ant* dry

wet *vb* • to make wet *Syn* bathe, douse, drench, soak, souse, wash, water *Rel* damp, dampen, humidify, hydrate, moisten *Ant* dry

wet *n* *Syn* RAIN (sense 1), cloudburst, deluge, downpour, rainstorm, storm

whack *Syn* ATTEMPT, crack, endeavor, essay, fling, go, pass, shot, stab, trial, try

whacking *Syn* VERY, awful, awfully, beastly, deadly, especially, exceedingly, extra, extremely, far, frightfully, full, greatly, heavily, highly, hugely, jolly, mightily, mighty, mortally, most, much, particularly, rattling, real, right, so, something, super, terribly, too *Ant* little, negligibly, nominally, slightly

whale *Syn* GIANT, behemoth, blockbuster, colossus, jumbo, leviathan, mammoth, monster, titan, whopper *Ant* dwarf, midget, mini, miniature, peewee, pygmy, runt, shrimp

wharf • a structure used by boats and ships for taking on or landing cargo or passengers *Syn* berth, dock, jetty, levee, pier, quay, slip

wheedle *Syn* COAX, blandish, blarney, cajole, soft-soap

wheel *Syn* TURN (sense 1), circle, eddy, gyrate, pirouette, revolve, rotate, spin, swirl, twirl, whirl

when *Syn* ALTHOUGH, albeit, howbeit, though, while

whet *Syn* SHARPEN, edge, grind, hone, strop *Ant* blunt, dull

while *vb* • to pass time, and especially leisure time, without boredom or in pleasant ways *Syn* beguile, fleet, wile *Rel* amuse, divert, entertain

while *conj* *Syn* ALTHOUGH, albeit, howbeit, though, when

whilom *Syn* FORMER, erstwhile, late, old, onetime, past, sometime

whim • a sudden impulsive and apparently unmotivated idea or action *Syn* caprice, fancy, freak, notion, vagary, whimsy *Rel* capriciousness, freakishness, whimsicality

whimper *Syn* CRY, blubber, keen, wail, weep

whimsical • prone to sudden illogical changes of mind, ideas, or actions *Syn* capricious, freakish, impulsive *Rel* mercurial, moody, temperamental, volatile

whimsy *Syn* WHIM, caprice, fancy, freak, notion, vagary

whine *Syn* COMPLAIN, beef, bellyache, carp, crab, croak, fuss, gripe, grouse, growl, grumble, kick, moan, murmur, mutter, repine, squawk, wail, yammer *Ant* rejoice

whiner *Syn* GROUCH, bear, complainer, crab, crank, croaker, curmudgeon, fusser, griper, grouser, growler, grumbler, grump, murmurer, mutterer

whirl *n* *Syn* COMMOTION, bother, bustle, clatter, disturbance, furor, furore, fuss, hubbub, hullabaloo, hurly-burly, pandemonium, pother, row, ruckus, ruction, rumpus, shindy, squall, stew, stir, storm, to-do, tumult, turmoil, uproar, welter

whirl *vb* **1** *Syn* HURRY (sense 2), barrel, bolt, bowl, breeze, career, course, dash, fly, hasten, hotfoot (it), hump, hurtle, hustle, pelt, race, rip, rocket, run, rush, rustle, scoot, scurry, scuttle, shoot, speed, step (along), tear, trot, whisk, zip, zoom *Ant* crawl, creep, poke **2** *Syn* REEL, stagger, totter **3** *Syn* TURN (sense 1), circle, eddy, gyrate, pirouette, revolve, rotate, spin, swirl, twirl, wheel

whirlpool *Syn* EDDY, maelstrom, vortex

whisk **1** *Syn* HURRY (sense 1), accelerate, hasten, quicken, rush, speed (up) *Ant* decelerate, retard, slow (down) **2** *Syn* HURRY (sense 2), barrel, bolt, bowl, breeze, career, course, dash, fly, hasten, hotfoot (it), hump, hurtle, hustle, pelt, race, rip, rocket, run, rush, rustle, scoot, scurry, scuttle, shoot, speed, step (along), tear, trot, whirl, zip, zoom *Ant* crawl, creep, poke

whisper *Syn* RUMOR, bruit (about), circulate, noise (about)

whistling *Syn* SHRILL, acute, high-pitched, piping, screeching, shrieking, squeaking, squeaky, treble *Ant* bass, deep, low, throaty

whit *Syn* PARTICLE, atom, bit, iota, jot, mite, smidgen, tittle

white *Syn* COLORLESS, uncolored, undyed, unpainted, unstained *Ant* colored, dyed, painted, stained, tinged, tinted

whiten **1** • to make white or whiter by removing color *Syn* blanch, bleach, blench, decolorize, dull, fade, pale, wash out *Rel* brighten, lighten *Ant* blacken, darken, deepen **2** *Syn* PALLIATE, extenuate, gloss, gloze, whitewash

whitewash *Syn* PALLIATE, extenuate, gloss, gloze, whiten

whiz *Syn* EXPERT, ace, adept, artist, authority, crackerjack, maestro, master, past master, scholar, shark, virtuoso, wizard *Ant* amateur

whole *adj* **1** • having every constituent element or individual *Syn* all, entire, gross, total *Ant* partial **2** *Syn* PERFECT, entire, intact *Ant* imperfect

whole *n* *Syn* SUM, aggregate, amount, number, quantity, total

wholehearted *Syn* SINCERE, heartfelt, hearty, unfeigned, whole-souled *Ant* insincere

wholeness *Syn* HEALTH, fitness, healthiness, heartiness, robustness, soundness, wellness, wholesomeness *Ant* illness, sickness, unhealthiness, unsoundness

wholesale *Syn* INDISCRIMINATE, sweeping *Ant* discriminating, selective

wholesome **1** *Syn* HEALTHFUL, healthy, hygienic, salubrious, salutary, sanitary **2** *Syn* HEALTHY, hale, robust, sound, well *Ant* unhealthy

wholesomeness *Syn* HEALTH, fitness, healthiness, heartiness, robustness, soundness, wellness, wholeness *Ant* illness, sickness, unhealthiness, unsoundness

whole-souled *Syn* SINCERE, heartfelt, hearty, unfeigned, wholehearted *Ant* insincere

whoop *vb* *Syn* SHOUT, holler, scream, screech, shriek, squeal, yell

whoop *n* *Syn* SHOUT, holler, scream, screech, shriek, squeal, yell

whopper *Syn* GIANT, behemoth, blockbuster, colossus, jumbo, leviathan, mammoth, monster, titan, whale *Ant* dwarf, midget, mini, miniature, peewee, pygmy, runt, shrimp

wicked *Syn* BAD (sense 1), evil, ill, naughty *Ant* good

wide **1** *Syn* BROAD, deep *Ant* narrow **2** *Syn* EXTENSIVE, broad, expansive, extended, far-flung, far-reaching, widespread *Ant* narrow

wide-awake **1** *Syn* WAKEFUL, awake, sleepless *Ant* asleep, dormant, dozing, napping, resting, sleeping, slumbering **2** *Syn* WATCHFUL, alert, vigilant

widespread *Syn* EXTENSIVE, broad, expansive, extended, far-flung, far-reaching, wide *Ant* narrow

wield **1** *Syn* EXERT, apply, exercise, ply, put out **2** *Syn* HANDLE, manipulate, ply, swing

wig *Syn* SCOLD, bawl, berate, chew out, jaw, rail, rate, revile, tongue-lash, upbraid, vituperate

wild *Syn* FURIOUS, delirious, frantic, frenetic, frenzied, rabid

wilderness *Syn* WASTE, badlands, desert

wile **1** *Syn* TRICKERY, artifice, chicanery, hanky-panky, jugglery, legerdemain, subterfuge **2** *Syn* TRICK, artifice, feint, gambit, maneuver, ploy, ruse, stratagem

will *n* • the power or act of making or effecting a choice or decision *Syn* conation, volition *Rel* design, intent, intention, purpose

will *vb* • to give to another by will *Syn* bequeath, devise, leave, legate

willful **1** *Syn* VOLUNTARY, deliberate, intentional, willing *Ant* instinctive, involuntary **2** *Syn* DISOBEDIENT, balky, contrary, defiant, froward, insubordinate, intractable, rebellious, recalcitrant, refractory, restive, ungovernable, unruly, untoward, wayward *Ant* amenable, compliant, docile, obedient, tractable **3** *Syn* OBSTINATE, adamant, adamantine, dogged, hard, hardened, hardheaded, hardhearted, headstrong, immovable, implacable, inflexible, mulish, obdurate, opinionated, ossified, pat, peevish, pertinacious, perverse, pigheaded, rigid, self-willed, stubborn, unbending, uncompromising, unrelenting, unyielding *Ant* acquiescent, agreeable, amenable, compliant, complying, flexible, pliable, pliant, relenting, yielding **4** *Syn* UNCONTROLLABLE, froward, headstrong, intractable, recalcitrant, refractory, ungovernable, unmanageable, unruly, untoward, wayward *Ant* controllable, governable, tractable **5** *Syn* UNRULY, headstrong, intractable, recalcitrant, refractory, ungovernable *Ant* docile, tractable

willfully *Syn* INTENTIONALLY, consciously, deliberately, designedly, knowingly, purposefully, purposely, wittingly *Ant* inadvertently, unconsciously, unintentionally, unknowingly, unwittingly

willfulness *Syn* DISOBEDIENCE, contrariness, defiance, frowardness, insubordination, intractability, rebelliousness, recalcitrance, refractoriness, unruliness *Ant* amenability, compliance, docility, obedience

willing *Syn* VOLUNTARY, deliberate, intentional, willful *Ant* instinctive, involuntary

willingness *Syn* ALACRITY, amenability, gameness, goodwill

willowy • able to bend easily without breaking *Syn* flexible, limber, lissome, lithe, pliable, pliant, supple *Rel* adaptable, ductile, elastic, fluid, malleable, modifiable, plastic, variable, yielding *Ant* inflexible, rigid, stiff

wilt *Syn* DROOP, flag, sag

wily *Syn* SLY, artful, crafty, cunning, foxy, guileful, insidious, tricky

win **1** *Syn* EARN, acquire, attain, capture, carry, draw, gain, garner, get, land, make, obtain, procure, realize, secure *Ant* forfeit, lose **2** *Syn* GET, gain, obtain, procure, secure

wince *Syn* RECOIL, blench, flinch, quail, shrink *Ant* confront, defy

wind • to follow a circular, spiral, or writhing course *Syn* coil, curl, entwine, twine, twist, wreathe *Rel* bend, curve

winding **1** • curving repeatedly first one way and then another *Syn* flexuous, serpentine, sinuous, tortuous *Rel* bending, curving, twisting *Ant* straight **2** *Syn* SPIRAL, coiling, corkscrew, helical, screwlike

window • an opening in the wall of a building that is usually covered with glass and serves to admit light and air *Syn* casement, oriel

windup *Syn* FINALE, close, closing, conclusion, consummation, end, ending, finis, finish *Ant* beginning, dawn, opening, start

wing **1** *Syn* ANNEX, ell, extension **2** *Syn* FACTION, bloc, body, coalition, party, sect, set, side

wink *Syn* INSTANT, flash, jiffy, minute, moment, second, shake, split second, trice, twinkle, twinkling

winner *Syn* VICTOR, champion, conqueror, vanquisher

winning **1** *Syn* LOVABLE, adorable, darling, dear, disarming, endearing, precious, sweet *Ant* abhorrent, abominable, detestable, hateful, odious, unlovable **2** *Syn* SWEET, dulcet, engaging, winsome *Ant* bitter, sour

win (over) *Syn* PERSUADE, argue, convince, get, induce, move, prevail (on *or* upon), satisfy, talk (into)

winsome *Syn* SWEET, dulcet, engaging, winning *Ant* bitter, sour

wipe *Syn* EXTERMINATE, deracinate, eradicate, extirpate, uproot

wire *Syn* CORD, cable, lace, lacing, line, rope, string

wisdom **1** *Syn* COMMON SENSE, discreetness, discretion, horse sense, levelheadedness, prudence, sense, sensibleness, wit *Ant* imprudence, indiscretion **2** *Syn* SENSE, common sense, good sense, gumption, horse sense, judgment

wise **1** • exercising or involving sound judgment *Syn* judicious, prudent, sage, sane, sapient, sensible *Rel* discreet, foresighted, prudent *Ant* simple **2** *Syn* EXPEDIENT, advisable, desirable, judicious, politic, prudent, tactical *Ant* imprudent, inadvisable, inexpedient, injudicious, unwise

wiseacre *Syn* SMART ALECK, smarty (*or* smartie), wise guy

wisecrack *vb Syn* JOKE, banter, fool, fun, jest, jive, josh, kid, quip

wisecrack *n Syn* JOKE, crack, gag, jape, jest, quip, witticism

wise guy *Syn* SMART ALECK, smarty (*or* smartie), wiseacre

wise (up) *Syn* ENLIGHTEN (sense 1), acquaint, advise, apprise, brief, clue, familiarize, fill in, inform, instruct, tell

wish *Syn* DESIRE, covet, crave, want

wishy-washy *Syn* INSIPID, banal, flat, inane, jejune, vapid *Ant* sapid, zestful

wit **1** • a mode of expression intended to arouse amusement *Syn* humor, irony, repartee, sarcasm, satire *Rel* alertness, brightness, brilliancy, cleverness, intelligence, quick-wittedness, smartness **2** *Syn* COMMON SENSE, discreetness, discretion, horse sense, levelheadedness, prudence, sense, sensibleness, wisdom *Ant* imprudence, indiscretion **3** *Syn* MIND, brain, intellect, intelligence, psyche, soul

witch *Syn* MAGICIAN (sense 1), charmer, conjurer (*or* conjuror), enchanter, necromancer, sorcerer, voodoo, wizard

witchcraft *Syn* MAGIC, alchemy, sorcery, thaumaturgy, witchery, wizardry

witchery *Syn* MAGIC, alchemy, sorcery, thaumaturgy, witchcraft, wizardry

with **1** *Syn* BECAUSE OF, due to, owing to, through **2** *Syn* BY, through

withdraw *Syn* GO, depart, leave, quit, retire *Ant* come

wither • to lose freshness and substance by or as if by loss of natural moisture *Syn* shrivel, wizen *Rel* desiccate, dry, parch

withhold *Syn* KEEP (sense 2), detain, hold back, keep back, keep out, reserve, retain *Ant* relinquish

without *Syn* BEYOND (sense 2), outside, outside of *Ant* within

withstand *Syn* RESIST, antagonize, combat, conflict, contest, fight, oppose *Ant* abide, submit

witness *vb* **1** *Syn* CERTIFY, attest, vouch **2** *Syn* TESTIFY, attest, depose, swear

witness *n* *Syn* SPECTATOR, beholder, bystander, eyewitness, kibitzer, looker-on, observer, onlooker

witticism *Syn* JOKE, crack, gag, jape, jest, quip, wisecrack

wittingly *Syn* INTENTIONALLY, consciously, deliberately, designedly, knowingly, purposefully, purposely, willfully *Ant* inadvertently, unconsciously, unintentionally, unknowingly, unwittingly

witty • provoking or intended to provoke laughter *Syn* facetious, humorous, jocose, jocular *Rel* amusing, diverting, entertaining

wizard **1** *Syn* EXPERT, ace, adept, artist, authority, crackerjack, maestro, master, past master, scholar, shark, virtuoso, whiz *Ant* amateur **2** *Syn* MAGICIAN (sense 1), charmer, conjurer (*or* conjuror), enchanter, necromancer, sorcerer, voodoo, witch

wizardry *Syn* MAGIC, alchemy, sorcery, thaumaturgy, witchcraft, witchery

wizen *Syn* WITHER, shrivel

wobble *Syn* SHAKE (sense 1), dither, quake, quaver, quiver, shimmy, shiver, shudder, teeter, totter, tremble

wobbling *Syn* HESITATION, faltering, hesitance, hesitancy, indecision, irresolution, shilly-shallying, vacillation, wavering

woe *Syn* SORROW, anguish, grief, heartache, heartbreak, regret *Ant* joy

woebegone *Syn* SAD (sense 1), bad, blue, brokenhearted, crestfallen, dejected, depressed, despondent, disconsolate, doleful, down, downcast, downhearted, droopy, forlorn, gloomy, glum, heartbroken, heartsick, heartsore, inconsolable, joyless, low, low-spirited, melancholy, miserable, mournful, saddened, sorrowful, sorry, unhappy, woeful, wretched *Ant* blissful, buoyant, buoyed, cheerful, cheery, chipper, delighted, glad, gladdened, gladsome, gleeful, happy, joyful, joyous, jubilant, sunny, upbeat

woeful **1** *Syn* REGRETTABLE, deplorable, distressful, distressing, grievous, heartbreaking, heartrending, lamentable, unfortunate **2** *Syn* SAD (sense 1), bad, blue, brokenhearted, crestfallen, dejected, depressed, despondent, disconsolate, doleful, down, downcast, downhearted, droopy, forlorn, gloomy, glum, heartbroken, heartsick, heartsore, inconsolable, joyless, low, low-spirited, melancholy, miserable, mournful, saddened, sorrowful, sorry, unhappy, woebegone, wretched *Ant* blissful, buoyant, buoyed, cheerful, cheery, chipper, delighted, glad, gladdened, gladsome, gleeful, happy, joyful, joyous, jubilant, sunny, upbeat

woman **1** • an adult female human being *Syn* FEMALE, lady **2** *Syn* GIRLFRIEND, gal, lady

womanish *Syn* FEMALE, feminine, ladylike, womanlike, womanly *Ant* male

womanlike *Syn* FEMALE, feminine, ladylike, womanish, womanly *Ant* male

womanly *Syn* FEMALE, feminine, ladylike, womanish, womanlike *Ant* male

wonder **1** • something that causes astonishment or admiration *Syn* marvel, miracle, phenomenon, prodigy **2** • the complex emotion aroused by the incomprehensible and especially the awe-inspiring *Syn* admiration, amazement, awe, wonderment *Rel* awe, fear, reverence

wonderful *Syn* EXCELLENT, A1, bang-up, banner, capital, classic, crackerjack, dandy, divine, fabulous, fine, first-class, first-rate, grand, great, groovy, heavenly, jim-dandy, keen, marvelous (*or* marvellous), mean, neat, nifty, noble, par excellence, prime, sensational, splendid, stellar, sterling, superb, superior, superlative, supernal, swell, terrific, tip-top, top, top-notch, unsurpassed *Ant* poor

wonderment *Syn* WONDER (sense 2), admiration, amazement, awe

wont *adj* *Syn* ACCUSTOMED, given, habituated, used *Ant* unaccustomed, unused

wont *n* *Syn* HABIT, custom, fashion, pattern, practice, trick, way

wonted *Syn* USUAL, accustomed, customary, habitual

woo *Syn* INVITE, bid, court, solicit

wooden *Syn* STIFF, inflexible, rigid, stark, tense *Ant* relaxed, supple

woolgathering *Syn* REVERIE, daydreaming, study, trance

woolly **1** *Syn* HAIRY (sense 1), bristly, fleecy, furry, hirsute, rough, shaggy, unshorn *Ant* bald, furless, hairless, shorn, smooth **2** *Syn* HAIRY (sense 2), furry, fuzzy, rough, shaggy

word *n* **1** • a pronounceable sound or combination of sounds that expresses and symbolizes an idea *Syn* term, vocable *Rel* expression, idiom, locution, phrase **2** *Syn* NEWS, information, intelligence, item, story, tidings **3** *Syn* PROMISE, oath, pledge, troth, vow

word *vb Syn* PHRASE, articulate, clothe, couch, express, formulate, put, say, state

wordless **1** *Syn* IMPLICIT, implied, tacit, unexpressed, unspoken, unvoiced *Ant* explicit, express, expressed, spoken, stated **2** *Syn* SILENT (sense 3), dumb, mum, mute, speechless, uncommunicative *Ant* communicative, speaking, talking

wordy • using or marked by the use of more words than are necessary to express the thought *Syn* diffuse, prolix, redundant, verbose *Rel* flatulent, inflated, tumid, turgid *Ant* compact, concise, crisp, pithy, succinct, terse

work *n* **1** • strenuous activity that involves difficulty and effort and usually affords no pleasure *Syn* drudgery, grind, labor, toil, travail *Rel* effort, exertion, pains, trouble *Ant* fun, play **2** • a sustained activity that affords one a livelihood *Syn* business, calling, employment, occupation, pursuit *Rel* art, craft, handicraft, profession, trade **3** • something brought into being by the exertion of effort and the exercise of skill *Syn* artifact, opus, product, production *Rel* article, object, thing **4** *Syn* OCCUPATION, calling, employment, line, profession, trade, vocation **5** *Syn* ROLE, capacity, function, job, part, place, position, purpose, task

work *vb* **1** *Syn* ACT (sense 1), behave, function, operate, react **2** *Syn* EFFECT, bring about, cause, create, effectuate, engender, generate, induce, make, produce, prompt, result (in), spawn, yield **3** *Syn* FUNCTION, act, perform, serve **4** *Syn* LABOR, drudge, endeavor, grub, hump, hustle, moil, peg (away), plod, plow, plug, slave, slog, strain, strive, struggle, sweat, toil, travail *Ant* dabble, fiddle (around), fool (around), mess (around), putter (around) **5** *Syn* SOLVE, answer, break, crack, dope (out), figure out, puzzle (out), resolve, riddle, unravel, work out

worker **1** • one who earns his living by labor and especially by manual labor *Syn* artisan, craftsman, hand, handicraftsman, laborer, mechanic, operative, roustabout, workingman, workman *Ant* idler **2** *Syn* SLAVE (sense 2), drudge, drudger, grubber, laborer, peon, plugger, slogger, toiler *Ant* freeman

workingman *Syn* WORKER, artisan, craftsman, hand, handicraftsman, laborer, mechanic, operative, roustabout, workman *Ant* idler

workman *Syn* WORKER, artisan, craftsman, hand, handicraftsman, laborer, mechanic, operative, roustabout, workingman *Ant* idler

work out *Syn* SOLVE, answer, break, crack, dope (out), figure out, puzzle (out), resolve, riddle, unravel, work

world *Syn* EARTH, globe, planet

worldly **1** *Syn* EARTHLY, earthy, mundane, sublunary, terrestrial **2** *Syn* WORLDLY-WISE, cosmopolitan, smart, sophisticated *Ant* ingenuous, innocent, naive, unsophisticated, unworldly, wide-eyed

worldly-wise • having a wide and refined knowledge of the world especially from personal experience *Syn* cosmopolitan, smart, sophisticated, worldly *Rel* suave, urbane *Ant* ingenuous, innocent, naive, unsophisticated, unworldly, wide-eyed

worn *Syn* HAGGARD, cadaverous, careworn, pinched, wasted

worried • distressed or troubled usually about something anticipated *Syn* anxious, careful, concerned, solicitous *Rel* afraid, apprehensive, fearful

worrisome *Syn* TROUBLESOME, discomforting, discomposing, disquieting, distressing, disturbing, perturbing, troubling, troublous, unsettling, upsetting *Ant* reassuring, untroublesome

worry *vb* • to disturb one or destroy one's peace of mind by repeated or persistent tormenting attacks *Syn* annoy, harass, harry, pester, plague, tantalize, tease *Rel* agitate, discompose, disquiet, disturb, perturb, upset

worry *n Syn* CARE, anxiety, concern, solicitude

worsen *Syn* DETERIORATE, crumble, decay, decline, degenerate, descend, ebb, rot, sink *Ant* ameliorate, improve, meliorate

worship *n* **1** • excessive admiration of or devotion to a person *Syn* adulation, deification, idolatry, idolization, worshipping *Rel* adoration, deference, glorification, reverence, veneration **2** *Syn* REVERENCE (sense 1), adoration, veneration

worship *vb* **1** *Syn* IDOLIZE, adore, adulate, canonize, deify, dote (on) **2** *Syn* REVERE, adore, reverence, venerate *Ant* flout

worshipping *Syn* WORSHIP, adulation, deification, idolatry, idolization

worthy • having sufficient worth or merit to receive one's honor, esteem, or reward *Syn* deserving, good, meritorious *Rel* admirable, commendable, creditable, laudable, praiseworthy *Ant* no-good, undeserving, valueless, worthless

wound • an injury to the body *Syn* bruise, contusion, lesion, trauma, traumatism *Rel* hurt, injury

wraith *Syn* GHOST, apparition, bogey, phantasm, phantom, poltergeist, shade, shadow, specter (*or* spectre), spirit, spook, vision

wrangle *Syn* QUARREL, altercation, bickering, spat, squabble, tiff

wrap *Syn* COVER, envelop, overspread, shroud, veil *Ant* bare
wrap up *Syn* SUMMARIZE, abstract, digest, encapsulate, epitomize, outline, recap, recapitulate, sum up
wrath *Syn* ANGER, angriness, furor, fury, indignation, irateness, ire, outrage, rage, spleen, wrathfulness *Ant* delight, pleasure
wrathful *Syn* ANGRY, angered, apoplectic, enraged, foaming, fuming, furious, incensed, indignant, inflamed, infuriated, irate, ireful, mad, outraged, rabid, riled, roiled, sore, steaming, wroth *Ant* delighted, pleased
wrathfulness *Syn* ANGER, angriness, furor, fury, indignation, irateness, ire, outrage, rage, spleen, wrath *Ant* delight, pleasure
wreathe *Syn* WIND, coil, curl, entwine, twine, twist
wreck *Syn* RUIN, dilapidate
wreckage *Syn* DESTRUCTION, annihilation, decimation, demolishment, demolition, desolation, devastation, extermination, extinction, havoc, loss, obliteration, ruin, ruination, wastage *Ant* building, construction, erection, raising
wrench • to turn or twist forcibly *Syn* wrest, wring *Rel* bend, curve, twist
wrest *Syn* WRENCH, wring
wrestle • to struggle with an opponent at close quarters *Syn* grapple, scuffle, tussle *Rel* battle, contend, fight, war
wretched *Syn* SAD, bad, blue, brokenhearted, crestfallen, dejected, depressed, despondent, disconsolate, doleful, down, downcast, downhearted, droopy, forlorn, gloomy, glum, heartbroken, heartsick, heartsore, inconsolable, joyless, low, low-spirited, melancholy, miserable, mournful, saddened, sorrowful, sorry, unhappy, woebegone, woeful *Ant* blissful, buoyant, buoyed, cheerful, cheery, chipper, delighted, glad, gladdened, gladsome, gleeful, happy, joyful, joyous, jubilant, sunny, upbeat
wring *Syn* WRENCH, wrest
writhe • to twist or turn in physical or mental distress *Syn* agonize, squirm *Rel* bend, curve, twist
wrong *adv* • off the desired or intended path or course *Syn* afield, amiss, astray, awry *Rel* badly *Ant* aright, right, well
wrong *vb* • to inflict injury without just cause or in an outrageous manner *Syn* aggrieve, oppress, persecute *Rel* abuse, ill-treat, maltreat, mistreat, outrage
wrong *adj* **1** *Syn* BAD (sense 2), poor *Ant* good **2** *Syn* INAPPROPRIATE, graceless, improper, inapt, incongruous, incorrect, indecorous, inept, infelicitous, unapt, unbecoming, unfit, unhappy, unseemly, unsuitable *Ant* appropriate, becoming, befitting, correct, decorous, felicitous, fit, fitting, genteel, happy, meet, proper, right, seemly, suitable
wrong *n* **1** *Syn* DISSERVICE, injury, injustice, raw deal *Ant* justice **2** *Syn* EVIL, bad, evildoing, ill, immorality, iniquity, sin, villainy *Ant* good, morality, right, virtue
wrongdoing *Syn* MISCONDUCT, malfeasance, misbehavior, misdoing
wroth *Syn* ANGRY, angered, apoplectic, enraged, foaming, fuming, furious, incensed, indignant, inflamed, infuriated, irate, ireful, mad, outraged, rabid, riled, roiled, sore, steaming, wrathful *Ant* delighted, pleased

Y

yammer *Syn* COMPLAIN, beef, bellyache, carp, crab, croak, fuss, gripe, grouse, growl, grumble, kick, moan, murmur, mutter, repine, squawk, wail, whine *Ant* rejoice
yank *Syn* JERK, snap, twitch
yap *Syn* BARK, bay, growl, howl, snarl, yelp
yardstick *Syn* STANDARD, criterion, gauge, touchstone
yarn *Syn* STORY, anecdote, narrative, tale
yearn *Syn* LONG, hanker, hunger, pine, thirst
yeast *Syn* FOAM, froth, lather, scum, spume, suds
yell *vb* **1** *Syn* SCREAM, howl, screech, shriek, shrill, squall, squeal, yelp **2** *Syn* SHOUT, holler, scream, screech, shriek, squeal, whoop
yell *n* *Syn* SHOUT, holler, scream, screech, shriek, squeal, whoop
yellow *Syn* COWARDLY, chicken, chickenhearted, craven, dastardly, lily-livered, pusillanimous, recreant, spineless, unheroic *Ant* brave, courageous, daring, dauntless, doughty, fearless, gallant, greathearted, gutsy, hardy, heroic, intrepid, lionhearted, stalwart, stout, stouthearted, valiant, valorous
yelp **1** *Syn* BARK, bay, growl, howl, snarl, yap **2** *Syn* SCREAM, howl, screech, shriek, shrill, squall, squeal, yell
yesterday *Syn* PAST, auld lang syne, history, yesteryear, yore
yesteryear *Syn* PAST, auld lang syne, history, yesterday, yore
yield **1** • to give way before a force that one cannot further resist *Syn* bow, capitulate, cave, defer, relent, submit, succumb *Rel*

cede, relinquish, surrender, waive **2** *Syn* BEAR (sense 1), produce, turn out **3** *Syn* EFFECT, bring about, cause, create, effectuate, engender, generate, induce, make, produce, prompt, result (in), spawn, work **4** *Syn* RELINQUISH, abandon, cede, leave, resign, surrender, waive *Ant* keep

yielding *Syn* PASSIVE, acquiescent, nonresistant, resigned, tolerant, tolerating, unresistant, unresisting *Ant* protesting, resistant, resisting, unyielding

yoke *Syn* COUPLE, brace, pair

yokel *Syn* HICK, bumpkin, clodhopper, countryman, provincial, rustic *Ant* cosmopolitan, sophisticate

yore *Syn* PAST, auld lang syne, history, yesterday, yesteryear

young *adj* • being in the early stage of life, growth, or development *Syn* adolescent, immature, juvenile, youngish, youthful *Rel* minor, underage *Ant* adult, full-grown, mature, matured

young *n Syn* OFFSPRING, descendants, issue, posterity, progeny

youngish *Syn* YOUNG, adolescent, immature, juvenile, youthful *Ant* adult, full-grown, mature, matured

youth • the period in life when one passes from childhood to maturity *Syn* adolescence, puberty, pubescence *Ant* age

youthful *Syn* YOUNG, adolescent, immature, juvenile, youngish *Ant* adult, full-grown, mature, matured

yo-yo *Syn* FOOL (sense 2), booby, goose, halfwit, jackass, lunatic, nincompoop, ninny, nitwit, nut, simpleton, turkey

Z

zeal *Syn* PASSION, ardor, enthusiasm, fervor

zealot **1** • one who is intensely or excessively devoted to a cause *Syn* crusader, fanatic, militant, partisan *Rel* activist **2** *Syn* ENTHUSIAST, fanatic

zenith *Syn* SUMMIT, acme, apex, apogee, climax, culmination, meridian, peak, pinnacle

zip *Syn* HURRY (sense 2), barrel, bolt, bowl, breeze, career, course, dash, fly, hasten, hotfoot (it), hump, hurtle, hustle, pelt, race, rip, rocket, run, rush, rustle, scoot, scurry, scuttle, shoot, speed, step (along), tear, trot, whirl, whisk, zip, zoom *Ant* crawl, creep, poke

zone **1** *Syn* AREA, belt, region, tract **2** *Syn* REGION, area, demesne, field

zoom *Syn* HURRY (sense 2), barrel, bolt, bowl, breeze, career, course, dash, fly, hasten, hotfoot (it), hump, hurtle, hustle, pelt, race, rip, rocket, run, rush, rustle, scoot, scurry, scuttle, shoot, speed, step (along), tear, trot, whirl, whisk, zip *Ant* crawl, creep, poke

CANADA
MEXICO
PACIFIC OCEAN
ATLANTIC OCEAN
Gulf of Mexico
ROCKY MOUNTAINS
GREAT BASIN
GREAT PLAINS
CUBA
BAHAMAS
RUSSIA
BERING SEA
ALEUTIAN ISLANDS
Gulf of Alaska
HAWAII
CHICAGO Cities over 1,000,000
Memphis Cities 500,000 to 1,000,000
Charlotte Cities 100,000 to 500,000
Harlingen Cities 50,000 to 100,000
Monterey Cities under 50,000
Capital
City
Point of interest
Dam
Intermittent river
National park
Indian reservations
Scale 1: 31,655,000
Albers Equal-Area
Scale 1: 25,839,000
Scale 1: 72,547,000
NEW YORK CITY
LOS ANGELES
CHICAGO
HOUSTON
PHOENIX
PHILADELPHIA
SAN DIEGO
DALLAS
DETROIT
Washington, D.C.

WORLD

ARCTIC
QUEEN ELIZABETH ISLANDS
Greenland (Denmark)
GREENLAND SEA
Baffin Bay
Baffin I.
Victoria I.
CHUKCHI SEA
BEAUFORT SEA
BROOKS RANGE
Alaska (U.S.)
Arctic Circle
Yukon
Fairbanks
ALASKA RANGE
Mt. Denali
BERING SEA
Anchorage
Mackenzie
Great Bear L.
Great Slave L.
Peace
Hudson Bay
LABRADOR SEA
Reykjavík
ICELAND
Gulf of Alaska
ALEUTIAN ISLANDS
C A N A D A
Edmonton
Saskatoon
Calgary
Winnipeg
Vancouver
Seattle
Portland
L. Superior
L. Huron
L. Michigan
Minneapolis
Chicago
Detroit
Toronto
Ottawa
Quebec
Montreal
Boston
Halifax
Island of Newfoundland
St. John's
Gulf of St. Lawrence
IRELAND
Dublin
U.K.
London
FRANCE
PORTUGAL
Lisbon
Madrid
SPAIN
U N I T E D S T A T E S
Snake
Missouri
Ohio
APPALACHIAN MTS.
New York City
Philadelphia
Washington, D.C.
San Francisco
Las Vegas
Colorado
Denver
Arkansas
Kansas City
St. Louis
Memphis
Oklahoma City
Dallas
Mississippi
Los Angeles
San Diego
Phoenix
Atlanta
Bermuda (U.K.)
ATLANTIC OCEAN
AZORES (Portugal)
MADEIRA IS. (Portugal)
Rabat
Casablanca
MOROCCO
CANARY IS. (Spain)
El Aaiún
Western Sahara (Morocco)
MAURITANIA
Juárez
Rio Grande
Houston
Baja California
SIERRA MADRE OCCIDENTAL
MEXICO
Monterrey
Gulf of Mexico
Miami
Nassau
THE BAHAMAS
TURKS AND CAICOS (U.K.)
Havana
CUBA
Santo Domingo
Puerto Rico (U.S.)
VIRGIN IS. (U.S.-U.K.)
ANTIGUA AND BARBUDA
ST. KITTS AND NEVIS
Guadeloupe (Fr.)
DOMINICA
Martinique (Fr.)
ST. LUCIA
BARBADOS
Tropic of Cancer
HAWAIIAN IS. (U.S.)
Guadalajara
Bay of Campeche
Mexico City
JAMAICA
HAITI
Port-au-Prince
Kingston
DOMINICAN REPUBLIC
Belmopan
BELIZE
Tegucigalpa
HONDURAS
Guatemala City
GUATEMALA
San Salvador
EL SALVADOR
NICARAGUA
Managua
CARIBBEAN SEA
ST. VINCENT AND THE GRENADINES
GRENADA
TRINIDAD AND TOBAGO
Barranquilla
Maracaibo
Caracas
San José
COSTA RICA
Panama City
PANAMA
Orinoco
LLANOS
VENEZUELA
GUYANA
Georgetown
SURINAME
Paramaribo
Cayenne
French Guiana (FR.)
GUIANA HIGHLANDS
Nouakchott
CAPE VERDE
Praia
GAMBIA
Dakar
SENEGAL
Banjul
Bamako
Bissau
GUINEA-BISSAU
Conakry
GUINEA
Freetown
SIERRA LEONE
Monrovia
LIBERIA
BURKINA FASO
Ouagadougou
CÔTE D'IVOIRE
GHANA
Abidjan
Accra
N
PACIFIC OCEAN
Palmyra Atoll (U.S.)
Cali
Bogotá
COLOMBIA
Equator
GALÁPAGOS IS. (Ecuador)
Quito
ECUADOR
Guayaquil
Iquitos
Manaus
Amazon
Belém
Fortaleza
Gulf of Guinea
KIRIBATI
Madeira
Tapajós
Xingu
Tocantins
São Francisco
Recife
B R A Z I L
PERU
ANDES
Ucayali
COOK IS. (N.Z.)
SAMOA
AMERICAN SAMOA (U.S.)
FRENCH POLYNESIA (France)
Lima
L. Titicaca
La Paz
BRAZILIAN HIGHLANDS
Brasília
Salvador
Arequipa
BOLIVIA
Sucre
TONGA
Tropic of Capricorn
Belo Horizonte
PARAGUAY
Paraná
Rio de Janeiro
Antofagasta
ATACAMA DESERT
GRAN CHACO
Asunción
São Paulo
San Felix I.
San Ambrosia I.
Córdoba
Porto Alegre
Mt. Aconcagua
Rosario
URUGUAY
Montevideo
Buenos Aires
PAMPAS
JUAN FERNÁNDEZ ISLANDS
Santiago
Concepción
ARGENTINA
ATLANTIC OCEAN
CHILE
Chiloé I.
PATAGONIA
Scale at equator
1: 125,202,000
0 500 1000 1500 2000 mi
0 1000 2000 3000 km
Robinson
FALKLAND IS. (U.K.)
SOUTH GEORGIA (U.K.)
Tierra del Fuego
Cape Horn
Antarctic Circle
Alexander I.
ANTARCTIC PEN.
WEDDELL SEA
Berkner I.
MARIE BYRD LAND
TRANSANTARCTIC MOUNTAINS
150° W
120° W
90° W
60° W
30° W
60° N
30° N
0°
30° S
60° S

OCEAN
30° E
60° E
90° E
120° E
150° E
FRANZ JOSEF LAND
SVALBARD (Norway)
NORWEGIAN SEA
NOVAYA ZEMLYA
KARA SEA
NEW SIBERIAN IS.
EAST SIBERIAN SEA
VERKHOYANSK MTS.
Arctic Circle
KOLYMA MTS.
URAL MOUNTAINS
WEST SIBERIAN PLAIN
RUSSIA
Lower Tunguska
Yenisey
Lena
Kolyma
Arkhangelsk
NORWAY
SWEDEN
FINLAND
Helsinki
Stockholm
Oslo
St. Petersburg
EST.
Tallinn
LAT.
LITH.
Vilnius
Moscow
Nizhniy Novgorod
Kazan
Perm
Yekaterinburg
Chelyabinsk
Ufa
Samara
Omsk
Novosibirsk
Krasnoyarsk
Novokuznetsk
Barnaul
Yakutsk
Irkutsk
Chita
Lake Baikal
STANOVOY MTS.
SEA OF OKHOTSK
KAMCHATKA PEN.
BERING SEA
60° N
NORTH SEA
DEN.
Copenhagen
NETH.
Berlin
POL.
Minsk
BELARUS
GER.
CZ. REP.
Warsaw
Kiev
UKRAINE
BEL.
Paris
SW.
AUS.
HUN.
SLVK.
MOL.
ROM.
Bucharest
SERB.
B.-H.
SL.
CR.
ITALY
MONT.
KOS.
BUL.
ALB.
MAC.
Rome
GREECE
Athens
Ankara
TURKEY
GEORGIA
Tbilisi
ARMENIA
AZERBAIJAN
Volgograd
KAZAKHSTAN
Astana
ARAL SEA
L. Balkhash
CASPIAN SEA
BLACK SEA
UZBEKISTAN
TURKMENISTAN
Ashkhabad
Tashkent
Bishkek
Almaty
KYRGYZSTAN
TAJIKISTAN
TIAN SHAN
GOBI DESERT
MONGOLIA
Ulaanbaatar
Amur
Khabarovsk
Sakhalin
Harbin
Vladivostok
Hokkaido
Shenyang
NORTH KOREA
Pyongyang
Beijing
Tianjin
Seoul
SOUTH KOREA
JAPAN
Honshu
Tokyo
Pusan
Osaka
Kyushu
Shikoku
YELLOW SEA
Huang He
KUNLUN MTS.
CHINA
Lanzhou
Xi'an
PACIFIC OCEAN
Algiers
MTNS.
Tunis
TUNISIA
Tripoli
MEDITERRANEAN SEA
CYPRUS
LEBANON
SYRIA
Damascus
ISRAEL
Jerusalem
JORDAN
IRAQ
Baghdad
Tehran
IRAN
ZAGROS MOUNTAINS
AFGHANISTAN
Kabul
Islamabad
Lahore
PAKISTAN
PLATEAU OF TIBET
Chang (Yangtze)
Nanjing
Wuhan
Shanghai
Chongqing
Alexandria
Cairo
KUWAIT
Kuwait
BAHRAIN
Riyadh
QATAR
U.A.E.
Masqat
OMAN
Persian Gulf
SAUDI ARABIA
Jiddah
RUB' AL KHALI DESERT
ALGERIA
LIBYA
EGYPT
SAHARA
L. Nasser
Nile
RED SEA
AHAGGAR MTS.
TIBESTI MTS.
NIGER
SAHEL
CHAD
L. Chad
Niamey
N'Djamena
Khartoum
SUDAN
Asmara
ERITREA
Sanaa
YEMEN
Gulf of Aden
Socotra (Yemen)
DJIBOUTI
Djibouti
Cape Gwardafuy
Addis Ababa
ETHIOPIA
ETHIOPIAN PLATEAU
SOMALIA
Mogadishu
NIGERIA
Abuja
BENIN
TOGO
Porto-Novo
CAMEROON
Yaoundé
C.A.R.
Bangui
Malabo
EQ. GUINEA
GABON
REP. OF THE CONGO
Congo
Libreville
Brazzaville
Kinshasa
Cabinda (ANGOLA)
UGANDA
Kampala
KENYA
Nairobi
RWANDA
Kigali
BURUNDI
Bujumbura
Lake Victoria
Kilimanjaro
DEM. REP. OF THE CONGO
Dodoma
Dar es Salaam
TANZANIA
Lake Tanganyika
Luanda
ANGOLA
MALAWI
Lake Malawi
Lilongwe
Moroni
COMOROS
ZAMBIA
Lusaka
Kubango
MOZAMBIQUE
Mozambique Channel
Antananarivo
MADAGASCAR
NAMIBIA
Windhoek
NAMIB DESERT
ZIMBABWE
Harare
BOTSWANA
Gaborone
Pretoria
Johannesburg
Maputo
Mbabane
SWAZILAND
Maseru
LESOTHO
Orange
SOUTH AFRICA
Cape Town
Cape of Good Hope
Victoria
SEYCHELLES
BRITISH INDIAN OCEAN TERRITORY (U.K.)
MALDIVES
Male
Colombo
SRI LANKA
ARABIAN SEA
Mumbai
Hyderabad
Bengaluru
Chennai
Ahmadabad
Karachi
Delhi
New Delhi
Indus
Ganges
INDIA
Nagpur
Kolkata
NEPAL
Mount Everest
Kathmandu
BHUTAN
Thimphu
Lhasa
BANGLADESH
Dhaka
Bay of Bengal
ANDAMAN IS. (India)
NICOBAR IS. (India)
MYANMAR
Naypyidaw
Yangon
LAOS
Vientiane
Hanoi
THAILAND
Bangkok
CAMBODIA
Phnom Penh
VIETNAM
Ho Chi Minh City
Xi
Guangzhou
HONG KONG
TAIWAN
Taibei
Gaoxiong
Tropic of Cancer
SOUTH CHINA SEA
PHILIPPINE SEA
Luzon
Manila
PHILIPPINES
Mindanao
Melekeok
PALAU
NORTHERN MARIANA IS. (U.S.)
Guam (U.S.)
MIDWAY IS. (U.S.)
30° N
FEDERATED STATES OF MICRONESIA
Palikir
MARSHALL IS.
Majuro
Bairiki
KIRIBATI
Equator
0°
Medan
Kuala Lumpur
MALAYSIA
BRUNEI
Bandar Seri Begawan
SINGAPORE
Sumatra
Borneo
Sulawesi
Palembang
INDONESIA
Jakarta
Bandung
Semarang
Surabaya
Java
Dili
EAST TIMOR
ARAFURA SEA
New Guinea
PAPUA NEW GUINEA
Port Moresby
SOLOMON ISLANDS
Honiara
TUVALU
Funafuti
VANUATU
Port-Vila
FIJI
Suva
New Caledonia (Fr.)
Tropic of Capricorn
CORAL SEA
Great Barrier Reef
ARNHEM LAND
GREAT DIVIDING RANGE
GREAT SANDY DESERT
GREAT ARTESIAN BASIN
AUSTRALIA
GREAT VICTORIA DESERT
Darling
Brisbane
Perth
Sydney
Adelaide
Canberra
Melbourne
Great Australian Bight
Tasmania
Hobart
TASMAN SEA
Auckland
NEW ZEALAND
Wellington
30° S
INDIAN OCEAN
KEELING IS. (Austl.)
MAURITIUS
Port Louis
Réunion (Fr.)
Amsterdam I. (Fr.)
Saint Paul I. (Fr.)
CROZET IS. (Fr.)
PRINCE EDWARD IS. (South Africa)
Kerguelen I. (Fr.)
AUCKLAND IS. (N.Z.)
60° S
Antarctic Circle
Abbreviations for European countries:
ALB. Albania
AUS. Austria
BEL. Belgium
B.-H. Bosnia and Herzegovina
BUL. Bulgaria
CR. Croatia
CZ. REP. Czech Republic
DEN. Denmark
EST. Estonia
GER. Germany
HUN. Hungary
KOS. Kosovo
LAT. Latvia
LITH. Lithuania
MAC. Macedonia
MOL. Moldova
MONT. Montenegro
NETH. Netherlands
POL. Poland
ROM. Romania
SERB. Serbia
SLVK. Slovakia
SL. Slovenia
SW. Switzerland
U.K. United Kingdom
ENDERBY LAND
QUEEN MAUD LAND
WILKES LAND
VICTORIA LAND
ROSS SEA
ANTARCTICA
© 2010 Encyclopædia Britannica, Inc.

ATLAS

NORTH AMERICA

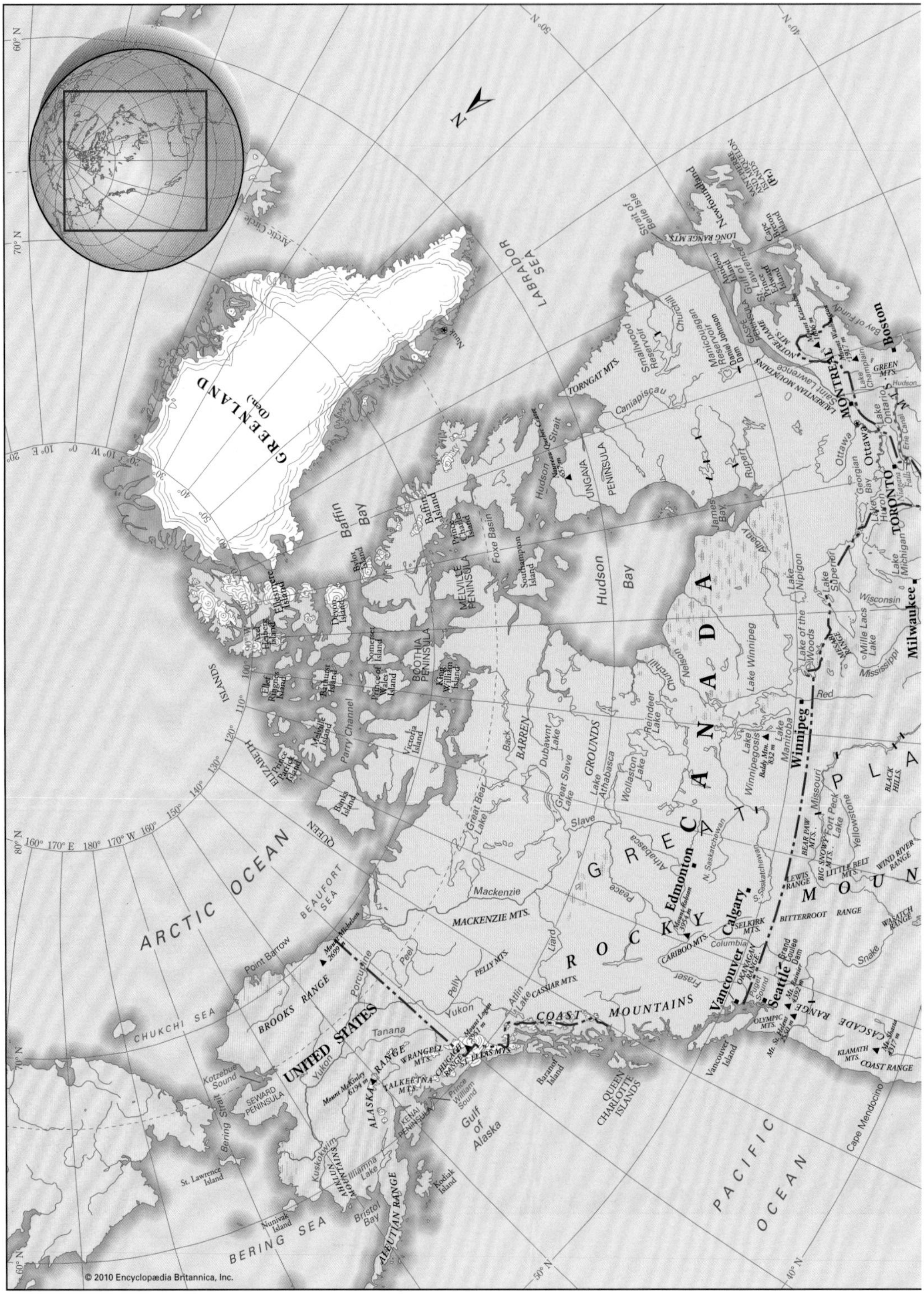

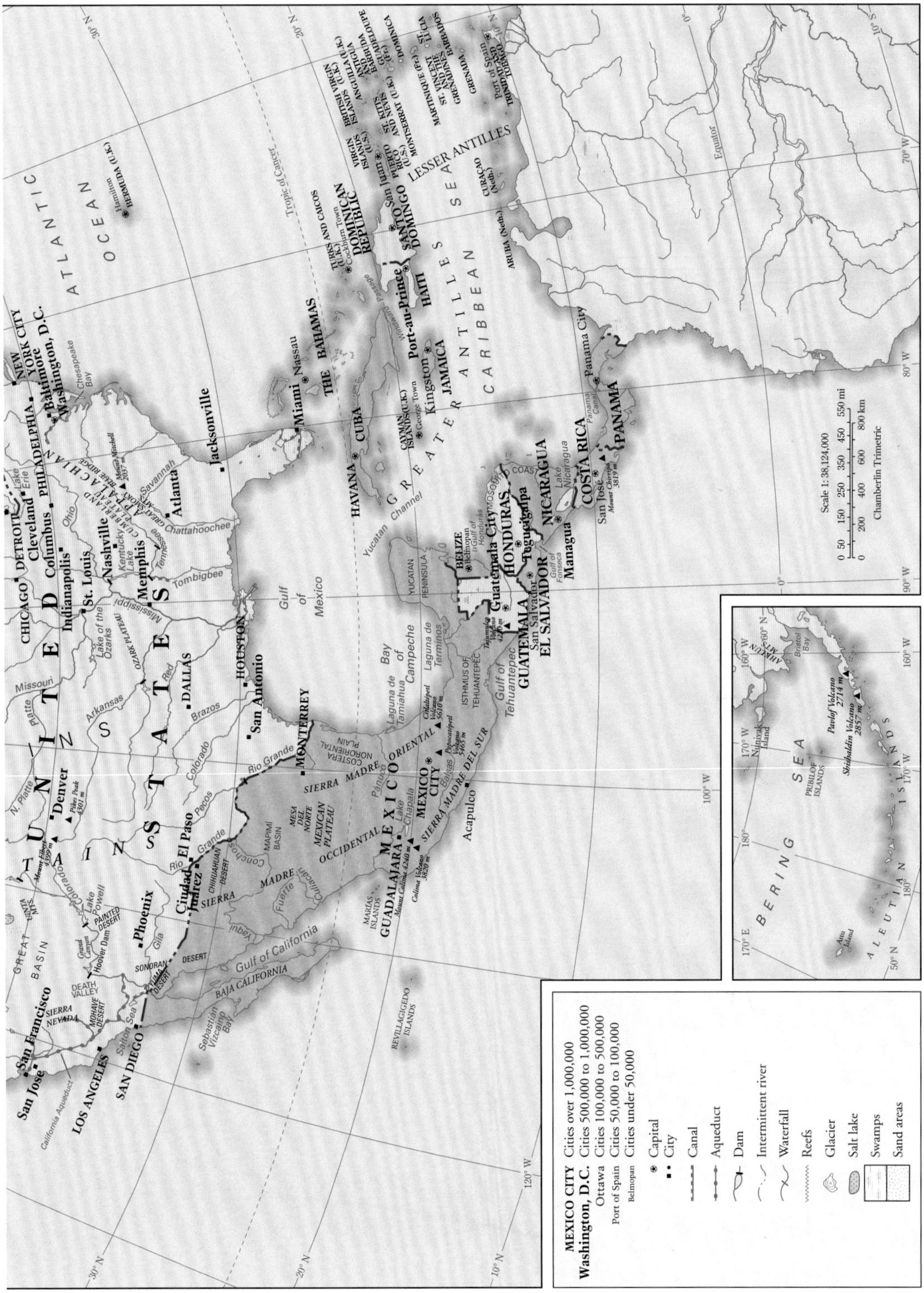
MEXICO CITY Cities over 1,000,000
Washington, D.C. Cities 500,000 to 1,000,000
Ottawa Cities 100,000 to 500,000
Port of Spain Cities 50,000 to 100,000
Belmopan Cities under 50,000
Capital
City
Canal
Aqueduct
Dam
Intermittent river
Waterfall
Reefs
Glacier
Salt lake
Swamps
Sand areas
Scale 1: 38,124,000
Chamberlin Trimetric
UNITED STATES
MEXICO
ATLANTIC OCEAN
CARIBBEAN SEA
Gulf of Mexico
BERMUDA (U.K.)
THE BAHAMAS
CUBA
HAITI
DOMINICAN REPUBLIC
JAMAICA
GREATER ANTILLES
LESSER ANTILLES
BELIZE
GUATEMALA
HONDURAS
EL SALVADOR
NICARAGUA
COSTA RICA
PANAMA
BERING SEA
ALEUTIAN ISLANDS
PRIBILOF ISLANDS
Tropic of Cancer
Equator
San Francisco
LOS ANGELES
SAN DIEGO
Phoenix
Denver
El Paso
Ciudad Juárez
DALLAS
HOUSTON
San Antonio
MONTERREY
GUADALAJARA
MEXICO CITY
Acapulco
CHICAGO
DETROIT
Cleveland
Columbus
Indianapolis
St. Louis
Memphis
Nashville
Atlanta
Jacksonville
Miami
PHILADELPHIA
NEW YORK CITY
Baltimore
Washington, D.C.
HAVANA
Nassau
Kingston
Port-au-Prince
SANTO DOMINGO
San Juan
Panama City
San José
Managua
Tegucigalpa
Guatemala City
San Salvador
Belmopan

ATLAS

CANADA

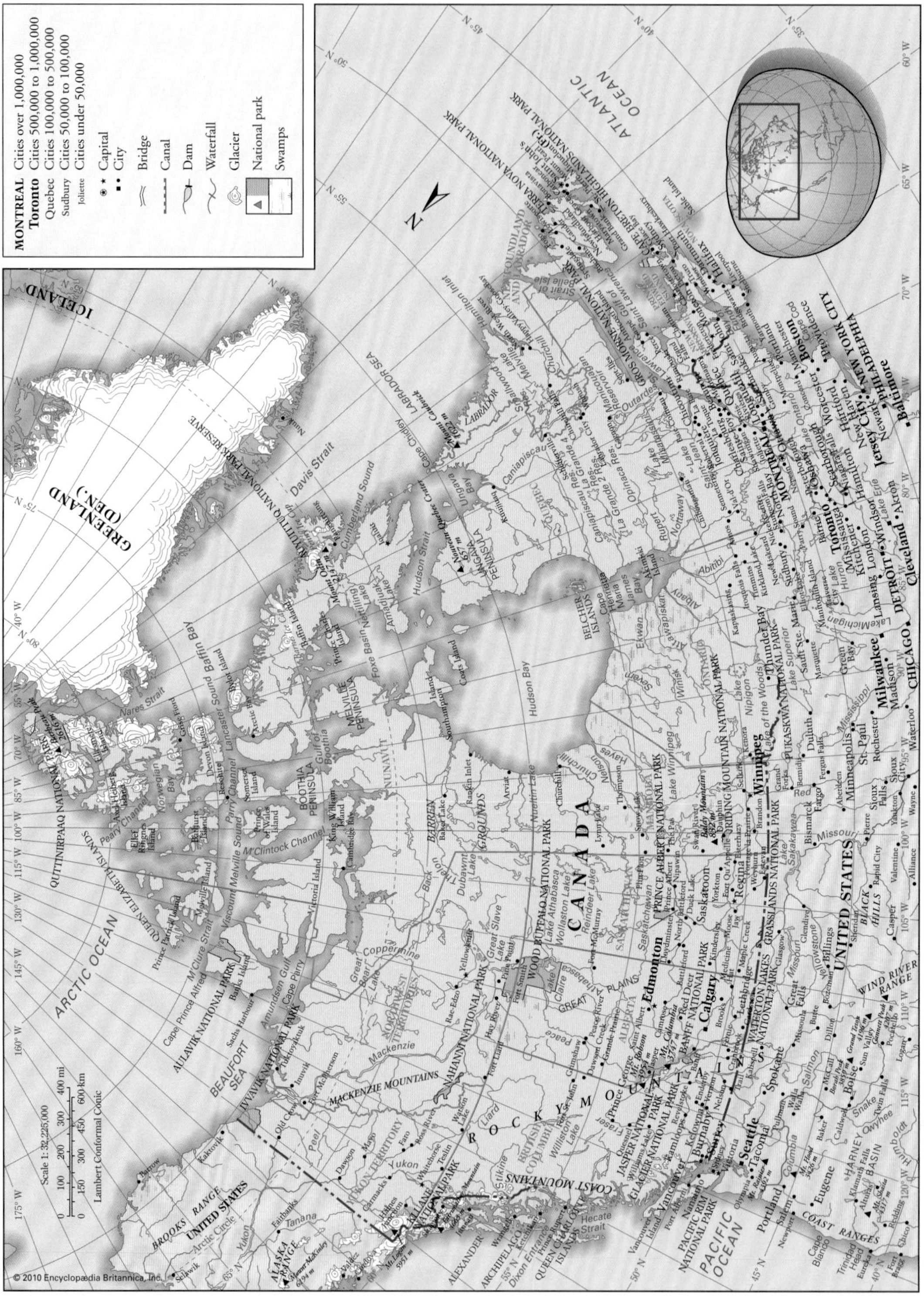

MONTREAL Cities over 1,000,000
Toronto Cities 500,000 to 1,000,000
Quebec Cities 100,000 to 500,000
Sudbury Cities 50,000 to 100,000
Joliette Cities under 50,000
Capital
City
Bridge
Canal
Dam
Waterfall
Glacier
National park
Swamps
Scale 1: 32,225,000
Lambert Conformal Conic
ARCTIC OCEAN
ATLANTIC OCEAN
PACIFIC OCEAN
BEAUFORT SEA
LABRADOR SEA
GREENLAND (DEN.)
ICELAND
Hudson Bay
Baffin Bay
Davis Strait
Hudson Strait
CANADA
UNITED STATES
ROCKY MOUNTAINS
MACKENZIE MOUNTAINS
COAST MOUNTAINS
GREAT PLAINS
QUEEN ELIZABETH ISLANDS
NUNAVUT
QUEBEC
MONTREAL
Toronto
Winnipeg
Edmonton
Calgary
Vancouver
Seattle
Regina
Saskatoon
Thunder Bay
Quebec
Halifax
CHICAGO
DETROIT
Cleveland
Boston
NEW YORK CITY
PHILADELPHIA
Baltimore
Milwaukee
© 2010 Encyclopædia Britannica, Inc.

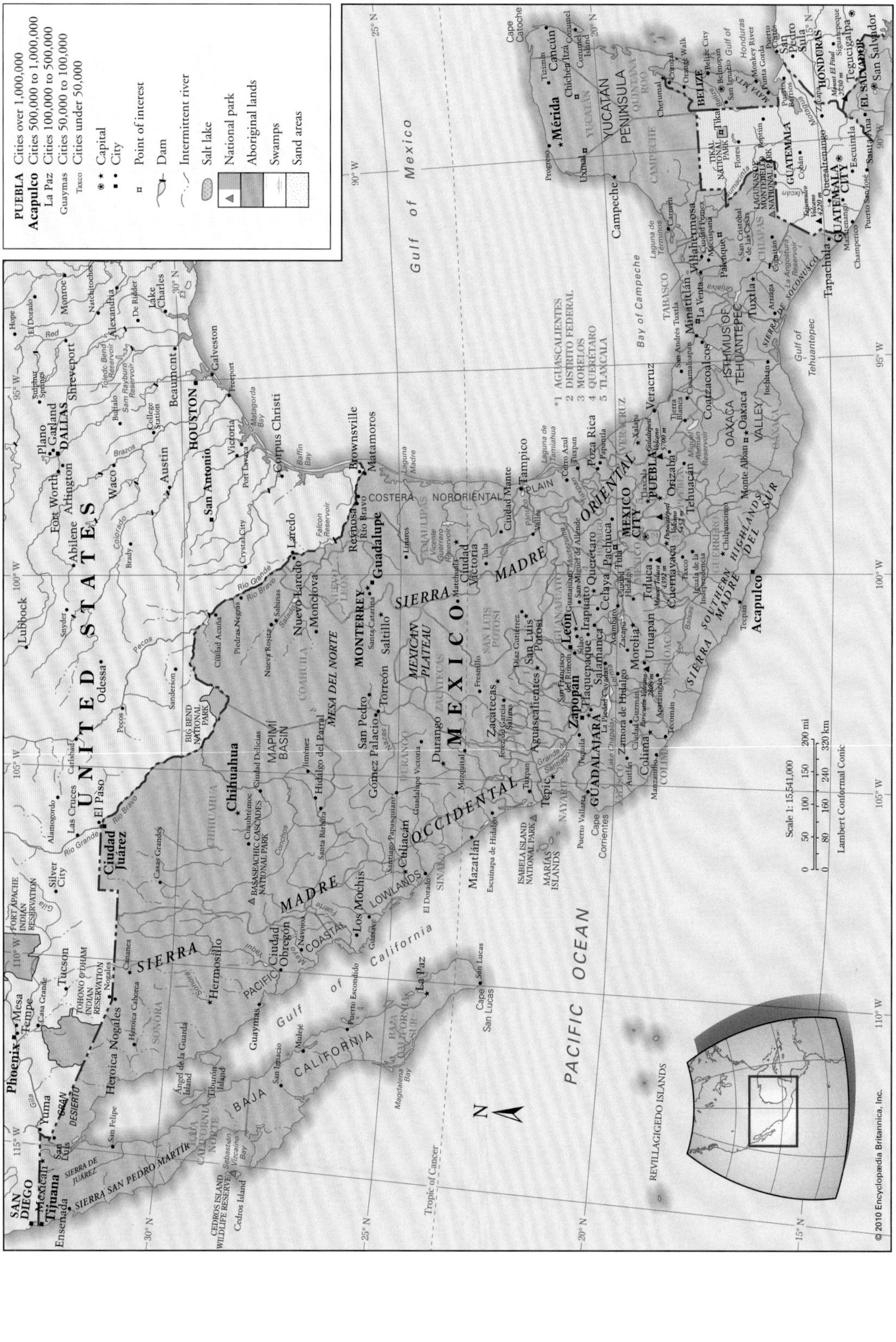
PUEBLA Cities over 1,000,000
Acapulco Cities 500,000 to 1,000,000
La Paz Cities 100,000 to 500,000
Guaymas Cities 50,000 to 100,000
Taxco Cities under 50,000
Capital
City
Point of interest
Dam
Intermittent river
Salt lake
National park
Aboriginal lands
Swamps
Sand areas
UNITED STATES
MEXICO
Gulf of Mexico
PACIFIC OCEAN
Gulf of California
BAJA CALIFORNIA
SIERRA MADRE OCCIDENTAL
SIERRA MADRE ORIENTAL
SIERRA MADRE DEL SUR
MEXICAN PLATEAU
YUCATAN PENINSULA
Bay of Campeche
Gulf of Tehuantepec
ISTHMUS OF TEHUANTEPEC
MEXICO CITY
GUADALAJARA
MONTERREY
PUEBLA
Acapulco
Mérida
Cancún
Chihuahua
Ciudad Juárez
Tijuana
Hermosillo
HOUSTON
DALLAS
San Antonio
GUATEMALA
BELIZE
HONDURAS
EL SALVADOR
REVILLAGIGEDO ISLANDS
Tropic of Cancer
Scale 1: 15,541,000
Lambert Conformal Conic
© 2010 Encyclopædia Britannica, Inc.

THE CARIBBEAN

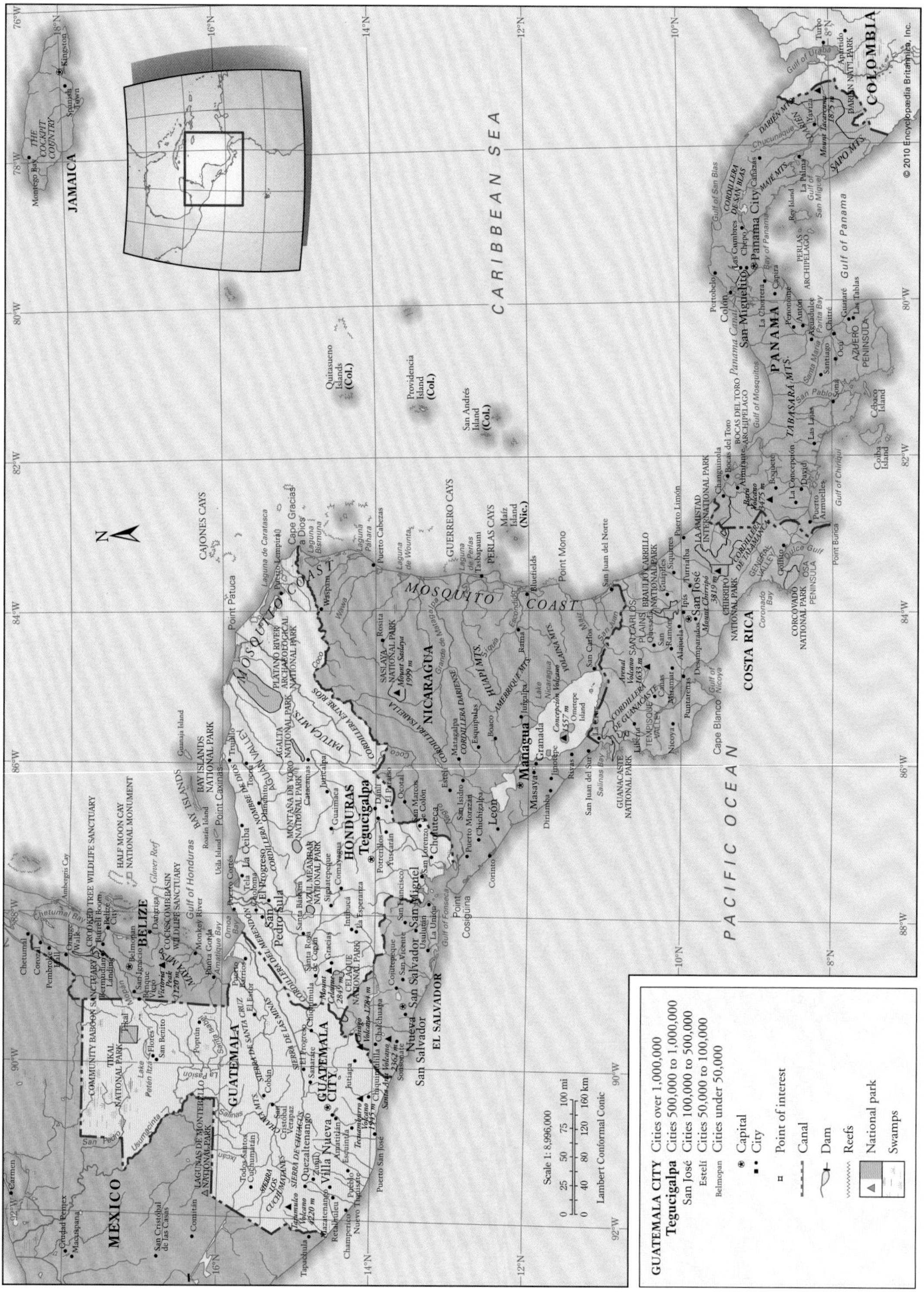
GUATEMALA CITY Cities over 1,000,000
Tegucigalpa Cities 500,000 to 1,000,000
San José Cities 100,000 to 500,000
Estelí Cities 50,000 to 100,000
Belmopan Cities under 50,000
Capital
City
Point of interest
Canal
Dam
Reefs
National park
Swamps
Scale 1: 8,996,000
0 25 50 75 100 mi
0 40 80 120 160 km
Lambert Conformal Conic
MEXICO
BELIZE
GUATEMALA
HONDURAS
EL SALVADOR
NICARAGUA
COSTA RICA
PANAMA
COLOMBIA
JAMAICA
CARIBBEAN SEA
PACIFIC OCEAN
GUATEMALA CITY
Tegucigalpa
San Salvador
Managua
San José
Panama City
Belmopan
Kingston
MOSQUITO COAST
© 2010 Encyclopædia Britannica, Inc.

SOUTH AMERICA

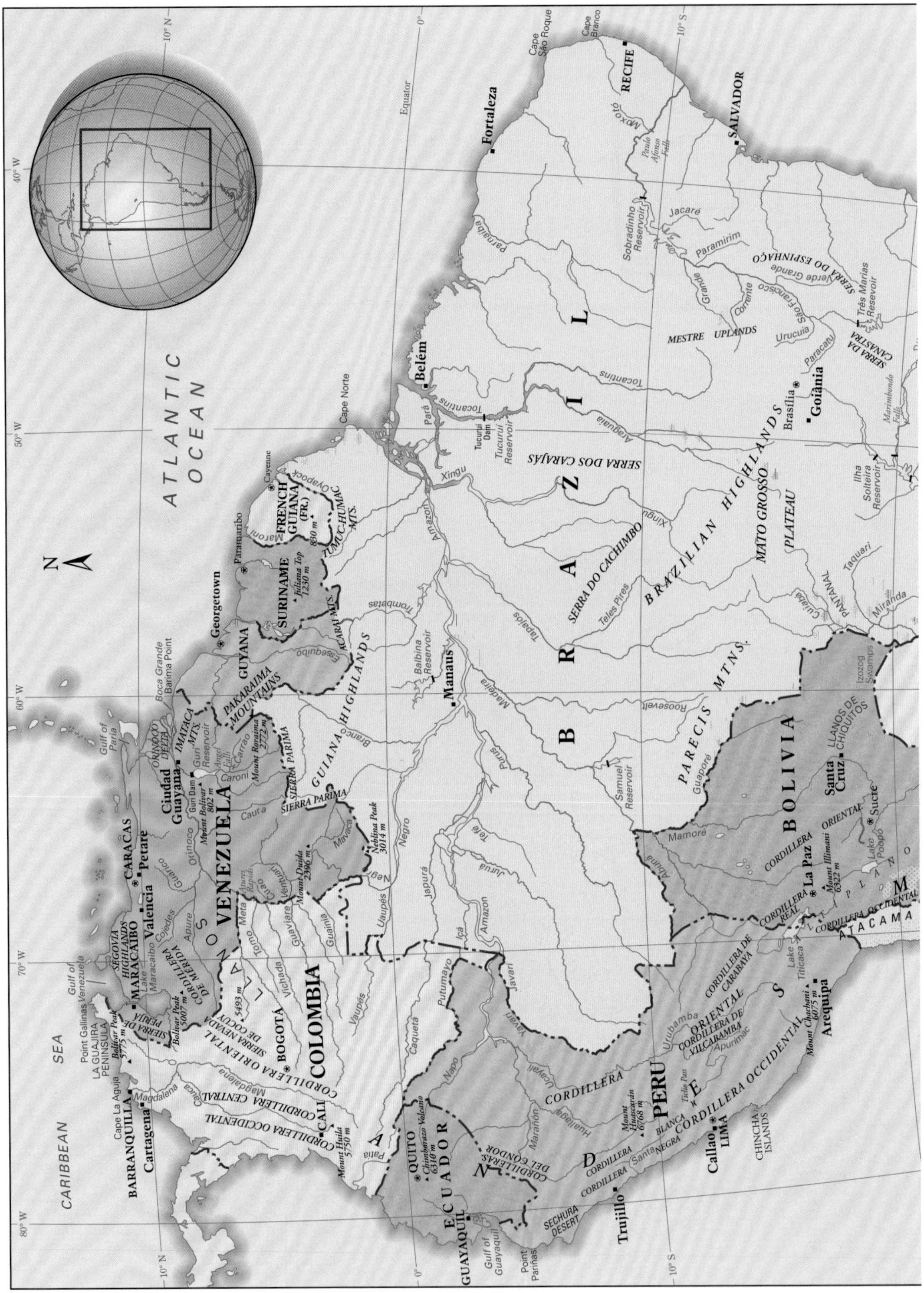

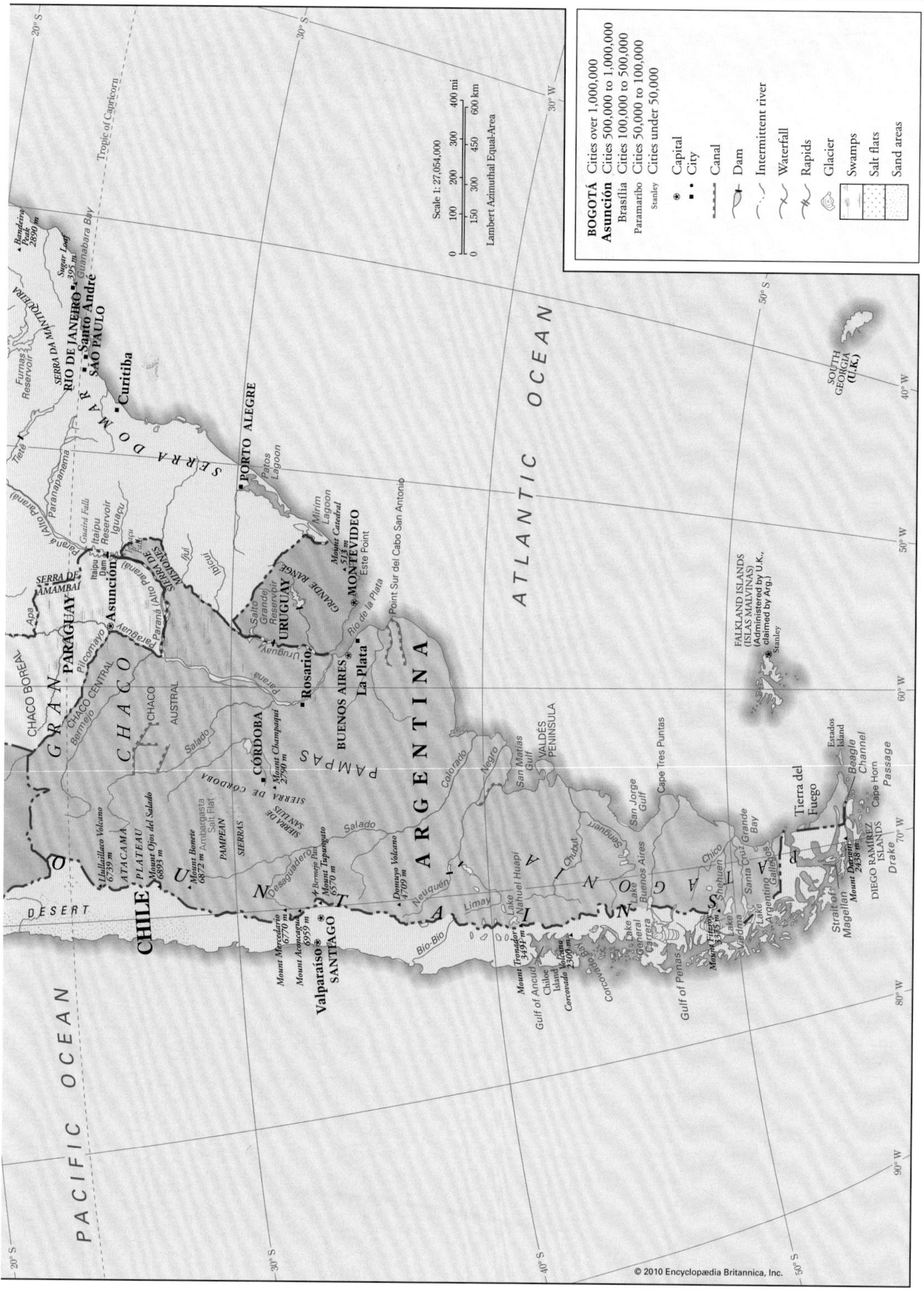
BOGOTÁ Cities over 1,000,000
Asunción Cities 500,000 to 1,000,000
Brasília Cities 100,000 to 500,000
Paramaribo Cities 50,000 to 100,000
Stanley Cities under 50,000
Capital
City
Canal
Dam
Intermittent river
Waterfall
Rapids
Glacier
Swamps
Salt flats
Sand areas
Scale 1: 27,054,000
Lambert Azimuthal Equal-Area
PACIFIC OCEAN
ATLANTIC OCEAN
ARGENTINA
CHILE
PARAGUAY
URUGUAY
GRAN CHACO
PATAGONIA
PAMPAS
SANTIAGO
Valparaíso
BUENOS AIRES
La Plata
Rosario
CÓRDOBA
MONTEVIDEO
Asunción
PORTO ALEGRE
Curitiba
SÃO PAULO
Santo André
RIO DE JANEIRO
Tropic of Capricorn
FALKLAND ISLANDS (ISLAS MALVINAS) (Administered by U.K., claimed by Arg.)
Stanley
SOUTH GEORGIA (U.K.)
Tierra del Fuego
Strait of Magellan
Drake Passage
Cape Horn
Mount Aconcagua 6959 m
Mount Mercedario 6770 m
Mount Tupungato 6570 m
Mount Ojos del Salado 6893 m
Llullaillaco Volcano 6739 m
Mount Bonete 6872 m
Río de la Plata
Valdés Peninsula
San Matías Gulf
San Jorge Gulf
Grande Bay
Gulf of Penas
Gulf of Ancud
Chiloe Island
Beagle Channel
Estados Island
Lake Nahuel Huapi
Lake Buenos Aires
Lake Argentino
Lake Viedma
Mirim Lagoon
Patos Lagoon
Salto Grande Reservoir
Itaipu Dam
Itaipu Reservoir
SERRA DO MAR
SERRA DA MANTIQUEIRA
SIERRA DE CÓRDOBA
ATACAMA PLATEAU
ATACAMA DESERT

ATLAS

BRAZIL, BOLIVIA, AND PARAGUAY

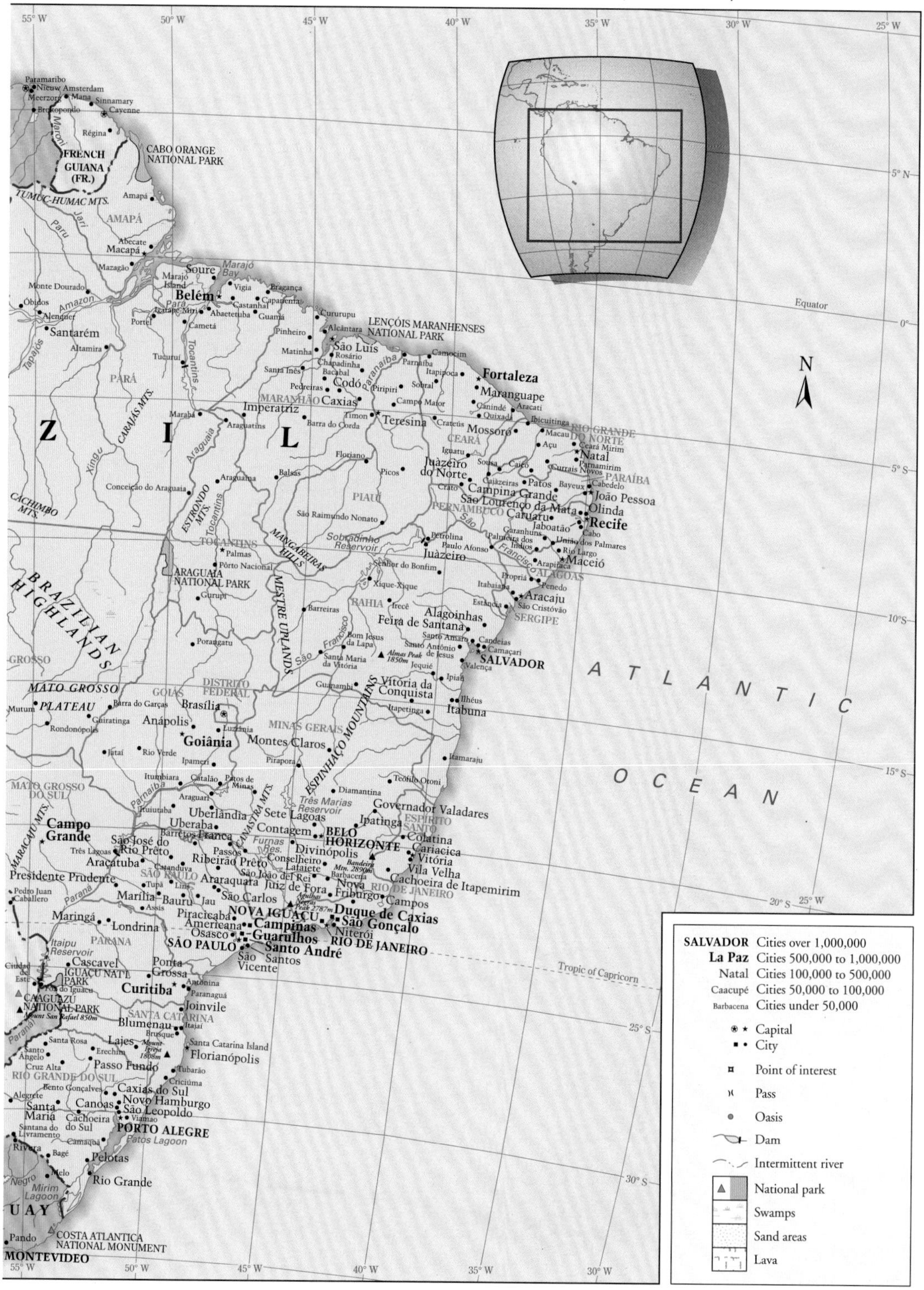
55° W
50° W
45° W
40° W
35° W
30° W
25° W
5° N
Equator
0°
5° S
10° S
15° S
20° S
25° S
30° S
Tropic of Capricorn
N
Paramaribo
Nieuw Amsterdam
Meerzorg
Mana
Sinnamary
Brokopondo
Cayenne
Régina
FRENCH GUIANA (FR.)
CABO ORANGE NATIONAL PARK
TUMUC-HUMAC MTS.
Amapá
AMAPÁ
Macapá
Mazagão
Soure
Marajó Island
Marajó Bay
Belém
Vigia
Bragança
Capanema
Castanhal
Abaetetuba
Cametá
Monte Dourado
Óbidos
Alenquer
Amazon
Santarém
Altamira
Portel
Tucuruí
Tocantins
PARÁ
Xingu
Tapajós
CARAJÁS MTS.
Marabá
Imperatriz
Araguatins
Araguaína
Conceição do Araguaia
CACHIMBO MTS.
ESTRONDO MTS.
TOCANTINS
Palmas
Pôrto Nacional
ARAGUAIA NATIONAL PARK
Gurupi
Porangatu
BRAZILIAN HIGHLANDS
MATO GROSSO PLATEAU
Cururupu
Alcântara
LENÇÓIS MARANHENSES NATIONAL PARK
São Luís
Rosário
Pinheiro
Matinha
Santa Inês
Chapadinha
Bacabal
Pedreiras
Codó
Caxias
MARANHÃO
Barra do Corda
Timon
Teresina
Parnaíba
Camocim
Itapipoca
Fortaleza
Maranguape
Sobral
Piripiri
Campo Maior
Crateús
Canindé
Quixadá
Aracati
Mossoró
CEARÁ
Iguatu
Floriano
Picos
PIAUÍ
Balsas
Juàzeiro do Norte
Crato
Sousa
Cajazeiras
Patos
Caicó
Currais Novos
Açu
Macau
Ceará Mirim
Natal
Parnamirim
RIO GRANDE DO NORTE
PARAÍBA
Cabedelo
João Pessoa
Bayeux
Campina Grande
São Lourenço da Mata
Olinda
Caruaru
Jaboatão
Recife
Cabo
PERNAMBUCO
São Raimundo Nonato
Sobradinho Reservoir
Petrolina
Paulo Afonso
Juàzeiro
Garanhuns
Palmeira dos Índios
União dos Palmares
Rio Largo
Maceió
Arapiraca
ALAGOAS
Propriá
Penedo
Itabaiana
Estância
Aracaju
São Cristóvão
SERGIPE
Senhor do Bonfim
Xique-Xique
BAHIA
Irecê
Barreiras
Alagoinhas
Feira de Santana
Santo Amaro
Santo Antônio de Jesus
Candeias
Camaçari
SALVADOR
Valença
Bom Jesus da Lapa
Santa Maria da Vitória
Almas Peak 1850m
Jequié
Guanambi
Vitória da Conquista
Ipiaú
Ilhéus
Itabuna
Itapetinga
MANGABEIRAS HILLS
MESTRE UPLANDS
São Francisco
ESPINHAÇO MOUNTAINS
DISTRITO FEDERAL
GOIÁS
Brasília
Barra do Garças
Mutum
Guiratinga
Rondonópolis
Anápolis
Goiânia
Luziânia
Jataí
Rio Verde
Ipameri
MINAS GERAIS
Montes Claros
Pirapora
Itamaraju
Teófilo Otoni
Diamantina
Itumbiara
Catalão
Patos de Minas
MATO GROSSO DO SUL
Araguari
Três Marias Reservoir
Governador Valadares
Ituiutaba
Uberlândia
Sete Lagoas
Ipatinga
ESPÍRITO SANTO
Uberaba
Contagem
BELO HORIZONTE
Colatina
Campo Grande
Franca
Barretos
Furnas Res.
Divinópolis
Cariacica
Vitória
Vila Velha
MARACAJU MTS.
CANASTRA MTS.
Três Lagoas
São José do Rio Prêto
Passos
Conselheiro Lafaiete
Bandeira Mtn. 2890m
Cachoeira de Itapemirim
Araçatuba
Ribeirão Prêto
São João del Rei
Barbacena
Presidente Prudente
Catanduva
SÃO PAULO
Araraquara
Juiz de Fora
Nova Friburgo
RIO DE JANEIRO
Pedro Juan Caballero
Marília
Tupã
Lins
São Carlos
Campos
Bauru
Jau
Agulhas Negras Peak 2787m
Assis
Piracicaba
NOVA IGUAÇU
Duque de Caxias
São Gonçalo
Maringá
Londrina
Americana
Campinas
Niterói
Osasco
Guarulhos
RIO DE JANEIRO
Paraná
PARANÁ
SÃO PAULO
Santo André
Itaipu Reservoir
São Vicente
Santos
Cascavel
Ponta Grossa
Ciudad del Este
IGUAÇU NAT'L PARK
Foz do Iguaçu
CAAGUAZU NATIONAL PARK
Mount San Rafael 850m
Curitiba
Antonina
Paranaguá
Joinvile
SANTA CATARINA
Blumenau
Itajaí
Brusque
Santa Rosa
Lajes
Mount Areya 1808m
Santa Catarina Island
Erechim
Florianópolis
Santo Ângelo
Cruz Alta
Passo Fundo
RIO GRANDE DO SUL
Tubarão
Criciúma
Bento Gonçalves
Caxias do Sul
Alegrete
Canoas
Novo Hamburgo
Santa Maria
Cachoeira do Sul
São Leopoldo
Viamão
PORTO ALEGRE
Santana do Livramento
Camaquã
Patos Lagoon
Rivera
Bagé
Pelotas
Melo
Rio Grande
Negro
Mirim Lagoon
UAY
Pando
COSTA ATLANTICA NATIONAL MONUMENT
MONTEVIDEO
ATLANTIC OCEAN
SALVADOR Cities over 1,000,000
La Paz Cities 500,000 to 1,000,000
Natal Cities 100,000 to 500,000
Caacupé Cities 50,000 to 100,000
Barbacena Cities under 50,000
Capital
City
Point of interest
Pass
Oasis
Dam
Intermittent river
National park
Swamps
Sand areas
Lava

ARGENTINA, CHILE, AND URUGUAY

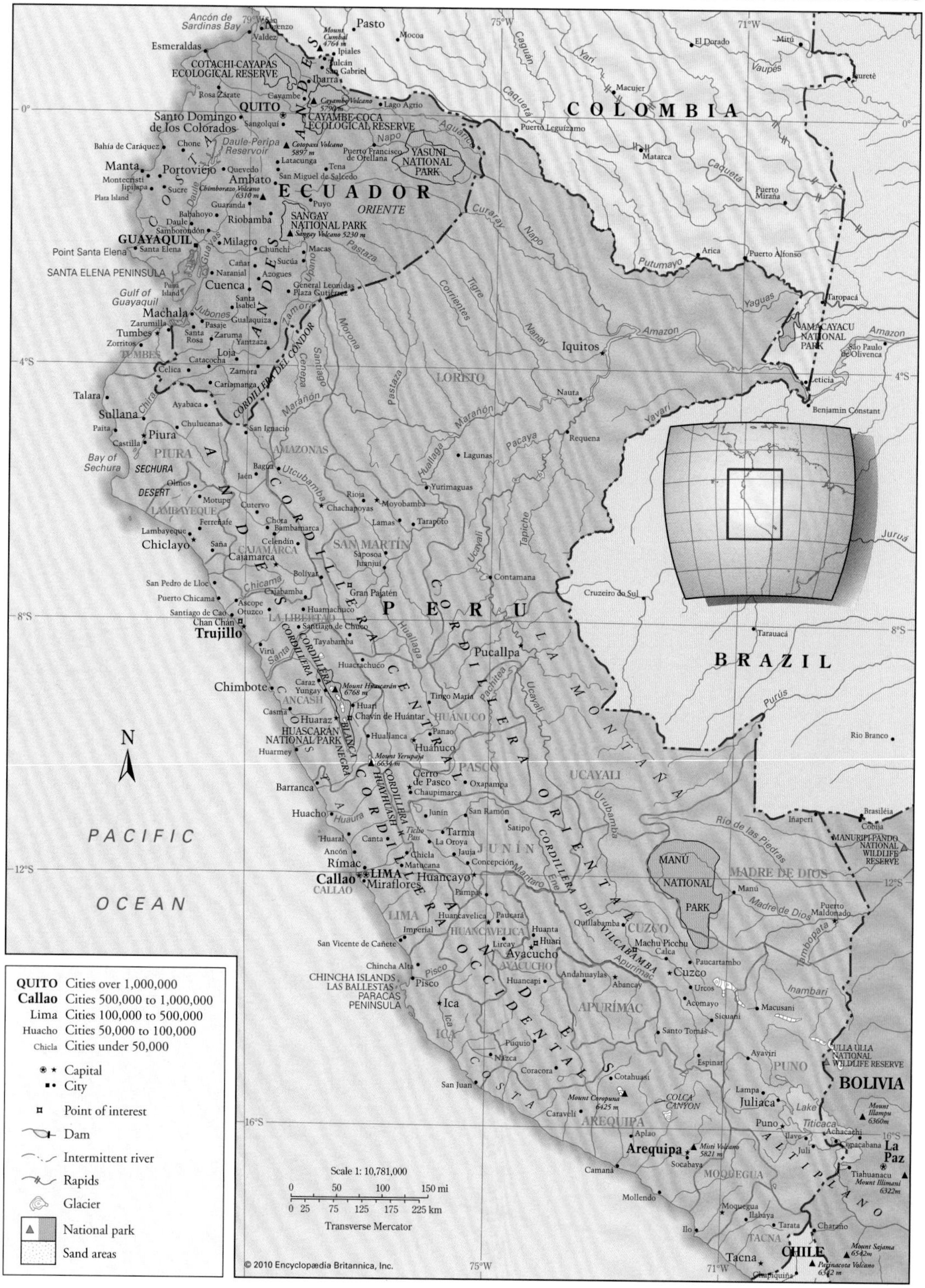
COLOMBIA
ECUADOR
PERU
BRAZIL
BOLIVIA
CHILE
PACIFIC
OCEAN
QUITO
GUAYAQUIL
LIMA
Callao
Trujillo
Chiclayo
Piura
Arequipa
Cuzco
Iquitos
Pucallpa
Huancayo
Chimbote
Ica
Tacna
Juliaca
Puno
La Paz
Cuenca
Ambato
Machala
Manta
Portoviejo
Santo Domingo de los Colorados
Esmeraldas
Riobamba
Milagro
Loja
Tumbes
Sullana
Talara
Cajamarca
Ayacucho
Huánuco
Huaraz
Pisco
Cerro de Pasco
Huacho
Tarma
Pasto
Leticia
Tabatinga
Rio Branco
Cruzeiro do Sul
Benjamin Constant
YASUNI NATIONAL PARK
SANGAY NATIONAL PARK
COTACHI-CAYAPAS ECOLOGICAL RESERVE
CAYAMBE-COCA ECOLOGICAL RESERVE
HUASCARÁN NATIONAL PARK
MANÚ NATIONAL PARK
AMACAYACU NATIONAL PARK
MANURIPI-PANDO NATIONAL WILDLIFE RESERVE
ULLA ULLA NATIONAL WILDLIFE RESERVE
CORDILLERA DEL CONDOR
CORDILLERA BLANCA
CORDILLERA CENTRAL
CORDILLERA ORIENTAL
CORDILLERA OCCIDENTAL
CORDILLERA DE VILCABAMBA
LA MONTAÑA
ALTIPLANO
ANDES
COSTA
ORIENTE
SECHURA DESERT
Lake Titicaca
Amazon
Marañón
Ucayali
Huallaga
Napo
Putumayo
Purús
Madre de Dios
Urubamba
Mount Huascarán 6768 m
Mount Yerupajá 6634 m
Chimborazo Volcano 6310 m
Cotopaxi Volcano 5897 m
Cayambe Volcano 5790 m
Sangay Volcano 5230 m
Misti Volcano 5821 m
Mount Coropuna 6425 m
Mount Illampu 6360 m
Mount Illimani 6322 m
Mount Sajama 6542 m
Parinacota Volcano 6342 m
0°
4°S
8°S
12°S
16°S
79°W
75°W
71°W
QUITO Cities over 1,000,000
Callao Cities 500,000 to 1,000,000
Lima Cities 100,000 to 500,000
Huacho Cities 50,000 to 100,000
Chicla Cities under 50,000
Capital
City
Point of interest
Dam
Intermittent river
Rapids
Glacier
National park
Sand areas
Scale 1: 10,781,000
0 50 100 150 mi
0 25 75 125 175 225 km
Transverse Mercator
© 2010 Encyclopædia Britannica, Inc.

ATLAS

COLOMBIA AND VENEZUELA

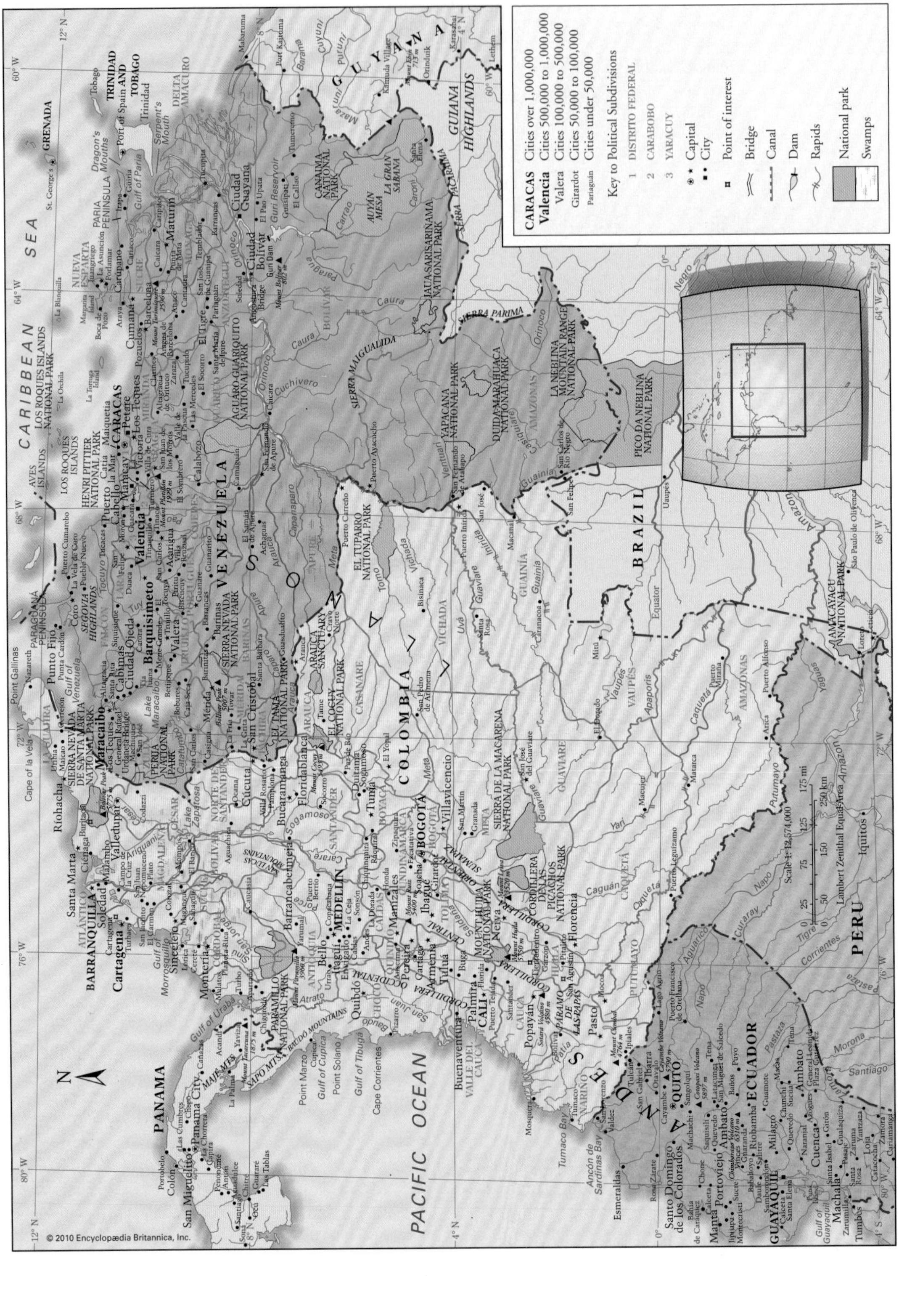

UNITED KINGDOM AND IRELAND

ATLAS

EUROPE

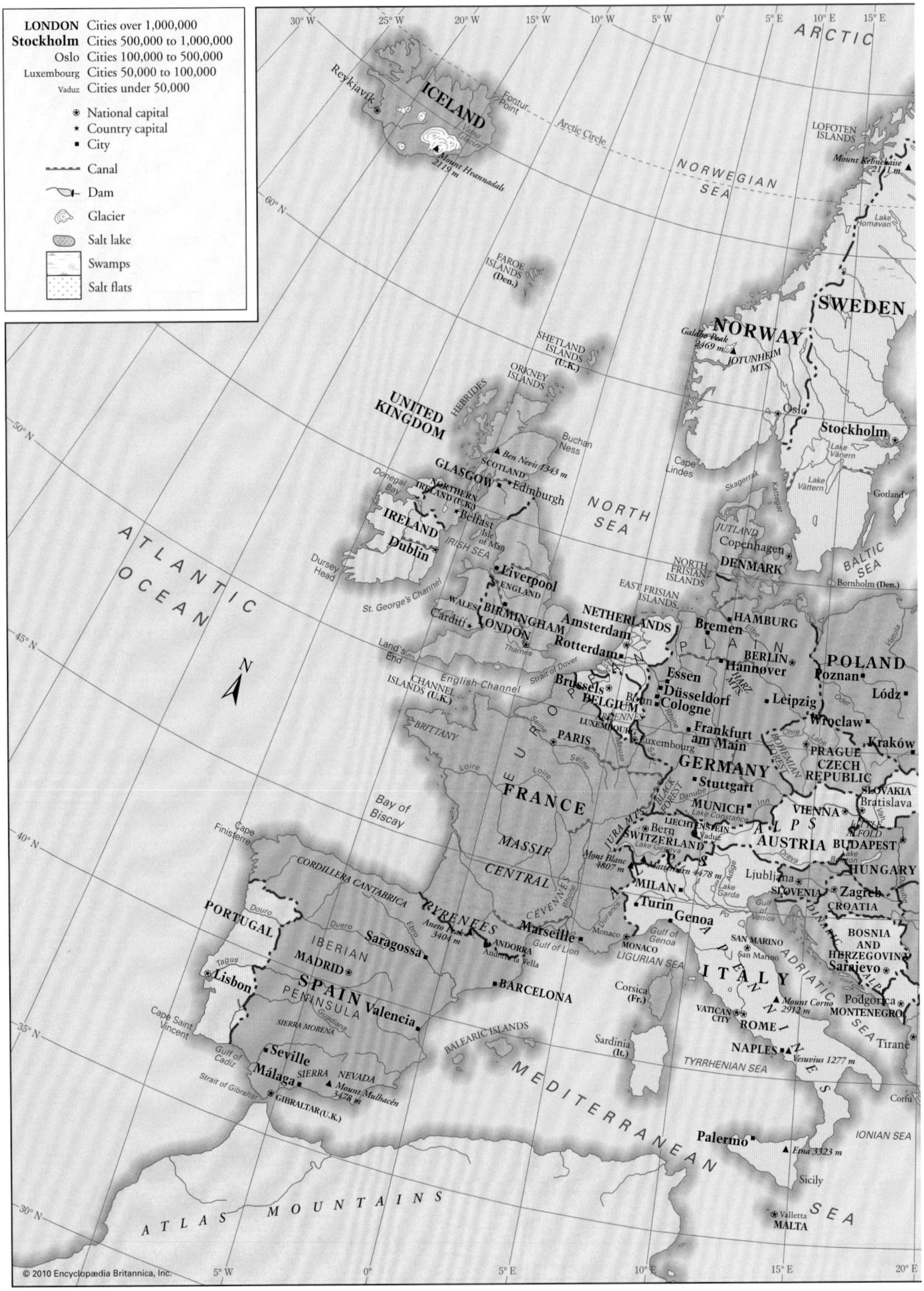

LONDON Cities over 1,000,000
Stockholm Cities 500,000 to 1,000,000
Oslo Cities 100,000 to 500,000
Luxembourg Cities 50,000 to 100,000
Vaduz Cities under 50,000
National capital
Country capital
City
Canal
Dam
Glacier
Salt lake
Swamps
Salt flats
ARCTIC
ICELAND
Reykjavík
Fontur Point
Arctic Circle
Mount Hvannadals 2119 m
NORWEGIAN SEA
LOFOTEN ISLANDS
Mount Kebnekaise 2111 m
FAROE ISLANDS (Den.)
SWEDEN
NORWAY
Galdhø Peak 2469 m
JOTUNHEIM MTS.
SHETLAND ISLANDS (U.K.)
ORKNEY ISLANDS
HEBRIDES
UNITED KINGDOM
Oslo
Stockholm
Lake Vänern
Lake Vättern
Gotland
Buchan Ness
Cape Lindes
Skagerrak
Kattegat
Ben Nevis 1343 m
SCOTLAND
GLASGOW
Edinburgh
Donegal Bay
NORTHERN IRELAND (U.K.)
Belfast
IRELAND
Dublin
Isle of Man
IRISH SEA
NORTH SEA
JUTLAND
Copenhagen
DENMARK
BALTIC SEA
Bornholm (Den.)
NORTH FRISIAN ISLANDS
EAST FRISIAN ISLANDS
ATLANTIC OCEAN
Dursey Head
Liverpool
ENGLAND
St. George's Channel
WALES
BIRMINGHAM
Cardiff
LONDON
Thames
NETHERLANDS
Amsterdam
Rotterdam
Bremen
HAMBURG
Elbe
BERLIN
Hannover
POLAND
Poznan
Lódz
Land's End
Strait of Dover
English Channel
CHANNEL ISLANDS (U.K.)
Brussels
BELGIUM
Essen
Düsseldorf
Cologne
Bonn
HARZ MTS.
Leipzig
Wroclaw
Kraków
BRITTANY
Seine
PARIS
LUXEMBOURG
Luxembourg
Frankfurt am Main
BOHEMIAN FOREST
PRAGUE
CZECH REPUBLIC
GERMANY
Stuttgart
Loire
FRANCE
Bay of Biscay
Danube
BLACK FOREST
MUNICH
SLOVAKIA
Bratislava
VIENNA
LIECHTENSTEIN
Vaduz
Lake Constance
Bern
SWITZERLAND
JURA MTS.
AUSTRIA
BUDAPEST
ALPS
Cape Finisterre
MASSIF CENTRAL
Mont Blanc 4807 m
Lake Geneva
Matterhorn 4478 m
Ljubljana
HUNGARY
SLOVENIA
Zagreb
CROATIA
MILAN
Lake Garda
CORDILLERA CANTABRICA
PYRENEES
CÉVENNES
Turin
Genoa
PORTUGAL
Douro
Duero
Ebro
Aneto Peak 3404 m
Marseille
Monaco
MONACO
Gulf of Genoa
LIGURIAN SEA
SAN MARINO
San Marino
ADRIATIC SEA
BOSNIA AND HERZEGOVINA
Sarajevo
IBERIAN PENINSULA
Saragossa
ANDORRA
Andorra la Vella
Gulf of Lion
MADRID
SPAIN
Tagus
Lisbon
BARCELONA
Corsica (Fr.)
ITALY
APENNINES
Mount Corno 2912 m
Podgorica
MONTENEGRO
Valencia
SIERRA MORENA
Guadiana
Cape Saint Vincent
BALEARIC ISLANDS
VATICAN CITY
ROME
Sardinia (It.)
NAPLES
Vesuvius 1277 m
Tirane
Gulf of Cadiz
Seville
Málaga
SIERRA NEVADA
Mount Mulhacén 3478 m
Strait of Gibraltar
GIBRALTAR (U.K.)
MEDITERRANEAN SEA
TYRRHENIAN SEA
Corfu
IONIAN SEA
Palermo
Etna 3323 m
Sicily
ATLAS MOUNTAINS
Valletta
MALTA
30° W
25° W
20° W
15° W
10° W
5° W
0°
5° E
10° E
15° E
20° E
60° N
50° N
45° N
40° N
35° N
30° N
N
© 2010 Encyclopædia Britannica, Inc.

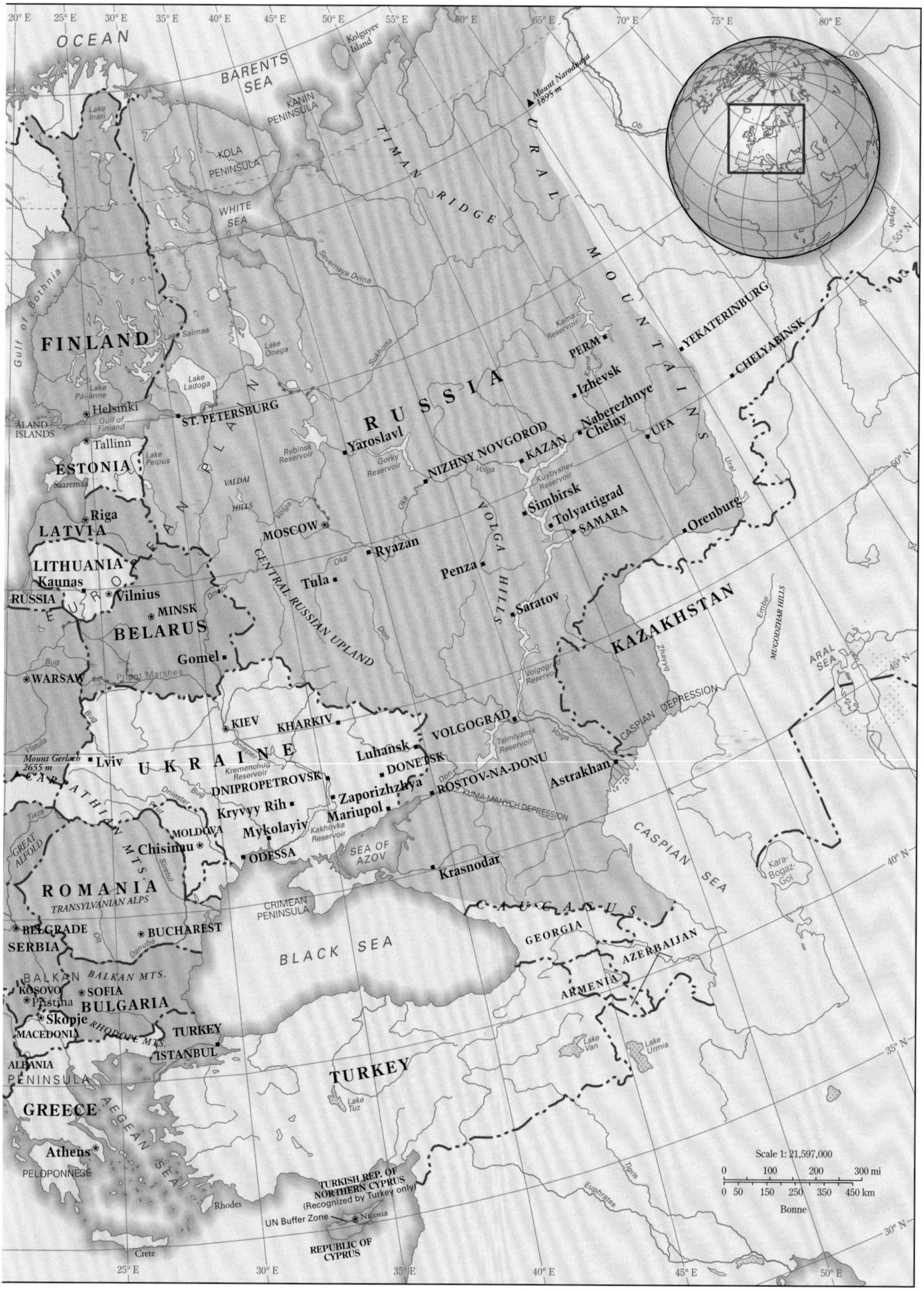
BARENTS SEA
OCEAN
FINLAND
RUSSIA
ESTONIA
LATVIA
LITHUANIA
BELARUS
UKRAINE
MOLDOVA
ROMANIA
SERBIA
BULGARIA
KOSOVO
MACEDONIA
ALBANIA
GREECE
TURKEY
GEORGIA
ARMENIA
AZERBAIJAN
KAZAKHSTAN
BLACK SEA
CASPIAN SEA
SEA OF AZOV
ARAL SEA
WHITE SEA
KOLA PENINSULA
KANIN PENINSULA
CRIMEAN PENINSULA
URAL MOUNTAINS
TIMAN RIDGE
VOLGA HILLS
CENTRAL RUSSIAN UPLAND
CAUCASUS
CARPATHIAN MTS.
TRANSYLVANIAN ALPS
BALKAN MTS.
RHODOPE MTS.
Helsinki
Tallinn
Riga
Kaunas
Vilnius
MINSK
WARSAW
Lviv
KIEV
KHARKIV
ST. PETERSBURG
MOSCOW
Yaroslavl
NIZHNY NOVGOROD
KAZAN
Naberezhnye Chelny
Izhevsk
PERM
YEKATERINBURG
CHELYABINSK
UFA
Orenburg
SAMARA
Tolyattigrad
Simbirsk
Penza
Saratov
Tula
Ryazan
Gomel
VOLGOGRAD
Luhansk
DONETSK
ROSTOV-NA-DONU
Astrakhan
Krasnodar
DNIPROPETROVSK
Zaporizhzhya
Kryvyy Rih
Mariupol
Mykolayiv
ODESSA
Chisinau
BUCHAREST
BELGRADE
SOFIA
Pristina
Skopje
ISTANBUL
Athens
Nicosia
TURKISH REP. OF NORTHERN CYPRUS (Recognized by Turkey only)
UN Buffer Zone
REPUBLIC OF CYPRUS
Mount Narodnaya 1895 m
Mount Gerlach 2655 m
Scale 1: 21,597,000
0 100 200 300 mi
0 50 150 250 350 450 km
Bonne

ATLAS

SPAIN AND PORTUGAL

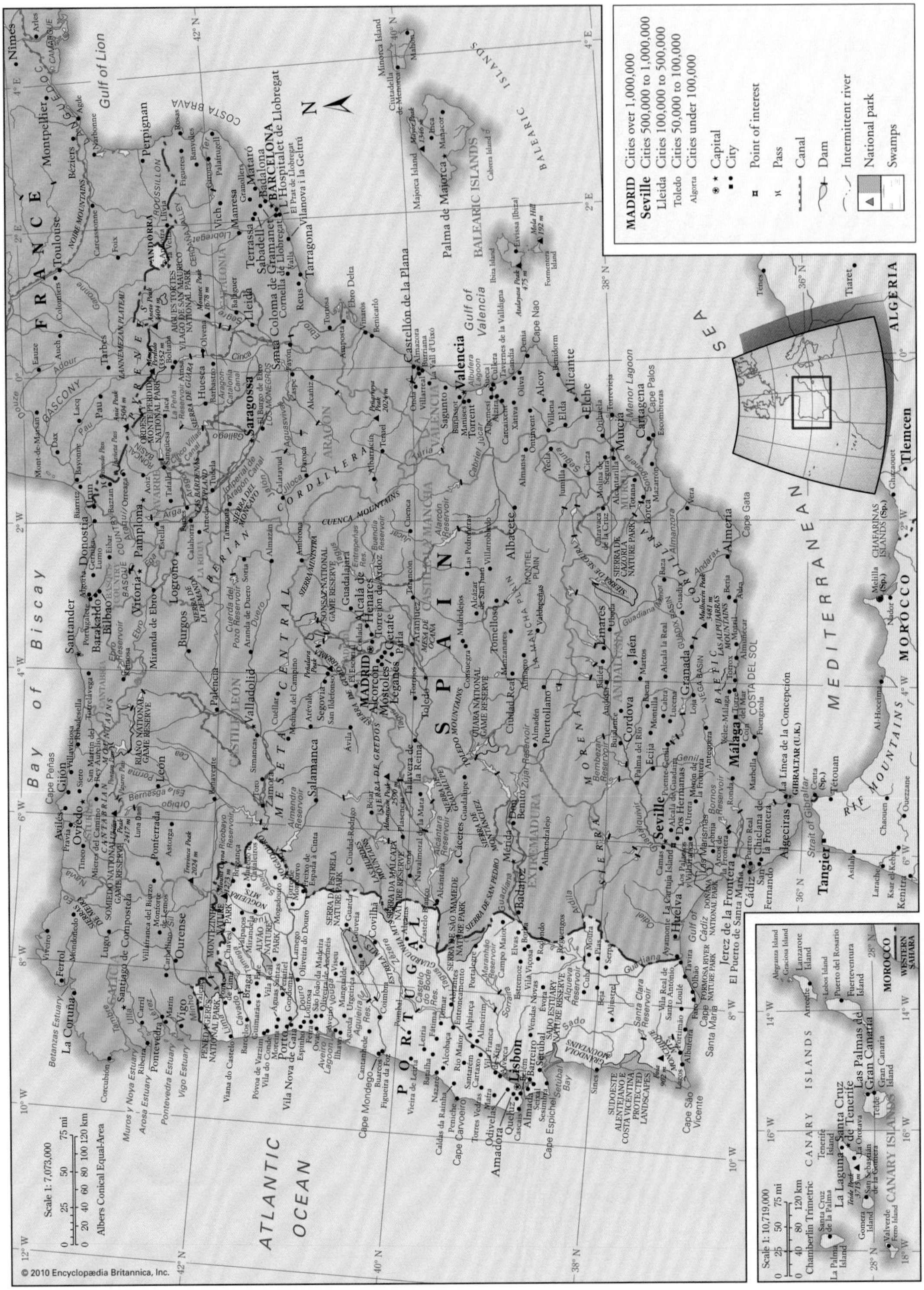

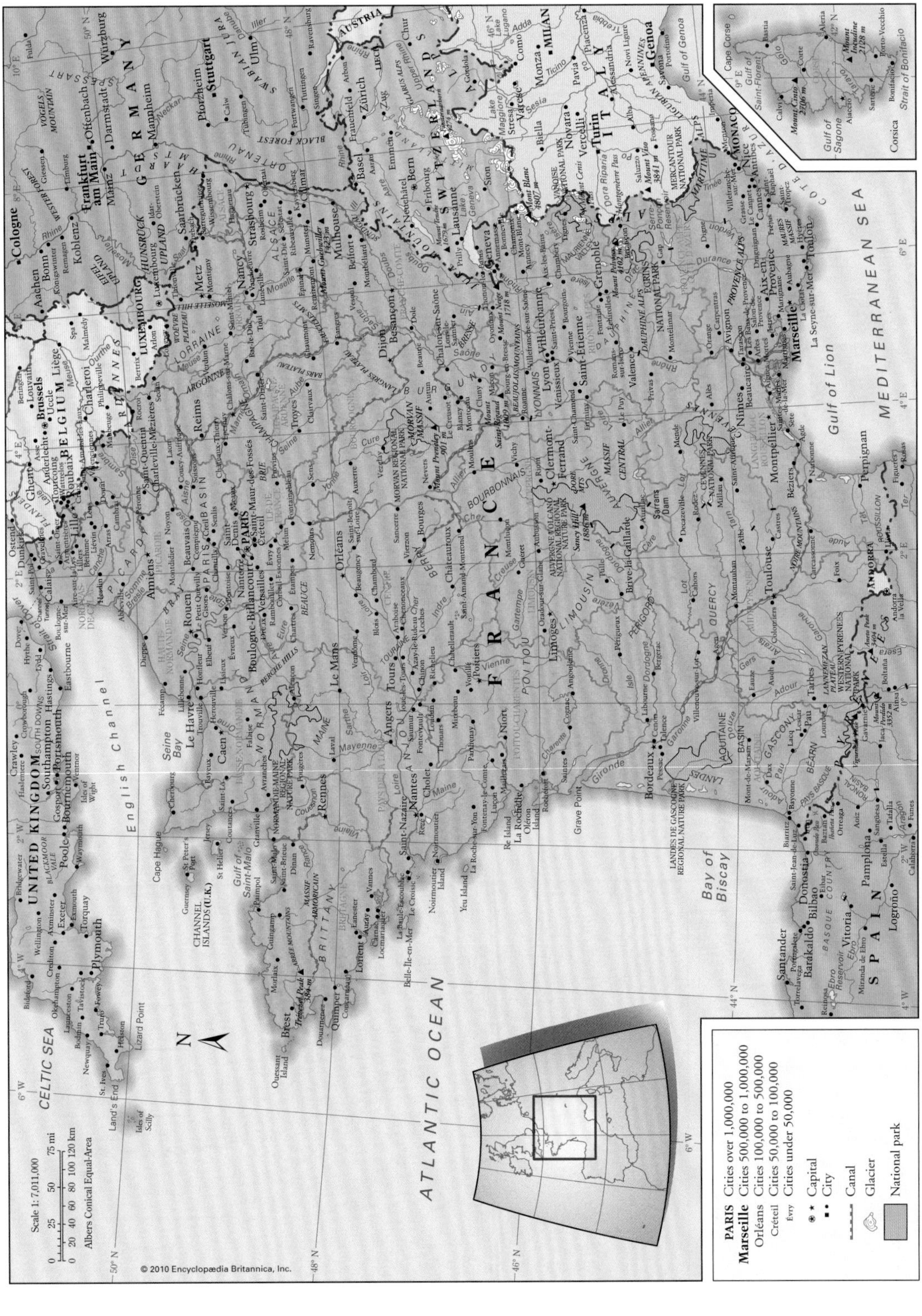
Scale 1: 7,011,000
0 25 50 75 mi
0 20 40 60 80 100 120 km
Albers Conical Equal-Area
© 2010 Encyclopædia Britannica, Inc.
PARIS Cities over 1,000,000
Marseille Cities 500,000 to 1,000,000
Orléans Cities 100,000 to 500,000
Créteil Cities 50,000 to 100,000
Évry Cities under 50,000
Capital
City
Canal
Glacier
National park
ATLANTIC OCEAN
CELTIC SEA
English Channel
Bay of Biscay
MEDITERRANEAN SEA
Gulf of Lion
Gulf of Genoa
UNITED KINGDOM
BELGIUM
LUXEMBOURG
GERMANY
SWITZERLAND
ITALY
SPAIN
ANDORRA
MONACO
AUSTRIA
FRANCE
PARIS
Marseille
Lyon
Toulouse
Nice
Nantes
Strasbourg
Montpellier
Bordeaux
Lille
Rennes
Corsica
Strait of Bonifacio

ITALY, SLOVENIA, AND CROATIA

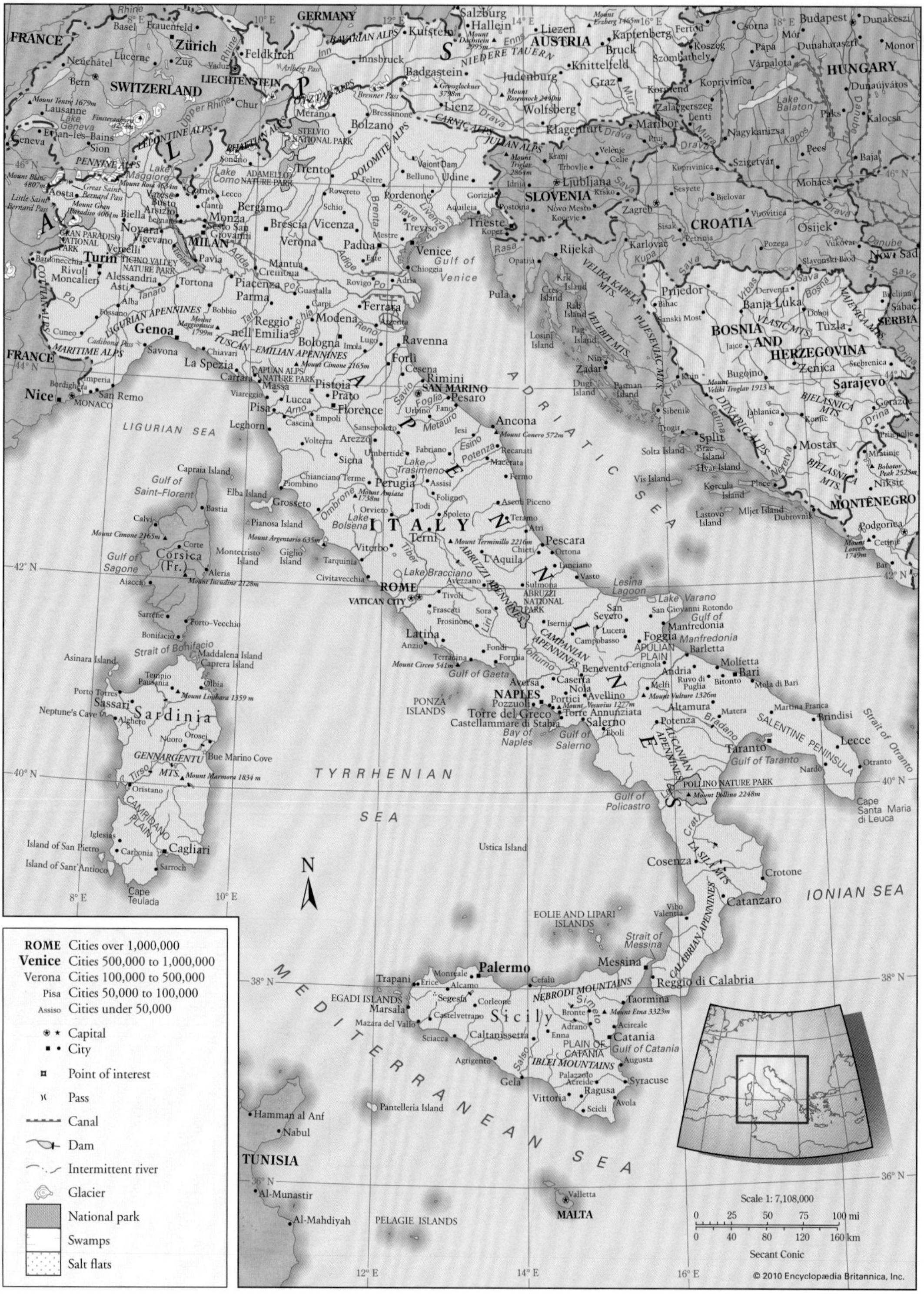

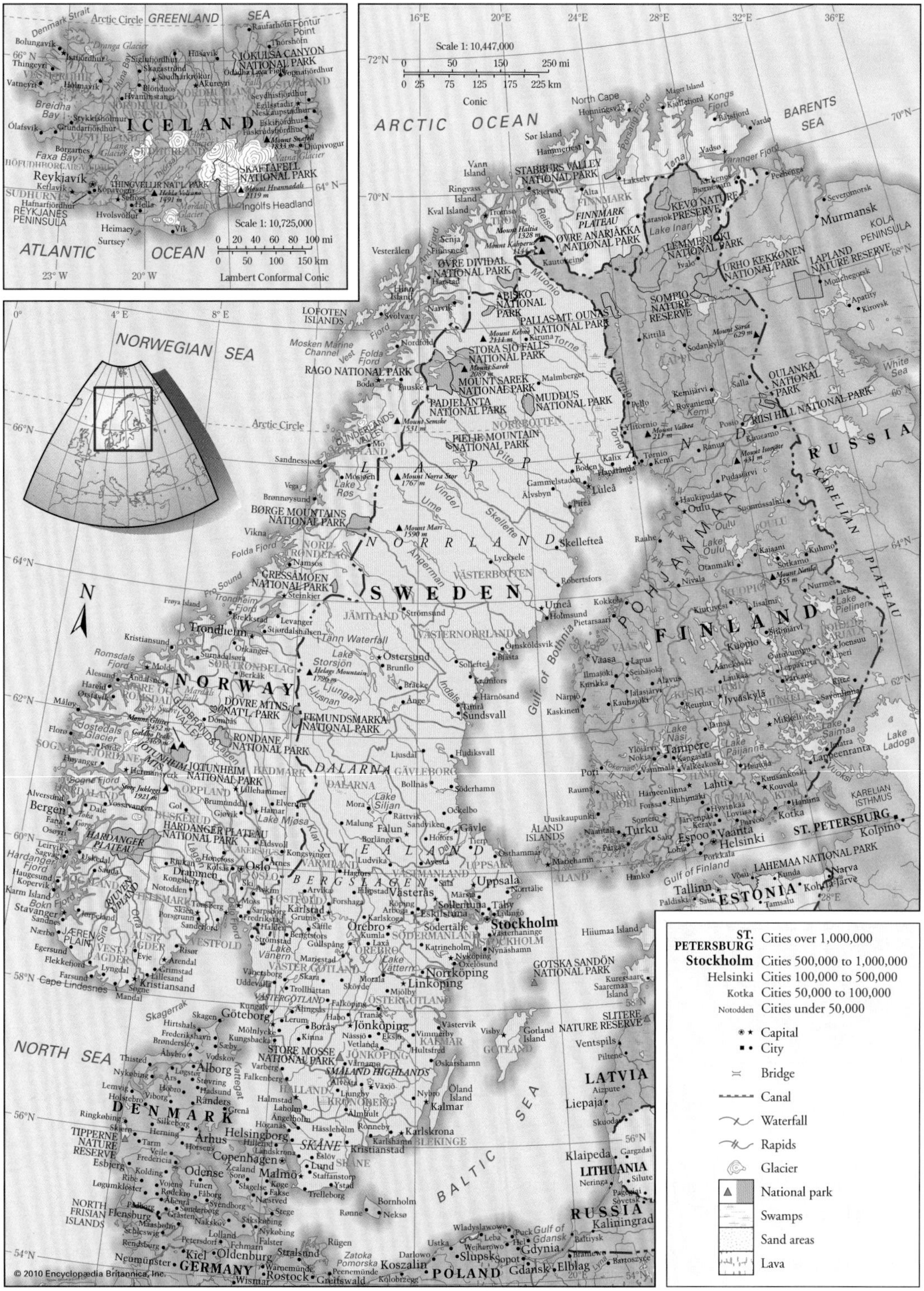
ICELAND
Scale 1: 10,725,000
Lambert Conformal Conic
GREENLAND SEA
ATLANTIC OCEAN
Denmark Strait
Arctic Circle
Reykjavík
Akureyri
Húsavík
Ísafjördhur
Keflavík
Hafnarfjördhur
Heimaey
Surtsey
Vík
Hella
Selfoss
Egilsstadir
Seydhisfjördhur
Neskaupstadhur
Eskifjördhur
Djúpivogur
Faxa Bay
Breidha Bay
Ingólfs Headland
Mount Hvannadals 2119 m
Mount Snaefell 1833 m
Hekla Volcano 1491 m
JÖKULSÁ CANYON NATIONAL PARK
SKAFTAFELL NATIONAL PARK
THINGVELLIR NAT'L PARK
REYKJANES PENINSULA
Scale 1: 10,447,000
Conic
ARCTIC OCEAN
NORWEGIAN SEA
BARENTS SEA
White Sea
NORTH SEA
BALTIC SEA
Skagerrak
Kattegat
Gulf of Bothnia
Gulf of Finland
Gulf of Gdansk
North Cape
KOLA PENINSULA
NORWAY
SWEDEN
FINLAND
RUSSIA
DENMARK
ESTONIA
LATVIA
LITHUANIA
POLAND
GERMANY
LAPPLAND
NORRLAND
SVEALAND
POHJANMAA
KARELIAN PLATEAU
KARELIAN ISTHMUS
LOFOTEN ISLANDS
ÅLAND ISLANDS
NORTH FRISIAN ISLANDS
SMÅLAND HIGHLANDS
HARDANGER PLATEAU
Lake Inari
Lake Ladoga
Lake Saimaa
Lake Vänern
Lake Vättern
Lake Siljan
Lake Mjøsa
Lake Storsjön
Oslo
Stockholm
Helsinki
Copenhagen
Tallinn
St. Petersburg
Bergen
Trondheim
Göteborg
Malmö
Turku
Tampere
Oulu
Murmansk
Kaliningrad
Gdańsk
Gdynia
Uppsala
Västerås
Örebro
Norrköping
Linköping
Jönköping
Umeå
Luleå
Kiruna
Narvik
Tromsø
Stavanger
Kristiansand
Ålborg
Århus
Odense
Kiel
Rostock
Klaipeda
Liepaja
Ventspils
Narva
Lahti
Espoo
Vantaa
Kuopio
Jyväskylä
Rovaniemi
Joensuu
Lappeenranta
Kotka
Pori
Vaasa
© 2010 Encyclopædia Britannica, Inc.
ST. PETERSBURG Cities over 1,000,000
Stockholm Cities 500,000 to 1,000,000
Helsinki Cities 100,000 to 500,000
Kotka Cities 50,000 to 100,000
Notodden Cities under 50,000
Capital
City
Bridge
Canal
Waterfall
Rapids
Glacier
National park
Swamps
Sand areas
Lava

ATLAS

WESTERN AND CENTRAL EUROPE

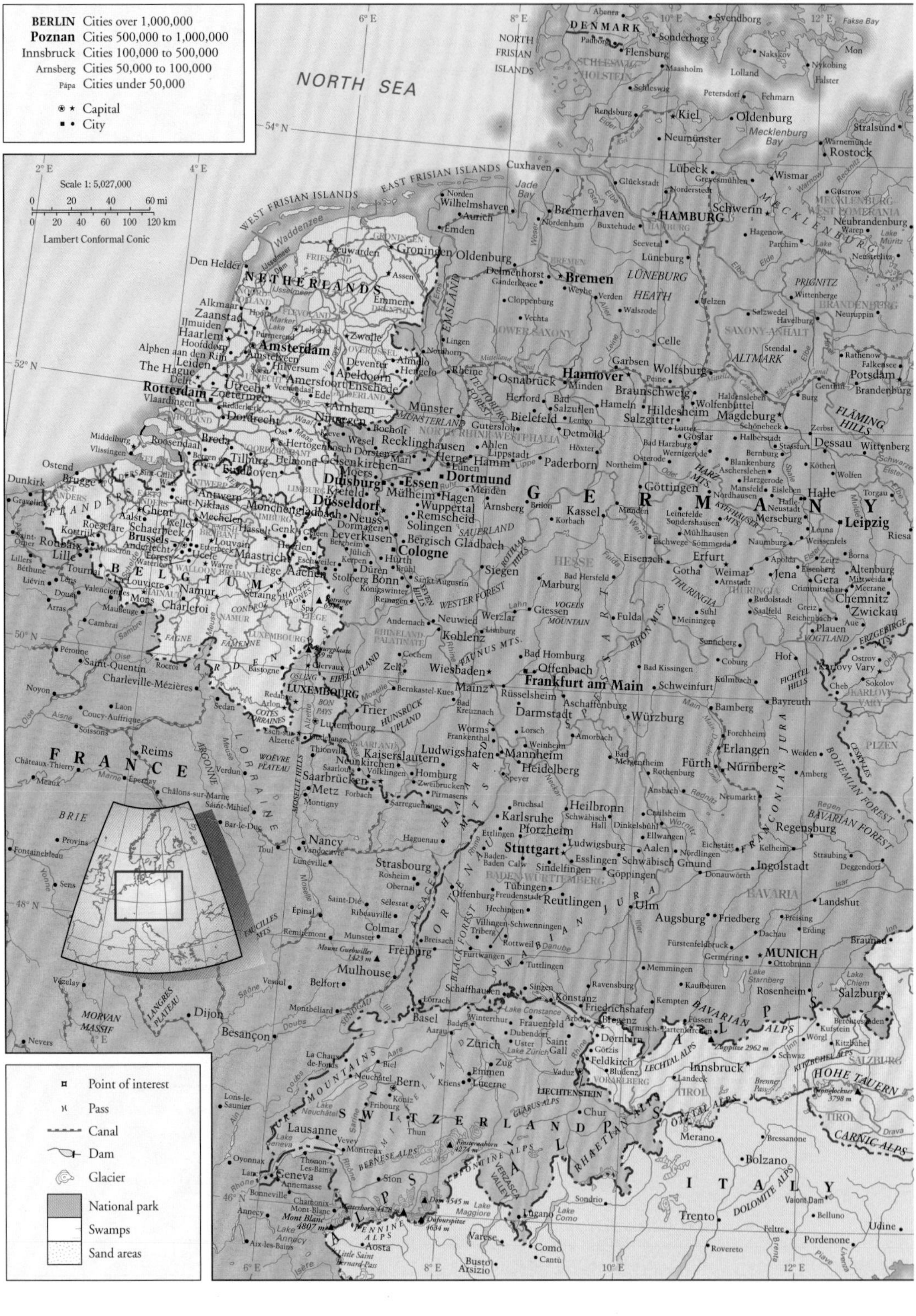

BALTIC SEA
Gulf of Gdansk
Bornholm (Den.)
RUSSIA
Kaliningrad
LITHUANIA
BELARUS
POLAND
WARSAW
BERLIN
UKRAINE
SLOVAKIA
CZECH REPUBLIC
PRAGUE
AUSTRIA
VIENNA
HUNGARY
BUDAPEST
ROMANIA
SLOVENIA
Ljubljana
CROATIA
Zagreb
SERBIA
CARPATHIAN MTS
BESKIDS MTS
SUDETEN MTS
Gdansk
Gdynia
Sopot
Elblag
Olsztyn
Bialystok
Grodno
Szczecin
Koszalin
Slupsk
Bydgoszcz
Torun
Grudziadz
Wloclawek
Plock
Poznan
Lódz
Radom
Lublin
Kielce
Czestochowa
Katowice
Kraków
Rzeszów
Tarnów
Przemysl
Wroclaw
Opole
Legnica
Zielona Góra
Gorzów Wielkopolski
Kalisz
Konin
Brest
Lviv
Chelm
Zamosc
Dresden
Leipzig
Cottbus
Frankfurt
Görlitz
Liberec
Ústí nad Labem
Hradec Králové
Pardubice
Plzen
Ceské Budejovice
Jihlava
Brno
Olomouc
Ostrava
Zlín
Zilina
Trencín
Banská Bystrica
Presov
Kosice
Uzhhorod
Bratislava
Nitra
Trnava
Linz
Sankt Pölten
Graz
Klagenfurt
Villach
Maribor
Miskolc
Nyíregyháza
Debrecen
Eger
Gyor
Sopron
Szombathely
Székesfehérvár
Veszprém
Kecskemét
Szolnok
Szeged
Pécs
Kaposvár
Nagykanizsa
Békéscsaba
Oradea
Arad
Timisoara
Satu Mare
Baia Mare
Subotica
Mount Sniezka 1602 m
Gerlachovsky Peak 2655 m
Mount Kékes 1015 m
Mount Triglav 2864 m
Mount Bihor 1849 m
Lake Balaton
JULIAN ALPS
LITTLE ALFOLD
TRANSDANUBIA
GREAT ALFOLD
14° E
16° E
18° E
20° E
22° E
24° E
54° N
52° N
50° N
48° N
46° N
© 2010 Encyclopædia Britannica, Inc.

ATLAS

SOUTHEASTERN EUROPE

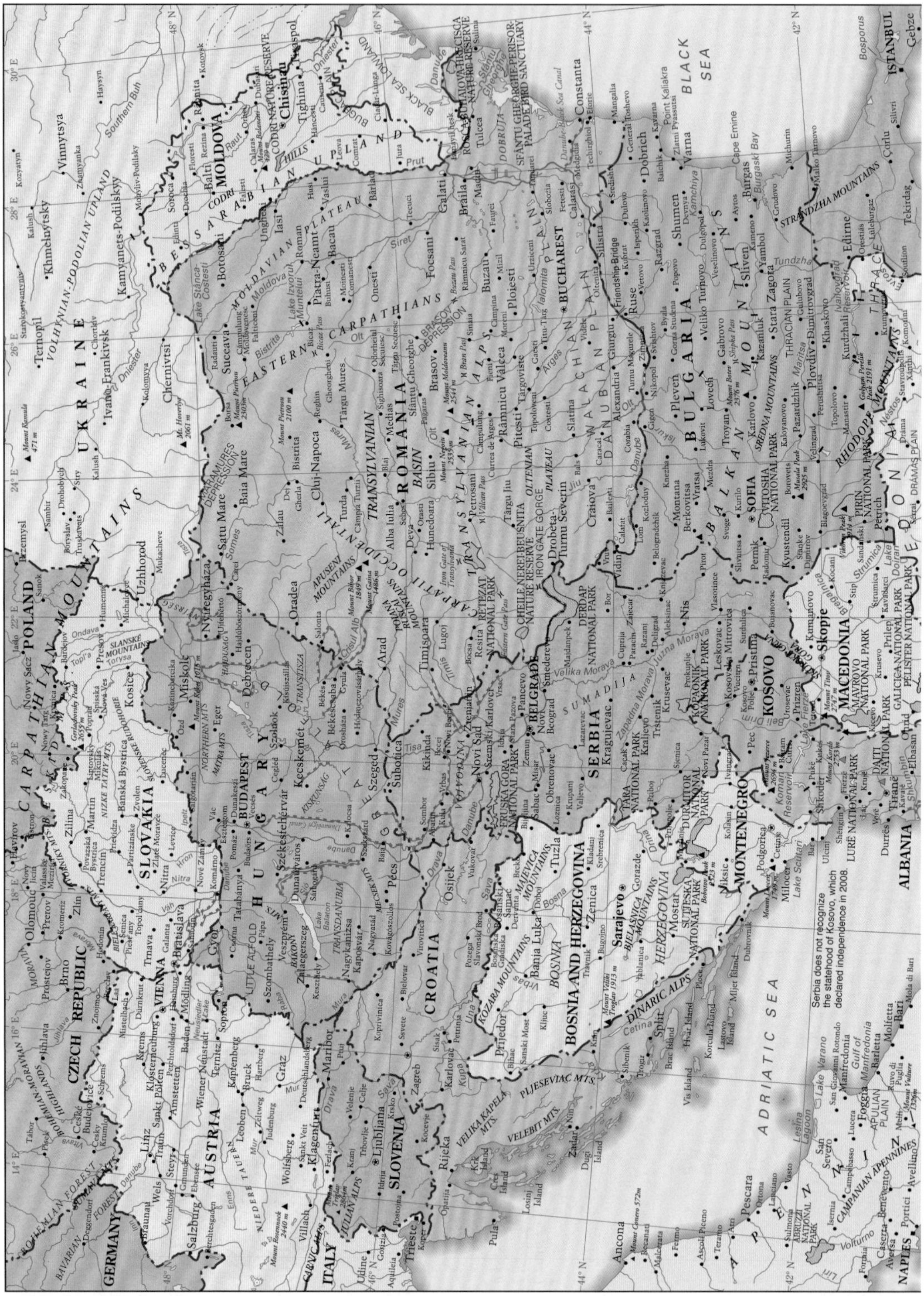

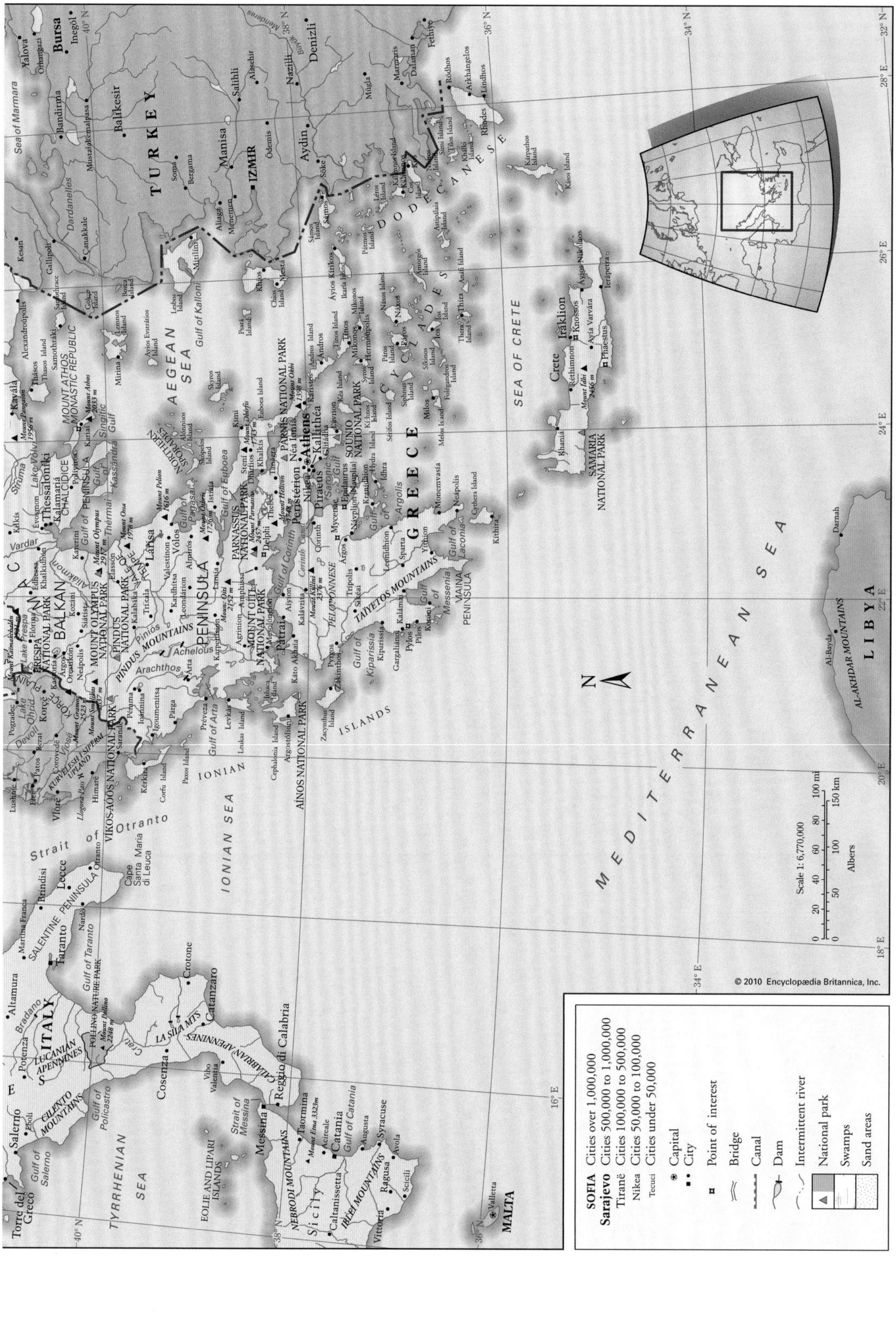
SOFIA Cities over 1,000,000
Sarajevo Cities 500,000 to 1,000,000
Tiranë Cities 100,000 to 500,000
Nikea Cities 50,000 to 100,000
Tecuci Cities under 50,000
Capital
City
Point of interest
Bridge
Canal
Dam
Intermittent river
National park
Swamps
Sand areas
Scale 1: 6,770,000
0 20 40 60 80 100 mi
0 50 100 150 km
Albers
© 2010 Encyclopædia Britannica, Inc.
TURKEY
GREECE
ITALY
LIBYA
MALTA
BALKAN PENINSULA
PELOPONNESE
AEGEAN SEA
IONIAN SEA
MEDITERRANEAN SEA
SEA OF CRETE
TYRRHENIAN SEA
Sea of Marmara
Strait of Otranto
Athens
Thessaloníki
Izmir
Bursa
Crete
Sicily
Rhodes

RUSSIA AND KAZAKHSTAN

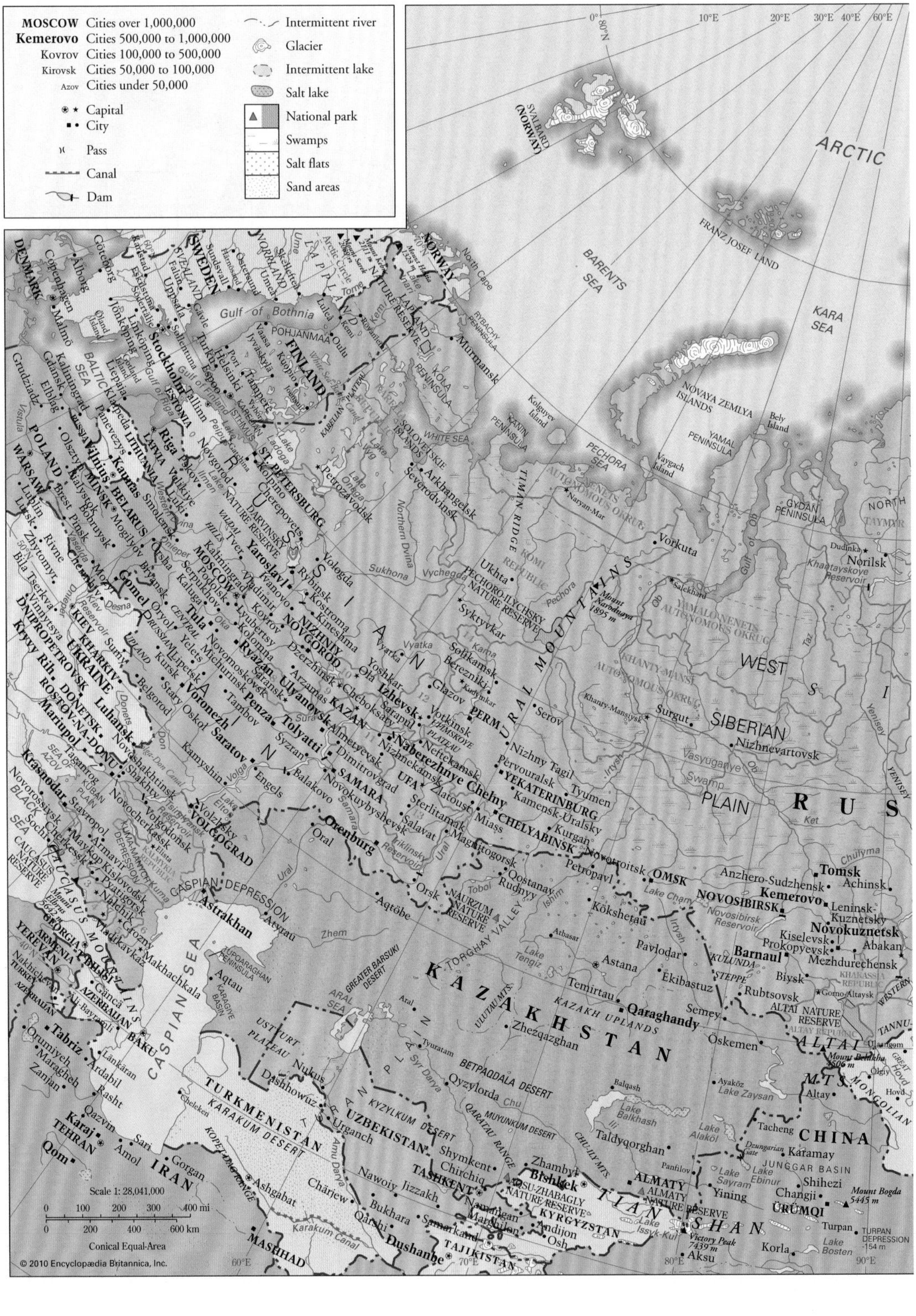

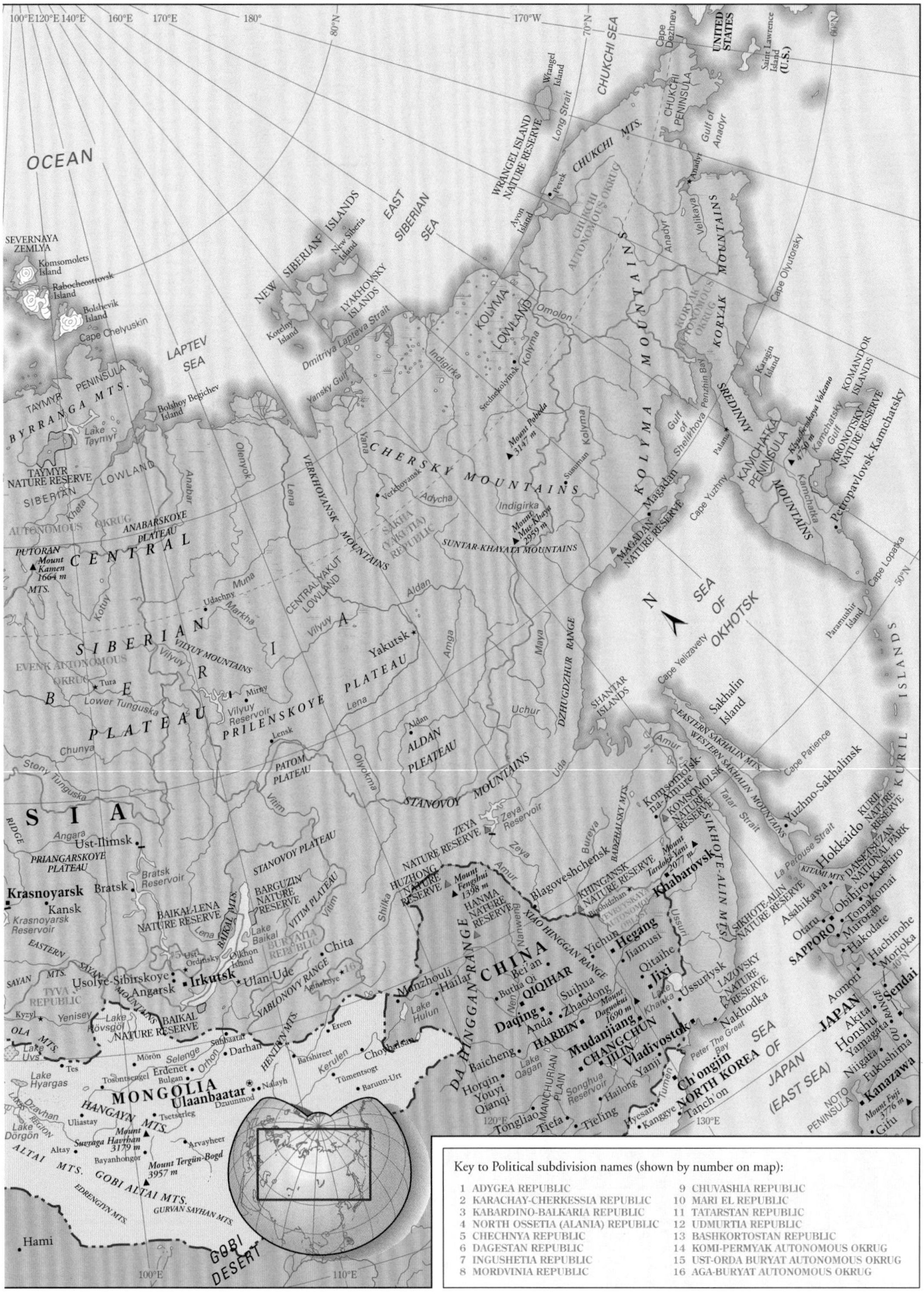

Key to Political subdivision names (shown by number on map):

1 ADYGEA REPUBLIC
2 KARACHAY-CHERKESSIA REPUBLIC
3 KABARDINO-BALKARIA REPUBLIC
4 NORTH OSSETIA (ALANIA) REPUBLIC
5 CHECHNYA REPUBLIC
6 DAGESTAN REPUBLIC
7 INGUSHETIA REPUBLIC
8 MORDVINIA REPUBLIC
9 CHUVASHIA REPUBLIC
10 MARI EL REPUBLIC
11 TATARSTAN REPUBLIC
12 UDMURTIA REPUBLIC
13 BASHKORTOSTAN REPUBLIC
14 KOMI-PERMYAK AUTONOMOUS OKRUG
15 UST-ORDA BURYAT AUTONOMOUS OKRUG
16 AGA-BURYAT AUTONOMOUS OKRUG

EASTERN EUROPE

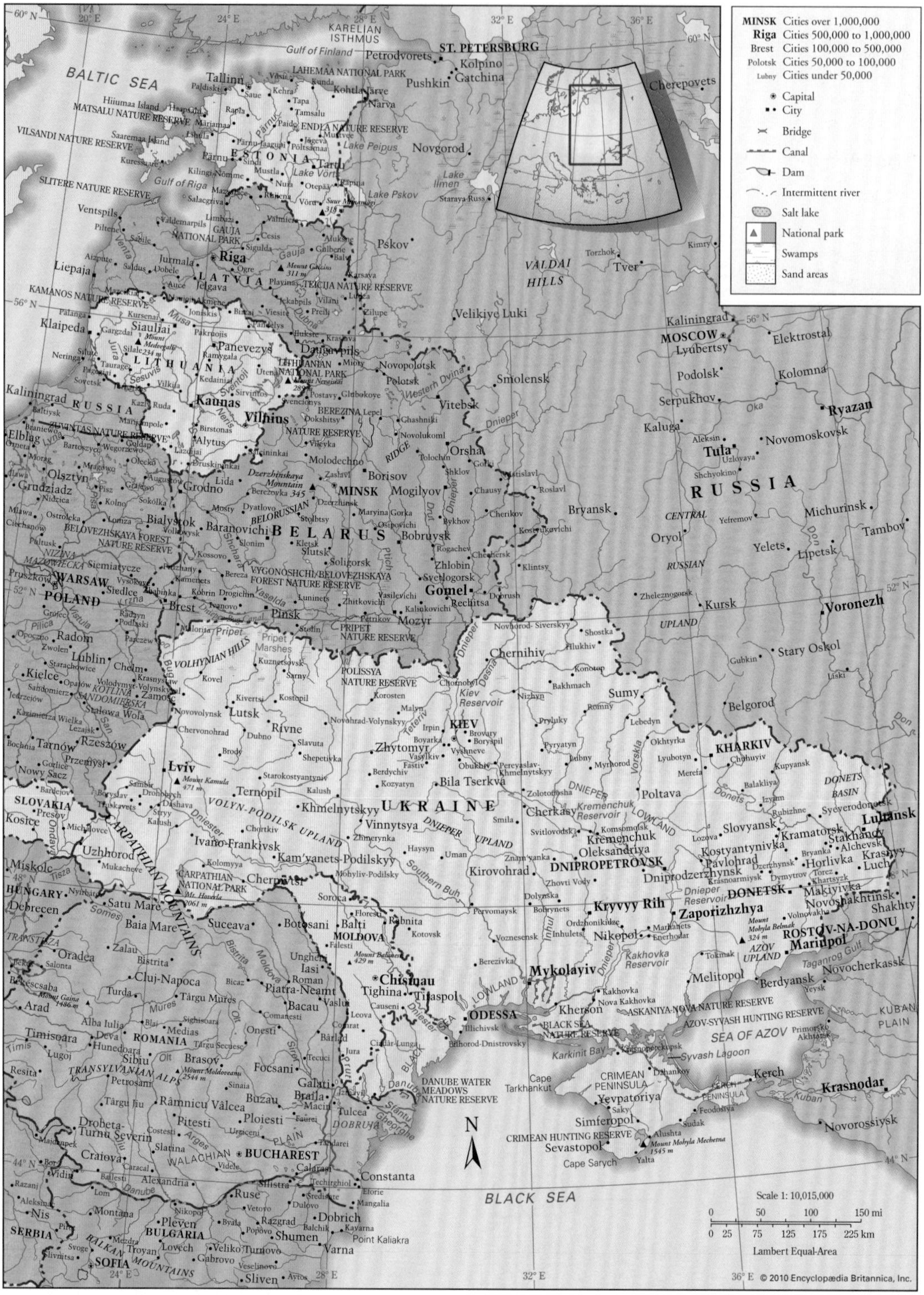

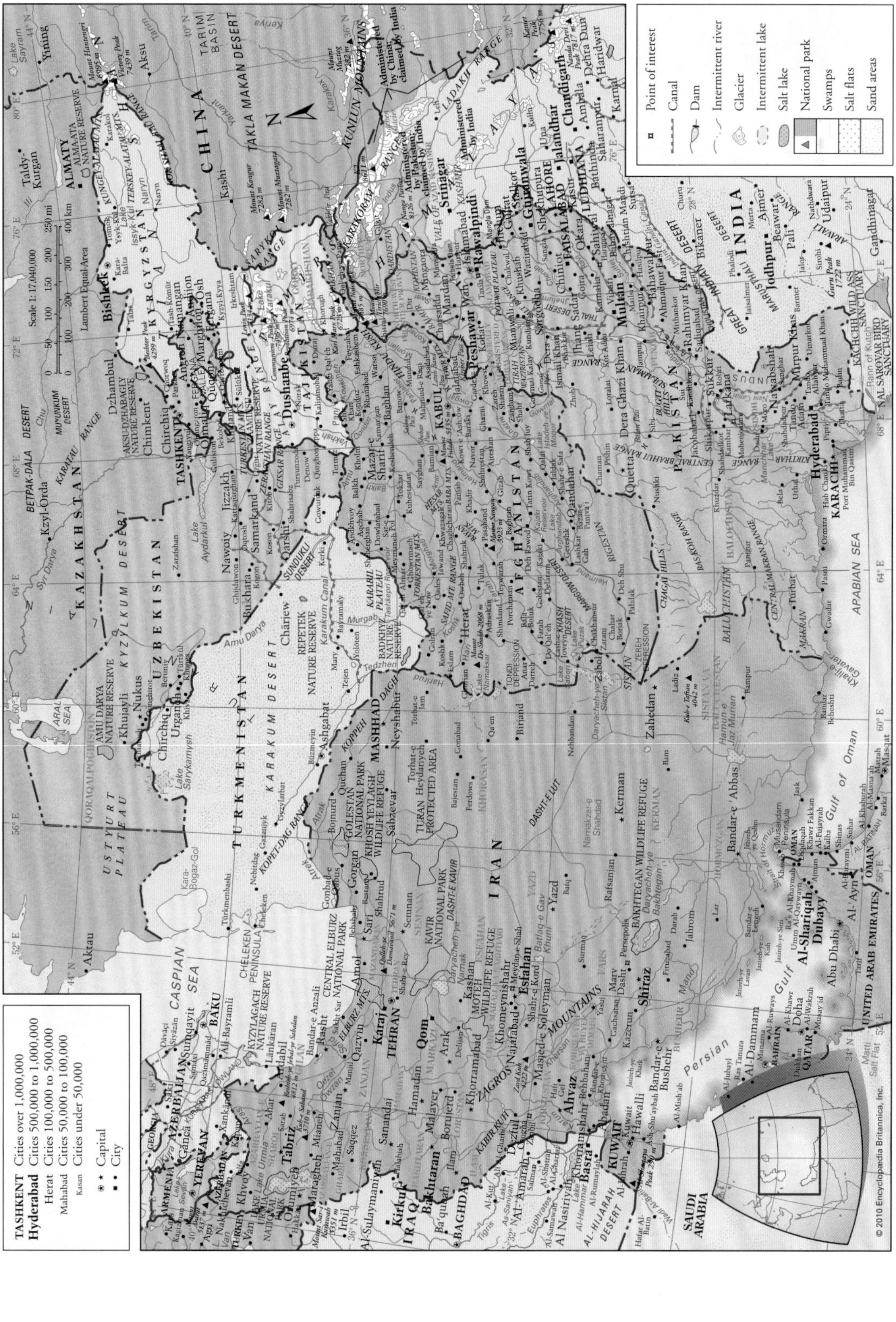
TASHKENT Cities over 1,000,000
Hyderabad Cities 500,000 to 1,000,000
Herat Cities 100,000 to 500,000
Mahabad Cities 50,000 to 100,000
Kasan Cities under 50,000
Capital
City
Point of interest
Canal
Dam
Intermittent river
Glacier
Intermittent lake
Salt lake
National park
Swamps
Salt flats
Sand areas
Scale 1:17,040,000
Lambert Equal-Area
KAZAKHSTAN
UZBEKISTAN
TURKMENISTAN
KYRGYZSTAN
TAJIKISTAN
AFGHANISTAN
PAKISTAN
INDIA
CHINA
IRAN
IRAQ
KUWAIT
SAUDI ARABIA
QATAR
UNITED ARAB EMIRATES
OMAN
CASPIAN SEA
ARABIAN SEA
© 2010 Encyclopædia Britannica, Inc.

ASIA

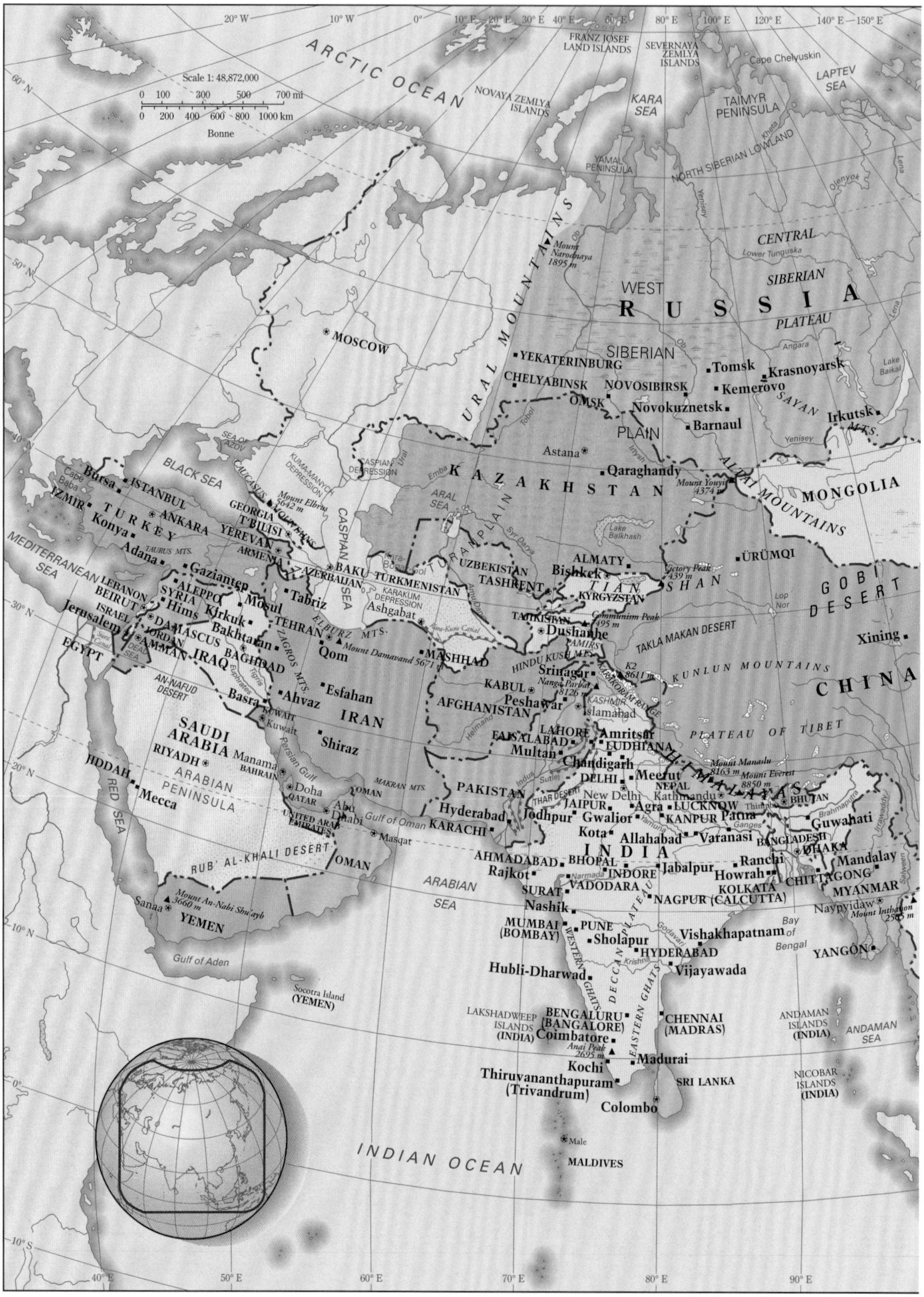
ARCTIC OCEAN
Scale 1: 48,872,000
0 100 300 500 700 mi
0 200 400 600 800 1000 km
Bonne
FRANZ JOSEF LAND ISLANDS
SEVERNAYA ZEMLYA ISLANDS
Cape Chelyuskin
LAPTEV SEA
NOVAYA ZEMLYA ISLANDS
KARA SEA
TAIMYR PENINSULA
NORTH SIBERIAN LOWLAND
YAMAL PENINSULA
Mount Narodnaya 1895 m
URAL MOUNTAINS
CENTRAL SIBERIAN PLATEAU
WEST SIBERIAN PLAIN
RUSSIA
MOSCOW
YEKATERINBURG
CHELYABINSK
NOVOSIBIRSK
OMSK
Tomsk
Kemerovo
Krasnoyarsk
Novokuznetsk
Barnaul
Irkutsk
SAYAN MTS.
Lake Baikal
Astana
Qaraghandy
KAZAKHSTAN
Mount Younyi 4374 m
ALTAI MOUNTAINS
MONGOLIA
BLACK SEA
SEA OF AZOV
KUMA-MANYCH DEPRESSION
CASPIAN DEPRESSION
CAUCASUS MOUNTAINS
Mount Elbrus 5642 m
ARAL SEA
Lake Balkhash
TURAN PLAIN
CASPIAN SEA
Bursa
ISTANBUL
IZMIR
TURKEY
ANKARA
Konya
Adana
TAURUS MTS.
GEORGIA
T'BILISI
YEREVAN
ARMENIA
AZERBAIJAN
BAKU
TURKMENISTAN
UZBEKISTAN
TASHKENT
ALMATY
Bishkek
KYRGYZSTAN
Victory Peak 7439 m
TIAN SHAN
ÜRÜMQI
GOBI DESERT
Lop Nor
MEDITERRANEAN SEA
LEBANON
BEIRUT
SYRIA
ALEPPO
Gaziantep
Hims
ISRAEL
Jerusalem
JORDAN
DAMASCUS
AMMAN
Mosul
Kirkuk
Tabriz
TEHRAN
Bakhtaran
IRAQ
BAGHDAD
ELBURZ MTS.
Mount Damavand 5671 m
Qom
ZAGROS MTS.
KARAKUM DEPRESSION
Ashgabat
TAJIKISTAN
Dushanbe
Communism Peak 7495 m
PAMIRS
TAKLA MAKAN DESERT
Xining
MASHHAD
HINDU KUSH MTS.
Srinagar
K2 8611 m
KUNLUN MOUNTAINS
CHINA
EGYPT
Suez Canal
DEAD SEA
AN-NAFUD DESERT
Esfahan
Ahvaz
Basra
KUWAIT
Kuwait
IRAN
KABUL
AFGHANISTAN
Peshawar
Nanga Parbat 8126 m
KASHMIR
KARAKORAM RANGE
Islamabad
SAUDI ARABIA
RIYADH
Manama
BAHRAIN
Persian Gulf
Shiraz
LAHORE
Amritsar
FAISALABAD
Multan
LUDHIANA
PLATEAU OF TIBET
JIDDAH
Mecca
ARABIAN PENINSULA
RED SEA
Doha
QATAR
MAKRAN MTS.
OMAN
Abu Dhabi
UNITED ARAB EMIRATES
Gulf of Oman
Masqat
PAKISTAN
Hyderabad
KARACHI
Chandigarh
DELHI
New Delhi
Meerut
NEPAL
Kathmandu
HIMALAYAS
Mount Manaslu 8163 m
Mount Everest 8850 m
Thimphu
BHUTAN
THAR DESERT
JAIPUR
Agra
LUCKNOW
Jodhpur
Gwalior
KANPUR
Patna
Guwahati
RUB' AL-KHALI DESERT
Kota
Allahabad
Varanasi
BANGLADESH
DHAKA
INDIA
AHMADABAD
BHOPAL
Jabalpur
Ranchi
Mandalay
Rajkot
INDORE
Howrah
CHITTAGONG
ARABIAN SEA
SURAT
VADODARA
KOLKATA (CALCUTTA)
NAGPUR
MYANMAR
Mount An-Nabi Shu'ayb 3660 m
Sanaa
YEMEN
Nashik
Naypyidaw
Mount Inthanon 2565 m
MUMBAI (BOMBAY)
PUNE
Sholapur
Vishakhapatnam
Bay of Bengal
WESTERN GHATS
DECCAN PLATEAU
HYDERABAD
YANGON
Gulf of Aden
Hubli-Dharwad
Vijayawada
EASTERN GHATS
Socotra Island (YEMEN)
LAKSHADWEEP ISLANDS (INDIA)
BENGALURU (BANGALORE)
CHENNAI (MADRAS)
ANDAMAN ISLANDS (INDIA)
ANDAMAN SEA
Coimbatore
Anai Peak 2695 m
Madurai
Kochi
Thiruvananthapuram (Trivandrum)
SRI LANKA
NICOBAR ISLANDS (INDIA)
Colombo
Male
MALDIVES
INDIAN OCEAN

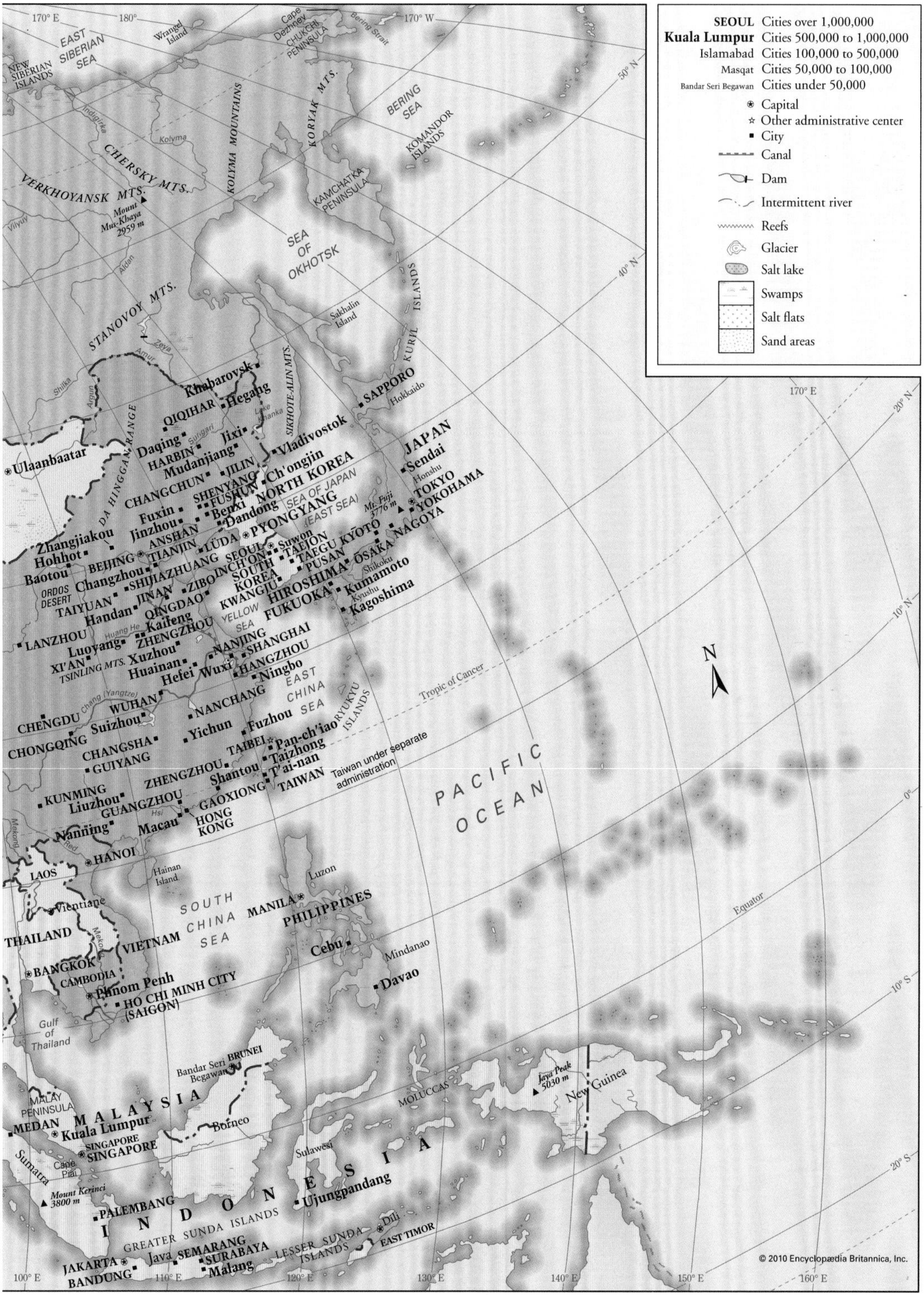
SEOUL Cities over 1,000,000
Kuala Lumpur Cities 500,000 to 1,000,000
Islamabad Cities 100,000 to 500,000
Masqat Cities 50,000 to 100,000
Bandar Seri Begawan Cities under 50,000
Capital
Other administrative center
City
Canal
Dam
Intermittent river
Reefs
Glacier
Salt lake
Swamps
Salt flats
Sand areas
EAST SIBERIAN SEA
NEW SIBERIAN ISLANDS
Wrangel Island
Cape Dezhnev
CHUKCHI PENINSULA
Bering Strait
BERING SEA
KOMANDOR ISLANDS
KORYAK MTS.
KOLYMA MOUNTAINS
Kolyma
CHERSKY MTS.
VERKHOYANSK MTS.
Mount Mus-Khaya 2959 m
KAMCHATKA PENINSULA
SEA OF OKHOTSK
Sakhalin Island
KURIL ISLANDS
STANOVOY MTS.
Amur
Zeya
Khabarovsk
SIKHOTE-ALIN MTS.
Hokkaido
SAPPORO
QIQIHAR
Hegang
Daqing
HARBIN
Jixi
Mudanjiang
Vladivostok
Ulaanbaatar
DA HINGGAN RANGE
JILIN
CHANGCHUN
Ch'ongjin
NORTH KOREA
JAPAN
Sendai
Honshu
SHENYANG
FUSHUN
SEA OF JAPAN (EAST SEA)
TOKYO
YOKOHAMA
Mt. Fuji 3776 m
Fuxin
Benxi
Dandong
PYONGYANG
Jinzhou
ANSHAN
Zhangjiakou
Hohhot
Baotou
BEIJING
TIANJIN
LÜDA
SEOUL
INCH'ON
Suwon
TAEJON
TAEGU
PUSAN
SOUTH KOREA
KWANGJU
KYOTO
OSAKA
NAGOYA
Shikoku
HIROSHIMA
FUKUOKA
Kyushu
Kumamoto
Kagoshima
Changzhou
SHIJIAZHUANG
ZIBO
ORDOS DESERT
TAIYUAN
JINAN
Handan
QINGDAO
YELLOW SEA
LANZHOU
Huang He
Kaifeng
ZHENGZHOU
Luoyang
Xuzhou
NANJING
SHANGHAI
XI'AN
TSINLING MTS.
Huainan
Wuxi
HANGZHOU
Hefei
Ningbo
EAST CHINA SEA
RYUKYU ISLANDS
Tropic of Cancer
CHENGDU
Chang (Yangtze)
WUHAN
NANCHANG
Suizhou
Yichun
Fuzhou
CHONGQING
CHANGSHA
TAIBEI
Pan-ch'iao
Taizhong
T'ai-nan
TAIWAN
Taiwan under separate administration
GUIYANG
ZHENGZHOU
Shantou
GAOXIONG
KUNMING
Liuzhou
GUANGZHOU
Macau
HONG KONG
Hsi
Nanning
Mekong
Red
HANOI
PACIFIC OCEAN
Hainan Island
Luzon
LAOS
Vientiane
SOUTH CHINA SEA
MANILA
PHILIPPINES
THAILAND
Mekong
VIETNAM
Cebu
Mindanao
Equator
BANGKOK
CAMBODIA
Phnom Penh
HO CHI MINH CITY (SAIGON)
Davao
Gulf of Thailand
Bandar Seri Begawan
BRUNEI
Jaya Peak 5030 m
New Guinea
MOLUCCAS
MALAY PENINSULA
MALAYSIA
MEDAN
Kuala Lumpur
Borneo
SINGAPORE
Sulawesi
Sumatra
Cape Prai
INDONESIA
Mount Kerinci 3800 m
PALEMBANG
Ujungpandang
GREATER SUNDA ISLANDS
Dili
EAST TIMOR
JAKARTA
Java
SEMARANG
SURABAYA
LESSER SUNDA ISLANDS
BANDUNG
Malang
© 2010 Encyclopædia Britannica, Inc.
170° E
180°
170° W
50° N
40° N
20° N
10° N
0°
10° S
20° S
100° E
110° E
120° E
130° E
140° E
150° E
160° E
170° E

CHINA, MONGOLIA, KOREA, AND JAPAN

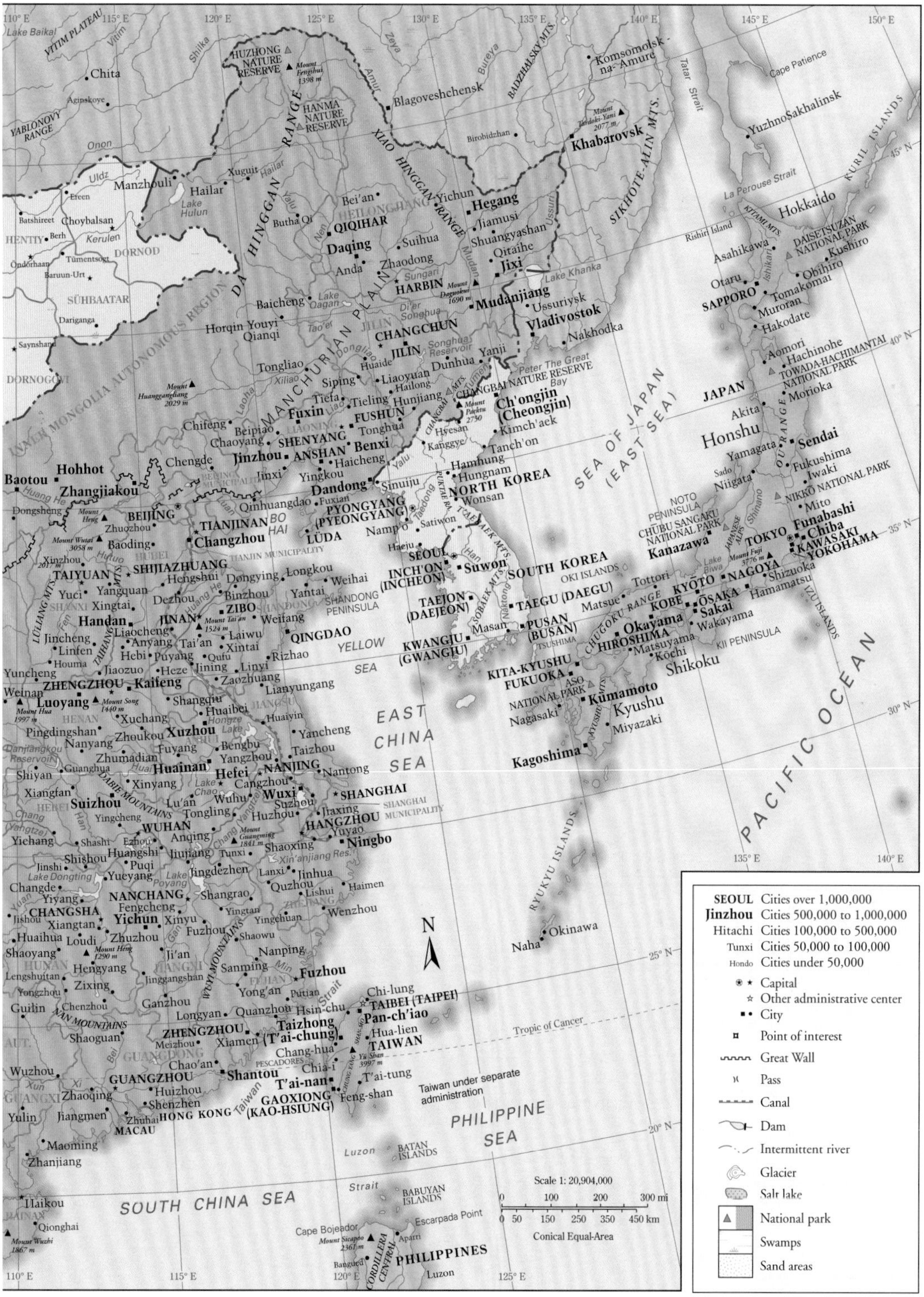
110° E
115° E
120° E
125° E
130° E
135° E
140° E
145° E
150° E
Lake Baikal
VITIM PLATEAU
Vitim
Chita
Aginskoye
YABLONOVY RANGE
Onon
Shilka
HUZHONG NATURE RESERVE
Mount Fengshui 1398 m
HANMA NATURE RESERVE
Amur
Zeya
Blagoveshchensk
Bureya
BADZHALSKIY MTS.
Komsomolsk-na-Amure
Tatar Strait
Cape Patience
YuzhnoSakhalinsk
Mount Tardoki-Yani 2077 m
Khabarovsk
Birobidzhan
SIKHOTE-ALIN MTS.
KURIL ISLANDS
45° N
La Perouse Strait
Hokkaido
KITAMI MTS.
Rishiri Island
DAISETSUZAN NATIONAL PARK
Asahikawa
Kushiro
Obihiro
Otaru
SAPPORO
Tomakomai
Muroran
Hakodate
Aomori
Hachinohe
TOWADA-HACHIMANTAI NATIONAL PARK
Morioka
40° N
XIAO HINGGAN RANGE
DA HINGGAN RANGE
Xuguit
Hailar
Manzhouli
Uldz
Ereen
Lake Hulun
Batshireet
Choybalsan
HENTIY
Berh
Kerulen
DORNOD
Öndörhaan
Tümentsogt
Baruun-Urt
SÜHBAATAR
Dariganga
Saynshand
DORNOGOVI
INNER MONGOLIA AUTONOMOUS REGION
Mount Huanggangliang 2029 m
Bei'an
HEILONGJIANG
Butha Qi
QIQIHAR
Nen
Yichun
Hegang
Jiamusi
Shuangyashan
Ussuri
Qitaihe
Jixi
Daqing
Suihua
Anda
Zhaodong
Sungari
HARBIN
Mount Daguokui 1690 m
Mudan
Lake Khanka
Mudanjiang
Ussuriysk
Vladivostok
Nakhodka
Baicheng
Lake Qagan
Di'er Songhua
Tao'er
JILIN
Horqin Youyi Qianqi
MANCHURIAN PLAIN
CHANGCHUN
Songhua Reservoir
Huaide
Tongliao
Xiliao
Liaoyuan
Dunhua
Yanji
Hailong
Peter The Great Bay
CHANGBAI NATURE RESERVE
Siping
Laoha
Tiefa
Tieling
Hunjiang
Mount Paektu 2750
Ch'ongjin (Cheongjin)
Fuxin
LIAONING
FUSHUN
Tonghua
CHANGBAI MTS.
Hyesan
Kimch'aek
Chifeng
Beipiao
Chaoyang
SHENYANG
Benxi
Kanggye
Tanch'on
Jinzhou
ANSHAN
Haicheng
Hamhung
Hungnam
Chengde
Yalu
Yingkou
Jinxi
Dandong
Sinuiju
NORTH KOREA
Hohhot
Baotou
Zhangjiakou
BEIJING MUNICIPALITY
Huang He
Dongsheng
Mount Heng
BEIJING
Qinhuangdao
Fuxian
PYONGYANG (PYEONGYANG)
Taedong
Wonsan
TAEBAEK MTS.
Zhuozhou
TIANJIN
BO HAI
Nampo
Satiwon
Mount Wutai 3058 m
Baoding
Changzhou
LÜDA
TIANJIN MUNICIPALITY
Haeju
SEOUL
Han
Xinzhou
Hutuo
HEBEI
INCH'ON (INCHEON)
Suwon
SOUTH KOREA
TAIYUAN
SHIJIAZHUANG
Hengshui
Dongying
Longkou
Weihai
Yuci
Yangquan
Binzhou
Yantai
Dezhou
SHANDONG PENINSULA
SHANXI
Xingtai
ZIBO
SHANDONG
TAEJON (DAEJEON)
SOBAEK MTS.
Naktong
TAEGU (DAEGU)
Handan
JINAN
Mount Tai'an 1524 m
Weifang
QINGDAO
Liaocheng
Laiwu
Masan
PUSAN (BUSAN)
Jincheng
Anyang
Tai'an
Xintai
YELLOW SEA
KWANGJU (GWANGJU)
TSUSHIMA
Linfen
Hebi
Puyang
Qufu
Rizhao
Houma
TAIHANG MTS.
LÜLIANG MTS.
Fen
Yuncheng
Jiaozuo
Heze
Jining
Linyi
Weinan
ZHENGZHOU
Kaifeng
Zaozhuang
Lianyungang
Luoyang
Mount Song 1440 m
Shangqiu
Mount Hua 1997 m
Huaibei
JIANGSU
Xuchang
Xuzhou
Huaiyin
HENAN
Hongze Lake
Pingdingshan
Zhoukou
Yancheng
Nanyang
Fuyang
Bengbu
Danjiangkou Reservoir
Zhumadian
Taizhou
Huai
Yangzhou
Guanghua
Huainan
NANJING
Nantong
Shiyan
Hefei
Xinyang
Lake Chao
Cangzhou
DABIE MOUNTAINS
Xiangfan
Suizhou
Lu'an
Wuhu
Wuxi
SHANGHAI
Suzhou
SHANGHAI MUNICIPALITY
HUBEI
Tongling
Jiaxing
Han
Yingcheng
Huzhou
Chang (Yangtze)
WUHAN
HANGZHOU
Yichang
Shashi
Ezhou
Anqing
Mount Guangming 1841 m
Yuyao
Ningbo
Shaoxing
Huangshi
Jiujiang
Tunxi
Xin'anjiang Res.
Jinshi
Shishou
Puqi
Lake Dongting
Yueyang
Lake Poyang
Jingdezhen
Lanxi
Jinhua
Haimen
Changde
Quzhou
Lishui
Yuan
Yiyang
NANCHANG
Shangrao
Fengcheng
ZHEJIANG
Jishou
CHANGSHA
Yichun
Xinyu
Yingtan
Yingchuan
Wenzhou
Xiangtan
Fuzhou
Gan
Huaihua
Loudi
Zhuzhou
Shaowu
WUYI MOUNTAINS
Shaoyang
Mount Heng 1290 m
Ji'an
HUNAN
Nanping
Hengyang
JIANGXI
Min
Lengshuitan
Sanming
Fuzhou
Jinggangshan
FUJIAN
Zixing
Yongzhou
Yong'an
Putian
Ganzhou
Strait
Chi-lung
Guilin
Chenzhou
Longyan
Quanzhou
Hsin-chu
TAIBEI (TAIPEI)
Pan-ch'iao
NAN MOUNTAINS
ZHENGZHOU
Taizhong (T'ai-chung)
Hua-lien
TAIWAN
Shaoguan
Meizhou
Xiamen
Chang-hua
Bei
GUANGDONG
Chao'an
PESCADORES
Yu Shan 3997 m
Chia-i
CHUNG YANG SHAN MO
Wuzhou
GUANGZHOU
Shantou
T'ai-nan
T'ai-tung
Xun
Xi
Zhaoqing
Huizhou
GAOXIONG (KAO-HSIUNG)
Feng-shan
GUANGXI
Shenzhen
Taiwan
Taiwan under separate administration
Yulin
Jiangmen
Zhuhai
HONG KONG
MACAU
PHILIPPINE SEA
20° N
Maoming
Zhanjiang
Luzon
BATAN ISLANDS
Strait
BABUYAN ISLANDS
SOUTH CHINA SEA
Haikou
HAINAN
Qionghai
Mount Wuzhi 1867 m
Cape Bojeador
Escarpada Point
Mount Sicapoo 2361 m
Aparri
Bangued
CORDILLERA CENTRAL
PHILIPPINES
Luzon
110° E
115° E
120° E
125° E
EAST CHINA SEA
SEA OF JAPAN (EAST SEA)
JAPAN
Akita
Honshu
OU RANGE
Sendai
Yamagata
Fukushima
Sado
Niigata
Iwaki
NIKKO NATIONAL PARK
Mito
NOTO PENINSULA
CHUBU SANGAKU NATIONAL PARK
JAPANESE ALPS
Shinano
TOKYO
Funabashi
Chiba
KAWASAKI
YOKOHAMA
Kanazawa
Mount Fuji 3776 m
35° N
OKI ISLANDS
Tottori
Lake Biwa
NAGOYA
Shizuoka
Matsue
CHUGOKU RANGE
KYOTO
KOBE
OSAKA
Hamamatsu
Sakai
IZU ISLANDS
Okayama
HIROSHIMA
Wakayama
Matsuyama
KII PENINSULA
Kochi
Shikoku
KITA-KYUSHU
FUKUOKA
ASO NATIONAL PARK
Kumamoto
KYUSHU MTS.
Kyushu
Nagasaki
Miyazaki
Kagoshima
30° N
PACIFIC OCEAN
RYUKYU ISLANDS
Okinawa
Naha
25° N
Tropic of Cancer
135° E
140° E
N
SEOUL Cities over 1,000,000
Jinzhou Cities 500,000 to 1,000,000
Hitachi Cities 100,000 to 500,000
Tunxi Cities 50,000 to 100,000
Hondo Cities under 50,000
Capital
Other administrative center
City
Point of interest
Great Wall
Pass
Canal
Dam
Intermittent river
Glacier
Salt lake
National park
Swamps
Sand areas
Scale 1: 20,904,000
0 100 200 300 mi
0 50 150 250 350 450 km
Conical Equal-Area

ATLAS

SOUTHEASTERN ASIA

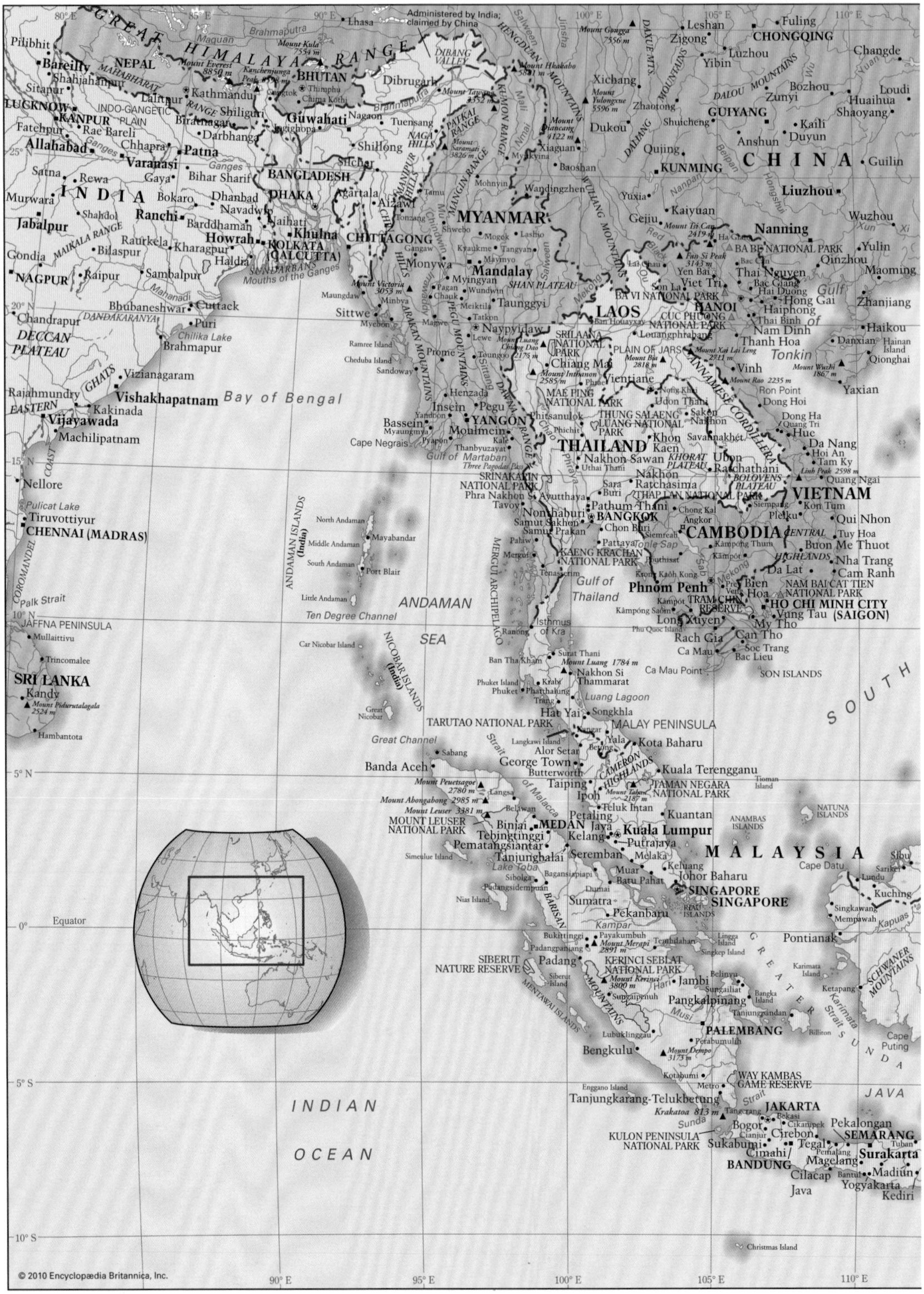

SOUTHEASTERN ASIA

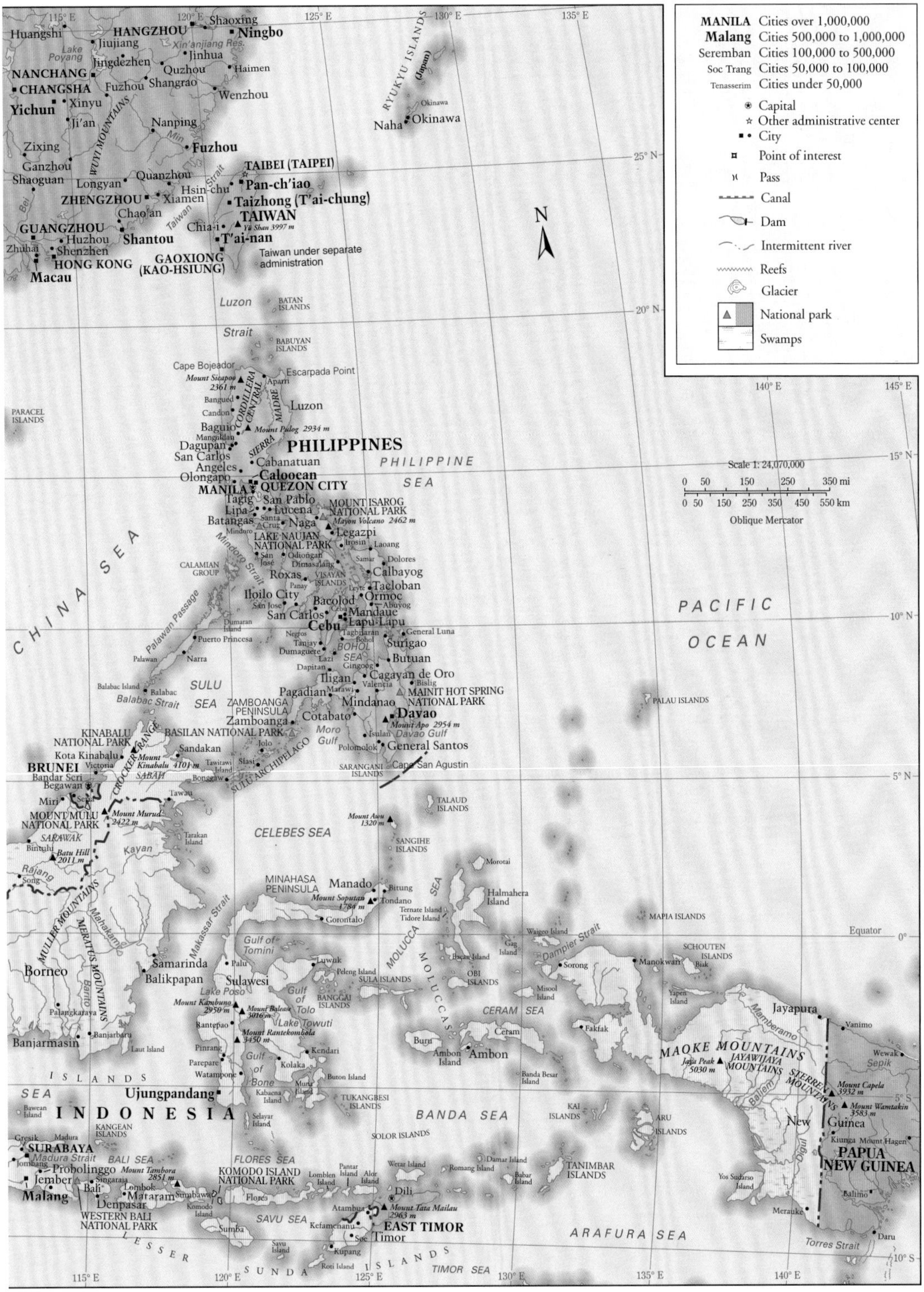

ATLAS

INDIA

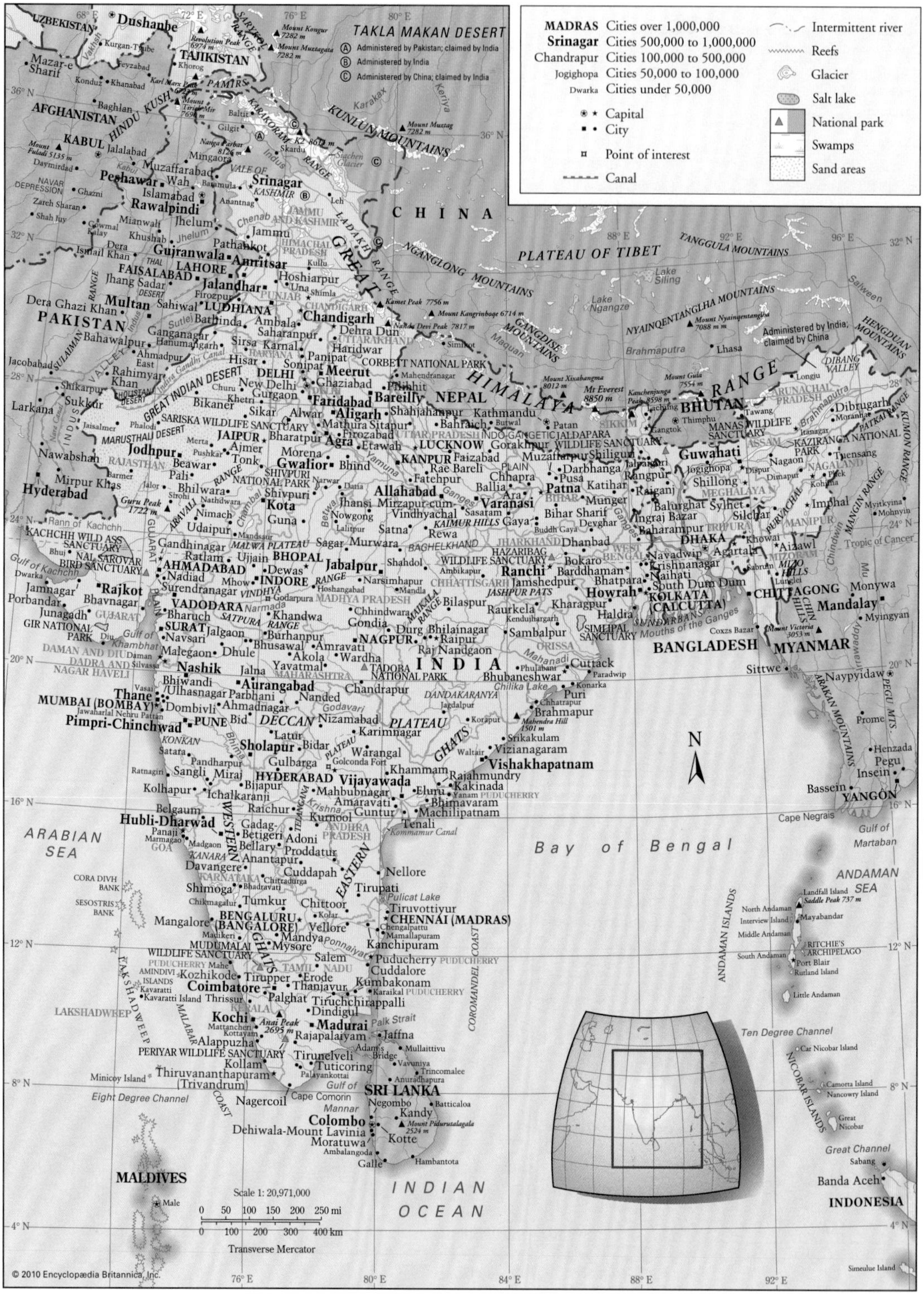
MADRAS Cities over 1,000,000
Srinagar Cities 500,000 to 1,000,000
Chandrapur Cities 100,000 to 500,000
Jogighopa Cities 50,000 to 100,000
Dwarka Cities under 50,000
Capital
City
Point of interest
Canal
Intermittent river
Reefs
Glacier
Salt lake
National park
Swamps
Sand areas
TAKLA MAKAN DESERT
Ⓐ Administered by Pakistan; claimed by India
Ⓑ Administered by India
Ⓒ Administered by China; claimed by India
Administered by India; claimed by China
UZBEKISTAN
Dushanbe
TAJIKISTAN
AFGHANISTAN
KABUL
Mazar-e Sharif
HINDU KUSH
PAMIRS
KARAKORAM
KUNLUN MOUNTAINS
Mount Kongur 7282 m
Mount Muztagata 7282 m
Mount Muztag 7282 m
K2 8611 m
Nanga Parbat 8126 m
Peshawar
Islamabad
Rawalpindi
Srinagar
KASHMIR
JAMMU AND KASHMIR
Jammu
C H I N A
PLATEAU OF TIBET
TANGGULA MOUNTAINS
NGANGLONG MOUNTAINS
GANGDISE MOUNTAINS
NYAINQENTANGLHA MOUNTAINS
HENGDUAN MOUNTAINS
Lhasa
Brahmaputra
GREAT HIMALAYA RANGE
Mount Xixabangma 8012 m
Mt Everest 8850 m
Kanchenjunga Peak 8598 m
Kamet Peak 7756 m
Mount Kangrinboqe 6714 m
Nanda Devi Peak 7817 m
Gujranwala
Amritsar
LAHORE
FAISALABAD
Jalandhar
Multan
LUDHIANA
Chandigarh
PAKISTAN
Dehra Dun
Haridwar
Meerut
DELHI
New Delhi
Ghaziabad
Faridabad
Bareilly
NEPAL
Kathmandu
BHUTAN
Thimphu
ARUNACHAL PRADESH
Dibrugarh
GREAT INDIAN DESERT
THAR DESERT
Bikaner
Aligarh
Agra
JAIPUR
Jodhpur
LUCKNOW
KANPUR
Gwalior
Guwahati
Shillong
Hyderabad
Kota
Allahabad
Varanasi
Patna
DHAKA
BANGLADESH
Ahmadabad
AHMADABAD
Rajkot
Bhopal
BHOPAL
Jabalpur
INDORE
Ranchi
Howrah
KOLKATA (CALCUTTA)
CHITTAGONG
Mandalay
MYANMAR
Tropic of Cancer
Mouths of the Ganges
VADODARA
SURAT
NAGPUR
Nashik
I N D I A
Aurangabad
Thane
MUMBAI (BOMBAY)
Pimpri-Chinchwad
PUNE
DECCAN PLATEAU
Cuttack
Bhubaneshwar
Solapur
HYDERABAD
Vijayawada
Vishakhapatnam
Naypyidaw
YANGON
ARABIAN SEA
Bay of Bengal
Hubli-Dharwad
WESTERN GHATS
EASTERN GHATS
Nellore
Tirupati
CHENNAI (MADRAS)
BENGALURU (BANGALORE)
Mysore
Salem
Coimbatore
Kochi
Madurai
Tiruchchirappalli
Thiruvananthapuram (Trivandrum)
Cape Comorin
COROMANDEL COAST
MALABAR COAST
LAKSHADWEEP
ANDAMAN SEA
ANDAMAN ISLANDS
NICOBAR ISLANDS
Port Blair
Ten Degree Channel
Eight Degree Channel
Great Channel
SRI LANKA
Jaffna
Kandy
Colombo
MALDIVES
Male
INDIAN OCEAN
INDONESIA
Banda Aceh
N
Scale 1: 20,971,000
0 50 100 150 200 250 mi
0 100 200 300 400 km
Transverse Mercator
© 2010 Encyclopædia Britannica, Inc.

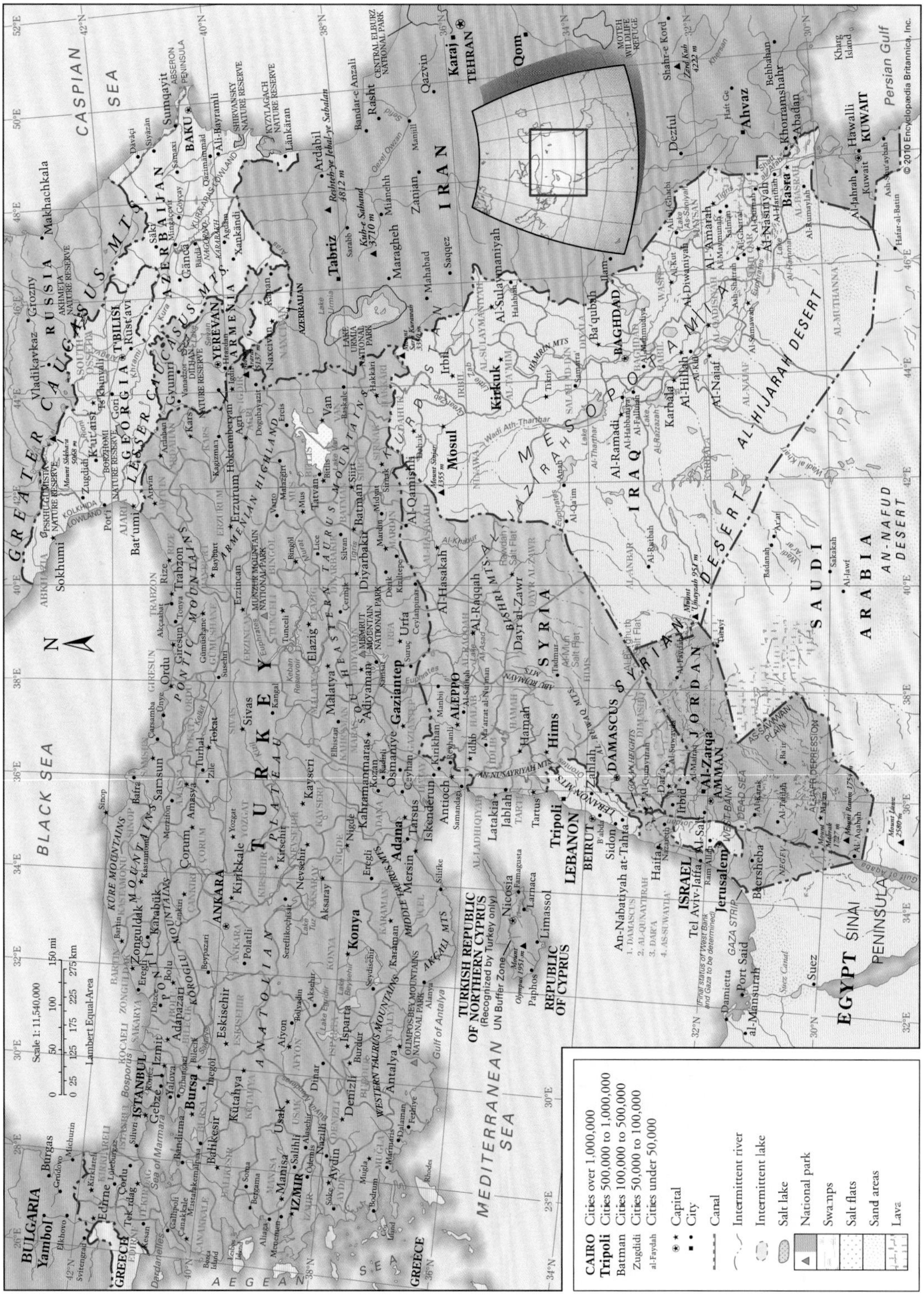
CAIRO Cities over 1,000,000
Tripoli Cities 500,000 to 1,000,000
Batman Cities 100,000 to 500,000
Zugdidi Cities 50,000 to 100,000
al-Faydah Cities under 50,000
Capital
City
Canal
Intermittent river
Intermittent lake
Salt lake
National park
Swamps
Salt flats
Sand areas
Lava
Scale 1: 11,540,000
Lambert Equal-Area
BLACK SEA
CASPIAN SEA
MEDITERRANEAN SEA
AEGEAN SEA
Persian Gulf
TURKEY
IRAN
IRAQ
SYRIA
JORDAN
SAUDI ARABIA
LEBANON
ISRAEL
EGYPT
GEORGIA
ARMENIA
AZERBAIJAN
RUSSIA
BULGARIA
GREECE
KUWAIT
REPUBLIC OF CYPRUS
TURKISH REPUBLIC OF NORTHERN CYPRUS (Recognized by Turkey only)
ANKARA
ISTANBUL
BAGHDAD
DAMASCUS
BEIRUT
AMMAN
TEHRAN
BAKU
YEREVAN
T'BILISI
Jerusalem
© 2010 Encyclopædia Britannica, Inc.

ATLAS

AFRICA

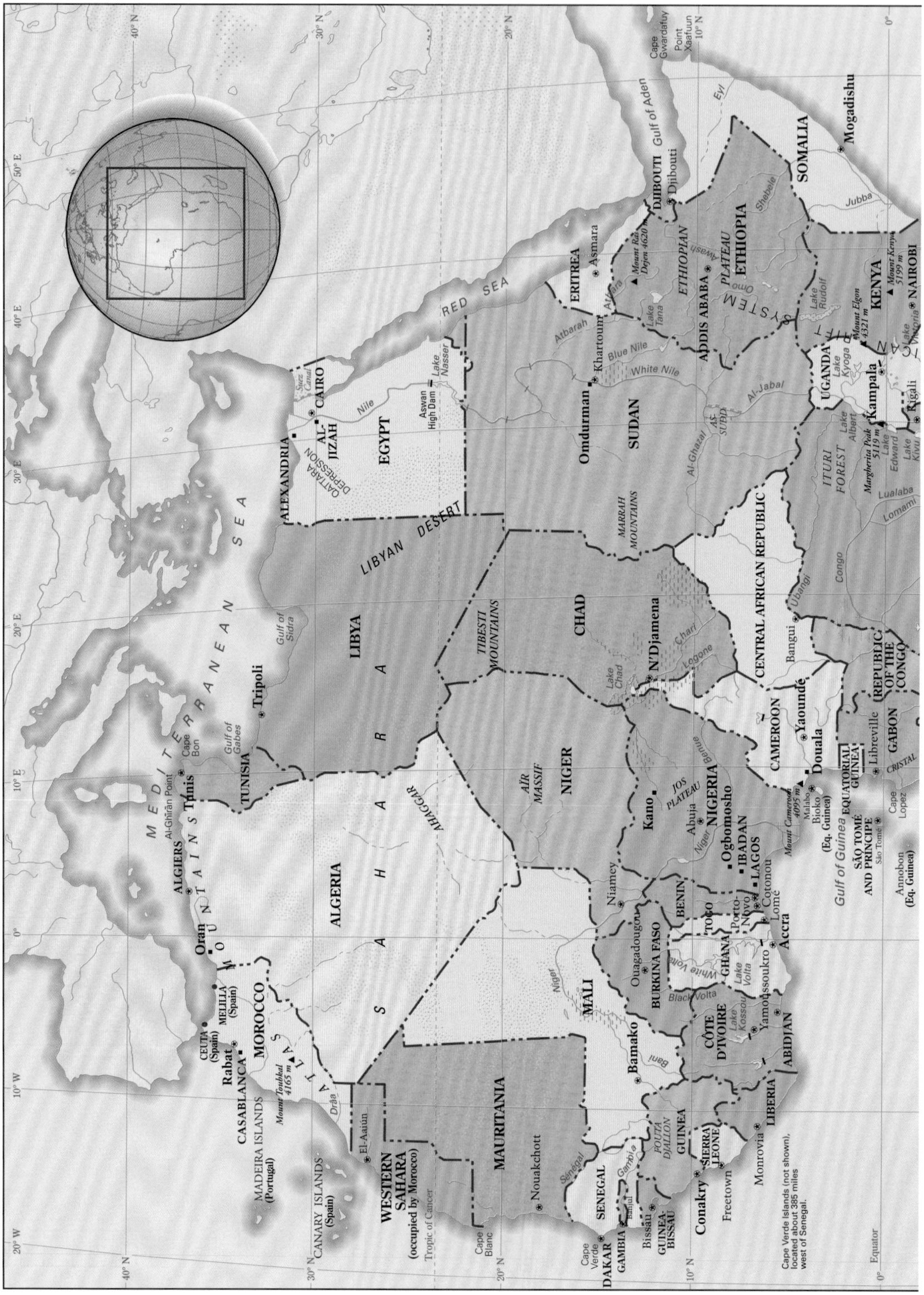

MEDITERRANEAN SEA
RED SEA
Gulf of Aden
Gulf of Guinea
SAHARA
LIBYAN DESERT
MOROCCO
ALGERIA
TUNISIA
LIBYA
EGYPT
SUDAN
ERITREA
DJIBOUTI
ETHIOPIA
SOMALIA
KENYA
UGANDA
WESTERN SAHARA
(occupied by Morocco)
MAURITANIA
MALI
NIGER
CHAD
SENEGAL
GAMBIA
GUINEA-BISSAU
GUINEA
SIERRA LEONE
LIBERIA
CÔTE D'IVOIRE
BURKINA FASO
GHANA
TOGO
BENIN
NIGERIA
CAMEROON
CENTRAL AFRICAN REPUBLIC
EQUATORIAL GUINEA
GABON
REPUBLIC OF THE CONGO
SÃO TOMÉ AND PRINCIPE
CANARY ISLANDS
(Spain)
MADEIRA ISLANDS
(Portugal)
CEUTA
(Spain)
MELILLA
(Spain)
Rabat
CASABLANCA
Oran
ALGIERS
Tunis
Tripoli
ALEXANDRIA
CAIRO
AL JIZAH
Khartoum
Omdurman
Asmara
Djibouti
ADDIS ABABA
Mogadishu
NAIROBI
Kampala
Kigali
El-Aaiún
Nouakchott
DAKAR
Banjul
Bissau
Conakry
Freetown
Monrovia
Bamako
Ouagadougou
Niamey
Yamoussoukro
ABIDJAN
Accra
Lomé
Porto-Novo
Cotonou
LAGOS
IBADAN
Ogbomosho
Abuja
Kano
N'Djamena
Yaoundé
Douala
Malabo
Libreville
Bangui
ATLAS MOUNTAINS
AHAGGAR
AÏR MASSIF
TIBESTI MOUNTAINS
MARRAH MOUNTAINS
JOS PLATEAU
ETHIOPIAN PLATEAU
QATTARA DEPRESSION
ITURI FOREST
FOUTA DJALLON
Nile
Blue Nile
White Nile
Niger
Congo
Tropic of Cancer
Equator
Cape Verde Islands (not shown), located about 385 miles west of Senegal.

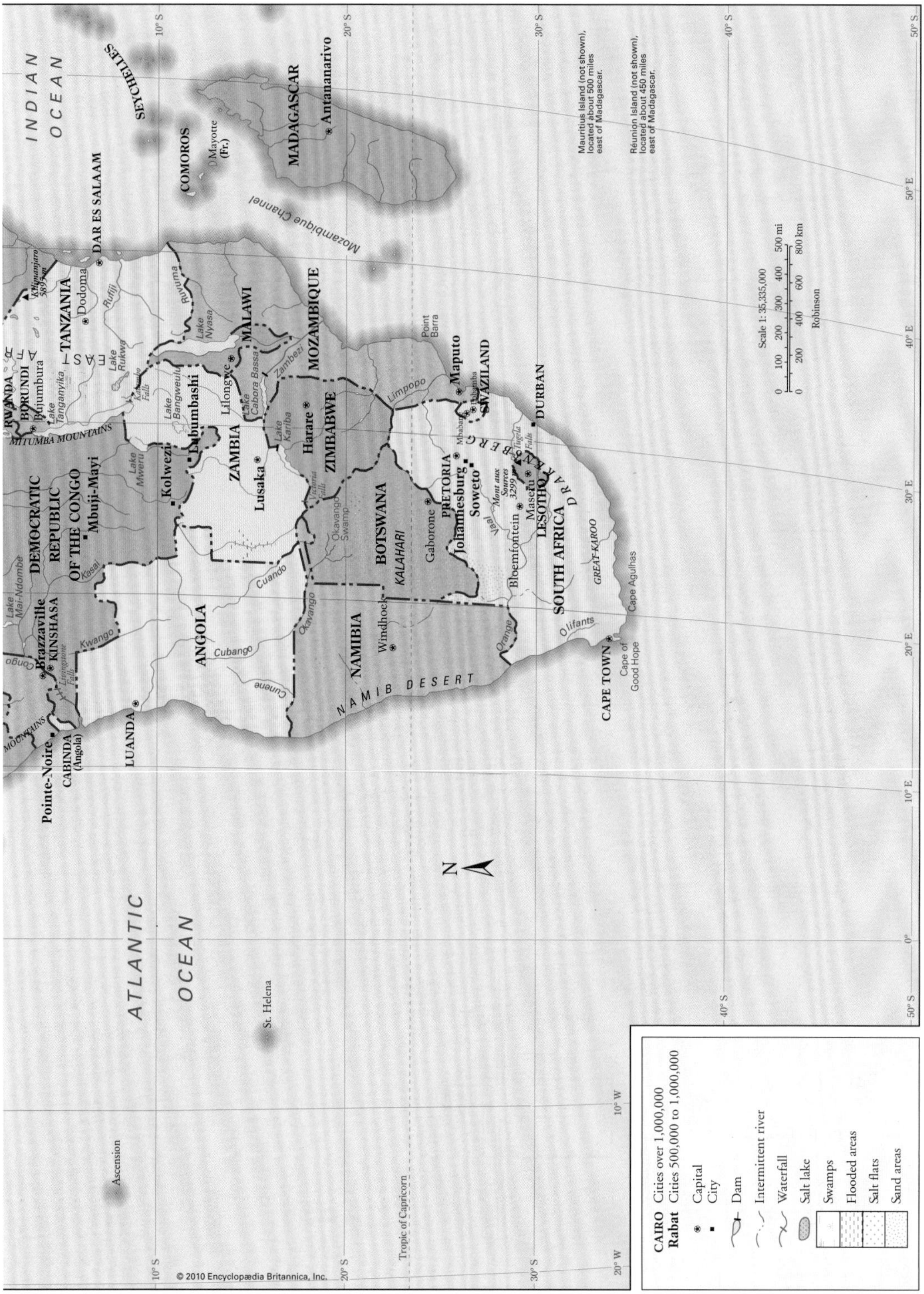
INDIAN OCEAN
ATLANTIC OCEAN
SEYCHELLES
COMOROS
Mayotte (Fr.)
MADAGASCAR
Antananarivo
Mozambique Channel
DAR ES SALAAM
TANZANIA
Dodoma
Kilimanjaro 5895 m
Rufiji
Ruvuma
Lake Nyasa
MALAWI
Lilongwe
Lake Rukwa
RWANDA
BURUNDI
Bujumbura
Lake Tanganyika
MITUMBA MOUNTAINS
Kalambo Falls
Lake Bangweulu
Lubumbashi
Lake Mweru
Kolwezi
DEMOCRATIC REPUBLIC OF THE CONGO
Mbuji-Mayi
Kasai
Lake Mai-Ndombe
Brazzaville
KINSHASA
Congo
Livingstone Falls
Kwango
Pointe-Noire
CABINDA (Angola)
LUANDA
ANGOLA
Cubango
Cuando
Cunene
ZAMBIA
Lusaka
Lake Kariba
Lake Cabora Bassa
Zambezi
Victoria Falls
ZIMBABWE
Harare
MOZAMBIQUE
Maputo
Point Barra
Limpopo
SWAZILAND
Mbabane
Lobamba
BOTSWANA
Gaborone
Okavango
Okavango Swamp
KALAHARI
NAMIBIA
Windhoek
NAMIB DESERT
PRETORIA
Johannesburg
Soweto
Vaal
Mont aux Sources 3299 m
Bloemfontein
Maseru
LESOTHO
Tugela Falls
DRAKENSBERG
DURBAN
SOUTH AFRICA
GREAT KAROO
Orange
Olifants
CAPE TOWN
Cape of Good Hope
Cape Agulhas
St. Helena
Ascension
Tropic of Capricorn
Mauritius Island (not shown), located about 500 miles east of Madagascar.
Réunion Island (not shown), located about 450 miles east of Madagascar.
Scale 1: 35,335,000
0 100 200 300 400 500 mi
0 200 400 600 800 km
Robinson
N
10° S
20° S
30° S
40° S
50° S
20° W
10° W
0°
10° E
20° E
30° E
40° E
50° E
CAIRO Cities over 1,000,000
Rabat Cities 500,000 to 1,000,000
Capital
City
Dam
Intermittent river
Waterfall
Salt lake
Swamps
Flooded areas
Salt flats
Sand areas
© 2010 Encyclopædia Britannica, Inc.

NORTHERN AFRICA

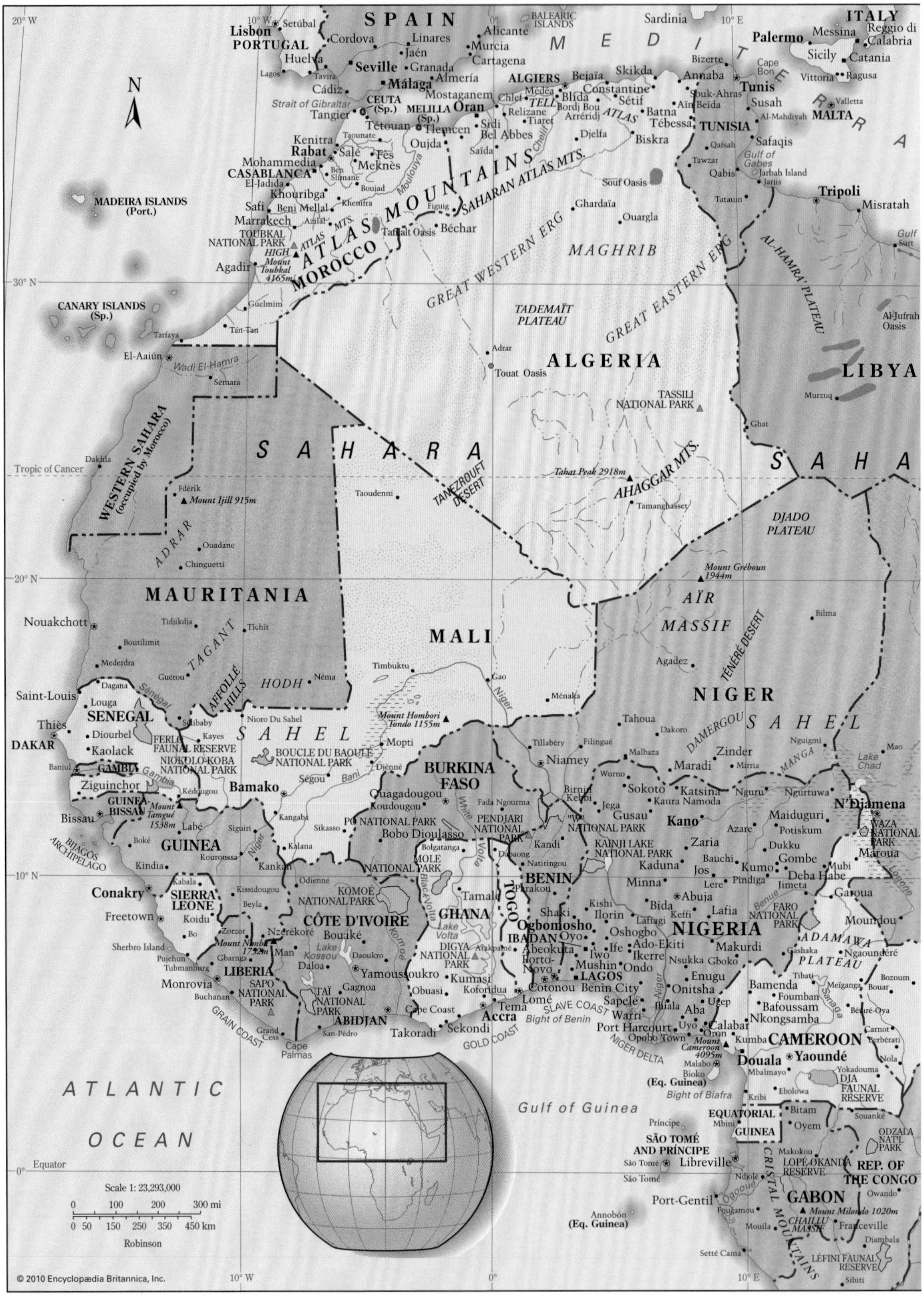

NORTHERN AFRICA

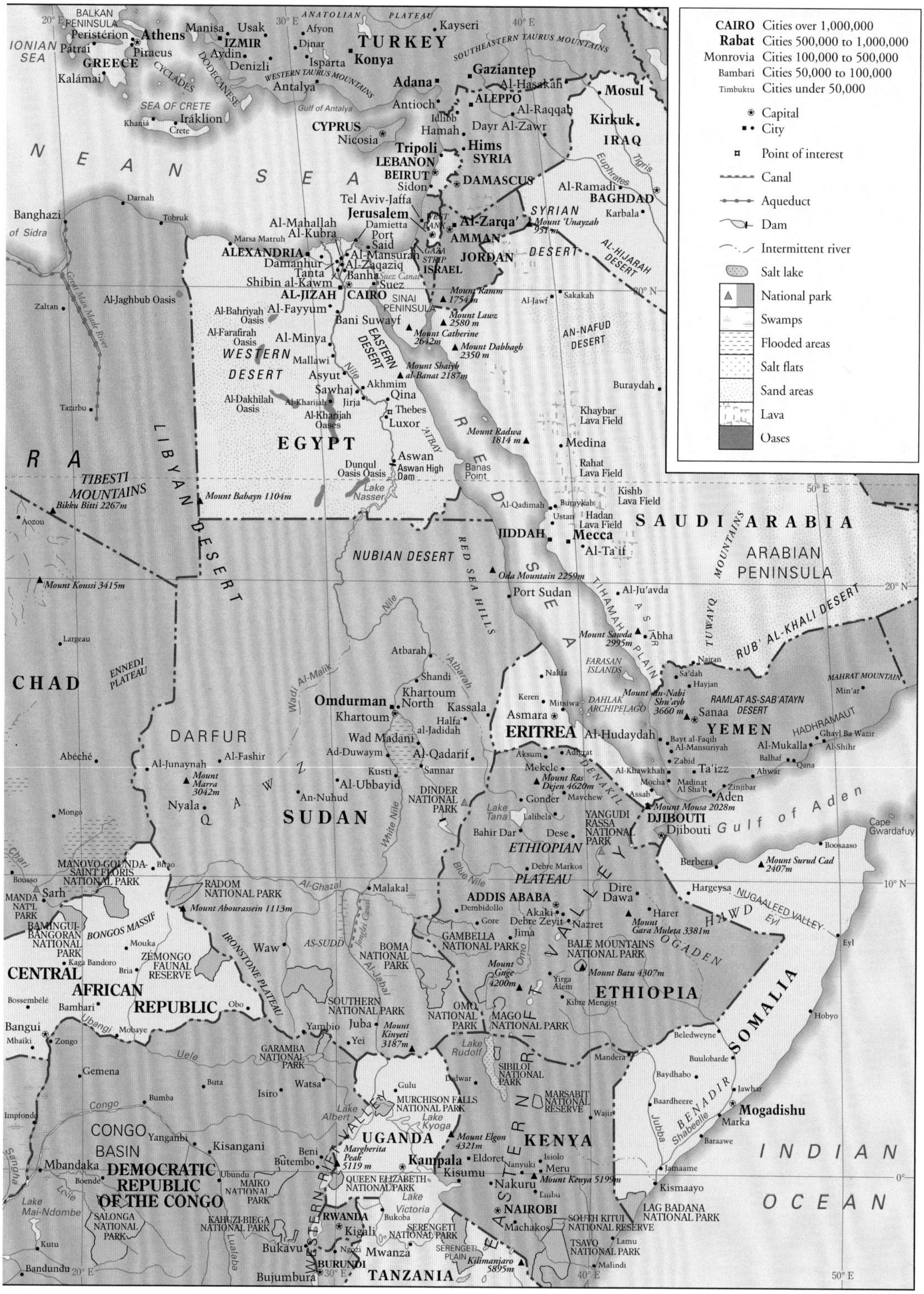

ATLAS

SOUTHERN AFRICA

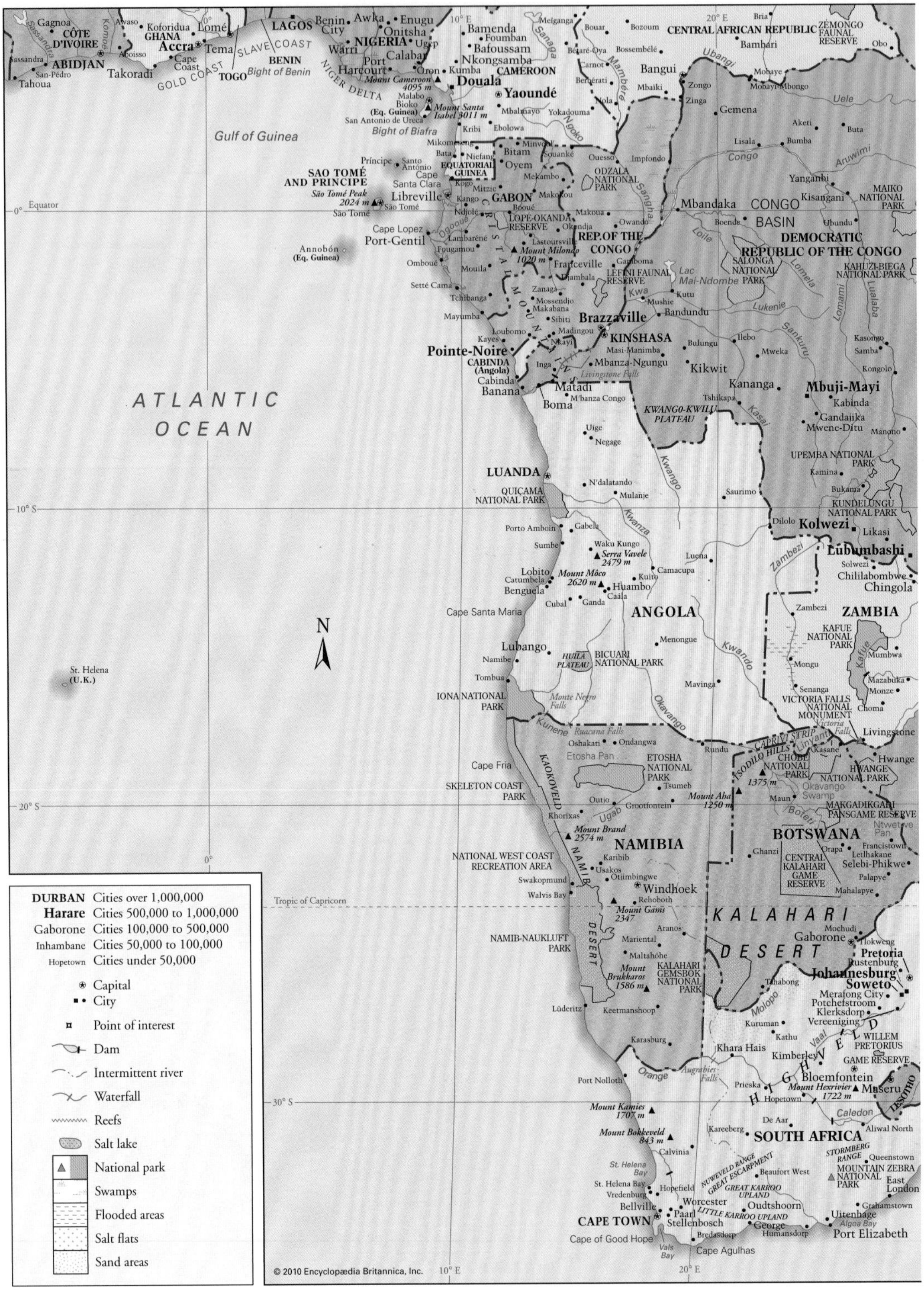

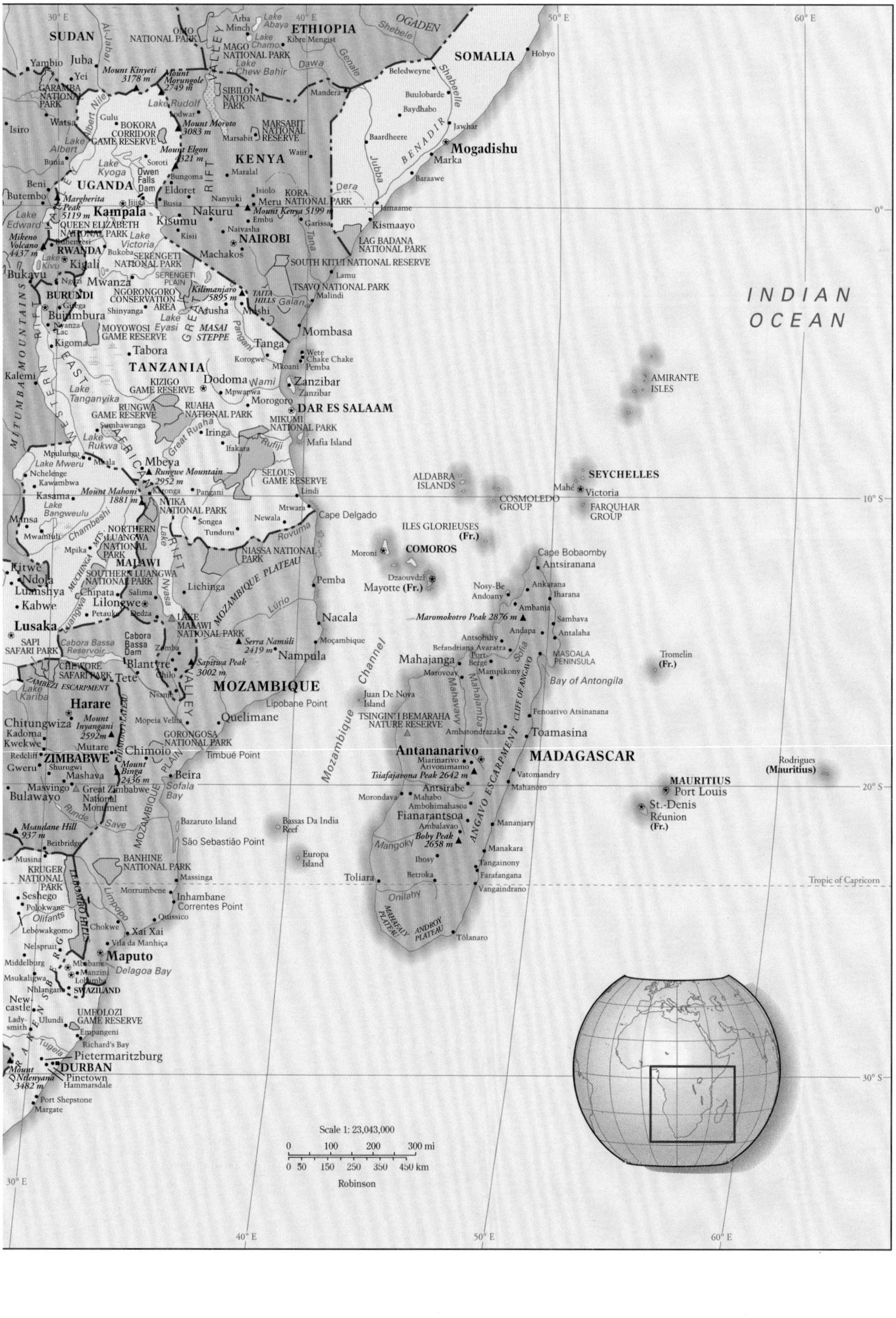
SUDAN
ETHIOPIA
SOMALIA
KENYA
UGANDA
RWANDA
BURUNDI
TANZANIA
MALAWI
MOZAMBIQUE
ZIMBABWE
SWAZILAND
COMOROS
SEYCHELLES
MADAGASCAR
MAURITIUS
INDIAN OCEAN
Mogadishu
Kampala
NAIROBI
Kigali
Bujumbura
Dodoma
DAR ES SALAAM
Zanzibar
Mombasa
Lilongwe
Lusaka
Harare
Maputo
DURBAN
Pietermaritzburg
Antananarivo
Port Louis
St.-Denis
Réunion (Fr.)
Victoria
Moroni
Mayotte (Fr.)
Tromelin (Fr.)
Rodrigues (Mauritius)
AMIRANTE ISLES
ALDABRA ISLANDS
COSMOLEDO GROUP
FARQUHAR GROUP
ILES GLORIEUSES (Fr.)
Juan De Nova Island
Bassas Da India Reef
Europa Island
Mozambique Channel
Lake Victoria
Lake Tanganyika
Lake Rudolf
Lake Nyasa
Mount Kenya 5199 m
Kilimanjaro 5895 m
Mount Elgon 4321 m
Maromokotro Peak 2876 m
Tsiafajavona Peak 2642 m
Boby Peak 2658 m
Toamasina
Mahajanga
Fianarantsoa
Toliara
Tôlanaro
Antsiranana
Cape Delgado
Tropic of Capricorn
0°
10° S
20° S
30° S
30° E
40° E
50° E
60° E
Scale 1: 23,043,000
0 100 200 300 mi
0 50 150 250 350 450 km
Robinson

ARABIAN PENINSULA

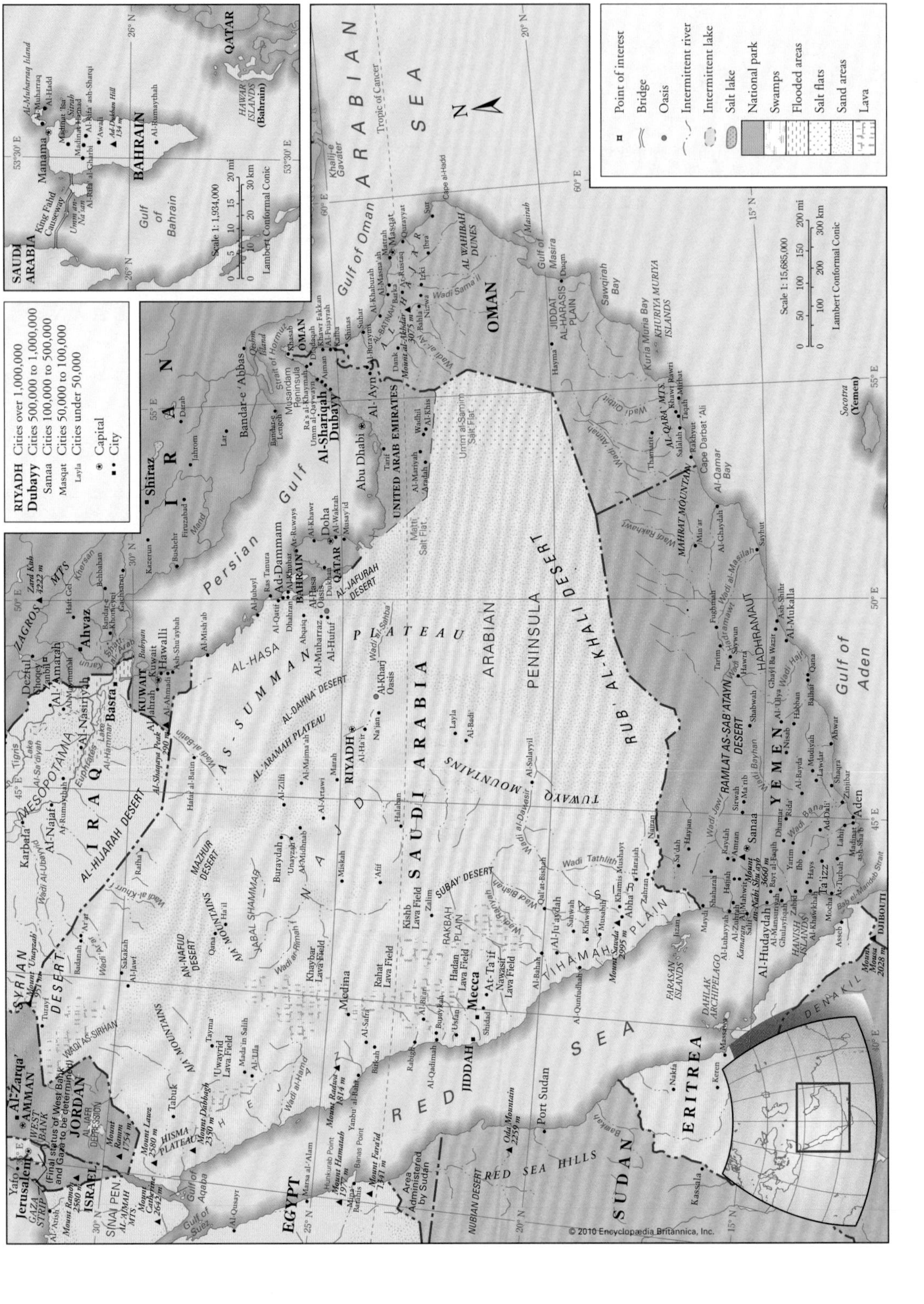

SYDNEY Cities over 500,000
Canberra Cities 100,000 to 500,000
Alice Springs Cities 50,000 to 100,000
Winton Cities under 50,000
Capital
City
Dam
Intermittent river
Reefs
Glacier
Intermittent lake
Salt lake
National park
Aboriginal lands
Swamps
Sand areas
Scale 1:31,952,000
0 50 100 200 300 400 mi
0 150 300 450 600 km
Conic
© 2010 Encyclopædia Britannica, Inc.
AUSTRALIA
NEW ZEALAND
PAPUA NEW GUINEA
INDONESIA
PACIFIC OCEAN
INDIAN OCEAN
TASMAN SEA
CORAL SEA
TIMOR SEA
ARAFURA SEA
Great Australian Bight
GREAT DIVIDING RANGE
GREAT SANDY DESERT
GIBSON DESERT
GREAT VICTORIA DESERT
NULLARBOR PLAIN
SIMPSON DESERT
WESTERN AUSTRALIA
NORTHERN TERRITORY
QUEENSLAND
SOUTH AUSTRALIA
NEW SOUTH WALES
VICTORIA
TASMANIA
PERTH
ADELAIDE
MELBOURNE
SYDNEY
BRISBANE
Canberra
Hobart
Darwin
Alice Springs
Auckland
Wellington
Christchurch
North Island
South Island

ATLAS

OCEANIA

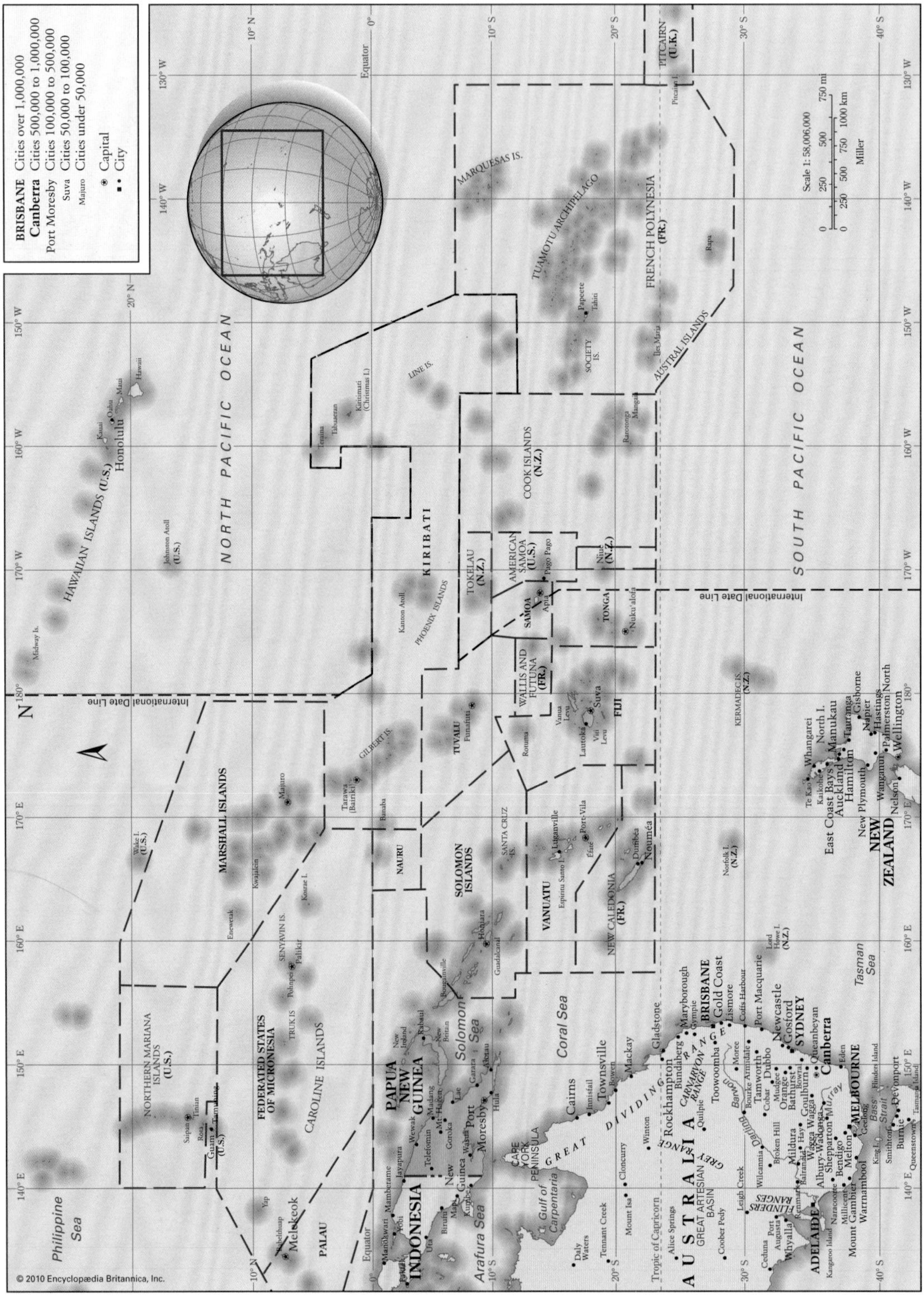
BRISBANE Cities over 1,000,000
Canberra Cities 500,000 to 1,000,000
Port Moresby Cities 100,000 to 500,000
Suva Cities 50,000 to 100,000
Majuro Cities under 50,000
Capital
City
Scale 1: 58,006,000
0 250 500 750 mi
0 250 500 750 1000 km
Miller
NORTH PACIFIC OCEAN
SOUTH PACIFIC OCEAN
HAWAIIAN ISLANDS (U.S.)
Honolulu
KIRIBATI
MARSHALL ISLANDS
NORTHERN MARIANA ISLANDS (U.S.)
FEDERATED STATES OF MICRONESIA
CAROLINE ISLANDS
PALAU
PAPUA NEW GUINEA
INDONESIA
SOLOMON ISLANDS
NAURU
TUVALU
VANUATU
NEW CALEDONIA (FR.)
FIJI
TONGA
SAMOA
AMERICAN SAMOA (U.S.)
TOKELAU (N.Z.)
WALLIS AND FUTUNA (FR.)
COOK ISLANDS (N.Z.)
FRENCH POLYNESIA (FR.)
PITCAIRN (U.K.)
MARQUESAS IS.
TUAMOTU ARCHIPELAGO
AUSTRAL ISLANDS
AUSTRALIA
NEW ZEALAND
SYDNEY
MELBOURNE
BRISBANE
ADELAIDE
Canberra
Coral Sea
Tasman Sea
Arafura Sea
Philippine Sea
Solomon Sea
International Date Line
Equator
Tropic of Capricorn